How to use your Connected Casebook

Step 1: Go to **www.CasebookConnect.com** and redeem your access code to get started.

Access Code:  SMILLCRP41097474

Step 2: Go to your **BOOKSHELF** and select your Connected Casebook to start reading, highlighting, and taking notes in the margins of your e-book.

Step 3: Select the **STUDY** tab in your toolbar to access a variety of practice materials designed to help you master the course material. These materials may include explanations, videos, multiple-choice questions, flashcards, short answer, essays, and issue spotting.

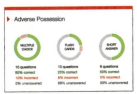

Step 4: Select the **OUTLINE** tab in your toolbar to access chapter outlines that automatically incorporate your highlights and annotations from the e-book. Use the My Notes area for copying, pasting, and editing your book notes or creating new notes.

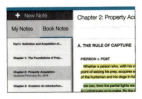

Step 5: If your professor has enrolled your class, you can select the **CLASS INSIGHTS** tab and compare your own study center results against the average of your classmates.

PIN: 10050922-0002 MLCRP6

CRIMINAL PROCEDURES

ASPEN CASEBOOK SERIES

CRIMINAL PROCEDURES

Cases, Statutes, and Executive Materials

Sixth Edition

MARC L. MILLER
Dean & Ralph W. Bilby Professor of Law
The University of Arizona James E. Rogers College of Law

RONALD F. WRIGHT
Needham Y. Gulley Professor of Criminal Law
Wake Forest University School of Law

JENIA I. TURNER
Amy Abboud Ware Centennial Professor in Criminal Law
Southern Methodist University, Dedman School of Law

KAY L. LEVINE
Professor of Law and Associate Dean of Faculty
Emory University School of Law

Published by Wolters Kluwer in New York.

Wolters Kluwer Legal & Regulatory U.S. serves customers worldwide with CCH, Aspen Publishers, and Kluwer Law International products. (www.WKLegaledu.com)

To contact Customer Service, e-mail customer.service@wolterskluwer.com, call 1-800-234-1660, fax 1-800-901-9075, or mail correspondence to:

> Wolters Kluwer
> Attn: Order Department
> PO Box 990
> Frederick, MD 21705

Printed in the United States of America.

2 3 4 5 6 7 8 9 0

ISBN 978-1-4548-9794-1

Library of Congress Cataloging-in-Publication Data

Names: Miller, Marc L. (Marc Louis), 1959- author | Wright, Ronald F., 1959-
    author. | Turner, Jenia I., author. | Levine, Kay L., author.
Title: Criminal procedures : cases, statutes, and executive materials / Marc
    L. Miller, Dean & Ralph W. Bilby, Professor of Law, The University of
    Arizona James E. Rogers College of Law; Ronald F. Wright, Needham Y.
    Gulley Professor of Criminal Law, Wake Forest University School of Law;
    Jenia I. Turner, Amy Abboud Ware Centennial Professor in Criminal Law,
    Southern Methodist University, Dedman School of Law; Kay L. Levine,
    Professor of Law and Associate Dean of Faculty, Emory University School of Law.
Description: Sixth edition. | New York : Wolters Kluwer, [2019] | Series:
    Aspen casebook series | Includes bibliographical references and index.
Identifiers: LCCN 2018056730 | ISBN 9781454897941
Subjects: LCSH: Criminal procedure—United States. | LCGFT: Casebooks (Law)
Classification: LCC KF9619 .M528 2019 | DDC 345.73/05–dc23
LC record available at https://lccn.loc.gov/2018056730

About Wolters Kluwer Legal & Regulatory U.S.

Wolters Kluwer Legal & Regulatory U.S. delivers expert content and solutions in the areas of law, corporate compliance, health compliance, reimbursement, and legal education. Its practical solutions help customers successfully navigate the demands of a changing environment to drive their daily activities, enhance decision quality and inspire confident outcomes.

Serving customers worldwide, its legal and regulatory portfolio includes products under the Aspen Publishers, CCH Incorporated, Kluwer Law International, ftwilliam.com and MediRegs names. They are regarded as exceptional and trusted resources for general legal and practice-specific knowledge, compliance and risk management, dynamic workflow solutions, and expert commentary.

Summary of Contents

Contents	ix
Preface	xxxi
Acknowledgments	xxxvii

PART ONE ■ GATHERING INFORMATION   1

I.	The Border of Criminal Procedure: Daily Interactions Between Citizens and Police	3
II.	Brief Police-Citizen Encounters	41
III.	Full Searches of People and Places: Basic Concepts	135
IV.	Searches in Recurring Contexts	223
V.	Arrests	297
VI.	Remedies for Unreasonable Searches and Seizures	345
VII.	Technology and Privacy	411
VIII.	Interrogations	471
IX.	Identifications	581
X.	Complex Investigations	629

PART TWO ■ EVALUATING CHARGES   667

XI.	Defense Counsel	669
XII.	Pretrial Release and Detention	747
XIII.	Charging	783
XIV.	Jeopardy and Joinder	861

PART THREE ■ RESOLVING GUILT AND INNOCENCE   **913**
    XV.   Discovery and Speedy Trial   915
    XVI. Pleas and Bargains   979
    XVII. Decisionmakers at Trial   1067
    XVIII. Witnesses and Proof   1137

PART FOUR ■ MEASURING PUNISHMENT AND REASSESSING GUILT   **1203**
    XIX. Sentencing   1205
    XX.   Appeals   1291

Table of Cases   *1333*
Index   *1353*

Contents

Preface   *xxxi*
Acknowledgments   *xxxvii*

PART ONE
■

GATHERING INFORMATION   1

   I.   ***The Border of Criminal Procedure: Daily Interactions***
       Between Citizens and Police   *3*

       A.   Police as Community Caretakers   4
             Oregon Revised Statutes §133.033   4
             Indianapolis Police Department Job
               Description: Patrol Officer   5
             Commonwealth v. Victoria Livingstone   6
             Notes   11
             Problem 1-1. I'm from the Government and I'm
               Here to Help   13
       B.   Policing Philosophies   13
             Seth W. Stoughton, Principled Policing: Warrior
               Cops and Guardian Officers   14
             COPS Program (Community-Oriented
               Policing Services)   20
             Fairfield Police Department Community
               Policing Programs   22

ix

				Tracey L. Meares, Norms, Legitimacy and Law	
				Enforcement	23
				Notes	27
				Problem 1–2. Loitering With No Apparent Purpose	30
				Problem 1–3. If You Can't Give 'Em a Rap, Give 'Em a Ride	30
				Problem 1–4. Juvenile Curfews	31
	C.	Policing Organizations			32
				Bureau of Justice Statistics, Local Police Departments, 2013: Personnel, Policies, and Practices	33
				Herbert L. Packer, Two Models of the Criminal Process	34
				Notes	38

II.   *Brief Police-Citizen Encounters*   **41**

A.	Searches and Seizures				43
	1.	What Is a Search?			43
			Charles Katz v. United States	43
			United States v. Antoine Jones	46
			Notes	50
			Problem 2-1. Peep-Hole Observations	54
			Problem 2-2. A Jurisprudence of Squeezes	55
			Problem 2-3. Plain View from a Ladder or Drone	55
			Problem 2-4. The Friendly Skies	56
	2.	What Is a Seizure?		56
			Delaware Code Tit. 11, §1902	57
			Notes	57
			United States v. Sylvia Mendenhall	58
			Wesley Wilson v. State	61
			Notes	64
			Problem 2-5. Tickets, Please	67
	3.	State Action Requirement		68
			Problem 2-6: Private Viewing	68
			Notes	69
B.	Reasonable Suspicion			70
	1.	Grounds for Stops: Articulable, Individualized Reasonable Suspicion		70
			State v. Theodore Nelson	71
			State v. David Dean	72
			Notes	74
			Jamal Sizer v. State	77
			Notes	81
	2.	Pretextual Stops		82
			People v. Frank Robinson	82
			Notes	87
			Problem 2-7. Asset Management	89

3.	Criminal Profiles and Race	90
	Uriel Harris v. State	90
	Attorney General of Maryland Ending Discriminatory Profiling in Maryland	94
	Notes	97
	Problem 2-8. Goatee and Dark Skin	99
4.	Collecting and Reporting Stop Data	100
	Nebraska Crime Commission 2017 Traffic Stops in Nebraska: A Report to the Governor and the Legislature on Data Submitted by Law Enforcement	100
	Notes	103
	Problem 2-9. Borderline State	105
C.	Brief Searches of Individuals	106
1.	Frisks for Weapons	107
	John Terry v. Ohio	107
	Notes	114
2.	The Scope of a *Terry* Search	116
	Commonwealth v. Roosevelt Wilson	116
	Arkansas Rule of Criminal Procedure 3.4	119
	Montana Code §46-5-401(2)	119
	Notes	120
	Problem 2-10. Frisking Car and Driver	123
D.	Brief Administrative Stops and Searches	123
	City of Indianapolis v. James Edmond	124
	Iowa Code §321k.1	129
	Notes	129

III.	***Full Searches of People and Places: Basic Concepts***	**135**
A.	Warrant Requirements	136
1.	General Search Warrants and the History of the Fourth Amendment	136
	John Entick v. Nathan Carrington	137
	The Writs of Assistance	138
	Notes	139
2.	Particularity in Warrants	143
	Christopher Wheeler v. State	143
	Notes	147
	Problem 3-1. Errors in a Facially Valid Warrant	151
3.	Probable Cause	151
a.	Standards for Defining Probable Cause	151
	Virgil Brinegar v. United States	153
	Problem 3-2. Applying Different Probable Cause Standards	157
	Notes	158
	Problem 3-3. A New Look	161

| | | b. | Sources of Information to Support Probable Cause | 162 |

b. Sources of Information to Support Probable Cause 162
    State v. Timothy Barton 162
    State v. Randall Utterback 168
    Notes 171
    Problem 3-4. Assessing Anonymous Tips 174
c. Can a Statute or Rule Clarify the Assessment
   of Probable Cause? 175
    Iowa Code §808.3 175
    Iowa Rule of Criminal Procedure 2.36, Form 2 175
    Iowa Rule of Criminal Procedure 2.36, Form 3 176
    Notes 177
4. Other Warrant Requirements 178
  a. Neutral and Detached Magistrate 178
    State ex rel. Eustace Brown v. Jerry Dietrick 178
    Notes 181
  b. Execution of Warrants 181
    State v. Tanya Marie Anyan 182
    Notes 188
B. Warrantless Searches 190
  1. Exigent Circumstances 191
    State v. Rashad Walker 191
    Notes 196
  2. Searches Based on Special Needs 198
    Roland Camara v. Municipal Court of San Francisco 199
    Notes 202
C. Consensual Searches 203
  1. Components of a Voluntary Choice 203
    Merle Schneckloth v. Robert Bustamonte 204
    Chicago Police Department Consent to Search
      Form, CPD-11.483 208
    Philadelphia Police Department Directive 7,
      Appendix A 208
    Notes 208
    Problem 3-5. Scope of Consent 212
  2. Third-Party Consent 212
    Arkansas Rule of Criminal Procedure 11.2 213
    Problem 3-6. Co-tenant Consenting
      for Co-tenant 213
    Problem 3-7. Parent Consenting for Child 213
    Problem 3-8. Child Consenting for Parent 213
    Notes 214
    Commonwealth v. Porter P. 215
    Notes 219
    Problem 3-9. Divide and Conquer 221
    Problem 3-10. Consent Through
      Lease Provisions 221

IV. *Searches in Recurring Contexts*   **223**

   A. "Persons"   224
      1. Searches Incident to Arrest   224
             Arkansas Rule of Criminal Procedure 12.2   224
             Annotated Laws of Massachusetts Ch. 276, §1   224
             Danny Birchfield v. North Dakota   225
             Notes   229
             Problem 4-1. Lunging in Handcuffs   232
             Problem 4-2. Search Incident to (but After)
                Arrest   232
             Problem 4-3. Sweeping Authority   232
      3. Body Searches at the Jail   233
             Maryland v. Alonzo J. King, Jr.   234
             Revised Code of Washington §§10.79.080,
                10.79.130, 10.79.140   237
             Notes   239
             Problem 4-4. Blood Test Consent   242
             Problem 4-5. Personal Inventories   243
             Problem 4-6. Body Cavity Search Away from the
                Jail   243
   B. "Houses" and Other Places   243
      1. The Outer Boundaries of Houses   244
             Constitution of Michigan Art. I, §11   244
             State v. Gregory Fisher   244
             Notes   249
             Problem 4-7. No Hunting in Open Fields   252
      2. Workplaces   252
             People v. Carlos Christopher Galvadon   253
             Notes   256
      3. Schools and Prisons   257
             Oklahoma Statutes Tit. 70, §24-102   257
             State v. Marzel Jones   258
              *Hugh and Lee Hageman v. Goshen County School
                District No. 1*   263
             Notes   267
             Problem 4-8. Jail Cell Search   270
             Problem 4-9. Gun Lockers   271
   C. "Papers"   271
             Edward Boyd v. United States   272
             Notes   274
   D. "Effects"   276
      1. Search of a Car Incident to Arrest   277
             Clarence Robinson v. State   277
             Notes   280
             Problem 4-10. Mobile Homes   283
      2. Inventory Searches   283
             People v. Curtis Gipson   284
             Notes   287
             Problem 4-11. The Other Gun   289

              3.   Containers, In and Out of Cars   290
                        California v. Charles Acevedo   290
                        Notes   296

V. *Arrests*   **297**

        A.   Stop or Arrest?   297
                        Nevada Revised Statutes §171.123   298
                        Arkansas Rule of Criminal Procedure 3.1   298
                        Robert Bailey v. State   298
                        Notes   303
        B.   Arrest Warrants   305
                        William Blackstone, Commentaries on the Laws
                           of England   306
                        State v. Steven Thomas   306
                        Notes   310
                        Problem 5-1. Indoor-Outdoor Arrest   311
                        Problem 5-2. Warrant Sweeps   311
        C.   Police Discretion in the Arrest Decision   312
                        William Blackstone, Commentaries on the Laws
                           of England   312
                        Connecticut General Statutes §46b-38b   313
                        Iowa Code §236.12   313
                        Lawrence Sherman & Richard Berk, The
                           Minneapolis Domestic Violence Experiment   314
                        Notes   316
                        Problem 5-3. Racial Patterns in Arrests   319
        D.   Paper Arrests: Citations   319
                        New York Criminal Procedure Law §§150.10,
                           150.20, 150.60   320
                        Revised Statutes of Nebraska §§29-435, 29-427   321
                        State v. Rico Bayard   321
                        Notes   324
        E.   Use of Force in Making Arrests   326
                        William Blackstone, Commentaries on the Laws
                           of England   327
                        Tennessee v. Edward Garner   327
                        Notes   334
                        Problem 5-4. Ruby Ridge   338
                        Notes   340
                        Problem 5-5. Subduing Motorcycle Rider   342
                        Problem 5-6. High-Speed Chase   343

VI. *Remedies for Unreasonable Searches and Seizures*   **345**

        A.   Origins of the Exclusionary Rule   345
                        Fremont Weeks v. United States   346
                        Notes   348
                        People v. Charles Cahan   349
                        Dollree Mapp v. Ohio   354
                        Notes   358

B.	Limitations on the Exclusionary Rule		361
	1.	Evidence Obtained in "Good Faith"	362
		Commonwealth v. Richard Johnson	362
		Colorado Revised Statutes §16-3-308	369
		Notes	369
		Problem 6-1. Objective Good Faith	372
		Problem 6-2. Unwarranted Good Faith	373
	2.	Causation Limits: Inevitable Discovery and Independent Source	373
		Michael Wehrenburg v. State	374
		Notes	379
		Problem 6-3. The Search Party	382
		Problem 6-4. Illegal Stop vs. Outstanding Warrant	382
		Problem 6-5. Breaking the Chain of Causation?	383
	3.	Standing to Challenge Illegal Searches and Seizures	383
		Louisiana Constitution Art. I., §5	384
		State v. John Bruns	384
		Notes	388
		Problem 6-6. Privacy Interests of Social Guests	390
C.	Additions and Alternatives to the Exclusionary Rule		391
	1.	Administrative Remedies	391
		Investigation of the Chicago Police Department	391
		Notes	396
		Problem 6-7. The Mayor's Next Move	398
	2.	Tort Actions and Criminal Prosecutions	399
		Office of the Attorney General, State of Arkansas, Opinion No. 2004-188	400
		Consent Decree, *United States v. City of Los Angeles*	402
		Notes	404
		Problem 6-8. Checking with the Boss	408
		Problem 6-9. Legislative Remedies	409

VII.	*Technology and Privacy*		**411**
A.	Enhancement of the Senses		412
		United States v. Antoine Jones	412
		Timothy Ivory Carpenter v. United States	418
		Notes	425
		Problem 7-1. Prescription Privacy	428
		Problem 7-2. ShotSpotter	428
		Problem 7-3. Eye in the Sky	429
		Problem 7-4. Reversing Time to Solve Crime	430
		Florida v. Joelis Jardines	430
		Notes	434

B. Wiretapping   435
    1. Judicial Limits on Wiretaps   436
            Roy Olmstead v. United States   436
            Notes   437
    2. Statutory Wiretapping Procedures   439
            18 U.S.C. §2511   440
            New Jersey Statutes §2A:156A-4   440
            Problem 7-5. Minimization   441
            Notes   442
            Problem 7-6. Number, Please   447
    3. Bugs on Agents   447
            State v. Michael Thaddeus Goetz   447
            Notes   454
C. Government Access to Databases   455
            People v. Mark Buza   456
            Notes   466
            Problem 7-7. Access to Private DNA Databases   469

VIII. *Interrogations*   *471*

A. Voluntariness of Confessions   472
    1. Physical Abuse and Deprivations   472
            Ed Brown v. Mississippi   473
            Notes   475
    2. Promises and Threats   478
            State v. Jami Del Swanigan   478
            Notes   483
    3. Police Lies   485
            People v. Adrian Thomas   486
            Notes   492
B. *Miranda* Warnings   494
    1. The *Miranda* Revolution   496
            Ernesto Miranda v. Arizona   496
            Louisiana Constitution Art. 1, §13   506
            Massachusetts General Laws, Ch. 276, §33A   506
            Notes   506
    2. The "Custody" Precondition for *Miranda* Warnings   508
            State v. Kevin Franklin Elmarr   508
            Notes   514
            Problem 8-1. Noncustody During Police
                Assistance   515
            Problem 8-2. Blunt Questions   516
    3. The "Interrogation" Precondition for *Miranda* Warnings 516
            Rhode Island v. Thomas Innis   517
            Notes   522
            Problem 8-3. Blurting   523
            Problem 8-4. Public Safety Motivation   524
    4. Form of Warnings   524
            Notes   525

C.   Invocation and Waiver of *Miranda* Rights   526
       Vermont Statutes Tit. 13, §§5234, 5237   526
       Commonwealth v. Clarke   527
       Notes   533
       Problem 8-5. Your Lawyer Is Standing Outside   537
       Problem 8-6. Invocation or Waiver?   538
       Problem 8-7. Capacity to Waive   538
D.   Post-invocation Activity by Police   539
       Charles Globe v. State   539
       Tevin Benjamin v. State   542
       Notes   548
E.   Sixth Amendment Right to Counsel During Investigations 549
       Robert Rubalcado v. State   550
       Notes   555
       Problem 8-8. Christian Burial Speech   557
       Problem 8-9. Cellmate Confession   559
F.   The Impact of Unlawful Interrogations   560
   1.   The Result of Interrogation Violations at the Case Level 560
       Missouri v. Patrice Seibert   560
       Notes   564
       Problem 8-10. Physical Fruits Discovered   566
   2.   Systemwide Impacts *of Miranda's* Warning/Waiver Regime 567
       Saul M. Kassin, Richard A. Leo et al.,
          Police Interviewing and Interrogation: A Self-
          Report Survey of Police Practices and Beliefs   567
       Notes   572
G.   Preventing Unlawful Interrogations: Other Approaches? 574
       Texas Code of Criminal Procedure Art. 38.22   575
       Policy Concerning Electronic Recording of
          Statements   575
       Notes   577
       Problem 8-11. Supplementing *Miranda*   579

IX.   *Identifications*   **581**

A.   Risks of Mistaken Identification   581
       Ralph Norman Haber & Lyn Haber,
          Experiencing, Remembering and
          Reporting Events   582
       Notes   586
B.   Exclusion of Identification Evidence   587
   1.   Exclusion on Right to Counsel Grounds   588
       United States v. Billy Joe Wade   588
       People v. Jonathan Hickman   592
       Notes   595
   2.   Exclusion on Due Process Grounds   597

			State v. Larry Henderson	598
			Problem 9-1. The Pizza Hut Robbery	606
			Notes	607
			Problem 9-2. Photo Lineups	610
	C.	Other Remedies for Improper Identification Procedures		611
		1.	Jury Instructions	611
			State v. Bryan Allen	611
			Notes	617
		2.	Expert Testimony and Other Remedies	618
			Problem 9-3. Help for the Jury	618
			Notes	619
			Problem 9-4. Videorecorded Lineups	621
	D.	Preventing Mistaken Identification		622
			Texas Code of Criminal Procedure	622
			U.S. Department of Justice, Office of Justice Programs	624
			Notes	625
			Problem 9-5. Drafting a Policy	627

X. *Complex Investigations*   *629*

	A.	The Investigative Grand Jury		629
		1.	Grand Jury Secrecy	630
			Federal Rule of Criminal Procedure 6	631
			Colorado Revised Statutes §16-5-204(4)(d)	631
			Notes	631
			Problem 10-1. The View from Trenton	634
		2.	Immunity for Witnesses and the Scope of the Privilege Against Self-Incrimination	635
			Commonwealth v. Patricia Swinehart	636
			Notes	640
		3.	Document Subpoenas	643
			George Tiller v. Michael Corrigan	643
			Ohio Revised Code §2939.12	649
			Arkansas Statutes §16-43-212	649
			Notes	649
			Problem 10-2. Compelling Passwords and Fingerprints	653
	B.	Undercover Investigations		654
			People v. Jessie Johnson	654
			Model Penal Code §2.13	660
			Missouri Revised Statutes §562.066	660
			Cincinnati Police Department, Procedure Manual §12.131 Confidential Informant Management and Control	661
			Notes	661
			Problem 10-3. Outrageous Government Conduct	665

PART TWO
■

EVALUATING CHARGES   667

XI.   *Defense Counsel*   669

   A. When Will Counsel Be Provided?   670
      1. Types of Charges   670
         Clarence Earl Gideon v. Louie Wainwright   672
         Florida Rule of Criminal Procedure 3.111   675
         Vermont Statutes Tit. 13, §§5231, 5201   676
         Notes   676
         Problem 11-1. Advice on Counsel   679
         Problem 11-2. Lawyers and Experts   680
         Problem 11-3. Universal Appointment   680
      2. Type of Proceedings   681
         Alabama Rule of Criminal Procedure 6.1(a)   682
         Missouri Supreme Court Rules 31.01, 31.02   682
         State v. John Arthur Senn, Jr.   682
         Notes   689
         Problem 11-4. Lawyers in Psychiatric
          Examinations   692
   B. Selection and Rejection of Counsel   692
         State v. Joseph Spencer   693
         Notes   698
         Problem 11-5. Competence to Stand Trial,
          Competence to Waive Counsel   702
   C. Adequacy of Counsel   703
         Charles Strickland v. David Washington   703
         Blaine Lafler v. Anthony Cooper   710
         Notes   715
         Problem 11-6. *Cronic* Errors   718
         American Bar Association, Criminal Justice
          Standards for the Defense Function   719
         Rule 33, Court of Common Pleas, Cuyahoga
          County, Ohio   721
         Notes   721
         Problem 11-7. More Objective Competence
          Standards   723
   D. Systems for Providing Counsel   723
         Donald J. Farole & Lynn Langton,
          County-Based and Local Public Defender
          Offices, 2007   724
         State v. Leonard Peart   726
         Kimberly Hurrell-Harring v. State   729
         American Bar Association, Model Rule of
          Professional Conduct 1.5(d)   733
         Notes   733

		Problem 11-8. Rights of Counsel	737
		Problem 11-9. Flat Fees for Service	738
		Problem 11-10. The Neighborhood Defender	739
E.	The Ethics of Defending Criminals		740
		Speeches of Lord Erskine	740
		John Dos Passos, The American Lawyer: As He Was—As He Is—As He Can Be	740
		American Bar Association and Association of American Law Schools, Professional Responsibility: Report of the Joint Conference (1958)	741
		John Kaplan, Defending Guilty People	743
		Letter from William Townsend	744
		Notes	744

XII.   *Pretrial Release and Detention*   747

A.	Pretrial Release		748
	1.	Standard Release Practices	748
		American Bar Association: Pretrial Release Standards	749
		Alabama Rules of Criminal Procedure 7.2, 7.3	750
		Thomas H. Cohen & Brian A. Reaves, Pretrial Release of Felony Defendants in State Courts	751
		Notes	753
		Problem 12-1. Automatic Delay	756
	2.	Bail Reform Efforts	757
		Vera Institute of Justice, Fair Treatment for the Indigent: The Manhattan Bail Project	757
		Megan Stevenson & Sandra G. Mayson, Pretrial Detention and Bail, 3 Reforming Criminal Justice: Pretrial and Trial Processes 21-47	761
		Notes	765
B.	Pretrial Detention		768
		U.S. Constitution Amendment VIII	769
		Tennessee Constitution Art. I, §§15, 16	769
		United States v. Anthony Salerno	769
		New Mexico Constitution Art. II, §13	776
		Virginia Code §19.2-120	776
		Problem 12-2. The Next Danger	777
		Notes	778

XIII.   *Charging*   783

A.	Individual Prosecutor Discretion Not to Charge		784
		Revised Code of Washington §9.94a.411(1)	784
		Notes	785
		Problem 13-1. Three Variations on a Theme	788
		Problem 13-2. Passing a School Bus	790

B. Policies to Encourage or Mandate Charges 790
      Florida Statutes §741.2901 791
      Wisconsin Statutes §968.075 792
      Italian Constitution Art. 112 792
      German Code of Criminal Procedure 152(2) 792
      West Virginia Code §7-4-1 792
      The Question on the Application of
         Peter Dennis v. DPP 793
      Notes 796
C. Policies to Discourage Charges 799
      District Attorney's Office, City of Philadelphia 799
      Florida State Attorney's Office, Fourth Judicial
         Circuit, Homicide Policies and Procedures 800
      Principles of Federal Prosecution of Business
         Organizations 803
      Notes 806
D. Diversion of Charges 808
      Montana Code §46-16-130 809
      Kitsap County Prosecuting Attorney Mission
         Statement and Standards and Guidelines 810
      Notes 811
      Problem 13-3. Diversion Policies and
         Exceptions 813
E. Selection Among Charges 814
      U.S. Department of Justice, Principles of Federal
         Prosecution 814
      Minnesota Statutes §388.051 815
      People v. Jaleh Wilkinson 815
      Notes 819
      Problem 13-4. Available Charges 822
F. Selection of System 822
   1. Juvenile versus Adult Justice System 823
         Howard N. Snyder, Melissa Sickmund & Eileen
            Poe-Yamagata, Juvenile Transfers to Criminal
            Court in the 1990s: Lessons Learned from
            Four Studies 823
         State v. Jonas Dixon 825
         Notes 829
   2. Federal versus State Justice System 831
         Alberto R. Gonzales v. Angel Mcclary Raich 832
         Problem 13-5. Federal Day 836
   3. Crime Committed on Tribal Lands 836
         James D. Diamond, Practicing Indian Law in
            Federal, State, and Tribal Criminal
            Courts: An Update About Recent Expansion
            of Criminal Jurisdiction over Non-Indians 836
G. Victim Input into Charging Decisions 839
      Wisconsin Statutes §968.02 839

		Joseph Kennedy, Private Financing of Criminal Prosecutions and the Differing Protections of Liberty and Equality in the Criminal Justice System	839
		Notes	841
		Problem 13-6. Involved Citizens	843
H.	Selective Prosecution		844
		United States v. Christopher Armstrong	844
		Notes	849
I.	Pretrial Screening		852
		New York Constitution Art. I, §6	853
		Illinois Annotated Statutes Ch. 725, Para. 5/111-2	853
		Commonwealth v. Khari Wilcox	853
		Notes	856

XIV. *Jeopardy and Joinder* — *861*

A.	Double Jeopardy		861
	1.	Multiple Sovereigns	862
		Alfonse Bartkus v. Illinois	863
		U.S. Attorneys' Manual §9-2.031, Dual Prosecution and Successive Prosecution Policy (*Petite* Policy)	868
		New Jersey Statutes §2C:1-11	870
		Ohio Revised Code §2925.50	871
		Notes	871
		Problem 14-1. When Do Successive Prosecutions Make Sense?	874
	2.	"Same Offence"	874
		Robert Taylor v. Commonwealth	875
		People v. Melissa Nutt	878
		New York Criminal Procedure Law §40.20	882
		Notes	883
		Problem 14.2. Multiplicity	887
	3.	Collateral Estoppel	888
		Ex parte Philip Taylor	888
		Notes	893
B.	Joinder		894
	1.	Discretionary Joinder and Severance of Offenses	895
		Federal Rule of Criminal Procedure 8(a)	895
		Federal Rule of Criminal Procedure 13	895
		Federal Rule of Criminal Procedure 14	896
		Vermont Rule of Criminal Procedure 8(a)	896
		Vermont Rule of Criminal Procedure 14	896
		Damian Long v. United States	897
		Notes	903
		Problem 14-3. Compulsory Joinder	905
		Problem 14-4. Protective Order	906

2. Joint Trials of Defendants   907
        Federal Rule of Criminal Procedure 8(b)   907
        Vermont Rule of Criminal Procedure 8(b)   908
        Vermont Rule of Criminal Procedure 14(b)(2)   908
        Notes   910
        Problem 14-5. Antagonistic Brothers   910

PART THREE
■
RESOLVING GUILT AND INNOCENCE   913

XV. *Discovery and Speedy Trial*   915

A. Discovery   915
    1. Prosecution Disclosure of Exculpatory Information   916
            People v. Alan Beaman   917
            Utah Criminal Procedure Rule 16   923
            Notes   924
            Problem 15.1. Preserving Evidence   928
            American Bar Association, Model Rule of
                Professional Conduct 3.8   929
            U.S. Department of Justice, Memorandum for
                Department Prosecutors   929
            Notes   933
    2. Prosecution Disclosure of Inculpatory Information   934
            Problem 15-2. Exchanging Words   935
            South Carolina Rule of Criminal
                Procedure 5(A)   935
            North Carolina General Statutes §15a-903   936
            Notes   938
    3. Defense Disclosures   941
            Pennsylvania Rule of Criminal
                Procedure 573(C)   941
            Pennsylvania Rule of Criminal
                Procedure 567(A)   942
            Commonwealth v. Patrick Durham   942
            Notes   945
    4. Discovery Ethics   946
            Standing Committee on Professional
                Responsibility and Conduct, State Bar of
                California, California Formal Ethics
                Opinion 1984-76   947
            North Carolina State Bar, Receipt of Evidence
                of Crime by Lawyer for Defendant, Ethics
                Opinion 221   948
            Notes   950
            Problem 15-3. Defense Attorney as Repository   951

B.	Speedy Trial Preparation		952
	1.	Pre-Accusation Delay	953
		New York Criminal Procedure Law §30.10	953
		Commonwealth v. Stephen Scher	954
		Notes	958
		Problem 15-4. Child Victims	960
	2.	Constitutional Protections for Speedy Trial After Accusation	961
		Vermont v. Michael Brillon	962
		Notes	967
	3.	Statutory Protections for Speedy Trial After Accusation	969
		California Penal Code §1382	970
		California Penal Code §1387	971
		Problem 15-5. The Fierce Urgency of Now	971
		18 U.S.C. §3161	973
		18 U.S.C. §3162	974
		Notes	974
		Problem 15-6. Voluminous Discovery	976

XVI. *Pleas and Bargains* — 979

A.	Bargain About What?		980
		Federal Rule of Criminal Procedure 11(a), (c)	980
		North Carolina Defender Manual	981
		State v. Ahmad Bey	982
		Notes	986
		Problem 16-1. Waiving the Right to Appeal a Sentence	989
B.	Validity of Guilty Pleas		990
	1.	Lack of Knowledge	990
		Federal Rule of Criminal Procedure 11(b)	991
		Missouri v. Galin Frye	991
		Notes	998
		Problem 16-2. Direct and Collateral Effects	1001
		Problem 16-3. Pre-Plea Discovery	1002
	2.	Involuntary Pleas	1002
		a. Large Plea Discounts	1003
		Robert Brady v. United States	1003
		Notes	1005
		b. Judicial Overinvolvement	1007
		State v. Landour Bouie	1007
		Notes	1012
		c. *Alford* Pleas: Voluntariness and Factual Basis	1014
		Federal Rule of Criminal Procedure 11(b)	1015
		State v. Edwin Urbina	1015
		Notes	1020
C.	Categorical Restrictions on Bargaining		1022
	1.	Legislative Limits	1022
		California Penal Code §1192.7	1022

New York Criminal Procedure Law §220.10   1024
Revised Code of Washington §§9.94a.450,
    9.94a.460   1024
Notes   1025

2. Judicial Rules   1026
Problem 16-4: Rejecting Plea Bargains   1027
Notes   1029

3. Prosecutorial Plea Negotiation Guidelines   1030
U.S. Department of Justice, Principles of
    Federal Prosecution   1031
Notes   1033
U.S. Sentencing Guidelines §§6b1.2, 6b1.4
    (Policy Statements)   1035
Prosecutors' Handbook on Sentencing
    Guidelines ("The Redbook")   1036
Charging and Plea Decisions ("Reno
    Bluesheet")   1037
Notes   1038
State v. Christopher Brimage   1040
Problem 16-5. Statewide Bargaining
    Guidelines   1044
Problem 16-6. Sharkfest   1045
Notes   1046

4. Victim Consultation   1047
Maine Revised Statutes Tit. 15, §812; Tit. 17-A,
    §§1172, 1173   1047
State v. Patrick William Casey   1048
Notes   1052

D. Alternatives to Plea Bargaining   1053
Albert Alschuler, Implementing the Criminal
    Defendant's Right to Trial: Alternatives
    to the Plea Bargaining System   1053
Frank Easterbrook, Plea Bargaining As
    Compromise   1055
Ronald Wright & Marc Miller, The Screening/
    Bargaining Tradeoff   1057
Notes   1063

XVII. *Decisionmakers at Trial*   *1067*

A. Judge or Jury?   1068
Jean-Baptiste Bado v. United States   1068
Maryland Courts and Judicial Proceedings
    Code §12-401   1075
Notes   1075
Problem 17-1. Judge Shopping and Jury Trial
    Waivers   1079

		B.	Selection of Jurors	1080
		1.	Voir Dire	1081
			Keith Filmore v. State	1083
			Notes	1085
			Problem 17-2. Defendant Bias and Voir Dire	1087
		2.	Dismissal for Cause	1088
			Texas Code of Criminal Procedure Art. 35.16	1088
			State v. Reche Smith	1089
			Notes	1092
		3.	Peremptory Challenges	1093
			James Batson v. Kentucky	1094
			People v. Rene Gutierrez, Jr.	1100
			Washington General Rule 37, Jury Selection	1108
			Notes	1109
			Problem 17-3. The Reach of *Batson*	1112
	C.	Jury Deliberations and Verdicts		1113
			State v. Ronald Bean	1113
			Notes	1116
			Problem 17-4. Someone Is Not Talking or Someone Is Not Listening	1123
			Problem 17-5. Non-Unanimous Verdicts	1124
			Problem 17-6. Jury Nullification and Social Justice	1125
	D.	The Public as Decisionmaker		1126
			State v. Manuel Turrietta	1126
			Notes	1132
			Problem 17-7. Measures for Justice	1135

XVIII.	*Witnesses and Proof*			*1137*
	A.	Confrontation of Witnesses		1138
		1.	The Value of Confrontation	1138
			Israel Romero v. State	1139
			Désiré Doorson v. Netherlands	1143
			Notes	1148
			Problem 18-1. Child Testimony	1150
		2.	Out-of-Court Statements by Unavailable Witnesses	1151
			Michael Crawford v. Washington	1151
			Notes	1158
		3.	Statements by Co-Defendants	1160
			Commonwealth v. John Bacigalupo	1160
			Notes	1164
	B.	Self-Incrimination Privilege at Trial		1167
			Eddie Dean Griffin v. California	1168
			Kevin Sean Murray v. United Kingdom	1171
			Notes	1177
			Problem 18-2. Telling the Jury	1181
			Problem 18-3. Pre-Arrest Silence	1182

C. Ethics and Lies at Trial   1183
        People v. Derek Andrades   1183
        Notes   1187
        Problem 18-4. The Do-Not-Call List   1188
D. Burden of Proof   1189
        State v. Denise Frei   1189
        Notes   1194
        Problem 18-5. Words and Numbers   1199
        Problem 18-6. A Doubt with a Reason   1199
        Problem 18-7. Presumption in the Fire   1200

PART FOUR

■

MEASURING PUNISHMENT AND REASSESSING GUILT   1203

XIX. *Sentencing*   *1205*
        Code of Hammurabi   1205
A. Who Sentences?   1206
    1. Indeterminate Sentencing   1206
        Samuel Williams v. New York   1207
        Notes   1209
    2. Legislative Sentencing   1212
        U.S. Sentencing Commission, Mandatory
            Minimum Penalties in the Federal Criminal
            Justice System   1212
        Problem 19-1. The Golf Club Odyssey   1214
        Notes   1215
    3. Sentencing Commissions   1218
        Dale Parent, Structuring Criminal Sentencing   1218
        Richard S. Frase, State Sentencing
            Guidelines: Diversity, Consensus, and
            Unresolved Policy Issues   1223
        Notes   1226
B. New Information About the Offender and the Victim   1228
    1. Offender Information   1229
        a. Criminal History   1229
            Washington State Sentencing Guidelines   1229
            Federal Rules of Criminal Procedure, Rule 32   1230
            Notes   1231
            Problem 19-2. Personal History and Prospects   1233
        b. Cooperation in Other Investigations   1235
            Taggart Parrish v. State   1235
            U.S. Sentencing Guidelines §5k1.1   1239
            Notes   1239

        2.   New Information About the Victim and the Community   1240
                  Michigan Constitution Article I, §24   1241
                  Notes   1241
                  Problem 19-3. The Community as Victim   1243
                  Problem 19-4. Sentencing Hearings, Guilty
                       Plea Hearings   1244
   C.   Revisiting Points in the Criminal Process   1245
        1.   Revisiting Investigations   1245
                  People v. Deon Lamont Claypool   1246
                  Notes   1249
                  Problem 19-5. Learning a Lesson   1250
                  Problem 19-6. Reversing the Exclusion   1250
        2.   Revisiting Charging Decisions: Relevant Conduct   1250
                  U.S. Sentencing Guidelines §1B1.3(a)   1251
                  Florida Rule of Criminal
                       Procedure 3.701(d)(11)   1252
                  State v. Douglas McAlpin   1252
                  Notes   1255
        3.   Revisiting Proof at Trial   1257
                  Ralph Blakely v. Washington   1258
                  Notes   1267
        4.   Revisiting Jury Verdicts and Guilty Pleas   1269
                  U.S. Sentencing Guidelines §3E1.1   1269
                  Notes   1269
                  Problem 19-7. Trial Penalty or
                       Reward for Plea?   1272
   D.   Race and Sentencing   1272
        1.   Race and the Victims of Crime   1273
                  Warren Mccleskey v. Ralph Kemp   1274
                  Notes   1280
        2.   Race and Discretionary Decisions Affecting Punishment   1281
                  Freddie Stephens v. State   1282
                  Notes   1287
                  Problem 19-8. The Crack-Powder Differential   1289

XX.   *Appeals*   *1291*

   A.   Who Appeals?   1291
        1.   Right to Appeal   1291
                  Arkansas Statutes §16-91-101   1292
                  Arkansas Rule of Criminal Procedure 24.3(b)   1292
                  California Penal Code §1237.5   1292
                  California Rule of Court 8.304(b)(4)   1292
                  Notes   1292
        2.   Appeals by Indigent Defendants   1294
                  Bryan Mosley v. State   1294
                  Notes   1297
        3.   Interlocutory Appeals   1298
                  Delaware Code Tit. 10, §§9902, 9903   1299
                  State v. Matthew Medrano   1300
                  Notes   1302

	B.	Appellate Review of Factual Findings	1304
		Kelvin Brooks v. State	1305
		Notes	1309
		Problem 20-1. Edited Trials	1310
	C.	Harmless Error	1310
		Federal Rule of Criminal Procedure 52	1312
		Tennessee Rule of Appellate Procedure 36(b)	1312
		Kentel Weaver v. Massachusetts	1313
		Notes	1320
		Problem 20-2. Preserving Error	1322
	D.	Retroactivity	1323
		George Membres v. State	1323
		Notes	1329

Table of Cases	*1333*
Index	*1353*

Preface

The American criminal justice system is huge, complex, and varied. Federal, state, and local governments together spend over $200 billion each year on policing, prosecution, trial, and punishment. About 2.3 million persons are incarcerated in federal and state prisons, and in state and local jails, in the United States at any one time. Another 4.5 million are on probation or parole.

There are more than 18,000 separate police agencies in the United States, with around 800,000 sworn officers. There are even more "private police" and security agents than sworn officers. In an average year, these officers and agents make more than 10 million arrests.

Criminal cases are prosecuted by more than 2,400 prosecutors' offices, employing about 35,000 attorneys and more than 50,000 additional staff. They obtain about 1 million felony convictions every year, and many more misdemeanor convictions. Thousands of attorneys work as public defenders or as defense counsel in private practice. Thousands of judges hear criminal cases in trial and appellate courts. Lawyers often find their first jobs in the criminal justice system. Some stay for life.

Criminal procedure is the body of law—drawn from many sources—that governs this collection of systems. The law of criminal procedure attempts to direct the actions of police officers, prosecutors, defense attorneys, judges, and other government officials. The law prescribes the way the government may interact with residents, suspects, defendants, convicted offenders, and victims.

The federal government, every state government, and many local governments operate criminal justice systems. Although the federal system is one of the largest systems standing alone, the state and local systems collectively are much larger. Virtually all misdemeanors are processed in state courts, along with almost 95 percent of all felony convictions. Criminal justice in the United States is overwhelmingly a state and local function.

There is no single criminal procedure: Each system follows its own set of rules, controlled to different degrees by outside authorities. Procedural rules come from many sources, including constitutions, legislatures, courts, and executive branch agencies. Because the issues of criminal procedure are common and accessible—unlike, say, antitrust or international law—a wealth of less formal constraints, including community views and the media, also shape procedure. We have titled this casebook "Criminal Procedures" to reflect these multiple layers and sources of law.

The Approach in This Casebook

A criminal procedure casebook must impose some order on the morass of cases, rules, and practices that characterize criminal justice systems. One accepted way to make this material accessible for newcomers is to focus on the role of one important institution, the United States Supreme Court, and on one important source of law, the United States Constitution.

Since the days of the Warren Court, starting in 1953, the Supreme Court has influenced criminal justice systems in profound ways. It made the Bill of Rights in the federal Constitution a shaping force for every criminal justice system. The Warren Court made the story of criminal procedure, told from the point of view of the Supreme Court, compelling. The main topics of controversy were police practices: stops, searches, and interrogations. Other decisions of the Court created a basic framework for providing defendants with counsel and for conducting criminal trials. For years, the focus on the Supreme Court's constitutional rulings guided students through the questions that most concerned judges and lawyers.

But the story of this one institution has offered less explanatory power over time. Traditional issues on the Court's constitutional criminal procedure docket now occupy less of the attention of judges, attorneys, defendants, victims, and others concerned with criminal justice. Most criminal defendants do not go to trial. Many have no complaints about illegal searches or coerced confessions. These defendants and their lawyers care about pretrial detention, the charges filed, the plea agreements they can reach with the prosecutor, and their sentences.

The central questions have shifted in light of changes in the workload, politics, funding, and structure of criminal justice institutions. For example, the question of *whether* indigent defendants will get counsel has become a question of *what* counsel they will get. New crime-fighting strategies—such as community policing and curfews—advances in technology, and changes in the political and social order raise new questions and place old questions in a new light. For judges, sentencing questions in particular have attained higher priority: Determining the proper sentence in some systems now requires more time from court personnel than resolution of guilt or innocence.

The U.S. Supreme Court leaves important dimensions of most procedural issues unresolved and thus leaves other institutions free to innovate; they have done so. The issues of current importance in criminal procedure are being shaped in multiple institutions, including state courts, legislatures, and executive branch agencies.

This book adopts a panoramic view of criminal procedure, emphasizing the interaction among, and variety within, criminal justice systems. In our opinion, students in an upper-level course such as criminal procedure can and should move well beyond the skills of case synthesis and develop the ability to appreciate the role of multiple institutions. Our materials emphasize the following themes and objectives:

- *Procedural variety.* In each area we present competing rules from the federal and state systems. We also occasionally examine procedures from earlier times or from non-U.S. systems. Reviewing different possible procedural rules encourages critical analysis and helps identify the assumptions and judgments made in the design of each criminal system.
- *Materials from multiple institutions.* In addition to leading U.S. Supreme Court cases, we make extensive use of state high court cases, statutes, rules of procedure, and police and prosecutorial policies, and we encourage readers to consider the interactions among multiple institutions. Examining the efforts of different institutions to achieve similar goals highlights the reality of procedural innovation and reform.
- *Street-level federalism.* Federal law, typically in the form of constitutional decisions by the U.S. Supreme Court, still plays an important role in guiding the investigation and prosecution of high-volume street crimes. The impact of abstract constitutional doctrine on daily police actions in the real world raises important theoretical questions about federal-state relations and interactions among governmental institutions.
- *Political context.* Materials trace the political environment surrounding different institutions and issues. We explore the impact on procedural rules of public concerns such as drug trafficking, domestic abuse, race and wealth disparities, and treatment of crime victims. Funding decisions with regard to criminal justice systems offer a window into the political setting. We devote the most attention to the issues arising in the largest number of cases, and to those issues now shaping criminal justice.
- *Impact of procedures.* We consider the effects that different procedures have on law enforcers, lawyers, courts, communities, defendants, and victims. We emphasize primary materials but include social science studies as well, especially when they have been the basis for procedural reform. This experimental perspective keeps in mind the managerial needs of criminal justice: Any legal rule must apply to multitudes of defendants in overcrowded systems.

By studying the various ways in which state and local systems have answered crucial procedural questions, students become aware of a broader range of policy alternatives. They form a more complete picture of the interactive workings of the criminal justice system. Our goal in emphasizing the variety within criminal procedure is to produce lawyers who know both the current law and the way to shape better law down the road.

Conceptual Anchors

Our emphasis on variety does not mean that we will survey the practices of all 50 states on each issue; this casebook is not a treatise. Rather, the materials highlight the majority and minority views on each topic, as well as the federal view. The major positions on a topic are usually summarized in the first note following the principal materials. Truly distinctive answers to problems are mentioned occasionally as a point of comparison with the leading approach and to illuminate alternatives, but we always highlight the uniqueness of the position.

The book addresses a wide range of U.S. Supreme Court precedents, including the recognized core of essential cases and many of the most recent important decisions. State supreme court decisions summarizing and critiquing a U.S. Supreme Court decision, or a line of cases, represent effective teaching tools since the state cases tend to highlight the competing doctrinal positions. State supreme court opinions by and large show less interest in the positions of individual justices than do U.S. Supreme Court decisions and devote less attention to questions about consistency with past decisions. State supreme court opinions often provide provocative settings that show how principles operate in practice. They tend to present succinctly the textual and institutional arguments favoring a procedural requirement, the values furthered by the rules, and their likely effects on police, suspects, and communities.

Studying a variety of possible answers to important procedural questions has an unexpected effect: through criticism and contrast, students finish with a firmer grasp of federal constitutional criminal procedure than they would obtain through study of federal law alone. We believe students emerge from this book better able to represent clients and to pass bar examinations. Short "problems" throughout the book also enable readers to apply and integrate basic concepts.

The state cases appearing in this book take every conceivable position with respect to Supreme Court precedent, ranging from total agreement to complete rejection, and encompassing subtle variations in interpretation and emphasis. For a large number of state cases that focus on state constitutional or statutory questions, the position of the U.S. Supreme Court is simply irrelevant. The case selection does not favor decisions merely because they reject the U.S. Supreme Court view—the "new federalism" approach. These materials are not a battle cry for state court independence; they simply reflect the vibrancy of state supreme courts and state law.

The Sixth Edition

The sixth edition of this book marks the arrival of two new editors: Jenia Turner and Kay Levine. With her doctoral training in Socio-Legal Studies and her balanced experience as a prosecutor and a defense attorney in state court, Professor Levine sharpens the focus of the book on the real-world operation of courtroom actors in high-volume state systems. With her background in international criminal tribunals and comparative criminal procedure, Professor Turner strengthens the comparisons between court systems in the U.S. and those around the world.

The new edition responds to changes in the field, incorporating emerging themes and major issues. Such themes and issues—the turning points in the law—result at least as often from dramatic events outside the courtroom as from blockbuster judicial decisions. Such dramatic "drivers" of change in criminal procedure over the years since the first edition of this book appeared include increasing attention to issues of race. Public and institutional debate about so-called DWB (driving while black) stops on American highways raise these questions in a setting that many students find familiar. Highly publicized wrongful convictions have reframed legal debates about eyewitness identification procedures and about enforcement of prosecutor discovery obligations. Changing public attitudes about criminal enforcement of marijuana laws have prompted some fascinating prosecutor office policies on declinations in those cases. And a growing awareness of the heavy use of prison in the United States, captured under the label "mass incarceration," calls for a rethinking of many procedural rules.

The sixth edition also explores police–community relations and the use of force by police that fuel protests after each new and tragic incident that plays out on YouTube. Such cases provoke national debate over the use of force, police rules and practices, the transfer of military equipment and practices to local police, the dramatic increase in the use of body-worn cameras by police, and the pervasive impact of cell phones to record police–citizen interactions.

We have made changes in every chapter. Our attention to developments in the states provides a large pool of new cases, statutes, and rules, keeping the discussion anchored to current reality in criminal justice. For example, many of the cases in this book were decided after 2010. Recent federal developments also find their place in these pages. Significant U.S. Supreme Court cases added to this edition include Birchfield v. North Dakota, Riley v. California, Utah v. Strieff, Carpenter v. United States, Perry v. New Hampshire, Gonzales v. Raich, McCoy v. Louisiana, Foster v. Chatman, Peña-Rodriguez v. Colorado, and Weaver v. Massachusetts.

The overall goal of these changes has been to produce a book that remains fresh and engaging while retaining those materials that work especially well in the classroom.

Procedure, Politics, and Reform

Students who appreciate the handful of basic political struggles that time and again shape procedural debates will be better able to direct changes in the system and to influence decisions in close cases. The struggles center on questions such as these: What are the purposes of the criminal justice system? In particular, what is the relevance of criminal law and procedure to the social goals of crime control and prevention? How does the theory and practice of federalism inform criminal justice theory and practice? Can we trust the police? How vital is the adversary system and the role of defense counsel to the success of that system? Are we comfortable with the broad discretion exercised on a daily basis by police and prosecutors? How important is it to treat suspects similarly? Should we explicitly consider the costs of procedures?

The priorities inherent in this textbook suggest a return to the study of criminal procedure as a genuine procedure course, not a course in constitutional adjudication. The constitutional component remains an indispensable part of the course but is not the sum total of criminal procedure.

The return to a fuller conception of criminal procedure offers enormous opportunities to those who study the system and to those who will soon participate in its operation and evolution. When many institutions are able to shape a legal system, there are many opportunities for change. We hope each student will leave this course ready to create procedures more sound than those that exist today.

Marc Miller
Ron Wright
Jenia Turner
Kay Levine

Tucson, Arizona
Winston-Salem, North Carolina
Dallas, Texas
Atlanta, Georgia
January 2019

Acknowledgments

Creating a new edition of this book powerfully reminded us of how communities make work more fun and make final products better. Our debts extend to our friends and colleagues, our institutions, our students, our teachers, and our families.

Some of the teachers who use this book have suggested improvements over the years. They include Raquel Aldana, Tom Alongi, Laura Appleman, Valena Beety, Doug Berman, Will Berry, Stephanos Bibas, Frank Bowman, Irus Braverman, Darryl Brown, Jenny Carroll, Steve Chanenson, Kami Chavis, Jack Chin, Jennifer Collins, Phyllis Crocker, Deborah Denno, Steve Easton, Nancy Gertner, Aya Gruber, Rachel Harmon, Jeanne Hauch, Thaddeus Hoffmeister, Maureen Howard, Jim Jacobs, Sam Kamin, Elizabeth Ludwin King, Tamara Lave, Margaret Lewis, Wayne Logan, Dan Markel, William Marsh, Tracey Meares, Alan Michaels, Tommy Miller, Janet Moore, Kenneth Nunn, Mark Rabil, Song Richardson, Anna Roberts, Jenny Roberts, Siera Russell, Jason Sabio, Laurie Serafino, Jonathan Simon, Shandrea Solomon, Kate Stith, Paul Stokstad, Andrew Taslitz, Sandra Guerra Thompson, Dean Valore, Ozan Varol, Robert Wagner, Jonathan Witmer-Rich, David Yellen, Tung Yin, and Stewart Young. It is a great joy for us as editors to learn from them what is happening in classrooms all over the world.

Scholars who provided wise counsel on earlier editions, which is still very evident in the revised volume, include Albert Alschuler, Akhil Amar, Barbara Babcock, Adolph Dean, Nora Demleitner, George Fisher, Dan Freed, Mark Hall, Mark Harris, Lenese Herbert, Andrew Kull, Gerard Lynch, William Mayton, David Orentlicher, Leonard Orland, Alan Palmiter, Anne Poulin, Aaron Rappaport, Sadiq Reza, Natsu Saito, Stephen Schulhofer, Charles Shanor, Rick Singer, Michael Smith, Bert Westbrook, and Deborah Young. We have also learned from two extensive published reviews of this book. See Robert Weisberg, A New Legal Realism for Criminal

Procedure, 49 Buff. L. Rev. 909 (2001), and Stephanos Bibas, The Real-World Shift in Criminal Procedure, 93 J. Crim. L. & Criminology 789 (2003).

We have all been graced with great teachers, many of whom became friends. We can trace in these pages the influence of Norval Morris, Frank Zimring, Edward Levi, Richard Epstein, Philip Kurland, David Currie, James Boyd White, Kate Stith, Owen Fiss, Robert Burt, Peter Schuck, Steven Duke, Sandy Kadish, Chuck Weisselberg, and Judges Frank Johnson and John Godbold.

Over the years we have worked on this project with many fine students whose energy renewed our own. They include Jeff Allcorn, Khashayar Attaran, Tammie Banko, Jason Brierley, Jordan Cassino, Lenae Davis, Chris Edwards, Nora Fakhri, Abed Fakhoury, Nicola Hines, Brian Hingston, Katie Hughes, Tori Kepes, Sarah Lee, Alison Lester, Elizabeth Lyons, Amanda Parker, Rachel Shields, Emily Thornton, and Tom Watkins. Exceptional research help on earlier editions came from Roger Abramson, Nathan Adams, Liz Asplund, Amber Byers, Wes Camden, Ryan Carter, Pablo Clarke, Perry Coumas, Don Donelson, Ben Durie, Joseph Ezzo, Heather Gaw, Jennifer Gibbons, Kaitlyn Girard, Elizabeth Goodwin, Whitney Hendrix, Christopher Lewis, Antoine Marshall, Shawn Mihill, Sean Monaghan, Tyronia Morrison, Sophia Pappalardo, Emily Parish, Rachel Raimondi, Russ Rotondi, Alice Shanlever, Matt Silverstein, Brad Simon, Sarah Spangenburg, Rebecca Stahl, Kyle Stocks, Daniel Terner, Paige Tucker, Aaron Vodicka, and Hannah Wannall.

We have made heavy demands on our libraries and technology experts, and owe thanks to Marcia Baker, Tim Gallina, Terry Gordon, Sarah Gotschall, Will Haines, Elizabeth Johnson, Deborah Keene, Tom Kimbrough, Lori Levy, William Morse, Stuart Myerberg, Holliday Osborne, John Perkins, and Erika Wayne. Steve Turner, the former director of the Wilsonville, Oregon, public library, helped us achieve greater clarity throughout the book. Kristie Gallardo, Barbara Lopez, Beverly Marshall, Radine Robinson, Pat Starkey, Sharon Thompson, Laura Tysinger, and Marissa White provided timely administrative support for this edition and earlier ones: It is a miracle they did not ask to work with faculty other than us.

We also have debts to many of the hard-working and visionary lawyers and judges in the criminal justice system. A few who provided special assistance are Russell Hauge of the Kitsap County Prosecutor's Office in Washington; Peter Gilchrist, Bart Menser, and Bruce Lillie of the District Attorney's Office in Mecklenburg County, North Carolina; Ed Rheinheimer of the County Attorney's Office in Cochise County, Arizona; John Chisholm of the Milwaukee County District Attorney's Office; Ben David of the District Attorney's Office in New Hanover County, North Carolina; Barbara LaWall and Amelia Craig Cramer of the County Attorney's Office in Pima County, Arizona; Harry Connick and Tim McElroy of the District Attorney's office in New Orleans; Kim Foxx, State's Attorney for Cook County, Illinois; Karen Friedman-Agnifilo of the District Attorney's Office in New York County, New York; Eric Gonzalez and Meg Reiss of the District Attorney's Office in Kings County, New York; Dan Satterberg, the Prosecuting Attorney in King County, Washington; Melissa Nelson, the State Attorney in Jacksonville, Florida; Andrew Warren, the State Attorney in Tampa, Florida; Numa Bertel of the Orleans Indigent Defender Program; Judge Camille Buras of the District Court in New Orleans; Lawson Lamar and William Vose of the State Attorney's office in Orange County, Florida; Patricia Jessamy of the State's Attorney's office in Baltimore, Maryland; and Chief Judge James Carr of the U.S. District Court for the Northern District of Ohio. We have also gained insight from our conversations with skilled reporters and criminal justice reformers, including Kevin Corcoran and Andrew Pantazi.

Family debts for so consuming a project are hard to recognize in print, and even harder to repay in life. Our spouses, children, parents, siblings, and grand-children have reminded us at every turn about the value of curiosity, skepticism, and lively questions for all students of this world. This book sits between covers only because of their daily encouragement and advice.

———

Albert Alschuler, Implementing the Criminal Defendant's Right to Trial: Alternatives to the Plea Bargaining System, 50 U. Chi. L. Rev. 931 (1983). Copyright © 1983 by the University of Chicago Law Review. Reprinted with permission.

American Bar Association, ABA Standards for Criminal Justice, Third Edition: Pretrial Release. Copyright © 2007 American Bar Association. Reprinted with permission of the American Bar Association.

American Bar Association, Criminal Justice Standards for the Defense Function, Fourth Edition. Copyright © 2015 American Bar Association. Reprinted with permission of the American Bar Association.

James D. Diamond, Practicing Indian Law in Federal, State, and Tribal Criminal Courts: An Update About Recent Expansion Of Criminal Jurisdiction Over Non-Indians, 32 Criminal Justice 8 (Winter 2018). Copyright © 2018 by the American Bar Association. Reprinted with permission. All rights reserved. This information or any or portion thereof may not be copied or disseminated in any form or by any means or stored in an electronic database or retrieval system without the express written consent of the American Bar Association.

Frank Easterbrook, Plea Bargaining as Compromise, 101 Yale L.J. 1969 (1992). Copyright © 1992 by The Yale Law Journal Company. Reprinted by permission of The Yale Law Journal Company and Fred B. Rothman & Company.

Richard S. Frase, State Sentencing Guidelines: Diversity, Consensus, and Unresolved Policy Issues, 105 Colum. L. Rev. 1190 (2005). Copyright © 2005 by the author. Reprinted with permission.

John Griffiths, Ideology in Criminal Procedure, or a Third "Model" of the Criminal Process, 79 Yale L.J. 359 (1970). Copyright © 1970 by The Yale Law Journal Company. Reprinted by permission of The Yale Law Journal Company and Fred B. Rothman & Company.

Ralph Norman Haber & Lyn Haber, Experiencing, Remembering and Reporting Events, 6 Psychol. Pub. Pol'y & L. 1057-1091 (2000). Copyright © 2000 by the American Psychological Association. Reprinted with permission of American Psychological Association via Copyright Clearance Center.

John Kaplan, Defending Guilty People, 7 U. Bridgeport L. Rev. 223 (1986). Copyright © 1986 by the University of Bridgeport Law Review Association. Reprinted by permission of the Quinnipiac Law Review.

Saul M. Kassin, Richard A. Leo, et al. Police Interviewing and Interrogation: A Self-Report Survey of Police Practices and Beliefs, 31 Law and Human Behavior 381 (2007). Copyright © 2007 by the American Psychological Association. Reprinted with permission of American Psychological Association via Copyright Clearance Center.

Joseph Kennedy, Private Financing of Criminal Prosecutions and the Differing Protections of Liberty and Equality in the Criminal Justice System, 24 Hastings Constitutional Law Quarterly 665 (1997). Reprinted with permission from UC Hastings College of the Law and the author.

Tracey L. Meares, Norms, Legitimacy, and Law Enforcement, 79 Or. L. Rev. 391 (2000). Copyright © 2000 by the Oregon Law Review. Reprinted with permission.

Herbert Packer, Two Models of the Criminal Process, 113 U. Pa. L. Rev. 1 (1964). Copyright © 1964 by the Trustees of the University of Pennsylvania. Reprinted with permission of University of Pennsylvania Law Review via Copyright Clearance Center.

Dale Parent, Structuring Criminal Sentences: The Evolution of Minnesota's Sentencing Guidelines (1988). Copyright © 1988 by Butterworth Legal Publishers. Reprinted with permission from LEXIS Law Publishing. All Rights Reserved.

Reena Raggi, Local Concerns, Local Insights, 5 Fed. Sent'g Rep. 306 (1993). Copyright © 1993, Vera Institute of Justice. Reprinted with permission of the author.

Lawrence W. Sherman & Richard A. Berk, The Minneapolis Domestic Violence Experiment. Washington, D.C., Police Foundation, 1984. Reprinted with permission of the Police Foundation.

Abbe Smith, Can You Be a Good Person and a Good Prosecutor?, 14 Geo. J. Legal Ethics 355 (2001). Copyright © 2001 Georgetown Journal of Legal Ethics. Reprinted with permission of the publisher.

Megan Stevenson & Sandra G. Mayson, Pretrial Detention and Bail, in 3 Reforming Criminal Justice: Pretrial and Trial Processes 21 (Erik Luna ed., 2017). Reprinted with permission of the editor.

Seth W. Stoughton, Principled Policing: Warrior Cops and Guardian Officers, 51 Wake Forest L. Rev. 611 (2016). Reprinted with permission from Wake Forest Law Review.

Barbara Underwood, Ending Race Discrimination in Jury Selection: Whose Right Is It, Anyway? 92 Colum. L. Rev. 725 (1992). Reprinted by permission of the author and the Columbia Law Review.

Vera Institute of Justice, Fair Treatment for the Indigent: The Manhattan Bail Project, in Ten-Year Report, 1961-1971. Reprinted by permission of Vera Institute of Justice, Inc.

Ronald Wright & Marc Miller, The Screening/Bargaining Tradeoff, 55 Stan. L. Rev. 29 (2002). Copyright © 2002 by the Board of Trustees of the Leland Stanford Junior University. Reprinted with permission.

PART ONE

GATHERING INFORMATION

I

The Border of Criminal Procedure: Daily Interactions Between Citizens and Police

Many institutions create procedural rules to regulate the criminal justice process. Those rules—the laws of "criminal procedure"—shape the behavior of the police, prosecutors, defense attorneys, and judges who manage complex systems that operate at different levels of government.

Looking at police work, for example, there are rules about when police can stop, search, and arrest suspects. But not all police activities are subject to rules. For example, no state has a body of law telling police officers how they should talk with people on their rounds. Why not? Legal systems are supposed to prevent extraordinary and undesirable police actions. Thus, when a legal system allows some kinds of police activities to fall outside the bounds of formal legal rules, it indicates what society considers to be ordinary and desirable policing.

A society's vision of ordinary and desirable police behavior determines the "border" of criminal procedure—that is, the point where the law, in the form of rules from whatever source, starts to guide and limit police activity. This chapter explores that border. It suggests that assumptions about the *ordinary* behavior of the police shape the procedures we will study in later chapters, procedures that govern the *exceptional* confrontations between citizens and officers.

Modern criminal procedure assumes that the police initiate contact with citizens while "engaged in the often competitive enterprise of ferreting out crime." Johnson v. United States, 333 U.S. 10 (1948). But the police do many things in addition to ferreting out crime. The cases in section A involve police-initiated actions that pursue some purpose other than enforcing the criminal law—actions often referred to as the "community caretaker" function of police. Should police and citizens have different powers and responsibilities when the police act outside their law enforcement mode? In section B, we consider different philosophies of policing that guide the ordinary work of law enforcement officers, and the ways that philosophies change over time. In particular, we examine the proliferation of the "community policing" model. In section C, we look at the way that law enforcement agencies are typically organized and the ways that they train and support their officers. The chapter closes with a classic description of the values that might inform the work of the police.

A.　POLICE AS COMMUNITY CARETAKERS

Any description of police work (and, therefore, any set of procedural rules to control the police) must reckon with the wide variety of functions that the police perform. Most of the time, police officers interact with citizens without giving a thought to making an arrest or gathering evidence of a crime. Police officers devote more than half of their time to matters other than criminal law enforcement. The following materials—drawn from statutes, police department manuals, and cases— offer concrete images of police trying to accomplish something other than enforcing the criminal law. The police might view their task as defusing domestic disputes, or moving people out of dangerous or unhealthy situations, or offering guidance to young people, or something else. How should procedural rules that apply to the police account for these different functions? Should there be different rules for the police when they pursue "community caretaker" objectives rather than "law enforcement" objectives?

■ OREGON REVISED STATUTES §133.033

(1) [Any] peace officer is authorized to perform community caretaking functions.

(2) As used in this section, "community caretaking functions" means any lawful acts that are inherent in the duty of the peace officer to serve and protect the public. "Community caretaking functions" includes, but is not limited to:

(a) The right to enter or remain upon the premises of another if it reasonably appears to be necessary to:

(A) Prevent serious harm to any person or property;

(B) Render aid to injured or ill persons; or

(C) Locate missing persons.

(b) The right to stop or redirect traffic or aid motorists or other persons when such action reasonably appears to be necessary to:

(A) Prevent serious harm to any person or property;

(B) Render aid to injured or ill persons; or

(C) Locate missing persons....

■ INDIANAPOLIS POLICE DEPARTMENT
JOB DESCRIPTION: PATROL OFFICER

% TIME   CRITICAL TASKS

15%   1. Patrols assigned area in vehicle and on foot; maintains high patrol visibility to assist in crime prevention; actively performs routine beat patrol, concentrating on high incident areas, to detect possible criminal activities or needs for service; regularly checks businesses and residential areas; monitors radio broadcasts by Communications and other officers to ensure awareness of activities in area and to provide assistance, if needed; identifies, reports, and responds to suspicious activities or needs for service.

14%   2. Performs variety of police–community relations functions; meets and talks with citizens, providing information and advising of safety measures; visits local businesses to determine needs for service; assists motorists, providing directions; talks with juveniles in district to establish rapport; makes presentations to neighborhood organizations and block clubs....

12%   3. Performs duties relating to service and assistance (lost child, injured persons, walk-aways, prowlers, abandoned vehicles, dog bites, civil law disputes, vehicle inspections, etc.)....

10%   4. Receives emergency and non-emergency radio runs and information from Communications; ... responds to run, using siren and/or red lights in emergencies....

10%   5. Prepares reports (incident reports, capias information sheets, probable cause affidavits, accident reports, arrest slips, [uniform traffic tickets], property slips, inter-departments, etc.) relating to activities in accordance with General Orders/Department Directives; observes and records events....

8%   6. Performs duties relating to criminal investigation and apprehension; responds to scenes of possible criminal activity through radio runs, notification, or observation; assesses scene to determine situation needs (assistance from other officers, ambulance, detective, K-9, etc.); provides assistance to victim(s); searches and secures crime scene; interviews victims and witnesses to determine and verify nature of offense and identify suspect(s); notifies Communications of descriptions for broadcast; assists in pursuit (foot and vehicular) and/or apprehension of suspects; interrogates suspects, advising of Constitutional rights; makes arrests using only that force necessary; conducts search of arrested suspects; ensures suspects are transported to appropriate detention area and evidence is secured; advises victims of procedures to follow in prosecution.

6%   7. Performs duties relating to disturbances and domestic violence; ... evaluates situation to determine needs (assistance from other officers, ambulance, etc.); administers first aid, if needed; assists in resolution of conflicts; subdues violent subject using only that physical force necessary; makes arrests as needed to preserve peace; ... advises victim of possible courses of action.

% TIME	CRITICAL TASKS
5%	8. Performs duties relating to traffic enforcement; observes traffic violations; stops vehicles; checks registration and licenses for status; advises driver of violation committed and need to maintain safe driving practices; conducts or requests breathalyzer tests, if indicated; issues citations and makes arrests to enforce law, advising violator of rights....
5%	9. Performs duties relating to accident investigation and assistance; ... assists in extraction of victims and provision of first aid; secures scene to prevent further incidents; conducts investigation, gathering evidence, taking statements, and preparing diagrams; conducts or requests breathalyzer tests, if indicated; issues citations and makes arrests to enforce law, advising violator of rights....
5%	10. Testifies in court; prepares for testimony, reviewing reports and notes; meets with victims, witnesses, detectives, defense attorneys, and representatives from Prosecutor's Office to review case; ... presents testimony in accordance with Department policy....

■ COMMONWEALTH v. VICTORIA LIVINGSTONE
174 A.3d 609 (Pa. 2017)

Todd, J.

We granted review in this matter to consider whether Appellant, Victoria Livingstone, who was in a stopped vehicle on the side of the road, was subjected to an investigatory detention without reasonable suspicion of criminal activity when a police officer, ostensibly seeking only to inquire about her need for assistance, pulled his patrol car, with its emergency lights activated, alongside her vehicle. For the reasons set forth below, we conclude that Appellant was subjected to an illegal investigatory detention. Furthermore, although we take this opportunity to recognize the public servant "exception" to the warrant requirement under the community caretaking doctrine, which in certain circumstances will permit a warrantless seizure, we conclude that the doctrine does not justify the detention of Appellant under the facts of this case. . . .

On June 14, 2013, at approximately 9:30 P.M., Pennsylvania State Trooper Jeremy Frantz was traveling northbound on Interstate 79 in his marked police cruiser when he observed a vehicle pulled over onto the right shoulder of the road; the engine was running, but the hazard lights were not activated. Trooper Frantz activated his emergency lights and, with his passenger window down, pulled alongside the stopped vehicle. Appellant, the sole occupant of the vehicle, was sitting in the driver's seat and appeared to be entering an address into her vehicle's navigation system. According to Trooper Frantz's testimony at the suppression hearing, when he first made eye contact with Appellant, she gave him a "hundred mile stare," which Trooper Frantz described as "glossy eyes" and "looking through [him]." Trooper Frantz motioned for Appellant to roll down her window, and he asked her if she was okay. Appellant answered affirmatively. When asked where she was going, Appellant stated that she was traveling to New York for a dragon boat race. At that point, Trooper Frantz pulled his cruiser in front of Appellant's vehicle, exited the cruiser, and approached Appellant's vehicle on foot. At approximately the same time, another trooper pulled behind Appellant's vehicle, but, when he exited his vehicle, that trooper remained in front of his police cruiser and did not make contact with Appellant. . . .

Trooper Frantz asked to see Appellant's driver's license, and, when asked if she had been drinking, Appellant replied that she had not, but that she would like to once she arrived at her destination. She explained that she had finished working at 8:00 p.m., and had been driving for approximately 90 minutes. The audio of Trooper Frantz's dashboard camera video, which was introduced at the suppression hearing, reveals that Appellant repeatedly told Trooper Frantz that she was "a CEO of five companies" and worked long hours. She also repeatedly stated that she had two sons at the Citadel, and she told Trooper Frantz that she was afraid of him, and afraid that her sons would get in trouble because of her being stopped. Based on the appearance of her eyes and the fact that she was acting "confused," Trooper Frantz asked Appellant to exit her vehicle so that he could perform field sobriety tests. He indicated that, at that point, she was "an emotional wreck. She was crying, constantly repeating herself about the fact that she's a CEO of five companies." Trooper Frantz then advised Appellant that he intended to administer a portable breathalyzer test ("PBT"), and, assuming it was clear, he would help her get to her destination. As neither of the troopers had a PBT in their cruisers, another officer brought one to the scene. The results of the PBT indicated the presence of alcohol in Appellant's system. As a result, Trooper Frantz placed Appellant under arrest, and transported her to the police barracks where an EMT administered a blood test. The test revealed that Appellant had a blood alcohol content (BAC) of .205%. Accordingly, Appellant was charged with DUI. . . .

Appellant filed a pre-trial motion to suppress evidence of her BAC on the basis that, once Trooper Frantz activated his emergency lights and pulled alongside her vehicle, she was subjected to an investigative detention unsupported by reasonable suspicion. [Following an evidentiary hearing, the trial court denied the motion. Livingstone was convicted.]

[We agree with Appellant] that when Trooper Frantz pulled alongside her vehicle, with his emergency lights activated, Appellant was subjected to an investigative detention. . . . Given that it is undisputed that the seizure was not supported by any degree of suspicion of criminal activity, we will proceed to determine whether it was otherwise justified under the Fourth Amendment.

THE COMMUNITY CARETAKING DOCTRINE

In order to protect individuals against unreasonable searches and seizures, a right guaranteed by the Fourth Amendment, law enforcement generally must obtain a warrant prior to conducting a search: "A search warrant indicates that the police have convinced a neutral magistrate upon a showing of probable cause, which is a reasonable belief, based on the surrounding facts and totality of circumstances, that an illegal activity is occurring or evidence of a crime is present." Commonwealth v. Petroll, 738 A.2d 993 (Pa. 1999).

[The Commonwealth maintains that the seizure of Appellant by Trooper Frantz] was reasonable under the community caretaking "exception" to the Fourth Amendment's warrant requirement. . . . The United States Supreme Court first recognized a community caretaking exception to the warrant requirement in

Cady v. Dombrowski, 413 U.S. 433 (1973). Therein, the Court considered whether police officers violated a vehicle owner's Fourth Amendment rights when, without obtaining a warrant, they searched the trunk of a parked vehicle because they reasonably believed that the trunk contained a loaded service revolver that could endanger the public if left unsecured. The vehicle owner had been arrested one day earlier for drunk driving and identified himself as a police officer. In determining that the search of the trunk was reasonable, the Court observed that police officers "frequently investigate vehicle accidents in which there is no claim of criminal liability and engage in what, for want of a better term, may be described as community caretaking functions, totally divorced from the detection, investigation, or acquisition of evidence relating to the violation of a criminal statute." . . .

The community caretaking doctrine has been characterized as encompassing three specific exceptions: the emergency aid exception; the automobile impoundment/inventory exception; and the public servant exception, also sometimes referred to as the public safety exception. Each of the exceptions contemplates that the police officer's actions be motivated by a desire to render aid or assistance, rather than the investigation of criminal activity.

[We have not addressed the public servant or the emergency aid exceptions under the community caretaking doctrine, although more than half of our sister states have done so. The Tennessee Supreme Court] observed that the "widespread adoption of the community caretaking doctrine as an exception to the warrant requirement reflects the reality that modern society expects police officers to fulfill various responsibilities," noting:

> Police officers wear many hats: criminal investigator, first aid provider, social worker, crisis intervener, family counselor, youth mentor and peacemaker, to name a few. They are charged with the duty to protect people, not just from criminals, but also from accidents, natural perils and even self-inflicted injuries. We ask them to protect our property from all types of losses—even those occasioned by our own negligence. They counsel our youth. They quell disputes between husband and wife, parent and child, landlord and tenant, merchant and patron and quarreling neighbors. Although they search for clues to solve crime, they also search for missing children, parents, dementia patients, and occasionally even an escaped zoo animal. They are society's problem solvers when no other solution is apparent or available.

State v. McCormick, 494 S.W.3d 673 (Tenn. 2016). This Court likewise recognizes that the role of police is not limited to the detection, investigation, and prevention of criminal activity.... However, even community caretaking activity must be performed in accordance with Fourth Amendment protections. . . .

In recognition of the overarching requirements of the Fourth Amendment, courts have adopted a variety of tests for determining whether the public servant exception justifies a warrantless search or seizure. In State v. Anderson, 362 P.3d 1232 (Utah 2015), the Utah Supreme Court opined that the same balancing test used in determining whether a seizure is reasonable under the Fourth Amendment—balancing an individual's interest in being free from police intrusion and the State's legitimate interest in the public welfare—is applicable to determining whether a seizure is justified pursuant to the community caretaking doctrine. [Courts] must first evaluate the degree to which an officer intrudes upon a citizen's freedom of movement and privacy. In doing so, courts should look to both the degree of overt authority and force displayed in effecting the seizure, and the length of the seizure. Second, courts must determine whether the degree of the public interest and the exigency of the situation justified the seizure for community caretaking purposes. In other words, how serious was the perceived emergency and what was the likelihood that the motorist may need aid? If the level of the State's interest in investigating whether a motorist needs aid justifies the degree to which an officer interferes with the motorist's freedoms in order to perform this investigation, the seizure is not "unreasonable" under the Fourth Amendment.

Applying this test, the [Utah] court first concluded that police officers' "seizure" of a motorist who was in a parked car on the side of a highway, at night and in below-zero temperatures, with his vehicle's hazard lights on, was "minimally invasive" of the motorist's right to be free from arbitrary interferences by police because (1) the vehicle was parked, not traveling down the highway; (2) there was no unduly excessive display of authority or force, in that the only show of authority was the trooper's use of his overhead flashing lights and he did not draw his weapon or shout commands; and (3) the officers detained the motorist only long enough to approach his vehicle and ask whether he needed aid. With regard to the second inquiry—the seriousness of the perceived emergency and the likelihood that the motorist needed aid—the court opined that a "reasonable officer would have cause to be concerned about the welfare of a motorist [who was] parked on the side of a highway with his hazard lights flashing just before 10:00 P.M." in very cold temperatures. Accordingly, the court held that the seizure was justified under the community caretaking doctrine. . . .

While [some] courts utilize a balancing test to determine whether a seizure was justified under the community caretaking doctrine, many state courts have adopted variations of what has been referred to as a "reasonableness test." Montana, for example, has adopted [a] three-part test. . . . First, as long as there are objective, specific, and articulable facts from which an experienced officer would suspect that a citizen is in need of help or is in peril, then that officer has the right to stop and investigate. Second, if the citizen is in need of aid, then the officer may take appropriate action to render assistance or mitigate the peril. Third, once, however, the officer is assured that the citizen is not in peril or is no longer in need of assistance or that the peril has been mitigated, then any actions beyond that constitute a seizure implicating . . . the protections provided by the Fourth Amendment. State v. Lovegren, 51 P.3d 471 (Mont. 2002). In *Lovegren*, a police officer observed a legally parked vehicle on the side of a highway, with its motor running but its headlights off. He approached the vehicle, and, seeing that the driver appeared to be asleep, knocked on the window. When the driver did not respond, the officer opened the vehicle door and the driver woke up and stated that he'd been drinking. The Montana Supreme Court concluded that the officer "had objective, specific and articulable facts suggesting that Lovegren might be in need of assistance. While Lovegren might simply have been asleep, he might just as likely have been ill and unconscious and in need of help." . . .

After careful consideration, we conclude that the reasonableness test best accommodates the interests underlying the public servant exception while simultaneously protecting an individual's Fourth Amendment right to be free from unreasonable searches and seizures. Specifically, we first hold that, in order for the public servant exception of the community caretaking doctrine to apply, police officers must be able to point to specific, objective, and articulable facts that would reasonably suggest to an experienced officer that a citizen is in need of assistance. [Requiring an officer to articulate specific and objective facts that would suggest to a reasonable officer that assistance is needed will cabin reliance on the exception and enable courts to properly assess its employment.]

As Appellant suggests, there are many reasons why a driver might pull to the side of a highway: the driver may need to look at a map, answer or make a telephone call, send a text message, pick something up off the floor, clean up a spill, locate something in her purse or in his wallet, retrieve something from the glove compartment, attend to someone in the back seat, or, as in the instant case, enter an address into the vehicle's navigation system. Pulling to the side of the road to perform any of these activities is encouraged, as a momentary distraction while driving may result in catastrophic consequences. . . .

Second, we hold that, in order for the public servant exception of the community caretaking doctrine to apply, the police caretaking action must be independent from the detection, investigation, and acquisition of criminal evidence. [The] police officer's action [must] be based on specific and articulable facts which, viewed objectively and independent of any law enforcement concerns, would suggest to a reasonable officer that assistance is needed.

We are not suggesting, however, that an officer's contemporaneous subjective concerns regarding criminal activity will preclude a finding that a seizure is valid under the community caretaking function. [It] is not realistic or wise to expect an officer to ignore the nature of his or her role in law enforcement—or its inherent dangers—in order for the public servant exception of the community caretaking doctrine to apply. Thus, so long as a police officer is able to point to specific, objective, and articulable facts which, standing alone, reasonably would suggest that his assistance is necessary, a coinciding subjective law enforcement concern by the officer will not negate the validity of that search under the public servant exception to the community caretaking doctrine. . . .

Finally, we hold that, in order for the public servant exception to apply the level of intrusion must be commensurate with the perceived need for assistance. Such a determination requires an assessment of the circumstances surrounding the seizure, including, but not necessarily limited to, the degree of authority or force displayed, the length of the seizure, and the availability of alternative means of assistance.

To summarize, in order for a seizure to be justified under the public servant exception to the warrant requirement under the community caretaking doctrine, the officer must point to specific, objective, and articulable facts which would reasonably suggest to an experienced officer that assistance was needed; the police action must be independent from the detection, investigation, and acquisition of criminal evidence; and, based on a consideration of the surrounding circumstances, the action taken by police must be tailored to rendering assistance or mitigating the peril. Once assistance has been provided or the peril mitigated, further police action will be evaluated under traditional Fourth Amendment jurisprudence.

Applying the standard we have adopted today, we must now determine whether the seizure of Appellant was justified under the public servant exception. . . . We have no reason to doubt Trooper Frantz's statement that he pulled alongside Appellant's vehicle simply to check to see whether she needed assistance. However, regardless of his intentions, based on our review of the record, Trooper Frantz was unable to articulate any specific and objective facts that would reasonably suggest that Appellant needed assistance. Indeed, Trooper Frantz conceded that he had not received a report of a motorist in need of assistance, and did not observe anything that outwardly suggested a problem with Appellant's vehicle. Moreover, although it was dark, the weather was not inclement. Finally, Appellant, who was inside her vehicle, did not have her hazard lights on. Thus, we are constrained to hold that Trooper Frantz's seizure of Appellant was not justified under the public servant exception, and, therefore, that the evidence obtained as a result of that seizure should have been suppressed at trial. . . .

BAER, J., concurring and dissenting.

I agree with the majority's . . . adoption of a discrete exception to the Fourth Amendment, which permits the seizure [of a motorist] when an officer is acting pursuant to his community caretaking function. I write separately, however, because I would hold that under the factual predicate before us, the seizure in the case sub judice was justified pursuant to the community caretaker exception.

[The] specific and articulable facts (that Appellant's car was stopped on the shoulder of a highway, rather than a rest stop, gas station, or the like) warranted the minimal intrusion of Trooper Frantz slowly approaching in his vehicle and peering at Appellant to ensure her well-being. Specifically, I would find that these facts presented an objective basis for concluding that Appellant may have been in peril. [In] addition to having grounds for believing that Appellant may have needed assistance, Trooper Frantz had an objective basis to be concerned for the overall safety of the highway because a parked vehicle located on the shoulder of an interstate highway without hazard lights obviously presents a potential safety risk to other motorists. . . .

DONOHUE, J., concurring and dissenting.

. . . I agree with the Majority that adopting a public servant exception is appropriate and I would also hold that the exception has no application under the facts presented here. I write separately because . . . I strongly disagree with the "independent from" language employed in the second prong of the Majority's "reasonableness" test. . . . Police officers can and do, in the line of duty, effectuate seizures for the sole purpose of rendering assistance and citizens of this Commonwealth have come to expect that police officers will not turn a blind eye to motorists in distress. [But to] allow any amount of criminal investigative motivation into a warrantless detention of a motorist is a sword to the heart of the Fourth Amendment, absent at least reasonable suspicion. I would hold that if an officer is motivated to any degree by a desire to investigate crime, the individual seized must be afforded his or her full panoply of Fourth Amendment rights. . . .

Notes

1. *Community caretakers: majority view.* The majority of the states have applied some form of the community caretaker doctrine to police. As we saw in *Livingstone*, this concept often arises when courts relax the usual restrictions on searches and seizures that apply during a criminal investigation. The community caretaker function has been used to justify entry into homes and stops of automobiles, with police officers pursuing various "caretaker" missions. See Laney v. State, 117 S.W.3d 854 (Tex. Crim. App. 2003) (officer entered trailer after midnight to determine where

two young boys lived); State v. Deneui, 775 N.W.2d 221 (S.D. 2009) (during investigation of theft of natural gas, officers noticed ammonia fumes emanating from home and entered based on concern that potential occupants may have succumbed to fumes). Does an energetic community caretaker function provide a convenient after-the-fact rationale for searches that would not otherwise be legal? Should statutes or ordinances, rather than judicial decisions, define the boundaries of community caretaker authority? Would the Oregon statute provide a different outcome in *Livingstone*?

The U.S. Supreme Court has also recognized the community caretaking function. In Brigham City v. Stuart, 547 U.S. 398 (2006), the Court held that the Fourth Amendment does not bar law enforcement officers from entering a residence without a warrant if they have "an objectively reasonable basis to believe that an occupant is seriously injured or imminently threatened" with a serious injury. See also Michigan v. Fisher, 558 U.S. 45 (2009) (officer entry into home without warrant was justified under "emergency aid" exception, when officers observed wrecked vehicle outside home and saw through windows a person inside screaming and throwing things, with cut on hand).

2. *Distinguishing community caretaker functions from criminal enforcement.* As suggested by the Oregon statute, the Indianapolis job description, and the *Livingstone* case, the community caretaker function of the police can cover a wide variety of activities. A community caretaker function can change along the way to a crime control function. What factors might identify such a shift in function? See Williams v. State, 962 A.2d 210 (Del. 2008) (officer who stopped person who appeared to need assistance did not convert the stop into an illegal detention by asking for person's name and date of birth; officer must have record of who receives assistance to respond to later claims of officer wrongdoing or to further later criminal investigations). If a police department receives a 911 call reporting unusual noises behind the neighbor's house, should that be treated as a "crime control" or a community caretaker episode? What if a patrol officer responds to a burglar alarm? What if 95 percent of burglar alarm calls are false calls? Review the job description of a patrol officer in Indianapolis and attempt to sort the various duties into the community caretaker or the crime control category. Courts usually declare that the officer's subjective intent when performing an action does not determine whether the courts will treat it as community caretaking or a criminal investigation. See State v. Kramer, 759 N.W.2d 598 (Wis. 2009). A few state courts disagree. See State v. Gibson, 267 P.3d 645 (Alaska 2012) (defining emergency aid doctrine more narrowly under state constitution than the federal constitution allows; requires courts to consider police officers' subjective motives for making warrantless entry of home).

There is debate among courts about whether the community caretaker doctrine should apply to the entry of homes, or whether it should remain limited to police encounters with individuals inside vehicles. For a survey of this debate about the proper boundaries of the community caretaker doctrine and a description of the related concept known as the "emergency aid" doctrine, see the web extension for this chapter at *http://www.crimpro.com/extension/ch01*.

3. *Adjusted procedural controls for different police roles.* The *Livingstone* court suggests that it is appropriate to have higher procedural requirements for police officers who are investigating a crime, and to apply more lax requirements to officers acting in a community caretaker function. What features of community caretaker functions might

justify this different treatment? Are caretaker functions less intrusive for citizens? Do those activities produce less severe consequences than a criminal investigation? Do police encounter a greater variety of situations during community caretaking, making it less amenable to general rules than the conduct of a criminal investigation? Could a legal system subject all police activity—whether or not directed toward criminal law enforcement—to the same procedural requirements? See Michael R. Dimino, Sr., Police Paternalism: Community Caretaking, Assistance Searches, and Fourth Amendment Reasonableness, 66 Wash. & Lee L. Rev. 1485 (2009).

Problem 1-1. I'm from the Government and I'm Here to Help

On July 4, two police officers responded to a call from the custodian of the apartment building in which Michael Dube lived with his family. Dube was not at home and the custodian needed to enter the apartment to stop sewage or water from leaking into the apartments below. The custodian had his own key but asked the police officers to accompany him to verify that he was only dealing with the emergency. When they entered the apartment, the officers noticed an intense smell of urine and feces. There was a puddle of urine on the kitchen floor, and an open diaper containing human feces that appeared to have been walked through by a baby. The feces had been tracked throughout the apartment. The officers watched the custodian work on toilets on the first and second floors. From where they stood on the second-floor landing, the officers could see into the three bedrooms. In the baby's bedroom and the children's bedroom, they saw clothes strewn on the floor covered with animal and human feces. There were at least 75–100 individual feces beside the baby's crib, and a similar number around the bunk beds and more in the hallway.

Officer Beaulieu called to request that the Department of Human Services (DHS) send a caseworker to the apartment. He also radioed for another police unit to bring a camera. The officers asked the custodian to "stand by," and when he finished with the repairs the custodian waited on the sidewalk. About five minutes later, two additional officers arrived with a camera and Officer Beaulieu took pictures of parts of the apartment, and then went outside to wait with the custodian. When two DHS workers arrived, Officer Beaulieu re-entered the apartment and showed them around. The state charged Dube with endangering the welfare of a child.

Dube argues that the initial entry into the apartment by the police officers was unlawful and a violation of the Fourth Amendment proscription against unreasonable searches. He also claims that even if the officers' initial entry was lawful, their continued presence at some point became unlawful. Were the officers acting within the bounds of the community caretaker function throughout their two visits inside the apartment, or did they need to obtain a warrant to justify their entry? Compare State v. Dube, 655 A.2d 338 (Me. 1995).

B. POLICING PHILOSOPHIES

The idea of what police do, and how they do it, is far from a static concept. The materials that follow describe the evolution from the Political Era, through the

Professional Era, to the current Community Policing Era. In its broadest outlines, community policing shifts control over police resources from central police management to the community level. The police listen to the community when they set their enforcement priorities. Community policing broadens the goals of policing to include community order and not just crime control; it recognizes that *fear* of crime is a serious matter in its own right. In these sweeping terms, most police departments have embraced this change.

The label of "community" policing, however, applies to a wide range of strategies and styles. Under this banner, some departments pursue "order maintenance" policing that calls for officers to target small signs of social disorder that are the precursors to crime. Others stress efforts by officers to help potential victims to make a crime more difficult to complete. Different communities may expect their police departments to pursue very different objectives.

As you read the description below of changing philosophies of policing, keep in mind the possible effects on procedural rules. If you were a city council member, would you pass an ordinance to give the police greater powers to "problem solve"? With the shift to community policing, are procedural controls on the police *less* important or feasible, or are they *more* important than ever—to prevent the officers from making arbitrary and discriminatory use of their more frequent interactions with the public?

■ SETH W. STOUGHTON, PRINCIPLED POLICING: WARRIOR COPS AND GUARDIAN OFFICERS

51 Wake Forest L. Rev. 611 (2016)

. . . Policing appeared in an early version of its modern form in 1829, when British Home Secretary Sir Robert Peel successfully lobbied for the legislative act that created London's Metropolitan Police Force.... The United States followed England's lead in the 1830s with municipal police agencies springing up as a response to rioting and civil unrest. The immediate precursors of these early police agencies—night watchmen and constabulary systems—had proven deeply unpopular, and it did not take long for municipal police agencies to supplant them. By the 1850s, police agencies were a common fixture of large cities. Police officers, however, were not readily identifiable; officers did not wear uniforms because of mutual distrust between the public and officers themselves. Critics condemned uniforms as undemocratic imitations of royal livery. [It] took municipal police agencies decades to adopt uniforms. Boston did so in 1858, New York in 1860, and Chicago in 1861. Officers also began carrying firearms at about this time, despite the prohibitions against guns most police agencies had in place. While police executives and the public were skeptical about the need for officers to have firearms, they eventually allowed the practice because doing so only recognized what was becoming standard behavior among officers.

[In] the United States policing was, and has since remained, a hyperlocalized endeavor, with each city having its own police agency. Unlike today, however, policing was intensely political. Both rank-and-file officers and police executives were deeply beholden to local politics, often owing their position to political patronage (which they often purchased) and, in return, using their position to support their patron. [Police] commanders consulted often with local political representatives about police priorities and progress.

This tight relationship with the political system . . . was not an unqualified evil. Good policing meant supporting the local political establishment, and that meant maintaining high levels of community satisfaction. Police officers and executives alike took a broad view of their mandate, engaging not just in preventative policing, primarily through foot patrols and the eventual introduction of automobiles, but also in social support services. Early police agencies established and operated soup kitchens and shelters for the homeless and for recent immigrants, helped immigrants find work, and provided shoes and medicines to the community.

Officers were part of the communities they served, typically living in the neighborhoods they patrolled. The close connections between officers and the communities they lived in and served paved the way for the underpolicing of certain people, particularly community insiders, and certain crimes, such as behaviors that were illegal but consistent with local norms. Police officers did not see their job as limited to defending the law-abiding members of the community from the criminal element; they also punished violations of the dominant social norms, leading to conflicts with community outsiders, especially minority ethnic and racial groups. This punishment could be as brutal as it was informal. . . . Outside of political pressures, there was little, if anything, in the way of police regulation. . . .

The Political Era of policing lasted for almost a century, from the establishment of the first police agencies until it began to give way to the Professional Era in the 1930s. The evolution of policing in this new era was marked by a concerted effort to distance police from the political machines of the day. Civil service systems were put into place to govern the selection and promotion of officers, and the power of politicians to hire and fire police commanders was eliminated or sharply curtailed. Policing's first principles shifted: political and public approval were no longer the measure of successful policing. Good policing was instead defined by officers' rigor and expertise in enforcing criminal law. Formal rules and informal norms were developed to prevent officers from pandering to community sensibilities, including a prohibition, in some cities, on officers living in the neighborhoods that they patrolled. Peace officers became law enforcers. Perhaps more importantly, policing became a self-regulated profession.

As policing's principles shifted, so too did officers' actions and attitudes. Officers became less involved in order maintenance and focused their efforts on crime control. Agencies no longer operated homeless shelters or soup kitchens. Using crime-fighting specialists to deal with generic social ills was considered a foolish waste of resources. Actions that did not directly prevent or respond to criminal incidents—derisively referred to as "social work"—were considered far outside the purview of the police. Professional policing was exemplified by detached, highly skilled experts who could dedicate themselves to crime fighting without being distracted by the social or emotional aspects of a specific victim or community. One of the era's most popular television shows, Dragnet, featured Detective Sergeant Joe Friday, a stone-faced LAPD detective whose tireless search for the "facts" typified the Professional Era image of the cool, effective, and no-nonsense crime fighter.

[Police] agencies became centrally organized. The foot patrols, substations, and local precincts that had been so accessible to the community were reduced or eliminated, replaced with vehicle-based, "preventative patrol" tactics and a central dispatch system that channeled calls for service to the appropriate "units" for rapid response to an incident. Indeed, the patrol car became the symbol of policing. . . .

The shift from politically responsive policing to professional policing reduced corruption, particularly political corruption, but it also detached policing from both politics and the community. Law enforcement agencies were no longer part of the local political structure; those ties were intentionally severed and policing recast as part of the criminal justice system. Agency priorities and officers' decisions were based not on political approval or community support, but on the knowledge, skills, and training believed to be exclusively available to members of the policing profession. Police were specialists, professionals who should be left alone to do what they and they alone knew how to do. Inevitably, this mindset affected the way that police officers interacted with and related to the public. Citizens could help by reporting crime and then stepping out of the way. . . .

The Professional Era of policing remained strong until the 1960s. During this time, crime increased despite the best efforts of the police to combat it, undermining the perception of police as uniquely knowledgeable specialists who were most effective when left alone. The image of police as neutral professionals was further called into question as officers came into conflict—often violent conflict—with minorities migrating to urban areas and anti-war protesters on the streets. . . .

The public's mounting distrust, along with experience and substantive research that called into question many of the assumptions about the relationship between police and crime, gave rise to the next evolution in law enforcement: the Community Policing Era. The policing profession found that it could not successfully control crime without addressing the underlying problems that caused crime. Those problems, however, did not always lend themselves to crime-fighting interventions. The relationships between officers and members of the public were vital; the information relayed through those relationships allowed police to prevent and investigate crime and apprehend criminals. But as the social unrest and political upheaval of the 1960s demonstrated, police agencies did not always have good relationships with their constituents. Changes to the police role and police regulation were necessary. External regulation was increasingly viewed as essential, and the police were called upon to become more than crime fighters. . . .

Social disorder, which had been ignored during the Professional Era, was now to be addressed as a cause of both crime and fear. But officers could not tackle this issue by relying solely on the authority provided by criminal law; disorder is, and was, often entirely legal. . . . Officers had to work cooperatively with civilians to identify problems, to craft solutions, and to evaluate those solutions. . . .

Community policing has failed to live up to its promise because of definitional failures, implementation and evaluation failures, and, most importantly, cultural resistance within law enforcement. Efforts to implement community policing principles have suffered, first and foremost, from a widespread failure to understand exactly what community policing entails. The phrase is more accurately used to refer to a loosely defined policing philosophy or set of philosophies that should permeate decision making by informing police commanders and officers about the practice of policing. Unfortunately, it is often used to describe a particular program, strategy, or tactic; certain police actions are designated as "community policing" while others are not. . . . Officers are left unsure of whom exactly they should be serving, which problems to focus on, and how to solve them. The lack of guidance about how to prioritize different community groups' various problems has proved particularly vexing given the disparity in different groups' political capital; solving the problems of the downtown business community, for example, may mean exacerbating the problems of the homeless population, and vice versa. . . .

Given the definitional problems, failures of implementation are inevitable. It is often unclear who should be responsible for community policing or whether community policing should be limited to trained specialists or implemented by officers more generally. [The] goals and methods of a specialized community-policing unit do not always align with the rest of the police agency. But adopting a more generalist approach is often no more successful. Properly instilling in every officer the principles of community policing takes time and resources that many agencies prefer to allocate to training in the "high-liability" areas: vehicle operations, the use of lethal and less-lethal force, and first aid. Without exposure to the underlying principles of community policing, officers are more likely to view community policing as extra work above and beyond their current duties, rather than a philosophy that should be incorporated into the way they perform every aspect of their jobs. . . .

Implementing an idealized version of community policing, in which officers are the first point of contact for a host of social problems and serve to coordinate non-law enforcement services, is relatively difficult. Officers are simply not trained, just as police agencies are not structured, to serve as liaisons for the range of public and private social services that a truly holistic solution may require. And so officers and agencies default to taking unilateral action using the authority that they have. All too often, that has involved aggressively policing minor offenses. That approach has proven counterproductive. Although widely adopted as a community policing tactic, order-maintenance policing reduces the potential of police-community partnerships and, ironically enough, may increase the very crime the police and community desire to suppress.

Further, the metrics by which community policing efforts are measured are often developed by stakeholders other than the disenfranchised community members themselves. These metrics often do not track the purported goals of the philosophy: to build and maintain positive partnerships between law enforcement and the community that can be leveraged to engage in problem-solving techniques that increase trust while decreasing crime, disorder, and fear. Lacking a reliable and timely way to measure police-community partnerships, perceived legitimacy and public trust, and perceptions of disorder and crime, police agencies tend to focus on quantifiable performance metrics, such as the number of arrests, stops, and frisks that an officer made or the number of calls that an officer responded to. . . .

THE WARRIOR IDEAL

. . . In the context of modern policing, the highly venerated Warrior concept is a simplified attempt to provide an ethical framework for an inherently violent job. The Warrior appeals to officers' self-image because it is a heroic and noble figure, imbued with the qualities that offi-cers most respect and admire. Although there are tremendous variations in exactly how those qualities are described, I believe they can be fairly condensed into four attributes: honor, duty, resolve, and the willingness to engage in righteous violence. . . .

Honor. Warriors serve others, not themselves, and do so only for honorable ends. Warriors pursue justice—the triumph of right over wrong—and they seek to defend the weak from those who would take advantage of them. But they are not free to do so in any way that they choose; like the Warrior's goals, the Warrior's methods must be honorable. Warriors must therefore adhere to a code of honor that governs their behavior. That standard is created not by law—which is often seen as frustrating, rather than furthering, justice—but by the norms of the Warrior brotherhood itself. . . .

Duty. Warriors commit themselves to their honorable mission. Because that mission has no end, no conclusive moment of triumph, Warriors must dedicate themselves to a cause, a calling, that they will never see completed. This commitment to duty demands self-sacrifice. For the Warrior, it is better to strive against overwhelming odds and suffer defeat than it is to forsake one's duty. . . .

Resolve. Warriors must be committed to their duty, but that commitment does not come easily. Warriors must . . . possess the mental tenacity to survive life-threatening situations and overwhelming odds, but that by itself is not enough; the need for resolve is not limited to surviving physical threats. Threats to Warriors' psychological and emotional well-being are just as prevalent as, if not more prevalent than, threats to their physical safety. Warriors must have the mental strength to survive these trials. They must also have the resolve to do their jobs to the best of their abilities even in the face of public criticism and when they believe that the legal and political systems have failed them. Further, they must have the resolve to complete tasks that they do not like or even strongly disagree with, such as enforcing laws they personally oppose and protecting individuals whom they personally despise.

Willingness to Engage in Righteous Violence. A Warrior must be capable of using violence in pursuit of his goals. . . . While most people want to close their eyes to the violence and evil of the world around them, the Warrior recognizes that evil exists and that violence is sometimes necessary to defend against it. Violence is not thrust upon the unwilling Warrior. Instead, it is a tool that the Warrior consciously chooses to use to protect himself and others from victimization. . . .

The Corruption of the Warrior Ideal

. . . The Warrior principles are admirable, but in practice, policing all too often fails to live up to those ideals. Troublingly, Warrior rhetoric is often invoked to explain or justify behaviors inconsistent with or outright contrary to policing's mission of public service and the Warrior's core values of honor, duty, and resolve. Despite the best of intentions, the Warrior concept promotes an adversarial style of policing that estranges the public and contributes to unnecessary conflict and violence. Further, it offers a way for officers to rationalize bad acts and resist criticism. . . .

Under a Warrior worldview, police legitimacy is founded in criminal law, the unique ability of officers to enforce it, and the code that officers must adhere to. Criminal law serves as an external source of legitimacy—officers, as many are often quick to point out, merely enforce the law; they do not make it. While public support for policing may be preferable in this worldview, it is not essential. . . .

In combination with the low value that many officers put on public trust, training that teaches officers to be hypervigilant to potential threats can lead officers to adopt an adversarial approach to civilian interactions that effectively precludes good police-community relations. . . . For their own safety, officers are taught that they need to take control of a scene—to exhibit an authoritative "command presence." . . .

From the officer's point of view, the officer is an authority figure that must be respected and obeyed. Indeed, officers may be taught formally or informally to demand respect. Under this worldview, disrespect is tantamount to resistance, and resistance indicates that an individual is one of the "bad guys," an "enemy." . . . But a civilian interacting with an officer may perceive the officer's expectation of deference as an entitled, unnecessary display of dominance, a sign of disrespect from the officer. Because the actors are not responding to each other as expected by either party to the encounter, the defiance between them escalates. . . .

The adversarial approach to policing that results largely from law enforcement's veneration of the Warrior metaphor does not just strain officer-civilian interactions; it also makes it more socially acceptable, among officers, to engage in or tolerate unprofessional conduct, misfeasance, malfeasance, and violations of law. . . . The Warrior brotherhood has its own code; it finds little merit in externally imposed regulations. Legal and administrative constraints thought up by lawyers or liability-sensitive administrators are viewed as unnecessary and unwise obstacles to effective law enforcement. For example, the Fourth Amendment's limitations on searches and seizures are viewed as artificial, serving only to protect the guilty at the expense of the crime-fighting mission. . . .

CREATING A GUARDIAN CULTURE

. . . If the Warrior is a problem, as I believe it is, then the Guardian may be a suitable replacement. . . . Guardian principles will lead to safer policing for three primary reasons. First, individuals in communities that trust the police are more likely to cooperate and less likely to resist officers, diminishing the risk to officers and the need for force. Second, Guardian policing seeks to avoid confrontations when it is possible to do so, which similarly minimizes the risk to officers and civilians alike. Third, Guardian policing increases the police agency social capital with the community, reducing suspicion of police actions and mitigating the negative effects of high-profile incidents, such as an egregious use of excessive force. . . .

A Guardian agency embraces the democratic ideal that the legitimacy of any government agency—and the moral right to impose the coercive power of the state—depends on the consent of the governed. . . . Guardian policing emphasizes cooperation over compliance, communication over commands, and legitimacy over authority.

It is important to recognize that the Guardian concept is not a lesser aspect of the police Warrior. In fact, the opposite is true. Guardian policing retains the four core principles of the Warrior—honor, duty, resolve, and a willingness to engage in righteous violence—but those requirements are joined by five additional, essential attributes: respect for human dignity, empathy, patience, inclusivity, and introspection.

Respect for Human Dignity. To protect members of the public from unnecessary indignity, Guardians must be attuned to human dignity. . . . The Guardian is aware that some police actions—especially the coercive use of authority to stop, frisk, search, arrest, or interrogate—inevitably impose some level of indignity. For that reason, Guardians must conduct themselves with an eye toward minimizing, to the extent possible given the situation, the potential for humiliation and harm. This principle is most valuable when officers have little reason to respect the person they are interacting with. [Respect] for human dignity must guide the officers as they interview or arrest rapists, work with protestors to set up the route of a march, or take a complaint from belligerent civilians. . . .

Empathy. As a counterpart to respect for human dignity, Guardians must have both the ability and, perhaps more relevantly, the willingness to take other people's perceptions of a given situation seriously. . . . Consider the differences between what individuals inside and outside of the police force consider a normal encounter. When a veteran officer conducts a traffic stop, makes a misdemeanor arrest, or responds to a report of a burglary, the officer's expectations and actions are guided by a long line of similar experiences. Traffic stops, low-level arrests, and burglaries are, to put it bluntly, business as usual. But to the motorist, arrestee, or burglary victim, the situation may be far outside the range of normal experiences. What is a routine aspect of an officer's working life may be nerve-racking for a civilian who feels confused, angry, and powerless. . . . Further, different civilians may have different perceptions of and responses to officers. A young black male may perceive an officer as officious and harassing, while an older white woman might not. It is incumbent on officers to be aware of those different perceptions and to calibrate their actions, expectations, and reactions accordingly. . . .

The Path Forward

[Such] a cultural shift will require changes that are both extrinsic and intrinsic to law enforcement agencies. Extrinsically, for example, communities will need to change the way that they evaluate successful policing. [Using] crime rates to assess a police agency or police executives creates perverse incentives that encourage the agency to adopt an aggressive approach that undermines police-community relations. Similarly, evaluating the success of a law enforcement agency by reviewing average response times to nonemergency calls can encourage dispatchers and officers to minimize the amount of time it takes to handle calls rather than maximize the potential for positive officer-civilian interactions. Intrinsically, police agencies will need to modify pre-service and in-service training and how supervisors evaluate officer performance. Just as relying on crime rates can create perverse incentives, so too can evaluating officers based on the number of enforcement-related actions they take, such as stops, arrests, or tickets. . . .

The idealization of the Warrior concept, ubiquitous in modern law enforcement, was adopted with the best of intentions, but has resulted in rhetoric, attitudes, and actions that fall far short of the principles it purports to venerate. [The] solution requires law enforcement to incorporate its previously cherished principles into a new Guardian culture that views as its highest priority the protection of civilians from unnecessary indignity and harm. . . .

■ COPS PROGRAM (COMMUNITY-ORIENTED POLICING SERVICES)
Community Policing Dispatch
U.S. Department of Justice (January 2008)

Community Policing Defined

Community policing is a philosophy that promotes organizational strategies, which support the systematic use of partnerships and problem solving techniques, to proactively address the immediate conditions that give rise to public safety issues, such as crime, social disorder, and fear of crime.

"Community policing is a philosophy"

Community policing is often misunderstood as a program or set of programs such as D.A.R.E.®, foot patrols, bike patrols, or police substations. Although each may be incorporated as part of a broader strategic community policing plan, these programs are not community policing. Rather, community policing is an overarching philosophy that informs all aspects of police business.

"that promotes organizational strategies"

Community policing emphasizes changes in organizational structures to institutionalize its adoption. Agencies should be aligned to support partnerships and proactive problem solving in areas such as training, hiring, reward and authority structures, technology, and deployment.

"which support the systematic use of partnerships"

Community policing recognizes that police can rarely solve public safety problems alone and encourages interactive partnerships with relevant stakeholders. The range of potential partners includes other government agencies, businesses, nonprofits, individual community members, and the media. These partnerships should be used to accomplish the two interrelated goals of developing solutions through collaborative problem solving and improving public trust.

"and problem solving techniques,"

Community policing emphasizes proactive problem solving in a systematic and routine fashion. Problem solving should be infused into all police operations and guide decision-making efforts. Agencies are encouraged to think innovatively about their responses and view making arrests as only one of a wide array of potential responses.

"to proactively address the immediate conditions that give rise to public safety issues,"

Rather than responding to crime only after it occurs, community policing encourages agencies to work proactively [to] develop solutions to the immediate underlying conditions contributing to public safety problems. Rather than addressing root causes, police and their partners should focus on factors that are within their reach, such as limiting criminal opportunities and access to victims, increasing guardianship, and associating risk with unwanted behavior.

"such as crime, social disorder and fear of crime."

Community policing recognizes that social disorder and fear of crime are also important issues to be addressed by the police. Both significantly affect quality of life and have been shown to be important contributors to crime. It is also important for the police and the communities they serve to develop a shared understanding of their primary mission and goals. The public should be involved in shaping the role of the police and the prioritization of public safety problems.

■ **FAIRFIELD POLICE DEPARTMENT COMMUNITY
POLICING PROGRAMS**
http://fpdct.com/community (July 2018)

Car Seat Safety Check and Installation. Our Certified Child Passenger Safety Technicians will demonstrate and explain to caregivers about the proper selection, installation and use of car seats, booster seats and proper use of seatbelts.

Safe Return Network. The Safe Return Network is a computer database developed to assist emergency personnel in locating community members who suffer from conditions which [make] them susceptible to "wandering" and safely returning them home.

Are You Okay? Program (RUOK). The Are You O.K. Program is an electronic reassurance system. It was implemented in 1998 for the elderly, handicapped or homebound on a daily basis to help guarantee their well-being and safety. It allows you to register with the Fairfield Police Department to receive a phone call at your residence, electronically at a predetermined time every day. If there is no answer the computer will make a second attempt and if there is still no answer the computer alerts the Emergency Communications Center and a police officer is dispatched to the residence to check on the welfare of the subscriber.

Internship Program. The Fairfield Police Department prides itself in offering a meaningful educational and work experience through an internship program. The internship program allows college students an opportunity to personally evaluate the profession of law enforcement. The Fairfield Police Department will make every attempt to allow students the opportunity to experience each division of our agency including but not limited to patrol, traffic, investigative, records, communications, marine (seasonal availability), and animal control.

Citizen Police Academy. The Fairfield Police Department's Citizen Police Academy is an interactive program designed to inform participants about the wide-range of services provided by the department and provides an inside look at law enforcement operations and personnel. The Citizen Police Academy is a 10-week program designed to get a glimpse at life within the police department. It provides deep insight into the relationship between law enforcement and the community it serves. Classes include presentations by all divisions of the police department. This course is designed to give the citizen student a chance to see life through the eyes of police personnel. The course of study will cover many aspects of police operations, including: Patrol Procedures, Crime Prevention, Criminal Investigations, Gangs, Narcotics, States Attorney Office, Processing Crime Scenes, Stolen Cars and other assorted topics. The program will also include an opportunity to ride along with a Fairfield Police Officer and to participate in firearms training.

Police Athletic League. The goals of PAL [are] to provide positive activities for the youth in town and to promote positive interaction with the police department.

Crisis Intervention Team. CIT is a team of Police Officers with special training in recognition of, and response to, a wide variety of Mental Health and Substance Abuse issues. In addition to exposure to many forms of moderate to severe Mental Health/Behavioral Conditions, this training involves further development of skills in interpersonal communications, de-escalation techniques, conflict resolution, and awareness of available Mental Health and Substance Abuse resources.

Neighborhood Watch Program. The Neighborhood Watch is a comprehensive crime prevention program intended to educate the community on matters of safety, emergency management and crime prevention. Team leaders are developed and thoroughly informed on important matters regarding specific problems in your neighborhood. The goal of this program is to effectively educate the public and promote a safe and security minded environment. The Neighborhood Watch prepares team leaders to identify suspicious activity, vehicles, and persons and provides them with the skills and information necessary to convey specific details to the emergency communications center. In turn, this ensures the prioritizing of calls for service and the appropriate officer response. . . .

The Office of Public Affairs also provides the following services and programs for residents and businesses within Fairfield. . . .

Home Security Survey. Home and business security assessments to prevent vulnerabilities. Practical and useful information to heighten security consciousness, and create an effective, target hardened environment designed to resist [a] crime opportunist.

Identity Theft Presentations. Highlighting current and past trends of I.D. thefts and scams carried out by criminals. Discussions geared toward reducing victimization and increasing knowledge. Proven techniques taught to reduce your chances of becoming a target of scammers.

Crime Informational Forum. Community meetings engaging topics of interest and or concerns to the citizens with regards to crime, safety, etc. These meetings are designed to engage the public in serious discussions involving community problems or changes with regards to police services rendered. These can include any member of the police department including the Chief and Deputy Chief of Police.

◼ TRACEY L. MEARES, NORMS, LEGITIMACY, AND LAW ENFORCEMENT
79 Or. L. Rev. 391 (2000)

Why do some communities exhibit high crime rates while others do not? As an answer, I have looked to social disorganization theory. This is a theory developed by Clifford Shaw and Henry McKay, [who] maintained that low economic status, ethnic heterogeneity and residential mobility led to the disruption of community social organization, which, in turn, accounted for variation in crime and delinquency rates in a given area. See Clifford R. Shaw & Henry D. McKay, Juvenile Delinquency and Urban Areas (rev. ed. 1969). To support this theory, the researchers demonstrated that high rates of juvenile delinquency were specific to certain areas in the cities they studied and that these rates persisted over time despite population turnover. This finding motivated the researchers to reject individual-level explanations of delinquency and focus instead on the features of the communities in which the juveniles lived in order to explain the high crime rates.

Contemporary researchers have applied Shaw and McKay's insights to the longstanding problematic observation that African-Americans are under criminal justice system control out of proportion to their representation in the general population. [They] have documented that major differences often exist between the ecological contexts in which poor African-Americans typically reside on the one hand, and those in which poor whites typically reside on the other. Poor white families tend to reside in communities that feature more family-stable contexts than poor black families.... Indeed, Professors Robert Sampson and William Julius Wilson have noted, "Racial difference in poverty and family disruption are so strong that the 'worst' urban contexts in which whites reside are considerably better than the average context of black communities." Robert J. Sampson & William Julius Wilson, Toward a Theory of Race, Crime, and Urban Inequality, in Crime and Inequality 37, 42 (John Hagan & Ruth D. Peterson eds., 1995).

In terms of social organization theory, these different contexts translate into different levels of capacity of neighborhoods to resist and reduce crime. This is in large part because ecological contexts affect the extent to which neighborhood residents exert social control—informal mechanisms rather than formal regulation imposed by police and courts—to achieve public order....

Norm enforcement is easier when individuals in a community have social linkages and trust one another. Individuals who reside in communities in which there are few social linkages and where distrust is rampant will have difficulty exerting social control over one another. Empirical work bears this out. While ecological factors such as poverty, joblessness and family disruption are associated with crime, criminologists have shown that such factors are mediated by community-type social capital factors such as prevalence of friendship networks, participation in formal and informal organizations like churches and PTAs and the like. Such social structural factors provide the linkages along which norms of law abidingness can travel. They are "norm highways."...

Because social capital factors appear to matter more to explaining high crime rates in communities than individual-level factors, it makes sense to engineer crime policy that takes account of this reality. The social capital thesis calls into question policies that attempt to control crime simply by manipulating an individual's calculus regarding whether "crime pays" in the particular instance. In fact, deterrence-based strategies directed toward individual law breakers may even exacerbate the very activity the strategy purports to curb. For example, if lawmakers choose to address illegal drug selling by increasing the number of those convicted for drug selling and by increasing prison sentences for those convicted of such activity (which is basically the current American approach to drug crimes), then one expected consequence is that more individuals will be imprisoned for longer periods of time. Although the standard economic conception of crime suggests that this strategy should make a dent in the level of illegal drug activity, social organization theory's emphasis on social capital and norms suggests that this strategy will backfire. The highest numbers of those caught under this approach will tend to be street-level dealers, who are not evenly distributed throughout a city, but who are geographically concentrated in disadvantaged, minority neighborhoods.... Removal of these individuals in large numbers from their communities will be associated with higher levels of joblessness, low economic status, and family disruption, which in turn will disrupt the social structural and cultural determinants of community-based social control....

The best norm-based strategies will maximize social organization benefits without visiting as high a cost on disadvantaged communities as high rates of imprisonment do. Drug enforcement strategies, such as reverse drug stings, redistribute enforcement costs to communities that have the capacity to absorb the consequences of possible imprisonment. These, and strategies that attempt to disrupt illegal drug markets without relying at all on imprisonment, such as using loitering ordinances to make it difficult for drug buyers to find street sellers, can address illegal drug markets without concentrating the costs of imprisonment on the communities least prepared to absorb those costs....

NORMS AND COMPLIANCE

Do people obey the law because they fear the consequences if they do not? Or, do they obey the law for other reasons? Focusing on the former question, economists have looked primarily to deterrence theory to explain compliance. The foundations of this theory are well-known. People rationally maximize their utility, and they, therefore, shape their behavior in response to incentives and penalties associated with the criminal code....

Social psychologists have offered another view of compliance with the law. By pointing to normative bases for compliance rather than instrumental ones, these researchers have connected voluntary compliance with the law to the fact that individuals believe the law is "just" or because they believe that the authority enforcing the law has the right to do so. See Tom R. Tyler, Why People Obey the Law 3-4 (1990).... In contrast to the individual who complies with the law because she is responding to externally imposed punishments, the individual who complies for normative reasons does so because she feels an internal obligation. [There] is empirical work demonstrating that legitimacy matters more to compliance than instrumental factors, such as sanctions imposed by authorities on individuals who fail to follow the law or private rules....

Legitimacy ... can be acquired simply by changing procedures and practices of current officials in ways that require almost no additional resources. For example, some research indicates that police who regularly treat arrestees with courtesy are more likely than those who do not to be viewed as legitimate. While police officers may not like to be told to be more polite to arrestees, this research suggests that law enforcement gains could be achieved more cheaply than through more instrumental means simply by telling officers to "be nice." ...

COMMUNITY PARTICIPATION IN POLICING

Generation of participation by stakeholders in criminal justice processes is a feature of ... law enforcement that should enhance legitimacy of government. [A key aspect of participation is] the leveling of authority between government officials and the governed. [The process described here] requires government officials to cede some of their exclusive power to enforce laws.

In an attempt to address the complaints of residents concerned about gang violence and open-air drug selling, the City of Chicago has recently adopted an ordinance that empowers police officers to approach groups of people involved in gang loitering or narcotics-related loitering, inform those individuals that they are engaged in prohibited loitering, order the individuals to disperse from within sight and hearing of the place which the order was issued, and inform the individuals ordered to disperse that they will be subject to arrest if they fail to obey the order or return to the area during the next three hours. This ordinance is a revised version of another anti-gang loitering ordinance adopted by Chicago. The original ordinance was struck down by the Supreme Court as unconstitutionally vague. While the original ordinance defined loitering as staying in one place "with no apparent purpose," the revised ordinance defines gang loitering as "remaining in any one place under circumstances that would warrant a reasonable person to believe that the purpose or effect of that behavior is to enable a criminal street gang to establish control over identifiable areas, to intimidate others from entering those areas, or to conceal illegal activities." Similarly, narcotics-related loitering means "remaining in any one place under circumstances that would warrant a reasonable person to believe that the purpose or effect of that behavior is to facilitate the distribution of substances in violation of the Cannabis Control Act or the Illinois Controlled Substances Act." The definitions of both types of loitering incorporate specific language from both Justice Stevens' opinion for the plurality and Justice O'Connor's concurrence, which was joined by Justice Breyer.

[The] revised ordinance contains language that has both social organization benefits and legitimacy benefits. Consider social organization first. The sociology explained above suggests that law enforcement strategies that depend on imprisonment of a large number of geographically concentrated individuals should be avoided if possible. Of course, some criminal offenses demand imprisonment, such as murder or robbery. But other offenses likely are better dealt with through norm-focused strategies. Open-air drug selling is an example. The anti-gang, anti-narcotics loitering ordinance adopted by Chicago empowers police officers to disrupt drug markets without arresting large numbers of low-level dealers who retail in open areas and who are concentrated in minority, poor areas of the City. These dealers depend on confederates to stand in strategic areas to advertise the drugs they are selling to the many buyers who come from outside the particular community in which the drugs are sold—often the suburbs. Without the "advertisers" these outsiders cannot find the dealers. So, enforcement of the anti-narcotics provision of the ordinance can disrupt the market without arrest and potential subsequent conviction and imprisonment of the dealer. This is a social organization benefit....

The City Council recognized that drug selling and gang clashes are intimately bound up in place. Therefore, the ordinance provides that the Superintendent of Police shall designate areas of the city for enforcement by written directive. In order to make this designation, the ordinance also provides that the Superintendent "shall consult as he or she deems appropriate with persons who are knowledgeable.... Such persons may include ... elected and appointed officials of the area [and] community-based organizations ... who are familiar with the area."...

The consultation provision provides a key opening for increased perceptions of legitimacy of Chicago police among the communities in which this ordinance will be enforced. By its very structure the ordinance reduces the hierarchy inherent to municipal policing. This ordinance creates a partnership in the law enforcement process, and through that process creates greater accountability of the police to the members of affected communities. [This] process provides both invitations to participation as well as meaningful signals to community members that their opinions count. . . .

Our current approach to crime control is basically inconsistent with the project of improving community capacity for social control—especially the capacity of those communities that possess the highest crime rates. The United States imprisons more people than any other country in the world, and the bulk of those imprisoned are African-American males, who likely come from urban areas. Social organization theory tells us that this approach is dangerously counterproductive.

Notes

1. *Community policing and day-to-day operations.* Externally, a police department that follows a community policing model will emphasize partnerships between the department and other community organizations, including neighborhood associations, nonprofits, businesses, other government agencies, and the media. Departments therefore assign officers to foot and bicycle patrols, based on fixed geographic beats; they ask officers to use outreach to neighborhood associations and other community organizations, and to survey citizens about their satisfaction with police services; community policing also emphasizes de-specialization of officers.

This strategy has implications for internal operations of the police department, as well. When it comes to internal operations, the department leadership sets general goals and policies but decentralizes more of the tactical planning to the officers in the field. Community policing utilizes computers for crime mapping and for interaction with the community.

2. *Community policing and measures of success.* There are theoretical reasons (such as those discussed by Tracey Meares above) to believe that community policing actually reduces crime. Some evaluations of programs in the field also offer reasons to be hopeful. Once the community policing model became firmly established in the 1990s, the United States also saw a remarkable drop in crime rates. Perhaps more effective policing can take credit for at least part of this good news. Community policing can claim credit in some cities for greater community satisfaction and less fear of crime, even when actual reductions in crime are harder to find.

On the other hand, the success or failure of community policing is terribly difficult to measure—especially when police administrators use the label "community policing" to describe virtually any change in management or department structure. Do the advocates of community policing make claims about its social effects that are measurable and verifiable? How would you measure the success of your local "community" police department?

3. *Control via legal rules versus politics.* Community policing tends to give more authority to the officer on the beat and to give supervisors less control over daily activities and choices of patrol officers. Does this development make it difficult to enforce procedural requirements? Is decentralized authority inconsistent with the very idea of uniform rules of procedure influencing all police officers?

The U.S. Supreme Court engaged with these questions in City of Chicago v. Morales, 527 U.S. 41 (1999). The Court struck down an anti-loitering ordinance that the city passed to suppress gang activity, holding that the ordinance was unconstitutionally vague. (The text of that ordinance appears below, in Problem 1-2.) The opinions of the justices in *Morales* reveal different visions of "ordinary" policing and the ordinary methods of controlling police. For the plurality and concurring justices, pre-announced rules of law are necessary to hold police discretion to an acceptable minimum; legislators and judges control the police through formal sources of law. An unduly vague criminal law could "authorize and even encourage arbitrary and discriminatory enforcement."

For the dissenting justices in *Morales*, however, police discretion is perfectly ordinary, even desirable. As Justice Thomas put it, control of the police comes from political pressure on elected officials at the local level rather than from pre-announced rules:

> Police officers are not, and have never been, simply enforcers of the criminal law. They wear other hats—importantly, they have long been vested with the responsibility for preserving the public peace. In order to perform their peace-keeping responsibilities satisfactorily, the police inevitably must exercise discretion. Indeed, by empowering them to act as peace officers, the law assumes that the police will exercise that discretion responsibly and with sound judgment. That is not to say that the law should not provide objective guidelines for the police, but simply that it cannot rigidly constrain their every action.... Just as we trust officers to rely on their experience and expertise in order to make spur-of-the-moment determinations about amorphous legal standards such as "probable cause" and "reasonable suspicion," so we must trust them to determine whether a group of loiterers contains individuals (in this case members of criminal street gangs) whom the city has determined threaten the public peace.

Professors Dan Kahan and Tracey Meares argue that doctrines granting broad discretion to police officers (including loitering laws) are more defensible today than in the 1960s because of the rising political power of African Americans in the nation's inner cities. Techniques formerly used to harass and exclude African Americans from public life could now become the tools of minority communities to free themselves from rampant criminality. Kahan & Meares, The Coming Crisis of Criminal Procedure, 86 Geo. L.J. 1153 (1998). Under what circumstances is their vision of democratic accountability realistic?

4. *Social norms and the sources of crime.* As the reading excerpt above implies, Professor Meares assigns only a secondary role to the police in the prevention of crime. The police (and the criminal procedure rules that structure their behavior) can contribute best to the control of crime if they ultimately strengthen the *community's* own ability to control crime. Thus, the "disorganization" of a community is the most salient source of crime, and the best rules for the police are built around an awareness of that source.

What are some other accounts of the sources of crime, and how might those accounts change your views on the proper role of the police? Several criminological theories over the years have emphasized the genetic and biological components of crime. (Sometimes this leads to searches for identifiable traits among a criminal "type," an enterprise that too often has degenerated into racial stereotyping or other unsound generalizations.) If you believe that some individuals have a biological or psychological predisposition to commit crimes, how might that affect the rules you would expect the police to follow? If the causes of female crime are different from the causes of male crime, does that have implications for policing?

Other criminological theories emphasize various aspects of the criminal's social environment. For instance, according to "strain theory," unemployment, poverty, and other sources of stress induce many people to commit crimes. "Social learning" theory suggests that many criminals learn to commit their crimes because the people around them reinforce criminal actions and attitudes. The influence of these theories and many other explanations for crime have waxed and waned among criminologists over the years. See Robert Agnew, Crime Causation: Sociological Theories, in Encyclopedia of Crime and Justice (Joshua Dressler ed., 2002). For each of these accounts of the sources of crime, how might the police best contribute

to the control of crime? For a survey of the leading criminological accounts of crime, see the web extension for this chapter at *http://www.crimpro.com/extension/ch01*.

5. *Police toleration of verbal abuse.* Police officers must deal with people who react to them in hostile ways, including verbal abuse and physical violence. Sometimes police arrest citizens for direct interference with their duties and charge them with obstruction or interfering with an arrest or assault, but in the absence of physical contact police more often respond with the indirect charge of disorderly conduct. Prosecutors refuse to charge some of these arrests, and trial courts dismiss others.

Most appellate decisions reverse disorderly conduct convictions based solely on profane insults directed toward police officers. See Jones v. State, 798 So. 2d 1241 (Miss. 2001); Patterson v. United States, 999 F.Supp. 2d 300 (D.D.C. 2013) (allowing trial of civil rights claim based on arrest for use of profanity during Occupy D.C. event in public park). But a few courts sustain such convictions. See Spry v. State, 396 Md. 682 (Md. 2007) (affirming arrest for disturbance of the peace one day after Spry initially refused an officer's request to leave the scene of a fight and said to the police officer, "Fuck you, bitch"). Problem 1-3 below calls for you to consider potential police responses to verbal abuse.

6. *Juvenile curfews as a community policing tool.* Many state and local governments have passed laws empowering the police to enforce a "curfew" on persons less than 18 years old. The practice is now commonplace, particularly in larger cities. See Emma G. Fitzsimmons, Baltimore Joins Cities Toughening Curfews, Citing Safety but Eliciting Concern, N.Y. Times, June 21, 2014. Children and parents who challenge the validity of these laws argue that the curfews are unconstitutionally vague and interfere with fundamental rights such as the "right to travel" or the right of parents to make basic parenting decisions without government interference. The state court response has been mixed, with the largest group of states upholding the statutes or ordinances, noting that they do not simply ban juveniles from being "present" in public after dark. Instead, they allow juveniles to be outdoors for certain legitimate reasons or in the company of a parent. See Ramos v. Town of Vernon, 761 A.2d 705 (Conn. 2000). A few state courts have struck down the juvenile curfew laws. See City of Sumner v. Walsh, 61 P.3d 1111 (Wash. 2003); State v. J.P., 907 So. 2d 1101 (Fla. 2004). To gain a better sense of this debate among state courts and lower federal courts, along with some historical background on the use of juvenile curfews, see the web extension for this chapter at *http://www.crimpro.com/extension/ch01*. Problem 1-4 below calls for you to evaluate curfews from the perspective of the community policing philosophy.

7. *Adult curfews.* There is a long and largely disreputable history of adult curfews in the United States. Before the Civil War, curfew laws in the South designated times when slaves could be on the streets. During the late 1800s, curfew ordinances flourished in places where there were large numbers of immigrants, because of fears that immigrants would not properly supervise their children. In 1941, emergency curfews were imposed on American citizens of Japanese ancestry. A variety of adult curfew, loitering, and vagrancy laws were invalidated in the late 1960s through the early 1980s as violations of the basic right of adult citizens to go where they want, whenever they want. See Papachristou v. City of Jacksonville, 405 U.S. 156 (1972) (striking down a vagrancy ordinance); Kolender v. Lawson, 461 U.S. 352 (1983) (rejecting a California statute requiring citizens who loiter to account for their presence and show "reasonable and reliable" identification when required by

a police officer; Lawson was detained about 15 times during a two-year period for walking in isolated areas at late hours). The Supreme Court reaffirmed this line of cases by striking down the gang loitering ordinance in Chicago v. Morales, 527 U.S. 41 (1999). In a society searching urgently for ways to control crime, should courts reconsider the validity of adult curfew laws? Is the right to prowl at 3 A.M. essential to a free country?

Problem 1-2. Loitering With No Apparent Purpose

The city of Chicago passed an ordinance, §8-4-015 of the Municipal Code, giving police authority to disrupt loitering by gang members.

(a) Whenever a police officer observes a person whom he reasonably believes to be a criminal street gang member loitering in any public place with one or more other persons, he shall order all such persons to disperse and remove themselves from the area. Any person who does not promptly obey such an order is in violation of this section....

(c) As used in this section:

(1) "Loiter" means to remain in any one place with no apparent purpose.

(2) "Criminal street gang" means any ongoing organization, association in fact or group of three or more persons, whether formal or informal, having as one of its substantial activities the commission of one or more [enumerated] criminal acts, ... and whose members individually or collectively engage in or have engaged in a pattern of criminal gang activity....

(e) Any person who violates this section is subject to a fine of not less than $100 and not more than $500 for each offense, or imprisonment for not more than six months, or both. In addition to or instead of the above penalties, any person who violates this section maybe required to perform up to 120 hours of community service....

During the three years of its enforcement, the police issued over 89,000 dispersal orders and arrested over 42,000 people for violating the ordinance. In 1997, the Illinois Supreme Court held that the ordinance violated the U.S. Constitution. City of Chicago v. Jesus Morales, 687 N.E.2d 53 (Ill. 1997). The U.S. Supreme Court agreed. City of Chicago v. Morales, 527 U.S. 41 (1999).

Imagine that you are a legal and policy advisor to a police department in a major city in the United States. How would you recommend revising the Chicago ordinance to overcome constitutional objections based on the "vagueness" doctrine? Would the enforcement of such an ordinance contribute to the objectives of community policing?

Problem 1-3. If You Can't Give 'Em a Rap, Give 'Em a Ride

At approximately 2 A.M. on December 7, Police Officer Finnegan stopped a car in Rockland, Maine, for having a license plate light out, illegal attachment of plates, and suspicion of operating under the influence (OUI). Finnegan smelled alcohol on the breath of the driver, Gifford Campbell, and asked Campbell to step out and walk to the front of Finnegan's cruiser for field sobriety tests. Campbell's passenger, Sharon Matson, came out of the car yelling, "No, no fucking way. You're not doing to him what you did to me," a reference to the fact that Finnegan had arrested her for OUI a few months before. Finnegan told Matson to sit in the car, to calm down, and not to interfere, but she refused and kept shouting.

Finnegan performed a horizontal gaze nystagmus test on Campbell but did no additional field sobriety tests because Matson continued yelling at him and no back-up officers were available. As Finnegan told Campbell he was under arrest for operating after suspension, Matson "charged forward," saying, "No, no fucking way. You're not arresting him." Matson stepped to within a couple of feet of Finnegan; as he began walking Campbell to the cruiser, she stepped in his way and refused to move, shouting all the while. Finnegan warned her she could be arrested for obstructing government administration and told her to step back, get out of the way, and stop interfering. She responded by saying, "Arrest me." He pushed her out of the way with his left hand, causing Matson to fall down. Finnegan continued walking with Campbell to the cruiser. Matson got up from the ground and followed them, shouting. Finnegan stopped to search Campbell, and then moved him toward the rear door of the cruiser. Matson stepped in front of them, stood with her back against the door, spread her arms, and said, "No, no way, you're not taking him to jail." Finnegan told her to get out of the way, and she refused and again told him to arrest her. He moved her aside again, this time with his right hand, put Campbell in the cruiser, and arrested her. Matson said, "Good, I wanted you to arrest me." Finnegan did not fear Matson at any time and she never struck him or threatened him.

Title 17-A M.R.S.A. §751(1) provides: "A person is guilty of obstructing government administration if the person uses force, violence or intimidation or engages in any criminal act with the intent to interfere with a public servant performing or purporting to perform an official function." As a trial judge, would you rule that the evidence described above is sufficient to support a conviction under this statute? Compare State v. Matson, 818 N.E.2d 213 (Me. 2003). Would your ruling change if Matson called the officer a crude name, such as "a fucking asshole"? How about if she were joined by a large crowd, all of them expressing verbal hostility to Finnegan's decision to arrest Campbell? Compare State v. Janisczak, 579 A.2d 736 (Me. 1990). Would you hold police officers to higher standards of tolerance than might be expected of ordinary citizens?

How upset do you think Officer Finnegan would be if the trial judge were to dismiss charges against Matson? Perhaps the answer comes from the observation made by some police officers that "If you can't give 'em a rap, you can still give 'em a ride."

If you were responsible for training police, would you recommend that officers enforce civility, both among citizens and toward officers? Would you draft a policy that offers guidance on this question?

Problem 1-4. Juvenile Curfews

At 10:35 P.M., 15-year-old David Simmons and a friend were skateboarding in a Panora, Iowa, shopping center. A police officer issued citations to them for violating a Panora juvenile curfew ordinance, which provided as follows:

1. It is unlawful for any minor [under 18] to be or remain upon any of the alleys, streets or public places or places of business and amusement in the city between the hours of 10 P.M. and 5 A.M. of the following day.
2. The curfew shall not apply to any minor who is accompanied by a guardian, parent or other person charged with the care and custody of such minor, or other responsible person over 18 years of age, nor shall the restriction apply to any minor who is traveling between his home or place of residence and the place where any approved place of employment, church, municipal or school function is being held.
3. It is unlawful for any parent, guardian or other person charged with the care and custody of any minor to allow or permit such minor to be in or upon any of the streets, alleys, places of business or amusement, or other public places within the curfew hours except as provided in subsection 2.
4. It is unlawful for any person, firm or corporation operating a place of business or amusement to allow or permit any minor to be in or upon any place of business or amusement operated by them within the curfew hours except as provided in subsection 2.
5. Any peace officer of this city while on duty is hereby empowered to arrest any minor who violates the curfew. Upon arrest, the minor shall be returned to the custody of the parent, guardian or other person charged with the care and custody of the minor.

Simmons was found guilty of violating the curfew ordinance. The penalty imposed was a $1 fine plus surcharge and costs. Simmons appealed the conviction, with strong support from his parents. The Simmons family also asked the city council to repeal or amend the curfew ordinance.

As an appellate court judge, how would you rule on his appeal? Is the ordinance constitutional? As a member of the city council, would you vote to repeal or amend the ordinance? Compare City of Panora v. Simmons, 445 N.W.2d 363 (Iowa 1989). As a parent, how would you feel about a local curfew law? Would your reaction depend on your view of the police purpose when enforcing a curfew? Are police pursuing a crime control function or a community caretaker function (or something else entirely) when they enforce a juvenile curfew?

C. POLICING ORGANIZATIONS

Law enforcement officers work in bureaucracies—more than 17,000 separate organizations in the United States. The statistical profile reprinted here, based on a recurring national survey, reveals some of the amazing variety among these organizations.

As we have seen in this chapter, a relatively small portion of police work involves the criminal law enforcement that we try to regulate through the law of criminal procedure. Given the huge range of routine activities of police officers, and the great variety in police organizations, is it even possible for regulators of the police—the lawyers, legislators, judges, budget makers, and citizens who create the criminal law procedure—to find any guiding principles that apply across these many settings? The Herbert Packer essay reprinted below offers two classic ways to answer this question.

■ BUREAU OF JUSTICE STATISTICS, LOCAL POLICE DEPARTMENTS, 2013: PERSONNEL, POLICIES, AND PRACTICES
NCJ 248677, May 2015

As of January 1, 2013, the more than 12,000 local police departments in the United States employed an estimated 605,000 persons on a full-time basis. This total included about 477,000 sworn officers (those with general arrest powers) and about 128,000 nonsworn employees.... In 2013, the 605,000 local police employees nationwide represented a majority (58%) of the full-time personnel working for general purpose state and local law enforcement agencies. [The 3,012 Sheriffs with primary law enforcement responsibility in their jurisdictions employed 34 percent of the full-time personnel, and the primary state agencies employed 8 percent.]

About 68% of local police officers were assigned to patrol operations, and about 16% worked in the investigations area. The 128,000 full-time nonsworn (or civilian) personnel in local police departments accounted for 21% of all full-time employees. [Most departments with 100 or more officers] reported that their nonsworn employees performed duties related to research and statistics (81% of departments), accounting (79%), dispatch (72%), information technology (57%), forensics (56%), and human resources (54%). In addition to full-time employees, local police departments employed about 57,000 persons on a part-time basis....

About half of local police departments employed fewer than 10 officers.... A total of 645 (5%) local police departments employed 100 or more officers in 2013. These departments employed 63% of all full-time officers.... The New York City Police Department remained the largest local police department in 2013, with 34,454 full-time officers.... More than half of local police officers were employed in jurisdictions with 100,000 or more residents....

In 2013, about 58,000 (12%) of the full-time sworn personnel in local police departments were female. From 2007 to 2013, female representation remained about the same. [The] percentage of female officers in jurisdictions with 250,000 or more residents (17%) was more than twice that in jurisdictions with fewer than 25,000 residents (7%).... An estimated 3% of local police chiefs were female, including about 7% of the chiefs in jurisdictions with 250,000 or more residents.

[More] than a quarter (27%) of full-time local police officers were members of a racial or ethnic minority. About 130,000 minority local police were employed in 2013. The total represented an increase of about 78,000 (up 150%) since 1987.... Departments serving larger jurisdictions were more diverse than departments serving smaller jurisdictions....

The overall average starting salary for entry-level local police officers in 2013 was $44,400, about the same as in 2003 after controlling for inflation. This amount represented a 7% increase from 1993, when newly hired entry-level officers earned the 2013 equivalent of about $41,500.... Starting salaries for officers were about 19% higher in departments with a collective bargaining agreement for sworn personnel, compared to departments without a collective bargaining agreement. In 2013, a majority of the local police departments serving a population of 10,000 or more residents had an active collective bargaining agreement. In some departments, officer salaries could be supplemented by certain types of special pay related to educational achievement, special skills, special duty assignments, and other circumstances....

In 2013, all local police departments serving a population of 100,000 or more, and nearly all departments in smaller jurisdictions, had a minimum education requirement for new officers. The most common requirement (84% of departments) was a high school diploma. An estimated 15% of departments had some type of college requirement, including 10% that required a 2-year degree and 1% that required a 4-year degree. An estimated 54% of departments with a degree requirement considered military service as an alternative.

[About] 7 in 10 local police departments, including about 9 in 10 departments serving a population of 25,000 or more, had a mission statement that included a community policing component. Departments with a community policing component employed 88% of all local police officers in 2013.... A majority of the local police departments serving 25,000 or more residents reported that they had one or more problem-solving partnerships or agreements with local organizations in their community in 2013. [These] partnerships and agreements were typically with other law enforcement agencies, school groups, neighborhood associations, local public agencies, business groups, advocacy groups, youth service organizations, senior citizen groups, or faith-based organizations. . . .

Most departments serving 25,000 or more residents, including more than 90% of those serving a population of 100,000 or more, used geographic beat assignments for patrol officers. A majority of the departments serving 50,000 or more residents actively encouraged patrol officer involvement in problem-solving projects.... A majority of the departments serving 10,000 or more residents trained all new recruits for 8 hours or more in community policing skills, such as problem-solving and developing community partnerships. . . .

In 2013, about 9 in 10 local police departments employing 100 officers or more had personnel designated (whether part of a specialized unit or not) to address child abuse (90%), and about 8 in 10 had personnel designated to address gangs (83%), juvenile crime (82%), and domestic violence (81%).... A majority of local police departments with 100 or more officers also had designated personnel to perform special operational tasks related to tactical operations (95%), terrorism or homeland security (71%), and fugitives or warrants (68%). . . .

■ HERBERT L. PACKER, TWO MODELS OF THE CRIMINAL PROCESS
113 U. Pa. L. Rev. 1 (1964)

... The kind of criminal process we have depends importantly on certain value choices that are reflected, explicitly or implicitly, in its habitual functioning. The kind of model we need is one that permits us to recognize explicitly the value choices that underlie the details of the criminal process. In a word, what we need is a *normative* model, or rather two models, to let us perceive the normative antinomy that runs deep in the life of the criminal law. These models may not be labeled Good and Bad, and I hope they will not be taken in that sense. Rather, they represent an attempt to abstract two separate value systems that compete for attention in the operation of the criminal process.... I call these two models the Due Process Model and the Crime Control Model....

CRIME CONTROL VALUES

The value system that underlies the Crime Control Model is based on the proposition that the repression of criminal conduct is by far the most important function to be performed by the criminal process. The failure of law enforcement to bring criminal conduct under tight control is viewed as leading to the breakdown of public order and thence to the disappearance of an important condition of human freedom.... The claim ultimately is that the criminal process is a positive guarantor of social freedom. In order to achieve this high purpose, the Crime Control Model requires that primary attention be paid to the efficiency with which the criminal process operates to screen suspects, determine guilt, and secure appropriate dispositions of persons convicted of crime....

The model, in order to operate successfully, must produce a high rate of apprehension and conviction and must do so in a context where the magnitudes being dealt with are very large, and the resources for dealing with them are very limited. There must then be a premium on speed and finality. Speed, in turn, depends on informality and on uniformity; finality depends on minimizing the occasions for challenge. The process must not be cluttered with ceremonious rituals that do not advance the progress of a case. Facts can be established more quickly through interrogation in a police station than through the formal process of examination and cross-examination in a court; it follows that extrajudicial processes should be preferred to judicial processes, informal to formal operations. Informality is not enough; there must also be uniformity. Routine stereotyped procedures are essential if large numbers are being handled. The model that will operate successfully on these presuppositions must be an administrative, almost a managerial, model. The image that comes to mind is an assembly line or a conveyor belt down which moves an endless stream of cases, never stopping, carrying the cases to workers who stand at fixed stations and who perform on each case as it comes by the same small but essential operation that brings it one step closer to being a finished product, or, to exchange the metaphor for the reality, a closed file.

The criminal process, on this model, is seen as a screening process in which each successive stage—prearrest investigation, arrest, post-arrest investigation, preparation for trial, trial or entry of plea, conviction, and disposition—involves a series of routinized operations whose success is gauged primarily by their tendency to pass the case along to a successful conclusion.

What is a successful conclusion? One that throws off at an early stage those cases in which it appears unlikely that the person apprehended is an offender and then secures, as expeditiously as possible, the conviction of the rest with a minimum of occasions for challenge, let alone postaudit. By the application of administrative expertness, primarily that of the police and prosecutors, an early determination of probable innocence or guilt emerges. The probably innocent are screened out. The probably guilty are passed quickly through the remaining stages of the process. The key to the operation of the model as to those who are not screened out is what I shall call a presumption of guilt....

The presumption of guilt allows the Crime Control Model to deal efficiently with large numbers. The supposition is that the screening processes operated by police and prosecutors are reliable indicators of probable guilt. Once a man has been investigated without being found to be probably innocent, or, to put it differently, once a determination has been made that there is enough evidence of guilt so that he should be held for further action rather than released from the process, then all subsequent activity directed toward him is based on the view that he is probably guilty....

It would be a mistake to think of the presumption of guilt as the opposite of the presumption of innocence. [The] two concepts embody different rather than opposite ideas.... The presumption of innocence is really a direction to the authorities to ignore the presumption of guilt in their treatment of the suspect. It tells them, in effect, to close their eyes to what will frequently seem to be factual probabilities....

For this model ... the preliminary screening processes operated by the police and the prosecuting officials contain adequate guarantees of reliable factfinding. Indeed, the position is a stronger one. It is that subsequent processes, particularly of a formal adjudicatory nature, are unlikely to produce as reliable factfinding as the expert administrative process that precedes them.... It becomes important, then, to place as few restrictions as possible on the character of the administrative factfinding processes and to limit restrictions to those that enhance reliability, excluding those designed for other purposes....

The complementary proposition is that the subsequent stages are relatively unimportant and should be truncated as much as possible. [There] have to be devices for dealing with the suspect after the preliminary screening process has resulted in a determination of probable guilt. The focal device ... is the plea of guilty; through its use adjudicative factfinding is reduced to a minimum. It might be said of the Crime Control Model that, reduced to its barest essentials and when operating at its most successful pitch, it consists of two elements: (a) an administrative factfinding process leading to exoneration of the suspect, or to (b) the entry of a plea of guilty.

DUE PROCESS VALUES

If the Crime Control Model resembles an assembly line, the Due Process Model looks very much like an obstacle course. Each of its successive stages is designed to present formidable impediments to carrying the accused any further along in the process....

The Due Process Model [takes] a view of informal, nonadjudicative factfinding that stresses the possibility of error: people are notoriously poor observers of disturbing events—the more emotion-arousing the context, the greater the possibility that recollection will be incorrect; confessions and admissions by persons in police custody may be induced by physical or psychological coercion, so that the police end up hearing what the suspect thinks they want to hear rather than the truth; witnesses may be animated by a bias or interest that no one would trouble to discover except one specially charged with protecting the interests of the accused—which the police are not. Considerations of this kind all lead to the rejection of informal factfinding processes as definitive of factual guilt and to the insistence on formal, adjudicative, adversary factfinding processes in which the factual case against the accused is publicly heard by an impartial tribunal and is evaluated only after the accused has had a full opportunity to discredit the case against him. Even then the distrust of factfinding processes that animates the Due Process Model is not dissipated. The possibilities of human error being what they are, further scrutiny is necessary, or at least must be available, lest in the heat of battle facts have been overlooked or suppressed.... The demand for finality is thus very low in the Due Process Model.

[Under the Due Process Model, if] efficiency suggests shortcuts around reliability, those demands must be rejected. The aim of the process is at least as much to protect the factually innocent as it is to convict the factually guilty. It somewhat resembles quality control in industrial technology: tolerable deviation from standard varies with the importance of conformity to standard in the destined use of the product. The Due Process Model resembles a factory that has to devote a substantial part of its input to quality control. This necessarily reduces quantitative output.

[The Due Process Model has evolved] from an original matrix of concern with the maximization of reliability into something quite different and more far-reaching. This complex of values can be symbolized although not adequately described by the concept of the primacy of the individual and the complementary concept of limitation on official power.

The combination of stigma and loss of liberty that is embodied in the end result of the criminal process is viewed as being the heaviest deprivation that government can inflict on the individual. Furthermore, the processes that culminate in these highly afflictive sanctions are in themselves coercive, restricting, and demeaning. Power is always subject to abuse, sometimes subtle, other times, as in the criminal process, open and ugly. Precisely because of its potency in subjecting the individual to the coercive power of the state, the criminal process must, on this model, be subjected to controls and safeguards that prevent it from operating with maximal efficiency. According to this ideology, maximal efficiency means maximal tyranny....

The most modest-seeming but potentially far-reaching mechanism by which the Due Process Model implements these antiauthoritarian values is the doctrine of legal guilt. According to this doctrine, an individual is not to be held guilty of crime merely on a showing that in all probability, based upon reliable evidence, he did factually what he is said to have done. Instead, he is to be held guilty if and only if these factual determinations are made in procedurally regular fashion and by authorities acting within competences duly allocated to them....

Another strand in the complex of attitudes that underlies the Due Process Model is the idea—itself a shorthand statement for a complex of attitudes—of equality.... Stated most starkly, the ideal of equality holds that "there can be no equal justice where the kind of trial a man gets depends on the amount of money he has." ... The demands made by a norm of this kind are likely by its very nature to be quite sweeping....

There is a final strand of thought in the Due Process Model whose presence is often ignored but which needs to be candidly faced if thought on the subject is not to be obscured. That is a mood of skepticism about the morality and the utility of the criminal sanction. [We] are told that the criminal law's notion of just condemnation and punishment is a cruel hypocrisy visited by a smug society on the psychologically and economically crippled; that its premise of a morally autonomous will with at least some measure of choice whether to comply with the values expressed in a penal code is unscientific and outmoded. [Doubts] about the ends for which power is being exercised create pressure to limit the discretion with which that power is exercised....

What assumptions do we make about the sources of authority to shape the real-world operations of the criminal process? ... Because the Crime Control Model is basically an affirmative model, emphasizing at every turn the existence and exercise of official power, its validating authority is ultimately legislative (although proximately administrative). Because the Due Process Model is basically a negative model, asserting limits on the nature of official power and on the modes of its exercise, its validating authority is judicial and requires an appeal to supra-legislative law, to the law of the Constitution. . . . That is at once the strength and the weakness of the Due Process Model: its strength because in our system the appeal to the Constitution provides the last and the overriding word; its weakness because saying no in specific cases is an exercise in futility unless there is a general willingness on the part of the officials who operate the process to apply negative prescriptions across the board. . . .

Notes

1. *Training for law enforcement agents.* Just as law enforcement agencies vary greatly in their size and level of specialization, they also differ from one another in the training they offer to new recruits and to veteran officers. About 45,000 recruits each year receive training in one of 664 state and local "academies." See Bureau of Justice Statistics, State and Local Law Enforcement Training Academies, 2013 (July 2016, NCJ 249784). Some police departments and sheriffs' offices operate their own academies, but educational institutions such as colleges or technical schools operate about half of all academies. About half of all academies train recruits based on a military model, emphasizing physical demands and psychological pressure. Others rely on a model that emphasizes academic achievement, physical training, and a more relaxed instructor-trainee relationship. The training programs last an average of 21 weeks, excluding any department-based field training. Major topics covered in training include firearms (71 hours), self-defense (60 hours), criminal and constitutional law (53 hours), patrol procedures (52 hours), investigations (42 hours), community-based problem solving (40 hours), emergency vehicle operations (38 hours), report writing (25 hours), traffic law (23 hours), and use of force and de-escalation tactics (21 hours). Would you expect the in-service training for veteran officers to follow this same mix of topics, or would you expect the topics to change?

2. *Herbert Packer's models of criminal procedure and the community policing philosophy.* Professor Herbert Packer created a way of thinking about criminal procedure that has remained influential to this day. His "Crime Control" and "Due Process" models offer a way to identify some of the values and assumptions associated with different approaches to procedural controversies. You might find it useful to refer to these models as organizing principles from time to time as you think about difficult procedural questions later in this course. How do Packer's two models differ in their description of police work? Do the two models share any assumptions about policing? Would a shift to community policing be more appealing to a Crime Control advocate or to a Due Process advocate? Or does community policing promote forms of policing that Packer's account does not address at all? Consider an alternative method of thinking about the criminal process, proposed by John Griffiths:

> Packer's [model] rests not upon two but upon a single, albeit unarticulated, basic conception of the nature of the criminal process—that it is a battleground of fundamentally hostile forces, where the only relevant variable is the "balance of advantage." [Packer] assumes disharmony, fundamentally irreconcilable interests, a state of war. We can start from an assumption of reconcilable—even mutually supportive—interests, a state of love. [There is] a "real-world" institution which occasionally

inflicts punishments on offenders for their offenses but which is nonetheless built upon a fundamental assumption of harmony of interest and love. [I therefore offer] a "Family Model" of the criminal process. [People operating within the Family Model would accept] the idea that criminals are just people who are deemed to have offended—that we are all ... both actual and potential criminals....

What other implications would follow from a Family Model? For one thing, that ideology would necessarily be accompanied by a basic faith in public officials; everyone would assume, as a general matter, that if a public official has a particular role or duty, he can be expected to carry it out in good faith and using his best judgment.... Basic faith in public officials would revolutionize American criminal procedure.... Our assumption that the state and the individual are in battle compels us to believe that any "discretion" ... will necessarily be exercised either on behalf of the individual's interest or on behalf of the state's. We see only Packer's two poles as the possible outcomes of discretion.

Griffiths, Ideology in Criminal Procedure, or a Third "Model" of the Criminal Process, 79 Yale L.J. 359 (1970). Is the "family" model more consistent with the realities of police-community relations in a world dominated by the community policing model? Does Packer's model suggest anything about different ways in which victims of alleged crimes might become involved in criminal investigations or adjudications? See Kent Roach, Four Models of the Criminal Process, 89 J. Crim. L. & Criminology 671 (1999) (proposing "punitive" and "non-punitive" models of victim involvement); Douglas Beloof, The Third Model of Criminal Process: The Victim Participation Model, 1999 Utah L. Rev. 289.

3. *Preview of the criminal process.* In those limited situations when the police investigate a crime and file charges (or recommend that prosecutors file charges), a complicated adjudication process begins. For these investigations destined to become criminal cases, it may be helpful to preview the most important stages in the criminal process. One famous visual tool for introducing the flow of cases through a typical criminal court system appears on the website for the Bureau of Justice Statistics, at *https://www.bjs.gov/content/largechart.cfm.* For a more elaborate survey of the common terminology and functions of state criminal court proceedings, see the web extension for this chapter at *http://www.crimpro.com/extension/ch01.*

II

Brief Police-Citizen Encounters

Police officers sometimes restrict the movement of individuals ("seize" them) or intrude into their privacy to obtain information ("search" them). But in most of these encounters, the stop or search does not last very long or intrude very deeply. Courts and legislatures have established rules to control these encounters between government agents and the public. Yet the restrictions on this police behavior are not as demanding as the rules that apply when government agents attempt to carry out a full-blown search or seizure. This chapter deals with efforts to regulate these lesser searches and seizures.

One of the most important legal constraints on these brief searches and seizures comes from the Fourth Amendment to the U.S. Constitution, which provides as follows:

> The right of the people to be secure in their persons, houses, papers, and effects, against unreasonable searches and seizures, shall not be violated, and no Warrants shall issue, but upon probable cause, supported by Oath or affirmation, and particularly describing the place to be searched, and the persons or things to be seized.

The Fourth Amendment and its analogs in state constitutions have spawned a huge and complex case law. They have also shaped many state and federal statutes, as well as prosecutorial office guidelines and police department directives and training manuals. To understand the complex law of search and seizure, it is helpful (and probably necessary) to approach the material with some general conceptual framework.

The threshold question in any police-citizen encounter is whether the encounter rises to the level of a "search" or a "seizure" under the Fourth Amendment. To determine whether a search has occurred, courts conduct two inquiries: (1) whether the police have trespassed onto one of the constitutionally protected areas under the Fourth Amendment ("persons, houses, papers, and effects") with the intent to obtain information; or (2) whether the police have invaded a person's reasonable expectation of privacy. To determine whether a seizure of a person has occurred, courts examine whether a reasonable person would "feel free to leave" or to terminate the encounter with the police under the circumstances. Part A shows how courts apply these fact-intensive tests.

Under the traditional framework, once a court determines that a search or seizure has occurred, it examines whether the search or seizure was authorized by a warrant. On this view, the Fourth Amendment incorporates a strong preference for warrants (that is, a judicial determination that a proposed search or seizure is justified), that warrantless searches and seizures are generally considered unreasonable, and that exceptions to the "warrant requirement" are "jealously and carefully drawn." State and federal courts invoke this theme. This preference for warrants grows out of the apparent emphasis on limited warrants in the constitutional text.

Before the late 1960s, the recognized exceptions to the warrant requirement were indeed fairly few. Most prominent were two umbrella categories: exigent circumstances and consent. Warrants were generally required unless the police could show exigent circumstances or consent to search or seize. Within the category of exigent circumstances, courts developed exceptions to the warrant requirement such as risk of flight or destruction of evidence.

A sensible approach for the study of search and seizure in such a legal system is to start with the foundational elements—the process for warrants and the standard of probable cause—and then to identify and study the exceptions. This would work well if the rules were ordinarily followed and the exceptions were modest. But in the modern law of search and seizure, the exceptions have swallowed the traditional rules. In doing so, they have changed the entire framework and the best way to study searches and seizures.

Modern search and seizure law is astoundingly complex and contradictory. A survey of current "exceptions" to the warrant requirement—some of which appear in this chapter, and others in Chapters 3 and 4—suggests how unwieldy the traditional framework has become. A partial list would include exigent circumstances, plain view, community caretaker functions, brief frisks for weapons, inventory searches, protective sweeps, automobile searches, border searches, school searches, prison searches, searches incident to arrest, fire investigations, and administrative searches. See Craig Bradley, Two Models of the Fourth Amendment, 83 Mich. L. Rev. 1468 (1985).

As you study the materials in the next few chapters, try to construct a coherent explanation for the cases and laws that govern searches and seizures. In particular, consider the explanatory value of a calculus that weighs three factors in determining the "reasonableness" of a search or seizure: (1) the privacy and property interests of the person subject to a search; (2) the government's interest in conducting the search; and (3) the degree of intrusion from the search. The balancing of these three factors may solve such crucial puzzles as the level of justification necessary to support the search (such as probable cause, reasonable suspicion, or no individualized suspicion) and the time when the government must give its justification (before the search to obtain a warrant, or after the fact when the target challenges the search). You will have the opportunity to test this conceptual framework, along with the more traditional framework that emphasizes probable cause and warrants, and to analyze a wide array of government efforts to collect information.

A. SEARCHES AND SEIZURES

1. *What Is a Search?*

In Katz v. United States, 389 U.S. 347 (1967), the U.S. Supreme Court changed the method of deciding whether a person had an interest that the Fourth Amendment would protect. It redefined the basic *conceptual framework* for deciding whether the government had engaged in a "search" that is subject to constitutional limitations. In doing so, the Court moved away from concepts of protected physical spaces (property) and toward concepts of individual privacy. As you read the case, consider the following questions: What are the implications of deciding that the Fourth Amendment "protects people, not places"? Does it expand the universe of cases where a "search" would be found? Does it make it easier, or more difficult, to determine whether a Fourth Amendment search has occurred?

While *Katz* introduced a privacy-oriented test for determining whether a search has occurred, the Supreme Court did not abandon the property-based trespass test. In United States v. Jones, 565 U.S. 400 (2012) the Court applied the centuries-old trespass test to examine whether a novel surveillance technology, tracking of a car through a Global-Positioning-System (GPS) device attached to its underside, constitutes a search.

■ CHARLES KATZ v. UNITED STATES
389 U.S. 347 (1967)

STEWART, J.*

The petitioner was convicted [of] transmitting wagering information by telephone from Los Angeles to Miami and Boston, in violation of a federal statute. At trial the Government was permitted, over the petitioner's objection, to introduce evidence of the petitioner's end of telephone conversations, overheard by FBI agents who had attached an electronic listening and recording device to the outside of the public telephone booth from which he had placed his calls. In affirming his conviction, the Court of Appeals rejected the contention that the recordings had been obtained in violation of the Fourth Amendment, because "there was no physical entrance into the area occupied by [the petitioner]."

[The] parties have attached great significance to the characterization of the telephone booth from which the petitioner placed his calls. The petitioner has strenuously argued that the booth was a "constitutionally protected area." The Government has maintained with equal vigor that it was not. But this effort to decide whether or not a given "area," viewed in the abstract, is "constitutionally protected" deflects attention from the problem presented by this case. For the Fourth Amendment protects people, not places. What a person knowingly exposes to the public, even in his own home or office, is not a subject of Fourth Amendment protection. But what he seeks to preserve as private, even in an area accessible to the public, may be constitutionally protected. . . .

---

* [Chief Justice Warren and Justices Brennan, Douglas, Fortas, Harlan, and White joined in this opinion.—EDS.]

No less than an individual in a business office, in a friend's apartment, or in a taxicab, a person in a telephone booth may rely upon the protection of the Fourth Amendment. One who occupies it, shuts the door behind him, and pays the toll that permits him to place a call is surely entitled to assume that the words he utters into the mouthpiece will not be broadcast to the world. To read the Constitution more narrowly is to ignore the vital role that the public telephone has come to play in private communication.

The Government contends, however, that the activities of its agents in this case should not be tested by Fourth Amendment requirements, for the surveillance technique they employed involved no physical penetration of the telephone booth from which the petitioner placed his calls. It is true that the absence of such penetration was at one time thought to foreclose further Fourth Amendment inquiry, Olmstead v. United States, 277 U.S. 438 (1928), for that Amendment was thought to limit only searches and seizures of tangible property. But the premise that property interests control the right of the Government to search and seize has been discredited. Thus, although a closely divided Court supposed in *Olmstead* that surveillance without any trespass and without the seizure of any material object fell outside the ambit of the Constitution, we have since departed from the narrow view on which that decision rested. Indeed, we have expressly held that the Fourth Amendment governs not only the seizure of tangible items, but extends as well to the recording of oral statements, overheard without any technical trespass under local property law. Silverman v. United States, 365 U.S. 505 (1961). Once this much is acknowledged, and once it is recognized that the Fourth Amendment protects people—and not simply "areas"—against unreasonable searches and seizures, it becomes clear that the reach of that Amendment cannot turn upon the presence or absence of a physical intrusion into any given enclosure.

[The] Government's position is that its agents acted in an entirely defensible manner: They did not begin their electronic surveillance until investigation of the petitioner's activities had established a strong probability that he was using the telephone in question to transmit gambling information to persons in other States, in violation of federal law. Moreover, the surveillance was limited, both in scope and in duration, to the specific purpose of establishing the contents of the petitioner's unlawful telephonic communications. The agents confined their surveillance to the brief periods during which he used the telephone booth,[14] and they took great care to overhear only the conversations of the petitioner himself. . . .

The Government urges that, because its agents . . . did no more here than they might properly have done with prior judicial sanction, we should retroactively validate their conduct. That we cannot do. It is apparent that the agents in this case acted with restraint. Yet the inescapable fact is that this restraint was imposed by the agents themselves, not by a judicial officer. . . . Over and again this Court has emphasized that the mandate of the Fourth Amendment requires adherence to judicial processes, and that searches conducted outside the judicial process, without prior approval by judge or magistrate, are per se unreasonable under the Fourth

---

14. Based upon their previous visual observations of the petitioner, the agents correctly predicted that he would use the telephone booth for several minutes at approximately the same time each morning. The petitioner was subjected to electronic surveillance only during this predetermined period. Six recordings, averaging some three minutes each, were obtained and admitted in evidence. They preserved the petitioner's end of conversations concerning the placing of bets and the receipt of wagering information.

Amendment—subject only to a few specifically established and well-delineated exceptions. . . . These considerations do not vanish when the search in question is transferred from the setting of a home, an office, or a hotel room to that of a telephone booth. Wherever a man may be, he is entitled to know that he will remain free from unreasonable searches and seizures. . . . It is so ordered.

HARLAN, J., concurring.

[As] the Court's opinion states, "the Fourth Amendment protects people, not places." The question, however, is what protection it affords to those people. Generally, as here, the answer to that question requires reference to a "place." My understanding of the rule that has emerged from prior decisions is that there is a twofold requirement, first that a person have exhibited an actual (subjective) expectation of privacy and, second, that the expectation be one that society is prepared to recognize as "reasonable." Thus a man's home is, for most purposes, a place where he expects privacy, but objects, activities, or statements that he exposes to the "plain view" of outsiders are not "protected" because no intention to keep them to himself has been exhibited. On the other hand, conversations in the open would not be protected against being overheard, for the expectation of privacy under the circumstances would be unreasonable. . . .

BLACK, J., dissenting.

[The Fourth Amendment's] first clause protects "persons, houses, papers, and effects, against unreasonable searches and seizures. . . ." These words connote the idea of tangible things with size, form, and weight, things capable of being searched, seized, or both. The second clause of the Amendment still further establishes its Framers' purpose to limit its protection to tangible things by providing that no warrants shall issue but those "particularly describing the place to be searched, and the persons or things to be seized." A conversation overheard by eavesdropping, whether by plain snooping or wiretapping, is not tangible and, under the normally accepted meanings of the words, can neither be searched nor seized. . . . Yet the Court's interpretation would have the Amendment apply to overhearing future conversations which by their very nature are nonexistent until they take place. . . .

Tapping telephone wires, of course, was an unknown possibility at the time the Fourth Amendment was adopted. But eavesdropping (and wiretapping is nothing more than eavesdropping by telephone) was . . . an ancient practice which at common law was condemned as a nuisance. In those days the eavesdropper listened by naked ear under the eaves of houses or their windows, or beyond their walls seeking out private discourse. There can be no doubt that the Framers were aware of this practice, and if they had desired to outlaw or restrict the use of evidence obtained by eavesdropping, I believe that they would have used the appropriate language to do so in the Fourth Amendment. They certainly would not have left such a task to the ingenuity of language-stretching judges. . . .

Since I see no way in which the words of the Fourth Amendment can be construed to apply to eavesdropping, that closes the matter for me. In interpreting the Bill of Rights, I willingly go as far as a liberal construction of the language takes me, but I simply cannot in good conscience give a meaning to words which they have never before been thought to have and which they certainly do not have in common ordinary usage. I will not distort the words of the Amendment in order to "keep the Constitution up to date" or "to bring it into harmony with the times." . . .

With this decision the Court has completed, I hope, its rewriting of the Fourth Amendment, which started only recently when the Court began referring incessantly to the Fourth Amendment not so much as a law against unreasonable searches and seizures as one to protect an individual's privacy. . . . Few things happen to an individual that do not affect his privacy in one way or another. . . .

■ UNITED STATES v. ANTOINE JONES
565 U.S. 400 (2012)

SCALIA, J.*
We decide whether the attachment of a Global-Positioning-System (GPS) tracking device to an individual's vehicle, and subsequent use of that device to monitor the vehicle's movements on public streets, constitutes a search or seizure within the meaning of the Fourth Amendment.

I.

In 2004 respondent Antoine Jones, owner and operator of a nightclub in the District of Columbia, came under suspicion of trafficking in narcotics and was made the target of an investigation by a joint FBI and Metropolitan Police Department task force. [Based on various sources, the government obtained a warrant authorizing installation of the GPS device] in the District of Columbia and within 10 days.

On the 11th day, and not in the District of Columbia but in Maryland, agents installed a GPS tracking device on the undercarriage of the Jeep while it was parked in a public parking lot. Over the next 28 days, the Government used the device to track the vehicle's movements, and once had to replace the device's battery when the vehicle was parked in a different public lot in Maryland. By means of signals from multiple satellites, the device established the vehicle's location within 50 to 100 feet, and communicated that location by cellular phone to a Government computer. It relayed more than 2,000 pages of data over the 4-week period.

The Government ultimately obtained a multiple-count indictment charging Jones and several alleged co-conspirators with . . . conspiracy to distribute and possess with intent to distribute five kilograms or more of cocaine and 50 grams or more of cocaine base. . . . Before trial, Jones filed a motion to suppress evidence obtained through the GPS device. The District Court granted the motion only in part, suppressing the data obtained while the vehicle was parked in the garage adjoining Jones's residence. It held the remaining data admissible, because "a person traveling in an automobile on public thoroughfares has no reasonable expectation of privacy in his movements from one place to another." [A jury convicted Jones] and the District Court sentenced Jones to life imprisonment. . . .

II.

. . . It is important to be clear about what occurred in this case: The Government physically occupied private property for the purpose of obtaining information.

*[Chief Justice Roberts and Justices Kennedy, Thomas, and Sotomayor joined this opinion.—EDS.]

We have no doubt that such a physical intrusion would have been considered a "search" within the meaning of the Fourth Amendment when it was adopted. Entick v. Carrington, 95 Eng. Rep. 807 (C.P. 1765), is a case we have described as a "monument of English freedom" undoubtedly familiar to "every American statesman" at the time the Constitution was adopted, and considered to be "the true and ultimate expression of constitutional law" with regard to search and seizure. In that case, Lord Camden expressed in plain terms the significance of property rights in search-and-seizure analysis: "[Our] law holds the property of every man so sacred, that no man can set his foot upon his neighbour's close without his leave; if he does he is a trespasser. . . ."

The text of the Fourth Amendment reflects its close connection to property, since otherwise it would have referred simply to "the right of the people to be secure against unreasonable searches and seizures"; the phrase "in their persons, houses, papers, and effects" would have been superfluous.

Consistent with this understanding, our Fourth Amendment jurisprudence was tied to common-law trespass, at least until the latter half of the 20th century. Thus, in Olmstead v. United States, 277 U.S. 438 (1928), we held that wiretaps attached to telephone wires on the public streets did not constitute a Fourth Amendment search because there was "no entry of the houses or offices of the defendants."

Our later cases, of course, have deviated from that exclusively property-based approach. In Katz v. United States, 389 U.S. 347 (1967), we said that "the Fourth Amendment protects people, not places," and found a violation in attachment of an eavesdropping device to a public telephone booth. Our later cases have applied the analysis of Justice Harlan's concurrence in that case, which said that a violation occurs when government officers violate a person's "reasonable expectation of privacy." . . .

The Government contends that the Harlan standard shows that no search occurred here, since Jones had no "reasonable expectation of privacy" in the area of the Jeep accessed by Government agents (its underbody) and in the locations of the Jeep on the public roads, which were visible to all. But we need not address the Government's contentions, because Jones's Fourth Amendment rights do not rise or fall with the *Katz* formulation. At bottom, we must assure preservation of that degree of privacy against government that existed when the Fourth Amendment was adopted. As explained, for most of our history the Fourth Amendment was understood to embody a particular concern for government trespass upon the areas ("persons, houses, papers, and effects") it enumerates.[3] [We do not] believe that *Katz*, by holding that the Fourth Amendment protects persons and their private conversations, was intended to withdraw any of the protection which the Amendment extends to the home. . . .[5]

3. Justice Alito's concurrence doubts the wisdom of our approach because "it is almost impossible to think of late-18th-century situations that are analogous to what took place in this case." But in fact it posits a situation that is not far afield—a constable's concealing himself in the target's coach in order to track its movements. . . . Whatever new methods of investigation may be devised, our task, *at a minimum*, is to decide whether the action in question would have constituted a "search" within the original meaning of the Fourth Amendment. Where, as here, the Government obtains information by physically intruding on a constitutionally protected area, such a search has undoubtedly occurred.

5. The concurrence notes that post-*Katz* we have explained that "an actual trespass is neither necessary *nor sufficient* to establish a constitutional violation." That is undoubtedly true, and undoubtedly irrelevant. . . . Trespass alone does not qualify, but there must be conjoined with that what was present here: an attempt to find something or to obtain information.

The concurrence faults our approach for presenting "particularly vexing problems" in cases that do not involve physical contact, such as those that involve the transmission of electronic signals. We entirely fail to understand that point. For unlike the concurrence, which would make *Katz* the *exclusive* test, we do not make trespass the exclusive test. Situations involving merely the transmission of electronic signals without trespass would *remain* subject to *Katz* analysis.

In fact, it is the concurrence's insistence on the exclusivity of the *Katz* test that needlessly leads us into "particularly vexing problems" in the present case. This Court has to date not deviated from the understanding that mere visual observation does not constitute a search. [Even] assuming that the concurrence is correct to say that "traditional surveillance" of Jones for a 4-week period "would have required a large team of agents, multiple vehicles, and perhaps aerial assistance," our cases suggest that such visual observation is constitutionally permissible. It may be that achieving the same result through electronic means, without an accompanying trespass, is an unconstitutional invasion of privacy, but the present case does not require us to answer that question.

And answering it affirmatively leads us needlessly into additional thorny problems. The concurrence posits that "relatively short-term monitoring of a person's movements on public streets" is okay, but that "the use of longer term GPS monitoring in investigations *of most offenses*" is no good. That introduces yet another novelty into our jurisprudence. There is no precedent for the proposition that whether a search has occurred depends on the nature of the crime being investigated. And even accepting that novelty, it remains unexplained why a 4-week investigation is "surely" too long and why a drug-trafficking conspiracy involving substantial amounts of cash and narcotics is not an "extraordinary" offense which may permit longer observation. What of a 2-day monitoring of a suspected purveyor of stolen electronics? Or of a 6-month monitoring of a suspected terrorist? We may have to grapple with these "vexing problems" in some future case where a classic trespassory search is not involved and resort must be had to *Katz* analysis; but there is no reason for rushing forward to resolve them here. . . .

SOTOMAYOR, J., concurring.

. . . In cases involving even short-term monitoring, some unique attributes of GPS surveillance relevant to the *Katz* analysis will require particular attention. GPS monitoring generates a precise, comprehensive record of a person's public movements that reflects a wealth of detail about her familial, political, professional, religious, and sexual associations. See, e.g., People v. Weaver, 909 N.E.2d 1195 (N.Y. 2009) ("Disclosed in [GPS data] will be trips the indisputably private nature of which takes little imagination to conjure: trips to the psychiatrist, the plastic surgeon, the abortion clinic, the AIDS treatment center, the strip club, the criminal defense attorney, the by-the-hour motel, the union meeting, the mosque, synagogue or church, the gay bar and on and on"). The Government can store such records and efficiently mine them for information years into the future. And because GPS

Related to this, and similarly irrelevant, is the concurrence's point that, if analyzed separately, neither the installation of the device nor its use would constitute a Fourth Amendment search. Of course not. A trespass on "houses" or "effects," or a *Katz* invasion of privacy, is not alone a search unless it is done to obtain information; and the obtaining of information is not alone a search unless it is achieved by such a trespass or invasion of privacy.

monitoring is cheap in comparison to conventional surveillance techniques and, by design, proceeds surreptitiously, it evades the ordinary checks that constrain abusive law enforcement practices: limited police resources and community hostility.

Awareness that the Government may be watching chills associational and expressive freedoms. And the Government's unrestrained power to assemble data that reveal private aspects of identity is susceptible to abuse. The net result is that GPS monitoring—by making available at a relatively low cost such a substantial quantum of intimate information about any person whom the Government, in its unfettered discretion, chooses to track—may alter the relationship between citizen and government in a way that is inimical to democratic society.

I would take these attributes of GPS monitoring into account when considering the existence of a reasonable societal expectation of privacy in the sum of one's public movements. . . . Resolution of these difficult questions in this case is unnecessary, however, because the Government's physical intrusion on Jones's Jeep supplies a narrower basis for decision. I therefore join the majority's opinion.

ALITO, J., concurring in the judgment.*

This case requires us to apply the Fourth Amendment's prohibition of unreasonable searches and seizures to a 21st-century surveillance technique, the use of a Global Positioning System (GPS) device to monitor a vehicle's movements for an extended period of time. Ironically, the Court has chosen to decide this case based on 18th-century tort law. By attaching a small GPS device to the underside of the vehicle that respondent drove, the law enforcement officers in this case engaged in conduct that might have provided grounds in 1791 for a suit for trespass to chattels. And for this reason, the Court concludes, the installation and use of the GPS device constituted a search.

This holding, in my judgment, is unwise. It strains the language of the Fourth Amendment; it has little if any support in current Fourth Amendment case law; and it is highly artificial. I would analyze the question presented in this case by asking whether respondent's reasonable expectations of privacy were violated by the long-term monitoring of the movements of the vehicle he drove.

[The] Court's reasoning largely disregards what is really important (the *use* of a GPS for the purpose of long-term tracking) and instead attaches great significance to something that most would view as relatively minor (attaching to the bottom of a car a small, light object that does not interfere in any way with the car's operation).

[The] Court's reliance on the law of trespass will present particularly vexing problems in cases involving surveillance that is carried out by making electronic, as opposed to physical, contact with the item to be tracked. For example, suppose that the officers in the present case had followed respondent by surreptitiously activating a stolen vehicle detection system that came with the car when it was purchased. . . .

The *Katz* expectation-of-privacy test avoids the problems and complications noted above, but it is not without its own difficulties. It involves a degree of circularity, and judges are apt to confuse their own expectations of privacy with those of the hypothetical reasonable person to which the *Katz* test looks. In addition, the *Katz* test rests on the assumption that this hypothetical reasonable person has a well-developed and stable set of privacy expectations. But technology can change those

---

* [Justices Ginsburg, Breyer, and Kagan joined this opinion.—EDS.]

expectations. Dramatic technological change may lead to periods in which popular expectations are in flux and may ultimately produce significant changes in popular attitudes. New technology may provide increased convenience or security at the expense of privacy, and many people may find the tradeoff worthwhile. And even if the public does not welcome the diminution of privacy that new technology entails, they may eventually reconcile themselves to this development as inevitable. . . .

In the pre-computer age, the greatest protections of privacy were neither constitutional nor statutory, but practical. Traditional surveillance for any extended period of time was difficult and costly and therefore rarely undertaken. The surveillance at issue in this case—constant monitoring of the location of a vehicle for four weeks—would have required a large team of agents, multiple vehicles, and perhaps aerial assistance. Only an investigation of unusual importance could have justified such an expenditure of law enforcement resources. Devices like the one used in the present case, however, make long-term monitoring relatively easy and cheap. In circumstances involving dramatic technological change, the best solution to privacy concerns may be legislative. A legislative body is well situated to gauge changing public attitudes, to draw detailed lines, and to balance privacy and public safety in a comprehensive way.

To date, however, Congress and most States have not enacted statutes regulating the use of GPS tracking technology for law enforcement purposes. The best that we can do in this case is to apply existing Fourth Amendment doctrine and to ask whether the use of GPS tracking in a particular case involved a degree of intrusion that a reasonable person would not have anticipated.

Under this approach, relatively short-term monitoring of a person's movements on public streets accords with expectations of privacy that our society has recognized as reasonable. But the use of longer term GPS monitoring in investigations of most offenses impinges on expectations of privacy. For such offenses, society's expectation has been that law enforcement agents and others would not—and indeed, in the main, simply could not—secretly monitor and catalogue every single movement of an individual's car for a very long period. In this case, for four weeks, law enforcement agents tracked every movement that respondent made in the vehicle he was driving. We need not identify with precision the point at which the tracking of this vehicle became a search. . . . We also need not consider whether prolonged GPS monitoring in the context of investigations involving extraordinary offenses would similarly intrude on a constitutionally protected sphere of privacy. In such cases, long-term tracking might have been mounted using previously available techniques. . . .

Notes

1. *Reasonable expectation of privacy test.* There are some government efforts to gather information from individuals that do not amount to a "search" at all. Where there is no search, there is no constitutional requirement for the government to justify its efforts to gather information. Under the approach heralded by *Katz* and followed by most states, no search occurs when the government intrudes into some place or interest without violating the person's "reasonable expectation of privacy." The definition of "reasonable expectation of privacy" contains both a subjective and an objective component, as described in Justice Harlan's concurring opinion. The

target of the search must actually expect privacy, and that expectation must be one that society is prepared to recognize as reasonable.

Later opinions of the U.S. Supreme Court and of state courts repeat this two-part formulation, but they also suggest that the objective component alone might be enough: A subjective expectation of privacy will not always be a precondition to a conclusion that a search has occurred. See United States v. White, 401 U.S. 745 (1971). Could you imagine courts holding otherwise, that is, insisting on a subjective expectation of privacy before finding that a search took place?

Keep in mind, however, that the "reasonable expectation of privacy" test is only part of the inquiry into whether a search has occurred under the Fourth Amendment. Under the *Jones* trespass test, courts also consider whether police investigation has physically intruded on a protected interest (person, house, papers, or effects) with the intent to obtain information.

2. *Observation of items in plain view.* One of the least intrusive forms of information-gathering occurs when the police simply notice what is out in the open for people to see. Under the Fourth Amendment and its equivalents, there is no reasonable expectation of privacy in matters left within plain view. Hence, if an officer sees an item in plain view and has not physically intruded on a protected interest, no search has occurred under state or federal law.

To qualify for plain view treatment, the police officer must view the item from a place where she has a right to be. The officer might have legal access to the place because it is open to the general public — some state courts, such as those in Florida and Hawaii, call this situation "open view" rather than "plain view." An officer might also have reason to view some item from a vantage point not open to the general public. For instance, the officer might be executing an arrest warrant or might be present in a "community caretaker" capacity. If the officer has a proper reason to be in that nonpublic location, the discovery of new information from that vantage point is not considered a search. In either setting, plain view or open view, the courts conclude that the target of the investigation has no reasonable expectation of privacy in the item within view of the officer.

What determines the "plain" nature of the view other than the location of the officer making the observation? First, the amount of police effort involved in reaching the location might matter. The use of technological enhancements such as flashlights makes a difference. The U.S. Supreme Court has indicated in several cases that any physical movement of an item makes it much more difficult to claim that the item observed was in plain view. See Arizona v. Hicks, 480 U.S. 321 (1987) (stereo receiver moved inches to observe serial number was not in plain view). Because of the many factors that bear on this question, it is sometimes difficult to determine whether an item is in "open" or "plain" view. Moreover, as *Jones* reminds us, the reasonable expectation of privacy test is only part of the inquiry as to whether a Fourth Amendment search has occurred. If the government trespasses on a protected area with the intent to obtain information, this is a search even if it does not violate a person's reasonable expectation of privacy.

3. *Plain smell and plain hearing.* If it is possible for an officer to notice an object in "plain view" without conducting a search, is it possible for the officer to notice a "plain smell" without conducting a search? There are cases in which the officer, standing in a proper location, smells something that creates some suspicion or evidence of a crime. State v. Rodriguez, 945 A.2d 676 (N.H. 2008) (officers who smell burning marijuana from the exterior of a residence need no warrant before

entering; court reviews divided case law on issue). The same can be said of an investigation based on something an officer hears when standing in a legally sanctioned location (plain hearing): There is no "search" here in the constitutional sense. We will consider the "plain feel" doctrine in section C of this chapter.

4. *Flyovers and reasonable expectations of privacy: majority position.* One difficult question about the definition of a search arises when government agents place themselves in unusual—but not necessarily illegal—positions for observing wrongdoing. A situation of this sort that appears frequently in appellate cases is the "flyover" of property by police officers searching for evidence of a crime.

In Florida v. Riley, 488 U.S. 445 (1988), the Supreme Court determined that police observing the defendant's backyard from a helicopter flying in legal airspace did not conduct a search for Fourth Amendment purposes. The defendant lived in a mobile home located on five acres of property. A greenhouse near the residence was obscured from ground-level view by a fence, trees, and shrubs. As the result of an anonymous tip, a police helicopter made two passes over the property at an altitude of 400 feet. The observing officer viewed what he thought was marijuana growing in the greenhouse, because two roof panels were missing. The Court stressed that the helicopter was flying in legal navigable airspace within the Federal Aviation Administration guidelines. The Court also considered the minimal intrusiveness of the observations: The helicopter never "interfered with respondent's normal use of the greenhouse or other parts of the curtilage." Furthermore, "no intimate details connected with the use of the home or curtilage were observed, and there was no undue noise, and no wind, dust, or threat of injury." See also California v. Ciraolo, 476 U.S. 207 (1986) (no search when police officer observes property from fixed-wing aircraft 1,000 feet above property in legal airspace). Do you believe the Supreme Court should have ruled in *Ciraolo* and *Riley* that the government conducted a search? Should the answer depend on whether the public has routine access to helicopters and planes?

Virtually all state courts have agreed with the U.S. Supreme Court's view that a flyover is not a "search" so long as the police aircraft stays within airspace where private aircraft could travel and does not create too much noise, dust, or threat of injury. But see State v. Bryant, 950 A.2d 467 (Vt. 2008) (police needed to obtain warrant before helicopter flyover of residential property in search of marijuana, based on reading of state constitution). How might a defendant dispute the government's factual claim about the flight pattern of the aircraft?

5. *Legal entitlement versus likelihood of observation.* Suppose a litigant could show that flyovers at 500 feet above the property in question are very rare. In what way would this be relevant to the definition of a search? Consider that five Justices in *Riley* agreed with the following proposition in Justice O'Connor's concurrence: "In determining whether Riley had a reasonable expectation of privacy from aerial observation, the relevant inquiry after *Ciraolo* is not whether the helicopter was where it had a right to be under FAA regulations. Rather . . . we must ask whether the helicopter was in the public airways at an altitude at which members of the public travel with sufficient regularity that Riley's expectation of privacy from aerial observation was not 'one that society is prepared to recognize as reasonable.'" Justice O'Connor nevertheless sided with the government in *Riley* because she believed that the defendant bore the burden of proof and failed to produce evidence that flyovers over his property were rare.

6. *Police observation versus public observation.* Let us assume that reasonable and law-abiding people leave some things visible to a few members of the public that

they would rather not expose to the sustained scrutiny of the police. Can police officers make observations from any place open to the public, or should they be expected to remain outside some areas open to some members of the public? Does the defendant's argument on the "search" issue get stronger when police officers flying over a property must apply their expertise to interpret what they see below (such as an assertion that a building is "typical" of those used to grow marijuana)?

7. *Other sense enhancements.* So long as the government agent remains in a position properly available to her, many state courts allow the agent to use various devices to get a clearer or closer look at the items in plain view. The clearest cases involve commonly used devices such as flashlights. See State v. Brooks, 446 S.E.2d 579 (N.C. 1994) (officer shining light inside a car is not a search). A few state and federal courts have been willing to go further, allowing government agents to use vision-enhancing devices not readily available to most viewers. See Dow Chemical Co. v. United States, 476 U.S. 227 (1986) (no search when agents in airplane over chemical plant use precision aerial-mapping camera). See Chapter 7.

8. *Garbage and abandoned property.* Reasonable expectations of privacy do not attach to property or activities in "plain view" or "open view." Thus, efforts to see such property are not searches in the constitutional sense. The same can be said for property that a person has abandoned, even though it does not lie within plain view of the public or government agents.

The U.S. Supreme Court in California v. Greenwood, 486 U.S. 35 (1988), held that there is no reasonable expectation of privacy in trash put out for collection; thus, there is no constitutionally relevant search if government agents inspect the trash. Over half the states have adopted this same view. See State v. Sampson, 765 A.2d 629 (Md. 2001) (officer collected trash left at curb by suspected drug dealer for six days; not a search). A smaller group (fewer than a dozen) have held in various contexts that there is a reasonable expectation of privacy in garbage, while a good number of high state courts still have not confronted the issue. See Beltz v. State, 221 P.3d 328 (Alaska 2009) (expectation of privacy in garbage placed by curb is reasonable under state constitution).

Privacy interests in a home or building also extend to the area under the eaves and immediately surrounding the building, an area known as the "curtilage." Thus, it could matter where the trash is placed. If the police inspect garbage containers standing beside a home prior to the day appointed for collection, have they conducted a "search"? Physical intrusion on the curtilage with the intent to obtain information is treated as a trespass under *Jones* and a subsequent Supreme Court case, Florida v. Jardines, 569 U.S.1 (2013), holding that a dog sniff of the curtilage was a search. For examples of various state court holdings regarding garbage searches, see the web extension for this chapter at *http://www.crimpro.com/extension/ch02*.

The collection of DNA and other sensitive information from trash raises interesting questions about the scope of the *Greenwood* doctrine. If police collect a discarded item and then test it for DNA, does this violate a person's reasonable expectation of privacy? If police collect a recycled smartphone and use a digital forensic tool to search the phone's files, does this constitute a search under the Fourth Amendment?

Some have pointed out that the government, under the reasoning of *Greenwood*, can defeat a widely shared expectation of privacy simply by announcing that it plans to conduct a particular form of investigation, thus defeating any expectation of privacy. See Anthony G. Amsterdam, Perspectives on the Fourth Amendment, 58 Minn.

L. Rev. 349, 384 (1974). If most Americans today still expect privacy in their curbside garbage bags, isn't there a reasonable expectation of privacy regardless of what the Supreme Court held in *Greenwood?* See Christopher Slobogin & Joseph Schumacher, Reasonable Expectations of Privacy and Autonomy in Fourth Amendment Cases: An Empirical Look at "Understandings Recognized and Permitted by Society," 42 Duke L.J. 727 (1993) (public survey measuring perceived intrusiveness of various investigative techniques). Should the courts announce decisions about reasonable expectations of privacy on a tentative basis, and overrule themselves if most people don't take the decision to heart?

9. *Computer "trash" cans.* Most electronic message systems allow the computer user to delete messages, but the deleted messages are recoverable until further events take place (e.g., the user turns off the system, or some manager of the computer system empties the electronic "trash can"). Similarly, it is possible under some circumstances to recover copies of electronic documents or files that a user has attempted to delete. If the government discovers evidence of a crime in these deleted but recoverable messages or files, was there a search at all? If there was a search, was it justified by implied consent?

Problem 2-1. Peep-Hole Observations

Detective Kelly Quirin became suspicious about auto thefts occurring in Seattle, Washington, and his investigation uncovered a possible connection between the thefts and storage facilities. Quirin obtained and executed a search warrant to examine certain units at Shurgard Storage facility. As Detective Quirin was searching the units, the facility's manager told Quirin that one of the units, unit E-71, might be connected with stolen vehicles.

One week later, Quirin went to the storage facility with another officer and asked to look at unit E-71, which was locked. The manager let the officers into an unrented, unlocked storage unit next door to unit E-71. Upon entering the unit, the officers saw a preexisting hole, "maybe big enough to stick your pinky finger in or a little bigger," about four feet off the ground. (The walls of the units extended up to the ceiling.) Quirin looked through the hole, and without aid of a flashlight was able to see items in unit E-71. Based on this information, Quirin obtained a search warrant for unit E-71 and recovered stolen goods.

Mihai Bobic was charged with theft, trafficking in stolen property, and conspiracy. Before trial, Bobic moved to suppress the evidence recovered during the search of unit E-71. During his pretrial suppression hearing, Bobic testified that a friend rented unit E-71, but he and the friend shared the unit. Bobic placed a lock on the door of the unit. The rental agreement permitted the manager to open a unit at any time to uncover illegal activities. The rental agreement states, "The Storage Unit may not be used for any unlawful purpose. Tenant represents to Landlord that all personal property to be stored by Tenant in the Storage Unit will belong to Tenant only, and not to any third parties. Tenant shall give the Landlord permission to enter the Storage Unit at any time for the purpose of removing and disposing of any property in the Storage Unit in violation of this provision."

Washington's constitution provides that "[no] person shall be disturbed in his private affairs . . . without authority of law." A violation of this right turns on whether the State has unreasonably intruded into a person's private affairs.

Did Detective Quirin's observations constitute a search under either the Fourth Amendment or the Washington constitution? Is the outcome clearer under one of the three tests applicable: (1) reasonable expectation of privacy, (2) trespass onto protected area with intent to obtain information, or (3) intrusion into a person's private affairs? Would the result differ if Detective Quirin had looked through a hole in a public restroom stall? Would it differ if Detective Quirin had looked through a hole in a residential garage or a home? See State v. Bobic, 996 P.2d 610 (Wash. 2000).

Problem 2-2. A Jurisprudence of Squeezes

Steven Dewayne Bond was a passenger on a Greyhound bus that left California bound for Little Rock, Arkansas. The bus stopped at the permanent Border Patrol checkpoint in Sierra Blanca, Texas. Border Patrol Agent Cesar Cantu boarded the bus to check the immigration status of its passengers. After reaching the back of the bus, having satisfied himself that the passengers were lawfully in the United States, Agent Cantu began walking toward the front. Along the way, he squeezed the soft luggage that passengers had placed in the overhead storage space.

Bond was seated four or five rows from the back of the bus. As Agent Cantu inspected the luggage in the compartment above Bond's seat, he squeezed a green canvas bag and noticed that it contained a "brick-like" object. Bond admitted that the bag was his and agreed to allow Agent Cantu to open it. Upon opening the bag, Agent Cantu discovered a "brick" of methamphetamine.

Bond was indicted for conspiracy to possess, and possession with intent to distribute, methamphetamine. He moved to suppress the drugs, arguing that Agent Cantu conducted an illegal search of his bag.

Did the initial manipulation of Bond's bag by Agent Cantu constitute a search under the Fourth Amendment? Is physically invasive inspection more intrusive than purely visual inspection? Bond conceded that "by placing his bag in the overhead compartment, he could expect that it would be exposed to certain kinds of touching and handling" but argued that Agent Cantu's physical manipulation of his luggage "far exceeded the casual contact" Bond could have expected from other passengers. If the court accepts this fact, how does the finding affect the analysis? Do the reasonable expectation of privacy test and the trespass test produce the same results? See Bond v. United States, 529 U.S. 334 (2000).

Problem 2-3. Plain View from a Ladder or Drone

Special Agent Forsythe became aware that football gambling forms were circulating in the town of Farrell. After receiving a tip about the source of the gambling forms, Forsythe began to keep watch at a local print shop. During one October evening, Forsythe noticed that the presses inside the shop were operating, but due to the location and size of the windows, he was unable to observe what was being printed from his position off the premises. The sills of the windows were 7 feet off the ground, so they prevented any view into the shop by someone standing on the ground outside the building. To remedy this problem, Forsythe mounted a 4-foot ladder that he placed on the railroad tracks abutting the print shop property. From a distance of 15 to 20 feet, he observed through a side window some "Las Vegas" football parlay sheets being run off the press. Did Agent Forsythe conduct a "search" within the meaning of state or federal constitutions? Compare Commonwealth v. Hernley, 263 A.2d 904 (Pa. Super. Ct. 1970). Would it constitute a search if Agent Forsythe operated a drone to hover outside the window and saw the gambling forms through the drone's camera?

Problem 2-4. The Friendly Skies

Stephen Bryant lived in a remote area in Vermont. His property was accessible through a locked gate on a U.S. Forest Service road; only Bryant, his partner, and the Forest Service had keys to that gate. Beyond the gate, the dirt road passed Bryant's homestead and continued a short distance into the National Forest. Bryant posted no-trespassing signs around his property and told local forest officials that he did not want the Forest Service or anyone else trespassing on his land.

A local forest official suspected that Bryant was responsible for marijuana plants that were reportedly growing in the National Forest because he found Bryant's insistence on privacy to be "paranoid." The forest official suggested to the State Police that a Marijuana Eradication Team (MERT) flight over Bryant's property might be a good idea. A state trooper scheduled a MERT flight and directed the pilot to Bryant's property, where two plots of marijuana were observed growing about 100 feet from the house. Pilots doing MERT flights in Vermont are told to stay at least 500 feet above the ground to avoid invasions of privacy.

A resident in the area witnessed the flight because she was working outside at the time of the flyover; she described the helicopter as being at twice the height of her house, or approximately 100 feet above ground level, and said that the noise was "deafening." She watched the helicopter spend "a good half-hour" in the area of Bryant's residence, where it circled "very low down to the trees." Although helicopters had flown in the area before, this one was different because "it was around so long and was so low and so loud." A second nearby resident saw the helicopter flying at about 120 feet, or at approximately twice the height of the trees. When he went outside, he felt the "concussion-like" feeling that is caused by air movement from a helicopter, and he could still feel the vibration when he returned inside the town offices in Goshen, where he was working.

After the flight, the state trooper prepared an application for a search warrant based solely on his observation during the aerial surveillance of what he believed to be marijuana plants. In the application, the trooper characterized the surveillance as having been from "an aircraft at least 500 feet above the ground." The warrant was issued and executed, and state troopers discovered three marijuana plots approximately 100 feet from Bryant's home. The defendant filed a motion to suppress the evidence. Will the judge grant it? Compare State v. Bryant, 950 A.2d 467 (Vt. 2008).

2. What Is a Seizure?

A Fourth Amendment seizure of an *object* occurs when law enforcement "meaningfully interfere[s] with an individual's possessory interests" in that property. United States v. Jacobsen, 466 U.S. 109, 113 (1984). Chapters 3 and 4 discuss the level of justification required for seizures of a person's effects in different circumstances. But in general, the preliminary question of whether a seizure of an item has occurred is not a difficult one.

By contrast, the question of whether an encounter between law enforcement and a person has become a Fourth Amendment "seizure" of that person is much more contested and complex. This section addresses the moment when police-citizen interactions cross the line between a "consensual encounter" and a "seizure" of a person, also known as a "stop."

Countless times each day, a police officer or some other government agent stops to talk with a member of the general public. Some citizens take part in these conversations willingly; others are more reluctant but feel obliged to stay and continue the conversation. A few do not cooperate at all. What authority does the officer have to insist that a citizen stop for a few moments during an investigation?

■ DELAWARE CODE TIT. 11, §1902

(a) A peace officer may stop any person abroad, or in a public place, who the officer has reasonable ground to suspect is committing, has committed or is about to commit a crime, and may demand the person's name, address, business abroad and destination.

(b) Any person so questioned who fails to give identification or explain the person's actions to the satisfaction of the officer may be detained and further questioned and investigated.

(c) The total period of detention provided for by this section shall not exceed 2 hours. The detention is not an arrest and shall not be recorded as an arrest in any official record. At the end of the detention the person so detained shall be released or be arrested and charged with a crime.

Notes

1. *Three types of encounters: voluntary conversations, stops, and arrests.* The Delaware statute sets out a typical set of requirements for police officers who stop a person in a vehicle or on foot in public. While most states codify these requirements in statutes or rules of criminal procedure, others announce the requirements in judicial opinions. Most are not recent innovations; for instance, the Delaware statute above was adopted in 1951 and is based on the Uniform Arrest Act of 1940. The Supreme Court ratified the constitutionality of this framework in Terry v. Ohio, 392 U.S. 1 (1968), a case we discuss later in this chapter. If you were a police officer, would you prefer explicit statutory authority to stop suspects, or would you rather see the power established and developed in case law?

These statutes create three different levels of controls on the officer. On the first level, where the police officer does not "stop" a person at all but merely engages in a voluntary conversation, the officer does not need to justify the decision to focus attention on one person. On the second level, where the officer "stops" a person for a brief time but not long enough to qualify as an arrest, the officer must have "reasonable suspicion" before making the stop. Reasonable suspicion has also been described as "individualized" or "articulable" suspicion. On the third level, where the officer detains a person for a longer time or in a more coercive way, there is an "arrest." Constitutions, statutes, and rules of procedure all require that the officer show "probable cause" that the arrestee has committed a crime.

Thus, for the brief encounters we are now exploring, there are two questions to resolve: Was the interaction between the police officer and the individual a consensual encounter, a limited "stop," or a full arrest? If the incident was a stop, did the government agent have the "reasonable suspicion" needed to justify the stop? This section discusses the first question; section B turns to the second question.

2. *The prevalence of stops and consensual encounters.* Consensual conversations and stops (particularly traffic stops) are the two most common forms of interaction between the police and the public. According to a 2008 national survey, about 17 percent of all persons age 16 or older had at least one contact with a police officer during the year. Just over 44 percent of those contacts occurred during a motor vehicle stop; another 21 percent of the contacts happened when people reported a crime to the police. Only 2.5 percent of the contacts occurred because the officer suspected the person of a crime. Bureau of Justice Statistics, Contacts Between Police and the Public, 2008 (October 2011, NCJ 234599).

3. *Ambiguous statutory language.* Will defense counsel and prosecutors in Delaware agree on what constitutes a "reasonable ground" for a stop under the statute? Will they agree on how long the "further" questioning can last under the statute? How should the trial court resolve their disagreements? What sources will be relevant? Is the court's task here the same as when parties dispute the meaning of some phrase that has developed through the common law? As you read further in this chapter, take special note of the methods courts use to resolve conflicts about the meaning of ambiguous statutory language.

4. *Conversations change direction.* Sometimes a conversation between a police officer and a member of the public will begin as a "consensual encounter" but will transform into a "stop" without the officer's announcement of this fact in so many words. What marks the difference between consensual encounters and coercive stops? The next case explores this question.

■ UNITED STATES v. SYLVIA MENDENHALL
446 U.S. 544 (1980)

STEWART, J.*

. . . I.

[Sylvia Mendenhall] arrived at the Detroit Metropolitan Airport on a commercial airline flight from Los Angeles early in the morning on February 10, 1976. As she disembarked from the airplane, she was observed by two agents of the Drug Enforcement Administration (DEA), who were present at the airport for the purpose of detecting unlawful traffic in narcotics. After observing the respondent's

---

* [Chief Justice Burger and Justices Blackmun and Powell concurred in part and joined in Parts I, IIB, IIC, and III of the opinion; Justice Rehnquist joined the opinion, including Part IA.—EDS.]

conduct, which appeared to the agents to be characteristic of persons unlawfully carrying narcotics,[1] the agents approached her as she was walking through the concourse, identified themselves as federal agents, and asked to see her identification and airline ticket. The respondent produced her driver's license, which was in the name of Sylvia Mendenhall, and, in answer to a question of one of the agents, stated that she resided at the address appearing on the license. The airline ticket was issued in the name of "Annette Ford." When asked why the ticket bore a name different from her own, the respondent stated that she "just felt like using that name." In response to a further question, the respondent indicated that she had been in California only two days. Agent Anderson then specifically identified himself as a federal narcotics agent and, according to his testimony, the respondent "became quite shaken, extremely nervous. She had a hard time speaking."

After returning the airline ticket and driver's license to her, Agent Anderson asked the respondent if she would accompany him to the airport DEA office for further questions. She did so, although the record does not indicate a verbal response to the request. The office, which was located up one flight of stairs about 50 feet from where the respondent had first been approached, consisted of a reception area adjoined by three other rooms. At the office the agent asked the respondent if she would allow a search of her person and handbag and told her that she had the right to decline the search if she desired. She responded: "Go ahead." She then handed Agent Anderson her purse, which contained a receipt for an airline ticket that had been issued to "F. Bush" three days earlier for a flight from Pittsburgh through Chicago to Los Angeles. The agent asked whether this was the ticket that she had used for her flight to California, and the respondent stated that it was.

A female police officer then arrived to conduct the search of the respondent's person. . . . The policewoman explained that the search would require that the respondent remove her clothing. . . . As the respondent removed her clothing, she took from her undergarments two small packages, one of which appeared to contain heroin, and handed both to the policewoman. The agents then arrested the respondent for possessing heroin. It was on the basis of this evidence that the District Court denied the respondent's motion to suppress. . . .

II.

A.

The Fourth Amendment's requirement that searches and seizures be founded upon an objective justification, governs all seizures of the person, including seizures that involve only a brief detention short of traditional arrest. Terry v. Ohio, 392 U.S. 1 (1968). Accordingly, if the respondent was "seized" when the DEA agents approached her on the concourse and asked questions of her, the agents'

---

1. The agent testified that the respondent's behavior fit the so-called "drug courier profile"—an informally compiled abstract of characteristics thought typical of persons carrying illicit drugs. In this case the agents thought it relevant that (1) the respondent was arriving on a flight from Los Angeles, a city believed by the agents to be the place of origin for much of the heroin brought to Detroit; (2) the respondent was the last person to leave the plane, "appeared to be very nervous," and "completely scanned the whole area where [the agents] were standing"; (3) after leaving the plane the respondent proceeded past the baggage area without claiming any luggage; and (4) the respondent changed airlines for her flight out of Detroit.

conduct in doing so was constitutional only if they reasonably suspected the respondent of wrongdoing. But "obviously, not all personal intercourse between policemen and citizens involves 'seizures' of persons. Only when the officer, by means of physical force or show of authority, has in some way restrained the liberty of a citizen may we conclude that a 'seizure' has occurred." *Terry*, 392 U.S., at 19, n.16. . . .

We adhere to the view that a person is "seized" only when, by means of physical force or a show of authority, his freedom of movement is restrained. Only when such restraint is imposed is there any foundation whatever for invoking constitutional safeguards. The purpose of the Fourth Amendment is not to eliminate all contact between the police and the citizenry, but to prevent arbitrary and oppressive interference by enforcement officials with the privacy and personal security of individuals. As long as the person to whom questions are put remains free to disregard the questions and walk away, there has been no intrusion upon that person's liberty or privacy as would under the Constitution require some particularized and objective justification.

Moreover, characterizing every street encounter between a citizen and the police as a "seizure," while not enhancing any interest secured by the Fourth Amendment, would impose wholly unrealistic restrictions upon a wide variety of legitimate law enforcement practices. The Court has on other occasions referred to the acknowledged need for police questioning as a tool in the effective enforcement of the criminal laws. Without such investigation, those who were innocent might be falsely accused, those who were guilty might wholly escape prosecution, and many crimes would go unsolved. In short, the security of all would be diminished.

We conclude that a person has been "seized" within the meaning of the Fourth Amendment only if, in view of all of the circumstances surrounding the incident, a reasonable person would have believed that he was not free to leave.[6] Examples of circumstances that might indicate a seizure, even where the person did not attempt to leave, would be the threatening presence of several officers, the display of a weapon by an officer, some physical touching of the person of the citizen, or the use of language or tone of voice indicating that compliance with the officer's request might be compelled. In the absence of some such evidence, otherwise inoffensive contact between a member of the public and the police cannot, as a matter of law, amount to a seizure of that person.

On the facts of this case, no "seizure" of the respondent occurred. The events took place in the public concourse. The agents wore no uniforms and displayed no weapons. They did not summon the respondent to their presence, but instead approached her and identified themselves as federal agents. They requested, but did not demand to see the respondent's identification and ticket. Such conduct without more, did not amount to an intrusion upon any constitutionally protected interest. The respondent was not seized simply by reason of the fact that the agents approached her, asked her if she would show them her ticket and identification, and posed to her a few questions. Nor was it enough to establish a seizure that the person asking the questions was a law enforcement official. In short, nothing in the record suggests that the respondent had any objective reason to believe that

6. We agree with the District Court that the subjective intention of the DEA agent in this case to detain the respondent, had she attempted to leave, is irrelevant except insofar as that may have been conveyed to the respondent.

she was not free to end the conversation in the concourse and proceed on her way, and for that reason we conclude that the agents' initial approach to her was not a seizure.

Our conclusion that no seizure occurred is not affected by the fact that the respondent was not expressly told by the agents that she was free to decline to cooperate with their inquiry, for the voluntariness of her responses does not depend upon her having been so informed. We also reject the argument that the only inference to be drawn from the fact that the respondent acted in a manner so contrary to her self-interest is that she was compelled to answer the agents' questions. It may happen that a person makes statements to law enforcement officials that he later regrets, but the issue in such cases is not whether the statement was self-protective, but rather whether it was made voluntarily. [The Court also held that Mendenhall had "voluntarily" walked to the DEA office and consented to the search of her person.]

■ WESLEY WILSON v. STATE
874 P.2d 215 (Wyo. 1994)

TAYLOR, J.

[Limping] severely, Wesley Wilson . . . walked rapidly eastbound on 12th Street in Casper, Wyoming on the morning of June 21, 1991. At 12:31 A.M., Officer Kamron Ritter . . . of the Casper Police Department watched Wilson's "lunging" steps and pulled his patrol car over to the sidewalk. Officer Ritter, believing that a fight may have taken place, asked if Wilson was okay and what happened to his leg. Wilson responded that he had twisted his ankle at a party. Smelling alcohol on Wilson's breath, Officer Ritter requested identification, which Wilson provided. Officer Ritter radioed for a routine warrants check with the National Crime Information Center (NCIC) and local files. This initial encounter with Wilson lasted about a minute and a half.

The conversation with Wilson was interrupted when Officer Ritter detected smoke coming from 12th Street, west of where he was standing. At the same time, two motorcyclists stopped and reported to Officer Ritter that a fire was burning in a building [one block] up the street. Before leaving to check on the fire, Officer Ritter told Wilson to "stay in the area."

Officer Ritter reported the fire to the police dispatcher. . . . After about eight minutes at the scene of the fire, Officer Ritter returned to check on Wilson. He had limped about 40 feet farther east and was attempting to cross 12th Street. As additional fire trucks approached, Officer Ritter helped Wilson cross the street. Officer Ritter then told Wilson to go to a nearby corner and "wait" while the officer returned to the fire scene.

As Officer Ritter provided traffic control, the police dispatcher radioed, at 12:41 A.M., that Wilson had two outstanding arrest warrants. Officer Ritter and Officer Terry Van Oordt then walked down the block to where Wilson was sitting on a lawn at the corner watching the fire. When the officers approached Wilson, they informed him of the outstanding warrants and asked him to stand. Wilson told the officers it was difficult to stand with his injured ankle. The officers noticed an oily patch on the right shoulder of the shirt Wilson was wearing. Both officers touched the stained area and found an oily substance. Wilson volunteered, "What are you doing? I don't smell like smoke." The officers proceeded to arrest Wilson on the outstanding warrants. The following morning, in custody, Wilson made a voluntary statement implicating himself in starting the fire.

At a suppression hearing, Officer Ritter testified about his concerns for Wilson's safety during their initial encounter and that he had no suspicions of Wilson's involvement in the fire or of arresting him for public intoxication. Officer Ritter stated he followed routine Casper Police Department procedure to get the names of subjects police come in "contact" with "at that time of night" and "always" run a warrants check. Officer Ritter said he wanted Wilson to wait until the results of the warrants check were received. During their second encounter, when Officer Ritter helped Wilson cross the street, the officer testified he still had no suspicion of Wilson's potential involvement in the fire but wanted Wilson to wait for the completion of the warrants check. . . .

Wilson, who did not testify at the hearing, argued that the stop was illegal and the evidence gathered from the stop [including his statements about smoke and his confession] should be suppressed.* [The district court denied the suppression motion, and the jury convicted Wilson of felony property destruction.]

[Three] categories or tiers of interaction between police and citizens may be characterized. The most intrusive encounter, an arrest, requires justification by probable cause to believe that a person has committed or is committing a crime. The investigatory stop represents a seizure which invokes Fourth Amendment safeguards, but, by its less intrusive character, requires only the presence of specific and articulable facts and rational inferences which give rise to a reasonable suspicion that a person has committed or may be committing a crime. The least intrusive police-citizen contact, a consensual encounter, involves no restraint of liberty and elicits the citizen's voluntary cooperation with non-coercive questioning.

The proper test for determining when a police-citizen encounter implicates Fourth Amendment rights as a seizure was initially outlined in United States v. Mendenhall, 446 U.S. 544 (1980). [The Court] found no seizure had occurred where federal drug agents approached a woman walking through an airport and requested her identification. [The *Mendenhall* standard] creates an objective test, which makes the subjective intent of the police officer irrelevant unless it is conveyed to the person being detained, and like all search and seizure cases, the inquiry is very fact oriented. The reasonable person standard also means the subjective perceptions of the suspect are irrelevant to the court's inquiry.

[An] analytical difficulty imposed by [this] standard lies in the determination of whether a reasonable person "would have believed that he was not free to leave" when being questioned by a police officer. We find useful instruction in the Model Code of Pre-Arraignment Procedure, §110.1 commentary at 259-60 (A.L.I. 1975):

> The motives that lead one to cooperate with the police are various. To put an extreme case, the police may in purely precatory language request a person to give information. Even if he is guilty, such a person might accede to the request because he has been trained to submit to the wishes of persons in authority, or because he fears that a refusal will focus suspicion, or because he believes that concealment is

---

* [The ordinary remedy for the violation of the defendant's constitutional rights is the exclusion of the evidence obtained as a result of the improper seizure during the prosecution's case at trial. Exclusion is not the only possible remedy. See discussion in Chapter 6.—Eds.]

no longer possible and a cooperative posture tactically or psychologically preferable. Regardless of the particular motive, the cooperation is clearly a response to the authority of the police. [The pressure to cooperate with a law enforcement officer is] a necessary condition of the police's capacity to operate reasonably effectively within their limited grant of powers.

The critical distinction between the position advanced by Wilson and that argued by the State is which type of encounter occurred in this case. Wilson basically contends that he was seized without reasonable suspicion during the period when his identification was being checked for possible warrants. The State asserts that Wilson was never seized in a manner that would implicate Fourth Amendment rights, until he was validly arrested on the outstanding warrants. . . .

The initial encounter between Officer Ritter and Wilson was prompted by the officer's concerns for the safety of a citizen. The officer conducted himself in a reasonable manner by simply pulling his patrol car to the curb to talk with Wilson. No flashing lights or siren sounds were used to signal Wilson to stop. The community caretaker function . . . permits police to act in a manner that enhances public safety. The police officer's observation of specific and articulable facts, Wilson's lunging walk with a severe limp, reasonably justified a brief inquiry into his condition and the possible cause, such as whether Wilson was a victim of criminal conduct. This portion of the initial encounter between Officer Ritter and Wilson occurred in a consensual atmosphere which implicates no Fourth Amendment interest.

When Officer Ritter requested Wilson's name and identification and Wilson complied, the encounter remained consensual. A request for identification is not, by itself, a seizure. Indeed, a reasonable person in physical distress should feel less intimidated by a police officer's offer to help and a request for identification than someone stopped at random. . . .

After obtaining Wilson's identification, Officer Ritter radioed for the NCIC and local warrants check. Despite the request for the computerized warrants check, the encounter remained consensual. Officer Ritter had not imposed any restriction on Wilson's freedom to leave as the warrants check was instituted. . . .

The initial encounter ended when Officer Ritter detected smoke and the two motorcyclists stopped to report a fire. At that point, Officer Ritter told Wilson to "stay in the area." [No seizure occurred at this point] because, when left unattended, [Wilson] limped away from the immediate area where the questioning had occurred. . . .

When Officer Ritter left the fire scene and returned to check on Wilson for the second time, [he] assisted Wilson across the street by grabbing him at the elbow and supporting his weight. [The] physical touching in this instance did not effect a seizure. A reasonable person would not believe that an officer's assistance in crossing a street would represent a restriction on the person's freedom to leave. The aid Officer Ritter provided ensured Wilson's safety by removing him from the path of emergency vehicles.

After Officer Ritter and Wilson crossed the street, the officer instructed Wilson to go to a specific street corner and wait. We hold a seizure occurred at the point when Wilson complied with the instruction to wait given by Officer Ritter in their second encounter. As Officer Ritter directed traffic, he could see Wilson sitting in front of a retail store at the specific corner the officer had directed. The persistence of Officer Ritter in returning to check on Wilson only supplements the determination that a seizure occurred. The show of authority by Officer Ritter restrained

Wilson's liberty. A reasonable person would have believed he or she was not free to leave. With his seizure, Wilson's Fourth Amendment right to be free of unreasonable intrusions was implicated. . . .

THOMAS, J., dissenting.

I must dissent from the majority opinion in this case. . . . The contact between the officer and Wilson never went beyond the elicitation of Wilson's voluntary cooperation so as to become a seizure. [Wilson never asked to leave.] The officer testified he would not have pursued Wilson if he had chosen to leave because he had no reason to detain him if Wilson did not consent. . . . Laying aside the question whether there was any constraint upon Wilson's freedom to leave, an elapsed period of ten minutes, during which the officer's attention was devoted to the fire and traffic direction, is not unreasonable. The record reveals, of the ten minutes, Wilson was in the presence of the officer less than three minutes. . . .

The American bench needs to understand that its invocation of the premise of protecting Constitutional rights in reversing criminal convictions has contributed to the development of a society in which violence stalks our streets and fear permeates our neighborhoods. Every decision that tightens the cuffs with which we shackle our law enforcement officers contributes to such evolution. We must remember this rule applies to serial killers and multiple rapists as well as to inept firebugs who are simply a nuisance to property, until someone dies in the fire. . . .

In my judgment, the real question to be addressed in this case is: What was going on that was wrong? The obvious answer is it was wrong for Wilson to set fire to another citizen's garage-workshop. . . . The conclusion Wilson's conviction should not be upheld because of an academic fascination with the supposed wrongful conduct of the police officer does not serve the interests of the citizens of Wyoming and their property rights, which are not constitutionally subordinated to the rights of their persons. . . . I most vigorously dissent.

Notes

1. *Definition of a "stop": majority position.* Most American jurisdictions define a "stop" along the lines set out in United States v. Mendenhall, 446 U.S. 544 (1980). An encounter between a police officer and a citizen becomes a "stop" when a reasonable person in that situation would not "feel free to leave" or to refuse to cooperate. Jurisdictions have generally adopted this definition in judicial decisions construing the state constitution rather than settling the question through statutes or rules of procedure. See Clark v. State, 994 N.E.2d 252 (Ind. 2013) (asking three men to sit on the ground, allowing officer to respond more quickly to any movements, converted consensual encounter into stop). The standard is said to be an "objective" one. Is this the same "reasonable person" you met in Torts? See State v. Ashbaugh, 244 P.3d 360 (Or. 2010) (suspect's subjective beliefs not relevant in establishing that a reasonable person would not feel free to leave).

2. *Does reality matter?* Empirical inquiries could help us answer the question of whether a reasonable person would "feel free to leave" in a given situation. How would you gather such information for a court to use? See David K. Kessler, Free to Leave? An Empirical Look at the Fourth Amendment's Seizure Standard, 99 J. Crim. L. & Criminology 51 (2009) (survey of Boston residents regarding encounters with

police). Did the Wyoming court in *Wilson* show any curiosity about the best method for finding a psychologically realistic answer to the question?

3. *The relevant pool.* The concept of the "reasonable person" is familiar in substantive criminal law. Courts applying the reasonable person concept are sometimes willing to consider particular features of the victim (age or gender, for instance) in their definition of a reasonable person. In effect, courts will sometimes narrow the relevant "pool" of persons from which the reasonable person is drawn.

Should the reasonable person standard for purposes of defining a "stop" consider the experiences and perceptions of different racial groups in their dealings with the police? Different genders? There is ample sociological and survey evidence that black males perceive the police to be more discriminatory and abusive than do white males. If a court is convinced that black males are more likely than other groups to submit passively to police encounters, should it account for this in the totality of the circumstances that go into the definition of a "stop"? See Devon W. Carbado, (E)Racing the Fourth Amendment, 100 Mich. L. Rev. 946, 974-1003 (2002).

4. *Routine check for warrants.* The court ultimately found that Ritter did not seize Wilson when he first requested a warrants check. Do you agree? Did Ritter "seize" Wilson without reasonable suspicion when he followed police department policy and requested an NCIC and warrants check on the person he "contacted" at night? The court concludes that Ritter later detained Wilson for the purpose of "completing" the warrants check. Did Ritter ever tell Wilson that he intended to complete the warrants check before releasing him? Does the status of a warrants check as a "stop" depend on how often police officers allow the individual to walk away before the check is complete? Or is it more important to know how this particular citizen (or a "reasonable" citizen) *believes* the officer would react? See State v. Martin, 79 So. 3d 951 (La. 2011) (reviewing cases and refusing to adopt a per se rule converting consensual encounter into seizure whenever police retain suspect's documentation for warrants check); Montague v. Commonwealth, 684 S.E.2d 583 (Va. 2009) (no "stop" when officers approached suspect in common area of apartment complex, asked for his identity and whether he lived in apartments, and ran a warrants check without informing suspect of that fact).

5. *Seizure by pursuit.* In California v. Hodari D., 499 U.S. 621 (1991), the Court assumed that a suspect's flight, standing alone, did not create reasonable suspicion. Nevertheless, the Court ruled that the officer needed no individualized suspicion to pursue Hodari because the pursuit did not amount to a "seizure" under the federal constitution. Two officers wearing police department jackets rounded a corner in their patrol car and saw four or five young men gathered around a small car parked at the curb. When the group saw the officers' car approaching, they ran away. The officers were suspicious and gave chase. One officer left the patrol car and took a route that placed him in front of one of the fleeing suspects. The suspect, looking behind as he ran, did not turn and see the officer until the two were quite close. At that point, he tossed away what appeared to be a small rock and ran in the opposite direction. A moment later, the officer tackled the suspect, handcuffed him, and radioed for assistance. The rock the suspect had discarded was crack cocaine. The Court held that there was no "stop" until the officer tackled Hodari; the pursuit by the officer was not enough. See also Michigan v. Chesternut, 486 U.S. 567 (1988) (police did not seize a pedestrian who ran at sight of police car, even though police pursued him, driving alongside him for a while without activating siren or flashers, as he emptied his pockets).

Courts in a majority of states, reviewing similar cases under their state constitutions, have reached the same conclusion. See State v. Smith, 39 S.W.3d 739 (Ark. 2001). However, most of the remaining states insist that pursuit might sometimes qualify as a seizure. Seizures occur when the totality of the circumstances reasonably indicate that the person is not free to leave. See State v. Garcia, 217 P.3d 1032 (N.M. 2009). How might a court reach the conclusion that a person can feel "free to leave," despite the fact that a police officer is chasing her and shouting "stop"? Is it because the suspect is in fact trying to leave? Would it matter if the suspect paused momentarily before or during flight? See State v. Rogers, 924 P.2d 1027 (Ariz. 1996).

6. *Asking for name and identification.* Does a stop occur whenever a police officer asks for a person to produce proof of identity? Does it matter how the officer asks for the identification card or how quickly she returns the card? How could anyone feel free to leave when an officer is holding his driver's license? More than 20 state legislatures have passed statutes empowering police officers to ask for identification. In other states, the judiciary has permitted the police to make this request without specific statutory authority. If a statute authorizes a request for identification only upon reasonable suspicion (as statutes typically do), does that suggest that any police request for a citizen's identification is a stop? Apart from asking for name and identification, are there certain questions a police officer might ask that should automatically convert a conversation into a stop?

Could a statute explicitly oblige citizens to comply with the request for identification and allow officers to restrain citizens who refuse to do so? The law in other countries, such as Germany and France, explicitly empowers police officers to insist that people identify themselves. The Supreme Court in Hiibel v. Sixth Judicial District Court, 542 U.S. 177 (2004), upheld a suspect's conviction for failure to provide his name to an officer during an otherwise valid investigative stop:

> The request for identity has an immediate relation to the purpose, rationale, and practical demands of a *Terry* stop. The threat of criminal sanction helps ensure that the request for identity does not become a legal nullity. On the other hand, the Nevada statute does not alter the nature of the stop itself: it does not change its duration or its location. A state law requiring a suspect to disclose his name in the course of a valid *Terry* stop is consistent with Fourth Amendment prohibitions against unreasonable searches and seizures.

Before *Hiibel*, there was surprisingly little precedent (in either state or federal courts) on the question of whether the state could punish a citizen's refusal to answer an officer's questions during an investigatory stop. Does an effort to investigate and prevent acts of terrorism—an objective of criminal law enforcement that gained new urgency after September 11, 2001—make this sort of questioning more common and more valuable?

Many states have enacted statutes that compel some level of cooperation with police officers during crime investigations. For a detailed discussion of these statutes, see Margaret Raymond, The Right to Refuse and the Obligation to Comply: Challenging the Gamesmanship Model of Criminal Procedure, 54 Buff. L. Rev. 1483 (2007). Related questions involve the subjects a police officer may discuss with occupants of a vehicle after making a stop. An exploration of these topics appears on the web extension for this chapter at *http://www.crimpro.com/extension/ch02.*

7. *Seizures in close quarters.* In Florida v. Bostick, 501 U.S. 429 (1991), the Supreme Court considered an encounter between police officers and a suspected drug courier who consented to a search of his luggage during questioning on a bus. Terrance Bostick was reclining on the back seat of the Greyhound bus bound from Miami to Atlanta when two officers wearing badges and sheriff's department jackets boarded the bus during a rest stop. The officers proceeded to the rear of the bus, stood in the aisle in front of Bostick, and questioned him about his destination. They asked to see his ticket and identification. After returning the documents, the officers stated that they were narcotics agents in search of illegal drugs. Then they asked for Bostick's consent to search his bag, telling him that he did not have to consent. He did consent, and they discovered cocaine in the bag. The Supreme Court decided that the agents did not "stop" Bostick when they questioned him on the bus. Although Bostick was not literally "free to leave" during the questioning because the officers were blocking the aisle of the bus, the Court concluded that a reasonable person in Bostick's position could have felt "free to decline the officers' requests or otherwise terminate the encounter." Compare United States v. Drayton, 536 U.S. 194 (2002) (no "stop" when two officers question passengers on bus while standing behind passenger's seat, one officer remains at front of bus watching passengers). Do the police "stop" the driver of a parked car when they position their patrol cars to block the vehicle from moving? Cases analyzing these and other potential stop scenarios appear on the web extension for this chapter at *http://www.crimpro.com/extension/ch02.*

8. *The reasonable person standard and the guilty suspect.* When trying to determine whether police seized a person during a conversation, courts say that the exchange amounts to a seizure only if a "reasonable person" would conclude that he is not free to go. In Florida v. Bostick, the defendant argued that any person carrying contraband in a piece of luggage would not freely consent to a search of the luggage in his presence. Hence, he argued, his agreement to allow the search of his bag demonstrated that he did not feel free to leave. The Court replied that the reasonable person standard "presupposes an innocent person." Does this standard lead to the conclusion that *any* refusal to engage in a conversation with a police officer amounts to reasonable suspicion for a stop?

Problem 2-5. Tickets, Please

At 3:30 A.M. on January 23, Mark Battaglia, an investigator from the Sheriff's Department, boarded a bus just as it arrived in Albany from New York City. Battaglia wore civilian clothing with his police badge displayed on his coat. Two uniformed officers accompanied him. Battaglia announced to the 15 passengers on board that he was conducting a drug interdiction. He said that he would ask everyone to produce bus tickets and identification. Battaglia then walked to the rear of the bus and saw Rawle McIntosh and a female companion sitting in the last row of seats. Battaglia noticed that McIntosh pushed a black jacket between himself and his companion. He asked McIntosh for his identification and bus ticket. Battaglia inspected the driver's license and ticket he provided and asked him about his travel plans. Battaglia then returned the identification and the ticket to McIntosh and asked the two passengers to stand. As they stood, the jacket remained on the seat. Noticing a bulge in the pocket of the jacket, Battaglia reached into the pocket and found cocaine.

Did Battaglia "stop" McIntosh? If so, exactly when did the stop happen? Would there be a stop if Battaglia questioned McIntosh about his identity and his travel plans without requesting or holding the ticket and identification document? See People v. McIntosh, 755 N.E.2d 329 (N.Y. 2001).

Now suppose that McIntosh refuses to provide the proof of his identity when Officer Battaglia requests it, and he is prosecuted under a statute punishing any person for refusing to provide proof of identity when a police officer makes such a request. The state legislature passed this statute in the aftermath of the terrorist attacks in New York City on September 11, 2001. Is the statute constitutional?

3. State Action Requirement

The federal and state constitutions reach only searches and seizures conducted by government agents. A private actor can conduct any sort of search she chooses without engaging in an "unreasonable" search or seizure within the meaning of the federal constitution. The foundational case for the "private search" doctrine is Burdeau v. McDowell, 256 U.S. 465 (1921). In that case, private parties who were investigating a potential fraud broke into McDowell's office in a bank building, drilled his safe, broke the locks on his desk, and removed papers from files elsewhere in the office. The private parties then informed federal prosecutors about their findings, and the prosecutors subpoenaed those documents from those private parties. The Supreme Court allowed the government to use the documents as evidence: "The papers having come into the possession of the government without a violation of petitioner's rights by governmental authority, we see no reason why the fact that individuals, unconnected with the government, may have wrongfully taken them should prevent them from being held for use in prosecuting an offense." 256 U.S. at 476.

However, if a private person acts at the government's behest, a search can become "state action." Courts examine a number of factors to determine whether a private actor is acting as an agent of the state in conducting a search or a seizure. They look at the motivation behind the search (whether the person had a motivation independent of helping law enforcement) and at the extent of law enforcement's knowledge, participation, or acquiescence in the search. See State v. Sines, 379 P.3d 502 (Or. 2016). The following problem gives you a chance to apply these doctrines.

Problem 2-6: Private Viewing

Joseph Wilkinson and Jessica Schultze shared an apartment; each had a separate bedroom. In her room, Schultze kept a computer with a webcam. Her boyfriend Harry Sadler was spending a lot of time at the apartment with her. Sadler discovered video files on Schultze's computer that made him suspect that Wilkinson was video-recording him and Schultze without their permission. Sadler called the City of Sacramento Police to report his concern. Officer James Walker came over to the house and spoke with Sadler and Schultze, then to Wilkinson. Officer Walker asked if he could look around Wilkinson's room, but Wilkinson refused consent. At that point, Officer Walker explained that he did not have authority to search Wilkinson's room. In response, Sadler asked if he himself could go into Wilkinson's room. Officer Walker responded, "Well, you can do whatever you want. It's your apartment. But keep in mind, you cannot act as an agent of my authority. I cannot ask you to go into the room, nor can you go into the room believing that you're doing this for me." Officer Walker also told Sadler and Schultze that Wilkinson had asked that they not go into his room.

Eventually, Sadler decided to go into Wilkinson's room to look for more evidence. He entered the room and picked up 15 compact discs he found strewn around the room. He viewed five of them on Schultze's computer, and he found intimate images and videos of him and Schultze on several of the CDs.

Sadler gave Officer Walker all 15 CDs and told him what he had seen on the five CDs. Officer Walker and Sadler went to Schultze's room, where Sadler showed the officer images on the five CDs he had already viewed. Officer Walker took the CDs to the police station, where he reviewed all of them and saw additional images with sexual content.

After Wilkinson was charged with unauthorized access, taking of computer data, and eavesdropping, he filed a motion to suppress. He argued that Sadler's taking of the disks amounted to an illegal search because Sadler was acting as a state agent; he further argued that Officer Walker's examination of the disks' content without a warrant at the police station was illegal. Under a previous standard, California courts examined whether law enforcement officers merely "stand silently by," that is, "*knowingly* permit the citizen to conduct an illegal search for their benefit and make no effort to protect the rights of the person being searched." Under a new standard, which follows the federal rule, California courts examine: (1) whether law enforcement actively participated in or encouraged the private search, and (2) whether the private individual intended to assist law enforcement or had some other independent motivation. How would the court rule under either of these standards on the question whether Sadler was a state agent? If the court finds no state agency, did Officer Walker's examination of the additional CDs at the police station exceed the scope of the private search? See People v. Wilkinson, 163 Cal. App. 4th 1554 (2008).

Notes

1. *The scope of the private search exception.* Under the private search exception, if the police view an item after a private person has already viewed the same item, the police view does not constitute a Fourth Amendment search as long as it is confined to the scope of the initial private search. United States v. Jacobsen, 466 U.S. 109 (1984). For example, if a computer technician has opened and viewed a file containing child pornography, and then a police officer views the same file, the officer has not conducted a Fourth Amendment search. But cf. Texas Code Crim. Proc. Article 38.23 ("No evidence obtained by an officer *or other person* in violation of any provisions of the Constitution or laws of the State of Texas, or of the Constitution or laws of the United States of America, shall be admitted in evidence against the accused on the trial of any criminal case.").

2. *The growth of private security.* The private security industry employs more personnel than federal, state, and local governments combined. As Professor David Sklansky points out, the growing number of private security forces might entail a shift in some of the most basic tenets of criminal procedure. He suggests that this trend will create a body of criminal procedure law that is deconstitutionalized, defederalized, tort-based, and heavily reliant both on legislatures and on juries.

See Sklansky, The Private Police, 46 UCLA L. Rev. 1165 (1999); Elizabeth Joh, Conceptualizing the Private Police, 2005 Utah L. Rev. 573; Seth W. Stoughton, The Blurred Blue Line: Reform in an Era of Public and Private Policing, 44 Am. J. Crim. L. 117 (2017).

B. REASONABLE SUSPICION

1. *Grounds for Stops: Articulable, Individualized Reasonable Suspicion*

To justify a "stop," the government agent must be able to articulate a reasonable suspicion that the person has committed or will commit a crime. Exactly how can an officer establish reasonable suspicion? This concept is among the most commonly invoked in criminal procedure. Judges and lawyers applying the concept speak with apparent assurance about its meaning. Yet it is surprisingly difficult to find a precise definition of reasonable suspicion. And even a precise standard will leave enormous difficulties when applied to varied circumstances.

Judicial decisions, statutes, and rules of procedure use somewhat different verbal formulations to describe the justification needed for a low-level stop. Some formulations, especially those of the U.S. Supreme Court, emphasize the difference between reasonable suspicion and probable cause (the level of proof necessary to justify an arrest or a full-blown search):

> The Fourth Amendment requires some minimal level of objective justification for making the stop [that] is considerably less than proof of wrongdoing by a preponderance of the evidence. We have held that probable cause means a fair probability that contraband or evidence of a crime will be found, and the level of suspicion required for [reasonable suspicion] is obviously less demanding than that for probable cause. The concept of reasonable suspicion, like probable cause, is not readily, or even usefully, reduced to a neat set of legal rules. . . . In evaluating the validity of a stop such as this, we must consider the totality of the circumstances—the whole picture. [United States v. Sokolow, 490 U.S. 1 (1989).]

Some formulations emphasize that reasonable suspicion must be more than a guess and that it must be based on objective and articulable facts about an individual:

> [In] justifying the particular intrusion the police officer must be able to point to specific and articulable facts which, taken together with rational inferences from those facts, reasonably warrant that intrusion. . . . And in determining whether the officer acted reasonably in such circumstances, due weight must be given, not to his inchoate and unparticularized suspicion or "hunch," but to the specific reasonable inferences which he is entitled to draw from the facts in light of his experience. [Terry v. Ohio, 392 U.S. 1 (1968).]

Still other formulations insist that the reasonable suspicion standard is fact-sensitive, and the facts necessary to meet the standard will change from one context to another.

> The following are among the factors to be considered in determining if the officer has grounds to "reasonably suspect": (1) The demeanor of the suspect; (2) The gait and manner of the suspect; (3) Any knowledge the officer may have of the suspect's

background or character; (4) Whether the suspect is carrying anything, and what he is carrying; (5) The manner in which the suspect is dressed, including bulges in clothing, when considered in light of all of the other factors; (6) The time of the day or night the suspect is observed; (7) Any overheard conversation of the suspect; (8) The particular streets and areas involved; (9) Any information received from third persons, whether they are known or unknown; (10) Whether the suspect is consorting with others whose conduct is "reasonably suspect"; (11) The suspect's proximity to known criminal conduct; (12) Incidence of crime in the immediate neighborhood; (13) The suspect's apparent effort to conceal an article; (14) Apparent effort of the suspect to avoid identification or confrontation by a law enforcement officer. [Ark. Stat. §16-81-203.]

■ STATE v. THEODORE NELSON
638 A.2d 720 (Me. 1994)

GLASSMAN, J.

Theodore Nelson appeals from the judgment entered . . . on a jury verdict finding him guilty of operating a motor vehicle while under the influence of intoxicating liquor. . . . We agree with Nelson that because the stop of his motor vehicle was unlawful, the District Court erred in not granting Nelson's motion to suppress the evidence secured as a result of the stop and we vacate the judgment. . . .

At the hearing before the District Court on Nelson's motion to suppress, the sole witness presented was Officer Michael Holmes, who testified as follows: On December 24, 1991, at approximately 1:30 A.M., while on patrol . . . he observed an unoccupied automobile he knew belonged to Bruce Moore, a former neighbor of his, in a well-lit parking lot at a housing complex for the elderly located on North Main Street. Because the police department within the prior two weeks had received several complaints of theft during the nighttime, Officer Holmes took up an observation post in a small parking lot adjacent to the driveway to the complex and approximately 50 to 100 yards from the Moore automobile. He observed a white pickup truck occupied by a driver, later identified as Nelson, and one passenger enter the driveway to the complex. The pickup was backed into a parking space beside the Moore vehicle, the motor was shut off, and the headlights extinguished leaving the parking lights illuminated. With the use of binoculars, Officer Holmes recognized the passenger as Moore. He observed each of the occupants of the pickup starting to drink from a 16-ounce Budweiser can. There was no evidence that Officer Holmes observed anything unusual about the appearance of either occupant. After approximately forty-five to fifty minutes, Moore left the pickup truck and entered his own vehicle. The headlights of the pickup truck were turned on and it was again driven past Officer Holmes onto North Main Street. As the pickup passed his observation site, Officer Holmes immediately "pulled out behind it, and turned on [his] blue lights, [and] made an enforcement stop." Nelson promptly brought the pickup to a stop. At no time did Officer Holmes observe anything unusual about the operation of the pickup. There was no evidence of mechanical defects to the pickup or of excessive speed. He stopped the pickup because he "observed the operator . . . drinking a can of beer [and suspected that] the person may be under the influence of intoxicating liquor." The District Court held "Officer Holmes had reasonable articulable suspicion to stop the Defendant's vehicle," and denied Nelson's motion to suppress evidence secured as a result of the claimed illegal stop. . . .

Every person is protected from unreasonable intrusions by police officers and other governmental agents by the Fourth Amendment to the United States Constitution and article I, section 5 of the Maine Constitution. An investigatory stop is justified if at the time of the stop the officer has an articulable suspicion that criminal conduct has taken place, is occurring, or imminently will occur, and the officer's assessment of the existence of specific and articulable facts sufficient to warrant the stop is objectively reasonable in the totality of the circumstances. . . . It is well established that the suspicion for the stop must be based on information available to the officer at the time of the stop and cannot be bolstered by evidence secured by the stop. . . .

In the instant case, we find a clear deficiency in the evidence supporting the reasonableness of the suspicion. The record reveals that the officer observed nothing to support his suspicion that Nelson was operating under the influence of alcohol other than Nelson's consumption of a single can of beer over the course of nearly one hour. An adult's consumption of liquor in a motor vehicle is neither a crime nor a civil violation. The reasonable suspicion standard requires more than mere speculation. There was no evidence that the officer observed indicia of physical impairment or anything unusual in Nelson's appearance. Officer Holmes testified that the pickup truck was not being operated in an erratic manner. The officer offered no reason for his stop of the motor vehicle other than his suspicion that Nelson was under the influence of alcohol.

Based on the whole picture presented by this case, it cannot be said that it was objectively reasonable to believe that criminal activity was afoot. Accordingly, the court should have granted Nelson's motion to suppress the evidence secured as a result of the illegal stop. Judgment vacated.

COLLINS, J., dissenting.

. . . The stop in this instance was not based on mere speculation that Nelson was driving while under the influence. Rather, the officer had observed Nelson drinking a 16-ounce beer, at 1:30 in the morning on Christmas Eve, while parked in the parking lot of a housing complex for the elderly from which several complaints of theft had been registered. These observed facts, in combination with the recognition of the common practice in American society of having a second beer, gave the officer an articulable suspicion that Nelson was operating his truck while under the influence of alcohol. The officer's suspicion was objectively reasonable given the totality of the circumstances. As such, I believe the stop was justified and I would affirm the trial court.

■ STATE v. DAVID DEAN
645 A.2d 634 (Me. 1994)

RUDMAN, J.

[David Dean entered a conditional plea of guilty to charges of operating a vehicle under the influence of alcohol. He now appeals on the ground that the stop was not justified by reasonable suspicion.] The underlying facts are undisputed. At approximately 11:00 P.M. on Tuesday, April 13, 1993, Officer Dennis Sampson of the South Paris Police Department spotted Dean's car while Sampson was patrolling a new residential development on Cobble Hill Road. The road is a dead end, and the development was uninhabited during weekdays. Sampson was patrolling the area at the request of the development's property owners after a number of complaints of vandalism. No complaint had been made that night, and Dean's driving was unremarkable. Sampson stopped him solely because of his presence at that particular time and place. Sampson "wanted to see what they was up to, see if they were landowners or property owners, get some names in case we did have problems up in that area." The District Court, in a well-reasoned opinion, ruled that Sampson had the necessary "reasonable suspicion" to justify the stop. . . .

Dean's contention is that Officer Sampson did not entertain any suspicion that Dean was engaged in criminal activity. Dean raises the specter of random stops in any high-crime area, justified solely by the fact that the person detained happens to be in that area. The District Court, however, understood Dean's contentions and explicitly made the required findings:

> Now, I'll point out that the facts in this case suggest that this particular defendant was driving along a dead-end road at nighttime. The—the structures in the area were uninhabited, and it had been an area which had been the scene of a variety of criminal behavior which, in fact, brought . . . if not residents then the property owners to the police. They asked for increased surveillance. Ordinarily, the officer could not have stopped this particular vehicle. But under the circumstances, given the fact that this occurred well after dark, that the place was virtually uninhabited, that it was a dead-end street and [an area] in which a substantial amount of crime had been perpetrated in the recent past—I find that the officer acted properly because he reasonably suspected, based on prior reports of criminal activity in the area, that this particular Defendant could be engaged in such behavior. . . .

The only real issue is whether the two articulable facts relied on by the court can yield a reasonable suspicion. Those two facts are: (1) Dean's presence in an area of recent crime reports; and (2) the apparent absence of any reason to be in an uninhabited area at night. It is well-settled that a person's mere presence in a high crime area does not justify an investigatory stop. However, the combination of the recent criminal activity with other articulable facts—in this case, the time of day and the fact that the area was uninhabited—creates a reasonable suspicion. Many cases uphold a finding of a reasonable suspicion on similar facts.

In a recent decision, also involving police surveillance of an area due to several complaints, we held that the District Court erred by failing to grant the defendant's motion to suppress. State v. Nelson (Me. 1994). . . . In the *Nelson* case, however, the defendant was sitting in a truck in the parking lot of an occupied housing complex. Dean, in contrast, was driving through an uninhabited development site on a dead end street at 11:00 at night. His situation is distinguishable from that of the defendant in *Nelson*.

Dean's situation is more analogous to that of the defendant in State v. Fitzgerald, 620 A.2d 874 (Me. 1993). After dark, a police officer spotted Fitzgerald's car entering a private turn-around, known to be the site of frequent illegal trash dumping, and posted with "no trespassing" signs by the owner. When the officer's vehicle drove into the turn-around, the defendant was standing next to his car. The defendant then got into his car and drove away. The officer stopped the defendant's vehicle, saw that the defendant displayed evidence of being under the influence of alcohol, and arrested him for operating under the influence. Although the officer never witnessed any illegality or impropriety (Fitzgerald never violated the no trespassing signs), we affirmed the finding that the officer had a reasonable and articulable suspicion, "based on the previous littering and trespassing," the fact that Fitzgerald was outside his car in the dark when the officer approached, and the fact that Fitzgerald tried to leave when he saw the cruiser. Similarly, Officer Sampson's suspicion of Dean was engendered by prior complaints combined with other facts—the time of night and the absence of any apparent reason to be in an uninhabited housing development.

But for Dean's intoxication, this would have been a brief investigatory stop. An investigatory stop of a motor vehicle is normally a minimal intrusion by the state into a person's affairs. Balancing the facts on which Officer Sampson relied to make the stop against Dean's right to be free from any arbitrary intrusions by the State, we find the District Court's findings that the officer's suspicion was reasonable and the stop was justified are not clearly erroneous.

GLASSMAN, J., dissenting.

I respectfully dissent. We have recently reemphasized that the reasonable articulable suspicion standard requires "more than mere speculation" on the part of the police officer to sustain an investigatory stop. State v. Nelson (Me. 1994). Dean's behavior in driving out of a dead-end street at 11:00 P.M. on a Tuesday was in no sense illegal or even inherently suspicious, and the officer's desire to "see what [Dean] was up to" stems, at best, from a hunch.[1] A mere hunch will not justify a stop, and the officer's reasons for stopping the vehicle must not be a mere pretext or ruse. . . .

As the court notes, it is well settled that a person's mere presence in a high-crime area does not justify an investigatory stop. What the court regards as "other articulable facts" justifying the stop, in reality, are mere speculations entertained by the officer because of Dean's presence on a public way in an area where there had been complaints of vandalism or other damage to property. Each of the cases cited by the court to support its position involves additional facts beyond the defendant's mere presence in a crime area, e.g., police observed unusual behavior by the defendant, intrusion onto private property, the unusual operation of a vehicle, or the vehicle's unusual location. The constitutional right to be free from an illegal stop should not be abridged solely on the basis of the day of the week or time of day a car is being operated on a public way. . . .

Notes

1. *Components of reasonable suspicion: majority position.* Courts typically do not specify the general categories of facts that could support a finding of reasonable suspicion. In virtually all cases, however, the suspect's suspicious conduct does not itself violate the criminal law. The observer must infer from the observed facts that there is some correlation between the legal conduct observed and the suspected criminal acts. The officer may observe something resembling criminal conduct (such as the

---

1. The court seeks to distinguish *Nelson* by noting that Nelson was sitting in a pickup truck parked in the parking lot of an occupied housing complex whereas Dean was observed driving a motor vehicle on a public way leading out of a largely uninhabited residential development site. This is inapposite because the surroundings in which the police observed Nelson were not at issue in that case, which turned on whether merely drinking a can of beer in a parked car provided a reasonably articulable suspicion that a crime had taken place. This case turns on the site of the stop.

legal acts necessary to prepare for a crime); she might also observe the suspect taking an action that could be designed to hide a crime or to avoid contact with the police (such as avoiding eye contact with the officer or running away from the scene). See Sibron v. New York, 392 U.S. 40 (1968); but cf. State v. Hall, 115 P.3d 908 (Or. 2005) (fact that suspect repeatedly turned to look at officer's patrol vehicle and then averted his gaze did not amount to reasonable suspicion). The surroundings of the suspect are another common component of reasonable suspicion: For instance, presence near a crime scene soon after the time of a crime would be significant, especially if the suspect has no other apparent reason to be in that location. See State v. Miller, 207 P.3d 541 (Alaska 2009) (officer observed man and woman in vehicle exiting parking lot of tavern soon after receiving 911 call about couple arguing loudly in parking lot). How strong should the correlation be between this innocent conduct and the suspected criminal conduct to establish reasonable suspicion? A study of stops in New York City gives us one indication of the level of certainty police officers believe in practice to be enough for reasonable suspicion. According to an annual ACLU analysis of police data, roughly 10 percent of all stops between 2002 and 2014 (stops presumably based on the officer's effort to establish reasonable suspicion) resulted in an arrest or the filing of criminal charges. See *http://www.nyclu.org/content/stop-and-frisk-data.* Do these figures indicate that police officers have 10 percent confidence that a crime has been or is about to be committed when they make a stop? If so, is that enough certainty?

2. *Do standards matter?* Are *Nelson* and *Dean* consistent? That is, do they reflect a single standard of reasonable suspicion? If you were representing Nelson and Dean, where would you rather argue the case: under the statutory definition of reasonable suspicion in Arkansas or the judicial definition in Maine? Do different formulations of the reasonable suspicion standard make any difference in the outcomes?

3. *Objective basis.* The basis for reasonable suspicion turns on the facts available to the officer; it does not matter whether the officer holds an actual suspicion. In fact, the officer might wrongly believe that reasonable suspicion exists for one crime, when in fact reasonable suspicion exists for another crime. Would a subjective "reasonable suspicion" standard promote more careful evaluation of facts by police officers?

4. *Seriousness of crime.* Would the reasonable suspicion determination in *Dean* have turned out differently if the suspected crime had been murder instead of vandalism of property? Was the police officer in *Nelson* concerned about a different crime from the one he ultimately charged? Should the seriousness of the crime committed or soon to be committed affect the determination of reasonable suspicion? See Commonwealth v. Hawkins, 692 A.2d 1068 (Pa. 1997) (rejects concept of fluctuating reasonable suspicion standard based on seriousness of crime suspected; no "gun exception" to reasonable suspicion requirement).

5. *Intrusiveness of policing technique.* Did it matter to the Maine Supreme Court that the police officer in *Nelson* watched two occupants in a parked vehicle through binoculars for 45–50 minutes on Christmas Eve? Should courts interpret reasonable suspicion to account for the intrusiveness of local police practices? See Jane R. Bambauer, Hassle, 113 Mich. L. Rev. 461 (2015) (arguing that reasonable suspicion standard must consider more than probability that crime was committed; because some investigation methods meet the relevant probability standard but nevertheless impose too many stops on the innocent, courts must consider the "hassle" aspect of stops separately).

6. *Anonymous tips as the basis for reasonable suspicion.* Ordinarily, the police obtain reasonable suspicion based on their own observations and investigations. But on occasion, the police receive information from an anonymous informant that might contribute later to a finding of "reasonable suspicion." The U.S. Supreme Court has stated that anonymous tips can contribute to a reasonable suspicion finding only if the police can find independent corroboration of "significant details," especially of predicted future actions of the suspect, in the informant's tip. Alabama v. White, 496 U.S. 325 (1990). The anonymous tip, standing alone without corroboration or with corroboration only of the suspect's appearance, cannot justify a brief seizure of the suspect. See Florida v. J.L., 529 U.S. 266 (2000) (anonymous tip says that young black male standing at a particular bus stop and wearing a plaid shirt was carrying a gun; not enough for reasonable suspicion); Navarette v. California, 134 S. Ct. 1683 (2014) (reasonable suspicion established, based on tip that a truck with stated license plate number ran the caller off the road, along with police identification of the truck within minutes near the location of caller).

You can get a flavor of the state court decisions regarding anonymous tips and reasonable suspicion on the web extension for this chapter at *http://www.crimpro. com/extension/ch02.*

7. *Role of appellate courts in defining reasonable suspicion.* Under the "totality of the circumstances" test, the factfinder at the trial level takes a central role in deciding whether reasonable suspicion exists. What contributions might an appellate court make? Could an appeals court bring more predictability to the process by describing the sorts of factors that should receive more or less weight? For instance, should an appellate court declare that conduct "as consistent with innocent activity as with criminal activity" should receive little or no weight? See State v. O'Meara, 9 P.3d 325 (Ariz. 2000) ("totality of circumstances" test for reasonable suspicion allows court to consider conduct susceptible of an innocent explanation; here, unusual meeting in parking lot with drivers switching among four vehicles established reasonable suspicion for stop).

In Ornelas v. United States, 517 U.S. 690 (1996), the U.S. Supreme Court held that appellate courts would determine for themselves, under a de novo standard, the presence or absence of reasonable suspicion. This standard, the Court said, would allow appellate courts to unify precedent and clarify the legal principles at stake, providing law enforcement officers with the tools to reach correct determinations beforehand. At the same time, the Court declared that a reviewing court must give "due weight" to factual inferences drawn by resident judges. In United States v. Arvizu, 534 U.S. 266 (2002), the Court applied this standard of review to affirm a trial judge's finding of reasonable suspicion. A Border Patrol agent stopped Arvizu while driving on an unpaved road in a remote area of southeastern Arizona, and discovered over 100 pounds of marijuana in the minivan. The officer became suspicious when the driver of the minivan slowed dramatically after the patrol car appeared, and the children in the back seat waved to the officer in an "abnormal" and "mechanical" fashion, off and on for about five minutes. While each of these facts was "susceptible to innocent explanations" when viewed in isolation, the trial judge nevertheless could consider them as part of the "totality of the circumstances" to establish reasonable suspicion. An appellate court should not "casually" reject factors such as these "in light of the District Court's superior access to the evidence and the well-recognized inability of reviewing courts to reconstruct what happened in the courtroom." Is this a de novo standard of review at work?

■ JAMAL SIZER v. STATE

174 A.3d 326 (Md. 2017)

GREENE, J.

In the case before us, we are asked to consider the constitutionality of the stop and the subsequent search incident to the arrest of Petitioner, Jamal Sizer. . . . On the evening of November 20, 2015, five or six officers, from the Howard County Police Department Pathway Patrol Unit . . . biked the footpaths that "lead all throughout Columbia, Maryland." While on the footpath, officers in the Patrol Unit observed a group of individuals "play fighting and passing around an alcoholic beverage back and forth." The Patrol Unit suspected that the beverage was alcohol because it was in a brown paper bag and the group's body language was "consistent with individuals drinking." The officers, from 25–35 yards away from the group, observed a bottle being thrown and heard it hit the ground, but could not see who threw the bottle. At that point, the officers approached the group to investigate. When the officers were approximately five feet away, Mr. Sizer fled on foot, away from the officers.

Officer Andrew Schlossnagle, one of the officers in the Patrol Unit, gave immediate chase and "physically took [Mr. Sizer] to the ground." As Mr. Sizer was being tackled to the ground, he revealed that he was carrying a handgun on his person. [Officers] performed a search of Mr. Sizer incident to his arrest. The officers recovered a .38 caliber handgun from Mr. Sizer's backpack and twenty-seven pills of oxycodone, a controlled dangerous substance, from Mr. Sizer's sock. . . .

Mr. Sizer moved to suppress the weapon and the pills, arguing that the evidence was obtained pursuant to an unlawful stop. . . . Officer Schlossnagle testified [at the hearing] that the Owen Brown, Long Reach, and Oakland Mills Village Centers "tend to have an increase in calls for service and just general issues. There tends to be more calls for service in that—in those congested areas." When asked about what types of crimes he had investigated in the Owen Brown Village Center, the officer responded, "We were tasked to Owen Brown because of the increased calls for service and on-going trends in the area." The Circuit Court judge interjected, "Is 'increased calls for service' a nice way of saying 'high crime'?" [and Officer Schlossnagle replied,] "Yes, Your Honor."

Officer Schlossnagle explained that at the time of the incident, there was "an ongoing robbery series" and that "business owners . . . were complaining of quality of life issues, such as controlled dangerous substance violations, loitering, drinking, where the business centers requested an increased presence." Officer Schlossnagle also explained that "there was a report of a subject displaying a handgun the day before in the footpaths and fields that abut up to the village center." . . . A second officer, Corporal James Zammillo, testified that the Owen Brown Village Center was a "high crime area" as compared to other parts of Columbia. . . .

The officers testified that they were concerned with the group's general disorderliness and possible open container violations. None of the officers testified that they believed the group was connected to the "ongoing robbery series," or that they suspected any member of the group was the individual who had displayed a gun on the previous night. [The trial judge suppressed the evidence because] "the fact that Mr. Sizer ran, in and of itself, based on the particular scenario that's being given here today, is not sufficient." . . . The State appealed the Circuit Court's decision to suppress the evidence. . . .

Fourth Amendment jurisprudence, as it pertains to stops and seizures, operates along an escalating plane that begins with unparticularized suspicions or hunches and crescendos at probable cause. Reasonable suspicion exists somewhere between unparticularized suspicions and probable cause. See Alabama v. White, 496 U.S. 325, 330 (1990). . . .

In Illinois v. Wardlow, 528 U.S. 119 (2000), which both parties rely on to advance their opposing views, the United States Supreme Court discussed the weight to be given unprovoked flight in a high crime area as one factor in the totality of the circumstances analysis. [A] team of eight officers, in a four car caravan, travelled through a Chicago neighborhood known for "heavy narcotics trafficking." The defendant, Wardlow, held an opaque bag in his hand, and upon noticing the last car in the police caravan, fled on foot from the outside area where he stood. Two officers chased him on foot, and when they finally caught him, they conducted a pat-down and search for weapons. The opaque bag he held contained a .38 caliber handgun. . . . The Supreme Court held that flight in a high crime area was relevant in a totality of the circumstances analysis. It opined that: "An individual's presence in an area of expected criminal activity, standing alone, is not enough to support a reasonable, particularized suspicion that the person is committing a crime. But officers are not required to ignore the relevant characteristics of a location in determining whether the circumstances are sufficiently suspicious to warrant further investigation. . . ." Specifically, the Supreme Court explained:

> In this case, moreover, it was not merely respondent's presence in an area of heavy narcotics trafficking that aroused the officers' suspicion, but his unprovoked flight upon noticing the police. Our cases have also recognized that nervous, evasive behavior is a pertinent factor in determining reasonable suspicion. Headlong flight—wherever it occurs—is the consummate act of evasion: It is not necessarily indicative of wrongdoing, but it is certainly suggestive of such.

In Bost v. State, 958 A.2d 356 (Md. 2008), we had occasion to consider whether a defendant's flight in a high crime area supplied officers with the necessary reasonable suspicion to stop him. Officers observed Mr. Bost and a group of people drinking alcohol and loitering on a sidewalk in a drug-trafficking area, located in Washington, D.C., three blocks from the Maryland border. As the officers approached Mr. Bost, he began briskly walking away and took flight "while clutching his right waistband." An officer pursued him on foot, under the suspicion that he was concealing a weapon and based on the officer's experience that Mr. Bost's clutching of his waistband was consistent with someone trying to conceal a weapon. Officers tackled him to the ground and then found a gun tied around his neck. . . . Upon review, we held that officers had reasonable suspicion to stop Mr. Bost because he was seen in a high crime, drug-trafficking area, he took off in unprovoked flight, and he was clutching his side, in what appeared to be an attempt to conceal a weapon. . . .

In Crosby v. State, 970 A.2d 894 (Md. 2009), we emphasized the need for hearing courts to consider the totality of the circumstances when wholly innocent actions take place in a high crime area. In that case, an arresting officer, at the suppression hearing, testified that he made the decision to approach a driver in a parked car because: the driver was in a high crime area, he pulled in and out of "parking pads," he was in an area where a recent homicide had occurred, he switched his left turn signal to a right turn signal, and he drove in a "big loop." [We held] that the factors the arresting officer relied on "did not constitute ingredients that were sufficiently potent enough" in that case "to enrich the porridge to the constitutionally required consistency of reasonable suspicion," because "the combination of innocent factors, viewed in their totality," were no more indicative of criminal activity than any one factor assessed individually.

[In the instant case, there was] no evidence at the suppression hearing that established that the parking lot was located [near] the Owen Brown Village Center or the area where the handgun violation had occurred. . . . The suppression hearing judge did not receive any testimony regarding whether the group was connected in any way to the Owen Brown Village Center. None of the officers testified that the group, or any member of the group, was seen leaving or approaching the Village Center at any time during the officers' patrol of the pathways. The officers did not observe anyone joining or leaving the group during their time of observation. Nor did they testify that they observed the group demonstrating behavior consistent with the nature of the crimes that led them to conclude that the Village Center was a high crime area. Furthermore, none of the officers testified that they suspected any member of Mr. Sizer's group to be connected to the weapon violation that had been reported the previous day. As was true for the location of the Village Center, the two officers who testified about the handgun violation did not provide any proximal description of the area where the violation had occurred and its relation to the parking lot where Mr. Sizer was observed.

Because we determine that the Circuit Court erred in its application of the totality of the circumstances analysis, we need not decide whether the Circuit Court's erred in finding that the parking lot was a "high or higher crime area." In her analysis, the suppression hearing judge did not consider other pertinent factors in their totality, such as the officers' suspicion of an open container violation or their attempt to investigate the littering. Instead she found that, "the fact that Mr. Sizer ran, in and of itself," [was not sufficient] to justify the stop. The hearing judge . . . overlooked the import of two possible crimes that had occurred in the officers' presence along with Mr. Sizer's unprovoked flight as officers approached to investigate. . . .

Upon our independent review of the factors that were before the hearing judge, we hold that under the totality of the circumstances, the officers had reasonable suspicion to stop Mr. Sizer to investigate a possible open container violation as well as the improper disposal of a glass container [which is a misdemeanor], whether he was in a high crime area or not. . . . Therefore, when officers observed that a bottle was passed among the group and then was discarded or thrown to the ground, they had reasonable suspicion to believe that criminal activity was afoot. Mr. Sizer's flight from the group as the officers approached to investigate probable crimes committed in their presence shifted their focus to Mr. Sizer, which could have reasonably heightened their suspicion that he was the individual responsible for throwing the bottle. . . . Based on these circumstances, we conclude that the officers had reasonable suspicion to stop Mr. Sizer. After being informed that he was armed with a weapon, the officers had reasonable suspicion to frisk him. . . .

ADKINS and HOTTEN, JJ., dissenting.

. . . The State relied heavily on Illinois v. Wardlow, 528 U.S. 119 (2000), as well as our own similar precedent, for the proposition that unprovoked flight in a "high crime area" provides sufficient reasonable suspicion to justify an investigatory detention in this case. The Majority rightfully appears skeptical of the evidence the State supplied that suggests that this incident took place in a "high crime" area, but avoids addressing the issue by deciding that the Circuit Court for Howard County erred in applying the totality of the circumstances analysis. . . .

Reasonable suspicion requires a determination that, under the totality of the circumstances, officers had a "particularized and objective basis for suspecting the particular person stopped of criminal activity." United States v. Cortez, 449 U.S. 411, 417-18 (1981). In evaluating the constitutionality of an investigatory detention, we consider "whether the officer's action was justified at its inception, and whether it was reasonably related in scope to the circumstances which justified the interference in the first place." Terry v. Ohio, 392 U.S. 1, 20 (1968). . . .

Whether an activity occurs in a high crime area can inform a police officer's analysis about the activity that is taking place. A suspect need not be connected to previous crimes in the area, Holt v. State, 78 A.3d 415 (Md. 2013), but the nature of the area is relevant to reasonable suspicion when the suspect's activities appear to be the kind of criminal activity that is likely to be occurring there. A generalized description of an area as "high crime," without a greater connection to the observed activities, does not support reasonable suspicion. Other Maryland cases addressing *Terry* stops in high crime areas demonstrate that the nexus between the nature of the area and the observed activities is significant in determining whether officers had reasonable suspicion. See Chase v. State, 144 A.3d 630 (Md. 2016) (detaining individuals for suspicion of drug trafficking based on behavior in area known for drug trafficking); Cox v. State, 871 A.2d 647 (Md. App. 2005) (individual suspected of drug dealing had been warned away from intersection known for heroin trafficking earlier, when officers saw him again, he fled, committing a traffic infraction). . . .

Applying these factors, I conclude that the State failed to show that the Owen Brown Village Center is a high crime area—a conclusion the Majority seems poised to reach, but then abandons. Increased calls for service and concerned business owners do not permit a conclusion that an area is "high crime." An ongoing series of robberies at unknown locations and times, as well as a single sighting of an individual with a handgun do not suffice absent greater specificity. Even assuming that these incidents could be sufficient for a finding that the area is "high crime," there is no nexus between these crimes and the activity in this case, or between these crimes and Mr. Sizer. For these reasons, I do not find sufficient evidence to support the State's contention that *Wardlow* is dispositive precedent. . . .

It is evident, upon review of the record that the hearing judge did apply the totality of the circumstances analysis. The officers observed a loud group in a parking lot from 25 to 35 yards away, and the officers thought that some individuals in the group might be consuming alcohol. The officers also testified that someone threw a bottle, but they did not know who threw it, or even where the bottle originated in the group. . . . The hearing judge considered all of these factors in reaching her decision that the seizure was unreasonable. She did not doubt what the officers had observed, but the officers never saw Mr. Sizer engaging in any of these activities. Thus, at the moment the officers reached the group, they had no reasonable articulable suspicion that Mr. Sizer was engaged in criminal activity. He was with a group of individuals, some of whom might have been engaging in misdemeanor activities. The hearing judge decided that this "scenario," combined with Mr. Sizer's flight, could not provide a sufficiently particularized reasonable suspicion to detain him. . . .

The Majority places too much weight on Mr. Sizer's flight. Unprovoked flight is a factor in the totality of the circumstances analysis. Based on the evidence presented, it appears that the officers had a hunch that Mr. Sizer was engaged in criminal activity because he ran at their approach.[9] We do not accord weight to an "inchoate and unparticularized suspicion or hunch." *Terry*, 392 U.S. at 27. Officers may certainly investigate ambiguities, but they must still be able to articulate a particularized basis for suspicion that comports with constitutional standards. . . .

I do not suggest officers should permit individuals suspected of committing crimes to escape. But at a suppression hearing, the State must demonstrate that the officers had a sufficient factual basis to stop a citizen — especially when that stop is a hard take-down. They failed to do so. This Court should not shoulder that burden.

Notes

1. *"High crime areas" and reasonable suspicion: majority position.* An officer trying to establish reasonable suspicion will at times rely on the amount of crime occurring recently in the neighborhood. The government typically does not support the assertion with any statistical analysis of reported crimes, but bases the claim on the impressions of the officer about neighborhoods. If you were a judge evaluating the claim of reasonable suspicion, would the reputation of the neighborhood for crime play any part in your decision? If you were a police officer, how might you strengthen such claims? See Brown v. Texas, 443 U.S. 47 (1979) ("The fact that appellant was in a neighborhood frequented by drug users, standing alone, is not a basis for concluding that appellant himself was engaged in criminal conduct.").

2. *Neighborhood as proxy for race?* The neighborhoods described in court as "high crime" areas are often the homes for poor and minority residents. Do the demographics of some neighborhoods make crimes committed or reported there easier to notice or remember? Do more crimes occur in poorer neighborhoods because of subtle signals that disorder is tolerated there — the so-called broken windows theory of policing? If this is true, then it would make sense to direct more stop-and-frisk activity in places where police find the greatest physical and social disorder. A study of New York City policing by Ben Grunwald and Jeffrey Fagan, however, found that officers call nearly every block in the city "high crime"; that their assessments of whether an area is high-crime are virtually uncorrelated with actual crime rates; and that the suspect's race, the racial and socioeconomic composition of the area, and the identity of the officer are all stronger predictors of whether an officer calls an area high-crime than the actual crime rate itself. See Grunwald and Fagan, The End of Intuition-Based High-Crime Areas, 106 Calif. L. Rev. (forthcoming 2019). If you were a police chief and a reporter called a similar study about your department to your attention, how would you respond?

3. *Avoiding or fleeing the police as basis for reasonable suspicion.* The officers in *Sizer* noted that the suspect tried to flee the scene and considered the flight to be one

9. Mr. Sizer's brief suggests that he may have run because he was startled. The officers approached out of darkness, and Officer Baker testified that the group first noticed the officers when they were five feet away from the group. The officers testified that they identified themselves as police during their approach, but they also described the group as "loud." Based on this evidence, it is not unreasonable to draw an inference that Mr. Sizer's flight may have not been entirely unprovoked.

factor contributing to reasonable suspicion. Would a suspect's flight from the police be enough, standing alone, to establish reasonable suspicion of criminal activity? A strong majority of state courts have decided that flight contributes to reasonable suspicion, but few cases arise in which flight alone is the basis for a claim of reasonable suspicion. See State v. Hicks, 488 N.W.2d 359 (Neb. 1992) (flight upon approach of police vehicle not sufficient to justify investigative stop).

4. *Discretion to stop and the definition of crimes.* There is a powerful relationship between reasonable suspicion and the substantive criminal law. If a legislature creates a crime such as "drug loitering," it empowers the police to stop people based on innocent behavior (such as standing on a corner or making signals) that is often a precursor to more harmful criminal activity, such as drug trafficking. See Mich. Comp. L. §750.167(1)(j) (disorderly conduct where a person knowingly loiters in or about a place where an illegal occupation or business is being conducted); Andrew D. Leipold, Targeted Loitering Laws, 3 U. Pa. J. Const. L. 474 (2001). And as we saw, open container laws and an anti-littering ordinance contributed to the outcome in *Sizer.* If you were counsel to a police department, would you ask the city council to pass such an ordinance, or would you rather formulate a profile within the department itself?

2. Pretextual Stops

An officer needs reasonable suspicion that a crime has been or will be committed before stopping a person for an investigation. But when the officer has multiple reasons to stop a person, including reasonable suspicion of one crime and a hunch that the person has committed another crime, must the suspicion and the purpose match? In other words, does the police officer invalidate a stop when the crime that she reasonably suspects is only a "pretext" to justify a stop that she intends to use while investigating some other crime? State courts were split on this subject until the U.S. Supreme Court addressed it in Whren v. United States, 517 U.S. 806 (1996). The case created a new shorthand term in criminal procedure: "*Whren* stops" refer to traffic stops based on reasonable suspicion of a traffic violation, but intended to further the investigation of some other crime. Now virtually all state courts addressing this question respond much like the New York court in the following case.

■ PEOPLE v. FRANK ROBINSON
767 N.E.2d 638 (N.Y. 2001)

Smith, J.

The issue [in these consolidated cases] is whether a police officer who has probable cause to believe a driver has committed a traffic infraction violates article I, §12 of the New York State Constitution when the officer, whose primary motivation is to conduct another investigation, stops the vehicle. We conclude that there is no violation, and we adopt Whren v. United States, 517 U.S. 806 (1996), as a matter of state law.

People v. Robinson. On November 22, 1993, New York City police officers in the Street Crime Unit, Mobile Taxi Homicide Task Force were on night patrol in a marked police car in the Bronx. Their main assignment was to follow taxicabs to make sure that no robberies occurred. After observing a car speed through a red light, the police activated their high intensity lights and pulled over what they suspected was a livery cab. After stopping the cab, one officer observed a passenger, the defendant, look back several times. The officers testified that they had no intention of giving the driver a summons but wanted to talk to him about safety tips. The officers approached the vehicle with their flashlights turned on and their guns holstered. One of the officers shined his flashlight into the back of the vehicle, where defendant was seated, and noticed that defendant was wearing a bullet proof vest. After the officer ordered defendant out of the taxicab, he observed a gun on the floor where defendant had been seated. Defendant was arrested and charged with criminal possession of a weapon and unlawfully wearing a bullet proof vest. Defendant moved to suppress the vest and gun, arguing that the officers used a traffic infraction as a pretext to search the occupant of the taxicab. The Court denied the motion, and defendant was convicted of both charges. . . .

People v. Reynolds. On March 6, 1999, shortly after midnight, a police officer, on routine motor patrol in the City of Rochester, saw a man he knew to be a prostitute enter defendant's truck. The officer followed the truck and ran a computer check on the license plate. Upon learning that the vehicle's registration had expired two months earlier, the officer stopped the vehicle. The resulting investigation did not lead to any charges involving prostitution. Nevertheless, because the driver's eyes were bloodshot, his speech slurred and there was a strong odor of alcohol, police performed various field sobriety tests, with defendant failing most. . . . Defendant was charged with driving while intoxicated, an unclassified misdemeanor, and operating an unregistered motor vehicle, a traffic infraction. Defendant's motion to suppress was granted by the Rochester City Court, which dismissed all charges.

People v. Glenn. On November 7, 1997, plainclothes police officers were on street crime patrol in an unmarked car in Manhattan. They observed a livery cab make a right hand turn without signaling. An officer noticed one of three passengers in the back seat lean forward. The police stopped the vehicle to investigate whether or not a robbery was in progress. A police officer subsequently found cocaine on the rear seat and, after he arrested defendant, found additional drugs on his person. Defendant was charged with criminal possession of a controlled substance in the third degree and criminally using drug paraphernalia in the second degree. He contended that the drugs should be suppressed, asserting that the traffic infraction was a pretext to investigate a robbery. After his motion to suppress was denied, he pleaded guilty to one count of criminal possession of a controlled substance. . . .

Discussion. The Supreme Court, in Whren v. United States, 517 U.S. 806 (1996), unanimously held that where a police officer has probable cause to detain a person temporarily for a traffic violation, that seizure does not violate the Fourth Amendment to the United States Constitution even though the underlying reason for the stop might have been to investigate some other matter. In *Whren*, officers patrolling a known drug area of the District of Columbia became suspicious when several young persons seated in a truck with temporary license plates remained at a stop sign for an unusual period of time, and the driver was looking down into the lap of the passenger seated on his right. After the car made a right turn without signaling, the police stopped it, assertedly to warn the driver of traffic violations, and saw two plastic bags of what appeared to be crack cocaine in Whren's hands.

After arresting the occupants, the police found several quantities of drugs in the car. The petitioners were charged with violating federal drug laws. The petitioners moved to suppress the drugs, arguing that the stop was not based upon probable cause or even reasonable suspicion that they were engaged in illegal drug activity and that the police officer's assertion that he approached the car in order to give a warning was pretextual. . . .

The Supreme Court held that the Fourth Amendment had not been violated because "as a general matter, the decision to stop an automobile is reasonable where the police have probable cause to believe that a traffic violation has occurred." . . . The Court rejected any effort to tie the legality of the officers' conduct to their primary motivation or purpose in making the stop, deeming irrelevant whether a reasonable traffic police officer would have made the stop. According to the Court, "Subjective intentions play no role in ordinary, probable-cause Fourth Amendment analysis." . . . More than forty states and the District of Columbia have adopted the objective standard approved by *Whren* or cited it with approval.

In each of the cases before us, defendant argues that the stop was pretextual and in violation of New York State Constitution, article I, §12. . . . We hold that where a police officer has probable cause to believe that the driver of an automobile has committed a traffic violation, a stop does not violate article I, §12 of the New York State Constitution. In making that determination of probable cause, neither the primary motivation of the officer nor a determination of what a reasonable traffic officer would have done under the circumstances is relevant. . . .

The real concern of those opposing pretextual stops is that police officers will use their authority to stop persons on a selective and arbitrary basis. *Whren* recognized that the answer to such action is the Equal Protection Clause of the Constitution. We are not unmindful of studies . . . which show that certain racial and ethnic groups are disproportionately stopped by police officers, and that those stops do not end in the discovery of a higher proportion of contraband than in the cars of other groups. The fact that such disparities exist is cause for both vigilance and concern about the protections given by the New York State Constitution. Discriminatory law enforcement has no place in our law. . . .

The alternatives to upholding a stop based solely upon reasonable cause to believe a traffic infraction has been committed put unacceptable restraints on law enforcement. This is so whether those restrictions are based upon the primary motivation of an officer or upon what a reasonable traffic police officer would have done under the circumstances. Rather than restrain the police in these instances, the police should be permitted to do what they are sworn to do—uphold the law. . . .

To be sure, the story does not end when the police stop a vehicle for a traffic infraction. Our holding in this case addresses only the initial police action upon which the vehicular stop was predicated. The scope, duration and intensity of the seizure, as well as any search made by the police subsequent to that stop, remain subject to the strictures of article I, §12, and judicial review. . . .

The dissenters concede that . . . an individualized determination of probable cause will generally provide an objective evidentiary floor circumscribing police conduct and thereby prevent the arbitrary exercise of search and seizure power. However, [the] dissenters assert that because motor vehicle travel is so much a part of our lives and is minutely regulated, total compliance with the law is impossible. We see no basis for this differentiation. While New Yorkers may ubiquitously disobey parts of the Vehicle and Traffic Law, that does not render its commands unenforceable. As noted by the unanimous United States Supreme Court, "we are aware of no principle that would allow us to decide at what point a code of law becomes so expansive and so commonly violated that infraction itself can no longer be the ordinary measure of the lawfulness of enforcement." *Whren*, 517 U.S. at 818. . . . An officer may choose to stop someone for a "minor" violation after considering a number of factors, including traffic and weather conditions, but the officer's authority to stop a vehicle is circumscribed by the requirement of a violation of a duly enacted law. . . .

The dissent also raises the spectre of "repeatedly documented" racial profiling in the search and seizure context. There is no claim in any of the three cases before us that the police officers engaged in racial profiling. But, if racial profiling is the analytical pivot of our colleagues' dissent, their remedy misses the mark. The dissenters' "reasonable police officer" standard does little to combat or reduce the likelihood of racially motivated traffic stops, since, in their view, an officer's primary motivation is irrelevant. . . .

The invention of the automobile has changed the fabric of American life. While the vast majority of New Yorkers own or drive vehicles, the frequency of their time on the road cannot recast the functional parameters of the Fourth Amendment or article 1, §12. . . . We are not confounded by the proposition that police officers must exercise their discretion on a daily basis. Nor are we surprised at the assertion that many New Yorkers often violate some provision of the Vehicle and Traffic Law. But we cannot equate the combination of police officer discretion and numerous traffic violations as arbitrary police conduct. . . . In the cases before us, [we have] a standard that constrains police conduct—probable cause under the Vehicle and Traffic Law and its related regulations that govern the safe use of our highways. . . .

LEVINE, J., dissenting.

[In] the context of pretextual traffic stops—traffic infraction stops that would not have been made but for the aim of the police to accomplish an otherwise unlawful investigative seizure or search—the existence of probable cause that the infraction was committed is manifestly insufficient to protect against arbitrary police conduct. That is so for two reasons. First, motor vehicle travel is one of the most ubiquitous activities in which Americans engage outside the home. Second, it is, by an overwhelming margin, the most pervasively regulated activity engaged in by Americans. . . .

The confluence of the foregoing factors—the dependency of the vast majority of Americans upon private automobile transportation and the virtual impossibility of sustained total compliance with the traffic laws—gives the police wide discretion to engage in investigative seizures, only superficially checked by the probable cause requirement for the traffic infraction that is the ostensible predicate for the stop. . . . Sadly, the pretext stop decisions in lower State and Federal courts confirm that the traffic infraction probable cause standard has left the police with the ability to stop vehicles at will for illegitimate investigative purposes. Typically, the stops are conducted as part of a drug interdiction program by a law enforcement agency. The vehicle and occupants appear to fit within a "drug courier" profile and the driver or occupants may have engaged in some other innocuous behavior which arouses a surmise of criminal conduct. The officer then follows the vehicle until some traffic code violation is observed. At that point, or even later, the vehicle is pulled over and the officer proceeds with the investigation. . . .

Moreover, as has been repeatedly documented, . . . drug courier interdiction through traffic infraction stops has a dramatically disproportionate impact on young African-American males. Yet both the majority and the *Whren* Court dismiss the relevance of such disparate treatment in the constitutional search and seizure context. They instead suggest that the remedy lies in invoking the Federal Constitution's Equal Protection Clause. The same studies that recognize the existence of a disparate racial impact, however, also demonstrate the inadequacy of the Equal Protection Clause as a remedy for those abuses. A racial profiling claim under the Equal Protection Clause is difficult, if not impossible, to prove. The Equal Protection Clause prohibits race-based selective enforcement of the law only when such enforcement "had a discriminatory effect and . . . was motivated by a discriminatory purpose." United States v. Armstrong, 517 U.S. 456 (1996). . . . Putting aside the unquestionably expensive and time-consuming process of assembling statistical evidence, it is debatable whether the requisite data would even be available.

[The petitioners in *Whren*] urged the adoption of an objective standard by which to judge police exploitation of arbitrary traffic code enforcement to conduct investigative stops: whether a reasonable police officer, under the circumstances, would have made the stop for the reasons given. Despite the objective nature of that test, the Supreme Court's primary reason for rejecting it was that it was "driven by subjective considerations"—that is, the improper motivation of the seizing officer to conduct an otherwise unjustified investigative stop. . . . This criticism, in our view, misses the mark. The petitioners in *Whren* claimed that the officers' seizure was unreasonable because it was arbitrary, not because it was either unjustified or improperly motivated. . . .

The *Whren* Court offered only two other reasons for rejecting the test suggested by the petitioners. The first was that "police enforcement practices, even if they could be practically assessed by a judge, vary from place to place and from time to time. We cannot accept that the search and seizure protections of the Fourth Amendment are so variable . . . and can be made to turn upon such trivialities." Under well-established Federal and State search and seizure doctrine, however, . . . the basic determination of reasonable suspicion or even probable cause to support a search or seizure will almost always vary from place to place and time to time, depending on the particular circumstances confronting an officer.

[The opinion in *Whren*] also claimed in substance that accepting petitioners' position would place Judges in the role of deciding what traffic code provisions are to be enforced at all. . . . Adoption of the [reasonable officer standard] would do nothing of the sort. It does nothing more than set an objective standard, the violation of which would deprive law enforcement officers only of the use of evidence of crimes unrelated to the traffic infraction obtained in investigative stops effected through arbitrary enforcement of the traffic laws. As to the infraction itself, . . . prosecution of the underlying traffic infraction is not based upon evidence obtained through exploitation of the initial stop, but upon observations made before the stop. . . .

Defendants urge that we adopt a subjective test, whether the "primary motivation" for the stop was to investigate criminal activity rather than to prosecute the traffic offense ostensibly justifying the seizure. We would reject that test [because] courts and commentators have noted the difficulty, if not futility, of basing the constitutional validity of searches or seizures on judicial determinations of the subjective motivation of police officers. . . . Thus, we prefer an objective [standard:] would a reasonable officer assigned to Vehicle and Traffic Law enforcement in the seizing officer's department have made the stop under the circumstances presented, absent a purpose to investigate serious criminal activity of the vehicle's occupants[?] Whether the stop was carried out in accordance with standard procedures of the officer's department would be a highly relevant inquiry in that regard. . . .

Notes

1. *Pretextual stops: majority position.* Under the federal constitution, courts refuse to question the legitimacy of allegedly pretextual stops, so long as the officer "could have" properly stopped the vehicle based on evidence of a traffic offense. According to the Supreme Court in Whren v. United States, 517 U.S. 806 (1996), any effort to determine whether a reasonable officer "would have" stopped a vehicle for traffic violations alone would be too uncertain: "While police manuals and standard procedures may sometimes provide objective assistance, ordinarily one would be reduced to speculating about the hypothetical reaction of a hypothetical constable—an exercise that might be called virtual subjectivity." The *Whren* decision convinced most states that at one time employed the "would have" doctrine to change approaches for purposes of the state constitution. At this point, over 40 states follow the *Whren* decision. See Mitchell v. State, 745 N.E.2d 775 (Ind. 2001).

One of the few remaining exceptions is the state of Washington. In State v. Ladson, 979 P.2d 833 (Wash. 1999), officers on proactive gang patrol noticed a driver who was rumored to be involved in gang and drug activity. They followed the car and stopped the driver after noticing that the license plate tags had expired. Their primary reason for the stop was to investigate drug activity, and they found drugs in the passenger's possession. The Washington Supreme Court called pretextual stops "a triumph of form over substance" and worried that approving such searches would mean that "nearly every citizen would be subject to a *Terry* stop simply because he or she is in his or her car." As for how to determine whether a given stop is pretextual, the court adopted a totality-of-the-circumstances approach. Trial courts may inquire both about the subjective intent of the officer as well as the objective reasonableness of the officer's behavior to determine whether a stop was pretextual or not. If you wanted to learn whether judicial controls of pretextual stops are workable in practice, what aspect of the Washington system would you study most closely?

2. *State constitutions and the federal constitution.* In *Robinson,* the New York court pointed out that both the state and federal constitutions contain provisions to limit police searches and seizures and to protect privacy. State courts must interpret both constitutional provisions when a litigant presents the issue. The state courts must adhere to the decisions of the U.S. Supreme Court as to the meaning of the federal constitution. State law enforcement officers must comply with certain provisions of the federal constitution—those applicable to the states because the Due Process Clause of the Fourteenth Amendment "incorporates" them. Today, most of the specific Bill of Rights protections for criminal defendants and for citizens generally have been "incorporated" to apply against the states and their agents. See Akhil Reed Amar, The Bill of Rights: Creation and Reconstruction (1998), and Michael Kent Curtis, No State Shall Abridge: The Fourteenth Amendment and the Bill of Rights (1986).

A state's supreme court, however, has the ultimate judicial authority over the meaning of its own state constitution. It might interpret the state constitution (or some other provision of state law, such as a statute) to place restrictions on law enforcement officers different from what the federal constitution might require. The federal courts, including the U.S. Supreme Court, must allow a state supreme court's decision in a criminal case to stand so long as the decision does not flatly conflict with binding federal law and rests on "independent and adequate" state law grounds. Periodically, we will consider cases about procedural issues in which state law gives different answers from federal law or asks different procedural questions altogether. This variety in criminal procedure in different jurisdictions makes it possible for lawyers to argue for procedural innovations that might not be apparent from studying federal law alone.

3. *Reading minds.* Do judicial controls on pretextual stops require the judge to read the officer's mind? Relevant "objective" evidence might include the prevalence of traffic stops in that situation, or the officer's compliance with a police department's internal rules about traffic stops. Perhaps a court's position on the pretext doctrine reflects an underlying assumption about the trustworthiness of police officers, rather than a factual finding about subjective or objective circumstances. If a court is unwilling to attempt to control pretextual stops, is it implicitly deciding that the police ordinarily make good faith decisions that ought to be encouraged? Is it making any implicit claims about the truthfulness of police testimony in the ordinary case? See Angela Davis, Race, Cops, and Traffic Stops, 51 U. Miami L. Rev. 425 (1997).

4. *Highways as a special arena.* The pretext issue takes on special urgency on the highways. Over half of all contacts between adults and police officers take place during traffic stops. In a given year, the police stop about 10 percent of all drivers. See Bureau of Justice Statistics, Police Behavior During Traffic and Street Stops, 2011 (September 2013, NCJ 242937). The vehicle's equipment and the driver's conduct are also regulated in minute detail, allowing a wide variety of stops. The potential grounds for stops cover everything from bumper height, to tire tread, to a burned-out license tag light, or the ever-popular "changing lanes without signaling." In 2011, speeding was the reason given to 47 percent of the stopped drivers; 14 percent were stopped for a burned-out light or other vehicle defect; 7 percent were stopped for a seatbelt or cell phone violation, and 7 percent for an improper turn or lane change.

Does a healthy legal system depend on lax enforcement of certain laws? In this imperfect world, how many cars and drivers can go for long without some minor violation, such as tag lights or lane violations? If police officers can develop reasonable suspicion against any driver if they persist in the effort, does the *Whren* decision effectively repeal the reasonable suspicion limit for police power on the highways? How does the majority opinion in the New York case answer this question?

5. *Police responses to pretext claims.* If you were legal counsel to a police department in a jurisdiction adopting the reasonable officer "would" test for pretext (such as Washington state), what advice would you give the department? For instance, what charges should the arresting officer file—the original offense justifying the stop or the more serious offense or both? What sorts of reasons should an officer give to justify an initial stop? Will the officer fare better if he identifies some grounds for stopping a car other than a traffic violation? See Scott v. State, 877 P.2d 503 (Nev. 1994) (officer stopped car because vehicle might have been stolen). Can the officer overcome the claim of pretext by arguing that he routinely stops several vehicles per month based on similar traffic violations? State v. Wilson, 867 P.2d 1175 (N.M.

1994) (officer testifies that he stops six to eight cars every month for failure to use seat belts; stop upheld).

6. *Department-level pretexts.* Are pretext claims by defendants stronger or weaker when the use of pretext (such as traffic stops to look for drugs) is a department policy instead of just an individual officer's decision? Other departments (for example, the Kansas City Police Department) use reasonable suspicion stops of cars and persons as a general policy with the goal of finding weapons and enforcing firearms laws. A study of the Kansas City program, which began in 1991, concluded that gun seizures in the 80-by-10-block target area increased by 65 percent, while seizures in a comparable beat went down slightly. Gun crimes in the target beat decreased by 49 percent and increased slightly in the comparison beat. See Lawrence Sherman, James Shaw & Dennis Rogan, The Kansas City Gun Experiment, National Institute of Justice, Research in Brief (Jan. 1995 NCJ 150855). Would a challenge to this Kansas City practice be more difficult than the challenges to the various individual stops in *Robinson*? See also Ashcroft v. al-Kidd, 563 U.S. 731 (2011) (after the government showed individualized suspicion that a person was a material witness to a federal crime who would soon disappear, the detainee could not invalidate the detention by showing that the true motive for his arrest was a Department of Justice policy to use the statute as a measure to strike preemptively against terrorism suspects).

7. *Technology and pretext.* As driverless cars start to appear on the roads, what effects do you anticipate on the patterns of traffic stops by police? Assume that driverless cars will unfailingly follow traffic regulations, and that the technology will be available first to drivers with more wealth. Does that mean the early phase of this technology will lead to greater socio-economic and racial disparities in stops? Consider surveillance technology, as well. If street cameras become ubiquitous and police rely on algorithms to identify suspicious behavior in the recordings as the basis for a stop, what effects would the technology have on racial disparities in pedestrian stops? See Bennett I. Capers, Race, Policing, and Technology, 95 N.C. L. Rev. 1241 (2017).

Problem 2-7. Asset Management

Under state and federal asset forfeiture laws, the police can seize any "proceeds" or "instrumentalities" of a crime. After a streamlined process to confirm that the assets are indeed connected to a crime, the assets typically are sold; if the asset is cash, it is converted to government use. Under most of these forfeiture laws, the proceeds from the sale go directly into the coffers of the law enforcement agency that seized the asset, not into general revenue to support all government operations. This arrangement allows some law enforcement agencies to purchase equipment and support programs without drawing on tax dollars.

In Barbour County, Alabama, Chief Deputy Eddie Ingram specializes in traffic stops that lead to asset forfeiture. He estimates that he and the officers he supervises have discovered more than $11 million in drug assets over the past 15 years. The sheriff's department has used asset forfeiture money to buy bulletproof vests, gun belts, guns, and 9 out of the 14 cars in the department's fleet.

When Ingram is deciding which cars to stop on the U.S. highway that serves as the main north-south thoroughfare through the county, he looks for "things that just are different, and there's no one way to explain it, there's no one indicator.

I just look for people that try to fit in that make themselves stand out." For instance, he says, if the speed limit is 65 mph, most people will drive 75 mph. But someone who is committing a crime will travel at 65 mph or less, and avoid eye contact with a deputy who pulls up alongside. Ingram calls these "stress-induced indicators."

Other departments in the region noticed the high levels of asset forfeiture in Barbour County and became interested in Ingram's techniques. He formed his own training academy, which allowed him to train thousands of officers. After the classroom portion of the training, the students in Ingram's academy go out on the highways in Barbour County to practice the techniques. If they make a stop and find hidden currency, the Barbour County Sheriff's Office keeps 40 percent of the cash.

Suppose you are a trial judge in Barbour County and you periodically hear claims from defendants about the alleged lack of reasonable suspicion to support a traffic stop that produced evidence of a drug crime. Would the larger pattern of reliance on asset forfeiture by the sheriff's department have any effect on your evaluation of reasonable suspicion in the case at hand? What other forum might be available for motorists to challenge the adequacy of reasonable suspicion to support a stop?

3. Criminal Profiles and Race

The police officer in the field is not left entirely to her own devices when deciding whether apparently innocent facts are actually indicators of criminal activity. Both police departments and legislative bodies offer guidance on the types of conduct that might create grounds for a stop. Police departments periodically create "criminal profiles," which are lists of personal characteristics and behaviors said to be associated with particular types of crime (most commonly drug trafficking). Sometimes these profiles are quite specific, while at other times they are relatively short and general. An officer hoping to explain after the fact why she stopped a person might describe the features of the profile that the suspect matched.

The criminal profiles developed in police departments often remain informal and unwritten. Do these "profiles"—collective judgments about suspicious activity—add any weight to the individual police officer's expert judgment in the field as the officer tries to establish reasonable suspicion? Does your response to a criminal profile change if it places some weight on the racial or ethnic identification of the suspect?

■ URIEL HARRIS v. STATE

806 A.2d 119 (Del. 2002)

VEASEY, C.J.

This case is about constitutional protections prohibiting unreasonable searches and seizures that the judicial branch of government is obligated to enforce for the protection of the rights of all citizens, including the law-abiding as well as reprehensible drug traffickers and other criminals. Thus, we consider whether the police in this case met the constitutional requirement of reasonable suspicion to stop a car. . . .

On April 30, 1997, Wilmington Police Detective Liam Sullivan, dressed in plain clothes, stationed himself on the Wilmington train station platform to monitor inbound trains from New York City for drug couriers. Sullivan had received no tips regarding any person or that there would even be drugs coming into Wilmington on a train that day. But he testified that "there's probably drugs on every train coming south from New York City."

That afternoon, Uriel Harris boarded a southbound train in Philadelphia. Harris testified [at the suppression hearing] that he planned to meet his friend Dale Green at the Wilmington train station. Green was to drive Harris back to Aberdeen, Maryland, where Green apparently originated his trip earlier that day. Harris' train arrived in Wilmington about twenty-five minutes late. After leaving the train along with about twenty other passengers, Harris, who carried a backpack, looked over his shoulder three times between the train and the platform's exit doors. Sullivan testified that he became suspicious because Harris looked over his shoulder three times. Harris testified that he had never been to the Wilmington train station before and was uncertain about where to meet Green. Harris stated he was looking for the appropriate exit and for Green.

At this point, Sullivan decided that he and his partner Sergeant Whalen would conduct a drug interdiction because Harris looked over his shoulder three times and fit a profile of a drug courier. Sullivan followed Harris down the platform exit steps into the station and observed Harris in the station lobby holding a green backpack, talking to another man and using a payphone. Sullivan left the train station to find Whalen and informed him that the target of an interdiction (who turned out to be the defendant, Harris) was on the phone and conversing as well with a man standing nearby, wearing a white bandanna (who turned out to be Green). Whalen responded that Green had just gotten out of a Ford Tempo with Maryland tags parked in front of Whalen's unmarked police vehicle. Whalen also told Sullivan that the car's driver was a woman, who remained in the car.

Just as Sullivan reentered the station and discovered that the two men, Harris and Green, were nowhere to be seen, Whalen radioed Sullivan to "get out here now." Sullivan testified that Whalen told him that, at first, he had not seen Harris in the vehicle but that Harris' head appeared or "popped up" in the backseat and looked toward the street corner when the car was approximately eighty feet away. Sullivan decided to pursue the Tempo and make a stop.

The Tempo entered Interstate 95 and headed south. Sullivan called for Wilmington and state police assistance in making the stop. The Tempo left the interstate to head west, but two marked state police cruisers had blocked the bottom of the exit ramp by placing their vehicles in a "V" position. Sullivan and Whalen stopped their vehicle directly behind the Tempo. Sullivan drew his gun to his side and approached the vehicle as two state troopers stood in front of the Tempo with guns drawn and shouted, "State Police, put your hands up."

Sullivan looked in the back window and noticed that Harris did not have his hands in the air and that he was holding one strap of the green backpack. Sullivan opened the door, pointed the gun at Harris and said, "Police officer, put your hands up." Harris complied by raising his hands and releasing the backpack strap. Sullivan asked Harris whether the backpack belonged to him. Harris replied, "No, that's not my bag. I don't know whose it is." Green and the woman driver also denied ownership of the bag. Sullivan ordered everyone out of the car to be frisked for weapons and declared the bag to be abandoned property. Sullivan then searched the bag and found three clear plastic bags that contained over 200 grams of crack cocaine.

Harris was charged with possession of cocaine with intent to deliver and trafficking in more than 100 grams of cocaine. Harris moved to suppress the cocaine found in the backpack. After the suppression hearing, the Superior Court denied that motion. Harris was tried three times. The first two trials in March 1998 and September 1998, ended in mistrials. The last trial ended March 11, 1999 and resulted in a conviction of Harris on both counts.

[We must determine] whether the police possessed the justification required for an investigatory stop to be lawful under either or both the Fourth Amendment of the United States Constitution and Article I, Section 6 of the Delaware Constitution. [An] automobile and its occupants may be subjected to a limited seizure by police based on reasonable suspicion.

Police suspicion of a person's involvement in criminal activity is reasonable if it is based on the detaining officer's ability to point to specific and articulable facts which, taken together with rational inferences from those facts, reasonably warrant the intrusion. Coleman v. State, 562 A.2d 1171, 1174 (Del. 1989). The United States Supreme Court has repeatedly noted that the reasonable suspicion standard is not readily, or even usefully, reduced to a neat set of legal rules and is somewhat abstract. Thus, a finding of reasonable suspicion depends on the concrete factual circumstances of individual cases. Reasonable suspicion also is a less demanding standard than probable cause and requires a showing considerably less than a preponderance of the evidence.

[The] totality of the circumstances process allows officers to draw on their own experience and specialized training to make inferences from and deductions about the cumulative information available to them that might well elude an untrained person. In Quarles v. State, 696 A.2d 1334 (Del. 1997), this Court stated that, in drug seizure cases, the totality of the circumstances review requires looking at the "whole picture, as viewed through the eyes of a police officer who is experienced in discerning the ostensibly innocuous behavior that is indicative of narcotics trafficking." In *Quarles*, as in this case, we considered whether a police officer had reasonable suspicion to stop the defendant based on the police's drug courier profile and the defendant's behavior after disembarking at Wilmington's bus terminal.

This Court articulated a two-pronged standard for reviewing the conduct of detaining officers . . . . First, courts must look at the totality of the circumstances, "including objective observations and consideration of the modes or patterns of operation of certain kinds of lawbreakers." Second, courts must consider "the inferences and deductions that a trained officer could make which might well elude an untrained person." In *Quarles*, the detaining officer testified that he viewed the following as "drug courier profile" characteristics: (1) the defendant [Samir Quarles] came into Wilmington via bus from New York, a known drug source city; (2) he and his companion carried no luggage; (3) he arrived at night, when law enforcement presence is at a minimum; and (4) he traveled with a companion. The "non-profile" characteristics relied upon by police in *Quarles* were that the defendant and his companion: (1) appeared startled and ended their conversation upon leaving the bus and seeing two uniformed police officers; (2) quickly left the bus terminal in a direction away from the officers; (3) repeatedly glanced over their shoulders to see if the officers were following them, before and after turning the street corner; (4) continued walking rapidly; and (5) abruptly turned around upon seeing a marked police car. This Court concluded that "Quarles' suspicious behavior and the 'drug profile,' when taken as a whole from the perspective of one who is trained in narcotics detection, produces a reasonable articulable suspicion that a crime was afoot" and concluded that the police officers had a sufficient basis upon which to support an initial stop to question Quarles.

In Reid v. Georgia, 448 U.S. 438 (1980), a case relied on and distinguished in *Quarles*, the United States Supreme Court considered whether a federal drug enforcement agent could lawfully stop the defendant in an airport because he fit a "drug courier profile." Specifically, the agent testified that (1) the petitioner had arrived from Fort Lauderdale, which the agent testified is a principal place of origin of cocaine sold elsewhere in the country, (2) the petitioner arrived in the early morning, when law enforcement activity is diminished, (3) he and his companion appeared to the agent to be trying to conceal the fact that they were traveling together, and (4) they apparently had no luggage other than their shoulder bags. In holding that the stop in *Reid* was not based on reasonable suspicion, the United States Supreme Court held:

> [The] agent could not as a matter of law, have reasonably suspected the petitioner of criminal activity on the basis of these observed circumstances. Of the evidence relied on, only the fact that the petitioner preceded another person and occasionally looked backward at him as they proceeded through the concourse relates to their particular conduct. The other circumstances describe a very large category of presumably innocent travelers, who would be subject to virtually random seizures were the Court to conclude that as little foundation as there was in this case could justify a seizure.

Thus, under *Reid*, an "inchoate and unparticularized suspicion or hunch" of experienced police officers is insufficient to support a finding of reasonable suspicion as a matter of law.

Harris concedes that, under *Quarles* and *Reid*, drug courier profile evidence is admissible to determine whether the police have reasonable suspicion or probable cause regarding a defendant. Harris contends, however, that the information the police had in this case was quantitatively and qualitatively less than the information the police had in *Quarles* and is akin to *Reid* where it was held that the officers lacked reasonable suspicion as a matter of law.[41] . . .

The totality of Harris' behavior at the train station and in the car was lawful and ostensibly innocent. Of course, there are circumstances in which wholly lawful conduct might justify the suspicion that "criminal activity is afoot" because it is possible for objective facts, meaningless to the untrained, to provide the basis for reasonable suspicion in the eyes of a reasonable, prudent, and experienced police officer. . . . The Fourth Amendment does not allow the law enforcement official to simply assert that apparently innocent conduct was suspicious to him or her; rather the officer must offer the factual basis upon which he or she bases the conclusion.

The detaining officer in this case testified that he profiles drug couriers "usually through the body language they display as they arrive or get off trains" and by watching individuals that "appear to be nervous, looking over their shoulders,

41. The American Civil Liberties Union filed amicus curiae briefs in this case. The ACLU contends that this Court should view this case as an opportunity to hold that Article I, Section 6 of the Delaware Constitution prohibits the State from using any type of profiling as factors to justify a warrantless search or seizure. The ACLU argues that this case demonstrates the danger of racial and drug courier profiling. Although both Harris and Green, the man he met at the station, are black, the police in this case did not testify that race was a factor in the drug courier profile or even a "non-profile" characteristic worthy of attention. Therefore, the issue of the constitutionality of racial profiling by law enforcement officials is not before us and we do not address it in this case. As for the specific issue of drug courier profiling, this Court in *Quarles* upheld the use of drug courier profile evidence to justify a search or seizure by law enforcement officials. . . .

seeing if they're being followed, constantly looking around for police presence." The detaining officer relied on the following observations to suspect that Harris was a drug courier: Harris (1) looked over his shoulder three times between leaving the train and descending the platform staircase into the station; (2) met another man in the lobby; (3) used a payphone; (4) "popped" his head up in the backseat; and (5) looked out the rear window of the Tempo. The detaining officer never stated that Harris appeared nervous or concerned about evading detection by police or others. Thus, the detaining officer never explained how Harris' behavior matched the characteristics of the police's drug courier profile.

Without a cogent explanation, Harris' seemingly innocent conduct provides no basis for a finding of reasonable suspicion even in the eyes of a reasonable, prudent, and experienced police officer. Rather, the detaining officer's belief that Harris was a drug courier fails the test of *Reid* because it "was more an inchoate and unparticularized suspicion or hunch than a fair inference in light of his experience [and] is simply too slender a reed to support the seizure in this case." Harris' behavior as described by the detaining officer, like that of the defendant in *Reid*, is consistent with "a very large category of presumably innocent travelers, who would be subject to virtually random seizures were the Court to conclude that as little foundation as there was in this case could justify a seizure." This is precisely what the constitutional prohibition against unreasonable searches and seizures was designed to prevent. Therefore, we hold that, as a matter of law under the Fourth Amendment of the United States Constitution and Article I, §6 of the Delaware Constitution, the police could not reasonably have suspected Harris of criminal activity based on the objective facts and the subjective interpretation of those facts described by the detaining officer in this case. . . .

It is vital that our society retains its balance by expecting that courts, enforcing the rule of law, will uphold our cherished constitutional liberties that protect both the innocent and guilty. Those constitutional protections, guaranteed by the Founders in the Eighteenth Century both in Delaware and nationally, must not be compromised or eroded because of the concerns of the moment, whether they be about drug traffic or even the safety of our society. As Benjamin Franklin declared contemporaneously with the establishment of these protections: "They that can give up essential liberty to obtain a little temporary safety deserve neither liberty nor safety." . . .

■ ATTORNEY GENERAL OF MARYLAND ENDING DISCRIMINATORY PROFILING IN MARYLAND
August 2015

. . . GOVERNING STANDARDS

Two distinct standards—applicable to two different sets of circumstances: routine law enforcement operations and law enforcement activities related to ongoing investigations—govern whether certain defining personal characteristics may be considered by police in the course of law enforcement activities and investigations. The first standard should guide law enforcement with respect to routine police activity (e.g., traffic stops) where no specific investigation is underway, while the second standard covers activities pertaining to pending investigations.

I. Standard for Routine Law Enforcement Activity

When conducting routine police activity unconnected to an investigation of a specific crime, organization, or scheme, law enforcement may not consider race, ethnicity, national origin, gender, gender identity, sexual orientation, disability or religion to any degree.

Every day, law enforcement officers in Maryland engage in important routine police work. They walk their beats and engage with the community, sometimes briefly detaining a person who has raised a reasonable, articulable suspicion. They stop speeding and reckless drivers and patrol for broken taillights and expired tags. Although this valuable work contributes to the body of police intelligence and sometimes leads to evidence of more serious crimes, these kinds of police activities generally are not connected to an investigation of a specific offense, gang or organization, or crime spree. Officers performing this work typically do not have information about the individuals they are pulling over or talking with apart from their observations. In these situations, a person's race, ethnicity, national origin, gender, gender identity, sexual orientation, disability and religion should play no part in a police officer's actions.

For one of these defining personal characteristics to bear on an officer's decision to make a traffic stop or to detain an individual for investigation is flatly improper and should not occur. The law enforcement officer should consider whether he or she would take the same action if the person were of a different race, ethnicity, national origin, gender, gender identity, sexual orientation, disability or religion. This does not preclude police from engaging in active enforcement in areas where greater enforcement is warranted. Nor should it discourage law enforcement from detaining individuals engaged in suspicious conduct or stopping drivers violating the law. Indeed, smart policing of locations that have experienced high rates of violence, drug trafficking, and other crimes has been a potent strategy in safeguarding specific neighborhoods. But decisions by police about whom to talk with, which vehicles to stop, and what areas to police should be made without regard to a person's race, ethnicity, national origin, gender, gender identity, sexual orientation, disability and religion.

> *Example.* An officer conducting traffic stops along a busy interstate believes that people of a certain ethnicity are more likely to be involved in the transportation of illegal narcotics. Based on that assumption, she focuses on drivers of that ethnicity, and when she witnesses a traffic violation, stops the vehicle. Even though the motorist is violating the traffic code, the officer's use of ethnicity in determining which motorists to stop is improper because a defining personal characteristic is one factor in the officer's actions.

Also, law enforcement may develop suspect profiles that do not incorporate race, ethnicity, national origin, gender, gender identity, sexual orientation, disability or religion, so long as a proxy for one of these traits is not being used as a pretext.

> *Example.* Officers develop a "drug courier profile" that focuses on the amount and type of luggage a traveler is carrying, how the traveler paid for his or her ticket, and when the traveler arrives at the airport. The officers then question people at BWI airport based upon this profile. This kind of routine police investigation is permissible because, while it targets certain individuals to the exclusion of others, it does not rely upon a defining personal trait, nor do the profiling characteristics operate as a proxy for an illegitimate consideration. See Grant v. State, 55 Md. App. 1, 7 (1983).

Example. Local law enforcement selectively approach individuals for consensual interviews and investigate their immigration status solely based upon how well they appear to speak English. Because English proficiency may operate as a proxy for race, ethnicity, or national origin, using this kind of superficial suspect profile is improper. See Santos v. Frederick County Board of Commissioners, 725 F.3d 451, 459 n.2 (4th Cir. 2013).

Thus, in routine police encounters where law enforcement are acting upon no additional information separate from their observations, the race, ethnicity, national origin, gender, gender identity, sexual orientation, disability and religion of the person in question should in no way influence the conduct of police. Maryland's commitment to equal protection under the law guarantees no less. . . .

II. *Standard for Investigative Law Enforcement Activity*

When investigating a specific criminal offense, criminal organization, or crime scheme, law enforcement may only consider race, ethnicity, national origin, gender, gender identity, sexual orientation, disability or religion if police are in possession of credible information that makes the defining personal characteristic directly relevant to the investigation of a specific offense, organization, or scheme. . . . Where, for example, an eyewitness to a shooting provides a description of the perpetrator that includes a particular characteristic, police can certainly narrow the search for the suspect to individuals possessing that trait. Similarly, if a reliable informant advises police that a narcotics organization or the "crew" responsible for a string of bank robberies is comprised of individuals who share some characteristic, law enforcement are permitted to take account of that information in conducting their investigation. Ending discriminatory profiling does not require law enforcement to ignore or reject bona fide leads and credible intelligence. It does require police to rely only upon information that is trustworthy and is relevant to the investigation of a specific offense, organization, or crime scheme.

As a threshold matter, police should be confident that the information implicating a potentially discriminatory personal characteristic is trustworthy. Many legal standards that govern police action (e.g., reasonable articulable suspicion to justify an investigatory stop or probable cause for a search warrant) already incorporate this requirement. Thus, law enforcement officers are not entitled to limit the scope of their investigation to individuals of a certain race, ethnicity, national origin, gender, gender identity, sexual orientation, disability or religion, when the information that would justify concentrating on a specific subgroup is unreliable and unspecific. . . .

Example. A confidential informant with a history of providing truthful information tells police that an individual of a certain nationality will be delivering narcotics to a particular place at a particular time. Law enforcement officers can properly consider nationality when investigating the suspected narcotics delivery.

The information upon which the police wish to act—even where that information satisfies the threshold requirement of being trustworthy—should also relate directly to the investigation of a certain crime, a particular criminal organization, or a specific crime scheme. . . .

CONCLUSION

. . . Unfortunately, many today do not appreciate the brave and important work of police. Frustration and misgivings have weakened the unspoken trust that once existed between law enforcement and the communities they serve. Correcting this will not happen overnight, but the end of discriminatory profiling—a practice that has long molded the views of groups who have been singled out—is essential to restoring that trust. The Office of the Attorney General issues this guidance with the hope that it assists in restoring the faith of all citizens, in every neighborhood and of every background, who form the rich mosaic of Maryland.

Notes

1. *Criminal profiles in the courts: majority position.* The strong majority of courts presented with stops based on facts listed in a police department's "criminal profile" will not allow the match with the profile, standing alone, to constitute reasonable suspicion. However, courts also often say that the appearance of an observed fact in a profile gives that fact added weight in the reasonable suspicion calculus. See State v. Staten, 469 N.W.2d 112 (Neb. 1991) (airline passengers fitting drug courier profile may be detained up to one hour). A significant minority of states have rejected or criticized any reliance on the use of profiles to add any weight to facts observed in the field. Commonwealth v. Lewis, 636 A.2d 619 (Pa. 1994). The federal law on profiles seems agnostic, placing no independent weight—positive or negative—on the existence of a profile. See United States v. Sokolow, 490 U.S. 1 (1989); Florida v. Royer, 460 U.S. 491 (1983) (reasonable suspicion established). Some state courts reject particular components of a profile (especially those components with a racial component) without rejecting the reliance on profiles generally. See State v. Gonzalez-Gutierrez, 927 P.2d 776 (Ariz. 1996) (characteristic of being Mexican did not add weight to reasonable suspicion analysis); Derricott v. State, 611 A.2d 592 (Md. 1992) (criticizing profile that apparently included race of suspect); Crockett v. State, 803 S.W.2d 308 (Tex. Crim. App. 1991) (no evidence that drug dealers purchase train tickets with cash more frequently than other people).

2. *Dueling profiles and discretion.* Courts seem especially skeptical about profiles phrased broadly enough to "describe a very large category of presumably innocent travelers, who would be subject to virtually random seizures" if a mere match to such a profile were enough to justify a search or seizure. Reid v. Georgia, 448 U.S. 438 (1980). Drug courier profiles sometimes are written broadly enough to attach suspicion both to a particular characteristic (such as exiting a plane first or making eye contact with another passenger) and to its opposite (exiting a plane last or avoiding eye contact with another passenger). What exactly is the problem with a declaration that a particular behavior and its opposite are both suspicious? Judicial opinions dealing with challenges to the use of a criminal profile almost never describe the provisions of a complete written departmental profile, depending instead on the police officer's testimony about the profile factors. What does this mean to the attorney hoping to challenge the reliability of the profile as a method of establishing reasonable suspicion? For examples of drug courier profiles, see the web extension for this chapter at *http://www.crimpro.com/extension/ch02.* The web extension also includes a discussion of the written profiles that the U.S. Postal Service uses to establish the reasonable suspicion necessary to detain a package for further investigation. See United States v. Van Leeuwen, 397 U.S. 249 (1970).

3. *Officer expertise and subjective standards.* Should the particular expertise of the investigating officer have any bearing on a finding of reasonable suspicion? See State v. Duhe, 130 So. 3d 880 (La. 2013) (experienced drug investigator had reasonable

suspicion to stop three individuals in car after they separately purchased cold medicine containing pseudoephedrine at pharmacy). Or should the court accept only those inferences that any "reasonable person" (that is, a citizen) would draw from the observed facts? If you are willing to account for the special experience of a particular police officer in establishing reasonable suspicion, is this consistent with your views on the "reasonable person" standard we encountered earlier, dealing with the "objective" definition of a "stop," or your views on pretextual stops?

4. *Collective judgments and expertise.* Stops based on criminal profiles differ from other reasonable suspicion stops because they attempt to give the officer on the street the benefit of the collective experience of other officers or the collective judgments of political authorities. The officer makes the stop not only based on his own expertise in law enforcement but also because the "profile" places significance on certain facts. Which is a stronger basis for believing that certain apparently innocent facts are actually indications of criminal activity: the individual training and experience of the officer making the stop, or the statistical and collective experience of police in the department? As the attorney for a person stopped, which of the two bases would you prefer to test on cross-examination? See Wayne LaFave, Controlling Discretion by Administrative Regulations: The Use, Misuse, and Nonuse of Police Rules and Policies in Fourth Amendment Adjudication, 89 Mich. L. Rev. 442 (1990).

5. *Efficiency in proof?* Is the problem with criminal profiles that the government has not written specific profiles and has not shown rigorously how the profile features are common to a great number of criminal defendants? Consider a profile constructed as follows. A group of more than 40 representatives from law enforcement agencies in the Phoenix area developed a profile for stopping suspected automobile thieves transporting stolen vehicles to Mexico. The profile was based on an analysis of 10,000 auto thefts in the area over a 17-month period. The profile indicated which vehicles the thieves targeted most often: sedans and pickup trucks manufactured by Ford and Chevrolet within the last three years. In addition, the records indicated that the driver of a stolen car would probably be a male between 17 and 27 years of age; he would usually be alone; he would have no apparent luggage; if there was a passenger, there would be no children; and the car's license plate would show a registration to either Tucson or Phoenix, the two largest cities in the state. Law enforcement teams were set up to patrol the highway between Tucson and the border town of Nogales, and only a small percentage of people driving on that highway fit the profile of a stolen car driver. See State v. Ochoa, 544 P.2d 1097 (Ariz. 1976). Could profiles, when carefully constructed and meticulously proven in early cases, prevent duplicative presentation of evidence in later cases? Cf. Andrew Ferguson, Big Data and Predictive Reasonable Suspicion, 163 U. Pa. L. Rev. 327 (2015).

6. *Race and witness descriptions.* Most courts allow the police to rely on race as one among many components of reasonable suspicion, particularly if the police use the racial element of a description received from a victim or witness of the crime. Note, Developments in the Law—Race and the Criminal Process, 101 Harv. L. Rev. 1473 (1988). Can you imagine a jurisdiction that would bar any use of race in establishing reasonable suspicion, thus requiring the police to point to other factors? For witness identifications, could the police rely on descriptions of clothing or facial hair, while being barred from using information about skin color?

On the other hand, police officers will at times rely on a suspect's race in cases where no witness has described the perpetrator, or even where there is no report of a crime at all. This most often occurs when a person appears to be "out of place": for instance, a black person walking in a predominantly white neighborhood. Courts have divided on whether such a fact can be the primary component of reasonable suspicion. See, e.g., State v. Dean, 543 P.2d 425 (Ariz. 1975) (Mexican male in dented car in predominantly white neighborhood, reasonable suspicion); State v. Mallory, 337 N.W.2d 391 (Minn. 1983) (black male stopped in white neighborhood where burglary by a black male had occurred recently, reasonable suspicion); State v. Barber, 823 P.2d 1068 (Wash. 1992) (presence of black person in white neighborhood can never amount to reasonable suspicion standing alone).

If most American jurisdictions allow race as one "factor" that contributes to a finding of reasonable suspicion, won't there necessarily be cases where race provides the extra marginal evidence to obtain reasonable suspicion? Would this be objectionable discrimination, or a plausible reaction to probabilities familiar to the police?

Problem 2-8. Goatee and Dark Skin

On February 21, at approximately 4:15 A.M., Nancy Henderson approached an automatic teller machine at a bank on Main Street. While she was operating the teller machine, but before completing her transaction, someone grabbed her from behind and said, "this is a stick-up" and "I want your money." During a brief struggle, the man pressed a hard, blunt object into her back. She gave her money to the man. The man then declared that he planned to rape Henderson. He ordered her to get into the driver's seat of her car, threatening to "blow her brains out" if she did not comply. The man positioned himself next to Henderson in the front passenger seat and directed her where to drive the car.

As Henderson drove, she noticed a pizza shop that appeared to be open. She accelerated the car in that direction and jumped the curb. Then she got out of the car and ran screaming for help. Several people emerged from the shop. During the confusion, the assailant walked away. The police were called and arrived at the pizza shop within minutes. Henderson described her assailant as "a black male, 5'11" to 6'2", wearing a ski cap, had a mustache, was wearing a light-colored coat, dark pants, white tennis shoes, and had medium to dark skin." The police dispatcher sent this description to all officers on patrol.

At 5:25 A.M., another officer on patrol stopped Daniel Coleman in the parking lot of a restaurant located approximately one-half of a mile from the pizza shop. Coleman fit the general description of the assailant, except that he had a goatee as well as a mustache and was not wearing a coat or a cap. The officer questioned Coleman briefly about his identity and destination. Coleman stated that he was coming from his girlfriend's home and that he was on his way to work. During this discussion, another officer drove by with Henderson in the car. She was unable to identify Coleman as her assailant. The officer detained Coleman for a total of about 10 minutes, then released him.

Later that morning, the police viewed a videotape taken by a camera installed near the automatic teller machine. Both of the police officers who had seen Coleman earlier that morning during his brief detention viewed the videotape and identified the assailant on the videotape as Coleman. Coleman was arrested at his place of employment and charged with robbery and attempted rape. When the officers first stopped Coleman, did they have reasonable suspicion? If they were to ignore information about the race of the suspect, would they have reasonable suspicion? See Coleman v. State, 562 A.2d 1171 (Del. 1989).

4. Collecting and Reporting Stop Data

Defendants have only rarely convinced courts to outlaw the use of pretextual stops or criminal profiles, but a related claim has achieved more success outside the courts. The related claim is that police stop motorists based at least partly on their race. Such claims are often described in public debates as the creation of a crime called "driving while black" or "DWB."

Claims of DWB, or of racial profiling more generally, are difficult for a criminal defendant to litigate, but state and federal governments now regularly investigate patterns of traffic and drug stops on highways. Some jurisdictions pass statutes that require law enforcement agencies to maintain statistics that could reveal such patterns of stops. Annual reports that analyze the statistical patterns in traffic stops have become a routine feature in police-community relations. Consider the following excerpts from one of these reports.

■ NEBRASKA CRIME COMMISSION 2017 TRAFFIC STOPS IN NEBRASKA: A REPORT TO THE GOVERNOR AND THE LEGISLATURE ON DATA SUBMITTED BY LAW ENFORCEMENT
Pages 4-23, March 30, 2018

INTRODUCTION

. . . The issues of fairness and any perception of unequal treatment are often at the forefront of our society but particularly as they relate to justice. Great attention is drawn to issues and reports of possible inequality in the criminal justice system. These issues can be very difficult to identify, as well as verify, and are critical for the public as well as for law enforcement. Traffic stops are one of the most common types of contact for the public. Perceptions derived from these contacts and the need for openness on the reasons for stops are paramount.

Potential profiling relating to traffic stops made by law enforcement has received broad attention in most states and localities. The Nebraska Legislature passed LB593 in 2001 to respond to possible issues relating to the way that traffic stops are made. The act specifically prohibited racial profiling and required law enforcement to implement policies prohibiting discriminatory practices as well as requiring the collection of prescribed data. . . .

Since the law took effect in 2001, and even prior to this law, students at the Nebraska Law Enforcement Training Center (NLETC) are taught that all traffic stops must be based on a legal justification and cannot be based solely upon the person's (or driver's) race or ethnic makeup. Any stop based solely upon the person's race or ethnicity would be unconstitutional. NLETC students compile racial profiling report forms with each simulated traffic stop conducted while in the training academy.

Proactive use of these data can assist in an agency's monitoring and adherence to legislation. They can provide opportunities for outreach with the community as well as examine processes and procedures. We strongly encourage agencies to examine their data and look at what is happening within their jurisdiction.

[The 2001 statute] 1) acknowledged the danger and impropriety of any practice that involves disparate treatment based on a person's skin color, apparent nationality or ethnicity; 2) defined racial profiling as the detaining of an individual or conducting a motor vehicle stop based upon disparate treatment of an individual [and] 3) required the collection of certain information relative to traffic stops, in that law enforcement agencies are required to collect, record, maintain and report [certain categories of information] to the NCC. [The categories include] A) the number of motor vehicle stops; B) the race or ethnicity of the people stopped; C) the nature of an alleged law violation that resulted in the motor vehicle stop [and] D) whether warnings or citations were issued, arrests made, or searches conducted as a result of the stops. . . . The bill prohibited revealing the identity of either the officer or the complainant. . . .

To collect the data required in a consistent and cost-effective manner the NCC convened a work group involving Nebraska State Patrol, Nebraska Sheriffs Association, Police Officers Association of Nebraska, Police Chiefs Association of Nebraska, and numerous local agencies including the Lincoln Police Department and the Omaha Police Department. This group reviewed possible data reporting formats to try to guarantee the most feasible, cost effective, and achievable method of reporting while meeting the mandates outlined above.

Data collection of this magnitude can be problematic in many ways. . . . Even for agencies that are automated the task of additional data collection by officers adds a level of complexity and additional workload that is significant. For those law enforcement agencies that are not automated it means an increase in the paper work for officers. . . .

Data Reporting Considerations

. . . To assess the effect race and/or ethnicity may have on decision-making, any study must exclude or control for factors other than race and/or ethnicity that might legitimately explain the stopping decision. For example, most jurisdictions disproportionally stop males. Does this indicate gender bias? Most would not jump to that conclusion because they can think of several factors other than bias that could explain the disproportionate stopping of male drivers. One possibility is that men drive more than women (a quantity factor). Another possibility is men violate traffic laws more often than women (a quality factor). A third possibility is that more males drive in areas where police stopping activity tends to occur (the location factor). We do not know if these possibilities are true, but we must consider these other alternative explanations as causal.

Unfortunately, we do not have the detailed traffic stop data that would allow a comprehensive research design that would rule out such other possibilities and therefore prohibits us from drawing definitive conclusions. We cannot say definitively whether there is or is not racial bias in traffic stops, we can only point to seeming disproportionality. . . .

It must be noted that disparities within this report are just that, disparities. Disparities alone do not prove bias or instances of racial profiling. By identifying disparity law enforcement agencies can and should make reasonable efforts to better understand the disparities within their data. It is recommended that law enforcement agencies and other interested parties examine disparity at the agency and local level to better understand possible reasons for the disproportionality. Agency specific results are available at the NCC website. . . .

Studies focusing on traffic stop reporting often compare data to racial distributions within a particular community or state. Some studies compare traffic stop data to the racial breakdown of the general population, of licensed drivers, of at-risk drivers or even to the racial breakdown of drivers actually observed on an area's roads by people stationed in the field. Each of these demographic comparisons has strengths and weaknesses, but there is no universally accepted method for analyzing at-risk populations compared to a reference group. Some studies draw conclusions that theoretically cannot be made given deficiencies in the available data. . . . All population data are obtained from the U.S. Census Bureau. Since the adult population more closely parallels the driving population than the overall population, primary tables and counts will be Nebraska's adult estimated population when available. . . .

DISPARITY INDEX

Over the past six years our state's population has changed in size and in specific dem-ographics. . . . By comparing the Nebraska Adult Population percentages with our Traffic Stop percentages outlined in the previous page we are able to produce a disparity index, seen below. To interpret the disparity index, a value greater than one indicates over-representation, a value of one indicates no disparity, and a value less than one indicates under-representation. The disparity index is calculated by dividing the proportion of stops by the proportion of population. . . .

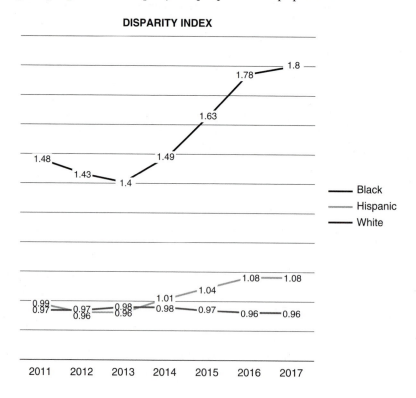

[While the figure above indicates the disparity index for all law enforcement agencies combined, the index numbers for the Nebraska State Police ranged from 0.82 to 1.15 for Black drivers, from 0.87 to 1.01 for Hispanic drivers, and from 1.01 to 1.06 for White drivers. The index figures for the Omaha Police Department ranged from 1.67 to 2.57 for Black drivers, from 0.51 to 0.78 for Hispanic drivers, and from 0.79 to 0.88 for White drivers. For the Lincoln Police Department, the figures ranged from 2.15 to 2.64 for Black drivers, from 0.80 to 0.90 for Hispanic drivers, and from 0.91 to 0.99 for White drivers. These last] two Police Departments collectively account for roughly twenty percent of the traffic stops reported each year. . . .

DISPOSITION OF TRAFFIC STOP

The Disposition of the Traffic Stop reports the primary outcome of the stop. A traffic stop may result in a variety of outcomes. A custodial arrest is not done when only a traffic violation is involved. Therefore, the stop could involve things such as a DUI arrest, a lack of identification, an outstanding warrant (discovered in a general license check) or some other criminal activity in the car or even by the occupants. However, the data are not detailed enough to know what specific violation caused a custodial arrest.

In 2017, 17.4% of Blacks stopped were taken into custodial arrest, compared to 4.2% of the general population. [Police arrested 5.9 percent of Hispanic drivers stopped and 2.5 percent of White drivers stopped.]

[In] 2017, 8.7% of all statewide traffic stops involving Black drivers included a search. [Police searched 5.3 percent of Hispanic drivers and 2.8 percent of White drivers.] Search counts do not include inventory arrests or those done incident to arrest. Instead they reflect searches done as part of the officer's processing of the traffic stop.

Notes

1. *Racial profiling constitutional claims.* Claims that police officers stop drivers because of their race and not their behavior are not new, but have become much more prominent over the years through civil litigation in many states. These civil lawsuits, along with defenses raised in criminal proceedings, have produced only modest success. Based on cases such as Whren v. United States, 517 U.S. 806 (1996), described above, most courts have found no constitutional violation.

2. *Racial profiling legislation.* With racial profiling in traffic stops making little or no headway as a constitutional claim, state legislatures took the lead in efforts to monitor, limit, and sanction racially biased traffic stops. See David A. Harris, Addressing Racial Profiling in the States: A Case Study of the "New Federalism" in Constitutional Criminal Procedure, 3 Pa. J. Const. L. 367 (2001). The statutes pursue different strategies. An Oklahoma statute, 22 Okla. Stat. §34.3, directly forbids the use of race as the "sole" basis for stopping or detaining a person and makes racial profiling a misdemeanor. The statute also calls for law enforcement agencies to adopt and publicize "a detailed written policy that clearly defines the elements constituting racial profiling." A California statute, Penal Code §13519.4, requires training of officers in topics related to cultural diversity. Statutes in many states

provide for mandatory collection and reporting of data about the race of motorists whom the police stop and search. Which of these strategies is most likely to reduce the amount of racial profiling?

3. *Executive branch policies and race.* Apart from legislation on the subject, many police departments have adopted internal guidelines calling on officers to record the age, gender, and race or ethnicity of every person they stop in traffic. See Bureau of Justice Statistics, Traffic Stop Data Collection Policies for State Police, 2004 (2005, NCJ 209156) (22 of 49 state police agencies require officers to record race or ethnicity of motorist in all traffic stops). What (or who) might convince a police department to adopt such a policy? It is now commonplace for law enforcement agencies to perform statistical analyses of their traffic stop patterns and to publish their findings. The reports typically show great variety among law enforcement agencies within the state in terms of racial disparities among drivers stopped, searched, and arrested. Matthew B. Ross et al., State of Connecticut, Traffic Stop Data Analysis and Findings, 2015-2016 November 2017); Institute for Municipal and Regional Policy, State of Rhode Island, Traffic Stop Data Analysis and Findings, 2016 (March 2018); Frank R. Baumgartner et al., Targeting Young Men of Color for Search and Arrest During Traffic Stops: Evidence from North Carolina, 2002-2013, 5 Politics, Groups, and Identities 107 (2017) (showing disparities in the rates at which black drivers, particularly young males, are searched and arrested as compared with similarly situated whites, women, or older drivers; rate at which searches lead to discover of contraband is consistently lower for blacks than whites).

To address the issue of an officer's ability to observe the race of a driver under conditions of limited visibility, some of the studies use a technique known as the "Veil of Darkness" or "Solar Visibility" analysis. This technique assesses relative differences in the ratio of minority to non-minority stops that occur in daylight as compared to darkness. It relies on the idea that, if police officers are profiling motorists, they are better able to do so during daylight hours when race and ethnicity is more easily observed.

4. *Crime rates and stop rates.* One of the first states to collect and analyze traffic stop data was New Jersey. In a 1999 report, law enforcement officials found that State Police units that exercised less discretion (such as the Radar Unit, focused on speeding violations) tended to produce smaller racial disparities in their stops. The authors of the report then explained their view that differential crime rates do not directly account for racial disparities in traffic stops:

> We turn now to the specific assumption that is at the heart of the racial profiling controversy: the notion that a disproportionate percentage of drug traffickers and couriers are black or Hispanic, so that race, ethnicity, or national origin can serve as a reliable, accurate predictor of criminal activity. The proponents of this view point to empirical evidence, usually in the form of arrest and conviction statistics, that would appear at first blush to demonstrate quite conclusively that minorities are disproportionately represented among the universe of drug dealers.
>
> The evidence for this conclusion is, in reality, tautological and reflects as much as anything the initial stereotypes of those who rely upon these statistics. . . . Arrest statistics, by definition, do not show the number of persons who were detained or investigated who, as it turned out, were not found to be trafficking drugs or carrying weapons.

Peter Verniero, Interim Report of the State Police Review Team Regarding Allegations of Racial Profiling (Apil 1999).

5. *Race and prevention of terrorism.* Note that the Department of Justice policy on racial profiling creates a special set of rules for terrorism investigations. What justification does the statement offer for creating an exception in this area? Does the legitimacy of such a policy depend on the actual number of terrorist acts committed by Muslim noncitizens, as compared to the number of terrorist acts committed by Christian citizens (such as the Oklahoma City bombing of 1995 or numerous school shootings)? The Department issued new draft rules in 2014 that included religion, national origin, and sexual orientation on the list of prohibited grounds for selection of investigative targets. The draft rules, however, still made special provisions for terrorism investigations. For the most recent federal law enforcement rules on racial profiling, see the web extension for this chapter at *http://www.crimpro.com/extension/ch02.*

6. *Race in immigration enforcement.* For enforcement of general criminal laws, such as drug crimes, race plays a shadowy, often implicit role as a factor in reasonable suspicion or probable cause determinations. For immigration enforcement, federal law allows *explicit* reliance on race or ethnicity. In United States v. Brignoni-Ponce, 422 U.S. 873, 886-887 (1975), the Supreme Court held that the U.S. Constitution allows race to be considered in immigration enforcement: "The likelihood that any given person of Mexican ancestry is an alien is high enough to make Mexican appearance a relevant factor." On the other hand, the Court maintains that some uses of race in the enforcement of immigration laws might violate the equal protection clause.

Problem 2-9. Borderline State

The Arizona legislature enacted a state immigration law known as SB 1070. Most public commentary centers on whether this law invites or forbids the use of race in police decisions whether to stop a suspect or investigate the person's immigration status. The leadership of the Tucson Police Department hired you to advise them on the relationship between SB 1070 and racial profiling.

Your client asks you to address separately two distinct conceptions of racial profiling: (1) when police officers use race as one element in a decision whether to stop or search, and (2) when race is an unconstitutional or otherwise illegal element in a decision whether to stop or search. With these two definitions in mind, consider the current text of A.R.S. §11-1051(B):

> For any lawful stop, detention or arrest made by a law enforcement official or a law enforcement agency . . . in the enforcement of any other law or ordinance of country, city or town or this state where reasonable suspicion exists that the person is an alien and is unlawfully present in the United States, a reasonable attempt shall be made, when practicable, to determine the immigration status of the person, except if the determination may hinder or obstruct an investigation. Any person who is arrested shall have the person's immigration status determined before the person is released. The person's immigration status shall be verified with the federal government. . . . A law enforcement official or agency of this state or a county, city, town or other political subdivision of this state may not consider race, color or national origin in implementing the requirements of this subsection except to the extent permitted by the United States or Arizona Constitution.

SB 1070 also prohibits government agencies from restricting enforcement of immigration law "to less than the full extent permitted by federal law." A.R.S. §1151(A). The statute creates a citizen suit provision, allowing a judicial challenge of any policy that interferes with the full enforcement of federal law. A.R.S. §11-1051(H).

The primary author of SB 1070, Arizona State Senator Russell Pearce, wrote that SB 1070 "explicitly prohibits racial profiling." The Arizona Police Office Standards and Training Board, AZPOST, which issues training materials but has no enforcement power, issued training materials and videos stating that race and ethnicity cannot be used in police decisions about whether to investigate immigration status. The materials list other factors officers can use to help determine a person's immigration status, including a car with foreign license plates, language of the car's occupants, along with their "demeanor." For instance, "you ask them where they live, they don't know. You ask them who else is in the car with them, they claim not to know anyone of the people in the car."

The Arizona Supreme Court has observed that race is relevant in determinations of reasonable suspicion during investigations of unauthorized immigration:

> Mexican ancestry alone, that is, Hispanic appearance, is not enough to establish reasonable cause, but if the occupants' dress or hair style are [sic] associated with people currently living in Mexico, such characteristics may be sufficient. The driver's behavior may be considered if the driving is erratic or the driver exhibits an "obvious attempt to evade officers." The type or load of the vehicle may also create a reasonable suspicion.

State v. Gonzalez-Gutierrez, 927 P.2d 776 (Ariz. 1996); but cf. United States v. Montero-Camargo, 208 F.3d 1122, 1131 (9th Cir. 2000) (en banc) (in a case arising in El Centro, 50 miles north of the Mexican border, the "likelihood that in an area in which the majority—or even a substantial part—of the population is Hispanic, any given person of Hispanic ancestry is in fact an alien, let alone an illegal alien, is not high enough to make Hispanic appearance a relevant factor in the reasonable suspicion calculus"). Notably, modern cases on the question of the explicit relevance of race to stops or searches arise in immigration cases and overwhelmingly involve persons of apparent Hispanic or Mexican origin.

Your counsel to the Tucson Police Department will likely expose the city to lawsuits, regardless of what you say. The Police Department plans to share your advice with other police departments and sheriff's offices throughout Arizona. What would you recommend?

C. BRIEF SEARCHES OF INDIVIDUALS

The police conduct a great variety of searches, ranging from brief and less intrusive searches of persons or property, up to extensive and very invasive searches. The number of legal standards—constitutional and otherwise—available to limit these searches is not nearly so large. As you read in this section about brief searches of individuals, consider whether the fit between police practices and available legal standards is sufficiently tight and whether different legal standards are likely to change actual behavior.

1. Frisks for Weapons

Police encounter people every day who carry hidden handguns. One time-honored police response to this threat is the "frisk," a brief search of a suspect's body. The frisk was a reality long before American courts resolved the question of whether or how the law would regulate the practice. The following case established the reasonable suspicion standard that we studied earlier in this chapter. It also laid out the constitutional controls over frisks for weapons that an officer may perform during some stops.

■ JOHN TERRY v. OHIO
392 U.S. 1 (1968)

WARREN, C.J.*

This case presents serious questions concerning the role of the Fourth Amendment in the confrontation on the street between the citizen and the policeman investigating suspicious circumstances.

Petitioner Terry was convicted of carrying a concealed weapon. [The] prosecution introduced in evidence two revolvers and a number of bullets seized from Terry and a codefendant, Richard Chilton, by Cleveland Police Detective Martin McFadden. At the hearing on the motion to suppress this evidence, Officer McFadden testified that while he was patrolling in plain clothes in downtown Cleveland at approximately 2:30 in the afternoon, [he noticed two men, Chilton and Terry, who "didn't look right"]. His interest aroused, Officer McFadden took up a post of observation in the entrance to a store 300 to 400 feet away from the two men. "I get more purpose to watch them when I seen their movements," he testified. [One of the men walked away from the corner and past some stores, paused for a moment and looked in a store window, then walked on a short distance, turned around and walked back toward the corner, pausing once again to look in the same store window. Then the second man went through the same series of motions. Each of the two men repeated this ritual five or six times. A third man, Katz, approached them and engaged them briefly in conversation, then walked away. Chilton and Terry resumed their earlier routine. After this had gone on for 10 to 12 minutes, the two men walked off together, following the route taken earlier by Katz.]

By this time Officer McFadden had become thoroughly suspicious. He testified that . . . he suspected the two men of "casing a job, a stick-up," and that he considered it his duty as a police officer to investigate further. He added that he feared "they may have a gun." Thus, Officer McFadden followed Chilton and Terry and saw them stop in front of Zucker's store to talk to [Katz]. Deciding that the situation was ripe for direct action, Officer McFadden approached the three men, identified himself as a police officer and asked for their names. . . . When the men "mumbled something" in response to his inquiries, Officer McFadden grabbed petitioner Terry, spun him around so that they were facing the other two, with Terry between McFadden and the others, and patted down the outside of his clothing. In the left breast pocket of Terry's overcoat Officer McFadden felt a pistol. He reached

---

* [Justices Black, Brennan, Stewart, Fortas, and Marshall joined in this opinion.—EDS.]

inside the overcoat pocket, but was unable to remove the gun. At this point, keeping Terry between himself and the others, the officer ordered all three men to enter Zucker's store. As they went in, he removed Terry's overcoat completely, removed a .38-caliber revolver from the pocket and ordered all three men to face the wall with their hands raised. Officer McFadden proceeded to pat down the outer clothing of Chilton and [Katz]. He discovered another revolver in the outer pocket of Chilton's overcoat, but no weapons were found on Katz. The officer testified that he only patted the men down to see whether they had weapons, and that he did not put his hands beneath the outer garments of either Terry or Chilton until he felt their guns. . . . Chilton and Terry were formally charged with carrying concealed weapons.

[The trial court concluded that McFadden did not have probable cause to search or arrest the men, but nonetheless upheld the validity of the search.] The court distinguished between an investigatory "stop" and an arrest, and between a "frisk" of the outer clothing for weapons and a full-blown search for evidence of crime. The frisk, it held, was essential to the proper performance of the officer's investigatory duties, for without it "the answer to the police officer may be a bullet, and a loaded pistol discovered during the frisk is admissible." [The court found Terry and Chilton guilty in a bench trial.]

I.

The Fourth Amendment provides that "the right of the people to be secure in their persons, houses, papers, and effects, against unreasonable searches and seizures, shall not be violated. . . ." This inestimable right of personal security belongs as much to the citizen on the streets of our cities as to the homeowner closeted in his study to dispose of his secret affairs. [However,] what the Constitution forbids is not all searches and seizures, but unreasonable searches and seizures. Unquestionably petitioner was entitled to the protection of the Fourth Amendment as he walked down the street in Cleveland. The question is whether in all the circumstances of this on-the-street encounter, his right to personal security was violated by an unreasonable search and seizure.

[It] is frequently argued that in dealing with the rapidly unfolding and often dangerous situations on city streets the police are in need of an escalating set of flexible responses, graduated in relation to the amount of information they possess. For this purpose it is urged that distinctions should be made between a "stop" and an "arrest" (or a "seizure" of a person), and between a "frisk" and a "search." Thus, it is argued, the police should be allowed to "stop" a person and detain him briefly for questioning upon suspicion that he may be connected with criminal activity. Upon suspicion that the person may be armed, the police should have the power to "frisk" him for weapons. If the "stop" and the "frisk" give rise to probable cause to believe that the suspect has committed a crime, then the police should be empowered to make a formal "arrest," and a full incident "search" of the person. This scheme is justified in part upon the notion that a "stop" and a "frisk" amount to a mere minor inconvenience and petty indignity, which can properly be imposed upon the citizen in the interest of effective law enforcement on the basis of a police officer's suspicion.

On the other side the argument is made that the authority of the police must be strictly circumscribed by the law of arrest and search as it has developed to date in the traditional jurisprudence of the Fourth Amendment. It is contended with some force that there is not—and cannot be—a variety of police activity which does not depend solely upon the voluntary cooperation of the citizen and yet which stops short of an arrest based upon probable cause to make such an arrest. The heart of the Fourth Amendment, the argument runs, is a severe requirement of specific justification for any intrusion upon protected personal security, coupled with a highly developed system of judicial controls to enforce upon the agents of the State the commands of the Constitution. Acquiescence by the courts in the compulsion inherent in the field interrogation practices at issue here, it is urged, would constitute an abdication of judicial control over, and indeed an encouragement of, substantial interference with liberty and personal security by police officers whose judgment is necessarily colored by their primary involvement in the often competitive enterprise of ferreting out crime. This, it is argued, can only serve to exacerbate police-community tensions in the crowded centers of our Nation's cities.

In this context we approach the issues in this case mindful of the limitations of the judicial function in controlling the myriad daily situations in which policemen and citizens confront each other on the street. . . . Street encounters between citizens and police officers are incredibly rich in diversity. They range from wholly friendly exchanges of pleasantries or mutually useful information to hostile confrontations of armed men involving arrests, or injuries, or loss of life. Moreover, hostile confrontations are not all of a piece. Some of them begin in a friendly enough manner, only to take a different turn upon the injection of some unexpected element into the conversation. Encounters are initiated by the police for a wide variety of purposes, some of which are wholly unrelated to a desire to prosecute for crime. . . .

II.

Our first task is to establish at what point in this encounter the Fourth Amendment becomes relevant. That is, we must decide whether and when Officer McFadden "seized" Terry and whether and when he conducted a "search." There is some suggestion in the use of such terms as "stop" and "frisk" that such police conduct is outside the purview of the Fourth Amendment because neither action rises to the level of a "search" or "seizure" within the meaning of the Constitution. We emphatically reject this notion. It is . . . nothing less than sheer torture of the English language to suggest that a careful exploration of the outer surfaces of a person's clothing all over his or her body in an attempt to find weapons is not a "search." . . . It is a serious intrusion upon the sanctity of the person, which may inflict great indignity and arouse strong resentment, and it is not to be undertaken lightly.

The danger in the logic which proceeds upon distinctions between a . . . "frisk" and a "search" is twofold. It seeks to isolate from constitutional scrutiny the initial stages of the contact between the policeman and the citizen. And by suggesting a rigid all-or-nothing model of justification and regulation under the Amendment, it obscures the utility of limitations upon the scope, as well as the initiation, of police action as a means of constitutional regulation. [A] search which is reasonable at its inception may violate the Fourth Amendment by virtue of its intolerable intensity and scope. The scope of the search must be strictly tied to and justified by the circumstances which rendered its initiation permissible. . . .

In this case there can be no question, then, that Officer McFadden "seized" petitioner and subjected him to a "search" when he took hold of him and patted down the outer surfaces of his clothing. We must decide whether at that point it was reasonable for Officer McFadden to have interfered with petitioner's personal security as he did. And in determining whether the seizure and search were "unreasonable" our inquiry is a dual one—whether the officer's action was justified at its inception, and whether it was reasonably related in scope to the circumstances which justified the interference in the first place.

III.

If this case involved police conduct subject to the Warrant Clause of the Fourth Amendment, we would have to ascertain whether "probable cause" existed to justify the search and seizure which took place. However, that is not the case. We do not retreat from our holdings that the police must, whenever practicable, obtain advance judicial approval of searches and seizures through the warrant procedure, or that in most instances failure to comply with the warrant requirement can only be excused by exigent circumstances. But we deal here with an entire rubric of police conduct—necessarily swift action predicated upon the on-the-spot observations of the officer on the beat—which historically has not been, and as a practical matter could not be, subjected to the warrant procedure. Instead, the conduct involved in this case must be tested by the Fourth Amendment's general proscription against unreasonable searches and seizures.

Nonetheless, the notions which underlie both the warrant procedure and the requirement of probable cause remain fully relevant in this context. In order to assess the reasonableness of Officer McFadden's conduct as a general proposition, it is necessary first to focus upon the governmental interest which allegedly justifies official intrusion upon the constitutionally protected interests of the private citizen, for there is no ready test for determining reasonableness other than by balancing the need to search [or seize] against the invasion which the search or seizure entails. And in justifying the particular intrusion the police officer must be able to point to specific and articulable facts which, taken together with rational inferences from those facts, reasonably warrant that intrusion. [When a judge assesses the reasonableness of a search or seizure,] it is imperative that the facts be judged against an objective standard: would the facts available to the officer at the moment of the seizure or the search warrant a man of reasonable caution in the belief that the action taken was appropriate? Anything less would invite intrusions upon constitutionally guaranteed rights based on nothing more substantial than inarticulate hunches, a result this Court has consistently refused to sanction. And simple good faith on the part of the arresting officer is not enough. If subjective good faith alone were the test, the protections of the Fourth Amendment would evaporate, and the people would be secure in their persons, houses, papers, and effects, only in the discretion of the police.

Applying these principles to this case, we consider first the nature and extent of the governmental interests involved. One general interest is of course that of effective crime prevention and detection; it is this interest which underlies the recognition that a police officer may in appropriate circumstances and in an appropriate manner approach a person for purposes of investigating possibly criminal behavior even though there is no probable cause to make an arrest. [In this case, it] would have been poor police work indeed for an officer of 30 years' experience in the detection of thievery from stores in this same neighborhood to have failed to investigate this behavior further.

The crux of this case, however, is not the propriety of Officer McFadden's taking steps to investigate petitioner's suspicious behavior, but rather, whether there was justification for McFadden's invasion of Terry's personal security by searching him for weapons in the course of that investigation. We are now concerned with more than the governmental interest in investigating crime; in addition, there is the more immediate interest of the police officer in taking steps to assure himself that the person with whom he is dealing is not armed with a weapon that could unexpectedly and fatally be used against him. Certainly it would be unreasonable to require that police officers take unnecessary risks in the performance of their duties. American criminals have a long tradition of armed violence, and every year in this country many law enforcement officers are killed in the line of duty, and thousands more are wounded. Virtually all of these deaths and a substantial portion of the injuries are inflicted with guns and knives.

In view of these facts, we cannot blind ourselves to the need for law enforcement officers to protect themselves and other prospective victims of violence in situations where they may lack probable cause for an arrest. When an officer is justified in believing that the individual whose suspicious behavior he is investigating at close range is armed and presently dangerous to the officer or to others, it would appear to be clearly unreasonable to deny the officer the power to take necessary measures to determine whether the person is in fact carrying a weapon and to neutralize the threat of physical harm.

We must still consider, however, the nature and quality of the intrusion on individual rights which must be accepted if police officers are to be conceded the right to search for weapons in situations where probable cause to arrest for crime is lacking. Even a limited search of the outer clothing for weapons constitutes a severe, though brief, intrusion upon cherished personal security, and it must surely be an annoying, frightening, and perhaps humiliating experience. . . .

Petitioner does not argue that a police officer should refrain from making any investigation of suspicious circumstances until such time as he has probable cause to make an arrest; nor does he deny that police officers in properly discharging their investigative function may find themselves confronting persons who might well be armed and dangerous. Moreover, he does not say that an officer is always unjustified in searching a suspect to discover weapons. Rather, he says it is unreasonable for the policeman to take that step until such time as the situation evolves to a point where there is probable cause to make an arrest. When that point has been reached, petitioner would concede the officer's right to conduct a search of the suspect for weapons, fruits or instrumentalities of the crime, or "mere" evidence, incident to the arrest.

[The problem with this line of reasoning, however, is that] it fails to take account of traditional limitations upon the scope of searches, and thus recognizes no distinction in purpose, character, and extent between a search incident to an arrest and a limited search for weapons. The former, although justified in part by the acknowledged necessity to protect the arresting officer from assault with a concealed weapon, is also justified on other grounds, and can therefore involve a relatively extensive exploration of the person. A search for weapons in the absence of probable cause to arrest, however, must, like any other search, be strictly circumscribed by the exigencies which justify its initiation. Thus it must be limited to that which is necessary for the discovery of weapons which might be used to harm the officer or others nearby, and may realistically be characterized as something less than a "full" search, even though it remains a serious intrusion. . . .

Our evaluation of the proper balance that has to be struck in this type of case leads us to conclude that there must be a narrowly drawn authority to permit a reasonable search for weapons for the protection of the police officer, where he has reason to believe that he is dealing with an armed and dangerous individual, regardless of whether he has probable cause to arrest the individual for a crime. The officer need not be absolutely certain that the individual is armed; the issue is whether a reasonably prudent man in the circumstances would be warranted in the belief that his safety or that of others was in danger. And in determining whether the officer acted reasonably in such circumstances, due weight must be given, not to his inchoate and unparticularized suspicion or "hunch," but to the specific reasonable inferences which he is entitled to draw from the facts in light of his experience.

IV.

We must now examine the conduct of Officer McFadden in this case to determine whether his search and seizure of petitioner were reasonable, both at their inception and as conducted. He had observed Terry, together with Chilton and another man, acting in a manner he took to be preface to a "stick-up." We think on the facts and circumstances Officer McFadden detailed before the trial judge a reasonably prudent man would have been warranted in believing petitioner was armed and thus presented a threat to the officer's safety while he was investigating his suspicious behavior. The actions of Terry and Chilton were consistent with McFadden's hypothesis that these men were contemplating a daylight robbery—which, it is reasonable to assume, would be likely to involve the use of weapons. . . . We cannot say his decision at that point to seize Terry and pat his clothing for weapons was the product of a volatile or inventive imagination, or was undertaken simply as an act of harassment; the record evidences the tempered act of a policeman who in the course of an investigation had to make a quick decision as to how to protect himself and others from possible danger, and took limited steps to do so.

The manner in which the seizure and search were conducted is, of course, as vital a part of the inquiry as whether they were warranted at all. The Fourth Amendment proceeds as much by limitations upon the scope of governmental action as by imposing preconditions upon its initiation. . . . We need not develop at length in this case, however, the limitations which the Fourth Amendment places upon a protective seizure and search for weapons. These limitations will have to be developed in the concrete factual circumstances of individual cases. Suffice it to note that such a search, unlike a search without a warrant incident to a lawful arrest, is not justified by any need to prevent the disappearance or destruction of evidence of crime. The sole justification of the search in the present situation is the protection of the police officer and others nearby, and it must therefore be confined in scope to an intrusion reasonably designed to discover guns, knives, clubs, or other hidden instruments for the assault of the police officer.

The scope of the search in this case presents no serious problem in light of these standards. Officer McFadden patted down the outer clothing of petitioner and his two companions. He did not place his hands in their pockets or under the outer surface of their garments until he had felt weapons, and then he merely reached for and removed the guns. He never did invade Katz' person beyond the outer surfaces of his clothes, since he discovered nothing in his pat-down which might have been a weapon. Officer McFadden confined his search strictly to what was minimally necessary to learn whether the men were armed and to disarm them once he discovered the weapons. He did not conduct a general exploratory search for whatever evidence of criminal activity he might find.

V.

We conclude that the revolver seized from Terry was properly admitted in evidence against him. . . . Each case of this sort will, of course, have to be decided on its own facts. We merely hold today that where a police officer observes unusual conduct which leads him reasonably to conclude in light of his experience that criminal activity may be afoot and that the persons with whom he is dealing may be armed and presently dangerous, where in the course of investigating this behavior he identifies himself as a policeman and makes reasonable inquiries, and where nothing in the initial stages of the encounter serves to dispel his reasonable fear for his own or others' safety, he is entitled for the protection of himself and others in the area to conduct a carefully limited search of the outer clothing of such persons in an attempt to discover weapons which might be used to assault him. Such a search is a reasonable search under the Fourth Amendment, and any weapons seized may properly be introduced in evidence against the person from whom they were taken. Affirmed.

HARLAN, J., concurring.

[If] the frisk is justified in order to protect the officer during an encounter with a citizen, the officer must first have constitutional grounds to insist on an encounter, to make a forcible stop. . . . Where such a stop is reasonable, however, the right to frisk must be immediate and automatic if the reason for the stop is, as here, an articulable suspicion of a crime of violence. Just as a full search incident to a lawful arrest requires no additional justification, a limited frisk incident to a lawful stop must often be rapid and routine. There is no reason why an officer, rightfully but forcibly confronting a person suspected of a serious crime, should have to ask one question and take the risk that the answer might be a bullet. . . . Upon the foregoing premises, I join the opinion of the Court.

DOUGLAS, J., dissenting.

[Frisking] petitioner and his companions for guns was a "search." But it is a mystery how that "search" . . . can be constitutional by Fourth Amendment standards, unless there was "probable cause" to believe that (1) a crime had been committed or (2) a crime was in the process of being committed or (3) a crime was about to be committed.

The opinion of the Court disclaims the existence of "probable cause." If loitering were in issue and that was the offense charged, there would be "probable cause" shown. But the crime here is carrying concealed weapons; and there is no basis for concluding that the officer had "probable cause" for believing that that crime was being committed. Had a warrant been sought, a magistrate would, therefore, have been unauthorized to issue one, for he can act only if there is a showing of "probable cause." We hold today that the police have greater authority to make a "seizure" and conduct a "search" than a judge has to authorize such action. We have said precisely the opposite over and over again.

In other words, police officers up to today have been permitted to effect arrests or searches without warrants only when the facts within their personal knowledge would satisfy the constitutional standard of probable cause. At the time of their "seizure" without a warrant they must possess facts concerning the person arrested that would have satisfied a magistrate that "probable cause" was indeed present. The term "probable cause" rings a bell of certainty that is not sounded by phrases such as "reasonable suspicion." Moreover, the meaning of "probable cause" is deeply imbedded in our constitutional history. . . .

The infringement on personal liberty of any "seizure" of a person can only be "reasonable" under the Fourth Amendment if we require the police to possess "probable cause" before they seize him. Only that line draws a meaningful distinction between an officer's mere inkling and the presence of facts within the officer's personal knowledge which would convince a reasonable man that the person seized has committed, is committing, or is about to commit a particular crime. . . .

To give the police greater power than a magistrate is to take a long step down the totalitarian path. Perhaps such a step is desirable to cope with modern forms of lawlessness. But if it is taken, it should be the deliberate choice of the people through a constitutional amendment. Until the Fourth Amendment . . . is rewritten, the person and the effects of the individual are beyond the reach of all government agencies until there are reasonable grounds to believe (probable cause) that a criminal venture has been launched or is about to be launched.

There have been powerful hydraulic pressures throughout our history that bear heavily on the Court to water down constitutional guarantees and give the police the upper hand. That hydraulic pressure has probably never been greater than it is today. Yet if the individual is no longer to be sovereign, if the police can pick him up whenever they do not like the cut of his jib, if they can "seize" and "search" him in their discretion, we enter a new regime. The decision to enter it should be made only after a full debate by the people of this country.

Notes

1. *Frisks for weapons: majority position.* The *Terry* opinion addressed both stops and frisks and approved a framework already in place in some states at that point. It allowed the police to seize a person for a short time based on reasonable suspicion. We explored this question in section A of this chapter. But the Court considered the brief search—the frisk—to be the "crux" of this case. On the question of frisks, *Terry* has been very influential in the state systems; all the states now approve of frisks for weapons based on some justification less than probable cause. The majority take this position by statute, while others authorize such frisks through judicial rulings. An elaborate body of law in the state courts defines the boundaries of where an officer may search during a frisk, and what techniques he or she may use to identify what he or she feels inside the clothing. An exploration of these topics appears on the web extension for this chapter at *http://www.crimpro.com/extension/ch02.*

2. *Grounds for a* Terry *search.* Exactly what justification must an officer have before she performs a pat-down search? Why do both Chief Justice Warren and Justice Harlan distinguish between the justification needed for the initial stop and

the justification needed for the brief search? Was Justice Douglas right to be concerned that government agents could manipulate too easily any standard less than probable cause?

Some state courts have declared that the police automatically have reasonable suspicion to frisk a person suspected of involvement in drug crimes and burglary. See State v. Evans, 618 N.E.2d 162, 169 (Ohio 1993); State v. Scott, 405 N.W.2d 829, 832 (Iowa 1987). Does the *Terry* opinion leave room for courts to make categorical judgments about reasonable suspicion to frisk, or does it require individualized findings in each case?

3. *The effect of gun laws on* Terry *stops and frisks.* In District of Columbia v. Heller, 554 U.S. 570 (2008) and McDonald v. City of Chicago, 561 U.S. 742 (2010), the Supreme Court interpreted the Second Amendment to prohibit blanket handgun bans. As a result, states have loosened restrictions on the ability of people to carry guns. If people have the right to carry a concealed weapon or even to carry the weapon openly in public, and they frequently do so, officers may no longer be able to cite the mere possession of a weapon as a reason for conducting a *Terry* stop and frisk. What other facts could a police officer rely upon to establish reasonable suspicion that someone who possesses a weapon may have committed or be in the process of committing a crime? What facts could an officer rely upon to show that the person is both armed *and* dangerous, justifying a frisk? See Jeffrey Bellin, The Right to Remain Armed, 93 Wash. U. L. Rev. 1 (2015); Nirej Sekhon, The Second Amendment in the Street, 112 Nw. U. L. Rev. Online 271 (2018).

4. *Prevalence of frisks.* How often do frisks happen? The use of frisks in major cities varies widely. For instance, police officers in New York City conducted 97,296 stop and frisks in 2002. Then the department started promoting this technique as a major crime control tool, and the numbers increased to 685,724 by 2011. By 2017, the policy fell out of favor and the numbers fell to 10,861 without any major increases in crime. See *http://www.nyclu.org/content/stop-and-frisk-data.* Much the same pattern played out in Philadelphia and other cities. Meanwhile, the police in Chicago followed the policy of increased stops, followed by later decreases; crime rates in that city increased there at about the same time that stops decreased.

5. *Racial disparities and frisks.* When the Supreme Court first considered the validity of stops based on reasonable suspicion, in Terry v. Ohio, 392 U.S. 1 (1968), advocates and commentators objected to the police practice, pointing to evidence that police used stops in a discriminatory manner to harass African Americans. It is still true that police stop and frisk young men of color in disproportionate numbers; in some neighborhoods, young black men are stopped and frisked multiple times every month.

This pattern of enforcement led to some successful litigation, challenging the use of stops on equal protection grounds. See Floyd v. City of New York, 959 F. Supp. 2d 540 (S.D.N.Y. 2013). These constitutional challenges explain the decreases in the use of stop and frisk in many major cities, as described above. For further background about this litigation and the New York City Police Department's stop-and-frisk practices, see the web extension for this chapter at http://www.crim-pro.com/extension/ch02.

6. *Frisks and officer self-preservation.* Do you believe that police officers frisked suspects based on something less than probable cause before Detective McFadden decided to do so in Cleveland in 1963? Police officers in some states had statutes or department rules explicitly authorizing them to search for weapons without

probable cause to arrest. The Uniform Arrest Act of 1942 provided that a "peace officer may search for a dangerous weapon any person whom he has stopped or detained to question . . . whenever he has reasonable ground to believe that he is in danger if the person possesses a dangerous weapon."

Only a handful of state courts before 1968 ever explicitly addressed whether police could perform these brief searches without probable cause, with a slight majority of courts approving of the practice. Why did the issue not arise in the Supreme Court until 1968? See Wayne LaFave, "Street Encounters" and the Constitution: *Terry, Sibron, Peters,* and Beyond, 67 Mich. L. Rev. 40 (1968).

Did the Supreme Court have any choice other than to approve of brief searches for weapons? If police officers felt that their lives were in jeopardy, would they not carry out the search regardless of the legal consequences? If Justice Douglas had written the opinion for the Court, what would have been the impact of the decision on police behavior and on the law of criminal procedure?

7. *Frisks in foreign systems.* In Great Britain, the Police and Criminal Evidence Act of 1984 provides that a constable can stop and search a person in a "public place" based on "reasonable grounds for suspecting" a search will reveal stolen or contraband articles. This level of justification is the same for a full-blown arrest, but it seems to correspond more closely to the American "reasonable suspicion" standard than to the "probable cause" standard. According to the government-issued Code of Practice for the Exercise by Police Officers of the Statutory Powers of Stop and Search, §3.5, a "search" occurring in a "public place" must be limited to a search of the outer garments, while a more thorough search can occur at the police station. In what ways do these legal provisions differ from the law of frisks in the United States? Do you believe that police practices in Great Britain reflect these differences in law? The law in France authorizes the police to conduct an identity check procedure that resembles the American stop and frisk, but the French procedure does not require individualized suspicion and may last up to four hours. See Richard S. Frase, Comparative Criminal Justice as a Guide to American Law Reform: How Do the French Do It, How Can We Find Out, and Why Should We Care?, 78 Cal. L. Rev. 542, 576 (1990).

2. *The Scope of a* Terry *Search*

The frisk for weapons in *Terry* proceeds on a reduced level of justification (reasonable suspicion) because of the especially urgent nature of the government's objective in that setting (the safety of the officer and others in the area) and the limited nature of the search. Could a search based on reasonable suspicion also serve other, non-safety purposes, such as collecting evidence of a crime? What if the search is a bit more intrusive than a weapons frisk? In short, how far do *Terry* searches extend?

■ COMMONWEALTH v. ROOSEVELT WILSON

805 N.E.2d 968 (Mass. 2004)

COWIN, J.

. . . On the night of October 24, 2000, the Brockton police received a telephone call from a person who stated, "This is Stella's Pizza." The caller reported that a person was being beaten with a hammer or being stabbed in a group of ten people huddled across the street from the small commercial area where the pizza parlor was located. A police radio dispatch was broadcast containing this information, and State Trooper Francis Walls, alone in his unmarked vehicle and dressed in plain clothes, was the first officer to arrive at the scene. Walls stopped a short distance from the commercial area, saw a group of nine or ten men standing in a circle, but detected no suspicious activity. He was familiar with the area as one where he had made numerous arrests for drug and weapon violations and fights.

When he saw a backup vehicle close by, Walls pulled up to the group of men. As he got out of his vehicle, Walls made eye contact with the defendant. On making eye contact, the defendant turned, started walking away from Walls, and put his hand "to his waist area." The defendant's back was toward Walls, who, at this point, was concerned that the defendant possessed a gun. Walls grabbed the defendant by the back of his shirt and simultaneously placed his hand on "the area of the defendant's waist" where the defendant's hand had been. As soon as Walls put his hand on the defendant's waist, he felt a bundle of smaller packages, which he recognized by feel as "dime" bags of marijuana. Walls immediately asked the defendant, "You did that for weed? I thought you were putting a gun in your pants." The defendant responded that he did not "mess with guns." Walls retrieved the bag from the defendant's waist and handcuffed him.

Two backup officers, also in an unmarked vehicle and in plain clothes, were getting out of their vehicle as Walls stopped and frisked the defendant. No evidence was found of the assault or beating that had been the subject of the radio dispatch. The defendant was arrested, and an inventory search revealed that in addition to the seized "dime" bags of marijuana, a pager, a cellular telephone, and $476 in cash were in his possession. . . .

The defendant claims that the police lacked the requisite reasonable suspicion to stop him and to initiate a patfrisk. In "stop and frisk" cases our inquiry is two-fold: first, whether the initiation of the investigation by the police was permissible in the circumstances, and, second, whether the scope of the search was justified by the circumstances. In both aspects, the inquiry is whether the police conduct was reasonable under the Fourth Amendment.

In regard to the stop, a police officer may make an investigatory stop where suspicious conduct gives the officer reasonable ground to suspect that a person is committing, has committed, or is about to commit a crime. Concerning the second part of the analysis, a *Terry*-type patfrisk incident to the investigatory stop is permissible where the police officer reasonably believes that the individual is armed and dangerous. Terry v. Ohio, 392 U.S. 1 (1968). The officer's action in both the stop and the frisk must be based on specific and articulable facts and reasonable inferences therefrom, in light of the officer's experience.

Applying these principles to the facts in this case, we first consider the stop. The defendant was seized (or stopped) when Walls grabbed the back of his shirt. At that time, specific and articulable facts supported Walls's belief that the defendant had committed a crime. Walls was responding to a radio dispatch that described ten people involved in a stabbing or beating with a weapon outside Stella's Pizza. On arriving at the location, an area of Brockton where Walls had made numerous arrests for fights and weapon violations, Walls's observations confirmed a group of men huddled on the sidewalk, just as the caller had described. As he left his vehicle, Walls made eye contact with the defendant, who immediately turned away from him, walked away from the group, and simultaneously moved his hand into his "waist area." [Walls testified at the motion hearing that "As soon as he looked at me, he turned around and took his right hand and placed it into his pant line. . . ."] The totality of these facts supports a reasonable belief that the defendant had been involved in a fight with a weapon, and therefore, the stop was proper. The same facts justify the patfrisk, as they establish a reasonable belief that the defendant was armed and dangerous and presented a threat to the officer or others. . . .

The defendant next argues that Walls exceeded the scope of the patfrisk by "exploring" and seizing the package of marijuana he discovered in the defendant's waistband after he had determined it contained no weapon. The scope of a *Terry* search cannot be general; rather it is strictly tied to the circumstances that render its initiation permissible. The Fourth Amendment permits a police officer to conduct a patfrisk for concealed weapons, provided that such a search is confined to what is minimally necessary to learn whether the suspect is armed and to disarm him should weapons be discovered. Terry v. Ohio, 392 U.S. 1, 29-30 (1968).

In Minnesota v. Dickerson, 508 U.S. 366 (1993), the Supreme Court concluded that a police officer may also seize nonthreatening contraband discovered during a *Terry*-type frisk if the "police officer lawfully pats down a suspect's outer clothing and feels an object whose contour or mass makes its identity [as contraband] immediately apparent." If the officer must manipulate or otherwise further physically explore the concealed object in order to discern its identity, then an unconstitutional search has occurred.

The scope of a *Terry* search is not exceeded if, during a lawful patfrisk, it is immediately apparent to the police officer, in light of the officer's training and experience, that a concealed item is contraband. The "plain feel" doctrine is grounded on the same premise that authorizes an officer to frisk the suspect for concealed weapons, i.e., that the weapon will be immediately detected through touch during the patfrisk. As long as the object's contraband identity is immediately apparent to the officer, there is no further "invasion of the suspect's privacy beyond that already authorized by the officer's search for weapons." The "plain feel" doctrine is limited; it does not permit an officer to conduct a general exploratory search for whatever evidence of criminal activity he might find. The contraband nature of the item must be immediately apparent on touch. For these reasons, we conclude that the "plain feel" doctrine is consistent with art. 14, as well as with the Fourth Amendment.

[Several states have adopted the "plain feel" doctrine. See, e.g., People v. Mitchell, 650 N.E.2d 1014 (Ill. 1995); People v. Champion, 549 N.W.2d 849 (Mich. 1996); Commonwealth v. Zhahir, 751 A.2d 1153 (Pa. 2000). Although the Court of Appeals of New York rejected the doctrine, that court did so prior to the Supreme Court's decision in Minnesota v. Dickerson. See People v. Diaz, 612 N.E.2d 298 (N.Y. 1993).]

We consider "plain feel" as analogous to "plain view." As long as the initial search is lawful, the seizure of an item whose identity is already known occasions no further invasion of privacy. The only difference between the two doctrines is the sensory perception used to identify the contraband nature of the object. The "plain feel" doctrine merely recognizes that if contraband is immediately apparent by sense of touch, rather than sight, the police are authorized to seize it.

The "plain feel" doctrine is no more susceptible to fabrication than the "plain view" doctrine. The initial requirement, that the officer be conducting a valid patfrisk of the suspect, ensures that the officer is lawfully in the position immediately to identify the contraband. Once an otherwise lawful search is in progress, the police may inadvertently discover contraband. Requiring an officer who recognizes contraband by "plain feel" to ignore this fact and walk away from the suspect without seizing the object flies in the face of logic. . . .

When we apply these principles to the facts here, Walls did not exceed the scope of the search because the judge found that it was immediately apparent to Walls when he touched the defendant's waist area that the object in the defendant's waistband was bundles of marijuana, and no manipulation was necessary to determine that fact. Contrast Minnesota v. Dickerson, 508 U.S. at 378-379 (scope of search unconstitutional where officer manipulated contents of defendant's pocket before discerning lump was contraband).

The defendant also contests the judge's finding that Walls knew the item in the defendant's waistband was drugs as soon as he touched it and did not manipulate it. The judge's finding is supported by record evidence. Walls repeatedly stated, despite thorough examination by the defense attorney, that he knew the identity of the object as soon as he touched it, without any manipulation ("The second I hit it, that's what I felt"). Other testimony by Walls supports this finding: his seven years of experience as a State trooper, and his inquiry to the defendant made immediately on touching the object, "You did that for weed?"

Contrary to the defendant's argument that there was no evidence concerning Walls's training and experience in tactile detection of marijuana or its packaging, Walls stated that he has made numerous arrests for drug violations, has seized drugs, and was serving in the "gang unit." From all of this evidence, the judge could reasonably infer that Walls had sufficient personal experience in narcotics packaging and detection to identify immediately the object in the defendant's waistband. . . .

■ ARKANSAS RULE OF CRIMINAL PROCEDURE 3.4

If a law enforcement officer who has detained a person under Rule 3.1 reasonably suspects that the person is armed and presently dangerous to the officer or others, the officer or someone designated by him may search the outer clothing of such person and the immediate surroundings for, and seize, any weapon or other dangerous thing which may be used against the officer or others. In no event shall this search be more extensive than is reasonably necessary to ensure the safety of the officer or others.

■ MONTANA CODE §46-5-401(2)

A peace officer who has lawfully stopped a person [may] frisk the person and take other reasonably necessary steps for protection if the officer has reasonable cause to suspect that the person is armed and presently dangerous to the officer or another person present. The officer may take possession of any object that is discovered during the course of the frisk if the officer has probable cause to believe that the object is a deadly weapon until the completion of the stop, at which time the officer shall either immediately return the object, if legally possessed, or arrest the person.

Notes

1. *"Plain feel": majority position.* Under the "plain feel" or "plain touch" doctrine, if an officer conducts a properly circumscribed *Terry* search for weapons and feels an object that is not a weapon, the officer can seize the item if it is "immediately apparent" that the item is contraband or evidence of a crime. Minnesota v. Dickerson, 508 U.S. 366 (1993). Most state courts to consider the question also have adopted a "plain feel" doctrine under their state constitutions. See People v. Champion, 549 N.W.2d 849 (Mich. 1996). While accepting the basic contours of the doctrine, courts in about half the states apply it strictly. Courts have declared that commonplace items touched during a frisk cannot be seized, because it cannot be "immediately apparent" that the item is contraband or evidence. Murphy v. Commonwealth, 570 S.E.2d 836 (Va. 2002) ("plain feel" doctrine does not permit seizure of baggie containing marijuana felt during pat of outside surface of pants pocket); but cf. State v. Rushing, 935 S.W.2d 30 (Mo. 1996) (applying doctrine more leniently; confiscation of roll of breath mints felt during pat-down was justified because officer's training and experience revealed that breath mint rolls were common cocaine containers).

The high court in New York rejected the "plain touch" doctrine entirely under its state constitution. The court in People v. Diaz, 612 N.E.2d 298 (N.Y. 1993), explained its position as follows:

> The identity and criminal nature of a concealed object are not likely to be discernible upon a mere touch or pat within the scope of the intrusion authorized by *Terry*. While in most instances seeing an object will instantly reveal its identity and nature, touching is inherently less reliable and cannot conclusively establish an object's identity or criminal nature. Moreover, knowledge concerning an object merely from feeling it through an exterior covering is necessarily based on the police officer's expert opinion. . . .
>
> Finally, an opinion of a police officer that the object touched is evidence of criminality will predictably, at least in some circumstances, require a degree of pinching, squeezing or probing beyond the limited intrusion allowed under *Terry*. The proposed "plain touch" exception could thus invite a blurring of the limits to *Terry* searches and the sanctioning of warrantless searches on information obtained from an initial intrusion which, itself, amounts to an unauthorized warrantless search.

What kind of training—formal and informal—would you expect to occur within police departments in jurisdictions that adopt a "plain feel" rule? Should courts evaluate plain feel cases based on what a reasonable officer would know or on what the officer in question knew?

2. *Reasonable suspicion for non-weapons frisks?* The Supreme Court has insisted that a frisk of a person designed to obtain evidence of a crime cannot be based on reasonable suspicion; the officer must have probable cause that the evidence will be on the person, even if the brief search is no more intrusive than a weapons frisk. See Ybarra v. Illinois, 444 U.S. 85 (1979) (frisk of customer in bar where search warrant was being executed). How exactly will the courts make the distinction between permissible weapons frisks and impermissible evidence frisks?

3. *Frisk statutes.* Would the court in *Wilson* have decided the case any differently if a statute identical to the Arkansas statute had been in effect in Massachusetts? What outcome under the Montana statute? Are the police in a better position, generally

speaking, in states with a frisk statute or in those where the authority to frisk is based entirely on judicial opinions?

4. *Are courts the agents of legislators or independent interpreters?* Suppose a court is convinced that a state statute regarding the scope of frisks is badly flawed because it does not authorize a frisk beyond the "outer clothing." Should the court feel free to "fix" the problem created by the legislature? Are there canons of construction that would allow a court to read this statute to allow more intrusive (and effective) frisks?

As we have seen earlier, courts look to several different sources of guidance in interpreting the meaning of ambiguous statutory language. They sometimes resort to canons of construction to determine the "plain meaning" of the statutory text. They also often consult the legislative history to determine the legislature's intent in passing the statute. Alternatively, they may refer to the statute's title or language to ascertain the legislative purpose. These different sources may point in different directions in a particular case. What weight will a court give to the various sources of guidance?

The answer to such a question depends on the court's objective: Does the court view itself as an agent of the legislature, or is the court to exercise its own best judgment about how to give meaning to the language? Courts have not agreed on this question. On the one hand, most probably adhere to the view that they interpret statutes as agents of the legislature, to put into effect what the legislators intended in a specific setting (or what they *would have* intended for the setting if they had thought of it). As Justice Oliver Wendell Holmes once stated, "If my fellow citizens want to go to Hell I will help them. It's my job." 1 Holmes-Laski Letters 249 (Mark DeWolfe Howe ed., 1953).

On the other hand, many courts *act* as if they have an independent responsibility to make sense of statutory language. Professor Ernst Freund captured this independent view of courts as interpreters of statutes with the following advice in 1917: "In cases of genuine ambiguity courts should use the power of interpretation consciously and deliberately to promote sound law and sound principles of legislation." Ernst Freund, Interpretation of Statutes, 65 U. Pa. L. Rev. 207 (1917). What objective of statutory interpretation would a court be endorsing if it were to interpret the Arkansas frisk statute to allow frisks of the person beyond the outer clothing?

5. *Purses, briefcases, and bags.* Police also commonly extend protective *Terry* searches to purses, briefcases, and other items a suspect might be holding at the time of a stop. Although the officer might reduce the danger of any weapons in a purse or bag by placing it well out of reach of the suspect, courts and police department rules have not uniformly required the police to do so. Cf. State v. Peterson, 110 P.3d 699 (Utah 2005) (officers could not pat down a jacket before giving it to detained person, who did not request jacket before going outdoors). The search must start with a "frisk" of the exterior of a cloth bag, and the officer may not open the bag to search its contents if the initial frisk confirms that there is no weapon inside.

6. *Duration of stop.* When an officer stops a car based on reasonable suspicion that a traffic violation has occurred, it creates an opportunity to investigate other crimes. But the opportunity is limited. It is clear that the stop can only last as long as it would ordinarily take to complete a routine traffic citation. See Rodriguez v. United States, 135 S. Ct. 1609 (2015) (officer stopped car for swerving out of lane, questioned driver and passenger, issued warning ticket, then after a seven- or

eight-minute delay walked a drug-sniffing dog around the car; extension of stop beyond the scope required for original stop must be supported by additional reasonable suspicion). For further discussion of stops based on suspicion of one crime that officers use to investigate a different crime, see section B of this chapter.

7. *Orders to exit a vehicle.* When an officer stops a vehicle, he will sometimes but not always ask the driver to get out of the vehicle, out of concern for his own safety. The U.S. Supreme Court has concluded that this intrusion on the driver is minimal and that the officer needs no justification (other than the reasonable suspicion necessary to stop the car) for ordering the driver to get out of the car. Pennsylvania v. Mimms, 434 U.S. 106 (1977); but see State v. Sprague, 824 A.2d 539 (Vt. 2003) (under state constitution, officer conducting routine traffic stop may not automatically order driver to exit vehicle). In Maryland v. Wilson, 519 U.S. 408 (1997), the court extended *Mimms* to hold that officers may order a *passenger* in the car to get out, without any grounds to believe that the passenger is dangerous. Some states previously had rejected that position. See State v. Smith, 637 A.2d 158 (N.J. 1994) (order to passenger to get out of car stopped for minor traffic infraction must be based on articulable suspicion that passenger poses danger). The great majority of state courts follow both *Mimms* and *Wilson*. Should the police treat the driver and the passenger differently? Is one any more or less dangerous than the other? Is the intrusion on drivers and passengers the same?

Arizona v. Johnson, 555 U.S. 323 (2009), confirms that passengers in a stopped vehicle are also subject to frisk if the officer has reasonable suspicion to believe a passenger is armed and dangerous, even if there is no reasonable suspicion that a passenger is involved in a crime. In that case, an officer frisked a passenger suspected of membership in a gang whose members frequently carried weapons.

8. Terry *searches of stopped cars.* Although a pat-down search of a person should expose any guns or other large weapons hidden in the clothing, a person stopped while riding in a car might hide a weapon somewhere in the vehicle. How can an officer protect herself from a suspect who keeps a weapon somewhere nearby, but not on his person? The U.S. Supreme Court, in Michigan v. Long, 463 U.S. 1032 (1983), stated that police officers who stop a vehicle and frisk the driver standing outside the car may conduct a further "protective" search of the passenger compartment and any containers inside it that might contain a large weapon such as a gun. Under the federal constitution, the police must have a reasonable suspicion that there may be weapons in the vehicle before the protective search takes place. Most state courts (all but about a half dozen) allow police to conduct protective searches of stopped cars, on terms identical to federal law. They allow the officers to conduct a protective search of the interior and any containers inside (but only those large enough to contain a weapon) if the officers reasonably suspect that there are dangerous weapons in the vehicle. These courts reason that the search of a vehicle is just as important to the officer's safety as a frisk of the person under *Terry*. See State v. Wilkins, 692 A.2d 1233 (Conn. 1997). However, the high court in New York decided in People v. Torres, 543 N.E.2d 61 (N.Y. 1989), that police officers could not search the interior of a stopped vehicle for weapons based only on reasonable suspicion. The *Torres* court suggested that the officer stopping the vehicle can reduce any risk by separating the suspect from the vehicle. How might the majority of courts respond to this argument? Would you draw a distinction between a pat-down search of the driver and placing the driver into the patrol car during the stop? See Wilson v. State, 745 N.E.2d 789 (Ind. 2001) (pat-down search of motorist prior to placing

him in police car during routine traffic stop violated Fourth Amendment; pat-down search was not supported by particularized reasonable suspicion that motorist was armed).

Problem 2-10. Frisking Car and Driver

Around 12:30 A.M., police officers Josephine Copland and Jess Segundo were patrolling West Oliwood, investigating narcotics sales in that area. As they waited at an intersection for a traffic signal to change, they saw a red Lexus drive through the intersection with a taillight burned out. Officers Copland and Segundo immediately stopped the Lexus, although they typically would not stop a car based only on a problem with the taillight.

When the driver, Steven Worth, pulled over and stopped, he started to move about the inside of the vehicle, back and forth in the front seat, and ducked down below the seat. When Officers Copland and Segundo exited their cruiser and approached on foot, they ordered Worth to step out of his vehicle.

Officer Copland ordered Worth to move away from his vehicle, and began examining the interior of the Lexus. She looked around and under the seats and found nothing suspicious. Officer Copland then opened the glove compartment and found what looked to her like a hand-rolled cigarette. Upon picking up and examining the cigarette, she discovered it was filled with tobacco. Officer Copland reached over and lifted the lever next to the driver's seat to disengage the trunk latch. Moving outside to the back of the car, she looked inside the trunk and found an expensive-looking set of golf clubs inside a golf bag. Officer Copland noticed a number of bulges within the golf bag, and she began to unzip the bag's various pockets. In the largest pocket, which ran the length of the bag, Copland discovered a sawed-off shotgun.

Meanwhile, Officer Segundo was examining Worth. She performed a pat-down search of Worth's outer clothing. As part of this frisk, Officer Segundo patted down the knit stocking cap Worth wore, which was rolled over on the edges. Officer Segundo felt a hard object on the right side of Worth's hat. Officer Segundo was not sure what this hard object was, and she reached inside the hat. Grabbing the hard object with her fingers, she felt what she believed (based upon her previous experience) to be crack cocaine. Officer Segundo then removed two pieces of suspected crack cocaine from the hat and arrested Worth for possession of that illegal substance.

Steven Worth was charged with possession of crack cocaine and with possession of an illegal firearm. He filed a motion prior to trial asking the court to suppress the gun recovered from the golf bag and the drugs recovered from his stocking cap. How would you argue in support of the motion?

D. BRIEF ADMINISTRATIVE STOPS AND SEARCHES

Among the brief stops and searches that government agents carry out, some are subject to less restrictive rules because of their routine administrative nature. These brief stops are carried out on large numbers of people and further government interests apart from criminal law enforcement. The U.S. Supreme Court determined, in Camara v. Municipal Court, 387 U.S. 523 (1967), that the Fourth Amendment could place limits on government activities even when they are not directed at enforcement of the criminal laws. These "administrative" or "special needs" stops and searches sometimes take place even when the government agents have no reasonable suspicion to believe that a law has been violated. To be lawful, such searches and seizures must primarily aim to advance an administrative, non-law-enforcement purpose. In addition, courts balance the individual interests implicated by the searches against the government interests at stake to determine whether the searches comply with the Fourth Amendment. To see how courts have applied these tests, we begin with non-individualized stops of drivers. Chapter 4 discusses the application of the balancing test in other "special needs search" areas, such as school searches and searches of prisoners, probationers, and parolees.

■ CITY OF INDIANAPOLIS v. JAMES EDMOND
531 U.S. 32 (2000)

O'CONNOR, J.*

. . . I.

. . . In August 1998, the city of Indianapolis began to operate vehicle checkpoints on Indianapolis roads in an effort to interdict unlawful drugs. The city conducted six such roadblocks between August and November that year, stopping 1,161 vehicles and arresting 104 motorists. Fifty-five arrests were for drug-related crimes, while 49 were for offenses unrelated to drugs. The overall "hit rate" of the program was thus approximately nine percent.

The parties stipulated to the facts concerning the operation of the checkpoints by the Indianapolis Police Department (IPD) for purposes of the preliminary injunction proceedings instituted below. At each checkpoint location, the police stop a predetermined number of vehicles. Approximately 30 officers are stationed at the checkpoint. Pursuant to written directives issued by the chief of police, at least one officer approaches the vehicle, advises the driver that he or she is being stopped briefly at a drug checkpoint, and asks the driver to produce a license and registration. The officer also looks for signs of impairment and conducts an open-view examination of the vehicle from the outside. A narcotics-detection dog walks around the outside of each stopped vehicle.

The directives instruct the officers that they may conduct a search only by consent or based on the appropriate quantum of particularized suspicion. The officers must conduct each stop in the same manner until particularized suspicion develops, and the officers have no discretion to stop any vehicle out of sequence. . . . According to Sergeant [Marshall] DePew, checkpoint locations are selected weeks in advance based on such considerations as area crime statistics and traffic flow. The checkpoints are generally operated during daylight hours and are identified with lighted signs reading, "NARCOTICS CHECKPOINT ___ MILE AHEAD, NARCOTICS K-9

---

* [Justices Stevens, Kennedy, Souter, Ginsburg, and Breyer joined in this opinion.—EDS.]

IN USE, BE PREPARED TO STOP." Once a group of cars has been stopped, other traffic proceeds without interruption until all the stopped cars have been processed or diverted for further processing. Sergeant DePew also stated that the average stop for a vehicle not subject to further processing lasts two to three minutes or less.

Respondents James Edmond and Joell Palmer were each stopped at a narcotics checkpoint in late September 1998. Respondents then filed a lawsuit on behalf of themselves and the class of all motorists who had been stopped or were subject to being stopped in the future at the Indianapolis drug checkpoints. Respondents claimed that the roadblocks violated the Fourth Amendment of the United States Constitution and the search and seizure provision of the Indiana Constitution. Respondents requested declaratory and injunctive relief for the class, as well as damages and attorney's fees for themselves. . . .

II.

The Fourth Amendment requires that searches and seizures be reasonable. A search or seizure is ordinarily unreasonable in the absence of individualized suspicion of wrongdoing. While such suspicion is not an irreducible component of reasonableness, we have recognized only limited circumstances in which the usual rule does not apply. For example, we have upheld certain regimes of suspicionless searches where the program was designed to serve "special needs, beyond the normal need for law enforcement." See, e.g., Vernonia School Dist. 47J v. Acton, 515 U.S. 646 (1995) (random drug testing of student-athletes); Treasury Employees v. Von Raab, 489 U.S. 656 (1989) (drug tests for United States Customs Service employees seeking transfer or promotion to certain positions). We have also allowed searches for certain administrative purposes without particularized suspicion of misconduct, provided that those searches are appropriately limited. See, e.g., New York v. Burger, 482 U.S. 691 (1987) (warrantless administrative inspection of premises of "closely regulated" business).

We have also upheld brief, suspicionless seizures of motorists at a fixed Border Patrol checkpoint designed to intercept illegal aliens, United States v. Martinez-Fuerte, 428 U.S. 543 (1976), and at a sobriety checkpoint aimed at removing drunk drivers from the road, Michigan Dept. of State Police v. Sitz, 496 U.S. 444 (1990). In addition, in Delaware v. Prouse, 440 U.S. 648 (1979), we suggested that a similar type of roadblock with the purpose of verifying drivers' licenses and vehicle registrations would be permissible. In none of these cases, however, did we indicate approval of a checkpoint program whose primary purpose was to detect evidence of ordinary criminal wrongdoing. . . .

In Sitz, we evaluated the constitutionality of a Michigan highway sobriety checkpoint program. The Sitz checkpoint involved brief suspicionless stops of motorists so that police officers could detect signs of intoxication and remove impaired drivers from the road. Motorists who exhibited signs of intoxication were diverted for a license and registration check and, if warranted, further sobriety tests. This checkpoint program was clearly aimed at reducing the immediate hazard posed by the presence of drunk drivers on the highways, and there was an obvious connection between the imperative of highway safety and the law enforcement practice at issue. The gravity of the drunk driving problem and the magnitude of the State's interest in getting drunk drivers off the road weighed heavily in our determination that the program was constitutional.

In *Prouse*, we invalidated a discretionary, suspicionless stop for a spot check of a motorist's driver's license and vehicle registration. The officer's conduct in that case was unconstitutional primarily on account of his exercise of "standardless and unconstrained discretion." We nonetheless acknowledged the States' "vital interest in ensuring that only those qualified to do so are permitted to operate motor vehicles, that these vehicles are fit for safe operation, and hence that licensing, registration, and vehicle inspection requirements are being observed." Accordingly, we suggested that "questioning of all oncoming traffic at roadblock-type stops" would be a lawful means of serving this interest in highway safety.

We further indicated in *Prouse* that we considered the purposes of such a hypothetical roadblock to be distinct from a general purpose of investigating crime. [We considered the state's primary interest in this setting to be roadway safety.] Not only does the common thread of highway safety thus run through *Sitz* and *Prouse*, but *Prouse* itself reveals a difference in the Fourth Amendment significance of highway safety interests and the general interest in crime control.

III.

It is well established that a vehicle stop at a highway checkpoint effectuates a seizure within the meaning of the Fourth Amendment. The fact that officers walk a narcotics-detection dog around the exterior of each car at the Indianapolis checkpoints does not transform the seizure into a search. See United States v. Place, 462 U.S. 696 (1983). Just as in *Place*, an exterior sniff of an automobile does not require entry into the car and is not designed to disclose any information other than the presence or absence of narcotics. . . . Rather, what principally distinguishes these checkpoints from those we have previously approved is their primary purpose.

As petitioners concede, the Indianapolis checkpoint program unquestionably has the primary purpose of interdicting illegal narcotics. In their stipulation of facts, the parties repeatedly refer to the checkpoints as "drug checkpoints" and describe them as "being operated by the City of Indianapolis in an effort to interdict unlawful drugs in Indianapolis." In addition, the [operating] directives instruct officers to "advise the citizen that they are being stopped briefly at a drug checkpoint." . . . Because the primary purpose of the Indianapolis narcotics checkpoint program is to uncover evidence of ordinary criminal wrongdoing, the program contravenes the Fourth Amendment.

Petitioners propose several ways in which the narcotics-detection purpose of the instant checkpoint program may instead resemble the primary purposes of the checkpoints in *Sitz* and *Martinez-Fuerte*. Petitioners state that the checkpoints in those cases had the same ultimate purpose of arresting those suspected of committing crimes. Securing the border and apprehending drunk drivers are, of course, law enforcement activities, and law enforcement officers employ arrests and criminal prosecutions in pursuit of these goals. If we were to rest the case at this high level of generality, there would be little check on the ability of the authorities to construct roadblocks for almost any conceivable law enforcement purpose. Without drawing the line at roadblocks designed primarily to serve the general interest in crime control, the Fourth Amendment would do little to prevent such intrusions from becoming a routine part of American life. . . .

Nor can the narcotics-interdiction purpose of the checkpoints be rationalized in terms of a highway safety concern similar to that present in *Sitz*. The detection and punishment of almost any criminal offense serves broadly the safety of the community, and our streets would no doubt be safer but for the scourge of illegal drugs. Only with respect to a smaller class of offenses, however, is society confronted with the type of immediate, vehicle-bound threat to life and limb that the sobriety checkpoint in *Sitz* was designed to eliminate. . . .

Of course, there are circumstances that may justify a law enforcement checkpoint where the primary purpose would otherwise, but for some emergency, relate to ordinary crime control. For example, . . . the Fourth Amendment would almost certainly permit an appropriately tailored roadblock set up to thwart an imminent terrorist attack or to catch a dangerous criminal who is likely to flee by way of a particular route. The exigencies created by these scenarios are far removed from the circumstances under which authorities might simply stop cars as a matter of course to see if there just happens to be a felon leaving the jurisdiction. . . .

Petitioners argue that our prior cases preclude an inquiry into the purposes of the checkpoint program. For example, they cite Whren v. United States, 517 U.S. 806 (1996) . . . to support the proposition that "where the government articulates and pursues a legitimate interest for a suspicionless stop, courts should not look behind that interest to determine whether the government's 'primary purpose' is valid." These cases, however, do not control the instant situation.

In *Whren*, we held that an individual officer's subjective intentions are irrelevant to the Fourth Amendment validity of a traffic stop that is justified objectively by probable cause to believe that a traffic violation has occurred. . . . In so holding, we expressly distinguished cases where we had addressed the validity of searches conducted in the absence of probable cause. [While] subjective intentions play no role in ordinary, probable-cause Fourth Amendment analysis, programmatic purposes may be relevant to the validity of Fourth Amendment intrusions undertaken pursuant to a general scheme without individualized suspicion. . . .

Petitioners argue that the Indianapolis checkpoint program is justified by its lawful secondary purposes of keeping impaired motorists off the road and verifying licenses and registrations. If this were the case, however, law enforcement authorities would be able to establish checkpoints for virtually any purpose so long as they also included a license or sobriety check. For this reason, we examine the available evidence to determine the primary purpose of the checkpoint program. While we recognize the challenges inherent in a purpose inquiry, courts routinely engage in this enterprise in many areas of constitutional jurisprudence as a means of sifting abusive governmental conduct from that which is lawful. . . .

Because the primary purpose of the Indianapolis checkpoint program is ultimately indistinguishable from the general interest in crime control, the checkpoints violate the Fourth Amendment. . . .

REHNQUIST, C.J., dissenting.*
The State's use of a drug-sniffing dog, according to the Court's holding, annuls what is otherwise plainly constitutional under our Fourth Amendment jurisprudence: brief, standardized, discretionless, roadblock seizures of automobiles, seizures which effectively serve a weighty state interest with only minimal intrusion on the privacy of their occupants. Because these seizures serve the State's accepted

* [Justice Thomas joined this opinion; Justice Scalia joined in Part I.—EDS.]

and significant interests of preventing drunken driving and checking for driver's licenses and vehicle registrations, and because there is nothing in the record to indicate that the addition of the dog sniff lengthens these otherwise legitimate seizures, I dissent.

I.

. . . Petitioners acknowledge that the "primary purpose" of these roadblocks is to interdict illegal drugs, but this fact should not be controlling. [The] question whether a law enforcement purpose could support a roadblock seizure is not presented in this case. The District Court found that another "purpose of the checkpoints is to check driver's licenses and vehicle registrations," and the written directives state that the police officers are to "look for signs of impairment." . . . That the roadblocks serve these legitimate state interests cannot be seriously disputed, as the 49 people arrested for offenses unrelated to drugs can attest. . . .

Because of the valid reasons for conducting these roadblock seizures, it is constitutionally irrelevant that petitioners also hoped to interdict drugs. In Whren v. United States, we held that an officer's subjective intent would not invalidate an otherwise objectively justifiable stop of an automobile. The reasonableness of an officer's discretionary decision to stop an automobile, at issue in *Whren*, turns on whether there is probable cause to believe that a traffic violation has occurred. The reasonableness of highway checkpoints, at issue here, turns on whether they effectively serve a significant state interest with minimal intrusion on motorists. . . . Once the constitutional requirements for a particular seizure are satisfied, the subjective expectations of those responsible for it, be it police officers or members of a city council, are irrelevant. It is the objective effect of the State's actions on the privacy of the individual that animates the Fourth Amendment. Because the objective intrusion of a valid seizure does not turn upon anyone's subjective thoughts, neither should our constitutional analysis. . . .

[The] checkpoints' success rate—49 arrests for offenses unrelated to drugs [or 4.2 percent of the motorists stopped]—only confirms the State's legitimate interests in preventing drunken driving and ensuring the proper licensing of drivers and registration of their vehicles. These stops effectively serve the State's legitimate interests; they are executed in a regularized and neutral manner; and they only minimally intrude upon the privacy of the motorists. They should therefore be constitutional.

II.

[Expectations] of privacy in an automobile and of freedom in its operation are significantly different from the traditional expectation of privacy and freedom in one's residence. This is because automobiles, unlike homes, are subjected to pervasive and continuing governmental regulation and controls. The lowered expectation of privacy in one's automobile is coupled with the limited nature of the intrusion: a brief, standardized, nonintrusive seizure. . . .

Because of these extrinsic limitations upon roadblock seizures, the Court's newfound non-law-enforcement primary purpose test is both unnecessary to secure Fourth Amendment rights and bound to produce wide-ranging litigation over the "purpose" of any given seizure. Police designing highway roadblocks can never be sure of their validity, since a jury might later determine that a forbidden purpose exists. . . .

■ IOWA CODE §321K.1

1. The law enforcement agencies of this state may conduct emergency vehicle roadblocks in response to immediate threats to the health, safety, and welfare of the public; and otherwise may conduct routine vehicle roadblocks only as provided in this section. Routine vehicle roadblocks may be conducted to enforce compliance with the law regarding any of the following:

    a. The licensing of operators of motor vehicles.

    b. The registration of motor vehicles.

    c. The safety equipment required on motor vehicles.

    d. The provisions of chapters 481A and 483A [dealing with fish and game conservation].

2. Any routine vehicle roadblock conducted under this section shall meet the following requirements:

    a. The location of the roadblock, the time during which the roadblock will be conducted, and the procedure to be used while conducting the roadblock, shall be determined by policymaking administrative officers of the law enforcement agency.

    b. The roadblock location shall be selected for its safety and visibility to oncoming motorists, and adequate advance warning signs, illuminated at night or under conditions of poor visibility, shall be erected to provide timely information to approaching motorists of the roadblock and its nature.

    c. There shall be uniformed officers and marked official vehicles of the law enforcement agency or agencies involved, in sufficient quantity and visibility to demonstrate the official nature of the roadblock.

    d. The selection of motor vehicles to be stopped shall not be arbitrary.

    e. The roadblock shall be conducted to assure the safety of and to minimize the inconvenience of the motorists involved.

Notes

1. *Automobile checkpoints: majority position.* As the opinion in *Edmond* makes clear, the federal constitution imposes different requirements on sobriety checkpoints and drug enforcement checkpoints. In Michigan Department of Police v. Sitz, 496 U.S. 444 (1990), the Court upheld a sobriety checkpoint where officers stopped vehicles without reasonable suspicion. The opinion emphasized the importance of neutral guidelines for carrying out the roadblock, formulated by supervisors or others besides the officers in the field. Those guidelines reduced both the "objective" intrusion (the duration of the stop and the intensity of the questioning) and the "subjective" intrusion of the stop (the anxiety of law-abiding drivers who are unaware of the purpose of the stop). On the other hand, after the ruling in *Edmond*, governments may not conduct suspicionless stops at drug enforcement checkpoints.

State courts are split on whether suspicionless sobriety checkpoints violate their state constitutions, with a strong majority (nearly 40 states) mirroring the federal position. See State v. Mikolinski, 775 A.2d 274 (Conn. 2001). A minority (about 10) require individualized suspicion before a vehicle stop may occur at a sobriety checkpoint. This group includes Michigan, the state whose appeals court decision was reversed in *Sitz*, which in turn rejected the U.S. Supreme Court's *Sitz* opinion on state constitutional grounds. Sitz v. Department of Police, 506 N.W.2d 209 (Mich. 1993).

2. *Driver's license and other safety reasons for checkpoints.* Police in many jurisdictions stop vehicles without individualized suspicion at a checkpoint to verify the validity of the operators' licenses, following much the same procedures for license checkpoints as they do for sobriety checkpoints. The Iowa statute above approves of roadblocks for purposes of enforcing safety equipment laws but not for purposes of enforcing drunk driving laws. Does this distinction make sense?

The U.S. Supreme Court has approved of license checkpoints so long as they are carried out in a way that does not leave officers in the field with discretion to select the vehicles to stop. Delaware v. Prouse, 440 U.S. 648 (1979). Some states have rejected license checkpoints under their state constitutions. State v. Sanchez, 856 S.W.2d 166 (Tex. Crim. App. 1993) (license and insurance checkpoint set up by four officers); State v. Hicks, 55 S.W.3d 515 (Tenn. 2001) (license checkpoint).

Government agents enforcing health and safety laws other than traffic laws also find it useful to stop and question motorists and persons outside their cars. See People v. McHugh, 630 So. 2d 1259 (La. 1994) (upholding statute authorizing suspicionless stops of hunters who are leaving state wilderness area to inspect hunting license and to request permission to inspect game); but see State v. Medley, 898 P.2d 1093 (Idaho 1995) (disallowing, in an opinion by Justice Trout, a game management checkpoint because of officer discretion in stopping vehicles and presence of criminal law enforcement officials). What set of safety and health concerns convinced the Iowa legislature to pass Section 321K.1?

3. *Which programmatic purpose?* Justice O'Connor, in her majority opinion in *Edmond,* says that "programmatic purposes may be relevant" even though an officer's subjective intentions normally do not matter in evaluating the reasonableness of a seizure. We encountered this issue earlier, in discussing "pretextual" stops. Is it any easier for courts to determine the purpose of a program than to determine the intentions of a particular officer? What sources of evidence are available to the court making this factual finding? See Crowell v. State, 994 P.2d 788 (Okla. Crim. App. 2000) (use of narcotics detection dog to sniff cars not enough to show that safety roadblock was a pretext for drug enforcement); State v. Sigler, 687 S.E.2d 391 (W. Va. 2009) (police conducting equipment safety checks must follow the same guidelines as they do for sobriety checkpoints; different rules for checkpoints carrying different labels would invite "pretextual" checkpoints).

4. *Balancing tests.* Sobriety checkpoints take place in the absence of any probable cause or reasonable suspicion to believe that a driver being stopped is violating the law. The Supreme Court in *Sitz* and the other courts that have upheld sobriety checkpoints have used a "balancing" methodology to determine that individualized suspicion is not necessary. These courts balance the needs of law enforcement against the intrusiveness of the search and the individual's interest in privacy. Did the majority opinion in *Edmond* also balance interests? Should courts engage in balancing at all when it comes to constitutionally protected privacy interests? Or should they conclude that the Fourth Amendment and its equivalents have already struck a balance for all cases, requiring individualized suspicion for any "seizure" or "search"? In thinking about this question, it is useful to keep in mind that the balancing methodology systematically produces more favorable outcomes for the government, sometimes based on judicial assumptions about government and individual interests that have no empirical basis. See Shima Baradaran, Rebalancing the Fourth Amendment, 102 Geo. L.J. 1 (2013).

5. *Effectiveness of checkpoints.* Is it relevant in weighing the government's interest to determine the effectiveness of a particular set of roadblock guidelines in catching drunk drivers or meeting the other objectives of the checkpoint? Would a roadblock that produces one arrest for every 100 cars stopped be more constitutionally suspect than a roadblock that produces one arrest for every 20 cars stopped? How might police supervisors change guidelines to increase the number of arrests? Perhaps courts, police, and legislatures could consider some measure of effectiveness besides the number of arrests. Would courts be more likely to validate sobriety checkpoints if the government shows decreases in alcohol-related fatal crashes?

Consider the type of evidence that supports a decision to establish a random checkpoint and the evidence that supports "individualized" suspicion. Don't both sorts of judgments depend on assessments of similar groups or situations from the past to predict a "hit rate" for future stops? See Christopher Slobogin, Government Dragnets, 73 Law & Contemp. Probs. 107 (2010); Bernard E. Harcourt & Tracey L. Meares, Randomization and the Fourth Amendment, 78 U. Chi. L. Rev. 809 (2011).

6. *Advance notice and neutral plans.* The guidelines for conducting roadblocks often provide for two types of notice. First, there are markers at the scene of the roadblock, announcing to oncoming drivers the purpose of the stop. Second, some guidelines require advance notice in the local media that roadblocks will be taking place in the area on particular days, without announcing the exact locations of the roadblocks. This advance notice is designed to increase the deterrent effect of the roadblocks by influencing the choices of all potential drivers who hear about the stops and to decrease the anxiety of drivers who encounter a roadblock. Such notice was part of the Michigan guidelines considered by the Supreme Court in *Sitz.*

Some courts have concluded that advance notice is not constitutionally required. See People v. Banks, 863 P.2d 769 (Cal. 1993). A few states modify the typical procedures by allowing random stops and giving officers more discretion. See State v. Mitchell, 592 S.E.2d 543 (N.C. 2004) (approves checkpoints based on standing permission from supervisor to operate under unwritten guidelines). The necessary conditions for valid automobile checkpoints have attracted the attention of many state and federal courts. For a sample of these debates, see the web extension for this chapter at *http://www.crimpro.com/extension/ch02.*

7. *Roadblocks to find particular criminal suspects.* Police will occasionally receive information about the location of a suspect for a serious crime and will search all vehicles leaving the area. At least 10 states give police explicit statutory authority to set up roadblocks to find criminal suspects. See Idaho Code §19-621. Courts evaluating these roadblocks tend to approve them more readily if the crime is serious and the officers administer the roadblock in an evenhanded way that minimizes the delay and other intrusions.

What if a car approaching a roadblock makes a U-turn or exits the highway in an apparent attempt to avoid the roadblock? Does that give the police reasonable suspicion to pursue and stop the vehicle? See Commonwealth v. Scavello, 734 A.2d 386 (Pa. 1999) (properly executed turn to avoid passing through roadblock not a basis for stop).

The Supreme Court created a specialized version of the checkpoint rules to apply when the roadblock is designed to obtain information about people other than the motorist stopped. In Illinois v. Lidster, 540 U.S. 419 (2004), a police department seeking information about a fatal hit-and-run accident stopped motorists passing by the scene of the accident several days later. Although one of the stopped motorists was discovered to be driving while intoxicated, the Court ruled that the suspicionless stop was reasonable because the checkpoint sought information rather than arrests of intoxicated drivers.

After this decision, is it still fair to characterize suspicionless searches as "exceptional" techniques that will be approved only under "special" circumstances? Or has the law now evolved (or devolved) to the point that suspicionless searches are regulated and approved on the same basis as more traditional searches?

8. *Fixed and roving stops for immigration enforcement.* Customs and immigration officials routinely stop vehicles crossing the border into the country, and vehicles passing fixed checkpoints near the border. There are criminal sanctions for certain violations of the immigration laws; indeed, immigration crimes have become some of the most common charges encountered in the federal courts (along with drug and fraud cases).

While the Supreme Court has disapproved of "roving" suspicionless stops of vehicles, it has upheld suspicionless stops of cars for brief questioning at fixed checkpoints at or near the border. See United States v. Martinez-Fuerte, 428 U.S. 543 (1976) (approves fixed checkpoint stops for brief questioning); United States v. Brignoni-Ponce, 422 U.S. 873 (1975) (disapproves roving stops in interior for questioning about immigration status); United States v. Ortiz, 422 U.S. 891 (1975) (disapproves roving immigration stops away from border to search interior of car); cf. United States v. Villamonte-Marquez, 462 U.S. 579 (1983) (approves suspicionless boarding of vessels at sea to inspect documentation). The Court has required reasonable suspicion for unusually long detentions of persons at the border. See United States v. Montoya de Hernandez, 473 U.S. 531 (1985); but cf. United States v. Flores-Montano, 541 U.S. 149 (2004) (Customs officials do not need individualized suspicion before removing, dismantling, and searching fuel tank of vehicle crossing the border, despite the fact that such searches were not routine).

9. *Airport and mass transit security checks.* Passengers who fly on commercial airlines must submit to unusually thorough inspections of their persons and belongings before they may approach the gate for boarding the airplane. What theory best explains this commonly accepted practice? Is it that the inspections do not amount to a "search" for Fourth Amendment purposes? That all passengers "consent" to the search when they purchase their tickets (including all the fine print buried on the back of the ticket or in the recesses of the airline websites)? See United States v. Hartwell, 296 F. Supp. 2d 596, 602 (E.D. Pa. 2003) ("No consensus has been reached as to the grounds justifying" an airport search). As we saw earlier, drivers do not consent to random searches for any and all of their travels on the road; some special justification is required for searches of cars that are not based on individualized suspicion. Would the rationale for airport searches apply equally well to searches of subway trains and other forms of mass transit? Does the choice of method of travel reflect different levels of privacy expectations?

10. *Changing airport security, changing reasonableness.* The security practices at airports change constantly, in response to the latest efforts by terrorists and criminals to bring weapons and explosives on board flights. If the consent of the people, at least in some broad sense, is necessary to make a search "reasonable," how might the government get feedback from the public about the reasonableness of its ever-changing intrusions into traveler privacy in airports? See Andrew E. Taslitz,

Fortune-Telling and the Fourth Amendment: Of Terrorism, Slippery Slopes, and Predicting the Future, 58 Rutgers L. Rev. 195 (2005).

11. *Warrant clause and reasonableness clause.* The materials in this chapter, dealing with *Terry* stops and frisks authorized on reasonable suspicion, as well as checkpoints authorized without suspicion, are all based on interpretations of the "reasonableness clause" of the Fourth Amendment. Recall that the text of the Fourth Amendment provides as follows: "The right of the people to be secure . . . against unreasonable searches and seizures, shall not be violated, and no Warrants shall issue, but upon probable cause. . . ." The first phrase (up to the word "violated") is known as the "reasonableness clause"; the second, the "warrant clause." What is the proper relationship between these clauses? Is the warrant clause a modifier to the reasonableness clause, defining the quintessential "reasonable" search and seizure, or do the clauses have independent meaning? If we are free to define reasonableness apart from the presence of a warrant and probable cause, then courts will need to determine in many different settings the proper measure of reasonableness. But if reasonableness is defined only in light of the warrant and probable cause requirements, then reasonableness in most settings becomes only a matter of determining how feasible it is to require police to show probable cause and obtain warrants. This is a question that we will revisit as we examine searches in several recurring contexts in Chapter 4.

III

Full Searches of People and Places: Basic Concepts

We now move from brief searches and stops to more extended and complete searches. This chapter describes the origins of the Fourth Amendment and the language of analogous provisions in state constitutions. Then it introduces key concepts that dominate the case law governing full searches: warrants, particularity, probable cause, warrantless searches in exigent circumstances, and consent searches.

Probable cause is the usual justification required to validate a full search. Courts have refused to provide a numerical threshold or categorical test for the probable cause standard, instead adopting a "common-sense," totality of circumstances approach. The judicial warrant is the procedure meant to ensure careful and early assessment of probable cause. To obtain a warrant, a government agent must demonstrate to a judge or magistrate, before the search happens, that the plan is justified. The warrant must also describe with particularity the place to be searched and the evidence to be seized. The particularity requirement reflects the historical concern with abusive general warrants and "writs of assistance," which allowed agents of the government to rummage indiscriminately through a person's belongings. After reviewing the historical underpinnings of the particularity requirement, the chapter discusses how particularity is difficult to enforce in contemporary searches, which often involve voluminous paper or digital evidence.

Courts have emphasized the importance of the warrant review as a disinterested check by a magistrate on the validity of searches and seizures. The Supreme Court has repeatedly held that "searches . . . without prior approval by judge or magistrate, are per se unreasonable under the Fourth Amendment—subject only to a few specifically established and well delineated exceptions." Katz v. United States, 389 U.S. 347 (1967). Yet the exceptions to the warrant requirement have been defined quite broadly over time. In practice, warrantless searches are the rule rather than the exception.

This chapter also examines two of the most commonly used exceptions to the warrant requirement: exigent circumstances and consent. Following this chapter's

135

survey of the most important tools for analyzing full searches, Chapter 4 applies these concepts in several contexts that recur time and again in judicial decisions and in the field.

A. WARRANT REQUIREMENTS

To be valid, warrants must be supported by probable cause and must particularly describe the place to be searched and the items to be seized. They must be issued by a neutral and detached magistrate and must be executed in a reasonable manner. This chapter reviews the requirements in greater detail and the concerns that each requirement reflects. To provide historical context, we begin by discussing the concerns that animated the drafters of the Fourth Amendment and led to the adoption of the particularity, probable cause, and warrant requirements.

1. General Search Warrants and the History of the Fourth Amendment

The police force is a nineteenth-century invention; the repressive government officers that most infuriated the colonists were tax and customs inspectors. These officials often carried out their work by using general warrants, which were broad grants of authority from the king of England or his representatives to search homes and businesses. One goal of this section is to identify the characteristics of government searches that constitutional drafters found most objectionable. Many historians and judges say that Americans were especially concerned with "general warrants." As you read, consider why general warrants were troubling to colonial lawyers.

In the 1760s, a series of English cases addressed the validity of general search warrants. The cases were civil tort actions against the individuals who issued and executed the warrants. The plaintiff in the following case, John Entick, published a series of pamphlets critical of the government. A minister of the government, Lord Halifax, considered the pamphlets libelous. He issued to his subordinates a "warrant" authorizing them to search for Entick (without specifying a place where they could look) and to seize him and his papers (without specifying which ones). Halifax's subordinates (or "messengers") executed the warrant and seized a great many of Entick's papers. Entick later brought a tort suit against Carrington, one of the messengers who had executed the warrant. The issue on appeal was whether the warrant was authorized by law (giving the searcher a legal defense) or was beyond the scope of the law, perhaps exposing those who created and executed the warrant to liability for the improper search.

After the opinion in *Entick*, we consider a type of general warrant used in the American colonies. Customs agents of the colonial governments, who enforced the highly unpopular and widely flouted tax laws for imports and exports, had all the powers of their English counterparts as they searched for taxable goods. Their power to search for goods sometimes took the form of "writs of assistance." Like a general warrant, the writ of assistance authorized the agent to search private premises, without specifying the place to search or the things to seize. These writs contained no real time limitation, for they expired only upon the death of the king. The writs also obligated all government officials and all subjects of the crown to assist the customs agent in the search. A reporter of proceedings in the court in the Massachusetts Bay colony describes below a 1755 application for a writ of assistance.

■ JOHN ENTICK v. NATHAN CARRINGTON
95 Eng. Rep. 807 (K.B. 1765)

In trespass; the plaintiff declares that the defendants . . . broke and entered the dwelling-house of the plaintiff . . . and continued there four hours without his consent and against his will, and all that time disturbed him in the peaceable possession thereof, and . . . searched and examined all the rooms, &c. in his dwelling-house, and all the boxes &c. so broke open, and read over, pryed into, and examined all the private papers, books, &c. of the plaintiff there found, whereby the secret affairs, &c. of the plaintiff became wrongfully discovered and made public; and took and carried away . . . printed pamphlets, &c. &c. of the plaintiff there found. [The defendants say] the plaintiff ought not to have his action against them, because they say, that before the supposed trespass . . . the Earl of Halifax was, and yet is, one of the Lords of the King's Privy Council, and one of his principal Secretaries of State, and that the earl . . . made his warrant under his hand and seal directed to the defendants, by which the earl did in the King's name authorize and require the defendants, taking a constable to their assistance, to make strict and diligent search for the plaintiff, mentioned in the said warrant to be the author . . . of several weekly very seditious papers . . . containing gross and scandalous reflections and invectives upon His Majesty's Government, and upon both Houses of Parliament, and him the plaintiff having found, to seize and apprehend and bring together with his books and papers in safe custody, before the Earl of Halifax to be examined. [The defendants argued that such warrants have frequently been granted by Secretaries of State since the Glorious Revolution of 1688 and have never been controverted. The jury found that the agents of Lord Halifax had committed the acts described by the plaintiff and was willing to award damages of 3,000 pounds if the court concluded that these facts constituted a trespass.]

[We] shall now consider the special justification, whether [the defense to a tort claim for trespass] can be supported in law, and this depends upon the jurisdiction of the Secretary of State; for if he has no jurisdiction to grant a warrant to break open doors, locks, boxes, and to seize a man and all his books, &c. in the first instance upon an information of his being guilty of publishing a libel, the warrant will not justify the defendants: it was resolved . . . in the case of Shergold v. Holloway, that a justice's warrant expressly to arrest the party will not justify the officer, there being no jurisdiction. The warrant in our case was an execution in the first instance, without any previous summons, examination, hearing the plaintiff, or proof that he was the author of the supposed libels; a power claimed by no other magistrate whatever . . . ; it was left to the discretion of these defendants to execute the warrant in the absence or presence of the plaintiff, when he might have no witness present to see what they did; for they were to seize all papers, bank bills, or any other valuable papers they might take away if they were so disposed; there might be nobody to detect them.

[In the case of Wilkes v. Wood (1763), involving a member of the House of Commons who had published an attack on the King and his ministers], all his books and papers were seized and taken away; we were told by one of these messengers that he was obliged by his oath to sweep away all papers whatsoever; if this is law it would be found in our books, but no such law ever existed in this country; our law holds the property of every man so sacred, that no man can set his foot upon his neighbour's close without his leave; if he does he is a trespasser, though he does no damage at all; if he will tread upon his neighbour's ground, he must justify it by law. [We] can safely say there is no law in this country to justify the defendants in what they have done; if there was, it would destroy all the comforts of society; for papers are often the dearest property a man can have. This case was compared to that of stolen goods; . . . but in that case the justice and the informer must proceed with great caution; there must be an oath that the party has had his goods stolen, and his strong reason to believe they are concealed in such a place; but if the goods are not found there, he is a trespasser; the officer in that case is a witness; there are none in this case, no inventory taken; if it had been legal many guards of property would have attended it. We shall now consider the usage of these warrants since the [Glorious] Revolution [of 1688]; if it began then, it is too modern to be law; the common law did not begin with the Revolution; the ancient constitution which had been almost overthrown and destroyed, was then repaired and revived; the Revolution added a new buttress to the ancient venerable edifice. [This] is the first instance of an attempt to prove a modern practice of a private office to make and execute warrants to enter a man's house, search for and take away all his books and papers in the first instance, to be law, which is not to be found in our books. It must have been the guilt or poverty of those upon whom such warrants have been executed, that deterred or hindered them from contending against the power of a Secretary of State and the Solicitor of the Treasury, or such warrants could never have passed for lawful till this time. We are . . . all of opinion that it cannot be justified by law. [If] a man is punishable for having a libel in his private custody, as many cases say he is, half the kingdom would be guilty in the case of a favourable libel, if libels may be searched for and seized by whomsoever and wheresoever the Secretary of State thinks fit. . . . Our law is wise and merciful, and supposes every man accused to be innocent before he is tried by his peers: upon the whole, we are all of opinion that this warrant is wholly illegal and void. One word more for ourselves; we are no advocates for libels, all Governments must set their faces against them, and whenever they come before us and a jury we shall set our faces against them; and if juries do not prevent them they may prove fatal to liberty, destroy Government and introduce anarchy; but tyranny is better than anarchy, and the worst Government better than none at all. Judgment for the plaintiff.

∎ THE WRITS OF ASSISTANCE
Quincy's Rep. (Mass.) App., 1:402-04, 453

To the Honourable his Majestys Justices of his Superiour Court for said Province to be held at York in and for the County of York on the third Tuesday of June 1755.

HUMBLY SHEWS Charles Paxton Esqr: That he is lawfully authorized to Execute the Office of Surveyor of all Rates Duties and Impositions arising and growing due to his Majesty at Boston in this Province & cannot fully Exercise said Office in such Manner as his Majestys Service and the Laws in such Cases Require Unless Your Honours who are vested with the Power of a Court of Exchequer for this Province will please to Grant him a Writ of Assistants, he therefore prays he & his Deputys may be Aided in the Execution of said office within his District by a Writ of Assistants under the Seal of this Superiour Court in Legal form & according to Usage in his Majestys Court of Exchequer & in Great Britain, & your Petitioner & Ca:

CHAS PAXTON

[The court issued the writ in the following form:]

GEORGE the Second by the Grace of God of Great Britain, France and Ireland King, Defender of the Faith &c — To all and singular Justices of the Peace, Sheriffs and Constables, and to all other our officers and Subjects within said Prov. & to each of you Greeting —

WHEREAS the Commissioners of our Customs have by their Deputation dated the 8th day of Jany 1752, assignd Charles Paxton Esqr Surveyor of all Rates, Duties, and Impositions arising and growing due within the Port of Boston in said Province as by said Deputation at large appears, WE THEREFORE command you and each of you that you permit ye said C.P. and his Deputies and Servants from Time to time at his or their Will as well in the day as in the Night to enter and go on board any Ship, Boat or other Vessell riding lying or being within or coming to the said Port or any Places or Creeks appertaining to said Port, such Ship, Boat or Vessell then & there found to View & Search & strictly to examine in the same, touching the Customs and Subsidies to us due, And also in the day Time together with a Constable or other public officer inhabiting near unto the Place to enter and go into any Vaults, Cellars, Warehouses, Shops or other Places to search and see whether any Goods, Wares or Merchandises, in ye same Ships, Boats or Vessells, Vaults, Cellars, Warehouses, Shops or other Places are or shall be there hid or concealed, having been imported, ship't or laden in order to be exported from or out of the said Port or any Creeks or Places appertain'g to the same Port; and to open any Trunks, Chests, Boxes, fardells [packages] or Packs made up or in Bulk, whatever in which any Goods, Wares, or Merchandises are suspected to be packed or concealed and further to do all Things which of Rt and according to Law and the Statutes in such Cases provided, is in this Part to be done: And We strictly command you and every of you that you, from Time to Time be aiding and assisting to the said C.P. his Deputies and Servants and every of them in the Execution of the Premises in all Things as becometh: Fail not at your Peril.

Notes

1. *The battle over general warrants and writs of assistance.* English judges were rejecting general warrants at the same time colonial officials in America were relying on such warrants more heavily. Lord Camden's decision in Entick v. Carrington is one of several decisions to declare that there was no statutory or other legal authority for general warrants in England. An equally famous decision, Wilkes v. Wood, 19 Howell's State Trials 1153 (C.P. 1763), involved a member of Parliament (John Wilkes) who wrote a series of pamphlets critical of the government and, like John Entick, became the target of government agents executing a general warrant. What concerns about general warrants does the *Entick* decision express? Did the *Entick* court simply want to encourage Parliament to enact clearer legislation authorizing such warrants? Or is it concerned more generally that the government agents had not provided an explanation for the proposed search before it began? Is the *Entick*

court troubled that a government official issued the warrant to his own subordinates? Why does it matter that the general warrants and writs of assistance name no particular target or place for a search? Notice also that the *Entick* court seemed troubled by the fact that the searches under these warrants took place with no witnesses present. What evils would witnesses help prevent? Try to identify, from these materials, a definition of general warrants that will enable you to spot their possible reemergence in modern doctrine and practice.

2. *American limits on general warrants.* Writs of assistance issued in the American colonies in the 1760s provoked arguments and protests similar to those found in the *Entick* decision. In a now famous (but at the time losing) argument against the validity of writs of assistance, James Otis criticized the writs in these terms:

> Now one of the most essential branches of English liberty, is the freedom of one's house. A man's house is his castle; and while he is quiet, he is as well guarded as a prince in his castle. This writ, if it should be declared legal, would totally annihilate this privilege. Custom house officers may enter our houses when they please—we are commanded to permit their entry—their menial servants may enter—may break locks, bars and every thing in their way—and whether they break through malice or revenge, no man, no court can inquire—bare suspicion without oath is sufficient.

2 Legal Papers of John Adams 113, 142 (L. Wroth & H. Zobel eds., 1965); see generally M. H. Smith, The Writs of Assistance Case (1978).

In June 1776, just before the American colonies declared their independence, Virginia adopted a Declaration of Rights that included this provision:

> That general warrants, whereby any officer or messenger may be commanded to search suspected places without evidence of a fact committed, or to seize any person or persons not named, or whose offense is not particularly described and supported by evidence, are grievous and oppressive, and ought not to be granted.

Other state constitutions imposed similar limits on searches and warrants. When the debate shifted from state constitutions to the new proposed federal constitution, many of the ratifying conventions in the states stipulated that they were approving the proposed federal constitution under the assumption that individual rights were implicit within the document and that an express Bill of Rights would soon be added. The First Congress elected under the new constitution immediately took up the task of drafting constitutional amendments dealing with basic liberties. James Madison presented to the House of Representatives a package of amendments, including one that addressed the problem of improper warrants:

> The rights of the people to be secured in their persons, their houses, their papers, and their other property, from all unreasonable searches and seizures, shall not be violated by warrants issued without probable cause, supported by oath or affirmation, or not particularly describing the places to be searched, or the persons or things to be seized.

After a House committee made some slight changes in language, the amendment came to the full House for a vote. At this point, some remarkable things happened. Rep. Egbert Benson of New York suggested that the provision was "good as far as it went" but was not sufficient. He proposed inserting the phrase "and no warrant shall issue" after the word "violated," so as to create two clauses, one addressing unreasonable searches and seizures generally and the other focused on warrants. Voting records of the convention showed that the House voted down Benson's proposed change "by a considerable majority." After the vote, the House appointed a committee to collect and summarize the various amendments it had approved over several days of debate. This so-called Committee of Three (which included Benson) placed on its list the search and seizure provision—as Benson had proposed amending it! The Senate and House both approved the language in this form, and the state conventions also ratified the text as follows:

> The right of the people to be secure in their persons, houses, papers, and effects, against unreasonable searches and seizures, shall not be violated, and no Warrants shall issue, but upon probable cause, supported by oath or affirmation, and particularly describing the place to be searched, and the persons or things to be seized.

See Nelson Lasson, The History and Development of the Fourth Amendment to the United States Constitution 100-103 (1937); Edward Dumbauld, The Bill of Rights and What It Means Today 35-42 (1957).

3. *Fourth Amendment history in the Supreme Court.* The concerns of the Constitution's framers figure into current interpretations of the Fourth Amendment. While the role of history rises and falls in different eras of the Supreme Court's search and seizure jurisprudence, history appears to be on the upswing. Consider this assertion by Justice Scalia in Wyoming v. Houghton, 526 U.S. 295, 299-300 (1999): "In determining whether a particular governmental action violates [the Fourth Amendment] provision, we inquire first whether the action was regarded as an unlawful search or seizure under the common law when the Amendment was framed. Where that inquiry yields no answer, we must evaluate the search or seizure under traditional standards of reasonableness . . . ." See David A. Sklansky, The Fourth Amendment and Common Law, 100 Colum. L. Rev. 1739, 1745-1770 (2000) (Justices in earlier periods focused on general warrants and writs of assistance and generalized from those controversies to the underlying evils; current justices read the Constitution in light of more particularized eighteenth-century common-law practices).

4. *Warranted searches and reasonable searches.* The incidents discussed most during constitutional debates involved *warranted* searches rather than warrantless searches. See Thomas Y. Davies, Recovering the Original Fourth Amendment, 98 Mich. L. Rev. 547, 551 (1999) ("[The] Framers understood 'unreasonable searches and seizures' simply as a pejorative label for the inherent illegality of any searches or seizures that might be made under general warrants"). Warrants issued from an authority with proper jurisdiction became a legal defense for the government officer in any tort suit against him for trespass during the search or seizure. As William Blackstone put it in his influential treatise on the common law of the period, "a lawful warrant will at all events indemnify the officer, who executes the same ministerially." 4 William Blackstone, Commentaries on the Laws of England *286. A messenger executing a warrant could defend against a tort suit by proving that the search was successful. Thus, warrants diminished the power of the jury in a tort suit to control government officers. See Akhil Reed Amar, Fourth Amendment First Principles, 107 Harv. L. Rev. 757 (1994); compare Ronald J. Alien & Ross M. Rosenberg, The Fourth Amendment and the Limits of Theory: Local Versus General Theoretical Knowledge, 72 St. John's L. Rev. 1149, 1169 (1998) (arguing that juries were not granted general power to determine reasonableness of searches).

The various uses of history in the interpretation of the Fourth Amendment will be a recurring theme over the next few chapters of this book. For additional resources in answering these questions, see the web extension for this chapter at *http://www.crimpro.com/extension/ch03*.

5. *Recent appearance of police departments.* The creators of the Fourth Amendment and the earliest analogs in state constitutions did not anticipate possible abuses by professional police officers, because police departments did not exist at the time. Most law enforcement was carried out by amateurs: citizens who volunteered (or who grudgingly took their turn) as constable or night watchman. There were local sheriffs, but they had no professional staff. Police departments as we think of them did not appear, even in the largest American cities, until late in the nineteenth century. See Lawrence M. Friedman, Crime and Punishment in American History 27-30 (1993); Carol Steiker, Second Thoughts About First Principles, 107 Harv. L. Rev. 820, 830-838 (1994). Does this major change in circumstance make history less relevant for interpreting the Fourth Amendment than it is for other constitutional language? See Anthony Amsterdam, Perspectives on the Fourth Amendment, 58 Minn. L. Rev. 349 (1974) (treating history as unhelpful).

6. *State analogs of the Fourth Amendment.* Courts did not treat the Fourth Amendment as a limit on the power of *state* governments (where most crimes are prosecuted) until Wolf v. Colorado, 338 U.S. 25 (1949). Although the federal Bill of Rights originally applied only to the federal government, the Fourteenth Amendment (passed after the Civil War) declared that "no state shall deprive any person of . . . liberty . . . without due process of law." During the 1940s and 1950s, the Supreme Court decided a series of cases, declaring that many of the rights guaranteed in the federal Bill of Rights were such a fundamental part of "due process" that they should apply to the states. The due process clause selectively "incorporated" these rights against state governments. See George C. Thomas, III, When Constitutional Worlds Collide: Resurrecting the Framers' Bill of Rights and Criminal Procedure, 100 Mich. L. Rev. 145 (2001). Before and after *Wolf,* however, states had their own constitutional limitations on state government action, parallel to the Fourth Amendment.

Today all states have a constitutional provision limiting the power of the government to conduct searches and seizures. About half of the states have a provision that tracks the language of the Fourth Amendment, some with only minor modifications. Other states have variations on the Fourth Amendment language that include additional procedural requirements. A typical requirement appears in article II, section 7 of the Colorado constitution, which says that affidavits must be in writing and that the person or thing to be seized must be described "as near as may be." A few states take aim at the specific problem of general warrants. For example, article I, section 7 of the Tennessee constitution states that "general warrants, whereby an officer may be commanded to search suspected places, without evidence of the fact committed, or to seize any person or persons not named, whose offenses are not particularly described and supported by evidence, are dangerous to liberty and ought not to be granted."

Other states emphasize the range of protected privacy rights of individuals. Article I, section 5 of the Louisiana constitution guarantees that the "person, property, communications, houses, papers, and effects" of every person shall be secure against "invasions of privacy." Arizona and Washington State frame the protection even more generally: "No person shall be disturbed in his private affairs, or his home invaded, without authority of law." The constitutions of about 10 states contain express protections for individual "privacy" rights. A number of these state constitutional provisions grew out of recent constitutional conventions, some as recent as the 1990s. See Robert Williams, Are State Constitutional Conventions a Thing of the Past? The Increasing Role of the Constitutional Commission in State Constitutional Change, 1 Hofstra L. & Pol'y Symp. 1 (1996).

7. *The interaction between probable cause and reasonableness.* Do the Fourth Amendment and its state constitutional analogs provide one standard to determine the validity of government searches and seizures? Is that standard probable cause or reasonableness? Are searches without probable cause presumptively (or conclusively) unreasonable? If reasonableness is not defined by reference to probable cause, how should it be defined?

2. Particularity in Warrants

Remember that the Fourth Amendment, in language echoed in many state provisions, says that "no Warrants shall issue, but upon probable cause, supported by Oath or affirmation, and particularly describing the place to be searched, and the persons or things to be seized." The following case explores the requirement that the warrant "particularly" describe the place to be searched and the persons or things to be seized. This "particularity" requirement captures an essential part of the distinction between valid warrants and invalid general warrants.

■ CHRISTOPHER WHEELER v. STATE
135 A.3d 282 (Del. 2016)

[Officers received information that Wheeler had sexually assaulted two minors (the W brothers) in the 1980s, as well as his own adopted son (NK, also a minor) at an unknown time. In July 2013, the two W brothers confronted Wheeler about the abuse, and he had email exchanges, phone conversations, and in-person discussions with them. Based on evidence received from the W brothers and NK, Wilmington police began investigating Wheeler for witness tampering charges in October 2013 and in the process obtained warrants authorizing the officers to search the following categories of items:]

3. Any personal computer, computer system, device or component to include desktop(s), laptop(s), notebook(s), PDA(s), or tower style systems capable of storing, retrieving, and/or processing magnetic, digital or optical data and in particular any such devices capable of connecting to or communicating with the Internet or Internet Service Providers by any means including dial-up, broadband, or wireless services.

4. Any digital or optical data storage device connected to, capable of being connected to, read by, or capable of being read by, any item described in paragraph 4, to include: internal or external hard drives (found within or without any item seized pursuant to paragraph 4), mass storage devices, pen drives, smart cards, compact disks (CD), compact disk—recordable (CD R)

or re-writable (CD RW), floppy diskettes, DVD+/- R or RW, or any other such device that stores digital data optically, electronically, or magnetically.

5. Any cellular telephone, to include the registry entries, call logs, pictures, video recordings, text messages, user names, buddy lists, screen names, telephone numbers, writings or other digital material as it relates to this investigation.

6. Any digital camera, digital video camera, optical camera, optical video camera, cell phone, or other device capable of capturing and storing to any media, photographs or images and the associated media there from [sic].

7. Any and all data, and the forensic examination thereof, stored by whatever means on any items seized pursuant to paragraphs 4, 5, and 6, as described above to include but not limited to: registry entries, pictures, images, temporary internet files, internet history files, chat logs, writings, passwords, user names, buddy names, screen names, email, connection logs, or other evidence.

8. Any file, writing, log, artifact, paper, document, billing record or other instrument, stored electronically or in printed form, which relates to or references the owner of items seized pursuant to paragraphs . . . 3, 4, 5, 6, 7 and 8, as described above. . . .

THE PARTICULARITY REQUIREMENT PRESENTS DIFFICULT CHALLENGES IN THE CONTEXT OF COMPUTER SEARCHES

Warrants directed to digital information present unique challenges in satisfying the particularity requirement, given the unprecedented volume of private information stored on devices containing such data. The expansive universe of digital and electronic information, and the intermingling data, complicates balancing the privacy interests of our citizens and the legitimate efforts of law enforcement in investigating criminal activity. . . .

The United States Constitution specifies only two matters that must be "particularly" described in the warrant: "the place to be searched" and "the persons or things to be seized." Satisfying the particularity requirement is difficult in the electronic search warrant context, given the commingling of relevant and irrelevant information and the complexities of segregating responsive files ex ante. [It] would be folly for a search warrant to structure the mechanics of the search because imposing such limits would unduly restrict legitimate search objectives. . . . Nonetheless, in an oft-quoted passage of Marron v. United States, 275 U.S. 192 (1927), the United States Supreme Court observed that "[the] requirement that warrants shall particularly describe the things to be seized makes general searches under them impossible and prevents the seizure of one thing under a warrant describing another. As to what is to be taken, nothing is left to the discretion of the officer executing the warrant." Accordingly, the United States Supreme Court has suggested that warrants that fail to describe the specific crime that has been or is being committed do not satisfy the particularity requirement. . . .

Warrants must be tested by courts in a commonsense and realistic fashion, and reviewing courts should avoid a hypertechnical approach. . . . Some irrelevant files may have to be at least cursorily perused to determine whether they are within the authorized search ambit. Accordingly, the proper metric of sufficient specificity is whether it was reasonable to provide a more specific description of the items at that juncture of the investigation.

Further, the propensity of criminals to disguise files must be balanced against the competing interest of avoiding unrestrained general searches: It is unrealistic to expect a warrant to prospectively restrict the scope of a search by directory, filename or extension or to attempt to structure search methods — that process must remain dynamic. [It] is clear that because criminals can — and often do — hide, mislabel, or manipulate files to conceal criminal activity, a broad, expansive search of the hard drive may be required. Consequently, it would likely unduly restrict law enforcement to require the crafting of specific keyword searches or identification of file names and extensions ex ante. In some instances, the technological reality may be that, in the end, there may be no practical substitute for actually looking in many (perhaps all) folders and sometimes at the documents contained within those folders, and that is true whether the search is of computer files or physical files. [No] tenet of the Fourth Amendment prohibits a search merely because it cannot be performed with surgical precision. . . .

We have considered how other courts have addressed similar claims. . . . Recently, in State v. Castagnola, 46 N.E.3d 638 (Ohio 2015), the Supreme Court of Ohio considered the application of the particularity requirement of the Fourth Amendment to the search of a computer. There, the initial search warrant related to the crimes of retaliation, criminal trespassing, criminal damaging, and possession of criminal tools. The warrant sought the following:

> Records and documents either stored on computers, ledgers, or any other electronic recording device to include hard drives and external portable hard drives, cell phones, printers, storage devices of any kind, printed out copies of text messages or emails, cameras, video recorders or any photo imaging devices and their storage media to include tapes, compact discs, or flash drives.

Looking for "evidence of intimidation" on the defendant's computer, the forensic examiner used a software program that goes through "documents, images, videos on the hard drive." The examiner also performed a keyword search that did not yield any responsive results, before proceeding to open a tab that maintained "all the images associated with the drive being examined." After accessing the tab, the examiner discovered images that she thought were child pornography, stopped her investigation, and applied for another warrant. When performing a search based on the second search warrant, the forensic examiner discovered "over a thousand videos and images of suspected child pornography."

In considering the defendant's motion to suppress, the Supreme Court of Ohio scrutinized the instrument's grant of authority to search and seize "records and documents . . . stored on computers," finding that its plain language demonstrated that there was "no limitation on what records and documents were to be searched for in [the defendant's] computer." The court held that the challenged search warrant failed to satisfy the particularity requirement for two reasons. First, the language of the search warrant did not "guide and control" the forensic examiner's judgment as to what was to be seized on the computer, leaving the determination as to what to seize within the discretion of the examiner. Second, "the broad language" of the search warrant clearly included items that were not subject to seizure, such that the instrument was not as specific as "the circumstances and the nature of the activity under investigation permitted. . . ."

The Ohio Supreme Court rejected the idea that the Fourth Amendment required a search warrant to specify restrictive search protocols. But it also recognized "that the Fourth Amendment does prohibit a sweeping comprehensive search of a computer's hard drive." The guiding metric applied by the court was that "officers must describe what they believe will be found on a computer with as much specificity as possible under the circumstances," and that this will "enable the searcher to narrow his or her search to only the items to be seized." With this guidance, we turn to the warrants at issue here. . . .

The Witness Tampering Warrants Have No Temporal Limitations, Despite Relevant Dates Being Available to the Police

A key principle distilled from the jurisprudence in this area is that warrants, in order to satisfy the particularity requirement, must describe what investigating officers believe will be found on electronic devices with as much specificity as possible under the circumstances. That principle simply was not followed here in several respects. One obvious respect was the failure to limit the search to the relevant time frame. . . .

We hesitate to prescribe rigid rules and instead reiterate that warrants must designate the things to be searched and seized as particularly as possible. Striking the correct balance when protecting against generality and overbreadth requires vigilance on the part of judicial officers who are on the front lines of preserving constitutional rights while assisting government officials in the legitimate pursuit of prosecuting criminal activity. Where, as here, the investigators had available to them a more precise description of the alleged criminal activity that is the subject of the warrant, such information should be included in the instrument and the search and seizure should be appropriately narrowed to the relevant time period so as to mitigate the potential for unconstitutional exploratory rummaging.

The State conceded that nothing relating to NK would be found on Wheeler's property identified in the Witness Tampering Warrants. And the Affidavits do not suggest otherwise. As to the only other potential victims, the W brothers, the Affidavits indicate that the alleged witness tampering occurred, if it did, in or after July 2013, since that was when the W brothers renewed contact with Wheeler. The Affidavits contain no facts suggesting that any tampering might have occurred prior to July 2013. Yet, the Witness Tampering Warrants were boundless as to time. Sergeant Perna testified that one of the first things he did in executing the search was determine when the iMac was last used. Proceeding under the Witness Tampering Warrants, he determined that the computer had last been powered on in September 2012. However, the State unsystematically sifted through Wheeler's digital universe, even though the iMac logically could not have contained material created or recorded during the relevant time period.

A failure to describe the items to be searched for and seized with as much particularity as the circumstances reasonably allow offends the constitutional protections against unreasonable searches and seizures. Because the State was able to more precisely describe the items to be searched and seized, the Witness Tampering Warrants violated the particularity requirement. . . .

*THE WITNESS TAMPERING WARRANTS LIKELY FAIL THE PARTICULARITY
REQUIREMENT FOR OTHER REASONS*

The Witness Tampering Warrants likely fail the particularity requirement in other respects. For example, nothing in the Affidavits supports an inference that evidence may be found on DVDs or optical cameras. The Affidavits do not allege that Wheeler was communicating with NK or any of the W brothers through videos or pictures. Nor do the Affidavits link witness tampering to these types of media. The likely reason that the Witness Tampering Warrants sought the search for and seizure of devices and items that cannot lead to evidence of witness tampering based on the Affidavits is that, as the State conceded, the language was essentially copied and pasted from a search warrant for child pornography. Although the parties agree that cutting and pasting search warrant language does not automatically invalidate the resulting instrument, that technique has led, in the context of this case, to search warrants that do not satisfy the particularity requirement.

Further, the Affidavits recite that the State was searching for "evidence of written communications," which it believed were relevant to the alleged witness tampering. Sergeant Perna wrote in his forensic report and testified that he was "looking for any files created and/or saved as word documents, emails, text messages, pdf [sic] or any other related file format." The portions of the Affidavits discussing the items sought refer to written communications. These observations suggest that the items for which there was probable cause to search and seize were written communications—not DVDs and optical cameras. Yet, by their terms, the Witness Tampering Warrants permitted the State to search for anything—from child pornography to medical records to consumer information to tax returns. In short, they permitted the species of wide-ranging, exploratory searches the Framers intended to prohibit. Because the lack of temporal limitations is sufficient to invalidate the Witness Tampering Warrants, we need not reach these other potential substantive challenges. Instead, we caution that the risk that warrants for digital and electronic devices take on the character of "general warrants" is substantial. This reality necessitates heightened vigilance, at the outset, on the part of judicial officers to guard against unjustified invasions of privacy.

The subject of this prosecution is an unsympathetic figure. And the sexual exploitation of children is a dreadful scourge in our society. But the principles laid down in this opinion affect the very essence of constitutional liberty and security. . . . There is always a temptation in criminal cases to let the end justify the means, but as guardians of the Constitution, we must resist that temptation.

Notes

1. *Particular description of place to be searched: majority position.* Both state and federal constitutions require that the warrant name with "particularity" the place to be searched and the things to be seized. Consider first how the particularity requirement applies to different dwellings. When a warrant lists property in an urban setting, the street address (including the apartment number, where relevant) is usually particular enough to allow the searching officer "with reasonable effort [to] ascertain and identify the place intended." Steele v. United States, 267 U.S. 498 (1925). Property in a rural setting might be described without an address. Could a warrant

listing more than one place to search ever be valid? Does it matter if different people own or occupy the properties? Compare State v. Mehner, 480 N.W.2d 872 (Iowa 1992) (validating warrant listing two house trailers with different occupants), with State v. Marshall, 974 A.2d 1038 (N.J. 2009) (warrant that listed address of house containing duplex units, leaving officers uncertain which unit to search, violated particularity requirement).

Warrants tend to be more specific about the place to be searched than about any persons to be searched. Why is that? If you were a magistrate, what sort of evidence would convince you to issue a warrant authorizing the search of a specific bar and "all persons" found on those premises? See State v. Thomas, 540 N.W.2d 658 (Iowa 1995) (invalidating warrant; application noted numerous prior arrests and controlled purchases of crack cocaine, and observations by undercover officers that most persons present in bar possessed narcotics or weapons).

2. *Particular description of things to be seized: majority position.* Warrants authorize searches for particular objects. The types of objects that may be seized include fruits, instrumentalities, and evidence of crime. The Fourth Amendment requirement of particularity makes general searches "impossible and prevents the seizure of one thing under a warrant describing another. As to what is taken, nothing is left to the discretion of the officer executing the warrant." Marron v. United States, 275 U.S. 192 (1927). What sort of description in the warrant would leave "nothing" to the discretion of the officer? See People v. Brown, 749 N.E.2d 170 (N.Y. 2001) (warrant naming four particular items plus authorizing search for "any other property the possession of which would be considered contraband" was overbroad).

Like the federal constitution, most state constitutions and statutes also require a description of the items (or persons) being sought and an explanation for why the applicant believes that the items (or persons) are at the location sought. See Ohio Rev. Code §2933.24(A) (search warrant shall "particularly name or describe the property to be searched for and seized, the place to be searched, and the person to be searched").

How can a warrant constrain the discretion of an officer during a digital search? As the *Wheeler* court noted, officers have to examine some files in a cursory fashion to determine whether they fall within the scope of the warrant. In addition, file names may be intentionally mislabeled to prevent a search from succeeding. Given these practical considerations, can magistrates impose meaningful restrictions on the search of digital devices?

The consequences are severe when the warrant fails to describe particularly the items to be seized. In Groh v. Ramirez, 540 U.S. 551 (2004), the Supreme Court held that a search warrant failing to describe the items to be seized from a home could not be cured by the agent's inclusion of a list of the items in an unincorporated warrant application, or by his oral description to the homeowners of the items to be seized.

3. *Plain view seizures.* You may recall, from Chapter 2, the "plain view" doctrine, which declares that the police do not conduct a "search" when they view an item out in the open, visible from a proper location. In addition to viewing the item, police may seize evidence, contraband, or the fruits or instrumentalities of crime that come within the "plain view" of police officers during proper execution of a valid warrant. See Horton v. California, 496 U.S. 128 (1990) (item in plain view is seizable if its incriminating character is immediately apparent to police). Under

the "plain view" doctrine, an officer must meet several requirements before seizing the item. The officer's ability to complete the seizure will depend primarily on where the item is located. If it is located in an unprotected area (such as the open bed of a pickup truck or an apartment where the officer already has obtained legal access) the officer may seize the item so long as there is probable cause to believe that it is contraband or evidence of a crime or otherwise subject to seizure. If the item is located in a protected area (such as the interior of a building that the officer observes from a point outside), most courts require the officer to obtain a search warrant or to explain why an exception to the warrant requirement is necessary. See Coolidge v. New Hampshire, 403 U.S. 443 (1971) (warrantless seizure of item in plain view is acceptable if officer observes item from lawful location, its incriminating nature is immediately apparent, and officer has lawful right of access to the object).

State and federal courts also require that the incriminating nature of the item in plain view be "immediately apparent" before the officer can seize an item in plain view. When the item in plain view is an illicit drug or other contraband, the incriminating nature of the item is easy to see. In other cases, the incriminating nature of the item might not be apparent to the average observer, but the police officer conducting the search will often know enough about the ongoing investigation to link the items she sees to the crime she is investigating. See State v. Chrisman, 514 N.W.2d 57 (Iowa 1994) (tennis shoes incriminating in light of footprints at crime scene). The incriminating nature of the item is "immediately apparent" if there is probable cause to believe that it is evidence of a crime.

Under federal law and the law of most states, the police may observe and seize an item in plain view, even if the officer intended to find it. See Horton v. California, 496 U.S. 128 (1990):

> Evenhanded law enforcement is best achieved by the application of objective standards of conduct, rather than standards that depend upon the subjective state of mind of the officer. The fact that an officer is interested in an item of evidence and fully expects to find it in the course of a search should not invalidate its seizure if the search is confined in area and duration by the terms of a warrant or a valid exception to the warrant requirement.

A strong minority of states take up a suggestion in older U.S. Supreme Court cases and insist that the police officer "inadvertently" discover the item in plain view before the officer can seize it. If the officer had reason to expect the discovery, he cannot seize the item. See Commonwealth v. Balicki, 762 N.E.2d 290 (Mass. 2002). Why don't most courts care about the motives of the police officer in obtaining the plain view? See State v. Nieves, 999 A.2d 389 (N.H. 2010). What police purpose might be objectionable? Is this debate over "inadvertence" the same as the disagreement reviewed above over "pretextual" stops, or are different interests at stake here?

4. *The advantage for police of warrants listing small items.* The nature of the items sought will determine the permissible scope of the search. If police are looking for an elephant, the search will be limited to places an elephant might hide. If police are looking for a field mouse, the scope of the search would be much broader. See, e.g., State v. Apelt, 861 P.2d 634 (Ariz. 1993) (because warrant included receipts, police could conduct a very detailed search and had a higher possibility of additional "plain view" discovery of evidence than in a more narrowly circumscribed

search). Would it be ethical to advise police to include small items such as receipts in all warrant applications?

Does the "plain view" authorization to seize items not named in the warrant effectively eliminate any requirement that the warrant "particularly name" the property to be seized? In digital search cases, some magistrates have imposed search protocols that prohibit the prosecution from using any incriminating evidence obtained under the "plain view" exception. Should appellate courts abolish the "plain view" exception altogether in digital search cases?

5. *The "four corners" rule.* If a defendant challenges the sufficiency of a warrant during a suppression hearing, statutes and court rules in most jurisdictions (and constitutional rulings in a few others) prevent the government from supplementing the warrant application itself with information that the officers knew at the time but failed to present to the magistrate. Some also prevent the government from relying on any information supplementing the application, even if it was actually presented to the magistrate. Greenstreet v. State, 898 A.2d 961 (Md. 2006). The government's defense of the warrant, in other words, must come from within the "four corners" of the application. Some states allow courts to supplement the "four corners" of the affidavit with information that could be "reasonably inferred" from the document, while a few others (about 10 states) go further and say that the court is free to use outside information at its discretion. See Moore v. Commonwealth, 159 S.W.3d 325, 328 (Ky. 2005). Various applications of the four corners rule can be found on the web extension for this chapter at *http://www.crimpro.com/extension/ch03.*

6. *Challenges to facially sufficient warrants.* Defendants sometimes concede that the facts set forth in the affidavit amount to probable cause but contend that the factual basis for the warrant is untrue. The Supreme Court has held (and state courts have largely agreed) that if a defendant makes a preliminary showing of false statements in the warrant application, the trial court must grant a hearing on the question. Under Franks v. Delaware, 438 U.S. 154 (1978), the defendant's preliminary showing must demonstrate that the government "knowingly and intentionally, or with reckless disregard for the truth," included a false statement in the warrant affidavit. The attack must be "more than conclusory," and must point out "specifically with supporting reasons" the portion of the warrant affidavit that is claimed to be false. It also must be accompanied by affidavits or reliable statements of witnesses, or a satisfactory explanation of their absence. If the unreliable evidence was necessary to the government's showing of probable cause, the defendant gets a hearing and must establish the claims by a preponderance of the evidence before the fruits of the search or seizure are excluded from evidence. See State v. Chenoweth, 158 P.3d 595 (Wash. 2007) (state constitution, like federal law, requires suppression of evidence only if officer seeking a search warrant makes an omission or misrepresentation through reckless or intentional disregard for the truth; negligence by affiant does not require suppression).

7. *Awareness of error in a warrant.* Does it make a difference whether the officer remains unaware of the inaccuracy until she has begun the search? In Maryland v. Garrison, 480 U.S. 79 (1987), the search warrant listed the third floor as a single apartment, when it was actually divided into separate apartments. The Court held that it was reasonable for officers to execute the warrant because they were reasonable in not discovering the inadvertent error in the warrant. What should police officers do when they obtain new information about the person or place

named in the warrant before they execute the warrant? Return to the magistrate for an updated finding of probable cause? See State v. Maddox, 98 P.3d 1199 (Wash. 2004) (officers must return to magistrate for updated ruling only if new facts negate probable cause).

8. *The wrong jurisdiction.* Is an otherwise valid warrant still valid if it is executed by police accidentally acting outside of their jurisdiction? See People v. Martinez, 898 P.2d 28 (Colo. 1995) (error in jurisdiction, despite violating statute, not fatal).

Problem 3-1. Errors in a Facially Valid Warrant

Officer Holden observed a confidential informant make two illegal purchases of weapons at 916 Varney Street. Both times, the informant entered the building, returned with the weapons, and told Holden that he made the purchases in the "last apartment, of two, on the left" in a hallway down a flight of stairs. With this information, Holden applied for and obtained a warrant to search the apartment. The affidavit accompanying the application described the premises as follows:

> First-floor corner apartment, 916 Varney Street, described as a four-story red-brick structure with a green-colored solid door, with the number 916 affixed to the outside of the main entryway. The corner apartment is described as down one flight of stairs where three apartment doors are situated with two on the left side and one on the right side, the door is tan in color and is the second door on the left side in the main hallway at the end of the hall.

Prior to executing the warrant, Holden sent the informant into the building for a third time. After returning outside, he told Holden that the apartment subject to the warrant had a rug in front of the door. When Holden entered the hallway of the building, he realized that the informant was mistaken: There were two doors on the right side of the hallway and only one on the left. Holden decided to search the sole apartment on the left because there was a rug outside the door. He discovered evidence of weapons violations.

In a suppression hearing, will the court treat the evidence as the product of a valid warranted search? Compare Buckner v. United States, 615 A.2d 1154 (D.C. 1992).

3. Probable Cause

The two most important standards in modern criminal procedure for justifying stops, searches, and seizures are reasonable suspicion (examined in Chapter 2) and probable cause. Probable cause is the central standard of traditional search and seizure law, and it continues to govern a large portion of full-fledged searches and seizures, including those based on warrants.

a. Standards for Defining Probable Cause

Probable cause is constantly applied but only rarely defined. Perhaps this is because the assessment of probable cause is an inherently fact-laden, case-specific sort of judgment. While some situations arise frequently enough for standards to develop (for example, how information from an unnamed informant should be assessed to determine probable cause), general principles are difficult to deduce.

A close analysis of case law and a handful of statutes suggest that general definitions of probable cause do exist and that there is some interesting variation among those definitions. The most common definition emerges from language used by the Supreme Court in Brinegar v. United States, 338 U.S. 160, 175-176 (1949), reprinted below. See Wesley Oliver, The Modern History of Probable Cause, 78 Tenn. L. Rev. 377 (2011). Four elements, not all of which are present in every definition, tend to capture the variation in definitions of probable cause.

Reasonable to whom. Most jurisdictions focus on the assessment that a "reasonably prudent" or "cautious" person would make in deciding whether probable cause exists. Some jurisdictions, however, focus on the information that a *police officer* knows. Would officers make the same connections and assessment as a citizen without law enforcement experience or training? Kentucky requires the assessment of probable cause to be reasonable to the magistrate. Would experienced magistrates make the same assessments as police?

Strength of inference. Several formulations define the required strength of the link between the facts offered and the conclusion that criminal activity has occurred. One common formulation says the magistrate must determine whether the facts suggest a "probability of criminal activity." Another says the magistrate must determine whether the facts are sufficient "to believe an offense has been committed." Yet another standard requires that the investigator "believe or consciously entertain a strong suspicion that the person is guilty." A few jurisdictions require merely that there be a "substantial basis for concluding that the articles mentioned are probably present" at the place to be searched.

Can these formulations be translated into probabilities of criminal activity? For example, do some of them mean less than 50 percent, while others mean a 50-50 chance, and still others mean more likely than not? Alone among the states, Oregon answers this question by statute. Oregon Rev. Stat. §131.005(11) states that probable cause "means that there is a substantial objective basis for believing that more likely than not an offense has been committed and a person to be arrested has committed it."

Comparison to other standards. Some jurisdictions not only define the probable cause standard but also suggest its limits through comparison with other procedural standards. For example, several states say that probable cause is "more than mere suspicion or possibility but less than certainty." Some states note that the determination of probable cause requires less confidence that a crime has occurred than is required for guilt (that is, proof beyond a reasonable doubt). As we saw in Chapter 2, the "reasonable suspicion" demands less of a showing by police than probable cause.

Quality of information. Some jurisdictions enhance their general definition of probable cause by requiring that the assessment be based on evidence that is reliable, trustworthy, or credible. The following chart excerpts typical language from the case law, constitutional provisions, and statutes in selected states. You can find further details about typical sources for such definitions on the web extension for this chapter at *http://www.crimpro.com/extension/ch03.*

State	Information to Be Considered	Quality of Information	Perspective	Nature of Belief	Degree of Certainty
Arizona	Facts and circumstances,	based on trustworthy information [such that a]	person of reasonable caution [would believe that]	items are related to criminal activity and likely to be found at the place described.	The showing is one of criminal activity, not the rigorous standard required for admissibility of evidence at trial.
California	A particularized suspicion or facts [sufficient]	to entertain a strong suspicion [such that a]	person of ordinary caution [would find that the]	object of the search is in the particular place to be searched.	The government need not demonstrate certainty.
Colorado	Sufficient facts [that a]		person of reasonable caution [would conclude that]	contraband or evidence of criminal activity is located at the place to be searched.	This judgment is one of reasonableness, not pure mathematical probability.
Connecticut	All information set forth in affidavit [such that the]	totality of the circumstances [could lead a]	magistrate [to conclude that]	contraband or evidence will be found in a particular place [with a]	fair probability.
South Dakota	The existence of facts and circumstances within the knowledge of the magistrate [such that a]		reasonable prudent man [would conclude that]	an offense has been or is being committed and the property exists at the place designated [to a]	probability.

■ VIRGIL BRINEGAR v. UNITED STATES
338 U.S. 160 (1949)

RUTLEDGE, J.*

. . . At about six o'clock on the evening of March 3, 1947, Malsed, an investigator of the Alcohol Tax Unit, and Creehan, a special investigator, were parked in a car beside a highway near the Quapaw Bridge in northeastern Oklahoma. The point was about five miles west of the Missouri-Oklahoma line. Brinegar drove past headed west in his Ford coupe. Malsed had arrested him about five months earlier for illegally transporting liquor; had seen him loading liquor into a car or truck in Joplin, Missouri, on at least two occasions during the preceding six months; and knew him to have a reputation for hauling liquor. As Brinegar passed, Malsed recognized both him and the Ford. He told Creehan, who was driving the officers' car, that Brinegar was the driver of the passing car. Both agents later testified that the

* [Chief Justice Vinson and Justices Black, Reed, Douglas, Burton, and Minton joined in this opinion. Justices Jackson, Frankfurter, and Murphy dissented.—EDS.]

car, but not especially its rear end, appeared to be "heavily loaded" and "weighted down with something." Brinegar increased his speed as he passed the officers. They gave chase. After pursuing him for about a mile at top speed, they gained on him as his car skidded on a curve, sounded their siren, overtook him, and crowded his car to the side of the road by pulling across in front of it. The highway was one leading from Joplin, Missouri, toward Vinita, Oklahoma, Brinegar's home. [The officers searched the car and found 13 cases of liquor. Brinegar was charged with importing intoxicating liquor into Oklahoma from Missouri in violation of the federal statute that forbids such importation contrary to the laws of any state. The trial judge denied the motion to suppress. Even though the facts described above did not constitute probable cause, the judge believed that certain statements Brinegar made after he was stopped gave the officers probable cause to search.]

The crucial question is whether there was probable cause for Brinegar's arrest, in the light of prior adjudications on this problem, more particularly Carroll v. United States, 267 U.S. 132 (1925), which on its face most closely approximates the situation presented here. The *Carroll* [court ruled] that the facts presented amounted to probable cause for the search of the automobile there involved.

In the *Carroll* case three federal prohibition agents and a state officer stopped and searched the defendants' car on a highway leading from Detroit to Grand Rapids, Michigan, and seized a quantity of liquor discovered in the search. About three months before the search, the two defendants and another man called on two of the agents at an apartment in Grand Rapids and, unaware that they were dealing with federal agents, agreed to sell one of the agents three cases of liquor. Both agents noticed the Oldsmobile roadster in which the three men came to the apartment and its license number. Presumably because the official capacity of the proposed purchaser was suspected by the defendants, the liquor was never delivered.

About a week later the same two agents, while patrolling the road between Grand Rapids and Detroit on the lookout for violations of the National Prohibition Act, were passed by the defendants, who were proceeding in a direction from Grand Rapids toward Detroit in the same Oldsmobile roadster. The agents followed the defendants for some distance but lost track of them. Still later, on the occasion of the search, while the officers were patrolling the same highway, they met and passed the defendants, who were in the same roadster, going in a direction from Detroit toward Grand Rapids. Recognizing the defendants, the agents turned around, pursued them, stopped them about sixteen miles outside Grand Rapids, searched their car and seized the liquor it carried.

This Court ruled that the information held by the agents, together with the judicially noticed fact that Detroit was "one of the most active centers for introducing illegally into this country spirituous liquors for distribution into the interior," constituted probable cause for the search.

I.

Obviously the basic facts held to constitute probable cause in the *Carroll* case were very similar to the basic facts here. . . . In each instance the officers were patrolling the highway in the discharge of their duty. And in each before stopping the car or starting to pursue it they recognized both the driver and the car, from recent personal contact and observation, as having been lately engaged in illicit liquor dealings. Finally, each driver was proceeding in his identified car in a direction from a known source of liquor supply toward a probable illegal market, under circumstances indicating no other probable purpose than to carry on his illegal adventure.

[There were also variations in details of the proof in the two cases.] In *Carroll* the agent's knowledge of the primary and ultimate fact that the accused were engaged in liquor running was derived from the defendants' offer to sell liquor to the agents some three months prior to the search, while here that knowledge was derived largely from Malsed's personal observation, reinforced by hearsay; . . . and in *Carroll* the Court took judicial notice that Detroit was on the international boundary and an active center for illegal importation of spirituous liquors for distribution into the interior, while in this case the facts that Joplin, Missouri, was a ready source of supply for liquor and Oklahoma a place of likely illegal market were known to the agent Malsed from his personal observation and experience as well as from facts of common knowledge. . . .

There were of course some legal as well as some factual differences in the two situations. Under the statute in review in *Carroll* the whole nation was legally dry. Not only the manufacture, but the importation, transportation and sale of intoxicating liquors were prohibited throughout the country. Under the statute now in question only the importation of such liquors contrary to the law of the state into which they are brought and in which they were seized is forbidden.

[The probable place of market for Brinegar may have been] the State of Oklahoma as a whole or its populous northeastern region. From the facts of record we know, as the agents knew, that Oklahoma was a "dry" state. At the time of the search, its law forbade the importation of intoxicating liquors from other states. . . . This fact, taken in connection with the known "wet" status of Missouri and the location of Joplin close to the Oklahoma line, affords a very natural situation for persons inclined to violate the Oklahoma and federal statutes to ply their trade. The proof therefore concerning the source of supply, the place of probable destination and illegal market, and hence the probability that Brinegar was using the highway for the forbidden transportation, was certainly no less strong than the showing in these respects in the *Carroll* case.

Finally, as for the most important potential distinction, namely, that concerning the primary and ultimate fact that the petitioner was engaging in liquor running, Malsed's personal observation of Brinegar's recent activities established that he was so engaged quite as effectively as did the agent's prior bargaining with the defendants in the *Carroll* case. He saw Brinegar loading liquor, in larger quantities than would be normal for personal consumption, into a car or a truck in Joplin on other occasions during the six months prior to the search. He saw the car Brinegar was using in this case in use by him at least once in Joplin within that period and followed it. And several months prior to the search he had arrested Brinegar for unlawful transportation of liquor and this arrest had resulted in an indictment which was pending at the time of this trial. . . .

II.

Guilt in a criminal case must be proved beyond a reasonable doubt and by evidence confined to that which long experience in the common-law tradition, to some extent embodied in the Constitution, has crystallized into rules of evidence consistent with that standard. These rules are historically grounded rights of our system, developed to safeguard men from dubious and unjust convictions, with resulting forfeitures of life, liberty and property. . . .

In dealing with probable cause, however, as the very name implies, we deal with probabilities. These are not technical; they are the factual and practical considerations of everyday life on which reasonable and prudent men, not legal technicians, act. The standard of proof is accordingly correlative to what must be proved.

The substance of all the definitions of probable cause is a reasonable ground for belief of guilt. And this means less than evidence which would justify condemnation or conviction. [It] has come to mean more than bare suspicion: Probable cause exists where the facts and circumstances within [the officers'] knowledge and of which they had reasonably trustworthy information [are] sufficient in themselves to warrant a man of reasonable caution in the belief that an offense has been or is being committed.

These long-prevailing standards seek to safeguard citizens from rash and unreasonable interferences with privacy and from unfounded charges of crime. They also seek to give fair leeway for enforcing the law in the community's protection. Because many situations which confront officers in the course of executing their duties are more or less ambiguous, room must be allowed for some mistakes on their part. But the mistakes must be those of reasonable men, acting on facts leading sensibly to their conclusions of probability. The rule of probable cause is a practical, nontechnical conception affording the best compromise that has been found for accommodating these often opposing interests. Requiring more would unduly hamper law enforcement. To allow less would be to leave law-abiding citizens at the mercy of the officers' whim or caprice.

The troublesome line posed by the facts in the *Carroll* case and this case is one between mere suspicion and probable cause. That line necessarily must be drawn by an act of judgment formed in the light of the particular situation and with account taken of all the circumstances. No problem of searching the home or any other place of privacy was presented either in *Carroll* or here. Both cases involve freedom to use public highways in swiftly moving vehicles for dealing in contraband, and to be unmolested by investigation and search in those movements. In such a case the citizen who has given no good cause for believing he is engaged in that sort of activity is entitled to proceed on his way without interference. But one who recently and repeatedly has given substantial ground for believing that he is engaging in the forbidden transportation in the area of his usual operations has no such immunity, if the officer who intercepts him in that region knows that fact at the time he makes the interception and the circumstances under which it is made are not such as to indicate the suspect going about legitimate affairs.

This does not mean, as seems to be assumed, that every traveler along the public highways may be stopped and searched at the officers' whim, caprice or mere suspicion. The question presented in the *Carroll* case lay on the border between suspicion and probable cause. But the Court carefully considered that problem and resolved it by concluding that the facts within the officers' knowledge when they intercepted the *Carroll* defendants amounted to more than mere suspicion and constituted probable cause for their action. We cannot say this conclusion was wrong, or was so lacking in reason and consistency with the Fourth Amendment's purposes that it should now be overridden. Nor, as we have said, can we find in the present facts any substantial basis for distinguishing this case from the *Carroll* case. Accordingly the judgment is affirmed.

Problem 3-2. Applying Different Probable Cause Standards

Consider the following two searches in light of the California and Connecticut standards described above.

Case 1: One afternoon, Captain Lee and Sergeant Hurter were on patrol in what they described as a "high crime area." Lee, Hurter, and four other officers in two other patrol cars stopped at 1225 6th Alley East, where five or six persons were gathered in front of a shot house (a private residence where illegal whiskey is sold by the shot). Officers had executed a search warrant at this residence two to three weeks earlier. As a result of that search, the owner of the residence had been arrested and charged with the illegal sale of alcohol. Officers during that earlier search found a small quantity of illegal drugs on the front porch, presumably left by people sitting there who dispersed when the police arrived at the house.

The house was located in a mostly African American neighborhood, and the people gathered in front of the house were African American men. Between the porch of the house and the roadway there was a small yard, and there was no sidewalk. Some of the men, including Eddie Tucker, were standing in the yard abutting the roadway, and some were in the roadway leaning on a parked car. There had been no calls or complaints to the police that day concerning any illegal activity at the house or pertaining to any of the people gathered in front of the house. Neither Lee nor Hurter knew Tucker at that point.

The officers testified that they were not aware of anything illegal occurring among the men, but as Lee exited the car, he noticed that Tucker (who was about three feet away from him) had a large bulge in one of his front pants pockets. For safety reasons, Lee asked Tucker what was in his pocket and told him to take whatever it was out so that it could be seen. Tucker took from his pocket a cell phone, a ring of keys, and a plastic box designed to hold Tic-Tac brand breath mints.

Lee then directed his attention to another of the persons present, and Hurter asked Tucker what was in the Tic-Tac container. In response, Tucker put the container behind his back. Sergeant Hurter then asked to see the plastic container. Tucker handed the box to Hurter, who opened it and found five pills with smiley faces on them. The pills field-tested positive for methamphetamine. Did Officer Hurter have probable cause to search the plastic container? Compare Ex parte Tucker, 667 So. 2d 1339 (Ala. 1995); Ex parte Kelley, 870 So. 2d 711 (Ala. 2003).

Case 2: On December 19, at 4 A.M., Detective Jon Gill and Deputy Justin Crafton were watching a house that the officers suspected of drug activity. When Robert Stevenson's vehicle left the house, the officers followed it until they observed the vehicle's turn signal engage as it approached a stop sign at the intersection of 14th and Broadway. The car was 30 feet from the stop sign when the blinker first engaged; state law requires a driver to signal continuously for 100 feet before a turn. The officers therefore stopped the car in an area well lit by street lights.

Deputy Crafton approached the vehicle's driver side, while Detective Gill approached the passenger side. Stevenson was the only occupant of the vehicle. Deputy Crafton noticed a "very strong odor of alcohol" coming from the open driver's side window and directed Stevenson to exit and proceed to the rear of his vehicle. While the deputy conducted field sobriety tests on Stevenson outside his vehicle, Detective Gill proceeded to the driver's side and put his head inside the car. Gill also noticed a very strong odor of alcohol, "as if possibly an alcohol container had spilled inside the vehicle."

The officers determined that Stevenson was not under the influence of alcohol and they permitted him to re-enter his vehicle. A records check indicated that Stevenson's driver's license was valid and clean. Nevertheless, the officers continued the detention because they believed they had probable cause to search Stevenson's vehicle for an open container of alcohol. Driving with an open container of alcohol is a misdemeanor in the state. Deputy Crafton first looked for an open container inside of the center console of the front seat, where he found two glass pipes containing methamphetamine. Crafton also noticed a large half-empty bottle of red wine on the floor in the backseat, with a closed screw-on top. He noticed a wet area on the floor mat beneath the wine bottle. Did Deputy Crafton have probable cause to support his search of the car? Compare State v. Stevenson, 321 P.3d 754 (Kan. 2014).

Notes

1. *Applying different standards?* Which of the cases described in Problem 3-2 offers a stronger basis—in other words, a stronger argument for probable cause—for a search? Does the relative strength of the cases depend on the standard applied to them, or are all the standards stronger for one of the cases? Consider the Connecticut standard. Can you add (or subtract) a fact that would make a weaker case for probable cause? Would you change different facts to make the case for finding probable cause stronger or weaker under the California standard?

2. *Probable cause and probabilities.* Does probable cause translate into a level of certainty the same as the preponderance of the evidence standard at trial? Courts in all jurisdictions have long insisted that probable cause is something less than "beyond a reasonable doubt" and something more than "mere suspicion," but they have shied away from equating it with the preponderance standard. See Illinois v. Gates, 462 U.S. 213 (1983) (probable cause requires "only the probability, and not a prima facie showing of criminal activity"). In a survey of more than 150 federal judges, about one-third believed that "probable cause" required 50 percent certainty, with the next largest groups of judges calling for 40 percent and 30 percent certainty. See C.M.A. McCauliff, Burdens of Proof: Degrees of Belief, Quanta of Evidence, or Constitutional Guarantees?, 35 Vand. L. Rev. 1293 (1982).

In general, however, courts have rejected quantifying the probable cause standard, holding that probable cause is a "flexible, common-sense" standard, "not reducible to precise definition or quantification." Florida v. Harris, 568 U.S. 237 (2013). Accordingly, the Supreme Court in *Harris* held that in establishing the reliability of a dog sniff, the state does not need to present records showing the dog's hits and misses in the field. A dog can be presumed to be reliable if the state shows it has satisfactorily completed a certification or training program.

In digital search cases, police officers may try to establish probable cause to believe that a person owns a cell phone or a computer by pointing to the high levels of cell phone or computer ownership among the general population. For a decision rejecting such a generalized approach to probable cause, see United States v. Griffith, 867 F.3d 1265 (D.C. Cir. 2017) (survey showing that more than 90 percent of American adults own a cell phone not enough to establish probable cause that Griffith had a cell phone).

3. *Probabilities and groups of suspects.* In Ybarra v. Illinois, 444 U.S. 85 (1979), police officers had a warrant to search a tavern and its bartender for evidence of drug possession. Upon entering the tavern, the officers conducted pat-down searches of the customers present in the tavern and found heroin inside Ybarra's pocket. The Court held that the search warrant did not permit the pat-down searches of all patrons in the tavern because "a person's mere propinquity to others independently suspected of criminal activity does not, without more, give rise to probable cause to search that person. [A] search or seizure of a person must be supported by probable cause particularized with respect to that person." But in a later case, Maryland v. Pringle, 540 U.S. 366 (2003), the Supreme Court held that officer who found $763 in glove compartment and cocaine behind armrest in back seat of a car had probable cause to arrest the driver, front seat passenger, and rear passenger when all three occupants of car denied knowledge of drugs. The Court explained that it was reasonable to believe that the car passengers and driver were involved in a common enterprise of drug dealing, given the amount of money and drugs and the fact that they were traveling together. Is it reasonable to assume that car passengers are involved in a common enterprise with the owner and driver of the car? Are there circumstances in which such an assumption would be unreasonable?

4. *Police expertise in assessing probable cause.* Courts often recognize that officers rely on their training and experience in assessing probable cause. See Ornelas v. United States, 517 U.S. 690 (1996) (reviewing court should give due weight to inferences drawn from historical facts by resident judges and local law enforcement officers; officer may draw inferences "based on his own experience"; the loose panel below the backseat armrest in the automobile in this case may suggest to a layman "only wear and tear, but to Officer Luedke, who had searched roughly 2,000 cars for narcotics, it suggested that drugs may be secreted inside the panel"); Commonwealth v. Thompson, 985 A.2d 928 (Pa. 2009) (officer observed defendant standing on street while exchanging small object for cash from driver; in such a setting, characterization of neighborhood as "high crime" and abstract assertion of police expertise would not suffice for probable cause, but officer here made the requisite connection between his experience and facts in case through testimony that he had observed hundreds of similar transactions that turned out to involve illegal narcotics).

Consider how an officer's experience might be used to establish probable cause in a child pornography case. In United States v. Mantha, the court credited the officer's experience that "individuals who repeatedly access and view child pornography by means of a computer will do so on any available computer" and that "child pornography images are often maintained for several years and are kept close by, usually at the possessor's residence, inside the possessor's vehicle, or, at times, on their person, to enable the individual to view the . . . images, which are valued highly." United States v. Mantha, 2018 WL 620088 (D. Mass. Jan. 30, 2018). As a trial judge in a suppression hearing, would you attribute the same level of expertise to all officers or to those within a particular unit of the police department (such as the narcotics squad)? Or would you insist on some particularized showing of experience from each police officer trying to establish probable cause? See Max Minzer, Putting Probability Back into Probable Cause, 87 Tex. L. Rev. 913 (2009) (proposal for the use of empirical evidence of the success of a given investigating officer or investigative technique in assessing the existence of probable cause to search or seize).

5. *Actual knowledge of officer.* Does one assess probable cause based on what the officer(s) on the scene actually relied on to justify the search or on facts that were available to the officer, whether or not she relied on them? Courts have not entirely agreed on this question, but the existence of probable cause usually depends on the facts available to the officer in the field, not just on facts the officer actually relied on to justify a search or seizure.

Most jurisdictions test probable cause based on the collective information the police have, even if the arresting or searching officer does not hold all of that information. See Grassi v. People, 320 P.3d 332 (Colo. 2014). Does this "collective knowledge" doctrine draw the wrong lessons from the institutional reality of police work? Should search and seizure doctrine generally try to account for the way that organizations (police departments) typically shape the actions of individuals (police officers)? For a comparison of the "collective knowledge" rule and the related "fellow officer" doctrine, see the web extension for this chapter at *http://www.crimpro.com/extension/ch03.*

Recall the discussion in Chapter 2 of "pretextual" stops and the choice discussed there between objective and subjective standards in criminal procedure. It is possible that the collective knowledge doctrine gives the police too much opportunity for post hoc rationalization of the individual officer's decision to conduct a search. What, if anything, is wrong with justifying a search after the fact, based on events that truly did occur?

6. *Anticipatory warrants.* The prototypical application for a search warrant describes events that have already occurred and infers from those facts the probable cause to believe that a crime has been committed and that the items sought will be found at the named location. But this creates a timing problem. The officer completes the application after gathering the relevant facts establishing probable cause and before the search takes place. The minutes or hours necessary to obtain a warrant may not be available after the confirmation of probable cause but before the search must happen. To get around this problem, officers can obtain an anticipatory warrant, which conditions the search on a specific future occurrence that provides probable cause for the search (for example, the delivery of a package that officers know contains drugs).

The courts in over half of the states have upheld the use of anticipatory search warrants. The Supreme Court addressed the question in United States v. Grubbs, 547 U.S. 90 (2006), and drew the following comparison between anticipatory warrants and traditional search warrants:

> In the typical case where the police seek permission to search a house for an item they believe is already located there, the magistrate's determination that there is probable cause for the search amounts to a prediction that the item will still be there when the warrant is executed. . . . Anticipatory warrants are, therefore, no different in principle from ordinary warrants. They require the magistrate to determine (1) that it is now probable that (2) contraband, evidence of a crime, or a fugitive will be on the described premises (3) when the warrant is executed. [For] a conditioned anticipatory warrant to comply with the Fourth Amendment's requirement of probable cause, two prerequisites of probability must be satisfied. It must be true not only that if the triggering condition occurs there is a fair probability that contraband or evidence of a crime will be found in a particular place, but also that there is probable cause to believe the triggering condition will occur. The supporting affidavit must provide the magistrate with sufficient information to evaluate both aspects of the probable-cause determination.

A number of state courts (about a half dozen) decided over the years that anticipatory warrants violated state *statutes* defining the use of search warrants. Dodson v. State, 150 P.3d 1054 (Okla. Crim. App. 2006). In some jurisdictions, the legislature responded right away with new statutory language authorizing the use of anticipatory warrants. See Ex parte Turner, 792 So. 2d 1141, 1151 (Ala. 2000).

7. *Predicting the future.* Do anticipatory warrants remove the magistrate from effective review of searches, or do they involve the magistrate even more closely than usual in examining warrant applications? Suppose that investigators plan to send a paid informant into two specific locations to purchase illegal drugs. They are confident that the informant will be able to purchase the drugs at one of the two locations, but they are uncertain which location is correct. Could they obtain an anticipatory search warrant for the two locations, conditioned on a positive field test showing that the substance purchased was indeed cocaine? See State v. Gillespie, 530 N.W.2d 446 (Iowa 1995). Would the names and addresses of the targets contribute to the showing of probable cause? Does this application amount to a request for the magistrate to pre-approve a standard police operating procedure?

Suppose you serve as counsel to the judicial conference of a state. What guidelines might you set for magistrates to avoid abuse of anticipatory warrants? Would you insist that the magistrate include as a condition in the warrant every detail that the police relate in the application? Over what time span might an anticipatory warrant remain valid?

Problem 3-3. A New Look

On July 1, an anonymous informant telephoned Detective Wygnanski of the Washoe County Consolidated Narcotics Unit. The informant told Wygnanski that Craig Parent would arrive at the Reno Airport on a Continental Airlines flight from New Orleans on July 3. The informant stated that Parent would be with two women named "Jody" and "Stephanie" and he would have cocaine concealed inside a baby powder bottle in his baggage. The informant also provided Wygnanski with a physical description of Parent, saying that he was 6'1" tall, with brown "wavy" hair, green eyes, and a moustache. The caller knew Parent's Social Security number, his FBI number, and his date of birth, and said that he had an extensive criminal record. Wygnanski confirmed the fact that Parent was scheduled to fly on Continental Airlines to Reno on July 3 and determined that he had several criminal convictions on his record. On July 2, Wygnanski obtained a search warrant. Execution of the warrant was conditioned upon the arrival of Continental Airlines flight number 781 from New Orleans on July 3.

On July 3, Parent and two women arrived at the Reno Airport. Police officers observed the threesome as they exited the airplane, and heard Parent call one of the two women "Karen." They noted that his hair was shortly trimmed rather than wavy, and he had no moustache, but Parent otherwise met the description that the informant had provided. The police officers arrested Parent shortly after he retrieved his luggage. A police officer found 3.7 grams of cocaine in a baby powder bottle located inside one of Parent's bags.

The state charged Parent with narcotics crimes, and Parent moved to suppress the evidence. He argues that the justice of the peace improperly issued the search warrant because the Nevada constitution prohibits anticipatory warrants under the circumstances presented in this case. As defense counsel, how would you distinguish the facts in this case from a controlled delivery case where officers obtain an anticipatory warrant conditioned on a delivery to a specific person of a package known to contain drugs? Cf. State v. Parent, 867 P.2d 1143 (Nev. 1994).

b. Sources of Information to Support Probable Cause

The information needed to show probable cause comes from sources as varied as victims, other witnesses, anonymous sources, confidential informants, and police officers themselves. In the abstract, which of these sources would you expect to be most reliable? Can we judge reliability in the abstract? This section considers how courts assess information from different sources, with particular attention to confidential informants and anonymous sources.

Much as the law of evidence shows a mistrust of hearsay, so the law of probable cause shows a mistrust of informants, who provide information to the police but are often not available to be questioned further when the time comes to assess probable cause. The U.S. Supreme Court has developed a specialized set of rules for judging the reliability of information from informants and anonymous tipsters. The following two cases describe changes in the Supreme Court's approach to such questions.

■ STATE v. TIMOTHY BARTON
594 A.2d 917 (Conn. 1991)

PETERS, J.

The sole issue in this appeal is whether . . . article first, §7, of the Connecticut constitution permits a court to determine the existence of probable cause on the basis of the "totality of the circumstances" when it reviews a search warrant application based on information provided to the police by a confidential informant. The state charged the defendant, Timothy Barton, with possession of over a kilogram of marihuana with intent to sell and with possession of marihuana . . . after police, acting under the authority of a warrant, had searched his home and had seized more than fifty pounds of marihuana there. The defendant moved to suppress the seized evidence, and the trial court granted the defendant's motion on the ground that the affidavit accompanying the search warrant application failed to state the informant's "basis of knowledge." The charges were subsequently dismissed with prejudice. [We] reverse.

[Officers] of the Winsted police department, acting on the authority of a search and seizure warrant obtained that day on the basis of information provided by a confidential informant, searched the defendant's apartment. . . . In the course of their search, the police found some fifty-two pounds of marihuana wrapped in clear plastic bags and kept in larger garbage bags in a bedroom. When the defendant returned home after midnight, the police arrested him.

[At the hearing on the defendant's motion to suppress this evidence, the trial court] applied the two-pronged analysis mandated by this court's decision in State v. Kimbro, 496 A.2d 498 (Conn. 1985), which requires a magistrate, in determining whether probable cause exists for a search or seizure, to evaluate both the "basis of knowledge" and the "veracity" or "reliability" of an informant upon whose information the police have relied. Spinelli v. United States, 393 U.S. 410 (1969); Aguilar

v. Texas, 378 U.S. 108 (1964). In the circumstances of this case, [the trial court] concluded that the affidavit in support of the search warrant did not adequately set forth the unnamed informant's basis of knowledge and therefore failed to establish probable cause. . . .

In the present appeal, the state urges us to overrule our holding in *Kimbro*, and to adopt the "totality of the circumstances" standard for determining probable cause used in the federal courts pursuant to the decision of the United States Supreme Court in Illinois v. Gates, 462 U.S. 213 (1983). . . . We agree with the state that application of the standards mandated by *Kimbro* has resulted at times in unduly technical readings of warrant affidavits, and we reject such an inappropriate methodology. . . .

In Illinois v. Gates, the United States Supreme Court rejected the "complex superstructure of evidentiary and analytical rules" that had evolved from its earlier decisions in Aguilar v. Texas and Spinelli v. United States. [The] "two-pronged" *Aguilar-Spinelli* test provides a method for evaluating the existence of probable cause consistent with the requirements of the fourth amendment when a search warrant affidavit is based upon information supplied to the police by a confidential informant. The issuing judge must be informed of (1) some of the underlying circumstances relied on by the informant in concluding that the facts are as he claims they are, and (2) some of the underlying circumstances from which the officer seeking the warrant concluded (a) that the informant, whose identity need not be disclosed, was credible, or (b) that the information was reliable. When the information supplied by the informant fails to satisfy the *Aguilar-Spinelli* test, probable cause may still be found if the warrant application affidavit sets forth other circumstances—typically independent police corroboration of certain details provided by the informant—that bolster the deficiencies.

The *Gates* court identified two principal flaws in the *Aguilar-Spinelli* test. First, because courts and commentators had generally regarded the two prongs of the test to be entirely independent of each other, courts had struggled to formulate rules regarding what types of information and what types of corroboration might satisfy each of the prongs. Specifically, some courts had concluded that independent police investigation might corroborate the "reliability" of the information, but could never satisfy the "basis of knowledge" prong of the test, while ample "self-verifying details" might establish that the informant had personal knowledge of the alleged activity and thus could satisfy the "basis of knowledge" prong, but could never compensate for a deficiency in the "veracity" or "reliability" prong. The "elaborate set of legal rules" that had resulted from this emphasis on the independent character of the two prongs had led courts, in many cases, to dissect warrant applications in an excessively technical manner, "with undue attention being focused on isolated issues that [could not] sensibly be divorced from the other facts presented to the magistrate." Such a result was inconsistent with the nature of a probable cause determination, which, as the *Gates* court noted, involves a "practical, non-technical conception."

The second principal flaw in the application of the *Aguilar-Spinelli* test, according to the *Gates* court, was that the test had caused reviewing courts, both at suppression hearings and at appellate levels, to test the sufficiency of warrant affidavits by de novo review. Such de novo review, in the view of the *Gates* majority, was inconsistent with the constitution's "strong preference for searches conducted pursuant to a warrant." A reviewing court should rather determine whether the magistrate issuing the warrant had a "substantial basis" for concluding that a search would uncover evidence of criminal activity.

In rejecting the complex structure of rules that had evolved from *Aguilar* and *Spinelli,* however, the *Gates* court did not reject out of hand the underlying concerns that had originally been expressed in *Aguilar.* In that case, the United States Supreme Court invalidated a search warrant supported by an affidavit that stated only that the affiants "have received reliable information from a credible person," without stating any of the underlying circumstances that would support a finding of probable cause. The *Aguilar* court ruled that such a conclusory affidavit failed to state a factual basis on which a neutral and detached magistrate could determine the existence of probable cause. In *Gates,* the court reaffirmed that the "veracity" or "reliability" and the "basis of knowledge" inquiries formulated in *Aguilar* remain "highly relevant" in the determination of probable cause and should be regarded as "closely intertwined issues that may usefully illuminate the commonsense, practical question" of the existence of probable cause to believe that contraband or evidence is located in a particular place. The *Gates* court abandoned only a "rigid compartmentalization" of the inquiries and denied that the court had ever intended them to be understood as "entirely separate and independent requirements to be rigidly exacted in every case."

In the place of the "compartmentalized" *Aguilar-Spinelli* test, the *Gates* court directed lower courts to apply a "totality of the circumstances" analysis more consistent with traditional assessments of probable cause. While still employing the analytical frame of reference established in *Aguilar,* a "totality of the circumstances" analysis permits a judge issuing a warrant greater freedom to assess "the relative weights of all the various indicia of reliability (and unreliability) attending an informant's tip." . . . The task of a subsequent court reviewing the magistrate's decision to issue a warrant is to determine whether the magistrate had a "substantial basis" for concluding that probable cause existed. The court's decision in *Gates* emphasized the necessity of a case-by-case analysis of probable cause based on all of the facts presented to the judge issuing the warrant, not merely on those capable of categorization as indicating the "veracity" or "basis of knowledge" of a particular informant.

[We turn now to a reconsideration of our 1985 decision in State v. Kimbro.] *Kimbro* did not rely upon historical analysis to determine the standard by which probable cause should be measured. We relied, rather, upon our determination that the *Aguilar-Spinelli* test, "with its two prongs of 'veracity' or 'reliability' and 'basis of knowledge,' offers a practical and independent test under our constitution that predictably guides the conduct of all concerned, including magistrates and law enforcement officials, in the determination of probable cause." We regarded the *Gates* "totality of the circumstances" analysis as an "amorphous standard" that inadequately safeguarded the rights of individuals to be free from unjustified intrusions. Upon careful review of that determination, we agree with the conclusion of the United States Supreme Court in *Gates* that the two prongs of the *Aguilar-Spinelli* test are highly relevant evidentiary questions that a magistrate issuing the warrant must consider in deciding whether probable cause for a search or seizure exists, but that they are not wholly independent and dispositive constitutional tests for which de novo review exists at a suppression hearing.

In reaching our present conclusion we return to first principles. Article first, §7, of our constitution . . . safeguards the privacy, the personal security, and the property of the individual against unjustified intrusions by agents of the government.

One of the principal means by which the warrant requirement protects the privacy and property of the individual is by the interposition of a neutral and detached magistrate who must judge independently the sufficiency of an affidavit supporting an application for a search warrant. Whether applying the fourth amendment or article first, §7, of our own constitution, we have frequently recognized that a magistrate issuing a warrant cannot form an independent opinion as to the existence of probable cause unless the affidavit supporting the warrant application sets forth some of the facts upon which the police have relied in concluding that a search is justified. . . .

When a police officer seeking a search warrant relies on hearsay information supplied by confidential informants rather than on personal knowledge and observations, certain additional facts are necessary to ensure that the magistrate's decision to issue the warrant is informed and independent. [The *Aguilar* decision began with the commonsensical premise] that confidential informants are themselves often "criminals, drug addicts, or even pathological liars" whose motives for providing information to the police may range from offers of immunity or sentence reduction, promises of money payments, or "such perverse motives as revenge or the hope of eliminating criminal competition." Because such an informant's reliance on rumors circulating on the street is not unlikely and the veracity of such an informant is questionable, a magistrate reviewing a search warrant application based on such an informant's word can best assess the probable reliability of the information if she or he is informed of some of the predicate facts that indicate how the informant gained his information and why the police officer believes that the information is reliable in order to decide, independently, whether the police officer's inferences from the informant's statements are reasonable.

In *Kimbro*, we expressed concern that the "fluid" totality of the circumstances analysis approved in the fourth amendment context of Illinois v. Gates would inadequately inform magistrates and law enforcement officials of their obligation to scrutinize the information gathered from confidential police informants with appropriate caution. In construing article first, §7, of our constitution to require continued application of the *Aguilar-Spinelli* test, we sought to make clear certain benchmarks to guide the discretion of our judges in reviewing ex parte applications for search and seizure warrants based on confidential informants' tips.

Nonetheless, over time, the case law applying the *Aguilar-Spinelli* test has come to be encrusted with an overlay of analytical rigidity that is inconsistent with the underlying proposition that it is the constitutional function of the magistrate issuing the warrant to exercise discretion in the determination of probable cause. That discretion must be controlled by constitutional principles and guided by the evidentiary standards developed in our prior cases, but it should not be so shackled by rigid analytical standards that it deprives the magistrate of the ability to draw reasonable inferences from the facts presented. To the extent that *Kimbro* stands for the proposition that the exercise of discretion by a magistrate is reviewable only according to fixed analytical standards, it is overruled.

Our adoption of a "totality of the circumstances" analysis does not mean, however, that a magistrate considering a search warrant application should automatically defer to the conclusion of the police that probable cause exists. Such deference would be an abdication of the magistrate's constitutional responsibility to exercise an independent and detached judgment to protect the rights of privacy and personal security of the people of Connecticut.

In essence, our adoption of a "totality of the circumstances" analysis of the probable cause requirement of article first, §7, of our constitution means simply this: When a search warrant affidavit is based on information provided to the police by confidential informants, the magistrate should examine the affidavit to determine whether it adequately describes both the factual basis of the informant's knowledge and the basis on which the police have determined that the information is reliable. If the warrant affidavit fails to state in specific terms how the informant gained his knowledge or why the police believe the information to be trustworthy, however, the magistrate can also consider all the circumstances set forth in the affidavit to determine whether, despite these deficiencies, other objective indicia of reliability reasonably establish that probable cause to search exists. In making this determination, the magistrate is entitled to draw reasonable inferences from the facts presented. When a magistrate has determined that the warrant affidavit presents sufficient objective indicia of reliability to justify a search and has issued a warrant, a court reviewing that warrant at a subsequent suppression hearing should defer to the reasonable inferences drawn by the magistrate. . . .

In adopting the *Gates* "totality of the circumstances" analysis, as we have here construed it, as the standard of analysis applicable to article first, §7, of our constitution, we do not intend to dilute the constitutional safeguards of the warrant requirement. This court has both the constitutional duty to construe article first, §7, in a way that adequately protects the rights of individuals in Connecticut and also the supervisory responsibility, as the overseer of the judiciary in Connecticut, to ensure that the standards adopted here require law enforcement officers to provide magistrates with adequate information on which to base their decisions in an ex parte context. . . .

We now consider the affidavit presented in this case in light of the proper constitutional standards. [The critical paragraph of the affidavit] provides: "That the affiants state on Sunday, August 7, 1988 Sgt. Gerald O. Peters received information from a confidential informant at police headquarters pertaining to Tim Barton who resides at 232 Perch Rock Trail, Winsted, Connecticut, first floor that Barton has in his apartment a large quantity of marijuana in plastic garbage bags, which are kept in a closet. That the informant also provided Sergeant Peters of [*sic*] a sample of the marijuana that is in the bags. A field test of the marijuana substance that was provided to Sgt. Peters was field tested and the test results was [*sic*] positive for cannibas [*sic*] substance. The informant further stated that Tim Barton operates a Texas registered vehicle and after being away for approximately one week Barton returned home on Saturday, August 6, 1988 and unloaded several large plastic bags in the evening hours. The informant further stated that shortly after that four to five people arrived at the Barton apartment and stayed a short while and then left with plastic garbage bags." . . .

Reviewing the allegations set forth in the third paragraph of the affidavit in this case, the Appellate Court concluded that the affidavit failed to establish probable cause because it was defective under the "basis of knowledge" prong of the *Aguilar-Spinelli* test mandated by *Kimbro*. The Appellate Court cited the following deficiencies: (1) the affidavit did not expressly indicate that the informant had ever been inside the defendant's apartment; (2) the details regarding the truck and the carrying in and out of garbage bags were "innocuous"; (3) the affidavit did not indicate that the informant had said that he had purchased the marihuana from the defendant, or that he had observed the defendant "constantly in possession" of marihuana in the apartment; and (4) the informant did not give a detailed description of the apartment but merely alleged that the garbage bags were in a closet. We agree that the affidavit does not expressly state that the informant had personal knowledge of the facts described. Legitimate law enforcement efforts, however, should not be unduly frustrated because a police officer, in the haste of a criminal investigation, fails to recite his information in particular formulaic phrases. Probable cause does not depend upon the incantation of certain magic words. Having reviewed the circumstances described by the informant, we conclude that the affidavit provided a substantial basis for the magistrate's inference that the informant was reporting events that he had personally observed.

[Details from the affidavit] support an inference that the informant was sufficiently acquainted with the defendant to have known of a week-long absence and to have been present to observe the defendant's activities upon his return. When considered together with the detail that the garbage bags were kept in a closet and with the fact that the informant provided the police with a marihuana sample purportedly from the same bags, these details support a reasonable, common-sense inference that the informant had personally observed the events he reported and had secured the marihuana sample directly from the defendant at his apartment. . . . Although the magistrate could have properly exercised his discretion to reject the warrant application or to require the affiants to supplement it or corroborate some of its details we conclude that the inference drawn by the magistrate that the informant had firsthand knowledge of the defendant's activities was not unreasonable.

[We also conclude] that the affidavit provided a substantial basis for the magistrate's inference that the informant's information was reliable. The first circumstance supporting an inference of "veracity" or "reliability" is the fact that the informant was not anonymous. . . . Because his identity was known to the police, the informant could expect adverse consequences if the information that he provided was erroneous. Those consequences might range from a loss of confidence or indulgence by the police to prosecution for the class A misdemeanor of falsely reporting an incident . . . had the information supplied proved to be a fabrication.

More significantly, however, the informant supplied the police with a sample of a substance that the police tested and confirmed to be marihuana. By entering the police station with the marihuana in his possession and by exhibiting the marihuana to the police, the informant rendered himself liable to arrest, conviction, and imprisonment. . . . Although the warrant application would have unquestionably been stronger if the affiants had bolstered the reliability of the informant by independently corroborating some of the details he reported we conclude that the affidavit sufficiently set forth some of the underlying circumstances from which the police could have concluded that the informant was credible or that his information was reliable.

As our discussion of this affidavit demonstrates, the determination of an informant's "veracity" or "reliability" and "basis of knowledge" remains highly relevant under the constitutional standard announced in this decision. . . . This is a marginal case; the magistrate could reasonably have demanded more information. We will not invalidate a warrant, however, merely because we might, in the first instance, have reasonably declined to draw the inferences that were necessary here. Having reviewed all the circumstances presented to the magistrate in this affidavit, we conclude that the affidavit provided a substantial basis for concluding that probable cause existed. We accordingly reverse the judgment of the Appellate Court [and] remand the case to the trial court for further proceedings.

GLASS, J., concurring in part, dissenting in part.

I concur in the result reached by the majority in this case because, unlike the majority, I conclude that the disputed warrant meets the established requirements of the time honored *Aguilar-Spinelli* test. Because I disagree with the majority's decision to scrap the *Aguilar-Spinelli* test by overruling State v. Kimbro . . . I write separately in dissent. . . .

Dressed today in Connecticut constitutional finery, the *Gates* approach relegates the principles pertinent to the "veracity" and "basis of knowledge" prongs of the *Aguilar-Spinelli* test to the status of "relevant considerations" among the amorphous "totality of the circumstances." The purported relevance of these "considerations," however, is belied by the majority's suggestion that despite "deficiencies" under both prongs of the *Aguilar-Spinelli* test, a warrant may yet derive sufficient sustenance from the "totality of the circumstances" to satisfy the mandates of our constitution. The majority thus appears to have strayed even further beyond the strictures of *Aguilar-Spinelli* than the *Gates* majority, which proposed that "a deficiency in one [of the prongs of the *Aguilar-Spinelli* test] may be compensated for . . . by a strong showing as to the other, or by some other indicia of reliability." Under the majority's evident reading of *Gates,* a warrant deficient under both prongs of the *Aguilar-Spinelli* test, nevertheless, complies with Connecticut constitutional requirements where the "totality of the circumstances" permit. [Magistrates and police officers,] unfettered by meaningful standards by which to discharge their respective functions in the warrant process, are now granted the unbridled play to accord weight to their subjective preferences in determining the "circumstances" whose "totality" permissibly adds up to probable cause. . . .

The *Aguilar-Spinelli* test, in my opinion, allows ample room for the application of common sense and the evaluation of the unique facts presented by particular cases. I do not, therefore, share the majority's desire to strip probable cause determinations of the "fixed, analytical standards" of *Aguilar-Spinelli* that have served to protect the free men and women of Connecticut from unreasonable government intrusion in a way that the standardless *Gates* approach, I submit, will never do. . . . In my view, the Connecticut constitution is not a document so fragile that a swift stroke of the federal pen suffices, as is allowed today, to erode the substantive protections found not six years ago to be afforded thereunder to the citizens of this state.

■ STATE v. RANDALL UTTERBACK
485 N.W.2d 760 (Neb. 1992)

PER CURIAM.

[A] search warrant, to be valid, must be supported by an affidavit establishing probable cause [founded on articulable facts]. When a search warrant is obtained on the strength of an informant's information, the affidavit in support of the issuance of the search warrant must (1) set forth facts demonstrating the basis of the informant's knowledge of criminal activity and (2) establish the informant's credibility, or the informant's credibility must be established in the affidavit through a police officer's independent investigation. The affidavit must affirmatively set forth the circumstances from which the status of the informant can reasonably be inferred.

To determine the sufficiency of an affidavit used to obtain a search warrant, this jurisdiction has adopted the "totality of the circumstances" test set forth by the U.S. Supreme Court in Illinois v. Gates, 462 U.S. 213 (1983). The issuing magistrate must make a practical, commonsense decision whether, given the totality of the circumstances set forth in the affidavit before him, including the veracity and basis of knowledge of the persons supplying hearsay information, there is a fair probability that contraband or evidence of a crime will be found in a particular place. . . .

At approximately 7 A.M. on March 1, 1990, a Fremont police detective and six or seven fellow law enforcement officers executed a no-knock search warrant at Utterback's home. Utterback shared his home with his wife and infant child. In various containers discovered at various locales in the Utterback house, police found 25 separate plastic bags which contained a total of 570 grams of marijuana. . . .

The warrant which the officers executed authorized a search for automatic weapons, drug paraphernalia, and various controlled substances. The police detective obtained the warrant on the previous day from a Dodge County judge. The sworn affidavit executed by the police detective to obtain the search warrant states in pertinent part:

> On February 28, 1990, your affiant was advised by an *individual who is neither a paid nor habitual informant* that a second individual named "Randy" was engaged in the distribution and sale of controlled substances at the residence [at 321 North K Street]. The informant advised that "Randy" lived at the above described residence with his wife. The informant gave a physical description of "Randy" which matches the physical description of Randy Utterback contained in Fremont Police Dept. files. *The informant advised your affiant that in the past six months (the informant) had purchased marijuana from "Randy" at the residence described above,* and had observed other sales of illegal drugs at said residence. The informant further advised your affiant that (the informant) had been inside said residence within the last five days, and had seen a large quantity of marijuana, and lesser quantities of hashish, cocaine, LSD, and PCP. The informant indicated to your affiant that (the informant) was very familiar with illegal drugs, and the information furnished to your affiant indicated such knowledge.
>
> The informant further indicated to your affiant that (the informant) had observed what (the informant) believed to be an AK 47 assault rifle and an Uzi submachine gun in said residence, together with other weapons. The informant advised your affiant that (the informant) had personally inspected these weapons, and that they were loaded with ammunition. The informant gave a description of these weapons to your affiant, and that description is consistent with an AK 47 assault rifle and an Uzi submachine gun.
>
> Your affiant personally drove by the above described residence and observed an older model blue station wagon parked in the driveway of said residence bearing Nebraska license plate No. 5-B8618. According to records of the Dodge County Treasurer said vehicle is registered to Randy and/or Maria Utterback. Your affiant personally checked the records of the Fremont Department of Utilities and determined that the utilities were registered to Maria Utterback. . . .

Utterback argues that the search warrant was invalid in that the affidavit failed to establish the veracity of the confidential informant. To credit a confidential source's information in making a probable cause determination, the affidavit should support an inference that the source was trustworthy and that the source's accusation of criminal activity was made on the basis of information obtained in a reliable way.

Among the ways in which the reliability of an informant may be established are by showing in the affidavit to obtain a search warrant that (1) the informant has given reliable information to police officers in the past, see State v. Hoxworth, 358 N.W.2d 208 (Neb. 1984); (2) the informant is a citizen informant, see State v. Duff, 412 N.W.2d 843 (Neb. 1987); (3) the informant has made a statement that is against his or her penal interest, see State v. Sneed, 436 N.W.2d 211 (Neb. 1989); and (4) a police officer's independent investigation establishes the informant's reliability or the reliability of the information the informant has given, see United States v. Stanert, 762 F.2d 775 (9th Cir. 1985).

Nowhere in the detective's affidavit to obtain the search warrant in this case is there an averment that the detective's informant had given reliable information in the past, nor is there an averment that the informant was a "citizen informant." [Our prior cases have defined a citizen informant as]

> a citizen who purports to be the victim of or to have been the witness of a crime who is motivated by good citizenship and acts openly in aid of law enforcement. [Experienced] stool pigeons or persons criminally involved or disposed are not regarded as "citizen-informants" because they are generally motivated by something other than good citizenship. . . .

The status of a citizen informant cannot attach unless the affidavit used to obtain a search warrant affirmatively sets forth the circumstances from which the existence of the status can reasonably be inferred. Here, there is nothing in the detective's affidavit used to obtain a search warrant even hinting that the informant was "motivated by good citizenship."

The State argues that the assertion in the detective's affidavit that "the informant advised your affiant that in the past six months (the informant) had purchased marijuana from 'Randy' at the residence described above" was a statement against the penal interest of the informant. An admission by an informant that he or she participated in the crime about which the informant is informing carries its own indicia of reliability, since people do not lightly admit a crime and place critical evidence of that crime in the hands of police.

The act of purchasing marijuana is not a statutorily proscribed act in Nebraska. [Statutes] prohibit the possession of marijuana and . . . being under its influence, but nowhere in the statutes of the State of Nebraska is the purchase of marijuana expressly prohibited. There is nothing in the affidavit used to obtain the search warrant in this case that would establish, unequivocally, that the informant could be prosecuted for the crimes of possession or being under the influence of marijuana. [When] the informant in this case admitted to purchasing marijuana he did not make a statement against his penal interest.

The fourth method of determining the veracity of a confidential informant is through corroboration. Here, the affidavit reveals only that the police corroborated that Utterback lived at the described address, that the car in the driveway was registered to him, that the utilities at the house were registered to Utterback's wife, and that Utterback's physical description matched that given by the informant. If the police had chosen to corroborate the information regarding any criminal activities of Utterback's rather than merely corroborating these innocent details of his life, or had the affidavit contained other corroborative sources of information about the same alleged criminal activity of Utterback's, the veracity of the informant might have been established in the affidavit. However, no such corroboration is reflected in the detective's affidavit used to obtain the search warrant in this case.

We conclude that the affidavit in support of obtaining the search warrant herein fails to establish the veracity and reliability of the confidential informant and that the county judge was clearly wrong in determining that it supported a finding of probable cause to issue a search warrant. . . .

Notes

1. Gates *versus* Aguilar-Spinelli: *majority position.* More than 40 states have adopted the *Gates* totality-of-the-circumstances standard, though a handful of states such as Massachusetts, New York, and Tennessee (fewer than 10) have retained the *Aguilar-Spinelli* analysis, relying on state constitutions or statutes. See, e.g., People v. Serrano, 710 N.E.2d 655 (N.Y. 1999); State v. Chenoweth, 158 P.3d 595 (Wash. 2007); State v. Arrington, 8 A.3d 483 (Vt. 2010). Why have these states rejected the *Gates* standard? A few jurisdictions have adopted a totality-of-the-circumstances test but have emphasized the continuing relevance of the *Aguilar-Spinelli* analysis. See People v. Leftwich, 869 P.2d 1260 (Colo. 1994). Is this a preferable compromise position?

The *Barton* court in Connecticut switched from its earlier choice of *Aguilar-Spinelli* to the *Gates* standard, saying the *Aguilar-Spinelli* analysis had become "encrusted with an overlay of analytical rigidity." What evidence did the court offer to support this conclusion? If the claim about "encrustation" is hyperbole, what other reasons might have moved the court to the *Gates* standard?

2. *Fact-based probable cause analysis.* Both *Barton* and *Utterback* adopt the totality-of-the-circumstances standard of *Gates.* Which set of facts provided stronger support for a finding of probable cause? Which confidential informant provided greater detail? Which description could a police officer verify more easily? Do you agree with the court in *Utterback* that an admitted purchase of marijuana is not an admission against penal interest because purchasing is not a crime? The web extension for this chapter, at *http://www.crimpro.com/extension/ch03*, offers photographs of Utterback's home.

The "totality" standard, as the court said in *Barton,* is designed to place more responsibility for the probable cause finding in the hands of the factfinder on the scene: the magistrate reviewing the application for a warrant. Should other institutions allow magistrates to make probable cause determinations by their own lights or should they attempt to standardize the probable cause determination? Do you imagine that magistrates see similar fact patterns repeatedly, ones amenable to legal rules? Or do the warrant applications present such different fact patterns that they cannot usefully be compared?

3. *Legal standards and legal cultures.* How different are the alternative legal standards at issue in these cases? If you were concerned about limiting police powers at a time of rising fear about crime, would you rather be in a state with the *Aguilar-Spinelli* standard or in a state with a legal culture suspicious of government abuses where the courts use the *Gates* standard? Attorneys and others who train police officers very often emphasize the facts central to the *Aguilar-Spinelli* standard, even in jurisdictions that have adopted the *Gates* standard under the state constitution. See Corey

Fleming Hirokawa, Making the "Law of the Land" the Law on the Street: How Police Academies Teach Evolving Fourth Amendment Law, 49 Emory L.J. 295 (2000). Why do they make such a choice?

4. *Prevalence of confidential informants.* While officers rely heavily on their own observations in unwarranted searches, cases involving search warrants more often turn on evidence obtained from confidential informants. A survey of warrants issued in drug cases in San Diego in 1998 found that 64 percent of the warrant applications included information from confidential informants, and a quarter of the applications offered information from anonymous tips. Most of the applications gave little information about the informant's reliability or track record; the information offered appeared in standard boilerplate language. However, in almost all cases depending on information from confidential informants (95 percent of them), the police corroborated the tip by conducting a "controlled buy" of narcotics. See Laurence A. Benner & Charles T. Samarkos, Searching for Narcotics in San Diego: Preliminary Findings from the San Diego Search Warrant Project, 36 Cal. W. L. Rev. 221, 238-243 (2000).

5. *The presumption in favor of "citizen informants."* As suggested in dicta in *Utterback*, most courts presume information provided by victims and witnesses to be sufficiently reliable to serve as a basis for finding probable cause without additional proof that the source is credible or the information reliable. See Bryant v. State, 901 So. 2d 810 (Fla. 2005). Why? Does a person lose the status of "citizen informant" if she receives a reward for the information? What if the police pay the citizen small amounts of cash for meals or transportation? See People v. Cantre, 95 A.D.2d 522 (N.Y. App. Div. 1983). Can victims or witnesses be liable to suspects for the torts of malicious prosecution or false arrest if they file a complaint with an intent other than the investigation or prosecution of the suspect?

6. *Informer's privilege.* Should suspects be able to challenge information provided by a confidential informant, even at the stage of establishing probable cause? Courts and legislatures have long recognized an "informer's privilege" that allows the government to withhold the name of a confidential informant. Drawing on well-established common-law roots in the law of evidence, the Supreme Court in McCray v. Illinois, 386 U.S. 300 (1967), explained the privilege in these terms: "Whether an informer is motivated by good citizenship, promise of leniency or prospect of pecuniary award, he will usually condition his cooperation on an assurance of anonymity—to protect himself and his family from harm, to preclude adverse social reactions."

Typically, the law allows a magistrate or judge (but not the suspect) to learn the informer's identity and to examine the informer in camera if there is some reason to disbelieve the informer's statements. Should the informer's privilege apply when *all* the information supporting a search warrant is withheld from the defendant as confidential? Justice Mosk of the California Supreme Court, in a dissenting opinion in People v. Hobbs, 873 P.2d 1246 (Cal. 1994), characterized this problem as follows:

> A search warrant containing no information other than the address of a home to be searched. Not a word as to what the government seeks to discover and seize. A government informer, his—or, indeed, her—identity kept secret from the suspect, the suspect's counsel, and the public. Both the suspect and counsel barred from a closed proceeding before a magistrate. No record of the proceeding given to the suspect or counsel. Based entirely on the foregoing, a court order approving an unrestricted search of the suspect's home. Did this scenario occur in a communist dictatorship? Under a military junta? Or perhaps in a Kafka novel? No, this is grim reality in California in the final decade of the 20th century.

What if another court reads Justice Mosk's observation, then re-reads Kafka and decides to eliminate the informer's privilege? Could a legal system function if it took the position that no deprivation of liberty, including a search or seizure, could take place without full disclosure to the suspect after the search or arrest?

7. *Anonymous tips and probable cause.* Courts do not adopt a special framework for assessing probable cause based on information from an anonymous tip. They usually apply the same basic framework—whether it be *Gates* or *Aguilar-Spinelli*—used to assess the reliability of named and confidential informants. A number of the classic cases on the sources of probable cause, including Illinois v. Gates, 462 U.S. 213 (1983) itself, involved tips from anonymous sources. Of course, the police in such cases face the major difficulty of establishing the reliability of the source without knowing the identity of the source. While a track record for the source might not be available, and an "admission against penal interest" cannot bolster the credibility of an anonymous source, it is still possible that the police will be able to corroborate some details of the tip. See State v. Griggs, 34 P.3d 101 (Mont. 2001) (corroborated facts in anonymous tip must be suspicious and associated with criminal activity to establish probable cause).

In a jurisdiction following the *Aguilar-Spinelli* approach to probable cause, how often will information from an anonymous informant satisfy both prongs? In a *Gates* jurisdiction, would you expect the showing for "basis of knowledge" to be much higher than usual in an anonymous informant case? Should courts treat anonymous sources like citizen informants, with presumptions of reliability, or like confidential informants, with a requirement that police show the informant is trustworthy or the information is accurate? Anonymous tips are not random or rare occurrences: Consider the common use of websites to collect information from the public about specific crimes or suspects, in exchange for reward money. See *http://crimetips.org/wanteds.aspx* (Crime Stoppers of Central Indiana). Or consider the many police departments that solicit on their websites anonymous tips about unspecified crimes or suspects. See *http://www.phillypolice.com/forms/submit-a-tip* (Philadelphia Police Department anonymous tips page). Governments, corporations, and "watchdog" organizations often maintain "whistle blower" sites on the Internet, to encourage employees and others who know about wrongdoing to share the information.

8. *Anonymous tips and reasonable suspicion to stop vehicles.* In Chapter 2, we considered the "reasonable suspicion" necessary to justify a police stop of a person or vehicle. Sometimes anonymous tips give the police a reason to stop a person. Typically, the officer confirms some of the details that the anonymous tipster related before making the stop based on reasonable suspicion. In one common fact pattern, an anonymous tip identifies a driver who might be driving while intoxicated. If the officer stops the vehicle on the basis of the anonymous tip without first developing some independent basis for reasonable suspicion, it presents a close question for reviewing courts. In Navarette v. California, 134 S. Ct. 1683 (2014), an anonymous 911 caller reported that a specific pickup truck had run her off the road at a specific place on the highway. The police pulled over the pickup truck shortly after the 911 call, about 18 miles down the highway. They smelled marijuana and in a subsequent search found 30 pounds of the drug in the bed of the pickup. The Supreme Court acknowledged that an anonymous tip alone "seldom demonstrates sufficient reliability" to support reasonable suspicion, but the tip was enough in this case. The caller claimed an eyewitness basis of knowledge and said she was calling immediately after

the traffic incident. The 911 system has the capacity to trace the identity of callers, making false reports less likely. See also Alabama v. White, 496 U.S. 325, 332 (1990) (upholding stop based on anonymous caller's information about the future travel plans of an alleged drug dealer; the tip, together with police efforts to corroborate the tip by following the vehicle for a time, amounted to reasonable suspicion). For a glimpse of the rich case law in the state courts on this question, see the web extension for this chapter at *http://www.crimpro.com/extension/ch03.*

Problem 3-4. Assessing Anonymous Tips

On May 3, the Bloomingdale, Illinois, Police Department received an anonymous handwritten letter implicating two Bloomingdale residents in drug trafficking:

> This letter is to inform you that you have a couple in your town who strictly make their living on selling drugs. They are Sue and Lance Gates, they live on Greenway, off Bloomingdale Rd. in the condominiums. Most of their buys are done in Florida. Sue his wife drives their car to Florida, where she leaves it to be loaded up with drugs, then Lance flys down and drives it back. Sue flys back after she drops the car off in Florida. May 3 she is driving down there again and Lance will be flying down in a few days to drive it back. At the time Lance drives the car back he has the trunk loaded with over $100,000 in drugs. Presently they have over $100,000 worth of drugs in their basement.
>
> They brag about the fact they never have to work and make their entire living on pushers. I guarantee if you watch them carefully you will make a big catch. They are friends with some big drugs dealers, who visit their house often.
>
> Lance & Susan Gates, Greenway in Condominiums

Detective Mader of the Bloomingdale Police Department pursued the tip. He found out that an Illinois driver's license had been issued to Lance Gates, residing in Bloomingdale. Examination of certain financial records revealed a more recent address for the Gates. Detective Mader also learned from a police officer assigned to O'Hare Airport that "L. Gates" had made a reservation on Eastern Airlines flight 245 to West Palm Beach, Florida, scheduled to depart from Chicago on May 5 at 4:15 P.M.

Mader then arranged with an agent of the Drug Enforcement Administration for surveillance of the May 5 Eastern Airlines flight. The agent later reported to Mader that Gates had boarded the flight, and that federal agents in Florida had observed him arrive in West Palm Beach and take a taxi to the nearby Holiday Inn. They also reported that Gates went to a room registered to one Susan Gates and that, at 7:00 A.M. the next morning, Gates and an unidentified woman left the motel in a Mercury bearing Illinois license plates and drove northbound on an interstate frequently used by travelers to the Chicago area. The license plate number on the Mercury was registered to a Hornet station wagon owned by Gates. The driving time between West Palm Beach and Bloomingdale was approximately 22 to 24 hours.

Based on these facts, Mader obtained a search warrant for the Gates' residence and for their Mercury automobile. The search of the Mercury uncovered approximately 350 pounds of marijuana, and a search of the home revealed marijuana, weapons, and other contraband. Did the facts provided in the anonymous letter, combined with the facts observed by law enforcement, provide sufficient probable cause to support the warrant? Would a court applying the *Gates* framework reach the same conclusion as a court applying the *Aguilar-Spinelli* test? See Illinois v. Gates, 462 U.S. 213 (1983).

c. Can a Statute or Rule Clarify the Assessment of Probable Cause?

If a jurisdiction were committed to consistent determinations of probable cause, would it help if a statute or criminal procedure rule specified the factors for assessing probable cause? Does the following statute adopt the *Aguilar-Spinelli* or the *Gates* standard? Apply the statute and rule of criminal procedure to the facts in *Barton* and *Utterback*. Would you reach a different outcome in either of those cases?

■ IOWA CODE §808.3

[The] magistrate shall endorse on the application the name and address of all persons upon whose sworn testimony the magistrate relied to issue the warrant together with the abstract of each witness' testimony, or the witness' affidavit. However, if the grounds for issuance are supplied by an informant, the magistrate shall identify only the peace officer to whom the information was given. The application or sworn testimony supplied in support of the application must establish the credibility of the informant or the credibility of the information given by the informant. The magistrate may in the magistrate's discretion require that a witness upon whom the applicant relies for information appear personally and be examined concerning the information.

■ IOWA RULE OF CRIMINAL PROCEDURE 2.36, FORM 2

An application for a search warrant shall be in substantially the following form: . . . Being duly sworn, I, the undersigned, say that at the place (and on the person(s) and in the vehicle(s)) described as follows:

In _____ County, there is now certain property, namely: _____
which is :
_____ Property that has been obtained in violation of law.
_____ Property, the possession of which is illegal.
_____ Property used or possessed with the intent to be used as the means of committing a public offense or concealed to prevent an offense from being discovered.
_____ Property relevant and material as evidence in a criminal prosecution.

The facts establishing the foregoing ground(s) for issuance of a search warrant are as set forth in the attachment(s) made part of this application.

ATTACHMENT
Applicant's name: _____
Occupation: _____ No. of years: _____
Assignment: _____ No. of years: _____
Your applicant conducted an investigation and received information from other officers and other sources as follows :
(_____ See attached investigative and police reports.) . . .

INFORMANT'S ATTACHMENT (Note: Prepare separate attachment for each informant.)

Peace Officer _____ received information from an informant whose name is:

_____ Confidential because disclosure of informant's identity would:

_____ Endanger informant's safety;

_____ Impair informant's future usefulness to law enforcement.

The informant is reliable for the following reason(s):

_____ The informant is a concerned citizen who has been known by the above peace officer for years and who:

_____ Is a mature individual.

_____ Is regularly employed.

_____ Is a student in good standing.

_____ Is a well-respected family or business person.

_____ Is a person of truthful reputation.

_____ Has no motivation to falsify the information.

_____ Has no known association with known criminals.

_____ Has no known criminal record.

_____ Has otherwise demonstrated truthfulness. (State in the narrative the facts that led to this conclusion.)

_____ Other:

_____ The informant has supplied information in the past _____ times.

_____ The informant's past information has helped supply the basis for _____ search warrants.

_____ The informant's past information has led to the making of _____ arrests.

_____ Past information from the informant has led to the filing of the following charges: _____

_____ Past information from the informant has led to the discovery and seizure of stolen property, drugs, or other contraband.

_____ The informant has not given false information in the past.

_____ The information supplied by the informant in this investigation has been corroborated by law enforcement personnel. (Indicate in the narrative the corroborated information and how it was corroborated.)

_____ Other: _____

The informant has provided the following information: _____

■ IOWA RULE OF CRIMINAL PROCEDURE 2.36, FORM 3

An endorsement on a search warrant shall be in substantially the following form: . . .

1. In issuing the search warrant, the undersigned relied upon the sworn testimony of the following person(s) together with the statements and information contained in the application and any attachments thereto. The court relied upon the following witnesses :

Name   Address

_____   _____

_____   _____

_____   _____

2. Abstract of Testimony. (As set forth in the application and the attachments thereto, plus the following information.)

3. The undersigned has relied, at least in part, on information supplied by a confidential informant (who need not be named) to the peace officer(s) shown on Attachment(s) _____.

4. The information appears credible because (select):

_____ A. Sworn testimony indicates this informant has given reliable information on previous occasions; or,

_____ B. Sworn testimony indicates that either the informant appears credible or the information appears credible for the following reasons (if credibility is based on this ground, the magistrate MUST set out reasons here):

_____

5. The information (is/is not) found to justify probable cause.

6. I therefore (do/do not) issue the warrant.

Notes

1. *Statutes and probable cause determinations: majority position.* Only one state (Oregon) offers a general statutory definition of probable cause. However, most states do have statutes or rules of procedure instructing magistrates how to determine whether probable cause exists before issuing a warrant. The statutes often specify the types of sources a magistrate may consider and the inquiries a magistrate must make when assessing "hearsay" information or other questionable sources. See, e.g., Ark. R. Crim. P. 13.1 (providing that "if an affidavit or testimony is based in whole or in part on hearsay, the affiant or witness shall set forth particular facts bearing on the informant's reliability and shall disclose, as far as practicable, the means by which the information was obtained").

Iowa courts have concluded that the state legislature, in passing section 808.3, was repudiating the decision of the Supreme Court in Illinois v. Gates, 462 U.S. 213 (1983). See State v. Swaim, 412 N.W.2d 568 (Iowa 1987) (interpreting language in statute, "shall include a determination that the information appears credible," as a rejection of *Gates*). What purposes might the other two provisions reprinted above serve?

2. *Rules as requirements versus rules as nonbinding guidance.* What should be the effect of a failure to check any boxes on the Iowa form to show why an informant was reliable, in a case where a reviewing court believes that the information provided to the magistrate was enough for probable cause? See State v. District Court of Black Hawk County, 472 N.W.2d 621 (Iowa 1991) (invalidating search warrant based on form application with no checks indicating informant's basis of knowledge). Such checklists are also developed as part of police and prosecutorial manuals. The lists often take the form of software or an app, used to prompt an officer to answer specific questions while constructing an application for a search warrant. Should failure to follow a written executive branch guideline have the same effect on review of probable cause as failure to follow an identical rule of criminal procedure? Should the question simply be whether probable cause exists, with the forms or checklists, whatever their origins, merely serving as evidence for the court assessing or reviewing the probable cause determination?

4. Other Warrant Requirements

a. Neutral and Detached Magistrate

In addition to probable cause and particularity, another constitutional requirement for a warrant is that it be by a "neutral and detached magistrate." A magistrate must not be involved in the activities of law enforcement while also sitting in judgment of those activities.

While there are occasional cases litigating the constitutional requirement of a "neutral and detached magistrate," issues of judicial neutrality are more often litigated under judicial ethics rules. Indeed, ethics rules provide a standard avenue for the regulation of lawyers and judges throughout the criminal process, as influential today in practical terms as constitutional provisions.

■ STATE EX REL. EUSTACE BROWN v. JERRY DIETRICK
444 S.E.2d 47 (W. Va. 1994)

MILLER, J.

[We] consider whether the Circuit Court of Jefferson County was correct in holding that a search warrant issued by a magistrate was void because the magistrate was married to the chief of police and one of his officers had procured the warrant. The lower court determined that because the magistrate was married to the chief of police there was a violation of Canon 3C(1) and 3C(1)(d) of the Judicial Code of Ethics. The former provision requires the recusal of a judge if his impartiality might reasonably be questioned; the latter requires disqualification where the judge's spouse has an interest in the proceeding.[3] We have not had occasion to consider this particular question.

Initially, we note that independent of the Judicial Code of Ethics, the United States Supreme Court has interpreted the Fourth Amendment to the United States Constitution to require that a search warrant be issued by a "neutral and detached magistrate." In Shadwick v. City of Tampa, 407 U.S. 345 (1972), the Supreme Court held that the office of magistrate, in order to satisfy the neutral and detached standard "requires severance and disengagement from activities of law enforcement." By way of illustration, the Supreme Court in *Shadwick* pointed to its earlier case of Coolidge v. New Hampshire, 403 U.S. 443 (1971), where it voided a search warrant issued by the state's attorney general because he "was actively in charge of the investigation and later was to be chief prosecutor at trial." Similarly, in Lo-Ji Sales, Inc. v. New York, 442 U.S. 319 (1979), the magistrate was found not to be neutral and

---

3. The applicable provisions in 1992 of the Judicial Code of Ethics . . . were in Canon 3C(1) and 3C(1)(d):

A judge should disqualify himself in a proceeding in which his impartiality might reasonably be questioned, including but not limited to instances where: . . .

(d) he or his spouse, or a person within the third degree of relationship to either of them, or the spouse of such a person:

(i) is a party to the proceeding, or an officer, director, or trustee of a party; . . .

(iii) is known by the judge to have an interest that could be substantially affected by the outcome of the proceeding;

(iv) is to the judge's knowledge likely to be a material witness in the proceeding. . . .

detached when he "allowed himself to become a member, if not the leader, of the search party which was essentially a police operation." In Connally v. Georgia, 429 U.S. 245 (1977), the Supreme Court determined that a magistrate who was compensated based on a fee for the warrants issued could not be considered neutral and detached. It relied on its earlier case of Tumey v. Ohio, 273 U.S. 510 (1927), which invalidated on due process principles the payment of the village mayor, when he acted as a judge, from costs collected in criminal cases brought before him in which there was a conviction.

We afforded the same protection for a neutral and detached magistrate under our search and seizure constitutional provision in . . . State v. Dudick, 213 S.E.2d 458 (W. Va. 1975):

> The constitutional guarantee under W. Va. Const., Article III, §6 that no search warrant will issue except on probable cause goes to substance and not to form; therefore, where it is conclusively proved that a magistrate acted as a mere agent of the prosecutorial process and failed to make an independent evaluation of the circumstances surrounding a request for a warrant, the warrant will be held invalid and the search will be held illegal.

As the foregoing law indicates, where there is a lack of neutrality and detachment in the issuance of the search warrant, it is void. Aside from the constitutional requirements for a neutral and detached magistrate as to warrants, similar standards are imposed by Canon 3C of the Judicial Code of Ethics relating to the disqualification of a judge. The Code defines those situations when a judge may be precluded from presiding over a case. The underlying rationale for requiring disqualification is based on principles of due process. . . .

Canon 3C(1) contains an initial general admonition that a "judge should disqualify himself in a proceeding in which his impartiality might reasonably be questioned." This admonition is followed by a number of specific instances when disqualification is required. . . . In this case, in addition to the general disqualification standard, it is claimed that the more specific disqualification test contained in Canon 3C(1)(d)(iii) applies. This provision requires disqualification if the judge's spouse has "an interest that could be substantially affected by the outcome of the proceeding." This disqualification is claimed to apply if Chief Boober appeared before his wife to seek a warrant. . . . We have no case law on this point, but we agree with cases from other jurisdictions that support the disqualification.

For example, the Louisiana court in State v. LaCour, 493 So. 2d 756 (La. Ct. App. 1986), set aside a criminal conviction because it found that the judge should have disqualified himself because his son was prosecuting the defendant on another criminal charge in a different county. . . . In Smith v. Beckman, 683 P.2d 1214 (Colo. Ct. App. 1984), the judge's wife was an assistant prosecutor. The record showed that the prosecutor's office had screened her from cases that were before her husband. The court concluded that his disqualification in all criminal cases was warranted because of the appearance of impropriety. . . . The critical point in the court's view was the perception of the closeness created by the marital relationship:

> A husband and wife generally conduct their personal and financial affairs as a partnership. In addition to living together, a husband and wife are also perceived to share confidences regarding their personal lives and employment situations. Generally, the public views married people as "a couple," as "a partnership," and as participants in a relationship more intimate than any other kind of relationship

between individuals. In our view the existence of a marriage relationship between a judge and a deputy district attorney in the same county is sufficient to establish grounds for disqualification, even though no other facts call into question the judge's impartiality. . . .

We believe that the foregoing cases and the language in Canon 3C(1) and 3C(1)(d)(i) of the Judicial Code of Ethics relating to the disqualification of a judicial official when his or her impartiality might reasonably be questioned if the official's spouse is a party to the proceeding would foreclose a magistrate from issuing a warrant sought by his or her spouse who is a police officer. However, this situation did not occur here.

The search warrant was issued at the request of Sergeant R. R. Roberts of the Ranson police force. At the hearing below, Magistrate Boober testified that she was the on-call magistrate for emergency matters that might occur after 4:00 P.M. and before 8:00 A.M. the next morning when the magistrate office would be open for normal business.

Magistrate Boober also stated that she was not related to Sergeant Roberts and had no contact with him except through the magistrate system. She also stated that she made an independent review of the affidavit for the search warrant. Her husband's name did not appear on the affidavit nor was there any discussion about her husband with Sergeant Roberts.

There was no evidence to show any actual bias or partiality on the part of Magistrate Boober. The entire argument centered on an implied partiality because of the magistrate's relationship to Chief Boober. We indicated earlier that any criminal matters which the magistrate's husband is involved with cannot be brought before her because of their spousal relationship. We decline to extend such a per se rule with regard to the other members of the Ranson police force. The fact that a magistrate's spouse is the chief of police of a small police force does not automatically disqualify the magistrate, who is otherwise neutral and detached, from issuing a warrant sought by another member of such police force. However, a small police force[14] coupled with the chief's active role in a given case may create an appearance of impropriety that would warrant a right to challenge the validity of a search warrant. Certainly, prudence dictates that Magistrate Boober's involvement with warrants from the Ranson police force should be severely curtailed. . . .

Finally, we are asked to extend the rule of necessity to allow Magistrate Boober to handle warrants when she is the on-call magistrate. The rule of necessity is an exception to the disqualification of a judge. It allows a judge who is otherwise disqualified to handle the case to preside if there is no provision that allows another judge to hear the matter. . . .

The rule of necessity is an exception to the general rule precluding a disqualified judge from hearing a matter. Therefore, it is strictly construed and applied only when there is no other person having jurisdiction to handle the matter that can be brought in to hear it. . . . We would not sanction the use of the rule were it to be offered if Chief Boober appeared seeking the search warrant. In the case of the other police officers from Ranson, we decline to utilize the rule simply because we do not find that Magistrate Boober is automatically barred from issuing warrants at their request.

---

14. The 1993 West Virginia Blue Book gives the population of the City of Ranson at 2,890. According to the [briefs], there are six other police officers in addition to the Chief of Police.

There may be circumstances that can be shown that would cast a shadow over the magistrate's impartiality. In that event, a motion to suppress the evidence obtained under the warrant may be made, and the issue will be resolved at a hearing. . . . The matter is remanded for a further hearing with regard to the warrant if the relators below desire to challenge it on the basis that there are additional facts, other than her marriage to Chief Boober, that demonstrate Magistrate Boober was not neutral and detached. . . .

Notes

1. *Who issues warrants? Majority view.* Most states (more than 30) allow only judges and magistrates to issue warrants. Some state statutes require that magistrates be lawyers, while others list no special qualifications. Judges generally appoint magistrates. They are thus subject to removal by judges or city officials and lack some of the usual privileges accorded to judicial officers. A smaller group of states allow functionaries—who go by titles such as "clerk magistrates," "ministerial recorders," clerks of court, or court commissioners—to issue search warrants. In West Virginia, mayors have the power to issue search warrants pursuant to violations of city ordinances. W. Va. Code §8-10-1.

As noted in *Dietrick*, the Supreme Court, in Connally v. Georgia, 429 U.S. 245 (1977), found unconstitutional a system that compensated magistrates for each warrant they issued. What if, to encourage protection of individual rights, magistrates were paid for warrants they *refused* to issue?

2. *Neutrality in outcomes.* What if a defendant can show that a particular magistrate has never refused a warrant or approves warrants 98 percent of the time? See Richard van Duizend, Paul Sutton & Charlotte Carter, The Search Warrant Process: Preconceptions, Perceptions, Practices 26-27 (1985). One study of warrant practices in one jurisdiction noted that some judges handled far more than their share of warrant applications. Of the 24 judges available for duty, six judges issued almost three-fourths of the search warrants. Laurence A. Benner & Charles T. Samarkos, Searching for Narcotics in San Diego: Preliminary Findings from the San Diego Search Warrant Project, 36 Cal. W. L. Rev. 221, 226 (2000). Could a defendant strengthen her challenge to the neutrality of a magistrate by demonstrating that the police apply to the particular magistrate in question for search warrants far more often than to other available magistrates?

When law enforcement officers submit warrants for electronic review, it is possible to track the amount of time that a magistrate spends between opening the document and approving it. If a magistrate spends 27 seconds reviewing a lengthy warrant application to search telephone records in a homicide case, how might defense counsel frame an argument that the warrant was not reviewed by a "neutral and detached" judicial officer? See Jessica Miller & Aubrey Weiber, Warrants Approved in Just Minutes: Are Utah Judges Really Reading Them Before Signing Off?, Salt Lake Tribune, Jan. 14, 2018.

b. Execution of Warrants

After the police obtain a valid warrant, they must "execute" it. That is, the police carry out a search within the limits described in the warrant, and "return" it to the magistrate who issued the warrant. The return serves as a report about the search.

Recall that the court in Entick v. Carrington expressed some concern about the lack of any return for a general warrant, and thus the enforcement officer who conducted the search would not be accountable for completing the job properly. Does a return actually prevent abuses by searchers?

Specific procedure rules and statutes address the details of executing warrants. For instance, rules determine the total time that can elapse between issuance and execution of a search warrant. All but three states prescribe a deadline for serving a warrant, at which time the warrant expires. This period ranges from two days (North Carolina and Pennsylvania) to 60 days (Arkansas). The typical time span is 10 days (the period employed in more than 30 states plus the federal system). As one might expect, searches are far more likely to produce the expected evidence if they are executed promptly. See Laurence A. Benner & Charles T. Samarkos, Searching for Narcotics in San Diego: Preliminary Findings from the San Diego Search Warrant Project, 36 Cal. W. L. Rev. 221, 223 (2000).

■ STATE v. TANYA MARIE ANYAN
104 P.3d 511 (Mont. 2004)

NELSON, J.

. . . ¶3 In late May 2000, Officer Christopher Nichols of the Thompson Falls Police Department was assigned to investigate suspected illegal drug activity occurring at a rented house in Thompson Falls. During the course of the investigation, Officer Nichols determined that the occupants of the house were involved in operating a clandestine methamphetamine lab. Hence, on July 11, 2000, Officer Nichols requested the assistance of Sergeant Allen Bardwell, an officer with the Kalispell Police Department and team leader of the Kalispell SWAT team, in serving a search warrant. After meeting with Officer Nichols and learning that the house to be searched was a large structure consisting of three levels with numerous rooms and that it might be occupied by as many as fifteen individuals, Sergeant Bardwell contacted the Flathead County Sheriff Department's SWAT team for assistance. The commander of the Flathead County SWAT team, Undersheriff Chuck Curry, agreed to assist in the service of the warrant.

¶4 On July 24, 2000, Officer Nichols obtained a warrant to search the residence. In his application for the search warrant, Officer Nichols related that "out of the ordinary traffic" was seen coming [to] and going from the residence and that a great number of the vehicles were from Washington state. Officer Nichols also stated that he checked the license plates on three of the vehicles that he had seen at the residence. One of them was registered to [Troy Klein]. Officer Nichols then checked with Spokane County and discovered that Klein had been charged in the past with committing drug offenses. According to Officer Nichols, Klein also had three active felony warrants.

¶5 Officer Nichols also related in his search warrant application that several other individuals that had been seen near the residence had been charged with drug offenses. In addition, one of the vehicles seen at the residence was registered to an individual who had felony convictions for burglary and child rape. Officer Nichols also related that during his investigation, he discovered that there was a surveillance camera located in the second story east window of the residence and that it appeared to be pointed at the driveway.

¶6 Officer Nichols had discovered during the course of his investigation that an individual matching Klein's description had purchased ammunition from a local hardware store. While he did not include this information in the application for the search warrant, Officer Nichols did share this information with Sergeant Bardwell and Undersheriff Curry. However, the two-and-a-half month investigation, which included surveillance of the home, had yielded no observation or reports of weapons sighted in the home or in the possession of any of the individuals in the home. Officer Nichols also discovered that Klein had a warrant for his arrest in connection with a nonviolent felony parole violation.

¶7 On the night of July 25, 2000, the two SWAT teams, totaling fifteen men, and officers from several other law enforcement agencies converged on Thompson Falls at approximately 1:45 A.M. . . . Officer Nichols ordered two officers to conduct surveillance on the residence from an upstairs bedroom of the house across the street. Officer Shawna Reinschmidt was watching the activities in the front of the house at 2:20 A.M. when a car, which had left the house about five minutes earlier, returned, and the male driver got out of the car and yelled at everyone to get inside and turn off the lights. Officer Reinschmidt reported her observations to the SWAT team assembled at the police department. . . . Officer Reinschmidt continued to observe the house and although she saw some movement in the kitchen, she later testified that her observations were entirely consistent with the occupants preparing to retire for the night.

¶9 Law enforcement officers executed their no-knock raid at 3:00 A.M. As the officers approached the house they observed that it was quiet and most of the lights were off. None of the officers detected any activity or heard anything consistent with attempts to escape or resist arrest. . . .

¶10 The officers approached the home from the west and the north, outside of the range of the surveillance camera located on the east side of the house. The Kalispell SWAT team was assigned to enter the house at the upper level from an outside stairway and the Flathead County SWAT team was assigned to enter the house from the ground floor. At least six officers from the Kalispell SWAT team entered the top floor by using a steel ram to break the doorjamb. They confronted four of the occupants of the house who were in various stages of sleep and preparation for sleep. Another seven or eight officers from the Flathead County SWAT team entered the house through the downstairs kitchen door confronting the two occupants residing in that portion of the house. Another five to ten officers surrounded the house. The officers did not knock and announce their presence prior to entering the house. . . .

¶12 [Several occupants of the house were charged] with conspiracy to manufacture dangerous drugs; criminal production or manufacture of dangerous drugs; criminal possession of dangerous drugs; and possession of dangerous drugs with intent to sell. [They] each filed motions to suppress the evidence seized during the search of the residence, based in part on the officers' failure to knock and announce their presence prior to entering the house to execute the search warrant. The District Court denied the motions. . . .

¶20 This is an issue of first impression in Montana. Montana has no statutory provisions or case law addressing the knock-and-announce rule. Consequently, we look to the relevant federal law and the laws of our sister states to decide this issue. We also look to the greater protections afforded to Montanans in search and seizure matters under Article II, Sections 10 and 11 of the Montana Constitution. . . .

¶22 Underlying the knock-and-announce rule are concerns for the protection of privacy, reduction in the potential for violence, and the prevention of the destruction of property of private citizens. There is nothing more terrifying to the occupants than to be suddenly confronted in the privacy of their home by a police officer decorated with guns and the insignia of his office. This is why the law protects its entrance so rigidly.

[As] a matter of policy, no-knock warrants are disfavored because of their staggering potential for violence to both the occupants of the residence and the police. "Unannounced breaking and entering into a home could quite easily lead an individual to believe that his safety was in peril and cause him to take defensive measures which he otherwise would not have taken had he known that a warrant had been issued to search his home." State v. Bamber, 630 So. 2d 1048, 1052 (Fla. 1994). . . .

¶25 Because the Fourth Amendment protects property as well as privacy, another purpose of the knock-and-announce rule is to prevent the needless destruction of property. . . .

¶29 [The United States Supreme Court addressed the knock-and-announce principle in Wilson v. Arkansas, 514 U.S. 927 (1995). The Supreme Court held that the common-law knock-and-announce principle forms a part of the Fourth Amendment reasonableness inquiry.] In making this determination, the Supreme Court examined in *Wilson* the history of the common-law knock-and-announce rule, noting that although common law generally protected a man's house as "his castle of defense and asylum," common-law courts long held that the sheriff, acting on behalf of the King, could enter a man's house to arrest him "or to do other execution of the King's process," but only after signifying the cause of his coming and requesting that the doors be opened. See 3 W. Blackstone, Commentaries; Semayne's Case, 77 Eng. Rep. 194 (K.B. 1603). . . . In addition, most of the states that ratified the Fourth Amendment enacted constitutional provisions or statutes generally incorporating English common law and a few states enacted statutes specifically embracing the common-law view that the breaking of the door of a dwelling was permitted once admittance was refused. . . . Hence, the Court held that the common-law knock-and-announce principle does form a part of the Fourth Amendment reasonableness inquiry.

¶32 The Court further held, however, that not every entry must be preceded by an announcement. [The] presumption in favor of announcement necessarily would give way to countervailing law enforcement interests. Those interests included circumstances presenting a threat of physical harm to officers, the fact that an officer is pursuing a recently escaped arrestee, and where officers have reason to believe that evidence would likely be destroyed if advance notice were given. . . .

EXIGENT CIRCUMSTANCES

¶34 Exigent circumstances [are] those circumstances that would cause a reasonable person to believe that entry (or other relevant prompt action) was necessary to prevent physical harm to the officers or other persons, the destruction of relevant evidence, the escape of a suspect, or some other consequence improperly frustrating legitimate law enforcement efforts. . . .

¶35 There are two types of exigencies, those that are foreknown and those unexpected that arise on the scene. . . . In the case before us on appeal, all of the factors that officers actually deemed exigent were actually known well in advance of applying for the search warrant. The SWAT teams became involved in this investigation almost two weeks prior to applying for a search warrant. It was at that point that the decision was made that there would be a no-knock forcible entry into the house. The court issuing the search warrant was never apprised of that decision, nor were any exigent circumstances laid out to the court when the search warrant was applied for.

¶36 Moreover, while peril to officers or the possibility of destruction of evidence or escape may well demonstrate an exigency, mere unspecific fears about those possibilities will not. Were they enough, the knock-and-announce [principle would be inapplicable to virtually all narcotics-based cases. The Supreme Court, however, has] held that the Fourth Amendment does not permit a blanket exception to the knock-and-announce requirement in felony drug investigations. Richards v. Wisconsin, 520 U.S. 385 (1997).

¶37 In *Richards*, law enforcement officers obtained a warrant to search Richards' motel room for drugs and related paraphernalia. One officer, dressed as a maintenance man, knocked on the door and stated that he was with maintenance. With the chain still on the door, Richards cracked it open, but slammed it closed again when he saw a uniformed officer standing behind the "maintenance man." After waiting two or three seconds, the officers kicked in the door. They claimed at trial that they identified themselves as police as they were kicking in the door. The officers caught Richards trying to escape through a window. They found cash and cocaine hidden in plastic bags in the bathroom ceiling.

¶38 Richards sought to have the evidence from his motel room suppressed on the ground that the officers failed to knock and announce their presence prior to forcing entry into the room. The trial court denied the motion. . . . The Wisconsin Supreme Court affirmed, concluding that . . . exigent circumstances justifying a no-knock entry are always present in felony drug cases; hence, police officers are never required to knock and announce their presence when executing a search warrant in a felony drug investigation.

¶39 The United States Supreme Court disagreed and determined that the Fourth Amendment does not permit a blanket exception to the knock-and-announce requirement for felony drug investigations. Rather, the Supreme Court held that to justify a no-knock entry, police must have a reasonable suspicion that knocking and announcing their presence, under the particular circumstances, would be dangerous or futile, or that it would inhibit effective investigation of the crime by, for example, allowing the destruction of evidence.

¶40 [The use of blanket exceptions] presented two serious concerns: (1) the exception contains considerable overgeneralization as not every drug investigation poses substantial risks to the officers' safety and the preservation of evidence; and (2) the reasons for creating an exception in one category can, relatively easily, be applied to others and thereby render meaningless the knock-and-announce element of the Fourth Amendment's reasonableness requirement.

¶41 Although the Supreme Court rejected the Wisconsin court's blanket exception to the knock-and-announce requirement in *Richards*, the Supreme Court agreed with the trial court that on the facts of that case, it was reasonable for the officers to believe that Richards knew, after he opened the door, that the men seeking entry to his room were the police and that once the officers reasonably believed that Richards knew who they were, it was reasonable for them to force entry immediately given the disposable nature of the drugs. . . .

SAFETY CONCERNS

. . . ¶44 [Evidence] that firearms are within the residence or that a particular defendant is armed is not by itself sufficient to create an exigency. There must be specific information to lead the officers to a reasonable conclusion that the presence of firearms raises concerns for the officers' safety. [Threats] to an officer's safety, a criminal record reflecting violent tendencies, or a verified reputation of a suspect's violent nature can be enough to provide law enforcement officers with justification to forgo the necessity of knocking and announcing their presence.

¶45 In the case sub judice, the officers had no information that any of the occupants of the house possessed weapons. Officer Nichols had information that a person matching Klein's description had purchased ammunition. However, even after months of surveillance, Officer Nichols had no information of weapons being in the residence and no report of anyone seeing any of the occupants of the house, including Klein, with weapons. There was no testimony indicating that any of the occupants of the house were prone to violence or the use of weapons or had ever made threats against law enforcement officers.

¶46 Prior to initiating the raid, Sergeant Bardwell completed a risk analysis report intended to assess the risk associated with specific individuals who the officers anticipate might be present during a raid. Sergeant Bardwell testified that Klein was the only person considered in conjunction with the risk analysis assessment and the only person about whom Sergeant Bardwell had any information prior to the raid. Sergeant Bardwell agreed that the only criterion that applied to Klein from the risk analysis checklist was that he was on probation or parole for a nonviolent offense. . . .

¶48 The State claims that another factor in determining exigency under the safety exception is the inherent danger in methamphetamine labs. In this case, although Officer Nichols expressed concerns regarding the safety of neighborhood residents, he made no attempt to evacuate any residences. . . .

DESTRUCTION OF EVIDENCE

¶58 We also conclude that in this case the possibility of destruction of evidence did not create an exigent circumstance justifying the no-knock entry into Appellants' house. [The] government must prove they had a reasonable belief that the loss or destruction of evidence was imminent. The mere possibility or suspicion that a party is likely to dispose of evidence when faced with the execution of a search warrant is not sufficient to create an exigency. . . . The larger the amount of drugs and the more complex the operation, the less likelihood there is that evidence will be destroyed during the period between the knock and announce and the subsequent entry.

¶60 In this case, both Sergeant Bardwell and Undersheriff Curry testified that the mere fact that the residence contained a meth lab would not justify a no-knock entry. Moreover, Sergeant Bardwell testified that the potential for the destruction of the meth lab was not a concern in deciding to take on the assignment. Both Sergeant Bardwell and Undersheriff Curry agreed that a meth lab cannot be destroyed in a matter of five to ten seconds.

CONCLUSION

. . . ¶63 [The] decision to make a no-knock entry should ordinarily be made by a neutral and detached magistrate as part of the application for search warrant. An investigating officer may, however, make this decision based on unexpected exigent circumstances that arise on the scene. When law enforcement officers contemplate a no-knock entry in executing a search warrant, that intention must be included in the application for the search warrant along with any foreknown exigent circumstances justifying the no-knock entry. . . .

¶65 In conclusion, we hold that the law enforcement officers' no-knock entry into Appellants' house to execute the search warrant violated Appellants' federal and state constitutional rights to be free from unreasonable searches and seizures. Consequently, the trial court erred in failing to suppress the evidence resulting from that search. . . .

¶72 [The dissent] objects to our analysis, complaining that we have taken the "totality" out of "totality of the circumstances." Contrary to the dissent's contention, in order to examine the "totality" of the circumstances, each circumstance must first be considered on its own strength. [We] cannot agree that just because there are a number of circumstances, not one of which standing alone would create an exigency, the sheer volume of circumstances without something more is sufficient to create exigent circumstances. [Simply] put, zero plus zero can never equal one. . . .

RICE, J., dissenting.

. . . ¶78 [The Supreme Court in] *Richards* held that, although police should be required to make the necessary showing whenever the reasonableness of a no-knock entry is challenged, the showing itself is "not high." Further, it is not necessary to establish a level of proof satisfying the probable cause standard.

¶79 Indeed, the *Richards* "reasonable suspicion" standard is the same standard applied for the reasonableness of an investigative stop. . . .

¶81 . . . Citing to *Richards'* holding that there can be no "blanket exceptions" to the knock-and-announce rule for felony drug investigations, the Court simply dismisses the nature of the crime here as irrelevant to the inquiry. This is an incorrect application of *Richards*, which also concluded that it is "indisputable that felony drug investigations may frequently involve both" the threat of physical violence and the likelihood of destruction of evidence. . . .

¶82 [The Court also] dismisses the significance of the kind of drugs involved here—a methamphetamine laboratory. The Court should well know by now that "meth labs" are inherently unstable and dangerous, presenting this additional danger to officers. Nonetheless, the Court concludes this factor is not relevant to the inquiry because police made no attempt to evacuate any residences. Unfortunately, the dismissal of this concern by the Court does not accurately reflect the evidence in the record. To the contrary, Officer Bardwell testified that the situation here—"a meth lab with multiple suspects and they had warrants"—weighed significantly in his mind. . . .

¶83 . . . Klein's ammunition purchase may by itself have been insufficient to establish an exigency, but that did not render this evidence irrelevant to the inquiry. The Court reasons as if the evidence did not exist or was completely inconsequential. To the contrary, Officer Bardwell testified that evidence of the ammunition purchase by Klein, a fugitive felon, was significant to his analysis, and the District Court found this fact to be significant. . . .

¶85 [The surveillance camera] would not have been rendered ineffective but for the no-knock entry. [Officer Bardwell testified] about the significance of the surveillance camera: . . . "if they have an operation that they deem the expense and trouble to put up counter-surveillance, it's probably a pretty substantial operation that they have." . . .

¶88 Additional factors could be analyzed, but this is enough. Clearly, there were specifically identifiable, objective factors which indicated to police that the situation required a no-knock entry. However, the Court, engaging in a "divide and conquer" analysis, systematically eliminates the effect of each factor. [The Court's analysis] separates and pigeonholes the factors which the police here considered, thereby eliminating all of them. In effect, it has taken the "totality" out of "totality of the circumstances."

¶90 Police here were faced with executing a felony drug warrant in a large structure in which numerous suspects with violent criminal backgrounds were staying. One suspect was known to have purchased ammunition. The suspects had mounted a surveillance camera. A meth lab was housed in the structure, and the size of the structure would inhibit the ability of police to locate and secure the lab. The numbers of suspects known to be inside could present safety and escape concerns. Shortly before the raid, one suspect yelled suspiciously. From a consideration of the totality of these circumstances, I would conclude that police had objective data from which they could reasonably infer, and from which a reasonable suspicion would arise, that a no-knock entry was necessary.

Notes

1. *Use of force in executing warrants and "knock and announce."* Most states have statutes requiring a police officer executing a search warrant to "knock and announce"—that is, to knock on the door before entering, to identify himself as a police officer, and to explain the purpose for seeking entry. See 18 U.S.C. §3109. Those with no statute on point have recognized the doctrine through judicial opinions. Only after entrance has been refused may the officer use force to enter. The knock-and-announce requirement derives from the common law. See Semayne's Case, 77 Eng. Rep. 194 (K.B. 1603). It also has constitutional dimensions: A failure to knock and announce can have some bearing on the constitutional "reasonableness" of a search or seizure. See Wilson v. Arkansas, 514 U.S. 927 (1995).

Once the officers have knocked on the door and announced their identity and purpose for wanting to enter, they may then enter by force after waiting a reasonable time for the occupants to respond to their knock. The amount of delay required in a given case depends on the nature of the evidence involved, the size of the dwelling, the time of day, and many other factors. In United States v. Banks, 540 U.S. 31 (2003), the Court approved of forceful entry by officers after they knocked, announced, and waited for 15 to 20 seconds. The evidence involved (cocaine) was easily disposable, and the apartment was small.

2. *No-knock entry.* There are important exceptions to the knock-and-announce requirement. Typically, the police may enter without notice if they have enough reason to believe that notice would endanger them or some other party, or would

allow for the destruction of evidence or the escape of a suspect. What common household sounds might justify a forcible no-knock entry to execute a search? See also United States v. Ramirez, 523 U.S. 65 (1998) ("no knock" searches that cause property damage subject to same reasonableness standard as those causing no damage). A number of courts allow police officers to enter without announcing their true intentions if they can gain entry through a ruse such as pretending to be the "pizza man." Adcock v. Commonwealth, 967 S.W.2d 6 (Ky. 1998); State v. Elerieki, 993 P.2d 1191 (Haw. 2000). Is entry through a ruse consistent with the rationale of the knock-and-announce principle?

According to the opinion in Richards v. Wisconsin, 520 U.S. 385 (1997), the exceptions to the knock-and-announce requirement should not be phrased too broadly. A blanket exception for "drug cases" will not stand; the police must show case-specific facts to demonstrate the need for a no-knock warrant. However, on the specific facts of that case, the officers' decision to enter the location unannounced might be constitutionally reasonable. An exploration of the cases that evaluate no-knock entry by the police appears on the web extension for this chapter at *http:// www.crimpro.com/extension/ch03.*

3. *Limits on nighttime searches.* Another common subject for statutes and codes of criminal procedure is the time of day or night an officer may execute a search warrant. More than a dozen states have rules or statutes explicitly authorizing the execution of a search warrant at night, without any special showing or procedures. See Ind. Code §35-33-5-7(c); Va. Code Ann. §19.2-56. However, more than 30 states have statutes or procedural rules imposing some legal limit on the execution of search warrants at night beyond the usual requirements for daytime warrants. These states often require the government agents to make some special showing to the magistrate before conducting a search at night. See Minn. Stat. §626.14 (search warrant may be served only between 7 A.M. and 8 P.M. unless court "determines on the basis of facts stated in the affidavits that a nighttime search outside those hours is necessary to prevent the loss, destruction, or removal of the objects of the search or to protect the searchers or the public"); State v. Jackson, 742 N.W.2d 163 (Minn. 2007) (Fourth Amendment incorporates common-law requirement that law enforcement officers have some justification for executing a search warrant at night); State v. Zeller, 845 N.W.2d 6 (S.D. 2014) (search warrant affidavit did not establish separate probable cause for nighttime search of defendant's resident). Where detailed statutes or procedure rules loom larger than any constitutional requirements, does that tend to make procedure clearer?

4. *Witnesses and returns.* The law in Germany and France requires searches of a home to be witnessed by a resident or someone else not working for the police. See Richard S. Frase & Thomas Weigend, German Criminal Justice as a Guide to American Law Reform: Similar Problems, Better Solutions?, 18 B.C. Int'l & Comp. L. Rev. 317 (1995). In the United States, officers executing a search warrant must fill out the "return," describing to the issuing judge the results of the search. Do these two requirements provide comparable protections to the owner of property that is searched?

5. *Burden of proof.* Most jurisdictions encourage greater police use of search warrants by shifting the burden of proof at a suppression hearing. While the government bears the burden of proof for warrantless searches that are challenged at a suppression hearing, the defendant must carry the burden of proof for warranted searches. Ford v. State, 158 S.W.3d 488 (Tex. Crim. App. 2005) (defendant bears

burden of production in motions to suppress, but burden of proof shifts to state if defendant shows that search was warrantless); People v. Syrie, 101 P.3d 219 (Colo. 2004). There is, however, a sizable group of states placing the burden of coming forward and the burden of persuasion on the prosecution for all motions to suppress. See Kan. Stat. Ann. §22-3216 ("the burden of proving that the search and seizure were lawful shall be on the prosecution").

6. *Physical detentions during execution of warrant.* Can the police insist that those present at the location of a warranted search remain there while the search goes forward? Can they use force to prevent those present from moving about? See Muehler v. Mena, 544 U.S. 93 (2005) (execution of search warrant was not unreasonable where officers entered home at 7 A.M., detained occupants of home in handcuffs during hours-long search of home for weapons and gang member, and questioned occupants about their immigration status); Michigan v. Summers, 452 U.S. 692 (1981); Cotton v. State, 872 A.2d 87 (Md. 2005) (officers executing search warrant at residence used to sell drugs may detain person found standing outside the home).

In Bailey v. United States, 568 U.S. 186 (2013), the Court addressed the outer geographical boundary of the *Summers* rule. Local police obtained a warrant to search a residence for a handgun. Officers watched from outside as two men (both of whom matched a very general description of the suspect) left the apartment in a car. Two detectives followed the car, while other officers remained behind to execute the search warrant. The detectives stopped the car about a mile from the apartment, ordered the two men out of the car, and did a pat-down search of both men. Then they handcuffed the men and returned them to the apartment. The Court, in an opinion by Justice Kennedy, held that any detention "incident" to the execution of a search warrant must be limited to the "immediate vicinity of the premises to be searched." Searches outside that area do not present the same dangers to officers or the same risks of evidence destruction that justifies detention of all occupants within the premises.

7. *Warrants for computer searches.* Some magistrates place specialized conditions on how computer warrants are executed. The conditions address the on-site seizure of computers, the timing of a later off-site search, the method of the off-site search, and the return of the seized computers after searches are complete. Does the nature of the storage medium for information justify a specialized set of practices for executing a warrant? See Orin S. Kerr, Ex Ante Regulation of Computer Search and Seizure, 96 Va. L. Rev. 1241 (2010).

B. WARRANTLESS SEARCHES

The U.S. Supreme Court and state supreme courts say it often: Searches and seizures ordinarily must be carried out under warrants obtained from neutral magistrates. See, e.g., Trupiano v. United States, 334 U.S. 699, 705 (1948) ("It is a cardinal rule that, in seizing goods and articles, law enforcement agents must secure and use search warrants wherever reasonably practicable"). Look back at the language of the Fourth Amendment and its equivalents. How would you respond to an argument that searches can be conducted only pursuant to warrants?

Even if an absolute warrant requirement is not plausible, the constitutional language and the oft-stated judicial "preference" for warrants might lead to the expectation that *most* searches are conducted pursuant to a warrant, with exceptions to the warrant requirement being just that—exceptions, and therefore uncommon. Does a judicial preference for warrants mean that warrants are common in practice? It is difficult to determine what proportion of searches are carried out based on warrants, but the current appellate case law suggests a great majority of searches in most contexts are conducted without first obtaining a warrant.

1. *Exigent Circumstances*

Perhaps the largest "exception" to the preference for warrants is the presence of exigent circumstances. When exigent circumstances appear, there is no need for police to obtain a warrant before conducting a search. Exigent circumstances include situations in which an immediate search or seizure is necessary to protect the safety of an officer or the public, or when the suspect might escape or destroy evidence. In what proportion of all searches and seizures would you imagine that there is some risk that one of these events might occur? How much risk must the government accept before the circumstances become "exigent"? Can the police take any actions that would provoke the suspect to flee or to destroy evidence, and therefore to create their own exigent circumstances?

■ STATE v. RASHAD WALKER
62 A.3d 897 (N.J. 2013)

RODRÍGUEZ, J.

This criminal appeal arises from a warrantless entry into defendant Rashad Walker's apartment, by undercover police officers who saw defendant smoking a marijuana cigarette during a brief interaction with him, while the apartment door was open. Defendant's motion to suppress evidence of possession of cocaine, heroin, and marijuana was denied. He entered into a plea agreement with the State to plead guilty to two counts of third-degree possession of controlled dangerous substances (CDS) with the intent to distribute and one count of third-degree possession of CDS with the intent to distribute while within 500 feet of public housing. The judge imposed three six-year extended terms, subject to a three-year period of parole ineligibility, to be served concurrently. . . .

I.

At the hearing on the motion to suppress, Newark Police Detective James Cosgrove, of the Narcotics Enforcement Team, testified that in the mid-morning of March 29, 2008, he received a tip from a confidential source. The informant had provided useful information to the Newark Police Department on at least ten occasions. The tip was that an African-American male was selling marijuana, cocaine, and heroin from a specified apartment in the Riverview Court public housing project in Newark. Around 11:00 P.M., Cosgrove and fellow officers Javier Rivera, Christopher Sigara, and James Rios, dressed in plain clothes, went to defendant's apartment. The officers intended to buy CDS from defendant, in order to corroborate the tip.

Officer Rios was chosen to be the buyer. Rios knocked at the apartment door. An African-American man, later identified as defendant, answered it. He was smoking a hand-rolled cigarette. Cosgrove, who was standing just outside the door, immediately recognized the smell of burning marijuana. Then defendant saw Rivera's police badge hanging around his neck. Defendant threw the cigarette into his apartment, retreated, and attempted to slam the door shut. Rios stopped the door from closing, followed defendant into the apartment, and arrested him. According to Cosgrove, he and the three officers entered the apartment to prevent defendant from fleeing, destroying evidence, retrieving a weapon, or in some other way impeding his arrest for possession of marijuana.

Defendant was searched in the living room. On his person, the officers found $99 in cash. In plain view in the living room, the officers saw a plastic bag containing 22.4 grams of marijuana, twenty-seven envelopes of heroin stamped "Horsepower," a plastic bag containing 4.2 grams of cocaine, a small Ziploc-style bag containing marijuana, a marijuana cigarette, a dark-colored plate with cocaine residue on it, a razor blade, and a digital scale. . . . The trial court denied the motion to suppress, concluding that probable cause to arrest defendant arose at the moment defendant opened the door smoking a marijuana cigarette, which is a disorderly persons offense. . . .

III.

. . . The warrant requirement provides citizens with protection from unreasonable arrests by having a neutral magistrate determine probable cause before an arrest is made. The warrant requirement is strictly applied to physical entry into the home because the primary goal of the Fourth Amendment and Article I, Paragraph 7 of the state constitution is to protect individuals from unreasonable home intrusions. . . .

Accordingly, a warrantless arrest in an individual's home is presumptively unreasonable. Nonetheless, we have adopted the principle that "exigent circumstances" in conjunction with probable cause may excuse police from compliance with the warrant requirement. Therefore, warrantless home arrests are prohibited absent probable cause and exigent circumstances. Without a warrant, the State has the burden of proving the overall reasonableness of an arrest. The State must show by a preponderance of the evidence that the warrantless arrest was valid.

First, we must determine whether the [police had probable cause to enter the apartment to arrest Walker]. The informant's history of providing reliable information to police on ten prior occasions was sufficient to support his veracity. However, the mere fact that the informant was reliable in the past cannot itself establish probable cause. There is no indication either directly from the source or in the details provided in the tip that specifies the informant's basis of knowledge. Nowhere did the informant indicate where he obtained the information or whether it was obtained in a reliable manner. . . . Also, the tip did not indicate any detail of when the information was obtained; even if accurate at one time, there was no guarantee that the contraband would still be in defendant's apartment when police went to investigate. Therefore, the tip lacked the requisite basis of knowledge to provide probable cause to believe defendant possessed CDS with intent to distribute. Nevertheless, the officers observed defendant smoking a marijuana cigarette in violation of N.J.S.A. 2C:35-10(a)(4) in their presence. At that point, the officers had probable cause to arrest defendant.

Despite the existence of probable cause to arrest defendant, a showing of exigent circumstances was required in order to comply with the Fourth Amendment; specifically, the exigencies of the situation must make a warrantless home arrest imperative. As the Supreme Court has held, this exception only "applies when the exigencies of the situation make the needs of law enforcement so compelling that a warrantless search is objectively reasonable." Kentucky v. King, 563 U.S. 452 (2011). Consequently, the application of the doctrine of exigent circumstances demands a fact-sensitive, objective analysis.

In determining whether exigency exists, courts consider many factors, including the degree of urgency and the amount of time necessary to obtain a warrant; the reasonable belief that the evidence was about to be lost, destroyed, or removed from the scene; the severity or seriousness of the offense involved; the possibility that a suspect was armed or dangerous; and the strength or weakness of the underlying probable cause determination. . . .

In Kentucky v. King, the United States Supreme Court explained that in response to a knock on their door by law enforcement, occupants have the right to refuse to answer the door or to refuse to speak with the officers. The Court held, however, that "occupants who choose not to stand on their constitutional rights but instead elect to attempt to destroy evidence have only themselves to blame for the warrantless exigent-circumstances search that may ensue." The possible destruction of evidence is of great concern when dealing with controlled dangerous substances because "drugs may be easily destroyed by flushing them down a toilet or rinsing them down a drain."

As noted above, the gravity of the underlying offense for which the arrest is being made is an important factor to be considered when determining whether any exigency exists. A number of cases address that factor. In Welsh v. Wisconsin, 466 U.S. 740 (1984), after a witness reported observing a car driving erratically, police checked the car's registration and obtained defendant's address. Without a warrant, law enforcement entered the defendant's home when his step-daughter answered the door, proceeded into the defendant's bedroom, and placed him under arrest for driving while under the influence. The Supreme Court held that the seizure violated the Fourth Amendment, focusing on the critical fact that under Wisconsin law, "driving while intoxicated was treated as a noncriminal violation subject to a civil forfeiture proceeding for a maximum fine of $200." The Supreme Court found that when the government's only interest in entering a home without a warrant "is to arrest for a minor offense, [the] presumption of unreasonableness that attaches to the officers' conduct is difficult to rebut."

In State v. Holland, 744 A.2d 656 (N.J. App. 2000), the Appellate Division consolidated two unrelated cases involving warrantless searches of homes. In one case, an officer knocked on the defendant Holland's door because he smelled burning marijuana emanating from the residence. Officers entered the home after they apprehended a person who attempted to leave through the back door. They conducted a search of the residence and found a large quantity of marijuana, drug paraphernalia, including equipment to grow marijuana, and a loaded gun. In the second case, a policeman on a bicycle patrolling the seaside town of Manasquan smelled burning marijuana as he rode past a home. He knocked on the front door of the home, and a woman inside consented to his entrance. When the officer entered, he saw defendant Califano and others smoking a marijuana cigarette on the back porch. The Appellate Division limited the issue in both cases to "whether the policeman's entry was authorized by what he knew before he went in."

In examining both cases, the court found that based on New Jersey precedent, the smell of burning marijuana gave officers probable cause that a criminal offense was being committed. However, the Appellate Division held that where the only evidence officers have before entering a premises is the smell of burning marijuana, law enforcement only has "probable cause to believe . . . that a disorderly persons offense was being committed," and exigent circumstances do not exist to justify law enforcement's warrantless entry into the home. . . .

The case law also addresses exigency manufactured by the police. In State v. Hutchins, 561 A.2d 1142 (N.J. 1989), Newark Police received a tip from a reliable informant that "a black male named Bob dressed in blue was dealing heroin from 118 Eleventh Avenue, Newark." Two officers went to the address to attempt a controlled buy, and a black male wearing a blue jogging suit answered the door. He did not respond to the officers' attempted solicitation, but his fist was clenched in a manner suggesting the possible concealment of narcotics. The officers identified themselves, and the defendant turned and fled into the house. The officers entered the home and arrested the defendant. The Court distinguished "between police-created exigent circumstances designed to subvert the warrant requirement and police-created exigencies that naturally arise in the course of an appropriate police investigation." Although the Court defined the limitations of the police-created exigency issue, it remanded to determine whether exigent circumstances existed.

Therefore, in order to justify the officers' warrantless home arrest here, the State must establish: (1) the existence of exigent circumstances, and (2) that those exigent circumstances were not police-created.

IV.

. . . We must examine the objective reasonableness of the police officers' conduct at each stage of their interaction with defendant. According to the testimony of Cosgrove, which the trial court credited, after the police knocked at the door, a significant event occurred. Defendant appeared at the door smoking a marijuana cigarette. Thus, a disorderly persons offense was being committed in the presence of police officers in the hallway of a public housing building, where the officers have a right to be. Defendant was standing inside his apartment. Nonetheless, defendant and the officers were within inches of each other. Clearly, defendant must have been aware that the officers knew that he was committing an offense. Such observations gave rise to probable cause and authorized the officers to arrest defendant for the disorderly persons offense.

Next, a second significant event occurred once again caused by defendant's action. He discarded the marijuana cigarette, retreated into his apartment, and attempted to close the door. At this point, because the officers directly observed defendant committing an offense in their presence and attempting to flee, they were compelled to act to prevent defendant from disposing of the marijuana cigarette, or eluding the officers.

Although the underlying offense here, possession of marijuana, is a disorderly persons offense, the circumstances indicate that the officers' warrantless entry into defendant's home was objectively reasonable for several reasons. First, the officers saw defendant commit the disorderly persons offense. Second, there was a reasonable belief that the evidence was about to be lost or destroyed. Third, the circumstances presented urgency. Any delay would certainly impede apprehension of defendant and seizure of evidence. These facts distinguish this matter from the factual bases presented in *Holland*, where an officer merely smelled marijuana smoke emanating from defendant Holland's house, and where an officer smelled marijuana from outside of a house where defendant Califano was staying. Moreover, these facts clearly distinguish this case from *Welsh*, where the probable cause to believe that the defendant committed motor vehicle violations was based on a witness's statement that the defendant was driving erratically.

Furthermore, this case is distinguishable on its facts from State v. Bolte, 560 A.2d 644 (N.J. 1989). In *Bolte*, a police officer noticed an automobile swerving on and off the road. The officer activated his police vehicle's lights and siren. However, the driver, later identified as defendant Bolte, ignored the signals to stop and continued to circle the neighborhood at increasing speeds. Thereafter, Bolte stopped in a private driveway, exited the vehicle, and entered his house through the garage. The officer followed Bolte into the house and to the bedroom door where the officer informed Bolte that he was under arrest. Bolte was taken to [the] police station where he refused to take a breathalyzer test. He was charged with reckless driving, driving while intoxicated, refusal to submit to a breathalyzer test, speeding, driving on an expired license, failure to maintain a single lane, disorderly conduct, eluding, and resisting arrest. Bolte moved to suppress the evidence of his refusal to take a breathalyzer test on the basis that his arrest was unlawful. The trial court denied the motion. [This Court reversed the denial of the motion] based on *Welsh*, holding that disorderly persons offenses, "individually and in the aggregate, are within the category of 'minor' offenses held by the *Welsh* Court to be insufficient to establish exigent circumstances justifying a warrantless home entry." However, in *Bolte*, this Court left an exception open to this general rule. "[If] under all the circumstances of a particular case, an officer has probable cause to believe that the delay involved in procuring an arrest warrant will gravely endanger the officer or other persons or will result in the suspect's escape, [we can] perceive no reason to disregard those exigencies on the ground that the offense for which the suspect is sought is a 'minor' one."

This case differs from *Bolte* in three ways. First, the warrantless police intrusion was significantly limited. Officer Rios went inside defendant's apartment only far enough to detain defendant and secure the marijuana cigarette. Second, defendant opened the door to his apartment while smoking a marijuana cigarette with the intent to interact with and expose himself to the scrutiny of whoever was outside. Third, the officers entered defendant's apartment to prevent the destruction of physical evidence that they observed defendant discard. If the officers did not act to preserve the evidence, defendant might well have escaped prosecution on the marijuana possession charge.

In contrast, defendant Bolte did not open the door to his house to interact with the police officer who attempted to stop his vehicle. Rather, he was trying to evade all contact with the officer. Moreover, the officer did not observe Bolte attempt to destroy any physical evidence. In *Bolte*, the officer's objective, based on the facts then known to him, was only to seize Bolte himself.

Accordingly, we hold that here the officers' entry was justified pursuant to the exigent circumstances exception to the warrant requirement. This exception did not authorize a broad search of the apartment, but justified a limited entry necessary to arrest defendant for the disorderly persons offense and to retrieve the marijuana cigarette.

Nevertheless, after entering, the officers saw in the living room CDS and other contraband in plain view. These items were subject to seizure as well. Our holding is limited to the precise facts before us. We do not suggest that, had no one come to the door, the mere smell of marijuana would have justified a forced entry into defendant's home. . . .

Notes

1. *Exigent circumstances: majority position.* Two of the most common grounds for arguing that the police need not obtain a judicial warrant are the potential destruction of evidence and the potential escape of suspects. Are there exigent circumstances—as a categorical matter—in all cases dealing with evidence (such as narcotics) that is easy to destroy or remove? In all cases where private parties will have access to the area while the police seek a warrant?

Exigent circumstances might also be based on possible danger to the investigating officers or to other people in the area where the search is to take place. The danger might involve the use of a weapon on the premises, an item creating a risk of fire or explosion, or the possible presence of persons needing medical care, among other things. See Michigan v. Fisher, 558 U.S. 45 (2009) (exigent circumstances allowed warrantless entry into home when occupant appeared to be injured and was screaming and throwing objects); Holder v. State, 847 N.E.2d 930 (Ind. 2006) (presence of child and adults in home used as methamphetamine lab, combined with health risk to neighbors when smell of ether was present throughout area). For a sample of the rich detail of the cases on this question, see the web extension for this chapter at *http://www.crimpro.com/extension/ch03.*

Exigent circumstances can vary with the seriousness of the crime; the showing becomes more difficult as the crime under investigation becomes less serious. See Welsh v. Wisconsin, 466 U.S. 740 (1984) ("application of the exigent-circumstances exception in the context of a home entry should rarely be sanctioned when there is probable cause to believe that only a minor offense [such as driving while intoxicated] has been committed").

2. *Police creation of exigent circumstances.* The police sometimes take actions during an investigation that cause the suspect to flee or to destroy evidence. They knock on the apartment door before a warrant is available or they announce their presence before detaining the suspect. Some courts declare that police may not "create their own exigent circumstances." Sometimes they ask if the police acted with the bad faith intent to provoke the suspect to flee or to destroy evidence; other courts ask if the police tactics made it reasonably foreseeable that the suspect would flee or destroy evidence. For some courts, it was relevant whether the police followed standard investigative tactics when they caused the exigency. Courts also discuss whether the police had time to secure a warrant before contacting the suspect.

The Supreme Court rejected each of these approaches in Kentucky v. King, 563 U.S. 452 (2011). Justice Alito's opinion for the majority limited the constitutional question to whether the police created an exigency "by engaging or threatening to engage in conduct that violates the Fourth Amendment." For instance, if the police knock on the door of a home and threaten to enter without a warrant or a legally sound basis for a warrantless entry, they could not rely on exigent circumstances to justify their entry. Cf. State v. Campbell, 300 P.3d 72 (Kan. 2013) (police officer improperly created concern for his own safety by knocking on door of suspected drug dealer, covering the peep hole in door with his finger, and "blading" himself to the side of the door with his gun drawn).

It is easy to misread the U.S. Supreme Court opinion in *King* and to conclude that police can now create exigent circumstances at will. The decision of the Kentucky Supreme Court on remand in that case, however, suggests that some limits will persist. In King v. Commonwealth, 386 S.W.3d 119 (Ky. 2012), the court on remand held that the government failed to meet its burden of proving exigent circumstances, even in light of the new constitutional standard. One of the officers at the scene expressed concern about the "possible" destruction of evidence and never specified the types of noises from inside the apartment that indicated the destruction of evidence, as compared to the "ordinary household sounds" of occupants "preparing to answer the door." This was not enough evidence to support an objectively reasonable conclusion that exigent circumstances were present.

Note also that *King* is based on the federal constitution. States that traditionally barred the use of "police-created exigency" may retain their tests as a matter of state constitutional law. If you were a district attorney advising police departments about the impact of *King*, how might you suggest that the officers tread warily around this complex area? Are there easy ways to find functional "safe harbors"? Cf. Emily Ayn Ward, From Pen to Patrol: How Arizona Law Enforcement Applied Carrillo v. Houser, 53 Ariz. L. Rev. 345 (2011).

3. *Maintaining the status quo while seeking a warrant.* May the police enter or remain on the premises long enough to prevent the destruction of evidence or other harms that could occur while they seek a warrant? See Illinois v. McArthur, 531 U.S. 326 (2001) (police obtained probable cause of presence of illegal narcotics in home; occupant required to remain outside home two hours with police officer present while other officers sought search warrant); Segura v. United States, 468 U.S. 796 (1984) (search valid where police officers remained in apartment 19 hours until warrant was obtained); Posey v. Commonwealth, 185 S.W.3d 170 (Ky. 2006) (officers speaking to occupant of home outside front door noticed through open door some marijuana inside the home, and stepped inside to secure evidence until warrant could be obtained for more thorough search). If it requires too many police officers too long to maintain the status quo, do the police then have exigent circumstances?

4. *Anticipatory warrants and exigent circumstances.* If anticipatory warrants are both allowed and encouraged in a particular state, how might that affect the state's doctrines regarding exigent circumstances? Should courts require police to obtain anticipatory search warrants and anticipate exigent circumstances that might arise? See Commonwealth v. Killackey, 572 N.E.2d 560 (Mass. 1991) (rejecting requirement that police obtain anticipatory warrant if they can). Will anticipatory warrants reinvigorate the warrant requirement?

5. *The special status of homes.* Courts strike down warrantless searches most often in the context of searches of homes. Many of the exceptions to the warrant requirement applicable outside the home do not apply in the same way within a home, and courts tend to demand greater justifications for warrantless searches of a house. Some courts extend the special protection provided homes to other areas. Indiana,

for example, has found a similar preference for warrants when the police search parked and impounded cars. Brown v. State, 653 N.E.2d 77 (Ind. 1995) ("Americans in general love their cars. It is, however, particularly important, in the state which hosts the Indy 500 automobile race, to recognize that cars are sources of pride, status, and identity that transcend their objective attributes. We are extremely hesitant to countenance their casual violation.").

6. *Warrants "in writing" and telephonic warrants.* A majority of states have statutes requiring that warrants be in writing. A number of state constitutions also expressly provide for written warrants. See R.I. Const. Art. 1, §6. Despite the prevalence of constitutional provisions and statutes calling for warrants obtained by testimony made under oath and "in writing," a growing number of states have statutes authorizing the police to obtain warrants over the telephone. Consider, for example, Kan. Stat. Ann. §22-2502(a):

> A search warrant shall be issued only upon the oral or written statement, including those conveyed or received by telefacsimile communication, of any person under oath or affirmation which states facts sufficient to show probable cause that a crime has been or is being committed and which particularly describes a person, place or means of conveyance to be searched and things to be seized. Any statement which is made orally shall be either taken down by a certified shorthand reporter, sworn to under oath and made part of the application for a search warrant, or recorded before the magistrate from whom the search warrant is requested and sworn to under oath. Any statement orally made shall be reduced to writing as soon thereafter as possible.

Why does Kansas insist that the person seeking the warrant swear to the statement under oath? Why does the state go to the trouble and expense of reducing the statements to writing? Does the availability of telephonic warrants mean that police can claim exigent circumstances in far fewer cases? One survey of warrant practices discovered that officers rarely used the available procedures for telephonic and electronic search warrants. Laurence A. Benner & Charles T. Samarkos, Searching for Narcotics in San Diego: Preliminary Findings from the San Diego Search Warrant Project, 36 Cal. W. L. Rev. 221, 223 (2000). Why might police officers decline to use such procedures when they are available?

7. *One exception among many.* Exigent circumstances are not the only cases in which courts will allow a warrantless search. As we saw in Chapter 2, many less intrusive searches may be conducted without a warrant. It is useful to make a list of the variety of justifications for warrantless searches. At different points in this volume, we will encounter warrant exceptions for automobile searches, searches incident to arrest, seizures of items in plain view, booking searches, inventory searches, special needs searches, consensual searches, and others.

2 Searches Based on Special Needs

One way to encourage the use of warrants is to allow a standard lower than probable cause for searches when the investigators obtain prior review and approval by magistrates for certain types of warrants. The following case is pivotal in Fourth Amendment jurisprudence. Not only did it open up the possibility of a reduced standard of probable cause for "administrative" warrants, but it also established the importance of "balancing" the competing interests in different categories of Fourth Amendment cases. The balancing methodology sometimes leads to the conclusion that "special needs" apart from criminal law enforcement justify a warrantless search.

■ ROLAND CAMARA v. MUNICIPAL COURT OF SAN FRANCISCO
387 U.S. 523 (1967)

WHITE, J.*

... On November 6, 1963, an inspector of the Division of Housing Inspection of the San Francisco Department of Public Health entered an apartment building to make a routine annual inspection for possible violations of the city's Housing Code. The building's manager informed the inspector that appellant, lessee of the ground floor, was using the rear of his leasehold as a personal residence. Claiming that the building's occupancy permit did not allow residential use of the ground floor, the inspector confronted appellant and demanded that he permit an inspection of the premises. Appellant refused to allow the inspection because the inspector lacked a search warrant.

[The inspector returned on several later occasions without a search warrant. When Camara refused to allow him to enter, he was charged with refusing to permit a lawful inspection, a misdemeanor. Camara argued that the charges against him were unconstitutional because they derived from illegitimate power of government agents to search without probable cause or a warrant.]

[In this Court's cases interpreting the Fourth Amendment,] one governing principle, justified by history and by current experience, has consistently been followed: except in certain carefully denned classes of cases, a search of private property without proper consent is "unreasonable" unless it has been authorized by a valid search warrant. . . .

In Frank v. Maryland, 359 U.S. 360 (1959), this Court upheld the conviction of one who refused to permit a warrantless inspection of private premises for the purposes of locating and abating a suspected public nuisance. . . . We proceed to a re-examination of the factors which persuaded the *Frank* majority to adopt this construction of the Fourth Amendment's prohibition against unreasonable searches.

To the *Frank* majority, municipal fire, health, and housing inspection programs "touch at most upon the periphery of the important interests safeguarded by the Fourteenth Amendment's protection against official intrusion," because the inspections are merely to determine whether physical conditions exist which do not comply with minimum [regulatory standards]. We may agree that a routine inspection of the physical condition of private property is a less hostile intrusion than the typical policeman's search for the fruits and instrumentalities of crime. . . . But we cannot agree that the Fourth Amendment interests at stake in these inspection cases are merely "peripheral." It is surely anomalous to say that the individual and his private property are fully protected by the Fourth Amendment only when the individual is suspected of criminal behavior. For instance, even the most law-abiding citizen has

---

* [Chief Justice Warren and Justices Black, Douglas, Brennan, and Fortas joined this opinion.—EDS.]

a very tangible interest in limiting the circumstances under which the sanctity of his home may be broken by official authority, for the possibility of criminal entry under the guise of official sanction is a serious threat to personal and family security. . . . Like most regulatory laws, fire, health, and housing codes are enforced by criminal processes. . . .

The *Frank* majority suggested, and appellee reasserts, two other justifications for permitting administrative health and safety inspections without a warrant. First, it is argued that these inspections are "designed to make the least possible demand on the individual occupant." The ordinances authorizing inspections are hedged with safeguards, and at any rate the inspector's particular decision to enter must comply with the constitutional standard of reasonableness even if he may enter without a warrant. [For instance, the San Francisco Code requires that the inspector display proper credentials, that he inspect "at reasonable times," and that he not obtain entry by force except in emergencies.] In addition, the argument proceeds, the warrant process could not function effectively in this field. The decision to inspect an entire municipal area is based upon legislative or administrative assessment of broad factors such as the area's age and condition. Unless the magistrate is to review such policy matters, he must issue a "rubber stamp" warrant which provides no protection at all to the property owner.

In our opinion, these arguments unduly discount the purposes behind the warrant machinery contemplated by the Fourth Amendment. Under the present system, when the inspector demands entry, the occupant has no way of knowing whether enforcement of the municipal code involved requires inspection of his premises, no way of knowing the lawful limits of the inspector's power to search, and no way of knowing whether the inspector himself is acting under proper authorization. These are questions which may be reviewed by a neutral magistrate without any reassessment of the basic agency decision to canvass an area. . . . The practical effect of [the current] system is to leave the occupant subject to the discretion of the official in the field. This is precisely the discretion to invade private property which we have consistently circumscribed by a requirement that a disinterested party warrant the need to search. . . .

In summary, we hold that administrative searches of the kind at issue here are significant intrusions upon the interests protected by the Fourth Amendment, [and] that such searches when authorized and conducted without a warrant procedure lack the traditional safeguards which the Fourth Amendment guarantees to the individual. . . . Because of the nature of the municipal programs under consideration, however, these conclusions must be the beginning, not the end, of our inquiry. . . .

The Fourth Amendment provides that, "no Warrants shall issue, but upon probable cause." Borrowing from more typical Fourth Amendment cases, appellant argues not only that code enforcement inspection programs must be circumscribed by a warrant procedure, but also that warrants should issue only when the inspector possesses probable cause to believe that a particular dwelling contains violations of the minimum standards prescribed by the code being enforced. We disagree.

In cases in which the Fourth Amendment requires that a warrant to search be obtained, "probable cause" is the standard by which a particular decision to search is tested against the constitutional mandate of reasonableness. To apply this standard, it is obviously necessary first to focus upon the governmental interest which allegedly justifies official intrusion upon the constitutionally protected interests of the private citizen. . . .

Unlike the search pursuant to a criminal investigation, the inspection programs at issue here are aimed at securing city-wide compliance with minimum physical standards for private property. The primary governmental interest at stake is to prevent even the unintentional development of conditions which are hazardous to public health and safety. Because fires and epidemics may ravage large urban areas, because unsightly conditions adversely affect the economic values of neighboring structures, numerous courts have upheld the police power of municipalities to impose and enforce such minimum standards even upon existing structures. . . . There is unanimous agreement among those most familiar with this field that the only effective way to seek universal compliance with the minimum standards required by municipal codes is through routine periodic inspections of all structures.

[Camara contends, first], that his probable cause standard would not jeopardize area inspection programs because only a minute portion of the population will refuse to consent to such inspections, and second, that individual privacy in any event should be given preference to the public interest in conducting such inspections. The first argument, even if true, is irrelevant to the question whether the area inspection is reasonable within the meaning of the Fourth Amendment. The second argument is in effect an assertion that the area inspection is an unreasonable search. Unfortunately, there can be no ready test for determining reasonableness other than by balancing the need to search against the invasion which the search entails. But we think that a number of persuasive factors combine to support the reasonableness of area code-enforcement inspections. First, such programs have a long history of judicial and public acceptance. Second, the public interest demands that all dangerous conditions be prevented or abated, yet it is doubtful that any other canvassing technique would achieve acceptable results. Many such conditions—faulty wiring is an obvious example—are not observable from outside the building and indeed may not be apparent to the inexpert occupant himself. Finally, because the inspections are neither personal in nature nor aimed at the discovery of evidence of crime, they involve a relatively limited invasion of the urban citizen's privacy. . . .

Having concluded that the area inspection is a "reasonable" search of private property within the meaning of the Fourth Amendment, it is obvious that "probable cause" to issue a warrant to inspect must exist if reasonable legislative or administrative standards for conducting an area inspection are satisfied with respect to a particular dwelling. Such standards, which will vary with the municipal program being enforced, may be based upon the passage of time, the nature of the building (e.g., a multi-family apartment house), or the condition of the entire area, but they will not necessarily depend upon specific knowledge of the condition of the particular dwelling.

[Most] citizens allow inspections of their property without a warrant. Thus, as a practical matter and in light of the Fourth Amendment's requirement that a warrant specify the property to be searched, it seems likely that warrants should normally be sought only after entry is refused unless there has been a citizen complaint or there is other satisfactory reason for securing immediate entry. . . .

In this case, [there was no emergency demanding immediate access, yet] no warrant was obtained and thus appellant was unable to verify either the need for or the appropriate limits of the inspection. [We] conclude that appellant had a constitutional right to insist that the inspectors obtain a warrant to search and that appellant may not constitutionally be convicted for refusing to consent to the inspection. . . .

CLARK, J., dissenting.*

Today the Court renders . . . municipal experience, which dates back to Colonial days, for naught by . . . striking down hundreds of city ordinances throughout the country and jeopardizing thereby the health, welfare, and safety of literally millions of people. But this is not all. It prostitutes the command of the Fourth Amendment that "no Warrants shall issue, but upon probable cause" and sets up in the health and safety codes area inspection a newfangled "warrant" system that is entirely foreign to Fourth Amendment standards. . . .

The Court then addresses itself to the propriety of warrantless area inspections. [These] boxcar warrants will be identical as to every dwelling in the area, save the street number itself. I daresay they will be printed up in pads of a thousand or more—with space for the street number to be inserted—and issued by magistrates in broadcast fashion as a matter of course. I ask: Why go through such an exercise, such a pretense? As the same essentials are being followed under the present procedures, I ask: Why the ceremony, the delay, the expense, the abuse of the search warrant? In my view this will not only destroy its integrity but will degrade the magistrate issuing them and soon bring disrepute not only upon the practice but upon the judicial process. . . .

Notes

1. *Do administrative warrants honor the Fourth Amendment or undermine it?* Does the majority or dissent in *Camara* do greater honor to the Fourth Amendment? Would the Court have been truer to the Fourth Amendment if it had allowed unwarranted administrative searches on the basis of their reasonableness, modest intrusion, and general applicability, subject to careful guidelines, rather than craft a new kind of warrant? Would the Court have been truer still to the Fourth Amendment if it had barred administrative searches absent consent or individualized suspicion of a civil or criminal violation?

Have you seen administrative warrants before, in another context? Review now the eighteenth-century writ of assistance reprinted earlier in this chapter. Are there significant differences between that writ and the administrative warrants described in the *Camara* decision? How do the facts and holding in *Camara* compare to City of Los Angeles v. Patel, 135 S. Ct. 2443 (2015)? There, the Court declared unconstitutional a city ordinance that requires hotel operators to record information about their guests in a registry and punishes those who refuse to provide the registry to police officers on demand. The Fourth Amendment requires some "opportunity for precompliance review before a neutral decisionmaker."

2. *Special needs searches.* One of the justifications for allowing administrative search warrants appears to be the modestly invasive nature of the searches they

---

* [Justices Harlan and Stewart joined this opinion.—EDS.]

justify. The Supreme Court has declared that the balancing method of determining the reasonableness of a search is available whenever there is a "special need" beyond the normal need for criminal law enforcement. New York v. Burger, 482 U.S. 691 (1987). If a court finds that special needs exist, it must determine next whether these special needs make the warrant and probable-cause requirement of the Fourth Amendment "impracticable" in a given context. Examples include sobriety checkpoints (covered in Chapter 2), airport searches, and international border searches.

3. *Administrative warrants in highly regulated industries.* There is an important exception to the requirement that the government obtain an administrative warrant. If the target of the search is engaged in a "highly regulated industry," the Supreme Court and an overwhelming number of state courts say that an administrative warrant is not necessary. Instead, the government must show that the warrantless search is necessary, that there is an adequate substitute for the warrant to limit the discretion of the field agent, and that the inspection is limited in time, place, and scope. Donovan v. Dewey, 452 U.S. 594 (1981) (statute authorizing warrantless safety inspections of coal mines). The regulation in question must apply to a focused group of people or enterprises; regulations covering all or most employers, however intrusive, do not eliminate the need for an administrative warrant. Marshall v. Barlow's, Inc., 436 U.S. 307 (1978) (warrantless inspection to enforce OSHA workplace safety rules invalid). Is this exception available because of the consent of the targets? That is, does a liquor or firearms retailer understand when going into the business that warrantless searches will occur? See State v. Larsen, 650 N.W.2d 144 (Minn. 2002) (conservation officer needed warrants to search recreational "ice fishing houses" on frozen lakes; court rejected analogy to closely regulated industries). Further details on the administrative warrant cases in varied contexts appear on the web extension for this chapter at *http://www.crimpro.com/ extension/ch03.*

C. CONSENSUAL SEARCHES

The police can conduct a full search *without a warrant and without probable cause* if the target of the search consents. In most jurisdictions, the police conduct far more consensual searches than those justified by probable cause or a search warrant. Indeed, one might ask whether a consensual search is a "search" (within the meaning of the constitution) at all, or whether instead a consensual search is one major category of warrantless searches. As you read these materials, compare consensual searches with intrusions, covered in Chapter 2, that are not considered "searches" at all.

1. Components of a Voluntary Choice

Any valid consent to search must be "voluntary," yet this choice rarely takes place in a setting ideally suited to rational deliberation of all available options. What are the minimum elements of voluntariness necessary to make a consensual search legally acceptable?

■ MERLE SCHNECKLOTH v. ROBERT BUSTAMONTE
412 U.S. 218 (1973)

Stewart, J.*

. . . *I.*

[While on routine patrol in Sunnyvale, California, at approximately 2:40 a.m., Police Officer James Rand stopped an automobile when he observed that one headlight and its license plate light were burned out. Six men were in the vehicle; Bustamonte was in the front passenger seat. When the driver, Joe Gonzalez, could not produce a driver's license, Rand asked the others for identification. Only Joe Alcala produced a license,] and he explained that the car was his brother's. After the six occupants had stepped out of the car at the officer's request and after two additional policemen had arrived, Officer Rand asked Alcala if he could search the car. Alcala replied, "Sure, go ahead." Prior to the search no one was threatened with arrest and, according to Officer Rand's uncontradicted testimony, it "was all very congenial at this time." [The police officer asked Alcala, "Does the trunk open?" Alcala said, "Yes," and opened up the trunk.] Wadded up under the left rear seat, the police officers found three checks that had previously been stolen from a car wash.

[Bustamonte was brought to trial in a California court on a charge of possessing a check with intent to defraud. The trial judge denied the motion to suppress the checks, and on the basis of the checks and other evidence he was convicted. After his failure to obtain relief on appellate review in state court, Bustamonte challenged his conviction in federal habeas corpus proceedings.]

II.

[The] State concedes that when a prosecutor seeks to rely upon consent to justify the lawfulness of a search, he has the burden of proving that the consent was, in fact, freely and voluntarily given. The precise question in this case, then, is what must the prosecution prove to demonstrate that a consent was "voluntarily" given. . . .

B.

[The] question whether a consent to a search was in fact "voluntary" or was the product of duress or coercion, express or implied, is a question of fact to be determined from the totality of all the circumstances. While knowledge of the right to refuse consent is one factor to be taken into account, the government need not establish such knowledge as the sine qua non of an effective consent. [Two] competing concerns must be accommodated in determining the meaning of a "voluntary" consent—the legitimate need for such searches and the equally important requirement of assuring the absence of coercion.

---

* [Chief Justice Burger and Justices White, Blackmun, Powell, and Rehnquist joined in this opinion.—Eds.]

In situations where the police have some evidence of illicit activity, but lack probable cause to arrest or search, a search authorized by a valid consent may be the only means of obtaining important and reliable evidence. . . . And in those cases where there is probable cause to arrest or search, but where the police lack a warrant, a consent search may still be valuable. If the search is conducted and proves fruitless, that in itself may convince the police that an arrest with its possible stigma and embarrassment is unnecessary, or that a far more extensive search pursuant to a warrant is not justified. In short, a search pursuant to consent may result in considerably less inconvenience for the subject of the search, and, properly conducted, is a constitutionally permissible and wholly legitimate aspect of effective police activity.

But the Fourth and Fourteenth Amendments require that a consent not be coerced, by explicit or implicit means, by implied threat or covert force. For, no matter how subtly the coercion was applied, the resulting "consent" would be no more than a pretext for the unjustified police intrusion against which the Fourth Amendment is directed. . . .

The problem of reconciling the recognized legitimacy of consent searches with the requirement that they be free from any aspect of official coercion cannot be resolved by any infallible touchstone. . . . In examining all the surrounding circumstances to determine if in fact the consent to search was coerced, account must be taken of subtly coercive police questions, as well as the possibly vulnerable subjective state of the person who consents. [There] is no reason for us to depart in the area of consent searches, from the traditional definition of "voluntariness."

The approach of [those courts ruling] that the State must affirmatively prove that the subject of the search knew that he had a right to refuse consent, would, in practice, create serious doubt whether consent searches could continue to be conducted. There might be rare cases where it could be proved from the record that a person in fact affirmatively knew of his right to refuse — such as a case where he announced to the police that if he didn't sign the consent form, "[you] are going to get a search warrant"; or a case where by prior experience and training a person had clearly and convincingly demonstrated such knowledge. But more commonly where there was no evidence of any coercion, explicit or implicit, the prosecution would nevertheless be unable to demonstrate that the subject of the search in fact had known of his right to refuse consent. . . .

One alternative that would go far toward proving that the subject of a search did know he had a right to refuse consent would be to advise him of that right before eliciting his consent. That, however, is a suggestion that has been almost universally repudiated by both federal and state courts, and, we think, rightly so. For it would be thoroughly impractical to impose on the normal consent search the detailed requirements of an effective warning. Consent searches are part of the standard investigatory techniques of law enforcement agencies. They normally occur on the highway, or in a person's home or office, and under informal and unstructured conditions. The circumstances that prompt the initial request to search may develop quickly or be a logical extension of investigative police questioning. . . . These situations are a far cry from the structured atmosphere of a trial where, assisted by counsel if he chooses, a defendant is informed of his trial rights. And, while surely a closer question, these situations are still immeasurably far removed from "custodial interrogation" where, in Miranda v. Arizona, 384 U.S. 436 (1966), we found that the Constitution required certain now familiar warnings as a prerequisite to police interrogation. . . .

C.

It is said, however, that a "consent" is a "waiver" of a person's rights under the Fourth and Fourteenth Amendments. The argument is that by allowing the police to conduct a search, a person "waives" whatever right he had to prevent the police from searching. It is argued that under the doctrine of Johnson v. Zerbst, 304 U.S. 458 (1938) to establish such a "waiver" the State must demonstrate "an intentional relinquishment or abandonment of a known right or privilege." But these standards were enunciated in *Johnson* in the context of the safeguards of a fair criminal trial [such as waiver of counsel at trial or] the right to confrontation, to a jury trial, and to a speedy trial, and the right to be free from twice being placed in jeopardy. . . .

The protections of the Fourth Amendment are of a wholly different order, and have nothing whatever to do with promoting the fair ascertainment of truth at a criminal trial. [The] Fourth Amendment protects the security of one's privacy against arbitrary intrusion by the police. . . . It is no part of the policy underlying the Fourth and Fourteenth Amendments to discourage citizens from aiding to the utmost of their ability in the apprehension of criminals. Rather, the community has a real interest in encouraging consent, for the resulting search may yield necessary evidence for the solution and prosecution of crime, evidence that may insure that a wholly innocent person is not wrongly charged with a criminal offense. [It] would be unrealistic to expect that in the informal, unstructured context of a consent search, a policeman, upon pain of tainting the evidence obtained, could make the detailed type of examination demanded by *Johnson*. . . .

D.

It is . . . argued that the failure to require the Government to establish knowledge as a prerequisite to a valid consent, will relegate the Fourth Amendment to the special province of "the sophisticated, the knowledgeable and the privileged." We cannot agree. The traditional definition of voluntariness we accept today has always taken into account evidence of minimal schooling, low intelligence, and the lack of any effective warnings to a person of his rights; and the voluntariness of any statement taken under those conditions has been carefully scrutinized to determine whether it was in fact voluntarily given.

E.

Our decision today is a narrow one. We hold only that when the subject of a search is not in custody and the State attempts to justify a search on the basis of his consent, the Fourth and Fourteenth Amendments require that it demonstrate that the consent was in fact voluntarily given, and not the result of duress or coercion, express or implied. Voluntariness is a question of fact to be determined from all the circumstances, and while the subject's knowledge of a right to refuse is a factor to be taken into account, the prosecution is not required to demonstrate such knowledge as a prerequisite to establishing a voluntary consent. . . .

MARSHALL, J., dissenting.

[I would] have thought that the capacity to choose necessarily depends upon knowledge that there is a choice to be made. But today the Court reaches the curious result that one can choose to relinquish a constitutional right—the right to be free of unreasonable searches—without knowing that he has the alternative of refusing to accede to a police request to search. I cannot agree, and therefore dissent.

[When] a search is justified solely by consent, . . . the needs of law enforcement are significantly more attenuated, for probable cause to search may be lacking but a search permitted if the subject's consent has been obtained. Thus, consent searches are permitted, not because such an exception to the requirements of probable cause and warrant is essential to proper law enforcement, but because we permit our citizens to choose whether or not they wish to exercise their constitutional rights. . . .

If consent to search means that a person has chosen to forgo his right to exclude the police from the place they seek to search, it follows that his consent cannot be considered a meaningful choice unless he knew that he could in fact exclude the police. . . . If one accepts this view, the question then is a simple one: must the Government show that the subject knew of his rights, or must the subject show that he lacked such knowledge? I think that any fair allocation of the burden would require that it be placed on the prosecution. . . . If the burden is placed on the defendant, all the subject can do is to testify that he did not know of his rights. And I doubt that many trial judges will find for the defendant simply on the basis of that testimony. [The government, however, might demonstrate the subject's knowledge of his rights by showing his responses at the time of the search.] Denials of knowledge may be disproved by establishing that the subject had, in the recent past, demonstrated his knowledge of his rights, for example, by refusing entry when it was requested by the police. The prior experience or training of the subject might in some cases support an inference that he knew of his right to exclude the police.

The burden on the prosecutor would disappear, of course, if the police, at the time they requested consent to search, also told the subject that he had a right to refuse consent and that his decision to refuse would be respected. . . .

The Court contends that if an officer paused to inform the subject of his rights, the informality of the exchange would be destroyed. I doubt that a simple statement by an officer of an individual's right to refuse consent would do much to alter the informality of the exchange, except to alert the subject to a fact that he surely is entitled to know. It is not without significance that for many years the agents of the Federal Bureau of Investigation have routinely informed subjects of their right to refuse consent, when they request consent to search. . . .

I must conclude, with some reluctance, that when the Court speaks of practicality, what it really is talking of is the continued ability of the police to capitalize on the ignorance of citizens so as to accomplish by subterfuge what they could not achieve by relying only on the knowing relinquishment of constitutional rights. Of course it would be "practical" for the police to ignore the commands of the Fourth Amendment, if by practicality we mean that more criminals will be apprehended, even though the constitutional rights of innocent people also go by the board. But such a practical advantage is achieved only at the cost of permitting the police to disregard the limitations that the Constitution places on their behavior, a cost that a constitutional democracy cannot long absorb. . . .

■ CHICAGO POLICE DEPARTMENT CONSENT TO SEARCH FORM, CPD-11.483

I, _____ [Print Full Name], have been advised of my constitutional right not to have a search made of the premises/vehicle described below without a search warrant first being obtained. I have also been advised that I do not have to consent to this warrantless search unless I wish to do so.

Having been advised that I do not have to consent to a warrantless search, I hereby authorize and give my consent to _____ [Officer] and _____ [Officer] who have identified themselves as Chicago Police Officers assigned to the _____ [Unit] to conduct a complete search at this time of the premises/vehicle under my lawful control and described as _____.

In addition, I hereby authorize and give my consent to the above named officers to obtain and remove from the searched premises/vehicle any materials, documents, or other items that may be used in connection with a legitimate law enforcement purpose.

By my signature on this document, I hereby state and certify that this consent to search is being given by me to the above named officers knowingly, voluntarily, and without having received any threats, promises, or duress of any kind.

_____ [Signature]

_____ [Witness, Non-Department Member if available]

■ PHILADELPHIA POLICE DEPARTMENT DIRECTIVE 7, APPENDIX A

[Officers] will ensure they provide the consenting party with the following warnings:

1. that the consenting party has the right to require the police to obtain a search warrant, and
2. that he/she has the right to refuse to consent to a search. . . .

If the person is in police custody, three additional warnings must be provided:

1. that any items found can and will be confiscated and may be used against them in court;
2. they have the right to consult with an attorney before making a decision to consent; and
3. that they have the right to withdraw their consent at any time.

Notes

1. *Voluntariness of consent: majority position.* Almost all state courts agree with *Bustamonte* that a "totality of the circumstances" determines whether a person consented to a search, and that it is not necessary to inform the person of the right to refuse consent. See Commonwealth v. Cleckley, 738 A.2d 427 (Pa. 1999); but see State v. Johnson, 346 A.2d 66 (N.J. 1975) (party consenting to search must

understand right to refuse consent). Whose perceptions of the totality of the circumstances will determine whether the choice was voluntary? Should a court adopt the viewpoint of the person being searched, the officer, or an objective "reasonable person"?

Both subjective and objective perspectives operate here. Courts ask about the subjective features of the target of the search, focusing specifically on the consenting person's age, education, and intelligence. Then the courts consider any objective evidence of coercion, deception, threats, or other undue influence by the police. In light of the police conduct and the defendant's particular subjective circumstances, the court ultimately decides whether the police conduct could have been coercive to a reasonable person in the defendant's circumstances. See Krause v. Commonwealth, 206 S.W.3d 922 (Ky. 2006) (consent to search was coerced when officer knocked at 4:00 A.M. and requested permission to enter apartment as part of an investigation of a roommate not present at the time, purportedly accused of raping a child; no sexual assault had occurred, officer's intent was to look for drugs in plain view, but knew that college-educated suspects would refuse consent to search for drugs). Should a person with more education and worldliness have more difficulty showing that her consent to a search was involuntary? Indeed, after taking this course, would you be able to claim your consent to a search was involuntary on any grounds short of torture?

Appellate courts treat the historical facts relevant to an assertion of consent as questions of fact that deserve deferential treatment under the clearly erroneous standard. On the other hand, the issue of whether those facts amount to genuine consent is an issue of law that an appellate court will answer de novo. See State v. Weisler, 35 A.3d 970 (Vt. 2011).

2. *Is consent rational?* Why would a "reasonable" person who knows that evidence of a crime is present on the premises ever consent to a search? There is considerable evidence in psychological studies that people unreflectively defer to the wishes of authority figures, including police officers. Is this a sufficient explanation? For a review of the empirical basis for consent doctrine, see Steven L. Chanenson, Get the Facts, Jack! Empirical Research and the Changing Constitutional Landscape of Consent Searches, 71 Tenn. L. Rev. 399 (2004).

3. *Proof of knowledge.* As a prosecutor, how would you prove that a person who consented to a search knew that she had the power to refuse? As police counsel, would you recommend that your officers use a written consent form in all cases when they wish to search on the basis of consent? Would it increase the chance that the courts would validate consent searches? Would this practice result in a loss of too many searches? Should the form contain explicit notice that the person can refuse to consent? Note that Directive 7 from the Philadelphia Police Manual provides for some warnings not required as a matter of federal constitutional law. The manual also calls for consent searches only when there is no probable cause and no chance to get a warrant. Why would a police manual contain such provisions?

4. *Consent based on inevitability of a search.* Is consent voluntary when the police claim to have the authority to search immediately, or as soon as they obtain a warrant? In Bumper v. North Carolina, 391 U.S. 543 (1968), the police officer said to a homeowner, "I have a warrant" and the homeowner therefore dropped her objections to the search; the prosecution later justified the search as a consensual search rather than relying on a warrant. The court held that the homeowner's consent to the search was not voluntary because it was induced by a "show

of authority" by the police. Was the consent involuntary because of some knowledge the homeowner did not have, such as the invalidity of the warrant? Or was it because the police affirmatively misrepresented the range of options open to her? Suppose the officer had said, "I can get a warrant if you don't consent." Would your answer change if she had said, "I will seek a warrant"? See State v. Brown, 783 P.2d 1278 (Kan. 1989).

5. *"Knock and talk" practices.* When police officers approach a home with no probable cause to search and request consent to search, this "knock and talk" practice raises difficult factual issues about whether the resident's consent is truly voluntary. Given the special sensitivity of searches in a home, a few jurisdictions declare that officers who approach a home for the sole purpose of obtaining consent to search the home must inform the resident that he or she does not have to consent. State v. Brown, 156 S.W.3d 722 (Ark. 2004) (state constitution requires police officers conducting "knock and talk" to inform home dweller that consent may be refused). Most jurisdictions, however, leave the voluntariness of such consensual searches to the factfinding of the trial judge in the individual case. State v. Smith, 488 S.E.2d 210 (N.C. 1997) ("knock and talk" policy of police department does not violate constitution per se). Would consent be voluntary if the police ask to search a home while saying that if the owner insists that they obtain a warrant, they plan to return with their "blue lights and sirens blazing" for the benefit of the neighbors?

6. *Consent while in custody.* Does the driver of a vehicle stopped for a traffic violation voluntarily consent to a search of the car if told that the alternative is to be arrested and taken to jail (and the officer has lawful authority to do just that for traffic violators)? Can a suspect already in custody consent to a search? In United States v. Watson, 423 U.S. 411 (1976), the court approved of a consensual search of a car owned by a person who had been taken into custody in a restaurant and was being held on a public street. The Court held that the lack of notice about the right to refuse consent did not make the choice involuntary in this setting. See also United States v. Drayton, 536 U.S. 194 (2002) (when armed and uniformed officers of drug interdiction team boarded bus and worked down the aisle questioning passengers, suspect agreed to allow pat-down search of his baggage and person; consent was valid).

7. *Consent after a traffic stop.* The Supreme Court held, in Ohio v. Robinette, 519 U.S. 33 (1996), that a police officer asking for consent to search the car at the conclusion of a valid traffic stop need not inform the motorist that he is free to leave and may refuse to consent to the search. However, the Ohio Supreme Court on remand held that the officer's failure to inform the motorist that the stop was over still amounted to one important factor showing lack of consent in the case. State v. Robinette, 685 N.E.2d 762 (Ohio 1997). Roughly 15 states follow Ohio's lead and list a lack of warning as one important component of the voluntariness issue. See Harris v. Commonwealth, 581 S.E.2d 286 (Va. 2003). Courts in other jurisdictions state that consent obtained at the end of any traffic stop deserves heightened review to ensure the voluntariness of the consent. Ferris v. State, 735 A.2d 491 (Md. 1999). In fact, a small group of states (fewer than a half dozen) insist that police may not request consent to search a car stopped for traffic violations unless they have reasonable suspicion of some criminal activity other than the traffic matter. See State v. Smith, 184 P.3d 890 (Kan. 2008). Are these decisions consistent with Schneckloth v. Bustamonte? Is knowledge about the power to refuse consent more important for

stopped automobile drivers than for others who are asked to consent to a search? Would your analysis of the consent question change if the police requested consent to collect a DNA sample from the driver and passengers of a stopped car? What if the driver and passengers are minors? See Lauren Kirchner, DNA Dragnet: In Some Cities, Police Go from Stop-and-Frisk to Stop-and-Spit, ProPublica, Sept. 12, 2016, *https://www.propublica.org/article/dna-dragnet-in-some-cities-police-go-from-stop-and-frisk-to-stop-and-spit.*

8. *Scope of consent: majority position.* A consent search is valid only if the government agent conducting the search remains within the bounds of the consent granted. The Supreme Court has held that the "standard for measuring the scope of a suspect's consent under the Fourth Amendment is that of 'objective' reasonableness—what would the typical reasonable person have understood by the exchange between the officer and the suspect?" Florida v. Jimeno, 500 U.S. 248 (1991). Virtually all state courts deciding this question have reached the same conclusion. See Commonwealth v. Ortiz, 90 N.E.3d 735 (Mass. 2018) (unless it is reasonably clear that consent to search extends beyond interior of vehicle, police must obtain explicit consent before vehicular search may extend beneath hood). You can explore further examples of this often-litigated doctrine on the web extension for this chapter at *http://www.crimpro.com/extension/ch03.*

A court will determine the exact coverage of the agreement by reviewing the language that the officer and the target of the search used, much as a court would examine the language used by contractual parties to determine the meaning of their agreement. Would the use of written consent forms tend to help or hurt police departments in this inquiry? If a person consents generally to a search of his "person" or his "vehicle," does that general statement include consent to search all areas within those bounds? A court will typically find it significant if the government agent tells the search target what she is looking for. If the officer is seeking illegal narcotics, the search might be more thorough and intrusive while still remaining within the bounds of the consent.

A person who has consented to a search can withdraw that consent (or restrict its scope) at any time before the completion of the search. However, the person must make an unequivocal withdrawal, through words or actions or both. An action withdrawing consent must be clearly inconsistent with the prior consent, such as a refusal to open a door or a container. See State v. Smith, 782 N.W.2d 913 (Neb. 2010) (person entering a nightclub requiring all patrons to submit to frisk withdrew that consent when officer tried to reach into his pocket and he grabbed officer's wrist and knocked his hand away).

9. *Duration of consent.* While it is clear that a person must withdraw consent through clear language or action, does that mean that a consent to search remains effective indefinitely, allowing a search several days after the grant of consent? Most courts conclude that an open-ended consent to search contains an implied time limitation: The search must be conducted as soon as it is reasonably possible to do so. Some circumstances suggest a consent with longer duration. In Caldwell v. State, 393 S.E.2d 436 (Ga. 1990), the defendant called the police at 3:00 P.M. to report the stabbing of her children, invited the police into her apartment, and asked them to search for evidence that would lead to the arrest of the murderer. She then left the premises to spend the night with relatives. The search continued until 10:00 P.M. the day of the murder, and for several hours the next day. The court concluded that the consent remained valid for the entire period of the search.

Problem 3-5. Scope of Consent

Just past midnight, Sergeant William Planeta and his partner, Officer Joseph Agresta, spotted a 10-year-old black Honda with tinted windows. A computer check on the car failed to turn up any negative information. After following the car for 20 blocks, the officers pulled it over for excessively tinted windows—a violation of the state motor vehicle code. While his partner spoke with the driver (Gomez), Planeta approached the vehicle, looked through the passenger window, and then inspected the undercarriage of the car for evidence of a hidden compartment. In Planeta's experience, the undercarriage of a vehicle can offer telltale signs of secret compartments used in narcotics trafficking.

Planeta noticed fresh undercoating around the gas tank. Meanwhile, the driver handed Agresta a registration card for the vehicle that showed signs of tampering. The word "Company" had been removed from the name on the card so that it read "Anna Teodora Fermin" rather than "Anna Teodora Fermin Company." The darkly tinted windows, fresh undercoating near the gas tank, and altered registration led Planeta to suspect that the vehicle was being used to transport drugs. Planeta then asked the driver whether he had any guns, knives, cocaine, heroin, or marijuana, and the driver responded, "No." Planeta then asked, "May I search your car, sir?" and the driver said, "Yeah."

Planeta instructed Gomez to stand at the rear of the car, where Officer Agresta patted him down; he then told him to sit on the rear bumper and wait. Planeta unlocked the rear seat and pulled it back. He observed gray "non-factory" carpet in the location above the area where he had spotted the fresh undercoating. He then pulled up the glued carpeting and discovered a cut in the floorboard. Planeta used his pocket knife to pry up the sheet metal. After struggling to reach what he thought was a plastic bag, Planeta returned to his cruiser and retrieved a crowbar, which he brought back to the Honda. Gomez remained silent as Sergeant Planeta began his search again. The crowbar finally enabled him to open part of the gas tank, where he discovered seven bags of cocaine weighing over 1.5 pounds in a hidden compartment.

Gomez has moved to suppress the drugs. He does not contest the voluntariness of his consent to search the vehicle but claims that Planeta's search went beyond the scope of his consent. Will the trial judge grant to motion? Cf. People v. Gomez, 838 N.E.2d 1271 (N.Y. 2005).

2. Third-Party Consent

The police can obtain the consent to search property either from the target of the search herself or from some third party. Of course, the third party's consent must be voluntary, just as with the target of the search. In addition, the third party must have the authority (or at least the apparent authority) to consent to the search. The third party's authority to consent to a search of property "does not rest upon the law of property, with its attendant historical and legal refinements, but rests rather on mutual use of the property by persons generally having joint access or control for most purposes." In such a setting, the target of the search has "assumed the risk" that another person with access to the property will consent to a search. United States v. Matlock, 415 U.S. 164 (1974). How might this standard apply in the following problems? Would any recurring fact make a difference to a reviewing court?

▮ ARKANSAS RULE OF CRIMINAL PROCEDURE 11.2

The consent justifying a search and seizure can only be given, in the case of: (a) search of an individual's person, by the individual in question or, if the person is under 14 years of age, by both the individual and his parent, guardian, or a person in loco parentis; (b) search of a vehicle, by the person registered as its owner or in apparent control of its operation or contents at the time consent is given; and . . . (c) search of premises, by a person who, by ownership or otherwise, is apparently entitled to give or withhold consent.

Problem 3-6. Co-tenant Consenting for Co-tenant

Gina owned a house, which she rented to her son Dale and another man, Thomas. At about 2:00 A.M. on August 30, several acquaintances of Dale and Thomas were at the house. Two of the guests left for about 30 minutes and returned with more than a half pound of marijuana. Thomas was upset that there was marijuana in the house and complained to Dale, but Dale seemed unconcerned.

Thomas went to the police, where he signed a consent to search the house for the marijuana. Several officers went to the house, drew their weapons, and entered the house without knocking or announcing their purpose or authority. They found marijuana in baggies in a black leather jacket in the kitchen and arrested the guest who owned the jacket. In plain view in the living room was a "sawed off" or "short barreled" shotgun belonging to Dale. Was this a valid consensual search? Compare In re Welfare of D.A.G., 474 N.W.2d 419 (Minn. 1991).

Problem 3-7. Parent Consenting for Child

During a murder investigation, police officers went to a suspect's house and asked his mother for consent to search his room. The suspect, who was 23 years old, slept and stored his clothes and other property in a bedroom upstairs in the house and sporadically paid his mother rent for the room. His mother had regular access to the room for purposes of collecting his laundry. She also stored her sewing machine in the room. Although the room was usually unlocked, on this day it was locked. The suspect's mother opened the door with a key and allowed the police to search his room. They found in the closet a jacket with blood stains matching the blood of the murder victim. Was this a valid consensual search?

Problem 3-8. Child Consenting for Parent

Deputy Sheriff Joe Brown and Officer Chris Nichols planned to arrest Jonathan Lowe. Nichols learned that Lowe was staying at the home of Karen Schwarz, so the two officers drove to Schwarz's home on a Friday night to carry out the arrest. Brittany Glazier, Schwarz's 13-year-old daughter, who had just arrived home from the movies with two girlfriends, answered the door. The three friends had been watching a video while waiting for one girl's ride home; the other friend had permission to spend the night at Brittany's house. Brittany had met Officer Brown at a Girl

Scout event. Officer Brown explained to Brittany, who he believed to be either 13 or 14 years old, that he was looking for Lowe. The officers asked for permission to come into the home and "look around" while they waited for Lowe. Brittany agreed.

During the search, Officer Nichols discovered a marijuana pipe and a small plastic container containing a white substance, later determined to be methamphetamine. At some point, Schwarz, who was out bowling, called home and learned of the officers' presence. She immediately drove home. When Schwarz arrived, Officer Nichols told her that he had discovered drugs. Schwarz admitted to owning the pipe and methamphetamine and provided written consent to another search of the entire house. Was this a valid consensual search? Cf. State v. Schwarz, 136 P.3d 989 (Mont. 2006).

Notes

1. *Presence or absence of target and consenting party.* It often happens that the target of a search is present during the search and does not consent, while some third party on the scene does consent. This situation arises frequently during investigations of alleged domestic abuse. In Georgia v. Randolph, 547 U.S. 103 (2006), Janet Randolph complained to the police that her husband, Scott, had taken their son away after a domestic dispute. She went with an officer to the home she shared with Scott to reclaim the child. When they arrived, Scott said that he had removed the child to a neighbor's house out of concern that Janet might take the boy out of the country. Janet mentioned that her husband used cocaine and left evidence of his use in the bedroom. She gave her consent for the police to search the home, but when an officer asked Scott for permission to search the house, he unequivocally refused. The Supreme Court held that "a physically present co-occupant's stated refusal to permit entry prevails" over the consent of the other occupant.

In Fernandez v. California, 134 S. Ct. 1126 (2014), the Court limited the reach of the *Randolph* holding. Police officers saw a robbery suspect run into an apartment building, and heard screams coming from inside. They knocked on the apartment door, and the woman who answered was bleeding. When the officers asked her to step out of the apartment so that they could conduct a protective sweep inside, the suspect came to the door and objected. Believing that he had assaulted the woman, the officers removed the suspect from the apartment and took him to the police station. An officer later returned to the apartment and obtained the woman's consent to search the apartment; he found several items linking the defendant to the robbery. The Supreme Court held that *Randolph* does not extend to a situation where the co-occupant's consent happens well after the objecting target of the search had been reasonably removed from the apartment. The consent here was valid.

2. *Unequal interests in property.* Parties with different legal interests in a location, such as landlords and tenants, will typically have powers to consent to a search only when contractual terms and other reasonable expectations allow such consent. See State v. Licari, 659 N.W.2d 243 (Minn. 2003) (landlord's contractual right to inspect rented storage unit did not provide actual or apparent authority to consent to police search); Stoner v. California, 376 U.S. 483 (1964) (unwarranted search of hotel room without consent of defendant was unlawful even though police obtained consent of hotel clerk). What happens if the consenting party has a clearly lesser

interest in the property than the target of the search? Suppose the target of the search pays rent on an apartment, while the consenting third party is a frequent long-term guest. Should the third party in that setting be able to override the objections of the party with the stronger claim on the property?

3. *Family member consent.* Family members frequently consent to a search of the shared family home during an investigation of some other occupant of the home, particularly when they are victims of the alleged crime. State v. Ellis, 210 P.3d 144 (Mont. 2009) (police obtained consent from 13-year-old to search her bedroom for evidence of sexual assault by father; state constitutional rule limiting third-party consent for search to those 16 and older provides for no exception for child's own bedroom).

Many third-party consent cases involve spouses or others in a similar relationship. Sometimes one spouse will consent to a search in an effort to injure a partner during a time of conflict. Is it reasonable for the police to rely on consent if it is clear that one party intends only to harm the target of the search? For a perusal of third-party consent cases from the family context, consult the web extension of this chapter at *http://www.crimpro.com/extension/ch03.*

4. *Consent forms and policies.* Would you advise a police department to adopt a special version of its consent-to-search forms for third-party consent searches? Would you advise the police to adopt any rules regarding the proper procedure for obtaining third-party consent?

■ COMMONWEALTH v. PORTER P.

923 N.E.2d 36 (Mass. 2010)

GANTS, J.

[The Juvenile Court suppressed a gun] seized by the police during a search of a room in a transitional family shelter occupied by the juvenile and a statement that he made after his arrest. Having been notified by the shelter's director that the juvenile allegedly possessed a gun, the police officers determined that the director had the authority to consent to their entry and conducted a warrantless search of the juvenile's room with her consent. After the police found the gun, the . . . juvenile was charged with delinquency by reason of the unlawful possession of a firearm and ammunition. . . . We affirm the allowance of the motion to suppress.

Background. . . . The juvenile and his mother moved into a room at the Roxbury Multi-Service Center, Inc., Family House Shelter in March, 2006. The shelter [contracts with the Commonwealth to provide] temporary housing for otherwise homeless families. . . . Families may remain at the shelter until they find a permanent living situation, unless they commit a violation of the shelter's rules and regulations. The typical stay is between four and eight months. Apart from a key deposit fee of thirty dollars, the families do not pay to live at the shelter.

Each new resident of the shelter, including the juvenile and his mother, as part of the intake procedure, is given a manual setting forth the shelter's rules and regulations. According to the manual, residents . . . are not permitted to enter another resident's room at any time for any purpose. Because residents must commit to being actively engaged at least twenty hours per week in employment, education, or job training, or looking for employment or housing, the residents are required to be out of the shelter from 9 A.M. to 3 P.M. every weekday. . . . Each resident and his or her family is provided a furnished room and given a key to his or her room. The director, however, has a master key that opens every door in the shelter, and the staff members have a master key that opens every resident's room. Members of the shelter's staff have the right to enter any room "for professional business purposes (maintenance, room inspections, etc.)," but only with the knowledge of the director. If a "business professional," such as a repair person or exterminator, requires entry to a resident's room, he or she must be escorted by a staff member, with the director's approval. The shelter staff may conduct "room checks" at any time without warning to monitor compliance with the shelter's "Good Housekeeping Standard" and other rules and regulations, including those affecting health and safety. The manual has a "zero tolerance policy in regards to violent acts committed by residents" and the possession of any weapon; "any resident in possession of a weapon will be terminated immediately." The shelter "reserves the right to contact the Police should the situation warrant," but the manual does not state that the shelter director or a staff member may consent to a police search of a resident's room.

On October 25, 2006, the shelter's director, Cynthia M. Brown, after having heard rumors that the juvenile had a gun, . . . contacted the Boston police department and arranged a meeting for the following morning "to figure out how to proceed." On October 26, 2006, at approximately 10:30 A.M., Detective Frank McLaughlin and four other police officers met with Brown at the shelter. . . . Brown told the officers that the resident's manual authorized her to enter residents' rooms to conduct room checks and that she had inspected residents' rooms several days earlier after reports of suspected drug use. The officers reviewed the portions of the manual authorizing staff to make controlled room entries. Detective McLaughlin confirmed with Brown that her authority to search residents' rooms included the ability to search closets, drawers, bureaus, and other places not in plain view. The detective testified at the evidentiary hearing that he "absolutely" believed that Brown had the authority to consent to a police search of the juvenile's room. He based this belief on the shelter's rules and regulations in the resident's manual, as well as Brown's possession of a master key to the residents' rooms.

Brown and the officers . . . proceeded upstairs to the room, where Brown knocked on the door and announced that she was conducting a room check. When no one answered, she used her master key to open the door. The juvenile was in the room, and it appeared that he had been lying in bed moments before. Brown explained that she was there to conduct a room check and had the police with her because of allegations that the juvenile had a gun in his possession. Detective McLaughlin asked the juvenile to step out of the room into the hallway, and the juvenile complied. Two or three officers began to search the room while the detective and Brown attempted to speak with the juvenile, who denied having a gun. When Brown asked why he was not in school, he stated that he was home sick that day. During their search of the room, the officers found a Glock .40 caliber firearm containing hollow point bullets in the clip underneath a duffel bag in the closet. The juvenile was then handcuffed and placed under arrest. . . .

Discussion. The juvenile argues that the warrantless search of his room at the shelter and the seizure of his firearm violated the Fourth Amendment to the United States Constitution; art. 14 of the Massachusetts Declaration of Rights; and G.L. c. 276, §1. . . .

2. . . . A third party has actual authority to consent to a warrantless search of a home by the police when the third party shares common authority over the home.

See Georgia v. Randolph, 547 U.S. 103 (2006); United States v. Matlock, 415 U.S. 164 (1974). The authority which justifies the third-party consent does not rest upon the law of property but rests rather on "mutual use of the property by persons generally having joint access or control for most purposes," so that it is reasonable to recognize that any of the co-inhabitants has the right to permit the inspection in his own right and that the others have assumed the risk that one of their number might permit the common area to be searched.

The reasonableness of a consent search is in significant part a function of commonly held understanding about the authority that co-inhabitants may exercise in ways that affect each other's interests. [Common] authority does not mean simply the right to enter the premises that the police wish to search. Landlords often contractually retain that right, and hotels routinely do, but that does not allow the landlord or hotel manager to consent to a police search of a defendant's apartment or hotel room. United States v. Jeffers, 342 U.S. 48 (1951) (hotel patron gives "implied or express permission [to enter] to such persons as maids, janitors or repairmen in the performance of their duties" but not to police). We have held that, when a college student executes a residence hall contract that permits college officials to enter the student's dormitory room "to inspect for hazards to health or personal safety," the college officials' authority to enter the room to conduct a health and safety inspection does not entitle those officials to consent to a police search for evidence of a crime. Commonwealth v. Neilson, 666 N.E.2d 984 (1996). Here, the shelter's manual allowed shelter staff to enter the room for "professional business purposes," such as to make repairs, exterminate insects and rodents, and monitor compliance with the shelter's "Good Housekeeping Standard," and to escort "business professionals" into the room to accomplish these purposes, but it did not permit shelter staff to allow the police to enter to search for and seize contraband or evidence. . . .

We understand that the police need clear guidance as to who has common authority over a residence and therefore who is entitled to give actual consent, because, as here, they rely on such consent in deciding to conduct a warrantless search, as opposed to securing the residence and applying for a search warrant. Therefore, we declare under art. 14 that a person may have actual authority to consent to a warrantless search of a home by the police only if (1) the person is a co-inhabitant with a shared right of access to the home, that is, the person lives in the home, either as a member of the family, a roommate, or a houseguest whose stay is of substantial duration and who is given full access to the home; or (2) the person, generally a landlord, shows the police a written contract entitling that person to allow the police to enter the home to search for and seize contraband or evidence. No such entitlement may reasonably be presumed by custom or oral agreement. . . .

Under this standard, Brown did not have actual authority to consent to the police entry into the room to search for a firearm. She was not a co-inhabitant of the room, and the shelter manual did not permit her to allow the police to enter the room to search for contraband or evidence. . . .

3. Having concluded that Brown did not have actual authority to consent to the search of the room by the police, we turn to whether she had the apparent authority to consent.

In Illinois v. Rodriguez, 497 U.S. 177, 179 (1990), the United States Supreme Court held that the Fourth Amendment's proscription of "unreasonable searches and seizures" is not violated when a warrantless entry of a home is based on the consent of a third party who the police, at the time of entry, reasonably, but mistakenly, believed had common authority over the premises. The Court reasoned, "to satisfy the reasonableness requirement of the Fourth Amendment, what is generally demanded of the many factual determinations that must regularly be made by agents of the government—whether the magistrate issuing a warrant, the police officer executing a warrant, or the police officer conducting a search or seizure under one of the exceptions to the warrant requirement—is not that they always be correct, but that they always be reasonable." The Court concluded that "the Constitution is no more violated when officers enter without a warrant because they reasonably (though erroneously) believe that the person who has consented to their entry is a resident of the premises, than it is violated when they enter without a warrant because they reasonably (though erroneously) believe they are in pursuit of a violent felon who is about to escape." Apparent authority is judged against an objective standard: "would the facts available to the officer at the moment . . . warrant a man of reasonable caution in the belief that the consenting party had authority over the premises?"

Federal courts have universally limited apparent authority to reasonable mistakes of fact, not mistakes of law. The *Rodriguez* decision thus applies to situations in which an officer would have had valid consent to search if the facts were as he reasonably believed them to be. An officer's mistaken belief as to the law, even if reasonable, cannot establish apparent authority.

The police officers' mistake in this case was one of law, not of fact. Detective McLaughlin and the other officers took considerable care to ascertain whether Brown had the authority to consent to a search of the room. Prior to entering the room, Detective McLaughlin conferred with Brown and reviewed the portions of the manual pertaining to staff searches of the rooms. They accurately understood the relevant facts regarding Brown's authority to consent to the search. They erred not in their understanding of the facts or in the diligence of their inquiry into Brown's authority to consent to the search, but in their understanding of the law; they believed that these facts gave them valid consent to search the room when, as a matter of law, they did not. Because Brown did not have actual or apparent authority to consent to the search, the warrantless search of the room was not reasonable under the Fourth Amendment or art. 14.

4. [Even] when the consenting individual explicitly asserts that he lives there, if the surrounding circumstances could conceivably be such that a reasonable person would doubt its truth, the police officer must make further inquiry to resolve the ambiguity. The police officer owes a duty to explore, rather than ignore, contrary facts tending to suggest that the person consenting to the search lacks actual authority. Police must not only thoroughly question the individual consenting to the search with respect to his or her actual authority, but also pay close attention to whether the surrounding circumstances indicate that the consenting individual is truthful and accurate in asserting common authority over the premises. . . .

COWIN, J., dissenting.

[Shelter rules regulate the] residents' use of their rooms. Residents "are not allowed access or permitted to enter another resident's room at any time," and they may meet with outside visitors only during stated times at designated locations in the building. The shelter's rules even forbid residents from rearranging the furniture in their rooms, limit the number of suitcases present in the room to "two . . . per family member," and prohibit residents from placing items "on the windowsills."

Alcohol and firearms are strictly forbidden in the facility, as are sexual activities (except between residents "coupled" together). [The] shelter requires residents to perform weekly chores and clean their rooms according to enumerated housekeeping standards.

The manual reveals a special concern for eliminating the presence of weapons in the shelter. The shelter forbids possession of "weapons of any kind." The manual defines a weapon as "any item that can be used to threaten or cause physical damage or harm."

[The] shelter director possessed sufficient common authority over the premises to consent to a police search. The staff's plenary authority in the circumstances, including the right to conduct unannounced inspections, meaningfully differentiates the shelter from hotels, apartments, and university dormitories.

The court does not dispute that the conditions of the manual grant shelter staff the authority to enter residents' rooms to search for contraband, but it holds that this power does not extend to granting consent to the police to do the same. This is an entirely unwarranted and impractical distinction, requiring that the shelter staff resort to self-help in order to obtain prompt enforcement of the prohibition on firearms. Shelter staff are not trained in dealing with guns or people armed with guns, and they cannot arrest those in possession of weapons. A commonsense reading of the provisions of the manual regarding weapons plainly communicates that shelter staff, at its choosing, may seek police assistance in undertaking their reserved right to control the premises. In sum, there was no objective basis in these circumstances for any expectation that the juvenile may have had that his room would be immune from the kind of entry that occurred.

Notes

1. *Apparent authority: majority position.* In a number of third-party consent cases, the third party does not actually have authority to consent to the search. Several state courts over the years concluded that these searches were still constitutional so long as the officer had a reasonable belief that the third party had authority to consent. The Supreme Court endorsed this "apparent authority" rule in Illinois v. Rodriguez, 497 U.S. 177 (1990). In that case, the police searched an apartment based on the consent of a former lover of the tenant, who did not have actual authority to consent to a search of the apartment; the Court held that the police were reasonable to search based on her apparent authority. The majority of states addressing this question both before and after *Rodriguez* have reached the same conclusion, approving of searches based on apparent rather than actual authority to consent. See State v. McCaughey, 904 P.2d 939 (Idaho 1995). A few states, however, have disagreed. See State v. McLees, 994 P.2d 683 (Mont. 2000).

The Massachusetts court in *Porter P.* was more explicit than most courts in specifying what the police must do when encountering a claim of authority to consent by a third party; most other courts simply say that the policy must act reasonably under the totality of the circumstances. Can you formulate an alternative description of the police officer's duty to investigate?

2. *Are consent searches reasonable?* One might view consent as a method of making any search a reasonable one. Alternatively, one might say that consent makes reasonableness irrelevant because the party consenting to the search decides not

to insist on the probable cause or valid warrant or other circumstances that would make a search reasonable. The latter view might lead a court to reject the apparent authority doctrine: If the search is unreasonable, then actual consent is necessary to salvage it. If, on the other hand, police act reasonably when they conduct a consensual search, then consent that is invalid for reasons not apparent to the police does not make their actions any less reasonable. Is there a principled basis for deciding between these two views?

3. *Voluntariness revisited.* While following *Bustamonte,* courts have stated that consent must still be voluntary, even if the consenting party lacks full knowledge of the nature of his rights. By allowing police to proceed on the apparent authority rather than the actual authority of third parties, have the majority of courts effectively eliminated the voluntariness requirement for a sizable group of cases? Are police training policies and practices likely to increase the number of consent searches based on the apparent authority of third parties?

4. *Prospective consent and conditioning of government benefits.* Courts limit the extent to which a landlord may waive a tenant's privacy rights and consent to police searches. They enforce lease terms allowing the landlord access only for inspections or emergencies. But suppose the lease includes an explicit clause giving prospective consent for weapons or drug searches. Would you allow tenants prospectively to give consent to searches? If so, should the consent be limited to searches of an individual's home or might it extend to searches of the person?

In Wyman v. James, 400 U.S. 309 (1971), the Supreme Court held that governments could condition the provision of social services (in this instance, Aid to Families with Dependent Children) on agreements to allow home access by aid workers on the grounds that home visits were not searches. To the extent the visits had the appearance of searches, they were reasonable. Finally, relying on *Camara,* the Court noted that the penalty for refusing caseworkers access was termination of benefits, not criminal sanctions.

What arguments would you make for and against applying Wyman v. James to a public housing lease condition allowing prospective searches? The general issue raised here—known as the doctrine of "unconstitutional conditions"—is whether the conditions that the government places on receipt of government support are unconstitutional. The question arises in a variety of contexts, including, for example, the ability of a state university to condition participation on an athletic team on a student's willingness to agree to random or periodic drug tests. See Lynn Baker, The Prices of Rights: Toward a Positive Theory of Unconstitutional Conditions, 75 Cornell L. Rev. 1185 (1990).

5. *Group consent.* Can a majority of a defined group consent for all members of the group? In the public housing situation, if a majority of residents sign leases allowing random searches, do the police have to check a list of who has agreed to the searches or can they treat the situation as one of "group consent"? Could a majority of residents agree to install a metal detector at the entrance to the complex? What percentage of residents would be needed to consent to searches in the common areas of the building?

If collective consent is not allowed as a basis to waive the rights of an entire group, could collective behavior, such as a series of gunshots in a project or a group fight, serve as an exigency that justifies multiple apartment searches? See Pratt v. Chicago Housing Authority, 848 F. Supp. 792 (N.D. Ill. 1994) (rejecting broad-scale searches and sweeps of multiple apartment units, including searches of "closets, drawers, refrigerators, cabinets and personal effects," days after multiple, random gunfire was heard throughout a complex, and despite consent from many tenants).

Problem 3-9. Divide and Conquer

New Jersey State Troopers Frank Trifari and Thomas Colella were patrolling the southbound lane of Interstate 95 when they observed a 1988 Oldsmobile with out-of-state license plates driving in the left-hand lane for approximately one-half mile. The troopers stopped the car for failing to keep right. The troopers approached the car and asked the driver, Gerald Green, for his license and registration. Both Green and the passenger, Reinaldo Maristany, appeared nervous as they searched for the papers. When Green failed to produce credentials, Trifari asked him to step out of the car and walk to the rear of the vehicle. The officers ordered Maristany to get out of the passenger seat and to sit on the front hood, facing forward.

Trifari and Colella questioned Green and Maristany separately. Green explained that he was returning from a visit with his sick aunt in New York. While Colella remained with Green at the rear of the car, Trifari walked to the front of the car to question Maristany, who claimed that he and Green had been visiting Maristany's children in New York. Because of the inconsistent responses and apparent nervousness, Trifari exchanged places with Colella and requested Green's consent to search the car and trunk. When asked if the trunk contained any luggage, Green indicated that a blue canvas bag and brown suitcase were inside.

After Trifari advised Green of his right to refuse consent, Green agreed to the search and signed a consent-to-search form that authorized Trifari to "conduct a complete search of trunk portion of vehicle including blue canvas bag, brown suitcase, also includes interior portion of vehicle." Maristany, still at the front of the car, did not hear Green consent to a search.

Trifari found no contraband in the car's interior. Green removed the keys from the ignition and opened the trunk for the trooper's inspection. In the blue canvas gym bag, Trifari found three kilograms of cocaine. The bag did not have any identification tags and was empty except for the cocaine. A search of the brown suitcase, likewise showing no identification tag, revealed no contraband. A further search of the car uncovered a rental agreement, indicating that the car had been rented to a Bernadette Harvey. After his arrest, Green claimed that the blue bag belonged to Maristany and that he had no knowledge of its contents.

At the suppression hearing, relying on Green's statement at headquarters, defense counsel argued that Green did not own the blue gym bag, and therefore his consent to search was invalid. According to the State, nothing had indicated that Maristany owned the gym bag, and the trooper saw only a driver who showed apparent ownership and control of the car and who consented to its search. How would you rule on the motion to suppress? Cf. State v. Maristany, 627 A.2d 1066 (N.J. 1993).

Problem 3-10. Consent Through Lease Provisions

In response to long-standing problems with drug trafficking and handgun violence in public housing developments in the city, organized groups of tenants urge the housing authority to require all public housing residents to sign leases consenting to police searches of their apartments for drugs or weapons at any time during the lease period. The housing authority tentatively agrees to the plan. In any public housing development where a majority of tenants vote to adopt the plan, the housing authority will include in every lease a provision consenting to searches of the apartment during the lease period.

As legal counsel for the housing authority, what advice would you offer about this plan? Would you amend it?

IV

Searches in Recurring Contexts

Chapters 2 and 3 introduced the basic elements of search and seizure analysis. This chapter explores the recurring situations in which courts, legislatures, and executive branch agencies apply those elements. Most of these situations actually happen quite often; others appear often in court opinions and statutes but happen less frequently in actual practice.

Review of these commonly encountered problems will give you the chance to practice using the concepts introduced in the previous two chapters. Will the government practice be considered a "search" within the meaning of the federal or state constitution? What showing does the government need to make to justify the search: reasonable suspicion, probable cause, or something else? Is a warrant necessary? Is the search acceptable because the target (or someone else with authority) consented to the search, either explicitly or implicitly? The theories we discuss in this chapter only become relevant when the government has no search warrant, and also cannot establish that a person with actual or apparent authority provided valid consent; many treatises and study aids address these topics under the umbrella of "exceptions to the Warrant Requirement."

This chapter is divided into categories identified in the text of the Fourth Amendment and many of its analogs. Remember that the Fourth Amendment secures the right of the people to be secure "in their persons, houses, papers, and effects, against unreasonable searches and seizures." Section A considers searches of "persons," along with searches of places or objects based on their proximity to persons. Section B considers issues that arise during searches of "houses" and then expands the inquiry to cover other searches where the location of the search matters in creating the relevant legal rules. Section C considers a historic debate (with modern echoes) about the proper treatment of private "papers," a debate that goes to the heart of the types of limits our legal system now places (and refuses to place) on government searches. Section D considers searches of personal property (or "effects"), especially searches of cars and containers, which are among the most common recurring situations in law enforcement.

A. "PERSONS"

Searches of the human body intrude into privacy more clearly than most other searches. When a government actor wants to intrude into or onto a suspect's body, the best option is to get a search warrant, explaining to the magistrate how probable cause supports the belief that an item subject to seizure is located in or on that person's body. The second option is to ask the suspect to consent to the search of his body. If the officer does not get a search warrant or obtain consent from the suspect, there are various ways the prosecutor can later try to justify the search during a suppression hearing. Depending on how deep the search goes, an officer might need reasonable suspicion, probable cause, or something more.

As you read the materials below, consider whether the legal rules about searches of the person reflect the special intrusiveness of these searches, and what distinctions in principle or policy explain the various search rules adopted.

1. Searches Incident to Arrest

When government agents arrest a person, it has long been clear that they may search the person "incident" to the arrest, without any probable cause or reasonable suspicion to believe that the search will produce any weapon or anything else connected to the crime. This automatic "search incident to arrest" was established in English common law and became part of the law of the American colonies from the very earliest times.

The "search incident to arrest" also extends beyond the body of the arrestee to include areas nearby. But just how near? As a matter of both common law and constitutional law, the answer to this question has fluctuated over time. As Judge Learned Hand once wrote, with typical understatement, "When a man is arrested, the extent to which the premises under his direct control may be searched has proved a troublesome question." United States v. Poller, 43 F.2d 911 (2d Cir. 1930).

■ ARKANSAS RULE OF CRIMINAL PROCEDURE 12.2

An officer making an arrest and the authorized officials at the police station or other place of detention to which the accused is brought may conduct a search of the accused's garments and personal effects ready to hand, the surface of his body, and the area within his immediate control.

■ ANNOTATED LAWS OF MASSACHUSETTS CH. 276, §1

A search conducted incident to an arrest may be made only for the purposes of seizing fruits, instrumentalities, contraband and other evidence of the crime for which the arrest has been made, in order to prevent its destruction or concealment; and removing any weapons that the arrestee might use to resist arrest or effect his escape. Property seized as a result of a search in violation of the provisions of this paragraph shall not be admissible in evidence in criminal proceedings.

◼ DANNY BIRCHFIELD v. NORTH DAKOTA

136 S. Ct. 2160 (2016)

Alito, J.*

Petitioner Danny Birchfield accidentally drove his car off a North Dakota highway on October 10, 2013. A state trooper arrived and watched as Birchfield unsuccessfully tried to drive back out of the ditch in which his car was stuck. The trooper approached, caught a strong whiff of alcohol, and saw that Birchfield's eyes were bloodshot and watery. Birchfield spoke in slurred speech and struggled to stay steady on his feet. At the trooper's request, Birchfield agreed to take several field sobriety tests and performed poorly on each. He had trouble reciting sections of the alphabet and counting backwards in compliance with the trooper's directions.

The state trooper arrested Birchfield for driving while impaired, gave the usual *Miranda* warnings, again advised him of his obligation under North Dakota law to undergo BAC testing, and informed him, as state law requires, that refusing to take the test would expose him to criminal penalties. . . . These criminal penalties apply to blood, breath, and urine test refusals alike. Although faced with the prospect of prosecution under this law, Birchfield refused to let his blood be drawn.

[Eventually Birchfield] pleaded guilty—to a misdemeanor violation of the refusal statute—but his plea was a conditional one: while Birchfield admitted refusing the blood test, he argued that the Fourth Amendment prohibited criminalizing his refusal to submit to the test. The State District Court rejected this argument and imposed a sentence that . . . included 30 days in jail . . . .

IV.

[Our] cases establish that the taking of a blood sample or the administration of a breath test is a search. See Skinner v. Railway Labor Executives', 489 U.S. 602, 616-617 (1989); Schmerber v. California, 384 U. S. 757, 767-768 (1966). The question, then, is whether the warrantless search at issue here [was] reasonable.

We have previously had occasion to examine whether one [warrant] exception—for "exigent circumstances"—applies in drunk-driving investigations. The exigent circumstances exception allows a warrantless search when an emergency leaves police insufficient time to seek a warrant. Michigan v. Tyler, 436 U. S. 499, 509 (1978). It permits, for instance, the warrantless entry of private property when there is a need to provide urgent aid to those inside, when police are in hot pursuit of a fleeing suspect, and when police fear the imminent destruction of evidence.

In *Schmerber*, we held that drunk driving may present such an exigency. . . . More recently, though, [in Missouri v. McNeely, 569 U.S. 141 (2013), we held] that the natural dissipation of alcohol from the bloodstream does not *always* constitute an exigency justifying the warrantless taking of a blood sample. While emphasizing that the exigent-circumstances exception must be applied on a case-by-case basis, the *McNeely* Court noted that other exceptions to the warrant requirement "apply categorically" rather than in a "case-specific" fashion. One of these . . . is the long-established rule that a warrantless search may be conducted incident to a lawful arrest.

* [Chief Justice Roberts and Justices Kennedy, Breyer, and Kagan joined this opinion.—Eds.]

V.

A.

The search-incident-to-arrest doctrine has an ancient pedigree. Well before the Nation's founding, it was recognized that officers carrying out a lawful arrest had the authority to make a warrantless search of the arrestee's person. . . . One Fourth Amendment historian has observed that, prior to American independence, "[any-one] arrested could expect that not only his surface clothing but his body, luggage, and saddlebags would be searched and, perhaps, his shoes, socks, and mouth as well." W. Cuddihy, The Fourth Amendment: Origins and Original Meaning: 602-1791, p. 420 (2009). No historical evidence suggests that the Fourth Amendment altered the permissible bounds of arrestee searches. . . .

The exception quickly became a fixture in our Fourth Amendment case law. But in the decades that followed, we grappled repeatedly with the question of the authority of arresting officers to search the area surrounding the arrestee, and our decisions reached results that were not easy to reconcile. See, e.g., United States v. Lefkowitz, 285 U.S. 452, 464 (1932) (forbidding "unrestrained" search of room where arrest was made); Harris v. United States, 331 U.S. 145, 149 (1947) (permitting complete search of arrestee's four-room apartment); United States v. Rabinowitz, 339 U.S. 56, 60-65 (1950) (permitting complete search of arrestee's office). We attempted to clarify the law regarding searches incident to arrest in Chimel v. California, 395 U.S. 752, 754 (1969), a case in which officers had searched the arrestee's entire three-bedroom house. *Chimel* endorsed a general rule that arresting officers, in order to prevent the arrestee from obtaining a weapon or destroying evidence, could search both "the person arrested" and "the area within his immediate control." No comparable justification, we said, supported "routinely searching any room other than that in which an arrest occurs—or, for that matter, for searching through all the desk drawers or other closed or concealed areas in that room itself."

Four years later, in United States v. Robinson, 414 U.S. 218 (1973), we elaborated on *Chimel*'s meaning. We noted that the search-incident-to-arrest rule actually comprises two distinct propositions: "The first is that a search may be made of the person of the arrestee by virtue of the lawful arrest. The second is that a search may be made of the area within the control of the arrestee." After a thorough review of the relevant common law history, we repudiated "case-by-case adjudication" of the question whether an arresting officer had the authority to carry out a search of the arrestee's person. The permissibility of such searches, we held, does not depend on whether a search of a particular arrestee is likely to protect officer safety or evidence . . . . Instead, the mere "fact of the lawful arrest" justifies a full search of the person. . . .

Our decision two Terms ago in Riley v. California, 134 S. Ct. 2473 (2014), reaffirmed *Robinson*'s categorical rule and explained how the rule should be applied in situations that could not have been envisioned when the Fourth Amendment was adopted. *Riley* concerned a search of data contained in the memory of a modern cell phone. . . . "Absent more precise guidance from the founding era," the Court wrote, "we generally determine whether to exempt a given type of search from the warrant requirement by assessing, on the one hand, the degree to which it intrudes upon an individual's privacy and, on the other, the degree to which it is needed for the promotion of legitimate governmental interests." [*Riley* concluded that searches of data from digital devices ordinarily require warrants, even when performed incident to arrest.]

Blood and breath tests to measure blood alcohol concentration are not as new as searches of cell phones, but here, as in *Riley*, the founding era does not provide any definitive guidance as to whether they should be allowed incident to arrest. Lacking such guidance, we engage in the same mode of analysis as in *Riley*: we examine the degree to which they intrude upon an individual's privacy and the degree to which [they are] needed for the promotion of legitimate governmental interests.

B.

We begin by considering the impact of breath and blood tests on individual privacy interests, and we will discuss each type of test in turn.

[Breath] tests do not implicate significant privacy concerns. . . . First, the physical intrusion is almost negligible. Breath tests do not require piercing the skin and entail a minimum of inconvenience. The process requires the arrestee to blow continuously for 4 to 15 seconds into a straw-like mouthpiece that is connected by a tube to the test machine. The effort is no more demanding than blowing up a party balloon. [There] is nothing painful or strange about this requirement. The use of a straw to drink beverages is a common practice and one to which few object. . . .

In prior cases, we have upheld warrantless searches involving physical intrusions that were at least as significant as that entailed in the administration of a breath test. Just recently we described the process of collecting a DNA sample by rubbing a swab on the inside of a person's cheek as a "negligible" intrusion. Maryland v. King, 569 U.S. 435 (2013). We have also upheld scraping underneath a suspect's fingernails to find evidence of a crime, calling that a "very limited intrusion." Cupp v. Murphy, 412 U.S. 291, 296 (1973). A breath test is no more intrusive than either of these procedures.

Second, breath tests are capable of revealing only one bit of information, the amount of alcohol in the subject's breath. In this respect, they contrast sharply with the sample of cells collected by the swab in Maryland v. King. Although the DNA obtained under the law at issue in that case could lawfully be used only for identification purposes, the process put into the possession of law enforcement authorities a sample from which a wealth of additional, highly personal information could potentially be obtained. A breath test, by contrast, results in a BAC reading on a machine, nothing more. . . .

Blood tests are a different matter. They require piercing the skin and [extracting] a part of the subject's body. And while humans exhale air from their lungs many times per minute, humans do not continually shed blood. It is true, of course, that people voluntarily submit to the taking of blood samples as part of a physical examination, and the process involves little pain or risk. Nevertheless, for many, the process is not one they relish. It is significantly more intrusive than blowing into a tube.

In addition, a blood test, unlike a breath test, places in the hands of law enforcement authorities a sample that can be preserved and from which it is possible to extract information beyond a simple BAC reading. Even if the law enforcement agency is precluded from testing the blood for any purpose other than to measure BAC, the potential remains and may result in anxiety for the person tested.

C.

Having assessed the impact of breath and blood testing on privacy interests, we now look to the States' asserted need to obtain BAC readings for persons arrested for drunk driving. . . . The States and the Federal Government have a paramount interest in preserving the safety of public highways. [Furthermore,] alcohol consumption is a leading cause of traffic fatalities and injuries. Petitioner [contends] that the States and the Federal Government could combat drunk driving in other ways that do not have the same impact on personal privacy. [Those] arguments are unconvincing.

The chief argument on this score is that an officer making an arrest for drunk driving should not be allowed to administer a BAC test unless the officer procures a search warrant or could not do so in time to obtain usable test results. The governmental interest in warrantless breath testing, [according to this argument], turns on whether the burden of obtaining a warrant is likely to frustrate the governmental purpose behind the search.

This argument contravenes our decisions holding that the legality of a search incident to arrest must be judged on the basis of categorical rules. In *Robinson*, for example, no one claimed that the object of the search, a package of cigarettes, presented any danger to the arresting officer or was at risk of being destroyed in the time that it would have taken to secure a search warrant. The Court nevertheless upheld the constitutionality of a warrantless search of the package, concluding that a categorical rule was needed to give police adequate guidance. . . .

Petitioner [also suggests] that requiring a warrant for BAC testing in every case in which a motorist is arrested for drunk driving would not impose any great burden on the police or the courts. But of course the same argument could be made about searching through objects found on the arrestee's possession, which our cases permit even in the absence of a warrant.

If a search warrant were required for every search incident to arrest that does not involve exigent circumstances, the courts would be swamped. And even if we arbitrarily singled out BAC tests incident to arrest for this special treatment . . . the impact on the courts would be considerable. . . . With a small number of judicial officers authorized to issue warrants in some parts of the State, the burden of fielding BAC warrant applications 24 hours per day, 365 days of the year would not be the light burden that petitioners . . . suggest.

In light of this burden and our prior search-incident-to-arrest precedents, petitioners would at a minimum have to show some special need for warrants for BAC testing. It is therefore appropriate to consider the benefits that such applications would provide. Search warrants protect privacy in two main ways. First, they ensure that a search is not carried out unless a neutral magistrate makes an independent determination that there is probable cause to believe that evidence will be found. Second, if the magistrate finds probable cause, the warrant limits the intrusion on privacy by specifying the scope of the search—that is, the area that can be searched and the items that can be sought.

How well would these functions be performed by the warrant applications that petitioners propose? In order to persuade a magistrate that there is probable cause for a search warrant, the officer would typically recite the same facts that led the officer to find that there was probable cause for arrest, namely, that there is probable cause to believe that a BAC test will reveal that the motorist's blood alcohol level is over the limit. As for the second function served by search warrants—delineating the scope of a search—the warrants in question here would not serve that function at all. In every case the scope of the warrant would simply be a BAC test of the arrestee. For these reasons, requiring the police to obtain a warrant in every case would impose a substantial burden but no commensurate benefit.

Having assessed the effect of BAC tests on privacy interests and the need for such tests, we conclude that the Fourth Amendment permits warrantless breath tests incident to arrests for drunk driving. The impact of breath tests on privacy is slight, and the need for BAC testing is great.

We reach a different conclusion with respect to blood tests. Blood tests are significantly more intrusive, and their reasonableness must be judged in light of the availability of the less invasive alternative of a breath test. Respondents have offered no satisfactory justification for demanding the more intrusive alternative without a warrant.

Because breath tests are significantly less intrusive than blood tests and in most cases amply serve law enforcement interests, we conclude that a breath test, but not a blood test, may be administered as a search incident to a lawful arrest for drunk driving. . . .

Notes

1. *Search incident to arrest: majority position.* Under the long-standing doctrine of "search incident to arrest" (or "SITA"), the police may search the person of an arrestee, along with some area near the arrestee, without any independent probable cause or warrant to support the search. Chimel v. California, 395 U.S. 752 (1969). The law defining the permissible scope of searches incident to arrest has gone through many changes over the past 70 years. Flexible as *Chimel* may seem, it narrowed the prior rule of Harris v. United States, 331 U.S. 145 (1947), and United States v. Rabinowitz, 339 U.S. 56 (1950), which allowed searches of multiple-room dwellings as searches incident to arrest. An earlier strand of Supreme Court cases—notably Go-Bart Importing Co. v. United States, 282 U.S. 344 (1931), and Trupiano v. United States, 334 U.S. 699 (1948) (rejected by *Rabinowitz*) —suggested that where a search warrant could be obtained before the arrest, it should be.

2. *The "wingspan" rule.* As for the amount of area the police may search "incident" to the arrest, the federal standard appears in Chimel v. California, 395 U.S. 752 (1969). The search may extend to the area within the "immediate control" of the arrestee, that is, the area in which the arrestee could reach a weapon or destroy evidence. State courts have by and large adopted this same "wingspan" standard under their state constitutions and statutes.

The majority of state courts determine the "wingspan" on a case-by-case basis and consider the fact that an arrestee was handcuffed at the time of a search when determining the area within the "immediate control" of an arrestee. A strong minority of states, however, follow the federal standard and use a more categorical approach. Rather than attempting to reconstruct a precise timeline of events during the arrest, these courts simply ask if the search happened within an area that was within the defendant's immediate control *in the moments before the arrest* began. For further exploration of the variety of state court applications of this standard, see the web extension for this chapter at *http://www.crimpro.com/extension/ch04.*

Whether a suspect is handcuffed at the time of a search incident to arrest is only one of a host of facts that state courts use to assess the validity of SITA searches in particular cases. Other factors include: (a) whether there are multiple defendants; (b) whether there are confederates of the suspect nearby who might destroy evidence; (c) whether the officers are between the suspect and the area or object

to be searched; (d) whether the officers have control over the area or object to be searched; and (e) whether there was any postarrest movement by the arrestee (for example, to get dressed). Which of these factors is subject to the control of the officer? Doesn't assessment of these factors depend on the justification underlying searches incident to arrest?

3. *Automatic authorization to search.* The distinctive feature of the search incident to arrest is its automatic quality: As the *Birchfield* court explained, the police need no justification for the search beyond the justification for the arrest. See United States v. Robinson, 414 U.S. 218 (1973). There is no need to suspect that the specific arrestee is holding a weapon or evidence of a crime; there is no need to suspect that the area within the arrestee's immediate control holds weapons, contraband, or evidence. Later in this chapter, when we consider SITA searches in the automobile context, note that the Supreme Court has recently gone in a different direction about the "automatic" nature of SITA search authority. See Arizona v. Gant, 556 U.S. 332 (2009).

Statutes in England regulate searches incident to arrest differently than American laws do; they reject the automatic search in favor of showing reasonable grounds for the search. Under section 18 of the Police and Criminal Evidence Act of 1984, the constable may search the *premises* of any arrested person (regardless of where the arrest takes place) if there are "reasonable grounds" to believe that the premises contain evidence of the offense that is the basis of the arrest or some similar offense. Section 32 of the Act allows the constable to search a *person*, if the person to be searched has been arrested at a place other than a police station, and if "the constable has reasonable grounds for believing that the arrested person may present a danger to himself or others." The constable may also search the arrested person for evidence of a crime, or for anything he or she might use to escape custody, but only if the constable has "reasonable grounds for believing" that such items will be found in the search. Finally, section 32 also allows the constable "to enter and search any premises in which [the arrested person] was when arrested . . . for evidence relating to the offence for which he has been arrested," but once again, only if the constable has "reasonable grounds for believing that there is evidence . . . on the premises." If an American jurisdiction were to adopt this statute, would it change the practices of the police during arrests in a significant way? Would the police face greater danger?

4. *Persons, purses, and phones.* Police making an arrest may search items "immediately associated" with the arrestee's person, such as purses, wallets, and luggage. See People v. Cregan, 10 N.E.3d 1196 (Ill. 2014) (officers searched wheeled suitcase of arrestee despite his request to allow his traveling companion to take custody of the luggage); State v. Byrd, 310 P.3d 793 (Wash. 2013) (search of purse that defendant set down upon arrest); State v. Hargis, 756 S.E.2d 529 (Ga. 2014) (search of wallet that arrestee removed from pocket and placed onto car seat at time of arrest). As for cell phones and other digital containers that a suspect carries at the time of arrest, consider Riley v. California, 134 S. Ct. 2473 (2014), mentioned in *Birchfield* and reprinted in Chapter 7.

5. *Comparison to* Terry *frisks.* Courts allow searches of the person incident to arrest to be more extensive than *Terry* frisks. See United States v. Robinson, 414 U.S. at 224-229, discussed in *Birchfield.* Why? How long can a search incident to arrest take? How many more pockets might it explore? After *Birchfield*, is there any kind of search, either of the person or of a place, that would not be allowed within the justification of a search incident to arrest?

6. *Protective sweeps.* Although *Chimel* rejected searches of entire rooms or multiple rooms as part of a search incident to arrest, such searches may still be allowed at the time of arrest on other grounds. One justification for a full-house search is to discover persons who may pose a threat to officers conducting the arrest. In Maryland v. Buie, 494 U.S. 325 (1990), the Supreme Court upheld two sorts of "protective sweeps" outside the area within the "immediate control" of the arrestee. First, the arresting officers may look in closets and other places *immediately adjoining* the place of the arrest from which another person might launch an attack on the officers. This search needs no justification beyond the simple fact of the arrest. Second, the officers may search other areas in the house for any persons who might pose a danger to them, but only if they have a reasonable suspicion that the "sweep" will reveal the presence of such a person. In either case, the search is limited to places where a person may be found.

Almost all state courts addressing this subject also allow police to make "protective sweeps" of the premises where an arrest takes place, under the same two-tier analysis that the *Buie* court used. See Commonwealth v. Robertson, 659 S.E.2d 321 (Va. 2008); cf. State v. Davila, 999 A.2d 1116 (N.J. 2010) (protective sweep also available in nonarrest situation if officers are lawfully on premises). Should multiple-room searches for potential accomplices be allowed even when there are no reasonable grounds to believe such accomplices pose a danger to officers but when there is a reasonable suspicion that parties to a multiparty offense are likely to be present or that persons in the house may destroy evidence?

7. *Subsequent searches: How much time?* The Supreme Court periodically declares that searches incident to arrest be "substantially contemporaneous with the arrest." See, e.g., Vale v. Louisiana, 399 U.S. 30 (1970); cf. People v. Jenkins, 20 N.E.3d 639 (N.Y. 2014) (police who entered apartment after seeing armed man flee inside had no authority to search for the missing gun in a closed box after they handcuffed suspect and secured the premises). Some state courts allow searches at the police station, well after the time of arrest, of objects "immediately associated with the person" that could have been searched at the time of arrest, including clothing, wallets, and purses. See Commonwealth v. Stallworth, 781 A.2d 110 (Pa. 2001); but see State v. Lamay, 103 P.3d 448 (Idaho 2004) (suspect first encountered in hotel room lying on bed next to backpack on floor, then ordered to step into hallway outside hotel room, where he was arrested; later search of backpack not justified as incident to arrest).

Professor Myron Moskovitz, based on telephone interviews with police officers and written training materials from various police departments, concluded that police officers typically handcuff a suspect before searching the vicinity. They usually obtain a warrant to search an area if they have already removed the arrestee from the scene. Moskovitz, A Rule in Search of a Reason: An Empirical Re-examination of *Chimel* and *Belton*, 2002 Wis. L. Rev. 657, 666-667. This practice, he concludes, is based on police views about the reasonableness of searches rather than their reading of what the courts might allow.

8. *Search incident to citation.* As we will discuss in Chapter 5, police officers often have the discretion to issue a citation (for example, a traffic ticket) rather than arresting a suspect. Can the officer search the suspect automatically after delivering such a citation? In Knowles v. Iowa, 525 U.S. 113 (1998), the Supreme Court ruled that the Fourth Amendment did not authorize an automatic search after a police officer cited a driver for speeding. There is relatively little case law on this subject,

but the few state court opinions on the topic tend to endorse *Knowles*. See *State v. Green*, 79 So. 3d 1013 (La. 2012).

Here, as with many issues surrounding arrest and detention, police department policies often supplement statutes and judicial doctrine. See Phoenix Police Manual Order No. B-5(5)(D) (prohibiting search incident to issuance of a citation). Does *Knowles* apply outside the traffic stop context? See *Lovelace v. Commonwealth*, 522 S.E.2d 856 (Va. 1999) (applies to brief detention of pedestrian to issue summons).

Problem 4-1. Lunging in Handcuffs

Marc Hufnagel was indicted on charges of selling cocaine and a warrant for his arrest was issued. That same afternoon, the sheriff and two deputies went to Hufnagel's condominium to execute the arrest warrant. The officers entered the condo without incident, asked Hufnagel to stand up, and told him that he was under arrest for selling cocaine.

The officers handcuffed him with his hands behind his back and patted him down for weapons shortly after he stood up. He was standing near the sofa and an adjacent, octagonal end table about 18 inches high. The sheriff then noticed that Hufnagel glanced at the end table, which was located less than 10 feet from where the arrestee stood. The sheriff opened a door in the table and saw a white lidless box inside, which contained several baggies of white powder. He picked up the box and examined its contents without removing them. The sheriff then put the box back into the end table and closed the door.

Later that same day, the sheriff obtained a search warrant based in part on his observation of the cocaine in the end table. The warranted search produced additional evidence.

Should the trial court grant Hufnagel's motion to suppress the evidence obtained from the end table? Cf. *State v. Hufnagel*, 745 P.2d 242 (Colo. 1987).

Problem 4-2. Search Incident to (but After) Arrest

An officer looking through binoculars saw a man with a plaid shirt and a blue backpack leaving a field of marijuana plants in a remote, unpopulated canyon. The officer and his partner followed the man in the plaid shirt, whose name turned out to be Howard Boff, and arrested him on a deserted dirt road after he sat down and placed the backpack on the ground about five feet from his body.

The officers drove Boff and his backpack to the sheriff's office, about 45 minutes away in Dove Creek. Three hours after placing Boff in custody, the police officers opened the backpack without a search warrant and found marijuana. Was the search valid as a search incident to arrest? Compare *People v. Boff*, 766 P.2d 646 (Colo. 1988).

Problem 4-3. Sweeping Authority

Deputy Sheriffs Hepperly and Ewalt learned that Terry McGrane, who was wanted on an arrest warrant for a parole violation, was present in a particular house. When they arrived at the house, Deputy Ewalt knocked on the side door, which leads directly into the kitchen. Melissa Schutz answered the door and initially denied that McGrane was in the home. When the deputies told her they had information that he was there, Schutz's demeanor changed and she allowed the deputies to enter the home. The three proceeded into the kitchen area. Around the corner of the kitchen, a stairwell led to the second floor of the two-story house. Schutz yelled up the stairs for McGrane. Deputy Hepperly heard someone moving around upstairs and started up the staircase. When Hepperly was about a third of the way up the stairs, McGrane appeared from behind a bed sheet curtain, which cordoned off a small storage area to the right of the top of the steps. Deputy Hepperly saw McGrane put something behind the curtain as he emerged from behind it. He informed McGrane of the arrest warrant and ordered him downstairs. McGrane walked down the stairs and into the kitchen. Deputy Ewalt searched him, placed him in hand-cuffs, and sat him down on a kitchen chair. McGrane was cooperative throughout this interaction.

Deputy Hepperly then went upstairs, leaving McGrane in Deputy Ewalt's cus-tody. The stairway led to an open area and did not include separate rooms or clos-ets. The living area included a bed, couch, coffee table, and computer stand. While upstairs, Deputy Hepperly observed drugs and paraphernalia strewn on the coffee table. The deputy also saw a scale, some baggies on the bed, and a pillow with a zip-per on it that had a baggie sticking out of it. Deputy Hepperly removed the baggie and found marijuana and cash. Meanwhile, from behind the bed sheet curtain, he retrieved a small leather pouch, which contained $60 in cash and thirteen small baggies of what appeared to be methamphetamine.

McGrane, charged with several counts of drug possession with intent to distribute, moves to suppress the evidence seized from the second floor. Did Deputy Hepperly conduct a search? Was it justified as a search incident to arrest? Was it a proper protective sweep? Compare State v. McGrane, 733 N.W.2d 671 (Iowa 2007).

2. Body Searches at the Jail

When a person is about to be booked into custody at the jail, she may be subject to a range of privacy invasions. She may have her cheek swabbed for DNA while get-ting her fingerprints taken as part of the booking process. She might also be subject to a strip search or a body cavity search before entering the jail; these latter types of searches are among the most intrusive searches that government agents perform, and require different justifications than the simple cheek swab.

In recent years, legislatures rather than courts have created the legal limits for these searches. Most states now have statutes placing some limits on the use of strip searches and body cavity searches, and courts have in turn largely ceased their efforts to regulate such searches. Reprinted below are a few examples of these stat-utes. They highlight how legislatures develop legal rules different from those that courts develop.

Consider the differences between the legislative and judicial rules governing pre-arrest and postarrest searches. Should the extremely intrusive nature of the search technique require some showing beyond probable cause and a judicial war-rant in any setting? Or should the regulation of strip searches be more substantial in the field (because of possible abuse), or in the station house (because of the more controlled setting)? Strip search statutes generally require that any allow-able strip or body cavity search take place in clean, private surroundings and that the police officers conducting the search must be of the same sex as the person being examined.

As you examine the three statutes reprinted below, consider (1) the different levels of justification required for such searches, (2) any special procedures or additional actors who must approve the search, and (3) the use of alternatives to body cavity and strip searches. Then, based on these elements, rank the following statutes in terms of their potential to minimize the number of strip and body cavity searches. What information would you collect to test your assumptions about the impact of different procedures in actual practice?

■ MARYLAND v. ALONZO J. KING, JR.
569 U.S. 435 (2013)

KENNEDY, J.*

. . . When King was arrested on April 10, 2009, he was processed for detention in custody at the Wicomico County Central Booking facility. Booking personnel used a cheek swab to take the DNA sample from him pursuant to provisions of the Maryland DNA Collection Act (or Act). On July 13, 2009, King's DNA record was uploaded to the Maryland DNA database, and three weeks later, on August 4, 2009, his DNA profile was matched to the DNA sample collected in [an] unsolved 2003 rape case. Once the DNA was matched to King, detectives presented the forensic evidence to a grand jury, which indicted him for the rape. . . . He moved to sup-press the DNA match on the grounds that Maryland's DNA collection law violated the Fourth Amendment. The Circuit Court Judge upheld the statute as constitutional. King . . . was convicted and sentenced to life in prison without the possibility of parole. . . .

III.

. . . The Maryland DNA Collection Act provides that, in order to obtain a DNA sample, all arrestees charged with serious crimes must furnish the sample on a buccal swab applied, as noted, to the inside of the cheeks. The arrestee is already in valid police custody for a serious offense supported by probable cause. The DNA collection is not subject to the judgment of officers whose perspective might be colored by their primary involvement in "the often competitive enter-prise of ferreting out crime." Johnson v. United States, 333 U.S. 10, 14 (1948). Here, the search effected by the buccal swab of respondent falls within the cat-egory of cases this Court has analyzed by reference to the proposition that the "touchstone of the Fourth Amendment is reasonableness, not individualized suspi-cion." Samson v. California, 547 U. S. 843 (2006). . . . This application of traditional standards of reasonableness requires a court to weigh the promotion of legitimate governmental interests against the degree to which the search intrudes upon an individual's privacy.

---

* [Chief Justice Roberts and Justices Thomas, Breyer, and Alito joined this opinion.—EDs.]

IV.

. . . The legitimate government interest served by the Maryland DNA Collection Act is . . . well established: the need for law enforcement officers in a safe and accurate way to process and identify the persons and possessions they must take into custody. . . . When probable cause exists to remove an individual from the normal channels of society and hold him in legal custody, DNA identification plays a critical role in serving those interests.

First, in every criminal case, it is known and must be known who has been arrested and who is being tried. . . . A suspect's criminal history is a critical part of his identity that officers should know when processing him for detention. It is a common occurrence that people detained for minor offenses "can turn out to be the most devious and dangerous criminals." . . . In this respect the only difference between DNA analysis and the accepted use of fingerprint databases is the unparalleled accuracy DNA provides. [Moreover,] the task of identification necessarily entails searching public and police records based on the identifying information provided by the arrestee to see what is already known about him.

Second, law enforcement officers bear a responsibility for ensuring that the custody of an arrestee does not create inordinate risks for facility staff, for the existing detainee population, and for a new detainee. [Officers] must know the type of person whom they are detaining, and DNA allows them to make critical choices about how to proceed.

Third, looking forward to future stages of criminal prosecution, the Government has a substantial interest in ensuring that persons accused of crimes are available for trials. A person who is arrested for one offense but knows that he has yet to answer for some past crime may be more inclined to flee the instant charges, lest continued contact with the criminal justice system expose one or more other serious offenses.

Fourth, an arrestee's past conduct is essential to an assessment of the danger he poses to the public, and this will inform a court's determination whether the individual should be released on bail. DNA identification of a suspect in a violent crime provides critical information to the police and judicial officials in making a determination of the arrestee's future dangerousness.

Finally, in the interests of justice, the identification of an arrestee as the perpetrator of some heinous crime may have the salutary effect of freeing a person wrongfully imprisoned for the same offense. . . .

In sum, there can be little reason to question the legitimate interest of the government in knowing for an absolute certainty the identity of the person arrested, in knowing whether he is wanted elsewhere, and in ensuring his identification in the event he flees prosecution. . . . In the balance of reasonableness required by the Fourth Amendment, therefore, the Court must give great weight both to the significant government interest at stake in the identification of arrestees and to the unmatched potential of DNA identification to serve that interest.

V.

. . . The government interest must outweigh the degree to which the search invades an individual's legitimate expectations of privacy. In considering those expectations in this case, however, the necessary predicate of a valid arrest for a serious offense is fundamental. [More-over,] the reasonableness of any search must be considered in the context of the person's legitimate expectations of privacy. The expectations of privacy of an individual taken into police custody necessarily are of a diminished scope. A search of the detainee's person when he is booked into custody may "involve a relatively extensive exploration," United States v. Robinson, 414 U. S. 218, 227 (1973), including "[requiring] at least some detainees to lift their genitals or cough in a squatting position," Florence v. Board of Chosen Freeholders of County of Burlington, 566 U.S. 318, 334 (2012). [In other words,] once an individual has been arrested on probable cause for a dangerous offense that may require detention before trial, his or her expectations of privacy and freedom from police scrutiny are reduced. [A] buccal swab involves an even more brief and still minimal intrusion. A gentle rub along the inside of the cheek does not break the skin, and it involves virtually no risk, trauma, or pain. . . .

In light of the context of a valid arrest supported by probable cause respondent's expectations of privacy were not offended by the minor intrusion of a brief swab of his cheeks. By contrast, that same context of arrest gives rise to significant state interests in identifying respondent not only so that the proper name can be attached to his charges but also so that the criminal justice system can make informed decisions concerning pretrial custody. Upon these considerations the Court concludes that DNA identification of arrestees is a reasonable search that can be considered part of a routine booking procedure. When officers make an arrest supported by probable cause to hold for a serious offense and they bring the suspect to the station to be detained in custody, taking and analyzing a cheek swab of the arrestee's DNA is, like fingerprinting and photographing, a legitimate police booking procedure that is reasonable under the Fourth Amendment. . . .

SCALIA, J., dissenting.*

The Fourth Amendment forbids searching a person for evidence of a crime when there is no basis for believing the person is guilty of the crime or is in possession of incriminating evidence. That prohibition is categorical and without exception; it lies at the very heart of the Fourth Amendment. Whenever this Court has allowed a suspicionless search, it has insisted upon a justifying motive apart from the investigation of crime. It is obvious that no such noninvestigative motive exists in this case. The Court's assertion that DNA is being taken, not to solve crimes, but to identify those in the State's custody, taxes the credulity of the credulous. . . .

The portion of the Court's opinion that explains the identification rationale is strangely silent on the actual workings of the DNA search at issue here. To know those facts is to be instantly disabused of the notion that what happened had anything to do with identifying King.

King was arrested on April 10, 2009, on charges unrelated to the case before us. That same day, April 10, the police searched him and seized the DNA evidence at issue here. What happened next? . . . Maryland officials did not even begin the process of testing King's DNA that day. Or, actually, the next day. Or the day after that. And that was for a simple reason: Maryland law forbids them to do so. A "DNA sample collected from an individual charged with a crime . . . may not be tested or placed in the statewide DNA data base system prior to the first scheduled arraignment date." And King's first appearance in court was not until three days after his

---

* [Justices Ginsburg, Sotomayor, and Kagan joined this opinion—EDS.]

arrest. This places in a rather different light the Court's solemn declaration that the search here was necessary so that King could be identified at "every stage of the criminal process." Does the Court really believe that Maryland did not know whom it was arraigning? . . .

It gets worse. King's DNA sample was not received by the Maryland State Police's Forensic Sciences Division until April 23, 2009 — two weeks after his arrest. It sat in that office, ripening in a storage area, until the custodians got around to mailing it to a lab for testing on June 25, 2009 — two months after it was received, and nearly three since King's arrest. After it was mailed, the data from the lab tests were not available for several more weeks, until July 13, 2009, which is when the test results were entered into Maryland's DNA database, together with information identifying the person from whom the sample was taken. Meanwhile, bail had been set, King had engaged in discovery, and he had requested a speedy trial — presumably not a trial of John Doe. It was not until August 4, 2009 — four months after King's arrest — that the forwarded sample transmitted (without identifying information) from the Maryland DNA database to the Federal Bureau of Investigation's national database was matched with a sample taken from the scene of an unrelated crime years earlier. . . .

That taking DNA samples from arrestees has nothing to do with identifying them is confirmed not just by actual practice (which the Court ignores) but by the enabling statute itself (which the Court also ignores). The Maryland Act at issue has a section helpfully entitled "Purpose of collecting and testing DNA samples." Md. Pub. Saf. Code Ann. §2-505. [The] law provides that DNA samples are collected and tested, as a matter of Maryland law, "as part of an official investigation into a crime."

So, to review: DNA testing does not even begin until after arraignment and bail decisions are already made. The samples sit in storage for months, and take weeks to test. When they are tested, they are checked against the Unsolved Crimes Collection — rather than the Convict and Arrestee Collection, which could be used to identify them. The Act forbids the Court's purpose (identification), but prescribes as its purpose what our suspicionless-search cases forbid ("official investigation into a crime"). . . .

Today's judgment will, to be sure, have the beneficial effect of solving more crimes; then again, so would the taking of DNA samples from anyone who flies on an airplane (surely the Transportation Security Administration needs to know the "identity" of the flying public), applies for a driver's license, or attends a public school. Perhaps the construction of such a genetic panopticon is wise. But I doubt that the proud men who wrote the charter of our liberties would have been so eager to open their mouths for royal inspection.

■ REVISED CODE OF WASHINGTON §§10.79.080, 10.79.130, 10.79.140

§10.79.080

(1) No person may be subjected to a body cavity search by or at the direction of a law enforcement agency unless a search warrant is issued. . . .

(2) No law enforcement officer may seek a warrant for a body cavity search without first obtaining specific authorization for the body cavity search from the ranking shift supervisor of the law enforcement authority. Authorization for the

body cavity search may be obtained electronically: PROVIDED, That such electronic authorization shall be reduced to writing by the law enforcement officer seeking the authorization and signed by the ranking supervisor as soon as possible thereafter.

(3) Before any body cavity search is authorized or conducted, a thorough pat-down search, a thorough electronic metal-detector search, and a thorough clothing search, where appropriate, must be used to search for and seize any evidence of a crime, contraband, fruits of crime, things otherwise criminally possessed, weapons, or other things by means of which a crime has been committed or reasonably appears about to be committed. No body cavity search shall be authorized or conducted unless these other methods do not satisfy the safety, security, or evidentiary concerns of the law enforcement agency.

(4) A law enforcement officer requesting a body cavity search shall prepare and sign a report regarding the body cavity search. . . .

§10.79.130

(1) No person [in custody at a holding, detention, or local correctional facility, regardless of whether an arrest warrant or other court order was issued before the person was arrested, may] be strip searched without a warrant unless:

(a) There is a reasonable suspicion to believe that a strip search is necessary to discover weapons, criminal evidence, contraband, or other thing concealed on the body of the person to be searched, that constitutes a threat to the security of a holding, detention, or local correctional facility;

(b) There is probable cause to believe that a strip search is necessary to discover other criminal evidence concealed on the body of the person to be searched, but not constituting a threat to facility security; or

(c) There is a reasonable suspicion to believe that a strip search is necessary to discover a health condition requiring immediate medical attention.

(2) For the purposes of subsection (1) of this section, a reasonable suspicion is deemed to be present when the person to be searched has been arrested for:

(a) A violent offense . . . ;

(b) An offense involving escape, burglary, or the use of a deadly weapon; or

(c) An offense involving possession of a drug or controlled substance. . . .

§10.79.140

(1) A person [in custody at a holding, detention, or local correctional facility, regardless of whether an arrest warrant or other court order was issued before the person was arrested or otherwise taken into custody] who has not been arrested for an offense within one of the categories specified in RCW 10.79.130(2) may nevertheless be strip searched, but only upon an individualized determination of reasonable suspicion or probable cause as provided in this section.

(2) With the exception of those situations in which reasonable suspicion is deemed to be present under RCW 10.79.130(2), no strip search may be conducted without the specific prior written approval of the jail unit supervisor on duty. Before any strip search is conducted, reasonable efforts must be made to use other less-intrusive means, such as pat-down, electronic metal detector, or clothing searches, to determine whether a weapon, criminal evidence, contraband, or other thing is concealed on the body, or whether a health condition requiring immediate medical

attention is present. The determination of whether reasonable suspicion or probable cause exists to conduct a strip search shall be made only after such less-intrusive means have been used and shall be based on a consideration of all information and circumstances known to the officer authorizing the strip search, including but not limited to the following factors:

(a) The nature of the offense for which the person to be searched was arrested;

(b) The prior criminal record of the person to be searched; and

(c) Physically violent behavior of the person to be searched, during or after the arrest.

Notes

1. *Booking searches.* When an arrestee arrives for booking in the jail, several searches routinely occur. The arrestee is searched, usually more thoroughly than a search incident to arrest performed in the field. Officers also inventory and store any personal items that the arrestee carries. Part of the booking process involves fingerprinting and, in some jurisdictions, DNA sampling. Courts generally treat these searches as automatic extensions of the decision to arrest a suspect.

2. *Strip search statutes.* In most places, state statutes and police department policies place special limits on strip searches and body cavity searches. Is it possible to bar all strip searches? Why does the Washington legislature provide so much detailed guidance for searches conducted once a person is in custody? Apart from responding to abuses in specific cases, what else might explain the willingness of so many legislatures to address this topic? If legislatures were to leave this question to courts, what standards would courts apply?

3. *Strip searches for misdemeanors and infractions.* Public attention is often drawn to strip searches conducted on people suspected only of minor offenses. See Florence v. Board of Chosen Freeholders, 566 U.S. 318 (2012) (arrestee for failure to appear at hearing to enforce a fine was subjected, like every other detainee entering the jail, to strip search that included inspection of genitals and body openings; search policy did not violate Fourth Amendment). Legislatures often claim to sharply limit strip searches for minor offenses. Consider the following illustration from California Penal Code §4030(e):

> A person arrested and held in custody on a misdemeanor or infraction offense, except those involving weapons, controlled substances or violence . . . shall not be subjected to a strip search or visual body cavity search prior to placement in the general jail population, unless a peace officer has determined there is reasonable suspicion based on specific and articulable facts to believe that person is concealing a weapon or contraband, and a strip search will result in the discovery of the weapon or contraband. A strip search or visual body cavity search, or both, shall not be conducted without the prior written authorization of the supervising officer on duty. The authorization shall include the specific and articulable facts and circumstances upon which the reasonable suspicion determination was made by the supervisor. . . .

How much protection for citizens suspected of minor offenses does this statute provide? Why do some legislatures create different presumptions for drug and violent offenders? In these states, how important for the ultimate impact of these rules is the definition of a drug or violent offender?

Other state legislatures have passed such statutes in response to notorious and newsworthy cases involving strip searches. See Mary Beth G. v. City of Chicago, 723 F.2d 1263 (7th Cir. 1983) (civil suit brought by women arrested for outstanding parking tickets, challenging city policy requiring a strip search and body cavity search of all women arrested and detained in city lockups, regardless of charges; Illinois legislature amended arrest statute to prohibit strip searches of persons arrested for traffic, regulatory, or misdemeanor offenses absent a reasonable belief that the arrestee is concealing weapons or controlled substances on her person). Often the motivation for these statutes is not the facts of a particular case but the judgment in a lawsuit. Hundreds of lawsuits based on strip suits have been filed over the years.

4. *The relative virtues of process and substantive standards.* Among the statutes addressing strip searches and body cavity searches, there are two distinct limiting techniques at work. Some of the statutory provisions contain substantive "standards," describing a subclass of cases not eligible for this type of search (such as those accused of particular offenses or cases where the police do not have adequate reason to believe that the search will succeed). For instance, Arkansas Rule of Criminal Procedure 12.3 places three requirements on an unwarranted search of an accused person's blood stream, body cavities, and subcutaneous tissues conducted incidental to an arrest. First, there must be a "strong probability" that the search will "disclose things subject to seizure and related to the offense for which the individual was arrested." Second, there must be reasonable grounds to believe that any delay in procuring a judicial search warrant "would probably result in the disappearance or destruction of the objects of the search." Finally, the search must be "otherwise reasonable under the circumstances of the case, including the seriousness of the offense and the nature of the invasion of the individual's person."

Other statutes, such as the Washington provision reprinted above, focus on the process of authorizing such a search (by requiring a judicial warrant or supervisor approval or a written record of any decision to conduct such a search). Which regulatory technique offers greater protection to citizens: more intricate process requirements or higher substantive standards?

5. *Consent to strip searches.* Some statutes bar consent to strip searches, others allow consent, still others require special procedures for obtaining consent, and several say nothing about consent. For instance, under Tenn. Code §40-7-121, a body cavity search by law enforcement officer prohibited unless based on search warrant or consent, and the statute specifies mandatory terms for an effective waiver, including this language: "I understand that a body cavity search may involve both visual and physical probing into my genitals and anus." In a jurisdiction whose statute says nothing about consent, what arguments would you make to a court that it should enforce special consent rules for strip and body cavity searches?

6. *Probable cause "plus": majority position.* Some courts require the government to justify the use of an especially intrusive bodily search with something more than probable cause. When the government uses invasive medical techniques to carry out a bodily search, the relevant standard under the federal constitution appears in Schmerber v. California, 384 U.S. 757 (1966), discussed briefly in *Birchfield*. There the Court approved the use of evidence derived from a blood sample that a physician had taken from a suspect. The Court found the search reasonable because (1) there was a "clear indication" that the blood sample would produce evidence of a crime; (2) the test was "commonplace" and involved almost no risk or trauma; and (3) the test was conducted in a "reasonable manner," carried out by a physician in

a hospital environment. See also Rochin v. California, 342 U.S. 165 (1952) (forced administration of emetic solution to induce vomiting in suspect who had swallowed capsules; barred by due process). Some state courts interpret *Schmerber* to require only probable cause, but most take this language to mean that the government must show exigent circumstances or evidence stronger than probable cause to justify the taking of blood. For further exploration of the variety of state court applications of this standard, see the web extension for this chapter at *http://www.crimpro.com/extension/ch04*. See also Missouri v. McNeely, 569 U.S. 141 (2013), discussed in *Birchfield*, in which the Court held that exigent circumstances for warrantless blood test was *not* established per se by natural metabolization of alcohol in bloodstream; exigency depends on facts of each case.

What role will police expertise play in jurisdictions where officers are left with some discretion to conduct highly intrusive searches in the field? For example, in People v. More, 764 N.E.2d 967 (N.Y. 2002), how could the police determine before the search whether or not any secreted drugs were in a form that might be destroyed or disappear with further delay? Would the plastic bag and its contents "inevitably" be discovered when a strip search was conducted at the station as part of standard processing before placing the suspect in a jail cell?

7. *Orders for nonintrusive identification evidence.* Should nonintrusive nontestimonial requests — for example, for handwriting, voice, saliva, and hair samples — and other evidence involving the physical state of the suspect be governed by a reasonable suspicion standard, since such information does not require intrusive body searches? See Iowa Code §§810.1-.6 (governing collection of nontestimonial identification evidence including "fingerprints, palm prints, footprints, measurements, hair strands, handwriting samples, voice samples, photographs, blood and saliva samples, ultraviolet or black-light examinations, paraffin tests, and lineups"). Under Iowa Code §810.6, nontestimonial identification orders require the government to establish each of the following:

1. That there is probable cause to believe that a felony described in the application has been committed.
2. That there are reasonable grounds to suspect that the person named or described in the application committed the felony and it is reasonable in view of the seriousness of the offense to subject that person to the requested nontestimonial identification procedures.
3. That the results of the requested nontestimonial identification procedures will be of material aid in determining whether the person named or described in the application committed the felony.
4. That such evidence cannot practicably be obtained from other sources.

In Bousman v. District Court, 630 N.W.2d 789 (Iowa 2001), the Iowa Supreme Court held that this statute and the federal and Iowa constitutions required only reasonable suspicion in support of an order to obtain saliva for a DNA test. The court also held that reasonable suspicion was all that is required to support a brief investigatory detention to gather this information. Is the compelled presence of a suspect at the police station for a physical sample an arrest?

8. *Noninvasive medical search techniques.* The pumping of a stomach is one medical technique that typically requires the probable cause "plus" showing. Would you require the probable cause "plus" only for physically invasive techniques? How

about the use of an X-ray, followed by administration of a laxative? See People v. Thompson, 820 P.2d 1160 (Colo. Ct. App. 1991) (higher justification required for laxative but not for X-ray). Would most people rather be subject to an unwanted X-ray or an unwanted laxative? Which of these procedures can go forward without the assistance of a doctor? A number of cases have approved the taking of a blood sample based only on a showing of probable cause. Would a justification higher than probable cause be necessary if the police officer uses a "stun gun" (a weapon that produces 0.00006 of an amp of electricity to cause muscle contractions and a resulting loss of balance) to disable a resisting suspect long enough to draw the blood sample? See McCann v. State, 588 A.2d 1100 (Del. 1991).

Problem 4-4. Blood Test Consent

Melissa Helton was admitted to the university hospital after the car she was driving crashed into a tree, killing four passengers. Two deputy sheriffs asked the medical staff to draw a blood sample from Helton for their investigation, in addition to the blood tests the medical staff was performing to prepare Helton for surgery. Helton was unconscious during the visit of the deputies and the drawing of her blood. The deputies did not have a warrant to support their request for a blood test. The sample showed that Helton had a blood alcohol content of 0.16 percent.

Helton was indicted for four counts of wanton murder and one count of first-offense driving under the influence. She moved to suppress the evidence of her blood alcohol level, arguing that the sample was taken in violation of state statutes and the state and federal constitutions. Section 189A.103 of the state code provides as follows:

> The following provisions shall apply to any person who operates a motor vehicle in this State:
>
> (1) He or she has given his or her consent to one or more tests of his or her blood, breath, and urine, for the purpose of determining alcohol concentration or presence of a substance which may impair one's driving ability, if an officer has reasonable grounds to believe that a violation of the impaired driving laws has occurred;
>
> (2) Any person who is dead, unconscious, or otherwise in a condition rendering him or her incapable of refusal is deemed not to have withdrawn the consent provided in subsection (1) of this section, and the test may be given.

A second statute specifies:

> (2) (b) Nothing in this subsection shall be construed to prohibit a judge of a court of competent jurisdiction from issuing a search warrant or other court order requiring a blood or urine test of a defendant charged with a violation of the impaired driving laws when a person is killed or suffers physical injury as a result of the incident in which the defendant has been charged. However, if the incident involves a motor vehicle accident in which there was a fatality, the investigating peace officer shall seek such a search warrant for blood, breath, or urine testing unless the testing has already been done by consent.

What will the prosecution have to prove to demonstrate compliance with all the relevant statutes and constitutional requirements? Will the judge suppress the evidence? Cf. Helton v. Commonwealth, 299 S.W.3d 555 (Ky. 2009).

Problem 4-5. Personal Inventories

Nancy Filkin was arrested and transported to the county jail by Deputy Richard McKinny.

Upon arrival at the county jail, McKinny took Filkin to the female booking area, removed her handcuffs, and remained present during the booking process. The standard operating procedure during the booking process at the county jail was to inventory personal items, to assure that the detainee carries no contraband objects into the jail, and to produce an accurate record so that the prisoner gets everything back when she is released. The search is also designed to protect the safety of the officers. The standard operating procedure for a purse is to remove all items to ensure that it contains no money or valuables.

A female corrections officer inventoried Filkin's closed purse under the watchful eye of McKinny. In the process, the officers discovered and opened a black film canister. The canister contained, among other things, a small self-seal bag holding .05 grams of methamphetamine.

Filkin has filed a motion to suppress the drugs found in the black film canister. How would you rule? Compare State v. Filkin, 494 N.W.2d 544 (Neb. 1993).

Problem 4-6. Body Cavity Search Away from the Jail

While lawfully present in an apartment, Detective Johns saw Eric More sitting on a couch with a crack pipe and small piece of white rocklike substance on a nearby table. Based upon his training and experience, the detective believed the substance was crack cocaine. The detective arrested More, handcuffed him, and conducted a "quick pat-down" search for weapons. He found no weapons. Detective Johns then took More into the bedroom and told him he would be strip-searched. More initially cooperated by taking off most of his clothes, but at some point he protested and scuffled with the detective. During the search, the detective saw a plastic bag protruding from More's rectum. He removed the bag and noticed that it contained several individually wrapped pieces of a white rock-like substance, which later tested positive for cocaine.

In his motion to suppress the drugs seized from his person, More claimed that the body cavity search was "illegal and effected in the absence of probable cause, in the absence of a warrant and in the absence of any exigency." If you are the trial judge hearing this motion, how would you rule? Compare People v. More, 764 N.E.2d 967 (N.Y. 2002).

B. "HOUSES" AND OTHER PLACES

We move now to searches of "houses" and other common searches in which the location of the search plays a major part in the legal analysis. Recall from Chapter 2 that the Fourth Amendment and most analogous state provisions protect a "reasonable expectation of privacy." Katz v. United States, 389 U.S. 347 (1967). In addition, a search occurs if a government agent performs a physical trespass on a person's property: a physical intrusion on a person's body, house, paper, or effect for the purpose of acquiring information is a search, even if the area is not protected by a reasonable expectation of privacy.

For a prosecutor attempting to justify the search of a location, the first step is to determine whether the searching officers obtained a search warrant based on probable cause. The prosecutor would next consider whether the officers obtained valid consent from someone with actual or apparent authority over the location. In the absence of a warrant and valid consent, the prosecutor will need to rely on other theories to explain the legality of the search. We consider in this section searches and seizures that take place in several important recurring locations: in or near homes, workplaces, and institutions such as schools and prisons.

1. The Outer Boundaries of Houses

Searches of homes have always presented some of the easiest cases for limiting the power of the government to search. Recall that the most infamous searches of the late eighteenth century—which most influenced the framers of the Fourth Amendment—were searches of homes. But it is not always so easy to tell where a home leaves off and where the rest of the world begins. The area immediately surrounding the home, known as the "curtilage," receives a similar level of protection to the home itself, and the Court in recent years has articulated more carefully the privacy interests protected within the curtilage. Areas beyond the curtilage, known as "open fields," traditionally received no Fourth Amendment protection at all because the Court believes nothing private happens there. The two cases reprinted in this section explore these two concepts.

■ CONSTITUTION OF MICHIGAN ART. I, §11

The person, houses, papers and possessions of every person shall be secure from unreasonable searches and seizures. No warrant to search any place or to seize any person or things shall issue without describing them, nor without probable cause, supported by oath or affirmation. The provisions of this section shall not be construed to bar from evidence in any criminal proceeding any narcotic drug, firearm, bomb, explosive or any other dangerous weapon, seized by a peace officer outside the curtilage of any dwelling house in this state.

■ STATE v. GREGORY FISHER
154 P.3d 455 (Kan. 2007)

Nuss, J.

Gregory C. Fisher was convicted of unlawful manufacture of methamphetamine, possession of ephedrine with the intent to manufacture methamphetamine, possession of anhydrous ammonia in an unapproved container for the production of methamphetamine, possession of methamphetamine, and possession of paraphernalia for use in the manufacture of methamphetamine. [The issue on appeal is as] follows: Did the district court err in failing to suppress evidence obtained pursuant to a search warrant partially based upon the contents of a trash bag seized from Fisher's property? . . .

FACTS

On August 20, 2001, Detective Shane Jager of the Pottawatomie County Sheriff's Department received information from fellow deputy Paul Hoyt concerning suspicious activity at 12420 Highway 63, Emmett, in Pottawatomie County. The property is bounded on the east by Highway 63 and by barbed wire fencing on the north, south, and west which separates the property from surrounding pasture. Photographs reveal . . . a large shed (barn) that is located 50 to 60 yards straight west of the house's western exterior near the barbed wire fence. A second, smaller shed sits equidistant between the house and the barn, but somewhat north, actually forming part of the north fence.

From Highway 63, a driveway runs from east to west on the south of the house, curving to the north and ending in a turn-around near the center of the area bounded by the three buildings. The only apparent walkway or sidewalk leads directly south from the house's front door to the driveway. According to photographs in the record, several large trees surround the house inside of the driveway.

According to Jager's suppression hearing testimony, Deputy Hoyt told him that a concerned citizen noticed a strong or peculiar odor emanating from trash being burned on the property and also observed numerous cars stopping there for short intervals of time. Hoyt further relayed to Jager that on August 28, 2001, he received information from another concerned citizen that a white female driving a van—that had been seen coming and going from the residence—drove to a shed located on the property, emptied boxes, placed more boxes in the van, and then left.

At approximately 1 A.M. on the day after Hoyt relayed the information about the delivery of boxes, Jager, Sergeant Chris Schmidt, and Deputy Shane Van Meter went to the area to determine if they could observe anything. While standing in a grass field to the west of the property, and approximately 30 yards west of the barn, Jager noticed a strong odor of ether. Based on his special training, coupled with the prior information of cars stopping at the residence, Jager suspected that methamphetamine was being manufactured and sold there.

Later that morning, Jager returned to the area twice more, once with the county attorney. From his parked position near Highway 63 about 50 yards south of Fisher's driveway, and once again off of Fisher's property, Detective Jager saw a burn barrel and a white translucent plastic trash bag near the barn. He then used binoculars to observe that the bag contained yellow containers. Based upon his training and experience, he associated the yellow bottles with the manufacture of methamphetamine, i.e., Heet bottles. Jager then walked to the field north of the property, where he again smelled ether. Jager testified that at that point he asked the county attorney how he felt about the trash bag. "He said . . . it was not on curtilage, that I could obtain the trash bag, and I advised him that I would like to try . . . to talk to the residents, see what we could obtain from them, and that's when I went to the door of the residence."

Jager testified that after this discussion with the county attorney he got back in his vehicle and

> I pulled my patrol vehicle in the driveway, went to the front door, knocked on the door several times. [After no answer,] I got back in my vehicle and there's a circle driveway that goes around the back side of the residence there, got in, drove by. When I was driving by the white trash bag I noticed Actifed blister packs, several Heet bottles, [and pseudoephedrine and] that's when I collected that white trash bag. . . .

Jager brought the bag to the sheriff's department for examination. In addition to the Heet bottles and 8 to 10 packs of ephedrine, the bag contained plastic gloves, coffee filters with a pinkish powder residue, and miscellaneous trash, including documents identifying Greg Fisher and Betty Harper. Based upon the tips and Jager's information observed and obtained at the scene, including the contents of the bag, he [obtained and executed a search warrant for the house, outbuildings, and vehicles. The search produced evidence of the manufacture of methamphetamine].

Fisher has consistently maintained that the State unlawfully seized the white trash bag from his property because it was within his curtilage. . . . Curtilage is the area surrounding the residence, to which historically the Fourth Amendment protection against unreasonable searches and seizures has been extended.

California v. Greenwood, 486 U.S. 35 (1988), is of guidance on the seizure issue. There, the Supreme Court addressed a situation where (1) the trash bag (2) was admittedly outside the curtilage; it determined seizure was proper. Despite the seizure of the bag from outside the curtilage, the Court nevertheless engaged in a reasonable expectation of privacy analysis. Since *Greenwood*, lower courts have struggled with exactly how the concept of curtilage fits into the analysis of trash seizures. In trash cases, this court has not only analyzed whether curtilage exists but also whether the owner has a reasonable expectation of privacy in the trash. . . . To analyze the parties' positions in the instant case, we will therefore examine both curtilage and reasonable expectation of privacy in trash.

CURTILAGE

[The] question of curtilage is a mixed question of fact and law. Accordingly, we review the district court's factual findings for substantial competent evidence and review de novo the district court's legal conclusion whether a particular seizure occurred within the curtilage.

Without elaboration, the district court in the instant case simply concluded that the trash bag was not within the cartilage. [United States v. Dunn, 480 U.S. 294 (1987) holds a central place in the curtilage analysis. The] extent of the curtilage is determined by factors that bear upon whether an individual reasonably may expect that the area in question should be treated as the home itself. [The] central component of this inquiry [is] whether the area harbors the "intimate activity associated with the sanctity of a man's home and the privacies of life." The *Dunn* Court held that curtilage questions should be resolved with particular reference to four factors:

> [1] The proximity of the area claimed to be curtilage to the home, [2] whether the area is included within an enclosure surrounding the home, [3] the nature of the uses to which the area is put, and [4] the steps taken by the resident to protect the area from observation by people passing by.

The *Dunn* Court was also quick to point out, however:

> We do not suggest that combining these factors produces a finely tuned formula that, when mechanically applied, yields a "correct" answer to all extent-of-curtilage questions. Rather, these factors are useful analytical tools only to the degree that, in any given case, they bear upon the centrally relevant consideration—whether the area in question is so intimately tied to the home itself that is should be placed under the home's "umbrella" of Fourth Amendment protection. . . .

The Fisher property is bounded on the east by the highway and on the west, north and south by a barbed wire fence. Outside the fence is farm ground in three directions. According to the photographs, inside the fence is short grass which appears to be mowed and maintained throughout. [Several] large trees surround the house inside of the driveway. Photographs show that vehicles are parked in the area formed by the three buildings. A garden apparently is between the barn and shed in the northwest corner of the property. A power pole with a readable electricity meter is near the curve (from west to north) in the driveway. A "Notice, No Trespassing" sign is on another pole near the entrance to the driveway from the highway. The bag was found between the house and the barn, i.e., within the area bounded by the three buildings.

We begin our determination by observing this is rural property, four miles from the nearest town. There are no other houses in the general vicinity of the house on the west side of the highway. On the east side of the highway, a neighbor's house sits approximately a quarter of a mile away. We next apply the *Dunn* factors.

(1) Proximity of the area claimed to be curtilage to the home: [There] is not any fixed distance at which curtilage ends. Here, although the barn is 50-60 yards west of the house's western edge, the exact distance of the trash bag from any feature is unknown, but it was found between the barn and house, albeit nearer the barn. Several courts have noted that in the context of a rural setting, the area extending to outbuildings may be in the curtilage.

(2) Whether the area is included within an enclosure surrounding the home: There is barbed wire fencing on three sides and highway on another. Moreover, the area within the barbed wire fence appears to be mowed and maintained.

(3) The nature of the uses to which the area is put: the bag was found between the barn and the driveway which splits the area between the house and the barn. Photographs show vehicles are parked on the driveway, between the driveway and the house, and between the driveway and the small shed. Additionally, the barbed wire fence-enclosed area also apparently includes a garden between the barn and shed.

(4) The steps taken by the resident to protect the area from observation by people passing by: The bag was found nearly 100 hundred yards from the highway, *i.e.*, behind the large two-story house whose eastern edge is 25 yards west of the highway and near the barn which, because of the size of the house, is more than 50-60 yards further west of the highway. According to the photographs, from the highway the house would have blocked a direct view of the bag, and the bag would have been observable only from obliques to the house, concomitantly from further distances. Outside of that distance, the house's placement, the remoteness of the house from other rural homes in the area, and a "No Trespassing" sign, however, there is nothing to suggest the residents took any particular precautions to prevent observation. [The] barbed wire fences do not prevent observation. Ether was smelled from outside the property. Yellow containers in the translucent bag were discovered through a detective's use of binoculars while parked near the highway and oblique to the house.

Based upon these facts, particularly this rural environment, we independently conclude the trash bag was found within the curtilage. We hold that in rural Kansas, Fisher's area harbors the "intimate activity associated with the sanctity of a person's home and the privacies of life."

REASONABLE EXPECTATION OF PRIVACY

Even though we have concluded that the trash bag was seized from within the curtilage, we still need to examine whether Fisher maintained a reasonable expectation of privacy in the bag. . . . An important inquiry in applying the *Greenwood* analysis to garbage within the curtilage is whether the garbage was so readily accessible to the public that its contents were exposed to the public for Fourth Amendment purposes. [In this case, the] trash bag was placed almost 100 yards from the public highway, blocked from the direct east view from the highway by the house, obscured from the direct north view by the small shed, and blocked from the direct west view by the barn; . . . the bag's yellow containers were visible only with use of binoculars. The bag was not exposed for the public to see; indeed, it was not left out for commercial trash collection. Rather, it was placed on the ground near a barrel for eventual disposition by Fisher. . . .

Under these circumstances, we conclude rural residents in Kansas would be quite surprised to learn that highway travelers, children, scavengers, snoops and other members of the public would be fully justified in pawing through the contents of a resident's trash bag placed approximately 100 yards from the highway and behind a rural home. In short, we conclude that Fisher maintained a reasonable expectation of privacy in his trash bag at its specific location—a subjective expectation that was objectively reasonable. Accordingly, the bag's warrantless seizure was per se unreasonable unless permissible under some recognized exception to the warrant requirement.

PLAIN VIEW

The State [argues that] even if the seizure occurred within the curtilage, as we have determined, that the plain view doctrine still justified the seizure. Under the facts of this case, we disagree for several reasons. . . .

It is first important to keep clear the distinctions between the different types of "plain view." As the Supreme Court has stated: "It is important to distinguish 'plain view' as used in Coolidge v. New Hampshire, 403 U.S. 443 (1971), to justify *seizure* of an object, from an officer's mere observation of an item left in plain view. Whereas the latter generally involves no Fourth Amendment search, . . . the former generally does implicate the Amendment's limitations upon seizures of personal property." Horton v. California, 496 U.S. 128, 133 n.5 (1990).

A number of courts have therefore used the term "open view doctrine" to refer to the rule that no Fourth Amendment search occurs where a law enforcement officer observes incriminating evidence or unlawful activity from a nonintrusive vantage point. Thus, the "open view" terminology distinguishes the analysis applicable to warrantless observations from the legally distinct "plain view" doctrine applicable to seizures. It is unclear, however, which of the doctrines the State applies to which events on the day of the seizure.

As for any State contention that the open view of the bag from the highway justified the seizure, we repeat that lawful observation does not equate to lawful seizure. [Absent] a justifiable intrusion onto Fisher's curtilage, the mere observation of the bag from the highway does not itself allow the bag's seizure.

As for any State contention that its justified intrusion was Jager's knock and talk and that the "plain view" of the bag obtained directly thereafter justified the seizure, we hold that the open observation of the bag from the highway—which led to the knock and talk—cannot also serve as a "plain view" of the bag from within the curtilage authorizing the seizure. . . . We specifically disapprove of any State attempt to "piggyback," i.e., to observe an object in open view from off the premises, to use knock and—in these cases, unsuccessful—talk for justified entry onto the premises, and then assert plain view while on the premises as a legal basis to seize the identical object that had been observed earlier. Such piggybacking under these facts would smear the careful distinctions drawn by the *Horton* Court between the right to merely observe an object (here, from off the premises) and the right to seize that object (on the premises). From a practical standpoint, this piggyback practice would grant law enforcement the right to seize virtually any object initially observed from a distance and subsequently located within plain view of a residential doorway by an officer purposely looking for that identical object.

An additional reason for us to reject the State's request to apply the plain view doctrine for justification of the seizure is that Jager's premises search and seizure of the bag exceeded the scope of his justified intrusion. . . . An officer is permitted the same license to intrude as a reasonably respectful citizen. However, a substantial and unreasonable departure from such an area, or a particularly intrusive method of viewing, will exceed the scope of the implied invitation and intrude upon a constitutionally protected expectation of privacy. [Once] Jager's knock and talk was complete, instead of driving away from the house to the highway, he simply drove deeper into the property on the driveway—according to the photographs, perhaps as much as 50 yards—directly to the previously observed bag. Once there, from his vehicle he noticed that it contained Actifed blister packs and, in confirmation of his earlier opinion, Heet bottles. He got out of the vehicle and seized the bag. . . .

Notes

1. *Open fields: majority position.* Under the federal constitution, there is no "search" when officers discover something in "open fields," land beyond the boundaries of a home and its curtilage. The decision in Oliver v. United States, 466 U.S. 170 (1984), affirming the traditional "open fields" doctrine, came as a surprise. After the Supreme Court declared in Katz v. United States, 389 U.S. 347 (1967), that the Fourth Amendment protected expectations of privacy rather than property interests, most lower courts assumed that the old per se rule allowing warrantless and suspicionless searches of open fields was no longer tenable. The *Oliver* decision, however, reaffirmed the traditional "open fields" doctrine (based on Hester v. United States, 265 U.S. 57 (1924)).

State courts considering the "open fields" question since 1984 are divided. A majority of state courts have followed the Supreme Court in *Oliver.* For items discovered on property outside the curtilage, no search takes place and no case-by-case consideration of "expectations of privacy" is necessary. See Commonwealth v. Russo, 934 A.2d 1199 (Pa. 2007) (seizure of bear stomach from ground 150 yards from cabin to obtain proof that hunting camp was baited). A handful of states, including New York, Oregon, Vermont, and Washington, have parted company with the federal rule. These courts have ruled that, under state statutes or constitutions, police must obtain a warrant to enter private property if the owner has taken enough measures to prevent entry onto the land by the public. The adequacy of the property owner's efforts to maintain privacy on the land might be measured case by case or with a relatively clear rule.

2. *Curtilage.* Many cases, both state and federal, have declared that the constitutional protection of privacy is at its highest in the home and the area immediately surrounding it, known as the "curtilage." Two U.S. Supreme Court cases reinforce the privacy protections afforded to the curtilage: in Florida v. Jardines, 569 U.S. 1 (2013), the Court held that officers cannot enter the curtilage to stand on the defendant's front porch for the purpose of conducting a dog sniff of the house. And in Collins v. Virginia, 138 S. Ct. 1663 (2018), the Court held that officers cannot walk up the driveway and examine a motorcycle hidden under a tarp in the carport to determine if it was stolen. In both instances, the Court held that the curtilage was protected by a shell of privacy that officers cannot invade—in order to acquire information about the home's residents —without a warrant, consent, or other warrant exception.

As the *Fisher* court indicated, United States v. Dunn, 480 U.S. 294 (1987), announced several factors that courts use widely to determine whether property falls inside the curtilage. In that case, federal agents suspected that the defendant was operating a drug laboratory in a barn on a ranch. The barn sat 60 yards from a house; a waist-high wooden fence with locked gates enclosed the front of the barn. A fence surrounded the perimeter of the property, and several barbed-wire fences crossed the interior of the property (including a fence surrounding the ranch house and running between the barn and the house). The agents crossed the perimeter fence, several of the barbed-wire fences, and the wooden fence in front of the barn. The court held that the barn was not within the curtilage of the ranch house. The web extension for this chapter, at *http://www.crimpro.com/extension/ch04*, offers diagrams of the properties in *Oliver, Fisher,* and *Dunn.*

The *Dunn* case and many others deal with searches of alleged "curtilage" areas in a rural or wooded setting. Are these definitions based on assumptions about land use and habits that do not apply in urban and suburban areas? For instance, would you conclude that a "search" of an item in the curtilage had occurred if police officers walked onto the front porch of a home, rang the doorbell, and then picked up a pair of boots, covered with plaster dust, sitting on a box on the porch (attempting to match the tread of the boots to white footprints found on the carpet at a burglary scene)? See State v. Portrey, 896 P.2d 7 (Or. Ct. App. 1995).

3. *Impermanent homes.* How long must a person occupy a temporary shelter before it can receive all the protections afforded to "houses" under the constitution? In Johnson v. United States, 333 U.S. 10 (1948), the Supreme Court held that a hotel room was a home for Fourth Amendment purposes, and thus officers needed a warrant before entering and searching it. See also State v. Pruss, 181 P.3d 1231 (Idaho 2008) (privacy expectation in "hooch," wooden frame enclosing a tent, on public land); State v. Mooney, 588 A.2d 145 (Conn. 1991) (privacy expectation in cardboard box hidden under bridge abutment containing effects of homeless man). Does it matter whether the occupant of the temporary shelter is otherwise homeless? For an argument that protections for traditional housing structures reach further than necessary to protect genuine privacy interests, see Stephanie Stern, The Inviolate Home: Housing Exceptionalism in the Fourth Amendment, 95 Cornell L. Rev. 905 (2010).

4. *Categories covered by constitutional texts.* The Fourth Amendment refers to "persons, houses, papers, and effects" that are protected from unreasonable searches and seizures. Some state constitutions follow this formulation, while others use different language. Does it matter what the constitutional framers considered to be the meaning of "effects" or "houses"? Where would a lawyer discover the framers' views on this question? Would it matter if the final category were called "possessions" instead of "effects"? See Falkner v. State, 98 So. 691 (Miss. 1924) (term "possessions" embraces "all of the property of the citizen"); State v. Pinder, 514 A.2d 1241 (N.H. 1986) (term "possessions" does not include real property beyond curtilage).

As we saw in Chapter 2, the Supreme Court has revived the trespass doctrine, which is a search theory grounded in the Fourth Amendment's text: government intrusions into constitutionally protected areas (persons, houses, papers, and effects) for the purpose of acquiring information are trespasses, which qualify as searches within the meaning of the Fourth Amendment. See United States v. Jones, 565 U.S. 400 (2012). Government agents thus need a warrant to perform them, regardless of whether these areas are protected by reasonable expectations of privacy. Open fields cannot be the subject of a trespass, however, because they are not included within "persons, houses, papers, and effects."

5. *Crime scene searches.* Police often search crime scenes. Do they need to obtain warrants at any point? Officers can secure a crime scene without a warrant. Officers can also conduct an initial search in response to emergency situations such as assisting a victim, searching for other victims, or searching for an offender. Police may also seize evidence in plain view during their emergency search and while securing the crime scene. However, in Mincey v. Arizona, 437 U.S. 385 (1978), the U.S. Supreme Court rejected a "crime scene exception" to the Fourth Amendment and said that police should have obtained a warrant before they conducted a detailed four-day search of an apartment following the murder of an undercover officer. In Flippo v. West Virginia, 528 U.S. 11 (1999), the U.S. Supreme Court reaffirmed *Mincey* and rejected the warrantless search of a briefcase found (closed) during a murder scene investigation of a vacation cabin in a state park. The briefcase belonged to the husband of the victim, who had called the police to investigate; it contained pictures that established his motive for the murder.

6. *Hot pursuit warrantless entry and search of homes.* Courts typically allow pre-arrest searches on the basis of "exigent circumstances," to find a suspect in a private location when police are otherwise lawfully within the premises. These searches often occur when officers are hot on the trail of a suspect believed to be dangerous and have probable cause to believe the suspect has entered a private home. The officer need not secure the consent of the homeowner to rush inside; hot pursuit justifies both the entry and the search for the felon. Warden v. Hayden, 387 U.S. 294 (1967) (officers a few minutes behind armed robbery suspect when he enters home; their entry is justified). Officers cannot rely on hot pursuit when they suspect the offender of only a minor crime. Welsh v. Wisconsin, 466 U.S. 740 (1984) (entry to pursue DUI suspect not justified, where DUI was an infraction in the state of Wisconsin at the time). State courts are split on hot pursuit authority where the suspected crime is a misdemeanor, with most states deciding such action is justified.

Courts may also allow pre-arrest searches of areas too small to conceal the offender but large enough to conceal weapons, when they are in hot pursuit of a defendant suspected to be dangerous and looking for his weapons. Warden v. Hayden, 387 U.S. 294 (1967) (during search for suspect, officer looks in toilet tank and washing machine and discovers evidence). Hot pursuit search authority for weapons ends as soon as the suspect is caught or it becomes clear the suspect is not in the home. The hot pursuit search warrant exception is distinct from SITA, as it always precedes the arrest of the suspect, but oftentimes a SITA search will justify officer behavior that occurs after the suspect has been apprehended.

Problem 4-7. No Hunting in Open Fields

Sheriff's deputies received an informant's tip that marijuana was growing on heavily forested land owned by the Rogge Lumber Company. The officers requested and received the company's permission to search the property for marijuana. They drove onto the property by way of a public road until they reached a dirt logging road the informant had described as leading to the marijuana. Unknown to the officers, this road extended onto property where Lorin and Theresa Dixson lived. The dirt road had fallen into disuse and no longer was passable by car. The trunk of a large tree lay across the road and, a little farther on, a wire cable with a "No Hunting" sign on it stretched across the road. The officers left their car and walked past the fallen tree and wire cable. Just past the cable was another dirt road running along a fence line. This road also had a wire cable and "No Hunting" sign stretched across it. The officers continued walking down this second road. At a bend in the road, they encountered another "No Hunting" sign. The area was rural and covered with thick brush. The officers were able to see marijuana plants only after pushing aside the brush. The plants, which were on the Dixsons' property, were not visible at ground level except from that property. The officers returned the next day and arrested the defendants near the plants. After charges were filed, the defendants filed a motion to suppress the evidence, based on both the state and federal constitutions.

The state of Oregon contends that the evidence should be admissible under the "open fields" doctrine as described in Oliver v. United States, 466 U.S. 170 (1984). The state argues that article I, section 9 of the Oregon Constitution, like the Fourth Amendment, expressly protects "persons, houses, papers, and effects." Therefore, the state says, the constitutional provision should be interpreted the same way that the United States Supreme Court has interpreted the Fourth Amendment. Prior Oregon cases establish that article I, section 9, does not protect property alone; in a broader sense, it also protects an individual's "privacy interest," which the court defines as an interest in freedom from certain forms of government scrutiny.

As a trial judge, how would you rule on the defendants' motion to suppress? Would it affect your analysis if the property owners had posted "No Trespassing" signs instead of "No Hunting" signs? Compare State v. Dixson, 766 P.2d 1015 (Or. 1988).

2. Workplaces

Although the Fourth Amendment and its state analogs extend to "homes," all courts have extended the protection against unreasonable searches and seizures to other locations. The nature of the place can profoundly influence the reasonableness of the search. Given the amount of time many people spend in the workplace, it should come as no surprise that police searches of the workplace generate plenty of disputes. In addition to the location of the search, these cases also sometimes raise questions about the relationship between the government and a private employer who participates to some degree in a search.

■ PEOPLE v. CARLOS CHRISTOPHER GALVADON
103 P.3d 923 (Colo. 2005)

MARTINEZ, J.

. . . Galvadon worked as the night manager of a liquor store owned by his mother-in-law. Galvadon and his mother-in-law were the only employees of the store.

As night manager, Galvadon was often left by himself to take care of the store. His responsibilities included ordering liquor, making bank deposits, writing checks for the store, and restocking shelves. Galvadon used the back room of the store to conduct all of these activities. [The back of the store is separated from the front of the store by a large refrigerator; the back room is . . . used for inventory storage, an office, and a bathroom. The only access to the back room from the front of the store is through a narrow corridor between the wall of the store and the refrigerator.] According to Galvadon, the only people who had unrestricted access to the back room were himself and the owner. Delivery persons were regularly permitted in the back room, but only if supervised or otherwise granted access. [The store had four video surveillance cameras, including one in the back room.]

On November 20, 2003, Galvadon was [on duty] as night manager. Two other people, Jeffery Hogan and David Flores, were at the store with him for about an hour. Shortly before midnight, Flores and Hogan were outside of the store standing in the parking lot [when] Flores was sprayed in the face with pepper spray by a stranger. [At about this time,] Sergeant Juhl of the Colorado Springs Police Department [happened to be driving] by the store. Hogan explained that he and Flores had been "assaulted" by someone around the corner and that Flores was sprayed with pepper spray. Hogan explained that he wanted to take Flores to get his face washed off and then began to escort Flores into the store. Sergeant Juhl followed them.

Once in the store, Hogan asked if he and Flores could use the bathroom. Galvadon stated that no one was allowed in the back. Hogan urged Galvadon that Flores was in pain and needed to use the bathroom to wash off his face. Galvadon again insisted, several times, that no one was allowed in the back room. Hogan, however, ignored Galvadon and escorted Flores to the back room. Sergeant Juhl followed them. . . .

While Flores was washing his face, backup officers arrived and went to the back room. While in the back room, one of the officers discovered a "brick" of marihuana sitting in the bottom of an open cardboard box. Shortly thereafter, another brick was discovered sitting in a bag on the floor of the bathroom. Later, the owner of the store arrived and consented to a search of the store. During the search a third brick of marihuana was discovered in the back room. . . .

Galvadon was subsequently charged with possession of marihuana and possession with intent to distribute marihuana. Prior to trial, Galvadon sought to suppress the evidence seized from the liquor store as the fruit of an illegal search. In response, the prosecution . . . claimed that because Galvadon was only an employee he could have no reasonable expectation of privacy. In addition, the prosecution asserted that because others had access to the back room and Galvadon was aware he was being videotaped by the in-store surveillance system while in the back room, . . . Galvadon could not have a reasonable expectation of privacy. The trial court disagreed and found that Galvadon had [a] reasonable expectation of privacy in the back room [and that] the warrantless intrusion into the back room could not be justified by any of the exceptions at law argued by the prosecution.

[In Katz v. United States, 389 U.S. 347 (1967), the U.S. Supreme Court] held that the Fourth Amendment protects people and their privacy from government intrusion, not simply places based upon a person's property interests or their right to be in that place. . . . Based upon privacy expectations set forth in *Katz*, the U.S. Supreme Court found that protection afforded by the Fourth Amendment is not limited to a literal reading of "houses," but instead extends beyond the home and may be asserted in the workplace. . . . In Mancusi v. DeForte, 392 U.S. 364 (1968), the defendant was a union official charged with misusing his office for coercion, extortion and conspiracy. The defendant shared an office with several other union officials. When the defendant refused to comply with a subpoena to produce union records, the state officials that served the subpoena searched the office and seized various records without a warrant. The defendant was present for the search and objected to it. The papers seized did not belong to the defendant. The Court applied the expectation of privacy analysis established in *Katz* to hold in *Mancusi* that the defendant could object to the search on Fourth Amendment grounds. . . . The Court found that despite sharing the office with several others, the defendant maintained a reasonable expectation of privacy from government intrusion in the office. . . .

Where the government search at issue takes place in a highly regulated industry such as the liquor business, under certain circumstances proprietors of such businesses might have a diminished expectation of privacy because of long-standing government oversight and consequently have less Fourth Amendment protection. The expectation of privacy in the liquor industry, however, is only diminished to the extent that searches are specifically authorized pursuant to constitutional administrative inspection regulations and conducted pursuant to the purpose of the regulatory scheme. Where, as here, the search of the liquor store was investigatory in nature and not an administrative search conducted pursuant to any regulation or statute, the defendant maintains his otherwise reasonable expectation of privacy. . . .

In examining the circumstances of a particular case [to determine if the defendant maintained a reasonable expectation of privacy in the place searched], courts have chosen to focus on different factors. Some courts look to the "nexus" between the area searched and the work space of the defendant. Other courts have looked to a defendant's right to exclude others from accessing the area for which the defendant asserts privacy. Regardless of the factors considered, an employee's expectation of privacy must be assessed in the context of the employment relation. O'Connor v. Ortega, 480 U.S. 709 (1987).

We look to several factors to determine whether Galvadon's expectation of privacy against government intrusion would exist absent the in-store surveillance system. . . . First, the back room of the liquor store is an exclusive area reserved for use by the owner and Galvadon. Its physical separation from the rest of the store indicates that public access is restricted in this area. The testimony of Sergeant Juhl indicates that even he assumed upon his first entry to the store that the public was not allowed in the back room. The room was specifically set apart as a private place for the owner and Galvadon to conduct the business affairs for the store shielded from the view and access of the public.

Second, Galvadon had the power to exclude access to the back room. As the night manager, and at the time of the police intrusion in this case, Galvadon was in charge and the only person in the store that controlled access to the back room. Because this incident occurred near midnight and Galvadon was left alone by the owner to manage the store, Galvadon could reasonably expect that only persons to whom he granted permission would be given access to the back room. Furthermore, Galvadon attempted several times to keep out Sergeant Juhl, Flores and Hogan, as well as the emergency medical technicians and other officers that arrived at the liquor store. This is a clear manifestation of Galvadon's belief that he could control access to the back room and maintain an expectation of privacy from intrusion of others into that area. . . .

Having found that Galvadon could maintain an expectation of privacy in absence of the in-store surveillance system, we now turn to the question of whether his expectation of privacy from government intrusion was diminished by the presence of the surveillance system. The surveillance system consists of four video cameras; one was located in the back room. The video monitor and tape machine were also located in the back room. The prosecution generally asserts that because Galvadon was aware that the back room was under in-store surveillance, any activities that occurred in the back room were "knowingly exposed" to the store owner and the public. . . . This general assertion, however, ignores the fundamental inquiry supporting Fourth Amendment standing—whether the defendant has a reasonable expectation of privacy from government intrusion. . . .

Galvadon's activities were not exposed to the public through the surveillance system. [There] is no indication that any monitors were viewable from the publicly accessible portions of the store or that the public had access to the video recordings under the normal operation of the store. The owner and Galvadon were the only store employees, the only persons with access to the back room, and thus the only persons with access to the video recording and video monitor located there. . . .

The parties do not dispute that the surveillance system exposed Galvadon's activities in the back room to the owner of the store. As such, we proceed with the analysis to determine if such exposure to the store owner eliminated Galvadon's reasonable expectation of privacy from government intrusion. The U.S. Supreme Court has found that defendant-employees may have little or no expectation of privacy from their employer, but may still maintain a reasonable expectation of privacy from government intrusion. In *Mancusi*, the defendant shared his office with several others. The Court found that this factor alone was insufficient to extinguish the defendant's expectation of privacy from government intrusion. . . . Similarly, we can assume here that because of the surveillance system, Galvadon had a diminished expectation of privacy from the owner of the store. . . . This, however, does not indicate that he had no reasonable expectation of privacy from government intrusion. . . .

We conclude under the totality of circumstances that the sole person in control of the store, the night manager, maintained a reasonable expectation of privacy from government intrusion in the back room of the store, an area without public access, such that he may assert protection of the Fourth Amendment. The use of a surveillance system reviewable only by the night manager and the owner of the store did not diminish his reasonable expectation of privacy from government intrusion. . . .

MULLARKEY, C.J., dissenting.

. . . I would find that Galvadon, as an employee of a retail liquor store, had no reasonable expectation in the store's back room because it was a liquor storage place subject to inspection at any time when the liquor store did business. . . . Determination of this question requires examining the law regulating searches of business premises in highly regulated industries and the law defining an employee's reasonable expectation of privacy in his workplace. With respect to highly regulated industries, the Supreme Court has recognized that searches may be conducted without warrants. The liquor business is perhaps the prime example of a highly regulated industry. In Colorado, a retail liquor store may operate only if it complies with the Liquor Code and its implementing regulations. The relevant regulations require a licensed retail liquor store to be open to warrantless inspection by administrative authorities and by peace officers during normal business hours and at all times when activity is occurring on the premises. 1 C.C.R. 203-2, §47-700 (2001). . . .

The Supreme Court has recognized that not all workplaces have identical levels of Fourth Amendment protection. Indeed, the Colorado regulation is consistent with Supreme Court case law that recognizes an explicit exception to the warrant requirement for inspections of business premises within highly regulated industries in Colonnade Catering Corp. v. United States, 397 U.S. 72 (1970) (warrant exception for inspections of the liquor industry); United States v. Biswell, 406 U.S. 311 (1972) (warrant exception applies to firearms industry); and Donovan v. Dewey, 452 U.S. 594 (1981) (extending exception to inspections conducted pursuant to the Federal Mine Safety and Health Act of 1977). . . .

In general, an employee's expectation of privacy in the workplace is subordinate to the employer's interests. See O'Connor v. Ortega, 480 U.S. 709, 717 (1987) ("The operational realities of the workplace, however, may make some employees' expectations of privacy unreasonable when an intrusion is by a supervisor rather than a law enforcement official."). Furthermore, when an employee knows, as Galvadon did, that he or she is being watched by an employer, the affected workers are on clear notice from the outset that any movements they might make and any objects they might display within the work area would be exposed to the employer's sight. . . .

Notes

1. *Privacy interests in the workplace: majority position.* American courts have overwhelmingly decided that workers can hold some reasonable expectation of privacy in items kept at their workplace and in their activities at the workplace. The crucial question, as identified in the *Galvadon* opinion from Colorado, is whether the workers have some control over access to the area. Yet the Fourth Amendment and its state analogs speak only about government searches of "persons, houses, papers, and effects." Is a workplace a "house"? What would a society be like that did not limit searches in workplaces? How does the growth of telecommuting affect the constitutional analysis of "houses" and "workplaces"?

The government has plenty of reasons to collect information in the workplace. What begins as routine regulatory enforcement might end in a criminal prosecution. For instance, immigration agents may question employees in their workplace about their immigration status. Because of the limited intrusion involved, the questioning does not amount to a "seizure," even if workplace rules require the employees to remain on the site when the government agents arrive. INS v. Delgado, 466 U.S. 210 (1984). Does the access of regulators to the workplace strengthen or weaken the privacy interest of workers in their place of employment?

2. *Workplace privacy in highly regulated industries.* As the dissenting opinion in *Galvadon* notes, specialized limits on searches apply to places of business in highly regulated industries such as mining, firearms sales, and liquor sales. Recall that Chapter 3 discusses the "administrative warrants" that apply to regulatory safety inspections in those settings.

3. *Government as employer.* If a government agent wishes to search a workplace in the private sector, she usually needs probable cause and a warrant, or consent. But if the government agent conducts a search of a *government* workplace, different constitutional rules apply. Neither a warrant nor probable cause is necessary when the government employer is conducting (1) a noninvestigatory work-related search (such as retrieving a file) or (2) an investigation of work-related misconduct. The Supreme Court in O'Connor v. Ortega, 480 U.S. 709 (1987), concluded that the reasonable suspicion standard was the best method of accommodating the employee's privacy interests with the public employer's interests apart from law enforcement. See also City of Ontario, Cal. v. Quon, 560 U.S. 746 (2010) (police chief ordered review of text messages sent by officers on alphanumeric pagers the department recently purchased to determine source of billing overruns, which revealed that officer used pager during work hours for personal messages; review was reasonable because it was motivated by legitimate work-related purpose, and not excessive in scope).

3. Schools and Prisons

When searches take place in institutions such as schools and prisons, courts tend to evaluate them much more generously than searches of homes or workplaces. These searches fall into a category sometimes known as "administrative" searches, where the government has purposes for its search other than enforcement of the criminal law. In such settings, warrants are often unnecessary, and the level of justification required does not rise to the level of probable cause. As you read the following materials, try to identify the elements of these searches that lead courts to place fewer controls on them than they do for searches in other settings. Could the arguments used to explain the looser supervision of searches in these contexts apply more broadly to others?

■ OKLAHOMA STATUTES TIT. 70, §24-102

The superintendent, principal, teacher, or security personnel of any public school in the State of Oklahoma, upon reasonable suspicion, shall have the authority to detain and search or authorize the search, of any pupil or property in the possession of the pupil when said pupil is on any school premises, or while in transit under the authority of the school, or while attending any function sponsored or authorized by the school, for dangerous weapons, controlled dangerous substances,

. . . intoxicating beverages, . . . or for missing or stolen property if said property be reasonably suspected to have been taken from a pupil, a school employee or the school during school activities. The search shall be conducted by a person of the same sex as the person being searched and shall be witnessed by at least one other authorized person, said person to be of the same sex if practicable.

The extent of any search conducted pursuant to this section shall be reasonably related to the objective of the search and not excessively intrusive in light of the age and sex of the student and the nature of the infraction. In no event shall a strip search of a student be allowed. No student's clothing, except cold weather outerwear, shall be removed prior to or during the conduct of any warrantless search. . . .

Pupils shall not have any reasonable expectation of privacy towards school administrators or teachers in the contents of a school locker, desk, or other school property. School personnel shall have access to school lockers, desks, and other school property in order to properly supervise the welfare of pupils. School lockers, desks, and other areas of school facilities may be opened and examined by school officials at any time and no reason shall be necessary for such search. Schools shall inform pupils in the student discipline code that they have no reasonable expectation of privacy rights towards school officials in school lockers, desks, or other school property.

■ STATE v. MARZEL JONES
666 N.W.2d 142 (Iowa 2003)

CADY, J.

. . . On December 20, 2001, teachers and administrators at Muscatine High School attempted to complete an annual pre-winter break cleanout of the lockers assigned to each student at the school. The students were asked three to four days before the cleanout to report to their locker at an assigned time to open it so a faculty member could observe its contents. The general purpose of the cleanout was to ensure the health and safety of the students and staff and to help maintain the school's supplies. Accordingly, faculty assigned to examine the lockers kept an eye out for overdue library books, excessive trash, and misplaced food items. They also watched for items of a more nefarious nature, including weapons and controlled substances. The cleanout functioned as expected for approximately 1400 of the 1700 students at the school. However, a sizeable minority—including the appellee, Marzel Jones—did not report for the cleanout at their designated time.

The next day, two building aides went around to the lockers that had not been checked the day before. Acting pursuant to rules and regulations adopted by the school board, the aides opened each locker to inspect its contents. The aides did not know the names of the students assigned to the lockers they were inspecting. One of the lockers they opened contained only one item: a blue, nylon coat, which hung from one of the two hooks in the locker. Apparently curious about its ownership and concerned that it might hold trash, supplies, or contraband, one of the aides manipulated the coat and discovered a small bag of what appeared to be marijuana in an outside pocket. The aides then returned the coat to the locker and contacted the school's principal.

After crosschecking the locker number with records kept by the administration, the principal determined the locker in which the suspected marijuana was found belonged to Jones. The principal and aides then went to Jones' classroom and escorted him to his locker. Jones was asked to open the locker and, after doing so, was further asked if anything in the locker "would cause any educational or legal difficulties for him." Jones replied in the negative. The principal then removed the coat from the locker. Jones grabbed the coat, struck the principal across the arms, broke free from him, and ran away. The principal gave chase and, after three attempts, captured and held Jones until the police arrived. The police retrieved the bag and determined that it held marijuana.

Jones was later charged with possession of a controlled substance in violation of Iowa Code section 124.401(5). He subsequently filed a motion to suppress the evidence—the marijuana—obtained during the search of his locker. He claimed that the search violated his right to be free from unreasonable search and seizure pursuant to the Fourth Amendment of the United States Constitution and article I, section 8 of the Iowa Constitution. . . . The district court granted the motion to suppress. It found that the school officials did not have reasonable grounds for searching Jones' coat pocket. . . .

FOUNDATIONAL PRINCIPLES OF SEARCH AND SEIZURE ANALYSIS

[We] have delineated a two-part test that applies in most cases requiring the determination of whether particular governmental action violates the constitutional search and seizure provisions. See State v. Naujoks, 637 N.W.2d 101, 106 (Iowa 2001) (describing our usual search and seizure analysis focused on the expectation of privacy and the reasonableness of an invasion of that privacy). However, we believe the specific facts of this case warrant an analysis that is more focused than our general approach.

[The] location of property seized by authorities may be of critical importance in determining whether the search and seizure were lawful. With this in mind, it is significant in this case that the search of Jones' locker occurred on school grounds. Although students maintain their constitutional rights within the school setting, the United States Supreme Court has acknowledged this setting "requires some easing of the restrictions to which searches by public authorities are ordinarily subject." New Jersey v. T.L.O., 469 U.S. 325, 340 (1985). The Court has provided specific commentary on this "easing of the restrictions" in three cases.

In the first case, New Jersey v. T.L.O. (1985), the Court articulated several baseline principles related to the search of a student in the school setting. However, *T.L.O.* focused on the search of a specific student whose property was searched based on some measure of individualized suspicion of her conduct [not amounting to probable cause]. In two subsequent cases, the Court considered the propriety of searches conducted in the absence of individualized suspicion of a particular student. See Bd. of Ed. of Indep. Sch. Dist. No. 92 v. Earls, 536 U.S. 822 (2002); Vernonia Sch. Dist. 47J v. Acton, 515 U.S. 646 (1995). In these cases, the search of the students was premised on generalized concerns about drug use prevention in light of the effect of the presence of drugs on the educational environment as a whole.

We believe the locker search conducted by the school officials in this case is most closely analogized to the broad searches conducted in *Acton* and *Earls.* Although this search eventually focused on Jones' locker, the process leading to that point was random and carried out with the purpose of protecting the health and safety of the whole student body to preserve a proper educational environment. Although *T.L.O., Acton,* and *Earls* each provide helpful insight on search and seizure in schools, it is the sum of their holdings, crystallized in the Court's opinion in *Earls,* from which our analysis must launch. Under the *Earls* analysis, we must consider three factors: (1) "the nature of the privacy interest allegedly compromised" by the search, (2) "the character of the intrusion imposed" by the search policy, and (3) "the nature and immediacy of the [school's] concerns and the efficacy of the [search policy] in meeting them." *Earls,* 536 U.S. at 830. . . . We turn now to our analysis of this appeal under the *Earls* factors. . . .

NATURE OF THE PRIVACY INTEREST

In assessing the nature of the privacy interest in this case, it is imperative to remember this controversy arose within the school context where the State is responsible for maintaining discipline, health, and safety. This reality has led the Court to acknowledge that "[securing] order in the school environment sometimes requires that students be subjected to greater controls than those appropriate for adults." Id. at 831. Although this may be the case, we do not believe it can be said that students have no expectation of privacy in a school setting, particularly in a location such as a locker.

The determination of the existence of a legitimate expectation of privacy is based on the unique facts of each case, focusing on whether the government's intrusion infringes upon the personal and societal values protected by the Fourth Amendment. In *T.L.O.,* the Court observed:

> Students at a minimum must bring to school not only the supplies needed for their studies, but also keys, money, and the necessaries of personal hygiene and grooming. In addition, students may carry on their persons or in purses or wallets such nondisruptive yet highly personal items as photographs, letters, and diaries. Finally, students may have perfectly legitimate reasons to carry with them articles of property needed in connection with extracurricular or recreational activities. In short, schoolchildren may find it necessary to carry with them a variety of legitimate, noncontraband items, and there is no reason to conclude that they have necessarily waived all rights to privacy in such items merely by bringing them onto school grounds.

469 U.S. at 339. However, the Court specifically avoided answering the question of whether a student "has a legitimate expectation of privacy in lockers, desks, or other school property provided for the storage of school supplies." Id. at 337 n. 5. Likely due in part to the absence of an authoritative statement on this issue, various courts considering it have produced a divergence of opinion. Some courts have concluded that there is no expectation of privacy in a student locker, particularly in situations in which there exists a school or state regulation specifically disclaiming any privacy right. See In re Patrick Y., 746 A.2d 405, 414 (Md. 2000). Other courts have concluded that a student does have a legitimate expectation of privacy in the contents of a school locker, even if a school or state regulation exists. See In re

Interest of S.C., 583 So. 2d 188, 191-192 (Miss. 1991). In this case, both Muscatine school district policy[4] and state law[5] clearly contemplate and regulate searches of school lockers. Nevertheless, we believe Jones maintained a legitimate expectation of privacy in the contents of his locker.

T.L.O. involved the search of a student's purse, but a student's locker presents a similar island of privacy in an otherwise public school. Numerous permissible items of a private nature are secreted away within a locker on a daily basis with the expectation that those items will remain private. In fact, Muscatine's school policy effectively presumes this to be the case and protects this interest: in those situations in which the school seeks to search a locker, the school's rules contemplate the presence of the student or at least a "waiver" of the student's opportunity to be present and supervising the search. Moreover, the school rules and state law related to search and seizure in schools are premised on a presumption of privacy; such legislation would likely be unnecessary if no expectation of privacy existed in the first place. Each of these factors indicates a broad societal recognition of a legitimate expectation of privacy in a school locker. Accordingly, we conclude that a student such as Jones has a measure of privacy in the contents of his locker. . . .

CHARACTER OF THE INTRUSION

We must next "consider the character of the intrusion imposed by the [search policy]." *Earls*, 536 U.S. at 832. The district court concluded the actions of the school officials were overly intrusive in light of what the court perceived to be unreasonable grounds to search Jones' particular locker. However, we believe the locker search was not overly intrusive, especially in light of the underlying governmental interest and broader purpose of the search.

The locker cleanout was premised on the need to maintain a proper educational environment, which school officials had determined was undermined by violations of school rules and potential violations of the law. Most students cooperated in the school's efforts to check the lockers for such violations. Although there was no indication that students on the day of the original cleanout had the contents of their lockers searched, the students were also present and supervised by a teacher who was responsible for observing the contents of the locker and ensuring the cleanout functioned as planned. Moreover, the teacher supervisors surely could have communicated with a student present at the locker about its contents and taken further steps if the situation warranted.

---

4. Muscatine Community School District policy 502.7 provides, in part: "All school property is held in public trust by the Board of Directors. School authorities may, without a search warrant, search students, student lockers, personal effects, desks, work areas or student vehicles. The search shall be in a manner reasonable in scope to maintain order and discipline in the schools, promote the educational environment, and protect the safety and welfare of students, employees and visitors to the school district facilities. . . . The school district has a reasonable and valid interest in insuring that the lockers are properly maintained. For this reason periodic inspections of lockers is permissible to check for cleanliness and vandalism. . . . The student's locker and its contents may be searched when a school official has reasonable and articulable suspicion that the locker contains illegal, or contraband items. Such searches should be conducted in the presence of another adult witness, when feasible." . . .

5. Iowa Code section 808A.2(2) provides, in part: "School officials may conduct periodic inspections of all, or a randomly selected number of, school lockers, desks, and other facilities or spaces owned by the school and provided as a courtesy to a student." . . .

The search on the second day came under different circumstances. The advantage of carrying out the cooperative cleanout and inspection of the previous day had passed. Students who had been advised that they were to report to their lockers for a cleanout had failed to do so, and caused the school to switch to an alternative method to ensure the cleanout was achieved. On entering Jones' locker, the only item in sight was the blue coat. The school officials believed that trash, supplies, or other items could be in the coat pockets, and did not have the advantage of turning to Jones to ask him about its contents, as they likely could have done the day before. For this reason, they decided to make a cursory check of the coat for such items. Although they found the bag of marijuana, they just as well could have found a banana peel. The scope of the search was supported by the underlying purpose of the search.

While it is possible that there would have been alternative ways to check the coat's contents, constitutional search and seizure provisions do not require the least intrusive action possible. Instead, they require a measure of "reasonableness, under all the circumstances." *T.L.O.*, 469 U.S. at 341. Under this standard, we conclude the search of the contents of Jones' locker was not overly intrusive. . . .

NATURE AND IMMEDIACY OF SCHOOL'S CONCERNS AND EFFICACY OF SEARCH POLICY IN MEETING THEM

The education of the students of the State of Iowa is a profound responsibility vested, ultimately, in the capable hands of local teachers, administrators, and school boards. What may be a daunting task to begin with is only made more difficult by the presence of various distractions ranging from excessive trash and missing supplies to—potentially—more troublesome items, such as controlled substances or weapons. What was observed by the Court in *T.L.O.* nearly twenty years ago remains true—if not truer—today: "Maintaining order in the classroom has never been easy, but in recent years, school disorder has often taken particularly ugly forms: drug use and violent crime in the schools have become major social problems." See id. at 339. These developments serve as the backdrop against which the conduct of school officials must be considered, especially as it relates to their duty to educate students while also protecting them from numerous threats to that mission.

The principal of the school testified that the annual winter break locker cleanout was conducted by the school to prevent violations of both school rules related to the accumulation of trash and school supplies and the sharing of lockers and the law related to possession of controlled substances and weapons. . . . To counteract the problems caused by these items, the school presented reasonable notice to the student body and attempted to check the lockers with student assistance. . . . Although the school did not have individualized suspicion of rule or law violations before the locker cleanout operation, constitutional search and seizure provisions include no irreducible requirement that such suspicion exist. Moreover, it would be contrary to the mission of our educational system to force schools to wait for problems to grow worse before allowing steps to be taken to prevent those problems. Given the public school context in which this controversy arose and the present realities of public education, we conclude that the search conducted by school officials was proper. . . .

■ HUGH AND LEE HAGEMAN v. GOSHEN COUNTY SCHOOL DISTRICT NO. 1

256 P.3d 487 (Wyo. 2011)

BURKE, J.

[¶1] In an effort to address a perceived drug and alcohol problem among its students, Goshen County School District No. 1 adopted a policy requiring all students who participate in extracurricular activities to consent to random testing for alcohol and drugs. Appellants initiated litigation, claiming that the Policy is unconstitutional. The district court granted summary judgment in favor of the School District. Appellants challenge that decision in this appeal. We affirm. . . .

[¶3] For the past several years, Goshen County School District No. 1 has participated in surveys of its students, known as the "Wyoming Youth Risk Surveys." According to the affidavit of the School District's Superintendent, the surveys revealed "a serious prevalence of alcohol and drug use among Goshen County School District No. 1 students. Goshen County has ranged at or near the top for alcohol and drug use for several of those surveys." . . .

Concern over the pervasiveness of drug and alcohol use among its students prompted the School District to hold a public forum on February 2, 2009, to discuss the possibility of requiring students to take random drug and alcohol tests. Following that forum, on April 14, 2009, the School District's Board of Trustees adopted a new policy requiring all students in grades 7 through 12 who participate in extracurricular activities to consent to random testing for drugs and alcohol. According to the School District's Superintendent, "the policy recognizes that many of the students participating in extracurricular activities are viewed as role models to other students."

[¶4] Appellants, referred to collectively as the Coalition, are a group of students and their parents or guardians who filed a declaratory judgment action in district court seeking to have the School District's Policy declared unconstitutional. After briefing and argument, the district court concluded that the drug testing program did not violate either the Wyoming Constitution or the United States Constitution. It granted summary judgment in favor of the School District, and the Coalition appealed. . . .

[¶7] The Coalition concedes that the Policy does not violate the Fourth Amendment to the United States Constitution. It contends, however, that Article 1, §4 of the Wyoming Constitution provides greater protections, under the facts of this case, than those afforded by the Fourth Amendment. . . .

[¶10] In Vernonia School Dist. 47J v. Acton, 515 U.S. 646 (1995), the United States Supreme Court rejected a Fourth Amendment challenge to a school district policy requiring drug testing for high school athletes. . . . To determine the reasonableness of these random, suspicionless searches, the Court applied a balancing test, weighing three factors: the nature of the privacy interest at issue, the character of the intrusion, and the nature of the governmental concern and the efficacy of the policy in addressing that concern. The Court concluded that public school students have a lower expectation of privacy than citizens in general, and that the expectation of privacy is even lower for student athletes. It found the search relatively unobtrusive. It determined that the school had a legitimate interest in deterring drug use, and noted that the school had presented evidence of a serious drug problem in the school, particularly among the student athletes. The drug testing program was considered an efficacious way to address the problem because it was aimed directly at the student athletes who were a major part of the problem.

[¶11] Seven years later, the Court decided Board of Education of Independent School Dist. No. 92 of Pottawatomie County v. Earls, 536 U.S. 822 (2002), again applying the basic standard of "reasonableness." This drug testing policy was not targeted at a specific group of problematical students with documented drug problems. Rather, like the Policy before us now, it subjected all students involved in extracurricular activities to random, suspicionless testing for drugs. The Court stated that all participants in extracurricular activities had a diminished expectation of privacy, and that the intrusion on that privacy was not significant. The Court concluded that the school's interest in deterring drug use prevailed over the insignificant intrusion on privacy, and thus rejected the constitutional challenge to the drug testing policy.

[¶12] In addition to *Vernonia* and *Earls*, we have reviewed decisions from several state courts. The majority of such cases have applied some version of the reasonableness test, and concluded that random, suspicionless drug testing of students involved in extracurricular activities did not violate the provisions of their respective state constitutions. . . .

[¶23] . . . In order to maintain safety and welfare, schools are afforded the flexibility to impose rules on students that might be inappropriate for adults. [The] school's role is custodial and tutelary, permitting a degree of supervision and control that could not be exercised over free adults. [Students] generally have diminished privacy expectations born of the government's duty to maintain safety, order, and discipline in the schools.

[¶24] The School District further points out that students participating in extracurricular activities are subject to rules and requirements not applicable to students in general. As set forth in the School District's Student Activity Code of Conduct: "Students who volunteer to participate in the Goshen County School District No. 1 extracurricular activities programs do so with the understanding that they must observe some regulations that are more restrictive than those relating to the general student community." These regulations vary according to the particular activity, but include requirements for medical releases and physical exams, academic standards, attendance rules, and compliance with specific rules pertaining to tobacco, alcohol, controlled substances, and offensive conduct. Because students who participate in extracurricular activities are already regulated more strictly, their reasonable expectations of privacy are even more limited than those of the general student population. . . .

[¶25] . . . The Coalition correctly contends that urination is a bodily function traditionally shielded by privacy. However, the degree to which the School District's Policy intrudes on the students' privacy depends largely upon the details of how the urine samples are collected.

[¶26] Under the School District's Policy, students to be tested are randomly selected by an independent testing company. Selected students are sent individually into a restroom to produce a sample. Each student enters the restroom alone, and remains unobserved while producing a sample. Direct observation of the students is not necessary, as tampering with the samples is prevented by measures such as rendering water faucets inoperable and placing dye in the water in the toilets. When a student exits the restroom, the sample is handed to a testing company employee, who splits the sample in two and marks them while the student observes. The student then returns to class.

[¶27] The School District's Policy is less intrusive than the one upheld by the United States Supreme Court in *Vernonia*, where male students were required to "produce samples at a urinal along a wall." [Female students produced] "samples in an enclosed stall, with a female monitor standing outside listening only for sounds of tampering." . . .

[¶31] There are additional measures taken under the School District's Policy to help preserve privacy. Testing is done for only a specified list of substances: alcohol, marijuana, cocaine, amphetamines, barbiturates, methadone, opiates, benzodiazepines (metabolites of Valium), and propoxyphene (metabolites of Darvon). Other information about, for example, any prescription medications a student might be taking, or other information about a student's health, is beyond the scope of testing under the School District's Policy. The results of testing under the School District's Policy serve only limited purposes. A student who tests positive may be suspended from extracurricular activities and required to participate in counseling and treatment programs. However, positive test results have no academic consequences, and do not lead to school discipline. Records of the testing are kept separately from the students' academic records, are held in confidence, and are destroyed when the student graduates. Records of the testing are turned over to law enforcement officials only by court order. . . .

[¶33] . . . As we turn to examine the efficacy of the means chosen by the School District to address that concern, it is important to note what it is that the School District must show. The Coalition appears to contend that the School District must prove that its Policy will achieve a specific level of success. We do not agree. Under such a stringent test, the School District would be limited to implementing only programs that have already been tried and proven. We do not think the Wyoming Constitution should preclude the School District from trying more innovative methods of deterring drug use. [It] is sufficient if the School District establishes that there is a rational connection between the Policy chosen and the problem identified.

[¶36] In this case, the School District has provided a factual basis to support its concerns regarding drug and alcohol usage by students in the district. As discussed previously, surveys identified relatively prevalent and widespread drug and alcohol use among students in Goshen County schools. . . . It is up to the School District to determine whether the problem is serious enough to require action. School districts in Wyoming have wide discretion in the management of the district's affairs, and this Court will not interfere with an honest exercise of discretion by public boards or officers. . . .

[¶39] The real difficulty in this case surrounds the efficacy of the School District's chosen means of addressing the problem it has identified. The School District has chosen to require drug and alcohol testing for all students involved in extracurricular activities. . . .

[¶44] The Coalition [argues that] there is no evidence that participants in all extracurricular activities are leaders of the drug culture, and there are no special health risks faced by those who participate in, for example, choir, drama club, or student council. For these reasons, the Coalition argues that there is, in effect, a disconnect between the problem identified by the School District—widespread drug and alcohol use among students—and the means chosen to address that problem—testing all students who participate in extracurricular activities. Based on this disconnect, the Coalition urges us to find the Policy unconstitutional.

[¶45] By a narrow margin, however, we believe that the School District has demonstrated a sufficient connection between the means chosen and the problem identified. The School District has explained that it chose to test students who participate in extracurricular activities in order to "undermine the effects of peer pressure by providing legitimate reasons for students to refuse use of illegal drugs and/or alcohol." The School District's Policy . . . offers the adolescent a nonthreatening reason to decline his friend's drug-use invitations, namely, that he intends to play baseball, participate in debate, join the band, or engage in any one of half a dozen useful, interesting, and important activities. There may be no guarantee that the Policy will achieve this purpose, but the School District has shown a rational basis for believing that it might. . . .

[¶47] The Coalition fervently stresses the importance of extracurricular activities, asserting that they are "critically important" in developing "the type of responsible students who will some day be leaders in our communities and in our State." The Coalition offered evidence that involvement in extracurricular activities is particularly significant to students who wish to pursue higher education. We readily acknowledge the importance of extracurricular activities in Wyoming's public schools. But we also recognize . . . that participation in extracurricular activities is a voluntary choice. . . .

[¶49] Finally, we note evidence that the School District did not adopt this Policy hastily or without careful consideration. Before the Policy was adopted, the Superintendent of Schools sent a letter to parents and guardians of school students. In this letter, the Superintendent summarized the survey results from the past several years as indicating "a serious prevalence of alcohol and drug use among our students." He explained previous efforts to address that problem, including educational and awareness programs, but said that "other school districts can and are doing more. Random drug testing of students involved in extra-curricular activities is an example of what other districts have successfully implemented to encourage youngsters to avoid the use of drugs and alcohol." He then invited recipients to a public forum in order to "hear from representatives from other school districts about the process of implementing a random drug and alcohol policy," and to receive "public comment on this issue."

[¶50] After engaging in this process to assess the Policy, the School District's board of trustees adopted the Policy by a vote of eight to one. . . .

[¶51] In sum, we acknowledge that Article 1, §4 of the Wyoming Constitution protects public school students from unreasonable searches and seizures. In considering whether the testing mandated by the School District's Policy is reasonable under all of the circumstances, we recognized that students, particularly those who participate in extracurricular activities, are already subject to more stringent rules and regulations than adults, and so have limited expectations of privacy in the school setting. We found that the School District's Policy adequately preserves the students' personal privacy rights, and appropriately limits the degree of invasion into those rights. We concluded that the School District has a compelling interest in providing for the safety and welfare of its students, and that it therefore has a legitimate interest in deterring drug and alcohol use among students. On the closest question of all, we determined that the School District showed that its Policy requiring random, suspicionless drug and alcohol testing for all students who participate in extracurricular activities is rationally related to furthering its interest in deterring drug and alcohol use among students.

[¶52] We conclude that the Coalition has not demonstrated that the School District's Policy subjects students to searches that are unreasonable under all of the circumstances. Accordingly, we hold that the School District's Policy does not violate Article 1, §4 of the Wyoming Constitution. . . .

Notes

1. *Lesser protections in school: majority position.* The decision of the U.S. Supreme Court in New Jersey v. T.L.O., 469 U.S. 325 (1985), reached the same conclusion as had many of the state courts considering earlier challenges to searches by school officials. Because of the special environment of the school, these courts concluded that neither a warrant nor probable cause was necessary to justify a search by school officials, even if the evidence found during the search ultimately led to a criminal or juvenile conviction. Instead, reasonable suspicion was all that was typically necessary to support a valid search of an individual student. Some highly intrusive searches in a school, however, might require a showing of probable cause. See Safford Unified School District #1 v. Redding, 557 U.S. 364 (2009) (search of 13-year-old student's underwear for prescription pain killer without probable cause was unreasonable).

State courts and legislatures continue to take the position that warrants and probable cause are usually not necessary in this environment; the Oklahoma statute printed above is typical in this respect. See State v. Best, 987 A.2d 605 (N.J. 2010) (reasonable suspicion can support search of automobile in school lot for drugs); cf. In re Randy G., 28 P.3d 239 (Cal. 2001) (reasonable suspicion not required to justify school security officer's temporary detention of student).

2. *Searches of school-owned areas.* School authorities grant students access to lockers and other areas for storage of personal property; sometimes school administrators inform students (either by posting signs or by providing individual notice) that they might search the lockers from time to time. See In re Patrick Y., 746 A.2d 405 (Md. 2000) (student has no reasonable expectation of privacy in locker); Md. Educ. Code §7-308 (authorizes searches of school-owned areas). Under such circumstances, is it reasonable for a student to expect any privacy at all in the locker area? What if the school assumes but does not announce its power to search lockers and exercises that power periodically? Would the same analysis apply to searches of dormitory rooms by school officials in state-supported universities?

3. *School officials as criminal law enforcers.* Part of the justification that courts often give for the relaxed requirements for valid searches in schools is the noncriminal purpose of the searches. Put another way, the school must show that its search meets a "special need" other than criminal law enforcement; school administrators can conduct searches based on reasonable suspicion of a violation of "either the law or the rules of the school." *T.L.O.*, 469 U.S. at 341.

But what happens if the police take the initiative and approach school officials, asking them to conduct the search? What if the law enforcement agent who initiates the search is stationed full time at the school? Most courts have used the probable cause standard for searches carried out by school officials at the request of the police. Courts use the reasonable suspicion standard for searches initiated by a police officer assigned full time or part time as a liaison to the school. See

State v. Meneese, 282 P.3d 83 (Wash. 2012); People v. Dilworth, 661 N.E.2d 310 (Ill. 1996). Should it matter whether the searching police officer has a regular relationship with the school? For further exploration of the variety of state court applications of this standard, including the permissible scope of searches in the school context, see the web extension for this chapter at *http://www.crimpro.com/ extension/ch04.*

Would your analysis change if school officials have a general duty to cooperate with criminal law enforcement rather than an intent to do so in a particular case? For instance, Tenn. Code Ann. §49-6-4209 imposes on school officials the legal duty to help enforce the criminal law: "It is the duty of a school principal who has reasonable suspicion to believe, either as a result of a search or otherwise, that any student is committing or has committed any violation of [criminal laws against possession of weapons or drugs], upon the school ground . . . to report [the] suspicion to the appropriate law enforcement officer." Searches in the school context have attracted the attention of about half of the state legislatures.

4. *Drug testing in schools: majority position.* When the Supreme Court first addressed drug testing in schools in Vernonia School District 47J v. Acton, 515 U.S. 646 (1995), the issue had received little attention in courts or legislatures. The existing statutes and cases validated drug testing of students based on reasonable suspicion of illegal drug use without addressing mandatory random testing. See Tenn. Code Ann. §49-6-4213 (reasonable suspicion testing). In the years between *Vernonia* and *Earls*, very few school districts adopted a policy of random drug testing. See Ronald F. Wright, The Abruptness of *Acton*, 36 Crim. L. Bull. 401 (2000). As the *Hageman* case discusses, courts have split on the validity of suspicionless drug tests for students under state constitutions; only a few state supreme courts have explicitly addressed the question. See York v. Wahkiakum School Dist. No. 200, 178 P.3d 995 (Wash. 2008) (random, suspicionless testing of student athletes violated their rights under the state constitution). What political or economic interests will press local school officials to adopt (or to reject) drug testing? Is it realistic for schools to limit drug tests to cases involving individual reasonable suspicion?

5. *Drug testing in other contexts.* Drug testing occurs more frequently in workplaces than in schools. Some employers require a drug test of all job applicants and probationary employees; among current employees, reasonable suspicion testing is more common. If the employer is a private party, the Fourth Amendment and its state analogs do not apply. Only statutes and common-law theories are available to limit the employer's choices, and those statutes tend to regulate but not bar use of random drug testing. See Ariz. Rev. Stat. §23-493.04 (allowing testing "for any job-related purposes"); Minn. Stat. §181.951 (allowing reasonable suspicion testing for all employees and random testing for "safety sensitive" employees). For further exploration of the variety of state court applications of this standard, see the web extension for this chapter at *http://www.crimpro.com/extension/ch04.*

As for public employers, courts have upheld testing programs against most challenges. It is clear that when a public employer has reasonable suspicion of drug use by an employee, drug testing is acceptable. Specific incidents (such as an accident involving a train) might give the employer reasonable suspicion, or at least some individualized suspicion, to test for drug use among the employees involved in the incident. See Skinner v. Railway Labor Executives' Association, 489 U.S. 602 (1989). Courts have even approved random or routine drug testing, at least for job categories in which drug use presents a special concern for the employer. In National Treasury Employees Union v. Von Raab, 489 U.S. 656 (1989), the Court upheld a program requiring a urinalysis from any Customs Service employee seeking a transfer to a position involving drug interdiction or the carrying of a firearm. Does this opinion suggest that a police department could insist on random drug testing for all of its officers? See McCloskey v. Honolulu Police Department, 799 P.2d 953 (Haw. 1990) (upholding such a program); Anchorage Police Department Employees Association v. Municipality of Anchorage, 24 P.3d 547 (Alaska 2001) (striking down such a program). For all members of the Narcotics Bureau within the department? See Delaraba v. Police Department, 632 N.E.2d 1251 (N.Y. 1994) (upholding such a program). Collective labor agreements will sometimes limit the power of an employer to implement drug testing. See Fraternal Order of Police, Miami Lodge 20 v. City of Miami, 609 So. 2d 31 (Fla. 1992).

6. *Searches of prison cells: majority position.* State and federal appellate courts have traditionally given latitude to the decisions of the administrators of prisons, jails, and other detention facilities. They point out the exceptional need for order in such a setting. The Supreme Court in Hudson v. Palmer, 468 U.S. 517 (1984), made a particularly strong statement of this view when it held that the Fourth Amendment does not place any limits on a prison guard's search of the prison cell of a convicted offender. The prisoner in that case claimed that a prison guard had searched his cell and destroyed his property solely to harass the prisoner. The Court replied:

> A right of privacy in traditional Fourth Amendment terms is fundamentally incompatible with the close and continual surveillance of inmates and their cells required to ensure institutional security and internal order. We are satisfied that society would insist that the prisoner's expectation of privacy always yield to what must be considered the paramount interest in institutional security.

468 U.S. at 527-528. A concern for the security and order of prisons led the Court to hold that "the Fourth Amendment has no applicability to a prison cell." Virtually all state courts to consider this question have followed the *Hudson* case and concluded that their analogous state constitutional provisions also have no application to searches of prison cells. Should the exemption from the Fourth Amendment apply only when searches are motivated by the need for order and security in the jail or prison? If so, how should a court determine what motivated the search?

7. *Pretrial detainees and parolees versus prisoners.* Some persons confined in a cell have been convicted of a crime, while others have only been accused of a crime. Should a pretrial detainee have a "reasonable expectation of privacy" in a cell when a convicted offender would not? The Supreme Court spoke indirectly to this issue in Bell v. Wolfish, 441 U.S. 520 (1979), when it held that the Fourth Amendment protects neither sentenced nor pretrial detainees from a prison policy requiring inmates to undergo strip and body cavity searches after all contact visits with non-inmates. The Court stated that the security concerns at issue for convicted offenders also exist for pretrial detainees. State courts have split on the question whether constitutional privacy protections apply differently to pretrial detainees and convicted offenders. See State v. Henderson, 517 S.E.2d 61 (Ga. 1999) (pretrial detainees have limited expectation of privacy in cell); State v. Martin, 367 S.E.2d 618 (N.C. 1988) (search of pretrial detainee's cell by jailer not subject to Fourth Amendment reasonableness test). Does the lack of a reasonable expectation of privacy, as announced in Hudson

v. Palmer, derive from the nature of the person's status (convicted of a crime) or from the nature of the place (a prison)?

Convicted individuals who serve their sentences outside of a prison or jail fall into their own category. In Samson v. California, 547 U.S. 843 (2006), the court heard a challenge to a state law that required parolees to submit to warrantless, suspicionless searches at any time. The Court held that the law did not violate the Fourth Amendment, drawing a parallel between parolees and prisoners, and saying that the public's strong interest in supervising parolees outweighs the parolees' diminished expectation of privacy. The Court also noted an element of consent involved when a parolee chooses the relatively greater freedom of a probation sentence over an active prison term.

8. *Places categorically out of reach of the constitution?* Do *Hudson* and the cases following its lead establish "Fourth-Amendment-free zones"? If prison officials are free to act without legal limits, how will this affect the present or future conduct of the prisoners being punished for violating the criminal law? Are there any alternatives? Consider State v. Berard, 576 A.2d 118 (Vt. 1990) (search and seizure provision in state constitution applies to prison searches, but "special needs" of prison environment allow warrantless random searches of cells). Is *Berard* an improvement over *Hudson* from a prisoner's point of view? From society's point of view? Compare United States v. Knights, 534 U.S. 112 (2001) (constitution allows police with reasonable suspicion of criminal behavior to conduct a warrantless search of home of a probationer who is subject to a probation condition authorizing warrantless searches) with Ferguson v. City of Charleston, 532 U.S. 67 (2001) (state hospital instructed staff to identify pregnant patients at risk for drug abuse, to test those patients for drug abuse, and to report positive tests to the police; Court held that this testing was an unreasonable search).

Problem 4-8. Jail Cell Search

McCoy's first two trials on charges of armed robbery and attempted murder of a police officer ended in mistrials. After his third trial, the jury convicted McCoy, but an appellate court reversed the conviction. On the eve of the scheduled date for the fourth trial, the assistant state attorney assigned to the case, Ketchum, and a police officer, Hagerman, went to McCoy's cell at the local pretrial detention facility.

Hagerman, following instructions from Ketchum, first removed McCoy and his cellmate and then searched the cell for anything McCoy may have written that might contain incriminating statements. As Hagerman searched, Ketchum stood in the doorway of the cell. Hagerman found on a table in the cell a number of depositions, transcripts, offense reports, and personal notes. He seized McCoy's copies of depositions of four state witnesses, which consisted of some 70 pages and included McCoy's copious handwritten notes in the margins. Several of the handwritten notes were incriminating.

McCoy presented no particular security problems at the detention facility, and there was no concrete information suggesting that the papers in his cell would contain incriminating information. How will the trial court rule on his motion to suppress the handwritten notes found on the depositions? Compare McCoy v. State, 639 So. 2d 163 (Fla. Dist. Ct. App. 1994).

Problem 4-9. Gun Lockers

One Friday night in November, students at Madison High School reported hearing gunshots as they left the school following a basketball game. School security guards found spent casings on school grounds the next day. By the following Monday morning, the school staff and security personnel were receiving more reports of guns present in the school building and on school buses, and rumors that a shootout would occur at the school that day. Some staff members and students asked to leave the school out of fear for their safety.

The school principal, Jude, ordered school security personnel to begin a random search of student lockers as a preventive measure while he interviewed selected students. The public school handbook indicates that "lockers are the property of the school system and subject to inspection as determined necessary or appropriate." Students are prohibited from putting private locks on their lockers.

Siena, a Madison High School security aide, searched the school lockers. Using a pass key, he opened the lockers and visually inspected the lockers' contents, moving some articles to see more clearly, and patted down coats in the lockers. Siena did not search every student locker. He chose lockers initially on the lower level of the building, where the largest crowds gathered. He also took care to search the lockers of any known "problem" students and any locker where he saw groups of students congregating.

Altogether, Siena conducted between 75 and 100 locker searches before he opened Baker's locker. At the time, Siena did not know who was assigned to the locker. Baker did not have a history of prior weapon violations, nor did the school officials suspect his involvement in the recent gun incidents. Siena removed a coat from the locker and immediately believed it to be unusually heavy. He found a gun in the coat.

Was the search legal? How would you resolve the case under typical constitutional standards? Under the Oklahoma statute reprinted above? Would your analysis change after hearing FBI estimates that nearly 100,000 students carry guns to school every day? See Isiah B. v. State, 500 N.W.2d 637 (Wis. 1993).

C. "PAPERS"

There are several methods available to the government to inspect "papers" during criminal law enforcement. One method, which we will explore in Chapter 10, is for a grand jury or administrative agency to issue a subpoena. The government might also rely on statutory requirements for certain types of businesses to maintain records and to allow the government access to those records. On the other hand, if the government attempts to search and seize papers without using a subpoena or a record-keeping requirement, it must comply with traditional Fourth Amendment requirements: showing probable cause to believe that the papers will provide evidence of a crime, and perhaps obtaining a warrant.

Are there some papers, however, that are so intimately personal that the government cannot obtain them, even if it demonstrates probable cause and obtains a warrant? We start with one of the most important early Supreme Court cases on the Fourth Amendment. The answer that the Court gave in 1886 to the question of "private papers" searches is not the same answer that legal institutions, by and large, give today. This classic opinion, however, does offer us a chance to consider an alternative form of privacy protection, in which rules would absolutely bar the government from searching some areas, regardless of the justifications it might have to conduct the search.

■ EDWARD BOYD v. UNITED STATES
116 U.S. 616 (1886)

BRADLEY, J.*

[The government brought this forfeiture action to obtain 35 cases of glass that Boyd and others allegedly imported from England without paying the proper customs duties. At trial, it became relevant to show the quantity and value of the glass contained in 29 cases previously imported. The trial court ordered Boyd to produce the invoices for the cases. Boyd objected to the constitutionality of the statute giving the judge the power to make such an order. Other provisions of the same statute empowered the judge to issue a warrant to a marshal or customs collector to enter private premises and obtain any papers, books, or invoices that might tend to prove the government's allegations in a civil forfeiture suit under the customs laws. The jury in this case heard the evidence relating to the invoices and rendered a verdict for the United States.]

The clauses of the Constitution, to which it is contended that these laws are repugnant, are the fourth and fifth amendments. . . . The fifth article, amongst other things, declares that no person "shall be compelled in any criminal case to be a witness against himself." . . .

Is a search and seizure, or, what is equivalent thereto, a compulsory production of a man's private papers, to be used in evidence against him in a proceeding to forfeit his property for alleged fraud against the revenue laws — is such a proceeding for such a purpose an "unreasonable search and seizure" within the meaning of the fourth amendment of the Constitution? Or, is it a legitimate proceeding?

[We] do not find any long usage, or any contemporary construction of the Constitution, which would justify any of the acts of Congress now under consideration. [The] act of 1863 was the first act in this country, and, we might say, either in this country or in England, so far as we have been able to ascertain, which authorized the search and seizure of a man's private papers, or the compulsory production of them, for the purpose of using them in evidence against him in a criminal case, or in a proceeding to enforce the forfeiture of his property. Even the act under which the obnoxious writs of assistance were issued did not go as far as this, but only authorized the examination of ships and vessels, and persons found therein, for the purpose of finding goods prohibited to be imported or exported, or on which the duties were not paid, and to enter into and search any suspected vaults, cellars, or warehouses for such goods.

The search for and seizure of stolen or forfeited goods, or goods liable to duties and concealed to avoid the payment thereof, are totally different things from a search for and seizure of a man's private books and papers for the purpose of obtaining

* [Justices Field, Harlan, Woods, Matthews, Gray, and Blatchford joined in this opinion.—EDS.]

information therein contained, or of using them as evidence against him. . . . In the one case, the government is entitled to the possession of the property; in the other it is not. The seizure of stolen goods is authorized by the common law; and the seizure of goods forfeited for a breach of the revenue laws . . . has been authorized by English statutes for at least two centuries past. [In] the case of excisable or dutiable articles, the government has an interest in them for the payment of the duties thereon, and until such duties are paid has a right to keep them under observation, or to pursue and drag them from concealment. . . . Whereas, by the proceeding now under consideration, the court attempts to extort from the party his private books and papers to make him liable for a penalty or to forfeit his property.

In order to ascertain the nature of the proceedings intended by the fourth amendment to the Constitution under the terms "unreasonable searches and seizures," it is only necessary to recall the contemporary or then recent history of the controversies on the subject, both in this country and in England. [The opinion of Lord Camden in the 1765 case of Entick v. Carrington] is regarded as one of the permanent monuments of the British Constitution, and is quoted as such by the English authorities on that subject down to the present time. . . . The principles laid down in [Entick v. Carrington] affect the very essence of constitutional liberty and security. They reach farther than the concrete form of the case then before the court, with its adventitious circumstances; they apply to all invasions on the part of the government and its employees of the sanctity of a man's home and the privacies of life. It is not the breaking of his doors, and the rummaging of his drawers, that constitutes the essence of the offence; but it is the invasion of his indefeasible right of personal security, personal liberty and private property [that violates the constitutional principle]. Breaking into a house and opening boxes and drawers are circumstances of aggravation; but any forcible and compulsory extortion of a man's own testimony or of his private papers to be used as evidence to convict him of crime or to forfeit his goods, is within the condemnation of that judgment. In this regard the fourth and fifth amendments run almost into each other. . . .

We have already noticed the intimate relation between the two amendments. They throw great light on each other. For the "unreasonable searches and seizures" condemned in the fourth amendment are almost always made for the purpose of compelling a man to give evidence against himself, which in criminal cases is condemned in the fifth amendment; and compelling a man "in a criminal case to be a witness against himself," which is condemned in the fifth amendment, throws light on the question as to what is an "unreasonable search and seizure" within the meaning of the fourth amendment. And we have been unable to perceive that the seizure of a man's private books and papers to be used in evidence against him is substantially different from compelling him to be a witness against himself. We think it is within the clear intent and meaning of those terms. . . .

Though the proceeding in question is divested of many of the aggravating incidents of actual search and seizure, yet, as before said, it contains their substance and essence, and effects their substantial purpose. . . . We think that the notice to produce the invoice in this case, the order by virtue of which it was issued, and the law which authorized the order, were unconstitutional and void, and that the inspection by the district attorney of said invoice, when produced in obedience to said notice, and its admission in evidence by the court, were erroneous and unconstitutional proceedings. . . .

Notes

1. *The erosion of* Boyd: *property and privacy.* The *Boyd* Court notes that the government could seize contraband or proceeds of a crime but not papers containing evidence of a crime, because only in the former cases does the government have a proprietary interest in the item stronger than that of the private party. The constitution, under this reading, reinforces the protections of property law.

The linkage between property law and unreasonable searches has changed. For one thing, as we have seen, a "search" now can be defined in two ways: a state action that intrudes on the "reasonable expectations of privacy" of the target of the search, or a state action that amounts to a physical trespass on any constitutionally protected property interest of the target. For another thing, most courts have now abandoned a traditional limitation on the search power known as the "mere evidence" rule. Under that rule, the government could search for and seize contraband, instrumentalities, or fruits of crime but not mere evidence of crime. Again, the reasoning was grounded in property law: The government had a superior claim to contraband and the like (which the private party had no right to own), but the private party had a superior claim to innocent property that provided evidence of a crime. The U.S. Supreme Court abandoned the mere evidence rule in Warden v. Hayden, 387 U.S. 294 (1967). Every state now interprets its own constitution to allow such searches. For further discussion of the relevance of property theory to Fourth Amendment jurisprudence, see Thomas K. Clancy, What Does the Fourth Amendment Protect: Property, Privacy, or Security, 33 Wake Forest L. Rev. 307 (1998); Morgan Cloud, The Fourth Amendment During the *Lochner* Era: Privacy, Property and Liberty in Constitutional Theory, 48 Stan. L. Rev. 555 (1996); William C. Heffernan, Property, Privacy, and The Fourth Amendment, 60 Brook. L. Rev. 633 (1994).

2. *The erosion of* Boyd: *self-incrimination and unreasonable searches.* The *Boyd* Court also suggested that the Fourth and Fifth Amendments throw light on each other, or provide mutually reinforcing protections. A search of a person's papers is equivalent to a demand that the person make incriminating testimony. This aspect of the *Boyd* case has also fallen by the wayside. In several cases, such as Andresen v. Maryland, 427 U.S. 463 (1976), the Supreme Court has declared that a search of a person's documents does not amount to compelled "testimony" because the person created the documents voluntarily and does not have to participate in the government's later search or seizure of the documents. Again, state courts have followed suit.

3. *The erosion of* Boyd: *private papers.* Federal and state courts have left more room to wonder if there is still an absolute bar to the search or seizure of private papers such as diaries. The Supreme Court has allowed searches and seizures of business records, as it did in Andresen v. Maryland, but has not squarely addressed private papers. See Daniel Solove, The First Amendment as Criminal Procedure, 82 N.Y.U. L. Rev. 112 (2007).

By and large, state courts have taken the next step to conclude that there is no absolute bar to the search of private papers. See State v. Andrei, 574 A.2d 295 (Me. 1990). Every so often, a court intimates that some private papers (so long as the papers themselves were not used to commit a crime) might be beyond the reach of a government search, even if supported by probable cause and a warrant. See State v. Bisaccia, 213 A.2d 185 (N.J. 1965). Georgia has an unusual statute protecting "private papers" from searches:

> [A judicial officer] may issue a search warrant for the seizure of the following: (1) Any instruments, articles, or things, *including* the private papers of any person, which are designed, intended for use, or which have been used in the commission of the offense in connection with which the warrant is issued; . . . or (5) Any instruments, articles or things, any information or data, and anything that is tangible or intangible, corporeal or incorporeal, visible or invisible evidence of the commission of the crime for which probable cause is shown, *other than* the private papers of any person.

Ga. Code Ann. §17-5-21(a) (emphasis added). Does this statutory protection from searches re-create the now-abandoned requirements of *Boyd?* Would it prevent a search for an illegal lottery ticket? For a list of telephone numbers of purchasers of illegal narcotics? If you were restricting the scope of this statute, how might you define "private" papers? See Sears v. State, 426 S.E.2d 553 (Ga. 1993) (interpreting section to bar search for documents only when covered by privilege, such as attorney-client or doctor-patient).

4. *Extra particularity in search warrants for private papers.* While it is not often that a legal system will absolutely bar all searches for private papers, it is more common to see judges insist on extra particularity in a warrant authorizing a search for books or papers. See Lo-Ji Sales, Inc. v. New York, 442 U.S. 319 (1979); Tattered Cover, Inc. v. City of Thornton, 44 P.3d 1044 (Colo. 2002); compare In re C.T., 999 A.2d 210 (N.H. 2010) (when law enforcement seeks privileged medical records, providers must comply with search warrant by producing records for in camera review, allowing patient and provider opportunity to object; state must demonstrate "essential need" for record).

5. *Private records held by third parties: banking records.* Many types of sensitive personal documents, such as banking records or medical records, are held by institutions on behalf of their customers. When government agents investigating a crime try to obtain these records, does the legal system allow the institution to deny the request? Under the Fourth Amendment, the Supreme Court in United States v. Miller, 425 U.S. 435 (1976), decided that a bank's customer has no reasonable expectation of privacy in records relating to the customer's account:

> All of the documents obtained, including financial statements and deposit slips, contain only information voluntarily conveyed to the banks and exposed to their employees in the ordinary course of business. . . . The depositor takes the risk, in revealing his affairs to another, that the information will be conveyed by that person to the Government.

Two years earlier, the California Supreme Court in Burrows v. Superior Court, 529 P.2d 590 (Cal. 1974), set out an argument in favor of giving bank customers standing to challenge unreasonable searches of bank records relating to their accounts:

> A bank customer's reasonable expectation is that, absent compulsion by legal process, the matters he reveals to the bank will be utilized by the bank only for internal banking purposes. . . . For all practical purposes, the disclosure by individuals or business firms of their financial affairs to a bank is not entirely volitional, since it is impossible to participate in the economic life of contemporary society without maintaining a bank account. In the course of such dealings, a depositor reveals many aspects of his personal affairs, opinions, habits and associations. . . .

State courts have divided on the constitutional question, with a strong minority following *Burrows.* See State v. Thompson, 810 P.2d 415 (Utah 1991) (following

Burrows); State v. Schultz, 850 P.2d 818 (Kansas 1993) (following *Miller*). See Stephen E. Henderson, Learning from All Fifty States: How to Apply the Fourth Amendment and Its State Analogs to Protect Third Party Information from Unreasonable Search, 55 Cath. U. L. Rev. 373 (2006).

Several legislatures have enabled banking customers to challenge the reasonableness of government efforts to search their banking records. Congress adopted the Right to Financial Privacy Act, 12 U.S.C. §§3401 et seq., as a repudiation of the *Miller* decision: "The Court did not acknowledge the sensitive nature of these records." 1978 U.S.C.C.A.N. 9305. The act requires that the bank customer have notice and an opportunity to object before the financial institution complies with a subpoena seeking the records. About one-third of the states have enacted an equivalent of the Right to Financial Privacy Act. See, e.g., Mo. Rev. Stat. §§408.683 et seq.

Do these statutes and cases provide enough protection by allowing the customer to insist that any search of records be reasonable? Should they provide instead for a much higher level of justification by the government to support a search of banking records (similar to bank secrecy provisions in some other nations)? Would a reinvigorated *Boyd* present an absolute bar to a search of banking records?

6. *Private papers and electronic devices.* Cell phones and other personal electronic devices hold many of the personal details and observations about a person's life that once could be found in "private papers." As we will see in Chapter 7, the regulation of searches of those devices is developing along new lines of precedent. See Carpenter v. United States, 138 S. Ct. 2206 (2018) (government's collection of cell phone site location information from wireless carrier to track customer's movement over a period of days amounted to search normally requiring a warrant); Riley v. California, 134 S. Ct. 2473 (2014) (collection of information from memory of cell phone obtained from arrestee amounts to separate search not justified automatically as part of search incident to arrest); United States v. Molina-Isidoro, 884 F.3d 287 (5th Cir. 2018) (discussion of *Boyd* in context of government agent search of cell phone apps Uber and WhatsApp). Do these cases effectively revive the tradition of *Boyd*, establishing higher protections for the government to respect when searching especially detailed and personal records?

D. "EFFECTS"

We now turn to the final interest mentioned in the text of the Fourth Amendment, "effects." Given the variety of property that falls within the meaning of this phrase, and the variety of places where a search of effects could take place, it is difficult to find a unifying theme for all these searches. This section will therefore focus on a very common — and very American — form of personal property: the automobile. In this section we survey the various theories prosecutors can use to justify police searches of cars, even when police officers did not first obtain a search warrant or consent. We begin with search incident to arrest. In the notes following the SITA discussion, we explain two other car search theories: (1) the automobile (or *Carroll-Chambers* probable cause) exception to the warrant requirement and (2) the frisk of a car during a traffic stop. We then address the inventory search exception, and finish with a broader discussion of containers found in and out of cars.

In a case involving a car search, the prosecution only needs to win on one of these theories (warrant, consent, SITA, *Carroll-Chambers*, inventory, or frisk) in order to justify the police action. The various theories, however, reach different areas of the car and apply to different time frames; these scope limitations might influence the government's choice of which theories to argue. When reading the following materials, be sure to distinguish the various rationales available to the police to search a car and its contents, the criteria necessary to establish each rationale, the scope limitations, and the ways that the search analysis changes because the search involves a car.

1. Search of a Car Incident to Arrest

■ CLARENCE ROBINSON v. STATE

754 S.E.2d 862 (S.C. 2014)

Toal, C.J.

. . . On February 26, 2008, at approximately 9:45 P.M., four men entered Benders Bar and Grill in the West Ashley area of Charleston, South Carolina, and robbed the patrons and the establishment, stealing approximately $875. . . . The men escaped out the front door of Benders, although no witness could attest whether they left in a vehicle or on foot. The police arrived at 9:51 P.M., within thirty-one seconds of the initial 911 call and two to three minutes of the robbery itself. The responding officer briefly interviewed the patrons and staff and issued an initial "be on the lookout" (BOLO) description to other patrolling officers via the police radio, describing the suspects as four armed African-American men, approximately twenty years old, and wearing all-black clothing.

At 10:06 P.M., a police officer spotted a parked vehicle with its lights off in the darkened, fenced-in parking lot of a closed church and decided to investigate, pulling his patrol car behind the parked vehicle and blocking it in. The officer was aware of the BOLO but testified that the BOLO did not include a description of the getaway vehicle, so he initially "thought maybe it was a couple that was parked there, or somebody from the church left a car there." He called in the car's license plate to dispatch and then approached the car. At that point, he noticed that there were four men in the vehicle who matched the approximate description of the BOLO—the correct number of men, the correct race, the correct age, and the correct approximate clothing color. Further, the testimony at trial established that the church is located within a short drive of Benders. The officer asked the driver, Petitioner, for his driver's license and walked back to his patrol vehicle and requested backup. . . .

At 10:09 P.M., two backup police officers arrived. These two officers also received the BOLO alert and knew there were four robbery suspects at large. One backup officer testified: . . . "when I approached and came around one side of the vehicle, and my partner went around the other side of the vehicle, everyone became really nervous and silent. And all four of them looked straight forward." The officers found the men's behavior suspicious. Therefore, the officers requested Petitioner exit the vehicle so they could pat him down for weapons. Next, they requested each passenger exit the vehicle, one-at-a-time, and patted each down for weapons. While the police found no weapons on any of the men, when the final passenger—seated in the rear passenger-side of the vehicle—exited the vehicle at the officers' request, a .22 caliber revolver with its serial number removed became immediately visible on the floorboard. Because none of the four men would admit who owned the gun, the officers arrested all four, including Petitioner. . . . At this point, several other officers responded to the scene to help secure the four suspects and search the vehicle.

At first, the officers detained the four suspects near the vehicle's trunk while other officers searched the car. [The initial search of the passenger area of the vehicle revealed a pair of black gloves, a yellow Nike knit hat, and a piece of red cloth tied into a bandana.] The trunk was locked, and the suspects claimed to be unaware of the key's location. The owner of the car (not Petitioner) stood with his back to the trunk while talking to the officers; however, every time an officer searched near or touched the back seat, the suspect "would turn his head around extremely quickly just to see what was going on." Once the officer stopped searching that area, "he would act completely normal again." After this pattern repeated several times, the officers noticed a gap between the top of the backseat and the flat paneling between the seat and the back windshield. The officers pulled the seat forward slightly to peer into the trunk and saw three more guns in an area that would have been accessible to the suspects had they still been in the vehicle.[5]

Petitioner and his three co-defendants proceeded to trial for armed robbery and possession of a firearm during the commission of a violent crime. At trial, Petitioner and his co-defendants moved to suppress the guns and all other evidence found from the search of the vehicle based on their claims that the police lacked a reasonable suspicion to stop them initially and that, even if the police did have a reasonable suspicion, the warrantless search of the car's trunk exceeded the scope of their permissible authority. The trial court . . . admitted all of the evidence, finding that (1) the officer had a reasonable suspicion that criminal activity was afoot when he stopped the car initially and (2) several exceptions to the warrant requirement justified the warrantless search. Ultimately, the jury found Petitioner and his co-defendants guilty. . . .

[A] warrantless search may nonetheless be proper under the Fourth Amendment if it falls within one of the well-established exceptions to the warrant requirement. . . . The trial court found that, because the police officers had reasonable suspicion of criminal activity afoot, the officers properly seized the gun with the serial numbers removed under the plain view exception. Additionally, the trial court found that the police officers did not need a warrant to search the rest of the vehicle after discovering the initial gun because: (1) under the search-incident-to-an-arrest exception, the officers had a reasonable belief that the vehicle contained evidence of the offense for which the co-defendants were arrested; [and] (2) under the automobile exception, the officers had probable cause to believe the vehicle contained contraband. . . . We agree. . . .

SEARCH INCIDENT TO A LAWFUL ARREST EXCEPTION

Petitioner contends that the evidence found in the trunk should have been excluded because the trunk search exceeded the scope of the search-incident-to-arrest exception. Specifically, Petitioner points out that he and his co-defendants

---

5. The officers also found a black hooded sweatshirt, two pairs of black gloves, a pair of clear latex gloves, a black and white knit hat, a black knit hat, a pair of black and red Nike Air Force One tennis shoes, and a piece of gray cloth tied into a bandana. . . . Between the four suspects, $870 was recovered.

were handcuffed and standing outside of the vehicle before the police officers searched the car after finding the gun with the serial number removed. Because we find the officers had a reasonable belief that the vehicle contained evidence of the criminal offense for which the co-defendants were arrested, we disagree. . . .

In Chimel v. California, 395 U.S. 752 (1969), the United States Supreme Court initially held that, in the cases of a lawful custodial arrest, the police may conduct a contemporaneous, warrantless search of the person arrested and the immediate surrounding area. . . . *Chimel's* rule proved difficult to apply, particularly in cases that involved searches inside of automobiles after the arrestees were no longer in them. The Supreme Court therefore clarified the *Chimel* rule in New York v. Belton, 453 U.S. 454 (1981), by outlining a bright-line rule concerning arrests of automobile occupants. Specifically, the Supreme Court held that, "when a policeman has made a lawful custodial arrest of the occupant of an automobile, he may, as a contemporaneous incident of that arrest, search the passenger compartment of that automobile." The Supreme Court justified the search on the grounds that the "articles inside the relatively narrow compass of the passenger compartment of an automobile are in fact generally, even if not inevitably, within the area into which an arrestee might reach in order to grab a weapon or evidentiary item." . . .

The *Belton* court specifically excluded the trunk from the permissible scope of a search incident to an arrest. . . . *Belton* prohibited trunk searches because the trunk is not within the control of the passengers either immediately before or during the process of arrest. However, subsequent courts found that, in certain situations, the trunk (in the traditional sense) constituted part of the passenger compartment for purposes of search incident to arrest. In general, courts would find the trunk part of the passenger compartment—and thus subject to a warrantless search incident to a lawful arrest—when the trunk was reachable without exiting the vehicle, without regard to the likelihood in the particular case that such a reaching was possible.

Courts faithfully applied the *Belton* rule for the next twenty-eight years and allowed the police to search the passenger compartment of a vehicle incident to the arrest of a recent occupant of the vehicle, even if the arrestee had been handcuffed and secured in the back of the officer's patrol car prior to the search. However, in Arizona v. Gant, 556 U.S. 332 (2009), the Supreme Court limited *Belton's* bright-line rule. There, the Supreme Court found that, if the arrestee was already secured and outside of reaching distance from the passenger compartment of the vehicle at the time of the search, a search could not be justified under the traditional rationale—protecting officer safety and preventing the destruction of evidence. Therefore, the Supreme Court set forth the new rule: police may search the passenger compartment of a vehicle incident to a recent occupant's arrest only if (1) the arrestee is "unsecured and within reaching distance of the passenger compartment at the time of the search," or (2) it is "reasonable to believe" the vehicle contains evidence of the crime of arrest. Absent either of those two instances, a search of an arrestee's vehicle will be unreasonable unless police obtain a warrant or show that another exception to the warrant requirement applies. . . .

We find that the first justification under the *Gant* rule (arrestee unsecured and within reach of area to be searched) does not apply here. Several officers had handcuffed Petitioner and his co-defendants at the back of the vehicle and were closely supervising them while other officers searched the car. . . .

However, we find that the second justification under *Gant* (reasonable to believe vehicle contains evidence of a crime) does apply in this instance. The officers arrested the suspects for the unlawful possession of a handgun with its serial number removed. Finding this gun, in conjunction with their knowledge of the BOLO and their suspicion that Petitioner and his co-defendants were in fact the four men involved in the armed robbery at Benders, provided the officers probable cause to likewise arrest them for armed robbery. Because there were four men involved in the armed robbery, and only one gun had thus far been recovered, it was reasonable to believe the vehicle contained further evidence of the armed robbery.

Furthermore, although *Belton*—and thus presumably *Gant*—excluded the trunk from the permissible scope of a search incident to a lawful arrest, we have not previously had the opportunity to address the issue of whether the trunk may, at times, be part of the passenger compartment, as many other courts have likewise found. We hereby adopt the view that the trunk may be considered part of the passenger compartment and may therefore be searched pursuant to a lawful arrest when the trunk is reachable without exiting the vehicle, as it was in this case. . . . We therefore find that the trial court properly admitted the evidence in the trunk as part of the search of the passenger compartment. . . .

PLEICONES, J., concurring.

. . . As the parties acknowledge, the search here could only be upheld under the second *Gant* scenario.[14] However, a *Gant* search is limited to the passenger compartment itself and the containers located therein, and the trunk is not within the permissible scope of an "evidence of the arrest" search. If this search is to be sustained, then it must be pursuant to a different exception to the Fourth Amendment's warrant requirement.

Gant recognizes the continued validity of the automobile exception, citing United States v. Ross, 456 U.S. 798 (1982). Here, the trial judge held the officers had probable cause to search the vehicle for evidence of the bar robbery under *Ross*'s automobile exception. This unchallenged ruling, whether correct or not, is the law of the case. . . .

Notes

1. *Search of automobile incident to arrest: majority position.* As the *Robinson* case from South Carolina indicates, the federal constitutional limits on searches incident to arrest in the automobile context followed a twisted road. In most settings, the rules for search incident to arrest allow the officer to search the arrestee's body, any nearby personal items associated with the arrestee (such as a purse), and the space within the arrestee's "immediate control." Chimel v. California, 395 U.S. 752 (1969). The authority to conduct such a search flows automatically from a valid arrest; it does not depend on any showing of reasonable suspicion to believe that evidence or weapons are actually present. At the same time, the purpose of the traditional search incident to arrest is to protect officer safety and to prevent the destruction of evidence. A specialized version of the *Chimel* search incident to arrest applies when

---

14. The majority . . . recognizes the weakness of upholding a vehicle search for evidence of a no-serial-number handgun which has already been seized. It thus transmogrifies the arrest for the weapon into one for the armed robbery, despite the arresting officer's testimony that "After we found the altered .22 they were all placed under arrest for that weapon."

the arrestee is in a car at the time of arrest. Under New York v. Belton, 453 U.S. 454 (1981), the arresting officer could search the person of the arrestee and the passenger compartment of the car, even if the officer did not make contact with the arrestee until after he or she left the car. See Thornton v. United States, 541 U.S. 615 (2004). As with *Chimel,* the *Belton* search was automatic, and required no showing of probable cause or reasonable suspicion to believe that weapons or evidence were present in the car. Most state courts read *Belton* as a bright-line rule that allowed a vehicle search incident to the arrest of a recent occupant, even if there was no possibility the arrestee could gain access to the vehicle at the time of the search.

The holding in Arizona v. Gant, 556 U.S. 332 (2009), placed tighter limits on searches incident to arrest in the automobile setting. There are now two possible justifications for a search of the vehicle incident to the arrest of a driver or passenger. An officer can search the car only (1) "when the arrestee is unsecured and within reaching distance of the passenger compartment at the time of the search" or (2) "when it is reasonable to believe evidence relevant to the crime of arrest might be found in the vehicle."

2. *Second prong application.* Most of the cases applying *Gant* focus on the second prong, because routine police procedures make the first prong inapplicable. Courts have debated the meaning of the "reasonable to believe" standard; most have concluded that it equates with reasonable suspicion under Terry v. Ohio, 392 U.S. 1 (1968). See United States v. Taylor, 49 A.3d 818 (D.C. App. 2012). Because the second prong only applies to evidence of "the crime of arrest," it has become newly important for trial courts to make factual findings about the precise crime that formed the basis for the arrest. Which crimes of arrest would give officers the most latitude to justify a car search after the arrest?

Another topic of frequent litigation involves the circumstances that can form a "reasonable" basis to believe that the car contains evidence. Which "furtive movements" create a suspicion that an arrestee is armed, and which "furtive movements" create reason to believe that evidence will be found in the car? See State v. Scheett, 845 N.W.2d 885 (N.D. 2014). To what extent will the probable cause to arrest be enough to establish a reasonable belief that evidence is in the car?

3. *Passengers and searches of cars incident to arrest.* There was some doubt over the years whether a search of a car incident to the arrest of the driver could also reach property that clearly belonged to a passenger who is not arrested. The Supreme Court resolved this question in Wyoming v. Houghton, 526 U.S. 295 (1999). In that case, an officer stopped a vehicle for speeding and noticed a hypodermic syringe in the driver's shirt pocket. When the driver admitted that he used the syringe to take drugs, the officer arrested him and ordered two female passengers out of the car. He searched the passenger compartment of the car for contraband and discovered drugs in a purse on the back seat belonging to one of the passengers. The Court upheld the search, emphasizing once again the need for bright-line rules that are easy for officers to apply in the field. Do you imagine that state courts tend to follow *Houghton* as they interpret their own constitutions? See State v. Ray, 620 N.W.2d 83 (Neb. 2000) (officer may inspect passenger's knapsack found in passenger compartment, although passenger not arrested at the time).

4. *Changing search-incident landscape.* The many variations on car searches will doubtlessly lead to a new wave of litigation on these questions in state and federal courts. For instance, will the second prong of the rule apply to searches of hatchback and trunk areas? You can track developments in this fast-changing area of

the law by consulting the web extension of this chapter at *http://www.crimpro.com/ extension/ch04.*

Persons who were not passengers in the car might attempt to retrieve a weapon or evidence from the car while the officer is still on the scene. How would you counsel a police department to respond to these situations? What are the prospects that *Gant* will influence the search-incident-to-arrest doctrine beyond the vehicle context? See State v. Henning, 209 P.3d 711 (Kan. 2009) (suppressing evidence obtained from search of automobile console after arrest of passenger on outstanding arrest warrant; court overturned statute allowing search incident to arrest for evidence of any crime).

5. *Alternative ground for searching cars: automobile exception to the warrant requirement.* In Carroll v. United States, 267 U.S. 132 (1925), the Supreme Court upheld a warrantless search by two federal prohibition agents looking for liquor hidden in the upholstery of an automobile. The Court allowed warrantless searches, based on probable cause, of automobiles and other vehicles because "the vehicle can be quickly moved out of the locality or jurisdiction." A second theory justifying reduced Fourth Amendment protection for cars, developed in a series of later cases, is that cars are subject to public view and to pervasive state regulation. Car owners have lower reasonable expectations of privacy than, for example, homeowners.

The power of the police to search cars and other conveyances without a warrant has become known as the "automobile exception" or the "*Carroll-Chambers* exception." This is an exception to the warrant requirement but not to the probable cause requirement: To exercise this power, police must have probable cause to believe that the car contains evidence or contraband. If police have probable cause, under the automobile exception they may stop the car and conduct a search of the car and any container in the car they have probable cause to believe contains the item they are looking for. See Chambers v. Maroney, 399 U.S. 42 (1970). A search may be rejected if it exceeds the scope justified by probable cause. That is, if officers have probable cause to believe the car contains a stolen tuba, they would have no cause to open the glove compartment.

The largest group of state courts (more than half) have fully embraced the federal view and require no warrant for any search of an automobile. In effect, these courts conclusively presume that exigent circumstances are present for any search of a car, even if the particular car in question was unlikely to move while the officers sought a warrant. A minority of state courts (about a dozen) still explicitly or implicitly require the government to show exigent circumstances to support a warrantless search of a car. The mobility of a car makes this showing quite easy in the ordinary case, but defendants can rebut a presumption of exigency by showing that the car was parked and locked or was otherwise not mobile. See State v. Tibbles, 236 P.3d 885 (Wash. 2010). For a glimpse of the rich case law in the state courts on the automobile exception to the warrant requirement, see the web extension for this chapter at *http://www.crimpro.com/extension/ch04.*

6. *Alternative ground for searching cars: the application of* Terry. A separate justification for car searches stems from the application of *Terry* searches to cars. As we saw in Chapter 2, the Supreme Court approved such searches in Michigan v. Long, 463 U.S. 1032 (1983). Such searches must satisfy the requirements of *Terry.* In other words, the officer must have a proper basis for stopping the car. Then the officer may automatically order the driver and any passengers out of the car. At that point, if the officer has reasonable suspicion to believe there are weapons in the

car, she can search in the passenger compartment, in any areas that could contain an accessible weapon, such as under the seats and inside containers large enough for a weapon. How would this doctrine apply in a case where the driver of a vehicle informs a police officer during a vehicle stop that he is carrying a concealed weapon under the terms of a license allowing him to do so?

7. *Viewing the exterior of cars.* The rules for searching the interior of cars do not apply to examination of the exterior of cars. Following the familiar expectation of privacy analysis of *Katz*, courts have held that no Fourth Amendment issue is raised when police examine the outside of a car or take a picture of it. Courts have also typically refused to apply the Fourth Amendment to examinations of the tread, tire wear, and even the removal of dirt or small samples of paint. See, e.g., Cardwell v. Lewis, 417 U.S. 583 (1974); State v. Skelton, 795 P.2d 349 (Kan. 1990). Examination of the contents of a car from the outside, including the use of sight, smell, or even a flashlight to enhance the view, usually falls outside the limits of the Fourth Amendment so long as the car is parked in a place that is otherwise accessible to the police.

What about the viewing of the VIN (vehicle identification number)? In cases involving police efforts to obtain the VIN, courts agree that if the VIN is visible through the front windshield (as it is on all modern cars), and the officer simply reads it, there is no search. If the officer must reach into the car, open the door, lift the hood, or look under the vehicle to read the VIN or inspect some other feature of the car, some courts (a minority) still hold that no search has occurred. See, e.g., New York v. Class, 475 U.S. 106 (1986); Wood v. State, 632 S.W.2d 734 (Tex. Crim. App. 1982). About twice as many states, however, conclude that probable cause is required to move items inside a car, open a door, or lift a hood before viewing a VIN. See State v. Larocco, 794 P.2d 460 (Utah 1990).

Problem 4-10. Mobile Homes

Robert Williams, an agent of the Drug Enforcement Administration, received information that a man in a motor home, parked at the curb near the San Diego courthouse, was exchanging sex for drugs with teenage boys. At the agent's request, a youth (who had previously been in the motor home) returned to the motor home and knocked on its door; Carney stepped out. Williams and his partner identified themselves as law enforcement officers. Without a warrant or consent, one agent entered the motor home and observed marijuana, plastic bags, and a scale of the kind used in weighing drugs on a table.

Assess the validity of the warrantless search. Is this a SITA search? Is it justified by probable cause under the automobile exception? Is it a frisk? Compare California v. Carney, 471 U.S. 386 (1985); State v. Otto, 840 N.W.2d 589 (N.D. 2013) (automobile exception applied to detached camper parked with stabilizing legs extended and power cords plugged in).

2. Inventory Searches

When police officers take a person into custody, some of his personal property comes with him. When the government holds a person's property, it must use ordinary care to maintain the property; the department therefore may need to keep records of the property. This process of examining and storing personal property can often produce evidence of a crime.

■ PEOPLE v. CURTIS GIPSON

786 N.E.2d 540 (Ill. 2003)

THOMAS, J.

At issue are two questions concerning inventory searches: (1) whether a police officer's unrebutted testimony about police policy on inventory searches can be sufficient evidence of such a policy if the State does not introduce a written policy into evidence; and (2) whether a policy requiring the police to inventory items of value is sufficient to allow the opening of closed containers if the policy does not specifically mention closed containers.

BACKGROUND

. . . Defendant moved to quash his arrest and to suppress the evidence that was found during a search of his car. At the hearing on the motion to suppress, [the] State presented the testimony of Sergeant David Byrd of the Illinois State Police. Byrd testified that he initially began following defendant's car because it had a cracked windshield. A "registration response" on defendant's license plate revealed that the owner's name was Curtis Gipson and that Gipson's driver's license had been revoked. Byrd pulled over defendant and informed him that the reason for the stop was that the car had a defective windshield and that the car's owner had a revoked license. When defendant confirmed that he was Curtis Gipson, Byrd placed defendant in the back of his squad car.

Once defendant was in the car, Byrd called a tow truck and conducted an inventory search of defendant's vehicle. Byrd explained that the State Police policy is to tow the vehicle when someone is arrested for driving on a revoked license. When a vehicle is towed following an arrest, the police policy is that a tow inventory search should be conducted. When asked to explain the police policy on tow inventory searches, Byrd responded: "We are required to check the passenger compartment and trunk area for any valuables, or just for our own—we don't want anything to leave us that might be of value without checking it first and putting it down on the tow sheet."

When Byrd opened the trunk, he found a yellow Ameritech bag. He opened the bag and noticed two smaller bags inside. He opened these and observed what appeared to be crack cocaine. Byrd testified that he never told defendant that he would be free to go at some point. Rather, defendant was arrested and taken into custody. Byrd gave defendant a ticket for having a cracked windshield and driving on a revoked license.

Following arguments by the attorneys, the trial judge recalled Sergeant Byrd to the stand. The following colloquy ensued:

> *The Court:* You are still under oath, sergeant. Is there a printed procedure regarding towing by the Illinois State police?
> *The Witness:* Yes, there is, your Honor. It's in our policy manual.
> *The Court:* It's in the policy manual?

The Witness: Right, and we teach it to all our cadets when they come out on the road.

The Court: Is it a manual that you might have handy?

The Witness: No, it's a—

The Court: Big?

The Witness: Six hundred pages.

The Court: But it is printed in the police procedure?

The Witness: It is printed, tow searches and vehicles being towed and if I may, the reason we do that is because even if somebody is revoked and if they just said, okay, okay, you are going to write the ticket—

Mr. Draper [defendant's attorney]: Objection, judge.

The Court: Okay, all right.

. . . Two months later, the court granted defendant's motion to suppress. The trial judge stated that the police had no right to tow the car and that State Police policy could not supersede the law. [Moreover, the judge said] that he was not sure what the State Police policy was because he had never seen it and the officer might have just given his own interpretation. The trial judge then stated that the police could not use a minor traffic ticket to create a basis for a search and that defendant had only been stopped for "a little, minor thing like a cracked windshield." . . .

ANALYSIS

. . . The State first argues . . . that there is no constitutional requirement that the State produce the actual written policy. We agree with the State.

An inventory search of a lawfully impounded vehicle is a judicially created exception to the warrant requirement of the fourth amendment. In South Dakota v. Opperman, 428 U.S. 364 (1976), the Supreme Court identified three objectives that are served by allowing inventory searches: (1) protection of the owner's property; (2) protection of the police against claims of lost or stolen property; and (3) protection of the police from potential danger.

In conducting such a search, the police must be acting pursuant to standard police procedures. Colorado v. Bertine, 479 U.S. 367 (1987). A single familiar standard is essential to guide police officers, who have only limited time and expertise to reflect on and balance the social and individual interests involved in the specific circumstances they confront. However, as Professor LaFave has noted, the courts have generally not read *Bertine* as requiring that these procedures be in writing. 3 W. LaFave, Search & Seizure §7.4(a), at 550 (3d ed. 1996). Rather, a police officer's testimony that he was following standard procedure is generally deemed to be sufficient. . . . Although it may be easier for the State to show that it was acting in accordance with standard procedures if it can produce a written policy, the Supreme Court has not required, as a matter of constitutional law, that such policies be reduced to writing.

The precise issue we face here is somewhat different. Here, the issue is whether, if the police do have a written policy on inventory searches, the policy itself has to be admitted into evidence, or if an officer's testimony describing the standard procedure can be sufficient. . . . Defendant argues that Officer Byrd's testimony was insufficient.

[We] disagree with defendant's assertion that the State did not meet its burden in this case. The defendant bears the burden of proof at a hearing on a motion to suppress. A defendant must make a prima facie case that the evidence was obtained by an illegal search or seizure. If a defendant makes a prima facie case, the State has the burden of going forward with evidence to counter the defendant's prima facie case. However, the ultimate burden of proof remains with the defendant.

Here, defendant made his prima facie case by showing that Sergeant Byrd searched the trunk of defendant's car without a warrant. The State, however, met its burden of going forward with the evidence by establishing that Sergeant Byrd searched defendant's trunk as part of a routine tow inventory search. Sergeant Byrd gave clear, unrebutted testimony of the standard procedures for inventory searches that he was following. Sergeant Byrd testified that it was department policy to tow the vehicle whenever a person is arrested for driving on a revoked license. Before the vehicle is towed, the arresting officer is supposed to do an inventory search of the vehicle and to record anything of value on the tow inventory sheet. The officer is supposed to check the passenger compartment and trunk area for valuables.

Defendant never attempted to challenge this testimony. His attorney did not ask a single question of Sergeant Byrd about the policy and presented no rebuttal testimony on the issue. The attorney did absolutely nothing to cast doubt on Sergeant Byrd's testimony. . . . The trial court, not the defense attorney, asked further questions about the policy. But the trial court seemed satisfied with Sergeant Byrd's answer. . . .

The court later ruled that it did not know what the police policy was because it had not seen the policy. This was error. Sergeant Byrd explained the police policy and defendant did not cross-examine him on the issue or offer any rebuttal to the testimony. The State met its burden of going forward with evidence to rebut the defendant's prima facie case. . . . Of course, it would be the better practice for the State to produce the written policy. If it does not, the State leaves itself open to the possibility that the defense will be able to cast doubt on the officer's testimony either through cross-examination or rebuttal testimony. Here, defense counsel did not attempt to do so.

[The defendant also contends] that Sergeant Byrd was not entitled to open the plastic bags because the State failed to produce any evidence that the inventory search policy allowed the opening of closed containers. In Florida v. Wells, 495 U.S. 1 (1990), the United States Supreme Court upheld the suppression of marijuana found in the trunk of a car during an inventory search. The marijuana was in a locked suitcase in the trunk, and the police forced open the suitcase as part of the inventory search. The record contained no evidence of a police policy on the opening of closed containers during inventory searches. The Supreme Court held that it would be permissible for the police policy to mandate the opening of all containers or no containers, or to allow the police the discretion to decide which containers should be opened, based on the nature of the search and the characteristics of the container. However, because there was no evidence of any policy with respect to closed containers in that case, the Supreme Court held that the search was not sufficiently regulated to satisfy the fourth amendment.

In People v. Hundley, 619 N.E.2d 744 (Ill. 1993), this court held that the general order of the State Police was sufficient to allow the opening of closed containers during an inventory search. The policy introduced into evidence in *Hundley* . . . did not use the words "closed containers." Rather, it required the police to inventory the contents of towed vehicles and to look wherever the owner or operator would ordinarily place or stow property. The officer testified in *Hundley* that he opened a cigarette case because, in his experience, women often put their drivers' licenses and money in such cases. This court held that the general order of the State Police was "adequate to the situation."

Hundley is controlling on this issue. Although defendant is correct that Sergeant Byrd did not specifically mention a closed container policy, he did testify that the policy required the police to check the passenger compartment and the trunk for valuables and to list any valuables on the tow inventory sheet. Obviously, such a policy requires the police to open any containers that might contain valuables. The policy that Sergeant Byrd testified to was more specific than the one at issue in *Hundley*. The *Hundley* policy merely referred to an inventory of the contents of the vehicle. Here, Sergeant Byrd specifically testified that he was supposed to search the trunk and passenger area for "valuables" and to inventory anything of value on the tow sheet. We believe this policy was sufficient to allow Sergeant Byrd to open the plastic bags in the trunk of defendant's car. . . .

Notes

1. *Inventory searches: majority position.* Inventory searches serve "administrative caretaking functions" of protecting against property damage claims and protecting police from dangerous items rather than enforcing criminal law. As a result, the Supreme Court has held that the federal constitution allows a routine (and warrantless) inventory search of impounded automobiles or other personal property without probable cause or individualized suspicion. South Dakota v. Opperman, 428 U.S. 364 (1976). The government must satisfy three requirements for a valid warrantless inventory search of a vehicle: (1) the original impoundment of the vehicle must be lawful; (2) the purpose of the inventory search must be to protect the owner's property or to protect the police from claims of lost, stolen, or vandalized property and to guard the police from danger; and (3) the inventory search must be conducted in good faith pursuant to reasonable standardized police procedures and not as a pretext for an investigatory search. The Supreme Court, in cases such as Colorado v. Bertine, 479 U.S. 367 (1987), has insisted that the inventory search occur under the guidance of "standardized" regulations. According to Florida v. Wells, 495 U.S. 1 (1990), the rules must address the proper treatment of containers found in a car, although those rules may leave some discretion to the officer conducting the inventory to open some containers and to leave others unopened. Most state courts also allow the police to conduct inventory searches without any special justification, so long as the inventory proceeds according to standard rules. The recurring issues in litigation deal with the specificity of the inventory rules and the amount of discretion those rules leave to the police officer in deciding whether to impound a vehicle and whether to open containers.

The issue is not as straightforward as it sounds. Consider this policy of the Illinois State Police, mentioned in the *Gipson* case:

> An examination and inventory of the contents of all vehicles/boats towed or held by authority of Division personnel shall be made by the officer who completes the Tow-In Recovery Report. This examination and inventory shall be restricted to those

areas where an owner or operator would ordinarily place or store property or equipment in the vehicle/boat; and would normally include front and rear seat areas, glove compartment, map case, sun visors, and trunk and engine compartments.

Different officers, with different levels of experience, might have very different ideas about where owners "ordinarily" place property. What property do owners normally store in the engine compartment? Do police departments need inventory rules at all? Would consensual inventory searches (and routine requests for that consent) address the problems of safeguarding property in vehicles?

2. *The impoundment decision.* Some jurisdictions address the inventory process at the first possible point and impose various limits on the initial decision whether to impound a vehicle or to leave it at the scene. See Fair v. State, 627 N.E.2d 427 (Ind. 1993) (prosecution must demonstrate (1) that the belief that the vehicle posed some threat or harm to the community or was itself imperiled was consistent with objective standards of sound policing, and (2) that the decision to combat that threat by impoundment was in keeping with established departmental routine or regulation); Commonwealth v. Lagenella, 83 A.3d 94 (Pa. 2013) (interpreting state statute to allow law enforcement officer to "immobilize" vehicle of arrestee; inventory search may only take place later, at "impoundment," after arrestee fails to obtain release of vehicle within 24 hours). Others, such as the Colorado rules reviewed in *Bertine*, leave some discretion to the individual officer to act within guidelines in deciding whether to impound a car in the first place.

3. *Least intrusive means and investigatory intent.* Defendants often argue that their vehicle was impounded, or the contents inventoried, despite less intrusive means to achieve the stated goals of inventory searches, such as leaving the car where it sits, leaving it with another person, or getting the defendant to sign liability waivers (thus removing the interest in protecting officers against a lawsuit for harm to the personal property). Only a handful of jurisdictions (fewer than a half dozen) recognize such claims when it comes to closed containers; similarly, a few require police to give an arrestee a reasonable chance to provide for alternative custody of a vehicle before it is impounded. See, e.g., State v. Perham, 814 P.2d 914 (Haw. 1991) (closed containers). Most courts focus only on whether the administrative rules were followed and whether those rules provide adequate guidance. Isn't a "least intrusive means" test one way to guarantee that officers do not use inventory searches to investigate crimes? Are less intrusive methods easier to see in hindsight than at the moment of decision? The Supreme Court has rejected the argument that the "least intrusive means" is a requirement of the federal constitution. Illinois v. Lafayette, 462 U.S. 640 (1983).

In Colorado v. Bertine, the Supreme Court said that inventory searches could be challenged if they were conducted "in bad faith or for the sole purpose of investigation." Is examination of "bad faith" consistent with the general rejection of "pretext" claims? See Chapter 2. Most state courts discussing inventory searches require that the officer conducting the inventory show "good faith" and prohibit use of the inventory as a "pretext" for a search for incriminating evidence. See State v. West, 862 P.2d 192 (Ariz. 1993). How will this "bad faith" come to light? What if an officer admits to "dual" purposes for an inventory search? See State v. Hauseman, 900 P.2d 74 (Colo. 1995).

4. *Inventory searches of personal belongings during booking.* Inventory searches apply to personal items carried by a person who is arrested and placed in detention; these

are the booking searches we discussed earlier in this chapter. What arguments can you make that the justification for inventory searches is stronger for inventory of personal belongings than for cars? What arguments can you make that the privacy interest of the individual is stronger for personal belongings, especially those held in pockets, outside of public view (such as the content of wallets or purses)? Most states impose fewer restrictions on inventory searches of personal belongings than on inventory searches of cars. See Oles v. State, 993 S.W.2d 103 (Tex. Crim. App. 1999) (police did not need probable cause or warrant to take a second look at clothing that had been seized from a defendant a week earlier as part of inventory of his belongings after his arrest). Should similar rules apply to the personal property of civil detainees, such as those who are extremely intoxicated or who suffer from mental illness? See State v. Carper, 876 P.2d 582 (Colo. 1994).

5. *Procedures whose validity turns on the adequacy of executive rules.* There are several types of searches, like inventory searches, in which courts have approved of procedures only when there is a regularized process for police to follow. Consider, for example, the legitimacy of sobriety checkpoints, where the U.S. Supreme Court and state courts have approved only of checkpoints governed by detailed rules. See Chapter 2; Wayne LaFave, Controlling Discretion by Administrative Regulations: The Use, Misuse, and Nonuse of Police Rules and Policies in Fourth Amendment Adjudication, 89 Mich. L. Rev. 442 (1990). Who should issue inventory rules? Should they be determined by statute? If you were the general counsel to a police department, and police officers complain about the length and complexity of the inventory forms and process, how might you address that concern?

Problem 4-11. The Other Gun

Winston-Salem police officers were dispatched to 1412 West Academy Street in response to a 911 call placed by Sala Hall. Hall reported that a black male, who was driving a red Ford Escape, was parked in his driveway. The man was armed with a black handgun and wearing a yellow shirt. Hall added that the same man had "shot up" his house the previous night.

Officers Walley and Horsley arrived at the scene within six minutes of the 911 call. They saw a black male (later identified as Omar Mbacke), who was wearing a yellow shirt, backing a red Ford Escape out of the driveway at the reported address. The officers parked behind him, got out of their patrol cars, drew their weapons, and moved toward Mbacke while ordering him to put his hands in the air.

At first, Mbacke rested his hands on his steering wheel, but then lowered his hands toward his waist. The officers shouted louder commands to Mbacke to keep his hands in sight and to exit his vehicle. Mbacke raised his hands and stepped out of his car, kicking the driver's door shut behind him as he stepped away from the car. The officers ordered Mbacke to lie on the ground and then handcuffed him. The officers asked if he was armed, and Mbacke told them that he had a gun in his waistband. Officer Walley lifted defendant's shirt and saw a black handgun. After the officers retrieved the pistol and rendered it safe, they arrested Mbacke for the offense of carrying a concealed gun without a license.

The officers placed the handcuffed Mbacke in the locked back seat of a patrol car, then returned to the Escape and opened the front door on the driver's side. Officer Horsley immediately saw a white brick wrapped in green plastic protruding from beneath the driver's seat. As Officer Horsley was showing Officer Walley what he had found, Mbacke slipped one hand out of his handcuffs, reached through the partially opened window of the police car, and tried to open the vehicle door by using the exterior handle. After re-securing Mbacke, the officers searched the entirety of his car but found no other contraband. A field test of powdery material from the white brick was positive for cocaine.

The car was later towed to the impound lot at the police station. An officer in the lot went through the interior of the car to check for personal belongings. Between the back seat cushions he found a wad of cash totaling $387.

Mbacke filed a motion to suppress the evidence obtained from his car. Assess the prosecution's ability to justify this search under the six theories available: warrant, consent, SITA, probable cause, frisk, and inventory. Pay particular attention to which evidence (the handgun, the white brick, and the cash) would be admissible under which theory. Cf. State v. Mbacke, 721 S.E.2d 218 (N.C. 2012).

3. Containers, In and Out of Cars

Recall that the government may search an automobile based on probable cause, without obtaining a warrant, under the *Carroll-Chambers* "automobile exception" to the warrant requirement. See Carroll v. United States, 267 U.S. 132 (1925); Chambers v. Maroney, 399 U.S. 42 (1970). At the same time, the ordinary warrant requirement applies to police searches of closed containers such as suitcases. The government either must obtain a warrant prior to the search or must invoke a pertinent exception to the warrant requirement. What happens, then, when the police encounter a container (warrant required) inside a car (no warrant required)?

■ CALIFORNIA v. CHARLES ACEVEDO
500 U.S. 565 (1991)

BLACKMUN, J.*
This case requires us once again to consider the so-called "automobile exception" to the warrant requirement of the Fourth Amendment and its application to the search of a closed container in the trunk of a car.

I.

On October 28, 1987, Officer Coleman of the Santa Ana Police Department received a telephone call from a federal drug enforcement agent in Hawaii. The agent informed Coleman that he had seized a package containing marijuana which was to have been delivered to the Federal Express Office in Santa Ana and which was addressed to J. R. Daza at 805 West Stevens Avenue in that city. The agent arranged to send the package to Coleman instead. Coleman then was to take the package to the Federal Express office and arrest the person who arrived to claim it.

---

* [Chief Justice Rehnquist and Justices O'Connor, Kennedy, and Souter joined in this opinion.—EDS.]

Coleman received the package on October 29, verified its contents, and took it to the Senior Operations Manager at the Federal Express office. At about 10:30 A.M. on October 30, a man, who identified himself as Jamie Daza, arrived to claim the package. He accepted it and drove to his apartment on West Stevens. He carried the package into the apartment.

At 11:45 A.M., officers observed Daza leave the apartment and drop the box and paper that had contained the marijuana into a trash bin. Coleman at that point left the scene to get a search warrant. About 12:05 P.M., the officers saw Richard St. George leave the apartment carrying a blue knapsack which appeared to be half full. The officers stopped him as he was driving off, searched the knapsack, and found one and a half pounds of marijuana.

At 12:30 P.M., respondent Charles Steven Acevedo arrived. He entered Daza's apartment, stayed for about 10 minutes, and reappeared carrying a brown paper bag that looked full. The officers noticed that the bag was the size of one of the wrapped marijuana packages sent from Hawaii. Acevedo walked to a silver Honda in the parking lot. He placed the bag in the trunk of the car and started to drive away. Fearing the loss of evidence, officers in a marked police car stopped him. They opened the trunk and the bag, and found marijuana.

Respondent was charged in state court with possession of marijuana for sale. . . . He moved to suppress the marijuana found in the car. The motion was denied. He then pleaded guilty but appealed the denial of the suppression motion. We granted certiorari to reexamine the law applicable to a closed container in an automobile, a subject that has troubled courts and law enforcement officers since it was first considered in United States v. Chadwick, 433 U.S. 1 (1977). . . .

II.

. . . In Carroll v. United States, 267 U.S. 132 (1925), this Court established an exception to the warrant requirement for moving vehicles, for it recognized "a necessary difference between a search of a store, dwelling house or other structure in respect of which a proper official warrant readily may be obtained, and a search of a ship, motor boat, wagon or automobile, for contraband goods, where it is not practicable to secure a warrant because the vehicle can be quickly moved out of the locality or jurisdiction in which the warrant must be sought." It therefore held that a warrantless search of an automobile, based upon probable cause to believe that the vehicle contained evidence of crime in the light of an exigency arising out of the likely disappearance of the vehicle, did not contravene the Warrant Clause of the Fourth Amendment. . . .

In United States v. Ross, 456 U.S. 798 (1982), we held that a warrantless search of an automobile under the *Carroll* doctrine could include a search of a container or package found inside the car when such a search was supported by probable cause. The warrantless search of Ross' car occurred after an informant told the police that he had seen Ross complete a drug transaction using drugs stored in the trunk of his car. The police stopped the car, searched it, and discovered in the trunk a brown paper bag containing drugs. We decided that the search of Ross' car was not unreasonable under the Fourth Amendment. [If] probable cause justifies the search of a lawfully stopped vehicle, it justifies the search of every part of the vehicle and its contents that may conceal the object of the search. . . .

Ross distinguished the *Carroll* doctrine from the separate rule that governed the search of closed containers. The Court had announced this separate rule, unique to luggage and other closed packages, bags, and containers, in United States v. Chadwick, 433 U.S. 1 (1977). In *Chadwick*, federal narcotics agents had probable cause to believe that a 200-pound double-locked footlocker contained marijuana. The agents tracked the locker as the defendants removed it from a train and carried it through the station to a waiting car. As soon as the defendants lifted the locker into the trunk of the car, the agents arrested them, seized the locker, and searched it. In this Court, the United States did not contend that the locker's brief contact with the automobile's trunk sufficed to make the *Carroll* doctrine applicable. Rather, the United States urged that the search of movable luggage could be considered analogous to the search of an automobile. The Court rejected this argument because, it reasoned, a person expects more privacy in his luggage and personal effects than he does in his automobile. Moreover, it concluded that as "may often not be the case when automobiles are seized," secure storage facilities are usually available when the police seize luggage.

In Arkansas v. Sanders, 442 U.S. 753 (1979), the Court extended *Chadwick's* rule to apply to a suitcase actually being transported in the trunk of a car. In *Sanders*, the police had probable cause to believe a suitcase contained marijuana. They watched as the defendant placed the suitcase in the trunk of a taxi and was driven away. The police pursued the taxi for several blocks, stopped it, found the suitcase in the trunk, and searched it. Although the Court had applied the *Carroll* doctrine to searches of integral parts of the automobile itself (indeed, in *Carroll*, contraband whiskey was in the upholstery of the seats), it did not extend the doctrine to the warrantless search of personal luggage "merely because it was located in an automobile lawfully stopped by the police." Again, the *Sanders* majority stressed the heightened privacy expectation in personal luggage and concluded that the presence of luggage in an automobile did not diminish the owner's expectation of privacy in his personal items. . . .

The facts in this case closely resemble the facts in *Ross*. In *Ross*, the police had probable cause to believe that drugs were stored in the trunk of a particular car. Here, the [California courts] concluded that the police had probable cause to believe that respondent was carrying marijuana in a bag in his car's trunk. Furthermore, for what it is worth, in *Ross*, as here, the drugs in the trunk were contained in a brown paper bag. . . . We now must decide the question deferred in *Ross*: whether the Fourth Amendment requires the police to obtain a warrant to open the sack in a movable vehicle simply because they lack probable cause to search the entire car. We conclude that it does not.

IV.

[A] container found after a general search of the automobile and a container found in a car after a limited search for the container are equally easy for the police to store and for the suspect to hide or destroy. In fact, we see no principled distinction in terms of either the privacy expectation or the exigent circumstances between the paper bag found by the police in *Ross* and the paper bag found by the police here. Furthermore, by attempting to distinguish between a container for which the police are specifically searching and a container which they come across in a car, we have provided only minimal protection for privacy and have impeded effective law enforcement.

The line between probable cause to search a vehicle and probable cause to search a package in that vehicle is not always clear, and separate rules that govern the two objects to be searched may enable the police to broaden their power to make warrantless searches and disserve privacy interests. . . . At the moment when officers stop an automobile, it may be less than clear whether they suspect with a high degree of certainty that the vehicle contains drugs in a bag or simply contains drugs. If the police know that they may open a bag only if they are actually searching the entire car, they may search more extensively than they otherwise would in order to establish the general probable cause required by *Ross*. . . . We cannot see the benefit of a rule that requires law enforcement officers to conduct a more intrusive search in order to justify a less intrusive one. . . .

Finally, the search of a paper bag intrudes far less on individual privacy than does the incursion sanctioned long ago in *Carroll*. In that case, prohibition agents slashed the upholstery of the automobile. This Court nonetheless found their search to be reasonable under the Fourth Amendment. If destroying the interior of an automobile is not unreasonable, we cannot conclude that looking inside a closed container is. In light of the minimal protection to privacy afforded by the *Chadwick-Sanders* rule, and our serious doubt whether that rule substantially serves privacy interests, we now hold that the Fourth Amendment does not compel separate treatment for an automobile search that extends only to a container within the vehicle.

V.

. . . The discrepancy between the two rules has led to confusion for law enforcement officers. For example, when an officer, who has developed probable cause to believe that a vehicle contains drugs, begins to search the vehicle and immediately discovers a closed container, which rule applies? The defendant will argue that the fact that the officer first chose to search the container indicates that his probable cause extended only to the container and that *Chadwick* and *Sanders* therefore require a warrant. On the other hand, the fact that the officer first chose to search in the most obvious location should not restrict the propriety of the search. The *Chadwick* rule, as applied in *Sanders*, has devolved into an anomaly such that the more likely the police are to discover drugs in a container, the less authority they have to search it. . . .

VI.

The interpretation of the *Carroll* doctrine set forth in *Ross* now applies to all searches of containers found in an automobile. In other words, the police may search without a warrant if their search is supported by probable cause. [However, probable] cause to believe that a container placed in the trunk of a [vehicle] contains contraband or evidence does not justify a search of the entire [vehicle]. In the case before us, the police had probable cause to believe that the paper bag in the automobile's trunk contained marijuana. That probable cause now allows a warrantless search of the paper bag. The facts in the record reveal that the police did not have probable cause to believe that contraband was hidden in any other part of the automobile and a search of the entire vehicle would have been without probable cause and unreasonable under the Fourth Amendment. . . .

Until today, this Court has drawn a curious line between the search of an automobile that coincidentally turns up a container and the search of a container that coincidentally turns up in an automobile. The protections of the Fourth Amendment must not turn on such coincidences. We therefore interpret *Carroll* as providing one rule to govern all automobile searches. . . .

SCALIA, J., concurring in the judgment.

I agree with the dissent that it is anomalous for a briefcase to be protected by the "general requirement" of a prior warrant when it is being carried along the street, but for that same briefcase to become unprotected as soon as it is carried into an automobile. On the other hand, I agree with the Court that it would be anomalous for a locked compartment in an automobile to be unprotected by the "general requirement" of a prior warrant, but for an unlocked briefcase within the automobile to be protected. I join in the judgment of the Court because I think its holding is more faithful to the text and tradition of the Fourth Amendment, and if these anomalies in our jurisprudence are ever to be eliminated that is the direction in which we should travel.

The Fourth Amendment does not by its terms require a prior warrant for searches and seizures; it merely prohibits searches and seizures that are "unreasonable." What it explicitly states regarding warrants is by way of limitation upon their issuance rather than requirement of their use. For the warrant was a means of insulating officials from personal liability assessed by colonial juries. An officer who searched or seized without a warrant did so at his own risk; he would be liable for trespass, including exemplary damages, unless the jury found that his action was "reasonable." If, however, the officer acted pursuant to a proper warrant, he would be absolutely immune. See Bell v. Clapp, 10 Johns. 263 (N.Y. 1813). By restricting the issuance of warrants, the Framers endeavored to preserve the jury's role in regulating searches and seizures. . . .

Even before today's decision, the "warrant requirement" had become so riddled with exceptions that it was basically unrecognizable. . . . Our intricate body of law regarding "reasonable expectation of privacy" has been developed largely as a means of creating these exceptions, enabling a search to be denominated not a Fourth Amendment "search" and therefore not subject to the general warrant requirement. . . . In my view, the path out of this confusion should be sought by returning to the first principle that the "reasonableness" requirement of the Fourth Amendment affords the protection that the common law afforded. . . .

STEVENS, J., dissenting.*

. . . The Fourth Amendment is a restraint on Executive power. The Amendment constitutes the Framers' direct constitutional response to the unreasonable law enforcement practices employed by agents of the British Crown. . . . This history is, however, only part of the explanation for the warrant requirement. The requirement also reflects the sound policy judgment that, absent exceptional circumstances, the decision to invade the privacy of an individual's personal effects should be made by a neutral magistrate rather than an agent of the Executive.

[In United States v. Chadwick, we] concluded that neither of the justifications for the automobile exception could support a similar exception for luggage. We first held that the privacy interest in luggage is substantially greater than in an automobile. Unlike automobiles and their contents, we reasoned, luggage contents are not open to public view, except as a condition to a border entry or common carrier travel; nor is luggage subject to regular inspections and official scrutiny on a continuing basis. Indeed, luggage is specifically intended to safeguard the privacy

_____

* [Justice Marshall joined this opinion.—EDS.]

of personal effects, unlike an automobile, whose primary function is transportation. We then held that the mobility of luggage did not justify creating an additional exception to the Warrant Clause. Unlike an automobile, luggage can easily be seized and detained pending judicial approval of a search. . . .

In its opinion today, the Court recognizes that the police did not have probable cause to search respondent's vehicle and that a search of anything but the paper bag that respondent had carried from Daza's apartment and placed in the trunk of his car would have been unconstitutional. Moreover, as I read the opinion, the Court assumes that the police could not have made a warrantless inspection of the bag before it was placed in the car. Finally, the Court also does not question the fact that, under our prior cases, it would have been lawful for the police to seize the container and detain it (and respondent) until they obtained a search warrant. Thus, all of the relevant facts that governed our decisions in *Chadwick* and *Sanders* are present here whereas the relevant fact that justified the vehicle search in *Ross* is not present.

The Court does not attempt to identify any exigent circumstances that would justify its refusal to apply the general rule against warrantless searches. Instead, it advances these three arguments: First, the rules identified in the foregoing cases are confusing and anomalous. Second, the rules do not protect any significant interest in privacy. And, third, the rules impede effective law enforcement. None of these arguments withstands scrutiny. . . .

THE PRIVACY ARGUMENT

. . . To support its argument that today's holding works only a minimal intrusion on privacy, the Court suggests that if the police "know that they may open a bag only if they are actually searching the entire car, they may search more extensively than they otherwise would in order to establish the general probable cause required by *Ross*." [This] fear is unexplained and inexplicable. Neither evidence uncovered in the course of a search nor the scope of the search conducted can be used to provide post hoc justification for a search unsupported by probable cause at its inception. . . .

THE BURDEN ON LAW ENFORCEMENT

The Court's suggestion that *Chadwick* and *Sanders* have created a significant burden on effective law enforcement is unsupported, inaccurate, and, in any event, an insufficient reason for creating a new exception to the warrant requirement. Despite repeated claims that *Chadwick* and *Sanders* have "impeded effective law enforcement," [in] the years since *Ross* was decided, the Court has heard argument in 30 Fourth Amendment cases involving narcotics. . . . And, in all except three, the Court upheld the constitutionality of the search or seizure.

In the meantime, the flow of narcotics cases through the courts has steadily and dramatically increased. No impartial observer could criticize this Court for hindering the progress of the war on drugs. On the contrary, decisions like the one the Court makes today will support the conclusion that this Court has become a loyal foot soldier in the Executive's fight against crime.

Even if the warrant requirement does inconvenience the police to some extent, that fact does not distinguish this constitutional requirement from any other procedural protection secured by the Bill of Rights. It is merely a part of the price that our society must pay in order to preserve its freedom. . . . I respectfully dissent.

Notes

1. *Searches of containers in cars: majority position.* In California v. Acevedo, an officer with probable cause to believe a container holds an item subject to seizure can do the following, when that container is placed in a car: stop the car, open the car, seize the container, and search the container—all without a warrant. In so holding, the Supreme Court extended the container rule it had adopted in United States v. Ross to a new situation. (Recall that *Ross* allowed warrantless searches of containers within automobiles so long as the police have probable cause to believe that the car contains an item subject to seizure, and the container is capable of concealing that item.) Very few state courts have rejected the Court's holding in *Acevedo* as they have interpreted their state constitutions. But see State v. Savva, 616 A.2d 774 (Vt. 1991). Even in the handful of courts that do require exigent circumstances for containers in cars, the rule applies only to containers in the trunk or in other areas not covered by a search incident to arrest.

The Court made it clear in Wyoming v. Houghton, 526 U.S. 295 (1999), that the *Ross* rule applied to any containers in the car, whether owned by passengers or the driver. Police officers with probable cause to search a car may inspect belongings inside the car if they are capable of concealing the object of the search; officers need not determine ownership of those belongings before the search, and ownership doesn't matter. Any container, when placed in a car, is subject to the car's reduced expectation of privacy. Would requiring a warrant in this setting encourage drivers to hide contraband in containers belonging to passengers?

2. *Containers (effects) not in cars.* The decision in the federal courts to apply the automobile exception to containers in cars creates an inconsistency between the status of the containers inside and outside a car. For containers outside of cars, the default rule about warrants applies; for a container that is out in public and not in the wingspan of an arrestee, police need probable cause to seize that container and a warrant to search it. (This is what remains of *Chadwick.*) In jurisdictions that follow the federal rule, a container becomes subject to warrantless search as soon as it is placed in a car, assuming the officers have probable cause to search either the car or the container. Will this wrinkle in the law change a police officer's strategy for the timing of an arrest of a suspect holding a container?

3. *Warrants reconsidered: What is the exception and what is the rule?* After studying the automobile exception, searches of cars incident to arrest, and inventory searches, look again at the following oft-repeated statement, quoted here from United States v. Ross, 456 U.S. 798 (1982): "The Fourth Amendment proscribes all unreasonable searches and seizures, and it is a cardinal principle that searches conducted outside the judicial process, without prior approval by judge or magistrate, are per se unreasonable under the Fourth Amendment—subject only to a few specifically established and well-delineated exceptions." Consider also Justice Scalia's observation in *Acevedo*, that the warrant requirement has become "so riddled with exceptions" that it is "basically unrecognizable." Is this a problem courts and legislatures should care about, or have they developed acceptable replacements for a strong warrant requirement? See Joseph Grano, Rethinking the Fourth Amendment Warrant Requirement, 19 Am. Crim. L. Rev. 603 (1982); Tracey Maclin, The Central Meaning of the Fourth Amendment, 35 Wm. & Mary L. Rev. 197 (1993).

V

![black square]

Arrests

Every year, police in the United States make about 15 million arrests. Arrests are a serious intrusion on liberty, and our legal systems place several types of controls on them. The constraints come from constitutions, statutes, police department rules, the common law of torts, and elsewhere. Despite these multiple limits, police officers in the field still make the most important decisions about arrests.

This chapter surveys the legal rules and institutions that limit the arrest power and studies the operation of that power within (and sometimes outside) those legal boundaries. Section A considers the distinction between arrests and the lesser restraints on liberty known as "stops." Section B identifies the limited situations in which a warrant is necessary to complete a valid arrest. Section C focuses on legal rules dealing with the police officer's decision *not* to make an arrest in certain settings. Section D continues with the theme of police discretion in the arrest decision, looking to the use of the citation power as an alternative to arrests. And finally, section E introduces the limits on the officer's use of force in carrying out an arrest.

A. STOP OR ARREST?

Police often find it necessary to restrain an individual from moving away from a particular place. They might do so to protect themselves or others from harm. They might do so to investigate a completed crime or to prevent an ongoing or future one. As we saw in Chapter 2, not all of these restraints are equally intrusive, and the different levels of restraint are subject to different legal controls. Some are consensual encounters, some are stops, and some are arrests. How do legal systems distinguish the different types of police efforts to control the movement of citizens? Answers to this question appear in statutes, in cases, and in the interaction between the two.

■ NEVADA REVISED STATUTES §171.123

1. Any peace officer may detain any person whom the officer encounters under circumstances which reasonably indicate that the person has committed, is committing or is about to commit a crime. . . .

4. A person must not be detained longer than is reasonably necessary to effect the purposes of this section, and in no event longer than 60 minutes. The detention must not extend beyond the place or the immediate vicinity of the place where the detention was first effected, unless the person is arrested.

■ ARKANSAS RULE OF CRIMINAL PROCEDURE 3.1

A law enforcement officer lawfully present in any place may, in the performance of his duties, stop and detain any person who he reasonably suspects is committing, has committed, or is about to commit (1) a felony, or (2) a misdemeanor involving danger of forcible injury to persons or of appropriation of or damage to property, if such action is reasonably necessary either to obtain or verify the identification of the person or to determine the lawfulness of his conduct. An officer acting under this rule may require the person to remain in or near such place in the officer's presence for a period of not more than 15 minutes or for such time as is reasonable under the circumstances. At the end of such period the person detained shall be released without further restraint, or arrested and charged with an offense.

■ ROBERT BAILEY v. STATE
987 A.2d 72 (Md. 2010)

Greene, J.

In this case, we are asked to determine whether the search and seizure of the petitioner, Robert Bailey, violated the Fourth Amendment to the United States Constitution and the Maryland Declaration of Rights. . . .

On the night of August 16, 2006, Officer Rodney Lewis of the Prince George's County Police Department was patrolling the 6800 block of Hawthorne Street in Landover, Maryland. The area was known for drug activity, though there were no specific complaints on the night in question. At approximately 11:35 P.M., while patrolling on foot, Officer Lewis spotted the petitioner, Robert Bailey, standing alone on the side of 6890 Hawthorne Street. Officer Lewis testified about the encounter at the suppression hearing:

> I observed the defendant standing on the side of a home, . . . just standing in the shadows, at which time I yelled out to him, "Excuse me, sir, do you live there?" I didn't get any acknowledgment from the individual, at which time I assumed that he probably didn't hear me. I repeated the same thing, "Excuse me, sir, do you live there," which again I received no acknowledgment from the suspect, at which time myself, along with another officer, walked over to the individual. At that time, I just happened to step out of the shallow [sic] area on the sidewalk where I could visibly see his hands. And from the area at which he was standing at the time, I could smell a strong odor of ether.

When Officer Lewis smelled the odor of ether, he was within a few feet of the petitioner, close enough to "reach out and touch him." The odor was emanating from the petitioner's "body odor." The odor of ether, according to Officer Lewis's testimony, is associated with phencyclidine, more commonly known as PCP. Officer Lewis acknowledged on cross-examination that it is not illegal to possess ether and that ether is a solvent that is used in several household products. Upon smelling the odor of ether, Officer Lewis "reached over and grabbed both of [the petitioner's] hands and . . . had him place them over top of his head." Officer Lewis then conducted a search of the petitioner, which uncovered a glass vial, approximately three to four inches in length and one inch in diameter, half-full of liquid, in the petitioner's right front pants pocket. Field tests confirmed that the liquid contained PCP, and the petitioner was subsequently taken into custody and charged with possession of a controlled dangerous substance. . . .

In addition to observing the odor of ether, Officer Lewis noted that the petitioner had "glossy eyes" and that the petitioner failed to respond to the inquiries about whether he lived in the house. Officer Lewis did not, however, indicate whether he observed the petitioner's glossy eyes before or after he initially seized the petitioner.

The petitioner moved to suppress the physical evidence recovered from the search, asserting that the glass vial was the fruit of an illegal search and seizure under the Fourth Amendment, as well as the Maryland Declaration of Rights. Following a suppression hearing at which Officer Lewis was the sole witness, the trial court found that Officer Lewis had reasonable articulable suspicion to stop and question the petitioner based on the smell of ether, the petitioner's failure to respond to Officer Lewis's questions, and the petitioner's presence in a "high crime drug area with a number of complaints from citizens." The suppression court also determined that Officer Lewis conducted a valid pat-down of the petitioner for "officer safety" and that, based on the totality of the circumstances, the search and seizure were valid.

The petitioner proceeded to trial on an Agreed Statement of Facts. [The] Circuit Court for Prince George's County entered [a] verdict of guilty to . . . possession of a controlled dangerous substance. This Court analyzed the applicability of the Fourth Amendment to varying levels of police interaction in Swift v. State, 899 A.2d 867 (Md. 2006):

> Many courts have analyzed the applicability of the Fourth Amendment in terms of three tiers of interaction between a citizen and the police. The most intrusive encounter, an arrest, requires probable cause to believe that a person has committed or is committing a crime. The second category, the investigatory stop or detention, known commonly as a *Terry* stop, is less intrusive than a formal custodial arrest and must be supported by reasonable suspicion that a person has committed or is about to commit a crime and permits an officer to stop and briefly detain an individual. . . . The least intrusive police-citizen contact, a consensual encounter, . . . involves no restraint of liberty and elicits an individual's voluntary cooperation with non-coercive police contact. A consensual encounter need not be supported by any suspicion [because an individual in this situation] is not considered to have been "seized" within the meaning of the Fourth Amendment.

We will consider how the petitioner's encounter with Officer Lewis proceeded from consensual encounter to custodial arrest, in light of settled Fourth Amendment precedent. . . .

Consensual Encounter or Investigatory Stop

. . . Officer Lewis's initial questioning of the petitioner was not an investigative stop, but rather a "consensual encounter" or accosting. [A] consensual encounter does not implicate the Fourth Amendment because the individual with whom the police are interacting is free to leave at any time. . . .

When the police officers asked the petitioner if he lived at the house in whose shadows he was standing, the petitioner could not have reasonably believed that the police were doing anything more than making a routine inquiry. The officers' inquiry was a request for basic information, not an order. Officer Lewis "yelled" the question because of the distance between the officers and the petitioner, and the officers began to walk toward the petitioner only after he did not respond to their questions, presumably to find out why he had not. In sum, the petitioner was not seized by the officers but merely was accosted at the point at which the officers began to approach him. . . .

Seizure and Search

An encounter has been described as a fluid situation, and one which begins as a consensual encounter may lose its consensual nature and become an investigatory detention or arrest once a person's liberty has been restrained and the person would not be free to leave. Officer Lewis's testimony indicates that his encounter with the petitioner proceeded quickly from an accosting, in which he shouted questions to the petitioner from the street, to a physical detention, when he grabbed the petitioner's hands.

As the Supreme Court observed in *Terry*, 392 U.S. at 19 n. 16, when the officer, "by means of physical force or a show of authority, has in some way restrained the liberty of a citizen [we may] conclude that a 'seizure' has occurred." In determining whether a person has been seized, the crucial test is whether, taking into account all of the circumstances surrounding the encounter, the police conduct would have communicated to a reasonable person that he was not at liberty to ignore the police presence and go about his business. . . .

In the present case, it is clear that, once Officer Lewis grabbed the petitioner's hands and placed them over his head, a reasonable person in the petitioner's position would have understood that he was physically detained and thus not free to leave or go about his business. Thus, when Officer Lewis grabbed the petitioner's hands, he seized the petitioner for purposes of the Fourth Amendment.

Because the officer seized and searched the petitioner without a warrant, the seizure was presumptively invalid unless it was supported by a reasonable, articulable suspicion of a threat to officer safety or by an exception to the warrant requirement. We must consider whether this seizure of the petitioner was a temporary detention and protective frisk pursuant to *Terry* . . . or a lawful arrest of the petitioner. . . .

Terry *Frisk*

We disagree with the Circuit Court's conclusion that the search and seizure of the petitioner was an investigatory stop and protective frisk pursuant to *Terry*. The purpose of a protective *Terry* frisk is not to discover evidence, but rather to protect the police officer and bystanders from harm. Pat-down frisks are proper when the officer has reason to believe that he is dealing with an armed and dangerous individual, regardless of whether he has probable cause to arrest the individual for a crime. The officer has reason to believe that an individual is armed and dangerous if a reasonably prudent person, under the circumstances, would have felt that he was in danger, based on reasonable inferences from particularized facts in light of the officer's experience.

Even if we were to assume that the encounter with the Officer Lewis was a *Terry* stop, the reasonableness of a *Terry* stop is determined by considering whether the officer's action was justified at its inception, and whether it was reasonably related in scope to the circumstances which justified the interference in the first place. Further, assuming *arguendo* that Officer Lewis had reasonable, articulable suspicion to believe that criminal activity was afoot and, accordingly, detain the petitioner, he still lacked the basis for a protective *Terry* frisk. At the suppression hearing, Officer Lewis indicated that he searched the petitioner to "check for weapons," but did not provide any basis for his suspicion that the petitioner was armed and dangerous. Officer Lewis did not testify as to any factors that would lead to a suspicion that the petitioner was carrying a weapon. Further, there are no objective factors in the record that indicate that the petitioner was armed and dangerous. Although the encounter took place at nighttime, the petitioner was alone and the officer "could visibly see his hands," which, presumably because the officer did not indicate otherwise, were empty. There is no indication in the record that the petitioner made any threatening movements, or any movements at all, nor is there any indication that Officer Lewis suspected that the petitioner was dealing drugs. Thus, we . . . hold that Officer Lewis had no basis to conduct a protective frisk.

Even if Officer Lewis had reasonably believed that the petitioner was armed and dangerous, therefore providing the basis for a proper *Terry* frisk, the search in the present case exceeded the scope of a proper protective frisk. A proper *Terry* frisk is limited to a pat-down of the outer clothing not to discover evidence of a crime, but rather to protect the police officer and bystanders from harm by checking for weapons. . . .

In the present case, Officer Lewis testified that he patted down the petitioner's right front pocket and that he did not manipulate the object contained therein. Officer Lewis testified that he "felt and recognized a glass vial" in the petitioner's pocket. He further testified that generally, in his experience, PCP is "contained in a glass vial." Based on Officer Lewis's testimony, however, the incriminating nature of the object in the defendant's pocket was not immediately apparent upon his initial touch of the object in the pat-down. Rather, Officer Lewis testified that he field-tested the liquid contained in the vial after removing it from the petitioner's pocket, thereby determining that the liquid contained PCP. The removal of the vial from the petitioner's pocket and field test of the liquid contained in the vial constituted a general exploratory search exceeding the permissible scope of a protective *Terry* frisk. . . .

ARREST

We must consider, alternatively, whether Officer Lewis's seizure of the petitioner in the present case constituted a de facto arrest. . . . This Court analyzed what constitutes an arrest in Bouldin v. State, 350 A.2d 130, 133 (Md. 1976).

It is generally recognized that an arrest is the taking, seizing, or detaining of the person of another . . . by touching or putting hands on him. . . . It is said that four elements must ordinarily coalesce to constitute a legal arrest: (1) an intent to arrest; (2) under a real or pretended authority; (3) accompanied by a seizure or detention of the person; and (4) which is understood by the person arrested.

In Belote v. State, 981 A.2d 1247, 1254 (Md. 2009), this Court further analyzed the factors set forth in *Bouldin*: . . . when an arresting officer's "objective conduct, which provides significant insight into the officer's subjective intent, is unambiguous, courts need not allocate significant weight to an officer's subjective intent. [The] officer's objective conduct, in effect, will have made his subjective intent clear."

A show of force is objective conduct demonstrating the officer's intent to make an arrest. Generally, a display of force by a police officer, such as putting a person in handcuffs, is considered an arrest. . . . Although the display of force often involves placing the individual who is seized in handcuffs, application of handcuffs is not a necessary element of an arrest. See Grier v. State, 718 A.2d 211, 217 (Md. 1998) ("Once Petitioner was on the ground and in custody and control of the officers, he was certainly under arrest"); Morton v. State, 397 A.2d 1385, 1388 (Md. 1979) ([arrest occurred] where an officer removed the individual from a recreation center and placed him under guard in a patrol car . . .); Dixon v. State, 758 A.2d 1063, 1073 (Md. App. 2000) (officers exceeded the permissible scope of an investigative *Terry* stop and "arrested appellant at the time they blocked his car, removed him from his vehicle, and handcuffed him").[8]

[Before] the Supreme Court's landmark decision in *Terry*, the Fourth Amendment's guarantee against unreasonable seizures of persons was analyzed in terms of arrest, and probable cause for arrest. *Terry* constituted a limited departure from the requirement of probable cause to support a seizure.[9] If a seizure [amounts to an arrest, it] must be supported by probable cause in order to be lawful.

---

8. Conversely, even if the officers' physical actions are equivalent to an arrest, the show of force is not considered to be an arrest if the actions were justified by officer safety or permissible to prevent the flight of a suspect. In re David S., 789 A.2d 607, 616 (Md. 2002) (holding that a "hard take down" in which officers forced the individual to the ground and handcuffed him was a limited *Terry* stop, not an arrest, when the "conduct was not unreasonable because the officers reasonably could have suspected that the respondent posed a threat to their safety"). The use of handcuffs in a seizure is not a dispositive factor in determining whether the seizure was a *Terry* stop or an arrest.

9. The Supreme Court of the United States discussed the distinction between an arrest and a *Terry* stop in United States v. Robinson, 414 U.S. 218, 228 (1973):

An arrest is a wholly different kind of intrusion upon individual freedom from a limited search for weapons, and the interests each is designed to serve are likewise quite different. An arrest is the initial stage of a criminal prosecution. It is intended to vindicate society's interest in having its laws obeyed, and it is inevitably accompanied by future interference with the individual's freedom of movement, whether or not trial or conviction ultimately follows. The protective search for weapons, on the other hand, constitutes a brief, though far from inconsiderable, intrusion upon the sanctity of the person.

The distinction between a *Terry* stop and an arrest is not defined simply by the length of the detention, the investigative activities during the detention, and whether the suspect was removed to a detention or interrogation area. [An] arrest is distinguishable from a *Terry* detention because the *Terry* stop is not only limited in duration, but also has a limited permissible scope. The scope of a *Terry* stop is limited to brief investigatory stops or detentions conducted in furtherance of the goal of protecting the safety of the officer, or the safety of bystanders.

In this case, Officer Lewis's conduct constituted an unambiguous show of force. He approached the petitioner while in uniform, physically restrained the petitioner, conducted a search of the petitioner's person, and ultimately took the petitioner into physical police custody. [Although] Officer Lewis testified at the suppression hearing that he was checking the petitioner for weapons, this statement is given less weight than his objective conduct on the night in question. . . .

Officer Lewis's conduct on the night in question exceeded the permissible boundaries of an investigative *Terry* stop, both in scope and in duration. A *Terry* stop must be justified both at its inception and be limited in scope, for the specific purpose of searching for weapons to protect the officer's safety, or the safety of bystanders. In the present case, the officer took complete control of the situation in conducting a general exploratory search of the petitioner, removing the vial from his pocket and taking him into custody. . . .

Grabbing the petitioner's wrists when he was not suspected of being armed and dangerous, then conducting a search and removing the vial from his pocket, and, finally, taking him into custody as the initial action leading up to a criminal prosecution, constituted a de facto arrest. Thus, we hold that Officer Lewis's seizure, in which he physically restrained the petitioner and ultimately took him into custody, constituted an arrest.

[The Court went on to conclude that the circumstances present in this case did not create probable cause to support an arrest. Because] Officer Lewis did not make a lawful arrest when he seized the petitioner, the subsequent warrantless search of the petitioner was not within an exception to the warrant requirement and therefore violated the Fourth Amendment. . . .

Notes

1. *Arrest versus stop: majority position.* The difference between a seizure that amounts to an arrest (requiring probable cause) and a seizure that is merely an investigative detention (requiring reasonable suspicion) turns on several different factors. Courts look to the amount of time the detention lasts, the techniques (such as handcuffs) used to restrain the suspect, the location of the suspect (including the distance covered during any transportation of the suspect), and what the police officers say to the suspect about the purposes of the detention. The judicial opinions often say, using a circular definition, that an arrest takes place when a reasonable person would believe that he or she is under arrest, even if the officer has not used the word "arrest." Medford v. State, 13 S.W.3d 769 (Tex. 2000) (arrest is complete "only if a reasonable person in the suspect's position would have understood the situation to constitute a restraint on freedom of movement of the degree which the law associates with formal arrest"). This is known as the doctrine of "constructive arrest."

The interaction among all these relevant facts is typically important to assessing what sort of seizure occurred. In Kaupp v. Texas, 538 U.S. 626 (2003), for example, police officers awakened a 17-year-old boy in his bedroom at 3:00 A.M., saying, "We need to go and talk." He was taken out in handcuffs, without shoes, dressed only in his underwear in January, driven in a patrol car to the scene of a crime and then to the sheriff's offices, and then taken into an interrogation room and questioned for 10-15 minutes before admitting to participation in a murder. The Court concluded that such police actions were "sufficiently like arrest to invoke the traditional rule that arrests may constitutionally be made only on probable cause."

The Supreme Court has validated the use of investigative detentions for misdemeanors in progress and for misdemeanors that haven't yet begun, as well as for felonies at every stage of development. But it has been silent on the propriety of using a *Terry* stop to confirm or dispel suspicion of a completed misdemeanor. The lower federal circuits have, for the most part, provided the validation the Supreme Court has avoided: while the Sixth Circuit holds on to a bright-line rule that *Terry* stops may not be justified based on completed misdemeanors, the Eighth, Ninth, and Tenth Circuits hold that *Terry* stops based on completed misdemeanors may be justified by the "totality of the circumstances." Gaddis ex rel. Gaddis v. Redford Twp., 364 F.3d 763 (6th Cir. 2004) (adopting per se rule against use of *Terry* for completed misdemeanors), but see United States v. Grigg, 498 F.3d 1070 (9th Cir. 2007) (rejecting per se rule), United States v. Moran, 503 F.3d 1135 (10th Cir. 2007) (same), and United States v. Hughes, 517 F.3d 1013 (8th Cir. 2008) (same). The Arizona statute printed above is an example of state legislative authority for detentions based on suspicion of a completed misdemeanor. In those jurisdictions that have adopted the per se rule against using *Terry* stops for completed misdemeanors, officers must have probable cause to arrest for the misdemeanor before they approach the suspect.

2. *Time of detention.* The amount of time that the police detain a person is among the most important facts in determining whether a seizure amounted to an arrest or merely a stop. In Florida v. Royer, 460 U.S. 491 (1983), the Supreme Court stated that an investigative detention "must be temporary and last no longer than is necessary to effectuate the purpose of the stop." Most states allow for a flexible determination of the time necessary to convert a stop into an arrest. Why might Nevada and Arkansas choose such different time limits (60 minutes and 15 minutes)? While the absolute number of minutes in a detention is important, courts also judge the length of the detention in light of the purposes of the stop and the time reasonably needed to effectuate those purposes, including the diligence of officers in pursuing the investigation. See United States v. Sharpe, 470 U.S. 675 (1985) (approves of 20-minute automobile stop for purpose of investigating potential narcotics violations); People v. Garcia, 11 P.3d 449 (Colo. 2000) (length of valid investigatory stop measured as time required for officers to diligently complete investigation given complexity of situation and protection of personal safety).

Is the amount of time allowed for an investigative stop the kind of factor amenable to bright-line rules rather than general standards such as "reasonableness"? If you were to draft a bright-line rule, would you include an "escape" valve for exceptional situations? If you prefer a rule in this situation, would you want that rule to be determined by the legislature or the courts?

3. *Conditions of detention.* What can be more typical of arrest than being handcuffed and placed in the back of a police cruiser? State and federal cases suggest that handcuffing ordinarily is improper as part of a stop (see, e.g., El-Ghazzawy v. Berthiaume, 636 F.3d 452 (8th Cir. 2011); People v. King, 16 P.3d 807 (Colo. 2001)), but may be used when necessary to thwart the suspect's attempt "to frustrate further inquiry." United States v. Hood, 774 F.3d 638 (10th Cir. 2014). Likewise, placing the suspect in the back of a patrol car is also usually out of bounds for a stop, but such a step is permissible when dictated by special circumstances. United States v. Manbeck, 744 F.2d 360 (4th Cir. 1984); State v. Williams, 240 Conn. 489 (1997).

For a sampling of the rich case law on this question, consult the web extension for this chapter at *http://www.crimpro.com/extension/ch05*.

Are officers allowed to fingerprint a suspect during a detention, or would that turn the detention into a full arrest? The Supreme Court, in Hayes v. Florida, 470 U.S. 811 (1985), said fingerprinting "in the field" would not turn a detention into an arrest, but a significant delay caused by fingerprinting, or taking a suspect to the police station to be fingerprinted, would be problematic. Various states have legislatively authorized police to temporarily detain someone for the purpose of fingerprinting her. Vermont Rule of Criminal Procedure 41.1, for example, provides that a Nontestimonial Identification Order (NTO) for identifying information such as fingerprints can be issued by a judicial officer, based on a sworn affidavit establishing that: (1) there is probable cause to believe that an offense has been committed; (2) there are reasonable grounds, that need not amount to probable cause to arrest, to suspect that the person named or described in the affidavit committed the offense; and (3) the results of specific nontestimonial identification procedures will be of material aid in determining whether the person named in the affidavit committed the offense. V.R.Cr.P. 41.1(c). Arizona and Colorado have similar statutes. A.R.S. §13-3905(a); People v. Madson, 638 P.2d 18, 21 (Colo. 1981). Would a DNA swab fall within the scope of a *Terry* stop, or would it convert the detention into an arrest?

4. *Location of detention.* Why do both the Arkansas rule and the Nevada statute require that the detained person remain in the vicinity of the initial stop? Most of the cases on this question allow officers to transport a suspect to some other location nearby to complete an investigation, but longer trips can convert the stop into an arrest. Taking a suspect to the police station is also a key factor in the cases. Can a person be taken to the police station and still not be under arrest? See Dunaway v. New York, 442 U.S. 200 (1979) (recognizing possibility of nonarrest detention during questioning at police station, but concluding that where defendant was taken from home to police station for questioning, constructive arrest had occurred).

5. *Probable cause to believe what?* What happens when an officer (incorrectly) arrests a suspect for one crime, but probable cause actually existed at that time for some other crime? Does it matter which crime the officer has in mind when making the arrest? In Devenpeck v. Alford, 543 U.S. 146 (2004), officers stopped a driver and ultimately arrested him for unlawful audio-taping of a police conversation during the stop, which was later determined not to be a crime. However, the officers on the scene had probable cause to arrest the suspect for impersonating an officer, a sufficient basis to support arrest even though it was not the crime the officers relied upon. The Court found the arrest was not unconstitutional, because objective facts supported probable cause as to the second crime. Are the arguments in this setting precisely the same as the arguments we encountered in the discussion of "pretextual" stops?

B. ARREST WARRANTS

In Chapter 3, we explored the various ways that the law supposedly encourages the use of a judicial warrant to authorize an officer to conduct a full search, even though most searches take place without a warrant. The same is true for arrests: There are legal rules encouraging or requiring warrants before a police officer can arrest a person in some settings (in particular, arrests made in a home), but because most arrests take place in public, most of them are warrantless. As you read the following materials on the coverage of the warrant requirement for arrests, keep in mind the types of arrests that these rules do not cover.

■ WILLIAM BLACKSTONE, COMMENTARIES ON THE LAWS OF ENGLAND

Vol. 3, p. 288 (1768)

An arrest must be by corporal seising or touching the defendant's body; after which the bailiff may justify breaking open the house in which he is, to take him: otherwise he has no such power; but must watch his opportunity to arrest him. For every man's house is looked upon by the law to be his castle of defence and asylum, wherein he should suffer no violence. Which principle is carried so far in the civil law, that for the most part not so much as a common citation or summons, much less an arrest, can be executed upon a man within his own walls.

■ STATE v. STEVEN THOMAS

124 P.3d 48 (Kan. 2005)

Luckert, J.

[Just before midnight on March 26, 2002, the Sedgwick County Sheriff's Department received information from a confidential informant that Brandon Prouse was trying to sell an informant 5 or 6 quarts of anhydrous ammonia (a chemical used in making methamphetamine). Prouse was wanted on a felony arrest warrant for a probation violation in an aggravated battery case. The sheriff's office began surveillance on the house where the informant indicated Prouse might be found; they did not know the home's owner and did not get a search warrant. When Prouse stepped out of the house and walked into the front yard, the uniformed deputies ordered him to stop. Prouse ran back into the residence and four deputies followed him inside. They pursued Prouse through different rooms and then arrested him.

While they were inside the house, the deputies smelled a strong chemical odor and saw in plain view various items that they believed were consistent with a methamphetamine lab. Seven people, including Prouse and the defendant (Thomas), were also inside; the deputies ordered them to wait on the front lawn. Once the occupants of the house were outside, deputies patted them down individually. During the pat-down search, Thomas admitted owning the house and said, "You might as well get [my] dope," and indicated that he had methamphetamine in his left front pants pocket. The deputy reached into Thomas' pocket and pulled out a bag containing smaller baggies filled with white rocks. Thomas was then placed under arrest.]

Thomas argues that the arrest warrant upon which the deputies based their chase of Prouse did not authorize their entry without a search warrant into the home of a third party. Further, Thomas contends there were no exigent circumstances to support the entry. . . .

The Fourth Amendment prohibits law enforcement officers from making a warrantless and nonconsensual entry into a home in order to make a routine felony arrest absent exigent circumstances. Payton v. New York, 445 U.S. 573 (1980). The majority in *Payton* noted it was a basic principle of Fourth Amendment law that searches and seizures inside a home without a warrant are "presumptively unreasonable," while "objects . . . found in a public place may be seized by the police without a warrant." The Court concluded that "this distinction has equal force when the seizure of a person is involved" because "an entry to arrest and an entry to search for and to seize property implicate the same interest in preserving the privacy and the sanctity of the home, and justify the same level of constitutional protection." Thus, the Court concluded: "In terms that apply equally to seizures of property and to seizures of persons, the Fourth Amendment has drawn a firm line at the entrance to the house. Absent exigent circumstances, that threshold may not reasonably be crossed without a warrant." . . .

ARREST WARRANT AUTHORIZES ENTRY INTO SUSPECT'S HOME

However, in *Payton* the United States Supreme Court recognized that a search warrant was not constitutionally required if the entry was made into a home where one who was the subject of a felony arrest warrant resided if there was [reason] to believe the subject was present in the home. The Court stated:

> It is true that an arrest warrant requirement may afford less protection than a search warrant requirement, but it will suffice to interpose the magistrate's determination of probable cause between the zealous officer and the citizen. If there is sufficient evidence of a citizen's participation in a felony to persuade a judicial officer that his arrest is justified, it is constitutionally reasonable to require him to open his doors to the officers of the law. Thus, for Fourth Amendment purposes, an arrest warrant founded on probable cause implicitly carries with it the limited authority to enter a dwelling in which the suspect lives when there is reason to believe the suspect is within.

Thus, had the officers followed Prouse into a house in which he resided in order to serve the warrant, the entry would have been constitutional. . . . In the present case, however, there is nothing in the record to indicate that the officers believed Prouse owned or resided at the house.

THIRD PARTY'S HOUSE

An arrest warrant, standing alone, is not a sufficient basis to enter the home of a third party. The United States Supreme Court reached this holding in Steagald v. United States, 451 U.S. 204 (1981). In *Steagald*, a confidential informant contacted an agent of the Drug Enforcement Administration, suggesting he might be able to locate Ricky Lyons, a federal fugitive wanted on drug charges. Agents found the address where they thought Lyons was located and, 2 days later, drove to the residence. Gary Steagald and Hoyt Gaultney stood outside of the house. After the agents frisked the two men and discovered that neither man was Lyons, they went to the front door. Gaultney's wife answered the door and told the agents she was alone. The agents proceeded, without consent, into the house and searched for Lyons. Although they did not find Lyons, the agents found cocaine. They subsequently obtained a search warrant, and ultimately found 43 pounds of cocaine. Steagald was arrested on federal drug charges.

The Supreme Court stated that the agents had neither consent nor exigent circumstances when they made their initial, warrantless search. The Court phrased its narrow issue for consideration as "whether an arrest warrant—as opposed to a search warrant—is adequate to protect the Fourth Amendment interests of persons not named in the warrant, when their homes are searched without their consent and in the absence of exigent circumstances." The *Steagald* Court recognized that different interests are protected by arrest warrants and search warrants. Arrest warrants protect individuals from unreasonable seizures; search warrants protect against the unjustified intrusion of police into one's home. The Court found that the agents wrongly relied on Lyons' arrest warrant to give them the legal authority to enter into a third persons' home. Thus, the third person's privacy interests were left unprotected.

The *Steagald* Court feared that allowing officers, without consent or exigent circumstances, to enter into a third party's residence to search for the subject of an arrest warrant would create a significant potential for abuse and pointed out that officers would then be able to use arrest warrants as a pretext for entering the residences of a suspect's friends and acquaintances or as a pretext for entering residences in which police have mere suspicion, not probable cause, that illegal activity is being committed. The Court held that, under the facts of the case, the warrantless search was unconstitutional.

However, the United States Supreme Court was careful to exempt two circumstances from its holding: consent and exigent circumstances. In this case, the State does not allege there was consent. Rather, the State relies upon exigent circumstances. . . .

Exigent Circumstances

The Court of Appeals, in holding that the deputies' conduct was justified by exigent circumstances, found that the present case is similar to United States v. Santana, 427 U.S. 38 (1976). Dominga Santana stood in the doorway of her own house when officers arrived to arrest her. When she saw the police, the defendant went inside the vestibule of the house. The officers followed the defendant inside and arrested her.

Santana filed a motion to suppress the incriminating evidence found during and after her arrest. The federal district court granted Santana's motion, [but the Supreme Court] disagreed with the lower court and determined that Santana's pursuit originated in a public place. Further, "the fact that the pursuit here ended almost as soon as it began did not render it any the less a [hot pursuit] sufficient to justify the warrantless entry into Santana's house." As for the police officers' entry into the defendant's house, the Court concluded: "A suspect may not defeat an arrest which has been set in motion in a public place . . . by the expedient of escaping into a private place."

Santana addressed a situation involving police entry into the suspect's house. The current set of facts involves the warrantless entry of police into a third party's house while trying to apprehend a suspect on an arrest warrant. [The *Steagald* Court discussed] the historical basis for the "hot pursuit doctrine," [and] concluded that English common-law "suggests that forcible entry into a third party's house was permissible only when the person to be arrested was pursued to the house." Later in the decision, the Court dismissed the government's argument that practical problems would arise if law enforcement were required to obtain a search warrant before entering the home of a third party. The Court noted these practical problems were largely ameliorated because "the situations in which a search warrant will be necessary are few." As examples, the Court noted that (1) "an arrest warrant alone will suffice to enter a suspect's own residence"; (2) "if probable cause exists, no warrant is required to apprehend a suspected felon in a public place"; (3) "the subject of an arrest warrant can be readily seized before entering or after leaving the home of a third party"; and (4) under the exigent circumstances doctrine, "a warrantless entry of a home would be justified if the police were in [hot pursuit] of a fugitive." . . .

APPLICATION OF HOT PURSUIT DOCTRINE

Without specific discussion of the hot pursuit exception, Thomas contends there were no exigent circumstances and cites to the list of factors this court has recognized which may be considered in determining if exigent circumstances existed, including: (1) the gravity or violent nature of the offense with which the suspect is to be charged; (2) whether the suspect is reasonably believed to be armed; (3) a clear showing of probable cause; (4) strong reasons to believe that the suspect is in the premises; (5) a likelihood that the suspect will escape if not swiftly apprehended; and (6) the peaceful circumstances of entry. The possible destruction of evidence is also a factor which may be considered. . . .

Here, the deputies had an arrest warrant for Prouse, began surveillance of the house where they reasonably believed he could be found, and then spotted Prouse as he first exited and then reentered the house. The district court found that the deputies initially intended to wait for Prouse and to arrest him outside. There is no evidence, or assertion by Thomas, that the deputies used the arrest warrant as a pretext for entering Thomas' house or for searching it for incriminating evidence.

The district court found the doctrine of hot pursuit applied and also found it was impractical to expect the officers to obtain a warrant once Prouse took refuge in Thomas' house. The district court expressed doubt that a search warrant could have been obtained quickly at 2 o'clock in the morning. Unquestionably, if the officers had sought a search warrant, there was a high possibility that the fugitive named in the arrest warrant would escape apprehension. Indeed, requiring such police conduct would negate the essence of the hot pursuit doctrine. . . .

Furthermore, certain facts in this particular case are important to a conclusion that the officers were justified in making a warrantless entry into a third-party residence. The initial entry and search was limited to the apprehension of Prouse, the suspect named in the arrest warrant. Thomas does not contest the officers' quick protective sweep of the home once they discovered that Prouse was not alone. There is no indication that the deputies dug into drawers or looked into places where the suspect obviously could not hide.

In addition, the evidence pertaining to the methamphetamine lab was in plain view as the deputies pursued Prouse and made a protective sweep of the residence. It is clear that any evidence seized in plain view must be located in places lawfully accessible to officers. The strong smell of anhydrous ammonia was prevalent throughout the house, and various items consistent with the manufacture of methamphetamine sat in plain view in the kitchen area. . . . The Court of Appeals' decision affirming the district court's denial of Thomas' motion to suppress evidence based upon the alleged unauthorized entry into a third-party residence is affirmed.

Notes

1. *Warrants for arrests in a home: majority position.* The federal constitution allows a police officer to make an arrest in a public place without an arrest warrant. When the arrest takes place in a home, however, warrants are required. As the *Thomas* decision from Kansas explained, the federal constitution requires an arrest warrant to justify entry into a suspect's home to carry out the arrest, along with some "reason to believe" the suspect is inside. Payton v. New York, 445 U.S. 573 (1980); Kirk v. Louisiana, 536 U.S. 635 (2002) (reaffirms *Payton*). The "reason to believe" standard is less than probable cause, and is likely akin to "reasonable suspicion" in the Terry stop context. When an officer enters a third party's home to arrest a suspect, he or she must have (in addition to the arrest warrant) a search warrant for the third-party home, alleging probable cause to believe that the suspect (the object of the search) is present in that location. Virtually all state courts have used this same framework under their state constitutions. See State v. Chippero, 987 A.2d 555 (N.J. 2009).

In what ways are arrest warrants different from search warrants? Do separate requirements for search warrants and arrest warrants accomplish anything meaningful for suspects? For nonsuspects?

2. *Warrantless arrests in public places.* The U.S. Constitution does not require warrants for arrests made in a public place, even if the arresting officer could easily have obtained a warrant. In United States v. Watson, 423 U.S. 411 (1976), the Court upheld statutes and regulations granting Postal Service officers the power to make warrantless arrests for felonies. The Court deferred to Congress's judgment about the meaning of the Fourth Amendment and also relied on "the ancient common-law rule that a peace officer was permitted to arrest without a warrant for a misdemeanor or felony committed in his presence as well as for a felony not committed in his presence if there was reasonable ground for making the arrest," noting that the common-law rule (allowing warrantless arrests for misdemeanors only when they are committed in the presence of the arresting officer) had prevailed under state and federal law.

3. *Arrest warrant procedures.* The arrest warrant procedure requires an officer to contact the magistrate in advance, to establish that she has probable cause to believe a crime was committed, and that this is a person responsible. For defendants arrested without warrants, magistrates review the existence of probable cause to support the arrest immediately after the arrest has taken place. This "*Gerstein* Hearing" must be held within 48 hours of the arrest; if the magistrate finds no probable cause, the suspect must be released from custody. The prosecution can continue to gather evidence to use against him, however; the finding has no prejudicial effect on the viability of the prosecution itself. County of Riverside v. McLaughlin, 500 U.S. 44 (1991); Gerstein v. Pugh, 420 U.S. 103 (1975).

4. *Is crime seriousness a basis for exigency when officers enter a suspect's home to arrest him?* In Welsh v. Wisconsin, 466 U.S. 740 (1984), the Supreme Court considered the validity of a night entry of a person's home to arrest him for a nonjailable traffic offense. The Court held that no exigent circumstances could support the arrest in Welsh's home, particularly "when the underlying offense for which there is probable cause to arrest is relatively minor." See also State v. Kiper, 532 N.W.2d 698 (Wis. 1995) (officer executing arrest warrant for failure to pay fine for allowing minor to drive; no exigent circumstances). Why should exigent circumstances for entering homes vary based on the seriousness of the alleged crime committed? For a sense of the interaction among arrest warrants, search warrants, and the exigent

circumstances doctrine, consult the web extension for this chapter at *http://www. crimpro.com/extension/ch05*.

5. *The dark side to arrest warrants.* Unlike search warrants, which must be executed in a short amount of time or go stale, arrest warrants have no expiration date and never go stale. They can be executed years after they were issued. As a result, there are many people in inner city neighborhoods walking around with outstanding warrants for minor crimes, failures to pay fines, failures to appear, and other instances of noncompliance with court orders. (There are others whose warrants are for serious offenses.) Police can and do use outstanding arrests warrants as a basis to hassle individuals. Alice Goffman, On the Run: Fugitive Life in an American City (2014). Nirej Sekhon calls them "dangerous warrants" for this reason—people get further entangled in the criminal justice system, and police have more and more bases to conduct stops to do warrant checks. Nirej Sekhon, Dangerous Warrants, 93 Wash. L. Rev. 967 (2018).

Problem 5-1. Indoor-Outdoor Arrest

Officer Roy Gows of the Boston Police Department responded to the hospital emergency room to investigate the report of a rape. The victim of the alleged rape told Officer Gows that she had been living in an apartment with Antonio Molina for six weeks. She said that Molina had raped her at knifepoint the previous night in the apartment, using a very large knife drawn from a brown sheath. The victim then gave Officer Gows the address of the apartment. Along with Detective Martin Nee, Gows proceeded to Molina's apartment to make an arrest. They did not first get an arrest warrant.

When they arrived at the apartment, Officer Gows knocked on the front door. When Molina opened the door, the officers noticed that he fit the physical description provided by the victim and, when asked, identified himself as Molina. Detective Nee and Officer Gows stepped into the living room, which is accessible directly from the front door, and handcuffed Molina while saying that he was under arrest. At that point, a young woman who was also standing in the living room became very angry and began screaming at the officers. Concerned that she might have access to Molina's handgun that was sitting on a table in the living room, Detective Nee moved Molina 10 feet through an adjacent doorway into the kitchen while instructing Officer Gows to deal with the young woman.

While in the kitchen, Nee noticed a two-foot-long knife on the counter. The officers then told Molina that he would be spending the night at the station, and asked if he wanted to retrieve a sweater to wear over his muscle shirt. He agreed, and led the officers to his third-floor bedroom. While in the bedroom, the officers saw a brown knife sheath.

Before his trial for rape, Molina filed a motion to suppress the knife and the sheath as evidence. Will the trial court grant the motion? Cf. Commonwealth v. Molina, 786 N.E.2d 1191 (Mass. 2003).

Problem 5-2. Warrant Sweeps

Rivertown, a mid-size city in the Northeast, has been experiencing a backlog of arrest warrants—when the clerk last checked, there were more than 10,000 unserved arrest warrants in the city's database. About 80 percent of those warrants are for low-level offenses, including traffic cases, misdemeanor probation violations, and failures to appear in court. The other 20 percent are for outstanding felony charges.

The two candidates running for mayor of Rivertown have proposed radically different responses to this problem. Mr. Darcy suggests that the police force ought to conduct warrant sweeps every weekend, to attempt to locate as many of the suspects as they can find. This approach, he says, will not only clear the backlog but also send a strong message to suspects that they cannot evade justice by evading the courts. Ms. Marple suggests instead that the court ought to purge the database of all of the warrants for probation violations and failures to appear; law enforcement resources, she says, ought to be used to pursue serious offenders and not to hassle the city's residents over issues of noncompliance with court orders. Both candidates believe their approach will be the fiscally responsible one.

You are a single-issue voter in Rivertown and care deeply about the backlog of warrants. How will you vote and why?

C. POLICE DISCRETION IN THE ARREST DECISION

This section considers recent legal reforms that could have contradictory effects on police discretion in arrests. First, statutes have expanded the power of the police to arrest a person without adhering to traditional common-law and statutory requirements that the police obtain an arrest warrant in some contexts. In most states, these statutory reforms override the common-law requirement for an arrest warrant. Second, while police officers generally have discretion to decide whether to arrest, statutes and police department rules in special areas now guide the officers in their arrest decisions once there is probable cause to believe that the person has committed a crime. Prominent examples of both of these trends—one expanding the officer's discretion to arrest and the other restricting it—appear in cases involving domestic violence. We begin with the traditional common-law rule, which requires a warrant to arrest a person for lesser crimes committed outside the officer's presence.

■ WILLIAM BLACKSTONE,
COMMENTARIES ON THE LAWS OF ENGLAND
Vol. 4, p. 287 (1769)

A warrant may be granted . . . ordinarily by justices of the peace. This they may do in any cases where they have a jurisdiction over the offence [and] this extends undoubtedly to all treasons, felonies, and breaches of the peace; and also to all such offences as they have power to punish by statute. [The constable] may, without warrant, arrest any one for a breach of the peace, committed in his view, and carry him before a justice of the peace. And, in case of felony actually committed, or a dangerous wounding whereby felony is likely to ensue, he may upon probable suspicion arrest the felon.

■ CONNECTICUT GENERAL STATUTES §46B-38B

(a) Except as provided in subsections (b) and (c) of this section, whenever a peace officer determines upon speedy information that a family violence crime has been committed within such officer's jurisdiction, such officer shall arrest the person or persons suspected of its commission and charge such person or persons with the appropriate crime. The decision to arrest and charge shall not (1) be dependent on the specific consent of the victim, (2) consider the relationship of the parties between persons suspected of committing a family violence crime, or (3) be based solely on a request by the victim. . . .

(b) When complaints of family violence are made by two or more opposing persons, a peace officer is not required to arrest both persons. The peace officer shall evaluate each complaint separately to determine which person is the dominant aggressor. In determining which person is the dominant aggressor, the peace officer shall consider the need to protect victims of domestic violence, whether one person acted in defense of self or a third person, the relative degree of any injury, any threats creating fear of physical injury, and any history of family violence between such persons, if such history can reasonably be obtained by the peace officer. The peace officer shall arrest the person whom the officer believes to be the dominant aggressor.

(c) If a peace officer believes probable cause exists for the arrest of two or more persons, in lieu of arresting or seeking a warrant for the arrest of any person determined not to be the dominant aggressor, such peace officer may submit a report detailing the conduct of such person during the incident to the state's attorney for the judicial district in which the incident took place for further review and advice. The provisions of this section shall be construed to discourage, when appropriate, but not prohibit, dual arrests.

■ IOWA CODE §236.12

1. If a peace officer has reason to believe that domestic abuse has occurred, the officer shall use all reasonable means to prevent further abuse including but not limited to the following:

a. If requested, remaining on the scene as long as there is a danger to an abused person's physical safety without the presence of a peace officer, including but limited to staying in the dwelling unit, or if unable to remain on the scene, assisting the person in leaving the residence.

b. Assisting an abused person in obtaining medical treatment necessitated by an assault. . . .

c. Providing an abused person with immediate and adequate notice of the person's rights.

2. a. A peace officer may, with or without a warrant, arrest a person . . . if, upon investigation, . . . the officer has probable cause to believe that a domestic abuse assault has been committed which did not result in any injury to the alleged victim.

b. Except as otherwise provided in subsection 3, a peace officer shall, with or without a warrant, arrest a person [if] the officer has probable cause to believe that a domestic abuse assault has been committed which resulted in the alleged victim's suffering a bodily injury.

    c. Except as otherwise provided in subsection 3, a peace officer shall, with or without a warrant, arrest a person [if] the officer has probable cause to believe that a domestic abuse assault has been committed with the intent to inflict a serious injury.

    d. Except as otherwise provided in subsection 3, a peace officer shall, with or without a warrant, arrest a person [if] the officer has probable cause to believe that a domestic abuse assault has been committed and that the alleged abuser used or displayed a dangerous weapon in connection with the assault.

    3. The peace officer shall arrest the person whom the peace officer believes to be the primary physical aggressor. . . . Persons acting with justification . . . are not subject to mandatory arrest. In identifying the primary physical aggressor, a peace officer shall consider the need to protect victims of domestic abuse, the relative degree of injury or fear inflicted on the persons involved, and any history of domestic abuse between the persons involved. A peace officer's identification of the primary physical aggressor shall not be based on the consent of the victim to any subsequent prosecution or on the relationship of the persons involved in the incident, and shall not be based solely upon the absence of visible indications of injury or impairment.

■ LAWRENCE SHERMAN & RICHARD BERK, THE MINNEAPOLIS DOMESTIC VIOLENCE EXPERIMENT
(1984)

[The] Minneapolis domestic violence experiment was the first scientifically controlled test of the effects of arrest for any crime. It found that arrest was the most effective of three standard methods police use to reduce domestic violence. The other police methods—attempting to counsel both parties or sending assailants away from home for several hours—were found to be considerably less effective in deterring future violence in the cases examined.

POLICING DOMESTIC ASSAULTS

Police have typically been reluctant to make arrests for domestic violence, as well as for a wide range of other kinds of offenses, unless a victim demands an arrest, a suspect insults an officer, or other factors are present. [Two surveys] of battered women who tried to have their domestic assailants arrested report that arrest occurred in only ten percent [and] three percent of the cases. Surveys of police agencies in Illinois and New York found explicit policies against arrest in the majority of the agencies surveyed.

The apparent preference of many police for separating the parties rather than arresting the offender has been attacked from two directions over the past 15 years. The original critique came from clinical psychologists who agreed that police should rarely make arrests in domestic assault cases and argued that police should mediate the disputes responsible for the violence. . . . By the mid 1970's, police practices were criticized from the opposite direction by feminist groups. Just as psychologists succeeded in having many police agencies respond to domestic violence as "half social work and half police work," feminists began to argue that police put "too much emphasis on the social work aspect and not enough on the criminal." . . . The feminist critique was bolstered by a study showing that for 85 percent of a sample of spouse killings, police had intervened at least once in the preceding two years. For 54 percent of those homicides, police had intervened five or more times.

HOW THE EXPERIMENT WAS DESIGNED

[To] find which police approach was most effective in deterring future domestic violence, . . . the Minneapolis Police Department agreed to conduct a classic experiment. . . . [A] lottery determined which of the three responses police officers would use on each suspect in a domestic assault case. According to the lottery, a suspect would be arrested, or sent from the scene of the assault for eight hours, or given some form of advice, which could include mediation at an offender's discretion. . . . The design called for a six-month follow-up period to measure the frequency and seriousness of any future domestic violence in all cases in which the police intervened.

The design applied only to simple (misdemeanor) domestic assaults, where both the suspect and the victim were present when the police arrived. . . . Police need not have witnessed the assault. Cases of life-threatening or severe injury, usually labeled as a felony (aggravated assault), were excluded from the design.

CONDUCT OF THE EXPERIMENT

As is common in field experiments, the actual process in Minneapolis suffered some slippage from the original plan. [The experiment ran from March 17, 1981] until August 1, 1982, and produced 314 case reports. . . . Ninety-nine percent of the suspects targeted for arrest actually were arrested; 78 percent of those scheduled to receive advice did; and 73 percent of those to be sent out of the residence for eight hours actually were sent. One explanation for this pattern . . . is that mediating and sending were more difficult ways for police to control a situation. There was a greater likelihood that an officer might have to resort to arrest as a fallback position. . . .

RESULTS

[Two] measures of repeat violence were used in the experiment. One was a police record of an offender repeating domestic violence during the six-month follow-up period. . . . A second kind of measure came from the interviews in which victims were asked if there had been a repeat incident with the same suspect, broadly defined to include an assault, threatened assault, or property damage. . . .

[The] police records on subsequent violence [show that] the arrest treatment is clearly an improvement over sending the suspect away, which produced two and a half times as many repeat incidents as arrest. [Ten percent of those arrested at the scene engaged in subsequent violence, compared to 19 percent of those advised and 24 percent of those sent away.] . . . [Even] according to the victims' reports of repeat violence, arrest is . . . the most effective police action. [According to the victims, 19 percent of those arrested originally engaged in subsequent violence, compared to 37 percent of those advised and 33 percent of those sent away.] . . . [Moreover,] these findings were basically the same for all categories of suspects. Regardless of the race, employment status, educational level, criminal history of the suspect, or how long the suspect was in jail when arrested, arrest still had the strongest violence reduction effect. There was one factor, however, that seemed to govern the effectiveness of arrest: whether the police showed interest in the victim's side of the story.

If police do listen [to the victim], that reduces the occurrence of repeat violence even more [9 percent instead of 19 percent]. But if the victims think the police did not take the time to listen, then the level of victim-reported violence is much higher [26 percent]. One interpretation of this finding is that by listening to the victim, the police "empower" her with their strength, letting the suspect know that she can influence their behavior. If police ignore the victim, the suspect may think he was arrested for arbitrary reasons unrelated to the victim and be less deterred from future violence.

Notes

1. *Common-law arrest powers and domestic abuse.* As the passage from Blackstone indicates, officers at common law did not have authority to make a warrantless arrest of a person who committed a misdemeanor out of the presence of the officer, even if the officer had probable cause to believe that the person had committed the crime. The modern view suggests that the officer needs only probable cause to believe the offense is occurring in her presence (judging based on the facts as they appeared, not on how they turned out), see, e.g., Drago v. State, 553 S.W.2d 375 (Tex. Crim. App. 1977); State v. Baysinger, 470 N.W.2d 840 (S.D. 1991); moreover, she may acquire such probable cause using any of her senses, or any form of technology (such as binoculars or a radar gun). See, e.g., Taylor v. United States, 259 A.2d 835 (D.C. 1969). This limitation makes it difficult for police officers, without some special statutory authority, to make arrests in the typical low-level misdemeanor domestic abuse call, because there was no officer witness to the crime. In this situation, the legally proper response is a citizen's arrest, followed by a transfer of custody to the police officer who responds. Note that other states have dropped the "presence" requirement entirely, and still others allow arrests for misdemeanors committed outside the officer's presence when exigent circumstances suggest arrest is appropriate.

2. *The variety of legislative solutions.* Many statutes, like those reprinted above, expand the authority of the officer to arrest an assailant in a domestic abuse setting. Note the different limits that states (for instance, Connecticut) place on this expanded arrest power. Why do the statutes address the time elapsed between the injury and the arrival of the police? See N.H. Stat. §594:10 (authority to arrest without warrant for misdemeanor domestic abuse occurring within 12 hours of arrest). Why do some require evidence of a physical injury? See 18 Pa. Cons. Stat. §2711; W. Va. Code §48-27-1002 (listing examples of "credible corroborative evidence," such as contusions, missing hair, torn clothing, damaged furnishings on premises).

In addition to expanding police authority to arrest in the domestic abuse setting, some of the statutes encourage or require officers to respond in ways other than arresting the assailant. For instance, about a dozen states require the officer on the scene to provide the victim with information about health care and legal protection from further abuse. It is also common for statutes to require the officer responding to the call to report the incident to the prosecutor's office, regardless of the arrest decision.

Finally, more than a dozen states have passed statutes encouraging or mandating arrest as the proper police response to evidence of domestic violence. While a few statutes only require probable cause that a domestic violence offense has occurred, other statutes impose a number of different preconditions on the mandatory arrest duty of the police. See Utah Code Ann. §77-36-2.2 ("shall arrest" if there is evidence of recent serious injury, or use of dangerous weapon, or probable cause to believe there is potential of continued violence toward victim); Mo. Rev. Stat. §455.085 ("shall" arrest for second incident within 12 hours). Why does Iowa direct a police officer to arrest the person the officer believes to be the "primary physical aggressor," and how does the statute define that term?

The statutes reprinted here do not exhaust the legislative responses to this problem. Other relevant approaches include a Florida statute directing state agencies to collect detailed annual statistics about the enforcement of that state's domestic violence arrest policy and subsequent incidents of violence. See Fla. Stat. §943.1702. Some statutes emphasize training of officers that stresses the criminal nature of domestic abuse rather than the "social work" approach to the problem; Idaho Code §39-6316 is one example of this approach.

Local ordinances or police department policies might adopt a mandatory arrest policy, or a strong preference for arrests, even when state statutes do not. Indeed, over 90 percent of all police departments have policies dealing with domestic violence. See Bureau of Justice Statistics, Local Police Departments, 2007 (December 2010, NCJ 231174).

3. *Arrest quotas.* Police department policies *other* than those calling for automatic or presumed arrests in some situations can have a powerful effect on individual officers' arrest decisions. How will officers respond to a departmental policy that evaluates and rewards officers based on the number of arrests they make? Is there a plausible legal basis for challenging a system of "arrest quotas" in court? Disputes over these policies more often arise during labor negotiations between police officer unions and department administrators.

4. *History, social science, and changes in legal rules.* One of the notable aspects of the Sherman and Berk policy paper is its effective use of recent history (the past 30 years) and social science to build an argument for a particular approach to domestic violence. How persuasive is the bottom line in the analysis of the Minneapolis experiment? If you were the police chief in another city or a legislator in another state, would you change policy on the basis of this publication?

This policy brief, and the movement it captured, is a notable example of the possible influence of social science on criminal procedure. Many states and police departments adopted some version of an "automatic" arrest policy (although most are not truly mandatory arrest policies but strongly encourage such arrests). Despite the warnings about the need for further research, the Minneapolis study was central in promoting these policy changes. The story told by Sherman and Berk also offers a cautionary tale: Prior policies were passionately supported by smart and principled people, and those policies, too, were bolstered by varying amounts of research.

This realization should serve as a warning against assuming that current policies are necessarily an improvement over earlier ones and that the current policy is the best possible policy—the end of the line.

5. *"More research is needed": an important caveat.* A series of further experiments over the years made it harder to predict how mandatory arrest policies affect domestic violence. Replication experiments in six cities only partially confirmed the dramatic findings in Minneapolis. In three cities, the use of arrest actually *increased* later domestic violence. The use of arrest had more of a deterrent effect on suspects who were employed than on those who were unemployed. Arrest also had a positive effect in *neighborhoods* with high rates of employment, and negative effects in neighborhoods with low employment rates. See, e.g., Lawrence W. Sherman, The Police, in James Q. Wilson & Joan Petersilia, eds., Crime 327, 336-338 (1995) (describing replication studies in Omaha, Charlotte, Milwaukee, Colorado Springs, Bade County); Lawrence W. Sherman & Heather M. Harris, Increased Death Rates of Domestic Violence Victims from Arresting vs. Warning Suspects in the Milwaukee Domestic Violence Experiment (MilDVE), J. Experimental Criminology (2014). Criminologists remain interested in this topic and continue to generate new data and updated analyses. For references to this sociological literature and a discussion of its ongoing significance, go to the web extension for this chapter at *http://www.crimpro.com/extension/ch05.*

Despite the mixed outcomes of replication studies, policies favoring arrest in domestic assault situations generally have remained in force, and new policies encouraging arrest are still being adopted. Why hasn't the more recent research on domestic assaults and arrest policies produced more targeted policies (for instance, a policy calling for arrest only if the suspect is employed)?

7. *Tracking arrest rates based on race.* For most crimes that generate large numbers of arrests in this country, African Americans are arrested in numbers disproportionate to their percentage of the general population. The differences are present for many crimes in many different places (but not for all crimes or places). How might one explain this persistent and discomfiting fact?

Some have postulated racial bias, whether conscious or unconscious, on the part of arresting police officers. See Coramae Richey Mann, Unequal Justice (1993). Consistent with this view, one study found that police forces with larger numbers of white officers produced higher arrest rates for nonwhite suspects, while police forces with larger numbers of nonwhite officers produced more arrests of white suspects, especially for minor crimes. John J. Donahue III & Steven D. Levitt, The Impact of Race on Policing and Arrests, 44 J.L. & Econ. 367 (2001).

Others conclude that blacks are arrested more often because they more often violate the criminal law. Alfred Blumstein, On the Racial Disproportionality of the United States' Prison Populations, 73 J. Crim. L. & Criminology 1259 (1982). Those who rely on this explanation point to surveys of victims regarding the race of the offenders in their cases (regardless of whether the police were ever involved or whether an arrest was ever made): The information from victims about the race of criminal perpetrators roughly corresponds to the racial makeup of arrestees.

Another line of explanation suggests that police arrest black suspects more frequently because black complainants (who are most often the victims of crimes by black perpetrators) request arrest more often than white complainants. See Richard Lundman, Richard Sykes & John Clark, Police Control of Juveniles: A Replication,

15 J. Res. Crime & Delinq. 74 (1978). Others suggest that blacks are more likely to encounter police officers in poorer neighborhoods and that police officers are more likely to use their discretion to arrest in such neighborhoods. Katherine Beckett, Kris Nyrop & Lori Pfingst, Race, Drugs, and Policing: Understanding Disparities in Drug Delivery Arrests, 44 Criminology 105 (2006); see also James Forman, Jr. Locking Up Our Own: Crime and Punishment in Black America (2017). Do these various explanations for racial disparity in arrest rates conflict with one another or are they reconcilable? Further studies of the interaction of race and arrest practices receive attention on the web extension for this chapter at *http://www.crimpro.com/ extension/ch05*.

Problem 5-3. Racial Patterns in Arrests

Law enforcement officials in one city in Georgia decided to increase their emphasis on enforcement of the narcotics laws. As a result, the number of white suspects arrested each year on drug charges increased slightly, while a much steeper increase occurred in arrests of black suspects. Over a five-year period, black suspects accounted for about 119,000 drug arrests; white suspects accounted for about 58,000 arrests, less than a third of the total. The disparity was stronger for cocaine cases than for marijuana cases. About 85 percent of all cocaine arrestees were black, while just over 40 percent of the marijuana arrestees were black.

When these figures are adjusted for the number of blacks and whites in the general population of the city, the arrest rate for African-Americans was more than 6 times the rate for whites. Even for marijuana arrests, where the racial disparities were less pronounced, the adjusted rate of arrest for blacks was about double the rate for whites. National surveys at the time suggested that a slightly larger proportion of blacks than whites used illicit drugs, but the numbers were nowhere close to the arrest rates produced by the department.

You are the mayor of this city and decide to investigate. Officers in the department tell you that more blacks are arrested for drug sales because they tend to make more sales on street corners and other places visible to the public, while white users and sellers tend more often to conduct their operations indoors. Are you convinced that this distinction accounts for the disparity?

D. PAPER ARRESTS: CITATIONS

An arrest is not the only method available to initiate a criminal prosecution or to secure a defendant's presence at judicial proceedings. There are some circumstances when a police officer will issue a "citation" or "appearance ticket" to a person, requiring the person to appear in court regarding a crime the officer believes the person has committed. As in other areas of police discretion, legal reforms in this field are moving in different directions. On the one hand, the range of offenses where the officer can use citation rather than arrest is expanding, giving the officer more options. On the other hand, in some limited circumstances the law restricts the officer to using a citation instead of an arrest.

■ NEW YORK CRIMINAL PROCEDURE LAW §§150.10, 150.20, 150.60

§150.10

An appearance ticket is a written notice issued and subscribed by a police officer or other public servant, . . . directing a designated person to appear in a designated local criminal court at a designated future time in connection with his alleged commission of a designated offense. . . .

§150.20

1. Whenever a police officer is authorized . . . to arrest a person without a warrant for an offense other than a class A, B, C or D felony, [the officer may] instead issue to and serve upon such person an appearance ticket.
2. (a) Whenever a police officer has arrested a person without a warrant for an offense other than a class A, B, C or D felony . . . such police officer may, instead of bringing such person before a local criminal court and promptly filing or causing the arresting peace officer or arresting person to file a local criminal court accusatory instrument therewith, issue to and serve upon such person an appearance ticket. The issuance and service of an appearance ticket under such circumstances may be conditioned upon a deposit of pre-arraignment bail. . . .

§150.60

If after the service of an appearance ticket and the filing of a local criminal court accusatory instrument charging the offense designated therein, the defendant does not appear in the designated local criminal court at the time such appearance ticket is returnable, the court may issue a summons or a warrant of arrest based upon the local criminal court accusatory instrument filed.

*COMMISSION STAFF NOTES ON DESK APPEARANCE TICKET PROVISIONS (1970 COMMENT)**

[An appearance ticket] is issued and served by a police officer or other public servant who has observed the commission of a minor offense, and it requires the offender to appear in a designated court upon a designated return date to answer a charge which the issuer of the ticket will formally file in the court some time after the issuance. In terms of basic function, an appearance ticket is used in some minor cases as a compassionate substitute for an arrest without a warrant, which is also employed to require or compel the court appearance of an offender against whom no formal charges have as yet been lodged.

On a state-wide basis, the use of appearance tickets is at present largely confined to traffic infraction cases. In New York City, however, numerous non-police public officials and employees, such as those of the Sanitation, Fire, Building and Markets Departments, are authorized to issue and serve such tickets in cases involving offenses peculiarly within their ambits. . . .

* [This is considered the legislative history for these provisions. The following excerpts mix paragraphs from the report for different statutory sections.—EDS.]

The theory of the proposed section is that under present law the virtues and advantages of the appearance ticket have not been sufficiently exploited. . . . The results to be expected from the new appearance ticket scheme are (1) an immense saving of police time, (2) elimination of much expense and embarrassment to defendants charged with minor offenses who are excellent risks to appear in court when required, and (3) above all, a significant reduction of that portion of our jail population consisting of unconvicted defendants awaiting trial or other disposition of their cases.

The advantages to the police may be partly appreciated by picturing the predicament of a police officer who observes the commission of a misdemeanor or petty offense by a person whom he either knows to be a resident of the community or whom he finds to have solid roots therein. Absent the appearance ticket device, two very awkward and unsatisfactory courses of action are available to the officer. Normal procedure requires him to arrest the defendant and, dropping his regular duties, take him to the station house to book him, and then to take him to a local criminal court where a formal information must be filed, the defendant arraigned, bail set, and so on. The even less appealing and equally time consuming alternative entails the officer first going to the court himself, filing an information against the defendant, obtaining a summons or a warrant of arrest and then returning to find the defendant and serve or execute such process; and all this in a case in which the simple issuance of an appearance ticket would almost certainly accomplish the same end result.

■ REVISED STATUTES OF NEBRASKA §§29-435, 29-427

§29-435

Except as provided in section 29-427, for any offense classified as an infraction, a citation shall be issued in lieu of arrest or continued custody. . . .

§29-427

Any peace officer having grounds for making an arrest may take the accused into custody or, already having done so, detain him further when the accused fails to identify himself satisfactorily, or refuses to sign the citation, or when the officer has reasonable grounds to believe that (1) the accused will refuse to respond to the citation, (2) such custody is necessary to protect the accused or others when his continued liberty would constitute a risk of immediate harm, (3) such action is necessary in order to carry out legitimate investigative functions, (4) the accused has no ties to the jurisdiction reasonably sufficient to assure his appearance, or (5) the accused has previously failed to appear in response to a citation.

■ STATE v. RICO BAYARD
71 P.3d 498 (Nev. 2003)

PER CURIAM.
Reno Police Officer Ty Sceirine witnessed Bayard commit two minor moving traffic violations. Bayard turned left onto a two-lane thoroughfare and instead of taking the closest lane to the center line Bayard drove immediately to the outside

lane, which is an illegal left turn. The second violation occurred when Bayard changed lanes abruptly. The officer followed the vehicle and observed a pedestrian waving at it. When the pedestrian spotted the patrol vehicle, he acted like he did not want to be seen flagging down the vehicle. At this point, Sceirine activated his lights and Bayard pulled his vehicle over to the side of the road. A male passenger seated beside Bayard was allowed to leave.

Bayard produced identification and cordially asked why he had been stopped. Sceirine told Bayard to step out of the vehicle. When Bayard exited the vehicle, he voluntarily informed Sceirine that he had a gun in his waistband and produced a valid concealed weapons permit. Bayard consented to a search of his person which yielded $116 in cash. Sceirine then arrested Bayard for violating local traffic ordinances. During the booking procedure, police strip-searched Bayard and bindles of cocaine and marijuana fell on the floor when he removed his underwear.

Bayard was charged with (1) trafficking in a controlled substance (cocaine), (2) possession of a controlled substance for the purpose of sale (marijuana), and (3) possession of a controlled substance for the purpose of sale (cocaine). After a preliminary hearing and arraignment, Bayard filed a motion to suppress the drugs based on the allegedly illegal arrest. The district court conducted a hearing and granted Bayard's motion, stating:

> The court finds that defendant's arrest violated [Nevada statutes] because he was arrested instead of being issued a citation even though there were no facts and circumstances which would cause a person of reasonable caution to believe that the defendant would disregard a written promise to appear. The evidence seized in the search incident to this arrest must be suppressed. . . .

The United States Supreme Court addressed the constitutional implications of a warrantless arrest for a misdemeanor offense in Atwater v. Lago Vista, 532 U.S. 318 (2001). In that case, an officer pulled over Gail Atwater, a small-town soccer mom with only one prior traffic citation and no criminal record, verbally berated her in front of her two small children, placed her in handcuffs behind her back, and took her to the police station. While at the station, police took away her jewelry, eyeglasses, shoes, and other personal possessions, took her "mug shot," and kept her in a jail cell for an hour. Atwater was forced to undergo this humiliation for committing the fine-only offense of failing to wear a seatbelt. In a controversial 5-4 decision, the United States Supreme Court upheld Atwater's arrest stating that if an officer "has probable cause to believe that an individual has committed even a very minor criminal offense in his presence, he may, without violating the Fourth Amendment, arrest the offender." The Court recognized, however, the states' power to legislatively restrict arrests for such minor offenses. The Court stated, "It is of course easier to devise a minor-offense limitation by statute than to derive one through the Constitution, simply because the statute can let the arrest power turn on any sort of practical consideration without having to subsume it under a broader principle." The Court also said it is "only natural that States should resort to this sort of legislative regulation [because] it is in the interest of the police to limit petty-offense arrests, which carry costs that are simply too great to incur without good reason." Numerous states have statutorily imposed more restrictive safeguards than those provided by the Fourth Amendment, [including Alabama, California, Kentucky, Louisiana, Maryland, South Dakota, Tennessee, and Virginia].

The *Atwater* dissent criticized the majority's opinion stating that providing "officers constitutional carte blanche to effect an arrest whenever there is probable cause to believe a fine-only misdemeanor has been committed is irreconcilable with the Fourth Amendment's command that seizures be reasonable." The dissent further states,

> The majority . . . acknowledges that "Atwater's claim to live free of pointless indignity and confinement clearly outweighs anything the City can raise against it specific to her case." But instead of remedying this imbalance, the majority allows itself to be swayed by the worry that "every discretionary judgment [by police] in the field [will] be converted into an occasion for constitutional review." It therefore mints a new rule that . . . is not only unsupported by our precedent, but runs contrary to the principles that lie at the core of the Fourth Amendment.

In Nevada, the Legislature has not forbidden warrantless arrests for minor traffic offenses. NRS 484.795 requires officers to perform an arrest in certain situations[15] and provides the officer with discretion to make an arrest or issue a citation in all other situations. The discretionary provision of NRS 484.795 states that when a person is halted by a peace officer for any violation of NRS Chapter 484 and is not required to be taken before a magistrate, the "person may, in the discretion of the peace officer, either be given a traffic citation, or be taken without unnecessary delay before the proper magistrate." The discretionary provision applies to the instant case. Bayard was stopped and arrested by Officer Sceirine for making an illegal left turn and lane change, violations of the Reno Municipal Traffic Code. He was cooperative, provided adequate identification, and was not under the influence of alcohol or a controlled substance. There is also no indication in the record that Officer Sceirine claimed a reasonable basis for concluding that Bayard would not respond to a traffic summons in municipal court. Thus, the mandatory provisions of NRS 484.795 do not apply.

The primary issue is whether Officer Sceirine abused his discretion by performing a full custodial arrest under the circumstances. Although the Legislature has given officers "discretion" in determining when to issue a citation or make an arrest for a traffic code violation, that discretion is not unfettered. Discretion "means power to act in an official capacity in a manner which appears to be *just and proper* under the circumstances." Black's Law Dictionary 419 (5th ed. 1979) (emphasis added). It also "means the capacity to distinguish between what is right and wrong, lawful or unlawful, wise or foolish, sufficiently to render one amenable and responsible for his acts." Id. An officer abuses his or her discretion when the officer exercises discretion in an arbitrary or unreasonable manner.

Both the Fourth Amendment of the United States Constitution and Article 1, Section 18 of the Nevada Constitution provide citizens with a right "to be secure in their persons, houses, papers and effects against unreasonable seizures and searches." Although the Nevada Constitution and the United States Constitution

---

15. The mandatory arrest procedures pertinent to this case are invoked when the driver provides insufficient identification or when the officer has reasonable grounds to conclude that the cited driver will not appear in court to respond to the citation or when the individual is charged with driving under the influence. NRS 484.795(1), (4). The officer's discretion to formally arrest is implicated when the above mandatory requirements are not met; that is, absent insufficient identification, if there is not a reasonable belief that the cited driver will not appear in court or is under the influence, the officer is statutorily empowered with discretion to arrest or cite the driver.

contain similar search and seizure clauses, the United States Supreme Court has noted that states are free to interpret their own constitutional provisions as providing greater protections than analogous federal provisions." . . .

We hold that an arrest made in violation of NRS 484.795 violates a suspect's right to be free from unlawful searches and seizures under Article 1, Section 18, even though the arrest does not offend the Fourth Amendment. An officer violates NRS 484.795 if the officer abuses his or her discretion in making a full custodial arrest instead of issuing a traffic citation. We adopt the test set forth by the Montana Supreme Court in State v. Bauer, 36 P.3d 892 (Mont. 2001), for determining the proper exercise of police discretion to arrest under NRS 484.795. To make a valid arrest based on state constitutional grounds, "an officer's exercise of discretion must be reasonable." Reasonableness requires probable cause that a traffic offense has been committed and circumstances that require immediate arrest. Absent special circumstances requiring immediate arrest, individuals should not be made to endure the humiliation of arrest and detention when a citation will satisfy the state's interest. Such special circumstances are contained in the mandatory section of NRS 484.795 or exist when an officer has probable cause to believe other criminal misconduct is afoot. This rule will help minimize arbitrary arrests based on race, religion, or other improper factors and will benefit law enforcement by limiting the high costs associated with arrests for minor traffic offenses.

In applying this test, we hold that Officer Sceirine abused his discretion because he had no legitimate reason to subject Bayard to the humiliation of a full custodial arrest instead of issuing him a citation. Bayard was cooperative at all times, provided the customary identification, volunteered that he was carrying a concealed weapon and furnished a valid permit, and even agreed to a search of his person for potential drugs and other weapons. The officer was not permitted to arrest Bayard based on a "hunch" or "whim" that Bayard was engaged in other illegal activity that might be revealed through a subsequent strip search or car search. The arrest was unlawful and violated Bayard's state constitutional right to be free from an unlawful search or seizure. . . . While in jail, Bayard was strip searched and narcotics were found on his person. [The] illegal drugs must be excluded from evidence because they were the product of an unlawful search and seizure in violation of Bayard's state constitutional rights. . . .

Notes

1. *Citations as supplement to arrest: majority position.* Every state gives its law enforcement officers the authority to issue citations (or "appearance tickets") for the violation of some criminal laws. Citations are ordinarily available to address traffic violations, but they are increasingly available for minor nontraffic violations of the criminal law—sometimes all "infractions" or specified misdemeanors. See Cincinnati Police Department Procedure Manual §12.555 (adults charged with misdemeanor offenses are eligible for Notice to Appear, except for specified misdemeanors such as weapons offense, second DUI offense, and three pending summons).

Some foreign jurisdictions make extensive use of devices such as citations to give police officers an alternative to custodial arrest. For instance, in Queensland, Australia, police can issue a "notice to appear" (NTA) for any criminal offense. The NTA can be issued in the field or after taking the person into custody. It is used most frequently for traffic violations, prostitution, drugs, and weapons charges. If police officers in the United States had similarly broad powers to use citations, do you believe they would use it in similar categories of cases? Would citation in the field or at the station prove more popular?

2. *Citations as replacement for arrest.* Many states now have statutes that attempt to control the choice between citations and arrests for certain traffic offenses. Some simply state that the officer "shall" use the citation, while others (such as the Nebraska statute reprinted above) require the citation unless the officer can demonstrate one of the designated exceptions. Will a law such as the Nebraska statute effectively limit the use of arrest?

On the constitutional level, the U.S. Supreme Court in Atwater v. City of Lago Vista, 532 U.S. 318 (2001), held that the federal constitution does not limit a police officer's power to arrest for a minor crime, where a state statute authorizes arrest for the offense. Before *Atwater*, state courts were reluctant to declare that state constitutions required use of a citation rather than an arrest. Relatively few state courts have addressed this question under state law, but about half the courts that took up the question after *Atwater* parted ways with the Supreme Court, as in the *Bayard* opinion from Nevada. See also State v. Askerooth, 681 N.W.2d 353 (Minn. 2004); State v. Brown, 792 N.E.2d 175 (Ohio 2003); but see People v. Fitzpatrick, 986 N.E.2d 1163 (Ill. 2013) (adopting *Atwater* under state constitution). There was no significant trend in state legislatures to expand police officer discretion over the use of citation versus arrest, even after *Atwater* made it clear that broad discretion was tolerable under the Fourth Amendment. For a sampling of the rich case law on this question, consult the web extension for this chapter at *http://www.crimpro.com/extension/ch05*.

In Virginia v. Moore, 553 U.S. 164 (2008), the U.S. Supreme Court explained that its holding in *Atwater* reaches broadly, such that even where state law *required* the officer to issue a summons rather than arrest a suspect for a traffic violation, the officer's decision to arrest was not unreasonable under the Fourth Amendment. As a matter of federal constitutional law, when an officer has probable cause to believe a person committed a crime, the arrest is constitutionally reasonable, regardless of whether a state statute authorizes the arrest.

3. *Choosing arrest vs. citation in practice.* If officers have discretion to choose between citation and arrest, why might they choose one over the other? What problems might result from extensive use of arrests? From extensive use of citations? In answering these questions, consider the issue from a number of different perspectives—police, courts, civil rights groups, minority groups, and various kinds of possible defendants. Also keep in mind the downstream effects of the officer's choice: Citations make it easier for the police to charge people with minor criminal law violations, because they don't have to go through the entire hassle of arresting and processing them. On the other hand, an arrest allows officers to conduct a full-blown search.

An empirical study of citation practices found that 87 percent of the agencies studied used citations in lieu of arrests for nearly a third of all incidents, most often for disorderly conduct, theft, trespassing, driving under suspension, and possession of marijuana cases. International Association of Chiefs of Police, Citation in Lieu of Arrest: Examining Law Enforcement's Use of Citation Across the United States (April 2016), at *http://www.iacp.org/citation*.

4. *Search incident to citation.* While officers are authorized to conduct a search incident to arrest, in Knowles v. Iowa, 525 U.S. 113 (1998), the Supreme Court held

that officers may not conduct a search incident to citation, even in cases where the officer had the discretion to either arrest or issue a citation. Before the Supreme Court's 1998 ruling in *Knowles,* very few courts addressed the question of whether police could conduct a search incident to citation. Why did state courts develop so little case law on this subject? Was the practice of "search incident to citation" simply too rare to generate much litigation? Or was the practice common but unchallenged because prosecutors used other techniques to avoid appellate rulings on the subject? The few state court opinions on the topic tend to endorse *Knowles.* See State v. Green, 79 So. 3d 1013 (La. 2012).

Here, as with many issues surrounding arrest and detention, police department policies often supplement statutes and judicial doctrine. See Phoenix Police Department Operations Order 4.11(7)(E)) (prohibiting search incident to issuance of a citation). Does *Knowles* apply outside the traffic stop context? See Lovelace v. Commonwealth, 522 S.E.2d 856 (Va. 1999) (applies to brief detention of pedestrian to issue summons).

5. *Pretextual arrests and limiting factors.* Recall the discussion from Chapter 2 about pretextual stops. Are the arguments any stronger or weaker to place controls on pretextual arrests—arrests motivated by some factor other than a desire to enforce some law that the officer has probable cause to believe the suspect has violated? Courts have given comparable treatment to claims about pretextual stops and arrests. See Arkansas v. Sullivan, 532 U.S. 769 (2001) (arrest based on probable cause does not violate Fourth Amendment even if arrest was motivated by desire to conduct search incident to arrest); State v. Hofmann, 537 N.W.2d 767 (Iowa 1995); but see State v. Sullivan, 74 S.W.3d 215 (Ark. 2002) (state constitution bars pretextual arrests for misdemeanor punishable by 90 days in jail).

There are several practical limits on the willingness of police officers to arrest for minor crimes, including the amount of time and effort it takes to process an arrest. Does the arrest actually have to happen before the search incident? Could the officer announce an arrest, conduct the search, and then convert the arrest to a citation? See Wayne A. Logan, An Exception Swallows a Rule: Police Authority to Search Incident to Arrest, 19 Yale L. & Pol'y Rev. 381, 406-414 (2001) (distinguishes custodial and noncustodial arrests; argues that search incident should only happen if the officer actually does carry out a custodial arrest).

6. *Arrests for minor crimes and race.* Does the officer's discretion to choose between arrest and citation for minor crimes create more risk of racial discrimination in enforcement? If you were advising a police department about a proposed campaign to stop and ticket more drivers who fail to use seat belts, and you had information that drivers from certain demographic groups use seat belts less frequently than other drivers, what advice would you give about carrying out this program? In the context of drug crimes, could you exercise arrest discretion in a way that equalizes the impact of enforcement on suburban and urban neighborhoods?

E. USE OF FORCE IN MAKING ARRESTS

The prior sections of this chapter have focused on *whether* an officer should make an arrest. In addition, the legal system pays attention to *how* a police officer makes an arrest. Legal controls are most vigorous when a suspect resists the officer's effort to make the arrest and the officer must use force — either deadly or nondeadly — to complete the arrest.

■ WILLIAM BLACKSTONE, COMMENTARIES ON THE LAWS OF ENGLAND

Vol. 4, p. 289 (1769)

[In] case of felony actually committed, or a dangerous wounding whereby felony is likely to ensue, [the constable] may upon probable suspicion arrest the felon; and for that purpose is authorized (as upon a justice's warrant) to break open doors, and even to kill the felon if he cannot otherwise be taken.

■ TENNESSEE v. EDWARD GARNER

471 U.S. 1 (1985)

WHITE, J.*

This case requires us to determine the constitutionality of the use of deadly force to prevent the escape of an apparently unarmed suspected felon. We conclude that such force may not be used unless it is necessary to prevent the escape and the officer has probable cause to believe that the suspect poses a significant threat of death or serious physical injury to the officer or others.

I.

At about 10:45 P.M. on October 3, 1974, Memphis Police Officers Elton Hymon and Leslie Wright were dispatched to answer a "prowler inside call." Upon arriving at the scene they saw a woman standing on her porch and gesturing toward the adjacent house. She told them she had heard glass breaking and that "they" or "someone" was breaking in next door. While Wright radioed the dispatcher to say that they were on the scene, Hymon went behind the house. He heard a door slam and saw someone run across the backyard. The fleeing suspect, who was [Edward Garner], stopped at a 6-feet-high chain link fence at the edge of the yard. With the aid of a flashlight, Hymon was able to see Garner's face and hands. He saw no sign of a weapon, and, though not certain, was "reasonably sure" and "figured" that Garner was unarmed. He thought Garner was 17 or 18 years old and about 5'5" or 5'7" tall.[2] While Garner was crouched at the base of the fence, Hymon called out "police, halt" and took a few steps toward him. Garner then began to climb over the fence. Convinced that if Garner made it over the fence he would elude capture,[3] Hymon shot him. The bullet hit Garner in the back of the head. Garner was taken by ambulance to a hospital, where he died on the operating table. Ten dollars and a purse taken from the house were found on his body.

---

* [Justices Brennan, Marshall, Blackmun, Powell, and Stevens joined in this opinion.—EDS.]

2. In fact, Garner, an eighth-grader, was 15. He was 5'4" tall and weighed somewhere around 100 or 110 pounds.

3. When asked at trial why he fired, Hymon stated . . . that the area beyond the fence was dark, that he could not have gotten over the fence easily because he was carrying a lot of equipment and wearing heavy boots, and that Garner, being younger and more energetic, could have outrun him.

In using deadly force to prevent the escape, Hymon was acting under the authority of a Tennessee statute and pursuant to Police Department policy. The statute provides that "[if], after notice of the intention to arrest the defendant, he either flee or forcibly resist, the officer may use all the necessary means to effect the arrest." Tenn. Code §40-7-108. The Department policy was slightly more restrictive than the statute, but still allowed the use of deadly force in cases of burglary. The incident was reviewed by the Memphis Police Firearm's Review Board and presented to a grand jury. Neither took any action.

Garner's father then brought this action, [seeking damages for asserted violations of Garner's constitutional rights]. After a 3-day bench trial, the District Court entered judgment for all defendants. [The trial court concluded that] Hymon had employed the only reasonable and practicable means of preventing Garner's escape. Garner had "recklessly and heedlessly attempted to vault over the fence to escape, thereby assuming the risk of being fired upon." . . .

II.

Whenever an officer restrains the freedom of a person to walk away, he has seized that person. While it is not always clear just when minimal police interference becomes a seizure there can be no question that apprehension by the use of deadly force is a seizure subject to the reasonableness requirement of the Fourth Amendment.

A police officer may arrest a person if he has probable cause to believe that person committed a crime. [The state argues] that if this requirement is satisfied the Fourth Amendment has nothing to say about how that seizure is made. This submission ignores the many cases in which this Court, by balancing the extent of the intrusion against the need for it, has examined the reasonableness of the manner in which a search or seizure is conducted. To determine the constitutionality of a seizure "[we] must balance the nature and quality of the intrusion on the individual's Fourth Amendment interests against the importance of the governmental interests alleged to justify the intrusion." We have described "the balancing of competing interests" as "the key principle of the Fourth Amendment." Because one of the factors is the extent of the intrusion, it is plain that reasonableness depends on not only when a seizure is made, but also how it is carried out.

[The balancing process] demonstrates that, notwithstanding probable cause to seize a suspect, an officer may not always do so by killing him. The intrusiveness of a seizure by means of deadly force is unmatched. The suspect's fundamental interest in his own life need not be elaborated upon. The use of deadly force also frustrates the interest of the individual, and of society, in judicial determination of guilt and punishment. Against these interests are ranged governmental interests in effective law enforcement. It is argued that overall violence will be reduced by encouraging the peaceful submission of suspects who know that they may be shot if they flee. Effectiveness in making arrests requires the resort to deadly force, or at least the meaningful threat thereof. "Being able to arrest such individuals is a condition precedent to the state's entire system of law enforcement."

Without in any way disparaging the importance of these goals, we are not convinced that the use of deadly force is a sufficiently productive means of accomplishing them to justify the killing of nonviolent suspects. The use of deadly force is a self-defeating way of apprehending a suspect and so setting the criminal justice mechanism in motion. If successful, it guarantees that that mechanism will not be set in motion. And while the meaningful threat of deadly force might be thought to lead to the arrest of more live suspects by discouraging escape attempts, the presently available evidence does not support this thesis. The fact is that a majority of police departments in this country have forbidden the use of deadly force against nonviolent suspects. If those charged with the enforcement of the criminal law have abjured the use of deadly force in arresting nondangerous felons, there is a substantial basis for doubting that the use of such force is an essential attribute of the arrest power in all felony cases. Petitioners and appellant have not persuaded us that shooting nondangerous fleeing suspects is so vital as to outweigh the suspect's interest in his own life.

The use of deadly force to prevent the escape of all felony suspects, whatever the circumstances, is constitutionally unreasonable. It is not better that all felony suspects die than that they escape. Where the suspect poses no immediate threat to the officer and no threat to others, the harm resulting from failing to apprehend him does not justify the use of deadly force to do so. It is no doubt unfortunate when a suspect who is in sight escapes, but the fact that the police arrive a little late or are a little slower afoot does not always justify killing the suspect. A police officer may not seize an unarmed, nondangerous suspect by shooting him dead. The Tennessee statute is unconstitutional insofar as it authorizes the use of deadly force against such fleeing suspects.

It is not, however, unconstitutional on its face. Where the officer has probable cause to believe that the suspect poses a threat of serious physical harm, either to the officer or to others, it is not constitutionally unreasonable to prevent escape by using deadly force. Thus, if the suspect threatens the officer with a weapon or there is probable cause to believe that he has committed a crime involving the infliction or threatened infliction of serious physical harm, deadly force may be used if necessary to prevent escape, and if, where feasible, some warning has been given. As applied in such circumstances, the Tennessee statute would pass constitutional muster.

III.

It is insisted that the Fourth Amendment must be construed in light of the common-law rule, which allowed the use of whatever force was necessary to effect the arrest of a fleeing felon, though not a misdemeanant. As stated in Hale's posthumously published Pleas of the Crown:

> [If] persons that are pursued by these officers for felony or the just suspicion thereof . . . shall not yield themselves to these officers, but shall either resist or fly before they are apprehended or being apprehended shall rescue themselves and resist or fly, so that they cannot be otherwise apprehended, and are upon necessity slain therein, because they cannot be otherwise taken, it is no felony.

2 M. Hale, Historia Placitoram Coronae 85 (1736). See also 4 W. Blackstone, Commentaries *289. Most American jurisdictions also imposed a flat prohibition against the use of deadly force to stop a fleeing misdemeanant, coupled with a general privilege to use such force to stop a fleeing felon.

The State and city argue that because this was the prevailing rule at the time of the adoption of the Fourth Amendment and for some time thereafter, and is still in force in some States, use of deadly force against a fleeing felon must be "reasonable." It is true that this Court has often looked to the common law in evaluating the reasonableness, for Fourth Amendment purposes, of police activity. On the other hand, it "has not simply frozen into constitutional law those law enforcement practices that existed at the time of the Fourth Amendment's passage." Because of sweeping change in the legal and technological context, reliance on the common-law rule in this case would be a mistaken literalism that ignores the purposes of a historical inquiry.

It has been pointed out many times that the common-law rule is best understood in light of the fact that it arose at a time when virtually all felonies were punishable by death. Though effected without the protections and formalities of an orderly trial and conviction, the killing of a resisting or fleeing felon resulted in no greater consequences than those authorized for punishment of the felony of which the individual was charged or suspected. Courts have also justified the common-law rule by emphasizing the relative dangerousness of felons.

Neither of these justifications makes sense today. Almost all crimes formerly punishable by death no longer are or can be. And while in earlier times the gulf between the felonies and the minor offences was broad and deep, today the distinction is minor and often arbitrary. Many crimes classified as misdemeanors, or nonexistent, at common law are now felonies. These changes have undermined the concept, which was questionable to begin with, that use of deadly force against a fleeing felon is merely a speedier execution of someone who has already forfeited his life. They have also made the assumption that a "felon" is more dangerous than a misdemeanant untenable. Indeed, numerous misdemeanors involve conduct more dangerous than many felonies.

There is an additional reason why the common-law rule cannot be directly translated to the present day. The common-law rule developed at a time when weapons were rudimentary. Deadly force could be inflicted almost solely in a hand-to-hand struggle during which, necessarily, the safety of the arresting officer was at risk. Handguns were not carried by police officers until the latter half of the last century. Only then did it become possible to use deadly force from a distance as a means of apprehension. As a practical matter, the use of deadly force under the standard articulation of the common-law rule has an altogether different meaning—and harsher consequences—now than in past centuries. . . .

In evaluating the reasonableness of police procedures under the Fourth Amendment, we have also looked to prevailing rules in individual jurisdictions. The rules in the States are varied. Some 19 States have codified the common-law rule, though in two of these the courts have significantly limited the statute. Four States, though without a relevant statute, apparently retain the common-law rule. Two States have adopted the Model Penal Code's provision verbatim.[8] Eighteen others allow, in

8. [Section 3.07(2) (b) of the Model Penal Code provides:

The use of deadly force is not justifiable . . . unless (i) the arrest is for a felony; and (ii) the person effecting the arrest is authorized to act as a peace officer or is assisting a person whom he believes to be authorized to act as a peace officer; and (iii) the actor believes that the force employed creates no substantial risk of injury to innocent persons; and (iv) the actor believes that (1) the crime for which the arrest is made involved conduct including the use or threatened use of deadly force; or (2) there is a substantial risk that the person to be arrested will cause death or serious bodily harm if his apprehension is delayed. —Eds.]

slightly varying language, the use of deadly force only if the suspect has committed a felony involving the use or threat of physical or deadly force, or is escaping with a deadly weapon, or is likely to endanger life or inflict serious physical injury if not arrested. . . .

It cannot be said that there is a constant or overwhelming trend away from the common-law rule. In recent years, some States have reviewed their laws and expressly rejected abandonment of the common-law rule. Nonetheless, the long-term movement has been away from the rule that deadly force may be used against any fleeing felon, and that remains the rule in less than half the States.

This trend is more evident and impressive when viewed in light of the policies adopted by the police departments themselves. Overwhelmingly, these are more restrictive than the common-law rule. The Federal Bureau of Investigation and the New York City Police Department, for example, both forbid the use of firearms except when necessary to prevent death or grievous bodily harm. For accreditation by the Commission on Accreditation for Law Enforcement Agencies, a department must restrict the use of deadly force to situations where "the officer reasonably believes that the action is in defense of human life . . . or in defense of any person in immediate danger of serious physical injury." A 1974 study reported that the police department regulations in a majority of the large cities of the United States allowed the firing of a weapon only when a felon presented a threat of death or serious bodily harm. Overall, only 7.5 percent of departmental and municipal policies explicitly permit the use of deadly force against any felon; 86.8 percent explicitly do not. In light of the rules adopted by those who must actually administer them, the older and fading common-law view is a dubious indicium of the constitutionality of the Tennessee statute now before us.

Actual departmental policies are important for an additional reason. We would hesitate to declare a police practice of long standing "unreasonable" if doing so would severely hamper effective law enforcement. But the indications are to the contrary. There has been no suggestion that crime has worsened in any way in jurisdictions that have adopted, by legislation or departmental policy, rules similar to that announced today. . . .

Nor do we agree with [the state] that the rule we have adopted requires the police to make impossible, split-second evaluations of unknowable facts. We do not deny the practical difficulties of attempting to assess the suspect's dangerousness. However, similarly difficult judgments must be made by the police in equally uncertain circumstances. See, e.g., Terry v. Ohio, 392 U.S. 1 (1968). Nor is there any indication that in States that allow the use of deadly force only against dangerous suspects, the standard has been difficult to apply or has led to a rash of litigation involving inappropriate second-guessing of police officers' split-second decisions. Moreover, the highly technical felony/misdemeanor distinction is equally, if not more, difficult to apply in the field. An officer is in no position to know, for example, the precise value of property stolen, or whether the crime was a first or second offense. . . .

IV.

The [district court did not determine whether Garner presented a danger of physical harm to Officer Hymon or others]. The court did find, however, that Garner appeared to be unarmed, though Hymon could not be certain that was the case. Restated in Fourth Amendment terms, this means Hymon had no articulable basis to think Garner was armed.

[These facts do not justify the use of deadly force.] Officer Hymon could not reasonably have believed that Garner—young, slight, and unarmed—posed any threat. Indeed, Hymon never attempted to justify his actions on any basis other than the need to prevent an escape. [The] fact that Garner was a suspected burglar could not, without regard to the other circumstances, automatically justify the use of deadly force. Hymon did not have probable cause to believe that Garner, whom he correctly believed to be unarmed, posed any physical danger to himself or others.

The dissent argues that the shooting was justified by the fact that Officer Hymon had probable cause to believe that Garner had committed a nighttime burglary. While we agree that burglary is a serious crime, we cannot agree that it is so dangerous as automatically to justify the use of deadly force. The FBI classifies burglary as a "property" rather than a "violent" crime. Although the armed burglar would present a different situation, the fact that an unarmed suspect has broken into a dwelling at night does not automatically mean he is physically dangerous. This case demonstrates as much. In fact, the available statistics demonstrate that burglaries only rarely involve physical violence. During the 10-year period from 1973-1982, only 3.8 percent of all burglaries involved violent crime.[23] . . .

V.

[We] hold that the statute is invalid insofar as it purported to give Hymon the authority to act as he did. [The] case is remanded for further proceedings consistent with this opinion. So ordered.

O'CONNOR, J., dissenting.*

[Although] the circumstances of this case are unquestionably tragic and unfortunate, our constitutional holdings must be sensitive both to the history of the Fourth Amendment and to the general implications of the Court's reasoning. By disregarding the serious and dangerous nature of residential burglaries and the longstanding practice of many States, the Court effectively creates a Fourth Amendment right allowing a burglary suspect to flee unimpeded from a police officer who has probable cause to arrest, who has ordered the suspect to halt, and who has no means short of firing his weapon to prevent escape. I do not believe that the Fourth Amendment supports such a right, and I accordingly dissent.

I.

The facts below warrant brief review because they highlight the difficult, split-second decisions police officers must make in these circumstances. . . . As Officer

---

23. The dissent points out that three-fifths of all rapes in the home, three-fifths of all home robberies, and about a third of home assaults are committed by burglars. These figures mean only that if one knows that a suspect committed a rape in the home, there is a good chance that the suspect is also a burglar. That has nothing to do with the question here, which is whether the fact that someone has committed a burglary indicates that he has committed, or might commit, a violent crime. The dissent also points out that this 3.8% adds up to 2.8 million violent crimes over a 10-year period, as if to imply that today's holding will let loose 2.8 million violent burglars. The relevant universe is, of course, far smaller. At issue is only that tiny fraction of cases where violence has taken place and an officer who has no other means of apprehending the suspect is unaware of its occurrence.

* [Chief Justice Burger and Justice Rehnquist joined in this opinion.—EDS.]

Hymon walked behind the house, he heard a door slam. He saw Edward Eugene Garner run away from the house through the dark and cluttered backyard. Garner crouched next to a 6-foot-high fence. Officer Hymon thought Garner was an adult and was unsure whether Garner was armed because Hymon "had no idea what was in the hand [that he could not see] or what he might have had on his person." In fact, Garner was 15 years old and unarmed. Hymon also did not know whether accomplices remained inside the house. . . .

The precise issue before the Court deserves emphasis. . . . The issue is not the constitutional validity of the Tennessee statute on its face or as applied to some hypothetical set of facts. Instead, the issue is whether the use of deadly force by Officer Hymon under the circumstances of this case violated Garner's constitutional rights. Thus, the majority's assertion that a police officer who has probable cause to seize a suspect "may not always do so by killing him," is unexceptionable but also of little relevance to the question presented here. . . . The question we must address is whether the Constitution allows the use of such force to apprehend a suspect who resists arrest by attempting to flee the scene of a nighttime burglary of a residence.

II.

[We must balance] the important public interest in crime prevention and detection and the nature and quality of the intrusion upon legitimate interests of the individual. In striking this balance here, it is crucial to acknowledge that police use of deadly force to apprehend a fleeing criminal suspect falls within the "rubric of police conduct . . . necessarily [involving] swift action predicated upon the on-the-spot observations of the officer on the beat." Terry v. Ohio, 392 U.S. 1 (1968). The clarity of hindsight cannot provide the standard for judging the reasonableness of police decisions made in uncertain and often dangerous circumstances. . . .

The public interest involved in the use of deadly force as a last resort to apprehend a fleeing burglary suspect relates primarily to the serious nature of the crime. Household burglaries not only represent the illegal entry into a person's home, but also "[pose] real risk of serious harm to others." According to recent Department of Justice statistics, "[three-fifths] of all rapes in the home, three-fifths of all home robberies, and about a third of home aggravated and simple assaults are committed by burglars." During the period 1973-1982, 2.8 million such violent crimes were committed in the course of burglaries. Victims of a forcible intrusion into their home by a nighttime prowler will find little consolation in the majority's confident assertion that "burglaries only rarely involve physical violence." Moreover, even if a particular burglary, when viewed in retrospect, does not involve physical harm to others, the "harsh potentialities for violence" inherent in the forced entry into a home preclude characterization of the crime as [innocuous or nonviolent].

Because burglary is a serious and dangerous felony, the public interest in the prevention and detection of the crime is of compelling importance. Where a police officer has probable cause to arrest a suspected burglar, the use of deadly force as a last resort might well be the only means of apprehending the suspect. With respect to a particular burglary, subsequent investigation simply cannot represent a substitute for immediate apprehension of the criminal suspect at the scene. Indeed, the Captain of the Memphis Police Department testified that in his city, if apprehension is not immediate, it is likely that the suspect will not be caught. Although some law enforcement agencies may choose to assume the risk that a criminal will remain at large, the Tennessee statute reflects a legislative determination that the [provision will] assist the police in apprehending suspected perpetrators of serious crimes and provide notice that a lawful police order to stop and submit to arrest may not be ignored with impunity. . . .

Against the strong public interests justifying the conduct at issue here must be weighed the individual interests implicated in the use of deadly force by police officers. The majority declares that "[the] suspect's fundamental interest in his own life need not be elaborated upon." This blithe assertion hardly provides an adequate substitute for the majority's failure to acknowledge the distinctive manner in which the suspect's interest in his life is even exposed to risk. [The] officer's use of force resulted because the suspected burglar refused to heed [his command to halt] and the officer reasonably believed that there was no means short of firing his weapon to apprehend the suspect. Without questioning the importance of a person's interest in his life, I do not think this interest encompasses a right to flee unimpeded from the scene of a burglary. The legitimate interests of the suspect in these circumstances are adequately accommodated by the Tennessee statute: to avoid the use of deadly force and the consequent risk to his life, the suspect need merely obey the valid order to halt.

A proper balancing of the interests involved suggests that use of deadly force as a last resort to apprehend a criminal suspect fleeing from the scene of a nighttime burglary is not unreasonable within the meaning of the Fourth Amendment. Admittedly, the events giving rise to this case are in retrospect deeply regrettable. No one can view the death of an unarmed and apparently nonviolent 15-year-old without sorrow, much less disapproval. Nonetheless, the reasonableness of Officer Hymon's conduct for purposes of the Fourth Amendment cannot be evaluated by what later appears to have been a preferable course of police action. [Instead], the question is whether it is constitutionally impermissible for police officers, as a last resort, to shoot a burglary suspect fleeing the scene of the crime. . . .

IV.

I cannot accept the majority's creation of a constitutional right to flight for burglary suspects seeking to avoid capture at the scene of the crime. Whatever the constitutional limits on police use of deadly force in order to apprehend a fleeing felon, I do not believe they are exceeded in a case in which a police officer has probable cause to arrest a suspect at the scene of a residential burglary, orders the suspect to halt, and then fires his weapon as a last resort to prevent the suspect's escape into the night. I respectfully dissent.

Notes

1. *Deadly force: majority position.* In the wake of *Garner,* most states now have statutes either meeting or surpassing the constitutional minimum described in that decision. More than 35 states follow the Model Penal Code provisions on the use of force; more than a dozen of these states adopted (or reaffirmed) this position after the decision in *Garner.* Other states enforce the constitutional requirements through judicial decisions. Chad Flanders & Joseph C. Welling, Police Use of Deadly Force: State Statutes 30 Years after *Garner,* St. Louis U. L.J. Online (Jan. 15, 2016),

http://www.slu.edu/colleges/law/journal/police-use-of-deadly-force-state-statues-30-years-after-garner/. Police departments now routinely adopt written policies regarding the use of deadly force, even departments that ordinarily do not maintain written operational guidelines. In fact, 100 percent of the police departments serving jurisdictions with populations greater than 10,000 have adopted written deadly force policies. About 90 percent of all police departments have written policies on nondeadly force. Bureau of Justice Statistics, Local Police Departments, 2007 (December 2010, NCJ 231174).

Are the situations in which police can use deadly force after *Garner* sufficiently clear to allow police to anticipate and train for those situations? Does *Garner* create an incentive for perjury by officers being sued for their use of force?

2. *Excessive nondeadly force.* The police need not use deadly force to provoke a claim that they used force improperly to carry out an arrest. Many civil damage claims are founded on incidents involving nondeadly force used during arrests. The use of nondeadly force raises potential claims under the Fourth Amendment that an unreasonable seizure occurred. But in much of the litigation over nondeadly force, traditional doctrines of tort law govern. Claims are made under state tort law, federal civil rights laws, or both. The question in such cases is often whether the officer reasonably believed such force to be necessary to accomplish a legitimate police purpose. Are civil juries less capable of evaluating claims of negligence or gross negligence by the police than they are in other types of tort cases?

3. *Changing times.* What societal changes since 1985 might be the basis for arguing that the Supreme Court should reverse *Garner*? What about the emergence of methamphetamine or the presence of Uzis and Mac 10s? The increase in the number of homicides among youth? What if researchers found an increase in the number of killings committed by burglars?

Since the early 1970s, in a trend that *Garner* has reinforced, killings of citizens by police have decreased substantially, as have killings of police by citizens. Documentation of this trend is available on the web extension for this chapter at *http://www.crimpro.com/ extension/ch05*. These changes occurred despite a largely stable, high homicide rate nationwide and dramatically increasing levels of homicide among youth in urban centers. To the extent the reduction in police killings (and killings of police) can be attributed to *Garner*, does this positive social change justify the original decision? Should courts intentionally conduct experiments, or is experimentation the sole province of legislatures, executive branch agencies, nonprofit foundations, and academics?

4. *Racial patterns in the use of excessive force.* Criminologists have extensively studied police use of deadly force; decades ago, one researcher summarized the thrust of the studies as follows: "The literature on police use of deadly force has produced two major findings. First, researchers report extreme variation in rates of police shooting among American jurisdictions. Second, regardless of its geographic scope, the research invariably reports that the percentage of police shootings involving black victims far exceeds the percentage of blacks in the population." James Fyfe, Blind Justice: Police Shootings in Memphis, 73 J. Crim. L. & Criminology 707 (1982); see also Jerome Skolnick & James Fyfe, Above the Law: Police and the Excessive Use of Force (1993). In some places, this pattern might be explained by the disproportionate number of black suspects involved in the most serious violent crimes. In other places, such as Memphis (the location of the shooting in *Garner*) between 1969 and

1976, African Americans were more likely to be injured or killed, even after controlling for seriousness of the suspected crime.

More recent studies have produced mixed results, with about half of the studies concluding that the race of the suspect influenced police use of force, in at least some settings, after controlling for other factors. Charles F. Klahm & Rob Tillyer, Understanding Police Use of Force: A Review of the Evidence, 7 Sw. J. Crim. Justice 214, 216-218 (2010) (8 of 17 studies show no relationship); see also Bureau of Justice Statistics, Contacts Between Police and the Public, 2008 at 12 (2011, NCJ 234599) ("Blacks were more likely than whites or Hispanics to experience use or threat of force.").

———

Police departments have devoted much attention to their policies for the use of force, both deadly and nondeadly. Their efforts go far beyond the constitutional requirements set out in *Garner* or in state constitutional decisions. The following materials suggest, both directly and more obliquely, the forces that compel police departments to develop these rules.

CHARLOTTE-MECKLENBURG POLICE DEPARTMENT 600-020 INTERACTIVE DIRECTIVES GUIDE USE OF FORCE CONTINUUM *EFFECTIVE DATE 05/12/2016*

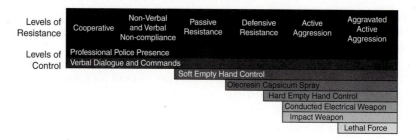

The Use of Force Continuum is a guideline for officers in making critical use of force decisions. The above image illustrates the options that an officer has at each level of resistance. It should be noted that professional presence and verbal interaction are present at every level of resistance.

Both State and Federal law require that all force be reasonable. In Graham v. Connor, the United States Supreme Court stated, "the test of reasonableness under the Fourth Amendment is not capable of precise definition or mechanical application, however, its proper application requires careful attention to the facts and circumstances of each particular case including the severity of the crime at issue, whether the suspect poses an immediate threat to the safety of the officers or others and whether he is actively resisting arrest or attempting to evade arrest by flight." In addition, an officer should take into account his or her abilities to handle the situation without force, or with lower levels of force.

The reasonableness of a particular use of force must be evaluated from the perspective of a reasonable officer on the scene, rather than with the 20/20 vision of hindsight. Determining reasonableness must include the fact that police officers are often forced to make split-second decisions about the amount of force necessary in a particular situation. Additionally, these split-second decisions occur in tense, uncertain, and rapidly evolving circumstances.

In deciding which level of control an officer should use, the officer should reasonably believe that a lower level of control is not sufficient and a higher level of control is not reasonably necessary. The level of control must be based on the current level of resistance when the control is applied. The Use of Force Continuum is not designed to be a step-by-step progression; the escalation and de-escalation by the officer or the subject may not be sequential. Moreover, in circumstances where a directive conflicts with the continuum, an officer should rely upon the directive. For example, officers are prohibited from shooting at a moving vehicle unless the officer believes that no other option is reasonably available.

Levels of Resistance:

- *Nonverbal and Verbal Noncompliance*: The subject expresses his intentions not to comply through verbal and nonverbal means. Statements by a subject ranging from pleading to physical threats may be encountered. This also includes physical gestures, stances, and subconscious mannerisms. The subject's actions at this stage do not equate to a risk of immediate danger to the officer, another person, or themselves.
- *Passive Resistance*: The subject does not cooperate with an officer's commands, and does not take action to prevent being taken into custody. An example of this would be a subject is taken into custody and the subject goes limp. The subject must then be carried away upon arrest. The subject's actions at this stage do not equate to a risk of immediate danger to the officer, another person, or themselves.
- *Defensive Resistance*: The subject is actively taking measures to prevent being taken into custody. This action may include twisting, pulling, holding onto fixed objects, or running away. The subject's actions at this stage do not equate to a risk of immediate danger to the officer, another person, or themselves.
- *Active Aggression*: At this level of resistance, the subject poses a risk of immediate danger to the officer, another person, or themselves. This aggression may manifest itself through punching, kicking, striking, or any other action when apparent that the subject has the immediate means to injure an officer, another person, or themselves.
- *Aggravated Active Aggression*: Aggravated Active Aggression includes actions that are likely to result in the death or serious bodily injury to an officer. These actions may include discharge of a firearm, use of a blunt or bladed weapon, and extreme physical force.

Levels of Control:

- *Professional Presence*: The displays of visual images of authority as well as a professional manner are present at every level of resistance. This includes all symbols of police authority including the badge, uniform, and marked police vehicle.
- *Verbal Dialogue and Commands*: Communication is critical to any potential use of force situation. This level of control includes any verbal requests, directions, or commands from the officer to a subject. Verbal interaction is present at every level of resistance.

- *Soft Empty Hand Control:* These techniques are not impact oriented and may be appropriate when a subject is engaged in passive or defensive resistance. The most appropriate response to passive resistance may include simply grabbing onto a subject, applying pressure points, handcuffing a subject to maintain control, or applying a joint lock to control a subject's movement. The most appropriate soft empty hand control response to defensive resistance may include arm bar takedowns, leg sweeps, and team takedowns.
- *Oleoresin Capsicum (OC) Spray:* OC spray is approved for use in situations where the officer believes that the attempts to control a subject may result in injury to the subject or the officer. OC should be utilized at a range of 3 to 8 feet, and should be accompanied by loud verbal commands.
- *Hard Empty Hand Control:* These techniques are impact oriented and include knee strikes, elbow strikes, punches, and kicks. Control strikes are used to get a subject under control and include strikes to pressure points such as the common peronneal (side of the leg), radial nerve (top of the forearm), or brachial plexus origin (side of neck). Defensive strikes are used by an officer to protect him- or herself from attack and may include strikes to other areas of the body including the abdomen or head.
- *Conducted Electrical Weapon (CEW):* The TASER device is used in situations where a subject presents an imminent physical threat to an officer, themselves, or another person.
- *Impact Weapon:* Less Lethal impact weapon strikes are targeted toward major muscle groups. The common peroneal nerve on the side of the leg is the primary target for impact weapon strikes.
- *Lethal Force:* Lethal force is any manner of force that is reasonably likely to cause death or serious injury. This includes, but is not limited to, the use of a firearm, striking the head or neck area with an impact weapon, or the choking of an arrestee.

Problem 5-4. Ruby Ridge

When Randy Weaver failed to appear in court on federal weapons charges, federal marshals decided to arrest him at his home in Ruby Ridge, Idaho. While several agents were walking around the property before approaching the house, a gun battle erupted between the marshals and Weaver's 14-year-old son, who was out walking and carrying a rifle when he encountered the agents. Weaver's son and one of the marshals died in the firefight.

The federal government was aware that other adults and children were on the Weaver property and that Weaver and his family owned and used a large number of firearms. As a result, the FBI sent several SWAT teams and a hostage rescue team to support the marshals in their effort to apprehend Weaver.

The FBI has general policies regarding the use of deadly force by its agents. The standard FBI rules at that time stated that an agent could use deadly force if the agent or some third party is threatened with "grievous" bodily injury. However, when FBI tactical teams are deployed, specialized "rules of engagement" can supplement the general policy. Rules of engagement are instructions that clearly indicate what action agents should take when confronted, threatened, or fired upon by someone. The on-scene commander formulates the rules of engagement. The special rules of engagement in effect at Ruby Ridge stated:

> If any adult in the compound is observed with a weapon after the surrender announcement is made, deadly force can and should be employed to neutralize this individual. If any adult male is observed with a weapon prior to the announcement, deadly force can and should be employed, if the shot can be taken without endangering any children.

The on-scene commander discussed these rules of engagement with supervisors within the FBI but not with legal counsel for the agency.

There were many interpretations of the rules of engagement among the FBI SWAT teams deployed to the Ruby Ridge site. One SWAT team leader recalled the rules as "if you see Weaver or Harris outside with a weapon, you've got the green light." Another member of a SWAT team remembered the rules as, "if you see 'em, shoot 'em."

During the ensuing siege, a member of the FBI's hostage rescue team shot and killed Weaver's wife while she was standing behind a door, holding her 10-month-old baby. Kevin Harris, a member of the Weaver household, was also shot. After the siege ended, Weaver was acquitted of criminal charges. He brought a civil suit against the government and settled the case for $3.1 million. Kevin Harris also filed a civil action against the government and its agents. See Harris v. Roderick, 126 F.3d 1189 (9th Cir. 1997). During Senate hearings on the matter, the FBI announced a new policy on deadly force. The new policy read as follows:

> *Use of Deadly Force Policy*
> a. Deadly Force. Officers may use deadly force only when necessary, that is, when the officer has a reasonable belief that the subject of such force poses an imminent danger of death or serious physical injury to the officer or to another person.
> b. Fleeing Felons. Deadly force may be used to prevent the escape of a fleeing subject if there is probable cause to believe:
> (1) the subject has committed a felony involving the infliction or threatened infliction of serious physical injury or death; and
> (2) the escape of the subject would pose an imminent danger of death or serious physical injury to the officer or to another person.
> *Use of Nondeadly Force*
> If force other than deadly force reasonably appears to be sufficient to accomplish an arrest or otherwise accomplish the law enforcement purpose, deadly force is not necessary.
> *Verbal Warnings*
> If feasible and if to do so would not increase the danger to the officer or others, a verbal warning to submit to the authority of the officer shall be given prior to the use of deadly force.

See Treasury Order No. 105-12, 60 Fed. Reg. 54,569 (October 24, 1995) (reaffirmed in 2000). The policy applies to all federal law enforcement agents. Is each component of the new federal deadly force policy required by *Garner*? Were the Ruby Ridge rules of engagement consistent with *Garner*? Would you recommend the same deadly force policy for the police officers in Memphis responding to calls about crimes in progress?

Notes

1. *Detailed guidance.* Almost all major metropolitan police departments have adopted policies dealing with the use of force, and most of them describe a "continuum" of force similar to the one used by the Charlotte-Mecklenburg Police Department. They vary, however, in the amount of detail they offer to guide police officers in the field. We provide several examples on the web extension for this chapter at *http://www.crimpro.com/extension/ch05.*

How do you suppose the law enforcement community received the Charlotte-Mecklenburg guidelines on the use of force? If you were one of the attorneys asked to review the guidelines during the drafting process, would you have suggested more or fewer categories? Would you change any of the boxes to add or eliminate a particular response level to a particular resistance level? If you were chief of police in Charlotte-Mecklenburg, would you issue cards with this chart for every member of the force? Would you publish this chart in the local newspaper?

A recent study found that many agencies lacked guidance on the need to provide verbal warnings before using force. At the same time, the study noted a consistent approach among prominent agencies that adopt detailed policies—they incorporate methods to de-escalate and minimize the need to use force. Brandon L. Garrett & Seth W. Stoughton, A Tactical Fourth Amendment, 102 Va. L. Rev. 211 (2017). Another recent study found that departmental policies do in fact affect how readily police officers use force. Officers in Charlotte-Mecklenburg, who were working under a more restrictive departmental policy, used force less readily than officers in Colorado Springs and Albuquerque, who operated under a more permissive policy. William Terrill & Eugene A. Paoline III, Police Use of Less Lethal Force: Does Administrative Policy Matter?, 34 Justice Q. 193 (2017).

2. *Extent of the use of force.* The prescribed responses in the lower and middle range of the grid prove just as important as the higher levels of force and resistance because police officers use the lower levels of force much more frequently. The Department of Justice collects statistics regarding use of "excessive force by law enforcement officers," as required by section 210402 of the Violent Crime Control and Law Enforcement Act of 1994. In 2008, an estimated 40 million persons had face-to-face contact with a police officer. The police used or threatened to use force against an estimated 776,000 persons in 2008, or about 1.9 percent of the total group. In 53.5 percent of use of force incidents, the police pushed or grabbed the suspect; in 17.2 percent, the officer kicked or hit the suspect; in 25.6 percent, the officer pointed a gun (up from 15 percent in 2005). Bureau of Justice Statistics, Contacts Between Police and the Public, 2008 at 12-13 (October 2011, NCJ 234599).

3. *High-speed chases.* Sometimes police officers must pursue suspects in automobiles, and those pursuits at high speed sometimes result in injuries to the police officers, the suspect, and third parties. Public scrutiny of police departments often centers on the use of force, particularly the damage that officers cause to third parties during high-speed chases. Newspapers routinely publish articles about high-visibility cases, especially those resulting in the payment of tort damages by the city.

More than 90 percent of law enforcement agencies have policies restricting the use of high-speed chases. Most of those policies appeared in the 1970s; about half of the policies have been updated since then to place tighter controls on the occasions for engaging in a high-speed chase. These policies allow high-speed chases more readily to chase suspects involved in more dangerous crimes. Several years ago the Bureau of Justice Statistics issued a report, *Police Vehicle Pursuits, 2012-2013*, discussing various agency policies, if you would like to read more.

Some departments also prohibit the use of more dangerous methods, such as roadblocks or Precision Immobilization Techniques, to prevent a pursuit from occurring, and instead provide for the use of less drastic measures, such as tire deflation devices (also known as "stop sticks"). See, e.g., Charlotte-Mecklenburg Police Department, Interactive Directives Guide, §600-022. But while even stop sticks pose dangers to the public and the driver when a vehicle is speeding, a newer technology—GPS darts—helps police track a car without engaging in a risky pursuit. The darts are shot from the police vehicle and attach onto the fleeing vehicle without damaging it; they then allow police to track the fleeing vehicle through GPS technology. See Cops' Latest Tool in High-Speed Chases: GPS Projectiles, CBS News, May 16, 2016, *https://www.cbsnews.com/news/police-test-gps-tracking-bullets-high-speed-chase-starchase/*. Should police department guidelines require the use of GPS darts, where available, before riskier pursuit-ending techniques are deployed? Should courts require the use of such less drastic measures?

Federal law is not hospitable to constitutional tort claims based on high-speed chases. In Sacramento County, California v. Lewis, 523 U.S. 833 (1998), the Court affirmed the lower court's dismissal of a suit brought by the estate of a passenger on a motorcycle who was killed after the police and the driver of the motorcycle engaged in a high-speed chase. The Court held that the high-speed police chase there did not amount to a Fourth Amendment "seizure" because the chase did not terminate the passenger's "freedom of movement through means intentionally applied." A plaintiff must show that the officers have an "intent to harm suspects physically." See also Plumhoff v. Rickard, 134 S. Ct. 2012 (2014) (officer did not perform an unreasonable seizure by firing three shots into moving car of suspect during high-speed chase, given the public danger that the suspect created; even if the force amounted to an unreasonable seizure, officer was entitled to qualified immunity because there was no robust consensus of cases of persuasive authority); Scott v. Harris, 550 U.S. 372 (2007) (officer did not unreasonably seize a fleeing motorist during a high-speed chase when the officer applied his push bumper to the speeding car, causing the car to crash and overturn; suspect was culpable in creating serious danger to the public by fleeing at a high speed).

4. *Resisting unlawful arrest.* Although the common law recognized a privilege for citizens to use reasonable force to resist an unlawful arrest, most states now require citizens to submit to unlawful arrests by police officers—about a dozen through judicial opinions and roughly another 20 states through statutes. See State v. Crawley, 901 A.2d 924 (N.J. 2006) (resisting an unlawful arrest or an unsupported stop by a known officer is a violation of state law); Haw. Rev. Stat. §703-304(4)(a) (use of force not justifiable to "resist an arrest which the actor knows is being made by a law enforcement officer, although the arrest is unlawful"). Courts typically address this criminal procedure topic when interpreting the outer boundaries of the substantive criminal law, such as a statute or ordinance making it a crime to "obstruct a police

officer lawfully performing an official function by means of flight." What is the case for allowing citizens to use reasonable efforts to resist an unlawful arrest by a police officer?

Problem 5-5. Subduing Motorcycle Rider

Around midnight on January 21, 2013, the Round Rock Police Department received a 911 call about an individual who was intoxicated and had crashed his motorcycle after leaving a bar. When police officers arrived at the scene, Officer Kevin Fruge observed a man, George Trammel, standing near a parked motorcycle in a parking lot. Officer Fruge detected a strong odor of alcohol coming from the man's breath. Officer Fruge instructed Trammel to "step away from the motorcycle." Because Trammel was on the phone and did not hear well, he did not respond to this command. The officer again asked Trammel to step away from the motorcycle, and Trammel eventually complied. As a body camera recording revealed, Officer Fruge and Trammel then had the following exchange:

Officer Fruge:	"What's goin' on? What's goin' on?"
Trammel:	"Nothing. I parked my bike."
Officer Fruge:	"Let me ask you a question, sir. How much have you had to drink tonight?"
Trammel:	"A whole lot of nothin'."
Officer Fruge:	"A whole lot of nothing? How much is that?"
Trammel:	"I'm not going to answer."

Officer Fruge then asked Trammel, "Well, can you walk toward me?" Trammel said "No." Officer Fruge then commanded Trammel to place his hands behind his back. Trammel again told Officer Fruge, "I'm not answering your questions," and did not comply with Officer Fruge's request. Then Trammel took off the jacket he was wearing and said, "I'm not going to jail."

At this point, Officer Fruge believed he had probable cause to arrest Trammel for public intoxication, and he grabbed Trammel's right arm as he told him to put his hands behind his back. Trammel immediately pulled back and told Officer Fruge that it hurt and not to grab him there. A second officer grabbed Trammel's left arm, but Trammel again pulled away. Officer Fruge executed a knee strike on Trammel's right thigh, and Trammel lost his balance. A third officer put Trammel in a headlock as he and two more officers pulled Trammel to the ground. Trammel states that he initially had his arms in front of his body because he was trying to keep from falling, but as the officers were grabbing at his arms and landed on top of his body, he hit the pavement face first.

While Trammel was on the ground, the officers tried to grab hold of his arms. The officers repeatedly asked Trammel to put his hands behind his back, and he refused to comply. As the officers commanded Trammel to "stop resisting," he was repeatedly heard yelling that his arm is fused. During this time, the officers administered knee strikes to Trammel's arms, thighs, and ribs so that they could subdue and handcuff him.

Six days after the arrest, Trammel was diagnosed with "mildly displaced right L1, L2, and L3 transverse process fractures." The incident caused Trammel to have "very limited mobility." He had to get a "new vehicle with a scooter" and began using a wheelchair while at home.

Trammel filed suit against the City of Round Rock and the police officers for excessive force. How is a court likely to evaluate the claim? How severe was the crime at issue? Did the suspect pose an immediate threat to the officers or others? Was he actively resisting or attempting to evade arrest? If so, was he resisting passively or actively? Should the court consider whether officers had less intrusive measures available at their disposal in arresting Trammel?

See Trammell v. Fruge, 868 F.3d 332 (5th Cir. 2017).

Problem 5-6. High-Speed Chase

Around 11 P.M. on a weekday night in March 2001, a Georgia police officer observed a car traveling at 73 miles per hour in a 55-mile-per-hour zone. The officer activated his flashing lights to pull the driver over. But the driver, Victor Harris, sped away, initiating a chase at speeds exceeding 85 miles per hour on a road that was mostly two-lane. Another officer, Timothy Scott, joined the chase. Mid-way through the chase, the driver was briefly boxed in by police cars in a parking lot, but he escaped by making a sharp turn and bumping into Officer Scott's cruiser. Officer Scott then took the lead in the pursuit. Six minutes after the chase had begun, Scott radioed a supervisor for permission to terminate the chase by using a "Precision Intervention Technique (PIT)" maneuver, which causes a moving vehicle to spin to a stop. He received permission to do so, but because he concluded that the cars were moving too quickly to execute a PIT safely, he instead applied his push bumper to Harris's car. This caused the car to crash and overturn, rendering Harris quadriplegic. Harris filed suit against Officer Scott and others alleging the use of excessive force. The incident was captured by Scott's dashboard camera and was available for review by the court: *https://www.youtube.com/watch?v= qrVKSgRZ2GY.*

What factors should the court consider in deciding the case and how is it likely to rule? How should the court weigh the risk the chase posed to potential bystanders against the risk that the end of the pursuit posed to the driver? Should the court take into account the culpability of the driver who engaged in a "reckless, high-speed flight"? Should the court consider whether police could reasonably have employed less drastic measures, such as the use of "stop sticks" or a warning through a loudspeaker? Is it relevant to consider whether departmental policy encouraged or required such less drastic measures? See Scott v. Harris, 550 U.S. 372 (2007).

VI

Remedies for Unreasonable Searches and Seizures

We have seen how the Fourth Amendment and its analogs, along with many statutes, rules, and internal police policies, condemn certain searches and seizures as unreasonable. We now consider various ways to remedy the government's violations of law.

The questions of whether and how to remedy a constitutional violation can arise at different stages of the criminal process—from search and seizure to interrogation to eyewitness identification to discovery and trial. The exclusionary rule, which is first discussed here in the context of searches and seizures, is also used to cure violations of the Fifth Amendment privilege against self-incrimination, the due process clause, the Sixth Amendment right to counsel, and related statutory provisions. Some of the themes first raised in this chapter therefore reappear in Chapter 8, which deals with remedies for violations of the law on interrogation, and in Chapter 9, which deals with remedies in the context of eyewitness identifications.

As you read through the materials, consider whether the exclusionary rule is more robust in some of these areas than in others, and if so, why that might be. Does the Constitution or statutory text provide stronger basis for exclusion in one or more of these areas? Does the case law assign different values to the underlying rights that exclusion protects? Or is the exclusionary rule a more fitting or necessary remedy in one context than another?

A. ORIGINS OF THE EXCLUSIONARY RULE

The texts of the Fourth Amendment and its state constitutional analogs do not usually specify the remedy for the victim of an illegal search or seizure. Up until the twentieth century, courts remedied these violations of the law by allowing the victims to sue the offending government agents in tort (typically for trespass). But when criminal defendants also asked the courts during criminal proceedings to exclude the wrongfully obtained evidence, state and federal courts rejected the sug-gestion unanimously. As Justice Joseph Story once put it:

> If it is competent or pertinent evidence, and not in its own nature objectionable, as having been created by constraint, or oppression, such as confessions extorted by threats or fraud, the evidence is admissible on charges for the highest crimes, even though it may have been obtained by a trespass upon the person, or by any other forcible and illegal means. The law deliberates not on the mode, by which it has come to the possession of the party, but on its value in establishing itself as satisfactory proof.

United States v. La Jeune, 26 F. Cas. 832 (C.C.D. Mass. 1822). The Supreme Court suggested for the first time in Boyd v. United States, 116 U.S. 616 (1886), that exclu-sion of evidence might be the proper remedy for evidence obtained through a viola-tion of both the Fourth and Fifth Amendments. A later case, Adams v. New York, 192 U.S. 585 (1904), curtly dismissed the exclusion remedy for a Fourth Amendment violation alone. The following case was the Court's next word on the subject of rem-edies for illegal searches and seizures.

■ FREMONT WEEKS v. UNITED STATES
232 U.S. 383 (1914)

DAY, J.*

[The defendant was convicted of using the mails for the purpose of transport-ing lottery tickets, in violation of section 213 of the Criminal Code. At the time of his arrest at the Union Station in Kansas City, Missouri, police officers went to the defendant's house to search it. A neighbor told them where to find the key, and they entered the house and took various papers from his room. Later in the same day police officers returned with the United States Marshal, who thought he might find additional evidence,] and, being admitted by someone in the house, probably a boarder, in response to a rap, the Marshal searched the defendant's room and car-ried away certain letters and envelopes found in the drawer of a chiffonier. Neither the marshal nor the police officers had a search warrant.

The defendant filed in the cause before the time for trial a "Petition to Return Private Papers, Books and Other Property" [claiming that officers of the govern-ment had seized his books and papers] "in violation of Sections 11 and 23 of the Constitution of Missouri and of the 4th and 5th Amendments to the Constitution of the United States." [He further argued that the District Attorney's plans to use the papers and property as evidence in the case against him would violate his constitu-tional rights. The trial court denied the petition.] Among the papers retained and put in evidence were a number of lottery tickets and statements with reference to the lottery, taken at the first visit of the police to the defendant's room, and a num-ber of letters written to the defendant in respect to the lottery, taken by the Marshal upon his search of defendant's room. . . .

The effect of the Fourth Amendment is to put the courts of the United States and Federal officials, in the exercise of their power and authority, under limitations

---

* [All the Justices joined in this opinion.—EDS.]

and restraints as to the exercise of such power and authority, and to forever secure the people, their persons, houses, papers and effects against all unreasonable searches and seizures under the guise of law. This protection reaches all alike, whether accused of crime or not, and the duty of giving to it force and effect is obligatory upon all entrusted under our Federal system with the enforcement of the laws. The tendency of those who execute the criminal laws of the country to obtain conviction by means of unlawful seizures and enforced confessions, the latter often obtained after subjecting accused persons to unwarranted practices destructive of rights secured by the Federal Constitution, should find no sanction in the judgments of the courts which are charged at all times with the support of the Constitution and to which people of all conditions have a right to appeal for the maintenance of such fundamental rights.

[This case] involves the right of the court in a criminal prosecution to retain for the purposes of evidence the letters and correspondence of the accused, seized in his house in his absence and without his authority, by a United States Marshal holding no warrant for his arrest and none for the search of his premises. . . . If letters and private documents can thus be seized and held and used in evidence against a citizen accused of an offense, the protection of the Fourth Amendment declaring his right to be secure against such searches and seizures is of no value, and, so far as those thus placed are concerned, might as well be stricken from the Constitution. The efforts of the courts and their officials to bring the guilty to punishment, praiseworthy as they are, are not to be aided by the sacrifice of those great principles established by years of endeavor and suffering which have resulted in their embodiment in the fundamental law of the land. The United States Marshal . . . acted without sanction of law, doubtless prompted by the desire to bring further proof to the aid of the Government, and under color of his office undertook to make a seizure of private papers in direct violation of the constitutional prohibition against such action. . . . To sanction such proceedings would be to affirm by judicial decision a manifest neglect if not an open defiance of the prohibitions of the Constitution, intended for the protection of the people against such unauthorized action.

The [government contends that the correct rule of law is] that the letters having come into the control of the court, it would not inquire into the manner in which they were obtained, but if competent would keep them and permit their use in evidence. Such proposition, the Government asserts, is conclusively established by certain decisions of this court. [This doctrine,] that a court will not in trying a criminal cause permit a collateral issue to be raised as to the source of competent testimony, has the sanction of so many state cases that it would be impracticable to cite or refer to them in detail. [The editor of one legal publication has explained the rule as follows:] "Such an investigation is not involved necessarily in the litigation in chief, and to pursue it would be to halt in the orderly progress of a cause, and consider incidentally a question which has happened to cross the path of such litigation, and which is wholly independent thereof."

It is therefore evident that [our prior cases] afford no authority for the action of the court in this case, when applied to in due season for the return of papers seized in violation of the Constitutional Amendment. [Prior cases were distinguishable, however, because they involved] application of the doctrine that a collateral issue will not be raised to ascertain the source from which testimony, competent in a criminal case, comes. . . . The right of the court to deal with papers and documents in the possession of the District Attorney and other officers of the court and subject to its authority [is clearly established]. That papers wrongfully seized should be turned over to the accused has been frequently recognized in the early as well as later decisions of the courts.

We therefore reach the conclusion that the letters in question were taken from the house of the accused by an official of the United States acting under color of his office in direct violation of the constitutional rights of the defendant; that having made a seasonable application for their return, which was heard and passed upon by the court, there was involved in the order refusing the application a denial of the constitutional rights of the accused, and that the court should have restored these letters to the accused. In holding them and permitting their use upon the trial, we think prejudicial error was committed. . . .

Notes

1. *Evidentiary fruits of illegal searches.* Would the exclusionary rule described in the *Weeks* case prevent the government from introducing evidence *derived* from illegally obtained papers rather than the papers themselves? In Silverthorne Lumber Co. v. United States, 251 U.S. 385 (1920), the government had illegally seized corporate papers, returned them before trial, and then issued a subpoena duces tecum to obtain the documents through proper means. The Court declared that the exclusionary rule prevented such a method of curing the effects of an illegal seizure: Exclusion means "that not merely evidence [illegally] acquired shall not be used before the Court but that it shall not be used at all." This is known as the "fruit of the poisonous tree" doctrine.

2. *The states and the exclusionary rule after 1949.* Because the *Weeks* opinion was based on the federal Bill of Rights, which did not at that time apply to the states, state courts and legislatures were free to adopt or reject the exclusionary remedy. Only a handful of states adopted an exclusionary rule prior to the *Weeks* opinion. See State v. Sheridan, 96 N.W. 730 (Iowa 1903). The *Weeks* opinion did not change this trend in the state courts. Most took the view of Judge Benjamin Cardozo in People v. Defore, 150 N.E. 585 (N.Y. 1926), in which he tartly summarized the exclusionary rule as follows: "There has been no blinking the consequences. The criminal is to go free because the constable has blundered. . . . The pettiest peace officer would have it in his power through overzeal or indiscretion to confer immunity upon an offender for crimes the most flagitious."

Thus, for the first half of this century the exclusionary remedy applied only in the federal system and a handful of states. As of 1926, fewer than 15 states had adopted the exclusionary rule and more than 30 had rejected it. Even after the Supreme Court decided to apply the Fourth Amendment to state law enforcement officers in Wolf v. Colorado, 338 U.S. 25 (1949), it did not insist that state courts exclude improperly seized evidence. They were still free to adopt remedies other than the exclusionary rule. About half of the states continued to rely on civil remedies for victims of illegal searches and on criminal charges against police officers who violated the law. But by the 1950s, judges and commentators started having doubts about the success of alternatives to the exclusionary rule—at that time, not just alternatives but the only remedies available in many states.

■ PEOPLE v. CHARLES CAHAN
282 P.2d 905 (Cal. 1955)

TRAYNOR, J.

Defendant and 15 other persons were charged with conspiring to engage in horse-race bookmaking and related offenses. [After a trial without a jury, the court found one defendant not guilty, and all the other defendants, including Cahan, guilty.]

Most of the incriminatory evidence introduced at the trial was obtained by officers of the Los Angeles Police Department in flagrant violation of the United States Constitution (4th and 14th Amendments), the California Constitution (art. I, §19), and state and federal statutes. Gerald Wooters, an officer attached to the intelligence unit of that department testified that after securing the permission of the chief of police to make microphone installations* at two places occupied by defendants, he, Sergeant Keeler, and Officer Phillips one night at about 8:45 entered one "house through the side window of the first floor," and that he "directed the officers to place a listening device under a chest of drawers." Another officer made recordings and transcriptions of the conversations that came over wires from the listening device to receiving equipment installed in a nearby garage. . . . Section 653h of the Penal Code does not and could not authorize violations of the Constitution. . . .

The evidence obtained from the microphones was not the only unconstitutionally obtained evidence introduced at the trial over defendants' objection. In addition there was a mass of evidence obtained by numerous forcible entries and seizures without search warrants. [The officers testified that they obtained evidence by kicking open a door in one location, and by breaking a window at another.]

Thus, without fear of criminal punishment or other discipline, law enforcement officers, sworn to support the Constitution of the United States and the Constitution of California, frankly admit their deliberate, flagrant acts in violation of both Constitutions and the laws enacted thereunder. It is clearly apparent from their testimony that they casually regard such acts as nothing more than the performance of their ordinary duties for which the city employs and pays them.

[Both] the United States Constitution and the California Constitution make it emphatically clear that important as efficient law enforcement may be, it is more important that the right of privacy guaranteed by these constitutional provisions be respected. [The] contention that unreasonable searches and seizures are justified by the necessity of bringing criminals to justice cannot be accepted. It was rejected when the constitutional provisions were adopted and the choice was made that all the people, guilty and innocent alike, should be secure from unreasonable police intrusions, even though some criminals should escape. Moreover, the constitutional provisions make no distinction between the guilty and the innocent, and it would be manifestly impossible to protect the rights of the innocent if the police were permitted to justify unreasonable searches and seizures on the ground that they assumed

* [Section 653h of the Penal Code provided: "Any person who, without consent of the owner, lessee, or occupant, installs or attempts to install or use a dictograph in any house . . . is guilty of a misdemeanor; provided, that nothing herein shall prevent the use and installation of dictographs by a regular salaried police officer expressly authorized thereto by the head of his office . . . when such use and installation are necessary in the performance of their duties in detecting crime and in the apprehension of criminals."—EDS.]

their victims were criminals. Thus, when consideration is directed to the question of the admissibility of evidence obtained in violation of the constitutional provisions, it bears emphasis that the court is not concerned solely with the rights of the defendant before it, however guilty he may appear, but with the constitutional right of all of the people to be secure in their homes, persons, and effects.

The constitutional provisions themselves do not expressly answer the question whether evidence obtained in violation thereof is admissible in criminal actions. Neither Congress nor the Legislature has given an answer, and the courts of the country are divided on the question. The federal courts and those of some of the states exclude such evidence. In accord with the traditional common-law rule, the courts of a majority of the states admit it, and heretofore the courts of this state have admitted it.

The decision of the United States Supreme Court in Wolf v. Colorado, 338 U.S. 25 (1949), that the guarantee of the Fourth Amendment applies to the states through the Fourteenth [Amendment,] does not require states like California that have heretofore admitted illegally seized evidence to exclude it now. The exclusionary rule is not "an essential ingredient" of the right of privacy guaranteed by the Fourth Amendment, but simply a means of enforcing that right, which the states can accept or reject. . . .

The rule admitting the evidence has been strongly supported by both scholars and judges. Their arguments may be briefly summarized as follows:

The rules of evidence are designed to enable courts to reach the truth and, in criminal cases, to secure a fair trial to those accused of crime. Evidence obtained by an illegal search and seizure is ordinarily just as true and reliable as evidence lawfully obtained. The court needs all reliable evidence material to the issue before it, the guilt or innocence of the accused, and how such evidence is obtained is immaterial to that issue. It should not be excluded unless strong considerations of public policy demand it. . . .

Exclusion of the evidence cannot be justified as affording protection or recompense to the defendant or punishment to the officers for the illegal search and seizure. It does not protect the defendant from the search and seizure, since that illegal act has already occurred. If he is innocent or if there is ample evidence to convict him without the illegally obtained evidence, exclusion of the evidence gives him no remedy at all. Thus the only defendants who benefit by the exclusionary rule are those criminals who could not be convicted without the illegally obtained evidence. Allowing such criminals to escape punishment is not appropriate recompense for the invasion of their constitutional rights; it does not punish the officers who violated the constitutional provisions; and it fails to protect society from known criminals who should not be left at large. For his crime the defendant should be punished. For his violation of the constitutional provisions the offending officer should be punished. As the exclusionary rule operates, however, the defendant's crime and the officer's flouting of constitutional guarantees both go unpunished. . . .

Opponents of the exclusionary rule also point out that it is inconsistent with the rule allowing private litigants to use illegally obtained evidence, and that as applied in the federal courts, it is capricious in its operation, either going too far or not far enough. So many exceptions to the exclusionary rule have been granted the judicial blessing as largely to destroy any value it might otherwise have had. . . .

Finally it has been pointed out that there is no convincing evidence that the exclusionary rule actually tends to prevent unreasonable searches and seizures and that the disciplinary or educational effect of the court's releasing the defendant for police misbehavior is so indirect as to be no more than a mild deterrent at best.

Despite the persuasive force of the foregoing arguments, we have concluded that evidence obtained in violation of the constitutional guaranties is inadmissible. We have been compelled to reach that conclusion because other remedies have completely failed to secure compliance with the constitutional provisions on the part of police officers with the attendant result that the courts under the old rule have been constantly required to participate in, and in effect condone, the lawless activities of law enforcement officers.

When, as in the present case, the very purpose of an illegal search and seizure is to get evidence to introduce at a trial, the success of the lawless venture depends entirely on the court's lending its aid by allowing the evidence to be introduced. . . . Out of regard for its own dignity as an agency of justice and custodian of liberty the court should not have a hand in such dirty business.

Courts refuse their aid in civil cases to prevent the consummation of illegal schemes of private litigants; a fortiori, they should not extend that aid and thereby permit the consummation of illegal schemes of the state itself. It is morally incongruous for the state to flout constitutional rights and at the same time demand that its citizens observe the law. The end that the state seeks may be a laudable one, but it no more justifies unlawful acts than a laudable end justifies unlawful action by any member of the public. Moreover, any process of law that sanctions the imposition of penalties upon an individual through the use of the fruits of official lawlessness tends to the destruction of the whole system of restraints on the exercise of the public force that are inherent in the concept of ordered liberty. . . . "Our Government is the potent, the omnipresent teacher. For good or for ill, it teaches the whole people by its example. Crime is contagious. If the Government becomes a lawbreaker, it breeds contempt for law, it invites everyman to become a law unto himself; it invites anarchy." Olmstead v. United States, 277 U.S. 438 (1928) (Brandeis, J., dissenting).

[If the constitutional guaranties against unreasonable searches and seizures] were being effectively enforced by other means than excluding evidence obtained by their violation, a different problem would be presented. If such were the case there would be more force to the argument that a particular criminal should not be redressed for a past violation of his rights by excluding the evidence against him. Experience has demonstrated, however, that neither administrative, criminal nor civil remedies are effective in suppressing lawless searches and seizures. The innocent suffer with the guilty, and we cannot close our eyes to the effect the rule we adopt will have on the rights of those not before the court. "The difficulty with [other remedies] is in part due to the failure of interested parties to inform of the offense. No matter what an illegal raid turns up, police are unlikely to inform on themselves or each other. If it turns up nothing incriminating, the innocent victim usually does not care to take steps which will air the fact that he has been under suspicion." Irvine v. California, 347 U.S. 128 (1954). Moreover, even when it becomes generally known that the police conduct illegal searches and seizures, public opinion is not aroused as it is in the case of other violations of constitutional rights. Illegal searches and seizures lack the obvious brutality of coerced confessions and the third degree and do not so clearly strike at the very basis of our civil liberties as do unfair trials or the lynching of even an admitted murderer. . . . There is thus all the more necessity for courts to be vigilant in protecting these constitutional rights if they are to be protected at all. People v. Mayen, 205 P. 435 (Cal. 1922) [rejecting the exclusionary rule in California] was decided over 30 years ago. Since then case after case has appeared in our appellate reports describing unlawful searches and seizures against the defendant on trial, and those cases undoubtedly reflect only a small fraction of the violations of the constitutional provisions that have actually occurred. On the other hand, reported cases involving civil actions against police officers are rare, and those involving successful criminal prosecutions against officers are nonexistent. In short, the constitutional provisions are not being enforced.

Granted that the adoption of the exclusionary rule will not prevent all illegal searches and seizures, it will discourage them. Police officers and prosecuting officials are primarily interested in convicting criminals. Given the exclusionary rule and a choice between securing evidence by legal rather than illegal means, officers will be impelled to obey the law themselves since not to do so will jeopardize their objectives. [If] courts respect the constitutional provisions by refusing to sanction their violation, they will not only command the respect of law-abiding citizens for themselves adhering to the law, they will also arouse public opinion as a deterrent to lawless enforcement of the law by bringing just criticism to bear on law enforcement officers who allow criminals to escape by pursuing them in lawless ways.

It is contended, however, that the police do not always have a choice of securing evidence by legal means and that in many cases the criminal will escape if illegally obtained evidence cannot be used against him. This contention is not properly directed at the exclusionary rule, but at the constitutional provisions themselves. It was rejected when those provisions were adopted. In such cases had the Constitution been obeyed, the criminal could in no event be convicted. He does not go free because the constable blundered, but because the Constitutions prohibit securing the evidence against him. . . .

In developing a rule of evidence applicable in the state courts, this court is not bound by the decisions that have applied the federal rule, and if it appears that those decisions have developed needless refinements and distinctions, this court need not follow them. . . . Under these circumstances the adoption of the exclusionary rule need not introduce confusion into the law of criminal procedure. Instead it opens the door to the development of workable rules governing searches and seizures and the issuance of warrants that will protect both the rights guaranteed by the constitutional provisions and the interest of society in the suppression of crime. . . .

SPENCE, J., dissenting.

I dissent. The guilt of the appellant is clearly demonstrated by the record before us. . . . In adopting and adhering to the nonexclusionary rule, the law of the State of California has thereby been kept in harmony with the law of the great majority of the other states and of all the British commonwealths; as well as in line with the considered views of the majority of the most eminent legal scholars. Only the federal courts and the courts of a relatively few states have adopted the judicially created exclusionary rule. . . .

The experience of the federal courts in attempting to apply the exclusionary rule does not appear to commend its adoption elsewhere. The spectacle of an obviously guilty defendant obtaining a favorable ruling by a court upon a motion to suppress evidence or upon an objection to evidence, and thereby, in effect, obtaining immunity from any successful prosecution of the charge against him, is a picture which has been too often seen in the federal practice. . . . Furthermore, under the present federal practice, the trial of the accused is interrupted to try the question of whether the evidence was in fact illegally obtained. This question is often a delicate one, and the main trial is at least delayed while the question of whether some other person has committed a wrong in obtaining the evidence has been judicially determined. . . .

[I cannot] ascertain from the majority opinion in the present case the nature of the rule which is being adopted to supplant the well established nonexclusionary rule in California. Is it the exclusionary rule as interpreted in the federal courts with all its technical distinctions, exceptions, and qualifications . . . ? [Neither] the federal courts nor the courts of any of the few states which adopted the exclusionary rule have apparently found a satisfactory solution to [the] problem of developing "workable rules," and it seems impossible to contemplate the possibility that this court can develop a satisfactory solution. At best, this court would have to work out such rules in piecemeal fashion as each case might come before it. In the meantime, what rules are to guide our trial courts in the handling of their problems? If the nonexclusionary rule can be said to have one unquestioned advantage, it is the advantage of certainty. . . .

If, however, reasons may be said to exist for a change in the established policy of this state, I believe that the Legislature, rather than the courts, should make such change. This is particularly true in a situation such as the present one, when the change of policy should be accompanied by "workable rules" to implement such change. . . . In this connection, it is worthy of note that bills have frequently been introduced in the Legislature to accomplish precisely that which is accomplished by the majority opinion, to wit: the supplanting of the nonexclusionary rule by the so-called exclusionary rule, without prescribing any "workable rules" for the latter's application. In the recent legislative sessions of 1951 and of 1953, such bills have been introduced but none has ever been brought to a vote in either house. Under the circumstances, it would be far better for this court to allow the Legislature to deal with this question of policy. . . .

Returning to the precise situation presented by the record before us, it may be conceded that the illegality in obtaining the evidence was both clear and flagrant. It may be further conceded that the crimes which defendants conspired to commit were not in the class of the more serious public offenses. The fact remains, however, that the exclusionary rule, as adopted by the majority, is a rule for all cases and that it deprives society of its remedy against the most desperate gangster charged with the most heinous crime merely because of some degree of illegality in obtaining the evidence against him. . . .

In my opinion, the cost of the adoption of the exclusionary rule is manifestly too great. It would be far better for this state to adhere to the nonexclusionary rule, and to reexamine its laws concerning the sanctions to be placed upon illegal searches and seizures. If the present laws are deemed inadequate to discourage illegal practices by enforcement officers, the Legislature might well consider the imposition of civil liability for such conduct upon the governmental unit employing the offending officer, in addition to the liability now imposed upon the officer himself. It might also consider fixing a minimum amount to be recovered as damages in the same manner that a minimum has been fixed for the invasion of other civil rights. These methods would be far more effective in discouraging illegal activities on the part of enforcement officers and such methods would not be subject to the objection, inherent in the adoption of the exclusionary rule, that "It deprives society of its remedy against one lawbreaker because he has been pursued by another." Irvine v. California, 347 U.S. 128 (1954). . . .

■ DOLLREE MAPP v. OHIO
367 U.S. 643 (1961)

CLARK, J.*

On May 23, 1957, three Cleveland police officers arrived at appellant's residence in that city pursuant to information that "a person [was] hiding out in the home, who was wanted for questioning in connection with a recent bombing, and that there was a large amount of policy paraphernalia being hidden in the home." Miss Mapp and her daughter by a former marriage lived on the top floor of the two-family dwelling. Upon their arrival at that house, the officers knocked on the door and demanded entrance but appellant, after telephoning her attorney, refused to admit them without a search warrant. They advised their headquarters of the situation and undertook a surveillance of the house.

The officers again sought entrance some three hours later when four or more additional officers arrived on the scene. When Miss Mapp did not come to the door immediately, at least one of the several doors to the house was forcibly opened[2] and the policemen gained admittance. Meanwhile Miss Mapp's attorney arrived, but the officers, having secured their own entry, and continuing in their defiance of the law, would permit him neither to see Miss Mapp nor to enter the house. It appears that Miss Mapp was halfway down the stairs from the upper floor to the front door when the officers, in this highhanded manner, broke into the hall. She demanded to see the search warrant. A paper, claimed to be a warrant, was held up by one of the officers. She grabbed the "warrant" and placed it in her bosom. A struggle ensued in which the officers recovered the piece of paper and as a result of which they hand-cuffed appellant because she had been "belligerent" in resisting their official rescue of the "warrant" from her person. Running roughshod over appellant, a policeman "grabbed" her, "twisted [her] hand," and she "yelled [and] pleaded with him" because "it was hurting." Appellant, in handcuffs, was then forcibly taken upstairs to her bedroom where the officers searched a dresser, a chest of drawers, a closet and some suitcases. They also looked into a photo album and through personal papers belonging to the appellant. The search spread to the rest of the second floor including the child's bedroom, the living room, the kitchen and a dinette. The basement of the building and a trunk found therein were also searched. The obscene [books and pictures] for possession of which she was ultimately convicted were discovered in the course of that widespread search.

At the trial no search warrant was produced by the prosecution, nor was the failure to produce one explained or accounted for. [The Ohio Supreme Court affirmed the conviction because] the evidence had not been taken "from defendant's person by the use of brutal or offensive physical force against defendant." The State says

---

* [Chief Justice Warren and Justices Black, Douglas, and Brennan joined in this opinion.—EDS.]

2. A police officer testified that "we did pry the screen door to gain entrance"; the attorney on the scene testified that a policeman "tried . . . to kick in the door" and then "broke the glass in the door and somebody reached in and opened the door and let them in. . . ."

that even if the search were made without authority, or otherwise unreasonably, it is not prevented from using the unconstitutionally seized evidence at trial. . . .

I.

[In] the year 1914, in the *Weeks* case, this Court for the first time held that in a federal prosecution the Fourth Amendment barred the use of evidence secured through an illegal search and seizure. This Court has ever since required of federal law officers a strict adherence to that command which this Court has held to be a clear, specific, and constitutionally required—even if judicially implied—deterrent safeguard without insistence upon which the Fourth Amendment would have been reduced to a form of words. . . .

II.

[Thirty-five years later, in Wolf v. Colorado, 338 U.S. 25 (1949)], the Court decided that the *Weeks* exclusionary rule would not then be imposed upon the States as "an essential ingredient of the right." The Court's reasons for not considering essential to the right to privacy, as a curb imposed upon the States by the Due Process Clause, that which decades before had been posited as part and parcel of the Fourth Amendment's limitation upon federal encroachment of individual privacy, were bottomed on factual considerations.

While they are not basically relevant to a decision that the exclusionary rule is an essential ingredient of the Fourth Amendment as the right it embodies is vouchsafed against the States by the Due Process Clause, we will consider the current validity of the factual grounds upon which *Wolf* was based.

The Court in *Wolf* first stated that "the contrariety of views of the States" on the adoption of the exclusionary rule of *Weeks* was "particularly impressive"; and, in this connection, that it could not "brush aside the experience of States which deem the incidence of such conduct by the police too slight to call for a deterrent remedy by overriding the States' relevant rules of evidence." While in 1949, prior to the *Wolf* case, almost two-thirds of the States were opposed to the use of the exclusionary rule, now, despite the *Wolf* case, more than half of those since passing upon it, [including California], by their own legislative or judicial decision, have wholly or partly adopted or adhered to the *Weeks* rule.

[The] second basis elaborated in *Wolf* in support of its failure to enforce the exclusionary doctrine against the States was that "other means of protection" have been afforded the right to privacy.[7] The experience of California [described in People v. Cahan] that such other remedies have been worthless and futile is buttressed by the experience of other States. . . . It, therefore, plainly appears that the factual considerations supporting the failure of the *Wolf* Court to include the *Weeks* exclusionary rule when it recognized the enforceability of the right to privacy against the States in 1949, while not basically relevant to the constitutional consideration, could not, in any analysis, now be deemed controlling. . . .

---

7. Less than half [23] of the States have any criminal provisions relating directly to unreasonable searches and seizures. . . .

III.

. . . Today we once again examine *Wolf*'s constitutional documentation of the right to privacy free from unreasonable state intrusion, and, after its dozen years on our books, are led by it to close the only courtroom door remaining open to evidence secured by official lawlessness in flagrant abuse of that basic right, reserved to all persons as a specific guarantee against that very same unlawful conduct. We hold that all evidence obtained by searches and seizures in violation of the Constitution is, by that same authority, inadmissible in a state court.

IV.

Since the Fourth Amendment's right of privacy has been declared enforceable against the States through the Due Process Clause of the Fourteenth, it is enforceable against them by the same sanction of exclusion as is used against the Federal Government. Were it otherwise, then just as without the *Weeks* rule the assurance against unreasonable federal searches and seizures would be "a form of words," valueless and undeserving of mention in a perpetual charter of inestimable human liberties, so too, without that rule the freedom from state invasions of privacy would be so ephemeral and so neatly severed from its conceptual nexus with the freedom from all brutish means of coercing evidence as not to merit this Court's high regard as a freedom "implicit in the concept of ordered liberty." . . . Therefore, in extending the substantive protections of due process to all constitutionally unreasonable searches—state or federal—it was logically and constitutionally necessary that the exclusion doctrine—an essential part of the right to privacy—be also insisted upon as an essential ingredient of the right newly recognized by the *Wolf* case. . . . To hold otherwise is to grant the right but in reality to withhold its privilege and enjoyment. . . .

This Court has not hesitated to enforce as strictly against the States as it does against the Federal Government the rights of free speech and of a free press, the rights to notice and to a fair, public trial, including, as it does, the right not to be convicted by use of a coerced confession, however logically relevant it be, and without regard to its reliability. And nothing could be more certain than that when a coerced confession is involved, "the relevant rules of evidence" are overridden. . . . Why should not the same rule apply to what is tantamount to coerced testimony by way of unconstitutional seizure of goods, papers, effects, documents, etc.? . . .

V.

Moreover, our holding that the exclusionary rule is an essential part of both the Fourth and Fourteenth Amendments is not only the logical dictate of prior cases, but it also makes very good sense. There is no war between the Constitution and common sense. Presently, a federal prosecutor may make no use of evidence illegally seized, but a State's attorney across the street may, although he supposedly is operating under the enforceable prohibitions of the same Amendment. Thus the State, by admitting evidence unlawfully seized, serves to encourage disobedience to the Federal Constitution which it is bound to uphold. Moreover, . . . the very essence of a healthy federalism depends upon the avoidance of needless conflict between state and federal courts. . . . Federal-state cooperation in the solution of crime under constitutional standards will be promoted, if only by recognition of their now mutual obligation to respect the same fundamental criteria in their approaches. . . .

There are those who say, as did Justice (then Judge) Cardozo, that under our constitutional exclusionary doctrine "the criminal is to go free because the constable has blundered." In some cases this will undoubtedly be the result. But . . . there is another consideration—the imperative of judicial integrity. The criminal goes free, if he must, but it is the law that sets him free. Nothing can destroy a government more quickly than its failure to observe its own laws, or worse, its disregard of the charter of its own existence. . . .

The ignoble shortcut to conviction left open to the State tends to destroy the entire system of constitutional restraints on which the liberties of the people rest. Having once recognized that the right to privacy embodied in the Fourth Amendment is enforceable against the States, and that the right to be secure against rude invasions of privacy by state officers is, therefore, constitutional in origin, we can no longer permit that right to remain an empty promise. Because it is enforceable in the same manner and to like effect as other basic rights secured by the Due Process Clause, we can no longer permit it to be revocable at the whim of any police officer who, in the name of law enforcement itself, chooses to suspend its enjoyment. Our decision, founded on reason and truth, gives to the individual no more than that which the Constitution guarantees him, to the police officer no less than that to which honest law enforcement is entitled, and, to the courts, that judicial integrity so necessary in the true administration of justice. . . .

HARLAN, J., dissenting.*

. . . *II.*

[It] cannot be too much emphasized that what was recognized in *Wolf* was not that the Fourth Amendment as such is enforceable against the States as a facet of due process, . . . but the principle of privacy "which is at the core of the Fourth Amendment." It would not be proper to expect or impose any precise equivalence, either as regards the scope of the right or the means of its implementation, between the requirements of the Fourth and Fourteenth Amendments. [Unlike the Fourteenth, which states a general principle only, the Fourth] is a particular command, having its setting in a pre-existing legal context on which both interpreting decisions and enabling statutes must at least build. . . .

I would not impose upon the States this federal exclusionary remedy. . . . Our concern here, as it was in *Wolf,* is not with the desirability of that rule but only with the question whether the States are Constitutionally free to follow it or not as they may themselves determine, and the relevance of the disparity of views among the States on this point lies simply in the fact that the judgment involved is a debatable one. . . .

The preservation of a proper balance between state and federal responsibility in the administration of criminal justice demands patience on the part of those who might like to see things move faster among the States in this respect. Problems of criminal law enforcement vary widely from State to State. One State, in considering

---

* [Justices Frankfurter and Whittaker joined in this opinion.—EDS.]

the totality of its legal picture, may conclude that the need for embracing the *Weeks* rule is pressing because other remedies are unavailable or inadequate to secure compliance with the substantive Constitutional principle involved. Another, though equally solicitous of Constitutional rights, may choose to pursue one purpose at a time, allowing all evidence relevant to guilt to be brought into a criminal trial, and dealing with Constitutional infractions by other means. Still another may consider the exclusionary rule too rough-and-ready a remedy, in that it reaches only unconstitutional intrusions which eventuate in criminal prosecution of the victims. Further, a State after experimenting with the *Weeks* rule for a time may, because of unsatisfactory experience with it, decide to revert to a non-exclusionary rule. And so on. . . . For us the question remains, as it has always been, one of state power, not one of passing judgment on the wisdom of one state course or another. . . .

I regret that I find so unwise in principle and so inexpedient in policy a decision motivated by the high purpose of increasing respect for Constitutional rights. But in the last analysis I think this Court can increase respect for the Constitution only if it rigidly respects the limitations which the Constitution places upon it, and respects as well the principles inherent in its own processes. In the present case I think we exceed both, and that our voice becomes only a voice of power, not of reason.

Notes

1. *Power and reason.* Was *Mapp* an appropriate interpretation of the due process clause? Do you believe that conditions had changed significantly between 1949 (the date of the *Wolf* decision) and 1961 (the date of *Mapp*)? Mapp's attorney did not ask the court to overturn the *Wolf* decision, but the American Civil Liberties Union, appearing as *amicus curiae*, raised the issue. Professor Richard Re has argued that by the mid-twentieth century, changes in law and practice had recast the Fourth Amendment as a source of pretrial "process" analogous to in-trial procedural guarantees such as the confrontation clause. Richard M. Re, The Due Process Exclusionary Rule, 127 Harv. L. Rev. 1885 (2014).

2. *Empirical evidence on the benefits of the exclusionary rule.* The *Cahan* court stated that "there is no convincing evidence that the exclusionary rule actually tends to prevent unreasonable searches and seizures" and that it was "a mild deterrent at best." It is quite difficult to estimate the real impact of the exclusionary rule on police and magistrate practices because the effect of the rule (if any) would produce a nonevent. That is, the exclusionary rule would, in theory, prevent improper searches and seizures from occurring. Some have attempted to measure the effects of the exclusionary rule by tracking either the number of search and arrest warrants sought or the number of arrests completed in the same location before and after the exclusionary rule took effect. In some locations, the number of warrants sought went up and the number of arrests went down after *Mapp*, but in other locations there was little or no change. See Albert W. Alschuler, Studying the Exclusionary Rule: An Empirical Classic, 75 U. Chi. L. Rev. 1365 (2008).

Others have estimated the deterrent effect of the exclusionary rule by asking police officers themselves how the prospect of losing evidence in a case would affect their decisions in the field. A survey of law enforcement officers in Ventura County, California, offered equivocal evidence about the deterrent effects of the exclusionary rule. About 20 percent of the officers responding to the survey said that the risk of exclusion of evidence was their primary concern in deciding whether to conduct a search or seizure, while nearly 60 percent considered suppression to be an "important" concern. Officers who had "lost" evidence because of improper searches or seizures in past cases were no more likely than other officers to give correct answers to hypothetical search and seizure questions. See Timothy Perrin et al., If It's Broken, Fix It: Moving Beyond the Exclusionary Rule—A New and Extensive Empirical Study of the Exclusionary Rule and a Call for a Civil Administrative Remedy to Partially Replace the Rule, 83 Iowa L. Rev. 669 (1998).

3. *Empirical evidence on the costs of the exclusionary rule.* More effort has gone into measuring the "costs" of the exclusionary rule. A number of studies have estimated the number of convictions that the government loses because of concerns about exclusion of evidence obtained from an improper search or seizure. The estimates of arrests lost range from 0.6 percent to 2.35 percent of all felony arrests, with a higher proportion (in the range of 3 to 5 percent) of arrests on drug and weapons charges. Thomas Davies, A Hard Look at What We Know (and Still Need to Learn) about the "Costs" of the Exclusionary Rule: The NIJ Study and Other Studies of "Lost" Arrests, 1983 Am. B. Found. Res. J. 611. For an attempt to measure the effects of the exclusionary rule on crime rates (as opposed to conviction rates), see Raymond A. Atkins & Paul H. Rubin, Effects of Criminal Procedure on Crime Rates: Mapping Out the Consequences of the Exclusionary Rule, 46 J.L. & Econ. 157 (2003).

4. *The imperative of judicial integrity.* The courts in *Mapp* and *Cahan* each mentioned that the exclusionary rule would serve multiple purposes. In addition to deterring violations of the Constitution, it would also protect judicial integrity. See Melanie D. Wilson, Improbable Cause: A Case for Judging Police by a More Majestic Standard, 15 Berkeley J. Crim. L. 259 (2010) (conducting empirical study of one federal district court over two years and concluding that judges probably perpetuate police perjury). Is the exclusionary rule necessary to protect the integrity of courts? Do courts undermine their own integrity when they accept evidence in *civil* cases that was obtained contrary to law? Is the "truth seeking" function of the criminal process the best guarantee of judicial integrity, and does the exclusionary rule harm the truth-seeking function?

5. *Deterrence and balancing the costs and benefits of exclusion.* Today, the Supreme Court describes the purpose of the exclusionary rule solely in terms of deterrence. See United States v. Janis, 428 U.S. 433, 458 (1976) ("considerations of judicial integrity do not require exclusion of the evidence"). In fact, the Court has used the singular focus on deterrence to justify narrowing the scope of the exclusionary rule. In United States v. Calandra, 414 U.S. 338 (1974), the Court held that the exclusionary rule does not apply in grand jury proceedings, reasoning that "the application of the rule has been restricted to those areas where its remedial objectives are thought most efficaciously served." The Court therefore weighs the benefit of excluding evidence in a particular context (e.g., grand jury proceedings, immigration proceedings, impeachment of witnesses at trial, and so on) against the costs of exclusion (impairing truth seeking and undermining criminal law enforcement). It typically finds that excluding the evidence from the prosecution's case-in-chief provides sufficient deterrent benefit and that exclusion in other contexts is disproportionately costly and therefore unnecessary.

Does the deterrence approach accurately reflect the incentives guiding individual police officers? Or does "deterrence" operate more effectively at the organizational level, encouraging police departments to provide better training on search and seizure law to their officers?

6. *What counts as a cost?* Are criminal convictions lost because the exclusionary rule is the chosen remedy or are the lost convictions simply the cost of having the Fourth Amendment and its analogs? Since the exclusionary rule arguably returns the parties to their relative positions before the constitutional violation took place, one might consider it a backward-looking "tort" remedy. On the other hand, if one is convinced that the value of the remedy to the defendant (avoiding a criminal conviction) far exceeds the value of any lost privacy, then the difference in value between the loss to the defendant and the loss to the government might be considered a "cost" of the exclusionary rule rather than a cost of the constitutional provision. One might prefer a remedy that more closely matches the defendant's actual loss. See Sharon Davies, The Penalty of Exclusion — A Price or Sanction?, 73 S. Cal. L. Rev. 1275 (2000) (describing competing views of exclusionary rule as a "sanction" to signal that conduct is wrong and completely intolerable, or as a "price" that tolerates some of the behavior so long as it produces more good than harm overall). Which is the most appropriate measure?

7. *Exclusion for violation of state constitutions, statutes, and procedure rules.* When a state court concludes that a search or seizure violated the state constitution rather than the federal constitution, exclusion is almost always the remedy the court adopts. Although exclusion is not required by federal law in such a case, state courts will typically choose exclusion as the proper remedy under state law.

When a search or seizure violates the provisions of a statute (state or federal) rather than a constitution, courts try to determine which remedy the legislature intended. Sometimes an explicit provision in a statute makes this relatively easy. See Ill. Stat. Ann. ch. 720, 5/14-5 (exclusion of any evidence obtained in violation of eavesdropping statute). . . . In other cases, the statutory language does not address remedies, and the legislative history is unhelpful. In such cases, courts tend to use the exclusion remedy for statutory violations when the search or seizure infringed in a "significant" way on "substantial" rights of the defendant. Compare People v. McKinstry, 843 P.2d 18 (Colo. 1993) (no exclusion for failure to include affiant's name in warrant application, as required by statute) with People v. Taylor, 541 N.E.2d 386 (N.Y. 1989) (exclusion required for violation of statutory requirement of contemporaneous recording of evidence supporting warrant application). What remedy would you expect state courts to select when police officers violate departmental policies as they gather evidence?

8. *Silver platters.* It is clear that a federal court cannot receive evidence that state officers obtain in violation of federal law. That is, the state officers may not present the evidence to their federal counterparts on a "silver platter." See Elkins v. United States, 364 U.S. 206 (1960). The same rule prevents federal officers from presenting evidence to a state court if they obtained it in violation of the federal constitution. But the "silver platter doctrine" does not operate in all possible combinations. Officers from some other jurisdiction (federal or state) may obtain evidence in violation of state law (constitutional or statutory) and present that evidence in the federal courts or in the courts of another state. Local rules about search and seizure do not export to the courts of other jurisdictions. As the reach of federal criminal law grows and the overlap between state and federal criminal justice increases, does the argument get stronger for applying local search and seizure rules in the courts of other jurisdictions? See State v. Torres, 262 P.3d 1006 (Haw. 2011) (where state seeks to admit evidence obtained in another jurisdiction, court must give "due consideration" to state constitution; court declines to declare categorically that

evidence obtained elsewhere in violation of Hawaii state constitution must always be excluded). How would traditional conflicts of laws doctrine resolve this issue?

9. *International adoption of exclusionary rule.* Although judges in the United States sometimes claim that no other country in the world uses an exclusionary rule, the claim is not true. For instance, in Germany, judges must consider whether admission of evidence obtained illegally would violate the constitutionally protected privacy interests of the defendant. German judges balance in each case the defendant's interests in privacy against the importance of the evidence and the seriousness of the offense charged. In practice, however, German judges rarely exclude evidence obtained through improper searches. Kay L. Levine et al., Evidence Laundering in a Post-*Herring* World, 106 J. Crim. L. & Criminology 627, 666 (2016). The balancing approach may expand the range of responses to government violations of the law. In the Netherlands, for example, courts can pick from several different remedies, ranging from a declaration of illegality to a sentence reduction to exclusion of the evidence. See Matthias J. Bogers & Lonneke Stevens, The Netherlands: Statutory Balancing and a Choice of Remedies, in Exclusionary Rules in Comparative Law 183 (Stephen C. Thaman ed. 2013). Would a sentencing reduction be a desirable alternative to exclusion in some cases under U.S. law as well? For an argument along those lines, see Guido Calabresi, The Exclusionary Rule, 26 Harv. J.L. & Pub. Pol'y 111 (2003).

In Canada, where courts have also embraced a balancing approach, exclusion happens more frequently. The constitutionally based Charter of Rights and Freedoms gives the accused a basis for excluding evidence that was obtained improperly. Evidence is excluded only if a breach of a Charter right or freedom is demonstrated and if the admission of the evidence in the trial would tend to bring the administration of justice "into disrepute." More serious violations are more likely to result in exclusion. R. v. Grant [2009] SCC 32; Ariane Asselin, Trends for Exclusion of Evidence in 2012, 1 C.R. (7th) 74 (2013) (finding a 73 percent rate of exclusion at the trial level in Canada in 2012).

In yet another group of countries, past experience with authoritarian rule has focused public attention on the danger of a powerful executive who exercises power arbitrarily. The exclusionary rule in these countries is therefore adopted, at least in part, because it embodies the idea of restraining government power and promoting the rule of law. Jenia I. Turner, The Exclusionary Rule as a Symbol of the Rule of Law, 67 SMU L. Rev. 821 (2014). The web extension for this chapter, at *http://www.crimpro.com/extension/ch06*, offers further examples of the use of the exclusionary remedy in other countries.

On the whole, foreign systems have resisted the deterrence approach to evidence exclusion and have focused instead on goals such as protecting judicial integrity, promoting the rule of law, and vindicating individual rights. If courts in the United States were to emphasize such goals, how might that change the scope or content of the exclusionary rule?

B. LIMITATIONS ON THE EXCLUSIONARY RULE

We have traced the history of the adoption of the exclusionary rule as a remedy for illegal searches and seizures. The exclusionary rule was a controversial choice of remedies at the time of *Weeks, Cahan,* and *Mapp,* and it remains so today.

Reservations about the exclusionary rule have not yet led any U.S. legal system to abandon the remedy, but they have led to some serious limitations on its applicability and effects.

Accordingly, the U.S. Supreme Court has restricted the application of the rule only to those areas where its deterrent purpose is seen to outweigh most clearly the social costs of exclusion. In United States v. Leon, 468 U.S. 897 (1984), the Court established the "good faith" exception to the exclusionary rule: where a police officer conducts a search in objective good faith reliance upon a duly issued warrant, the exclusionary rule does not apply. The Court reasoned that the exclusionary rule would not deter officers who act in an objectively reasonable belief that their conduct is lawful.

Subsequent cases expanded the scope of the "good faith" exception to cover certain negligent conduct by law enforcement officers. Herring v. United States, 555 U.S. 135 (2009). Separately, the Court carved out exceptions to the exclusionary rule in noncriminal proceedings, at the grand jury stage, at trial when the evidence is used solely to impeach the defendant, and in various areas where the connection between the original violation and the ultimate seizure of the evidence is too attenuated. As you read the materials, consider whether the exceptions to the exclusionary rule have now swallowed the rule itself.

1. Evidence Obtained in "Good Faith"

■ COMMONWEALTH v. RICHARD JOHNSON
86 A.3d 182 (Pa. 2014)

CASTILLE, C.J.

This matter turns upon whether the Superior Court erred in affirming the trial court's suppression of physical evidence seized incident to an arrest based on an invalid (expired) arrest warrant, where the police officer reasonably and in good faith believed that the arrest warrant was valid. We hold that the evidence was properly suppressed under Article I, Section 8 of the Pennsylvania Constitution and this Court's decision in Commonwealth v. Edmunds, 586 A.2d 887 (Pa. 1991) (rejecting federal good faith exception to exclusionary rule in case involving evidence seized pursuant to defective search warrant). Accordingly, we affirm the Superior Court's order.

On March 8, 2010, appellee Richard Allen Johnson was a passenger in a vehicle in Wilkes-Barre which was stopped by State Trooper James Knott, who had previously received a radio communication that the vehicle in question had been involved in a drug transaction, and who then observed that the vehicle had a broken tail light. Upon requesting identification and processing appellee's name through his patrol car computer, Trooper Knott received a "hit" message advising that there was an active arrest warrant for appellee. Trooper Knott then placed appellee under arrest and conducted a pat-down search during which he discovered thirty-seven packets of suspected heroin, two cell phones and $1,674 in cash. Trooper Knott placed appellee in the back of a police car and transported him to the police barracks. . . . Appellee made several statements to Trooper Knott. In one statement, appellee indicated that he is a drug dealer and that the driver of the vehicle bought drugs from him. In a later statement, appellee claimed he is a user of drugs, not a seller, and that the cash he carried at the time of the arrest and patdown search was a tax refund.

Trooper Knott subsequently determined that the warrant notification he relied upon when he arrested appellee was no longer valid and should have been recalled, since it had previously been served on appellee nine days earlier. . . . Appellee was nonetheless charged with three violations of the Controlled Substance, Drug, Device and Cosmetic Act. Appellee moved to suppress the physical evidence recovered during the search incident to his arrest, as well as the incriminating statements he made to Trooper Knott. Appellee alleged that his underlying arrest was unlawful under both the Fourth Amendment of the U.S. Constitution and Article I, Section 8 of the Pennsylvania Constitution. [The trial court] granted appellee's motion and ordered suppression of the evidence under Article I, Section 8. The court found as a fact that Trooper Knott had acted in good faith in arresting appellee on the basis of what Knott mistakenly believed was an active warrant, but the court reasoned that there is no good faith exception to the exclusionary rule under the Pennsylvania Constitution. The court concluded that the physical evidence, as well as the statements obtained later at the police barracks, were the fruits of an illegal arrest based on an invalid warrant, and therefore must be suppressed. . . .

Article I, Section 8 explicitly addresses seizures of persons (here, by an arrest) no less than searches of a person's houses, papers or possessions:

> Security from searches and seizures. The people shall be secure in their persons, houses, papers and possessions from unreasonable searches and seizures, and no warrant to search any place or to seize any person or things shall issue without describing them as nearly as may be, nor without probable cause, supported by oath or affirmation subscribed to by the affiant.

Pa. Const. art. I, §8. The established remedy for illegal seizures and searches, in criminal cases, is exclusion of the fruits of the illegal police conduct—under both the Fourth Amendment and under Article I, Section 8. That general rule of exclusion, of course, is subject to numerous exceptions. The U.S. Supreme Court recognized a new such exception to the Fourth Amendment's exclusionary rule in United States v. Leon, 468 U.S. 897 (1984). *Leon* held that, where a police officer conducts a search in objective good faith reliance upon a search warrant duly issued by a magistrate or judge, the Fourth Amendment does not require exclusion of evidence found pursuant to the warrant, even if it is later determined that there was no probable cause for the warrant to issue. The High Court considered that the deterrence goal of the federal exclusionary rule based on the Fourth Amendment would not be served by applying it in circumstances where officers have properly relied on a subsequently invalidated search warrant.

In its subsequent decision in Herring v. United States, 555 U.S. 135 (2009), the High Court considered the good faith exception in an expired arrest warrant context, ultimately adopting a conditional application of the good faith exception, turning upon the reason why the expired warrant was erroneously deemed valid, i.e., whether the error in failing to purge the warrant was systemic or not. [Since the failure to purge the expired warrant in *Herring* was the result of isolated negligence rather than systemic errors or intentional wrongdoing, the Court held that the evidence was sufficiently attenuated from the official error to justify the use of the good faith exception.]

This Court's consideration and rejection of the *Leon* good faith exception as a matter of state constitutional law in Commonwealth v. Edmunds did not turn upon the nature of the intrusion—*i.e.*, whether a search was at issue or a seizure was at issue—but rather upon the perceived values furthered by the exclusionary rule applied under Article I, Section 8 of Pennsylvania's Constitution. By way of background, Edmunds was convicted of drug related charges, after the admission into evidence of marijuana seized at his property pursuant to a search warrant, a warrant later determined to have been unsupported by probable cause because the warrant affidavit "failed to set forth with specificity the date upon which the anonymous informants observed the marijuana."

[This Court rejected] *Leon* as an Article I, Section 8 matter, . . . holding that Section 8 does not incorporate a good faith exception to the exclusionary rule. The *Edmunds* Court examined the question by considering: (1) the text of the provision of the Pennsylvania Constitution; (2) the history of the provision, including the caselaw of this Commonwealth; (3) relevant caselaw from other jurisdictions; and (4) policy considerations, "including unique issues of state and local concern, and applicability within modern Pennsylvania jurisprudence." After applying this state constitutional paradigm . . . to the facts at hand, the Court concluded that the evidence seized from Edmunds's property based on an invalid search warrant should have been suppressed. *Edmunds* turned on a determination that, under Article I, Section 8, the exclusionary rule in Pennsylvania serves other values besides deterrence; it also vindicates an individual's right to privacy:

> [Given] the strong right of privacy which inheres in Article 1, Section 8, as well as the clear prohibition against the issuance of warrants without probable cause, or based upon defective warrants, the good faith exception to the exclusionary rule would directly clash with those rights of citizens as developed in our Commonwealth over the past 200 years. To allow the judicial branch to participate, directly or indirectly, in the use of the fruits of illegal searches would only serve to undermine the integrity of the judiciary in this Commonwealth. From the perspective of the citizen whose rights are at stake, an invasion of privacy, in good faith or bad, is equally as intrusive. This is true whether it occurs through the actions of the legislative, executive or the judicial branch of government.

[The Commonwealth has not] argued that *Edmunds* itself should be modified or rejected. Indeed, the Commonwealth cites to *Edmunds* only once in its three-page argument, while arguing that this Court's failure to adopt a good faith exception to the exclusionary rule there "does not lead to the exclusion of evidence in every case where the police act on a mistaken belief that they are entitled to seize certain evidence." Of course, every decision must be read against its facts, and it may well be true that this Court will come to recognize exceptions to various general rules in the Article I, Section 8 area—no less than in other areas of the law. . . .

The Commonwealth has not explained why exclusion of the evidence seized here, unlike the exclusion of the evidence seized in *Edmunds*, would not vindicate the privacy interests of Pennsylvania citizens, or would forward some other value that was not at issue or sufficiently acknowledged in *Edmunds*. Indeed, under the rationale articulated in *Edmunds*, there is at least as much reason to afford an exclusionary remedy in the expired arrest warrant scenario as in the defective search warrant scenario. The mistake in *Edmunds* was made by the magistrate assessing probable cause; the executive branch (there, embodied by the police executing the warrant) did nothing wrong. This case involves an arrest warrant, not a search warrant, but the defect leading to suppression below did not involve a mistake in the judicial issuance of a warrant without probable cause. Rather, the lapse arose somewhere in the executive branch — not with the arresting officer, but with whoever was responsible for purging executed warrants in a timely fashion.

Thus, this case, unlike *Edmunds*, involves a situation where application of the exclusionary rule would not only serve the same privacy-based function it was deemed to serve in *Edmunds*, but also would serve some generalized deterrence function. In this regard, it is worth noting that appellee already suffered the authorized compromise of his liberty via a prior arrest on the same warrant. Application of the exclusionary rule may encourage the executive to adopt more efficient measures to purge executed arrest warrants and thereby to better ensure the privacy rights of Pennsylvanians. . . . We therefore affirm the Superior Court's order affirming the trial court's suppression of the physical evidence seized incident to appellee's illegal arrest.

McCAFFERY, J., dissenting.

The question before the Court is whether evidence found during a search incident to arrest is admissible at trial under Article I, Section 8 of the Pennsylvania Constitution even though the warrant for the arrest was subsequently found to have already been served and thus was no longer valid. In Herring v. United States, 555 U.S. 135 (2009), the United States Supreme Court held that when police mistakes in the execution of an expired arrest warrant are the result of negligence, rather than systemic error or reckless disregard of constitutional requirements, the exclusionary rule should not apply. I would hold that Article I, Section 8 does not require greater privacy protection than the high Court afforded in *Herring*. Accordingly, I dissent.

FOURTH AMENDMENT JURISPRUDENCE

. . . Twenty-three years after *Mapp* was decided, the United States Supreme Court limited the scope of the exclusionary rule, holding that evidence obtained by police officers acting in reasonable reliance on a search warrant subsequently found to be unsupported by probable cause was not barred from use at trial. United States v. Leon, 468 U.S. 897 (1984). In promulgating this "good faith exception" to the exclusionary rule, the . . . *Leon* Court explained that it had re-examined the purposes of the exclusionary rule and concluded that its primary purpose is to deter police misconduct, i.e., "willful, or at the very least negligent, [police] conduct which has deprived the defendant of some right." When the police have not engaged in any misconduct, but rather have acted with objectively reasonable reliance on a search warrant that is subsequently determined to be invalid, then the benefits of applying the exclusionary rule are "marginal or nonexistent." Under such circumstances, the *Leon* Court held, the costs of applying the exclusionary rule outweigh the benefits, and, pursuant to the good faith exception, determined that the rule is inapplicable.

The U.S. Supreme Court employed a similar balancing approach to decide Herring v. United States, [a case] with facts and circumstances closely resembling the case currently before us. The defendant-petitioner was arrested on a warrant, and a search incident to arrest revealed drugs on his person and an illegally possessed firearm in his motor vehicle. Very shortly after the arrest, the warrant was found to have been recalled months earlier, and thus it was invalid. After the defendant-petitioner was indicted for illegal possession of the drugs and the firearm, he moved to suppress the evidence, contending that his arrest was illegal under the Fourth Amendment because the warrant had been rescinded. [The district court denied the suppression motion and the U.S. Supreme Court ultimately] affirmed, reiterating that the exclusionary rule is a judicially created rule, not an individual right; is not a necessary consequence of a Fourth Amendment violation; and applies only where it has the potential to result in the deterrence of future Fourth Amendment violations. . . . Recognizing that the cases that had given rise to the exclusionary rule involved intentional, flagrant, patently unconstitutional conduct, the high Court made clear that the "exclusionary rule serves to deter deliberate, reckless, or grossly negligent conduct, or in some circumstances recurring or systemic negligence."

In applying these principles to the facts and circumstances of *Herring*, the high Court determined that the conduct of the law enforcement officers "was not so objectively culpable as to require exclusion" of the evidence. There was no evidence that record-keeping errors in the sheriff's office were routine or widespread; rather, the testimony suggested that such errors were rare. . . .

In the three decades immediately following *Mapp* . . . this Court decided numerous search and seizure cases. In many, this Court's rulings were aligned with federal jurisprudence. See, e.g., Commonwealth v. Musi, 404 A.2d 378, 385 (Pa. 1979) (accepting "the wisdom of [the federal] approach" in holding that a violation of a procedural rule for the execution and return of warrants should not render an otherwise valid search illegal unless the defendant can show prejudice). It is therefore apparent that this Court, from its earliest days up through most of the 20th century, discerned no additional or strengthened protections in the Pennsylvania Constitution as compared to the Fourth Amendment with regard to search and seizure cases.

In the late 1970s, however, a line of cases began to emerge from this Court that departed from federal search and seizure jurisprudence, based on our discernment of greater protection for individual privacy rights in Article I, Section 8 of the Pennsylvania Constitution than in the Fourth Amendment to the U.S. Constitution. In Commonwealth v. DeJohn, 403 A.2d 1283 (Pa. 1979), this Court declined to follow the U.S. Supreme Court's decision in United States v. Miller, 425 U.S. 435 (1976), in which the high Court held that a depositor had no reasonable expectation of privacy in his or her bank records. [The opinion also reviewed two similar Pennsylvania cases, dealing with standing to challenge police searches and the use of pen registers.]

COMMONWEALTH V. EDMUNDS

[This] Court in Commonwealth v. Edmunds, 586 A.2d 887 (Pa. 1991), again departed from U.S. Supreme Court precedent, and declined to adopt the "good faith" exception to the exclusionary rule as inconsistent with the guarantees embodied in Article I, Section 8 of the Pennsylvania Constitution. . . . In reaching this holding, *Edmunds* set forth a methodology to be used in analyzing issues that arise under the Pennsylvania Constitution. Specifically, the Court determined that it was "important" for the litigants in any future case implicating a provision of the Pennsylvania Constitution, to brief and analyze at least the following four factors: 1) text of the Pennsylvania constitutional provision; 2) history of the provision including Pennsylvania case-law; 3) related case-law from other states; 4) policy considerations, including unique issues of state and local concern, and applicability within modern Pennsylvania jurisprudence.

[In applying these four factors, the *Edmunds* Court] concluded that the exclusionary rule in Pennsylvania "served to bolster the twin aims of Article I, Section 8; to wit, the safeguarding of privacy and the fundamental requirement that warrants shall only be issued upon probable cause." *Edmunds* explicitly rejected the U.S. Supreme Court's view in *Leon* that the sole purpose of the exclusionary rule was to deter police misconduct. . . .

Edmunds also drew support from rulings in other states that had declined to adopt a good faith exception. More specifically, *Edmunds* briefly summarized rulings from the highest courts of New Jersey, Connecticut, and North Carolina, each of which had concluded that the exclusionary rule serves broader purposes than merely the deterrence of police misconduct, and therefore had rejected the good faith exception.

Finally, *Edmunds* addressed the fourth factor, to wit, policy considerations. *Edmunds* concluded that adoption of a good faith exception would "effectively nullify" Pa. R. Crim. P. 2003, which requires that an inquiry into probable cause for a search warrant be confined to the written affidavit and warrant, "in order to avoid any doubt as to the basis for probable cause." *Edmunds* stressed the requirement that an independent magistrate make a determination of probable cause prior to the issuance of any search warrant. *Edmunds* also questioned the magnitude of the costs of applying the exclusionary rule in practice and the concerns attached to the alternative remedy, *i.e.*, allowing victims of improper searches to sue police officers directly. Finally, *Edmunds* noted that Pennsylvania's adoption of the flexible, totality of the circumstances standard for determining probable cause eliminated concerns that the exclusionary rule might be applied in an overly rigid manner. . . .

APPLICATION OF EDMUNDS FACTORS TO THIS CASE

. . . The question now before us is whether Article I, Section 8 requires greater privacy protection than the high Court afforded in *Herring*. This can be determined only after consideration and analysis of the circumstances of this case in light of the relevant factors set forth by this Court in *Edmunds*.

With respect to the text of Article I, Section 8, this Court has noted many times that it is similar to that of the Fourth Amendment. There are no textual differences between the two provisions that would suggest greater protection under the Pennsylvania Constitution for a defendant who has been arrested under an expired warrant.

With regard to the history of Article I, Section 8, [no] case stands on all fours with the instant case. Our discernment, over the past few decades, of heightened protection of privacy interests under Article I, Section 8 for certain circumstances does not automatically support the extension of heightened protection to the instant circumstances. . . . Indeed, we have stated that there should be "compelling reasons" to interpret our state Constitution to afford defendants greater protections than those granted by the U.S. Constitution. Commonwealth v. Gray, 503 A.2d 921, 926 (Pa. 1985). Under the circumstances of the instant case, I have not discerned "compelling reasons" to grant greater protections than those afforded by the Fourth Amendment. . . .

In the cases where this Court has discerned enhanced protection for individual privacy interests under Article I, Section 8, we have articulated a broad view of the purpose of the exclusionary rule. [It serves the twin aims of safeguarding privacy] and the fundamental requirement that warrants shall only be issued upon probable cause.

Our articulation of these broad goals of the exclusionary rule in Pennsylvania does not and cannot alter the rule's prospective nature, an inherent characteristic that circumscribes the rule's remedial function. Once an unreasonable, illegal search or seizure has taken place, the constitutional violation is accomplished; exclusion of evidence pursuant to the exclusionary rule does nothing to repair or redress the unconstitutional invasion of privacy that has already occurred. . . . Even when focusing on the right to privacy or the mandate of probable cause, goals emphasized by this Court in *Edmunds*, we must be mindful that the exclusionary rule looks ahead to the next case, seeking to prevent future violations of the right to privacy and future issuance of warrants unsupported by probable cause. Accordingly, the exclusionary rule is of marginal value under circumstances where its application is unlikely to yield future benefits with regard to the right to privacy and/or the mandate of probable cause. Furthermore, we must consider not only the marginal value of the rule under such circumstances, but also the costs of the rule with respect to prosecution of the accused and protection of society. . . .

In any given case, balancing the individual right of privacy and/or the mandate of probable cause against the public interest in truth-determination at trial and conviction of the guilty, requires a fact-specific inquiry operating between wide parameters. [It is notable] that the exclusionary rule provides no relief whatsoever for an individual who is the subject of an unreasonable search or seizure that has not led to the discovery of any incriminating evidence. An innocent victim of an illegal search and seizure has suffered as grievous an invasion of privacy as an accused, but only the accused has any possibility of direct and individual benefit from the exclusionary rule. . . .

I conclude that when police make an illegal arrest on an expired warrant as a result of an error in record-keeping reflecting nothing more than a non-systemic instance of administrative negligence, the exclusionary rule should not apply to suppress evidence discovered incident to the arrest. This conclusion logically follows from the marginal impact that application of the exclusionary rule would have on deterring a rare instance of negligent record-keeping. When the slim likelihood of benefit under such circumstances is balanced against the high price of loss of evidence, I conclude that the exclusionary rule should not apply. However, if the error in record-keeping reflects a systemic or institutional administrative problem leading to repeated errors in the recording and transmission of information as to the status of warrants, then application of the exclusionary rule would be appropriate because of its deterrent effect and consequent promotion of individual privacy. Likewise, and for the same reasons, if law enforcement agents exhibit intentional or reckless disregard of constitutional rights by arresting an individual on a warrant the agents knew or reasonably should have known was expired, application of the exclusionary rule is appropriate. . . .

Here, the trial court specifically determined that there was no misconduct on the part of the arresting officer, who acted on what he, the State Police and the Wilkes-Barre City Police all believed to be an active warrant. However, the trial court made no findings as to the nature of the error that led to the misidentification of the warrant as active, and thus, on the record before us, it is impossible to determine if the exclusionary rule should have been applied. I would, therefore, vacate the order of the Superior Court and remand to the trial court to conduct further proceedings to determine the nature of the error that led to the incorrect characterization of the warrant as active. I would suggest that the trial court consider the relevant administrative procedures in place for tracking arrest warrants and informing police as to the viability of a particular warrant, and the time that elapsed between when the arrest warrant should have been withdrawn and when the accused was arrested.

■ COLORADO REVISED STATUTES §16-3-308

(1) Evidence which is otherwise admissible in a criminal proceeding shall not be suppressed by the trial court if the court determines that the evidence was seized by a peace officer . . . as a result of a good faith mistake or of a technical violation.

(2) As used in subsection (1) of this section:

(a) "Good faith mistake" means a reasonable judgmental error concerning the existence of facts or law which if true would be sufficient to constitute probable cause.

(b) "Technical violation" means a reasonable good faith reliance upon a statute which is later ruled unconstitutional, a warrant which is later invalidated due to a good faith mistake, or a court precedent which is later overruled. . . .

(4) (a) It is hereby declared to be the public policy of the state of Colorado that, when evidence is sought to be excluded from the trier of fact in a criminal proceeding because of the conduct of a peace officer leading to its discovery, it will be open to the proponent of the evidence to urge that the conduct in question was taken in a reasonable, good faith belief that it was proper, and in such instances the evidence so discovered should not be kept from the trier of fact if otherwise admissible. . . .

(b) It shall be prima facie evidence that the conduct of the peace officer was performed in the reasonable good faith belief that it was proper if there is a showing that the evidence was obtained pursuant to and within the scope of a warrant, unless the warrant was obtained through intentional and material misrepresentation.

Notes

1. *Good faith exception: majority position.* More than a dozen states have decided, like Pennsylvania, not to adopt a good faith exception to exclusionary rules under their state constitutions. A majority of states have explicitly adopted *Leon* under state constitutions. See State v. Eason, 629 N.W.2d 625 (Wis. 2001). For a richer account of the courts that accept or reject *Leon,* consult the web extension for this chapter at *http://www.crimpro.com/extension/ch06.* Do you agree with the Pennsylvania court that a state rejecting the good faith exception will maintain stronger privacy protections and stronger control over the quality of warranted searches? If you were directing a police training program in a state that had adopted *Leon,* would that decision affect your training priorities or your recommendations to police officers?

2. *Objective good faith and perjury.* The officer's good faith reliance on the warrant under *Leon* must be "objectively reasonable." There is no objective good faith when (1) the officer gives to the magistrate information that the officer knew or should

have known was false; (2) the magistrate "wholly abandon[s]" the judicial role; (3) the affidavit is "so lacking in indicia of probable cause" that it would be "entirely unreasonable" for a well-trained officer to believe probable cause existed; or (4) the warrant is so facially deficient that the officer could not reasonably believe it is valid. *Leon,* 468 U.S. at 923. See Messerschmidt v. Millender, 565 U.S. 535 (2012) (fact that detective asked for review of warrant application by police supervisors and prosecutor before submitting it to magistrate is relevant in determining objective good faith reliance on warrant); People v. Miller, 75 P.3d 1108 (Colo. 2003) (well-trained officer could not rely on month-old tip with no mention of ongoing activity as basis for probable cause in warrant; no good faith exception). How could a magistrate approve a warrant that is so lacking in probable cause or particularity that it would be "entirely unreasonable" for a well-trained officer to believe it was valid?

How would a criminal defendant prove that an officer gave false information to the magistrate? The "four corners" rule is one traditional technique to prevent perjury or other inaccurate police testimony. Under this rule, the state may not rely on evidence not included in the affidavit or the warrant application submitted to the magistrate. Is it possible to adopt the good faith exception while continuing to insist that any facts related to the reasonableness of the search appear within the "four corners" of the warrant application and supporting affidavits? See State v. Davidson, 618 N.W.2d 418 (Neb. 2000) (inquiry into officers' good faith is not limited to four corners of warrant affidavit).

3. *Good faith reliance on negligent police action.* The *Leon* decision allows police officers to rely on determinations by a magistrate. In Arizona v. Evans, 514 U.S. 1 (1995), the Court allowed a good faith exception to the exclusionary rule when an officer relied on an inaccurate record showing an outstanding arrest warrant for a person he had stopped. The record was inaccurate because an employee of the clerk of the court had failed to update a computer database. In Herring v. United States, 555 U.S. 135 (2009), the Court extended this decision and held that the exclusionary rule does not apply when an illegal search is based on "isolated [police] negligence attenuated from the search." In *Herring,* police relied on a faulty police report of an outstanding arrest warrant for failure to appear on a felony change. This false report led to an arrest, a search incident to arrest, and the discovery of methamphetamine in Herring's pocket and an illegal pistol in his car. According to the *Herring* court, "the exclusionary rule serves to deter deliberate, reckless, or grossly negligent conduct, or in some circumstances recurring or systemic negligence." It does not apply outside that context.

Is *Herring* a logical extension of *Leon* and *Evans*? Or is it another example of death (to exclusion) by a thousand small (doctrinal) cuts? Thomas K. Clancy, The Irrelevancy of the Fourth Amendment in the Roberts Court, 85 Chi.-Kent L.J. 191 (2010) (attributing decline in the number of cases addressing Fourth Amendment questions in part to *Herring*). Most state courts have accepted the expanded good faith exception of *Herring* under state constitutional analysis.

4. *Good faith reliance on legislatures and appellate courts.* Rules or statutes can also work in favor of a good faith exception. In Illinois v. Krull, 480 U.S. 340 (1987), the court extended the good faith exception of *Leon* to include searches by officers who relied in good faith during a search or seizure on a statute later declared to be unconstitutional. See State v. De La Cruz, 969 A.2d 413 (N.H. 2009) (adopting *Krull* while rejecting *Leon*). Does the exclusionary rule help to "deter" the legislature from passing unconstitutional legislation regarding searches and seizures?

Do the arguments for the good faith exception change when the police rely on established interpretations of the Fourth Amendment by appellate courts that are later overturned? In Davis v. United States, 564 U.S. 229 (2011), the police conducted a search in compliance with New York v. Belton, 453 U.S. 454 (1981), before it was modified by the new search-incident-to-arrest rule of Arizona v. Gant, 556 U.S. 332 (2009), as discussed in Chapter 4. According to the *Davis* court, the exclusionary rule does not apply to evidence from a search conducted "in objectively reasonable reliance on binding appellate precedent" that "specifically authorized" the search at the time it was conducted. How closely should the circumstances of a search match those in the binding precedent to come within the case law good faith exception?

5. *Statutory exclusion.* A number of states have passed statutes calling in general terms for the exclusion of evidence obtained through illegal searches or seizures. Would this sort of statute make it more difficult for a court to justify the creation of good faith exceptions or other limitations on the state's exclusionary rule? On the other hand, several jurisdictions have passed statutes allowing admission of evidence obtained illegally, so long as the officer acted in good faith. See Colo. Rev. Stat. §16-3-308; see also Zarychta v. State, 44 S.W.3d 155 (Tex. App. 2001) (noting the narrow interpretation of "good faith" under Texas statute, under which "it is not enough for an officer to believe he was acting pursuant to a warrant based on probable cause; rather, the warrant must, in fact, be supported by probable cause"). Further examples of statutory exclusionary rules and statutory limits to the remedy appear on the web extension for this chapter at *http://www.crimpro.com/extension/ch06.*

6. *Evidence excluded in which proceedings?* The statutes printed above all address admission of evidence in criminal proceedings. Federal and state constitutions require the exclusion of evidence from the government's case-in-chief at a criminal trial. However, the exclusionary rule usually does not operate in other proceedings. For instance, the government can use such evidence in grand jury proceedings and in most administrative proceedings. See INS v. Lopez-Mendoza, 468 U.S. 1032 (1984) (exclusion does not apply in civil deportation proceedings). Likewise, most federal and state courts have refused to extend the exclusionary rule to the sentencing stage, though some have stated they would exclude evidence at sentencing if the police engaged in gross or shocking misconduct or conducted the unlawful search or seizure for the purpose of influencing the sentence. See, e.g., Elson v. State, 659 P.2d 1195 (Alaska 1983); State v. Habbena, 372 N.W.2d 450 (S.D. 1985).

Courts deciding whether to follow the exclusionary rule in various types of proceedings have often relied on the reasoning of the Supreme Court in United States v. Calandra, 414 U.S. 338 (1974). The Court there decided that the exclusionary rule would not apply to grand jury proceedings because the rule would have little additional deterrent effect on police, given that the evidence was already excludable from any criminal trial. Would this reasoning apply to investigators for the Immigration and Naturalization Service, or others like them, whose principal task is to enforce civil laws? The exclusionary rule is generally applied to "quasi-criminal" proceedings before judges or administrative agencies such as proceedings to forfeit property (because of its connection with criminal activity). See, e.g., Commonwealth v. One 1985 Ford Thunderbird Automobile, 624 N.E.2d 547 (Mass. 1993). But see Pennsylvania Board of Probation and Parole v. Scott, 524 U.S. 357 (1998) (parole boards are not required by federal law to exclude evidence obtained in violation of Fourth Amendment). Is the deterrent value of the exclusionary rule in quasi-criminal proceedings any greater than in other civil proceedings? A number of state statutes and court rules clarify whether illegally obtained evidence may be admitted in various types of proceedings. See, e.g., La. Code Evid. art. 1101.

7. *Impeachment.* The government can also use improperly obtained evidence as the basis for impeaching a defendant if she testifies at a criminal trial. The Court in United States v. Havens, 446 U.S. 620 (1980), reasoned that exclusion in such cases would not deter police because the usefulness of evidence for impeachment purposes is so difficult to predict. At the same time, allowing the evidence to form the basis of impeachment questions would discourage defendants from committing perjury. See also James v. Illinois, 493 U.S. 307 (1990) (illegally obtained evidence may *not* be used to impeach defense witnesses other than defendant; such impeachment is not necessary to discourage perjury of witnesses other than defendant).

Problem 6-1. Objective Good Faith

The Drug Squad of the Boulder Police Department received an anonymous letter, postmarked from Kansas City, which read as follows:

> This letter is to inform you that the person described below is an active drug dealer and warrants investigation. This is based on firsthand knowledge and eyewitness accounts by me and others. Below are some facts that may help you.
>
> Name: Jeff; Age: 35-40; Height: 5′9″; Weight: 170 lbs.; Race: white; Features: Bald on the top of his head. Crooked front teeth. Address: Lives in Boulder, Colorado, and is a student at the university.
>
> Vehicle: Two-door van with a large window on the driver's side. The passenger side has a sliding door. Color is steel blue. License plate number is MXS 518 or MSX 518, Colorado.
>
> Drugs are collected at a music store located in Kansas City just north of the intersection of 39th and Main on the east side of the street. The collection times may coincide with the vacation times of the university in Colorado. The drugs are then taken to Boulder for resale.
>
> We hope that this information will help you and are sorry that we must remain anonymous as other innocent people may get involved.
>
> Your friends in Kansas City.

Detective Kurt Weiler began an investigation, and confirmed that the vehicle described was registered to Jeffrey Leftwich, that Leftwich was 37 years old, and that his appearance matched the description in the letter. A call to the Kansas City Police Department confirmed that the music store described in the letter was in a "high drug" area.

During spring break at the university, officers noted that no vehicles were parked outside Leftwich's trailer residence. The day after spring break ended, an officer observed a car parked in the driveway of the residence. The parked car belonged to a person who had been convicted two years earlier of possessing cocaine. The next day, officers noted that Leftwich's Ford van was parked in the driveway. Further inquiries confirmed that Leftwich had traveled to Kansas City during spring break.

Detective Weiler then prepared an affidavit for a search warrant for Leftwich's home. The chief deputy district attorney reviewed the affidavit and advised Detective Weiler that the affidavit presented a close case and that a judge might not sign it.

Weiler nonetheless filed the application and a district court judge issued a warrant. During the search of Leftwich's home, Weiler found a triple-beam balance and some marijuana.

Assuming that a reviewing court would conclude that the warrant was not supported by probable cause, would the good faith exception apply? Recall that the officer's good faith must be "objectively" reasonable. If this officer did not qualify for the good faith exception, how often will the exception apply in those states adopting it? Compare People v. Leftwich, 869 P.2d 1260 (Colo. 1994).

Problem 6-2. Unwarranted Good Faith

Three undercover police officers went to the Brook Hollow Inn to set up surveillance of possible illegal activities in one of the rooms. The manager checked the officers into a room that she believed to be vacant. However, when the officers entered the room they noticed that clothing and luggage had been left in the room. One officer called the registration desk to confirm that they were in the right room. Another officer opened the doors of the television cabinet and found cocaine there. After the officers had left the room, Charles Farmer arrived at the room and let himself in with his key. He called the manager from the phone in the room and told her that he had paid for another day and still occupied the room. The manager told Farmer that a terrible mistake had been made.

In light of the statute reprinted above, would a court in Colorado exclude from evidence the cocaine found in the room? Would this evidence be admissible under *Leon* or *Herring*? Compare Fanner v. State, 759 P.2d 1031 (Okla. Crim. App. 1988).

2. Causation Limits: Inevitable Discovery and Independent Source

Long before *Wolf* and *Mapp*, it was clear that the exclusionary rule applied not only to evidence obtained during an improper search or seizure but also to any "fruits," that is, evidence the government later developed on the basis of leads obtained during an improper search or seizure. A common phrase presents a powerful image: The exclusionary rule, it is said, applies to the "fruit of the poisonous tree." But there must be some end to the consequences of error; a government error early in an investigation cannot bar all subsequent investigation. Courts have wrestled over how far to extend the impact of government errors—what harms can be said to be "caused" by, or fairly attributed to, the initial violation?

Federal and state courts have placed several causal limitations on the fruit-of-the-poisonous-tree doctrine. Two widely acknowledged limitations are known as the "independent source" and "inevitable discovery" rules. Though these are often described as "exceptions" to the exclusionary rule, each amounts to a conclusion that the government would have obtained the evidence in question even without the illegal enforcement activity; thus, the violation did not "cause" the government to hold the evidence. Application of the "inevitable discovery" and "independent source" rules raise a host of questions, many spurred by the fundamental problem of asking judges to decide what could or would have happened in a case, rather than what did in fact happen.

■ MICHAEL WEHRENBERG v. STATE

416 S.W.3d 458 (Tex. Crim. App. 2013)

ALCALA, J.

Is the federal independent source doctrine, which excepts from the exclusionary rule evidence initially observed during an unlawful search but later obtained lawfully through independent means, applicable in Texas? [We conclude that] the independent source doctrine poses no conflict with Article 38.23 of the Texas Code of Criminal Procedure, the statutory exclusionary rule in Texas that requires suppression of evidence "obtained" in violation of the law. . . .

FACTS AND TRIAL PROCEEDING

A police anti-narcotics unit had been conducting surveillance of a Parker County residence for approximately thirty days when officers received a call from a confidential informant advising them that the occupants were preparing to manufacture methamphetamine that night. Several hours after receiving that call, at approximately 12:30 A.M., officers entered the residence without a search warrant and without consent. Upon entering the residence, the officers encountered several individuals, including appellant, whom they handcuffed and escorted to the front yard. Officers performed a protective sweep of the residence, determined that no methamphetamine was being "cooked" at that time, and then went back outside the residence. Two investigators then prepared the search-warrant affidavit. The affidavit relied only on information provided by the confidential informant and did not mention the officers' warrantless entry into the residence. In relevant part, the affidavit stated that the informant had "provided information detailing narcotics manufacture and trafficking" at appellant's residence and had, within the past 72 hours, "personally observed the suspected parties in possession of certain chemicals with intent to manufacture a controlled substance." The affidavit additionally stated that, according to the confidential informant, the subjects were planning to use the "shake and bake" method of manufacturing methamphetamine, which the affiant described as "fast" and "often utilized to prevent detection of the illicit laboratory by law enforcement personnel."

At 1:50 A.M., approximately one-and-a-half hours after the officers' initial entry into the residence, the magistrate signed the search warrant. Police officers conducted a search of the residence and discovered methamphetamine and implements for manufacturing methamphetamine. Appellant was arrested and charged with possession of chemicals with intent to manufacture methamphetamine and possession of methamphetamine weighing more than 4 but less than 200 grams. . . .

At the hearing on the motion to suppress, the trial court heard testimony from Investigator Montanez, one of the officers who had prepared the search-warrant affidavit. Regarding the initial entry, Montanez stated that upon receiving the informant's tip that the subjects were "fixing to cook methamphetamine," the officers decided to "pull everybody out of the house and place them in the front yard" in order to "keep from evidence being destroyed." Montanez additionally explained that it was necessary to "secure the residence" because the process of "cooking" methamphetamine via the "shake-and-bake method" is "volatile" and "hazardous" in that it can cause explosions and/or fire, and he was afraid that the subjects "would begin making methamphetamine and then a fire would break out." Regarding the search warrant, Montanez testified that the affidavit's contents were based solely on the confidential informant's tip. He stated that he left to go get the warrant signed "immediately" after appellant and his co-defendants were detained, and that he returned to the scene around 2 A.M., at which time the search warrant was executed.

The trial court granted in part and denied in part appellant's motion to suppress. [The] trial judge stated that the officers' initial entry into the residence was "without a lawful warrant, exigent circumstances, or other lawful basis," and that, therefore, "any evidence from that search and seizure during that entry and detention at the initial entry to the home is suppressed." The trial judge went on to explain, however, that evidence seized pursuant to the search warrant was not subject to suppression because the search-warrant affidavit did not "allude to or mention the previous entry of the home, nor the detention of the suspect inhabitant defendants," and, therefore, the warrant was "untainted by the previous entry and detention." . . .

GENERAL SCOPE OF INDEPENDENT SOURCE DOCTRINE

Before answering the question of whether the independent source doctrine is consistent with the plain terms of the Texas exclusionary rule, we must first define the scope of that doctrine. We initially note that the federal exclusionary rule generally requires suppression of both primary evidence obtained as a direct result of an illegal search or seizure, as well as derivative evidence acquired as an indirect result of unlawful conduct. The Supreme Court has, however, developed several exceptions to this rule, including the independent source doctrine. That doctrine was first referred to by the Supreme Court in Silverthorne Lumber Company v. United States, 251 U.S. 385 (1920), in which the Court recognized that facts do not become "sacred and inaccessible" simply because they are first discovered unlawfully; rather, if knowledge of facts is gained "from an independent source they may be proved like any others." . . .

At its core, the independent source doctrine provides that evidence derived from or obtained from a lawful source, separate and apart from any illegal conduct by law enforcement, is not subject to exclusion. Thus, in determining whether challenged evidence is admissible under the independent source doctrine, the central question is whether the evidence at issue was obtained by independent legal means. [When the challenged evidence is actually obtained through a source independent of a separate instance of unlawful police conduct, exclusion of such evidence would put the police in a worse position than they would have been in absent any error or violation. A proper balance between deterring unlawful police action and the use of probative evidence is achieved by putting the police in the same position that they would have been in if no police misconduct had occurred.]

Segura v. United States, 468 U.S. 796 (1984), established that, notwithstanding a prior instance of unlawful police conduct, evidence actually discovered and obtained pursuant to a valid search warrant is not subject to suppression, so long as the police would have sought the warrant regardless of any observations made during the illegal entry. In Segura, the question before the Supreme Court was whether suppression was required after the police, acting on a tip regarding possible drug-trafficking activity, entered the defendant's apartment without his consent and conducted a security sweep of the residence. No search warrant was obtained until the next day, 19 hours after the initial entry, at which point a search was conducted and several items of evidence were discovered and seized, including weapons, cash, and several pounds of cocaine. None of these items was observed by officers during the initial entry; rather, they were discovered for the first time during the subsequent search pursuant to the warrant. After determining that the initial entry into the defendant's apartment had been unlawful, the Supreme Court nevertheless concluded that the evidence seized pursuant to the search warrant need not be excluded "as derivative or fruit of the poisonous tree" because of the existence of an "independent source."

Explaining its ruling, the Court stated that suppression was not warranted because the evidence was discovered "during the subsequent search of the apartment the following day pursuant to the valid search warrant," and the warrant was "issued wholly on information known to the officers before the entry into the apartment." It further observed that "none of the information on which the warrant was secured was derived from or related in any way to the initial entry into petitioners' apartment." The information supporting the search warrant instead "came from sources wholly unconnected with the entry and was known to the agents well before the initial entry." . . . *Segura* instructs that the existence of an independent source makes the exclusionary rule inapplicable because it breaks the causal chain between the constitutional violation alleged and the discovery of the evidence challenged. . . .

Subsequent to *Segura*, the Supreme Court has explained that the independent source doctrine is broad enough to encompass both (1) evidence observed and obtained for the first time during an independent lawful search following a previous instance of unlawful police conduct, which was the factual situation in *Segura*, and (2) evidence observed in plain view during an initial unlawful entry but later "obtained independently from activities untainted by the initial illegality," the situation presented in Murray v. United States, 487 U.S. 533 (1988). In *Murray*, after receiving a tip from an informant, federal drug-enforcement agents entered a warehouse by force and without a warrant, at which time they observed drugs in plain view. The officers then left the warehouse without disturbing the drugs, but kept the location under surveillance. Eight hours later, the agents secured a search warrant based solely on information already in their possession prior to the initial entry. They then re-entered the warehouse and seized 270 bales of marijuana. In holding that the drugs were not tainted by the initial entry and not subject to suppression, the Supreme Court explained that, although "knowledge that the marijuana was in the warehouse was assuredly acquired at the time of the unlawful entry," it was "also acquired at the time of entry pursuant to the warrant, and if that later acquisition was not the result of the earlier entry there is no reason why the independent source doctrine should not apply." . . .

INDEPENDENT SOURCE DOCTRINE CONSISTENT WITH TEXAS EXCLUSIONARY RULE

. . . The Texas exclusionary rule provides in relevant part that "No evidence obtained . . . in violation of any provisions of the Constitution or laws of the State of Texas, or of the Constitution or laws of the United States of America, shall be admitted in evidence against the accused on the trial of any criminal case." Tex. Code Crim. Proc. art. 38.23. To determine the meaning of this provision, we examine its plain language.

Evidence is "obtained" if it is "possessed," "gained or attained," usually "by planned action or effort." Webster's New Collegiate Dictionary 816 (9th ed. 1988).

Applying this definition in the context of the Texas exclusionary rule, the word "obtained" means that evidence is acquired by planned action or effort, or, more specifically, by seizure. Applying this ordinary definition, this Court has previously interpreted Article 38.23 to mean that evidence is "obtained" in violation of the law only if there is some causal connection between the illegal conduct and the acquisition of evidence. Roquemore v. State, 60 S.W.3d 862 (Tex. Crim. App. 2001). Conversely, if there is no causal connection, then the evidence cannot be said to have been "obtained" in violation of the law and thus is not subject to exclusion under the statute. . . .

Furthermore, this Court has long recognized that evidence is not "obtained" in violation of the law within the plain meaning of Article 38.23 if the taint from the illegality has dissipated by the time the evidence is acquired. In Johnson v. State, 871 S.W.2d 744 (Tex. Crim. App. 1994), this Court adopted the federal attenuation doctrine as being consistent with the express provisions of Article 38.23 because "evidence sufficiently attenuated from the violation of the law is not considered to be 'obtained' therefrom." The Court further reasoned that the attenuation doctrine was not an impermissible non-statutory exception to the exclusionary rule, but rather was "a method of determining whether evidence was 'obtained' in violation of the law, with 'obtained' being included in the plain language of the statute." . . .

Because the independent source doctrine by definition applies only to situations in which there is no causal connection between the illegality and the obtainment of evidence, we conclude that an ordinary person would not consider evidence seized pursuant to an independent source to be "obtained" in violation of the law. The independent source doctrine, therefore, is consistent with the plain terms of the Texas exclusionary rule.

INDEPENDENT SOURCE DOCTRINE DISTINCT FROM INEVITABLE DISCOVERY

In a related argument, appellant [argues] that the independent source doctrine must be rejected on the basis that it is the functional equivalent of the inevitable discovery doctrine, which has been disavowed in Texas. [This] Court has previously concluded that the inevitable discovery doctrine is inapplicable in Texas based on that doctrine's inconsistency with the plain language of the statutory exclusionary rule. See Garcia v. State, 829 S.W.2d 796 (Tex. Crim. App. 1992). In *Garcia*, a plurality of this Court observed that the inevitable discovery doctrine is "a species of harmless error rule which holds that constitutional violations in the seizure of evidence are inconsequential for purposes of admissibility . . . when the outcome of police investigation was probably unaffected by it." In reaching its conclusion that the doctrine was inapplicable, the *Garcia* plurality noted that the inevitable discovery doctrine, by its terms, applies only to situations that involve actual unlawful seizures of evidence. This aspect of the doctrine, it observed, could not be squared with the statutory exclusionary rule's absolute requirement of exclusion of all evidence seized in violation of the Fourth Amendment. . . .

Although we recognize that the independent source and inevitable discovery doctrines are closely related, . . . the independent source and inevitable discovery doctrines are not functionally the same. [The] independent source doctrine applies to situations involving a seizure or discovery of evidence "by means wholly independent of any constitutional violation" following a prior instance of unlawful police conduct. The independent source doctrine thus removes from the scope of the exclusionary rule evidence actually obtained pursuant to an independent source, so long as the source (such as a valid search warrant) is truly independent and untainted by the prior police conduct. The doctrine is distinct from other exceptions to the exclusionary rule because it requires that there be a complete break in the causal chain between the illegality and the acquisition of evidence; it asks a court to decide whether the evidence was actually discovered lawfully through an independent source. If so, exclusion is not required.

By contrast, the inevitable discovery doctrine applies to situations involving an actual unlawful seizure or discovery of evidence and serves to permit use of that evidence when the evidence would have eventually been discovered in a lawful manner had it not first been seized unlawfully. Unlike the independent source doctrine, inevitable discovery involves an inquiry into what might have, as opposed to what actually, happened. . . .

We conclude that this difference is significant in the context of deciding whether each doctrine may be applied consistently with the statutory exclusionary rule, the application of which hinges on whether evidence was "obtained" in violation of the law. . . . We therefore conclude that our adoption of the independent source doctrine, which applies only to lawfully obtained evidence, is logically consistent with our prior rejection of the inevitable discovery doctrine. . . . We remand this cause to the court of appeals for further consideration of appellant's argument that the trial court erroneously denied his motion to suppress.

MEYERS, J., dissenting.

[It] is obvious to me that this search warrant was obtained based upon the officers' unlawful entry into Appellant's residence. According to testimony of the investigator who secured the warrant, he spoke to the informant three to four hours before the officers went to "secure" Appellant's residence. This is completely inconsistent with the idea that the officers had to conduct the unwarranted entry because of exigent circumstances or to prevent destruction of evidence. Had such circumstances actually existed, the officers would have proceeded immediately to the residence rather than delaying for the number of hours that they did. There was more than enough time to secure a search warrant before the officers' intrusion into the premises, but they deliberately chose not to attempt to obtain it until after they had conducted the unlawful entry. Further, had the officers entered the home and found the occupants only baking cupcakes, the officers would not have bothered to then obtain the warrant at all. It was only after unlawfully entering and finding suspicious activity that they felt the need to then secure the warrant in order to cover their tracks and collect the evidence without the taint of their entry.

[The] officers in Appellant's case should have explained, when the warrant was obtained, that they had already entered the home. Concealing this information from the magistrate further indicates that the officers were trying to sidestep the fact that the warrant was actually based on their unlawful entry.

PRICE, J., concurring.

[It] might better serve our purposes to eschew terminology such as "inevitable discovery" and "independent source" and to simply inquire in every case: Was the evidence "obtained" by virtue of the primary illegality? As a practical matter, if the evidence was acquired by means that had no causal connection whatsoever to that primary illegality, then the answer is "no." If, on the other hand, there was a direct and undeniable causal connection between the primary illegality and the acquisition of the evidence, then the answer is "yes," regardless of what might plausibly have happened later. Although federal case law may prove to be persuasive authority on the facts of a particular case, there is no compelling need for us to complicate the statutory inquiry by importing the often-confusing terminology attending the federal exclusionary rule — at least not with those relatively rare cases that reside on the far peripheries of the spectrum that extends from direct-causality to no-causality-at-all.

The hard cases, as always, will be those that fall somewhere in the middle — those for which there is at least some "but/for" causal connection between the primary illegality and the subsequent acquisition of evidence. In that context, application of case law, both state and federal, that describes and applies the factors that inform the attenuation of taint doctrine, will have a definite utility. . . . I say that about this case because it is not altogether clear to me that there is not at least some "but/for" relationship between the initial, unlawful entry into the house — and, more to the point, the unlawful seizure of its occupants — and the later acquisition of evidence, albeit by virtue of an untainted warrant. . . .

Notes

1. *Independent source: majority position.* All but a few states have declared that the exclusionary rule does not apply to evidence obtained after an improper search or seizure if the government also learned of the evidence through an "independent source." The government must show that an untainted source actually did lead the police to the evidence in question, rather than a source or process that hypothetically might have done so. For instance, a search that begins without a warrant might benefit from the independent source rule if officers later in fact obtain a warrant based on information in their possession before they entered the building the first time. The basis for the proper warranted search is "independent" of anything the police learned during the improper search. See Murray v. United States, 487 U.S. 533 (1988); Segura v. United States, 468 U.S. 796 (1984); compare People v. Weiss, 978 P.2d 1257 (Cal. 1999) (prosecution does not have to show that particular magistrate would have issued warrant if affidavit had not contained illegally obtained information; independent source applies if police would have sought warrant even without tainted information, and redacted affidavit was sufficient for probable cause). Other courts reject this reasoning, because they are concerned that police have nothing to lose by routinely conducting a "preliminary" search before seeking a search warrant. See Wilder v. State, 717 S.E.2d 457 (Ga. 2011) (initial warrantless seizure of briefcase during child molestation investigation, followed by warranted search of briefcase based on same information used to justify seizure; independent source exception not available); William Stuntz, Warrants and Fourth Amendment Remedies, 77 Va. L. Rev. 881 (1991).

2. *Inevitable discovery: majority position.* As discussed in Nix v. Williams, 467 U.S. 431 (1984), the federal courts recognize an "inevitable discovery" exception to exclusion; the same is true for every state except Texas and Washington. See State v. Winterstein, 220 P.3d 1226 (Wash. 2009). Under this doctrine, a court may use evidence obtained as the fruit of an illegal search or seizure if the government *would have* learned about the evidence through proper techniques or channels without

the illegal search or seizure ever taking place. The inevitable discovery exception is a potentially huge limit on exclusion, particularly if one is willing to presume that the police (or interested citizens) are often capable of solving important crimes. The government must argue more than "if we hadn't done it wrong, we would have done it right." State v. Topanotes, 76 P.3d 1159 (Utah 2003). The level of certainty required in predicting the "inevitability" of the discovery is a key issue.

Under federal law, the government must prove by a preponderance of the evidence the underlying facts necessary to conclude that the discovery was inevitable. Most states have embraced the federal position and use a preponderance standard, but a few states require the government to show that discovery was inevitable by "clear and convincing" evidence. See Smith v. State, 948 P.2d 473 (Alaska 1997). Some states distinguish between the standard of proof necessary to establish the underlying facts and the level of certainty necessary to reach the conclusion that discovery was "inevitable." Compare State v. Sugar, 527 A.2d 1377 (N.J. 1987) (body buried in shallow ground would have inevitably been discovered because defendant was attempting to sell the property and prospective buyers would have smelled decomposing body; meets clear and convincing evidence requirement of state law) with State v. Rodrigues, 286 P.3d 809 (Haw. 2012) (no inevitable discovery when illegal frisk preceded arrest, because defendant could have disposed of baggie between arrest and inventory search at police station).

In the typical pretrial motion to suppress (for claims other than inevitable discovery), the standard of proof is a preponderance of the evidence. The defendant carries the burden of proof for warranted searches; the government carries the burden for warrantless searches. Do the factual and legal questions surrounding inevitable discovery justify changes in the ordinary rules about standard of proof and burden of proof?

3. *Potential limits on inevitable discovery doctrine.* A number of state courts endorsing the inevitable discovery exception to the exclusionary rule take great pains to say that they do not consider it a "blanket" exception and that it might be used in some circumstances but not in others. See, e.g., State v. Ault, 724 P.2d 545 (Ariz. 1986) (inevitable discovery doctrine does not apply to illegal search or seizure of items in a home); People v. Stith, 506 N.E.2d 911 (N.Y. 1987) (inevitable discovery exception does not apply to "primary evidence" obtained at time of illegal search; applies only to indirect fruits of illegal search). The web extension for this chapter, at *http://www.crimpro.com/extension/ch06*, offers a richer view of the state cases marking limits on the use of inevitable discovery.

What if the police deliberately conduct an illegal search, knowing that discovery of any evidence is inevitable (say, during a later inventory search)? Should courts apply the inevitable discovery exception only when the police act in "good faith"? How regularized must the investigative process be to count as "inevitable"? Consider State v. Notti, 71 P.3d 1233 (Mont. 2003) (inevitable discovery of identification of suspect who was in state DNA database and who left DNA on cigarette at murder scene, either through a DNA database computer check or when a Crime Lab employee compared profiles in the "forensic unknown" database with the State's DNA Identification Index).

4. *Attenuation.* Even when there is a causal linkage between an improper search or seizure and some evidence obtained later, the evidence can still be admitted if the link is sufficiently "attenuated." An analogy from the law of torts might be the concept of "proximate cause." For instance, in United States v. Ceccolini, 435 U.S.

268 (1978), a police officer during a conversation with a friend at her workplace wrongfully peered into an envelope in the room and discovered gambling paraphernalia, which belonged to the friend's boss. The friend agreed months later to testify against her boss in criminal proceedings. Even though the improper search of the package was a "but for" cause of the government's access to this testimony, it was not excluded because the witness's willingness to testify was more important than the improper search. In this type of case, courts will not exclude the evidence because, they say, police are unlikely to anticipate the chain of events linking their illegal search to some later source of evidence and therefore will not be deterred by the threat of exclusion. Could the officer in *Ceccolini* have anticipated that an unlawful search of the envelope might create an opportunity for his friend to provide evidence in a criminal trial? See also State v. Guillen, 223 P.3d 658 (Ariz. 2010) (possibly improper dog sniff of garage cured by later consent of homeowner unaware of dog sniff; consent was sufficiently attenuated from tainted conduct).

In Hudson v. Michigan, 547 U.S. 586 (2006), the Supreme Court held that violation of the "knock-and-announce" rule does not require suppression. Justice Scalia, writing for the majority, found the connection between the constitutional violation (knocking, but not waiting long enough before entering) and the harm too attenuated to suppress the evidence. He explained the doctrine in terms of causation:

> [Exclusion] may not be premised on the mere fact that a constitutional violation was a "but-for" cause of obtaining evidence. Our cases show that but-for causality is only a necessary, not a sufficient, condition for suppression. [But-for cause], or causation in the logical sense alone, can be too attenuated to justify exclusion. . . . Attenuation can occur, of course, when the causal connection is remote. Attenuation also occurs when, even given a direct causal connection, the interest protected by the constitutional guarantee that has been violated would not be served by suppression of the evidence obtained. . . .

5. *Improper stops and arrests that produce additional information.* If an arrest is improper, the defendant might argue that his very presence in the courtroom is the result of illegal government action, and a conviction would be barred. Both state and federal courts have uniformly rejected this argument because the use of properly obtained evidence to obtain a conviction in criminal proceedings cures any error in the arrest. United States v. Crews, 445 U.S. 463 (1980) (illegal arrest does not taint otherwise valid eyewitness identification of arrestee); Frisbie v. Collins, 342 U.S. 519 (1952) (illegal arrest is no bar to prosecution); People v. Jones, 810 N.E.2d 415 (N.Y. 2004) (police improperly arrested defendant in his home without arrest warrant; identification during lineup conducted while in custody was admissible).

Like the inevitable discovery and independent source rules, the *Frisbie* rule is based on the idea that the illegal government action was not a legally sufficient "cause" of any harm to the defendant. In Utah v. Strieff, 136 S. Ct. 2056 (2016), the Supreme Court held that the discovery of a valid arrest warrant cured the preceding unlawful investigatory stop. The Court concluded that the initial violation was not flagrant, and that the discovery of the arrest warrant attenuated the connection between the initial unlawful stop and the evidence seized incident to a lawful arrest pursuant to the warrant. Consistent with *Strieff*, state courts hold that discovery of an outstanding warrant and subsequent arrest and search are attenuated from the initial illegal stop that led to the identification and warrant check; this holds true even though the warrant check or search would not have occurred but for that stop. See, e.g., Myers v. State, 909 A.2d 1048 (Md. 2006).

Problem 6-3. The Search Party

Pamela Powers, a 10-year-old child, disappeared from a YMCA building in Des Moines, Iowa, where she had accompanied her parents to watch an athletic contest. Shortly after she disappeared, Robert Williams was seen leaving the YMCA carrying a large bundle wrapped in a blanket; a 14-year-old boy who had helped Williams open his car door reported that he had seen "two legs in it and they were skinny and white."

Williams's car was found the next day 160 miles east of Des Moines in Davenport, Iowa. Later several items of clothing belonging to the child, some of Williams's clothing, and an army blanket like the one used to wrap the bundle that Williams carried out of the YMCA were found at a rest stop on Interstate 80 near Grinnell, between Des Moines and Davenport. A warrant was issued for Williams's arrest.

Police surmised that Williams had left Pamela Powers or her body somewhere between Des Moines and the Grinnell rest stop, where some of the girl's clothing had been found. On December 26, the Iowa Bureau of Criminal Investigation initiated a large-scale search. Two hundred volunteers divided into teams began the search 21 miles east of Grinnell, covering an area several miles to the north and south of Interstate 80. A snowstorm threatened as the volunteers moved westward from Poweshiek County, in which Grinnell was located, into Jasper County. Searchers were instructed to check all roads, abandoned farm buildings, ditches, culverts, and any other place in which the body of a small child could be hidden.

Suppose that police officers learned the location of the body through an illegal search of Williams's home. The officers found the child's body next to a culvert in a ditch beside a gravel road in Polk County, about two miles south of Interstate 80. At that time, one search team near the Jasper-Polk county line was only two and one-half miles from the location of the body. Will the trial court exclude from trial the evidence obtained from the body? Cf. Nix v. Williams, 467 U.S. 431 (1984).

Problem 6-4. Illegal Stop vs. Outstanding Warrant

A Florida officer observed a person make a left turn without signaling, and then saw a white light emanating from a crack in the plastic lens covering the tail light of the left rear of the defendant's vehicle. On these two grounds, the officer stopped the vehicle, checked the driver's identification, and learned that there was an outstanding warrant for his arrest for failure to appear in another proceeding. As a result of the outstanding warrant, the officer arrested the driver. A search incident to the arrest revealed a firearm, which formed the basis for criminal charges against the driver.

The initial traffic stop was unlawful under Florida law. See State v. Riley, 638 So. 2d 507 (Fla. 1994) (failure to use turn signal without driver's conduct creating reasonable safety concern does not constitute violation of statute), and Doctor v. State, 596 So. 2d 442 (Fla. 1992) (cracked tail light was not violation of law). The arrest warrant also turned out to be erroneous: A later investigation determined that the arrest warrant was issued due to another person's failure to appear.

Imagine that the defendant moves to suppress the seizure of the firearm, contending that: (1) the traffic stop preceding the arrest was unlawful, and (2) the warrant that provided the basis for his arrest was wrongfully issued, and therefore that the government should not be allowed to use the fruits of the search incident to arrest. You are the trial judge. How would you rule? See State v. Frierson, 926 So. 2d 1139 (Fla. 2006).

Problem 6-5. Breaking the Chain of Causation?

As Richard Brown was climbing the stairs leading to his Chicago apartment around 7:45 P.M., he saw a stranger inside the apartment pointing a gun at him through the window. The man said: "Don't move, you are under arrest." Another man, also with a gun, came up behind Brown and repeated the statement that he was under arrest. The two men, Detectives William Nolan and William Lenz of the Chicago police force, had broken into Brown's apartment and searched it, and when Brown arrived, they arrested him. They did all this without probable cause and without any warrant. They later testified that they made the arrest for the purpose of questioning Brown as part of their investigation of the murder of a man named Roger Corpus.

The two detectives took Brown to the police station and placed him in the interrogation room. They left him alone for some minutes. When the officers returned, they warned Brown of his rights to remain silent and to counsel (rights established under Miranda v. Arizona, 384 U.S. 436 (1966)), and told him about some of the evidence in the case. At this point, around 8:45 P.M., and for the next 20-25 minutes, Brown answered questions about the murder and said he had helped another man, Jimmy Claggett, kill Corpus. About 9:30 P.M., the two detectives and Brown left the station house to look for Claggett. After finding and arresting Claggett, the detectives and the arrestees returned to the station about 12:15 A.M.

Brown was again placed in the interrogation room. Officers gave him coffee and left him alone, for the most part, until 2 A.M., when the prosecutor in the case reminded Brown about his rights to silence and to counsel, and then started asking him further questions about the murder. Brown gave a second statement, largely consistent with his first statement to the detectives.

Brown filed a motion to suppress the statements he gave to the police officers and the prosecutor, arguing that they were the fruit of the unlawful arrest. The prosecution argued that the statements were sufficiently attenuated from the unlawful arrest because enough time had elapsed between the arrest and the confession and the *Miranda* warnings broke the chain of causation between the unlawful arrest and the subsequent statements. How is a court likely to rule? See Brown v. Illinois, 422 U.S. 590 (1975).

3. Standing to Challenge Illegal Searches and Seizures

One other major limitation on the exclusionary rule restricts the number of people who can challenge an allegedly illegal search or seizure. In some jurisdictions, this is known as the "standing" doctrine. This limitation applies when the government improperly intrudes on a reasonable privacy expectation of one person and finds evidence implicating a second person in a crime. Can the second person challenge the unreasonable intrusion?

■ LOUISIANA CONSTITUTION ART. I, §5

Any person adversely affected by a search or seizure conducted in violation of this Section shall have standing to raise its illegality in the appropriate court.

■ STATE v. JOHN BRUNS
796 A.2d 226 (N.J. 2002)

STEIN, J.

. . . In the early morning hours of July 27, 1997, Officer John Seidler stopped a vehicle for speeding in Lakewood Township. After effectuating the stop, Seidler [determined that the driver, Barbara Edwards, was operating the car with a suspended license. He also discovered two outstanding arrest warrants for Edwards.] Based on the outstanding warrants, Seidler placed Edwards under arrest, handcuffed her, searched her, and seated her in his patrol car.

Seidler next asked the sole passenger in the vehicle, Walter Evans, to step out of the car. Officer Regan, who had been called to the scene as backup, placed Evans in his patrol car. Seidler conducted a search of the passenger compartment after Evans exited the vehicle. He found a handgun and a large knife under the front passenger seat. The object that appeared to be a handgun was later determined to be a toy handgun. [Those two items later became relevant evidence in the investigation of an armed robbery that Evans and John Bruns allegedly committed seven days before the search of Edwards' car.]

In his subsequent trial for armed robbery defendant made a motion to suppress the evidence seized during the search of Edwards' car, alleging that Seidler's search of the vehicle and seizure of the toy handgun and knife were unlawful. The motion judge concluded that the search was incident to Edwards' lawful arrest and that "the steps that the officers took were necessary given the particular circumstances." . . .

The State argues that defendant did not have a proprietary, possessory, or participatory interest in the vehicle searched or the evidence retrieved from it. Therefore, it asserts that defendant did not have standing to move to suppress the evidence. . . .

II.

In order to contest at trial the admission of evidence obtained by a search or seizure, a defendant must first demonstrate that he has standing. Generally speaking, that requires a court to inquire whether defendant has interests that are substantial enough to qualify him as a person aggrieved by the allegedly unlawful search and seizure.

In Rakas v. Illinois, 439 U.S. 128 (1978), the United States Supreme Court held that a defendant must have a legitimate expectation of privacy in the place searched or items seized to establish Fourth Amendment standing. In State v. Alston, 440 A.2d 1311 (N.J. 1981), this Court established a broader standard to determine when a defendant has the right to challenge an illegal search or seizure, rejecting the line of United States Supreme Court cases culminating with Rakas v. Illinois that effectively resolved standing issues only on the basis of a defendant's expectations of privacy. Instead, before reaching the substantive question whether a defendant has a reasonable expectation of privacy, our courts first determine whether that defendant has a proprietary, possessory or participatory interest in the place searched or items seized.

For the twenty years preceding the United States Supreme Court's adoption of the "legitimate expectation of privacy" standard the leading Fourth Amendment standing case was Jones v. United States, 362 U.S. 257 (1960). In *Jones*, the defendant was arrested for the possession and sale of narcotics after federal officers executed a search warrant for narcotics in an apartment in which the defendant was present. The Court rejected the Government's contention that the defendant lacked standing because he did not claim either ownership of the seized narcotics or a property interest in the apartment, but rather was simply a guest in the apartment. Recognizing the predicament a defendant faces when attempting to establish Fourth Amendment standing by demonstrating that he owned or possessed the seized property while at the same time defending against a charge in which an essential element is possession, the Court adopted the so-called "automatic standing rule." The Court . . . concluded that the allegations of possession that led eventually to defendant's conviction afforded him sufficient standing to challenge the search. In addition, acknowledging that the interests of law enforcement would not "be hampered by recognizing that anyone legitimately on premises where a search occurs may challenge its legality by way of a motion to suppress, when its fruits are proposed to be used against him," the Court concluded that his friend's consent to his presence also gave defendant sufficient standing to challenge the search under the Fourth Amendment. That portion of the *Jones* holding became known as the "legitimately on the premises test."

In Rakas v. Illinois . . . the defendants argued that any person who was a "target" of a search should have standing to object to the search. Reaffirming the principle that Fourth Amendment rights cannot be vicariously asserted, the Court rejected the defendants' argument and [endorsed the "better analysis" that] forthrightly focuses on the extent of a particular defendant's rights under the Fourth Amendment, rather than any theoretically separate, but invariably intertwined concept of standing. The Court in *Rakas* also considered the appropriate scope of the interest protected by the Fourth Amendment. It determined that the "legitimately on the premises" standard applied in *Jones* was too broad, and instead adopted the standard established in Katz v. United States, 389 U.S. 347 (1967), stating that a defendant must have a "legitimate expectation of privacy in the invaded place." Based on that standard the Court held that the defendants had failed to demonstrate that they had a legitimate expectation of privacy in the glove compartment or the area under the front seat of the car in which they were passengers.

In United States v. Salvucci, 448 U.S. 83 (1980), shortly after its decision in *Rakas*, the Court also abolished the "automatic standing" rule of *Jones* and held that defendants who are charged with crimes that have an element of possession can invoke the exclusionary rule only if their own Fourth Amendment rights have in fact been violated. The defendants in *Salvucci* were charged with unlawful possession of stolen mail, and relied solely on the *Jones* automatic standing rule without asserting that they had a legitimate expectation of privacy in the place where the stolen mail was seized. In assessing the trial court's decision to suppress the evidence the Court concluded: "We are convinced that the automatic standing rule of *Jones* has outlived its usefulness in the Court's Fourth Amendment jurisprudence. The doctrine now serves only to afford a windfall to defendants whose Fourth Amendment rights have not been violated. . . ."

In Rawlings v. Kentucky, 448 U.S. 98 (1980), the companion case to *Salvucci*, the Court addressed an argument by the defendant that his ownership of drugs seized by the police entitled him to invoke his Fourth Amendment rights although he claimed no expectation of privacy in the area from which the drugs were seized. The Court rejected defendant's argument, relying on the Court's observation in *Rakas* that "arcane" concepts of property law should not control the analysis of Fourth Amendment standing. [The Court] explained that prior to *Rakas* the defendant "might have been given 'standing' in such a case to challenge a 'search' that netted those drugs but probably would have lost his claim on the merits. After *Rakas*, the two inquiries merge into one: whether governmental officials violated any legitimate expectation of privacy."

Concluding that the United States Supreme Court's decisions such as *Rakas*, *Salvucci*, and *Rawlings* insufficiently guarded against unreasonable searches and seizures, this Court's decision in State v. Alston, 440 A.2d 1311 (N.J. 1981), applied Article I, paragraph 7 of the New Jersey State Constitution to the standing issue in order to afford our citizens greater protection. . . . The more protective approach adopted by this Court was based on the belief that "adherence to the vague 'legitimate expectation of privacy' standard, subject as it is to the potential for inconsistent and capricious application, will in many instances produce results contrary to commonly held and accepted expectations of privacy. . . ."

In *Alston* four defendants charged with the unlawful carrying and possession of weapons moved to suppress the weapons seized as the result of the warrantless search of the vehicle in which they were the driver and passengers. The State argued that the passengers had no standing to challenge the search because they had no ownership interest in the vehicle, and that the driver legitimately possessed the car but lacked a reasonable expectation of privacy in the areas of the vehicle that were searched. The Court rejected the State's arguments, finding that the privacy interests protected by the federal constitution and our State Constitution "flow from some connection with or relation to the place or property searched" and that "it serves the purposes of clarity to emphasize an accused's relationship to property rather than to attempt a definition of expectations in terms of the person." Accordingly, we reiterated our traditional standing rule that requires a defendant to show "he has a proprietary, possessory, or participatory interest in either the place searched or the property seized," and found that the automatic standing rule conferred standing on all four defendants.

In State v. Mollica, 554 A.2d 1315 (N.J. 1989), we elaborated on the participatory interest portion of our standing rule. Defendants Mollica and Ferrone were charged with various gambling offenses after the state police discovered bookmaking paraphernalia in their hotel rooms. The warrants to search the rooms were based in part on the telephone records for Ferrone's hotel room that the Federal Bureau of Investigation had previously obtained without a warrant as part of its own bookmaking investigation. The State argued that Mollica had no standing to object to the seizure of Ferrone's telephone records even though those records provided the basis for a search warrant that included his hotel room. The Court acknowledged that our standing rule does not automatically provide a defendant charged with a possessory crime "standing to object to prior or antecedent state action that was directed against another person," and observed that Mollica's standing to object to the search and seizure of evidence found in his hotel room did not necessarily give him standing to object to the seizure of Ferrone's telephone records. Nonetheless, the Court considered whether Mollica had a participatory interest in the seized telephone records, noting that a participatory interest "stresses the relationship of the evidence to the underlying criminal activity and defendant's own criminal role in the generation and use of such evidence," and confers standing on a person who "had some culpable role, whether as a principal, conspirator, or accomplice, in a criminal activity that itself generated the evidence." Based on the State's allegation that Mollica participated in illegal bookmaking that included the use of Ferrone's hotel room telephone and resulted in the generation of the telephone records in question, the Court concluded that [there was a] "sufficient connection between the telephone toll records and the underlying criminal gambling for which this defendant is charged, and a sufficient relationship between the defendant and the gambling enterprise, to establish a participatory interest on the part of defendant in this evidence. . . ."

III.

We see no reason to depart from the broad standing rule that entitles a criminal defendant to challenge an unreasonable search and seizure under Article I, paragraph 7 of the New Jersey Constitution if he or she can demonstrate a proprietary, possessory, or participatory interest in the place searched or items seized. Nonetheless, applying that standard to the facts of this case we find that defendant has failed to demonstrate an interest sufficient to give him standing. In reaching that conclusion, we need not specifically delineate the contours of the interest in evidence seized that will justify standing. Defendant's alleged connection to the place searched and items seized simply is far too attenuated to support a constitutional right to object to the search and seizure.

To begin with, based on the record before us defendant cannot claim a proprietary or possessory interest in the vehicle that was searched. During the suppression hearing defense counsel made a vague claim that Edwards had at one point indicated that the vehicle belonged to Bruns. However, the claim was never substantiated and the record confirms that the vehicle was registered in Edwards' name at the time of the search.

Moreover, defendant has failed to demonstrate either an ownership or possessory interest in the weapons seized. We note defense counsel's assertion that there is no reason to believe defendant divested himself of any possessory interest in the weapons, and his hypothetical statement that "for all we know, Mr. Bruns placed the toy gun under the seat ten minutes before the car was stopped and asked those in the car to keep a close watch on it." However, the record contains no evidence whatsoever to support the contention that defendant retained any interest in the weapons at the time of the search.

With no proprietary or possessory interest established, defendant nevertheless asserts that he had a participatory interest in the weapons seized because they were used to commit the robbery for which he was charged. We note first that the toy handgun and knife seized from Edwards' vehicle implicated defendant and Evans in a robbery that took place seven days before the contested search. The evidence was seized as a result of the search incident to Edwards' arrest that occurred after she was pulled over for speeding and a police officer discovered that there were two outstanding warrants for her arrest. Moreover, defendant was not a passenger in the vehicle and he was not in the vicinity of the vehicle at the time it was searched. In *Mollica*, the only case in which we have had occasion to consider whether a defendant's participatory interest was sufficient to confer standing, the Court emphasized the relationship between the evidence seized and the underlying criminal activity with which the defendant was charged, as well as the extent to which a co-defendant played a role in generating and using that evidence.

Defendant points to the relationship between the weapons seized from Edwards' car and the crime with which he was charged. Accepting that generalized connection, however, we are unpersuaded that that connection is adequate to confer standing based on a participatory interest. That evidence implicates a defendant in a crime is not, in and of itself, sufficient to confer standing. There also must be at a minimum some contemporary connection between the defendant and the place searched or the items seized. [Suppression] of the product of a Fourth Amendment violation can be successfully urged only by those whose rights were violated by the search itself, not by those who are aggrieved solely by the introduction of damaging evidence. . . .

Likewise, the weapons seized in this matter did not relate to any ongoing criminal activity between Edwards and defendant, or between Evans and defendant, at the time the allegedly illegal search occurred. The robbery for which defendant was charged occurred seven days before the items were found in Edwards' vehicle. . . .

Although we recognize that in most cases in which the police seize evidence implicating a defendant in a crime that defendant will be able to establish an interest in the property seized or place searched, our broad standing rule necessarily has limits. If substantial time passes between the crime and the seizure of the evidence, and a proprietary connection between defendant and the evidence no longer exists, the defendant's basis for being aggrieved by the search will have diminished. In addition to the temporal aspects of a specific search or seizure, a showing that the search was not directed at the defendant or at someone who is connected to the crime for which he has been charged also will diminish a defendant's interest in the property searched or seized. . . .

Notes

1. *Standing: majority position.* A majority of states follow the federal "legitimate expectation of privacy" approach when they determine who may invoke the exclusionary rule to remedy an illegal search or seizure. Others, like the New Jersey court in *Bruns*, use some form of the older "legitimately on the premises" test for standing. Often, these courts say that a defendant challenging an illegal search or seizure must demonstrate a "proprietary, possessory, or participatory interest" in the premises searched or the property seized. Try to imagine situations in which the federal test and the "legitimately on the premises" test produce different results.

The Supreme Court attempted, in Rakas v. Illinois, 439 U.S. 128 (1978), to eliminate any distinction between a person's "standing" to challenge an illegal search
and the "extent of a particular defendant's rights" under the Fourth Amendment.
Rights against unreasonable searches and seizures, said the Court, are personal
rights and third parties may not assert them. See Brendlin v. California, 551 U.S. 249
(2007) (when police officer makes traffic stop, passenger in car is seized and may
challenge constitutionality of stop). What would be the consequences of allowing
a criminal defendant to challenge an allegedly improper search of a third party's
property? Consider the Louisiana constitutional provision reprinted above. Why
require standing *at all* for a litigant who hopes to challenge governmental misconduct, particularly if deterrence of government wrongdoing is the central purpose of
the exclusionary rule?

2. *Standing for searches of residences and business premises.* Even though a defendant, under the federal (and majority) rule, must show a "legitimate" expectation
of privacy in the premises searched or the property seized, this does not preclude
challenges by those who do not own or lease property. The easier cases to decide
involve the search of a residence, where the defendant lives full time even though
another person owns or leases the residence. Courts in that setting have no trouble
in concluding that the person living in the house may challenge a search of any
common area in the house or any area within the special control of the defendant.
How might these residential cases apply to business premises?

More difficult cases involve guests and others who are present in a residence for
shorter periods. In Minnesota v. Olson, 495 U.S. 91 (1990), the Court recognized
standing for an overnight guest at an apartment: staying overnight in another's
home "is a longstanding social custom that serves functions recognized as valuable
by society." On the other hand, the Court in Minnesota v. Carter, 525 U.S. 83 (1998),
concluded that defendants present in an apartment only for a few hours and purely
for a business transaction did not have a "legitimate expectation of privacy" in the
premises. What could be said in favor of allowing dinner guests to challenge the
admission of evidence obtained when the police make a warrantless entry of a home
to arrest the guest or search her possessions? What if the police illegally search
the purse of one person and find inside some contraband belonging to another
person? See Rawlings v. Kentucky, 448 U.S. 98 (1980) (denying standing in such a
setting). What if the nature of the social arrangement between the resident and a
guest is unclear at the time of the search? See State v. Hess, 680 N.W.2d 314 (S.D.
2004) (tenant of apartment testified that she had an intimate relationship with
owner of drugs found during search, and he had spent the night at her apartment
on previous nights, but on this night her plans were unclear and it was "possible" he
would spend night); State v. Filion, 966 A.2d 405 (Me. 2009) (long-time friend of
lessee of apartment who was frequent social visitor does not have reasonable privacy
expectation; key inquiry is defendant's relationship to property, not to the tenant;
defendant had never spent the night at apartment, held no key to dwelling, and
never visited apartment when friend was absent).

3. *"Automatic" standing for possessory crimes.* Special rules sometimes apply to
defendants charged with possessory offenses, such as possession of stolen property
or narcotics. The defendant in such a case faces a dilemma. For purposes of standing, she often must establish some ownership interest in the premises that were illegally searched, but for purposes of defending against the charges, she would prefer
to deny any connection with the contraband or the premises searched. At one time,

most American courts responded to this difficulty by granting "automatic" standing to any defendant who chose to challenge a search or seizure in a possessory crime case. See Jones v. United States, 362 U.S. 257 (1960). Later, the Supreme Court took a different approach to the problem. It held, in Simmons v. United States, 390 U.S. 377 (1968), that the government could not use at trial the defendant's testimony at a suppression hearing, if it was given for the purpose of establishing standing. Because of this "immunity" for the defendant's testimony, the Court decided that "automatic" standing was no longer necessary to protect a defendant. In addition, a defendant might establish a "legitimate" expectation of privacy in some premises searched without necessarily admitting ownership of contraband. See United States v. Salvucci, 448 U.S. 83 (1980). A sizable minority of states have retained the "automatic" standing rule for possessory offenses. See State v. Carvajal, 996 A.2d 1029 (N.J. 2010) (bus passenger who denied ownership of checked luggage abandoned that property and could not later invoke state's automatic standing rule). Some have explained that the "immunity" for the defendant's testimony at a suppression hearing is not adequate because the testimony still might be used to impeach the defendant's trial testimony. Can you think of any other reasons to retain the "automatic" standing rule?

4. *"Target" standing.* Should a court give any special treatment to a claim that the police *intentionally* conducted an illegal search against one party for the purpose of obtaining evidence against another party? In United States v. Payner, 447 U.S. 727 (1980), the Supreme Court applied its usual rules of standing in such a case. A few other courts, however, have responded to purposefully illegal searches of this sort by granting standing to the "target" of the search, even if the target had no legitimate expectation of privacy (or any other interest) in the premises that were searched. See Waring v. State, 670 P.2d 357 (Alaska 1983). What difficulties might a court encounter in applying the "target" standing rule? How often will the doctrine be relevant?

Problem 6-6. Privacy Interests of Social Guests

A citizen in Eagen, Minnesota, was walking by a ground-floor apartment and saw through the window a party in progress. Some people in the apartment were dancing, others were drinking, and several people appeared to be snorting white powder. He called the police, and Officer James Thielen went to Apartment 103 to investigate. Thielen looked in the same window through a gap in the closed blinds and observed Wayne Carter and Melvin Johns snorting white powder and Kimberly Thompson shooting a substance into her veins. While other officers began to prepare affidavits for a search warrant, Thielen remained at the apartment building to keep watch. He then saw Carter and Johns leave the building and drive away. Police stopped the car and noticed in the passenger compartment some drug paraphernalia and a handgun. They arrested Carter and Johns; an inventory search of the vehicle uncovered 47 grams of cocaine in plastic sandwich bags.

After seizing the car, the police returned to Apartment 103 and arrested Thompson. A warranted search of the apartment revealed cocaine residue on the kitchen table and plastic bags similar to those found in the car. Thompson was the lessee of the apartment. Carter and Johns lived in Chicago and had come to the apartment solely to attend the party, on Thompson's invitation. They had never been to the apartment before and were in the apartment for less than three hours.

Carter and Johns were charged with narcotics crimes, and they moved to suppress all evidence obtained from the apartment and the car. Do they have a sufficient privacy interest in the apartment to challenge any illegal search that may have happened there? Compare Minnesota v. Carter, 525 U.S. 83 (1998) and Minnesota v. Olson, 495 U.S. 91 (1990).

C. ADDITIONS AND ALTERNATIVES TO THE EXCLUSIONARY RULE

As we have seen, the exclusionary rule is not available in many cases to enforce rights against unreasonable searches and seizures. Are there any credible alternatives to the exclusionary rule? Would you embrace any (or all) of these remedies as replacements to the exclusionary rule, or would you adopt them as *additional* remedies and wait for proof of their viability?

1. Administrative Remedies

Police officers swear to uphold the law, and supervisors within a police department must ensure that the rank-and-file officers obey the law. Many police departments hire legal counsel to train and advise investigating officers. What other steps might a police department or a local government adopt to discourage illegal searches and seizures?

Events in Chicago in the 2010s offer a fascinating window into a police department's efforts to punish and prevent misbehavior by individual officers. The following report summarizes the city's complex system of discipline, one that combines input from organizations located both inside and outside the Chicago Police Department. The report also details how those organizations failed to provide accountability or effective policing.

■ INVESTIGATION OF THE CHICAGO POLICE DEPARTMENT
United States Department of Justice
January 13, 2017

On December 7, 2015, the United States Department of Justice (DOJ), Civil Rights Division, Special Litigation Section, and the United States Attorney's Office for the Northern District of Illinois, jointly initiated an investigation of the City of Chicago's Police Department (CPD). . . . We opened this investigation pursuant to the Violent Crime Control and Law Enforcement Act of 1994, 42 U.S.C. § 14141. . . . Section 14141 prohibits law enforcement agencies from engaging in a pattern or practice of conduct that violates the Constitution or laws of the United States. . . . This investigation was initiated as Chicago grappled with the aftermath of the release of a video showing a white police officer fatally shooting black teenager Laquan McDonald. This aftermath included protests, murder charges for the involved officer, and the resignation of Chicago's police superintendent. The

McDonald incident was widely viewed as a tipping point—igniting longstanding concerns about CPD officers' use of force, and the City's systems for detecting and correcting the unlawful use of force. . . .

During the year it took us to complete this investigation, the City of Chicago took action of its own. . . . In June of 2016, the City issued a new "transparency policy" mandating the release of videos and other materials related to certain officer misconduct investigations. CPD also pledged to establish an anonymous hotline for CPD members to report misconduct; began an ambitious process to develop an early intervention system; and developed a draft disciplinary matrix to guide CPD in assigning appropriate discipline for various misconduct violations.

[The] City began a pilot program for body-worn cameras, and reported recently that the expansion of the program will be accelerated. [CPD recently] began an important force mitigation/de-escalation training course for officers, and revised several policies related to use of force. The City also committed to providing additional training on how officers and emergency dispatchers respond to individuals in mental health crisis, and to improving CPD's training more broadly. . . . The City is also undertaking recruitment efforts aimed at increasing CPD's diversity. . . .

Force

[We] found that CPD officers engage in a pattern or practice of using force, including deadly force, that is unreasonable. [This] pattern is largely attributable to systemic deficiencies within CPD and the City. CPD has not provided officers with adequate guidance to understand how and when they may use force, or how to safely and effectively control and resolve encounters to reduce the need to use force. CPD also has failed to hold officers accountable when they use force contrary to CPD policy or otherwise commit misconduct. . . .

*Accountability**

Chicago's police accountability system is currently divided among three investigative entities: (1) the Independent Police Review Authority (IPRA); (2) CPD's Bureau of Internal Affairs (BIA); and (3) CPD district offices. IPRA . . . is intended to operate as a civilian disciplinary body that is independent from CPD. IPRA serves two main functions: it receives and registers all complaints against CPD officers and assigns them to either BIA or itself, depending on the claim; and it investigates specific categories of complaints as well as other non-complaint police incidents and recommends discipline where appropriate.

IPRA investigates four types of complaints: (1) excessive force; (2) domestic violence; (3) coercion; and (4) bias-based verbal abuse. It also conducts mandatory investigations, regardless of alleged misconduct for: (1) officer weapon discharges (including gun, Taser, or pepper spray); and (2) death or serious injury in police custody. Over the last five years, IPRA has received almost 7,000 citizen complaints per year and retained investigative authority over approximately 30% of them as falling within IPRA's jurisdiction. In addition, it receives notification of

---

* [The following six paragraphs were originally placed later in the report. We moved the material to this location—EDS.]

approximately 800 mandatory investigations a year. IPRA is headed by the Chief IPRA Administrator . . . who is appointed by Chicago's Mayor and operates with an 80-person civilian staff.

BIA investigates complaints that are outside of IPRA's jurisdiction, which consists of approximately 70% of all police complaints. [The] BIA Chief reports directly to the Superintendent. BIA is responsible for investigating four types of officer misconduct: (1) criminal misconduct; (2) bribery and other forms of corruption; (3) drug or other substance abuse; and (4) driving under the influence, as well as all operational and other violations of CPD rules. BIA receives approximately 4,500 complaints per year from IPRA and refers approximately 40% of the less serious investigations to the 22 individual police districts for investigation. . . .

After IPRA and BIA complete their investigations, the investigator issues a finding of "sustained," "not sustained," "unfounded" [when the investigator concludes that the alleged events did not occur], or "exonerated" [when the investigator concludes that the alleged events occurred but the officer acted appropriately]. If one or more of the allegations of misconduct is sustained, the investigator's supervisor makes a discipline recommendation. [Historically], the recommended discipline is not pursuant to any applicable guidelines, but rather is based only upon experience and historical precedence. The investigation concludes with a summary report by the investigator.

Investigators' findings . . . and discipline recommendations for all sustained cases at either IPRA or BIA are subject to several layers of CPD review before they become final decisions. [Supervisors] in the accused officer's chain of command review and comment on the recommended discipline [before the recommendations] are forwarded to the Superintendent for review. . . . If the Superintendent approves the recommendations, the decision is final, but if not, it is subject to another process before the Chicago Police Board, which is made up of nine private citizens appointed by Chicago's Mayor with the City Council's consent. If the Superintendent disagrees with IPRA's recommendations, the Superintendent has the burden of convincing a three-person panel from the Chicago Police Board that the Superintendent is justified in departing from those recommendations.

[Officers] also can challenge final CPD discipline decisions through arbitration, which can either be a summary disposition on the record or a full evidentiary hearing, depending on the officer's rank and the level of discipline recommended. Decisions of the Police Board and arbitrators are subject to administrative review in the Circuit Court of Cook County and can then be appealed to the Illinois Appellate Court and the Illinois Supreme Court. . . .

The City received over 30,000 complaints of police misconduct during the five years preceding our investigation, but fewer than 2% were sustained, resulting in no discipline in 98% of these complaints. This is a low sustained rate. In evaluating the City's accountability structures, we looked beneath these and other disconcerting statistics and attempted to diagnose the cause of the low sustained rates. . . .

The City does not investigate the majority of cases it is required by law to investigate. Most of those cases are uninvestigated because they lack a supporting affidavit from the complaining party, but the City also fails to investigate anonymous and older misconduct complaints as well as those alleging lower level force and non-racial verbal abuse. Finally, and also contrary to legal mandates, IPRA does not investigate most Taser discharges and officer-involved shootings where no one is hit. Some of these investigations are ignored based on procedural hurdles in City agreements with its unions, but some are unilateral decisions by the accountability agencies to reduce caseloads and manage resources. And many misconduct complaints that avoid these investigative barriers are still not fully investigated because they are resolved through a defective mediation process, which is actually a plea bargain system used to dispose of serious misconduct claims in exchange for modest discipline. . . .

Those cases that are investigated suffer from serious investigative flaws that obstruct objective fact finding. Civilian and officer witnesses, and even the accused officers, are frequently not interviewed during an investigation. The potential for inappropriate coordination of testimony, risk of collusion, and witness coaching during interviews is built into the system, occurs routinely, and is not considered by investigators in evaluating the case. . . . Questioning is often marked by a failure to challenge inconsistencies and illogical officer explanations, as well as leading questions favorable to the officer. Investigators routinely fail to review and incorporate probative evidence from parallel civil and criminal proceedings based on the same police incident. And consistent with these biased investigative techniques, the investigator's summary reports are often drafted in a manner favorable to the officer by omitting conflicts in testimony or with physical evidence that undermine the officer's justification or by exaggerating evidence favorable to the officer, all of which frustrates a reviewer's ability to evaluate for investigative quality and thoroughness.

Investigative fact-finding into police misconduct and attempts to hold officers accountable are also frustrated by police officers' code of silence. The City, police officers, and leadership within CPD and its police officer union acknowledge that a code of silence among Chicago police officers exists, extending to lying and affirmative efforts to conceal evidence. [Our] investigation found that IPRA and BIA treat such efforts to hide evidence as ancillary and unexceptional misconduct, and often do not investigate it, causing officers to believe there is not much to lose if they lie to cover up misconduct. . . .

TRAINING AND SUPERVISION

. . . Both at the outset and through the duration of their careers, CPD officers do not receive the quality or quantity of training necessary for their jobs. Pre-service Academy training relies on outmoded teaching methods and materials, and does not equip recruits with the skills, knowledge, and confidence necessary to serve Chicago communities. For example, we observed an Academy training on deadly force—an important topic, given our findings regarding CPD's use of force—that consisted of a video made decades ago, which was inconsistent with both current law and CPD's own policies. The impact of this poor training was apparent when we interviewed recruits who recently graduated from the Academy: only one in six recruits we spoke with came close to properly articulating the legal standard for use of force. Post-Academy field training is equally flawed. . . .

CPD provides only sporadic in-service training, and does not think proactively about training needs Department-wide. . . . The recently-mandated Department-wide Taser training exemplifies CPD's problematic approach to in-service training. Large numbers of officers were cycled through this important training quickly in order to meet a deadline set by the City, without proper curriculum, staff, or equipment. This left many officers who completed the training uncomfortable with how to use Tasers effectively as a less-lethal force option. . . .

We found that deficiencies in officer training are exacerbated by the lack of adequate supervision CPD provides to officers in the field, which further contributes to CPD's pattern or practice of unconstitutional policing. . . . Overall, CPD does not hold supervisors accountable for performing certain basic supervisory tasks, including guiding officer behavior or reporting misconduct. Additionally, structural deficiencies in how CPD organizes supervision prevent effective oversight of officer activities. CPD requires supervisors to engage in non-supervisory tasks and manage too many officers at a time. CPD also structures its shift system in such a way that supervisors do not consistently work with the same groups of officers, which inhibits supervisors from learning the needs of officers under their watch. And, much like the deficiencies in CPD's officer training, CPD does not adequately train supervisors on how to provide appropriate supervision. Compounding its supervision problems, CPD does not have a meaningful early intervention system (EIS) to effectively assist supervisors in identifying and correcting problematic behavior. . . .

DATA COLLECTION AND TRANSPARENCY

A lack of transparency regarding CPD's and IPRA's activities has contributed to CPD's failure to identify and correct unlawful practices and to distrust between CPD and the public. . . . Currently, CPD's data collection systems are siloed and do not allow for meaningful cross-system data collection, evaluation, and tracking. As a result, CPD is unable to easily use the data at its disposal to identify trends, including trends in misconduct complaints, training deficiencies, and more. . . .

The data that is collected and publicly reported by the City is also incomplete, and at times, inaccurate. IPRA reports only on how investigations are resolved by that agency; but, as discussed in this Report, the findings of IPRA investigators can be set aside, and its discipline recommendations greatly reduced. IPRA's reporting, therefore, does not give a full picture of how misconduct investigations are ultimately resolved. . . . Currently, very little information is published about [investigations by the BIA and the districts], even though those entities handle roughly 70% of all misconduct complaints. Finally, the City should also release more information regarding settlements of officer misconduct lawsuits; publicly available data is, at present, limited to the general nature of the allegation (e.g., "excessive force" or "false arrest") and the settlement amount. . . .

COMMUNITY-FOCUSED POLICING

. . . CPD has the officers it needs to make community policing work. During our investigation we observed many instances of diligent, thoughtful, and selfless policing, and we heard stories of officers who police this way every day. We know that there are many dedicated CPD officers who care deeply about the community, are affected by the violence they see, and work hard to build trust between the community and the Department. We heard about officers and command staff who are well-respected and beloved in the neighborhoods they patrol. But for community policing to really take hold and succeed in Chicago, CPD must ensure that its supervision, training, promotions, and accountability systems incentivize and support officers who police in a manner that conveys to community members that CPD officers can be a trusted partner in protecting them, their families, and their neighborhoods.

[The] City must address serious concerns about systemic deficiencies that disproportionately impact black and Latino communities. CPD's pattern or practice of unreasonable force and systemic deficiencies fall heaviest on the predominantly black and Latino neighborhoods on the South and West Sides of Chicago, which are also experiencing higher crime. Raw statistics show that CPD uses force almost ten times more often against blacks than against whites. As a result, residents in black neighborhoods suffer more of the harms caused by breakdowns in uses of force, training, supervision, accountability, and community policing. . . .

Our review of complaints of racially discriminatory language found repeated instances where credible complaints were not adequately addressed. Moreover, we found that some Chicago police officers expressed discriminatory views and intolerance with regard to race, religion, gender, and national origin in public social media forums, and that CPD takes insufficient steps to prevent or appropriately respond to this animus. As CPD works to restore trust and ensure that policing is lawful and effective, it must recognize the extent to which this type of misconduct contributes to a culture that facilitates unreasonable force and corrodes community trust. . . .

Finally, during our investigation, we heard allegations that CPD officers attempt to gain information about crime using methods that undermine CPD legitimacy and may also be unlawful. In some instances, we were told, CPD will attempt to glean information about gang activity or other crime by arresting or detaining individuals, and refusing to release the individual until he provides that information. In other instances, CPD will take a young person to a rival gang neighborhood, and either leave the person there, or display the youth to rival members, immediately putting the life of that young person in jeopardy by suggesting he has provided information to the police. . . . CPD must root out these practices that harm CPD's interaction with the community. Doing so will better support lawful policing, and allow CPD to gain legitimacy in the eyes of the public and more effectively address crime. . . .

Notes

1. *Police review boards and internal disciplinary measures.* Most police departments of any size have a division (often called "Internal Affairs" or "IAD") that reviews police officer conduct. Sometimes cities establish external review boards, composed of civilian residents of the city, to advise internal affairs divisions or to reconsider the IAD findings. What are the advantages of an external review board? Who should be its members? What powers should the board have? Review boards have now operated in some jurisdictions for decades, and policy experts have evaluated their work across several dimensions. You can find a sample of those evaluations on the web extension for this chapter at *http://www.crimpro.com/ extension/ch06*.

2. *Patrol officers and supervisors.* When explosive evidence of police conduct becomes public (often through reporting in local news media), people who work in different positions with the police department often have different diagnoses of the problem. Events in Los Angeles in the late 1990s illustrate the typical debate between line officers and their bosses about the causes and proper responses to police misconduct.

In 1998, eight pounds of cocaine were found missing from a police evidence locker in the Los Angeles Police Department's Rampart division. Investigations led to officer Raphael Perez, a member of Rampart's elite anti-gang unit known as

CRASH, for Community Resources Against Street Hoodlums. Officer Perez agreed with prosecutors to trade information about other officers for a reduced sentence. The information from Officer Perez (much of it later confirmed from independent sources) revealed one of the largest patterns of police misconduct in U.S. history. He described police conspiring to frame innocent suspects, beating suspects, and covering up unjustified shootings. Hundreds of felony cases were tainted by alleged police misconduct. Dozens of officers were fired, relieved of duty, suspended, or quit. The city faced possible civil damages of hundreds of millions of dollars.

In response to these revelations, the LAPD assembled a Board of Inquiry to study the corruption scandal. A 362-page Board of Inquiry report blamed the calamity on poor hiring, the isolation of the special CRASH unit, and "rogue cops." The police chief responded to the report by restructuring the supervision of gang units and firing additional officers. At this point, the Police Protective League (an organization representing police officers) hired a local law professor, Erwin Chemerinsky, to conduct an independent analysis. The Chemerinsky Report criticized the Board of Inquiry report as "the management account" of the scandal, an account that wrongly focused on the individual misconduct of a "few" officers. Instead, the Chemerinsky Report argued, the central problem with LAPD was a "culture" that emphasized "exclusion of scrutiny by outsiders" and "control over the rank and file officers through a highly stratified, elaborate discipline system that enforces voluminous rules and regulations, some of them very petty." This culture generated hostility from officers to the management of the Department and produced a code of silence and toleration of excessive force. Instead of changes in police hiring, the Chemerinsky Report called for changes in management, improvements in the internal disciplinary system, and external oversight of the department.

3. *Early warning systems.* Police chiefs have a slogan: Ten percent of the officers cause ninety percent of the problems. How can police managers identify the officers who need special training or removal from the field? Some departments (just over a fourth of all departments nationwide) use "early warning" systems (also known as "early intervention" systems) to select officers who might benefit from training or other intervention. Data collection systems flag officers for special attention if they are involved in some requisite number of citizen complaints, firearm discharges, use-of-force reports, civil litigation, high-speed pursuits, or vehicular damage. The supervisor of an officer so identified reviews the incident and counsels the officer; sometimes the department sends the officer to special training classes. Assuming that plaintiffs in civil lawsuits could subpoena this data about individual officers, does it help or hurt the department during the litigation? Do early warning systems encourage inactive policing?

4. *Revocation of officer's license.* State and local police departments hire only individuals who are certified by state licensing authorities to serve as law enforcement officers. Administrative bodies in many states review allegations of police misconduct and sometimes revoke the license of an officer based on that misconduct; the licensing body in Florida is among the most active. The revocation of a license prevents other police forces in the same state from hiring an officer after he or she is fired for misconduct. One database, tracking the work of licensing authorities in 11 states going back to 1973, shows over 5,600 revocations during that time. See Roger L. Goldman, State Revocation of Law Enforcement Officers' Licenses and Federal Criminal Prosecution: An Opportunity for Cooperative Federalism, 22 St. Louis U. Pub. L. Rev. 121 (2003).

5. *Nonconstitutional "law of policing."* As we have seen, various institutions like police review boards and state licensing authorities operate alongside the constitutional exclusionary rule to shape police behavior. In the next section, we consider the impact of tort suits against police officers and departments. Consider, as well, how other bodies of law might come together to form a "law of policing." In particular, what might be the impact on police conduct of the civil service law in a state? What about collective bargaining law, employment discrimination law, and the law relevant to municipal annexation and municipal bonds? See Seth W. Stoughton, The Incidental Regulation of Police, 98 Minn. L. Rev. 2179 (2014), Rachel Harmon, The Problem of Policing, 110 Mich. L. Rev. 761 (2012); Stephen Rushin, Police Union Contracts, 66 Duke L.J. 1191 (2017).

Problem 6-7. The Mayor's Next Move

Police officers in Albuquerque killed 23 people and wounded 14 others with gunfire between 2010 and 2014. Some of these uses of force received media attention and created public discontent. In one notorious case, Albuquerque police officers fired a stun gun at a deranged man who had doused himself in gasoline, setting him ablaze. Another time, they fired a stun gun at a man who yelled, "Bang, bang," as the officers approached. Police fired one at a 75-year-old homeless man for refusing to leave a bus stop, at a 16-year-old boy for refusing to lie on a floor covered in broken glass, and at a young man so drunk he could not get up from a couch. Officers also frequently kicked, punched, and violently restrained nonthreatening people. About 75 percent of the shooting victims suffered from mental illnesses, and some were disabled, elderly, or drunk. Leadership in the department seldom reprimanded officers for excessive use of force.

One of the incidents involved the killing of James Boyd, a homeless man with a long history of violent outbursts and mental instability. Heavily armed police officers shot and killed him. The Police Department released video footage of the Boyd shooting, taken from a camera mounted on an officer's helmet. By releasing the video in the name of transparency, the APD stoked outrage in many residents, setting off protests that brought hundreds of people to the streets. Demonstrators at one protest pelted officers with rocks and doughnuts, tried to block freeway ramps, and marched on busy streets. Advocates from around Albuquerque called for massive reforms of the police department.

The APD has written policies to govern the use of force. The policy requires officers to report to superiors any incident that involves the "use of force," but the policy does not define the term any more specifically. The department also has some general procedures for handling people with mental illness, aimed at minimizing the use of "unnecessary force" against them. Only a few officers in the APD have been trained to work with people who suffer from mental illness.

The Civil Rights Division of the U.S. Department of Justice has opened an investigation into the practices of the APD. Meanwhile, the city's mayor is considering a range of responses to the situation. You serve as the mayor's chief of staff. She has asked for your recommendations about several possible courses of action.

First, the mayor could enter negotiations with the Department of Justice to enter a consent order in a federal civil rights action. The disposition of that lawsuit might require specific police department reforms and the appointment of a monitor to ensure proper implementation of the order.

Second, the mayor might propose changes in the city ordinances that regulate the powers or operations of the Police Oversight Commission (POC). The POC is composed of nine community representatives. It oversees the "full investigation and/or mediation" of all citizen complaints about the Albuquerque police. The Commission can also "audit and monitor all investigations and/or police shootings under investigation by APD's Internal Affairs." The POC can recommend disciplinary measures to the police chief, but the chief retains final authority to decide what discipline, if any, to impose. Finally, the POC is responsible for submitting quarterly reports that detail the number and status of all complaints about the police, "statistical ethnicity of subject officers, statistical ethnicity of complainants," and "ongoing disciplinary trends of the Police Department." The reports then offer suggested policy or procedural changes.

Third, the mayor might request changes in training or licensing practices from the statewide board for police officer standards and training. The New Mexico Department of Public Safety's Training and Recruiting Division is responsible for certifying the adequacy of the training for any individual who serves as a "certified peace officer" in the state.

Which strategy (or combination of strategies) will you recommend to the mayor? Is the problem in Albuquerque explained by bad cops and weak supervision, or is there a wider problem with a renegade culture of policing? What different responses are called for by the two kinds of problems? Compare Fernando Santos, Justice Department Accuses Albuquerque Police of Excessive Force, N.Y. Times, April 10, 2014.

2. Tort Actions and Criminal Prosecutions

The most common private remedy for illegal searches prior to the use of the exclusionary rule was a tort action against the officer who violated the law during the search. Any victim of a wrongful search (not just those who later face criminal charges) can, in theory, bring a lawsuit against the officer conducting the search, or against the police department or other governmental units, requesting damages or other relief. The search victim might sue in state court based on state common law torts such as false imprisonment or trespass; she might also look to a state statute granting a civil cause of action for wrongful searches or seizures. Some victims also rely on a federal statute, 42 U.S.C. §1983, which creates a cause of action in federal court against any "person" who acts "under color of" state law to deprive another person of federal constitutional or statutory rights.

These lawsuits have not become a common method of dealing with improper searches or seizures. The plaintiffs in such cases face several substantial legal obstacles: The most important are the doctrines of "sovereign immunity" protecting the state or local government from suit, and "qualified immunity," which protects individual police officers who act with "good faith."

The theory behind the tort suit as a remedy for illegal searches and seizures is that civil damages can more precisely measure the violation and the harm. In terms of deterrence, the remedy imposes costs on the officer, the police department, or both; unlike suppression, a tort remedy can apply whether or not the suspect faces criminal charges.

Whether financial costs imposed as result of successful tort claims in fact deter police officers or police departments from unconstitutional actions may turn in part on whether the individual officer (who will often be judgment-proof) or the department (or the county or state government) will pay the damages. One related issue is whether the government is obligated through contract or state law to indemnify the police officer for the costs of defense and any judgment against the officer.

Private enforcement is not the only possibility. In 1994, Congress passed legislation (now codified at 42 U.S.C. §14141) that prohibits state and local governments from engaging in "a pattern or practice of conduct by law enforcement officials" that deprives persons of "rights, privileges, or immunities secured or protected by the Constitution or laws of the United States." The statute authorizes the U.S. Department of Justice to sue in federal court for injunctive and declaratory relief to eliminate the pattern or practice. The Civil Rights Division of the Justice Department filed such a suit against the Los Angeles Police Department; the consent decree resolving that suit is excerpted below. What are the relative merits of public and private civil enforcement?

■ OFFICE OF THE ATTORNEY GENERAL, STATE OF ARKANSAS, OPINION NO. 2004-188
(September 8, 2004)

The Honorable Larry Jegley
Prosecuting Attorney, Sixth Judicial District
Little Rock, Arkansas

Dear Mr. Jegley:

You have requested my opinion on certain issues related to chemical testing for the purpose of determining alcohol and drug levels in a suspect's body. You indicate that your questions are related to situations in which police officers arrive at the scene of a motor vehicle accident and find a dead or dying victim of a suspected drunk driver. The suspected drunk driver refuses to submit to chemical testing pursuant to A.C.A. §5-65-208. . . . Your questions are: . . .

(2) [What] action should police take to enforce the provisions of Section 208? (Should they seek a court order or warrant if a driver refuses consent to testing (although dissipating drugs or alcohol create a time crunch, often late at night)?) May officers use reasonable force, if needed to obtain the sample, either with or without court order or warrant?

(3) If force is permitted either with or without a warrant, are there any civil liability issues for police agencies enforcing the requirements of A.C.A. §5-65-208, assuming it is mandatory? . . .

RESPONSE

[*Question 2.*] The Arkansas Supreme Court recently stated: "The law is settled that the taking of blood by a law enforcement officer amounts to a Fourth Amendment search and seizure." Haynes v. State, 127 S.W.3d 456, 461 (Ark. 2003), citing Schmerber v. California, 384 U.S. 757 (1966). Accordingly, a warrant is required unless an exception to the warrant requirement can be established. For example, a warrant is not necessary if the suspect gives his consent to the test. Another example of a situation in which a warrant may not be necessary is a situation involving certain exigent circumstances, such as those in which the opportunity to administer the test will exist only for a short time. . . .

[*Question 3.*] The answer to this question will depend upon the type of liability to which you are referring. Law enforcement officers, as employees of the state or of political subdivisions of the state, are entitled to certain limited immunity from suit for some types of acts that are performed in the course of their official duties. Law enforcement officers who are employees of the State fall within the provisions of A.C.A. §19-10-305(a), which states: "Officers and employees of the State of Arkansas are immune from liability and from suit, except to the extent that they may be covered by liability insurance, for damages for acts or omissions, other than malicious acts or omissions, occurring within the course and scope of their employment."

It should be noted that the above-quoted grant of immunity applies generally to nonmalicious acts, but that it contains an exception to the extent of liability insurance coverage. Therefore, while law enforcement officers generally cannot be held liable for nonmalicious acts, they can be held liable for such acts to the extent that such acts are covered by liability insurance. They can also, of course, be held liable for malicious acts.

Law enforcement officers who are employees of cities and counties fall within the provisions of A.C.A. §21-9-301, which states:

> It is declared to be the public policy of the State of Arkansas that all counties, municipal corporations, school districts, special improvement districts, and all other political subdivisions of the state shall be immune from liability and from suit for damages, except to the extent that they may be covered by liability insurance. No tort action shall lie against any such political subdivision because of the acts of its agents and employees.

Although A.C.A. §21-9-301 speaks only in terms of the immunity of the political subdivision itself, the Arkansas Supreme Court has interpreted the statute as extending immunity to officers and employees of the political subdivisions as well when they negligently commit acts or omissions in their official capacities. Accordingly, a claimant may be able to sue city or county law enforcement officers personally for intentional or malicious acts, or for negligent acts not committed in their official capacities. However, the claimant cannot sue the city or county officer for negligence that was committed in the officer's official capacity (except to the extent that such acts are covered by liability insurance).

In addition to these two types of statutory immunity, law enforcement officers may be entitled to "qualified immunity." Under the doctrine of qualified immunity, an individual is immune from suit if the actions complained of were taken in good faith in the performance of one's duties, and the acts do not violate any clearly established constitutional right. Harlow v. Fitzgerald, 457 U.S. 800 (1982). The test for the applicability of qualified immunity turns upon the "objective legal reasonableness of the action," assessed in light of legal rules that were "clearly established" at the time the action was taken. See Anderson v. Creighton, 483 U.S. 635 (1987). The immunity is "qualified" because it does not obtain where the activity is in violation of clearly established law that a reasonable person would have known.

The question of whether a law enforcement officer is entitled to any type of immunity from a claim arising out of the execution of the testing requirements of A.C.A. §5-65-208 will depend largely upon the facts of each case, including the particular damage claimed, whether that damage resulted from an act committed by the officer in his official capacity, and whether the officer acted negligently or maliciously. . . .

Sincerely,
Mike Beebe, Attorney General

■ CONSENT DECREE, UNITED STATES v. CITY OF LOS ANGELES
Civil No. 00-11769 GAF, June 15, 2001

1. The United States and the City of Los Angeles, a chartered municipal corporation in the State of California, share a mutual interest in promoting effective and respectful policing. They join together in entering this settlement in order to promote police integrity and prevent conduct that deprives persons of rights, privileges, or immunities secured or protected by the Constitution or laws of the United States.

2. In its Complaint, plaintiff United States alleges that the City of Los Angeles, the Los Angeles Board of Police Commissioners, and the Los Angeles Police Department (collectively, "the City defendants") are violating 42 U.S.C. §14141 by engaging in a pattern or practice of unconstitutional or otherwise unlawful conduct that has been made possible by the failure of the City defendants to adopt and implement proper management practices and procedures. In making these allegations, the United States recognizes that the majority of Los Angeles police officers perform their difficult jobs in a lawful manner. . . .

MANAGEMENT AND SUPERVISORY MEASURES TO PROMOTE CIVIL RIGHTS INTEGRITY

39. The City . . . shall establish a database containing relevant information about its officers, supervisors, and managers to promote professionalism and best policing practices and to identify and modify at-risk behavior (also known as an early warning system). This system shall be a successor to, and not simply a modification of, the existing computerized information processing system known as the Training Evaluation and Management System ("TEAMS"). The new system shall be known as "TEAMS II." . . .

41. TEAMS II shall contain information on the following matters:

a. all non-lethal uses of force that are required to be reported in LAPD "use of force" reports or otherwise are the subject of an administrative investigation by the Department; . . .

c. all officer-involved shootings and firearms discharges, both on-duty and off-duty; . . .

d. all other lethal uses of force;

e. all other injuries and deaths that are reviewed by the LAPD Use of Force Review Board; . . .

f. all vehicle pursuits and traffic collisions; . . .

i. all written compliments received by the LAPD about officer performance;

j. all commendations and awards;

k. all criminal arrests and investigations known to LAPD of, and all charges against, LAPD employees;

l. all civil or administrative claims filed with and all lawsuits served upon the City or its officers . . . resulting from LAPD operations and known by the City, the Department, or the City Attorney's Office; . . .

p. training history and any failure of an officer to meet weapons qualification requirements; and

q. all management and supervisory actions taken pursuant to a review of TEAMS II information, including non-disciplinary actions. . . .

47. The protocol for using TEAMS II shall include the following provisions and elements:

a. The protocol shall require that, on a regular basis, supervisors review and analyze all relevant information in TEAMS II about officers under their supervision to detect any pattern or series of incidents that indicate that an officer, group of officers, or an LAPD unit under his or her supervision may be engaging in at-risk behavior. . . .

g. The protocol shall require that all relevant and appropriate information in TEAMS II be taken into account when [deciding matters of] pay grade advancement, promotion, assignment as . . . a Field Training Officer, or when preparing annual personnel performance evaluations. . . .

INCIDENTS, PROCEDURES, DOCUMENTATION, INVESTIGATION, AND REVIEW

78. The Department shall continue to require officers to report to the LAPD without delay: any conduct by other officers that reasonably appears to constitute (a) an excessive use of force or improper threat of force; (b) a false arrest or filing of false charges; (c) an unlawful search or seizure; (d) invidious discrimination; (e) an intentional failure to complete forms required by LAPD policies and in accordance with procedures; (f) an act of retaliation for complying with any LAPD policy or procedure; or (g) an intentional provision of false information in an administrative investigation or in any official report, log, or electronic transmittal of information. . . . Failure to voluntarily report as described in this paragraph shall be an offense subject to discipline if sustained. . . .

97. [The] City shall develop and initiate a plan for organizing and executing regular, targeted, and random integrity audit checks, or "sting" operations . . . to identify and investigate officers engaging in at-risk behavior, including: unlawful stops, searches, seizures (including false arrests), [or] uses of excessive force. . . . These operations shall also seek to identify officers who discourage the filing of a complaint or fail to report misconduct or complaints. . . . The Department shall use the relevant TEAMS II data, and other relevant information, in selecting targets for these sting audits. . . .

104. [The] Department shall require LAPD officers to complete a written or electronic report each time an officer conducts a motor vehicle stop. . . . The report shall include the following: (i) the officer's serial number; (ii) date and approximate time of the stop; (iii) reporting district where the stop occurred; (iv) driver's apparent race, ethnicity, or national origin; (v) driver's gender and apparent age; (vi) reason for the stop . . . (vii) whether the driver was required to exit the vehicle; (viii) whether a pat-down/frisk was conducted; (ix) action taken, to include check boxes for warning, citation, arrest, completion of a field interview card, with

appropriate identification number for the citation or arrest report; and (x) whether the driver was asked to submit to a consensual search of person, vehicle, or belongings, and whether permission was granted or denied. . . .

105. [The] Department shall require LAPD officers to complete a written or electronic report each time an officer conducts a pedestrian stop. . . .

COMMUNITY OUTREACH AND PUBLIC INFORMATION

155. For the term of this Agreement, the Department shall conduct a Community Outreach and Public Information program for each LAPD geographic area. The program shall require . . . at least one open meeting per quarter in each of the 18 geographic Areas for the first year of the Agreement, and one meeting in each Area annually thereafter, to inform the public about the provisions of this Agreement, and the various methods of filing a complaint against an officer. . . .

156. The LAPD shall prepare and publish on its website semiannual public reports. . . . Such reports shall include aggregate statistics broken down by each LAPD geographic area and for the Operations Headquarters Bureau, and broken down by the race/ethnicity/national origin of the citizens involved, for arrests, information required to be maintained pursuant to paragraphs 104 and 105, and uses of force. Such reports shall include a brief description of [audits completed] and any significant actions taken as a result of such audits or reports, (ii) a summary of all discipline imposed during the period reported by type of misconduct, broken down by type of discipline, bureau and rank, and (iii) any new policies or changes in policies made by the Department to address the requirements of this Agreement. . . .

Notes

1. *The availability of tort remedies for police misconduct.* All states and the federal system offer some kind of tort (or tort-like) remedies for some kinds of police misconduct. In the federal system, private claims can arise under 42 U.S.C. §1983 (civil rights), the Federal Tort Claims Act, or directly under the Constitution in suits known as *Bivens* actions, after Bivens v. Six Unknown Named Agents of Federal Bureau of Narcotics, 403 U.S. 388 (1971). Remedies in federal court may include money damages, injunctive relief, or consent decrees entered between parties in lieu of further litigation. In many states recovery is allowed under statutes providing generally for tort claims against the government and its agents, subject to limitations for sovereign immunity (for governments) and official immunity (for individual officers). Claims may also be made under specialized tort statutes. Surprisingly, few states have promulgated statutes specifically addressing actions by citizens against the police.

2. *The invisibility of tort claims.* Despite the long history of tort actions to remedy unconstitutional and excessive police action, it is extremely difficult to find any reported cases involving successful claims. Indeed, there are more law review articles discussing tort actions than reported decisions about successful recoveries. See, e.g., John C. Jeffries, Jr., Disaggregating Constitutional Torts, 110 Yale L.J. 259 (2000); Susan Bandes, Patterns of Injustice: Police Brutality in the Courts, 47 Buff. L. Rev. 1275-1341 (1999).

The rarity of reported decisions might suggest that tort remedies are entirely illusory, and that the legal barriers to recovery are too high (at least too high to make tort suits a plausible remedy, either for the purposes of the claimant or as a behavior-shaping device). But some plaintiffs who sue the government for improper police conduct do recover damages, despite immunities and other obstacles. Newspapers regularly carry stories of settlements or jury verdicts in civil suits dealing with officer misconduct. The most frequent basis for these claims is excessive use of force.

Cities tend to settle most of these suits for relatively small amounts, with a few high-visibility cases receiving larger settlements or jury verdicts after trial. The unadorned numbers show some large total payments in some cities and much smaller total payments elsewhere. For example, newspapers in Chicago and Dallas have tracked trends in civil rights suits against the police. See Andrew Schroedter, Police-Related Suits Cost City More Than $500 Million Since '04, Chicago Sun-Times, April 3, 2014 (2013 payout of $84.6 million was largest in decade and more than triple the amount budgeted); Tristan Hallman, Lawsuits Against Dallas Police Costing City Millions, Dallas News, May 10, 2014 (video is playing an increased role in police suits). Would you devote a major portion of your private practice to representing such clients? What would you need to know before concluding that such a practice would be financially viable?

The news accounts of settlements raise the classic tort question whether civil suits have any impact on police practices. Many of the settlements include a provision keeping the settlement terms secret. The settlements are often paid from the city's general budget rather than the police department budget, and the officer whose conduct led to the lawsuit is not routinely disciplined as a result of the city's financial loss. Despite these limits, does the amount of money that cities pay to tort plaintiffs each year suggest that civil liability is working reasonably well? See John Rappaport, How Private Insurers Regulate Public Police, 130 Harv. L. Rev. 1539 (2017); Joanna C. Schwartz, Myths and Mechanics of Deterrence: The Role of Lawsuits in Law Enforcement Decisionmaking, 57 UCLA L. Rev. 1023 (2010) (finding that officials rarely have probative information about suits alleging misconduct by their officers).

3. *Costs and indemnity for judgments.* Almost all states have statutes that allow the state or local government to pay for the police officer's legal representation so long as the officer was acting within the scope of authority. Many states go further, allowing the state or local government to indemnify the officer for the amount of any judgment paid to the plaintiff. See, e.g., Ky. Code §16.185. Do such statutes compromise the power of tort suits to deter officers from making improper searches and seizures? Some states also have statutes authorizing the trial court to order a losing plaintiff to pay the attorney's fees and costs of the defendants if the suit was not substantially justified. See, e.g., Md. State Govt. Code §12-309.

4. *Qualified good faith immunity for individuals.* The legal barriers to tort claims are very high. State and federal courts have created protections known as a "qualified good faith immunity" or "official immunity" for police officers sued in tort for the illegal acts they commit during the course of their employment. An individual is immune from suit if the illegal actions were performed in good faith and did not violate any "clearly established" constitutional right. Harlow v. Fitzgerald, 457 U.S. 800 (1982). The immunity is "qualified" because an officer loses it when she subjectively knows that she is violating the rights of the victim, or when she objectively should know that she is violating those rights. Does the doctrine of qualified

immunity mean that damages will be unavailable in all cases where *Leon* would create a good faith exception to the exclusionary rule? Does it leave plaintiffs without a remedy? See Malley v. Briggs, 475 U.S. 335 (1986) (officer's good faith immunity from tort liability for improper warranted search is same scope as *Leon* good faith exception to exclusionary rule); Hope v. Pelzer, 536 U.S. 730 (2002) (new factual situations calling for new application earlier legal principles could nonetheless violate "clearly established" rights); Plumhoff v. Rickard, 134 S. Ct. 2012 (2014) (officer who fired three shots into moving car of suspect during high-speed chase, was entitled to qualified immunity because there was no robust consensus of cases declaring the practice unconstitutional).

5. *Sovereign immunity and waiver.* Often the victim of an improper search or seizure will prefer to sue the state or local government rather than the judgment-proof individual officer who violated the law. Under traditional common law principles, such a suit is not possible under state law because of the doctrine of "sovereign immunity," which insulates the government from any monetary claims. Most states have passed statutes that partially waive their sovereign immunity, so they will pay for some wrongdoing committed by state employees (on a respondeat superior basis). Under these tort claims acts, the lawsuit against the state or local government usually becomes the only cause of action for the wrongdoing; the plaintiff can no longer sue the individual employee. However, almost all of these statutes contain exceptions. For instance, most provide that the state or local government will not be liable for "discretionary" actions of officials. Some also exempt any action by officials engaged in the "enforcement" of any law or judicial order. See S.C. Code §15-78-60. Section 1983 does not create respondeat superior liability for state or local government. A plaintiff can sue a local government based on the actions of its police officers only if the officer was acting pursuant to a "policy" or "practice" endorsed by the government.

Beyond the perspective of individual claimants, a more general issue for remedies other than suppression is whether the substantive and procedural barriers to relief make tort claims a plausible and functional alternative. The materials in this chapter only hint at the complexity of section 1983 and state civil rights and tort claims. Entire books and law school courses—and entire legal practices—can be built around specialization in these areas. See, e.g., Joseph Cook & John Sobieski, Civil Rights Actions (seven-volume treatise); Sheldon Nahmod, Civil Rights and Civil Liberties Litigation: The Law of Section 1983 (three-volume treatise).

6. *Who benefits from a damages remedy?* Unlike the exclusion remedy, a tort suit can benefit victims of illegal searches and seizures who commit no crime or who are not charged with a crime. This feature of tort suits could make them a better remedy for those injured in the past. Which remedy—the exclusionary rule or tort suits—is more likely to prevent future violations? Think about the connection between remedies and rights. If tort suits were the primary method for enforcing the Fourth Amendment, would courts see different types of parties raising these claims? Would the scope of privacy rights change if the remedy were to change?

7. *Limitations on equitable relief.* Sometimes plaintiffs want injunctive relief rather than, or in addition to, money damages. Although injunctions are now considered a legitimate response to some search and seizure violations, they are still not as widely used as exclusion or damages. When relief is sought in federal court for actions of state actors, federal courts may be reluctant to order or affirm injunctive relief on federalism grounds. Another limitation on the availability of injunctions is the

standing doctrine. Who has standing to challenge a police policy or practice? When a plaintiff seeks injunctive relief rather than damages, the Supreme Court has held that the plaintiff must show a likelihood of future harm. In City of Los Angeles v. Lyons, 461 U.S. 95 (1983), a plaintiff who was challenging the use of "chokeholds" by the police department had no standing to obtain injunctive or declaratory relief (as opposed to damages). Although the police had used the chokehold on Adolph Lyons in a situation where the officers faced no threat of injury, Lyons could not demonstrate a "substantial likelihood" that he personally would be choked again in the future. Is this standing limitation applicable mostly to use of force policies?

State courts may not be constrained by similarly strict standing doctrines, and the federalism concerns will not be present. Is an injunction inherently more intrusive than damage awards or exclusion of evidence in criminal proceedings? Should it be reserved for certain types of violations by law enforcement officials? Keep in mind that an injunction gives a court continuing jurisdiction over the controversy; the court can impose contempt sanctions on any defendant violating the terms of an injunction.

8. *Federal involvement in police review.* Over the past several years, the U.S. Department of Justice (DOJ) has entered into a series of consent decrees with local and state police departments around the country, focusing on issues such as racial bias in stops, use of deadly force, and mistreatment of citizens. Under 42 U.S.C. §14141, known as the "Police Misconduct Provision," the Department can sue in federal court to prohibit state and local governments from engaging in "a pattern or practice of conduct by law enforcement officials" that deprives persons of "rights, privileges, or immunities secured or protected by the Constitution or laws of the United States." Since 1994, DOJ has investigated dozens of matters under the authority of 14141, and entered several settlements, including the consent decree in Los Angeles. See Stephen Rushin, Structural Reform Litigation in American Police Departments, 99 Minn. L. Rev. 1343 (2015) (use of quantitative and qualitative methods to evaluate structural police reform prompted by federal litigation).

The Los Angeles Consent Decree reprinted above requires a lot of data, recordkeeping, and monitoring. Can you access this information? See Mary Fan, Panopticism for Police: Structural Reform Bargaining and Police Regulation by Data-Driven Surveillance, 87 Wash. L. Rev. 93 (2012) (remedies fashioned in shadow of threatened civil litigation can concentrate on data collection and access for greatest impact).

9. *Criminal charges.* It is possible for a prosecutor to file criminal charges against an officer who conducts an illegal search or seizure, either under general criminal statutes (such as false imprisonment or trespass) or under statutes expressly covering police violations of civil rights. See 18 U.S.C. §§241, 242. U.S. Attorneys have to get central DOJ clearance to bring criminal charges against a police officer. Does the potential for criminal charges help prevent illegal searches and seizures? Would these criminal statutes become more effective if they were amended to compel prosecutors to file charges whenever there is probable cause? Local prosecutors are charged with the duty of prosecuting crimes, whether they are committed by citizens or officers. But do local prosecutors aggressively prosecute police officers, with whom they work on a daily basis? For a thorough consideration of the obstacles to the investigation and prosecution of police officers, see Kate Levine, How We Prosecute the Police, 104 Geo. L.J. 745 (2016); Kate Levine, Police Suspects, 116 Colum. L. Rev. 1197 (2016).

Problem 6-8. Checking with the Boss

Shelly Kelly decided to break off her romantic relationship with Jerry Ray Bowen and move out of her apartment, to which Bowen had a key. Bowen had assaulted Kelly in the past and had been convicted of several violent felonies. She therefore asked officers from the Los Angeles County Sheriff's Department to accompany her while she gathered her things from the apartment. Deputies from the Sheriff's Department came to assist Kelly but were called away to respond to an emergency before the move was complete.

As soon as the officers left, an enraged Bowen appeared at the bottom of the stairs to the apartment, yelling "I told you never to call the cops on me, bitch!" Bowen then ran up the stairs to Kelly and tried to throw her over the railing of the second-story landing. Kelly managed to escape and ran to her car. By that time, Bowen had retrieved a black sawed-off shotgun with a pistol grip. He ran in front of Kelly's car, pointed the shotgun at her, and told Kelly that if she tried to leave he would kill her. Kelly sped away, while Bowen fired at the car five times, blowing out the car's left front tire in the process.

Kelly quickly located police officers and reported the assault. She told Detective Curt Messerschmidt about Bowen's assault that day, his previous assaults on her, and mentioned that he was an active member of the "Mona Park Crips," a local street gang. Kelly said that she thought Bowen was staying at the home of his former foster mother, Augusta Millender.

Based on a search of government records, Messerschmidt confirmed that Bowen had some current connection to Millender's home, that he was an active gang member, and that he had been arrested and convicted for numerous violent and firearm-related offenses. On this basis, Messerschmidt prepared a warrant to authorize the search of Millender's house. An attachment to the search warrant described the property that would be the object of the search:

> All handguns, rifles, or shotguns of any caliber, or any firearms capable of firing ammunition, or firearms or devices modified or designed to allow it [*sic*] to fire ammunition. All caliber of ammunition, miscellaneous gun parts, gun cleaning kits, holsters which could hold or have held any caliber handgun being sought. Any receipts or paperwork, showing the purchase, ownership, or possession of the handguns being sought. Any firearm for which there is no proof of ownership. Any firearm capable of firing or chambered to fire any caliber ammunition.
>
> Articles of evidence showing street gang membership or affiliation with any Street Gang to include but not limited to any reference to "Mona Park Crips," including writings or graffiti depicting gang membership, activity or identity. Articles of personal property tending to establish the identity of person [*sic*] in control of the premise or premises. Any photographs or photograph albums depicting persons, vehicles, weapons or locations, which may appear relevant to gang membership, or which may depict the item being sought and or believed to be evidence in the case being investigated on this warrant, or which may depict evidence of criminal activity. Additionally to include any gang indicia that would establish the persons being sought in this warrant, affiliation or membership with the "Mona Park Crips" street gang.

Two affidavits accompanied Messerschmidt's warrant application. The first affidavit described Messerschmidt's extensive law enforcement experience, including that he had served as a peace officer for 14 years, that he was then assigned to a specialized unit investigating gang related crimes, that he had been involved in "hundreds of gang related incidents, contacts, and or arrests" during his time on the force, and that he had "received specialized training in the field of gang related crimes" and training in "gang related shootings."

The second affidavit explained why Messerschmidt believed there was sufficient probable cause to support the warrant. That affidavit described the facts of the incident involving Kelly and Bowen in great detail, including the weapon used in the assault. It described the crime as a "domestic assault." The affidavit also reported that a background check based on government records gave Messerschmidt reason to believe that Bowen resided at Millender's home. The affidavit requested that the search warrant be endorsed for night service because Bowen had ties to the Mona Park Crips gang and that "night service would provide an added element of safety to the community as well as for the deputy personnel serving the warrant."

Messerschmidt submitted the warrants to two supervisors at the police department for review. A Deputy District Attorney also reviewed the materials and initialed the search warrant, indicating that she agreed with Messerschmidt's assessment of probable cause. At that point, Messerschmidt submitted the warrants to a magistrate, who approved the warrants and authorized night service.

The search warrant was served two days later by a team of officers. Sheriff's deputies forced open the front door and encountered Augusta Millender—a woman in her 70s—and Millender's daughter and grandson. All three of them lived in the home, along with seven other sporadic residents, including Bowen. The Millenders went outside while the residence was secured but remained in the living room while the search was conducted. Officers did not find Bowen in the residence. The search resulted in the seizure of Augusta Millender's shotgun, a letter addressed to Bowen from a state social services agency, and a box of .45-caliber ammunition.

If Millender files a tort suit against the Sheriff's Department and Messerschmidt for an invasion of property and privacy, will she obtain a favorable judgment, despite immunity doctrines? Will Millender collect any damages? Cf. Messerschmidt v. Millender, 565 U.S. 535 (2012).

Problem 6-9. Legislative Remedies

You work as an adviser to a state senator who wants to limit or abolish the exclusionary rule and to replace it with a genuinely effective, alternative set of tort remedies. Draft a statute creating, to the extent possible, effective remedies for illegal searches and seizures. The remedies can include tort damages, injunctions, and police department training requirements and promotion rules, among other options. The senator has always valued your candid opinion. When you submit this proposal to her, will you recommend that the array of new remedies replace the exclusionary rule?

VII

Technology and Privacy

> *There was of course no way of knowing whether you were being watched at any given moment. . . . It was even conceivable that they watched everybody all the time. . . . You had to live — did live, from habit that became instinct — in the assumption that every sound you made was overheard, and . . . every moment scrutinized.*
>
> George Orwell, 1984
> (published 1949)

The cases, statutes, and executive branch policies we have examined thus far have revealed social forces at work, shaping the basic rules constraining searches and seizures. At times and in places where protection of privacy or individual liberty are paramount or where the police are perceived skeptically, the rules of criminal procedure tend to be more restrictive. Where crime control takes the upper hand or where the police are perceived as largely benign, police are given greater power and discretion.

The collective attitudes that influence criminal procedures are constantly shifting. One tectonic force that has been changing perspectives on state power and privacy is technology, which alters the ability both to conceal and to detect information. Indeed, as both government and private actors collect more and more information about more and more people, and then store that information into databases to be mined indefinitely, the fundamental principles of criminality, process, proof, and punishment, and even more deeply of autonomy and freedom of thought, all come into question. Consider that technological advances will soon allow law enforcement to replay the locations and actions of people with great precision from ground, satellite, and personal device data. Predictive policing advocates further suggest that we will soon be able to establish highly precise, data-based triggers for certain crimes. These possibilities move us from the realm of criminal law and procedure into the larger realm of the theory and structure of our political and social order.

But before we move to 2049 (and perhaps in a time of rapid change much sooner than that), we consider how typical rules governing searches and seizures change when the government uses various existing and emerging technologies to enhance its powers to collect information that no human sense could otherwise detect.

411

A. ENHANCEMENT OF THE SENSES

What is the relevance of eighteenth-century text to twenty-first-century technologies? For every new technology that police use to seize or search objects or individuals, courts must wrestle with this puzzle. This was true in the early twentieth century with wiretaps, and then later with bugs, beepers, pen registers (how quaint), cell phones, and computers. You should consider not only whether the limits on today's devices have been resolved wisely but also whether there is a solid foundation of principle and practice that can resolve questions about the flood of new observation and search technologies on the horizon.

Under the widely adopted test in Katz v. United States, 389 U.S. 347 (1967), a "search" subject to constitutional limitations takes place when the government intrudes into a person's "reasonable expectation of privacy." Applying this test, when a government agent sees something in plain view, there is no "search" that is subject to constitutional limits. See Chapter 2. But can the same be said of an item that an officer sees (or smells or hears) with the aid of some device that offers a clearer or closer view or a louder sound or a stronger smell? Since the *Katz* standard first appeared in 1967, federal and state courts have wrestled with a variety of investigative technologies, often on a technology-by-technology basis. More recently, as a result of dissatisfaction with the *Katz* test by some Justices, the Supreme Court has also revived a property-oriented approach to the question whether technologically enhanced police investigation constitutes a search.

Consider whether either of the following two cases provides a useful framework for assessing high technology searches and whether the privacy-based or the property-based approach is better suited for a techno-data age.

■ UNITED STATES v. ANTOINE JONES
565 U.S. 400 (2012)

SCALIA, J.*
We decide whether the attachment of a Global-Positioning-System (GPS) tracking device to an individual's vehicle, and subsequent use of that device to monitor the vehicle's movements on public streets, constitutes a search or seizure within the meaning of the Fourth Amendment.

I.

In 2004 respondent Antoine Jones, owner and operator of a nightclub in the District of Columbia, came under suspicion of trafficking in narcotics and was made the target of an investigation by a joint FBI and Metropolitan Police Department task force. Officers employed various investigative techniques, including visual surveillance of the nightclub, installation of a camera focused on the front door of the club, and a pen register and wiretap covering Jones's cellular phone.

Based in part on information gathered from these sources, in 2005 the Government applied to the United States District Court for the District of Columbia

---

* [Chief Justice Roberts and Justices Kennedy, Thomas, and Sotomayor joined this opinion.—EDS.]

for a warrant authorizing the use of an electronic tracking device on the Jeep Grand Cherokee registered to Jones's wife. A warrant issued, authorizing installation of the device in the District of Columbia and within 10 days.

On the 11th day, and not in the District of Columbia but in Maryland, agents installed a GPS tracking device on the undercarriage of the Jeep while it was parked in a public parking lot. Over the next 28 days, the Government used the device to track the vehicle's movements, and once had to replace the device's battery when the vehicle was parked in a different public lot in Maryland. By means of signals from multiple satellites, the device established the vehicle's location within 50 to 100 feet, and communicated that location by cellular phone to a Government computer. It relayed more than 2,000 pages of data over the 4-week period.

The Government ultimately obtained a multiple-count indictment charging Jones and several alleged co-conspirators with . . . conspiracy to distribute and possess with intent to distribute five kilograms or more of cocaine and 50 grams or more of cocaine base. . . . Before trial, Jones filed a motion to suppress evidence obtained through the GPS device. The District Court granted the motion only in part, suppressing the data obtained while the vehicle was parked in the garage adjoining Jones's residence. It held the remaining data admissible, because "a person traveling in an automobile on public thoroughfares has no reasonable expectation of privacy in his movements from one place to another." [A jury convicted Jones] and the District Court sentenced Jones to life imprisonment. . . .

II.

. . . It is important to be clear about what occurred in this case: The Government physically occupied private property for the purpose of obtaining information. We have no doubt that such a physical intrusion would have been considered a "search" within the meaning of the Fourth Amendment when it was adopted. Entick v. Carrington, 95 Eng. Rep. 807 (C.P. 1765), is a case we have described as a "monument of English freedom" undoubtedly familiar to "every American statesman" at the time the Constitution was adopted, and considered to be "the true and ultimate expression of constitutional law" with regard to search and seizure. In that case, Lord Camden expressed in plain terms the significance of property rights in search-and-seizure analysis: "[Our] law holds the property of every man so sacred, that no man can set his foot upon his neighbour's close without his leave; if he does he is a trespasser. . . ."

The text of the Fourth Amendment reflects its close connection to property, since otherwise it would have referred simply to "the right of the people to be secure against unreasonable searches and seizures"; the phrase "in their persons, houses, papers, and effects" would have been superfluous.

Consistent with this understanding, our Fourth Amendment jurisprudence was tied to common-law trespass, at least until the latter half of the 20th century. Thus, in Olmstead v. United States, 277 U.S. 438 (1928), we held that wiretaps attached to telephone wires on the public streets did not constitute a Fourth Amendment search because there was "no entry of the houses or offices of the defendants."

Our later cases, of course, have deviated from that exclusively property-based approach. In Katz v. United States, 389 U.S. 347 (1967), we said that "the Fourth Amendment protects people, not places," and found a violation in attachment of an eavesdropping device to a public telephone booth. Our later cases have applied the analysis of Justice Harlan's concurrence in that case, which said that a violation occurs when government officers violate a person's "reasonable expectation of privacy." See, e.g., Bond v. United States, 529 U.S. 334 (2000).

The Government contends that the Harlan standard shows that no search occurred here, since Jones had no "reasonable expectation of privacy" in the area of the Jeep accessed by Government agents (its underbody) and in the locations of the Jeep on the public roads, which were visible to all. But we need not address the Government's contentions, because Jones's Fourth Amendment rights do not rise or fall with the *Katz* formulation. At bottom, we must assure preservation of that degree of privacy against government that existed when the Fourth Amendment was adopted. As explained, for most of our history the Fourth Amendment was understood to embody a particular concern for government trespass upon the areas ("persons, houses, papers, and effects") it enumerates.[3] [We do not] believe that *Katz*, by holding that the Fourth Amendment protects persons and their private conversations, was intended to withdraw any of the protection which the Amendment extends to the home. . . .[5]

United States v. Knotts, 460 U.S. 276 (1983), upheld against Fourth Amendment challenge the use of a "beeper" that had been placed in a container of chloroform, allowing law enforcement to monitor the location of the container. We said that there had been no infringement of Knotts' reasonable expectation of privacy since the information obtained — the location of the automobile carrying the container on public roads, and the location of the off-loaded container in open fields near Knotts' cabin — had been voluntarily conveyed to the public. But as we have discussed, the *Katz* reasonable-expectation-of-privacy test has been *added to*, not *substituted for*, the common-law trespassory test. The holding in *Knotts* addressed only the former, since the latter was not at issue. The beeper had been placed in the container before it came into Knotts' possession, with the consent of the then-owner. Knotts did not challenge that installation, and we specifically declined to consider its effect on the Fourth Amendment analysis. . . .

The concurrence faults our approach for presenting "particularly vexing problems" in cases that do not involve physical contact, such as those that involve the transmission of electronic signals. We entirely fail to understand that point. For unlike the concurrence, which would make *Katz* the *exclusive* test, we do not make trespass the exclusive test. Situations involving merely the transmission of electronic signals without trespass would *remain* subject to *Katz* analysis.

---

3. Justice Alito's concurrence doubts the wisdom of our approach because "it is almost impossible to think of late-18th-century situations that are analogous to what took place in this case." But in fact it posits a situation that is not far afield—a constable's concealing himself in the target's coach in order to track its movements. . . . Whatever new methods of investigation may be devised, our task, *at a minimum*, is to decide whether the action in question would have constituted a "search" within the original meaning of the Fourth Amendment. Where, as here, the Government obtains information by physically intruding on a constitutionally protected area, such a search has undoubtedly occurred.

5. The concurrence notes that post-*Katz* we have explained that "an actual trespass is neither necessary *nor sufficient* to establish a constitutional violation." That is undoubtedly true, and undoubtedly irrelevant. . . . Trespass alone does not qualify, but there must be conjoined with that what was present here: an attempt to find something or to obtain information.

Related to this, and similarly irrelevant, is the concurrence's point that, if analyzed separately, neither the installation of the device nor its use would constitute a Fourth Amendment search. Of course not. A trespass on "houses" or "effects," or a *Katz* invasion of privacy, is not alone a search unless it is done to obtain information; and the obtaining of information is not alone a search unless it is achieved by such a trespass or invasion of privacy.

In fact, it is the concurrence's insistence on the exclusivity of the *Katz* test that needlessly leads us into "particularly vexing problems" in the present case. This Court has to date not deviated from the understanding that mere visual observation does not constitute a search. [Even] assuming that the concurrence is correct to say that "traditional surveillance" of Jones for a 4-week period "would have required a large team of agents, multiple vehicles, and perhaps aerial assistance," our cases suggest that such visual observation is constitutionally permissible. It may be that achieving the same result through electronic means, without an accompanying trespass, is an unconstitutional invasion of privacy, but the present case does not require us to answer that question.

And answering it affirmatively leads us needlessly into additional thorny problems. The concurrence posits that "relatively short-term monitoring of a person's movements on public streets" is okay, but that "the use of longer term GPS monitoring in investigations *of most offenses*" is no good. That introduces yet another novelty into our jurisprudence. There is no precedent for the proposition that whether a search has occurred depends on the nature of the crime being investigated. And even accepting that novelty, it remains unexplained why a 4-week investigation is "surely" too long and why a drug-trafficking conspiracy involving substantial amounts of cash and narcotics is not an "extraordinary" offense which may permit longer observation. What of a 2-day monitoring of a suspected purveyor of stolen electronics? Or of a 6-month monitoring of a suspected terrorist? We may have to grapple with these "vexing problems" in some future case where a classic trespassory search is not involved and resort must be had to *Katz* analysis; but there is no reason for rushing forward to resolve them here. . . .

SOTOMAYOR, J., concurring.

. . . In cases involving even short-term monitoring, some unique attributes of GPS surveillance relevant to the *Katz* analysis will require particular attention. GPS monitoring generates a precise, comprehensive record of a person's public movements that reflects a wealth of detail about her familial, political, professional, religious, and sexual associations. See, e.g., People v. Weaver, 909 N.E.2d 1195 (N.Y. 2009) ("Disclosed in [GPS data] will be trips the indisputably private nature of which takes little imagination to conjure: trips to the psychiatrist, the plastic surgeon, the abortion clinic, the AIDS treatment center, the strip club, the criminal defense attorney, the by-the-hour motel, the union meeting, the mosque, synagogue or church, the gay bar and on and on"). The Government can store such records and efficiently mine them for information years into the future. And because GPS monitoring is cheap in comparison to conventional surveillance techniques and, by design, proceeds surreptitiously, it evades the ordinary checks that constrain abusive law enforcement practices: limited police resources and community hostility.

Awareness that the Government may be watching chills associational and expressive freedoms. And the Government's unrestrained power to assemble data that reveal private aspects of identity is susceptible to abuse. The net result is that GPS monitoring—by making available at a relatively low cost such a substantial quantum of intimate information about any person whom the Government, in its unfettered discretion, chooses to track—may alter the relationship between citizen and government in a way that is inimical to democratic society.

I would take these attributes of GPS monitoring into account when considering the existence of a reasonable societal expectation of privacy in the sum of one's public movements. . . . More fundamentally, it may be necessary to reconsider the premise that an individual has no reasonable expectation of privacy in information voluntarily disclosed to third parties. E.g., United States v. Miller, 425 U.S. 435 (1976). This approach is ill suited to the digital age, in which people reveal a great deal of information about themselves to third parties in the course of carrying out mundane tasks. . . . Resolution of these difficult questions in this case is unnecessary, however, because the Government's physical intrusion on Jones' Jeep supplies a narrower basis for decision. I therefore join the majority's opinion.

ALITO, J., concurring in the judgment.*

This case requires us to apply the Fourth Amendment's prohibition of unreasonable searches and seizures to a 21st-century surveillance technique, the use of a Global Positioning System (GPS) device to monitor a vehicle's movements for an extended period of time. Ironically, the Court has chosen to decide this case based on 18th-century tort law. By attaching a small GPS device to the underside of the vehicle that respondent drove, the law enforcement officers in this case engaged in conduct that might have provided grounds in 1791 for a suit for trespass to chattels. And for this reason, the Court concludes, the installation and use of the GPS device constituted a search.

This holding, in my judgment, is unwise. It strains the language of the Fourth Amendment; it has little if any support in current Fourth Amendment case law; and it is highly artificial. I would analyze the question presented in this case by asking whether respondent's reasonable expectations of privacy were violated by the long-term monitoring of the movements of the vehicle he drove.

[The] Court's reasoning largely disregards what is really important (the *use* of a GPS for the purpose of long-term tracking) and instead attaches great significance to something that most would view as relatively minor (attaching to the bottom of a car a small, light object that does not interfere in any way with the car's operation). . . .

[The] Court's reliance on the law of trespass will present particularly vexing problems in cases involving surveillance that is carried out by making electronic, as opposed to physical, contact with the item to be tracked. For example, suppose that the officers in the present case had followed respondent by surreptitiously activating a stolen vehicle detection system that came with the car when it was purchased. . . .

The *Katz* expectation-of-privacy test avoids the problems and complications noted above, but it is not without its own difficulties. It involves a degree of circularity, and judges are apt to confuse their own expectations of privacy with those of the hypothetical reasonable person to which the *Katz* test looks. In addition, the *Katz* test rests on the assumption that this hypothetical reasonable person has a well-developed and stable set of privacy expectations. But technology can change those expectations. Dramatic technological change may lead to periods in which popular expectations are in flux and may ultimately produce significant changes in popular attitudes. New technology may provide increased convenience or security at the expense of privacy, and many people may find the tradeoff worthwhile. And even if the public does not welcome the diminution of privacy that new technology entails, they may eventually reconcile themselves to this development as inevitable.

---

* [Justices Ginsburg, Breyer, and Kagan joined this opinion—EDS.]

On the other hand, concern about new intrusions on privacy may spur the enactment of legislation to protect against these intrusions. This is what ultimately happened with respect to wiretapping. After *Katz*, Congress did not leave it to the courts to develop a body of Fourth Amendment case law governing that complex subject. Instead, Congress promptly enacted a comprehensive statute, see 18 U.S.C. §§2510-2522, and since that time, the regulation of wiretapping has been governed primarily by statute and not by case law. . . .

Recent years have seen the emergence of many new devices that permit the monitoring of a person's movements. [Cell] phones and other wireless devices now permit wireless carriers to track and record the location of users. . . . For example, when a user activates the GPS on such a phone, a provider is able to monitor the phone's location and speed of movement and can then report back real-time traffic conditions after combining ("crowdsourcing") the speed of all such phones on any particular road. Similarly, phone-location-tracking services are offered as "social" tools, allowing consumers to find (or to avoid) others who enroll in these services. The availability and use of these and other new devices will continue to shape the average person's expectations about the privacy of his or her daily movements. . . .

In the pre-computer age, the greatest protections of privacy were neither constitutional nor statutory, but practical. Traditional surveillance for any extended period of time was difficult and costly and therefore rarely undertaken. The surveillance at issue in this case — constant monitoring of the location of a vehicle for four weeks — would have required a large team of agents, multiple vehicles, and perhaps aerial assistance. Only an investigation of unusual importance could have justified such an expenditure of law enforcement resources. Devices like the one used in the present case, however, make long-term monitoring relatively easy and cheap. In circumstances involving dramatic technological change, the best solution to privacy concerns may be legislative. A legislative body is well situated to gauge changing public attitudes, to draw detailed lines, and to balance privacy and public safety in a comprehensive way.

To date, however, Congress and most States have not enacted statutes regulating the use of GPS tracking technology for law enforcement purposes. The best that we can do in this case is to apply existing Fourth Amendment doctrine and to ask whether the use of GPS tracking in a particular case involved a degree of intrusion that a reasonable person would not have anticipated.

Under this approach, relatively short-term monitoring of a person's movements on public streets accords with expectations of privacy that our society has recognized as reasonable. But the use of longer term GPS monitoring in investigations of most offenses impinges on expectations of privacy. For such offenses, society's expectation has been that law enforcement agents and others would not — and indeed, in the main, simply could not — secretly monitor and catalogue every single movement of an individual's car for a very long period. In this case, for four weeks, law enforcement agents tracked every movement that respondent made in the vehicle he was driving. We need not identify with precision the point at which the tracking of this vehicle became a search. . . . We also need not consider whether prolonged GPS monitoring in the context of investigations involving extraordinary offenses would similarly intrude on a constitutionally protected sphere of privacy. In such cases, long-term tracking might have been mounted using previously available techniques. . . .

■ TIMOTHY IVORY CARPENTER v. UNITED STATES

138 S. Ct. 2206 (2018)

ROBERTS, J.*

This case presents the question whether the Government conducts a search under the Fourth Amendment when it accesses historical cell phone records that provide a comprehensive chronicle of the user's past movements.

I.

. . . There are 396 million cell phone service accounts in the United States — for a Nation of 326 million people. Cell phones perform their wide and growing variety of functions by connecting to a set of radio antennas called "cell sites." Although cell sites are usually mounted on a tower, they can also be found on light posts, flagpoles, church steeples, or the sides of buildings. Cell sites typically have several directional antennas that divide the covered area into sectors.

Cell phones continuously scan their environment looking for the best signal, which generally comes from the closest cell site. Most modern devices, such as smartphones, tap into the wireless network several times a minute whenever their signal is on, even if the owner is not using one of the phone's features. Each time the phone connects to a cell site, it generates a time-stamped record known as cell-site location information (CSLI). The precision of this information depends on the size of the geographic area covered by the cell site. The greater the concentration of cell sites, the smaller the coverage area. As data usage from cell phones has increased, wireless carriers have installed more cell sites to handle the traffic. That has led to increasingly compact coverage areas, especially in urban areas.

Wireless carriers collect and store CSLI for their own business purposes, including finding weak spots in their network and applying "roaming" charges when another carrier routes data through their cell sites. In addition, wireless carriers often sell aggregated location records to data brokers, without individual identifying information of the sort at issue here. While carriers have long retained CSLI for the start and end of incoming calls, in recent years phone companies have also collected location information from the transmission of text messages and routine data connections. Accordingly, modern cell phones generate increasingly vast amounts of increasingly precise CSLI.

[Prosecutors suspected Carpenter and a group of 15 accomplices of robbing a series of Radio Shack and T-Mobile stores in Detroit. Based on information received from one of the suspects, the prosecutors applied for court orders under the Stored Communications Act to obtain cell phone records for petitioner Timothy Carpenter and several other suspects.] That statute, as amended in 1994, permits the Government to compel the disclosure of certain telecommunications records when it "offers specific and articulable facts showing that there are reasonable grounds to believe" that the records sought "are relevant and material to an ongoing criminal investigation." U.S.C. §2703(d). Federal Magistrate Judges issued two orders directing Carpenter's wireless carriers — MetroPCS and Sprint — to disclose "cell/site sector information for Carpenter's telephone at call origination

---

* [Justices Ginsburg, Breyer, Sotomayor, and Kagan joined this opinion — EDS.]

and at call termination for incoming and outgoing calls" during the four-month period when the string of robberies occurred. The first order sought 152 days of cell-site records from MetroPCS, which produced records spanning 127 days. The second order requested seven days of CSLI from Sprint, which produced two days of records covering the period when Carpenter's phone was "roaming" in northeastern Ohio. Altogether the Government obtained 12,898 location points cataloging Carpenter's movements — an average of 101 data points per day.

[Before trial, Carpenter moved to suppress the cell site location data, but the trial court denied the motion. Based in part on the cell site location data, Carpenter was convicted of robbery and carrying a firearm during a federal crime of violence. The Court of Appeals for the Sixth Circuit affirmed.]

II.

. . . We have kept [our] attention to Founding-era understandings in mind when applying the Fourth Amendment to innovations in surveillance tools. As technology has enhanced the Government's capacity to encroach upon areas normally guarded from inquisitive eyes, this Court has sought to assure preservation of that degree of privacy against government that existed when the Fourth Amendment was adopted.

[Requests] for cell-site records lie at the intersection of two lines of cases, both of which inform our understanding of the privacy interests at stake. The first set of cases addresses a person's expectation of privacy in his physical location and movements. . . . In United States v. Jones, 565 U.S. 400 (2012), FBI agents installed a GPS tracking device on Jones's vehicle and remotely monitored the vehicle's movements for 28 days. The Court decided the case based on the Government's physical trespass of the vehicle. At the same time, five Justices agreed that related privacy concerns would be raised by, for example, "surreptitiously activating a stolen vehicle detection system" in Jones's car to track Jones himself, or conducting GPS tracking of his cell phone. . . . Since GPS monitoring of a vehicle tracks "every movement" a person makes in that vehicle, the concurring Justices concluded that "longer term GPS monitoring in investigations of most offenses impinges on expectations of privacy" — regardless whether those movements were disclosed to the public at large. . . .

In a second set of decisions, the Court has drawn a line between what a person keeps to himself and what he shares with others. We have previously held that "a person has no legitimate expectation of privacy in information he voluntarily turns over to third parties." Smith v. Maryland, 442 U.S. 735, 743-744 (1979). That remains true "even if the information is revealed on the assumption that it will be used only for a limited purpose." United States v. Miller, 425 U.S. 435, 443 (1976). As a result, the Government is typically free to obtain such information from the recipient without triggering Fourth Amendment protections. . . .

III.

The question we confront today is how to apply the Fourth Amendment to a new phenomenon: the ability to chronicle a person's past movements through the record of his cell phone signals. Such tracking partakes of many of the qualities of the GPS monitoring we considered in *Jones.* Much like GPS tracking of a vehicle, cell phone location information is detailed, encyclopedic, and effortlessly compiled.

At the same time, the fact that the individual continuously reveals his location to his wireless carrier implicates the third-party principle of *Smith* and *Miller*. But while the third-party doctrine applies to telephone numbers and bank records, it is not clear whether its logic extends to the qualitatively different category of cell-site records. After all, when *Smith* was decided in 1979, few could have imagined a society in which a phone goes wherever its owner goes, conveying to the wireless carrier not just dialed digits, but a detailed and comprehensive record of the person's movements.

We decline to extend *Smith* and *Miller* to cover these novel circumstances. Given the unique nature of cell phone location records, the fact that the information is held by a third party does not by itself overcome the user's claim to Fourth Amendment protection. Whether the Government employs its own surveillance technology as in *Jones* or leverages the technology of a wireless carrier, we hold that an individual maintains a legitimate expectation of privacy in the record of his physical movements as captured through CSLI. The location information obtained from Carpenter's wireless carriers was the product of a search.

A person does not surrender all Fourth Amendment protection by venturing into the public sphere. To the contrary, "what [one] seeks to preserve as private, even in an area accessible to the public, may be constitutionally protected." United States v. Katz, 389 U.S. 347, 351-352 (1967). A majority of this Court has already recognized that individuals have a reasonable expectation of privacy in the whole of their physical movements. . . . Mapping a cell phone's location over the course of 127 days provides an all-encompassing record of the holder's whereabouts. As with GPS information, the timestamped data provides an intimate window into a person's life, revealing not only his particular movements, but through them his "familial, political, professional, religious, and sexual associations." . . . And like GPS monitoring, cell phone tracking is remarkably easy, cheap, and efficient compared to traditional investigative tools. With just the click of a button, the Government can access each carrier's deep repository of historical location information at practically no expense.

In fact, historical cell-site records present even greater privacy concerns than the GPS monitoring of a vehicle we considered in *Jones*. Unlike the bugged container in United States v. Knotts, 460 U.S. 276 (1983), or the car in *Jones*, a cell phone — almost a "feature of human anatomy," . . . — tracks nearly exactly the movements of its owner. While individuals regularly leave their vehicles, they compulsively carry cell phones with them all the time. A cell phone faithfully follows its owner beyond public thoroughfares and into private residences, doctor's offices, political headquarters, and other potentially revealing locales. . . . Accordingly, when the Government tracks the location of a cell phone it achieves near perfect surveillance, as if it had attached an ankle monitor to the phone's user.

Moreover, the retrospective quality of the data here gives police access to a category of information otherwise unknowable. In the past, attempts to reconstruct a person's movements were limited by a dearth of records and the frailties of recollection. With access to CSLI, the Government can now travel back in time to retrace a person's whereabouts, subject only to the retention polices of the wireless carriers, which currently maintain records for up to five years. Critically, because location information is continually logged for all of the 400 million devices in the United States — not just those belonging to persons who might happen to come under investigation — this newfound tracking capacity runs against everyone. Unlike with the GPS device in *Jones*, police need not even know in advance whether they want to follow a particular individual, or when. Whoever the suspect turns out to be, he has effectively been tailed every moment of every day for five years, and the police may — in the Government's view — call upon the results of that surveillance without regard to the constraints of the Fourth Amendment. Only the few without cell phones could escape this tireless and absolute surveillance. . . .

Accordingly, when the Government accessed CSLI from the wireless carriers, it invaded Carpenter's reasonable expectation of privacy in the whole of his physical movements. . . .

The Government's primary contention to the contrary is that the third-party doctrine governs this case. In its view, cell-site records are fair game because they are "business records" created and maintained by the wireless carriers. The Government (along with Justice Kennedy) recognizes that this case features new technology, but asserts that the legal question nonetheless turns on a garden-variety request for information from a third-party witness. . . . The Government's position fails to contend with the seismic shifts in digital technology that made possible the tracking of not only Carpenter's location but also everyone else's, not for a short period but for years and years. Sprint Corporation and its competitors are not your typical witnesses. Unlike the nosy neighbor who keeps an eye on comings and goings, they are ever alert, and their memory is nearly infallible. There is a world of difference between the limited types of personal information addressed in *Smith* and *Miller* and the exhaustive chronicle of location information casually collected by wireless carriers today. . . .

Neither does the second rationale underlying the third-party doctrine — voluntary exposure — hold up when it comes to CSLI. Cell phone location information is not truly "shared" as one normally understands the term. In the first place, cell phones and the services they provide are "such a pervasive and insistent part of daily life" that carrying one is indispensable to participation in modern society. . . . Second, a cell phone logs a cell-site record by dint of its operation, without any affirmative act on the part of the user beyond powering up. Virtually any activity on the phone generates CSLI, including incoming calls, texts, or e-mails and countless other data connections that a phone automatically makes when checking for news, weather, or social media updates. Apart from disconnecting the phone from the network, there is no way to avoid leaving behind a trail of location data. As a result, in no meaningful sense does the user voluntarily "assume the risk" of turning over a comprehensive dossier of his physical movements. *Smith*, 442 U.S., at 745.

We therefore decline to extend *Smith* and *Miller* to the collection of CSLI. Given the unique nature of cell phone location information, the fact that the Government obtained the information from a third party does not overcome Carpenter's claim to Fourth Amendment protection. The Government's acquisition of the cell-site records was a search within the meaning of the Fourth Amendment. . . .

Our decision today is a narrow one. We do not express a view on matters not before us:

> real-time CSLI or "tower dumps" (a download of information on all the devices that connected to a particular cell site during a particular interval). We do not disturb the application of *Smith* and *Miller* or call into question conventional surveillance techniques and tools, such as security cameras. Nor do we address other business records that might incidentally reveal location information. . . .

IV.

Having found that the acquisition of Carpenter's CSLI was a search, we also conclude that the Government must generally obtain a warrant supported by probable cause before acquiring such records. Although the ultimate measure of the constitutionality of a governmental search is "reasonableness," our cases establish that warrantless searches are typically unreasonable where "a search is undertaken by law enforcement officials to discover evidence of criminal wrongdoing." Vernonia School Dist. 47J v. Acton, 515 U.S. 646, 652-653 (1995). . . .

Justice Alito contends that the warrant requirement simply does not apply when the Government acquires records using compulsory process. Unlike an actual search, he says, subpoenas for documents do not involve the direct taking of evidence; they are at most a "constructive search" conducted by the target of the subpoena. . . . But this Court has never held that the Government may subpoena third parties for records in which the suspect has a reasonable expectation of privacy. . . .

If the choice to proceed by subpoena provided a categorical limitation on Fourth Amendment protection, no type of record would ever be protected by the warrant requirement. Under Justice Alito's view, private letters, digital contents of a cell phone — any personal information reduced to document form, in fact — may be collected by subpoena for no reason other than "official curiosity. . . ."

This is certainly not to say that all orders compelling the production of documents will require a showing of probable cause. The Government will be able to use subpoenas to acquire records in the overwhelming majority of investigations. We hold only that a warrant is required in the rare case where the suspect has a legitimate privacy interest in records held by a third party. . . .

As Justice Brandeis explained in his famous dissent, the Court is obligated — as "[subtler] and more far-reaching means of invading privacy have become available to the Government" — to ensure that the "progress of science" does not erode Fourth Amendment protections. Olmstead v. United States, 277 U.S. 438, 473-474 (1928). Here the progress of science has afforded law enforcement a powerful new tool to carry out its important responsibilities. At the same time, this tool risks Government encroachment of the sort the Framers, "after consulting the lessons of history," drafted the Fourth Amendment to prevent. . . .

We decline to grant the state unrestricted access to a wireless carrier's database of physical location information. In light of the deeply revealing nature of CSLI, its depth, breadth, and comprehensive reach, and the inescapable and automatic nature of its collection, the fact that such information is gathered by a third party does not make it any less deserving of Fourth Amendment protection. The Government's acquisition of the cell-site records here was a search under that Amendment.

The judgment of the Court of Appeals is reversed, and the case is remanded for further proceedings consistent with this opinion.

KENNEDY, J., dissenting.[*]

. . . The Court has twice held that individuals have no Fourth Amendment interests in business records which are possessed, owned, and controlled by a third party.

---

[*] [Justices Thomas and Alito joined this opinion. — EDS.]

United States v. Miller, 425 U.S. 435 (1976); Smith v. Maryland, 442 U.S. 735 (1979). This is true even when the records contain personal and sensitive information. So when the Government uses a subpoena to obtain, for example, bank records, telephone records, and credit card statements from the businesses that create and keep these records, the Government does not engage in a search of the business's customers within the meaning of the Fourth Amendment. . . .

Cell-site records . . . are no different from the many other kinds of business records the Government has a lawful right to obtain by compulsory process. Customers like petitioner do not own, possess, control, or use the records, and for that reason have no reasonable expectation that they cannot be disclosed pursuant to lawful compulsory process. . . .

Miller and *Smith* set forth an important and necessary limitation on the *Katz* framework. They rest upon the commonsense principle that the absence of property law analogues can be dispositive of privacy expectations. The defendants in those cases could expect that the third-party businesses could use the records the companies collected, stored, and classified as their own for any number of business and commercial purposes. The businesses were not bailees or custodians of the records, with a duty to hold the records for the defendants' use. The defendants could make no argument that the records were their own papers or effects. . . . The records were the business entities' records, plain and simple. The defendants had no reason to believe the records were owned or controlled by them and so could not assert a reasonable expectation of privacy in the records.

The second principle supporting *Miller* and *Smith* is the longstanding rule that the Government may use compulsory process to compel persons to disclose documents and other evidence within their possession and control. . . . A subpoena is different from a warrant in its force and intrusive power. While a warrant allows the Government to enter and seize and make the examination itself, a subpoena simply requires the person to whom it is directed to make the disclosure. A subpoena, moreover, provides the recipient the "opportunity to present objections" before complying, which further mitigates the intrusion. . . .

For those reasons this Court has held that a subpoena for records, although a "constructive" search subject to Fourth Amendment constraints, need not comply with the procedures applicable to warrants — even when challenged by the person to whom the records belong. . . . Rather, a subpoena complies with the Fourth Amendment's reasonableness requirement so long as it is "'sufficiently limited in scope, relevant in purpose, and specific in directive so that compliance will not be unreasonably burdensome.'" . . . Persons with no meaningful interests in the records sought by a subpoena, like the defendants in *Miller* and *Smith*, have no rights to object to the records' disclosure — much less to assert that the Government must obtain a warrant to compel disclosure of the records. . . .

Technological changes involving cell phones have complex effects on crime and law enforcement. Cell phones make crimes easier to coordinate and conceal, while also providing the Government with new investigative tools that may have the potential to upset traditional privacy expectations. . . . How those competing effects balance against each other, and how property norms and expectations of privacy form around new technology, often will be difficult to determine during periods of rapid technological change. In those instances, and where the governing legal standard is one of reasonableness, it is wise to defer to legislative judgments like the one embodied in §2703(d) of the Stored Communications Act. . . .

GORSUCH, J. dissenting.

. . . Can the government demand a copy of all your e-mails from Google or Microsoft without implicating your Fourth Amendment rights? Can it secure your DNA from 23andMe without a warrant or probable cause? *Smith* and *Miller* say yes it can — at least without running afoul of *Katz*. But that result strikes most lawyers and judges today — me included — as pretty unlikely. In the years since its adoption, countless scholars, too, have come to conclude that the "third-party doctrine is not only wrong, but horribly wrong." . . .

What if we dropped *Smith* and *Miller*'s third party doctrine and retreated to the root *Katz* question whether there is a "reasonable expectation of privacy" in data held by third parties? Rather than solve the problem with the third party doctrine, I worry this option only risks returning us to its source: After all, it was *Katz* that produced *Smith* and *Miller* in the first place. . . . *Katz* has yielded an often unpredictable — and sometimes unbelievable — jurisprudence. . . .

There is another way. From the founding until the 1960s, the right to assert a Fourth Amendment claim didn't depend on your ability to appeal to a judge's personal sensibilities about the "reasonableness" of your expectations or privacy. It was tied to the law. Florida v. Jardines, 569 U.S. 1, 11 (2013); United States v. Jones, 565 U.S. 400, 405 (2012). The Fourth Amendment protects "the right of the people to be secure in their persons, houses, papers and effects, against unreasonable searches and seizures." True to those words and their original understanding, the traditional approach asked if a house, paper or effect was yours under law. . . . Under this more traditional approach, Fourth Amendment protections for your papers and effects do not automatically disappear just because you share them with third parties.

Given the prominence *Katz* has claimed in our doctrine, American courts are pretty rusty at applying the traditional approach to the Fourth Amendment. We know that if a house, paper, or effect is yours, you have a Fourth Amendment interest in its protection. But what kind of legal interest is sufficient to make something yours? And what source of law determines that? Current positive law? The common law at 1791, extended by analogy to modern times? Both? . . . Much work is needed to revitalize this area and answer these questions. . . .

First, the fact that a third party has access to or possession of your papers and effects does not necessarily eliminate your interest in them. Ever hand a private document to a friend to be returned? Toss your keys to a valet at a restaurant? Ask your neighbor to look after your dog while you travel? You would not expect the friend to share the document with others; the valet to lend your car to his buddy; or the neighbor to put Fido up for adoption. Entrusting your stuff to others is a bailment. A bailment is the "delivery of personal property by one person (the bailor) to another (the bailee) who holds the property for a certain purpose." . . . A bailee normally owes a legal duty to keep the item safe, according to the terms of the parties' contract if they have one, and according to the "implication[s] from their conduct" if they don't. . . . A bailee who uses the item in a different way than he's supposed to, or against the bailor's instructions, is liable for conversion. . . .

It seems to me entirely possible a person's cell-site data could qualify as his papers or effects under existing law. Yes, the telephone carrier holds the information. But 47 U. S. C. §222 designates a customer's cell-site location information as "customer proprietary network information" (CPNI), §222(h)(1)(A), and gives customers certain rights to control use of and access to CPNI about themselves. The statute generally forbids a carrier to "use, disclose, or permit access to individually identifiable" CPNI without the customer's consent, except as needed to provide the customer's telecommunications services. §222(c)(1). It also requires the carrier to disclose CPNI "upon affirmative written request by the customer, to any person designated by the customer." §222(c)(2). Congress even afforded customers a private cause of action for damages against carriers who violate the Act's terms. §207. Plainly, customers have substantial legal interests in this information, including at least some right to include, exclude, and control its use. Those interests might even rise to the level of a property right.

The problem is that we do not know anything more. Before the district court and court of appeals, Mr. Carpenter pursued only a *Katz* "reasonable expectations" argument. He did not invoke the law of property or any analogies to the common law, either there or in his petition for certiorari. Even in his merits brief before this Court, Mr. Carpenter's discussion of his positive law rights in cell-site data was cursory. He offered no analysis, for example, of what rights state law might provide him in addition to those supplied by §222. In these circumstances, I cannot help but conclude — reluctantly — that Mr. Carpenter forfeited perhaps his most promising line of argument. . . .

Notes

1. *Definition of "search" for new technologies: majority position.* *Jones* is a fascinating case doctrinally: While the Court unanimously finds that the use of the GPS in this instance was an unconstitutional search, different Justices offered different takes on the role of *Katz* in determining whether a search occurred. It is also a fascinating case for what it suggests and asks about the competence of judges and legislators to respond to changing technology.

The side-stepping of *Katz* by the majority in *Jones* is a surprising development, as 44 years and countless citations attest. In the long run, the relevance of physical trespass to searches using technology may be quite limited. The holding in this case may matter less over time than the larger issues about the challenges of technology to the Fourth Amendment and the questions about which institution is best positioned to respond to such developments. Justice Alito's uncharacteristic doctrinal suggestion that a complex balancing test under *Katz* should decide when the use of an attached GPS device is a search is balanced by his compelling observation that courts are poorly situated either to weigh the values that should govern the uses of technology, or to regulate technologies.

2. *"Digital trespass."* In finding that law enforcement had conducted a search, the *Jones* majority focused on the physical intrusion on Jones's car. But as Justice Alito's concurrence points out, the "Court's reliance on the law of trespass will present particularly vexing problems in cases involving surveillance that is carried out by making electronic, as opposed to physical, contact with the item to be tracked." Should the Court develop a doctrine of "digital trespass" to address such surveillance? How does Justice Gorsuch in *Carpenter* propose that courts update property-based approaches to the Fourth Amendment?

3. *The "mosaic theory" of surveillance.* Both the *Jones* concurrences and *Carpenter* majority appear to accept that while short-term surveillance of public movements is not a search, long-term tracking is (defined in *Jones* as four weeks of GPS tracking

and in *Carpenter* as one week of cell site location information records). According to Orin Kerr, this reflects a "mosaic theory" of surveillance: Even if individual steps of surveillance do not represent searches on their own, the collection of such steps does. Orin S. Kerr, The Mosaic Theory of the Fourth Amendment, 111 Mich. L. Rev. 311 (2012). What might be the benefits and the challenges of the "mosaic" approach?

4. *Thermal imaging.* Thermal imagers detect infrared radiation, which virtually all objects emit but which is not visible to the naked eye. The imager converts radiation into images based on relative warmth — black is cool, white is hot, shades of gray connote relative differences; the device operates like a video camera showing heat images. State and federal law enforcement authorities started using thermal imaging — also commonly referred to as forward-looking infrared radar, or "FLIR" — in the late 1980s. Federal circuit courts mostly upheld the constitutionality of thermal imaging without a warrant, analogizing the examination of the heat emitted from the house to examination of garbage left at the curb, and to the molecules sniffed by a dog during the warrantless external examination of a bag, approved by the Supreme Court in United States v. Place, 462 U.S. 696 (1983). In Kyllo v. United States, 533 U.S. 27 (2001), the Supreme Court held that thermal imaging of a home is a search under the Fourth Amendment. The Court stressed the fact that police used thermal imaging to gather information about a home, which it called the "prototypical" area of protected privacy. The majority also qualified its holding by observing that the image there provided information "that would previously have been unknowable without physical intrusion."

5. *Technology in general use.* Some of the Supreme Court decisions in this area, including *Kyllo* and *Jones*, ask about the common or unusual nature of the technology involved. Will this "general use" factor pose the same kind of continual erosion as the original "expectation" doctrine of *Katz*, since technology often becomes cheaper and more widespread over time? Consider, for example, satellite imaging. Commercial satellite cameras supplement the government's spy satellite cameras, and they monitor domestic as well as foreign sites. Given enough commercial and spy satellites, intelligence and law enforcement agencies could realistically achieve constant surveillance of the entire planet. Combine this network of satellite cameras with street-level surveillance cameras, and it becomes possible to record much of daily living — particularly urban living — on camera. Do you expect the law that governs satellites to change as the presence of the cameras becomes more ubiquitous and access to the images grows? For a flavor of the active news media coverage of surveillance cameras for law enforcement, see the web extension for this chapter at *http://www.crimpro.com/extension/ch07*.

6. *Personal information held by third parties.* The third-party doctrine holds that when a person shares information with others (whether individuals or businesses), he or she assumes the risk that the information might further be shared with law enforcement and loses any "legitimate expectation of privacy" in the information. Today, private parties hold a large range of personal information, including banking and other financial records, health and medical records, and electronic communications records. As Justice Sotomayor notes in her concurrence in *Jones*, "people reveal a great deal of information about themselves to third parties in the course of carrying out mundane tasks."

Carpenter expressly declined to disturb the judgments in *Miller* and *Smith*, which held that by sharing certain information with a business (banking information in

Miller and phone number dialing records in *Smith*), a person assumes the risk that the information might be shared with law enforcement. At the same time, *Carpenter* suggested that the third-party doctrine does not apply to certain business records that provide "an exhaustive chronicle of location information." What is the scope of the third-party doctrine after *Carpenter*? How would it apply, for example, to exhaustive credit card records that reveal daily purchases? To pharmaceutical records?

Even before *Carpenter*, state courts had divided on the question of constitutional privacy rights in banking records and pharmaceutical records. See State v. Skinner, 10 So. 3d 1212 (La. 2009); State v. McAllister, 875 A.2d 866 (N.J. 2005); Stephen E. Henderson, Learning from All Fifty States: How to Apply the Fourth Amendment and Its State Analogs to Protect Third Party Information from Unreasonable Search, 55 Cath. U. L. Rev. 373 (2006).

7. *Email privacy.* If your employer opens mail that you send from work, the employer may be subject to criminal prosecution under 18 U.S.C. §1702 ("Whoever takes any letter, postal card, or package out of any post office or any authorized depository for mail matter . . . before it has been delivered to the person to whom it was directed, with the design to obstruct the correspondence, or to pry into the business or secrets of another, or opens, secretes, embezzles, or destroys the same, shall be fined under this title or imprisoned not more than five years, or both."). The employer may also be subject to a statutory or common-law civil suit for privacy infringement. Add an "e" to the word "mail," however, and the employer can — and, in the case of many larger employers, probably does — read and review it. See City of Ontario, Cal. v. Quon, 560 U.S. 746 (2010) (review of text messages sent by police officers on departmental pagers to determine source of billing overruns revealed that officer used pager during work hours for personal messages; review was reasonable because it was motivated by legitimate work-related purpose, and not excessive in scope). The only significant limits on the authority of employers to read employee email come in the contractual relationships between the employee and employer. Of course, employers are not the only potential uninvited readers of a person's email.

The analogy of email to "snail mail" has some vitality with respect to third parties — including the government — seeking to read email without the permission of employers or Internet service providers. However, the analogy has fared poorly with regard to employers or Internet service providers, where the privacy of an individual's communication depends largely on the contract. See Meir S. Hornung, Think Before You Type: A Look at Email Privacy in the Workplace, 11 Fordham J. Corp. & Fin. Law (2005). Should individuals have enforceable privacy interests against nongovernment parties with respect to email that resides on third-party or corporate computers? Should the answer depend on social norms or laws beyond the scope of any contract between the person and her employer? Limits on employer review of employee email or web usage may come from quasi-contractual relationships defining professional association, such as the relationship of faculty and students to a university under the principles of academic freedom.

8. *An area ripe for statutory precision?* Do questions about the use of technological enhancement of the senses require answers too precise for judges to give? Can statutes better limit the misuse of technology? Statutes have become the most common method of regulating some technological search devices. These include wiretapping and pen registers, which are topics covered later in this

chapter. To explore further examples of legislative regulation of access to sensitive personal information, consult the web extension for this chapter at *http://www.crimpro.com/extension/ch07.*

Problem 7-1. Prescription Privacy

Marcus Brown, a DEA agent, suspected that Nicholas Russo was abusing prescription medicines. Rumor suggested that Santo Buccheri, a Hartford physician, overprescribed pain killers to Russo and failed to maintain proper records. Brown therefore went to pharmacies located near Buccheri's office and Russo's home. Although Brown had no search warrant or probable cause to believe a crime had occurred, he asked each of the pharmacies to provide him with Russo's prescription records. The records contained information about prescriptions that each pharmacy had filled for Russo, including the name of the prescribing physician, the date Russo submitted the prescription to the pharmacy, the type and quantity of drug prescribed, and the price of the drug. The pharmacies complied with Brown's requests. Those records indicated that Russo had obtained a large amount of Tylenol 3, about 8,000 tablets. Brown therefore returned to each pharmacy and requested copies of the actual prescription forms that Russo presented to the pharmacies. Again, the pharmacists cooperated with Brown's request. The state filed an information charging Russo with 32 counts of obtaining Tylenol with Codeine No. 3 (the active ingredient in Tylenol 3), a controlled substance, by forging a prescription. Russo moved to suppress the records of his prescriptions that the state obtained from the pharmacies without a warrant and without his consent. Russo contended that he had a reasonable expectation of privacy in his prescription records and, therefore, that the state obtained those records in violation of his rights under the federal and state constitutions. A state statute declares that "prescriptions shall be open for inspection only to federal, state, county and municipal officers, whose duty it is to enforce the laws of this state or of the United States relating to controlled substances." How would you rule on the motion to suppress? See State v. Russo, 790 A.2d 1132 (Conn. 2002).

Problem 7-2. ShotSpotter

Concerned about the rise in school shootings, Alpha University has decided to install a gunshot detection system called ShotSpotter on campus. The University installs ShotSpotter's microphones across campus to monitor for gunshot sounds. When the microphones detect what the ShotSpotter algorithm considers to be gunfire, the system sends an audio recording to a 24-hour monitoring center, where it's reviewed by experts. The results are then transmitted to local police officers. According to ShotSpotter, the process takes about 30 seconds — significantly faster than the typical 3-5 minutes for a 911-call after a gunshot is heard. The company claims that private conversations would not trigger the system. In a few cases, conversations were in fact recorded and used to corroborate witness statements, but in those cases, as ShotSpotter explains on its website, "the words were yelled loudly, in a public place, at the scene of a gunfire-related crime, and within a few seconds of that event." A 2013 investigation of ShotSpotter devices in Newark, New Jersey, found that

75 percent of the gunshot alerts by ShotSpotter devices had been for false alarms, meaning that audio clips were recorded even in the absence of gunshots.

Could the deployment of ShotSpotter devices on campus constitute a Fourth Amendment search? If yes, under what circumstances? What, if anything, could university administrators do to ensure that the installation of ShotSpotter does not violate students' Fourth Amendment rights?

Problem 7-3. Eye in the Sky

Advances in technology are making it easier for police to use video cameras for surveillance of pedestrian areas and busy street intersections. Earlier technologies used analog videotape and were wired to monitoring locations through fiber-optic cable. New cameras use digital images that can be stored and manipulated more easily. The new cameras can be operated by radio commands and can transmit images wirelessly, saving the cost of installing cable.

Police in many jurisdictions are experimenting with video cameras posted in public places. Many cities in the United States have installed cameras at intersections to record the license plates of drivers who disobey traffic signals; private firms operate the cameras in exchange for a large portion of the revenues from traffic tickets issued.

In Washington, D.C., the police department now has dozens of cameras mounted in downtown areas, monitoring such sites as the White House, the National Mall, and Union Station, as well as cameras attached to police helicopters. Eventually, the system could include more than 200 cameras in stations of the Washington Metro system, another 200 cameras in public schools, and 100 more to be installed by the city traffic department at busy intersections. The first neighborhood to add camera surveillance will probably be Georgetown, a shopping district popular with tourists and college students.

The signals from the cameras all feed into a control room in police headquarters, called the Joint Operations Command Center. The center has 40 video stations angled around a wall of floor-to-ceiling screens. The cameras are programmed to scan public areas automatically, and officers can assume manual control if they see something they want to examine more closely. Eventually, the system could include "biometric" software that will permit an automated match between a face in the crowd and a computerized photo of a suspect contained in a database consisting of photos of arrestees and prison inmates. While some facial recognition technology reaches 99 percent accuracy for white males, the same technology can have an error rate as high as 35 percent for darker-skinned women. Steve Lohr, Facial Recognition Is Accurate, If You Are a White Guy, N.Y. Times, Feb. 9, 2018, at *https://www.nytimes.com/2018/02/09/technology/facial-recognition-race-artificial-intelligence.html*. Furthermore, the technology currently used by the Federal Bureau of Investigation has a lower accuracy rate of about 85 percent.

In addition to facial recognition, D.C. authorities are considering whether to follow the example of the Newark Police Department, which has created a web portal through which ordinary citizens can log in and watch a live feed coming from the city's surveillance cameras. Karen Rouse, Newark Police Camera System Relies on Residents, Stirring Privacy Concerns, Nat'l Pub. Radio, May 26, 2018, *https://www.npr.org/2018/05/26/614387170/newark-police-camera-system-relies-on-residents-stirring-privacy-concerns*.

If you were asked to testify before a state legislature about the legal implications of camera surveillance, what would you say? Does the sheer number of existing cameras make it easier or harder to justify further additions to the surveillance area? What Fourth Amendment implications, if any, might the addition of facial recognition add to the surveillance system? Would it matter what the accuracy rate of the technology is and whether it is equally accurate across different races? Would it matter whether the database contains photos of convicted offenders only, or also those of arrestees, or also those of drivers' license holders? Finally, are there additional Fourth Amendment implications flowing from the decision to make the live video feed available to members of the public?

Whatever your testimony about the pervasive or targeted collection and use of face recognition technology in Boston (for Massachusetts) or Boise (for Idaho), would you offer the same testimony in Beijing (for China)? See Paul Mazur, Inside China's Dystopian Dreams: A.I., Shame and Lots of Cameras, New York Times, July 8, 2018, *https://www.nytimes.com/2018/07/08/business/china-surveillance-technology.html.*

Problem 7-4. Reversing Time to Solve Crime

The National Public Radio program Radiolab describes a powerful technology in a 2015 podcast:

> Ross McNutt has a superpower — he can zoom in on everyday life, then rewind and fast-forward to solve crimes in a shutter-flash. But should he?
>
> In 2004, when casualties in Iraq were rising due to roadside bombs, Ross McNutt and his team came up with an idea. With a small plane and a 44 mega-pixel camera, they figured out how to watch an entire city all at once, all day long. Whenever a bomb detonated, they could zoom onto that spot and then, because this eye in the sky had been there all along, they could scroll back in time and see — literally see — who planted it. After the war, Ross McNutt retired from the Air Force, and brought this technology back home with him from Juarez, Mexico, to Dayton, Ohio.

Listen at *https://www.wnycstudios.org/story/eye-sky/.* The same technology is being used in some U.S. cities. As drones, cameras, databases, and artificial-intelligence analytic tools become ever faster and cheaper, the deployment of this pervasive "time reconstruction" technology could become pervasive. At what point does technology not just enhance human senses, but transform what it means to be human, or at least what it means to be a member of a community? At what point do we need to reconsider the very foundations of what it means to commit, combat—and prevent—crime?

■ FLORIDA v. JOELIS JARDINES
569 U.S. 1 (2013)

SCALIA, J.*

We consider whether using a drug-sniffing dog on a homeowner's porch to investigate the contents of the home is a "search" within the meaning of the Fourth Amendment.

* [Justices Thomas, Ginsburg, Sotomayor, and Kagan joined this opinion.—EDS.]

I.

In 2006, Detective William Pedraja of the Miami-Dade Police Department received an unverified tip that marijuana was being grown in the home of respondent Joelis Jardines. One month later, the Department and the Drug Enforcement Administration sent a joint surveillance team to Jardines' home. Detective Pedraja was part of that team. He watched the home for fifteen minutes and saw no vehicles in the driveway or activity around the home, and could not see inside because the blinds were drawn. Detective Pedraja then approached Jardines' home accompanied by Detective Douglas Bartelt, a trained canine handler who had just arrived at the scene with his drug-sniffing dog. The dog was trained to detect the scent of marijuana, cocaine, heroin, and several other drugs, indicating the presence of any of these substances through particular behavioral changes recognizable by his handler.

Detective Bartelt had the dog on a six-foot leash, owing in part to the dog's "wild" nature, and tendency to dart around erratically while searching. As the dog approached Jardines' front porch, he apparently sensed one of the odors he had been trained to detect, and began energetically exploring the area for the strongest point source of that odor. As Detective Bartelt explained, the dog "began tracking that airborne odor by . . . tracking back and forth," engaging in what is called "bracketing," "back and forth, back and forth." Detective Bartelt gave the dog "the full six feet of the leash plus whatever safe distance [he could] give him" to do this—he testified that he needed to give the dog "as much distance as I can." And Detective Pedraja stood back while this was occurring, so that he would not "get knocked over" when the dog was "spinning around trying to find" the source.

After sniffing the base of the front door, the dog sat, which is the trained behavior upon discovering the odor's strongest point. Detective Bartelt then pulled the dog away from the door and returned to his vehicle. He left the scene after informing Detective Pedraja that there had been a positive alert for narcotics.

On the basis of what he had learned at the home, Detective Pedraja applied for and received a warrant to search the residence. When the warrant was executed later that day, Jardines attempted to flee and was arrested; the search revealed marijuana plants, and he was charged with trafficking in cannabis.

At trial, Jardines moved to suppress the marijuana plants on the ground that the canine investigation was an unreasonable search. The trial court granted the motion, and [the Florida Supreme Court upheld that decision].

II.

The Fourth Amendment . . . establishes a simple baseline, one that for much of our history formed the exclusive basis for its protections: When "the Government obtains information by physically intruding" on persons, houses, papers, or effects, a "search" within the original meaning of the Fourth Amendment has "undoubtedly occurred." United States v. Jones, 565 U.S. 400, 406 n.3 (2012). By reason of our decision in Katz v. United States, 389 U.S. 347 (1967), property rights "are not the sole measure of Fourth Amendment violations"—but though *Katz* may add to the baseline, it does not subtract anything from the Amendment's protections when the Government *does* engage in a physical intrusion of a constitutionally protected area.

That principle renders this case a straightforward one. The officers were gathering information in an area belonging to Jardines and immediately surrounding his house—in the curtilage of the house, which we have held enjoys protection as part of the home itself. And they gathered that information by physically entering and occupying the area to engage in conduct not explicitly or implicitly permitted by the homeowner.

[When] it comes to the Fourth Amendment, the home is first among equals. At the Amendment's very core stands "the right of a man to retreat into his own home and there be free from unreasonable governmental intrusion." *Silverman v. United States*, 365 U.S. 505 (1961). This right would be of little practical value if the State's agents could stand in a home's porch or side garden and trawl for evidence with impunity; the right to retreat would be significantly diminished if the police could enter a man's property to observe his repose from just outside the front window.

We therefore regard the area immediately surrounding and associated with the home—what our cases call the curtilage—as part of the home itself for Fourth Amendment purposes. . . . The front porch is the classic exemplar of an area adjacent to the home and to which the activity of home life extends. . . .

Since the officers' investigation took place in a constitutionally protected area, we turn to the question of whether it was accomplished through an unlicensed physical intrusion. While law enforcement officers need not "shield their eyes" when passing by the home on public thoroughfares, an officer's leave to gather information is sharply circumscribed when he steps off those thoroughfares and enters the Fourth Amendment's protected areas. . . . As it is undisputed that the detectives had all four of their feet and all four of their companion's firmly planted on the constitutionally protected extension of Jardines' home, the only question is whether he had given his leave (even implicitly) for them to do so. He had not.

"A license may be implied from the habits of the country," notwithstanding the "strict rule of the English common law as to entry upon a close." *McKee v. Gratz*, 260 U.S. 127 (1922) (Holmes, J.). We have accordingly recognized that the knocker on the front door is treated as an invitation or license to attempt an entry, justifying ingress to the home by solicitors, hawkers and peddlers of all kinds. This implicit license typically permits the visitor to approach the home by the front path, knock promptly, wait briefly to be received, and then (absent invitation to linger longer) leave. Complying with the terms of that traditional invitation does not require fine-grained legal knowledge; it is generally managed without incident by the Nation's Girl Scouts and trick-or-treaters. Thus, a police officer not armed with a warrant may approach a home and knock, precisely because that is no more than any private citizen might do.

But introducing a trained police dog to explore the area around the home in hopes of discovering incriminating evidence is something else. There is no customary invitation to do *that*. An invitation to engage in canine forensic investigation assuredly does not inhere in the very act of hanging a knocker. To find a visitor knocking on the door is routine (even if sometimes unwelcome); to spot that same visitor exploring the front path with a metal detector, or marching his bloodhound into the garden before saying hello and asking permission, would inspire most of us to—well, call the police. . . .

III.

The State argues that investigation by a forensic narcotics dog by definition cannot implicate any legitimate privacy interest. The State cites for authority our decisions in United States v. Place, 462 U.S. 696 (1983), United States v. Jacobsen, 466 U.S. 109 (1984), and Illinois v. Caballes, 543 U.S. 405 (2005), which held, respectively, that canine inspection of luggage in an airport, chemical testing of a substance that had fallen from a parcel in transit, and canine inspection of an automobile during a lawful traffic stop, do not violate the "reasonable expectation of privacy" described in *Katz*. . . .

[We] need not decide whether the officers' investigation of Jardines' home violated his expectation of privacy under *Katz*. One virtue of the Fourth Amendment's property-rights baseline is that it keeps easy cases easy. That the officers learned what they learned only by physically intruding on Jardines' property to gather evidence is enough to establish that a search occurred. . . . The government's use of trained police dogs to investigate the home and its immediate surroundings is a "search" within the meaning of the Fourth Amendment. . . .

KAGAN, J., concurring.*

For me, a simple analogy clinches this case—and does so on privacy as well as property grounds. A stranger comes to the front door of your home carrying super-high-powered binoculars. He doesn't knock or say hello. Instead, he stands on the porch and uses the binoculars to peer through your windows, into your home's furthest corners. It doesn't take long (the binoculars are really very fine): In just a couple of minutes, his uncommon behavior allows him to learn details of your life you disclose to no one. Has your "visitor" trespassed on your property, exceeding the license you have granted to members of the public to, say, drop off the mail or distribute campaign flyers? Yes, he has. And has he also invaded your "reasonable expectation of privacy," by nosing into intimacies you sensibly thought protected from disclosure? Yes, of course, he has done that too.

That case is this case in every way that matters. Here, police officers came to Joelis Jardines' door with a super-sensitive instrument, which they deployed to detect things inside that they could not perceive unassisted. The equipment they used was animal, not mineral. But contra the dissent, that is of no significance in determining whether a search occurred. Detective Bartelt's dog was not your neighbor's pet, come to your porch on a leisurely stroll. [Drug-detection] dogs are highly trained tools of law enforcement, geared to respond in distinctive ways to specific scents so as to convey clear and reliable information to their human partners. They are to the poodle down the street as high-powered binoculars are to a piece of plain glass. . . .

ALITO, J., dissenting.**

. . . The law of trespass generally gives members of the public a license to use a walkway to approach the front door of a house and to remain there for a brief time. This license is not limited to persons who intend to speak to an occupant or who actually do so. (Mail carriers and persons delivering packages and flyers are examples of individuals who may lawfully approach a front door without intending to

---

* [Justices Ginsburg and Sotomayor joined this opinion.—EDS.]
** [Chief Justice Roberts and Justices Breyer and Kennedy joined this opinion.—EDS.]

converse.) Nor is the license restricted to categories of visitors whom an occupant of the dwelling is likely to welcome. . . . And the license even extends to police officers who wish to gather evidence against an occupant (by asking potentially incriminating questions).

According to the Court, however, the police officer in this case, Detective Bartelt, committed a trespass because he was accompanied during his otherwise lawful visit to the front door of respondent's house by his dog, Franky. Where is the authority evidencing such a rule? Dogs have been domesticated for about 12,000 years; they were ubiquitous in both this country and Britain at the time of the adoption of the Fourth Amendment; and their acute sense of smell has been used in law enforcement for centuries. Yet the Court has been unable to find a single case—from the United States or any other common-law nation — that supports the rule on which its decision is based. Thus, trespass law provides no support for the Court's holding today.

The Court's decision is also inconsistent with the reasonable-expectations-of-privacy test that the Court adopted in Katz v. United States. A reasonable person understands that odors emanating from a house may be detected from locations that are open to the public, and a reasonable person will not count on the strength of those odors remaining within the range that, while detectible by a dog, cannot be smelled by a human.

For these reasons, I would hold that no search within the meaning of the Fourth Amendment took place in this case, and I would reverse the decision below. . . .

Notes

1. *Are dog sniffs searches? Majority position.* In United States v. Place, 462 U.S. 696 (1983), the Supreme Court held that dog sniffs are not searches and therefore are not subject to the constraints of the Fourth Amendment. The Court confirmed this position in Illinois v. Caballes, 543 U.S. 405 (2005), holding that a dog sniff performed on the exterior of a vehicle during a valid traffic stop requires no justification because the dog reveals only the presence or absence of contraband and does not intrude on a reasonable expectation of privacy.

The largest group of state courts read their state constitutions and statutes in a similar fashion to conclude that the use of canines to sniff items in public places does not qualify as a "search." See, e.g., State v. Nguyen, 841 N.W.2d 676 (N.D. 2013) (use of drug-sniffing dog in common hallways of apartment building was not a search). A strong minority, however, treat a canine sniff as a "search" under the state constitution. These holdings tend to appear in cases in which the dog is brought into a residence or to the front door of a home. These courts typically require the police to demonstrate reasonable suspicion—not probable cause—to carry out the canine sniff search. See People v. Devone, 931 N.E.2d 70 (N.Y. 2010) (dog sniff of automobile classified as "search" under state constitution, but the government needs only "founded suspicion," less demanding standard than reasonable suspicion, to justify dog sniff). You can sample the state court variety in dealing with canine sniffs on the web extension for this chapter at *http://www.crimpro.com/extension/ch07*.

2. *Dog versus house.* The *Jardines* case could easily be retitled "dog v. house." Notice what a minor role United States v. Place, 462 U.S. 696 (1983), plays in *Jardines*. In the past decade, the Supreme Court has amplified the special standing of the home in

Fourth Amendment jurisprudence, perhaps most notably in Kyllo v. United States, 533 U.S. 27 (2001). The opinions in this case all wrestle with categorical questions about the proper analytical framework (property versus privacy), when enhancement of the senses turns "plain view" observations into a search, and the impact of technology on the Fourth Amendment. Only time will tell, but the relatively simple facts and setting in *Jardines* suggest some of the new dogs (*Kyllo* and *Jones*) can, indeed, hunt.

3. *Plain view and sense enhancements: majority position.* Remember that it is no search for an officer to view objects within "plain" view when the officer is justified in being in a particular place—whether in a home during execution of a warrant or in an area based on consent or some exception to the warrant requirement. See Chapter 2. Most courts draw an analogy between "plain view" and the use of familiar tools that enhance human senses of sight or hearing to provide light, or to change or magnify a view. They often ask whether the officer (or a group of officers) could have made the observation by using normal senses from a permissible location. If the answer to this question is "yes," courts often conclude that the evidence collection is not a search at all; if not, they are more inclined to consider it a search and then evaluate whether the search was reasonable.

More often than not, a court reviewing a police officer's use of sense-enhancing devices will conclude that the officer did not conduct a "search." See Dow Chemical Co. v. United States, 476 U.S. 227 (1986) (no search when government uses $22,000 aerial mapping camera during overflight of industrial plant suspected of environmental crimes). As with other aspects of search and seizure doctrine, the shift in *Katz* from a property-based conception to a privacy-based conception of the Fourth Amendment makes it more difficult for courts to reach categorical conclusions about the use of any particular technological sense-enhancement. The amount of effort a government agent expends in obtaining a "plain" view, the nature of the location observed, the place from which the observation is made, and the public familiarity with a device may all be relevant. For a sample of state court rulings on the use of sense enhancing devices such as high-powered binoculars, flashlights, starscopes, and others, consult the web extension for this chapter at *http://www.crim-pro.com/extension/ch07*. Remember that even when use of a sense-enhancing device constitutes a search, a court must address further questions: It must determine what level of justification the government must have to support the search, and then it must evaluate whether the search was reasonable given those particular facts.

B. WIRETAPPING

Wiretapping is just one of many technologies that provide the capacity to observe or hear more than would be possible with human senses. This section considers the evolution of the procedures governing wiretapping, from judicial doctrine to statute. The first subsection looks at Olmstead v. United States, one of the earliest wiretapping cases. This case, along with Katz v. United States, invited Congress and state legislatures to occupy the wiretapping field, largely unrestricted by precedent and other limits on judicial authority. The remainder of this section highlights the recurring features of these wiretapping statutes, and reviews some difficult choices about how to extend this regulation to some specialized settings.

1. Judicial Limits on Wiretaps

■ ROY OLMSTEAD v. UNITED STATES
277 U.S. 438 (1928)

TAFT, C.J.[*]

The petitioners were convicted . . . of a conspiracy to violate the National Prohibition Act by unlawfully possessing, transporting and importing intoxicating liquors and maintaining nuisances, and by selling intoxicating liquors. Seventy-two others in addition to the petitioners were indicted. Some were not apprehended, some were acquitted and others pleaded guilty.

The evidence in the records discloses a conspiracy of amazing magnitude to import, possess and sell liquor unlawfully. . . . Olmstead was the leading conspirator and the general manager of the business. . . . Of the several offices in Seattle the chief one was in a large office building. In this there were three telephones on three different lines. There were telephones in an office of the manager in his own home, at the homes of his associates, and at other places in the city. . . .

The information which led to the discovery of the conspiracy and its nature and extent was largely obtained by intercepting messages on the telephones of the conspirators by four federal prohibition officers. Small wires were inserted along the ordinary telephone wires from the residences of four of the petitioners and those leading from the chief office. The insertions were made without trespass upon any property of the defendants. They were made in the basement of the large office building. The taps from house lines were made in the streets near the houses. The gathering of evidence continued for many months. . . .

The [Fourth] Amendment itself shows that the search is to be of material things—the person, the house, his papers or his effects. The description of the warrant necessary to make the proceeding lawful, is that it must specify the place to be searched and the person or things to be seized. . . . It is plainly within the words of the Amendment to say that the unlawful rifling by a government agent of a sealed letter is a search and seizure of the sender's papers or effects. The letter is a paper, an effect, and in the custody of a Government that forbids carriage except under its protection. The United States takes no such care of telegraph or telephone messages as of mailed sealed letters. The Amendment does not forbid what was done here. There was no searching. There was no seizure. The evidence was secured by the use of the sense of hearing and that only. There was no entry of the houses or offices of the defendants.

By the invention of the telephone, 50 years ago, and its application for the purpose of extending communications, one can talk with another at a far distant place. The language of the Amendment cannot be extended and expanded to include telephone wires reaching to the whole world from the defendant's house or office. The intervening wires are not part of his house or office any more than are the highways along which they are stretched. . . .

Congress may of course protect the secrecy of telephone messages by making them, when intercepted, inadmissible in evidence in federal criminal trials, by direct legislation, and thus depart from the common law of evidence. But the courts

---

[*] [Justices McReynolds, Sanford, Sutherland, and Van Devanter joined in this opinion.—EDS.]

may not adopt such a policy by attributing an enlarged and unusual meaning to the Fourth Amendment. . . .

BRANDEIS, J., dissenting.

[At least six] prohibition agents listened over the tapped wires and reported the messages taken. Their operations extended over a period of nearly five months. The typewritten record of the notes of conversations overheard occupies 775 typewritten pages. [The Government concedes] that if wire-tapping can be deemed a search and seizure within the Fourth Amendment, such wire-tapping as was practiced in the case at bar was an unreasonable search and seizure, and that the evidence thus obtained was inadmissible. . . .

When the Fourth and Fifth Amendments were adopted, [force] and violence were then the only means known to man by which a Government could directly effect self-incrimination. It could compel the individual to testify—a compulsion effected, if need be, by torture. It could secure possession of his papers and other articles incident to his private life—a seizure effected, if need be, by breaking and entry. Protection against such invasion of the sanctities of a man's home and the privacies of life was provided in the Fourth and Fifth Amendments by specific language. . . . Subtler and more far-reaching means of invading privacy have become available to the Government. Discovery and invention have made it possible for the Government, by means far more effective than stretching upon the rack, to obtain disclosure in court of what is whispered in the closet.

Moreover, in the application of a constitution, our contemplation cannot be only of what has been but of what may be. The progress of science in furnishing the Government with means of espionage is not likely to stop with wire-tapping. Ways may some day be developed by which the Government, without removing papers from secret drawers, can reproduce them in court, and by which it will be enabled to expose to a jury the most intimate occurrences of the home. Advances in the psychic and related sciences may bring means of exploring unexpressed beliefs, thoughts and emotions. . . . Can it be that the Constitution affords no protection against such invasions of individual security?

[The] tapping of one man's telephone line involves the tapping of the telephone of every other person whom he may call, or who may call him. As a means of espionage, writs of assistance and general warrants are but puny instruments of tyranny and oppression when compared with wire-tapping.

The makers of our Constitution undertook to secure conditions favorable to the pursuit of happiness. They recognized the significance of man's spiritual nature, of his feelings and of his intellect. . . . They conferred, as against the Government, the right to be let alone — the most comprehensive of rights and the right most valued by civilized men. To protect that right, every unjustifiable intrusion by the Government upon the privacy of the individual, whatever the means employed, must be deemed a violation of the Fourth Amendment. . . .

Notes

1. *Constitutional interpretation.* Recall that the Supreme Court overruled *Olmstead* in Katz v. United States, 389 U.S. 347 (1967). Despite their great differences in doctrine and bottom line, *Olmstead* and *Katz* are both splendid examples

of constitutional decision-making. They each raise some of the foundational issues in any difficult constitutional context: What do the words of the various provisions mean? Should interpretation be limited to the words? If not, what principles limit the power of the court from acting as a superlegislature by interpreting words? As for the role a court plays when interpreting the meaning of constitutional terms such as "persons," "houses," or "effects"—much less concepts such as "privacy" and "reasonableness"—consider the following exchange:

> "There's glory for you!"
>
> "I don't know what you mean by 'glory,' " Alice said.
>
> Humpty Dumpty smiled contemptuously. "Of course you don't—till I tell you. I meant there's a nice knock-down argument for you."
>
> "But 'glory' doesn't mean 'a nice knock-down argument,' " Alice objected.
>
> "When I use a word," Humpty Dumpty said in rather a scornful tone, "it means just what I choose it to mean—neither more nor less."
>
> "The question is," said Alice, "whether you can make words mean so many different things."
>
> "The question is," said Humpty Dumpty, "which is to be the master—that's all."

Lewis Carroll, Through the Looking-Glass and What Alice Found There 269 (Martin Gardner ed., 1960).

2. *Wiretap cases between* Olmstead *and* Katz. Even before *Katz*, the Supreme Court had begun to place limits on electronic eavesdropping. In Silverman v. United States, 365 U.S. 505 (1961), the Court found that the government violated the Fourth Amendment when it inserted a "spike mike" into a heating duct. Although the Court concluded that the government had committed a trespass, it emphasized that its decision did "not turn upon the technicality of a trespass upon a party wall as a matter of local law. It is based upon the reality of an actual intrusion into a constitutionally protected area."

3. *Computer searches.* During investigations of certain crimes (think, for instance, of fraud or pornography cases), investigators need to learn about the contents of personal computers. The computer search context calls for some adjustments to traditional search and seizure doctrine. Just as courts in the wiretap context eventually placed less emphasis on whether investigators carried out a physical intrusion of a protected place, courts that regulate computer searches have placed less weight over time on the physical location where the information is stored.

When the police want access to a personal computer, they typically obtain a warrant. Should the warrant describe the nature of the storage device, or the files or data to be accessed during a later analysis of the storage device? When the government copies data, does that constitute a "search" or a "seizure," or does a search occur only when a human being views or analyzes the data? Does the opening or analysis of the data have to occur within a reasonable time from the issuance of the warrant, or is timing relevant only to the physical seizure of the storage device? Thus far, the federal case law is decidedly more developed than the appellate decisions in the state courts. See Orin Kerr, Searches and Seizures in a Digital World, 119 Harv. L. Rev. 531 (2005). For a glimpse at the evolving answers that courts offer to these questions, see the web extension for this chapter at *http://www.crimpro.com/ extension/ch07.*

2. Statutory Wiretapping Procedures

Congress took up the Supreme Court's invitation in the *Olmstead* opinion to regulate wiretapping by statute. Indeed, Congress followed the specific recommendation in Chief Justice William Howard Taft's opinion that wiretap evidence be made inadmissible in federal court. Section 605 of the Federal Communications Act of 1934 stated that no person "shall intercept any communication *and* divulge or publish" that communication to any other person, unless the sender authorizes the interception. This ban on divulging wiretap information barred the use in federal court of most intercepted telephone conversations of criminal defendants. Because Congress focused on the admissibility of the evidence and not on its collection, federal agents continued to use wiretaps in investigations. Where the evidence could be used in state prosecutions, federal agents would provide it to the state under what was known as the "silver platter" doctrine (because the federal agents could offer the tainted evidence to the state prosecutors "on a silver platter").

The 1934 statutory limits on federal law enforcement changed when the United States Congress enacted Title III of the Omnibus Crime Control and Safe Streets Act of 1968, which established procedures for authorized wiretapping. The provisions in Title III reflected not only the new constitutional emphasis on privacy in *Katz*, but the specific concerns that led the United States Supreme Court in 1967—the same year as *Katz*—to reject New York's wiretap statute in Berger v. New York, 388 U.S. 41 (1967). For a discussion of the *Berger* opinion and the guidance it offered for creators of the federal wiretapping statute, see the web extension for this chapter at *http://www.crimpro.com/extension/ch07.*

Wiretap statutes treat government searches through electronic surveillance differently from other searches. First, the wiretap statutes decide for all cases the question debated as a matter of Fourth Amendment interpretation in *Olmstead* and *Katz*: They declare that wiretaps are searches. Second, Congress and the state legislatures have left little room for the many varieties of exigent circumstances that government agents rely on every day to conduct warrantless searches: If agents want to use wiretaps, they must seek a warrant.

The federal and state statutes do not cover every "intercepted communication." First, most statutes exclude from the wiretap warrant process conversations that are recorded with the consent of one of the parties. Second, the statutes do not apply to all kinds of communications, though the coverage of wiretap statutes has expanded well beyond traditional taps such as those seen in *Olmstead* and *Katz*. The federal wiretap statute originally applied to communications transmitted over a wire, but now it protects wire, oral, and electronic communications, as do most of the state statutes. A wire communication includes any transfer of the human voice by means of a wire, cable, or other connection between the sender and the recipient. See 18 U.S.C. §§2510(4), (18). Electronic communications include those not carried by sound waves, such as electronic mail, video teleconferences, and other data transfers. 18 U.S.C. §2510 (12). Under the federal statute, an "interception" of one of these types of communications occurs when a person uses "any electronic, mechanical, or other device" to make an "aural acquisition" of the "contents" of the communication. How well do these statutory definitions account for future technological changes in communications?

Third, the statutes may not apply to recording of conversations outside the governing jurisdiction or in another country. This question often arises when

prosecutors wish to introduce conversations between a party in a different jurisdiction and a second party in the prosecutors' jurisdiction. Should a state statute
control law enforcement efforts to intercept calls placed to or from another state?
Between two other states? The following two statutes illustrate common features of
wiretap statutes.

■ 18 U.S.C. §2511

(1) Except as otherwise specifically provided in this chapter any person who —
    (a) intentionally intercepts, endeavors to intercept, or procures any other
person to intercept or endeavor to intercept, any wire, oral, or electronic communication; . . .
    (c) intentionally discloses, or endeavors to disclose, to any other person the
contents of any wire, oral, or electronic communication, knowing or having reason to know that the information was obtained through the interception of a
wire, oral, or electronic communication in violation of this subsection;
    (d) intentionally uses, or endeavors to use, the contents of any wire, oral,
or electronic communication, knowing or having reason to know that the information was obtained through the interception of a wire, oral, or electronic communication in violation of this subsection; . . . shall be punished as provided
[elsewhere in this statute] or shall be subject to suit. . . .
    (2) (c) It shall not be unlawful under this chapter for a person acting under
color of law to intercept a wire, oral, or electronic communication, where such person is a party to the communication or one of the parties to the communication has
given prior consent to such interception.
    (d) It shall not be unlawful under this chapter for a person not acting
under color of law to intercept a wire, oral, or electronic communication where
such person is a party to the communication or where one of the parties to
the communication has given prior consent to such interception unless such
communication is intercepted for the purpose of committing any criminal or
tortious act in violation of the Constitution or laws of the United States or of
any State.

■ NEW JERSEY STATUTES §2A:156A-4

It shall not be unlawful under this act for . . .
    b. Any investigative or law enforcement officer to intercept a wire, electronic
or oral communication, where such officer is a party to the communication or
where another officer who is a party to the communication requests or requires
him to make such interception;
    c. Any person acting at the direction of an investigative or law enforcement
officer to intercept a wire, electronic or oral communication, where such person
is a party to the communication or one of the parties to the communication has
given prior consent to such interception; provided, however, that no such interception shall be made without the prior approval of the Attorney General or his
designee or a county prosecutor or his designee. . . .

Problem 7-5. Minimization

The Harford County Narcotics Task Force and Baltimore County authorities jointly investigated Carl Briscoe for suspected cocaine distribution. Along the way, the investigators began to suspect that Roland Mazzone, who lived in Baltimore County, was involved in the distribution ring. On June 19, the State's Attorney for Baltimore County filed ex parte applications with the circuit court to intercept and record conversations on two telephones (one at Mazzone's home, the other at his business, the Valley View Inn) from June 20 to July 20. A circuit court judge approved the applications and, on June 19, signed orders authorizing the interceptions. The orders authorized the wiretaps and placed certain conditions on the operation of the wiretap, including a statement in the orders that the interceptions be conducted "in such a way as to minimize the interception of communications not otherwise subject to interception under Title III or the Maryland wiretap provisions."

At the time the orders were signed, the court also approved written "minimization guidelines," formulated by the State's Attorney. The guidelines included a section on privileged communications:

> Under Maryland Law, we will be concerned with privileged communications involving lawyer-client, husband-wife, priest-penitent, accountant-client and psychologist-patient relationship. Contact the above listed Assistant State's Attorneys for Baltimore County for instructions if you anticipate that you are about to monitor such a conversation and cannot affirmatively decide to minimize it completely. If it appears that the communication does discuss the commission of a designated crime itself, the privilege is breached and the whole conversation is to be monitored. If it appears that the communication might discuss the commission of a designated crime then spot monitoring shall be employed. If the communication does not involve the commission of a crime then the privilege applies absolutely and must be completely minimized as soon as the speakers identify themselves. All husband and wife communications are privileged; but discussions which involve the commission of the designated crime may be intercepted. All other communications must be minimized and spot monitoring must be employed carefully.

On July 12, after the State's Attorney filed further ex parte applications, the court issued new orders to continue the interceptions for an additional 30 days. The court approved a new set of written minimization guidelines, prepared by the State's Attorney, which stated that the minimization guidelines approved on June 19 "will also apply to the operational procedures" authorized on July 12, except for the following changes:

> Information garnered from the wiretaps conducted over Roland Mazzone's residence telephone as well as the business telephone of the Valley View Inn has identified Mazzone's wife, Elizabeth Ann, as being involved in this illegal controlled dangerous substance operation. Thus the privilege that is afforded to them under Maryland Law as husband and wife is breached during the interception of conversations that pertain to Mazzone's illegal drug activity.

During the investigation, the investigating officers learned that David Vita was Mazzone's supplier. Specifically, the officers collected evidence that on June 30, Mazzone paid Vita $14,000 and received from Vita a kilo of cocaine. Agents recorded dozens of phone calls between Roland and Elizabeth. Two provided incriminating evidence. In the first conversation, Roland called Elizabeth and she told him that he should not "come home empty-handed," meaning that he should bring some cocaine home with him. In the second conversation, Elizabeth called Roland at his business to inform him that Vita had arrived at their house.

Before trial, Mazzone moved to suppress all communications intercepted pursuant to the wiretap orders. He argued that the wiretap orders were illegal because the minimization guidelines misstated Maryland law on the marital communication privilege and therefore illegally authorized interception of privileged communications. The marital communications privilege is codified at section 9-105. It provides that "one spouse is not competent to disclose any confidential communication between the spouses occurring during their marriage." As Mazzone suggests, Maryland courts have indeed interpreted the marital communications privilege to apply even when the communication furthers a crime.

As the trial judge in this case, you must rule on Mazzone's motion to suppress. Section 10-408(i) of the state wiretap law permits suppression of "any intercepted wire, oral, or electronic communication, or evidence derived therefrom" when "the interception was not made in conformity with the order of authorization."

When evaluating the validity of a wiretap order, Maryland courts distinguish between "preconditions" and "post conditions." Preconditions include the actions that investigators must take before a judge may issue an ex parte wiretap order and the inclusion of certain provisions required to be in the wiretap order. One such precondition is the requirement in section 10-408(e)(3) that "every order and extension thereof shall contain a provision that the authorization to intercept . . . shall be conducted in such a way as to minimize the interception of communications not otherwise subject to interception under this subtitle." Maryland courts say that failure of a precondition requires suppression of all the evidence obtained under the wiretap.

Post conditions are the actions that must be taken after the judge issues a valid wiretap order, including compliance with the minimization mandate in the order. Imperfect compliance with a post condition does not require suppression of the evidence obtained under the wiretap order, so long as the level of compliance is "reasonable under the circumstances." Maryland case law designates the following ten factors to be considered in determining the reasonableness of minimization:

> (1) the nature and scope of the crime being investigated; (2) the sophistication of those under suspicion and their efforts to avoid surveillance through such devices as coded conversations; (3) the location and the operation of the subject telephone; (4) government expectation of the contents of the call; (5) the extent of judicial supervision; (6) the duration of the wiretap; (7) the purpose of the wiretap; (8) the length of the calls monitored; (9) the existence of a pattern of pertinent calls, which the monitoring agents could discern so as to eliminate the interception of non-pertinent calls; (10) the absence of monitoring of privileged conversations.

As the trial judge, how would you rule? Would you suppress all the wiretap evidence? Only the recorded calls between husband and wife? None of the statements? Compare State v. Mazzone, 648 A.2d 978 (Md. 1994).

Notes

1. *Special showing of probable cause.* The court issuing a wiretap order under the typical statute must be convinced that probable cause exists as to several facts: (a) an

individual has committed, is committing, or is about to commit a crime designated in the statute; (b) communications about that offense will be obtained through an interception; and (c) the particular facility to be monitored will be used in connection with the offense. See 18 U.S.C. §2518(3); Or. Rev. Stat. §133.724(3). How does this compare to the probable cause finding to support an ordinary search warrant?

Wiretap orders are available only to investigate crimes designated in the statute. While the federal statute includes an extensive list of federal and state crimes, some state statutes are far more selective. Most state statutes extend to violent crimes and narcotics offenses. The applicant has an incentive to list as many crimes as possible to increase the scope of the permissible interceptions that may take place.

2. *Specifying the targeted person and facility.* Wiretap statutes typically require that applications specify the identity of the person whose communications are to be intercepted, "if known." See, e.g., 18 U.S.C. §2518(1)(b)(iv). Do statutory provisions such as these mean that a person specified in the application must take part in every intercepted conversation, or can the government intercept conversations at the specified facility between two people who were not specified in the application? See United States v. Kahn, 415 U.S. 143 (1974) (approving of interception of conversation between two persons not named in application, where application mentioned "others unknown").

Wiretap statutes also require the application to describe the "nature and location" of the facility from which the communication is to be intercepted. In 1986, Congress amended the federal wiretap statute to allow applications for "roving wiretaps" and "roving oral intercepts." See 18 U.S.C. §2518(11). The USA PATRIOT Act, passed soon after the terrorist attacks of September 11, 2001, expanded the authority for roving wiretaps. More than a dozen states followed suit. See, e.g., Fla. Stat. Ann. §§934.09(10), (11). Under these provisions, the government may intercept any communication of a designated individual about a suspected crime, wherever the communication takes place. The application for a roving wiretap must specify, to a greater extent than an ordinary wiretap application, the targeted individuals. It must also set out facts demonstrating that a wiretap at a specific facility would be ineffective because the target has a purpose to thwart interception by changing facilities. Is the "roving wiretap" the equivalent of a search warrant that fails to "particularly describe" the place to be searched?

3. *Necessity requirement.* Some items included in the wiretap application are analogous to the kinds of information government agents present in typical applications for search warrants. But some of the information required for wiretaps is entirely new. One important example is the requirement in 18 U.S.C. §2518(c) that government agents describe any "other investigative procedures" that have been tried and an explanation of why those procedures failed or why they "reasonably appear" unlikely to succeed or are "likely" to be too dangerous. The provisions are designed to encourage the government to try measures other than wiretapping as the initial steps in an investigation. As the Court stated in United States v. Kahn, 415 U.S. 143 (1974), interceptions should not be permitted if "traditional investigative techniques would suffice to expose the crime." Courts often note that the "other procedures" provisions do not require the government to show that no other means would work, or that all other means have been tried and failed, but only that some reasonable effort has been made. You can find examples of state courts working in the investigative trenches of the wiretapping laws on the web extension for this chapter at *http://www.crimpro.com/extension/ch07.*

4. *Duration of wiretaps.* All wiretap statutes limit the total length of surveillance allowed. For example, 18 U.S.C. §2518(5) provides that wiretap orders should not authorize interceptions "for any period longer than is necessary to achieve the objective of the authorization, nor in any event longer than thirty days." The judge can grant extensions of a wiretap order if the government renews the application, again for no longer than 30 days. Some state statutes authorize shorter periods of time for surveillance. The average duration of a wiretap in 2016 was 44 days.

5. *Consensual intercepts: majority view.* Most state wiretap statutes follow the federal lead and do not protect interceptions of communications if at least one of the parties to the communication consents to the interception. About a dozen states require the consent of both parties before a conversation maybe recorded (absent judicial authorization). The New Jersey statute reprinted above takes the unusual position of allowing consensual interceptions only when a government agent provides the consent or directs the interception. Why did the New Jersey legislature require only executive branch review of these interceptions? Will the state attorney general or county prosecutor ever rebuff a police request to seek third-party consent to record a conversation?

6. *The statutory exclusion remedy.* If a government wiretap violates a constitutional provision, then the constitutional remedy (exclusion of the evidence) will take hold. But what if the government violates statutory limits on wiretapping that are not mandated by the Constitution? The state and federal wiretap statutes almost uniformly contain their own exclusionary remedy for at least some statutory violations. See 18 U.S.C. §2515 (designating exclusion as the remedy for unlawful interceptions of wire and oral communications but not electronic communications). In United States v. Giordano, 416 U.S. 505 (1974), the Supreme Court interpreted the federal remedial statute to apply only to violations of provisions that play "a central role in the statutory scheme." How does a court determine which statutory provisions are "central" if the statute itself does not say so? Does it depend on the number of cases in which the government is likely to violate the provision? Is the intent of the investigating officer relevant? Note that the federal statute reprinted above and most state statutes also provide for civil and criminal sanctions against individuals who intentionally violate those statutes.

7. *Minimization: majority view.* Wiretap statutes require the government to "minimize" the number of conversations "intercepted." This limitation prevents the government from listening to all conversations at a given telephone. Instead, agents must stop listening to a call if it does not fall within the coverage of the wiretap order. Reviewing courts, however, rarely invalidate a wiretap on the basis of improper minimization. In Scott v. United States, 436 U.S. 128 (1978), the Supreme Court held that the monitoring and recording of the entirety of virtually all calls received on a tapped phone over a 30-day period was reasonable under the Fourth Amendment and was not a violation of the statute. The Court noted that the extent of the criminal activity under investigation, the extent to which the phone was used for illegal purposes, and the frequent use of ambiguous language in the conversations justified the full monitoring of every call. Admittedly, the officers knew about the "minimization" requirement contained in the statute and in the judge's order and took no steps to reduce the number of conversations they intercepted. Nevertheless, the Supreme Court decided that the relevant question was not the good faith of the officers (or the lack thereof) but the "objective" reasonableness of the scope of the interceptions. If a target suspects the government is listening to her

communications, how could she take advantage of a minimization requirement in jurisdictions where it is enforced more strictly?

8. *Statutes and federalism.* The language of the federal wiretap statute in Title III applies both to federal and state law enforcement officers. The supremacy clause in Article VI of the U.S. Constitution declares that federal legislation is "the supreme Law of the Land." Thus, federal legislation can create binding legal obligations on state law enforcement officials. But is the converse true? Can state statutes (for instance, those regulating wiretaps more stringently than federal law) create binding obligations on federal law enforcement officers operating within the state? Does it matter whether the evidence that the federal agents collect is presented in a state or federal prosecution? See 18 U.S.C. §2516(2).

State wiretap statutes also apply to some communication activities in other states. How important would a state wiretap statute be if it applied only to monitoring of calls between two people located within the state where the crime was committed? Consider also whether a state court might allow law enforcement agents to follow the law of a foreign jurisdiction, but insist that prosecutors within the state follow domestic law regarding wiretap evidence, such as an obligation to provide defendants with copies of the wiretap warrant. See State v. Capolongo, 647 N.E.2d 1286 (N.Y. 1995). Would the outcome change if both callers were located in the foreign country during the telephone call and discussed a crime that had occurred in the state?

9. *Statutory procedure.* Congress and state legislatures have taken an active hand in criminal procedure questions. Hardly a legislative session goes by without the passage of some new statute affecting the investigation and prosecution of crime. Wiretap statutes were one of the earliest and most prominent examples of "statutory procedure": an area in which legislatures take the leading role in setting the legal limits on practices in the field.

Legislatures have considerably greater flexibility than courts to fashion procedural rules. Legislatures can, for example, create new institutions or allocate funds to support new procedures. Are there characteristics of new technologies that make them especially strong candidates for legislative procedure?

Are courts interpreting a wiretap statute more likely to be guided more by their own judicial view of prudent legal controls on government investigations, and consider themselves less obliged to carry out the expressed views of legislators who voted for the bill? In other words, does a constitutional aura around a statute increase the judiciary's interpretive powers?

10. *National security warrants.* To explore the related area of national security wiretaps and warrants, go to the web extension at *http://www.crimpro.com/extension/ch07*. An important question is how closely related national security warrants issued by the special Foreign Intelligence Surveillance Court (FISC) are to domestic statutory regulation. At what point do approvals for wiretaps over time and space become virtual writs of assistance and general warrants that were the very reason for enacting the Fourth Amendment? Should procedures and searches in the national security realm have any impact on domestic search and seizure law? Does the response to national security and terrorism operate in a different constitutional realm? *Inter arma enim silent leges* ("In times of war, the laws fall silent")? See William H. Rehnquist, All the Laws But One—Civil Liberties in Wartime (1998). Given the special nature of national security wiretaps and investigations, what institution is best situated to regulate the special needs of national security, and national security review?

As a way to interest you in the web extension, consider the following information provided by the Electronic Privacy Information Center (EPIC) on the number of FISC requests, modifications, denials, and warrants issued.

Year	# Applications Submitted	# Modified	# Denied
1979–1999	12,082		0
2001	932	2	0
2003	1,727	79	4
2005	2,074	61	0
2007	2,371	86	4
2009	1,329	14	2
2011	1,676	30	0
2013	1,588	34	0
2015	1,457	80	5
2017	1,372	310	34

11. *Statutes governing pen registers.* In Smith v. Maryland, 442 U.S. 735 (1979), the Supreme Court held that the FBI's installation of a pen register, which records the phone numbers dialed from a residence, does not constitute a Fourth Amendment search. (In the more recent decision in Carpenter v. United States, 138 S. Ct. 2206 (2018), the Court expressly stated that it stands by *Smith*'s holding that pen registers are not a search. The Court explained that there is "a world of difference between the limited types of personal information addressed in *Smith* and *Miller* and the exhaustive chronicle of location information casually collected by wireless carriers today").

Concerned about the privacy interests implicated by pen registers, however, in 1986, Congress enacted the Pen Register Act (as part of the broader Electronic Communications Privacy Act), requiring government agents to obtain a court order before installing a pen register. To obtain such an order, the agents must certify "that the information likely to be obtained is relevant to an ongoing criminal investigation." 18 U.S.C. §3122(b).

Unlike the U.S. Supreme Court, most state supreme courts have concluded that use of a pen register is a "search" within the meaning of the constitution. The cases also conclude that it is a search for the government to compel a telephone company to provide access to *existing* records, as opposed to the creation of new records, which takes place with a pen register. But see Saldana v. State, 846 P.2d 604 (Wyo. 1993) (no violation of state constitution to subpoena toll records for unlisted number).

Yet state statutes often authorize the use of a pen register after obtaining a court order, based on a showing that the pen register is "likely" to produce information that is "material" or "relevant" to a criminal investigation. See Fla. Stat. §934.33. Are statutes such as these consistent with the conclusion of many state courts that using a pen register is a constitutionally regulated "search"? These statutes also compel the telephone company to cooperate with the government in placing an authorized pen-register device on a telephone. Would telephone companies oppose the passage of a pen-register statute?

Problem 7-6. Number, Please

Officers of the Texas Department of Public Safety were involved in an extensive investigation of a suspected drug ring operating in Lubbock County. The investigation centered on Damon Richardson, who was in the Lubbock County Jail awaiting trial for capital murder, and several other individuals living at the Seven Acres Lodge, a motel in Lubbock. Despite Richardson's incarceration, officers had a hunch that he was controlling a cocaine and crack distribution organization using the telephones located in the county jail, by placing calls to a private telephone located at the Seven Acres Lodge.

On March 30, in accordance with the provisions of a state statute, Article 18.21, the officers obtained a court order authorizing the installation of a pen register to catalogue the telephone numbers dialed from 555-4729, a telephone at the Seven Acres Lodge. The officers then combined this information with other information outlined in a 56-page affidavit signed by Officer J.A. Randall, and on April 13, received a court order authorizing the wiretapping and recording of communications on the same telephone line. The wiretap intercepted numerous incriminating telephone conversations involving Richardson and other targeted suspects.

Prior to trial, Richardson moved to suppress the evidentiary fruit of the pen register, arguing that the use of this device was a search under Article I, section 9 of the Texas Constitution which is similar but not identical to the Fourth Amendment to the U.S. Constitution. Assuming that the officers did not have any probable cause or reasonable suspicion to support their use of the pen register, how do you predict the trial court would rule on a federal constitutional claim? A state constitutional claim? Cf. Richardson v. State, 865 S.W.2d 944 (Tex. Crim. App. 1993) (en banc).

3. Bugs on Agents

Katz firmly established that a search occurs when a government agent plants an electronic bug in a flower vase and leaves the vase in a person's home. But what if a government agent attaches the bug to a flower, places the flower in his lapel, and then converses with a suspect? Which should be the determinative fact—that a conversation is taking place between two people (one of whom could be an agent or could choose to recount that conversation to authorities) or that electronic devices are recording the conversation?

■ STATE v. MICHAEL THADDEUS GOETZ
191 P.3d 489 (Mont. 2008)

GRAY, C.J.:

. . . ¶5 On May 19, 2004, Matt Collar, a detective with the Missouri River Drug Task Force, made contact with Suzanne Trusler, who previously had agreed to act as a confidential informant for the Task Force. Trusler informed Collar she had arranged to purchase a gram of methamphetamine from Goetz. Trusler then met with Collar and Detective Travis Swandal and allowed them to outfit her with a body wire receiving device. The detectives did not seek or obtain a search warrant authorizing use of the body wire. Collar gave Trusler $200 with which to purchase the drug. Trusler then went to Goetz's residence and purchased methamphetamine from him. The conversation between Goetz and Trusler during the drug transaction was monitored and recorded by the detectives via Trusler's body wire. Goetz was unaware of, and did not consent to, the electronic monitoring and recording of his conversation with Trusler.

¶6 The State of Montana subsequently charged Goetz by information with the offense of felony criminal distribution of dangerous drugs. : . . . Goetz moved the District Court to suppress the evidence derived from the electronic monitoring and recording of the conversation on the basis that it violated his rights to privacy and to be free from unreasonable searches and seizures as guaranteed by Article II, Sections 10 and 11 of the Montana Constitution. The District Court held a hearing and subsequently denied the motion to suppress. [The court consolidated this appeal with a similar one by defendant Hamper.]

¶13 . . . The Defendants do not dispute that, pursuant to United States Supreme Court jurisprudence, warrantless electronic monitoring of face-to-face conversations, with the consent of one party to the conversation, does not constitute a search and, therefore, does not violate the Fourth Amendment. See, e.g., United States v. White, 401 U.S. 745 (1971). They assert, however, that Article II, Sections 10 and 11 of the Montana Constitution afford citizens a greater right to privacy which, in turn, provides broader protection than the Fourth Amendment in situations involving searches and seizures occurring in private settings. . . .

II. Analysis Under Current Montana Constitutional Search and Seizure and Right to Privacy Jurisprudence . . .

¶27 We determine whether a state action constitutes an "unreasonable" or "unlawful" search or seizure in violation of the Montana Constitution by analyzing three factors: 1) whether the person challenging the state's action has an actual subjective expectation of privacy; 2) whether society is willing to recognize that subjective expectation as objectively reasonable; and 3) the nature of the state's intrusion. The first two factors are considered in determining whether a search or seizure occurred, thus triggering the protections of Article II, Sections 10 and 11. . . . Under the third factor, we determine whether the state action complained of violated the Article II, Section 10 and 11 protections because it was not justified by a compelling state interest or was undertaken without procedural safeguards such as a properly issued search warrant or other special circumstances. . . .

A. Did the Defendants Have an Actual Subjective Expectation of Privacy? . . .

¶29 . . . What a person knowingly exposes to the public is not protected, but what an individual seeks to preserve as private, even in an area accessible to the public, may be constitutionally protected. Indeed, in Montana, . . .

> when a person takes precautions to place items behind or underneath seats, in trunks or glove boxes, or uses other methods of ensuring that those items may not be accessed and viewed without permission, there is no obvious reason to believe that any privacy interest with regard to those items has been surrendered simply because those items happen to be in an automobile.

State v. Elison, 14 P.3d 456 (Mont. 2000). While *Elison* involved physical items stowed within a vehicle, the same rationale applies to a conversation with another person in a vehicle which cannot be overheard by the public outside the vehicle. Thus, where a person has gone to considerable trouble to keep activities and property away from prying eyes, the person evinces a subjective expectation of privacy in those activities and that property. . . .

¶30 Here, the face-to-face conversations between the Defendants and one other individual were within the Defendants' private homes and, in Hamper's case, in the confines of a vehicle. . . . We conclude the Defendants exhibited actual subjective expectations of privacy in the face-to-face conversations they held in private settings.

B. Is Society Willing to Recognize the Defendants' Expectations of Privacy as Reasonable?

. . . ¶33 We have on prior occasions quoted extensively from—and discussed the debates of—the delegates to the constitutional convention with regard to the inclusion of the right to privacy in the 1972 Montana Constitution. Delegate Campbell stated that the Bill of Rights committee "felt very strongly that the people of Montana should be protected as much as possible against eavesdropping, electronic surveillance, and such type of activities. [We] found that the citizens of Montana were very suspicious of such type of activity." Delegate Dahood reported even more strongly: "It is inconceivable to any of us that there would ever exist a situation in the State of Montana where electronic surveillance could be justified. [Within] the area of the State of Montana, we cannot conceive of a situation where we could ever permit electronic surveillance." Thus, the Constitutional Convention delegates were aware of the great value Montana citizens place on the right to privacy and the clear risk to that privacy engendered by the existence and advancement of electronic technology as used by law enforcement. . . .

¶35 The express statements of the delegates to the 1972 Montana Constitutional Convention regarding the government's use of electronic surveillance against Montana's citizens provide direct support for a conclusion that society is willing to recognize as reasonable the expectation that conversations held in a private setting are not surreptitiously being electronically monitored and recorded by government agents. We are convinced that Montanans continue to cherish the privacy guaranteed them by Montana's Constitution. Thus, while we recognize that Montanans are willing to risk that a person with whom they are conversing in their home or other private setting may repeat that conversation to a third person, we are firmly persuaded that they are unwilling to accept as reasonable that the same conversation is being electronically monitored and recorded by government agents without their knowledge.

¶36 Nor should the underlying purpose or content of the conversations at issue reflect upon society's willingness to accept a subjective expectation of privacy in those conversations as reasonable. [All] of us discuss topics and use expressions with one person that we would not undertake with another and that we would never broadcast to a crowd. Few of us would ever speak freely if we knew that all our words were being captured by machines for later release before an unknown and potentially hostile audience. No one talks to a recorder as he talks to a person. . . .

It is, of course, easy to say that one engaged in an illegal activity has no right to complain if his conversations are broadcast or recorded. If, however, law enforcement officials may lawfully cause participants secretly to record and transcribe private conversations, nothing prevents monitoring of those persons not engaged in illegal activity, who have incurred displeasure, have not conformed or have espoused unpopular causes.

¶37 Based on the foregoing, we conclude each Defendant's expectation of privacy in the conversations at issue here is one society is willing to accept as reasonable. . . . Thus, we further conclude that the electronic monitoring and recording of the Defendants' in-person conversations constituted searches within the contemplation of the Article II, Sections 10 and 11 rights to privacy and to be free from unreasonable searches.

C. Nature of the State's Intrusion . . .

¶39 [The] Article II, Section 10 right to privacy is not absolute, but may be infringed upon a showing of a compelling state interest to do so. Even upon the showing of a compelling state interest, however, state action which infringes upon an individual's privacy right must be closely tailored to effectuate that compelling interest. Thus, the State may not invade an individual's privacy unless the procedural safeguards attached to the right to be free from unreasonable searches and seizures are met.

¶40 . . . Where, as here, a warrantless search has been conducted, the State bears the burden of establishing that an exception to the warrant requirement justifies the search. The State advances alternative arguments in this regard and we address them in turn.

1. Consent

¶41 The State first argues that the warrantless searches at issue here were authorized by the confidential informants' consent to the monitoring and recording of the conversations. . . .

¶42 . . . While we interpret Montana's Constitution to provide greater protections for individuals in the context of search and seizure issues than does the Fourth Amendment to the United States Constitution, we use some federal Fourth Amendment analysis in addressing issues under the Montana Constitution. In that regard, we observe that the Supreme Court recently refined the third-party consent exception in Georgia v. Randolph, 547 U.S. 103 (2006).

¶43 In *Randolph*, the defendant's wife contacted law enforcement regarding a domestic dispute she had with Randolph. The wife informed the officers upon their arrival that Randolph was a drug user and items of drug use were located in the house. Randolph, who was present in the house at the time, denied his wife's allegations and unequivocally refused the officers' request for his consent to search the house. The officers then obtained the wife's consent to search. During the search, the officers observed and seized evidence of drug use. Upon being charged with possession of cocaine, Randolph moved to suppress the evidence on the basis that his wife's consent, given over his express refusal to consent, rendered the searches unlawful. . . .

¶44 The United States Supreme Court . . . held that "a warrantless search of a shared dwelling for evidence over the express refusal of consent by a physically present resident cannot be justified as reasonable as to him on the basis of consent given to the police by another resident."

¶45 . . . Under the *Randolph* rationale . . . the confidential informants' consent to the electronic monitoring and recording of the conversations could not override any objection expressed by the Defendants. Furthermore, because both parties to the conversations were present at the time the searches were conducted, both parties must have the opportunity to object to the search. As the Supreme Court observed, law enforcement may not avoid a refusal of consent by removing a potentially objecting individual from the premises prior to requesting consent. . . .

¶46 Similarly, here, the State cannot justify a search under the consent exception as a result of the simple expedient of failing to inform the potential — and physically present — objecting party that the search is being conducted. We conclude that the warrantless searches of the conversations at issue here cannot be justified by the consent exception to the warrant requirement.

2. Particularized Suspicion Standard

¶47 Alternatively, the State contends that [the] intrusion into the Defendants' privacy expectations by the electronic monitoring and recording of their conversations was minimal and, therefore, did not rise to a level of requiring probable cause.

¶48 [Throughout] this country, but especially in Montana, . . . a person's residence and his homestead are secure from unwarranted government intrusion, be it by physical or technological means. In two of the searches at issue here, the State intruded into the sanctity of the Defendants' homes for the purpose of performing those searches by technological means. We will not countenance such an intrusion under a lesser standard than probable cause.

¶49 We turn, then, to the State's argument that the particularized suspicion standard should apply to the search of the conversation between Hamper and the confidential informant which took place in the confidential informant's vehicle. . . .

¶52 [We have held that] the dog sniff of the exterior of a vehicle constituted a search, but that such a search may be justified by particularized suspicion of wrongdoing, rather than probable cause sufficient for issuance of a search warrant. State v. Tackitt, 67 P.3d 295 (Mont. 2003). Here, the State asserts that, because the electronic monitoring and recording of a conversation is even less intrusive than a dog sniff, particularized suspicion is a sufficient standard here. We disagree.

¶53 In *Tackitt*, law enforcement officers used a drug-detecting canine to sniff the exterior of the defendant's vehicle parked outside his residence and the canine alerted on the trunk of the vehicle, indicating the presence of drugs. [We] determined that, although warrantless searches generally are *per se* unreasonable, the purpose and minimally intrusive nature of such a canine sniff warranted an exception to the warrant requirement, but would "still require particularized suspicion when the area or object subject to the canine sniff is already exposed to the public." Here, however, the private face-to-face conversation in the vehicle was not exposed to the public. Consequently, we decline to adopt a particularized suspicion standard to justify the warrantless electronic monitoring and recording of a one-on-one conversation occurring in a vehicle. . . .

¶54 For the above-stated reasons, we hold that the electronic monitoring and recording of the Defendants' conversations with the confidential informants, notwithstanding the consent of the confidential informants, constituted searches subject to the warrant requirement of Article II, Section 11 of the Montana Constitution. The electronic monitoring and recording of those conversations without a warrant or the existence of an established exception to the warrant requirement violated the Defendants' rights under Article II, Sections 10 and 11. . . .

LEAPHART, J., specially concurring.

¶56 I specially concur in the court's conclusion that evidence obtained through warrantless, consensual participant recording of a conversation in a home or automobile is not admissible in court. Although the court ties its rationale to the private settings (home and automobile) involved in these cases, I would not limit a Montana citizen's reasonable expectation of conversational privacy to "private settings."

¶57 In my view, Montanans do not have to anticipate that a conversation, no matter what the setting, is being secretly recorded by agents of the state acting without benefit of a search warrant. As Justice Harlan noted in his dissent in United States v. White, 401 U.S. 745, 777 (1971), "it is one thing to subject the average citizen to the risk that participants in a conversation with him will subsequently divulge its contents to another, but quite a different matter to foist upon him the risk that unknown third parties may be simultaneously listening in." . . .

¶58 Article II, Section 11, like the Fourth Amendment, protects people not places. . . . Although an individual's expectation of privacy may be more compelling in one setting (e.g., a home) than another, that is not to say that an individual conversing in a more public setting has no expectation of privacy and must reasonably anticipate the risk of warrantless consensual monitoring. As Justice Harlan observed in *White*, warrantless consensual monitoring undermines "that confidence and sense of security in dealing with one another that is characteristic of individual relationships between citizens in a free society." A "free society" is precisely what Article 10, Section 10, was designed to foster. . . .

¶61 . . . There is a theme throughout the dissent that someone who chooses to engage in discourse about criminal endeavors has no expectation of privacy. The examples and rationales cited are all circuitous in that they assume the "risky" or illegal "nature" of the conversation in question. An officer does not know that a call is obscene or that the conversation relates to a drug sale until after the officer listens in or hears the tape of the conversation. If the officer does have prior reason to believe that an individual has already engaged in obscene calling or drug sales, then the officer has probable cause to obtain a warrant. . . .

RICE, J., dissenting. . . .

¶79 . . . The Court's error springs from an incorrect analytical approach to the issue, resulting in an unnecessarily broad and sweeping decision not predicated on the specific facts of this case. . . .

¶88 The facts of this case do not involve the exercise of "complete discretion" by police to wire someone "just to snoop" or to gather information that might be used or not used at all. The facts here do not involve situations where police did not have particularized suspicion and probable cause. Even before wiring the informants, police had probable cause to believe that both defendants had already committed the crime of criminal distribution of dangerous drugs. Authority to wire aside, the police could have *arrested* the defendants because they had already committed a crime. . . .

¶91 This was a commercial transaction. . . . As in the typical commercial transaction, the sellers here offered their product to members of the public — they intentionally exposed and sold their product to customers who were non-confidants. The length of each transaction is reflective of its impersonal and commercial nature as each lasted only moments — similar to other retail purchases. These meetings were not social occasions between friends or family. . . . Thus, in these transactions, the defendants first "knowingly exposed" their business by offering to sell and then

B. Wiretapping

453

exposed their product during the actual exchange to someone who was not a confidant to them.

¶93 The place of the transaction is also a relevant fact, though not necessarily determinative. Goetz invited Trusler, described by the District Court as a "mere visitor," into his home on Main Street and there conducted the brief sales transaction. Hamper met Ms. White first in a parking lot on Main Street, where he got into *her* car for the brief conversation and sale. . . .

¶96 The public and commercial nature of the criminal enterprise at issue here— the sale of illegal drugs to strangers—separates this case from other kinds of crimes, even drug-related, and further illustrates the necessity of a close factual analysis. For instance, a person joining others at a friend's house to smoke pot, though an illegal act, would have a different privacy expectation than a person who undertakes the risk of meeting with a member of the public to consummate a drug transaction. . . .

¶97 Consistent with its approach of over-generalizing, the Court attempts to summarize the statements of the delegates to the 1972 Montana Constitutional Convention in a manner which appears to provide support for its holding. . . . However, the Court considers only some of the delegates' words, and ignores other specifically applicable words altogether, thereby covering up the reality that the delegates' primary concern was over electronic surveillance and eavesdropping undertaken by the government *without the consent of any party.* [The delegates addressed the factual scenario at issue here. As Delegate Campbell put it:]

> I feel that with "oral communications" you are not excluding the legitimate law enforcement people, who, with the consent of one party, the person who is being threatened by phone calls and things like this, to act on behalf of the victim. The privacy of that individual certainly could be waived with his or her consent, and there's certainly no privacy toward the obscene caller. . . .

¶99 [The] Court appears to distinguish between the risk that a conversation will be repeated and the risk that the same conversation will be consensually electronically monitored by government agents. However, if this is the Court's distinction, it is without a constitutional difference because society would not consider a privacy interest in a non-private commercial drug transaction to be reasonable. Indeed, our constitutional convention delegates did not, and neither did some of the greatest legal minds of our time. . . . Accordingly, I would join them and conclude that no "search" took place.

¶100 However, even assuming *arguendo* that a search did occur, the Court's analysis of the "nature of the State's intrusion" again further ignores the facts of the present case and mischaracterizes the role of consent in our search and seizure jurisprudence. . . .

¶101 . . . The *Randolph* situation cannot fairly be likened to the instant case. [A] conversation, unlike a home, is not a shared space. Once the conversation commences, it becomes the individual property of each participant. Neither participant can prevent the other (absent privilege) from sharing or repeating the conversation because each has full control over it. A conversation is not the same as a dwelling space and, accordingly, consent of both conversationalists is not required in order to monitor the conversation. . . .

¶105 [There are other pertinent details about the nature of the state's intrusion here.] First and foremost, the recording did not produce any evidence beyond what the informant herself could have relayed. . . . The facts clearly distinguish the monitoring here from the "sense enhancing" technologies [that] could be used to surreptitiously monitor the heat signatures generated by activities conducted within the confines of Montanans' private homes and enclosed structures for the purpose of drawing inferences about the legality of such activities.

¶108 [What is the likely impact of this intrusion] on the individual's sense of security? . . . As Goetz stated while selling drugs to Trusler: "[The] real deal is with this sh__, they are all over. The Feds are f___ing everywhere in this town. The DTF, the FBI, there's reason to be superultra-f___ing-freaked!"

¶109 [The] impact of consensual monitoring upon the "sense of security" of people commercially marketing illegal drugs to the public in an environment of active law enforcement is, respectfully, *very* minimal. This activity is a highly risky venture, and, indeed, one engaging in it truly has good reason to be "freaked" because, consistent with Goetz's knowledge of the risk, law enforcement is engaged. . . .

¶111 Truly, it is a different world today, not only in terms of technological advances, but also in the expectation of the use of technology. I would submit . . . that our citizens, especially young people in today's society who have been raised in the age of *Law and Order* and *CSI,* would think it unusual that a drug dealer would have a *reasonable* expectation that his conversations during a drug sale to a non-confidant were not being consensually monitored. . . .

¶114 . . . Our right of privacy has been hijacked by those engaging in activities which the right was clearly not meant to protect, and has thus been devalued — becoming the new refuge of meth dealers selling to the public by means they well knew risked law enforcement involvement. The delegates to the Constitutional Convention did not countenance such a distortion of the right they found "essential to the well-being of a free society." . . .

CotTer, J., concurring . . . .

¶125 While the Dissent complains that the Court's decision is unnecessarily broad and sweeping, so too is its own reach. If the Dissent's rationale is intended to apply equally to the criminal and the law-abiding alike—which I submit, it must— then it stands for the proposition that virtually any commercial transaction may be surreptitiously recorded without a warrant and with only one party's consent, with the resulting recording being admissible in evidence against the speaker. It would, in essence, gut any expectation of privacy one might reasonably have in his commercial conversation, regardless of the lawfulness of the transaction. If, on the other hand, the analysis is intended to apply to only those transactions that are criminal in nature . . . then it runs afoul of our duty to treat all persons the same before the law, without distinction for criminal/non-criminal behavior. Respectfully, either result is unacceptable. . . .

Notes

1. *Bugs on government agents: majority position.* A substantial majority of the states take the federal position as stated in United States v. White, 401 U.S. 745 (1971). Under this reasoning, a conversation between a government agent and a suspect does not become a "search," subject to constitutional limitations, when the agent uses a device to transmit or record the conversation. State courts that reject *White*

often rely on distinctive language in a state constitution or a distinctive state constitutional history. State v. Geraw, 795 A.2d 1219 (Vt. 2002); State v. Mullens, 650 S.E.2d 169 (W. Va. 2007).

A number of state courts that originally rejected *White* have reconsidered their decision (sometimes many years later) and have embraced the federal position. See People v. Collins, 475 N.W.2d 684 (Mich. 1991) (overruling 1975 decision that had rejected *White*); Melanie Black Dubis, The Consensual Electronic Surveillance Experiment: State Courts React to *United States v. White*, 47 Vand. L. Rev. 857 (1994). If a state court has rejected the federal view on a constitutional question, does that decision remain a questionable authority for its entire life span? Is there something special about the issue of consensual electronic surveillance that made these courts willing to reconsider their earlier independent stances?

2. *Confusing bugs and people.* Is the tape recording or transmission of a conversation with a government agent a consensual search, or is it no search at all? When a recording device is on an agent, doesn't the microphone simply serve as a more accurate way to capture and re-create statements? Should the rules be different when the technological enhancement changes the listener's capacity for recollection, but not the capacity to hear the evidence in the first place?

C. GOVERNMENT ACCESS TO DATABASES

Just as technology enables government investigators to monitor a suspect's conversations, it can also enable the government to make the most of the available information by assembling small bits of scattered information into larger patterns. At other times the government collects highly identifying information—speaking digitally or literally, not in bits, but in massive bytes. Sometimes the government assembles the data itself, for purposes other than criminal law enforcement. In other situations, the target of the search might cooperate with a third party—such as a health care provider or a communications provider—to collect and store data. In Carpenter v. United States, 138 S. Ct. 2206 (2018), for example, the government collected cell phone location data from wireless carriers. Government access to such records may allow collection of a huge range of information because of the sheer quantity of data that business databases contain and the ability to search the databases.

But current data collection, storage, and analytics only hint at what is possible in terms of information gathering and use, and indeed there are countries creating vast digital archives, observation, listening, and identification capacity, often in real time. Pervasive collection of information, big data, and analytics may change not only how we prove crimes, but how we define crimes. To pick a simple example, but one that would apply to most adults, if every time you pass the speed limit a compelling record of your violation is recorded, would legislators change speeding laws?

DNA databases can be used to search for or exonerate suspects. The case below explores the trend toward the expansion of the categories of people from whom DNA is collected to be stored in government databases. As you read in Chapter 4, in Maryland v. King, 569 U.S. 435 (2013), the U.S. Supreme Court upheld a state statute that authorized the collection of DNA from people arrested for certain serious felony offenses. The Court held that both the initial collection of the DNA and the subsequent testing of the sample against existing databases were reasonable booking procedures that were justified by special law enforcement needs. But why stop at collecting DNA from those arrested for serious offenses? What about broader efforts at getting DNA samples with consent? What about DNA samples in return for various rights and privileges, such as driving? What about connecting government and private DNA databases?

DNA databases are important in their own right, but also illustrate a broader trend toward the collection, storage, retrieval, and analysis of vast amounts of identifying records and a vast range of behaviors. How should the law regulate the use of "big data" for law enforcement purposes?

■ PEOPLE v. MARK BUZA
413 P.3d 1132 (Cal. 2018)

KRUGER, J.

In 2004, California voters passed Proposition 69, known as the "DNA Fingerprint, Unsolved Crime and Innocence Protection Act" (DNA Act), to expand existing requirements for the collection of DNA identification information for law enforcement purposes. The DNA Act requires law enforcement officials to collect DNA samples, as well as fingerprints, from all persons who are arrested for, as well as those who have been convicted of, felony offenses. Penal Code, § 296.1, subd. (a)(1)(A).

Defendant Mark Buza was arrested for arson and related felonies and transported to jail. At booking, a jail official informed defendant that he was required to provide a DNA sample by swabbing the inside of his cheek. He refused. A jury later convicted him of both the arson-related felonies and the misdemeanor offense of refusing to provide a specimen required by the DNA Act. . . .

Defendant raises a number of questions about the constitutionality of the DNA Act as it applies to various classes of felony arrestees. But the question before us is a narrower one: Whether the statute's DNA collection requirement is valid as applied to an individual who, like defendant, was validly arrested on "probable cause to hold for a serious offense"—here, the felony arson charge for which defendant was ultimately convicted—and who was required to swab his cheek as part of a routine booking procedure at county jail. Under the circumstances before us, we conclude the requirement is valid under both the federal and state Constitutions, and we express no view on the constitutionality of the DNA Act as it applies to other classes of arrestees. . . .

I.

A.

For decades before the DNA Act, California law had required the collection of biological samples from individuals convicted of certain offenses. In 1983, the Legislature enacted legislation requiring certain sex offenders to provide blood and saliva samples before their release or discharge. In 1998, the Legislature enacted the "DNA and Forensic Identification Data Base and Data Bank Act," which required the collection of DNA samples from persons convicted of certain felony offenses, including certain sex offenses, homicide offenses, kidnapping, and felony assault or battery.

When the California electorate voted to pass Proposition 69 on the 2004 general election ballot, it substantially expanded the scope of DNA sampling to include individuals who are arrested for any felony offense, as well as those who have been convicted of such an offense. In People v. Robinson, 224 P.3d 55 (Cal. 2010), this court upheld the expanded DNA collection requirement as applied to persons convicted of felony offenses. The question now before us concerns the application of the DNA Act to persons who have been arrested for, but not yet convicted of, a felony offense.

In its statutory findings and declarations of purpose, Proposition 69 explained [with] respect to arrestees in particular [that the state] "has a compelling interest in the accurate identification of criminal offenders"; that "DNA testing at the earliest stages of criminal proceedings for felony offenses will help thwart criminal perpetrators from concealing their identities and thus prevent time-consuming and expensive investigations of innocent persons"; and "it is reasonable to expect qualifying offenders to provide forensic DNA samples for the limited identification purposes set forth in this chapter."

The DNA Act provides that, as of January 1, 2009, all adult felony arrestees "shall provide buccal swab samples, right thumbprints, and a full palm print impression of each hand, and any blood specimens or other biological samples required pursuant to this chapter for law enforcement identification analysis." Providing a buccal swab sample requires the arrestee to apply a swab to the inside of his or her cheek to collect the "inner cheek cells of the mouth," which contain DNA. The statute provides that these specimens, samples, and print impressions shall be collected "immediately following arrest, or during the booking . . . process or as soon as administratively practicable . . . but, in any case, prior to release on bail or pending trial or any physical release from confinement or custody." Refusal to provide any of the required specimens is punishable as a misdemeanor.

Collected DNA samples are sent to California Department of Justice's DNA Laboratory for forensic analysis. The laboratory uses the samples to create a unique DNA identification profile, using genetic loci that are known as "junk" or "noncoding" DNA, because the loci have no known association with any genetic trait, disease, or predisposition. This profile is stored in California's DNA databank. California's DNA databank is part of the Combined DNA Index System (CODIS), a nationwide database that enables law enforcement to search DNA profiles collected from federal, state, and local collection programs. DNA profiles stored by the DNA Laboratory may be accessed by law enforcement agencies. The DNA Laboratory must "store, compile, correlate, compare, maintain, and use" DNA profiles for forensic casework, for comparison with samples found at crime scenes, and for identification of missing persons.

Information obtained from an arrestee's DNA is confidential and may not be disclosed to the public. DNA samples and the biological material from which they are obtained may not be used "as a source of genetic material for testing, research, or experiments, by any person, agency, or entity seeking to find a causal link between genetics and behavior or health." . . .

The DNA Act provides that if an arrestee is cleared of charges and there is no other basis for keeping the information, the arrestee "shall have his or her DNA specimen and sample destroyed and searchable database profile expunged from the databank program." An arrestee may request expungement if he or she is released without being charged, if all qualifying charges against the arrestee are dismissed, or if the arrestee is found not guilty or factually innocent of all qualifying charges. The federal legislation establishing CODIS likewise requires participating states to "promptly expunge" the DNA profile of any person who is cleared of qualifying charges. 34 U.S.C. § 12592(d)(2)(A)....

B.

On the afternoon of January 21, 2009, a San Francisco police officer saw defendant running away from a police car that had burning tires. Police found defendant hiding nearby and searched him. Matches were found in defendant's pocket, a container of oil was found in his backpack, and a road flare and a bottle containing a liquid that smelled like gasoline were discovered in the area where he had been hiding.

Defendant was arrested and taken to county jail. There, several hours after the initial arrest, a San Francisco sheriff's deputy asked defendant to swab the inside of his cheek for purposes of providing a sample of his DNA. The deputy told defendant he was required by law to provide the sample, asked defendant to read a form that described the pertinent requirements, and warned defendant that refusing to provide a DNA sample was a misdemeanor. Defendant refused.

[Defendant was charged with felony arson, possession of combustible material or incendiary device, vandalism, and refusal to provide a DNA specimen. At trial, Buza] admitted to setting the police car on fire; he testified that while he regarded setting the fires as a justified protest against government overreach, he knew his act was regarded as illegal. Defendant also admitted to refusing to provide a DNA sample. [The jury convicted Buza of all charges and the court sentenced him to a prison term of 16 months on the arson charge, imposing concurrent sentences on the charges of possession of combustible material and misdemeanor refusal to provide a DNA specimen.]

On appeal, the Court of Appeal reversed defendant's conviction for refusing to provide a DNA sample. . . . We granted review to decide whether the collection and analysis of forensic identification DNA database samples from felony arrestees, as required by Proposition 69, violates either article I, section 13 of the California Constitution or the Fourth Amendment to the United States Constitution.

II.

. . . The question before us is whether it was unreasonable within the meaning of [the Fourth Amendment of the U.S. Constitution or Article I, section 13 of the California Constitution] to require defendant to use a cheek swab to provide a DNA sample to jail officials as part of the booking process following his arrest for arson. If so, defendant cannot be penalized for failure to comply, and his misdemeanor refusal conviction must be reversed. . . .

[The United States Supreme Court in Maryland v. King, 569 U.S. 435 (2013), upheld a DNA collection requirement against Fourth Amendment challenge. Defendant argues] that *King* should be either distinguished on its facts or rejected as a matter of state constitutional law. . . . .

B.

[The defendant highlights three features of California's DNA Act] that, in his view, distinguish this case from *King*: (1) the DNA Act applies to a broader category of arrestees than the Maryland law; (2) the DNA Act, unlike the Maryland law, authorizes both collection and testing of DNA samples before an accusatory pleading is filed in court and before a judicial determination has been made that the charges are valid; and (3) the DNA Act, unlike the Maryland law, does not provide for automatic destruction of the DNA sample if the arrestee is cleared of felony charges.

Although these differences between the California and Maryland laws may be relevant in another case involving a differently situated arrestee, this case involves a defendant who was validly arrested on probable cause to believe he had committed felony arson, and who was promptly charged with (and ultimately convicted of) that offense. In the context of the particular case before us, we conclude that none of the differences to which defendant points meaningfully alters the constitutional balance struck in *King*.

[First, Buza] observes that the Maryland law at issue in *King* authorized DNA collection only from those accused of specified serious crimes, including a category defined as "crimes of violence" under state law, whereas the DNA Act authorizes DNA collection from all felony arrestees. Defendant argues that this difference is important because the seriousness of the crime of arrest figures prominently in the high court's balancing analysis: The high court's opinion states that "the necessary predicate of a valid arrest for a serious offense is fundamental" and elsewhere uses language that suggests the court was particularly concerned with persons arrested for "violent" or "dangerous" crimes. Such a limitation makes sense, defendant contends, because such crimes are the kinds of crimes that typically yield DNA evidence.

Defendant appears to read too much into the language on which he relies. The high court identified the question before it more generally as "whether the Fourth Amendment prohibits the collection and analysis of a DNA sample from persons arrested, but not yet convicted, on felony charges." [And even if] the federal Constitution permitted states to mandate collection of DNA samples only from persons arrested for felonies classified as particularly serious or violent, defendant in this case was arrested for felony arson . . . a crime that is classified as a "serious felony" under California law. . . .

Although defendant himself was charged and convicted, we acknowledge defendant's concern about the collection of DNA samples from other individuals who are booked into custody but who ultimately will never be charged with a qualifying crime, or against whom qualifying charges will ultimately be dismissed. Voters responded to that concern by providing for a particular remedy—expungement of the DNA sample and associated records—when the suspect is cleared of qualifying charges. . . .

This brings us to defendant's final point, concerning the adequacy of the DNA Act's expungement procedures. As defendant notes, under the Maryland law at issue in *King*, an arrestee who is later exonerated is entitled to automatic destruction of his or her DNA sample and associated records. Under the DNA Act, by contrast, an exonerated arrestee ordinarily must file a written request for expungement of DNA records. Provisions of the Act can be read to suggest, moreover, that a trial court may not act on such a request before 180 days have elapsed, and the court has unreviewable discretion to grant or deny the request. . . . What is more, he argues, the provisions make it possible for the state to retain the DNA sample and associated records for an extended period of time—perhaps even indefinitely—after the prosecutor has declined to file or has dismissed charges, or after those charges have failed to yield a conviction. . . .

[The] retention of an arrestee's fingerprints, photographs, and other identifying information in law enforcement files generally has not been thought to raise constitutional concerns, even though the arrestee may later be exonerated. But the question defendant raises is whether, given the uniquely sensitive nature of DNA information, a different rule should apply here: one that calls not only for expungement, but for automatic expungement of an arrestee's DNA sample, DNA identification profile, or both after an arrest has been shown to be invalid or after an arrestee is cleared of charges, or both.

Whether the Fourth Amendment requires this added protection for the wrongly arrested or exonerated is, however, a question we must leave for another day, because defendant in this case is neither. Defendant has not been found to have been wrongly arrested; indeed, he has never challenged the validity of his arrest. Nor was he cleared of the charges that formed the basis for his arrest; he was promptly charged with that offense and was later convicted as charged. . . . In short, although the DNA Act differs in some ways from the Maryland law at issue in *King*, none of those differences affects the Fourth Amendment analysis in the specific case before us.

III.

Defendant argues . . . that even if requiring him to furnish a DNA sample as part of the booking process did not violate the Fourth Amendment, it violated the parallel prohibition on unreasonable searches and seizures in article I, section 13 of the California Constitution.

We evaluate the constitutionality of searches and seizures under our state Constitution by employing the same mode of analysis that the high court applied in *King*. That is, we determine whether the intrusion on the defendant's expectation of privacy is unreasonable by applying a general balancing test "weighing the gravity of the governmental interest or public concern served and the degree to which the [challenged government conduct] advances that concern against the intrusiveness of the interference with individual liberty."

[Although] decisions of the United States Supreme Court interpreting parallel federal text are not binding, we have said they are "entitled to respectful consideration." . . . The question is whether adequate reasons are present here to conclude, despite *King*, that California voters exceeded constitutional bounds in mandating the collection of DNA sample from an individual arrested and booked on probable cause to believe he had committed a serious offense.

Defendant argues there are several such reasons. To begin with, he argues that *King* should be rejected because its central premise is faulty. *King* concluded that DNA collection from persons arrested for serious offenses serves a legitimate governmental interest in safely and accurately processing and identifying the persons they take into custody. Defendant argues, however, that arrestee DNA information is not used to determine an arrestee's identity, but "solely for investigation of possible other crimes." . . .

In evaluating defendant's argument, we do not write on a blank slate. As noted, in People v. Robinson, 224 P.3d 55 (Cal. 2010), this court upheld against a Fourth Amendment challenge the practice of mandatory collection of DNA samples from convicted felons. This . . . court concluded that the search was reasonable because

DNA testing is, like fingerprinting, a means of identification, and "individuals in lawful custody cannot claim privacy in their identification."

Robinson, like *King*, recognized that suspects can change their names, assume a false identity using forged documents, change their hair color, have tattoos removed, have plastic surgery, and change their eye color with contact lenses. But it is impossible to alter a DNA profile. . . . A genetic code describes a person with "far greater precision than a physical description or a name." . . .

California law, like federal law, has also recognized that identification of arrestees is not an end in itself; rather, the primary purpose of identification is to facilitate the gathering of information about the arrestee contained in police records, which in turn informs decisions about how to proceed with the arrestee. . . . In this respect the use of DNA for identification is no different than matching an arrestee's face to a wanted poster of a previously unidentified suspect; or matching tattoos to known gang symbols to reveal a criminal affiliation; or matching the arrestee's fingerprints to those recovered from a crime scene. DNA testing uses a different form of identification than a name or fingerprint, but its function is the same.

[Defendant] does not dispute that it is reasonable for officers to check an arrestee's fingerprints against electronic databases of known criminals and unsolved crimes. This, he says, is because fingerprints are capable of serving a "genuine" identification purpose, while a DNA profile is not. To be sure, a DNA profile is not, at least under present technological conditions, generated immediately or nearly immediately, in the manner of fingerprints. . . .

Even if a DNA profile is not generated until weeks or months after the initial booking, the information it yields about the arrestee and his criminal history can still have an important bearing on the processing of the arrestee—whether, for example, to revisit an initial determination to release the arrestee or to impose new release conditions. Information obtained after initial booking may also influence the jailer's decision about where to house the arrestee. . . .

Defendant also argues that . . . *King* "ignored the highly sensitive nature of the genetic data contained in the collected DNA," and "did not address . . . the more significant privacy implications posed by the state's subsequent analysis and retention of the sensitive information contained in DNA." The criticism is misplaced. Contrary to defendant's characterization, the court in *King* recognized that the privacy interests at stake extended beyond the "minimally invasive" physical collection of the DNA sample by buccal swab. [The Court] explained that CODIS testing is designed to reveal nothing more about the arrestee than his or her identity, and that state law forbade the use of DNA information for nonidentification purposes. But the court acknowledged that if scientific advances or other developments mean that CODIS testing will now lead to discovery of personal medical information, a new Fourth Amendment analysis will be required.

We, too, are mindful of the heightened privacy interests in the sensitive information that can be extracted from a person's DNA. These interests implicate not only article I, section 13, but the privacy rights enjoyed by all Californians under the explicit protection of article I, section 1 of the California Constitution. But our cases have also recognized that safeguards against the wrongful use or disclosure of sensitive information may minimize the privacy intrusion when the government accesses personal information, including sensitive medical information. Here, the DNA Act makes the misuse of a DNA sample a felony, punishable by years of imprisonment and criminal fines. These strong sanctions substantially reduce the likelihood of an unjustified intrusion on the suspect's privacy. . . .

Defendant next argues that this court should reject *King* because article I, section 13, gives arrested suspects greater privacy rights than they possess under the Fourth Amendment. Defendant points to decisions of this court holding that article I, section 13 forbids officers from conducting so-called "accelerated booking searches" in the field at the time of arrest; from conducting full body searches of arrested suspects before determining whether they will be cited and released without being booked; and from conducting searches of personal effects incident to a citation or arrest for a traffic violation, absent reason to believe the effects contain weapons or contraband. In the latter cases, we rejected the rule of United States v. Robinson, 414 U.S. 218 (1973), which . . . permits "full body searches of all individuals subjected to custodial arrest," as well as their effects, "regardless of the offense, and regardless of whether the individual is ultimately to be incarcerated."

But what motivated these decisions was not principally a difference in opinion with the federal courts about the scope of legitimate privacy rights of persons subject to custodial arrest. . . . Rather, the cases on which defendant relies all turn on a different evaluation of legitimate law enforcement needs when arresting suspects in the field. . . .

The question before us, by contrast, does not concern the constitutionality of a booking search conducted immediately upon arrest, but a booking search conducted at *the time of booking*, and justified by an interest in accurate identification that applies to all persons who are taken into police custody following a valid arrest for a serious offense. Cases concluding that full booking searches are inappropriate for arrestees who will never be booked into jail are thus of limited relevance here. . . .

IV.

Our holding today is limited. The sole question before us is whether it was reasonable, under either the Fourth Amendment or article I, section 13 of the California Constitution, to require the defendant in this case to swab his cheek as part of a routine jail booking procedure following a valid arrest for felony arson. Because we conclude the requirement was reasonable as applied to defendant, we hold he is subject to the statutory penalties prescribed in Penal Code section 298.1. . . .

Liu, J., dissenting.

According to today's opinion, the "sole question before us is whether it was reasonable, under either the Fourth Amendment or article I, section 13 of the California Constitution, to require the defendant in this case to swab his cheek as part of a routine jail booking procedure *following a valid arrest for felony arson*." This statement of the issue is misleading.

The DNA Fingerprint, Unsolved Crime and Innocence Protection Act (DNA Act) requires collection of DNA from all adult felony arrestees "immediately following arrest" and requires samples to be "forwarded immediately" to the laboratory for analysis. Buza was arrested on January 21, 2009. At booking a few hours later, a police officer requested a cheek swab from Buza under penalty of law. Buza refused. It was not until the next day, January 22, 2009, that a judge found probable cause to believe Buza committed arson. On January 23, 2009, the district attorney filed a complaint charging Buza with arson and related offenses as well as unlawful refusal to provide a DNA specimen on January 21, 2009. The question is whether Buza can be convicted of refusing to provide his DNA at booking *prior to any judicial determination of whether he was validly arrested.* Today's opinion does not explain why the fact that Buza was found "validly arrested on probable cause to believe he had committed felony arson, and . . . was promptly charged with (and ultimately convicted of) that offense" has any bearing on whether it was lawful to require him to provide his DNA *before any of those determinations were made.*

The court says that a "valid arrest" in this context does not require a judicial determination of its validity. But this assertion, even if true, does not disturb the main premise of the question presented: *For purposes of constitutional analysis, Buza is no different than any felony arrestee who has not been charged, convicted, or found by a neutral magistrate to be lawfully detained.* This point is critical because it brings into focus the startling breadth of DNA collection and retention authorized by the statute. This is not a scheme carefully calibrated to identify felony offenders. Instead, it can be fairly described as a biological dragnet. . . .

According to the Office of the Attorney General, there are 200,000 to 300,000 felony arrests in California every year. But not all arrests end in convictions; far from it. [From] 2009 to 2016, nearly one in five felony arrests did not result in prosecution, and almost one in three—a total of 724,492 arrests—did not result in a conviction.

Each of those arrests triggered the requirement to provide a DNA sample. Yet the state has no legal basis for retaining the DNA sample or profile if no charges are filed, if the charges are dismissed, if the person is acquitted or found not guilty or factually innocent, or if the conviction is reversed and the case is dismissed, unless there is some other basis such as a prior offense that qualifies the person for inclusion in the state DNA database. . . .

The statute sets forth a process for expungement, but this process is not adequate to allay constitutional concerns. . . . The Department of Justice has sought to expedite the process by creating a "Streamlined DNA Expungement Application Form." But the reality is that few DNA samples, once collected, are ever removed. . . .

The state's retention of DNA is troubling not only because of its sheer magnitude but also because it predictably burdens certain groups. African Americans, who are 6.5 percent of California's population, made up 20.3 percent of adult felony arrestees in 2016. Non-Hispanic whites, by contrast, comprised 31.2 percent of felony arrestees but only 27.0 percent of felony arrestees released by law enforcement or the prosecuting attorney. The fact that felony arrests of African Americans disproportionately result in no charges or dropped charges means that African Americans are disproportionately represented among the thousands of DNA profiles that the state has no legal basis for retaining.

[The] court says collecting DNA from an arrestee before a judge has determined the validity of the arrest is analogous to a search incident to arrest, where a valid arrest is also essential and there is no such preapproval requirement. But a search incident to arrest is justified and limited by the immediate need to protect arresting officers and safeguard any evidence of the offense of arrest that an arrestee might conceal or destroy. DNA collection upon arrest does not serve any similarly pressing purpose. Moreover, when an arrest is later found invalid by a neutral magistrate, a search incident to the arrest is deemed unlawful, and the evidence obtained is subject to suppression. The DNA Act does not deem unlawful the collection of DNA pursuant to an arrest that is later found invalid; such DNA may be retained and used by law enforcement so long as there is no request for expungement. . . .

I have no doubt that law enforcement is aided by the collection and retention of massive numbers of DNA profiles, whether those profiles are used to confirm a person's identity, to facilitate access to criminal history or other information about a person, or to help solve unsolved crimes. But if those interests are enough to justify the collection and retention of DNA from persons who are arrested but not convicted, not charged, or not even found to be lawfully detained so long as they do not seek expungement, then it is not that far a step for the state to collect and retain DNA from law-abiding people in general, including anyone who "applies for a driver's license" or "attends a public school." Such broad-based policies would similarly aid law enforcement while having the virtue of being less discriminatory in their effects.

Indeed, the court's analogy to fingerprinting, a less invasive and less powerful technology, should give us pause. State law already requires individuals to provide a fingerprint in order to get a driver's license, to become a school teacher, to be a professional engineer, to be a practicing attorney, or to join many other occupations [California law requires] a full set of fingerprints for purposes of conducting criminal history record checks from applicants to 29 state licensing boards, including nurses, pharmacists, physicians, court reporters, funeral directors, guide dog instructors, contractors, and accountants. These requirements serve important public safety and law enforcement purposes. But if DNA matching is constitutionally justified by its unparalleled efficacy in serving the "same" identification function as fingerprinting, then it is not clear what constitutional principle stands in the way of requiring a DNA sample in every context where the law now requires a fingerprint. One need not be a diehard civil libertarian to have serious qualms about where all of this may lead. . . .

CUÉLLAR, J., dissenting.

. . . Our state Constitution provides heightened protections for the privacy rights of individuals, including arrestees. Those protections do not vanish merely because someone is arrested. An arrest itself requires probable cause—but such cause, however probable, is a far cry from a conviction. Indeed, the underlying logic of our system of criminal investigation and enforcement is grounded in the distinction between the relatively low-threshold probable cause determination and the onerous burden the government must carry to achieve a criminal conviction. The government may justify a variety of investigative activities without probable cause—from routine patrol of a particular geographic location to following up on tips or information from undercover agents. But when the Act compels the collection of a DNA sample before a determination of probable cause, the government's rationale for seeking DNA samples for all felony arrestees is not sufficiently compelling to outweigh the intrusion on an arrestee's privacy that accompanies the collection and storage of his personal genetic information. . . .

The California Constitution is not some minor codicil to the United States Constitution. . . . Our cases have described the "core value" of article I, section 1 [of the California Constitution] as protecting so-called "informational privacy," meaning the privacy interest in sensitive and confidential personal information. We have found that article I, section 1 grew out of the electorate's fears of "increased surveillance and data collection activity in contemporary society" and was intended to address the potential collection, stockpiling, and use of individuals' most personal information in an arbitrary and unjustified fashion. Article I, section 1 provides special protection for what we have deemed "autonomy," or dignitary privacy, which we have described as protecting the interest in making "personal decisions or conducting personal activities without observation, intrusion, or interference." We have found dignitary privacy to embrace a person's interest in retaining control over his or her own body and "bodily integrity." Finally, it has not escaped our attention that article I, section 1 addresses the unique harms that can occur when the government intrudes on a person's privacy. The proponents of the provision warned of the possibility of the government assembling "personal information" and referred specifically to the possibility that private information could be permanently stored in government records.

Given the nature of these concerns, the machinery of the DNA Act appears to epitomize the sort of intrusion relevant under article I, section 1. The collection of DNA—whether it is via cheek swab or any of the other collection processes the Act permits—violates the subject's bodily integrity. And the use of that sample to create and store a DNA profile gives the government long-term access to the subject's genetic code—some of the most personal information imaginable. The DNA Act's processes thus seem to fall close to the heart of article I, section 1's scope. . . .

Crime-solving through identification of [perpetrators of unsolved crimes] can certainly constitute a legitimate government interest. At issue here is not whether the government can have a legitimate interest in solving crimes, but whether such a generalized interest—without more—is sufficient to overcome the privacy rights of individuals subject to arrest. We have made clear that where the primary purpose of a search or seizure is to detect crime or gather evidence of crime, the government must ordinarily have individualized suspicion that the person to be searched has committed a specific offense for the search or seizure to be valid. Such individualized suspicion is utterly missing when the government searches all arrestees for evidence that, at some unknown time in some unknown place under unknown circumstances, they might have committed some other unidentified crime. . . .

The detection of legal wrongdoing is perhaps the preeminent justification for all policing activity, making such a generalized interest virtually always loom in the background when any law enforcement search is attempted. To allow such an interest to tip the balance and allow for, first, an intrusion into the body; second, analysis of the information seized therefrom; and, finally, potentially indefinite retention of the results (regardless of the outcome of the initial arrest that served as justification for the search), is to permit such an interest to become not only omnipresent but also omnipotent. . . .

Nor should we ignore that fingerprinting remains available to advance many of the very interests that allegedly support the DNA Act. The existence of fingerprints as a fast and accurate means to ascertain the identity of an arrestee further diminishes the state's interest in identifying individuals by their DNA. Undoubtedly there are some instances where a DNA sample may help to solve a cold case but a set of fingerprints would not. Nonetheless, just as the reasonableness of blood tests must be judged in light of the availability of the less invasive alternative of a breath test, DNA tests must be judged in light of the availability of the less invasive alternative of fingerprints—even if the alternative is not a perfect substitute. . . .

A DNA sample stored by the state contains an arrestee's entire genetic code—information that has the capacity to reveal the individual's race, biological sex, ethnic background, familial relationships, behavioral characteristics, health status, genetic diseases, predisposition to certain traits, and even the propensity to engage in violent or criminal behavior. . . . One can scarcely imagine personal information that falls more closely to the core of the "realm of guaranteed privacy" that constitutional protections against searches and seizures aim to protect. . . .

Waiting for a neutral determination of probable cause would add, at most, 48 hours to the 30 days needed on average to process a DNA sample. In view of the delays already associated with DNA processing, postponing the process until a detached and neutral magistrate has found probable cause would diminish none of the state's interests furthered by the DNA Act, since the state would be as able to "identify" arrestees after a 32-day waiting period as it would after a 30-day period. The amendment, however, would significantly cut down on the number of people whose privacy is invaded due to the analysis, storage, and comparison of their DNA samples. . . .

Notes

1. *DNA slippery slope.* Every state in the country has passed legislation to create a DNA database made up of samples from various categories of citizens, most often groups of criminal offenders or suspects. All states and the federal government require the gathering of DNA samples from persons convicted of felony offenses. More than half the states allow collection of DNA from some or all arrestees. The military obtains genetic information from every member of the armed services. Some states collect identifying information, such as fingerprints, as part of providing basic services, such as a driver's license. It may not be long until the basic elements of citizenship and commerce obligate individuals to provide a sample of their DNA. And DNA can be obtained from trace sources—trash, or even door handles. See Mary Graw Leary, Touch DNA and Chemical Analysis of Skin Trace Evidence: Protecting Privacy While Advancing Investigations, 26 Wm. & Mary Bill Rts. J. 251, 269-270 (2017).

Buza reviews the decision of the U.S. Supreme Court in Maryland v. King, 569 U.S. 435 (2013), which turned aside a constitutional challenge to Maryland's statute and was excerpted in Chapter 4. Are *King* and decisions like *Buza* steps toward a national DNA database? If so, has the long-standing debate over a national identification card or national identification system now become passé?

2. *Distinguishing collection and use of DNA.* Should courts pay more attention to the distinction between the collection and the use of DNA information? Would most people be more concerned about the invasion of privacy associated with the warrantless buccal swab, or the retention and use of the DNA information obtained? As both a policy and constitutional matter, what limits should governments place on the access and use of DNA databases? While Maryland does not allow searches for familial matches, other states do—for instance, searching a database for any samples from people who are likely to be close relatives of the person who left a DNA sample at the scene of an unsolved crime. Is this use of the DNA database for investigatory purposes wise? Constitutional?

3. *Reducing the risk of misuse of private information.* The majority opinions in *King* and in *Buza* emphasize that the harm to privacy interests from the DNA testing statutes is reduced because such testing only reveals the identity of the arrestee and state law criminalizes the use of DNA information for any other purposes. Is this a sufficient protection against the misuse of DNA information? Note that both the California and U.S. Supreme Courts further acknowledged that "if scientific advances or other developments mean that CODIS testing will now lead to discovery of personal medical information, a new Fourth Amendment analysis will be required."

4. *Cell phone review incident to arrest. Buza* and *King* addressed the question whether the government could collect DNA samples from persons arrested for certain serious offenses. Upon balancing the individual's privacy interests and state's law enforcement interests at stake, the DNA collection scheme was upheld as a reasonable feature of the booking procedure for serious crimes. Might the balancing come out differently depending on the nature of the information collected and the express limits on the use of the collected information? Consider that in Riley v. California, 134 S. Ct. 2473 (2014), the Supreme Court held that, even after a person has been lawfully arrested and has a cell phone in his possession or nearby, police may not search information on the person's cell phone without a warrant. The Court recognized that modern cell phones, even the flip phone at issue in one of the *Riley* cases, with "all they contain and all they may reveal, they hold for many Americans the privacies of life." The Court emphasized that "a cell phone search would typically expose to the government far more than the most exhaustive search of a house." The privacy interests at stake in a cell phone search were therefore very weighty. On the other hand, the government's interests in searching the phone on the spot and without a warrant were minimal as there is no risk of harm to officers from waiting to search information on phones. The Court therefore concluded that "officers must generally secure a warrant before conducting" a search of the screen or contents of a cell phone. Does it make sense that the government must obtain a warrant before searching a cell phone incident to arrest but not before obtaining and processing a DNA sample incident to booking?

5. *Private DNA databases.* Consider that DNA information is held in private, as well as government, databases. Genealogy websites like Ancestry.com and 23andMe. com are increasing in popularity. These websites help individuals who upload DNA information learn about their own ancestors and relatives. But are they also treasure troves for law enforcement authorities seeking to identify a suspect? The problem below pursues this question further. As you review the problem, consider that a recent study found that 60% of Americans of North European descent can already be identified through the DNA uploaded to genealogical databases, even if they have not personally uploaded a sample. The researchers estimate that this number will go up to 90% in five years. Yaniv Ehrlich et al., Identity Inference of Genomic Data Using Long-Range Familial Searches, Science, Oct. 11, 2018.

6. *Combinations of government-held information.* Once the government gains access to information, is any search or seizure issue involved in how the government uses the information? The U.S. Department of the Treasury runs an investigative program, known as "FinCEN," designed to make the most of the information scattered in various government files. The records that FinCEN reviews are based on reports that banks and other institutions and individuals must submit to comply with federal statutes and regulations. By using computers to combine and analyze the

information held legitimately in various government files, law enforcers can obtain a more complete picture of an individual's activities or can note trends among certain groups of people that could justify closer scrutiny. This particular program focuses on financial crimes, such as tax evasion or money laundering. Does this technique hold promise for other sorts of investigations? How might one construct an argument that the assembling of many existing bits of data about an individual, contained in different records, creates new information that should be deemed a "search" regulated by the constitution?

Most search and seizure law relates to the government's initial access to information. The FinCEN program offers an example of government *use* of information to which it has undeniable access. Is the use of information relevant to the constitutional requirement of "reasonableness"? See Harold Krent, Of Diaries and Data Banks: Use Restrictions Under the Fourth Amendment, 74 Tex. L. Rev. 49 (1995). If a legislature, or some executive policymaker, decided to place some limit on the government's use of legitimately obtained information, what sort of limit would be feasible? Should the statute or policy impose a time limit on the use of the information? Should it force the government to use the information only in the enforcement of specified laws?

7. *Nongovernmental infringement of privacy (or "private privacy").* Criminal procedure and its constitutional superstructure speak to the relationship between citizens' privacy and their government's power to invade that privacy. On the other hand, infringement of privacy rights by nongovernmental actors has historically been left to private law. Tort claims for trespass, conversion, assault, battery, libel, slander, and invasion of privacy allow private parties to recover damages, and a handful of criminal charges reinforce those privacy interests.

There are various private actors who might collect information about criminal suspects, including family members, friends, employers, teachers, or roommates. Private security firms employ a growing number of people to prevent and ferret out crime. Since traditional constitutional limits on searches and seizures do not apply to "private" searches, police and prosecutors might simply encourage private actors to conduct searches and interrogations, and then turn over their evidence to the authorities. However, courts hold private searchers to public standards when the private action is conducted "at the behest of" or "in partnership with" government authorities.

Courts uniformly assess whether there is a sufficiently close link between a private search and government agents in deciding whether evidence found or obtained from a private search should be admitted. Courts look to a variety of factors, including prior agreements between private actors and government agents that a private agent will conduct a search. The application of this loose standard, however, leads  to varying outcomes, both across and within jurisdictions. For an exploration of the wide range of issues involving "private privacy," see Chapter 2 and the web extension for this chapter at *http://www.crimpro.com/extension/ch07.*

8. *Privacy torts in partnership with criminal procedure.* Every state except Rhode Island provides a cause of action for "intentional intrusion upon the solitude or seclusion of another." Some states allow the action as part of common-law tort doctrine; in others a cause of action for invasion of privacy appears in state statutes. For instance, Nebraska Statute §20-203 provides that any "person, firm, or corporation that trespasses or intrudes upon any natural person in his or her place of solitude or seclusion, if the intrusion would be highly offensive to a reasonable person, shall be liable for invasion of privacy." Whether based in common law or statutory causes of

actions, the law of intentional intrusion on seclusion is relatively unformed. Is this an area of social interaction generally in need of greater legal regulation? If not, are there avenues other than civil tort claims to bolster a sense (and perhaps the reality) of individual privacy, and to limit invasions of privacy by private actors? Are there some actors in particular, such as firms that gather and sell information about individuals, that merit particular regulation?

More familiar than claims for physical invasion of privacy are claims that someone, often a media outlet, has published information that invades the claimant's privacy. It is important to distinguish such claims from claims that another person has reported false information or portrayed the claimant in a false light, which includes causes of action for defamation, libel, and slander.

9. *Web privacy.* Few users of the World Wide Web—a technology whose full name is already an anachronism—know how much information is conveyed when they access a website. Companies and individuals, both legitimate and shady, use the web to gain information about consumers as a group, and as individuals. The range of issues is substantial. See Daniel J. Solove, Marc Rotenberg & Paul Schwartz, Information Privacy Law (Aspen 2006); The Privacy Law Sourcebook (Marc Rotenberg ed., EPIC 2004). It is helpful to think in terms of the interests and claims that different actors might make in asserting a right to gather information, or the uses of that information, or a right to withhold information. Many websites have privacy policies; when did you last read one?

Problem 7-7. Access to Private DNA Databases

In April 2018, after year-long investigations, California detectives tracked the Golden State killer by matching a DNA sample found at one of the crime scenes to a sample in a genealogy site. Kristen V. Brown, DNA Website Had Unwitting Role in Golden State Manhunt, Bloomberg, May 29, 2018, *https://www.bloomberg. com/news/articles/2018-05-29/killer-app-dna-site-had-unwitting-role-in-golden-state-manhunt.* Consider the following hypothetical related to the Golden State killer investigation: Inspired by the success of their California counterparts, Dallas Police Department officers employed a similar method to solve cold cases. The first case the officers decided to reopen was the unsolved rape of A.B. in 1999. Police officers had collected DNA from the crime scene and decided to use it to find the perpetrator with the help of GEDmatch, the same open-source genealogy site that California investigators used to solve the Golden State killer case.

According to its website, "GEDmatch provides DNA and genealogical analysis tools for amateur and professional researchers and genealogists." Users "need to upload DNA and or genealogical . . . data to make use of the tools." The GEDmatch Privacy Policy advises users that "while the results presented on this Site are intended solely for genealogical research, we are unable to guarantee that users will not find other uses, including both current and new genealogical and non-genealogical uses. For example, some of these possible uses of Raw Data, personal information, and/or Genealogy Data by any registered user of GEDmatch include but are not limited to . . . familial searching by third parties such as law enforcement agencies to identify the perpetrator of a crime."

In May 2018, Dallas police officers went to the GEDmatch website and uploaded the DNA sample information. After searching almost 930,000 DNA profiles voluntarily uploaded by users of the website, the officers obtained over a thousand "matches" of distant relatives of the rape suspect. The closest relatives were identified by GEDmatch's algorithm as third cousins of the perpetrator. After more than a two-months-long additional investigation, which involved tracking down the third cousins and their relatives, and working with a DNA expert to determine what the DNA profile suggested about the appearance of the suspect (e.g., that he was likely to be bald and that he was likely to suffer from a unique skin condition), the Dallas Police Department detectives concluded that Dane Daniels, a Dallas resident, had raped A.B. They arrested Daniels in early August and charged him with rape.

Daniels's defense attorney moved to suppress evidence resulting from the GEDmatch inquiry, arguing that it was the product of an unreasonable search in violation of the Fourth Amendment. Was the Dallas Police Department's use of the GEDmatch website in the Daniels case a search under the Fourth Amendment? Should the state legislature regulate such investigative tactics?

VIII

■

Interrogations

Some crimes go unsolved unless the perpetrator confesses. Confessions are especially important in some violent crimes, such as murder and robbery; they are less important in possession crimes or transactional crimes (such as drug offenses or fraud), where a greater range of testimonial and physical evidence is often available. Beyond these general observations, however, it is hard to determine the exact number and types of cases in which police interrogation is necessary to solve the crime.

Many police officers are convinced that interrogations and confessions are indispensable in a broad range of cases. Field studies have confirmed that the police interrogate the great majority of all suspects in custody—roughly 80 to 90 percent of them. See Paul Cassell & Bret Hayman, Police Interrogation in the 1990s: An Empirical Study of the Effects of *Miranda*, 43 UCLA L. Rev. 839 (1996); Project, Interrogations in New Haven: The Impact of *Miranda*, 76 Yale L.J. 1519 (1967). If a suspect does provide the police with incriminating information, this has a considerable effect on the later processing of her case: people who confess to the police are more likely to be charged with a crime, less likely to have the charges against them dismissed, more likely to plead guilty, more likely to be convicted, and more likely to receive a more serious punishment. See Richard Leo, Inside the Interrogation Room, 86 J. Crim. L. & Criminology 266 (1996). Moreover, jurors consider evidence of a confession by the defendant to be among the most important types of information that a prosecutor can present. See Saul Kassin & Katherine Neumann, On the Power of Confession Evidence: An Experimental Test of the Fundamental Difference Hypothesis, 21 Law & Hum. Behav. 469 (1997).

In short, the confession of a criminal suspect can be a pivotal moment in the investigation and processing of a criminal case. For that reason, we focus your attention in this chapter on three central questions: What are the legal obligations of the police and other government agents who interrogate suspects in the hope of obtaining incriminating evidence? What remedies are available when officers violate a suspect's rights during an interrogation? How can such violations be prevented in the first place?

A. VOLUNTARINESS OF CONFESSIONS

Courts have long declared that an involuntary confession cannot be a valid source of prosecution evidence, but the factors that can demonstrate the involuntariness of the confession have shifted over the years. The following materials consider the impact of physical abuse, promises, threats, and lies on courts considering whether a confession is voluntary.

1. Physical Abuse and Deprivations

Not so long ago, police in the United States used physical violence widely when they interrogated suspects. In 1931, the National Commission on Law Observance and Enforcement (known as the Wickersham Commission) collected evidence from current and former police officers and from many observers of police interrogation practices. The Commission concluded as follows:

> The third degree—the inflicting of pain, physical or mental, to extract confessions or statements—is widespread throughout the country. Physical brutality is extensively practiced. The methods are various. They range from beating to harsher forms of torture. The commoner forms are beating with the fists or with some implement, especially the rubber hose, that inflicts pain but is not likely to leave permanent visible scars.
>
> The method most commonly employed is protracted questioning. By this we mean questioning—at times by relays of questioners—so protracted that the prisoner's energies are spent and his powers of resistance overcome. . . . Methods of intimidation adjusted to the age or mentality of the victim are frequently used alone or in combination with other practices. The threats are usually of bodily injury. They have gone to the extreme of procuring a confession at the point of a pistol or through fear of a mob. . . .
>
> In considerably over half of the States, instances of the third degree practice have occurred in the last 10 years. . . . Fifteen representative cities were visited during the last 12 months by our field investigators. In 10 of them there was no doubt as to the existence of third-degree practices at that time.

Some police officers argued that third-degree tactics were justified, for a number of reasons (again, as summarized by the Wickersham Commission):

- [The] third degree is used only against the guilty.
- [Obstacles] in the way of the police make it almost impossible to obtain convictions except by third-degree methods. [Through] intimidation, bribery, and all kinds of political connections criminals are often set free. . . . Consequently they hope to build up such a solid case on the basis of a confession that the prisoner will, in spite of all obstacles, be convicted.
- [Police] brutality is an inevitable and therefore an excusable reaction to the brutality of criminals.
- [Restrictions] on the third degree may impair the morale of the police.
- [The] existence of organized gangs in large cities renders traditional legal limitations outworn.

Five years after the Wickersham Commission report appeared, the Supreme Court issued a major ruling on the question of coerced confessions. As early as 1897, the Court had considered the validity of confessions obtained by federal law enforcement officers, concluding in Bram v. United States, 168 U.S. 532 (1897), that the Fifth Amendment's self-incrimination clause limited coercive police interrogations. However, the Fifth Amendment did not apply to the states at that point, and it was unclear whether federal law placed any limits on the use of an involuntary confession in state court.

■ ED BROWN v. MISSISSIPPI
297 U.S. 278 (1936)

HUGHES, C.J.[*]
The question in this case is whether convictions, which rest solely upon confessions shown to have been extorted by officers of the State by brutality and violence, are consistent with the due process of law required by the Fourteenth Amendment of the Constitution of the United States.

[Ed Brown, Henry Shields, and Yank Ellington] were indicted for the murder of one Raymond Stewart, whose death occurred on March 30, 1934. They were indicted on April 4, 1934, and were then arraigned and pleaded not guilty. Counsel were appointed by the court to defend them. Trial was begun the next morning and was concluded on the following day, when they were found guilty and sentenced to death.

Aside from the confessions, there was no evidence sufficient to warrant the submission of the case to the jury. [Defendants testified] that the confessions were false and had been procured by physical torture. The case went to the jury with instructions, upon the request of defendants' counsel, that if the jury had reasonable doubt as to the confessions having resulted from coercion, and that they were not true, they were not to be considered as evidence.

[The state supreme court refused to overturn the convictions on appeal.] The grounds of the decision were (1) that immunity from self-incrimination is not essential to due process of law, and (2) that the failure of the trial court to exclude the confessions after the introduction of evidence showing their incompetency, in the absence of a request for such exclusion, did not deprive the defendants of life or liberty without due process of law. . . .

That the evidence established that [the confessions] were procured by coercion was not questioned. . . . There is no dispute as to the facts upon this point and as they are clearly and adequately stated in the dissenting opinion of Judge Griffith . . .—showing both the extreme brutality of the measures to extort the confessions and the participation of the state authorities—we quote this part of his opinion in full, as follows:

> The crime with which these defendants, all ignorant negroes, are charged, was discovered about one o'clock P.M. on Friday, March 30, 1934. On that night one Dial, a deputy sheriff, accompanied by others, came to the home of Ellington, one of the

---

[*] [Justices Van Devanter, McReynolds, Brandeis, Sutherland, Butler, Stone, Roberts, and Cardozo joined in this opinion.—EDS.]

defendants, and requested him to accompany them to the house of the deceased, and there a number of white men were gathered, who began to accuse the defendant of the crime. Upon his denial they seized him, and with the participation of the deputy they hanged him by a rope to the limb of a tree, and having let him down, they hung him again, and when he was let down the second time, and he still protested his innocence, he was tied to a tree and whipped, and still declining to accede to the demands that he confess, he was finally released and he returned with some difficulty to his home, suffering intense pain and agony. The record of the testimony shows that the signs of the rope on his neck were plainly visible during the so-called trial. A day or two thereafter the said deputy, accompanied by another, returned to the home of the said defendant and arrested him, and departed with the prisoner towards the jail in an adjoining county, but went by a route which led into the State of Alabama; and while on the way, in that State, the deputy stopped and again severely whipped the defendant, declaring that he would continue the whipping until he confessed, and the defendant then agreed to confess to such a statement as the deputy would dictate, and he did so, after which he was delivered to jail.

The other two defendants, Ed Brown and Henry Shields, were also arrested and taken to the same jail. On Sunday night, April 1, 1934, the same deputy, accompanied by a number of white men, one of whom was also an officer, and by the jailer, came to the jail, and the two last named defendants were made to strip and they were laid over chairs and their backs were cut to pieces with a leather strap with buckles on it, and they were likewise made by the said deputy definitely to understand that the whipping would be continued unless and until they confessed, and not only confessed, but confessed in every matter of detail as demanded by those present; and in this manner the defendants confessed the crime, and as the whippings progressed and were repeated, they changed or adjusted their confession in all particulars of detail so as to conform to the demands of their torturers. When the confessions had been obtained in the exact form and contents as desired by the mob, they left with the parting admonition and warning that, if the defendants changed their story at any time in any respect from that last stated, the perpetrators of the outrage would administer the same or equally effective treatment. . . .

The evidence upon which the conviction was obtained was the so-called confessions. Without this evidence a peremptory instruction to find for the defendants would have been inescapable. The defendants were put on the stand, and by their testimony the facts and the details thereof as to the manner by which the confessions were extorted from them were fully developed, and it is further disclosed by the record that the same deputy. Dial, under whose guiding hand and active participation the tortures to coerce the confessions were administered, was actively in the performance of the supposed duties of a court deputy in the courthouse and in the presence of *the* prisoners during what is denominated, in complimentary terms, the trial of these defendants. This deputy was put on the stand by the state in rebuttal, and admitted the whippings. It is interesting to note that in his testimony with reference to the whipping of the defendant Ellington, and in response to the inquiry as to how severely he was whipped, the deputy stated, "Not too much for a negro; not as much as I would have done if it were left to me." Two others who had participated in these whippings were introduced and admitted it—not a single witness was introduced who denied it. . . .

I.

The State stresses the statement in Twining v. New Jersey, 211 U.S. 78 (1908), that "exemption from compulsory self-incrimination in the courts of the States is not secured by any part of the Federal Constitution." . . . But the question of the

right of the State to withdraw the privilege against self-incrimination is not here
involved. The compulsion to which the quoted statements refer is that of the processes of justice by which the accused may be called as a witness and required to
testify. Compulsion by torture to extort a confession is a different matter.

The State is free to regulate the procedure of its courts in accordance with its
own conceptions of policy, unless in so doing it "offends some principle of justice
so rooted in the traditions and conscience of our people as to be ranked as fundamental." The State may abolish trial by jury. It may dispense with indictment by a
grand jury and substitute complaint or information. But the freedom of the State
in establishing its policy is the freedom of constitutional government and is limited
by the requirement of due process of law. Because a State may dispense with a jury
trial, it does not follow that it may substitute trial by ordeal. The rack and torture
chamber may not be substituted for the witness stand. The State may not permit
an accused to be hurried to conviction under mob domination—where the whole
proceeding is but a mask—without supplying corrective process. The State may not
deny to the accused the aid of counsel. Nor may a State, through the action of its
officers, contrive a conviction through the pretense of a trial which in truth is "but
used as a means of depriving a defendant of liberty through a deliberate deception
of court and jury by the presentation of testimony known to be perjured." Mooney
v. Holohan, 294 U.S. 103 (1935). And the trial equally is a mere pretense where
the state authorities have contrived a conviction resting solely upon confessions
obtained by violence. . . . It would be difficult to conceive of methods more revolting
to the sense of justice than those taken to procure the confessions of these petitioners, and the use of the confessions thus obtained as the basis for conviction and
sentence was a clear denial of due process. . . .

II.

. . . In the instant case, the trial court was fully advised by the undisputed evidence of the way in which the confessions had been procured. The trial court knew
that there was no other evidence upon which conviction and sentence could be
based. Yet it proceeded to permit conviction and to pronounce sentence. The conviction and sentence were void for want of the essential elements of due process. . . .

Notes

1. *Disappearance of the third degree.* Thirty-six years after the appearance of the
Wickersham Commission report, another national commission reported the virtual disappearance of physical coercion as an interrogation technique: "[T]oday
the third degree is almost non-existent," declared the President's Commission on
Criminal Justice and the Administration of Justice, The Challenge of Crime in a
Free Society (1967). Physical brutality and intimidation disappeared in part because
of political pressure from the public, outraged by the findings of the Wickersham
Commission and countless similar news accounts. Would these practices have disappeared, even without the Supreme Court's ruling in *Brown*? During the 30 years
following *Brown*, due process claims of involuntary confessions became a staple of
the Supreme Court docket. The Court ultimately decided more than 30 such cases.
Over time, the nature of the police conduct in question shifted away from physical

violence or threats of violence to more subtle physical deprivations and psychological coercion. However, the move away from physical deprivation happened slower in some places than others. In particular, physical abuse of black defendants in Southern states continued through the 1940s. See Michael Klarman, Is the Supreme Court Sometimes Irrelevant? Race and the Southern Criminal Justice System in the World War II Era, 89 J. Am. Hist. 119 (2002). The allegations also still arise in rare cases. See People v. Richardson, 917 N.E.2d 501 (Ill. 2009) (confession from teenage suspect was voluntary, even though it was obtained a few hours after he was punched by an officer in the jail; interrogating officers worked with separate subdivision of department and in different part of the building from the jail).

2. *Physical deprivations: modern limits.* Although physical abuse such as striking a suspect has largely disappeared from interrogations in this country, one can still find examples of physical deprivations, such as depriving a suspect of food or sleep for some period of time. Courts find some deprivations of sleep or food tolerable while others are not. See Payne v. Arkansas, 356 U.S. 560 (1958) (confession coerced resulted when defendant was given only two sandwiches during 40-hour detention and interrogations). Is deprivation of cigarettes equivalent to deprivation of food or water? What about medication?

3. *Mental coercion.* After the physical coercion in police interrogations withered away, the legal system still faced questions about psychological manipulation during interrogations. Because the *Brown* court prohibited the use of "coerced" or "involuntary" confessions, courts needed to address what types of psychological pressures might qualify under that standard. The notes below focus on physical coercion, while the subsequent two sections discuss in greater detail tactics that may constitute mental coercion, such as police lies, threats, or promises.

4. *Length of interrogation.* How long should an interrogation take? In one survey, 631 police investigators estimated that the mean length of interrogations of suspects is 1.6 hours. See Saul M. Kassin et al., Police Interviewing and Interrogation: A Self-Report Survey of Police Practices and Beliefs, 31 Law and Hum. Beha. 381-400 (2007). Criminologist Richard Leo, who observed about 180 police interrogations, concluded that the length of an interrogation is one of the strongest determinants of its success (defined as procuring an admission from the suspect). Richard Leo, Inside the Interrogation Room, 86 J. Crim. L. & Criminology 266 (1996). At the same time, lengthy interrogations create a risk that a court will later find any confession to be involuntary. Ashcraft v. Tennessee, 322 U.S. 143 (1944) (continuous 36-hour interrogation, confession involuntary); cf. State v. Harris, 105 P.3d 1258 (Kan. 2005) (detention of a suspect by shackling him to floor of interrogation room for seven hours did not render his subsequent confession involuntary; suspect was questioned for two and a half hours and denied access to telephone, but allowed to take bathroom breaks). There is no clear time limit that will create an involuntary confession under the "totality of the circumstances," but studies have found that most false confessions occur during interrogations that last six or more hours. Richard A. Leo, Police Interrogation and American Justice 311 (2008). Police interrogators affirm that they rarely need more than four hours to obtain a valid confession, and commentators have proposed a limit of four or six hours on all custodial interrogations. Richard A. Leo, Interrogation and Confessions, in Reforming Criminal Justice 233, 257 (Erik Luna ed. 2017).

5. *Delay in presenting a suspect to a judicial officer.* Can the length of detention influence a suspect's decision to give an incriminating statement? The Supreme

Court has held that, if a person is arrested without a warrant, he or she must be promptly presented to a magistrate to determine whether the arrest was based on probable cause. Gerstein v. Pugh, 420 U.S. 103 (1975). Promptly generally means within 48 hours, unless extraordinary circumstances require further delay. County of Riverside v. McLaughlin, 500 U.S. 44 (1991). [These rules also appear in Chapter 5, Arrests.]

The rules of criminal procedure in most jurisdictions likewise require the police to arrange for the suspect's prompt appearance before a judicial officer. The rules in some states specify a time period. See Ariz. R. Crim. Proc. 4.1 ("An arrested person must be promptly taken before a magistrate. . . . If the initial appearance does not occur within 24 hours after arrest, the arrested person must be immediately released from custody."); Cal. Penal Code §825 (defendant shall "be taken before the magistrate without unnecessary delay, and, in any event, within 48 hours after his or her arrest, excluding Sundays and holidays").

Federal Rule of Criminal Procedure 5(a) requires that an arrestee be presented before a magistrate "without unnecessary delay." Any violation of this Rule will require suppression of confessions obtained as a result of presentment delay. This requirement (declared under the Supreme Court's so-called supervisory power over federal law enforcement) is known as the *McNabb-Mallory* rule, after McNabb v. United States, 318 U.S. 332 (1943), and Mallory v. United States, 354 U.S. 449 (1957).

Although most states have a time-limit provision in their rules of procedure, most state courts have rejected the *McNabb-Mallory* rule and have declared instead that a violation of the timeliness requirement will not lead to automatic suppression but will be one part of the "totality of the circumstances" that could indicate an involuntary confession. Fewer than 10 states follow the per se federal rule. See Commonwealth v. Perez, 845 A.2d 779 (Pa. 2004) (disavowed state's bright-line rule with a "totality of the circumstances" test for determining the admissibility of statements made during delays in arraignment). Some states have special rules (embodied in statutes, court rules, or constitutional due process rulings) requiring prompt presentation of *juveniles* to a judicial officer. See W. Va. Code, §49-4-705; In re Steven William T., 499 S.E.2d 876 (W. Va. 1997). Even if a lengthy detention rises to the level of violating the constitutional rule set out in *Gerstein* and *McLaughlin* (as opposed to merely a violation of rules of procedure), courts do not always suppress confessions obtained during the unlawfully extended detention. Some courts consider delay as merely one factor in assessing the voluntariness of the confession, whereas other courts focus on the causal connection between the delay and the confession. People v. Jenkins, 122 Cal. App. 4th 1160, 1177–1178 (2004) (reviewing these different approaches).

6. *Vulnerability of suspect.* The Court in *Brown* mentioned the "ignorance" of the suspects. Many other cases assessing the voluntariness of a confession for due process purposes have also considered the vulnerability of the suspect. A suspect who is especially young or who is suffering from illness or injury will be more likely to succeed in claiming that a confession was involuntary. See Beecher v. Alabama, 408 U.S. 234 (1972) (suspect confesses while under influence of morphine and in pain from gunshot wound, confession involuntary); Haley v. Ohio, 332 U.S. 596 (1948) (15-year-old interrogated with no advice from family or friends, confession involuntary). Conversely, a suspect who is mature and well educated will find it more difficult to sustain a claim of involuntariness. One recurring source of psychological pressure that has been influential with courts has been the extended isolation

of the defendant from family, friends, legal counsel, and other support. See Fikes v. Alabama, 352 U.S. 191 (1957) (isolation for more than a week, confession involuntary).

7. *Torture, truth, and need.* Exactly what is objectionable about relying on confessions obtained through torture? If the problem is unreliable information, could that be cured by an evidentiary rule requiring independent corroboration of anything learned through physical abuse of a suspect? If the objection is abuse of police powers, could that risk be addressed through procedures specifying when physical coercion would be allowed, and the types of physical techniques the police could use? Are there situations in criminal law enforcement that could justify torture? What if the life of a hostage is at stake, or there is a possibility of great loss of life from an act of terror? See John Langbein, Torture and the Law of Proof (1977).

These questions are not merely academic. In the aftermath of the terrorist attacks in New York City and Washington on September 11, 2001, lawyers and government officials started to anticipate settings where torture might be appropriate. During military operations in Afghanistan in 2001 and 2002, U.S. armed forces captured enemy combatants. Agents of the Central Intelligence Agency interrogated the detainees at locations near the fighting, and for months after their capture at the military detention facility at Guantanamo Bay in Cuba. The interrogators used "stress and duress" and "waterboarding" techniques. For instance, detainees who refused to cooperate were kept standing or kneeling for hours while wearing black hoods or spray-painted goggles. Some were allegedly held in awkward and painful positions, or were subjected to 24-hour lighting to disrupt their sleep. In some cases, the United States turned captured combatants over to foreign governments known to use torture during interrogations. News developments related to this topic appear on the web extension for this chapter at *http://www.crimpro. com/extension/ch08.* Do the techniques described above make any confessions of the detainees involuntary? Are such techniques acceptable so long as the government pursues no criminal charges against the detainee, but merely uses the information to stop further violence? Does the Constitution turn a blind eye to interrogations that take place outside the territory of the United States?

2. Promises and Threats

Only rarely does a suspect volunteer a confession without any effort by the police to extract that statement. While trying to convince a suspect of the value of a confession, is it proper for the officer to make promises or threats of any type? Are these techniques objectionable for the same reasons that one might object to physical torture during interrogations?

■ STATE v. JAMI DEL SWANIGAN
106 P.3d 39 (Kan. 2005)

Nuss, J.

. . . Shortly before 4 A.M. on October 26, 2000, the Kwik Shop on West Cloud Street in Salina was robbed. According to clerk Krystal Keefer, she saw a black man put his hand up to the glass of the front window and look inside. He then rushed in the front door with a gun. Several times the robber told her to hurry and at one point told her that he would shoot her or kill her if she did not go faster. She opened the cash drawer, grabbed the bills, and handed them to the robber. As she began to grab the change, the robber turned and ran out the front door to the east. The robber stole $100 to $102. . . . Surveillance cameras at the Kwik Shop captured video images of the robber.

Five days after the robbery, [when attention began to focus on Jami Swanigan as the person in the video, Officer Shari Lanham went to Swanigan's home and asked] if he would come to the police department to answer questions about this robbery and other recent convenience store robberies in Salina. He agreed and rode in a patrol car to the station. Upon his arrival, he was placed in a locked waiting room for 30 to 45 minutes before the interrogation began.

The interrogation lasted from 5:03 P.M. until 6:20 P.M., with all but the first few minutes recorded on audiotape. . . . Swanigan first denied knowing anything about the robberies, but eventually said he had heard Marcus Brown was involved. Lanham falsely told Swanigan that his fingerprints had been found at the scene. She also informed him that he had been caught on the surveillance camera. Swanigan had no explanation for either fact, except that he had possibly been at the store before.

After Swanigan took a bathroom break, Lieutenant Mike Sweeney, who was in charge of criminal investigations and who supervised Lanham, joined the interrogation. Swanigan gave Sweeney and Lanham several different stories, but each version contained facts that were contrary to what the officers knew from the eyewitnesses. When confronted with the discrepancies, Swanigan then denied any involvement in the robbery.

Investigator James Feldman then joined the interrogation. Right after Feldman's comments, Swanigan confessed to the robbery. When a discrepancy arose over the clothes the robber had worn, Feldman showed Swanigan a photo from the surveillance video. Swanigan immediately denied the photo was of him and denied that he had any involvement in the robbery. Based primarily upon his interrogation—since latent fingerprints taken from the store, including the front window, were found not to be his—he was arrested and charged with aggravated robbery. . . .

In Swanigan's motion to suppress, he alleged that his statements were not voluntary, knowing, or intelligent under the totality of the circumstances. Specifically, Swanigan alleged that the police used coercive and deceptive tactics, including providing him false information that his fingerprints matched those found at the crime scene and promising that his cooperation in the investigation would help him. [The court denied his motion to suppress the confession.]

In reviewing a district court's decision regarding suppression, this court reviews the factual underpinnings of the decision by a substantial competent evidence standard and the ultimate legal conclusion by a de novo standard with independent judgment. This court does not reweigh evidence, pass on the credibility of witnesses, or resolve conflicts in the evidence. We stated additional considerations specifically concerning confessions in State v. Sanders, 33 P.3d 596 (Kan. 2001):

> In determining whether a confession is voluntary, a court is to look at the totality of the circumstances. The burden of proving that a confession or admission is admissible is on the prosecution, and the required proof is by a preponderance of the evidence. Factors bearing on the voluntariness of a statement by an accused include the duration and manner of the interrogation; the ability of the accused

on request to communicate with the outside world; the accused's age, intellect, and background; and the fairness of the officers in conducting the interrogation. The essential inquiry in determining the voluntariness of a statement is whether the statement was the product of the free and independent will of the accused.

[The court heard] evidence at the suppression hearing concerning the officers' alleged promises, threats, or both. Regarding promises, the trial court found that "Swanigan was told several times that if he cooperated that that would be conveyed to anybody who might pursue the case." The court further found that although "there was . . . an allegation made that you were promised leniency," that "no specific promises of leniency were made," and that several times "Lieutenant Sweeney indicated that there couldn't be any promises made by those in authority." . . .

Regarding threats, the trial court found: "At no time were any threats uttered." We agree no express threats were uttered, but find that evidence of implied threats exists on the audiotape. The implicit threats are occasionally intertwined with the officers' urgings that Swanigan cooperate. Examples from both categories of interrogation techniques are italicized below:

> [Lanham:] So you need to come clean. You know what's gonna happen after I get done talking with you Jami. I've gotta do a report. Right? You know that. That's all we do here is reports. *And I need to go and put in my report that Jami cooperated. I need to be able to tell Parrish that you, that you cooperated with me and that you came clean and that you got it straight. And that you weren't involved in all of them because you know what Jami? I don't think you're involved in all of them. I think you had a small part in one of them, and that's what I want from you. That's what we need to know from you so that you don't go down for all these robberies. We just want to know your involvement in yours. That's all we want to know from you, so that you don't get charged with all of them.* . . .

Later in the interview Lanham said: "I just need you to tell me how you was involved. Jami, you know it's the right thing to do. *It's gonna help you in the long run and you know it. 'Cause I guarantee there's a lot of difference between going to jail for five robberies than there is for one.*"

[When] Investigator Feldman entered the room, he told Swanigan:

> *You're going to jail. It's guaranteed. You are going to jail. You got one of two options. You can sit there and B.S. and act like we're, we're idiots and tell these lame stories and we'll write every word you say down and send it over to the county attorney and you'll have every lawyer reading that going, "Jesus Christ, this is bullshit!" And you know what they're [county attorney] gonna say? Well, when your lawyer comes up and goes, "Hey, can we get a deal?" You know what they're gonna say? "Read the report. He, he played games the whole time. He doesn't deserve a break. He hasn't learned from any of the mistakes he made."* . . .
>
> *You can show that you made a mistake and you want to take responsibility for your actions and you apologize for it. Or you sit there and play stupid. And then you're gonna fry. Because when the county attorney comes to Sweeney or Lanham and goes, "What do you think? Here's the deal [plea bargain] that I'm being offered." You know what we're gonna say if you're playing games? "Screw ya."*

Lanham then told Swanigan, "And if you don't think they [county attorney] ask our opinion you're crazy cause they do."

Immediately after these comments by officers Feldman and Lanham, the following exchange occurred:

> [*Swanigan:*] Everything happened so fast. I was standing up at the window. I looked in, put my hand up on the window and looked in. I walked inside the store with a gun in my hand. And I pointed it at the um, clerk and asked, and tell him give me all your money. . . . "Give me your money or I'll kill you." So he finally gave me the money. . . .
>
> *F:* What were you wearing?
>
> *S:* I was wearing, I was wearing tan pants and, um, tan shirt that's over at Jessica's house. . . .
>
> *L:* So that outfit that you have on, the other one. There's another outfit there just like this one you have on, right? That what you were wearing?
>
> *S:* Yeah. . . .

In an apparent attempt to wrap up Swanigan's confession, Feldman produced a photograph of the robber from the surveillance video and asked, "That you?" Swanigan vehemently denied it: "Hell no! I can tell you that's not me. I can tell you that's not me." Among other things, Swanigan pointed out that the figure in the photograph was not wearing tan pants and a tan shirt, contrary to what he had just confessed.

From that point until the interrogation ended, Swanigan denied that he was involved in the robbery. When Lanham asked Swanigan how he would therefore know exactly how the robbery happened, he replied, "Because you guys done gave me tips behind how it done happened." When Lanham asked why he would make up the story that he committed the robbery when he actually had not, Swanigan responded, "Because you guys are forcing me to do this." When she denied forcing him into saying anything, he said, "When I try to tell you the truth you guys say it's me."

[The court also heard evidence at the suppression hearing concerning Swanigan's intellect and psychological state.] Dr. Schulman's report on Swanigan was reviewed by the trial court, and in a section titled "examination findings" it states:

> *Estimated intellectual functioning is in the borderline range of intellectual abilities with an estimated IQ of 76.* He says that he missed a lot of school, that he was in regular classes and did not enjoy going to high school. The clinical examination is essentially within normal limits. *He shows some mild depression. He also shows difficulty in dealing with anxiety and is susceptible to being overcome by anxiety but in this setting he shows good control.* There are no indications of any underlying associative thought disturbance. . . .

Swanigan argues the police used [unfair tactics] to overbear his will [by] repeatedly telling him that he would be helping or hurting himself by what he told them. According to him, they urged him to confess to the crime so that they could report that he had cooperated. He claims that when he told them he did not commit the crime, they threatened to report that he was not cooperating, occasionally suggesting that he would be charged with more robberies if he did not confess. At the time, Swanigan was on probation.

Investigator Lanham mentioned the other robberies and the need for Swanigan's cooperation, adding she "needed" to put in her report that he cooperated. . . . Sweeney repeated the need for police to show that Swanigan had cooperated and indicated what would happen if Swanigan did not. "We can write the report where it shows that you're willing to get this straightened out" and, if not,

"Jami, we're going to charge you with aggravated robbery. We're gonna show [the county attorney] that you're not cooperating with us." . . .

Like Lanham and Sweeney, Feldman suggested positive consequences for Swanigan admitting his mistake, i.e., confessing to the robbery, but suggested negative consequences if he did not so "cooperate." He specifically mentioned the influence the interrogators have with the county attorney's office, including what they write in their report. . . .

This court has held that, without more, a law enforcement officer's offer to convey a suspect's cooperation to the prosecutor is insufficient to make a confession involuntary. State v. Banks, 927 P.2d 456 (Kan. 1996) ("it will be noted by the authorities that you did cooperate"). Likewise, we have declined to find a confession involuntary when the police encourage the accused to tell the truth. Kansas appellate courts, however, have not addressed the other side of the same coin, law enforcement conveying a suspect's lack of cooperation to the prosecutor. A growing number of courts have disapproved this tactic. Those not finding that it is coercive per se regard it as another circumstance to be considered in determining the voluntariness of the confession.

[We] fail to see how law enforcement can be . . . allowed to warn [Swanigan] of punishment for his "noncooperation" when [the Fifth Amendment gives him a privilege against self-incrimination]. On the other hand, we do not regard this tactic as one which makes the confession involuntary per se, but rather as one factor to be considered in the totality of circumstances.

Turning now to the assertion that detectives told Swanigan he would be charged for five convenience store robberies instead of just one unless he confessed, we first examine general statements of Kansas law. K.S.A. 60-460(f) provides in relevant part:

> Evidence of a statement which is made other than by a witness while testifying at the hearing, offered to prove the truth of the matter stated, is hearsay evidence and inadmissible except: . . .
>
> (f) *Confessions.* In a criminal proceeding as against the accused, a previous statement by the accused relative to the offense charged, but only if the judge finds that the accused . . . (2) was not induced to make the statement . . . (B) *by threats or promises concerning action to be taken by a public official with reference to the crime, likely to cause the accused to make such a statement falsely, and made by a person whom the accused reasonably believed to have the power or authority to execute the same.*

No Kansas cases have addressed this specific issue. However, Aguilar v. State, 751 P.2d 178 (N.M. 1988), is directly on point. Among other things, during Aguilar's interrogation the police chief implied that if Aguilar did not confess to the burglary, he would be charged in connection with unrelated incidents of vandalism in town. Aguilar then confessed. In examining interrogation techniques quite similar to those in the instant case, the New Mexico Supreme Court held:

> Chief Barela's interrogation alternated between threatening the defendant with charges in connection with unrelated incidents of vandalism in Dexter and assuring the defendant that a confession to the burglary would be looked upon favorably by all concerned. In the totality of the circumstances, this interrogation technique is preponderant. In comparison with all evidence to the contrary, these implied

threats and promises, especially when knowingly made to a defendant with diminished mental capacity, rendered the confession involuntary as a matter of law.

[The] trial court did not specifically assess Swanigan's IQ of 76 as a factor in the voluntariness determination. Nor did the court consider his psychological state during the interrogation, finding only that it was insufficient to make the police interrogation improper at all. Our review of the record, including the audiotape of the October 31 interrogation, discloses that Swanigan's relatively low IQ and his susceptibility to being overcome by anxiety played a part in his alternating denials and confessions (which themselves varied considerably). His confession began to unravel for the last time when the robber in the photo was wearing the wrong clothes. . . .

Although any one of these factors which Swanigan asserts—his low intellect and susceptibility to being overcome by anxiety, the officers' repeated use of false information, and their threats and promises—may not be sufficient to show coercion, the combination of all of them in this case leads us to conclude as a matter of law that Swanigan's October 31 statement was not the result of his free will, but was involuntary. . . .

We acknowledge that there must be a link between the coercive conduct of the State and the confession. A thorough review of the record, as partly evidenced by the facts set forth in this opinion, clearly shows that Swanigan's numerous changes in story, whether in denial or in confession, usually occurred shortly after the officers lied to or threatened him. As such, his October 31 statement should have been excluded as evidence at trial. . . .

Notes

1. *Police promises: majority position.* Most jurisdictions have not taken literally the Supreme Court's prohibition on the use of confessions obtained through "any sort of threats or . . . any direct or implied promises, however slight." Bram v. United States, 168 U.S. 532 (1897). Some promises or threats, standing alone, are indeed enough to render a confession "involuntary." These would include promises to reduce (or decline to file) charges, threats to file more serious charges, or promises to seek more or less serious punishment for the crime. See Lynumn v. Illinois, 372 U.S. 528 (1963) (suspect told that cooperation could lead to lesser charges; failure to cooperate would mean loss of custody of children, confession involuntary); State v. Rezk, 840 A.2d 758 (N.H. 2004) (interrogator said that if defendant confessed, the officer "wouldn't charge him with all the felonies"; confession was involuntary because defendant and police engaged in "station house plea-bargaining" without benefit of defense counsel for the suspect). Improper statements could also include threats to refuse to protect the suspect from mob violence or from a dangerous co-conspirator, or promises to protect an inmate from violence by fellow prisoners in exchange for a confession (thereby implying that harm would come to the inmate if he remained quiet). Arizona v. Fulminante, 499 U.S. 279 (1991) (undercover government agent's offer to protect inmate from credible threats of violence by fellow prisoners if the prisoner confessed rendered the subsequent confession involuntary, due to implicit threat of harm); Bond v. State, 9 N.E.3d 134 (Ind. 2014) (interrogator suggested that suspect tell his side of story rather than

going to trial before a "racist jury" that would convict him on sight; confession was involuntary).

Interrogators can, however, make many other promises or threats without invalidating a confession. They can promise to inform the prosecutor about the defendant's cooperation in making a statement, to ask the prosecutor to discuss lesser charges, or to arrange for treatment programs or similar activities. What distinguishes the acceptable from the unacceptable promises? See People v. Holloway, 91 P.3d 164 (Cal. 2004) (detectives' mention of a possible death penalty and suggestions that defendant would benefit from giving a truthful, mitigated version of the crimes was not an improper promise or threat; court compared these facts to improper interrogations where detectives falsely suggested that suspect would be subject to death penalty, or that statements could not be used in court).

When the police make promises or threats to a *juvenile* suspect, the government has a somewhat more difficult burden to meet in showing that the confession was voluntary. See State v. Presha, 748 A.2d 1108 (N.J. 2000) (courts should consider parent's absence during interview as a highly significant factor in judging voluntariness of juvenile's statement); In re G.O., 727 N.E.2d 1003 (Ill. 2000) (juvenile's confession should not be suppressed simply because he was denied the opportunity to confer with a parent during interrogation, but that factor may be relevant in determining voluntariness).

2. *Proving causation.* The government carries the burden of proving that a confession was voluntary, and the standard of proof is preponderance of the evidence. State v. Agnello, 593 N.W.2d 427 (Wis. 1999) (voluntariness of confession need be shown only by a preponderance, not beyond reasonable doubt). As the Kansas court in *Swanigan* indicated, even after a defendant demonstrates that the police made an improper promise or threat, his statement still might be admissible if the promise or threat did not "induce" or "cause" the confession. What factors would be relevant to the assessment of a causal link between the threat or promise and the confession?

3. *Do innocent people confess?* Do innocent people really confess to crimes they did not commit? The use of DNA evidence to identify clear cases of wrongful convictions allows careful assessments of confessions in cases that go wrong. Some research indicates that false confessions account for a substantial number of wrongful conviction cases, and those confessions include many convincing details about the crime that  were likely suggested to the suspect by the questioners. See Brandon Garrett, The Substance of False Confessions, 62 Stan. L. Rev. 1051 (2010). For a review of the sources, effects, and frequency of false confessions, consult the web extension for this chapter at *http://www.crimpro.com/extension/ch08*. More than 25 percent of the DNA exoneration cases involved a false confession or admission. See *https://www. innocenceproject.org/causes/false-confessions-admissions.*

A number of psychologists have investigated the circumstances that lead people to make false confessions. A Royal Commission in Great Britain summarized the findings as follows:

> [There] is now a substantial body of research which shows that there are four distinct categories of false confession:
>
> (i) people may make confessions entirely voluntarily as a result of a morbid desire for publicity or notoriety; or to relieve feelings of guilt about a real or imagined previous transgression; or because they cannot distinguish between reality and fantasy;

(ii) a suspect may confess from a desire to protect someone else from interrogation and prosecution;

(iii) people may see a prospect of immediate advantage from confessing (e.g., an end to questioning or release from the police station), even though the long-term consequences are far worse (the resulting confessions are termed "coerced-compliant" confessions); and

(iv) people may be persuaded temporarily by the interrogators that they really have done the act in question (the resulting confessions are termed "coerced-internalized" confessions).

Report of the Royal Commission on Criminal Justice 57 (1993) (Runciman Commission); see also Saul M. Kassin, Inside Interrogation: Why Innocent People Confess, 32 Am. J. Trial Advoc. 525 (2009).

The availability of video recordings has created a rich field for psychological and sociological research on this topic. Richard Ofshe and Richard Leo have used these materials to develop a model of true and false confessions that emphasizes the misuse of standard interrogation techniques as a major cause of false confessions. They pay particular attention to the "post-admission" portion of an interrogation, when a suspect provides the details that can corroborate or repudiate the suspect's admission of guilt. See Ofshe & Leo, The Decision to Confess Falsely: Rational Choice and Irrational Action, 74 Denv. U. L. Rev. 979 (1997).

4. *Central Park jogger case.* A tragic combination of forces came together in a wrongful conviction case in the New York courts in 1990. After the assault and rape of a young woman who was jogging in New York City's Central Park, police arrested several teenage boys who were in the park that night, at a time when several robberies and other crimes were taking place. The boys were told their *Miranda* rights (which they waived), and all but one had a parent or guardian present at the station. But the interrogations stretched for prolonged periods of time, some more than 20 hours. There was a dispute as to whether the officers had used coercive tactics, but one officer did admit lying to one of the juveniles about the evidence in the case. Steven A. Drizin & Richard A. Leo, The Problem of False Confessions in the Post-DNA World, 82 N.C. L. Rev. 891 (2004). In the end, four of the boys confessed to involvement in the rape but retracted their statements within a few weeks: They claimed that police lies and prosecutor coercion had produced false confessions. No DNA or other strong physical evidence linked them to the crime, but five defendants were convicted in 1990. The last of those convictions was vacated in 2002 after the confession of the actual rapist (confirmed by DNA evidence). The Manhattan District Attorney's office supported the motion to vacate the sentences, based on inconsistencies among the confessions of the five suspects, and the city ultimately settled a civil lawsuit brought by the suspects. A documentary film offers a look back on the events, and allows us today to reconstruct what went wrong. See *The Central Park Five* (IFC Films, 2012).

3. Police Lies

Police often know facts that suspects do not know and can use those facts to expose a suspect's false story or to encourage a silent suspect to talk. Sometimes police only pretend to know something: They make assertions that are untrue or unsupported, such as stating that a co-defendant has confessed or that a victim has died. Other times police create props, in the form of physical evidence, to increase the chance of obtaining a confession. Are all police lies in the interrogation room a fair and legal part of the "often competitive enterprise of ferreting out crime"? If not, where should courts or police agencies draw the line?

■ PEOPLE v. ADRIAN THOMAS
8 N.E.3d 308 (N.Y. 2014)

LIPPMAN, C.J.

Defendant was convicted by a jury of murdering his four-month-old son, Matthew Thomas. The evidence considered by the jury included a statement in which he admitted that on three occasions during the week preceding the infant's death he "slammed" Matthew down on a mattress just 17 inches above the floor and a videotape of defendant's interrogation, near the end of which defendant, a particularly large individual [who weighed well over 300 pounds], demonstrated how he raised the infant above his head and threw him down with great force on the low-lying mattress. The jury also heard testimony from the child's treating doctors from Albany Medical Center, the medical examiner who performed the autopsy on Matthew, and an expert on child abuse from Brown Medical School. These witnesses, citing radiologic and postmortem findings of subdural fluid collections, brain swelling and retinal hemorrhaging, as well as defendant's account of what he had done, said that Matthew died from intracranial injuries caused by abusively inflicted head trauma. . . .

I.

On the morning of September 21, 2008, defendant's wife, Wilhelmina Hicks, awoke to discover that the couple's four-month-old, prematurely born infant, Matthew, was limp and unresponsive. [He was rushed to the hospital where the treating doctor noted that the most likely diagnosis was septic shock, although intracranial injuries were also listed as a possible cause.]

In the early afternoon, Matthew was transferred to the Pediatric Intensive Care Unit at Albany Medical Center, where he continued to be treated for sepsis. The child's treating physician concluded that his patient had been a victim of blunt force trauma—indeed, that the by-then moribund child had been "murdered." [At the trial of the case, this doctor and other prosecution experts testified that blunt force trauma was indeed the cause of death; defense experts disputed this, attributing the death to sepsis, and the defense suggested that the treating doctor was misled by his initial impression, later proved wrong, that the child's skull was fractured.]

[Shortly after Matthew's death, based on a report by the treating physician that Matthew had been physically abused, Troy Police Sergeant Adam Mason] accompanied child protective workers to defendant's home and assisted in the removal of defendant's six other children. Defendant, who had been caring for the children while his wife was at the hospital with Matthew, remained at his residence subsequent to the removal. Hours later, the police returned and escorted defendant to an interrogation room at the Troy Central Police Station. There, they read the evidently distraught father his rights and commenced a course of videotaped interrogation.

The interrogation lasted about nine and one half hours, broken into an initial two-hour and a subsequent seven and one half hour session. In between, defendant, having expressed suicidal thoughts during the initial interview, was involuntarily hospitalized . . . for some 15 hours in a secure psychiatric unit. By pre-arrangement, he was released back to his interrogators who immediately escorted him back to the police station where the interrogation resumed.

The premise of the interrogation was that an adult within the Thomas-Hicks household must have inflicted traumatic head injuries on the infant. Indeed one of the interrogating officers told defendant that he had been informed by Matthew's doctor that Matthew had been "slammed into something very hard. It's like a high speed impact in [a] vehicle. This baby was murdered. [This] baby is going to die and he was murdered." The interrogators, however, repeatedly reassured defendant that they understood Matthew's injuries to have been accidental. They said they were not investigating what they thought to be a crime and that once defendant had told them what had happened he could go home. He would not, they reassured over and again, be arrested. When, however, defendant continued to deny having hurt Matthew, even accidentally, the officers falsely represented that his wife had blamed him for Matthew's injuries and then threatened that, if he did not take responsibility, they would "scoop" Ms. Hicks out from the hospital and bring her in, since one of them must have injured the child. By the end of the initial two-hour interrogation, defendant agreed to "take the fall" for his wife. He said that he had not harmed the child and did not believe that his wife had either because "she is a good wife," but that he would take responsibility to keep her out of trouble.

Before the interrogation recommenced on the evening of September 22nd, Matthew was pronounced brain dead. Nonetheless, the interrogating officers told defendant that he was alive and that his survival could depend on defendant's disclosure of how he had caused the child's injuries:

> SERGEANT MASON: The doctors need to know this. Do you want to save your baby's life, all right? Do you want to save your baby's life or do you want your baby to die tonight?
>
> [DEFENDANT]: No, I want to save his life.
>
> SERGEANT MASON: Are you sure about that? Because you don't seem like you want to save your baby's life right now. You seem like you're beating around the bush with me.
>
> [DEFENDANT]: I'm not lying.
>
> SERGEANT MASON: You better find that memory right now Adrian, you've got to find that memory. This is important for your son's life man. You know what happens when you find that memory? Maybe if we get this information, okay, maybe he's able to save your son's life. Maybe your wife forgives you for what happened. Maybe your family lives happier ever after. But you know what, if you can't find that memory and those doctors can't save your son's life, then what kind of future are you going to have? Where's it going to go? What's going to happen if Matthew dies in that hospital tonight, man?

About four hours into the second interrogation session defendant gave a statement. He said that, about 10 or 15 days before, he accidentally dropped Matthew five or six inches into his crib and Matthew hit his head "pretty hard." He supposed that that impact caused Matthew's brain injury. He also recalled accidentally bumping Matthew's head with his head on the evening of September 20th. He noticed that Matthew's breathing became labored, but was afraid to tell his wife what happened. Defendant would expand upon this statement, but before he did so a second officer, Sergeant Colaneri, entered the interrogation room. He claimed to have had experience with head injuries during his military service in Operation Desert Storm, and angrily accused defendant of lying—he said that Matthew's injuries could only have resulted from a far greater application of force than defendant had described. Matthew's doctors, he reported, had stated that the child's head injuries were comparable to those that would have been sustained by a passenger in a high-speed car collision. After Colaneri left, Sergeant Mason said that he felt betrayed by defendant's untruthfulness and that he was doing all he could to stop his superior from having defendant arrested. Although he would acknowledge in his hearing testimony that he did not then have probable cause for defendant's arrest, he represented to defendant that he was defendant's last hope in forestalling criminal charges. He said that he could not help defendant unless defendant told him how he had caused Matthew's injuries. He proposed that defendant had been depressed and emotionally overwhelmed after having been berated by his wife over his chronic unemployment and that, out of frustration, he had, without intending to harm the infant, responded to his crying by throwing him from above his head onto a low-lying mattress. [The officer suggested that defendant had thrown the child down on his mattress after defendant adamantly denied throwing the child against a hard surface, e.q., the wall or the floor.] He emphasized several times that, according to the doctor at the hospital, the child would have had to hit the mattress at a speed of 60 miles per hour to sustain the injuries from which he was suffering. He had defendant demonstrate with a clip-board how he threw the child down on the mattress, instructing:

> Move that chair out of the way. Here hold that like you hold the baby. Turn around, look at me. Now here's the bed right here, all right. Now like I said, the doctor said that this injury is consistent with a 60 mile per hour vehicle crash, all right, all right. That means it was a very severe acceleration. It means he was going fast and stopped suddenly, all right, so think about that. Don't try to downplay this and make like it's not as severe as it is. Because [we] both know now you are finally starting to be honest, okay, all right. Maybe this other stuff you said is the truth.

> *[DEFENDANT]:*   That is.
> *SERGEANT MASON:*   For what the information that I need to know we both know now you are starting to finally be honest with that, all right. Hold that like you hold that baby, okay and start thinking about them negative things that your wife said to you, all right, start thinking about them kids crying all day and all night in your ear, your mother-in-law nagging you and your wife calling you a loser, all right, and let that aggression build up and show me how you threw Matthew on you bed, all right. Don't try to sugar coat it and make it like it wasn't that bad. Show me how hard you threw him on that bed.

The ensuing enactment conforming to the Sergeant's directions was captured on the interrogation video. Defendant then enlarged upon his prior statement, now admitting that, under circumstances precisely resembling those specified by Mason, he threw Matthew down on his mattress on the Wednesday, Thursday and Saturday preceding the child's hospitalization.

Defendant's motion to suppress his written and videotaped statements on the ground that they were not voluntary, but had been extracted by means of threats and misrepresentations to which he was specially vulnerable by reason of physical and emotional exhaustion, and upon the ground that the police tactics used during the interrogation created a substantial risk of false incrimination, was denied. . . .

II.

It is the People's burden to prove beyond a reasonable doubt that statements of a defendant they intend to rely upon at trial are voluntary. To do that, they must show that the statements were not products of coercion, either physical or psychological, or, in other words, that they were given as a result of a "free and unconstrained choice by their maker." Culombe v. Connecticut, 367 U.S. 568, 602 (1961). The task is the same where deception is employed in the service of psychologically oriented interrogation; the statements must be proved, under the totality of the circumstances—necessarily including any potentially actuating deception — the product of the maker's own choice. The choice to speak where speech may incriminate is constitutionally that of the individual, not the government, and the government may not effectively eliminate it by any coercive device. It is well established that not all deception of a suspect is coercive, but in extreme forms it may be. Whether deception or other psychologically directed stratagems actually eclipse individual will, will of course depend upon the facts of each case, both as they bear upon the means employed and the vulnerability of the declarant. There are cases, however, in which voluntariness may be determined as a matter of law—in which the facts of record permit but one legal conclusion as to whether the declarant's will was overborne. This, we believe, is such a case. What transpired during defendant's interrogation was not consonant with, and, indeed, completely undermined, defendant's right not to incriminate himself—to remain silent.

III.

Most prominent among the totality of the circumstances in this case is the set of highly coercive deceptions. They were of a kind sufficiently potent to nullify individual judgment in any ordinarily resolute person and were manifestly lethal to self-determination when deployed against defendant, an unsophisticated individual without experience in the criminal justice system.

It is established that interrogators may not threaten that the assertion of Fifth Amendment rights will result in harm to the interrogee's vital interests. In Garrity v. New Jersey, 385 U.S. 493 (1967), police officers were convicted of conspiracy to obstruct justice on the basis of confessions made after the officers were threatened with the loss of their jobs if they asserted their Fifth Amendment rights. The Court held that the confessions were "infected by the coercion inherent in the scheme of questioning" and thus impossible to sustain as voluntary. In People v. Avant, 307 N.E.2d 230 (N.Y. 1973), this Court, following *Garrity*, held that municipal contractors could not be pressured to make incriminating disclosures by threatening forfeiture of the right to bid on municipal contracts if they did not. . . .

It was not consistent with the rule of *Garrity* and *Avant* to threaten that if defendant continued to deny responsibility for his child's injury, his wife would be arrested and removed from his ailing child's bedside. While the People [argue that this threat is] "reasonable," the issue is not whether it reflected a reasonable investigative option, but whether it was permissibly marshaled to pressure defendant to speak against his penal interest. It was not. [Although the] defendant did not finally provide a complete confession until many hours had passed, it is clear that defendant's agreement to "take the fall"—an immediate response to the threat against his wife—was pivotal to the course of the ensuing interrogation and instrumental to his final self-inculpation.

Another patently coercive representation made to defendant—one repeated some 21 times in the course of the interrogation—was that his disclosure of the circumstances under which he injured his child was essential to assist the doctors attempting to save the child's life. [These] were representations of a sort that would prompt any ordinarily caring parent to provide whatever information they thought might be helpful, even if it was incriminating. Perhaps speaking in such a circumstance would amount to a valid waiver of the Fifth Amendment privilege if the underlying representations were true, but here they were false. These falsehoods were coercive by making defendant's constitutionally protected option to remain silent seem valueless and respondent does not plausibly argue otherwise. Instead, it is contended that they did not render defendant's ensuing statements involuntary because there was no substantial risk that appealing to defendant's fatherly concern would elicit a false confession. It has long been established that what the Due Process Clause of the Fourteenth Amendment forbids is a coerced confession, regardless of whether it is likely to be true. In Rogers v. Richmond, 365 U.S. 534 (1961), [Justice Frankfurter] explained:

> [Convictions] following the admission into evidence of confessions which are involuntary, i.e., the product of coercion, either physical or psychological, cannot stand. This is so not because such confessions are unlikely to be true but because the methods used to extract them offend an underlying principle in the enforcement of our criminal law: that ours is an accusatorial and not an inquisitorial system—a system in which the State must establish guilt by evidence independently and freely secured and may not by coercion prove its charge against an accused out of his own mouth. . . .

Additional support for the conclusion that defendant's statements were not demonstrably voluntary, under the totality of the circumstances, can be found in the ubiquitous assurances offered by defendant's interrogators, that whatever had happened was an accident, that he could be helped if he disclosed all, and that, once he had done so, he would not be arrested, but would be permitted to return home. In assessing all of the attendant circumstances, these assurances cannot be minimized on the basis that the eventual confession admitted behavior that could not be characterized as accidental. It is plain that defendant was cajoled into his inculpatory demonstration by these assurances—that they were essential to neutralizing his often expressed fear that what he was being asked to acknowledge and demonstrate was conduct bespeaking a wrongful intent. Defendant unquestionably relied upon these assurances, repeating with each admission that what he had done was an accident. These assurances, however, were false. From its inception, defendant's interrogation had as its object obtaining a statement that would confirm the hypothesis that the infant had been murdered through physical abuse. That objective was incompatible with any true intermediate representation that what defendant did was just an accident.

Had there been only a few such deceptive assurances, perhaps they might be deemed insufficient to raise a question as to whether defendant's confession had been obtained in violation of due process. This record, however, is replete with false assurances. Defendant was told 67 times that what had been done to his son was an accident, 14 times that he would not be arrested, and eight times that he would be going home. These representations were, moreover, undeniably instrumental in the extraction of defendant's most damaging admissions. When Sergeant Mason suggested that defendant had thrown Matthew down on the bed, defendant protested repeatedly that he was being asked to admit that he had intentionally harmed his son. To each such protest, Mason responded that what defendant had done was not intentional, often adding an elaborate explanation of why that was so. In this way, and after a final appeal from Mason to provide the "proper information to relate to the hospital and talk to the doctors to keep your son alive," defendant at last agreed that he argued with Ms. Hicks and then threw Matthew down on the bed. Based on that admission, he would be prosecuted for murder. We do not decide whether these police techniques would themselves require suppression of defendant's statements, but that they, taken in combination with the threat to arrest his wife and the deception about the child, reinforce our conclusion that, as a matter of law, defendant's statements were involuntary.

IV.

Defendant's inculpating statements were also inadmissible as "involuntarily made" within the meaning of CPL 60.45(2)(b)(i) [which treats as "involuntarily made" a statement elicited "by means of any promise or statement of fact, which promise or statement creates a substantial risk that the defendant might falsely incriminate himself"]. The various misrepresentations and false assurances used to elicit and shape defendant's admissions manifestly raised a substantial risk of false incrimination. Defendant initially agreed to take responsibility for his son's injuries to save his wife from arrest. His subsequent confession provided no independent confirmation that he had in fact caused the child's fatal injuries. Every scenario of trauma induced head injury equal to explaining the infant's symptoms was suggested to defendant by his interrogators. Indeed, there is not a single inculpatory fact in defendant's confession that was not suggested to him. He did not know what to say to save his wife and child from the harm he was led to believe his silence would cause. It was at Mason's request and pursuant to his instructions that defendant finally purported to demonstrate how he threw the child. And after Mason said that he must have thrown the child still harder and after being exhorted not to "sugar coat" it, he did as he was bid. Shortly after this closely directed enactment, defendant was arrested.

Defendant's admissions were not necessarily rendered more probably true by the medical findings of Matthew's treating physicians. The agreement of his inculpatory account with the theory of injury advanced by those doctors can be readily understood as a congruence forged by the interrogation. The attainment of the interrogation's goal, therefore, cannot instill confidence in the reliability of its result. . . .

Notes

1. *Police lies: majority position.* Most jurisdictions take the view that some police lies will produce a per se "coerced" confession, while others will ordinarily not be enough standing alone to make the confession inadmissible under the "totality of the circumstances." See Frazier v. Cupp, 394 U.S. 731 (1969) (confession voluntary even though police lied to defendant in telling him that another suspect had already confessed and implicated him). Sometimes courts say that police lies are especially likely to produce false confessions if they are unrelated to the government's evidence of guilt and relate instead to "extrinsic" considerations. See State v. Kelekolio, 849 P.2d 58 (Haw. 1993) (treating "extrinsic" lies as per se violations of due process and leaving more latitude for police to tell lies regarding matters "intrinsic" to their investigation); Brisbon v. United States, 957 A.2d 931 (D.C. App. 2008).

Some courts are especially troubled about police lies that relate to the purpose of the interrogation. See State v. McConkie, 755 A.2d 1075 (Me. 2000) (involuntary statement when officer said during police station interview that suspect's statement would "stay confidential"; officers may not affirmatively mislead suspects about the uses to which their statements may be put). Are police falsehoods of this sort more likely to coerce a confession? More detailed treatment of the categories of deception that produce a skeptical judicial response appears on the web extension for this chapter at *http://www.crimpro.com/extension/ch08*.

2. *False physical evidence and false friends.* Is there any relevant difference between verbal lies about evidence against a defendant and the creation of false physical evidence against a suspect (for instance, forging a report from the forensics laboratory)? Courts seem especially concerned about the latter form of deception. See Commonwealth v. DiGiambattista, 813 N.E.2d 516 (Mass. 2004) (confession coerced by use of fake videotape and forged documentary evidence); Wilson v. State, 311 S.W.3d 452 (Tex. Crim. App. 2010) (use of fictional fingerprint report requires suppression of confession under statutory bar).

Another type of lie that especially troubles courts is the use of "false friends," when the questioner asks the suspect to confess out of friendship or sympathy. In Spano v. New York, 360 U.S. 315 (1959), the questioner was a friend of the suspect and stated (falsely) that if he did not obtain a statement, he would lose his job and his source of support for his family. The resulting confession was held to be involuntary.

3. *Bad confessions or bad police?* Over time the Supreme Court has shifted its views on the role of blameworthy police conduct in evaluating an "involuntary" confession. In Bram v. United States, 168 U.S. 532 (1897), the Court concluded that a coerced confession was a violation of the Fifth Amendment's self-incrimination clause. Hence, the emphasis was on the suspect's state of mind—the question was whether the statement was "compelled." By 1936, in Brown v. Mississippi, the Court had shifted its emphasis to the due process clause as the relevant limitation on the use of coerced confessions. But the Court still seemed most concerned with interrogation practices, such as physical torture, that made the confession "involuntary" and therefore quite possibly false. Later decisions shifted the focus of analysis from the reliability of the statement obtained to the conduct of the police in extracting confessions. In cases such as Rogers v. Richmond, 365 U.S. 534 (1961), the Court barred use of confessions that were obtained through trickery (a false order to arrest the suspect's ill wife). Hence, even if police conduct does not create a risk

of false confession from the defendant, some morally objectionable interrogation tactics might still lead a court to conclude that the confession was "involuntary" based on the totality of the circumstances.

But in Colorado v. Connelly, 479 U.S. 157 (1986), the Supreme Court went further and held that wrongful police coercion is "a necessary predicate" to the finding that a confession is not voluntary under federal law. In *Connelly*, a suspect suffering from psychosis confessed to murder because he heard the "voice of God" urging him to do so. Even though his statement was a "command hallucination" (and not the product of his "rational intellect" and "free will"), the Court concluded that the officers who took his statements had not acted wrongfully (for instance, in taking advantage of his mental illness). For that reason, the due process clause was not violated by the use of the statement to convict him. *Connelly* confirmed that a violation of the due process clause requires state action—so if a family member or clergy member induces a suspect to confess, the subsequent use of the confession by the state does not deprive the defendant of due process.

4. *How common is police lying?* One criminologist who observed more than 180 police interrogations noted that police officers lied to the suspect in about 30 percent of all the interrogations he observed. This technique, he concluded, was among the most effective methods of obtaining a confession or admission but it was less effective than appealing to the suspect's conscience, identifying contradictions in the story the suspect was telling, or offering excuses for the suspect's alleged conduct. Richard Leo, Inside the Interrogation Room, 86 J. Crim. L. & Criminology 266, 278 (1996). See also Laurie Magid, Deceptive Police Interrogation Practices: How Far Is Too Far?, 99 Mich. L. Rev. 1168 (2001) (arguing that deception should be permitted unless it creates an unreasonable risk that an innocent person would falsely confess; until statistically sound research on random sample of confession cases demonstrates the size of this problem, no drastic limit on deceptive techniques is justified).

What ethical boundaries should limit police lies or unenforceable (but legally valid) promises? What would be the impact of a legal rule barring the use of a confession obtained because of police lies of *any* sort? See Deborah Young, Unnecessary Evil: Police Lying in Interrogations, 28 Conn. L. Rev. 425 (1996).

5. *Training police to lie.* A widely used training manual for police interrogators (known as the Reid Manual) advises readers to accuse the suspect of committing the crime and, if necessary, to lie about the evidence available to the police or about other matters: Such "trickery and deceit" is necessary to successful interrogations in the majority of cases, say the authors. Fred Inbau et al., Criminal Interrogation and Confessions 484 (5th ed. 2011). The authors also promote the use of a claustrophobic room, repeated accusations of guilt, presentation of real or invented evidence, and the slow build-up of pressure.

Wicklander-Zulawski & Associates, a consulting group that works with many U.S. police departments, announced in 2017 that it would stop training detectives in the "Reid technique" of interrogation. The firm concluded, based on feedback from police departments, that the technique created too many false confessions. See Radley Balko, Big Changes May Be Coming to Police Interrogations, Washington Post, Mar. 10, 2017.

6. *Police deception and interrogation techniques abroad.* In the 1990s, to address the problem of false confessions produced by manipulative interrogations following the Reid Technique, researchers working with police officers in England and Wales developed a new method of investigative interviewing known under the acronym

PEACE. It encourages officers to build rapport with the suspect and to question him or her without deception, preconception of guilt, or coercion. Instead of aiming to get a confession, officers are supposed to elicit the suspect's account and then to check it against other evidence and any additional statements. The PEACE interview–based method is now being taught to police in a number of countries, including Canada, Australia, and Germany. Aside from the PEACE technique, section 136a of the German Code of Criminal Procedure expressly prohibits a number of interrogation tactics, including "ill treatment, induced fatigue, physical interference, administration of drugs, torment, deception, . . . hypnosis [and] . . . measures that impair the memory of suspects or their ability to understand." Deception is disfavored as an interrogation technique in other European jurisdictions as well. For an overview of interrogation law and practice in other countries, see David Dixon, Interrogation Law and Practice in Common Law Jurisdictions, in Oxford Handbook of Criminal Process (Darryl Brown, Jenia Turner & Bettina Weisser eds., forthcoming 2019); Marijke Malsch & Meike M. De Boer, Interviews of Suspects of Crime: Law and Practice in European Countries, in Oxford Handbook of Criminal Process (Darryl Brown, Jenia Turner & Bettina Weisser eds., forthcoming 2019).

B. *MIRANDA* WARNINGS

It can be very difficult for a court to determine after the fact whether a confession was "voluntary" within the meaning of the due process clause. In a series of cases between 1936 and 1964, the Supreme Court attempted to highlight various facts that might, in the "totality of the circumstances," deprive the suspect of the "power of resistance." Fikes v. Alabama, 352 U.S. 191 (1957). But as the cases proliferated, it became clear that a great many facts could be relevant to the question of voluntariness, which meant that every case was decided on its unique facts and the jurisprudence had little predictive value. The Supreme Court, perhaps out of frustration with the repeated and difficult application of the "voluntariness" test it had created under the due process clause, began a search in the late 1950s for a more effective and easily administered method of stopping interrogation abuses.

The Court turned first to the possibility of requiring defense lawyers to be present during at least some interrogations. In a series of opinions, several members of the Court indicated that due process required that any suspect in custody should be able to obtain an attorney from the moment of arrest. See Spano v. New York, 360 U.S. 315 (1959). These tentative suggestions soon led to a holding, under the Sixth Amendment right to counsel (rather than the due process clause), that defendants in at least some interrogations had the right to have an attorney present. For instance, in Massiah v. United States, 377 U.S. 201 (1964), the defendant had already been indicted for violating narcotics laws and had retained defense counsel when the government recruited his friend/co-defendant to collect more evidence against him. The government placed a radio transmitter in his friend's car, and then the friend struck up a conversation with Massiah in the car about the crimes. The Court invalidated the use of the confession that Massiah made in the car. The use of the confession at trial, the Court said, violated Massiah's Sixth Amendment right to counsel in all "criminal proceedings." Although these circumstances did not amount to physical or psychological coercion under due process analysis, the

Court said that an effective right to counsel "must apply to indirect and surreptitious interrogations as well as those conducted in the jailhouse."

The *Massiah* decision created a method for courts to invalidate confessions on the basis of a clear rule, one that could apply regardless of the conditions during the interrogation. But if the rule were applied only to suspects who have already been indicted or to those who are tricked into a confession outside the police station, its impact would be small.

The right to counsel during custodial interrogations occurring *before* indictment received its clearest declaration in Escobedo v. Illinois, 378 U.S. 478 (1964), decided just weeks after *Massiah*. The investigators in that murder case obtained a confession from Escobedo by preventing him from consulting with his retained attorney (who was present at the police station) during the interrogation. The investigators kept Escobedo handcuffed and standing during the interrogation, and they arranged a confrontation with a second suspect, who accused Escobedo of the killing.

Some of the language in the opinion referred broadly to the importance of the presence of counsel at interrogation, which the Court now called a "critical stage" in the criminal process and which was thus covered by the Sixth Amendment right to counsel during a "prosecution." The opinion suggested that all interrogations of persons in custody would have to take place in the presence of counsel:

> The right to counsel would indeed be hollow if it began at a period when few confessions were obtained. There is necessarily a direct relationship between the importance of a stage to the police in their quest for a confession and the criticalness of that stage to the accused in his need for legal advice. [No] system worth preserving should have to fear that if an accused is permitted to consult with a lawyer, he will become aware of, and exercise, these rights. [378 U.S. at 488.]

However, the opinion also lent itself to a narrower reading by emphasizing some of the distinctive facts of the case in its holding:

> We hold, therefore, that where, as here, the investigation is no longer a general inquiry into an unsolved crime but has begun to focus on a particular suspect, the suspect has been taken into police custody, the police carry out a process of interrogations that lends itself to eliciting incriminating statements, the suspect has requested and been denied an opportunity to consult with his lawyer, and the police have not effectively warned him of his absolute constitutional right to remain silent, the accused has been denied "the Assistance of Counsel" in violation of the Sixth Amendment to the Constitution . . . and that no statement elicited by the police during the interrogation may be used against him at a criminal trial. [378 U.S. at 490-491.]

Escobedo suggested the possibility that the Sixth Amendment might require the government to provide suspects with counsel before any interrogation, and the decision sparked a national debate among state courts. Most states restricted the holding to situations in which a defendant had requested counsel, but some states tried to forecast the direction of the Supreme Court and required the government to provide counsel when an interrogation reached the "accusatory" or "critical" stage. See People v. Dorado, 394 P.2d 952 (Cal. 1964) ("The defendant who does not realize his rights under the law and who therefore does not request counsel is the very defendant who most needs counsel."); Neuenfeldt v. State, 138 N.W.2d 252 (Wis. 1965). A few states went in a different direction, requiring police to advise suspects about their right to assistance of counsel and their right to remain silent. See State v. Mendes, 210 A.2d 50 (R.I. 1965). In 1966, two years after *Escobedo*, the Supreme Court decided Miranda v. Arizona.

1. The *Miranda* Revolution

■ ERNESTO MIRANDA v. ARIZONA
384 U.S. 436 (1966)

WARREN, C.J.[*]

The cases before us raise questions which go to the roots of our concepts of American criminal jurisprudence: the restraints society must observe consistent with the Federal Constitution in prosecuting individuals for crime. More specifically, we deal with the admissibility of statements obtained from an individual who is subjected to custodial police interrogation and the necessity for procedures which assure that the individual is accorded his privilege under the Fifth Amendment to the Constitution not to be compelled to incriminate himself. . . .

Our holding will be spelled out with some specificity in the pages which follow but briefly stated it is this: the prosecution may not use statements, whether exculpatory or inculpatory, stemming from custodial interrogation of the defendant unless it demonstrates the use of procedural safeguards effective to secure the privilege against self-incrimination. By custodial interrogation, we mean questioning initiated by law enforcement officers after a person has been taken into custody or otherwise deprived of his freedom of action in any significant way. As for the procedural safeguards to be employed, unless other fully effective means are devised to inform accused persons of their right of silence and to assure a continuous opportunity to exercise it, the following measures are required. Prior to any questioning, the person must be warned that he has a right to remain silent, that any statement he does make may be used as evidence against him, and that he has a right to the presence of an attorney, either retained or appointed. The defendant may waive effectuation of these rights, provided the waiver is made voluntarily, knowingly and intelligently. If, however, he indicates in any manner and at any stage of the process that he wishes to consult with an attorney before speaking there can be no questioning. Likewise, if the individual is alone and indicates in any manner that he does not wish to be interrogated, the police may not question him. The mere fact that he may have answered some questions or volunteered some statements on his own does not deprive him of the right to refrain from answering any further inquiries until he has consulted with an attorney and thereafter consents to be questioned.

I.

The constitutional issue we decide in each of these cases is the admissibility of statements obtained from a defendant questioned while in custody or otherwise deprived of his freedom of action in any significant way. In each, the defendant was questioned by police officers, detectives, or a prosecuting attorney in a room in

---

[*] [Justices Black, Douglas, Brennan, and Fortas joined in this opinion.—EDS.]

which he was cut off from the outside world. In none of these cases was the defendant given a full and effective warning of his rights at the outset of the interrogation process. In all the cases, the questioning elicited oral admissions, and in three of them, signed statements as well which were admitted at their trials. They all thus share salient features—incommunicado interrogation of individuals in a police-dominated atmosphere, resulting in self-incriminating statements without full warnings of constitutional rights.

An understanding of the nature and setting of this in-custody interrogation is essential to our decisions today. . . . From extensive factual studies undertaken in the early 1930's . . . it is clear that police violence and the "third degree" flourished at that time. [These practices] are undoubtedly the exception now, but they are sufficiently widespread to be the object of concern. Unless a proper limitation upon custodial interrogation is achieved—such as these decisions will advance—there can be no assurance that practices of this nature will be eradicated in the foreseeable future. [Furthermore, this] Court has recognized that coercion can be mental as well as physical, and that the blood of the accused is not the only hallmark of an unconstitutional inquisition.

Interrogation still takes place in privacy. Privacy results in secrecy and this in turn results in a gap in our knowledge as to what in fact goes on in the interrogation rooms. A valuable source of information about present police practices, however, may be found in various police manuals and texts which document procedures employed with success in the past, and which recommend various other effective tactics. These texts are used by law enforcement agencies themselves as guides. . . .

The officers are told by the manuals that the "principal psychological factor contributing to a successful interrogation is privacy—being alone with the person under interrogation." The efficacy of this tactic has been explained as follows:

> [The subject] is more keenly aware of his rights and more reluctant to tell of his indiscretions or criminal behavior within the walls of his home. Moreover his family and other friends are nearby, their presence lending moral support. In his own office, the investigator possesses all the advantages. The atmosphere suggests the invincibility of the forces of the law.

To highlight the isolation and unfamiliar surroundings, the manuals instruct the police to display an air of confidence in the suspect's guilt and from outward appearance to maintain only an interest in confirming certain details. The guilt of the subject is to be posited as a fact. The interrogator should direct his comments toward the reasons why the subject committed the act, rather than court failure by asking the subject whether he did it. Like other men, perhaps the subject has had a bad family life, had an unhappy childhood, had too much to drink, had an unrequited desire for women. The officers are instructed to minimize the moral seriousness of the offense, to cast blame on the victim or on society. These tactics are designed to put the subject in a psychological state where his story is but an elaboration of what the police purport to know already—that he is guilty. Explanations to the contrary are dismissed and discouraged. . . .

The manuals also contain instructions for police on how to handle the individual who refuses to discuss the matter entirely, or who asks for an attorney or relatives. The examiner is to concede him the right to remain silent. "This usually has a very undermining effect. [A] concession of this right to remain silent impresses the subject with the apparent fairness of his interrogator." After this psychological conditioning, however, the officer is told to point out the incriminating significance of the suspect's refusal to talk:

> Joe, you have a right to remain silent. That's your privilege and I'm the last person in the world who'll try to take it away from you. . . . But let me ask you this. Suppose you were in my shoes and I were in yours and you called me in to ask me about this and I told you, "I don't want to answer any of your questions." You'd think I had something to hide, and you'd probably be right in thinking that. That's exactly what I'll have to think about you, and so will everybody else. So let's sit here and talk this whole thing over. . . .

In the event that the subject wishes to speak to a relative or an attorney, the following advice is tendered:

> The interrogator should respond by suggesting that the subject first tell the truth to the interrogator himself rather than get anyone else involved in the matter. If the request is for an attorney, the interrogator may suggest that the subject save himself or his family the expense of any such professional service, particularly if he is innocent of the offense under investigation. The interrogator may also add, "Joe, I'm only looking for the truth, and if you're telling the truth, that's it. You can handle this by yourself."

From these representative samples of interrogation techniques, the setting prescribed by the manuals and observed in practice becomes clear. . . . Even without employing brutality, the "third degree" or the specific stratagems described above, the very fact of custodial interrogation exacts a heavy toll on individual liberty and trades on the weakness of individuals. . . .

In these cases, we might not find the defendants' statements to have been involuntary in traditional terms. Our concern for adequate safeguards to protect precious Fifth Amendment rights is, of course, not lessened in the slightest. In each of the cases, the defendant was thrust into an unfamiliar atmosphere and run through menacing police interrogation procedures. The potentiality for compulsion is forcefully apparent, for example, in State v. Miranda, 401 P.2d 721 (Ariz. 1965), where the indigent Mexican defendant was a seriously disturbed individual with pronounced sexual fantasies, and in People v. Stewart, 400 P.2d 97 (Cal. 1965), in which the defendant was an indigent Los Angeles Negro who had dropped out of school in the sixth grade. [In] none of these cases did the officers undertake to afford appropriate safeguards at the outset of the interrogation to insure that the statements were truly the product of free choice. . . .

The current practice of incommunicado interrogation is at odds with one of our Nation's most cherished principles — that the individual may not be compelled to incriminate himself. Unless adequate protective devices are employed to dispel the compulsion inherent in custodial surroundings, no statement obtained from the defendant can truly be the product of his free choice. From the foregoing, we can readily perceive an intimate connection between the privilege against self-incrimination and police custodial questioning. . . .

II.

[The] constitutional foundation underlying the privilege is the respect a government—state or federal—must accord to the dignity and integrity of its citizens. To maintain a fair state-individual balance, to require the government to shoulder the entire load, to respect the inviolability of the human personality, our accusatory system of criminal justice demands that the government seeking to punish an individual produce the evidence against him by its own independent labors, rather than by the cruel, simple expedient of compelling it from his own mouth. In sum, the privilege is fulfilled only when the person is guaranteed the right to remain silent unless he chooses to speak in the unfettered exercise of his own will.

The question in these cases is whether the privilege is fully applicable during a period of custodial interrogation. . . . An individual swept from familiar surroundings into police custody, surrounded by antagonistic forces, and subjected to the techniques of persuasion described above cannot be otherwise than under compulsion to speak. As a practical matter, the compulsion to speak in the isolated setting of the police station may well be greater than in courts or other official investigations, where there are often impartial observers to guard against intimidation or trickery. . . .

Without the protections flowing from adequate warnings and the rights of counsel, all the careful safeguards erected around the giving of testimony, whether by an accused or any other witness, would become empty formalities in a procedure where the most compelling possible evidence of guilt, a confession, would have already been obtained at the unsupervised pleasure of the police. . . .

III.

It is impossible for us to foresee the potential alternatives for protecting the privilege which might be devised by Congress or the States in the exercise of their creative rule-making capacities. Therefore we cannot say that the Constitution necessarily requires adherence to any particular solution for the inherent compulsions of the interrogation process as it is presently conducted. Our decision in no way creates a constitutional straitjacket which will handicap sound efforts at reform, nor is it intended to have this effect. . . . However, unless we are shown other procedures which are at least as effective in apprising accused persons of their right of silence and in assuring a continuous opportunity to exercise it, the following safeguards must be observed.

At the outset, if a person in custody is to be subjected to interrogation, he must first be informed in clear and unequivocal terms that he has the right to remain silent. For those unaware of the privilege, the warning is needed simply to make them aware of it—the threshold requirement for an intelligent decision as to its exercise. More important, such a warning is an absolute prerequisite in overcoming the inherent pressures of the interrogation atmosphere. It is not just the subnormal or woefully ignorant who succumb to an interrogator's imprecations, whether implied or expressly stated, that the interrogation will continue until a confession is obtained or that silence in the face of accusation is itself damning and will bode ill when presented to a jury. . . . The Fifth Amendment privilege is so fundamental to our system of constitutional rule and the expedient of giving an adequate warning as to the availability of the privilege so simple, we will not pause to inquire in individual cases whether the defendant was aware of his rights without a warning being given. . . .

The warning of the right to remain silent must be accompanied by the explanation that anything said can and will be used against the individual in court. This warning is needed in order to make him aware not only of the privilege, but also of the consequences of forgoing it. It is only through an awareness of these consequences that there can be any assurance of real understanding and intelligent exercise of the privilege. Moreover, this warning may serve to make the individual more acutely aware that . . . he is not in the presence of persons acting solely in his interest.

The circumstances surrounding in-custody interrogation can operate very quickly to overbear the will of one merely made aware of his privilege by his interrogators. Therefore, the right to have counsel present at the interrogation is indispensable to the protection of the Fifth Amendment privilege under the system we delineate today. Our aim is to assure that the individual's right to choose between silence and speech remains unfettered throughout the interrogation process. A once-stated warning, delivered by those who will conduct the interrogation, cannot itself suffice to that end among those who most require knowledge of their rights. . . . Even preliminary advice given to the accused by his own attorney can be swiftly overcome by the secret interrogation process. Thus, the need for counsel to protect the Fifth Amendment privilege comprehends not merely a right to consult with counsel prior to questioning, but also to have counsel present during any questioning if the defendant so desires.

The presence of counsel at the interrogation may serve several significant subsidiary functions as well. If the accused decides to talk to his interrogators, the assistance of counsel can mitigate the dangers of untrustworthiness. With a lawyer present the likelihood that the police will practice coercion is reduced, and if coercion is nevertheless exercised the lawyer can testify to it in court. The presence of a lawyer can also help to guarantee that the accused gives a fully accurate statement to the police and that the statement is rightly reported by the prosecution at trial.

[An individual's] failure to ask for a lawyer does not constitute a waiver. No effective waiver of the right to counsel during interrogation can be recognized unless specifically made after the warnings we here delineate have been given. The accused who does not know his rights and therefore does not make a request may be the person who most needs counsel. . . .

Accordingly we hold that an individual held for interrogation must be clearly informed that he has the right to consult with a lawyer and to have the lawyer with him during interrogation under the system for protecting the privilege we delineate today. As with the warnings of the right to remain silent and that anything stated can be used in evidence against him, this warning is an absolute prerequisite to interrogation. . . .

If an individual indicates that he wishes the assistance of counsel before any interrogation occurs, the authorities cannot rationally ignore or deny his request on the basis that the individual does not have or cannot afford a retained attorney. The financial ability of the individual has no relationship to the scope of the rights involved here. The privilege against self-incrimination secured by the Constitution applies to all individuals. . . . In fact, were we to limit these constitutional rights to those who can retain an attorney, our decisions today would be of little significance. The cases before us as well as the vast majority of confession cases with which we have dealt in the past involve those unable to retain counsel. . . .

In order fully to apprise a person interrogated of the extent of his rights under this system then, it is necessary to warn him not only that he has the right to consult with an attorney, but also that if he is indigent a lawyer will be appointed to represent him. Without this additional warning, the admonition of the right to consult with counsel would often be understood as meaning only that he can consult with a lawyer if he has one or has the funds to obtain one. . . .

Once warnings have been given, the subsequent procedure is clear. If the individual indicates in any manner, at any time prior to or during questioning, that he wishes to remain silent, the interrogation must cease. At this point he has shown that he intends to exercise his Fifth Amendment privilege; any statement taken after the person invokes his privilege cannot be other than the product of compulsion, subtle or otherwise. Without the right to cut off questioning, the setting of in-custody interrogation operates on the individual to overcome free choice in producing a statement after the privilege has been once invoked. If the individual states that he wants an attorney, the interrogation must cease until an attorney is present. At that time, the individual must have an opportunity to confer with the attorney and to have him present during any subsequent questioning. If the individual cannot obtain an attorney and he indicates that he wants one before speaking to police, they must respect his decision to remain silent.

This does not mean, as some have suggested, that each police station must have a "station house lawyer" present at all times to advise prisoners. It does mean, however, that if police propose to interrogate a person they must make known to him that he is entitled to a lawyer and that if he cannot afford one, a lawyer will be provided for him prior to any interrogation. . . . If the interrogation continues without the presence of an attorney and a statement is taken, a heavy burden rests on the government to demonstrate that the defendant knowingly and intelligently waived his privilege against self-incrimination and his right to retained or appointed counsel. . . .

An express statement that the individual is willing to make a statement and does not want an attorney followed closely by a statement could constitute a waiver. But a valid waiver will not be presumed simply from the silence of the accused after warnings are given or simply from the fact that a confession was in fact eventually obtained. . . . Moreover, where in-custody interrogation is involved, there is no room for the contention that the privilege is waived if the individual answers some questions or gives some information on his own prior to invoking his right to remain silent when interrogated.

Whatever the testimony of the authorities as to waiver of rights by an accused, the fact of lengthy interrogation or incommunicado incarceration before a statement is made is strong evidence that the accused did not validly waive his rights. . . . Moreover, any evidence that the accused was threatened, tricked, or cajoled into a waiver will, of course, show that the defendant did not voluntarily waive his privilege. The requirement of warnings and waiver of rights is a fundamental with respect to the Fifth Amendment privilege and not simply a preliminary ritual to existing methods of interrogation. . . .

The principles announced today deal with the protection which must be given to the privilege against self-incrimination when the individual is first subjected to police interrogation while in custody at the station or otherwise deprived of his freedom of action in any significant way. It is at this point that our adversary system of criminal proceedings commences, distinguishing itself at the outset from the inquisitorial system recognized in some countries. . . .

Our decision is not intended to hamper the traditional function of police officers in investigating crime. When an individual is in custody on probable cause, the police may, of course, seek out evidence in the field to be used at trial against him.

Such investigation may include inquiry of persons not under restraint. General on-the-scene questioning as to facts surrounding a crime or other general questioning of citizens in the fact-finding process is not affected by our holding. . . .

In dealing with statements obtained through interrogation, we do not purport to find all confessions inadmissible. Confessions remain a proper element in law enforcement. Any statement given freely and voluntarily without any compelling influences is, of course, admissible in evidence. . . .

IV.

In announcing these principles, we are not unmindful of the burdens which law enforcement officials must bear, often under trying circumstances. [Our] decision does not in any way preclude police from carrying out their traditional investigatory functions. Although confessions may play an important role in some convictions, the cases before us present graphic examples of the overstatement of the "need" for confessions. In each case authorities conducted interrogations ranging up to five days in duration despite the presence, through standard investigating practices, of considerable evidence against each defendant. . . .

Over the years the Federal Bureau of Investigation has compiled an exemplary record of effective law enforcement while advising any suspect or arrested person, at the outset of an interview, that he is not required to make a statement, that any statement may be used against him in court, that the individual may obtain the services of an attorney of his own choice and, more recently, that he has a right to free counsel if he is unable to pay. . . .

The experience in some other countries also suggests that the danger to law enforcement in curbs on interrogation is overplayed. The English procedure since 1912 under the Judges' Rules is significant. As recently strengthened, the Rules require that a cautionary warning be given an accused by a police officer as soon as he has evidence that affords reasonable grounds for suspicion; they also require that any statement made be given by the accused without questioning by police. The right of the individual to consult with an attorney during this period is expressly recognized. . . .

V.

Because of the nature of the problem and because of its recurrent significance in numerous cases, we have to this point discussed the relationship of the Fifth Amendment privilege to police interrogation without specific concentration on the facts of the cases before us. We turn now to these facts to consider the application to these cases of the constitutional principles discussed above. . . .

On March 13, 1963, petitioner, Ernesto Miranda, was arrested at his home and taken in custody to a Phoenix police station. He was there identified by the complaining witness. The police then took him to Interrogation Room No. 2 of the detective bureau. There he was questioned by two police officers. The officers admitted at trial that Miranda was not advised that he had a right to have an attorney present. Two hours later, the officers emerged from the interrogation room with a written confession signed by Miranda. At the top of the statement was a typed paragraph stating that the confession was made voluntarily, without threats or promises of immunity and "with full knowledge of my legal rights, understanding any statement I make may be used against me." [One of the officers testified that he read this paragraph to Miranda. Apparently, however, he did not do so until after Miranda had confessed orally.]

At his trial before a jury, the written confession was admitted into evidence over the objection of defense counsel, and the officers testified to the prior oral confession made by Miranda during the interrogation. Miranda was found guilty of kidnapping and rape. . . . . On appeal, the Supreme Court of Arizona held that Miranda's constitutional rights were not violated in obtaining the confession and affirmed the conviction. In reaching its decision, the court emphasized heavily the fact that Miranda did not specifically request counsel.

We reverse. From the testimony of the officers and by the admission of respondent, it is clear that Miranda was not in any way apprised of his right to consult with an attorney and to have one present during the interrogation, nor was his right not to be compelled to incriminate himself effectively protected in any other manner. Without these warnings the statements were inadmissible. The mere fact that he signed a statement which contained a typed-in clause stating that he had "full knowledge" of his "legal rights" does not approach the knowing and intelligent waiver required to relinquish constitutional rights. . . .

HARLAN, J., dissenting.*

[The] new rules are not designed to guard against police brutality or other unmistakably banned forms of coercion. Those who use third-degree tactics and deny them in court are equally able and destined to lie as skillfully about warnings and waivers. Rather, the thrust of the new rules is to negate all pressures, to reinforce the nervous or ignorant suspect, and ultimately to discourage any confession at all. The aim in short is toward "voluntariness" in a Utopian sense, or to view it from a different angle, voluntariness with a vengeance. To incorporate this notion into the Constitution requires a strained reading of history and precedent and a disregard of the very pragmatic concerns that alone may on occasion justify such strains. . . .

It is most fitting to begin an inquiry into the constitutional precedents by surveying the limits on confessions the Court has evolved under the Due Process Clause of the Fourteenth Amendment. This is so because these cases show that there exists a workable and effective means of dealing with confessions in a judicial manner. . . .

The earliest confession cases in this Court emerged from federal prosecutions and were settled on a nonconstitutional basis, the Court adopting the common-law rule that the absence of inducements, promises, and threats made a confession voluntary and admissible. [A] new line of decisions, testing admissibility by the Due Process Clause, began in 1936 with Brown v. Mississippi, and must now embrace somewhat more than 30 full opinions of the Court. While the voluntariness rubric was repeated in many instances, the Court never pinned it down to a single meaning but on the contrary infused it with a number of different values. To travel quickly over the main themes, there was an initial emphasis on reliability, supplemented by concern over the legality and fairness of the police practices, in an "accusatorial" system of law enforcement, and eventually by close attention to the individual's state of mind and capacity for effective choice. The outcome was a continuing re-evaluation on the facts of each case of how much pressure on the suspect was permissible.

---

* [Justices Stewart and White joined in this opinion. — Eds.]

Among the criteria often taken into account were threats or imminent danger, physical deprivations such as lack of sleep or food, repeated or extended interrogation, limits on access to counsel or friends, length and illegality of detention under state law, and individual weakness or incapacities. Apart from direct physical coercion, however, no single default or fixed combination of defaults guaranteed exclusion, and synopses of the cases would serve little use because the overall gauge has been steadily changing, usually in the direction of restricting admissibility. . . .

There are several relevant lessons to be drawn from this constitutional history. The first is that with over 25 years of precedent the Court has developed an elaborate, sophisticated, and sensitive approach to admissibility of confessions. It is "judicial" in its treatment of one case at a time, flexible in its ability to respond to the endless mutations of fact presented, and ever more familiar to the lower courts. . . . The second point is that in practice and from time to time in principle, the Court has given ample recognition to society's interest in suspect questioning as an instrument of law enforcement. . . .

I turn now to the Court's asserted reliance on the Fifth Amendment, an approach which I frankly regard as a *trompe l'oeil*. The Court's opinion in my view reveals no adequate basis for extending the Fifth Amendment's privilege against self-incrimination to the police station. Far more important, it fails to show that the Court's new rules are well supported, let alone compelled, by Fifth Amendment precedents. . . .

Examined as an expression of public policy, the Court's new regime proves so dubious that there can be no due compensation for its weakness in constitutional law. . . . Without at all subscribing to the generally black picture of police conduct painted by the Court, I think it must be frankly recognized at the outset that police questioning allowable under due process precedents may inherently entail some pressure on the suspect and may seek advantage in his ignorance or weaknesses. . . . The Court's new rules aim to offset these minor pressures and disadvantages intrinsic to any kind of police interrogation. . . .

What the Court largely ignores is that its rules impair, if they will not eventually serve wholly to frustrate, an instrument of law enforcement that has long and quite reasonably been thought worth the price paid for it. There can be little doubt that the Court's new code would markedly decrease the number of confessions. To warn the suspect that he may remain silent and remind him that his confession may be used in court are minor obstructions. To require also an express waiver by the suspect and an end to questioning whenever he demurs must heavily handicap questioning. And to suggest or provide counsel for the suspect simply invites the end of the interrogation. . . .

While passing over the costs and risks of its experiment, the Court portrays the evils of normal police questioning in terms which I think are exaggerated. Albeit stringently confined by the due process standards interrogation is no doubt often inconvenient and unpleasant for the suspect. However, it is no less so for a man to be arrested and jailed, to have his house searched, or to stand trial in court, yet all this may properly happen to the most innocent given probable cause, a warrant, or an indictment. Society has always paid a stiff price for law and order, and peaceful interrogation is not one of the dark moments of the law. . . .

No State in the country has urged this Court to impose the newly announced rules, nor has any State chosen to go nearly so far on its own. [The] FBI falls sensibly short of the Court's formalistic rules. For example, there is no indication that FBI agents must obtain an affirmative "waiver" before they pursue their questioning. . . .

In closing this [discussion] of policy considerations attending the new confession rules, some reference must be made to their ironic untimeliness. There is now in progress in this country a massive re-examination of criminal law enforcement procedures on a scale never before witnessed. [Legislative] reform is rarely speedy or unanimous, though this Court has been more patient in the past. But the legislative reforms when they come would have the vast advantage of empirical data and comprehensive study, they would allow experimentation and use of solutions not open to the courts, and they would restore the initiative in criminal law reform to those forums where it truly belongs. . . .

WHITE, J., dissenting.*

Decisions like these cannot rest alone on syllogism, metaphysics or some ill-defined notions of natural justice, although each will perhaps play its part. . . . First, we may inquire what are the textual and factual bases of this new fundamental rule. [The] Court concedes that it cannot truly know what occurs during custodial questioning, because of the innate secrecy of such proceedings. It extrapolates a picture of what it conceives to be the norm from police investigatorial manuals. . . . Judged by any of the standards for empirical investigation utilized in the social sciences the factual basis for the Court's premise is patently inadequate. . . .

Even if one were to postulate that the Court's concern is not that all confessions induced by police interrogation are coerced but rather that some such confessions are coerced and present judicial procedures are believed to be inadequate to identify the confessions that are coerced and those that are not, it would still not be essential to impose the rule that the Court has now fashioned. Transcripts or observers could be required, specific time limits, tailored to fit the cause, could be imposed, or other devices could be utilized to reduce the chances that otherwise indiscernible coercion will produce an inadmissible confession.

On the other hand, even if one assumed that there was an adequate factual basis for the conclusion that all confessions obtained during in-custody interrogation are the product of compulsion, the rule propounded by the Court would still be irrational, for, apparently, it is only if the accused is also warned of his right to counsel and waives both that right and the right against self-incrimination that the inherent compulsiveness of interrogation disappears. But if the defendant may not answer without a warning a question such as "Where were you last night?" without having his answer be a compelled one, how can the Court ever accept his negative answer to the question of whether he wants to consult his retained counsel or counsel whom the court will appoint? . . .

The obvious underpinning of the Court's decision is a deep-seated distrust of all confessions. As the Court declares that the accused may not be interrogated without counsel present, absent a waiver of the right to counsel, and as the Court all but admonishes the lawyer to advise the accused to remain silent, the result adds up to a judicial judgment that evidence from the accused should not be used against him in any way, whether compelled or not. . . . I see nothing wrong or immoral, and certainly nothing unconstitutional, in the police's asking a suspect whom they have reasonable

* [Justices Harlan and Stewart joined in this opinion. — EDS.]

cause to arrest whether or not he killed his wife or in confronting him with the evidence on which the arrest was based, at least where he has been plainly advised that he may remain completely silent. . . . Particularly when corroborated, as where the police have confirmed the accused's disclosure of the hiding place of implements or fruits of the crime, such confessions have the highest reliability and significantly contribute to the certitude with which we may believe the accused is guilty. . . .

Much of the trouble with the Court's new rule is that it will operate indiscriminately in all criminal cases, regardless of the severity of the crime or the circumstances involved. It applies to every defendant, whether the professional criminal or one committing a crime of momentary passion. [If] further restrictions on police interrogation are desirable at this time, a more flexible approach makes much more sense than the Court's constitutional straitjacket which forecloses more discriminating treatment by legislative or rule-making pronouncements. . . .

■ LOUISIANA CONSTITUTION ART. 1, §13

When any person has been arrested or detained in connection with the investigation or commission of any offense, he shall be advised fully of the reasons for his arrest or detention, his right to remain silent, his right against self incrimination, his right to the assistance of counsel and, if indigent, his right to court appointed counsel.

■ MASSACHUSETTS GENERAL LAWS, CH. 276, §33A

The police official in charge of the station or other place of detention having a telephone wherein a person is held in custody, shall permit the use of the telephone, at the expense of the arrested person, for the purpose of allowing the arrested person to communicate with his family or friends, or to arrange for release on bail, or to engage the services of an attorney. Any such person shall be informed forthwith upon his arrival at such station or place of detention, of his right to so use the telephone, and such use shall be permitted within one hour thereafter.

Notes

1. *The constitutional basis for* Miranda. What is the legal basis of the *Miranda* decision? The Court in *Miranda* indicated that the warnings and the right to counsel it was announcing were requirements of the Fifth Amendment's self-incrimination clause. Why do you suppose the Court based its ruling on the Fifth Amendment rather than the Sixth Amendment's right to counsel? In the decades following, the Court refined its position and stated that *Miranda* rights were "prophylactic" rules that were not, strictly speaking, required by the Fifth Amendment but were necessary to prevent violations of the self-incrimination privilege. See Michigan v. Tucker, 417 U.S. 433 (1974); New York v. Quarles, 467 U.S. 649 (1984). If the *Miranda* warnings really are a prophylactic rule rather than a constitutional requirement, did the Court have the authority to impose this requirement on state as well as federal law enforcement officers? Moreover, could Congress overrule *Miranda?*

Soon after the *Miranda* decision, Congress enacted 18 U.S.C. §3501, stating that the admissibility of statements made by federal defendants while in police custody should turn only on whether they were voluntarily made. While the statute instructed the judge to consider any warnings given to the suspect about his right to silence or his right to consult an attorney, the "presence or absence" of any such warnings "need not be conclusive on the issue of voluntariness of the confession." For many years and through many administrations, federal prosecutors made only modest use of section 3501. See Paul Cassell, The Statute That Time Forgot: 18 U.S.C. §3501 and the Overhauling of *Miranda*, 85 Iowa L. Rev. 175, 197-225 (1999). Why was it overlooked? The most likely explanation is that section 3501 was such a stark rejection of the Supreme Court's decision that most federal prosecutors felt they should not, and perhaps could not, rely upon it, since they are sworn to uphold the Constitution.

The Supreme Court finally spoke to the constitutionality of section 3501 in Dickerson v. United States, 530 U.S. 428 (2000). The defendant in the case gave incriminating evidence against himself in an interview that proceeded without proper *Miranda* warnings (although the interrogation was not otherwise coercive). The key question was whether *Miranda* announced a constitutional rule or was merely a regulation of evidence used in federal court. The Court held that *Miranda* was "a constitutional decision of this Court," as proven by the fact that it had been applied to the states, and for that reason "may not be in effect overruled by an Act of Congress." And the Court declined to overrule *Miranda* even though the government invited it to do so.

2. *Detailed guidance.* The opinion in *Miranda* creates a relatively detailed set of obligations. Even before 1966, some states and law enforcement agencies used warnings to increase the likelihood that a confession would be found voluntary. Would the Court have been wiser to announce more general principles and hope for legislation or police rules to appear before providing any needed specification? See Mark A. Godsey, Rethinking the Involuntary Confession Rule: Toward a Workable Test for Identifying Compelled Self-Incrimination, 93 Cal. L. Rev. 465 (2005) (argues for replacing voluntariness with self-incrimination as basic criterion for admission of confessions; proposes asking whether confession was obtained by using an objective penalty on the suspect to punish silence or provoke speech).

3. *State adoption and modification of* Miranda. The *Miranda* requirements apply to law enforcement officials in all the states. A few states, such as Louisiana and Massachusetts, have independently adopted state constitutional provisions or statutes that specify a set of required warnings similar to those in *Miranda*. See Traylor v. State, 596 So. 2d 957 (Fla. 1992). Others declare that *Miranda* has no basis in the state constitution. See State v. Bleyl, 435 A.2d 1349 (Me. 1981). Does the Louisiana provision reprinted above impose any requirements different from what the Court required in *Miranda*?

4. *Real* Miranda *reforms.* Again and again courts and commentators have noted that the *Miranda* Court left open "potential alternatives for protecting the privilege which might be devised by Congress or the States," and allowed legislative solutions different from *Miranda* warnings, so long as the alternatives were "at least as effective in apprising accused persons of their right of silence and in assuring a continuous opportunity to exercise it." If *Miranda* warnings are problematic for law enforcement, why hasn't Congress or a state legislature enacted alternatives more substantial than section 3501? What form might this legislation take? Subsection

4 of this chapter discusses the variations on the language of the warnings that the Supreme Court has tolerated in the decades since *Miranda* was decided.

5. *The coercive environment and the "infinite regress" problem.* The *Miranda* opinion rests on the premise that interrogation of a suspect in a custodial setting is inherently coercive. Do you agree with this premise? If so, what makes the interrogation coercive? Consider again the words of the Fifth Amendment: Are you convinced that interrogation in a police station "compels" a person to be a "witness" against himself? As you answer these questions, keep in mind the physical environment of a typical custodial interrogation. Interrogation rooms are designed to isolate suspects, for instance; they tend to be located in the rear of the building and rarely have windows for viewing persons outside the room. The room will usually contain only a table and a few chairs. Consider also the subject matter of the conversation, and the assertions a questioner will often make. If interrogation is inherently coercive, isn't the decision to waive the right to counsel also made in the same setting? Could the Court respond to this problem by requiring a more specific warning about waiver? A warning about the warning?

2. The "Custody" Precondition for Miranda Warnings

Miranda warnings do not need to be given before every conversation between police and citizens. They are only required when two conditions are met: First, the suspect must be *in custody*, and second, the officers must be conducting an *interrogation*. Even though judges, police, and commentators often join the concepts in the phrase "custodial interrogation," it is important to evaluate custody and interrogation separately.

To begin, the police are required to give *Miranda* warnings only to suspects who are interrogated while in "custody," which is a term of art in criminal procedure. As you read below, consider how custody for Miranda analysis purposes compares with seizure analysis for 4th amendment purposes.

■ STATE v. KEVIN FRANKLIN ELMARR
181 P.3d 1157 (Colo. 2008)

RICE, J.

In this interlocutory appeal . . . we review an order from the Boulder County District Court suppressing statements the defendant made in response to police interrogation. We find that the trial court properly suppressed the defendant's statements because the defendant was in custody while interrogated, and it is conceded that he did not receive proper *Miranda* warnings before that custodial interrogation. . . .

I. FACTS AND PROCEDURAL HISTORY

On Sunday, May 24, 1987, Detectives Ferguson and Haugse of the Boulder Sheriff's Department and Officer Stiles of the Longmont Police Department visited Defendant Kevin Franklin Elmarr at his home to inform him that his ex-wife, Carol Murphy, was found dead the day before. According to the testimony before the trial court, the detectives were not in uniform, and their weapons were holstered. Officer Stiles was in uniform, but was present more as a friend of Elmarr's family to aid in the notification of death. Two other police officers—Captain Epp and Lieutenant Hopper—later arrived at Elmarr's home in another unmarked police car and were seen there by Elmarr, but they stayed outside.

Detectives Ferguson and Haugse spoke with Elmarr at his home and Elmarr disclosed that he had visited with his ex-wife the day before she was found dead, and had taken her for a ride on his motorcycle. Shortly after this disclosure, Detective Ferguson said the police had more questions for him, and asked him if he would mind accompanying them to the Sheriff's Department at the Boulder Justice Center for further questioning; Elmarr agreed. The detectives drove Elmarr to the Sheriff's Department in their unmarked police car, with Elmarr in the back seat. The detectives did not provide Elmarr the option of driving himself to the station. Elmarr was not handcuffed.

During the drive to the Sheriff's Department, Elmarr volunteered that he had not been entirely truthful in his earlier conversation with the detectives, and provided further information regarding his meeting with his ex-wife the day before she was found dead. The detectives did not say anything while in the car.

The detectives arrived at the Sheriff's Department through the garage in the basement, which is a secure area not open to the public. They escorted Elmarr into an elevator that led to the Sheriff's Department Detective Bureau, which is also not open to the public. Witnesses were unable to recall whether Elmarr was searched before entering the building, but Captain Epp testified that it was standard procedure for persons to be patted down before being transported. Based on this testimony, the trial court found that Elmarr was subjected to a pat-down search upon arrival at the Sheriff's Department. The trial court also found that Elmarr was then placed in a closed interview room measuring seven by ten feet, and told to stay there until officers returned. Captain Epp and Lieutenant Hopper subsequently interrogated Elmarr in that interview room. During the interrogation, Elmarr was seated against the wall, while Captain Epp and Lieutenant Hopper were seated in front of the door. The officers were dressed casually, but the trial court found that they were carrying their weapons. . . . Though the interview room door had a lock on it, no one could recall if it was locked while Elmarr was in the room.

Witnesses testified that Elmarr was never handcuffed or otherwise directly physically restrained, but no one ever told Elmarr that he was free to leave or that he was not under arrest. The interrogation was audio- and video-taped, and the recording shows that Captain Epp began his interrogation by advising Elmarr that he did not have to talk to the police, that he had a right to remain silent, that anything he said that incriminated him would be taken down, and that he had a right to an attorney. Captain Epp then asked if Elmarr wanted to talk to them then. Elmarr answered "sure," and then began speaking about the last time he saw his ex-wife.

Captain Epp then questioned Elmarr about the details of that last meeting with his ex-wife. Though Captain Epp spoke rather slowly and softly, he soon began expressing his doubts about Elmarr's story. For instance, early in the interview Captain Epp told Elmarr, "I hope you're telling me the truth." Later he inspected what he thought were scratches on Elmarr's arms.

Approximately halfway into the interview, Lieutenant Hopper took over much of the questioning, and his tone was more aggressive. He asked Elmarr if he ever thought of hurting his ex-wife; why witnesses would say they saw his ex-wife on a motorcycle matching Elmarr's near the place where her body was found; and whether his ex-wife was "all right" the last time he saw her. Lieutenant Hopper again asked Elmarr why he initially lied when interviewed at his house. [Elmarr said] that he felt he was being accused of murder, and Lieutenant Hopper answered, "You've lied to us already. . . . Put yourself in our place. What would you, what would you think if you were us?"

The recording also shows that near the end of the interrogation, which lasted almost an hour, Captain Epp resumed his questioning, telling Elmarr, "I just get the feeling that you are holding something back." When Elmarr wondered aloud whether he should get a lawyer and protested that he was telling the truth, Captain Epp responded, "Well, I'm not sure. I've got reason to believe that something, that some points here that you're not." Shortly thereafter Lieutenant Hopper explicitly asked Elmarr whether he killed his ex-wife, and Elmarr denied it. Elmarr then said, "I think I would like to talk to a lawyer." At this point the officers stated the interview was over, opened the door, and left the room. They testified that the entire interrogation lasted approximately fifty minutes.

However, Elmarr remained in the Sheriff's Department. The recording shows that he was kept in the interview room for a period of time, after which one of the officers returned and asked him if he would like to take a polygraph test. Elmarr demurred and again stated he wanted to talk to an attorney. The officer left. After a further wait, yet another officer entered the interview room, stated that he wanted to take some photographs of Elmarr, and asked if Elmarr would mind removing his clothes for those pictures, adding, "You really don't have a choice right now." Elmarr complied, after which he asked, "When do I get to go home?" The officer responded, "Shortly here, I hope." Elmarr then asked to make some calls to his family and the officer left, returning later to escort Elmarr out of the interview room to make his calls. Afterwards, Elmarr was escorted back into the interview room, and in the videotape one can hear the door close again. Elmarr again asked how long he would be there, and was told, "At least until your lawyer calls." After a further wait, Elmarr's attorney entered the interview room and the videotape ended, almost an hour after Captain Epp and Lieutenant Hopper had terminated their formal interrogation. . . .

Elmarr was not charged with a crime until almost twenty years later, when in January 2007 he was arrested and charged with first degree murder for the murder of his ex-wife Carol Murphy. [The trial court] suppressed all of the statements Elmarr made at the Sheriff's Department, finding that they were all the product of custodial interrogation. . . .

II. ANALYSIS

In their interlocutory appeal, the People . . . argue that Elmarr was not in custody when he was interrogated at the Sheriff's Department. . . . We find that the trial court erroneously considered the police officers' subjective intent in determining whether Elmarr was in custody, but that the court's other factual findings are supported by the record. We hold that those findings, coupled with the undisputed evidence in the record, establish that Elmarr was in custody when he was interrogated at the Sheriff's Department. . . .

For purposes of determining whether *Miranda* warnings are required, a suspect is in custody when his or her "freedom of action is curtailed to a degree associated with formal arrest." People v. Polander, 41 P.3d 698, 705 (Colo. 2001) (quoting Berkemer v. McCarty, 468 U.S. 420 (1984)). In assessing the question of custody, we consider such factors as the time, place, and purpose of the interrogation; the persons present during the interrogation; the words the officers spoke to the suspect; the officers' tone of voice and general demeanor; the length and mood of the interrogation; whether any restraint or limitation was placed on the suspect's movement during interrogation; the officers' response to any of the suspect's questions; whether directions were given to the suspect during interrogation; and the suspect's verbal or nonverbal responses to such directions. None of these factors is determinative, and the question of custody is determined in light of the totality of the circumstances.

However, because the test of custody is an objective one, unarticulated thoughts or views of the officers and suspects are irrelevant. See Stansbury v. California, 511 U.S. 318 (1994) (The "initial determination of custody depends on the objective circumstances of the interrogation, not on the subjective views harbored by either the interrogating officers or the person being questioned."). Thus, . . . the trial court erred when, in determining whether Elmarr was in custody, it relied (in part) upon the finding that Captain Epp likely suspected that Elmarr was involved in Carol Murphy's murder and attempted to elicit incriminating statements from him. That finding has no relevance to the custody question. We therefore review de novo whether the trial court's other factual findings, and the undisputed evidence in the record, establish that Elmarr was in custody.

Our analysis is guided by precedent considering somewhat analogous facts. For instance, in California v. Beheler, 463 U.S. 1121 (1983), officers asked the suspect to accompany them to the police station, transported him there, informed him he was not under arrest, and questioned him for less than thirty minutes before he voluntarily left the police station. The court found that these facts established that the suspect was not in custody. Similarly, in Oregon v. Mathiason, 429 U.S. 492 (1977), the officers asked the suspect to come to the police station to be interviewed. The suspect drove himself to the station, was immediately told he was not under arrest, was told that he was a suspect in a crime, and interviewed for approximately thirty minutes behind closed doors in an interview room before he left the station voluntarily. Again, the court found the suspect was not in custody. We came to the same conclusion in People v. Matheny, 46 P.3d 453 (Colo. 2002), where the suspect was asked to come to the police station to be interviewed, drove himself and the police officers to the station, was escorted to an interview room, was told he was free to leave and not under arrest, and then was interviewed for approximately an hour and a half.

In People v. Trujillo, 784 P.2d 788 (Colo. 1990), however, we found that a suspect was in custody where he was asked to come to the police station for an interview and drove himself to the station; upon arrival, he was never told he was free to leave or not under arrest, was asked accusatory questions for over an hour and a half, was asked to submit to a mug shot and a polygraph test, and was asked to produce certain evidence to the police. Similarly, in People v. Dracon, 884 P.2d 712 (Colo. 1994), we found the suspect was in custody where she agreed to accompany officers to the police station, riding in the front seat of the police car, and was taken through a non-public area to an office and questioned for almost three hours; she was never told she was free to leave or not under arrest, and was made to wait for another three hours in the police station before being interviewed yet again. Finally, we found that a suspect was in custody in People v. Minjarez, 81 P.3d 348 (Colo. 2003), where police officers came to the hospital where the suspect's child was being treated, asked nurses to bring him to a hospital interview room the officers had procured, directed the suspect to sit in a chair away from the closed door, and told the suspect he was free to go but then subjected him to aggressive interrogation—consisting of leading questions and accusations of guilt—for twenty of the forty-five minutes of the interview.

Precedent does not provide a neat formula for deciding the case at hand, and indeed there can be no such formula as each case will present novel factual patterns not previously addressed. We have provided some general rules, however. On the one hand, we have heeded the warning that one is not in custody simply because the questioning takes place in the station house. On the other hand, an officer's statement that a suspect is "free to leave" is not sufficient to establish that an interview is non-custodial, when all the external circumstances appear to the contrary.

Though the case at hand presents a close question, we find that Elmarr was in custody while interrogated by officers in the Sheriff's Department in 1987. No one fact leads us to this conclusion, but rather the totality of the circumstances combine to create a custodial atmosphere. Though Elmarr was asked to accompany police officers to the station for questioning, such a question does not necessarily make the event voluntary, as one could interpret the question to be one where "no" is not an available answer—especially in the circumstances present here. It is significant that Elmarr was transported in the back of a police car to the non-public area of the Sheriff's Department, where he was directed to wait and then interrogated in a small, closed-door interview room. Importantly, he was never told he was not under arrest, or that he was free to leave. In fact, the trial court found that Elmarr was instructed to wait for officers in a closed room, and was thereafter interrogated at length in that room.

Furthermore, it is significant that Elmarr was subjected to aggressive interrogation, where the interrogators expressed doubts regarding his truthfulness, discounted his denials, confronted him with potential evidence of his guilt, and accused him of committing murder. Such interrogation by multiple officers in a small room isolated from others helped create a sense of custody. The custodial atmosphere continued after Elmarr requested an attorney—even then, he was kept in the closed-door interview room and was asked about his willingness to submit to a polygraph test, and then was directed to disrobe for photographs, about which he was told, "You really don't have a choice." All of these factors combined to prompt Elmarr to ask the reasonable question, "When do I get to go home?" All of these facts lead to the conclusion that Elmarr's freedom of action was curtailed to a degree associated with formal arrest, and a reasonable person under those circumstances would feel that he was in custody.[5]

We conclude that all of Elmarr's statements to the police at the Boulder Sheriff's Department in 1987 were the product of custodial interrogation. Because it is conceded that Elmarr did not receive a proper *Miranda* warning, all of those statements

---

5. The People argue that if the interrogation of Elmarr was custodial, it only became so toward the end of the interview, so that only statements after that point could be suppressed. However, there is no discrete point at which one could say that a non-custodial interview suddenly became custodial. It is the totality of the circumstances, from the time Elmarr was put in a police car until the time he was finally released hours later, that makes the encounter custodial.

must be suppressed. Accordingly, we affirm the trial court's suppression order, and remand for further proceedings consistent with this opinion.

COATS, J., dissenting.

Almost a quarter-century ago, the United States Supreme Court made clear that a suspect is not placed in custody for purposes of the *Miranda* requirements merely by being seized and subjected to an investigatory stop. Berkemer v. McCarty, 468 U.S. 420 (1984). Rather, the prophylactic *Miranda* warnings are triggered only when a suspect's liberty has been infringed upon to an extent commensurate with a formal arrest. And interrogation at a police station, as long as it is consensual, does not constitute a seizure of any kind, much less a seizure tantamount to an arrest.

[The majority] fails to distinguish objective indications that a suspect has effectively been arrested from indications of a potential suspect's interest in avoiding that eventuality. In the former case, any statements made without an effective waiver of *Miranda* warnings are presumptively the product of police coercion. In the latter, whether motivated more by a desire to assist the investigation or to avoid attracting further suspicion, no such presumption arises. Comparing voluntary witness statements and real evidence is not only a legitimate but in fact a highly desirable and effective technique for solving crimes.

In the absence of actual indicia of an arrest, the majority marshals a laundry list of circumstances or factors, indicative of little more than an interview at the police station. The fact that interview rooms are typically neither large nor public, that two officers are present for an interview, or that they close the door for privacy indicate virtually nothing about the voluntariness of an interviewee's presence. As the Supreme Court has expressly noted, the fact that questioners carry holstered side-arms indicates only that they are police officers, which is understood by the interviewee when he consents to a stationhouse interview. And rather than being an indication of arrest, riding in a police car, only after giving consent and without having been patted-down or handcuffed, would suggest to any reasonable person precisely the opposite.

In the absence of an objectively manifested change in circumstances, the fact that a defendant who is present by agreement is not expressly told that he is free to leave has little meaning; and it seems more than a little disingenuous to suggest it as a worthy practice in light of the trial court's adverse reaction to the police reminder that the defendant was free not to speak with them. To the extent that circumstances actually did change at some point as a result of the defendant's responses, he clearly felt free to, and did, terminate the interview, and only his earlier statements are at issue here. In fact, the majority's substantial reliance on events following termination of the interview is a further indication of its failure to grasp, or at least its failure to apply, the objective standard dictated by the Supreme Court. In the absence of any indication that they already intended, and had already communicated their intent, to arrest him, the subsequent actions of the officers could have no bearing whatsoever on the defendant's perception of his status at the time of his statements. . . .

I believe the majority's holding today conflicts with the Supreme Court's interpretation of the United States Constitution; can serve only to dissuade law enforcement officers from seeking and preserving a record of voluntary witness interviews; and needlessly hinders the search for truth in the criminal process. I therefore respectfully dissent.

Notes

1. *Subjective versus objective test for custody: majority position.* Federal and state courts determine whether a suspect is in "custody" for purposes of *Miranda* by using an objective test: Would a reasonable person in the suspect's position believe that she has been constrained in a manner akin to an arrest? See Berkemer v. McCarty, 468 U.S. 420 (1984). The particular officer's intentions about the suspect's freedom to leave, and the suspect's actual views about whether she was free to leave, are not controlling under this approach. Many circumstances—the location of the interrogation, the suspect's reason for coming there, the number of officers present, the defendant's conduct after the interrogation—can have a bearing on this objective test. An event does not have to occur in a police station to be custodial. See Orozco v. Texas, 394 U.S. 324 (1969) (custodial interrogation when four police officers wake suspect in bedroom at 4 A.M. and question him). By the same token, an interrogation does not become custodial whenever it occurs within a police station. See California v. Beheler, 463 U.S. 1121 (1983) (no custody where suspect arrives at station voluntarily, is told he is not under arrest, and leaves after brief interrogation); cf. Howes v. Fields, 565 U.S. 499 (2012) (rejecting categorical rule that any questioning of a prisoner isolated from the general prison population about an alleged crime is custodial; no "custody" here based on totality of circumstances surrounding interrogation in prison conference room by sheriff's deputies).

When a suspect is "asked" to come to the station, is it necessarily a voluntary appearance? If a police officer asks a suspect "to have a seat" in the patrol car, is the suspect necessarily in custody? See People v. Taylor, 41 P.3d 681 (Colo. 2002) (roadside stop of driver became custodial for *Miranda* purposes after passenger was arrested on outstanding warrant, officers searched car without consent, and one officer kept driver standing in one place outside car). The dizzying level of detail that seems relevant in answering the custody question gets further attention in the web extension for this chapter at *http://www.crimpro.com/extension/ch08.*

While the Colorado Supreme Court seems to apply a relatively broad definition of "custody," it is equally easy to find high state courts more skeptical of custody determinations. See State v. Smith, 546 N.W. 2d 916 (Iowa 1996) (no custody where four juveniles under probation in Missouri were brought to a juvenile center by their mothers, where they were interviewed by Iowa officers about a murder; while the interviews took place over many hours, the interview center was "family-centered" and "warm" and had a fish tank, food and drinks were provided, and the questioning was "non-coercive"); Herrera v. State, 241 S.W.3d 520 (Tex. Crim. App. 2007) (simply pointing out that interrogation occurred in jail, where suspect was already in jail on unrelated charges, is not enough to meet burden of showing that suspect was in custody for purposes of *Miranda*).

2. *Age and experience as custody factors.* In the context of juvenile suspects, the labels "objective" and "subjective" may not be a reliable guide to which facts will shape the outcome of the court's custody analysis. On the one hand, the Supreme Court tries to avoid any definition of "custody" that would require interrogators to learn about the particular suspect's "actual mindset." See Yarborough v. Alvarado, 541 U.S. 652 (2004) (defendant's age or experience with law enforcement did not qualify as "objective circumstances of the interrogation" in determining the question of custody). On the other hand, when the officer does know (or reasonably should know) the age of a young suspect, courts may treat the child's age as relevant

to the custody analysis. The court treats this as a categorical analysis rather than an observation about the mindset of a single suspect. In J.D.B. v. North Carolina, 564 U.S. 261 (2011), a uniformed police officer removed a 13-year-old student from a seventh-grade classroom and questioned him for an hour in a closed-door conference room in the school. Although the state courts refused to consider the defendant's age as a relevant factor, the Supreme Court reversed and remanded, seeing "no reason for police officers or courts to blind themselves" to the "commonsense reality" that children "often feel bound to submit to police questioning when an adult in the same circumstances would feel free to leave."

3. *"Arrest" versus "custody."* A suspect who is arrested is in custody for purposes of *Miranda*. But custodial interrogation may occur even if the suspect is not formally arrested, and even if the interrogation does not take place at the police station. For example, the Colorado Supreme Court in *Elmarr* notes that custodial interrogation took place in People v. Minjarez, 81 P.3d 348 (Colo. 2003), where police officers "aggressively" interrogated a suspect in a hospital interview room for 20 of the 45 minutes of interrogation. See also State v. McKenna, 103 A.3d 756 (N.H. 2014) (defendant was in custody even though he was in his own yard when police questioned him, because defendant was told he was not free to walk away, the questioning was confrontational and accusatory, and the entire episode lasted an hour and 15 minutes).

4. *"Stop" versus "custody."* Recall that, for purposes of the Fourth Amendment, a "stop" occurs when a reasonable innocent person would not "feel free to leave" or to otherwise terminate the encounter, and has submitted to the officer's show of authority (see Chapter 2). If an officer questions a person during such an investigative stop, has a custodial interrogation occurred for purposes of *Miranda?* In Berkemer v. McCarty, 468 U.S. 420 (1984), the Supreme Court decided that a traffic stop does *not* amount to "custody" under *Miranda*. State courts both before and after *Berkemer* have reached the same conclusion. How is questioning during an investigative stop different from interrogation in the police station? How are they similar?

5. *Compelled appearances in legal proceedings.* Is a person in "custody" when a court orders her to appear in legal proceedings to answer questions? Under the U.S. Constitution, the courts have concluded that compulsory process is not "custody" for purposes of *Miranda*. See United States v. Mandujano, 425 U.S. 564 (1976) (no *Miranda* warnings required for witnesses compelled to appear before grand jury); State v. Monteiro, 632 A.2d 340 (R.I. 1993) (same); Minnesota v. Murphy, 465 U.S. 420 (1984) (no warnings necessary during required interview with probation officer); but see Estelle v. Smith, 451 U.S. 454 (1981) (suspect is in custody when compelled to attend interview with state-paid psychologist who will testify at sentencing). Given that a refusal to comply with an order to appear can lead to a jail term for contempt, how is this situation different from custodial interrogation in a police station?

Problem 8-1. Conversation During Police Assistance

Shortly after midnight, Police Officer Gene Sheldon was dispatched to the residence of Marvin and Linda Dyer on an emergency call, because Ms. Dyer was reportedly suffering from a medical problem. Officer Sheldon arrived at the same time as an ambulance. After the rescue unit had left to take Ms. Dyer to the medical clinic, Officer Sheldon asked Mr. Dyer what had happened, and Mr. Dyer admitted that he had hit his wife. After a few moments of conversation, Mr. Dyer said that he wanted to go to bed and "if anybody comes back to the bedroom, all they are going to hear is a loud bang." Sheldon stopped Mr. Dyer from leaving the room by standing in the hallway. He convinced Mr. Dyer to sit down and relax. About two hours later Ms. Dyer returned home, and Officer Sheldon placed Mr. Dyer under arrest. Did Mr. Dyer make his statements while in custody? See State v. Dyer, 513 N.W.2d 316 (Neb. 1994).

Problem 8-2. Blunt Questions

Joseph Turmel was driving north on Interstate 89 when he was passed by Trooper James Mayers at about 70 mph. The officer noticed that Turmel appeared to be smoking a marijuana cigarette as he drove by. Mayers radioed for a marked police cruiser to assist him, and soon Sgt. Scott Sweet caught up to pursue. The officers eventually pulled over Turmel's car.

Sgt. Sweet approached on the driver's side and asked Turmel to step out of the car; he then escorted Turmel to the back of the car. Mayers smelled marijuana coming from the interior of the car. Mayers introduced himself to Turmel as an officer with the Narcotics Investigation Unit of the State Police, and explained that he had watched him smoking marijuana in the car. Mayers told Turmel that he wanted him to cooperate and asked him if he had been smoking marijuana. Turmel replied, "Yes." Mayers told him that he was not under arrest and asked him whether there were any weapons or drugs in the car. Turmel said there were none, and then Mayers asked for consent to search the vehicle, saying that if no weapons or drugs were found in the car, Turmel would "probably" be free to leave. Mayers told Turmel that he did not have to consent to the search, but if he did not consent, Mayers would pursue "other avenues" to search the car. Turmel consented to the search.

Mayers' initial search did not produce any contraband. But following the discovery of a large amount of cash in the trunk, the officers summoned a trooper with a drug-sniffing dog, who arrived at the scene 10 minutes later. They eventually found the butt of a marijuana cigarette in the car's ashtray. Neither Sweet nor Mayers read a *Miranda* warning to Turmel before the questioning or before his consent to search the car. Will the trial court grant a motion to suppress the cash and the marijuana cigarette butt? Does the legal analysis here differ at all from the "stop versus arrest" question explored in Chapter 5? Cf. State v. Turmel, 838 A.2d 1279 (N.H. 2003).

3. The "Interrogation" Precondition for Miranda Warnings

A suspect's conversations with police while in custody might not rise to the level of interrogation and therefore might not require *Miranda* warnings. Of the many conversations taking place between police officers and suspects, which qualify as "interrogations" that trigger *Miranda* warnings in custodial settings? Have the courts drawn the line wisely?

■ RHODE ISLAND v. THOMAS INNIS

446 U.S. 291 (1980)

STEWART, J.[*]

In Miranda v. Arizona, 384 U.S. 436 (1966), the Court held that, once a defendant in custody asks to speak with a lawyer, all interrogation must cease until a lawyer is present. The issue in this case is whether the respondent was "interrogated" in violation of the standards promulgated in the *Miranda* opinion.

I.

[Shortly] after midnight, the Providence police received a telephone call from Gerald Aubin, . . . a taxicab driver, who reported that he had just been robbed by a man wielding a sawed-off shotgun [near Mount Pleasant]. While at the Providence police station waiting to give a statement, Aubin noticed a picture of his assailant on a bulletin board [on a poster relating to the murder of a taxicab driver five days earlier. That picture was of Innis].

At approximately 4:30 A.M. on the same date, Patrolman Lovell, while cruising the streets of Mount Pleasant in a patrol car, spotted [Innis, arrested him, and advised him of his *Miranda* rights. Within minutes, Sergeant Sears and Captain Leyden arrived at the scene, and each of them also gave Innis *Miranda* warnings.] The respondent stated that he understood those rights and wanted to speak with a lawyer. Captain Leyden then directed that the respondent be placed in a "caged wagon," a four-door police car with a wire screen mesh between the front and rear seats, and be driven to the central police station. Three officers, Patrolmen Gleckman, Williams, and McKenna, were assigned to accompany the respondent to the central station. They placed the respondent in the vehicle and shut the doors. Captain Leyden then instructed the officers not to question the respondent or intimidate or coerce him in any way. The three officers then entered the vehicle, and it departed.

While en route to the central station, Patrolman Gleckman initiated a conversation with Patrolman McKenna concerning the missing shotgun. As Patrolman Gleckman later testified:

> At this point, I was talking back and forth with Patrolman McKenna stating that I frequent this area while on patrol and [that because a school for handicapped children is located nearby,] there's a lot of handicapped children running around in this area, and God forbid one of them might find a weapon with shells and they might hurt themselves.

Patrolman McKenna apparently shared his fellow officer's concern: "I more or less concurred with him [Gleckman] that it was a safety factor and that we should, you know, continue to search for the weapon and try to find it." While Patrolman Williams said nothing, he overheard the conversation between the two officers: "He [Gleckman] said it would be too bad if the little—I believe he said a girl—would pick up the gun, maybe kill herself." The respondent then interrupted the conversation, stating that the officers should turn the car around so he could show them

---

[*] [Justices White, Blackmun, Powell, and Rehnquist joined in this opinion.—EDS.]

where the gun was located. . . . At the time the respondent indicated that the officers should turn back, they had traveled no more than a mile, a trip encompassing only a few minutes. The police vehicle then returned to the scene of the arrest where a search for the shotgun was in progress. There, Captain Leyden again advised the respondent of his *Miranda* rights. The respondent replied that he understood those rights but that he "wanted to get the gun out of the way because of the kids in the area in the school." The respondent then led the police to a nearby field, where he pointed out the shotgun under some rocks by the side of the road.

[The trial court denied Innis's motion to suppress the evidence regarding the gun, concluding that Innis had waived his *Miranda* rights. The jury returned a verdict of guilty on all counts.] We granted certiorari to address for the first time the meaning of "interrogation" under Miranda v. Arizona. . . .

II.

. . . The starting point for defining "interrogation" in this context is, of course, the Court's *Miranda* opinion. There the Court observed that "[by] custodial interrogation, we mean questioning initiated by law enforcement officers after a person has been taken into custody or otherwise deprived of his freedom of action in any significant way." This passage and other references throughout the opinion to "questioning" might suggest that the *Miranda* rules were to apply only to those police interrogation practices that involve express questioning of a defendant while in custody.

We do not, however, construe the *Miranda* opinion so narrowly. The concern of the Court in *Miranda* was that the "interrogation environment" created by the interplay of interrogation and custody would "subjugate the individual to the will of his examiner" and thereby undermine the privilege against compulsory self-incrimination. The police practices that evoked this concern included several that did not involve express questioning. For example, [the Court mentioned] the use of psychological ploys, such as to posit "the guilt of the subject," to "minimize the moral seriousness of the offense," and "to cast blame on the victim or on society." It is clear that these techniques of persuasion, no less than express questioning, were thought, in a custodial setting, to amount to interrogation.

This is not to say, however, that all statements obtained by the police after a person has been taken into custody are to be considered the product of interrogation. [It is clear] that the special procedural safeguards outlined in *Miranda* are required not where a suspect is simply taken into custody, but rather where a suspect in custody is subjected to interrogation. "Interrogation," as conceptualized in the *Miranda* opinion, must reflect a measure of compulsion above and beyond that inherent in custody itself.

We conclude that the *Miranda* safeguards come into play whenever a person in custody is subjected to either express questioning or its functional equivalent. That is to say, the term "interrogation" under *Miranda* refers not only to express questioning, but also to any words or actions on the part of the police (other than those normally attendant to arrest and custody) that the police should know are reasonably likely to elicit an incriminating response from the suspect. The latter portion of this definition focuses primarily upon the perceptions of the suspect, rather than the intent of the police. This focus reflects the fact that the *Miranda* safeguards were designed to vest a suspect in custody with an added measure of protection against coercive police practices, without regard to objective proof of the underlying intent of the police. A practice that the police should know is reasonably likely to evoke an incriminating response from a suspect thus amounts to interrogation.[7] But, since the police surely cannot be held accountable for the unforeseeable results of their words or actions, the definition of interrogation can extend only to words or actions on the part of police officers that they should have known were reasonably likely to elicit an incriminating response.[8]

Turning to the facts of the present case, we conclude that the respondent was not "interrogated" within the meaning of *Miranda*. It is undisputed that the first prong of the definition of "interrogation" was not satisfied, for the conversation between Patrolmen Gleckman and McKenna included no express questioning of the respondent. Rather, that conversation was, at least in form, nothing more than a dialogue between the two officers to which no response from the respondent was invited.

Moreover, it cannot be fairly concluded that the respondent was subjected to the "functional equivalent" of questioning. It cannot be said, in short, that Patrolmen Gleckman and McKenna should have known that their conversation was reasonably likely to elicit an incriminating response from the respondent. There is nothing in the record to suggest that the officers were aware that the respondent was peculiarly susceptible to an appeal to his conscience concerning the safety of handicapped children. Nor is there anything in the record to suggest that the police knew that the respondent was unusually disoriented or upset at the time of his arrest.

The case thus boils down to whether, in the context of a brief conversation, the officers should have known that the respondent would suddenly be moved to make a self-incriminating response. Given the fact that the entire conversation appears to have consisted of no more than a few offhand remarks, we cannot say that the officers should have known that it was reasonably likely that Innis would so respond. This is not a case where the police carried on a lengthy harangue in the presence of the suspect. Nor does the record support the respondent's contention that, under the circumstances, the officers' comments were particularly "evocative." It is our view, therefore, that the respondent was not subjected by the police to words or actions that the police should have known were reasonably likely to elicit an incriminating response from him. . . .

MARSHALL, J., dissenting.*

I am substantially in agreement with the Court's definition of "interrogation" within the meaning of Miranda v. Arizona, 384 U.S. 436 (1966). In my view, the *Miranda* safeguards apply whenever police conduct is intended or likely to produce a response from a suspect in custody. [The] Court requires an objective inquiry into

---

7. This is not to say that the intent of the police is irrelevant, for it may well have a bearing on whether the police should have known that their words or actions were reasonably likely to evoke an incriminating response. In particular, where a police practice is designed to elicit an incriminating response from the accused, it is unlikely that the practice will not also be one which the police should have known was reasonably likely to have that effect.

8. Any knowledge the police may have had concerning the unusual susceptibility of a defendant to a particular form of persuasion might be an important factor in determining whether the police should have known that their words or actions were reasonably likely to elicit an incriminating response from the suspect.

* [Justice Brennan joined in this opinion. —EDS.]

the likely effect of police conduct on a typical individual, taking into account any special susceptibility of the suspect to certain kinds of pressure of which the police know or have reason to know.

I am utterly at a loss, however, to understand how this objective standard as applied to the facts before us can rationally lead to the conclusion that there was no interrogation. . . . Since the car traveled no more than a mile before Innis agreed to point out the location of the murder weapon, Officer Gleckman must have begun almost immediately to talk about the search for the shotgun. . . . One can scarcely imagine a stronger appeal to the conscience of a suspect—any suspect—than the assertion that if the weapon is not found an innocent person will be hurt or killed. And not just any innocent person, but an innocent child—a little girl—a helpless, handicapped little girl on her way to school. The notion that such an appeal could not be expected to have any effect unless the suspect were known to have some special interest in handicapped children verges on the ludicrous. . . . I firmly believe that this case is simply an aberration, and that in future cases the Court will apply the standard adopted today in accordance with its plain meaning.

STEVENS, J., dissenting.

. . . *I.*

[In] my view any statement that would normally be understood by the average listener as calling for a response is the functional equivalent of a direct question, whether or not it is punctuated by a question mark. The Court, however, takes a much narrower view. It holds that police conduct is not the "functional equivalent" of direct questioning unless the police should have known that what they were saying or doing was likely to elicit an incriminating response from the suspect. This holding represents a plain departure from the principles set forth in *Miranda.*

[Once a suspect cuts off questioning,] the police are prohibited from making deliberate attempts to elicit statements from the suspect. Yet the Court is unwilling to characterize all such attempts as "interrogation," noting only that "where a police practice is designed to elicit an incriminating response from the accused, it is unlikely that the practice will not also be one which the police should have known was reasonably likely to have that effect."[8]

[In] order to give full protection to a suspect's right to be free from any interrogation at all, the definition of "interrogation" must include any police statement or conduct that has the same purpose or effect as a direct question. Statements that appear to call for a response from the suspect, as well as those that are designed to do so, should be considered interrogation. By prohibiting only those relatively few statements or actions that a police officer should know are likely to elicit an incriminating response, the Court today accords a suspect considerably less protection. Indeed, since I suppose most suspects are unlikely to incriminate themselves even when questioned directly, this new definition will almost certainly exclude every statement that is not punctuated with a question mark from the concept of "interrogation."

---

8. This factual assumption is extremely dubious. I would assume that police often interrogate suspects without any reason to believe that their efforts are likely to be successful in the hope that a statement will nevertheless be forthcoming.

The difference between the approach required by a faithful adherence to *Miranda* and the stinted test applied by the Court today can be illustrated by comparing three different ways in which Officer Gleckman could have communicated his fears about the possible dangers posed by the shotgun to handicapped children. He could have:

1. directly asked Innis: "Will you please tell me where the shotgun is so we can protect handicapped schoolchildren from danger?"
2. announced to the other officers in the wagon: "If the man sitting in the back seat with me should decide to tell us where the gun is, we can protect handicapped children from danger," or
3. stated to the other officers: "It would be too bad if a little handicapped girl would pick up the gun that this man left in the area and maybe kill herself."

In my opinion, all three of these statements should be considered interrogation because all three appear to be designed to elicit a response from anyone who in fact knew where the gun was located. Under the Court's test, on the other hand, the form of the statements would be critical. The third statement would not be interrogation because in the Court's view there was no reason for Officer Gleckman to believe that Innis was susceptible to this type of an implied appeal; therefore, the statement would not be reasonably likely to elicit an incriminating response. Assuming that this is true, then it seems to me that the first two statements, which would be just as unlikely to elicit such a response, should also not be considered interrogation. But, because the first statement is clearly an express question, it would be considered interrogation under the Court's test. The second statement, although just as clearly a deliberate appeal to Innis to reveal the location of the gun, would presumably not be interrogation because (a) it was not in form a direct question and (b) it does not fit within the "reasonably likely to elicit an incriminating response" category that applies to indirect interrogation.

As this example illustrates, the Court's test creates an incentive for police to ignore a suspect's invocation of his rights in order to make continued attempts to extract information from him. If a suspect does not appear to be susceptible to a particular type of psychological pressure, the police are apparently free to exert that pressure on him despite his request for counsel, so long as they are careful not to punctuate their statements with question marks. And if, contrary to all reasonable expectations, the suspect makes an incriminating statement, that statement can be used against him at trial. The Court thus turns *Miranda*'s unequivocal rule against any interrogation at all into a trap in which unwary suspects may be caught by police deception. . . .

II.

. . . In any event, I think the Court is clearly wrong in holding, as a matter of law, that Officer Gleckman should not have realized that his statement was likely to elicit an incriminating response. The Court implicitly assumes that, at least in the absence of a lengthy harangue, a criminal suspect will not be likely to respond to indirect appeals to his humanitarian impulses. [This assumption] is directly contrary to the teachings of police interrogation manuals, which recommend appealing to a suspect's sense of morality as a standard and often successful interrogation technique. . . .

Moreover, there is evidence in the record to support the view that Officer Gleckman's statement was intended to elicit a response from Innis. Officer Gleckman, who was not regularly assigned to the caged wagon, was directed by a police captain to ride with respondent to the police station. . . . The record does not explain why, notwithstanding the fact that respondent was handcuffed, unarmed, and had offered no resistance when arrested by an officer acting alone, the captain ordered Officer Gleckman to ride with respondent. It is not inconceivable that two professionally trained police officers concluded that a few well-chosen remarks might induce respondent to disclose the whereabouts of the shotgun. This conclusion becomes even more plausible in light of the emotionally charged words chosen by Officer Gleckman. . . .

Notes

1. *Interrogation by known government agents: majority position.* Virtually all jurisdictions follow the *Innis* definition of "interrogation": words or actions that the police "should know are reasonably likely to elicit an incriminating response from the suspect." See State v. Grant, 944 A.2d 947 (Conn. 2008) (statement to defendant that defendant's blood had been found at murder scene did not constitute interrogation; conduct here was of the sort "normally attendant to arrest" and "a per se rule that confronting a suspect with incriminating evidence constitutes interrogation is not required under *Innis*"). Did the Court apply this test appropriately to the facts of *Innis?* This definition applies not only in those cases when the police initiate a conversation; it also reaches some cases in which the suspect asks a question or makes a statement, and the officer responds in a way that leads the suspect to make an incriminating reply. In such cases, the reply is subject to interrogation analysis, even if the first statement is exempt.

2. *Booking questions.* The definition of an "interrogation" sometimes becomes an issue when a police officer who processes the routine paperwork and fingerprints as part of the suspect's detention makes some comment that elicits an incriminating response from the suspect. In Pennsylvania v. Muniz, 496 U.S. 582 (1990), the Supreme Court determined that some, but not all, of the questions asked of a defendant during a routine booking on DWI charges were "interrogations" that required *Miranda* warnings. *Routine questions* asking for the suspect's name, address, height, weight, eye color, date of birth, and current age were not considered interrogations. When, however, the booking officer asked the suspect the date of his sixth birthday and the suspect was unable to calculate it, the officer's question qualified as an interrogation. What is it about most of the booking questions that takes them outside the coverage of *Miranda?* See State v. Goseland, 887 P.2d 1109 (Kan. 1994) (during booking paperwork, officer remarks to suspect in narcotics case, "You need to find something else to do with your life" and suspect replies, "No, I'll not stop selling dope, because then you all would not have anything to do"; no interrogation, because officer always makes this remark to suspects being booked).

3. *Interrogation by unknown government agents: majority position.* In all the interrogations we have considered so far, the suspect was aware that the person asking questions was a police officer. But can there be an "interrogation" when a suspect in custody is talking with a person whom he does not believe to be an agent of the police? The Supreme Court and state high courts say no. In Illinois v. Perkins,

496 U.S. 292 (1990), the Supreme Court held that no *Miranda* warnings were necessary when police placed an undercover agent in same cellblock with a murder suspect, and the agent asked if the suspect had ever "done" anybody, leading the suspect to confess to the murder. The Court held that conversations between suspects and undercover agents "do not implicate the concerns underlying *Miranda*." But weren't the undercover agent's words "reasonably likely to elicit an incriminating response"? If so, what explains the inapplicability of *Miranda* when undercover agents ask the questions?

4. *"Public safety" exception to* Miranda: *majority position.* In New York v. Quarles, 467 U.S. 649 (1984), a woman reported to police officers around midnight that she had just been raped by a man and said that the man, who was armed, had entered a nearby supermarket. One of the officers went into the supermarket and spotted a man, later determined to be Benjamin Quarles, fitting the description given by the woman. The officer frisked Quarles and discovered an empty shoulder holster. After handcuffing Quarles, the officer asked him where the gun was. Quarles nodded in the direction of some empty cartons and responded, "The gun is over there." Quarles subsequently argued that the statement about the gun had been obtained in violation of *Miranda*.

The Supreme Court concluded that even though the officer had conducted a custodial interrogation without giving *Miranda* warnings, the suspect's statement was not obtained contrary to the Constitution. The officer's questions about the gun were necessary not only to solve a completed crime but to prevent future crimes or accidents involving the missing gun. The need for "answers to questions in a situation posing a threat to the public safety outweighs the need for the prophylactic rule protecting the Fifth Amendment's privilege against self-incrimination." 467 U.S. at 657. Even if the officer did not ask the questions with the actual purpose of preventing a future mishap with the weapon, a court could later infer a public safety purpose for the questions from the surrounding circumstances.

More than half the states allow a "public safety" or related "rescue" exception to *Miranda*. See People v. Davis, 208 P.3d 78 (Cal. 2009) (state's "rescue doctrine" still applies after more than two months elapsed between abduction of young girl and interrogation of suspect, because defendant told others he was "only doing this for the money," raising possibility that victim might still be alive). A 2011 empirical study of the application of the public safety exception (PSE) in federal and state cases found that 83 percent of PSE cases involve firearms, 10 percent involve other weapons, 4 percent involve a second suspect, and 3 percent involve a bomb or explosive device. Joanna Wright, Mirandizing Terrorists? An Empirical Analysis of the Public Safety Exception, 111 Colum. L. Rev. 1296 (2011).

Problem 8-3. Blurting

A suspect in a shooting was taken into custody. The suspect asked to talk with the detectives investigating the case, but they told him that he could do so only after his fingerprints were taken and after he had executed a written waiver of his *Miranda* rights. While a different detective was taking the prints, the suspect blurted out, "This is really going to f*** me up." The detective immediately asked why, and the suspect said that he had handled the gun in question on the previous day but that it had jammed. The detective stopped the defendant from saying anything further.

Later tests of the gun yielded no identifiable fingerprints. Was the suspect "interrogated" at the time he made this statement? Compare Commonwealth v. Diaz, 661 N.E.2d 1326 (Mass. 1996).

Problem 8-4. Public Safety Motivation

On November 26, 2011, police in Monroe County, Pennsylvania, received a 911 call reporting a domestic dispute at a neighbor's home. Officers Matthew Tretter and Joel Rutter arrived at the scene, and the caller told them that she had heard a loud noise and a high-pitched scream ("Help me!") outside of her door. When she looked outside, she saw someone being dragged across her front lawn into the neighbor's residence. The officers noticed that there was a smear of blood on the neighbor's front door and that a wooden porch railing had been broken.

When the troopers knocked on the door and announced their presence, Manuel Sepulveda opened the door. He initially denied knowledge of any incident, but then stated that he had been assaulted by two men. At this time, the officers arrested Sepulveda and placed him in the back of the police cruiser. Believing that a domestic assault had occurred, the officers asked Sepulveda where the woman was. He responded, "There is no 'she.' They are in the basement. I shot them." Subsequently, police found two bodies in the basement and charged Sepulveda with two counts of murder. Sepulveda moved to suppress the statements he gave to the officers in the police car, claiming that they were obtained in violation of Miranda v. Arizona. How is a court likely to rule? See Commonwealth v. Sepulveda, 855 A.2d 783 (Pa. 2004).

4. Form of Warnings

The *Miranda* decision designated four topics that warnings would need to cover before a custodial interrogation could take place. However, the Court did not specify the precise language that the police must use to convey these warnings. How much variation in the language of the warnings is tolerable?

In California v. Prysock, 453 U.S. 355 (1981), the Supreme Court confirmed that a "verbatim recital" of the words in the *Miranda* opinion is not necessary to give an adequate warning to a suspect before an interrogation. The warning in that case told the suspect of his right to have an attorney present prior to and during questioning, and of his "right to have a lawyer appointed at no cost if he could not afford one." This was sufficient, even though it might have left the suspect with the impression that an appointed lawyer would become available only after questioning. In Duckworth v. Eagan, 492 U.S. 195 (1989), the Supreme Court considered the constitutionality of an Indiana *Miranda* warning that said, among other things, "we have no way of giving you a lawyer, but one will be appointed for you, if you wish, if and when you go to court." The Court held the warning complied with *Miranda*, noting that "*Miranda* does not require that attorneys be producible on call, but only that the suspect be informed, as here, that he has the right to an attorney before and during questioning, and that an attorney would be appointed for him if he could not afford one."

In Florida v. Powell, 559 U.S. 50 (2010), the police informed a suspect before a custodial interrogation that "You have the right to talk to a lawyer before answering any of our questions" and "You have the right to use any of these rights at any time you want during this interview." The suspect waived *Miranda* rights and admitted ownership of a firearm. Although the warning informed a suspect about access to an attorney *before* questioning rather than *during* an interrogation, the Supreme Court held that this combination of warnings satisfied the requirements of *Miranda*. The Court reiterated its view that no particular formulation of words is necessary to convey the essential information about rights of a suspect during custodial interrogation. The two statements that police used in this case, taken together, address the *Miranda* Court's concern that the "circumstances surrounding in-custody interrogation can operate very quickly to overbear the will of one merely made aware of his privilege [to remain silent] by his interrogators."

State courts have also determined that their constitutions allow for some variety (and some ambiguity) in the way the warnings are phrased. A few state statutes provide for additional warnings to some suspects (especially juveniles) before interrogation, but state courts have hesitated to conclude that statutes dealing with warnings for suspects require a particular verbal formula. See, e.g., State v. Bittick, 806 S.W.2d 652 (Mo. 1991) (interpreting warnings listed in Mo. Rev. Stat. §600.048.1). Why haven't more state courts insisted on a uniform and unambiguous method of conveying the *Miranda* warnings? Wouldn't an "inflexible" rule be both realistic and easy to administer because police officers could simply read the warnings from a pocket-sized card?

Notes

1. *Other variations in the warning.* Some police officers tell suspects that anything they say during an interrogation can be used "for or against" the suspect. Why do you suppose they phrase the warning this way? Is it an acceptable variation on the *Miranda* warnings? See State v. Stanley, 613 A.2d 788 (Conn. 1992) (approving of "for or against" statement on printed waiver form when it is accompanied by other "against" statements); Dunn v. State, 721 S.W.2d 325 (Tex. Crim. App. 1986) (error to give "for or against" warning).

The *Miranda* opinion, after describing the four warnings now known as the *Miranda* warnings, added the following: If the suspect "indicates in any manner that he does not wish to be interrogated, the police may not question him." 384 U.S. at 445. The opinion also refers to "the right to refrain from answering any further inquiries." Should the police be expected to warn suspects about this "fifth right" to cut off questioning? Courts considering this question have almost uniformly said no. See, e.g., State v. Mitchell, 482 N.W.2d 364 (Wis. 1992). But see Tex. Code Crim. P. 38.22(2) (requiring police to inform defendants of "the right to terminate the interview at any time."). If the suspect does indeed have the right to cut off questioning, why should the police be obliged to tell suspects about some of their rights but not this one? Would warnings about this right have any greater effect than the four existing warnings? Cf. United States v. Lombera-Camorlinga, 206 F.3d 882 (9th Cir. 2000) (failure to inform arrested noncitizen of Vienna Convention right to contact consul does not require suppression of statement).

For an exploration of other variations in the precise wording of the *Miranda* warnings, see the web extension for this chapter at *http://www.crimpro.com/extension/ch08.*

2. *Translation of* Miranda *warnings.* A suspect who has difficulty understanding English must receive the warnings in her own language. For this reason, some police departments maintain a standardized translation of the *Miranda* warnings in languages commonly spoken in the area. See State v. Santiago, 556 N.W.2d 687 (Wis. 1996).

3. Miranda *warnings for vulnerable suspects.* Should *Miranda* warnings be adapted for vulnerable suspects, such as the mentally disabled, who are less likely to comprehend the standard warnings? Empirical studies have found that defendants with mental disorders have serious difficulties comprehending *Miranda* warnings. See, e.g., Richard Rogers et al., Knowing and Intelligent: A Study of *Miranda* Warnings in Mentally Disordered Defendants, 31 Law & Hum. Behav. 401 (2007).

C. INVOCATION AND WAIVER OF *MIRANDA* RIGHTS

After the police give a *Miranda* warning, a suspect may invoke the right to counsel or to silence, or waive these rights and submit to the interrogation. Most suspects waive the right to counsel and the right to silence after receiving *Miranda* warnings; studies show that waiver occurs in at least three-quarters of all custodial interrogations (and probably more). In this section, we review how courts determine whether a suspect has invoked or waived *Miranda* rights.

Suspects typically use language that leaves some doubt about their invocation or waiver of the right to counsel or silence. The rules for handling ambiguous words or actions suggesting invocation or waiver can have a huge practical impact: If only crystal clear invocation is valid, there will be more waivers, while if courts insist that government agents treat a range of ambiguous statements or actions as assertions of *Miranda* rights, invocation will be more common. Police actions during times of ambiguity have given rise to a range of cases in state and federal courts.

■ VERMONT STATUTES TIT. 13, §§5234, 5237

§5234

(a) If a person who is being detained by a law enforcement officer . . . is not represented by an attorney under conditions in which a person having his own counsel would be entitled to be so represented, the law enforcement officer, magistrate, or court concerned shall:

(1) Clearly inform him of the right of a person to be represented by an attorney and of a needy person to be represented at public expense; and

(2) If the person detained or charged does not have an attorney and does not knowingly, voluntarily and intelligently waive his right to have an attorney when detained or charged, notify the appropriate public defender that he is not so represented. . . .

(d) Information . . . given to a person by a law enforcement officer under this section gives rise to a rebuttable presumption that the information was effectively communicated if:

(1) It is in writing or otherwise recorded;

(2) The recipient records his acknowledgment of receipt and time of receipt of the information; and

(3) The material so recorded under paragraphs (1) and (2) of this subsection is filed with the court next concerned.

§5237

A person who has been appropriately informed under section 5234 of this title may waive in writing, or by other record, any right provided by this chapter, if the court, at the time of or after waiver, finds of record that he has acted with full awareness of his rights and of the consequences of a waiver and if the waiver is otherwise according to law. The court shall consider such factors as the person's age, education, and familiarity with the English language, and the complexity of the crime involved.

▇ COMMONWEALTH v. CLARKE
960 N.E. 2d 306 (Mass. 2012)

LENK, J.

The question for decision is whether the defendant, by his conduct, had invoked the right to remain silent guaranteed under the Fifth Amendment to the United States Constitution and art. 12 of the Massachusetts Declaration of Rights and, if so, whether the police sufficiently honored that right. We conclude that, under both the Fifth Amendment and art. 12, the right to remain silent was invoked but was not "scrupulously honored," and that suppression of the subsequent incriminating statements was accordingly warranted. In so concluding, we hold that, in the pre-waiver context, art. 12 does not require a suspect to invoke his right to remain silent with the utmost clarity, as required under Federal law. See Berghuis v. Thompkins, 560 U.S. 370 (2010).

1. BACKGROUND AND PRIOR PROCEEDINGS

On October 10, 2008, Detectives Christopher Ahlborg and Audrina Lyles of the Massachusetts Bay Transportation Authority (MBTA) transit police arrested the defendant for an indecent assault and battery that had occurred at a subway station. After the arrest, Ahlborg and Lyles placed the defendant in an interrogation room at MBTA headquarters. The detectives informed the defendant that their conversation would be video recorded.

At the outset of the interrogation, Ahlborg provided the defendant with a waiver form, which described the defendant's rights under Miranda v. Arizona, 384 U.S. 436 (1966). On being given the *Miranda* waiver form, the defendant immediately began to sign it. Ahlborg stopped the defendant, informing him that he first wanted to review with him verbally the rights described in the form before obtaining the defendant's written waiver of those rights. After reviewing those rights with the defendant, Ahlborg asked him whether he wanted to discuss the charges. The following exchange ensued:

The defendant: "[Inaudible] speak with you, or?"

Ahlborg: "Nope, you don't have to speak with me at all if you don't want to. It's completely up to you."

The defendant: "What happens if I don't speak with you?"

Ahlborg: "Nothing."

The defendant: "I just want to go home."

Ahlborg: "You just want to go home? So you don't want to speak?"

At this point in the interrogation, as found by the motion judge, the defendant "shook his head back and forth in a negative fashion." Ahlborg responded to this head motion by saying, "Okay." During the motion hearing, Ahlborg testified that he interpreted the defendant's head motion to mean that "he didn't want to speak."

Lyles, however, stated that she "really didn't interpret that headshake at the time," although she did characterize the motion as a "headshake." Instead, she began to correct a misapprehension that she thought had resulted from the earlier exchange. When Ahlborg told the defendant "nothing" would happen to him if he did not speak to the detectives, Lyles thought the defendant understood that statement to indicate that he would be free to leave. So she continued: "But that 'nothing' does not exclude you still being charged and us detaining you here. You'll either be bailed, or you'll have to go to court in the morning to answer to what you're being charged with. So it doesn't mean you'll get to walk up out of here and go home right now."

In the subsequent portion of the interrogation, the defendant made a number of statements indicating his confusion. He at different times stated, "I don't know what's going on. I'm really lost about what's going on"; "I just wanna know what's going on"; and "I'm just really scared." The defendant also cried at various points during the interrogation. After further discussion between the detectives and the defendant, the following exchange occurred:

Lyles: "Well we can't talk to you about anything until you make a decision."

The defendant: "Like yeah, I want to talk about it, but I'm just not sure what it is about."

Ahlborg: "Ok, so you want to talk to us?"

The defendant: "Yeah."

Ahlborg: "You do. Ok. If you want to talk to us, sign the paper and indicate that you do want to talk to us."

The defendant then signed and dated the *Miranda* waiver form, but did not grant the detectives permission to record the remainder of the interrogation. During this unrecorded portion of the interrogation, the defendant admitted that he had repeatedly brushed his hand against a man on the subway car.

The defendant was charged with one count of assault and battery, and two counts of indecent assault and battery on a person fourteen or over. He moved to suppress the incriminating statements made during the interrogation, arguing that he had invoked his right to remain silent by shaking his head in a negative fashion at the outset of the interview.

After an evidentiary hearing at which Ahlborg and Lyles both testified, a Boston Municipal Court judge allowed the motion to suppress. In doing so, the judge held that the defendant had unambiguously invoked his right to remain silent. The judge found that the defendant "shook his head back and forth in a negative fashion" in response to the question, "You don't want to speak with us?" The judge based his decision also on the defendant's over-all reluctance to speak with the detectives, as demonstrated by questions such as "Do I have to speak with you?" and "What will happen if I don't speak to you?" In examining the totality of the circumstances of the interrogation, including that the defendant was a "young man in his early twenties" with no prior arrests, the judge concluded that it was "clear that [the defendant] invoked his right to remain silent." . . .

3. DISCUSSION

a. Fifth Amendment

The Fifth Amendment provides that "[n]o person . . . shall be compelled in any criminal case to be a witness against himself . . . ." In *Miranda*, the United States Supreme Court held that this privilege against self-incrimination extends to State custodial interrogations; the Court reasoned that without proper safeguards, "the possibility of coercion inherent in custodial interrogations unacceptably raises the risk that a suspect's privilege against self-incrimination might be violated." United States v. Patane, 542 U.S. 630, 639 (2004). As a result, in circumstances of custodial interrogation, *Miranda* requires that the defendant "be warned prior to any questioning that he has the right to remain silent, that anything he says can be used against him in a court of law, that he has the right to the presence of an attorney, and that if he cannot afford an attorney one will be appointed for him prior to any questioning if he so desires." Unless the government can prove voluntary, knowing, and intelligent waiver of these rights after such warnings are given, any statements made by the suspect are inadmissible. See Commonwealth v. Simon, 923 N.E.2d 58 (Mass. 2010). Although waiver and invocation of the rights described in the *Miranda* warning are "entirely distinct inquiries," Smith v. Illinois, 469 U.S. 91, 98 (1984), there is an important relationship between the two insofar as any "waiver, express or implied, may be contradicted by an invocation at any time." Berghuis v. Thompkins, 560 U.S. 370 (2010).

Responsibility for invoking the protections guaranteed by *Miranda* and art. 12 "rests squarely in the hands of criminal defendants." Commonwealth v. Collins, 799 N.E.2d 1251 (Mass. 2003). The United States Supreme Court's decision in *Miranda* set a low bar for invocation of the right to remain silent: "If the individual indicates in any manner, at any time prior to or during questioning, that he wishes to remain silent, the interrogation must cease." More recently, however, the Court [held in *Thompkins*] that, under the Federal Constitution, in order for criminal defendants to invoke their right to remain silent, whether before or after waiving their *Miranda* rights, they must "unambiguously" announce their desire to be silent. This test is an objective one, requiring "that a reasonable police officer in the circumstances would understand the statement" to be an invocation of the *Miranda* right. Davis v. United States, 512 U.S. 452, 459 (1994). In *Thompkins*, the defendant's two hours and forty-five minutes of near-total prewaiver silence was insufficient to meet this heightened requirement of "unambiguous" invocation.

On sufficiently clear invocation, the right to remain silent must be "scrupulously honored." Michigan v. Mosley, 423 U.S. 96, 104 (1975). See Commonwealth v. Brant, 406 N.E.2d 1021 (Mass. 1980). The right to remain silent described in

Miranda includes "not only the right to remain silent from the beginning [of questioning] but also a continuing right to cut off, at any time, any questioning that does take place." Commonwealth v. Bradshaw, 431 N.E.2d 880 (Mass. 1982). Absent such "scrupulous" protection of the right to remain silent, statements made after invocation of the right are inadmissible in the prosecution's case-in-chief. See Harris v. New York, 401 U.S. 222, 224-226 (1971).

Here, the record supports the motion judge's determination that the defendant met the heightened *Thompkins* standard and invoked his right to remain silent as a matter of Federal law. In response to a direct question — "So you don't want to speak?" — the motion judge found, reasonably, that the defendant shook his head, indicating a negative response. Ahlborg's question was not investigatory in nature but, instead, directly concerned the defendant's desire to invoke his *Miranda* rights; Ahlborg himself understood the gesture to mean that the defendant did not want to speak. Unlike in *Thompkins*, where the defendant sat in silence for almost three hours, the defendant here engaged in affirmative conduct indicating his desire to end police questioning.

Relying on *Thompkins*, the Commonwealth argues that the defendant must actually speak to invoke the right to remain silent. *Thompkins*, however, does not go quite so far, and we are satisfied that a suspect's nonverbal expressive conduct can suffice to invoke the right to remain silent. In fact, *Miranda* itself provides that the right to remain silent may be invoked "[if] the individual [so] indicates in any manner. . . ."

Moreover, given the nature of the right at issue — the right to remain silent — it seems sensible to recognize that a suspect may well communicate through conduct other than speech. "Advising a suspect that he has a 'right to remain silent' is unlikely to convey that he must speak (and must do so in some particular fashion) to ensure the right will be protected." *Thompkins*, *supra* at 409 (Sotomayor, J., dissenting). Here, the defendant's conduct—an explicit headshake in response to a direct question—is sufficiently communicative so as to invoke his right to remain silent. See Commonwealth v. Marrero, 766 N.E.2d 461 (Mass. 2002) (recognizing that head nods and shakes in response to questioning constitute "deliberate nonverbal expression").

Because the defendant invoked his Fifth Amendment right to remain silent, we must determine whether the officers "scrupulously honored" that right. In Michigan v. Mosley, 423 U.S. 96 (1975), the United States Supreme Court explored the question whether and in what circumstances the prosecution is prohibited from using a defendant's in-custody statement obtained after the right to remain silent had been invoked. In concluding that the officers had scrupulously honored the defendant's right to remain silent, the *Mosley* Court highlighted three factors: the police (1) had immediately ceased questioning; (2) resumed questioning "only after the passage of a significant period of time and the provision of a fresh set of warnings"; and (3) limited the scope of the later interrogation "to a crime that had not been a subject of the earlier interrogation." *Mosley*, *supra* at 106.

None of these factors is present here. In response to the defendant's invocation of his right to cut off questioning, Lyles immediately began describing what the defendant could expect would follow. Although the motion judge found, and we agree, that the detectives were "very patient with the defendant in explaining his rights," they did not immediately cease questioning in the face of the defendant's unambiguous invocation of his right not to speak with them, there was no pause in the interrogation, and the questioning that did ensue concerned the crimes for which the defendant had been arrested. Because the detectives did not scrupulously honor the defendant's right to remain silent and thereby elicited the incriminating response that is the subject of the defendant's motion to suppress, the motion judge was correct in concluding that the defendant's statements must be suppressed.

b. Article 12

While the *Miranda* rule protects both Fifth Amendment rights and rights guaranteed under art. 12, we have not had occasion since the *Thompkins* decision to consider the scope of the analogous art. 12 protection in situations involving prewaiver invocations of the right to remain silent. If the defendant's conduct were to be construed as not meeting the heightened Federal standard, articulated in *Thompkins*, for invocation of the right to remain silent, the question becomes whether art. 12 affords greater protection than the rule of *Thompkins* would provide. We take this occasion to address that question.

"[State] courts cannot rest when they have afforded their citizens the full protections of the federal Constitution. State constitutions, too, are a font of individual liberties, their protections often extending beyond those required by the Supreme Court's interpretation of federal law." William Brennan, State Constitutions and the Protection of Individual Rights, 90 Harv. L. Rev. 489, 491 (1977). . . . Both the text and history of art. 12 support the view that it provides greater protection against self-incrimination than the Fifth Amendment. In assessing our pre-*Thompkins* jurisprudence, we must recall that the requirement of heightened clarity imposed in *Thompkins* derives from the 1994 United States Supreme Court decision in *Davis*. Yet in *Davis*, the suspect had already waived his *Miranda* rights when, after one and one-half hours of questioning, he stated that "[maybe he] should talk to a lawyer." The *Davis* Court held that, after suspects waive their rights, law enforcement officers may continue questioning them unless the suspects clearly request counsel. Unlike the postwaiver request for counsel at issue in *Davis*, the circumstances here involve the prewaiver invocation of the fundamental right to remain silent.

We have previously considered a suspect's waiver of his or her rights and concomitant willingness to talk to the police to be a critical factor in determining whether that suspect subsequently invoked his or her right to remain silent. Even before *Davis*, in Commonwealth v. Pennellatore, 467 N.E.2d 820 (Mass. 1984), we concluded that a defendant had not invoked his right to cut off questioning by saying, "I guess I'll have to have a lawyer for this," because he had been willing to talk before making the isolated comment and had thereby waived his rights. In *Davis*, the Supreme Court recognized the vital importance of this distinction and predicated its requirement of heightened clarity on the fact that the alleged invocation of the right to counsel had occurred "after a knowing and voluntary waiver of the *Miranda* rights." Subsequent to and consistent with the 1994 *Davis* decision, where we have held statements to be insufficient to invoke the right to remain silent, we have emphasized the postwaiver context in which those statements were made.

Our pre-*Thompkins* jurisprudence accords with the view that the fundamental purpose of *Miranda* is "to assure that the individual's right to choose between speech and silence remains unfettered throughout the interrogation process." Connecticut v. Barrett, 479 U.S. 523, 528 (1987). In the postwaiver context, a suspect has already made this choice. As a result, our case law recognizes that it makes sense to expect heightened clarity from a suspect who wants to change course and cease interrogation after having already indicated a desire to continue questioning. Prewaiver, however, the suspect has yet to exercise the choice between speech and silence that underlies *Miranda*. To require a suspect, before a waiver, to invoke his or her right to remain silent with the utmost clarity, as called for by *Thompkins*, would ignore this long-standing precedent and provide insufficient protection for residents of the Commonwealth under art. 12.

Furthermore, a suspect's failure to invoke the right to remain silent with heightened clarity, particularly in the absence of a prior waiver, does not necessarily reflect uncertainty. There are a number of other reasons a suspect might speak imprecisely. As Justice Souter observed in *Davis*, criminal suspects "who may (in *Miranda*'s words) be 'thrust into an unfamiliar atmosphere and run through menacing police interrogation procedures,' would seem an odd group to single out for the Court's demand of heightened linguistic care. A substantial percentage of them lack anything like a confident command of the English language, . . . many are 'woefully ignorant,' . . . and many more will be sufficiently intimidated by the interrogation process or overwhelmed by the uncertainty of their predicament that the ability to speak assertively will abandon them." In addition, "discrete segments of the population—particularly women and ethnic minorities—are far more likely than others to adopt indirect speech patterns." Ainsworth, In a Different Register: The Pragmatics of Powerlessness in Police Interrogation, 103 Yale L.J. 259, 261 (1993). Suspects falling into such categories should not be denied a constitutional right by reason of their hesitance ab initio to state their intent with perfect clarity.

This is especially important because, if the initial statement is intended as an actual invocation of the right to remain silent but fails to meet the heightened *Thompkins* standard, a suspect may not try later to reassert his or her rights if the police appear to ignore the invocation by continued questioning. "When a suspect understands his (expressed) wishes to have been ignored . . . in contravention of the 'rights' just read to him by his interrogator, he may well see further objection as futile and confession (true or not) as the only way to end his interrogation." *Davis, supra* at 472-473 (Souter, J., concurring in the judgment). That is precisely what the requisite preinterrogation recitation of *Miranda* warnings to suspects is meant to guard against.

We therefore hold that, even if the defendant's conduct was insufficient to meet the Federal *Thompkins* standard, the defendant acted with sufficient clarity to invoke his art. 12 right to remain silent. We decline to adopt the *Thompkins* approach to invocation, which permits police to continue questioning a person in custody who has never waived his right to remain silent until such time as that person articulates with utmost clarity his desire to remain silent. Such a rule "turns *Miranda* upside down" by placing too great a burden on the exercise of a fundamental constitutional right. *Thompkins, supra* at 2278 (Sotomayor, J., dissenting). When law enforcement officials reasonably do not know whether or not a suspect wants to invoke the right to remain silent, there can be no dispute that it is a good police practice for them to stop questioning on any other subject and ask the suspect to make his choice clear. Although we do not today mandate it, such clarification, the intuitively sensible course, has the benefit both of ensuring protection of the right if invoked and of minimizing the chance of suppression of subsequent statements at trial if not. Far from creating any "wholly irrational obstacles" to police investigation, *Mosley, supra* at 102, moreover, the process of asking, in a brief and even-handed fashion, simple clarifying questions does not burden the police.

Here, for the reasons discussed, the officers did not "scrupulously honor" the defendant's invocation of his right to remain silent. Accordingly, his subsequent incriminating statements were correctly suppressed. . . .

Notes

1. *Unambiguous assertion of* Miranda *rights: majority position.* Over the years, the Supreme Court has changed the legal test for courts to use in deciding whether a suspect has invoked the *Miranda* right to silence or right to counsel. According to *Miranda* itself, a "heavy burden rests on the government to demonstrate that the defendant knowingly and intelligently waived" the self-incrimination privilege. A "valid waiver" of the privilege "will not be presumed simply from the silence of the accused after warnings are given or simply from the fact that a confession was in fact actually obtained." Lengthy interrogation before a suspect makes a statement is "strong evidence" that the accused did not waive his rights. Later cases, however, have made it easier for police and courts to conclude that the defendant waived *Miranda* rights. In Davis v. United States, 512 U.S. 452 (1994), for example, the Court declared that a suspect must make an "unambiguous" and "unequivocal" statement to invoke the *Miranda* right to counsel; absent invocation, the court is inclined to find waiver.

The opinion in Berghuis v. Thompkins, 560 U.S. 370 (2010), cited in *Clarke*, expanded the unequivocality requirement of *Davis* to cover both the right to silence and the right to counsel. Now, in the face of ambiguity waiver is often presumed, and state courts and lower federal courts are wrestling with the question of which words or actions of a suspect amount to an "unambiguous" invocation of the right to silence. Will the courts encounter greater ambiguity in the invocation of the right to silence than they find in the invocation of the right to counsel? Is it too much to expect criminal suspects to speak with such clarity? You can track current developments on this question on the web extension for this chapter at *http://www.crimpro. com/extension/ch08.*

As the Massachusetts Supreme Court mentioned in *Clarke*, some state courts adopt a more defendant-friendly standard under their state constitutions. A few courts treat any reference by the suspect to silence or an attorney as an invocation of *Miranda* rights, even if the statement is ambiguous. Others require interrogators to "stop and clarify" the suspect's intentions after hearing an ambiguous statement about a possible desire to consult an attorney. Courts sometimes require interrogators to respond to clear questions from the suspect, even if the question does not clearly invoke *Miranda* rights. See Almeida v. State, 737 So. 2d 520 (Fla. 1999) (when suspect asks, "Well, what good is a lawyer going to do?" questioner must reply that decision belongs to suspect).

2. *Timing of invocation.* Even if the suspect uses unambiguous words, she must use them at the right time. Courts have not allowed suspects to make "anticipatory assertions" of rights, before interrogation begins. See, e.g., Sapp v. State, 690 So. 2d 581 (Fla. 1997); People v. Villalobos, 737 N.E.2d 639 (Ill. 2000). Moreover, invocation mid way through an interrogation does not have retroactive effect.

Some courts, like the *Clarke* majority, apply different tests for invocation, depending on whether the invocation happens at the start of the interrogation or in mid-stream, after an initial waiver of *Miranda* rights. Does the nature of the interaction between the suspect and questioner change during an interview in ways that justifies a change in the standard for invoking *Miranda* rights?

3. *Ambiguous waiver: majority position.* There are many instances in which a defendant says or does something that might be interpreted to constitute a waiver (rather than an assertion) of *Miranda* rights. This could be something as simple as refusing to answer any questions about waiver but discussing the crime with the interrogating officer. In North Carolina v. Butler, 441 U.S. 369 (1979), a precursor to Berghuis v. Thompkins, the Court said that "an explicit statement of waiver is not invariably necessary to support a finding that the defendant waived the right to remain silent or the right to counsel guaranteed by the *Miranda* case." Virtually all state courts have agreed that a suspect can implicitly waive *Miranda* rights through conduct or ambiguous statements. Garvey v. State, 873 A.2d 291 (Del. 2005) (suspect who responded to *Miranda* advisory by saying, "Depends on what you ask me," effectively waived interrogation rights, indicating intent to selectively waive rights and an understanding of those rights).

Consider how legislation on the topic of waiver might look different from constitutional rulings on the subject. Does the Vermont statute reprinted above prevent the use of a confession obtained after a suspect orally waives his rights but refuses to sign any waiver form? See State v. Caron, 586 A.2d 1127 (Vt. 1990). The Vermont statute is taken in large part from the Model Public Defender Act, adopted in 1970 by the National Conference of Commissioners on Uniform State Laws.

4. *Standard of proof for waiver.* In Lego v. Twomey, 404 U.S. 477 (1972), the Court ruled that the Constitution requires the government to show that a confession was voluntary by a preponderance of the evidence. The same standard of proof applies when the government must prove the existence of a knowing and intelligent waiver of *Miranda* rights. Colorado v. Connelly, 479 U.S. 157 (1986). In both cases, the Court emphasized the distinction between proving the essential elements of a crime (which bears directly on the reliability of the jury's verdict) and establishing the voluntariness of a confession (which bears on the admissibility of evidence). Most state courts have also adopted the preponderance standard. See, e.g., People v. Clark, 857 P.2d 1099 (Cal. 1993), but see State v. Gerald, 549 A.2d 792 (N.J. 1988) (beyond reasonable doubt). How might doubts about the validity of a waiver of *Miranda* rights translate into doubts about the accuracy of the prosecution's evidence of the underlying crime?

5. *Why do suspects waive their rights?* Can a suspect gain anything by talking to the police? Perhaps suspects believe they can convince the officers to look elsewhere for the culprit or to drop the investigation. Observers of interrogations say that it is standard practice for police interrogators at the beginning of an interrogation to encourage the suspect to speak with the officer as a way of telling "his side" of the story and to learn more about the evidence the police have collected. The officer will be careful to engage in small talk, to cover routine booking questions, and to talk about the advantages of waiver before allowing the suspect to answer any questions about *Miranda* rights. At that point, the questioner will often speak of the *Miranda* waiver as a formality that is surely very familiar to the suspect. If the suspect announces a decision about waiver too early, the officer has no opportunity to persuade the suspect to waive, and the relevant legal rules make it difficult to follow up after an invocation of rights. David Simon, Homicide: A Year on the Killing Streets (1991). The web extension for this chapter, at *http://www.crimpro.com/extension/ch08*, reviews the legal and criminological studies of interrogation practices. In hindsight,

if the Warren Court was concerned about the coercive nature of the interrogation environment in the police station, was it a mistake to allow a suspect to waive the right to silence without an attorney present?

6. *Capacity to waive under* Miranda: *majority position.* Analysis of the capacity of suspects to waive their *Miranda* rights is highly case-specific. Courts assess a variety of factors to resolve these frequently litigated claims of incapacity, such as the defendant's prior experience with the criminal justice system, the defendant's intelligence and education, mental illness, vocabulary and literacy, state of intoxication, and emotional state. Courts also look at the conduct of the police in eliciting a confession. For example, the U.S. Supreme Court in Colorado v. Connelly, 479 U.S. 157 (1986), considered a case involving the confession of a suspect who suffered from a psychosis. Because the police could not reasonably have known about the condition and did not engage in any "overreaching" conduct during the interrogation, the Court held that the waiver of *Miranda* rights was knowing and voluntary. See also State v. Chapman, 605 A.2d 1055 (N.H. 1992). How can police interrogators determine whether and to what degree a suspect is mentally disabled to the point of incapacity?

Note that a suspect's capacity to waive *Miranda* rights is distinct from the voluntariness of the confession. The mental illness of a suspect might interfere with that person's ability to understand *Miranda* rights even if the police do nothing blameworthy to affect the voluntariness of the confession. Capacity questions are also connected to the accuracy of confessions. The availability of DNA evidence has uncovered a number of wrongful convictions over the years, some based substantially on false confessions. It is quite common in these false-confession cases to find that the defendant had some form of mental impairment that raised questions about the capacity to waive *Miranda* rights as well. Richard Rogers et al., Knowing and Intelligent: A Study of *Miranda* Warnings in Mentally Disordered Defendants, 31 Law & Hum. Behav. 401 (2007); Steven A. Drizin & Richard A. Leo, The Problem of False Confessions in the Post-DNA World, 82 N.C. L. Rev. 891 (2004).

Appellate courts defer to trial court judgments of capacity; the appellate case law is full of decisions affirming a trial court's finding of waiver, even on fairly dramatic facts. Is a per se rule or rebuttable presumption of incapacity appropriate for some defendants? See Morgan Cloud et al., Words Without Meaning: The Constitution, Confessions, and Mentally Retarded Suspects, 69 U. Chi. L. Rev. 495 (2002) (authors tested sample of mentally impaired individuals to determine if they could understand *Miranda* warnings; mentally impaired suspects do not understand legal consequences of confessing or meaning of sentences comprising warnings).

7. *Intoxication and capacity to waive.* Suspects under the influence of alcohol or drugs very rarely convince a court that they did not have the capacity to waive their *Miranda* rights. In State v. Keith, 628 A.2d 1247 (Vt. 1993), for example, the court affirmed a finding of valid waiver where defendant had a blood-alcohol level of .203 at the time he was interrogated and gave several inconsistent stories of his whereabouts at the time of a suspicious fire. Courts in these cases often point out that the defendant voluntarily got himself into the intoxicated condition. Does the blameworthiness of the defendant have any bearing on her capacity to waive rights?

8. *Juveniles and* Miranda *waivers.* The youth of a suspect in custody can be an important factor for courts determining whether the suspect has the capacity to make a knowing and voluntary waiver. Most states follow the totality-of-the-circumstances rule of Fare v. Michael C., 442 U.S. 707 (1979). See Commonwealth v. Williams,

475 A.2d 1283 (Pa. 1984). A few states, however, require that a juvenile consult with an "interested adult" before she can waive *Miranda* rights. See In re Interest of J.L.H., 488 SW 3d 689 (Mo. App. 2016), transfer denied (May 3, 2016) (discussing Section 211.059 of the Montana Penal Code); Conn. Gen. Stat. Ann. §46b-137(a). California recently passed a statute requiring any suspect 15 years old or younger to consult specifically with legal counsel (in person or by phone or video conference); the consultation requirement cannot be waived, but it is subject to the public safety exception. Cal. Welf. & Inst. Code 625.6 (2017). Is a per se consultation rule appropriate for juveniles as a group? One empirical study, which sought to determine the capacity of juveniles to comprehend the meaning and significance of their *Miranda* rights, concluded that juveniles younger than 15 years old typically did not adequately comprehend their *Miranda* rights and that one-third to one-half of 15 year-olds showed an inadequate understanding of the *Miranda* warnings. See Thomas Grisso, Juveniles' Capacities to Waive *Miranda* Rights: An Empirical Analysis, 68 Cal. L. Rev. 1134 (1980).

9. *Language barriers.* Courts have also treated language barriers as one circumstance that might contribute to a finding of incapacity. See People v. Jiminez, 863 P.2d 981 (Colo. 1993) (suspect spoke no English and little Spanish, mostly Kickapoo; no valid waiver when warnings were delivered in Spanish). Could or should courts design a rule for language-barrier cases even if they remain confounded by the alcohol, mental disability, or youthfulness claims?

10. *Valid waiver: voluntary, knowing, and intelligent. Miranda* requires that a waiver be voluntary, knowing, and intelligent. The voluntariness requirement is essentially the same as the standard for confessions. But how much information are police required to provide to a suspect before she can make a knowing and intelligent decision to waive her rights? The Supreme Court has not required officers to provide information beyond that contained in the warnings. For example, officers need not inform a suspect about the scope of the interrogation. Colorado v. Spring (1987) (suspect gave a valid waiver of *Miranda* even though agents had not told him they would question him about a murder; they had only told him they would ask him about transporting stolen firearms).

11. *Informing a suspect about an available retained attorney.* What happens if counsel for the suspect arrives at the police station and offers to advise the suspect, even though the suspect has not yet requested an attorney? Must the interrogators tell the suspect that his or her attorney has arrived? The Supreme Court decided in Moran v. Burbine, 475 U.S. 412 (1986), that the police had no obligation to tell a suspect about an available attorney if the suspect has already waived the *Miranda* rights. In *Moran*, the defendant was already in custody for a burglary investigation when the police received information connecting him with a murder. The police interrogated the defendant about the murder, even though they knew that the defendant's sister had retained a public defender in connection with the burglary charge. The attorney had called to say that she would act as the defendant's attorney if the police placed him in a lineup or interrogated him. The police assured the public defender that they had no plans to question the defendant that evening; the police, however, did interrogate the defendant about the murder that night. They never informed the defendant that his sister had retained a public defender to assist him or that the public defender was trying to reach him. The Supreme Court held that the failure to inform the defendant of the attorney's efforts to reach him did not deprive the defendant of information essential to his ability to knowingly waive

his *Miranda* rights. The Court reasoned that while this information would have been useful to the defendant in deciding whether to waive his right to remain silent and right to counsel, the Constitution does not require the police to "supply a suspect with a flow of information to help him calibrate his self-interest in deciding whether to speak or stand by his rights."

Supreme courts in most states have now faced this issue, and a clear majority have disagreed with the Supreme Court; they hold that failure to advise about an available attorney prevents the waiver from being "knowing." Compare Commonwealth v. Mavredakis, 725 N.E.2d 169 (Mass. 2000) (rejecting *Moran*), with State v. Fox, 868 N.W.2d 206 (Minn. 2015) (following *Moran*). In the jurisdictions that reject *Moran*, some public defender offices have reorganized to provide attorneys to suspects during interrogations. See Commonwealth v. McNulty, 937 N.E.2d 16 (Mass. 2010) (appointed defense attorney telephoned police station while driving to location to advise client; confession excluded because police did not immediately inform defendant of attorney's call or relay his advice not to talk with police).

Problem 8-5. Your Lawyer Is Standing Outside

Fran Varga called the police Monday at 8:00 A.M. to inform them that her boyfriend, John Reed, had just found the dead body of Susan Green, one of Reed's coworkers, on the floor of her own apartment with 53 stab wounds. When detectives Shedden and Importico arrived at the scene, they asked Reed some questions and then asked him to go to the prosecutor's office to give a statement and provide "elimination" fingerprints. Varga drove him to the prosecutor's office, where they arrived just before 11:00 A.M. The detectives isolated Reed in an interrogation room and asked Varga to remain in the waiting room. Varga called an attorney and told him that she and Reed were at the prosecutor's office, that the police were about to question Reed, and that she and Reed needed an attorney. The attorney, Mr. Aitken, agreed to come to the station immediately. Varga informed an officer that Attorney Aitken was on the way.

Meanwhile, Chief Richard Thornburg instructed detectives Shedden and Importico to move Reed to the Major Crimes Building, located a few blocks away. In the MCB, Reed signed a *Miranda* waiver form, then gave a different account of the events than he had given earlier.

At approximately 11:25 A.M., Aitken arrived at the prosecutor's office and consulted with Varga. He approached the prosecutor who would eventually present the case against Reed and told him that he was there to represent both Varga and Reed. The prosecutor informed Aitken that Reed was a witness and not a suspect, and stated that, in any event, Aitken had "no right to walk into an investigation." Aitken gave the prosecutor a business card, and the prosecutor assured Aitken that the police would call him if and when Reed requested an attorney. No one informed Reed that a lawyer retained by Varga was waiting to see him.

After a second waiver of *Miranda* rights around noon, Reed spoke with another interrogator, Lt. Mazzei, and told a story markedly different from the second account he had provided. He eventually admitted that he had killed Green. After waiving his *Miranda* rights for a third time, Reed confessed on tape. The time was 3:52 P.M.

Reed has moved to suppress his confession because he did not knowingly, voluntarily, and intelligently waive his *Miranda* rights. What result would be consistent with Supreme Court jurisprudence on waiver? Imagine the state court wants to depart from the Supreme Court approach by using its state constitution. In crafting a different rule, should it focus on whether the police take affirmative steps to deceive the attorney about the location or status of the client? Should it focus on whether attorneys are present at the location of the interrogation, or also extend to attorneys who place a telephone call or send some other message to the police about their client? Should the police be obligated to pass along to the suspect any messages from the attorneys, such as "Your attorney advises you not to speak any more with us until she gets here"?

Problem 8-6. Invocation or Waiver?

Danny Ortega was arrested by Officer O'Leary for the murder of his landlord, Pat Ulrich. Shortly after O'Leary brought Ortega into the interrogation room and moved to turn on the recording equipment (but before *Miranda* warnings were read), Ortega said, "Well, am I supposed to have a lawyer here?" O'Leary answered, "I'm about to explain all of that to you," and then read the *Miranda* warnings out loud to Ortega. After this reading, he asked Ortega to sign a form indicating that he had received the warnings, and then to initial the line next to "I am willing to talk." Ortega signed the form but would not initial it, repeating his earlier question: "Aren't I supposed to have a lawyer here?" If O'Leary questions Ortega about the murder at this point, would he be in compliance with *Miranda* and *Thompkins*? See State v. Ortega, 798 N.W.2d 59 (Minn. 2011).

Problem 8-7. Capacity to Waive

Donald Cleary forced his way into a home, held the occupant at gunpoint, and fled. About an hour later, Cleary was arrested for a traffic offense and officers noticed he fit the description of the burglar that the occupant had provided. The sergeant read Cleary his *Miranda* rights twice, and Cleary signed a statement purporting to waive those rights. He then confessed, admitting that he had entered the victim's house and accosted her, and that he had intended to rape her.

At the hearing on the defense motion to suppress this statement, the court received testimony from a psychiatrist, Dr. Robert Linder, who had evaluated Cleary in connection with several prior criminal charges. He estimated that Cleary had an IQ of 65, which translated into a mental age between 10 and 12, and only a limited ability to read and write. Dr. Linder testified that Cleary had difficulty thinking abstractly and anticipating future events, which would limit his ability to comprehend the language of the *Miranda* warnings. He conceded, however, that Cleary could understand that he did not have to talk to the police, that he could speak with an attorney if he wished, and that he could stop answering questions whenever he chose. He also conceded that the defendant had undergone a learning process through his prior contacts with the police and court system. (Cleary had been declared incompetent to stand trial for one of the prior charges, but the arresting officer did not know this.) Cleary himself testified at the hearing that he spoke to the officers because he thought they would help him and because he thought he could not leave until he spoke to them.

The prosecutor mentioned that Cleary operated his own logging business for seven years. He purchased and maintained equipment for the business and negotiated bank loans, timber contracts, and truck transportation for his timber. Cleary had a driver's license, maintained a vehicle, was knowledgeable about how it worked, and purchased parts for it.

If you are the trial judge, would you conclude that Cleary voluntarily waived his *Miranda* rights? Cf. State v. Cleary, 641 A.2d 102 (Vt. 1994).

D. POST-INVOCATION ACTIVITY BY POLICE

The *Miranda* opinion appeared to bar police efforts to change a suspect's decision after he or she invoked *Miranda* rights during an interrogation: "If the individual indicates in any manner, at any time prior to or during questioning, that he wishes to remain silent, the interrogation must cease. At this point, he has shown that he intends to exercise his Fifth Amendment privilege; any statement taken after the person invokes his privilege cannot be other than the product of compulsion, subtle or otherwise." It later became clear, however, that a suspect could waive *Miranda* rights even after initially invoking them. Indeed, the police in some circumstances can take actions to encourage this later waiver.

The U.S. Supreme Court has distinguished between the effects of invoking the *right to silence* and the *right to counsel*. In Michigan v. Mosley, 423 U.S. 96 (1975) (discussed in the *Clarke* decision), the Court upheld the use of a confession despite the fact that the suspect earlier invoked his right to silence. Under the circumstances of that case, the Court concluded that the police "scrupulously honored" Mosley's initial invocation of the privilege because they immediately ceased the interrogation when Mosley invoked his right to silence, resumed questioning only after the passage of a significant period of time and the provision of a fresh set of *Miranda* warnings, and restricted the second interrogation to a crime that had not been a subject of the earlier interrogation. In Edwards v. Arizona, 451 U.S. 477 (1981), however, the Court insisted on a different rule for those who invoke the right to counsel: Such a person "is not subject to further interrogation, by the authorities until counsel has been made available to him, unless the accused himself initiates further communication, exchanges or conversations with the police." 451 U.S. at 484. The *Edwards* rule applies to all crimes, to all law enforcement officers, and even after a break in the interrogation; it is thus a stronger protective shell than the *Mosley* rule. Consider the following judicial efforts to apply these rules regarding obtaining a waiver after an initial invocation.

■ CHARLES GLOBE v. STATE
877 So. 2d 663 (Fla. 2004)

PER CURIAM.

. . . Globe was convicted of the July 3, 2000, first-degree murder of Elton Ard, a fellow inmate at the Columbia Correctional Institution (CCI). On the morning of July 3, 2000, Globe slipped into the prison cell shared by Ard and Andrew Busby. After locking the cell door and covering the window, Globe grabbed Ard around the neck and they began to struggle. [At the end of the struggle, Ard was dead.]

Several hours after the murder, Agent Bill Gootee met with Globe, advised him of his *Miranda* rights, and asked Globe if he wanted to make a statement. Globe replied, "Not at this time," but did not request an attorney. Gootee terminated the interview and passed this information on to Agent Don Ugliano. Approximately seven hours later, Ugliano was standing in a hallway and heard Globe say something to the effect of "that guy doesn't need to be here," [apparently referencing Busby, who was a short distance away]. Ugliano asked Globe "why," and Globe said, "The whole place is just screwed up. It is all messed up." Ugliano then asked Globe if he was willing to make a statement. Globe answered that he would, if he could be with Busby. After Globe and Busby were advised of their *Miranda* rights, they gave a tape recorded statement in which they admitted to killing Ard. After the statement was taken, Globe was moved to Florida State Prison. Inspector Jack Schenck, a senior inspector with the Florida Department of Corrections, Office of the Inspector General, interviewed Globe on July 7, 2000, at Florida State Prison. Schenck was present for Globe's July 3, 2000, statement to Ugliano. After being advised of his *Miranda* rights, Globe discussed how he had been planning to murder an inmate and how he had actually murdered Ard. Counsel was appointed for Globe, and he was arraigned on September 7, 2000. The jury convicted Globe of first-degree murder on September 11, 2001, and on September 14, 2001, recommended death by a vote of nine to three. Globe argues that the trial court erred by denying his motion to suppress the July 3 and July 7 statements. The court denied Globe's motion to suppress his statements "upon a finding that the statements were made freely, voluntarily, and knowingly after full and complete advisal and waiver of *Miranda* rights."

[Police-initiated] questioning of a person in custody is not absolutely foreclosed if he or she invokes the right to remain silent but not the right to counsel. We implicitly recognized the distinction between assertion of the two rights in Traylor v. State, 596 So. 2d 957, 966 (Fla. 1992):

> If the suspect indicates in any manner that he or she does not want to be interrogated, interrogation must not begin or, if it has already begun, must immediately stop. If the suspect indicates in any manner that he or she wants the help of a lawyer, interrogation must not begin until a lawyer has been appointed and is present or, if it has already begun, must immediately stop until a lawyer is present. Once a suspect has requested the help of a lawyer, no state agent can reinitiate interrogation on any offense throughout the period of custody unless the lawyer is present, although the suspect is free to volunteer a statement to police on his or her own initiative at any time on any subject in the absence of counsel.

In Michigan v. Mosley, 423 U.S. 96 (1975), the United States Supreme Court held that resolution of the question of the admissibility of statements obtained after a person in custody has invoked his or her right to remain silent depends upon whether the person's decision to assert his or her "right to cut off questioning" was "scrupulously honored." In holding that no *Miranda* violation occurred in *Mosley*, the Court stated:

> This is not a case, therefore, where the police failed to honor a decision of a person in custody to cut off questioning, either by refusing to discontinue the interrogation upon request or by persisting in repeated efforts to wear down his resistance and make him change his mind. In contrast to such practices, the police here

immediately ceased the interrogation, resumed questioning only after the passage of a significant period of time and the provision of a fresh set of warnings, and restricted the second interrogation to a crime that had not been a subject of the earlier interrogation.

We applied *Mosley* in Henry v. State, 574 So. 2d 66, 69 (Fla. 1991), when analyzing the resumption of questioning on the same offense after invocation of the right to silence. We recognized that in *Mosley* the Supreme Court neither set out "precise guidelines" for what constitutes scrupulous adherence to *Miranda* nor stated that "any factor standing by itself would be dispositive of the issue." However, we recognized five factors the Court in *Mosley* found to be relevant:

> First, Mosley was informed of his rights both times before questioning began. Second, the officer immediately ceased questioning when Mosley unequivocally said he did not want to talk about the burglaries. Third, there was a significant lapse of time between the questioning on the burglary and the questioning on the homicide. Fourth, the second episode of questioning took place in a different location. Fifth, the second episode involved a different crime.

In *Henry*, we determined that variance as to one or more of the five factors was not dispositive, and therefore applied a totality of the circumstances approach. We apply the same analysis in this case.

Globe argues that his right to remain silent was not "scrupulously honored" because of Agent Ugliano's request for a statement approximately seven hours after he declined to give a statement to Agent Gootee. Applying the five factors set out in *Mosley* and *Henry* to the facts in this case, it is evident that four of the five factors are present: (1) *Miranda* warnings were given several times, including right before each request for a statement; (2) interrogations ceased immediately when Globe expressed his desire to remain silent; (3) there was a significant time lapse between the questioning in that the second request for a statement was made seven and a half hours after the first request; and (4) the second questioning took place at a different location. We conclude that it is not dispositive that the second questioning involved the same crime. We consider not only that four of the five factors weigh in favor of admissibility but also that when Globe initially invoked his right to silence he said only that he did not want to make a statement "at this time," leaving open the prospect of future questioning on the crime. We hold that Globe's right to remain silent was scrupulously honored. Accordingly, the trial court did not err when it denied Globe's motion to suppress the July 3, 2000, statement.

The July 7 statement was taken at Florida State Prison, where Globe had been moved for security reasons. Globe alleges that the July 7 statement was the fruit of the illegally obtained July 3 statement; that it was not made voluntarily, intelligently, or knowingly; and that it was taken in violation of Florida Rule of Criminal Procedure 3.130.

Globe's first argument fails because the July 3 statement was not illegally obtained, as discussed above. Globe's second argument also is without merit. Before making his July 7 statement, Globe was advised of his *Miranda* rights by Agent Ugliano. [The] proper inquiry is whether the "totality of the circumstances surrounding the interrogation" reveal both an uncoerced choice and the requisite level of comprehension. In this case, Globe was read his rights. He was asked if he understood his rights and responded, "Sure." He was then asked, "With your rights in mind, would you like to answer questions and make a statement at this time?" Although Globe's response was inaudible on the tape recording, he proceeded to make a statement. All of this occurred after Globe had been read his rights twice before on July 3. The totality of the circumstances in this case demonstrate that Globe voluntarily waived his rights and was fully aware of the consequences of his decision. Globe's right to remain silent was scrupulously honored.

■ TEVIN BENJAMIN v. STATE
116 So. 3d 115 (Miss. 2013)

CHANDLER, J.

¶1. A Jackson County jury found Tevin James Benjamin guilty of capital murder with the underlying felony of robbery [for fatally shooting Michael Porter while he was stopped at a gas station]. We find that Benjamin's statement to the police was taken in violation of his rights under Miranda v. Arizona, 384 U.S. 436 (1966).

WHETHER BENJAMIN'S STATEMENT WAS OBTAINED IN VIOLATION OF MIRANDA

¶7. Benjamin was fourteen years old at the time of the crime. A few days after the shooting, Officer Miller questioned Benjamin in the presence of his mother and a second, unidentified police officer. The conversation was recorded on audio and video. Officer Miller read Benjamin his *Miranda* rights, but Benjamin asked for his youth-court attorney. Officer Miller stated that Benjamin would not be in youth court because he was being charged in the "capital murder out at the Conoco gas station." Benjamin expressed surprise that he was being charged with capital murder. Then, the following occurred:

Miller: Who is your lawyer?

Benjamin: Mrs. Brenda Lotts.

Miller: Brenda Lott is a . . .

Officer: I know Brenda. Down in Youth Court.

Miller: She's, she's, you're gonna have to talk to uh, I don't think she can come down here but I don't know. I think she's a public defender down at the Youth Court. You won't be going to Youth Court.

Benjamin: Where I'm gonna be staying the night at?

Miller: Right here in the jail.

Mother: You better think about it baby. I'm telling you cause you know dern well I don't have no money for no lawyer.

Benjamin: So ya'll saying if I don't talk to ya'll, ya'll just going to charge me with it.

Miller: We're going to detain you, yes.

Benjamin: It's just that I don't even know nothing about no murder.

Miller: OK.

Benjamin: That's what I'm saying.

Miller: OK. You'll have to tell your lawyer.

Benjamin: I ain't trying to stay the night here, so could I, you know, I ain't did nothing.

Miller: OK, you'll have to tell your lawyer all of that and then they'll tell us all of that.

Officer: OK. That's all we can do. He asked for his lawyer, so.

At that point, Miller looked at Benjamin's mother and said "The only way that anything will change is if he request a, you know, request it. And uh, I can't, I can't pressure him into changing his tune about wanting a lawyer, you know, and that kind of stuff. So, if you want to speak to him for a few minutes then, you know, we'll go from there." Miller and the officer exited the room, leaving Benjamin alone with his mother.

¶8. As shown by the following excerpts from their conversation, Benjamin's mother immediately began pressuring Benjamin into relinquishing his request for an attorney and talking to the police:

> *Mother:*   T.J. I'm telling you now. If you know something, you did something, you better let them know.
> *Benjamin:*   Know what, I ain't did nothing. That's what I'm telling, that's what I'm steady trying to say. . . .
> *Mother:*   See, see what I told you. If you'd just learn to listen to me. That's why I keep telling you and Trell. Ya'll put me in predicaments. You know I ain't got no money for no lawyer. And then if they get a public defender you know how they work. . . . Should have do the questioning and told what you know.
> *Benjamin:*   What I know about what?
> *Mother:*   I don't know. You have to let them go through the questions with you.

After a few minutes, Miller returned to the room. Benjamin's mother asked what Benjamin had to do if he was going to talk. Miller responded:

> Well he's gonna have to probably request it that he talks to somebody at this point. But uh, it may be best to just wait until tomorrow and talk, you know, you know, and let him stay back there in jail tonight. Well uh, we got all we need. We don't really need to talk to him. We just wanted his side of it. And if he don't want to give it to us that's fine you know. We'll eventually uh, eventually I'm sure that he'll either tell his attorney or tell the judge or tell somebody while. . . .

When Miller said that Benjamin would stay the night in jail, he looked directly at Benjamin. Miller said he was trying to get Benjamin's side of the story, but that they had no problems with it if he wanted to work through it with an attorney. Then, the following occurred:

> *Mother:*   So what, why, what you, oh so you just saying let him stay here?
> *Miller:*   He's going to have to stay here with us, yes ma'am. It's a capital offense and that's happened. It's a capital murder, OK. Uh, and it's our position at this point uh, that he had some involvement in it, to the extent we're not 100% sure that was what was going on. We're going to let him line that out for us. Um, and you know um, we, if he wants a lawyer, that's what we're going to honor. So you can probably uh, go ahead and say your goodbyes I guess and he'll be in the big boy jail tonight.

Miller and the officer again left Benjamin alone with his mother. Their further conversation was not recorded.

¶9. Miller testified at the suppression hearing that Benjamin's mother emerged from the interview room and said that Benjamin wanted to talk. The police recorded his subsequent interview with Officers Miller and Roberts. At the beginning of the interview, Miller said, "What's the deal? You want to talk to us?" Benjamin responded, "I just want to let you know sir, I don't, you said ya'll charge me." Miller read Benjamin his *Miranda* rights, and Benjamin said he understood. Then, Miller continued questioning Benjamin about whether he wanted to talk. Benjamin said that he wanted to talk and had requested to talk to the police. Then, the following occurred:

> *Benjamin:*   Can I say something right quick sir?
> *Miller:*   You can say anything you want to buddy, it's your interview.
> *Benjamin:*   So uh, when we get done am I still gonna be getting locked up?
> *Miller:*   Well that has a lot to do with what you talk about and everything. Uh, that has a lot to do with that dude.

Miller testified that, although he told Benjamin that whether he stayed in jail depended on what he said to the police, in fact it was a virtual certainty that Benjamin would be incarcerated that night no matter what he told the police. Benjamin gave a statement in which he claimed that he was at the fair on the night of the shooting. . . . Although the officers and Benjamin's mother continued to pressure Benjamin to "tell the truth," Benjamin did not depart from his statement that he had been at the fair, and the interview concluded. At the end of the interview, Officer Miller thanked Benjamin's mother "for your help." He also said, "Thank you ma'am, we appreciate ya."

¶10. Benjamin filed a pretrial motion to suppress his statement. He argued that, because the police unconstitutionally reinitiated interrogation after he invoked his right to counsel, his statement was given in violation of *Miranda*. Benjamin claimed that the police had used his mother to prompt his reinitiation of interrogation, and that his waiver of rights was not knowing, intelligent, and voluntary. After hearing the testimony of Officer Miller and viewing the recording of Benjamin's statement, the trial court denied Benjamin's motion to suppress. The trial court found that, after Benjamin had invoked his right to counsel, the officers had made no statements in an attempt to elicit a response, and that Benjamin's waiver of rights was freely, knowingly, and voluntarily made. Benjamin attacks the trial court's ruling.

¶11. For the accused's statement to be admissible in evidence, the prosecution must prove beyond a reasonable doubt that the statement was given after a valid waiver.

¶12. In *Miranda*, the United States Supreme Court held that the Fifth and Fourteenth Amendments' privilege against compelled self-incrimination requires that, before any custodial interrogation may occur, the accused must be informed of his right to counsel and right to remain silent. Once the accused is informed of these rights, custodial interrogation may proceed provided the accused knowingly, intelligently, and voluntarily waives the rights. If the accused chooses to remain silent, then interrogation must cease. If the accused invokes his right to counsel, then interrogation must cease until an attorney is present.

¶13. "If the accused invoked his right to counsel, courts may admit his responses to further questioning only on finding that he (a) initiated further discussions with the police, and (b) knowingly and intelligently waived the right he had invoked." Smith v. Illinois, 469 U.S. 91, 95 (1984); Edwards v. Arizona, 451 U.S. 477 (1981). Additional safeguards are necessary when the accused asks for counsel. When an accused has invoked his right to counsel a valid waiver of that right cannot be established by showing only that he responded to further police-initiated custodial interrogation even if he has been advised of his rights. An accused, having expressed his desire to deal with the police only through counsel, is "not subject to further interrogation by the authorities until counsel has been made available to him, unless the accused himself initiates further communication, exchanges, or conversations with the police." *Edwards*, 451 U.S. at 484-85. Once an accused has invoked his right to counsel, any subsequent waiver of rights carries a presumption of involuntariness that ensures "police will not take advantage of the mounting coercive pressures of prolonged police custody by repeatedly attempting to question a suspect who previously requested counsel until the suspect is badgered into submission." Maryland v. Shatzer, 559 U.S. 98 (2010).

¶14. It is undisputed that Benjamin was in custody and invoked his right to counsel. He contends that, after he invoked his right to counsel, he was subjected to further interrogation by the police and that his mother acted as an agent for the police for the purpose of extracting his statement. "Interrogation" is not limited to express questioning of a suspect while in custody. Rhode Island v. Innis, 446 U.S. 291 (1980). The concept also embraces any words and conduct of the police that are the functional equivalent of interrogation. Thus, "interrogation" encompasses express questioning and "any words or actions on the part of the police (other than those normally attendant to arrest and custody) that the police should know are reasonably likely to elicit an incriminating response from the suspect." The determination of whether the police should have known a particular practice was reasonably likely to elicit an incriminating response focuses on the perceptions of the suspect, not the intent of the police.

¶15. This Court has held that a private third party may, without realizing that he or she is doing so, act as an agent for the police to induce a defendant's statement. In Arizona v. Mauro, 481 U.S. 520 (1987), the United States Supreme Court held that Mauro, who had invoked his right to counsel, was not subjected to the functional equivalent of interrogation when the police allowed him to speak with his wife in the presence of an officer and recorded the conversation. The police allowed Mauro to speak with his wife in response to her insistent demands. They informed Mr. and Mrs. Mauro that an officer would be present and placed a tape recorder in plain sight. During the conversation, Mauro told his wife not to answer questions until a lawyer was present. The State used Mauro's statement to rebut his claim that he was insane on the day of the crime.

¶16. The Court found that there was no evidence that the police decision to allow Mauro's wife to see him was a psychological ploy that was the functional equivalent of interrogation. The Court found Mauro had not been subjected to compelling influences or direct questioning. Nor was there any evidence that the police had allowed Mrs. Mauro to see her husband for the purpose of eliciting incriminating statements. Viewing the situation from Mauro's perspective, the Court found that "a suspect, told by officers that his wife will be allowed to speak to him, would [not] feel that he was being coerced to incriminate himself in any way." The Court held that the conduct of the police was not the functional equivalent of interrogation.

¶17. This case stands in contrast with *Mauro*. After Benjamin invoked his right to counsel, interrogation had to cease until an attorney was present. Instead, the police continued to interact with Benjamin and with his mother, who repeatedly expressed the desire that Benjamin forego an attorney and talk to the police. Officer Miller announced that Benjamin was being charged with capital murder and that Benjamin was going to spend the night in jail. Although Benjamin repeatedly requested confirmation of his erroneous belief that if he talked, he would not have to spend the night in jail, Officer Miller never corrected Benjamin's false assumption that he could avoid spending the night in jail by talking. Then, with knowledge that Benjamin's mother wanted Benjamin to waive his right to counsel and talk, Officer Miller informed Benjamin's mother exactly what Benjamin would have to do in order to reinitiate questioning, and left her alone with Benjamin. Officer Miller explained that he could not "pressure him into changing his tune about wanting a lawyer," and allowed his mother to speak with Benjamin "for a few minutes," and "we'll go from there." Predictably, Benjamin's mother used her time alone with Benjamin to pressure him to talk. Then, Officer Miller returned to the interview room to assess the situation, and Benjamin's mother asked for clarification on what Benjamin had to do to talk. When Benjamin did not relent, officers readied him for incarceration and again left him with his mother to say goodbye. After that conversation, Benjamin announced that he was ready to talk.

¶18. Benjamin's immaturity is revealed by the fact that his main concern at being charged with capital murder was avoiding a night in jail. When the police encourage a parent to pressure a fourteen-year-old suspect to talk, and the police foster the suspect's mistaken belief that talking would allow him to avoid a night in jail, the police should know their conduct is reasonably likely to elicit an incriminating response. By encouraging Benjamin's belief that, by talking to the police, he could avoid a night in jail, and by allowing Benjamin's mother to speak with him after instructing her on how Benjamin could reinitiate questioning, the police used psychological ploys and compelling influences to elicit Benjamin's statement. These tactics constituted the functional equivalent of interrogation, because they were reasonably likely to elicit an incriminating response from fourteen-year-old Benjamin. We find that Benjamin was subjected to interrogation after invoking his right to counsel in violation of Edwards v. Arizona.

¶19. Under *Edwards*, Benjamin's waiver was presumptively involuntary because it was made in response to interrogation after Benjamin had invoked his right to counsel. Further, the facts condemn any notion that the prosecution proved beyond a reasonable doubt that Benjamin's waiver was knowing and intelligent. A knowing and intelligent waiver must be made with a full awareness both of the nature of the right being abandoned and the consequences of the decision to abandon it. Benjamin's mother was under the false impression that it would be helpful to Benjamin to cooperate and waive his rights. She also communicated that he should talk to the police because they could not afford an attorney. It is manifestly apparent that Benjamin conceded to pressure from his mother and to his desire to avoid a night in jail in deciding to waive his rights. Benjamin's youth rendered him particularly susceptible to parental pressure. Under these circumstances, we cannot say that the record demonstrates that Benjamin's waiver was made with full awareness of the nature of the right and the consequences of abandoning it.

¶20. For the foregoing reasons, we find that the trial court manifestly erred in failing to suppress Benjamin's statement to the police. The record reflects that the police subjected Benjamin to interrogation after he had invoked his right to counsel and that the State failed to prove his waiver of rights was knowing, intelligent, and voluntary. We reverse and remand for a new trial consistent with this opinion. . . .

PIERCE, J., dissenting.

¶24 Based on my review of the video-recorded interview, I can no more factually infer the use of psychological or compelling influence on Officer Miller's part from this portion of the video, than if the video had instead—hypothetically—shown Officer Miller abruptly halting the proceeding and immediately escorting Benjamin's mother out of the room, leaving fourteen-year-old Benjamin alone to await the booking process. Further, I find nothing inherently coercive in the fact that Officer Miller told Benjamin's mother what Benjamin would have to do if he wanted to talk after having asserted his right to counsel. This was an accurate statement by Officer Miller . . . and Officer Miller made no promises or threats in conjunction with it.

¶25. Afterward, Benjamin and his mother spoke to one another alone. [When Benjamin's mother asked Officer Miller what Benjamin would have to do to talk], Officer Miller equivocated with his response. [He] nonetheless bluntly informed Benjamin and his mother that it was the police's position that Benjamin was involved with the murder, and Officer Miller unequivocally told Benjamin and his mother that Benjamin was going to be detained.

¶26. [After Benjamin and his mother again spoke alone, Benjamin asked if he was going to be detained in the jail. Miller replied], "Well that has a lot to do with what you talk about and everything. Uh, that has a lot to do with that dude." I can see how, by isolating this exchange in a vacuum, it could be interpreted as deceptive. But there is more. Officer Miller immediately qualified his response as follows:

Miller: But I'm going to tell you this right now, and I'm not here to be, nobody's going to be mean to you, mistreat you, or nothing else, OK. But, I don't want you wasting my time, and I'm not going to waste your time, OK.
Benjamin:Yes, sir.
Miller: I don't want you to lie to me or nothing else. We've already interviewed a bunch of boys that was involved in this thing. We know that you're not the shooter, you know. We have no doubts that you're not the shooter. But, you're either going to have to tell your side of the story or we're going to go with what everybody else is saying, OK. Tell me what happened last Thursday evening.

¶27. We cannot look at statements made by the police in a vacuum in determining whether interrogation occurred; rather, we must view them in light of the circumstances of the interaction between the suspect and the police on the occasion in question. Although Benjamin was fourteen years old at the time in question, Benjamin, as shown by the record, was not unfamiliar with how the system worked, having been exposed to it in the past. He requested his youth-court attorney at the outset of the interview. When Benjamin asked if he was going to be spending the night in jail, Officer Miller . . . truthfully informed Benjamin of the current state of the investigation. Prior to that, Officer Miller expressly informed Benjamin through the advice of rights form—which, again, Benjamin confirmed he understood—that Benjamin still had the right to stop answering questions at any time until he talked to a lawyer. Benjamin elected to proceed with the interview.

¶28. The record, based on my review of it, does not affirmatively show that Benjamin did not voluntarily and intelligently withdraw his previous request for counsel and waive his *Miranda* rights. Accordingly, I would affirm the trial court's decision not to suppress Benjamin's statement as well as Benjamin's conviction and sentence.

Notes

1. *Effect of invoking right to counsel: majority position.* The Supreme Court now applies the two-part test elaborated in Oregon v. Bradshaw, 462 U.S. 1039 (1983), to determine whether a suspect's statement is admissible when made after an earlier invocation of the right to counsel. First, the court asks who "initiated" any post-invocation conversation about the crime. If the police initiate the conversation (by word or deed) in the absence of the suspect's attorney, then they violate Edwards v. Arizona, 451 U.S. 477 (1981), and the confession must be suppressed. If the suspect initiates "a generalized discussion about the investigation," a court will proceed to the second step and ask whether the defendant waived the right to counsel knowingly and intelligently, despite the earlier invocation of the right.

In *Bradshaw*, the defendant "initiated" the conversation by asking, "Well, what is going to happen to me now?" This basic approach has also met with approval in most state courts. See, e.g., State v. McKnight, 319 P.3d 298 (Haw. 2013); Ex parte Williams, 31 So. 3d 670 (Ala. 2010). However, it is not always easy to determine who "initiates" a "generalized" conversation about the investigation. For instance, what should a police officer do if a suspect who has invoked the right to counsel asks, after a lineup procedure, "What happened?" See Hartman v. State, 988 N.E.2d 785 (Ind. 2013) (police initiated renewed interrogation by reading search warrants to defendant and asking if he had any questions).

Does the *Edwards* rule sufficiently protect the suspect's privilege against self-incrimination? New York provides that a suspect who has invoked the right to counsel should never be allowed to initiate a conversation with the police about the crime unless counsel is present. See People v. Cunningham, 400 N.E.2d 360 (N.Y 1980) (barring any interrogation after invocation of right to counsel unless waiver made with attorney present). This position has attracted virtually no following among the other states. State v. Piorkowski, 700 A.2d 1146 (Conn. 1997) (rejects New York rule on waiver, defendant may make post-arraignment waiver of counsel in counsel's absence).

2. *Time and place limits on the effects of invoking right to counsel.* The right to counsel invocation, once unambiguously made, applies to all law enforcement officers and to all crimes, while the defendant is in custody. It is a very broad protective shell and it is difficult to move past the suspect's invocation of the right to counsel once it happens. According to Arizona v. Roberson, 486 U.S. 675 (1988), the invocation stays in place even if the police approach the suspect for a waiver in connection with an entirely different crime. Further, the Court held in Minnick v. Mississippi, 498 U.S. 146 (1990), the invocation remains effective even after the detained suspect consults with an attorney, for the duration of custody. Cf. People v. Elliott, 833 N.W.2d 284 (Mich. 2013) (*Edwards* rule does not apply to noncustodial interrogations; jailhouse meeting with parole officer was not custodial).

In Maryland v. Shatzer, 559 U.S. 98 (2010), however, the Court did create an outer temporal boundary on the effects of invocation. The Court ruled that an invocation of the right to counsel no longer blocks the government from initiating a conversation with the suspect if there has been a "break in custody" and 14 days or more have passed. In *Shatzer*, such a "break in custody" occurred when a prisoner serving a sentence for a different crime was returned to the general prison population after he had asserted the right to counsel in a new criminal investigation. See also State v. Edler, 833 N.W.2d 564 (Wis. 2013).

3. *Effect of invoking right to silence: majority position.* As the *Globe* case from Florida indicates, it is easier for the police to initiate a new interrogation after a suspect has invoked the right to silence, as opposed to the right to counsel. Most state courts have read their state constitutions to reach results consistent with the holding in Michigan v. Mosley, 423 U.S. 96 (1975). As the *Globe* case suggests, it is still not entirely clear which of the various facts in *Mosley* were essential to the holding there. See Wilson v. State, 562 S.E.2d 164 (Ga. 2002) (reinterrogation under *Mosley* not available for same crime after 17-hour interval; later interrogation must address different crime). A sampling of the complex state court rulings on this topic appear on the web extension for this chapter at *http://www.crimpro.com/extension/ch08.*

Is it appropriate to place different obligations on the police, depending on which right the defendant invokes? Should suspects be told of the differing impacts their words might have? Consider People v. Pettingill, 578 P.2d 108 (Cal. 1978) (rejecting the *Mosley* rule and disallowing any government initiation of interrogation after invocation of right to silence).

4. *The right to consult counsel before and during interrogation: foreign practice.* Throughout Europe, the right of a suspect to consult with counsel before and during interrogation was established in a 2009 decision of the European Court of Human Rights, Salduz v. Turkey, App. No. 36391/02, 49 Eur. H.R. Rep. 421 (2008). The Court held that "as a rule, access to a lawyer should be provided as from the first interrogation of a suspect by the police, unless it is demonstrated in the light of the particular circumstances of each case that there are compelling reasons to restrict this right." The right may be waived only if the suspect is first adequately informed of the right to counsel; the waiver must be unequivocal and "be attended by minimum safeguards commensurate to its importance."

A number of European countries have had to amend their laws to bring them in conformity with *Salduz*. For a discussion of the effects of *Salduz* on national laws relating to interrogations and the right to counsel, see John D. Jackson, Responses to *Salduz*: Procedural Tradition, Change and the Need for Effective Defence, 79 Modern L. Rev. 987 (2016); Thomas Weigend, Defense Rights in European Legal Systems under the Influence of the European Court of Human Rights, in Oxford Handbook of Criminal Process (Darryl Brown, Jenia Turner & Bettina Weisser eds., forthcoming 2019).

E. SIXTH AMENDMENT RIGHT TO COUNSEL DURING INVESTIGATIONS

The Fifth Amendment to the U.S. Constitution, as interpreted in *Miranda*, is not the only source of a right to counsel during the investigative stage of the criminal process. Indeed, the Sixth Amendment provides an explicit right to counsel: "In all criminal prosecutions, the accused shall enjoy the right to . . . have the Assistance of Counsel for his defence." Recall that shortly before it decided *Miranda*, the U.S. Supreme Court suggested, in Escobedo v. Illinois, 378 U.S. 478 (1964), that the Sixth Amendment right to counsel might apply before the start of any formal criminal process. But it eventually became clear that the Sixth Amendment right to counsel attaches only after the initiation of formal proceedings, which typically means some form of charging or court appearance (initial arraignment, indictment, or information). State courts have given the same meaning to state constitutional right to counsel provisions.

The Sixth Amendment thus provides the accused an alternative—a clear, textually based alternative—right to counsel after charging. This separate source of a right to counsel for some defendants raises the fundamental question whether the scope and impact of the Fifth and Sixth Amendment rights to counsel are the same. For example, must defendants be informed of the Sixth Amendment right to counsel, or is the notice regarding the Fifth Amendment right to counsel— through *Miranda*—sufficient? Must a defendant assert the Sixth Amendment right, or does it automatically attach after charging? Will the detailed rules that govern notice, assertion, and waiver of the right to counsel under *Miranda* also apply after indictment?

Section D of this text examined the effect of assertion of the Fifth Amendment right to counsel under *Miranda*. The following case and problem examine the effect of asserting a Sixth Amendment right to counsel after charges are filed. Notice any differences between the standards applied under the two constitutional clauses. The specific legal question is whether a government agent can ask questions to an accused after the Sixth Amendment right attaches.

■ ROBERT RUBALCADO v. STATE

424 S.W.3d 560 (Tex. Crim. App. 2014)

KELLER, J.

Appellant, arrested pursuant to an Ector County complaint, made bail and was released from incarceration. Afterwards, at the behest of Midland County law enforcement, the complaining witness in the Ector County case contacted appellant and elicited incriminating statements from him. The question before us is whether appellant's Sixth Amendment right to counsel was violated when these statements were later used as primary evidence of guilt in the Ector County case.

I. BACKGROUND

. . . In 2002, appellant began a romantic relationship with J.S.'s mother and moved into her home in Midland, in Midland County. In 2004, the family moved to Odessa, in Ector County. J.S. subsequently accused appellant of sexually abusing her, and on March 12, 2009, a complaint was filed in Ector County that accused appellant of aggravated sexual assault of a child. The next day, appellant was arrested pursuant to a warrant, and soon thereafter he was released on bail. A criminal investigation also began in Midland County, and Midland police officers subsequently asked J.S. to make pretextual phone calls to appellant in an effort to induce appellant to confess to committing crimes against J.S. [in both Ector County and Midland County].

J.S. agreed to make the phone calls. The Midland police department supplied recording equipment that J.S. could connect to her cell phone and operate. J.S. connected the equipment herself and called appellant on three different days. At least one Midland police officer was with J.S. during each call, but the police did not tell J.S. what to say.

In all three phone calls, J.S. and appellant engaged in innocuous banter about how they were doing and about their activities. Often, J.S. would just respond "yeah," "right," or "okay" to comments made by appellant, but there were some occasions in which J.S. made comments that were designed, or possibly designed, to elicit incriminating responses. [For example, in one call] J.S. asked, "Can I ask you a question?" Appellant responded, "Sure." J.S. then asked, "Can I ask why you were doing those things to me?" Appellant responded, "Do what? What things?" J.S. replied, "The way you were touching me and stuff like that." Appellant responded that appellant, J.S., and J.S.'s mother would have to get together and "see what is going on." . . . Then J.S. asked, "Can I ask you something else?" Appellant responded affirmatively, and J.S. asked, "Why did you have sex with me?" Appellant responded evasively: "We will get with your mom and see [inaudible] because I already got this thing over. If you don't want to do it—I mean, if you want to come, I mean." J.S. replied, "I do, but I want everything to be different." Appellant responded, "It is going to be different." . . .

On November 16, 2009, appellant was indicted in Ector County for various sex offenses against [J.S.]. During its case-in-chief, the State offered the three recorded phone conversations. Defense counsel objected that the recordings violated the right to counsel. . . .

II. ANALYSIS

A. Massiah

In Massiah v. United States, 377 U.S. 201 (1964), a co-defendant agreed to cooperate with the police in obtaining information from Massiah after Massiah had been released on bail. Massiah was unaware of this cooperation. The police installed a radio transmitter under the front seat of the co-defendant's car and secretly listened while the co-defendant elicited incriminating statements from Massiah. The Supreme Court held that Massiah was denied the basic protections of his Sixth Amendment right to counsel "when there was used against him at his trial evidence of his own incriminating words, which federal agents had deliberately elicited from him after he had been indicted and in the absence of his counsel." That the interrogation was "indirect and surreptitious," instead of being conducted at the jailhouse, did not preclude the application of the Sixth Amendment. In fact, Massiah was more seriously imposed upon . . . because he did not even know that he was under interrogation by a government agent."

Maine v. Moulton, 474 U.S. 159 (1985), involved similar facts. Moulton and his co-defendant were on bail, the co-defendant was secretly cooperating with the government, law enforcement personnel secretly recorded telephone conversations and an in-person meeting between the two, and the co-defendant deliberately elicited incriminating statements from Moulton. The State argued that Massiah was distinguishable because government agents set up the encounter in that case while Moulton initiated the telephone calls and requested the in-person meeting. The Court rejected that argument, holding that the identity of the party who instigated the meeting at which the incriminating statements were obtained was not decisive or even important to its decision in Massiah. The Court observed that the Sixth Amendment guarantees the accused, after the initiation of formal charges, the right to rely on counsel as a "medium" between him and the State. The State has an affirmative obligation not to act in a manner that circumvents this protection, and the knowing exploitation of an opportunity to confront the accused without counsel is as much a breach of this obligation as the intentional creation of the opportunity." Accordingly, the Sixth Amendment is violated when the State obtains incriminating statements by knowingly circumventing the accused's right to have counsel present in a confrontation between the accused and a state agent." . . .

From this discussion, we conclude that the *Massiah* inquiry is whether, after the Sixth Amendment right to counsel has attached, the government has knowingly circumvented the defendant's right to counsel by using an undisclosed government agent to deliberately elicit incriminating information. We turn to the various *Massiah* issues implicated in the present case.

B. Attachment

1. Attached in Ector County

The Sixth Amendment right to counsel does not apply until it has attached, and it attaches when the prosecution has commenced. The prosecution commences for Sixth Amendment right to-counsel purposes "at the first appearance before a judicial officer at which the defendant is told of the formal accusation against him and restrictions are imposed on his liberty." Under this test for attachment, appellant's Sixth Amendment right to counsel with respect to the Ector County charges had attached before the recorded phone conversations took place.

2. Not Attached to Midland County Offenses

But the Sixth Amendment right to counsel is "offense specific." It attaches only to an offense for which a prosecution has been initiated. . . . The question, then, is whether the recorded conversations in this case involved offenses that were separate from the Ector County charges, and if so, to what extent.

In determining what constitutes an "offense" for Sixth Amendment right-to-counsel purposes, and consequently, whether separate offenses are involved, the Supreme Court has resorted to double-jeopardy law. The Court has explained that this means that offenses are considered separate for right-to-counsel purposes if they would be considered separate under the Blockburger same-elements test, i.e. each statutory provision proscribing the respective charges requires proof of a fact that the other does not. . . .

Separate instances of sexual assault are separate offenses. The same is true of the offense of indecency with a child by contact. So, multiple incidents in Ector County would be included in the Ector County complaint and arrest warrant, but any sexual offenses committed solely in Midland County would be separate, for double-jeopardy purposes, from the sexual offenses that were the subject of prosecution in Ector County. No one contends that a prosecution was pending in Midland County at the time of the recorded phone conversations. The Sixth Amendment right to counsel, therefore, had not attached to any offenses committed solely in Midland County. . . .

4. Dual-Use Evidence

In her questions on the recording, J.S. made no attempt to distinguish between the offenses that occurred in Midland and those that occurred in Odessa [Ector County]. She was simply trying to get appellant to admit that he had committed sexual offenses against her. Appellant's evasive answers also failed to provide any distinction between Midland and Odessa offenses. Just as the Moulton decision recognized that some criminal investigations have "dual purposes," relating to both charged and uncharged crimes, we recognize that evidence elicited in criminal investigations can sometimes have dual uses, being evidence of both charged and uncharged crimes.... Consequently, appellant's Sixth Amendment right to counsel had attached with respect to the recordings insofar as [information about other crimes, and statements about those crimes, became] relevant to [prove] the Ector County [crimes].

C. Knowing Circumvention

In Moulton, the Supreme Court indicated that a *Massiah* violation occurs only if the State "knowingly circumvented" the right to counsel. The court of appeals' opinion suggests that a knowing circumvention did not occur because Midland law enforcement was unaware that appellant had counsel. Appellant's position is that the knowledge of Ector County law enforcement should be imputed to Midland County law enforcement.

Appellant has the better of the argument. In Michigan v. Jackson, 475 U.S. 625 (1986), the Supreme Court held that the State is responsible, in the Sixth Amendment context, for the knowledge of all of its actors: "Sixth Amendment principles require that we impute the State's knowledge from one state actor to another. For the Sixth Amendment concerns the confrontation between the State and the individual. One set of state actors (the police) may not claim ignorance of defendants' unequivocal request for counsel to another state actor (the court)."...

It is true that, in Montejo v. Louisiana, 556 U.S. 778 (2009), the Supreme Court overruled Jackson insofar as it imposed a prophylactic rule forbidding interrogation once the accused has requested counsel. But the *Montejo* decision expressly stated that it was not concerned with the substantive scope of the Sixth Amendment right to counsel, and in so saying it cited both *Moulton* and *Massiah*.

D. Government Agent

Having determined that the right to counsel had attached with respect to the recordings and that knowledge of that attachment, and that appellant had counsel, must be imputed to Midland law enforcement, we now address whether J.S. was a government agent. The rule in *Massiah* applies only if the person who elicited statements from the defendant was a government agent.

In Manns v. State, 122 S.W.3d 171 (Tex. Crim. App. 2003), we observed that there were some differences in the approaches of various jurisdictions regarding this issue, but the jurisdictions were unified by at least one common principle: "to qualify as a government agent, the informant must at least have some sort of agreement with, or act under instructions from, a government official." We were not required to specify in greater detail what makes someone a government agent for *Massiah* purposes because the informant in *Manns* had acted entirely on his own volition, without any promises, encouragement, or instructions from the government, and was therefore not a government agent. We must now explore in more detail the issue of what makes someone a government agent.

As we observed in *Manns*, some of the federal circuits espouse a bright-line test that an informant becomes a government agent "when the informant has been instructed by the police to get information about a particular defendant." The

Supreme Court of California has suggested that an informant becomes a government agent if he acts "under the direction of the government pursuant to a preexisting arrangement, with the expectation of some resulting benefit or advantage." People v. Dement, 264 P.3d 292, 318 (Cal. 2011). The Fifth Circuit held that the informant in one case was not a government agent because the evidence failed to show a quid pro quo and it failed to show instruction or control by the State. Creel v. Johnson, 162 F.3d 385, 394 (5th Cir. 1998). . . . Other jurisdictions have said that someone was not a government agent if he was not instructed by the police or not promised something of value for the information. . . . Similarly, the Ninth Circuit has held that an agreement to compensate the informant for his services was not required. It is enough, the court held, that "the State made a conscious decision to obtain [the informant's] cooperation and that [the informant] consciously decided to provide that cooperation." Randolph v. California, 380 F.3d 1133, 1144 (9th Cir. 2004).

We conclude that J.S. was a government agent. The Midland police encouraged J.S. to call appellant for the purpose of eliciting a confession. They also supplied J.S. with the recording equipment, and an officer was present during the calls. . . .

E. Deliberately Elicit

The next question is whether J.S. "deliberately elicited" incriminating statements from appellant. In State v. Maldonado, 259 S.W.3d 184 (Tex. Crim. App. 2008), we surveyed the Supreme Court's cases regarding the meaning of the Sixth Amendment's "deliberately elicited" requirement and concluded that it encompassed a broader range of activity than the Fifth Amendment concept of interrogation. Interrogation would certainly qualify as deliberate elicitation for *Massiah* purposes, but it is not required. "Deliberate elicitation" simply involves "some conduct designed to obtain incriminating statements." Such conduct has not occurred if the informant is merely a passive "listening post" who relates any statements the defendant makes of his own volition. In *Maldonado*, we further concluded that a police officer's act of introducing himself was not sufficient to constitute deliberate elicitation.

There were times on the recording when J.S. engaged in explicit interrogation, such as when she asked appellant why he had touched her and why he had sex with her. At other times, J.S. made statements that fell short of interrogation but were nevertheless designed to invoke incriminating responses. After all, the purpose of the calls was to elicit incriminating evidence. Although some of the statements made by J.S. on the recordings were entirely innocuous, the incriminating relevance of the recordings flowed from J.S.'s attempts to elicit incriminating admissions. We readily conclude that deliberate elicitation has been shown.

F. Waiver

The State cites *Montejo* for the proposition that a defendant who invokes his right to counsel by requesting an appointed attorney . . . can still waive his right to counsel. . . . The State then . . . claims that appellant's "conversations with J.S. were purely voluntary on his part and he would certainly have been free to decline to speak to her at all." In saying that appellant was free to decline to speak to J.S., the State implicitly suggests that appellant waived his right to counsel by choosing to speak to her.

The Supreme Court, however, has indicated that waiver does not apply in the *Massiah* [undercover] context:

[The] concept of a knowing and voluntary waiver of Sixth Amendment rights does not apply in the context of communications with an undisclosed undercover informant acting for the Government. In that setting, [the defendant], being unaware that [the informant] was a Government agent expressly commissioned to secure evidence, cannot be held to have waived his right to the assistance of counsel.

Nevertheless, some courts have held or suggested that a waiver can occur when the informant is the complaining witness. [For instance, in] People v. Wojtkowski, 167 Cal. App. 3d 1077 (1985), a California appellate court held *Massiah* to be inapplicable where the defendant called the complaining witness, his wife. The court explained that "no one twisted [the defendant's] arm to place telephone calls to his wife." The defendant "knew that his wife was a prosecution witness, and the very purpose of his call was to dissuade her from proceeding with the prosecution." Moreover, the complaining witness's few references to the crime were in response to the defendant's suggestion that she discourage prosecution of the offense. The court concluded that the wife "was not an agent provocateur." . . .

Unlike the defendant in *Wojtkowski*, appellant did not initiate the calls to the complaining witness. The complaining witness initiated the calls, and she made statements during the calls that were designed to lull appellant into believing that she was not adverse to him. And unlike the authorities in Berry, the Midland police encouraged J.S. to contact appellant for the purpose of eliciting a confession, and they provided recording equipment to her to memorialize any incriminating statements. We conclude that appellant did not waive his right to counsel. . . .

The recordings were made in violation of appellant's right to counsel with respect to the Ector County prosecution. We reverse the judgment of the court of appeals and remand the case to that court for further proceedings consistent with this opinion.

Notes

1. *The Sixth Amendment right to counsel and "deliberately eliciting" a confession.* The Sixth Amendment to the U.S. Constitution provides for a right to counsel "in all criminal prosecutions." The U.S. Supreme Court, along with most states applying analogous state constitutional provisions, has held that Sixth Amendment counsel rights attach automatically after the initiation of formal proceedings, whether by way of indictment, information, or initial arraignment. "Automatically" means the accused need not assert a request for counsel in order for the Sixth Amendment to protect her. In this regard, the Sixth Amendment right to counsel is broader than the Fifth Amendment right to counsel under the *Miranda* line of cases.

The Sixth Amendment is violated when a law enforcement agent, uniformed or undercover, "deliberately elicits" information from an accused without her attorney present, about the crimes for which she has been charged, without first securing a valid waiver. Deliberate elicitation means the officer intentionally tried to extract information from the accused about the crimes in the indictment; unlike the Fifth Amendment setting, it is *not* judged against whether a reasonable officer would have thought his behavior would produce information. Deliberate elicitation can occur through words or deeds. In Fellers v. United States, 540 U.S. 519 (2004), for example, an officer went to the home of an indicted defendant, told him he had been indicted for drug conspiracy, mentioned the names of the co-conspirators, and then arrested him. The officer did not ask him any questions. The Supreme Court held the officer's actions violated the Sixth Amendment right to counsel because the officer discussed Fellers' charges with him in the absence of an attorney, even though this contact did not amount to constructive interrogation under *Miranda.*

2. *Waiver and invocation of Sixth Amendment rights.* In Michigan v. Jackson, 475 U.S. 625 (1986), the Court explained that Sixth Amendment rights deserve at least as much protection as Fifth Amendment rights, and held that government agents could not seek a valid waiver of the Sixth Amendment right to counsel after it had attached, unless the defendant re-initiated the conversation with police. In Montejo v. Louisiana, 556 U.S. 778 (2009), however, the Court reversed course on the waiver issue. Overruling *Jackson,* the Court held that a defendant may waive the Sixth Amendment right to counsel—so long as relinquishment of the right is voluntary, knowing, and intelligent—even if the government initiates the conversation after the assignment of counsel to the defendant. The majority considered the *Edwards* rule to be sufficient to prevent police from badgering a defendant into waiving his previously asserted *Miranda* rights; the Court did not consider it necessary to create any separate protection for Sixth Amendment interests. Of course, the Court noted, an accused's prior request for counsel, or an existing relationship with counsel, will make the government's claim of waiver harder to support, and as the *Rubalcaldo* opinion mentions, waiver is not possible when the law enforcement agent is undercover. Some states reject *Montejo* for purposes of their state constitutions, preferring the *Jackson* approach instead. See State v. Bevel, 745 S.E.2d 237 (2013) (after suspect has requested counsel, it cannot later be waived before meeting with counsel).

3. *Sixth Amendment right to counsel and undercover agents.* In Kuhlmann v. Wilson, 477 U.S. 436 (1986), the U.S. Supreme Court addressed whether the Sixth Amendment rights of the accused could be violated by an undercover agent (like a jail cellmate), or whether only uniformed officers were subject to Sixth Amendment scrutiny. The Court held that the Sixth Amendment governs the behavior of both types of agents, but only if they deliberately elicit information about crimes for which charges have been filed. Undercover agents who merely passively listen to the accused (without asking questions) are not deliberately eliciting information. From this line of cases we can distinguish between agents who are acting as "mouths" and those who are acting as "ears"; if the court believes the agent was only an "ear," there is no Sixth Amendment violation. In this fact-sensitive area, one can find enormous variety in the decisions of state and lower federal courts; a review of some representative holdings appear on the web extension for this chapter at *http://www.crimpro.com/ extension/ch08.* Why is there a different standard for assessing undercover agents' behavior under the Fifth Amendment and Sixth Amendment rights to counsel?

4. *Scope of the Sixth Amendment right to counsel for "other" offenses.* Can government agents interrogate a defendant about a crime other than an offense for which the government has initiated formal proceedings? In McNeil v. Wisconsin, 501 U.S. 171 (1991), the Court explained that the Sixth Amendment right to counsel "is offense specific. It cannot be invoked once for all future prosecutions, for it does not attach until a prosecution is commenced, that is, at or after the initiation of adversary judicial criminal proceedings — whether by way of formal charge, preliminary hearing, indictment, information, or arraignment." In Texas v. Cobb, 532 U.S. 162 (2001), the Court addressed the issue of what constituted the "same offense." Some state court and lower federal court decisions treated "factually related" crimes as the "same offense." The Supreme Court, however, held that the determination

E. Sixth Amendment Right to Counsel During Investigations

of whether a second offense was the "same offense" under the Sixth Amendment should be determined under the narrow standards applied under federal law to determine whether double jeopardy barred the filing of two separate charges for the "same offence." See Blockburger v. United States, 284 U.S. 299 (1932), discussed in Chapter 14. Thus, a second offense would not be considered the "same offense" and would allow subsequent interrogation when each of two statutory provisions "requires proof of a fact which the other does not."

A number of state courts have refused to follow Texas v. Cobb when interpreting their state constitutions. See Jewell v. State, 957 N.E.2d 625 (Ind. 2011) (interrogation without counsel is barred when police ask suspect about uncharged offense that is factually interrelated with another charged offense for which an attorney represents the suspect); People v. Lopez, 947 N.E.2d 1155 (N.Y. 2011) (right to counsel under state constitution bars interrogation of in-custody suspect about any offense if investigators know that suspect has counsel for the offense that is the basis for custody; investigators also must ask suspect about counsel if "there is a probable likelihood" that suspect has counsel for the custodial offense). Note that if officers begin to question about an unrelated offense but elicit information about the same offense, the latter statements will be blocked by the Sixth Amendment if the officers should have reasonably expected the conversation to take this turn. Maine v. Moulton, 474 U.S. 159 (1985).

5. *Does a valid waiver of* Miranda *rights amount to a waiver of the Sixth Amendment right to counsel?* Yes, but only as to crimes for which the defendant has been charged! In Patterson v. Illinois, 487 U.S. 285 (1988), the U.S. Supreme Court made clear that the same standards for voluntary waiver in the *Miranda* context apply in the Sixth Amendment context, thereby adopting the standard that was already common in several of the circuits. See, e.g., United States v. Karr, 742 F.2d 493 (9th Cir. 1984); Tinsley v. Purvis, 731 F.2d 791 (11th Cir. 1984). But remember, an accused can only waive his Sixth Amendment rights if they've attached. Thus, any *Miranda* waiver secured before formal charges have been filed for certain crimes cannot be construed as a waiver of the Sixth Amendment right to counsel on those crimes.

6. *Rate of success on* Massiah *claims?* Wayne Logan examined how often defendants succeed when they raise *Massiah*-type claims in state and federal courts. Considering cases both before and after *Montejo* was decided, he concluded that the government wins these challenges 85 percent of the time. Thus he argues that the various components of the *Massiah* claim—that the Sixth Amendment right has attached to these specific charges, that the government agent deliberately elicited information about these charges, and that there was no waiver first—have proven to be significant hurdles for most defendants. Wayne A. Logan, False *Massiah*: The Sixth Amendment Revolution That Wasn't, 50 Tex. Tech. L. Rev. 153 (2017). There is, of course, no way to measure how much police have conformed their behavior to the dictates of *Massiah*, thereby avoiding the creation of Sixth Amendment problems in the first place.

Problem 8-8. Christian Burial Speech

On the afternoon of December 24, 1968, 10-year-old Pamela Powers disappeared from the YMCA in Des Moines, Iowa. An arrest warrant was issued for Robert Williams in Des Moines for the abduction of Pamela Powers.

On the morning of December 26, a Des Moines lawyer named Henry McKnight went to the Des Moines police station and informed the officers present that he had just received a long-distance call from Williams and that he had advised Williams to turn himself in to the Davenport police. Williams did surrender that morning to the police in Davenport, and they booked him on the charge specified in the arrest warrant and gave him the warnings required by Miranda v. Arizona. The Davenport police then telephoned their counterparts in Des Moines to inform them that Williams had surrendered. McKnight, the lawyer, was still at the Des Moines police headquarters, and Williams spoke with McKnight on the telephone. McKnight advised Williams that Des Moines police officers would be driving to Davenport to pick him up, that the officers would not interrogate him or mistreat him, and that Williams was not to talk to the officers about Pamela Powers until after consulting with McKnight upon his return to Des Moines. As a result of these conversations, McKnight and the Des Moines police officials agreed that Detective Learning and a fellow officer would drive to Davenport to pick up Williams, that they would bring him directly back to Des Moines, and that they would not question him during the trip.

In the meantime, Williams was arraigned before a judge in Davenport on the outstanding arrest warrant. The judge advised him of his *Miranda* rights and committed him to jail. Before leaving the courtroom, Williams conferred with a lawyer named Thomas Kelly, who advised him not to make any statements until consulting with McKnight back in Des Moines.

Soon after Detective Learning and his fellow officer arrived in Davenport, they met with Williams and Kelly. Detective Learning repeated the *Miranda* warnings and told Williams: "We both know that you're being represented here by Mr. Kelly and you're being represented by Mr. McKnight in Des Moines, and I want you to remember this because we'll be visiting between here and Des Moines." Kelly reiterated to Detective Learning that Williams was not to be questioned about the disappearance of Pamela Powers until after he had consulted with McKnight back in Des Moines. When Learning expressed some reservations, Kelly firmly stated that the agreement with McKnight was to be carried out—that there was to be no interrogation of Williams during the journey to Des Moines. Kelly was denied permission to ride in the police car back to Des Moines with Williams and the two officers. The two detectives, with Williams in their charge, then set out on the 160-mile drive. Williams said several times during the trip that "when I get to Des Moines and see Mr. McKnight, I am going to tell you the whole story."

Detective Learning knew that Williams was a former mental patient, and knew also that he was deeply religious. Learning and Williams soon embarked on a conversation covering a variety of topics, including the subject of religion. Learning addressed Williams as "Reverend." He then made this speech:

> I want to give you something to think about while we're traveling down the road. Number one, I want you to observe the weather conditions, it's raining, it's sleeting, it's freezing, driving is very treacherous, visibility is poor, it's going to be dark early this evening. They are predicting several inches of snow for tonight, and I feel that you yourself are the only person that knows where this little girl's body is, that you yourself have only been there once, and if you get a snow on top of it you yourself may be unable to find it. And, since we will be going right past the area on the way into Des Moines, I feel that we could stop and locate the body, that the parents of this little girl should be entitled to a Christian burial for the little girl who was

snatched away from them on Christmas Eve and murdered. And I feel we should stop and locate it on the way in rather than waiting until morning and trying to come back out after a snow storm and possibly not being able to find it at all.

Learning then added, "I do not want you to answer me. I don't want to discuss it any further. Just think about it as we're riding down the road."

As the car approached Grinnell, a town approximately 100 miles west of Davenport, Williams asked whether the police had found the victim's shoes. When Detective Learning replied that he was unsure, Williams directed the officers to a service station where he said he had left the shoes; a search for them proved unsuccessful. As they continued toward Des Moines, Williams asked whether the police had found the blanket, and directed the officers to a rest area where he said he had disposed of the blanket. Nothing was found. The car continued toward Des Moines, and as it approached Mitchellville, Williams said that he would show the officers where the body was. He then directed the police to the body of Pamela Powers.

Williams was indicted for first-degree murder. Before trial, his counsel moved to suppress all evidence resulting from any statements Williams had made during the automobile ride from Davenport to Des Moines. Should the judge grant the motion on Sixth Amendment grounds? Would the officer's action also violate *Miranda/Edwards* under the Fifth Amendment? Compare Brewer v. Williams, 430 U.S. 387 (1977), and Yale Kamisar, *Brewer v. Williams*—A Hard Look at a Discomfiting Record, 66 Geo. L.J. 209 (1977).

Problem 8-9. Cellmate Confession

Josiah has been indicted on two counts of grand theft auto for stealing a Chevy Camaro and a Pontiac Firebird from two different mall parking lots. He is arrested and placed in a jail cell with Eli, who is awaiting trial on drug charges. Eli decides to start chatting with Josiah to see if he can get Josiah to talk about his crimes, because Eli has traded information for lesser punishment in the past and has a long-standing agreement with the cops to share what he knows. But Josiah seems pretty closed off and stays quiet about most things on the outside. All Josiah says is that he's "done some stupid things to get money to buy an engagement ring" for his girlfriend.

Eli keeps his ears open for Josiah to say more. A few days later, Josiah mumbles something in his sleep about a car, and Eli hears it. Eli says in the morning, "You were talking in your sleep last night, buddy—said something about a car?" Josiah sighs and says, "I never should have stolen that first car." Eli asks, "How many have you stolen?" Josiah responds, "Two—a Camaro and a Firebird." Eli says, "Ever stolen anything else?" Josiah looks at his feet and then murmurs, "Those two cars, plus some jewelry from the shop around the corner from my house, but that's all."

Eli reports these statements to correctional officer Ufficio, who shares them with the deputy district attorney on Josiah's case. The DDA includes these statements in the discovery packet he gives to Josiah's lawyer on the grand theft auto case. The DDA then looks into the jewelry store burglary that Josiah referenced. The police had opened an investigation into the burglary but had not yet located a suspect. The police run Josiah's fingerprints against the fingerprints found at the scene, and they are a match.

Can Josiah's statements about stealing the cars be used in his grand theft auto prosecution? Answer according to *Miranda* and Sixth Amendment right to counsel jurisprudence.

Can Josiah's statement about the jewelry store be used in a future burglary prosecution? Answer according to *Miranda* and Sixth Amendment right to counsel jurisprudence.

F. THE IMPACT OF UNLAWFUL INTERROGATIONS

The decades-long debate over the wisdom of *Miranda* and the Sixth Amendment right to counsel interrogation jurisprudence turns in part on how much of an impact these doctrines have had on criminal investigations and prosecutions. The first part of this section considers the extent to which an interrogation error can affect the prosecution's evidence in the criminal case. The second part considers the effects of *Miranda* on the criminal justice system as a whole, in terms of lost convictions and system credibility.

1. The Result of Interrogation Violations at the Case Level

In the ordinary case, a violation of *Miranda*, the Sixth Amendment, or the Fifth Amendment due process clause will mean that the confession extracted during the tainted interrogation will be inadmissible as evidence. But what about physical evidence or testimony of witnesses obtained as a result of the improper interrogation? Will this derivative evidence — the "fruit of the poisonous tree" — be admissible? There are a number of circumstances under which courts will admit evidence obtained after a *Miranda* violation, or after a Sixth Amendment violation, even if the improper interrogation was the "but for" cause of the police obtaining the evidence. Evidence obtained from a due process violation, by contrast, is blocked for all purposes.

■ MISSOURI v. PATRICE SEIBERT
542 U.S. 600 (2004)

SOUTER, J.*

This case tests a police protocol for custodial interrogation that calls for giving no warnings of the rights to silence and counsel until interrogation has produced a confession. Although such a statement is generally inadmissible, since taken in violation of Miranda v. Arizona, 384 U.S. 436 (1966), the interrogating officer follows it with *Miranda* warnings and then leads the suspect to cover the same ground a second time. The question here is the admissibility of the repeated statement. Because this midstream recitation of warnings after interrogation and unwarned confession

---

* [Justices Stevens, Ginsburg, and Breyer joined in this opinion; Justice Kennedy concurred in the judgment. — EDS.]

could not effectively comply with *Miranda*'s constitutional requirement, we hold that a statement repeated after a warning in such circumstances is inadmissible.

Respondent Patrice Seibert's 12-year-old son Jonathan had cerebral palsy, and when he died in his sleep she feared charges of neglect because of bedsores on his body. In her presence, two of her teenage sons and two of their friends devised a plan to conceal the facts surrounding Jonathan's death by incinerating his body in the course of burning the family's mobile home, in which they planned to leave Donald Rector, a mentally ill teenager living with the family, to avoid any appearance that Jonathan had been unattended. Seibert's son Darian and a friend set the fire, and Donald died.

Five days later, the police awakened Seibert at 3 A.M. at a hospital where Darian was being treated for burns. In arresting her, Officer Kevin Clinton followed instructions from [another officer] that he refrain from giving *Miranda* warnings. After Seibert had been taken to the police station and left alone in an interview room for 15 to 20 minutes, Hanrahan questioned her without *Miranda* warnings for 30 to 40 minutes, squeezing her arm and repeating, "Donald was also to die in his sleep." After Seibert finally admitted she knew Donald was meant to die in the fire, she was given a 20-minute coffee and cigarette break. Officer Hanrahan then turned on a tape recorder, gave Seibert the *Miranda* warnings, and obtained a signed waiver of rights from her. He resumed the questioning with "Ok, 'trice, we've been talking for a little while about what happened on Wednesday the twelfth, haven't we?," and confronted her with her prewarning statements:

> *Hanrahan:* Now, in discussion you told us, you told us that there was an understanding about Donald.
> *Seibert:* Yes. . . .
> *Hanrahan:* And what was the understanding about Donald?
> *Seibert:* If they could get him out of the trailer, to take him out of the trailer. . . .
> *Hanrahan:* 'Trice, didn't you tell me that he was supposed to die in his sleep?
> *Seibert:* If that would happen, 'cause he was on that new medicine, you know. . . .
> *Hanrahan:* The Prozac? And it makes him sleepy. So he was supposed to die in his sleep?
> *Seibert:* Yes.

After being charged with first-degree murder for her role in Donald's death, Seibert sought to exclude both her prewarning and postwarning statements. At the suppression hearing, Officer Hanrahan testified that he made a "conscious decision" to withhold *Miranda* warnings, thus resorting to an interrogation technique he had been taught: question first, then give the warnings, and then repeat the question "until I get the answer that she's already provided once." He acknowledged that Seibert's ultimate statement was "largely a repeat of information . . . obtained" prior to the warning.

The trial court suppressed the prewarning statement but admitted the responses given after the *Miranda* recitation. A jury convicted Seibert of second-degree murder. . . .

[Giving *Miranda*] warnings and getting a waiver has generally produced a virtual ticket of admissibility; maintaining that a statement is involuntary even though given after warnings and voluntary waiver of rights requires unusual stamina, and litigation over voluntariness tends to end with the finding of a valid waiver. To point out the obvious, this common consequence would not be common at all were it not that *Miranda* warnings are customarily given under circumstances allowing for a real choice between talking and remaining silent.

The technique of interrogating in successive, unwarned and warned phases raises a new challenge to *Miranda*. Although we have no statistics on the frequency of this practice, it is not confined to Rolla, Missouri. [The] Police Law Institute, for example, instructs that "officers may conduct a two-stage interrogation. . . . At any point during the pre-*Miranda* interrogation, usually after arrestees have confessed, officers may then read the *Miranda* warnings and ask for a waiver. If the arrestees waive their *Miranda* rights, officers will be able to repeat any *subsequent* incriminating statements later in court." Police Law Institute, Illinois Police Law Manual 83 (Jan. 2001-Dec. 2003) (hereinafter Police Law Manual). . . .

The inquiry is simply whether the warnings reasonably convey to a suspect his rights as required by *Miranda*. The threshold issue when interrogators question first and warn later is thus whether it would be reasonable to find that in these circumstances the warnings could function "effectively" as *Miranda* requires. Could the warnings effectively advise the suspect that he had a real choice about giving an admissible statement at that juncture? Could they reasonably convey that he could choose to stop talking even if he had talked earlier? For unless the warnings could place a suspect who has just been interrogated in a position to make such an informed choice, there is no practical justification for accepting the formal warnings as compliance with *Miranda*, or for treating the second stage of interrogation as distinct from the first, unwarned and inadmissible segment. . . .

By any objective measure, applied to circumstances exemplified here, it is likely that if the interrogators employ the technique of withholding warnings until after interrogation succeeds in eliciting a confession, the warnings will be ineffective in preparing the suspect for successive interrogation, close in time and similar in content. After all, the reason that question-first is catching on is as obvious as its manifest purpose, which is to get a confession the suspect would not make if he understood his rights at the outset; the sensible underlying assumption is that with one confession in hand before the warnings, the interrogator can count on getting its duplicate, with trifling additional trouble. . . . What is worse, telling a suspect that "anything you say can and will be used against you," without expressly excepting the statement just given, could lead to an entirely reasonable inference that what he has just said will be used, with subsequent silence being of no avail. Thus, when *Miranda* warnings are inserted in the midst of coordinated and continuing interrogation, they are likely to mislead and deprive a defendant of knowledge essential to his ability to understand the nature of his rights and the consequences of abandoning them. . . .

Missouri argues that a confession repeated at the end of an interrogation sequence envisioned in a question-first strategy is admissible on the authority of Oregon v. Elstad, 470 U.S. 298 (1985), but the argument disfigures that case. In *Elstad*, the police went to the young suspect's house to take him into custody on a charge of burglary. Before the arrest, one officer spoke with the suspect's mother, while the other one joined the suspect in a "brief stop in the living room," where the officer said he "felt" the young man was involved in a burglary. The suspect acknowledged he had been at the scene. This Court noted that the pause in the living room "was not to interrogate the suspect but to notify his mother of the reason for his arrest," and described the incident as having "none of the earmarks of coercion." The Court, indeed, took care to mention that the officer's initial failure to warn was an "oversight" that "may have been the result of confusion as to whether the brief exchange qualified as 'custodial interrogation' or . . . may simply have reflected . . . reluctance to initiate an alarming police procedure before [an officer] had spoken with respondent's mother." At the outset of a later and systematic station house interrogation going well beyond the scope of the laconic prior admission, the suspect was given *Miranda* warnings and made a full confession. In holding the second statement admissible and voluntary, *Elstad* rejected the "cat out of the bag" theory that any short, earlier admission, obtained in arguably innocent neglect of *Miranda*, determined the character of the later, warned confession; on the facts of that case, the Court thought any causal connection between the first and second responses to the police was "speculative and attenuated." Although the *Elstad* Court expressed no explicit conclusion about either officer's state of mind, it is fair to read *Elstad* as treating the living room conversation as a good-faith *Miranda* mistake, not only open to correction by careful warnings before systematic questioning in that particular case, but posing no threat to warn-first practice generally.

The contrast between *Elstad* and this case reveals a series of relevant facts that bear on whether *Miranda* warnings delivered midstream could be effective enough to accomplish their object: the completeness and detail of the questions and answers in the first round of interrogation, the overlapping content of the two statements, the timing and setting of the first and the second, the continuity of police personnel, and the degree to which the interrogator's questions treated the second round as continuous with the first. In *Elstad*, it was not unreasonable to see the occasion for questioning at the station house as presenting a markedly different experience from the short conversation at home; since a reasonable person in the suspect's shoes could have seen the station house questioning as a new and distinct experience, the *Miranda* warnings could have made sense as presenting a genuine choice whether to follow up on the earlier admission.

At the opposite extreme are the facts here, which by any objective measure reveal a police strategy adapted to undermine the *Miranda* warnings.[6] The unwarned interrogation was conducted in the station house, and the questioning was systematic, exhaustive, and managed with psychological skill. When the police were finished there was little, if anything, of incriminating potential left unsaid. The warned phase of questioning proceeded after a pause of only 15 to 20 minutes, in the same place as the unwarned segment. [The] police did not advise that her prior statement could not be used. Nothing was said or done to dispel the oddity of warning about legal rights to silence and counsel right after the police had led her through a systematic interrogation. . . . The impression that the further questioning was a mere continuation of the earlier questions and responses was fostered by references back to the confession already given. It would have been reasonable to regard the two sessions as parts of a continuum, in which it would have been unnatural to refuse to repeat at the second stage what had been said before. . . .

Because the question-first tactic effectively threatens to thwart *Miranda*'s purpose of reducing the risk that a coerced confession would be admitted, and because

---

6. Because the intent of the officer will rarely be as candidly admitted as it was here (even as it is likely to determine the conduct of the interrogation), the focus is on facts apart from intent that show the question-first tactic at work.

the facts here do not reasonably support a conclusion that the warnings given could have served their purpose, Seibert's postwarning statements are inadmissible. . . .

KENNEDY, J., concurring in the judgment.

The plurality concludes that whenever a two-stage interview occurs, admissibility of the postwarning statement should depend on "whether the *Miranda* warnings delivered midstream could have been effective enough to accomplish their object" given the specific facts of the case. This test envisions an objective inquiry from the perspective of the suspect, and applies in the case of both intentional and unintentional two-stage interrogations. In my view, this test cuts too broadly. *Miranda*'s clarity is one of its strengths, and a multifactor test that applies to every two-stage interrogation may serve to undermine that clarity. I would apply a narrower test applicable only in the infrequent case, such as we have here, in which the two-step interrogation technique was used in a calculated way to undermine the *Miranda* warning. . . .

O'CONNOR, J., dissenting.*

The plurality devours Oregon v. Elstad, 470 U.S. 298 (1985), even as it accuses petitioner's argument of "disfiguring" that decision. I believe that we are bound by *Elstad* to reach a different result, and I would vacate the judgment of the Supreme Court of Missouri. . . . I would analyze the two-step interrogation procedure under the voluntariness standards central to the Fifth Amendment and reiterated in *Elstad*. . . .

Notes

1. *Out-of-court statements obtained after earlier* Miranda *violations: majority position.* Unlike illegal searches and seizures, an unwarned interrogation will not necessarily require a later court to exclude all the evidence derived from the tainted statement. Although any statement made during an unwarned interrogation must not come into evidence, later statements of the suspect might still be admissible—because the Supreme Court does not regard a *Miranda* violation as causing a "poisonous tree" in the same way that constitutional violations do.

In Oregon v. Elstad, 470 U.S. 298 (1985), the Supreme Court held that, even after a *Miranda* violation produced a first unwarned statement, the state could use as evidence a subsequent confession as long as that subsequent confession was voluntary. According to the Court, when the initial unwarned statement was given voluntarily,

> a careful and thorough administration of *Miranda* warnings serves to cure the condition that rendered the unwarned statement inadmissible. The warning conveys the relevant information and thereafter the suspect's choice whether to exercise his privilege to remain silent should ordinarily be viewed as an act of free will.

470 U.S. at 310. *Seibert* clearly changed the standard, even though the majority worked hard to keep *Elstad*'s factual holding intact. Courts now require the

prosecution to show that the second statement was the product of a different inter-rogation, not merely that it was voluntary, such that receiving *Miranda* warnings mid-stream can be regarded as effective from the reasonable suspect's point of view. Before *Seibert* was decided, a significant minority of states (around 15) had rejected the *Elstad* decision, placing a burden on the government to overcome a presumption of compulsion for subsequent confessions. See, e.g., Commonwealth v. Smith, 593 N.E.2d 1288 (Mass. 1992). Is this presumption of compulsion a bet-ter standard than the "distinct interrogation" multifactor formula designed by the *Seibert* majority? For a glimpse of the vigorous state court rulings on the question of "cures" for improper *Miranda* warnings, see the web extension for this chapter at *http://www.crimpro.com/extension/ch08*.

What if the earlier statement was obtained in violation of the Sixth Amendment, but the interrogation did not violate *Miranda*? Do courts use the standard atten-uation analysis designed in the Fourth Amendment context (as discussed in Chapter 6), or the special attenuation analysis set forth in *Seibert* to handle *Miranda* violations? The U.S. Supreme Court had the opportunity to decide this question in Fellers v. United States, 540 U.S. 519 (2004), but it declined to answer, sending the case back to the Eighth Circuit. Lower courts have mostly followed standard attenuation analysis but have used some of the factors identified in *Seibert* to assess when the taint has dissipated, in accordance with the Eighth Circuit's *Fellers II* anal-ysis. See Fellers v. United States, 397 F.3d 1090, 1097-1098 (8th Cir. 2005) (applying the *Seibert* plurality test to hold that Fellers's post-warned statement was admissible because the prior unwarned statement was elicited at Fellers's home, the jailhouse interrogation took place almost one hour later, post-warned questioning addressed different allegations, and there was no evidence that the officers employed a delib-erate strategy to evade the accused's right to counsel). For a state supreme court case invoking the fruit of the poisonous tree analysis, see State v. Barron, 16 A.3d 620 (Vt. 2011).

2. *Use of statements for impeachment at trial.* Although state and federal courts exclude *Miranda*-tainted statements from the prosecution's case in chief, they allow the prosecution to use such statements (and the evidentiary fruit of those state-ments) to impeach a defendant's testimony at trial. See Oregon v. Hass, 420 U.S. 714 (1975); Harris v. New York, 401 U.S. 222 (1971). Again, not all states agree. See State v. Santiago, 492 P.2d 657 (Haw. 1971).

Even statements obtained in violation of the Sixth Amendment right to counsel can be used to impeach the defendant if she testifies. Michigan v. Harvey, 494 U.S. 344 (1990) (impeachment use allowed after invalid waiver); Kansas v. Ventris, 556 U.S. 586 (2009) (impeachment use allowed after no waiver). Justice Scalia's opinion for the Court in *Ventris* distinguished between "core" or "substantive" protections and "prophylactic" protections. For the latter category, he said, impeachment uses of illegally obtained evidence are allowed, as they are necessary to prevent defen-dant perjury. If a statement is obtained in violation of due process, however, no impeachment use is allowed. Mincey v. Arizona, 437 U.S. 385 (1978). According to Justice Scalia's formula, due process rights are core protections that would be undermined if the prosecution were permitted to use coerced statements for any reason.

3. *Tainted leads to witnesses and physical evidence.* An improper interrogation might give the authorities information that can lead them to other witnesses or to physical evidence. Where the interrogators violate the Sixth Amendment in obtaining the

defendant's statement, physical fruits and new witnesses found because of the statement would normally be excluded under the fruits of the poisonous tree doctrine. See, e.g., United States v. Terzado-Madruga, 897 F.2d 1099 (11th Cir. 1990) (citing U.S. v. Wade, 388 U.S. 218 (1967)).

A different rule applies when the alleged violation concerns *Miranda.* In Michigan v. Tucker, 417 U.S. 433 (1974), the Supreme Court allowed the use of prosecution witnesses whose names had been obtained during an interrogation where proper *Miranda* warnings had not been given. While recognizing that a truly involuntary confession, obtained in violation of the due process clause, could be remedied only by complete exclusion of all evidentiary "fruits" of the confession (see, e.g., Kastigar v. United States, 406 U.S. 441 (1972)), this was not such a case. The failure to give proper *Miranda* warnings was merely a violation of a "prophylactic" rule rather than a constitutional violation as such. Because *Miranda* violations do not create a factually involuntary (and thus unconstitutional) confession, the Court believed that exclusion of evidence would be too costly. This conclusion applies to physical evidence as well as to new witnesses. United States v. Patane, 542 U.S. 630 (2004) (physical evidence produced through unwarned but voluntary statements was admissible, even though police deliberately violated *Miranda*).

Many state courts have not rejected this analysis explicitly, but rather seem to assume that any evidentiary "fruit" from a confession obtained in violation of *Miranda* must be excluded unless one of the traditional exceptions to the "fruits" rule is present. A deliberate violation of *Miranda* by interrogators also has led some state courts to limit the use of evidentiary fruit. See Commonwealth v. Martin, 827 N.E.2d 198 (Mass. 2005) (rejecting *Patane*; holding that state constitution requires suppression of physical evidence derived from unwarned statements); State v. Peterson, 923 A.2d 585 (Vt. 2007) (state constitution requires suppression of tangible fruits of *Miranda* violation).

4. *Harmless error.* There are some constitutional errors in a trial that an appellate court will consider "harmless" because the verdict likely would have remained the same even if the errors had not occurred. Other errors can never be harmless. For a number of years after the *Miranda* decision, courts said that the introduction into evidence of a coerced confession could never be harmless error, because it involved a right so basic to a fair trial that harm was a virtual certainty. In Arizona v. Fulminante, 499 U.S. 279 (1991), however, the Supreme Court decided that the introduction of a coerced confession could, in certain circumstances, be seen as a harmless error after all. We discuss this issue further in Chapter 20, dealing with appeals.

Problem 8-10. Physical Fruits Discovered

Elizabeth Reed, an attendant at a county landfill, died from a shotgun wound fired at close range as she was preparing to leave work. The killer left Reed's body hidden in some brush beside a dirt road, approximately 95 feet from the landfill office. The police soon began to focus their investigation on Kenneth DeShields, who had been seen that day driving Reed's car. They arrested him the morning after the murder.

Before any questioning began, DeShields requested an attorney and said that he did not wish to speak about the incident. However, the investigating officers persisted in their questions, and DeShields ultimately gave a series of statements.

He eventually told the police that he had killed Reed during an attempt to rob her. DeShields also said that after he had left the landfill, he had thrown a rake and several items from the robbery into a ditch. Detective Hudson then searched the dirt road that DeShields had described. He found a ditch containing a rake, an expended shotgun shell casing and the victim's wallet approximately 15 feet east of the dirt road and approximately 1,000 feet from the dump site.

At trial, the state did not introduce any of DeShields's postarrest statements into evidence. However, the shell casing and wallet were admitted into evidence, and an expert testified that the shell casing had been fired from DeShields's shotgun. The shell casing was the only direct evidence linking the killing to his shotgun.

How should the trial court rule on the admissibility of the shell casing and wallet? Would your answer change if the prosecution could establish that the ditch and the dirt road were well within the search perimeter used by the officers in this case, and that the team of searchers were within a few hundred yards of the ditch at the time DeShields made his statement? Compare DeShields v. State, 534 A.2d 630 (Del. 1987).

2. Systemwide Impacts of Miranda's Warning/Waiver Regime

Miranda has been criticized on both doctrinal and practical grounds. The practical critiques take many forms, but they boil down to the question of how many convictions are "lost" because *Miranda* warnings were given. Is it possible to reach a conclusion about the impact of *Miranda*, either 30 years ago or today? Can the benefits of *Miranda* be quantified? For example, did the *Miranda* decision effectively reduce the coerciveness of police interrogations? Or did it legitimize police interrogation through the use of a routine and inconsequential warning and foreclose more intrusive and less predictable judicial supervision of interrogation techniques? What has been the effect of post-*Miranda* case law? Have the various exceptions to the exclusionary rule provided an incentive for police officers to routinely violate *Miranda* or the Sixth Amendment, simply to provide the prosecutor with potential impeachment evidence or useful "fruits" of the interrogation?

■ SAUL M. KASSIN, RICHARD A. LEO ET AL., POLICE INTERVIEWING AND INTERROGATION: A SELF-REPORT SURVEY OF POLICE PRACTICES AND BELIEFS

31 Law and Human Behavior 381 (2007)

INTRODUCTION

Forty years ago, the United States Supreme Court lamented the relative absence of empirical information about what constituted common or routine police interrogation practices. In its landmark decision in Miranda v. Arizona (1966), the Court wrote that, "Interrogation still takes place in privacy. Privacy results in secrecy and this in turn results in a gap in our knowledge as to what in fact goes on in the interrogation room." To fill this gap in its own analysis, this Court surveyed and critiqued then-existing police interrogation training manuals—most notably, Inbau and Reid's Criminal Interrogation and Confessions, which is now in its fourth edition. . . .

Since *Miranda*, researchers have used an array of methods to fill in this empirical gap. This literature is comprised of individual case studies, archival analyses of actual case documents, observations of taped interrogations, retrospective self-reports of suspects, and laboratory and field experiments. In addition, a number of social scientists, journalists, and legal scholars have directly observed police practices "inside the interrogation room." . . .

A number of issues have attracted attention in recent research. One concerns the extent to which law enforcement professionals can accurately distinguish between truthful and deceptive statements. Police investigators have confidence in their ability to make such judgments during a pre-interrogation interview, judgments that often determine whether they interrogate suspects or send them home. . . . For example, John E. Reid and Associates claims that trained investigators can achieve an 85% level of accuracy through the use of various verbal cues (e.g., qualified or rehearsed responses), nonverbal cues (e.g., gaze aversion, frozen posture, slouching) and behavioral attitudes (e.g., lack of concern, anxiousness, and guardedness) presumably diagnostic of truth or deception. . . . The bulk of research indicates that this faith is misplaced. Over the years, numerous studies have demonstrated that individuals perform no better than chance at detecting deception, that training tends to produce only small and inconsistent increments in performance, and that "experts" perform only slightly better than ordinary people, if at all. . . .

A second issue concerns *Miranda* rights. In 1966, the U.S. Supreme Court ruled that prior to commencing interrogation police must inform custodial suspects of their Constitutional rights to silence and to appointed counsel, and that anything they say can be used against them. This Court further held that suspects must voluntarily, knowingly, and intelligently waive those rights in order for their statements to be admissible at trial. Subsequent rulings have carved out exceptions to this rule and limited the consequences for non-compliance. . . . Over the years, police have adapted a number of strategies to circumvent or nullify *Miranda* and its invocation rules. For example, they may avoid the need for warnings by questioning suspects in settings that appear noncustodial. Or they may read the rights but then proceed to question suspects as though they had no choice in the matter, eliciting what some courts have called an "implicit waiver." Sometimes police properly read the *Miranda* rights and invocation rules but then downplay their significance and persuade suspects that it is in their own self interest to waive these rights. In some cases, they interrogate "outside *Miranda*" by tricking suspects into talking after they had invoked their rights—producing "off the record" disclosures that may be used to generate other admissible evidence and to impeach the defendant at trial if he or she chooses to testify.

Consistently, research has revealed that custodial suspects waive their rights approximately 80% of the time. This high waiver rate stems not only from use of the aforementioned techniques but from the fact that many suspects— such as juveniles, people who are mentally retarded, and those who are under stress—do not fully understand their *Miranda* rights and how to apply them. Even among suspects who are competent, it appears that those who are innocent may be particularly disposed to waive their precious rights out of a naive belief in the transparency of their innocence.

A third issue concerns the interrogation tactics that are used to elicit confessions. The stated objective of interrogation is to move a presumed guilty suspect from denial to admission. The techniques used are thus designed to overcome a suspect's resistance and to induce him or her to confess. [Studies] have shown that police use many of the [professional manual's] recommended techniques—such as physical isolation, positive confrontations with evidence, and minimization. . . .

A fourth issue concerns the amount of time suspects spend in the interrogation room, a factor of relevance to evaluating the voluntariness of the statements that are made. Observational studies have suggested that routine interrogations tend to be relatively brief encounters, with the modal duration ranging from 20 minutes to an hour. These findings stand in stark contrast to Drizin and Leo's archival study of 125 proven false confessions, where 34% of interrogations lasted 6 to 12 hours, 39% lasted 12 to 24 hours, and the mean was 16.3 hours. This latter finding is not surprising in light of prominent case studies of false confessions, so many of which were taken at night and after lengthy interrogations. . . .

A fifth issue concerns the rate at which suspects make incriminating statements to police in the form of admissions and full narrative confessions. Confession rates have always factored prominently into debates concerning law enforcement practices in the United States and elsewhere. Researchers have sought to determine confession rates to gauge how successful interrogators are. Interrogation outcomes also represent an obvious "bottom line" for detectives who are largely evaluated by their ability to solve and close cases. The rate at which police elicit incriminating statements is also highly consequential for individual suspects and the criminal justice system as a whole. People who confess are treated differently at every subsequent stage of the criminal process than those who do not. They are more likely to be charged by prosecutors; more likely to be charged with more crimes; less likely to have their cases dismissed; more likely to have their cases resolved by plea bargaining; more likely to be found guilty, especially of more serious charges; and more likely to receive severe punishment upon conviction.

In the United States, research has suggested that the confession rate ranges from 46% to 68%. Based on their own observations, Cassell and Hayman reported a confession rate of 54% in Utah; Leo reported a confession rate of 64% in Northern California. . . . On the question of interrogation outcomes, false confessions are a particular source of concern, arising with disturbing frequency in DNA exoneration cases. . . .

A sixth issue concerns the ways in which police interrogations and confessions are recorded. Investigators are trained to convert the oral admissions they elicit into full written, audiotaped, or videotaped confessions that can later be presented in court. As more and more wrongful convictions based on false confessions are discovered, however, there has emerged a lively debate in state legislatures and in the courts about these record-keeping practices. Increasingly, there are calls for mandating the electronic recording of entire interrogations—a requirement that would arguably deter egregious interrogation tactics, reduce the number of false confessions, inhibit frivolous defense claims of coercion, and increase the fact-finding accuracy of judges and juries. . . . It is interesting that police who have videotaped interrogations as a matter of policy or on a voluntary basis have reacted favorably to the practice. . . .

THE PRESENT SURVEY

Although researchers have learned a great deal about interviewing, interrogation, and the elicitation of confessions, to date there has been no published survey of police interrogators themselves. In light of the steady stream of false confession stories in the news—some of which feature horrific tales of lengthy interrogations and the use of high pressure tactics—it is important to gain insight into police perspectives on how common the problem is, as well as the methods they use most often. To help fill this gap in our knowledge we designed a survey, the purpose of which was to describe the law enforcement perspective.

The participants in this study were 631 investigators from 16 police departments in five American states (N=574) and customs officials from two Canadian provinces (N=57). . . . Participants were not asked for identifying information other than sex, age, and state of residence; whether they were employed at the local, state or federal level; and whether they had received any special training (seminars, workshops, etc.) on how to conduct interviews and interrogations. To address the specific issues and controversies previously described, we asked participants to estimate, rate, and otherwise self-report on six aspects of their work: (1) their ability to detect truth and deception; (2) *Miranda* warnings and waivers; (3) the use of various interrogation techniques; (4) the frequency, length, and timing of interviews and interrogations; (5) the rates of true and false confessions; and (6) their own practices and opinions with regard to the recording of interrogations and confessions. Across the board, our goal was to obtain reports directly from police investigators themselves, to distinguish, albeit imperfectly, common practices and beliefs from those that may be uncommon if not extraordinary, and to triangulate what has been found in other types of empirical research.

Discussion

On the subject of deception detection, we asked investigators about their accuracy at judging the veracity of suspects—a pivotal judgment, regularly made, that can determine whether they proceed to interrogate suspects or send them home. . . . When we asked participants in this study to rate their own deception detection skills, they estimated a 77% level of accuracy, a figure that substantially exceeds human lie detection performance and parallels these earlier findings. . . .

Ever since the U.S. Supreme Court imposed the *Miranda* warning and waiver requirements, questions have been raised about the practical effects, or lack of effects, on police and suspects. Research suggests that roughly four out of five people waive their rights. In our survey, participants' self-reported experiences were highly consistent with this finding, as they estimated an overall waiver rate of 81%—a figure that closely tracks naturalistic data, representing the exact midpoint between the waiver rate found in Leo's observational study in Northern California (78%) and Cassell and Hayman's study of interrogations through prosecutorial screening sessions in Utah (84%). Interestingly, our respondents estimated that 68% waived their rights fully, whereas 13% initially waived their rights but later invoked. This estimated high rate of initial waiver followed by invocation had not previously been observed. Our result thus suggests that police perceive *Miranda* as more of a safeguard during interrogation (i.e., after initially waived) than is actually the case. In their estimates, respondents also exhibited the belief that innocent suspects are more likely than offenders to waive their rights (84% to 74%).

When participants self-reported on their use of various interrogation techniques, the results closely paralleled Wald et al.'s early observational study in which "the most common approach was to confront the suspect with evidence or with the assertion that there was a witness. . . . The confrontation might be accompanied with the admonition that the detectives had all the information they needed to convict the suspect, and that he would make it easier for all concerned if he would fill in the rest of the story." The present results are also generally consistent with Leo's observation that interrogators tend to use the techniques found in training manuals and seldom resort to tactics that the courts have deemed coercive—most notably, threats and the use of physical intimidation. . . .

We also examined the conceptual clustering of techniques used by respondents in everyday practice. Results of an exploratory factor analysis demonstrated that techniques involving "Confrontation" were employed most frequently followed, respectively, by "Isolation, Rapport, and Minimization," "Presentation of Evidence," and "Threatening the Suspect." We also conducted several regression models to assess the predictive nature of investigator background characteristics. Consistent with previous research indicating that prior training and experience are associated with a propensity to make judgments of deception and guilt, these models indicated that more years of law enforcement experience, special training, greater confidence in one's deception detection ability, and a history of conducting more and longer interrogations all predicted greater endorsement of one or more sets of interrogation techniques. Thus it would appear that investigator characteristics associated with a tendency to presume guilt are predictive of more frequent use of psychologically manipulative and confrontational techniques in everyday practice. . . .

When it comes to the outcomes of interrogation, participants estimated that 68% of suspects had made self-incriminating statements, a number that is high but consistent with prior observational studies with confession rates ranging from 46% to 68% (in our survey, the estimate included both partial admissions and full confessions). This result indicates that detectives see themselves as generally quite successful at eliciting admissions and confessions. Regardless of how accurate these estimates are, they suggest that law enforcement officers of the twenty-first century do not feel "handcuffed," as their predecessors had once feared, by the *Miranda* warning and waiver requirements. Indeed, this result parallels two generations of empirical "*Miranda* impact" studies suggesting that *Miranda* does not hinder police in their efforts to interrogate suspects and elicit confessions.

Of particular interest were the results obtained when we asked participants to separately estimate the self-incrimination rates for guilty and innocent suspects. As one would reasonably expect, participants reported a far higher rate among suspects who were guilty (69%). The reported self-incrimination rate among innocent suspects also exceeded zero by a substantial margin, at 24%. However, omission of outliers to normalize the distribution lowered the mean false confession rate to 4.78%, which was significantly greater than 0. Within this group, 3.80% provided a partial admission and only 0.97% provided a full confession. We also asked respondents to more directly indicate the number of times they had seen an innocent person confess—to investigators, friends or others. To this question, they reported an average lifetime total of 2.97 false confessions, down to 0.71 when outliers were omitted—an estimate that was also significantly greater than 0.

On the important policy question of whether police investigators themselves favor or oppose the videotaping of interrogations, our results clearly corroborate the recent strong law enforcement support for electronic recording that has been reported elsewhere. Indeed, although only 16% of the participants in our survey worked in jurisdictions where the electronic recording of interrogations was required (none were in states in which it was mandatory), 81% believed that interviews and interrogations should be fully recorded, from start to finish. . . .

While the present survey provides new information about investigators' self-reported interrogation practices, beliefs, and perceptions, our knowledge of contemporary police interrogation remains incomplete. Over the last forty years, researchers have made great strides in addressing the "gap problem" that the U.S. Supreme Court inveighed against in Miranda v. Arizona. The *Miranda* Court noted that this problem stems from secrecy in the interrogation room. As electronic recording becomes increasingly commonplace, however, there should be less and less secrecy about the process. In an era of electronic recording, the ideal way for scholars to measure and study actual police practices and their outcomes—and thus the best way to find out what is common practice and what is extraordinary—is to observe large numbers of videotaped interrogations, randomly selected from across the country, involving a full range of crimes. . . .

Notes

1. *Number of waivers.* The most current studies have concluded that roughly 80 percent of all suspects waive their *Miranda* rights and make statements without counsel present. Some studies have found waiver rates in excess of 90 percent. See Paul Cassell, *Miranda's Social Costs: An Empirical Reassessment*, 90 Nw. U. L. Rev. 387 (1996) (collecting studies of waiver rate). A study in Great Britain suggested that about 68 percent of suspects in 1991 requested legal advice, after receiving warnings similar to those in *Miranda*. David Brown, Tom Ellis & Karen Larcombe, Changing the Code: Police Detention Under the Revised PACE Codes of Practice, Home Office Research and Planning Unit, London HMSO (1992). The tendency to waive the right to counsel or the right to silence is especially strong among suspects with no prior criminal convictions. Richard Leo, Inside the Interrogation Room, 86 J. Crim. L. & Criminology 266 (1996). Would the repeat offenders who tend more often to invoke their rights be more or less likely than the average offender to provide an incriminating statement in the absence of a warning? If so many suspects waive their rights, is that an indication of *Miranda's* failure or success? See George Thomas, Is *Miranda* a Real-World Failure? A Plea for More (and Better) Empirical Evidence, 43 UCLA L. Rev. 821 (1996).

2. *Number of confessions or admissions.* The major concern of *Miranda's* critics is that the warnings change the dynamic between the questioner and the suspect and reduce the number of successful interrogations, even when the suspect agrees to talk to the police. A number of empirical studies attempt to measure the "success rate" for interrogations immediately before and after the *Miranda* decision. A "Seaside City" (California) study pointed to a pre-*Miranda* confession rate of 68.9 percent and a post-*Miranda* rate of 66.9 percent. This study included only suspects who were arrested and incarcerated; it excluded cases in which suspects were detained for questioning but never incarcerated. James Witt, Non-Coercive Interrogation and the Administration of Justice: The Impact of *Miranda* on Police Effectuality, 64 J. Crim. L. & Criminology 320 (1973). A Salt Lake City study, based on cases investigated in 1994, found a success rate of 33.3 percent overall and 42.2 percent of cases where questioning actually occurred. In contrast, a study of interrogations in three California cities in 1992-1993 concluded that 64 percent of all the observed

interrogations produced a confession or incriminating admission. Richard Leo, Inside the Interrogation Room, 86 J. Crim. L. & Criminology 266 (1996).

One difficulty in studying this issue is defining what constitutes a "successful" interrogation. The studies all include outright confessions, in which the suspect tells the police that he committed the crime. Many also include some partially successful interrogations leading to "admissions": statements that police and prosecutors can use to prove one or more elements of the crime. Should the extraction of admissions (that fall short of confessions) be included in measures of *Miranda*'s impact? Moreover, for some suspects, the warnings and a request for waiver create a more cooperative atmosphere; in this instance, the *Miranda* regime is likely to lead to more (or more damaging) admissions. George Thomas reviewed the available empirical studies and concluded that they are inconclusive, but still consistent with the view that *Miranda* helps as much as it hurts. Thomas, Plain Talk About the *Miranda* Empirical Debate: A "Steady-State" Theory of Confessions, 43 UCLA L. Rev. 933 (1996).

A related difficulty in this debate comes from the (possibly) changing effects of *Miranda* in the nearly 50 years since the decision appeared. Is it plausible to think that the confession rate "rebounded" after an initial drop, once police officers adjusted their practices to the new requirements and found the best ways to prevent lost confessions? A reporter who spent one year with homicide detectives in Baltimore (research that later formed the basis for the television series *The Wire*) concluded that the police are able to use the *Miranda* warnings to create an atmosphere of cooperation with at least some suspects. He observed cases in which the suspect's act of acknowledging an understanding of the rights, followed by a waiver of those rights, created some momentum for cooperation during the interrogation. David Simon, Homicide: A Year on the Killing Streets (1991). Paul Cassell, in contrast, asserts that the depressed confession rate has remained quite consistent over time, thereby criticizing *Miranda*'s long-term effect of "handcuffing" the police. Paul Cassell & Richard Fowles, "Still Handcuffing the Cops? A Review of Fifty Years of Empirical Evidence of *Miranda*'s Harmful Effects on Law Enforcement," 97 B.U. L. Rev. 685 (2018). When confessions cannot be obtained due to *Miranda*, this is not a neutral effect: It jeopardizes the police's ability to make arrests and to clear cases. Cassell and Fowles's review of the FBI's Uniform Crime Rate data since 1950 shows that the clearance rate for most violent crimes and most property crimes has dropped since the *Miranda* decision was announced. Homicide, assault, rape, and burglary stand out as exceptions to this trend. But clearance rates can be affected by far more than interrogation doctrine, particularly since only a certain percentage of cases will require a statement from the defendant in order for the police to make an arrest. See Floyd Feeney, Police Clearances: A Poor Way to Measure the Impact of *Miranda* on the Police, 32 Rutgers L.J. 1 (2000).

3. *Number of convictions.* Another measurement of *Miranda*'s effects might come from estimating its impact on the conviction rate. There are two methods of arriving at this number. First, one might compare the percentage of all suspects convicted of crimes in the same location immediately before and after the Court's decision, and presume that some or all of the change in conviction rates was attributable to *Miranda*. The Seaside City study found a 9 percent decline in the conviction rate (from 92 percent to 83 percent). Is there any problem with this method of estimating the decision's impact on convictions? Second, one might start with an estimate of the number of confessions lost and combine it with some estimate of the proportion

of cases in which a confession is essential to obtain a conviction. Multiplying the lost confessions by the number of cases in which confessions are necessary results in a final estimate. A researcher might estimate the number of cases in which a confession is important by asking for the opinion of prosecutors and others involved in the case. She might also review the case files herself to imagine which cases might have ended differently if a confession were or were not available. Using these methods (or a combination of them), most studies have estimated that confessions are essential in 13 percent to 28 percent of all cases. See Paul Cassell, *Miranda's* Social Costs, 90 Nw. U. L. Rev. 387 (1996) (summarizing studies and reaching average of 23.8 percent). In choosing which studies of this question are most reliable, what would you want to know?

4. *Number of reversals on appeal.* Yet another measure of *Miranda's* effects is the number of convictions overturned on appeal because of *Miranda* violations. All the evidence suggests that a trivial number of cases are lost on appeal because of *Miranda.* Peter Nardulli, The Societal Costs of the Exclusionary Rule Revisited, 1987 U. Ill. L. Rev. 223 (confessions suppressed in 0.04 percent of all cases). Why might this be the case when other measures show evidence of a larger *Miranda* impact?

5. *Acceptable costs and benefits.* After resolving all the factual disputes about the actual case-level effects of the *Miranda* decision, one is left with a different type of question: Why is the effect on case outcomes the only effect we study? A complete empirical assessment of *Miranda's* impact should ask whether and how much *Miranda* has fostered trust among the public, created goodwill with, and reinforced the dignity of, suspects, inspired police officers to pursue other investigative techniques, and deterred crime in the first place. Meghan J. Ryan, Is *Miranda* Good News or Bad News for the Police? The Usefulness of Empirical Evidence, 50 Tex. Tech L. Rev. 81, 95 (2017).

G. PREVENTING UNLAWFUL INTERROGATIONS: OTHER APPROACHES?

For decades, the principal deterrent for the use of improper interrogation techniques has been exclusion of the confession itself. As we have seen in the pages above, many courts refuse to exclude the physical fruits of a tainted confession, or the testimony of witnesses derived from the suspect's statement, or even the suspect's subsequent statements, when the interrogators violated *Miranda* or the Sixth Amendment. Only when a confession is actually coerced (as opposed to merely obtained in violation of the *Miranda* requirements), will any evidentiary fruits of the confession be inadmissible.

Because the penalty for conducting an illegal interrogation has generally been limited to the exclusion of just the confession, there is widespread disagreement about whether these interrogation doctrines do much to deter officers from illegally extracting statements from suspects in the first place. Some scholars suggest that damage suits, injunctions, or administrative sanctions could serve as workable alternatives to better protect our constitutional values.

Could a legislature draft an alternative approach? The Court in *Miranda* expressly invited legislatures to find alternative methods for protecting the privilege against self-incrimination, "so long as they are fully as effective as those described above in informing accused persons of their right of silence and in affording a continuous opportunity to exercise it." The Court in Dickerson v. United States, 530 U.S. 428 (2000), struck down one such legislative effort, a federal statute instructing judges to judge the admissibility of confessions only by the traditional standards of voluntariness.

Perhaps a legislature could revise the *Miranda* warning to remove aspects most often criticized as obstacles to proper crime-solving techniques. Perhaps interrogations should occur before a judicial officer. Or perhaps a trial jury might later be told of any refusal to make a statement to the magistrate, or the refusal to make a statement to the judicial officer might be punishable as contempt of court. See Akhil Amar & Renee Lettow, Fifth Amendment First Principles: The Self-Incrimination Clause, 93 Mich. L. Rev. 857 (1995); Donald Dripps, Foreword: Against Police Interrogation—And the Privilege Against Self-Incrimination, 78 J. Crim. L. & Criminology 699 (1988).

Or perhaps we should use technology to provide clearer evidence of what happens in the interrogation room; creating a permanent record of the interrogation might be the best way to bolster a suspect's self-incrimination right and to ensure that only those who want to speak to the police will speak to the police.

■ TEXAS CODE OF CRIMINAL PROCEDURE ART. 38.22

Sec. 3. (a) No oral or sign language statement of an accused made as a result of custodial interrogation shall be admissible against the accused in a criminal proceeding unless:[*]

(1) an electronic recording, which may include motion picture, video tape, or other visual recording, is made of the statement; (2) prior to the statement but during the recording the accused is given the warning in Subsection (a) of Section 2 above and the accused knowingly, intelligently, and voluntarily waives any rights set out in the warning; (3) the recording device was capable of making an accurate recording, the operator was competent, and the recording is accurate and has not been altered; (4) all voices on the recording are identified; and (5) not later than the 20th day before the date of the proceeding, the attorney representing the defendant is provided with a true, complete, and accurate copy of all recordings of the defendant made under this article. . . .

■ POLICY CONCERNING ELECTRONIC RECORDING OF STATEMENTS

Memorandum from James M. Cole, Deputy Attorney General of the United States May 12, 2014

This policy establishes a presumption that the Federal Bureau of Investigation (FBI), the Drug Enforcement Administration (DEA), the Bureau of Alcohol, Tobacco, Firearms, and Explosives (ATF), and the United States Marshals Service

---

[*] Section 9 of the Article makes an exception when the state shows good cause that making the recording was infeasible.

(USMS) will electronically record statements made by individuals in their custody in the circumstances set forth below. This policy also encourages agents and prosecutors to consider electronic recording in investigative or other circumstances where the presumption does not apply. . . . This policy is solely for internal Department of Justice guidance. It is [does not] create any rights or benefits, substantive or procedural, enforceable at law or in equity. . . .

I. PRESUMPTION OF RECORDING

There is a presumption that the custodial statement of an individual in a place of detention with suitable recording equipment, following arrest but prior to initial appearance, will be electronically recorded, subject to the exceptions defined below. . . .

a. *Electronic recording.* This policy strongly encourages the use of video recording to satisfy the presumption. When video recording equipment considered suitable under agency policy is not available, audio recording may be utilized.

b. *Custodial interviews.* The presumption applies only to interviews of persons in FBI, DEA, ATF or USMS custody. Interviews in non-custodial settings are excluded from the presumption.

c. *Place of detention.* A place of detention is any structure where persons are held in connection with federal criminal charges where those persons can be interviewed. This includes not only federal facilities, but also any state, local, or tribal law enforcement facility, office, correctional or detention facility, jail, police or sheriff's station, holding cell, or other structure used for such purpose. Recording under this policy is not required while a person is waiting for transportation, or is en route, to a place of detention.

d. *Suitable recording equipment.* The presumption is limited to a place of detention that has suitable recording equipment. With respect to a place of detention owned or controlled by FBI, DEA, ATF, or USMS, suitable recording equipment means: (i) an electronic recording device deemed suitable by the agency for the recording of interviews that (ii) is reasonably designed to capture electronically the entirety of the interview.

Each agency will draft its own policy governing placement, maintenance and upkeep of such equipment, as well as requirements for preservation and transfer of recorded content.

With respect to an interview by FBI, DEA, ATF, or USMS in a place of detention they do not own or control, but which has recording equipment, FBI, DEA, ATF, or USMS will each determine on a case by case basis whether that recording equipment meets or is equivalent to that agency's own requirements or is otherwise suitable for use in recording interviews for purposes of this policy.

e. *Timing.* The presumption applies to persons in custody in a place of detention with suitable recording equipment following arrest but who have not yet made an initial appearance before a judicial officer under Federal Rule of Criminal Procedure 5.

f. *Scope of offenses.* The presumption applies to interviews in connection with all federal crimes.

g. *Scope of recording.* Electronic recording will begin as soon as the subject enters the interview area or room and will continue until the interview is completed.

h. *Recording may be overt or covert.* Recording under this policy may be covert or overt. Covert recording constitutes consensual monitoring, which is allowed by federal law. Covert recording in fulfilling the requirement of this policy may be carried out without constraint by the procedures and approval requirements prescribed by other Department policies for consensual monitoring.

Notes

1. *Video recording as a constitutional requirement: majority position.* Only the Alaska Supreme Court has required that interrogations be recorded as a constitutional matter. Stephan v. State, 711 P.2d 1156 (Alaska 1985); cf. In re Jerrell C.J., 699 N.W.2d 110 (Wis. 2005) (under judicial supervisory power, court requires all station house custodial interrogations of juveniles to be electronically recorded). While the argument has been made in a number of jurisdictions, courts typically have not received it with any sympathy. See, e.g., Brashars v. Commonwealth, 25 S.W.3d 58 (Ky. 2000); State v. Lockhart, 4 A.3d 1176 (Conn. 2010). After *Stephan* was decided, the Minnesota Supreme Court, relying on its supervisory authority, mandated recordings of "custodial interrogations" when they occur "at a place of detention." See State v. Scales, 518 N.W.2d 587, 592 (Minn. 1994); State v. Castillo-Alvarez, 836 N.W.2d 527 (Minn. 2013) (unrecorded out-of-state interrogation can be used in Minnesota prosecution if prosecution was contemplated in the other state and confession was admissible under rules of other state). Other courts have indicated that recording will weigh strongly in favor of findings of voluntariness.

2. *Video recording as a state statutory requirement.* A recent report surveying state approaches concluded that "the total number of states that either legally or voluntarily record custodial interrogations statewide, under certain conditions, [is] 27 (53%). However, the legal route to the implementation of the law, the offense criteria under which the law applies, and the possible remedy that is utilized if the police violate the law varies considerably by state." For further study into this, see *http://journals.sagepub.com/doi/abs/10.1177/1461355717750172.*

3. *Police discretion to video record interrogations and confessions.* Periodic surveys of law enforcement agencies find that they record interrogations most often in homicide and rape investigations and for other serious crimes. The officers in jurisdictions that use video recording believe that it leads to better preparation by detectives and better monitoring of detectives' work by supervisors. They also believe that it produces stronger evidence of guilt and induces more guilty pleas. It also leads to fewer claims against police that they had coerced or intimidated a suspect or fabricated a confession. Prosecutors are generally more supportive of video recording interrogations than are defense attorneys, who find video recordings harder to attack than written or audio recorded confessions. The use of DNA evidence to establish definitively that false confessions led to a surprising number of wrongful convictions has added momentum to the voluntary adoption of video recording by police departments. See Jeremy W. Peters, Wrongful Conviction Prompts Detroit Police to Videotape Certain Interrogations, N.Y. Times, Apr. 11, 2006 (at least 450

police departments in United States record interrogations, in some cases prompted by concerns about false confessions).

So why not video record every interrogation and confession? Most agencies are concerned that suspects would be less willing to talk when video recording takes place. But these concerns have proven to be unfounded, and once police officers experience the use of video recording, they tend to endorse it. See Thomas P. Sullivan et al., The Case for Recording Police Interrogations, Litigation, Volume 34, Number 3 (Spring 2008) (telephone survey of more than 600 departments that record interrogations).

4. *Administrative issues in recording.* Most police departments record interrogations openly or ask the subject about recording. Some police departments, however, use surreptitious recording equipment. Such practices reduce the chance that the use of video recording will discourage suspects from confessing (since they will not know they are being recorded). What reasons might there be not to record surreptitiously? See Matthews v. Commonwealth, 168 S.W.3d 14 (Ky. 2005) (police interrogators may lie to suspect about whether they are recording his statements). Must police record the whole interrogation, or is it necessary to record only the defendant's confession and summary after interrogation? Suppose the interrogation takes seven hours but the summary is only 30 minutes. Should the cost of the recording medium factor into the decision whether to record the entire confession? What about the cost of making transcripts? See State v. Barnett, 789 A.2d 629 (N.H. 2001) (under supervisory power, court requires any video recording of interrogation admitted into evidence to be complete). In some jurisdictions defense counsel are not given immediate access to recorded interrogations and confessions. Some prosecutors show defense counsel recorded confessions but object to making copies. Other jurisdictions do not give defense counsel access to video recordings until after indictment or for a period of time after the interrogation.

5. *Is video recording an acceptable "alternative" to* Miranda? Can a legislature pass a mandatory recording statute expressly to take the place of *Miranda* warnings in protecting each suspect's Fifth Amendment rights? Is there any reason not to record interrogations and confessions *along with* providing *Miranda* warnings? Would you expect foreign jurisdictions, without the constraints or protections of *Miranda*, to be more or less hesitant to adopt recording procedures? The 1991 Code of Practice for Interrogation in England requires that all interviews be recorded, wherever they occur, unless it is impracticable to do so. See M. McConville & P. Morrell, Recording the Interrogation: Have the Police Got It Taped?, 1983 Crim. L. Rev. 159 (noting an increase after appearance of Code of Practice in spontaneous confessions allegedly spoken before the video was running); Paul Marcus & Vicki Waye, Australia and the United States: Two Common Criminal Justice Systems Uncommonly at Odds, 12 Tul. J. Int'l & Comp. L. 27 (2004).

6. *Confessions, lies, and video recording.* Recording interrogations and confessions seems to solve a number of problems, such as reducing or eliminating the frequent claims by suspects that they were threatened or that they did not in fact confess or say what the police say they did. But does recording make all confessions look voluntary even when they have been compelled by forces not visible (or audible) on the recording? Won't recording create a whole new set of factual issues about whether the recording is complete? Is taping of interrogations and confessions a

great reform for a past era, since now tapes can be altered without leaving much trace of the editing?

Problem 8–11. Supplementing *Miranda*

You are the Governor of a small state that is considering a range of criminal justice reforms; you are, in particular, concerned about the recent social science evidence documenting the relative ineffectiveness of *Miranda* warnings at conveying the self-incrimination right to suspects. You have read the studies about video-recording procedures and are about to sign a bill requiring law enforcement in your state to record all interrogations from this point forward. But then your legislative aide brings you information about how certain European countries are handling interrogation warnings these days. For example, in England, a "duty solicitor" is available at police stations to help suspects who want advice, and German courts prohibit the police from making affirmative misrepresentations during interrogations.

Do you believe either of these approaches, either by itself or in combination with each other, would yield more benefits than the recording procedure you were considering? Would these approaches be supplements to the video-recording procedure, or would they be alternatives to it?

IX

Identifications

Eyewitnesses to crime can provide some of the most convincing evidence to support a conviction. This is especially true when the physical evidence linking the defendant to the crime is thin, or when the offender is a stranger to others at the scene (as in many robbery cases). All too often, however, this important evidence turns out to be unreliable. In fact, mistaken identifications are the leading cause of wrongful convictions of innocent defendants.

How do legal institutions respond to the special value and risks of eyewitness identifications? This chapter explores that question. Section A reviews some of the psychological literature detailing the risks of eyewitness identifications. Section B surveys the conditions that lead courts to exclude evidence coming from in-person identifications (both in the field and at the police station) and from identifications of photographs. Section C considers the remedies other than exclusion of evidence that are available to a defendant who believes that an identification procedure was unreliable. Section D reviews strategies for preventing mistaken identifications before they even occur.

A. RISKS OF MISTAKEN IDENTIFICATION

Eyewitnesses are wrong in a disturbing number of cases. One famous example involves the case of Ronald Cotton. One night a man broke into the apartment of Jennifer Thompson, a 22-year-old college student in Burlington, North Carolina. The intruder raped Thompson. When police received an anonymous tip in the case, they showed Thompson several photographs of potential suspects, and she picked the photograph of Ronald Cotton. Cotton was a plausible suspect, who had been convicted four years earlier of attempted rape and had recently been released from prison. Although there was no physical evidence linking Cotton to the crime, the jury convicted him based on Thompson's confident identification of Cotton during the trial as the man who had raped her. The judge sentenced him to 50 years in prison. Eleven years later, lawyers for Cotton arranged for DNA tests on some of the physical evidence in the case. The tests conclusively established that Cotton was the wrong man. The evidence pointed instead to Bobby Poole—already convicted and serving a prison term for another sexual assault—and Poole later confessed to the rape of Thompson. Jennifer Thompson-Cannino, Ronald Cotton & Erin Torneo, Picking Cotton: Our Memoir of Injustice and Redemption (2010).

One famous example, of course, does not tell us how often the problem arises in criminal justice systems that produce millions of criminal convictions each year. How often does a mistaken identification lead to an erroneous conviction? Nobody really knows since we have no convincing way to identify all the wrongful convictions.

It is possible, however, to estimate the importance of mistaken identifications *relative to other causes* of the wrongful convictions we have learned about over the years. Over the last few years, the widespread availability of DNA testing has confirmed many examples of wrongful convictions. Far and away the most common cause of these errors is mistaken identifications by eyewitnesses. See Brandon L. Garrett, Convicting the Innocent: Where Criminal Prosecutions Go Wrong (2011).

Psychologists have studied witness memory in great detail over the years. The following summary of psychological research may suggest some of the reasons why eyewitness identifications sometimes lead to erroneous convictions. Given the commonplace nature of these identification errors, what changes in the legal rules might address these predictable failures of witnesses?

■ RALPH NORMAN HABER & LYN HABER, EXPERIENCING, REMEMBERING AND REPORTING EVENTS
6 Psychol. Pub. Pol'y & L. 1057-1091 (2000)

[Consider] the following description of a bank robbery, drawn from actual cases. Several men entered a bank, tied up the only guard in the lobby, told the customers to lie down on the floor, and demanded that the tellers hand over all their money. The robbers then left. There were five tellers, two officers, one guard, and five customers in the bank at the time. When the police took their statements over the next hour, there was little consensus among the thirteen witnesses as to the number of robbers, what they looked like, what they did, the presence of weapons, or the duration of the robbery.

Video cameras in the bank recorded the robbery. Comparing these recordings to the descriptions provided by the witnesses, it was found that no single witness gave an accurate report of the sequence of events, nor did any single witness provide a consistently accurate description of any of the robbers. Further, in subsequent photo identification line-ups, half of the witnesses made serious errors: Four of the thirteen witnesses erroneously selected as a perpetrator one of the other people who had been in the bank at the time of the robbery (a teller or a customer), and three of the thirteen erroneously selected a photograph of someone who had not been there at all at the time. All seven of these witnesses asserted that they were sure they had correctly identified one of the robbers and that they were willing to so testify. . . .

The purpose of this article is to summarize the scientific evidence on the accuracy of eyewitness testimony, with specific attention to the factors that enhance or impair the likelihood of accuracy. . . .

OBSERVING AND ENCODING EVENTS INTO MEMORY

In this first section, we consider the factors that might lead witnesses to make and remember differing observations of the same event. . . .

Observational point of view. In the bank robbery described earlier, the customers forced to lie down on the floor had less opportunity to view from the front those robbers who approached the teller booths, whereas some of the tellers had frontal views. Therefore, those tellers should be able to give more detailed descriptions of the appearance of those robbers, and in the absence of other factors, those descriptions are more likely to be accurate. . . . In addition to distance, lighting conditions, especially back lighting, reflections, and shadows impact the ability to see fine details. . . .

Allocation of Attention. Attention is memory's gatekeeper. [The] deployment of attention has two consequences: it allows you to encode and retain memory of some aspects of what happens to you, and it allows the remainder to slip away and be lost forever.

[You] can switch attention quickly. Any change in stimulation, such as a loud noise, or a movement off to the side, will cause you to orient your attention to it. That re-orientation allows you to encode sudden changes in what is happening, though at the expense of what you had been attending to just previously, which then stops being accessible for encoding into memory. When driving comfortably, it is possible to divide your attention so you can control the car while conversing with a passenger. However, a sudden squeal of brakes refocuses your attention exclusively on the emergency, and you cannot remember what your passenger said during that interval. [What] you as an observer will encode about an event depends on where and how your attention is focused, not just where you happen to be looking. . . .

Bias in Attentional Focus. [Frequently] some aspect of an event causes an involuntary narrowing of attention to some particular detail, so much so that other parts of the event are not attended to at all, and therefore not encoded into memory. One area of great legal importance concerns the narrowing of attention that occurs for most witnesses when they detect the presence of a weapon. . . . Specifically, scientific research on "weapon focus" has shown that, when a weapon is present, witnesses are far less able to remember distinctive features of the people present, including those of the person holding the weapon. Hence, a witness's chances of making a correct identification of a person are reduced if that person held a weapon. It is equally likely that a narrowing of attention will occur, with its concomitant loss in encoding, whenever any component of the event is highly dramatic, frightening, violent, or distasteful to the witness. . . .

Knowledge, Familiarity, and Expertise with the Content of the Event. In the course of everyday life, you are highly familiar with aspects of your work, both inside your home and at your jobsite. If you work as a supermarket clerk, you are likely to be far more knowledgeable than most people about a wide range of edible products; if you are a car salesman, you know a lot about the makes of cars. Within your own sphere, you are an expert. Bystander-witnesses are often required to testify about details of what they observed, such as the characteristics of a vehicle or a weapon. If the eyewitness has little knowledge of that class of objects, the witness's reports about the object are often incomplete or simply wrong. . . .

Similarly, lack of familiarity has been demonstrated in scientific experiments to lead to inaccurate identification of people. The adage that "all Asians look alike (to non-Asians)" is in fact mostly true. In experiments on cross-racial identification, in which the race of the criminal is different from that of the witness and the witness has few close interactions with people of that race, the witness cannot provide as many identifying features of the criminal he observed, thereby making it less likely that subsequent identifications will be accurate. . . .

Witness Expectations and Interpretation of the Event. Research has shown that the beliefs of the witness produce fundamental changes in the reports of what was observed. For example, one study [from 1947] concerned with racial prejudice asked subjects/witnesses to view a scene depicting two men in which one man held a knife: The witnesses were to describe the scene to other people who had not seen it. The two critical contents of the scene that were varied were whether both men were the same race and which one held the knife. When both men were of the same race, nearly all witnesses correctly described the critical element of who held the knife, as well as most of the details of dress and the position of the two men. However, if one man was Black and one White, most witnesses (Black and White alike) reported that the Black man held the knife even when it was held by the White man. Some witnesses who correctly described who held the knife incorrectly added that the White man was defending himself (there was nothing in either man's posture or position to suggest this conclusion). All of the witnesses stated that they believed that crimes were more likely to be committed by Blacks than by Whites. The results suggest that eyewitnesses sometimes encode and remember the event so as to be consistent with their beliefs rather than the way it actually happened. . . .

REMEMBERING EVENTS

Experts on memory research refer to a witness's first report of an observed event, when it is given after the event, as an independent memory. . . . A witness's independent memory report of an event is normally the most accurate description the witness will ever be able to produce. . . .

In normal life, your own independent memories often undergo influences that, in psychological parlance, "taint" them: You dress your stories up for your listeners who did not observe the events, and you discuss the events with other people who also observed them and you incorporate what they say as part of your memory. A tainted memory is not necessarily a false or inaccurate memory, but it is no longer your own, original, independent encoding of the event. . . .

The Inevitably Wrong Focus of Autobiographical Memory. . . . Typically, as an event unfolds, you as an observer are not thinking about describing the other people and their actions: you see the event in terms of how it affects you. The event has all of the properties of a story, with a beginning, middle, and end, and a sequence of actions with one or more actors. The most important actor—the protagonist in your story—is you. . . . As an example of how an eyewitness describes events from a personal point of view, consider one of the eyewitness accounts from a woman who was in the bank described above:

> I stopped at the bank to cash a check. I was putting the money in my purse when armed men ran into the bank, waved their guns at everyone and ordered me to lie down on the floor. One gigantic man, who looked like a football player, stepped over me and I was afraid he would take all of the money I just got I was so scared he

would hurt me. He went to the same teller who had just helped me, threatened her with his pistol, and stuffed what she handed him into his bag. After what seemed like hours of terror, all the robbers ran out. They didn't take my money.

This report has little helpful content for the policeman who wants to identify the robbers. The policeman asked her: How many robbers were there? Which ones had guns? What did each of the robbers look like? What were they wearing? What did each of the other robbers do? Every investigator and every interrogator forces the witness to switch from "What happened to you?" to "What happened in the bank?" Hence, almost immediately, the eyewitness is required to change from an autobiographical and psychological focus to an objective focus. This translation usually produces changes in the report, changes that may introduce inaccuracies about the physical reality. . . . In trying to answer the interrogator's questions, the witness often adds content and details that "must have happened"—details not present in independent memory. . . .

Systematic Changes in the Content of Memory with Each Repetition. Unlike a video recording, which remains the same each time it is played, memory undergoes changes with rehearsal. [Each] further repetition of the report produces predictable changes in the report. These predictable changes are, first, that many of the details drop out of the subsequent reports altogether and are never reported again and, second, that other details are altered or additions are made to fit more consistently with the overall description provided by the observer. . . .

By the time the witness reaches the stand and is questioned by counsel, she has told her story dozens of times. Often, the first time the story is told is to other observers or to the first new arrivals at the scene. That description, the closest one available from the independent memory of the observer, is usually unrecorded. The first recorded description, taken down by one of the officers at the scene, may already have undergone many changes after several prior rehearsals, each with its smoothings, rearrangements of facts, and attempts to be congruent with what has been learned from other witnesses. This is only the beginning of the rehearsals required of the witness. More than one policeman will demand a repetition; then come the investigators and the lawyers. . . .

Post-Event Information Can Create New (and Potentially) False Memories. The single most dramatic finding in recent memory research concerns changes in reports made by witnesses when other people give them information. Two insidious facts have emerged: First, witnesses are unaware that they have acquired new information from somebody else—the information is treated as if it were part of what they themselves originally observed; and second, witnesses usually are unaware that they have changed their report based on that new information. . . .

Consider some findings from recent research: (a) Embedding a false presupposition into a question (asking "Did the red car stop or run the light just before the crash?" when the car's color has not been previously specified) will often change the witness's subsequent testimony as to the color of the car; (b) varying the intensity of verbs in a question (asking "Did the car hit . . . Did the car collide . . . Did the car smash . . . Did the car demolish . . . ?") will often change the witness's subsequent testimony about the speed of the car; (c) showing a witness line-up pictures of people not involved in the observed event will often result in the witness subsequently choosing one of those innocent people as the criminal, even when the real criminal is present in the later line-up. . . .

Encoding, Remembering, and Identifying Strangers

[Now we can summarize] what is known about the accuracy of a witness's identification of unfamiliar people from memory. [Consider] identification accuracy for research line-ups that are constructed with the known perpetrator present. The first kind of accuracy of concern is whether the witness can discriminate between the true perpetrator and the remaining foils who are innocent of the crime. Based on a large number of experiments, about 75% of the time the perpetrator is correctly selected (true positive); the remaining 25% of the time the witness identifies someone who either was not present at the crime scene, or was a bystander at the scene, but not the criminal (false positive). If no weapon is present, no violence, no bystanders, no post-event contamination, and little delay, true-positive rates can approach 90% (with false-positive rates dropping to a low of about 10%). Conversely, if a weapon is present, the scene is violent, bystanders are present, post-event information is available, the witness feels great stress, and there is a long time delay between observation and identification, the true-positive rate for correct identification of the perpetrator drops well below 50%, with the false-positive rate exceeding 50%. . . .

The fallibility of the eyewitness becomes even more evident when results of lineup research are considered in which the perpetrator is known not to be in the lineup. Now the correct response for the eyewitness is to say "no," none of the people in the line-up is the perpetrator. The results show that, on average, under normal observation conditions, eyewitnesses still say "yes" (that someone present is the perpetrator) about 60% of the time when the perpetrator is known to be absent! All of these "yes" responses are false positives: The eyewitness has identified an innocent person. . . .

Notes

1. *The stages of observation and memory problems.* A committee of the National Research Council (a branch of the National Academy of Sciences) published a summary of the psychological research on eyewitness identifications. That report reviewed the limitations on the "three functional stages of visual processing—sensation, attention, and perception." The "sensation" stage is "the initial stage of detecting light and extracting basic image features." Attention involves the selection of a subset of information for further processing, and perception is "the process by which attended visual information is integrated, linked to environmental cause, made coherent, and categorized." In addition to limitations on the witness's vision of events, the report discussed three "core" processes of memory: "encoding, storage, and retrieval . . . which refer to the placement of items in memory, their maintenance therein, and subsequent access to the stored information." Errors in vision and memory can occur at each of these stages. National Research Council, Identifying the Culprit: Assessing Eyewitness Identification 46-47, 59 (2014). For a sampling of the rich psychological literature on eyewitness observation and memory, consult the web extension for this chapter at *http://www.crimpro.com/extension/ch09.*

The psychological experiments in this field often take place in a setting different from what an actual crime victim might face. What might those differences be? Would they make a crime witness more or less likely than an experimental "subject" to give an accurate identification?

2. *Individual recognition skills and witness certainty.* It is important to remember that these difficulties with memory address only trends and averages: Any individual witness might be affected less (or more) by such problems. Unfortunately, it is difficult to determine whether a particular witness is above average or below average in her ability to identify a crime suspect. The age of a witness is one of the few consistently helpful indicators: Children tend to make less accurate identifications, mostly because they are substantially more suggestible than adults.

One might be tempted to rely on the witness's level of certainty to identify the most "able" witnesses, i.e., the witness who says, "I'm absolutely sure it was him." But researchers have gone back and forth on the importance of witness certainty. For several decades, scholars declared that the correlation between witness certainty and witness accuracy was quite weak. Later, however, the scholarly consensus shifted. Empirical research now finds that witnesses who express more certainty about their opinion when they first identify a witness also tend, on average, to be more accurate. See John Wixted et al., "Initial Eyewitness Confidence Reliably Predicts Eyewitness Identification Accuracy," 70 American Psychologist 515 (September 2015).

3. *Police officers as witnesses.* Sometimes the witness to a crime is a police officer. Does the special training and experience of police officers increase their accuracy as eyewitnesses? The evidence on this question is equivocal. On the one hand, police officers (as well as untrained witnesses) tend to have more complete and accurate memories if they are able to anticipate an event and know that they will later need to recall it accurately. A police officer may be in a good position to anticipate the need for later recall. On the other hand, a number of studies have concluded that police officers and others with special training fare no better than other witnesses under realistic eyewitness conditions.

4. *Early forgetting.* Some of the earliest research in memory showed that more forgetting happens early. We forget very rapidly immediately after an event—usually within a few hours—but forgetting becomes more and more gradual as time passes. See Elizabeth F. Loftus, Eyewitness Testimony 21-83 (1996). What are the implications of this research for police work?

B. EXCLUSION OF IDENTIFICATION EVIDENCE

Witnesses identify potential suspects in several settings. The most formal identification procedures occur in the police station. The "live lineup" places a small group of persons before the witness; the witness is asked if any person in the lineup is the person who committed the crime. In another identification technique that often takes place in a police station, the witness reviews photographs of different people to identify a suspect, a process known as a "photographic array." Finally, there are "confrontations" or "showups," in which the police ask the witness to view the suspect alone. This sort of identification occurs most frequently in the field, near the crime scene, but it can also occur at the station. One version of a showup takes place when a police officer shows a photograph of a single suspect to a witness, asking the witness to confirm the identity of the suspect.

Until the mid-1960s, the legal system relied on adversarial testing of evidence to control these identification procedures. If a "showup" produced unreliable evidence, defense counsel was expected to point this out to the jury. Over the years, however, federal and state courts started interpreting their constitutions to require the exclusion of some evidence obtained during identification procedures. The constitutional controls derive from (1) the right to counsel clauses and (2) the due process clauses of the federal and state constitutions. Courts declared a small group of identification procedures invalid unless they take place with counsel for the defendant present. For a larger group of identification procedures, defendants make claims based on the due process clause, arguing that the identifications were too unreliable to be admitted as evidence. The following materials explore the right-to-counsel and due process limitations in several common settings.

1. Exclusion on Right to Counsel Grounds

The Sixth Amendment to the U.S. Constitution provides that "In all criminal prosecutions, the accused shall . . . have the Assistance of Counsel for his defence." Every state constitution except one (Virginia's) also provides explicitly for legal counsel in criminal cases. A number describe the point at which the right to counsel attaches by using phrases such as "appear" or "defend," as in New York's article I, section 6: "In any trial in any court whatever the party accused shall be allowed to appear and defend in person and with counsel. . . ." Others speak in terms of a right to be "heard" through counsel, as in New Hampshire's article 15: "Every subject shall have a right . . . to be fully heard in his defense, by himself, and counsel." In what way are these constitutional provisions relevant to police efforts to obtain eyewitness identifications of suspects?

■ UNITED STATES v. BILLY JOE WADE
388 U.S. 218 (1967)

BRENNAN, J.[*]

The question here is whether courtroom identifications of an accused at trial are to be excluded from evidence because the accused was exhibited to the witnesses before trial at a post-indictment lineup conducted for identification purposes without notice to and in the absence of the accused's appointed counsel.

The federally insured bank in Eustace, Texas, was robbed on September 21, 1964. A man with a small strip of tape on each side of his face entered the bank, pointed a pistol at the female cashier and the vice president, the only persons in the bank at the time, and forced them to fill a pillowcase with the bank's money. [Wade was indicted for the robbery on March 23, 1965, and arrested on April 2. Counsel was appointed to represent him on April 26.] Fifteen days later an FBI agent, without notice to Wade's lawyer, arranged to have the two bank employees observe a

---

* [Justice Clark joined in this opinion. Chief Justice Warren and Justices Douglas and Fortas joined in this opinion except for Part I, which is not reprinted here. Justice Black joined in Parts II through IV of this opinion. Justices White, Harlan, and Stewart joined in Parts I and III of this opinion.—EDS.]

lineup made up of Wade and five or six other prisoners and conducted in a courtroom of the local county courthouse. Each person in the line wore strips of tape such as allegedly worn by the robber and upon direction each said something like "put the money in the bag," the words allegedly uttered by the robber. Both bank employees identified Wade in the lineup as the bank robber.

At trial, the two employees, when asked on direct examination if the robber was in the courtroom, pointed to Wade. The prior lineup identification was then elicited from both employees on cross-examination. At the close of testimony, Wade's counsel moved for a judgment of acquittal or, alternatively, to strike the bank officials' courtroom identifications on the ground that conduct of the lineup, without notice to and in the absence of his appointed counsel, violated his . . . Sixth Amendment right to the assistance of counsel. The motion was denied, and Wade was convicted. . . .

II.

. . . The Framers of the Bill of Rights envisaged a broader role for counsel than under the practice then prevailing in England of merely advising his client in "matters of law," and eschewing any responsibility for "matters of fact." The constitutions in at least 11 of the 13 States expressly or impliedly abolished this distinction. . . .

When the Bill of Rights was adopted, there were no organized police forces as we know them today. The accused confronted the prosecutor and the witnesses against him, and the evidence was marshalled, largely at the trial itself. In contrast, today's law enforcement machinery involves critical confrontations of the accused by the prosecution at pretrial proceedings where the results might well settle the accused's fate and reduce the trial itself to a mere formality. In recognition of these realities of modern criminal prosecution, our cases have construed the Sixth Amendment guarantee to apply to "critical" stages of the proceedings. The guarantee reads: "In all criminal prosecutions, the accused shall enjoy the right . . . to have the Assistance of Counsel for his defence." The plain wording of this guarantee thus encompasses counsel's assistance whenever necessary to assure a meaningful "defence." . . . The presence of counsel at such critical confrontations, as at the trial itself, operates to assure that the accused's interests will be protected consistently with our adversary theory of criminal prosecution. . . .

III.

The Government characterizes the lineup as a mere preparatory step in the gathering of the prosecution's evidence, not different—for Sixth Amendment purposes—from various other preparatory steps, such as systematized or scientific analyzing of the accused's fingerprints, blood sample, clothing, hair, and the like. We think there are differences which preclude such stages being characterized as critical stages at which the accused has the right to the presence of his counsel. Knowledge of the techniques of science and technology is sufficiently available, and the variables in techniques few enough, that the accused has the opportunity for a meaningful confrontation of the Government's case at trial through the ordinary processes of cross-examination of the Government's expert witnesses and the presentation of the evidence of his own experts. . . .

IV.

But the confrontation compelled by the State between the accused and the victim or witnesses to a crime to elicit identification evidence is peculiarly riddled with innumerable dangers and variable factors which might seriously, even crucially, derogate from a fair trial. The vagaries of eyewitness identification are well-known; the annals of criminal law are rife with instances of mistaken identification. . . . A major factor contributing to the high incidence of miscarriage of justice from mistaken identification has been the degree of suggestion inherent in the manner in which the prosecution presents the suspect to witnesses for pretrial identification. [It] is a matter of common experience that, once a witness has picked out the accused at the lineup, he is not likely to go back on his word later on, so that in practice the issue of identity may (in the absence of other relevant evidence) for all practical purposes be determined there and then, before the trial.

[As] is the case with secret interrogations, there is serious difficulty in depicting what transpires at lineups and other forms of identification confrontations. [The] defense can seldom reconstruct the manner and mode of lineup identification for judge or jury at trial. Those participating in a lineup with the accused may often be police officers; in any event, the participants' names are rarely recorded or divulged at trial. The impediments to an objective observation are increased when the victim is the witness. Lineups are prevalent in rape and robbery prosecutions and present a particular hazard that a victim's understandable outrage may excite vengeful or spiteful motives. In any event, neither witnesses nor lineup participants are apt to be alert for conditions prejudicial to the suspect. . . . Improper influences may go undetected by a suspect, guilty or not, who experiences the emotional tension which we might expect in one being confronted with potential accusers. Even when he does observe abuse, if he has a criminal record he may be reluctant to take the stand and open up the admission of prior convictions. Moreover, any protestations by the suspect of the fairness of the lineup made at trial are likely to be in vain; the jury's choice is between the accused's unsupported version and that of the police officers present. In short, the accused's inability effectively to reconstruct at trial any unfairness that occurred at the lineup may deprive him of his only opportunity meaningfully to attack the credibility of the [witness's] courtroom identification. . . .

The potential for improper influence is illustrated by the circumstances, insofar as they appear, surrounding the prior identifications in the three cases we decide today. [The companion cases were Gilbert v. California, 388 U.S. 263 (1967), and Stovall v. Denno, 388 U.S. 293 (1967).] In the present case, the testimony of the identifying witnesses elicited on cross-examination revealed that those witnesses were taken to the courthouse and seated in the courtroom to await assembly of the lineup. The courtroom faced on a hallway observable to the witnesses through an open door. The cashier testified that she saw Wade "standing in the hall" within sight of an FBI agent. . . . The lineup in *Gilbert* was conducted in an auditorium in which some 100 witnesses to several alleged state and federal robberies charged to Gilbert made wholesale identifications of Gilbert as the robber in each other's presence, a procedure said to be fraught with dangers of suggestion. And the vice of suggestion created by the identification in *Stovall*, was the presentation to the witness of the suspect alone handcuffed to police officers. It is hard to imagine a situation more clearly conveying the suggestion to the witness that the one presented is believed guilty by the police. . . .

The trial which might determine the accused's fate may well not be that in the courtroom but that at the pretrial confrontation, with the State aligned against the accused, the witness the sole jury, and the accused unprotected against the over-reaching, intentional or unintentional, and with little or no effective appeal from the judgment there rendered by the witness—"that's the man." . . .

No substantial countervailing policy considerations have been advanced against the requirement of the presence of counsel. Concern is expressed that the require-ment will forestall prompt identifications and result in obstruction of the confron-tations. As for the first, we note that in the two cases in which the right to counsel is today held to apply, counsel had already been appointed and no argument is made in either case that notice to counsel would have prejudicially delayed the confron-tations. [Law] enforcement may be assisted by preventing the infiltration of taint in the prosecution's identification evidence. That result cannot help the guilty avoid conviction but can only help assure that the right man has been brought to justice.[29] Legislative or other regulations, such as those of local police departments, which eliminate the risks of abuse and unintentional suggestion at lineup proceedings and the impediments to meaningful confrontation at trial may also remove the basis for regarding the stage as "critical." But neither Congress nor the federal authorities have seen fit to provide a solution. What we hold today in no way creates a constitu-tional straitjacket which will handicap sound efforts at reform, nor is it intended to have this effect.

V.

We come now to the question whether the denial of Wade's motion to strike the courtroom identification by the bank witnesses at trial because of the absence of his counsel at the lineup required . . . the grant of a new trial at which such evidence is to be excluded. We do not think this disposition can be justified without first giv-ing the Government the opportunity to establish by clear and convincing evidence that the in-court identifications were based upon observations of the suspect other than the lineup identification. [The] appropriate procedure to be followed is to vacate the conviction pending a hearing to determine whether the in-court identi-fications had an independent source, or whether, in any event, the introduction of the evidence was harmless error, and for the District Court to reinstate the convic-tion or order a new trial, as may be proper. . . .

WHITE, J., dissenting in part and concurring in part.[*]
. . . The Court's opinion is far-reaching. . . . It matters not how well the witness knows the suspect, whether the witness is the suspect's mother, brother, or long-time associate, and no matter how long or well the witness observed the perpetrator at the scene of the crime. . . .

---

29. Many other nations surround the lineup with safeguards against prejudice to the suspect. In England the suspect must be allowed the presence of his solicitor or a friend; Germany requires the presence of retained counsel; France forbids the confrontation of the suspect in the absence of his counsel; Spain, Mexico, and Italy provide detailed procedures prescribing the conditions under which confrontation must occur under the supervision of a judicial officer who sees to it that the proceedings are officially recorded to assure adequate scrutiny at trial.

* [Justices Harlan and Stewart joined in this opinion.—EDS.]

To find the lineup a "critical" stage of the proceeding and to exclude identifications made in the absence of counsel, the Court must [assume] that there is now no adequate source from which defense counsel can learn about the circumstances of the pretrial identification in order to place before the jury all of the considerations which should enter into an appraisal of courtroom identification evidence. But [I am not willing to assume] that the police and the witnesses will forget or prevaricate, that defense counsel will be unable to bring out the truth and that neither jury, judge, nor appellate court is a sufficient safeguard against unacceptable police conduct occurring at a pretrial identification procedure. I am unable to share the Court's view of the willingness of the police and the ordinary citizen-witness to dissemble.

[The] absolute rule requiring the presence of counsel will cause significant delay and it may very well result in no pretrial identification at all. . . . Nor do I think the witnesses themselves can be ignored. They will now be required to be present at the convenience of counsel rather than their own. Many may be much less willing to participate if the identification stage is transformed into an adversary proceeding not under the control of a judge. . . .

Finally, I think the Court's new rule is vulnerable in terms of its own unimpeachable purpose of increasing the reliability of identification testimony. Law enforcement officers have the obligation to convict the guilty and to make sure they do not convict the innocent. . . . To this extent, our so-called adversary system is not adversary at all; nor should it be. But defense counsel has no comparable obligation to ascertain or present the truth. Our system assigns him a different mission. [As] part of our modified adversary system and as part of the duty imposed on the most honorable defense counsel, we countenance or require conduct which in many instances has little, if any, relation to the search for truth. [Defense counsel] will not only observe what occurs and develop possibilities for later cross-examination but will hover over witnesses and begin their cross-examination then, menacing truthful factfinding as thoroughly as the Court fears the police now do. . . . In my view, the State is entitled to investigate and develop its case outside the presence of defense counsel. . . .

■ PEOPLE v. JONATHAN HICKMAN

684 N.W.2d 267 (Mich. 2004)

CORRIGAN, C.J.

In this case, we must determine when the right to counsel attaches to corporeal identifications. We adopt the analysis of Moore v. Illinois, 434 U.S. 220 (1977), and hold that the right to counsel attaches only to corporeal identifications conducted at or after the initiation of adversarial judicial criminal proceedings. To the extent that People v. Anderson, 205 N.W.2d 461 (Mich. 1973), goes beyond the constitutional text and extends the right to counsel to a time before the initiation of adversarial criminal proceedings, it is overruled. . . .

Defendant was convicted of possession of a firearm during the commission or attempted commission of a felony, conspiracy, and armed robbery, for robbing the complainant of $26 and two two-way radios. The complainant testified that two men approached him from behind and robbed him. He testified that one of the men, later identified as defendant, pointed a gun at his face while the other person took the radios and money. The complainant then called the police and gave a description of the two men, as well as a description of the gun.

An officer soon saw a man fitting the description of the man with the gun. The man, later identified as defendant, was caught after a foot chase. During the chase, the police saw defendant throw something and they later recovered a chrome handgun that matched the complainant's description of the gun. Defendant was carrying one of the two-way radios.

Approximately ten minutes later, an officer took the complainant to a police car in which defendant was being held. The officer asked the complainant if the person sitting in the police car was involved in the robbery. The complainant immediately responded that defendant was the man who had the gun.

Defendant's motion to suppress an on-the-scene identification by the victim on the ground that defendant was not represented by counsel at the time of the identification was denied, and defendant was convicted. . . . Defendant appealed, and this Court granted leave, limited to the issue whether counsel is required before an on-the-scene identification can be admitted at trial. . . .

In People v. Anderson, 205 N.W.2d 461 (Mich. 1973), the right to counsel was extended to all pretrial corporeal identifications, including those occurring before the initiation of adversarial proceedings. This extension of United States v. Wade, 388 U.S. 218 (1967), to all pretrial identification procedures was based on "psychological principles," and "social science." Notably absent was any grounding in our federal constitution or state constitution. In People v. Jackson, 217 N.W.2d 22 (Mich. 1974), this Court acknowledged that the *Anderson* rules were not [mandated under the federal constitution]. The *Jackson* Court affirmed the *Anderson* rules, however, as an exercise of the Court's "constitutional power to establish rules of evidence applicable to judicial proceedings in Michigan courts and to preserve best evidence eyewitness testimony from unnecessary alteration by unfair identification procedures." Thus, the *Anderson* rules lack a foundation in any constitutional provision, whether state or federal. Instead, the rules reflect the policy preferences of the *Anderson* Court. . . .

In Moore v. Illinois, 434 U.S. 220 (1977), the United States Supreme Court adopted the plurality opinion in Kirby v. Illinois, 406 U.S. 682 (1972), holding:

> [The] right to counsel announced in *Wade* and Gilbert v. California, 388 U.S. 263 (1967), attaches only to corporeal identifications conducted at or after the initiation of adversary judicial criminal proceedings—whether by way of formal charge, preliminary hearing, indictment, information, or arraignment . . . because the initiation of such proceedings marks the commencement of the criminal prosecutions to which alone the explicit guarantees of the Sixth Amendment are applicable.

The Court further noted that identifications conducted before the initiation of adversarial judicial criminal proceedings could still be challenged: "In such cases, however, *due process* protects the accused against the introduction of evidence of, or tainted by, unreliable pretrial identifications obtained through unnecessarily suggestive procedures." Therefore, it is now beyond question that, for federal Sixth Amendment purposes, the right to counsel attaches only at or after the initiation of adversarial judicial proceedings.

This conclusion is also consistent with our state constitutional provision, Const. 1963, art. 1, §20, which provides: "*In every criminal prosecution*, the accused shall have the right . . . to have the assistance of counsel for his or her defense. . . ." This Court has already noted . . . that a defendant's right to counsel under art. 1, §20 attaches only at or after the initiation of adversarial judicial proceedings. . . . Both the federal and the state provisions originated from the same concerns and to protect the same rights.

[The] *Anderson* decision generated considerable confusion regarding its proper application. . . . In People v. Dixon, 271 N.W.2d 196 (Mich. App. 1978), the Court held that if the police have "more than a mere suspicion" that the suspect is wanted for the crime, there can be no on-the-scene corporeal identification; rather, the suspect must be taken to the police station and participate in a lineup with counsel present. In People v. Turner, 328 N.W.2d 5 (Mich. App. 1982), however, the Court found the *Dixon* rule too difficult and, instead, held that police may conduct on-the-scene identifications without counsel unless the police have "very strong evidence" that the person stopped is the perpetrator. "Very strong evidence" was defined as "where the suspect has himself decreased any exculpatory motive, *i.e.*, where he has confessed or presented the police with either highly distinctive evidence of the crime or a highly distinctive personal appearance." . . .

Rather than perpetuate the confusion in this area, we take this opportunity to adopt the *Moore* analysis and clarify that the right to counsel attaches only to corporeal identifications conducted at or after the initiation of adversarial judicial criminal proceedings. This eliminates any unwarranted confusion and allows the focus to be on whether the identification procedure used violates due process. . . .

KELLY, J., dissenting.

To the casual reader, the rationale for today's majority decision may be elusive. After all, as the majority correctly notes, the case deals with law that has been relatively well-settled for close to thirty years: a potential criminal defendant does not have a Sixth Amendment right to counsel during identifications that occur before the initiation of adversarial judicial proceedings, such as a formal charge or preliminary hearing. . .

Nor has this Court held that the protective rules enumerated by People v. Anderson and its progeny apply to on-the-scene identification procedures and require counsel during those procedures. In fact, the opposite is true.

Yet the majority undertakes today ostensibly to resolve these issues. Its purpose is to take away the potential defendant's entitlement to counsel during all preindictment proceedings by overruling *Anderson* and its progeny. Hereafter, a defendant, in custody but not yet indicted, will no longer have the practical ability to challenge photographic or corporeal identification procedures. The police will be able to conduct such procedures without allowing a defendant's attorney to be present. Moreover, even after the initiation of adversarial judicial procedures, a criminal defendant will no longer have the right to counsel during a photographic showup. Because I do not see any good reason to depart from longstanding precedent, I must respectfully dissent. . . .

Anderson, which itself dealt with the right to counsel for pretrial custodial photographic showup procedures, set forth "justified" exceptions, albeit arguably in dicta, for the absence of counsel at eyewitness identification procedures. Notably included as exceptions were emergency situations requiring immediate identification and "prompt, on-the-scene corporeal identifications within minutes of the crime. . . ."

The majority could reaffirm the *Anderson* exception for prompt on-the-scene identifications, or perhaps enlarge the explanation of the exception to provide a workable framework for the lower courts. Instead, it unnecessarily chooses to remove the *Anderson* protections from all preindictment identification procedures. It is an ill-conceived decision that ignores principles of stare decisis. It also fails to consider the adverse effect on defendants' rights to be assured that pretrial identifications are not obtained through mistake or unnecessarily suggestive procedures. . . .

Unlike the majority, I believe *Anderson* was decided with due deference to the practical problems of ensuring accurate identifications. . . . *Anderson* discussed at length the scope of the problem of misidentifications, particularly in the use of photographic identification procedures. These concerns have certainly not diminished with time. [The] past century has seen the accumulation of literally thousands of studies on the weakness of eyewitness testimony. . . .

The fact that the majority has seen fit to unnecessarily overturn *Anderson* creates a Catch-22 for defendants during other preindictment identification procedures. Until today, a defendant who was not "formally" charged but in custody was entitled to an attorney during any identification procedure. Now, the only required persons in the room will be the investigating officer and the witness. Where the defendant is presented to a potential witness during an on-the-scene identification, the defendant himself is present to observe the actions and words of the officer. Arguably, a defendant who has been subjected to an unnecessarily suggestive on-the-scene identification procedure has the opportunity to present a coherent rationale for his arguments.

In contrast, a defendant who seeks to challenge a corporeal identification procedure will be effectively unable to do so. He must stand before the one-way glass and trust the competence and conscience of the investigating officer. I doubt that J.R.R. Tolkien's image of Wormtongue whispering quietly into the ear of Theoden, King of Rohan will be one that is frequently repeated in practice. However, even an inadvertent suggestion will be imperceptible to a defendant who remains precluded from witnessing it. The majority is essentially creating a black box into which the defendant will not be allowed to peer. . . .

Notes

1. *Availability of counsel during in-person identifications: majority position.* The decisions in *Wade* and Gilbert v. California, 388 U.S. 263 (1967), gave a dramatic debut to the constitutional right to counsel for identification procedures. The Supreme Court spoke broadly of the unreliability of this type of evidence and of the need for defense counsel to help counter this problem. But five years later, in Kirby v. Illinois, 406 U.S. 682 (1972), the Court sharply limited the type of lineup procedures in which counsel would be required under the Constitution: The *Wade-Gilbert* rule, according to *Kirby*, applied only to lineups occurring at or after the initiation of "adversary judicial criminal proceedings." See also Moore v. Illinois, 434 U.S. 220 (1977). Most states have adopted the *Kirby* rule to determine which identification procedures fall within the reach of the constitutional right to counsel. But see State v. Mitchell, 593 S.W.2d 280 (Tenn. 1980) (right to counsel applies after all warranted arrests).

No state has applied the right to counsel to field confrontations or showups, in which the police bring the crime victim together with a single suspect near the time and place where the crime occurred. To require counsel in such a setting would amount to a constitutional ban on the use of evidence from a field confrontation.

The overwhelming majority of live identification procedures, such as showups and live lineups, happen before the state files charges against a particular suspect. For that reason, the Sixth Amendment right to counsel for post-indictment lineups holds far less practical importance than the due process challenges to identification procedures that we explore in the next section.

2. *Initiation of criminal proceedings.* The Sixth Amendment requires the presence of counsel for live lineups that occur after the "initiation" of adversary judicial criminal proceedings. In *Moore*, the Court clarified that this "initiation" point arrives as early as the pre-indictment "preliminary hearing" in which a magistrate determines if there is probable cause to bind the defendant over to the grand jury. Later, in Rothgery v. Gillespie County, 554 U.S. 191 (2008), the Court clarified that an initial appearance before a magistrate can qualify as the start of the criminal proceedings even if no prosecutor is present—so long as the defendant could lose a procedural advantage or defense by failing to assert it at the initial appearance.

3. *The role of counsel in creating a record.* What should an attorney do at a lineup? Silently observe any suggestive police practices, or object to them? If the attorney takes an observer role, does he have to terminate representation of the defendant later in order to become a witness in the case? If you were a lawyer, would you want to know where the witness had been in the station prior to the lineup? Whom she had seen? What route your client took to get to the station? In light of the importance of what the witness has to say immediately after the lineup, can a defense attorney be excluded from the interview? Cases that address this question generally uphold police efforts to exclude defense counsel from these conversations.

If the primary function of the defense counsel is to create a record for possible challenges to the use of the identification evidence at trial, could a state conduct a post-indictment lineup without counsel present, so long as it is recorded? See Utah Code §77-8-4: "The entire lineup procedure shall be recorded, including all conversations between the witnesses and the conducting peace officers. The suspect shall have access to and may make copies of the record and any photographs taken of him or any other persons in connection with the lineup."

4. *Counsel's role at trial.* Although the presence of counsel at pretrial identification procedures is now extremely limited, the defense attorney still plays a critical role at trial in testing the reliability of an out-of-court identification. The attorney must point out to the jury any suggestive features of the process—if the attorney ever learns about such problems. A failure to raise these questions for the jury could result in a later challenge to the conviction, alleging constitutional ineffectiveness of the lawyer.

5. *The exclusion remedy and identification at trial.* If police fail to allow counsel to be present during identification when such presence is constitutionally required, then the judge must exclude at trial any evidence of the pretrial identification. In addition, any identification of the defendant by the witness *at trial* is excludable unless the prosecution can demonstrate that the witness's ability to recognize the defendant at trial has an "independent basis" apart from the tainted pretrial identification. Justice White's dissent in *Wade* predicted that trial identifications would rarely meet this standard, but one limited survey of case law in the years immediately after *Wade* found that courts still routinely allowed at-trial identifications. Joseph Quinn, In the Wake of *Wade*: The Dimensions of the Eyewitness Identification Cases, 42 U. Colo. L. Rev. 135 (1970) (citing six cases).

Technically speaking, the rules of evidence could bar any testimony at trial about the witness's out-of-court identification as improper hearsay. The Federal Rules of Evidence (and the counterpart rules that operate in state court) create a special exemption from the definition of hearsay for this type of statement, reasoning that the out-of-court identification is more important and better suited to adversarial testing than the in-court identification. See Fed. R. Evid. 801(d)(1)(C).

6. *Right to counsel for photographic identifications: majority position.* Rather than arranging an acceptable in-person encounter, it is often easier for police investigators to show pictures of potential suspects to a witness. Furthermore, pictures can be matched on more features. Photo lineups have become the most common identification technique. Are concerns about the reliability of the witness's identification different when investigators use photographs or other recorded images of a suspect?

In United States v. Ash, 413 U.S. 300 (1973), the Court held that the federal constitution does not require the presence of counsel at *any* photographic identification, whether it is conducted before or after the start of adversarial criminal proceedings. It reasoned that a photographic display, unlike an in-person lineup, does not involve a "trial-like confrontation" between the defendant and the witness. Thus, the presence of a lawyer is less important to a defendant whose picture is used in a photo array. Is this distinction convincing?

Most state courts have followed *Ash* and concluded that there is no right to counsel for photographic identifications. See Barone v. State, 866 P.2d 291 (Nev. 1993) (reversing a 1969 decision that had granted right to counsel for photo identification).

7. *Counsel at identification procedures in foreign practice.* Several legal systems outside the United States rely on counsel at formal identification procedures more heavily than the U.S. system does. For instance, in England and Wales, Code D of the Police and Criminal Evidence Act of 1984 provides for defense counsel at any formal "identification parade." Case law in Israel provides that a suspect must be informed of the right to counsel during a lineup. See Eliahu Harnon & Alex Stein, Israel, in Criminal Procedure: A Worldwide Study (Craig Bradley ed., 2d ed. 2007). In civil law systems (said to be less "adversarial" than common-law systems), the rules on defense counsel participation vary greatly. In some countries, such as Argentina, both the Code of Criminal Procedure and case law require a judge (who is responsible for scheduling a lineup) to notify defense counsel of the procedure. In the Netherlands, and under the European Court of Human Rights law, counsel is not required to be present at identification procedures, but counsel's presence helps establish the reliability of the identification. See Aya Gruber et al., Practical Global Criminal Procedure: United States, Argentina, and the Netherlands 196-205 (2012).

2. Exclusion on Due Process Grounds

As we saw in the preceding subsection, federal and state constitutions generally require the presence of counsel only for lineups taking place after the initiation of adversary criminal proceedings. This accounts for a small number of the identification procedures that take place. Are there any limitations—constitutional or otherwise—on the larger number of lineups and "field confrontations" that occur earlier in the investigative process?

Courts have insisted for decades that due process will prevent the use of the least reliable identification procedures, regardless of the presence or absence of counsel. In Stovall v. Denno, 388 U.S. 293 (1967), decided the same day as United States v. Wade, the Supreme Court refused to exclude evidence of a pretrial identification under the due process clause. While investigating a stabbing case, the police entered the victim's hospital room with the suspect handcuffed to an officer and asked the victim if the suspect was the person who had committed the crime. Although the Court acknowledged that unduly "suggestive" lineups in some cases might lead to an exclusion of the evidence under the due process clause, the procedure used here was not "unnecessarily suggestive" because the police had no viable alternative.

The Supreme Court appeared to shift its emphasis in two later cases, Neil v. Biggers, 409 U.S. 188 (1972), and Manson v. Brathwaite, 432 U.S. 98 (1977). Even though the police had used suggestive "showups" to identify suspects in those cases, the Court reasoned that a witness with an adequate memory of the original crime could reliably identify the criminal despite the suggestive procedure followed at the time of the identification. The Court went on to describe the factors it would consider, as part of the "totality of the circumstances," that could outweigh a suggestive identification procedure. These include: (1) the "opportunity of the witness to view the criminal at the time of the crime"; (2) "the witness's degree of attention"; (3) "the accuracy of his prior description of the criminal"; (4) "the level of certainty demonstrated at the time of the confrontation"; and (5) "the time between the crime and the confrontation." Thus, the Supreme Court rejected a "per se" rule that would exclude all evidence obtained through unduly suggestive identification procedures, in favor of a "reliability test" that would allow some identification evidence to stand because other factors supported its accuracy.

The Supreme Court in Perry v. New Hampshire, 565 U.S. 228 (2012), declined an invitation to update the legal framework that governs due process claims in this area. The Court held that due process does not require a trial judge to determine the reliability of eyewitness testimony unless a defendant establishes as a preliminary matter that the identification procedure was "unduly suggestive."

The following case describes the U.S. Supreme Court's "totality" approach to identification evidence obtained at the police station, but then offers a more demanding test for the admissibility of eyewitness testimony for purposes of the state constitution.

■ STATE v. LARRY HENDERSON

27 A.3d 872 (N.J. 2011)

RABNER, C.J.

. . . In the thirty-four years since the United States Supreme Court announced a test for the admission of eyewitness identification evidence, which New Jersey adopted soon after, a vast body of scientific research about human memory has emerged. That body of work . . . calls into question the vitality of the current legal framework for analyzing the reliability of eyewitness identifications. See Manson v. Brathwaite, 432 U.S. 98 (1977); State v. Madison, 536 A.2d 254 (N.J. 1988).

In this case, defendant claims that an eyewitness mistakenly identified him as an accomplice to a murder. Defendant argues that the identification was not reliable because the officers investigating the case intervened during the identification process and unduly influenced the eyewitness. After a pretrial hearing, the trial court found that the officers' behavior was not impermissibly suggestive and admitted the evidence. [We] appointed a Special Master to evaluate scientific and other evidence about eyewitness identifications. The Special Master presided over a hearing that probed testimony by seven experts and produced more than 2,000 pages of transcripts along with hundreds of scientific studies. . . . That evidence offers convincing proof that the current test for evaluating the trustworthiness of eyewitness identifications should be revised. It does not offer an adequate measure for reliability or sufficiently deter inappropriate police conduct. It also overstates the jury's inherent ability to evaluate evidence offered by eyewitnesses who honestly believe their testimony is accurate.

Two principal steps are needed to remedy those concerns. First, when defendants can show some evidence of suggestiveness, all relevant system and estimator variables should be explored at pretrial hearings. . . . Second, the court system should develop enhanced jury charges on eyewitness identification for trial judges to use. We anticipate that identification evidence will continue to be admitted in the vast majority of cases. To help jurors weigh that evidence, they must be told about relevant factors and their effect on reliability. To that end, we have asked the Criminal Practice Committee and the Committee on Model Criminal Jury Charges to draft proposed revisions to the current model charge on eyewitness identification and address various system and estimator variables. . . .

FACTS AND PROCEDURAL HISTORY . . .

In the early morning hours of January 1, 2003, Rodney Harper was shot to death in an apartment in Camden. James Womble witnessed the murder but did not speak with the police until they approached him ten days later.

Womble and Harper were acquaintances who occasionally socialized at the apartment of Womble's girlfriend, Vivian Williams. On the night of the murder, Womble and Williams brought in the New Year in Williams' apartment by drinking wine and champagne and smoking crack cocaine. [Soon after Harper joined them at 2:00 to 2:30 A.M.], two men forcefully entered the apartment. Womble knew one of them, co-defendant George Clark, who had come to collect $160 from Harper. The other man was a stranger to Womble.

While Harper and Clark went to a different room, the stranger pointed a gun at Womble and told him, "Don't move, stay right here, you're not involved in this." He remained with the stranger in a small, narrow, dark hallway. Womble testified that he "got a look at" the stranger, but not "a real good look." Womble also described the gun pointed at his torso as a dark semiautomatic. Meanwhile, Womble overheard Clark and Harper argue over money in the other room. At one point, Harper said, "do what you got to do," after which Womble heard a gunshot. Womble then walked into the room, saw Clark holding a handgun, offered to get Clark the $160, and urged him not to shoot Harper again. As Clark left, he warned Womble, "Don't rat me out, I know where you live."

Harper died from the gunshot wound to his chest on January 10, 2003. Camden County Detective Luis Ruiz and Investigator Randall MacNair were assigned to investigate the homicide, and they interviewed Womble the next day. Initially, Womble told the police that he was in the apartment when he heard two gunshots outside, that he left to look for Harper, and that he found Harper slumped over in his car in a nearby parking lot, where Harper said he had been shot by two men he did not know.

The next day, the officers confronted Womble about inconsistencies in his story. Womble claimed that they also threatened to charge him in connection with the murder. Womble then decided to "come clean." He admitted that he lied at first because he did not want to "rat" out anyone and "didn't want to get involved" out of fear of retaliation against his elderly father. Womble led the investigators to Clark, who eventually gave a statement about his involvement and identified the person who accompanied him as defendant Larry Henderson.

The officers had Womble view a photographic array on January 14, 2003. . . . Womble identified defendant from the array. . . . Upon arrest, defendant admitted to the police that he had accompanied Clark to the apartment where Harper was killed, and heard a gunshot while waiting in the hallway. But defendant denied witnessing or participating in the shooting. . . .

The trial court conducted a pretrial *Wade* hearing to determine the admissibility of [Womble's] identification. United States v. Wade, 388 U.S. 218 (1967). Investigator MacNair, Detective Ruiz, and Womble all testified at the hearing. Cherry Hill Detective Thomas Weber also testified. Detective Weber conducted the identification procedure because, consistent with guidelines issued by the Attorney General, he was not a primary investigator in the case. According to the Guidelines . . . primary investigators should not administer photo or live lineup identification procedures "to ensure that inadvertent verbal cues or body language do not impact on a witness."

Ruiz and MacNair gave Weber an array consisting of seven "filler" photos and one photo of defendant Henderson. The eight photos all depicted headshots of African-American men between the ages of twenty-eight and thirty-five, with short hair, goatees, and, according to Weber, similar facial features. . . . The identification procedure took place in an interview room in the Prosecutor's Office. At first, Weber and Womble were alone in the room. Weber began by reading [cautionary] instructions off a standard form. . . . Detective Weber pre-numbered the eight photos, shuffled them, and showed them to Womble one at a time. Womble quickly eliminated five of the photos. He then reviewed the remaining three, discounted one more, and said he "wasn't 100 percent sure of the final two pictures." At the *Wade* hearing, Detective Weber recalled that Womble "just shook his head a lot. He seemed indecisive." But he did not express any fear to Weber.

Weber left the room with the photos and informed MacNair and Ruiz that the witness had narrowed the pictures to two but could not make a final identification. MacNair and Ruiz testified at the hearing that they did not know whether defendant's picture was among the remaining two photos. MacNair and Ruiz entered the interview room to speak with Womble. [They believed] Womble was "nervous, upset about his father." In an effort to calm Womble, MacNair testified that he "just told him to focus, to calm down, to relax and that any type of protection that [he] would need, any threats against [him] would be put to rest by the Police Department." Ruiz added, "just do what you have to do, and we'll be out of here." In response, according to MacNair, Womble said he "could make [an] identification."

MacNair and Ruiz then left the interview room. Ruiz testified that the entire exchange lasted less than one minute; Weber believed it took about five minutes. When Weber returned to the room, he reshuffled the eight photos and again displayed them to Womble sequentially. This time, when Womble saw defendant's photo, he slammed his hand on the table and exclaimed, "that's the mother [------] there." From start to finish, the entire process took fifteen minutes.

Womble did not recant his identification, but during the *Wade* hearing he testified that he felt as though Detective Weber was "nudging" him to choose defendant's photo, and "that there was pressure" to make a choice. After hearing the testimony, the trial court . . . concluded that the photo identification was reliable. The court . . . noted that Womble displayed no doubts about identifying defendant Henderson, that he had the opportunity to view defendant at the crime scene, and that Womble fixed his attention on defendant "because he had a gun on him." . . .

The following facts—relevant to Womble's identification of defendant—were adduced at trial after the court determined that the identification was admissible: Womble smoked two bags of crack cocaine with his girlfriend in the hours before the shooting; the two also consumed one bottle of champagne and one bottle of wine; the lighting was "pretty dark" in the hallway where Womble and defendant interacted; defendant shoved Womble during the incident; and Womble remembered looking at the gun pointed at his chest. Womble also admitted smoking about two bags of crack cocaine each day from the time of the shooting until speaking with police ten days later.

At trial, Womble elaborated on his state of mind during the identification procedure. He testified that when he first looked at the photo array, he did not see anyone he recognized. As he explained, "my mind was drawing a blank . . . so I just started eliminating photos." To make a final identification, Womble said that he "really had to search deep." He was nonetheless "sure" of the identification. . . . Neither Clark nor defendant testified at trial. The primary evidence against defendant, thus, was Womble's identification and Detective MacNair's testimony about defendant's post-arrest statement. [The] jury acquitted defendant of murder and aggravated manslaughter, and convicted him of reckless manslaughter, aggravated assault, and two weapons charges.

CURRENT LEGAL FRAMEWORK

The current standards for determining the admissibility of eyewitness identification evidence derive from the principles the United States Supreme Court set forth in Manson v. Brathwaite, 432 U.S. 98 (1977); State v. Madison, 536 A.2d 254 (N.J. 1988). . . . *Madison* succinctly outlined *Manson*'s two-step test as follows:

> [A] court must first decide whether the procedure in question was in fact impermissibly suggestive. If the court does find the procedure impermissibly suggestive, it must then decide whether the objectionable procedure resulted in a "very substantial likelihood of irreparable misidentification." In carrying out the second part of the analysis, the court will focus on the reliability of the identification. If the court finds that the identification is reliable despite the impermissibly suggestive nature of the procedure, the identification may be admitted into evidence. . . .

To assess reliability, courts must consider five factors adopted from Neil v. Biggers, 409 U.S. 188 (1972): (1) the "opportunity of the witness to view the criminal at the time of the crime"; (2) "the witness's degree of attention"; (3) "the accuracy of his prior description of the criminal"; (4) "the level of certainty demonstrated at the time of the confrontation"; and (5) "the time between the crime and the confrontation." Those factors are to be weighed against the corrupting effect of the suggestive identification itself. [A proper record convinces us now that a different approach is required.]

SCOPE OF SCIENTIFIC RESEARCH

[The] Special Master estimated that more than two thousand studies related to eyewitness identification have been published in the past thirty years. [Identification] statistics from across the studies were remarkably consistent: [the studies of all types consistently found that approximately] 24% of witnesses identified fillers. Those statistics are similar to data from real cases. [In] police investigations in Sacramento and London [examined later by researchers], roughly 20% of eyewitnesses identified fillers. Thus, although lab and field experiments may be imperfect proxies for real-world conditions, certain data they have produced are relevant and persuasive.

[Eyewitness identification research] reveals that an array of variables can affect and dilute memory and lead to misidentifications. Scientific literature divides those variables into two categories: system and estimator variables. System variables are factors like lineup procedures which are within the control of the criminal justice system. Estimator variables are factors related to the witness, the perpetrator, or the event itself—like distance, lighting, or stress—over which the legal system has no control.

[Several system variables increase the likelihood of misidentification. These include a failure to perform blind lineup procedures; a failure to give proper pre-lineup instructions to the witness; a lineup that does not place the suspect in an array of look-alikes; a lineup with less than five fillers, or featuring more than one suspect; providing confirmatory feedback to the witness after he or she identifies the suspect; giving a witness more than one viewing of the same suspect in different identification efforts; and use of showups conducted more than two hours after an event.

Several estimator variables are likely to affect the reliability of an identification. These include high levels of stress for the witness during the event; the presence of a visible weapon during a brief interaction; brief or fleeting time available to observe an event; reliance on a witness who is intoxicated, or a witness who is a child; a large age gap between the witness and the observed party; the use of a disguise by the perpetrator; a large time gap between the event and the identification; cross-racial identifications; and feedback from co-witnesses.]

RESPONSES TO SCIENTIFIC STUDIES

Beyond the scientific community, law enforcement and reform agencies across the nation have taken note of the scientific findings. In turn, they have formed task forces and recommended or implemented new procedures to improve the reliability of eyewitness identifications.

New Jersey has been at the forefront of that effort. In 2001, under the leadership of then–Attorney General John J. Farmer, Jr., New Jersey became the first state in the Nation to officially adopt the recommendations issued by the Department of Justice and issue guidelines for preparing and conducting identification procedures. . . .

Other state and local authorities have instituted similar changes to their eye-witness identification procedures. In 2005, for example, the Attorney General of Wisconsin issued a set of identification guidelines recommending, among other things, "double-blind, sequential photo arrays and lineups with non-suspect fill-ers chosen to minimize suggestiveness, non-biased instructions to eyewitnesses, and assessments of confidence immediately after identifications." See also Dallas Police Dep't, Dallas Police Department General Order §304.01 (2009); Denver Police Dep't, Operations Manual §104.44 (2006). North Carolina was among the first states to pass legislation mandating, among other things, pre-lineup instruc-tions and blind and sequential lineup administration. Illinois, Maryland, Ohio, West Virginia, and Wisconsin have passed similar laws regarding lineup practices. . . .

Because eyewitness identification science is probabilistic—meaning that it can-not determine if a particular identification is accurate—the State . . . argues that the legal system should continue to rely on jurors to assess the credibility of eyewit-nesses. To guide juries, the State favors appropriate, flexible jury instructions. The State maintains that expert testimony is not advisable because the relevant subjects are not beyond the ken of the average juror. . . .

With regard to the *Manson/Madison* test, defendant and amici argue that more than thirty years of scientific evidence undercut the assumptions underlying the Supreme Court's decision in *Manson*. [They] urge this Court to require a reli-ability hearing in every case in which the State intends to present identification evidence. At the hearing, they submit that a wide range of system and estimator variables would be relevant, and the State should bear the burden of establishing reliability. . . .

Legal Conclusions . . .

To protect due process concerns, the *Manson* Court's two-part test rested on three assumptions: (1) that it would adequately measure the reliability of eyewit-ness testimony; (2) that the test's focus on suggestive police procedure would deter improper practices; and (3) that jurors would recognize and discount untrustworthy eyewitness testimony. We remanded this case to determine whether those assump-tions and other factors reflected in the two-part *Manson/Madison* test are still valid. We conclude from the hearing that they are not. . . .

First, under *Manson/Madison*, defendants must show that police procedures were "impermissibly suggestive" before courts can consider estimator variables that also bear on reliability. As a result, although evidence of relevant estimator vari-ables tied to the *Neil v. Biggers* factors is routinely introduced at pretrial hearings, their effect is ignored unless there is a finding of impermissibly suggestive police conduct. In this case, for example, the testimony at the *Wade* hearing related princi-pally to the lineup procedure. Because the court found that the procedure was not "impermissibly suggestive," details about the [witness's] use of drugs and alcohol, the dark lighting conditions, the presence of a weapon pointed at the [witness's] chest, and other estimator variables that affect reliability were not considered at the hearing. (They were explored later at trial.)

Second, [three of the five reliability] factors—the opportunity to view the crime, the [witness's] degree of attention, and the level of certainty at the time of the identification—rely on self-reporting by eyewitnesses; and research has shown that those reports can be skewed by the suggestive procedures themselves and thus may not be reliable. . . . The irony of the current test is that the more suggestive the procedure, the greater the chance eyewitnesses will seem confident and report better viewing conditions.

[Finally], the *Manson/Madison* test addresses only one option for questionable eyewitness identification evidence: suppression. Yet few judges choose that ultimate sanction. An all-or-nothing approach does not account for the complexities of eyewitness identification evidence. . . .

Remedying the problems with the current *Manson/Madison* test requires an approach that addresses its shortcomings: one that allows judges to consider all relevant factors that affect reliability in deciding whether an identification is admissible; that is not heavily weighted by factors that can be corrupted by suggestiveness; that promotes deterrence in a meaningful way; and that focuses on helping jurors both understand and evaluate the effects that various factors have on memory—because we recognize that most identifications will be admitted in evidence. . . .

First, to obtain a pretrial hearing, a defendant has the initial burden of showing some evidence of suggestiveness that could lead to a mistaken identification. That evidence, in general, must be tied to a system—and not an estimator—variable. Second, the State must then offer proof to show that the proffered eyewitness identification is reliable—accounting for system and estimator variables—subject to the following: the court can end the hearing at any time if it finds from the testimony that defendant's threshold allegation of suggestiveness is groundless. . . .

Third, the ultimate burden remains on the defendant to prove a very substantial likelihood of irreparable misidentification. . . . Fourth, if after weighing the evidence presented a court finds from the totality of the circumstances that defendant has demonstrated a very substantial likelihood of irreparable misidentification, the court should suppress the identification evidence. If the evidence is admitted, the court should provide appropriate, tailored jury instructions. . . .

To evaluate whether there is evidence of suggestiveness to trigger a hearing, courts should consider the following non-exhaustive list of system variables:

1. *Blind Administration.* Was the lineup procedure performed double-blind? If double-blind testing was impractical, did the police use a technique . . . to ensure that the administrator had no knowledge of where the suspect appeared in the photo array or lineup?

2. *Pre-identification Instructions.* Did the administrator provide neutral, pre-identification instructions warning that the suspect may not be present in the lineup and that the witness should not feel compelled to make an identification?

3. *Lineup Construction.* Did the array or lineup contain only one suspect embedded among at least five innocent fillers? Did the suspect stand out from other members of the lineup?

4. *Feedback.* Did the witness receive any information or feedback, about the suspect or the crime, before, during, or after the identification procedure?

5. *Recording Confidence.* Did the administrator record the [witness's] statement of confidence immediately after the identification, before the possibility of any confirmatory feedback?

6. *Multiple Viewings.* Did the witness view the suspect more than once as part of multiple identification procedures? Did police use the same fillers more than once?

7. *Showups.* Did the police perform a showup more than two hours after an event? Did the police warn the witness that the suspect may not be the perpetrator and that the witness should not feel compelled to make an identification?

8. *Private Actors.* Did law enforcement elicit from the eyewitness whether he or she had spoken with anyone about the identification and, if so, what was discussed?

9. *Other Identifications Made.* Did the eyewitness initially make no choice or choose a different suspect or filler?

[Courts] should consider the above system variables as well as the following non-exhaustive list of estimator variables to evaluate the overall reliability of an identification and determine its admissibility:

1. *Stress.* Did the event involve a high level of stress?
2. *Weapon focus.* Was a visible weapon used during a crime of short duration?
3. *Duration.* How much time did the witness have to observe the event?
4. *Distance and Lighting.* How close were the witness and perpetrator? What were the lighting conditions at the time?
5. *Witness Characteristics.* Was the witness under the influence of alcohol or drugs? Was age a relevant factor under the circumstances of the case?
6. *Characteristics of Perpetrator.* Was the culprit wearing a disguise? Did the suspect have different facial features at the time of the identification?
7. *Memory decay.* How much time elapsed between the crime and the identification?
8. *Race-bias.* Does the case involve a cross-racial identification? . . .

The above factors are not exclusive. Nor are they intended to be frozen in time. We recognize that scientific research relating to the reliability of eyewitness evidence is dynamic; the field is very different today than it was in 1977, and it will likely be quite different thirty years from now. . . . But to the extent the police undertake new practices, or courts either consider variables differently or entertain new ones, they must rely on reliable scientific evidence that is generally accepted by experts in the community.

[We] anticipate that eyewitness identification evidence will likely not be ruled inadmissible at pretrial hearings solely on account of estimator variables. For example, it is difficult to imagine that a trial judge would preclude a witness from testifying because the lighting was "too dark," the witness was "too distracted" by the presence of a weapon, or he or she was under "too much" stress while making an observation. How dark is too dark as a matter of law?

[Courts] cannot affect estimator variables; by definition, they relate to matters outside the control of law enforcement. More probing pretrial hearings about suggestive police procedures, though, can deter inappropriate police practices.

[We] are mindful of the practical impact of today's ruling. Because defendants will now be free to explore a broader range of estimator variables at pretrial hearings to assess the reliability of an identification, those hearings will become more intricate. They will routinely involve testimony from both the police and eyewitnesses, and that testimony will likely expand as more substantive areas are explored. Also, trial courts will retain discretion to allow expert testimony at pretrial hearings.

In 2009, trial courts in New Jersey conducted roughly 200 *Wade* hearings, according to the Administrative Office of the Courts. If estimator variables alone could trigger a hearing, that number might increase to nearly all cases in which eyewitness identification evidence plays a part. We have to measure that outcome in light of the following reality that the Special Master observed: judges rarely suppress eyewitness evidence at pretrial hearings. Therefore, to allow hearings in the majority of identification cases might overwhelm the system with little resulting benefit. . . .

Expert testimony may also be introduced at trial, but only if otherwise appropriate. The Rules of Evidence permit expert testimony to "assist the trier of fact to understand the evidence or to determine a fact in issue." N.J.R.E. 702. . . . Finally, in rare cases, judges may use their discretion to redact parts of identification testimony. . . . For example, if an [eyewitness's] confidence was not properly recorded soon after an identification procedure, and evidence revealed that the witness received confirmatory feedback from the police or a co-witness, the court can bar potentially distorted and unduly prejudicial statements about the [witness's] level of confidence from being introduced at trial. . . .

We return to the facts of this case. After Womble, the eyewitness, informed the lineup administrator that he could not make an identification from the final two photos, the investigating officers intervened. They told Womble to focus and calm down, and assured him that the police would protect him from retaliation. "Just do what you have to do," they instructed. . . .

The suggestive nature of the officers' comments entitled defendant to a pretrial hearing, and he received one. Applying the *Manson/Madison* test, the trial judge admitted the evidence. We now remand to the trial court for an expanded hearing consistent with the principles outlined in this decision. . . . In addition to suggestiveness, the trial court should consider Womble's drug and alcohol use immediately before the confrontation, weapon focus, and lighting, among other relevant factors. We express no view on the outcome of the hearing. . . .

Problem 9-1. The Pizza Hut Robbery

Shortly before 1:00 A.M., Kathy Davis was preparing to leave the Pizza Hut where she worked as manager. Her husband, John Davis, and her brother, Gerald Wilson, had come to visit her and accompany her home. As they left the building, they were accosted by a man wearing a white scarf across his face and carrying a metal pipe ("the pipe man"). He demanded that they give him the bank bag with the day's receipts. Gerald attempted to grapple with the pipe man. The pipe man hit Gerald with the pipe and then told a second robber ("the gunman") that if Gerald moved again, the gunman should kill him.

This was the first indication that a second robber was present. The gunman was crouched near the corner of the building, about 25 feet away from the victims, holding a gun. The man, who wore a hat and covered the lower part of his face with a scarf, held the gun on Gerald while Kathy and John went back into the building. They brought the bank bag out to the robbers, who then fled. The victims reported the robbery to the police, who responded within a few minutes.

Gerald (who is white, as are Kathy and John) described the gunman as a male Mexican, 5'9" to 6'0" tall, wearing a blue sweater and jeans, with a white scarf around the lower part of his face. He described the pipe man in more detail: male Mexican,

21 to 22 years old, 5'7" to 5'8" tall, 155 to 160 pounds, shaggy brown hair, brown eyes, wearing a blue sweater and Levi's and a white scarf over the lower part of his face, one front tooth missing, and a bald spot on the side of his head.

A short time after the robbery, police officers apprehended Livio Ramirez, who had been walking with another man, who fled at the sight of a police car. Ramirez was wearing jeans, a blue sweatshirt with paint spattered on the front, and a brown baseball cap. Ramirez also had readily visible tattoos on his arms. They searched Ramirez and handcuffed him to the fence by placing a second set of handcuffs through the fence and attaching them to the handcuffs Ramirez was wearing.

Roughly 45 minutes after the end of the robbery, the police drove Kathy, John, and Gerald to the location where Ramirez was handcuffed to the fence to determine whether they could identify him as one of the robbers. The police told them they had found someone who matched the description of one of the robbers.

Ramirez, a dark-complexioned Apache Indian with long hair, was the only suspect present and was surrounded by police officers. The police turned the headlights and spotlights from the police cars on Ramirez to provide adequate light. The witnesses viewed Ramirez by looking at him from the back seat of a police car. Of the three witnesses, only Gerald identified Ramirez as the masked man with the gun; the other two witnesses were unable to identify him as one of the robbers. Following the identification, Ramirez was placed under arrest and was charged with the robbery. During a later suppression hearing, Gerald mentioned for the first time that the gunman had tattoos and a hat.

How is a court likely to resolve this case under the federal standard? Under the New Jersey standard? Compare State v. Ramirez, 817 P.2d 774 (Utah 1991).

Suppose now that Kathy, John, and Gerald had their first opportunity to identify a suspect during a lineup at the police station two days after the Pizza Hut robbery. Would either the federal or the state due process clause (the latter as the *Henderson* court interpreted it) bar the introduction at trial of any evidence of the pretrial identification or an at-trial identification under the following circumstances?

(a) Before the lineup takes place, a police officer mentions to the witnesses that "we have arrested someone for this crime and have included that person in this lineup."

(b) During the lineup, John says (in the presence of Kathy and Gerald), "It's definitely the third guy—I can tell by his eyes." Kathy and Gerald agree that the third lineup participant was the gunman in the robbery.

(c) After the three witnesses have identified a lineup participant as the gunman, a detective says, "You picked out the guy we had arrested for the crime."

Notes

1. *Due process limits on suggestive identifications: majority position.* Most states follow the federal position set out in *Biggers* and in Manson v. Brathwaite, 432 U.S. 98 (1977). When applying state constitutions to suggestive identifications, courts look to the totality of the circumstances, emphasizing the five factors listed in *Biggers* to determine the "reliability" of an identification despite suggestiveness in the identification procedure. Appellate courts applying this test refuse to overturn convictions

in the overwhelming majority of due process challenges to "suggestive" identifications, although there are exceptions.

Massachusetts employs a per se rule and excludes from evidence *any* identification produced by an unduly suggestive process. See Commonwealth v. Johnson, 650 N.E.2d 1257 (Mass. 1995). The *Johnson* court explained that juries are unduly receptive to eyewitness evidence and are not able to discount unreliable identifications. A per se rule is therefore necessary to reduce the risk that a mistaken eyewitness identification results in a wrongful conviction. Most states, however, refuse to adopt this per se rule based on suggestiveness. Cf. State v. Dubose, 699 N.W.2d 582 (Wis. 2005) (evidence from showup is inherently suggestive; evidence is admissible only if the prosecution shows that the procedure was necessary). Does the per se rule make a defendant better off than she would have been in the absence of any suggestive identification procedure at all?

2. *Unreliable measures of reliability.* Some state courts have criticized the federal "reliability" factors from Neil v. Biggers, 409 U.S. 188 (1972), because they are inconsistent with "empirical" findings of psychologists studying eyewitness memory. See Young v. State, 374 P.3d 395 (Alaska 2016); State v. Lawson, 291 P.3d 673 (Oregon 2012). Is the New Jersey court's modified test more empirically grounded? Will it lead to different results?

3. *Showups and lineups.* All other factors being equal, showups are thought to be more suggestive than lineups. Does the due process limitation on the use of identification evidence give police enough reason to avoid showups in favor of lineups whenever possible?

According to one survey, only 21 percent of police departments use live lineups, while 62 percent of departments use showups. Departments using these techniques conducted an average of two live lineups per year; they used an average of 30 showups per year. Police Executive Research Forum, A National Survey of Eyewitness Identification Procedures in Law Enforcement Agencies (2013). In light of the rapid deterioration of human memory, does the short time lapse between the crime and the identification make the showup, on balance, as reliable as a lineup occurring several hours, days, or weeks later? See Nancy Steblay, Jennifer Dysart, Solomon Fulero & R.C.L. Lindsay, Eyewitness Accuracy Rates in Police Showup and Lineup Presentations: A Meta-Analytic Comparison, 27 Law & Hum. Behav. 523 (2003) (in target-present conditions, showups and lineups yield approximately equal hit rates, whereas in target-absent conditions, showups produce a higher level of correct rejections).

If a witness identifies a defendant for the first time in court, is that the equivalent of an unduly suggestive showup? See Commonwealth v. Crayton, 21 N.E.3d 157 (Mass. 2014) (if an eyewitness has not participated before trial in an identification procedure, court will admit in-court identifications only where there is "good reason" for the admission, such as where the witness knew the defendant before the crime).

4. *Detention for identification.* Do the police have the power to compel a person who is not currently in custody to participate in a lineup? Many states do address this question by statute and court-issued rules of procedure. See Model Code of Pre-Arraignment Criminal Procedure, art. 170. Nebraska Revised Statutes §29-3303 is typical. It authorizes a judge to order a person to submit to a lineup or some other identification procedure (such as fingerprinting). The order may issue upon a showing that (1) there is probable cause to believe that an offense has been committed; (2) identification procedures may contribute to the identification of the

individual who committed the offense; and (3) the identified or described individual has refused, or will refuse, to participate voluntarily.

Such a court order is not necessary if a suspect is already in police custody. A few state rules and statutes allow the detention of persons for the purpose of participating in lineups or other identification procedures, even in the absence of probable cause to believe the detained person committed the crime. See State v. Rodriguez, 921 P.2d 643 (Ariz. 1996). Are identification procedures sufficiently similar to fingerprinting to allow a judicial order of detention based on less than probable cause? Note that detention for fingerprinting at the station house, based on less than probable cause, would likely be an unconstitutional "seizure" if it took place without a judicial order. See Davis v. Mississippi, 394 U.S. 721 (1969).

In a state allowing the police to detain a suspect for identification purposes, should a defendant have a comparable power to obtain a court order forcing *another* suspect to attend a lineup? Should citizens generally have an obligation to take part in a lineup along with a suspect who physically resembles them? Would you willingly take part in a lineup? For modest compensation, say, $100?

5. *Due process limits on photo identifications.* As with in-person identifications, the due process clause creates a second constitutional restraint on photographic identifications. If the photo array is unduly suggestive, *and* if the totality of the circumstances suggests that the improper identification procedure created an undue risk of misidentification, the court will exclude at trial any evidence based on that tainted identification. See Commonwealth v. Silva-Santiago, 906 N.E.2d 299 (Mass. 2009) (court described the preferred procedures for presenting photographic arrays to eyewitnesses and declared that it expected law enforcement agencies to follow these protocols in future; double-blind procedure is best practice but not required in every case; no suppression of identification in this case).

Many of the claims of unduly "suggestive" photo arrays derive from the showing of multiple photo arrays to the witness when the suspect's picture appears in each of the arrays. Courts virtually always reject challenges based on these claims. See, e.g., State v. Rezk, 609 A.2d 391 (N.H. 1992) (approves an identification in second photo lineup when defendant was the only subject pictured also in first photo lineup and was the only person pictured in prison overalls).

6. *Whose pictures?* When the police have no suspect, they will sometimes ask the witness to review a large number of photos in the hope that the perpetrator's picture will appear. Which pictures can the police show to a witness? Can the photos include only those who have been convicted of a crime similar to the one now at issue? Any arrested person? Any person at all? Suppose the police collect pictures of persons from one ethnic group, awaiting those occasions when a crime victim is attempting to identify, say, an Asian perpetrator? See San Jose Recorder, Jan. 31, 1996 (lawsuit settlement by the town of San Jose, California, paying $150,000 in damages to person who spent three months in jail after being identified by witness to armed robbery; witness selected photograph from mug book containing pictures only of Asians, many of whom—like plaintiff—had never been arrested or convicted).

7. *Identifications and new technology.* Computer programs have enabled the police to create a digitized image based on the description by a witness, and to match that digitized image to photographs in existing databases such as arrest files or drivers' license pictures. For a survey of the typical features of this software, see the web extension of this chapter at *http://www.crimpro.com/extension/ch09.* Conversely, in cases where officers have a photo of the suspect from surveillance, they have used

facial recognition databases to generate a match. As a defense attorney, what kind of information about the facial recognition databases would you want to know when deciding whether to challenge the reliability of the match? See Benjamin Conarck, How a Jacksonville Man Caught in the Drug War Exposed Details of Police Facial Recognition, Fla. Times-Union, May 26, 2017.

Problem 9-2. Photo Lineups

On August 8, a man robbed the People's Bank in Port Huron, Michigan, of more than $22,000 (including approximately $600 in Canadian currency). Three bank tellers, the branch manager, and a customer witnessed the robbery and gave descriptions of the robber and his car to investigators. Bank teller Mary Kamendat described the robber as approximately 45 or 46 years old, almost six feet tall, weighing about 210 pounds, with dust or some other substance on his face. She also described him as needing a haircut. Another bank teller, Cindy Dortman, noticed that the robber was wearing a light-colored shirt, a baseball cap, dark sunglasses, and had longer hair than normal for a man of his age. She also described him as wearing flared jeans, with a chain hanging out of his pocket and his shirt pulled over his pants. She said that the robber had a "long, very distinguished" nose.

The bank's surveillance camera took photographs of the robber. After the local newspaper published two of the surveillance photographs a few days after the crime, the Sheriff's Department received several phone calls regarding the robbery. One caller identified Albin Kurylczyk as the man in the photographs. This information prompted a detective and an FBI agent to visit Kurylczyk at his home on August 17. At their request, Kurylczyk permitted the officers to search his house and his car, which was similar to the getaway car the eyewitnesses had described. He also agreed to accompany the investigators to the local police station for further interviews. Once there, he consented to be photographed. At that time, he was not represented by counsel, nor did he request an attorney.

On the same day, other deputies responded to a call from the bank. The bank tellers Dortman and Kamendat believed the robber had returned when a customer dressed like the robber entered the bank and attempted to exchange some Canadian currency. The tellers detained him by delaying his transaction until the deputies arrived. However, after an investigation, the law enforcement authorities were satisfied that this customer was not the bank robber. He was not included in any of the identification procedures used later in the investigation.

Two days later, a detective assembled an array of six photographs, including the photograph he had taken of Kurylczyk and one of another suspect. Kurylczyk was the only man in the photographic array dressed in clothing that matched the description of the eyewitnesses. In particular, his photo showed him wearing a chain attached to his belt and extending to a wallet in the rear pocket of his jeans. None of the others in the photographic lineup wore such a trucker's wallet. This same type of wallet was visible in the bank's surveillance photographs, as published in the local paper. In addition, Kurylczyk's photograph was taken from a closer distance, so that his image appeared larger than the others. Three of the men in the array had mustaches; Kurylczyk did not have a mustache, and none of the witnesses described the robber as having a mustache.

The detective showed the photo array to Kamendat and Dortman, and both identified Kurylczyk as the bank robber. As a result, the government charged him with the crime. Before trial, Kurylczyk moved to exclude the identification testimony of the eyewitnesses. First, he contended that he was entitled to the assistance of counsel during the photographic lineup. Second, he argued that the photographic lineup was impermissibly suggestive in violation of his Fourteenth Amendment right of due process. How should the trial court rule? Compare People v. Kurylczyk, 505 N.W.2d 528 (Mich. 1993).

C. OTHER REMEDIES FOR IMPROPER IDENTIFICATION PROCEDURES

As we have seen, one remedy for improper pretrial identification procedures is the exclusion at trial of any evidence of the pretrial identification, along with the possible exclusion of any at-trial identification based on the earlier procedure. But the exclusion remedy is extreme. Recall that identifications tend to be important to the prosecution in cases charging very serious crimes such as rape and robbery. Perhaps for this reason, courts invoke the remedy in only a small number of cases. Whatever problems might be present with the identification procedure, courts have concluded most of the time that the improper identification method was a "harmless error" of sorts—that it did not cause the witness to make an improper identification.

In sum, the exclusion remedy is available to very few defendants who have legitimate complaints about improper identification procedures. Is there some way other than exclusion for these defendants to reduce the chances of an erroneous conviction?

1. Jury Instructions

The following case considers the need for a jury instruction that highlights the difficulties of cross-racial identifications. Will jury instructions of the sort described in this opinion actually change juror conduct?

■ **STATE v. BRYAN ALLEN**
294 P.3d 679 (Wash. 2013)

C. JOHNSON, J.

. . . ¶2 Gerald Kovacs, who is white, was walking near the University of Washington at dusk when he was approached by two young African American men who offered to sell Kovacs marijuana. Irritated, he told them to "Fuck off." The men screamed and cursed Kovacs, and then followed him. One of the men told Kovacs, "I'm going to kill you, you Bitch," and lifted up his shirt to display what Kovacs believed to be a gun. Kovacs ran to the nearest gas station and called the police.

¶3 During the 911 call, Kovacs described the man with the gun as an African American in his mid-20s, wearing a black hooded sweatshirt, a hat, and big, gold-framed sunglasses. Kovacs also described the man as being around 5'9" and between 210-220 pounds. He described the other man as an African American in his teens, around 5'5", wearing a "red kind of shirt," though he could not remember the color exactly. Several minutes later, based on Kovacs' description, a University of Washington patrol officer attempted to stop two African American men near the scene of the crime. One of the men, wearing a white T-shirt, fled. The other, Bryan Allen, did not. Seattle City Police detained Allen and Kovacs was transported to the location of the arrest for a show-up identification procedure. Though Allen matched Kovacs' description of the man with the gun as to race, clothing, hat, and sunglasses, physically he was larger at 6'1" and 280 pounds. Kovacs identified Allen as the man who threatened him. The police searched Allen incident to arrest but found no gun, marijuana, or cash.

¶4 The State charged Allen with felony harassment. Prior to trial, Allen requested the court to instruct the jury regarding cross-racial identifications.[1] The court refused Allen's request. No expert testimony on the reliability of cross-racial eyewitness testimony was given at trial. The only testimony given on the subject was by Officer Bennett, the officer in charge of directing the show-up identification, who, on cross-examination, agreed that he was "aware of studies suggesting that cross-racial identifications can be more difficult for people." . . . Allen's defense counsel, in closing argument, challenged the reliability of such evidence. . . . The jury found Allen guilty. . . .

¶7 Concerns and discussions over the reliability of eyewitness identifications, and more specifically cross-racial eyewitness identifications, have arisen in cases for some time. . . . The United States District Court for the District of Columbia, in United States v. Telfaire, 469 F.2d 552 (D.D.C. 1972) . . . discussed the importance of, and need for, a special instruction on the issue of identification in order to safe-guard the presumption of innocence. The court in *Telfaire* crafted a special identification instruction for use in future cases, to specifically instruct the jury to assess the value of eyewitness testimony based on several considerations. [The *Telfaire* instruction asks the jury to consider whether the witness had the capacity and opportunity to observe the offender, whether the identification made by the witness subsequent to the offense was the product of his or her own recollection, whether the witness

---

1. Allen proposed two identification instructions. The first stated: "In this case, the identifying witness is of a different race than the defendant. In the experience of many, it is more difficult to identify members of a different race than members of one's own. Psychological studies support this impression. In addition, laboratory studies reveal that even people with no prejudice against other races and substantial contact with persons of other races still experience difficulty in accurately identifying members of a different race. Quite often people do not recognize this difficulty in themselves. You should consider these facts in evaluating the witness's testimony, but you must also consider whether there are other factors present in this case that overcome any such difficulty of identification."

The second proposed instruction mirrored an instruction endorsed by the American Bar Association, and stated: "In this case, the defendant, Bryan Allen, is of a different race than Gerald Kovacs, the witness who has identified him. You may consider, if you think it is appropriate to do so, whether the fact that the defendant is of a different race than the witness has affected the accuracy of the [witness's] original perception or the accuracy of a later identification. You should consider that in ordinary human experience, some people may have greater difficulty in accurately identifying members of a different race than they do in identifying members of their own race. You may also consider whether there are other factors present in this case which overcome any such difficulty of identification."

made an inconsistent identification, and the credibility of the witness.] This model instruction did not specifically address cross-racial eyewitness identification; however, in his concurring opinion, Chief Judge Bazelon urged that juries be charged specifically on the pitfalls of cross-racial identification and also proposed sample instruction language.

¶8 After *Telfaire*, jurisdictions have developed three general approaches to address the problems perceived to be inherent in eyewitness identification testimony. Some have accepted the rationale underlying *Telfaire* and have required or encouraged a particularized instruction to be given. See People v. Wright, 755 P.2d 1049 (Calif. 1988) (approving a condensed *Telfaire*-type instruction and requiring that such an instruction be given when requested in a case in which identification is a central issue and there is little corroborative evidence).

¶9 In other jurisdictions, the decision has been left up to the discretion of the trial court. See Wallace v. State, 701 S.E.2d 554 (Ga. App. 2010) (holding the trial court did not abuse its discretion in refusing the defendant's requested jury instruction on the reliability of cross-racial eyewitness identification where, by general instructions, the jury was informed that it was required to determine whether the eyewitness identification was sufficiently reliable to help satisfy the State's burden of proof and other corroborating evidence existed).

¶10 The final approach adopted by some jurisdictions has been to reject outright a requirement for *Telfaire*-like instructions. The courts in these jurisdictions have held that the other general instructions on witness credibility and the government's burden of proof are adequate and/or that the identification instructions impermissibly comment on the evidence. See Nevius v. State, 699 P.2d 1053 (Nev. 1985).

¶11 Our cases suggest we have aligned somewhere between the second and third categories mentioned above. . .

¶12 In State v. Jordan, 564 P.2d 340 (Wash. App. 1977), the Court of Appeals reviewed a *Telfaire*-type instruction and held the trial judge did not err in rejecting the instruction. In that case the court recognized "the focus and emphasis of the instruction is upon the credibility of identification witnesses. . . . Witness credibility is more properly tested by examination and cross-examination in the forum of the trial court." . . .

¶14 Allen argues our case law . . . is outdated. He argues the scientific data regarding the unreliability of eyewitness identification, and of cross-racial eyewitness identification in particular, is now irrefutable. [The] State does not provide contrary evidence or research nor seriously question the scientific data relied upon by Allen. Based on this data, Allen asks us to adopt a rule of general application, founded in notions of due process, that in cases involving cross-racial eyewitness identification it is reversible error to fail to instruct on cross-racial identification when requested. Allen argues the world has changed, and we must change along with it. We are not convinced, however, that the constitutionality of our case law on this issue has changed.

¶15 A problem with the studies Allen relies upon is that none of them support the conclusion that the giving of a cautionary cross-racial identification instruction solves the purported unreliability of cross-racial eyewitness identification, any more than would cross-examination, expert evidence, or arguments to the jury. As the Supreme Court has recognized, the United States Constitution "protects a defendant against a conviction based on evidence of questionable reliability . . . by affording the defendant means to persuade the jury that the evidence should be discounted as unworthy of credit." Perry v. New Hampshire, 132 S. Ct. 716 (2012). In *Perry*, the Supreme Court addressed the issue of whether due process requires judicial inquiry into the reliability of a suggestive eyewitness identification that was not the result of police arrangement, and held it does not. As part of its analysis, the Court listed safeguards, built into our adversary system, that caution juries against placing undue weight on eyewitness testimony of questionable reliability, including the right to confront witnesses, the right to counsel, eyewitness jury instructions adopted by many federal and state courts, expert evidence, the government's burden to prove guilt beyond a reasonable doubt, and state rules of evidence. Many of these safeguards were at work in Allen's trial.

¶16 For example, a defendant has a right to effective assistance of counsel, who can expose the unreliability in [eyewitness's] testimony during cross-examination and focus the jury's attention on the fallibility of eyewitness identification during opening and closing arguments. Allen's counsel did just that. On cross-examination he questioned Kovacs regarding his mental state during the encounter, regarding the time of day the encounter took place (dusk), and regarding the discrepancy between Allen's actual height and weight, and the description Kovacs gave the 911 dispatcher. Allen's counsel also questioned Officer Bennett regarding the potential suggestiveness of show-up identifications, the problems associated with cross-racial identifications, and the lack of other witnesses to the crime. Then, in closing argument, Allen's counsel discussed how emotion and stress can affect the reliability of identifications, and discussed the risk of police influence on identifications. He further discussed the "dangers of cross-racial identification" and explained how cross-racial identification may have impacted this case.

¶17 The requirement that the State prove a defendant's guilt beyond a reasonable doubt also protects against convictions based on dubious identification evidence. The jury in Allen's case was instructed on the State's burden of proof and on witness credibility generally. Taken together, these instructions charged the jury with deciding whether the State has proven beyond a reasonable doubt that Kovacs correctly identified Allen as the man with the gun. In conjunction with competent defense counsel, the instructions focused the jury's attention to the issue of identification and the reliability of Kovacs' testimony. . . .

¶ 19 Applying that standard, we find no abuse of discretion here. Providing a cautionary cross-racial identification instruction would not have added to the safeguards operating in Allen's case, a case involving an eyewitness identification based on general physique, apparel, and sunglasses, and not on facial features. During the 911 call, Kovacs described the man with the gun by approximate age, height, and weight. Beyond these general characteristics, Kovacs' description was limited to the man's apparel: "black hoodie," "jeans," "baseball cap," and "big sunglasses" with "gold on the frames." . . . Kovacs did not make an in-court identification of Allen. In fact, Kovacs testified Allen looked different at trial because he was not wearing the same clothes. Thus, Kovacs did not base the identification on facial features, specific physical characteristics, or merely the fact that Allen is African American. . . .

¶21 We decline to adopt a general rule requiring the giving of a cross-racial instruction in cases where cross-racial identification is at issue, and the trial court did not abuse its discretion by refusing to give a cautionary cross-racial jury instruction under the facts of this case. . . .

MADSEN, C.J., concurring.

¶ 31 [I agree] that the trial court did not abuse its discretion in this case because there was no indication that Gerald Kovacs' identification of Bryan Allen was based upon facial features or other specific physical characteristics beyond the mere fact that Allen is African American.

¶32 I write separately because I believe in a hypothetical case where a victim makes a cross-racial identification based on a suspect's facial features, hair, or other physical characteristic implicating race, a trial judge likely would abuse his or her discretion if he or she refused to provide a cross-racial identification instruction. The dissent properly recognizes that cross-examination, expert testimony, and closing argument may not provide sufficient safeguards against cross-racial misidentification because the very nature of the problem is that witnesses believe their identification is accurate. . . .

¶33 However, the dissent's concerns are misplaced in this case. The identification here simply did not implicate the type of physical characteristics that give rise to erroneous cross-racial identifications or the need for an instruction. Besides reporting the suspect to be African American, Kovacs described the man in race-neutral terms: mid-20s; about 5'9" in height and 210-220 pounds; wearing a black hooded sweatshirt, dark blue jeans, big gold-framed sunglasses, and a dark baseball cap; and possessing a gun. When asked by the 911 operator if the man had any facial hair, Kovacs responded vaguely, "Not that I remember," signaling a lack of attention to facial features. At trial, when Kovacs described how he identified Allen as the man who had threatened him, he referred to Allen's hat, clothes, and sunglasses. Indeed, Kovacs did not even mention Allen's facial features, hair, or other physical characteristics. While one might infer from Kovacs' estimate of the older suspect's age and the lengthy encounter between Kovacs and both suspects that Kovacs must have considered facial features at some point, this would be purely speculative. Instead, the record in this case supports the lead opinion's conclusion that the identification here was based primarily on race-neutral factors.

¶34 Therefore, I agree with the lead opinion that the trial court did not abuse its discretion when it refused to give an instruction on cross-racial identification in this case. . . .

WIGGINS, J., dissenting.

. . . ¶41 I agree with the lead opinion that we need not adopt an across-the-board rule requiring a cross-racial identification instruction in every case potentially raising the issue. But courts should be required to give an instruction where eyewitness identification is a central issue in a case, there is little evidence corroborating the identification, and the defendant specifically asks for an instruction. . . .

¶42 When all relevant facts are taken into account, it is plain that this is precisely the factual scenario calling for a jury instruction on the dangers of cross-racial identification. Consider the facts:

1. The case involved a cross-racial identification of a black suspect by a white victim, the racial combination accounting for most identification errors.

2. There is barely any evidence corroborating the identification of the State's witness, Gerald Kovacs:

   a. The person who was with Bryan Allen when he was stopped did not match the description of the armed suspect's companion.

b. Allen himself did not match Kovacs' description, being four or five inches taller and 60 pounds heavier than Kovacs' description.

c. No gun, weapon, or other item that could be mistaken for a gun was found on Allen.

d. No drugs or other evidence were recovered on Allen to corroborate Kovacs' claim that Allen was selling drugs.

3. The identification occurred under circumstances calling its accuracy into question.

a. The incident occurred at dusk, limiting Kovacs' ability to identify the suspect.

b. A weapon was involved, making it harder for Kovacs to accurately identify the suspect due to "weapon focus."

c. The suspect wore a cap and sunglasses. The use of disguises compromises identification accuracy.

d. The identification was based in part on the cap and sunglasses, which the police required Allen to wear for the show-up so that he more closely resembled the suspect. The police also instructed Allen to pull his cap low over his face before the showup. . . .

¶46 The lead opinion . . . suggests that cross-examination, expert testimony, and closing argument sufficiently guard against the problem. But cross-examination is a useless tool for educating jurors about cross-racial bias. The very nature of the cross-racial problem is that witnesses are unaware of it; witnesses believe their identification is accurate, making traditional impeachment methods inadequate for ferreting out the truth. Social science confirms this logic: studies show that cross-examination fails to increase juror sensitivity to the inaccuracy of eyewitness testimony.

¶47 Nor is expert testimony a practical solution. Expert testimony seems like a natural way to educate jurors about cross-racial bias, except that it is far too costly. Experts are both scarce and expensive. Most felony defendants in state court are indigent, and public defenders cannot afford to pay expert fees either. This being the case, expert testimony for all defendants is not a solution but a pipe dream.

¶48 Likewise, it is a hollow exercise to educate jurors about faulty cross-racial identification in closing argument where an attorney has been deprived of the raw materials integral to building an effective defense. Without evidence or some other form of authority, it is difficult to imagine why jurors would believe defense counsel's unsupported assertions about cross-racial identification.

¶49 The lead opinion also argues that a reasonable doubt instruction safeguards against the dangers of cross-racial identification, but I do not see how this can be. The implication here seems to be that since the State's burden of proof is so high in a criminal case, it is not harmful to permit the State to use inaccurate and misleading evidence. . . .

¶51 The lead opinion is also mistaken in assuming that a jury instruction on the inaccuracy of cross-racial identifications is unhelpful. Jury instructions are in many ways an ideal way to deal with this disparity; the heart of the problem is that jurors believe cross-racial identification is equally or more accurate than same-race identification, when in fact it is far less accurate. Thus, educating jurors is precisely what is called for. Consider the benefits of a jury instruction. First, it costs nothing. Second, jury instructions are focused, concise, and authoritative (jurors hear them from a trial judge, not from a witness called by one side). Third, a jury instruction avoids the problem of dueling experts and eliminates the risk of an expert invading the jury's role or opining on an eyewitness's credibility. Fourth, jurors may be more likely to discuss racial differences and the cross-racial problem in deliberation if bolstered by the credibility of an instruction.

¶52 There are benefits beyond the juror box as well. For the courts to recognize that cross-racial eyewitness identification is frequently erroneous would encourage police and prosecutors to approach these identifications cautiously when making charging and investigative decisions. . . . For example, law enforcement personnel might try to find more corroborating evidence where the only link between a suspect and a crime is a cross-racial identification. . . .

¶53 Once the lead opinion's false assumptions are cleared away, little reason remains to reject the palliative measure proposed by the petitioners. I would embrace a version of the rule adopted in other jurisdictions, holding that a court must give the instruction where cross-racial eyewitness identification is a central issue in the case, where there is little corroborating evidence, and where the defendant asks for the instruction. . . .

Notes

1. *Jury instructions about eyewitness testimony: majority position.* Judicial instructions to the jury can remind jurors about the vagaries of human memory. Such instructions are sometimes called *Telfaire* instructions, after one of the first cases to approve of their use. See United States v. Telfaire, 469 F.2d 552 (D.C. Cir. 1972) (describing a suggested jury instruction). About 30 states allow (but do not require) the trial judge to grant a request for such jury instructions. More than a dozen states do require jury instructions, at least when there is some special reason to question the identification. See State v. Cabagbag, 277 P.3d 1027 (Haw. 2012); State v. Ledbetter, 881 A.2d 290 (Conn. 2005) (under supervisory power, court requires jury instructions whenever police fail to tell witness that suspect might not be present in the lineup).

2. *Cross-racial identifications.* Unfortunately, there is some truth to the distasteful phrase, "They [people of another race] all look alike." Research studies over the years have found an empirical basis for saying that people of one race find it more difficult to identify people of another race. A witness's difficulty in making such identifications seems to be tied to unfamiliarity: People who have more regular contact with those of another race have less difficulty making such identifications. The so-called own-race bias accounts for about 15 percent of the variation in the ability of witnesses to identify another person. See Christian A. Meissner & John C. Brigham, Eyewitness Identification: Thirty Years of Investigating the Own-Race Bias in Memory for Faces: A Meta-Analytic Review, 7 Psychol. Pub. Pol'y & L. 3 (2001).

A few courts have held that specialized jury instructions are required if the defense requests the instruction in a case that places particular weight on a cross-racial identification. See People v. Boone, 91 N.E.3d 1194 (N.Y. 2017); cf. Smith v. State, 880 A.2d 288 (Md. 2005) (defense counsel must be free to argue to jury about special difficulties of cross-racial identification). However, several other states prohibit the use of such instructions as an interference with the jurors' duty to evaluate the evidence for themselves. See Graham v. Commonwealth, 459 S.E.2d

97 (Va. 1995). If jury instructions provide enough specific information about the circumstances that tend to produce less reliable eyewitness testimony, are they an adequate replacement for exclusion?

2. Expert Testimony and Other Remedies

Another possible remedy for improper identification procedures would permit parties to introduce expert testimony about eyewitness identification. Courts increasingly allow judges to permit such testimony—and leave it within their discretion whether to do so. Rules of evidence generally require that such expert testimony should help jurors "understand the evidence or to determine a fact in issue," be "based on sufficient facts or data," be "the product of reliable principles and methods," and reliably apply these principles and methods to the facts of the case. See Fed. R. Evid. 702.

Judges could also exclude eyewitness identification unless it is corroborated by other evidence; prosecutors might account for the risks of eyewitness identification when charging the defendant or when negotiating the outcome of the case. How do these remedies compare in terms of their potential to prevent wrongful convictions? In terms of their costs to enforcing the criminal law?

Problem 9-3. Help for the Jury

One night around 3:00 A.M., university students Jonathan Ghitis and Kristina Leone were walking on the street in a residential area, where several lampposts lined the street. Two men walked toward the students. As the men approached the couple, one of them moved to the side and flashed a silver handgun, approximately 6–8 inches long. Leone began to scream. The man with the handgun threw her to the ground and ordered her to be quiet. At the same time, the second man threw Ghitis down onto steps of a nearby residence. The men demanded whatever property the victims had. Leone immediately gave them her pocketbook, and Ghitis handed them his wallet, watch, and cell phone. Leone continued to cry and scream, so the man with the gun repeatedly struck her on the back of her head with his gun. He also ordered Ghitis to calm Leone, which he did. The two men fled the scene.

At 3:30 A.M., after calling the police, both victims gave their account of the events and described their assailant to a detective with the University Police Department. They met with the detective at headquarters three hours later. There, the detective separated the victims and showed three separate photo arrays of individuals who had similar characteristics. Leone looked at the first array and told the detective that she could not recognize anyone. Upon viewing the second array, Leone immediately identified Benjamin Walker as her assailant, viscerally reacting to his picture. Leone was shown a third array, which included an individual the police suspected was Walker's co-conspirator, but she could not identify him. Leone spent three to four minutes looking at the arrays. The detective did not comment to her as to whether Walker was a suspect after she made her identification. The police conducted the same procedure with Ghitis. He pointed out Walker from the array but was less than 100 percent positive. Again, the detective did not comment to Ghitis whether Walker was the suspect after he made his identification. The sole evidence connecting Walker to the robberies was eyewitness identification by the victims.

Walker was arrested and charged with robbery and related charges. Walker filed a pretrial motion in limine to present the expert testimony of Dr. Solomon Fulero regarding the fallibility of human memory, the science as to human recall, and scientific studies related to the reliability of eyewitness testimony generally. The court denied the motion. After trial, the jury found Walker guilty of five charges relating to the robbery of the two students.

How could expert testimony have helped Walker? On what grounds might the trial court have denied the motions? On appeal, what arguments could Walker make in requesting the appellate court to reverse the lower court's decision? See Commonwealth v. Walker, 92 A.3d 766 (Pa. 2014).

Notes

1. *Admissibility of expert testimony on eyewitness memory.* Starting in the 1980s, a few defendants asked courts to allow experts to testify about recurring problems with witness memory. At first, very few courts allowed those experts to testify. Since then, the trend has been toward allowing such testimony. The high state courts addressing this question fall into several different groups. Appellate courts in fewer than 10 states still instruct trial courts that such expert testimony is not admissible in the ordinary criminal case because it invades the province of the jury. Most appellate courts (over 30 states) now allow the trial court the discretion to admit or exclude the testimony. See State v. Guilbert, 49 A.3d 705 (Conn. 2012); State v. Clopten, 223 P.3d 1103 (Utah 2009) (expert testimony regarding the reliability of eyewitness identification is admissible under the general standard that governs all expert testimony). There are still a few appellate courts that will overturn a trial court's decision to exclude such testimony as an abuse of discretion. Under what circumstances might a court conclude that such testimony is necessary to a fair trial? See People v. LeGrand, 867 N.E.2d 374 (N.Y. 2007) (it can be an abuse of discretion for the trial court to exclude expert testimony about "weapon focus" if guilt or innocence turns on accuracy of eyewitness identifications and there is little or no corroborating evidence connecting defendant to the crime).

2. *The expert's role.* The rules of evidence in every jurisdiction place limits on the use of opinion evidence, including the testimony of expert witnesses. Under Rule 702 of the Federal Rules of Evidence (and comparable language typically found in state court evidence rules), a qualified expert can testify in the form of an opinion only if the expert's specialized knowledge "will help the trier of fact to understand the evidence or to determine a fact in issue." The expert cannot "invade the province of the jury" by offering an opinion about some matter that a juror could decide based on common experience, such as the resemblance between the defendant and a photo of the perpetrator taken from a nearby surveillance camera.

3. *The experts on expert testimony.* Social scientists have concluded that there is a great need for expert testimony about eyewitness identifications. Studies of jurors have indicated (with the usual ambiguity of social science studies) that jurors (1) place great weight on eyewitness testimony as they deliberate and reach their verdicts and (2) often have misconceptions about the reliability of eyewitness testimony and the conditions that pose the greatest risks for misidentification. See Brian

Cutler, Steven Penrod & Hedy Dexter, Juror Sensitivity to Eyewitness Identification Evidence, 14 Law & Hum. Behav. 185 (1990) (study showing jurors remain unaffected by factors that should influence accuracy of witness's memory); but cf. Rogers Elliott, Beth Farrington & Holly Manheimer, Eyewitnesses Credible and Discredible, 18 J. Appl. Soc. Psychol. 1411 (1988) (recounts difficulty in replicating early studies showing that jurors rely heavily on eyewitness testimony). Social scientists are split on the question of whether expert testimony can correct juror misconceptions about eyewitness memory without affecting their overall willingness to believe eyewitness testimony. Compare Brian L. Cutler, Steven D. Penrod & Hedy Red Dexter, The Eyewitness, the Expert Psychologist, and the Jury, 13 Law & Hum. Behav. 311 (1989), with E. B. Ebbesen & V. J. Konecni, Eyewitness Memory Research: Probative v. Prejudicial Value, 5 Expert Evidence 2-28 (1997) (prejudicial outweighs probative value).

4. *Corroboration.* Would it make sense to exclude identification evidence—regardless of any violations of due process or right to counsel—unless there is independent evidence to corroborate the identification evidence? See Regina v. Turnbull, [1977] 1 Q.B. 224 (1976):

> When, in the judgment of the trial judge, the quality of the identifying evidence is poor, as for example when it depends solely on a fleeting glance or on a longer observation made in difficult conditions, [the] judge should then withdraw the case from the jury and direct an acquittal unless there is other evidence which goes to support the correctness of the identification. [For] example, X sees the accused snatch a woman's handbag; he gets only a fleeting glance of the thief's face as he runs off but he does see him entering a nearby house. [Although this is poor identification evidence, the judge need not withdraw the case from the jury] if there was evidence that the house into which the accused was alleged by X to have run was his father's.

In the United States, no state has adopted a general corroboration requirement for eyewitness testimony. However, as Sandra Guerra Thompson explains, such a requirement does exist with respect to perjury charges:

> [The] federal criminal perjury statute does include a requirement of two witnesses or one witness with sufficient corroborating evidence. According to one author, the two-witness rule for perjury is "deeply rooted in past centuries, and is designed to prevent a defendant from being convicted on the strength of his oath versus that of another." Numerous state statutes also contain provisions requiring two witnesses, sometimes including the option of corroborating testimony, for convictions of perjury.

Thompson notes that corroboration requirements have been used in other areas of criminal procedure (for example, to support accomplice testimony or confessions) where the reliability of the evidence is considered weak. How might a corroboration requirement work with respect to eyewitness testimony? See Sandra Guerra Thompson, Beyond a Reasonable Doubt? Reconsidering Uncorroborated Eyewitness Identification Testimony, 41 U.C. Davis L. Rev. 1487, 1535 (2008).

5. *Prosecutors as the cure.* Is the prosecutor's power to decline to file charges against a defendant the ultimate remedy for weak identification evidence? Do prosecutors have adequate incentives and ability to screen out cases with the most questionable eyewitness-identification evidence? When Samuel Gross studied the

records available in a large number of misidentification cases, he reached the following conclusions:

> (1) More often than not, a misidentified defendant was originally suspected because of his appearance. (2) A misidentified defendant is more likely to be cleared before his case comes to trial than after. (3) If he is not exonerated before trial, a misidentified defendant will almost certainly go to trial rather than plead guilty, even in return for an attractive plea bargain. (4) A misidentified defendant who is convicted at trial may still be exonerated, but the chances decrease over time.

Gross, Loss of Innocence: Eyewitness Identification and Proof of Guilt, 16 J. Legal Stud. 395 (1987). See also Heather D. Flowe, Amrita Mehta & Ebbe B. Ebbesen, The Role of Eyewitness Identification Evidence in Felony Case Dispositions, 17 Psychol. Pub. Pol'y & L. 140 (2011) (examining role of eyewitness identification evidence in felony issuing decisions in one large district attorney's office); Kathy Pezdek & Matthew O'Brien, Plea Bargaining and Appraisals of Eyewitness Evidence by Prosecutors and Defense Attorneys, 20 Psychology, Crime & Law 222 (2013) (finding that prosecutors and defense attorneys generally agreed on the influence that different eyewitness identification factors have on the case and that the strength of eyewitness identification evidence affected plea bargaining decisions of both prosecutors and defense attorneys).

Problem 9-4. Videorecorded Lineups

At 2:20 A.M., a man entered a gas station and asked Roy Beals, the attendant, for permission to use the telephone. He was followed by a second man, holding what appeared to be a .45-caliber automatic pistol, and by a third man, whom Beals was unable to see. The three men robbed the gas station. Beals told police after the robbery that the gunman was approximately 5'6" or 5'7" tall, and wore a knee-length brown vinyl coat, with a fleecy lining and collar. From the loose fit of the coat, Beals assumed the man was thin. The man wore what appeared to be uniform pants and a security guard's cap, with a badge, and had a second badge pinned on his collar. The fleecy coat collar was turned up around the man's face, and the bill of his cap came down to his eyebrows. Beals was therefore able to observe only a portion of the man's face. From his observation, Beals (who was white) could tell that the gunman was a black man and that he was not wearing glasses. He could not describe the man's hair or estimate his age.

The gunman told Beals to turn around, go into a back room, and lie face down on the floor. Following Beals into the backroom, the gunman then asked where "the money" was. Beals answered that the money was in a locked box on a post outside. The man demanded a key, but Beals did not have one. At one point, the gunman struck him with the weapon he was carrying. The robbers were in the station for about five minutes, and Beals spent most of this time face down on the floor.

Later that same day, the police stopped a car containing four young black men, including Oscar McMillian. The four occupants of the car were taken into custody. At some point, the police staged a lineup, consisting of these four men, in connection with the investigation of an unrelated crime, a purse-snatching. The lineup was recorded on videotape with an audio recording of the men speaking. No attorney was present at this lineup.

Several days later, McMillian was charged with armed robbery. Soon thereafter, the police showed the videotaped lineup to Beals. McMillian was given no notice that Beals was to view the recorded lineup, and defense counsel was not present at the viewing.

Based on the defendant's height, build, and voice, Beals identified McMillian as the gunman in the gas station robbery. Beals explained that he made the visual identification of McMillian by comparing McMillian's height with that of another man in the lineup, whom Beals recognized as the first robber, who had asked to use the telephone. The relative heights of the defendant and this man corresponded to the relative heights of the robbers, Beals said. At trial, however, Beals was shown a photograph of the men in the lineup and was unable to positively identify the first robber, whose height he had used in identifying the defendant.

Imagine you are McMillian's defense attorney. What actions *could* you take to contest the eyewitness identification of your client? Which of these actions *would* you take? As a matter of litigation strategy, does the timing of your objection affect the chances of success for your client? Compare McMillian v. State, 265 N.W.2d 553 (Wis. 1978).

D. PREVENTING MISTAKEN IDENTIFICATION

The previous sections focused on court-imposed limits on identification procedures. Court intervention occurs after an identification procedure has concluded, and a defendant is claiming that the identification violated his right to counsel or due process. Accordingly, courts are limited to remedying the problems in the identification process through exclusion, expert testimony, or jury instructions. They can only hope that the remedy will lead police departments to reform identification procedures in response. By contrast, the legislative and executive branches can directly regulate identification procedures and enact safeguards to prevent mistaken eyewitness identifications. This section reviews some state and federal efforts in this regard.

Read the Texas statute and the Department of Justice policy reprinted below and consider whether they do enough to prevent mistaken identifications. Or do they attempt too much? If you could amend the provisions, what changes would you make?

■ TEXAS CODE OF CRIMINAL PROCEDURE
Article 38.20

Sec. 3. (a) Each law enforcement agency shall adopt, implement, and as necessary amend a detailed written policy regarding the administration of photograph and live lineup identification procedures in accordance with this article. A law enforcement agency may adopt [a model policy developed at Sam Houston State University in consultation with law enforcement agencies and scientific experts, or] the agency's own policy that, at a minimum, conforms to the requirements of Subsection (c). . . .

(c) The . . . policy adopted by a law enforcement agency under Subsection (a) must:

(1) be based on:

(A) credible field, academic, or laboratory research on eyewitness memory;

(B) relevant policies, guidelines, and best practices designed to reduce erroneous eyewitness identifications and to enhance the reliability and objectivity of eyewitness identifications; and

(C) other relevant information as appropriate; and

(2) include the following information regarding evidence-based practices:

(A) procedures for selecting photograph and live lineup filler photographs or participants to ensure that the photographs or participants:

(i) are consistent in appearance with the description of the alleged perpetrator; and

(ii) do not make the suspect noticeably stand out;

(B) instructions given to a witness before conducting a photograph or live lineup identification procedure that must include a statement that the person who committed the offense may or may not be present in the procedure;

(C) procedures for documenting and preserving the results of a photograph or live lineup identification procedure, including the documentation of witness statements, regardless of the outcome of the procedure;

(D) procedures for administering a photograph or live lineup identification procedure to an illiterate person or a person with limited English language proficiency;

(E) for a live lineup identification procedure, if practicable, procedures for assigning an administrator who is unaware of which member of the live lineup is the suspect in the case or alternative procedures designed to prevent opportunities to influence the witness;

(F) for a photograph identification procedure, procedures for assigning an administrator who is capable of administering a photograph array in a blind manner or in a manner consistent with other proven or supported best practices designed to prevent opportunities to influence the witness; and

(G) any other procedures or best practices supported by credible research or commonly accepted as a means to reduce erroneous eyewitness identifications and to enhance the objectivity and reliability of eyewitness identifications.

(d) A witness who makes an identification based on a photograph or live lineup identification procedure shall be asked immediately after the procedure to state, in the witness's own words, how confident the witness is in making the identification. A law enforcement agency shall document in accordance with Subsection (c)(2)(C) any statement made under this subsection. . . .

Sec. 5. (a) Any evidence or expert testimony presented by the state or the defendant on the subject of eyewitness identification is admissible only subject to compliance with the Texas Rules of Evidence. Except as provided by Subsection (c), evidence of compliance with the model policy or any other policy adopted under this article is not a condition precedent to the admissibility of an out-of-court eyewitness identification.

(b) [Except] as provided by Subsection (c), a failure to conduct a photograph or live lineup identification procedure in substantial compliance with the model policy or any other policy adopted under this article does not bar the admission of eyewitness identification testimony in the courts of this state.

(c) If a witness who has previously made an out-of-court photograph or live lineup identification of the accused makes an in-court identification of the accused, the eyewitness identification is admissible into evidence against the accused only if the evidence is accompanied by the details of each prior photograph or live lineup identification made of the accused by the witness, including the manner in which the identification procedure was conducted.

■ U.S. DEPARTMENT OF JUSTICE, OFFICE OF JUSTICE PROGRAMS

Eyewitness Evidence: A Trainer's Manual for Law Enforcement
September 2003, NCJ 188678

FIELD IDENTIFICATION PROCEDURE (SHOWUP)

A. Conducting Showups . . .

Procedure: When conducting a showup, the investigator should—

1. Determine and document, prior to the showup, a description of the perpetrator.
2. Consider transporting the witness to the location of the detained suspect to limit the legal impact of the suspect's detention. There are likely to be legal restrictions concerning trans-porting suspects to the scene. . . . Other issues that may be involved with bringing the suspect to the scene include potential contamination of the scene or exposure to media or multiple witnesses.
3. When multiple witnesses are involved [separate] witnesses and request that they avoid discussing details of the incident with other witnesses. Witnesses should not hear others' accounts because they may be influenced by that information. If a positive identification is obtained from one witness, consider using other identification procedures (e.g., lineup or photo array) for remaining witnesses. Because showups can be considered inherently suggestive, once an identification is obtained at a showup and probable cause for arrest has been achieved, less suggestive procedures can be used with other witnesses to obtain their identifications.
4. Caution the witness that the person he/she is looking at may or may not be the perpetrator. This instruction to the witness can lessen the pressure on the witness to make an identification solely to please the investigator or because the witness feels it is his/her duty to do so. The investigator should assure the witness that the investigation will continue regard-less of whether an identification is obtained at the showup. Keep in mind that it is just as important to clear innocent parties; a nonidentification can help to refocus the investigation.
5. Obtain and document a statement of certainty for both identifications and nonidentifications. It can be helpful to have some indication of how certain

the witness is at the time of an identification (or nonidentification). This can be useful in assessing the likelihood of whether or not the identification is accurate. Later, the witness's certainty might be influenced by other factors. It is not necessary for the witness to give a number to express his/her certainty. Some witnesses will spontaneously include information about certainty (e.g., "That's him, I KNOW that's him," or, "It could be him"). If the witness does not volunteer information about certainty, then the witness can be asked to state certainty in his/her own words. A question such as, "How do you know this individual?" will often lead the witness to express his/her certainty. If a statement of certainty is not obtained, then the investigator can follow up with the question, "How certain are you?" . . .

B. Recording Showup Results . . .

Procedure: When conducting a showup, the investigator should—

1. Document the time and location of the procedure.
2. Record both identification and nonidentification results in writing, including the witness's own words regarding how certain he/she is. . . .

Notes

1. *Statutory limits on lineups.* For many years, few jurisdictions passed statutes or court rules addressing the use of identification procedures by police. Exonerations based on DNA evidence, however, pointed to identification procedures as a major source of errors in criminal justice and convinced many state legislatures to address the question. The Texas statute reprinted above is an example of this trend. North Carolina also adopted a statute that lays out "warning" statements to be given to witnesses before making identification and requires extensive documentation of identification procedures used during investigation. North Carolina General Statutes §15A-284.52. For other legislative developments in this field, see the web extension for this chapter at *http://www.crimpro.com/extension/ch09.* How do legislatures compare to state appellate courts as the institution to take the lead in changing identification procedures? See Sandra Guerra Thompson, Eyewitness Identifications and State Courts as Guardians Against Wrongful Conviction, 7 Ohio St. J. Crim. Law 603 (2010).

2. *Delegated monitoring of best practices.* The best practices as indicated in the research in applied psychology are always shifting. The Texas statute reprinted above calls for biannual review and revision of the state's "model" policy by the Bill Blackwood Law Enforcement Management Institute of Texas located at Sam Houston State University. The policy also instructs the Institute to create and revise training materials connected to the model policy. Why didn't the Texas legislature reserve for itself the power to revisit the model policy every two years? What advantages does an administrative agency (or an institute located in a state university) have over a legislature in developing policies for identification procedures?

3. *Executive guidelines and policies.* While legislatures have been reluctant to impose detailed requirements on law enforcement identification practices, law

enforcement agencies have promulgated extensive guidelines and policies of their own. The Department of Justice set the standard with its Guide (and later Manual) for Law Enforcement. The New Jersey Attorney General adopted many of the specific recommendations from the U.S. Department of Justice in connection with photo identifications, and required all state-controlled law enforcement agencies in the state to follow those guidelines. In most instances, however, individual law enforcement agencies create their own guidance documents, sometimes based on the standards and ideas from the national or state level.

4. *Best practices during lineups.* The most important policies deal with field identifications and photo lineups, because investigators rely on those techniques more often than on live lineups. Over 94 percent of all law enforcement agencies use photo lineups, but only 35 percent of agencies have adopted written policies about the construction or administration of photo lineups. See Police Executive Research Forum, A National Survey of Eyewitness Identification Procedures in Law Enforcement Agencies (NIJ Grant No. 2010-IJ-CX0032, 2013).

The extensive academic research on the subject of eyewitness testimony produces a long list of possible improvements to current police practices. The U.S. Department of Justice sponsored a Technical Working Group that published the recommended practices (a portion of the document is reprinted above). Under those guidelines, witnesses should be told that the perpetrator "may or may not be present" in the lineup. Research indicates that this latter instruction greatly decreases the number of false positives. See Gary L. Wells, Police Lineups: Data, Theory, and Policy, 7 Psychol. Pub. Pol'y & L. 791 (2001). Over 88 percent of the law enforcement agencies that use live lineups now routinely give this instruction to witnesses.

However, the Department of Justice recommendations stop short of imposing two further requirements that find support in the academic research. It is clear that "blind presentations" of the lineup (that is, the officer conducting the lineup procedure does not know which participant is the suspect) improve the accuracy of witness identification. Officers who know the identity of the suspect can signal to the witness, either through words or subtle body language, which is the "correct" choice. Nevertheless, it is difficult for some smaller law enforcement agencies to make the logistical arrangements for a blind presentation, so the Justice Department stopped short of recommending this measure for all live identification procedures. According to a national survey, less than 10 percent of the law enforcement agencies that use live lineup procedures provide for blind lineups.

A second technique involves "sequential" lineups, where the officer presents to the witness one person at a time, asking each time whether he or she is the perpetrator. Sequential lineups encourage witnesses to compare each person to their memory of the events, rather than asking which lineup participant (relatively speaking) most closely resembles the original description. The field research on sequential lineups has produced mixed results. For research suggesting that sequential lineups are less accurate than simultaneous lineups, see Steven E. Clark, Eyewitness Identification: California Reform Redux (2015); but cf. Dawn McQuiston-Surrett, Roy S. Malpass & Colin G. Tredoux, Sequential vs. Simultaneous Lineups: A Review of Methods, Data, and Theory, 12 Psychol. Pub. Pol'y & L. 137 (2006).

Problem 9-5. Drafting a Policy

The U.S. Department of Justice amended in 2017 its guidelines to law enforcement for conducting photo arrays. The revised guidelines appear on the web extension for this chapter at *http://www.crimpro.com/extension/ch09*. The Deputy Attorney General prefaced the new guidelines by noting the changes in research and practice since the DOJ had previously addressed procedures for photo arrays, back in 1999, and described the proper uses of the guidance document: "These procedures are not a step-by-step description of how to conduct photo arrays, but rather set out principles and describe examples of how to perform them. The heads of the Department's law enforcement components should review these procedures and, to the extent necessary, update their own internal policies to ensure that they are consistent with the procedures described in this document." The revised procedures address the location of the photo array, the selection of photographs, the method of presenting photographs, the administrator's knowledge of the suspect, instructions to the witness, presentations to multiple witnesses, administrator feedback to the witness, and documentation of the process. For a summary of additional scientific findings and recommendations for improving eyewitness identification, see Chapter 6 in the 2014 report of the National Academy of Sciences, Identifying the Culprit: Assessing Eyewitness Identification, at *https://www.innocenceproject.org/wp-content/uploads/2016/02/NAS-Report-ID.pdf*.

Imagine that you are legal counsel for a police department in a major city. The chief of your department asks you to read the revised guidance from the U.S. Department of Justice and to draft new guidelines for the police in your city. What identification procedures will you recommend for field investigations and for photo lineups? Who will you consult (and in what contexts) as you draft the new guidelines? Should your guidelines mandate blind or double-blind administration of photo arrays? Should they require sequential or simultaneous presentation of the photos? Should they require that officers administering the photo array read certain instructions about the procedure to the witness? Should they require that the photo array have a certain composition (e.g., no more than one suspect per array, a minimum number of fillers)? Should they regulate the feedback that officers provide to suspects? Should they require that the identification result and the certainty of the witness be recorded?

How do your recommendations (and your consultation process) change if you work for a law enforcement agency in a small town or a rural area?

X

Complex Investigations

Most crime investigations last for a short time and involve the efforts of only a few law enforcement officers. Different procedural issues crop up when criminal investigations last longer and involve more people. In this chapter, we consider two central issues that arise in proactive, complex investigations. In the first section, we consider the power of the grand jury to investigate crimes and the legal and practical limits on that power. In the second section, we consider whether the legal system places any limits on the government's use of undercover agents and confidential informants to gather information.

A. THE INVESTIGATIVE GRAND JURY

Efforts by police officers to gather information about criminal suspects have occupied most of our attention thus far. The police are indeed the government agents who gather information in most criminal law enforcement. But in more complex investigations, other institutions such as grand juries and regulatory bodies, often acting under prosecutorial guidance, become important players in the effort to build a file that could lead to criminal charges. These investigations typically pursue suspicions about alleged white-collar crimes such as fraud. Such complex investigations, although making up only a tiny fraction of the criminal cases ultimately filed, require an enormous amount of resources for both the prosecution and defense, and receive much media attention.

The grand jury is the central investigative tool in these complex cases. Unlike police departments, which emerged in this country late in the nineteenth century, the grand jury is an ancient institution. It can trace its heritage at least as far back as twelfth-century England. The grand jury began as a body of citizens that the courts empowered to investigate criminal violations in the vicinity. Initially, the criminal charges that the grand jury issued were based on the personal knowledge of grand jurors. Only later did they acquire the power to call witnesses and to consider evidence that representatives of the Crown placed before them.

The grand jury thrived when first transplanted to England's American colonies. Each state entering the Union prior to the Civil War created grand juries and gave them broad powers to call witnesses and to gather documents. Later in the nineteenth century, voters grew less enthusiastic about the institution (especially in new states, such as Colorado and Nebraska) and passed constitutional provisions allowing the legislature to abolish the grand jury altogether. Although many of the newer states no longer *required* indictments as the method of initiating charges in serious criminal cases, they retained the grand jury as one method of investigating important cases, particularly those involving political corruption, where the independence of the police or prosecutor might be in question. Because of special investigative powers given to grand juries, prosecutors found it convenient to rely on them to gather evidence in cases, such as those involving conspiracies and documentary material, where routine police work could not produce enough evidence.

The grand jury is technically an arm of the court, and a judge supervises some of its activities. For instance, a judge hears any motions to quash a grand jury subpoena and will enforce a subpoena if a witness refuses to comply. The court instructs the grand jurors at the beginning of their term about their general responsibilities. Despite this supervisory power, the judge is generally not present during grand jury proceedings, and state and federal courts have proven reluctant to interfere in the affairs of the grand jury.

In this section, we consider issues relating to the special investigative powers of grand juries and similar government bodies to subpoena testimony and evidence. We postpone until Chapter 13 our discussion of the charging functions of the grand jury.

1. Grand Jury Secrecy

A witness who receives a subpoena to testify before a grand jury enters an unfamiliar room where the prosecuting attorney asks most of the questions, the grand jurors listen, and the stenographer records everything said. The witness usually knows very little about the grand jury's overall investigation or her place in that investigation. In this setting, most of the information flows in one direction. The grand jury can obtain a lot of information without revealing much of its investigative strategy.

Witnesses, however, often have legal counsel who can make the grand jury less intimidating. In an ordinary criminal case, an attorney enters the scene only after the government already has gathered most of its evidence. But lawyers have the opportunity to become involved earlier in more complex investigations because of the long time period involved: A white-collar crime case will often take months, or even years, to investigate. Lawyers also get involved earlier in the more complex cases because larger amounts of money are often at stake, and the targets of the investigation can afford to hire an attorney. As you read the statutes and notes below, consider the intricate game that occurs when counsel and sophisticated grand jury witnesses face off against prosecutors trying to get the most information from witnesses without revealing too much about the grand jury's investigation.

■ FEDERAL RULE OF CRIMINAL PROCEDURE 6

. . . **(d) Who May Be Present.**

(1) While the Grand Jury Is in Session. The following persons may be present while the grand jury is in session: attorneys for the government, the witness being questioned, interpreters when needed, and a court reporter or an operator of a recording device.

(2) During Deliberations and Voting. No person other than the jurors, and any interpreter needed to assist a hearing-impaired or speech-impaired juror, may be present while the grand jury is deliberating or voting.

(e) Recording and Disclosing the Proceedings.

(1) Recording the Proceedings. Except while the grand jury is deliberating or voting, all proceedings must be recorded by a court reporter or by a suitable recording device. But the validity of a prosecution is not affected by the unintentional failure to make a recording. Unless the court orders otherwise, an attorney for the government will retain control of the recording, the reporter's notes, and any transcript prepared from those notes.

(2) Secrecy. . . .

(B) Unless these rules provide otherwise, the following persons must not disclose a matter occurring before the grand jury: (i) a grand juror; (ii) an interpreter; (iii) a court reporter; (iv) an operator of a recording device; (v) a person who transcribes recorded testimony; (vi) an attorney for the government; or (vii) [government personnel who assists the attorney for the government].

■ COLORADO REVISED STATUTES §16-5-204(4)(d)

Any witness subpoenaed to appear and testify before a grand jury or to produce books, papers, documents, or other objects before such grand jury shall be entitled to assistance of counsel during any time that such witness is being questioned in the presence of such grand jury, and counsel may be present in the grand jury room with his client during such questioning. However, counsel for the witness shall be permitted only to counsel with the witness and shall not make objections, arguments, or address the grand jury. Such counsel may be retained by the witness or may, for any person financially unable to obtain adequate assistance, be appointed in the same manner as if that person were eligible for appointed counsel. An attorney present in the grand jury room shall take an oath of secrecy. If the court, at an in camera hearing, determines that counsel was disruptive, then the court may order counsel to remain outside the courtroom when advising his client. No attorney shall be permitted to provide counsel in the grand jury room to more than one witness in the same criminal investigation, except with the permission of the grand jury.

Notes

1. *Grand jury secrecy.* The proceedings of grand juries traditionally are secret. The federal rules of criminal procedure, like the rules and statutes of most states,

codify the traditional practice: Only the grand jurors, attorneys for the government, the witness, and (sometimes) a court reporter can be present in the room. Each of these parties except for the witness has an obligation not to disclose what happens in the grand jury room. A classic explanation for the secrecy of grand jury proceedings appears in United States v. Amazon Industrial Chemical Corp., 55 F.2d 254, 261 (D. Md. 1931):

> The reasons which lie behind the requirement of secrecy may be summarized as follows: (1) To prevent the escape of those whose indictment may be contemplated; (2) to insure the utmost freedom to the grand jury in its deliberations, and to prevent persons subject to indictment or their friends from importuning the grand jurors; (3) to prevent subornation of perjury or tampering with the witnesses who may testify before the grand jury and later appear at the trial of those indicted by it; (4) to encourage free and untrammeled disclosures by persons who have information with respect to the commission of crimes; (5) to protect the innocent accused who is exonerated from disclosure of the fact that he has been under investigation, and from the expense of standing trial where there was no probability of guilt.

About 20 states have statutes or court rules, like the Colorado statute reprinted above, that allow a grand jury witness to bring an attorney into the grand jury room. See also Fla. Stat. §§905.17(1)(2). Rules of evidence do not apply to grand jury proceedings, and the witness's attorney typically may not object to any questions. What, then, is the attorney's function? Will the presence of an attorney in the grand jury room influence the type of questions asked or the witnesses selected to testify?

2. *Makeup and selection of the grand jury.* At common law, a grand jury had anywhere between 12 and 23 members. Federal grand juries have 16 to 23 members, and most state grand juries stay within the common-law size limits. See Alaska Stat. §12.40.020 (12 to 18 jurors). Some jurisdictions have grand juries that sit routinely, and the court impanels such a grand jury on its own initiative; elsewhere, the prosecutor requests the court to impanel a grand jury for some special purpose. The clerk of the court summons the potential grand jurors, typically from lists of registered voters and licensed drivers. The judge may excuse some potential jurors if service would be particularly burdensome to them. What sorts of document requests will an investigative body of this type tend to make? How might the grand jury's requests for testimony and documents change if the court assigned staff members or experts to advise the grand jurors?

3. *Witness debriefing.* Although attorneys for grand jury witnesses are not allowed in the grand jury room in a majority of American jurisdictions, they still obtain information about the grand jury's questions and the witness's answers by debriefing their clients immediately after the testimony. Many attorneys also encourage their clients to step outside the grand jury room periodically (perhaps after each question) for a consultation. See Sara Sun Beale et al., Grand Jury Law and Practice §6:28 (2d ed. 1997) (surveying statutory and common-law protections for witnesses' ability to consult counsel outside grand jury room). Some attorneys attempt to debrief witnesses who are not their clients. Statutes and rules of criminal procedure typically impose an obligation of secrecy on the grand jurors and the government attorneys but not on grand jury witnesses. See Fed. R. Crim. P. 6(e)(2); 725 Ill. Comp. Stat. §5/112-6. About a dozen states have statutes or rules that prevent a grand jury witness from discussing her testimony with anyone other than her attorney. See N.C. Gen. Stat. §§15A-623(e)(g). What would be the likely attitude of government attorneys about

witness debriefing? Is there anything government attorneys can or should do about it? See In re Grand Jury Proceedings, 558 F. Supp. 532 (W.D. Va. 1983) (defense lawyers may debrief all witnesses, but government attorneys may request grand jury witnesses not to discuss their testimony with others).

4. *Warnings to grand jury witnesses: constitutional requirements.* The witness who receives a subpoena to testify before the grand jury can be held in contempt of court for failing to appear, even if the witness plans only to invoke the Fifth Amendment privilege. Despite this element of coercion, the Supreme Court has decided (along with the great majority of state courts) that prosecutors need not give *Miranda* warnings to grand jury witnesses. United States v. Mandujano, 425 U.S. 564 (1976); State v. Driscoll, 360 A.2d 857 (R.I. 1976). Would you require a warning only for those witnesses who become "targets" of a grand jury investigation? Again, most jurisdictions have not required such warnings as a constitutional matter. See United States v. Washington, 431 U.S. 181 (1977) (no warning of "target" status is required by federal Constitution); People v. J.H., 554 N.E.2d 961 (Ill. 1990) (same for Illinois constitution); but see People ex rel. Gallagher v. District Court, 601 P.2d 1380 (Colo. 1979) (Colorado constitution requires warnings).

5. *Nonconstitutional requirements of warnings.* Despite a lack of success on the constitutional front, witnesses still often receive various warnings before appearing in front of the grand jury. In the federal system, the U.S. Attorney's Manual requires prosecutors to inform witnesses of their right to silence, the fact that statements to the grand jury can be used against the witness, and the fact that those who have retained attorneys may consult with their attorneys outside the grand jury room. See §9-11.151. The manual also requires prosecutors to inform grand jury witnesses (and some nonwitnesses) of their status as "targets" of the investigation. See §§9-11.151 to 155. What would be the remedy for a violation of this written prosecutorial policy? In a strong minority of states, statutes require the prosecutor to inform grand jury witnesses of their right to silence, especially when the witness is a target of the investigation. 725 Ill. Comp. Stat. §5/112-4(b); Tex. Code Crim. Proc. art. 20.17. Some state statutes also require the state to notify subpoena recipients if they are targets of the investigation. See Ind. Code Ann. §35-34-2-5. Why would a potential witness want to know if he is a target of the investigation? Some state statutes provide certain advantages (such as the right to consult with counsel in the grand jury room) only to targets and not to other witnesses.

6. *Grand jury witnesses versus police interrogation.* The question of warnings for grand jury witnesses calls for a comparison between interrogation during grand jury proceedings and custodial interrogation in a police station. There are certain similarities in the two experiences: In both cases, the witness is confined against her will, and the questioning takes place in isolation and in an unfamiliar setting. The two forms of questioning are also different: A person in police custody can end all questioning by invoking the right to silence, while a grand jury witness has no general right to silence and can be imprisoned for contempt of court for refusing to answer questions (unless the answers would be self-incriminating). Can you think of other parallels and differences between the two forms of questioning? Who goes to the grand jury and who goes to the police station?

7. *The legal ethics of contacting represented persons.* There may be times when a prosecutor would prefer to speak to witnesses outside the grand jury room. Such an interview can save the witness the trouble of appearing at a specific time and place to testify, and it allows the prosecutor to screen out all but the most relevant

inculpatory evidence from the grand jury. But if the witness is represented by counsel, can the prosecutor accomplish these purposes? Can the prosecutor (or an investigator working with the prosecuting attorney) interview the witness without the witness's attorney present? The Model Rule of Professional Conduct 4.2 has some bearing on this question: "In representing a client, a lawyer shall not communicate about the subject of the representation with a person the lawyer knows to be represented by another lawyer in the matter, unless the lawyer has the consent of the other lawyer or is authorized to do so by law or a court order."

In light of this ethical rule, will criminal suspects be able to protect themselves from interrogation by placing a lawyer on retainer and notifying the government of that fact? There is a lively debate about whether state bar authorities can appropriately enforce this rule against federal prosecutors. For a sample of the arguments, see the web extension for this chapter at *http://www.crimpro.com/extension/ch10*.

8. *Strategy in representing grand jury witnesses.* What are some of the strategic questions for counsel advising a grand jury witness? A practice manual on representing witnesses before a grand jury advises the following:

> Going into the grand jury appearance, there are numerous questions that must be answered, such as: Who are the prosecutors really after? What gaps in their knowledge are they trying to fill? The answers to such questions are vital to counsel's ability to advise and protect his or her client. In addition, the answers to such questions will guide the attorney in assuming a bargaining position, if that becomes necessary. . . .
>
> If the client has been served a subpoena duces tecum . . . the subpoena itself may provide counsel with invaluable insight into the thrust of the government's investigation. If financial records are called for, are they the company's records or the client's personal records? What type of corporate records are sought? What contracts, and with whom? Assuming the subpoena is clearly targeted toward specific information, counsel may well get a good idea of the concern of the prosecution and be able to react immediately. Unfortunately, ... it will almost surely be the case that the subpoena is so wide-ranging and inconclusive that not only will it be of little help in clarifying the issues for counsel, it will also suggest to counsel that preliminary litigation in the form of a motion to quash is called for.

Thomas J. Cox, Representing the Grand Jury Target Witness, 38 Am. Jur. Trials 651 (1989) (2018 update). How is counsel's advice to her client likely to differ if she expects her client to be a target as opposed to a mere witness?

Problem 10-1. The View from Trenton

A grand jury has begun an investigation of the governor of New Jersey, Carl Carter, for possible corruption. Although the precise topics of the investigation remain undisclosed, news stories raise a number of possibilities. Reporters asked questions about the decision by Carter's appointee to the Port Authority, Bill Bacon, to close lanes on the George Washington Bridge, causing traffic jams in Fort Lee, a town on the New Jersey side of the bridge. The reporters speculated that the lane closure was political retribution against the mayor of Fort Lee for his failure to endorse Carter in a recent reelection campaign.

Other stories asked whether Carter arranged to divert bond money from the Port Authority to fund public-private development projects in New Jersey, outside the scope of the Port Authority's jurisdiction. Still other reports focus on the award of a multimillion dollar contract to operate New Jersey's halfway houses to a private firm run by Dell Davis, a close friend and advisor of Carter.

Consider the distinct interests of several potential witnesses in this grand jury investigation: (1) Amy Able, the governor's deputy chief of staff, who was the contact person in the governor's office for the halfway house contract and the public-private development projects; (2) Bill Bacon, the governor's appointee to the Port Authority Commission; (3) Dell Davis, the president of the halfway-house management firm; and (4) Ed Egland, a contractor who received one of the New Jersey development contracts funded by Port Authority bond money.

Divide into groups, with each student in the group taking the role of defense counsel for one of the witnesses listed above, and discuss the following questions. Which types of witnesses will likely receive the first subpoenas? What types of documents will the grand jury likely request from each witness? Will each witness invoke the Fifth Amendment privilege against self-incrimination? What will determine whether each witness chooses to join a "joint defense agreement" with the other potential witnesses? What could the government offer to each witness as an inducement to cooperate in the investigation? Do you anticipate that government agents will attempt to interview any witnesses outside the presence of the grand jury?

2. Immunity for Witnesses and the Scope of the Privilege Against Self-Incrimination

Although the grand jury can ask for a very broad range of testimony and documents, there is still some evidence beyond its reach. For instance, a grand jury cannot obtain information protected by common-law privileges, such as the attorney-client privilege. There is also an important constitutional limit on the statements that a grand jury may obtain from a witness. The Fifth Amendment to the U.S. Constitution, and analogous provisions in almost every state constitution (all but two), create a privilege against self-incrimination:

> No person . . . shall be compelled in any criminal case to be a witness against himself. [U.S. Const., amend. 5]

> No subject shall be . . . compelled to accuse or furnish evidence against himself. [N.H. Const., pt. I, art. 15]

A witness who receives a subpoena to appear and testify before a grand jury (or before a magistrate, administrative agency, or congressional committee, as the case may be) can invoke this constitutional privilege and refuse to answer questions when the answers would incriminate the witness. But this does not end the matter. Once the witness has invoked the privilege against self-incrimination, the prosecutor has another option. She can ask a court to order the witness to testify despite the risk of self-incrimination; in exchange, the prosecutor promises that no government agent will use the "compelled" testimony to further a later criminal prosecution against the witness. This promise is known as "immunity."

The question of immunity offers a useful vantage point for studying the privilege against self-incrimination. Just as the nature of a contract can be understood by exploring remedies for breach of contract, so the nature of the privilege against self-incrimination becomes clear when one explores the nature of the immunity necessary to overcome that privilege. The following case explores exactly what sort of promises a prosecutor must make to an immunized witness. Although the case deals with witnesses at trial, the same constitutional reasoning would apply to the immunity offered to grand jury witnesses.

■ COMMONWEALTH v. PATRICIA SWINEHART
664 A.2d 957 (Pa. 1995)

CAPPY, J.

This case presents the question of whether the use and derivative use immunity provided in 42 Pa. C.S. §5947,[1] is consistent with the Pennsylvania constitutional privilege at Article I, Section 9, against compelled self-incrimination. For the reasons that follow we find that use and derivative use immunity is consistent with the protection provided under our state constitution.

[After the murder of David Swinehart, authorities charged his nephew, Thomas DeBlase, with the crime. Preliminary rulings and interlocutory appeals delayed his trial for several years. In the meantime,] Patricia Swinehart, the wife of the decedent, was arrested and charged with the murder of her husband, and with being a co-conspirator of DeBlase. DeBlase was subpoenaed as a witness in the Patricia Swinehart trial and offered a grant of immunity pursuant to 42 Pa. C.S. §5947. DeBlase moved to quash the subpoena and objected to the grant of immunity. . . . The trial court refused to quash the subpoena, approved the grant of immunity to DeBlase, and then when DeBlase still refused to answer, found him to be in both civil and criminal contempt. [Without DeBlase's testimony, the trial of Patricia Swinehart resulted in an acquittal. This is DeBlase's appeal of his contempt conviction.]

DeBlase asserts that the Act, which grants an immunized witness use and derivative use immunity, offers insufficient safeguards in exchange for the considerable protection guaranteed under Article I, Section 9 of the Pennsylvania Constitution which the immunized witness is forced to forsake. DeBlase acknowledges that the United States Supreme Court has upheld use and derivative use immunity as sufficient protection under the Fifth Amendment to the United States Constitution in Kastigar v. United States, 406 U.S. 441 (1972). He argues, however, that the Pennsylvania Constitutional protection is broader and can only be satisfied by a grant of transactional immunity.[5]

---

1. The pertinent portions of the immunity statute that are at issue provide: . . .

    (c) Whenever a witness refuses, on the basis of his privilege against self-incrimination, to testify or provide other information in a [judicial proceeding, and the judge] communicates to the witness an immunity order, that witness may not refuse to testify based on his privilege against self-incrimination.

    (d) No testimony or other information compelled under an immunity order, or any information directly or indirectly derived from such testimony or other information, may be used against a witness in any criminal case, except that such information may be used . . . in a prosecution [for perjury or false swearing].

5. Generally three types of immunity are recognized, although some scholars treat "use" and "use and derivative use" immunity as one and the same. "Use" immunity provides immunity only for the testimony actually given pursuant to the order compelling said testimony. "Use and derivative use" immunity enlarges the scope of the grant to cover any information or leads that were derived from the actual testimony given under compulsion. Thus, under either "use" or "use and derivative use" immunity a

[We] will begin our analysis with a review of the text of the constitutional provision at issue, the history of that provision as related through legislative enactments and prior decisions of this Court, related case law from our sister states, and finally, policy considerations which include matters unique to our Commonwealth.

Article I, Section 9 [says that] "In all criminal prosecutions the accused . . . cannot be compelled to give evidence against himself. . . . A comparison of the actual language in Article I, Section 9 and the Fifth Amendment does not reveal any major differences in the description of the privilege against self-incrimination within the two Constitutions. As the words themselves are not persuasive of either interpretation on the issue at bar, we turn to the prior decisions of this Court which interpreted the right against self-incrimination as contained within the Pennsylvania Constitution.

[It] was not until after the United States Supreme Court decision in *Counselman v. Hitchcock*, 142 U.S. 547 (1892), that this Court addressed the question of immunity in relation to the privilege against self-incrimination. In *Counselman*, the United States Supreme Court rejected a federal statute which conferred only use immunity as being an insufficient substitute for the privilege guaranteed under the Fifth Amendment. . . . The Court then went on to conclude that a statutory grant of immunity, in order to be valid as against the Fifth Amendment, "must afford absolute immunity against future prosecution for the offense to which the question relates." In the wake of *Counselman*, only those legislative grants of immunity which compelled testimony from a witness in exchange for transactional immunity were found to be valid.

Thus, from 1892 until 1978, Pennsylvania recognized only transactional immunity as a sufficient exchange for compelling a witness to forsake the privilege against self-incrimination. The courts in Pennsylvania followed the lead of the United States Supreme Court on this issue.

The Pennsylvania Legislature also adhered to the dictates of the United States Supreme Court when drafting legislation on the issue of immunity grants for witnesses. Prior to the 1978 revisions, which are at issue in this case, the immunity conferred under the Act was transactional immunity. This shift in the type of immunity authorized by the Act can easily be traced to the United States Supreme Court decision in Kastigar v. United States, 406 U.S. 441 (1972).

In *Kastigar*, the United States Supreme Court found use and derivative use immunity to adequately protect the privilege against compulsory self-incrimination contained within the Fifth Amendment. The Court reconsidered its opinion in *Counselman* and determined that although use immunity offers insufficient protection under the Fifth Amendment, transactional immunity offers greater protection than is necessary and thus concluded that use and derivative use immunity would thereafter be sufficient.

> [The] privilege has never been construed to mean that one who invokes it cannot subsequently be prosecuted. Its sole concern is to afford protection against being forced to give testimony leading to the infliction of penalties affixed to criminal

---

prosecution against the witness is not foreclosed; any prosecution must, however, arise from evidence unrelated to the information which is derived from the witness's own mouth. "Transactional" immunity is the most expansive, as it in essence provides complete amnesty to the witness for any transactions which are revealed in the course of the compelled testimony.

acts. Immunity from the use of compelled testimony, as well as evidence derived directly and indirectly therefrom, affords this protection. It prohibits the prosecutorial authorities from using the compelled testimony in any respect, and it therefore insures that the testimony cannot lead to the infliction of criminal penalties on the witness.

[Following the *Kastigar* decision and our 1975 decision commenting favorably on *Kastigar*,] the immunity statute was revised to its present form wherein transactional immunity was replaced with use and derivative use immunity. [It] is clear that Pennsylvania, for the most part, followed the lead of the United States Supreme Court. . . .

Turning to our sister states, we find that they are evenly split on the issue of whether their state constitutions afford protection against compulsory self-incrimination greater than the Fifth Amendment in the wake of *Kastigar*. The six states that have rejected *Kastigar* and found their constitutions to require transactional immunity are [Alaska, Hawaii, Massachusetts, Mississippi, Oregon, and South Carolina].[13]

In each of [these six states], the state courts, relying upon their constitutional self-incrimination clauses, rejected legislation that had been developed post-*Kastigar* replacing transactional immunity with use/derivative use immunity. South Carolina and Alaska found the protection of use/derivative use immunity to be too cumbersome to enforce, citing the practical problems in determining whether or not later prosecutions stemmed from the immunized testimony. . . . Mississippi more bluntly phrased the problem as being one of having to rely upon the good faith of the prosecutor in use/derivative use situations. . . . Oregon found the rationale of *Kastigar* unpersuasive and chose to remain consistent with their case law which had always followed the reasoning of *Counselman*. . . .

The six states which have found use and derivative use immunity consistent with the self-incrimination clauses in their state constitutions are [Arizona, Indiana, Maryland, New Jersey, New York, and Texas].[14] [These courts] accepted use and derivative use immunity grants as consistent with their state constitutions [because they] found the state constitutional privilege at issue to be coextensive with the Fifth Amendment. In reviewing the relevant opinions and legislation from our sister states we find no clear preference among the jurisdictions. . . .

This case involves the juxtaposition of the privilege against self-incrimination and the need to compel testimony. The inherent conflict between these two important concepts is the heart of this case. Each of these concepts [carries] historical baggage of considerable proportion. Our system of jurisprudence abhors the ancient star chamber inquisitions which forced a witness into "the cruel trilemma of self-accusation, perjury or contempt." On the other hand, of equal importance to our system of justice is the ancient adage that "the public has a right to every man's evidence." The concept of compelling a witness to testify has been recognized in

---

13. Eleven jurisdictions provide for transactional immunity through legislation. [These include California, Idaho, Illinois, Maine, Michigan, Nevada, New Hampshire, Rhode Island, Utah, Washington, and West Virginia.]

14. Eighteen jurisdictions have provided for use/derivative use immunity through legislation passed after *Kastigar*. [These include Arkansas, Colorado, Connecticut, Delaware, Florida, Georgia, Iowa, Kansas, Louisiana, Minnesota, Montana, Nebraska, New Mexico, North Carolina, North Dakota, South Dakota, Vermont, and Wisconsin.]

Anglo-American jurisprudence since the Statute of Elizabeth, 5 Eliz. 1, c.9, §12 (1562). Immunizing a witness has always been a feature of Pennsylvania jurisprudence. The dilemma in balancing these competing concerns centers on the type of immunity which can best provide the public with the information to which it is entitled in order to ferret out criminal activity and at the same time protect the rights of the witness being forced to testify under compulsion.

In urging this Court to declare the present immunity statute unconstitutional, DeBlase places great emphasis on the fact that Pennsylvania has historically required transactional immunity as the only adequate safeguard for compelling a witness's testimony in violation of the right against self-incrimination. As with most critics of use/derivative use immunity, DeBlase asserts that only transactional immunity can truly protect a witness from later being condemned by his own words. The strongest argument for rejecting use/derivative use immunity is what has been commonly referred to as the "web effect." . . .

In fact in the instant case DeBlase argues that if forced to testify against his co-conspirator he will forever be caught within the web and his ability to receive a fair trial forever tainted. Specifically, the untraceable effects of his immunized testimony will impact upon the selection of his jury, the presentation of a defense, the ability to utilize character witnesses and infringe upon his decision to testify in his own behalf. . . .

On the other hand, there is no dispute that immunization of a witness is a necessary, effective and ancient tool in law enforcement. As the United States Supreme Court stated in *Kastigar*, "many offenses are of such a character that the only persons capable of giving useful testimony are those implicated in the crime." The very nature of criminal conspiracies is what forces the Commonwealth into the Hobson's choice of having to grant one of the parties implicated in the criminal scheme immunity in order to uncover the entire criminal enterprise. Thus, in order to serve justice an accommodation must be made; however, that arrangement should not place the "witness" in a better position as to possible criminal prosecution than he had previously enjoyed. A grant of immunity should protect the witness from prosecution through his own words, yet it should not be so broad that the witness is forever free from suffering the just consequences of his actions, if his actions can be proven by means other than his own words.

Clearly, there are compelling "pros" and "cons" on the question of the right against self-incrimination versus the need to immunize the witness. However, to elevate the right against self-incrimination above the right of the public to every person's evidence would not achieve a proper balance of these competing interests. Transactional immunity offers complete amnesty to the witness, a measure of protection clearly greater than the privilege against self-incrimination. The practical consequences, otherwise known as the "web effect," created by immunizing a witness should not tip the balance so far in favor of the witness that the Commonwealth is only left with the option of granting complete amnesty to a witness in order to fully investigate criminal enterprises and serve the public need for justice. Use/derivative use immunity strikes a better balance between the need for law enforcement to ferret out criminality and the right of the witness to be free of self-incrimination.

In this case we find that Article I, Section 9 is, in fact, more expansive than the Fifth Amendment; it is not, however, so expansive that the privilege against self-incrimination would require greater protection than that provided within the Act. . . . Recognizing the serious practical concerns which almost always accompany a later prosecution of the immunized witness, we hold that in the later prosecution, the evidence offered by the Commonwealth shall be reviewed with the most careful scrutiny. That is, the Commonwealth must prove, of record, by the heightened standard of clear and convincing evidence, that the evidence upon which a subsequent prosecution is brought arose wholly from independent sources. . . .

Notes

1. *Transactional and use immunity: majority position.* As the *Swinehart* court indicates, "use/derivative use" immunity is sufficient to satisfy the federal Constitution, while states are divided over the type of immunity that prosecutors must offer to witnesses before a court will compel the witness to give self-incriminating testimony. Roughly 20 states require use immunity, while a slightly smaller group requires transactional immunity. In other states, the type of immunity needed varies, depending on factors such as the seriousness of the offense being investigated. Note that more states resolve this question by statute than by a constitutional court ruling. Immunity orders do not occur in a large number of cases.

2. *Simple use immunity.* The Supreme Court's *Kastigar* decision approved of "use/derivative use" immunity: Later prosecution of an immunized witness is possible, but only if the prosecution's case is not based on the witness's statements or on any investigative leads obtained from that testimony. But was the Court correct to insist on this form of immunity, instead of "simple" use immunity? Simple use immunity would prevent use of immunized testimony in a later prosecution, but it would leave the prosecution free to use evidence obtained from investigative leads created by the witness's compelled testimony. For instance, the judicially compelled testimony of a murder suspect could not be introduced at the suspect's trial, but the murder weapon found through leads obtained during compelled testimony might come into evidence. Simple use immunity was an acceptable form of overcoming the self-incrimination privilege in most states during the nineteenth century. See People v. Kelly, 24 N.Y. 74 (1861). Courts in England today do not exclude the fruits of testimony compelled under an immunity order. Does this approach, which bars only the use of a witness's actual statements, make the most sense of the Fifth Amendment's language: "No person . . . shall be compelled . . . to be a *witness* against himself"? Would your attitude about simple use immunity be different if you were interpreting a state provision such as the one in Texas, "[The] accused . . . shall not be compelled to give evidence against himself"? Tex. Const, art. I, §10. For a constitutional defense of simple use immunity, see Akhil Amar & Renee Lettow, Fifth Amendment First Principles: The Self-Incrimination Clause, 93 Mich. L. Rev. 857 (1995).

3. *The history of the privilege against self-incrimination.* What exactly does the privilege against self-incrimination—in a federal or state constitution—protect? Because an immunity order must substitute for the privilege against self-incrimination, it creates an occasion for addressing this question. What are the relevant sources for an answer? The precise words of the constitutional provision surely should have some role. What is the relevance of the *history* of the self-incrimination concept?

The Latin maxim *nemo tenetur seipsum prodere* ("no one is obliged to accuse himself") originated in the medieval law of the Roman Catholic Church: It confirmed that even though a believer had a duty to confess sins to a priest, that obligation did not extend to criminal proceedings. The concept first became prominent in England in the ecclesiastical courts which were investigating and prosecuting those who resisted Anglican religious practice and belief. Puritans and other non-conformists invoked the concept to prevent their investigation and prosecution by ecclesiastical courts. See Michael Macnair, The Early Development of the Privilege Against Self-Incrimination, 10 Oxford J. Legal Stud. 66 (1990).

Despite these early uses in ecclesiastical courts, an evidentiary privilege against the use of self-incriminating statements did not operate in the English common-law criminal courts until late in the eighteenth century, when defense counsel first became widely available and it was possible for a defendant to offer a defense without testifying himself. See John Langbein, The Historical Origins of the Privilege Against Self-Incrimination at Common Law, 92 Mich. L. Rev. 1047 (1994).

The American drafters of constitutions in the late eighteenth century all included a privilege against self-incrimination as part of a cluster of rights designed to reinforce the importance of the jury in a criminal trial as the central guarantee against oppressive government. But the typical criminal process at the time included widespread techniques to encourage an accused to testify. Defendants in custody had to appear before a magistrate who would routinely question the defendant about his involvement in the alleged crime. If the defendant confessed, the confession could form the basis for a summary conviction before the magistrate (for lesser offenses) or could be introduced at a later trial. If the defendant refused to answer a magistrate's questions, that fact could be revealed at trial. Does this history point in the direction of transactional immunity, use/derivative use immunity, or simple use immunity?

4. *The purpose of the privilege.* If the text and history leave some doubt about the proper scope of the privilege, should legislators (who draft immunity statutes) and judges (who apply them) engage in some form of moral or political philosophy to flesh out the meaning of the privilege that is most attractive, or one most in keeping with our governmental structure and traditions? David Dolinko summarized the philosophical support for the privilege as follows:

> The rationales for the privilege fall, very roughly, into two categories. Systemic rationales are policies their proponents believe to be crucial to our particular kind of criminal justice system. Individual rationales are principles claimed to be entailed by a proper understanding of human rights or by a proper respect for human dignity and individuality. Among systemic rationales are the suggestions that the privilege encourages third-party witnesses to appear and testify by removing the fear that they might be compelled to incriminate themselves and removes the temptation to employ short cuts to conviction that demean official integrity. Individual rationales include the arguments that compelled self-incrimination works an unacceptable cruelty or invasion of privacy, as well as the notion of respect for the inviolability of the human personality, and the belief that punishing an individual for silence or perjury when he has been placed in a position in which his natural instincts and personal interests dictate that he should lie is an intolerable invasion of his personal dignity.

Dolinko, Is There a Rationale for the Privilege Against Self-Incrimination?, 33 UCLA L. Rev. 1063 (1986). The philosopher Jeremy Bentham criticized some of the leading arguments in favor of the privilege. He listed them as follows:

> 2. The old woman's reason. The essence of this reason is contained in the word *hard*: 'tis hard upon a man to be obliged to criminate himself. Hard it is upon a man, it must be confessed, to be obliged to do any thing that he does not like. That

he should not much like to do what is meant by his criminating himself, is natural enough; for what it leads to, is, his being punished. [But] did it ever yet occur to a man to propose a general abolition of all punishment, with this hardship for a reason for it? . . . You know of such or such a paper; tell us where it may be found. A request thus simple, your tenderness shudders at the thoughts of putting to a man: his answer might lead to the execution of that justice, which you are looking out for pretences to defeat. This request, you abhor the thought of putting to him: but what you scruple not to do (and why should you scruple to do it?) is, to dispatch your emissaries in the dead of night to his house, to that house which you call his castle, to break it open, and seize the documents by force. . . .

3. The fox-hunter's reason. This consists in introducing upon the carpet of legal procedure the idea of *fairness*, in the sense in which the word is used by sportsmen. The fox is to have a fair chance for his life: he must have . . . leave to run a certain length of way, for the express purpose of giving him a chance for escape. . . . In the sporting code, these laws are rational, being obviously conducive to the professed end. Amusement is that end. [The] use of a fox is to be hunted; the use of a criminal is to be tried. . . .

4. Confounding interrogation with torture: with the application of physical suffering, till some act is done; in the present instance, till testimony is given to a particular effect required. [The] act of putting a question to a person whose station is that of defendant in a cause, is no more an act of torture than the putting the same question to him would be, if, instead of being a defendant, he were an extraneous witness. [If] any thing he says should be mendacious, he is liable to be punished for it. . . .

5. Reference to unpopular institutions. Whatever Titius did was wrong: but this is among the things that Titius did; therefore this is wrong: such is the logic from which this sophism is deduced. In the apartment in which the court called the Court of Star-chamber sat, the roof had stars in it for ornaments. [The] judges of this court conducted themselves very badly: therefore judges should not sit in a room that has had stars in the roof. [Using this reasoning, lawyers claim that the Star Chamber was a bad court because of its] abominable practice of asking questions, by the abominable attempt to penetrate to the bottom of a cause.

5 Bentham, Rationale of Judicial Evidence 230-243 (1827). Which of the possible rationales can best explain limitations on the applicability of the concept (i.e., its use to protect a person from criminal but not civil consequences of wrongdoing, or its application only to "testimony" and not other forms of compelled cooperation with a prosecution, such as participation in a lineup)? Which of the "principled" rationales described above might support transactional immunity?

5. *Prosecution based on independent sources.* As the *Swinehart* court indicates, the government might successfully prosecute an immunized witness for the crime that is the subject of the testimony, but only under limited circumstances. The prosecutors must show that the evidence upon which a subsequent prosecution is brought "arose wholly from independent sources" and that they did not use the compelled testimony "in any respect." If you were a prosecutor in such a case, how would you attempt to prove that your evidence was based on "independent" sources? Consider this policy from the U.S. Department of Justice Criminal Resource Manual, §726:

[Prosecutors] should take the following precautions in the case of a witness who may possibly be prosecuted for an offense about which the witness may be questioned during his/her compelled testimony: (1) Before the witness testifies, prepare for the file a signed and dated memorandum summarizing the existing evidence against the witness and the date(s) and source(s) of such evidence; (2) ensure that the witness's immunized testimony is recorded verbatim and thereafter maintained in a secure location to which access is documented; and (3) maintain a record of the date(s) and source(s) of any evidence relating to the witness obtained after the witness has testified pursuant to the immunity order.

How often will these procedures be feasible? How often will they suffice when the defendant raises a constitutional challenge to the prosecution?

6. *Effect of immunity in other jurisdictions.* If a state prosecutor immunizes a grand jury witness and compels self-incriminating testimony, what assurance does the witness have that federal prosecutors will not use the testimony as a basis for federal criminal charges? The Supreme Court has declared that the Fifth Amendment requires federal prosecutors to respect the immunity grants of state governments. Murphy v. Waterfront Commission of New York Harbor, 378 U.S. 52 (1964). Does this ruling create a potential source of conflict between state and federal authorities? If so, how might the various actors respond to the conflict?

7. *Invoking the privilege based on potential future prosecutions.* Although the Fifth Amendment speaks of a privilege "in any criminal case," a person need not testify in a criminal courtroom to invoke the privilege. In fact, it is extraordinarily easy to invoke Fifth Amendment protections, because they apply to any legally compelled statements that *could* lead to the discovery of incriminating evidence, even though the statements themselves are not incriminating and are not introduced into evidence. Such statements would include grand jury testimony or testimony in a civil trial. For further discussion of the invocation and effects of the privilege in grand jury investigations, see the web extension for this chapter at *http://www.crimpro.com/extension/ch10.*

3. Document Subpoenas

Documents are the stock-in-trade of an investigative grand jury. The grand jury obtains documents by issuing subpoenas to document holders, compelling them to appear before the grand jury with the documents in hand. In reality, the prosecutor who advises the grand jury draws up the subpoena duces tecum describing the documents the grand jury demands. The terms of the subpoena are often very broad, and courts and legislatures have placed few if any bounds on the document requests. There is no requirement for the grand jury to show probable cause or reasonable suspicion that the documents they request will contain evidence of a crime. Historically, the documents needed only to be relevant to some legitimate grand jury inquiry.

■ GEORGE TILLER v. MICHAEL CORRIGAN
182 P.3d 719 (Kan. 2008)

Johnson, J.

These . . . consolidated original actions in mandamus were prompted by subpoenas duces tecum issued by a Sedgwick County grand jury summoned in response to a citizen petition under K.S.A. 22-3001, which called for investigation of alleged illegal abortions and other violations of the law by George R. Tiller, M.D., and others performing professional services at Women's Health Care Services, Inc. (WHCS), in Wichita. The respective Petitioners are: (1) George R. Tiller, M.D., and WHCS; [and] (2) Jane Doe, Ann Roe, Sarah Coe, and Paula Poe, on behalf of themselves and similarly situated patients (Patients). . . . The subpoenas duces tecum that remain under challenge in this consolidated action are as follows:

A. A subpoena signed by Judge Michael Corrigan on or about January 22, 2008, identifying Ann Swegle (Deputy District Attorney) as attorney for the plaintiff, and directing the records custodian for WHCS to appear at the Sedgwick County Courthouse on February 1, 2008, at 9 A.M. to testify on behalf of the plaintiff, and further reciting:

> DUCES TECUM:
> Copies of all health care records of each patient who received an abortion at Women's Health Care Services, Inc., or Women's Health Care Services, P.A., from July 1, 2003, through January 18, 2008, when the gestational age of each patient's fetus was determined to be 22 weeks or more, specifically including all records required to be made or maintained pursuant to K.S.A. 65-6703. . . .
> Counsel for Women's Health Care Services, Inc., may redact all personal identity indicators from the copies of the records for each patient including patient name; the day and month of the patient's birth; patient's social security number; photocopies of any patient identity documents; any insurance policy information; identification of any individuals accompanying the patient to Women's Health Care Services; patient's residential address; patient's telephone number(s); patient's occupation; and patient's emergency contact information.

The subpoena specifically stated that it required the personal attendance of the business records custodian and the production of original records and that delivering copies of the records to the court clerk would not be deemed sufficient compliance with the subpoena. . . .

B. A subpoena signed by Judge Michael Corrigan on January 23, 2008, identifying Swegle as attorney for the plaintiff, and directing the records custodian for WHCS to appear at the Sedgwick County Courthouse on February 1, 2008, at 9 A.M. to testify on behalf of the plaintiff. [The subpoena also requested "all health care records of each patient" at WHCS during the dates described in the first subpoena, "when the gestational age of each patient's fetus was determined to be 22 weeks or more but the patient did not receive an abortion because there was not a determination that a continuation of the patient's pregnancy would cause a substantial and irreversible impairment of a major bodily function." The second subpoena allowed for redaction of the same personal identity indicators that the first subpoena described.] As with the first subpoena, this one specifically required the personal attendance of the business records custodian and the production of the original records. . . .

Tiller and WHCS moved to quash the two subpoenas directed at WHCS's records custodian, claiming they encompassed more than 2,000 patient records and thus subjected the recipient to an undue burden, as contemplated by K.S.A. 60-245(c)(3)(A)(iv). . . . Separately, the Patients moved to intervene and to quash the subpoenas because they imposed an unjustified and profound intrusion on all similarly situated patients' privacy rights. . . . Judge Paul Buchanan overruled both motions to quash. . . .

We discern, collecting all of the Petitioners' arguments, that the Petitioners believe the subpoenas should be quashed for the following reasons:

(1) [There is no] reasonable suspicion to believe the subpoenaed records will contain evidence of a crime and that the basis for the alleged criminal conduct is on firm legal ground.

(2) The number of records which are encompassed by the subpoenas makes compliance unduly burdensome, especially in light of the time, money, and effort required to redact patient-identifying information prior to production.

(3) Tiller and WHCS have been targeted for investigation out of malice, and the subpoenas have been issued with an intent to harass.

(4) The subpoenas invade the patients' constitutional privacy interests in their confidential abortion clinic records.

RELEVANCE

The Respondents, as well as the other parties, rely heavily on cases dealing with federal grand juries. The federal system has some significant differences from our state grand jury system. For instance, in the federal system the prosecutor has the responsibility for deciding which witnesses to call, which evidence to subpoena, and which portions of the evidence will be presented to the grand jury. Thus the federal prosecutor, a licensed attorney subject to professional and ethical obligations, operates as the initial gatekeeper on the propriety of a particular subpoena. Furthermore, our grand jury provisions do not contain a counterpart to Federal Rule of Criminal Procedure 17(c), which specifically controls the issuance of subpoenas duces tecum and provides in relevant part: . . . "The court on motion made promptly may quash or modify the subpoena if compliance would be unreasonable or oppressive."

Notwithstanding the differences in the federal and state systems, we do find some guidance in the manner in which the United States Supreme Court has viewed the reasonableness requirement of Federal Rule of Criminal Procedure 17(c). In United States v. R. Enterprises, Inc., 498 U.S. 292 (1991), a federal grand jury had been investigating allegations of interstate transportation of obscene materials for approximately 2 years. It issued a series of subpoenas to three companies, seeking a variety of corporate books and records, as well as copies of videotapes alleged to have been shipped to retailers in the area. All three companies moved to quash the subpoenas, arguing that the subpoenas called for the production of materials which were irrelevant to the grand jury's investigation and that the enforcement of the subpoenas would likely infringe upon the companies' First Amendment rights. The trial court refused to quash the subpoenas.

Previously, in United States v. Nixon, 418 U.S. 683 (1974), the Supreme Court had held that in order for a Rule 17(c) trial subpoena to be valid, the prosecutor had the burden of clearing three hurdles: (1) relevancy, (2) admissibility, and (3) specificity. In the *R. Enterprises* case, the Court of Appeals for the Fourth Circuit found that the *Nixon* standards were equally applicable to grand jury subpoenas; determined that the Government had failed to carry its burden on relevancy, admissibility, and specificity; and quashed the subpoenas. . . .

The Supreme Court looked to the unique role that a grand jury occupies as an investigatory body charged with the responsibility of determining whether a crime has been committed. Accordingly, the Court determined that a grand jury subpoena "is thus much different from a subpoena issued in the context of a prospective criminal trial, where a specific offense has been identified and a particular defendant charged." After reviewing its precedent, the Court opined that the "teaching of the Court's decisions is clear: A grand jury may compel the production of evidence or the testimony of witnesses as it considers appropriate, and its operation generally is unrestrained by the technical procedural and evidentiary rules governing the conduct of criminal trials." In other words, the multi-factor test announced in *Nixon* did not apply in the context of a grand jury subpoena.

However, the Supreme Court announced that the "investigatory powers of the grand jury are nevertheless not unlimited. Grand juries are not licensed to engage in arbitrary fishing expeditions, nor may they select targets of investigation out of malice or an intent to harass." The Court then proceeded to define the extent to which Rule 17(c) imposed a reasonableness limitation on grand jury subpoenas. The Court began "by reiterating that the law presumes, absent a strong showing to the contrary, that a grand jury acts within the legitimate scope of its authority," and that "the burden of showing unreasonableness must be on the recipient who seeks to avoid compliance." The Court then concluded that where the subpoena is challenged on relevance grounds, "the motion to quash must be denied unless the district court determines that there is no reasonable possibility that the category of materials the Government seeks will produce information relevant to the general subject of the grand jury's investigation."

Interestingly, the Court acknowledged that the burden on the challenging party to show unreasonableness may be difficult without knowing the general subject matter of the investigation. Accordingly, the Court noted that a district court "may be justified in a case where unreasonableness is alleged in requiring the Government to reveal the general subject of the grand jury's investigation before requiring the challenging party to carry its burden of persuasion."

[The] record does not suggest that Judge Buchanan applied any relevance standard at all in considering the motions to quash. Therefore, upon remand, the district court is directed to determine and make specific findings on the record as to whether there is no reasonable possibility that the patients' records being sought will produce information relevant to the general subject of the grand jury's investigation. Consistent with the procedure described in *R. Enterprises*, if necessary, the judge may require the prosecuting attorney to share with the court, in camera, the nature of the information the grand jury is seeking from the patients' records.

By way of example, neither the Respondents nor the Deputy District Attorney proffered to this court any compelling reason why the grand jury needs the records of any woman who did not have an abortion because two independent physicians did not make the requisite medical findings. . . . To clarify, the first step for the district court will be to assess whether each of the subpoenas meets the relevance threshold as articulated in this opinion. If not, the court should quash the subpoena or modify it to comport with the relevance standard. If a subpoena passes muster under the relevance test, the court will then move on to consider the remaining challenges to that subpoena.

UNDUE BURDEN

[In his concurring opinion in *R. Enterprises*, Justice Stevens noted] that the burden of establishing that compliance would be unreasonable or oppressive rests on the subpoena recipient, who must move to quash. Justice Stevens then described the movant's task:

> The moving party has the initial task of demonstrating to the Court that he has some valid objection to compliance. This showing might be made in various ways. Depending on the volume and location of the requested materials, the mere cost in terms of time, money, and effort of responding to a dragnet subpoena could satisfy the initial hurdle. Similarly, if a witness showed that compliance with the subpoena would intrude significantly on his privacy interests, or call for the disclosure of trade secrets or other confidential information, further inquiry would be required. Or, as in this case, the movant might demonstrate that compliance would have First Amendment implications.

[Once] a showing was made that a subpoena was intrusive or burdensome, it appears the concurrence would depart from the majority's strict "no reasonable possibility of relevance" standard. The concurrence would opt for a more flexible standard, e.g., "the degree of need sufficient to justify denial of the motion to quash will vary to some extent with the burden of producing the requested information."

We find this approach to be persuasive. If the challenge to a subpoena is based solely on the material being irrelevant, the motion to quash must be denied unless there is no reasonable possibility that the category of materials sought will produce information relevant to the general subject of the grand jury's investigation. However, if the subpoena recipient makes an initial showing that the subpoena is overly burdensome or intrudes on a privacy interest, the district court must balance the grand jury's need for the subpoenaed material against the burden or intrusion upon the subpoena recipient.

At the district court hearing, Tiller and WHCS argued that they estimated, from previous experience in redacting and copying patient records, it would take 5,000 person hours to prepare the 2,000 patient records subject to the subpoenas. They estimated the cost to redact and copy those records would be $250,000. While the Deputy District Attorney and the Respondents question the accuracy of those estimates, one simply cannot deny that the time, money, and effort required to redact and copy 2,000 patient records is burdensome. Likewise, their argument that the grand jury would accept fewer than all of the subpoenaed records is unsupported by the record. Although Judge Buchanan ruled that Tiller and WHCS could incrementally comply with the subpoena by providing the patient records in groups of 50, the subpoenas have not been modified and still command the production of all of the patients' records encompassed by the descriptions in the subpoenas.

Accordingly, we direct the district court to assess the degree of need the grand jury has in obtaining the material described in each subpoena and to balance that need against the burden imposed upon Tiller and WHCS. To accomplish that balancing analysis, the court may need to know what information the grand jury is seeking from the patients' records and the crime(s) which the grand jurors believe may be revealed by that information. If so, such information may be presented to the court in camera through the prosecuting attorney.

If the district court determines that the scales tip toward the subpoenas being overly burdensome, the judge should quash the subpoenas or modify them accordingly. If the district court determines that the State's interest is compelling enough to outweigh the burden on the subpoena recipient, the court should move to the next issue.

HARASSMENT

Tiller and WHCS complain that they have been maliciously targeted for investigation and that the subpoenas are intended to harass the recipients and disparage their reputation. These Petitioners point out that they were the targets of a 2004 inquisition commenced by the AG and a 2006 grand jury investigation which was also charged with investigating, inter alia, illegal late-term abortions. For factual support, they point to the declarations of the special interest groups that spearheaded the petition drive to summon this grand jury. For legal support, they rely on the language in the *R. Enterprises* majority opinion that grand juries may not "select targets of investigation out of malice or an intent to harass." . . .

In this case, Judge Buchanan correctly noted that the grand jurors are not the same persons who led the petition drive. However, the court should consider that some of the records have been subject to discovery in the 2004 inquisition and that the previous grand jury investigation in 2006 resulted in no indictment. In other words, the court should satisfy itself that the grand jury has not engaged in an arbitrary fishing expedition and that the targets were not selected and subpoenas issued out of malice or with intent to harass. If so, the court should quash the subpoenas. Otherwise, the court should move to the final issue of the patients' privacy interests.

PATIENTS' PRIVACY INTERESTS

The foregoing steps could pertain to any grand jury subpoena duces tecum. The constitutional privacy interests implicated by these subpoenas present a unique circumstance requiring additional analysis. [Three] federal constitutional privacy interests [are] subject to infringement by a subpoena for the production of abortion clinic patient records: (1) the right to maintain the privacy of certain information, (2) the right to obtain confidential health care, and (3) the fundamental right of a pregnant woman to obtain a lawful abortion without government imposition of an undue burden on that right. [An] individual's right to informational privacy is not necessarily absolute; rather, it is a conditional right which may be infringed upon a showing of proper governmental interest. [The] State's right to invade patient privacy for investigative purposes is likewise not absolute. . . .

Accordingly, we hold that the district court must consider the competing interests of the State and the patients. . . . This means that if and when the district court settles on the scope of records for which there is a compelling State interest that justifies intrusions upon the patients' constitutional privacy rights, the court must permit WHCS to redact all patient-identifying information from the records to be produced. Contrary to Judge Buchanan's blanket ruling, patient-identifying information may include the number assigned each patient by WHCS, depending on how that number is designed. Obviously, this redaction requirement would preclude the production of the original patient records, and that portion of the original subpoenas must be modified in any event.

Upon receipt of the redacted patient records, the court shall refer the records to an independent attorney and independent physician. The attorney and physician shall be advised of the information the grand jury is seeking from the records and the possible crimes under consideration, so that they may redact all irrelevant information from the files, regardless of whether such additional redactions would be considered patient-identifying information. . . .

In conclusion, the petitions for writs mandamus are granted in part. The matter is remanded to the district court for further proceedings in accordance with this opinion.

■ OHIO REVISED CODE §2939.12

When required by the grand jury, prosecuting attorney, or judge of the court of common pleas, the clerk of the court of common pleas shall issue subpoenas and other process to any county to bring witnesses to testify before such jury.

■ ARKANSAS STATUTES §16-43-212

(a) The prosecuting attorneys and their deputies may issue subpoenas in all criminal matters they are investigating and may administer oaths for the purpose of taking the testimony of witnesses subpoenaed before them. Such oath when administered by the prosecuting attorney or his deputy shall have the same effect as if administered by the foreman of the grand jury. . . .

Notes

1. *Breadth of document subpoena.* A recipient of a grand jury subpoena can challenge both the breadth of the subpoena and the burden of compliance. The Supreme Court stated in Oklahoma Press Publishing Co. v. Walling, 327 U.S. 186 (1946), that an unreasonably indefinite or overbroad subpoena might violate the Fourth Amendment or perhaps due process; in many states, such a subpoena would also violate statutes or rules of procedure. In United States v. R. Enterprises, 498 U.S. 292 (1991), Federal Rule of Criminal Procedure 17(c) placed the most pertinent limit on the range of documents requested: Compliance must not be "unreasonable or oppressive." What specific facts might convince a court that a particular subpoena is overbroad or too indefinite? Does the subject matter of the grand jury's investigation matter? How about the cost of collecting relevant documents? The proportion of a business's documents falling within the terms of the subpoena (as opposed to the absolute number of documents)?

2. *The justification needed for a subpoena.* In the strong majority of states and in the federal system, the prosecution does not need to make any preliminary showing of the relevance of testimony or other evidence sought through a grand jury subpoena. The probable cause necessary to support a search warrant is not a prerequisite for a grand jury subpoena. As the Court reasoned in United States v. Dionisio, 410 U.S. 1 (1973), a subpoena is different from an arrest, or even a more limited "stop," because the subpoena is served like any other legal process and involves no stigma and no force. Although the recipient of a subpoena to testify before a grand jury might challenge it on relevance grounds, it is very difficult to succeed on such a claim, in light of the breadth of the grand jury's duties to investigate any violations of the criminal law. The *Tiller* court in Kansas is typical in its willingness to allow the grand jury to obtain documents and testimony relevant to a broad range of *potentially* criminal conduct.

A few jurisdictions have required a modest grand jury showing of relevance. A grand jury subpoena in these courts is enforceable only if the grand jury (or the prosecutor on behalf of the grand jury) affirms that the testimony or documents it seeks will be relevant to a legitimate subject of inquiry. See In re Grand Jury Proceeding, Schofield I, 486 F.2d 85 (3d Cir. 1973). Would this preliminary statement from the grand jury make it any easier for the subpoena recipient to show that the subpoena is not relevant to some possible investigation? Should the level of justification to support a grand jury subpoena turn on the type of document involved? See State v. Nelson, 941 P.2d 441 (Mont. 1997) (state constitution requires state to show probable cause to support investigative subpoena for discovery of medical records).

3. *The prosecutor and grand jury subpoenas.* The subpoenas requiring witnesses to appear before a grand jury are, strictly speaking, issued under the authority of the grand jury itself. In practice, however, the prosecutor coordinating the grand jury's investigation has virtually complete control over the subpoenas that issue. Some statutes, such as the Ohio statute above, give independent authority to the prosecutor to issue grand jury subpoenas. Others give the prosecutor the power to subpoena a witness only if the grand jury approves of the request, either before or after the subpoena issues.

The Arkansas statute reprinted above is an unusual one, giving the prosecutor the subpoena power completely separate from the grand jury. See also Mich. Comp. Laws §§767A.1 et seq. (empowers prosecutors to issue investigatory subpoenas; judge must find probable cause that felony has been committed and that the person subpoenaed "may have knowledge regarding the commission of the felony," before authorizing investigative subpoena); Oman v. State, 737 N.E.2d 1131 (Ind. 2000) (prosecutor acting without grand jury must get court approval to subpoena documents). In the many states where prosecutors have no such subpoena power, do they miss significant investigative opportunities? Must they conduct all their witness interviews in front of the grand jury? How do prosecutors ever speak in private with hostile witnesses during an investigation? Some states (fewer than a dozen) allow a magistrate to issue a subpoena to witnesses during an investigation, requiring the witness to appear before the magistrate rather than a grand jury. This system is sometimes called the "one-man grand jury." See Idaho Code §19-3004. Would you insist on secrecy in such proceedings, as in grand jury proceedings? Would you allow the witness to have counsel present during the testimony?

4. *Subpoenas and search warrants.* A prosecutor advising a grand jury during an investigation may have the choice of obtaining documents through a subpoena or a search warrant. What considerations will help the prosecutor make the choice? As we have seen, a subpoena requires the government to show no reasonable suspicion or probable cause to believe that the subpoena will produce evidence of a crime, and it requires virtually no showing of relevance. A search warrant, of course, must be based on probable cause and must particularly describe the place to be searched and the things to be seized. In Carpenter v. United States, 585 U.S. __ (2018) (excerpted in Chapter 7), the Supreme Court suggested that the prosecution could not subpoena third parties for records in which the owner of the records has a reasonable expectation of privacy (in that case, records of Carpenter's cell site location); the records may only be obtained through a search warrant. The dissenters criticized this position, arguing that it would hamstring government investigations and that it departs from traditional doctrine on subpoenas: "A subpoena . . . permits a subpoenaed individual to conduct the search for the relevant documents

himself, without law enforcement officers entering his home or rooting through his papers and effects. As a result, subpoenas avoid the many incidental invasions of privacy that necessarily accompany any actual search."

Does a subpoena give the government a way to bypass all the ordinary restraints on searches and seizures? Is the deference to grand jury requests a relic, or are grand jury investigations truly different from investigations that would require a search warrant? Which method is likely to produce more evidence? Which will be more intrusive and which will cost the recipient more to comply with? State and federal statutes make it a crime for a person to destroy or alter documents that have been subpoenaed by a grand jury. How might these statutes affect a prosecutor's choice about the timing, scope, and recipients of subpoenas?

5. *Searches and freedom of the press.* In Zurcher v. Stanford Daily, 436 U.S. 547 (1978), the Supreme Court considered the validity of a search warrant authorizing the search of a newspaper's offices for photographs of demonstrators who had injured several police officers. The Court concluded that the Constitution imposed no special requirements for "third party" searches: The probable cause necessary to obtain a warrant was sufficient justification for a search, even if the target of the search was a newspaper not itself involved in wrongdoing. Congress responded to this decision by passing the Privacy Protection Act of 1980, 42 U.S.C. §2000aa. The statute, recognizing the special threats to the constitutional freedom of the press that are involved with searches of newspaper offices, creates a presumption in favor of subpoenas rather than search warrants to obtain documents from publishers. It prevents all criminal law enforcement agents (both state and federal) from searching for or seizing any "work-product materials" possessed by a publisher or broadcaster, unless there is probable cause to believe that the publisher has committed a crime relating to the documents or that immediate seizure is necessary to prevent death or serious bodily injury. Is this statute sufficient to protect the special First Amendment concerns involved in the search of newspaper offices? Cf. Branzburg v. Hayes, 408 U.S. 665 (1972) (enforcing grand jury subpoena for testimony of news reporter despite claim of privilege for news sources).

6. *Attorneys as subpoena and search targets.* Internal guidelines at the Department of Justice require special authorization before seeking a subpoena of an attorney to obtain information about that attorney's representation of a client. Before a federal prosecutor may request such a subpoena, the U.S. Attorneys' Manual §9-13.410 requires certification of the following: (1) information is not privileged, (2) information is reasonably necessary to complete investigation, (3) alternative sources of the information are not available, and (4) need for information outweighs "potential adverse effects" on attorney-client relationship. What sorts of harms might flow from issuing a subpoena to an attorney? One of the ABA Model Rules of Professional Conduct, Rule 3.8(e), at one time required a prosecutor to obtain judicial approval after an adversarial hearing before she could issue a grand jury subpoena to a lawyer. The rule has since been revised to remove the requirement of judicial approval, but ethics rules in a handful of states still retain it. Is the requirement consistent with the guidelines in the U.S. Attorneys' Manual?

Section 9-13.420 of the U.S. Attorney's Manual creates special rules for the use of search warrants to search the offices of attorneys who are suspects, subjects, or targets of a criminal investigation. The application may go forward only if there is a "strong need" for material and if alternatives (such as a subpoena) will not work because of a risk of destroyed documents. The rules call for the creation of a "privilege team" consisting of agents and lawyers not involved in the investigation, who must review seized documents to identify those containing possibly privileged information. The privilege team cannot reveal the contents of privileged documents to the investigating agents and attorneys. In special cases, such as the high-profile investigation of Michael Cohen, President Donald Trump's personal attorney, the court may appoint a "special master"—an independent third party (often a retired magistrate judge), to review documents subpoenaed or seized by federal authorities and determine whether any of them contain potentially privileged information. Cohen v. United States, In the Matter of Search Warrants Executed on April 9, 2018, Case 1:18-mj-03161-KMW (S.D.N.Y. April 27, 2018). Should a special master be appointed in all cases concerning searches or subpoenas of documents from attorneys?

7. *Negotiations over terms of compliance.* If your client receives a grand jury subpoena for documents, and you conclude that there is no viable constitutional basis for objecting to the subpoena, is there anything left to do except collect the documents and turn them over? Can you negotiate some less onerous form of compliance? What negotiating leverage do you have, if any?

8. *The contents of incriminating documents.* When a grand jury forces a witness to provide documents, including some that the witness created personally, is it forcing him to "witness" against himself? Should the privilege against self-incrimination apply to the contents of all documents a suspect creates? Under federal law, it is now clear that the privilege against self-incrimination generally cannot stop the grand jury from obtaining such documents. This is because the contents of these documents, while testimonial and potentially incriminating, was not produced under government compulsion; rather, the witness wrote the contents before the subpoena was issued and under no official pressure. See Fisher v. United States, 425 U.S. 391 (1976). All the states addressing this question have followed the federal lead. How much documentary evidence would be beyond the reach of a grand jury if the contents of documents were considered privileged when self-incriminating? If the government can force a person to turn over written statements that incriminate, does a privilege against oral testimony mean much at all?

9. *Act of production doctrine.* There is an exception to the *Fisher* rule regarding the contents of incriminating documents. Compliance with a subpoena is an implicit admission that the records requested in the subpoena exist, that they are in the possession or control of the subpoena recipient, and that they are authentic. The U.S. Supreme Court and all the state courts to address the issue recognize that the *act* of producing documents under a grand jury subpoena can give the government valuable information that might ultimately help convict the document holder of a crime. The contents of the documents, as opposed to the act of producing the documents, remains a valid source of evidence. See United States v. Doe, 465 U.S. 605 (1984) (act of producing incriminating business records is itself testimonial self-incrimination); Braswell v. United States, 487 U.S. 99 (1988) (individual representative of legal entity must submit subpoenaed documents to grand jury, but prosecution may not use act of production evidence against individual).

This area of law is nuanced, including complex fields such as the "collective entity" doctrine, the self-incrimination privilege for corporate entities, and the "required records" doctrine. For a review of these interconnected doctrines and practices, see the web extension for this chapter at *http://www.crimpro.com/extension/ ch10.*

10. *Testimonial vs. non-testimonial evidence.* The Supreme Court has held that "in order to be testimonial, an accused's communication must itself, explicitly or implicitly, relate a factual assertion or disclose information." Doe v. United States, 487 U.S. 201, 210 (1988). The Court has further described an action as testimonial when it requires a person to make "use of the contents of his own mind." United States v. Hubbell, 530 U.S. 27, 43 (2000). As the Court explained in *Hubbell,* by asking Hubbell to identify hundreds of documents responsive to the requests in the grand jury subpoena, the government made "extensive use of the 'contents of his own mind.' . . . The assembly of those documents was like telling an inquisitor the combination to a wall safe, not like being forced to surrender the key to a strongbox."

Is a person serving as a "witness" against herself if the grand jury asks for a blood sample for testing? Handwriting exemplars? Are these actions any different from the act of producing documents? In Schmerber v. California, 384 U.S. 757 (1966), the Court held that there is no compelled self-incrimination when a grand jury orders a witness to provide a blood sample. Some states make an exception to the grand jury's broad subpoena power when it comes to the most intrusive grand jury requests for evidence. For instance, grand juries will sometimes subpoena witnesses and ask for fingerprints, hair samples, or voice exemplars. Compare Woolverton v. Multi-County Grand Jury Oklahoma County, 859 P.2d 1112 (Okla. Crim. App. 1993) (requiring showing of probable cause to support request for blood samples, reasonable suspicion for palm prints), with United States v. Dionisio, 410 U.S. 1 (1973) (upholding subpoena for voice exemplar with no special government justification). Is there an argument for treating voice exemplars differently from palm prints? From blood samples? What about the results of a brain scan that could tell authorities whether a person is telling the truth (an MRI "lie detector")?

11. *Foregone conclusion exception.* Even when the act of production may be testimonial and incriminating, the government may nonetheless be able to compel a person to produce the document if it shows by reasonable particularity that it has independent knowledge of all the matters that the act of production communicates. In other words, the government must show that it already knows that the subpoenaed documents exist, that the person being subpoenaed has custody of the documents, and that they are authentic. As the Supreme Court explained in *Fisher,* in this case, the "existence and location of the papers are a foregone conclusion and the [person subpoenaed] adds little or nothing to the sum total of the Government's information by conceding that he in fact has the papers." Fisher v. United States, 425 U.S. 391 (1976). One way the prosecution can show that the existence and location of the documents are a "foregone conclusion" is if it can point to a previous admission by the person being subpoenaed that he has the papers being sought. The prosecution would also have to find an independent means of authenticating the documents sought (e.g., by calling an expert or a corporate custodian).

Problem 10-2. Compelling Passwords and Fingerprints

David Baust was indicted for strangling his girlfriend at his house. Pursuant to his girlfriend's complaint, in which she suggested that Baust videorecorded the assault, the police obtained a search warrant for Baust's home and were able to recover Baust's phone, several recording devices, assorted discs, flash drives, and computer equipment belonging to Baust. The victim and Baust both affirmed to the officers at the scene that a home recording device, connected to Baust's cell phone "could have possibly" recorded the assault and the recording "may exist" on the phone. Entry to the phone is possible only by password or fingerprint.

May the police compel Baust to produce the password to his phone? If the state can show that the existence of the password and Baust's possession of the *password* are a "foregone conclusion," does that change the analysis? Or must the state show that it has independent knowledge that Baust has possession and control of the relevant *cell phone*? Alternatively, does the state have to show that the existence of the *recording* on the phone is a "foregone conclusion"?

May the state compel Baust to provide his fingerprints to decrypt the phone? If the phone could be unlocked via "FaceID"—i.e., a scan of the owner's facial features—could the state compel Baust to have his face scanned to unlock the phone? See Commonwealth v. Baust, 89 Va. Cir. 267 (Va. Cir. Ct. 2014).

B. UNDERCOVER INVESTIGATIONS

Some crimes, such as prostitution, drug trafficking, or price fixing, involve voluntary transactions that are difficult for anyone other than the participants to observe. Sometimes government agents investigate such crimes through "undercover" operations, not revealing to their targets the fact that they are law enforcement officers. The undercover agent might pretend to participate in a crime as it takes place rather than inquiring after a crime has happened. The agent might also create the opportunity for some person to commit a crime under "simulated" conditions. How should judges, legislators, and enforcement officials respond to the dangers—and perhaps the necessity—of these enforcement techniques? When will a defendant escape a conviction because the government "entrapped" him?

■ PEOPLE v. JESSIE JOHNSON
647 N.W.2d 480 (Mich. 2002)

YOUNG, J.

This case involves the defense of entrapment. The circuit court found that defendant was entrapped by the police and dismissed two charges of possession with intent to deliver more than 225, but less than 650, grams of cocaine. The Court of Appeals affirmed in a split decision. We conclude that the lower courts clearly erred in finding that defendant was entrapped under Michigan's current entrapment test. . . .

FACTS AND PROCEEDINGS

Defendant was a police officer in the city of Pontiac. He also owned a house in the city of Pontiac that he rented out as a residence.

Defendant became the subject of a criminal investigation after one of defendant's former tenants turned informant and reported to the Pontiac police department that defendant was instrumental in operating his rented house as a drug den. The informant indicated that he sold crack cocaine from defendant's house with defendant's full knowledge and consent. Further, according to the informant, defendant arranged, oversaw, and protected the drug-selling operation. In exchange, defendant received a substantial portion of the profits from the drug sales.

The Pontiac police called in the state police for assistance in their investigation of defendant. An undercover officer from the state police department, Lieutenant Sykes, was introduced by the informant to defendant as a major drug dealer in Detroit and Mount Clemens who wished to expand his operations into Pontiac. Defendant agreed to meet with Sykes, but not pursuant to any police investigation he was conducting himself. Defendant was propositioned by Sykes to serve as protection and security from "rip-offs" and police raids for Sykes' drug operations, as well as to identify potential locations for drug dens in Pontiac. Defendant was to be compensated for his services. Defendant agreed to participate only after he determined that Sykes was not an undercover officer known to defendant's fellow Pontiac officers. Defendant made no attempt to arrest Sykes or report his illegal activities for further investigation.

At Sykes' request, defendant agreed to accompany Sykes to a mall on February 7, 1992, to assist him in purchasing drugs from a supplier. The supplier was in reality another undercover state police officer.

Defendant and Sykes arrived at the mall parking lot in different vehicles. After some preliminary discussions, Sykes drove over to the undercover officer to make the staged drug deal, while defendant walked. Armed with a gun in his pocket, defendant stood one and a half car lengths from the passenger side of the second undercover officer's vehicle. After the transaction began, Sykes directed defendant to come to the driver's side of the undercover officer's vehicle. Sykes then handed defendant the package of drugs received from the supplier in the staged drug deal. Defendant took the package and returned to Sykes' vehicle and waited for Sykes. At that time, defendant expressed some confusion regarding the exact procedures he was to follow, stating that he needed to know what to do "from A to Z." Sykes testified, and audiotapes of the February 7, 1992, drug deal confirm, that Sykes wanted defendant to take the drugs back to his car, check them, ensure that the package was correct, and notify Sykes of any problems. Sykes stated that in order for defendant to fulfill his duty to protect against "rip-offs," defendant would be required to hold and examine the drugs purchased. Sykes explained that he could not watch the supplier and the package at the same time. After this conversation, while defendant and Sykes weighed the cocaine, defendant indicated that as a result of their discussion he had a better understanding of what Sykes wanted him to do. Defendant did not express his unwillingness to perform the duties explained by Sykes. Sykes then paid defendant $1,000 for his assistance.

Sometime after this first drug deal, Sykes asked defendant if he wished to participate in future drug deals and told him that it was okay if he no longer wanted to participate. Defendant indicated that he wanted to be included in future transactions. As a result, a second, similarly staged drug deal occurred on March 4, 1992, immediately after which defendant was arrested.

Defendant was charged with two counts of possession with intent to deliver more than 225, but less than 650, grams of cocaine. [Johnson] moved to dismiss the charges on the basis of an entrapment theory. The trial court granted defendant's motion to dismiss, reasoning that Sykes had changed defendant's duty during the first transaction from one of protection to one of actual drug possession, thus entrapping defendant into the drug possessions.

As indicated, the Court of Appeals affirmed in a split decision. The majority wrote that "because many of the factors indicative of entrapment existed in this case, we hold that defendant has met his burden of proving that the police conduct would have induced an otherwise law-abiding person in similar circumstances as defendant to commit the offenses charged." It also concluded that "Sykes' conduct in this case was so reprehensible as to constitute entrapment." . . .

ANALYSIS

Under the current entrapment test in Michigan, a defendant is considered entrapped if either (1) the police engaged in impermissible conduct that would induce a law-abiding person to commit a crime in similar circumstances or (2) the police engaged in conduct so reprehensible that it cannot be tolerated. People v. Ealy, 564 N.W.2d 168 (Mich. App. 1997). However, where law enforcement officials present nothing more than an opportunity to commit the crime, entrapment does not exist.

INDUCING CRIMINAL CONDUCT

When examining whether governmental activity would impermissibly induce criminal conduct, several factors are considered: (1) whether there existed appeals to the defendant's sympathy as a friend, (2) whether the defendant had been known to commit the crime with which he was charged, (3) whether there were any long time lapses between the investigation and the arrest, (4) whether there existed any inducements that would make the commission of a crime unusually attractive to a hypothetical law-abiding citizen, (5) whether there were offers of excessive consideration or other enticement, (6) whether there was a guarantee that the acts alleged as crimes were not illegal, (7) whether, and to what extent, any government pressure existed, (8) whether there existed sexual favors, (9) whether there were any threats of arrest, (10) whether there existed any government procedures that tended to escalate the criminal culpability of the defendant, (11) whether there was police control over any informant, and (12) whether the investigation was targeted. People v. Juillet, 475 N.W.2d 786 (Mich. 1991).

In holding that defendant was entrapped, the Court of Appeals found that defendant had not previously committed the possession with intent to deliver offenses charged, the procedures employed by the government escalated defendant's conduct to the charged offense, and the offer of consideration was excessive. On the basis of these three factors, it held that "because many of the factors indicative of entrapment existed," the defendant "met his burden of proving that the police conduct would have induced an otherwise law-abiding person in similar circumstances as defendant to commit the offenses charged." We respectfully disagree.

First, while the Court of Appeals noted that defendant had "merely owned" a crack house and that no evidence existed that defendant was a drug dealer or even a drug user, it ignored ample evidence presented that defendant had in fact previously committed the offense of possession with intent to deliver. To be convicted of the charge of possession with intent to deliver, the defendant must have knowingly possessed a controlled substance, intended to deliver that substance to someone else, and the substance possessed must have actually been cocaine and defendant must have known it was cocaine. Actual physical possession is unnecessary for a conviction of possession with intent to deliver; constructive possession will suffice. Constructive possession exists when the totality of the circumstances indicates a sufficient nexus between defendant and the contraband. Possession is attributed not only to those who physically possess the drugs, but also to those who control its disposition. In addition, possession may be either joint or exclusive.

Defendant owned a home that he rented to tenants who operated it as a drug house. Despite being a police officer in the jurisdiction in which the house was located, defendant knew and consented to the house being used for drug sales. Further, defendant provided protection for the operation and received a portion of the profits from the drug sales, specifically $200 for each quarter ounce of drugs sold from the house. . . .

Under these circumstances, it is clear these alleged previous actions by defendant could serve as the foundation for a conviction for possession with intent to deliver under a constructive possession theory. Defendant had a duty to arrest the informant, yet not only did he permit the informant to sell drugs, he accepted money to provide protection for the operation. Without such protection, drugs would not have been sold from the house. Accordingly, defendant controlled the disposition of drugs at the house he owned and shared in the profits in so doing. For these reasons, we find clear error in the lower court's deduction that there was insufficient evidence to surmise that defendant had not previously committed the offense of possession with intent to deliver cocaine. [The] defendant's prior actions, at the very least, are sufficient to establish the charge of possession with intent to deliver cocaine as an aider and abettor. . . .

Therefore, no conduct by the state police in the undercover operation could serve to escalate defendant's prior criminal activity. Rather, the government simply provided defendant with an additional opportunity to commit a crime that he had previously committed. . . .

Similarly, defendant's culpability was not escalated at the scene of the first transaction in regard to the role defendant agreed to play in the undercover drug transaction. The touchstone of the Court of Appeals opinion in this regard was that placing the drugs in the hands of defendant at the scene of the first drug deal was a violation of what defendant had agreed to do. However, our review of the record leads us to conclude that touching the drugs should not have come as a surprise to defendant.

Although the taped recording of the first drug transaction suggests that defendant was unsure precisely what he was to do beyond providing "protection," that confusion was not based on defendant's lack of agreement to do more. [Defendant] was hired by Sykes to protect and secure against arrests, police raids, and "rip-offs." While the Court of Appeals construed "rip-off" as narrowly as possible by equating it with "theft," protecting against a "rip-off" would seem to include ensuring that drug packages received at drug deals contain actual drugs in the negotiated quantity and quality, a task that necessarily requires taking possession of the drugs in order to properly inspect them. . . .

In addition, defendant's willingness to participate in the crimes charged is evidenced by his agreement to participate in further transactions after he participated in the first transaction, which included his taking possession of the drugs. We further note that the second drug transaction between defendant and the undercover police officers exposes a consideration that the lower courts appear to have overlooked during their review. Initial entrapment does not immunize a defendant from criminal liability for subsequent transactions that he readily and willingly undertook. . . .

For these reasons, it is apparent that Sykes' handing the drugs to defendant for inspection during the first transaction failed to escalate defendant's criminal culpability. As a result, the Court of Appeals clearly erred in concluding otherwise.

Finally, the Court of Appeals majority clearly erred in holding that the amount of money offered for defendant's services was excessive and unusually attractive. [Given] defendant's understanding that he would receive $1,000 for each transaction, the compensation was neither excessive or unusually attractive. Each transaction involved approximately ten ounces of cocaine, which had an estimated street value of $75,000. A $1,000 fee for a transaction involving almost $75,000, roughly one percent of the street value, is not excessive. . . .

In sum, we have concluded that the Court of Appeals clearly erred in regard to each of the three factors that persuaded that Court to conclude that the police engaged in conduct that would induce a law-abiding person to commit a crime in similar circumstances. Therefore, because none of the remaining *Juillet* factors are at issue, we hold that defendant failed to establish by a preponderance of the evidence that the police engaged in conduct that would induce a law-abiding person to commit a crime in similar circumstances.

REPREHENSIBLE CONDUCT

The Court of Appeals alternatively held that the police conduct was so reprehensible that, as a matter of public policy, it could not be tolerated regardless of its relationship to the crime and therefore constituted entrapment. [Defendant willingly participated in the criminal enterprise and even met with Sykes at the Pontiac police department station before these drug deals in order to determine whether Sykes was an undercover officer who would be recognized by defendant's fellow officers.] Given our conclusion that defendant had previously committed the offense of possession with intent to deliver and that he agreed to provide protection against "rip-offs," which clearly includes handling the drugs in order to inspect them, the police did nothing more than provide defendant with an opportunity to commit a crime. Such conduct was not reprehensible and does not establish entrapment.

For these reasons, we conclude that the Court of Appeals clearly erred in finding that defendant established by a preponderance of the evidence that the police conduct in this case was so reprehensible as to constitute entrapment.

THE ENTRAPMENT TEST IN MICHIGAN

We originally granted leave to appeal in this case to consider whether the current entrapment test in Michigan, a modified objective test, is the most appropriate one. Accordingly, we asked the parties to address whether this Court should adopt the federal subjective test for entrapment. Sorrells v. United States, 287 U.S. 435 (1932). However, because defendant's case fails to meet even the current, more lenient modified objective test, we do not need to reach that question.

Nevertheless, after review of our entrapment defense law, we note that Chief Justice Corrigan has raised serious questions regarding the constitutionality of any judicially created entrapment test in Michigan. People v. Maffett, 633 N.W.2d 339 (Mich. 2001) (Corrigan, C.J., dissenting). Accordingly, we urge the Legislature to consider these questions and determine whether a legislative response is warranted. . . .

CAVANAGH, J., dissenting.

I concur in the majority's holding that the police conduct did not entrap defendant into the second transaction. However, I would conclude that the police conduct did entrap defendant into the first transaction; therefore, I respectfully dissent.

The majority's conclusion that defendant constructively possessed cocaine and, therefore, was not entrapped into committing the possession crimes is based on repeated references to the informant's claim that defendant "arranged, oversaw, and protected" the drug sales at the home defendant owned. [The informant, however,] did not testify at the entrapment hearing. Rather, the information that the informant allegedly relayed to the police came into evidence through the police officer the informant contacted about defendant. This officer testified as follows:

> Q. Now did this [informant] tell you how he [defendant] was involved? . . .
> A. He said he was running a dope house. [The defendant] owned the house and [the informant] was selling crack out of the house with [defendant's] full knowledge and consent and more or less participation; not in the actual sale, but in setting it up and providing protection and in running the operation. . . .

The most crucial part of the officer's testimony, which sheds light on the Court of Appeals reasoning, is omitted.

> Q. Did you ever run across any . . . evidence other than [the informant's] statements that [defendant] had been involved in the — this purported dope house? . . .
> A. Yes.
> Q. And what was that?
> A. I checked records on the house that was pointed out and [defendant] did in fact own that house; to me that was corroboration. . . .

The police officer initially stated that the informant told him defendant set up, ran, and supervised the drug house. However, when asked what information corroborated what the informant allegedly said, the officer pointed to only the fact that defendant owned the home and accepted money to look the other way. The trial court made its credibility determination on this testimony that defendant had no other involvement beyond owning the drug house and bribery. Contrary to the picture the majority paints of defendant's part in the drug sales occurring in the home he owned, the record supports the Court of Appeals conclusion that defendant did nothing more than own a crack house and accept money to keep silent. Thus, the majority's mischaracterization of defendant's involvement directly conflicts with this Court's duty to give deference to credibility determinations in light of direct testimony supporting them. . . .

I cannot join a decision that not only mischaracterizes the facts in favor of a result, but also strips the deference that is due credibility determinations made by lower courts in such a way as the majority does today. Accordingly, I would reverse in part the decision of the Court of Appeals holding defendant was entrapped into the second possession transaction and affirm in part the decision of the Court of Appeals holding defendant was entrapped into the first.

■ MODEL PENAL CODE §2.13
American Law Institute (1962)

(1) A public law enforcement official or a person acting in cooperation with such an official perpetrates an entrapment if for the purpose of obtaining evidence of the commission of an offense, he induces or encourages another person to engage in conduct constituting such offense by either:

(a) making knowingly false representations designed to induce the belief that such conduct is not prohibited; or

(b) employing methods of persuasion or inducement that create a substantial risk that such an offense will be committed by persons other than those who are ready to commit it.

(2) Except as provided in Subsection (3) of this Section, a person prosecuted for an offense shall be acquitted if he proves by a preponderance of evidence that his conduct occurred in response to an entrapment. The issue of entrapment shall be tried by the Court in the absence of the jury.

(3) The defense afforded by this Section is unavailable when causing or threatening bodily injury is an element of the offense charged and the prosecution is based on conduct causing or threatening such injury to a person other than the person perpetrating the entrapment.

■ MISSOURI REVISED STATUTES §562.066

1. The commission of acts which would otherwise constitute an offense is not criminal if the actor engaged in the prescribed conduct because he or she was entrapped by a law enforcement officer or a person acting in cooperation with such an officer.

2. An "entrapment" is perpetuated if a law enforcement officer or a person acting in cooperation with such an officer, for the purpose of obtaining evidence of the commission of an offense, solicits, encourages or otherwise induces another person to engage in conduct when he or she was not ready and willing to engage in such conduct.

3. The relief afforded by subsection 1 of this section is not available as to any crime which involves causing physical injury to or placing in danger of physical injury a person other than the person perpetrating the entrapment.

4. The defendant shall have the burden of injecting the issue of entrapment.

■ CINCINNATI POLICE DEPARTMENT, PROCEDURE MANUAL §12.131 CONFIDENTIAL INFORMANT MANAGEMENT AND CONTROL

A. A person must meet three criteria to establish them as a CI: (1) the person is in a unique position to help the Department in a present or future investigation, (2) the person will not compromise Department interests or activities, (3) the person will accept the direction necessary to effectively use their services.

B. Precautions when dealing with CIs:

1. Never provide CIs with knowledge of police facilities, operations, activities, or personnel.

2. Two police officers must be capable of contacting a CI. Two officers will be present at all contact with CIs unless otherwise approved by a supervisor. [When] dealing with CIs of the opposite sex or homosexual CIs, two officers will always be present. [Two] officers will always be present when paying CIs.

3. Immediately document initial debriefing contacts with CIs on Form 277, CI Registration and Reliability Report.

4. Document all significant contacts with CIs on Form 277A, Controlling District/Section/Unit Debriefing Report. Examples of significant contact are: (a) receiving information about criminals or criminal activity including information from phone conversations, (b) any compensation made to CIs, (c) any contact resulting in an arrest or the execution of a search warrant. . . .

D. Undesirable CIs are those who (1) commit an act which could endanger the life or safety of a police officer, (2) reveal the identity of a police officer to suspects, or in any other way compromise an official investigation, (3) try to use the Department to further criminal goals, (4) provide false or misleading information to police officers, (5) engage in conduct that brings discredit or embarrassment upon the Department. . . .

L. Controlled Purchases Using Confidential Informants:

(1) Get permission from an immediate supervisor before making controlled purchases.

(2) When possible, use CIs to introduce police officers to make purchases.

(3) Use a concealed body transmitting device and/or recording devices on CIs whenever possible. Never destroy recordings before the conclusion of court proceedings, including appeals.

(4) Search all CIs before and after conducting a controlled purchase of drugs. The Strip Search Law does not apply to the voluntary search of CIs. . . .

(5) Currency used in controlled purchases: (a) make an enlarged photocopy and record serial numbers, (b) two officers will witness buy money given to CIs.

(6) When possible, use two or more officers for surveillance of CIs during controlled purchases.

Notes

1. *Entrapment: majority position.* The Supreme Court first recognized an entrapment defense in Sorrells v. United States, 287 U.S. 435 (1932). In that case, a government

agent posed as a tourist and befriended Sorrells. The agent asked Sorrells to get him some illegal liquor. At first, Sorrells declined. Eventually, however, Sorrells obtained a half gallon of whiskey for the agent. The Supreme Court stated that improper entrapment occurs when "the criminal design originates with the officials of the Government, and they implant in the mind of an innocent person the disposition to commit the alleged offense and induce its commission in order that they may prosecute." The concurring opinions focused on the objective conduct of law enforcement personnel rather than on the subjective predisposition of the defendant.

The opinions in *Sorrells* were the origins of the "subjective" and "objective" approaches to entrapment. See also Sherman v. United States, 356 U.S. 369 (1958) (improper entrapment sets a "trap for the unwary innocent [rather than a] trap for the unwary criminal"); United States v. Russell, 411 U.S. 423 (1973) (also recognizing due process defense of "outrageous governmental conduct"). The *Sorrells* and *Sherman* cases were not constitutional rulings. The courts instead based the entrapment defense on the presumed intent of the legislators that had passed the criminal statutes involved. The courts reasoned that Congress did not mean to criminalize acts that were entirely the creations of government action.

More than 30 states follow the "subjective" test developed in the federal courts. Roughly 10 states apply the "objective" approach, exemplified in the Michigan opinion in *Johnson*. See People v. Barraza, 591 P.2d 947 (Cal. 1979). Another group of about half a dozen states use a "hybrid" approach, combining both subjective and objective elements. England v. State, 887 S.W.2d 902 (Tex. Crim. App. 1994); State v. Vallejos, 945 P.2d 957 (N.M. 1997). The subjective component of this mixed test requires evidence that the accused himself was actually induced to commit the charged offense by the persuasiveness of the police conduct. As for the objective component, the issue becomes whether the persuasion was enough to cause an ordinarily law-abiding person nevertheless to commit the offense.

If you were a prosecutor, would you systematically prefer one test over the other or would you guess that each test will be favorable to you in some factual settings and not in others? State courts sometimes adopt the entrapment doctrine (whether subjective or objective) through constitutional rulings or through their supervisory powers, whereas in many states the legislature codifies the defense. Section 2.13 of the Model Penal Code, which opts for the objective approach, has been influential. What might lead a legislature to adopt instead the subjective standard for entrapment? Could it be that those who are entrapped lack the criminal intent that the legislature was targeting when it defined the crime? If one reason to adopt an objective entrapment standard is to protect the integrity of the courts, should the legislatures attempt to address this question or should they leave it to the courts themselves?

2. *The pliability of subjective standards.* Under the "subjective" version of the entrapment defense, a defendant must demonstrate that the government "induced" him to commit the crime and that he was not "predisposed" to commit the crime. In Jacobson v. United States, 503 U.S. 540 (1992), the Supreme Court applied once again its subjective standard of entrapment. The opening words of the opinion tell the reader right away about the Court's view of the case:

> In February 1984, petitioner, a 56-year-old veteran-turned-farmer who supported his elderly father in Nebraska, ordered two magazines and a brochure from a California adult bookstore. The magazines . . . contained photographs of nude preteen and teenage boys. The contents of the magazines startled petitioner, who testified that

he had expected to receive photographs of "young men 18 years or older." [Postal] inspectors found petitioner's name on the mailing list of the California bookstore. . . . There followed over the next two and one half years, repeated efforts by two Government agencies, through five fictitious organizations and a bogus pen pal, to explore petitioner's willingness to break the new [child pornography] law by ordering sexually explicit photographs of children through the mail.

The Court explained that the evidence must demonstrate predisposition both prior to and independent of the government's acts. On the evidence presented, the Court found that neither Jacobson's prior behavior nor his response to the agencies' inducements was enough to establish predisposition. Does this mean that the government must have reasonable suspicion of wrongdoing before proceeding with a sting operation against a target? See Foster v. State, 13 P.3d 61 (Nev. 2000) (undercover police need not have grounds for believing that target is predisposed; overrules earlier case requiring reasonable cause).

3. *Entrapment and trial strategy.* When a defendant raises the entrapment defense, it has some important consequences at trial. Perhaps most important is the effect on the usual rules of evidence. Once a defendant claims entrapment, the rules barring the introduction of evidence of a defendant's prior criminal conduct are suspended. That evidence becomes relevant to proving predisposition; it also may be relevant to the reasonableness of the government's actions if government agents knew about the conduct. Because of this change in the rules of evidence, many defense lawyers consider entrapment to be a high-risk defense. Raising entrapment also affects the instructions a trial jury could receive about possible defenses, the allocation of authority between judge and jury, and other procedural issues. For an exploration of these trial issues, see the web extension for this chapter at *http://www. crimpro.com/extension/ch10.*

4. *Outrageous conduct: majority position.* Most state and federal courts recognize, at least theoretically, a constitutional defense to criminal charges based on the overly aggressive tactics of government investigators. In some jurisdictions, it is called "due process entrapment," while in others (including the federal system) it is known as "outrageous governmental conduct." United States v. Russell, 411 U.S. 423 (1973). However, the defense rarely succeeds. There is no clear consensus among courts on the elements necessary to prove the defense, although many courts consider the four issues raised by the New Jersey Supreme Court in State v. Johnson, 606 A.2d 315, 323 (N.J. 1992):

> Relevant factors are (1) whether the government or the defendant was primarily responsible for creating and planning the crime, (2) whether the government or the defendant primarily controlled and directed the commission of the crime, (3) whether objectively viewed the methods used by the government to involve the defendant in the commission of the crime were unreasonable, and (4) whether the government had a legitimate law enforcement purpose in bringing about the crime. [The] factors most invoked center around two major recurrent concerns: the justification for the police in targeting and investigating the defendant as a criminal suspect; and the nature and extent of the government's actual involvement in bringing about the crime.

The defense commonly appears in drug cases because it would be difficult to prosecute many narcotics violations (which are often consensual transactions leaving behind little evidence and few willing witnesses) without undercover operations.

Most courts and commentators note that there is some overlap between the defenses of subjective entrapment, objective entrapment, and due process "outrageous conduct." See Elizabeth E. Joh, Breaking the Law to Enforce It: Undercover Police Participation in Crime, 62 Stan. L. Rev. 155 (2009). The various tests all allow for some inquiry into both the predisposition of the defendant and the reasonableness of the government's conduct.

5. *Regulation or ban on undercover operations?* Are undercover operations simply too corrosive to tolerate in an open and democratic society? Consider this description of the use of informants in Communist East Germany: "Of all aspects of the MfS [Ministry for State Security], the generation of an army of individuals, willing to report suspicious information about acquaintances, friends, and family roused the fiercest resentment—and fear. The end result was to turn citizens against one another and to create an atmosphere of debilitating apprehension." Nancy Travis Wolfe, Policing a Socialist Society: The German Democratic Republic 78 (1992).

Police forces in nations other than the United States have been slower to adopt undercover techniques in the enforcement of ordinary criminal laws. For instance, Italian law evaluates the actions of government agents under the ordinary complicity doctrines of criminal law, meaning that an agent must not aid or abet a crime. See Jacqueline E. Ross, Impediments to Transnational Cooperation in Undercover Policing: A Comparative Study of the United States and Italy, 52 Am. J. Comp. Law 569 (2004). What would a society look like if the law prohibited undercover police operations? Conversely, what if the law gave judges no role in regulating undercover operations? See Richard H. McAdams, The Political Economy of Entrapment, 96 J. Crim. L. & Criminology 107 (2005).

6. *Confidential informant and undercover guidelines.* The use of a confidential informant raises special difficulty for law enforcement agencies because the government has less control over the actions of its agent. The problem is most pronounced when the informant participates in a crime while being paid by the government, as opposed to simply telling a police officer about past crimes. The Cincinnati police guidelines regarding confidential informants illustrate how executive branch agencies respond to these special concerns. What dangers were the drafters of the Cincinnati guidelines trying to prevent? See Alexandra Natapoff, Snitching: The Institutional and Communal Consequences, 73 U. Cin. L. Rev. 645 (2004) (use of informants is usually framed as a threat to accuracy, but in light of plea bargaining and prosecutorial discretion, threat extends to principles of accountability, predictability, and other rule of law precepts).

Most large police departments also have policies that address undercover operations, especially for narcotics and vice officers. For instance, the narcotics division of the Dallas Police Department requires written approval for all "long-term undercover operations" (longer than one to two hours). The undercover officer works with a partner whenever possible; when the officer must work undercover alone, a partner is still assigned to maintain daily contact, "cover" the undercover officer during sales, and maintain records and chain of custody for all evidence. The policy also forbids the officer to consume any narcotic unless forced to do so "under threat of immediate bodily injury." If you were drafting police guidelines on the subject of undercover investigations, what criteria would you set out for selecting the targets of undercover investigations?

7. *Supervision by prosecutors.* Prosecutors are often involved in planning and executing undercover operations. Although prosecutors have absolute immunity from any

tort suit for their "prosecutorial" decisions, that immunity does not extend to a prosecutor's actions when advising criminal investigators about an undercover operation. See Burns v. Reed, 500 U.S. 478 (1991) (granting qualified "good faith" immunity but not absolute immunity to prosecutors for participation in investigations). What tort claims might arise against a prosecutor who is advising criminal investigators?

Problem 10-3. Outrageous Government Conduct

Jerome Johnson, a New Jersey state trooper, and Wanda Bonet, Johnson's girlfriend, met a person who became their cocaine supplier. On one occasion, Johnson told his supplier, "I would like to rip off a drug dealer with a lot of cocaine and then I could turn around and sell it and make some money." Some months later, Johnson's supplier was arrested while delivering a large quantity of cocaine to an undercover agent of the Drug Enforcement Administration Task Force. The supplier decided to cooperate with law enforcement authorities by becoming an informant. He told DEA agents that Johnson was willing to "rip off" drugs from a drug dealer and then sell those drugs for money.

The federal agents and the New Jersey State Police jointly developed a plan to give Johnson the opportunity to steal drugs from a drug dealer and to sell those drugs. The plan contemplated that the informant would tell Johnson that he knew of an opportunity for Johnson to steal drugs from a drug courier and make a lot of money; that he, the informant, was acting as a broker for the sale of a kilogram of cocaine; that he had arranged for a "mule," a paid courier, to transport the drugs by car to a meeting place with a prospective buyer; and that the informant and the seller of the cocaine would be in a second car following the mule. According to the plan, Johnson, wearing his state trooper uniform, would pretend to make a traffic stop of the mule's car at a prearranged location and then would seize the cocaine. The seller of the cocaine, following in the car with the broker-informant, would see the seizure and chalk up the loss of the cocaine as a cost of doing business. Johnson then would meet the broker at Johnson's apartment and sell the cocaine to the mule for $5,000.

When the informant presented and explained the scheme to Johnson, he agreed to participate and added new elements to the plan. He requested $1,000 cash in advance, an unmarked car, and a portable flashing red light to use to make the traffic stop. Johnson also indicated he would change shifts so that he would be off-duty at the time of the stop. The informant and a detective, acting as the mule, met with Johnson and Bonet in their Newark apartment. The parties reviewed and discussed the details of the plan. The next day Johnson stopped the mule as planned and seized one kilogram of cocaine. The informant and a special agent, posing as the seller, drove off. Johnson drove to his apartment, followed by the mule. On his arrival at approximately 12:05 P.M., Johnson was arrested.

Johnson was indicted for drug offenses and for crimes related to the abuse of his office. He moved to dismiss the indictment on two grounds. First, he argued that the sting involved such outrageous government conduct that it violated state due process standards. Second, he claimed that the sting violated the New Jersey statutory entrapment defense, N.J. Stat. Ann. §2C:2-12, which provides as follows:

> A public law enforcement official or a person engaged in cooperation with such an
> official or one acting as an agent of a public law enforcement official perpetrates

an entrapment if for the purpose of obtaining evidence of the commission of an offense, he induces or encourages and, as a direct result, causes another person to engage in conduct constituting such offense by [employing] methods of persuasion or inducement which create a substantial risk that such an offense will be committed by persons other than those who are ready to commit it.

How would you rule? Compare *State v. Johnson*, 606 A.2d 315 (N.J. 1992).

PART TWO

EVALUATING CHARGES

XI

Defense Counsel

During the earliest phases of the criminal process, defense lawyers are rarely to be seen. But as the prosecution and police formulate and file charges against some suspects, and as the courts begin to process those charges, defense lawyers get involved.

In this chapter, we introduce the various sources of law that make it possible for a criminal defendant to get a lawyer. We also consider the practical value of these legal entitlements to the ordinary criminal defendant. Does having an attorney really matter to defendants? What do defense lawyers do?

The role of the defense attorney looks quite different in various criminal justice systems around the world. In the United States and other countries within the common-law tradition, the defense attorney takes the lead in testing the quality of the evidence and in protecting the rights of the defendant. Judges depend on adversarial parties—the prosecutor and the defense attorney—to frame legal issues and to develop the facts and legal arguments. Other criminal justice systems, operating within the "civil law" tradition, assign a less pivotal job to the defense lawyer and give the judge a more active "inquisitorial" role in developing evidence and presenting legal issues. See Jacqueline Hodgson, The Role of the Criminal Defence Lawyer in an Inquisitorial Procedure: Legal and Ethical Constraints, 9 Legal Ethics 125 (2006).

In short, the role that a defense attorney plays in a given system can tell you a lot about the assumptions built into criminal adjudication in that system. The legal rules and institutions that shape the work of defense lawyers, in a sense, reveal the values that take highest priority in criminal justice. Rules that address the work of defense attorneys also have ripple effects on the work of prosecutors and judges. Materials that preview the adjudicative process in a typical state court system in the United States, while developing the contrast between adversarial procedure and "inquisitorial" or "accusatorial" procedure, appear on the web extension for this chapter at *http://www.crimpro.com/extension/ch11.*

A. WHEN WILL COUNSEL BE PROVIDED?

Not every person charged with a crime consults a lawyer. The most common reason for a defendant to face charges alone, without a lawyer, is financial—defendants often cannot afford counsel. But our legal systems do not leave matters there. The same government that pays the judge, the prosecutor, and the investigators will also (at least in some cases) pay for the defendant's lawyer.

The question that has persisted over many decades is when the state will pay for defense counsel and when it will not. Some cases involve charges that are not serious enough to require counsel; some proceedings are too early or late in the process to require counsel. This section reviews the law on (1) the types of charges necessary to invoke constitutional and statutory rights to counsel and (2) the types of criminal proceedings that trigger a defendant's right to counsel.

1. Types of Charges

Constitutions have much to say about the availability of defense counsel. The Sixth Amendment to the federal constitution states, "In all criminal prosecutions, the accused shall enjoy the right . . . to have the assistance of counsel for his defence." Almost every state constitution has an equivalent provision.

The most important early decision regarding the Sixth Amendment right to counsel was Powell v. Alabama, 287 U.S. 45 (1932). The defendants were nine young black men who were accused of raping two young white women on a train near Scottsboro, Alabama. The case against the defendants attracted much local attention: Soldiers escorted the defendants to and from their proceedings to protect them from hostile mobs. None of the defendants was literate, and none was a resident of Alabama.

The defendants were divided into three groups for trial. The first trial began six days after indictment, and each of the three trials was completed within one day. Until the morning of the first trial, the court named no particular lawyer to represent the defendants. The trial judge instead appointed all the members of the Scottsboro bar "for the limited purpose of arraigning" the defendants. Some members of the bar consulted with the defendants in jail but did nothing further. A colloquy on the morning of the trial left it unclear which attorney, if any, would represent the defendants at trial. An attorney sent from Tennessee by people concerned about the defendants' situation was unprepared to serve as lead counsel, but members of the Scottsboro bar were quick to say they would "assist" the newly arrived lawyer. The juries found all the defendants guilty and imposed the death penalty upon each of them.

The Supreme Court concluded that appointment of a primary defense lawyer, at least under these circumstances, was a requirement of due process. The Court made some general observations about the value of legal counsel:

> The right to be heard would be, in many cases, of little avail if it did not comprehend the right to be heard by counsel. Even the intelligent and educated layman has small and sometimes no skill in the science of law. If charged with crime,

he is incapable, generally, of determining for himself whether the indictment is good or bad. He is unfamiliar with the rules of evidence. Left without the aid of counsel he may be put on trial without a proper charge, and convicted upon incompetent evidence, or evidence irrelevant to the issue or otherwise inadmissible. He lacks both the skill and knowledge adequately to prepare his defense, even though he had a perfect one. He requires the guiding hand of counsel at every step in the proceedings against him. Without it, though he be not guilty, he faces the danger of conviction because he does not know how to establish his innocence.

287 U.S. at 68-69. The opinion also stressed some of the more compelling facts in the case:

In the light [of] the ignorance and illiteracy of the defendants, their youth, the circumstances of public hostility, the imprisonment and the close surveillance of the defendants by the military forces, the fact that their friends and families were all in other states and communication with them [was] necessarily difficult, and above all that they stood in deadly peril of their lives, . . . the necessity of counsel was so vital and imperative that the failure of the trial court to make an effective appointment of counsel was . . . a denial of due process within the meaning of the Fourteenth Amendment. Whether this would be so in other criminal prosecutions, or under other circumstances, we need not determine. . . . In a case such as this, whatever may be the rule in other cases, the right to have counsel appointed, when necessary, is a logical corollary from the constitutional right to be heard by counsel.

287 U.S. at 71. The Scottsboro case became an international *cause célèbre*. A crusading New York lawyer, Samuel Leibowitz, participated in the defense during the second trial, which also ended in the conviction of all defendants by an all-white jury. After the later convictions were overturned on appeal in the state system, the government agreed to a plea agreement allowing for the release of four defendants and prison terms for the other five. See James Goodman, Stories of Scottsboro (1994); Michael J. Klarman, *Powell v. Alabama*: The Supreme Court Confronts "Legal Lynchings," in Criminal Procedure Stories (Carol Steiker ed., 2006).

After a series of later Supreme Court cases considering the right to appointed counsel at trial, Betts v. Brady, 316 U.S. 455 (1942), settled on the "special circumstances" test to govern the appointment of counsel; that is, counsel would be constitutionally required only under "special circumstances," and not in every criminal case. Betts was indicted for robbery. Due to lack of funds, he was unable to employ counsel, and asked the judge to appoint counsel for him. The judge refused because the local practice was to appoint counsel only in prosecutions for murder and rape. Betts then pleaded not guilty and elected to be tried without a jury. Witnesses were summoned on his behalf. He cross-examined the State's witnesses and examined his own alibi witnesses. Betts did not take the witness stand. The judge found him guilty and sentenced him to eight years in prison. The Court concluded that due process did not require the appointment of counsel under these circumstances.

In the following case, the Supreme Court returned to the question of appointed counsel, this time giving a different answer.

■ CLARENCE EARL GIDEON v. LOUIE WAINWRIGHT
372 U.S. 335 (1963)

BLACK, J.*

Petitioner was charged in a Florida state court with having broken and entered a poolroom with intent to commit a misdemeanor. This offense is a felony under Florida law. Appearing in court without funds and without a lawyer, petitioner asked the court to appoint counsel for him. [When the Court denied his request, Gideon objected: "The United States Supreme Court says I am entitled to be represented by Counsel."]

Put to trial before a jury, Gideon conducted his defense about as well as could be expected from a layman. He made an opening statement to the jury, cross-examined the State's witnesses, presented witnesses in his own defense, declined to testify himself, and made a short argument "emphasizing his innocence to the charge contained in the Information filed in this case." The jury returned a verdict of guilty, and petitioner was sentenced to serve five years in the state prison. [The state supreme court later denied habeas corpus relief.] Since 1942, when Betts v. Brady, 316 U.S. 455, was decided by a divided Court, the problem of a defendant's federal constitutional right to counsel in a state court has been a continuing source of controversy and litigation in both state and federal courts. To give this problem another review here, we granted certiorari. . . .

I.

The facts upon which Betts claimed that he had been unconstitutionally denied the right to have counsel appointed to assist him are strikingly like the facts upon which Gideon here bases his federal constitutional claim. Betts was indicted for robbery in a Maryland state court. On arraignment, . . . Betts was advised that it was not the practice in that county to appoint counsel for indigent defendants except in murder and rape cases. He then pleaded not guilty, had witnesses summoned, cross-examined the State's witnesses, examined his own, and chose not to testify himself. He was found guilty by the judge, sitting without a jury. [Upon review of the conviction, this Court] held that a refusal to appoint counsel for an indigent defendant charged with a felony did not necessarily violate the Due Process Clause of the Fourteenth Amendment. . . . The Court said: "Asserted denial [of due process] is to be tested by an appraisal of the totality of facts in a given case. That which may, in one setting, constitute a denial of fundamental fairness, shocking to the universal sense of justice, may, in other circumstances . . . fall short of such denial."

Treating due process as "a concept less rigid and more fluid than those envisaged in other specific and particular provisions of the Bill of Rights," the Court held that refusal to appoint counsel under the particular facts and circumstances in the *Betts* case was not so "offensive to the common and fundamental ideas of fairness" as to amount to a denial of due process. Since the facts and circumstances of the two cases are so nearly indistinguishable, we think the Betts v. Brady holding if left standing would require us to reject Gideon's claim that the Constitution guarantees

*[Chief Justice Warren and Justices Douglas, Brennan, Stewart, White, and Goldberg joined this opinion.—EDS.]

him the assistance of counsel. Upon full reconsideration we conclude that Betts v. Brady should be overruled.

II.

The Sixth Amendment provides, "In all criminal prosecutions, the accused shall enjoy the right . . . to have the Assistance of Counsel for his defence." We have construed this to mean that in federal courts counsel must be provided for defendants unable to employ counsel unless the right is competently and intelligently waived. [In *Betts*, the Court] set out and considered "relevant data on the subject . . . afforded by constitutional and statutory provisions subsisting in the colonies and the States prior to the inclusion of the Bill of Rights in the national Constitution, and in the constitutional, legislative, and judicial history of the States to the present date." On the basis of this historical data the Court concluded that appointment of counsel is not a fundamental right, essential to a fair trial, [and thus was not a due process requirement applicable to the States].

We accept Betts v. Brady's assumption, based as it was on our prior cases, that a provision of the Bill of Rights which is "fundamental and essential to a fair trial" is made obligatory upon the States by the Fourteenth Amendment. We think the Court in *Betts* was wrong, however, in concluding that the Sixth Amendment's guarantee of counsel is not one of these fundamental rights. Ten years before Betts v. Brady, this Court, after full consideration of all the historical data examined in *Betts*, had unequivocally declared that "the right to the aid of counsel is of this fundamental character." Powell v. Alabama, 287 U.S. 45, 68 (1932). While the Court at the close of its *Powell* opinion did by its language, as this Court frequently does, limit its holding to the particular facts and circumstances of that case, its conclusions about the fundamental nature of the right to counsel are unmistakable. Several years later, in 1936, the Court reemphasized what it had said about the fundamental nature of the right to counsel in this language:

> We concluded that certain fundamental rights, safeguarded by the first eight amendments against federal action, were also safeguarded against state action by the due process of law clause of the Fourteenth Amendment, and among them the fundamental right of the accused to the aid of counsel in a criminal prosecution.

Grosjean v. American Press Co., 297 U.S. 233, 243-44 (1936). [Similar statements appear in several other decisions. In] deciding as it did—that "appointment of counsel is not a fundamental right, essential to a fair trial"—the Court in Betts v. Brady made an abrupt break with its own well-considered precedents. In returning to these old precedents, sounder we believe than the new, we but restore constitutional principles established to achieve a fair system of justice.

Not only these precedents but also reason and reflection require us to recognize that in our adversary system of criminal justice, any person haled into court, who is too poor to hire a lawyer, cannot be assured a fair trial unless counsel is provided for him. This seems to us to be an obvious truth. Governments, both state and federal, quite properly spend vast sums of money to establish machinery to try defendants accused of crime. Lawyers to prosecute are everywhere deemed essential to protect the public's interest in an orderly society. Similarly, there are few defendants charged with crime, few indeed, who fail to hire the best lawyers they can get to prepare and present their defenses. That government hires lawyers to prosecute and defendants who have the money hire lawyers to defend are the strongest indications of the widespread belief that lawyers in criminal courts are necessities, not luxuries. The right of one charged with crime to counsel may not be deemed fundamental and essential to fair trials in some countries, but it is in ours. From the very beginning, our state and national constitutions and laws have laid great emphasis on procedural and substantive safeguards designed to assure fair trials before impartial tribunals in which every defendant stands equal before the law. This noble ideal cannot be realized if the poor man charged with crime has to face his accusers without a lawyer to assist him. . . .

The Court in Betts v. Brady departed from the sound wisdom upon which the Court's holding in Powell v. Alabama rested. Florida, supported by two other States, has asked that Betts v. Brady be left intact. Twenty-two States, as friends of the Court, argue that *Betts* was "an anachronism when handed down" and that it should now be overruled. We agree. . . .

HARLAN, J., concurring.

I agree that Betts v. Brady should be overruled, but consider it entitled to a more respectful burial than has been accorded, at least on the part of those of us who were not on the Court when that case was decided. I cannot subscribe to the view that Betts v. Brady represented "an abrupt break with its own well-considered precedents." In 1932, in Powell v. Alabama, a capital case, this Court declared that under the particular facts there presented—"the ignorance and illiteracy of the defendants, their youth, the circumstances of public hostility . . . and above all that they stood in deadly peril of their lives"—the state court had a duty to assign counsel for the trial as a necessary requisite of due process of law. It is evident that these limiting facts were not added to the opinion as an afterthought; they were repeatedly emphasized, and were clearly regarded as important to the result.

Thus when this Court, a decade later, decided Betts v. Brady, it did no more than to admit of the possible existence of special circumstances in noncapital as well as capital trials, while at the same time insisting that such circumstances be shown in order to establish a denial of due process. The right to appointed counsel had been recognized as being considerably broader in federal prosecutions, but to have imposed these requirements on the States would indeed have been "an abrupt break" with the almost immediate past. . . .

The principles declared in *Powell* and in *Betts*, however, have had a troubled journey throughout the years that have followed first the one case and then the other. . . . In noncapital cases, the "special circumstances" rule has continued to exist in form while its substance has been substantially and steadily eroded. [Since 1950] there have been not a few cases in which special circumstances were found in little or nothing more than the "complexity" of the legal questions presented, although those questions were often of only routine difficulty. The Court has come to recognize, in other words, that the mere existence of a serious criminal charge constituted in itself special circumstances requiring the services of counsel at trial. In truth the Betts v. Brady rule is no longer a reality. This evolution, however, appears not to have been fully recognized by many state courts, in this instance charged with the front-line responsibility for the enforcement of constitutional rights. To continue a rule which is honored by this Court only with lip service is not a healthy thing and in the long run will do disservice to the federal system.

The special circumstances rule has been formally abandoned in capital cases, and the time has now come when it should be similarly abandoned in noncapital cases, at least as to offenses which, as the one involved here, carry the possibility of a substantial prison sentence. (Whether the rule should extend to all criminal cases need not now be decided.) This indeed does no more than to make explicit something that has long since been foreshadowed in our decisions. . . .

■ FLORIDA RULE OF CRIMINAL PROCEDURE 3.111

(a) A person entitled to appointment of counsel as provided herein shall have counsel appointed when the person is formally charged with an offense, or as soon as feasible after custodial restraint, or at the first appearance before a committing judge, whichever occurs earliest.

(b) (1) Counsel shall be provided to indigent persons in all prosecutions for offenses punishable by incarceration including appeals from the conviction thereof. In the discretion of the court, counsel does not have to be provided to an indigent person in a prosecution for a misdemeanor or violation of a municipal ordinance if the judge, at least 15 days prior to trial, files in the cause a written order of no incarceration certifying that the defendant will not be incarcerated in the case pending trial or probation violation hearing, or as part of a sentence after trial, guilty or nolo contendere plea, or probation revocation. This 15-day requirement may be waived by the defendant or defense counsel.

> (A) If the court issues an order of no incarceration after counsel has been appointed to represent the defendant, the court may discharge appointed counsel unless the defendant is incarcerated or the defendant would be substantially disadvantaged by the discharge of appointed counsel. . . .
>
> (C) If the court withdraws its order of no incarceration, it shall immediately appoint counsel if the defendant is otherwise eligible for the services of the public defender. The court may not withdraw its order of no incarceration once the defendant has been found guilty or pled nolo contendere.

(2) Counsel may be provided to indigent persons in all proceedings arising from the initiation of a criminal action against a defendant, including post-conviction proceedings and appeals therefrom, extradition proceedings, mental competency proceedings, and other proceedings that are adversary in nature, regardless of the designation of the court in which they occur or the classification of the proceedings as civil or criminal.

(3) Counsel may be provided to a partially indigent person on request, provided that the person shall defray that portion of the cost of representation and the reasonable costs of investigation as he or she is able without substantial hardship to the person or the person's family, as directed by the court.

(4) "Indigent" shall mean a person who is unable to pay for the services of an attorney, including costs of investigation, without substantial hardship to the person or the person's family; "partially indigent" shall mean a person unable to pay more than a portion of the fee charged by an attorney, including costs of investigation, without substantial hardship to the person or the person's family.

■ VERMONT STATUTES TIT. 13, §§5231, 5201

§5231

A needy person who is being detained by a law enforcement officer without charge or judicial process, or who is charged with having committed or is being detained under a conviction of a serious crime, is entitled:

(1) To be represented by an attorney to the same extent as a person having his own counsel; and

(2) To be provided with the necessary services and facilities of representation. Any such necessary services and facilities of representation that exceed $1,500 per item must receive prior approval from the court after a hearing involving the parties. . . . This obligation and requirement to obtain prior court approval shall also be imposed in like manner upon the Attorney General or a State's Attorney prosecuting a violation of the law. . . .

§5201

In this chapter, the term . . .

(4) "Serious crime" includes: (A) A felony; (B) A misdemeanor the maximum penalty for which is a fine of more than $1,000 or any period of imprisonment unless the judge, at the arraignment but before the entry of a plea, determines and states on the record that he or she will not sentence the defendant to a fine of more than $1,000 or period of imprisonment if the defendant is convicted of the misdemeanor. . . .

(5) "Serious crime" does not include the following misdemeanor offenses unless the judge at arraignment but before the entry of a plea determines and states on the record that a sentence of imprisonment or a fine over $1,000 may be imposed on conviction: [big game violations, simple assault by mutual consent, bad checks, petty larceny, theft of services under $500, retail theft under $900, unlawful mischief, unlawful trespass, disorderly conduct, possession of marijuana first offense, violation of municipal ordinance].

Notes

1. *Constitutional right to appointed defense counsel in minor cases: majority position.* The reach of *Gideon*'s rule has expanded over time. *Gideon* itself talked about access to counsel in felony cases. A few years later, in Argersinger v. Hamlin, 407 U.S. 25 (1972), access to appointed counsel broadened to include any criminal proceeding—felony, misdemeanor, or petty offense—if the conviction "actually leads to imprisonment even for a brief period." On the other hand, under this rule, counsel need not be appointed for misdemeanor convictions that result in a fine, but not "actual imprisonment." Scott v. Illinois, 440 U.S. 367 (1979).

The scope of the constitutional rule expanded again in Alabama v. Shelton, 535 U.S. 654 (2002). Shelton was convicted of third-degree assault, a misdemeanor, and was sentenced to a jail term of 30 days, which the trial court immediately suspended, placing him on probation for two years. The Court held that a suspended sentence that may "end up in the actual deprivation of a person's liberty" may not be imposed unless the defendant was accorded "the guiding hand of counsel" during the criminal proceedings. This holding expanded the constitutional right to counsel to a much larger group of defendants; there are reasons to believe that some states still are not in compliance with *Shelton.*

What do the courts in *Gideon* and in *Shelton* believe that lawyers do? Are attorneys indispensable to criminal justice, or an impediment to criminal justice, or both? Consider, in this connection, what happened to Clarence Gideon. After the Supreme Court reversed Gideon's conviction, an attorney defended Gideon at his retrial on the charges. He was acquitted. See Anthony Lewis, Gideon's Trumpet 223-238 (1964).

2. *Statutory right to appointed counsel in minor cases.* There is more variation among state statutes providing counsel than among state constitutional interpretations. Some states have statutes or rules that simply track the federal and state constitutional requirements. States such as Vermont, however, add to the list of crimes for which the state must provide counsel for indigent defendants. Some states also provide counsel for some cases involving large criminal fines.

Perhaps the most important statutory provisions and rules on this subject are the ones (like the Florida rule above) giving a trial judge the *discretion* to appoint counsel in any criminal proceedings, regardless of the crime involved. The critical decisions in these jurisdictions are funding decisions, which are often made at the local rather than state level. Will a city provide enough money to fund attorneys for all those accused of violating its criminal ordinances? As a trial judge, can you identify any class of cases where you would not routinely appoint counsel even if the funds were available? Funding for indigent criminal defense takes place against a complex political background, which receives fuller attention on the web extension for this chapter at *http://www.crimpro.com/extension/ch11.*

3. *Determination of indigence.* The trial court typically determines, in a hearing soon after charges are filed, whether or not the defendant qualifies as an indigent to receive state-provided counsel. The trial judge must consult factors listed in appellate opinions, statutes, or procedure rules, but those factors tend to be general enough to leave the trial judge with much discretion in deciding which defendants qualify. The judge often must consider such factors as the seriousness of the crime, the amount of bail bond required, and the defendant's income. See Tenn. Code §40-14-202(c). The state might provide counsel and later attempt to collect the attorney's fees from defendants who have more resources than they originally appeared to have. In the end, the great majority of felony defendants are indigents who receive public defenders or appointed counsel. By some estimates, more than three-quarters of all defendants charged with eligible crimes are provided with counsel.

4. *Recoupment of fees.* State statutes typically allow the government to recoup some fees for the services of the defense attorney if the defendant is convicted and the court later finds that the defendant has the funds for at least a partial payment of the attorney's fees. See State v. Dudley, 766 N.W.2d 606 (Iowa 2009) (statute requiring acquitted indigent defendants to reimburse cost of defense, if applied without means test, violates right to counsel). In most jurisdictions, judges tell the defendant about these recoupment laws when asking whether the defendant wants

to waive counsel. Exactly how would you word this notice to defendants if you were a trial judge?

5. *Distribution of offenses.* The decision to provide counsel for different classes of misdemeanants has serious consequences, not the least of them fiscal. If felonies rest at the top of a "pyramid" of criminal charges, the least serious misdemeanors are the charges at the broad bottom of the pyramid: In most systems, they are by far the most numerous charges. See Bureau of Justice Statistics, Prosecutors in State Courts, 2005 at 6 (July 2006, NCJ 213799) (prosecutors' offices close three times more misdemeanor cases than felony cases). As a result, choices about the appointment of counsel for the lowest-level charges will generally have the largest impact on the system for providing counsel. The federal system is atypical on this score, since only about a quarter of all charges filed in a given year are misdemeanors. Many states create special court systems to handle the lowest-level offenses, with names such as "misdemeanor court" or "district court."

6. *Constitutional sources of the right to counsel.* Keep in mind the different constitutional sources for the right to counsel. In some settings (a "criminal prosecution"), the Sixth Amendment requires counsel to be available. When it comes to police station interrogations, the Fifth Amendment requires that a defendant be told about the right to have counsel present. In others (such as some postconviction proceedings), the due process clause requires counsel. In still other settings, the equal protection clause requires the state to provide counsel to all if it allows counsel for some. Recall also that most states have analogs to these federal constitutional provisions. What constitutional source was the basis for the *Gideon* decision?

What does the text of the Sixth Amendment suggest about the types of cases in which the state must provide counsel? On the one hand, the amendment does provide for a right to counsel "in *all* criminal prosecutions." Thus, it would seem to cover any misdemeanor. On the other hand, the Sixth Amendment was originally thought to address access to *retained* counsel, not defense counsel provided by the state. The Sixth Amendment right to counsel apparently was drafted as a repudiation of the common law of England, which prevented those accused of most felonies from relying upon retained counsel to conduct their defense at trial.

7. *Incorporation.* Long before *Gideon*, the Supreme Court declared that the Sixth Amendment required the government to appoint counsel for all criminal defendants in *federal* court. See Johnson v. Zerbst, 304 U.S. 458 (1938). The language of the Sixth Amendment and the rest of the Bill of Rights applied only to the federal government, not to the states. Thus, the *Gideon* Court had to resolve the larger question (given the relative sizes of the federal and state criminal systems) of whether the due process clause of the Fourteenth Amendment—which did apply to the states—"incorporated" the specific guarantees of the Bill of Rights.

The majority in *Gideon* argued that the *Betts* rule was an aberration and a departure from earlier cases dealing with the incorporation of the right to counsel; Justice John Marshall Harlan suggested instead that the *Betts* case was a plausible but impracticable extension of earlier cases. Who was right?

The Supreme Court has decided that due process "selectively" incorporates some Bill of Rights guarantees. *Gideon* was an important development in this broader constitutional trend. While there has been debate over the years about the extent to which the framers and adopters of the Fourteenth Amendment intended to incorporate provisions of the Bill of Rights, the current consensus seems to be that the Court was substantially correct to incorporate most, if not all, of the provisions.

See Michael Kent Curtis, No State Shall Abridge: The Fourteenth Amendment and the Bill of Rights (1986); Akhil Amar, The Bill of Rights and the Fourteenth Amendment, 101 Yale L.J. 1193 (1992).

8. *Appointment of experts.* In Ake v. Oklahoma, 470 U.S. 68 (1985), the Supreme Court held that the due process and equal protection clauses (but not the Sixth Amendment) require a state to provide an indigent defendant with access to a psychiatrist if the defendant makes a preliminary showing that his sanity will be a "significant issue" at trial. Later litigation focused on the question of when an appointed expert is one of the "raw materials integral to building an effective defense." See Caldwell v. Mississippi, 472 U.S. 320 (1985) (trial court properly denied an indigent defendant's requests for the appointment of a criminal investigator, a fingerprint expert, and a ballistics expert). Most courts that have considered the appointment of a non-psychiatric expert have held that state constitutions require the appointment of non-psychiatric experts to indigent defendants where they make a "particularized" showing of the need for the assistance. See Rey v. State, 897 S.W.2d 333 (Tex. Crim. App. 1995) (requiring appointment of pathologist to assist in cross-examination of state pathologist regarding autopsy). Some states determine the "particularized need" by asking the defendant to show prejudice if the expert is not available. See Dowdy v. Commonwealth, 686 S.E.2d 710 (Va. 2009) (defendant failed to show adequate prejudice from failure of state to provide investigator to locate alibi witnesses).

Problem 11-1. Advice on Counsel

The governor of Rhode Island is drafting his budget request to the state legislature and hopes to spend less in the category of indigent criminal defense. He wonders whether the state constitution will allow him to reduce the operating budget for defense lawyers.

The Rhode Island constitutional analog to the Sixth Amendment guarantee of the right to counsel is found in article I, section 10, of the Rhode Island Constitution. This section protects a defendant's right to assistance of counsel in terms almost identical to those of its federal counterpart: "In all criminal prosecutions, accused persons shall . . . have the assistance of counsel in their defense."

The Rhode Island Supreme Court, in State v. Holliday, 280 A.2d 333 (R.I. 1971), extended the right to counsel for indigent defendants charged with serious *misdemeanors* that could subject them to an imposition of penalty in excess of six months' imprisonment. Then in State v. Moretti, 521 A.2d 1003 (R.I. 1987), the court held that if an indigent criminal defendant faces a *potential* sentence of more than six months, Rhode Island constitutional law guarantees to a defendant appointed counsel, even if the trial justice predetermines that no prison sentence will be imposed.

The state constitution allows the governor to request an "advisory opinion" from the Rhode Island Supreme Court to clarify the meaning of state law. The governor has certified this question to the Justices: "Is the State of Rhode Island required by the Rhode Island Constitution to provide free counsel to indigents notwithstanding that the trial justice determines that no incarceration will be imposed?"

The court invited briefing from the state's Department of Justice, the Administrative Office of the Courts, the state's public defender organization, and various other organizations. Some of the briefs urged the court to provide heightened constitutional protection to indigent criminal defendants who, although they may face no threat of imprisonment, may suffer such consequences as denial of public housing and loss of professional licenses. Others warned that the court should not "interpret article I, section 10 of the Rhode Island Constitution in such fashion as further to subordinate societal interests in effective prosecution of the guilty."

Imagine yourself as a Justice on the Rhode Island Supreme Court. What responses to the governor's question are possible under current federal constitutional law? What answers are embodied in existing state case law? If you were to modify state law in some way, how would you explain that decision? Cf. In re Advisory Opinion to the Governor (Appointed Counsel), 666 A.2d 813 (R.I. 1995).

Problem 11-2. Lawyers and Experts

Paul Husske was charged with rape. Part of the government's case against him was a DNA analysis of tissue obtained from the rape victim. Several months before trial, the defendant filed a motion asserting his indigence and requesting that the trial court appoint an expert, at the government's expense, to help him challenge the DNA evidence that the prosecution intended to use. Husske asserted that because DNA evidence is "of a highly technical nature," it is "difficult for a lawyer to challenge DNA evidence without expert assistance." He expressed concern about the use of DNA evidence because the state's laboratory in the Division of Forensic Science had a "well-known record" for incompetent or biased testing. He also attached an affidavit from a local attorney who had read extensively on the subject of DNA and who also asserted the need for expert assistance to test the reliability of such evidence. Even though the trial court denied the defendant's motion, the court appointed the local attorney as co-counsel to assist the defendant, because he was "the most knowledgeable member of the local bar in the area of forensic DNA application."

A researcher from the Division of Forensic Science and a faculty member from a nearby state university testified at trial for the government as expert witnesses on the subject of DNA analysis. The experts each testified that the defendant's DNA profile matched the profile of the individual who had attacked the victim. They said that the DNA analysis did not exclude the defendant as a contributor of the genetic material that the assailant left on the victim's body and clothing. They also stated that the statistical probability of randomly selecting a person unrelated to the defendant in the Caucasian population with the same DNA profile was 1 in 700,000. Was the trial judge obliged to appoint an expert to assist defense counsel? Compare Husske v. Commonwealth, 476 S.E.2d 920 (Va. 1996).

Problem 11-3. Universal Appointment

The director of the Indigent Defense Services office for the largest county in the state would like to expand the coverage of the service. Currently about three-quarters of the criminal defendants in the state court are eligible to receive services from IDS. She would like to convince judges in the county to make appointments of counsel available to all criminal defendants, regardless of their income levels, the seriousness of the crimes charged, or the types of punishments they face. If they were to do so, she believes the overall quality of representation for defendants would increase, and public satisfaction with public services would improve. The county might have to increase funding for the office by modest amounts—experience would determine the necessary funding levels over time—but the current rules for recoupment of fees from defendants who are financially capable of paying should keep any budget shortfall within reasonable limits. Defendants would remain free, of course, to hire private defense counsel if they want to reject the appointment of an attorney from IDS. Defendants could also waive counsel if they prefer not to wait for the attorney to prepare for the representation.

What are the prospects for the director's idea? Which arguments might be most persuasive to the local judges? Which other figures in local government, state government, the local bar, and the community might determine the type of reception that the director's proposal receives? The director's favorite analogy when talking about universal appointment of counsel is the Medicare program: The federal program that provides basic medical services to older citizens is broadly popular and is thought to deliver cost-effective medical care. Will this argument resonate with the relevant actors?

2. Type of Proceedings

For typical crimes, it would probably be unworkable to provide counsel as soon as a person becomes a suspect or interacts with the police. Consider, in this regard, the great variety of interactions between citizens and police. The right to counsel more plausibly could attach whenever a person is arrested, though no jurisdiction has found a right to appointed counsel based simply on the fact of arrest. Perhaps no right to counsel should attach until a person appears in court and is asked to plead guilty or not guilty, or at some other point in the standard criminal process.

Courts trying to determine when the right to counsel attaches have concluded that different constitutional provisions create obligations arising at different points in the process. There are at least two distinct counsel rights—one based on the Sixth Amendment and its state analogs, the other based on the Fifth Amendment privilege against self-incrimination.

The Fifth Amendment right to counsel—a right derived from the inherently compulsory nature of custodial interrogation and from the need to protect against compulsory self-incrimination—was recognized in Miranda v. Arizona, 384 U.S. 436 (1966). The Fifth Amendment right to counsel arises whenever the police conduct a custodial interrogation. Because interrogations usually occur before charging (since they are used to gather evidence), the Fifth Amendment right to counsel will often arise before any Sixth Amendment right to counsel.

The Sixth Amendment provides that in "all criminal prosecutions, the accused shall . . . have the assistance of counsel for his defense." The language raises the question: What is a "criminal prosecution"? The legal test of when a Sixth Amendment right to counsel attaches turns on whether the procedure is considered (1) a "critical stage" of the criminal process, (2) taking place after the "initiation" of the adversarial judicial proceedings. We saw one application of the right to counsel in Chapter 9—the U.S. Supreme Court considers post-indictment lineups to be a "critical stage" of the criminal process. What is it that makes a police technique or judicial hearing a "critical stage" after the initiation of adversarial proceedings?

■ ALABAMA RULE OF CRIMINAL PROCEDURE 6.1(a)

A defendant shall be entitled to be represented by counsel in any criminal proceedings held pursuant to these rules and, if indigent, shall be entitled to have an attorney appointed to represent the defendant in all criminal proceedings in which representation by counsel is constitutionally required. The right to be represented shall include the right to consult in private with an attorney or the attorney's agent, as soon as feasible after a defendant is taken into custody, at reasonable times thereafter, and sufficiently in advance of a proceeding to allow adequate preparation therefor.

■ MISSOURI SUPREME COURT RULES 31.01, 31.02

31.01

Every person arrested and held in custody by any peace officer in any jail, police station or any other place, upon or without a warrant or other process for the alleged commission of a criminal offense, or upon suspicion thereof, shall promptly, upon request, be permitted to consult with counsel or other persons in his behalf, and, for such purpose, to use a telephone.

31.02

(a) In all criminal cases the defendant shall have the right to appear and defend in person and by counsel. If any person charged with an offense, the conviction of which would probably result in confinement, shall be without counsel upon his first appearance before a judge, it shall be the duty of the court to advise him of his right to counsel, and of the willingness of the court to appoint counsel to represent him if he is unable to employ counsel. Upon a showing of indigency, it shall be the duty of the court to appoint counsel to represent him. If after being informed as to his rights, the defendant requests to proceed without the benefit of counsel, and the court finds that he has intelligently waived his right to have counsel, the court shall have no duty to appoint counsel. . . .

■ STATE v. JOHN ARTHUR SENN, JR.

882 N.W.2d 1 (Iowa 2016)

WATERMAN, J.

Iowa Code § 804.20 provides a limited statutory right to counsel that allows persons who have been arrested to make phone calls to lawyers or family members and to meet alone and in private with their lawyer at the place of detention. While the statute allows private in-person consultations, it permits the police officer or jailer to be present for the detainee's phone calls. We must decide whether this statute is unconstitutional as applied to a person arrested, but not yet formally charged, for operating a motor vehicle while intoxicated (OWI) who wants to speak privately by phone with a lawyer before deciding whether to submit to a chemical breath test. . . .

I. BACKGROUND FACTS AND PROCEEDINGS

In the early morning hours of Labor Day, September 1, 2014, Officer Brian Cuppy was on patrol in downtown Des Moines when he saw a truck eastbound on Court Avenue stop for a red light in the middle of the intersection with Water Street with its "back tires . . . more than five feet past the cross walk." Officer Cuppy followed the truck, activated his police cruiser's flashing lights, and initiated a traffic stop nearby. The driver, John Arthur Senn Jr., age twenty-nine, told Officer Cuppy that he did not realize he had stopped in the middle of the intersection. Officer Cuppy noted that Senn had bloodshot watery eyes, slurred speech, and a "staggered gait" and smelled of alcohol. Senn initially denied that he had been drinking that night. Officer Cuppy administered field sobriety tests, which Senn failed. Senn then admitted that he had been drinking but said he had stopped over twenty minutes earlier. Senn took a preliminary breath test, which showed an alcohol concentration of 0.165, more than double the legal limit. Senn was arrested for failing to obey the traffic control signal and for operating while intoxicated and was transported to the Des Moines metro police station for chemical testing.

Around 2:30 A.M., Officer Cuppy led Senn to the DataMaster testing room and gave Senn a copy of the implied-consent advisory [explaining the potential consequences if a driver refuses to allow a breath or blood test after a lawful request from law enforcement]. At 2:34 A.M., Officer Cuppy requested a breath specimen.

Senn asked to call a lawyer. Officer Cuppy remained in the room while Senn made phone calls. Senn had trouble contacting counsel. Officer Cuppy offered to let Senn use the phone book. Senn declined. Around 2:46 A.M., Officer Cuppy asked if Senn was trying to call a lawyer and offered the phone book again. Senn explained he had a lawyer, but she had not answered her after-hours phone number. Senn eventually reached an attorney at 2:49 A.M. Senn, in Officer Cuppy's presence, told the attorney on the phone he was being investigated for his "second first" OWI. Senn explained that his first OWI was "relinquished at the state's expense" in 2009 or 2010. Senn answered the attorney's questions. Senn then asked Officer Cuppy for "attorney-client privilege please." Officer Cuppy responded that he could not have attorney-client privilege while on the phone but that he could if the attorney came to the jail. Senn repeated that comment to his attorney. . . .

Senn explained to the attorney that he worked as an electrician, so his license was "imperative" to his work. . . . Senn asked the attorney to come to the police station and said he was able to pay for the trip. . . . Officer Cuppy then said Senn had thirty-two minutes left for private consultation. Senn said he understood the consequences of his choice to take or refuse the breathalyzer. . . . While Senn was on the phone, he said, "I'd like to expunge any legal options I have at this point because I was downtown on a good faith gesture picking up a friend, so it's not like I was being—obviously I was legally intoxicated, but . . . ." The attorney was unable to meet with Senn in person. . . . Senn asked for attorney references, and she gave him some. Their conversation ended at 3:17 A.M. Senn then tried to call the recommended attorneys and left messages.

Officer Cuppy escorted Senn to the restroom upon his request. When Senn returned, he called another lawyer and asked Officer Cuppy for a glass of water. Officer Cuppy explained he could not have any water until he decided whether he would take the breath test. Senn left two more voice mails explaining his situation and asking for legal help. Officer Cuppy told Senn that because of his prior license revocation, this time his license would be suspended for one year if he failed the test and it would be suspended for two years if he refused to take the test. Senn called a friend to let him know he would be booked soon. He expressed frustration about not being able to get an attorney to come to the station. He said he was willing to pay $5000 but no one was willing to come. He was afraid of losing his job. He said he was "playing for the good team" and hoped the officer would let him go. At 3:39 A.M., Officer Cuppy told Senn he had to make a decision. Senn consented to take the breathalyzer test. At 3:41 A.M., Senn took the test, and his blood alcohol content was 0.140.

Officer Cuppy submitted a complaint to the county attorney, and it was approved at 6:14 A.M. Eleven days later, on September 12, Senn was charged by trial information with operating while intoxicated. . . . On November 20, Senn filed a motion to suppress, contesting the legality of the stop and the interference with his right to counsel under article I, § 10 of the Iowa Constitution. [The district court denied the motion. Following the denial of his motion, Senn waived jury trial and was convicted.] He was fined $1250 plus surcharges and court costs and incarcerated for one year with all but three days suspended. . . .

III. ANALYSIS

Senn asks us to hold for the first time that the right to counsel under article I, § 10 of the Iowa Constitution attached before the State filed criminal charges against him while he was under arrest for suspicion of drunk driving and faced with the decision of whether to submit to a chemical breath test that measures his blood alcohol level. . . . Senn argues that the provision in § 804.20 allowing the officer to be present for the defendant's phone call with a lawyer is unconstitutional because he was entitled under article I, § 10 to a private telephone consultation with his lawyer. . . . In State v. Vietor, 261 N.W.2d 828 (Iowa 1978), we rejected the argument that the right to counsel under the Sixth Amendment had attached when the arrestee was asked to submit to the breathalyzer test. . . .

A. Constitutional Construction . . .

Article I, § 10 is entitled "Rights of persons accused." It contains two clauses that do not appear in the Sixth Amendment, which are italicized below:

> In all criminal prosecutions, *and in cases involving the life, or liberty of an individual* the accused shall have a right to a speedy and public trial by an impartial jury; to be informed of the accusation against him, *to have a copy of the same when demanded*; to be confronted with the witnesses against him; to have compulsory process for his witnesses; and, to have the assistance of counsel.

In State v. Young, 863 N.W.2d 249 (Iowa 2015), we relied on the textual differences between the state and federal provisions to hold that the right to counsel under article I, § 10 applies to misdemeanor charges with the possibility of imprisonment. But we have never held the right to counsel under the Iowa Constitution attaches before the filing of formal criminal charges. . . .

We begin with the plain meaning of the words of article I, § 10, which by its terms applies to "criminal prosecutions" and in "cases involving the life, or liberty of an individual." Section 10 expressly provides "the accused" with eight enumerated rights: (1) a speedy trial, (2) a public trial, (3) a trial by an impartial jury, (4) to be informed of the accusation, (5) to obtain a copy of the accusation, (6) to confront witnesses, (7) to have compulsory process for the accused's witnesses, and (8) to have the assistance of counsel. The first seven of these enumerated rights make sense only in the context of a formal legal proceeding leading to a trial. The final enumerated right—to counsel—should be construed together with the seven preceding rights in § 10 that ensure a fair trial in criminal proceedings and cases involving the liberty of the accused. We read words not in isolation, but rather in context. . . . This canon has been colorfully explained by Lord Macmillan as "words of a feather flock together." It makes sense to construe the right to counsel as attaching when the State files charges in court. . . .

A prosecution is defined as "the commencement, including the filing of a complaint, and continuance of a criminal proceeding, and pursuit of that proceeding to final judgment on behalf of the state." Iowa Code § 801.4(13). A "case" is a "civil or criminal proceeding, action, suit, or controversy at law or in equity." Black's Law Dictionary (2014). A criminal proceeding does not begin until a document is filed with the court. The grammatical subject in article I, § 10 is "the accused." An "accused" is "one charged with an offense, especially the defendant in a criminal case." Webster's Third New International Dictionary (2002). By contrast, the other sections of article I provide rights more broadly to "persons" or "the people." We may infer from the unique word choice in § 10—"the accused"—that the framers intended to limit the rights therein to persons accused in formal criminal proceedings. . . .

Senn was not a defendant in a criminal prosecution when he took the chemical breath test. The State was not seeking "to punish the offender by fine or imprisonment" when Officer Cuppy administered the test. Instead, the police were investigating a crime. The State had not yet committed itself to prosecution based on the investigation to that point. There was not yet a prosecution or case against Senn. . . . Our caselaw indicates Senn did not have a right to counsel at the time of his chemical breath test. . . .

C. Other Jurisdictions

. . . The Supreme Court employs a two-part test to determine whether the accused has a right to counsel. First, the right must have attached, which means that "formal judicial proceedings have begun." Rothgery v. Gillespie County, 554 U.S. 191 (2008). Second, it must be a "critical stage" of the prosecution. In United States v. Wade, 388 U.S. 218 (1967), a defendant argued he had a right to counsel during a postindictment lineup at a courtroom. During the lineup, each person wore strips of tape like the ones worn by the robber and was forced to say something like "put the money in the bag." The Court explained that the Sixth Amendment right to counsel is not limited to the trial:

> [In] addition to counsel's presence at trial, the accused is guaranteed that he need not stand alone against the State at any stage of the prosecution, formal or informal, in court or out, where counsel's absence might derogate from the accused's right to a fair trial. The security of that right is as much the aim of the right to counsel as it is of the other guarantees of the Sixth Amendment—the right of the accused to a speedy and public trial by an impartial jury, his right to be informed

of the nature and cause of the accusation, and his right to be confronted with the witnesses against him and to have compulsory process for obtaining witnesses in his favor. The presence of counsel at such critical confrontations, as at the trial itself, operates to assure that the accused's interests will be protected consistently with our adversary theory of criminal prosecution.

The Court focused on whether potential substantial prejudice to defendant's rights inheres in the particular confrontation and the ability of counsel to help avoid that prejudice. The *Wade* Court found a right to counsel because there was "grave potential for prejudice, intentional or not, in the pretrial lineup, which may not be capable of reconstruction at trial," and because presence of counsel itself can often avert prejudice and assure a meaningful confrontation at trial. . . . But the Court agreed with the government that gathering scientific evidence does not implicate the right to counsel:

> [A] mere preparatory step in the gathering of the prosecution's evidence [is] not different—for Sixth Amendment purposes—from various other preparatory steps, such as systematized or scientific analyzing of the accused's fingerprints, blood sample, clothing, hair, and the like. We think there are differences which preclude such stages being characterized as critical stages at which the accused has the right to the presence of his counsel. Knowledge of the techniques of science and technology is sufficiently available, and the variables in techniques few enough, that the accused has the opportunity for a meaningful confrontation of the Government's case at trial through the ordinary processes of cross-examination of the Government's expert witnesses and the presentation of the evidence of his own experts. [There] is minimal risk that his counsel's absence at such stages might derogate from his right to a fair trial.

In our view, the DataMaster breathalyzer test is an example of scientific evidence gathering. . . .

In Rothgery v. Gillespie County, 554 U.S. 191 (2008), the Court gave further guidance on when a prosecution commences. Walter Rothgery was arrested [for the crime of possession of a firearm by a felon] based on an erroneous record that he had been convicted of a felony. Rothgery was brought before a magistrate because the officers did not have an arrest warrant. The arresting officer submitted an affidavit that claimed that Rothgery was charged with a felony. The magistrate determined there was probable cause for the arrest and set a $5000 bond. Rothgery posted the bond, which stated that "Rothgery stands charged by complaint." Rothgery did not have money for a lawyer, and his requests for one were denied. Six months later, a lawyer was appointed for Rothgery, who assembled the relevant paperwork and relayed the information to the district attorney, who dismissed the indictment. . . . The Court held the prosecution had commenced against Rothgery when he was brought before the judicial magistrate because

> an accusation filed with a judicial officer is sufficiently formal, and the government's commitment to prosecute it sufficiently concrete, when the accusation prompts arraignment and restrictions on the accused's liberty to facilitate the prosecution. From that point on, the defendant is faced with the prosecutorial forces of organized society, and immersed in the intricacies of substantive and procedural criminal law that define his capacity and control his actual ability to defend himself against a formal accusation that he is a criminal. . . .

It is irrelevant whether a public prosecutor is aware or involved in the initiated proceedings. In sum, the Court concluded [that] a criminal defendant's initial appearance before a judicial officer, where he learns the charge against him and his liberty is subject to restriction, "marks the start of adversary judicial proceedings that trigger attachment of the Sixth Amendment right to counsel." The Supreme Court has never held that the Sixth Amendment provides a right to counsel before submitting to chemical testing. . . .

The vast majority of courts deciding the issue conclude there is no state constitutional right to counsel at the time the motorist must decide whether to submit to chemical testing. [The court cites decisions from Georgia, Hawaii, Kansas, Massachusetts, Maine, Montana, Nebraska, New Jersey, New Mexico, North Carolina, Pennsylvania, Rhode Island, Tennessee, Wyoming, and Virginia.] Our sister courts give several reasons why the right to counsel does not attach during an implied-consent proceeding. The Massachusetts Supreme Court focused on the inherent practical problems in concluding there is no right to counsel before submitting to a breathalyzer test: . . . "If an attorney is not available, a delay may ensue and the test results may then be stale and inaccurate. The same result follows for one who has no attorney or has no money to retain an attorney." Commonwealth v. Brazelton, 537 N.E.2d 143, 143 (Mass. 1989). . . . If we hold the right to counsel attaches during an implied-consent proceeding, we will also need to determine whether that right, like the federal constitutional right to counsel, includes the right to an attorney at state expense if the motorist is indigent.

The Georgia Supreme Court rejected a defendant's right to counsel before deciding whether to take a chemical breath test because it would be unlikely that an attorney would be able to meaningfully assist the driver before the test: [because] the officer who administers the test must advise the driver of his implied consent rights pursuant to [the Georgia implied consent statute], "there is very little that a lawyer could add that would substantially affect the fairness of the trial." Rackoff v. State, 637 S.E.2d 706 (Ga. 2006). . . .

These authorities are persuasive. We too want to avoid creating an unworkable rule for determining when the right to counsel attaches. If we expand the right to counsel to include implied-consent chemical breath tests before any criminal case is filed, what is the limiting principle? Why stop there? Why not expand the right further to include noncustodial questioning by police or police requests for consent searches before any charges are filed? The text of our constitution provides a clear starting point for the attachment of the right to counsel—the court filing that commences the criminal proceeding or other case putting liberty at risk. . . .

Only four jurisdictions—Florida, Oregon, Minnesota, and New York—have recognized a broader right to counsel under their state constitutions. . . . Senn relies primarily on the Minnesota Supreme Court's decision in Friedman v. Commissioner of Public Safety, 473 N.W.2d 828 (Minn. 1991). Joy Friedman was arrested in Minneapolis when she failed a preliminary breath test. The police officer took her to the police station to take an intoxilyzer test. The machine was in use, so they waited twenty-five minutes at the station. During this time, Friedman asked what her rights were and whether she could consult an attorney. The officer did not allow her to contact an attorney. A different officer took Friedman into a videotaping room and read her the implied-consent advisory three times. The implied-consent advisory stated she had a right to consult an attorney after testing. Friedman said she did not understand the advisory and that she had been tested in the squad car. The police considered Friedman's response a refusal to be tested, which resulted in a one-year revocation of her drivers' license.

The Minnesota Supreme Court . . . concluded a defendant is guaranteed a "limited right to counsel within a reasonable time before submitting to testing . . . provided that such a consultation does not unreasonably delay the administration of the test." . . . The right to counsel will be considered vindicated if the person is provided with a telephone prior to testing and given a reasonable time to contact and talk with counsel. [Under the Minnesota rule, evidence] of the driver's telephonic statements with counsel may be suppressed during the criminal trial. This does not help Senn. Senn was tried on the minutes of testimony. He made inculpatory statements during his phone call, but none of those admissions were included in the minutes. . . .

Senn likely would fare better under Oregon's broader state constitutional right to counsel. [Under State v. Spencer, 750 P.2d 147 (Or. 1988) (en banc)], an arrested driver has the "right upon request to a reasonable opportunity to obtain legal advice before deciding whether to submit to a breath test." . . . This right encompasses the ability to "consult with counsel in private" [but] the Oregon right to counsel is not absolute because that state will not provide a lawyer at the state's expense for indigent persons during chemical testing, and the right may be forfeited. The right to counsel in Oregon is limited to those who can afford lawyers.

New York has extended its state constitutional right to counsel to persons who are taken into custody, whether as an "accused," a "suspect," or a "witness." People v. Hobson, 348 N.E.2d 894 (N.Y. 1976). The detainee is generally entitled to speak privately with counsel by phone. Senn does not cite or rely on New York precedent, presumably because of the textual differences in that state's constitution, which combines multiple rights—including due process, self-incrimination, and the right to counsel—into one provision. . . . Senn would be entitled to reversal under the caselaw of only two other states—Oregon and New York. We are not persuaded to follow those outliers.

D. Practical Problems

We also consider the practical problems that would arise by recognizing a broader independent state constitutional right to counsel during implied-consent chemical testing. . . . First, any Iowa constitutionally based right to counsel should apply equally to rich and poor alike. Iowa has recognized the right to appointed counsel for indigents at government expense in felony cases since 1850. We recently extended that right to indigents facing misdemeanor charges with potential incarceration. A first offense OWI carries a potential jail sentence. Thus, if we hold an individual is constitutionally entitled to a private consultation with legal counsel at the time the State invokes implied consent, the State would need to ensure that public defenders or court-appointed lawyers are available twenty-four hours a day to field calls from detained motorists, typically late at night. . . .

Second, if Senn was entitled to a private consultation with counsel over the phone, the police or jailers would have to determine who is on the other end of the line for each phone call made. Iowa Code § 804.20 applies to all detainees, not just motorists suspected of impaired driving. It is easy to imagine detainees taking advantage of private phone calls to inform confederates to flee or get rid of evidence. . . .

For these reasons, we conclude the right to counsel under article I, § 10 of the Iowa Constitution does not attach until formal charges have been filed by the state in court. Accordingly, the arresting officer in this case did not violate Senn's constitutional right to counsel by remaining in the room during Senn's phone call with a lawyer. . . .

CADY, C.J., concurring specially.

I concur in the result, but not because the right to counsel under the Iowa Constitution did not attach at the time the State initiated the implied-consent process. Even assuming the right to counsel did attach under the Iowa Constitution, I conclude Senn was not deprived of the right . . . . Senn was in fact provided an opportunity to consult with an attorney before making the decision [about testing]. He also took advantage of the opportunity by talking to an attorney on the telephone for twenty-eight minutes before making a decision. [No] evidence was introduced to explain how the conversation was inadequate in light of its purpose. . . .

It may be understandable that some attorneys want to personally assess the condition of a person arrested for operating while intoxicated before giving advice on whether or not to submit to the request for a chemical test. However, this in-person assessment does not establish a minimum constitutional standard of counsel. . . . Senn was not denied any constitutional right to counsel because the facts of the case do not reveal that he failed to receive advice from counsel to assist in deciding to take a chemical test. . . .

WIGGINS, J., dissenting.

[It] is time we recognized that the phrase "in cases involving the life, or liberty of an individual" in article I, § 10 extends the right to counsel under the Iowa Constitution at least to arrested individuals suspected of crimes with respect to which their guilt or innocence will be determined in a judicial proceeding under the jurisdiction of our state courts. . . . I believe Senn's right to counsel attached when he was arrested for suspicion of driving under the influence . . . a serious misdemeanor. At that point, Senn faced a case involving his liberty within the meaning of article I, § 10.

[Next, I] consider whether Senn faced a critical stage in the criminal process associated with his case when Officer Cuppy read him the implied-consent advisory and asked him to submit to a chemical test. . . . When an individual suspected of driving under the influence submits to a chemical test that will determine his or her blood-alcohol concentration, that individual may be providing the government with nearly conclusive evidence of a serious crime. In a prosecution for OWI under Iowa Code § 321J.2, the State may prove its case merely by showing beyond a reasonable doubt (1) that the defendant operated a motor vehicle (2) while having a blood-alcohol concentration of .08 or more. . . .

Notes

1. *Initiation of adversarial proceedings: majority position.* The federal constitutional right to counsel applies only when two preconditions are met. First, the right attaches only after the initiation of an "adversarial proceeding." Second, even after the initiation of adversarial proceedings, the government must allow a defense

attorney to participate only during a "critical stage" of those proceedings. Most state courts adopt this same two-part test to determine when the right to counsel under the state constitution applies. The precise methods for filing criminal charges and the exact functions of early judicial hearings differ from state to state; as the U.S. Supreme Court confirmed in Rothgery v. Gillespie County, 554 U.S. 191 (2008), the "initiation" prong of the test does not depend on the involvement of the prosecutor or the potential contributions of defense counsel at the proceeding. The federal constitutional right to counsel does not begin with arrest, or even with a postarrest probable cause hearing required by Gerstein v. Pugh, 420 U.S. 103 (1975).

Some high state courts have read their state constitutions to provide for a right to counsel earlier than in the federal system. See Page v. State, 495 So. 2d 436 (Miss. 1986) (right to counsel attaches before arraignment, when proceedings reach "accusatory" stage); cf. McCarter v. State, 770 A.2d 195 (Md. 2001) (statute gives defendant right to counsel at initial appearance; not necessary to decide if initial appearance is "critical stage" for constitutional counsel right). A minority of states have concluded that a postarrest identification lineup or photo identification can qualify as a "critical stage" that triggers the right to counsel. See, e.g., Commonwealth v. Richman, 320 A.2d 351 (Pa. 1974) (lineup). Some states also conclude that it is a violation of the right to counsel to fail to inform a suspect during interrogation that his attorney is trying to make contact. See Haliburton v. State, 514 So. 2d 1088 (Fla. 1987).

The Supreme Court in Turner v. Rogers, 564 U.S. 431 (2011), considered the right to appointed counsel during civil proceedings that can lead to imprisonment for a spouse who fails to make court-ordered child support payments and as a result is held in contempt of court. Michael Turner failed to make numerous child support payments. A judge in the Family Court ultimately found him in contempt of court and ordered him to serve a 12-month jail term. The Supreme Court concluded that appointed counsel is not strictly necessary for the respondent in such civil proceedings, so long as the complaining party is also unrepresented by counsel, the respondent receives notice that his ability to pay the arrears will be the critical issue, and the court creates adequate opportunities to learn about his ability to pay. Because Turner received neither appointed counsel nor such "alternative procedural safeguards" in the civil contempt proceedings in this case, the Court ruled that his imprisonment violated due process.

2. *Critical stages before trial: majority position.* The second prong of the Sixth Amendment test depends on the value that defense counsel might contribute during a particular proceeding, with the ultimate objective of ensuring a fair trial. The right to counsel extends to preliminary hearings in which the government must demonstrate a prima facie case against the defendant, Coleman v. Alabama, 399 U.S. 1 (1970), because defense counsel at such a hearing can obtain discovery of the state's evidence, make a record for later impeachment of state witnesses at trial, and preserve defense witness testimony. See also Cooks v. State, 240 S.W.3d 906 (Tex. Crim. App. 2007) (period of 30 days for filing of motion for new trial is a "critical stage").

State constitutions are almost always interpreted to cover the same pretrial proceedings as the federal constitution. Typically, a state's rules of criminal procedure will track these constitutional boundaries and will provide for the appointment of legal counsel at the defendant's initial appearance before a magistrate, when the defendant is informed of the charges. The Missouri rule reprinted above is typical.

3. *Defense counsel for initial bail determination.* Defense attorneys are usually not available when the judge makes the first determination of bail or pretrial detention at the initial appearance. About half the states, however, do provide counsel at the time of bail in urban centers, even though defense lawyers are not available elsewhere in the state. A few state courts have ruled that access to counsel at a bail hearing is required under the state constitution. See DeWolfe v. Richmond, 76 A.3d 1019 (Md. 2013) (state must provide defense counsel to indigent defendants at initial appearance); John Gross, The Right to Counsel but Not the Presence of Counsel: A Survey of State Criminal Procedures for Pre-Trial Release, 69 Fla. L. Rev. 831 (2017). A study of the Baltimore courts compared defendants who were all charged with similar nonviolent offenses, some represented by counsel and others not. The presence of counsel made an enormous difference in outcomes: two and a half times as many represented defendants were released on recognizance as unrepresented defendants. More than twice as many represented defendants had their bail reduced to affordable amounts. See Douglas L. Colbert, Ray Paternoster & Shawn D. Bushway, Do Attorneys Really Matter? The Empirical and Legal Case for the Right of Counsel at Bail, 23 Cardozo L. Rev. 1719 (2002).

4. *Are psychiatric examinations a "critical stage"?* Should there be a rule governing whether all psychiatric examinations are a critical stage in the proceedings, or should it depend on the use of the information gained by the examination? Courts in a few states have concluded that there is a right to counsel during at least some psychiatric exams, and these opinions typically state that the examination might be a "critical stage" in some cases but not in others. More than 20 states have declared that there is no constitutional right to counsel during any psychiatric exams. Should competency examinations be treated differently from examinations used to undermine potential defenses? Those used at sentencing? Those used to establish aggravating factors for a capital sentence? In Estelle v. Smith, 451 U.S. 454 (1981), the Supreme Court held that use of a psychiatrist's testimony at a capital sentencing proceeding based on a pretrial psychiatric examination at which defendant had not been represented by counsel violated defendant's Fifth Amendment rights against compulsory self-incrimination. What would a lawyer do at a psychiatric examination? Would a lawyer have a right to review a psychiatrist's questions before the examination?

5. *Right to counsel at sentencing.* The Sixth Amendment and its state constitutional analogs apply to sentencing hearings; the government must provide the defendant with an attorney at these hearings. Mempa v. Rhay, 389 U.S. 128 (1967); State v. Alspach, 554 N.W.2d 882 (Iowa 1996) (right to counsel at postconviction hearing to challenge amount of restitution). However, counsel is not required if the trial court sentences a defendant to probation and the state later attempts to convince the judge to revoke the defendant's probation (and send the defendant to prison) because she has violated the conditions of probation. Gagnon v. Scarpelli, 411 U.S. 778 (1973). If the end result is the same for the offender (a prison term), what is the constitutional distinction between sentencing hearings and probation revocation hearings?

6. *Right to counsel on appeal.* The criminal prosecution ends with a conviction and sentence. If the defendant appeals the case, the government is defending the judgment rather than "prosecuting" the case. As a result, courts say, the Sixth Amendment right to counsel does not apply to criminal appeals. The federal constitutional right to counsel on the first appeal as of right is based instead on both

due process and equal protection principles. See Douglas v. California, 372 U.S. 353 (1963). The federal constitutional right does not extend to discretionary appeals. Ross v. Moffitt, 417 U.S. 600 (1974). The government also has no federal constitutional obligation to supply counsel for postconviction proceedings such as habeas corpus. See Murray v. Giarratano, 492 U.S. 1 (1989). Once again, state courts have by and large followed the federal lead when interpreting their own constitutional provisions. Nevertheless, many states do appoint counsel for at least some defendants during these postconviction proceedings. See, e.g., Mont. Code Ann. §§46-8-103, 46-8-104 (providing for appointment of counsel "upon direct appeal to the Montana supreme court" and "in any postconviction criminal action or proceeding").

7. *Right to counsel in juvenile court proceedings.* State court systems operate special divisions to handle allegations of misconduct by juveniles, actions that would be considered a crime if an adult were to commit them. The U.S. Supreme Court in In re Gault, 387 U.S. 1 (1967), declared that youthful offenders in juvenile delinquency proceedings must receive many of the basic process rights that protect adult defendants in criminal court: the right to timely notification of the charges, the right to confront witnesses, the right against self-incrimination, and the right to counsel.

Problem 11-4. Lawyers in Psychiatric Examinations

Raymond Larsen was charged with murder in Illinois. He admitted that he killed the victim but relied on the affirmative defense of insanity at the time of the slaying. The state filed a written pretrial motion to require Larsen to submit to examination by a state-designated psychiatrist as provided by statute. The court appointed Dr. Robert Reifman, assistant director of the Psychiatric Institute of the Circuit Court of Cook County, to conduct an examination "on August 23, or on any date subsequent, necessary to complete such examination." The defendant's counsel did not receive notice of the location and time, or of the name of the psychiatrist, prior to the examination, which was conducted on August 24.

Based on the court-ordered psychiatric examination, Dr. Reifman testified for the state on rebuttal at trial. He opined that the defendant had an antisocial personality but did not suffer from a mental defect or disease and had substantial capacity to conform his conduct to the requirement of the law and to appreciate the criminality of his conduct. On appeal the defendant argues that the psychiatric examination was a "critical stage" of the proceedings and that he had the right to notice and presence of counsel. How would you rule? See People v. Larsen, 385 N.E.2d 679 (Ill. 1979).

B. SELECTION AND REJECTION OF COUNSEL

Although the government may have an obligation to offer an attorney to most criminal defendants, not all defendants accept the offer. Some will insist on representing themselves, while others will be unhappy with the assigned lawyer and will ask for some other attorney. Which legal institutions must respond to these sorts of requests?

The U.S. Supreme Court, for one, has declared a general principle that the Sixth Amendment right to counsel includes a right to self-representation. In Faretta v. California, 422 U.S. 806 (1975), the Court pointed to historical practices giving the defendant power to waive counsel. The Sixth Amendment made the assistance of counsel "an aid to a willing defendant—not an organ of the State interposed between an unwilling defendant and his right to defend himself personally." A great many defendants exercise this *Faretta* right and waive their access to appointed counsel during pretrial proceedings and entry of a guilty plea; far fewer represent themselves at trial.

The right to self-representation, however, is far different from what most defendants might prefer: the right to select the attorney who will be appointed to represent them. Most defendants who choose to represent themselves at trial do so after a frustrating experience with an attorney assigned to their case (or an attorney assigned to some earlier case). But it is clear that poor defendants do not have the legal right to select which attorney will represent them. Courts do not grant indigent defendants such a power, nor do most managers of public defender organizations. The decision about self-representation, then, is part of a broader negotiation between the defendant, the judge, the former attorney, and a prospective new attorney about who will represent the defendant. What interests will each of these parties bring to the negotiation?

■ STATE v. JOSEPH SPENCER
519 N.W.2d 357 (Iowa 1994)

McGiverin, C.J.

The question presented here is whether a criminal defendant suffered a violation of his sixth amendment right to self-representation when the district court appointed counsel for him over his objection. . . . On July 18, 1990, Monona County Sheriff Dennis Smith went to Joseph Spencer's rural home to investigate complaints that Spencer was discharging firearms on his property. Sheriff Smith [observed marijuana growing in Spencer's garden, obtained a search warrant, and seized marijuana plants, cocaine, and firearms from the house]. On August 20, trial informations were filed charging Spencer with possession of marijuana with intent to manufacture, unauthorized possession of firearms, possession of cocaine, and possession of marijuana. . . .

Defendant Spencer retained a private attorney, Richard Mock of Onawa, to represent him and pleaded not guilty. Attorney Mock filed a motion to suppress drugs and weapons seized during the execution of the search warrant. After an evidentiary hearing, the district court overruled the motion.

A trial date was set. On May 17, 1991, a few days before trial, attorney Mock moved to withdraw from his representation of defendant Spencer. During the hearing on that motion, the question arose as to who would represent defendant at trial. Defendant Spencer told the court he wished to represent himself but admitted he did not know legal procedures or how to object to improper evidence. After a lengthy colloquy, the district court stated, "As far as I'm concerned, although he indicates he wants to do it himself, I don't see that he's competent and qualified to do it himself." The district court then appointed attorney Richard McCoy of Sioux City to represent Spencer. The case was continued and went to trial about one year later. Attorney McCoy fully represented defendant prior to and during the trial. Spencer was found guilty by a jury and was sentenced on the four charges. Spencer appealed, contending through new counsel that the district court denied his right to self-representation. [He] contends that the district court forced counsel upon him, contrary to his rights under the sixth amendment of the federal constitution. . . .

The sixth amendment provides that an accused "shall enjoy the right . . . to have the assistance of counsel for his defence." The fourteenth amendment of the federal constitution extends this right to state prosecutions. In Faretta v. California, 422 U.S. 806 (1975), the Supreme Court held that the right to self-representation to make one's own defense is necessarily implied by the structure of the Sixth Amendment. However, the Supreme Court also recognized an important limitation on that right: Although the defendant may elect to represent himself (usually to his detriment), the trial court "may—even over objection by the accused—appoint a 'standby counsel' to aid the accused if and when the accused requests help, and to be available to represent the accused in the event that termination of the defendant's self-representation is necessary." Such an appointment serves "to relieve the judge of the need to explain and enforce basic rules of courtroom protocol or to assist the defendant in overcoming routine obstacles that stand in the way of the defendant's achievement of his own clearly indicated goals." McKaskle v. Wiggins, 465 U.S. 168 (1984). . . .

Moreover, a defendant waives his right to self-representation unless he asserts that right by "knowingly and intelligently forgoing his right to counsel." This waiver may occur despite the defendant's statement that he wishes to represent himself if he makes that statement merely out of brief frustration with the trial court's decision regarding counsel and not as a clear and unequivocal assertion of his constitutional rights. In addition, a waiver [of the right to self-representation] may be found if it reasonably appears to the court that defendant has abandoned his initial request to represent himself.

We believe that the trial court did not err in appointing an attorney for Spencer. The intent behind the appointment, from the comments of both the court and Mock, defendant's withdrawing attorney, was to provide Spencer with "standby counsel" as envisioned in *Faretta* and *McKaskle*. The following comments were made at the hearing on attorney Mock's application to withdraw:

> *The Court:* Well, I don't think that you're [the defendant] in the position of being able to defend yourself. And the least I would do is have somebody appointed to sit and be available as your counsel. But, frankly, I'm not going to put the court in the position whereby you defend yourself and then it's reversed if there is a conviction, just because there was no attorney present. It's as simple as that. Now, do you have any other person in mind?
>
> *The Defendant:* No, sir. . . .
>
> *The Court:* Well, what familiarity do you have with the legal system?
>
> *The Defendant:* I don't have any, Your Honor. . . .
>
> *The Court:* An ordinary citizen can defend himself, but frankly an ordinary citizen is going to have a little difficulty following the procedures, making the proper objections and defending his own interests, unless he's familiar with the procedure in court. That's the problem I have. If you think you can do that, that's one thing; otherwise, what will happen is, if there is a conviction, it will be appealed and they will say you should have had somebody here to protect your rights.

The court thus properly appointed attorney McCoy over defendant's objection. If defendant had wished to treat this appointed attorney as standby counsel, he could have done so. The record here, however, evinces Spencer's initial desire to be represented by counsel (in employing attorney Mock), leading us to conclude that even if he wished to proceed pro se at the time of the withdrawal hearing, he waived and abandoned that right by acquiescing to attorney McCoy's full representation of his case for the following year leading up to and during the jury trial. . . .

Spencer's request for self-representation came out of frustration rather than a distinct and unequivocal request for that constitutional right. When Spencer was first charged in August 1990, he hired a private attorney (Richard Mock). Spencer worked with him until his motion to suppress evidence was overruled. Then, in May 1991, Mock moved to withdraw. Defendant was exasperated and did not want to pay for another attorney. Yet he willingly accepted attorney McCoy's name and address from the court and clearly relied on McCoy's representation during the following year and throughout trial. Spencer never attempted to try the jury case himself with McCoy as standby counsel. He never again raised the self-representation issue in the trial court. . . . Finally, defendant Spencer has pointed to nothing that he would have done differently had he represented himself at trial, nor has he demonstrated any way in which attorney McCoy denied him "a fair chance to present his case in his own way." *McKaskle*, 465 U.S. at 177. . . .

We believe that the trial court's appointment of attorney McCoy to be available as standby counsel satisfied Spencer's request to represent himself but ensured that Spencer's other rights were protected as well. By his later acts Spencer waived and abandoned any right to self-representation that he may have had. . . .

LAVORATO, J., dissenting.

In a state criminal trial, a defendant has a Sixth and Fourteenth Amendment right under the federal Constitution to self-representation. Faretta v. California, 422 U.S. 806 (1975). Before the right attaches, the defendant must voluntarily elect to proceed without counsel by "knowingly and intelligently" waiving his Sixth Amendment right to counsel. In addition, the defendant's request to proceed without counsel must be "clear and unequivocal." Before a trial court accepts the request, the court must make the defendant aware of the dangers and disadvantages of self-representation, so that the record will establish that "he knows what he is doing and his choice is made with eyes open." *Faretta*, 422 U.S. at 835. A trial court may not bar a defendant from proceeding without counsel even though the defendant is not technically competent in the law. The defendant must only be competent to make the choice to proceed without counsel. . . .

I easily infer from the record that Spencer is above average in intelligence. He has college training in electronics and math. His work experience included several years in the Air Force. He also worked as an electronics technician at General Dynamics. . . .

Unlike the majority, I believe the following colloquy between the court and Spencer shows that (1) Spencer made a clear and unequivocal request—not once, but several times—to proceed without counsel, (2) his request was knowingly and intelligently made, and (3) the trial court understood Spencer was making a clear and unequivocal request to proceed without counsel: . . .

The Court: . . . Do you want to get another attorney or do you want to go to trial tomorrow with him?

The Defendant: I feel I would be better off defending myself, Your Honor. He doesn't want to listen to what I'm telling him. . . . I'll have to go pro—I'll have to defend myself.

The Court: Before I would let you do that, I would appoint somebody. If your status is as it appears to be, that you have property, those will be assessed—the fees of whoever is appointed will be assessed against that.

The Defendant: I don't see how you can force me to do that, Your Honor.

The Court: Well, I don't think that you're in the position of being able to defend yourself. And the least I would do is have somebody appointed to sit and be available as your counsel. But, frankly, I'm not going to put the court in the position whereby you defend yourself and then it's reversed if there is a conviction, just because there was no attorney present. It's as simple as that. [What] familiarity do you have with the legal system?

The Defendant: I don't have any, Your Honor. Shouldn't make the legal system that way where I can't defend myself. I'm the one that's familiar with the case. I'm the one that's arrested. I know what my best interest is.

The Court: Well, if I understand your complaint, [Mr. Mock] wanted to plead it and you wanted to fight it. Now, the question is, how are you going to fight it in the courtroom? My problem with it is that I don't want you to sit in the courtroom not being prepared for the procedures and end up with a verdict against you because you weren't familiar with the procedures. Do you understand what I'm saying?

The Defendant: I understand what you're saying, but I don't understand why you make them that way.

The Court: Why do we make what that way?

The Defendant: Court procedures that way. Ordinary citizen can't come in and defend himself. . . .

The Court: Okay. During the interim, the court has attempted to contact an attorney to represent the defendant in this case. I have contacted Richard McCoy in Sioux City. He practices in criminal court and he's . . . tried a lot of cases and I feel that he's a good attorney. He's indicated that he would be willing to take your case. . . . Does that meet with your approval?

The Defendant: Doesn't meet with my approval, Your Honor, but if you're going to force it on me, I'm going to have to take it. . . .

The Prosecutor: The appointment of Mr. McCoy is pursuant to [section] 815.10(2) then?

The Court: That's right. And I can appreciate that it says, "if a person desires legal assistance and is not indigent." As far as I'm concerned, although he indicates he wants to do it himself, I don't see that he's competent and qualified to do it himself. There should be somebody there. And on that basis, [the] court interprets that section to apply. . . .

Spencer captured the essence of *Faretta* when he insisted that we "shouldn't make the legal system that way where I can't defend myself. I'm the one that's familiar with the case. I'm the one that's arrested. I know what my best interest is." On this point, *Faretta* eloquently says:

> . . . To force a lawyer on a defendant can only lead him to believe that the law contrives against him. Moreover, it is not inconceivable that in some rare instances, the defendant might in fact present his case more effectively by conducting his own

defense. Personal liberties are not rooted in the law of averages. The right to defend is personal. [Although the defendant] may conduct his own defense ultimately to his own detriment, his choice must be honored out of "that respect for the individual which is the lifeblood of the law.

The majority . . . attempts to finesse the trial court's denial of Spencer's request to defend himself by simply characterizing the court's actions as appointment of standby counsel. [However, the] role of standby counsel is limited to assisting a pro se defendant when such defendant wants assistance. A pro se defendant has the right to control the case the defendant chooses to present to the jury. That means a trial court must permit the pro se defendant to control the organization and content of the defense, to make motions, to argue points of law, to participate in voir dire, to question witnesses, and to address the court and jury at appropriate points in the trial. . . . If the trial court permits standby counsel to participate in the defense over the defendant's objections, such participation effectively allows counsel to make or substantially interfere with any significant tactical decisions, or to control questioning of witnesses, or to speak instead of the defendant on any matter of importance. Such interference is a denial of the pro se defendant's right to self-representation. . . .

These stringent limitations were recently spelled out in McKaskle v. Wiggins, 465 U.S. 168 (1984), the first case in which the Supreme Court has described the role of standby counsel. Because the role of standby counsel is severely restricted, trial courts contemplating appointment of standby counsel should—at a minimum—explain the limitations I have sketched out above from *McKaskle*. The reason is obvious: if the right to self-representation is to mean anything, a defendant who is appointed standby counsel should know how far the defendant can go in defending himself or herself without interference.

Here the trial court should have granted Spencer's request to defend himself. If the court was still concerned, the court should have then explicitly told Spencer he was appointing standby counsel and should have explained the limitations on standby counsel's role. Although above average in intelligence, Spencer is still a layperson untrained in the intricacies of criminal law. . . . After the colloquy between the court and himself, Spencer could only have had one thought: appointed counsel was being forced upon him and he was not going to be allowed to defend himself. . . .

At English common law the insistence upon a right of self-representation was the rule, rather than the exception. It is ironic that in the long history of British criminal jurisprudence there was only one tribunal that ever adopted the practice of forcing counsel upon an unwilling criminal defendant. That tribunal was the Star Chamber, a tribunal that for centuries symbolized the disregard of basic human rights. And the insistence upon a right to self-representation was, if anything, more fervent in the American colonies than at English common law. As *Faretta* points out, [the] "value of state-appointed counsel was not unappreciated by the Founders, yet the notion of compulsory counsel was utterly foreign to them. And whatever else may be said of those who wrote the Bill of Rights, surely there can be no doubt that they understood the inestimable worth of free choice." In sum, I would hold that the trial court denied Spencer the right to represent himself. I would therefore reverse and remand for a new trial.

Notes

1. *Knowing and voluntary waiver of counsel: majority position.* Once the right to counsel has attached, the defendant can waive that right, but only if the choice is "knowing and voluntary." Johnson v. Zerbst, 304 U.S. 458 (1938). In Faretta v. California, 422 U.S. 806 (1975), the Supreme Court declared that the right to "assistance" of counsel logically implied a defendant's right to represent herself at trial without counsel. How does this square with the Court's observation in *Gideon* that a lawyer is a "necessity, not a luxury"?

As *Spencer* indicates, there is no simple answer to the question of how a trial court will determine that the defendant's request is a knowing and voluntary waiver of the right to counsel. Typically, courts say that the defendant can waive counsel and invoke the *Faretta* right to self-representation only if (1) the trial court informs the defendant about the dangers of such a strategy, or (2) it otherwise appears from the record that the defendant understood the dangers. See People v. Adkins, 551 N.W.2d 108 (Mich. 1996) (waiver of counsel requires an unequivocal request by defendant, offer by trial court to appoint counsel, explanation of dangers of self-representation and the punishment for the crime charged, and a finding that self-representation will not disrupt trial). Courts often say that a waiver hearing expressly addressing the disadvantages of a pro se defense is much preferred but not absolutely necessary. The ultimate test, they say, is not the trial court's express advice but the defendant's understanding.

Defendants who represent themselves sometimes claim after conviction that the trial judge did not adequately warn them about the perils of acting as their own counsel. What warnings should judges give? State v. Cornell, 878 P.2d 1352 (Ariz. 1994) (no reversible error where court did not warn defendant that self-representation would undermine his planned insanity defense). Should courts, legislatures, or drafters of procedural rules design the standard *Faretta* warnings? See People v. Arguello, 772 P.2d 87 (Colo. 1989) (model inquiry); Michigan Court Rules 6.005(D), (E) (court must advise the defendant of the charge, the maximum possible prison sentence for the offense, any mandatory minimum sentence required by law, and the risk involved in self-representation).

2. *Timeliness and manner of request.* Trial judges commonly explain their denial of a defendant's motion for self-representation on timeliness grounds. If the request arrives too close to the start of trial, a continuance might become necessary to allow the defendant to prepare for trial. People v. Lynch, 237 P.3d 416 (Cal. 2010) (timeliness of defendant's request to represent himself is not merely a matter of calendar days remaining before trial; trial judge may consider age of alleged victims, complexity of case, and any factor that makes it more or less feasible to delay trial); cf. Coleman v. Johnsen, 330 P.3d 952 (Ariz. 2014) (recognizing right to self-representation on appeal and imposing time limit of 30 days within filing of appeal to waive counsel). Under what circumstances do you imagine that trial judges would grant a self-representation motion filed after the start of the trial? Commonwealth v. El, 977 A.2d 1158 (Pa. 2009) (request for self-representation was not timely when submitted after motion for bench trial and motion to bar admission of evidence).

Defendants sometimes take actions that amount to a request for self-representation, including physical attacks against the appointed attorney. State v. Holmes, 302 S.W.3d 831 (Tenn. 2010) (trial judge compelled defendant to stand trial with only standby counsel after he attacked his attorney by knocking his glasses askew; while defendant's actions were serious, they fell short of "extremely serious misconduct" that would justify sanction of total forfeiture of Sixth Amendment right to counsel; court suggested appointment of new counsel and warning to defendant regarding consequences of further misconduct).

3. *Reasons for waiver of counsel.* The old bromide says that "the man who represents himself has a fool for a client." Is the decision to waive an attorney indeed a foolish choice in most cases? See State v. Jones, 228 P.3d 394 (Kan. 2010) (pretrial denial of *Faretta* rights can never amount to harmless error because exercise of the right normally increases likelihood of outcome unfavorable to defendant). It is difficult to answer such a question at the system level. A study of federal pro se defendants determined that very few of them showed signs of mental illness, and the outcomes in their cases compared favorably with the outcomes for defendants represented by counsel. See Erica Hashimoto, Defending the Right of Self Representation: An Empirical Look at the Felony Pro Se Defendant, 85 N.C. L. Rev. 423 (2007). Is it possible to conclude from this observation that defendants waive counsel in cases where the evidence is especially strong or especially weak? Or that defendants who waive have realistic concerns about the quality of the effort that busy defense lawyers can offer?

Another study, based on state court data, noted that defendants waive counsel far more often in misdemeanor cases (even those misdemeanors where the law requires the government to provide counsel upon request) than in felony cases. The study found no evidence to confirm the hypothesis that concerns about money—either an up-front "application fee" or later recoupment of a portion of the attorney's fees—influenced the waiver decision. Ronald F. Wright & Wayne A. Logan, The Political Economy of Application Fees for Indigent Criminal Defense, 47 Wm. & Mary L. Rev. 2045 (2006). How might an observer learn whether costs influence some defendants who waive counsel?

4. *Standby counsel.* Often a judge will respond to a request for self-representation by appointing "standby counsel." Even if the standby counsel gives the defendant unwelcome advice and direction, a conviction can be upheld. See McKaskle v. Wiggins, 465 U.S. 168 (1984) (appointment of standby counsel does not violate self-representation right unless counsel interferes with substantial tactical decisions of defendant); Partin v. Commonwealth, 168 S.W.3d 23 (Ky. 2005) (rights to self-representation and confrontation satisfied even though trial court prohibited defendant from personally cross-examining his wife during trial on domestic violence charges; cross-examination conducted by standby counsel). Is the obligation of the trial judge to warn the defendant about the dangers of self-representation lower when the defendant's lawyer accepts "standby counsel" status at the time defendant asks to represent herself? See State v. Layton, 432 S.E.2d 740 (W. Va. 1993) (allowing less extensive warning about self-representation when standby counsel played relatively active role at trial); Anne Bowen Poulin, The Role of Standby Counsel in Criminal Cases: In the Twilight Zone of the Criminal Justice System, 75 N.Y.U. L. Rev. 676 (2000).

The law in some states allows a defendant to partially waive the right to counsel; the defendant may rely on an appointed lawyer for some purposes, but also serve as co-counsel and examine some witnesses himself or herself. See Allen v. Commonwealth, 410 S.W.3d 125 (Ky. 2013) (trial judge's decision to allow standby counsel but not defendant to participate in bench conferences amounted to violation of *Faretta* rights).

5. *The constituency for* Faretta *rights.* In *Spencer,* what could the defendant have said to the trial judge to convince the appellate court that he had tried to exercise his right to represent himself? If trial judges can appoint counsel over requests like Spencer's, how vibrant is the right to self-representation? Which constituency, if any, keeps *Faretta* rights alive? If you were a prosecutor, would you argue on behalf of defendants who want to represent themselves?

If lawyers are essential to justice, shouldn't *Faretta* be reversed? In Martinez v. Court of Appeal of California, 528 U.S. 152 (2000), the Supreme Court refused to extend the *Faretta* right of self-representation to a direct appeal. The appellate courts may properly appoint counsel for the appellant, even if the appellant objects. Are trial judges better able than appellate judges to manage the difficulties presented by defendants who represent themselves? Are a defendant's interests in self-representation stronger at trial than during an appeal? See State v. Rafay, 222 P.3d 86 (Wash. 2009) (state constitution guarantees right to represent oneself on appeal; rejects *Martinez*).

6. *Client autonomy and control over the objective of representation.* The Sixth Amendment right to reject the assistance of counsel entirely also applies to a client's choice of the "objective" of the representation. According to McCoy v. Louisiana, 138 S. Ct. 1500 (2018), an attorney violates the Sixth Amendment rights of a defendant when the attorney insists on conceding guilt during a capital trial, despite the client's objections. Even when the lawyer's decision is based on a reasonable strategic choice to concentrate on the penalty phase of the trial, the defendant holds a constitutional right to choose the objective of the representation; the decision whether or not to contest guilt at trial goes directly to the objective of the defense. As the Court put it, "The choice is not all or nothing: to gain assistance, a defendant need not surrender control entirely to counsel." The rules of professional conduct in all states similarly instruct attorneys to "abide by a client's decisions concerning the objectives of representation." Model Rules of Professional Conduct, Rule 1.2(a).

7. *Competence to stand trial and to waive the right to counsel.* According to Drope v. Missouri, 420 U.S. 162 (1975), the Constitution does not permit trial of an individual who lacks "mental competency." The trial judge must determine (1) whether the defendant has "a rational as well as factual understanding of the proceedings against him" and (2) whether the defendant "has sufficient present ability to consult with his lawyer with a reasonable degree of rational understanding." A person who lacks the capacity to understand the nature and object of the proceedings against him, to consult with counsel, and to assist in preparing his defense may not be subjected to a trial.

A second competency determination involves the defendant's "knowing and voluntary waiver" of the right to counsel. In Godinez v. Moran, 509 U.S. 389 (1993), the Supreme Court held that a defendant who was marginally competent to stand trial could also plead guilty after waiving his rights to counsel and trial. According to the Court, the decision to plead guilty "is no more complicated than the sum total of decisions that a [represented] defendant may be called upon to make during the course of a trial." As a result, "there is no reason to believe that the decision to waive counsel requires an appreciably higher level of mental functioning than the decision to waive other constitutional rights." Thus, due process does not require a state to set the standard for competence to waive the right to trial or the right to counsel at a level higher than the standard for competence to stand trial.

In *Indiana v. Edwards*, 554 U.S. 164 (2008), however, the Court ruled that a state can declare a defendant incompetent to conduct his or her own defense at trial, even if the state also concluded that the defendant was competent to stand trial. As the Court explained:

> Mental illness itself is not a unitary concept. It varies in degree. It can vary over time. It interferes with an individual's functioning at different times in different ways. . . . In certain instances an individual may well be able to satisfy [the trial] competence standard, for he will be able to work with counsel at trial, yet at the same time he may be unable to carry out the basic tasks needed to present his own defense without the help of counsel.

Is there a convincing way to reconcile *Edwards* and *Godinez*? See *State v. Barnes*, 753 S.E.2d 545 (S.C. 2014) (declining to follow *Edwards*). For a more thorough treatment of competence hearings, see the web extension for this chapter at *http://www.crimpro.com/extension/ch11.*

8. *Performance standards for pro se counsel.* In practice, trial courts appear to give some leeway to lay lawyers, but appellate cases consistently hold that the ordinary standards of practice and evidence are to be applied to defendants who appear pro se. See *Commonwealth v. Jackson*, 647 N.E.2d 401 (Mass. 1995). Should judges assist pro se litigants in questioning witnesses? Should judges give pro se litigants miniature "lessons" in trial procedure and the rules of evidence? See Sharon Finegan, Pro Se Criminal Trials and the Merging of Inquisitorial and Adversarial Systems of Justice, 58 Cath. U. L. Rev. 445 (2009) (procedures followed during pro se criminal trials have evolved to look less like classic adversarial trial and more like inquisitorial model of justice with more active role for judge).

9. *Selection of appointed counsel.* Defendants who retain their own lawyers may retain any lawyer they can afford who will agree to take the case (assuming the lawyer has no conflict of interest). This ability of the client to choose a particular lawyer helps to create a cooperative relationship. The lawyer is urged to "establish a relationship of trust and confidence with the accused." ABA Standards for Criminal Justice 4-3.1 (1980). An indigent defendant, however, may not choose his appointed counsel. In the homely phrase of the Nebraska trial judge in *State v. Green*, 471 N.W.2d 402 (Neb. 1991), "beggars can't be choosey." This is a fair, if blunt, assessment of the law in almost every jurisdiction. See *Morris v. Slappy*, 461 U.S. 1 (1983) (upholds trial court's refusal to grant continuance necessary to allow original counsel to represent defendant; trial proceeded with new appointed counsel). Does this rule suggest we are committed to providing counsel only in the most minimal sense to indigent defendants? If you were a supervisor in a public defender's office, would you institute a rule that allowed clients to take part in the choice of their lawyers?

Should a judge appointing defense counsel place any weight on a defendant's request to work with an attorney with specific qualities? Consider this possible conversation between a lawyer and client:

> "I want a Black lawyer to represent me." These are the first words you hear after you introduce yourself to your new client. . . . You are white. He is Black. You answer that you are an experienced criminal lawyer and will represent him to the best of your ability, regardless of his or your race. He responds that he too is experienced with the criminal justice system—a system that targets Black men, like himself, for prosecution far more than whites, that sentences Black men to prison more frequently

and for a longer duration than whites, and that fails to acknowledge or address the role that race and racism play in the development, enforcement, and execution of the criminal laws established by "the system." . . . He explains that an African-American lawyer will be better able to understand and appreciate the circumstances that resulted in the bringing of these charges and that he, the client, can trust a Black lawyer more than a white one.

Kenneth P. Troccoli, "I Want a Black Lawyer to Represent Me": Addressing a Black Defendant's Concerns with Being Assigned a White Court-Appointed Lawyer, 20 Law and Inequality: A Journal of Theory and Practice 1 (Winter 2002). See also Marcus T. Boccaccini & Stanley L. Brodsky, Characteristics of the Ideal Criminal Defense Attorney from the Client's Perspective: Empirical Findings and Implications for Legal Practice, 25 Law & Psychol. Rev. 81, 116 (2001) (client survey lists the following, in descending order, as most desired attorney characteristics: advocates for client's interest, works hard, keeps client informed, cares about the client, honest, gets favorable outcome, "would not do whatever prosecution says," listens to client, spends time with client before court date).

10. *Law students as counsel.* Almost every state allows some law students to participate in the defense of criminal cases. Statutes and court rules typically allow law students to represent indigent criminal defendants, so long as the defendant is informed that the representative is a law student and consents to the representation, and a licensed attorney supervises the student's efforts. See Rules Regulating the Florida Bar 11-1.2(b); Miss. Code Ann. §73-3-207. What would you say to a defendant to convince her to allow a law student to "practice" on her case?

Problem 11-5. Competence to Stand Trial and to Waive Counsel

Ahmad Edwards tried to steal a pair of shoes from a department store. After he was discovered, he drew a gun, fired at a store security officer, and wounded a bystander. He was arrested and charged with attempted murder, battery with a deadly weapon, criminal recklessness, and theft.

Several months after Edwards' arrest, his court-appointed counsel asked for a psychiatric evaluation of the defendant's competence to stand trial. During this first competency hearing, Edwards' counsel presented psychiatric and neuropsychological evidence showing that Edwards was suffering from serious thinking difficulties and delusions. A testifying psychiatrist reported that Edwards could understand the charges against him, but he was "unable to cooperate with his attorney in his defense because of his schizophrenic illness"; his "delusions and his marked difficulties in thinking" made it "impossible for him to cooperate with his attorney." The court concluded that Edwards was not then competent to stand trial and ordered his recommitment to the state hospital.

Seven months after his commitment, doctors reported that Edwards' condition had improved and the court ruled that he was competent to stand trial. Almost one year after that hospital report, just before his trial started, Edwards asked to represent himself. He also asked for a continuance to give him enough time to prepare for pro se representation. The judge refused the continuance; Edwards then proceeded to trial represented by counsel. The jury convicted him of criminal recklessness and theft but failed to reach a verdict on the charges of attempted murder and battery.

The State decided to retry Edwards on the attempted murder and battery charges. Just before the retrial, six months after his first trial ended, Edwards again asked the court to permit him to represent himself. Referring to the lengthy record of psychiatric reports, the judge noted that Edwards still suffered from schizophrenia and concluded that "he's competent to stand trial but I'm not going to find he's competent to defend himself." The court denied Edwards' self-representation request. Edwards was represented by appointed counsel at his retrial. The jury convicted Edwards on both of the remaining counts.

Edwards appeals from this conviction after the second trial and argues that the trial court's refusal to permit him to represent himself at his retrial deprived him of his constitutional right of self-representation. How could you argue on behalf of the state that the trial court's denial of Edwards' motion to represent himself was correct? What sort of pretrial factual submissions and factual findings by the trial judge could most effectively bolster your position?

C. ADEQUACY OF COUNSEL

Constitutions and other laws not only govern the availability of a lawyer; they also address the quality of the legal representation that the attorney must give the client. So long as lawyers make mistakes, courts and other legal institutions must decide whether the client will be the one who pays. The next case lays down a legal standard now followed almost uniformly by courts trying to determine whether an attorney has provided a client with the "effective assistance of counsel" necessary for a constitutionally acceptable criminal conviction.

■ CHARLES STRICKLAND v. DAVID WASHINGTON
466 U.S. 668 (1984)

O'CONNOR, J.[*]

This case requires us to consider the proper standards for judging a criminal defendant's contention that the Constitution requires a conviction or death sentence to be set aside because counsel's assistance at the trial or sentencing was ineffective.

I.

A.

During a 10-day period in September 1976, respondent planned and committed three groups of crimes, which included three brutal stabbing murders, torture, kidnapping, severe assaults, attempted murders, attempted extortion, and theft. After his two accomplices were arrested, respondent surrendered to police and voluntarily gave a lengthy statement confessing to the third of the criminal episodes. The

---

[*] [Chief Justice Burger and Justices White, Blackmun, Powell, Rehnquist, and Stevens joined in this opinion.—EDS.]

State of Florida indicted respondent for kidnapping and murder and appointed an experienced criminal lawyer to represent him.

Counsel actively pursued pretrial motions and discovery. He cut his efforts short, however, and he experienced a sense of hopelessness about the case, when he learned that, against his specific advice, respondent had also confessed to the first two murders. [Respondent also acted against counsel's advice in pleading guilty to all charges and waiving the right to an advisory jury at his capital sentencing hearing.]

In preparing for the sentencing hearing, counsel spoke with respondent about his background. He also spoke on the telephone with respondent's wife and mother, though he did not follow up on the one unsuccessful effort to meet with them. He did not otherwise seek out character witnesses for respondent. Nor did he request a psychiatric examination, since his conversations with his client gave no indication that respondent had psychological problems. [To establish his claim of "emotional stress" as a "mitigating factor" against a death sentence, counsel decided to rely on the defendant's statements at the guilty plea colloquy about his emotional state, and not to introduce further evidence on the question. By forgoing the opportunity to present new evidence on these subjects, counsel prevented the State from cross-examining respondent on his claim and from putting on psychiatric evidence of its own.]

Counsel also excluded from the sentencing hearing other evidence he thought was potentially damaging. He successfully moved to exclude respondent's "rap sheet." Because he judged that a presentence report might prove more detrimental than helpful, as it would have included respondent's criminal history and thereby would have undermined the claim of no significant history of criminal activity, he did not request that one be prepared.

[Because the sentencing judge had a reputation as a person who thought it important for a convicted defendant to own up to his crime, counsel argued at sentencing that Washington's remorse and acceptance of responsibility justified sparing him from the death penalty. Counsel also argued that respondent had no history of criminal activity and that respondent committed the crimes under extreme mental or emotional disturbance, thus coming within the statutory list of mitigating circumstances. The trial judge found numerous aggravating circumstances and no significant mitigating circumstances, and sentenced respondent to death on each of the three counts of murder.]

B.

Respondent subsequently sought collateral relief in state court on numerous grounds, among them that counsel had rendered ineffective assistance at the sentencing proceeding. Respondent challenged counsel's assistance in six respects. He asserted that counsel was ineffective because he failed to move for a continuance to prepare for sentencing, to request a psychiatric report, to investigate and present character witnesses, to seek a presentence investigation report, to present meaningful arguments to the sentencing judge, and to investigate the medical examiner's reports [about the condition of the victims' bodies] or cross-examine the medical experts. [The state trial court, the state appellate courts, and the federal district court all refused to find ineffective assistance of counsel, and therefore refused to grant postconviction relief. The federal appeals court announced a new legal standard for claims of ineffective assistance of counsel and remanded the case for further factfinding under the new standards. This appeal followed.]

II.

In a long line of cases that includes Powell v. Alabama, 287 U.S. 45 (1932) . . . and Gideon v. Wainwright, 372 U.S. 335 (1963), this Court has recognized that the Sixth Amendment right to counsel exists, and is needed, in order to protect the fundamental right to a fair trial [in the adversary system. It has also] recognized that the right to counsel is the right to the effective assistance of counsel. . . .

The Court has not elaborated on the meaning of the constitutional requirement of effective assistance in [cases] presenting claims of "actual ineffectiveness." In giving meaning to the requirement, however, we must take its purpose—to ensure a fair trial—as the guide. The benchmark for judging any claim of ineffectiveness must be whether counsel's conduct so undermined the proper functioning of the adversarial process that the trial cannot be relied on as having produced a just result. . . .

III.

A convicted defendant's claim that counsel's assistance was so defective as to require reversal of a conviction or death sentence has two components. First, the defendant must show that counsel's performance was deficient. This requires showing that counsel made errors so serious that counsel was not functioning as the "counsel" guaranteed the defendant by the Sixth Amendment. Second, the defendant must show that the deficient performance prejudiced the defense. This requires showing that counsel's errors were so serious as to deprive the defendant of a fair trial, a trial whose result is reliable. Unless a defendant makes both showings, it cannot be said that the conviction or death sentence resulted from a breakdown in the adversary process that renders the result unreliable. . . .

A.

. . . When a convicted defendant complains of the ineffectiveness of counsel's assistance, the defendant must show that counsel's representation fell below an objective standard of reasonableness. More specific guidelines are not appropriate. The Sixth Amendment refers simply to "counsel," not specifying particular requirements of effective assistance. It relies instead on the legal profession's maintenance of standards sufficient to justify the law's presumption that counsel will fulfill the role in the adversary process that the Amendment envisions. The proper measure of attorney performance remains simply reasonableness under prevailing professional norms.

Representation of a criminal defendant entails certain basic duties. Counsel's function is to assist the defendant, and hence counsel owes the client a duty of loyalty, a duty to avoid conflicts of interest. Cuyler v. Sullivan, 446 U.S. 335 (1980). From counsel's function as assistant to the defendant derive the overarching duty to advocate the defendant's cause and the more particular duties to consult with the defendant on important decisions and to keep the defendant informed of important developments in the course of the prosecution. Counsel also has a duty to bring to bear such skill and knowledge as will render the trial a reliable adversarial testing process.

These basic duties neither exhaustively define the obligations of counsel nor form a checklist for judicial evaluation of attorney performance. In any case presenting an ineffectiveness claim, the performance inquiry must be whether counsel's assistance was reasonable considering all the circumstances. Prevailing norms of practice as reflected in American Bar Association standards and the like, e.g., ABA Standards for Criminal Justice 4-1.1 to 4-8.6 (2d ed. 1980), are guides to determining what is reasonable, but they are only guides. No particular set of detailed rules for counsel's conduct can satisfactorily take account of the variety of circumstances faced by defense counsel or the range of legitimate decisions regarding how best to represent a criminal defendant. Any such set of rules would interfere with the constitutionally protected independence of counsel and restrict the wide latitude counsel must have in making tactical decisions. Indeed, the existence of detailed guidelines for representation could distract counsel from the overriding mission of vigorous advocacy of the defendant's cause. Moreover, the purpose of the effective assistance guarantee of the Sixth Amendment is not to improve the quality of legal representation, although that is a goal of considerable importance to the legal system. The purpose is simply to ensure that criminal defendants receive a fair trial.

Judicial scrutiny of counsel's performance must be highly deferential. It is all too tempting for a defendant to second-guess counsel's assistance after conviction or adverse sentence, and it is all too easy for a court, examining counsel's defense after it has proved unsuccessful, to conclude that a particular act or omission of counsel was unreasonable. A fair assessment of attorney performance requires that every effort be made to eliminate the distorting effects of hindsight, to reconstruct the circumstances of counsel's challenged conduct, and to evaluate the conduct from counsel's perspective at the time. Because of the difficulties inherent in making the evaluation, a court must indulge a strong presumption that counsel's conduct falls within the wide range of reasonable professional assistance; that is, the defendant must overcome the presumption that, under the circumstances, the challenged action might be considered sound trial strategy. There are countless ways to provide effective assistance in any given case. Even the best criminal defense attorneys would not defend a particular client in the same way.

The availability of intrusive post-trial inquiry into attorney performance or of detailed guidelines for its evaluation would encourage the proliferation of ineffectiveness challenges. Criminal trials resolved unfavorably to the defendant would increasingly come to be followed by a second trial, this one of counsel's unsuccessful defense. Counsel's performance and even willingness to serve could be adversely affected. . . .

B.

An error by counsel, even if professionally unreasonable, does not warrant setting aside the judgment of a criminal proceeding if the error had no effect on the judgment. The purpose of the Sixth Amendment guarantee of counsel is to ensure that a defendant has the assistance necessary to justify reliance on the outcome of the proceeding. Accordingly, any deficiencies in counsel's performance must be prejudicial to the defense in order to constitute ineffective assistance under the Constitution.

In certain Sixth Amendment contexts, prejudice is presumed. Actual or constructive denial of the assistance of counsel altogether is legally presumed to result in prejudice. So are various kinds of state interference with counsel's assistance. Prejudice in these circumstances is so likely that case-by-case inquiry into prejudice is not worth the cost. Moreover, such circumstances involve impairments of the Sixth Amendment right that are easy to identify and, for that reason and because the prosecution is directly responsible, easy for the government to prevent.

One type of actual ineffectiveness claim warrants a similar, though more limited, presumption of prejudice. In Cuyler v. Sullivan, 446 U.S. 335 (1980), the Court held that prejudice is presumed when counsel is burdened by an actual conflict of interest. In those circumstances, counsel breaches the duty of loyalty, perhaps the most basic of counsel's duties. Moreover, it is difficult to measure the precise effect on the defense of representation corrupted by conflicting interests. Given the obligation of counsel to avoid conflicts of interest and the ability of trial courts to make early inquiry in certain situations likely to give rise to conflicts, it is reasonable for the criminal justice system to maintain a fairly rigid rule of presumed prejudice for conflicts of interest. . . .

Conflict of interest claims aside, actual ineffectiveness claims alleging a deficiency in attorney performance are subject to a general requirement that the defendant affirmatively prove prejudice. . . . It is not enough for the defendant to show that the errors had some conceivable effect on the outcome of the proceeding. Virtually every act or omission of counsel would meet that test, and not every error that conceivably could have influenced the outcome undermines the reliability of the result of the proceeding. . . .

On the other hand, we believe that a defendant need not show that counsel's deficient conduct more likely than not altered the outcome in the case. [The "more likely than not altered the outcome" test, which is used to decide whether to grant a new trial based on new evidence,] is not an apt source from which to draw a prejudice standard for ineffectiveness claims. The high standard for newly discovered evidence claims presupposes that all the essential elements of a presumptively accurate and fair proceeding were present in the proceeding whose result is challenged. An ineffective assistance claim asserts the absence of one of the crucial assurances that the result of the proceeding is reliable, so finality concerns are somewhat weaker and the appropriate standard of prejudice should be somewhat lower. The result of a proceeding can be rendered unreliable, and hence the proceeding itself unfair, even if the errors of counsel cannot be shown by a preponderance of the evidence to have determined the outcome.

Accordingly, the appropriate test for prejudice finds its roots in the test for materiality of exculpatory information not disclosed to the defense by the prosecution, and in the test for materiality of testimony made unavailable to the defense by Government deportation of a witness. The defendant must show that there is a reasonable probability that, but for counsel's unprofessional errors, the result of the proceeding would have been different. A reasonable probability is a probability sufficient to undermine confidence in the outcome. . . .

IV.

Although we have discussed the performance component of an ineffectiveness claim prior to the prejudice component, there is no reason for a court deciding an ineffective assistance claim to approach the inquiry in the same order or even to address both components of the inquiry if the defendant makes an insufficient showing on one. In particular, a court need not determine whether counsel's performance was deficient before examining the prejudice suffered by the defendant as a result of the alleged deficiencies. The object of an ineffectiveness claim is not to grade counsel's performance. If it is easier to dispose of an ineffectiveness claim on the ground of lack of sufficient prejudice, which we expect will often be so, that course should be followed. . . .

V.

Having articulated general standards for judging ineffectiveness claims, we think it useful to apply those standards to the facts of this case in order to illustrate the meaning of the general principles. . . . With respect to the performance component, the record shows that respondent's counsel made a strategic choice to argue for the extreme emotional distress mitigating circumstance and to rely as fully as possible on respondent's acceptance of responsibility for his crimes. . . . The trial judge's views on the importance of owning up to one's crimes were well known to counsel. The aggravating circumstances were utterly overwhelming. Trial counsel could reasonably surmise from his conversations with respondent that character and psychological evidence would be of little help. Respondent had already been able to mention at the plea colloquy the substance of what there was to know about his financial and emotional troubles. Restricting testimony on respondent's character to what had come in at the plea colloquy ensured that contrary character and psychological evidence and respondent's criminal history, which counsel had successfully moved to exclude, would not come in. On these facts, there can be little question, even without application of the presumption of adequate performance, that trial counsel's defense, though unsuccessful, was the result of reasonable professional judgment.

With respect to the prejudice component, the lack of merit of respondent's claim is even more stark. The evidence that respondent says his trial counsel should have offered at the sentencing hearing would barely have altered the sentencing profile presented to the sentencing judge. [At] most this evidence shows that numerous people who knew respondent thought he was generally a good person and that a psychiatrist and a psychologist believed he was under considerable emotional stress that did not rise to the level of extreme disturbance. Given the overwhelming aggravating factors, there is no reasonable probability that the omitted evidence would have changed the conclusion that the aggravating circumstances outweighed the mitigating circumstances and, hence, the sentence imposed. Indeed, admission of the evidence respondent now offers might even have been harmful to his case: his "rap sheet" would probably have been admitted into evidence, and the psychological reports would have directly contradicted respondent's claim that the mitigating circumstance of extreme emotional disturbance applied to his case.

[Respondent] has made no showing that the justice of his sentence was rendered unreliable by a breakdown in the adversary process caused by deficiencies in counsel's assistance. . . .

MARSHALL, J., dissenting.

[State] and lower federal courts have developed standards for distinguishing effective from inadequate assistance. Today, for the first time, this Court attempts to synthesize and clarify those standards. For the most part, the majority's efforts are unhelpful. . . .

I.

A.

My objection to the performance standard adopted by the Court is that it is so malleable that, in practice, it will either have no grip at all or will yield excessive variation in the manner in which the Sixth Amendment is interpreted and applied by different courts. To tell lawyers and the lower courts that counsel for a criminal defendant must behave "reasonably" . . . is to tell them almost nothing. In essence, the majority has instructed judges called upon to assess claims of ineffective assistance of counsel to advert to their own intuitions regarding what constitutes "professional" representation, and has discouraged them from trying to develop more detailed standards governing the performance of defense counsel. In my view, the Court has thereby not only abdicated its own responsibility to interpret the Constitution, but also impaired the ability of the lower courts to exercise theirs.

The debilitating ambiguity of an "objective standard of reasonableness" in this context is illustrated by the majority's failure to address important issues concerning the quality of representation mandated by the Constitution. . . . Is a "reasonably competent attorney" a reasonably competent adequately paid retained lawyer or a reasonably competent appointed attorney? It is also a fact that the quality of representation available to ordinary defendants in different parts of the country varies significantly. Should the standard of performance mandated by the Sixth Amendment vary by locale? The majority offers no clues as to the proper responses to these questions. . . .

I agree that counsel must be afforded wide latitude when making tactical decisions regarding trial strategy, but many aspects of the job of a criminal defense attorney are more amenable to judicial oversight. For example, much of the work involved in preparing for a trial, applying for bail, conferring with one's client, making timely objections to significant, arguably erroneous rulings of the trial judge, and filing a notice of appeal if there are colorable grounds therefor could profitably be made the subject of uniform standards.

B.

I object to the prejudice standard adopted by the Court for two independent reasons. First, it is often very difficult to tell whether a defendant convicted after a trial in which he was ineffectively represented would have fared better if his lawyer had been competent. Seemingly impregnable cases can sometimes be dismantled by good defense counsel. On the basis of a cold record, it may be impossible for a reviewing court confidently to ascertain how the government's evidence and arguments would have stood up against rebuttal and cross-examination by a shrewd, well-prepared lawyer. The difficulties of estimating prejudice after the fact are exacerbated by the possibility that evidence of injury to the defendant may be missing from the record precisely because of the incompetence of defense counsel. . . .

Second and more fundamentally, the assumption on which the Court's holding rests is that the only purpose of the constitutional guarantee of effective assistance of counsel is to reduce the chance that innocent persons will be convicted. In my view, the guarantee also functions to ensure that convictions are obtained only through fundamentally fair procedures. The majority contends that the Sixth Amendment is not violated when a manifestly guilty defendant is convicted after a trial in which he was represented by a manifestly ineffective attorney. I cannot agree. Every defendant is entitled to a trial in which his interests are vigorously and conscientiously advocated by an able lawyer. [I would hold] that a showing that the performance of a defendant's lawyer departed from constitutionally prescribed standards requires a new trial regardless of whether the defendant suffered demonstrable prejudice thereby. . . .

IV.

[I must also] dissent from the majority's disposition of the case before us. It is undisputed that respondent's trial counsel made virtually no investigation of the possibility of obtaining testimony from respondent's relatives, friends, or former employers pertaining to respondent's character or background. Had counsel done so, he would have found several persons willing and able to testify that, in their experience, respondent was a responsible, nonviolent man, devoted to his family, and active in the affairs of his church. . . . Had this evidence been admitted, respondent argues, his chances of obtaining a life sentence would have been significantly better. . . .

The State makes a colorable — though in my view not compelling — argument that defense counsel in this case might have made a reasonable "strategic" decision not to present such evidence at the sentencing hearing on the assumption that an unadorned acknowledgment of respondent's responsibility for his crimes would be more likely to appeal to the trial judge, who was reputed to respect persons who accepted responsibility for their actions. But however justifiable such a choice might have been after counsel had fairly assessed the potential strength of the mitigating evidence available to him, counsel's failure to make any significant effort to find out what evidence might be garnered from respondent's relatives and acquaintances surely cannot be described as "reasonable." . . . If counsel had investigated [and presented the available mitigating evidence], there is a significant chance that respondent would have been given a life sentence. . . .

■ BLAINE LAFLER v. ANTHONY COOPER
566 U.S. 156 (2012)

Kennedy, J.[*]

In this case . . . a criminal defendant seeks a remedy when inadequate assistance of counsel caused non-acceptance of a plea offer and further proceedings led to a less favorable outcome. [A] favorable plea offer was reported to the client but, on advice of counsel, was rejected. [After a jury conviction], the defendant received a sentence harsher than that offered in the rejected plea bargain. . . .

---

* [Justices Ginsburg, Breyer, Sotomayor, and Kagan joined this opinion.—Eds.]

I.

On the evening of March 25, 2003, respondent pointed a gun toward Kali Mundy's head and fired. From the record, it is unclear why respondent did this, and at trial it was suggested that he might have acted either in self-defense or in defense of another person. In any event the shot missed and Mundy fled. Respondent followed in pursuit, firing repeatedly. Mundy was shot in her buttock, hip, and abdomen but survived the assault.

Respondent was charged under Michigan law with assault with intent to murder, possession of a firearm by a felon, possession of a firearm in the commission of a felony, misdemeanor possession of marijuana, and for being a habitual offender. On two occasions, the prosecution offered to dismiss two of the charges and to recommend a sentence of 51 to 85 months for the other two, in exchange for a guilty plea. In a communication with the court respondent admitted guilt and expressed a willingness to accept the offer. Respondent, however, later rejected the offer on both occasions, allegedly after his attorney convinced him that the prosecution would be unable to establish his intent to murder Mundy because she had been shot below the waist. On the first day of trial the prosecution offered a significantly less favorable plea deal, which respondent again rejected. After trial, respondent was convicted on all counts and received a mandatory minimum sentence of 185 to 360 months' imprisonment. [After the Michigan courts denied Cooper's claim of ineffective assistance of counsel, the defendant sought federal habeas corpus review of his conviction.]

II.

A.

Defendants have a Sixth Amendment right to counsel, a right that extends to the plea-bargaining process. During plea negotiations defendants are entitled to the effective assistance of competent counsel. In Hill v. Lockhart, 474 U.S. 52 (1985), the Court held "the two-part Strickland v. Washington test applies to challenges to guilty pleas based on ineffective assistance of counsel." . . . In this case all parties agree the performance of respondent's counsel was deficient when he advised respondent to reject the plea offer on the grounds he could not be convicted at trial. In light of this concession, it is unnecessary for this Court to explore the issue. The question for this Court is how to apply *Strickland's* prejudice test where ineffective assistance results in a rejection of the plea offer and the defendant is convicted at the ensuing trial.

B.

To establish *Strickland* prejudice a defendant must "show that there is a reasonable probability that, but for counsel's unprofessional errors, the result of the proceeding would have been different." In the context of pleas a defendant must show the outcome of the plea process would have been different with competent advice. In *Hill,* when evaluating the petitioner's claim that ineffective assistance led to the improvident acceptance of a guilty plea, the Court required the petitioner to show "that there is a reasonable probability that, but for counsel's errors, [the defendant] would not have pleaded guilty and would have insisted on going to trial."

In contrast to *Hill,* here the ineffective advice led not to an offer's acceptance but to its rejection. Having to stand trial, not choosing to waive it, is the prejudice alleged. In these circumstances a defendant must show that but for the ineffective advice of counsel there is a reasonable probability that the plea offer would have been presented to the court (*i.e.,* that the defendant would have accepted the plea and the prosecution would not have withdrawn it in light of intervening circumstances), that the court would have accepted its terms, and that the conviction or sentence, or both, under the offer's terms would have been less severe than under the judgment and sentence that in fact were imposed. . . .

Petitioner and the Solicitor General propose a different, far more narrow, view of the Sixth Amendment. They contend there can be no finding of *Strickland* prejudice arising from plea bargaining if the defendant is later convicted at a fair trial. The . . . reasons petitioner and the Solicitor General offer for their approach are unpersuasive.

First, petitioner and the Solicitor General claim that the sole purpose of the Sixth Amendment is to protect the right to a fair trial. Errors before trial, they argue, are not cognizable under the Sixth Amendment unless they affect the fairness of the trial itself. The Sixth Amendment, however, is not so narrow in its reach. The Sixth Amendment requires effective assistance of counsel at critical stages of a criminal proceeding. . . .

In the instant case respondent . . . received a more severe sentence at trial, one three and a half times more severe than he likely would have received by pleading guilty. Far from curing the error, the trial caused the injury from the error. Even if the trial itself is free from constitutional flaw, the defendant who goes to trial instead of taking a more favorable plea may be prejudiced from either a conviction on more serious counts or the imposition of a more severe sentence. . . .

It is, of course, true that defendants have no right to be offered a plea, nor a federal right that the judge accept it. In the circumstances here, that is beside the point. If no plea offer is made, or a plea deal is accepted by the defendant but rejected by the judge, the issue raised here simply does not arise. . . .

The constitutional rights of criminal defendants . . . are granted to the innocent and the guilty alike. Consequently, we decline to hold either that the guarantee of effective assistance of counsel belongs solely to the innocent or that it attaches only to matters affecting the determination of actual guilt. [A contrary ruling, that a fair trial wipes clean any deficient performance by defense counsel during plea bargaining, would ignore] the reality that criminal justice today is for the most part a system of pleas, not a system of trials. Ninety-seven percent of federal convictions and ninety-four percent of state convictions are the result of guilty pleas. [The] right to adequate assistance of counsel cannot be defined or enforced without taking account of the central role plea bargaining plays in securing convictions and determining sentences.

C.

Even if a defendant shows ineffective assistance of counsel has caused the rejection of a plea leading to a trial and a more severe sentence, there is the question of what constitutes an appropriate remedy. . . . Sixth Amendment remedies should . . . neutralize the taint of a constitutional violation while at the same time not grant a windfall to the defendant or needlessly squander the considerable resources the State properly invested in the criminal prosecution.

The specific injury suffered by defendants who decline a plea offer as a result of ineffective assistance of counsel and then receive a greater sentence as a result of trial can come in at least one of two forms. In some cases, the sole advantage a defendant would have received under the plea is a lesser sentence. This is typically the case when the charges that would have been admitted as part of the plea bargain are the same as the charges the defendant was convicted of after trial. In this situation the court may conduct an evidentiary hearing to determine whether the defendant has shown a reasonable probability that but for counsel's errors he would have accepted the plea. If the showing is made, the court may exercise discretion in determining whether the defendant should receive the term of imprisonment the government offered in the plea, the sentence he received at trial, or something in between.

In some situations it may be that resentencing alone will not be full redress for the constitutional injury. If, for example, an offer was for a guilty plea to a count or counts less serious than the ones for which a defendant was convicted after trial, or if a mandatory sentence confines a judge's sentencing discretion after trial, a resentencing based on the conviction at trial may not suffice. In these circumstances, the proper exercise of discretion to remedy the constitutional injury may be to require the prosecution to reoffer the plea proposal. Once this has occurred, the judge can then exercise discretion in deciding whether to vacate the conviction from trial and accept the plea or leave the conviction undisturbed. . . .

Principles elaborated over time in decisions of state and federal courts, and in statutes and rules, will serve to give more complete guidance as to the factors that should bear upon the exercise of the judge's discretion. At this point, however, it suffices to note two considerations that are of relevance.

First, a court may take account of a defendant's earlier expressed willingness, or unwillingness, to accept responsibility for his or her actions. Second, it is not necessary here to decide as a constitutional rule that a judge is required to prescind (that is to say disregard) any information concerning the crime that was discovered after the plea offer was made. The time continuum makes it difficult to restore the defendant and the prosecution to the precise positions they occupied prior to the rejection of the plea offer, but that baseline can be consulted in finding a remedy that does not require the prosecution to incur the expense of conducting a new trial. . . .

III.

The standards for ineffective assistance of counsel when a defendant rejects a plea offer and goes to trial must now be applied to this case. . . . Respondent has satisfied *Strickland*'s two-part test. [In this case], the fact of deficient performance has been conceded by all parties. . . . As to prejudice, respondent has shown that but for counsel's deficient performance there is a reasonable probability he and the trial court would have accepted the guilty plea. In addition, as a result of not accepting the plea and being convicted at trial, respondent received a minimum sentence three and one half times greater than he would have received under the plea. The standard for ineffective assistance under *Strickland* has thus been satisfied.

As a remedy, the District Court ordered specific performance of the original plea agreement. The correct remedy in these circumstances, however, is to order the State to reoffer the plea agreement. Presuming respondent accepts the offer, the state trial court can then exercise its discretion in determining whether to vacate the convictions and resentence respondent pursuant to the plea agreement, to vacate only some of the convictions and resentence respondent accordingly, or to leave the convictions and sentence from trial undisturbed. . . .

SCALIA, J., dissenting.*

[The] Court today opens a whole new field of constitutionalized criminal procedure: plea-bargaining law. The ordinary criminal process has become too long, too expensive, and unpredictable, in no small part as a consequence of an intricate federal Code of Criminal Procedure imposed on the States by this Court in pursuit of perfect justice. The Court now moves to bring perfection to the alternative in which prosecutors and defendants have sought relief. . . . And it would be foolish to think that "constitutional" rules governing *counsel*'s behavior will not be followed by rules governing the *prosecution*'s behavior in the plea-bargaining process. . . . Is it constitutional, for example, for the prosecution to withdraw a plea offer that has already been accepted? Or to withdraw an offer before the defense has had adequate time to consider and accept it? Or to make no plea offer at all, even though its case is weak . . . ?

Anthony Cooper received a full and fair trial, was found guilty of all charges by a unanimous jury, and was given the sentence that the law prescribed. The Court nonetheless concludes that Cooper is entitled to some sort of habeas corpus relief (perhaps) because his attorney's allegedly incompetent advice regarding a plea offer *caused* him to receive a full and fair trial. That conclusion is foreclosed by our precedents. . . .

As the Court notes, the right to counsel does not begin at trial. It extends to "any stage of the prosecution, formal or informal, in court or out, where counsel's absence might derogate from the accused's right to a fair trial." United States v. Wade, 388 U.S. 218, 226 (1967). Applying that principle, we held that the entry of a guilty plea, whether to a misdemeanor or a felony charge, ranks as a "critical stage" at which the right to counsel adheres. Iowa v. Tovar, 541 U.S. 77, 81 (2004); see also Hill v. Lockhart, 474 U.S. 52 (1985). And it follows from this that *acceptance* of a plea offer is a critical stage. [Our decisions have never required] the advice of competent counsel before the defendant rejects a plea bargain and stands on his constitutional right to a fair trial. The latter is a vast departure from our past cases, protecting not just the constitutionally prescribed right to a fair adjudication of guilt and punishment, but a judicially invented right to effective plea bargaining. . . .

Since the right to the effective assistance of counsel is recognized not for its own sake, but because of the effect it has on the ability of the accused to receive a fair trial, the benchmark inquiry in evaluating any claim of ineffective assistance is whether counsel's performance so undermined the proper functioning of the adversarial process that it failed to produce a reliably just result. . . . Impairment of fair trial is how we distinguish between unfortunate attorney error and error of constitutional significance. . . .

It is impossible to conclude discussion of today's extraordinary opinion without commenting upon the remedy it provides for the unconstitutional conviction. It is

* [Justice Thomas joined this opinion; Chief Justice Roberts joined all but Part IV of the opinion.—EDS.]

a remedy unheard-of in American jurisprudence—and, I would be willing to bet, in the jurisprudence of any other country.

The Court requires Michigan to "reoffer the plea agreement" that was rejected because of bad advice from counsel. That would indeed be a powerful remedy—but for the fact that Cooper's acceptance of that reoffered agreement is not conclusive. Astoundingly, "the state trial court can then *exercise its discretion* in determining whether to vacate the convictions and resentence respondent pursuant to the plea agreement, to vacate only some of the convictions and resentence respondent accordingly, *or to leave the convictions and sentence from trial undisturbed.*" (emphasis added). . . .

I suspect that the Court's squeamishness in fashioning a remedy, and the incoherence of what it comes up with, is attributable to its realization, deep down, that there is no real constitutional violation here anyway. The defendant has been fairly tried, lawfully convicted, and properly sentenced, and *any* "remedy" provided for this will do nothing but undo the just results of a fair adversarial process. . . .

I am less saddened by the outcome of this case than I am by what it says about this Court's attitude toward criminal justice. The Court today embraces the sporting-chance theory of criminal law, in which the State functions like a conscientious casino-operator, giving each player a fair chance to beat the house, that is, to serve less time than the law says he deserves. And when a player is excluded from the tables, his *constitutional rights* have been violated. I do not subscribe to that theory. No one should, least of all the Justices of the Supreme Court. . . .

Notes

1. *The test for ineffective assistance of counsel: majority position.* The *Strickland* opinion was the Supreme Court's first substantial effort to define the quality of representation required by the Sixth Amendment. In *Strickland*, the court announced its two-part standard: (1) counsel's performance must be "reasonably effective" and cannot fall below an "objective standard" of reasonableness, and (2) the defendant must show a "reasonable probability" that the outcome in the proceedings changed because of the attorney's deficient performance. The *Strickland* opinion has been enormously influential, with states overwhelmingly adopting its framework under state constitutions. Why did it take until 1984 (almost 200 years) to get a square decision from the U.S. Supreme Court on standards of attorney competence? Note that the Court did not explicitly require access to counsel as an element of due process in state criminal trials until Powell v. Alabama, 287 U.S. 45 (1932), and it was not until Gideon v. Wainwright, 372 U.S. 335 (1963), that state-provided attorneys became the rule rather than the exception. See David Cole, *Gideon v. Wainwright* and *Strickland v. Washington*: Broken Promises, in Criminal Procedure Stories (Carol Steiker ed., 2006).

In *Strickland*, Justice O'Connor describes the effectiveness standard as an "objective" standard. What makes a standard "objective" or "subjective"? Why does the Court create a "strong presumption" of sound lawyering? Is that an objective standard?

2. *Measuring performance.* The defendant has the burden of proving unreasonable performance, by a preponderance of the evidence. The most straightforward cases of substandard performance involve an attorney's failure to consult a client (or

failure to follow client instructions) over the basic direction of the litigation, such as a decision whether to file a notice of appeal, or a decision to concede guilt and concentrate on the sentencing phase of a capital case. See Roe v. Flores-Ortega, 528 U.S. 470 (2000) (ineffectiveness often present but not presumed when counsel fails to consult client about appeal and misses deadline for filing); Padilla v. Kentucky, 559 U.S. 356 (2010) (when immigration consequences of criminal conviction are clear, competent counsel must inform defendant about those consequences prior to entry of guilty plea).

The more common and more difficult claims about attorney performance involve questionable choices about trial preparation and presentation of evidence. The U.S. Supreme Court has applied the *Strickland* standard lately to emphasize the reasonableness of the investigation that *precedes* an attorney's trial choices, rather than focusing on the reasonableness of the trial decision itself. See Rompilla v. Beard, 545 U.S. 374 (2005) (unreasonable performance during pretrial investigation of prior related conviction that prosecution would emphasize as aggravating fact in capital case); Porter v. McCollum, 558 U.S. 30 (2009) (defense counsel in capital case was deficient; attorney failed to uncover and present during penalty phase any mitigating evidence regarding client's mental health, family background, or military service). Does the legal standard in *Strickland* prevent a finding of unreasonable performance in any case where the attorney (or an appellate court) can construct a *post hoc* justification for the choice? When a defendant complains about a large collection of attorney decisions, does the standard require a court to consider them one at a time, or can the court consider the collective impact of many borderline attorney choices?

With sad regularity, attorneys are accused of sleeping, practicing while drunk or drugged, or otherwise being physically unable to present an effective defense. Courts sometimes hold that such impairments do not deny defendants effective counsel without specific proof about faulty legal decisions caused by the impairment. See, e.g., McFarland v. Texas, 928 S.W.2d 482 (Tex. Crim. App. 1996) (72-year-old lawyer who said he "customarily" takes a "short nap in the afternoon" held not to be ineffective assistance where napping might have been a "strategic" move to generate jury sympathy and where co-counsel remained awake). Are attorneys impaired if they do not know the most basic law governing the case? Should courts give experienced attorneys a stronger presumption of reasonable performance than newer attorneys?

3. *Performance and collateral consequences.* Just as the right to effective assistance of counsel extends to the attorney's actions during plea negotiations, it also reaches attorney advice to their clients about certain "collateral" consequences of a criminal conviction—that is, legal consequences carried out by decisionmakers other than the sentencing judge. For instance, in Padilla v. Kentucky, 559 U.S. 356 (2010), the Court held that a defense attorney engages in deficient performance by failing to give the defendant accurate advice about "succinct, clear, and explicit" provisions of immigration law that require removal of noncitizens after certain types of criminal convictions. Where immigration consequences of a criminal conviction are unclear, effective defense counsel must inform the defendant that pending charges may carry a risk of adverse immigration charges.

4. *Public and private incompetence.* Should the judicial standards for ineffective assistance of counsel be the same for public defenders and private attorneys practicing criminal defense? There was a time when courts in some jurisdictions used

different standards for publicly provided and privately retained defense counsel, applying a less demanding standard when reviewing the work of privately retained counsel because the work of such an attorney was not considered "state action." See People v. Stevens, 53 P.2d 133 (Cal. 1935). However, in Cuyler v. Sullivan, 446 U.S. 335, 344-345 (1980), the Supreme Court rejected the idea that private attorneys are to be judged by some lesser standard of constitutional scrutiny: "Since the State's conduct of a criminal trial itself implicates the State in the defendant's conviction, we see no basis for drawing a distinction between retained and appointed counsel that would deny equal justice to defendants who must choose their own lawyers."

Although it is clear that retained attorneys cannot be scrutinized less carefully than appointed counsel, could they be scrutinized *more* carefully? On average, which type of attorney do you suppose would be more effective? Does your answer change for different types of criminal cases?

5. *Measuring prejudice.* The prejudice standard under *Strickland,* requiring a "reasonable probability" of a different outcome absent attorney error, calls for a counterfactual inquiry into what the outcome would have been in a hypothetical trial without attorney error. Is the prejudice standard too restrictive or too liberal? How can courts best account for the effects of what counsel *failed* to do? In Sears v. Upton, 561 U.S. 945 (2010), defense counsel selected one theory of mitigation in a capital trial but failed to investigate others. Although the chosen mitigation theory was a reasonable one, the Supreme Court held that prejudice still might flow from the failure to investigate alternatives.

Should a court insist on reaching the difficult and counterfactual prejudice issue only after finding substandard attorney performance? The bulk of the appellate cases on ineffective assistance (and it is indeed a bulky body of cases) turn on prejudice rather than ineffectiveness. You can find a sampling of these cases from the state courts on the web extension of this chapter at *http://www.crimpro.com/extension/ch11.*

6. *Prejudice during plea negotiations.* How should the standard for prejudice change when the defendant alleges that counsel's error affected plea negotiations? As the Court explained in *Lafler,* a defendant must show that "the outcome of the plea process would have been different" with competent performance by the lawyer. A defendant who *fails* to enter a guilty plea because of substandard performance by the defense attorney during plea negotiations must show a "reasonable probability" that (1) the defendant would have accepted the plea offer and the prosecution would not have withdrawn it, (2) the court would have accepted its terms, and (3) the sentence under the offer's terms would have been less severe than the sentence that in fact was imposed. On the other hand, a defendant who accepts a guilty plea on the basis of substandard lawyer performance must show "that there is a reasonable probability that, but for counsel's errors, [the defendant] would not have pleaded guilty and would have insisted on going to trial." Hill v. Lockhart, 474 U.S. 52 (1985). See Jenny M. Roberts, Proving Prejudice, Post-*Padilla,* 54 How. L.J. 693 (2011). Are these counterfactuals related to the plea negotiation process any more difficult to reconstruct than the counterfactuals about what might have happened at trial?

7. *Structural ineffectiveness and presumed prejudice.* In a few settings, the trial might occur in a setting so likely to produce error that prejudice can be presumed; no attorney is likely to provide adequate defense in these settings. Examples of

"structural" ineffectiveness appear in conflict of interest cases, in which an attorney represents multiple clients and runs the risk of harming one client while furthering the interests of the other. If defense counsel raises at trial the issue of potential conflict of interest, and the trial court fails to appoint new counsel or to hold a hearing to determine the risk of a conflict, prejudice is presumed. See People v. Hernandez, 896 N.E.2d 297 (Ill. 2008) (defendant whose attorney had been retained by victim of alleged offense, in a crime allegedly committed against the current defendant years earlier, could now rely on presumption of prejudice, and would not have to show that attorney was "actively" representing the victim). If the defendant raises the issue after trial, she must prove that there was an "actual conflict of interest" that "adversely affected" her lawyer's performance, but there is no need to prove that the adverse effects on lawyer performance changed the outcome at trial. See Cuyler v. Sullivan, 446 U.S. 335 (1980); but see Mickens v. Taylor, 535 U.S. 162 (2002) (defendant must show prejudice where defense lawyer had *potential* conflict of interest based on former representation of murder victim in juvenile proceedings).

Structural ineffectiveness (and the presumption of prejudice) is more difficult to establish in other settings. In United States v. Cronic, 466 U.S. 648 (1984), a companion case to *Strickland*, the Court rejected a presumption of ineffectiveness when an inexperienced lawyer was appointed shortly before a complex case. However, the court noted that such a presumption could be found "if the accused is denied counsel at a critical stage of his trial," or "if counsel entirely fails to subject the prosecution's case to meaningful adversarial testing." See McCoy v. Louisiana, 138 S. Ct. 1500 (2018) (attorney's refusal to contest defendant's guilt in capital trial, over objection of defendant, ranked as "structural" error with no required showing of prejudice).

Problem 11-6. *Cronic* Errors

Joe Elton Nixon was convicted of first-degree murder, kidnapping, robbery, and arson; the court sentenced him to death. Nixon's trial counsel made the following remarks during his opening statement in the guilt phase:

> In this case, there will be no question that Jeannie Bickner died a horrible, horrible death. In fact, that horrible tragedy will be proved to your satisfaction beyond any reasonable doubt. In this case, there won't be any question, none whatsoever, that my client, Joe Elton Nixon, caused Jeannie Bickner's death. This case is about the death of Joe Elton Nixon and whether it should occur within the next few years by electrocution or maybe its natural expiration after a lifetime of confinement.

During his closing argument, Nixon's counsel said:

> Ladies and gentlemen of the jury, I wish I could stand before you and argue that what happened wasn't caused by Mr. Nixon, but we all know better. I know what you will decide will be unanimous. You will decide that the State of Florida, through Mr. Hankinson and Mr. Guarisco, has proved beyond a reasonable doubt each and every element of the crimes charged, first-degree premeditated murder, kidnapping, robbery, and arson.

Nixon filed a motion for collateral review, claiming that his trial counsel was ineffective during the guilt phase of the trial. Nixon argues that these comments were the equivalent of a guilty plea by his attorney. He claims that he did not give his attorney consent to enter a guilty plea or to admit guilt as part of a trial strategy.

Nixon argues that his counsel's conduct in this case amounted to per se ineffective assistance of counsel and that the proper test for assessing counsel arises under United States v. Cronic, 466 U.S. 648 (1984), rather than Strickland v. Washington. In *Cronic*, decided the same day as *Strickland*, the Supreme Court created an exception to the *Strickland* standard for ineffective assistance of counsel and acknowledged that certain circumstances are so egregiously prejudicial that ineffective assistance of counsel will be presumed. In *Cronic*, the Supreme Court stated:

> [There are] circumstances that are so likely to prejudice the accused that the cost of litigating their effect in a particular case is unjustified. Most obvious, of course, is the complete denial of counsel. [A] trial is unfair if the accused is denied counsel at a critical stage of his trial. Similarly, if counsel entirely fails to subject the prosecution's case to meaningful adversarial testing, then there has been a denial of Sixth Amendment rights that makes the adversary process itself presumptively unreliable.

How would you rule on Nixon's motion? Compare Nixon v. Singletary, 758 So. 2d 618 (Fla. 2000); Florida v. Nixon, 543 U.S. 175 (2004).

■ AMERICAN BAR ASSOCIATION, CRIMINAL JUSTICE STANDARDS FOR THE DEFENSE FUNCTION
(4th ed. 2015)

STANDARD 4-1.8 APPROPRIATE WORKLOAD

(a) Defense counsel should not carry a workload that, by reason of its excessive size or complexity, interferes with providing quality representation, endangers a client's interest in independent, thorough, or speedy representation, or has a significant potential to lead to the breach of professional obligations. A defense counsel whose workload prevents competent representation should not accept additional matters until the workload is reduced, and should work to ensure competent representation in counsel's existing matters. Defense counsel within a supervisory structure should notify supervisors when counsel's workload is approaching or exceeds professionally appropriate levels.

(b) Defense organizations and offices should regularly review the workload of individual attorneys, as well as the workload of the entire office, and adjust workloads (including intake) when necessary and as permitted by law to ensure the effective and ethical conduct of the defense function.

(c) Publicly-funded defense entities should inform governmental officials of the workload of their offices, and request funding and personnel that are adequate to meet the defense caseload. Defense counsel should consider seeking such funding from all appropriate sources. If workload exceeds the appropriate professional capacity of a publicly-funded defense office or other defense counsel, that office or counsel should also alert the court(s) in its jurisdiction and seek judicial relief.

Standard 4-4.1 Duty to Investigate

(a) Defense counsel has a duty to investigate in all cases, and to determine whether there is a sufficient factual basis for criminal charges.

(b) The duty to investigate is not terminated by factors such as the apparent force of the prosecution's evidence, a client's alleged admissions to others of facts suggesting guilt, a client's expressed desire to plead guilty or that there should be no investigation, or statements to defense counsel supporting guilt.

(c) Defense counsel's investigative efforts should commence promptly and should explore appropriate avenues that reasonably might lead to information relevant to the merits of the matter, consequences of the criminal proceedings, and potential dispositions and penalties. Although investigation will vary depending on the circumstances, it should always be shaped by what is in the client's best interests, after consultation with the client. Defense counsel's investigation of the merits of the criminal charges should include efforts to secure relevant information in the possession of the prosecution, law enforcement authorities, and others, as well as independent investigation. Counsel's investigation should also include evaluation of the prosecution's evidence (including possible re-testing or re-evaluation of physical, forensic, and expert evidence) and consideration of inconsistencies, potential avenues of impeachment of prosecution witnesses, and other possible suspects and alternative theories that the evidence may raise.

(d) Defense counsel should determine whether the client's interests would be served by engaging fact investigators, forensic, accounting or other experts, or other professional witnesses such as sentencing specialists or social workers, and if so, consider, in consultation with the client, whether to engage them. Counsel should regularly re-evaluate the need for such services throughout the representation.

(e) If the client lacks sufficient resources to pay for necessary investigation, counsel should seek resources from the court, the government, or donors. Application to the court should be made ex parte if appropriate to protect the client's confidentiality. Publicly funded defense offices should advocate for resources sufficient to fund such investigative expert services on a regular basis. If adequate investigative funding is not provided, counsel may advise the court that the lack of resources for investigation may render legal representation ineffective.

Standard 4-6.1 Duty to Explore Disposition Without Trial

(a) Defense counsel should be open, at every stage of a criminal matter and after consultation with the client, to discussions with the prosecutor concerning disposition of charges by guilty plea or other negotiated disposition. Counsel should be knowledgeable about possible dispositions that are alternatives to trial or imprisonment, including diversion from the criminal process.

(b) In every criminal matter, defense counsel should consider the individual circumstances of the case and of the client, and should not recommend to a client acceptance of a disposition offer unless and until appropriate investigation and study of the matter has been completed. Such study should include discussion with the client and an analysis of relevant law, the prosecution's evidence, and potential dispositions and relevant collateral consequences. Defense counsel should advise against a guilty plea at the first appearance, unless, after discussion with the client, a speedy disposition is clearly in the client's best interest.

■ RULE 33, COURT OF COMMON PLEAS, CUYAHOGA COUNTY, OHIO

No attorney will be assigned to defend any indigent person in a criminal case unless his or her name appears on the applicable list of approved trial counsel. . . . The approved trial counsel list shall remain in effect for a period of two years. . . . Counsel whose name appears on the approved trial counsel list may file an application for renewal to serve as appointed counsel to sustain eligibility. . . . The following experience qualifications shall be a prima facie basis for the inclusion of a lawyer on the lists designated below:

(1) Assigned counsel for murder cases (including charges of murder, aggravated murder and aggravated murder with specifications).

(a) Trial counsel in a prior murder trial; or

(b) Trial counsel in four first degree felony jury trials; or

(c) Trial counsel in any ten felony or civil jury trials; or

(d) No lawyers may appear on the list for murder cases unless they are also listed as counsel for major felony cases described below. . . .

(2) Assigned counsel for major felony cases (first, second, and third degree felonies).

(a) Trial counsel in two previous major felony jury trials (first, second, or third degree felonies); or

(b) Trial counsel in any four previous criminal jury trials; or

(c) Trial counsel in any previous six criminal or civil jury trials; or

(d) Trial counsel in any two criminal jury trials plus assistant trial counsel in any two criminal jury trials.

(3) Assigned counsel for fourth and fifth degree felony cases.

(a) Trial counsel in any previous criminal or civil jury trial; or

(b) Assistant counsel in any two civil or criminal jury trials. . . .

To assist attorneys in obtaining trial experience in criminal cases, and for the purposes of obtaining experience necessary for inclusion on one of the above lists, this Court will cooperate with programs organized by local bar associations in which interested attorneys may be assigned as assistant trial counsel on a non-fee basis in cooperation with regularly retained or assigned counsel in criminal case trials in this county, under the supervision of the trial judge. . . .

The office of the Cuyahoga County Public Defender shall be assigned 35 percent defendants for which counsel are selected for indigent defendants. The assigned Public Defender, before being assigned to represent an indigent defendant, shall also meet the established criteria. . . .

Notes

1. *Rules and standards.* The majority in *Strickland* said that "specific guidelines are not appropriate." Was Justice O'Connor correct in concluding that courts should not specify what is adequate representation of a criminal defendant? What is the significance of the fact that a few states had begun to announce specific expectations for defense counsel to meet? Is any institution other than the judiciary more capable of specifying the standards for effective assistance of counsel, or is lawyering

an activity that simply cannot be reduced to enforceable standards? Cf. Bobby v. Van Hook, 558 U.S 4 (2009) (reversing a grant of habeas corpus relief for ineffective assistance that was based heavily on defense counsel's failure to satisfy 2003 ABA standards for uncovering and presenting mitigating evidence during preparation for a trial years earlier).

2. *Performance standards versus experience standards.* The Cuyahoga County rules take a fairly typical approach to the problem of attorney competence: Like the court rules in many other local jurisdictions, these rules focus on the prior experience of attorneys rather than specifying the tasks a competent attorney should perform. Are the approaches embodied in the ABA Standards and the Cuyahoga County standards compatible? Were both standards drafted based on the same goals or assumptions? Do prospective standards for appointment prevent incompetent representation better than retrospective claims by disgruntled clients? For further examples of performance standards adopted by the ABA and other professional organizations to promote effective representation in criminal cases, go to the web extension for this chapter at *http://www.crimpro.com/extension/ch11.*

3. *Caseload limits as a competence strategy.* The seeming numerical gold standard for indigent defense caseloads was established in 1973 by the National Advisory Council of the Federal Law Enforcement Assistance Administration. The council's Standard 13.12 provides that the caseload of a public defender attorney "should not exceed" 150 felonies per year, 400 misdemeanors, 200 juvenile cases, 200 mental commitment cases, or 25 appeals. Those numbers have been cited and adopted as a rough measure of appropriate caseloads by the American Bar Association and by many state-level professional organizations. It is common to find evaluations of criminal defense services that point out the excessive caseload of defense attorneys, using these numbers as benchmark.

What enforcement mechanisms are available to prevent violations of these caseload targets? According to ABA Formal Opinion 06-441 (2006), lawyers who represent indigent criminal defendants have an ethical obligation to refuse new cases if their workloads are so excessive that they cannot competently represent their clients. The opinion states that many factors determine when a caseload becomes excessive, including these numerical standards as well as the complexity of cases, availability of support services, the experience and ability of individual lawyers, and the lawyer's duties other than representing clients.

4. *Malpractice liability for defense attorneys.* If substandard work by criminal defense counsel injures a client, can the client sue for malpractice? While malpractice suits in criminal cases are possible, they face more obstacles than civil malpractice claims. For suits against publicly financed attorneys, sovereign immunity and various official immunities block the suit unless state law waives those defenses. Often state law allows criminal defendants to bring malpractice suits only if they can prove they were actually innocent; it is not enough to claim that the attorney caused an overly severe sentence. See Meredith J. Duncan, Criminal Malpractice: A Lawyer's Holiday, 37 Ga. L. Rev. 1251 (2003); Schreiber v. Rowe, 814 So. 2d 396 (Fla. 2002) (public defenders cannot assert judicial immunity in malpractice cases, but former defendant must prove actual innocence to maintain suit).

5. *Disqualification as an early remedy.* If the defense attorney discovers a conflict of interest, she must file a motion to withdraw. The same is arguably true when the attorney is not capable of preparing adequately to represent the defendant, perhaps because of the complexity of the case or the overwhelming nature of the attorney's

caseload. Under what circumstances might the prosecutor file a motion to disqualify the defense attorney? Should a judge view such a motion as an attempt to weaken the defense or to strengthen it?

Problem 11-7. More Objective Competence Standards

Assume that you are chief counsel to the senate rules committee in a state where the legislature promulgates rules of criminal procedure. The chair of the committee, with the support of the chief justice of the state supreme court, has asked you to draft specific competence standards for the pretrial process. In particular, you are directed to research and draft standards providing guidance on the following three questions:

- How soon must attorneys see a new client?
- How much time must attorneys have, at a minimum, to prepare for plea negotiations?
- What obligations, if any, should counsel have with respect to researching alibi or character witnesses?

How specific can such rules be without interfering with effective defense in some cases? Do nonbinding guidelines accomplish anything? Would you recommend ultimate adoption of these types of rules, or would you encourage the committee and the courts to rely on the *Strickland* standards without additional guidance?

D. SYSTEMS FOR PROVIDING COUNSEL

We have surveyed the legal standards designed to ensure that individual defense counsel will provide effective assistance of counsel. The methods the government uses to fund and deliver legal services to the indigent also have a powerful effect on the performance of the defense counsel in individual cases. Which institutions and sources of law shape entire systems for providing counsel?

The first method of providing defense counsel to indigent defendants in this country was the appointment of a private attorney to the case. The attorney might have handled the case as an unpaid volunteer or might have received some small compensation from the government. Early in the twentieth century, however, organizations of full-time defense attorneys began to spring up in major urban areas. The first appeared in Los Angeles in 1914. Supporters of these "defender organizations" (public agencies and private charitable groups) hoped that they would provide criminal defense at less expense to the public and would avoid the distracting and needlessly confrontational style of the "shyster" lawyers who often accepted court appointments. As one prominent defense attorney put it, the publicly accountable defense attorney could join forces with the prosecutor to see that "no innocent man may suffer or guilty man escape." Mayer Goldman, The Need for a Public Defender, 8 J. Crim. L. & Criminology 273 (1917-1918).

Today, most places still use more than one method of providing defense counsel, but the "organizational" defenders have become the most important piece of the puzzle. Those who create and fund the defender organizations hope to control the costs of providing adequate criminal defense and to do so without compromising either the fairness or the efficiency of the criminal justice system. As you read the following materials, think about how to determine the proper goals of a system for delivering criminal defense services. Do the different systems provide defense counsel with different incentives to handle criminal cases in particular ways, such as choosing between plea bargains and trials?

■ DONALD J. FAROLE & LYNN LANGTON, COUNTY-BASED AND LOCAL PUBLIC DEFENDER OFFICES, 2007

Bureau of Justice Statistics, September 2010 (NCJ 231175)

In 2007, 49 states and the District of Columbia had public defender offices to provide legal representation for some or all indigent defendants. In 27 states and the District of Columbia, counties or local jurisdictions funded and administered public defender offices. In the remaining 22 states, one office oversaw indigent defense operations throughout the state. . . . County-based public defender offices employed 71% of the nation's 15,026 public defenders in 2007. . . .

In 1963 the United States Supreme Court ruled in Gideon v. Wainwright that state courts are required to ensure that the provisions of the right to counsel under the Sixth and Fourteenth Amendments apply to indigent defendants. Since the *Gideon* ruling, states, counties, and jurisdictions have established varying means of providing public representation for defendants unable to afford a private attorney. Indigent defense systems typically provide representation through some combination of three methods:

1. A public defender office.
2. An assigned counsel system in which the court schedules cases for participating private attorneys.
3. A contract system in which private attorneys contractually agree to take on a specified number of indigent defendants or indigent defense cases. . . .

The 27 states and the District of Columbia with county-based public defender offices operated a total of 530 offices. . . . In 2007, 83% of county-based public defender offices reported using formal criteria to determine if a defendant qualified as indigent and was eligible for public representation. . . . Judges (52%) and public defenders (47%) were the most common entities responsible for screening potential clients for indigency in jurisdictions served by county-based public defender offices. . . .

Public defender offices had various procedures to handle cases in which there was a conflict of interest, such as a co-defendant already handled by the defender office. The majority (52%) of county-based public defender offices reported handling conflict cases through a court administered assigned counsel program; about a quarter (23%) of offices handled conflict cases through previously established contracts with private attorneys. Less than 1 in 10 (7%) county-based public defender offices used an ethical screen, whereby an office would take a case regardless of the conflict but preclude an attorney with conflicting connections from involvement in the case. . . .

Vertical representation refers to the practice of one attorney representing a client from arraignment through the duration of the case. It is distinguished from horizontal representation in which a different attorney represents the same client at various stages of the case. Sixty percent of county-based public defender offices had a written policy requiring vertical representation of indigent cases. About 7 in 10 (71%) offices reported providing primarily vertical representation in felony, non-capital cases (these offices may or may not have had written policies requiring vertical representation). . . . The majority of county-based public defender offices had formal policies that required the most experienced attorneys to handle the most complex cases (58%) and about a quarter (28%) required that an attorney be appointed to the case within 24 hours of client detention. . . .

Eighty-two percent of county-based public defender offices allowed for some form of cost recoupment for public defender services in 2007. Among the offices that permitted cost recoupment, the most widely available fee was a charge based on the cost for the defender's services (69% of offices). . . . More than 2 in 5 (44%) offices charged an up-front application or administrative fee, which typically ranged from $10 to $200 depending on the state and the type of case. . . .

In 2007, 15% of county-based public defender offices had formal caseload limits, and 36% had the authority to refuse appointments due to excessive caseloads. About 6 in 10 (59%) offices reported having neither caseload limits nor the authority to refuse cases. About half (49%) of offices that received more than 5,000 cases reported having the authority to refuse appointments due to excess caseload, compared to 28% of offices that received fewer than 1,000 cases in 2007. . . .

County-based public defender offices received a median of 853 felony non-capital cases and 1,000 misdemeanor cases, and employed a median of 7 full-time equivalent (FTE) litigating public defenders per office in 2007. . . . The National Advisory Commission (NAC) guidelines recommend a caseload for each public defender's office, not necessarily each attorney in the office. They state that "the caseload of a public defender office should not exceed the following: felonies per attorney per year: not more than 150; misdemeanors (excluding traffic) per attorney per year: not more than 400; juvenile court cases per attorney per year: not more than 200; Mental Health Act cases per attorney per year: not more than 200; and appeals per attorney per year: not more than 25." . . . One way to examine the numeric caseload guideline is to assess the number of cases received per FTE litigating attorney. . . . Using this estimation method, a public defender office would meet the guideline for cases received in 2007 if the FTE litigating attorneys received no more than 75 felony non-capital and 200 misdemeanor cases.

This conservative measure also assumes that attorneys did not have any cases pending from previous years and did not handle any other type of case. Still, 36% of county-based public defender offices met the guideline for felony non-capital cases per attorney, and 66% met the guideline for the number of misdemeanor cases per attorney. Offices with larger overall caseloads were more likely than those with smaller caseloads to exceed the maximum recommended limit for both felony and misdemeanor cases. About 4 in 5 offices that received more than 2,500 cases in 2007 failed to meet the national guideline of felony non-capital cases per attorney.

Another way to examine caseloads is to calculate the number of defenders needed to meet the nationally accepted caseload guideline. . . . To meet this guideline in 2007, the median office would have needed 11 attorneys who only handled the median number of felony, misdemeanor, juvenile-related, or appellate cases reported. . . . The median office reported employing 7 FTE litigating attorneys, approximately 64% of the estimated number needed. Twenty-seven percent of county-based public defender offices reported sufficient numbers of litigating attorneys to handle the cases received in those offices in 2007. About a quarter (23%) of all offices reported less than half of the number of litigating attorneys required to meet the professional guidelines for the number of cases received in 2007.

[Professional guidelines recommend 1 managerial attorney for every 10 staff attorneys.] The 273 county-based offices with 5 or more litigating attorneys reported a median of 1.7 managerial attorneys for every 10 assistant public defenders. [Professional guidelines recommend 1 investigator per 3 litigating attorneys.] County-based public defender offices employed about 1,500 investigators and 800 paralegals. . . . In 2007, 7% of the 469 county-based public defender offices with at least 1.5 FTE litigating attorneys met the accepted professional guideline for the ratio of investigators to attorneys. . . . Forty percent of all county-based offices employed no investigators. Among offices receiving less than 1,000 cases in 2007, nearly 9 in 10 (87%) had no investigators on staff. . . .

The median salary for entry-level assistant public defenders ranged from $42,000 to $45,000. With 6 years or more experience, assistant public defenders earned a median salary in the range of $54,000 to $68,000. Assistant public defenders in higher caseload offices received higher salaries in general. . . .

■ STATE v. LEONARD PEART
621 So. 2d 780 (La. 1993)

CALOGERO, C.J.

[The legislature established Louisiana's indigent defender system, creating Indigent Defender Boards to oversee indigent defense operations in each judicial district. The funds for indigent defender systems come from parish governments and from the city of New Orleans. Almost all of the funds for indigent defense come from criminal violation assessments in amounts ranging from $17.50 to $25.00 for each violation. Parking violations are excepted.] In New Orleans, the Indigent Defender Board ("IDB") has created the Orleans Indigent Defender Program ("OIDP"). OIDP operates under a public defender model.

[Leonard Peart was charged with armed robbery, aggravated rape, aggravated burglary, attempted armed robbery, and first degree murder. Because Peart is indigent, the] trial court appointed Rick Teissier, one of the two OIDP attorneys assigned to Section E, to defend Peart against all the above charges except first degree murder. . . .

At the time of his appointment, Teissier was handling 70 active felony cases. His clients are routinely incarcerated 30 to 70 days before he meets with them. In the period between January 1 and August 1, 1991, Teissier represented 418 defendants. Of these, he entered 130 guilty pleas at arraignment. He had at least one serious case set for trial for every trial date during that period. OIDP has only enough funds to hire three investigators. They are responsible for rendering assistance in more than 7,000 cases per year in the ten sections of Criminal District Court, plus cases in Juvenile Court, Traffic Court, and Magistrates' Court. In a routine case Teissier receives no investigative support at all. There are no funds for expert witnesses. OIDP's library is inadequate.

The court found that Teissier was not able to provide his clients with reasonably effective assistance of counsel because of the conditions affecting his work, primarily the large number of cases assigned to him. The court further ruled that "the system of securing and compensating qualified counsel for indigents" in LSA-R.S. 15:145, 15:146 and 15:304 was "unconstitutional as applied in the City of New Orleans" because it does not provide adequate funding for indigent defense and because it places the burden of funding indigent defense on the city of New Orleans. The trial judge ordered short and long term relief. In the short term, he ordered Teissier's caseload reduced; ordered the legislature to provide funding for an improved library and for an investigator for Teissier; and announced his intention to appoint members of the bar to represent indigents in his court. For the long term, he ordered that the legislature provide funds to OIDP to pay additional attorneys, secretaries, paralegals, law clerks, investigators, and expert witnesses.

[While the State's appeal of this ruling was pending, Peart was tried and acquitted of armed robbery.] In a second trial, in which he was represented by other counsel, he was acquitted on the murder charge. He is awaiting trial on the aggravated rape charge. Teissier again represents him.

[The] language of La. Const. art. 1 sec. 13 is unequivocal: "At each stage of the proceedings, every person is entitled to the assistance of counsel . . . appointed by the court if he is indigent and charged with a crime punishable by imprisonment." That assistance must be reasonably effective. Article 1 sec. 13 also provides that "the legislature shall provide for a uniform system for securing and compensating qualified counsel for indigents." As noted above, the legislature has enacted statutes responsive to these constitutional requirements.

[This] system has resulted in wide variations in levels of funding, both between different IDB's and within the same IDB over time. The general pattern has been one of chronic underfunding of indigent defense programs in most areas of the state. The system is so underfunded that [one recent study committee, appointed by the state judiciary, concluded that] there is a "desperate need to double the budget for indigent defense in Louisiana in the next two years." The unique system which funds indigent defense through criminal violation assessments, mostly traffic tickets, is an unstable and unpredictable approach.[10] . . .

The conditions in Section E should be contrasted with the American Bar Association Standards for Criminal Justice (1991). These conditions routinely violate the standards on workload (Std. 4-1.3(e)) ("defense counsel should not carry a workload that, by reason of its excessive size, interferes with the rendering of quality representation"); initial provision of counsel (Std. 5-6.1) ("counsel should be provided to the accused . . . at appearance before a committing magistrate, or when criminal charges are filed, whichever occurs earliest"); investigation (Std. 4-4.1) ("defense counsel should conduct a prompt investigation of the circumstances of the case and explore all avenues leading to facts relevant to the merits of the case"); and others. We know from experience that no attorney can prepare for one felony trial per day, especially if he has little or no investigative, paralegal, or clerical assistance. As the trial judge put it, "not even a lawyer with an S on his chest could effectively handle this docket." We agree. . . . In light of the unchallenged evidence

---

10. Examples of the approach's unpredictability abound. One particularly stark example: when the City of East Baton Rouge ran out of pre-printed traffic tickets in the first half of 1990, the indigent defender program's sole source of income was suspended while more tickets were being printed.

in the record, we find that because of the excessive caseloads and the insufficient support with which their attorneys must work, indigent defendants in Section E are generally not provided with the effective assistance of counsel the constitution requires.

REMEDIES

Having found that indigent defendants in Section E cannot all be receiving effective assistance of counsel, we must decide what remedy this Court should impose. . . . By virtue of this Court's constitutional position as the final arbiter of the meaning of the state constitution and laws, we have a duty to interpret and apply the constitution. In addition, the constitution endows this Court with general supervisory jurisdiction over all other courts. . . . Acting pursuant to the established sources of authority . . . we find that a rebuttable presumption arises that indigents in Section E are receiving assistance of counsel not sufficiently effective to meet constitutionally required standards. This presumption is to apply prospectively only; it is to apply to those defendants who were represented by attorney Teissier when he filed the original "Motion for Relief" who have not yet gone to trial; and it will be applicable to all indigent defendants in Section E who have OIDP attorneys appointed to represent them hereafter, so long as there are no changes in the workload and other conditions under which OIDP assigned defense counsel provide legal services in Section E. If legislative action is not forthcoming and indigent defense reform does not take place, this Court, in the exercise of its constitutional and inherent power and supervisory jurisdiction, may find it necessary to employ the more intrusive and specific measures it has thus far avoided to ensure that indigent defendants receive reasonably effective assistance of counsel. We decline at this time to undertake these more intrusive and specific measures because this Court should not lightly tread in the affairs of other branches of government and because the legislature ought to assess such measures in the first instance. . . .

We instruct the judge of Section E, when trying Leonard Peart's motion and any others which may be filed, to hold individual hearings for each such moving defendant and, in the absence of significant improvement in the provision of indigent defense services to defendants in Section E, to apply a rebuttable presumption that such indigents are not receiving assistance of counsel effective enough to meet constitutionally required standards. If the court, applying this presumption and weighing all evidence presented, finds that Leonard Peart or any other defendant in Section E is not receiving the reasonably effective assistance of counsel the constitution requires, and the court finds itself unable to order any other relief which would remedy the situation, then the court shall not permit the prosecution to go forward until the defendant is provided with reasonably effective assistance of counsel. . . . Reversed and remanded.

DENNIS, J., dissenting.

[The] conditions that affect indigent services in Orleans Parish obviously are not limited to Section E. To deny this is as whimsical as saying that a person in early term is "only a little bit pregnant." . . . I respectfully decline to join the majority's decision because it does not realistically and thoroughly address or attempt to remedy the systemic constitutional deficiencies affecting the provision of indigent defense services in Orleans and perhaps other parishes. . . .

The Legislature and the Executive branch of Louisiana have a duty to correct the constitutional deficiencies in the system. However, without a clear explanation by this court of the controlling constitutional principles and standards, the legislature cannot know exactly what is required to bring the indigent defender system into constitutional alignment; and it is unlikely that the legislature will be inspired or impelled to take satisfactory action without adequate guidance from this court. . . .

This court should establish standards by setting limits on the number of cases handled by indigent defense attorneys, by requiring a minimum number of investigators to be assigned to each defender, and by requiring specified support resources for each attorney. If a defendant demonstrates future error due to funding and resource deficiencies, the courts should be instructed to view the harm as state-imposed error, which would require reversal of the conviction unless the state demonstrates that the error was harmless. . . .

KIMBERLY HURRELL-HARRING v. STATE
930 N.E.2d 217 (N.Y. 2010)

Lippman, C.J.

. . . Gideon v. Wainwright, 372 U.S. 335 (1963), is not now controversial either as an expression of what the Constitution requires or as an exercise in elemental fair play. Serious questions have, however, arisen in this and other jurisdictions as to whether *Gideon*'s mandate is being met in practice.

In New York, the Legislature has left the performance of the State's obligation under *Gideon* to the counties, where it is discharged, for the most part, with county resources and according to local rules and practices. Plaintiffs in this action, defendants in various criminal prosecutions ongoing at the time of the action's commencement in Washington, Onondaga, Ontario, Schuyler and Suffolk counties, contend that this arrangement, involving what is in essence a costly, largely unfunded and politically unpopular mandate upon local government, has functioned to deprive them and other similarly situated indigent defendants in the aforementioned counties of constitutionally and statutorily guaranteed representational rights. They seek a declaration that their rights and those of the class they seek to represent are being violated and an injunction to avert further abridgment of their right to counsel; they do not seek relief within the criminal cases out of which their claims arise.

[Defendants claim that the action is not justiciable, because there is no cognizable claim for ineffective assistance of counsel apart from one seeking relief from a conviction. They argue that the case law conditions] relief for constitutionally ineffective assistance upon findings that attorney performance, when viewed in its total, case specific aspect, has both fallen below the standard of objective reasonableness, see Strickland v. Washington, 466 U.S. 668, 687-688 (1984), and resulted in prejudice, either with respect to the outcome of the proceeding or, under this Court's somewhat less outcome oriented standard of "meaningful assistance," to the defendant's right to a fair trial. People v. Benevento, 697 N.E.2d 584 (N.Y. 1998). Defendants reason that the prescribed, deferential and highly context sensitive inquiry into the adequacy and particular effect of counsel's performance cannot occur until a prosecution has concluded in a conviction, and that, once there is a conviction, the appropriate avenues of relief are direct appeals and the various other established means of challenging a conviction. . . .

These arguments possess a measure of merit. A fair reading of *Strickland* and our relevant state precedents supports defendants' contention that effective assistance is a judicial construct designed to do no more than protect an individual defendant's right to a fair adjudication; it is not a concept capable of expansive application to remediate systemic deficiencies. The cases in which the concept has been explicated are in this connection notable for their intentional omission of any broadly applicable defining performance standards. . . .

Having said this, however, we would add the very important caveat that *Strickland*'s approach is expressly premised on the supposition that the fundamental underlying right to representation under *Gideon* has been enabled by the State in a manner that would justify the presumption that the standard of objective reasonableness will ordinarily be satisfied. The questions properly raised in this Sixth Amendment–grounded action, we think, go not to whether ineffectiveness has assumed systemic dimensions, but rather to whether the State has met its foundational obligation under *Gideon* to provide legal representation. . . .

According to the complaint, 10 of the 20 plaintiffs—two from Washington, two from Onondaga, two from Ontario and four from Schuyler County—were altogether without representation at the arraignments held in their underlying criminal proceedings. Eight of these unrepresented plaintiffs were jailed after bail had been set in amounts they could not afford. It is alleged that the experience of these plaintiffs is illustrative of what is a fairly common practice in the aforementioned counties of arraigning defendants without counsel and leaving them, particularly when accused of relatively low level offenses, unrepresented in subsequent proceedings where pleas are taken and other critically important legal transactions take place. . . .

In addition to the foregoing allegations of outright nonrepresentation, the complaint contains allegations to the effect that although lawyers were eventually nominally appointed for plaintiffs, they were unavailable to their clients—that they conferred with them little, if at all, were often completely unresponsive to their urgent inquiries and requests from jail, sometimes for months on end, waived important rights without consulting them, and ultimately appeared to do little more on their behalf than act as conduits for plea offers, some of which purportedly were highly unfavorable. It is repeatedly alleged that counsel missed court appearances, and that when they did appear they were not prepared to proceed, often because they were entirely new to the case, the matters having previously been handled by other similarly unprepared counsel. . . .

The allegations of the complaint must at this stage of the litigation be deemed true and construed in plaintiffs' favor, affording them the benefit of every reasonable inference, the very limited object being to ascertain whether any cognizable claim for relief is made out. . . . The above summarized allegations, in our view, state cognizable Sixth Amendment claims.

[The right to counsel] attaches at arraignment and entails the presence of counsel at each subsequent "critical" stage of the proceedings. As is here relevant, arraignment itself must under the circumstances alleged be deemed a critical stage since . . . it is clear from the complaint that plaintiffs' pretrial liberty interests were on that occasion regularly adjudicated with most serious consequences, both direct and collateral, including the loss of employment and housing, and inability to support and care for particularly needy dependents. There is no question that a bail hearing is a critical stage of the State's criminal process. . . .

These allegations state a claim, not for ineffective assistance under *Strickland,* but for basic denial of the right to counsel under *Gideon.* . . . While it may turn out after further factual development that what is really at issue is whether the representation afforded was effective — a subject not properly litigated in this civil action — at this juncture . . . the complaint states a claim for constructive denial of the right to counsel by reason of insufficient compliance with the constitutional mandate of *Gideon.* See United States v. Cronic, 466 U.S. 648 (1984). The dissent's conclusion that these allegations assert only performance based claims, and not claims for nonrepresentation, seems to us premature. . . .

Strickland itself, of course, recognizes the critical distinction between a claim for ineffective assistance and one alleging simply that the right to the assistance of counsel has been denied and specifically acknowledges that the latter kind of claim may be disposed of without inquiring as to prejudice:

> In certain Sixth Amendment contexts, prejudice is presumed. Actual or constructive denial of the assistance of counsel altogether is legally presumed to result in prejudice. So are various kinds of state interference with counsel's assistance. Prejudice in these circumstances is so likely that case-by-case inquiry into prejudice is not worth the cost. Moreover, such circumstances involve impairments of the Sixth Amendment right that are easy to identify and, for that reason and because the prosecution is directly responsible, easy for the government to prevent.

The allegations before us state claims falling precisely within this described category. It is true, as the dissent points out, that claims, even within this category, have been most frequently litigated postconviction, but it does not follow from this circumstance that they are not cognizable apart from the postconviction context. Given the simplicity and autonomy of a claim for nonrepresentation, as opposed to one truly involving the adequacy of an attorney's performance, there is no reason . . . why such a claim cannot or should not be brought without the context of a completed prosecution.

[We] perceive no real danger that allowing these claims to proceed would impede the orderly progress of plaintiffs' underlying criminal actions. Those actions have, for the most part, been concluded, and we have, in any event, removed from the action the issue of ineffective assistance, thus eliminating any possibility that the collateral adjudication of generalized claims of ineffective assistance might be used to obtain relief from individual judgments of conviction. Here we emphasize that our recognition that plaintiffs may have claims for constructive denial of counsel should not be viewed as a back door for what would be nonjusticiable assertions of ineffective assistance seeking remedies specifically addressed to attorney performance, such as uniform hiring, training and practice standards. To the extent that a cognizable Sixth Amendment claim is stated in this collateral civil action, it is to the effect that in one or more of the five counties at issue the basic constitutional mandate for the provision of counsel to indigent defendants at all critical stages is at risk of being left unmet because of systemic conditions, not by reason of the personal failings and poor professional decisions of individual attorneys. . . .

It is, of course, possible that a remedy in this action would necessitate the appropriation of funds and perhaps, particularly in a time of scarcity, some reordering of legislative priorities. But this does not amount to an argument upon which a court might be relieved of its essential obligation to provide a remedy for violation of a fundamental constitutional right. See Marbury v. Madison, 5 U.S. 137 (1803) ("every right, when withheld, must have a remedy, and every injury its proper redress"). We have consistently held that enforcement of a clear constitutional or statutory mandate is the proper work of the courts, and it would be odd if we made an exception in the case of a mandate as well-established and as essential to our institutional integrity as the one requiring the State to provide legal representation to indigent criminal defendants at all critical stages of the proceedings against them. . . . Accordingly, the order of the Appellate Division should be modified . . . by reinstating the complaint in accordance with this opinion. . . .

PIGOTT, J., dissenting.

[United States v. Cronic, 466 U.S. 648 (1984), recognizes a narrow exception] to *Strickland*'s requirement that a defendant asserting an ineffective assistance of counsel claim must demonstrate a deficient performance and prejudice. . . . *Cronic*'s "narrow exception" applies to individual cases where: (1) there has been a "complete denial of counsel"; i.e., the defendant is denied counsel at a critical stage of the trial; (2) "counsel entirely fails to subject the prosecution's case to meaningful adversarial testing"; or (3) "the likelihood that any lawyer, even a fully competent one, could provide effective assistance is so small that a presumption of prejudice is appropriate without inquiry into the actual conduct of the trial." *Cronic*'s holding is instructive, if only to point out that the Supreme Court was reaching the obvious conclusion that, in *individual cases*, the absence or inadequacy of counsel must generally fall within one of those three narrow exceptions. Constructive denial of counsel is a branch from the *Strickland* tree, with *Cronic* applying only when the appointed attorney's representation is so egregious that it's as if defendant had no attorney at all. Therefore, whether a defendant received ineffective assistance of counsel under *Strickland* or is entitled to a presumption of prejudice under *Cronic* is a determination that can only be made *after* the criminal proceeding has ended. . . .

That is not to say that a claim of constructive denial could never apply to a class where the State effectively deprives indigent defendants of their right to counsel, only that the various claims asserted by plaintiffs here do not rise to that level. Here, plaintiffs' complaint raises basic ineffective assistance of counsel claims in the nature of *Strickland* (i.e., counsel was unresponsive, waived important rights, failed to appear at hearings, and was unprepared at court proceedings) and not the egregious type of conduct found in *Cronic*. Plaintiffs' mere lumping together of 20 generic ineffective assistance of counsel claims into one civil pleading does not ipso facto transform it into one alleging a systemic denial of the right to counsel. . . .

Giving plaintiffs the benefit of every favorable inference, the complaint nevertheless fails to state a cause of action for the deprivation of the right to counsel at arraignment. One reason is that there is no allegation that the failure to have counsel at one's first court appearance had an adverse effect on the criminal proceedings. . . . There is nothing in New York law which in any way prevents counsel's later taking advantage of every opportunity or defense which was originally available to a defendant upon his initial arraignment. . . . As pleaded, none of the 10 plaintiffs arraigned without counsel entered guilty pleas and, indeed, in compliance with the strictures of CPL 180.10, all met with counsel shortly after the arraignment. . . .

While the perfect system of justice is beyond human attainment, plaintiffs' frustration with the deficiencies in the present indigent defense system is understandable. Legal services for the indigent have routinely been underfunded, and appointed counsel are all too often overworked and confronted with excessive caseloads, which affects the amount of time counsel may spend with any given client. [The Legislature is] the proper forum for weighing proposals to enhance indigent defense services in New York. This complaint is, at heart, an attempt to convert what are properly policy questions for the Legislature into constitutional claims for the courts. . . .

■ AMERICAN BAR ASSOCIATION, MODEL RULE OF PROFESSIONAL CONDUCT 1.5(d)

A lawyer shall not enter into an arrangement for, charge, or collect . . . a contingent fee for representing a defendant in a criminal case.

Notes

1. *Local variety in indigent defense systems.* Jurisdictions use several different systems to provide defense counsel to indigent criminal defendants. These include government public defender offices, government "conflict" public defender offices (which receive cases after the primary public defender office declines them on the basis of a conflict of interest), nongovernment public defender offices (typically operated by nonprofit organizations), contract systems, and assigned or appointed counsel systems. Public defender offices handle about two-thirds of the cases in state courts, while assigned counsel handle 20 percent and contract counsel account for 13 percent. Bureau of Justice Statistics, State-Administered Indigent Defense Systems, 2013 (November 2016, NCJ 250249). The federal system continues to rely on different systems from district to district. This local variation in the federal system is the legacy of one of the great justice reform reports in U.S. history, the Report of the Attorney General's Committee on Poverty and the Administration of Federal Criminal Justice (1963), known after its chair as the "Allen Report." The Allen Report led to the federal Criminal Justice Act of 1964, which provided a framework for funding indigent defense in the federal system.

In most states, local governments choose and finance systems of indigent defense. A growing group of states—currently over 20 of them—fund and operate statewide indigent defender services with full authority to provide legal services. See Mary Sue Backus & Paul Marcus, The Right to Counsel in Criminal Cases: A National Crisis, 57 Hastings L.J. 1031, 1046-1053 (2006). Other states create a statewide commission to provide uniform policies and training for public defenders but leave the choice and funding of systems to the local government. There is more statewide uniformity for police practices and trial procedures (through state statutes, constitutional rulings, and procedural rules) than for the provision of defense counsel. Why have the local governments rather than the state governments remained the focal point for choices about defense counsel?

2. *Caseloads and legal challenges to public defender systems.* On a regular basis, criminal defendants or civil plaintiffs litigate claims of systemic failure of the public defender system. As the Louisiana and New York opinions indicate above, the doctrinal challenge for these claims is to demonstrate how they are different from

individual claims of ineffective assistance of counsel under the federal constitution. The litigation tends to be filed in jurisdictions during acute funding crises. For surveys of some recent litigation to challenge system conditions for public defender offices, go to the web extension for this chapter at *http://www.crimpro.com/extension/ch11*. In particular, the web extension offers a case study of the turmoil in the Georgia system in recent years.

On those relatively rare occasions when defendants challenge the overall effectiveness of a public defender program, the caseload of the attorneys is always a key variable. See Cara H. Drinan, The Third Generation of Indigent Defense Litigation, 33 N.Y.U. Rev. L. & Social Change 427 (2009) (first-generation suits were reactive and sought limited relief from the courts for extraordinary workloads; second-generation suits were marked by their empirical grounding, extensive alliances of support, and requests for sweeping reform). The ABA standards recommend annual caseloads of no more than 150 noncapital felonies per attorney, 400 misdemeanors, 200 juvenile cases, or 25 appeals. ABA Standards for Criminal Justice, Providing Defense Services §5-5.3 cmt. (3d ed. 1992). How do these standards compare with the workload of Rick Teissier, the defense attorney in *Peart*? Several states have statutes directing public defenders not to accept additional cases if the heavier caseload would prevent them from providing effective representation. A handful of states have statutes adopting specific annual caseload caps for public defender programs. See N.H. Rev. Stat. §604-B:6; Wash. Rev. Code §10.101.030; Wis. Stat. §977.08(5)(bn).

3. *Volunteer lawyers and conscripted lawyers.* Almost all jurisdictions rely on volunteer attorneys to represent some indigent defendants. Sometimes these attorneys take cases when the public defender organization has a conflict of interest; in other places, the court appoints attorneys for all cases from a list of volunteers. The amount of compensation varies. A volunteer attorney can ordinarily expect some compensation for "overhead" expenses and some reduced compensation for her time. But payment in some systems is discretionary, and the lawyers on the list do not have complete freedom to accept or refuse appointments from the court, depending on schedule and income needs. In a companion case to *Peart*, the Louisiana court in State v. Clark, 624 So. 2d 422 (La. 1993), upheld a contempt finding against an attorney who had refused to accept an appointment to represent a criminal defendant. The attorney, who had placed himself on the volunteer list, had been appointed to five felony cases over a four-month period; he refused to represent the fifth defendant because his private practice was suffering from neglect. The Louisiana court said that attorneys must represent indigents unless a court decides that the appointment is "unreasonable and oppressive," and that these circumstances were not enough to meet the standard. See also State ex rel. Missouri Public Defender Comm'n v. Pratte, 298 S.W.3d 870 (Mo. 2009) (reaffirms traditional power of court to appoint any lawyer in the state to represent indigent criminal defendants, with exception of public defenders, who are prohibited by statute from private practice and therefore cannot be appointed to cases that defender office cannot accept through ordinary means).

Broad-based challenges to appointment systems do not occur routinely. A few systemic lawsuits have produced more funding and better organization for appointed counsel systems, including litigation in New York City. See New York County Lawyer's Assn. v. State, 763 N.Y.S.2d 397, 400 (N.Y. Sup. 2003). More often, however, courts conclude that the level of compensation at issue, while perhaps in need of an increase, does not create a constitutional problem. Why are systemic judicial challenges to public defender systems more common than systemic challenges to appointed systems? Do lawyers simply decline to participate in the appointment system (when the choice is theirs) rather than litigate over the adequacy of the compensation?

4. *Judicial and legislative remedies.* The most vexing question in much of the litigation challenging systems for providing defense counsel is the question of remedy. What should the court do if local practices make it difficult or impossible for an attorney to provide effective assistance? Overturn individual convictions of those who challenge the effectiveness of their attorneys? Order the legislature to provide additional funding? Mandate a minimally acceptable caseload or fee schedule? Order the prosecutor to stop filing new criminal charges for the remainder of the fiscal year? See Mike Carter, Judge: Mt. Vernon, Burlington Failing Poor Defendants, Seattle Times, Dec. 4, 2013 (federal court order for two cities to hire supervisor to monitor public defense operations; retains jurisdiction for three years).

After *Peart* was decided, the Louisiana legislature created the Louisiana Indigent Defender Board and gave it a $10 million budget to use for studying problems with indigent defense in the state and for granting operating funds in trouble areas, such as appointment of defense experts in particular cases. It also transferred fiscal responsibility for indigent defense from the parishes to the state. The legislature later cut the budget in half, and it soon became clear that funding from the state would not improve the workload situation for most public defenders. In State v. Citizen, 898 So. 2d 325 (2005), the court reviewed the anemic state funding and ruled that an appointed attorney could file a motion to determine the availability of funds for payment of fees. If the revenue is not available, the judge must order the state to cease its prosecution. Does this aftermath of the *Peart* litigation tell you anything about the remedies a court should impose? Do judicial interventions in indigent defense systems have to occur regularly, say, every 10 years?

5. *Self-help for public defenders.* Sometimes the remedy for inadequate funding of a defense system occurs without any judicial order, when the leaders of a public defense organization refuse to accept additional cases until the caseload on its attorneys becomes lighter. See Erik Eckholm, Public Defenders, Bolstered by a Work Analysis and Rulings, Push Back Against a Tide of Cases, Feb. 18, 2014, N.Y. Times (Missouri public defender refusals to accept additional cases). Indeed, ABA guidelines adopted in 2009 call for public defense providers to "file motions asking a court to stop the assignment of new cases and to withdraw from current cases, as may be appropriate, when workloads are excessive and other adequate alternative are unavailable." American Bar Association, Eight Guidelines of Public Defense Related to Excessive Workloads, Guideline 6 (2009).

6. *Incentives for aggressive representation.* Which system—public defender organizations, appointed counsel, or contract attorneys—provides an acceptable defense for the least amount of money? The best defense for an acceptable amount of money? There is no single answer to these questions. As the Bureau of Justice Statistics indicates, the funding, staffing, and caseloads for public defender offices vary quite a lot. One often hears the assertion that defender organizations are funded at a level that compels the attorneys to urge their clients to plead guilty in most cases. Is it inevitable that defense attorneys who regularly accept money from the government will, in the long run, moderate their demands on prosecutors, police, and judges?

Some believe that "organizational" defenders are more cost-efficient because they represent many defendants at once and work in criminal justice full time. Thus, legislatures tend to create public defender programs because of potential cost savings. Are public defenders more efficient than appointed counsel, or do they choose certain cases and issues to pursue aggressively while allowing the other cases and clients to suffer from neglect? Would an appointed attorney be better able to represent each client more thoroughly, without trading off one client's needs against those of another? Are attorneys who spend all their time representing criminal defendants in the best position to bring systemwide challenges to the practices of police, prosecutors, or judges?

7. *Funding parity.* If popular support for prosecution of crimes is higher than the support for funding criminal defense, is the answer to require parity of funding between prosecution and defense? How would you accomplish this most effectively—through a constitutional ruling, a statute, or a local ordinance?

There is little doubt that the total resources available for the investigation and prosecution of crime are greater than those available for defending against criminal charges. See David Luban, Are Criminal Defenders Different? 91 Mich. L. Rev. 1729 (1993) (resources for prosecution versus public and private defense counsel may be at roughly comparable levels, but only when ignoring prosecutorial access to police and forensic expert support). If it is true that prosecutors and police combined receive more resources than defense counsel, is that a problem? Perhaps one might respond that prosecutors have more funding because they perform a wider range of functions than defense counsel. For instance, they make screening decisions on cases that are never charged. Alternatively, one might ask whether the increased demands on defense counsel really translate into worse outcomes for clients. Apart from the question of funding for entire offices, is there any justification for paying individual prosecutors a higher salary than individual defense attorneys? See Ariz. Stat. §11-582 (chief public defender salary to be at least 70 percent of chief prosecutor salary).

8. *Challenges to adequacy of payments to appointed lawyers.* Lawyers raising constitutional challenges to the adequacy of payments for their work as appointed or contract counsel in individual criminal cases have found modest but consistent success. Courts do sometimes recognize that lawyers can be asked to perform enough services for so little compensation that a due process or takings clause violation occurs. See State v. Young, 172 P.3d 138 (N.M. 2007) (fees in complex capital case amounted to less than $73 per hour; court ruled the compensation inadequate and presumed ineffectiveness without inquiry into actual performance). The challenge could also be based on a violation of the client's constitutional right to counsel or on violations of the ethical obligations of attorneys. See People v. Doolin, 198 P.3d 11 (Cal. 2009) (rejecting capital defendant's claim that county's compensation system for appointed counsel violated state constitutional right to conflict-free counsel by allowing attorney to keep any funds from flat fee not spent on defense).

9. *Challenges to contract attorney systems.* In contract attorney programs, the government (typically at the county level) agrees with a private law firm, bar association, or nonprofit organization to provide indigent defense. The contract may cover all criminal cases or specific classes of cases (such as all juvenile cases or adult cases in which the public defender's office has a conflict of interest). These contracts become especially attractive in jurisdictions where the costs of appointed attorneys have increased.

The method of pricing the services is the difficult issue. Some jurisdictions use a fixed price contract, in which the provider agrees to perform defense services at the stated price, regardless of the number of cases that actually arise. Although this method of setting the contract amount is relatively common, it has only rarely been challenged on constitutional grounds. In State v. Smith, 681 P.2d 1374 (Ariz. 1984), a defendant convicted of burglary argued that he was denied effective assistance of counsel because of his attorney's "shocking, staggering and unworkable" caseload, which was the product of a fixed price contract. The county had granted the contract to the lowest bidder, but the contract did not allow for support costs such as investigators, paralegals, and secretaries and did not consider the experience or competence of the attorney. Smith's attorney handled a "part time" caseload of 149 felonies, 160 misdemeanors, 21 juvenile cases, and 33 other cases in the year Smith was convicted, in addition to a private civil practice. The court therefore found that the bid system violated the rights of defendants to due process and the right to counsel. Would a government avoid these problems by entering a contract that pays a fixed fee per case, with provisions to fund some investigative and forensic expenses?

10. *Contingent fees.* Would private defense attorneys be more willing to represent criminal defendants if they could make contingent fee arrangements with their clients, calling for different levels of compensation depending on the outcome of the proceedings? The ABA standard reprinted above, barring the use of contingent fees in criminal cases, reflects the law of all the states. Why are contingent fees prohibited in criminal cases when they have been such an effective method (some might say too effective) for providing counsel to civil litigants?

Problem 11-8. Rights of Counsel

The district court in Oklahoma appointed two lawyers, Jack Mattingly and Rob Pyron, to represent Delbert Lynch, an indigent defendant charged with first degree murder in 1990. Although the State sought the death penalty, after a complicated trial that lasted 11 days, the jury returned a guilty verdict and gave Lynch a life sentence. Following Lynch's sentencing, the lawyers petitioned the court for fees and expenses.

At the hearing on counsel fees, Mattingly testified that he had spent 169 hours on the case, and incurred $173 in out of pocket expenses, requesting a $17,073 fee. Pyron spent 109.5 hours on Lynch's behalf, and he sought a $10,995 fee. Mattingly submitted a statement documenting his hourly overhead rate during the three years of this litigation, a rate that ranged from $46 to $54. Pyron submitted his overhead figures for a single year, reflecting an average hourly rate of $48. Had the two lawyers split the maximum statutory fee of $3,200, Mattingly would have received $9.47 per hour, with Pyron receiving $14.61 per hour. Based on these computations, Mattingly and Pyron would lose in overhead expenses for every hour that they worked on Lynch's defense.

Mattingly and Pyron challenge the constitutionality of the statutory cap on defense attorney fees, as applied in this case. The Oklahoma Constitution, art. 2, §7, provides that "No person shall be deprived of life, liberty, or property without due process of law." The lawyers contend that under this constitutional provision mandatory representation without just compensation is unconstitutional.

The attorneys also argue that the statutory fee cap conflicts with the rules of professional ethics. According to Model Rules of Professional Conduct, Rule 6.2, a lawyer may refuse an appointment for the representation of an indigent upon a showing of good cause. Judicial precedent in Oklahoma defines "good cause" to include any representation that "will result in a conflict of interest." Rule 1.16 of the Model Rules of Professional Conduct provides that a lawyer may refuse to represent a client if the representation would violate the Rules of Professional Conduct or other law.

Finally, the attorneys argue that the State's appointment system results in unequal treatment of attorneys in the state, in violation of the federal and state constitution. Practically speaking, attorneys who practice in counties which have public defenders' offices are exempt from representing indigent defendants in state courts. Lawyers in these counties are subject to appointment only when a conflict of interest arises in the public defender's office.

You are the judge who will decide what fees to award Mattingly and Pyron. Will you award attorney's fees higher than the statutory maximum of $3,200? Do you want to link the hourly rate of the defense attorneys to the compensation of the prosecutors? All chief prosecutors in the state currently receive $56,180 per year or $29.26 per hour. And what is the relevance of the overhead rate of these two attorneys? Cf. State v. Lynch, 796 P.2d 1150 (Okla. 1990).

Problem 11-9. Flat Fees for Service

The Detroit Recorder's Court used an "event based" fee system to compensate counsel assigned to represent indigent criminal defendants. Under this system, a separate fee was paid for pre-preliminary examination jail visits, preliminary examinations, two post-preliminary examination jail visits, investigation and trial preparation, written motions filed and heard, calendar conferences, arraignments on the information, final conferences, evidentiary hearings, pleas, and forensic hearings. The system also provided compensation for each day of trial necessary to dispose of any particular case, and for counsel appearances in court for sentencing of the defendant.

In an effort to reduce jail overcrowding, a jail oversight committee of the city council asked the clerk of the Detroit Recorder's Court to devise a compensation system that would promote docket efficiency without reducing the overall level of compensation paid to assigned counsel. The clerk then proposed a fee system that would pay attorneys a flat fee for representing a defendant, regardless of the number of "events" the attorney performed. Assigned counsel would be entitled to the full fee, regardless of whether the case is dismissed at the preliminary examination, the defendant pleads guilty at the arraignment on the information, or the case is ultimately disposed of after a jury trial. The flat fee would vary for different types of offenses and would reflect the average fees paid for defending such cases under the old system. The fixed rates would range from $475 for a 24-month maximum crime to $1,400 for a first-degree murder case.

The local court adopted the fixed fee system, and it succeeded in speeding up the docket. By shortening the time between arrest and disposition, the system alleviated some of the pressure for more jail space. A lawyer could earn $100 an hour for a guilty plea, typically three to four hours of work. If she went to trial the earnings could be $15 an hour or less. Prosecutors also noted a decrease in the number of "frivolous" defense motions and increased pressure from the defense bar for the prosecutor to dismiss weak cases at an earlier stage.

The fee system permitted assigned counsel to petition the chief judge of the Recorder's Court for payment of extraordinary fees in cases requiring above-average effort. While more than 3,000 indigent criminal defense assignments were made in the Court during the first year of the new system, only 29 petitions were filed for extraordinary fees, of which 23 were granted, totaling $11,175. This is approximately 1.6 percent of the total indigent attorney fees paid for that year.

In Michigan, assigned counsel have a statutory right to compensation for providing criminal defense services to the indigent. The controlling statute provided that the appointed attorney "shall be entitled to receive from the county treasurer, on the certificate of the chief judge that the services have been rendered, the amount which the chief judge considers to be reasonable compensation for the services performed." Mich. Comp. Laws §775.16. Does the fixed fee system provide assigned counsel "reasonable compensation for the services performed"? Does it violate indigent defendants' right to effective assistance of counsel? Compare Recorder's Court Bar Assn. v. Wayne Circuit Court, 503 N.W.2d 885 (Mich. 1993).

Problem 11-10. The Neighborhood Defender

The Neighborhood Defender Service (NDS) of Harlem created a new method of organizing public defense resources. The differences between NDS and the more typical public defender's office were manifest in the outreach efforts of the office, the range of legal services offered to clients, and the assignment of staff to clients.

Rather than placing its offices in one location near the courthouse, NDS placed several offices around the community to make the organization more visible and available to its clients. The service also placed posters, business cards, and other outreach devices in the community so that people in the neighborhood would be familiar with the service before they or their family members needed legal representation in a criminal matter. NDS hoped that this would help attorneys establish a relationship with their clients earlier in the criminal process and would give clients more reason to trust and cooperate with their attorneys.

NDS also shifted its focus from trial to the early stages of cases (sometimes even before arrest), emphasizing investigation and early resolution of charges. Through mediation, attorneys in NDS could sometimes resolve conflicts between victims and defendants, leading the victim to ask the prosecutor to drop charges. The service also continued to advise clients after conviction, to avoid problems during probation or parole. On occasion, NDS would represent clients or their family members in civil matters closely connected to a criminal charge (for instance, possible eviction from public housing based on drug trafficking charges).

As for assignment of staff to the clients, NDS moved away from the typical arrangement of placing one attorney alone in charge of a proportional share of cases the office receives. Each NDS client is represented by a team, consisting of a lead attorney, secondary attorneys, community workers, an investigator, and an administrative assistant. Each NDS attorney is assigned to more total cases than he would handle alone under the traditional arrangement, but the attorneys share the workload on each of the cases. If a client ever has a second case, the same team handles the client's case again. The strategy is to assign more tasks to nonlawyers and to ensure continuity of representation over time and more widespread responsibility for making early progress on the cases.

Is this organizational model for public defender services likely to work in many different communities? If not, what are the conditions necessary for a neighborhood defender service to succeed? See National Inst. of Justice, Public Defenders in the Neighborhood: A Harlem Law Office Stresses Teamwork, Early Investigation (1997, NCJ 163061).

E. THE ETHICS OF DEFENDING CRIMINALS

If you are a defense lawyer, you may often hear the question, "How can you defend those people?" Should all lawyers be required to defend criminals, regardless of the crime of which the defendant is accused or the lawyer's view of the defendant's guilt? The following selections represent a range of time-honored answers to this question. As you read them, try to come up with a short phrase to describe the position suggested in each passage. Which of the positions reflects the current mainstream of thought among American lawyers? Among law students? What are the institutional and ethical implications of each position?

■ SPEECHES OF LORD ERSKINE
(James High ed., 1876)

In every place where business or pleasure collects the public together, day after day, my name and character have been the topics of injurious reflection.[*] And for what? Only for not having shrunk from the discharge of a duty which no personal advantage recommended, but which a thousand difficulties repelled. Little indeed did they know me, who thought that such calumnies would influence my conduct. I will forever, at all hazards assert the dignity, independence and integrity of the English Bar, without which impartial justice, the most valuable part of the English Constitution, can have no existence. From the moment that any advocate can be permitted to say that he will or will not stand between the Crown and the subject arraigned in the court where he daily sits to practice, from that moment the liberties of England are at an end. If the advocate refuses to defend, from what he may think of the charge or of the defense, he assumes the character of the judge; nay he assumes it before the hour of judgment; and in proportion to his rank and reputation puts the heavy influence of perhaps a mistaken opinion into the scale against the accused in whose favor the benevolent principles of English law makes all presumptions. . . .

■ JOHN DOS PASSOS, THE AMERICAN LAWYER: AS HE WAS—AS HE IS—AS HE CAN BE
158 (1907)

I do not place the right of the lawyer to defend a client when he believes him to be guilty upon the ground that he cannot know that his client is guilty until his guilt

---

* [Lord Erskine was defense counsel for Thomas Paine, the influential pamphleteer.—Eds.]

has been officially and finally declared by a court and jury, because he often does know, in the sense that he has a moral conviction of the guilt of his client which he has derived through the ordinary channels of information. I place the right of the lawyer upon the ground that he is an officer of the law, and that it is his *duty* to see that the forms of law are carried out, quite irrespective of individual knowledge.

■ AMERICAN BAR ASSOCIATION AND ASSOCIATION OF AMERICAN LAW SCHOOLS, PROFESSIONAL RESPONSIBILITY: REPORT OF THE JOINT CONFERENCE (1958)

The Joint Conference on Professional Responsibility** was established in 1952 by the American Bar Association and the Association of American Law Schools. [Those] who had attempted to teach ethical principles to law students found that the students were uneasy about the adversary system, some thinking of it as an unwholesome compromise with the combativeness of human nature, others vaguely approving of it but disturbed by their inability to articulate its proper limits. . . . Confronted by the layman's charge that he is nothing but a hired brain and voice, the lawyer often finds it difficult to convey an insight into the value of the adversary system. . . . Accordingly, it was decided that the first need was for a reasoned statement of the lawyer's responsibilities, set in the context of the adversary system. . . .

THE LAWYER'S ROLE AS ADVOCATE IN OPEN COURT

The lawyer appearing as an advocate before a tribunal presents, as persuasively as he can, the facts and the law of the case as seen from the standpoint of his client's interest. . . . In a very real sense it may be said that the integrity of the adjudicative process itself depends upon the participation of the advocate. This becomes apparent when we contemplate the nature of the task assumed by any arbiter who attempts to decide a dispute without the aid of partisan advocacy.

Such an arbiter must undertake, not only the role of judge, but that of representative for both of the litigants. Each of these roles must be played to the full without being muted by qualifications derived from the others. When he is developing for each side the most effective statement of its case, the arbiter must put aside his neutrality and permit himself to be moved by a sympathetic identification. . . . When he resumes his neutral position, he must be able to view with distrust the fruits of this identification and be ready to reject the products of his own best mental efforts. The difficulties of this undertaking are obvious. If it is true that a man in his time must play many parts, it is scarcely given to him to play them all at once.

It is small wonder, then, that failure generally attends the attempt to dispense with the distinct roles traditionally implied in adjudication. What generally occurs in practice is that at some early point a familiar pattern will seem to emerge from the evidence; an accustomed label is waiting for the case and, without further proofs, this label is promptly assigned to it. [What] starts as a preliminary diagnosis

---

** [The conference was chaired by Lon Fuller, a law professor at Harvard University, and John Randall, an Iowa attorney and president of the ABA.—EDS.]

designed to direct the inquiry tends, quickly and imperceptibly, to become a fixed conclusion, as all that confirms the diagnosis makes a strong imprint on the mind, while all that runs counter to it is received with diverted attention.

An adversary presentation seems the only effective means for combating this natural human tendency to judge too swiftly in terms of the familiar that which is not yet fully known. The arguments of counsel hold the case, as it were, in suspension between two opposing interpretations of it. While the proper classification of the case is thus kept unresolved, there is time to explore all of its peculiarities and nuances. . . .

Viewed in this light, the role of the lawyer as a partisan advocate appears not as a regrettable necessity, but as an indispensable part of a larger ordering of affairs. The institution of advocacy is not a concession to the frailties of human nature, but an expression of human insight in the design of a social framework within which man's capacity for impartial judgment can attain its fullest realization. . . .

THE REPRESENTATION OF UNPOPULAR CAUSES

One of the highest services the lawyer can render to society is to appear in court on behalf of clients whose causes are in disfavor with the general public. . . . Where a cause is in disfavor because of a misunderstanding by the public, the service of the lawyer representing it is obvious, since he helps to remove an obloquy unjustly attaching to his client's position. But the lawyer renders an equally important, though less readily understood, service where the unfavorable public opinion of the client's cause is in fact justified. It is essential for a sound and wholesome development of public opinion that the disfavored cause have its full day in court, which includes, of necessity, representation by competent counsel. Where this does not occur, a fear arises that perhaps more might have been said for the losing side and suspicion is cast on the decision reached. Thus, confidence in the fundamental processes of government is diminished.

The extent to which the individual lawyer should feel himself bound to undertake the representation of unpopular causes must remain a matter for individual conscience. The legal profession as a whole, however, has a clear moral obligation with respect to this problem. . . . No member of the Bar should indulge in public criticism of another lawyer because he has undertaken the representation of causes in general disfavor. Every member of the profession should, on the contrary, do what he can to promote a public understanding of the service rendered by the advocate in such situations. . . .

These are problems each lawyer must solve in his own way. But in solving them he will remember, with Whitehead, that moral education cannot be complete without the habitual vision of greatness. And he will recall the concluding words of a famous essay by Holmes:

> Happiness, I am sure from having known many successful men, cannot be won simply by being counsel for great corporations and having an income of fifty thousand dollars. An intellect great enough to win the prize needs other food besides success. The remoter and more general aspects of the law are those which give it universal interest. It is through them that you not only become a great master in your calling, but connect your subject with the universe and catch an echo of the infinite, a glimpse of its unfathomable process, a hint of the universal law.

█JOHN KAPLAN, DEFENDING GUILTY PEOPLE
7 U. Bridgeport L. Rev. 223 (1986)

I would like to address an often asked, many times answered, but still extremely complex question: Why would lawyers want to defend guilty people? I will try to do so by examining first a somewhat different issue: Why should society as a whole want guilty people to be represented by lawyers? . . . The first means of approach is to ask two related questions: "Why do we want lawyers to represent criminal defendants at all?" and, second, "How does this rationale change in the case when we know that the defendant is guilty?" . . .

The first of the questions seems simple, but there are three quite different reasons why we wish those accused of crimes to be defended by lawyers. The most obvious reason is that defense lawyers improve the accuracy of the fact-finding process in which they are engaged. Many people may dispute this, since over the years the adversary system has played, at best, to mixed reviews. . . . Often it was said that a system where each of the two sides was trying to put something over on the decision maker was a crazy method of deciding important questions. . . .

The second major reason why we want defendants in criminal cases to be defended by counsel is much more complex. [The] basic idea is that one major characteristic of the due process model of criminal litigation is the use of the criminal process to check and regulate its own institutions. [The] lawyer also will be making sure that the arms of the state have complied with the many legal rules which bind them. . . .

The third major reason for providing an attorney for those accused of crimes involves the symbolic statement that it makes about us and our society; it is a multi-faceted statement. It says that we are a compassionate people and that in our society even the worst off (and it is hard to think of any who, as a class, are worse off than those accused of crimes) are entitled to have one person in their corner to help them. It underlines the value we place upon equality, because though lawyers vary considerably in their ability to manipulate our complex system of jury trials, their variation is far less than that among criminal defendants. [Our] trial system makes the statement that in our society the individual has rights against the state which can actually be enforced through the legal system. . . .

Next we move to the second question—which of these three reasons for having the defendant represented by an attorney no longer applies when we know that the defendant is guilty. [It] seems that only the first reason, improving the accuracy of the fact-finding process, loses its force. . . . With respect to the second reason, checking the operation of the institutions of the criminal law, [there] is a thin line between arguing that a defendant is innocent—a matter that goes to fact-finding— and arguing that the police and prosecutors improperly brought the case on insufficient evidence—a matter involving the checking function. . . .

We must remember that when prosecutors and police do their jobs well, they do so in part because of the discipline imposed upon them by the fact that they will have to prove their case against a defendant represented by a lawyer. If that should cease, it may be impossible to guarantee that the police and prosecutors will continue at the same level of competence, energy, and integrity. The perhaps apocryphal example of a mountain village may be instructive: it is said that the town fathers took down the "dangerous curve ahead" sign because no one had gone off the road there. They had therefore concluded that the curve was no longer dangerous. . . .

Similarly, the third major reason for having attorneys represent criminal defendants is not affected by whether the defendant is guilty. Indeed, the symbolic value of having an attorney represent a defendant may even be increased when we know the accused is guilty. The statement, then, becomes that much louder that the rights of those defendants whose guilt has not been officially and fairly determined are so fixed and important that, even if we knew they were guilty, these rights would remain. . . .

The last question we need to ask is, "Why would anyone want to make a living this way?" The answer to that question involves a very different kind of discourse, but my answer is simple. The question should not be asked. It is important to remember that, for one reason or another, criminal lawyers want to defend criminal defendants. Their taste may be as baffling to us as is the proctologist's, but we need both and should not try to dissuade either from pursuing his or her profession. Instead, we ought to encourage both because, whether they realize it or not—or even care— they are doing exactly what we want them to do.

■ LETTER FROM WILLIAM TOWNSEND
4 N.Y. L. Rev. 173 (1926)

[William H. Townsend, of the Lexington, Kentucky, bar, shed some interesting light on Abraham Lincoln's views about the duties of defense counsel]:

> Lincoln was regarded as a really formidable antagonist only when he was thoroughly convinced of the justice of his cause. He seemed utterly incapable of that professional partisanship that enlisted the best efforts of his colleagues at the bar, regardless of the side they were on. He would never argue a case before a jury when he believed he was wrong. His associate, Henry C. Whitney, says of him in this respect: "No man was stronger than he when on the right side, and no man weaker than he when on the opposite. A knowledge of this fact gave him additional strength before a court or a jury."
>
> Leonard Swett (one of Lincoln's closest friends) and Lincoln were once defending a man charged with murder, and, after all the evidence was in, Lincoln believed their man was guilty. "You speak to the jury," he said to Swett, "if I say a word they will see from my face that the man is guilty and convict him."
>
> In another murder case, the circumstantial evidence of guilt seemed almost conclusive and, when Lincoln, who had never wavered in his masterly defense, arose to address the jury, he frankly conceded that the testimony for the State was exceedingly strong. He said, in his slow, drawling way, that he had thought a great deal about the case and that the guilt of his client seemed probable. "But I am not sure," he said as his honest gray eyes looked the jury squarely in the face, "are you?" It was an application of the rule of reasonable doubt which secured an acquittal.

Notes

1. *The line between obligation and excuse.* In England the question appears to be not whether lawyers should choose to represent those who are guilty but whether any advocate can or should ever refuse to represent a defendant. A barrister cannot refuse to take a case, whether to act as an advocate or to advise, "unless the barrister

is professionally committed already, has not been offered a proper fee, is professionally embarrassed by a prior conflict of interest or lacks sufficient experience or competence to handle the matter." Anthony Thornton, Responsibility and Ethics of the English Bar, in Legal Ethics and Professional Responsibility 68 (Ross Cranston ed., 1995). In the United States, lawyers can choose whether to take a case and then are asked to defend this choice. Is the English practice the best way, in the end, to reduce public criticism of criminal defense work?

The ethics of defending criminals is a topic that commands the attention of attorneys in criminal practice, and not just legal ethicists. See Lisa J. McIntyre, The Public Defender: The Practice of Law in the Shadows of Repute 139-170 (1987) (based on interviews with public defenders in Cook County, Illinois). For some attorneys who represent criminal defendants, no line of argument about the defense lawyer's specialized role can counter the emotional costs of defending people accused of terrible crimes. For others, a more heroic conception of the defense attorney supplements the traditional need to test factual and legal claims through an adversarial system. See Margareth Etienne, The Ethics of Cause Lawyering: An Empirical Examination of Criminal Defense Lawyers as Cause Lawyers, 95 J. Crim. L. & Criminology 101 (2005) (based on data from interviews with 40 criminal defense attorneys, concludes that many criminal defense attorneys consider themselves to be "cause lawyers" who are committed to individual clients but also to the cause of legal reform in criminal law); Monroe Friedman & Abbe Smith eds., How Can You Represent Those People? (2013).

2. *Asking the question.* Some of the justifications for representing potentially guilty defendants depend on the possibility (however slim) that a client could be innocent of the charges. If a defense lawyer learns that a particular client did indeed commit the crime as charged, what justifications remain for going forward with the case? Should a defense lawyer ever ask a client, "Are you guilty?" Experienced lawyers give different answers to this question. Some insist on asking their clients, because they believe they cannot prepare a good defense unless they know "the whole truth." Others do not ask, because they believe the answer would be irrelevant to the defense.

3. *Ethical deliberation for lawyers.* Even if a theory supporting the strong defense of criminal defendants, including those clients a lawyer believes to be guilty, provides general justification for an individual lawyer to defend criminals, these theories hardly answer the difficult questions that arise in actually defending clients. There are more than a few difficult questions of application. What ought a defense attorney to do if she believes her client is lying? Is it appropriate for a defense attorney to use procedural tactics or create scheduling conflicts to increase the chance that the state's case will weaken and that the memory of witnesses will fade? Some of these questions will receive further attention in later chapters. Each deserves considered reflection by a lawyer before the moment of decision. As Monroe Freedman explains: "In making a series of ethical decisions, we create a kind of moral profile of ourselves. You should be conscious, therefore, of how your own decisions on issues of lawyers' ethics establish your moral priorities and thereby define your own moral profile. In understanding lawyers' ethics, you may come to better understand your moral values, and yourself." Freedman, Understanding Lawyers' Ethics (1990).

4. *The question for prosecutors.* Defense attorneys often hear the question, "How can you defend those people?" Less frequently, prosecutors encounter questions about their choice of career: "How can you prosecute people within such an unjust

system?" Consider this framing of the question by defense attorney (and professor) Abbe Smith:

> Prosecutors and would-be prosecutors must acknowledge who it is they are seeking to lock up and for what. They must acknowledge that those who are locked up remain there for longer and longer periods of time, no matter the circumstance: drug users and drug sellers, first-time offenders and those who have been in trouble before, the violent and nonviolent. Although prosecutors are not responsible for the conditions that spawn crime, [they] uphold the banishment of a generation of African American men simply by playing their role in the context of today's criminal justice system. The government has devoted an arsenal of resources to a mean-spirited and misguided criminal justice policy that has literally stolen hope for the next generation from entire communities. There is no redemption under this policy, no belief that people who have done wrong could ever rise above their pasts and contribute something of value. There is only the prison cell. It is the role of the prosecutor, the government's lawyer, to carry out these policies.
>
> The most mundane prosecutorial duties maintain the current regime: charging decisions, plea offers, disclosure of evidence, pretrial and trial advocacy, and sentencing arguments. This is so for prosecutors who see themselves as mere players in an imperfect system, hard-working government lawyers just trying to do their jobs. Because of the context in which they are practicing, even prosecutors who claim to be concerned about racial and social justice are helping to lock up scores of young black men for years.
>
> I believe there are moral implications to choosing sides in this context. The only question is whether well-intentioned prosecutors—prosecutors who are conscientious, prudent, and socially-conscious—can make enough of a difference to overcome this context.

Abbe Smith, Can You Be a Good Person and a Good Prosecutor?, 14 Geo. J. Legal Ethics 355 (2001).

Prosecutors themselves give a variety of answers to the question of why they pursue a job that pays less and sometimes offers more frustrations than other forms of legal practice. Interviews from more than 260 prosecutors in nine different offices revealed four principal career motivations for working state prosecutors: (1) reinforcing one's core identity as a rule-enforcer or advocate of accountability for wrongdoing; (2) gaining trial skills; (3) performing a valuable public service, including service for criminal defendants and their families; and (4) sustaining a work-life balance. Ronald F. Wright & Kay L. Levine, Career Motivations for State Prosecutors, 86 Geo. Wash. L. Rev. __ (2018).

In what ways do the moral dilemmas of entering prosecution parallel the dilemmas of entering a criminal defense practice? In what ways are the questions different?

XII

Pretrial Release and Detention

Not long after the police arrest a suspect, the government must decide what charges (if any) to file against the suspect. At about the same time, the court must decide whether to release the suspect from custody. These questions about charging and release arise, sometimes repeatedly, in a group of preliminary proceedings that differ in title and in detail from jurisdiction to jurisdiction. This chapter explores the decision whether to release or detain a suspect, and Chapter 13 considers the related decision of what charges to file.

As we saw in Chapter 5, a police officer will sometimes issue a citation instead of arresting a suspect. For many other suspects, the release decision is resolved at the police station, without any appearance before a judicial officer. Most jurisdictions allow "station-house bail" for minor crimes: An administrative official within the law enforcement agency (or perhaps an administrative employee of the courts) releases the suspect by following routine requirements. For instance, the suspect might make a written promise to appear at later proceedings or might pay a modest amount of money "bail" that would be forfeited upon a failure to appear.

Release decisions may also occur a few hours later, when the suspect appears before a judge or magistrate. This "initial appearance" before a judicial officer combines several functions: (1) a determination of whether the government had probable cause to support an arrest of the suspect, (2) an inquiry into whether the court must assign defense counsel to the defendant, and (3) the decision whether to release the suspect (if he has been in jail since his arrest). The release decision might be the first determination of a bail amount (or other conditions of release), or it might involve an adjustment of a bail amount set earlier.

Finally, the release decision can occur at a later proceeding, when a judge reconsiders the bail amount or other conditions of release. The later proceeding might be a "preliminary hearing," when a judge also determines whether there is enough evidence to hold the defendant for trial; the later proceeding might also be a "bail hearing," devoted exclusively to the question of release or detention. Defense counsel could be involved at the earliest judicial determination of bail amounts, but usually counsel has little opportunity to become familiar with the defendant's circumstances and to make an effective argument at that point. Only when the court revisits the release decision (often several days after the arrest) can defense counsel develop and present relevant facts.

A great deal is at stake in pretrial release decisions. Most obviously, the liberty of a person who is presumed innocent is weighed against the risk of flight or the possibility that the suspect will commit further crimes after being released. The costs of pretrial detention are also relevant here. The jail facilities required to house pretrial detainees are expensive to build and operate; there were over 475,000 pretrial detainees in local jails on an average day in 2016, about 65 percent of the total jail inmates. Bureau of Justice Statistics, Jail Inmates in 2016 (February 2018, NCJ 251210). Any laws or practices that might change those numbers will drive (or at least take account of) major budget choices, especially at the local government level. Perhaps most significantly, social scientists have documented a strong correlation between detention before trial, the risk of conviction at trial, and the length of sentence after conviction. In other words, being detained rather than released before trial does not just cause a temporary disruption in a person's life—it can have a major impact on her freedom for a much longer period.

Section A describes the factors that influence the release decision and the institutions most responsible for making that choice. Section B then traces a related movement to expand the state's power to detain some defendants until the time of trial in an effort to protect the public from further crimes the defendant might commit.

A. PRETRIAL RELEASE

The release decision has changed dramatically over the past few generations, and it is still in flux. This section highlights a reform movement, begun more than 50 years ago and still a vibrant part of state law, to make it easier for defendants to gain release from custody before trial.

1. Standard Release Practices

Many legal actors have something to say about the pretrial release of a defendant. Judges are ultimately responsible for the release order, but judges delegate some of those choices to police or court administrators, defer sometimes to prosecutors, respond to defense attorney arguments, and interpret legislative and constitutional limits on their power to release the defendant. The interaction among these actors reflects the classic tension between rule-based uniformity and individualized judgments.

As you read the advisory standards, rule, and government report excerpted below, consider the interaction between the judge and other system actors. To what extent is the judge the principal decisionmaker?

■ AMERICAN BAR ASSOCIATION, PRETRIAL RELEASE STANDARDS

(3d ed. 2007)

STANDARD 10-1.2, RELEASE UNDER LEAST RESTRICTIVE CONDITIONS; DIVERSION AND OTHER ALTERNATIVE RELEASE OPTIONS

In deciding pretrial release, the judicial officer should assign the least restrictive condition(s) of release that will reasonably ensure a defendant's attendance at court proceedings and protect the community, victims, witnesses or any other person. Such conditions may include participation in drug treatment, diversion programs or other pre-adjudication alternatives. The court should have a wide array of programs or options available to promote pretrial release on conditions that ensure appearance and protect the safety of the community, victims and witnesses pending trial and should have the capacity to develop release options appropriate to the risks and special needs posed by defendants, if released to the community.

STANDARD 10-1.7, CONSIDERATION OF THE NATURE OF THE CHARGE IN DETERMINING RELEASE OPTIONS

Although the charge itself may be a predicate to pretrial detention proceedings, the judicial officer should exercise care not to give inordinate weight to the nature of the present charge in evaluating factors for the pretrial release decision except when, coupled with other specified factors, the charge itself may cause the initiation of a pretrial detention hearing. . . .

STANDARD 10-1.10, THE ROLE OF THE PRETRIAL SERVICES AGENCY

Every jurisdiction should establish a pretrial services agency or program to collect and present the necessary information, present risk assessments, and, consistent with court policy, make release recommendations required by the judicial officer in making release decisions, including the defendant's eligibility for diversion, treatment or other alternative adjudication programs, such as drug or other treatment courts. Pretrial services should also monitor, supervise, and assist defendants released prior to trial, and review the status and release eligibility of detained defendant for the court on an ongoing basis.

STANDARD 10-5.12, RE-EXAMINATION OF THE RELEASE OR DETENTION DECISION: STATUS REPORTS REGARDING PRETRIAL DETAINEES

(a) Upon motion by the defense, prosecution or by request of the pretrial services agency supervising released defendants alleging changed or additional circumstances, the court should promptly reexamine its release decision including any conditions placed upon release or its decision authorizing pretrial detention. . . .

■ ALABAMA RULES OF CRIMINAL PROCEDURE 7.2, 7.3

RULE 7.2

(a) Before conviction. Any defendant charged with an offense bailable as a matter of right may be released pending or during trial on his or her personal recognizance or on an appearance bond unless the court or magistrate determines that such a release will not reasonably assure the defendant's appearance as required, or that the defendant's being at large will pose a real and present danger to others or to the public at large. If such a determination is made, the court may impose the least onerous condition or conditions contained in Rule 7.3(b) that will reasonably assure the defendant's appearance or that will eliminate or minimize the risk of harm to others or to the public at large. In making such a determination, the court may take into account the following:

(1) The age, background and family ties, relationships and circumstances of the defendant.

(2) The defendant's reputation, character, and health.

(3) The defendant's prior criminal record, including prior releases on recognizance or on secured appearance bonds, and other pending cases.

(4) The identity of responsible members of the community who will vouch for the defendant's reliability.

(5) Violence or lack of violence in the alleged commission of the offense.

(6) The nature of the offense charged, the apparent probability of conviction, and the likely sentence, insofar as these factors are relevant to the risk of nonappearance. . . .

(11) Residence of the defendant, including consideration of real property ownership, and length of residence in his or her place of domicile.

(12) In cases where the defendant is charged with a drug offense, evidence of selling or pusher activity should indicate a substantial increase in the amount of bond.

(13) Consideration of the defendant's employment status and history, the location of defendant's employment, e.g., whether employed in the county where the alleged offense occurred, and the defendant's financial condition. . . .

RULE 7.3

(a) Mandatory conditions. Every order of release under this rule shall contain the conditions that the defendant:

(1) Appear to answer and to submit to the orders and process of the court having jurisdiction of the case;

(2) Refrain from committing any criminal offense;

(3) Not depart from the state without leave of court; and

(4) Promptly notify the court of any change of address.

(b) Additional conditions. An order of release may include any one or more of the following conditions reasonably necessary to secure a defendant's appearance:

(1) Execution of an appearance bond in an amount specified by the court, either with or without requiring that the defendant deposit with the clerk security in an amount as required by the court;

(2) Execution of a secured appearance bond;

(3) Placing the defendant in the custody of a designated person or organization agreeing to supervise the defendant;

(4) Restrictions on the defendant's travel, associations, or place of abode during the period of release;

(5) Return to custody after specified hours; or

(6) Any other conditions which the court deems reasonably necessary.

■ THOMAS H. COHEN & BRIAN A. REAVES, PRETRIAL RELEASE OF FELONY DEFENDANTS IN STATE COURTS
Bureau of Justice Statistics (November 2007, NCJ 214994)

. . . From 1990 to 2004, an estimated 62% of State court felony defendants in the 75 largest counties were released prior to the disposition of their case (table 1). Defendants were about as likely to be released on financial conditions requiring the posting of bail (30%) as to be granted a non-financial release (32%). Among the 38% of defendants detained until case disposition, about 5 in 6 had a bail amount set but did not post the financial bond required for release.

[A pronounced trend] was observed in the type of release used. From 1990 to 1998, the percentage of released defendants under financial conditions rose from 24% to 36%, while non-financial releases dropped from 40% to 28%. From 1990 to 2004, surety bond (33%) and release on recognizance (32%) each accounted for about a third of all releases. . . . The trend away from non-financial releases to financial releases was accompanied by an increase in the use of surety bonds and a decrease in the use of release on recognizance (ROR). From 1990 through 1994,

Table 1. Type of pretrial release or detention for State court felony defendants in the 75 largest counties, 1990-2004

Detention-release outcome	*Number [of defendants]*	*Percent*
. . . **Released before case disposition**	264,604	62
Financial conditions	125,650	30
Surety bond	86,107	20
Deposit bond	23,168	6
Full cash bond	12,348	3
Property bond	4,027	1
Non-financial conditions	136,153	32
Personal recognizance	85,330	20
Conditional release	32,882	8
Unsecured bond	17,941	4
Emergency release	2,801	1
Detained until case disposition	159,647	38
Held on bail	132,572	32
Denied bail	27,075	6

ROR accounted for 41% of releases, compared to 24% for surety bond. In 2002 and 2004, surety bonds were used for 42% of releases, compared to 23% for ROR. . . .

COMMERCIAL BAIL AND PRETRIAL RELEASE

An estimated 14,000 commercial bail agents nationwide secure the release of more than 2 million defendants annually. . . . Bond forfeiture regulations and procedures vary by jurisdiction, but most States regulate commercial bail and license bail agents through their departments of insurance. Four States do not allow commercial bail: Illinois, Kentucky, Oregon, and Wisconsin. Also, the District of Columbia, Maine, and Nebraska have little commercial bail activity.

Bail agents generally operate as independent contractors using credentials of a surety company when posting appearance bond for their client. For a fee, the surety company allows the bail agent to use its financial standing and credit as security on bonds. In turn, the bail agent charges the defendant a fee (usually 10% of the bail amount) for services. In addition, the bail agent often requires collateral from the defendant.

A bail agent usually has an opportunity to recover a defendant if they fail to appear. If the defendant is not returned, the agent is liable to the court for the full bail amount. Most jurisdictions permit revocation of the bond, which allows the agent to return the defendant to custody before the court date, freeing the agent from liability. The agent may be required to refund the defendant's fee in such cases. Courts can also set aside forfeiture judgments if good cause is shown as to why a defendant did not appear.

MANY FACTORS INFLUENCE THE PRETRIAL RELEASE DECISION

[Courts typically use an offense-based schedule when setting bail. After assessing the likelihood that a defendant, if released, will not appear in court and assessing any danger the defendant may present to the community, the court may adjust the bail higher or lower. In the most serious cases, the court may deny bail altogether. The use of a high bail amount or the denial of bail was most evident in cases involving serious violent offenses.]

Murder defendants (19%) had the lowest probability of being released, followed by those charged with robbery (44%), burglary (49%), motor vehicle theft (49%), or rape (53%). Defendants charged with fraud (82%) were the most likely to be released.

Female defendants (74%) were more likely than males (60%) to be released pretrial. By race and Hispanic origin, non-Hispanic whites (68%) had a higher probability of release than Hispanics (55%). Pretrial detention rates for Hispanics may have been influenced by the use of immigration holds to detain those illegally in the U.S.

Defendants on parole (26%) or probation (43%) at the time of their arrest for the current offense were less likely to be released than those without an active criminal justice status (70%). Defendants who had a prior arrest, whether they had previously failed to appear in court (50%) or not (59%), had a lower probability of release than those without a prior arrest (79%).

Defendants with a prior conviction (51%) . . . had a lower probability of being released than those without a conviction (77%). This was true even if the prior convictions were for misdemeanors only (63%). . . .

A THIRD OF RELEASED DEFENDANTS WERE CHARGED WITH PRETRIAL MISCONDUCT WITHIN 1 YEAR AFTER RELEASE

From 1990 through 2004, 33% of defendants were charged with committing one or more types of misconduct after being released but prior to the disposition of their case. A bench warrant for failure to appear in court was issued for 23% of released defendants. An estimated 17% were arrested for a new offense, including 11% for a felony. Overall misconduct rates varied only slightly from 1990 through 2004, ranging from a high of 35% to a low of 31% for surety bond releases (19%). . . .

By type of release, the percent of the defendants who were fugitives after 1 year ranged from 10% for unsecured bond releases to 3% of those released on surety bond. Overall, 28% of the defendants who failed to appear in court and had a bench warrant issued for their arrest were still fugitives at the end of a 1-year study period. This was 6% of all defendants released pretrial. . . . Compared to the overall average, the percentage of absconded defendants who remained a fugitive was lower for surety bond releases (19%). . . .

Defendants who had an active criminal justice status at the time of arrest— such as pretrial release (48%), parole (47%), or probation (44%)—had a higher misconduct rate than those who were not on a criminal justice status (27%). This difference was observed for both failure to appear and rearrest.

Defendants with a prior failure to appear (49%) had a higher misconduct rate than defendants who had previously made all court appearances (30%) or had never been arrested (23%). Defendants with a prior failure to appear (35%) were about twice as likely to have a bench warrant issued for failing to appear during the current case than other defendants (18%).

Defendants with at least one prior felony conviction (43%) had a higher rate of pretrial misconduct than defendants with misdemeanor convictions only (34%) or no prior convictions (27%).

Notes

1. *Bail schedules.* The earliest available point of release, "station-house bail," often depends on officers' use of a "bail schedule," a listing of the presumptive amount of bail to require from various types of offenders. Most often, the presumptive bail is linked to the criminal charge a defendant is facing. For example, a Los Angeles County bail schedule made $60,000 the presumptive bail amount for voluntary manslaughter; for kidnapping for ransom, $500,000; and for bookmaking, $2,500. For additional examples of bail schedules and a discussion of how they operate in practice, see the web extension for this chapter at *http://www.crimpro.com/extension/ch12.*

2. *Rules and discretion in bail.* Most systems give judges substantial discretion to set bail amounts, allowing them to adjust the default amounts in the bail schedule. See, e.g., Mont. Code §46-9-302 ("A judge may establish and post a schedule of bail for offenses over which the judge has original jurisdiction"). Tennessee allows magistrates substantial discretion but imposes statewide caps on bail amounts based on the nature of the offense. See Tenn. Code §40-11-105.

Which crimes are likely to create the most pressure on the judges and other actors with power to release arrestees before trial? Are specific bail guidelines useful?

Who should develop guidelines? Would evidence of discriminatory bail practices by judges support strict adherence to bail schedules?

3. *Appellate court controls on bail.* There are constitutional limits on the amount of bail a trial court can set. According to Stack v. Boyle, 342 U.S. 1 (1951), the "excessive bail" clause of the Eighth Amendment prevents a trial court from setting bail "higher than an amount reasonably calculated to fulfill the purpose" of ensuring the accused's presence at trial. A slight majority of states have an even stronger constitutional provision guaranteeing a right to bail. Do these constitutional provisions suggest that the appellate courts are the institution with the ultimate authority in setting bail? What impact would bail guidelines have on appellate review of individual cases?

4. *Consultation with victims.* All 50 states have passed statutes offering protections to victims during the criminal justice process, and most have given some of these protections constitutional status. These provisions all require authorities to provide information to victims, such as explaining the possibility of pretrial release, notifying victims after a suspect is arrested, and notifying victims about the time and place of release hearings. See, e.g., Cal. Penal Code §4024.4 (granting power to local governments to contract for victim notification). About half of the states require that victims be notified of a suspect's release, and the terms of release, including the amount of any bail, though many states require the victim to make a written request for such information. A few "victims' rights" provisions indicate that the judge should consider the concerns of the victim of the alleged crime when determining the conditions to place upon the defendant during pretrial release. See Texas Code Crim. Proc. art. 56.02 ("A victim, guardian of a victim, or close relative of a deceased victim [has] the right to have the magistrate take the safety of the victim or his family into consideration as an element in fixing the amount of bail for the accused."). A few states allow the victim to have some input prior to the bail decision. See, e.g., Mo. Const. art. I, §32 (crime victims have the right "to be informed of and heard" at bail hearings "unless in the determination of the court the interests of justice require otherwise"). Are such provisions likely to change the release decisions that judges make? Are they consistent with the practice of station-house bail?

5. *Prosecutors and bail.* Statutes and rules tell judges what they should consider in their bail and pretrial release decisions. What factors actually influence judges the most? Judges are less likely to release a defendant already on parole or probation at the time of the current charges; the same is true for defendants with prior arrests or convictions, and those currently charged with violent offenses. In particular, less than 10 percent of murder defendants are released before trial.

Some observers of bail practices contend that the recommendation of the prosecutor is the single most influential variable as judges make bail and release decisions. A classic study of San Diego judges reached this conclusion. When researchers presented the judges with several hypothetical case files and asked them to set bail, the local ties of the defendant was the most important variable. However, when observers watched judges decide actual cases, the recommendation of the prosecutor became the most important variable in setting bail amounts—more important than severity of the crime, prior record, defense attorney recommendation, or local ties. The prosecutors, for their part, were most heavily influenced by the severity of the crime and (to a lesser extent) the defendant's local ties. See Ebbe Ebbeson & Vladimir Konecni, Decision Making and Information Integration in the Courts: The Setting of Bail, 32 J. Personality & Soc. Psychol. 805 (1975). Why did the researchers observe judges in the courtroom in addition to asking them about simulated case files?

6. *Bond dealers and bounty hunters.* In jurisdictions requiring payment of the full amount of money bail prior to release (known as full cash bond) or the posting of a surety bond, many defendants rely on the services of bail bond dealers. Surety bonds remain the most common form of financial release, and the trend over the last two decades has been toward greater use of surety bonds. The bond dealer makes the required payment to the court in the form of a bond obligating the dealer to pay the amount of the bail if the defendant does not appear for court proceedings. The dealer charges the defendant a nonrefundable fee, often around 10 percent of the total bond amount, although it varies with the dealer's assessment of the risk that a particular defendant will flee. In practice, the bond dealer does not pay the full amount for every defendant who fails to appear. For instance, the average collection rate in New Jersey in 2012 was less than 9 percent. See State of New Jersey Commission of Investigation, Inside Out: Questionable and Abusive Practices in New Jersey's Bail-Bond Industry (May 2014).

About half of the states grant express authority to the dealer and their agents—often called "bounty hunters"—to arrest a defendant who tries to flee. See Ala. Code §15-13-117. Nineteenth-century authority confirms the substantial powers of bond dealers and bounty hunters, which in some respects exceeds that of government agents trying to recapture a fugitive. Reese v. United States, 76 U.S. 13 (1869); Taylor v. Taintor, 83 U.S. 366 (1872). This authority creates a potential for rough practices—and for adventures that have occasionally become the subject of front-page stories and the plot lines for movies, classic and otherwise. For photos, graphics, and other multimedia materials related to the bail bond industry, see the web extension for this chapter at *http://www.crimpro.com/extension/ch12.*

7. *Abolition of surety bonds.* Critics of the surety bond system argue that it fosters violence and leaves defendants with no financial incentive to appear in court after their release. Jurisdictions have taken a number of steps to reduce the importance of bond dealers. A handful of states have directly outlawed the offering of surety bonds. See Wis. Stat. §969.12. Around 20 states have made the surety bond less attractive to defendants by using "deposit" bonds, allowing defendants themselves to deposit with the court a portion of their bail—usually 10 percent—comparable to the rates charged by sureties. See, e.g., Cal. Penal Code §1295; Ohio R. Crim. P. 46. Because the cash deposit to the state is refundable and the fee to the bond dealer is not, defendants have little reason to call on the dealer. The State can also profit from the use of cash bail because courts often do not collect bonds from sureties when the defendant fails to appear. Given all these advantages of cash bail, why does the surety bond system remain the most common form of financial release?

8. *Nonfinancial release conditions.* A defendant's pretrial release might be conditioned not on payment of bail but on performance of certain nonfinancial conditions. The most common nonfinancial release condition is a requirement that the defendant maintain regular contact with a pretrial program. It is also common for the judge to insist that the defendant avoid any contact with the victim of the alleged crime. As defense counsel, how might you respond to a judicial order that a defendant in a domestic violence case buy his wife flowers and take her out for bowling and a nice dinner, as conditions of pretrial release? See Dan Markel & Eric J. Miller, Bowling, as Bail Condition, N.Y. Times, July 13, 2012.

An increasingly common condition of release is regular drug monitoring or treatment. See Kan. Stat. §22-2802 (drug testing limited to those charged with felonies). Testing positive for some drugs (particularly cocaine) is a predictor, according to some studies, of a higher rate of nonappearance and arrests for crimes committed after release. Peggy Tobolowsky & James Quinn, Drug-Related Behavior as a Predictor of Defendant Pretrial Misconduct, 25 Tex. Tech L. Rev. 1019 (1994). If positive drug tests do not predict a failure to appear, should the tests still be administered? What is the rationale for requiring drug treatment?

Another increasingly common nonfinancial condition of release is acceptance of electronic monitoring. An electronic device attached to the defendant's person (often a wrist or an ankle bracelet) allows the government to monitor his proximity to home or to some other location. Should electronic monitoring be used primarily for those who receive release on their own recognizance, or for those who would otherwise remain in jail?

Problem 12-1. Automatic Delay

During the most recent meeting of the county judges, the Chief Judge for the District Courts in Spokane, Christine Cary, proposed to the other judges that they issue a General Order regarding bail for domestic violence offenses. A draft of her proposed order, entitled "Domestic Violence Offense—Mandatory Court Appearance—No Bail," provides as follows:

> Any person arrested for a crime as Domestic Violence shall be held in jail without bail pending their first appearance. This order shall apply to all offenses listed under Chapter 10.99, irrespective of their classification as a Felony, Gross Misdemeanor, or Misdemeanor.

Chief Judge Cary argued to her colleagues that her proposed General Order would exercise authority granted to the trial judges under Rule 3.2(a) of the Criminal Rules for Courts of Limited Jurisdiction: "A court of limited jurisdiction may adopt a bail schedule for persons who have been arrested on probable cause but have not yet made a preliminary appearance before a judicial officer. With the exception of [certain traffic offenses], the adoption of such a schedule or whether to adopt a schedule, is in the discretion of each court of limited jurisdiction."

Under current practices in Spokane County, jail personnel determine bail according to a preset bail schedule and grant release to some defendants prior to any preliminary court appearance. The practical effect of the new General Order, therefore, would be to delay the release of most persons arrested for domestic violence crimes until the arrestee's first appearance before a judge or magistrate, typically on the day after the arrest, because the majority of domestic violence arrests occur in the evening.

After the judges' meeting ended, word of Chief Judge Cary's proposal spread to other government officials and community figures. Within two days, the District Attorney for Spokane County urged the judges not to adopt the proposed General Order. He believes that the order would violate the state constitutional right to bail and would expose the county to tort liability. The Spokane County public defender's office also wrote a letter opposing the order. The Sheriff, who is responsible for operating the county jail, told the judges that the new General Order would increase operating expenses at the jail, given the large number of domestic violence arrestees. Officials from the Young Women's Christian Association (YWCA), an organization that operates a shelter for battered women, sent a letter to the judges in favor of the General Order, arguing that a forced overnight separation of a couple during a domestic violence event can prevent additional violence against the victim.

You are one of the District Court judges in Spokane County. How do you plan to vote on Chief Judge Cary's proposed General Order at the next meeting of the judges?

2. Bail Reform Efforts

Bail procedures have been the subject of extensive social science research. The researchers' interest in bail stems from the relative ease of quantifying bail determinations and the moral problems raised by detaining those who have not yet been tried (and are, therefore, presumptively innocent). Furthermore, the cost of keeping hundreds or thousands of pretrial defendants in county jail is exorbitant, thus providing a financial motivation for jurisdictions to consider alternatives. More recently, strong connections between pretrial detention and case outcomes have captured the interest of social science researchers in a number of disciplines. For example, Paul Heaton and his colleagues tracked hundreds of thousands of misdemeanor cases in Harris County, Texas; they found that detained defendants are 25 percent more likely than released defendants to plead guilty, 43 percent more likely to be sentenced to jail, and receive jail sentences that are twice as long as those imposed on released defendants. Paul S. Heaton, Sandra G. Mayson & Megan T. Stevenson, The Downstream Consequences of Misdemeanor Pretrial Detention, 69 Stan. L. Rev. 711 (2017). Similar data was recorded in a study of New York City. Emily Leslie & Nolan G. Pope, The Unintended Impact of Pretrial Detention on Case Outcomes: Evidence from New York City Arraignments, 60 J.L. & Econ. 529 (2017).

Social scientists don't just study the bail systems as they operate today; sometimes they propose reforms. A classic illustration of the use of social science as an engine of reform is the Manhattan Bail Project conducted by the Vera Institute of Justice. More recently, scientists have been studying risk assessment software that uses algorithms to determine which populations present higher risks of flight and re-offending. As you read the following materials, consider whether this new software represents a significant improvement over the basic formula developed by the Vera staff in the 1960s, in terms of its ability to distinguish high risk from low risk offenders.

■ VERA INSTITUTE OF JUSTICE, FAIR TREATMENT FOR THE INDIGENT: THE MANHATTAN BAIL PROJECT
Ten-Year Report, 1961-1971 (May 1972)

There are many penalties imposed upon an accused person who is detained in jail because he is too poor to post bail. [The] detainee is more apt to be convicted than if he were free on bail; and, if convicted, he is more apt to receive a tougher sentence. [Detainees] lose income while they are away from their jobs, and suffer dislocation and sometimes even permanent rupture in their family lives. They frequently suffer social stigmatization and loss of self respect because of their confinement—even though they have not been convicted of anything and must be presumed innocent, and may eventually be acquitted. . . .

In a large city like New York, these people can also expect to be detained in jails where conditions are comparable to maximum security prisons. . . . Meanwhile, detained persons' defense preparations suffer as it is difficult or impossible for them to consult with attorneys, communicate with family or friends, locate witnesses, or gather evidence.

VERA TAKES ACTION

Real reform was indeed possible. . . . This was the idea of encouraging judges to release far more accused persons on their honor pending trial, and providing the judges with verified information about the accused on which such releases could be based. It was an obvious, but . . . daring idea: find out who can be trusted, and trust them to appear for trial. . . . A project based on these concepts quickly took form:

1. Indigent defendants awaiting arraignment in Manhattan's criminal courts would be questioned by Vera staff interviewers to determine how deep their community roots were and thus whether they could be relied upon to return to court for trial if they were released without bail.
2. The test of indigency would be representation by a Legal Aid lawyer.
3. Questioners would develop information about the defendant's length of residence in the city, his family ties, and his employment situation.
4. Responses of the defendant would be verified immediately in personal or telephone interviews with family, friends, and employers.
5. When verified information indicated that an individual was trustworthy and could be depended on to return for trial, the Vera staff member would appear at arraignment and recommend to the judge that the accused be released on his own recognizance (R.O.R. or pretrial parole) pending trial.

A DEMONSTRATION PROJECT IS SET UP

The experiment was scheduled to begin in the fall of 1961 in the arraignment part of the Manhattan Magistrate's Felony Court. [Students] from the School of Law at New York University were recruited as Vera staff interviewers and received a period of training during which they learned how the arraignment court functioned. On October 16, 1961 after months of detailed planning, the Manhattan Bail Project began operations. Specifics attending the launching were carefully arranged:

1. No publicity was given the inauguration of the venture, on grounds that it would be most effective as a demonstration to the community if the results could later speak for themselves. . . .

2. The answers sought through the project were limited and precise: (a) Would judges release more defendants on their own recognizance if they were given verified information about the defendants than they would without such information? (b) Would released defendants return for trial at the same rate as those released on bail? (c) How would the cases of released defendants compare with a control group not recommended for release, both in convictions and in sentencing? . . .

3. All magistrates who would be sitting in court during the project were visited personally by Vera staff members prior to its initiation so that they would understand fully what was happening and why.

4. Since a primary function of the project was to demonstrate to the public and to those within the criminal justice system that pretrial parole was a device that could serve the public's interest as well as the defendant's, some offenders were excluded at the outset from the experiment. These were homicide, forcible rape, sodomy involving a minor, corrupting the morals of a child, and carnal abuse—crimes that were all thought to be too sensitive and controversial to be associated with a release program; narcotics offenses, because of special medical problems and . . . a greater risk of flight; and assault on a police officer, where intervention by Vera might, it was feared, arouse police hostility.

5. Comprehensive follow-up procedures were devised to be sure that released defendants knew when they were expected in court for further appearances in connection with their trials. These procedures included mailed reminders, telephone calls, visits at home or work, and special notifications in the defendant's language, if he did not speak English.

[The] law students began their interviews in the detention pens in the arraignment court. At first, they were asked to make subjective evaluations of the defendant's eligibility for pretrial parole after they had verified their community ties. [Then] a weighted system of points was developed and the sole determinant as to whether or not a defendant would be recommended for release without bail was his achieving a point score of five or above. This development of a set of objective criteria on which to base release recommendations proved to be an important innovation. . . .

POINT SCORING SYSTEM: MANHATTAN BAIL PROJECT

To be recommended, defendant needs [a] New York area address where he can be reached and [a] total of five points from the following categories:

Prior Record

  1   No convictions.
  0   One misdemeanor conviction.
−1   Two misdemeanor or one felony conviction.
−2   Three or more misdemeanors or two or more felony convictions.

Family Ties (in New York Area)

  3   Lives in established family home AND visits other family members (immediate family only).

2   Lives in established family home (immediate family).
1   Visits others of immediate family.

Employment or School

3   Present job one year or more, steadily.
2   Present job 4 months. . . .
1   Has present job which is still available,
    or Unemployed 3 months or less and 9 months or more steady prior job,
    or Unemployment Compensation,
    or Welfare.
3   Presently in school, attending regularly.
2   Out of school less than 6 months but employed or in training.
1   Out of school 3 months or less, unemployed and not in training.

Residence (in New York Area steadily)

3   One year at present residence.
2   One year at present [and] last prior residence or 6 months at
    present residence.
1   Six months at present and last prior residence or in New York City
    5 years or more.

Discretion

1   Positive, over 65, attending hospital, appeared on some previous case.
0   Negative—intoxicated—intention to leave jurisdiction.

COMPARING THE EXPERIMENTAL AND THE CONTROL GROUPS

. . . Vera was especially anxious to compare the experiences of those who had been recommended for release with the experiences of the control group, a statistically identical group for which recommendations had not been made to the judges. It found that 59 percent of its pretrial parole recommendations were followed by the court and that only 16 percent of the control group was released without bail by the judges acting on their own. Judges were clearly basing their actions on the availability of reliable information about the defendants. More significantly, *60 percent of those released pending trial during the first year eventually were acquitted or had their case dismissed, compared with only 23 percent of the control group. And only 16 percent of the released defendants who were convicted were sentenced to prison, where 96 percent of those convicted in the control group received prison sentences.* Unquestionably, detention was resulting in a higher rate of convictions and in far more punitive dispositions. At the end of the second year, the control group was dropped. . . .

MODIFICATIONS IN PROJECT PROCEDURES

[In] the fall of 1964, the New York City Office of Probation took over the administration of the Vera project. . . . During the three years [of the Bail Project] 3,505 defendants had been released on their own recognizance following the recommendations of Vera staff members, out of a total of some 10,000 defendants who had been interviewed. *Only 56 of these parolees, or 1.6 percent of the total, willfully failed to appear in court for trial. During the same period, 3 percent of those released on bail failed to appear, or nearly twice as many as had been released without bail.* The figures strongly suggested that bail was not as effective a guarantee of court appearance as was release on verified information.

Over the thirty-five months, a little less than half—48 percent—of those released through the Vera project were acquitted or had their cases dismissed, while the remaining 52 percent were found guilty. Of those found guilty, 70 percent received suspended sentences, 10 percent were given jail terms, and 20 percent were given the alternative of a fine or jail sentence.

During the Vera operation, staff recommendations became increasingly liberal as experience established that more and more persons could be released safely on their assurances that they would return for trial. Also judicial acceptance of the recommendations rose sharply. At the outset, Vera urged release for 28 percent of the defendants interviewed, while two and a half years later the figure was 65 percent. Judges were following Vera's advice 55 percent of the time in 1961, and 70 percent of the time in 1964. . . .

■ MEGAN STEVENSON & SANDRA G. MAYSON, PRETRIAL DETENTION AND BAIL
3 REFORMING CRIMINAL JUSTICE: PRETRIAL AND TRIAL PROCESSES 21-47
(Eric Luna ed., 2017)

. . . In the last few years, the hefty costs of pretrial detention have generated growing interest in bail reform. Jurisdictions around the country are now rewriting their pretrial law and policy. They aspire to reduce pretrial detention rates, as well as racial and socioeconomic disparities in the pretrial system, without increasing rates of non-appearance or pretrial crime. The overarching reform vision is to shift from the "resource-based" system of money bail to a "risk-based" system, in which pretrial interventions are tied to risk rather than wealth. To accomplish this, jurisdictions are implementing actuarial risk assessment and reducing the use of money bail as a mediator of release. The idea is that defendants who pose little statistical risk of flight (i.e., fleeing the jurisdiction) or committing pretrial crime can be released without money bail or onerous conditions. . . .

IMPROVING PRETRIAL PROCESS . . .

Jurisdictions can reduce the number of people who require a bail hearing in the first place by increasing the use of citation rather than arrest, and by authorizing direct release from the police station (station-house release). The process of arrest is obtrusive, time-consuming, expensive, and potentially damaging to community-police relations. Jurisdictions such as Philadelphia, New York, New Orleans, and Ferguson have recently begun substituting citations or summons for arrest for some categories of crime. Even for crimes that require arrest, defendants who pose little risk of flight or serious pretrial crime should be identified rapidly and released. Risk-assessment tools may be helpful in identifying good candidates. Kentucky, for example, uses a risk-assessment tool to identify defendants who are eligible for station-house release. . . .

Currently, bail hearings in many jurisdictions are shockingly short: only a few minutes per case. It is hard to imagine that two minutes are sufficient to effectively evaluate the risk of flight, risk of serious crime, whether detention or conditions of release are necessary, and, if money bail is used, ability to pay. Taking more care during the bail hearing is likely to improve the courts' ability to evaluate risk and determine appropriate pretrial conditions. While slowing down the bail hearing would, barring other changes, increase costs, a bail hearing should only be required for defendants at risk of losing liberty. . . .

Currently, many jurisdictions do not provide counsel to indigent defendants at the bail hearing. . . . While providing counsel at the bail hearing would come at some expense, the presence of counsel is also useful to the system as a whole: lawyers can provide information that may help a judge determine which defendants can be safely released. . . .

The judges and magistrates who set bail may not be fully aware of how their decisions translate into detention rates. It may surprise some to learn how high detention rates can be even at relatively low amounts of bail. For example, 40% of Philadelphia defendants with bail set at $500—who need only pay a $50 deposit to secure their release—remain detained pretrial. While it is conceivable that these detention rates are the result of well-considered policies, it is possible that the magistrates are unaware of how difficult it can be for defendants to come up with even relatively small sums of money. . . .

There are many reasons why a defendant may not appear in court beyond willful flight from justice. A defendant may not know when her court date is, have forgotten about it, or struggle to make adequate preparations (such as arranging transportation, child care, or time off from work). For these defendants, court reminders in the form of mail notifications, phone calls, or automated text messages may greatly increase appearance rates. The available research shows that phone-call reminders can increase appearance rates by as much as 42%, and mail reminders can increase appearance rates by as much as 33%. Entrepreneurial technology firms now offer automated, individually customized text-message reminders. . . .

Jurisdictions striving to reduce pretrial detention rates can also reinvest the savings by expanding supportive pretrial services. A pretrial services agency can connect defendants to a range of social services to address underlying risk factors like homelessness, joblessness, and addiction. It can also help defendants manage the logistics of attending court (transportation, child care, work leave, etc.). . . .

EVALUATING RISK

Actuarial risk assessment is a common theme in contemporary bail reform. Reformers aspire to improve the accuracy and consistency of pretrial decisionmaking by assessing each defendant's statistical risk of non-appearance and rearrest in the pretrial period, and providing this assessment to judges along with a recommendation for pretrial intervention. Pretrial risk assessment holds great promise, but also raises concerns. . . .

There is reason to be optimistic about the actuarial turn in pretrial practice. Risk-assessment tools should reduce the subjective, irrational bias that distorts judicial decision-making. They may also mitigate judicial incentives to overdetain by absolving judges of personal responsibility for "mistaken" release decisions. They have the potential to bring consistency to pretrial decisionmaking and ensure that like defendants are treated alike. So long as the tools are not opaque, they may improve the transparency of pretrial release decisions. Risk-assessment tools also offer a mechanism of accountability: risk scores and defendants' outcomes can be monitored, and if the tool or its implementation is resulting in unnecessary detention, inappropriate release or unwarranted disparities, the tool or implementation rules can be adjusted.

Several recent studies argue that tying pretrial detention directly to statistical risk can minimize detention rates while maximizing appearance rates, public safety, or both. Analyzing a dataset from the 75 largest urban counties in the U.S., Baradaran and McIntyre found that the counties could have released 25% more felony defendants pretrial and reduced pretrial crime if detention decisions had been made on the basis of statistical risk. In Philadelphia, Richard Berk and colleagues concluded that deferring to the detention recommendations of a machine-learned algorithm in domestic violence (DV) cases could cut the rearrest rate on serious DV charges (over two years) from 20% to 10%. Jon Kleinberg and colleagues, working with New York City data, found that delegating detention decisions to a machine-learned algorithm could "reduce crime by up to 24.8% with no change in jailing, or reduce jail populations by 42.0% with no increase in crime," while also reducing racial disparities in detention.

These are studies of policy simulations, not actual policy changes. There has been very little research evaluating the effectiveness of risk assessment in practice. One recent study showed that a law requiring judges to consider the risk assessment in the pretrial release decision led to a small increase in pretrial release, but it also led to an increase in failures-to-appear, and possibly in pretrial crime. Furthermore, the study showed that judges ignored the recommendations associated with the risk tool more often than not. While risk assessments have promise, realizing their benefits in practice is not simple.

CONCERNS OVER ACCURACY, RACIAL EQUALITY, AND CONTESTABILITY

Pretrial risk assessment has also sparked controversy in the popular press. In 2016, news outlet ProPublica published a study that claimed to have discovered that the COMPAS, a prominent risk-assessment tool, was "biased against blacks." It also opined that the COMPAS was "remarkably unreliable in forecasting violent crime," and only "somewhat more accurate than a coin flip" in predicting pretrial rearrest generally. Finally, the article noted that statistical generalization may be at odds with individualized justice, and that proprietary risk-assessment tools like the COMPAS pose transparency concerns. These critiques—regarding accuracy, racial equality, and contestability—represent core concerns with actuarial assessment.

Debate about accuracy would benefit from an acknowledgement that no method of prediction is 100% accurate. It is particularly hard to predict low frequency events like violent crime. The ProPublica article concluded that the COMPAS was "remarkably unreliable" on the basis that "[only] 20 percent of the people predicted to commit violent crimes actually went on to do so [in a two-year window]." But that is much higher than the base rate. An algorithm that can identify people with a 20% chance of rearrest for violent crime provides useful knowledge. The policy-relevant question is not whether a tool is "accurate," but rather what statistical information it provides, whether that information represents an improvement over the status quo, and whether it can justifiably guide pretrial decision-making.

The concern for racial equality is similarly complex. The most obvious source of racial bias in prediction would be if an algorithm treated race as an independently predictive factor, or over-weighted factors that correlate with race, like ZIP code, relative to their predictive power. But none of the pretrial risk-assessment tools in current use utilize race as an input factor; the dominant tool, the Public Safety Assessment, relies exclusively on criminal history information. Two people of different races with the same criminal history will thus receive the same risk score. Nonetheless, risk assessment can have disparate impact across racial groups.

This was the source of the disparity that ProPublica documented: The black defendants in its dataset had higher arrest-risk profiles, on average, than the white. There is no easy way to prevent this result. Nor is it a good reason to reject actuarial risk assessment, because subjective risk assessment will have the same effect. It is possible to modify an algorithm to equalize outcomes across racial groups, but [that] usually requires treating defendants with the same observable risk profiles differently on the basis of race.

The third set of concerns with pretrial risk assessment is procedural. If people cannot meaningfully contest the basis of their risk score, actuarial risk assessment might violate due process by denying a meaningful opportunity to be heard. This problem arises with proprietary algorithms like the COMPAS and other "black box" machine-learned algorithms, although there are ways to make machine-learned algorithms more transparent. A related concern is that no algorithm will take account of every relevant fact about a given individual. For this reason, most scholars believe that judges must retain discretion to vary from the recommendations of a risk-assessment tool, and jurisdictions have universally followed this practice.

BEST PRACTICE IN RISK ASSESSMENT

Given these concerns and the limitations of existing research, jurisdictions implementing pretrial risk assessment should keep a number of best practices in mind. First, risk-assessment tools should be intelligible to the people whose lives they affect. To the greatest extent possible, the identity and weighting of risk factors should be public. Relatedly, tools that rely on objective data are preferable to tools that include subjective components. Second, stakeholders should take care in determining what risks to assess. At present, many tools measure pretrial "failure," a composite of flight risk and crime risk. But these two risks are different in kind and call for different responses. Within each category, moreover, further divisions are warranted. Some people are at high risk for flight because they have powerful incentives to abscond. Others are just likely to struggle with the logistics of attending court. The response to these two groups should be different. Likewise, most tools currently define crime risk as the likelihood of arrest for anything at all, including minor offenses. If society's core concern is violent crime, then assessing the risk of any arrest is counterproductive; people at highest risk for any arrest are not at highest risk of arrest for violent crime in particular, and vice versa.

[In addition], criminal justice stakeholders should confront the value judgments that a detention regime guided by risk assessment will entail. Someone must decide what degree of statistical risk justifies detention—if any does. Either the developers of risk-assessment tools will make that judgment implicitly, by choosing the "cut point" at which a risk is determined to be high and detention is recommended, or stakeholders can make it and direct the design of the tool accordingly.

Similarly, any predictive system (including subjective risk assessment) will perpetuate underlying racial and socioeconomic disparities in the world, and stakeholders should determine how best to respond to this reality. . . .

IMPLEMENTING NONMONETARY CONDITIONS OF RELEASE

In order to limit the use of money bail and reduce detention rates, bail reformers advocate non-financial conditions of release as an alternative for defendants who pose some pretrial risk. . . .

The requirement of meeting periodically (in person or over the phone) with a pretrial officer is one of the most common conditions of release. Pretrial supervision is an expensive intervention, as it requires the time of a salaried employee of the state. It imposes time burdens on the defendant, and, in increasing the requirements of release, increases the likelihood that the defendant will fail to fulfill them. There is no good evidence to support this practice. A small experiment conducted by John Goldkamp, in which defendants were randomly assigned to low-supervision or high-supervision conditions, found no difference in appearance rates or rearrest across the two groups. . . . More high-quality research on the effectiveness of pretrial supervision is needed. At the moment, the practice is far from "evidence-based," and the best available research shows no benefits. . . .

The use of drug testing during the pretrial period has been shown to be ineffective at reducing failure-to-appear rates or pretrial rearrest rates in a number of randomized control trials. These studies mostly date from around the time when drug testing was broadly implemented (in the late 1980s and 1990s). . . .

There is limited high-quality research on the effectiveness of electronic monitoring (EM) in the pretrial period. However, there is growing evidence that electronic monitoring reduces criminal activity for defendants in the probation or parole context. . . . Electronic monitoring has been found to reduce crime relative to traditional parole for gang members and sex offenders in California, although it increased the likelihood of returning to custody for gang members, due to an increased likelihood of technical violations.

Whatever benefit EM provides comes at substantial cost. EM is a significant burden on a person's liberty. It places strain on family relationships, makes it difficult to find employment, and can lead to shame and stigma. Surveys of people serving sentences find that EM is considered only slightly less onerous than incarceration. EM is also costly to the state. Purchasing the equipment, monitoring individuals, and responding to violations entails considerable expense. . . . In conclusion: EM should be used selectively, and only as an alternative to detention.

Notes

1. *Bail and crowded jails.* In some jurisdictions, a large number of defendants fail to "make bail"—that is, the defendant finds no way to meet the financial conditions for release that the judge imposes. These defendants can account for a significant share of the total jail population, and increase the total operating expense for local governments. For instance, in New Jersey, approximately 12 percent of the county jail population consists of defendants who cannot post bail of $2,500 or less. Report

of the Joint Committee on Criminal Justice (March 2014), available at *http://www. judiciary.state.nj.us/pressrel/2014/FinalReport_3_20_2014.pdf.* The high cost of operating jails, one of the single largest components in the budgets of many local governments, is an important driver in efforts to improve bail and other release practices.

2. *Rates of failure to appear.* Some of the defendants released before trial or the entry of a guilty plea fail to appear at their later court proceedings. Statistics compiled every two years between 1990 and 2009 in large urban jurisdictions show consistent results: between 17 and 24 percent of the felony defendants who were released before case disposition failed to appear. Bureau of Justice Statistics, Felony Defendants in Large Urban Counties, 2009—Statistical Tables (December 2013, NCJ 243777). These statistics, however, include "technical defaults" where defendants miss the initial court date but come voluntarily at a later time (as well as those who purposely flee the jurisdiction). The Stevenson and Mayson report indicates that algorithms and courts ought to distinguish between different kinds of flight risks, and devise responses that are appropriate to each type of risk rather than lumping them all together.

3. *Racial and gender bias in release and bail decisions.* Evidence periodically surfaces to suggest that black and Hispanic defendants receive less favorable bail and release decisions than white defendants. One study of bail practices in Connecticut by Professors Ian Ayres and Joel Waldfogel revealed that bond dealers charged lower bond rates to black and Hispanic defendants than to white defendants, suggesting that judges set the bail amounts for black and Hispanic defendants higher than the real risk of flight. The "competitive market"—in the form of the bond dealers—thus was able to discount the rate for minority defendants and still make a profit. Ian Ayres, Pervasive Prejudice? Unconventional Evidence of Race and Gender Discrimination (2001). An econometric analysis of nationwide statistics, however, reached the opposite conclusion. Frank McIntyre & Shima Baradaran, Race, Prediction, and Pretrial Detention, 10 J. Empirical Legal Studies 741 (2013) (11 percent racial gap in "hold rate" nearly disappears after controlling for probability of future commission of violent felony, based on type of felony in original arrest, age, and prior record). Based on the Stevenson and Mayson report, would you expect algorithm-based software to correct for these kinds of biases based on race?

Studies have consistently indicated that female defendants are more likely than male defendants to obtain pretrial release and to receive nonfinancial conditions of release. Why might a judge make more "lenient" release decisions for female defendants? Stephen Demuth & Darrell Steffensmeier, The Impact of Gender and Race-Ethnicity in the Pretrial Release Process, 51 Social Problems 222 (2004) (white females most likely to be released; black and Hispanic male defendants most likely to be detained, in part because of inability to post bail).

4. *Effects of pretrial release on acquittal rates.* Bail researchers have long believed that a defendant's odds of acquittal at trial go down if the defendant fails to obtain pretrial release. They reason that a defendant who remains in jail is less able to locate witnesses and otherwise prepare a defense. Caleb Foote's study of bail practices in Philadelphia in the 1950s observed that 67 percent of the defendants charged with violent crimes were acquitted if they were released before trial, while only 25 percent of jailed defendants were acquitted. Foote, Compelling Appearance in Court: Administration of Bail in Philadelphia, 102 U. Pa. L. Rev. 1031 (1954). A number of later studies found a causal relationship (and not just a statistical association) between pretrial release and acquittal rates. Among more recent studies, the trend (although not uniform) is to conclude that pretrial release is correlated

with—but does not necessarily cause—high acquittal rates. For instance, the seriousness of a charge is a factor both in making release less likely and in making conviction more likely because (among other reasons) prosecution witnesses are more likely to show up. See Gerald Wheeler & Carol Wheeler, Bail Reform in the 1980s: A Response to the Critics, 18 Crim. L. Bull. 228 (1982).

5. *Effects of pretrial release on sentences.* There is stronger evidence of a causal linkage between the pretrial release decision and the choice of punishment after a conviction. The best evidence indicates that defendants not released before their conviction are more likely to receive prison sentences than those who are released. For instance, one analysis of data from Kentucky found that defendants held for the entire pretrial period were three times more likely to be sentenced to prison than other defendants who were similar in terms of age, gender, race, marital status, risk level, offense type, and incarceration history. The prison sentences for detained defendants were also twice as long as the prison sentences for comparable defendants who were released pretrial. Christopher T. Lowenkamp, Marie VanNostrand & Alexander Holsinger, Investigating the Impact of Pretrial Detention on Sentencing Outcomes (November 2013), available at *http://www.arnoldfoundation.org/sites/default/files/pdf/LJAF_Report_state-sentencing_FNL.pdf.*

6. *Self-incrimination risk?* In order for a defendant to get evaluated for bail, she has to provide information about herself, her work history, her home life, and prior criminal record. Can these statements later be used against her in a criminal proceeding? If she admits to prior criminal behavior that had not previously been charged, should the prosecution be able to use this information to justify a new case filing?

7. *Shift to nonfinancial techniques during 1960s bail reform.* Changes to the bail system in the 1950s and 1960s increased the use of nonfinancial techniques, such as release on recognizance, and standardized the criteria used for release decisions as a way of preventing the wealth of defendants from dominating the release decision. See Daniel Freed & Patricia Wald, Bail in the United States (1964). One example of these changes was the 1966 Federal Bail Reform Act. Unlike the federal statute at work until that time, which gave virtually no guidance to the judge on release and bail decisions, the 1966 statute required courts to consider standard criteria in reaching their decisions. The statutory factors included "(1) the nature of the offense charged; (2) the weight of the evidence against the accused; (3) the accused's family ties; (4) employment; (5) financial resources; (6) character; (7) mental health; (8) the length of residence in the community; (9) a record of convictions; and (10) a record of failure to appear at court appearances or of flight to avoid prosecution." The ABA Standards on Criminal Justice, Pretrial Release (1968), also embodied many of the aspirations of critics of the money bail system. Both the 1966 Bail Reform Act and the ABA standards influenced state legislatures to revise their criteria for making release decisions; most states have a similar (though not identical) list of factors. See, e.g., Cal. Penal Code §1275. This era of federal and state legislation, together with changes in local practices, resulted in higher numbers of defendants being released before trial or guilty plea.

8. *Shift to risk assessment techniques during 2010s bail reform.* Later reform efforts put less emphasis on nonfinancial conditions of release. They aim instead to reduce the use of financial release devices through the use of "risk assessment" instruments, which identify criminal defendants most likely to fail to appear for later criminal proceedings, and those most likely to commit additional crimes. See Shima

Baradaran Baughman, The Bail Book: A Comprehensive Look at Bail in America's Criminal Justice System (2017). These risk assessment systems collect information about each offender and predict, on the basis of a statistical formula that weighs those selected inputs, the risk of nonappearance or rearrest within a designated time period. These instruments come from many different sources, including agencies of state government, nonprofit organizations, and for-profit firms. For tables that summarize the different characteristics of the leading competitors in the market for risk assessment instruments, see Sandra G. Mayson, Dangerous Defendants, 127 Yale L.J. 490, 512-514 (2018).

9. *Constitutional litigation over disparate impact of bail practices.* Some criminal defendants have challenged pretrial release practices on constitutional equal protection and due process grounds because in practice, the release of misdemeanor arrestees depends entirely on their wealth. These claims have found mixed success. Compare O'Donnell v. Harris County, 892 F.3d 147 (5th Cir. 2018) (preliminary injunction appropriate in civil suit alleging that county's system for setting bail for indigent misdemeanor arrestees violated equal protection and due process clauses, because it resulted in detention of indigent arrestees solely due to their inability to pay bail) and People ex rel. Desgranges on Behalf of Kunkeli v. Anderson, 59 Misc.3d 238, 72 N.Y.S.3d 328 (N.Y. Sup. 2018) (failure to consider a defendant's financial situation when imposing bail violates defendant's right to equal protection), with Walker v. City of Calhoun, 901 F.3d 1245 (11th Cir. 2018) (plaintiff did not make necessary showing for preliminary injunction in suit claiming equal protection violation by city operating bail system in a manner that systematically detained poor defendants for longer periods than wealthy defendants), and Holland v. Rosen, 895 F.3d 272 (3d Cir. 2018) (denying preliminary injunction to person accused of assault, released pending trial subject to conditions including electronic monitoring, and bail bond provider; New Jersey statute that subordinated monetary bail to nonmonetary conditions of release did not unconstitutionally deny presumptively innocent criminal defendants the opportunity to post monetary bail for pretrial release).

B. PRETRIAL DETENTION

Until the 1980s, a substantial majority of state constitutions guaranteed a right to bail except in capital cases. Earlier in our history, the capital case exception applied to a large number of defendants because a wide range of crimes (from murder to burglary) were punishable by death. Once capital punishment became available only for a subset of murders, however, the state constitutional right to bail extended to a much larger group—indeed, to most criminal defendants.

These constitutional provisions never meant that all defendants were to be released before trial. A judge could, consistent with these constitutional provisions, deny bail altogether or set bail in prohibitively high amounts when necessary to ensure a defendant's appearance at trial or to prevent the defendant from threatening witnesses or otherwise undermining the integrity of the judicial process. These hard-to-identify practices blunted the practical impact of the constitutional provisions and statutes declaring in broad terms the "right to bail."

However, decreasing use of money bail and the increased number of defendants released before trial gave new visibility and urgency to an old question: What are the purposes of pretrial release and detention? Should systems refuse to release a defendant before trial only when necessary to preserve the integrity of the judicial process? Or could a judge deny bail altogether if necessary to serve different purposes, such as protecting the public from further wrongdoing by the defendant before trial?

In 1970, only four years after the 1966 Bail Reform Act, Congress passed a controversial pretrial detention law for the District of Columbia that allowed detention on the basis of the threat of additional criminal acts by the defendant before trial. Then in 1984 Congress declared, in a new Bail Reform Act, that prevention of future wrongdoing was indeed a proper basis for detaining a defendant in custody before trial. That declaration gave momentum to a movement that has now become the law in over half the states.

The federal statute creates a rebuttable presumption of detention for some defendants. For a detailed analysis of the complex provisions of the federal statute, see the web extension for this chapter at *http://www.crimpro.com/extension/ch12.*

■ U.S. CONSTITUTION AMENDMENT VIII

Excessive bail shall not be required, nor excessive fines imposed, nor cruel and unusual punishments inflicted.

■ TENNESSEE CONSTITUTION ART. I, §§15, 16

15. That all prisoners shall be bailable by sufficient sureties, unless for capital offences, when the proof is evident or the presumption great. And the privilege of the writ of habeas corpus shall not be suspended, unless when in case of rebellion or invasion, the General Assembly shall declare the public safety requires it.

16. That excessive bail shall not be required, nor excessive fines imposed, nor cruel and unusual punishments inflicted.

■ UNITED STATES v. ANTHONY SALERNO
481 U.S. 739 (1987)

REHNQUIST, C.J.*

The Bail Reform Act of 1984 allows a federal court to detain an arrestee pending trial if the Government demonstrates by clear and convincing evidence after an adversary hearing that no release conditions "will reasonably assure . . . the safety of any other person and the community." . . . We hold that, as against the facial attack mounted by these respondents, the Act fully comports with constitutional requirements. . . .

---

* [Justices White, Blackmun, Powell, O'Connor, and Scalia joined this opinion.—EDS.]

I.

Responding to "the alarming problem of crimes committed by persons on release," S. Rep. No. 98-225, p.3 (1983), Congress formulated the Bail Reform Act of 1984, 18 U.S.C. §3141 et seq., as the solution to a bail crisis in the federal courts. . . . Congress hoped to give the courts adequate authority to make release decisions that give appropriate recognition to the danger a person may pose to others if released.

To this end, §3141(a) of the Act requires a judicial officer to determine whether an arrestee shall be detained. Section 3142(e) provides that "if, after a hearing pursuant to the provisions of subsection (f), the judicial officer finds that no condition or combination of conditions will reasonably assure the appearance of the person as required and the safety of any other person and the community, he shall order the detention of the person prior to trial." . . . If the judicial officer finds that no conditions of pretrial release can reasonably assure the safety of other persons and the community, he must state his findings of fact in writing, §3142(i), and support his conclusion with "clear and convincing evidence," §3142(f).

The judicial officer is not given unbridled discretion in making the detention determination. Congress has specified the considerations relevant to that decision. These factors include the nature and seriousness of the charges, the substantiality of the Government's evidence against the arrestee, the arrestee's background and characteristics, and the nature and seriousness of the danger posed by the suspect's release. §3142(g). Should a judicial officer order detention, the detainee is entitled to expedited appellate review of the detention order. §§3145(b), (c).

Respondents Anthony Salerno and Vincent Cafaro were arrested on March 21, 1986, after being charged in a 29-count indictment alleging various Racketeer Influenced and Corrupt Organizations Act (RICO) violations, mail and wire fraud offenses, extortion, and various criminal gambling violations. The RICO counts alleged 35 acts of racketeering activity, including fraud, extortion, gambling, and conspiracy to commit murder. At respondents' arraignment, the Government moved to have Salerno and Cafaro detained pursuant to §3142(e), on the ground that no condition of release would assure the safety of the community or any person. The District Court held a hearing at which the Government made a detailed proffer of evidence. The Government's case showed that Salerno was the "boss" of the Genovese crime family of La Cosa Nostra and that Cafaro was a "captain" in the Genovese family. According to the Government's proffer, based in large part on conversations intercepted by a court-ordered wiretap, the two respondents had participated in wide-ranging conspiracies to aid their illegitimate enterprises through violent means. The Government also offered the testimony of two of its trial witnesses, who would assert that Salerno personally participated in two murder conspiracies. Salerno opposed the motion for detention, challenging the credibility of the Government's witnesses. He offered the testimony of several character witnesses as well as a letter from his doctor stating that he was suffering from a serious medical condition. Cafaro presented no evidence at the hearing, but instead characterized the wiretap conversations as merely "tough talk."

The District Court granted the Government's detention motion, concluding that the Government had established by clear and convincing evidence that no condition or combination of conditions of release would ensure the safety of the community or any person. . . . Respondents appealed, contending that to the extent that the Bail Reform Act permits pretrial detention on the ground that the arrestee is likely to commit future crimes, it is unconstitutional on its face. . . .

II.

A facial challenge to a legislative Act is, of course, the most difficult challenge to mount successfully, since the challenger must establish that no set of circumstances exists under which the Act would be valid. . . . We think respondents have failed to shoulder their heavy burden to demonstrate that the Act is "facially" unconstitutional.

Respondents present two grounds for invalidating the Bail Reform Act's provisions permitting pretrial detention on the basis of future dangerousness. First, they [argue] that the Act exceeds the limitations placed upon the Federal Government by the Due Process Clause of the Fifth Amendment. Second, they contend that the Act contravenes the Eighth Amendment's proscription against excessive bail. We treat these contentions in turn.

A.

The Due Process Clause of the Fifth Amendment provides that "No person shall . . . be deprived of life, liberty, or property, without due process of law. . . ." Respondents first argue that the Act violates substantive due process because the pretrial detention it authorizes constitutes impermissible punishment before trial. The Government, however, has never argued that pretrial detention could be upheld if it were "punishment." The Court of Appeals assumed that pretrial detention under the Bail Reform Act is regulatory, not penal, and we agree that it is. . . .

To determine whether a restriction on liberty constitutes impermissible punishment or permissible regulation, we first look to legislative intent. Unless Congress expressly intended to impose punitive restrictions, the punitive/regulatory distinction turns on whether an alternative purpose to which the restriction may rationally be connected is assignable for it, and whether it appears excessive in relation to the alternative purpose assigned to it.

We conclude that the detention imposed by the Act falls on the regulatory side of the dichotomy. The legislative history of the Bail Reform Act clearly indicates that Congress did not formulate the pretrial detention provisions as punishment for dangerous individuals. Congress instead perceived pretrial detention as a potential solution to a pressing societal problem. There is no doubt that preventing danger to the community is a legitimate regulatory goal.

Nor are the incidents of pretrial detention excessive in relation to the regulatory goal Congress sought to achieve. The Bail Reform Act carefully limits the circumstances under which detention may be sought to the most serious of crimes. See 18 U.S.C. §3142(f) (detention hearings available if case involves crimes of violence, offenses for which the sentence is life imprisonment or death, serious drug offenses, or certain repeat offenders). The arrestee is entitled to a prompt detention hearing, and the maximum length of pretrial detention is limited by the stringent time limitations of the Speedy Trial Act. Moreover, . . . the conditions of confinement envisioned by the Act appear to reflect the regulatory purposes relied upon by the Government. [The] statute at issue here requires that detainees be housed in a facility "separate, to the extent practicable, from persons awaiting or serving sentences or being held in custody pending appeal." 18 U.S.C. §3142(i)(2). We conclude, therefore, that the pretrial detention contemplated by the Bail Reform Act is regulatory in nature, and does not constitute punishment before trial in violation of the Due Process Clause.

[The] Government's regulatory interest in community safety can, in appropriate circumstances, outweigh an individual's liberty interest. [We] have found no absolute constitutional barrier to detention of potentially dangerous resident aliens pending deportation proceedings. Carlson v. Landon, 342 U.S. 524 (1952). We have also held that the government may detain mentally unstable individuals who present a danger to the public, Addington v. Texas, 441 U.S. 418 (1979), and dangerous defendants who become incompetent to stand trial, Jackson v. Indiana, 406 U.S. 715 (1972). We have approved of postarrest regulatory detention of juveniles when they present a continuing danger to the community. Schall v. Martin, 467 U.S. 253 (1984). Even competent adults may face substantial liberty restrictions as a result of the operation of our criminal justice system. If the police suspect an individual of a crime, they may arrest and hold him until a neutral magistrate determines whether probable cause exists. Gerstein v. Pugh, 420 U.S. 103 (1975). Finally, . . . an arrestee may be incarcerated until trial if he presents a risk of flight . . . or a danger to witnesses. . . .

Given the well-established authority of the government, in special circumstances, to restrain individuals' liberty prior to or even without criminal trial and conviction, we think that the present statute providing for pretrial detention on the basis of dangerousness must be evaluated in precisely the same manner that we evaluated the laws in the cases discussed above.

The government's interest in preventing crime by arrestees is both legitimate and compelling. In *Schall*, we recognized the strength of the State's interest in preventing juvenile crime. This general concern with crime prevention is no less compelling when the suspects are adults. . . . The Bail Reform Act of 1984 responds to an even more particularized governmental interest than the interest we sustained in *Schall*. The statute we upheld in *Schall* permitted pretrial detention of any juvenile arrested on any charge after a showing that the individual might commit some undefined further crimes. The Bail Reform Act, in contrast . . . operates only on individuals who have been arrested for a specific category of extremely serious offenses. Congress specifically found that these individuals are far more likely to be responsible for dangerous acts in the community after arrest. Nor is the Act by any means a scattershot attempt to incapacitate those who are merely suspected of these serious crimes. The Government must first of all demonstrate probable cause to believe that the charged crime has been committed by the arrestee, but that is not enough. In a full-blown adversary hearing, the Government must convince a neutral decisionmaker by clear and convincing evidence that no conditions of release can reasonably assure the safety of the community or any person. While the Government's general interest in preventing crime is compelling, even this interest is heightened when the Government musters convincing proof that the arrestee, already indicted or held to answer for a serious crime, presents a demonstrable danger to the community. Under these narrow circumstances, society's interest in crime prevention is at its greatest.

On the other side of the scale, of course, is the individual's strong interest in liberty. We do not minimize the importance and fundamental nature of this right. But, as our cases hold, this right may, in circumstances where the Government's interest is sufficiently weighty, be subordinated to the greater needs of society. We think that

Congress' careful delineation of the circumstances under which detention will be permitted satisfies this standard. When the Government proves by clear and convincing evidence that an arrestee presents an identified and articulable threat to an individual or the community, we believe that, consistent with the Due Process Clause, a court may disable the arrestee from executing that threat. . . .

B.

Respondents also contend that the Bail Reform Act violates the Excessive Bail Clause of the Eighth Amendment. . . . The Eighth Amendment addresses pretrial release by providing merely that "excessive bail shall not be required." This Clause, of course, says nothing about whether bail shall be available at all. Respondents nevertheless contend that this Clause grants them a right to bail calculated solely upon considerations of flight. They rely on Stack v. Boyle, 342 U.S. 1, 5 (1951), in which the Court stated that "bail set at a figure higher than an amount reasonably calculated [to ensure the defendant's presence at trial] is 'excessive' under the Eighth Amendment." In respondents' view, since the Bail Reform Act allows a court essentially to set bail at an infinite amount for reasons not related to the risk of flight, it violates the Excessive Bail Clause. Respondents concede that the right to bail they have discovered in the Eighth Amendment is not absolute. A court may, for example, refuse bail in capital cases. [A] court may [also] refuse bail when the defendant presents a threat to the judicial process by intimidating witnesses. Respondents characterize these exceptions as consistent with what they claim to be the sole purpose of bail—to ensure the integrity of the judicial process.

While we agree that a primary function of bail is to safeguard the courts' role in adjudicating the guilt or innocence of defendants, we reject the proposition that the Eighth Amendment categorically prohibits the government from pursuing other admittedly compelling interests through regulation of pretrial release. The above-quoted dictum in Stack v. Boyle is far too slender a reed on which to rest this argument. [The] statute before the Court in that case in fact allowed the defendants to be bailed. Thus, the Court had to determine only whether bail, admittedly available in that case, was excessive if set at a sum greater than that necessary to ensure the arrestees' presence at trial.

The holding of *Stack* is illuminated by the Court's holding just four months later in Carlson v. Landon, 342 U.S. 524 (1952). In that case, remarkably similar to the present action, the detainees had been arrested and held without bail pending a determination of deportability. The Attorney General refused to release the individuals, "on the ground that there was reasonable cause to believe that [their] release would be prejudicial to the public interest and would endanger the welfare and safety of the United States." The detainees brought the same challenge that respondents bring to us today: the Eighth Amendment required them to be admitted to bail. The Court squarely rejected this proposition: "The bail clause was lifted with slight changes from the English Bill of Rights Act. In England that clause has never been thought to accord a right to bail in all cases, but merely to provide that bail shall not be excessive in those cases where it is proper to grant bail." [342 U.S. at 545.]

Nothing in the text of the Bail Clause limits permissible Government considerations solely to questions of flight. The only arguable substantive limitation of the Bail Clause is that the Government's proposed conditions of release or detention not be "excessive" in light of the perceived evil. Of course, to determine whether the Government's response is excessive, we must compare that response against the interest the Government seeks to protect by means of that response. Thus, when the Government has admitted that its only interest is in preventing flight, bail must be set by a court at a sum designed to ensure that goal, and no more. We believe that when Congress has mandated detention on the basis of a compelling interest other than prevention of flight, as it has here, the Eighth Amendment does not require release on bail.

III.

In our society liberty is the norm, and detention prior to trial or without trial is the carefully limited exception. We hold that the provisions for pretrial detention in the Bail Reform Act of 1984 fall within that carefully limited exception. The Act authorizes the detention prior to trial of arrestees charged with serious felonies who are found after an adversary hearing to pose a threat to the safety of individuals or to the community which no condition of release can dispel. The numerous procedural safeguards detailed above must attend this adversary hearing. We are unwilling to say that this congressional determination, based as it is upon that primary concern of every government—a concern for the safety and indeed the lives of its citizens—on its face violates either the Due Process Clause of the Fifth Amendment or the Excessive Bail Clause of the Eighth Amendment. The judgment of the Court of Appeals is therefore reversed.

MARSHALL, J., dissenting.*

This case brings before the Court for the first time a statute in which Congress declares that a person innocent of any crime may be jailed indefinitely, pending the trial of allegations which are legally presumed to be untrue, if the Government shows to the satisfaction of a judge that the accused is likely to commit crimes, unrelated to the pending charges, at any time in the future. Such statutes, consistent with the usages of tyranny and the excesses of what bitter experience teaches us to call the police state, have long been thought incompatible with the fundamental human rights protected by our Constitution. . . .

II.

[In connection with the due process challenge,] the majority concludes that the Act is a regulatory rather than a punitive measure. The ease with which the conclusion is reached suggests the worthlessness of the achievement. . . . Let us apply the majority's reasoning to a similar, hypothetical case. After investigation, Congress determines (not unrealistically) that a large proportion of violent crime is perpetrated by persons who are unemployed. It also determines, equally reasonably, that much violent crime is committed at night. From amongst the panoply of "potential solutions," Congress chooses a statute which permits, after judicial proceedings, the imposition of a dusk-to-dawn curfew on anyone who is unemployed. Since this is not a measure enacted for the purpose of punishing the unemployed, and since the

---

* [Justice Brennan joined this opinion.—EDS.]

majority finds that preventing danger to the community is a legitimate regulatory goal, the curfew statute would, according to the majority's analysis, be a mere "regulatory" detention statute, entirely compatible with the substantive components of the Due Process Clause.

The absurdity of this conclusion arises, of course, from the majority's cramped concept of substantive due process. The majority proceeds as though the only substantive right protected by the Due Process Clause is a right to be free from punishment before conviction. The majority's technique for infringing this right is simple: merely redefine any measure which is claimed to be punishment as "regulation," and, magically, the Constitution no longer prohibits its imposition. . . .

The logic of the majority's Eighth Amendment analysis is equally unsatisfactory. . . . If excessive bail is imposed the defendant stays in jail. The same result is achieved if bail is denied altogether. Whether the magistrate sets bail at $1 billion or refuses to set bail at all, the consequences are indistinguishable. It would be mere sophistry to suggest that the Eighth Amendment protects against the former decision, and not the latter. Indeed, such a result would lead to the conclusion that there was no need for Congress to pass a preventive detention measure of any kind; every federal magistrate and district judge could simply refuse, despite the absence of any evidence of risk of flight or danger to the community, to set bail. . . .

III.

The essence of this case may be found, ironically enough, in a provision of the Act to which the majority does not refer. Title 18 U.S.C. §3142(j) provides that "nothing in this section shall be construed as modifying or limiting the presumption of innocence." But the very pith and purpose of this statute is an abhorrent limitation of the presumption of innocence. . . .

The statute does not authorize the Government to imprison anyone it has evidence is dangerous; indictment is necessary. But let us suppose that a defendant is indicted and the Government shows by clear and convincing evidence that he is dangerous and should be detained pending a trial, at which trial the defendant is acquitted. May the Government continue to hold the defendant in detention based upon its showing that he is dangerous? The answer cannot be yes, for that would allow the Government to imprison someone for uncommitted crimes based upon "proof" not beyond a reasonable doubt. The result must therefore be that once the indictment has failed, detention cannot continue. But our fundamental principles of justice declare that the defendant is as innocent on the day before his trial as he is on the morning after his acquittal. Under this statute an untried indictment somehow acts to permit a detention, based on other charges, which after an acquittal would be unconstitutional. The conclusion is inescapable that the indictment has been turned into evidence, if not that the defendant is guilty of the crime charged, then that left to his own devices he will soon be guilty of something else. . . .

IV.

Throughout the world today there are men, women, and children interned indefinitely, awaiting trials which may never come or which may be a mockery of the word, because their governments believe them to be "dangerous." Our Constitution, whose construction began two centuries ago, can shelter us forever from the evils of such unchecked power. Over 200 years it has slowly, through our efforts, grown more durable, more expansive, and more just. But it cannot protect us if we lack the courage, and the self-restraint, to protect ourselves. Today a majority of the Court applies itself to an ominous exercise in demolition. Theirs is truly a decision which will go forth without authority, and come back without respect. I dissent.

STEVENS, J., dissenting.

There may be times when the Government's interest in protecting the safety of the community will justify the brief detention of a person who has not committed any crime. [It] is indeed difficult to accept the proposition that the Government is without power to detain a person when it is a virtual certainty that he or she would otherwise kill a group of innocent people in the immediate future. Similarly, I am unwilling to decide today that the police may never impose a limited curfew during a time of crisis. These questions are obviously not presented in this case, but they lurk in the background and preclude me from answering the question that is presented in as broad a manner as Justice Marshall has. Nonetheless, I firmly agree with Justice Marshall that the provision of the Bail Reform Act allowing pretrial detention on the basis of future dangerousness is unconstitutional. . . . If the evidence of imminent danger is strong enough to warrant emergency detention, it should support that preventive measure regardless of whether the person has been charged, convicted, or acquitted of some other offense. . . .

■ NEW MEXICO CONSTITUTION ART. II, §13

All persons shall, before conviction, be bailable by sufficient sureties, except for capital offenses when the proof is evident or the presumption great and in situations in which bail is specifically prohibited by this section. Excessive bail shall not be required, nor excessive fines imposed, nor cruel and unusual punishment inflicted.

Bail may be denied by a court of record pending trial for a defendant charged with a felony if the prosecuting authority requests a hearing and proves by clear and convincing evidence that no release conditions will reasonably protect the safety of any other person or the community. . . . A person who is not detainable on grounds of dangerousness nor a flight risk in the absence of bond and is otherwise eligible for bail shall not be detained solely because of financial inability to post a money or property bond. . . .

■ VIRGINIA CODE §19.2-120

. . . A. A person who is held in custody pending trial or hearing for an offense, civil or criminal contempt, or otherwise shall be admitted to bail by a judicial officer, unless there is probable cause to believe that:

1. He will not appear for trial or hearing or at such other time and place as may be directed, or

2. His liberty will constitute an unreasonable danger to himself or the public.

B. The judicial officer shall presume, subject to rebuttal, that no condition or combination of conditions will reasonably assure the appearance of the person or the safety of the public if the person is currently charged with:

1. An act of violence as defined in [this Code];

2. An offense for which the maximum sentence is life imprisonment or death;

3. A violation . . . involving a Schedule I or II controlled substance if (i) the maximum term of imprisonment is ten years or more and the person was previously convicted of a like offense or (ii) the person was previously convicted as a "drug kingpin" as defined in [this Code];

4. A violation . . . which relates to a firearm and provides for a mandatory minimum sentence;

5. Any felony, if the person has been convicted of two or more offenses described in subdivision 1 or 2 . . . ;

6. Any felony committed while the person is on release pending trial for a prior felony under federal or state law or on release pending imposition or execution of sentence or appeal of sentence or conviction;

7. [Felony sexual assault] and the person had previously been convicted of [felony sexual assault] and the judicial officer finds probable cause to believe that the person who is currently charged with one of these offenses committed the offense charged;

8. A violation of [the statutes prohibiting the activities of criminal street gangs, acts of terrorism, or acts of bioterrorism against agricultural crops or animals]; or

9. A violation [involving driving while intoxicated] and the person has, within the past five years of the instant offense, been convicted three times on different dates of a violation of any combination of these Code sections, or any [similar ordinance or statute], and has been at liberty between each conviction. . . .

C. The judicial officer shall presume, subject to rebuttal, that no condition or combination of conditions will reasonably assure the appearance of the person or the safety of the public if the person is being arrested pursuant to [the enforcement of federal immigration laws].

Problem 12-2. The Next Danger

Yaser Mohammed Jawad was charged in Virginia with first degree murder and the use of a firearm in the commission of first degree murder. At the bail hearing, Antwoin Boyd, an eyewitness to the shooting, testified for the prosecution. Boyd testified that he saw Jawad come out of the store he owns and attempt to separate two men who were fighting. Jawad was yelling and cursing at the men. One of the men involved in the fighting, Benjamin Jones, started "fussing with Jawad face to face." The men yelled and spat at each other. At some point Jawad went back into his store and Jones started to walk to his car. But Jawad came back outside holding a handgun and shot the gun once in the air, then pinned Jones against the car. After Jones dared him three times to shoot, Jawad stepped back and shot Jones in the face, killing him. Jawad's attorney told the trial court that there would be a factual question at trial about "whether or not the defendant was the aggressor or whether the alleged victim engaged in conduct that brought about his own demise."

Jawad testified on his own behalf at the bail hearing. According to his testimony, he has never "failed to appear for anything in court" and intends "to appear for all court appearances" in this case. He is married to an American citizen and lives with his wife, 14 month-old son, father, mother, and brother in a home in Chesapeake. He has lived in the United States consistently for eight years and in Chesapeake for three years. He has no immediate family still living in Pakistan and owns no property there. Nearly 32 years of age, he is in good physical health, has never been treated for any mental conditions, and has never abused drugs or alcohol. He has no prior criminal record, and he voluntarily surrendered his passport.

Robert Lindemann, the family's business attorney who had been practicing law for 23 years, testified to Jawad's reputation for honesty and fair dealing. He opined that Jawad would not flee and would comply with all terms of bond.

Imagine that you are the trial judge in this case, and you must decide whether to set bail under the terms of Virginia Code §19.2-120, reprinted above. Subsection (b) of the statute creates a presumption against the granting of bail. How would that presumption figure into your ruling on Jawad's release? Jawad's attorney has argued that a "presumption" against bail based simply on the seriousness of the charge he faces is inconsistent with the due process protections discussed in United States v. Salerno, 481 U.S. 739 (1987). Is this argument consistent with your reading of *Salerno*?

If you decide to release Jawad, what factual findings will best insulate that ruling from reversal on appeal? What financial and nonfinancial conditions would you place on his release? For a comparison point of typical bail amounts, see *http://www.bjs.gov/content/pub/pdf/fdluc09.pdf*, at Table 15. Cf. Commonwealth v. Jawad, 2002 WL 31655285 (Va. App. 2002).

Notes

1. *Preventive detention: majority position.* Like the federal system, most states authorize courts to detain defendants before trial for the purpose of preventing the commission of new crimes ("preventive detention"). See, e.g., Mass. Gen. L. ch. 276, §58A. On the other hand, a substantial minority of states have constitutional provisions that guarantee the right to bail in non-capital cases. See Fry v. State, 990 N.E.2d 429 (Ind. 2013) (strikes down law requiring defendant to show that guilt is not evident, because allocation of burden to accused is inconsistent with state constitution's presumption of bail); Ariana Lindermayer, What the Right Hand Gives: Prohibitive Interpretations of the State Constitutional Right to Bail, 78 Fordham L. Rev. 267 (2009).

Among states that authorize detention, the details of their statutes and constitutions vary substantially. Some states limit preventive detention to "serious crimes"; others limit detention to offenders with specific combinations of prior record and sufficiently serious current charges. A handful of states have enacted limits on the maximum time a defendant may be detained to prevent crimes. See, e.g., Mass. Gen. L. ch. 276, §58A (120 days); Wis. Stat. §969.035 (60 days). For a taxonomy of the state statutes that authorize pretrial detention and an analysis of trends, see the web extension for this chapter at *http://www.crimpro.com/extension/ch12*.

2. *Presumption of innocence.* The justices in *Salerno* disagreed about the meaning of the presumption of innocence. See Daniel Richman, *United States v. Salerno*: The

Constitutionality of Regulatory Detention, in Criminal Procedure Stories (Carol Steiker ed., 2006). A critic of the majority opinion might draw a comparison to the following passage from Lewis Carroll's *Through the Looking Glass*, where the Queen and Alice discuss the consequences of having a memory that works both ways:

> "What sort of things do you remember best?" Alice ventured to ask.
>
> "Oh, things that happened the week after next," the Queen replied in a careless tone.
>
> "For instance, now," she went on, sticking a large piece of plaster on her finger as she spoke, "there's the King's Messenger. He's in prison now, being punished: and the trial doesn't even begin till next Wednesday: and of course the crime comes last of all."
>
> "Suppose he never commits the crime?" said Alice.
>
> "That would be all the better, wouldn't it?" the Queen said, as she bound the plaster round her finger with a bit of ribbon.
>
> Alice felt there was no denying that. "Of course it would be all the better," she said: "but it wouldn't be all the better his being punished."
>
> "You're wrong there, at any rate," said the Queen: "Were you ever punished?"
>
> "Only for faults," said Alice.
>
> "And you were all the better for it, I know!" the Queen said triumphantly.
>
> "Yes, but then I had done the things I was punished for," said Alice: "that makes all the difference."
>
> "But if you hadn't done them," the Queen said, "that would have been better still; better, and better, and better!" . . .

Is this the message of the *Salerno* opinion? If not, in what sense can we say that *Salerno* respects the presumption of innocence? See Sandra G. Mayson, Dangerous Defendants, 127 Yale L.J. 490 (2018) (describing a "third generation" of bail reform that relies less on money bail and more on risk assessment tools to reduce pretrial detention; arguing that status of detainee as criminal defendant should add no weight to the determination of level of risk that supports detention).

3. *Limitation to serious felonies and repeat offenders.* Most of the states passing new statutory or constitutional provisions to allow preventive detention have limited its use to criminal defendants who are accused of committing a select group of serious or violent felonies. See Mendonza v. Commonwealth, 673 N.E.2d 22 (Mass. 1996) (upholding revised statute under federal and state constitutions because it applies to felonies involving the use, or threatened use, of violence or abuse, or the violation of protective orders). Some, like the New Mexico constitutional provision above, apply only to those accused of a felony who have also been convicted of one or more felonies in the past. See also Colo. Const. art. II, §19 (new bail denied to those accused of committing violent crime while on prior bail, parole, or probation for previous charges of violent crime). Do both the "serious crime" and "repeat offender" limitations serve the same purpose? Another variety of selective detention statutes applies only to defendants accused of a particularly high-priority crime, such as stalking or domestic violence. See Ill. Rev. Stat. ch. 725, para. 5/110-4.

Imagine that you are a state legislator, serving on a committee to consider changes to pretrial detention practices in your state. Do you read *Salerno* to impose any limits on the seriousness of crimes that can form the basis for pretrial detention? Do you prefer the Virginia statute, the New Mexico constitutional provision, or the Tennessee constitutional provision (all reprinted above)? What particular facts would you like your staff to gather for you before you vote on any proposed changes?

4. *How many defendants are detained?* The number of defendants detained in the federal system is creeping upward. Among federal defendants in 1983 (the year before the passage of the Bail Reform Act), 24 percent remained in custody until their prosecutions were completed. In 1985 the figure rose to 29 percent (including those who failed to make bail and those who were ordered detained). In 2014 over 71 percent of federal defendants were detained until the disposition of their cases. Bureau of Justice Statistics, Federal Justice Statistics, 2014—Statistical Tables, at Table 3.1 (March 2017, NCJ 250183). The story is quite different in the state systems: In large counties in 2009, only 38 percent of felony defendants were detained until case disposition. See *https://www.bjs.gov/content/pub/pdf/fdluc09.pdf*, at Table 12. These national average statistics obscure some real differences among jurisdictions.

What is the proper practical balance between the 1960s reform encouraging presumptive release and the 1980s reform encouraging open detention for those who threaten harm? Does detention until trial of almost two-thirds of those charged with felonies in the federal system seem too high? Does the federal system reflect the victory of candor? Is open preventive detention preferable to continued sub rosa detention through unrealistically high bail requirements in states where there is no legal authority to detain defendants for the purpose of protecting the public from the commission of additional crimes?

The rate of pretrial detention varies from country to country. For instance, Canada detains a higher proportion of its defendants than the United States, while Germany, England, and Finland detain a smaller percentage. See Justice Policy Institute, Fact Sheet: Pretrial Detention and Remand to Custody (April 2011). What features of a legal system (or what other social characteristics) might best explain international variations in pretrial detention? For further background to compare practices in other nations, see the web extension for this chapter at *http://www.crim-pro.com/extension/ch12*.

5. *Compensation for wrongful detention.* Should the government compensate people who are detained under the Bail Reform Act or analogous state statutes and are later found at trial to be not guilty? See Masson v. Netherlands, 22 EHRR 491 (1996) (European Court of Human Rights reviewing domestic law that allows civil court, after a failure to convict a suspect in criminal proceedings, to grant compensation at expense of the state for damage suffered as a result of wrongful pretrial detention).

6. *Civil detention after completion of sentence.* States now use post-sentence detention to extend their control over some persons convicted of sex offenses. Statutes commonly authorize the government to request continued detention of convicted sex offenders after they have completed their sentences. These statutes typically require the government to demonstrate, on a year-to-year basis, that the offender remains "dangerous." The Supreme Court has upheld statutes against challenges based on the due process, ex post facto, and double jeopardy clauses of the federal constitution. Kansas v. Hendricks, 521 U.S. 346 (1997). Employing the same distinction that it used in *Salerno*, the Court said that this detention was "regulatory" rather than "punitive." See also Kansas v. Crane, 534 U.S. 407 (2002) (Constitution does not require judicial finding of total or complete lack of control to support regulatory detention of sexual offender, but Constitution does require a showing that person lacks some control over his or her behavior); United States v. Comstock,

560 U.S. 126 (2010) (necessary and proper clause gives Congress authority to enact civil commitment statute that authorizes detention of sexually dangerous, mentally ill federal prisoners).

7. *Detention of excludable aliens.* In Zadvydas v. Davis, 533 U.S. 678 (2001), the Supreme Court interpreted a statute that, according to the government, allowed an alien who is subject to a final order of removal to be detained beyond a 90-day statutory "removal period" at the discretion of the attorney general. The Court construed the statute narrowly to avoid constitutional problems, and observed that as a matter of due process aliens could not be detained indefinitely following a final order of removal and that the attorney general had to justify continued detention. Two years later, however, the Court in Demore v. Kim, 538 U.S. 510 (2003), upheld a statute requiring mandatory detention for deportable criminal aliens, as applied to a lawful permanent resident who entered the United States at age six and was convicted of burglary and "petty theft with priors." Might it have been significant that the Court decided *Demore* a year and a half after the terrorist attack of September 11, 2001?

8. *Detention in the terrorism context.* The ongoing efforts to resolve the questions surrounding detainees at Guantanamo Bay, together with the lively debate about the legitimacy of the government's use of the material witness statute as a detention device, receive fuller treatment on the web extension to this chapter at *http://www. crimpro.com/extension/ch12.*

To what extent do government practices that develop in response to threats from terrorists ultimately spread to more ordinary anti-crime contexts? Scholars sometimes try to answer this question historically, by studying government responses to various emergencies around the world over the years. For instance, some criminologists characterize the government response to violence in Northern Ireland as a "contagion." According to this thesis, Northern Ireland served as a testing ground for repressive police practices that would later spread elsewhere to extend the authority of the state. See Aogàn Mulcahy, The "Other" Lessons from Ireland? Policing, Political Violence and Policy Transfer, 2 Eur. J. Criminology 185 (2005) (based on qualitative interview data about impact of Northern Ireland conflict, assessing both the contagion thesis and more positive lessons other jurisdictions learned from the conflict); Oren Gross, Chaos and Rules: Should Responses to Violent Crises Always Be Constitutional?, 112 Yale L.J. 1011 (2003) (collecting studies of impact of conflict in Northern Ireland and other prolonged "emergency" settings).

9. *The revenge of social science.* Social science studies were the driving force behind legal changes to make pretrial release easier and less dependent on money bail. Similarly, social science figured prominently in the movement to expand the power of judges to detain defendants before trial. Later, social science supported the movement away from money bail toward risk assessment instruments.

Over the decades, we have reduced (and then increased, and then reduced) the number of people who are detained. Moreover, we have changed the acceptable reasons for detaining persons, allowing the detention of some defendants who at one time would have been released on bail. Do we now have it just about right? Are we now detaining the right people?

XIII

![black square]

Charging

Soon after arrest, suspects learn why they have been detained. Most often, this occurs when the arresting officer files a form (sometimes called a complaint, sometimes an investigation report) proposing criminal charges to be filed against the arrestee. Those charges are subject to change at many points later in the process. A prosecutor ordinarily decides whether to accept the police officer's proposed charge and files a "complaint" or an "information." In some states, and for some types of cases, a grand jury hears the evidence and issues an indictment to initiate the charges.

A judicial officer reviews the charges at an initial appearance, a hearing that is given various names in different jurisdictions. This hearing takes place within a short period (typically 48 hours, or some other time defined by rule or statute). See Gerstein v. Pugh, 420 U.S. 103 (1975) (Fourth Amendment requires judicial hearing shortly after arrest to determine probable cause to support that arrest). The charges can change at a later hearing known as an arraignment, when the defendant indicates how he or she will plead, or at a hearing to test the adequacy of the evidence for trial, sometimes known as a "preliminary examination" or "probable cause hearing."

You might think of the charging process as a set of screens following investigation: Various government institutions help decide which persons in custody will become criminal defendants and which charges they will face. The arresting police officer and the officer's supervisor have some input into the charging decision. Prosecuting attorneys usually have the most important voice in determining whether to charge and what charges to select.

Courts are usually less involved in the charging decision than in most other procedural choices. Much of the time, courts review charging decisions only to confirm that there is a minimal amount of evidence supporting the charge, enough to justify "binding over" the case for trial. Judges explain their reluctance to become involved in charging decisions on three grounds: (1) under the separation of powers doctrine, the executive branch has the responsibility to enforce the criminal law; (2) judges are poorly situated to make judgments about allocation of limited prosecutorial resources; and (3) overbroad provisions in criminal codes require selection from among the possible charges that could be filed, based on grounds apart from the sufficiency of the evidence.

The prosecutor might follow personal criteria, policies and principles established for the office, or (less frequently) statutes dictating the charging decision. Because the prosecutor's choices dominate the charging phase, we concentrate in this chapter on sources of law other than appellate opinions, statutes, and rules. As you survey the charging process, ask whether the various executive branch guidelines and practices at work here are comparable in any way—in origins, function, evolution, and so on—to the way legislatures and courts craft rules.

A. INDIVIDUAL PROSECUTOR DISCRETION NOT TO CHARGE

Prosecutors (who go by various names, such as "district attorneys," "county attorneys," "state's attorneys," or simply "prosecuting attorneys") have the most to say about whether to file charges against a suspect and which charges to select. Granted, they react to an initial charge proposed by the police, and they may have to convince a judge or a grand jury that there is enough evidence to justify going forward with a prosecution. But in the end, the prosecutor can overrule police charging decisions without interference, and judges and grand juries only rarely refuse to support the prosecutor's charging decisions.

■ REVISED CODE OF WASHINGTON §9.94A.411(1)

STANDARD

A prosecuting attorney may decline to prosecute, even though technically sufficient evidence to prosecute exists, in situations where prosecution would serve no public purpose, would defeat the underlying purpose of the law in question or would result in decreased respect for the law.

GUIDELINE/COMMENTARY

. . . The following are examples of reasons not to prosecute which could satisfy the standard.

(a) Contrary to Legislative Intent—It may be proper to decline to charge where the application of criminal sanctions would be clearly contrary to the intent of the legislature in enacting the particular statute.

(b) Antiquated Statute—It may be proper to decline to charge where the statute in question is antiquated in that: (i) it has not been enforced for many years; and (ii) most members of society act as if it were no longer in existence; and (iii) it serves no deterrent or protective purpose in today's society; and (iv) the statute has not been recently reconsidered by the legislature. This reason is not to be construed as the basis for declining cases because the law in question is unpopular or because it is difficult to enforce.

(c) De Minimis Violation—It may be proper to decline to charge where the violation of law is only technical or insubstantial and where no public interest or deterrent purpose would be served by prosecution.

(d) Confinement on Other Charges—It may be proper to decline to charge because the accused has been sentenced on another charge to a lengthy period of confinement; and (i) conviction of the new offense would not merit any additional direct or collateral punishment; (ii) the new offense is either a misdemeanor or a felony which is not particularly aggravated; and (iii) conviction of the new offense would not serve any significant deterrent purpose.

(e) Pending Conviction on Another Charge—It may be proper to decline to charge because the accused is facing a pending prosecution in the same or another county; and (i) conviction of the new offense would not merit any additional direct or collateral punishment; (ii) conviction in the pending prosecution is imminent; (iii) the new offense is either a misdemeanor or a felony which is not particularly aggravated; and (iv) conviction of the new offense would not serve any significant deterrent purpose.

(f) High Disproportionate Cost of Prosecution—It may be proper to decline to charge where the cost of locating or transporting, or the burden on, prosecution witnesses is highly disproportionate to the importance of prosecuting the offense in question. This reason should be limited to minor cases and should not be relied upon in serious cases.

(g) Improper Motives of Complainant—It may be proper to decline charges because the motives of the complainant are improper and prosecution would serve no public purpose, would defeat the underlying purpose of the law in question or would result in decreased respect for the law.

(h) Immunity—It may be proper to decline to charge where immunity is to be given to an accused in order to prosecute another where the accused's information or testimony will reasonably lead to the conviction of others who are responsible for more serious criminal conduct or who represent a greater danger to the public interest.

(i) Victim Request—It may be proper to decline to charge because the victim requests that no criminal charges be filed and the case involves the following crimes or situations: (i) assault cases where the victim has suffered little or no injury; (ii) crimes against property, not involving violence, where no major loss was suffered; (iii) where doing so would not jeopardize the safety of society. Care should be taken to insure that the victim's request is freely made and is not the product of threats or pressure by the accused. . . . The prosecutor is encouraged to notify the victim, when practical, and the law enforcement personnel, of the decision not to prosecute.

Notes

1. *Two charging questions.* Prosecutors in the United States think about the charging decision in two stages. First, they ask whether there is enough admissible evidence to predict a reasonable likelihood of success at trial, proving each element of the charged crime beyond a reasonable doubt. Second, they ask whether a criminal conviction in the case would do justice: Would it further the purposes of the criminal justice system, promote public safety, and make the best available use of limited

resources in the courts and the prosecutor's office? Put another way, a prosecutor asks not only, "Am I authorized to file charges?" but also "Should I file charges?" Prosecutors in many different regions and types of offices use this two-stage process to describe their thinking at the point of charging. The same considerations remain on the prosecutor's mind when deciding whether to dismiss charges after filing, or whether to propose a plea agreement. See Bruce Frederick & Don Stemen, The Anatomy of Discretion: An Analysis of Prosecutorial Decision Making—Technical Report (National Institute of Justice 2012); Ronald F. Wright & Kay L. Levine, The Cure for Young Prosecutors' Syndrome, 56 Ariz. L. Rev. 1065 (2014) (describing the emphasis that mature prosecutors place on the second question).

2. *Reasons for declinations.* Over the years, several scholars, commissions, and associations have described some common reasons for individual prosecutors to choose not to file criminal charges in a particular case. Frank Miller offered one such list of reasons why prosecutors decline to file charges: negative attitude of the victim, cost to the system, undue harm to the suspect, adequacy of alternative procedures, and willingness of the suspect to cooperate in achieving other enforcement goals. See Frank Miller, Prosecution: The Decision to Charge a Suspect with a Crime (1969). The National District Attorneys Association, in its National Prosecution Standards manual, §42.3 (2d ed. 1991), advances several possible grounds for a prosecutor to decline a criminal case, including "doubt as to the accused's guilt," "possible improper motives of a victim or witness," "undue hardship caused to the accused," "the expressed desire of an accused to release potential civil claims against victims, witnesses, law enforcement agencies and their personnel, and the prosecutor and his personnel," and "any mitigating circumstances." How do these reasons compare to those in the Washington statute reprinted above?

How often do prosecutors actually rely on these plausible reasons for declination? Taking the federal landscape first, in 2003, federal prosecutors gave the following reasons for their declinations: no crime committed (22 percent of the declinations), matter handled in other prosecutions (21 percent), pretrial diversion (1.6 percent), weak evidence (22 percent), minimal federal interest (3.6 percent), U.S. Attorney policy (2.7 percent), lack of resources (5.7 percent), and several others. See Michael Edmund O'Neill, Understanding Federal Prosecutorial Declinations: An Empirical Analysis of Predicative Factors, 41 Am. Crim. L. Rev. 1439 (2004).

Data for state systems are sketchier. According to one study of prosecution data from New Orleans during the 1990s, prosecutors explained that 38 percent of the charges they declined to prosecute were not necessary because they were "prosecuting on other charges." Various evidentiary flaws in the charges accounted for 26 percent of the declinations, while concerns about the victim of the crime explained 18 percent of the charges declined. Marc L. Miller & Ronald F. Wright, The Black Box, 94 Iowa L. Rev. 125 (2008).

3. *Number of declinations.* The precise number of criminal matters that are declined for prosecution each year is hard to pin down, but in the federal system, where the best data are available, U.S. Attorneys' offices decline to prosecute a large proportion of criminal matters they receive. In 2010, for example, federal prosecutors filed charges in only 49 percent of the "criminal matters" referred to them for investigation or prosecution; they declined to prosecute 16 percent of the matters

and referred 35 percent of the suspects to federal magistrates (who handle misdemeanors and charges that are ultimately sent to state court).

The percentage of police reports that result in declinations in the typical state system is similarly significant. In large urban counties in 2009, for instance, charges were dismissed for 25 percent of all defendants initially arrested on a felony charge. Bureau of Justice Statistics, Felony Defendants in Large Urban Counties, 2009, Table 21 (December 2013, NCJ 243777). Of course, the dismissal rate does not capture the total number of *arrests* declined for prosecution.

4. *Judicial review of declinations and decisions to file charges.* At common law, each local prosecutor had complete discretion to refuse to file charges or to dismiss charges after they had been filed. See Wilson v. Renfroe, 91 So. 2d 857 (Fla. 1956). Judges might overturn a prosecutor's decision to file charges or not to file charges, but only in rare circumstances. See State v. Foss, 556 N.W.2d 540 (Minn. 1996) (acknowledging power of trial court to stay adjudication of guilt over prosecutor's objection in "special circumstances"; such circumstances existed in an earlier case involving consensual sex with 14-year-old when victim and her mother did not desire criminal prosecution, but no special circumstances exist in typical misdemeanor assault case).

5. *Dismissals after charges are filed.* At English common law, the power of the prosecutor to dismiss a charge—to enter a plea of *nolle prosequi*—was every bit as broad as the discretion to file charges initially. An illustration of this power appears in the following conversation between an advocate, Lacy, and Chief Justice John Holt in seventeenth-century England. Lacy asked the chief justice to dismiss seditious libel charges against other members of his religious sect:

> *Lacy:* I come to you, a prophet from the Lord God, who has sent me to thee, and would have thee grant a nolle prosequi for John Atkins, His servant, whom thou hast cast into prison.
>
> *Chief Justice Holt:* Thou art a false prophet, and a lying knave. If the Lord God had sent thee, it would have been to the attorney general, for He knows that it belongeth not to the Chief Justice to grant a nolle prosequi; but I, as Chief Justice, can grant a warrant to commit thee to bear him company.

See 2 Francis Wharton, A Treatise on Criminal Procedure §1310 (10th ed. 1918). This common-law rule on dismissals took hold in the United States and was especially useful in systems that allowed private prosecutors to file charges without consulting the public prosecutor. Today, however, a strong majority of jurisdictions (more than 30) give prosecutors less control over dismissals than over the initial decision whether to charge. They require the prosecutor to state reasons and obtain the court's permission before dismissing charges. See Mich. Comp. Laws §767.29; Fed. R. Crim. P. 48(a) (indictment, information or complaint can be dismissed "with leave of court"). For reasons you can well imagine, judges rarely deny a prosecutor's motion to dismiss charges.

6. *Police screening.* Police departments screen some cases out of the system before they ever send an investigative file to the prosecutor's office. Many police departments do not openly acknowledge that officers screen cases *after* arrest, even though almost all police officials recognize the substantial discretion of police officers in making arrest decisions. Some departments train officers to select certain kinds

of charges from among different possible charges. Other departments institute a formal screening process, either at the scene of an arrest or as part of the booking process at jail. This screening can take the form of review by a supervisor or by an officer trained to examine the facts of cases and the charges filed.

Many departments establish methods of pretransfer review by prosecutors. In Houston, for instance, trial lawyers staff the charging unit to answer inquiries from the police 24 hours a day. Police call from crime scenes and roadside stops for advice. Typically, the officers will not arrest or charge a suspect if the consulting prosecutor will not agree to accept charges. From the prosecutors' vantage point, this process serves the purpose of educating police officers about the proof required for conviction of various crimes; it also strengthens cases when the prosecutor advises the officer to take pictures, record statements, or pursue other investigative leads. Because the line prosecutors who receive the calls from the police must sign the charges they accept, they have some professional stake in the viability of the charges. They sometimes must persuade officers who are frustrated with belligerent suspects not to file charges based on that short-term frustration.

7. *Police-prosecutor cooperation in the charging decision.* In some jurisdictions, the police and the prosecutors pursue conflicting visions of the best charging practices. The police might evaluate cases in light of the probable cause standard necessary to support an arrest, indictment, or information, while the prosecutor might evaluate the case in light of the higher standard of proof required at trial. At a deeper level, police officers and prosecutors might differ about the value of courtroom expertise versus the value of investigative expertise. In jurisdictions that authorize police to file their proposed charges directly with the court, prosecutors still request early review of the proposed charges. See Natasha Lindstrom, Allegheny County DA Zappala Wants Police to Seek Prosecutor's Approval on Felony Charges, Pittsburgh Tribune-Review, Feb. 9, 2017. Why would prosecutors favor early review of charges, given that they have undisputed power to revise charges after the police file them? For examples of struggles between police and prosecutors over the initial filing of charges, see the web extension for this chapter at *http://www.crimpro.com/extension/ch13.*

8. *Police cautions in England.* Because the police in England make the initial decision whether to prosecute a criminal case, a practice has grown up (without a statutory basis) known as a "police caution." The caution is a warning to an arrested person, delivered by a senior police officer. If the person accepts the caution, the police agree not to refer the case to the Crown Prosecution Service. The caution becomes part of the offender's prior record. The Home Secretary has issued "National Standards for Cautioning" to guide police decisions in this area. See Home Office Circular 18/1994, The Cautioning of Offenders; Andrew Ashworth, The Criminal Process (2d ed. 1998). How does this "caution" differ from the common practice by law enforcement officers in the United States to issue a "warning" to a person without arresting or issuing a citation?

Problem 13-1. Three Variations on a Theme

You serve as an assistant district attorney assigned to the drug task force. Three files just landed on your desk.

- Brent Acheson: Arrested for selling five marijuana cigarettes to an undercover officer at a local bus station. Each cigarette weighed .15 ounces. Suspect is a 19-year-old student at the nearby community college and amateur competitive skateboarder. He graduated from a series of foster homes with his GED two years ago. He has one prior adult conviction for misdemeanor theft but local officers have heard a rumor that he may be involved in a major marijuana distribution ring. You also suspect he has a juvenile record, but it's sealed so you cannot access it.
- Freda Malledo: Arrested for possession with intent to sell six rocks of crack cocaine. Each rock weighed slightly less than one ounce. Suspect is a 22-year-old single mother of a 4-year-old son. She dropped out of high school. She has one prior conviction for possession with intent to sell a small amount of crack (stemming from a case in which her abusive boyfriend forced her to sell drugs to make money for him); she also has several prior arrests (but no convictions) for shoplifting.
- Jonas Gyllenson: Arrested for purchasing six rocks of crack cocaine from Malledo. Suspect is 45 years old, married, with four children. He is employed as a manager at a local grocery story. He has no prior record. When arrested, suspect said at first that he did not know what the rocks were, then said he did not know how they got into his pocket. Then he said he was buying the cocaine for a co-worker, then finally admitted that he has an addiction. The suspect's brother is a police officer in the jurisdiction.

What charges, if any, would you file? What sentencing outcomes, if any, would do justice as you see it? Consult the statutes below as you consider your choices.

Section 1. Possession of controlled substance, less than one ounce
Intentional possession of less than one ounce of any controlled substance is punishable by up to six months in county jail.

Section 2. Simple possession
Intentional possession of any amount of any controlled substance is punishable by up to one year in county jail or a term of imprisonment not more than two years in state prison.

Section 3. Transportation
Intentional transportation on pubic roadways of any controlled substance is punishable by up to one year in county jail or a term of imprisonment not more than four years in state prison. Transportation can occur on one's person or in a motorized or unmotorized vehicle.

Section 4. Possession with intent to distribute
Intentional possession of any controlled substance with the intent to distribute that substance to another person is a felony, punishable by a term of imprisonment not more than five years. For second offenses occurring within five years of the first conviction under this section, the maximum punishment shall be a term of imprisonment not more than eight years. It is no defense to this charge that the intended distribution was a gift. Intent to distribute may be inferred from the quantity of controlled substance the person possesses.

Section 5. Sales
Intentional sale of any controlled substance is a felony, punishable by a term of imprisonment not more than six years. For second offenses occurring within

five years of the first conviction under this section, the maximum punishment shall be a term of imprisonment not more than eight years.

Section 6. Operating a drug cartel

Any person who knowingly operates a sales enterprise to distribute controlled substances, consisting of three or more persons, shall be punished by a term of imprisonment not more than fifteen years.

Section 7. Affirmative defense

It shall be an affirmative defense to any possession crime charged under this article that the defendant possessed a valid prescription for the product in question, or was a licensed pharmacist acting within the scope of his or her employment. It shall be an affirmative defense to any distribution or sales crime charged under this article that the defendant was a licensed pharmacist acting within the scope of his or her employment.

Problem 13-2. Passing a School Bus

Helena Bannister is an 82-year-old grandmother with diabetes and a heart condition. On the afternoon of December 9, she was driving her sedan to the grocery store. She came up behind a school bus that was lawfully stopped to let children off. The bus was flashing its red lights and displaying stop signs on both sides. Bannister passed the school bus while children were crossing the road to reach the opposite curb. One such child was Javi Ramirez; Bannister's car struck and killed him. There is some dispute about whether Bannister's car first struck Javi while he was in the roadway or while he was on the sidewalk; when police arrived, they found his body on the sidewalk, several feet from Bannister's car.

The jurisdiction makes it a misdemeanor, punishable by up to one year in county jail, to pass a school bus that is displaying its flashing lights and stop signs. The jurisdiction also recognizes the misdemeanor-manslaughter rule for unintentional deaths that result from the commission of a misdemeanor. Misdemeanor-manslaughters are felonies, punishable by up to three years in prison.

You are an assistant district attorney. Bannister's attorney tells you that she is completely broken up about this and swears that she didn't see any children outside the bus. She promises not to drive again and has given up her license. What charges, if any, would you file against Bannister?

B. POLICIES TO ENCOURAGE OR MANDATE CHARGES

Should prosecutors pursue every crime brought to them? Could they?

This question has become particularly important in domestic violence cases. Many jurisdictions have restricted the power of prosecutors to decline or divert domestic assault cases, because these cases present distinctive challenges for prosecutors. "No-drop" prosecutorial policies combine with other systemwide policy initiatives regarding domestic assaults, including mandatory arrest policies, detention policies, and sentencing policies.

The scope of the domestic violence problem is daunting. Domestic violence is found at all socio-economic levels, among all races and age groups, and among people with all levels of education. More than one million American women are battered each year by their husbands or partners. National Institute of Justice, Crime, Violence and Victimization Research Division's Compendium of Research on Violence Against Women 1993-2013 (December 2013, NCJ 223572), available at https://www.ncjrs.gov/pdffiles1/nij/223572/223572.pdf.

Victims of abuse are often reluctant to testify in criminal cases against their partners, preferring that prosecutors drop the charges. Immediately following an assault, an abusive spouse is typically apologetic and attentive, promising to change. Later, tension builds and the abusive spouse becomes unpredictable and threatening again, often leading to another episode of battering. Victim advocates report that an abused woman will return to her partner an average of six times before she leaves permanently. A battered spouse is often isolated, having few friends or sources of support. She also might find the criminal process to be daunting and frustrating, particularly if the prosecutor fails to file serious charges in the case or delays its progress.

A prosecutor's office can address some of these problems by adopting a "no-drop" policy, mandating prosecution for all domestic violence cases filed. Such a policy takes the victim "off the hook" and insulates her from pressure to drop the case coming from her partner, family, and friends. These policies also emphasize that society at large has an interest in deterring domestic violence. Domestic violence can lead to murder or to injuries that require medical treatment. Children growing up in violent families are more likely to suffer from alcohol or drug abuse, and are more likely to commit violent crimes themselves later in life.

The Florida and Wisconsin statutes reprinted below offer different responses to the special problems of domestic violence. The remaining materials in this section—from Italy, Germany, West Virginia, and the United Kingdom—place the issue of mandatory prosecution in a more general context. They reveal the unique discretion of prosecutors in the United States to decline to file charges, and explore how judges or other actors might exercise greater supervision over the prosecutor's declination decision.

■ FLORIDA STATUTES §741.2901

(1) Each state attorney shall develop special units or assign prosecutors to specialize in the prosecution of domestic violence cases, but such specialization need not be an exclusive area of duty assignment. These prosecutors, specializing in domestic violence cases, and their support staff shall receive training in domestic violence issues.

(2) It is the intent of the Legislature that domestic violence be treated as a criminal act rather than a private matter. . . . The state attorney in each circuit shall adopt a pro-prosecution policy for acts of domestic violence. . . . The filing, nonfiling, or diversion of criminal charges, and the prosecution of violations of injunctions for protection against domestic violence by the state attorney, shall be

determined by these specialized prosecutors over the objection of the victim, if necessary. . . .

■ WISCONSIN STATUTES §968.075

(7) Each district attorney's office shall develop, adopt and implement written policies encouraging the prosecution of domestic abuse offenses. The policies shall include, but not be limited to, the following:

(a) A policy indicating that a prosecutor's decision not to prosecute a domestic abuse incident should not be based:

1. Solely upon the absence of visible indications of injury or impairment;

2. Upon the victim's consent to any subsequent prosecution of the other person involved in the incident; or

3. Upon the relationship of the persons involved in the incident.

(b) A policy indicating that when any domestic abuse incident is reported to the district attorney's office, including a report [which police officers are required by law to submit after responding to a domestic abuse incident], a charging decision by the district attorney should, absent extraordinary circumstances, be made not later than two weeks after the district attorney has received notice of the incident. . . .

(9) Each district attorney shall submit an annual report to the department of justice listing [the] number of arrests for domestic abuse incidents in his or her county as compiled and furnished by the law enforcement agencies within the county [and the] number of subsequent prosecutions and convictions of the persons arrested for domestic abuse incidents. . . .

■ ITALIAN CONSTITUTION ART. 112

The public prosecutor has the duty to exercise criminal proceedings.

■ GERMAN CODE OF CRIMINAL PROCEDURE 152(2)

[The public prosecutor] is required . . . to take action against all judicially punishable . . . acts, to the extent that there is a sufficient factual basis. [Translator: John Langbein]

■ WEST VIRGINIA CODE §7-4-1

It shall be the duty of the prosecuting attorney to attend to the criminal business of the State in the county in which he is elected and qualified, and when he has information of the violation of any penal law committed within such county, he shall institute and prosecute all necessary and proper proceedings against the offender, and may in such case issue or cause to be issued a summons for any witness he may deem material. . . .

■ THE QUESTION ON THE APPLICATION OF PETER DENNIS v. DPP

High Court of Justice Queen's Bench Division Administrative Court [2006]
EWHC 3211 (Admin)

LORD JUSTICE WALLER:

1 This is an application for judicial review by the claimant Mr Peter Dennis in respect of the decision of the Crown Prosecution Service Gwent Area . . . not to bring prosecutions for gross negligence manslaughter arising out of the death of the claimant's son, Daniel Dennis, in an industrial accident on the 8th April 2003.

2 Daniel Dennis was 17 years of age when, on the 1st April 2003, he started work as a labourer with Roy Clarke, who traded under the name of North Eastern Roofing. Work was being carried out on the refurbishment of buildings at a retail park in Cwmbran, Gwent, South Wales. . . Daniel Dennis was in his second week of working for North Eastern Roofing when he fell through a roof light to his death. . . .

5 The claimant maintains that this was his son's first job working at heights or on roofs, that he had no experience of so doing . . . . He is critical of the fact that no training, relevant to working at heights or on roofs or round roof lights, was provided, no safety equipment was provided, nor were there any safety measures in place to restrict access to the roof or to mark off particular dangerous areas of the roof. It is said that no steps had been taken to comply with statutory obligations including those relating to designated safe walkways, fencing off of vulnerable points and the provision of suitable safety equipment.

6 On the 15th March 2005 an inquest was held before the Coroner for Gwent and a jury. The inquest heard evidence from the claimant, Mr Clarke, [Mr Dennis's co-workers Jason Ryan and Cain Hayes], a pathologist and Mr Baker of the Health and Safety Executive (HSE). [The jury] were directed that their verdict could not identify any individuals having criminal or civil responsibility and that the criminal standard of proof was to be applied in considering whether the death was an unlawful killing. The jury returned a unanimous verdict of unlawful killing.

7 In August 2004 the HSE took a decision to prosecute . . . North East Roofing for offences under the Health and Safety at Work Act 1974. . . .

8 Even before the inquest solicitors acting for the family of Daniel Dennis had raised with the defendant the possibility of criminal charges arising out of his death. On the 6th April 2005, following the verdict of the Coroner's jury, the claimant's solicitors made detailed submissions to the defendant to the effect that there was an abundance of evidence to support manslaughter charges against Mr Clarke. On the 23rd August 2005 Mr Ian Griffiths, a solicitor in the Crown Prosecution Service, wrote to the claimant's solicitors stating that the case failed to satisfy the evidential test of the Code for Crown Prosecutors. Mr Griffiths . . . had advised the police that there was no realistic prospect of a successful conviction and he had not gone on to consider the public interest test under the applicable Code. [Mr Griffiths explained his decision as follows]:

> Whilst I am satisfied that Roy Clarke and Jason Ryan had a duty of care towards the deceased and, further, whilst I am satisfied that Clarke and Ryan were in breach of that duty, I remain firmly of the opinion that the degree of negligence exhibited was not such as to amount to criminal negligence. The following factors were of influence: . . .

1. The suggestion that the deceased had some experience in the building trade. I accept that this was a suggestion made by Roy Clarke in his [interview with authorities under the Police and Criminal Evidence Act 1984, or "PACE" interview]. I also accept that there was no other evidence to this effect. . . .

2. That both Clarke and Caine Hayes indicated that the deceased had been told specifically not to go anywhere near the sky lights. Both Caine Hayes and Jason Ryan gave evidence to the inquest jury that they believed they had told the deceased specifically not to go near sky lights. Although their evidence was somewhat "watered down" from their PACE interviews they both believed that they had made reference to sky lights and the dangers inherent in going on or near them. Roy Clarke in his PACE interview clearly indicates that the deceased had been told not to go near the sky lights. Even if it is accepted that the deceased received general advice rather than a direction this again goes to the degree of negligence and would not have changed my opinion. . . .

4. That there was no reason for the deceased to have gone onto the roof in any event. Again, there is no evidence available that the deceased was instructed to go onto the roof or that it was suggested that he might do so to render assistance to his colleagues. There may have been "nothing unusual" about him going onto the roof and it may have been foreseeable that he might go onto the roof but again this goes to the degree of negligence involved. . . .

20 Mr Hermer, [appellate counsel for the family of the deceased], submitted that he could show that the CPS had failed to follow their own procedures and had failed to consider important evidence or had clearly wrongly analysed important evidence. He submitted that in the result he could establish a failure to act in accordance with the CPS code and he submitted that that would entitle the claimant to succeed in obtaining an order requiring the CPS to reconsider the matter. . . .

22 The code demonstrates that the decision to prosecute follows a two stage process: the evidential stage and then, if the evidence is sufficient, the public policy stage. In this case we are concerned with the evidential stage, the decision of the CPS in this case being that the evidence was not sufficient to warrant prosecution. The relevant paragraphs of the code read as follows:—

5.2 Crown Prosecutors must be satisfied that there is enough evidence to provide a "realistic prospect of conviction" against each defendant on each charge. They must consider what the defence case may be, and how that is likely to affect the prosecution case.

5.3 A realistic prospect of conviction is an objective test. It means that a jury or bench of magistrates or judge hearing a case alone, properly directed in accordance with the law, is more likely than not to convict the defendant of the charge alleged. This is a separate test from the one that the criminal courts themselves must apply. A court should only convict if satisfied so that it is sure of a defendant's guilt.

5.4 When deciding whether there is enough evidence to prosecute, Crown prosecutors must consider whether the evidence can be used and is reliable. . . . What explanation has the defendant given? Is a court likely to find it credible in the light of the evidence as a whole? Does it support an innocent explanation? . . . Is the witness's background likely to weaken the prosecution case? For example, does the witness have any motive that may affect his or her attitude to the case, or a relevant previous conviction? . . .

30 My approach to the arguments in the instant case, guided by the above authorities, is as follows. First, if it can be demonstrated on an objective appraisal

of the case that a serious point or serious points supporting a prosecution have not been considered, that will give a ground for ordering reconsideration of the decision. Second, if it can be demonstrated that in a significant area a conclusion as to what the evidence is to support a prosecution is irrational, that will provide a ground. Third, the points have to be such as to make it seriously arguable that the decision would otherwise be different, but the decision is one for the prosecutor and not for this court. Indeed it is important to bear that fact in mind at all stages. Fourth, where an inquest jury has found unlawful killing the reasons why a prosecution should not follow need to be clearly expressed. . . .

32 Mr Hermer took us to evidence that was before Mr Griffiths [in the form of police interviews] to the following effect (i) that Roy Clarke owned North East Roofing and was the boss . . . (ii) that on the morning of the accident Roy Clarke had instructed Daniel Dennis to go onto the roof to work with Caine Hayes and that Roy Clarke had told Daniel to work on the roof on a number of occasions since 1st April when Daniel started . . . (iii) that the scaffold had been used as a means of access by Roy Clarke, Jason Ryan, Caine Hayes and Daniel and that Daniel had been on the roof on at least two occasions . . . (iv) Daniel had received no induction course or training . . .

33 He took us to the PACE interview of Roy Clarke. Roy Clarke began by asserting that he was not Daniel's employer; he also asserted that Daniel had worked in the building trade before; he asserted that Daniel was told not to go near the roof lights; he asserted that the only time Daniel went on the roof was at the time of the accident, and he asserted that there was no need for Daniel to go on the roof as the timber was in the gutter near the scaffolding.

34 It was then put to Roy Clarke that there were statements saying that Daniel was on the roof earlier and that Clarke had given instructions to clear the roof. He then accepted that he had given instructions to Daniel to go onto the roof to tidy. . . .

37 Mr Hermer then came back to the [factors described by Mr Griffiths in his letter to Mr Dennis. He began with factor 4]. He submitted that there was evidence of reasons why Daniel might go on the Matalan roof; Roy Clarke had instructed him to go on the roof as part of his job and had never instructed him not to go on the roof. The scaffolding up to the . . . roof had been used by Roy Clarke, with Daniel . . . . It was obviously foreseeable that he would go on the [roof].

39 As regards factor (1), the suggestion that Daniel had "some experience in the building trade" was a suggestion of Roy Clarke's and contrary to the evidence.

40 As regards factor (2), the factor has an oddity in that why would Daniel be told not to go near skylights if Roy Clarke was otherwise asserting that he was being told not to go on the roof? But, in any event, the evidence that he was ever told about the danger of skylights was very weak and not in the language of an instruction. It is evidence, in any event, which a jury might well not accept. . . .

41 Mr Jarman defended Mr Griffiths' . . . factors. He took us to a file note made by Mr Griffiths [and] demonstrated by reference to that note that Mr Griffiths was aware of the possibility that Daniel had been instructed by Roy Clarke to go on the roof as part of his work. Mr Griffiths was sceptical of the assertion that Daniel had been told specifically not to go any where near skylights, picking up the point that if the new roof did not have skylights, why was this warning being given? Further Mr Jarman submitted that if one focused on the particular moment when Daniel went up on the roof just before his accident, "there was no reason for [him] to have got onto the roof." . . .

43 It seems to me that, whatever the file note may show, Mr Griffiths has not dealt in his reasons with the real thrust of any case that might be brought against Mr Clarke. There was evidence of a reason why Daniel might have gone on the roof—he had been instructed to do so as part of his duties as an employee, without any training or induction course, or any serious warning about roof lights, and had not been told not to do so prior to receiving that induction course. There is, furthermore, force in the point that by focusing on the particular moment before the accident, Mr Griffiths is failing to take account of the seriousness of a failure to give proper instruction not to go on the roof prior to induction or proper instruction in relation to working on a roof and particularly a roof with roof lights. . . .

46 I have concluded that the failures identified do provide a basis on which it would be right to refer the matter back to the CPS. My view is that it is seriously arguable that a different decision might be made once account is taken of those matters. I would stress that I am by no means prejudging the decision, which remains one for the CPS. Indeed, despite the failures identified, I have given anxious consideration as to whether in the light of the time that has gone by and the further anxiety which will be visited on the family and those that are awaiting the final decision as to whether to prosecute, it is right to send this matter back when it cannot be put more highly than seriously arguable. I have, however, formed the conclusion that, for the reasons I have endeavoured to give, it is right to do so, but I stress again that it must still be appreciated that the matter is one for the prosecuting authority.

Notes

1. *No-drop policies for domestic abuse cases.* Several states, including Florida and Wisconsin, have enacted laws encouraging or requiring the development of plans and policies to increase prosecutions and convictions in domestic abuse cases. Many jurisdictions, however, have implemented written or unwritten guidelines within the prosecutor's office about domestic abuse cases in the absence of specific legislative guidance. A growing group of state attorneys general (for instance, in New Jersey and North Carolina) have adopted statewide policies discouraging local prosecutors from dropping domestic violence charges. Policies like the one set out in the Florida statute, encouraging the prosecutor to proceed over the victim's objections, are known as "hard no-drop" policies; the more common policies, focusing on victim support and encouragement, are known as "soft no-drop" policies. Other approaches require the prosecutor to consult with the victim or with other individuals or agencies before dismissing a prosecution. Should the decision be left to the police, or should it depend on the victim's willingness to make an initial complaint?

Academic researchers and policy innovators devote considerable attention to the effects of no-drop policies. Advocates of no-drop policies for domestic violence cases start with the observation that the rate of prosecution for domestic violence complaints remains lower than the rate of prosecution for other types of complaints. They devise various methods of measuring whether these prosecutorial policies change the prosecution rate. They also inquire about the effects of no-drop policies on later stages of the criminal process, and of course, the effects of the policy on the actual levels of domestic violence. For some selections from the ever-growing body of research on this question, go to the web extension for this chapter at *http://www. crimpro.com/extension/ch13.*

2. *Case "attrition."* The phenomenon of cases "falling out" of the criminal justice process is commonly referred to as case "attrition." One possible reaction to the level of case attrition is to claim that police and prosecutors are failing in their obligation to protect the public. What are other possible implications of case attrition? A famous study conducted in the 1970s closely examined case attrition for felony cases in New York City. Vera Institute of Justice, Felony Arrests: Their Prosecution and Disposition in New York City's Courts (Malcolm Feeley ed., rev. ed. 1980). It found an unexpectedly high level of prior relationships throughout felony crime categories, and it attributed the bulk of case attrition to the relationships between the parties involved.

> [Criminal] conduct is often the explosive spillover from ruptured personal relations among neighbors, friends and former spouses. Cases in which the victim and defendant were known to each other constituted 83 percent of rape arrests, 69 percent of assault arrests, 36 percent of robbery arrests, and 39 percent of burglary arrests. The reluctance of the complainants in these cases to pursue prosecution (often because they were reconciled with the defendants or in some cases because they feared the defendants) accounted for a larger portion of the high dismissal rate than any other factor.

Does this study suggest that the problems with domestic abuse victims as reliable complainants are also commonplace for other crimes? Does this study suggest reasons to hesitate in implementing a no-drop policy for domestic abuse cases, or does it offer a reason to consider no-drop policies for some other crimes? From another perspective, is there a proper ratio of convictions to complaints (or arrests) for most types of crimes?

3. *Specialized units or new policies in prosecutors' offices.* Although the criminal code might give prosecutors huge amounts of discretion over whether to file criminal charges, the legislature or the chief prosecutor might structure the prosecutor's office in ways that will encourage the filing of some criminal charges and discourage the filing of others. For instance, the office leadership might create specialized units whose work is easy to monitor. Line items in budgets offer strong incentives to pursue certain charges. See Kay L. Levine, "The State's Role in Prosecutorial Politics," in The Changing Role of the American Prosecutor (John L. Worrall & M. Elaine Nugent-Borakave eds., 2008). Some investigative techniques or charging decisions require special authorization from those high in the prosecutorial hierarchy. These office structures establish predictable limits on the reach of substantive criminal laws, even when those criminal laws are drafted very broadly and delegate nominally large powers to the prosecutor.

Sometimes the chief prosecutor will announce a new policy to structure the decisionmaking of the line prosecutors who work for him, to significantly increase the amount of attention and resources they devote to a particular crime. For example, Attorney General Jeff Sessions released a memorandum in 2017 urging federal prosecutors to increase their efforts to make immigration offenses a higher priority. The "urging" took multiple forms. First, the memorandum made clear that AUSAs had to consider charging a full range of border crimes, including the misdemeanor crime of illegal entry (which had previously been neglected in favor of multiple reentry charges). Second, the memorandum ordered U.S. Attorneys in the American Southwest to factor deterrence into their filing strategies; third, it created a "border security coordinator" to oversee the investigation and prosecution of immigration crime for each border district. For federal prosecutors who previously had regarded immigration crimes as less important than financial crimes, drug crimes, or violent crimes, the memorandum forced a restructuring of office priorities to coordinate with the immigration policy objectives of the President.

4. *Written reasons, public reasons.* Most larger prosecutors' offices require a prosecutor who declines to file charges to give reasons in some written form in the case file. What purposes might the requirement of written reasons serve? If, as chief prosecutor, you supervised an office that required line prosecutors to record their reasons, would you reveal to the public the prosecutor's reasoning in each case? Would you release aggregate statistics that reveal the reasons used in multiple cases? A few states have statutes requiring a prosecutor to explain in writing each refusal to prosecute a case. See Mich. Stat. §767.41; Neb. Rev. Stat. §29-1606.

5. *Charging discretion in foreign legal systems.* The civil law tradition that prevails in most legal systems of the world nominally denies the prosecutor discretion in charging. The "legality" principle requires the prosecutor to file charges whenever they have evidence to support the charges. Studies of such systems—especially the Italian, German, and French systems, which have received relatively close examination—suggest that prosecutors, in fact, exercise a substantial degree of discretion in charging. See, e.g., Kay Levine & Malcolm Feeley, Prosecution, 19 Int'l Encyclopedia of the Social & Behavioral Sciences 210, 213 (2d ed. 2015). As the volume increases in criminal justice systems, the prosecutors divert more cases from full adjudication. Some civil law systems now recognize a principle of "expediency" that ratifies this prosecutorial power to set priorities among cases. See Jorg-Martin Jehle & Marianne Wade, Coping with Overloaded Criminal Justice Systems: The Rise of Prosecutorial Power Across Europe (2006).

The highly bureaucratized prosecutor services in some countries give victims and others the ability to pursue an "appeal" of the initial prosecutor declination. The appeal is resolved by supervisors working in the prosecutor's organization (typically the national Ministry of Justice), who apply standardized charge selection criteria during their review. See David T. Johnson, The Japanese Way of Justice: Prosecuting Crime in Japan 119-143 (2002).

Meanwhile, as we saw in the *Dennis* case reprinted above, judges in some common-law jurisdictions such as England hold more influence over charging decisions than they do in the United States. Judges can review the reasonableness of a prosecutor's decision not to prosecute, a decision to prosecute, or a police decision to issue a formal "caution" instead of forwarding the case to the prosecutorial service. See R. v. Chief Constable of Kent ex rel. L, (1991) 93 Cr. App. R. 416 (review of juvenile case based on prosecutors' own Code for Crown Prosecutors policy); R. v. DPP ex rel. Kebilene, [2000] 2 AC 326 (review of decision to prosecute adults in a select set of offenses).

6. *Mandatory charging statutes in the United States.* The West Virginia Code creates what seems to be a nondiscretionary charging obligation, in sync with the provisions from Italy and Germany. However, prosecutors retain substantial discretion in West Virginia despite the mandatory language of the statute. See State ex rel. Bailey v. Facemire, 413 S.E.2d 183 (W. Va. 1991). The Colorado Criminal Code permits a person to challenge the district attorney's decision not to charge, but the Colorado Supreme Court has warned that the statute does not permit a judge to substitute her judgment for that of the prosecutor. Colo. Rev. Stat. §16-5-209. The court must

find that the "district attorney's decision was arbitrary or capricious and without reasonable excuse" before it will step in. Landis v. Farish, 674 P.2d 957, 958 (Colo. 1984). Are there universal realities of justice systems that make mandatory charging provisions unlikely to succeed?

C. POLICIES TO DISCOURAGE CHARGES

The initial question that a prosecutor faces is whether to file criminal charges at all. Many times when the police believe a person has committed a crime, the prosecutor "declines" to file charges. Declinations are typically based on a prosecutor's ad hoc discretionary decision that the pursuit of criminal charges is not a good use of the limited resources of the office or is not a proper use of the criminal sanction. Sometimes, however, these discretionary decisions will develop into a pattern that may become formalized in internal office policies or rules. Chief prosecutors will at times create declination policies to control the decisions of the attorneys in the office. On rare occasions, statutes or judicial rulings require the creation of general policies to govern declinations.

Three examples of declination policies for prosecutor offices appear below. One involves the charging of low-level offenses in the high-volume work of a local prosecutor's office. The second involves charges in homicide cases. The third document—created at the national level and implemented in almost 100 separate offices around the country—deals with the more rarified atmosphere of federal criminal charges against corporate defendants. What common ground do you notice among the guidelines that grew out of these strikingly different contexts?

■ **OFFICE OF THE DISTRICT ATTORNEY'S, CITY OF PHILADELPHIA**
February 15, 2018

These policies are an effort to end mass incarceration and bring balance back to sentencing. All policies are presumptive, not mandatory requirements. Where extraordinary circumstances suggest that an exception is appropriate, specific supervisory approval must be obtained. . . .

DECLINE CERTAIN CHARGES

1. Do not charge possession of marijuana (cannabis) regardless of weight.
2. Do not charge any of the offenses relating to paraphernalia or buying from a person (BFP) where the drug involved is marijuana.
3. Do not charge prostitution cases against sex workers where a person who has been arrested has two, one or no prostitution convictions. . . .
4. Individuals who have three or more prostitution convictions will be charged with prostitution and immediately referred to DAWN Court.

CHARGE LOWER GRADATIONS FOR CERTAIN OFFENSES

Rationale: summary gradation greatly reduces pre-trial incarceration rates as no bail is required and the shorter time required for hearings expedites Municipal Court and Common Pleas dockets.

1. Charge and dispose of Retail Theft cases as summary offenses unless the value of the item(s) stolen in a particular case exceeds $500 or where the defendant has a very long history of theft and retail theft convictions.
2. You must seek supervisory approval to charge and dispose of retail theft cases at misdemeanor or felony levels.
3. Remember that a summary conviction permits a sentence of 90 days incarceration, fines of up to $250, and full restitution. These penalties are sufficient to hold a retail thief accountable.
4. In all cases seek full restitution.

DIVERT MORE

All attorneys are directed to approach diversion and re-entry with greater flexibility and an eye toward achieving accountability and justice while avoiding convictions where appropriate. For example:

1. An otherwise law-abiding, responsible gun owner who is arrested because he does not have a permit to carry a firearm may apply for individualized consideration for diversion.
2. An otherwise law-abiding, first DUI (driving under the influence) defendant who has no driver's license (regardless of whether or not that defendant's immigration status interferes with obtaining a license under Pennsylvania law) may apply for individualized consideration for diversion with a requirement of efforts to overcome license impediments where possible as an aspect of any diversionary program.
3. A defendant charged with marijuana (cannabis) delivery or PWID (Possession with the Intent to Deliver) may apply for diversion.

This is not a comprehensive list. . . .

■ HOMICIDE POLICIES AND PROCEDURES
Florida State Attorney's Office, Fourth Judicial Circuit (2017)

1.010 – PURPOSES FOR WRITTEN POLICIES

These written policies and procedures are to ensure the fair, uniform, efficient, and transparent handling of all homicide cases by the office of the State Attorney, Fourth Judicial Circuit, Florida; . . . to provide meaningful and appropriate supervisory review of the manner in which homicide cases in the Fourth Judicial Circuit are investigated, charged, and prosecuted; and to ensure that similarly-situated defendants are treated similarly by this office after review of individual cases, taking into account the unique facts and circumstances of each case. . . .

1.012 – HOMICIDE ROTATION

The Director of the Homicide Division shall be responsible for maintaining a rotating list of qualified Assistant State Attorneys to handle all homicide investigations and prosecutions in the Fourth Judicial Circuit as well as an on-call calendar ("the Homicide Rotation"). . . . When an Assistant State Attorney on the Homicide Rotation is notified of a new homicide, the general expectation of this office is for that lawyer to respond to the homicide scene and work closely with homicide detectives to provide support and prosecutorial guidance as soon as feasibly possible. . . .

1.017 – CHARGING NON-CAPITAL HOMICIDES

Members of the Homicide Rotation shall consult early and often with the Director and Deputy Directors of the Homicide Division regarding the investigation of, and potential charges lodged against, any particular defendant. The Director and Deputy Directors of the Homicide Division have full authority to approve formal charges for any non-capital homicide. . . .

1.019 – REVIEW PROCESS FOR HOMICIDE TRIALS

The Director and Deputy Directors of the Homicide Division shall convene regular, meaningful, and thorough homicide trial round table meetings or staffing meetings. . . . As soon as possible prior to a realistic trial date, but not later than 120 days after arraignment, the assigned Assistant State Attorney shall prepare a trial memo in a format designated by the Homicide Director, circulate it to the members of the round table or staffing team, and meet to ensure the particular case is ready for trial. . . .

1.020 – FORMATION AND OPERATION OF THE GRAND JURY INDICTMENT REVIEW PANEL

. . . The Grand Jury Indictment Review Panel shall consist of five permanent members and four rotating members. . . . The GJIRP shall review all cases in which the assigned Assistant State Attorney seeks an indictment for capital murder. In reviewing cases, the GJIRP shall act in a fact-finding role to the State Attorney concerning each particular case reviewed. At all times, the State Attorney retains all authority and discretion to approve indictments for capital murder and to seek or not seek the death penalty. The death penalty shall not be sought, and no Assistant State Attorney shall threaten to seek it, solely for the purpose of obtaining a more advantageous negotiating position or as a matter of trial strategy or tactics.

1.021 – PURPOSE OF THE GRAND JURY INDICTMENT REVIEW PANEL

. . . The overriding goal of the review process is to allow proper, individualized consideration of the facts and law relevant to each particular case, set within a framework of consistent and even-handed application of Florida law. Arbitrary or legally impermissible factors—like a defendant's race, gender, ethnicity, sexual orientation, or religion—will play no role in the decision to seek or waive the death penalty. . . .

1.023 – GRAND JURY MEMORANDUM

A Grand Jury Memo shall be submitted to the GJIRP for any case in which an Assistant State Attorney seeks the return by a grand jury of an indictment charging capital murder. . . . The GJ Memo shall constitute attorney work product and shall be kept confidential pursuant to the laws governing Florida grand juries. The GJ Memo shall contain the following sections:

[Procedural] history section. Here, the assigned Assistant State Attorney should outline the procedural history of the case, to include date of arrest, current charges, and the status of speedy trial. The Assistant State Attorney should also detail any prior submissions of the case to the GJIRP and the results of those submissions.

[Summary] of the defendant's history and characteristics. Here, the assigned Assistant State Attorney should outline what is known of the history and characteristics of the defendant, to include known physical, mental, and familial history, education level, employment history, and criminal record.

[Listing] of key, non-law enforcement witnesses. This section should identify all key non-law-enforcement witnesses, their expected testimony, the form of any prior statements (e.g., recorded, written, interview, etc.), any known record of the witness, to include any impeachable offenses, [and] any known bias of the witness.

[Listing] of key physical evidence. Here, the assigned Assistant State Attorney should summarize the key physical evidence and outline all forensic testing that has been completed on that evidence.

[Listing] of key law enforcement witnesses. Here, the assigned Assistant State Attorney should outline the key law enforcement witnesses, [and] provide a summary of their anticipated testimony.

[Analysis] of all statutory aggravating factors. Here, the assigned Assistant State Attorney will address each of Florida's statutory aggravating factors, whether each factor is present, and the anticipated proof that will establish that factor. . . .

[Analysis] of all known mitigating factors. Here, the assigned Assistant State Attorney will outline all known mitigating factors. Minimally, this section shall include discussion of the defendant's prior criminal history, age, and level of participation in the offense. This section shall also address any mitigating circumstances known to be present or suggested to be present by the defendant's attorney, including the following: the extent to which the victim participated in the conduct that resulted in the homicide; that the defendant was acting under duress or domination by another person; that the defendant was under the influence of drugs or alcohol at the time of the offense; that the defendant was under extreme mental or emotional disturbance at the time of the offense, such that the defendant's diminished capacity to appreciate the criminality of his or her conduct or to conform his or her conduct to the requirements of the law was substantially impaired; or any other factors that would mitigate against the imposition of the death penalty.

[Statement] of law enforcement's recommendation. Here, the assigned Assistant State Attorney shall provide the recommendation of the investigating agency.

[Statement] of the recommendation of the victim's family. In this section, the assigned Assistant State Attorney shall detail the position of the victim's family and shall note all significant contact to date with the victim's family. If the assigned Assistant State Attorney has been unable to reach the victim's family, the assigned Assistant State Attorney shall outline all steps taken to attempt that contact.

[Statement] of the assigned Assistant State Attorney's recommendation. Here, the assigned Assistant State Attorney should recommend to the GJIRP whether the office should seek or not seek the death penalty and the principal reasons why. . . .

1.026 – MEETINGS OF THE GRAND JURY INDICTMENT REVIEW PANEL

. . . In accord with its fact-finding role, the GJIRP shall provide legal and factual analysis on matters such as the following: strength of the guilt phase evidence, whether the evidence supports a finding that one or more aggravators exist, whether substantial mitigation in the case outweighs the aggravators likely to be proven, whether facts would disqualify the defendant from the death penalty (e.g., age or intellectual disability) . . . and whether any other considerations relevant to the State Attorney's ultimate decision are present (e.g., family members' wishes, consistency within the circuit, etc.). . . . The ultimate decision to seek or waive the death penalty at all time rests with the State Attorney. . . .

1.031 – EFFECT OF NONCOMPLIANCE

While these policies shall guide the handling of homicide cases by this office, any failure to comply with these policies create no rights for defendants, and any failure to comply with these policies creates no legal claims or defenses for any defendant.

■ PRINCIPLES OF FEDERAL PROSECUTION OF BUSINESS ORGANIZATIONS
United States Attorney Manual, Chapter 9-28.000 et seq. (2015)

9-28.010 FOUNDATIONAL PRINCIPLES OF CORPORATE PROSECUTION

The prosecution of corporate crime is a high priority for the Department of Justice. By investigating allegations of wrongdoing and bringing charges where appropriate for criminal misconduct, the Department promotes critical public interests. These interests include, among other things: (1) protecting the integrity of our economic and capital markets by enforcing the rule of law; (2) protecting consumers, investors, and business entities against competitors who gain unfair advantage by violating the law; (3) preventing violations of environmental laws; and (4) discouraging business practices that would permit or promote unlawful conduct at the expense of the public interest. . . .

9-28.210 - FOCUS ON INDIVIDUAL WRONGDOERS

A. *General Principle.* Prosecution of a corporation is not a substitute for the prosecution of criminally culpable individuals within or without the corporation. Because a corporation can act only through individuals, imposition of individual criminal liability may provide the strongest deterrent against future corporate wrongdoing. Provable individual culpability should be pursued, particularly if it relates to high-level corporate officers, even in the face of an offer of a corporate guilty plea or some other disposition of the charges against the corporation, including a deferred prosecution or non-prosecution agreement, or a civil resolution. . . .

B. *Comment*: . . . If a decision is made at the conclusion of the investigation to pursue charges or some other resolution with the corporation but not to bring criminal or civil charges against the individuals who committed the misconduct, the reasons for that determination must be memorialized and approved by the United States Attorney or Assistant Attorney General whose office handled the investigation, or their designees. . . .

9-28.300 – FACTORS TO BE CONSIDERED

A. *General Principle*: Generally, prosecutors apply the same factors in determining whether to charge a corporation as they do with respect to individuals. Thus, the prosecutor must weigh all of the factors normally considered in the sound exercise of prosecutorial judgment: the sufficiency of the evidence; the likelihood of success at trial; the probable deterrent, rehabilitative, and other consequences of conviction; and the adequacy of noncriminal approaches. However, due to the nature of the corporate "person," some additional factors are present. In conducting an investigation, determining whether to bring charges, and negotiating plea or other agreements, prosecutors should consider the following factors in reaching a decision as to the proper treatment of a corporate target:

- the nature and seriousness of the offense, including the risk of harm to the public, and applicable policies and priorities, if any, governing the prosecution of corporations for particular categories of crime;
- the pervasiveness of wrongdoing within the corporation, including the complicity in, or the condoning of, the wrongdoing by corporate management;
- the corporation's history of similar misconduct, including prior criminal, civil, and regulatory enforcement actions against it;
- the corporation's willingness to cooperate in the investigation of its agents;
- the existence and effectiveness of the corporation's pre-existing compliance program;
- the corporation's timely and voluntary disclosure of wrongdoing;
- the corporation's remedial actions, including any efforts to implement an effective corporate compliance program or to improve an existing one, to replace responsible management, to discipline or terminate wrongdoers, to pay restitution, and to cooperate with the relevant government agencies;
- collateral consequences, including whether there is disproportionate harm to shareholders, pension holders, employees, and others not proven personally culpable, as well as impact on the public arising from the prosecution;
- the adequacy of remedies such as civil or regulatory enforcement actions; and
- the adequacy of the prosecution of individuals responsible for the corporation's malfeasance.

B. *Comment*: The factors listed in this section are intended to be illustrative of those that should be evaluated and are not an exhaustive list of potentially relevant considerations. Some of these factors may not apply to specific cases, and in some cases one factor may override all others. . . . In most cases, however, no single factor will be dispositive. . . .

9-28.700 THE VALUE OF COOPERATION

Cooperation is a mitigating factor, by which a corporation—just like any other subject of a criminal investigation—can gain credit in a case that otherwise is appropriate for indictment and prosecution. Of course, the decision not to cooperate by a corporation (or individual) is not itself evidence of misconduct, at least where the lack of cooperation does not involve criminal misconduct or demonstrate consciousness of guilt (e.g., suborning perjury or false statements, or refusing to comply with lawful discovery requests). . . .

A. *General Principle*: In order for a company to receive any consideration for cooperation under this section, the company must identify all individuals involved in or responsible for the misconduct at issue, regardless of their position, status or seniority, and provide to the Department all facts relating to that misconduct. . . . To be clear, a company is not required to waive its attorney-client privilege and attorney work product protection in order satisfy this threshold. . . .

B. *Comment*: In investigating wrongdoing by or within a corporation, a prosecutor may encounter several obstacles resulting from the nature of the corporation itself. It may be difficult to determine which individual took which action on behalf of the corporation. Lines of authority and responsibility may be shared among operating divisions or departments, and records and personnel may be spread throughout the United States or even among several countries. Where the criminal conduct continued over an extended period of time, the culpable or knowledgeable personnel may have been promoted, transferred, or fired, or they may have quit or retired. Accordingly, a corporation's cooperation may be critical in identifying potentially relevant actors and locating relevant evidence, among other things, and in doing so expeditiously.

[Cooperation] can be a favorable course for both the government and the corporation. Cooperation benefits the government by allowing prosecutors and federal agents, for example, to avoid protracted delays, which compromise their ability to quickly uncover and address the full extent of widespread corporate crimes. With cooperation by the corporation, the government may be able to reduce tangible losses, limit damage to reputation, and preserve assets for restitution. At the same time, cooperation may benefit the corporation — and ultimately shareholders, employees, and other often blameless victims — by enabling the government to focus its investigative resources in a manner that will not unduly disrupt the corporation's legitimate business operations. In addition, cooperation may benefit the corporation by presenting it with the opportunity to earn credit for its efforts. . . .

9-28.1400 SELECTING CHARGES

. . . Once a prosecutor has decided to charge a corporation, the prosecutor at least presumptively should charge, or should recommend that the grand jury charge, the most serious offense that is consistent with the nature of the defendant's misconduct and that is likely to result in a sustainable conviction. . . .

Notes

1. *Declination policies versus ad hoc judgments.* Although most declination decisions fall within the discretion of the individual prosecutor, many offices develop written policies to govern the declination decision for at least some types of cases. We have already seen one type of declination policy earlier in this chapter: "no-drop" policies for domestic violence crimes. It is quite common to find such articulated (often written) office policies that declare certain crimes to be a high priority for the office.

Just as important, many offices articulate general policies that declare certain crimes to hold a low priority for the office. For example, the District Attorney's office in Kings County (Brooklyn), New York issued a policy in 2014 that limited the prosecution of low-level possession of marijuana cases against persons with only minimal criminal records. The policy still allowed the filing of possession cases if the person "is smoking marijuana around other people in a public space, especially in a location frequented by families, or when the possessor of the marijuana is himself or herself still a youth." The District Attorney explained the rationale for this rebuttable presumption in favor of dismissal as follows:

> The goal of this new policy is to ensure that: (1) the limited resources of this Office are allocated in a manner that most enhances public safety; and (2) individuals, and especially young people of color, do not become unfairly burdened and stigmatized by involvement in the criminal justice system for engaging in non-violent conduct that poses no threat of harm to persons or property. . . . We recognize that the possession of marihuana is illegal in this State, and that the police, when acting in a constitutional manner, have authority to arrest offenders who break the law. This Office and the NYPD have a shared mission of public safety, and we have collaborated, and will continue to collaborate on many initiatives, that advance that goal. But a District Attorney has the additional duty "to seek justice, and not merely convict" and the important function of trying "to reform and improve the administration of justice" (American Bar Association, Criminal Justice Standards on the Prosecution Function, Standard 3-1.2), and it is bearing those obligations in mind, that I am instituting the new policy.
>
> If the conduct in which the individual has engaged is the mere possession of a small amount of marihuana in public, it would not, under most circumstances, warrant saddling that individual with a new criminal conviction and all of its attendant collateral consequences related to employment, education, and housing. Moreover, given the vast number of community members who, regardless of race, have engaged at some point in their lives in this non-violent conduct with impunity, the imposition of a conviction for such conduct may perpetuate the public's perception that the criminal justice system as a whole and law enforcement in particular is neither colorblind, nor class-blind. . . .
>
> More than two-thirds of [all low-level possession] cases ended up being dismissed, most often because the defendant was offered an adjournment in contemplation of dismissal at his or her criminal court arraignment. . . . Given that these cases are ultimately (and predictably) dismissed, the burdens that they pose on the system and the individual are difficult to justify.

For another example, the prosecutor's office in Kitsap County, Washington, issues "standards and guidelines" stating explicitly that the office will devote relatively fewer resources to crimes and activities, such as "economic crime" and "confiscation of the fruits of drug crime" that appear toward the bottom of the declared priority list. The charging standards also explicitly state a more demanding standard for charging crimes against property (evidence that "would justify conviction") than for charging crimes against persons (evidence that makes conviction "probable"). These detailed and substantive charging policies are posted on the web extension for this chapter at *http://www.crimpro.com/extension/ch13.*

Declination policies also address categories of criminal suspects. For instance, many offices adopt specialized charging rules for juvenile suspects and for repeat felony offenders. As we saw above, the U.S. Department of Justice has created written guidelines to govern the charging of corporate entities in particular.

2. *Declination policies that require internal consultation.* A declination policy is only one method of discouraging the use of criminal charges for specific types of cases. Prosecutors' offices will sometimes adopt policies requiring the "line" prosecutors to consult with supervisors or others in the office with special expertise before filing criminal charges under certain statutes. See U.S. Attorneys' Manual §9-2.400 (requiring line prosecutor to consult with supervisors before filing charges against member of news media or for desecration of flag, draft evasion, obscenity, RICO, and other offenses). Is it possible to predict which offenses are most likely to be singled out for a prior consultation requirement?

3. *Prosecutorial policy and office size.* The size and structure of the prosecutor's office determines to some extent whether explicit declination policies will be in place and what topics the policies will address. The chief prosecutors in 45 of the 50 states are elected locally, most for four-year terms. Full-time prosecutors' offices in jurisdictions with large populations (one million persons or more) have a median of about 140 assistant prosecutors; offices in jurisdictions serving populations between 250,000 and one million residents employed a median of about 35 assistant prosecutors; smaller offices employed a median of three assistant prosecutors. Bureau of Justice Statistics, Prosecutors in State Courts, 2005 (July 2006, NCJ 213799). There are 2,344 separate prosecutor offices that try felony cases in the state courts. What effects does a decentralized structure have on the declination policies to be adopted or followed in prosecutors' offices? See Kay L. Levine & Ronald F. Wright, Prosecution in 3D, 102 J. Crim. L. & Criminology 1119 (2013) (illustrating the effects of centralized supervisory structure on prosecutor professional self-image and prosecutor decisions).

4. *Judicial enforcement of prosecutor charging policies.* If an individual prosecutor appears to be violating a known office policy by filing criminal charges when the policy calls for declination, can the defendant convince a court to enforce the policy? Most prosecutor policies about charging declare that they provide "internal" guidance only, without creating any judicially enforceable rights. See United States v. Caceres, 440 U.S. 741 (1979) (defendant may not enforce internal rules of law enforcement agency, such as IRS rule requiring internal approval before eavesdropping). Are written policies a meaningful limit on prosecutorial choices if defendants cannot enforce them? See Kenneth Culp Davis, Discretionary Justice (1969); Gerard E. Lynch, Our Administrative System of Criminal Justice, 66 Fordham L. Rev. 2117 (1998).

5. *Declinations and the community prosecution model.* Ideally, the cases that a prosecutor's office accepts or declines for prosecution reflect some coherent set of priorities for the office. Cases that reinforce the highest priorities for the office would, of

course, be the least likely to be declined. To what extent do you imagine you could reconstruct the priorities of an office by analyzing the pattern of declinations?

Some prosecutors talk about a shift in philosophy, moving to a "community prosecution" model that parallels the "community policing" model that is now at least one generation old. According to this approach, prosecutors place less emphasis on obtaining convictions in the courtroom or through plea agreements. Instead, the prosecutor mobilizes legal resources and leads other government agencies to address community problems to prevent crime before it happens, rather than respond to crime after the fact. They use their legal authority to motivate slumlords to comply with housing codes, prevent liquor law violators from obtaining new liquor licenses, and place high priorities on crimes committed in public parks and other areas where the public is highly aware of crime. See Walter J. Dickey & Peggy A. McGarry, The Search for Justice and Safety Through Community Engagement: Community Justice and Community Prosecution, 42 Idaho L. Rev. 313 (2006). If a new chief prosecutor were to embrace a community prosecution approach, what specific changes in declination patterns would you expect to see?

6. *Corporations and declinations.* The U.S. Department of Justice first issued instructions in 1999 for line prosecutors around the country regarding the decision of whether to charge a corporate entity with a crime. The Department revised the charging policies several times over the years, after federal legislators, business groups, bar associations, and civil liberties advocates complained that the guidelines placed such heavy weight on the "cooperation" of a corporation under investigation that the policy unfairly forced a corporation to waive its attorney-client and work-product privileges. The version reprinted above was published in 2015.

Can you think of any comparable examples of the targets of criminal investigations successfully pressuring the prosecutor to clarify the limits on its charging authority? Do the relevant factors discussed in the DOJ policy on corporations differ from the factors relevant to deciding whether to charge an individual? Are guidelines in the federal system more likely to be revised on a regular basis than guidelines of local prosecutors in the state courts?

D. DIVERSION OF CHARGES

Prosecutors file charges in some cases and decline to charge in others, but they have other options as well. The prosecutor may, for example, "divert" the suspect from the criminal justice system into an alternative program for rehabilitation and restitution. Diversion occurs in some states before charges are ever filed: The prosecutor agrees to withhold any criminal charges, provided the suspect successfully completes the designated program or other conditions that the prosecutor specifies. Diversion can also take place after charges are filed, in which case the prosecution is suspended while the defendant completes the diversion program. If the defendant succeeds, the prosecutor dismisses the criminal charges. The archetypal "diversion" case involves a first-time offender who has committed a nonviolent crime. Some diversion programs explicitly focus on classes of offenders, such as nonviolent drug offenders.

As you read the following materials, consider whether the prosecutor is properly situated to identify "good" cases for diversion and to set the proper conditions for a successful diversion program. Will a prosecutor systematically place requirements on a defendant that a judge at sentencing would not? Will defendants respond differently to diversion programs than they would to requirements imposed at sentencing after a conviction?

■ MONTANA CODE §46-16-130

(1) (a) Prior to the filing of a charge, the prosecutor and a defendant who has counsel or who has voluntarily waived counsel may agree to the deferral of a prosecution for a specified period of time based on one or more of the following conditions:

(i) that the defendant may not commit any offense;

(ii) that the defendant may not engage in specified activities, conduct, and associations bearing a relationship to the conduct upon which the charge against the defendant is based;

(iii) that the defendant shall participate in a supervised rehabilitation program, which may include treatment, counseling, training, or education;

(iv) that the defendant shall make restitution in a specified manner for harm or loss caused by the offense; or

(v) any other reasonable conditions. . . .

(d) The agreement must be terminated and the prosecution automatically dismissed with prejudice upon expiration and compliance with the terms of the agreement. . . .

(3) After a charge has been filed, a deferral of prosecution may be entered into only with the approval of the court.

(4) A prosecution for a violation of [laws that prohibit driving while impaired] may not be deferred.

MONTANA COMMISSION ON CRIMINAL PROCEDURE: COMMENTS

A provision regulating pretrial diversion, sometimes called deferred prosecution, is new to Montana, although the practice has been statutorily recognized since at least 1979. The Commission believed a pretrial diversion provision was necessary because prosecutors have long employed diversion on an informal, individual basis by deferring prosecution if, for example, the accused agreed to undergo rehabilitative treatment. Since the President's Commission on Law Enforcement and Administration of Justice recommended such programs in its 1967 report, many states have formalized diversion by statute or court rule. Pretrial diversionary programs are premised on the belief that it is not always necessary and, in fact, may often be detrimental to pursue formal courtroom prosecution for every criminal violation. In most situations, the criminal prosecution is suspended subject to the defendant's consent to treatment, rehabilitation, restitution, or other noncriminal or nonpunitive alternatives.

The statute contemplates that the decision to divert lies with the prosecutor in an exercise of his powers and is not ordinarily subject to judicial review. This conforms with existing practice in that several Montana County Attorneys conduct formal diversion programs, yet no Montana case has been found that discusses the practice. However, some litigation has occurred in other jurisdictions. . . .

■ KITSAP COUNTY PROSECUTING ATTORNEY MISSION STATEMENT AND STANDARDS AND GUIDELINES
(2007)

. . . In this office we utilize three kinds of diversion programs. In dealing with juvenile offenders, the legislature has obligated us to divert all youth the first time they commit a minor offense. In the District and Municipal Courts, we use pretrial diversion agreements (PDAs) to relieve court congestion by diverting first-time offenders and defendants in problematic cases. Our adult felony diversion program offers an opportunity to avoid felony conviction to certain low risk property offenders and to select drug offenders.

Juvenile Diversions: "Diversion—A first time misdemeanor offender will be sent to the Juvenile Department Diversion Unit. A second misdemeanor offense may be sent to diversion if the circumstances warrant. Factors the charging deputy shall consider in determining whether to divert the second offense include: length, seriousness, and recency of the alleged offender's criminal history and the circumstances surrounding the commission of the alleged offense." RCW 13.40.050. Following the law, we cooperate with the Superior Court Juvenile Department by determining which offenders qualify under the statute.

Pre-Trial Diversion Agreements (PDAs), District and Municipal Courts: The decision when to PDA a case is less-than-scientific. Generally, most non-DV or non-DUI/Physical Control cases will be PDA'd if no aggravating factors are present. PDAs may also be offered the morning of trial due to court congestion and/or speedy trial problems. However, when faced with the need to choose among a number of cases all set for trial on the same day, priority should be given to the most aggravated Domestic Violence and DUI cases. . . .

DUI cases may be offered a PDA if a first offense, no aggravating factors are present, and a BAC of 0.12 or less. DUI PDA cases will not be dismissed, however. The typical DUI PDA will be to amend the charge to first degree negligent driving upon successful PDA compliance.

DV cases can and do become more problematic over time so evidence problems often result in a PDA being offered even with the presence of aggravating factors. The DPA, if possible, should speak with a Division Chief or a Senior DPA if significant aggravating factors are present, however, prior to offering a PDA in a DV case based upon proof problems.

If aggravating factors are present but a case is problematic (i.e. conviction by jury is unlikely), less-than-one-year DPAs are expected to speak with a Division Chief or a Senior DPA prior to offering a PDA if possible. Of course, if in a time crunch in court, the DPA should always make his or her best call and thereafter speak with the Division Chief to discuss the DPA's decision. Continuing cases for a DPA to speak with a Division Chief or Senior DPA (or to permit the defense attorney to speak with a Division Chief or a Senior DPA) is discouraged due to court congestion problems.

Felony Diversions: Many minor non-violent felony offenses are committed by first time offenders as a result of substance abuse and/or unusually bad judgment. If an offender is addicted to controlled substances, criminal behavior is likely to continue unless the offender receives treatment. In other minor felony cases involving first time offenders, less expensive alternatives to costly incarceration exist, and those alternatives may succeed at lessening the risk of further criminal behavior. In addition, the conditions of diversion will allow more supervision than currently available for a minor felony conviction.

One alternative is Drug Court. We screen the referrals of felony possession of controlled substances for prior sex offenses or violent crimes, including burglary and eluding a police vehicle. If there are none, in most cases we will offer the offender the opportunity to take judicially supervised treatment instead of going to jail. If the offender completes the program, the charge is dismissed. If they fail, having already confessed to the crime, they are convicted of the underlying offense and sentenced. . . .

Felony Diversion Screening Factors: To identify offenders who will be offered diversion either through Drug Court or some other option, we will use the following criteria.

1. The Seriousness of the Current Offense. No sex crimes or violent crime, including eluding a police vehicle, will be considered for diversion. First Degree Burglary (a violent offense) and Residential Burglary are excluded from consideration. Second Degree Burglary generally will not be considered for diversion. However, it may be considered if approved by the Chief of Case Management or the Prosecutor. If a case of second degree burglary is considered, particular attention will be paid to the likelihood that the offender would have encountered another person in the course of the crime.

2. Criminal History. Generally a history of sex or violent offenses, including eluding a police vehicle, will disqualify an offender. A history of Residential Burglary will also generally disqualify an offender unless the offense was disposed of in Juvenile Court. Exceptions must be approved by the Chief Deputy supervising the program or by the Prosecutor.

3. Strength of the Case. In considering Drug Court, the strength of the State's case should generally not be a factor. However, in diversion other than Drug Court, if, in the opinion of the Chief of Case Management or the Prosecutor, there would be value in exerting some control over the offender through a diversion program, a problematic case may be considered.

4. Ability to Pay Associated Costs. No person shall be denied diversion solely on present inability to pay the associated costs. However, the willingness to commit to pay future costs or to perform alternative community service is a factor that may be used in determining eligibility for a diversion program.

Notes

1. *Prevalence of diversion.* Diversion of arrestees is not as common as the outright rejection of criminal charges or the filing of felony charges. Prosecutors are most likely to offer diversion to suspects who face misdemeanor charges. About 9 percent of all felony arrestees in the largest urban counties in 2009 took part in diversion or "deferred adjudication" programs. Bureau of Justice Statistics, Felony Defendants in Large Urban Counties, 2009 (December 2013, NCJ 243777).

2. *Authority for diversion.* Prosecutors do not always have clear legal authority to take part in diversion programs. In some states, programs have statewide statutory

authority (illustrated by the Montana statute reprinted above). Elsewhere, judges establish and supervise diversion programs. In a few jurisdictions, prosecutors send offenders into diversion programs without any explicit statutory authority to do so. Combinations of these situations are also possible: A statute might authorize diversion of offenders only after the filing of charges, yet the prosecutor may decide unilaterally to send some offenders into diversion programs before filing charges. For a sample of these state statutes, rules, and judicial decisions, go to the web extension for this chapter at *http://www.crimpro.com/extension/ch13*. Would the source of authority affect the level of funding for the program or the prosecutor's control over the conditions that program participants must meet?

3. *Who decides who enters the program?* State statutes dealing with pretrial diversion programs most often empower judges to approve of prosecutorial recommendations of individual offenders. In practice, however, prosecutors decide which defendants or suspects will enter a pretrial diversion program, and a court will give great deference to the prosecutor's decision. Indeed, in many states courts refuse to review the prosecutor's decision on whether to offer diversion to a suspect unless the prosecutor relies on unconstitutional grounds such as race. Flynt v. Commonwealth, 105 S.W.3d 415 (Ky. 2003) (court must have prosecutor's approval to admit defendant into diversion program; separation-of-powers doctrine requires this reading of statute). Prosecutors' offices sometimes create policies to govern eligibility for diversion, at least for some types of cases.

Legislatures also create some preconditions for defendants or suspects to participate in pretrial diversion programs. See, e.g., Ind. Code §33-39-1-8 (prosecutor "may" withhold prosecution against a person charged with a misdemeanor if person agrees to listed conditions of pretrial diversion program). If the prosecutor and the suspect disagree about the proper interpretation of the statute defining eligibility requirements, can a court review the prosecutor's decision based on its independent interpretation of the statute? Or must it defer to the prosecutor's reading of the statute?

4. *Who decides whether the defendant has completed the program?* Suppose a defendant believes she has fulfilled all the conditions of the diversion program but the prosecutor disagrees and files criminal charges. Will a court review the prosecutor's conclusion that the defendant failed to complete the program? Is there any reason to treat this question differently from the question of who will enter a diversion program? Among states with statutes addressing this question, most require court approval for a decision to remove an offender from a diversion program, but a few states have statutes granting this decision exclusively to the prosecutor. See Fla. Stat. §948.08. What circumstances might enable a court to make an independent judgment about the defendant's success or failure in the program?

5. *Statement of reasons.* A few diversion programs require the prosecutor to provide an applicant to the program with written notice of rejection, along with the reasons for the rejection. The statement of reasons facilitates judicial review of the prosecutor's decision and is thought to help the courts identify arbitrary and abusive denials by the prosecutor. However, fewer than 10 states have a statewide legal requirement that the prosecutor give written reasons. Reconsider the case studies in Problem 13-1; would you consider diversion for any of the three defendants?

6. *Youth courts and other diversion courts.* Many states authorize nonprofit organizations to operate "youth courts" that provide prosecutors, police, and schools with an alternative to juvenile courts. Police, prosecutors, or school officials divert juvenile

offenders out of the courts and into these programs. Often the volunteer "judges" in youth courts are not lawyers; sometimes they are not even adults, but rather the offender's peers. State law typically limits their authority to minor offenses. The offender must consent to enter the program and admit his or her guilt. The judge in youth court can impose dispositions such as "community service; participation in law-related educational classes, appropriate counseling, treatment, or other educational programs; providing periodic reports to the Youth Court; participating in mentoring programs; participation by the youth as a member of a Youth Court; letters of apology; [or] essays." Utah Code Ann. §78A-6-1203.

Does the creation of diversion courts (as opposed to diversion programs) exacerbate, undermine, or sidestep concerns about prosecutorial power and discretion? If you were a district attorney, would you encourage the development and use of youth courts in your state? What other kinds of offenders or offenses might be handled with similar group diversion models? For additional examples of diversion courts, go to the web extension for this chapter at *http://www.crimpro.com/extension/ch13*.

Problem 13-3. Diversion Policies and Exceptions

At 5:30 P.M., Wallace Baynes purchased .44 grams of heroin from Jose Morales outside of the Rainbow Liquor Store, which was under police surveillance at the time. The store was located about 900 feet from the Garfield Primary School in Middletown, New Jersey. Police arrested Baynes and prosecutors charged him with possession of heroin within 1,000 feet of a school zone.

Baynes applied to the prosecutor's office for admission into the Monmouth County Pretrial Intervention Program ("PTI" program). His application shows that he is 43 years old, employed, living with and supporting his elderly mother and his 17-year-old son. Baynes has worked for the same employer for the previous nine years. He has no prior criminal record. Baynes claims that he purchased the heroin because he was having difficulty dealing with the serious illness of his mother.

The Director of the PTI program, an attorney in the prosecutor's office, accepted Baynes's application for admission. The police officer who arrested Baynes did not object to Baynes's diversion. The chief prosecutor, however, advised Baynes in a memorandum that his PTI application was rejected because of that prosecutor's general policy to deny PTI admission to defendants charged with "school zone offenses," including those involving possession of small amounts of controlled substances for personal use.

The PTI program in New Jersey has unusual origins. The state supreme court established the program by promulgating Rule 3:28 in 1970. The legislature later authorized a statewide PTI program as part of the Criminal Code of Justice, codifying the program that the court had created. The court later promulgated criteria for making PTI decisions in its Guidelines for Operation of Pretrial Intervention. Guideline 1 sets forth the purposes of PTI:

> (1) to enable defendants to avoid ordinary prosecution by receiving early rehabilitative services expected to deter future criminal behavior; (2) to provide defendants who might be harmed by the imposition of criminal sanctions with an alternative to prosecution expected to deter criminal conduct; (3) to avoid burdensome

prosecutions for "victimless" offenses; (4) to relieve overburdened criminal cal-
endars so that resources can be expended on more serious criminal matters; and
(5) to deter future criminal behavior of PTI participants.

Guideline 2 provides that any defendant "accused of crime shall be eligible
for admission into a PTI program." Guideline 3 refers to and supplements N.J.S.A.
2C:43-12(e), which presents 17 criteria that prosecutors and criminal division managers are to consider in formulating their PTI recommendation. Guideline 3(i)
clarifies that the "nature of the crime" is only one factor to be considered in the
admissions decision. Moreover, Guideline 3(i) states that there is a presumption
against acceptance into a program when "the crime was (1) part of organized criminal activity; or (2) part of a continuing criminal business or enterprise; or (3) deliberately committed with violence or threat of violence against another person; or
(4) a breach of the public trust." A presumption against acceptance into a PTI program also exists when the defendant is charged with a sale of narcotic drugs "and
is not drug dependent." Finally, Guideline 8 requires a prosecutor, when making
a PTI decision, to provide the defendant with a statement of reasons justifying the
decision and describing the facts considered.

Imagine that you are a trial judge in the Superior Court. Baynes files suit, asking
you to overturn the prosecutor's decision to exclude him from the PTI program.
What would you decide? What standard of review, if any, would be most appropriate? Cf. State v. Baynes, 690 A.2d 594 (N.J. 1997).

E. SELECTION AMONG CHARGES

Up to this point, we have focused on prosecutorial choices that would place
a suspect either "in" or "out" of the criminal justice system. But once prosecutors
decide to file a case, they also have to select among a range of criminal charges that
could apply to the facts.

■ U.S. DEPARTMENT OF JUSTICE, PRINCIPLES OF FEDERAL PROSECUTION
(1980)

SELECTING CHARGES

1. Except as hereafter provided, the attorney for the government should charge,
or should recommend that the grand jury charge, the most serious offense that is
consistent with the nature of the defendant's conduct, and that is likely to result in
a sustainable conviction.

2. Except as hereafter provided, the attorney for the government should also
charge, or recommend that the grand jury charge, other offenses only when, in his
judgment, additional charges:

   (a) are necessary to ensure that the information or indictment: (i) adequately reflects the nature and extent of the criminal conduct involved; and (ii)

provides the basis for an appropriate sentence under all the circumstances of the case; or

(b) will significantly enhance the strength of the government's case against the defendant or a codefendant.

3. The attorney for the government may file or recommend a charge or charges without regard to the provisions of paragraphs 1 and 2, if such charge or charges are the subject of a pre-charge plea agreement. . . .

■ MINNESOTA STATUTES §388.051

(1) The county attorney shall [prosecute] felonies, including the drawing of indictments found by the grand jury, and, to the extent prescribed by law, gross misdemeanors, misdemeanors, petty misdemeanors, and violations of municipal ordinances, charter provisions and rules or regulations. . . .

(3) [Each] county attorney shall adopt written guidelines governing the county attorney's charging . . . policies and practices. The guidelines shall address, but need not be limited to, the . . . factors that are considered in making charging decisions. . . .

■ PEOPLE v. JALEH WILKINSON
94 P.3d 551 (Cal. 2004)

GEORGE, C.J.

[In] the early morning hours of February 27, 1999, a motorist observed defendant driving erratically on a street in the City of Santa Monica. Defendant's vehicle crossed over the center divider, struck a parked car, and continued down the street, swerving between lanes. [When the police stopped her, the defendant could not complete a field sobriety test. At the police station, she] was belligerent during booking and resisted a patsearch. At one point, defendant grabbed a custodial officer's arm with both hands, causing a visible welt. When taken to a holding cell, defendant charged at an officer and yelled, kicked, and banged at the door. After the police reminded defendant that she would have to submit to a blood or breath test, defendant covered her ears, stated "I can't hear you," and began running around inside the cell. . . .

Defendant testified in her own defense as follows. On the night in question, defendant, a bank vice-president, went to a bar, where she met a man who offered to buy her a drink. She accepted and eventually consumed two glasses of wine. The man invited defendant to dinner, and they agreed to meet at a Santa Monica restaurant. At the restaurant, defendant consumed three alcoholic beverages over the course of three hours while she waited for the man, but he never arrived. . . . She eventually left the restaurant, driving away without feeling any signs of intoxication. The next thing she remembered was waking up in jail, with no recollection of her encounter with the officers. After her release from custody, defendant filed a police complaint alleging she had been drugged. [A toxicologist who reviewed her case concluded that she was under the influence of a "date rape" drug.]

Defendant was convicted of violating Penal Code section 243.1, which states in full: "When a battery is committed against the person of a custodial officer as defined in Section 831 of the Penal Code, and the person committing the offense knows or reasonably should know that the victim is a custodial officer engaged in the performance of his or her duties, and the custodial officer is engaged in the performance of his or her duties, the offense shall be punished by imprisonment in the state prison." Section 831, subdivision (a), in turn, defines a "custodial officer" as "a public officer, not a peace officer, employed by a law enforcement agency of a city or county who has the authority and responsibility for maintaining custody of prisoners and performs tasks related to the operation of a local detention facility used for the detention of persons usually pending arraignment or upon court order either for their own safekeeping or for the specific purpose of serving a sentence therein." [A violation of section 243.1] is punishable "by imprisonment in any of the state prisons for 16 months, or two or three years. . . ."

[Another relevant statute, section 243, includes four distinct crimes], with subdivision (a) covering simple battery (punishable as a misdemeanor with a maximum jail sentence of six months), subdivision (b) covering battery on a person who the defendant knows or should know is a peace officer, firefighter, etc. (punishable as a misdemeanor with a maximum jail sentence of one year), subdivision (c) covering battery on a peace officer, firefighter, etc., that results in the infliction of injury ([punishable as either a felony or a misdemeanor, commonly known as a "wobbler,"] with a possible state prison term of 16 months, two years, or three years), and subdivision (d) covering battery that results in serious bodily injury (a wobbler with a possible prison term of two, three, or four years). [Six years after the passage of section 243.1 in 1976], the Legislature added a reference to custodial officers to subdivisions (b) and (c) of section 243, defining custodial officers by reference to section 831. . . .

On appeal, defendant [contends] that the current statutory scheme pertaining to battery on a custodial officer is "irrational" and violates the federal and state guarantees of equal protection because one who commits the "lesser" offense of battery on a custodial officer without injury can receive felony punishment under section 243.1 while a person committing the "greater" offense of battery on a custodial officer with injury can be convicted of a wobbler offense under section 243, subdivision (c)(1) and can receive a misdemeanor sentence. . . .

We begin our discussion with an overview of relevant case authority. . . . In People v. Chenze, 97 Cal. App. 4th 521 (Cal. App. 2002), the defendant contended that he was improperly charged and convicted under section 243.1 because that provision had been "impliedly repealed" when the Legislature amended section 243 to include references to custodial officers. . . . The Court of Appeal in *Chenze* disagreed that the two statutes were in irreconcilable conflict and thus rejected the claim of implied repeal. The court cited an enrolled bill report . . . which explained the need for an amendment to section 243 to include references to custodial officers notwithstanding the existence of section 243.1: "According to the bill's sponsors, simple battery charges against custodial officers are rarely pursued by local prosecutors because the present law only provides for felony charges with imprisonment in a state prison. Thus, these violators are rarely, if ever, punished. By providing for the option of county jail and/or fine for such violations, proponents hope that simple battery charges will be prosecuted more vigorously. Felony battery charges can still be pursued for the more serious cases." . . . But the Legislature also apparently envisioned that there might be circumstances under which no or only slight injury was inflicted, but felony charges would nonetheless still be appropriate. . . .

The United States Supreme Court's decision in United States v. Batchelder, 442 U.S. 114 (1979), . . . concluded that the defendant properly could be sentenced under one federal firearms statute, although an almost identical statute prescribed a lesser punishment. In *Batchelder*, the court took note of legislative history indicating that Congress "intended to enact two independent gun control statutes, each fully enforceable on its own terms." The court in *Batchelder* then stated that . . . "when an act violates more than one criminal statute, the Government may prosecute under either so long as it does not discriminate against any class of defendants. . . . The prosecutor may be influenced by the penalties available upon conviction, but this fact, standing alone, does not give rise to a violation of the Equal Protection or Due Process Clause." . . .

Batchelder instructs us that neither the existence of two identical criminal statutes prescribing different levels of punishments, nor the exercise of a prosecutor's discretion in charging under one such statute and not the other, violates equal protection principles. Thus, defendant may not complain that she was charged with a felony violation under section 243.1 even though section 243, subdivision (b) is an identical statute prescribing a lesser punishment. [Numerous] factors properly may enter into a prosecutor's decision to charge under one statute and not another, such as a defendant's background and the severity of the crime, and so long as there is no showing that a defendant has been singled out deliberately for prosecution on the basis of some invidious criterion [such as race or religion], that is, one that is arbitrary and thus unjustified because it bears no rational relationship to legitimate law enforcement interests, the defendant cannot make out an equal protection violation. Defendant does not allege that her prosecution was motivated by improper considerations.

[Defendant's argument] is based upon the questionable premise that battery on a custodial officer without injury always is a less serious offense than battery with injury, so as to warrant inevitably a lesser punishment. [Consider, however,] whether a hypothetical defendant who, in the course of grabbing the arm of a correctional officer, inflicts a puncture wound with her fingernail that requires medical attention would be more culpable than a defendant who repeatedly hits and kicks the correctional officer, intending to cause serious injury but does not do so through no lack of effort. [The Legislature amended section 243] to allow misdemeanor prosecutions of batteries committed on custodial officers, and the Legislature did not repeal section 243.1 to allow felony prosecutions for more serious cases, even if no injury was inflicted. . . .

A rational basis for these statutes exists; the Legislature reasonably could have concluded that reduction of the section 243.1 offense is not appropriate in cases of a battery on a custodial officer that is deemed serious enough by the prosecutor to warrant felony prosecution under the latter statute. . . . Because a rational basis exists for the statutory scheme pertaining to battery on a custodial officer, these statutes are not vulnerable to challenge under the equal protection clause. . . .

KENNARD, J., dissenting.

[The] statutory scheme lacks any rational basis, in my view, and thereby violates the constitutional guarantee of equal protection of the laws. [The] current scheme encourages arbitrary, irrational charging. In the case of a battery on a custodial officer that causes injury, there would be no incentive for the prosecutor to charge the defendant under section 243(c). [Under section 243.1], the prosecutor is spared the burden of proving the injury and the trial court is precluded from treating the offense as a misdemeanor, an option that would be available to the court if the defendant had been charged with, and convicted of a violation of section 243(c). . . .

Other consequences of the statutory scheme are even more perplexing, as illustrated by the problems involved in instructing a jury in the trial of a defendant charged with a violation of section 243(c). [When] a defendant is charged with a battery on a custodial officer with injury or serious bodily injury, and there is a question whether the injury occurred, the trial court must instruct [the jury] on the necessarily included offense of battery in violation of section 243.1 (battery on a custodial officer without injury). If the jury then found the defendant guilty as charged of a battery on a custodial officer causing injury (§243(c)), the court would have discretion to impose a misdemeanor sentence. But if the jury, because it entertained a reasonable doubt that the battery had caused an injury to the custodial officer, found the defendant guilty only of the necessarily included offense of battery on a custodial officer (§243.1), the trial court would be required to sentence the defendant as a felon.

I can perceive no rational basis for this rather startling statutory scheme. The majority does, however. . . . It observes that if we compare two different batteries, it is possible that a particular battery without injury could be more heinous than another battery that did cause an injury. By the same reasoning, however, a particular petty theft could, depending on the circumstances, be more serious than a particular grand theft, and a particular grand theft could be more serious than a particular robbery, and so forth. Under this reasoning, the legal classification of crimes as inherently "greater" or "lesser" becomes meaningless and a rational ordering of crimes and punishment in the penal law becomes impossible. In deciding which of two crimes is the greater, the only meaningful comparison is between the elements of each crime, . . . not the particular circumstances of their commission. . . .

The majority holds that section 243.1 (battery on a custodial officer without injury) does not violate the principle of equal protection of the laws because the Legislature could have rationally concluded that reduction of this offense to a misdemeanor is not appropriate whenever the prosecutor deems the offense serious enough for felony prosecution. This reasoning misses the point. Equal protection analysis requires comparing two statutes. . . . The majority offers no rational basis for the distinction between them.[4] . . . Could the Legislature rationally believe that some batteries without injury are so serious that the prosecutor must be given unfettered, unreviewable power to ensure that they are prosecuted as felonies, but that this is not the case for batteries causing injury? Conversely, could the Legislature rationally believe that the courts could be trusted to determine when batteries causing injury should be treated as felonies rather than misdemeanors, but could not

4. The majority mistakenly relies on United States v. Batchelder, 442 U.S. 114 (1979), a case involving a federal statutory scheme that defined two crimes with essentially the same elements but different penalties. . . . The court was not faced with a statutory scheme like the one at issue here, which defines two closely related crimes and permits lesser punishment for the crime that differs only in requiring one additional aggravating element. . . . I note, moreover, that the Colorado Supreme Court found the reasoning in Batchelder unpersuasive and declined to follow it in construing the equal protection clause of its own state constitution. People v. Estrada, 601 P.2d 619 (Colo. 1979).

be trusted to make the same determination as to batteries that did not cause injury? The answer is inescapable: the statutory distinction has no rational basis, thus denying defendant the equal protection of the laws. . . .

Here, after charging defendant with a felony battery under section 243.1, the prosecutor offered to dismiss the felony charge if defendant would plead guilty to a misdemeanor battery, which would be further reduced to an infraction if she successfully completed probation. Defense counsel refused the offer. The prosecutor then offered to dismiss the battery charge if defendant would plead guilty to the misdemeanor of driving under the influence of alcohol or drugs. Defense counsel rejected this offer as well. The case was then prosecuted as a felony. The trial court expressed dismay that the case had not been settled, and, after the jury found defendant guilty as charged, the court placed defendant on probation instead of sending her to prison for the felony conviction.

[These] facts show that the prosecutor did not consider defendant's conduct so egregious as to require felony punishment. A prosecutor taking that view would not have been so eager to induce defendant to plead guilty to crimes punishable only as misdemeanors. But because defendant was charged under section 243.1, a mandatory felony, the trial court was prevented from exercising the discretion the Legislature gave it to treat the more serious crime of battery on a custodial officer with injury (§243(c)) as a misdemeanor. This kind of injustice is the predictable result of the current irrational statutory scheme. . . .

Notes

1. *Selection among charges: majority view.* According to judges in the United States, prosecutors may select among all applicable statutes in deciding what charges to bring, with no outside interference. The occasional claim by defendants that one crime better fits the offense and offender than another virtually always fails. In United States v. Batchelder, 442 U.S. 114 (1979), the Supreme Court considered two overlapping criminal statutes. Although both statutes prohibited convicted felons from possessing firearms, one provision imposed only a two-year maximum penalty while the second imposed a maximum penalty of five years. The Court held that Batchelder's conviction and sentence to the maximum term under the five-year statute did not violate the due process, equal protection, or separation of powers doctrine. While some courts reach this result as a matter of constitutional doctrine, others rely on statutory interpretation. These courts apply a technique of statutory interpretation or "rule of construction" referred to by its Latin name, *in pari materia*, which leads courts to presume that all related statutes make up a single, coherent statutory scheme, regardless of when they were enacted.

Such a hands-off judicial attitude is easiest to explain when the two statutes involve a greater offense and a lesser included offense. It is more difficult to justify, however, when two statutes with different penalties require the prosecutor to prove precisely the same elements. A few courts create rules of statutory interpretation that apply the lesser penalty in a situation where two identical statutes impose different penalties, assuming that the legislature made an error. See State v. McAdam, 83 P.3d 161 (Kan. 2004).

2. *Structuring the charging discretion.* Does the absence of judicial regulation of charge selection create the need for detailed charging guidelines? What institutions

could develop charging policies? Should legislatures draft policies or should they follow the Minnesota legislature's approach, simply directing that each chief prosecutor draft charging policies?

Consider again the Justice Department's Principles of Federal Prosecution. Do they give any meaningful direction to a prosecutor making a charging decision? The National District Attorneys Association lists the following among the appropriate factors for a prosecutor to consider in selecting charges: "the probability of conviction," "the willingness of the offender to cooperate with law enforcement," "possible improper motives of a victim or witness," "excessive cost of prosecution in relation to the seriousness of the offense," "recommendations of the involved law enforcement agency," and "any mitigating circumstances." National Prosecution Standards §43.6 (2d ed. 1991). Does this list differ in emphasis or in particulars from the federal standards? For examples of local prosecutorial office policies that govern the selection among charges, go to the web extension for this chapter at *http://www.crimpro.com/extension/ch13.*

3. *Repeat offenders are subject to significant sentence increases.* Habitual felon laws typically leave prosecutors with charging discretion that can make exceptionally large differences in the sentence. For instance, under Florida's "habitual offender" statute, a prosecutor's unreviewable decision to charge an eligible defendant as a habitual offender translated into longer prison sentences. Within a few years of the passage of this law, defendants began to complain that prosecutors were using their new charging power in an arbitrary and racially discriminatory manner. Legislative committees asked for a study of the use of the habitual offender statute. The study concluded as follows:

> [First, in] most circuits, and certainly on a statewide basis, the statute has not been limited to use against the very worst offenders but has been applied more frequently to the less serious offenders. . . . Second, the circuit in which an offender is prosecuted is of enormous importance to the risk of habitualization. This means that for the roughly one third of all guilty adjudications who are eligible for habitualization, Florida does not have a single statewide system of reasonably uniform sentencing. For this group of offenders . . . there are effectively 20 separate sentencing systems that vary widely in their treatment of offenders eligible for habitualization.
>
> Third, in all but two circuits [those encompassing Miami and Sarasota], the habitual offender sanctions are much more likely to be used against black offenders than non-black offenders, even after adjusting for prior record, the nature of the current offense and a variety of other factors that might have a bearing on the decision to habitualize. It was also found that, on a statewide basis, prosecutors were much more likely to use the statute against male offenders than similarly situated female offenders. . . .

After receiving this report, several state legislators called for revisions to the statute that would restrict or remove the prosecutor's power to decide when to charge an offender as a habitual felon. The Florida Prosecuting Attorneys' Association (FPAA) promptly issued a "Statement Concerning Implementing of Habitual Offender Laws." In an effort to discourage the legislature from repealing the habitual offender laws, the prosecutors voluntarily adopted "criteria" for use of those laws. In addition to the statutory prerequisites for the invocation of habitual violent felon punishments, the prosecutors imposed several nonstatutory elements:

A. Charged offense must be a second degree felony or higher, . . . AND

B. Charged offense must be an enumerated violent felony, AND

C. Defendant must have at least one prior conviction for an enumerated violent felony, AND

D. The felony for which the defendant is to be sentenced was committed within five years of the date of the conviction for the last enumerated violent felony or within five years of the defendant's release, on parole or otherwise, from a prison sentence or other commitment imposed as a result of the prior enumerated felony conviction.

The FPAA Statement also noted that there could be cases that would justify habitual offender treatment, even when they do not meet these extra criteria. In such cases, the prosecutors committed to record their reasons. You might think of this incident as an example of "political" or "legislative" review of charge selection. How does this form of prosecutor accountability compare to judicial review of the prosecutor's charge selection?

4. *Charges of overcharging.* Defense attorneys and many observers of the criminal justice system claim that prosecutors routinely "overcharge" cases in anticipation of plea bargain negotiations. Standard 3-3.9 of the ABA Standards for Criminal Justice (3d ed. 1993) advises prosecutors against bringing charges greater than necessary "to reflect the gravity of the offense" or charges where there is not "sufficient admissible evidence to support a conviction." How can we know when prosecutors are "overcharging" for strategic reasons? The baseline for declaring appropriate charges in a given case might be (1) the typical charges filed in factually similar cases, or (2) any charge that is supported by probable cause, or (3) any charge that presents a reasonable likelihood of success at trial, using the beyond a reasonable doubt standard. If it is difficult to prove that an abuse is taking place at all, is there any hope of reducing the amount of any abuse?

Should prosecutors evaluate their charging options differently when certain crimes carry mandatory minimums and others do not? Should prosecutors file the most readily provable charge irrespective of sentence impact, or instead should they consider whether the mandatory minimum appropriately fits the defendant's behavior? They might take this "fit" factor into account if confronted with evidence that racial disparities have resulted from reflexive application of the mandatory minimum scheme. See, e.g., M.M. Rehavi & Sonia Starr, Mandatory Sentencing and Racial Disparity, Assessing the Role of Prosecutors and the Effects of *Booker,* 123 Yale L.J. 2 (2013). Should they take the "fit" factor into account if confronted with evidence that prosecutorial overcharging has played a significant role in producing mass incarceration in recent decades? John Pfaff, Locked In: The True Causes of Mass Incarceration and How to Achieve Real Reform (2017).

5. *Statutory limits on multiple convictions.* A few states have statutes that approach the question of charge selection at the "back end" of convictions rather than the "front end" of charges. These statutes limit the number of convictions that can result from overlapping charges. Consider Mo. Ann. Stat. §556.041:

When the same conduct of a person may establish the commission of more than one offense he may be prosecuted for each such offense. He may not, however, be convicted of more than one offense if [the] offenses differ only in that one is defined to prohibit a designated kind of conduct generally and the other to prohibit a specific instance of such conduct. . . .

But cf. Ill. Ann. Stat. ch. 720, para. 5/3-3 ("When the same conduct of a defendant may establish the commission of more than one offense, the defendant may be prosecuted for each such offense"). Is a statute directed to the trial judge who enters final judgment more likely to produce consistent punishment for similar conduct than any effort to influence the charging decision more directly? Constitutional limits on "double jeopardy" also place some limits on prosecutor charging decisions here, a topic we explore in Chapter 14.

6. *Criminal code reform.* Criminal codes often include hundreds or, in some cases, thousands of separate crimes. Would a well-drafted criminal code reduce concerns about consistent and fair charging? Are there fewer overlaps and conflicts between statutes in states with a uniform criminal code? Imagine the practices or institutions that might produce well-drafted criminal codes. Whenever there is an apparent conflict between two statutory provisions, should the courts (or the lawyers) notify the appropriate legislative committees? Consider again the overlapping statutes in the *Wilkinson* case from California. Why do you suppose the state legislatures passed these overlapping statutes? Was it an oversight?

Problem 13-4. Available Charges

On the evening of January 9, Ida County deputy sheriff Randy Brown was on patrol in Ida Grove. He observed three snowmobiles traveling on a downtown sidewalk and then on the streets in a careless and reckless manner. Once Brown began pursuit, the trio split up. With the aid of another deputy, Brown eventually stopped and arrested Mitch Peters.

At the time of arrest, Peters had a strong odor of alcohol on his breath. The deputies took him to the Ida County sheriff's office, where they administered sobriety tests. Peters failed the horizontal gaze nystagmus test and the preliminary breath test, registering above .10. Peters was charged with operating a motor vehicle while intoxicated, second offense, under Iowa Code §321J.2, which provides as follows:

> A person commits the offense of operating while intoxicated if the person operates a motor vehicle in this state [while] under the influence of an alcoholic beverage or other drug or a combination of such substances, [or while] having an alcohol concentration . . . of .10 or more.

Peters objects to the charge, claiming that he could be prosecuted only under section 321G.13(3), which provides as follows: "A person shall not drive or operate an all-terrain vehicle or snowmobile [while] under the influence of intoxicating liquor or narcotics or habit-forming drugs." This statute carries a lesser punishment than §321J.2. The trial court rejected Peters's claim. After conviction Peters appealed, claiming that §321J.2 did not apply to his conduct. How would you rule? Compare State v. Peters, 525 N.W.2d 854 (Iowa 1994); People v. Rogers, 475 N.W.2d 717 (Mich. 1991).

F. SELECTION OF SYSTEM

The use of the phrase "the justice system" to portray an institution that processes people accused of crime in the United States is actually a misnomer. There are in fact many justice systems operating in varied and intersecting ways across the country, and prosecutors have to choose which system handles which case in the event of concurrent jurisdiction. The procedures (and the substantive law) can vary across these different systems, so the choice of system can have a significant impact on how the accused is treated throughout. In this part, we discuss first the choice to place a juvenile arrestee into juvenile court or adult court. We then turn to the interplay between the federal justice system and the state courts where the crime occurs, noting the complexities of multijurisdictional task forces. Finally, we discuss the intersection of tribal courts with federal and state courts in Indian Country.

1. Juvenile versus Adult Justice System

Most of the crimes committed by defendants under 18 years old are handled in specialized juvenile courts as "delinquency" cases. Juvenile courts (which go by various names, such as "Family Court" or "Delinquency Court") tend to have more informal processes than adult courts and do not include jury trials; juvenile proceedings are considered civil (rather than criminal) and are designed to emphasize rehabilitation and to avoid the stigma associated with adult criminal punishment. The juvenile justice system loses its authority over offenders when they reach age 18 or 21.

While most juvenile offenders have their cases adjudicated in the juvenile system, about 5 percent are transferred to the adult criminal justice system based on the nature of the crime and the offender's age. States have created a variety of mechanisms and presumptions to direct juvenile offenders into one system or the other. As with other charging decisions, the prosecutor is the key decisionmaker over this transfer decision, while the legislature also sets some important parameters. Do the limitations on the prosecutor's choice between systems differ from the limits on other prosecutorial charging decisions?

■ HOWARD N. SNYDER, MELISSA SICKMUND & EILEEN POE-YAMAGATA, JUVENILE TRANSFERS TO CRIMINAL COURT IN THE 1990s: LESSONS LEARNED FROM FOUR STUDIES
National Center for Juvenile Justice (August 2000)

The legal mechanisms for "transferring" juveniles from the juvenile to the criminal justice system differ from State to State. . . . These mechanisms, while having different labels across the States, fall into three general categories, according to who makes the transfer decision. The three mechanisms are judicial waiver, statutory exclusion, and concurrent jurisdiction; the decisionmakers are, respectively, the juvenile court judge, the legislature, and the prosecutor.

Judicial waiver (the juvenile court judge). In judicial waivers, a hearing is held in juvenile court, typically in response to the prosecutor's request that the juvenile court judge "waive" the juvenile court's jurisdiction over the matter and transfer the juvenile to criminal court for trial in the "adult" system. Most State statutes limit judicial waiver by age and offense criteria and by "lack of amenability to treatment" criteria. Amenability determinations are typically based on a juvenile's offense history and previous dispositional outcomes but may also include psychological assessments. Under many State statutes, a court making an amenability determination must also consider the availability of dispositional alternatives for treating the juvenile, the time available for sanctions (for older juveniles), public safety, and the best interests of the child.

Regardless of the degree of flexibility accorded to the court, the waiver process must adhere to certain constitutional principles of fairness. The U.S. Supreme Court, in Kent v. United States (1966), held that juvenile courts must provide "the essentials of due process" when transferring juveniles to criminal court. In 1996, approximately 10,000 cases—or 1.6 percent of all formally processed delinquency cases disposed in juvenile courts that year—were judicially waived to criminal court.

Statutory exclusion (the legislature). In a growing number of States, legislatures have statutorily excluded certain young offenders from juvenile court jurisdiction based on age and/or offense criteria. Perhaps the broadest such exclusion occurs in States that have defined the upper age of juvenile court jurisdiction as 15 or 16 and thus excluded large numbers of youth under age 18 from the juvenile justice system. . . .

Many States also exclude certain individuals charged with serious offenses from juvenile court jurisdiction. Such exclusions are typically limited to older youth. The offenses most often targeted for exclusion are capital and other murders and violent offenses; however, an increasing number of States are excluding additional felony offenses. . . .

Concurrent jurisdiction (the prosecutor). Under this transfer option, State statutes give prosecutors the discretion to file certain cases in either juvenile or criminal court because original jurisdiction is shared by both courts. State concurrent jurisdiction provisions, like other transfer provisions, typically are limited by age and offense criteria.

Prosecutorial transfer, unlike judicial waiver, is not subject to judicial review and is not required to meet the due process requirements established in *Kent.* According to some State appellate courts, prosecutorial transfer is an "executive function" equivalent to routine charging decisions. Some States, however, have developed guidelines for prosecutors to follow in "direct filing" cases. . . .

WHAT CRITERIA ARE USED IN THE TRANSFER DECISION?

[Recent studies of juvenile justice in South Carolina, Utah, and Pennsylvania offer insight into the factors that influence the assignment of cases to the juvenile or criminal system.] Judges concurred with most waiver requests made by prosecutors (solicitors) in South Carolina and Utah. Two factors distinguished cases that were waived from those that were not: the extent of a juvenile's court history and the seriousness of his or her offense. . . . In South Carolina, offense seriousness was . . . a key determinant in the waiver decision. Regardless of a youth's court history, cases involving serious person offenses were more likely to be approved for waiver than other types of cases. Although the seriousness of the offense category alone was not as key in Utah as it was in South Carolina, [characteristics] of the crime incident were important in decisions to waive in Utah. Waiver was most likely to be granted in cases involving serious person offenders who used weapons and seriously injured someone, regardless of the offenders' court history. Even first-time offenders in Utah were waived if they seriously injured their victim. For other types of cases, the court looked to a youth's court history to decide whether to waive the matter to criminal court. In these cases, youth with long histories were more likely to be waived than those with shorter histories. . . .

WHAT WAS THE IMPACT OF NEW LEGISLATION THAT EXCLUDES ADDITIONAL OFFENDERS FROM JUVENILE COURT JURISDICTION?

Findings from the project's four transfer studies can be summarized as follows:

Juvenile court judges largely concur with prosecutors as to which juveniles should be transferred to criminal court. These studies show that the juvenile court supports the prosecutor's request for transfer in approximately four out of five cases—indicating that these two key decisionmakers generally agree about who should be waived and who should not. Anecdotal evidence from the Utah study, in fact, indicates that in many cases in which a waiver petition was denied, the denial was based on a prosecutor's recommendation to withdraw the petition (following a plea bargaining agreement). It may be that the high proportion of judicial approval of waiver requests indicates that prosecutors are able to gauge which cases juvenile court judges will agree to waive and request waivers in only those cases. However, the study of exclusions in Pennsylvania implies that criminal court judges agree with juvenile court judges as to which youth should receive criminal court sanctions. . . .

The system adapts to large changes in structure. The structure of transfer decisions has changed in response to the public's concern over the increase in juvenile violence. Data in these studies confirm that the decisionmaking process will adapt to changing legal conditions and social pressure. For example, the study of the implementation of Pennsylvania's exclusion law found that even though the justice system adopted the State's new set of rules and followed new paths, case processing resulted in the same outcomes that would have occurred if the rules had not changed. There had been an expectation that the changed statutory exclusion provision would result in many, many more juveniles being tried in criminal court and in many of these youth ending up incarcerated in adult correctional facilities. However, Pennsylvania's exclusion legislation has had little overall impact on either the number of juveniles handled in criminal court or the proportion incarcerated in adult correctional facilities.

There was also an underlying assumption that transfer decisionmaking by juvenile court judges in Pennsylvania tended to favor juveniles and that decisionmaking by criminal court judges under the new provisions would be different. However, this study found that, in Pennsylvania, the decisionmaking process followed by criminal court judges regarding decertification was much the same as that followed by juvenile court judges regarding waiver. . . .

■ STATE v. JONAS DIXON
967 A.2d 1114 (Vt. 2008)

REIBER, C.J.

¶1. In this interlocutory appeal, defendant appeals from the district court's denial of his motion to transfer his trial for second-degree murder to juvenile court. We conclude that the district court erred in several respects in evaluating the transfer motion. Accordingly, we reverse and remand.

¶2. . . . On January 27, 2007, shortly before 1:00 A.M., defendant, then fifteen years old, shot and killed a man in the living room of defendant's home, a trailer in Sutton, Vermont. The man, who was intoxicated at the time, had arrived around 11:30 P.M. on January 26, 2007 to have sexual relations with defendant's mother. Defendant heard the two having sex and became angry. Soon after, he loaded a twelve-gauge shotgun that he kept in his room for turkey hunting and confronted the man in the living room in an effort to get him to leave. A struggle ensued, and defendant shot the man in the chest at close range; the man died at the scene.

[Defendant's mother had previously been diagnosed with bipolar disorder; she was also the victim of physical and verbal abuse by her ex-husband, the defendant's father, until his death in 2004. Her mental health had been deteriorating since early 2006; she had stopped taking her medication and was experiencing significant delusions on a regular basis. Defendant noticed men coming to the house to have sex with his mother; he told his grandmother that he thought these men were perverts and that they were taking advantage of his mother. He also told his grandmother that he had thought about shooting bottle rockets into his mother's bedroom on one occasion when she had a man over. Defendant told his sister that he would get mad about the men coming over to have sex with his mother, and that he was going to "do something" if any of the men came to the house again.]

¶9. At approximately 12:57 A.M. on January 27, 2007, defendant's mother called 911, indicating that someone had been shot and that an ambulance was needed. She stayed on the phone for about a minute and was then replaced by defendant. Defendant stayed on the phone with the dispatcher until police arrived, approximately twenty-seven minutes later. Defendant was hyperventilating, moaning, and repeating, "Oh my God, oh my God. What have I done? I don't know what the f—— I just did! I don't know what the f—— I just did!" He told the dispatcher, "I was so f——ing pissed, I don't know! I wanted him out of the house—I wanted him out!" When asked where the man had been shot, defendant stated, "I don't know. I just f——ing pulled the shotgun on him and told him to get the f—— out. Then he tried to attack [to] take it away and I pulled the trigger! I just f——ing told him to leave. . . . He tried to f——ing take it and I shot him! Oh no, my life is over. I'm just going to f——ing go and kill myself. I'm not going to go to f——ing jail. I told him to get out and he f——ing tried to get the gun! It wasn't my fault. I was scared!"

¶10. When asked why he wanted the man out, he exclaimed, "Because he was f——ing my mom! I wanted him out! I wanted him out!" Defendant told the dispatcher that he had shot the man with a shotgun and that, "It was four shot. I'm not sure that is strong enough to kill anybody. It probably is. I don't know." . . .

¶11. Defendant was charged with second-degree murder and committed to the custody of Vermont's juvenile-detention facility. On March 27, 2007, he was released into his grandparents' custody, and has been on conditional release ever since. He has not violated the conditions of that release, and is receiving academic tutoring and psychotherapy at this time. Because defendant was between the ages of fourteen and sixteen at the time of the killing, the district court had discretion to transfer the case to the juvenile court. See 33 V.S.A. §5505(b) ("If it appears to any court of this state in a criminal proceeding . . . that the defendant had attained the age of 14 but not the age of 16 at the time an offense specified in [§5506(a)] was alleged to have been committed, that court may forthwith transfer the proceeding to the juvenile court").

¶12. In connection with defendant's motion to transfer, at the request of his counsel, defendant was examined by Dr. Kinsler, a clinical psychologist. . . . Dr. Kinsler's testing and interviews showed that defendant has an IQ of 118, no brain damage, and no mental illness. He opined that defendant is bright, with outstanding academic abilities. Dr. Kinsler found defendant to be introverted, sad, depressed, doleful, and self-deprecating. He indicated that defendant is not a chronically angry person.

¶13. Defendant gave Dr. Kinsler a lengthy account of the shooting. Defendant told Dr. Kinsler that, on the night of the shooting, he and his sister watched a movie with their mother in separate rooms through a common hook-up. Later that night, the shooting victim came to the house, and defendant knew that he was there to have sex with his mother. Defendant heard the two having sex and was extremely angry at the man for taking advantage of his mother. Defendant told Dr. Kinsler that he contemplated killing himself, but instead decided to use the gun to scare the man away. He loaded the gun and went out to the living room, where the man ran at defendant and grabbed the gun barrel and defendant's shoulder. Defendant told Dr. Kinsler that he felt the man would shoot him if he got the gun away from him, and defendant got scared. He took the safety off, and the two struggled for the gun. Feeling that he was about to lose the gun, defendant pulled the trigger. Defendant told Dr. Kinsler that he was hoping only to scare the man, and was not intending to shoot him.

¶14. Dr. Kinsler concluded that defendant's decision to come out with a loaded gun was a very poor and immature one. . . . He felt that defendant was emotionally delayed by about two years due to his mother's mental illness and to the mental and physical abuse defendant had suffered. Dr. Kinsler concluded that defendant did not act aggressively or with any intention to kill and that defendant's use of a shotgun to scare was an error in judgment. In Dr. Kinsler's opinion, in defendant's mind he was defending his mother, not acting aggressively. Dr. Kinsler concluded that defendant should be treated in the juvenile justice system, and that being in the adult system would "harden" defendant. He also concluded that there was sufficient time to treat defendant in the juvenile system.

¶15. The State's expert, Dr. Linder, met with defendant and his counselor for a two-hour interview. . . . Although Dr. Linder had not affirmatively diagnosed defendant, he felt that defendant may have had post-traumatic stress disorder (PTSD) prior to the shooting and that his PTSD may be prolonged as a result of this event. Dr. Linder stated that getting upset was a typical response for defendant, and that this may be a symptom of PTSD. Dr. Linder stated that PTSD is difficult and time-consuming to treat, and that defendant cannot get the proper treatment during the limited time that he will be subject to juvenile supervision. Dr. Linder believed that the extent of defendant's need for mental health services may not be fully known at this time, further supporting his opinion that defendant will need treatment beyond the age of eighteen, when the juvenile court's jurisdiction will end.

¶16. As noted, defendant moved to transfer his case to juvenile court. After the contested hearing at which the above expert testimony was introduced, the trial court denied defendant's motion. In making its conclusions, the trial court considered the eight *Kent* factors for evaluating when a case should be tried in juvenile court, as well as three non-*Kent* factors. See Kent v. United States, 383 U.S. 541 (1966); State v. Buelow, 587 A.2d 948 (Vt. 1990) (noting factors with approval, but holding that they are neither mandatory nor exclusive considerations for the court).

¶26. The court ultimately concluded that a transfer to juvenile court would be inappropriate, because defendant had not met his burden of showing that transfer was warranted. . . .

¶29. [The] factual backdrop to defendant's actions is important as the context within which the trial court's discretion must be exercised. By any measure, the events leading up to the shooting involved the nearly total disruption of defendant's security in his own home and family. While the factual setting properly evoked the district court's attention and concern, the court did not assign it any particular weight. Similarly, the case must be considered in the context of this youthful defendant's increasing frustration at his inability to control the escalating events at home—events of the most humiliating and degrading nature for a child. That these events may have combined to overwhelm his youthful judgment should inform the district court's discretion in light of the special status accorded juvenile cases by the Legislature. We now turn to the factors considered by the district court in ruling on the transfer motion.

¶30. First, we conclude that the district court erred in weighing the non-*Kent* factor titled "System Breakdown" against defendant. As the court noted, DCF plainly failed in its duty to protect or remove defendant and his sister from the deplorable living situation they endured in their mother's house. . . . Their pleas for help from the adults in positions of authority in their lives had had no effect on the deplorable living situation. Just the day before the shooting, according to grandmother, she was told that nothing could be done to help defendant and his sister after business hours, and that they would therefore have to pass another weekend in their mother's home. As the trial court noted, this representation was incorrect. . . .

¶32. The court also appears to have denied the motion to transfer in part to protect "the ability of the public to follow the case through the judicial system." . . . This was not a proper consideration, and was not entitled to independent weight as a matter of law. The Legislature has determined that a primary purpose of the juvenile court system is to protect juveniles from the "taint of criminality" that inevitably results from the publicity and permanence of convictions in the district court. See 33 V.S.A. §5501. [The] district court also rested its decision on five of the *Kent* factors. We consider them in turn.

¶33. First, the court relied on the seriousness of the alleged offense. The court was plainly correct that second-degree murder is a serious offense, among the most harshly punished in our criminal code. There was certainly no abuse of discretion in so concluding.

¶34. Second, the court concluded that the alleged offense was committed in an aggressive, violent, premeditated or willful manner. This conclusion rested on several findings: (1) "the only reason for defendant loading the gun was the possibility of using it"; (2) "threatening another with a loaded shotgun was an inherently aggressive action"; (3) "defendant did not claim that the discharge of the weapon was accidental"; and (4) defendant's "response that evening was the result of anger which had been increasing over many months." On the other side of this factor, as defendant points out, was the evidence that there was a struggle over the gun; that defendant claimed to believe that the man would shoot him if defendant lost control of the gun; that defendant said he did not intend to shoot the man, but only to scare him. Further, defendant argues, the trial court did not credit Dr. Kinsler's opinion that defendant's choice to confront the man with a loaded weapon was the result of emotional immaturity. Defendant's contentions on this point, at their core, amount to an argument with the factfinder's assessment of witness credibility and the weight given to testimony. It was within the province of the trial court to determine that weight, and we will not reevaluate the conflicting testimony or the credibility of witnesses. We find no error in the court's conclusion that the shooting was committed in an aggressive, violent, or premeditated manner. . . .

¶36. The fourth *Kent* factor, which the court also found militated against transfer, is the prosecutive merit of the charge. . . . In cases like the one before us today, however, this fourth factor cannot bear much, if any, dispositive weight. By definition, in all cases in which a juvenile defendant seeks transfer from the district court to the juvenile court, the "prosecutive merit" question has already been decided by the court's finding of probable cause. . . .

¶39. The final *Kent* factor that augured against transfer, according to the district court, was the prospect for adequate protection of the public and the likelihood of reasonable rehabilitation of defendant. The district court found that there was no evidence in the record that the services available in juvenile court were different in kind from those available in district court, and found that prosecution in district court was unlikely to result in defendant's being "hardened." Thus, the court's focus was on the temporal differences between the two courts; in this regard, the court concluded that defendant's "supervisory needs . . . will exceed the temporal grasp of the juvenile court." This statement is supported by the testimony of the State's expert, and we will not question on appeal the factfinder's decision to credit that testimony over the contrary testimony of defendant's expert. [The] fact that defendant has now been maintained on conditions of release, and has been receiving outpatient treatment for well over a year, can only support the conclusion that public protection does not require adult prosecution. Nonetheless, it was within the district court's discretion to conclude that, despite there being no public-protection basis for retaining jurisdiction, the need for more time to rehabilitate defendant supported trial in district court.

¶40. Accordingly, we reverse and remand so that the district court may reevaluate defendant's transfer motion in light of this opinion. We do not dictate here how the trial court should rule. Rather, we remand in recognition that the trial court has seen the witnesses, heard their testimony, viewed the exhibits, and is therefore in a better position than this Court to reweigh the factors pertinent to transfer in light of our decision today. . . .

Notes

1. *Choice of system for juvenile offenders: majority position.* The choice between the adult and juvenile systems is cluttered with various starting presumptions, shifting burdens of proof or persuasion, and opportunities to reconsider the choice of systems. In the end, the statutes in almost every state (along with the federal juvenile system) initially assign the great majority of juveniles to the juvenile court, and then allow a judge in the juvenile court to "waive" jurisdiction after an investigation, a hearing, and a statement of reasons by the court. See Kent v. United States, 383 U.S. 541 (1966).

Almost half the states give prosecutors the power in some cases to select between the adult and juvenile systems when there is "concurrent" jurisdiction (ordinarily for the most serious offenses and the oldest juveniles). Most states initially place into the adult system the oldest juveniles who commit the most serious crimes, and place into the juvenile system (at least initially) the youngest juveniles and those who commit the least serious crimes.

Various studies of juvenile justice suggest that major changes in the laws dealing with the assignment of juveniles to the adult criminal justice system have made little difference in the numbers of juvenile cases actually resolved in the adult system. In 2002, two-thirds of the juveniles transferred to criminal court were charged with a violent offense. The proportion of delinquency cases that were waived into the adult system was 1.4 percent in 1985; the proportion reached 1.5 percent in 1991 and then dropped to 0.8 percent by 2002. Howard N. Snyder & Melissa Sickmund, Juvenile Offenders and Victims: 2006 National Report 187 (2006).

Where the law gives the prosecutor the initial choice of systems, that decision is usually subject to judicial review, and the burden of proof usually falls on the party seeking to transfer the case (that is, the juvenile attempting to move into the juvenile court). In many states, such as North Dakota, the trial court in the adult system retains jurisdiction if there are "reasonable grounds" (in essence, probable cause) to believe that the juvenile committed the crime as charged and would not be "amenable to rehabilitation" in the juvenile system. See In the Interest of A.E., 559 N.W.2d 215 (N.D. 1997). Thus, the judge decides whether to transfer the juvenile during an "amenability" hearing. See State v. Fernandes, 12 A.3d 925 (Conn. 2011) (statute empowers criminal court judge in serious cases to decide whether defendant should transfer into juvenile system).

2. *Constitutional challenges to charging of juveniles.* Juveniles in several states have challenged the constitutionality of statutes that mandate the choice of the adult system for some cases or that give prosecutors the discretion to file charges in the adult system. These challenges are based on many different clauses in state constitutions, most frequently due process and equal protection clauses. See In re William M., 196 P.3d 456 (Nev. 2008) (statute that creates rebuttable presumption that certain juveniles are certifiable for trial in adult court offends the constitutional privilege against self-incrimination). More often than not, however, the challenges have failed. See State v. Angilau, 245 P.3d 745 (Utah 2011) (upholds constitutionality of statutory assignment to adult system for designated serious crimes); Manduley v. Superior Court, 41 P.3d 3 (Cal. 2002) (upholds constitutionality of system allowing prosecutor to choose juvenile versus adult system for certain defendants).

3. *Right to counsel and right to jury in juvenile delinquency proceedings.* The right to retained counsel in delinquency proceedings was made a federal constitutional requirement in In re Gault, 387 U.S. 1 (1967). Because counsel is not appointed or is often waived, less than half of all juveniles are represented by attorneys in their delinquency proceedings. Barry Feld, Criminalizing the American Juvenile Court 222 (1993). Statutes in many states have created systems for appointing counsel in some juvenile proceedings. Roughly 10 states have mandatory appointment statutes; about half the states make appointment of counsel discretionary. See Tory Caeti, Craig Hemmens & Velmer Burton, Jr., Juvenile Right to Counsel: A National Comparison of State Legal Codes, 23 Am. J. 611 (1996).

Jury trials are typically not available in the juvenile system, even when they would be required for comparable charges in the adult system. But see In re L.M., 186 P.3d 164 (Kan. 2008) (because the goals and processes of the revised juvenile justice code are now patterned on the adult criminal system, with a reduced emphasis on rehabilitation and the State's parental role in providing guidance and discipline, procedural protections in juvenile proceedings must now include a jury trial, not just bench trial). In situations where transfer into the adult criminal courts means that the state will appoint an attorney and provide a jury, will a juvenile welcome the transfer?

4. *Abolition of juvenile court?* The first juvenile court was created in Chicago after the Illinois legislature passed the Illinois Juvenile Court Act of 1899. By 1925, 46 states, 3 territories, and the District of Columbia had separate juvenile courts. See Robert E. Shepherd, The Juvenile Court at 100 Years: A Look Back, Juv. Just. (Dec. 1999) at 13. About 20 states have created "family courts" with broader jurisdiction to handle the full range of criminal and civil issues involving children. Now, 100 years after their creation, the basic premises that support the creation of juvenile courts are in doubt. Are children who commit crimes better served by having a separate system for adjudicating their crimes and imposing sentences? Or would they be better off in a single criminal justice system, perhaps with special allowances made for their age?

5. *Disparate racial impact in juvenile justice.* The juvenile justice system entrusts prosecutors and judges with even larger zones of discretion than they utilize in the adult criminal justice system. As a result, a great deal of research has taken place in the juvenile justice system. One topic of continuing concern is the presence of any racial disparities in the outcomes of the juvenile system. On the whole, the research has found racial disparities that are larger than disparities found in some studies of the adult criminal justice system. As a legislator, how would you respond to research findings of this sort study? Would you argue to transfer fewer juveniles into the adult system (even though the racial disparities in the adult system might be smaller overall)? To make the juvenile system less discretionary? For a sample of the voluminous research about the operation of the juvenile justice systems in various states, go to the web extension for this chapter at *http://www.crimpro.com/extension/ch13*.

2. *Federal versus State Justice System*

Turning now to the federal versus state system choice, it is often said that criminal justice remains primarily a state and local function, and in terms of volume that remains true. The federal courts still produce less than 10 percent of the felony convictions in this country each year, and virtually all misdemeanor convictions come out of the state courts. But the areas of potential overlap between the federal and state criminal justice systems have been growing. The federal government has been exerting more authority and money on criminal matters during the last few decades than at any previous point in the nation's history. In particular, the federal presence in narcotics enforcement has grown enormously over the years. See Michael M. O'Hear, Federalism and Drug Control, 57 Vand. L. Rev. 783 (2004).

The 1999 report of the American Bar Association's Task Force on Federalization of Criminal Law documents various aspects of this growth. Federal crime legislation has become more common: "[More] than forty percent of the federal criminal provisions enacted since the Civil War have been enacted since 1970." The number of federal investigators and prosecutors has expanded along with the number of available federal crimes. The report lists some negative consequences of federalization: "diminution of the stature of the state courts in the perception of citizens" and "disparate results for the same conduct."

Informal discussions between federal and state prosecutors normally determine whether a case will be routed through the federal or the state system. The federal system can normally devote more resources to a case, and a federal conviction normally produces a more severe sentence than would result from a state conviction. For these reasons, combined with the overwhelming volume of cases in the state system, the federal prosecutor normally can take her choice of cases that violate the criminal laws of both jurisdictions. Speaking in generalities, federal prosecutors do tend to accept cases involving the largest losses and the defendants with the most serious prior convictions for violent crimes. See Susan Klein et al., Why Federal Prosecutors Charge: A Comparison of Federal and New York State Arson and Robbery Filings, 2006-2010, 51 U. Hous. L. Rev. 1381 (2014).

Informal working groups of state and federal investigators and prosecutors, known as "inter-agency task forces" or some comparable label, might develop over time some predictable criteria for assignment of prosecutions to the state or federal systems. In order to combat drug trafficking, for example, some states employ multi-jurisdictional drug task forces, which are made up of law enforcement officers from state, county, and local police departments to pool resources across multiple jurisdictions. See, e.g., *http://www.icjia.state.il.us/assets/articles/MEGTF_FINAL_REPORT_120517.pdf.* For further exploration of the devices used to coordinate federal and state law enforcement (along with the related questions of coordination among different states), go to the web extension for this chapter at *http://www.crimpro.com/extension/ch13.*

Some restraint on the growth of federal criminal law might come from various constitutional provisions, such as the commerce clause, that were designed to limit the authority of the federal government and to preserve essential areas of state authority. Those constitutional limits, however, have produced very few rulings that in fact limit congressional authority to create federal crimes. In United States v. Lopez, 514 U.S. 549 (1995), the Supreme Court held that possession of a gun near a school is not an economic activity that has a "substantial effect" on interstate commerce; thus, Congress went beyond its constitutional authority in passing a federal crime to cover this activity. More typical of recent cases, however, is Sabri v. United States, 541 U.S. 600 (2004), where the Court held that Congress had constitutional authority to make it a federal crime to bribe officials of a local organization or government that receives federal program funds, even when the bribe has nothing to do with the federal funds. Even a remote connection to federal funds makes such a law a valid exercise of Congress's authority under the Constitution's spending clause.

■ ALBERTO R. GONZALES v. ANGEL McCLARY RAICH
545 U.S. 1 (2005)

STEVENS, J.*

I.

In 1996, California voters passed Proposition 215, now codified as the Compassionate Use Act of 1996. The proposition was designed to ensure that

---

*[Justices Scalia, Kennedy, Souter, Ginsburg, and Breyer joined this opinion.—EDS.]

"seriously ill" residents of the State have access to marijuana for medical purposes, and to encourage Federal and State Governments to take steps toward ensuring the safe and affordable distribution of the drug to patients in need. The Act creates an exemption from criminal prosecution for physicians, as well as for patients and primary caregivers who possess or cultivate marijuana for medicinal purposes with the recommendation or approval of a physician. A "primary caregiver" is a person who has consistently assumed responsibility for the housing, health, or safety of the patient.

Respondents Angel Raich and Diane Monson are California residents who suffer from a variety of serious medical conditions and have sought to avail themselves of medical marijuana pursuant to the terms of the Compassionate Use Act. They are being treated by licensed, board-certified family practitioners, who have concluded, after prescribing a host of conventional medicines to treat respondents' conditions and to alleviate their associated symptoms, that marijuana is the only drug available that provides effective treatment. Respondent Monson cultivates her own marijuana, and ingests the drug in a variety of ways including smoking and using a vaporizer. Respondent Raich, by contrast, is unable to cultivate her own, and thus relies on two caregivers, litigating as "John Does," to provide her with locally grown marijuana at no charge.

On August 15, 2002, county deputy sheriffs and agents from the federal Drug Enforcement Administration (DEA) came to Monson's home. After a thorough investigation, the county officials concluded that her use of marijuana was entirely lawful as a matter of California law. Nevertheless, after a three-hour standoff, the federal agents seized and destroyed all six of her cannabis plants.

Respondents thereafter brought this action against the Attorney General of the United States and the head of the DEA seeking injunctive and declaratory relief prohibiting the enforcement of the federal Controlled Substances Act (CSA), 21 U.S.C. § 801 et seq., to the extent it prevents them from possessing, obtaining, or manufacturing cannabis for their personal medical use. In their complaint and supporting affidavits, Raich and Monson described the severity of their afflictions, their repeatedly futile attempts to obtain relief with conventional medications, and the opinions of their doctors concerning their need to use marijuana. Respondents claimed that enforcing the CSA against them would violate the Commerce Clause, the Due Process Clause of the Fifth Amendment, the Ninth and Tenth Amendments of the Constitution, and the doctrine of medical necessity. The District Court denied respondents' motion for a preliminary injunction. . . .

The case is made difficult by respondents' strong arguments that they will suffer irreparable harm because, despite a congressional finding to the contrary, marijuana does have valid therapeutic purposes. The question before us, however, is not whether it is wise to enforce the statute in these circumstances; rather, it is whether Congress' power to regulate interstate markets for medicinal substances encompasses the portions of those markets that are supplied with drugs produced and consumed locally. Well-settled law controls our answer. The CSA is a valid exercise of federal power, even as applied to the troubling facts of this case. . . .

II.

Marijuana . . . was not significantly regulated by the Federal Government until 1937 when accounts of marijuana's addictive qualities and physiological

effects, paired with dissatisfaction with enforcement efforts at state and local levels, prompted Congress to pass the Marihuana Tax Act, 50 Stat. 551 (repealed
1970). [The] Marihuana Tax Act did not outlaw the possession or sale of marijuana
outright. Rather, it imposed registration and reporting requirements for all individuals importing, producing, selling, or dealing in marijuana, and required the
payment of annual taxes in addition to transfer taxes whenever the drug changed
hands. Moreover, doctors wishing to prescribe marijuana for medical purposes
were required to comply with rather burdensome administrative requirements.
Noncompliance exposed traffickers to severe federal penalties, whereas compliance
would often subject them to prosecution under state law. Thus, . . . the prohibitively
expensive taxes, and the risks attendant on compliance practically curtailed the
marijuana trade.

Then in 1970, after declaration of the national "war on drugs," federal drug
policy underwent a significant transformation. [Prompted] by a perceived need to
consolidate the growing number of piecemeal drug laws and to enhance federal
drug enforcement powers, Congress enacted [the CSA]. The main objectives of
the CSA were to conquer drug abuse and to control the legitimate and illegitimate
traffic in controlled substances. Congress was particularly concerned with the need
to prevent the diversion of drugs from legitimate to illicit channels.

To effectuate these goals, Congress devised a closed regulatory system making it
unlawful to manufacture, distribute, dispense, or possess any controlled substance
except in a manner authorized by the CSA. 21 U.S.C. §§ 841(a)(1), 844(a). The CSA
categorizes all controlled substances into five schedules. The drugs are grouped
together based on their accepted medical uses, the potential for abuse, and their
psychological and physical effects on the body. Each schedule is associated with
a distinct set of controls regarding the manufacture, distribution, and use of the
substances listed therein. The CSA and its implementing regulations set forth strict
requirements regarding registration, labeling and packaging, production quotas,
drug security, and recordkeeping. 21 CFR § 1301 et seq. By classifying marijuana as
a Schedule I drug, as opposed to listing it on a lesser schedule, the manufacture,
distribution, or possession of marijuana became a criminal offense, with the sole
exception being use of the drug as part of a Food and Drug Administration preap-
proved research study.

III.

Respondents in this case do not dispute that passage of the CSA . . . was well
within Congress' commerce power. Nor do they contend that any provision or section of the CSA amounts to an unconstitutional exercise of congressional authority.
Rather, respondents' challenge is actually quite limited; they argue that the CSA's
categorical prohibition of the manufacture and possession of marijuana as applied
to the intrastate manufacture and possession of marijuana for medical purposes pursuant to California law exceeds Congress' authority under the Commerce Clause.

Our case law firmly establishes Congress' power to regulate purely local activities that are part of an economic "class of activities" that have a substantial effect on
interstate commerce. See Perez v. United States, 402 U.S. 146, 151 (1971); Wickard
v. Filburn, 317 U.S. 111, 128-129 (1942). As we stated in *Wickard*, "even if appellee's
activity be local and though it may not be regarded as commerce, it may still, whatever its nature, be reached by Congress if it exerts a substantial economic effect on

interstate commerce." *Id.*, at 125. We have never required Congress to legislate with scientific exactitude. When Congress decides that the "total incidence" of a practice poses a threat to a national market, it may regulate the entire class. In this vein, we have reiterated that when "a general regulatory statute bears a substantial relation to commerce, the de minimis character of individual instances arising under that statute is of no consequence." United States v. Lopez, 514 U.S. 549, 558 (1995). . . .

Findings in the introductory sections of the CSA explain why Congress deemed it appropriate to encompass local activities within the scope of the CSA. The submissions of the parties and the numerous amici all seem to agree that the national, and international, market for marijuana has dimensions that are fully comparable to those defining the class of activities regulated by the Secretary pursuant to the 1938 statute. Respondents nonetheless insist that the CSA cannot be constitutionally applied to their activities because Congress did not make a specific finding that the intrastate cultivation and possession of marijuana for medical purposes based on the recommendation of a physician would substantially affect the larger interstate marijuana market. Be that as it may, we have never required Congress to make particularized findings in order to legislate. . . .

In assessing the scope of Congress' authority under the Commerce Clause, we stress that the task before us is a modest one. We need not determine whether respondents' activities, taken in the aggregate, substantially affect interstate commerce in fact, but only whether a "rational basis" exists for so concluding. Given the enforcement difficulties that attend distinguishing between marijuana cultivated locally and marijuana grown elsewhere, and concerns about diversion into illicit channels, we have no difficulty concluding that Congress had a rational basis for believing that failure to regulate the intrastate manufacture and possession of marijuana would leave a gaping hole in the CSA. That the regulation ensnares some purely intrastate activity is of no moment.

[The] fact that marijuana is used for personal medical purposes on the advice of a physician cannot itself serve as a distinguishing factor. The CSA designates marijuana as contraband for any purpose; in fact, by characterizing marijuana as a Schedule I drug, Congress expressly found that the drug has no acceptable medical uses. Moreover, the CSA is a comprehensive regulatory regime specifically designed to regulate which controlled substances can be utilized for medicinal purposes, and in what manner. Indeed, most of the substances classified in the CSA "have a useful and legitimate medical purpose." 21 U.S.C. § 801(1). Accordingly, the mere fact that marijuana—like virtually every other controlled substance regulated by the CSA—is used for medicinal purposes cannot possibly serve to distinguish it from the core activities regulated by the CSA.

Second, limiting the activity to marijuana possession and cultivation "in accordance with state law" cannot serve to place respondents' activities beyond congressional reach. The Supremacy Clause unambiguously provides that if there is any conflict between federal and state law, federal law shall prevail. It is beyond peradventure that federal power over commerce is superior to that of the States to provide for the welfare or necessities of their inhabitants, however legitimate or dire those necessities may be.

[Respondents raised in the lower courts several alternative theories of relief. We do not address] the question whether judicial relief is available to respondents on these alternative bases. We do note, however, the presence of another avenue of relief. [The] statute authorizes procedures for the reclassification of Schedule

I drugs. But perhaps even more important than these legal avenues is the democratic process, in which the voices of voters allied with these respondents may one day be heard in the halls of Congress. . . .

Problem 13-5. Federal Day

In Manhattan, federal prosecutors operated a program known as "Federal Day." One day each week chosen at random, all drug arrests obtained by state and local police agencies were processed in federal court, where sentences for drug crimes were much higher than in the state courts. Prosecutors said that the program was designed to help the overwhelmed state courts and to deter criminal activity by imposing the stiffer sentences. The federal court in the district adjudicated between 100 and 200 indictments per year in cases that the local police developed. For instance, 231 cases went to federal district court under the Federal Day program between January 2008 and May 2010. During that same period, New York police made 5,837 felony narcotics arrests. Of the 5,606 cases sent to the state prosecutor in Manhattan, 1,172 resulted in state felony indictments. A total of 1,043 other cases were reduced to state misdemeanors.

A U.S. senator heard about the Federal Day program and introduced legislation requiring all U.S. Attorneys' offices to institute such programs. Would you advise the U.S. Attorney for Manhattan to continue the program? Under what conditions?

3. Crimes Committed on Tribal Lands

Lastly, turning to the issue of crimes committed on tribal lands, by tribe members and outsiders, three justice systems might express interest: tribal authority, state authority, and federal authority.

■ JAMES D. DIAMOND, PRACTICING INDIAN LAW IN FEDERAL, STATE, AND TRIBAL CRIMINAL COURTS: AN UPDATE ABOUT RECENT EXPANSION OF CRIMINAL JURISDICTION OVER NON-INDIANS
32 Criminal Justice 8 (Winter 2018)

. . . Indian law in the United States is a complex maze depending on what the subject is, the pinpoint precise location of where an offense is committed, and the particular indigenous people affected. The state attorney general of Washington once said, "One reason that the State of Washington and its Indian citizens have frequently been in court is because no one truly understands exactly what position an Indian tribe occupies within the federal system." And Comanche activist LaDonna Harris said, "We are part of the federal system, not part of the states. Our political relationship is not well-known and little is understood, which causes a great deal of problems." . . .

Lawyers appearing in tribal courts working in either prosecution or defense quickly learn that the place to start analyzing any case is to determine where jurisdiction lies. A case may be brought in one forum or more than one, in cases where concurrent jurisdiction exists. Attacking a jurisdiction problem can be complex, and requires attention.

Indian tribes, as sovereigns, historically have inherent jurisdictional power over everything occurring within their territory. Tribal courts are courts of general jurisdiction that continue to have broad criminal jurisdiction. Any analysis of tribal criminal jurisdiction should begin with this sovereign authority and determine whether there has been any way in which this broad overarching sovereign authority has been reduced. . . .

Defining terms. . . . The term "Indian country" was first defined by the Indian Country Crimes Act (ICCA) and now applies to most federal Indian law. The term includes (1) all land within the limits of any Indian reservation under the jurisdiction of the United States government, (2) dependent Indian communities, and (3) all Indian allotments, where the Indian titles have not been extinguished.

[There] is no single statute that defines "Indian" for federal Indian law purposes. The most widely accepted test evolved after the 1846 United States Supreme Court case of United States v. Rogers. This test considers Indian descent as well as recognition by a federally recognized tribe. No single percentage of Indian ancestry has been established to satisfy the descent prong of the test. Congress has often deferred to tribal determinations of establishing their own membership, which sometimes impose actual blood quantum parameters. Tribal membership often requires formal enrollment. Where this is the case, the tribe's own list of enrolled members is the easiest source of determining Indian status. . . . In cases where there is not a tribal enrollment list, other factors may be considered, including whether the person holds himself or herself out to be an Indian, lives on an Indian reservation, attends Indian schools, or receives tribal or federal benefits for being an Indian.

Criminal jurisdiction over non-Indians. With very limited exceptions that are outlined here, tribal courts no longer have criminal jurisdiction over non-Indians, unless Congress delegates such power to them. . . .

Sentencing limitations. The ICRA provides that tribal courts cannot "impose for conviction of any one offense any penalty or punishment greater than imprisonment for a term of one year or a fine of $5,000, or both." However, in 2010 Congress enacted amendments to ICRA (referred to as the Tribal Law and Order Act of 2010) whereby tribes are permitted to sentence defendants up to a term of three years for any one offense and fines of up to $15,000, if the tribes guarantee defendants certain constitutional rights. These constitutional rights include the rights of indigent defendants to tribal paid counsel, their cases to be presided over by judges "licensed to practice law," and other guarantees.

Charging defendants in both federal and tribal court is not a violation of double jeopardy. The U.S. Supreme Court held that the source of the power to punish offenders is an inherent part of tribal sovereignty and not a grant of federal power. United States v. Wheeler, 435 U.S. 313 (1978). Consequently, when two prosecutions are by separate sovereigns (e.g., the Navajo Nation and the United States), the subsequent federal prosecution does not violate the defendant's right against double jeopardy.

Federal criminal jurisdiction. . . . Congress granted criminal jurisdiction in Indian country to the federal courts in certain circumstances. [Under the General Crimes

Act, 18 U.S.C. §1152, enacted in 1817], the federal courts have jurisdiction over interracial crimes committed in Indian country as follows:

> Except as otherwise expressly provided by law, the general laws of the United States as to the punishment of offenses committed in any place within the sole and exclusive jurisdiction of the United States, except the District of Columbia, shall extend to the Indian country. This section shall not extend to offenses committed by one Indian against the person or property of another Indian, nor to any Indian committing any offense in the Indian Country who has been punished by the local law of the tribe, or to any case where, by treaty stipulations, the exclusive jurisdiction over such offenses is or may be secured to the Indian tribes respectively.

The Major Crimes Act, 18 U.S.C. § 1153, enacted following the U.S. Supreme Court's 1883 decision in Ex parte Crow Dog, provides for federal criminal jurisdiction over seven major crimes when committed by Indians in Indian country. Over time, the original seven offenses have been increased and now include 16 offenses: murder, manslaughter, kidnapping, maiming, felony sexual abuse, incest, assault with intent to commit murder, assault with a dangerous weapon, assault resulting in serious bodily injury, assault against an individual under the age of 16, felony child abuse, arson, burglary, robbery, felony embezzlement, and theft. . . .

State criminal jurisdiction. The states generally do not have jurisdiction over crimes occurring in Indian country, [with limited exceptions. Under Public Law 280, enacted in 1953], Congress authorized states to exercise jurisdiction over offenses by or against Indians. 18 U.S.C. § 1162. Public Law 280 provided for broad state concurrent criminal jurisdiction on those states and reservations impacted by the law. Some states have mandatory Public Law 280 status and others opted to assume it. . . .

Non-Indian vs. non-Indian crimes. The U.S. Supreme Court ruled in United States v. McBratney, 104 U.S. 621 (1882), and Draper v. United States, 164 U.S. 240 (1896), that state courts have jurisdiction to punish wholly non-Indian crimes in Indian country. . . .

Some cases that might be treated as criminal actions in federal or state court may need to be treated as civil cases in tribal courts. This may be due to many factors, including legal jurisdictional limitations such as the lack of tribal jurisdiction over non-Indians, practical jurisdictional limitations (e.g., Public Law 280), and resource limitations. Consequently, it is more difficult to determine individual victim's rights in Indian country than would be necessary in federal and state courts. . . .

Domestic Violence Exception. In 2013, President Obama signed into law the reauthorization of the Violence Against Women Act (VAWA), a federal statute that addresses domestic violence and other crimes against women. When originally enacted in 1994, VAWA created new federal offenses and sanctions, provided training for federal, state, and local law enforcement and courts to address these crimes, and funded a variety of community services to protect and support victims. Most significantly, the amended version of VAWA recognizes that tribal courts have jurisdiction over criminal cases brought by tribes against nonmembers, including non-Indians, that arise under VAWA. . . . This change in the law represents a major change for native communities and especially native women, [because] Native American and Alaska Native women experience sexual violence at a rate two and a half times higher than other women in the United States.

G. VICTIM INPUT INTO CHARGING DECISIONS

If prosecutors won't prosecute, perhaps an aggrieved citizen will. Indeed, there is a long tradition of private rather than public prosecution. Public prosecutors—like many of the institutions of criminal justice, including police and public defense counsel—are a modern invention. Throughout much of the eighteenth and nineteenth centuries, it was common for private citizens to bring complaints to a grand jury or a magistrate, *and* to hire private attorneys to assist the public prosecutor or to prosecute the criminal case alone. Only at the start of the twentieth century did the public prosecutor become the primary method for initiating criminal charges.

Remnants of true private prosecution exist still in United States law. The "victim's rights" concept has strengthened the accountability of public prosecutors to victims of crime. Prosecutors also reflect the political priorities of the voters or the executive who appoints them, and the legislature that funds them.

As traditional and well recognized as interest group politics may be, the link between private preferences and public prosecution is not widely recognized. Consider the legal and policy dimensions of the modern forms of private prosecution described in the following statute and journal article.

■ WISCONSIN STATUTES §968.02

(1) Except as otherwise provided in this section, a complaint charging a person with an offense shall be issued only by a district attorney of the county where the crime is alleged to have been committed. A complaint is issued when it is approved for filing for the district attorney. . . .

(3) If a district attorney refuses or is unavailable to issue a complaint, a circuit judge may permit the filing of a complaint, if the judge finds there is probable cause to believe that the person to be charged has committed an offense after conducting a hearing. If the district attorney has refused to issue a complaint, he or she shall be informed of the hearing and may attend. The hearing shall be ex parte without the right of cross-examination.

■ JOSEPH KENNEDY, PRIVATE FINANCING OF CRIMINAL PROSECUTIONS AND THE DIFFERING PROTECTIONS OF LIBERTY AND EQUALITY IN THE CRIMINAL JUSTICE SYSTEM
24 Hastings Constitutional Law Quarterly 665 (1997)

. . . Private financing of a government prosecution in a criminal case frames a unique set of questions about what role equality should play in a prosecutor's decisions. Should a prosecutor be able to consider the willingness of a victim to finance a prosecution in choosing which cases to prosecute or to what extent a case should be prosecuted? Would such victims enjoy preferential access to justice? By expanding the resources available to a government prosecutor on a selective basis, private financing introduces a new tension into prosecutorial decisionmaking: Society's interest in punishing the guilty must compete with society's interest in equal treatment by government.

In allocating their limited time and resources, prosecutors choose which crimes to prosecute based on the type of crime, the nature of the victim, and the nature of the potential defendants. Prosecutors are expected to be guided in these choices by the "public interest," but embedded in the prosecutor's conception of the public interest are trade-offs among competing public goods and competing private interests. Is it more in the public interest to prosecute insurance fraud or environmental crime? To prosecute fraud committed against businesses or against consumers? To invest heavily in a single death penalty prosecution or to spread the same investment of time and money over all crimes of violence? Currently, such choices are entrusted to the sole discretion of the prosecutor. Private financing raises the question of whether taking voluntary contributions from victims or other private groups creates a conflict of interest—a conflict between the prosecutor's obligation to be impartial in making these choices and the prosecutor's institutional interest in the monies received.

Private financing of criminal prosecutions also raises the question of whether institutions, as opposed to people, can be biased by money. Prosecutorial conflict of interest typically involves a prosecutor who has some personal interest—sometimes pecuniary—in the prosecution of a given criminal case. A paradigm example is the prosecutor who prosecutes a defendant in a criminal case and simultaneously represents the victim of the crime in a civil suit against the same defendant. Private financing arguably involves no such personal interest because the money does not flow directly into the pockets of any individual prosecutor—instead, it flows into the coffers of the prosecutor's office.

Private financing has taken a number of different forms. In California's Silicon Valley, a district attorney prosecuting a trade secret case allowed the victim corporation to pay more than $13,000 for independent expert investigators and was recused by the trial judge, who found that receipt of the funds created a conflict of interest. Local businesses in California's Ventura County voluntarily contributed $150,000 to a fund used by the district attorney to prosecute workers' compensation fraud, a fund that has operated with the California Attorney General's blessing. In Portland, Oregon, local businesses have funded the salary and office expenses of a "neighborhood district attorney." In Philadelphia, the district attorney established a nonprofit corporation for the purpose of accepting private contributions for a variety of purposes, which include financing certain prosecutions. In an unusual case not involving contributions from business interests, a number of people from all parts of the country sent donations to help finance the costs of the prosecution against Susan Smith for the murder of her two sons after the media reported that the rural South Carolina county might not be able to afford the expense of a death penalty prosecution.

The trend toward private financing is driven in part by chronic fiscal pressures. Prosecutors at all levels of government face budget cutbacks at the same time that public concern about crime is at an all-time high. Taxes, the traditional means of financing government prosecutions, are seen as politically unpopular. Allowing some sort of private financial contribution arguably helps to close the gap between supply and demand for the prosecution of crime.

Private financing may also be seen as a way to make government more efficient in prosecuting crime. Partnering public with private dollars is an increasingly popular form of "reinventing government," through which public resources are directed toward the problems that concern society most. In some cases, private financing could be seen as a "user's fee" for those victims of crime who wish to use the criminal justice system.

However, private financing is driven by more than just monetary concerns. Private financing taps into powerful pressures for a greater involvement of the victim in the criminal justice system. A view exists that both society's interest in punishment and the individual interests of the victim lose out to the interests of the criminal justice system's repeat players—the judges, prosecutors, and defense counsel who deal with one another on a daily basis. Some believe that only through greater participation of the victim in the charging and disposition of crimes will criminals get their just deserts and victims their recompense due. From this latter perspective, private financing could be seen as a means both of squeezing more punishment out of a criminal justice system in which institutional players are too often willing to compromise and of shaping the course of the prosecution in a manner beneficial to the victim.

Notes

1. *Private filing of complaints.* Most states give the public prosecutor exclusive authority to file criminal complaints. See Cal. Govt. Code §26500 ("The public prosecutor shall attend the courts, and within his or her discretion shall initiate and conduct on behalf of the people all prosecutions"). The same is true in the federal system. The court in Harman v. Frye, 425 S.E.2d 566 (W. Va. 1992), considered criminal complaints for battery that two participants in a fight filed against each other. The opinion summarized the reasons why most states have required the public prosecutor to approve of the filing of any criminal charges:

> [Citizens] can misuse the right to file a criminal complaint before a magistrate by exaggerating the facts or omitting relevant facts they disclose to the magistrate so as to transform a noncriminal dispute into a crime. The magistrate, who must remain neutral, is not in the same position as the prosecuting attorney or law enforcement officers to ascertain whether all of the relevant facts have been disclosed accurately. . . . When citizens file criminal complaints before the magistrate which later prove to be frivolous, retaliatory or unfounded, the prosecuting attorney is required to take the time to investigate the complaint before moving a nolle pros to dismiss. . . . Moreover, additional time and expense are also incurred when either the public defender or an attorney-at-law must be appointed to represent indigent persons against whom frivolous, retaliatory or unfounded charges have been filed. . . . Finally, private citizens have not undergone the same professional training as prosecuting attorneys or law enforcement officers nor are they subject to the same rules of professional conduct and discipline which are imposed on prosecuting attorneys and law enforcement officers.

In a few states, statutes authorize citizens to file criminal complaints even when the prosecutor has declined to do so. Most of these statutes (like the Wisconsin statute reprinted above) allow the private complaint to occur only after the public prosecutor has affirmatively decided not to file charges, and they require the citizen to obtain approval for the charges from a judge or grand jury. A few of the statutes apply only to particular crimes, such as domestic violence or issuance of a worthless check. See W. Va. Code §§48-27-902, 61-3-39a. What do you anticipate might happen if citizens could prosecute criminal matters without the assistance of an attorney? See In re Richland County Magistrate's Court, 699 S.E.2d 161 (S.C. 2010) (state law that authorizes nonlawyers to represent business in civil actions does not extend to nonlawyers prosecuting misdemeanor charges on behalf of business). Note that in some civil law countries, citizens can direct criminal charges against other people, although not always successfully. See, e.g., *https://www.chronicle.com/article/French-Court-Finds-in-Favor-of/126599.* Can the public prosecutor prevent any abuses of private complaints simply by dismissing charges once they are filed? If the prosecutor retains the power to dismiss charges filed by a private citizen, has the mechanism accomplished anything other than creating paperwork?

2. *Historical roots of victim rights during prosecution.* By the turn of the twentieth century the public prosecutor became the primary method for initiating criminal charges. Private prosecutions became the exception rather than the rule as public prosecutors became more professionalized and independent of the courts, professional police departments became more common in metropolitan areas, and acquittal rates rose for privately initiated complaints.

Traces of the older private prosecution system remain visible today, and are gaining renewed attention as a method of empowering the victims of crime. More than half the states still have statutes or constitutional provisions that allow private counsel, retained by a crime victim, to participate in criminal proceedings. In most jurisdictions, the private prosecutor may only assist the prosecutor, while in a few the private prosecutor has more authority to direct the criminal proceedings. See, e.g., Pa. Stat. tit. 16, §1409 (the court may "direct any private counsel employed by [a complainant] to conduct the entire proceeding").

Most states, however, do not give the victim any right to "consult" with the prosecutor about the charges to be filed. They simply instruct the prosecutor to inform the victim about the charges to be filed or about the decision not to file charges. See Ariz. Stat. §13-4408 (prosecutor to give victim notice of the charge against defendant and concise statement of procedural steps in criminal prosecution, and to inform victim of decision to decline prosecution, with reasons for declination). Are these "notice" statutes an inevitable response to the abandonment of private prosecutions? To get a sense of the range of these efforts to allow victim representation in the criminal process, go to the web extension for this chapter at *http://www.crimpro. com/extension/ch13.*

3. *Private financial aid to public prosecution.* What is wrong with private parties funding public prosecutions so long as the public prosecutor makes the decisions? As the Kennedy excerpt suggests, one might treat private prosecutions of crime as a way to supplement the limited resources of a public prosecutor, much as we rely on "private attorneys general" to help enforce some civil statutes. See Roger A. Fairfax, Jr., Delegation of the Criminal Prosecution Function to Private Actors, 43 U.C. Davis L. Rev. 411 (2009). In Commonwealth v. Ellis, 708 N.E.2d 644 (Mass. 1999), the Massachusetts Supreme Court upheld the statutory industry funding scheme for insurance and fraud prosecutions, finding no appearance of conflict. The court observed: "[W]here the question is whether the appearance of an arrangement may support a determination of unconstitutionality, the fact that the Legislature has endorsed the plan, has supervisory authority over it, and appropriates funds for it substantially changes appearances." How does this differ from the examples that Kennedy gives? Should we reach a different conclusion if the movie industry

cooperates with federal law enforcement to enforce laws against video piracy? See *https://www.ice.gov/news/releases/federal-law-enforcement-agencies-join-movie-industry-unveil-new-anti-piracy-warning.*

4. *Special prosecutors.* Almost all states have statutes empowering a judge (or a prosecuting attorney) to appoint a "special prosecutor" to file and prosecute criminal charges. The court appoints the special prosecutor when the district attorney "refuses to act" or "neglects" to perform a duty. See Ala. Code §12-17-186; Tenn. Const. art. 6, §5 ("In all cases where the Attorney for any district fails or refuses to attend and prosecute according to law, the Court shall have power to appoint an Attorney pro tempore"). Courts will also order the use of a special prosecutor when the prosecuting attorney has a conflict of interest regarding a suspect, a complainant, or some other person involved in a potential criminal case. If an independent official who decides whether to file criminal charges does not operate within a limited budget and does not compare the current case to all other potential criminal cases that an office might prosecute, will the quality of the prosecutorial decision improve?

Problem 13-6. Involved Citizens

Larry Parrish, an attorney in Memphis, Tennessee, was approached by the executive director of an organization known as the Citizens for Community Values, Inc., ("CCV"), who asked him to meet with two Shelby County assistant district attorneys, Amy Weirich and Jennifer Nichols, regarding the prosecution of obscenity cases. Parrish, a former Assistant United States Attorney, was experienced in the prosecution of such cases.

Parrish met with Weirich and Nichols for three hours. On the following day, then–Shelby County District Attorney John Pierotti contacted Parrish and requested his assistance. Pierotti told Parrish that his office could not pay for Parrish's services but could reimburse expenses. When Parrish asked if he could be compensated by outside sources, Pierotti agreed.

Parrish then conducted an extensive investigation into sexually oriented businesses in Shelby County, with the assistance of two assistant district attorneys, an investigator from the District Attorney General's office, and investigators from the Tennessee Bureau of Investigation and the Department of Revenue. Parrish met with these employees in his law firm office on a daily basis for several months. The group's investigation consisted of conducting surveillance of sexually oriented establishments and taking statements from a large number of witnesses. Although Parrish testified that it was "understood" that John Pierotti had the ultimate decision-making authority, there were no procedures or guidelines establishing Parrish's specific duties or Pierotti's oversight.

The initial agreement called for the District Attorney General's office to pay for expenses incurred during the investigation, but Parrish began to pay expenses from contributions by CCV and numerous members of the community. Parrish testified that CCV received a monthly statement itemizing his time and expenses, just like any other client. Parrish's expenses included the use of court reporters to take statements, copying and courier expenses, video monitors, special telephone lines, and various office supplies and equipment. The trial court later found that Parrish received $410,932 for his services from CCV and other private contributors over an 18-month period. Of this amount, Parrish's expenses exceeded $100,000.

Later that year, the grand jury returned an 18-count indictment against Donald Culbreath, including ten counts of promoting prostitution, six counts of prostitution, and two counts of public indecency. All of the evidence against Mr. Culbreath was collected by Mr. Parrish and his staff.

If Mr. Culbreath files a motion to disqualify the District Attorney's Office on the basis of conflict of interest, how should the court rule? Cf. State v. Culbreath, 30 S.W.3d 309 (Tenn. 2000).

H. SELECTIVE PROSECUTION

We began this chapter explaining the various ways that judges refuse to second-guess the exercise of charging discretion. A prosecutor might make very different charging decisions in two similar cases and will not have to explain those choices. We now pivot to consider two important constraints on the prosecutor's filing discretion: the equal protection clause and the use of pretrial screening procedures.

Pursuant to the equal protection clause, a judge may be asked to review the prosecutor's decision if it appears to be based on some constitutionally suspect grounds—such as the defendant's race or gender. Similarly, the prosecutor cannot file a charge (or increase the charges) in order to punish a defendant for taking constitutionally protected action, such as exercising free speech or filing a successful appeal. Thus, a prosecutor can have many different reasons for a charging decision, but she cannot rely on a limited set of constitutionally improper reasons.

■ UNITED STATES v. CHRISTOPHER ARMSTRONG
517 U.S. 456 (1996)

REHNQUIST, C.J.[*]

In this case, we consider the showing necessary for a defendant to be entitled to discovery on a claim that the prosecuting attorney singled him out for prosecution on the basis of his race. We conclude that respondents failed to satisfy the threshold showing: They failed to show that the Government declined to prosecute similarly situated suspects of other races.

In April 1992, respondents were indicted in the United States District Court for the Central District of California on charges of conspiring to possess with intent to distribute more than 50 grams of cocaine base (crack) and conspiring to distribute the same, [and federal firearms offenses]. In response to the indictment, respondents filed a motion for discovery or for dismissal of the indictment, alleging that they were selected for federal prosecution because they are black. In support of their motion, they offered only an affidavit by a "Paralegal Specialist," employed by the Office of the Federal Public Defender representing one of the respondents. The only allegation in the affidavit was that, in every one of the 24 [narcotics] cases closed by the office during 1991, the defendant was black. Accompanying the

*[Justices O'Connor, Scalia, Kennedy, Souter, Thomas, and Ginsburg joined this opinion. Justice Breyer concurred in part and concurred in the judgment.—EDS.]

affidavit was a "study" listing the 24 defendants, their race, whether they were prosecuted for dealing cocaine as well as crack, and the status of each case.

The Government opposed the discovery motion, arguing, among other things, that there was no evidence or allegation "that the Government has acted unfairly or has prosecuted non-black defendants or failed to prosecute them." The District Court granted the motion. It ordered the Government (1) to provide a list of all cases from the last three years in which the Government charged both cocaine and firearms offenses, (2) to identify the race of the defendants in those cases, (3) to identify what levels of law enforcement were involved in the investigations of those cases, and (4) to explain its criteria for deciding to prosecute those defendants for federal cocaine offenses.

The Government moved for reconsideration of the District Court's discovery order. With this motion it submitted affidavits and other evidence to explain why it had chosen to prosecute respondents and why respondents' study did not support the inference that the Government was singling out blacks for cocaine prosecution. The federal and local agents participating in the case alleged in affidavits that race played no role in their investigation. An Assistant United States Attorney explained in an affidavit that the decision to prosecute met the general criteria for prosecution, because

> there was over 100 grams of cocaine base involved, over twice the threshold necessary for a ten year mandatory minimum sentence; there were multiple sales involving multiple defendants, thereby indicating a fairly substantial crack cocaine ring; . . . there were multiple federal firearms violations intertwined with the narcotics trafficking; the overall evidence in the case was extremely strong, including audio and videotapes of defendants; . . . and several of the defendants had criminal histories including narcotics and firearms violations.

The Government also submitted sections of a published 1989 Drug Enforcement Administration report which concluded that large-scale, interstate trafficking networks "controlled by Jamaicans, Haitians and Black street gangs dominate the manufacture and distribution of crack." In response, one of respondents' attorneys submitted an affidavit alleging that an intake coordinator at a drug treatment center had told her that there are "an equal number of caucasian users and dealers to minority users and dealers." Respondents also submitted an affidavit from a criminal defense attorney alleging that in his experience many nonblacks are prosecuted in state court for crack offenses. . . . The District Court denied the motion for reconsideration. When the Government indicated it would not comply with the court's discovery order, the court dismissed the case. [The Court of Appeals affirmed the order.]

A selective-prosecution claim is not a defense on the merits to the criminal charge itself, but an independent assertion that the prosecutor has brought the charge for reasons forbidden by the Constitution. Our cases delineating the necessary elements to prove a claim of selective prosecution have taken great pains to explain that the standard is a demanding one. These cases afford a "background presumption" that the showing necessary to obtain discovery should itself be a significant barrier to the litigation of insubstantial claims.

A selective-prosecution claim asks a court to exercise judicial power over a "special province" of the Executive. The Attorney General and United States Attorneys retain "broad discretion" to enforce the Nation's criminal laws. Wayte v. United

States, 470 U.S. 598 (1985). They have this latitude because they are designated by statute as the President's delegates to help him discharge his constitutional responsibility to "take Care that the Laws be faithfully executed." U.S. Const., Art. II, §3. . . .

Of course, a prosecutor's discretion is subject to constitutional constraints. One of these constraints, imposed by the equal protection component of the Due Process Clause of the Fifth Amendment, is that the decision whether to prosecute may not be based on "an unjustifiable standard such as race, religion, or other arbitrary classification," Oyler v. Boles, 368 U.S. 448, 456 (1962). A defendant may demonstrate that the administration of a criminal law is "directed so exclusively against a particular class of persons . . . with a mind so unequal and oppressive" that the system of prosecution amounts to "a practical denial" of equal protection of the law. Yick Wo v. Hopkins, 118 U.S. 356, 373 (1886).

In order to dispel the presumption that a prosecutor has not violated equal protection, a criminal defendant must present clear evidence to the contrary. We explained in *Wayte* why courts are "properly hesitant to examine the decision whether to prosecute." Judicial deference to the decisions of these executive officers rests in part on an assessment of the relative competence of prosecutors and courts. "Such factors as the strength of the case, the prosecution's general deterrence value, the Government's enforcement priorities, and the case's relationship to the Government's overall enforcement plan are not readily susceptible to the kind of analysis the courts are competent to undertake." It also stems from a concern not to unnecessarily impair the performance of a core executive constitutional function. "Examining the basis of a prosecution delays the criminal proceeding, threatens to chill law enforcement by subjecting the prosecutor's motives and decisionmaking to outside inquiry, and may undermine prosecutorial effectiveness by revealing the Government's enforcement policy."

The requirements for a selective-prosecution claim draw on ordinary equal protection standards. The claimant must demonstrate that the federal prosecutorial policy had a discriminatory effect and that it was motivated by a discriminatory purpose. To establish a discriminatory effect in a race case, the claimant must show that similarly situated individuals of a different race were not prosecuted. This requirement has been established in our case law since Ah Sin v. Wittman, 198 U.S. 500 (1905). Ah Sin, a subject of China, petitioned a California state court for a writ of habeas corpus, seeking discharge from imprisonment under a San Francisco county ordinance prohibiting persons from setting up gambling tables in rooms barricaded to stop police from entering. He alleged in his habeas petition "that the ordinance is enforced solely and exclusively against persons of the Chinese race and not otherwise." We rejected his contention that this averment made out a claim under the Equal Protection Clause, because it did not allege "that the conditions and practices to which the ordinance was directed did not exist exclusively among the Chinese, or that there were other offenders against the ordinance than the Chinese as to whom it was not enforced."

The similarly situated requirement does not make a selective-prosecution claim impossible to prove. Twenty years before *Ah Sin*, we invalidated an ordinance, also adopted by San Francisco, that prohibited the operation of laundries in wooden buildings. *Yick Wo*, 118 U.S. at 374. The plaintiff in error successfully demonstrated that the ordinance was applied against Chinese nationals but not against other laundry-shop operators. The authorities had denied the applications of 200 Chinese subjects for permits to operate shops in wooden buildings, but granted the applications of 80 individuals who were not Chinese subjects to operate laundries in wooden buildings "under similar conditions." . . .

Having reviewed the requirements to prove a selective-prosecution claim, we turn to the showing necessary to obtain discovery in support of such a claim. If discovery is ordered, the Government must assemble from its own files documents which might corroborate or refute the defendant's claim. Discovery thus imposes many of the costs present when the Government must respond to a prima facie case of selective prosecution. It will divert prosecutors' resources and may disclose the Government's prosecutorial strategy. The justifications for a rigorous standard for the elements of a selective-prosecution claim thus require a correspondingly rigorous standard for discovery in aid of such a claim.

The parties [describe] the requisite showing to establish entitlement to discovery . . . with a variety of phrases, like "colorable basis," "substantial threshold showing," "substantial and concrete basis," or "reasonable likelihood." However, the many labels for this showing conceal the degree of consensus about the evidence necessary to meet it. The Courts of Appeals require some evidence tending to show the existence of the essential elements of the defense, discriminatory effect and discriminatory intent.

In this case we consider what evidence constitutes "some evidence tending to show the existence" of the discriminatory effect element. . . . The vast majority of the Courts of Appeals require the defendant to produce some evidence that similarly situated defendants of other races could have been prosecuted, but were not, and this requirement is consistent with our equal protection case law.

The Court of Appeals [in this case] reached its decision in part because it started "with the presumption that people of all races commit all types of crimes—not with the premise that any type of crime is the exclusive province of any particular racial or ethnic group." It cited no authority for this proposition, which seems contradicted by the most recent statistics of the United States Sentencing Commission. Those statistics show that: More than 90 percent of the persons sentenced in 1994 for crack cocaine trafficking were black, 93.4 percent of convicted LSD dealers were white, and 91 percent of those convicted for pornography or prostitution were white. Presumptions at war with presumably reliable statistics have no proper place in the analysis of this issue.

The Court of Appeals also expressed concern about the "evidentiary obstacles defendants face." But . . . if the claim of selective prosecution were well founded, it should not have been an insuperable task to prove that persons of other races were being treated differently than respondents. For instance, respondents could have investigated whether similarly situated persons of other races were prosecuted by the State of California, were known to federal law enforcement officers, but were not prosecuted in federal court. We think the required threshold—a credible showing of different treatment of similarly situated persons—adequately balances the Government's interest in vigorous prosecution and the defendant's interest in avoiding selective prosecution.

In the case before us, respondents' "study" did not constitute some evidence tending to show the existence of the essential elements of a selective-prosecution claim. The study failed to identify individuals who were not black, could have been prosecuted for the offenses for which respondents were charged, but were not so prosecuted. This omission was not remedied by respondents' evidence in opposition to the Government's motion for reconsideration. . . . Respondents' affidavits, which recounted one attorney's conversation with a drug treatment center employee and the experience of another attorney defending drug prosecutions in state court, recounted hearsay and reported personal conclusions based on anecdotal evidence. The judgment of the Court of Appeals is therefore reversed, and the case is remanded for proceedings consistent with this opinion. It is so ordered.

Stevens, J., dissenting.

Federal prosecutors are respected members of a respected profession. Despite an occasional misstep, the excellence of their work abundantly justifies the presumption that they have properly discharged their official duties. Nevertheless, the possibility that political or racial animosity may infect a decision to institute criminal proceedings cannot be ignored. For that reason, it has long been settled that the prosecutor's broad discretion to determine when criminal charges should be filed is not completely unbridled. . . .

The Court correctly concludes that in this case the facts presented to the District Court in support of respondents' claim that they had been singled out for prosecution because of their race were not sufficient to prove that defense. Moreover, I agree with the Court that their showing was not strong enough to give them a right to discovery, either under Rule 16 or under the District Court's inherent power to order discovery in appropriate circumstances. [However], I am persuaded that the District Judge did not abuse her discretion when she concluded that the factual showing was sufficiently disturbing to require some response from the United States Attorney's Office. Perhaps the discovery order was broader than necessary, but I cannot agree with the Court's apparent conclusion that no inquiry was permissible.

The District Judge's order should be evaluated in light of three circumstances that underscore the need for judicial vigilance over certain types of drug prosecutions. First, the Anti-Drug Abuse Act of 1986 and subsequent legislation established a regime of extremely high penalties for the possession and distribution of so-called "crack" cocaine. Those provisions treat one gram of crack as the equivalent of 100 grams of powder cocaine. The distribution of 50 grams of crack is thus punishable by the same mandatory minimum sentence of 10 years in prison that applies to the distribution of 5,000 grams of powder cocaine. . . . Second, the disparity between the treatment of crack cocaine and powder cocaine is matched by the disparity between the severity of the punishment imposed by federal law and that imposed by state law for the same conduct. For a variety of reasons, often including the absence of mandatory minimums, the existence of parole, and lower baseline penalties, terms of imprisonment for drug offenses tend to be substantially lower in state systems than in the federal system. The difference is especially marked in the case of crack offenses. . . . Finally, it is undisputed that the brunt of the elevated federal penalties falls heavily on blacks. While 65 percent of the persons who have used crack are white, in 1993 they represented only 4 percent of the federal offenders convicted of trafficking in crack. Eighty-eight percent of such defendants were black. . . . Those figures represent a major threat to the integrity of federal sentencing reform, whose main purpose was the elimination of disparity (especially racial) in sentencing. . . .

The extraordinary severity of the imposed penalties and the troubling racial patterns of enforcement give rise to a special concern about the fairness of charging practices for crack offenses. Evidence tending to prove that black defendants charged with distribution of crack in the Central District of California are prosecuted in federal court, whereas members of other races charged with similar offenses are prosecuted in state court, warrants close scrutiny by the federal judges in that District. In my view, the District Judge, who has sat on both the federal and the state benches in Los Angeles, acted well within her discretion to call for the development of facts that would demonstrate what standards, if any, governed the choice of forum where similarly situated offenders are prosecuted. . . .

The majority discounts the probative value of the [defendant's] affidavits, claiming that they recounted "hearsay" and reported "personal conclusions based on anecdotal evidence." But [it] was certainly within the District Court's discretion to credit the affidavits of two members of the bar of that Court, at least one of whom had presumably acquired a reputation by his frequent appearances there, and both of whose statements were made on pains of perjury. The criticism that the affidavits were based on "anecdotal evidence" is also unpersuasive. I thought it was agreed that defendants do not need to prepare sophisticated statistical studies in order to receive mere discovery in cases like this one. . . .

Even if respondents failed to carry their burden of showing that there were individuals who were not black but who could have been prosecuted in federal court for the same offenses, it does not follow that the District Court abused its discretion in ordering discovery. There can be no doubt that such individuals exist, and indeed the Government has never denied the same. In those circumstances, I fail to see why the District Court was unable to take judicial notice of this obvious fact and demand information from the Government's files to support or refute respondents' evidence. The presumption that some whites are prosecuted in state court is not "contradicted" by the statistics the majority cites, which show only that high percentages of blacks are convicted of certain federal crimes, while high percentages of whites are convicted of other federal crimes. Those figures are entirely consistent with the allegation of selective prosecution. The relevant comparison, rather, would be with the percentages of blacks and whites who commit those crimes. But, as discussed above, in the case of crack far greater numbers of whites are believed guilty of using the substance. The District Court, therefore, was entitled to find the evidence before her significant and to require some explanation from the Government.[6] I therefore respectfully dissent. . . .

Notes

1. *Selective prosecution: majority position.* The U.S. Supreme Court makes it clear from time to time that it is possible, at least in theory, for a court to overturn a prosecutor's charging decision when it is based on a constitutionally impermissible ground such as race, religion, or sex. A defendant who makes such a claim must establish that (a) the prosecutor made different charging decisions for similarly situated suspects (a discriminatory effect), and (b) the prosecutor intentionally made the decision on the basis of an "arbitrary" classification (a discriminatory intent). Arbitrary classifications would include "suspect classes" under equal protection

6. Also telling was the Government's response to respondents' evidentiary showing. It submitted a list of more than 3,500 defendants who had been charged with federal narcotics violations over the previous 3 years. It also offered the names of 11 nonblack defendants whom it had prosecuted for crack offenses. All 11, however, were members of other racial or ethnic minorities. . . .

doctrine and those exercising their constitutional liberties such as freedom of speech or religion. See Oyler v. Boles, 368 U.S. 448 (1962); Wayte v. United States, 470 U.S. 598 (1985).

Although a selective prosecution claim remains theoretically available, the claim is very difficult for a defendant to win. The *Wayte* decision made it clear that the government must choose the defendant for prosecution "because of" and not "despite" the protected conduct or status of the defendant. In that case, the government had prosecuted for draft evasion a person who had publicly criticized the military draft. The government had chosen to prosecute the case under a "passive enforcement" policy, in which the government filed charges only when told about a person's refusal to register for the draft and only when the person refused to comply with the law after a specific request. The government carried out this policy in Wayte's case, despite (and not because of) his speech criticizing the draft. This basic federal framework for analyzing constitutional challenges to discriminatory charging policies has also been very influential in state courts. See, e.g., Salaiscooper v. Eighth Judicial District Court ex rel. County of Clark, 34 P.3d 509 (Nev. 2001) (disparate treatment of prostitutes and customers is not discrimination on basis of sex); but see In re D.B., 950 N.E.2d 528 (Ohio 2011) (application of statutory rape provision to a child under age 13 who engages in sexual conduct with another child under age 13 violates the equal protection clause mandate that persons similarly circumstanced be treated alike).

2. *Discovery to support selective prosecution claims.* According to the opinion in *Armstrong*, a court hearing a claim of selective prosecution may grant discovery to the defendant if there is "some evidence" to support each of the elements of the claim. Do you agree with the court that the defendants in *Armstrong* failed to produce "some evidence"? See also United States v. Bass, 536 U.S. 862 (2002) (overturns trial court order for discovery concerning capital charging practices; defendant failed to show disparate treatment of similarly situated persons).

What sort of evidence is likely to be available to support a selective prosecution claim? To show disparate treatment, a defendant must prove that he is "similarly situated" to a pool of other suspects who were not prosecuted. Those who are similarly situated would have committed basically the same act as the defendant. Further, there could be no significant difference in the harm caused by these similar acts, and prosecution of one case could not be significantly less costly or difficult than the others. Where can a defendant get information about this pool of unprosecuted suspects?

Will it ever be possible to prove disparate impact in those prosecutorial offices (the overwhelming majority) in which the prosecuting attorneys keep no records of the cases they decline to charge or of the reasons for the declination? Cf. Commonwealth v. Washington W., 928 N.E.2d 908 (Mass. 2010) (juvenile charged with homosexual statutory rape was entitled to discovery of prosecutor office statistics on charges brought in other juvenile cases; juvenile records, unlike those in adult courts, are closed to public and would prevent investigation of potential claim of selective prosecution). Very few courts have reversed convictions on selective prosecution grounds, and no Supreme Court opinions have done so on racial grounds except for Yick Wo v. Hopkins, 118 U.S. 356 (1886). Does this pattern prove anything? What did the claimants in *Yick Wo* do that claimants today might emulate?

3. *Racial patterns in charging.* It is clear that racial minorities are charged with crimes at a rate disproportionate to their numbers. But is the rate higher after

accounting for different levels of participation in crime? Criminologists addressing this question have studied records of large numbers of cases using statistical techniques (especially "regression" analysis) to compare similar cases and sort out racial and nonracial influences over charging decisions. For instance, one study by Richard Berk analyzed the correlation between race and crack cocaine charging practices in Los Angeles. The study indicates that the U.S. Attorney prosecuted black offenders at a higher rate than comparable white offenders. Richard Berk & Alec Campbell, Preliminary Data on Race and Crack Charging Practices in Los Angeles, 6 Fed. Sentencing Rep. 36 (1993). For more recent evidence reaching the same conclusion, see Sonia Starr & M.M. Rehavi, Racial Disparity in Federal Criminal Sentences, 122 J. Pol. Econ. 1320 (2014); Mona Lynch, Hard Bargains (2016) (assessing data from three different U.S. district courts); Quattrone Center, Racial Disparities in Outcomes for Indigent Defendants (2017), available at *https://www.law.upenn.edu/ live/files/6793-examining-racial-disparities-may-2017-full* (examining case outcomes in San Francisco).

Does any of this analysis support the conclusion that selective prosecution doctrine fails to control biased prosecution? If racial discrimination in charging is indeed widespread, is it unrealistic to ask a defendant to make a prediscovery showing?

For an exploration of other studies of racial disparities in charging decisions, go to the web extension for this chapter at *http://www.crimpro.com/extension/ch13*. The methodological issues involved in designing a credible study in this field are serious, and receive some attention on the web extension.

4. *Prosecutorial vindictiveness.* If all criminal defendants were to insist on exercising all of their constitutional and statutory procedural rights, they could make life difficult for a prosecutor. Can a prosecutor charge defendants more severely if they insist on a jury trial, an appeal, or some other procedural right? In Blackledge v. Perry, 417 U.S. 21 (1974), a defendant was initially charged in state district court with misdemeanor assault. After conviction, he requested a trial de novo on the charges in state superior court, and the prosecutor changed the charges to felony assault. The Supreme Court concluded that a prosecutor in such a situation would have an incentive to "retaliate" against the defendant for taking an action that the prosecutor finds inconvenient. Thus, the prosecutor would have to demonstrate on the record that the change in charges was based on some factor other than the defendant's exercise of procedural rights. The limit on "prosecutorial vindictiveness" set out in Blackledge v. Perry does not apply, however, to a prosecutor's *pretrial* decision to add or reduce charges based on a defendant's willingness to waive procedural rights. See United States v. Goodwin, 457 U.S. 368 (1982) (no presumption of vindictiveness where prosecutor changes misdemeanor charges to felony after defendant requests jury trial); State v. Knowles, 239 P.3d 129 (Mont. 2010) (during plea negotiations following hung jury in first trial, increase of charges from 5-year maximum statute to 20-year maximum statute because of defendant's rejection of prosecutor's plea offer constituted vindictive prosecution; no new factual information was uncovered after first trial). Is this distinction a meaningful one?

5. *Prosecution in the sunshine.* Would prosecutors benefit or lose more from the collection and publication of data on the race of every defendant and victim for every criminal matter the office encounters? If a chief prosecutor were to carry out this policy (either voluntarily or pursuant to a statute), would she want to show the data broken down by type of crime and by the action the office chose to pursue?

If you believe prosecutors would resist the collection and publication of such data, what arguments might they raise against this proposal? What if the legislature were willing to provide funds for any extra personnel needed to collect and analyze the data? See Angela J. Davis, Prosecution and Race: The Power and Privilege of Discretion, 67 Fordham L. Rev. 13 (1998) (proposing a requirement that prosecutors publish "racial impact studies").

I. PRETRIAL SCREENING

> The grand jury would indict a hamburger.
> — Traditional courthouse wisdom

Pretrial judicial hearings that go by names such as "initial appearance" and "preliminary examination" serve multiple functions. At the initial appearance, the magistrate informs the defendant about the nature of the charges, the right to remain silent, the right to appointed counsel, and other features of the criminal process. An initial appearance also gives the magistrate an occasion to assign counsel to indigent defendants (or at least to ascertain whether a defendant is eligible for appointed counsel) and to set bail or other conditions of pretrial release.

For our present purposes, we focus on the ability of judges in these pretrial hearings to screen out charges without enough factual support. The prosecutor (in consultation with the police, as we have seen) can file charges through a charging instrument known as the "complaint" or "information." Then the charges are tested in judicial proceedings. If the prosecutor, in the adversarial "preliminary examination," is not able to produce evidence showing probable cause to believe that the defendant committed the crime as charged, then the charges are dismissed and the defendant released. If probable cause is present, the magistrate will "bind over" the defendant for arraignment and trial in a court with jurisdiction to try the offense.

There are alternatives to the use of the preliminary judicial hearing as the initial filter in the accusatory process. In just under half of the states, a defendant can insist that the prosecutor seek the permission of a grand jury before filing felony charges. If the grand jury agrees with the prosecutor's request to charge an individual, the charges appear in a grand jury "indictment." In Chapter 10 we studied the role of the grand jury in investigating crimes—the grand jury as a "sword." Now we consider the grand jury's function as a "shield" against unfounded prosecutions, and the interaction between the grand jury and the judicial "preliminary examination" as screening devices.

The traditional image of the grand jury as a shield might be misleading. By all accounts, grand juries indict in virtually all cases when a prosecutor requests the indictment. There are several possible reasons for this, all built into the structure of the grand jury. First, the grand jury's review standard is quite low: It must determine only whether there is probable cause to believe that the accused has committed the crime that the prosecutor has specified. Second, the grand jury proceedings are not adversarial. Only the prosecutor presents evidence to the grand jury, and he has no obligation (in most states) to present any exculpatory evidence. In most jurisdictions, no representatives of the grand jury witnesses or targets are even present in the grand jury room during testimony or deliberations.

NEW YORK CONSTITUTION ART. I, §6

No person shall be held to answer for a capital or otherwise infamous crime . . . unless on indictment of a grand jury, except that a person held for the action of a grand jury upon a charge for such an offense, other than one punishable by death or life imprisonment, with the consent of the district attorney, may waive indictment by a grand jury and consent to be prosecuted on an information filed by the district attorney; such waiver shall be evidenced by written instrument signed by the defendant in open court in the presence of his or her counsel. . . .

The power of grand juries to inquire into the wilful misconduct in office of public officers, and to find indictments or to direct the filing of informations in connection with such inquiries, shall never be suspended or impaired by law. . . .

ILLINOIS ANNOTATED STATUTES CH. 725, PARA. 5/111-2

(a) All prosecutions of felonies shall be by information or by indictment. No prosecution may be pursued by information unless a preliminary hearing has been held or waived . . . and at that hearing probable cause to believe the defendant committed an offense was found. . . .

(b) All other prosecutions may be by indictment, information or complaint. . . .

(f) Where the prosecution of a felony is by information or complaint after preliminary hearing, or after a waiver of preliminary hearing in accordance with paragraph (a) of this Section, such prosecution may be for all offenses, arising from the same transaction or conduct of a defendant even though the complaint or complaints filed at the preliminary hearing charged only one or some of the offenses arising from that transaction or conduct.

COMMONWEALTH v. KHARI WILCOX

767 N.E.2d 1061 (Mass. 2002)

Greaney, J.

After hearing six days of evidence during a three-month period, a Suffolk County grand jury indicted the defendant on charges of armed robbery and home invasion. The defendant moved for discovery of the grand jury attendance records to ascertain whether at least twelve of the grand jurors who voted to indict him had heard "all of the evidence" presented against him. (Of particular concern to the defendant was whether fewer than the required minimum of twelve grand jurors voting to indict him had heard certain exculpatory evidence, including evidence suggesting that he had been erroneously identified.) A judge in the Superior Court allowed the defendant's motion, but stayed discovery to give the Commonwealth an opportunity to seek interlocutory review of her order. . . .

The grand jury as known to the common law always has been regarded as a bulwark of individual liberty and a fundamental protection against despotism and persecution. It is an institution preserved by our State Constitution, which asserts the "great principle . . . that no man shall be put to answer a criminal charge [for a capital or otherwise infamous offense] until the criminating evidence has been laid before a grand jury," Commonwealth v. Holley, 69 Mass. 458 (1855). See Mass. R. Crim. P. 3(b)(1), 378 Mass. 847 (1979) ("A defendant charged with an offense punishable by imprisonment in state prison shall have the right to be proceeded against by indictment except when the offense charged is within the concurrent jurisdiction of the District and Superior Courts and the District Court retains jurisdiction"). For an indictment to stand, the grand jury must hear sufficient evidence to establish the identity of the accused and probable cause to arrest him.

The defendant's discovery motion is predicated on the argument that the requirement in Mass. R. Crim. P. 5(e), 378 Mass. 850 (1979), of a "concurrence" of at least twelve grand jurors to return an indictment, mandates that a core of at least twelve grand jurors heard all of the evidence and voted to indict. He asserts that the word "concurrence" presumes that a grand juror has been present to hear all of the evidence presented before joining in a decision to indict, and that such an obligation is necessitated by the grand jurors' oath. The defendant urges us to follow the "better-reasoned decisions from other jurisdictions" that "recognize that an informed grand jury that truly concurs to indict, based on hearing all of the evidence, ensures the integrity of the grand jury process." We decline to add such a requirement to rule 5.

Rule 5(e) has its origins in the common law. By the common law, a grand jury "may consist of not less than thirteen, nor more than twenty-three persons," Crimm v. Commonwealth, 119 Mass. 326 (1876), and a concurrence of at least twelve was required to return an indictment. Both the maximum number of grand jurors and the minimum number required to indict prescribed by the common law [were] kept intact by statute and rule. See G.L. c. 277, §§1, 2A-2G (twenty-three grand jurors shall be selected to serve); Mass. R. Crim. P. 5(a), 378 Mass. 850 (1979) ("the court shall select not more than twenty-three grand jurors to serve"); Mass. R. Crim. P. 5(e) ("An indictment may be found only upon the concurrence of twelve or more jurors"). The common law quorum requirement of thirteen remains in place, unaltered by statute or rule.

Rule 5 is modeled in large part on its Federal counterpart, Fed. R. Crim. P. 6. The Federal rule requires that every grand jury session be attended by "not less than 16 nor more than 23 members," Fed. R. Crim. P. 6(a)(1), and, for an indictment to be found, requires "the concurrence of 12 or more jurors," Fed. R. Crim. P. 6(f). Federal courts have nearly uniformly rejected the argument raised by the defendant that the grand jurors voting to indict be required to hear all of the evidence presented. See United States v. Byron, 994 F.2d 747, 748 (10th Cir. 1993); but see United States v. Provenzano, 688 F.2d 194, 202-203 (3d Cir. 1982) (expressing uneasiness with approach followed by other Federal courts and providing procedure whereby replacement and absentee grand jurors are given transcript of missed proceedings as well as an opportunity to recall witnesses for questioning). Often quoted and relied on in these Federal decisions is the reasoning stated by Judge Learned Hand, writing for the court in United States ex rel. McCann v. Thompson, 144 F.2d 604, 607 (2d Cir. 1944):

> Since all the evidence adduced before a grand jury—certainly when the accused does not appear—is aimed at proving guilt, the absence of some jurors during some

part of the hearings will ordinarily merely weaken the prosecution's case. If what the absentees actually hear is enough to satisfy them, there would seem to be no reason why they should not vote. Against this we can think of nothing except the possibility that some of the evidence adduced by the prosecution might conceivably turn out to be favorable to the accused; and that, if the absentees had heard it, they might have refused to vote a true bill. No one can be entirely sure that this can never occur; but it appears to us so remote a chance that it should be left to those instances in which it can be made to appear that the evidence not heard was of that character, in spite of the extreme difficulty of ever proving what was the evidence before a grand jury. Indeed, the possibility that not all who vote will hear all the evidence, is a reasonable inference from the fact that sixteen is a quorum. Were the law as the relator argues, it would practically mean that all jurors present at the beginning of any case, must remain to the end, for it will always be impossible to tell in advance whether twelve will eventually vote a true bill, and if they do, who those twelve will be. The result of such a doctrine would therefore be that in a long case, or in a case where there are intervals in the taking of evidence, the privilege of absence would not exist. That would certainly be an innovation, for the contrary practice has, so far as we are aware, been universal; and it would be an onerous and unnecessary innovation.

We reject the defendant's contention that the reasoning stated in the *Thompson* case is "unpersuasive." In most instances, grand jurors hear only inculpatory evidence. Commonwealth v. O'Dell, 466 N.E.2d 828 (Mass. 1984) (stating that prosecutors are not required "to bring exculpatory evidence to the attention of grand juries"). It is only when the prosecutor possesses exculpatory evidence that would greatly undermine either the credibility of an important witness or evidence likely to affect the grand jury's decision, or withholds exculpatory evidence causing the presentation to be "so seriously tainted," that the prosecutor must present such evidence to the grand jury. See Commonwealth v. Vinnie, 698 N.E.2d 896 (Mass. 1998). On the occasion when a grand juror "misses" inculpatory evidence, such a circumstance, as stated by Judge Hand, may work in the accused's favor if that grand juror has not otherwise heard sufficient evidence to establish the probable cause standard. On the other hand, the "missed" evidence may have been cumulative of other evidence presented.

Provisions governing grand jurors, which we decline to change, take into account the lengthy terms for which many grand juries sit, usually a number of months. The provisions also, as acknowledged by the defendant, insure that the grand jury can continue functioning despite absent members. Adoption of the rule the defendant proposes may cause the prosecution to seek to indict an accused on the basis of whatever evidence it can present in one day. In such circumstances, the prosecution may not be able to present the direct testimony of several witnesses, relying instead on the hearsay statements of one witness. While proceedings conducted in this manner would not be impermissible, see Commonwealth v. O'Dell, 466 N.E.2d 828 (Mass. 1984) ("an indictment may be based solely on hearsay"), they would run contrary to our "preference for the use of direct testimony before grand juries," Commonwealth v. St. Pierre, 387 N.E.2d 1135 (Mass. 1979), which inures to the accused's benefit. The defendant's rule would also be disruptive of witnesses, police and their schedules, court sessions, and the daily encumbered lives of grand jurors and their families.

Although the defendant correctly identifies that other States, either by statute, rule, or decision, have adopted the requirement that the grand jurors voting to indict have heard all the evidence presented, see, e.g., Ariz. Rev. Stat. Ann. §21-406(B); Me. R. Crim. P. 6(j); N.D. Cent. Code §29-10.1-20; Or. Rev. Stat. §132.360; Commonwealth v. Levinson, 389 A.2d 1062 (Pa. 1978) (explaining when "a substantial percentage of the total membership of the jury is absent from a significant portion of the presentation of evidence, it can no longer be said with confidence that the deliberations were not affected"), some State courts have followed the Federal approach. See, e.g., People v. Martin-Trigona, 444 N.E.2d 527 (Ill. App. 1982); State v. Blyth, 226 N.W.2d 250 (Iowa 1975); Johnston v. State, 822 P.2d 1118 (Nev. 1991). We join this latter group of courts.

Notes

1. *Which crimes require an indictment?* The grand jury requirement is one of the few provisions of the federal Bill of Rights that has not yet been "incorporated" against the states through the due process clause of the Fourteenth Amendment. Hurtado v. California, 110 U.S. 516 (1884). Further, there is no federal constitutional requirement that either a judge or a grand jury determine whether probable cause supports the criminal charges filed against a defendant. Lem Woon v. Oregon, 229 U.S. 586 (1913) (upholding statute providing for no preliminary examination after information). And yet all states have statutes offering at least some defendants a determination of probable cause underlying the charges, whether the determination comes from a judge in a preliminary hearing or from a grand jury indictment. See State v. Hernandez, 268 P.3d 822 (Utah 2011) (defendant charged with class A misdemeanor entitled to preliminary hearing under state constitution). Why would states provide this extra hearing if not constitutionally required?

In almost half the states, known as "indictment jurisdictions," a grand jury indictment rather than a prosecutor's information is necessary for at least some charges. In some of these jurisdictions, such as New York, the state constitution requires a grand jury indictment; in others, the state constitution allows the legislature to decide which if any crimes must be charged through grand jury indictment. For the most part, the "indictment" states have retained the traditional requirement embodied in the Fifth Amendment to the federal constitution: Indictment must occur in all capital and "infamous" crimes—that is, felonies. A few require indictments only for crimes punishable by death or life imprisonment.

In most states and for most charges, the grand jury is optional. Prosecutors can decide whether to proceed under an information or a grand jury indictment (as in Illinois, under the statute reprinted above). In these "information" states that offer prosecutors a choice, indictments have become one weapon in the prosecutor's arsenal of ways to investigate and charge crimes. For example, prosecutors often use grand juries to charge politically sensitive crimes (to share responsibility for the charging decision) or to charge crimes that come to light as the result of grand jury investigations.

2. *Grand jury versus preliminary examinations.* In cases where the prosecutor files an information rather than seeking an indictment from the grand jury, the factual and legal basis for the prosecutor's charge is usually tested before trial in a judicial proceeding, usually called a "preliminary examination" or "preliminary hearing" or

"prelim." Some defendants might actually prefer a preliminary examination over a grand jury indictment because of several features. First, at prelim the judge might evaluate the evidence more skeptically than the grand jury, given that the grand jurors only hear the prosecution's side of the case. Second, defendants and their attorneys may attend the preliminary examination, giving them discovery and cross examination opportunities that are not generally available from the grand jury. Although the use of a preliminary examination might give such practical advantages to the defendant, the government usually holds the power to choose between the grand jury and preliminary examination options. The majority view is that there is no constitutional right to a preliminary hearing once a prosecutor has decided to seek an indictment. See People v. Glass, 627 N.W.2d 261 (Mich. 2001) (overruling earlier case granting right to preliminary examination to all defendants, including indictees).

3. *Waiver of indictment.* In the jurisdictions requiring indictment for some crimes, defendants often waive their right to indictment and proceed without any grand jury or judicial screening of the charges. Are there times when the legal system might want to discourage defendants from waiving the right to indictment? See N.Y. Crim. Proc. Law §195.20(a) (waiver must be written, executed in open court in presence of counsel); N.C. Gen. Stat. §15A-642(b) (waiver allowed except for offenses punishable by death or cases in which defendant waives counsel).

4. *Nonadversarial proceedings.* Time and again, judicial opinions point out that grand jury proceedings are not adversarial and are not a "mini-trial." Truer words have never been spoken. To begin with, the grand jury's task is far different from that of a trial jury: The grand jury need only decide whether the prosecutor has demonstrated probable cause to believe that the defendant committed the crime charged. In most jurisdictions, only the prosecutor presents testimony and documents to the grand jury, and none of it is subject to cross-examination or the rules of evidence. Costello v. United States, 350 U.S. 359 (1956). In a strong minority of states, defense attorneys for some grand jury witnesses may observe the testimony of their clients, but the attorneys may not question the witness or make any statements to the grand jury. See, e.g., Ill. Ann. Stat. ch. 725, para. 5/112-4.1. The one-sidedness of this practice, and the one-sided outcomes it produces, have garnered significant criticism from scholars in the United States. See, e.g., Roger Fairfax, Grand Jury Innovation: Toward a Functional Makeover of the Ancient Bulwark of Liberty, 19 William & Mary Bill of Rights Journal 339-368 (2010).

5. *What about exculpatory evidence?* In most systems, the prosecutor has no obligation to present exculpatory evidence. The Supreme Court, in United States v. Williams, 504 U.S. 36 (1992), declared that such evidence is not necessary for the grand jurors to decide the sufficiency of the charge (although it is necessary to decide ultimate guilt, which is the province of the trial jury). Support for this traditional position is eroding, though; about one-third of the states now have statutes or judicial rulings that require the prosecutor to present exculpatory evidence under some circumstances. In states without statutes on point, courts have relied on due process analysis or the court's supervisory authority over grand jury procedures. For an example of a statutory jurisdiction, see Schuster v. Eighth Judicial District Court, 160 P.3d 873 (Nev. 2007) (state statute requires district attorney to subject to grand jury any evidence that will "explain away the charge," but statute does not impose duty on district attorney to explain to jurors the importance of the evidence). For examples of due process analysis, see State v. Chong, 949 P.2d 122 (Haw.

1997); State v. Herrera, 601 P.2d 75 (N.M. App. 1979); State v. Olkon, 299 N.W.2d 89 (Minn. 1980). For examples of the court exercising supervisory authority, see State v. Hogan, 676 A.2d 533 (N.J. 1996); Mayes v. City of Columbus, 664 N.E.2d 1340, 1348 (Ohio App. 1995); State v. Hall, 235 N.W.2d 702, 712 (Iowa 1975). Jurisdictions recognizing the obligation commonly give it teeth by allowing a defense challenge to any subsequent indictment based upon the prosecutor's failure to inform the grand jury of such exculpatory evidence. See, e.g., United States v. Roberts, 481 F. Supp. 1385 (C.D. Cal. 1980) (case dismissed because prosecutor did not make good on promise to provide exculpatory evidence).

To supplement these formal law rules, prosecutorial office or association policies sometimes recognize the obligation of a prosecutor to present exculpatory evidence that would lead the grand jury to refuse to indict. See U.S. Attorneys' Manual §9-11.233; see also ABA Standards for Criminal Justice, Prosecution Function Standard 3-3.6(b) ("No prosecutor should knowingly fail to disclose to the grand jury evidence which tends to negate guilt or mitigate the offense"). Sometimes the target of a grand jury investigation must have notice and an opportunity to testify before the grand jury can indict. See Sheriff of Humboldt County v. Marcum, 783 P.2d 1389 (Nev. 1989).

6. *Judicial review of indictments.* As you might imagine based on the other materials in this chapter, judicial dismissal of charges contained in an indictment is a rare event. The U.S. Supreme Court decided decades ago that courts ought not to entertain challenges to either the competency or sufficiency of the evidence used to support an indictment, based largely on the history of the grand jury as an institution. Costello v. United States, 350 U.S. 359 (1956). A substantial majority of the states agree, although there is broader agreement on the competency point than on the sufficiency point. Just over a dozen states depart entirely from the *Costello* rule, and instead insist that the trial court act with caution in reviewing the sufficiency of the evidence before the grand jury. Challenges based on prosecutorial misconduct are only slightly more successful as a basis for dismissal of an indictment.

Assuming that a court is willing to review an indictment, will there be a record of the proceedings sufficient to allow judicial review? Statutes and rules of procedure in the federal system and in a majority of the states require recording of at least the testimony that a grand jury hears, and a strong minority also require recording of other statements made to the grand jury, such as the commentary of the prosecutor. Virtually nowhere are the deliberations and votes of the grand jury recorded. Moreover, indictments and other charging documents are usually quite thin when it comes to reciting relevant facts. They provide very little notice to defendants of the sum total of evidence that will be introduced against them.

7. *Police defendants at grand jury.* In the wake of some high-profile cases in which police officer suspects were not indicted, state rules for grand jury procedures have come into the spotlight. See, e.g., Roger Fairfax, The Grand Jury's Role in the Prosecution of Unjustified Police Killings: Challenges and Solutions, 52 Harv. C.R.-C.L. L. Rev. 397 (2017). Some states have taken steps to reform their grand jury procedures in police-involved crimes, but not always with success. Compare *http://www.pacga.org/site/content/321* (including special provisions for treatment of police officer defendants) with *http://rightoncrime.com/2018/07/texas-legislature-could-restore-justice-through-grand-jury-reform/* (documenting efforts to restart reform in Texas because bills the previous year did not pass).

8. *Staff for grand jury.* The grand jury depends on the prosecutor for legal advice and most of the logistics of its operation. Would grand juries assert more independence in the evaluation of criminal charges if they could employ their own legal counsel and other experts and staff? Fewer than 10 states have statutes authorizing support staff for grand juries, such as legal counsel, accountants, or detectives. See Kan. Stat. §22-3006; Hawaii Const. art. 1, §11; State v. Kahlbaun, 64 Haw. 197, 638 P.2d 309 (1981). More frequently, statutes authorize the prosecutor to provide legal advice to the grand jury. See, e.g., Fla. Stat. §905.19. The supervising judge for the grand jury is also available to provide legal advice, although his or her primary role is to charge the jury as it begins work, telling the grand jurors to act as an independent body in screening charges, to view prosecutors as "advocates for the government," to request the production of additional witnesses if they deem this necessary, and to apply the appropriate level of proof needed to indict.

But other sources of staff support for the grand jury have not developed in most places. Given the complexity of governance, what institution of government could survive without support staff? Could Congress or the president perform their duties without the benefit of their own counsel? For an exploration of the idea of grand jury staff and other innovations to revitalize this ancient institution, go to the web extension for this chapter at *http://www.crimpro.com/extension/ch13.*

Jeopardy and Joinder

Chapter 13 addressed the legal forces at work when a prosecutor chooses whether to charge a suspect and which charges to select. We concentrate now on cases that might involve multiple charges. When several related criminal incidents happen, a prosecutor might file a single count or multiple counts in a single prosecution against one or more defendants, or she might instead file separate criminal cases leading to separate trials.

Several sources of law shape the prosecutor's grouping of multiple charges. First, the constitutional bar against "double jeopardy," embodied in the Fifth Amendment of the U.S. Constitution and in most state constitutions, puts some pressure on the prosecutor to include more charges and more conduct within a single initial prosecution, because double jeopardy might bar any later attempt to pursue the related charges. Section A considers these double jeopardy issues. Prosecutors must also consider statutes and procedural rules on the conceptually related concepts of "joinder" and "severance" of charges and defendants. These rules define both the maximum and minimum range of charges that a prosecutor can join together into a single proceeding. Under the joinder and severance rules, both the prosecutor and the trial court decide whether to include or exclude charges or defendants in a single proceeding. Section B explores these rules.

A. DOUBLE JEOPARDY

A prosecutor must plan for the future when filing charges. If she chooses not to combine related charges in an initial set of proceedings and instead files some of the charges later, there is a risk that the court will bar the later charges. The legal basis for this limitation is the double jeopardy clause of the federal constitution and of most state constitutions. The Fifth Amendment to the federal constitution provides: "No person shall . . . be subject for the same offence to be twice put in jeopardy of life or limb. . . ."

Double jeopardy, it is often said, protects criminal defendants from (1) a second prosecution after acquittal, (2) a second prosecution after conviction, and (3) multiple punishments for the same offense within the same proceeding. You can see the ordinary operation of the double jeopardy rule in a foundational case, Ball v. United States, 163 U.S. 662 (1896). In 1889, a federal grand jury indicted Millard Fillmore Ball, John C. Ball, and Robert E. Boutwell for the murder of William T. Box in the "Indian Territory" of the Chickasaw Nation. The indictment alleged that the defendants shot Box, inflicting on him "ten mortal wounds, of which mortal wounds the said William T. Box did languish, and languishing did die." At trial, the jury acquitted Millard Fillmore Ball and convicted John Ball and Robert Boutwell. On appeal, the U.S. Supreme Court vacated the convictions because the indictment did not allege the time or place of Box's death.

In 1891, the grand jury returned a new indictment against all three defendants, this time alleging a time and place of Box's death. In the second trial, the jury convicted all three men and the judge sentenced them to death. The Supreme Court held that double jeopardy barred the conviction of Millard Fillmore Ball, even though the original indictment was legally defective: "[A] general verdict of acquittal upon the issue of not guilty to an indictment undertaking to charge murder, and not objected to before the verdict as insufficient in that respect, is a bar to a second indictment for the same killing." The jury verdict acquitted Millard Fillmore Ball of "the whole charge, of murder, as well as of any less offense included therein." As for the other two defendants, the first jury trial did not produce any valid conviction that would bar a second indictment and trial: "[I]t is quite clear that a defendant who procures a judgment against him upon an indictment to be set aside may be tried anew upon the same indictment, or upon another indictment, for the same offense of which he had been convicted."

The materials in this part touch on some prominent double jeopardy issues that flow from the charging decision. First, we consider a controversial and revealing limitation on the operation of the double jeopardy principle—the "dual sovereign" exception. Second, we consider which charges in a later proceeding amount to the "same offence" that was charged in a prior proceeding.

1. Multiple Sovereigns

Federal and state governments have overlapping responsibilities for enforcing criminal laws. Many economic and other activities cross state lines, and the criminal codes of most states and the federal government now reach much of the same conduct. Often a person who engages in criminal behavior could face charges in two states, or in both state and federal systems.

The overlap between the federal and state criminal laws is a recurring issue for double jeopardy purposes. In United States v. Lanza, 260 U.S. 377 (1922), several defendants were convicted under state law in Washington for manufacturing, transporting, and possessing liquor and were fined $750 each. When the federal government also brought criminal charges under the National Prohibition Act, Lanza raised a double jeopardy objection to the federal prosecution. He noted that the Eighteenth Amendment, prohibiting the manufacture, sale, or transportation of intoxicating liquors, gave both Congress and the states "concurrent power to enforce" the prohibition. According to Lanza, the state and the federal criminal statutes were punishing the "same offense" because they each derived from the same constitutional authority.

The Court rejected this argument and embraced instead the doctrine known as the "dual sovereign" exception to double jeopardy:

> We have here two sovereignties, deriving power from different sources, capable of dealing with the same subject-matter within the same territory. Each may, without interference by the other, enact laws to secure prohibition. . . . Each government in determining what shall be an offense against its peace and dignity is exercising its own sovereignty, not that of the other.

260 U.S. at 382.

The following materials trace the continuing vitality of the "dual sovereign" doctrine during a time when the overlap between federal and state criminal laws has grown larger.

■ ALFONSE BARTKUS v. ILLINOIS
359 U.S. 121 (1959)

FRANKFURTER, J.[*]

Petitioner was tried in the Federal District Court for the Northern District of Illinois on December 18, 1953, for robbery of a federally insured savings and loan association, the General Savings and Loan Association of Cicero, Illinois, in violation of 18 U.S.C. §2113. The case was tried to a jury and resulted in an acquittal. On January 8, 1954, an Illinois grand jury indicted Bartkus. The facts recited in the Illinois indictment were substantially identical to those contained in the prior federal indictment. The Illinois indictment charged that these facts constituted a violation of [the Illinois robbery statute. Bartkus entered a plea of autrefois acquit, which the trial court rejected. Bartkus was tried, convicted, and sentenced to life imprisonment.]

The state and federal prosecutions were separately conducted. It is true that the agent of the Federal Bureau of Investigation who had conducted the investigation on behalf of the Federal Government turned over to the Illinois prosecuting officials all the evidence he had gathered against the petitioner. Concededly, some of that evidence had been gathered after acquittal in the federal court. The only other connection between the two trials is to be found in a suggestion that the federal sentencing of the accomplices who testified against petitioner in both trials was purposely continued by the federal court until after they testified in the state trial. The record establishes that the prosecution was undertaken by state prosecuting officials within their discretionary responsibility. . . . It establishes also that federal officials acted in cooperation with state authorities, as is the conventional practice between the two sets of prosecutors throughout the country. It does not support the claim that the State of Illinois in bringing its prosecution was merely a tool of the federal authorities, who thereby avoided the prohibition of the Fifth Amendment against a retrial of a federal prosecution after an acquittal. It does not sustain a conclusion that the state prosecution was a sham and a cover for a federal prosecution. . . . Since

---

[*] [Justices Clark, Harlan, Whittaker, and Stewart joined this opinion.—EDS.]

the new prosecution was by Illinois, and not by the Federal Government, the claim of unconstitutionality must rest upon the Due Process Clause of the Fourteenth Amendment. . . .

Time and again this Court has attempted by general phrases not to define but to indicate the purport of due process and to adumbrate the continuing adjudicatory process in its application. The statement by Mr. Justice Cardozo in Palko v. Connecticut, 302 U.S. 319, 324-325 (1937), has especially commended itself and been frequently cited in later opinions. Referring to specific situations, he wrote:

> In these and other situations immunities that are valid as against the federal government by force of the specific pledges of particular amendments have been found to be implicit in the concept of ordered liberty, and thus, through the Fourteenth Amendment, become valid as against the states.

[He suggested that due process] prohibited to the States only those practices "repugnant to the conscience of mankind." In applying these phrases in *Palko*, the Court ruled that, while at some point the cruelty of harassment by multiple prosecutions by a State would offend due process, the specific limitation imposed on the Federal Government by the Double Jeopardy Clause of the Fifth Amendment did not bind the States. [*Palko* sustained a first-degree murder conviction returned in a second trial after an appeal by the State from an acquittal of first-degree murder.]

The Fifth Amendment's proscription of double jeopardy has been invoked and rejected in over twenty cases of real or hypothetical successive state and federal prosecution cases before this Court. While United States v. Lanza, 260 U.S. 377 (1922), was the first case in which we squarely held valid a federal prosecution arising out of the same facts which had been the basis of a state conviction, the validity of such a prosecution by the Federal Government has not been questioned by this Court since the opinion in Fox v. Ohio, 46 U.S. 410 (1847), more than one hundred years ago.

In Fox v. Ohio, argument was made to the Supreme Court that an Ohio conviction for uttering counterfeit money was invalid. This assertion of invalidity was based in large part upon the argument that since Congress had imposed federal sanctions for the counterfeiting of money, a failure to find that the Supremacy Clause precluded the States from punishing related conduct would expose an individual to double punishment. Mr. Justice Daniel, writing for the Court [recognized] a possibility of double punishment, but denied that from this flowed a finding of pre-emption, concluding instead that both the Federal and State Governments retained the power to impose criminal sanctions, the United States because of its interest in protecting the purity of its currency, the States because of their interest in protecting their citizens against fraud. . . .

The experience of state courts in dealing with successive prosecutions by different governments is obviously also relevant in considering whether or not the Illinois prosecution of Bartkus violated due process of law. Of the twenty-eight States which have considered the validity of successive state and federal prosecutions as against a challenge of violation of either a state constitutional double-jeopardy provision or a common-law evidentiary rule of autrefois acquit and autrefois convict, twenty-seven have refused to rule that the second prosecution was or would be barred. These States were not bound to follow this Court and its interpretation of the Fifth Amendment. The rules, constitutional, statutory, or common law which bound them, drew upon the same experience as did the Fifth Amendment, but were and are of separate and independent authority. . . .

With this body of precedent as irrefutable evidence that state and federal courts have for years refused to bar a second trial even though there had been a prior trial by another government for a similar offense, it would be disregard of a long, unbroken, unquestioned course of impressive adjudication for the Court now to rule that due process compels such a bar. A practical justification for rejecting such a reading of due process also commends itself in aid of this interpretation of the Fourteenth Amendment. In Screws v. United States, 325 U.S. 91 (1945), defendants were tried and convicted in a federal court under federal statutes with maximum sentences of a year and two years respectively. But the state crime there involved was a capital offense. Were the federal prosecution of a comparatively minor offense to prevent state prosecution of so grave an infraction of state law, the result would be a shocking and untoward deprivation of the historic right and obligation of the States to maintain peace and order within their confines. It would be in derogation of our federal system to displace the reserved power of States over state offenses by reason of prosecution of minor federal offenses by federal authorities beyond the control of the States.[25] . . .

The entire history of litigation and contention over the question of the imposition of a bar to a second prosecution by a government other than the one first prosecuting is a manifestation of the evolutionary unfolding of law. Today a number of States have statutes which bar a second prosecution if the defendant has been once tried by another government for a similar offense. A study of the cases under the New York statute, which is typical of these laws, demonstrates that the task of determining when the federal and state statutes are so much alike that a prosecution under the former bars a prosecution under the latter is a difficult one. [Experience] such as that of New York may give aid to Congress in its consideration of adoption of similar provisions in individual federal criminal statutes or in the federal criminal code.

Precedent, experience, and reason alike support the conclusion that Alfonse Bartkus has not been deprived of due process of law by the State of Illinois.

Affirmed.

BLACK, J., dissenting.[*]

. . . Fear and abhorrence of governmental power to try people twice for the same conduct is one of the oldest ideas found in western civilization. Its roots run deep into Greek and Roman times. Even in the Dark Ages, when so many other principles of justice were lost, the idea that one trial and one punishment were enough remained alive through the canon law and the teachings of the early Christian writers. By the thirteenth century it seems to have been firmly established in England, where it came to be considered as a "universal maxim of the common law." [Some] writers have explained the opposition to double prosecutions by emphasizing the injustice inherent in two punishments for the same act, and others have stressed

---

25. Illinois had an additional and unique interest in Bartkus beyond the commission of this particular crime. If Bartkus was guilty of the crime charged he would be an habitual offender in Illinois and subject to life imprisonment. The Illinois court sentenced Bartkus to life imprisonment on this ground.

* [Chief Justice Warren and Justice Douglas joined this opinion.—EDS.]

the dangers to the innocent from allowing the full power of the state to be brought against them in two trials. . . .

The Court apparently takes the position that a second trial for the same act is somehow less offensive if one of the trials is conducted by the Federal Government and the other by a State. Looked at from the standpoint of the individual who is being prosecuted, this notion is too subtle for me to grasp. If double punishment is what is feared, it hurts no less for two "Sovereigns" to inflict it than for one. If danger to the innocent is emphasized, that danger is surely no less when the power of State and Federal Governments is brought to bear on one man in two trials, than when one of these "Sovereigns" proceeds alone. In each case, inescapably, a man is forced to face danger twice for the same conduct.

The Court, without denying the almost universal abhorrence of such double prosecutions, nevertheless justifies the practice here in the name of "federalism." This, it seems to me, is a misuse and desecration of the concept. Our Federal Union was conceived and created "to establish Justice" and to "secure the Blessings of Liberty," not to destroy any of the bulwarks on which both freedom and justice depend. We should, therefore, be suspicious of any supposed "requirements" of "federalism" which result in obliterating ancient safeguards. I have been shown nothing in the history of our Union, in the writings of its Founders, or elsewhere, to indicate that individual rights deemed essential by both State and Nation were to be lost through the combined operations of the two governments. . . .

The Court's argument also ignores the fact that our Constitution allocates power between local and federal governments in such a way that the basic rights of each can be protected without double trials. The Federal Government is given power to act in limited areas only, but in matters properly within its scope it is supreme. It can retain exclusive control of such matters, or grant the States concurrent power on its own terms.

[This] practice, which for some 150 years was considered so undesirable that the Court must strain to find examples, is now likely to become a commonplace. For, after today, who will be able to blame a conscientious prosecutor for failing to accept a jury verdict of acquittal when he believes a defendant guilty and knows that a second try is available in another jurisdiction and that such a second try is approved by the Highest Court in the Land? Inevitably, the victims of such double prosecutions will most often be the poor and the weak in our society, individuals without friends in high places who can influence prosecutors not to try them again. The power to try a second time will be used, as have all similar procedures, to make scapegoats of helpless, political, religious, or racial minorities and those who differ, who do not conform and who resist tyranny.

There are some countries that allow the dangerous practice of trying people twice. [Such practices] are not hard to find in lands torn by revolution or crushed by dictatorship. I had thought that our constitutional protections embodied in the Double Jeopardy and Due Process Clauses would have barred any such things happening here. Unfortunately, [today's decision causes] me to fear that in an important number of cases it can happen here. I would reverse.

BRENNAN, J., dissenting.*

Bartkus was tried and acquitted in a Federal District Court of robbing a federally insured savings and loan association in Cicero, Illinois. He was indicted for the

---

* [Chief Justice Warren and Justice Douglas joined this opinion.—EDS.]

same robbery by the State of Illinois less than three weeks later, and subsequently convicted and sentenced to life imprisonment. The single issue in dispute at both trials was whether Bartkus was the third participant in the robbery along with two self-confessed perpetrators of the crime.

The Government's case against Bartkus on the federal trial rested primarily upon the testimony of two of the robbers, Joseph Cosentino and James Brindis, who confessed their part in the crime and testified that Bartkus was their confederate. The defense was that Bartkus was getting a haircut in a barber shop several miles away at the time the robbery was committed. The owner of the barber shop, his son and other witnesses placed Bartkus in the shop at the time. The federal jury in acquitting Bartkus apparently believed the alibi witnesses and not Cosentino and Brindis.

The federal authorities were highly displeased with the jury's resolution of the conflicting testimony, and the trial judge sharply upbraided the jury for its verdict. The federal authorities obviously decided immediately after the trial to make a second try at convicting Bartkus, and since the federal courthouse was barred to them by the Fifth Amendment, they turned to a state prosecution for that purpose. It is clear that federal officers solicited the state indictment, arranged to assure the attendance of key witnesses, unearthed additional evidence to discredit Bartkus and one of his alibi witnesses, and in general prepared and guided the state prosecution. . . .

I think that the record before us shows that the extent of participation of the federal authorities here [made this state prosecution into] a second federal prosecution of Bartkus. The federal jury acquitted Bartkus late in December 1953. Early in January 1954 the Assistant United States Attorney who prosecuted the federal case summoned Cosentino to his office. Present also were the FBI agent who had investigated the robbery and the Assistant State's Attorney for Cook County who later prosecuted the state case. The Assistant State's Attorney said to Cosentino, "Look, we are going to get an indictment in the state court against Bartkus, will you testify against him?" Cosentino agreed that he would. Later Brindis also agreed to testify. Although they pleaded guilty to the federal robbery charge in August 1953, the Federal District Court postponed their sentencing until after they testified against Bartkus at the state trial, which was not held until April 1954. . . . Both Cosentino and Brindis were also released on bail pending the state trial, Brindis on his own recognizance.

In January, also, an FBI agent who had been active in the federal prosecution purposefully set about strengthening the proofs which had not sufficed to convict Bartkus on the federal trial. . . . He uncovered a new witness against Bartkus, one Grant Pursel. . . . The first time that Pursel had any contact whatsoever with a state official connected with the case was the morning that he testified. . . .

Given the fact that there must always be state officials involved in a state prosecution, I cannot see how there can be more complete federal participation in a state prosecution than there was in this case. I see no escape from the conclusion that this particular state trial was in actuality a second federal prosecution—a second federal try at Bartkus in the guise of a state prosecution. If this state conviction is not overturned, then, as a practical matter, there will be no restraints on the use of state machinery by federal officers to bring what is in effect a second federal prosecution. . . .

Of course, cooperation between federal and state authorities in criminal law enforcement is to be desired and encouraged, for cooperative federalism in this field can indeed profit the Nation and the States in improving methods for carrying out the endless fight against crime. But the normal and healthy situation consists of state and federal officers cooperating to apprehend law-breakers and present the strongest case against them at a single trial, be it state or federal. . . .

■ U.S. ATTORNEYS' MANUAL §9-2.031, DUAL PROSECUTION AND SUCCESSIVE PROSECUTION POLICY (*PETITE* POLICY)

A. Statement of Policy: This policy establishes guidelines for the exercise of discretion by appropriate officers of the Department of Justice in determining whether to bring a federal prosecution based on substantially the same act(s) or transactions involved in a prior state or federal proceeding. See Rinaldi v. United States, 434 U.S. 22, 27 (1977); Petite v. United States, 361 U.S. 529 (1960). Although there is no general statutory bar to a federal prosecution where the defendant's conduct already has formed the basis for a state prosecution, Congress expressly has provided that, as to certain offenses, a state judgment of conviction or acquittal on the merits shall be a bar to any subsequent federal prosecution for the same act or acts. See 18 U.S.C. §§659 [interstate or foreign shipments by carrier], 660 [embezzling carrier's funds derived from commerce], 2101 [travel in interstate commerce to incite a riot].

The purpose of this policy is to vindicate substantial federal interests through appropriate federal prosecutions, to protect persons charged with criminal conduct from the burdens associated with multiple prosecutions and punishments for substantially the same act(s) or transaction(s), to promote efficient utilization of Department resources, and to promote coordination and cooperation between federal and state prosecutors.

This policy precludes the initiation or continuation of a federal prosecution, following a prior state or federal prosecution based on substantially the same act(s) or transaction(s) unless three substantive prerequisites are satisfied: first, the matter must involve a substantial federal interest; second, the prior prosecution must have left that interest demonstrably unvindicated; and third, applying the same test that is applicable to all federal prosecutions, the government must believe that the defendant's conduct constitutes a federal offense, and that the admissible evidence probably will be sufficient to obtain and sustain a conviction by an unbiased trier of fact. In addition, there is a procedural prerequisite to be satisfied, that is, the prosecution must be approved by the appropriate Assistant Attorney General. . . .

In order to insure the most efficient use of law enforcement resources, whenever a matter involves overlapping federal and state jurisdiction, federal prosecutors should, as soon as possible, consult with their state counterparts to determine the most appropriate single forum in which to proceed to satisfy the substantial federal and state interests involved, and, if possible, to resolve all criminal liability for the acts in question.

B. Types of Prosecution to Which This Policy Applies: [This] policy applies whenever the contemplated federal prosecution is based on substantially the same act(s) or

transaction(s) involved in a prior state or federal prosecution. This policy constitutes an exercise of the Department's prosecutorial discretion, and applies even
where a prior state prosecution would not legally bar a subsequent federal prosecution under the Double Jeopardy Clause because of the doctrine of dual sovereignty
(see Abbate v. United States, 359 U.S. 187 (1959)), or a prior prosecution would not
legally bar a subsequent state or federal prosecution under the Double Jeopardy
Clause because each offense requires proof of an element not contained in the
other. See United States v. Dixon, 509 U.S. 688 (1993); Blockburger v. United States,
284 U.S. 299 (1932).

This policy does not apply, and thus prior approval is not required, where the
prior prosecution involved only a minor part of the contemplated federal charges.
For example, a federal conspiracy or RICO prosecution may allege overt acts or
predicate offenses previously prosecuted as long as those acts or offenses do not represent substantially the whole of the contemplated federal charge, and, in a RICO
prosecution, as long as there are a sufficient number of predicate offenses to sustain
the RICO charge if the previously prosecuted offenses were excluded. . . .

D. Substantive Prerequisites for Approval of a Prosecution Governed by This Policy: As
previously stated there are three substantive prerequisites that must be met before
approval will be granted for the initiation or a continuation of a prosecution governed by this policy.

The first substantive prerequisite is that the matter must involve a substantial
federal interest. This determination will be made on a case-by-case basis, applying
the considerations applicable to all federal prosecutions. See Principles of Federal
Prosecution, USAM 9-27.230. Matters that come within the national investigative or
prosecutorial priorities established by the Department are more likely than others
to satisfy this requirement.

The second substantive prerequisite is that the prior prosecution must have
left that substantial federal interest demonstrably unvindicated. In general, the
Department will presume that a prior prosecution, regardless of result, has vindicated the relevant federal interest. That presumption, however, may be overcome
when there are factors suggesting an unvindicated federal interest.

The presumption may be overcome when a conviction was not achieved because
of the following sorts of factors: first, incompetence, corruption, intimidation, or
undue influence; second, court or jury nullification in clear disregard of the evidence or the law; third, the unavailability of significant evidence, either because
it was not timely discovered or known by the prosecution, or because it was kept
from the trier of fact's consideration because of an erroneous interpretation of the
law; fourth, the failure in a prior state prosecution to prove an element of a state
offense that is not an element of the contemplated federal offense; and fifth, the
exclusion of charges in a prior federal prosecution out of concern for fairness to
other defendants, or for significant resource considerations that favored separate
federal prosecutions.

The presumption may be overcome even when a conviction was achieved in
the prior prosecution in the following circumstances: first, if the prior sentence was
manifestly inadequate in light of the federal interest involved and a substantially
enhanced sentence—including forfeiture and restitution as well as imprisonment
and fines—is available through the contemplated federal prosecution, or second,
if the choice of charges, or the determination of guilt, or the severity of sentence

in the prior prosecution was affected by the sorts of factors listed in the previous paragraph. An example might be a case in which the charges in the initial prosecution trivialized the seriousness of the contemplated federal offense, for example, a state prosecution for assault and battery in a case involving the murder of a federal official.

The presumption also may be overcome, irrespective of the result in a prior state prosecution, in those rare cases where the following three conditions are met: first, the alleged violation involves a compelling federal interest, particularly one implicating an enduring national priority; second, the alleged violation involves egregious conduct, including that which threatens or causes loss of life, severe economic or physical harm, or the impairment of the functioning of an agency of the federal government or the due administration of justice; and third, the result in the prior prosecution was manifestly inadequate in light of the federal interest involved.

The third substantive prerequisite is that the government must believe that the defendant's conduct constitutes a federal offense, and that the admissible evidence probably will be sufficient to obtain and sustain a conviction by an unbiased trier of fact. This is the same test applied to all federal prosecutions. See Principles of Federal Prosecution, USAM 9-27.200 et seq. . . .

E. Procedural Prerequisite for Bringing a Prosecution Governed by This Policy: Whenever a substantial question arises as to whether this policy applies to a prosecution, the matter should be submitted to the appropriate Assistant Attorney General for resolution. Prior approval from the appropriate Assistant Attorney General must be obtained before bringing a prosecution governed by this policy. The United States will move to dismiss any prosecution governed by this policy in which prior approval was not obtained, unless the Assistant Attorney General retroactively approves it on the following grounds: first, that there are unusual or overriding circumstances justifying retroactive approval, and second, that the prosecution would have been approved had approval been sought in a timely fashion. Appropriate administrative action may be initiated against prosecutors who violate this policy.

F. . . . No Substantive or Procedural Rights Created: This policy has been promulgated solely for the purpose of internal Department of Justice guidance. It is not intended to, does not, and may not be relied upon to create any rights, substantive or procedural, that are enforceable at law by any party in any matter, civil or criminal, nor does it place any limitations on otherwise lawful litigative prerogatives of the Department of Justice.

■ NEW JERSEY STATUTES §2C:1-11

When conduct constitutes an offense within the concurrent jurisdiction of this State and of the United States, a prosecution in the District Court of the United States is a bar to a subsequent prosecution in this State under the following circumstances:

a. The first prosecution resulted in an acquittal or in a conviction, or in an improper termination . . . and the subsequent prosecution is based on the same conduct, unless (1) the offense of which the defendant was formerly convicted or acquitted and the offense for which he is subsequently prosecuted each requires proof of a fact not required by the other and the law defining each of such offenses is intended to prevent a substantially different harm or evil or (2) the offense for which the defendant is subsequently prosecuted is intended to prevent a substantially more serious harm or evil than the offense of which he was formerly convicted or acquitted or (3) the second offense was not consummated when the former trial began; or

b. The former prosecution was terminated, after the information was filed or the indictment found, by an acquittal or by a final order or judgment for the defendant which has not been set aside, reversed or vacated and which acquittal, final order or judgment necessarily required a determination inconsistent with a fact which must be established for conviction of the offense of which the defendant is subsequently prosecuted.

■ OHIO REVISED CODE §2925.50

If a violation of this chapter is a violation of the federal drug abuse control laws . . . a conviction or acquittal under the federal drug abuse control laws for the same act is a bar to prosecution in this state.

Notes

1. *Double jeopardy and dual sovereigns: majority position.* The Supreme Court ultimately decided, in Benton v. Maryland, 395 U.S. 784 (1969), that the due process clause of the Fourteenth Amendment incorporates double jeopardy requirements against state governments. The Supreme Court, however, never repudiated its 1959 decision in *Bartkus,* despite all the changes in state-federal relations that it wrought through its incorporation decisions from that same era. See United States v. Lara, 541 U.S. 193 (2004) (dual sovereign doctrine permits federal government to prosecute Native Americans for offenses after they have already been convicted of similar offenses in tribal courts). See Anthony J. Colangelo, Double Jeopardy and Multiple Sovereigns: A Jurisdictional Theory, 86 Wash. U. L. Rev. 769 (2009).

A substantial majority of states follow the U.S. Supreme Court and hold, under state constitutional provisions, that the double jeopardy bar does not prohibit a second prosecution by a different sovereign, even for an offense defined by identical elements that would be considered the "same offence" within one jurisdiction. See State v. Franklin, 735 P.2d 34 (Utah 1987) (avowed racist killed two black men who were jogging in park with two white women; federal conviction for civil rights crime does not bar state murder trial under state statute or constitution). A few states have extended their constitutional double jeopardy provisions to bar a second prosecution for the same offense—or sometimes a similar offense—if it has been prosecuted in another jurisdiction.

2. *Dual sovereign statutes.* In contrast to the narrow constitutional rulings, more than a dozen states reject the dual sovereignty doctrine by statute. See, e.g., Cal. Penal Code §656 ("Whenever on the trial of an accused person it appears that upon a criminal prosecution under the laws of another State, Government, or country, founded upon the act or omission in respect to which he is on trial, he has been acquitted or convicted, it is a sufficient defense."). Most statutory limits on second

prosecutions are limited to particular categories of offenses, such as the Ohio statute relating to drug offenses. Typically, these statutes are based on either the Uniform Narcotic Drug Act or the Uniform Controlled Substances Act. Unif. Narcotic Drug Act 21, 9B U.L.A. 284 (1958); Unif. Controlled Substances Act 418, 9 U.L.A. 596 (1990). See State v. Hansen, 627 N.W.2d 195 (Wis. 2001) (state statute applicable to controlled substance offenses bars prosecution of defendant by state officials for offenses arising out of the same conduct for which the defendant has been federally prosecuted). Why might legislatures restrict statutory double jeopardy provisions to specified types of crimes?

The statutes are intended to prevent the unfairness of multiple prosecutions and to avoid the unnecessary use of state resources to prosecute cases already adequately prosecuted in federal courts. They often provide for exceptions when a reprosecution serves a different purpose or addresses a different evil from the earlier prosecution. See Ga. Code Ann. §16-1-8(c) (barring reprosecution except to prevent a "substantially more serious" or different harm or evil). For an exploration of the variety of state statutes on dual prosecutions, see the web extension for this chapter at *http://www.crimpro.com/extension/ch14.*

3. *Silver platters and dual sovereigns.* When more than one system can prosecute a criminal case, choice of law questions will crop up. For instance, which system's rules will be used to evaluate the work of the government agents who collected the evidence? Will the agents of one sovereign, acting in violation of the rules of their own government, be able to offer any evidence they obtain on a "silver platter" to prosecutors in another jurisdiction? When the federal constitution creates the obligations for the government agents, the answer is clear: No court (state or federal) may rely on evidence obtained by any state or federal agents in violation of the federal constitution. But what happens when the states have different rules from the federal government? If a state has its own rules (constitutional or statutory) to control government agents, and its agents violate those rules and offer the tainted evidence to federal prosecutors, the federal courts will admit the evidence, so long as the agent's actions comported with the Fourth Amendment. See United States v. Master, 614 F.3d 236 (6th Cir. 2010). A number of state courts also accept evidence from government agents in another jurisdiction that violate the rules of that other jurisdiction. See Burge v. State, 443 S.W.2d 720 (Tex. Crim. App. 1969). Some states, however, use an interest-based approach or a policy-based approach (tied to the policy behind the exclusionary rule) in deciding whether to admit evidence obtained in violation of another state's rules. For a discussion of the different approaches adopted by states, see Jenia Iontcheva Turner, Interstate Conflict and Cooperation in Criminal Cases: An American Perspective, 4 Eur. Crim. L. Rev. 114 (2014). Should a prosecutorial office policy dealing with prosecutions by multiple jurisdictions also address the use of evidence obtained in violation of law in another jurisdiction?

4. *Creation of the federal* Petite *policy.* Some jurisdictions that do not have constitutional or statutory limitations on filing cases already prosecuted in another jurisdiction nonetheless have *internal* prosecutorial rules or guidelines limiting successive prosecutions. The best-known illustration is the federal *Petite* policy. One week after the decision in *Bartkus,* which made it clear that the "dual sovereign" exception to the constitutional doctrine of double jeopardy would allow both state and federal prosecutions of the same crime, the Department of Justice issued a policy limiting federal prosecution after a state prosecution. The policy allows a federal prosecution

following a state prosecution only when necessary to advance compelling interests of federal law enforcement. The policy later took its name from Petite v. United States, 361 U.S. 529 (1960), in which the Court noted with approval the existence of the policy. It was designed to limit successive prosecutions for the same offense to situations involving distinct federal and state interests. In announcing the policy, Attorney General William Rogers stated:

> We should continue to make every effort to cooperate with state and local authorities to the end that the trial occur in the jurisdiction, whether it be state or federal, where the public interest is best served. If this be determined accurately, and is followed by efficient and intelligent cooperation of state and federal law enforcement authorities, then consideration of a second prosecution very seldom should arise.

Dept. of Justice Press Release, Apr. 6, 1959, at 3. The policy creates internal guidance only and does not create any rights that a defendant can enforce in court. See United States v. Snell, 592 F.2d 1083 (9th Cir. 1979). Are such policies properly considered "law"?

5. *Double jeopardy and international extradition.* The law in some other nations clearly rejects any dual sovereignty exception. As global legal regimes emerge, should double jeopardy principles bar multiple prosecutions by different countries? Is the principle barring double jeopardy an essential element of human rights? A partial answer to this question may be worked out on a bilateral basis as part of extradition treaties, for if a country cannot obtain control over the defendant, it is difficult to conduct a trial or to punish a person.

The European Union (EU) Convention implementing the Schengen Agreement of 1985 states in Article 54 that "[a] person who has been finally judged by a Contracting Party may not be prosecuted by another Contracting Party for the same offences provided that, where he is sentenced, the sentence has been served or is currently being served or can no longer be carried out under the sentencing laws of the Contracting Party." In two consolidated cases, the European Court of Justice held in 2003 that under this provision a person cannot be prosecuted in another member state even if (1) his case was discontinued by the prosecution after payment of a certain amount of money (based on a procedure of discontinuation) or (2) the case was settled out of court through a monetary payment (also based on national procedure). C-187/01 *Hyüseyin Gözütok* and C-385/01 *Klaus Brügge* (Feb. 11, 2003). Article 54 sweeps far more broadly than internal United States double jeopardy barriers. The decision is noteworthy because it equates the discontinuation of procedures through a decision by the public prosecutor with a trial (or other judicial action).

6. *Double jeopardy and the Interstate Agreement on Detainers.* Even in the domestic U.S. context, one state's refusal to extradite a suspect could limit the capacity of another state to try that person regardless of the double jeopardy law in either jurisdiction. The possibility of such conflicts, however, has been reduced through the Interstate Agreement on Detainers, which provides a regular method of processing criminal charges filed by more than one state. The IAD is an interstate compact that most state legislatures have adopted. See Cal. Penal Code §1389. It allows prosecutors to notify officials holding a criminal defendant in an out-of-state facility that the state wishes to pursue criminal charges against the defendant; such notice is called a "detainer." The IAD also allows the defendant to request that the state issuing the detainer dispose of the charges promptly.

Problem 14-1. When Do Successive Prosecutions Make Sense?

How would you apply the *Petite* policy in each of the following situations?

(1) Several police officers take an African American man into custody on the streets of Baltimore; he dies while in their custody. The state criminal trials of the officers result in acquittals, after the officers convince the trial judge that they were not the cause of the man's death. Should the federal government initiate a prosecution against the officers?

(2) A man bombs the federal building in Oklahoma City; the bomb kills 160 people, including dozens of children in the day care center for employees' children. In a federal prosecution, he is convicted of hundreds of crimes and receives multiple punishments of death. Should the State of Oklahoma thereafter try him for 160 counts of homicide?

(3) Working with a juvenile accomplice, a man shoots various people from hidden locations in Maryland, Virginia, and neighboring states. Virginia prosecutes him for multiple counts of homicide and he receives the death penalty. Following the close of the Virginia case, should Maryland initiate a prosecution against him for the homicides committed within its borders?

(4) A man being prosecuted for rape in Atlanta escapes his confinement and kills multiple people, including a state court judge and a federal agent trying to apprehend him. He is convicted of felony murder in the state court system, but the jury verdict is for life without parole instead of the death penalty. Should the federal government initiate a prosecution for the murder of the federal agent, which carries the death penalty?

2. "Same Offence"

The limitations on double jeopardy apply only when a person is placed twice in jeopardy for the "same offence." Determining whether a second offense is the "same" offense as the first one raises difficult challenges. First, many criminal codes include hundreds or even thousands of crimes with overlapping elements, aimed at punishing similar harms. The federal code, for example, includes more than 3,000 separate offenses. Because of the intricacy of most criminal codes (to put it kindly), courts have conceded that charges need not be brought twice under precisely the same statute before concluding that the prosecutions are for the "same" offense. The topic of this subsection is how courts determine whether charges under different code provisions count as the same offense.

The dominant test for answering this question appears in Blockburger v. United States, 284 U.S. 299 (1932). The defendant in that case was convicted of three counts of violating the Harrison Narcotics Act based on the sale of small amounts of morphine hydrochloride. One of the counts of conviction charged a sale of eight grains of the drug not from the original stamped package; another count alleged that the same sale was not made according to a written order of the purchaser, as required by the statute. The court sentenced Blockburger to five years in prison and imposed a fine of $2,000 upon each count, the terms of imprisonment to run consecutively. Blockburger asserted that these two counts constituted one offense for which only a single penalty could be imposed. The Court disagreed, holding that "where the same act or transaction constitutes a violation of two distinct statutory provisions, the test to be applied to determine whether there are two offenses or only one is whether each provision requires proof of an additional fact which the other does not." 284 U.S. at 304.

Consider this application of the *Blockburger* rule. Suppose that Ralph, during a heated argument with Alice, shakes his fist at her angrily and says, "I am sending you to the moon, Alice!" He then draws his arm back to prepare for a punch, hits her in the face, and breaks her nose. Prosecutors file three charges against him: assault on a female, simple assault, and communicating threats. The state criminal code defines simple assault as "knowingly placing a person in fear of an immediate physical attack." The more serious crime of assault on a female requires proof that "a male person at least 18 years of age assaults a female." A person commits the crime of communicating threats when "(1) the person willfully threatens to physically injure another person or that person's property; (2) the threat is communicated to the other person, orally, in writing, or by any other means; and (3) the person threatened believes that the threat will be carried out." Under the *Blockburger* test, the prosecution could not simultaneously charge simple assault and assault on a female, because simple assault is a lesser included offense to assault on a female; in other words, assault on a female starts with the proof necessary for simple assault, and then adds two more elements. As for communicating threats, the charge can co-exist with simple assault or with assault on a female. The "communicating threats" statute requires proof of communication, while the assault crimes require proof that the victim feared an "immediate" attack.

The *Blockburger* test is often criticized because the government can so easily obtain multiple convictions based on the same conduct. The Supreme Court experimented briefly with a more demanding test. In Grady v. Corbin, 495 U.S. 508 (1990), the Court added a "same conduct" test on top of the *Blockburger* "same elements" test for those cases when the government pursues successive prosecutions. Under this expanded test, the double jeopardy principle "bars any subsequent prosecution in which the government, to establish an essential element of an offense charged in that prosecution, will prove conduct that constitutes an offense for which the defendant has already been prosecuted."

Three years later, however, the Court overruled *Grady* and reinstated the "same elements" test as the basic way to identify double jeopardy violations in United States v. Dixon, 509 U.S. 688 (1993). For a more detailed comparison of the facts and holdings in these three Supreme Court cases, see the web extension for this chapter at *http://www.crimpro.com/extension/ch14.*

The first of the following two cases shows the *Blockburger* test at work. The second case discusses the choices among different tests for the "same offense" and illustrates the response of state courts to the leadership of the U.S. Supreme Court in this difficult area.

■ ROBERT TAYLOR v. COMMONWEALTH
995 S.W.2d 355 (Ky. 1999)

COOPER, J.

. . . On the afternoon of October 9, 1996, Appellant, then seventeen years of age, his girlfriend, Lucy Cotton, and Cotton's infant son had attended the Daniel Boone Festival and were traveling through rural Knox County in a 1985 Buick owned by Cotton's mother. They had with them a .22 rifle, a .38 Derringer handgun, and two shotguns. When the vehicle stalled, Appellant sought assistance from Herman McCreary, who lived nearby. McCreary agreed to help and drove his 1984 Ford pickup truck to the location of the stalled vehicle. Upon arrival, he observed Cotton sitting in the passenger seat of the Buick holding a child in her lap. Several attempts to jump-start the Buick failed. According to Cotton, Appellant told her, "If it don't start this time, I'm gonna take his truck," and armed himself with the .22 rifle and the .38 handgun. According to Appellant, Cotton pointed the .38 handgun at him and threatened to shoot him if he did not steal McCreary's truck.

When a final attempt to jump-start the Buick was unsuccessful, Appellant got out of the vehicle, pointed the .22 rifle at McCreary, and ordered him to lie on the ground. When McCreary complied, Appellant fired a round from the rifle into the ground near McCreary's head. According to Cotton, Appellant then struck McCreary in the head with the stock of the rifle. McCreary temporarily lost consciousness. Upon regaining consciousness, McCreary experienced dizziness and noticed blood coming from the left side of his head. Appellant then told McCreary to get into the ditch beside the road or he would "blow his head off." McCreary again complied, whereupon Appellant, Cotton and the child departed the scene in McCreary's truck. McCreary walked to a neighbor's house and called the police. [Taylor and Cotton were later apprehended and Taylor was convicted of assault in second degree, robbery in first degree, and possession of handgun by a minor. He was sentenced to two ten-year prison terms, to be served consecutively, for the assault and robbery charges, along with a twelve-month term for the weapons charge, to be served concurrently. Taylor] asserts that his convictions violated the constitutional proscription against double jeopardy. U.S. Const. amend. V; Ky. Const. §13.

In Commonwealth v. Burge, 947 S.W.2d 805, 809-11 (1997), we reinstated the "*Blockburger* rule," Blockburger v. United States, 284 U.S. 299 (1932), as incorporated in KRS §505.020, as the sole basis for determining whether multiple convictions arising out of a single course of conduct constitutes double jeopardy. The test in this case is not whether all three convictions were premised upon the use or possession of a firearm, or whether both the assault and the robbery occurred in the course of a single transaction. Where the "same act or transaction constitutes a violation of two distinct statutory provisions, the test to be applied to determine whether there are two offenses or only one is whether each provision requires proof of an additional fact which the other does not." Blockburger v. United States, 284 U.S. 299, 304 (1932).

KRS §515.020(1) defines robbery in the first degree as follows:

> A person is guilty of robbery in the first degree when, in the course of committing a theft, he uses or threatens the immediate use of physical force upon another person with intent to accomplish the theft and when he:
> (a) Causes physical injury to any person who is not a participant in the crime; or
> (b) Is armed with a deadly weapon; or
> (c) Uses or threatens the use of a dangerous instrument upon any person who is not a participant in the crime.

The first paragraph of the statute sets forth three elements which must be proven in any robbery case, viz.: (1) In the course of committing a theft, (2) the defendant used or threatened the immediate use of physical force upon another person (3) with the intent to accomplish the theft. Subsections (a), (b), and (c) of the statute then describe three separate and distinct factual situations, any one of which could constitute the fourth element of the offense. The indictment of Appellant for robbery in the first degree in this case charged that he committed the offense "by being armed with a deadly weapon." The jury was instructed that it could convict Appellant of robbery in the first degree only if it believed beyond a reasonable doubt that "when he did so, he was armed with a .22 rifle." Thus, both the indictment and the instruction were predicated upon a violation of KRS 515.020(1)(b). Neither the indictment nor the instruction required Appellant to have caused a physical injury to McCreary or to have used or threatened the use of a dangerous instrument upon McCreary.

KRS 508.020(1) defines assault in the second degree as follows:

> A person is guilty of assault in the second degree when:
> (a) He intentionally causes serious physical injury to another person; or
> (b) He intentionally causes physical injury to another person by means of a deadly weapon or a dangerous instrument; or
> (c) He wantonly causes serious physical injury to another person by means of a deadly weapon or a dangerous instrument.

The statute sets forth three alternative factual situations by which the offense can be committed. Although the indictment charged Appellant with having committed the offense "by striking Herman McCreary with a pistol," the jury instruction conformed to the testimony of Lucy Cotton, who provided the only evidence with respect to this offense:

> You will find the defendant guilty under this instruction if, and only if, you believe from the evidence beyond a reasonable doubt all of the following: (a) that in this county on or about October 9, 1996 and before the finding of the indictment herein, he inflicted an injury upon Herman McCreary by striking him with a .22 rifle, a deadly weapon; AND (b) that in so doing, the defendant intentionally caused physical injury to Herman McCreary.[1]

Thus, conviction of either the assault or the robbery of McCreary required proof of an element not required to prove the other. The conviction of robbery required proof of a theft, which was not required to convict of assault. The conviction of assault required proof of a physical injury to McCreary, whereas the conviction of robbery required proof only that Appellant used or threatened the use of physical force upon McCreary while armed with a .22 rifle. . . .

STUMBO, J., dissenting.

Respectfully, I must dissent. I believe Appellant's convictions for both assault and robbery violated the prohibition against double jeopardy. . . . As written, the indictment did not violate the double jeopardy prohibition. The indictment charged

---

1. Appellant did not object to the variance of this instruction from the language of the indictment. The indictment described the weapon used to inflict the injury as a pistol, whereas the instruction described the weapon as a .22 rifle. Generally, instructions should be based on the evidence introduced at trial, and any variance between the language of the indictment and the language of the instruction is not deemed prejudicial unless the defendant was misled.

Appellant with "Assault in the Second Degree by striking Herman McCreary with a pistol" and "Robbery in the First Degree by being armed with a deadly weapon while in the course of committing a theft of Herman McCreary." Clearly, these offenses arise from two distinct statutes. As charged, each would have required proof of a fact which the other did not. For the assault, the prosecution would have had to prove that Appellant struck McCreary with the .38 pistol causing a physical injury. For the robbery, the prosecution would have had to prove Appellant used or threatened to use physical force on McCreary while armed with a deadly weapon (presumably the .22 rifle) during the course of the theft of his truck.

In the end, however, the prosecution was unable to maintain this logically sound but practically impossible distinction. By the time the jury was instructed, the assault had merged into the robbery so that one was clearly included within the other. This is so because the jury instruction on second-degree assault required the jury to find the offense was accomplished "by striking him with a .22 rifle, a deadly weapon." The jury instruction on first-degree robbery required the jury to find Appellant "used or threatened the immediate use of physical force upon Herman McCreary; AND (c) that when he did so, he was armed with a .22 rifle." This melding of the charges allowed the jury to consider any assault with the .22 rifle during the incident as an element of the robbery and thus made the assault charge a lesser included offense of the robbery charge. . . .

■ PEOPLE V. MELISSA NUTT

677 N.W.2d 1 (Mich. 2004)

YOUNG, J.

The United States and Michigan Constitutions protect a person from being twice placed in jeopardy for the same offense. The prohibition against double jeopardy provides three related protections: (1) it protects against a second prosecution for the same offense after acquittal; (2) it protects against a second prosecution for the same offense after conviction; and (3) it protects against multiple punishments for the same offense. The first two of these three protections concern the "successive prosecutions" strand of the Double Jeopardy Clause, which is implicated in the case before us. In particular, because our Double Jeopardy Clause is essentially identical to its federal counterpart, we must determine whether the term "same offense" in our Constitution was, in *White*, properly accorded a meaning that is different from the construction of that term in the federal Constitution. . . .

FEDERAL SUCCESSIVE PROSECUTIONS PROTECTION AND THE
SAME-ELEMENTS TEST

Application of the same-elements test, commonly known as the "*Blockburger* test," is the well-established method of defining the Fifth Amendment term "same offence." The test, which has deep historical roots, focuses on the statutory elements of the offense. If each requires proof of a fact that the other does not, the *Blockburger* test is satisfied, notwithstanding a substantial overlap in the proof offered to establish the crimes. . . .

Although Justice William Brennan was a persistent advocate of the same transaction test, see Werneth v. Idaho, 449 U.S. 1129 (1981) (Brennan, J., dissenting), the idea that crimes arising from the same criminal episode constitute the same offenses for double jeopardy purposes has been consistently rejected by the United States Supreme Court. Instead, the . . . *Blockburger* same-elements analysis was consistently applied by the Court . . . until the Court in Grady v. Corbin, 495 U.S. 508 (1990), adopted a "same-conduct" rule—a somewhat compromised version of Justice Brennan's "same transaction" test—as an additional step to be performed in addressing successive prosecutions claims. In an opinion authored by Justice William Brennan, the Court held that "the Double Jeopardy Clause bars a subsequent prosecution if, to establish an essential element of an offense charged in that prosecution, the government will prove conduct that constitutes an offense for which the defendant has already been prosecuted."

Justice Scalia dissented, noting that the majority's holding was wholly without historical foundation and that it created a procedural mandatory joinder rule: "In practice, [the majority's holding] will require prosecutors to observe a rule we have explicitly rejected in principle: that all charges arising out of a single occurrence must be joined in a single indictment." Looking to the text of the Double Jeopardy Clause and its origins in the common law, Justice Scalia opined that the *Blockburger* rule best gave effect to the plain language of the Clause, "which protects individuals from being twice put in jeopardy 'for the same offense,' not for the same conduct or actions."

The *Grady* same-conduct test was short-lived. In United States v. Dixon, 509 U.S. 688 (1993), the Court overruled *Grady* as wrongly decided for the reasons expressed in Justice Scalia's *Grady* dissent and returned to the *Blockburger* formulation of the test for both successive prosecutions and multiple punishments. . . .

MEANING OF "SAME OFFENSE" IN MICHIGAN'S DOUBLE JEOPARDY PROVISION

. . . In accordance with the principle that our double jeopardy provision was intended to embody English common-law tenets of former jeopardy, this Court more than one hundred years ago rejected the "same transaction" approach and instead embraced the federal same-elements test as supplying the functional definition of "same offense" under our Constitution's Double Jeopardy Clause. In People v. Parrow, 45 N.W. 514 (Mich. 1890), this Court held that Const. 1850, art. 6, §29 did not preclude the defendant's prosecution for larceny of money stolen during an alleged burglary where the defendant had previously been acquitted of burglary. . . .

However, in People v. White, 212 N.W.2d 222 (Mich. 1973), the majority . . . adopted the same transaction test advocated unsuccessfully by Justice William Brennan—one even more expansive than the defunct compromise *Grady* test. We noted that several other states had adopted the same transaction test, either under their own constitutions or under statutes requiring mandatory joinder, and that . . . the same transaction test was necessary to effectuate the intent of the framers that the state not be allowed to make repeated attempts to convict a defendant. Without reference to our Constitution, its text, or its ratification process, the *White* Court opined that the same transaction test fostered sound policy:

> In a time of overcrowded criminal dockets, prosecutors and judges should attempt to bring to trial a defendant as expeditiously and economically as possible. A far more basic reason for adopting the same transaction test is to prevent harassment of a defendant. The joining of all charges arising out of the same criminal episode at one trial . . . will enable a defendant to consider the matter closed and save the costs of redundant litigation. It will also help . . . to equalize the adversary capabilities of grossly unequal litigants and prevent prosecutorial sentence shopping.

The *White* Court also noted that the equivalent of the same transaction test had long been the standard applied to civil actions by the court rule governing joinder and by the doctrines of collateral estoppel and res judicata. Finally, the Court concluded that the three crimes committed by the defendant were all part of a single criminal transaction because they "were committed in a continuous time sequence and displayed a single intent and goal—sexual intercourse with the complainant." . . .

In our 1963 Constitution the narrower language of the 1850 and 1908 double jeopardy provisions was replaced with language similar to that of the original Constitution of 1835 and the Fifth Amendment: "No person shall be subject for the same offense to be twice put in jeopardy." Art. 1, §15.

It is immediately striking that the plain language of the provision provides no support for the conclusion that the term "same offense" should be interpreted by reference to whether a crime arises out of the "same transaction" as another. Rather, we believe that the plain and obvious meaning of the term "offense" is "crime" or "transgression." . . .

The ultimate inquiry, of course, is the meaning ascribed to the phrase "same offense" by the ratifiers of our 1963 Constitution. Examination of the record of the Constitutional Convention of 1961 provides the historical context and persuasive support for our decision to return to the original meaning given to the Fifth Amendment–based double jeopardy language in art. 1, §15. . . .

In 1973, this Court disregarded decades of precedent and, without consideration of the will of the people of this state in ratifying the Double Jeopardy Clause in our 1963 Constitution, adopted Justice William Brennan's long-rejected "same transaction" test. . . . In the absence of any evidence that the term "offense" was understood by the people to comprise all criminal acts arising out of a single criminal episode, we are compelled to overrule *White*. [The] same-elements test best gives effect to the intent of the ratifiers of the 1963 Constitution.[28]

APPLICATION

Defendant's Oakland County prosecution for possession of stolen firearms, following her conviction for second-degree home invasion in Lapeer County, withstands constitutional scrutiny under the same-elements test. Defendant was convicted of home invasion pursuant to MCL 750.110a(3), which provided: "A person who breaks and enters a dwelling with intent to commit a felony or a larceny in the dwelling or a person who enters a dwelling without permission with intent to commit a felony or a larceny in the dwelling is guilty of home invasion in the second degree." Required for a conviction of this offense was proof that defendant (1) entered a dwelling, either by a breaking or without permission, (2) with the intent to commit a felony or a larceny in the dwelling.

---

28. [Principles] of collateral estoppel and properly adopted procedural joinder rules might well compel the dismissal of charges in certain circumstances. Nevertheless, collateral estoppel and joinder are discrete, nonconstitutional concepts that should not be conflated with the constitutional double jeopardy protection. [We] will be requesting the Committee on the Rules of Criminal Procedure to consider whether our permissive joinder rule, MCR 6.120(A), should be amended to impose mandatory joinder of all the charges against a defendant arising out of the same transaction. . . .

Defendant now stands charged with receiving and concealing a stolen firearm in violation of MCL 750.535b(2), which provides: "A person who receives, conceals, stores, barters, sells, disposes of, pledges, or accepts as security for a loan a stolen firearm or stolen ammunition, knowing that the firearm or ammunition was stolen, is guilty of a felony. . . ." Thus, the Oakland County Prosecutor is required to prove that defendant (1) received, concealed, stored, bartered, sold, disposed of, pledged, or accepted as security for a loan (2) a stolen firearm or stolen ammunition (3) knowing that the firearm or ammunition was stolen.

Clearly, there is no identity of elements between these two offenses. Each offense requires proof of elements that the other does not. Because the two offenses are nowise the same offense under either the Fifth Amendment or art. 1, §15, we . . . hold that defendant is not entitled to the dismissal of the Oakland County charge.

CAVANAGH, J., dissenting.

. . . This Court's decision to overrule *White* is grounded in the improper belief that the same elements test is the sole test used by the United States Supreme Court to protect citizens' constitutional rights under the United States Constitution. However, the same elements test, also referred to as the *Blockburger* test, is not as entrenched in federal jurisprudence as the majority claims. . . .

In numerous cases, the United States Supreme Court has used other tests because it recognized that the same elements test is not an adequate safeguard to protect a citizen's constitutional right against double jeopardy. In Ashe v. Swenson, 397 U.S. 436 (1970), the United States Supreme Court held that the double jeopardy clause includes a collateral estoppel guarantee. . . . As stated in Albernaz v. United States, 450 U.S. 333, 340 (1981), "The *Blockburger* test is a rule of statutory construction, and because it serves as a means of discerning congressional purpose the rule should not be controlling where, for example, there is a clear indication of contrary legislative intent." Further, in In re Nielsen, 131 U.S. 176 (1889), a conviction for unlawful cohabitation precluded a subsequent charge of adultery because the incident occurred during the same two and a half year period as that for unlawful cohabitation. In Harris v. Oklahoma, 433 U.S. 682 (1977), the defendant was convicted of felony murder after a store clerk was killed during a robbery. After the defendant's conviction for felony murder, the defendant was tried and convicted of robbery with firearms. The United States Supreme Court held that when "conviction of a greater crime . . . cannot be had without conviction of the lesser crime, the Double Jeopardy Clause bars prosecution for the lesser crime after conviction of the greater one." And in Brown v. Ohio, 432 U.S. 161 (1977), double jeopardy barred a subsequent prosecution for a greater offense even though the greater offense required proof of an additional element. . . .

Our Double Jeopardy Clause is meant to protect our citizens from government zeal and overreaching; yet, the same elements test permits multiple prosecutions stemming from a single incident. "The same-elements test is an inadequate safeguard, for it leaves the constitutional guarantee at the mercy of a legislature's decision to modify statutory definitions." United States v. Dixon, 509 U.S. 688, 735 (1993) (White, J., dissenting). Notably, a technical comparison of the elements is neither constitutionally sound nor easy to apply. While the same elements test appears at first glance to be easy to apply, this Court's recent struggle with whether materiality is an element of perjury in People v. Lively, 664 N.W.2d 223 (Mich. 2003), provides proof to the contrary. . . . If our courts struggle with the basics of determining what elements constitute a crime, it is inevitable that these struggles will continue when courts attempt to determine whether two crimes contain the same elements.

In contrast to the same elements test, the same transaction test requires the government to join at one trial all the charges against a defendant arising out of a continuous time sequence, when the offenses shared a single intent and goal. Although a single transaction can give rise to distinct offenses, the charges must be joined at one trial. However, the same transaction test also offers flexibility for certain circumstances, such as when facts necessary to sustain a charge have not yet occurred or have not been discovered despite due diligence. . . .

In this case, defendant pleaded guilty of second-degree home invasion, MCL 750.110a(3). She was subsequently charged with receiving and concealing stolen firearms, MCL 750.535b. Notably, defendant was the driver in the home invasion during which the guns were stolen. She also admitted that the guns concealed were the ones stolen during the home invasion. Defendant's actions represent a single intent and goal, as well as the events being part of a continuous time sequence. Almost universally, inherent in stealing an item is receiving it and concealing it, if only for a brief time. Defendant's intent when she participated in the home invasion was to successfully steal the guns. Defendant's intent when she participated in the concealing of the guns was to successfully steal the guns. The subsequent prosecution for receiving and concealing stolen firearms violated defendant's double jeopardy rights. . . .

Without double jeopardy protections, our citizens are at risk of facing multiple prosecutions by the government, regardless of a prior acquittal. Further, because the state can devote its resources to improving the presentation of its case, the probability of a conviction may increase with each retrial. Accordingly, [after] pleading guilty of second-degree home invasion, defendant's subsequent prosecution for receiving and concealing stolen firearms violated her double jeopardy rights.

■ NEW YORK CRIMINAL PROCEDURE LAW §40.20

1. A person may not be twice prosecuted for the same offense.

2. A person may not be separately prosecuted for two offenses based upon the same act or criminal transaction unless:

(a) The offenses as defined have substantially different elements and the acts establishing one offense are in the main clearly distinguishable from those establishing the other; or

(b) Each of the offenses as defined contains an element which is not an element of the other, and the statutory provisions defining such offenses are designed to prevent very different kinds of harm or evil; or

(c) One of such offenses consists of criminal possession of contraband matter and the other offense is one involving the use of such contraband matter, other than a sale thereof; or

(d) One of the offenses is assault or some other offense resulting in physical injury to a person, and the other offense is one of homicide based upon the death of such person from the same physical injury, and such death occurs after a prosecution for the assault or other non-homicide offense; or

(e) Each offense involves death, injury, loss or other consequence to a different victim; or

(f) One of the offenses consists of a violation of a statutory provision of another jurisdiction, which offense has been prosecuted in such other jurisdiction and has there been terminated by a court order expressly founded upon insufficiency of evidence to establish some element of such offense which is not an element of the other offense, defined by the laws of this state; or

(g) The present prosecution is for a consummated result offense . . . which occurred in this state and the offense was the result of a conspiracy, facilitation or solicitation prosecuted in another state. . . .

Notes

1. *Determining whether two charges are for the "same offence": majority position.* The Supreme Court's decision in United States v. Dixon, 509 U.S. 688 (1993), reestablished the "same elements" test of Blockburger v. United States, 284 U.S. 299 (1932). Under this test, if the two offenses *each* have at least one distinct "element," they are not treated as the same offense. Hence, multiple trials or multiple punishments based on these offenses do not violate the protection against double jeopardy.

About 30 state courts follow *Dixon* and have adopted (or readopted) the *Blockburger* "same elements" test under state law. See, e.g., State v. Alvarez, 778 A.2d 938 (Conn. 2001). About 10 jurisdictions have interpreted their state constitutions to employ the *Grady* "same conduct" test (or the closely related "same evidence" test) in addition to the *Blockburger* analysis as a limit on multiple prosecutions. See State v. Feliciano, 115 P.3d 648 (Haw. 2005) (successive prosecution cases). A smaller group of states (about a half dozen) apply a test that places even stronger limits on government attempts to bring multiple prosecutions: the "same transaction" test (also called the "same episode" or "same incident" test) suggested by Justice Brennan in his concurring opinion in Ashe v. Swenson, 397 U.S. 436 (1970). See, e.g., State v. Farley, 725 P.2d 359 (Or. 1986). Around 15 states have adopted statutory tests for whether a second charge is for the "same offense"; some statutes mirror the *Blockburger* test, Fla. Stat. §775.021(4)(a), while others add a "same facts" or "same conduct" test.

Trial judges pay close attention to their jury instructions relating to the "same elements" test; as a result, these instructions offer some of the clearest available descriptions of the doctrine. Samples of such instructions appear on the web extension for this chapter at *http://www.crimpro.com/extension/ch14*. The extension also explores some of the suggestions in the academic literature for reworking this doctrine from the ground up.

2. *Punishment for greater and lesser included offenses.* A lesser included offense is one that is necessarily included within the statutory elements of another offense. Thus, if Crime 1 has elements A and B, it is a lesser included offense for Crime 2, with elements A, B, and C (for example, Crime 1 = kidnapping; Crime 2 = kidnapping with intent to rape). In a straightforward application of the *Blockburger* test, a prosecution for either Crime 1 or Crime 2 would prevent a later prosecution or punishment for the second crime. An exception to this bar would allow a prosecution for Crime 2 after a prosecution for Crime 1, if the additional element C had not yet occurred at the time of the Crime 1 prosecution (for instance, if an assault victim dies after the trial for assault goes forward). See Brown v. Ohio, 432 U.S. 161, 169 n.7 (1977).

But the courts have gone beyond this literal understanding of lesser included offenses. Both federal and state courts declare that double jeopardy limits for the "same offense" also apply to "a species of lesser included offense." In Harris v. Oklahoma, 433 U.S. 682 (1977), the court held that a conviction for felony murder barred a later trial of the defendant for the underlying robbery. Strictly speaking, the robbery and felony murder statutes pass the *Blockburger* test: Felony murder requires proof of a killing (robbery does not), and robbery requires proof of forcible taking of property (which felony murder does not necessarily require). But the court was willing to treat robbery and felony murder as the "same offense" because in the *case at hand*, the prosecution was relying on forcible taking of property to establish the predicate felony for felony murder. See also United States v. Dixon, 509 U.S. 688, 697-700 (1993) (criminal contempt of court for violation of judicial order not to commit "any criminal offense" and possession of cocaine with intent to distribute are the same offense); State v. Quick, 206 P.3d 985 (N.M. 2009) (double jeopardy prevents use of single act of drug possession to form basis for possession and possession with intent to distribute convictions; government may not divide stash of drugs into subgroups to support both convictions). On the other hand, the same logic does not seem to apply to conspiracy or "continuing criminal enterprise" crimes. See United States v. Felix, 503 U.S. 378, 387-392 (1992) (conspiracy to manufacture narcotics is not same offense as manufacturing narcotics); Garrett v. United States, 471 U.S. 773, 777-786 (1985) (distribution of marijuana is not same offense as conducting a continuing criminal enterprise to distribute marijuana). It also does not apply to RICO prosecutions—a defendant can be prosecuted successively for the predicate offenses in a RICO prosecution. See United States v. Luong, 393 F.3d 913 (9th Cir. 2004) (allowing successive prosecutions for RICO and predicate offenses, even when predicate offense is conspiracy).

3. *The "multiple punishment" prong of double jeopardy.* Unlike the relatively clear rule against multiple *prosecutions* for the same offense, there are looser limits when the prosecutor files multiple charges in a *single proceeding*, and the defendant claims that the charges are actually an attempt to impose multiple punishments for what is really a single offense. In this setting, the legislature sets the constraints on the prosecutor. In Missouri v. Hunter, 459 U.S. 359 (1983), the Supreme Court held that "the Double Jeopardy Clause does no more than prevent the sentencing court from prescribing greater punishment than the legislature intended." The defendant in *Hunter* was convicted after a single trial for robbery and armed criminal action. The armed criminal action statute explicitly provided that any penalty imposed for the crime "shall be in addition to any punishment provided by law" for any other crime committed with the weapon in question. The Court upheld the convictions and sentences even though the two crimes would be considered the "same offence" for *Blockburger* purposes, citing legislative history as the basis for enhancing the punishment. This holding is puzzling, to say the least, given our Constitution's Supremacy Clause: If the double jeopardy rule is constitutional, how can the legislature circumvent it with purposeful action?

Most states follow Missouri v. Hunter and hold that in the context of a single prosecution, the *Blockburger* test (or an alternative test) only helps determine whether the legislature intended to allow separate convictions and punishments for a single criminal episode or event. See, e.g., State v. Adel, 965 P.2d 1072 (Wash. 1998); People v. Miller, 869 N.W.2d 204 (Mich. 2015) (convicting a man of both drunken driving and drunken driving that caused serious injury to another person violated the double jeopardy clauses of the U.S. Constitution and the Michigan Constitution; statutes do not explicitly authorize multiple punishments). The courts reason that the legislature can select from a wide range of punishments for any particular offense. Other states have rejected the majority rule and have applied state law to limit cumulative punishments regardless of the legislature's intent. In one especially difficult area, states are split on whether punishment is acceptable for both felony murder and the underlying felony when they are tried together. See, e.g., Todd v. State, 917 P.2d 674 (Alaska 1996) (allowing multiple punishment); cf. Boulies v. People, 770 P.2d 1274 (Colo. 1989) (state merger rule barring multiple punishment).

What reasons might justify the different treatment of "multiple proceedings" on the one hand, and "multiple punishment" for the same conduct in a single proceeding on the other hand? Does this distinction make sense? See Nancy King, Portioning Punishment: Constitutional Limits on Successive and Excessive Penalties, 144 U. Pa. L. Rev. 101 (1995) (points to illogic of cases allowing multiple punishments in a single trial but not in successive trials; argues for limiting Eighth Amendment to a remedy for excessive punishments imposed in multiple proceedings).

4. *When do double jeopardy claims arise?* Double jeopardy claims can arise at a variety of points in the criminal justice process. A defendant can raise double jeopardy claims as soon as she is charged with multiple counts in a single proceeding. A defendant might challenge even a single count, claiming that jeopardy already attached at an earlier proceeding. Jeopardy "attaches" at an initial trial when the jury is sworn in (for jury trials) or when the first witness is sworn in (for a bench trial) or when the court accepts a guilty plea. See Martinez v. Illinois, 134 S. Ct. 2070 (2014). The defendant also might raise a double jeopardy challenge at the time of sentencing, claiming that the state has requested multiple punishments for the same offense.

It is important to recognize that double jeopardy influences the work of all three branches of government. Double jeopardy rules have a substantial impact on what kinds of charges the prosecution chooses to file. Principles of prior jeopardy may also shape the actions of judges at sentencing, when the judge can group together charges to produce a single sentence lower than what technically could be imposed for each separate conviction. Finally, legislators will have a powerful effect on the grouping of crimes when they define the elements of different crimes. Ultimately, are double jeopardy principles anything more than instructions to legislatures to draft cleanly?

5. *Double jeopardy after mistrial.* When major errors occur during a criminal trial, the judge might declare a mistrial. Most mistrials do not bar a retrial, even though jeopardy has attached; retrial is possible so long as the earlier declaration of mistrial was a "manifest necessity." Mistrials declared after a jury deadlocks typically fall into this category. See Renico v. Lett, 559 U.S. 766 (2010) (trial court declaration of mistrial after jury deadlocked was based on manifest necessity). Errors that happen during the trial itself are more difficult to classify. If *every* declaration of mistrial could bar subsequent prosecution, defense attorneys could manipulate the outcome. Whenever a trial starts to go badly, their own misconduct in the later stages of a trial could gain the defendant a second chance in a new trial. As a result, most declarations of mistrial based on defense errors are considered to be manifest necessities. The same risk of manipulation would hold true for prosecutors if *no* mistrial ever barred subsequent prosecution. Thus, mistrials declared after prosecutorial

misconduct at trial or other errors within the control of the prosecutor are less likely to be classified as "manifest necessities."

6. *Consistency and respect.* What principles of decision making underlie the Supreme Court's boomerang from *Grady* (1990) to *Dixon* (1993)? All courts offer words of respect for stare decisis. Should courts have a different stare decisis rule with respect to constitutional and nonconstitutional decisions? Should all constitutional decisions have a natural life span? Should readers discount all constitutional decisions by the age of the justices and the number of justices who decided the case who are still active—a kind of actuarial jurisprudence?

7. *Multiplicity: majority view.* At what point does the commission of one offense end and the commission of a second offense begin? This can be a very difficult question with criminal acts that occur in several locations (such as drug sales), through multiple events (such as conspiracies based on a series of conversations), or over extended periods of time. All jurisdictions must face claims that multiple, identical charges are applied to what is only a single event. See State v. Leyda, 138 P.3d 610 (Wash. 2006) (when defendant obtained victim's credit card and used it to make four purchases, the "unit of prosecution" for crime of identity theft was the act of obtaining identification of another person with criminal intent, rather than each discrete use); Commonwealth v. Horne, 995 N.E.2d 773 (Mass. 2013) (defendant can be convicted twice for possessing the same gun in public without a license on two different days).

In fact, in *Blockburger* itself the defendant claimed that two drug sales on successive days constituted one offense. Shortly after delivery of the drug that was the subject of the first sale, the purchaser paid for an additional quantity to be delivered the next day. The defendant argued that these two sales to the same purchaser, with no substantial interval of time between the delivery of the drug in the first transaction and the payment for the second quantity sold, constituted a single continuing offense. 284 U.S. at 301. The Court rejected the claim: "The Narcotic Act does not create the offense of engaging in the business of selling the forbidden drugs, but penalizes any sale made. . . . Each of several successive sales constitutes a distinct offense, however closely they may follow each other." 284 U.S. at 302.

Some courts refer to the issue of dividing one offender's behavior into distinct offenses as the problem of "multiplicity." Though not all jurisdictions use the term, the question of multiplicity is common to all jurisdictions. See Vincent v. Commonwealth, 281 S.W.3d 785 (Ky. 2009) (defendant not prejudiced when prosecutor alleged 294 counts of sexual offenses; prosecutor did not intentionally stack indictment to prejudice defendant, because victims of alleged crimes were uncertain of number and location of incidents). To what extent does application of the *Blockburger* test answer the question of how many different crimes can be charged? Beyond the scope of *Blockburger*, what principles should govern?

8. *The special problem of conspiracies.* The puzzle of determining how many separate charges are possible is especially difficult in the context of conspiracies—especially drug conspiracies—which tend to take place over time and space and to involve multiple participants. To determine whether criminal conduct amounted to one conspiracy or two, courts consult the "totality of the circumstances," with special emphasis on (1) the time of the conduct, (2) the persons acting as co-conspirators, (3) the overlap among the statutory offenses charged in the indictments, (4) the overt acts charged by the government or any other description of the offenses charged that indicate the nature and scope of the activity that the government

sought to punish in each case, and (5) places where the events alleged as part of the conspiracy took place. The procedural difficulties regarding the parsing of conspiracies reflect the substantive battles over the scope of conspiracy law. See State v. Gallegos, 254 P.3d 655 (N.M. 2011) (defendant's convictions under one statute for conspiracy to murder, conspiracy to kidnap, and conspiracy to commit arson violated double jeopardy).

Problem 14-2. Multiplicity

On December 11, Ronald Gardner, Cato Peterson, Amir Wilson, and Aaron Banks were traveling in a white Cougar automobile from Detroit to Muskegon. Muskegon County Sheriff Deputy Al VanHemert received a tip from a confidential informant that Aaron Banks and several other persons would be transporting crack cocaine to a Muskegon Heights neighborhood that afternoon. Two deputies executed a legal stop and search of the vehicle. They seized 222 grams of crack cocaine and arrested the occupants of the car.

Ronald Gardner, Cato Peterson, and Amir Wilson each made statements to the officers. Gardner said that Ricky Franklin paid him $200 to drive Peterson, Wilson, and Banks to the Muskegon Heights area. He admitted that he had previously transported sellers and drugs to that area. Gardner also stated he had picked up money at the home of "Miss Louise" in Muskegon and transported the cash back to Detroit. He stated that cocaine was sometimes transported in the spare tire in the trunk. Gardner called Franklin the head of the organization, while Banks was the boss of the Muskegon portion of the operation.

Peterson stated to the officers that he was traveling to Muskegon to sell crack cocaine, that this was his second trip to Muskegon, and that Franklin was the head of the organization.

Wilson also made a statement to the Muskegon authorities after his arrest. He stated that he sold crack cocaine for Ricky Franklin and that he had sold drugs on three previous trips to Muskegon. He stated that Banks would stay at Miss Louise's house and dispense the crack baggies to the sellers there. The cocaine was transported in the spare tire in the trunk. Robert Johnson was also involved in the sale of cocaine.

On June 6, a Muskegon County jury convicted Amir Wilson of possession with intent to deliver and conspiracy to deliver between 50 and 225 grams of cocaine. On July 3, Wilson was sentenced to two concurrent prison terms of 8 to 20 years.

On July 5, police arrested Gerald Hill in Southfield (in Oakland County, near Muskegon County) for possession with intent to deliver between 225 and 649 grams of cocaine. Southfield police made the arrest after a routine traffic stop of the vehicle in which Hill and Ricky Franklin were passengers. The police allowed Hill to go into a store across the street from where the vehicle was stopped. After Hill left the area, store employees alerted police officers that they had found cocaine in a jacket behind the store. The Muskegon and Oakland County Sheriff Departments joined efforts to investigate the "Franklin organization."

In November, an Oakland County grand jury indicted Wilson, Banks, Hill, Johnson, and another individual, Terrence Moore, on charges of conspiring over a 26-month period to possess with intent to deliver over 650 grams of cocaine. Wilson moved to set aside the indictment on the basis of a violation of double jeopardy.

Should the trial judge in Oakland County grant the motion? Compare People v. Wilson, 563 N.W.2d 44 (Mich. 1997).

3. Collateral Estoppel

The common-law doctrine of collateral estoppel raises a question related to double jeopardy: When has an issue or a fact been resolved in one proceeding in a way that will bind the parties in later disputes? The prototypical case illustrating this doctrine is Ashe v. Swenson, 397 U.S. 436 (1970). During a late-night poker game in a basement, three or four masked men entered with weapons and robbed the six men playing cards. In Ashe's trial for robbing one of the card players, defense counsel cross-examined the prosecution witnesses on the identification of Ashe as one of the robbers and offered no other defense to the charges. The jury found him not guilty. When the government brought Ashe to trial again six weeks later for the robbery of the second card player, the defendant moved to dismiss the charge, based on his previous acquittal. The Supreme Court later agreed that the jury's verdict in the first trial prevented a second robbery trial.

■ EX PARTE PHILIP TAYLOR
101 S.W.3d 434 (Tex. Crim. App. 2002)

COCHRAN, J.

Appellant lost control of his car on a rural road and collided with an oncoming car. Appellant's two passengers died in the accident. A jury acquitted appellant of intoxication manslaughter in causing the death of one passenger. The State had alleged that appellant was intoxicated by alcohol. The State now seeks to prosecute appellant for intoxication manslaughter in causing the death of his second passenger. This time, however, the State alleges that appellant was intoxicated by either alcohol and marijuana or by marijuana alone. We must determine whether the appellant's acquittal in the first trial, of intoxication manslaughter, prevents the State from attempting to prove, in another criminal proceeding, an alternate theory of intoxication for causing the death of his second passenger. . . .

I.

. . . The evidence showed that appellant was driving his Ford Thunderbird on a rural road in Brazos County late one afternoon. His fiancee, Kyla Blaisdell, sat in the front passenger seat and her best friend, Michelle James, sat in the back seat. It was not disputed that appellant was speeding, but witnesses' estimates of his actual speed varied widely. As appellant came out of a curve, the Thunderbird's right front wheel left the paved surface and veered onto a grassy, gravely area. [Taylor] lost control of the car, which veered into the left lane and collided with [Patricia] Varner's oncoming Suburban. . . . Kyla Blaisdell and Michelle James died in the collision. Ms. Varner and appellant were both seriously injured.

At the hospital, medical technicians drew a sample of appellant's blood to determine its blood alcohol concentration ("BAC"). Their analysis resulted in a .137

BAC reading. The DPS twice reanalyzed this blood sample, using more sensitive equipment. Its analysis returned BAC readings of .124 and .119. DPS took another blood sample from appellant more than three hours after the first sample. This second sample indicated a BAC of .06. Appellant's blood also tested positive for the presence of marijuana, but there was no evidence that he had smoked marijuana on that particular day. The prosecutor, agreeing that traces of marijuana may linger in the body for days after its actual use, did not oppose appellant's motion in limine barring any mention of marijuana during the trial. Kyla Blaisdell tested negative for both alcohol and drugs; Michelle James tested negative for drugs, but .04 for alcohol; and Ms. Varner tested negative for both drugs and alcohol. Appellant's toxicology expert testified that, according to his calculations, appellant's BAC at the time of the accident must have been between .07 and .09.

Kelsey Blaisdell, Kyla's brother, testified that the trio spent most of the afternoon at his parent's home. He said that they came over to do laundry and to "hang out." They had some wine with them and were drinking from about 2:30 until 6:00 P.M. Kelsey testified that appellant did not seem drunk or otherwise intoxicated: appellant did not slur his speech or have poor balance. . . .

At the conclusion of all evidence, the trial judge charged the jury that, if it believed from the evidence, beyond a reasonable doubt, that appellant [operated a motor vehicle] while intoxicated, "either by not having the normal use of his mental or physical faculties by reason of the introduction of alcohol into his body or by having an alcohol concentration of .10 or more, and by reason of that intoxication, if any, by accident or mistake, caused the death of Michelle James, you will find [appellant] guilty of intoxication manslaughter." The jury was also instructed, as an alternate basis for a finding of guilt, that if it believed from the evidence, beyond a reasonable doubt, that appellant [recklessly caused the death of Michelle James] by "operating a motor vehicle at an excessive speed and by driving into a motor vehicle occupied by Patricia Varner, you will find [appellant] guilty of manslaughter." . . .

The jury acquitted appellant of all counts of intoxication manslaughter and reckless manslaughter of Michelle James. The State subsequently dismissed appellant's indictment for causing Kyla Blaisdell's death. But later the State learned that appellant, sometime after the trial, allegedly told Kyla Blaisdell's mother that he and the girls had been smoking marijuana cigarettes on the afternoon of the accident. Based upon this newly discovered evidence, the State re-indicted appellant for intoxication manslaughter in causing the death of Kyla Blaisdell, alleging that he had lost the normal use of his mental and physical faculties by reason of the introduction of alcohol, marijuana, or a combination of alcohol and marijuana.

Appellant filed an application for a pretrial writ of habeas corpus, contending that the doctrine of collateral estoppel barred any further State efforts to prosecute him for causing this accident based upon his alleged intoxication. The trial court largely denied appellant relief, concluding that only the issue of intoxication by reason of alcohol had been litigated in the first trial, but not the distinct factual question of whether marijuana, either alone or in combination with alcohol, had rendered him intoxicated. Appellant then filed a pretrial appeal [to the intermediate appellate court, which disagreed with the trial court and concluded that the ultimate issue of fact decided by the jury was that appellant was not intoxicated; therefore, the issue of intoxication could not be relitigated in any further criminal proceeding. The government appealed this ruling.]

II.

At issue in this appeal is the scope of the factual finding that the jury made when it acquitted appellant. The State assumes that the first jury concluded that appellant was not intoxicated because of alcohol. It contends that this finding does not preclude the State from prosecuting appellant for the death of a second accident victim, when the State alleged intoxication by alcohol and marijuana or by marijuana alone. . . .

The first prosecution was for killing Michelle James; the second, for killing Kyla Blaisdell. For double jeopardy purposes, the unlawful killing of each victim is a separate offense. In its seminal case on collateral estoppel, Ashe v. Swenson, 397 U.S. 436 (1970), the Supreme Court noted that the defendant's reprosecution was not barred by double jeopardy under the usual *Blockburger* test because the second prosecution was for a different offense, namely the robbery of a different victim attending the same poker party. Thus, the Supreme Court had to turn to the related doctrine of collateral estoppel, which prevents a party who lost a fact issue in the trial of one cause of action from relitigating the same fact issue in another cause of action against the same party. The situation is the same in this case. If the State had prosecuted appellant for the same offense (causing the death of Michelle James) on a different theory, we would not have to resort to collateral estoppel. Reprosecution would be barred by autrefois acquit under *Blockburger*.

In Ashe v. Swenson, the Supreme Court stated that collateral estoppel "means simply that when an issue of ultimate fact has once been determined by a valid and final judgment, that issue cannot again be litigated between the same parties in any future lawsuit." To determine whether collateral estoppel bars a subsequent prosecution (or permits prosecution but bars relitigation of certain specific facts) courts employ a two-step analysis. Courts must determine: (1) exactly what facts were "necessarily decided" in the first proceeding; and (2) whether those "necessarily decided" facts constitute essential elements of the offense in the second trial.

In each case, courts must review the entire trial record to determine—"with realism and rationality"—precisely what fact or combination of facts the jury necessarily decided and which will then bar their relitigation in a second criminal trial. In Ashe v. Swenson, the Supreme Court emphasized that:

> the rule of collateral estoppel is not to be applied with the hypertechnical and archaic approach of a 19th century pleading book, but with realism and rationality. . . . Any test more technically restrictive would, of course, simply amount to a rejection of the rule of collateral estoppel in criminal proceedings, at least in every case where the first judgment was based upon a general verdict of acquittal.

Although Texas courts have rarely discussed the scope of a fact barred by collateral estoppel, cases from other jurisdictions have held that collateral estoppel operates only if the "very fact or point now in issue" was determined in the prior proceeding. It must be precisely the same issue in both cases. Thus, issue preclusion is limited to cases where the legal and factual situations are identical. . . . On the other hand, issue preclusion cannot be defeated simply by advancing new or different evidence to support the same issue already litigated. Thus, a party who neglects to submit the evidence that would support a legal theory that the party withheld in a first proceeding, cannot later point to its own omission as justification for pursuing a second proceeding.

In sum, there are no hard and fast rules concerning which factual issues are legally identical and thus barred from relitigation in a second criminal proceeding. . . . In each case, the entire record—including the evidence, pleadings, charge, jury arguments, and any other pertinent material—must be examined to determine precisely the scope of the jury's factual findings. In one case, for example, a jury's acquittal might rest upon the proposition that the defendant was "not intoxicated," while in another, that same verdict might rest upon the narrower proposition that the defendant was "not intoxicated" by a particular substance, but he might well have been intoxicated by a different substance. Generally, then, the scope of the facts that were actually litigated determines the scope of the factual finding covered by collateral estoppel.

Given the pleadings, the jury charge, the disputed issues, and the evidence presented by both the State and the defense at the trial, the jury in this particular case necessarily concluded that, at the time of the accident: 1) Appellant had not lost the normal use of his mental or physical faculties by reason of the introduction of alcohol; 2) Appellant did not have an alcohol concentration of .10 or more; and 3) Appellant did not recklessly drive at an excessive speed into another vehicle.

Thus, these three facts have been established, and they cannot be relitigated in any future criminal proceeding against appellant. But do these discrete factual findings leave open the possibility that appellant was intoxicated, but by some substance other than alcohol?

Not here. The only witness who testified to appellant's possible loss of normal use of mental or physical faculties was Kelsey Blaisdell, the brother of one of the victims. He stated that appellant and the two girls had some wine that afternoon. . . . Because the trial court granted appellant's unopposed motion in limine, there was no mention at trial of any other possible source of intoxication and no other evidence that appellant had lost the normal use of his mental or physical faculties.

The source of appellant's intoxication was not a disputed issue in the first trial. It was only the more general issue of intoxication—was he or wasn't he—that was disputed, and upon this issue, the appellant prevailed. Had appellant's defense been one of conceding the fact of intoxication, but contesting the manner in which he became intoxicated, the situation would, of course, be different. Thus, considering the question in a practical, common-sense manner, it is evident that there is no reasonable possibility that the jury in the first trial could have decided, based upon this evidence, that appellant was intoxicated but not because of alcohol. . . .[29]

The State argues that it now possesses more and different evidence—namely that appellant admitted to Mrs. Blaisdell, after his acquittal, that both he and the girls had smoked marijuana that day. But here, as in Harris v. Washington, 404 U.S. 55 (1971), when an ultimate issue has been decided, the constitutional guarantee of collateral estoppel applies "irrespective of whether the jury considered all relevant evidence, and irrespective of the good faith of the State in bringing successive prosecutions." [In Harris v. Washington, a jury acquitted the defendant of murder,

29. The dissent argues that the jury could have decided that appellant was, in fact, intoxicated but that "his intoxication was not a contributing factor to the accident." This is, of course, a possibility, but that factual finding would not prevent the application of collateral estoppel. Quite the reverse. . . . If that were the fact that the jury necessarily decided, then collateral estoppel would apply to causation, rather than intoxication. [If an acquittal could have been based on either fact A or fact B, and the government is required to prove both fact A and fact B in a subsequent trial, collateral estoppel bars relitigation of either fact.]

finding that the defendant had not mailed the bomb that killed the victim and his infant son and seriously injured the victim's wife. The Supreme Court found that the State could not reprosecute the defendant for killing the infant based upon additional evidence, namely a threatening letter that the defendant had allegedly sent to the victim's family.]

[The State argues that] resolving whether collateral estoppel applies depends entirely upon the precise indictment allegations, regardless of the actual evidence or the facts "necessarily" found by the jury. But application of collateral estoppel depends not merely upon the pleadings, but also upon the evidence, charge, jury argument, and any other relevant material. The State fails to point to any evidence, argument, or other material in this record which would support its theory that this jury could have concluded appellant was intoxicated, but not by alcohol. . . . Therefore, we affirm the court of appeals.

HERVEY, J., dissenting.

. . . The State's theory was that appellant's alcohol intoxication caused him to drive recklessly at an excessive rate of speed which caused the accident resulting in the victim's death. Appellant's theory was that he was not intoxicated by any of the two manner and means submitted to the jury but that, if he was, his intoxication was not a contributing factor to the accident. . . . Appellant's accident reconstructionist supported these assertions at trial [and] contradicted other aspects of the prosecution's theory of how the accident occurred such as when appellant began to lose control of his vehicle (before the curve at a lower speed limit or after the curve at a higher speed limit). . . .

During closing jury arguments, the defense argued that . . . the prosecution failed to prove that appellant's intoxication, if any, caused the fatal accident. The last thing the defense told the jury was that it should still acquit appellant even if the jury found that he was intoxicated.

> [What] could have caused this accident? . . . Could be that the Varner vehicle was towards the middle of the road. It could be inattentiveness. It could be an animal ran out. . . . We will never know what caused that accident. . . . Even if you find he was intoxicated, if you don't find that intoxication beyond a reasonable doubt caused this accident, you must return a verdict of not guilty. . . .

These portions of the record demonstrate that the jury could have acquitted appellant . . . because it did not believe that this intoxication was a contributing factor to the accident which the record reflects was one of the theories appellant urged at the first trial. . . .

The Court's opinion concedes that it is "a possibility" that the jury did not necessarily find that appellant was not intoxicated by alcohol. This should be fatal to appellant's collateral estoppel claim. But, the Court still concludes that this prosecution is jeopardy-barred because, even if the jury found that appellant was intoxicated, it nevertheless could have found that the "intoxication itself was not a contributing factor to the accident" in which case "collateral estoppel would apply to causation, rather than intoxication."

But, in analyzing the collateral estoppel issue this way, the Court concludes that this prosecution is jeopardy-barred even though it is unable to decide what the jury necessarily found in the first trial. In other words, the Court apparently bases its decision on what the jury could have found without deciding what the jury necessarily found. My understanding of collateral estoppel law, however, is that for the collateral estoppel bar to apply, the Court must be able to decide what the jury necessarily found in the first trial, not what it could have found.

The Court's analysis involving what the jury could have found in appellant's first trial also fails to take into account that it is entirely possible that the jury did not speak with one voice in acquitting appellant. For example, it is possible that some of the jurors believed that appellant was not intoxicated, some of the jurors believed that he was intoxicated but his intoxication was not a contributing factor to the accident, and some of the jurors believed that appellant should have been acquitted for other reasons. Cf. Schad v. Arizona, 501 U.S. 624 (1991) (Scalia, J., concurring) (stating the general rule that "when a single crime can be committed in various ways, jurors need not agree upon the mode of commission"). Under these circumstances, it cannot be said that the jury necessarily found anything in the first trial except possibly that it had a reasonable doubt of appellant's guilt. . . .

Notes

1. *Collateral estoppel: majority position.* The U.S. Supreme Court declared in Ashe v. Swenson, 397 U.S. 436 (1970), that the federal guarantee against double jeopardy includes the concept of collateral estoppel: "[W]hen an issue of ultimate fact has once been determined by a valid and final judgment, that issue cannot again be litigated between the same parties in any future lawsuit." There are several limitations, however, that prevent collateral estoppel from having an impact in a wide range of cases. First, the doctrine typically does not apply to matters resolved by guilty plea. Federal and state courts agree that collateral estoppel applies only after an "adjudication on the merits after full trial." Ohio v. Johnson, 467 U.S. 493, 500 (1984).

Second, as *Ex parte Taylor* illustrates, it is often difficult, based on a jury's general verdict, to determine exactly what factual findings were the basis for a jury's acquittal. This problem is commonplace because defendants are prone to give the jury more than one possible theory for an acquittal. See Yeager v. United States, 557 U.S. 110 (2009) (in original trial, jury acquitted Yeager of securities fraud counts, and was unable to reach verdict on additional counts; collateral estoppel bars retrial because acquittal necessarily reflected finding by jury that Yeager did not possess relevant information, and courts should treat the deadlock on other counts as a nonevent). Would the use of special interrogatories to the jury (to be completed only after the jury has delivered its general verdict) make the collateral estoppel doctrine a more meaningful limitation on multiple criminal trials?

In Bravo-Fernandez v. United States, 137 S. Ct. 352 (2016), a unanimous Court answered a narrow question, and held that when a jury issues inconsistent verdicts, and where the guilty verdicts are vacated on appeal, ultimate issues of fact may again be litigated in a future lawsuit—in other words, while the acquittal precludes prosecution for the same offense, issue preclusion does not attach. In this case a jury convicted defendants of the federal bribery statute (18 U.S.C. §666) and simultaneously acquitted them of conspiracy to violate the same statute. Since the additional elements of conspiracy were uncontested, the verdicts were inconsistent. The Court explained that issue preclusion does not apply when verdict inconsistency renders unanswerable "what the jury necessarily decided."

2. *Parties and proceedings covered.* Although collateral estoppel binds the government, most courts say that the doctrine is asymmetrical; that is, it does not bind defendants. If a factfinder determines some fact against a defendant in one criminal proceeding, the defendant may still ask a factfinder in some later criminal case to find that same fact in his favor. State v. Allen, 31 A.3d 476 (Md. 2011) (after conviction of felony murder and armed robbery, appeals court vacated felony murder conviction; on retrial for felony murder, it was error to instruct jury that defendant was already convicted of robbery, thus establishing the precondition to felony murder). On the other hand, in most jurisdictions the collateral estoppel doctrine benefits the defendant only at the first trial, and does not extend to any co-defendants. A jury's finding concerning a factual issue at the trial of one co-defendant does not preclude the prosecution from relitigating the same issue at a subsequent trial of another co-defendant.

Can a finding of fact made in an administrative or civil proceeding be the basis for collateral estoppel in a later criminal proceeding? Typically, the courts do not apply the doctrine to bar such prosecutions. For instance, if a defendant in license revocation proceedings convinces the factfinder that some critical factual element of drunken driving charges is missing, that finding generally does not bar a later criminal prosecution for driving while impaired. Courts point out that the two proceedings operate under two different standards of proof: preponderance of the evidence in the administrative proceedings, and beyond a reasonable doubt in the criminal proceedings.

These arguments about the reach of collateral estoppel to parties and proceedings beyond the prototypical setting of two criminal trials involving a single criminal defendant generate a complex case law. You can work through some of the implications of this doctrine on the web extension for this chapter at *http://www.crimpro. com/extension/ch14.*

3. *Collateral estoppel and dual sovereigns.* It is common to find the collateral estoppel principle embodied in state statutes barring or limiting multiple prosecutions. Around 10 states have statutes recognizing collateral estoppel based on adverse factual findings made in criminal proceedings in another jurisdiction. See Colo. Rev. Stat. §18-1-303(1)(b). Recall that the common-law doctrine of collateral estoppel required "mutuality of parties"—that is, the same two parties had to be involved in both the original proceedings and the later relitigation of the same factual issue. Is there any reason to insist on "mutuality of parties" when it comes to dual sovereigns prosecuting the same person for crimes based on the same factual premise? In other words, should one government's loss in a criminal trial prevent another government from relitigating the same factual issue?

B. JOINDER

Constitutional and statutory double jeopardy rules require prosecutors to choose carefully when grouping together the potential charges to be brought against a defendant. We now look at some doctrinal cousins to double jeopardy: the statutory and court rules that govern "joinder" and "severance" of potentially related charges. As you read the following materials, consider to what extent the joinder and severance rules further interests different from the constitutional or statutory bar on double jeopardy.

The most common joinder rules (exemplified by Rule 8 of the Federal Rules of Criminal Procedure) are known as "permissive" joinder rules. They define the outer boundaries of the prosecutor's power to join charges together for a single trial, that is, the *maximum* range of charges that can be grouped together. These rules address both the joinder of separate offenses filed against a single defendant and joinder of multiple defendants in a single trial. Some states also have "compulsory" or "mandatory" joinder rules. These rules identify the *minimum* range of charges that the prosecutor must group together for a single trial. Like the doctrines of double jeopardy and collateral estoppel, these compulsory joinder rules require dismissal of charges if they should have been tried in an earlier proceeding dealing with related charges. Rules on "severance" address the power of the court to override a prosecutor's joinder decisions and order separate trials for charges that were otherwise properly joined. This is sometimes necessary to prevent an undue prejudicial effect on the defense.

The joinder rules may on first inspection seem dry and technical. But joinder and severance rules are enormously important to defendants and prosecutors because they define the possible strategies at trial and very often determine the outcome of the case. The issues appeal to lawyers who enjoy puzzles.

1. Discretionary Joinder and Severance of Offenses

When a prosecutor files multiple charges against a defendant, the charges usually fall within the minimum and maximum range of charges that a prosecutor has the power to group together in a single case. If the prosecutor fails to join the charges and the defendant wishes to resolve them in one trial, the court has the discretion to join the charges even though the prosecutor did not file them together. The parties can also urge the trial court to sever the joined charges as a discretionary matter to avoid prejudice. Review the federal rules and Vermont rules reprinted below, then read the following case. Would the outcome of the case change under the Vermont rules?

■ FEDERAL RULE OF CRIMINAL PROCEDURE 8(A)

The indictment or information may charge a defendant in separate counts with two or more offenses if the offenses charged—whether felonies or misdemeanors or both—are of the same or similar character, or are based on the same act or transaction, or are connected with or constitute parts of a common scheme or plan.

■ FEDERAL RULE OF CRIMINAL PROCEDURE 13

The court may order that separate cases be tried together as though brought in a single indictment or information if all offenses . . . could have been joined in a single indictment or information.

■ FEDERAL RULE OF CRIMINAL PROCEDURE 14

(a) Relief. If the joinder of offenses or defendants in an indictment, an information, or a consolidation for trial appears to prejudice a defendant or the government, the court may order separate trials of counts, sever the defendants' trials, or provide any other relief that justice requires.

(b) Defendant's Statements. Before ruling on a defendant's motion to sever, the court may order an attorney for the government to deliver to the court for in camera inspection any defendant's statement that the government intends to use as evidence.

■ VERMONT RULE OF CRIMINAL PROCEDURE 8(A)

Two or more offenses may be joined in one information or indictment, with each offense stated in a separate count, when the offenses, whether felonies or misdemeanors or both,

(1) are of the same or similar character, even if not part of a single scheme or plan; or

(2) are based on the same conduct or on a series of acts connected together or constituting parts of a single scheme or plan.

■ VERMONT RULE OF CRIMINAL PROCEDURE 14

(a) The court may order a severance of offenses or defendants before trial if a severance could be obtained on motion of a defendant or the prosecution under subdivision (b) of this rule.

(b) (1) Severance of Offenses.

(A) Whenever two or more offenses have been joined for trial solely on the ground that they are of the same or similar character, the defendant shall have a right to a severance of the offenses.

(B) The court, on application of the prosecuting attorney, or on application of the defendant other than under subparagraph (A), shall grant a severance of offenses whenever,

(i) if before trial, it is deemed appropriate to promote a fair determination of the defendant's guilt or innocence of each offense; or

(ii) if during trial upon consent of the defendant, or upon a finding of manifest necessity, it is deemed necessary to achieve a fair determination of the defendant's guilt or innocence of each offense.

VERMONT REPORTER'S NOTES—1995 AMENDMENT

[Rule 8] is taken from ABA Minimum Standards (Joinder and Severance) §§1.1, 1.2, and is similar to Federal Rule 8. Rule 8(a) permits joinder of offenses either because they are of similar character though factually unrelated or because they are factually related. Note that each offense must be pleaded in a separate count. . . . Under the federal rule the phrase "same character" adopted for Rule 8(a)(1) has been ordinarily held to mean the same crime committed against distinct objects upon distinct occasions. Although joinder of similar offenses has been criticized as tending to prejudice the defendant through its cumulative effect, the ABA recommends the provision, because it may actually work to the defendant's advantage in preventing multiple trials and facilitating concurrent sentencing. Prejudice will be avoided because under Rule 14(b)(1)(A) defendant has an absolute right to severance of such offenses for trial. ABA Minimum Standards §1.1(a), Commentary. . . .

Rule 8(a)(2) is, of course, a rule of permissive joinder. As a practical matter, if the same facts are centrally involved in two offenses, joinder is virtually compelled. Otherwise, acquittal of the defendant upon one offense will bar prosecution for the second offense by virtue of the Fifth Amendment's Double Jeopardy Clause, which includes the principles of collateral estoppel. Ashe v. Swenson, 397 U.S. 436 (1970).

[Rule 14] is based on ABA Minimum Standards (Joinder and Severance) §§2.1-2.4, 3.1, with variations reflecting Vermont practice. It is similar in effect to the more complicated provisions of Federal Rule 14. Note that Rule 14 is a grant of discretion to sever a joinder otherwise proper under Rule 8 in the interests of fairness or to avoid prejudice. If a joinder is improper under Rule 8, a severance must be granted or it is reversible error. Rule 14(a) is based on ABA Minimum Standards §3.1(b). A power in the court to sever on its own motion, like the comparable power to join under Rule 13(a), is necessary to allow the court to carry out its responsibilities for the orderly conduct of the trial. The federal courts have recognized a power in the court to act on its own motion under Federal Rule 14. . . . Rule 14(b)(1), dealing with severance of offenses, is taken from ABA Minimum Standards §2.2. Subparagraph (A), conferring an absolute right of severance where offenses have been joined solely by virtue of Rule 8(a)(1) because they are of the same or similar character, is a necessary protection for defendants against what would otherwise be potential prejudice in such joinders. That prejudice may consist in the defendant's fear of testifying in his own behalf on one count because of the effect of such testimony on the other count, or in the danger that proof of one count will have prejudicial effect on the other count as inadmissible evidence of another crime. In requiring severance in these circumstances the rule is stricter than Federal Rule 14, although individual decisions under the latter rule have allowed severance for similar purposes. The rule is stricter than prior Vermont practice, which gave the court discretion as to severance even where unrelated offenses were involved. See State v. Dopp, 255 A.2d 186 (Vt. 1969). Severance of offenses joined under Rule 8(a)(2) as arising from the same or connected conduct or a single scheme is available to either party under Rule 14(b)(1)(A) when necessary in the interests of fair trial. . . .

■ DAMIAN LONG v. UNITED STATES
687 A.2d 1331 (D.C. 1996)

FERREN, J.

A jury found appellant, Damian Long, guilty of assault with intent to rob three victims while armed on September 8, 1992, at about 10:30 P.M., at 12th and Orren Streets, N.E. He also was found guilty of attempted robbery while armed and felony murder while armed of another victim several minutes later on Trinidad Avenue, N.E., a block away from the first crime. Long contends . . . the trial court erroneously joined the Orren Street and Trinidad Avenue offenses for trial and then abused its discretion in denying the defense motion for severance. . . . We affirm in part, reverse in part, and remand for reconsideration of Long's severance motion.

[Around 5:30 to 6:00 P.M. on September 8], appellant Long left the apartment of Scholethia Monk, located at Holbrook Terrace, N.E., where he had been spending time with Ms. Monk, her brother (David), and Kimberly Bridgeford. Long was dressed in a black suede jacket with fringe, a black shirt, black jeans, black boots, and a black silk-stocking skull cap. The Holbrook Terrace apartment was only a few blocks from the area where the Orren Street and Trinidad Avenue incidents at issue here took place.

Several hours later, at about 10:30 P.M., a man dressed in a black fringed jacket, black pants, and black shoes—later identified as Damian Long—approached the three Orren Street victims, Sabrina Fox, Carla Davis, and Guy Foster, who were standing in the street on the driver's side of the car that was parked against the curb in front of Fox's home. They were attempting to open the door and window of the car with a coat hanger because they had inadvertently locked the keys inside. Long crossed over to them from the opposite side of the street, pointed a revolver at them, and said something to the two women that sounded like "get the fuck out of here." He then pressed the pistol against Foster's head and demanded his money. When Foster protested that he had none, Long put his hand in Foster's pants pockets and satisfied himself that this was true. Long then ordered Foster to crawl under the car, and Long walked away in the direction of Trinidad Avenue.

Fox and Davis had fled in the same direction. They feared that their assailant was following them, so they hid in an alleyway a few blocks away from where the car was parked. Fox and Davis then heard gunshots and unsuccessfully tried to flag down a passing police cruiser. They hailed a taxi and went to a nearby police precinct where they told their story and gave a description of the perpetrator.

In the meantime, Fox's mother, Penelope Boyd-Fox, who had witnessed the assault on the three from the porch of her home on Orren Street, had immediately telephoned "911" for help. While she was still on the phone to the police department emergency number, she heard gunshots nearby. At about the same time, Foster came out from under the car and fled to his home on Orren Street. He telephoned the police to report the crime. While on the phone with the police, he heard gunshots and reported that as well.

Deborah Alford . . . was sitting on her front porch [on Trinidad Avenue] with several family members at approximately 10:30 P.M. the same night. A few minutes earlier, she had seen [her neighbor Louis Johnson] park his Suzuki sports vehicle on the street and enter his home several doors away. Apparently returning home from work, Johnson had been wearing his Army uniform. Shortly thereafter, Alford saw Johnson walking from his home, dressed in his bathrobe, and returning to his Suzuki. At this moment, Alford saw a man dressed in a black jacket ("I didn't know it had suede fringes on it"), black pants, and a black skull cap walking in Trinidad Street alongside the parked cars. Alford saw the man in black, after he had passed by Johnson, take out a pistol from his jacket and turn back toward Johnson as Johnson put the keys into the car's doorlock. Alford next saw the man in black and her neighbor "tussling." Frightened by the sight of the pistol, she and the others fled into their home. A few seconds later, Alford heard a series of gunshots. Johnson was later pronounced dead of gunshot wounds.

Kimberly Bridgeford testified that at around 5:00 P.M. on September 8, 1992, she and her boyfriend, David Monk, had gone with Damian Long to David's sister's,

Scholethia Monk's, apartment on Holbrook Terrace. After awhile, Long left the apartment and, shortly thereafter, Bridgeford and David Monk left to go to the store. On the way to the store, Bridgeford heard gunshots, saw an ambulance, and walked by the Trinidad Avenue murder scene where she saw Johnson lying on the street with blood all over him. Bridgeford and David Monk then returned to the Holbrook Terrace apartment and found Long on the front porch. Long told Bridgeford that he had "shot a man on Trinidad Avenue because the man tried to rob him with a knife."

Scholethia Monk testified that Long returned later to her Holbrook Terrace apartment on September 8, 1992, "panicking and sweating." Long had told Monk that "two dudes" had tried to rob him on Trinidad Avenue and that he had just shot one of them. There was blood on Long's face, he no longer wore a skull cap, and he was carrying a pistol. Long put the gun under a couch. Monk told Long to get his pistol out of her apartment. He then wrapped it in a plastic bag and took it outside. Ten days later, the police recovered a gun from under the seat of the car where Long's close friend, Monk's brother, had been sitting just before they found the gun. A ballistics expert was "positive" that a bullet recovered from the scene of the murder on Trinidad Avenue had been fired by that pistol.

Homicide detective Willie Toland investigated the Trinidad Avenue case. When he arrived at the scene, he noticed a black skull cap seven feet from the place where Johnson had been shot, and Johnson's keys were still in the Suzuki's passenger door lock. As Toland investigated the crime scene, Foster arrived and informed Toland of what had happened earlier on Orren Street. Toland spoke with Davis and Fox later the same night and a few days later conducted a video lineup in which they identified Long as their attacker. . . .

Long's argument, raised before trial and renewed at the end of the government's case, [is] that the Orren Street and Trinidad Avenue charges had been improperly joined for trial. Specifically, Long protested joinder because the offenses were "not similar offenses, [nor] offenses committed in a single act or transaction, nor a series of offenses that [were] sufficiently connected to each other."

Super. Ct. Crim. R. 8(a) provides for joinder of offenses when the offenses charged "are of the same or similar character or are based on the same act or transaction or on two or more acts or transactions connected together or constituting parts of a common scheme or plan." We review the trial court's joinder decision de novo.

The government urges that joinder was proper because the Orren Street offenses had been "connected together" with the Trinidad Avenue offenses in the sense that proof of the Orren Street offenses "constituted a substantial portion of the proof" of the Trinidad Avenue offenses. The facts, however, do not support the government's argument. None of the witnesses to the Orren Street incident saw the Trinidad Avenue incident, and neither crime depended on the other for its furtherance or success.

The government also argues that the Orren Street and Trinidad Avenue offenses had been properly joined as part of a "common scheme or plan," because Long had been "walking the neighborhood in search of people to rob." We have previously rejected such an argument when considering joinder of defendants under Super. Ct. Crim. R. 8(b), and we reject the argument in this context as well. See Jackson v. United States, 623 A.2d 571 (D.C. 1993) ("The goal of obtaining property from others, here money and guns, was too general for joinder of offenses under Rule 8(b).").

The government contends, finally, that the Orren Street offenses were similar in character to the Trinidad Avenue offenses, and we agree. The "similarity of offenses [under Rule 8(a)] is determined by the content of the indictment"; it is not dependent on whether evidence of one crime would be admissible in the trial of the other. In this case . . . the two crimes, as charged, "both involved armed robberies which were closely related in time and place." Accordingly, it cannot plausibly be maintained that they are insufficiently similar to one another to warrant initial joinder under Rule 8(a). We must conclude that the two sets of offenses were properly joined.

Long contends the trial court erred nonetheless in denying his severance motion under Super. Ct. Crim. R. 14. He says the Orren Street offenses should have been severed from the Trinidad Avenue charges because the evidence of each would be inadmissible in a separate trial of the other. Long adds he was further prejudiced because he was "precluded from presenting separate defenses" to each group of charges.[4]

We have noted that

> even when offenses are properly joined, it is within the trial court's discretion to sever counts and order separate trials if the defendant would be prejudiced by joinder. Our standard of review of such rulings is abuse of discretion, and appellant must make a showing of compelling prejudice to show such error. Of course, there is a potential for prejudice whenever similar, but unrelated offenses are charged. However, the requisite prejudicial effect for a severance will not be found where the evidence [1] can be kept separate and distinct at trial or [2] is mutually admissible at separate trials. [Cox v. United States, 498 A.2d 231, 235 (D.C. 1985).]

Because the incidents were not tried separately and distinctly,[5] resolution of the severance issue turns on mutual admissibility: whether the evidence of each joined offense would be admissible at a separate trial of the other. The first sentence of Super. Ct. Crim. R. 14 provides:

> [If] it appears that a defendant or the government is prejudiced by a joinder of offenses or of defendants in an indictment or information or by such joinder for trial together, the Court may order an election or separate trials of counts, grant a severance of defendants or provide whatever other relief justice requires.

In response to Long's contention, the government argues that the severance motion was properly denied because evidence of each group of offenses would have been admissible in a separate trial of the other "to explain the immediate

---

4. Long apparently wanted to present a misidentification defense as to Orren Street and to claim self-defense at Trinidad Avenue, but realistically separate defenses appeared to be possible only if the offenses were tried separately. . . .

5. The evidence as to each offense was not "kept separate and distinct such that it would not be amalgamated in the jury's mind into a single inculpatory mass." Although the prosecutor attempted to structure the trial to separate the incidents, calling first the Orren Street witnesses and then the Trinidad Avenue witnesses, the evidence of the two crimes was closely tied together by some of the witnesses whose testimony pertained to both crimes, e.g., Scholethia Monk, Kimberly Bridgeford, and the homicide investigator, Willie Toland. Moreover, the government's closing argument also brought together evidence of the two crimes. Finally, the strong identification evidence and intent-to-rob evidence from the Orren Street incident served to supply identification and motive evidence for the Trinidad Avenue incident, so there was a substantial likelihood that the jury would cumulate the evidence. Accordingly, we cannot uphold the denial of severance based on the "separate and distinct"—sometimes known as the "simple and distinct"—theory.

circumstances surrounding the offense charged." Technically speaking, such evidence "is not other crimes evidence because it is too intimately entangled with the charged criminal conduct."[6] Alternatively, the government argues that the evidence of each incident would be admissible in a trial of the other as "other crimes" evidence tending to prove "identity."[7]

Commonly, the question is whether uncharged criminal conduct shall be admitted in a trial of the charged crime, but in this case the question is the admissibility of a charged crime in the trial of another charged crime. If each would be admissible in the other, then there would be no reason why the two should not be tried together; but, if one or both would not meet the test for admissibility in the other, then severance is required. . . .

In this case, Long presented a misidentification defense at trial. Thus, identity was a contested issue. . . . We therefore believe it appropriate to scrutinize the evidence of each incident, as it bears on proving identity of the assailant in the other. . . . The Orren Street evidence informed the jury that, at about 10:30 P.M., on September 8, 1992, a man identified as Damian Long, dressed entirely in black (including a fringe jacket and skull cap) and carrying a gun, had . . . attempted a robbery at gunpoint. After the assault, the witnesses saw Long headed toward nearby Trinidad Avenue. They heard gunshots soon thereafter.

As for Trinidad Avenue, earlier on the same day at about 5:30 to 6:00 P.M., Scholethia Monk and Kimberly Bridgeford saw Long, dressed entirely in black (including a fringe jacket and skull cap), leave Monk's apartment. Bridgeford saw Long depart in the direction of Trinidad Avenue. Later that evening shortly after 10:30 P.M., Deborah Alford, from her front porch on Trinidad Avenue, saw a man dressed in a black jacket (she did not notice fringe on it), black pants, and a black skull cap walk past her neighbor, Louis Johnson, who was standing next to his car. . . . Alford never identified the assailant. Both Monk and Bridgeford, however, witnessed Long's return to Monk's apartment "panicking and sweating," admitting he had "shot a man on Trinidad Avenue because the man tried to rob him with a knife." Long had blood on his face and was carrying a pistol. His skull cap was missing. The police later found a black skull cap seven feet from where Johnson had been shot. Monk's apartment on Holbrook Terrace was but a few blocks away from where the offenses occurred on Orren Street and Trinidad Avenue.

We believe that the testimony of the Orren Street witnesses, Davis and Fox (who identified Long as a would-be robber), that they saw Long heading in the direction of Trinidad Avenue nearby, and then heard gunshots—all around 10:30 P.M., on September 8, 1992—provided powerful evidence of the Trinidad Avenue assailant's identity. Indeed, this evidence was particularly significant for the Trinidad Avenue

---

6. The trial court accepted the government's . . . theory in denying Long's renewed motion to sever: "This matter is so inextricably intertwined each with each other that there is no way the Government can separate it all and make sense of the whole matter. They absolutely need for identification purposes, if for nothing else, they absolutely have to have these cases tried together, they should be tried together temporally. And by temporally, I mean both time and place they are as connected as can be." Recently our en banc court discerned three subcategories of evidence embraced by the "immediate circumstances" rationale: such evidence (1) is direct and substantial proof of the charged crime, (2) is closely intertwined with the evidence of the charged crime, or (3) is necessary to place the charged crime in an understandable context.

7. "Other crimes" evidence is admissible only if [it is introduced to show] motive, intent, absence of mistake or accident, common scheme or plan, or identity as reflected in Fed. R. Evid. 404(b).

prosecution, when coupled with Monk's and Bridgeford's testimony about Long's admission that he had shot a man on Trinidad Avenue, because the only person who saw the assailant approach Johnson, Deborah Alford, was unable to identify Johnson's killer (although Alford provided a description consistent with Fox's, Davis's, Monk's, and Bridgeford's description of Long). The Orren Street evidence also revealed the assailant's possible motive for approaching Johnson on Trinidad Avenue (robbery).

We also recognize that the Trinidad Avenue evidence was probative of the identity of the Orren Street attacker. Alford's description of an unidentified, black-jacketed, gun-carrying assailant on Trinidad Avenue, combined with the Monk/Bridgeford testimony that Damian Long had come to Monk's apartment with a gun, "panicking and sweating," tended to identify Long as the Orren Street assailant dressed in black seen heading toward Trinidad Avenue just before shots were fired around 10:30 P.M. The fact that Monk testified that Long's skull cap was missing when he returned to her apartment, coupled with the police officer's finding a skull cap on Trinidad Avenue, adds to Long's connection with the Orren Street attack by a man wearing a black skull cap.

Accordingly, without regard to the required probative value/prejudicial impact analysis, we can say that the Orren Street and Trinidad Avenue offenses [would be mutually admissible] in separate trials (and thus would not be joined prejudicially if prosecuted in a joint trial).

We turn to the ruling on probative value/prejudicial impact. The motions judge said, "I don't see prejudice under [Super. Ct. Civ. R.] 14 that would justify severance." The trial judge, in considering the renewed severance motion at trial, referred to the motions judge's ruling and then added his own belief that [a joint trial was permissible] because the cases were "inextricably intertwined."

The trial judge, therefore, said not a word about probative value relative to prejudice. That was unfortunate. At least as to admissibility of Trinidad Avenue evidence in an Orren Street trial, we see a serious question whether probative value outweighs prejudicial impact. Monk and Bridgeford identified the man—Damian Long—whom Alford apparently had seen accosting Johnson: a man fitting the description of the person who had attempted the robbery only blocks away on Orren Street minutes earlier. This identification evidence from Trinidad Avenue, however, was cumulative of—and of far less probative value than—the direct eyewitness testimony from Fox and Davis . . . that Long was the would-be bandit on Orren Street. Furthermore, this weaker identification evidence includes the powerfully prejudicial testimony that Long had committed a murder, not merely an assault, on Trinidad Avenue.

The trial judge, after a pretrial severance motion has been denied, has a continuing obligation to grant a severance if undue prejudice arises as a result of joinder at any time during trial. The trial judge recognized this obligation: "the Court of Appeals seems to indicate that I have to listen [to severance motions] again and again and again and again." Here, however, in denying the renewed severance motion, the trial judge, for his prejudice analysis, merely referred to the ruling of the motions judge, who did not "see prejudice" from a pretrial perspective. . . .

The probative/prejudicial analysis is a discretionary evaluation which an appellate court cannot undertake itself when the trial court fails to do so unless it is clear from the record, as a matter of law, that the trial court had "but one option." In this case, admissibility of the Trinidad Avenue murder evidence in an Orren Street trial appears to be a more difficult discretionary call than admissibility of the Orren Street assault in a Trinidad Avenue trial, but as to either case we find no sound basis on the record for this court to take over the trial court's function by ruling on probative value/prejudicial impact.

We, therefore, must remand the case for the trial judge to make a probative/prejudicial ruling for each case and thus to rule once again on the severance motion—including consideration of Long's contention that he was prejudiced by his inability, in a single trial, to present separate defenses (Orren Street, misidentification; Trinidad Avenue, self-defense). The judge shall order a new trial of the Orren Street prosecution if he concludes that the murder evidence from Trinidad Avenue should have been omitted from the Orren Street trial. Otherwise, the Orren Street convictions . . . shall stand, without prejudice to Long's right to appeal the severance ruling on remand.[10] Similarly, the judge shall make a probative/prejudice ruling on admissibility of Orren Street evidence in the Trinidad Avenue trial, and also shall rule on Long's claim of prejudice from his practical inability to claim self-defense for Trinidad Avenue at a joint trial. The judge shall order a new trial, or not, as indicated. Absent a new trial order, the Trinidad Avenue conviction shall stand, subject to Long's right of appeal of that severance ruling. . . .

Notes

1. *Permissive joinder of offenses: majority view.* The rules governing joinder and severance work together to define the permissible bounds for single prosecutions and the extent of judicial discretion. A slight majority of states track the federal rule on permissive joinder and allow prosecutors or judges to join offenses for trial, whether they are "related" charges ("based on the same act or transaction or on two or more acts or transactions connected together or constituting parts of a common scheme or plan") or similar but "unrelated" charges (having the "same or similar character"). A significant minority of states authorize joinder only for "related" offenses utilizing a variety of formulations. See, e.g., Fla. R. Crim. P. 3.150; Ill. Ann. Stat. ch. 725, para. 5/111-4; State v. Ramos, 818 A.2d 1228 (N.H. 2003) (adopts ABA standards for joinder, because former, more permissive approach produced

---

10. We have indicated that other crimes evidence on occasion should be tailored to minimize prejudice. Theoretically, it would be possible to sanitize the Trinidad Avenue evidence for a separate Orren Street trial. In such a trial, the Trinidad Avenue identification testimony would have to be trimmed to leave out reference to a murder, and Deborah Alford would be limited to testifying that an unidentifiable man in black had accosted Johnson with a gun at about 10:30 P.M. Scholethia Monk and Kimberly Bridgeford would be limited to saying that Long—dressed in black—had returned to the apartment shortly after 10:30 P.M., admitting he had just assaulted someone on Trinidad Avenue. The police could then testify about finding a black skull cap on Trinidad Avenue nearby.

The trial court will have to decide, as part of the required probative value/prejudicial impact analysis, (1) whether the preferred approach would be admission of sanitized Trinidad Avenue evidence in a separate Orren Street trial, in order to keep prejudicial homicide evidence from that jury, or (2) whether, because (a) the Fox/Davis identification evidence was strong, (b) the Monk/Bridgeford testimony could be limited to identification of Long as the man who returned "panicking and sweating" at about 10:30 P.M., (c) the murder evidence was highly prejudicial, and (d) sanitizing the evidence would be complicated, the Trinidad Avenue murder evidence should be kept out of the Orren Street trial altogether, or (3) whether sanitizing the Trinidad Avenue evidence would not work, and the probative value of that evidence outweighs prejudice. If either of the first two instances applies, the court should grant the severance motion; in the third, the court should deny it.

inconsistent results; when two or more unrelated offenses are joined for trial, both prosecution and defense have absolute right to severance). Given that "related" offenses can include two or more acts "connected together or constituting parts of a common scheme or plan," will the results of this rule be much different from the results of a rule allowing joinder of acts with the "same or similar character"?

2. *The effects of joinder.* Joinder may offer some benefits for defendants, since an attorney can charge less money to represent a defendant at a single trial than at multiple trials. Generally speaking, however, the conventional wisdom is that joint trials provide more advantages to the prosecution. What particular advantages might the prosecutor gain by combining related charges into a single trial?

One careful study of joinder in the federal courts compared outcomes at trial for joined offenses and separately tried offenses. After controlling for the seriousness of the charges and other variables, the study concluded that trial defendants who face multiple counts are roughly 10 percent more likely to be convicted of the most serious charge than a defendant who stands trial on a single count. Andrew D. Leipold & Hossein A. Abbasi, The Impact of Joinder and Severance on Federal Criminal Cases: An Empirical Study, 59 Vand. L. Rev. 101 (2006). If you were studying the effects of joinder in a state felony court system, what variables other than the number of counts would you want to investigate?

3. *Severance of offenses: majority view.* A majority of states have rules or statutes that address severance separately from the joinder question. Most states with severance provisions require severance upon a finding of prejudice, or if necessary to promote a "fair determination of innocence or guilt." A few authorize severance in the "interests of justice." A group of about a half dozen states (represented by the Vermont rule reprinted above) follow the recommendations of the ABA Standards for Criminal Justice by giving the defendant the absolute right to sever "unrelated but similar" offenses. This approach bars the joinder of the unrelated but similar offenses unless the defendant consents. See, e.g., Mich. R. Crim. P. 6.121. What reasons might lead a defendant to accept joinder of unrelated but similar offenses?

The *Long* decision from the District of Columbia reviews the most important sources of prejudice to defendants during a trial of properly joined offenses. First, a defendant might want to pursue separate and inconsistent defenses to the different charges. Was Long asking for the opportunity to mislead two different juries? A second common source of prejudice to defendants from a joint trial of separate offenses involves "other crimes" evidence. The rules of evidence limit the prosecutor's ability to introduce evidence of one crime during the trial of another crime, because the jury might infer that a person who committed one crime is more likely to have committed a second crime. Joinder of offenses might allow a prosecutor to overcome this evidentiary rule; thus, severance is often granted when a court determines that the rules of evidence would exclude evidence of one charge in a separate trial of the other charge. Federal Rule of Evidence 404(b) governs such questions in the federal system. Evidence of "other crimes" is admissible to show a defendant's motive, intent, absence of mistake or accident, common scheme or plan, or identity, but not her propensity to commit a crime.

Even when the rules of evidence might exclude evidence of one crime during a separate trial for the other crime, the charges can still be joined if the evidence remains "simple and distinct" at trial. See United States v. Lotsch, 102 F.2d 35 (2d Cir. 1939) (Hand, J.) ("Here we can see no prejudice from the joining of the three charges: The evidence to each was short and simple; there was no reasonable ground for thinking that the jury would not keep separate what was relevant to each").

"Simple and distinct" (or "separate and distinct") refers both to the content of the evidence and to the method the prosecution uses to present it. If witnesses for one crime are presented together, followed by a different set of witnesses for the other crime, the evidence is more likely to be considered "simple and distinct."

4. *Appellate review of joinder and severance decisions.* Appellate courts rarely overturn a trial court's joinder and severance decisions. The standard of review in virtually all jurisdictions is "abuse of discretion." Did the trial court in *Long* abuse its discretion? Given that most joinder and severance decisions are resolved before trial and are based on the charges in the indictment or information rather than testimony of witnesses at trial, are trial courts really better situated to resolve these claims than an appellate court?

5. *Mandatory joinder: majority position.* About 10 states have adopted a "mandatory" or "compulsory" joinder requirement, either by statute, procedural rule, or judicial ruling. See N.Y. Crim. Proc. Law §40.40 ("Where two or more offenses are joinable in a single accusatory instrument against a person by reason of being based upon the same criminal transaction . . . such person may not . . . be separately prosecuted for such offenses"); Va. Code §19.2-294. A larger group of states, following the federal approach embodied in Fed. R. Crim. P. 8(a), maintain a "permissive" joinder rule, which defines the maximum range of charges that the prosecutor can bring together in the same trial but does not speak to any minimum range of charges that the prosecutor must join together. Note that in a permissive joinder jurisdiction, double jeopardy principles and the related doctrine of collateral estoppel still define a minimum range of charges that must be resolved in a single criminal proceeding. Thus, the mandatory joinder jurisdictions have supplemented double jeopardy and collateral estoppel principles.

6. *Misjoinder.* The converse of mandatory joinder is "misjoinder." When a defendant believes that a prosecutor has grouped together more charges than the permissive joinder rules will allow, she can request the trial court to declare misjoinder. The remedy is separate trials, not dismissal of the charges. Misjoinder can occur in any jurisdiction, whether it has a permissive or compulsory joinder rule, because all jurisdictions define the maximum range of charges that may be grouped together. But not all jurisdictions declare the same maximum. Some follow the model of Fed. R. Crim. P. 8(a), allowing joinder of offenses based on (1) acts that are of the same or similar character or (2) the "same act or transaction" or (3) two or more acts or transactions connected together or constituting parts of a common scheme or plan. Another group of states do not include the first ground for joinder, acts of the "same or similar character." Can you imagine a class of cases in which this first ground for joinder would make a difference in the outcome on a motion to declare misjoinder, or do you expect the different formulations to produce essentially the same results?

The relationships among the doctrines of permissive joinder, mandatory joinder, misjoinder, and severance are complex. You can find diagrams to sort out these overlapping spheres on the web extension for this chapter at *http://www.crimpro.com/extension/ch14.*

Problem 14-3. Compulsory Joinder

Matthew Hensley was involved in a bar fight in Kanawha County, West Virginia on November 16, 1991. Hensley and four other people were arrested at the scene and were immediately charged in magistrate court with public intoxication and destruction of property, both misdemeanors. Although one of the victims of the fight, Barbara Lane, told detectives that Hensley threw a cue ball, hitting her in her left eye, causing bone fractures and resulting in plastic and reconstructive surgery, no additional charges were brought against Hensley for these injuries prior to his trial in magistrate court on March 13, 1992. He was acquitted of both misdemeanors at the trial in magistrate court.

The Sheriff's Department did not tell the prosecutor's office about the nature of Lane's injuries until January 1994, over two years after the bar fight and nearly two years after the acquittal in magistrate court. Soon after learning about the severity of Lane's injuries, the prosecutor charged Hensley with malicious assault, a felony. Hensley moved to dismiss the indictment under Rule 8(a) of the West Virginia Rules of Criminal Procedure based on the failure of the State to join the felony charge with the misdemeanor charges prior to the trial in magistrate court in March 1992. Rule 8(a) of West Virginia Rules of Criminal Procedure provides in relevant part:

> Joinder of Offenses.—All offenses based on the same act or transaction or on two or more acts or transactions connected together or constituting parts of a common scheme or plan shall be charged in the same indictment or information . . . , whether felonies or misdemeanors or both.

West Virginia courts have developed several exceptions to the application of the rule despite the absence of explicit language within the rule. The first exception is that all offenses, even though based on the same act or transaction or constituting parts of a common scheme or plan, must have occurred in the same jurisdiction. The second exception applies when the prosecuting attorney does not know and has no reason to know about all the offenses. The third exception happens when the prosecuting attorney had no opportunity to attend the proceeding where the first offense is presented.

If you were the trial judge in Hensley's felony case, what issues would you ask the parties to address during the hearing on the motion to dismiss? How would you expect to rule? Would the outcome change if West Virginia had adopted a rule identical to Federal Rule of Criminal Procedure 8(a)? Compare State ex rel. Forbes v. Canady, 475 S.E.2d 37 (W. Va. 1996).

Problem 14-4. Protective Order

Aurelio Chenique-Puey and Susan Lake cohabited from 1983 until 1987, and they had a daughter in 1986. After their separation in 1987, Chenique-Puey harassed Lake repeatedly. Lake obtained a domestic violence restraining order, which prohibited Chenique-Puey from "returning to the scene of the domestic violence" and "from having any contact with the plaintiff or harassing plaintiff or plaintiff's relatives in any way." It also curtailed his child-visitation rights.

Chenique-Puey was convicted and imprisoned on unrelated charges, so Lake did not have any further contact with him until 1991. Five days after his release from prison, Chenique-Puey came to Lake's apartment to see his daughter. Lake refused to admit Chenique-Puey and told him to leave. According to Lake, Chenique-Puey then taunted her through an open rear window and waved a knife at her. He then threatened to return to the apartment with a shotgun to kill her and her boyfriend before driving away.

Lake called the police and filed a criminal complaint against him. He was indicted on charges of third-degree terroristic threats and fourth-degree contempt of a judicial restraining order. At the start of trial, the defendant moved for a severance of the contempt charge. He argued that joinder of this offense would prejudice him because evidence of the restraining order would convince the jury that he had in fact made the alleged terroristic threats against Lane.

In New Jersey, joinder of offenses is governed by Rule 3:7-6, which provides that two or more offenses may be charged together if they are "of the same or similar character or are based on the same act or transaction or on two or more acts or transactions connected together or constituting parts of a common scheme or plan." Mandatory joinder under Rule 3:15-1(b) is required when multiple criminal offenses charged are "based on the same conduct or arise from the same episode." Rule 3:15-2(b) vests a trial court with discretion to order separate trials if a defendant or the State is "prejudiced" by permissive or mandatory joinder of offenses.

As a trial court judge, would you grant the motion to sever the offenses? Compare State v. Chenique-Puey, 678 A.2d 694 (N.J. 1996).

2. Joint Trials of Defendants

The joinder and severance questions we have considered thus far all deal with multiple offenses and an individual defendant. Related questions arise when prosecutors charge two or more defendants with committing essentially the same crime. Under what circumstances will the co-defendants receive separate trials?

The key phrases in procedural rules such as the ones reprinted below are framed generally and require further elaboration by courts presented with recurring factual situations. Cases have generally held that a defendant should obtain severance from a co-defendant when: (1) evidence admitted against one defendant is facially incriminating to the other defendant, such as a prior statement of one co-defendant that incriminates the other co-defendant; (2) evidence admitted against one defendant influences the jury so strongly that it has a harmful "rub-off effect" on the other defendant; (3) there is a significant disparity in the amount of evidence introduced against each of the two defendants; or (4) co-defendants present defenses that are so antagonistic that they are mutually exclusive.

Only clear examples of these types of prejudice will convince an appellate court to reverse a trial court's decision to require a joint trial. For instance, to determine if a "rub off" problem exists, the court must ask whether the jury can keep separate the evidence that is relevant to each defendant and render a fair and impartial verdict as to each. Even in some cases where such prejudicial factors are strong enough to warrant a severance, courts sometimes decide that curative jury instructions can remove any risk of prejudice that might result from a joint trial.

■ FEDERAL RULE OF CRIMINAL PROCEDURE 8(b)

The indictment or information may charge two or more defendants if they are alleged to have participated in the same act or transaction, or in the same series of acts or transactions, constituting an offense or offenses. The defendants may be charged in one or more counts together or separately. All defendants need not be charged in each count.

■ VERMONT RULE OF CRIMINAL PROCEDURE 8(b)

Two or more defendants may be joined in the same information or indictment:

(1) when each of the defendants is charged with accountability for each offense included;

(2) when each of the defendants is charged with conspiracy and some of the defendants are also charged with one or more offenses alleged to be in furtherance of the conspiracy; or

(3) when, even if conspiracy is not charged and all of the defendants are not charged in each count, it is alleged that the several offenses charged

(A) were part of a common scheme or plan; or

(B) were so closely connected in respect to time, place, and occasion that it would be difficult to separate proof of one charge from proof of others.

■ VERMONT RULE OF CRIMINAL PROCEDURE 14(b)(2)

Whenever two or more defendants have been joined together in the same information or indictment,

(A) On motion of the prosecuting attorney or a defendant before trial, the court shall grant severance of one or more defendants if the court finds that they are not joinable under Rule 8(b)(2).

(B) On motion of the prosecuting attorney before trial, other than under subparagraph (A) of this paragraph, the court shall grant severance of one or more defendants if the court finds that there is no reasonable likelihood of prejudice to any defendant. On motion of the prosecuting attorney during trial, the court shall grant severance of one or more defendants only with the consent of the defendant or defendants to be severed or upon a finding of manifest necessity.

(C) On motion of a defendant for severance because an out-of-court statement of a codefendant makes reference to, but is not admissible against, the moving defendant, the court shall determine whether the prosecution intends to offer the statement in evidence as part of its case in chief. If so, the court shall require the prosecuting attorney to elect one of the following courses:

(i) a joint trial at which the statement is not admitted into evidence:

(ii) a joint trial at which the statement is admitted into evidence only after all references to the moving defendant have been deleted, provided that the court finds that the statement, with the references deleted, will not prejudice the moving defendant; or

(iii) severance of the moving defendant.

(D) On motion of a defendant other than under subparagraph (A) or (C) of this paragraph, the court shall grant severance of the moving defendant unless the court finds that there is no reasonable likelihood that that defendant would be prejudiced by a joint trial.

(E) In determining whether there is no reasonable likelihood that a defendant would be prejudiced, the court shall consider among other factors whether, in view of the number of offenses and defendants charged and the complexity of the evidence to be offered, the trier of fact will be able to distinguish the evidence and apply the law intelligently as to each offense and as to each defendant.

(F) The court may, at any time, grant severance of one or more defendants with the consent of the prosecution and the defendant or defendants to be severed.

VERMONT REPORTER'S NOTES—1995 AMENDMENT

Rule 14(b)(2) is amended to eliminate the absolute right of severance for a defendant in a felony case and to provide guidelines under which a motion for severance of defendants is to be considered. Under the prior rule, in misdemeanor cases severance or whatever other relief justice required was to be granted when either a defendant or the State was prejudiced by joinder. The amended rule applies to both felonies and misdemeanors. The amendment is based on ABA Standard 13-3.2. The purposes of the amendment are to give the court flexibility and to strike a proper balance between avoidance of multiple trials for victims and the right of defendants to a fair trial. . . .

When two or more defendants have been joined, the first issue for determination is whether the joinder is proper under the terms of that rule. Amended Rule 14(b)(2)(A) requires the court to grant a pretrial request by either prosecution or defense for severance on grounds of misjoinder, regardless of whether there is prejudice. If a defect in joinder appears during trial, a severance on that ground is to be considered in accordance with the standards of subparagraphs (B) and (D).

Under Rule 14(b)(2)(B), even if joinder is proper pursuant to Rule 8(b), the prosecutor will be granted a severance on motion before trial if the court finds "no reasonable likelihood" that any defendant would be prejudiced by the severance. . . . On an appropriate motion by a defendant under Rule 14(b)(2)(C), the court must determine whether Bruton v. United States, 391 U.S. 123 (1968), affects the severance decision. Under *Bruton*, the trial court must protect the confrontation rights of a nonconfessing defendant where a codefendant has confessed and that confession is admissible only against the confessing defendant. Rule 14(b)(2)(C)(i)-(iii) set out the options which must be followed for compliance with *Bruton*. . . .

If a defendant moves for severance before trial on grounds other than misjoinder or the potential use of a codefendant's confession, the court under Rule 14(b)(2)(D) is to sever the moving defendant unless it finds that there is no reasonable likelihood of prejudice to that defendant from the joinder. The standard for determining prejudice is set forth in Rule 14(b)(2)(E). That standard departs from the formulation, "fair determination of guilt or innocence," found in ABA Standard 13-3.2(b)(i), (ii). In deciding the question, the court is to consider "prejudice" in terms of the impact of the challenged joinder on each defendant's right to a fair trial where the prosecution makes the motion and on the moving defendant's fair trial right where a defendant makes the motion. [There] is a reasonable likelihood of prejudice where the jury might consider evidence against one defendant that is properly offered only against a codefendant, either on the merits or as to character or credibility. Where the evidence against both defendants is substantially similar, however, they may be tried jointly in the absence of other factors giving rise to a reasonable likelihood of prejudice. . . .

Notes

1. *Joinder of defendants: majority view.* Joint trials account for almost one-third of all federal criminal trials, a rate much higher than in most state systems. As a result, the federal courts have dealt extensively with severance issues. See Richardson v. Marsh, 481 U.S. 200 (1987). In general, the federal courts have shown a strong preference for joint trials. This preference has become even more pronounced in recent years, and severance requests in the federal courts are now routinely denied. Interestingly, one empirical study of the joinder of federal defendants concluded that joining co-defendants in a single trial had virtually no impact on the likelihood of conviction. Andrew D. Leipold & Hossein A. Abbasi, The Impact of Joinder and Severance on Federal Criminal Cases: An Empirical Study, 59 Vand. L. Rev. 101 (2006).

A majority of states leave decisions on the joinder and severance of trials for multiple defendants to the discretion of the trial judge. Defendants in these jurisdictions find courts generally unreceptive when they request separate trials based on the special legal and practical difficulties of defending against conspiracy charges. As the reporter's notes to Vermont Rule 14(b)(2) indicate, Vermont had a mandatory severance rule but amended it in 1995, in line with the dominant view, allowing the trial judge some discretion over whether to order joint trials. See Kan. Stat. §22-3204. A significant minority of states, including Vermont, provide more detailed rules to guide courts in assessing out-of-court statements by co-defendants. See, e.g., Fla. R. Crim. P. 3.152(b).

2. *Remedies short of severance.* Courts take several approaches short of severing trials to deal with conflicts among co-defendants. The most common is simply to issue cautionary instructions to the jury before it retires to consider the case. Sometimes the judge also instructs the jury at the beginning of the trial or when particular evidence is presented. Occasionally courts will bar the use of evidence that would be admissible at a trial of a co-defendant tried separately. A more complex option, which has been tried in a number of states, is the use of "dual" juries to hear the same case. Each jury considers the charges against one defendant. The court will excuse one of the juries when evidence is presented against one defendant that could not be presented against the other. For a general discussion of "mega-trials" in the federal courts, see James Jacobs et al., Busting the Mob: United States v. Cosa Nostra (1994).

Problem 14-5. Antagonistic Brothers

Brothers Durid and Kafan Hana were arrested following a controlled narcotics purchase that took place at the Sterling Heights home in which the brothers lived with their parents. Yuri Alsarih went to the door of the Hana home and spoke with Durid about buying some drugs for a friend (who turned out to be an undercover officer). Later that evening, Alsarih returned to the home; Kafan admitted him and then walked to a back bedroom where Durid was sleeping. Durid awoke when Kafan turned on the light. Kafan removed a plastic bag from a safe in the bedroom, mixed it with the contents from some other bags and gave it to Alsarih. They returned to the front of the house, and Kafan watched while Alsarih went out to his parked car. Durid was watching from the living room window. A subsequent search of the home, pursuant to a search warrant, disclosed that the safe contained three kilograms of cocaine, miscellaneous jewelry and papers, a telephone recorder, and a telephone beeper. Both Kafan and Durid initially denied knowing the combination to the safe, but Kafan later supplied the combination, and Durid admitted that the safe was his.

Both Durid and Kafan filed pretrial motions for separate trials. Each brother claimed that the controlled substances in the safe were the sole property of the other brother. During oral argument on the motions. Durid's attorney said that "the two defenses could not be more antagonistic. Two people are pointing the finger at each other and the case is clear that severance must be granted." The prosecutor argued that it took more than "a mere allegation of pointing fingers at one another" to warrant separate trials. The trial court denied the motion.

In his opening statement at trial, Kafan's attorney told jurors that their deliberations necessarily pitted brother against brother. In closing arguments, Kafan's attorney disputed the theory that his client had control over the three kilograms of cocaine seized from the safe:

> We know he used the house, we know he used the safe, but we know he didn't own the house and own the safe. Everybody who has ever shared a locker in school or anybody who's ever shared an apartment, everybody who's ever lived in a rooming house and had to share a bathroom knows that you can share special areas and have absolutely no right to control something that belongs to somebody else.

Neither defendant testified at trial. The jury convicted both of them. Durid appeals, alleging that the trial court erred in denying his motion for a separate trial given the antagonistic defenses of the two brothers. He argues that the events at trial support his claim of antagonistic defenses. How would you rule? Suppose the jurisdiction has adopted joinder and severance rules with language identical to Federal Rules of Criminal Procedure 8(b) and 14, related to joinder and severance of defendants? Would it change the outcome if the rules in the jurisdiction tracked the language of Vermont Rules of Criminal Procedure 8(b) and 14(b)(2), reprinted above? Compare People v. Hana, 524 N.W.2d 682 (Mich. 1994).

PART THREE

RESOLVING GUILT AND INNOCENCE

XV

Discovery and Speedy Trial

The most critical task for the attorney preparing for trial is to gather information about the events in question. Some of the best information is in the hands of the other party. The rules of discovery govern how and when the parties exchange information that may be relevant in resolving the charges, whether through trial or guilty plea. These rules are grounded in constitutions, statutes, court rules, and local policies and practices.

Adequate preparation takes time. But all the while, the defendant must live with the shame of accusation and the inconvenience and expense of preparing for trial. For defendants who are detained, even a short period awaiting trial can destroy employment prospects and personal relationships. For these reasons, many defendants, and especially those in detention, want a "speedy" trial. In this chapter, we review the tools for discovering information and the many sources of law that give parties the ability, and the incentive, to speed up or slow down the trial date.

A. DISCOVERY

In all litigation, there are rules about exchanging information among the parties and gathering information from nonparties. What the parties learn during discovery determines in large part the evidence they will have at their disposal at trial. Even more important for most defendants, discovery allows them to estimate their chances of success at trial and to enter plea bargain negotiations with that information in mind.

Two sets of interrelated questions dominate the law of discovery in criminal cases. First, discovery rules must resolve whether shared information or independent information is the norm — that is, do the rules allow "broad" or "narrow" discovery? The answer to this question reflects the expected relationship among prosecutors, judges, and defense attorneys. Less exchange of information reflects a more adversarial and independent model, where each side develops its own evidence; more exchange reflects a more cooperative model of litigation, with the court taking a stronger role in coordinating a collective search for truth. As you read and discuss the materials in this section, try to draw comparisons to civil discovery techniques and to identify trends over time toward more or less extensive criminal discovery.

The second set of questions deals with the symmetry of discovery. Do prosecution and defense have an equal ability to obtain information from the opposing side? In a system with other asymmetries built into it (such as the "beyond a reasonable doubt" standard of proof, the privilege against self-incrimination, and the government's funding of prosecutors, investigators, and crime labs), are asymmetrical discovery rights necessary or desirable?

Our discussion of discovery begins with the prosecutor's constitutional obligation to share material exculpatory and impeachment information with the defense before trial. Pay particular attention to the role "materiality" plays in setting the boundaries of this obligation, as well as to the nature of the temporal requirement—that material information need be shared only *before trial.* Constitutional obligations are only the floor of discovery obligations, however; in the second section we consider how state and federal statutory schemes enlarge the prosecutor's obligation to share information with the defense. In the final section, we examine the extent of defense obligations to share information with the prosecution.

1. Prosecution Disclosure of Exculpatory Information

Although the U.S. Constitution does not have a specific provision related to disclosure, the Supreme Court has interpreted the due process clause to require disclosure of several types of information to the defense, even if the defense lawyer never asks for the information. Such disclosure is regarded as necessary to ensure a fair trial.

One disclosure duty that courts place on prosecutors involves perjured testimony of government witnesses. If the prosecutor knows or should know that government witnesses are presenting false testimony or evidence, due process requires the prosecutor to disclose this fact to the defendant and to the court. A conviction must be set aside if there is any reasonable likelihood that the false testimony could have affected the judgment of the jury. See Mooney v. Holohan, 294 U.S. 103 (1935); Napue v. Illinois, 360 U.S. 264 (1959).

A second constitutional duty to disclose derives from Brady v. Maryland, 373 U.S. 83 (1963). In that case, a defense attorney in a murder case asked to review all the extrajudicial statements of a co-conspirator, but the prosecutor withheld a statement in which the co-conspirator admitted to shooting the victim. The Supreme Court ruled that the Constitution's due process clause requires the prosecution to disclose "evidence favorable to an accused" if that evidence is "material either to guilt or to punishment." The Court expanded this disclosure duty in United States v. Agurs, 427 U.S. 97 (1976). The obligation to disclose all *material* evidence favorable to the accused, the Court said, applies even when the defendant makes only a general request for exculpatory information or makes no discovery request at all. Such material evidence includes evidence that the defense might use to impeach prosecution witnesses, along with evidence that more directly points to the defendant's innocence. See United States v. Bagley, 473 U.S. 667 (1985). Failure to disclose *nonmaterial* evidence does not violate *Brady,* regardless of whether defense counsel requested disclosure.

Appellate and postconviction litigation over *Brady* issues remains quite common. Courts struggle to identify which prosecutorial failures to disclose are important enough to justify overturning a conviction. This difficult question necessarily calls for the court to speculate: What would have happened if the prosecutor had disclosed the material? How certain does the reviewing court have to be that a different outcome would have occurred if these facts were shared before trial?

A third constitutional duty relates to evidence that may cast doubt on the credibility of a prosecution witness. In Giglio v. United States, 405 U.S. 150 (1972), the Court overturned a conviction based on the prosecutor's failure to disclose a promise made to its key witness that he would not be prosecuted if he testified for the government. Such "*Giglio* material" is now a routine part of the disclosure obligations of the prosecutor, because it goes to impeachment.

In the following case, the Illinois Supreme Court unanimously found that the government had committed a *Brady* violation. Could lower courts have reached a different result on these facts? What office practices became necessary for Illinois prosecutors as a result of this case?

■ PEOPLE v. ALAN BEAMAN
890 N.E.2d 500 (Ill. 2008)

KILBRIDE, J.

The petitioner, Alan Beaman, appeals the dismissal of his postconviction petition. His petition stems from a first degree murder conviction, and sentence of 50 years. [Petitioner] asserts several claims, including that the State violated his constitutional right to due process of law by failing to disclose information about a viable alternative suspect in the murder. We conclude that the State violated petitioner's right to due process under Brady v. Maryland, 373 U.S. 83 (1963), by failing to disclose material information about the alternative suspect. . . .

I. BACKGROUND

Jennifer Lockmiller, an Illinois State University student, was found dead in her apartment in Normal, Illinois, on August 28, 1993. Seven fingerprints were recovered from the scene. Two of the fingerprints were from petitioner, four belonged to Jennifer's boyfriend Michael Swaine, and one was unidentified. The State asserted the murder occurred between 12 P.M. and 2 P.M. on that date.

Prior to trial, the State filed a motion *in limine* seeking to exclude evidence of Jennifer's relationships with men other than petitioner and Michael Swaine. The State argued that petitioner should not be allowed to offer alternative-suspect evidence unless he could establish it was not remote or speculative. The prosecutor informed the court that the State did not possess nonspeculative evidence of a third-party suspect. The court reserved ruling on the motion.

Before the jury trial, the prosecutor and defense counsel discussed Jennifer's relationship with a person identified as John Doe. The prosecutor informed the court that Doe had "nothing to do with this case." Petitioner conceded that he did not have any specific evidence showing that another person committed the offense. The trial court then granted the motion *in limine*, ruling that petitioner could not present any evidence of an alternative suspect.

At trial, petitioner testified that he began dating Jennifer in July of 1992. During the following year, petitioner and Jennifer ended and then restarted their relationship a number of times. Petitioner was a student at Illinois Wesleyan University in Bloomington during that time. In several letters to Jennifer, petitioner expressed his desire to have a monogamous relationship. The letters indicated that petitioner believed Jennifer was involved with other men. . . .

Petitioner testified that one night in the spring of 1993, Jennifer called and told him that she wanted to end their relationship. He went to Jennifer's apartment to get his compact disc player. When he arrived, he saw John Doe's car in the parking lot. Petitioner pounded on the door to Jennifer's apartment, but she refused to let him inside. Petitioner continued pounding and kicking the door until it broke. After he discovered Jennifer and Doe inside, he took his compact disc player from the apartment and left. Petitioner was yelling while inside the apartment, but he did not touch either Jennifer or Doe.

Additionally, Jennifer and petitioner's roommate, Michael Swaine, began a relationship during the summer of 1993. One night in early July, petitioner suspected that Swaine was at Jennifer's apartment. Petitioner pounded and kicked the door until it broke. He entered the apartment, but could not find Swaine. Petitioner did not touch Jennifer, but confronted her verbally and left after 30 to 45 minutes.

On July 25, 1993, petitioner searched Swaine's room and discovered letters that Jennifer had written to Swaine. Petitioner located Swaine and screamed at him about "seeing" Jennifer. Petitioner then went to Jennifer's apartment, pounded on her door, and when she let him inside, he confronted her by reading the letters. At that point, petitioner considered the relationship to be over. Petitioner then moved back to his parents' home in Rockford, Illinois.

Jennifer called petitioner at his home in Rockford several times, including a call on August 23, 1993. Petitioner testified that Jennifer asked him if they could get back together when the school year began. Petitioner told her "no, we're through," and hung up the telephone. . . .

After Jennifer's body was found in her apartment, police detectives interviewed petitioner several times. Petitioner denied any involvement in the murder. Petitioner testified that he worked a night shift at his uncle's grocery store, ending at 9 A.M. on August 25. He went home, picked up some cash and a check, and drove to his bank to make a deposit. A bank security videotape showed petitioner leaving the bank at 10:11 A.M. After returning from the bank, petitioner went to sleep in his room until approximately 5 P.M. Petitioner also presented testimony that he drove 305.6 miles that week in his daily activities in Rockford to show that he could not have driven approximately 140 miles to Normal on August 25. The parties presented conflicting testimony on whether petitioner's odometer had been subject to tampering.

Telephone records showed that calls were made from the Beaman residence to their church at 10:37 A.M. and to Mitchell Olson's residence at 10:39 A.M. Olson was the church's director of music and youth ministries. The evidence showed that only petitioner or his mother, Carol Beaman, could have made those calls. Petitioner testified that he did not remember making the calls, but it was "entirely possible" that he made them.

Carol Beaman testified that she did not make the phone calls from her residence at 10:37 and 10:39 A.M. She left home around 7 o'clock that morning and did errands much of the day. When she arrived home around 2:15, she said, petitioner's car was in the driveway and his dog was sitting in front of his bedroom door. She woke petitioner for dinner at approximately 6 P.M.

Normal Police Detective Timothy Freesmeyer testified about drive times and distances relevant to defendant's opportunity to commit the murder. Freesmeyer testified that the distance from petitioner's bank to Jennifer's apartment was 126.7 miles. Freesmeyer's drive time test indicated that petitioner could have arrived at Jennifer's apartment just before noon if he left the bank at 10:11 A.M. and drove 10 miles per hour over the speed limit. The distance from petitioner's home to Jennifer's apartment was 139.7 miles. Petitioner could have driven from Jennifer's apartment to his residence in Rockford in just under two hours, driving 10 miles per hour over the speed limit. . . .

In terms of other possible suspects, the State presented evidence that Swaine was working at his former high school's bookstore in Elmhurst, Illinois, on August 25. Jennifer's former long-term boyfriend, Stacey Gates, also known as "Bubba," testified that he was employed as a teacher in Peoria, Illinois, and he worked that day.

In closing argument, the State maintained that the evidence clearly established petitioner's motive and opportunity to commit the offense. According to the State, petitioner drove to Normal after he left the bank at 10:11 A.M., arriving at around noon. When he walked into Jennifer's apartment, he saw Swaine's property. At that point, he "snapped" and committed the murder. Petitioner left the apartment by 12:15 P.M. and drove back to Rockford, arriving home around 2:10 P.M. The State argued that petitioner's guilt was also shown by his immediate focus on August 25 when asked to account for his time that week.

The State further argued that petitioner did not make the telephone calls from the Beaman residence at 10:37 and 10:39 A.M. According to the State, Carol Beaman could have driven home in between running errands. The State concluded that the circumstantial evidence "weaves around this defendant a web . . . that's so powerful that you can rest assured that you have the right person here."

Defense counsel responded that the evidence against petitioner was almost non-existent, and the State had improperly focused its investigation on him to the exclusion of other potential suspects. Defense counsel explained that petitioner began with the evening of August 25 in accounting for the week because certain events stood out in his memory that day, including a church event, his music rehearsal, and a party. The rest of the week was, for the most part, routine. Counsel argued that the evidence against Swaine was as strong as the evidence presented against petitioner. . . .

In rebuttal, the prosecutor defended the State's investigation. He argued, "Alibis, we proved up everybody else's, but—we just jumped right in there and cleared all these other people, and we just didn't do the same for him." The prosecutor further argued, "Did we look at Mr. Swaine? You bet we did. Did we look at Bubba? You bet we did. Did we look at a lot of people and interview a lot of witnesses? You bet we did. And guess who sits in the courtroom . . . with the gap in his alibi still unclosed even after all this?" . . .

The jury found petitioner guilty of first degree murder and the trial court sentenced him to 50 years' imprisonment. The appellate court affirmed the trial court's judgment. . . . Petitioner then filed a postconviction petition [alleging that] the State violated his constitutional right to due process of law under *Brady* by failing to disclose material information supporting John Doe's viability as a suspect. . . .

At the evidentiary hearing, retired Normal Police Lieutenant Tony Daniels testified about the John Doe evidence. Doe and Jennifer had previously been involved in a romantic relationship. He lived in Bloomington, approximately 1.5 miles from Jennifer's apartment. Daniels testified that it would take Doe four to six minutes to drive to Jennifer's apartment and back. Doe told police officers that he and Jennifer were about to renew their relationship before her death. Jennifer and Michael Swaine came to his apartment a few days before the murder. Doe stated that he had supplied Jennifer with marijuana and other drugs, and she owed him money.

Daniels interviewed Doe twice in early September 1993 and found him to be "somewhat evasive" and "very nervous." In his first interview, Doe stated that he went out of town on August 24, the day before the murder. In the second interview a few days later, Doe informed Daniels that he did not leave Bloomington until 4 P.M. on August 25. He was in his apartment until 4 P.M. that day. Doe's girlfriend stated that she was with him from just after 1 P.M. until 4 P.M. that day. Doe did not provide any verification of his location before his girlfriend arrived around 1 P.M.

Daniels explained that he asked Doe to take a polygraph examination, but the examiner was unable to start the test because Doe failed to follow his directions. The polygraph examiner testified that the failure to follow the instructions could have been an intentional avoidance tactic. He further testified that Doe was being examined as a suspect in the murder. Daniels asked Doe to try again. Doe initially agreed, but the polygraph examination never occurred due to Doe's lack of cooperation.

Daniels further testified that Doe was charged with domestic battery and possession of marijuana with intent to deliver prior to petitioner's trial. A witness to the domestic battery indicated that Doe had his girlfriend on the floor and was elbowing her in the chest. Doe's girlfriend stated that Doe had physically abused her on numerous previous occasions. Additionally, she stated that Doe was using steroids, causing him to act erratically. Daniels testified that he considered Doe a viable suspect in the murder at the time of petitioner's trial, and he believed that Doe remained a viable suspect. . . .

Following the evidentiary hearing, the circuit court concluded that . . . petitioner's *Brady* claim failed because the undisclosed information on Doe's polygraph and his domestic battery charge was inadmissible at trial. Additionally, the court found that the evidence pointing to Doe as a viable suspect was remote and speculative. The court found that petitioner had "not provided enough evidence that if presented at the [motion *in limine* hearing], the trial court would have allowed the defense to present John Doe I as a suspect." . . .

II. ANALYSIS

. . . We first address petitioner's claim under Brady v. Maryland that the State violated his right to due process by failing to disclose material information on a viable alternative suspect. Petitioner argues that the State's evidence based on his motive and opportunity to commit the offense was entirely circumstantial. He contends there is a reasonable probability that the jury would have acquitted him had it known there was another suspect with motive and opportunity to commit the murder. The State responds that the withheld evidence was not favorable to petitioner's defense or material to his guilt or punishment. Accordingly, the State argues petitioner's right to due process was not violated by the failure to disclose the evidence. . . .

In *Brady*, the Supreme Court held that the prosecution violates an accused's constitutional right to due process of law by failing to disclose evidence favorable to the accused and material to guilt or punishment. This rule encompasses evidence known to police investigators, but not to the prosecutor. To comply with *Brady*, the prosecutor has a duty to learn of favorable evidence known to other government actors, including the police. The Supreme Court has, therefore, noted "the special role played by the American prosecutor in the search for truth in criminal trials." The prosecutor's interest in a criminal prosecution "is not that it shall win a case, but that justice shall be done."

A *Brady* claim requires a showing that: (1) the undisclosed evidence is favorable to the accused because it is either exculpatory or impeaching; (2) the evidence was suppressed by the State either willfully or inadvertently; and (3) the accused was prejudiced because the evidence is material to guilt or punishment. Evidence is material if there is a reasonable probability that the result of the proceeding would have been different had the evidence been disclosed. To establish materiality, an accused must show "the favorable evidence could reasonably be taken to put the whole case in such a different light as to undermine confidence in the verdict."

In making the materiality determination, courts must consider the cumulative effect of all the suppressed evidence rather than considering each item of evidence individually. After a reviewing court has found a *Brady* violation, the constitutional error cannot be found harmless.

Here, the undisclosed evidence consists of four points: (1) John Doe failed to complete the polygraph examination; (2) Doe was charged with domestic battery and possession of marijuana with intent to deliver prior to petitioner's trial; (3) Doe had physically abused his girlfriend on numerous prior occasions; and (4) Doe's use of steroids had caused him to act erratically. Petitioner's attorney testified at the evidentiary hearing that he did not receive this evidence. In its brief to this court, the State does not dispute that it knew of the evidence and failed to disclose it. In fact, the State refers to the evidence as being "withheld." Accordingly, petitioner has established that the evidence was suppressed by the State.

The State, however, argues that the evidence was not favorable to petitioner or material to his guilt or punishment. Initially, we note that the circuit court held the State did not violate *Brady* by failing to disclose the polygraph evidence and the domestic battery charge because that evidence would not have been admissible at trial. In addressing whether the undisclosed evidence was favorable to petitioner, however, we need not decide whether each of the individual items of undisclosed evidence would have been admissible at trial. In this case, petitioner's essential claim is that he could have used the undisclosed evidence, along with the disclosed evidence tending to show Doe's possible involvement in the offense, to present Doe as an alternative suspect. Thus, even if some of the undisclosed evidence would have been inadmissible at trial, it still may have been favorable to petitioner in gaining admission of critical alternative suspect evidence. . . .

An accused in a criminal case may offer evidence tending to show that someone else committed the charged offense. Evidence of an alternative suspect should be excluded as irrelevant, however, if it is too remote or speculative. Generally, evidence is relevant if it tends to make the existence of any fact in consequence more or less probable than it would be without the evidence.

The undisclosed evidence is clearly favorable to petitioner in establishing Doe as an alternative suspect. First, the circumstances of the polygraph examination indicate that Doe intentionally avoided the test. He did not comply with the polygraph examiner's instructions during the first attempt and failed to cooperate in scheduling a second attempt. Moreover, the polygraph examiner testified that the police had identified Doe as a suspect in the murder. . . .

The evidence that Doe was charged with domestic battery and had physically abused his girlfriend on many prior occasions also could have been used by petitioner at a pretrial hearing to establish Doe as a viable suspect. That evidence is relevant to Doe's likelihood to commit a violent act against his girlfriend. The evidence that Doe had physically abused his girlfriend on numerous occasions, together with the evidence that he was in the process of renewing his romantic relationship with Jennifer prior to her death, provided additional support of Doe as a viable suspect. Further, the undisclosed evidence of Doe's steroid abuse may have explained his violent outbursts toward his girlfriend and supported an inference of a tendency to act violently toward others.

Finally, the undisclosed evidence that Doe had been charged with possession of marijuana with intent to deliver could have been used by petitioner as part of Doe's motive to commit the murder. That evidence tends to establish Doe as a drug dealer and, with evidence of Jennifer owing Doe money for drugs, it could have been offered to support a motive to commit the murder.

In analyzing whether the undisclosed evidence is favorable to petitioner, we also note that the Supreme Court recently examined the constitutionality of a rule of evidence restricting a criminal defendant from introducing proof of "third-party guilt" in cases where the prosecution offered forensic evidence that, if believed, strongly supported a guilty verdict. Holmes v. South Carolina, 547 U.S. 319 (2006). In finding the rule of evidence unconstitutional, the Court concluded that "by evaluating the strength of only one party's evidence, no logical conclusion can be reached regarding the strength of contrary evidence offered by the other side to rebut or cast doubt." This observation is applicable to whether the undisclosed evidence here is favorable and material. The impact or strength of the undisclosed evidence can only be determined by also viewing the strength of the evidence presented against petitioner.

Here, the State summarizes its evidence against petitioner as resting "on more than mere opportunity: petitioner's fingerprints were on the murder weapon; petitioner demonstrated knowledge of when Jennifer was murdered; and petitioner had every reason to kill Jennifer when he arrived at her apartment and saw, for the first time, definitive proof that Jennifer and Swaine had been sleeping together." In our view, the State's evidence against petitioner was not particularly strong. The State essentially presented evidence of motive, evidence of opportunity that was strongly disputed by petitioner, inferences from petitioner's statements to police officers that he knew the date of the murder, and fingerprints on the clock radio that were explained by petitioner's relationship with Jennifer and made less important by the State's concession that it would not have been necessary to touch the clock radio in committing the murder. This evidence is tenuous and supports admission by petitioner of the similarly probative alternative suspect evidence on Doe. We conclude that the evidence withheld by the State is favorable to petitioner because it supports Doe's viability as an alternative suspect. . . .

Having found that the withheld evidence is favorable to petitioner, we must next determine whether it is material. As noted, evidence is material if there is a reasonable probability that the result would have been different had it been disclosed. An accused must show "the favorable evidence could reasonably be taken to put the whole case in such a different light as to undermine confidence in the verdict." Again, the impact of the alternative-suspect evidence on the verdict cannot be determined without viewing the strength of the evidence presented by petitioner as well as the evidence presented by the State.

The State's evidence against petitioner showed that he had a motive to commit the murder based on his jealousy. Additionally, the State established that petitioner had been violent toward objects, but not people, on several occasions during his involvement with Jennifer. The evidence of petitioner's opportunity to commit the offense was strongly disputed. . . . The State's timeline depended on petitioner driving 10 miles per hour over the speed limit to Normal and back to Rockford. Additionally, the timeline required petitioner to commit the offense and stage the crime scene in an extremely quick and efficient manner. . . .

The State's other evidence against petitioner was based on inferences from his statements to police officers and his fingerprints on the clock radio. That evidence, however, was explained by petitioner. Petitioner explained that he began with August 25 in accounting for his time the week of the murder because he had events that day that stood out in his memory. The rest of the week was routine. . . .

We also note that the State's argument relied upon the assertion that all other potential suspects had been eliminated from consideration. The prosecutor informed the jury that the State had "proved up everybody else's" alibi and petitioner was the one "who sits in the courtroom . . . with the gap in his alibi still unclosed." The prosecution presented testimony to establish the alibis of two named suspects, Swaine and Gates. The prosecution's argument that all other potential suspects had been eliminated from consideration was a key part of the State's case given the tenuous circumstantial evidence of petitioner's guilt. . . .

We conclude that there is a reasonable probability that the result of the trial would have been different if petitioner had presented the evidence establishing Doe as an alternative suspect. We cannot have confidence in the verdict finding petitioner guilty of this crime given the tenuous nature of the circumstantial evidence against him, along with the nondisclosure of critical evidence that would have countered the State's argument that all other potential suspects had been eliminated from consideration. Accordingly, we conclude that the State's suppression of the withheld evidence violated petitioner's constitutional right to due process under *Brady*. Based on this record, the circuit court's dismissal of petitioner's *Brady* claim was manifest error.

A *Brady* violation cannot be found harmless. Petitioner's conviction must, therefore, be reversed and the matter remanded for further proceedings. . . .

■ UTAH CRIMINAL PROCEDURE RULE 16

(a) Except as otherwise provided, the prosecutor shall disclose to the defense upon request the following material or information of which he has knowledge: . . . (4) evidence known to the prosecutor that tends to negate the guilt of the accused, mitigate the guilt of the defendant, or mitigate the degree of the offense for reduced punishment. . . .

(b) The prosecutor shall make all disclosures as soon as practicable following the filing of charges and before the defendant is required to plead. The prosecutor has a continuing duty to make disclosure.

Notes

1. *Disclosure of evidence favorable to the accused: majority position.* The Supreme Court decision in Brady v. Maryland, 373 U.S. 83 (1963), remains central to discovery practice in American criminal justice. Because the disclosure duty described in *Brady* is a requirement of federal due process, it applies in every criminal case unless the defendant expressly waives the disclosure. As illustrated by the Utah rules reprinted above, over 40 states have passed rules or statutes codifying the *Brady* disclosure requirement, although many of these rules and statutes (unlike the constitutional requirement) only take effect after a request from the defense. See Ohio R. Crim. P. 16(A) (disclosure upon defendant's request).

Defendants often win *Brady* claims that are appealed in the state courts, at least when those claims are the focus of the appeal (as opposed to one in a laundry list of claims, especially in capital cases). See, e.g., State v. Huggins, 788 So. 2d 238 (Fla. 2001) (prosecutors failed to turn over a statement by a minor witness that a prosecution witness might herself have been seen driving the victim's vehicle). But *Brady* claims appear to be appealed infrequently, so the relative success of defendants in this context says little if anything about discovery practices in the mine run of cases.

2. *Exculpatory evidence in government hands.* The defendant who seeks dismissal of charges because of a *Brady* violation need not show bad faith by the prosecutor. The prosecutor does not even have to know about the evidence that must be disclosed: Evidence in the hands of government agents (such as criminal investigators) who regularly report to the prosecutor form the basis for a *Brady* violation because the prosecutor has a duty to inquire about such information. See Kyles v. Whitley, 514 U.S. 419 (1995); Banks v. Dretke, 540 U.S. 668 (2004) (reiterating the affirmative duty on prosecutors to disclose *Brady* material and observing that a rule "declaring 'prosecutor may hide, defendant must seek,' is not tenable").

3. *Impeachment as a form of "favorable" evidence.* The *Brady* disclosure duty reaches both exculpatory evidence and evidence that the defense might use to impeach a prosecution witness. While the potential impeachment evidence might take many forms, much litigation centers on disclosure of any rewards that the prosecution offers to its witnesses. See Smith v. Cain, 565 U.S. 73 (2012) (statements by the eyewitness contradicting his testimony was material for *Brady* purposes because testimony was the only evidence linking defendant to the crime, and the eyewitness's undisclosed statements contradicted his testimony).

In addition to any *Brady* disclosures of impeachment evidence to defense counsel, the prosecution must disclose to the *jury* the fact that its witness expects to receive lenient treatment from the government as a result of cooperating. Attorneys who practice in this arena refer to such evidence as *Giglio* material, named for Giglio v. United States, 405 U.S. 150 (1972). In that case, the Court declared that reversal is required when a witness falsely denies any arrangement for lenient treatment, even though the promise of leniency came from another prosecutor and was unknown to the government attorney at trial. The test for materiality under *Giglio* is whether there is a "reasonable likelihood" that the false evidence may have affected the judgment of the jury. Even if the prosecution witness does not lie at trial about any promise of leniency, the existence of such deals with witnesses typically qualifies as *Brady* material. See United States v. Bagley, 473 U.S. 667 (1985) (evidence of government agreement to pay money to witnesses commensurate with the information they furnished did qualify as impeachment evidence, but it did not satisfy materiality requirement).

4. *Materiality of exculpatory evidence.* The major limit on the *Brady* disclosure duty is the requirement that the undisclosed evidence be "material" to the defense. Under federal law, all *Brady* violations share a uniform materiality standard: The defendant must show a "reasonable probability" that the verdict would have been different if the prosecution had disclosed the exculpatory evidence. It does not affect the standard one way or the other if the defendant requests the disclosure.

State courts have split over the proper materiality standard. Most have adopted the federal "uniform" standard, but a strong minority grant defendants a more favorable materiality standard in cases where the defense makes specific requests for the information. People v. Vilardi, 555 N.E.2d 915 (N.Y. 1990). Does a specific request for discovery from the defense change the legitimate expectations of both parties? Note also that many state rules of criminal procedure (like the Utah rule reprinted above), include something similar to the *Brady* disclosure duty without including any materiality requirement; most of these rules, however, depend on a request from the defense.

5. Brady *and plea bargaining.* While *Brady* information might affect the outcome at trial, it could also affect the negotiating strength of the defendant during plea bargaining. Given the dominance of guilty pleas and plea bargaining in American criminal justice, it is critical to know whether a defendant can challenge the validity of a guilty plea if she discovers later that the prosecutor failed to disclose *Brady* material during the negotiations. A few states have statutes or rules that explicitly link the prosecutor's disclosure obligation to a defendant's not-guilty plea at arraignment. See N.H. R. Crim. P. 12(b) (prosecutor to disclose exculpatory material within 45 days from a not-guilty plea). The U.S. Supreme Court addressed one aspect of this question in United States v. Ruiz, 536 U.S. 622 (2002), stating that "the Constitution does not require the Government to disclose material impeachment evidence prior to entering a plea agreement with a criminal defendant." Ruiz was challenging a provision in a proposed plea agreement that required her to waive certain *Brady* rights as part of the arrangement, but the Court's statement appears broad enough to cover guilty pleas reached without any explicit waiver of *Brady* rights in a plea agreement. Note that the ruling applies to impeachment material, but it is not clear whether it extends to exculpatory material.

State courts are split over whether *Brady* violations by the prosecution invalidate a defendant's guilty plea. The web extension for this chapter, at *http://www.crimpro. com/extension/ch15*, explores the range of state court rulings on this critical topic. See State v. Harris, 680 N.W.2d 737, 741 (Wis. 2004) (imposes disclosure at the guilty plea stage as a matter of state law).

6. *Preservation of evidence.* It is sometimes said that the duty to disclose evidence would be meaningless if the prosecutor were free to destroy evidence. Is this true? The Supreme Court has addressed the government's obligation, under the due

process clause, to preserve some types of evidence. In Arizona v. Youngblood, 488 U.S. 51 (1988), the police failed to preserve semen samples from the victim's body and clothing. The defendant, accused of child molestation and sexual assault, argued that he could have performed tests on the samples that might have established his defense of mistaken identity. However, the Supreme Court noted that the state did not attempt to use the materials in its own case in chief, and it limited the government's duty to preserve evidence as follows:

> [Requiring] a defendant to show bad faith on the part of the police both limits the extent of the police's obligation to preserve evidence to reasonable bounds and confines it to that class of cases where the interests of justice most clearly require it, i.e., those cases in which the police themselves by their conduct indicate that the evidence could form a basis for exonerating the defendant. We therefore hold that unless a criminal defendant can show bad faith on the part of the police, failure to preserve potentially useful evidence does not constitute a denial of due process of law.

Years later, Youngblood was found to be innocent on the basis of other DNA evidence, and was released two days before completing his original sentence. See also Illinois v. Fisher, 540 U.S. 544 (2004) (holding that if destroyed evidence was only "potentially useful" and not factually exculpatory, then the defendant must show that the state acted in bad faith in destroying the evidence).

Once again, there is dissension among state courts on an important aspect of this discovery issue. Most states directly addressing the question have accepted the holding in *Youngblood*. About a dozen states, however, have declared that bad faith is not a necessary part of the defendant's showing because the destruction of evidence often reflects some negligence by the government and because the evidence could sometimes be crucial to the defense. See State v. Tiedemann, 162 P.3d 1106 (Utah 2007) (state due process claim does not require showing of bad faith by government officials when they destroy evidence that is potentially useful to defense); Cynthia E. Jones, The Right Remedy for the Wrongly Convicted: Judicial Sanctions for Destruction of DNA Evidence, 77 Fordham L. Rev. 2893 (2009). Why do state courts seem so willing to part ways with the Supreme Court on constitutional questions involving discovery? Do the state courts take more responsibility for their own litigation management, in light of the state's needs and practices?

The preservation of evidence has made a critical difference in more cases lately as DNA testing procedures become more widely available. These tests make it possible to reevaluate the convictions of some defendants in cases (such as rape and murder cases) where blood or other biological material from the perpetrator is available at the crime scene or from the victim. The incentive to test this material and to match it to the convicted defendant is very strong in capital cases, and some capital defendants have been released on the basis of DNA test information.

7. *The extent of disclosure violations.* How often do prosecutors and defense attorneys fail to disclose the information that they should to the opposing party? Periodic newspaper reports on "prosecutorial misconduct" focus on discovery violations; they suggest (inconclusively) that discovery violations by prosecutors occur regularly. Recent examples appear on the web extension for this chapter at *http://www. crimpro.com/extension/ch15*, exploring the range of state court rulings on this critical topic. How would you measure in a reliable way whether prosecutors are now

committing more discovery violations than in the past? If such a trend were proven, could it be traced to the number of new prosecutors hired in a given time period?

8. *Ethics remedies for prosecutorial disclosure violations.* As we have seen, courts might reverse criminal convictions if the prosecutor fails to disclose material information when required by law. Will the state bar authorities also sanction prosecutors who violate their legal obligations to disclose information, even when the evidence is not material? Examples of disciplinary proceedings against prosecutors for discovery violations do get reported from time to time. For example, disciplinary proceedings in 2007 served as a remedy for multiple violations of the discovery rules during criminal proceedings against several members of the Duke University lacrosse team members. Prosecutor Mike Nifong made inflammatory remarks to the press about the three indicted players and their teammates, withheld key DNA evidence, and lied to the court, all in violation of the North Carolina professional responsibility rules. The state bar revoked Nifong's license to practice law. See North Carolina State Bar v. Nifong, N.C. State Bar Disciplinary Hearing Commission, No. 06 DHC 35, June 16, 2007. However, state bar authorities discipline criminal prosecutors less often than they discipline private attorneys. See Fred C. Zacharias, The Professional Discipline of Prosecutors, 79 N.C. L. Rev. 721 (2001). What might explain the relatively infrequent disciplinary actions against criminal prosecutors? See Innocence Project, Prosecutorial Oversight: A National Dialogue in the Wake of *Connick v. Thompson* 14-15 (2016) (discussing why prosecutorial misconduct is underreported and still relatively rarely punished by state bar disciplinary authorities); see also Van de Kamp v. Goldstein, 555 U.S. 335 (2009) (prosecutors who fail to properly train and supervise subordinates in complying with discovery and disclosure obligations regarding impeachment material about confidential informers are protected from civil rights actions by absolute immunity).

9. *Monetary remedies for discovery violations.* However clear-cut the *Brady* violation may be, monetary damages for wronged defendants are extremely limited under the federal civil rights statute, 42 U.S.C. §1983. In Connick v. Thompson, 563 U.S. 51 (2011), the Supreme Court overturned a jury verdict for $14 million against the district attorney of Orleans Parish, Harry Connick. The plaintiff, John Thompson, was wrongly convicted of robbery and capital murder after prosecutors knowingly failed to disclose to defense attorneys the existence of a blood test confirming the innocence of the defendant, as well as tape recordings that impeached the credibility of key prosecution witnesses. He spent 18 years in prison (and 14 years on death row) before his investigator discovered the evidence and a reviewing court vacated his conviction. The district attorney's office retried Thompson for the murder despite the exculpatory evidence, but the jury acquitted him.

Recovery in tort against the individual prosecutors was impossible because of absolute prosecutorial immunity. According to the Supreme Court, recovery against the district attorney's office was also barred under the federal statute because there was no adequate proof that the *Brady* violation resulted from a "policy or custom" of the office. A failure by the office supervisors to train prosecutors about their discovery obligations would amount to a section 1983 violation only if that failure reflected a "deliberate indifference" to the violation of defendants' rights. The court characterized the failure of multiple prosecutors over many years to disclose the evidence in the case as a "single violation," and therefore not enough to prove the necessary pattern or practice. Although other prosecutors in the office had committed *Brady* violations during the 10 years prior to Thompson's trial (leading to four reversals of convictions in the appellate courts), Justice Thomas declared that those other violations were different in character and unrelated to the violation in Thompson's case. The *Brady* violations in the other cases, the Court explained, did not involve the failure to disclose physical evidence or crime lab reports.

Based on this holding, it appears that monetary damages under section 1983 will be available only in cases when plaintiffs can prove multiple closely related *Brady* violations in a single office over a short period of time. Given the difficulty of uncovering even a single *Brady* violation, such damages will prove to be a practical impossibility. Will any civil plaintiff in any case ever meet this standard, or ever even obtain discovery on the question? Cf. United States v. Armstrong, 517 U.S. 456 (1996) (establishing an extremely demanding standard for obtaining discovery on selective prosecution claims).

Problem 15-1. Preserving Evidence

Officers from the Bluefield Police Department began hearing rumors that someone had been shot at the Charlton home. Two detectives visited the home. Upon observing a stained couch, the detectives took samples from it and from the carpet surrounding it. They also discovered a bullet hole in it. Detective Ted Jones inserted a writing pen into the bullet hole to determine the trajectory of the bullet. He extracted a badly deformed bullet as well as some hair and bone fragments. The officers confiscated the couch and stored it at the police department.

Because the couch gave off an unpleasant odor and was both a fire and health hazard, the police (with the consent of the prosecutor's office) disposed of it at the county landfill. Before doing so, they did not measure either the proportions of the couch, the location of the bullet hole in the couch, or the trajectory of the bullet. Neither did they photograph the couch or the bullet hole.

Kenji Osakalumi was eventually arrested for killing Kevin Fleetwood on the couch that had been found in the Charlton home. He claimed that Fleetwood had shot himself, and that he and others buried him nearby after the fact. The only evidence that Fleetwood had been murdered was the trial testimony of Dr. Irvin Sopher, medical examiner for the state of West Virginia. Dr. Sopher testified that approximately 9 months after Fleetwood's death (but approximately 14 months before his body was found), Detective Ted Jones delivered to him the bullet, blood samples, and bone fragments. In addition, Detective Jones drew for Dr. Sopher a diagram of the couch, along with the location of the bullet hole and the position of the bullet when officers found it.

Although Jones's diagram of the couch was lost, Dr. Sopher drew Detective Jones's couch diagram from memory at trial. Dr. Sopher testified that based upon examination of the skull and the purported right-to-left, straight-line trajectory of the bullet through the couch, the manner of Fleetwood's death was homicide. Dr. Sopher testified that he came to this conclusion when he lined up the trajectory of the bullet through the skull with the right-to-left path of the bullet through the couch, as drawn by Detective Jones. Dr. Sopher determined that Fleetwood was held down on the couch and was shot through the head, with the bullet traveling in a straight line.

The jury convicted Osakalumi of first-degree murder. On appeal he claims that the trial court erred when it allowed Dr. Sopher to testify based on the condition of the couch. As the appellate court judge, how do you rule? Compare State v. Osakalumi, 461 S.E.2d 504 (W. Va. 1995).

■ AMERICAN BAR ASSOCIATION, MODEL RULES OF PROFESSIONAL CONDUCT

Rule 3.8, Special Responsibilities of a Prosecutor

The prosecutor in a criminal case shall: . . .

(d) make timely disclosure to the defense of all evidence or information known to the prosecutor that tends to negate the guilt of the accused or mitigates the offense, and, in connection with sentencing, disclose to the defense and to the tribunal all unprivileged mitigating information known to the prosecutor, except when the prosecutor is relieved of this responsibility by a protective order of the tribunal; . . .

(g) When a prosecutor knows of new, credible and material evidence creating a reasonable likelihood that a convicted defendant did not commit an offense of which the defendant was convicted, the prosecutor shall:

(1) promptly disclose that evidence to an appropriate court or authority, and

(2) if the conviction was obtained in the prosecutor's jurisdiction,

(i) promptly disclose that evidence to the defendant unless a court authorizes delay, and

(ii) undertake further investigation, or make reasonable efforts to cause an investigation, to determine whether the defendant was convicted of an offense that the defendant did not commit.

(h) When a prosecutor knows of clear and convincing evidence establishing that a defendant in the prosecutor's jurisdiction was convicted of an offense that the defendant did not commit, the prosecutor shall seek to remedy the conviction.

* * *

In 2008, U.S. Senator Ted Stevens was prosecuted by the Department of Justice for taking unfair advantage of his position; the government alleged that he had allowed a contractor to work on his home and then did not pay full value for the construction work. During the course of the prosecution, the government failed to turn over evidence the FBI had received from the contractor about the actual value of the work and the payments made by Senator Stevens; it also relied upon a witness whose background suggested serious credibility problems. Senator Stevens's conviction was ultimately overturned on *Brady* grounds. Following this result, the Department of Justice sought to re-educate its prosecutors about their disclosure obligations, and to emphasize the importance of fair play in federal prosecutions by outlining a set of steps that every prosecutor must take to avoid lapses of the sort that plagued the Stevens prosecution.

■ U.S. DEPARTMENT OF JUSTICE, MEMORANDUM FOR DEPARTMENT PROSECUTORS

January 4, 2010

FROM: David W. Ogden, Deputy Attorney General

SUBJECT: Guidance for Prosecutors Regarding Criminal Discovery

[It] is important for prosecutors to consider thoroughly how to meet their discovery obligations in each case. Toward that end, the Department has adopted the guidance for prosecutors regarding criminal discovery set forth below. . . . [This memorandum] provides prospective guidance only and is not intended to have the force of law or to create or confer any rights, privileges, or benefits. . . .

Step 1: Gathering and Reviewing Discoverable Information
A. Where to look — The Prosecution Team

Department policy states: "It is the obligation of federal prosecutors, in preparing for trial, to seek all exculpatory and impeachment information from all members of the prosecution team. Members of the prosecution team include federal, state, and local law enforcement officers and other government officials participating in the investigation and prosecution of the criminal case against the defendant." USAM §9-5.001. . . .

Many cases arise out of investigations conducted by multi-agency task forces or otherwise involving state law enforcement agencies. In such cases, prosecutors should consider (1) whether state or local agents are working on behalf of the prosecutor or are under the prosecutor's control; (2) the extent to which state and federal governments are part of a team, are participating in a joint investigation, or are sharing resources; and (3) whether the prosecutor has ready access to the evidence. Courts will generally evaluate the role of a state or local law enforcement agency on a case-by-case basis. . . .

Prosecutors are encouraged to err on the side of inclusiveness when identifying the members of the prosecution team for discovery purposes. Carefully considered efforts to locate discoverable information are more likely to avoid future litigation over *Brady* and *Giglio* issues and avoid surprises at trial. . . .

B. What to Review

To ensure that all discovery is disclosed on a timely basis, generally all potentially discoverable material within the custody or control of the prosecution team should be reviewed. The review process should cover the following areas:

1. *The Investigative Agency's Files:* With respect to Department of Justice law enforcement agencies, with limited exceptions, the prosecutor should be granted access to the substantive case file and any other file or document the prosecutor has reason to believe may contain discoverable information related to the matter being prosecuted. Therefore, the prosecutor can personally review the file or documents or may choose to request production of potentially discoverable materials from the case agents. With respect to outside agencies, the prosecutor should request access to files and/or production of all potentially discoverable material. ... Prosecutors should also discuss with the investigative agency whether files from other investigations or non-investigative files such as confidential source files might contain discoverable information. . . .

2. *Confidential Informant (CI)/Witness (CW)/Human Source (CHS)/Source (CS) Files:* The credibility of cooperating witnesses or informants will always be at issue if they testify during a trial. Therefore, prosecutors are entitled to access to the agency file for each testifying CI, CW, CHS, or CS. Those files should be reviewed for discoverable information and copies made of relevant portions for discovery purposes. The entire informant/source file, not just the portion relating to the current case, including all proffer, immunity and other agreements, validation assessments, payment information, and other potential witness impeachment information should be included within this review. . . .

Prosecutors should take steps to protect the non-discoverable, sensitive information found within a CI, CW, CHS, or CS file. . . .

3. *Evidence and Information Gathered During the Investigation:* Generally, all evidence and information gathered during the investigation should be reviewed, including anything obtained during searches or via subpoenas, etc. . . .

4. *Substantive Case-Related Communications:* "Substantive" case-related communications may contain discoverable information. Those communications that contain discoverable information should be maintained in the case file or otherwise preserved in a manner that associates them with the case or investigation. "Substantive" case-related communications are most likely to occur (1) among prosecutors and/or agents, (2) between prosecutors and/or agents and witnesses and/or victims, and (3) between victim-witness coordinators and witnesses and/or victims. . . . Prosecutors should also remember that with few exceptions (*see, e.g.,* Fed. R. Crim. P. 16(a)(1)(B)(ii)), the format of the information does not determine whether it is discoverable. For example, material exculpatory information that the prosecutor receives during a conversation with an agent or a witness is no less discoverable than if that same information were contained in an email. . . .

5. *Potential* Giglio *Information Relating to Non-Law Enforcement Witnesses:* . . . All potential *Giglio* information known by or in the possession of the prosecution team relating to non-law enforcement witnesses should be gathered and reviewed. That information includes, but is not limited to:

- Prior inconsistent statements . . .
- Statements or reports reflecting witness statement variations . . .
- Benefits provided to witnesses, including dropped or reduced charges, immunity, expectations of downward departures or motions for reduction of sentence, assistance in a state or local criminal proceeding, . . . stays of deportation or other immigration status considerations, . . . monetary benefits, non-prosecution agreements, letters to other law enforcement officials (*e.g.* state prosecutors, parole boards) setting forth the extent of a witness's assistance or making substantive recommendations on the witness's behalf, relocation assistance, [or] benefits to culpable or at risk third-parties
- Other known conditions that could affect the witness's bias such as . . . animosity toward defendant, animosity toward a group of which the defendant is a member or with which the defendant is affiliated, relationship with victim, [or] known but uncharged criminal conduct . . .
- Prior convictions under Fed. R. Evid. 609
- Known substance abuse or mental health issues or other issues that could affect the witness's ability to perceive and recall events

6. *Information Obtained in Witness Interviews:* Although not required by law, generally speaking, witness interviews should be memorialized by the agent. Agent and prosecutor notes and original recordings should be preserved, and prosecutors should confirm with agents that substantive interviews should be memorialized. . . .

a. *Witness Statement Variations and the Duty to Disclose:* Some witnesses' statements will vary during the course of an interview or investigation. For example, they may initially deny involvement in criminal activity, and the information they provide may broaden or change considerably over the course of time, especially if there are a series of debriefings that occur over several days or weeks. Material variances in a witness's statements should be memorialized, even if they are within the same interview, and they should be provided to the defense as *Giglio* information.

b. *Trial Preparation Meetings with Witnesses:* Trial preparation meetings with witnesses generally need not be memorialized. However, prosecutors should be particularly attuned to new or inconsistent information disclosed by the witness during a pre-trial witness preparation session. New information that is exculpatory or impeachment information should be disclosed. . . .

c. *Agent Notes:* Agent notes should be reviewed if there is a reason to believe that the notes are materially different from the memorandum, if a written memorandum was not prepared, if the precise words used by the witness are significant, or if the witness disputes the agent's account of the interview. . . .

STEP 2: CONDUCTING THE REVIEW

. . . It would be preferable if prosecutors could review the information themselves in every case, but such review is not always feasible or necessary. The prosecutor is ultimately responsible for compliance with discovery obligations. Accordingly, the prosecutor should develop a process for review of pertinent information to ensure that discoverable information is identified. . . . In cases involving voluminous evidence obtained from third parties, prosecutors should consider providing defense access to the voluminous documents to avoid the possibility that a well-intentioned review process nonetheless fails to identify material discoverable evidence. . . .

STEP 3: MAKING THE DISCLOSURES

[Prosecutors are] encouraged to provide discovery broader and more comprehensive than the discovery obligations. If a prosecutor chooses this course, the defense should be advised that the prosecutor is electing to produce discovery beyond what is required under the circumstances of the case but is not committing to any discovery obligation beyond the discovery obligations. . . .

A. *Considerations Regarding the Scope and Timing of the Disclosures:* Providing broad and early discovery often promotes the truth-seeking mission of the Department and fosters a speedy resolution of many cases. It also provides a margin of error in case the prosecutor's good faith determination of the scope of appropriate discovery is in error. . . . But when considering providing discovery beyond that required by the discovery obligations or providing discovery sooner than required, prosecutors should always consider any appropriate countervailing concerns in the particular case, including, but not limited to: protecting victims and witnesses from harassment or intimidation; protecting the privacy interests of witnesses; protecting privileged information; protecting the integrity of ongoing investigations; protecting the trial from efforts at obstruction; protecting national security interests; investigative agency concerns; enhancing the likelihood of receiving reciprocal discovery by defendants; any applicable legal or evidentiary privileges; and other strategic considerations that enhance the likelihood of achieving a just result in a particular case. . . .

Prosecutors should never describe the discovery being provided as "open file." Even if the prosecutor intends to provide expansive discovery, it is always possible that something will be inadvertently omitted from production and the prosecutor will then have unintentionally misrepresented the scope of materials provided. . . .

B. *Timing:* Exculpatory information, regardless of whether the information is memorialized, must be disclosed to the defendant reasonably promptly after discovery. Impeachment information, which depends on the prosecutor's decision on who is or may be called as a government witness, will typically be disclosed at a reasonable time before trial to allow the trial to proceed efficiently. [Witness] security, national security, or other issues may require that disclosures of impeachment information be made at a time and in a manner consistent with the policy embodied in the Jencks Act. . . .

Discovery obligations are continuing, and prosecutors should always be alert to developments occurring up to and through trial of the case that may impact their discovery obligations and require disclosure of information that was previously not disclosed. . . .

STEP 4: MAKING A RECORD

One of the most important steps in the discovery process is keeping good records regarding disclosures. Prosecutors should make a record of when and how information is disclosed or otherwise made available. . . .

CONCLUSION

Compliance with discovery obligations is important for a number of reasons. First and foremost, however, such compliance will facilitate a fair and just result in every case, which is the Department's singular goal in pursuing a criminal prosecution. . . . By evaluating discovery obligations pursuant to the methodical and thoughtful approach set forth in this guidance and taking advantage of available resources, prosecutors are more likely to meet their discovery obligations in every case and in so doing achieve a just and final result in every criminal prosecution. . . .

Notes

1. *Interaction among discovery obligations.* Consider the relationship between jurisdiction-wide and local court rules that define discovery obligations, constitutional obligations under *Brady* and *Giglio*, state ethics rules such as those embodied in Model Rule 3.8, and discovery policies internal to the prosecutor's office. Note, for instance, that the DOJ memorandum reprinted above adopts an expansive view of materiality—indeed, it does not even discuss a materiality limit on disclosure obligations. Meanwhile, Model Rule 3.8 covers more information than *Brady* but requires proof of a knowing violation to prove a violation of the rule. See ABA Formal Ethics Op. 09-454 (2009) ("Rule 3.8(d) is more demanding than the constitutional case law, in that it requires the disclosure of evidence or information favorable to the defense without regard to the anticipated impact of the evidence or information on a trial's outcome. . . . Further, this ethical duty of disclosure is not limited to admissible 'evidence,' . . . it also requires disclosure of favorable 'information.'"); In re Disciplinary Action Against Feland, 820 N.W.2d 672 (N.D. 2012). Some state courts, however, interpret Rule 3.8 to extend no further than the constitutional minimum of the *Brady* doctrine. See In re Riek, 834 N.W.2d 384 (Wis. 2013).

2. *Internal enforcement practices.* Prosecutors' offices sometimes evaluate the performance of their own attorneys and create systems to sanction wrongdoers and

to train less experienced attorneys to avoid discovery violations. One such mechanism is the Office for Professional Responsibility (OPR) within the U.S. Department of Justice. The office of the District Attorney of Los Angeles operates a "*Brady* Compliance Unit" that places certain police officers into a "*Brady* Alert System" for special monitoring after they fail to turn over evidence to the deputy district attorney working on the case. See *http://da.co.la.ca.us/pdf/bradyoperationsman.pdf.*

Suppose you are the senior career attorney in a prosecutor's office, and the chief prosecutor has asked you to take charge of the discovery practices in the office. What training programs would you create? Would you limit those training programs to new attorneys when they first join the office? Would you institute any supervisor review of discovery decisions of line prosecutors as their cases progress? See Kay L. Levine & Ronald F. Wright, Prosecutor Risk, Maturation, and Wrongful Conviction Practice, 42 L. & Soc. Inquiry 648 (2017). How about any auditing of discovery decisions after the conclusion of a case? Consider the resources and routines that the "discovery coordinators" mentioned in the DOJ memorandum might create for each U.S. Attorney's Office. See New Perspectives on *Brady* and Other Disclosure Obligations: Report of the Working Groups on Best Practices, 31 Cardozo L. Rev. 1961 (2010). Compliance with discovery obligations is a major quality-control topic for managers in prosecutors' offices. For a sampling of materials that supervisors develop and use to promote compliance, consult the web extension for this chapter at *http://www.crimpro.com/extension/ch15.*

2. Prosecution Disclosure of Inculpatory Information

A defense attorney with enough time, ingenuity, and resources could learn much about the government's evidence in a criminal case, even in the absence of *Brady* disclosures of material exculpatory information. Rules of procedure and statutes in most jurisdictions set out the obligations of the prosecution to disclose some of the incriminating evidence against the accused, but only after the defendant requests it. Local court rules sometimes supplement the statewide rules.

Despite these discovery rules, however, the defense attorney frequently knows much less than the prosecutor about the case at the time of plea bargaining or trial. Some of the functional limits on discovery are built into the rules themselves, and others stem from the defense attorney's limited time and resources.

The criminal discovery rules show remarkable variety from jurisdiction to jurisdiction. Federal Rule of Criminal Procedure 16 and the South Carolina rule reprinted below are typical of the more restrictive rules, which give the defendant access to only a handful of documents and tangible objects before trial. Most states go beyond these limited categories to allow defense discovery of a wider range of prosecution information. The ABA Standards for Criminal Justice have been an influential model for those states moving in the direction of wider discovery. The North Carolina statute reprinted below illustrates the broader scope of documents and other information that some states consider essential to the preparation of a defense.

Use the following problem as a setting for applying the North Carolina and South Carolina rules. Under each of these approaches to criminal discovery, what information gets exchanged? How will a plea negotiation or a trial progress if the defense lawyer does not have access to such information before trial? Can defense counsel develop the same information through different avenues?

Problem 15-2. Exchanging Words

Wayne Galvan and his friends got into a fight with Perry Sutton and his friends at a bar. During this fight Galvan drew a small handgun and fired two shots, the second of which killed Sutton. Galvan ran away after the shooting, but several of Sutton's friends knew Galvan by name and identified him to police officers. The officers later arrested Galvan and found the handgun.

You have been appointed to represent Galvan. Galvan tells you three things: (1) he had discussed the incident with two other detainees in the county jail, (2) he had only meant to frighten Sutton and his crew, and (3) he can give you the names and addresses of his friends who were there at the time of the shooting.

You call two of those friends first. You learn that one was interviewed within a week of the shooting by a police officer and an attorney from the district attorney's office, both of whom were taking notes. The second was interviewed by a police officer alone, and the officer did not take any notes. You learned from Galvan's friends the name of one of Sutton's friends who was present on the night of the shooting, but that person refuses to talk to you.

What sort of discovery will you request? Consider each of the following categories of potentially useful information:

- Any statements that Galvan made to police officers, prosecutors, his friends, or members of the rival group. Does it matter whether the statements have been recorded in a document?
- Any statements that members of the rival group made to police or prosecutors about what they saw or heard that night. Can you insist that the police tell you what they know about the background and reliability of these witnesses?
- Any statements that members of Galvan's group made to the police or prosecutors. Can the prosecutors gain discovery of these statements? Is there anything you can or should do to prepare these potential defense witnesses for an interview with the police or cross-examination at trial by the prosecutor?
- Any ballistics or other scientific tests performed on the gun, along with any medical examinations performed on Sutton.

Anticipate how the prosecutors might respond if the relevant discovery rules are similar to those in South Carolina. Then compare the government's response if the rules look like those in North Carolina.

■ SOUTH CAROLINA RULE OF CRIMINAL PROCEDURE 5(A)

(1) Information Subject to Disclosure.

(A) *Statement of Defendant.* Upon request by a defendant, the prosecution shall permit the defendant to inspect and copy or photograph: any relevant written or recorded statements made by the defendant, or copies thereof, within the possession, custody, or control of the prosecution, the existence of which is known, or by the exercise of due diligence may become known, to the attorney for the prosecution; the substance of any oral statement which the prosecution intends to offer in evidence at the trial made by the defendant whether before or after arrest in response to interrogation by any person then known to the defendant to be a prosecution agent.

(B) *Defendant's Prior Record.* Upon request of the defendant, the prosecution shall furnish to the defendant such copy of his prior criminal record, if any, as is within the possession, custody, or control of the prosecution, the existence of which is known, or by the exercise of due diligence may become known, to the attorney for the prosecution.

(C) *Documents and Tangible Objects.* Upon request of the defendant the prosecution shall permit the defendant to inspect and copy books, papers, documents, photographs, tangible objects, buildings, or places, or copies or portions thereof, which are within the possession, custody, or control of the prosecution, and which are material to the preparation of his defense or are intended for use by the prosecution as evidence in chief at the trial, or were obtained from or belong to the defendant.

(D) *Reports of Examinations and Tests.* Upon request of a defendant the prosecution shall permit the defendant to inspect and copy any results or reports of physical or mental examinations, and of scientific tests or experiments, or copies thereof, which are within the possession, custody, or control of the prosecution, the existence of which is known, or by the exercise of due diligence may become known, to the attorney for the prosecution, and which are material to the preparation of the defense or are intended for use by the prosecution as evidence in chief at the trial.

(2) *Information Not Subject to Disclosure.* Except as provided in paragraphs (A), (B), and (D) of subdivision (a)(1), this rule does not authorize the discovery or inspection of reports, memoranda, or other internal prosecution documents made by the attorney for the prosecution or other prosecution agents in connection with the investigation or prosecution of the case, or of statements made by prosecution witnesses or prospective prosecution witnesses provided that after a prosecution witness has testified on direct examination, the court shall, on motion of the defendant, order the prosecution to produce any statement of the witness in the possession of the prosecution which relates to the subject matter as to which the witness has testified; and provided further that the court may upon a sufficient showing require the production of any statement of any prospective witness prior to the time such witness testifies.

(3) *Time for Disclosure.* The prosecution shall respond to the defendant's request for disclosure no later than thirty days after the request is made, or within such other time as may be ordered by the court.

■ NORTH CAROLINA GENERAL STATUTES §15A-903

(a) Upon motion of the defendant, the court must order:

(1) The State to make available to the defendant the complete files of all law enforcement agencies, investigatory agencies, and prosecutors' offices involved in the investigation of the crimes committed or the prosecution of the defendant. . . .

a. The term "file" includes the defendant's statements, the codefendants' statements, witness statements, investigating officers' notes, results of tests and examinations, or any other matter or evidence obtained during the investigation of the offenses alleged to have been committed by the defendant. When any matter or evidence is submitted for testing or examination, in addition to any test or examination results, all other data, calculations, or writings of any kind shall be made available to the defendant, including, but not limited to, preliminary test or screening results and bench notes. . . .

c. Oral statements shall be in written or recorded form, except that oral statements made by a witness to a prosecuting attorney outside the presence of a law enforcement officer or investigatorial assistant shall not be required to be in written or recorded form unless there is significantly new or different information in the oral statement from a prior statement made by the witness.

d. The defendant shall have the right to inspect and copy or photograph any materials contained therein and, under appropriate safeguards, to inspect, examine, and test any physical evidence or sample contained therein.

(2) The prosecuting attorney to give notice to the defendant of any expert witnesses that the State reasonably expects to call as a witness at trial. Each such witness shall prepare, and the State shall furnish to the defendant, a report of the results of any examinations or tests conducted by the expert. The State shall also furnish to the defendant the expert's curriculum vitae, the expert's opinion, and the underlying basis for that opinion. The State shall give the notice and furnish the materials required by this subsection within a reasonable time prior to trial, as specified by the court. Standardized fee scales shall be developed by the Administrative Office of the Courts and Indigent Defense Services for all expert witnesses and private investigators who are compensated with State funds.

(3) The prosecuting attorney to give the defendant, at the beginning of jury selection, a written list of the names of all other witnesses whom the State reasonably expects to call during the trial. Names of witnesses shall not be subject to disclosure if the prosecuting attorney certifies in writing and under seal to the court that to do so may subject the witnesses or others to physical or substantial economic harm or coercion, or that there is other particularized, compelling need not to disclose. If there are witnesses that the State did not reasonably expect to call at the time of the provision of the witness list, and as a result are not listed, the court upon a good faith showing shall allow the witnesses to be called. Additionally, in the interest of justice, the court may in its discretion permit any undisclosed witness to testify. . . .

(c) On a timely basis, law enforcement and investigatory agencies shall make available to the prosecutor's office a complete copy of the complete files related to the investigation of the crimes committed or the prosecution of the defendant for compliance with this section and any disclosure under G.S. 15A-902(a). Investigatory agencies that obtain information and materials listed in subdivision (1) of subsection (a) of this section shall ensure that such information and materials are fully disclosed to the prosecutor's office on a timely basis for disclosure to the defendant.

(d) Any person who willfully omits or misrepresents evidence or information required to be disclosed pursuant to subdivision (1) of subsection (a) of this section, or required to be provided to the prosecutor's office pursuant to subsection (c) of this section, shall be guilty of a Class H felony. Any person who willfully omits or misrepresents evidence or information required to be disclosed pursuant to any other provision of this section shall be guilty of a Class 1 misdemeanor.

Notes

1. *Defendant and co-defendant statements.* Discovery rules in all jurisdictions allow defense counsel at least some access to the government's evidence regarding statements that the defendant made about the alleged crime. This does not mean, however, that the government must turn over all statements by a defendant. Under Fed. R. Crim. P. 16(a)(1)(A)-(B), the defense may obtain written or recorded statements of a defendant and written evidence of oral statements made by a defendant in response to interrogation by a known government agent. The ABA Standard for Criminal Justice, Discovery 11-2.1(a)(i) (3d ed. 1996) calls for the prosecutor to disclose "all written and all oral statements of the defendant or any co-defendant," along with any documents "relating to the acquisition of such statements." See also Fla. R. Crim. P. 3.220(b)(1)(C). What sorts of statements does the ABA standard cover that the Federal Rule does not? Does a defense attorney really need to obtain such statements from the government when he could simply ask his client about any statements he made? How would he use documents "relating to the acquisition" of a defendant's statement?

Note that Rule 16 makes no provision for the discovery of co-defendant's statements. Cf. Fla. R. Crim. P. 3.220(b)(1)(D) (discovery of "any written or recorded statements and the substance of any oral statements made by a co-defendant"). When might defense counsel use such a statement? Does defense counsel have an alternative method of preparing for any co-defendant statements that might be used at trial?

2. *Prosecution expert witnesses.* Criminal discovery rules, like their civil counterparts, recognize the special challenges of preparing for the trial testimony of expert witnesses. Fed. R. Crim. P. 16(a)(1)(G) calls for disclosure of a "written summary of any testimony that the government intends to use" from experts in its case in chief, which includes the expert's opinions, the bases and the reasons for the opinions, and the expert's qualifications. Once again, many states give the defense more information, by including disclosure of the reports or statements of any experts (such as the results of tests) made "in connection with" a particular case, whether or not the government plans to call the expert at trial. Fla. R. Crim. P. 3.220(b)(1)(J). The rules typically impose on both parties the same obligations of disclosure about their experts.

3. *Lay witnesses and potential witnesses.* Perhaps the greatest variety in discovery rules involves information about lay witnesses and potential witnesses. Federal Rule of Criminal Procedure 26.2 provides for disclosure *at trial* by both the prosecution and defense of written "statements" of any witnesses other than the defendant. Any disclosure of witness statements before trial results from negotiations between the parties. What impact would this timing question have on the course of plea negotiations?

What is the rationale for providing such limited discovery of potential witnesses? To some extent, such discovery rules endorse the classic adversarial model of justice. Rules that limit disclosure of prosecution witnesses also reflect worries that defendants will engage in witness tampering, bribery, and intimidation. To the extent that defendants can use broader discovery to fine-tune misleading or perjured defenses, broader discovery could undermine the basic truth-finding function of criminal adjudication.

Discovery rules in other jurisdictions treat information about potential witnesses as a matter that the defense cannot develop alone before trial. The rules commonly require the government to give the defense—before trial—the names and addresses of its witnesses and other persons who have knowledge of the events surrounding the alleged crime. See Fla. R. Crim. P. 3.220(b)(1)(A). The rules also oblige the government to provide the defense with potential impeachment material, such as the prior criminal record of any witnesses or the nature of any cooperation agreement between the government and the witness. The rules typically extend to any written summaries of witness statements, even if the statements are not "adopted" or "verbatim." See ABA Standard 11-2.1(a)(ii) (all written statements of witness in possession of government, relevant to case); Fla. R. Crim. P. 3.220(b)(1)(B). Is all of this discovery about witnesses necessary? Once a defense attorney has the name and address of a potential witness, can she obtain statements from the witness on equal terms with the government?

4. *Open file policies.* A few jurisdictions (such as North Carolina, as indicated in the provisions reprinted above) have embraced "open file" discovery—rules that require the prosecutor to keep any written records about the case completely open to the defense attorney. While such a position is unusual to find in statewide statutes or rules, it is commonplace to find individual prosecutors' offices that have committed themselves to open file discovery. Why would prosecutors create discovery rules that go well beyond the requirements of the applicable law? Does it save them the trouble of sorting through documents to comply with discovery requests? Does an open file policy best achieve the discovery objectives identified by the National District Attorneys Association: "to minimize surprise, afford the opportunity for effective cross-examination, expedite trials, and meet the requirements of due process"? National Prosecution Standards 4-9.1 (3d ed. 2009). For a discussion of the motivations for adopting open file policies and the effects of such policies, see Jenia I. Turner & Allison Redlich, Two Models of Pre-Plea Discovery in Criminal Cases: An Empirical Comparison, 73 Wash. & Lee L. Rev. 285 (2016); Ben Grunwald, The Fragile Promise of Open-File Discovery, 49 Conn. L. Rev. 771 (2017). Can a prosecutor's office count on the limited time available to a defense attorney in most smaller cases to minimize the impact of an open file policy? Cf. ABA Standard 11-1.2 (discovery "may be more limited" in cases involving minor offenses).

5. *Depositions.* Depositions of witnesses and other third parties, the lifeblood of civil discovery, does not hold an important place in criminal discovery. In the federal system and in most states, depositions are available only to preserve the testimony of a witness who is unlikely to be available at trial. A few states, however, have begun to make it easier to obtain depositions and to use them in criminal proceedings. These are sometimes called "discovery" depositions, as opposed to depositions used to preserve testimony. See Fla. R. Crim. P. 3.220(h). Why have criminal discovery innovators focused their attention on the available documents rather than the deposition or written interrogatory?

Despite the rarity of criminal depositions in most jurisdictions, the parties do interview witnesses before trial. Does this voluntary system of gathering evidence give the parties equal access to information? See ABA Standard 11-6.3 (neither prosecutor nor defense should advise persons other than defendant to refrain from speaking with counsel for opposing side).

6. *E-discovery.* As the volume of digital evidence in criminal cases has grown, defense attorneys and prosecutors have encountered difficulties managing the discovery of such evidence. In what format should the evidence be produced? Can prosecutors fulfill their *Brady* obligations simply by "dumping" gigabytes of evidence onto the defense, without any index or other guidance about where potentially exculpatory evidence might be located? How should the parties handle the storage of voluminous digital evidence and especially sensitive or confidential information? Neither state nor federal rules of criminal procedure have addressed the unique challenges of e-discovery in criminal cases. The only state so far to have promulgated e-discovery rules for criminal cases is New Jersey. New Jersey Court Rule 3:13-3 (b)(3) requires that digital files be disclosed in a publicly available format or with software that would allow the recipient to review the files. Where metadata is important to the case, the court can also order that files be produced in their original format, as well as in a searchable format. Finally, the rules require the producing party to list the disclosed digital evidence, and in case of multiple disks, the specific disks on which the evidence is located. At the federal level, a few federal districts have addressed e-discovery in local rules or standing orders. Daniel S. McConkie, The Local Rules Revolution in Criminal Discovery, 39 Cardozo L. Rev. 59, (2017). A joint working group of federal prosecutors and defense attorneys has also drafted a detailed protocol for disclosing electronically stored information (ESI Protocol), but the protocol is not binding and is not yet widely known or followed. Joint Working Group on Electronic Technology in the Criminal Justice System, Recommendations for Electronically Stored Information Discovery Production in Federal Criminal Cases (2012). For a discussion of the challenges presented by e-discovery in criminal cases, see Jenia I. Turner, Managing Digital Discovery in Criminal Cases, 109 J. Crim. L. & Criminology (forthcoming 2019).

7. *Remedies.* Discovery rules typically leave courts with a great deal of discretion in selecting a remedy for a violation of the law. The most common remedies are continuances (to allow the party time to develop a response to the evidence) and exclusion of the evidence that the party should have disclosed (particularly where the aggrieved party can show some prejudice flowing from the discovery violation). Trial courts have also dismissed charges for more serious discovery violations by a prosecutor. State ex rel. Rusen v. Hill, 454 S.E.2d 427 (W. Va. 1994). If an appellate court decides that a discovery violation occurred, it can reverse the conviction if the defendant shows prejudice. Contempt citations against the attorney or later disciplinary proceedings by the state bar are also possibilities.

8. *Discovery by any other name.* The rules of pretrial discovery are not the defendant's only method of finding out about the government's evidence. The preliminary hearing, where the government establishes probable cause to support the charges in the case, often gives defense counsel a glimpse of the government's theory of the case. Defendants will also on occasion request a "bill of particulars," a document that supplements the indictment or information when necessary to give proper notice to the defendant of the charges he must defend against.

3. Defense Disclosures

The trend over the past several decades has been toward broader criminal discovery rights for both the defense and the prosecution. The most potent arguments against expanding discovery at each juncture have pointed to some necessary limits on defense disclosures. There may be constitutional difficulties in forcing a defendant to disclose certain information to the prosecution. Among other things, forced disclosure might be considered self-incrimination in violation of the constitutional privilege. Faced with this sort of barrier, prosecutors have resisted the general expansion of criminal discovery on the basis of litigation fairness. If the defendant does not have to disclose evidence, prosecutors argue, then neither should they.

In the end, the arguments for limiting criminal discovery have lost more often than they have won—in part because the constitutional problems with compelling the defendant to disclose evidence have turned out to be surprisingly small. Where the Constitution has created no barrier, both defense and prosecution disclosures have increased.

If the Constitution will stop only a few types of defense disclosures, what are other possible grounds for evaluating discovery innovations? Are there some types of information that the prosecution will not develop if the defendant does not provide it? What, if anything, do we gain from a truly adversarial system of developing and presenting evidence?

■ PENNSYLVANIA RULE OF CRIMINAL PROCEDURE 573(C)

(1) In all court cases, if the Commonwealth files a motion for pretrial discovery, upon a showing of materiality to the preparation of the Commonwealth's case and that the request is reasonable, the court may order the defendant, subject to the defendant's rights against compulsory self-incrimination, to allow the attorney for the Commonwealth to inspect and copy or photograph any of the following requested items:

(a) results or reports of physical or mental examinations, and of scientific tests or experiments made in connection with the particular case, or copies thereof, within the possession or control of the defendant, that the defendant intends to introduce as evidence in chief, or were prepared by a witness whom the defendant intends to call at the trial, when results or reports relate to the testimony of that witness, provided the defendant has requested and received discovery under paragraph (B)(1)(e); and

(b) the names and addresses of eyewitnesses whom the defendant intends to call in its case-in-chief, provided that the defendant has previously requested and received discovery under paragraph (B)(2)(a)(i).

(2) If an expert whom the defendant intends to call in any proceeding has not prepared a report of examination or tests, the court, upon motion, may order that the expert prepare and the defendant disclose a report stating the subject matter on which the expert is expected to testify; the substance of the facts to which the expert is expected to testify; and a summary of the expert's opinions and the grounds for each opinion.

■ PENNSYLVANIA RULE OF CRIMINAL PROCEDURE 567(A)

A defendant who intends to offer the defense of alibi at trial shall file with the clerk of courts not later than the time required for filing the omnibus pretrial motion provided in Rule 579 a notice specifying an intention to offer an alibi defense, and shall serve a copy of the notice and a certificate of service on the attorney for the Commonwealth.

(1) The notice and a certificate of service shall be signed by the attorney for the defendant, or the defendant if unrepresented.

(2) The notice shall contain specific information as to the place or places where the defendant claims to have been at the time of the alleged offense and the names and addresses of the witnesses whom the defendant intends to call in support of the claim.

■ COMMONWEALTH v. PATRICK DURHAM

843 N.E.2d 1035 (Mass. 2006)

Greaney, J.

In issue is the order of a Superior Court judge that directed the defendant, as part of the reciprocal discovery authorized by Mass. R. Crim. P. 14(a), to furnish the Commonwealth with "statements" of witnesses whom the Commonwealth intended to call at trial and which were in the possession, custody, or control of the defendant or his attorney. . . . We find the order lawful; the discovery required is permitted by the rule and violates no Federal or State constitutional right of the defendant.

The procedural background is as follows. [The defendant requested] the names of all the Commonwealth's prospective trial witnesses and an opportunity to inspect all documentary and physical evidence that the Commonwealth intended to offer at trial. A Superior Court judge allowed the motion, contingent on the defendant providing the same discovery to the Commonwealth, and limiting the obligation to such evidence that pertained to each party's case-in-chief.

Subsequently, the Commonwealth filed a motion for additional reciprocal discovery. In its motion, the Commonwealth sought, among other requests, the disclosure of any written or recorded statement of any prospective witness, including potential witnesses for the Commonwealth, that the defendant intended to offer at trial for any purpose, including for impeachment. [The] judge allowed the request. [The] judge's order did not limit the required disclosure to statements that the defendant could use for impeachment purposes. Rather, the order is broader, compelling the defendant to furnish statements that the Commonwealth also possibly could use in its case-in-chief or that the defendant might use in establishing a defense. . . .

The defendant argued that the order violates Federal and State constitutional protections by impairing his right to confront the witnesses against him, his privilege against self-incrimination, and his right to a fair trial and the effective assistance of counsel.

(a) Both the Sixth Amendment to the United States Constitution and art. 12 of the Massachusetts Declaration of Rights guarantee a criminal defendant's right to confront the witnesses against him through cross-examination. There is no question that effective cross-examination is an important safeguard of liberty and a valuable tool for testing the reliability of evidence, thereby ensuring a truthful verdict. We also have no disagreement with the view that, as a tactical matter, surprise can be an important element of effective cross-examination. But neither of these propositions is affected by the order to a degree where it can be held that the defendant's constitutional right to confront witnesses against him would be violated.

The statements the defendant would have had to turn over under the order were presumably already known to the Commonwealth's witnesses who gave them. The defendant, if appropriate, might have received reciprocal discovery of written statements obtained by the Commonwealth from defense witnesses. As such, both sides are given a fair opportunity to investigate the veracity of statements and are not faced with confronting them for the first time at trial. See United States v. Nobles, 422 U.S. 225 (1975) ("The Sixth Amendment does not confer the right to present testimony free from the legitimate demands of the adversarial system; one cannot invoke the Sixth Amendment as a justification for presenting what might have been a half-truth"). Indeed, such investigation might even have revealed beneficial information for the defense. Had there been a trial, the defendant's trial counsel would have been afforded an adequate opportunity to cross-examine effectively the witnesses who gave the statements. In addition to asking each witness about the substance of his or her statement, defense counsel could have questioned the witness about pretrial preparation. Such questioning could negate any mistaken impression that the witness was encountering the material for the first time and also could suggest that the witness may have conveniently crafted an explanation for any variations in former testimony or statements. The right to confront and to cross-examine a witness is not absolute and may, in appropriate cases, bow to accommodate other legitimate interests in the criminal trial process. The trial process seeks to ascertain the truth. . . .

(b) There was no violation of the defendant's privilege against self-incrimination under either the Fifth Amendment to the United States Constitution or the broader protection afforded by art. 12. The defendant was not being compelled to state anything himself. Rather, the rule and order only permit discovery of statements made by other persons that the defendant intended to use at trial. In United States v. Nobles, 422 U.S. at 227-228, when defense counsel attempted to impeach the credibility of two prosecution witnesses with prior statements they allegedly had made to a defense investigator, the Federal trial judge ordered that the witnesses' prior statements be disclosed to the prosecutor for his use in cross-examining the investigator. In rejecting the defendant's Fifth Amendment challenge, the United States Supreme Court explained: "The court's order was limited to statements allegedly made by third parties who were available as witnesses to both the prosecution and the defense. [The defendant] did not prepare the report, and there is no suggestion that the portions subject to the disclosure order reflected any information that he conveyed to the investigator." . . . The reasoning applies to the disclosure of witnesses' statements prior to trial.

The timing of the disclosure has no relevance to the defendant's privilege against self-incrimination. The order merely accelerated disclosures that the defendant intended to make. See Williams v. Florida, 399 U.S. 78 (1970). The privilege does not entitle "a defendant as a matter of constitutional right to await the end of the State's case before announcing the nature of his defense, any more than it entitles him to await the jury's verdict on the State's case-in-chief before deciding whether or not to take the stand himself." This statement applies equally to disclosure of a defense, like alibi, where required by the criminal rules of procedure and to the disclosure required by the order.

(c) The order also did not diminish, in any legally significant way, the defendant's right to be represented by effective counsel or to have a fair trial. No production was required of statements that the defense did not intend to use at trial. As to statements intended to be used at trial, the order simply gives the prosecution fair notice of the information the defendant had obtained from prospective prosecution witnesses in the form of written or recorded statements. Under rule 14, the discovery is reciprocal, and the defendant was also, but first, entitled to statements of persons in the prosecutor's possession, custody, or control. The defendant's trial counsel would still have been able to cross-examine the prosecutor's witnesses and impeach their credibility. The statements may have contained information that provided substantive evidence that may have benefited the defense. The Commonwealth would be entitled to see that information as well. Nothing in the State or Federal Constitution guarantees a defendant a right so to defend as to deny the State a chance to check the truth of his position. . . . See Wardius v. Oregon, 412 U.S. 470, 474 (1973) ("The growth of [reciprocal] discovery devices is a salutary development which, by increasing the evidence available to both parties, enhances the fairness of the adversary system. [Nothing] in the Due Process Clause precludes States from experimenting with systems of broad discovery designed to achieve these goals").

Indeed, we have upheld reciprocal discovery obligations, despite their tendency to compel defense counsel to make strategic decisions before trial. See, e.g., Commonwealth v. Diaz, 730 N.E.2d 845 (Mass. 2000) (policy justifying reciprocal discovery, when defendant places his statements and mental state in issue, applies to alleged inability to premeditate or form specific intent to kill, and to lack of criminal responsibility defense); Commonwealth v. Blodgett, 386 N.E.2d 1042 & n.6 (Mass. 1979) (judge properly precluded defense from calling alibi witnesses until he disclosed their names to Commonwealth); Commonwealth v. Lewinski, 329 N.E.2d 738 (Mass. 1975) ("The judge may condition the right of the defense to secure a witness's statement from the prosecution, on the reciprocal discovery by the defense to the prosecution of all or part of a statement by the same witness given to the defense"). The due process clause speaks to the balance of forces between the accused and his accuser. That balance is satisfied here.

[In] summary, we acknowledge, as the defendant had emphasized, that cross-examination is important for determining credibility and assisting the trier of fact in arriving at a fair verdict. We acknowledge as well that some "imbalance" exists between the resources of the State and those of the defendant. The imbalance, however, has been considerably adjusted in modern criminal practice by requiring the State to assist the defense with full discovery, by the provision of considerable funds to hire an investigator and to retain experts to conduct evaluations and other tests (and then to testify), and by nonconstitutionally compelled prophylactic measures, such as permitting jury instruction on topics like the failure of the police to record a confession and mistaken identification. . . . The role of cross-examination, and the existence of an imbalance, should not override the right of the people, and the victims of crimes, to have the evidence evaluated by a fully informed trier of fact. . . . Our interpretation recognizes that criminal trials are matters of justice and not sporting events in which the side that has the strongest advocate (employing advantages to which he or she is not entitled) gains the upper hand. . . .

Notes

1. *Reciprocal discovery: majority position.* The trend in American jurisdictions is toward increasingly reciprocal discovery. These statutes usually survive constitutional challenges. See State v. Brown, 940 P.2d 546 (Wash. 1997). However, the full "two-way street" form of discovery is more rare. Some courts have struck down the most ambitious efforts to create reciprocal discovery, particularly those requiring the defendant to reveal information about potential witnesses that she does *not* plan to call at trial. Appellate courts typically focus on whether the material that the defense must disclose under the statute would be disclosed later at trial. The most common constitutional objections are based on the self-incrimination privilege, the right to cross-examination, the right to effective assistance of counsel, and due process. For a sampling of the wide-ranging state court decisions on defense disclosures in criminal discovery, consult the web extension for this chapter at *http://www.crim-pro.com/extension/ch15.*

Discovery rules in most states regulate specialized defenses such as alibis, self-defense, or insanity. The Supreme Court has upheld the constitutionality of such statutes in Williams v. Florida, 399 U.S. 78 (1970). The defenses must be reciprocal: The Supreme Court has struck down a statute that required the defense to provide notice of an alibi defense without requiring the prosecution to disclose its alibi-rebuttal witnesses. Wardius v. Oregon, 412 U.S. 470 (1973). Why are alibi, self-defense, and insanity the three types of defense evidence that appear most often in the statutes and rules regarding disclosure? At least two of these defenses (alibi and insanity) require the development of evidence unrelated to the events of the alleged crime. But why should the government obtain special notice about self-defense? And once the government knows that a defendant plans to pursue an insanity defense, why should the government have access to defense experts? Can't the prosecution hire its own experts?

2. *Consensual discovery.* Statutes in many states finesse the constitutional questions involved in compelling defendant disclosures by giving the defendant the choice of opting out of extensive discovery. Only if the defendant obtains full discovery rights against the government must she also comply with the disclosure duties. Does a defendant "waive" objections to disclosure in the same sense that he or she can "waive" the right to trial or to an appointed attorney? Does consensual discovery protect a true adversarial option?

3. *Work-product doctrine in criminal cases.* Recall that discovery rules usually include a privilege, developed at common law, for the "work product" of attorneys and their agents. The privilege limits the disclosures of both defense and prosecution. The U.S. Supreme Court recognized the work-product doctrine in Hickman v. Taylor, 329 U.S. 495 (1947), establishing a qualified privilege for certain materials prepared by an attorney in anticipation of litigation. The Court explained the decision as follows:

> Historically, a lawyer is an officer of the court and is bound to work for the advancement of justice while faithfully protecting the rightful interests of his clients. In performing his various duties, however, it is essential that a lawyer work with a certain degree of privacy, free from unnecessary intrusion by opposing parties and their counsel. Proper preparation of a client's case demands that he assemble information, sift what he considers to be the relevant from the irrelevant facts, prepare his

legal theories and plan his strategy without undue and needless interference. . . . This work is reflected, of course, in interviews, statements, memoranda, correspondence, briefs, mental impressions, personal beliefs, and countless other tangible and intangible ways—aptly though roughly termed . . . as the [work] product of the lawyer. Were such materials open to opposing counsel on mere demand, much of what is now put down in writing would remain unwritten. An attorney's thoughts, heretofore inviolate, would not be his own. Inefficiency, unfairness and sharp practices would inevitably develop in the giving of legal advice and in the preparation of cases for trial. The effect on the legal profession would be demoralizing. And the interests of the clients and the cause of justice would be poorly served.

329 U.S. at 510-511. There are two levels of "work-product" protections. An "absolute" privilege attaches to any mental impressions, conclusions, opinions or legal theories of an attorney; that is, any document containing such material must be redacted to remove it before disclosure to another party. On the other hand, a "qualified" privilege attaches to other materials created "in anticipation of litigation." An opposing party can obtain this material if there is a strong enough reason for the disclosure. Is a state that has embraced broad defense disclosures likely to weaken the work-product doctrine? Is the work-product privilege based on a view of an independent and adversarial development of information that is incompatible with extensive discovery?

4. *Effective advocacy and reciprocal discovery.* Which of the following sorts of information would an advocate most want to withhold from the other party before trial: information about fact witnesses, expert witnesses, or documents? Do the discovery rules in criminal cases provide the most protection to information that requires the most effort to develop? Or do they protect the information that will have the most impact at trial? Or is the objective instead to require disclosure of information precisely *because* it is likely to have an impact at trial or *because* it is difficult to develop?

Discovery rules that encourage the parties to share information with each other well in advance of trial might seem at odds with the traditional adversarial system. What about rules that require only the prosecution, and not the defense, to disclose evidence to the other side before trial? Are these rules more consistent with the adversarial or inquisitorial approach to criminal procedure? As you reflect on this question, consider that in Germany, a country with an inquisitorial tradition, the judge and the defense attorney have full access to the prosecution file, but the defense has no corresponding duty to disclose its information to the court or the prosecution. Likewise, Texas, which has an adversarial system, recently required the prosecution to provide open file discovery, but remains the only U.S. state not to require the defense to reciprocate by disclosing evidence in its case. Tex. Code Crim. P. 39.14. As you evaluate the rules of criminal discovery, try to anticipate how lawyers in the adversarial tradition will react to rules that attempt to shift that tradition toward reciprocal discovery.

4. Discovery Ethics

During discovery, defense attorneys could face one of the classic puzzles of legal ethics. If a client gives her lawyer incriminating physical evidence, what are the lawyer's obligations? Do the obligations change if the material comes from a third party? If the client or a third party tells the lawyer about the location of such material? Finally, does defense counsel have an affirmative ethical obligation to seek out incriminating evidence?

▮ STANDING COMMITTEE ON PROFESSIONAL RESPONSIBILITY AND CONDUCT, STATE BAR OF CALIFORNIA, CALIFORNIA FORMAL ETHICS OPINION 1984-76

Issue: What are the ethical obligations of a criminal defense attorney during the course of a pending criminal matter when the client places upon the attorney's desk or informs the attorney of the location of the instrumentality, fruits, or other physical evidence of the crime? . . .

Fundamental to this discussion is Section 954 of the Evidence Code, which provides that a client "has a privilege to refuse to disclose, and to prevent another from disclosing, a confidential communication between client and lawyer. . . ." Likewise, Business and Professions Code Section 6068, subdivision (e) places upon the attorney the duty "to maintain inviolate the confidence, and at every peril to himself to preserve the secrets, of his client." The rationale behind the evidentiary privilege and the professional obligation of the attorney is to allow the client to make disclosures to the attorney "without fear that his attorney may be forced to reveal the information confided to him." People v. Meredith, 29 Cal. 3d 682, 690 (1981).

On the other hand, by the provisions of Section 135 of the Penal Code, it is a violation of the law for one knowingly to conceal or destroy any "instrument in writing or other matter or thing [that] is about to be produced in evidence upon any trial, inquiry or investigation whatever, authorized by law . . .", and it is clear that the attorney-client privilege does not grant to the client the power permanently to "sequester physical evidence such as a weapon or any other article used in the perpetration of a crime by delivering it to his attorney." People v. Lee, 3 Cal. App. 3d 514, 526 (1970). Likewise, rule 7-107(A) of the California Rules of Professional Conduct states: "A member of the State Bar shall not suppress any evidence that he or his client has a legal obligation to reveal or produce."

The California Supreme Court in People v. Meredith has determined that physical evidence of a crime over which the lawyer has exercised dominion and control, thus taking possession, is not protected by the attorney-client privilege. Other jurisdictions have imposed a clear legal and ethical duty upon the lawyer to turn that evidence over to the prosecution. State v. Olwell, 394 P.2d 681 (Wash. 1964); Anderson v. State 297 So. 2d 871 (Fla. App. 1974). . . .

In considering the attorney's legal obligations to his client under the Sixth Amendment to provide effective counsel, the attorney should advise the client of the attorney's ethical as well as legal obligation with respect to the duty to deliver physical evidence of the crime to the prosecution if the attorney takes possession of such physical evidence. It is at this stage of representation that the impact upon the attorney-client relationship is at its greatest. The client is informed of the duties the attorney may have in the search-for-truth aspect of the adversary system, even to the extent of a legal duty imposed upon the attorney to participate in the very case against his client by delivering material evidence of the crime to the prosecution.

Although the fact of the delivery of the physical evidence of a crime by the client to the attorney is within the protection of the attorney-client privilege, the physical evidence itself is not. As a corollary, however, although it was held in Anderson v. State that the attorney acted properly under the circumstances that confronted him by turning the stolen items over to the police, "in order for the attorney-client privilege to be meaningfully preserved, the state cannot introduce evidence that it received the items from the attorney's office."

It was also held in State v. Olwell [that the] "attorney should not be a depository for criminal evidence. . . . Such evidence given the attorney during legal consultation . . . and used by the attorney in preparing the defense of his client's case . . . could clearly be withheld for a reasonable period of time. It follows that the attorney after a reasonable period, should, as an officer of the court, on his own motion turn the same over to the prosecution." The prosecution, however, must take "extreme precautions" to make certain that the source of the evidence is not disclosed at trial. Thus, in its *Olwell* decision, the court was seeking the proper balance between truth seeking by the prosecution, and the attorney-client privilege of the defense.

[The] criminal defense attorney, after holding for a reasonable time for the purpose of preparing his client's defense, the instrumentality, fruits, or other physical evidence of the crime placed upon his desk by the client, is thereafter both legally and ethically obligated on his own motion to turn such evidence over to the prosecution.

It is apparent, however, that there is a significant difference in the legal and ethical obligations of an attorney when given possession of the physical evidence of a crime, as opposed to merely being told by his client of the location of the physical evidence of the crime.

[In] the situation wherein the client informs the attorney of the location of the physical evidence of the crime, or the attorney merely observes it without taking possession, the attorney need not disclose to the prosecution either its location or his or his agent's physical observations of the same. When, however, the defense attorney removes the physical evidence from its original location or takes possession of it, the evidence must, after reasonable time for investigation, be delivered to the prosecution and the location of its discovery will be subject to disclosure.

A criminal defense attorney should give careful consideration to the consequences of his actions before accepting possession of physical evidence or revealing any oral or observation evidence to the prosecution in light of the client's Sixth Amendment right to effective counsel and Business and Professions Code Section 6068, subdivision (e), requiring confidentiality. [Case law suggests] that all investigation and examination by a criminal defense attorney (with the exception of possession of physical evidence) is within the self-incrimination privilege of the defendant. . . .

This opinion is . . . advisory only. It is not binding upon the courts, The State Bar of California, its Board of Governors, any persons or tribunals charged with regulatory responsibilities, or any member of the State Bar.

■ NORTH CAROLINA STATE BAR, RECEIPT OF EVIDENCE OF CRIME BY LAWYER FOR DEFENDANT, ETHICS OPINION 221 (1995)

Inquiry #1: Attorney A and Attorney B work for different law firms. They have been appointed to represent Defendant, who is charged with first-degree murder. Defendant's wife, W, was apparently present during the altercation that led to the victim's death. During Attorney A and Attorney B's investigation, Defendant implicated W in the matter and told the attorneys that he had knowledge of relevant physical evidence. The police detectives who investigated the death are in possession of a stick they believe Defendant used to commit the murder, but neither the police detectives nor the prosecutors are aware of the existence of other physical evidence.

Defendant brought the physical evidence to Attorney B's office. Attorney B took possession of the physical evidence for purposes of examination and consultation with Attorney A concerning the extent to which the physical evidence might incriminate or exculpate Defendant.

Attorney A and Attorney B interviewed W, who incriminated herself. The story W told Attorney A and Attorney B is different from the statement that she gave to the police officers during the initial investigation.

Must Attorney A or Attorney B notify the district attorney's office or the investigating law enforcement agency of the existence of the physical evidence?

Opinion #1: No. On the one hand, a lawyer has a duty to preserve the confidences of the client and to zealously represent the client within the bounds of the law. Rule 4 and Canon VII of the Rules of Professional Conduct. On the other hand, a lawyer is an officer of the court and should not engage in conduct that is prejudicial to the administration of justice. Rule 1.2(d). In the absence of a court order or a common law or statutory obligation to disclose the location or deliver an item of inculpatory physical evidence that is not contraband (the possession of which is in and of itself a crime, such as narcotics) to law enforcement authorities, a defense lawyer may take such evidence into his or her possession for the purpose of testing, examination, or inspection. The defense lawyer should return the evidence to the source from whom the lawyer received it. In returning the item to the source, the lawyer must advise the source of the legal consequences pertaining to the possession or destruction of the evidence by that person or others. This advice should include the advice to retain the evidence intact and not engage in conduct that might be a violation of criminal statutes relating to evidence. See generally ABA Standards for Criminal Justice: Prosecution Function and Defense Function (3rd ed.), Standard 4-4.6(a)-(c), "Physical Evidence," and Commentary. If a defense lawyer receives a subpoena for inculpatory physical evidence in his or her possession, the lawyer may take appropriate steps to contest the subpoena in order to protect the interests of the client. However, the lawyer must comply with a court order to produce the evidence.

Similarly, pursuant to N.C.G.S. §15A-905, a defense lawyer must comply with any order entered by the court to produce evidence the defendant intends to introduce at trial.

Inquiry #2: What specific information, if any, is Attorney A or Attorney B allowed to disclose to the district attorney or the law enforcement agency regarding the weapon or how it was obtained?

Opinion #2: See opinion #1 above.

Inquiry #3: W provided information to Attorney A and Attorney B which would assist Defendant in his defense. Since Attorney A and Attorney B might be witnesses for Defendant, do they have to withdraw from the representation of Defendant?

Opinion #3: No. Rule 5.2(b) requires a lawyer to withdraw from the representation of a client if, "after undertaking employment in contemplated or pending litigation, a lawyer learns or it is obvious that he or a lawyer in his firm ought to be called as a witness on behalf of his client." However, he may continue the representation and he or a lawyer in his firm may testify under the circumstances enumerated in Rule 5.2(a). It is not "obvious" that Attorney A or Attorney B "ought" to be called as a witness for their client. Any information gained by Attorney A and Attorney B during the professional relationship with Defendant, including information obtained from third parties such as W, is confidential information. Rule 4(a); see also N.C.G.S. §15A-906. Unless Defendant consents to disclosure of the information gained from W, the lawyers may not testify about what W told them. Even if Defendant consents to the use of this information, W may be called as a witness herself, thus avoiding the need for Attorney A or Attorney B to testify. A problem of this nature can be avoided by having a nonlawyer present at all interviews with prospective trial witnesses.

Inquiry #4: Defendant has consented to the disclosure by Attorney A and Attorney B of the substance of W's statements to them. At trial, W is called as a witness and testifies contrary to her earlier statements to Attorney A and Attorney B. If the testimony of Attorney A or Attorney B is necessary to rebut the testimony of W, must one or both of them withdraw from the representation?

Opinion #4: Withdrawal may not be required. It is possible that by aggressive cross-examination of W, the need for one of the lawyers to testify will be avoided. If Lawyer A or Lawyer B must testify in order to rebut the testimony of W, moreover, the lawyers might conclude that an exception in Rule 5.2(a)(4) applies which would allow the lawyer to testify without withdrawing from the representation. Rule 5.2(b). Rule 5.2(a)(4) allows a lawyer to continue the representation despite acting as a witness in the trial if withdrawal "would work a substantial hardship on the client because of the distinctive value of the lawyer . . . as counsel in the particular case."

If it is necessary for one of the lawyers to testify, the lawyer who testifies may have to withdraw from the representation but the other lawyer may remain in the case. Rule 5.2(b) only requires the lawyer who testifies for his client and the other members of his firm to withdraw from the representation.

Notes

1. *Ethical obligations to turn over physical evidence.* The rules governing a defense lawyer's obligations to disclose physical evidence are largely uniform. If a defense lawyer receives incriminating *testimony* from a client, the attorney-client privilege and the self-incrimination clause combine to prevent the attorney from revealing that information to the government. But if the defense lawyer receives incriminating *physical* evidence, the outcome is different. Discovery rules do not address this question. Instead, Rule 3.4 of the Model Rules of Professional Conduct, adopted as law in many states, provides the starting point for analyzing the attorney's duties:

> A lawyer shall not . . . unlawfully obstruct another party's access to evidence or unlawfully alter, destroy or conceal a document or other material having potential evidentiary value. A lawyer shall not counsel or assist another person to do any such act.

Hence, the key question is whether a lawyer's act is an "unlawful" obstruction of access or tampering with evidence. Most states have statutes that prohibit obstruction of investigations or tampering with evidence. In some places, an investigation must be pending before the destruction or concealment of potential evidence becomes unlawful, while elsewhere the intent to prevent detection of a crime is the critical element, regardless of the timing of the destruction or concealment. The courts addressing these situations have held that the attorney who takes possession of contraband relevant to a criminal investigation against a client must ordinarily give the evidence to the government. The attorney can return the evidence to its original location only if the return of the evidence does not create a risk that the evidence will be concealed or altered. See Rubin v. State, 602 A.2d 677 (Md. 1992). The National Legal Aid and Defender Association recommends that a lawyer deliver physical evidence to the government only if delivery is required by law or court order, or if "the item received is contraband, or if in the lawyer's judgment the lawyer cannot retain the item in a way that does not pose an unreasonable risk of physical harm to anyone."

What would you say to your client or a third party about incriminating physical evidence? If you decided to deliver the physical evidence to the government, exactly how would you proceed? Could you deliver the item to some third party (say, a member of the Ethics Committee of the state bar) and ask that person to deliver the evidence anonymously?

2. *Source and type of evidence.* As you read Problem 15-3 below, consider whether it matters that the wristwatch was not contraband (that is, it was not illegal for anyone to possess the watch)? Does it matter that the attorney learned of the location of the wristwatch from a third party rather than from the client? Can the prosecutor reveal to the jury that defense counsel was the source of the watch when it comes into evidence at trial? See State v. Olwell, 394 P.2d 681 (Wash. 1964) (if client provides defense counsel with evidence that must be given to government, attorney-client privilege prevents prosecutor from informing jury about source of evidence).

3. *Ethics rules and prosecutorial disclosures.* Rules of ethics often recognize a distinctive set of duties for prosecuting attorneys. How might these rules be relevant during the discovery process? Rule 3.8 of the ABA's Model Rules of Professional Conduct, the basis for most state bar ethics rules, is reprinted earlier in this chapter.

If you were a chief prosecutor in the district, what office policies would you consider to ensure that the trial attorneys in your office follow the requirements of *Brady* and other disclosure and discovery laws? Is it more important to hire good people as line prosecutors, or to establish proper routines, monitoring, and incentives for the people who work in the office? See Model Rule of Professional Conduct 5.1 ("A lawyer having direct supervisory authority over another lawyer shall make reasonable efforts to ensure that the other lawyer conforms to the Rules of Professional Conduct.").

Problem 15-3. Defense Attorney as Repository

Michael Hitch was indicted for first-degree murder and is currently awaiting trial on that charge. In the course of their investigation, the police interviewed Hitch's girlfriend, Diane Heaton, who told them that the victim was wearing a certain wristwatch shortly before his death. Later, an investigator for the Public Defender's Office contacted Ms. Heaton, and she informed the investigator that she had found a wristwatch in Hitch's suit jacket. She also stated that she did not want to turn the evidence over to the police. The investigator contacted the defendant's attorney, who told him to bring the watch to the attorney's office. The attorney indicated that he did this for two reasons. First, he wanted to examine the watch to determine whether it was the same one that Ms. Heaton had described to the police. Second, he was afraid that she might destroy or conceal the evidence. Shortly thereafter, Hitch informed the police that he had taken a watch from the victim. The police were, however, unaware of the location of that watch.

The defense attorney filed a petition with the Ethics Committee of the State Bar, requesting an opinion concerning his duties with respect to the wristwatch. You are a practicing attorney in the state and serve as a volunteer member of the Ethics Committee. After reviewing the California and North Carolina ethics opinions reprinted above, what guidance would you give to Hitch's attorney? If the attorney ignores the guidance from the committee, does that constitute grounds for discipline against him? Cf. Hitch v. Pima County Superior Court, 708 P.2d 72 (Ariz. 1985).

B. SPEEDY TRIAL PREPARATION

An old bromide reminds us that "justice delayed is justice denied." This can be true for both the prosecution and the defense in criminal cases. If preparations for trial last too long, the evidence becomes less reliable for both sides. The uncertainty about the criminal charges may harm the defendant's reputation and make it difficult for the defendants and the victims of the alleged crime to move ahead with their lives. The need for speedy resolution of criminal charges has been mentioned in some of the earliest documents in our legal tradition, including the Magna Carta of 1215, which states, "we will not deny or defer to any man either justice or right."

The right to a speedy trial appears in constitutional provisions, both state and federal. The Sixth Amendment guarantees a "speedy and public trial," and most states have similar provisions. The federal and state due process clauses prevent some extreme forms of delay. Recent constitutional amendments recognizing the rights of victims of crime have declared that victims, too, have a right to a speedy trial. Many state and federal statutes also hurry the criminal process along. These include statutes of limitations (requiring charges to be filed within a limited time from the events in question) and speedy trial acts (requiring the parties and the courts to bring the matter to trial within a specified period from the start of the process).

Despite all this emphasis on speed, another bromide reminds us that "haste makes waste." Both prosecution and defense have some reasons to slow down the process. Some of their reasons may be less than noble. If testimony is going to damage one side or another, a witness's fading memory may make the testimony less convincing and more susceptible to attack. If a defendant remains in custody before trial, a prosecutor may not be so anxious to risk an acquittal that would release the defendant from custody; a defendant not in custody may want to delay the day of reckoning. But other reasons for delay are surely necessary, even praiseworthy, including a desire to complete the discovery processes examined in the previous section.

1. *Pre-Accusation Delay*

Once a crime occurs and an investigation begins, the matter typically becomes the basis for criminal charges or criminal charges are declined within a matter of days. Among the handful of matters that take more time, a small proportion can remain active for many months or years after the events take place. What legal principles and institutions are available to limit the amount of time that can pass between the commission of a crime and the filing of criminal charges? Once a state legislature has passed a statute of limitations, is any further limitation necessary to avoid delays that might create hardship or unreliable outcomes?

■ NEW YORK CRIMINAL PROCEDURE LAW §30.10

1. A criminal action must be commenced within the period of limitation prescribed in the ensuing subdivisions of this section.

2. Except as otherwise provided in subdivision three:

(a) A prosecution for a class A felony or rape in the first degree . . . or aggravated sexual abuse in the first degree . . . or course of sexual conduct against a child in the first degree . . . may be commenced at any time;

(b) A prosecution for any other felony must be commenced within five years after the commission thereof;

(c) A prosecution for a misdemeanor must be commenced within two years after the commission thereof;

(d) A prosecution for a petty offense must be commenced within one year after the commission thereof.

3. Notwithstanding the provisions of subdivision two, the periods of limitation for the commencement of criminal actions are extended as follows in the indicated circumstances:

(a) A prosecution for larceny committed by a person in violation of a fiduciary duty may be commenced within one year after the facts constituting such offense are discovered or, in the exercise of reasonable diligence, should have been discovered by the aggrieved party or by a person under a legal duty to represent him who is not himself implicated in the commission of the offense. . . .

(f) For purposes of a prosecution involving a sexual offense . . . committed against a child less than 18 years of age [other than those delineated in paragraph (a)], the period of limitation shall not begin to run until the child has reached the age of 18 or the offense is reported to a law enforcement agency. . . .

4. In calculating the time limitation applicable to commencement of a criminal action, the following periods shall not be included:

(a) Any period following the commission of the offense during which (i) the defendant was continuously outside this state or (ii) the whereabouts of the defendant were continuously unknown and continuously unascertainable by the exercise of reasonable diligence. However, in no event shall the period of limitation be extended by more than five years beyond the period otherwise applicable under subdivision two.

(b) When a prosecution for an offense is lawfully commenced within the prescribed period of limitation therefor, and when an accusatory instrument upon which such prosecution is based is subsequently dismissed by an authorized court under directions or circumstances permitting the lodging of another charge for the same offense or an offense based on the same conduct, the period extending from the commencement of the thus defeated prosecution to the dismissal of the accusatory instrument does not constitute a part of the period of limitation applicable to commencement of prosecution by a new charge.

■ COMMONWEALTH v. STEPHEN SCHER
803 A.2d 1204 (Pa. 2002)

NEWMAN, J.

. . . Martin Dillon died of a gunshot wound to the chest on June 2, 1976. Scher was the only other individual present when Dillon died. How Dillon died, and whether that death was an accident or an intentional act of murder, is a story that evolved in fits and starts in the intervening two decades, culminating in murder charges being filed against Scher in 1996 and his conviction for first degree murder following a six-week jury trial in 1997 [more than 20 years after the homicide].

On appeal to the Superior Court, Scher [claimed] that the twenty-year delay in filing charges against him violated his right to due process of law as guaranteed by the United States and Pennsylvania Constitutions. The Superior Court reversed the Judgment of Sentence. . . .

THE DUE PROCESS STANDARD

. . . United States v. Marion, 404 U.S. 307 (1971), was the seminal case to address whether a defendant's federal constitutional rights are violated by an extensive delay between the occurrence of a crime and the indictment or arrest of a defendant for the crime. In *Marion*, the defendants were charged with having engaged in a fraudulent business scheme beginning in March of 1965 and ending in January of 1966. The federal prosecutor in *Marion* did not empanel a grand jury to investigate the scheme until September of 1969, and no indictment was returned until March of 1970. [The Supreme Court held that constitutional speedy trial claims do] not apply until "either a formal indictment or information or else the actual restraints imposed by arrest and holding to answer a criminal charge," which was not implicated in defendants' complaints of pre-arrest delay. Concerning the defendants' Fifth Amendment due process claims, the Court noted that the primary guarantee against the bringing of overly stale charges was whatever statute of limitations applied to the crime. The Court went on to note, however, "the statute of limitations does not fully define the appellees' rights with respect to the events occurring prior to indictment." The following passage from *Marion* is significant:

> Thus, the Government concedes that the Due Process Clause of the Fifth Amendment would require dismissal of the indictment if it were shown at trial that the pre-indictment delay in this case caused substantial prejudice to appellees' rights to a fair trial and that the delay was an intentional device to gain tactical advantage over the accused. Cf. Brady v. Maryland, 373 U.S. 83 (1963). However, we need not, and could not now, determine when and in what circumstances actual prejudice resulting from pre-accusation delays requires the dismissal of the prosecution. . . .

Six years after *Marion*, the United States Supreme Court revisited the due process implications of pre-arrest delay in United States v. Lovasco, 431 U.S. 783 (1977). Eugene Lovasco was indicted in March of 1975 for possessing firearms stolen from the mail beginning in July and ending in August of 1973. Lovasco moved to dismiss the indictment, claiming that the prosecutor's delay in bringing the indictment caused him prejudice through the deaths of two favorable witnesses and therefore violated his due process rights. [The Court stated that] the due process inquiry must consider the reasons for the delay as well as the prejudice to the accused. In [its] discussion of the "reasons for the delay," the Court stated, "in our view, investigative delay is unlike delay undertaken by the Government solely to gain a tactical advantage over the accused." . . .

We [read] *Marion* and *Lovasco* [to mean] that delay intentionally undertaken by the prosecution to gain a tactical advantage over the defendant is one case, but not the only case, where pre-arrest delay would violate due process. However, [there is no] obligation on the Commonwealth to conduct all criminal investigations pursuant to a due diligence or negligence standard, measured from the moment when criminal charges are filed and the defendant raises his due process claim. Such a standard would be too onerous, requiring judicial oversight of decisions traditionally entrusted to the prosecutor. Furthermore, a due diligence or negligence standard would require an inquiry into the methods, resources, and techniques of law enforcement in conducting a criminal investigation that would amount to judicial second-guessing of how the Commonwealth must build its case. We are mindful of the Supreme Court's admonition in *Lovasco* against placing too stringent a responsibility on the prosecution to justify the delay in the face of these claims: "The Due Process Clause does not permit courts to abort criminal prosecutions simply because they disagree with a prosecutor's judgment as to when to seek an indictment."

[The] test that we believe is the correct one must take into consideration all of the facts and circumstances surrounding the case, including: the deference that courts must afford to the prosecutor's conclusions that a case is not ripe for prosecution; the limited resources available to law enforcement agencies when conducting a criminal investigation; the prosecutor's motives in delaying indictment; and the degree to which the defendant's own actions contributed to the delay. Therefore, . . . in order to prevail on a due process claim based on pre-arrest delay, the defendant must first show that the delay caused him actual prejudice, that is, substantially impaired his or her ability to defend against the charges. The court must then examine all of the circumstances to determine the validity of the Commonwealth's reasons for the delay. Only in situations where the evidence shows that the delay was the product of intentional, bad faith, or reckless conduct by the prosecution, however, will we find a violation of due process. Negligence in the conduct of a criminal investigation, without more, will not be sufficient to prevail on a due process claim based on pre-arrest delay. With this clarification of the standard in mind, we turn to Scher's case.

ACTUAL PREJUDICE

. . . In order for a defendant to show actual prejudice, he or she must show that he or she was meaningfully impaired in his or her ability to defend against the state's charges to such an extent that the disposition of the criminal proceedings was likely affected. This kind of prejudice is commonly demonstrated by the loss of documentary evidence or the unavailability of an essential witness. It is not sufficient for a defendant to make speculative or conclusory claims of possible prejudice as a result of the passage of time. Where a defendant claims prejudice through the absence of witnesses, he or she must show in what specific manner missing witnesses would have aided the defense. Furthermore, it is the defendant's burden to show that the lost testimony or information is not available through other means.

Scher claims that he suffered prejudice because certain witnesses died and important evidence was lost by the time of trial that would have aided his defense that the shooting of Dillon was accidental, not intentional. Specifically, he . . . claims prejudice from the decomposition of Dillon's body that occurred during the twenty-year period, and from the Commonwealth's conduct of the second autopsy in 1995, which he claims interfered with his ability to present expert testimony in support of his position that Dillon's death was accidental. Further, Scher argues that the loss or destruction of other evidence, such as . . . the audio recording of the June 1976 autopsy; certain photographs taken of the scene; . . . and any bloodstains on the inside of the shotgun, impaired his ability to show that the shooting was accidental and not a premeditated act of murder.

In order to argue prejudice from the loss or destruction of evidence in these due process claims, the defendant must show that the loss or destruction of evidence related to the delay in filing charges. With respect to some of the items that Scher claims were lost or destroyed, the delay in filing charges clearly had no role in causing these items to be lost or destroyed. [The] repeated firing of the shotgun in 1976 by the police during testing of the weapon would have removed any bloodstains from inside the barrel [which would have tended to prove a close range of fire consistent with Scher's story]. Accordingly, the loss of this evidence cannot be attributed to the delay in indicting Scher for murder. . . .

Scher claims prejudice from the [death of the County Coroner, Dr. John Conarton]. Scher notes that Dillon's death certificate, completed by Conarton, lists the cause of Dillon's death as accidental. Scher contends that he was prejudiced when he lost the opportunity to have Conarton explain why he believed Dillon's death was accidental. What Scher ignores, however, is that in the section of the death certificate that asks, "How did injury occur?" Coroner Conarton wrote, "Running with gun, fell, gun went off." As Scher admitted in his trial testimony, this is not how Dillon died, and his stories to Conarton, Collier, and the other investigating officers to this effect were lies. Conarton was present when Scher gave his statement to Trooper Hairston at the scene, which related the false story of how Dillon tripped while running with the shotgun. The record strongly suggests that Conarton formed his opinion as to the cause of Dillon's death based mainly on Scher's false statement and a cursory review of the scene where Dillon's body lay positioned in a manner, with shoelaces untied, that Scher deliberately set to make it appear that Dillon tripped and fell while carrying the shotgun. . . . Consequently, we cannot credit Scher's complaints of prejudice from the absence of Conarton's testimony. . . .

The most serious claim of prejudice raised by Scher concerns the death of [Dr. James Grace, who conducted the autopsy,] and the loss of audio recordings from the June 3, 1976 autopsy performed by Dr. Grace, as well as the alteration of Dillon's body during the second autopsy in 1995. The critical issue to Scher's defense was whether the physical evidence was consistent with an accidental discharge of the weapon during a struggle. Evidence of the angle of Dillon's chest wound, . . . the presence or absence of gunpowder around the wound, and the size of the wound were relevant to the determination of whether Dillon was shot from a close range, consistent with a struggle, or a more distant range that could not have been caused by an accidental discharge during a struggle.

In support of his defense theory, Scher presented a number of expert witnesses. John Shane, M.D., a pathologist, reviewed, among other evidentiary items: twenty-seven black and white photographs of the scene; the clothes worn by Dillon, the photographs taken during Dr. Grace's autopsy; photographs taken during the second autopsy in 1995; forty-three microscopic slides of tissue taken from Dillon's body; Dr. Grace's autopsy report; and the shot cup retrieved from Dillon's body. . . . Dr. Shane testified that the presence of gunpowder residue in the wound tract signaled that the range of fire would have been within eighteen inches, due to the limited distance that gunpowder travels from the barrel when a firearm is discharged. [Scher also presented the testimony of two other expert witnesses who reviewed the available autopsy reports, photographs, clothing, and tissue samples; both concluded that the shot was fired from less than one foot from Dillon's body.] The ability of Scher's experts to support his defense by offering opinions to a reasonable degree of medical certainty based on a review of the evidence available to them demonstrates why Scher's claims of prejudice fail. . . .

REASONS FOR THE DELAY

[In] order for there to be a violation of due process, the Commonwealth's behavior must be more than merely negligent in causing the delay. Only where the Commonwealth has intentionally delayed in order to gain a tactical advantage or acted recklessly to such a degree as to shock one's conscience and offend one's sense of justice will we find a deprivation of due process. We do not find the Commonwealth's behavior in this case to be so outrageous as to meet that standard. There has been no allegation that the Commonwealth intentionally delayed indicting Scher in order to gain a tactical advantage over him, and the record contains credible denials from a succession of Susquehanna County District Attorneys that they ever intentionally employed delay tactics. Furthermore, we cannot accept the Superior Court's conclusion that the Commonwealth's actions were "grossly negligent." Astonishingly, the Superior Court's opinion makes no mention of the watershed moment in this case: when Scher admitted that he had lied to investigators about how Dillon's death occurred and that, for the past twenty years, he lied when he denied having had an affair with Patricia prior to the incident at Gunsmoke. [Scher] staged the scene and fabricated a story that gained some credence with investigators. Perhaps, as Scher argues, those investigators should have been more circumspect in accepting his tale and pursued their suspicions more thoroughly, but we cannot find the Commonwealth's actions towards Scher so egregious when, in a small town, in a rural part of Pennsylvania with a part-time District Attorney, those responsible for enforcing the law would find it difficult to disbelieve the word of a respected physician. Nor can we ignore the benefit that Scher gained by lying to authorities rather than remaining silent: he enjoyed his liberty for twenty years. In these circumstances, we cannot find that the Commonwealth's failure to charge Scher with murder sooner violated his right to due process of law. . . .

ZAPPALA, C.J., dissenting.

. . . The Commonwealth's inordinate and unexcused delay in filing charges against Dr. Scher resulted in actual prejudice to Dr. Scher's ability to defend himself against the charges. At trial, the pivotal issue was whether Mr. Dillon's death resulted from an accidental firing of the shotgun as he and Dr. Scher struggled with the shotgun or resulted from the intentional and deliberate firing of the shotgun by Dr. Scher at a distance of several feet away from Dillon. The Commonwealth premised its theory on the testimony of expert witnesses following an autopsy conducted 18 years after Dillon's death. The expert testimony sought to contradict the findings made by Dr. James Grace based upon the autopsy he conducted immediately after Dillon's death. During the trial, the competency of Dr. Grace to conduct the autopsy and the findings themselves were challenged by the Commonwealth. . . . While Dr. Grace's observations of the body and the shotgun wound were of paramount importance in determining whether the shotgun fired accidentally, the Commonwealth's delay in bringing the prosecution resulted in the unavailability of Dr. Grace as a witness. . . . While Dr. Grace lived for 19 years after the shooting incident, the Commonwealth lost the audio recording made during the 1976 autopsy performed by Dr. Grace and failed to subsequently preserve his recollection of the examination of crucial evidence. . . .

The resulting prejudice to Dr. Scher's defense due to the unavailability of this crucial witness was compounded by the Commonwealth's deliberate tactics at trial to disparage the findings made by Dr. Grace which were contrary to the prosecution's theory. In order to support its theory of the shooting, the Commonwealth attempted to flatly contradict Dr. Grace's observations by suggesting to the jury that as a physician he was incompetent to make even the simplest physical observations and claimed that the observations recorded by Dr. Grace in his autopsy report were not those that Dr. Grace actually intended to make.

[Throughout the 20 years that elapsed after the shooting, the Commonwealth possessed all] of the physical evidence that was collected after the shooting. This evidence included: the clothing worn by Dr. Scher and Mr. Dillon on the date of the shooting; Dr. Scher's 16-gauge shotgun, Mr. Dillon's 20-gauge shotgun, ammunition and shells found at the scene of the shooting, shooting glasses and ear protectors found at the scene, clay birds, bird thrower, and sections of a log. [Any of the witnesses interviewed by the troopers in the renewed investigation would have been available to be interviewed in 1976. The facilities and experts who conducted the testing were available to the Commonwealth when the investigation began. Any new tests performed by the Commonwealth and the Federal Bureau of Investigation failed to reveal any new and/or relevant information that could not have been discovered by testing procedures available to them in 1976.]

This record demonstrates that there was no ongoing investigation into the death of Mr. Dillon. The investigation was dormant for most of the 20 years of pre-arrest delay. Indeed, for 8 of those years, the "investigation" was non-existent. . . . There is no basis to conclude that the pre-arrest delay was required for further investigation. The record establishes that the Commonwealth did not have a proper reason for the inordinate delay. . . .

Notes

1. *Pre-accusation delay: majority position.* All state courts have interpreted the due process provisions of their state constitutions to limit a few types of pre-accusation delay, applying the test that the U.S. Supreme Court created in United States

v. Lovasco, 431 U.S. 783 (1977). A defendant raising a constitutional objection to a delay between the date of an alleged crime and the time of the indictment or information must show (1) the prejudice that the delay caused for the defense and (2) the reason for the delay. There are two basic approaches in the state courts on the burden of proving these elements. One group requires the defendant to prove both prejudice and an intentional prosecutorial delay to achieve a tactical advantage. See State v. Lacy, 929 P.2d 1288 (Ariz. 1996). A roughly equal number of states give the defendant the initial burden of proving prejudice and then require the government to prove a valid reason for the delay. See also People v. Nelson, 185 P.3d 49 (Cal. 2008) (pre-indictment delay between 1976 rape and murder and 2001 filing of charges in "cold-hit" DNA case did not cause unconstitutional prejudice; unavailability of defense witnesses and loss of other evidence is outweighed by prerogative of state to allocate investigative resources; record does not demonstrate prosecutorial negligence). In states that have passed statutes of limitations (as almost all states have), does the *Lovasco* analysis enable the courts to identify correctly the "stale" cases that the statute of limitations does not reach? Or does the constitutional analysis merely make the law less predictable, without systematically improving on the statutory limits? The breakdown among the state courts on this issue receives some attention on the web extension for this chapter at *http://www. crimpro.com/extension/ch15.*

2. *Reasons for delay.* The *Lovasco* Court declared categorically that there can be no due process violation if "good-faith investigative delay" is responsible for the timing of the charges. Courts also say that a delay created solely to gain a "tactical advantage" for the prosecution does create a due process problem. For example, if the prosecution has two potential cases against an accused and delays filing the second case in order to prevent the possibility of the accused receiving concurrent sentences, a court is likely to find a due process violation. Likewise, the prosecution may violate due process if it delays indicting the defendant until after a co-defendant's conviction has been affirmed, and this delay is based on the belief that the co-defendant would be a better witness at that time. United States v. Foxman, 87 F.3d 1220 (11th Cir. 1996). The longer the delay, the more willing courts are to find an improper reason for it. Did the prosecutors in *Scher* purposely delay filing charges, or did they each just change their minds about whether criminal charges were warranted?

A central question in the pre-accusation delay cases seems to be the good faith of the prosecutor. Compare this interpretation of the requirements of due process with the more general judicial reluctance to become involved in the prosecutor's charging decision in ordinary cases. See Chapter 13. Will an inquiry into the prosecutor's state of mind regarding a delay lead to more judicial scrutiny of prosecutorial charging decisions than traditional doctrine has allowed? In other words, is the test for pre-accusation delay more intrusive than the test for selective prosecution?

Problem 15-4 below illustrates one reason for delay: Crime victims in some cases—notably for intrafamily sexual assaults on children—do not make allegations for many years after the incidents. Should special constitutional rules apply to such cases? See State v. Gray, 917 S.W.2d 668 (Tenn. 1996) (dismissal of charges of sexual abuse brought 42 years after incident involving 8-year-old girl). Specialized statutes of limitations in many states address this type of case (as does the New York statute above).

3. *Source of constitutional protections.* Although the federal constitution and most state constitutions provide specifically for a "speedy trial," these provisions attach at a particular point in time: when charges are filed or when the defendant is arrested, whichever comes first. For a defendant who is not arrested, pre-accusation delays fall outside the bounds of the speedy trial clock. The U.S. Supreme Court took the lead on this question in United States v. Marion, 404 U.S. 307 (1971). A review of the text and history of the Sixth Amendment's speedy trial clause (which speaks of a speedy trial for the "accused") convinced the Court that only "a formal indictment or information or else the actual restraints imposed by arrest and holding to answer a criminal charge" would trigger the protections of the speedy trial clause. See also United States v. MacDonald, 456 U.S. 1 (1982) (no speedy trial protection for period between dismissal of first charges and second indictment). As you read further materials in this chapter and encounter cases decided under the Sixth Amendment or analogous state constitutional clauses, consider whether the due process cases dealing with pre-accusation delay would be decided differently if they were analyzed under the more specific constitutional language requiring a "speedy trial."

4. *Statutes of limitations.* The Court in *Marion* noted that statutes of limitations provide "the primary guarantee against bringing overly stale criminal charges." The New York statute above is typical in several respects. First, it provides longer limitation periods for more serious crimes. Second, it creates special rules for marking the beginning of the limitation period for certain crimes unlikely to be detected or reported immediately. The statute leaves it for judges to answer the difficult question of when a continuing crime, such as conspiracy, is "committed" in the sense necessary to trigger the statute. Finally, the statute defines certain events that can "toll" (i.e., suspend) the statute after it has begun to run. Should the drafters of the New York statute have included a provision that would allow judges to create additional "tolling" rules "in the interest of justice"?

Should statutes of limitations influence a court ruling on a constitutional challenge to pre-accusation delay? More specifically, if a statute gives extra latitude to a prosecutor in some cases, should that lead a court to give prosecutors extra latitude for delay under the due process clause? Or should the due process protections be strongest when legislatures have provided less statutory protection against delay?

Perhaps the rationale for a statute of limitations is based on something other than deterioration of evidence. Should we keep statutes of limitations because criminals tend to be more short-sighted than the general public, and the deterrent power of criminal charges is lost if the case is not filed relatively quickly? See Yair Listokin, Efficient Time Bars: A New Rationale for the Existence of Statutes of Limitations in Criminal Law, 31 J. Legal Stud. 99 (2002) (because potential criminals tend to discount the future at higher rates than society, punishing crimes long after they are committed will have only a nominal deterrent effect, while they may cost society substantial sums).

Problem 15-4. Child Victims

Gilbert Vernier is a 69-year-old grandfather. In July 1999, M.E., then 7 years old, supported by her sister, J.V., informed their mother, "Grandpa touched me in a bad way." The Wyoming Department of Family Services and the county sheriff's department investigated the claim. Two interviews of the victim and her sister were recorded on audiotape. A lieutenant in the sheriff's department who was present during the interview transcribed the second tape. No charges were filed at that time.

Ten years later, in 2009, another granddaughter, L.L., reported to the sheriff's department that in 1992 Vernier had molested her when she was 9 years old. Two weeks after L.L. made this report, M.E. again informed the sheriff's department that Vernier had sexually assaulted her in 1999, and J.V. corroborated M.E.'s statements. Shortly after L.L. came forward in 2009, Vernier's daughters also recounted repeated sexual abuse and rape by their father when they were young teenagers.

Following the 2009 investigation, the state charged Vernier with two counts of indecent liberties and one count of second-degree sexual assault based on the alleged incidents in 1999. At his arraignment, Vernier entered a plea of not guilty and filed a motion to dismiss, claiming the state intentionally had delayed filing charges. Although Wyoming has no statute of limitations for prosecuting crimes, Vernier claimed that the delay violated his due process rights. He argued that the 10-year delay impaired his efforts to defend himself against the charges. During that time, the government lost the two 1999 audiotapes of conversations between M.E. and investigators. The transcript of the second tape still exists, however, along with the deputy's notes reflecting her own observations about the interview. Vernier also argued that in 1999 he might have recalled an alibi that would have been helpful.

The district court denied the motion. How would you rule on appeal? How would you respond if Vernier asks your court to create a specific limitations period for crimes in the absence of a statute of limitations, either as a matter of constitutional law or as an exercise of the court's "supervisory" power over the state's criminal justice system? Compare Vernier v. State, 909 P.2d 1344 (Wyo. 1996).

2. Constitutional Protections for Speedy Trial After Accusation

Once the prosecution obtains an indictment or files an information against a defendant, a wider array of legal provisions become available to move the process along. The Sixth Amendment grants to "the accused" the right to a "speedy and public trial." Analogous state constitutional clauses announce such rights in similarly general terms. The federal Speedy Trial Act creates a more specific obligation for the government to process all criminal trials within 70 days of the indictment or information, although it provides several ways to exclude days from the tally. Most states have statutes limiting the time between an accusation and the start of trial (or entry of a guilty plea). Statutes and judicial orders also allocate judicial resources to keep criminal dockets moving.

The deadlines become relevant in a great number of cases. In large urban jurisdictions in 2006, the median time it took to adjudicate a felony case was 92 days (up from 79 days in 1998). Just under half the cases were adjudicated within three months. Twelve percent of the felony cases were still unresolved a year after the arrest. See Bureau of Justice Statistics, Felony Defendants in Large Urban Counties, 2006, at Table 10 (2010, NCJ 228944).

From its earliest opportunity, the U.S. Supreme Court has insisted that the constitutional guarantee of a "speedy" trial is a "necessarily relative" concept. See Beavers v. Haubert, 198 U.S. 77 (1905). The same length of time between accusation

and resolution of criminal charges might be acceptable in one case and unacceptable in another, depending on the prosecutor's reasons, the harm that the defendant suffered, and other circumstances. In Barker v. Wingo, 407 U.S. 514 (1972),
the Court settled on four circumstances that every court must consider when resolving a claim that the government has violated a defendant's constitutional right to a
speedy trial. As you read the following case, consider how the four factors interact
and ask whether some pertinent questions have now been placed out of view.

■ VERMONT V. MICHAEL BRILLON
556 U.S. 81 (2009)

GINSBURG, J.*

This case concerns the Sixth Amendment guarantee that in "all criminal prosecutions, the accused shall enjoy the right to a speedy . . . trial." Michael Brillon,
defendant below, respondent here, was arrested in July 2001 on felony domestic
assault and habitual offender charges. Nearly three years later, in June 2004, he was
tried by jury, found guilty as charged, and sentenced to 12 to 20 years in prison.
The Vermont Supreme Court vacated Brillon's conviction and held that the charges
against him must be dismissed because he had been denied his right to a speedy
trial. . . . We hold that the Vermont Supreme Court erred. . . .

I.

On July 27, 2001, Michael Brillon was arrested after striking his girlfriend.
Three days later he was arraigned in state court in Bennington County, Vermont
and charged with felony domestic assault. His alleged status as a habitual offender
exposed him to a potential life sentence. The court ordered him held without bail.

Richard Ammons, from the county public defender's office, was assigned on the
day of arraignment as Brillon's first counsel. In October, Ammons filed a motion
to recuse the trial judge. It was denied the next month and trial was scheduled for
February 2002. In mid-January, Ammons moved for a continuance, but the State
objected, and the trial court denied the motion.

On February 22, four days before the jury draw, Ammons again moved for a continuance, citing his heavy workload and the need for further investigation. Ammons
acknowledged that any delay would not count (presumably against the State) for
speedy-trial purposes. The State opposed the motion,[2] and at the conclusion of a
hearing, the trial court denied it. Brillon, participating in the proceedings through
interactive television, then announced: "You're fired, Rick." Three days later, the
trial court—over the State's objection—granted Ammons' motion to withdraw as
counsel, citing Brillon's termination of Ammons and Ammons' statement that he
could no longer zealously represent Brillon. The trial court warned Brillon that

---

* [Chief Justice Roberts and Justices Scalia, Kennedy, Souter, Thomas, and Alito joined this opinion.—EDS.]

2. . . . Under Vermont procedures, the judge presiding over the trial was scheduled to "rotate" out
of the county where Brillon's case was pending in March 2002. Thus, a continuance past March would
have caused a different judge to preside over Brillon's trial, despite the denial of his motion to recuse the
initial judge. Ammons requested a continuance until April.

further delay would occur while a new attorney became familiar with the case. The same day, the trial court appointed a second attorney, but he immediately withdrew based on a conflict.

On March 1, 2002, Gerard Altieri was assigned as Brillon's third counsel. On May 20, Brillon filed a motion to dismiss Altieri for, among other reasons, failure to file motions, "virtually no communication whatsoever," and his lack of diligence "because of heavy case load." At a June 11 hearing, Altieri denied several of Brillon's allegations, noted his disagreement with Brillon's trial strategy,[4] and insisted he had plenty of time to prepare. The State opposed Brillon's motion as well. Near the end of the hearing, however, Altieri moved to withdraw on the ground that Brillon had threatened his life during a break in the proceedings. The trial court granted Brillon's motion to dismiss Altieri, but warned Brillon that "this is somewhat of a dubious victory in your case because it simply prolongs the time that you will remain in jail until we can bring this matter to trial."

That same day, the trial court appointed Paul Donaldson as Brillon's fourth counsel. At an August 5 status conference, Donaldson requested additional time to conduct discovery in light of his caseload. A few weeks later, Brillon sent a letter to the court complaining about Donaldson's unresponsiveness and lack of competence. Two months later, Brillon filed a motion to dismiss Donaldson—similar to his motion to dismiss Altieri—for failure to file motions and "virtually no communication whatsoever." At a November 26 hearing, Donaldson reported that his contract with the Defender General's office had expired in June and that he had been in discussions to have Brillon's case reassigned. The trial court released Donaldson from the case without making any findings regarding the adequacy of Donaldson's representation.

Brillon's fifth counsel, David Sleigh, was not assigned until January 15, 2003; Brillon was without counsel during the intervening two months. On February 25, Sleigh sought extensions of various discovery deadlines, noting that he had been in trial out of town. On April 10, however, Sleigh withdrew from the case, based on "modifications to [his] firm's contract with the Defender General."

Brillon was then without counsel for the next four months. On June 20, the Defender General's office notified the court that it had received funding from the legislature and would hire a new special felony unit defender for Brillon. On August 1, Kathleen Moore was appointed as Brillon's sixth counsel. The trial court set November 7 as the deadline for motions, but granted several extensions in accord with the parties' stipulation. On February 23, 2004, Moore filed a motion to dismiss for lack of a speedy trial. The trial court denied the motion on April 19.

The case finally went to trial on June 14, 2004. Brillon was found guilty and sentenced to 12 to 20 years in prison. The trial court denied a post-trial motion to dismiss for want of a speedy trial, concluding that the delay in Brillon's trial was "in large part the result of his own actions" and that Brillon had "failed to demonstrate prejudice as a result of [the] pre-trial delay."

On appeal, the Vermont Supreme Court held 3 to 2 that Brillon's conviction must be vacated and the charges dismissed for violation of his Sixth Amendment

---

4. Specifically, Altieri appeared reluctant to follow Brillon's tactic that he "bring in a lot of people" at trial, "some of them young kids and relatives . . . in an attempt by Mr. Brillon—this is his theory—I don't want to use the words trash, [to] impeach [the victim]."

right to a speedy trial. Citing the balancing test of Barker v. Wingo, 407 U.S. 514 (1972), the majority concluded that all four of the factors described in *Barker*—length of delay, the reason for the delay, the defendant's assertion of his right, and prejudice to the defendant—weighed against the State.

The court first found that the three-year delay in bringing Brillon to trial was "extreme" and weighed heavily in his favor. In assessing the reasons for that delay, the Vermont Supreme Court separately considered the period of each counsel's representation. It acknowledged that the first year, when Brillon was represented by Ammons and Altieri, should not count against the State. But the court counted much of the remaining two years against the State for delays "caused, for the most part, by the failure of several of defendant's assigned counsel, over an inordinate period of time, to move his case forward." As for the third and fourth factors, the court found that Brillon "repeatedly and adamantly demanded to be tried," and that his "lengthy pretrial incarceration" was prejudicial, despite his insubstantial assertions of evidentiary prejudice. . . .

II.

The Sixth Amendment guarantees that in "all criminal prosecutions, the accused shall enjoy the right to a speedy . . . trial." . . . In *Barker*, the Court refused to quantify the right into a specified number of days or months or to hinge the right on a defendant's explicit request for a speedy trial. Rejecting such "inflexible approaches," *Barker* established a balancing test, in which the conduct of both the prosecution and the defendant are weighed. Some of the factors that courts should weigh include length of delay, the reason for the delay, the defendant's assertion of his right, and prejudice to the defendant.

Primarily at issue here is the reason for the delay in Brillon's trial. *Barker* instructs that "different weights should be assigned to different reasons," and in applying *Barker*, we have asked "whether the government or the criminal defendant is more to blame" for the delay. Doggett v. United States, 505 U.S. 647, 651 (1992). Deliberate delay to hamper the defense weighs heavily against the prosecution. More neutral reasons such as negligence or overcrowded courts weigh less heavily but nevertheless should be considered since the ultimate responsibility for such circumstances must rest with the government rather than with the defendant.

In contrast, delay caused by the defense weighs against the defendant: If delay is attributable to the defendant, then his waiver may be given effect under standard waiver doctrine. That rule accords with the reality that defendants may have incentives to employ delay as a defense tactic: delay may work to the accused's advantage because witnesses may become unavailable or their memories may fade over time.

Because the attorney is the defendant's agent when acting, or failing to act, in furtherance of the litigation, delay caused by the defendant's counsel is also charged against the defendant. Coleman v. Thompson, 501 U.S. 722, 753 (1991).[6] The same principle applies whether counsel is privately retained or publicly assigned, for once a lawyer has undertaken the representation of an accused, the duties and obligations are the same whether the lawyer is privately retained, appointed, or serving in

---

6. Several States' speedy-trial statutes expressly exclude from computation of the time limit continuances and delays caused by the defendant or defense counsel. [The Court cited statutes or rules of procedure from California, New York, Alaska, Arkansas, and Indiana.]

a legal aid or defender program. Except for the source of payment, the relationship between a defendant and the public defender representing him is identical to that existing between any other lawyer and client. Unlike a prosecutor or the court, assigned counsel ordinarily is not considered a state actor.

III.

Barker's formulation necessarily compels courts to approach speedy trial cases on an ad hoc basis, and the balance arrived at in close cases ordinarily would not prompt this Court's review. But the Vermont Supreme Court made a fundamental error in its application of *Barker* that calls for this Court's correction. The Vermont Supreme Court erred in attributing to the State delays caused by "the failure of several assigned counsel . . . to move his case forward," and in failing adequately to take into account the role of Brillon's disruptive behavior in the overall balance.

The Vermont Supreme Court's opinion is driven by the notion that delay caused by assigned counsel's "inaction" or failure "to move the case forward" is chargeable to the State, not the defendant. In this case, that court concluded, a significant portion of the delay in bringing defendant to trial must be attributed to the state, even though most of the delay was caused by the inability or unwillingness of assigned counsel to move the case forward.

We disagree. An assigned counsel's failure "to move the case forward" does not warrant attribution of delay to the State. Contrary to the Vermont Supreme Court's analysis, assigned counsel generally are not state actors for purposes of a speedy-trial claim. While the Vermont Defender General's office is indeed "part of the criminal justice system," the individual counsel here acted only on behalf of Brillon, not the State.

Most of the delay that the Vermont Supreme Court attributed to the State must therefore be attributed to Brillon as delays caused by his counsel. During those periods, Brillon was represented by Donaldson, Sleigh, and Moore, all of whom requested extensions and continuances. Their "inability or unwillingness" to move the case forward may not be attributed to the State simply because they are assigned counsel.

A contrary conclusion could encourage appointed counsel to delay proceedings by seeking unreasonable continuances, hoping thereby to obtain a dismissal of the indictment on speedy-trial grounds. Trial courts might well respond by viewing continuance requests made by appointed counsel with skepticism, concerned that even an apparently genuine need for more time is in reality a delay tactic. Yet the same considerations would not attend a privately retained counsel's requests for time extensions. We see no justification for treating defendants' speedy-trial claims differently based on whether their counsel is privately retained or publicly assigned.

In addition to making assigned counsel's "failure to move the case forward" the touchstone of its speedy-trial inquiry, the Vermont Supreme Court further erred by treating the period of each counsel's representation discretely. [The] Vermont Supreme Court failed appropriately to take into account Brillon's role during the first year of delay. . . .

Brillon sought to dismiss Ammons on the eve of trial. His strident, aggressive behavior with regard to Altieri, whom he threatened, further impeded prompt trial and likely made it more difficult for the Defender General's office to find replacement counsel. Even after the trial court's warning regarding delay, Brillon sought dismissal of yet another attorney, Donaldson. Just as a State's deliberate attempt to delay the trial in order to hamper the defense should be weighted heavily against the State, so too should a defendant's deliberate attempt to disrupt proceedings be weighted heavily against the defendant. Absent Brillon's deliberate efforts to force the withdrawal of Ammons and Altieri, no speedy-trial issue would have arisen. The effect of these earlier events should have been factored into the court's analysis of subsequent delay.

The general rule attributing to the defendant delay caused by assigned counsel is not absolute. Delay resulting from a systemic breakdown in the public defender system could be charged to the State. But the Vermont Supreme Court made no determination, and nothing in the record suggests, that institutional problems caused any part of the delay in Brillon's case.

In sum, delays caused by defense counsel are properly attributed to the defendant, even where counsel is assigned. Any inquiry into a speedy trial claim necessitates a functional analysis of the right in the particular context of the case, and the record in this case does not show that Brillon was denied his constitutional right to a speedy trial. . . .

BREYER, J., dissenting.*

We granted certiorari in this case to decide whether delays caused "solely" by a public defender can be "charged against the State pursuant to the test in Barker v. Wingo. The case, in my view, does not squarely present that question, for the Vermont Supreme Court, when it found Michael Brillon's trial unconstitutionally delayed, did not count such delays against the State. . . . Given these circumstances, I would dismiss the writ of certiorari as improvidently granted.

The relevant time period consists of slightly less than three years, stretching from July 2001, when Brillon was indicted, until mid-June 2004, when he was convicted and sentenced. In light of Brillon's improper behavior, the Vermont Supreme Court did not count months 1 through 12 (mid-July 2001 through mid-June 2002) against the State. Noting the objection that Brillon had sought to "intentionally sabotage the criminal proceedings against him," the Vermont Supreme Court was explicit that this time period "does not count against the State."

The Vermont Supreme Court did count months 13 through 17 (mid-June 2002 through November 2002) against the State. It did so under circumstances where (1) Brillon's counsel, Paul Donaldson, revealed that his contract with the defender general's office had expired in June 2002—shortly after (perhaps before!) he took over as Brillon's counsel, (2) he stated that this case was "basically the beginning of [his] departure from the contract," and (3) he made no filings, missed several deadlines, did "little or nothing" to "move the case forward," and made only one brief appearance at a status conference in mid-August. I believe it fairer to characterize this period, not as a period in which "assigned counsel" failed to move the case forward, but as a period in which Brillon, in practice, had no assigned counsel. And, given that the State conceded its responsibility for delays caused by another defender who resigned for "contractual reasons," it is hardly unreasonable that the Vermont Supreme Court counted this period of delay against the State.

* [Justice Stevens joined this opinion.—EDS.]

The Vermont Supreme Court also counted months 18 through 25 (the end of November 2002 through July 2003) against the State. It did so because the State conceded in its brief that this period of delay cannot be attributed to the defendant. This concession is not surprising in light of the fact that during much of this period, Brillon was represented by David Sleigh, a contract attorney, who during the course of his representation filed nothing on Brillon's behalf except a single motion seeking to extend discovery. The record reflects no other actions by Sleigh other than a letter sent to Brillon informing him that as a result of "modifications to our firm's contract with the Defender General, we will not be representing you in your pending case." Brillon was left without counsel for a period of nearly six months. The State explained in conceding its responsibility for this delay that Sleigh had been forced to withdraw "for contractual reasons," and that the defender general's office had been unable to replace him "for funding reasons."

Finally, the Vermont Supreme Court counted against the State the last 11 months—from August 2003 to mid-June 2004. But it is impossible to conclude from the opinion whether it did so because it held the State responsible for the defender's failure to "move the case forward," or for other reasons having nothing to do with counsel, namely the judge's unavailability, or the fact that the case files were incomplete and "additional documents were needed from the State."

[The] Vermont Supreme Court has considerable authority to supervise the appointment of public defenders. See Vt. Stat. Ann., Tit. 13, §§5204, 5272 (1998); see also Vt. Rule Crim. Proc. 44 (2003). It consequently warrants leeway when it decides whether a particular failing is properly attributed to assigned counsel or instead to the failure of the defender general's office properly to assign counsel. I do not believe the Vermont Supreme Court exceeded that leeway here. . . .

Notes

1. *Constitutional speedy trial rights: majority position.* The Supreme Court has incorporated the "speedy trial" clause of the Sixth Amendment as a component of the Fourteenth Amendment's due process clause that applies to the states. Klopfer v. North Carolina, 386 U.S. 213 (1967). As noted in the prior section, the speedy trial clock begins to run when the defendant is charged or arrested, whichever comes first. United States v. Marion, 404 U.S. 307 (1971). In addition, virtually all states have used the four-part test from Barker v. Wingo, 407 U.S. 514 (1972), to assess potential violations of the speedy trial rights of defendants under their state constitutions. As illustrated in the *Brillon* case, the analysis of constitutional speedy trial claims often requires courts to answer a series of questions, assigning responsibility for each period of delay. The first *Barker* factor (the length of the delay) is a necessary threshold. Only when the delay becomes long enough will the court analyze the other factors. Although the exact length of time necessary is a question for common-law development, a delay of just under one year is usually sufficient to obtain a full review of the four factors. Once the full inquiry takes place, often the most important factor is whether the defendant has been prejudiced.

2. *Ranking reasons for delay.* Courts in most jurisdictions have followed the *Barker* Court's suggestion that a "deliberate attempt to delay the trial in order to hamper the defense" is weighed heavily against the government, while a "valid reason" such as a missing witness would justify some delay. Reasons such as prosecutorial negligence

or lack of resources will count against the government, but not heavily. See State v. Spivey, 579 S.E.2d 251 (N.C. 2003) (delay of over four years in starting murder trial acceptable under *Barker*; reasons for delay included numerous homicide cases on docket, courthouse renovations). Prosecutors in the Bronx have been known to request continuances to accommodate their vacation plans, and some defense attorneys have asked to postpone court hearings because of birthday celebrations. Does it make sense to make defendants bear the cost of these sorts of conflicts? What about delays caused by inadequate public defender funding? Should a similar ranking system apply to a defendant's reasons for contributing to the delay? Will the defendant's actions only be weighed "heavily" against her claim if she has made a deliberate attempt to hamper the prosecution through delay? See State v. Azania, 865 N.E.2d 994 (Ind. 2007) (time elapsed during pursuit of collateral relief after first trial is attributed to defendant, the party with the obligation to go forward in such proceedings, and does not require dismissal of charges before retrial after grant of habeas relief).

3. *Prejudice.* The *Barker* Court listed three types of prejudice that a speedy trial could avoid: (a) "oppressive pretrial incarceration"; (b) "anxiety and concern of the accused"; and (c) "the possibility that the defense will be impaired." Courts routinely say that the third type of prejudice, which can include disappearance of witnesses or loss of memory, is the most serious. If there is a statistical relationship between pretrial detention and conviction for the charged crime, is it plausible to argue that any prejudice of the first type (pretrial detention) also must count as prejudice of the third type (impairment of defense)? Does it matter what grounds the government has for holding the defendant? Speedy trial rights extend to persons imprisoned for other offenses. See Smith v. Hooey, 393 U.S. 374 (1969). Will incarceration for another offense weigh less heavily in favor of the defendant than incarceration only for the current charges?

There are cases in which the other *Barker* factors create such a strong showing for the defendant that the court will presume prejudice. According to Doggett v. United States, 505 U.S. 647 (1992), the presumption of prejudice strengthens over time. The eight-year delay between indictment and arrest in *Doggett* was a product of the defendant's choice to leave the country (unaware that he was under indictment) and the government's negligence in pursuing him. The Court was willing to presume that such a lengthy delay would impair the defense. But see People v. Martinez, 996 P.2d 32 (Cal. 2000) (court refuses to adopt federal rule that defendant need not show specific prejudice if delay is sufficiently long; defendant must always show prejudice under state law).

4. *Remedy.* What should a court do if it is convinced that the government has violated a defendant's constitutional speedy trial rights? According to Strunk v. United States, 412 U.S. 434 (1973), dismissal of the charges with prejudice is the only proper remedy for a violation of the Sixth Amendment speedy trial right. State courts by and large have interpreted their own constitutions the same way. Can you imagine any alternative remedies that would effectively deter delay without losing convictions of guilty persons? How about a reduction of sentence to reflect the amount of improper delay? What about money damages for improper pretrial incarceration or prolonged anxiety? If these alternatives were available to state courts, would they become more willing to find a constitutional violation? Should a court be able to select a nondismissal remedy only for particular kinds of prejudice (such as anxiety

or loss of reputation) but not for others (such as impairment of defense)? See Akhil Amar, The Constitution and Criminal Procedure: First Principles 96-116 (1997).

5. *No right to speedy sentencing.* In 2017, the U.S. Supreme Court held that the speedy trial right does not apply to sentencing delays. "As a measure protecting the presumptively innocent, the speedy trial right—like other similarly situated measures—loses force upon conviction," the Court said in Betterman v. Montana, 136 S.Ct. 1609 (2016).

6. *The influence of pretrial hearings.* One reason why a trial may be delayed includes the consideration of various pretrial motions, such as motions to dismiss the indictment, to suppress evidence, to change venue, or to compel discovery, as well as interlocutory appeals of the court's decisions on these motions. Under speedy trial statutes, delays resulting from such motions and interlocutory appeals are typically excluded from the speedy trial calculation, regardless of which party has filed the motion or the appeal. See, e.g., 18 U.S.C. §3161(h)(1)(C)-(D); N.Y. Crim. Proc. Law §30.30(4)(a). Should delays resulting from motions, responses to motions, or interlocutory appeals filed by the prosecution be excluded? See United States v. Loud Hawk, 474 U.S. 302 (1986). Some states require the prosecution to show that it exercised due diligence in filing or responding to a motion or interlocutory appeal. Commonwealth v. Hill, 736 A.2d 578 (Pa. 1999).

7. *The victim's right to speedy trial.* Over the past generation, state constitutional amendments and statutes have recognized some of the interests and procedural rights of victims of alleged crimes. A majority of states now have statutory or constitutional provisions requiring the trial court to consider the interests of crime victims (especially youthful or elderly victims) when responding to requests for continuances. A few states declare more generally that victims have a right to a speedy trial. Take, for instance, Utah Code §77-38-7:

> (1) In determining a date for any criminal trial or other important criminal or juvenile justice hearing, the court shall consider the interests of the victim of a crime to a speedy resolution of the charges under the same standards that govern a defendant's or minor's right to a speedy trial. . . .
>
> (3)(a) In ruling on any motion by a defendant or minor to continue a previously established trial or other important criminal or juvenile justice hearing, the court shall inquire into the circumstances requiring the delay and consider the interests of the victim of a crime to a speedy disposition of the case. . . .

What assurance does a crime victim have that a trial court will carry out these directives? Is the statute enforceable on appeal?

3. Statutory Protections for Speedy Trial After Accusation

Almost all states now have statutes or procedural rules that oblige the government to complete criminal trials promptly. These "speedy trial acts" show some important differences from one another. First, these statutes and rules differ in how specifically they define the time period that may elapse between accusation and the start of trial. Most, like the federal Speedy Trial Act, give the state a specific number of days (70 days in the federal system) to process the case. Within the group of states that specify the time period, many allow more days to bring to trial a defendant who is not in custody than one who is in custody. See 725 ILCS 5/103-5 (120 days for defendants in custody, 160 days for defendants released pretrial). A smaller group of states do not specify a number of days at all, but simply require the trial to take place within a "reasonable" time. Mich. R. Crim. P. 6.004 (provides that the "defendant and the people are entitled to a speedy trial and to a speedy resolution of all matters before the court," but states no specific time period for trial of charges against defendants not in custody).

Second, the statutes differ from one another in the methods available to extend the number of days the parties may use to prepare for trial. Some, like the federal statute, exhaustively list the events that can add time to the available days; a number of statutes allow the trial court to extend the time period for "good cause" (or on some other generally phrased grounds). Third, the statutes differ from one another in the remedies they provide for violations. The federal statute is typical of one group, giving the trial judge considerable discretion to choose whether to dismiss the charges with or without prejudice. Other statutes make it clear that one form of dismissal or the other is strongly preferred or required.

Can you identify a combination of features described above that is likely to have the most effect on the amount of time available to prepare a case for trial? The least effect? As you reflect on these statutes, keep a close eye on the interaction between rights and remedies. Is there a relationship between the clarity of the speedy trial obligations that the government faces and the stringency of the remedy for violations? Do these statutes "codify" the constitutional analysis or do they pursue different objectives, using different means?

■ CALIFORNIA PENAL CODE §1382

(a) The court, unless good cause to the contrary is shown, shall order the action to be dismissed in the following cases: . . .

(2) In a felony case, when a defendant is not brought to trial within 60 days of the defendant's arraignment on an indictment or information, or reinstatement of criminal proceedings . . . or, in case the cause is to be tried again following a mistrial, an order granting a new trial from which an appeal is not taken, or an appeal from the superior court, within 60 days after the mistrial has been declared. . . . However, an action shall not be dismissed under this paragraph if either of the following circumstances exists:

(A) The defendant enters a general waiver of the 60-day trial requirement. . . .

(B) The defendant requests or consents to the setting of a trial date beyond the 60-day period. . . . Whenever a case is set for trial beyond the 60-day period by request or consent, expressed or implied, of the defendant without a general waiver, the defendant shall be brought to trial on the date set for trial or within 10 days thereafter. . . .

(c) If the defendant is not represented by counsel, the defendant shall not be deemed under this section to have consented to the date for the defendant's trial unless the court has explained to the defendant his or her rights under this section and the effect of his or her consent.

■ CALIFORNIA PENAL CODE §1387

(a) An order terminating an action pursuant to [section 1382] is a bar to any other prosecution for the same offense if it is a felony or if it is a misdemeanor charged together with a felony and the action has been previously terminated pursuant to [section 1382], or if it is a misdemeanor not charged together with a felony, except in those [cases in which] the judge or magistrate finds any of the following:

(1) That substantial new evidence has been discovered by the prosecution which would not have been known through the exercise of due diligence at, or prior to, the time of termination of the action.

(2) That the termination of the action was the result of the direct intimidation of a material witness, as shown by a preponderance of the evidence. . . .

(b) Notwithstanding subdivision (a), an order terminating an action pursuant to this chapter is not a bar to another prosecution for the same offense if it is . . . an offense based on an act of domestic violence, . . . and the termination of the action was the result of the failure to appear by the complaining witness, who had been personally subpoenaed. This subdivision shall apply only within six months of the original dismissal of the action, and may be invoked only once in each action. . . .

Problem 15-5. The Fierce Urgency of Now

In recent years, the Superior Court of fast-growing Riverside County, California, has been severely overburdened by the substantial number of criminal cases awaiting trial. Section 1382 of the Penal Code, reprinted above, establishes a presumptive time period of 60 days for bringing a felony case to trial. Nonetheless, a 2007 survey revealed that nearly 25 percent of jail inmates had been awaiting trial for more than one year. One hundred seventy-seven inmates had been awaiting trial for more than two years, thirty-two inmates were awaiting trial for more than four years, and in one case the delay was an astonishing eight years.

To address this problem, the Chief Justice of the California Supreme Court assigned numerous retired judges and active judges from outside the county to assist the Riverside Superior Court. Furthermore, the Riverside Superior Court itself devoted virtually all of its judges and courtrooms ordinarily intended for the trial of civil cases to the trial of criminal cases.

The case of Terrion Marcus Engram illustrates some of the delay issues in Riverside County. Engram initially was tried and convicted of burglary. His conviction was overturned on appeal and his case was remanded for a new trial. Engram was released from custody pending retrial and remained free from custody throughout the later proceedings. His second trial resulted in a hung jury on May 27. His third trial on the burglary charges was set for July 14. Here's what happened.

- July 14: the prosecution moved to postpone the trial until July 28, the last day for trial under the then-governing time waiver executed by defendant. The assigned deputy district attorney gave four reasons to support the request: (1) "I have a last-day case set for today," (2) "I also have two last-day cases on July 21," (3) "I need time to prepare one of these cases as a hand-off for another Deputy District Attorney to try," and (4) "I need time to coordinate witness schedules." The trial court granted the prosecution's motion.

- July 28: defendant moved to continue the trial to August 28, based on his counsel's declaration that he was unable to complete discovery and investigation pending receipt of the trial transcripts from the second trial. The court granted the motion without objection by the prosecution and continued the trial to the date requested. At that time, counsel stipulated that the last day for trial under defendant's then-applicable time waiver was September 8.

- August 28: the prosecution moved to continue the trial to September 8. A declaration filed by the deputy district attorney stated: (1) "I will be out of town the week of September 1-5," (2) "I recently finished trial" in another case, (3) "I have another case that has a current last day of September 8, and I need time to prepare this case as a 'hand off' for another Deputy District Attorney," and (4) "I need time to coordinate witness schedules and prepare for trial." The trial court, without a waiver of time by defendant, granted the motion and continued the trial to September 8.

- September 8: the prosecution moved to continue the trial, this time until September 17. A declaration filed in support of the motion stated that the deputy district attorney assigned to the case was out of the state and unavailable, attending to his brother who unexpectedly had been hospitalized. Without opposition by the defendant, the trial court granted the motion and continued the trial to September 17. At that point, counsel for both parties stipulated that the last day for trial was September 29.

- September 11: the prosecution moved to postpone the trial to September 29. The assigned deputy district attorney stated that the prosecution would be unable to proceed on the 17th because (1) "I will be out of town the week of September 15-18," (2) "I have two other cases that have a current last day of September 19 and September 22," (3) "I need time to prepare this or the other two cases as a 'hand off' for another Deputy District Attorney," and (4) "I need time to coordinate witness schedules and prepare for trial." When the case was called on September 17, the trial court, without a waiver of time by defendant, granted the prosecution's motion to postpone the trial until September 29.

- September 29: defense counsel announced he was ready for trial and that Engram objected to any further delay of trial. The elected district attorney appeared for the prosecution and informed the judge that in addition to the present case involving Engram, there were 17 other "last day" cases (one other felony case and 16 misdemeanor cases) that were before the court on September 29, each of which presented a statutory speedy trial issue. In each of the cases, the defense announced it was ready for trial and stated that the defendant objected to any further delay. The trial court informed counsel for both parties that there were no available courtrooms to which the case could be assigned for trial (including courtrooms regularly devoted to juvenile, probate, and family law matters). At that point, the defense attorney moved to dismiss, pursuant to section 1382 (reprinted above). The district attorney responded with a request for a "good cause" exception to the requirements of the speedy trial preparation statute: "If the Court doesn't have sufficient resources to try these cases and the Court has done everything that the Court can do to find courtrooms for these cases, that should amount to good cause to continue each of these matters at least one day."

Imagine that you are the trial judge in this case. Engram is seeking to dismiss and the prosecution is requesting a good cause continuance. How will you rule? See People v. Johnson, 606 P.2d 738 (Cal. 1980) (ordinary court congestion arising from inadequate resources is not good cause, but congestion arising from extraordinary and nonrecurring circumstances can qualify as good cause). Would your decision be different if the Chief Justice had not already devoted extra judicial resources to the county? Cf. People v. Engram, 240 P.3d 237 (Cal. 2010). If you grant the defendant's motion, will you dismiss the case with prejudice (prohibiting the prosecution from filing charges again), or without prejudice? What would be the outcome if the controlling statute were the federal Speedy Trial Act, reprinted below?

Consider the problem also from the perspective of the prosecutor. It is the duty of the prosecutor to stay on top of her calendar, and her career may suffer over unwarranted delay. Was this prosecutor diligently on top of her calendar? Consider also that victims generally want to see the case come to a resolution quickly. Notice that none of the continuances in *Engram* invoked the victim's position on whether the trial should be postponed. What should a prosecutor do if a victim disagrees with her decision to delay the trial, but the prosecutor otherwise has a strong reason to request a delay?

■ 18 U.S.C. §3161

(c) (1) In any case in which a plea of not guilty is entered, the trial of a defendant charged in an information or indictment with the commission of an offense shall commence within 70 days from the filing date (and making public) of the information or indictment, or from the date the defendant has appeared before a judicial officer of the court in which such charge is pending, whichever date last occurs. . . .

(h) The following periods of delay shall be excluded in computing the time within which an information or an indictment must be filed, or in computing the time within which the trial of any such offense must commence:

(1) Any period of delay resulting from other proceedings concerning the defendant. . . .

(2) Any period of delay during which prosecution is deferred by the attorney for the Government pursuant to written agreement with the defendant, with the approval of the court, for the purpose of allowing the defendant to demonstrate his good conduct.

(3) . . . Any period of delay resulting from the absence or unavailability of the defendant or an essential witness. . . .

(5) If the information or indictment is dismissed upon motion of the attorney for the Government and thereafter a charge is filed against the defendant for the same offense, or any offense required to be joined with that offense, any period of delay from the date the charge was dismissed to the date the time limitation would commence to run as to the subsequent charge had there been no previous charge.

(6) A reasonable period of delay when the defendant is joined for trial with a codefendant as to whom the time for trial has not run and no motion for severance has been granted.

(7) (A) Any period of delay resulting from a continuance granted by any judge on his own motion or at the request of the defendant or his counsel or at the request of the attorney for the Government, if the judge granted such continuance on the basis of [findings on the record] that the ends of justice served by taking such action outweigh the best interest of the public and the defendant in a speedy trial. . . .

(B) The factors, among others, which a judge shall consider in determining whether to grant a continuance under subparagraph (A) of this paragraph in any case are as follows:

(i) Whether the failure to grant such a continuance in the proceeding would be likely to make a continuation of such proceeding impossible, or result in a miscarriage of justice.

(ii) Whether the case is so unusual or so complex, due to the number of defendants, the nature of the prosecution, or the existence of novel questions of fact or law, that it is unreasonable to expect adequate preparation for pretrial proceedings or for the trial itself within the time limits established by this section. . . .

(iv) Whether the failure to grant such a continuance in a case which, taken as a whole, is not so unusual or so complex as to fall within clause (ii), would deny the defendant reasonable time to obtain counsel, would unreasonably deny the defendant or the Government continuity of counsel, or would deny counsel for the defendant or the attorney for the Government the reasonable time necessary for effective preparation, taking into account the exercise of due diligence.

(C) No continuance under subparagraph (A) of this paragraph shall be granted because of general congestion of the court's calendar, or lack of diligent preparation or failure to obtain available witnesses on the part of the attorney for the Government. . . .

■ 18 U.S.C. §3162

(a)(2) If a defendant is not brought to trial within the time limit required by section 3161(c) as extended by section 3161(h), the information or indictment shall be dismissed on motion of the defendant. The defendant shall have the burden of proof of supporting such motion but the Government shall have the burden of going forward with the evidence in connection with any exclusion of time under subparagraph 3161(h)(3). In determining whether to dismiss the case with or without prejudice, the court shall consider, among others, each of the following factors: the seriousness of the offense; the facts and circumstances of the case which led to the dismissal; and the impact of a reprosecution on the administration of this chapter and on the administration of justice. . . .

Notes

1. *Speedy trial statutes and the federal constitution.* Almost all states have statutes or court rules addressing speedy trial preparation. Some of these statutes are intended to implement the constitutional speedy trial right, while others serve the additional

purpose of clearing court dockets. Do these provisions add a new dimension to the constitutional analysis simply because they are more specific than a general right to a "speedy trial"? In the minority of states where statutes or rules use general language (such as a statutory bar against "unreasonable delay"), does the statute or rule add anything at all to the constitutional inquiry? Why would drafters of rules or statutes bother to pass a provision without specific time limits?

2. *Time allowed for preparation.* Speedy trial statutes select many different time periods to allow the parties to prepare for trial. The federal statute's 70-day limit is one of the shorter periods; some state statutes allow periods longer than six months. Most have tighter time limits for defendants in custody than for those who have been released before trial. It is also customary for these statutes to provide longer time limits for felonies than for misdemeanors, and some create even finer distinctions between the more serious and less serious offenses. See Ohio Rev. Stat. §2945.71. The statutes list several events that can start the speedy trial "clock." Under the federal statute, an arrest starts a time period that must end within 30 days in an indictment or information, while the indictment or information starts the 70-day countdown to the trial. Under most of the state statutes, an indictment or information starts the clock for felonies, and the filing of a complaint begins the period for misdemeanors. Trials that end in mistrials or in convictions reversed on appeal have their own specialized timing rules.

If you were drafting a speedy trial statute, would you anticipate the ways that the parties might try to manipulate the time periods? For instance, would you address the defendant's ability to enter a plea agreement and withdraw it near the arrival of the statutorily designated number of days from the filing of the charge? How would you respond to the prosecutor's power to enter a nolle prosequi as the deadline nears and to refile charges when the case is ready to try?

3. *Speedy trial rights for crime victims.* Generally speaking, the victims of alleged crimes prefer not to wait for trial to begin. What are the shortest preparation periods that a statute could grant to a defendant without being unconstitutional? Under the federal statute, a trial cannot commence "less than 30 days from the date on which the defendant first appears through counsel" unless the defendant consents to a quicker deadline. 18 U.S.C. §3161(c)(2). A minority of states have statutes setting a minimum time period for trial preparation. This question ordinarily arises as a constitutional challenge (based on due process or the right to counsel) to a trial court's refusal to grant a defense motion for a continuance; appellate courts almost always defer to the trial court's discretion on this question.

4. *Excluded time periods.* One major difference among speedy trial statutes appears in the method of identifying "excluded" days, those that do not count toward the speedy trial deadline. Most jurisdictions, represented by the federal statute reprinted above, list the particular events that can be excluded from the speedy trial countdown. See Bloate v. United States, 559 U.S. 196 (2010) (under federal Speedy Trial Act, days granted to defendant to prepare pretrial motions are not automatically excludable from the 70-day time limit for bringing defendant to trial; days may be excluded only if trial court makes case-specific findings that the ends of justice served by granting a continuance outweigh the best interest of the public and the defendant in a speedy trial); Commonwealth v. Denehy, 2 N.E.3d 161 (Mass. 2014) (speedy trial rules count against the state any days between a trial court's dismissal of charges and defendant's arraignment on new, identical charges).

A minority of states, represented by the California statute above, do not specify the grounds for excluding days, instead allowing judges to determine in a particular case whether "good cause" exists to allow an exclusion. See Bulgin v. State, 912 So. 2d 307 (Fla. 2005) (if state officials do not obtain express waiver of speedy trial rights, days that defendant spent cooperating with investigators must count against statutory limit of 175 days to begin trial). Some statutes say simply that any delay "caused" by the defendant is excluded from the countdown.

5. *Sanctions for violations of statutes.* Another major difference among speedy trial statutes is the remedy they require or encourage for statutory violations. As you saw in the federal statute reprinted above, dismissal without prejudice is the preferred remedy under some speedy trial statutes. Is dismissal without prejudice a toothless remedy? Consult again the New York statute of limitations reprinted at the beginning of this section and consider whether such provisions make the dismissal without prejudice remedy more effective. It is more common to find speedy trial statutes or rules of procedure that make dismissal with prejudice the preferred remedy. See Neb. Stat. §29-1208. Does the California statute reprinted above make dismissal with prejudice the preferred remedy?

Is the dismissal remedy for speedy trial violation similar to the exclusionary rule for unconstitutional searches and seizures because it rewards some guilty defendants out of proportion to the wrong that the state has committed? Would monetary damages be a better remedy, at least for defendants who make no showing that the delay impaired their defense? A Massachusetts statute offers compensation to some defendants whose cases are delayed beyond the statutory limits. See Commonwealth v. Bunting, 518 N.E.2d 1159 (Mass. 1988) (in action to recover damages for statutory speedy trial delays, state can still litigate question of whether defendant consented to delays, even after dismissal of criminal charges on speedy trial grounds).

Problem 15-6. Voluminous Discovery

Nearly two years ago, a federal grand jury indicted John Bravata for several offenses, including one count of conspiracy to commit wire fraud and fourteen counts of aiding and abetting wire fraud. Two of Bravata's associates were indicted for related offenses.

It is now one week before trial. The defendant is moving to dismiss the indictment with prejudice because of a violation of the Speedy Trial Act. Twenty months have elapsed since the grand jury indictment. Bravata charges that the government's disorganized and unsearchable discovery caused most of the delay: (1) the government produced hundreds of thousands of documents, consisting of millions of pages and hundreds of audio and video files, but not in any easily identifiable categories; (2) no technology is available to search the audio and video files, requiring attorneys to listen to the entire recordings, without guidance from the prosecution about where in the recordings the defense might find material evidence; and (3) the court failed to intervene to streamline the discovery process. Bravata argues that he was significantly prejudiced by the delay and that the government used the delay to interview new witnesses and develop additional evidence against him.

The prosecution argues that most of the delay resulted from pretrial motions filed by the defendant, as well as from Bravata's request for a new attorney. In addition, the prosecution submits that multiple defendants and voluminous discovery make the case more complex, excusing the remaining delay. Finally, the prosecution notes that all the documents it produced to the defendant were in a searchable format, as requested by Bravata's computer expert.

How is a court likely to rule on Bravata's claims? What factors is the court likely to consider? What can a trial judge do to prevent undue delays resulting from voluminous discovery and pretrial motions? See United States v. Graham, 2008 WL 2098044 (S.D. Ohio May 16, 2008); United States v. Bravata, 636 F. App'x 277 (6th Cir. 2016).

One last thought: Is Bravata's attorney risking his relationship with the prosecutor by filing this speedy trial motion? Should he consider that risk before he files? If he has previously agreed to postponements requested by the prosecution, (how) should that factor into the court's speedy trial analysis?

XVI

■

Pleas and Bargains

In criminal courts in this country, guilty pleas before trial occur far more often than verdicts after trial. In large urban counties in 2009, more than 9 of 10 felony convictions were based on a guilty plea rather than a trial. For many felony categories criminal trials were rarer still, to the point of disappearance. Only murder charges produced trials in more than 10 percent of the cases; the rate of guilty pleas was even higher than 90 percent for misdemeanor charges. Most of the time, in most places in this country, the overwhelming majority of criminal charges are resolved through guilty pleas.

Why do we see so few criminal trials? Plea bargains are the short—and incomplete—answer. A large proportion of felony defendants enter pleas of guilty only after they have reached an agreement with the prosecutor, obliging the prosecutor to make some concessions. Perhaps the prosecutor will agree to dismiss some pending charges or to reduce the pending charge to something less serious (this is known as a "charge bargain"). Or perhaps the prosecutor will agree to recommend a particular sentence or to refrain from making certain recommendations (a "sentence bargain"). Other agreement terms are possible, such as a promise not to file charges against third parties.

But plea agreements are not the only explanation for guilty pleas. Some defendants plead guilty as charged without extracting any promises at all from the prosecutor (an "open" plea). These defendants (and their attorneys) know that judges tend to impose less severe sentences on offenders who plead guilty, compared to those who go to trial. This "plea discount" is a reality in virtually every court, but it is rare to find formal acknowledgment of the practice in case law, statutes, or procedural rules.

Anyone who wants to understand American criminal justice must study both guilty pleas and plea bargains. The numbers suggest that these topics are more fundamental than criminal trials. Of course, it may be that plea bargaining takes place in the "shadow" of criminal trials, so that the terms of any agreement reflect the parties' predictions about what *would* have happened at a trial. But it is also possible that some types of cases are resolved by guilty pleas so often that the rules of trial have little relevance, while the trials that do occur represent some different, special universe of cases.

The materials in this chapter survey the boundaries that our legal institutions place on the practice of plea bargaining. We begin inside those boundaries, examining some of the typical topics for bargaining, the ordinary motives of parties who enter plea agreements, and the elements of a valid guilty plea. We then move out to the boundaries, looking at the types of bargains that the negotiating parties are willing to accept but the legal system as a whole rejects. Categorical constraints on plea bargains come from legislatures, the executive branch, and (less frequently) judges. As always, we will consider whether these different institutions create distinctive answers to the puzzle of what makes a fair plea bargain. Running throughout the chapter is a question about the controlling substantive principles: Does the common law of contracts provide the necessary guidance for determining which plea agreements are enforceable and which are not? The chapter closes with a discussion of the largest questions about plea bargaining: Is the practice inevitable, and is it desirable?

A. BARGAIN ABOUT WHAT?

Every defendant who pleads guilty gives up the right to a jury trial, and the concomitant rights to be represented by counsel, compel witnesses to testify, and confront adverse witnesses. Why would a defendant waive these key rights—essentially those guaranteed by the Fifth and Sixth Amendments to the federal constitution and their state analogs—along with the chance of an acquittal? And why would prosecutors be willing to bargain away the chance of a conviction in court, with the public affirmation of justice and the publicity that go along with it? The materials in this section explore the objectives of the prosecution and defense as they bargain over a possible plea of guilty. This section also pursues another theme: Are there certain rights that defendants cannot waive as part of a bargain? Are there terms in a bargain that courts should scrutinize more closely because of their potential to coerce a guilty plea or undermine the fairness or accuracy of the disposition? What are the proper limits on the parties' freedom to negotiate a criminal case?

■ FEDERAL RULE OF CRIMINAL PROCEDURE 11(a), (c)

(a) *Entering a Plea.*

(1) *In general.* A defendant may plead not guilty, guilty, or (with the court's consent) nolo contendere.

(2) With the consent of the court and the government, a defendant may enter a conditional plea of guilty or nolo contendere, reserving in writing the right to have an appellate court review an adverse determination of a specified pretrial motion. A defendant who prevails on appeal may then withdraw the plea.

(3) Before accepting a plea of nolo contendere, the court must consider the parties' views and the public interest in the effective administration of justice.

(4) If a defendant refuses to enter a plea or if a defendant organization fails to appear, the court must enter a plea of not guilty.

(c) *Plea Agreement Procedure.*

(1) *In general.* An attorney for the government and the defendant's attorney, or the defendant when proceeding pro se, may discuss and reach a plea agreement. The court must not participate in these discussions. If the defendant pleads guilty or nolo contendere to either a charged offense or a lesser or related offense, the plea agreement may specify that an attorney for the government will:

(A) not bring, or will move to dismiss, other charges;

(B) recommend, or agree not to oppose the defendant's request, that a particular sentence or sentencing range is appropriate or that a particular provision of the Sentencing Guidelines, or policy statement, or sentencing factor does or does not apply (such a recommendation or request does not bind the court); or

(C) agree that a specific sentence or sentencing range is the appropriate disposition of the case, or that a particular provision of the Sentencing Guidelines, or policy statement, or sentencing factor does or does not apply (such a recommendation or request binds the court once the court accepts the plea agreement).

(2) *Disclosing a Plea Agreement.* The parties must disclose the plea agreement in open court when the plea is offered, unless the court for good cause allows the parties to disclose the plea agreement in camera.

(3) *Judicial Consideration of a Plea Agreement.*

(A) To the extent the plea agreement is of the type specified in Rule 11(c)(1)(A) or (C), the court may accept the agreement, reject it, or defer a decision until the court has reviewed the presentence report.

(B) To the extent the plea agreement is of the type specified in Rule 11(c)(1)(B), the court must advise the defendant that the defendant has no right to withdraw the plea if the court does not follow the recommendation or request.

■ NORTH CAROLINA DEFENDER MANUAL

Chapter 23 (2d ed. 2012)

A valid plea bargain may include:

- an agreement by the prosecutor to dismiss or reduce charges;
- an agreement by the prosecutor not to charge an additional or more serious crime;
- specific sentencing arrangements;
- an agreement by the prosecutor not to recommend a sentence within the aggravated range;
- an agreement by the prosecutor not to oppose probation or other community or intermediate sentence;
- an agreement by the defendant to pay restitution, including the agreement to pay for rehabilitative treatment for the victim;

- an agreement by the defendant to testify truthfully for the prosecution against a codefendant in a related case or in another case;
- an agreement by the defendant not to appeal or not to seek post-conviction relief*

■ STATE v. AHMAD BEY
17 P.3d 322 (Kan. 2001)

McFarland, C.J.

Ahmad Bey appeals from the district court's denial of his motion to withdraw his nolo contendere plea to the reduced charge of aiding and abetting intentional second-degree murder . . . . Defendant and his brother, Yusif Bey, were each initially charged with premeditated first-degree murder in connection with the March 24, 1999, slaying of Victor Conger. The deceased was killed by a gunshot to the head and was found lying in a Pittsburg intersection. Defendant contends . . . the district court erred in not inquiring into the "package deal" involving the negotiated pleas of defendant and his brother. . . .

Both brothers were initially charged with premeditated first-degree murder in connection with the slaying of Victor Conger. Over a period of 2 to 3 weeks, extensive plea negotiations were conducted among the State and counsel for each of the brothers. Discussions were had between both counsel and the brothers. The county attorney advised that if the two cases proceeded to trial, the prosecution thereof would be in the hands of the Kansas attorney general. Any plea agreement involving the county attorney would be required to dispose of the cases against both brothers and would have to be concluded prior to the time the prosecution would be turned over to the attorney general's office.

Ultimately an agreement was reached whereby defendant would plead nolo contendere to aiding and abetting intentional second-degree murder with a life sentence and parole eligibility after 10 years. Brother Yusif would plead to first-degree felony murder with a life sentence serving a minimum of 15 years before becoming parole eligible. Under the original charges each brother, if convicted, would have been faced with life sentences serving either a 25-year or 40-year term before becoming parole eligible.

Although the negotiated pleas of both brothers were heard and accepted by the same court on the same day, apparently no reference was made to the court that disposal of both cases was a condition of the plea agreements. Defendant contends that the court's failure to inquire of him as to the package deal rendered his plea involuntary as the situation was coercive. Defendant contends his brother put pressure on him to accept the deal.

In his motion to enter into the plea agreement, defendant stated, *inter alia:*

> 13) I declare that no officer or agent of any branch of government (federal, state or local) has promised, suggested, or predicted that I will receive a lighter sentence, or probation, or any other form of leniency if I plead 'NO CONTEST', except as follows: refer to paragraph (15). If anyone else, including my attorney, made such

---

* [The scope of such waivers of the right to appeal or to seek post-conviction relief may be limited by federal or state law, as subsequent materials explain.—EDS.]

a promise, suggestion, or prediction, except as noted in the previous sentence, I know that he had no authority to do so. . . .

15) My plea of no contest is the result of a plea agreement entered into between the County Attorney, my attorney, and me. Since my plea of guilty is the result of a plea agreement, I hereby state that the terms of said agreement are as follows: The state agrees to amend the complaint to a charge of Intentional 2nd Degree Murder. I will enter a plea of "NO CONTEST" to Count I of the Amended Complaint/Information. Further, I understand the penalty will be mandatory life imprisonment without parole or post release supervision for a minimum of 10 years and that there is no guarantee that I will be released after the minimum 10 years. It is my understanding that life imprisonment will be the sentence despite my previous criminal history. Finally, the state agrees not to, now or forever in the future, file any other charges that may or could have been filed as a result of any and all events and activities that I may have been involved in which preceded the shooting of Victor Lee Conger on or about March 24, 1999 or that followed the shooting of Victor Lee Conger on or about March 24, 1999.

I fully understand that the Court is not bound by the terms of the plea agreement, and may accept or reject said agreement. If the Court rejects the agreement, I also understand the Court may *not* give me the opportunity to withdraw my plea of guilty.

At the plea hearing, in addition to the usual statements and questions going to voluntariness and understanding, there were extensive questions and answers between defense counsel and defendant. Included therein was the following:

> *MR. DOSH:* Okay. Do you have any questions about what you are doing or do you fully understand.
>
> *THE DEFENDANT:* I fully understand.
>
> *MR. DOSH:* And you and I have had numerous conversations both over the phone, letters that I've sent you and also several person-to-person meetings about what we are doing here today; is that correct.
>
> *THE DEFENDANT:* Yes, sir.
>
> *MR. DOSH:* Okay. And while it may be true that you are not particularly or completely happy with what we are doing here today, this is how you best decided to proceed with this case at this point; is that correct.
>
> *THE DEFENDANT:* Yes, sir.
>
> *MR. DOSH:* And this is something that you've done knowingly and voluntarily, nobody has forced you to do it; is that correct.
>
> *THE DEFENDANT:* Yes, sir.
>
> *MR. DOSH:* I told you if it was your desire to go through trial that we would take it to a trial; is that correct.
>
> *THE DEFENDANT:* Yes, sir.
>
> *MR. DOSH:* Again, do you have any questions about what you are pleading to today or what you are doing.
>
> *THE DEFENDANT:* No, sir.
>
> *MR. DOSH:* Okay. I don't think I have anything further, Your Honor.
>
> *THE COURT:* Actually you are reading my mind. I was going to ask, Mr. Bey, do you have any questions of myself or of Mr. Dosh with regard to what we've said today, what has occurred today, do you feel that you fully understand what is occurring.
>
> *THE DEFENDANT:* Yes, sir.
>
> *THE COURT:* Have you understood every question I've asked of you.
>
> *THE DEFENDANT:* Yes, sir.

Defendant contends that the State's plea offer, which was contingent upon both men accepting the offer and which was available for a limited time, was rendered involuntary by the court's failure to inquire about the nature of this "package deal." . . .

The State notes that the United States Supreme Court in Brady v. United States, 397 U.S. 742 (1970), held that the threatened invocation of the death penalty was not coercive so as to invalidate a plea. Further, defendant made no mention of this point during the plea hearing when being closely questioned as to the voluntariness of his plea and, in fact, indicated that the agreement was entered into of his own free will. The State contends that defendant simply changed his mind after the plea was entered, which is an insufficient basis to support a withdrawal of the plea.

In State v. Reed, 809 P.2d 553 (Kan. 1991), the defendant alleged he was under pressure to accept the plea. There, like here, Reed had indicated during the plea hearing that he understood the terms of the plea agreement and no one had made any threats or promises to him to induce him to plead nolo contendere. Reed also stated that he did not commit the crime but knew that there were people ready to testify against him at trial. Reed testified that he understood his rights but felt like it would be to his advantage to go ahead with the plea. Reed later sought to withdraw his plea, alleging it was involuntary and entered into under pressure.

We first noted in *Reed* that a defendant, while maintaining his or her innocence, may, for a variety of reasons, wish to enter a plea of nolo contendere . . . . Additionally, we noted that it was not surprising that Reed felt he was under stress. "It would be an unusual person who would not feel stressful when confronting a trial involving charges of the magnitude herein." In Reed's case, everything in the record indicated that the plea was his free and voluntary act.

Here the trial court held the following in denying defendant's motion to withdraw his plea:

> Secondly, was the defendant misled, coerced, mistreated or unfairly taken advantage of. I don't think he was, all things considered. I think this is simply a situation where the defendant has had second thoughts or cold feet. I think one of the cases I read in preparation for this hearing references buyer's remorse. I even read the *Reed* case, the Supreme Court says this is a situation involving buyer's remorse and seems to be what the present case is. Thirdly, was the plea fairly and understandably made. The Court finds that the plea was fairly and understandably made. The plea agreement is very extensive. It covers all the statutory requirements and I think the same is done in the plea hearing. The Court took great pains to make certain the defendant was doing this voluntarily and knowingly and with full awareness of the potential consequences.

Here, as in *Reed*, everything in the record indicates that defendant was informed of his rights, knew the consequences of entering a plea, understood the rights he was waiving by entering a plea, had ample opportunity to discuss the plea with his attorney and with his brother, and entered this plea voluntarily and knowingly. The district court did not abuse its discretion in denying the motion on this ground.

We do believe, however, that a discussion of the desirability of disclosure of package deals to the court hearing the plea is appropriate. In this regard we note the Minnesota case of State v. Danh, 516 N.W.2d 539 (Minn. 1994), cited by defendant. In *Danh*, 23 year old Danh and his three codefendants were charged with three counts of assault and three counts of burglary. One of the codefendants was

Danh's 19-year-old brother. Shortly before trial the prosecutor offered a plea agreement which was contingent upon all four codefendants pleading. Danh initially told his attorney that he would plead guilty but later informed his attorney that he had changed his mind. Danh's brother then asked to speak with him alone. After this conversation, Danh pled guilty. The trial court conducted a thorough inquiry wherein Danh stated that no promises other than those contained in the petition or stated in court had been made to him. He affirmed that he was not coerced into entering the plea. Neither party explicitly mentioned the contingent nature of the plea at any point in the guilty plea hearing. However, in its later findings denying Danh's motion to withdraw the plea, the judge stated that he "was aware that some sort of a package was being presented to all of the defendants" but "was not a party to the negotiations and did not become aware of the specific details until they were presented in court." . . . The Minnesota Supreme Court noted that it had never addressed the issue of a contingent plea agreement in which a defendant agrees to plead guilty in exchange for leniency for a third party. Providing a review of the issue and case law, the court then held:

> "Package deal" agreements are generally dangerous because of the risk of coercion; this is particularly so in cases involving related third parties, where there is a risk that a defendant, who would otherwise exercise his or her right to a jury trial, will plead guilty out of a sense of family loyalty.
>
> In Bordenkircher v. Hayes, 434 U.S. 357, 364 n.8 (1978), the U.S. Supreme Court stated that these types of agreements "might pose a greater danger of inducing a false guilty plea by skewing the assessment of the risks a defendant must consider." Other states and federal circuit courts hold that "package deal" agreements are not per se invalid. See In re Ibarra, 666 P.2d 980, 986 (Cal. 1983); United States v. Marquez, 909 F.2d 738, 741 (2d Cir. 1990). However, several courts hold that this type of plea is per se involuntary if the prosecutor did not have probable cause to charge the third party. See United States v. Nuckols, 606 F.2d 566, 569 (5th Cir. 1979). . . .
>
> We are not prepared at this time to adopt a rule that "package deal" plea agreements are per se invalid. We believe, however, that such agreements are fraught with danger, and that the standard Minn. R. Crim. P. 15.01 inquiry cannot adequately discover coercion in these cases. We therefore hold that the state must fully inform the trial court of the details of these agreements at the time a defendant enters a "package deal" plea, and the trial court must then conduct further inquiries to determine whether the plea is voluntarily made. In future cases, a defendant must be allowed to withdraw his or her guilty plea if the state fails to fully inform the trial court of the nature of the plea, or if the trial court fails to adequately inquire into the voluntariness of the plea at the time of the guilty plea. . . .

We conclude that, in keeping with the need for a court considering a plea to be fully informed of the terms of the plea agreement in making inquiry as to the voluntariness thereof, disclosure of any package deal terms should be made to the court. This would enable the court to make appropriate inquiry of the defendant as to whether the package deal aspect of the plea agreement renders the plea involuntary. This rule will apply to future cases. However, failure to do so will not automatically render the acceptance of the plea invalid. The greatest risk of coercive conduct lies where the State, in bad faith, threatens prosecution of a family member when there is no probable cause supporting such a charge. Even though such a package deal may rarely be considered coercive, it is desirable to have such terms before the court in order that appropriate inquiry can be made.

Disclosure of this aspect of the plea at the plea hearing would serve another worthwhile purpose. It would preclude a defendant from taking advantage of the plea agreement and then seeking to nullify a part of its terms by seeking to withdraw his or her plea after the third party's plea has been accepted. This would have been the effect herein as the brother's plea would be unaffected by the withdrawal of defendant's plea. Another beneficial effect of the disclosure of the package deal on the record is that such disclosure should head off any dispute as to exactly what the term was and whether the State had complied with the term.

Notes

1. *Common types of bargains.* Prosecutors and defendants are allowed to bargain over a wide variety of topics. What do prosecutors typically offer during plea negotiations? Under a "charge bargain" (see Federal Rule 11(c)(1)(A) above), the prosecutor agrees to reduce charges or to drop some counts entirely. When the prosecutor agrees to reduce the number of counts at a given level of seriousness, this is known as a "horizontal" charge bargain; an agreement to reduce the seriousness of the top charge is known as a "vertical" charge bargain. The prosecutor might also agree not to file charges in the future against the defendant or some third party based on the events in question. Under a "sentence bargain" (see Rule 11(c)(1)(B) above), a prosecutor agrees to ask the sentencing judge for a certain outcome, or to refrain from asking for a certain outcome, or to make no sentencing recommendation at all—that is, to "stand silent."

What does a defendant typically offer? The most important and obvious benefit the defendant can offer is to waive the trial and all its accompanying procedural protections, such as the right to confront witnesses. The waiver of a trial saves the government the expense of preparing and conducting a trial, along with the uncertainty about the outcome at trial. See Commonwealth v. Stagner, 3 S.W.3d 738 (Ky. 1999) (allowing defendant to plead guilty while jury is deliberating; some other jurisdictions prevent guilty pleas after the jury receives case because bargain no longer serves public function of clearing docket). A defendant can also offer to cooperate during investigations of other defendants and other crimes.

There are several ways for a defendant to give up some procedural options while preserving others. The "conditional plea" (see Rule 11(a) above) allows the defendant to plead guilty while reserving the right to appeal on a defined pretrial issue, such as the voluntariness of a confession. If the defendant succeeds on appeal, the guilty plea can be withdrawn. Although it is used less often than the conditional plea, the "slow plea" is another way for a defendant to preserve some options while waiving others. Under a slow plea, the defendant and the prosecution stipulate to the existence of some facts, and then go forward with an abbreviated bench trial to resolve the remaining factual and legal issues.

Finally, a defendant might offer a plea of nolo contendere rather than a plea of guilty. A plea of nolo contendere (meaning "I will not contest" the charges) allows the court to impose criminal sanctions, just as a guilty plea would, but the nolo plea cannot be used against the defendant in any later civil litigation as an admission of guilt. The court (and in some jurisdictions, the prosecutor) must agree before a defendant enters a nolo plea rather than a guilty plea.

2. *Why plead guilty? Plea discounts.* Defendants considering a guilty plea surely know the conventional wisdom that those who plead guilty receive less severe sentences than those who are convicted after a trial. The size of the so-called plea discount varies from place to place, and it is difficult to measure because where the plea discount is most effective (not necessarily where it is most generous), it results in very few trials as a point of comparison. One estimate placed the discount in the federal system at about 30 to 40 percent of the typical sentence imposed on those convicted after trial. See U.S. Sentencing Commission, Supplemental Report on the Initial Sentencing Guidelines and Policy Statements 48 (1987); Jeffery Todd Ulmer et al., Trial Penalties in Federal Sentencing: Extra-Guidelines Factors and District Variation, 27 Just. Q. 560 (2010). Many consider the fact of a plea bargain to be an illegitimate basis for sentencing some offenders less severely than others. See ABA Standards for Criminal Justice: Pleas of Guilty 14-1.8 (guilty plea alone is not sufficient grounds for leniency in sentence). For a more detailed examination of the empirical studies of the plea discount, go to the web extension for this chapter at *http://www.crimpro.com/extension/ch16.*

Would a legislature improve the certainty and honesty of criminal justice by specifying the proper size for a plea discount? The Italian criminal code offers an example of such an explicit plea discount. It provides for a one-third reduction in applicable sentence after guilty plea, provided that maximum sentence does not exceed two years; for more serious charges, the code offers an "abbreviated trial" with one-third reduction in applicable sentence upon conviction. See Codice di procedura penale art. 442, 444. In England and Wales, courts are required by statute to comply with guidelines set by the Sentencing Guidelines Council. The 2007 guidelines presumptively set plea discounts to one-third of the custodial term when a guilty plea is entered at the earliest reasonable opportunity and less if entered later. The Council stated that the recommended reduction should be given "unless there are good reasons for a lower amount." A 2015 empirical study found that English courts do in fact follow the guidelines and that "almost all cases where a plea was entered attracted reductions of one-third or less." Julian V. Roberts & Ben Bradford, Sentence Reductions for a Guilty Plea in England and Wales: Exploring New Empirical Trends, 12 J. Emp. Leg. Stud. 187 (2015).

3. *Presumed good faith in bargaining.* Courts in the United States, since at least the middle of the twentieth century, have generally presumed that plea bargaining is both an appropriate and necessary part of the criminal justice system. As the U.S. Supreme Court put it in Santobello v. New York, 404 U.S. 257 (1971), plea bargaining is "not only an essential part of the process but a highly desirable part for many reasons." The courts have also presumed, except in extraordinary cases, that a prosecutor who negotiates a plea bargain does so for proper reasons (such as faster disposition of cases and elimination of uncertainty) and not improper ones (such as obtaining convictions based on questionable evidence, or punishing the defendant's exercise of rights). For instance, the Supreme Court has rejected claims that a prosecutor acted "vindictively" and contrary to due process by increasing the charges against a defendant who rejected an initial offer of a plea bargain. Bordenkircher v. Hayes, 434 U.S. 357 (1978). As a practical matter, is it possible for courts to identify cases when the prosecutor's motives for offering a plea deal might be improper?

4. *Limits on the subjects of bargaining.* As the *Bey* decision suggests, courts generally give the parties great freedom to negotiate the disposition of criminal cases—including the disposition of cases of relatives. Do you agree with this laissez-faire approach to plea bargaining? Should courts put certain deals—such as package deals involving relatives—off limits, given the risk that they might be coercive? Even if the Supreme Court does not consider such deals to be inconsistent with due process, should a state court or legislature make a different choice under state law? Part B of this chapter considers further the voluntariness requirement of guilty pleas and the limits that it imposes on plea bargaining, and Part C considers additional constraints that courts and legislatures have placed on the practice.

5. *Waivable and nonwaivable procedural rights.* When defendants attempt to raise challenges in appellate or postconviction review on issues that they waived in plea agreements, claiming that the agreement is unenforceable, courts typically dismiss the challenge. Courts allow defendants to bargain away rights of all sorts. See United States v. Mezzanatto, 513 U.S. 196 (1995) (allowing defendant to waive protections of Rule 11(e)(6), which prevented later introduction into evidence of statements made during plea negotiations); People v. Stevens, 610 N.W.2d 881 (Mich. 2000) (statements made during plea negotiations are admissible in prosecution's case-in-chief); Cowan v. Superior Court, 926 P.2d 438 (Cal. 1996) (allowing waiver of statute of limitations). Most state and federal courts have also concluded that a defendant may explicitly waive the right to appeal a conviction as part of a plea agreement. See People v. Seaberg, 541 N.E.2d 1022 (N.Y. 1989).

There are a few legal challenges to a conviction that some courts say a defendant may not waive, even if the waiver appears explicitly in a plea agreement. Courts have taken this position on constitutional speedy trial rights, People v. Callahan, 604 N.E.2d 108 (N.Y. 1992). Courts are split on whether the parties can agree to a sentence outside the statutorily authorized range of punishments; often they enforce illegal sentences falling below the authorized range of punishments but not illegal sentences set above the authorized range. Ex parte Johnson, 669 So. 2d 205 (Ala. 1995) (enforces prosecutor's agreement to two-year prison term, even though prosecutor failed to account for sentencing enhancements requiring additional minimum sentences). The same is true for waivers of claims for ineffective assistance of counsel. See Peter A. Joy & Rodney J. Uphoff, Systemic Barriers to Effective Assistance of Counsel in Plea Bargaining, 99 Iowa L. Rev. 2103 (2014). Even where courts permit waivers of claims for ineffective assistance of counsel, defense attorneys and prosecutors may be prohibited by their states' ethical rules from negotiating such waivers. See, e.g., United States, ex rel. U.S. Attorneys ex rel. E., W. Districts of Kentucky v. Kentucky Bar Ass'n, 439 S.W.3d 136 (Ky. 2014). At the federal level, the Department of Justice has issued a policy prohibiting prosecutors from seeking waivers of ineffective assistance of counsel as part of a plea agreement. Deputy Attorney General James M. Cole, Department Policy on Waivers of Claims of Ineffective Assistance of Counsel, Oct. 14, 2014.

Is there any pattern that separates the waivable from the nonwaivable rights? Are the waivable rights the least important ones? See Nancy J. King, Priceless Process, 47 UCLA L. Rev. 113 (1999) (nonwaivable rights should focus on constitutional claims with impact on third parties, since legislature can decide whether to protect statutory rights from waiver).

6. *Forfeiture of claims.* In some contexts, a guilty plea will lead a court to conclude that the defendant forfeited a legal challenge, even though the defendant

did not knowingly and intelligently relinquish a known right. This "forfeiture" (as opposed to "waiver") of claims occurs most often when a defendant raises a claim in collateral proceedings such as habeas corpus, which take place after the direct appeal. A guilty plea will automatically bar most postconviction collateral challenges to the conviction based on events occurring before the entry of the plea, because those errors could be cured by recharging or trying the case. See United States v. Broce, 488 U.S. 563 (1989) (guilty plea bars later double jeopardy claim when further evidence is necessary to determine whether one conspiracy or two were present); Tollett v. Henderson, 411 U.S. 258 (1973) (forfeiture of claim of racial discrimination in grand jury selection); McMann v. Richardson, 397 U.S. 759 (1970) (forfeiture of claims regarding jury exposure to coerced confessions). For some exceptional claims, however, a defendant can raise the issue on collateral attack. See Blackledge v. Perry, 417 U.S. 21 (1974) (allowing petitioner for habeas corpus to raise claim of vindictive prosecutorial charging decision). The Supreme Court in *Blackledge* explained that these exceptional claims are not forfeited, despite the guilty plea, because they go to "the very power of the State" to charge the defendant. See also Menna v. New York, 423 U.S. 61 (1975) (allowing habeas petitioner to raise double jeopardy claim despite guilty plea).

Problem 16-1. Waiving the Right to Appeal a Sentence

The United States Attorney for your district adopted a policy to encourage defendants to waive the right to appeal. The new office policy states that any plea agreements with federal criminal defendants must include the following language:

> The defendant is aware that Title 18, United States Code, Section 3742 affords a defendant the right to appeal the sentence imposed. Acknowledging this, the defendant knowingly waives the right to appeal any sentence within the maximum provided in the statute(s) of conviction (or the manner in which that sentence was determined) on the grounds set forth in Title 18, United States Code, Section 3742 or on any ground whatever, in exchange for the concessions made by the United States in this plea agreement. The defendant also waives his right to challenge his sentence or the manner in which it was determined in any collateral attack. . . .

Any proposed plea agreements that do not include this language must receive approval from a supervisory committee, and the committee will grant these "exceptions" only under "extraordinary circumstances." The policy calls on prosecutors to negotiate for the government to retain its right to appeal any legal error in the application of the federal sentencing guidelines.

The policy recognizes that a sentencing appeal waiver provision does not waive all claims on appeal. The federal courts of appeals have held that appellate review of some claims cannot be waived, such as a defendant's claim that he was denied the effective assistance of counsel at sentencing, that he was sentenced on the basis of his race, or that his sentence exceeded the statutory maximum. The memo also warns that prosecutors must not use the appeal waiver provision "to promote circumvention of the sentencing guidelines."

You are the director of the office of the Federal Public Defender in this district. How will you respond to the new bargaining policy of the federal prosecutors? How do you predict the courts will respond to this new policy? Can you predict whether the policy will be difficult for the prosecutors to implement in particular types of cases? Develop some alternative bargaining strategies for the public defenders in your office to pursue. See United States v. Guevara, 941 F.2d 1299 (4th Cir. 1991); Memo from John Keeney, Acting Assistant Attorney General, October 4, 1995.

B. VALIDITY OF GUILTY PLEAS

Most of the statutes and judicial opinions on the subject of guilty pleas do not address plea bargaining as an institution. Instead, they focus on the validity of the guilty plea in an individual case. There are three essential ingredients for a valid plea of guilty, whether the plea is "open" or "negotiated": The plea must reflect a knowing waiver of trial rights, the defendant must waive those rights voluntarily, and there must be an adequate "factual basis" to support the charges to which the defendant pleads guilty.

1. Lack of Knowledge

A defendant who pleads guilty must know about the nature of the charges and some of the consequences of waiving the right to trial and accepting a conviction. In essence, the defendant must see two future paths. Down one path, she must visualize the events likely to occur at a trial and after a possible conviction; down another path, she must picture the events likely to occur after a conviction based on a plea of guilty. But predicting the future is no easy task. Courts do not require that a defendant know every single consequence of pleading guilty; the challenge is to select *which* consequences a defendant must understand before entering a valid plea of guilty. Traditional doctrine states that the defendant must understand the "direct" consequences of the conviction but not the "collateral" consequences. A rich case law has developed in an effort to sort out direct from collateral consequences.

The rules of criminal procedure give the trial judge the primary responsibility for ensuring that defendants understand the consequences of waiving trial and pleading guilty. This judicial responsibility is also grounded in the federal constitution. In Boykin v. Alabama, 395 U.S. 238 (1969), the Supreme Court declared that guilty pleas will not be constitutionally valid unless the record affirmatively shows that defendants understand their privilege against self-incrimination, their right to trial by jury, and their right to confront their accusers. During a *Boykin* hearing, the judge asks the defendant a routine set of questions about these rights and other matters before the court will accept a plea of guilty or nolo contendere.

The defense attorney, however, also carries important responsibilities in educating the defendant. A failure to explain to the client the nature of the charges and the relevant consequences of a conviction could amount to ineffective assistance of counsel and affect the validity of the guilty plea. Given the centrality of plea negotiations to modern criminal practice, an ability to explain a guilty plea to a client numbers among the most important skills for a defense lawyer.

◼ FEDERAL RULE OF CRIMINAL PROCEDURE 11(b)

(1) Before the court accepts a plea of guilty or nolo contendere, the defendant may be placed under oath, and the court must address the defendant personally in open court. During this address, the court must inform the defendant of, and determine that the defendant understands, the following:

(A) the government's right, in a prosecution for perjury or false statement, to use against the defendant any statement that the defendant gives under oath;

(B) the right to plead not guilty, or having already so pleaded, to persist in that plea;

(C) the right to a jury trial;

(D) the right to be represented by counsel—and if necessary have the court appoint counsel—at trial and at every other stage of the proceeding;

(E) the right at trial to confront and cross-examine adverse witnesses, to be protected from compelled self-incrimination, to testify and present evidence, and to compel the attendance of witnesses;

(F) the defendant's waiver of these trial rights if the court accepts a plea of guilty or nolo contendere;

(G) the nature of each charge to which the defendant is pleading;

(H) any maximum possible penalty, including imprisonment, fine, and term of supervised release;

(I) any mandatory minimum penalty;

(J) any applicable forfeiture;

(K) the court's authority to order restitution;

(L) the court's obligation to impose a special assessment;

(M) the court's obligation to apply the Sentencing Guidelines, and the court's discretion to depart from those guidelines under some circumstances;

(N) the terms of any plea-agreement provision waiving the right to appeal or to collaterally attack the sentence; and

(O) that, if convicted, a defendant who is not a United States citizen may be removed from the United States, denied citizenship, and denied admission to the United States in the future.

◼ MISSOURI v. GALIN FRYE

566 U.S. 134 (2012)

KENNEDY, J.[*]

. . . This case arises in the context of claimed ineffective assistance that led to the lapse of a prosecution offer of a plea bargain, a proposal that offered terms more lenient than the terms of the guilty plea entered later. The initial question is whether the constitutional right to counsel extends to the negotiation and consideration of plea offers that lapse or are rejected. If there is a right to effective assistance with respect to those offers, a further question is what a defendant must demonstrate in order to show that prejudice resulted from counsel's deficient performance. . . .

---

[*] [Justices Ginsburg, Breyer, Sotomayor, and Kagan joined this opinion.—EDS.]

I.

In August 2007, respondent Galin Frye was charged with driving with a revoked license. Frye had been convicted for that offense on three other occasions, so the State of Missouri charged him with a class D felony, which carries a maximum term of imprisonment of four years.

On November 15, the prosecutor sent a letter to Frye's counsel offering a choice of two plea bargains. The prosecutor first offered to recommend a 3-year sentence if there was a guilty plea to the felony charge, without a recommendation regarding probation but with a recommendation that Frye serve 10 days in jail as so-called "shock" time. The second offer was to reduce the charge to a misdemeanor and, if Frye pleaded guilty to it, to recommend a 90-day sentence. The misdemeanor charge of driving with a revoked license carries a maximum term of imprisonment of one year. The letter stated both offers would expire on December 28. Frye's attorney did not advise Frye that the offers had been made. The offers expired.

Frye's preliminary hearing was scheduled for January 4, 2008. On December 30, 2007, less than a week before the hearing, Frye was again arrested for driving with a revoked license. At the January 4 hearing, Frye waived his right to a preliminary hearing on the charge arising from the August 2007 arrest. He pleaded not guilty at a subsequent arraignment but then changed his plea to guilty. There was no underlying plea agreement. The state trial court accepted Frye's guilty plea. The prosecutor recommended a 3-year sentence, made no recommendation regarding probation, and requested 10 days shock time in jail. The trial judge sentenced Frye to three years in prison.

Frye filed for post-conviction relief in state court. He alleged his counsel's failure to inform him of the prosecution's plea offer denied him the effective assistance of counsel. At an evidentiary hearing, Frye testified he would have entered a guilty plea to the misdemeanor had he known about the offer.

A state court denied the post-conviction motion, but the Missouri Court of Appeals reversed. It determined that Frye met both of the requirements for showing a Sixth Amendment violation under *Strickland.* First, the court determined Frye's counsel's performance was deficient because the "record is void of any evidence of any effort by trial counsel to communicate the Offer to Frye during the Offer window." The court next concluded Frye had shown his counsel's deficient performance caused him prejudice because "Frye pled guilty to a felony instead of a misdemeanor and was subject to a maximum sentence of four years instead of one year."

To implement a remedy for the violation, the court deemed Frye's guilty plea withdrawn and remanded to allow Frye either to insist on a trial or to plead guilty to any offense the prosecutor deemed it appropriate to charge. This Court granted certiorari.

II.

A.

It is well settled that the right to the effective assistance of counsel applies to certain steps before trial. The Sixth Amendment guarantees a defendant the right to have counsel present at all "critical" stages of the criminal proceedings. Critical stages include arraignments, post-indictment interrogations, post-indictment line-ups, and the entry of a guilty plea.

With respect to the right to effective counsel in plea negotiations, a proper beginning point is to discuss two cases from this Court considering the role of counsel in advising a client about a plea offer and an ensuing guilty plea: Hill v. Lockhart, 474 U.S. 52 (1985); and Padilla v. Kentucky, 559 U.S. 356 (2010).

Hill established that claims of ineffective assistance of counsel in the plea bargain context are governed by the two-part test set forth in *Strickland.* . . . In *Hill*, the decision turned on the second part of the *Strickland* test. There, a defendant who had entered a guilty plea claimed his counsel had misinformed him of the amount of time he would have to serve before he became eligible for parole. But the defendant had not alleged that, even if adequate advice and assistance had been given, he would have elected to plead not guilty and proceed to trial. Thus, the Court found that no prejudice from the inadequate advice had been shown or alleged.

In *Padilla*, the Court again discussed the duties of counsel in advising a client with respect to a plea offer that leads to a guilty plea. *Padilla* held that a guilty plea, based on a plea offer, should be set aside because counsel misinformed the defendant of the immigration consequences of the conviction. The Court made clear that "the negotiation of a plea bargain is a critical phase of litigation for purposes of the Sixth Amendment right to effective assistance of counsel." It also rejected the argument made by petitioner in this case that a knowing and voluntary plea supersedes errors by defense counsel.

In the case now before the Court the State, as petitioner, points out that the legal question presented is different from that in *Hill* and *Padilla*. In those cases the claim was that the prisoner's plea of guilty was invalid because counsel had provided incorrect advice pertinent to the plea. In the instant case, by contrast, the . . . challenge is not to the advice pertaining to the plea that was accepted but rather to the course of legal representation that preceded it with respect to other potential pleas and plea offers. . . .

The State urges that there is no right to a plea offer or a plea bargain in any event. It claims Frye therefore was not deprived of any legal benefit to which he was entitled. Under this view, any wrongful or mistaken action of counsel with respect to earlier plea offers is beside the point.

The State is correct to point out that *Hill* and *Padilla* concerned whether there was ineffective assistance leading to acceptance of a plea offer, a process involving a formal court appearance with the defendant and all counsel present. Before a guilty plea is entered the defendant's understanding of the plea and its consequences can be established on the record. This affords the State substantial protection against later claims that the plea was the result of inadequate advice. . . .

When a plea offer has lapsed or been rejected, however, no formal court proceedings are involved. This underscores that the plea-bargaining process is often in flux, with no clear standards or timelines and with no judicial supervision of the discussions between prosecution and defense. Indeed, discussions between client and defense counsel are privileged. So the prosecution has little or no notice if something may be amiss and perhaps no capacity to intervene in any event. And, as noted, the State insists there is no right to receive a plea offer. For all these reasons, the State contends, it is unfair to subject it to the consequences of defense counsel's inadequacies, especially when the opportunities for a full and fair trial, or, as here, for a later guilty plea albeit on less favorable terms, are preserved.

The State's contentions are neither illogical nor without some persuasive force, yet they do not suffice to overcome a simple reality. Ninety-seven percent of federal convictions and ninety-four percent of state convictions are the result of guilty pleas. The reality is that plea bargains have become so central to the administration of the criminal justice system that defense counsel have responsibilities in the plea bargain process, responsibilities that must be met to render the adequate assistance of counsel that the Sixth Amendment requires in the criminal process at critical stages. Because ours is for the most part a system of pleas, not a system of trials, it is insufficient simply to point to the guarantee of a fair trial as a backstop that inoculates any errors in the pretrial process. "To a large extent . . . horse trading [between prosecutor and defense counsel] determines who goes to jail and for how long. That is what plea bargaining is. It is not some adjunct to the criminal justice system; it *is* the criminal justice system." Scott & Stuntz, Plea Bargaining as Contract, 101 Yale L.J. 1909, 1912 (1992). In today's criminal justice system, therefore, the negotiation of a plea bargain, rather than the unfolding of a trial, is almost always the critical point for a defendant.

To note the prevalence of plea bargaining is not to criticize it. The potential to conserve valuable prosecutorial resources and for defendants to admit their crimes and receive more favorable terms at sentencing means that a plea agreement can benefit both parties. In order that these benefits can be realized, however, criminal defendants require effective counsel during plea negotiations. . . .

B.

The inquiry then becomes how to define the duty and responsibilities of defense counsel in the plea bargain process. This is a difficult question. The art of negotiation is at least as nuanced as the art of trial advocacy and it presents questions farther removed from immediate judicial supervision. Bargaining is, by its nature, defined to a substantial degree by personal style. The alternative courses and tactics in negotiation are so individual that it may be neither prudent nor practicable to try to elaborate or define detailed standards for the proper discharge of defense counsel's participation in the process.

This case presents neither the necessity nor the occasion to define the duties of defense counsel in those respects, however. Here the question is whether defense counsel has the duty to communicate the terms of a formal offer to accept a plea on terms and conditions that may result in a lesser sentence, a conviction on lesser charges, or both.

This Court now holds that, as a general rule, defense counsel has the duty to communicate formal offers from the prosecution to accept a plea on terms and conditions that may be favorable to the accused. Any exceptions to that rule need not be explored here, for the offer was a formal one with a fixed expiration date. When defense counsel allowed the offer to expire without advising the defendant or allowing him to consider it, defense counsel did not render the effective assistance the Constitution requires.

Though the standard for counsel's performance is not determined solely by reference to codified standards of professional practice, these standards can be important guides. The American Bar Association recommends defense counsel "promptly communicate and explain to the defendant all plea offers made by the prosecuting attorney," ABA Standards for Criminal Justice, Pleas of Guilty 14-3.2(a) (3d ed. 1999), and this standard has been adopted by numerous state and federal courts over the last 30 years. The standard for prompt communication and consultation is also set out in state bar professional standards for attorneys.

The prosecution and the trial courts may adopt some measures to help ensure against late, frivolous, or fabricated claims after a later, less advantageous plea offer has been accepted or after a trial leading to conviction with resulting harsh consequences. First, the fact of a formal offer means that its terms and its processing can be documented so that what took place in the negotiation process becomes more clear if some later inquiry turns on the conduct of earlier pretrial negotiations. Second, States may elect to follow rules that all offers must be in writing, again to ensure against later misunderstandings or fabricated charges. Third, formal offers can be made part of the record at any subsequent plea proceeding or before a trial on the merits, all to ensure that a defendant has been fully advised before those further proceedings commence. At least one State [Arizona] often follows a similar procedure before trial.

Here defense counsel did not communicate the formal offers to the defendant. As a result of that deficient performance, the offers lapsed. Under *Strickland*, the question then becomes what, if any, prejudice resulted from the breach of duty.

C.

To show prejudice from ineffective assistance of counsel where a plea offer has lapsed or been rejected because of counsel's deficient performance, defendants must demonstrate a reasonable probability they would have accepted the earlier plea offer had they been afforded effective assistance of counsel. Defendants must also demonstrate a reasonable probability the plea would have been entered without the prosecution canceling it or the trial court refusing to accept it, if they had the authority to exercise that discretion under state law. To establish prejudice in this instance, it is necessary to show a reasonable probability that the end result of the criminal process would have been more favorable by reason of a plea to a lesser charge or a sentence of less prison time. . . .

Frye argues that with effective assistance he would have accepted an earlier plea offer (limiting his sentence to one year in prison) as opposed to entering an open plea (exposing him to a maximum sentence of four years' imprisonment). In a case, such as this, where a defendant pleads guilty to less favorable terms and claims that ineffective assistance of counsel caused him to miss out on a more favorable earlier plea offer, *Strickland*'s inquiry into whether "the result of the proceeding would have been different" requires looking . . . [at] whether he would have accepted the offer to plead pursuant to the terms earlier proposed.

In order to complete a showing of *Strickland* prejudice, defendants who have shown a reasonable probability they would have accepted the earlier plea offer must also show that, if the prosecution had the discretion to cancel it or if the trial court had the discretion to refuse to accept it, there is a reasonable probability neither the prosecution nor the trial court would have prevented the offer from being accepted or implemented. This further showing is of particular importance because a defendant has no right to be offered a plea, nor a federal right that the judge accept it. In at least some States, including Missouri, it appears the prosecution has some discretion to cancel a plea agreement to which the defendant has agreed. The Federal Rules, some state rules including in Missouri, and this Court's precedents give trial courts some leeway to accept or reject plea agreements. It can be assumed that in most jurisdictions prosecutors and judges are familiar with the boundaries of acceptable plea bargains and sentences. So in most instances it should not be difficult to make an objective assessment as to whether or not a particular fact or intervening circumstance would suffice, in the normal course, to cause prosecutorial withdrawal or judicial nonapproval of a plea bargain. The determination that there is or is not a reasonable probability that the outcome of the proceeding would have been different absent counsel's errors can be conducted within that framework.

III.

These standards must be applied to the instant case. As regards the deficient performance prong of *Strickland*, . . . it is evident that Frye's attorney did not make a meaningful attempt to inform the defendant of a written plea offer before the offer expired. The Missouri Court of Appeals was correct that "counsel's representation fell below an objective standard of reasonableness."

The Court of Appeals erred, however, in articulating the precise standard for prejudice in this context. As noted, a defendant in Frye's position must show not only a reasonable probability that he would have accepted the lapsed plea but also a reasonable probability that the prosecution would have adhered to the agreement and that it would have been accepted by the trial court. Frye can show he would have accepted the offer, but there is strong reason to doubt the prosecution and the trial court would have permitted the plea bargain to become final.

There appears to be a reasonable probability Frye would have accepted the prosecutor's original offer of a plea bargain if the offer had been communicated to him, because he pleaded guilty to a more serious charge, with no promise of a sentencing recommendation from the prosecutor. It may be that in some cases defendants must show more than just a guilty plea to a charge or sentence harsher than the original offer. For example, revelations between plea offers about the strength of the prosecution's case may make a late decision to plead guilty insufficient to demonstrate, without further evidence, that the defendant would have pleaded guilty to an earlier, more generous plea offer if his counsel had reported it to him. Here, however, that is not the case. The Court of Appeals did not err in finding Frye's acceptance of the less favorable plea offer indicated that he would have accepted the earlier (and more favorable) offer had he been apprised of it; and there is no need to address here the showings that might be required in other cases.

The Court of Appeals failed, however, to require Frye to show that the first plea offer, if accepted by Frye, would have been adhered to by the prosecution and accepted by the trial court. Whether the prosecution and trial court are required to do so is a matter of state law, and it is not the place of this Court to settle those matters. The Court has established the minimum requirements of the Sixth Amendment as interpreted in *Strickland*, and States have the discretion to add procedural protections under state law if they choose. A State may choose to preclude the prosecution from withdrawing a plea offer once it has been accepted or perhaps to preclude a trial court from rejecting a plea bargain. In Missouri, it appears a plea offer once accepted by the defendant can be withdrawn without recourse by the prosecution. The extent of the trial court's discretion in Missouri to reject a plea agreement appears to be in some doubt.

We remand for the Missouri Court of Appeals to consider these state-law questions, because they bear on the federal question of *Strickland* prejudice. If, as the Missouri court stated here, the prosecutor could have canceled the plea agreement, and if Frye fails to show a reasonable probability the prosecutor would have adhered to the agreement, there is no *Strickland* prejudice. Likewise, if the trial court could have refused to accept the plea agreement, and if Frye fails to show a reasonable probability the trial court would have accepted the plea, there is no *Strickland* prejudice. In this case, given Frye's new offense for driving without a license on December 30, 2007, there is reason to doubt that the prosecution would have adhered to the agreement or that the trial court would have accepted it at the January 4, 2008, hearing, unless they were required by state law to do so. . . .

SCALIA, J., dissenting.*

. . . Frye's conviction here was established by his own admission of guilt, received by the court after the usual colloquy that assured it was voluntary and truthful. . . .

Galin Frye's attorney failed to inform him about a plea offer, and Frye ultimately pleaded guilty without the benefit of a deal. Counsel's mistake did not deprive Frye of any substantive or procedural right; only of the opportunity to accept a plea bargain to which he had no entitlement in the first place. So little entitlement that, had he known of and accepted the bargain, the prosecution would have been able to withdraw it right up to the point that his guilty plea pursuant to the bargain was accepted.

[In future cases] it will not be so clear that counsel's plea-bargaining skills, which must now meet a constitutional minimum, are adequate. . . . What if an attorney's personal style is to establish a reputation as a hard bargainer by, for example, advising clients to proceed to trial rather than accept anything but the most favorable plea offers? It seems inconceivable that a lawyer could compromise his client's *constitutional rights* so that he can secure better deals for other clients in the future; does a hard-bargaining personal style now violate the Sixth Amendment? [This case presents] the necessity of confronting the serious difficulties that will be created by constitutionalization of the plea-bargaining process. It will not do simply to announce that they will be solved in the sweet by-and-by. . . .

Prejudice is to be determined, the Court tells us, by a process of retrospective crystal-ball gazing posing as legal analysis. First of all, of course, we must estimate whether the defendant *would have accepted* the earlier plea bargain. Here that seems an easy question, but as the Court acknowledges, it will not always be. Next, since Missouri, like other States, permits accepted plea offers to be withdrawn by the prosecution (a reality which alone should suffice, one would think, to demonstrate that Frye had no entitlement to the plea bargain), we must estimate whether the prosecution *would have withdrawn* the plea offer. And finally, we must estimate whether the trial court *would have approved* the plea agreement. These last two estimations may seem easy in the present case, since Frye committed a new infraction before the hearing at which the agreement would have been presented; but they assuredly will not be easy in the mine run of cases. . . .

Virtually no cases deal with the standards for a prosecutor's withdrawal from a plea agreement beyond stating the general rule that a prosecutor may withdraw any time prior to, but not after, the entry of a guilty plea or other action constituting detrimental reliance on the defendant's part. And cases addressing trial courts' authority to accept or reject plea agreements almost universally observe that a trial

---

* [Chief Justice Roberts and Justices Thomas and Alito joined this opinion.—EDS.]

court enjoys broad discretion in this regard. Of course after today's opinions there will be cases galore. . . . Whatever the "boundaries" ultimately devised (if that were possible), a vast amount of discretion will still remain, and it is extraordinary to make a defendant's constitutional rights depend upon a series of retrospective mind-readings as to how that discretion, in prosecutors and trial judges, *would have been* exercised.

The plea-bargaining process is a subject worthy of regulation, since it is the means by which most criminal convictions are obtained. It happens not to be, however, a subject covered by the Sixth Amendment, which is concerned not with the fairness of bargaining but with the fairness of conviction. [In this case] the Court's sledge may require the reversal of perfectly valid, eminently just, convictions. A legislature could solve the problems presented by these cases in a much more precise and efficient manner. It might begin, for example, by penalizing the attorneys who made such grievous errors. That type of sub-constitutional remedy is not available to the Court, which is limited to penalizing (almost) everyone else by reversing valid convictions or sentences. Because that result is inconsistent with the Sixth Amendment and decades of our precedent, I respectfully dissent.

Notes

1. *Knowledge of nature of charges and procedural rights.* The federal constitution requires a defendant to understand the nature of the charges before pleading guilty to them. Although defense counsel usually explains the elements of the offense to the client, the judge ordinarily confirms that the defendant understood what he was told. In Henderson v. Morgan, 426 U.S. 637 (1976), a defendant with below-average intelligence pleaded guilty to second-degree murder while insisting that he "meant no harm" to the victim. Because the judge during the plea colloquy did not explain to the defendant that intent was a "critical" element of the crime, the Court overturned the conviction, even though there was overwhelming evidence of the defendant's guilt. The *Henderson* decision, however, does not require the judge to explain every element of every crime to every defendant. The opinion addressed only "critical" elements of the offense. See Bradshaw v. Stumpf, 545 U.S. 175 (2005) (guilty plea is valid when "the record accurately reflects that the nature of the charge and the elements of the crime were explained to the defendant by his own, competent counsel").

Defendants must also understand the nature of trial rights they are waiving, such as confrontation of witnesses, representation by counsel, and jury factfinding. As with the nature of the charges, the judge need not describe every detail of the procedural rights that the defendant is waiving. In Iowa v. Tovar, 541 U.S. 77 (2004), the defendant pled guilty to a DUI charge after waiving the right to counsel. When the sentence for a later conviction was enhanced based on the earlier conviction, Tovar challenged the validity of his waiver of counsel in the initial proceedings because the trial judge had only explained the disadvantages of self-representation in general terms. The Supreme Court held that a trial court must inform the accused of the nature of the charges against him, of his right to be counseled regarding his plea, and of the range of allowable punishments. The judge is not required to advise the defendant more specifically that an attorney might identify a viable defense that a layperson might overlook, or that an attorney can offer an independent opinion on whether it is wise to plead guilty. Compare Hopper v. State, 934 N.E.2d 1086 (Ind. 2010) (under court's supervisory power, it requires trial court to inform defendants who propose to waive right to counsel and enter guilty plea about "the value of counsel's experience in bargaining for a plea and ability to identify chinks in the State's armor to fortify a negotiating position").

2. *Knowledge of direct penal consequences.* A valid plea of guilty does not require the defendant to understand each and every consequence of the sentence that could be imposed: in traditional terminology, the defendant must understand the "direct" consequences of the conviction but not the "collateral" consequences. In general terms, consequences that occur farther in the future and more contingent on later events or the decisions of other governmental actors are more likely to be declared "collateral." Direct consequences include the maximum sentence authorized and some information about the prison term a defendant should expect. See State v. Cozart, 897 N.E.2d 478 (Ind. 2008) (judicial explanation of maximum and minimum limits of sentence range was adequate, even without explanation that court had no discretion to suspend sentence below the minimum term). Most courts also conclude that any substantial restitution payments would be a direct consequence.

On the other hand, eligibility for parole tends to fall into the "collateral" category. The courts are split over requirements that sex offenders register with law enforcement officers near their residence after the completion of any prison term. State v. Bellamy, 835 A.2d 1231 (N.J. 2003) (court must advise a guilty-pleading defendant of possible future civil commitment as a sexually violent predator); but cf. People v. Gravino, 928 N.E.2d 1048 (N.Y. 2010) (judges need not advise defendants pleading guilty of sex crimes involving children about registration obligations or possible probation conditions that would prohibit contact with their own minor children); Ward v. State, 315 S.W.3d 461 (Tenn. 2010) (trial judge must inform defendant at guilty plea colloquy about mandatory lifetime community supervision component of sentence, but not mandatory sex offender registration requirement).

For a sampling of the many state court decisions that distinguish the "collateral" consequences of a conviction from the "direct" consequences, go to the web extension for this chapter at *http://www.crimpro.com/extension/ch16.*

3. *Guilty pleas and incompetent lawyers.* A defendant who pleads guilty must be represented by counsel or must waive the right to counsel. Moore v. Michigan, 355 U.S. 155 (1957). Furthermore, if a lawyer gives constitutionally inadequate representation that causes a defendant to enter a guilty plea, the defendant may later withdraw the plea. But this does not mean that any faulty legal advice will invalidate a plea. In Brady v. United States, 397 U.S. 742 (1970), counsel gave the defendant incorrect but competent advice about the constitutionality of the death penalty statute at issue in the case; the incorrect advice of counsel was not sufficient reason to invalidate the defendant's "knowing" waiver of trial rights. See also Davie v. People, 675 S.E.2d 416 (S.C. 2009) (when counsel fails to communicate plea offer to defendant, court should decide on case-by-case basis whether prejudice is inherent in failure and whether defendant needs to show evidence of prejudice to establish ineffective assistance and involuntary guilty plea; surveys fractured jurisprudence in other states).

Many state courts, state procedural rules, and professional standards address the question of whether the defense lawyer must inform the defendant about the immigration consequences of a guilty plea and conviction. According to Padilla v. Kentucky, 559 U.S. 356 (2010), attorneys have an affirmative obligation to inform clients about any "clear" immigration consequences that flow from a criminal conviction. In cases with immigration consequences that are less clear, the attorney must advise the defendant that such consequences are possible, and recommend a consultation with a qualified immigration attorney.

State institutions have also addressed the parallel obligations of the judge to inform the defendant about immigration consequences. The web extension for this chapter collects the pronouncements of these different institutions about the obligations of defense counsel and trial judges regarding immigration consequences of criminal convictions; you can find these materials on the web extension for this chapter at *http://www.crimpro.com/extension/ch16.*

4. *Guilty pleas before discovery.* If defendants must know about the nature of the charges and the direct consequences of a guilty plea, must they also know about the basic facts the prosecutor could present against them at trial? According to United States v. Ruiz, 536 U.S. 622 (2002), federal prosecutors are not constitutionally required, before entering into a binding plea agreement with a criminal defendant, to disclose "impeachment information relating to any informants or other witnesses." The Supreme Court's decision in *Ruiz* is typical in its refusal to declare a per se rule against bargaining away discovery rights. A few courts, however, have concluded that in some cases, accepting a guilty plea based on a plea agreement that prevents the defendant from engaging in discovery violates due process. See State v. Draper, 784 P.2d 259 (Ariz. 1989) (due process and right to counsel sometimes may prohibit plea agreement conditioned on defendant not interviewing victim of alleged crime; remand to determine defendant's access to state's evidence through other witnesses). Can you identify circumstances in which a defendant could make a "knowing" waiver of the right to a jury trial without taking advantage of a discovery right? The *Ruiz* court found it significant that the condition relating to discovery was nonmandatory because the defendant could choose to go forward with discovery and forgo the plea agreement. Are there any terms that prosecutors simply may not offer because they prevent the defendant from making a knowing waiver?

5. *Professional obligations during plea negotiations.* Several sources of law address the information that attorneys for the prosecution and defense reveal to each other and to the defendant during plea negotiations. First, ethics rules and aspirational standards instruct a defense lawyer to inform the defendant about the terms of any proposed plea agreement because the client must decide what plea to enter. See ABA Model Rule of Professional Conduct 1.4; ABA Standards for Criminal Justice: Defense Function 4-6.2(a), (b); see also People v. Whitfield, 239 N.E.2d 850 (Ill. 1968) (overturning conviction after trial because defense counsel failed to communicate plea bargain offer to client). These ethics rules and aspirational standards state that it is unprofessional conduct for an attorney (prosecution or defense) to knowingly make false statements during plea negotiations. ABA Model Rule 4.1 (lawyer shall not knowingly make a false statement of material fact or law to a third person); ABA Standards 3-4.1(c), 4-6.2. To what extent do discovery rules provide for disclosure of information before the entry of a guilty plea? Do professional obligations require greater or earlier disclosures than those required under the rules of discovery? See State v. Gibson, 514 S.E.2d 320 (S.C. 1999) (prosecutor's failure to disclose *Brady* information can undermine voluntariness of guilty plea).

6. *Hearing procedures.* The decision in Boykin v. Alabama, 395 U.S. 238 (1969), gave a constitutional foundation to some of the information a defendant must know before entering a guilty plea. The record must show the defendant's awareness of

three major constitutional rights waived through entry of a guilty plea: the privilege against self-incrimination, the right to jury trial, and the right to confront adverse witnesses. In addition to these constitutional requirements, many rules of procedure have added requirements such as knowledge regarding the nature of the charges, the direct consequences of a conviction, and the factual basis for the charge. Trial courts engage in lengthy (and elaborately scripted) "plea colloquies" to create a record establishing that a defendant knows what is necessary before pleading guilty. What happens if the trial court fails to cover one of the necessary questions and thereby violates a rule of procedure? Fed. R. Crim. P. 11(h) allows a federal court to uphold a plea if the violation of the rule's requirements was "harmless error." Compare State v. Hoppe, 765 N.W.2d 794 (Wis. 2009) (guilty plea was not knowing, even though trial court found that defendant read and understood a form that includes a guilty plea questionnaire and waiver of rights; plea colloquy must satisfy 10 requirements as described in state case law, and the form that the defendant read here failed to inquire into promises or threats that were made in connection with plea or about information regarding potential range of punishments).

Problem 16-2. Direct and Collateral Effects

Donald Ross pleaded guilty to three counts of second-degree child rape committed against his former stepdaughter. Those offenses carried a maximum sentence of 10 years and a $20,000 fine, a minimum sentence of 67 months, and a mandatory 12-month community placement. As part of the plea negotiations, the government agreed to recommend a prison term of 89 months. Ross did not receive an explicit warning of his mandatory one-year community placement term prior to entering his plea.

At the sentencing hearing, the judge imposed an 89-month sentence plus the mandatory one-year community placement. In addition to the standard community placement conditions, the court adopted special conditions recommended by the pre-sentence investigator: no contact with the victim; no contact with females under 16 years old; Department of Corrections approval of residence location and living arrangements; and urinalysis and polygraph at the will of his community corrections officer.

Ross then filed a motion to withdraw his guilty plea as involuntary. The state's rules of criminal procedure say this about knowing and intelligent pleas of guilt:

> The court shall not accept a plea of guilty, without first determining that it is made voluntarily, competently and with an understanding of the nature of the charge and the consequences of the plea. The court shall not enter a judgment upon a plea of guilty unless it is satisfied that there is a factual basis for the plea.

The trial court denied withdrawal, concluding that the omission of the mandatory 12-month community placement represented merely a "collateral" consequence of his plea. His lack of knowledge about this potential consequence, the court said, was not a sufficient basis for withdrawing the guilty plea.

Will an appellate court uphold the denial of the motion to withdraw the guilty plea? Appellate decisions in this state distinguish "direct" from "collateral" consequences by asking whether the component of the sentence represents "a definite, immediate and largely automatic effect on the range of the defendant's punishment." Cf. State v. Ross, 916 P.2d 405 (Wash. 1996).

Problem 16-3. Pre-Plea Discovery

Deputy Dawn Barkman stopped a vehicle for exceeding the speed limit and driving briefly onto the shoulder of a road. When Barkman approached the driver, David Secord, she smelled alcohol and investigated whether Secord had been driving under the influence. Barkman conducted three field sobriety tests, during which she observed Secord's gait, appearance, and speech. Barkman also questioned Secord about his consumption of alcohol. At the end of the investigation, Barkman wrote a report about her observations, noting that she had used a video camera to record her investigation.

The state indicted Secord on aggravated driving with an alcohol concentration level of .10 or more. The state later offered to permit Secord to plead guilty to endangerment, a lower-level felony, and DUI with one prior conviction, a class one misdemeanor. Defense counsel requested a copy of the police video before advising Secord whether he should accept the offer. In response to that request, the state withdrew the plea offer, provided a copy of the video to Secord, and transferred the case to a "trial team."

Secord nevertheless filed with the trial court a request for a change-of-plea hearing, saying he wanted to accept the plea offer and noting the state might oppose the request because he had asked for a copy of the video. He argued he was "entitled to review the video." The state opposed Secord's request to accept the plea offer but offered him a similar agreement that would have required him to serve more time in jail. Is a court likely to accept Secord's argument that he possessed a due process right to review the video before deciding whether to accept the original plea offer? Cf. State v. Secord, 88 P.3d 587 (Ariz. Ct. App. 2004). If, upon reading that the officer made a video recording of the sobriety tests, Secord's defense attorney nonetheless failed to request the videotape from the prosecution and instead counseled Secord to accept the first plea offer, would that constitute ineffective assistance of counsel? Would it matter to the resolution of either question above whether the tape contained potentially exculpatory evidence?

2. Involuntary Pleas

Time and again, procedural rules and judicial opinions say that a plea of guilty or nolo contendere must be "voluntary." The question of voluntariness raises a familiar theme in criminal procedure: In what sense can we say that a defendant *chooses* to waive procedural advantages such as a right to jury trial? Surely a defendant is choosing among unpleasant options when she decides to plead guilty. Is it possible for the government to restrict the defendant's options in such a way that the defendant's decision to plead guilty is no longer a "choice" in any meaningful sense? In this section, we consider three settings in which defendants have repeatedly claimed that their decision to plead guilty was not truly voluntary.

a. Large Plea Discounts

ROBERT BRADY v. UNITED STATES
397 U.S. 742 (1970)

White, J.

In 1959, petitioner was charged with kidnap[p]ing in violation of 18 U.S.C. §1201(a). Since the indictment charged that the victim of the kidnap[p]ing was not liberated unharmed, petitioner faced a maximum penalty of death if the verdict of the jury should so recommend. Petitioner, represented by competent counsel throughout, first elected to plead not guilty. Apparently because the trial judge was unwilling to try the case without a jury, petitioner made no serious attempt to reduce the possibility of a death penalty by waiving a jury trial. Upon learning that his codefendant, who had confessed to the authorities, would plead guilty and be available to testify against him, petitioner changed his plea to guilty. His plea was accepted after the trial judge twice questioned him as to the voluntariness of his plea. Petitioner was sentenced to 50 years' imprisonment, later reduced to 30.

In 1967, petitioner sought relief under 28 U.S.C. §2255, claiming that his plea of guilty was not voluntarily given because §1201(a) operated to coerce his plea, because his counsel exerted impermissible pressure upon him, and because his plea was induced by representations with respect to reduction of sentence and clemency. It was also alleged that the trial judge had not fully complied with Rule 11 of the Federal Rules of Criminal Procedure. . . .

That a guilty plea is a grave and solemn act to be accepted only with care and discernment has long been recognized. Central to the plea and the foundation for entering judgment against the defendant is the defendant's admission in open court that he committed the acts charged in the indictment. He thus stands as a witness against himself and he is shielded by the Fifth Amendment from being compelled to do so—hence the minimum requirement that his plea be the voluntary expression of his own choice. But the plea is more than an admission of past conduct; it is the defendant's consent that judgment of conviction may be entered without a trial—a waiver of his right to trial before a jury or a judge. Waivers of constitutional rights not only must be voluntary but must be knowing, intelligent acts done with sufficient awareness of the relevant circumstances and likely consequences. On neither score was Brady's plea of guilty invalid. . . .

The trial judge in 1959 found the plea voluntary before accepting it; the District Court in 1968, after an evidentiary hearing, found that the plea was voluntarily made; the Court of Appeals specifically approved the finding of voluntariness. We see no reason on this record to disturb the judgment of those courts. Petitioner, advised by competent counsel, tendered his plea after his codefendant, who had already given a confession, determined to plead guilty and became available to testify against petitioner. It was this development that the District Court found to have triggered Brady's guilty plea.

The voluntariness of Brady's plea can be determined only by considering all of the relevant circumstances surrounding it. One of these circumstances was the possibility of a heavier sentence following a guilty verdict after a trial. It may be that Brady, faced with a strong case against him and recognizing that his chances for acquittal were slight, preferred to plead guilty and thus limit the penalty to life imprisonment rather than to elect a jury trial which could result in a death penalty. But even if we assume that Brady would not have pleaded guilty except for the death penalty provision of §1201(a), this assumption merely identifies the penalty provision as a "but for" cause of his plea. That the statute caused the plea in this sense does not necessarily prove that the plea was coerced and invalid as an involuntary act.

The State to some degree encourages pleas of guilty at every important step in the criminal process. For some people, their breach of a State's law is alone sufficient reason for surrendering themselves and accepting punishment. For others, apprehension and charge, both threatening acts by the Government, jar them into admitting their guilt. In still other cases, the post-indictment accumulation of evidence may convince the defendant and his counsel that a trial is not worth the agony and expense to the defendant and his family. All these pleas of guilty are valid in spite of the State's responsibility for some of the factors motivating the pleas; the pleas are no more improperly compelled than is the decision by a defendant at the close of the State's evidence at trial that he must take the stand or face certain conviction.

Of course, the agents of the State may not produce a plea by actual or threatened physical harm or by mental coercion overbearing the will of the defendant. But nothing of the sort is claimed in this case; nor is there evidence that Brady was so gripped by fear of the death penalty or hope of leniency that he did not or could not, with the help of counsel, rationally weigh the advantages of going to trial against the advantages of pleading guilty. Brady's claim is of a different sort: that it violates the Fifth Amendment to influence or encourage a guilty plea by opportunity or promise of leniency and that a guilty plea is coerced and invalid if influenced by the fear of a possibly higher penalty for the crime charged if a conviction is obtained after the State is put to its proof.

Insofar as the voluntariness of his plea is concerned, there is little to differentiate Brady from (1) the defendant, in a jurisdiction where the judge and jury have the same range of sentencing power, who pleads guilty because his lawyer advises him that the judge will very probably be more lenient than the jury; (2) the defendant, in a jurisdiction where the judge alone has sentencing power, who is advised by counsel that the judge is normally more lenient with defendants who plead guilty than with those who go to trial; (3) the defendant who is permitted by prosecutor and judge to plead guilty to a lesser offense included in the offense charged; and (4) the defendant who pleads guilty to certain counts with the understanding that other charges will be dropped. In each of these situations, as in Brady's case, the defendant might never plead guilty absent the possibility or certainty that the plea will result in a lesser penalty than the sentence that could be imposed after a trial and a verdict of guilty. We decline to hold, however, that a guilty plea is compelled and invalid under the Fifth Amendment whenever motivated by the defendant's desire to accept the certainty or probability of a lesser penalty rather than face a wider range of possibilities extending from acquittal to conviction and a higher penalty authorized by law for the crime charged.

The issue we deal with is inherent in the criminal law and its administration because guilty pleas are not constitutionally forbidden, because the criminal law characteristically extends to judge or jury a range of choice in setting the sentence in individual cases, and because both the State and the defendant often find it advantageous to preclude the possibility of the maximum penalty authorized by law. For a defendant who sees slight possibility of acquittal, the advantages of pleading guilty and limiting the probable penalty are obvious—his exposure is reduced, the correctional processes can begin immediately, and the practical burdens of a trial are eliminated. For the State there are also advantages—the more promptly imposed punishment after an admission of guilt may more effectively attain the objectives of punishment; and with the avoidance of trial, scarce judicial and prosecutorial resources are conserved for those cases in which there is a substantial issue of the defendant's guilt or in which there is substantial doubt that the State can sustain its burden of proof. It is this mutuality of advantage that perhaps explains the fact that at present well over three-fourths of the criminal convictions in this country rest on pleas of guilty, a great many of them no doubt motivated at least in part by the hope or assurance of a lesser penalty than might be imposed if there were a guilty verdict after a trial to judge or jury. . . .

Brady first pleaded not guilty; prior to changing his plea to guilty he was subjected to no threats or promises in face-to-face encounters with the authorities. He had competent counsel and full opportunity to assess the advantages and disadvantages of a trial as compared with those attending a plea of guilty; there was no hazard of an impulsive and improvident response to a seeming but unreal advantage. His plea of guilty was entered in open court and before a judge obviously sensitive to the requirements of the law with respect to guilty pleas. Brady's plea . . . was voluntary.

The standard as to the voluntariness of guilty pleas must be essentially that defined by Judge Tuttle of the Court of Appeals for the Fifth Circuit:

> A plea of guilty entered by one fully aware of the direct consequences, including the actual value of any commitments made to him by the court, prosecutor, or his own counsel, must stand unless induced by threats (or promises to discontinue improper harassment), misrepresentation (including unfulfilled or unfulfillable promises), or perhaps by promises that are by their nature improper as having no proper relationship to the prosecutor's business (e.g. bribes).

Shelton v. United States, 246 F.2d 571 (5th Cir. 1957). Under this standard, a plea of guilty is not invalid merely because entered to avoid the possibility of a death penalty. . . .

Notes

1. *Sizeable plea discounts.* In Brady v. United States, 397 U.S. 742 (1970), the Supreme Court held that the threat of a significantly more severe penalty (even the death penalty) upon conviction is not so coercive as to invalidate a guilty plea. Subsequent cases—from the Supreme Court and lower courts—have found few government actions short of physical coercion to render a guilty plea involuntary. Yet empirical studies suggest that innocent defendants are at the greatest risk of pleading guilty in four situations: (1) when there is a significant differential between the negotiated sentence and the sentence expected upon conviction after trial; (2) when the plea offer is to probation, while the expected sentence post-trial entails imprisonment; (3) when the plea offer is to imprisonment, while capital punishment is a possibility after trial; and (4) when the defendant is detained, and a guilty plea results in release for time served. See Jenia I. Turner, Plea Bargaining, in

Reforming Criminal Justice: Trial and Pre-Trial Processes (Erik Luna ed., 2017). Do such findings suggest that courts should scrutinize more closely the size and type of plea discounts negotiated?

2. *"Package deals."* Can the prosecutor increase the cost of the trial by threatening to prosecute third parties, such as family members of the defendant? Courts have not announced any outright bans of "package deals" or "connected pleas," but as the *Bey* decision (reprinted above) suggests, they review them with some suspicion. What should a defendant emphasize to convince a court that her particular "package deal" produced an involuntary plea? How will the defendant obtain the evidence necessary to make this showing? Does the fact that a defendant's sentence is near the minimum available sentence help or hurt her claim that the plea was involuntary? Does the difficulty with package deals come from the defendant's reduced capacity to make decisions (because the package deal offers the defendant options that cannot be compared in a rational manner) or from the public's unease about using family or other intimate bonds to gain a litigation advantage?

3. *Coercive overcharging.* A prosecutor can make the decision to go to trial very costly, through a combination of serious charges and an attractive plea agreement. These decisions, however, will usually not provoke a court to rule that the defendant's guilty plea was involuntary. In *Brady*, the defendant's belief that a decision to go to trial would expose him to a possible death penalty was not enough to invalidate the guilty plea. Nonetheless, some statutes and aspirational standards instruct the prosecutor not to "overcharge." Take, for instance, a North Carolina statute, N.C. Gen. Stat. §15A-1021(b), which forbids state agents from placing "improper pressure" on a defendant to plead guilty. According to the drafters' commentary, the statute (based on the American Law Institute's Model Code of Pre-Arraignment Procedure) was meant to prevent the prosecutor from filing charges not supported by provable facts or charges not ordinarily filed based on the conduct in question. See also ABA Standards for Criminal Justice, Prosecution Function 3-3.9(f) (prosecutor should not bring charges greater than "can reasonably be supported with evidence at trial" or greater than necessary to reflect gravity of offense).

4. *Civil consequences.* Do the prosecutor's proposed bargain terms become coercive when they move beyond matters of criminal charges and sentences to include civil consequences, matters that other legal institutions ordinarily decide? State courts have not expressed any special concern about such agreements. See Gustine v. State, 480 S.E.2d 444 (S.C. 1997) (prosecutor offers plea agreement on child sex-abuse charges contingent on defendant's giving up parental rights to stepdaughter; court does not declare parental rights term coercive as a matter of law but calls for case-by-case inquiry into knowing and voluntary nature of guilty plea). Is it wise to assume that criminal consequences are the most serious problems facing a defendant?

5. *Breaching a contract and breaking a plea bargain.* Coercive negotiation techniques by a prosecutor call into question the authenticity of any "meeting of the minds" between the government and the defendant. Indeed, the law of plea bargains is often described by analogy to the law of contract. In both areas, courts must decide when an agreement is made, what terms the agreement includes, whether a breach has occurred, and the appropriate remedies.

The basic federal law for deciding when a bargain is made comes from the U.S. Supreme Court decisions in Santobello v. New York, 404 U.S. 257 (1971), and Mabry v. Johnson, 467 U.S. 504 (1984). In *Santobello*, the Supreme Court stated: "If the guilty plea is part of a plea bargain, the State is obligated to comply with any promises it makes." 404 U.S. 262. In *Mabry,* the Court explained that the enforceability of bargains was guaranteed by the due process clause, but that a plea was not binding until it was entered and accepted by a court: Until that point the plea bargain was a "mere executory agreement" without "constitutional significance." In general, therefore, a prosecutor can withdraw an offer any time before the formal plea is accepted by the court. A majority of state courts have adopted this framework.

Once it becomes clear that the parties have indeed entered a binding plea agreement, courts also must determine whether either of the parties has breached that agreement. Further, they wrestle with the question of proper remedies for breaches of a plea agreement. An extensive discussion of these interrelated questions appears on the web extension for this chapter at *http://www.crimpro.com/extension/ch16.* Along the way, this web material considers in more detail the contractual dimensions of plea bargains.

b. Judicial Overinvolvement

Earlier in this chapter we considered the individual judge's responsibility during a plea hearing to confirm and document that the defendant is entering the guilty plea knowingly and voluntarily. But what is the individual judge's role prior to the guilty plea? Rules of procedure paint very different portraits of the judge's involvement in plea negotiations. Some rules, such as Fed. R. Crim. P. 11(c)(1), state that the trial judge "shall not participate in any" plea discussions. Others do not tell the judge what to do during the negotiations. Rules and statutes in a few states authorize the trial judge to take part in negotiations. See N.C. Gen. Stat. §15A-1021(a) ("The trial judge may participate in the discussions"). Do these rules reflect profound differences in practice, or do they reflect an ambiguity about what qualifies as judicial "participation" in the plea negotiations?

■ STATE v. LANDOUR BOUIE
817 So. 2d 48 (La. 2002)

CALOGERO, C.J.

We granted this writ application to determine whether the district court abused its discretion in not allowing the defendant to withdraw his plea of guilty, given that the trial judge had previously interjected his own opinions into the plea negotiations as to whether the defendant would be acquitted or found guilty. . . .

The state charged the defendant and his co-defendant, Cornelius Johnson, with attempted second degree murder. . . . The charge arose out of the shooting of Eddie Hughes, who had intervened in an attempt by [Bouie] and Johnson to secure the services of a prostitute doing business near Hughes's home. Using a rifle that [Johnson] retrieved from [Bouie's] house, where the two men had driven after the initial dispute with Hughes, Johnson confronted Hughes on the street outside his home and fired a bullet that struck the victim in the throat, severing his spinal column. The victim survived. . . .

From the outset, the defendant indicated that he wanted to go to trial, and throughout the discussions, he consistently indicated that he believed he was innocent of the charge of attempted second degree murder. . . . At the outset of the day set for trial, the defendant, represented by appointed counsel, stated that he understood that he was going to trial, and asserted that he *wanted* to go to trial. Immediately, the trial judge told the defendant that he was being tried for attempted second degree murder and that "if you go to trial, the penalty for that charge is fifty years at hard labor." The trial judge followed up by telling the defendant that, because he had been on probation at the time of the offense, he could be found guilty of being a second felony offender and receive a sentence of up to 100 years. But if he pleaded guilty, . . . and if the state filed a multiple offender bill, the trial judge would give the defendant the minimum twenty-five years at hard labor, or as low as ten years if the state did not file the multiple offender bill.

When the defendant was asked if this information helped him to make up his mind, the defendant responded affirmatively, but he also asserted, "Your Honor—uh—I'm just going you know, I haven't did anything." The trial judge quickly responded with his view on the certainty that the defendant would be convicted if he chose to go to trial: . . .

> *Court:* You may be able to be found not guilty. . . . But I can tell you this, all of the years that I've been either a prosecutor or a judge, I don't think I've ever seen more than one or two people who went to trial found not guilty. The D.A. knows what they're doing when they try somebody, generally, and the jury seems to believe them, generally. And the odds are not in your favor of going to trial and winning a case. Do you understand that? Do you?
>
> *Bouie:* Yes, sir.
>
> *Court:* And when I say all the years I've been doing that, that's been since 1981, so how long is that? Sixteen years I've been doing this, either a judge or an assistant district attorney and I think I've found two people found not guilty—uh—seen two people found not guilty in felony trials. Now, if you go to trial, I'm telling you the odds are against you winning. Do you understand that?
>
> *Bouie:* Yes, sir.
>
> *Court:* All right, then if you lose, then you're looking at the hundred years. . . . If you plead guilty, you're looking at no more than twenty-five and maybe as low as ten. Do you understand that?
>
> *Bouie:* Yes, sir.

At this point, the defendant was allowed to confer with his counsel and the matter of his co-defendant was taken up by the trial judge. Johnson, too, expressed indecision and questioned the state's version of the facts, but, after discussions with the trial judge, in which the judge offered the same deal and stated that a hundred-year sentence meant that Johnson would die in prison, Johnson eventually entered a plea of guilty as charged in return for a sentencing commitment by the court of twenty-five years imprisonment at hard labor, the minimum term for a second offender convicted of attempted murder and sentenced as a multiple offender. In its recitation of the case, the state indicated that Johnson had given a video-taped statement in which he stated that the defendant had encouraged him to retrieve the weapon and to shoot the victim. According to the state, Johnson said that, on the way back to the scene, the two men had struck a bargain in which the defendant agreed to drive the getaway car and Johnson vowed to shoot the victim. Johnson, in court, disagreed with the state's recitation, but he conceded that there had been a shooting and that what the state had said had basically happened "in so many ways."

After Johnson's plea was completed, the defendant returned to court. [The] defendant was asked what he thought he was facing and he replied, "Whew, um, I really don't know." Expressing some frustration, "All right, that's why I keep trying to explain it to you," the trial judge reiterated that the defendant was charged with attempted second degree murder, which carries a sentence of up to 50 years at hard labor, that a jury was waiting upstairs and would return a verdict in a few days if he elected to go to trial that day, that the defendant in fact had a prior felony conviction, and that the sentence would be up to 100 years at hard labor as a second felony offender if he went to trial, but only 25 years if he pleaded guilty. After conferring with his attorney, the defendant agreed to plead guilty, and the *Boykin* examination commenced. See Boykin v. Alabama, 395 U.S. 238 (1969).

During the colloquy, the trial judge gave a similar response anytime the defendant vacillated. When the defendant indicated that he thought he had been promised 10 years, the trial judge responded that it was only if the state chose not to file a multiple offender bill would he impose a sentence between 10 and 25 years at hard labor. The trial judge then asked if the defendant wanted to plead guilty. When he received no response, the trial judge stated that if not, "we've got the people waiting upstairs to get the trial started." The defendant responded, "I—whew, um—." The trial judge again asked if the defendant wanted to finish the guilty plea and if he understood what was happening. The defendant said he did "in a way" and expressed doubt about the evidence against him. The trial judge then explained the law of principals, using the getaway driver of an armed robbery as an example. The trial judge [said that if the jury concluded that Bouie] provided a gun to Johnson, drove him back to the scene, and encouraged him to shoot the victim, then the defendant would be as guilty as if he had shot the victim.

The trial judge then had the state repeat its case against the defendant for the record. Unlike his co-defendant Johnson, the defendant expressed considerable doubt that he was guilty of any crime for transporting Johnson back and forth from the scene of the shooting. In his own statement to the police, the defendant had acknowledged only that he had been on the scene with Johnson to pick up a prostitute, that after the initial confrontation with the victim he had driven Johnson back to his (the defendant's) house where Johnson retrieved a rifle that he (Johnson) had hidden there earlier that evening, and that he (the defendant) had then returned with Johnson to the scene to "turn a trick" with the prostitute. The defendant had denied in his statement that he knew beforehand that Johnson would shoot the victim and he continued to insist in court that the two men had gone back "to see . . . where the trick was. [Johnson] got out the car and the only thing I heard was a shot. . . ." [After Bouie observed that "everything is pointing at me," the trial judge returned to the question of a guilty plea]:

Court: Do you think it's in your best interest at this point to go ahead and accept a guilty plea and get the lesser years that you've been offered rather than running the risk of going to trial and getting the Habitual Act charged against you and getting, maybe, up to a hundred years?

Bouie: (no answer)

Court: Do you think this guilty plea today, right now, is better than doing that? In other words, this is in your best interest at this point.

Bouie: It seems like, Your Honor.

The trial court then accepted the defendant's guilty plea.[2] However, after the state filed a multiple offender bill, but before sentencing, the defendant moved to withdraw his plea, alleging that he had been under "extreme emotional stress" when he entered the plea. At the hearing on the motion, the defendant testified that the court had, in effect, stampeded him into pleading guilty, not simply by the sentencing offer of 25 years imprisonment at hard labor but also by informing him, in effect, that "if I take you to trial, I was not going to win in your courtroom. You was going to give me fifty to a hundred years. So I feel as though I wasn't going to win no matter what." On the basis of that testimony, the attorney representing the defendant asked the court at the close of the hearing, "You saw [two acquittals] in nearly a twenty-year period. . . . How is he going to knowingly and intentionally plead guilty after he hears that, Your Honor?"

The trial judge denied the motion on grounds that it had spent over an hour and a half with the defendant in a painstaking effort to persuade him that a guilty plea was in his best interests "because he probably would have gotten convicted and been sentenced to fifty to a hundred years. [Instead] of doing that, I gave him twenty-five, and, certainly . . . that was in his best interest." The court . . . sentenced him to the promised term of 25 years imprisonment at hard labor. . . .

A trial judge has broad discretion in ruling on a defendant's motion to withdraw his guilty plea before sentencing. La. Code Crim. Proc. art. 559. When circumstances indicate that the plea was constitutionally invalid, the trial judge should allow the defendant to withdraw his plea. . . . However, as a general rule, an otherwise valid plea of guilty is not rendered involuntary merely because it was entered to limit the possible maximum penalty to less than that authorized by law for the crime charged.

[The] defendant contends that the nature and extent of the district court judge's participation in the plea agreement had a coercive effect on his decision to plead guilty. While this court has not directly addressed the issue of a judge's participation in negotiating a plea agreement, in State v. Chalaire, 375 So. 2d 107, fn.2 (La. 1979), albeit in dicta, we stated: "Although not objected to in this appeal, the judge's active participation in the plea negotiations evokes our concern. The ABA Standards recommend that the trial judge should not be involved with plea discussions before the parties have reached an agreement. ABA Standards, The Function of the Trial Judge §4.1 (Approved Draft 1972); accord, Fed. R. Crim. P. [11(c)(1)]." As we noted in *Chalaire*, the reasons for proscribing judicial participation in plea negotiations, according to the ABA Standards Commentary, are:

(1) judicial participation in the discussions can create the impression in the mind of the defendant that he would not receive a fair trial were he to go to trial before this judge; (2) judicial participation in the discussions makes it difficult for the judge objectively to determine the voluntariness of the plea when it is offered; (3) judicial participation to the extent of promising a certain sentence is inconsistent with the theory behind the use of the presentence investigation report; and (4) the risk of

2. Notably, the trial judge never explained to the defendant that, to prove him guilty of attempted second degree murder, the state was required to prove that the defendant, even as a principal, had possessed the requisite specific intent to kill the victim. Consequently, whether a jury accepting the defendant's story as true could have rationally found the requisite specific intent proved beyond a reasonable doubt appears less certain than the trial judge advocated.

not going along with the disposition apparently desired by the judge may seem so great to the defendant that he will be induced to plead guilty even if innocent. ABA Standards, Pleas of Guilty §3.3(a) Commentary 73 (Approved Draft 1968).

On the other hand, we also pointed out that . . . removal of the judge from the bargaining process usually places the sentencing prerogative in the district attorney's office. [We] concluded that . . . "any judge who directly participates in plea discussions should take extreme care to avoid the dangers described in the ABA commentary."

In our decision today, we do not adopt a rule absolutely prohibiting the participation of Louisiana trial judges in plea negotiations, such as that provided by the Federal Rules of Criminal Procedure [11(c)(1)] ("The court shall not participate in any such discussions"). Instead, we find that the interjection of the trial judge's personal knowledge and opinion in the plea discussions under the circumstances of this case did, or probably did, have a coercive effect on this particular defendant's decision that a guilty plea was in his best interest.

In the present case, the trial judge's explanations of the penalties the defendant faced if he went to trial and if he were convicted by a jury, and of the trial judge's discretion to impose greater penalties after conviction than offered in the course of plea negotiations, were not inherently coercive because the advice concerned information that an accused ought to possess to enter a knowing and intelligent guilty plea. Furthermore, the court's explanation of the law of principals under La. Rev. Stat. 14:24, which would form the basis of any verdict rendered by a jury, also served the same end.

However, when the trial judge coupled those lengthy explanations with his personal view that the result of a jury trial was all but a foregone conclusion, he went beyond simply facilitating the entry of a knowing and voluntary guilty plea. The trial judge's discussion of the chances of an acquittal at a jury trial conveyed the court's personal experience over the years in unrelated cases and its confidence in the soundness of the exercise of the charging discretion of the District Attorney's Office. No matter how benign the judge's intent, and no matter how solicitous of the defendant's interests, the trial judge clearly conveyed his opinion that this particular defendant had no realistic choice other than to plead guilty or face penalties ranging from two to four times as great as the court offered. Aside from the question of its reliability, such a message was inherently coercive because it came from the court, not from the prosecutor. . . . See Standley v. Warden, 990 P.2d 983, 985 (Nev. 1999) ("Appellant had good reason to fear offending the judge if he declined [the plea offer] because the same judge would have presided over the trial and, if the trial resulted in a conviction, the judge would have determined the appropriate sentence"). The defendant here voiced those concerns in his own words at the hearing on his motion to withdraw his guilty plea when he explained to the court that he took the sentencing offer because, "You told me, if I take you to trial, I'm not going to win in your courtroom."

We recognize that a defendant may enter a voluntary guilty plea even while he continues to protest his innocence. North Carolina v. Alford, 400 U.S. 25 (1970). . . . However, *Alford* presupposes that the defendant "must be permitted to judge for himself in this respect." Therefore, whether the offered plea agreement was in fact in the defendant's best interest was not for the court to decide, but for the defendant to determine with the advice of his counsel.

We concede that a fine line may at times separate a trial judge's attempts to insure that the defendant understands that a guilty plea might serve his best interest and the overbearing of a defendant's will to reach a result the court, with the best of intentions, deems appropriate. However, we find that the trial judge in this case, by stating his personal views on the virtual certainty that the defendant would be convicted by a jury, as well as on the prospect of a sentence much greater than that offered, when this judge would be determining the sentence to be imposed following the guilty verdict, overstepped his bounds and acted as more of an advocate than as a neutral arbiter of the criminal prosecution. We conclude that the defendant's guilty plea under these circumstances was not knowingly and voluntarily entered, such that the district court abused its discretion in not granting the defendant's motion to withdraw the guilty plea. . . .

WEIMER, J., dissenting.

. . . I do not believe the statements were sufficient to coerce the defendant or unreasonably persuade him to plead guilty. It has not been alleged that anything the trial court stated was inaccurate. . . . It should be noted that defendant's admitted behavior in the events surrounding the shooting subjected him to a risk of conviction. This risk of conviction was amplified when the statement of his co-defendant, which implicated the defendant, was considered. . . .

Certainly, the trial court can and must inform the defendant of the consequences of his plea. However, in doing so, the court must avoid the impression of coercing or persuading the defendant to plead guilty. Despite the defendant's allegations, I believe the court succeeded in avoiding that impression.

Notes

1. *Legal limits on judicial participation in plea negotiations.* States have addressed the role of the judge during plea negotiations through statutes, rules of criminal procedure, rules of judicial ethics, and in judicial opinions interpreting constitutional provisions. More than half of the states instruct the judge not to "participate" in the plea discussions, the position embodied in the Federal Rules of Criminal Procedure. See People v. Collins, 27 P.3d 726 (Cal. 2001) (judge's promise of "some benefit" for giving up jury trial right rendered guilty plea involuntary); State v. Wakefield, 925 P.2d 183 (Wash. 1996); Colo. Rev. Stat. §16-7-302; Ga. Unif. Super. Ct. R. 33.5(a); Mass. R. Crim. P. 12(b) (reporter's notes). Does this mean that a judge cannot even be present as an observer during such discussions?

Another group of states discourages judges from participating in plea negotiations but does not prohibit it. Judicial opinions in these states suggest that judicial participation in negotiations, while not the best practice, is not a reason to invalidate a conviction on constitutional or other grounds. State v. Niblack, 596 A.2d 407 (Conn. 1991); State v. Ditter, 441 N.W.2d 622 (Neb. 1989). A small but growing number of states (now over a dozen) have rules or statutes that do not discourage judicial participation, and some even authorize judges to take part. See Mont. Code §46-12-211; N.C. Gen. Stat. §15A-1021(a). Some of the laws authorizing judges to participate extend only to limited types of participation. For instance, some states allow judges to take part only when the parties extend an invitation. People v. Cobbs, 505 N.W.2d 208 (Mich. 1993). Others limit the judge to commenting on the acceptability of charges and sentences that the parties themselves propose. See Ill. Sup. Ct. R. 402(d); State v. Warner, 762 So. 2d 507, 514 (Fla. 2000) (once invited by parties, court may actively discuss potential sentences and comment on proposed plea agreements). Do these limits identify the judicial practices with the most potential for making a guilty plea involuntary?

The ABA Standards for Criminal Justice, Pleas of Guilty 14-3.3, have embodied over the years an ambivalence about judicial involvement in plea discussions. The original 1968 version of Standard 14-3.3 completely barred judicial participation in plea negotiations. The 1980 edition of the Standards established a more active role for judges as a participant in plea negotiations. The parties could request to meet with the judge to discuss a plea agreement, and the judge could "serve as a moderator in listening to their respective presentations" and could "indicate what charge or sentence concessions would be acceptable." On the other hand, "the judge should never through word or demeanor, either directly or indirectly, communicate to the defendant or defense counsel that a plea agreement should be accepted or that a guilty plea should be entered." The 1997 edition of the Standards set out a more limited role for the judge: "[A] judge may be presented with a proposed plea agreement negotiated by the parties and may indicate whether the court would accept the terms as proposed and, if relevant, indicate what sentence would be imposed."

2. *Judicial involvement in practice.* Judges do participate in plea negotiations. As the variety of legal rules on the subject suggests, the practice varies from place to place. One study from the late 1970s concluded that about a third of judges in felony and misdemeanor courts nationwide attended plea negotiations. Judges in states with rules clearly barring their participation in plea bargaining were much less likely to attend the negotiations than judges in other states. John Paul Ryan & James Alfini, Trial Judges' Participation in Plea Bargaining: An Empirical Perspective, 13 Law & Soc'y Rev. 479 (1979). A more recent study of judicial practice in ten states found that judicial involvement in negotiations is now routine and institutionalized in many court systems. The authors found that such participation occurs primarily in response to increasing pressure to manage dockets more efficiently, but judges, defense attorneys, and prosecutors also value the judge's involvement for reducing the uncertainty of plea negotiations and the potential compulsion of a prosecutor's early offer. Nancy J. King & Ronald F. Wright, The Invisible Revolution in Plea Bargaining: Managerial Judging and Judicial Participation in Negotiations, 95 Tex. L. Rev. 325 (2016); see also Jenia Iontcheva Turner, Judicial Participation in Plea Negotiations: A Comparative View, 54 Am. J. Comp. L. 199 (2006) (surveying judicial participation in plea negotiations in Germany, Florida, and Connecticut and arguing that a judge's early input into plea negotiations can render the final disposition more accurate and procedurally just).

3. *Judicial neutrality and plea negotiations.* Critics of judicial participation in plea negotiations have argued that a judge who proposes or ratifies the terms of a plea agreement cannot properly perform judicial duties later in the case. For instance, they say, such a judge cannot properly decide at the plea hearing whether the defendant is entering the guilty plea voluntarily. If the defendant rejects a proposed offer, it may be difficult for the negotiating judge to preside at the trial. The participating judge may also find it difficult at sentencing to give proper consideration to a pre-sentence investigation that recommends some sentence different from the negotiated recommendation. See Richard Klein, Due Process Denied: Judicial Coercion in the Plea Bargaining Process, 32 Hofstra L. Rev. 1349 (2004). Are these

concerns realistic? Are there ways to avoid these problems in systems that permit judges to participate in plea discussions? Should rules require different judges for the plea and the trial? See State v. D'Antonio, 877 A.2d 696 (Conn. 2005) (noting Connecticut case law holding that "it is improper for a trial judge to preside over a defendant's trial after having participated actively in unsuccessful plea negotiations in the case").

4. *Judicial coercion and plea negotiations.* The most common objection to judicial participation in plea discussions is that the judge will coerce the defendant into accepting a plea agreement. While the prosecutor does not hold ultimate authority to impose a sentence in most cases, the judge can say with certainty what sentence she will impose after trial or after a guilty plea. If the judge indicates that a particular outcome is a "good deal," does the defendant have much hope for a better outcome? One might conclude alternatively that judges who participate in plea discussions merely give the defendant more accurate and complete information about what will occur at sentencing. Their presence might prevent prosecutors from misrepresenting local sentencing practices or from proposing unreasonable outcomes. See United States v. Davila, 569 U.S. 597 (2013) (judicial involvement in plea negotiations, in violation of federal rules, does not result in automatic vacatur of guilty plea; defendant must show prejudice to the decision to plead guilty); Albert Alschuler, The Trial Judge's Role in Plea Bargaining (pt. 1), 76 Colum. L. Rev. 1059 (1976). For reasons such as these, a law reform commission in England and Wales has called for a return to the practice of "sentence canvassing," in which a judge can tell a defendant in private the most severe sentence he might expect after a guilty plea. Report of the Royal Commission on Criminal Justice 112-113 (1993) (Runciman Commission). Today, English judges may indicate to the advocates their "views of the viability of the case or the acceptability of pleas," but they can only do so on the request of the defendant, not on their own initiative. Furthermore, "this should be done in open court with a full recording of proceedings, in the absence of the jury but with both sides represented and the defendant present. Reporting restrictions can be applied in order to safeguard a situation where the indication is not accepted and the matter proceeds to trial." Crown Prosecution Service Legal Guidance, Sentencing: Overview, at *https://www.cps.gov.uk/legal-guidance/sentencing-overview.*

How does judicial participation in plea negotiations compare to other sources of coercion to plead guilty? If a defendant can voluntarily plead guilty while claiming innocence, and can voluntarily plead guilty when the prosecutor plans to seek more severe sanctions against the defendant's family members unless they all enter guilty pleas, why object to a judge who tells the defendant the going rate for an offense?

c. *Alford* Pleas: Voluntariness and Factual Basis

A defendant who pleads guilty stands ready to accept punishment for the crime as charged. Is this decision coerced if the defendant insists that he did not commit the crime? Even if the plea is held to be voluntary, does it meet the requirement that a plea be supported by sufficient factual basis? In North Carolina v. Alford, 400 U.S. 25 (1970), the U.S. Supreme Court held that a defendant may knowingly, intelligently, and voluntarily enter a guilty plea, even while he maintains his innocence, as long as the record establishes a strong factual basis for the guilty plea. As the decision below shows, however, some states do not permit defendants to enter *Alford* pleas.

◼ FEDERAL RULE OF CRIMINAL PROCEDURE 11(b)

(2) Before accepting a plea of guilty or nolo contendere, the court must address the defendant personally in open court and determine that the plea is voluntary and did not result from force, threats, or promises (other than promises in a plea agreement).

(3) Before entering judgment on a guilty plea, the court must determine that there is a factual basis for the plea.

◼ STATE v. EDWIN URBINA

115 A.3d 261 (N.J. 2015)

FERNANDEZ-VINA, J.

[In 2007, the defendant, Edwin Urbina, was identified as the shooter of Edwin Torres and was charged with an offense that, if committed by an adult, would constitute murder.] To avoid an indictment for first-degree murder carrying a potential life sentence with a mandatory parole disqualifier of thirty years, defendant entered into a negotiated plea agreement with the State. Under the terms of that plea arrangement, defendant agreed to proceed as an adult and to plead guilty to one count of first-degree aggravated manslaughter, in exchange for the State's recommendation of a sentence not to exceed seventeen-and-one-half years' incarceration subject to an eighty-five percent parole disqualifier and five years of post-release parole supervision under the No Early Release Act. . . .

At the plea hearing, defendant testified under oath that he had sufficient time to speak with his family and counsel before deciding to plead guilty. . . . To establish the factual basis for defendant's plea, the following colloquy took place. . . .

> *[DEFENSE COUNSEL]:* Edwin, on November 24th you were in the City of Camden, correct?
> *THE DEFENDANT:* Yes.
> *[DEFENSE COUNSEL]:* You came into contact at that time with Edwin Torres. Do you recall that?
> *THE DEFENDANT:* Yes.
> *[DEFENSE COUNSEL]:* And, Edwin, actually there was another young man with him, is that correct?
> *THE DEFENDANT:* Yes.
> *[DEFENSE COUNSEL]:* And at the time, you and Edwin Torres, would it be fair to say, got into an argument?
> *THE DEFENDANT:* Yes.
> *[DEFENSE COUNSEL]:* At some point during that argument did you produce a handgun and fire that at Edwin? Did you shoot the handgun?
> *THE DEFENDANT:* First he smacked me. When I was walking off, I looked behind me. He said I know you and I turn your back behind me. I looked behind me. Him and his cousin was pulling out their firearms. I went for mines. It was an automatic, so then the gun just went off. When it went off it dropped. When it

dropped I picked it up and I just ran. I ain't mean to kill him, your Honor. I just wanted to have him back up.

THE COURT: You discharged a firearm in his direction, right?

THE DEFENDANT: I shot, like, away from, but it hit and the gun took my hand.

THE COURT: Well, you didn't shoot it in the air and it went in the air and accidentally came down and hit him in the top of the head, right?

THE DEFENDANT: No.

THE COURT: You pointed it in his direction, right?

THE DEFENDANT: Yes.

THE COURT: You discharged it multiple times, right?

THE DEFENDANT: Yes.

THE COURT: You pulled it six times. It wasn't an automatic, right?

THE DEFENDANT: Yes—no, it was an automatic.

THE COURT: You pulled the trigger once and six bullets came out?

THE DEFENDANT: Yes.

THE COURT: That's right?

THE DEFENDANT: Yes.

THE COURT: You knew the pistol was an automatic?

THE DEFENDANT: No.

THE COURT: But you still shot in his direction six times, correct?

THE DEFENDANT: Yes.

THE COURT: And you struck him six times?

THE DEFENDANT: Yes.

[DEFENSE COUNSEL]:   Your Honor, for the record, I also have discovery. The postmortem indicates six bullet wounds to the victim, so I would just state that also. As far as—and I don't disagree at all with Edwin's recitation of the facts. However, as far as the disposition in this matter, in preparation of this matter, there was no handgun found on the victim at the time the police responded. We would have had to argue that someone disposed of it in order to proffer a viable self-defense argument and I took all that into account when we decided on that and, therefore, although it certainly was contemplated a possible self-defense, based on the lack of a weapon found at the scene and the six bullet wounds, it's my professional opinion that that would not have been a particularly viable defense.

THE COURT: You understand what your lawyer just said?

THE DEFENDANT: Yes.

THE COURT: And you agree with that assessment?

THE DEFENDANT: Yes.

[PROSECUTOR]:   If I may, Judge, there is an eyewitness and the eyewitness account does not include the victim having a handgun. The facts as the State understood them are different from the defense version. We ask that the plea paperwork be amended to show a waiver of self-defense as part of the plea.

THE COURT: You understand what [the prosecutor] said?

THE DEFENDANT: Yes.

THE COURT: You agree with that as well?

THE DEFENDANT: Yeah.

THE COURT: You reviewed everything with your lawyer and you reached this conclusion that this was the best thing to do under the circumstances, right?

THE DEFENDANT: Yes.

THE COURT: There's no doubt that you, in fact, discharged a firearm in the direction of Mr. Torres and caused his death, correct?

THE DEFENDANT: Yes.

> *THE COURT:* All right. And you do know that, again, by pleading guilty today,
> you've waived any potential utilization of self-defense, correct?
> *THE DEFENDANT:* Yes. . . .

The court thereafter found that defendant provided an adequate factual basis
for aggravated manslaughter, and accepted the plea. [The defendant subsequently
appealed arguing that] the trial court erred in accepting his guilty plea because the
factual basis elicited for that plea indicated that he was asserting a complete defense
to the charge of aggravated manslaughter. Defendant argues that accepting a guilty
plea despite a claim of self-defense runs afoul of this Court's disapproval of *Alford*
pleas. See North Carolina v. Alford, 400 U.S. 25 (1970). Therefore, according to
defendant, a plea generally should not be accepted unless there is a retraction or
disavowal of a "complete defense, like self-defense, which is an assertion of innocence."

Defendant additionally argues that the trial court failed to sufficiently engage
defendant both to determine whether there existed an adequate factual basis for his
guilty plea and to confirm that he understood the law of self-defense well enough to
make a truly voluntary and knowing decision to waive that defense. Defendant notes
that he was only sixteen years old, with a limited education, and no experience with
the adult criminal justice system when he entered his guilty plea. Defendant asserts
that the trial court did not give him appropriate advice regarding his rights.

In contrast, the State contends that defendant's guilty plea was supported by
an adequate factual basis. Noting that a challenge to the sufficiency of the factual
basis for a plea is generally premised upon a failure of a defendant to admit to all
of the elements of a crime, the State argues that it is beyond dispute that defendant's own admissions established all of the elements of aggravated manslaughter.
According to the State, defendant's testimony that the victim pulled out a gun first
did not negate his guilty plea, and did not constitute a contemporaneous claim of
innocence requiring that his plea be vacated. Rather, the State maintains that these
statements were nothing more than an unsupported, self-serving attempt by defendant to downplay his criminal culpability.

The State also insists that when confronted with defendant's testimony regarding this alleged act of the victim, the trial court appropriately explored the issue to
ensure that defendant's plea was knowing and voluntary, and that it was based on
facts sufficient to support the charge of aggravated manslaughter. Addressing the
claim that the trial court failed to adequately explain to defendant on the record
the nature of self-defense and the significance of his waiver, the State argues that
requiring a more detailed colloquy would place an improper burden on the trial
judge to become a second defense attorney in advising a defendant with respect
to his decision to enter a guilty plea. Specifically, the State argues that the dissent
"would require the trial judge to explore the merits of a potential self-defense claim
on the record with a defendant.". . .

A defendant who enters a plea of guilty "simultaneously waives several constitutional rights, including his privilege against compulsory self-incrimination, his right
to trial by jury, and his right to confront his accusers." McCarthy v. United States,
394 U.S. 459 (1969). While in some jurisdictions a guilty plea operates as a waiver
of all affirmative defenses . . . our courts have been hesitant to go to such extremes.

This is in line with our Rules of Court, which instruct courts not to accept a plea
of guilty

"without first questioning the defendant personally, under oath or by affirmation, and determining by inquiry of the defendant and others, in the court's discretion, that there is a factual basis for the plea and that the plea is made voluntarily, not as a result of any threats or of any promises or inducements not disclosed on the record, and with an understanding of the nature of the charge and the consequences of the plea."

R. 3:9-2.

Indeed, "it is essential to elicit from the defendant a comprehensive factual basis, addressing each element of a given offense in substantial detail." State v. Campfield, 61 A.3d 1258 (N.J. 2013). The "court must be satisfied from the lips of the defendant," State v. Smullen, 571 A.2d 1305 (N.J. 1990), that he committed every element of the crime charged.

The purpose of this factual foundation is multi-faceted. First, the factual basis enables a judge to ascertain the plea's voluntariness. "Because a guilty plea is an admission of all the elements of a formal criminal charge, it cannot be truly voluntary unless the defendant possesses an understanding of the law in relation to the facts." *McCarthy*, 394 U.S. at 466. Indeed, Rule 3:9-2 specifies that the court must determine that the "plea is made voluntarily . . . with an understanding of the nature of the charge." It is therefore the duty of the plea judge to ensure that a defendant pleading guilty "has a full understanding of what the plea connotes and of its consequence," and to thereby leave a "record adequate for any review that may be later sought." Boykin v. Alabama, 395 U.S. 238, 244 (1969).

Second, the requirement of a factual basis helps "to protect a defendant who is in the position of pleading voluntarily with an understanding of the nature of the charge but without realizing that his conduct does not actually fall within the charge." State v. Barboza, 558 A2d 1303 (N.J. 1989). In fact, in New Jersey, even if a defendant wished to plead guilty to a crime he or she did not commit, he or she may not do so. "No court may accept such a plea." *Smullen*, 571 A.2d at 1305. This is in stark contrast to the federal standard, which allows an individual accused of a crime to "voluntarily, knowingly, and understandingly consent to the imposition of a prison sentence even if he is unwilling or unable to admit his participation in the acts constituting the crime," so long as there is a "strong factual basis for the plea," *Alford*, 400 U.S. at 37-38. Our rationale for departure from the federal rule is clear:

> We are mindful that our system of justice is not perfect and that, at times, an accused, without the knowledge of the court, may enter a plea of guilty to a crime he did not commit to insulate himself from a potentially greater sentence if found guilty by a jury. That is something over which we have no control. It is another thing, however, for a court to say it is acceptable for a defendant to give a perjured plea. Our court rules and case law require a factual basis for a plea of guilty, that is, a truthful account of what actually occurred to justify the acceptance of a plea. That approach in the long-run is the best means of ensuring that innocent people are not punished for crimes they did not commit. It is an approach that is essential to the very integrity of our criminal justice system.
>
> Just because we are powerless to control or eliminate every negative practice in our criminal justice system does not mean that we must condone those practices. Though we recognize that sometimes an accused, unknown to the trial judge, will perjure himself to put through a plea agreement, a court cannot give official license to such a practice.

State v. Taccetta, 200 N.J. 183, 198, 975 A.2d 928 (2009). . . .

So long as the defendant does not factually contend that he acted in self-defense, a defendant may waive a claim of self-defense. As such, before allowing a defendant to waive a claim of self-defense, we require "a thorough and searching inquiry" into "his or her understanding of the nature of the right being waived and the implications that flow from that choice." State v. Handy, 73 A.3d 421 (N.J. 2013). . . . To this end, it is the responsibility of the plea judge to ensure that the waiver is knowing and voluntary, and to do so on the record. See *Boykin*, 395 U.S. at 244. Presuming waiver from a silent record is impermissible. Accordingly, during the plea colloquy, both the plea judge and defense counsel should ensure that the defendant has an understanding of self-defense in relation to the facts of his case, and should inform the defendant that the State has the burden to disprove the defense if asserted.

Here, the trial court's colloquy on aggravated manslaughter would have been appropriate if not for the failure to make further inquiry into the apparent assertion of self-defense. Furthermore, we are not satisfied that defendant's waiver of self-defense comported with the standard that we require.

After defendant stated during the plea colloquy that he pulled his handgun after the victim and his cousin pulled their guns, and that "I ain't mean to kill him, your Honor. I just wanted to have him back up," the trial court should have explored whether defendant was claiming he acted in self-defense. However, the plea judge did not ensure that defendant truly understood the law of self-defense, including the requirement of a reasonable and honest belief in the necessity of using force, or that he understood that the State had the burden to disprove self-defense once asserted. Absent such an inquiry on the record, it is unclear whether defendant's plea was truly knowing, intelligent, and voluntary. . . . As such, we cannot rightly conclude that a strong factual basis existed to support defendant's guilty plea.

Because we find that the factual basis was insufficient, we are constrained to vacate defendant's plea of guilty to aggravated manslaughter. . . .

SOLOMON, J., dissenting.

Defendant admitted under oath that he caused the death of the victim, who was standing in close proximity just before defendant fired a gun in the victim's direction, shooting him six times. The majority acknowledges that these admissions were sufficient to support defendant's conviction for aggravated manslaughter. . . . However, the majority believes that defendant did not knowingly, intelligently, and voluntarily waive the affirmative defense of self-defense. Because, in my view, defendant's express waivers were adequate to relinquish his self-defense claim, I respectfully dissent. . . .

At the plea hearing, defendant stated that he had a verbal disagreement with the victim, and that, as defendant was "walking off," he looked back and saw the victim and his cousin "pulling out their firearms." Because this statement suggested defendant was making a claim of self-defense, the plea judge directed further inquiry to determine whether defendant's plea was factually supported and whether he actually intended to assert or waive self-defense.

I agree with the majority that defendants are permitted to waive self-defense pursuant to a plea. [A] criminal defendant should be permitted to waive self-defense where waiver offers a strategic benefit to the defendant—including entering into a plea agreement—provided the waiver is knowing, voluntary, and intelligent. As stated by the majority, "so long as the defendant does not factually contend that he acted in self-defense a defendant may waive a claim of self-defense." . . .

Here, defendant did not factually contend that he acted in self-defense. Furthermore, after defendant intimated that his actions were justified, defense counsel stated that, because "there was no handgun found on the victim at the time the police responded," it was his "professional opinion that [self-defense] would not have been a particularly viable defense." Defendant agreed with his counsel's assessment.

Additionally, the prosecutor stated that an "eyewitness account" indicated that the victim was unarmed at the time of the shooting. Defendant not only agreed with that statement, but also acquiesced to the prosecutor's request to amend the plea agreement to include a waiver of self-defense, which defendant later signed.

Defendant also assented when, near the end of the plea colloquy, the judge asked if defendant "reached this decision with your family's and [defense counsel's] assistance." Moreover, the court specifically asked defendant if he understood that, "by pleading guilty today, you've waived any potential utilization of self-defense," to which defendant answered "Yes."

Any uncertainty about defendant's admission of guilt was resolved by the trial court's questioning and the admissions of defendant who unequivocally and emphatically adopted the statements of his counsel. . . .

The majority also fails to account for considerations first acknowledged by this Court in State v. Smullen, 571 A.2d 1305 (N.J. 1990), namely, a defendant's reasonable impulse to avoid directly admitting criminal conduct. In *Smullen*, this Court accepted that criminal defendants are often reluctant to recognize "the distasteful reality that makes the charged conduct criminal" during their plea hearing. Thus, defendants providing a factual basis often exhibit a "natural reluctance to elaborate on the details." . . .

This "natural reluctance" on the part of defendants has informed our approach to plea colloquies. For example, plea courts are permitted to elicit from defendants through leading questions admissions "necessary to ensure an adequate factual basis for the guilty plea." . . .

This record reveals that defendant agreed that no gun was found on the victim at the scene, an eyewitness to the crime stated the victim was unarmed, his claim of self-defense was "not viable," and he was waiving any claim of self-defense by pleading guilty. Based on those facts, I conclude that defendant's fleeting suggestion that he acted in self-defense was a product of his natural reluctance to admit to criminally culpable conduct, not a legitimate assertion of a self-defense claim. . . . Thus, in my view, defendant knowingly, intelligently, and voluntarily waived his right to raise a self-defense claim and proffered a sufficient factual basis to support his guilty plea. . . .

Notes

1. *Guilty pleas by defendants claiming innocence: majority position.* Although there was once a real dispute among state courts about the constitutionality of accepting guilty pleas from defendants who maintained their innocence, that dispute is now largely resolved. A substantial majority of states follow the lead of the U.S. Supreme Court and allow a defendant to plead guilty, despite claims of innocence, so long as the prosecution establishes a strong factual basis to support the conviction. See People v. Canino, 508 P.2d 1273 (Colo. 1973). Fewer than a half-dozen states follow

the approach of the New Jersey Supreme Court and prevent trial judges from accepting *Alford* pleas. See Ross v. State, 456 N.E.2d 420 (Ind. 1983). The military justice system and many foreign legal systems also forbid *Alford* pleas.

Even in those U.S. jurisdictions that do accept *Alford* pleas, however, a live question is whether the trial judge has discretion to *reject* such pleas. In a footnote in *Alford,* the Supreme Court suggested that an individual trial judge, or a state court system as a whole through its rules of procedure, might refuse to accept such guilty pleas. Many individual judges do refuse to accept *Alford* pleas, and the majority of appellate courts uphold their discretion to do so. See Albert Alschuler, The Defense Attorney's Role in Plea Bargaining, 84 Yale L.J. 1179 (1975). If a state system decides not to prohibit *Alford* pleas, should it place controls on the power of the trial judge to refuse to accept such pleas? Would this step ensure the equal treatment of defendants and prevent litigants from shopping for judges? See ABA Standards for Criminal Justice: Pleas of Guilty 14-1.6 (defendant's offer to plead guilty should not be refused "solely" because defendant refuses to admit culpability). What reasons might a judge give to refuse an offer of an *Alford* plea in a specific case, apart from a general ban on such pleas?

2. Alford *pleas and free will.* If a defendant is *not* coerced when she pleads guilty while insisting that she is innocent, who *is* coerced into pleading guilty? Defendants who offer an *Alford* plea have a very limited set of options. We can presume that defendants prefer to have the option of entering an *Alford* plea rather than face the expense or publicity of a trial, along with the risk of a more severe sentence after trial. Are there reasons why the public should deny this option to the bargaining parties?

As you might expect, a defendant who enters any guilty plea must be mentally competent; otherwise, the court cannot consider the plea to be knowing and voluntary. See Godinez v. Moran, 509 U.S. 389 (1993) (same competence standard used for entry of guilty plea and capacity to stand trial); State v. Engelmann, 541 N.W.2d 96 (S.D. 1995) (allows withdrawal of *Alford* plea based on lack of mental competence at arraignment).

3. Alford *pleas and the truth.* If trials always uncovered the truth about the events surrounding alleged crimes, would there be any reason to allow *Alford* pleas? Is a system that accepts such pleas implicitly admitting that trials often fail to uncover the truth and that an innocent defendant might be justifiably concerned about an erroneous conviction after trial? The factual basis for an *Alford* plea must come from sources other than the statements of the defendant. Compare State v. Case, 213 P.3d 429 (Kan. 2009) (defendant's *Alford* plea to aggravated endangering of child and admission of a factual basis for that charge did not amount to stipulation to prosecutor's characterization of the offense as sexual abuse; sentencing judge not authorized to increase period of supervised release under statute applicable to sexually motivated crimes).

Most courts say that it is not necessary that the factual basis establish guilt beyond a reasonable doubt. The Supreme Court's opinion in *Alford* called the factual basis in that case "strong" and "overwhelming"; state courts have suggested several formulations to describe the necessary level of proof. Clewley v. State, 288 A.2d 468 (Me. 1972) (not unreasonable to conclude guilt); Re Guilty Plea Cases, 235 N.W.2d 132, 145 (Mich. 1975) (might have been convicted at trial); State v. Hagemann, 326 N.W.2d 861 (N.D. 1982) ("strong" proof of guilt). Would the "beyond a reasonable doubt" standard seriously reduce the number of *Alford* pleas accepted? See Ala. Code §15-15-23 (adopting beyond-reasonable-doubt standard for acceptance of guilty pleas); Richard Uviller, Pleading Guilty: A Critique of Four Models, 41 Law & Contemp. Probs. 102 (1977) (clear and convincing evidence). It is also possible to view an *Alford* plea as the most honest route available in a system in which some defendants want to avoid a trial even though they believe in their own innocence. When a state bans *Alford* pleas, does it invite defendants to lie to their attorneys and to the court?

C. CATEGORICAL RESTRICTIONS ON BARGAINING

As we have seen, both the prosecution and the defense have reasons to make concessions during plea negotiations, and there are few categorical restrictions on topics for bargaining. In individual cases, courts may reject a bargain that renders the underlying guilty plea involuntary, uninformed, or not sufficiently grounded in facts. But are there broader and more systematic measures that courts, legislators, prosecutorial supervisors, or other government officials have taken to regulate plea bargains? What limits have these various institutions placed on the terms available to the negotiating parties during plea bargaining?

1. Legislative Limits

Until recently, legislatures did not explicitly limit the power of the prosecution and defense to enter plea agreements. Even now, it is unusual to find a statute that addresses the topic of plea agreements directly, except to authorize the prosecuting attorney in general terms to enter such agreements. It is common to find statutes setting out the procedures necessary to ensure that a defendant enters a guilty plea knowingly and voluntarily, but these procedures apply both to negotiated pleas and non-negotiated (or "open") pleas.

Yet, in many jurisdictions, statutes have profound—even if indirect—effects on plea bargaining. Most states have at least some statutes that specify mandatory minimum penalties for certain crimes. The statutes do not require the prosecutor to charge the crime in question whenever there is sufficient evidence, and they do not stop the prosecutor from reducing or dismissing charges when this crime occurs. Nevertheless, these statutes do influence bargaining, for once the prosecutor obtains a conviction for the designated crime, the prosecutor has limited influence over the sentence and the judge has fewer sentencing options.

In addition to these sentencing statutes, some state legislatures have addressed more directly the prosecutor's power to negotiate over charges and sentences. Three examples follow. In what ways do the statutes represent different strategies for limiting plea bargains? Which strategies are likely to have the most impact on actual charging and negotiating practices?

■ CALIFORNIA PENAL CODE §1192.7

(a)(1) It is the intent of the Legislature that district attorneys prosecute violent sex crimes under statutes that provide sentencing under a "one strike," "three strikes," or habitual sex offender statute instead of engaging in plea bargaining over those offenses.

(2) Plea bargaining in any case in which the indictment or information charges any serious felony, any felony in which it is alleged that a firearm was personally used by the defendant, or any offense of driving while under the influence of alcohol, drugs, narcotics, or any other intoxicating substance, or any combination thereof, is prohibited, unless there is insufficient evidence to prove the people's case, or testimony of a material witness cannot be obtained, or a reduction or dismissal would not result in a substantial change in sentence.

(3) If the indictment or information charges the defendant with a violent sex crime [such as rape, sexual penetration, sodomy, oral copulation, or continuous sexual abuse of a child], that could be prosecuted under [enhanced penalty provisions such as the "three strikes" habitual felon law], plea bargaining is prohibited unless there is insufficient evidence to prove the people's case, or testimony of a material witness cannot be obtained, or a reduction or dismissal would not result in a substantial change in sentence. At the time of presenting the agreement to the court, the district attorney shall state on the record why a sentence under one of those sections was not sought.

(b) As used in this section "plea bargaining" means any bargaining, negotiation, or discussion between a criminal defendant, or his or her counsel, and a prosecuting attorney or judge, whereby the defendant agrees to plead guilty or nolo contendere, in exchange for any promises, commitments, concessions, assurances, or consideration by the prosecuting attorney or judge relating to any charge against the defendant or to the sentencing of the defendant.

(c) As used in this section, "serious felony" means any of the following: (1) Murder or voluntary manslaughter; (2) mayhem; (3) rape; (4) sodomy by force, violence, duress, menace, threat of great bodily injury, or fear of immediate and unlawful bodily injury on the victim or another person; (5) oral copulation by force, violence, duress, menace, threat of great bodily injury, or fear of immediate and unlawful bodily injury on the victim or another person; (6) lewd or lascivious act on a child under 14 years of age; (7) any felony punishable by death or imprisonment in the state prison for life; (8) any felony in which the defendant personally inflicts great bodily injury on any person, other than an accomplice, or any felony in which the defendant personally uses a firearm; (9) attempted murder; (10) assault with intent to commit rape or robbery; (11) assault with a deadly weapon or instrument on a peace officer; (12) assault by a life prisoner on a non-inmate; (13) assault with a deadly weapon by an inmate; (14) arson; (15) exploding a destructive device or any explosive with intent to injure; (16) exploding a destructive device or any explosive causing bodily injury, great bodily injury, or mayhem; (17) exploding a destructive device or any explosive with intent to murder; (18) any burglary of the first degree; (19) robbery or bank robbery; (20) kidnapping; . . . (23) any felony in which the defendant personally used a dangerous or deadly weapon; (24) selling, furnishing, administering, giving, or offering to sell, furnish, administer, or give to a minor any heroin, cocaine, phencyclidine (PCP), or any methamphetamine-related drug, . . . (26) grand theft involving a firearm; (27) carjacking; . . . (31) assault with a deadly weapon, firearm, machinegun, assault weapon, or semiautomatic firearm or assault on a peace officer or firefighter . . . ; (32) assault with a deadly weapon against a public transit employee, custodial officer, or school employee . . . ; (33) discharge of a firearm at an inhabited dwelling, vehicle, or aircraft; . . . (37) intimidation of victims or witnesses . . . ; and (42) any conspiracy to commit an offense described in this subdivision.

■ NEW YORK CRIMINAL PROCEDURE LAW §220.10

The only kinds of pleas which may be entered to an indictment are those specified in this section:

1. The defendant may as a matter of right enter a plea of "not guilty" to the indictment.

2. Except as provided in subdivision five, the defendant may as a matter of right enter a plea of "guilty" to the entire indictment.

3. Except as provided in subdivision five, where the indictment charges but one crime, the defendant may, with both the permission of the court and the consent of the people, enter a plea of guilty of a lesser included offense.

4. Except as provided in subdivision five, where the indictment charges two or more offenses in separate counts, the defendant may, with both the permission of the court and the consent of the people, enter a plea of:

(a) Guilty of one or more but not all of the offenses charged; or

(b) Guilty of a lesser included offense with respect to any or all of the offenses charged; or

(c) Guilty of any combination of offenses charged and lesser offenses included within other offenses charged.

5. (a) (i) Where the indictment charges one of the class A felonies . . . or the attempt to commit any such class A felony, then any plea of guilty entered pursuant to subdivision three or four must be or must include at least a plea of guilty of class B felony. . . .

(iii) Where the indictment charges one of the class B felonies . . . then any plea of guilty entered pursuant to subdivision three or four must be or must include at least a plea of guilty of a class D felony.

■ REVISED CODE OF WASHINGTON §§9.94A.450, 9.94A.460

§9.94A.450

(1) Except as provided in subsection (2) of this section, a defendant will normally be expected to plead guilty to the charge or charges which adequately describe the nature of his or her criminal conduct or go to trial.

(2) In certain circumstances, a plea agreement with a defendant in exchange for a plea of guilty to a charge or charges that may not fully describe the nature of his or her criminal conduct may be necessary and in the public interest. Such situations may include the following:

(a) Evidentiary problems which make conviction on the original charges doubtful;

(b) The defendant's willingness to cooperate in the investigation or prosecution of others whose criminal conduct is more serious or represents a greater public threat;

(c) A request by the victim when it is not the result of pressure from the defendant;

(d) The discovery of facts which mitigate the seriousness of the defendant's conduct;

(e) The correction of errors in the initial charging decision;

(f) The defendant's history with respect to criminal activity;

(g) The nature and seriousness of the offense or offenses charged;

(h) The probable effect on witnesses.

§9.94A.460

The prosecutor may reach an agreement regarding sentence recommendations. The prosecutor shall not agree to withhold relevant information from the court concerning the plea agreement.

Notes

1. *Codifying plea considerations.* The Washington statute lists several considerations that prosecutors traditionally describe as reasons to reduce charges or to recommend a lesser sentence as part of a plea bargain. The National District Attorneys Association lists similar factors for a prosecutor to consider before negotiating a plea agreement, including the following: "the nature of the offense(s)"; "age, background, and criminal history of the defendant"; "expressed remorse or contrition of the defendant and his or her willingness to accept responsibility for the crime"; "sufficiency of admissible evidence to support a verdict"; "undue hardship caused to the defendant"; "possible deterrent value of trial"; "aid to other prosecution goals through non-prosecution"; "a history of non-enforcement of the statute violated"; "willingness of the defendant to waive (release) his right to pursue potential civil causes of action arising from his arrest"; and "availability and willingness [of witnesses] to testify." National Prosecution Standards 5-3.1 (3d ed. 2009). A few other states have similar statutes. See also Oregon Code §135.415 (nonexclusive list of criteria the prosecutor may consider in making plea agreements). Would the passage of such a statute alter any practices in a prosecutor's office? What would motivate a legislature to pass such a statute?

2. *Particular charges.* It has become more common for legislatures to instruct prosecutors not to dismiss or reduce charges for specific crimes. As you might imagine, the crimes involved are usually those that have become high priorities for the public. See Nev. Rev. Stat. §§483.560, 484C.420-430 (prosecutor may not dismiss charges for driving with suspended or revoked license, or for drunk driving offenses, unless there is no probable cause to support charge). Cf. Miss. Stat. §43-21-555 (no plea bargaining in youth court).

3. *Size of discount.* The New York statute does not bar plea bargains for any particular crimes. Rather, it defines the maximum reduction in charges and authorized sentences that the prosecutor may offer. A statute specifying the size of the discounts a prosecutor can offer may create a very visible incentive to plead guilty. For

instance, in Corbitt v. New Jersey, 439 U.S. 212 (1978), the Supreme Court upheld the constitutionality of a statute that required a mandatory term of life imprisonment for a conviction after trial; the same statute allowed either a life term or a 30-year term for a conviction under the statute based on a guilty or nolo plea. Compare United States v. Jackson, 390 U.S. 570 (1968) (overturning statute as undue burden on right to jury trial where death penalty is authorized only for defendants who go to trial); Shumpert v. Department of Highways, 409 S.E.2d 771 (S.C. 1991) (statute reducing period of driver's license suspension for those pleading guilty of drunk driving offenses is overturned as burden on trial rights).

4. *Exceptions under the California statute.* Section 1192.7 of the California Penal Code became law as a result of a voter referendum in 1982. Other provisions of the "victims' rights" referendum included greater admissibility of evidence of a defendant's prior convictions and increased penalties for repeat felony offenders. The statute has been amended often over the years, sometimes through ordinary legislation and at other times through voter initiatives (for instance, the "serious felonies" numbered higher than 27 were added as part of the 2000 Juvenile Crime Initiative). Subsection (a)(3) of the statute was not included in the original language. What does this portion of the statute change?

The plea bargain limitations for "serious felonies," however, never reduced the number of cases resolved through guilty pleas and plea negotiations in California. One study of California plea bargaining concluded that the statutory ban never reduced the use of guilty pleas because section 1192.7 applied only to cases in superior court. Since virtually all serious felonies are charged initially in municipal court and transferred to superior court only after the preliminary examination, the prosecution and defense can negotiate a plea bargain in almost any case during the first few days after the filing of the charge, before any preliminary examination and before much discovery has taken place. See Candace McCoy, Politics and Plea Bargaining: Victims' Rights in California (1993). Even if the bar on plea negotiations were to apply to all court systems, how many dismissals and reductions of charges would it prevent? Consider the exceptions in subsections (a)(2) and (a)(3), allowing plea bargaining when there is "insufficient evidence" or when a material witness is not available, or when no substantial reduction in sentence would result. How many cases would fall within these subsections, and who would determine the breadth of coverage for this statutory language?

2. Judicial Rules

Judges are pulled in two directions when it comes to plea bargains. On the one hand, plea bargaining appears to be an extension of the prosecutor's charging decision, and judges are reluctant to become involved in charging decisions. See Chapter 13. On the other hand, plea bargaining is a key determinant in sentencing, and judges have customarily considered sentencing to be a judicial function. As a result, judges usually accept the practice of negotiated guilty pleas and allow prosecutors to dismiss or reduce charges. But they resist more strenuously when plea bargaining takes the form of a sentence bargain.

What form does judicial resistance to sentence bargains take? It is rare to find judges creating rules of criminal procedure or making other general pronouncements that place whole categories of agreements out of bounds. But they do frequently insist on the power, in individual cases, to make an independent judgment about any sentence that the parties might have selected under their agreement. This means that judges have been especially skeptical about agreements that give the judge only one sentencing option (the one that the prosecution and the defense have negotiated) and allow the defendant to withdraw the plea if the judge does not enter the sentence specified in the agreement. See Fed. R. Crim. P. 11(c)(1)(C) (parties may "agree that a specific sentence or sentencing range is the appropriate disposition of the case").

Problem 16-4: Rejecting Plea Bargains

The five judges in one of four criminal divisions of the Maricopa County Superior Court issued a memorandum detailing a new plea agreement policy stating that they would no longer accept any plea agreements containing stipulated sentences because sentencing "is a judicial function which should not be subjected to limitations which are imposed by the parties, but are not required by law." The relevant section of that policy reads as follows:

> Plea agreements may stipulate to "probation," or "department of corrections" for felonies, or "county jail" for misdemeanors. Agreements may not stipulate to any term of years (other than lifetime probation in dangerous crimes against children) or to any non-mandatory terms and conditions of probation, or to sentences running concurrently or consecutively.

The only two exceptions to the policy are as follows:

> 1. Exceptions will be made for legitimate cooperation agreements. If the state wishes to make stipulated sentencing concessions in exchange for information, testimony or cooperation from a defendant, that fact should be made known to the judge in an appropriate manner prior to the change of plea.
> 2. Stipulations in capital murder cases to life imprisonment are viewed by the judges as charging concessions and not true sentencing stipulations. Therefore, such stipulations are unaffected by the policy.

Rule 17.4 of the Arizona Rules of Criminal Procedure provides: "The parties may negotiate concerning, and reach an agreement on, any aspect of the disposition of the case. The court shall not participate in any such negotiation." Rule 17.4 also grants trial courts considerable discretion in deciding whether to accept or reject such agreements. Rule 17.4(d) provides in part:

> After making such determinations [of the accuracy of the agreement and the voluntariness and intelligence of the plea] and considering the victim's view, if provided, the court shall either accept or reject the tendered negotiated plea. The court shall not be bound by any provision in the plea agreement regarding the sentence or the term and conditions of probation to be imposed, if, after accepting the agreement and reviewing a presentence report, it rejects the provision as inappropriate. . . . If an agreement or any provision thereof is rejected by the court, it shall give the defendant an opportunity to withdraw his or her plea, advising the defendant that if he or she permits the plea to stand, the disposition of the case may be less favorable to him or her than that contemplated by the agreement.

A defendant who wanted to enter a plea agreement with a stipulated sentence in this division of the Superior Court challenges the judges' policy as a violation of Rule 17.4. The defendant argues that while a judge has discretion to reject any plea offer, the judges do not have the power to categorically reject plea offers. How should the court rule on the challenge? See Espinoza v. Martin, 894 P.2d 688 (Ariz. 1995).

Compare the policy of the judges in Maricopa County Superior Court to that of Judge Joseph Goodwin in the South District of West Virginia. In United States v. Stevenson, No. 2:17-CR-00047, 2018 WL 1769371 (S.D. W. Va. Apr. 12, 2018), Judge Goodwin set out the following policy with respect to plea agreements before him:

> I have . . . reflected upon the near-total substitution of plea bargaining for the system of justice created by our nation's Founders, and I FIND that I should give great weight to the people's interest in participating in their criminal justice system when considering whether to accept or reject a proffered plea bargain in a particular case. I FIND that the scales of justice tip in favor of rejecting plea bargains unless I am presented with a counterbalance of case-specific factors sufficiently compelling to overcome the people's interest in participating in the criminal justice system.
>
> Therefore, in each case, I will consider the case-specific factors presented to me and weigh those competing factors against the people's participatory interest and then determine whether to accept or reject the plea bargain. . . .
>
> Before me is a plea bargain that trades four counts of opioid drug dealing, one count of cocaine base drug dealing, and one count of firearm possession by a felon, all returned by the grand jury, for a guilty plea to a single count of distributing heroin. I am puzzled that, in the face of the government's explicit admission that it has no evidentiary concerns in this case, the government would abandon six of the seven grand jury charges.
>
> The primary arguments advanced by the government in favor of the plea bargain in this case are generally applicable to every plea bargain and not case-specific. That is, the government points only to the standard justifications for plea bargaining. In the absence of any case-specific support for this capitulation on the bulk of indicted charges, I am left to conclude that this plea bargain is motivated by expediency and an abiding desire to avoid going to trial.
>
> [The] government believes that leaving the judge with broad sentencing discretion is the only interest to be considered in accepting or rejecting a plea bargain. The government repeatedly emphasizes the defendant's cooperation with respect to drug amounts and Guideline enhancements. Simply put, the government seems to think that all I care about is the length of the available Guideline sentence. Its premise is that if the defendant agrees to be incarcerated for what the government considers an appropriate amount of time, nothing else in the criminal justice process really matters. Why bother seeking an indictment from the grand jury if a defendant can be convinced to agree to plead guilty to an information? Why try to obtain convictions on other grand jury counts if the defendant admits the conduct qualifying as relevant under the Guidelines? Shouldn't the judge be completely satisfied? Why make the government prepare for and present its case at trial? Why make the government liable for defending against any appeal? . . .
>
> The Founders clearly intended and articulated a preeminent role for the people's direct participation in that criminal justice system. I do not see justice in the plea agreement proffered in this case. As with most plea bargains, it eliminates the people's participation entirely on the reasoning that the people have "an interest in the efficient and effective adjudication of criminal cases," and that is good enough. Plea bargains like this one perpetuate the ongoing metamorphosis of the criminal

justice system into nothing more than an administrative system controlled entirely by bureaucrats, where judge and jury are merely stage props to convince the general public that the criminal justice system they see nightly on television is being busily played out in the big courtroom downtown. . . .

Because I have concluded that the parties have not overcome the weighty interest of the people in participating in their criminal justice system, and because the plea bargain in this case reflects an agreement which erodes that interest without a compelling, case-specific reason beyond mere expediency, I REJECT the plea agreement.

What, if any, powers should individual judges or groups of judges have to categorically restrict plea practice? If such powers should be limited, can't the judges achieve the same end under current law in most if not all jurisdictions? Should legislatures explicitly authorize judges or courts (perhaps under state rule-making procedures) to regulate criminal plea practice? If not, why not?

Notes

1. *Reasons for rejection of a plea agreement.* Statutes and rules give judges the opportunity to approve or disapprove plea agreements. The court must decide whether to accept or reject the defendant's plea of guilty; if the plea grows out of an objectionable plea agreement, the court can simply refuse to accept the guilty plea. Further, rules and statutes in more than 30 states require prosecutors to obtain the consent of the court to dismiss a charge. Does the court need any justification, or any particular type of justification, to reject a guilty plea based on a plea agreement or to refuse to dismiss a charge? Almost all appellate courts allow trial courts to reject guilty pleas or dismissals of charges without any serious review of the judge's reasons for refusing. A few cases, however, have held that a trial judge must state reasons for rejecting a guilty plea; the judge may refuse the guilty plea or the dismissal of charges only if the prosecutor has abused his discretion by failing to consider facts important to the public interest in the case. Sandy v. District Court, 935 P.2d 1148 (Nev. 1997); United States v. Ammidown, 497 F.2d 615 (D.C. Cir. 1973). Limits on the judicial power to reject guilty pleas are based on separation of powers concepts and on judges' limited knowledge both about the relative strengths of individual cases and about the most efficient allocation of prosecutorial resources. Would you expect such limits on judicial power to apply equally to charging agreements and sentencing agreements?

2. *Stipulated sentences.* In the case that is the basis for Problem 16-4, the Arizona Supreme Court considered (and rejected) an amendment to the guilty plea rules dealing with "stipulated sentences," and the trial judges in one of the criminal divisions created their own rule about stipulated sentences. What exactly can a trial judge do when the parties present a stipulated or "negotiated" sentence? The details vary from place to place. Most jurisdictions (including the federal courts) allow the parties to choose the type of agreement they will present to the judge: They can agree either to recommend a sentence (leaving the judge free to accept or reject the recommendation) or to offer the judge only a stipulated sentence that the judge must simply accept or reject as a package with the guilty plea. See People v. Johnson, 929 N.E.2d 361 (N.Y. 2010) (judge's decision that stipulated sentence was inadequate invalidated waiver of appeal contained in plea agreement). A few states recognize only the "binding" form of sentencing agreements. See People v. Killebrew,

330 N.W.2d 834 (Mich. 1982) (when judge plans to impose sentence that exceeds sentence recommendation or agreement, defendant may withdraw guilty plea). Other states have statutes or rules to preserve the judge's power, in all cases, to accept a guilty plea but still depart from the sentence the parties recommend. See State v. Strecker, 883 P.2d 841 (Mont. 1994). For an overview of the cases on binding sentence bargains, go to the web extension for this chapter at *http://www.crimpro. com/extension/ch16.*

Even though most criminal procedure rules allow the parties to stipulate to a particular sentence, stipulated sentences are far less common in practice than charge bargains or nonbinding sentencing recommendations. Many judges declare that they will not accept "binding" sentence recommendations, even though the relevant rules of procedure authorize such agreements. Why does this pattern emerge in most places?

3. *Prosecutor's objection to guilty plea and sentence.* We have considered the situation in which the judge objects to a sentence that the parties have negotiated. Can a judge side with a defendant against a prosecutor and accept a guilty plea (and impose a sentence or dismiss a charge) over the prosecutor's objection? The prosecutor's ability to object to the sentence that the defendant proposes derives from a charge bargain or a binding sentence bargain. The prosecutor has no power to object to the sentence imposed when a defendant pleads to the court, and thus to the whole indictment.

Most courts give the prosecutor the power to block a guilty plea if the judge plans to dismiss charges or impose a sentence below what the plea agreement specifies. See State v. Vasquez-Aerreola, 940 S.W.2d 451 (Ark. 1997) (court may not dismiss charge of gang activity and accept guilty plea on other charges over prosecutor's objection); People v. Siebert, 537 N.W.2d 891 (Mich. 1995) (court may not accept a plea bargain containing a sentence agreement but impose a lower sentence than that agreed to; in such a case, prosecutor must be given opportunity to withdraw from agreement). Nonetheless, a few courts insist, at least for sentence bargains, that the prosecutor cannot prevent the judge from selecting the sentence to impose. See State v. Warren, 558 A.2d 1312 (N.J. 1989) (prohibits use of plea agreements in which prosecutor reserves right to withdraw from plea agreement if court-imposed sentence is more lenient than one agreed to by parties or recommended to court by prosecutor).

3. Prosecutorial Plea Negotiation Guidelines

Decisions whether to offer or accept plea bargains, like decisions about charging a suspect, are often governed by executive branch policies. These prosecutor plea bargaining policies vary in their level of detail; in many smaller offices, prosecutors follow consistent plea practices that may reflect unwritten (but articulated) guidelines, or they may simply reflect shared office culture and experience. Sometimes prosecutors develop formal plea review standards, describing substantively the types of bargains that are acceptable. Other times they create procedural review mechanisms, such as supervisory review or committee review of possible plea bargains. These guidelines or procedures might apply only for identified types of cases, such as those involving drugs or those likely to attract publicity.

Federal prosecutors, under the central control of the U.S. Attorney General, have developed a detailed set of written plea bargaining policies. In addition to the nationwide guidelines set out below, many of the U.S. Attorneys' offices in the 94 federal districts around the country have developed additional guidance to reflect the distinctive caseloads, resources, and other factors in each district.

The federal executive branch plea policies that follow were created against a background of major changes in sentencing law. At the time of the 1980 policy printed below, the federal system (and all but a handful of state systems) still had a highly discretionary sentencing system. Under discretionary sentencing systems the legislature defined most crimes to include a wide range of possible sentences, sometimes covering (for a single crime) everything from nonprison sanctions, such as fines or probation, to long prison terms. In theory, the law left huge discretion to the sentencing judge to set terms within the statutorily authorized range. The actual sentence to be served was often determined through "back-end" review by parole boards once the offender had spent a minimum required portion of the judicially imposed term in prison. In such systems, the charge might have only a modest binding effect. In practice, however, the processing of many cases by the same "working group" of attorneys and judges within the criminal court culture would lead to very firm expectations or "prices" for various crimes. See Milton Heumann, Plea Bargaining: The Experiences of Prosecutors, Judges, and Defense Attorneys (1978).

Remember as you read these policies that the Federal Rules of Criminal Procedure authorize three kinds of pleas: (1) agreements to enter a guilty plea to one or more charges in return for dismissal of other charges (a "charge" bargain under Rule 11(c)(1)(A)); (2) agreements to recommend a sentence in exchange for a guilty plea, subject to the judge's power to select the final sentence after accepting the guilty plea (a "sentence" bargain under Rule 11(c)(1)(B)); and (3) an agreement to a particular sentence in exchange for a guilty plea (a stipulated sentence plea under Rule 11(c)(1)(C)).

■ U.S. DEPARTMENT OF JUSTICE, PRINCIPLES OF FEDERAL PROSECUTION

(1980)

ENTERING INTO PLEA AGREEMENTS

1. The attorney for the government may, in an appropriate case, enter into an agreement with a defendant that, upon the defendant's plea of guilty or nolo contendere to a charged offense or to a lesser or related offense, he will move for dismissal of other charges, take a certain position with respect to the sentence to be imposed, or take other action.

2. In determining whether it would be appropriate to enter into a plea agreement, the attorney for the government should weigh all relevant considerations, including:

(a) the defendant's willingness to cooperate in the investigation or prosecution of others;

(b) the defendant's history with respect to criminal activity;

(c) the nature and seriousness of the offense or offenses charged;

(d) the defendant's remorse or contrition and his willingness to assume responsibility for his conduct;

(e) the desirability of prompt and certain disposition of the case;

(f) the likelihood of obtaining a conviction at trial;

(g) the probable effect on witnesses;

(h) the probable sentence or other consequences if the defendant is convicted;

(i) the public interest in having the case tried rather than disposed of by a guilty plea;

(j) the expense of trial and appeal; and

(k) the need to avoid delay in the disposition of other pending cases.

Comment: . . . The provision is not intended to suggest the desirability or lack of desirability of a plea agreement in any particular case. . . . A plea disposition in one case may facilitate the prompt disposition of other cases, including cases in which prosecution might otherwise be declined. This may occur simply because prosecutorial, judicial, or defense resources will become available for use in other cases, or because a plea by one of several defendants may have a "domino effect," leading to pleas by other defendants. In weighing the importance of these possible consequences, the attorney for the government should consider the state of the criminal docket and the speedy trial requirements in the district, the desirability of handling a larger volume of criminal cases, and the workloads of prosecutors, judges, and defense attorneys in the district.

3. If a prosecution is to be concluded pursuant to a plea agreement, the defendant should be required to plead to a charge or charges:

(a) that bears a reasonable relationship to the nature and extent of his criminal conduct;

(b) that has an adequate factual basis;

(c) that makes likely the imposition of an appropriate sentence under all the circumstances of the case; and

(d) that does not adversely affect the investigation or prosecution of others.

Comment: [The] considerations that should be taken into account in selecting the charge or charges to which a defendant should be required to plead guilty . . . are essentially the same as those governing the selection of charges to be included in the original indictment or information.

(a) Relationship to criminal conduct—The charge or charges to which a defendant pleads guilty should bear a reasonable relationship to the defendant's criminal conduct, both in nature and in scope. . . . In many cases, this will probably require that the defendant plead to the most serious offense charged. . . . The requirement that a defendant plead to a charge that bears a reasonable relationship to the nature and extent of his criminal conduct is not inflexible. There may be situations involving cooperating defendants in which [lesser charges may be appropriate].

(c) Basis for sentencing—[The] prosecutor should take care to avoid a "charge agreement" that would unduly restrict the court's sentencing authority. [If] restitution is appropriate under the circumstances of the case, a sufficient number of counts should be retained under the agreement to provide a basis for an adequate restitution order. . . .

Notes

1. *The shift away from discretionary sentencing.* Since the early 1980s the federal system and about half of the states have shifted to a more rule-bound sentencing process known as "guideline" or "structured" sentencing. The effect of such laws has been to take away some sentencing discretion from the judge. Sometimes the new laws also created more "determinate" systems that abolished or restricted the use of parole to adjust the sentence to be served. In such a system, the judge announces the sentence that corresponds closely to the sentence that the offender will actually serve.

2. *Federal sentencing guidelines.* In the Sentencing Reform Act of 1984, Congress designed a radically new sentencing system. In place of the indeterminate sentencing system that allowed judges to choose sentences from a broad range of available outcomes, Congress created a new agency — the United States Sentencing Commission — to draft detailed sentencing guidelines. The U.S. Sentencing Commission, following general statutory guidance, produced a lengthy set of guidelines in 1987. The guidelines direct federal judges in most cases to impose sentences from a much narrower range than before.

Under the sentencing guidelines, the trial judge calculates an "offense level" (ranging on a scale from 1 to 43) to measure the seriousness of the offense, and a "criminal history category" (ranging on a scale from 1 to 6) to account for the offender's prior criminal convictions. To combine these scores, the guidelines create a grid, placing the offense levels on a vertical axis, and the criminal history categories on the horizontal axis. Each combination of the two scores corresponds to one of the 258 boxes in the grid, and each box contains a presumptive sentencing range (expressed as months of imprisonment, such as 51-63 months) for that particular offense level and criminal history score.

The guidelines begin with a "base offense level" for each crime and instruct the judge to adjust that number up or down, in specified amounts, based on specific characteristics of the case. These factors focus mostly on offense information, such as the amount of drugs sold, whether the offender used a gun, or whether the offender played a leading or minor role in a multi-person offense. Because these particular factual findings can have such a clear impact on the sentence, the guidelines have spawned a new kind of bargaining — "fact bargaining" — in which the parties agree to the presence or absence of these relevant sentencing facts in a given case.

The offense levels are based not only on the elements of the offenses charged but also on other activities of the defendant (called "relevant conduct") that are related to the charged offense. Relevant conduct can include uncharged behavior, behavior underlying dismissed charges, and even behavior underlying prior acquittals. For instance, the government might charge a defendant with participating in one sale of a small amount of narcotics, although there is evidence that he participated in larger, related sales. The sentencing judge can consider both the sale that formed the basis for the charge and the uncharged sales in setting the sentence for the crime of conviction. Thus, charge bargains are less likely to have an impact on the ultimate sentence because the sentencing guidelines instruct the judge to consider the underlying conduct regardless of the charges.

Once the judge determines the designated sentencing range under the guidelines, she must also decide whether to "depart" up or down from the narrow range of sentences specified under the guidelines. A sentencing court departing from the guidelines can be overturned on appeal more easily if the ground for departure is not acceptable under the standard of 18 U.S.C. §3553(b) (part of the Sentencing Reform Act). Under that statute, departures may occur only in unusual cases, when "there exists an aggravating or mitigating circumstance of a kind, or to a degree, not adequately taken into consideration by the Sentencing Commission in formulating the guidelines."

3. *Guidance from Main Justice in 1987 and 1989.* The U.S. Department of Justice issued special guidance to prosecutors that appeared simultaneously with the guidelines. Excerpts from the 1987 "Redbook" are reprinted below. Is this internal guidance to prosecutors consistent with the statute and with the policy statements? What changes does it make to the 1980 Principles of Federal Prosecution?

After the first few months of practice under the new sentencing and plea bargaining rules, officials in the Department of Justice believed that federal prosecutors in the field were not adhering closely enough to the department's plea bargaining policies. Consequently, the leadership of the Department (housed in "Main Justice" in Washington, D.C.) revised the 1987 Redbook by issuing the 1989 "Thornburgh Bluesheet," named for Attorney General Richard Thornburgh. The revision of the policy was aimed at increasing compliance with the plea practices that the leadership of the department wanted.

The Thornburgh policy stresses transparency and honesty with the courts. Prosecutors must publicly disclose when they support a departure from the guideline sentence range: "[It] would be improper for a prosecutor to agree that a departure is in order, but to conceal the agreement in a charge bargain that is presented to a court as a fait accompli so that there is neither a record of nor judicial review of the departure." Federal prosecutors can only stipulate to facts that "accurately represent the defendant's conduct."

The Thornburgh policy also limits dismissal of charges. They are "not to be bargained away or dropped, unless the prosecutor has a good faith doubt as to the government's ability readily to prove a charge for legal or evidentiary reasons." There are two exceptions to this rule. First, a prosecutor can dismiss a readily provable charge as part of a plea bargain if the dismissal does not affect the sentence. Second, a federal prosecutor can dismiss a readily provable charge with specific approval from a supervisor. The supervisor might grant the exception if the office is "particularly overburdened" and the case "would be time-consuming to try."

4. *The 1992 Terwilliger Bluesheet.* After a few years of experience with the new system, officials in the Department of Justice remained unsatisfied with the plea bargaining practices of its attorneys in the field. In a 1992 revision of the plea bargaining policy, known as the "Terwilliger Bluesheet," the department moved away from an emphasis on describing the types of bargains that are acceptable. Instead, the revised policy strengthened the procedural review process for plea agreements:

> All negotiated plea agreements to felonies or misdemeanors negotiated from felonies shall be in writing and filed with the court. . . . There shall be within each office a formal system for approval of negotiated pleas. The approval authority shall be vested in at least a supervisory criminal Assistant United States Attorney . . . who will have the responsibility of assessing the appropriateness of the plea agreement under the policies of the Department of Justice pertaining to pleas. . . .

The 1992 policy allowed for categorical review of certain plea bargains. Fact situations that "arise with great frequency and are given identical treatment" could be handled through a "written instruction" that "describes with particularity the standard plea procedure to be followed, so long as that procedure is otherwise within Departmental guidelines." The policy listed as an example "a border district which routinely deals with a high volume of illegal alien cases daily." What do you suppose were the effects of these 1992 policy changes?

After the 1992 elections, the incoming Clinton administration appointed new leadership to the Department of Justice. The new Attorney General, Janet Reno, reviewed plea bargaining policies and issued a "Bluesheet" of her own. It is reprinted below. In most districts, this policy was carried out by newly appointed U.S. Attorneys, along with many career attorneys who had also served under the previous administration.

■ U.S. SENTENCING GUIDELINES §§6B1.2, 6B1.4 (POLICY STATEMENTS)

§6B1.2

(a) In the case of a plea agreement that includes the dismissal of any charges or an agreement not to pursue potential charges [under Rule 11(c)(1)(A)], the court may accept the agreement if the court determines, for reasons stated on the record, that the remaining charges adequately reflect the seriousness of the actual offense behavior and that accepting the agreement will not undermine the statutory purposes of sentencing or the sentencing guidelines. Provided, that a plea agreement that includes the dismissal of a charge or a plea agreement not to pursue a potential charge shall not preclude the conduct underlying such charge from being considered under the provisions of §1B1.3 (Relevant Conduct) in connection with the count(s) of which the defendant is convicted.

(b) In the case of a plea agreement that includes a nonbinding recommendation [under Rule 11(c)(1)(B)], the court may accept the recommendation if the court is satisfied either that: (1) the recommended sentence is within the applicable guideline range; or (2) the recommended sentence departs from the applicable guideline range for justifiable reasons.

(c) In the case of a plea agreement that includes a specific sentence [under Rule 11(c)(1)(C)], the court may accept the agreement if the court is satisfied either that: (1) the agreed sentence is within the applicable guideline range; or (2) the agreed sentence departs from the applicable guideline range for justifiable reasons.

§6B1.4

(a) A plea agreement may be accompanied by a written stipulation of facts relevant to sentencing. [Stipulations] shall: (1) set forth the relevant facts and circumstances of the actual offense conduct and offender characteristics; (2) not contain misleading facts; and (3) set forth with meaningful specificity the reasons why the sentencing range resulting from the proposed agreement is appropriate. . . .

(d) The court is not bound by the stipulation, but may with the aid of the presentence report, determine the facts relevant to sentencing.

■ PROSECUTORS' HANDBOOK ON SENTENCING GUIDELINES ("THE REDBOOK")
William Weld, Assistant Attorney General (1987)

[The] validity and use of the Commission's policy statements by prosecutors should depend upon whether the agreement reflects charge bargaining or sentence bargaining under [Rule 11(c)].

SENTENCE BARGAINING

A significant problem with the Commission's policy statements on plea bargains which include a specific sentence under [Rule 11(c)(1)(B) and (C)], §6B1.2(b) and (c), is that the standard they set forth for acceptance or rejection of a sentence that departs from the guidelines appears to be of doubtful validity under the Sentencing Reform Act (SRA). The standard for departure from the guidelines is set forth in the Act and requires a finding that an aggravating or mitigating circumstance exists that was not adequately taken into consideration by the Commission in formulating the guidelines. Yet the Commission's policy statements relating to sentence bargains authorize departure "for justifiable reasons." We do not believe it is possible to argue that the Commission has not adequately taken into consideration the value of a plea agreement as a mitigating factor so as to support a departure. . . . We recognize, nonetheless, that many judges might be tempted to take a realistic approach; a sentence outside the guidelines in the context of a plea agreement is unlikely to result in an appeal of the sentence. Therefore, if urged to accept a plea agreement that departs from the guidelines, they will follow the policy statements despite their questionable basis.

[Prosecutors] should not recommend or agree to a lower-than-guideline sentence merely on the basis of a plea agreement. They may, however, recommend or agree to a sentence at the low end of an applicable sentencing range [within the guidelines. Departure] from the guidelines may be warranted and may be included in the recommended or agreed-upon sentence if the [statutory standard] is met. That is, a mitigating circumstance must exist (other than the reaching of a plea agreement) that was not adequately taken into consideration by the Commission in formulating the guidelines and that should result in a sentence different from that described. Moreover, a departure from the guidelines may also be reflected in a plea agreement if the defendant provided substantial assistance in the investigation or prosecution of another person who has committed an offense. . . .

The basic reason for rejecting the Commission's policy statements on sentence bargains and treating sentences which are the subject of a sentence bargain in the same manner as sentences which result from conviction after trial is that any other result could seriously thwart the purpose of the SRA to reduce unwarranted disparity in sentencing [among defendants with similar records who have been found guilty of similar criminal conduct].

CHARGE BARGAINING

[It] is our view that moderately greater flexibility legally can and does attach to charge bargains than to sentence bargains. While, as indicated previously, the

Commission's quite liberal policy statements on sentence bargaining appear to be inconsistent with the controlling (and stricter) statutory departure standard, the statutory departure standard is not applicable in the charge-bargain context. . . .

Nevertheless, in order to fulfill the objectives of the Sentencing Reform Act prosecutors should conduct charge bargaining in a manner consistent with the direction in the applicable policy statement, §6B1.2(a), i.e., subject to the policy statement's instruction that the "remaining charges [should] adequately reflect the seriousness of the actual offense behavior" and that the agreement not undermine the statutory purposes of sentencing. In our view, this translates into a requirement that readily provable serious charges should not be bargained away. The sole legitimate ground for agreeing not to pursue a charge that is relevant under the guidelines to assure that the sentence will reflect the seriousness of the defendant's "offense behavior" is the existence of real doubt as to the ultimate provability of the charge. Concomitantly, however, the prosecutor is in the best position to assess the strength of the government's case and enjoys broad discretion in making judgments as to which charges are most likely to result in conviction on the basis of the available evidence. . . .

It is appropriate that the sentence for an offender who agrees to plead guilty to relatively few charges should be different from the sentence for an offender convicted of many charges since guilt has not been determined as to the dismissed charges. At the same time, however, sentence bargaining should not result in a vastly different sentence as compared to a sentence following trial. . . . The overriding principle governing the conduct of plea negotiations is that plea agreements should not be used to circumvent the guidelines. . . .

A subsidiary but nonetheless important issue concerns so-called "fact" bargaining or stipulations. [The policy statement §6B1.4] attaches certain conditions to such stipulations. The most important condition, with which the Department concurs, is that stipulations shall "not contain misleading facts." Otherwise, the basic purpose of the SRA to reduce unwarranted sentence disparity will be undermined. Thus, if the defendant can clearly be proved to have used a weapon or committed an assault in the course of the offense, the prosecutor may not stipulate, as part of a plea agreement designed to produce a lower sentence, that no weapon was used or assault committed. If, on the other hand, certain facts surrounding the offense are not clear, e.g., the extent of the loss or injury resulting from the defendant's fraud, the prosecutor is at liberty to stipulate that no loss or injury beyond that clearly provable existed. . . .

■ CHARGING AND PLEA DECISIONS ("RENO BLUESHEET")

Janet Reno, Attorney General (1993)

As first stated in the preface to the original 1980 edition of the Principles of Federal Prosecution, "they have been cast in general terms with a view to providing guidance rather than to mandating results. The intent is to assure regularity without regimentation, to prevent unwarranted disparity without sacrificing flexibility."

It should be emphasized that charging decisions and plea agreements should reflect adherence to the Sentencing Guidelines. However, a faithful and honest application of the Sentencing Guidelines is not incompatible with selecting charges or entering into plea agreements on the basis of an individualized assessment of the extent to which particular charges fit the specific circumstances of the case, are consistent with the purposes of the federal criminal code, and maximize the impact of federal resources on crime. Thus, for example, in determining "the most serious offense that is consistent with the nature of the defendant's conduct, that is likely to result in a sustainable conviction," it is appropriate that the attorney for the government consider, inter alia, such factors as the sentencing guideline range yielded by the charge, whether the penalty yielded by such sentencing range (or potential mandatory minimum charge, if applicable) is proportional to the seriousness of the defendant's conduct, and whether the charge achieves such purposes of the criminal law as punishment, protection of the public, specific and general deterrence, and rehabilitation. . . .

To ensure consistency and accountability, charging and plea agreement decisions must be made at an appropriate level of responsibility and documented with an appropriate record of the factors applied.

Notes

1. *Policies and political accountability.* In response to the Reno Bluesheet, Senator Orrin Hatch (R-Utah), the ranking minority member on the Judiciary Committee, sent Attorney General Janet Reno a letter strongly opposing her directive:

> The Department's new policy now permits prosecutors to make independent decisions about whether a prescribed guideline sentence or mandatory minimum charge is not "proportional to the seriousness of the defendant's conduct." In other words, this new policy increases the potential for the unwarranted softening of sentences for violent offenders. . . .
>
> I do not support the Department's announcement to drug traffickers and violent criminals that certain illegal conduct may not be charged because a Department employee may find the prescribed punishment too severe. If the Administration believes that existing sentences for drug cases and violent criminals are too severe, then it should seek to change the law or the relevant sentencing guidelines — not ignore them.

Reno responded:

> [It] remains the directive of the Department of Justice that prosecutors charge the most serious offense that is consistent with the nature of the defendant's conduct, that is likely to result in a sustainable conviction; that prosecutors adhere to the Sentencing Guidelines; and that charging and plea agreements be made at an appropriate level of responsibility with appropriate documentation. In short, contrary to what you suggest, individual prosecutors are not free to follow their own lights or to ignore legislative directives.

2. *The 2003 Ashcroft memos.* In 2003 Congress enacted the USA PROTECT Act, Public Law 108-21, 117 Stat. 650. Although the statute dealt primarily with crimes involving child abuse, it also changed several features of federal sentencing law more generally, making downward departures from the sentencing prescribed by the federal guidelines more difficult for judges to invoke. In response to the

PROTECT Act, Attorney General John Ashcroft issued a policy in 2003 dealing with selection of charges and plea agreements. The policy reaffirmed the traditional rule that federal prosecutors can only dismiss charges if they are not "readily provable." The innovation of this policy was to specify the basis for any exceptions that would allow dismissal of a provable charge. These exceptions included: (1) the sentence would be unaffected by the dismissal; (2) the dismissal happens under a Department-approved early dismissal or "fast-track" program, designed to handle the high volume of cases — particularly immigration cases — in some districts; (3) post-indictment circumstances cause a prosecutor to determine in good faith that the most serious offense is not readily provable, because of a change in the evidence; and (4) a supervisor determines that the office is particularly overburdened, the duration of the trial would be exceptionally long, and proceeding to trial would significantly reduce the total number of cases disposed of by the office. The policy stressed that case-by-case exceptions should be rare events, and that prosecutors are "strongly encouraged" to retain any charges that support automatic "statutory enhancements" to sentences. The memo also spotlighted the role of supervisor review and documentation of non-guideline sentences.

3. *The 2010 Holder memo.* With the arrival of the Obama administration in 2008, another change in charging and plea bargaining policy issued from Main Justice. This policy was issued in the context of a series of Supreme Court opinions, such as United States v. Booker, 543 U.S. 220 (2005), and Kimbrough v. United States, 552 U.S. 85 (2007), which loosened the binding effect of the federal sentencing guidelines on the decisions of federal sentencing judges, converting them into "advisory" guidelines. The new policy declared that a federal prosecutor should ordinarily charge the "most serious offense that is consistent with the nature of the defendant's conduct, and that is likely to result in a sustainable conviction." This determination, however, "must always be made in the context of "an individualized assessment of the extent to which particular charges fit the specific circumstances of the case, are consistent with the purpose of the Federal criminal code, and maximize the impact of Federal resources on crime." The Holder Memo, unlike the Reno Bluesheet, stressed supervisory control and documentation. Further evaluation and recent amendments of these Department policies appear on the web extension for this chapter at *http://www.crimpro.com/extension/ch16.*

4. *Written and unwritten guidance.* A striking feature of the plea bargaining policies in the federal system is the fact that they are written. Many other prosecutors' offices in state systems have pursued goals similar to those of the Department of Justice in creating its plea policies. They hope to maintain adequate control over prosecutors in the field and to send appropriate public signals about sentencing and plea bargaining. Nonetheless, within the state systems, such policies are rarely written, even when they are explicit. Why might a supervising prosecutor choose to keep such a critical office policy unwritten?

5. *Uniformity within a jurisdiction.* The federal plea bargaining policies reprinted above apply to U.S. Attorneys' offices throughout the country. While these offices still have a great deal of independence, and vary from one another in their plea bargaining practices, they are still subject to more centralized control than the various prosecutors' offices located throughout a given state. Since prosecutors often create plea bargaining policies for their own offices, shouldn't there be great variety in plea bargaining practices among the different prosecutors within a state? Or are there institutions or incentives that produce similar prosecutorial plea policies

throughout a state or even across different states? The following case addresses this topic.

■ STATE v. CHRISTOPHER BRIMAGE

706 A.2d 1096 (N.J. 1998)

GARIBALDI, J.

We are again presented with issues relating to Section 12 of the Comprehensive Drug Reform Act of 1987, N.J.S.A. 2C:35-1 to 36A-1 ("CDRA"). Under N.J.S.A. 2C:35-12 ("Section 12"), a prosecutor may, through a negotiated plea agreement or post-conviction agreement with a defendant, waive the mandatory minimum sentence specified for any offense under the CDRA. To satisfy the constitutional requirements of the separation of powers doctrine, N.J. Const. art. III, ¶1, this Court in State v. Vasquez, 609 A.2d 29 (N.J. 1992), held that prosecutorial discretion under Section 12 must be subject to judicial review for arbitrary and capricious action. To further that review, the Court held that prosecutors must adhere to written guidelines governing plea offers and state on the record their reasons for waiving or not waiving the parole disqualifier in any given case.

In response to that holding, the Attorney General promulgated plea agreement guidelines. . . . Although the Guidelines prescribe statewide minimum plea offers, they also direct each county prosecutor's office to adopt its own written plea agreement policy. . . . We must determine whether the Attorney General's Plea-Bargaining Guidelines are adequate to satisfy the separation of powers doctrine, as enunciated in *Vasquez*, and to meet the statutory goals of uniformity in sentencing.

I.

On May 12, 1995, the Franklin Township Police, armed with a search warrant, conducted a search of the Brimage residence. According to defendant's statements at the plea hearing, during the search defendant turned over to the police eighteen bags of cocaine totaling about six grams. . . . Defendant's residence was within 1000 feet of Franklin Township High School. In September 1995, defendant was indicted under the CDRA for possession of a controlled dangerous substance with intent to distribute . . . ; possession of a controlled dangerous substance with intent to distribute within 1000 feet of school property, contrary to N.J.S.A. 2C:35-7; and possession of a controlled dangerous substance, . . . all third degree offenses. . . .

The Somerset County Prosecutor's Office offered, in exchange for defendant's guilty plea, to recommend the presumptive sentence for a third degree crime — four years incarceration — plus the mandatory three-year period of parole ineligibility specified in N.J.S.A. 2C:35-7 for the school zone offense. The prosecutor proffered the following reasons for not waiving the parole ineligibility term of N.J.S.A. 2C:35-7: the proofs available to sustain a conviction of defendant were very strong, including defendant's taped confession that he intended to sell cocaine for profit; defendant did not offer to cooperate in any other drug-related investigations; and the Somerset County Prosecutor's Office had sufficient resources to litigate this matter, unlike various other counties that were plagued with a lack of resources or with case management problems. . . .

Defendant then accepted the prosecutor's original plea agreement offer and pled guilty to all counts in the indictment, although he reserved the right to challenge the validity of the Guidelines and the applicability of the mandatory three-year parole disqualifier to his case. [At the hearing on his motion for waiver of the mandatory minimum sentence, Brimage] argued that the standard plea offer required by the Attorney General's Guidelines for a school zone offense was . . . probation conditioned on 364 days in county jail . . . and that the prosecutor acted arbitrarily and capriciously by not making that offer to defendant. . . . Finding that nonwaiver of the mandatory parole disqualifier was standard policy in Somerset County for school zone cases and that the Guidelines' lesser plea offer was only applicable when the prosecutor in his discretion decided to waive that disqualifier, the court denied defendant's motion. [The] court sentenced defendant to four years imprisonment with three years of parole ineligibility, in accordance with the prosecutor's recommendation. . . .

II.

. . . N.J.S.A. 2C:35-7 of the CDRA ("Section 7") requires a mandatory minimum custodial sentence between one-third and one-half of the sentence imposed, but no less than three years for those convicted of dispensing or possessing with the intent to distribute drugs within a school zone. [The] Legislature's intention, as stated in its Declaration of Policy and Legislative Findings for the CDRA, [was] to "provide for the strict punishment, deterrence and incapacitation of the most culpable and dangerous drug offenders." N.J.S.A. 2C:35-1.1(c). To foster that policy, the Legislature included in the CDRA mandatory periods of parole ineligibility for various crimes.

Despite the nondiscretionary nature of N.J.S.A. 2C:35-7, that section, like other mandatory parole bar provisions in the CDRA, contemplates exceptions to its rule as provided by N.J.S.A. 2C:35-12 ("Section 12"). Section 12 allows a prosecutor to waive the period of parole ineligibility imposed under Section 7 as part of a plea or post-conviction agreement with a defendant. . . .

The primary purpose of the Section 12 waiver provision is to provide an incentive for defendants, especially lower and middle level drug offenders, to cooperate with law enforcement agencies in the war against drugs. Another goal of N.J.S.A. 2C:35-12, as enunciated in the Department of Law and Public Safety's report on the CDRA, is to encourage plea bargaining so as not to plague the courts with too many defendants who, without any incentive to plead guilty, demand jury trials and thus overburden and backlog the system. . . .

To achieve the Legislature's specific goal of encouraging cooperation and turning State's evidence and to prevent sentencing courts from undermining the effectiveness of prosecutors' strategies, N.J.S.A. 2C:35-12 requires the sentencing court to enforce all agreements reached by the prosecutor and a defendant under that section and prohibits the court from imposing a lesser term of imprisonment than that specified in the agreement. That shift in sentencing power from the judiciary to the prosecutor is uncommon. . . .

As a result of the atypical grant of sentencing power to the prosecutor in N.J.S.A. 2C:35-12, that statute has been the subject of various constitutional challenges on separation of powers grounds. We first considered the interaction of Section 7 and Section 12 in [State v. Vasquez]. In *Vasquez*, . . . we upheld the transfer of sentencing authority under Section 12, but stated that judicial oversight was "mandated to protect against arbitrary and capricious prosecutorial decisions." To enable judicial review, we required prosecutors to state on the record their reasons for waiving or not waiving the parole disqualifier in any given case and to promulgate written guidelines governing their exercise of discretion. [Only] those defendants who showed "clearly and convincingly that the exercise of discretion was arbitrary and capricious would be entitled to relief." . . .

The Guidelines

In response to this Court's ruling in *Vasquez,* on September 15, 1992 the Attorney General promulgated plea agreement guidelines for charges brought under the Comprehensive Drug Reform Act. . . . Recognizing the various goals of the Legislature in enacting the CDRA as well as the intentions of the Court in *Vasquez,* the Introduction to the 1992 Guidelines states: "In order to satisfy the principal goal of the Legislature to ensure a uniform, consistent and predictable sentence for a given offense, these decisions require that the prosecutorial decision-making process must be guided by uniform standards that channel the exercise of discretion and reduce the danger of uneven application." . . .

The Guidelines continue by asserting that the "specified mandatory term of imprisonment and minimum term of parole ineligibility" should be treated as norms and that prosecutors "should exercise caution and reluctance in deciding whether to waive the minimum sentence or parole ineligibility." §II.1. More specifically, in Section II.3 of those Guidelines, the Attorney General requires that all plea agreements for a CDRA offense impose on defendants a mandatory minimum term of incarceration, except where the agreement is or was necessary to obtain cooperation of "substantial value" to the State. That term must be a state prison term, except in the case of a school zone offense under N.J.S.A. 2C:35-7. The 1992 version of the Guidelines provides that the "minimum term of imprisonment for a school zone offense shall include the imposition of 364 days incarceration in a county jail as a condition of probation." . . . In Section II.9, the Guidelines specify various requirements for cooperation agreements. Finally, in Section II.5, the Guidelines outline criteria for deciding whether to approve or disapprove a plea agreement that incorporates an upward or downward departure from any plea agreement policy.

Despite those specific provisions in the Guidelines, Section II.4 directs each county prosecutor's office to adopt and implement its own written policy governing plea and post-conviction agreements, using the Guidelines as a model, and suggests that the counties may also promulgate their own "standardized plea offers for typical cases and offenders." The Guidelines state that the counties, in formulating those plea offers, may consider certain factors such as the nature and extent of the drug distribution and use problem, the number and type of drug arrests in the jurisdiction, and the backlog of drug and non-drug cases in the courts. They should also consider the seriousness of the offense, the role of the actor in the crime, the amount of time that has passed since the offense was committed, whether the defendant has previously been convicted of an offense, and the amount of resources already expended on the particular case. Finally, Section II.4 specifically states that "nothing contained in these guidelines shall preclude a prosecutor from adopting more stringent policies or standardized plea offers consistent with the needs, resources and enforcement priorities of each county." . . .

Although the Introduction to the Guidelines recognizes the need to "guard against sentencing disparity," the Guidelines actually generated such disparity. The inter-county disparity created by the Guidelines is evidenced in the actual policies that have been adopted throughout the jurisdictions. . . . Although the standard plea offer in Gloucester and Hudson Counties [for a person in Brimage's situation] would have been probation with 364 days in jail, the pre-indictment offer in Mercer and Salem Counties was one year without parole. Meanwhile, the plea in Camden and Cumberland Counties would have been three years flat and three to five years flat, respectively. . . .

The Supplemental Directive

Subsequent to Brimage's plea, the Attorney General issued additional guidelines in its 1997 Supplemental Directive; however, the Supplemental Directive fails to limit the discretion authorized by Section II.4 and thus maintains the resulting inter-county disparity. The Supplemental Directive was developed in response to Governor Christine Todd Whitman's Drug Enforcement, Education and Awareness Program, which required the Attorney General to issue new, revised guidelines concerning prosecutorial charging, case disposition, and plea bargaining policies to ensure that the CDRA is aggressively and uniformly enforced in court. The Supplemental Directive mandates, among other requirements, that each county reduce its plea policies to writing and review the policies at least once a year; that downward departures shall not be permitted except as provided in the Attorney General's Guidelines; that both downward and upward departures and all cooperation agreements shall be memorialized in writing; . . . and that offenders may be sentenced to treatment in lieu of imprisonment only if they meet a long list of explicit conditions. [While] the Directive states that the Guidelines are "intended and shall hereinafter be interpreted to establish drug prosecution policies that must be followed by every county prosecutor's office," the Directive nevertheless permits each county to adopt its own standards pursuant to Section II.4. . . .

III.

By permitting each county to adopt its own standard plea offers and policies, neither the former nor the current Guidelines serve as the universal, equitable prototype that the *Vasquez* line of cases had in mind. Although the guidelines adopted within each county may avoid arbitrariness with respect to decision-making among individual prosecutors, and while we concede that some disparity in sentencing is inevitable in the administration of criminal justice, the formalization of disparity from county to county is clearly impermissible. The inter-county disparity authorized by the Attorney General's Guidelines, both before and after their amendment, violates the goals of uniformity in sentencing and, thus, not only fails on statutory grounds, but also threatens the balance between prosecutorial and judicial discretion that is required under *Vasquez*. The Guidelines fail to appropriately channel prosecutorial discretion, thus leading to arbitrary and unreviewable differences between different localities. . . .

Accordingly, to meet the requirements of the *Vasquez* line of cases, the plea agreement guidelines for N.J.S.A. 2C:35-12 must be consistent throughout the State. [Prosecutors] must be guided by specific, universal standards in their waiver of mandatory minimum sentences under the CDRA.

Although the record does not indicate that the availability of county resources has been a significant factor in causing sentencing disparity between the counties, we recognize . . . the need for some flexibility among the different counties and some accommodation of local concerns and differences. The Declaration of Policy for the CDRA states that one of the goals of the Act is to "ensure the most efficient and effective dedication of limited investigative, prosecutorial, judicial and correctional resources," N.J.S.A. 2C:35-1.1. [Using] the waiver power to advance this legislative goal would not be an abuse of power. Consistent with that authority, we believe that differences in available county resources as well as varying backlog and caseload situations are legitimate factors that prosecutors may consider in deciding whether or not to waive a mandatory minimum sentence under N.J.S.A. 2C:35-12. However, before a prosecutor may take any such factors into account, those factors must be explicitly set forth in . . . the Attorney General's Guidelines, just as the requirements for cooperation agreements are precisely and distinctly enumerated. Although . . . flexibility among the prosecutors of different counties may sometimes be necessary, that does not justify the adoption of different guidelines in every county in contravention of the goals of uniformity and the *Vasquez* line of cases. Any flexibility on the basis of resources or local differences must be provided for and explicitly detailed within uniform, statewide guidelines. . . .

We therefore order the Attorney General to review and promulgate, within ninety days, new plea offer guidelines, which all counties must follow. . . . The new guidelines should specify permissible ranges of plea offers for particular crimes and should be more explicit regarding permissible bases for upward and downward departures. The Attorney General may, if he chooses, provide for differences in treatment among various offenders based on specific factors of flexibility among the counties, such as resources or backlog, in certain circumstances. As in all plea offers, the individual characteristics of the crime and of the defendant, such as whether the defendant is a first or second time offender, must be considered. Finally, to permit effective judicial review, prosecutors must state on the record their reasons for choosing to waive or not to waive the mandatory minimum period of parole ineligibility specified in the statute. Additionally, for proper judicial review, if a prosecutor departs from the guidelines, the reasons for such departure must be clearly stated on the record. . . .

Problem 16-5. Statewide Bargaining Guidelines

Soon after the New Jersey Supreme Court issued its decision in *Brimage*, the state attorney general created a 64-page set of "*Brimage* Guidelines." The drafters patterned their prosecutor guidelines after judicial sentencing guidelines, including a grid laying out the offense seriousness on a vertical axis and the defendant's criminal history on a horizontal axis. Each box of the grid showed three different plea agreements a prosecutor might offer, with more favorable outcomes going to those defendants accepting offers earlier before the start of trial.

The immediate effect of the guidelines was probably an increase in the seriousness of drug charges that urban defendants faced. The more severe charging practices of the less urban counties became more standard across the state, and the guidelines left urban prosecutors less room to negotiate in the initial filing of charges or in the disposition of cases.

A few years later, a new state attorney general considered potential changes in the *Brimage* Guidelines. After consultations with county prosecutors, defense attorneys, and judges, the attorney general became concerned about the fairness of sentences in cases involving drug sales in school zones. The urban-suburban divide (and thus a racial divide) was stark for these crimes. In most urban areas, virtually all drug sales happened within 1,000 feet of a school; in less densely populated parts of the state, many more drug sales happened outside the 1,000-foot boundary.

The new attorney general is now considering revised guidelines that depend less on the crime of conviction. The plea agreements that prosecutors would be authorized to offer account for more specific offense characteristics (such as the amount of drugs and the presence of a weapon) and offender characteristics (such as gang membership or prior criminal record). The revisions also increase the minimum "authorized plea offers" available in cases involving defendants who carry or use weapons, while making more lenient offers possible for other drug defendants with prior records, or those who sold drugs near a school but presented no particular threat of violence. Prosecutors could also "depart" from the presumptive charge or disposition that is preferred under the guidelines if the evidence in the case is weak or if the defendant offers cooperation in other cases.

Suppose you are advising the attorney general. Who is likely to support or oppose this collection of policy changes? What arguments will they present? See *http://www.state.nj.us/lps/dcj/pdfs/agdir.pdf.*

Problem 16-6. Sharkfest

In one county in Arizona, most of the plea bargaining takes place during what defense attorneys call "Sharkfest." On a designated day each week, the deputy county attorneys, deputy public defenders, and a few private defense attorneys gather in one large room. The location of Sharkfest alternates between the county attorney's office and the public defender's office.

Each defense attorney pulls out an open case file, finds the deputy county attorney assigned to the case, argues over the facts and the legal issues, and inquires about possible plea agreements. As the prosecutor and defense attorney make their arguments to one another, their colleagues might be listening — although they might also be engaged in their own negotiations at that moment — and chime in with their own thoughts. Colleagues might comment on the facts, note a similar case the attorney had in the past and the resolution to that case, or mention applicable case law. The defense attorneys generally rely on the input of their colleagues more often than the prosecutors do. The prosecutors generally operate within office policies about acceptable plea agreements, and must resolve the case within parameters set forth by the "charging department," unless new information about the case comes to light during the negotiation.

After the two attorneys reach a potential plea agreement in a case, but before the defense attorney can take that plea bargain to her client, the prosecutor takes the proposed plea bargain to the chief deputy county attorney for approval. Because there is only one chief deputy county attorney in the office, much of the attorney time spent at Sharkfest involves waiting for him to make his way around the room.

What motivates prosecutors and public defenders to attend Sharkfest every week? Why don't more private defense counsel attend? How might the results of Sharkfest resemble the results one might obtain from a carefully crafted set of written office guidelines for plea bargaining?

Notes

1. *Uniformity in guidelines.* The New Jersey decision in *Brimage* is unusual; courts do not often order prosecutors to create statewide policies on questions of plea bargaining or requests for sentencing enhancements. Prosecutors themselves do not often create statewide guidelines for such matters, either. Instead, it is more common to find policies about plea bargaining and related matters set at the local office level. See Pamela Utz, Settling the Facts (1978) (comparing practices in California jurisdictions).

How are prosecutors likely to respond to a judicial requirement that they create statewide guidelines? Is there such a thing as too much uniformity from office to office? Within a single office? See State v. Pettitt, 609 P.2d 1364 (Wash. 1980) (striking down prosecutor's office policy mandating the filing of habitual criminal complaints against any defendant who had three or more prior felonies as abuse of discretion where policy resulted in mandatory life sentence for a defendant with three nonviolent property crimes).

2. *Priority crimes.* Prosecutorial office policies on plea bargaining often restrict the power of the individual prosecutor to negotiate terms for a select group of high-priority crimes. While the line prosecutors remain free to reach plea agreements in less serious cases (which are by far the most numerous), the guidelines prohibit dismissal of charges or sentencing concessions in cases involving violent crimes such as murder, rape, or armed robbery. Alternatively, in such cases the guidelines may require special justifications for plea agreements or may limit the acceptable bargaining outcomes. How do supervising prosecutors choose the priority crimes that will be subject to these special bargaining limitations? Do they take their cues from crime legislation and limit bargaining whenever the legislature has emphasized the importance of a crime by enhancing its penalty? See Milton Heumann & Colin Loftin, Mandatory Sentencing and the Abolition of Plea Bargaining: The Michigan Felony Firearm Statute, 13 Law & Soc'y Rev. 393 (1979) (evaluating mandatory-minimum-sentence statute for firearms cases, and contemporaneous county prosecutor's no-plea-bargaining policy for crimes charged under the statute).

3. *Internal review.* One common prosecutorial policy on plea bargaining is procedural rather than substantive. Instead of banning plea bargains for some crimes or limiting the outcomes that a prosecutor can accept in certain cases, these policies simply require the line prosecutor to obtain approval from a supervisor (or some committee of supervisors) before entering a plea agreement. See Richard Kuh, Plea Bargaining: Guidelines for the Manhattan District Attorney's Office, 11 Crim. L. Bull. 48 (1975) (supervisor review for proposed agreements reducing charges to extent greater than ordinarily allowed under office policy). The web extension for this chapter, at *http://www.crimpro.com/extension/ch16*, offers examples of such office policies regarding plea negotiations.

4. Victim Consultation

Many prosecutors feel obliged to inform crime victims about their efforts to negotiate a guilty plea. But only recently have legal provisions and institutions reinforced this sense of obligation. Over the past generation, a majority of states have enacted statutes and constitutional provisions requiring prosecutors to inform or consult the victims of alleged crimes about any plea agreements in their case. These laws differ in the type of information the victim and the prosecutor must exchange and in the timing of the exchange. But they share the assumption that the involvement of a crime victim will change the outcomes in at least some plea negotiations. Will the timing of the victim's involvement make a difference in many plea negotiations?

■ **MAINE REVISED STATUTES TIT. 15, §812; TIT. 17-A, §§1172, 1173**

Title 15, §812

1. The Legislature finds that there is citizen dissatisfaction with plea bargaining which has resulted in some criticism of the criminal justice process. The Legislature further finds that part of the dissatisfaction is caused because victims of crimes and law enforcement officers who respond to those crimes have no subsequent contact with the cases as they proceed through the courts for judicial disposition. Victims and law enforcement officers are many times not informed by prosecutors of plea agreements which are to be submitted to the court for approval or rejection. . . . It is the intent of this section to alleviate these expressions of citizen dissatisfaction and to promote greater understanding by prosecutors of citizens' valid concerns. This is most likely to be accomplished by citizens and law enforcement officers being informed of the results of plea negotiations before they are submitted to the courts. This notification will in no way affect the authority of the judge to accept, reject or modify the terms of the plea agreement.

2. Whenever practicable, before submitting a negotiated plea to the court, the attorney for the State shall make a good faith effort to inform the relevant law enforcement officers of the details of the plea agreement reached in any prosecution where the defendant was originally charged with murder, a Class A, B or C crime or [an assault crime, sex offense, or kidnapping,] and, with respect to victims, shall comply with Title 17-A, section 1172, subsection 1, paragraphs A and B relative to informing victims of the details of and their right to comment on a plea agreement.

Title 17-A, §1172

1. When practicable, the attorney for the State shall make a good faith effort to inform each victim of a crime of the following: A) the details of a plea agreement . . . before it is submitted to the court; B) the right to comment on a plea agreement . . . pursuant to section 1173; B-1) the proposed dismissal or filing of an indictment, information or complaint . . . before that action is taken; C) the time and place of the trial; D) the time and place of sentencing; and E) the right to participate at sentencing. . . .

Title 17-A, §1173

When a plea agreement is submitted to the court . . . , the attorney for the State shall disclose to the court any and all attempts made to notify each victim of the plea agreement and any objection to the plea agreement by a victim. A victim who is present in court at the submission of the plea may address the court at that time.

■ STATE v. PATRICK WILLIAM CASEY
44 P.3d 756 (Utah 2002)

DURRANT, J.

¶1 The central issue presented in this appeal is whether the district court deprived M.R., a victim of sexual abuse, of his constitutional and statutory right to be heard at defendant's change of plea hearing. . . .

¶3 On November 3, 1999, the Tooele County Attorney's Office charged defendant with aggravated sexual abuse of a child, a first degree felony. . . .

¶4 A few weeks [after the preliminary hearing], the prosecutor handling defendant's case sent M.R.'s mother a letter explaining that defendant had requested a plea bargain. After receiving this letter, M.R.'s mother, according to her affidavit, met with the prosecutor and obtained an assurance that the first degree felony charge would not be reduced due to the strong evidence of guilt compiled against defendant.

¶5 Nevertheless, the prosecutor subsequently offered to reduce the first degree felony charge to lewdness involving a child, a class A misdemeanor, in return for a guilty plea. M.R.'s mother, upon learning [this], contacted the prosecutor and expressed a desire to tell the district court how her family, including M.R., felt about the proposed plea. The prosecutor advised her to attend the change of plea hearing scheduled for October 24, 2000.

¶6 M.R. and his mother appeared at this change of plea hearing as directed. [M.R.'s mother told the prosecutor that she wished to make a statement to the court, but the prosecutor failed to tell the court about this, and she also did not speak up.]

¶7 . . . Noting the "dramatic" reduction in the charge, the court refused to be limited to the four-month sentence recommended in the stipulated plea agreement. The State and defendant responded to the court's concern by agreeing to delete the stipulated sentence provision. The court then accepted defendant's guilty plea to the class A misdemeanor charge and set the matter for sentencing.

¶8 Subsequently, M.R.'s mother, acting on behalf of M.R., obtained legal assistance and filed two motions with the district court: a motion for a misplea and a motion to reject the plea bargain. In response, the prosecutor and defendant filed separate motions to strike M.R.'s pleadings, claiming that M.R. lacked standing to set aside the plea because he was not a party to the criminal proceeding.

¶9 Without ruling on whether M.R. had standing to challenge defendant's guilty plea, the district court held defendant's sentencing hearing on November 27, 2000. At the start of this hearing, M.R.'s counsel moved the court to set aside the accepted plea. . . .

¶10 M.R. and his mother testified that the court should have rejected the plea bargain. Specifically, M.R. declared, "I don't think it's right that defendant gets that less of a plea agreement because of what he's done. He's done it to me . . . and . . . he's hurt my whole family." M.R.'s mother testified that "the court should reject the plea bargain because a misdemeanor sentence did not truly reflect the seriousness of the offenses committed by defendant the same way that a felony conviction would." . . .

¶11 . . . M.R.'s counsel argued that the Victims' Rights Amendment of the Utah Constitution placed M.R. on equal footing with defendant and envisioned that M.R. could employ an attorney in exercising his legal rights. M.R.'s counsel then argued that (1) M.R. had the right to be heard before the court's acceptance of defendant's plea, (2) M.R.'s right to be heard had been violated, and (3) the court should grant a misplea and hear from M.R. before accepting any subsequent plea between the State and defendant. . . .

¶12 [The] court decided to "informally" reopen the plea hearing in order to accept the testimony that it had just heard from M.R. and his mother. Having accepted this testimony, the court "reaffirmed" defendant's plea at the class A level. The court then denied both of M.R.'s pending motions, sentenced defendant to eight months in jail on the class A misdemeanor charge, and fined him. . . .

¶14 On appeal, M.R., by and through his legal guardian, contends that (1) he had the right to seek appellate review of the district court's adverse rulings on his two motions, (2) he had the right to be heard through counsel with respect to legal issues related to the constitutional and statutory rights afforded him as a victim, (3) he had a constitutional and statutory right to be heard regarding the appropriateness of the plea bargain, (4) he properly invoked his right to be heard at defendant's change of plea hearing by submitting a request to the prosecutor, and (5) the court, through the negligence of the prosecutor, denied him his right to be heard by accepting the plea bargain without hearing from him. . . .

¶18 In 1987, the Utah Legislature enacted the Victims' Rights Act. See Utah Code Ann. §§77-37-1 to -5. This statute included, among other things, a bill of rights for victims, and declared that these rights must be "protected in a manner no less vigorous than protections afforded criminal defendants." §77-37-1. The Utah Legislature then passed the Victims' Rights Amendment, which was ratified by Utah citizens. . . . Utah Const. art. I, §28. This constitutional amendment bestowed specific rights upon crime victims and gave the Utah Legislature the power to "enforce and define [its terms] by statute." Acting pursuant to this authority, the Utah Legislature subsequently enacted the Rights of Crime Victims Act. Utah Code Ann. §§77-38-1 to -14. This act elaborated upon the rights afforded crime victims under the Victims' Rights Amendment and defined several terms included in the amendment. . . .

¶21 Applying the principles outlined above, we first address whether M.R. had the right to appeal the district court's rulings regarding his right to be heard. [We] conclude that M.R. had the right to seek appellate review pursuant to the plain meaning of [the Rights of Crime Victims Act].

¶23 We next address whether M.R. had the right to be heard at defendant's change of plea hearing. . . . In pertinent part, the Victims' Rights Amendment states as follows: "To preserve and protect victims' rights to justice and due process, victims of crimes have [the right, upon request, to be] heard at important criminal justice hearings related to the victim, either in person or through a lawful representative, once a criminal information or indictment charging a crime has been publicly filed in court." Utah Const. art. I, §28(1)(b). Using comparable language, section 77-38-4 of the Rights of Crime Victims Act similarly declares that the victim of a crime "shall have . . . the right to be heard at . . . important criminal . . . justice hearings." . . .

¶25 [The] question that arises is what constitutes an "important criminal justice hearing" under the Victims' Rights Amendment and the Utah Code. Section 77-38-2 of the Rights of Crime Victims Act answers this question with respect to both the Utah Constitution and the Utah Code; it defines "important criminal justice hearings" involving the disposition of charges in this way: "For the purposes of this chapter and the Utah Constitution, important criminal justice hearings [means] any court proceeding involving the disposition of charges against a defendant [except for] unanticipated proceedings to take an admission or a plea of guilty as charged to all charges previously filed or any plea taken at an initial appearance." . . .

¶26 Here, the change of plea hearing conducted by the district court fell within the definition of an important criminal justice hearing because it disposed of a first degree felony charge filed against defendant in return for a guilty plea on a class A misdemeanor. Further, neither exception applied because the hearing was not an initial appearance and the defendant did not accept responsibility for the first degree felony charge previously filed. . . .

¶27 While it is clear that the Utah Constitution and the Utah Code afforded M.R. the right to be heard upon request at defendant's change of plea hearing, neither the constitution nor the code mandates how M.R.'s request must be submitted. Relying on the Victims' Rights Act and the Rights of Crime Victims Act, M.R. argues that a request to be heard at a plea hearing suffices if it is submitted either to the district court or to the prosecutor. The State contends that the two statutes require a crime victim to petition the court directly. . . .

¶28 We begin our analysis with the Victims' Rights Amendment. This constitutional provision merely notes that the right to be heard is activated "upon request." Utah Const. art. I, §28(b). . . . The Victims' Rights Act states that victims have the "right to be informed and assisted as to their role in the criminal justice process," and all criminal justice agencies have "the duty to provide this information and assistance." Utah Code Ann. §77-37-3(1)(b). Additionally, the Victims' Rights Act declares that victims have a "right to clear explanations regarding relevant legal proceedings," and all "criminal justice agencies have the duty to provide these explanations." Id. §77-37-3(1)(c). Because prosecutors are a component of the criminal justice system and the Victims' Rights Act applies to "all criminal justice agencies," the aforementioned duties necessarily fall upon prosecutors. . . .

¶30 We further conclude that a prosecutor's obligation to provide "assistance" to the victim should mean, at a minimum, that a victim may submit a request to be heard at a plea hearing to a prosecutor and expect that the request will be forwarded to the court. Likewise, a prosecutor's obligation to provide a "clear explanation" of events occurring at a plea hearing should mean that a victim can rely on a prosecutor's statement indicating he or she will convey a request to be heard to the district court. . . .

¶32 In addition to having a duty to convey requests to be heard under the Victims' Rights Act and the Rights of Crime Victims Act, prosecutors also have a duty to convey requests to be heard as officers of the court. Prosecutors must convey such requests because they are obligated to alert the court when they know that the court lacks relevant information. This duty, which is incumbent upon all attorneys, is magnified for prosecutors because, as our case law has repeatedly noted, prosecutors have unique responsibilities. Specifically, a prosecutor is a minister of justice, possessing duties that rise above those of privately employed attorneys. The prosecutor "is the representative not of an ordinary party to a controversy, but of a sovereignty whose obligation to govern impartially is as compelling as its obligation to govern at all; and whose interest . . . in a criminal prosecution is not that it shall win . . . but that justice shall be done." State v. Emmett, 839 P.2d 781, 787 (Utah 1992). . . .

¶38 Based on the prosecutor's failure to relay M.R.'s request to be heard, the district court initially deprived M.R. of his right to speak at the change of plea hearing. At defendant's sentencing hearing, however, the court learned of M.R.'s earlier desire to be heard. The court then permitted M.R. and his mother to take the stand and testify regarding the appropriateness of defendant's plea bargain. The court also permitted extensive argument by M.R.'s counsel. Restricted in no respect by the court, all three individuals claimed that the plea bargain should have been rejected. After hearing this testimony and argument, the court "informally" reopened defendant's change of plea hearing and accepted the testimony that it had just heard from M.R. and his mother. The court then reaffirmed defendant's plea at the Class A level.

¶39 By taking these steps, the district court remedied its initial denial of M.R.'s right to be heard. Our conclusion is based on the following rationale. First, we note that the plea was subject to review up until the time of sentencing. Accordingly, in exercising its power to reopen the plea, the court permitted M.R. to be heard at a time when he could have persuaded the court to reject the proposed plea. Second, the record clearly demonstrates that the court reaffirmed the plea only after having accepted M.R.'s and his mother's testimony, and permitting argument by his counsel.

¶40 Thus, although M.R. was entitled to be heard at defendant's change of plea hearing, we conclude that he has enjoyed the fruits of the right he now claims he was denied. Accordingly, we hold that the district court, to its credit, cured the error initially committed at the change of plea hearing and honored M.R.'s right to be heard as soon as it discovered M.R. wished to be heard.[14] . . .

WILKINS, J., concurring.

. . . ¶44 [When] the trial court was finally informed of M.R.'s desire to be heard, it was clearly insufficient for the trial court to "informally" reopen the change of plea hearing and "consider" M.R.'s concerns before summarily reaffirming the "accepted" plea. Doing so merely compounded the error invited by the prosecution in failing to promptly inform the court of M.R.'s initial request to be heard at the change of plea hearing. [The] defendant's plea had not yet been finally accepted at the time the trial court became aware of M.R.'s desire to be heard on the matter. The correct course would have been for the trial court to reopen the hearing, after notice to all concerned. . . .

---

14. Because the district court upheld M.R.'s right to be heard in the present case, we decline to address what remedies are available for the hypothetical denial of a victim's right to be heard. We do note, however, that the Utah Legislature established a framework in which only three remedies were provided for the violation of a victim's right: injunctive relief, declaratory relief, and writ of mandamus. Utah Code Ann. §§77-38-11(1)-(2)(i). [Even] if the declaration of a misplea were assumed to be an available remedy, such a declaration would raise constitutional issues regarding the double jeopardy clauses of both the United States Constitution and the Utah Constitution.

¶46 The constitutional provisions granting M.R. his right to be heard, however, also limit this right. Subsection (2) of the Victims' Rights Amendment, Article I, Section 28 of the Utah Constitution, specifically prohibits construing the rights afforded M.R. in such a way as to provide "relief from any criminal judgment." The defendant's plea, once accepted by the court and sentence imposed, is a criminal judgment. . . . Only while the plea was still not final, that is, prior to the entry of sentence, could M.R.'s motion for misplea have been granted on the basis of M.R. having been denied his constitutional right to speak at the change of plea hearing. . . .

¶48 So, our hands are tied by the same constitutional and statutory provisions that gave M.R. his right to be heard in the first place. We cannot order the plea "undone" once the sentence and judgment have been entered by the trial court. We cannot impose any corrective action on the failure of the prosecutor to inform the court of the request to speak, or the failure of the trial court to fully reconsider the change of plea, with all due formality, thereby according M.R. his constitutional right to actually be heard.

¶49 As it works in practice, the right of a victim to be heard at a change of plea hearing is fragile at best, and may be made illusory by the intentional or unintentional mishandling of the situation by the prosecutor or the trial court, all without meaningful remedy. Perhaps the legislature may find it wise to reconsider the provisions of the statute addressing appellate review of the denial of a victim's request to assert the rights granted by the Victims' Rights Amendment. There may be other circumstances under which those rights may be just as easily and negligently denied as were M.R.'s in this case.

Notes

1. *Informing victims of plea agreements: majority position.* A majority of states now have statutes or constitutional provisions dealing with the rights of crime victims in the criminal process. Virtually all of these laws address plea bargains. The most common type of provision requires the prosecutor, when feasible, to inform a victim that the prosecutor plans to recommend that a court accept a guilty plea based on a plea agreement. The statutes also typically instruct the prosecutor to inform the victim of the time and place for the plea hearing. See U.S. Dept. of Justice, Victim Input into Plea Agreements (2002) (survey of state laws). Does a law requiring notice about a public document (the plea agreement) and a public hearing (the plea hearing) give crime victims anything of practical value? Would the notice requirement have a different effect if it were to apply before the prosecutor finalizes any plea negotiations? Does a notice requirement remain ineffective until the legislature authorizes funds to hire extra prosecutorial staff members to provide support to victims?

A smaller number of statutes require the prosecution to "consult" with the victim before recommending a plea agreement. See Ind. Code §35-35-3-5; W. Va. Code §61-11A-6(a)(5)(C). A few laws also authorize the victim to make a statement to the court during the plea hearing or require the prosecutor to inform the court about the victim's views on any proposed plea agreement. R.I. Gen. Laws §§12-28-3(14), 12-28-4.1. What might the victim say to the prosecutor or the judge that would provide new information relevant to the case?

2. *Responsiveness to victims.* Are prosecutors free to give controlling weight to the views of victims? The victims' rights laws described above all assume the validity

of a prosecutor's partial reliance on the wishes of crime victims. When defendants raise constitutional and other legal challenges to prosecutorial decisions based partly on the views of victims, courts have upheld the decisions. See Commonwealth v. Latimore, 667 N.E.2d 818 (Mass. 1996) (district attorney's decision not to accept defendant's offer of guilty plea to lesser offense, based in part on victim's family's desire to pursue murder conviction, was not prosecutorial misconduct). Would you predict the same result if a statute explicitly provided the victim with controlling authority — a "veto" power over any proposed plea agreement? What if a prosecutor adopted such a policy in the absence of a statute? Does the legitimacy of the victim's input change if he has filed a civil suit to recover monetary damages from the defendant? See N.D. Cent. Code §§29-01-16 and 29-01-17 (provides for "compromise" of a misdemeanor; victim accepts civil settlement, and there is no criminal conviction).

3. *The impact of victims' rights laws.* All 50 states have some statutory protections for the rights of victims during the criminal process, and about 30 states have amended their constitutions to provide for such rights. But some states have stronger requirements than others. Does the type of law at work in a state influence the way that government officials deal with the victim of an alleged crime? Does a stronger law change the likely reaction of the victim? Scholars from a variety of disciplines have studied the impact of victims' rights laws. For an overview of those empirical surveys, go to the web extension for this chapter at *http://www.crimpro. com/extension/ch16.*

D. ALTERNATIVES TO PLEA BARGAINING

Many scholars, judges, and lawyers believe that the routine use of trials to decide guilt or innocence would cause a meltdown of the justice system. But before we consider whether it is feasible to ban plea bargaining, we need to know whether an attempted ban would be worth the effort. Is plea bargaining legitimate? Would we keep it in an ideal world?

■ ALBERT ALSCHULER, IMPLEMENTING THE CRIMINAL DEFENDANT'S RIGHT TO TRIAL: ALTERNATIVES TO THE PLEA BARGAINING SYSTEM
50 U. Chi. L. Rev. 931 (1983)

. . . Plea bargaining makes a substantial part of an offender's sentence depend, not upon what he did or his personal characteristics, but upon a tactical decision irrelevant to any proper objective of criminal proceedings. In contested cases, it substitutes a regime of split-the-difference for a judicial determination of guilt or innocence and elevates a concept of partial guilt above the requirement that criminal responsibility be established beyond a reasonable doubt. This practice also deprecates the value of human liberty and the purposes of the criminal sanction by treating these things as commodities to be traded for economic savings—savings that, when measured against common social expenditures, usually seem minor.

Plea bargaining leads lawyers to view themselves as judges and administrators rather than as advocates; it subjects them to serious financial and other temptations to disregard their clients' interests; and it diminishes the confidence in attorney-client relationships that can give dignity and purpose to the legal profession and that is essential to the defendant's sense of fair treatment. In addition, this practice makes figureheads of court officials who typically prepare elaborate presentence reports only after the effective determination of sentence through prosecutorial negotiations. Indeed, it tends to make figureheads of judges, whose power over the administration of criminal justice has largely been transferred to people of less experience, who commonly lack the information that judges could secure, whose temperaments have been shaped by their partisan duties, and who have not been charged by the electorate with the important responsibilities that they have assumed. Moreover, plea bargaining perverts both the initial prosecutorial formulation of criminal charges and, as defendants plead guilty to crimes less serious than those that they apparently committed, the final judicial labeling of offenses.

The negotiation process encourages defendants to believe that they have, [in the words of a Chicago defense attorney], "sold a commodity and . . . in a sense, gotten away with something." It sometimes promotes perceptions of corruption. It has led the Supreme Court to a hypocritical disregard of its usual standards of waiver in judging the most pervasive waiver that our criminal justice system permits. The practice of plea bargaining is inconsistent with the principle that a decent society should want to hear what an accused person might say in his defense—and with constitutional guarantees that embody this principle and other professed ideals for the resolution of criminal disputes. Moreover, plea bargaining has undercut the goals of legal doctrines as diverse as the fourth amendment exclusionary rule, the insanity defense, the right of confrontation, the defendant's right to attend criminal proceedings, and the recently announced right of the press and the public to observe the administration of criminal justice. This easy instrument of accommodation has frustrated both attempts at sentencing reform and some of the most important objectives of the due process revolution.

Plea bargaining provides extraordinary opportunities for lazy lawyers whose primary goal is to cut corners and to get on to the next case; it increases the likelihood of favoritism and personal influence; it conceals other abuses; it maximizes the dangers of representation by inexperienced attorneys who are not fully versed in an essentially secret system of justice; it promotes inequalities; it sometimes results in unwarranted leniency; it merges the tasks of adjudication, sentencing, and administration into a single amorphous judgment to the detriment of all three; it treats almost every legal right as a bargaining chip to be traded for a discount in sentence; and it almost certainly increases the number of innocent defendants who are convicted. In short, an effort to describe comprehensively the evils that plea bargaining has wrought requires an extensive tour of the criminal justice system. . . .

At the end of a long investigation of plea bargaining, I confess to some bafflement concerning the insistence of most lawyers and judges that plea bargaining is inevitable and desirable. Perhaps I am wrong in thinking that a few simple precepts of criminal justice should command the unqualified support of fair-minded people:

- that it is important to hear what someone may be able to say in his defense before convicting him of crime;

- that, when he denies his guilt, it is also important to try to determine on the basis of all the evidence whether he is guilty;
- that it is wrong to punish a person, not for what he did, but for asking that the evidence be heard (and wrong deliberately to turn his sentence in significant part on his strategies rather than on his crime);
- and, finally, that it is wrong to alibi departures from these precepts by saying that we do not have the time and money to listen, that most defendants are guilty anyway, that trials are not perfect, that it is all an inevitable product of organizational interaction among stable courtroom work groups, and that any effort to listen would merely drive our failure to listen underground.

From my viewpoint, it is difficult to understand why these precepts are controversial; what is more, I do not understand why the legal profession, far from according them special reverence, apparently values them less than the public in general does. Daniel Webster thought it a matter of definition that "law" would hear before it condemned, proceed upon inquiry, and render judgment only after trial. Apparently the legal profession has lost sight of Webster's kind of law. . . .

■ FRANK EASTERBROOK, PLEA BARGAINING AS COMPROMISE
101 Yale L.J. 1969 (1992)

Is plea bargaining good or bad? Should we keep it or kick it? . . .

The analogy between plea bargains and contracts is far from perfect. Courts use contract as an analogy when addressing claims for the enforcement of plea bargains, excuses for nonperformance, or remedies for their breach. But plea bargains do not fit comfortably all aspects of either the legal or the economic model. Courts refuse to enforce promises to plead guilty in the future, although the enforcement of executory contracts is a principal mission of contract law.

On the economic side, plea bargains do not represent Pareto improvements. Instead of engaging in trades that make at least one person better off and no one worse off, the parties dicker about how much worse off one side will be. In markets persons can borrow to take advantage of good deals or withdraw from the market, wait for a better offer, and lend their assets for a price in the interim. By contrast, both sides to a plea bargain operate under strict budget constraints, and they cannot bide their time. They bargain as bilateral monopolists (defendants can't shop in competitive markets for prosecutors) in the shadow of legal rules that work suspiciously like price controls. Judges, who do not join the bargaining, set the prices, increasingly by reference to a table of punishments that looks like something the Office of Price Administration would have promulgated. Plea bargaining is to the sentencing guidelines as black markets are to price controls.

Black markets are better than no markets. Plea bargains are preferable to mandatory litigation—not because the analogy to contract is overpowering, but because compromise is better than conflict. Settlements of civil cases make both sides better off; settlements of criminal cases do so too. Defendants have many procedural and substantive rights. By pleading guilty, they sell these rights to the prosecutor, receiving concessions they esteem more highly than the rights surrendered. Rights that may be sold are more valuable than rights that must be consumed, just as money (which may be used to buy housing, clothing, or food) is more valuable to a poor person than an opportunity to live in public housing.

Defendants can use or exchange their rights, whichever makes them better off. So plea bargaining helps defendants. Forcing them to use their rights at trial means compelling them to take the risk of conviction or acquittal; risk-averse persons prefer a certain but small punishment to a chancy but large one. Defendants also get the process over sooner, and solvent ones save the expense of trial. Compromise also benefits prosecutors and society at large. In purchasing procedural entitlements with lower sentences, prosecutors buy that most valuable commodity, Time. With time they can prosecute more criminals. When [80] percent of defendants plead guilty, a given prosecutorial staff obtains five times the number of convictions it could achieve if all went to trial. Even so, prosecutors must throw back the small fish. The ratio of prosecutions (and convictions) to crimes would be extremely low if compromises were forbidden. Sentences could not be raised high enough to maintain deterrence, especially not when both economics and principles of desert call for proportionality between crime and punishment.

True, defense lawyers and prosecutors are imperfect agents of their principals. Of what agents is this not true? Real estate agents? Corporate managers? Agency costs are endemic and do not justify abandoning consensual transactions. . . . Monitoring the performance of agents is difficult, and serious monitoring means substantially increasing the time and number of lawyers devoted to each case. Critics of plea bargaining commit the Nirvana Fallacy, comparing an imperfect reality to a perfection achievable only in imaginary systems. . . .

Why should we interfere with compromises of litigation? If the accused is entitled to a trial at which all his rights are honored and the sentence is appropriate to the crime, yet prefers compromise, who are we to disagree? . . . Why is liberty too important to be left to the defendant whose life is at stake? Should we not say instead that liberty is too important to deny effect to the defendant's choice?

Every day people choose where (if at all) to obtain an education, what occupation to pursue, whom to marry, whether to bear children, and how to raise them. Often they choose in ignorance—not simply because they do not know whether Yale offers a better education than the University of Southern Mississippi, but also because they do not know what the future holds. Technological changes or fluctuations in trade with foreign nations will make some educations obsolete and raise the value of others. People may, without the approval of regulators, climb mountains, plummet down slopes at eighty miles per hour on waxed boards, fail to exercise, eat fatty foods, smoke cigarettes, skip physical checkups, anesthetize their minds by watching television rather than reading books, and destroy their hearing by listening to rock music at high volumes. Sometimes courts say that the Constitution protects the right to make these choices, precisely because they are so important. . . .

Courts give effect not only to life-and-death choices actually made but also to elections by inaction. When a defendant's lawyer fails to make an important motion or omits an essential line of argument, we treat the omission as a forfeiture. How bizarre for a legal system that routinely puts persons in jail for twenty years following their agents' oversight to deny them the right to compromise the same dispute, advertently, for half as much loss of liberty. . . .

Curtailing the discount for pleading guilty has been justified in the name of equality. Yet the greatest disparity in sentencing is between those convicted at trial and those not prosecuted. A reduction in the number of convictions attributable to a decline in the number of pleas would dramatically increase the effective disparity in the treatment of persons suspected of crime. . . .

Plea bargains are compromises. Autonomy and efficiency support them. "Imperfections" in bargaining reflect the imperfections of an anticipated trial. To improve plea bargaining, improve the process for deciding cases on the merits. When we deem that process adequate, there will be no reason to prevent the person most affected by the criminal process from improving his situation through compromise.

◼ RONALD WRIGHT & MARC MILLER, THE SCREENING/BARGAINING TRADEOFF
55 Stan. L. Rev. 29 (2002)

When it comes to plea bargaining, we have created a false dilemma. . . . Scholars, judges, prosecutors, defense lawyers, and politicians have offered only two basic responses to the fact that guilt is mostly resolved through negotiated guilty pleas: They take it or they leave it.

Some take the system more or less as it is. They accept negotiated pleas in the ordinary course of events, either because such a system produces good results or because it is inevitable. They might identify some exceptional cases that create an intolerable risk of convicting innocent defendants, or unusual cases where there are special reasons to doubt the knowing and voluntary nature of the defendant's plea. These special cases might call for some regulation. But the mine run of cases, in this view, must be resolved with a heavy dose of plea bargains and a sprinkling of trials.

Then there are those who leave it, arguing that our system's reliance on negotiated guilty pleas is fundamentally mistaken. Some call for a complete ban on negotiated guilty pleas. Others, doubting that an outright ban is feasible, still encourage a clear shift to more short trials to resolve criminal charges. Restoring the criminal trial to its rightful place at the center of criminal justice might require major changes in public spending, and it might take a lifetime, but these critics say the monstrosity of the current system demands such a change.

This dilemma about plea bargaining—take it or leave it—is a false one. It is based on a false dichotomy. It errs in assuming that criminal trials are the only alternative to plea bargains. In this erroneous view, fewer plea bargains lead inexorably to more trials; indeed, the whole point in limiting plea bargains is to produce more trials.

This paper offers a different choice, and points to prosecutorial "screening" as the principal alternative to plea bargains. Of course all prosecutors "screen" when they make any charging decision. By prosecutorial screening we mean a far more structured and reasoned charge selection process than is typical in most prosecutors' offices in this country. The prosecutorial screening system we describe has four interrelated features, all internal to the prosecutor's office: early assessment, reasoned selection, barriers to bargains, and enforcement.

First, the prosecutor's office must make an early and careful assessment of each case, and demand that police and investigators provide sufficient information before the initial charge is filed. Second, the prosecutor's office must file only appropriate charges. Which charges are "appropriate" is determined by several factors. A prosecutor should only file charges that the office would generally want to result in a criminal conviction and sanction. In addition, appropriate charges must reflect reasonably accurately what actually occurred. They are charges that the prosecutor can very likely prove in court. Third, and critically, the office must severely restrict all plea bargaining, and most especially charge bargains. Prosecutors should also recognize explicitly that the screening process is the mechanism that makes such restrictions possible. Fourth, the kind of prosecutorial screening we advocate must include sufficient training, oversight, and other internal enforcement mechanisms to ensure reasonable uniformity in charging and relatively few changes to charges after they have been filed. If prosecutors treat hard screening decisions as the primary alternative to plea bargaining, they can produce changes in current criminal practice that would be fundamental, attractive, and viable. . . .

TRADITIONAL ALTERNATIVES TO PLEA BARGAINING

. . . For those who wish to establish that plea bargaining is an inevitable and irrepressible force in American criminal justice, Philadelphia is a problem. The city has long operated a system that relies more on short bench trials than on pleas of guilty. A number of scholars conducted case studies in Philadelphia (and a few other cities with high rates of bench trials) and concluded that the trials in those cities were not truly adversarial trials. Instead, they were "slow pleas" of guilt. The brief trials allowed the defendant to present evidence about the circumstances of the case, not to obtain an acquittal, but to influence the judge at sentencing.

Stephen Schulhofer visited the Philadelphia courts and took away a different impression. [He] observed a large number of bench trials in the city and concluded that they were genuinely adversarial proceedings where defendants retained many of the constitutional protections sacrificed during plea bargaining. Schulhofer called for other jurisdictions to follow Philadelphia's lead and to treat short trials as a viable alternative to plea bargaining. . . .

Explicit efforts to shorten trials have not been the preferred technique among American prosecutors who want to limit the reach of negotiated pleas. Instead, the handful of prosecutors who aspire to "ban" plea bargaining—either for targeted crimes or for the entire criminal docket—have issued strong ukases against bargaining, enforced by more rigorous screening and modest staffing increases, as their most workable solution. . . .

Among the most famous American plea bargaining bans occurred in Alaska during the 1970s and 1980s. In 1975, state Attorney General Avrum Gross declared that prosecutors would no longer engage in charge bargaining or sentence bargaining. Attorney General Gross hoped to restore public confidence in the system, increase the number of trials, improve the litigation skills of prosecutors, and return prosecutors to their traditional roles of evaluating evidence and trying cases instead of negotiating.

Major studies in 1978 and 1991 evaluated the impact of the Alaska plea ban. By all accounts, both charge bargaining and sentence bargaining became rare events during the first ten years of the policy. During the late 1980s, charge bargains reappeared, but prosecutors continued to avoid sentence bargains. For a few years, the trial rate increased modestly. Seven percent of charged cases went to trial before the ban, and the rate moved to 10% before returning to 7% by the end of the 1980s.

Since the cases were not ending in negotiated pleas or trials, what was happening to them? The answer was a combination of aggressive screening and open guilty pleas. Before the ban, prosecutors in Fairbanks refused to prosecute about 4% of the felonies referred to them by the police or other investigators. After the ban, the proportion of felonies that prosecutors declined to prosecute increased to about 44%. A large portion of the case load (about 23%) was disposed of through open pleas of guilt. This was part of the Attorney General's thinking when he created the plea ban. More careful selection of cases would make it possible to stick with the initial charges, even in front of a judge or jury.

The Alaska experience received lackluster academic reviews. Some implied that the failure to increase trials proved that unseen bargains were still driving the system, and explained the high number of open guilty pleas. Others pointed to the reappearance of charge bargaining after ten years, and suggested that it is futile to place controls on the quintessential prosecutorial decision of charge selection. Some implied that Alaska was too unusual a jurisdiction to offer any guidance to prosecutors in most major American cities. However, other jurisdictions scattered around the country have duplicated pieces of the Alaska experience over the years. Some prosecutors in other locales have picked out priority crimes like homicide and banned plea bargains for those cases.[53] Some of the bans target particular forms of bargaining rather than particular crimes.[54] The reaction to these experiences, like the reaction to the Alaska plea ban, has been subdued. If these prosecutors were not increasing their trial rates, the critics found the effort unimportant.

These experiences do not mean that any ban on charge reductions will produce small trial increases and large numbers of open guilty pleas. If prosecutors do not change their screening principles to insist on more declinations of cases referred to the office, the dispositions shift in other directions. In El Paso County, Texas during the 1980s, the chief prosecutor announced an end to all plea bargaining in burglary cases. There was no organized effort to change the screening of such cases, and the number of trials increased enough to create a serious backlog of untried cases. Partial bans on plea bargaining appear regularly around the country. Most prosecutors today who plan to restrict plea negotiations focus on priority crimes, such as homicide or sex crimes. Some of the bans are limited to particular courts or phases of litigation, such as the statutory ban on plea bargains for most serious felonies in

53. In the 1970s, the prosecutor in Maricopa County (Phoenix), Arizona barred plea bargains in cases involving designated crimes such as drug sales, homicide, robbery, burglary, assault with a deadly weapon, and sexual misconduct. The policy did not increase trial rates for these crimes because more defendants pled guilty as charged. Moise Berger, *The Case Against Plea Bargaining*, 62 A.B.A. J. 621 (1976). Similar reports came after prosecutors in Multnomah County, Oregon and Black Hawk County, Iowa banned plea bargaining for selected crimes during the early 1970s. Note, The Elimination of Plea Bargaining in Black Hawk County: A Case Study, 60 Iowa L. Rev. 1053 (1975). . . .

54. In an example of one such effort to discourage some forms of bargaining, the District Attorney for Manhattan in the mid-1970s prohibited his attorneys from recommending sentences and established (and published!) a 1974 memorandum suggesting specific charge discounts to offer in exchange for guilty pleas. Richard H. Kuh, Plea Bargaining: Guidelines for the Manhattan District Attorney's Office, 11 Crim. L. Bull. 48 (1975). Thomas Church documented the efforts of a county in a Midwestern state during the early 1970s to eliminate charge bargaining in drug sale cases. Thomas Church, Jr., Plea Bargains, Concessions and the Courts: Analysis of a Quasi-Experiment, 10 Law & Soc'y Rev. 377 (1976). The prosecutor left sentence bargaining in place, and the proportion of the cases resolved through defendants pleading guilty as charged increased from 17 to 90% between 1972 and 1974. In Church's view, the county's experience demonstrated the inevitability of plea bargaining. But his interviewees believed that the concessions the defendants were promised after the ban were far less reliable and valuable than the concessions they negotiated before the ban.

Superior Court in California, or the ban on plea bargaining in the Supreme Court in the Bronx in the mid-1990s.

When plea bans are limited to a particular court (such as the highest trial court), the effects are usually minimal because the bargainers simply move to a different (typically earlier) point in the process. Plea bans exist today, but we know little about their effects on case dispositions and sentences. The attention of academic observers has strayed to other areas, even as prosecutors keep innovating. . . . Thirty years of scholarship has missed a fundamental perspective on plea bargaining: there are in fact many alternative points of comparison when assessing the wisdom and necessity of plea bargains. . . .

THE SCREENING/BARGAINING TRADEOFF IN PRACTICE: NODA DATA

A chief prosecutor attempting to change plea practices faces both administrative and political hurdles. Will her proposed policy actually change the use of negotiated guilty pleas? If so, can the office sustain it over the long haul? We do not believe that plea bargaining is inevitable, but plea bargaining surely is pervasive and deeply entrenched. Any effort to limit plea bargaining must confront the habits and relationships of prosecutors and defense attorneys.

Reform efforts emerging voluntarily from within one criminal justice institution may have a greater chance to succeed than reforms imposed externally. A single institution can set up review and reward systems, allowing for more supervision— and, we believe, more consistency—than external constraints can provide. Among the many virtues we see in the screening/bargaining tradeoff described in this paper is the authority of a chief prosecutor, acting alone, to set this change in motion.

What should we expect to happen when a prosecutor decides to shift the screening/bargaining tradeoff in the direction of screening? As for changes in case processing, the most direct effect should be measurable: fewer plea bargains. The kinds of plea bargains that are easiest to track are charge reductions after cases are filed. A jurisdiction with hard screening practices should produce fewer and smaller charge reductions than jurisdictions with weaker screening practices.

[We can] test the plausibility of the screening/bargaining tradeoff using previously unstudied and unreported data about one major urban prosecutor's office: the New Orleans District Attorney's Office, or NODA. This data exists because the District Attorney for Orleans Parish, Harry Connick, has remained committed to principled screening throughout his long term in office. . . .

Harry Connick was elected as the District Attorney for Orleans Parish in 1974. He has remained in that office for the past twenty-eight years. Connick first ran for office in 1969 against incumbent Jim Garrison, the flamboyant District Attorney made famous in the film JFK. His first unsuccessful campaign did not focus on plea bargaining. He promised faster prosecution and better tracking of defendants who failed to appear for trial. His 1973 campaign began with a similar emphasis on swift prosecution. As the campaign wore on, however, Connick's speeches began to feature attacks on plea bargaining. . . .

Connick told voters that widespread plea bargaining was wrong; years later, he explained that victims were right to resent it when cases were bargained away simply because of a "lazy" prosecutor. He promised to eliminate "baseless" plea bargaining and to hire full-time prosecutors who would not use plea bargains just to move cases from the docket.

As in other American cities, the criminal courts in New Orleans deal with enormous volume. In the face of this large urban caseload, Connick needed a strategy to carry out his campaign statements about plea bargaining. During the weeks between his election victory and taking office, he started speaking publicly about a plan with two central components. First, Connick planned to devote expertise and resources to screening. He proposed a screening procedure that "would weed out those cases really not worthy of being on the criminal docket, so more courtroom emphasis can be devoted to the violent offender." Second, he instructed his prosecutors not to engage in plea bargaining—particularly charge bargaining—except under very limited circumstances. . . .

The distinctiveness of the screening process in the NODA office is apparent from a closer examination of the path each new case takes through the system. Police officers develop a case folder after they complete an investigation and file charges with the magistrate. The first stop for the case folder in the NODA office is the Magistrate Section, where the least experienced assistants work. They typically have logged six months or fewer on the job. The ADA from the Magistrate Section appears for the state at the first appearance and bail hearing before the magistrate. A public defender is also present for the first appearance, but the case is reassigned immediately after the hearing and there is typically no further defense presence or participation in the case until after the DA files an information or obtains an indictment.

After any proceedings in the Magistrate Division, the folder moves to the Screening Section of the NODA office. Connick devotes extraordinary resources to this operation. For instance, in the late 1990s, about fifteen of the eighty-five attorneys in the office worked in Screening. . . . All attorneys in the Screening Section served previously (usually a couple of years) in the Trial Section. This level of experience comes at a premium in New Orleans, where the turnover among prosecuting attorneys is quite high. The average tenure of an ADA in the NODA office is around two years.

Within the Screening Section, designated cases such as homicide or rape get assigned to screeners with special expertise. Drug cases and a few other high-volume cases go to a subgroup known as Expedited Screening. Ordinary cases go to the Screening Attorney on duty for that day. The screener reviews the investigation file, speaks to all the key witnesses and the victims (often by telephone, but sometimes in person), and generally gauges the strength of the case. If the police report neglects to mention a factual issue that is likely to arise at trial, the screening attorney will speak directly with the police officer to resolve it. There is a powerful office expectation that the Screening Attorney will make a decision within ten days of receiving the folder.

NODA instituted a variety of measures to ensure reasonable uniformity in screening decisions. Connick committed his screening principles to writing in an office policy manual. The general office policy is to charge the most serious crime the facts will support at trial. The policy does not, on its face, allow individual prosecutors to consider for themselves the equities in the case when selecting the charge. By the same token, however, Connick insists that overcharging is unacceptable, because the charges chosen for the information will stay in place through the trial. If screening prosecutors overcharge cases too often, the Chief of the Trial Section might send the screening attorney back into the courtroom on at least one of those overcharged matters to "get his teeth kicked in."

Supervisors review all refusals to charge. Attorneys say they often compare notes, especially in early morning discussions, and this helps to educate and develop shared charging norms in the office. Office policy discourages refusal for select categories of crimes, notably domestic violence cases. For the most serious crimes, including rape and homicide, the office conducts "charge conferences" with senior prosecutors and police present to discuss the facts and potential charges.

Neither Connick nor any attorneys in his office claim to have abolished plea bargaining entirely from the New Orleans system. Prosecutors in the office acknowledge that sometimes new information appears and changes the value of a case. Witnesses leave town, victims decide not to testify, new witnesses appear, and investigators find new evidence. On occasion, the screening attorney makes a bad judgment and overcharges, and a plea could save the case.

Nevertheless, office policy tries to keep these changes in charges to a minimum. A supervisor must approve any decision to drop or change charges after the information is filed. The attorney requesting the change must complete a special form naming the screening and trial attorneys, and explaining the reason for the decision, drawing from a list of acceptable reasons. The ADAs believe there is a "stigma" involved in reducing charges, however strong the reasons for a reduction might be.

Attorneys from the NODA office believe that they decline to prosecute an exceptional number of cases. They view this as a necessary part of training police officers to investigate more thoroughly. The relatively high rate of declination also created a political challenge for Connick over the years. During each of his reelection campaigns—in 1978, 1984, 1990, and 1996—Connick's challengers criticized the number of cases that the NODA office declined to prosecute. As his opponent Morris Reed put it in many public debates, "the PD arrests them and the DA turns them loose." Connick had several replies. Poor police work made declinations necessary. Further, he pointed to specific examples of how his office dealt severely with defendants once they were charged. Connick also explicitly linked his screening policies to his plea bargaining policies: Tough screening, he said, made it possible to keep plea bargaining at low levels.

Connick drew on case data to make specific claims about low rates of plea bargaining in the office: He asserted that plea bargaining in Jim Garrison's day reached 60 to 70%, but fell to 7 or 8% of all cases filed under his office policy. He also routinely mentioned the high number of trials in New Orleans compared to other Louisiana jurisdictions. In addition, Connick pointed to his routine use of the habitual felon law to enhance sentences. By the end of each of the four reelection campaigns, Connick convinced the voters that it was possible both to decline many cases and to run a tough prosecutor's office at the same time. . . .

The data mostly support District Attorney Harry Connick's claims to have implemented a screening/bargaining tradeoff over the last thirty years. Several kinds of information bolster that judgment, but the most substantial and useful by far is the data that Connick has kept to assist in his administration of the office. New Orleans shows that the screening/bargaining tradeoff does not necessarily lead to a disabling number of trials. The office also shows that a committed prosecutor can implement the screening/bargaining tradeoff even without the conscious support of other actors in the system. . . . Plea bargaining's triumph, and the cynical products of that triumph, are simply not as absolute as a century of practice and study suggest.

Notes

1. *The arrival of plea bargaining.* Courts and commentators occasionally refer to plea bargaining as eternal and inevitable. It may be inevitable, though it is surely not eternal. Research suggests that plea bargaining was forbidden (at least formally) in the first two-thirds of the nineteenth century, and emerged in the last third of that century, becoming institutionalized and widespread in the twentieth century. See Lawrence Friedman, Plea Bargaining in Historical Perspective, 13 Law & Soc'y Rev. 247 (1979); Albert Alschuler, Plea Bargaining and Its History, 13 Law & Soc'y Rev. 211 (1979).

Professor George Fisher, through careful study of the origins of plea bargaining in nineteenth-century Massachusetts, revealed how plea bargaining first thrived for crimes that gave judges little choice over sentences (and therefore gave added importance to the prosecutor's choice of charges). Bargaining also became more attractive to prosecutors after the appearance of probation as a sentencing option. Judges became more amenable to plea bargaining after a flood of railroad tort suits created civil docket pressures. Fisher, Plea Bargaining's Triumph, 109 Yale L.J. 857 (2000).

A case from an earlier time reveals how much judicial attitudes toward plea negotiations have changed. In Commonwealth v. Battis, 1 Mass. 95 (1804), the defendant asked to plead guilty to a murder charge. Although the trial judge informed the defendant of the consequences of his plea and told him that he was "under no legal or moral obligation to plead guilty," the defendant did not retract his plea. At that point, "the Court told him that they would allow him a reasonable time to consider of what had been said to him" and returned him to prison. The defendant returned to court later that afternoon and asked again to plead guilty. The judge questioned the jailer and others "as to the sanity of the prisoner" and "whether there had not been tampering with him, either by promises persuasions, or hopes of pardon, if he would plead guilty." Only after determining that "nothing of that kind" occurred did the judge accept the guilty plea.

2. *Plea bargains: contract or charade?* Some scholars have accepted the essentially contractual nature of plea bargaining, and have suggested that the problem with plea bargaining law is that it does not take the contracting analogy seriously enough. Robert Scott and William Stuntz, for example, focus on the risk of convicting an innocent defendant, arguing that "by following appropriate contract models, one can devise different rules that reduce the harm to innocent defendants and meanwhile reduce transaction costs and inefficiency for everyone else." Scott & Stuntz, Plea Bargaining as Contract, 101 Yale L.J. 1909 (1992). Critics of plea bargaining, such as Professor Stephen Schulhofer, have rejected the notion that plea bargains are fair simply because the defendant agreed to the terms and because the agreement puts the defendant in a better position than if the defendant went to trial. Schulhofer, Plea Bargaining as Disaster, 101 Yale L.J. 1979 (1992). Schulhofer and other critics focus on the public interest in criminal justice that the contract model obscures. Does plea bargaining undermine public confidence in the criminal justice system? Stanley Cohen & Anthony Doob, Public Attitudes to Plea Bargaining, 32 Crim. L.Q. 85 (1989-1990) (1988 survey found that more than two-thirds of Canadians disapprove of plea bargaining). What is Judge Easterbrook's attitude toward the use of contract law to explain plea bargaining? Does he take account of the public interest arguments? Does Professor Alschuler account for the contractarian argument that

plea bargains are the fairest (most preferable) means for the defendant to address criminal charges, except in very limited circumstances? Would the fairness of plea bargaining be cast into doubt if there were no trials at all? See Malcolm Feeley, The Process Is the Punishment (1979) (of 1,640 misdemeanor cases, not one defendant requested jury trial). Is there such a thing as a "natural" rate of trials?

3. *The public interest in trials.* Judge Easterbrook treats plea bargains as the best way to honor the rights of the defendant, including the right to autonomy—to determine one's own destiny. But do offenders not forgo any such right when they commit a crime? Do criminal defendants have a constitutional right to bargain? Why should society care about giving free choice to a person who has acted in a way that denies rights (life, health, autonomy, ownership, and so forth) to others? Might the public have a greater interest in public trials than in more convictions? Might the public have an interest in convictions and sentences as close as possible to conceptions of what "really" happened, whether the conviction and sentence follow a trial or a nonbargained guilty plea?

4. *Bargaining and bribery.* Sometimes the government will enter a plea bargain with a defendant in exchange for the defendant's cooperation in other criminal investigations, including testimony against other criminal defendants. Does this sort of plea bargain amount to bribing a witness? Courts never took such an argument seriously until a panel of the U.S. Court of Appeals for the Tenth Circuit reversed a money laundering conviction on the ground that the government had bribed the cooperating witness. A few months later, the en banc court changed direction and upheld the conviction. The "anti-gratuity statute," 18 U.S.C. §201(c)(2), declares that whoever "directly or indirectly, gives, offers, or promises anything of value to any person, for or because of the testimony under oath or affirmation given or to be given by such person" has committed a crime. The en banc court read the word "whoever" to exclude prosecuting attorneys acting within the normal course of their authority. Any other result, the court said, would be "a radical departure from the ingrained legal culture of our criminal justice system." United States v. Singleton, 165 F.3d 1297 (10th Cir. 1999) (en banc). What would be the effects if prosecutors stopped promising to enter lenient plea agreements with cooperative witnesses? Try to formulate alternatives that prosecutors might adopt to obtain cooperation from witnesses who were involved in alleged crimes.

5. *The isolated popularity of bans.* Though a minor theme in current criminal justice debates, bans on plea bargaining occasionally become a topic of public concern, and they remain a subject of intense scholarly interest. Jurisdictions other than Alaska have experimented with formal plea bans, though none have been statewide; most are implemented by a single prosecutor with a particular vision for improving the criminal justice system. Other modern efforts to abolish plea bargaining include a ban in El Paso, Texas; a Detroit ban on bargaining in felony firearm cases; another effort in Michigan to abolish charge bargaining in drug trafficking cases; and a judge-imposed ban in Superior Court in New Hampshire. See Amy Fixsen, Plea Bargaining: The New Hampshire "Ban," 9 New Eng. J. on Crim. & Civ. Confinement 387 (1983); Robert Weninger, The Abolition of Plea Bargaining: A Case Study of El Paso County, Texas, 35 UCLA L. Rev. 265 (1987); see generally 13 Law & Soc'y Rev. (1979). In the 1990s, the Bronx District Attorney's office banned bargains in felony cases after indictment. See Kenneth Jost, Critics Blast New York Plea Ban, 9 CQ Researcher No. 6, at 124 (Feb. 12, 1999). Which aspect of plea bargaining do these reforms target? Is selective restriction on bargaining preferable to a total ban?

6. *Alternatives to plea bargaining.* If bargains are banned, what takes their place? The Alaska and New Orleans experiences suggest that guilty plea rates may remain quite high even in the absence of bargains. Why might this be so? Professor Schulhofer and others have argued that it is possible to offer meaningful trials in place of bargains, including greater use of bench rather than jury trials. See Stephen Schulhofer, Is Plea Bargaining Inevitable?, 97 Harv. L. Rev. 1037 (1984) (discussing use of short trials in Philadelphia). In an article excerpted at the beginning of this section, Professor Alschuler makes a particularly eloquent argument in favor of offering some kind of trial over any kind of bargain: "In providing elaborate trials to a minority of defendants while pressing all others to abandon their right to trial, our nation allocates its existing resources about as sensibly as a nation that attempted to solve its transportation problem by giving Cadillacs to ten percent of the population while requiring everyone else to travel by foot. [Less] would be more." Does the New Orleans District Attorney offer defendants, as a group, less procedural protection or less favorable outcomes than they might receive in a jurisdiction that negotiates more routinely for reduced charges?

Are bans likely to be effective only for a short time? Are plea bargains an inevitable answer to pressures within the justice system (whether political, legal, social, or economic)? See generally Milton Heumann, Plea Bargaining: The Experiences of Prosecutors, Judges, and Defense Attorneys (1978). Can individual lawyers or judges "ban" bargaining? For a ban to work, does there need to be a more proportional and modest system of punishments? Is plea bargaining a necessity or virtue in highly punitive times? In other words, does a world with no plea bargaining require penalties that judges and prosecutors are actually comfortable enforcing?

XVII

Decisionmakers at Trial

More than 90 percent of all criminal convictions are obtained through plea bargains and guilty pleas, leaving comparatively few cases for trial. Looking at trials from this vantage point, however, obscures four important points. First, for some kinds of offenses and offenders, the trial rate is considerably higher. For example, in 2009 in large urban counties, about 26 percent of murder convictions were obtained through trial. Generally, trial rates for violent offenses against persons are higher than for property, drug, and weapons offenses.

Second, only 5 to 10 percent of all convictions may seem small compared with the proportion of charges settled through plea bargains, but there are still large absolute numbers of criminal trials in most U.S. jurisdictions. A small change in the plea rate can have a major impact on the number of trials and the operation of court systems.

Third, there is not just one kind of trial. Public perception often seems to be shaped by long, high-profile trials. But in fact, most trials are short. Even in federal court, which conducts the most complex criminal trials, over half of the trials are completed in a single day. Just under half of state felony trials are handled by judges sitting without a jury. Judges try a much higher percentage of misdemeanor trials, though the rate varies enormously among the states and the proportion of the roughly 12 million misdemeanors each year that go to trial is difficult to determine.

Finally, plea bargaining practices do not develop in a vacuum: They reflect to some degree the availability, benefits, and costs of trials. For example, when sanctions imposed after trials start to resemble sanctions imposed after guilty pleas, more defendants are likely to go to trial since there is always some chance that the government will fail to prove the case or that a jury or judge will find the defendant not guilty for some other reason.

A useful perspective for studying the U.S. trial system is to consider the very different processes used in other countries. For example, the paradigm decisionmaker in U.S. criminal trials—the criminal jury—is virtually unknown in some other lands. Other countries employ institutions not familiar in the United States, such as multi-judge panels in criminal cases. In Germany lone judges try minor offenses, but more serious offenses are tried before panels made up of "professional" and "lay" judges.

The fact that other places conduct trials in other ways serves as a reminder that the U.S. justice system involves choices. One fundamental question about U.S. criminal trials is why they are relatively rare, compared with plea bargains, and whether that is a good or bad thing. If public criminal trials are preferred to plea bargains, will different rules produce more trials?

This chapter examines different decisionmakers at trial. The first section examines the choice between jury and judge trials. The second and third sections study the procedures for selecting jurors and guiding juries as they perform their function. The final section considers the role of a decisionmaker in a larger sense—the public—in watching and evaluating criminal trials.

A. JUDGE OR JURY?

Perhaps the most distinctive feature of American criminal trials is the criminal jury. But juries do not decide the outcomes of every criminal trial; in some situations, the judge sits as the factfinder in a bench trial. When is a jury trial available to a criminal defendant?

The Sixth Amendment provides in part: "In all criminal prosecutions, the accused shall enjoy the right to a speedy and public trial, by an impartial jury." The U.S. Supreme Court determined in Duncan v. Louisiana, 391 U.S. 145 (1968), that this fundamental right applies to the states through the due process clause of the Fourteenth Amendment. Despite the absolute language of the amendment ("*all* criminal prosecutions"), the right is not absolute; the constitutional guaranty of a jury trial does not cover "petty offenses." The *Duncan* Court explained that jury trials were not available historically for petty crimes and that nonjury trials are faster and less expensive than jury trials.

The question of which crimes qualify as "petty" crimes has enormous practical consequences because the largest number of cases in American criminal justice systems involve less serious (but not necessarily "petty") crimes. The Court in Baldwin v. New York, 399 U.S. 66 (1970), relied on the history of the Sixth Amendment in concluding that it was meant to protect jury trials only in cases that were triable by a jury at common law. In later cases, it has become clear that a "serious" offense covered by the federal right to jury trial must be punishable by a prison term of more than six months.

■ JEAN-BAPTISTE BADO v. UNITED STATES
186 A.3d 1243 (D.C. App. 2018)

Ruiz, Senior Judge.

. . . Appellant Jean-Baptiste Bado came to the United States on February 8, 2005, from Burkina Faso, where he was a pastor, fleeing at the time from "systematic prosecution and torture for his political and religious beliefs." Once in this country, he filed an application for asylum. His asylum proceeding continued for several years. It was halted in 2011, however, when he was charged by information with three counts of misdemeanor sexual abuse of a minor because, if convicted, under U.S. immigration law he would be barred from receiving political asylum and removed from the United States. Appellant pleaded not guilty and demanded a jury trial, which was denied. At the bench trial, appellant took the stand and contradicted the charges, calling into question the complainant's credibility. He was acquitted of two of the charges but convicted of one count. He was sentenced to 180 days and ordered to pay $50 to the Crime Victims Compensation Program Fund and register as a sex offender for ten years. The United States commenced deportation proceedings on the basis of the conviction. . . .

The Sixth Amendment guarantees a bundle of trial rights to the accused in "all criminal prosecutions." The first of these is "the right to a speedy and public trial, by an impartial jury." The Supreme Court has interpreted the scope of the jury trial right, in the light of the common law, as applying to criminal prosecutions for "serious offenses." Duncan v. Louisiana, 391 U.S. 145 (1968). Criminal prosecutions for offenses that are not serious, but deemed to be "petty," may be tried by a judge without violating the Sixth Amendment.

The Supreme Court has set the parameters of what constitutes a "serious" offense under the Sixth Amendment. It is settled that any offense "where imprisonment for more than six months is authorized" cannot be considered "petty" for purposes of the right to trial by jury. Baldwin v. New York, 399 U.S. 66 (1970). In Blanton v. City of North Las Vegas, 489 U.S. 538 (1989), the Court set out the analytical framework to determine whether a particular offense punishable by incarceration for six months or less is to be deemed "serious," triggering the constitutional right to a jury trial, or "petty," leaving the question of a jury trial to resolution under other applicable law. Noting that the maximum exposure to incarceration is usually the clearest indicator of the seriousness of an offense, the Court, following *Baldwin's* lead, stated that offenses with a maximum period of incarceration of six months are "presumptively" petty. The Court, however, declined to hold that all such offenses "automatically qualify" as petty offenses, and established that the presumption can be overcome if the accused "can demonstrate that any additional statutory penalties, viewed in conjunction with the maximum authorized period of incarceration, are so severe that they clearly reflect a legislative determination that the offense in question is a 'serious' one."

In *Blanton* the Court applied that test to a conviction for driving under the influence by assessing the statutorily authorized penalties that could be imposed upon conviction for DUI: incarceration from a minimum of two days to a maximum of six months, or alternatively, 48 hours of community service dressed in clothing identifying the convicted defendant as a DUI offender; a maximum penalty of $1000; a 90-day suspension of a driver's license; and mandatory attendance at an alcohol abuse education course at the offender's expense. The Court made clear that, in evaluating the seriousness of the offense, it considered the "maximum authorized prison sentence," and that it considered only those potential penalties that are actually faced by the particular defendant. The Court reasoned that, because the maximum period of incarceration did not exceed six months, the offense was presumptively petty. It then considered the additional statutory penalties. Of the distinctive garb required if the person were alternatively sentenced to a short period of community service, the Court stated that, even if it were "the source of some embarrassment," it would be "less embarrassing and less onerous than six months in jail." The Court considered the license suspension and concluded it was not "that significant" as a Sixth Amendment matter, in part because the record was unclear as to whether the suspension would be concurrent with the six-month incarceration, in which case it would be "irrelevant," and because a restricted license could be obtained after forty-five days. The Court dismissed the mandatory alcohol abuse education course as a "de minimis" requirement. After taking into account all of the possible maximum statutory penalties that could be applied to the defendant, the Court concluded that "viewed together, the statutory penalties are not so severe that DUI must be deemed a 'serious' offense for purposes of the Sixth Amendment." The Court applied a *Blanton* analysis one other time, in United States v. Nachtigal, 507 U.S. 1 (1993), another case that involved operating a motor vehicle while intoxicated. The possibility of a five-year probation and $5000 fine did not convert the presumptively petty offense to a serious one for jury trial purposes, the Court held, because they did not approximate or entail as great a loss of liberty as the possibility of imprisonment for more than six months.

We apply a *Blanton* analysis in this case. In light of the 180-day maximum exposure to incarceration for misdemeanor sexual abuse of a minor, we begin with the presumption that the offense is "petty" for Sixth Amendment purposes. The question before us is whether the possibility of deportation refutes that presumption. We note the obvious: there is no comparison between the penalty of deportation and the statutory penalties considered in *Blanton* (temporary license suspension, embarrassing clothing to be worn during two days of community service, and alcohol abuse education course) that were deemed not significant enough to render the DUI offense serious under the Sixth Amendment. Like incarceration, deportation separates a person from established ties to family, work, study, and community. In this forced physical separation, it is similar in severity to the loss of liberty that a prison term entails. . . . Once the actual sentence is served (which could be for a term less than the six-month maximum, or even only probation), a U.S. citizen can return home to family and community and take steps to resume and, possibly, redirect his life. But when a person faces deportation, serving the sentence is only the first step following conviction; once the sentence is completed, the person faces the burdens and anxiety that attend detention pending removal proceedings. Upon removal, the physical separation from family and community lasts at least ten years and, for some, including Mr. Bado, exclusion from the country becomes permanent. This disruption causes harm and suffering to those who are forced to leave and those who remain. Wrenching decisions might have to be made within the family, which could be left without an important source of emotional and financial support. . . .

The loss of liberty, akin to incarceration, that results from removal as well as the Court's repeated statements about its severity, lead us to conclude, under a *Blanton* analysis, that deportation is so onerous a penalty for conviction that it presents the "rare situation" that should ensure the availability of a jury trial in a criminal proceeding even though the penalty of incarceration does not puncture the six-month incarceration line.

[The government argues] that removal, even if it is triggered by a criminal conviction, is a "civil" sanction that should not be considered in a *Blanton* analysis. We disagree. [The *Blanton*] Court considered the possible penalty of license suspension following conviction for DUI relevant in deciding whether the Sixth Amendment guarantees that apply to criminal prosecutions required a jury trial. A license can be suspended, even in the absence of conviction, for purely regulatory reasons such as failure to renew or driving without prescribed vision correction, just as a person may be subject to removal for violating the terms of admission absent a criminal conviction. Yet, in *Blanton*, the Court took into account the possibility of a license suspension as part of its Sixth Amendment analysis because the statute provided that suspension of licensing privileges was a penalty for a DUI conviction. Similarly here, a statutory provision imposes deportation as a penalty for conviction.

[The] argument that deportation is simply a civil measure also overlooks that harsher substantive and procedural requirements apply when deportation is triggered by a criminal conviction than in "regulatory" deportations, such as when a person is out of status (e.g., a person who is working without authorization or enters on a student visa and is no longer in school). Those who are removed as a result of a criminal conviction are ineligible for reentry for a longer period or permanently barred, they are more likely to be detained pending removal proceedings, and, once a removal order has been entered, they are also streamlined through expedited removal proceedings, subjected to additional periods of detention, and extremely limited in their eligibility for relief from deportation. . . .

The government argues that removal should not be considered a penalty in a *Blanton* analysis because (1) the sentencing court does not have authority to order deportation upon conviction for a deportable offense and (2) there would be an "anomaly" if a noncitizen would be entitled to a jury trial but a citizen would not. Neither of these is a factor whose relevance can be gleaned from *Blanton*. [The] Court's consideration of the license suspension for the DUI conviction in *Blanton* was not dependent on whether it was imposed by the sentencing court. Moreover, by expressly declining to consider other enhanced penalties that were not faced by the accused individual, *Blanton* made clear that what is relevant to the Sixth Amendment analysis are the potential penalties to which the particular defendant is exposed upon conviction. In an analogous circumstance, we have rejected a claim that an enhanced penalty for recidivism triggers a jury trial right where the defendant was not "personally" facing the penalty. . . .

The government further argues that removal that is triggered by a criminal conviction should not be taken into account because it is a penalty that results from a congressional enactment and is not part of the penalty designated by the legislature that created the offense, in this case, the Council of the District of Columbia. This argument misapprehends *Blanton*'s meaning and is contrary to its purpose. In *Blanton*, the Court rejected the notion that a court may gauge the seriousness of an offense for Sixth Amendment purposes by coming to a subjective judgment about the "nature" of the offense. Instead, the seriousness of an offense is to be assessed by reference to objective standards—penalties—"resulting from state action, e.g., those mandated by statute or regulation." Through the penalties mandated by public officials and elected representatives, "the laws and practices of the community [are] taken as a gauge of its social and ethical judgments." Congress, as the national legislature, is presumed to reflect the nation's social and ethical judgments. . . .

The government points to cases holding that deportation is not "punishment" for a crime. . . . The cases on which the government relies are not on point because they did not present a Sixth Amendment claim, but arose under different constitutional provisions, the Double Jeopardy Clause of the Fifth Amendment and the Ex Post Facto Clause. This is a significant difference. Because the Constitution's text is silent as to how these Clauses are to be applied, the Court has ruled that the question turns on whether a law retroactively "alters the definition of a crime or increases the punishment for criminal acts," or whether the state is "punishing twice, or attempting a second time to punish criminally, for the same offense." The threshold question of whether either of these Clauses applies in a particular case therefore depends on whether the law or government action under judicial review involves a criminal offense or punishment for a crime. There is no similar threshold question here, however, because the Sixth Amendment by its terms applies to "all criminal prosecutions," and this case involves a criminal prosecution. . . .

Finally, the government asserts that there are "practicalities and uncertainties" as to whether conviction of an offense renders a defendant removable which could make application of a *Blanton* analysis difficult in some cases. The government does not argue that any such difficulties are presented in this case, as it agrees that appellant's conviction makes him deportable. . . . In a case where the prosecution and defense are in disagreement on the question of whether an accused will face the serious penalty of deportation if convicted, the trial court is not without resources to come to a sound resolution of the constitutional issue presented. Government counsel are part of the Department of Justice, which has deep expertise in immigration matters. . . . If necessary, the court presiding over a criminal prosecution can appoint its own expert advisor on immigration law.

We do not expect this to be a common occurrence in Superior Court. . . . Where a jury trial demand is made in a case with a truly vexing issue of deportability, the trial court can decide to default to recognition of the Sixth Amendment right, and avoid the risk of imperiling a conviction that may be obtained after a bench trial, should it eventually be determined that denial of the jury trial demand was based on a flawed judgment on the deportation question. The additional time required for a jury trial may well be offset by the time saved in pretrial argument. . . .

We conclude that the penalty of deportation, when viewed together with the 180-day maximum period of incarceration for misdemeanor sexual abuse of a minor, overcomes the presumption that appellant was charged with a petty offense and triggers the Sixth Amendment right to a trial by jury. As appellant was denied his rightful demand for a jury trial, the conviction is reversed and the case is remanded for further proceedings. So ordered.

WASHINGTON, Senior Judge, concurring.
. . . I write separately because I am concerned that our decision today, while faithful to the dictates of *Blanton*, creates a disparity between the jury trial rights of citizens and noncitizens that lay persons might not readily understand. That disparity is one that the legislature could and, in my opinion, should address. The failure to do so could undermine the public's trust and confidence in our courts to resolve criminal cases fairly.

[For] the first time, a majority of our court has relied on a collateral civil statutory penalty to transmogrify an otherwise petty offense into a serious crime and that means that the courts likely will be faced with new challenges in individual cases to the Act's limitation on the right to jury trials in misdemeanor cases. [There] are many other severe civil statutory penalties that have been attached to criminal convictions, in addition to deportation and, because it is the legislature's intent that must guide our analysis, the Council should speak clearly to the issue of whether the civil penalties that attach to certain misdemeanor crimes reflects a legislative judgment that the commission of those crimes is more serious than the potential criminal sentence might suggest.

Alternatively, the Council could reconsider its decision [in the D.C. Misdemeanor Streamlining Act] to value judicial economy above the right to a jury trial. Restoring the right to a jury trial in misdemeanor cases could have the salutary effect of elevating the public's trust and confidence that the government is more concerned with courts protecting individual rights and freedoms than in ensuring that courts are as efficient as possible in bringing defendants to trial. This may be an important message to send at this time because many communities, especially communities of color, are openly questioning whether courts are truly independent or are merely the end game in the exercise of police powers by the state. Those perceptions are fueled not only by reports that police officers are not being held responsible in the courts for police involved shootings of unarmed suspects but is likely also promoted by unwise decisions, like the one that authorized the placement of two large monuments to law enforcement on the plaza adjacent to the entrance to the highest court of the District of Columbia.

One of the ways that the founders sought to ensure that citizens were protected from overreaching by the government was to guarantee a right to a jury trial to anyone charged with a crime. John Adams is famously quoted as saying, "Representative government and trial by jury are at the heart and lungs of liberty," and Thomas Jefferson considered a trial by jury as "the only anchor . . . imagined by man by which a government can be held to the principles of its constitution." It is why the right to a jury trial is enshrined in the Sixth Amendment to the Constitution. And, while the D.C. Council complied with the letter of the law when it reduced the potential sentences for misdemeanor crimes to a level that made them non-jury demandable, that decision made us one of the few state court jurisdictions in the country that does not guarantee a right to a jury trial for those charged with criminal misdemeanors. Most states recognize that a jury trial in criminal cases is critically important because of the stigma that accompanies a criminal conviction and many of those states accept the fact that any period of incarceration, no matter how short, can have a devastating impact on one's life and livelihood.

So, perhaps the answer to the anomaly created by our decision today is to hew more closely to the plain language of the Sixth Amendment and make no distinction between serious and petty crimes when it comes to an individual's right to a jury trial. If the Council chooses this latter path, it will not only address the disparity created by our attempt to faithfully apply *Blanton* in this case, but the District would also be rejoining the majority of other states where a jury trial in a criminal case is the norm, and not the exception. To me, this latter approach has many virtues.

THOMPSON, Associate Judge, concurring in the judgment.

. . . In my view, we have no basis for concluding that Congress's prescription of deportation for non-citizens who are found to have committed any of the criminal offenses to which the deportation penalty is attached clearly reflects a determination by the legislature that all such offenses are serious ones. Congress has broadly declared as "deportable" offenses everything from possession of any more than 30 grams of marijuana to mass murder. Its declaration that conviction—of any of a long list of enumerated but quite different types of offenses—renders a non-citizen "deportable" is scant if any evidence that it views the offenses as serious in the Sixth Amendment sense. . . .

Congress has afforded non-citizens who have been convicted of some "deportable" offenses avenues of relief to avoid actual removal. This, I believe we can conclude, is a signal from Congress that some offenses that expose non-citizens to the threat of deportation are not so serious after all. . . . By contrast, with respect to one category of offenses—those that Congress has termed "aggravated felonies"— Congress has given what I believe are clear signals that it regards the offenses as serious. . . .

The parties agree that appellant Bado, a non-citizen, was convicted of an aggravated felony. At the time he made his jury demand, it was known that conviction of the crimes with which he was charged (three counts of misdemeanor sexual abuse of a child) would render him ineligible for cancellation of removal and ineligible for the asylum he was actively seeking before an immigration judge at the time he went to trial in the instant matter. Thus, he was charged with offenses that exposed him to inevitable statutory penalties, an inevitability by which Congress has clearly signaled that it regards the offenses as serious. For that reason, applying the teaching of *Blanton*, I conclude that Mr. Bado was entitled to a jury trial.

One final observation: The rationale I have set out above would afford non-citizens a jury trial when they are threatened almost inevitably with removal from this country (a fate that may be of greater concern to a convicted non-citizen than any jail sentence). It does so, however, without expanding the right to a jury trial to non-citizens in circumstances that may be impossible to distinguish from those of our fellow citizens who likely will face severe collateral consequences from misdemeanor convictions, but who, under our statutory and case law, have no right to a jury trial. . . .

FISHER, Associate Judge, dissenting.

According to the majority, a citizen charged with misdemeanor sexual abuse of a child does not have a right to a jury trial, but a noncitizen charged with the very same offense does. This is a startling result, neither compelled nor justified by Supreme Court precedent. . . . Under *Blanton*, the seriousness of the offense is not measured on a case-by-case basis. . . .

If the maximum term of imprisonment is six months or less, a crime "is presumptively a petty offense to which no jury trial right attaches." United States v. Nachtigal, 507 U.S. 1 (1993). A defendant may rebut this presumption, but "only if he can demonstrate that any additional statutory penalties, viewed in conjunction with the maximum authorized period of incarceration, are so severe that they clearly reflect a legislative determination that the offense in question is a 'serious' one." *Blanton*. This will be a "rare situation," the Court observed. Indeed, there has not yet been a case in which the Supreme Court found that an offense with a maximum authorized incarceration period of 6 months was a serious one so as to require a jury trial under the Sixth Amendment.

Under *Blanton* and related Supreme Court decisions, the right to a jury trial turns on the seriousness of the charged offense in the eyes of the legislature that created it, as indicated by the severity of the penalty authorized and made applicable across the board to anyone who commits it. In fixing the maximum penalty for a crime, a legislature includes within the definition of the crime itself a judgment about the seriousness of the offense. The seriousness of the offense is not measured on a case-by-case basis by the varying additional consequences an individual defendant might suffer based on his own circumstances unrelated to commission of the crime. . . .

Deportation or removal is not part of the criminal penalty. It is, rather, a result (serious, no doubt) of abusing the privilege of living in this country.

[The] majority's analysis enormously complicates the practice of criminal law. Immigration law can be complex, and it is a legal specialty of its own. . . . Trial judges and practitioners of criminal law will have to acquire the expertise to make these judgments.

[Further] complications are certain to follow. Defendants inevitably will rely upon the majority's flawed analysis in an effort to distinguish themselves from others charged with the same offense. Will a doctor who stands to lose his professional license if convicted be entitled to a jury trial although a day laborer will not? What about a defendant who may be evicted from public housing or lose (or be denied) other government benefits if he is convicted?

A citizen charged with this offense would not be entitled to a jury trial. The answer should be the same for Mr. Bado. I respectfully dissent.

■ MARYLAND COURTS AND JUDICIAL PROCEEDINGS CODE §12-401

(d) (1) A defendant who has been found guilty of a municipal infraction . . . or a Code violation . . . may appeal from the final judgment entered in the District Court. . . .

(f) [In any criminal case, including a] case in which sentence has been imposed or suspended following a plea of nolo contendere or guilty, and an appeal in a municipal infraction or Code violation case, an appeal shall be tried de novo [in the trial court of original jurisdiction for felonies, the Circuit Court].

(g) In a criminal appeal that is tried de novo: (1) There is no right to a jury trial unless the offense charged is subject to a penalty of imprisonment or unless there is a constitutional right to a jury trial for that offense. . . .

Notes

1. *Jury trials and petty offenses under state constitutions: majority position.* The federal courts look primarily to the length of imprisonment imposed as an "objective" measure of a crime's seriousness for purposes of the Sixth Amendment right to a jury trial. A crime whose punishment is more than six months' imprisonment is "presumptively" serious; any crime that is punished by a shorter term of imprisonment is difficult to establish as "serious" under the Sixth Amendment, even when coupled with substantial fines and other penalties.

Virtually all state constitutions guarantee the right to a jury trial, often by stating that the right "shall remain inviolate." Does this language suggest an effort to preserve a right in its limited historical form rather than an effort to declare a more extensive right based in natural law? Most state courts have concluded that the state constitution does not require a jury trial for all offenses, but only for "serious" (as opposed to "petty") offenses. However, most state courts disagree with the federal constitutional definition of a "petty" crime. Fewer than 10 states follow the federal approach and deny a jury trial to defendants charged with a crime punishable by 180 days or less of incarceration. See, e.g., State v. Smith, 672 P.2d 631 (Nev. 1983) (no jury trial for six-month prison term authorized for drunken-driving offense). A larger group of states adopt the federal methodology (focusing on the length of the prison term) but conclude that some shorter period of potential or actual imprisonment is enough to trigger the right to a jury trial. Many states declare that any defendant facing the possibility of any incarceration is entitled to a jury trial. See Opinion of the Justices (DWI Jury Trials), 608 A.2d 202 (N.H. 1992).

A substantial number of state courts reject the federal methodology for determining the scope of the right to a jury trial. Some of these courts continue to insist that jury trials are available only for the most serious crimes, but they give great weight to factors other than the length of potential or actual incarceration in deciding which crimes are serious. See State v. Benoit, 311 P.3d 874 (Or. 2013) (any defendant subjected to pretrial arrest and detention must be provided a jury trial because of "the stigma caused by criminal pre-charging procedures"); Fisher v. State, 504 A.2d 626 (Md. 1986) (considers historical treatment of offense, "infamous" nature of offense, maximum authorized sentence, and place of incarceration). Other courts inquire about the "punitive" nature of the fines imposed. A number of courts turn to history to determine whether the offense is analogous to some crime that was tried by jury at the time the federal constitution was adopted. Medlock v. 1985 Ford F-150 Pick Up, 417 S.E.2d 85 (S.C. 1992). State courts in more than 10 states have declared that the state constitution requires jury trials for all "offenses." The only exceptions involve crimes with trivial punishments or other characteristics that make them criminal offenses in name only. For an overview, see Adam M. Gershowitz, 12 Unnecessary Men: The Case for Eliminating Jury Trials in Drunk Driving Cases, 2011 U. Ill. L. Rev. 961 (2011).

2. *Statutory right to jury trials.* It is common to find state statutes that extend the right to a jury trial to a broader range of cases than the federal or state constitution requires. Some statutes provide a jury trial for a particular offense without declaring any general rule about the availability of jury trials. Others declare generally the minimum lengths of incarceration or minimum fine amounts that will create a statutory right to a jury. See Ohio Rev. Code §2945.17(B)(2) (jury trial for any offense punishable by incarceration or a fine exceeding $1,000); 725, ILCS §5/103-6 (jury trial for "[every] person accused of an offense"). Another type of statute grants a right to jury trial for less serious cases but places conditions on the exercise of the right, such as the payment of a fee. See Colo. Stat. §16-10-109 (granting jury trial for petty offenses, provided defendant pays $25 fee). One form of this "conditional" statutory right to a jury trial appears in two-tiered court systems; the Maryland statute offers an example. These laws allow defendants in some cases initially charged and tried in the misdemeanor-level trial court to "appeal" the case for a trial de novo (before a jury) in the felony-level court. This system, in effect, gives even those charged with misdemeanors a statutory right to a jury trial, but only for those who persist in an appeal from the misdemeanor court. See, e.g., Ark. Code §16-17-703. Do such "conditional" systems effectively deny the right to a jury trial to those defendants without the resources or persistence to jump through the proper hoops before receiving a jury? For further analysis of the variety of statutory jury trial rights in the states, go to the web extension for this chapter at *http://www. crimpro.com/extension/ch17.*

3. *Combining petty offenses.* Will a defendant receive a jury trial if she faces several "petty" charges, where convictions on the multiple counts would authorize

the judge to impose a sentence longer than six months? In Lewis v. United States, 518 U.S. 322 (1996), the Court held that a defendant who is prosecuted in a single proceeding for multiple petty offenses does not have a Sixth Amendment right to a jury trial. Lewis was charged with two counts of obstructing the mail, each charge carrying a maximum authorized prison sentence of six months. The Court concluded that Congress, by setting the maximum prison term at six months, had categorized the offense as petty. Congress's judgment, and not the punishment imposed in a particular case, determines the seriousness of an offense under the Sixth Amendment. See also People v. Foy, 673 N.E.2d 589 (N.Y. 1996).

4. *Trial at option of prosecutor or judge.* Judges in most courts can avoid a jury trial for some crimes that authorize prison or jail sentences if they commit before the trial not to incarcerate the defendants after conviction. Should courts consider suspended sentences as incarceration for purposes of the right to a jury trial? Is it appropriate to allow trial judges to "override" the legislature's decision to make a crime eligible for jury trials?

Prosecutors also have much to say about the availability of a jury trial. The prosecutor can charge a defendant with multiple counts of a petty offense rather than a more serious one, or charge the lesser of two alternative offenses if the more serious offense triggers a jury trial. See City of Casper v. Fletcher, 916 P.2d 473 (Wyo. 1996) (prosecutor in battery case could choose between municipal ordinance, for which jury trial did not attach, and state statute that would qualify for jury trial). Is there any problem with the prosecutor initially filing the more serious charge, and revising the charge to some lesser crime (a nonjury trial offense) only for defendants who insist on a jury trial?

5. *Prevalence of bench trials and jury trials.* The seemingly simple question of how many trials are resolved by juries and how many by judges is surprisingly difficult to answer because of the lack of uniform records and lack of interest in low-level cases. In 2006, about 4 percent of all felony convictions in state courts resulted from jury trials, while about 2 percent of the convictions resulted from bench trials. But this overall rate of felony bench trials hides real differences among types of crimes and among jurisdictions. Juries are much more likely to try violent offenses, and judges are more likely to try drug offenses. Fewer than 10 percent of the felony trials are before the bench in some states (such as Alaska and New Jersey), while more than two-thirds of the trials are before the bench in other states (such as Virginia). See Sean Doran, John D. Jackson & Michael L. Seigel, Rethinking Adversariness in Nonjury Criminal Trials, 23 Am. J. Crim. L. 1 (1995). Note that these figures deal only with felony trials. A much smaller proportion of misdemeanor cases are tried before juries.

6. *Waiver of jury trial: majority position.* Many defendants who could insist on a trial by jury instead waive the right and proceed to a bench trial with the judge as the sole factfinder. Sometimes the waiver of a jury trial will be welcome news to the government and to the public since jury trials are expensive and difficult to administer. Judges may even encourage some defendants to waive jury trials, perhaps by discounting the sentence in cases tried to the bench, a local practice that might result in lower overall levels of plea bargaining. However, there are times when the prosecutor or the judge will not share the defendant's desire to bypass the jury. The defendant may believe the judge will better understand a complex defense or will react with more restraint to an abhorrent crime.

Almost all jurisdictions allow a defendant to waive the right to a jury trial; more than 30 states, however, condition the defendant's waiver of the jury on the judge's agreement that a bench trial is appropriate. N.Y. Crim. Proc. Law §320.10; Or. Rev. Stat. §136.001(2). About 10 states give the defendant the unilateral power to select a bench trial over a jury trial. See, e.g., Iowa R. Crim. P. 2.17(1). About 30 states and the federal courts also empower the prosecutor to block the defendant's choice of a bench trial. Fed. R. Crim. P. 23(a); Cal. Const. art. I, §16 ("consent of both parties"); Fla. R. Crim. P. 3.260. For a graphic summary of the state positions on this issue, consult the web extension for this chapter at *http://www.crimpro.com/extension/ch17*.

Until the early twentieth century, very few states gave defendants facing felony charges the option to waive jury trial for bench trial; amendments to the rules allowing waiver of jury trial occurred at the same time that plea bargaining began to dominate criminal practice in the United States. Is there any connection between these developments? See George Fisher, Plea Bargaining's Triumph: A History of Plea Bargaining in America (2003).

Like the U.S. Supreme Court in Singer v. United States, 380 U.S. 24 (1965), most state courts have rejected constitutional challenges to rules and statutes that require the consent of the prosecution and the court before a waiver takes effect. People v. Kirby, 487 N.W.2d 404 (Mich. 1992); but see State v. Baker, 976 P.2d 1132 (Or. 1999) (statute granting the prosecution right to insist on jury trial despite defendant's waiver violates the waiver provision of Oregon Constitution's jury trial guarantee). In jurisdictions that permit the court to deny a defendant's request for a bench trial, the rules often say that a trial court has discretion to deny such a request, and an appellate court can review that decision for an abuse of discretion. What circumstances might amount to an abuse of discretion?

7. *Outcome differences between bench trials and jury trials.* The evidence is mixed on whether bench trials or jury trials result more often in acquittals. The most broad-based studies indicate that jurors acquit more often. Theodore Eisenberg et al., Judge-Jury Agreement in Criminal Cases: A Partial Replication of Kalven & Zeisel's The American Jury, 2 J. Empirical Legal Studies 171, 173 (2005) (arguing that a pro-acquittal tendency reflects jurors' insistence on a higher standard of proof). But there is contrary evidence, particularly from the federal court system, with its distinctive workloads and sentencing rules. See Andrew Leipold, Why Are Federal Judges So Acquittal Prone, 83 Wash. U. L.Q. 151 (2005) (finding that the conviction rate after bench trials was significantly lower than the conviction rate after jury trials); Kenneth S. Klein, Unpacking the Jury Box, 47 Hastings L.J. 1325 (1996) (juries convict at higher rates than judges in felony cases; the opposite is true in misdemeanor cases).

8. *Law-trained judges.* Most state court systems have different levels of trial courts, with "limited jurisdiction" courts to try misdemeanors and other minor offenses in the first instance, and "general jurisdiction" courts to try all felonies and (sometimes) the cases of defendants who appeal a conviction from the limited jurisdiction court. Judges in the general jurisdiction courts virtually always have legal training. However, a number of judges in limited jurisdiction courts do not have legal training. Courts have usually turned aside due process challenges to this arrangement, but the opinions often rely on the fact that cases tried before a nonlawyer judge will ultimately receive meaningful review by a law-trained judge. See North v. Russell, 427 U.S. 328 (1976); Amrein v. State, 836 P.2d 862 (Wyo. 1992); but see Gordon v. Justice Court for Yuba, 525 P.2d 72 (Cal. 1974) (criminal trials before nonlawyer

judges violate due process). What differences would you expect in the arguments that lawyers make to nonlawyer judges?

9. *Mixed panels and other decisionmakers.* Many other countries involve citizens on panels resembling juries to decide criminal cases. See Neil Vidmar, World Jury Systems (2000). Consider, for example, the use of multi-member panels in Germany to try serious offenses. The panels are made up of three "professional" and two "lay" judges. Japan and South Korea also employ a version of the German mixed court. The important question in designing such mixed panels is the division of authority between professional judges and lay jurors. What kinds of information do the lay jurors hear? Do they participate in sentencing?

Compared to judges presiding at trials in legal systems outside the United States, judges are relatively unconstrained when they preside at bench trials in this country. The same judge may decide a suppression motion and then later rule on guilt or innocence while being aware of the suppressed evidence. Judges in the United States typically do not write a reasoned judgment at the end of a criminal bench trial, while civil law systems require the judge to write a reasoned judgment, at least for more serious crimes. How would the choice between bench trial and jury trial change if bench trials were regulated more closely?

Problem 17-1. Judge Shopping and Jury Trial Waivers

Early in the morning of March 17, Tyeric Lamar Lessley, Lessley's cousin, and a friend finished their evening at a nightclub in Minneapolis. When the three men left the nightclub at closing time, the police were responding to an unrelated fight outside the nightclub and sprayed mace on the three men. All three of them got into a car and Lessley's cousin drove toward a service station to wash out their eyes. While on their way to the service station, their car collided with a pickup truck.

Four men, driving away from a nearby bar, occupied the pickup truck. After the collision, Lessley's cousin continued driving, prompting the occupants of the truck to follow the car. Lessley pulled out a handgun. The men in the truck eventually were able to stop the car. Lessley got out and began to walk away from the two vehicles. An occupant of the pickup truck, Darby Claar, got out of the truck and followed Lessley on foot. Claar caught up with Lessley and punched him twice, including once in the jaw. Armed with the handgun, Lessley shot twice at Claar and hit him once. Lessley then left the scene. Police officers investigating the traffic accident discovered Claar's body about a half-block from the scene of the traffic accident. An autopsy determined that Claar died from a single bullet wound.

There is some dispute about the distance from which Lessley shot Claar. Lessley said the men were about six feet apart, but the medical examiner estimated that the gun was fired from a range of anywhere from "two centimeters up to three feet." Lessley told the police that he shot Claar in self-defense. He also said that he fired twice at Claar after Claar tried to make him return to the scene of the accident. Lessley said that he left the shooting scene because he had a gun and was scared.

The State charged Lessley with murder in the second degree (intentional homicide) and murder in the second degree (unintentional homicide committed during a felony). The State exercised its right under Minn. R. Crim. P. 26.03, subd. 13(4) to remove the judge who was initially assigned to the case. The case was reassigned to a second judge and Lessley exercised his right under Rule 26.03 to remove that judge. Imagine that you are a trial judge in Minnesota, and this case was reassigned to you at this point in the proceedings.

Lessley filed a motion, asking you to allow him to plead guilty to the lesser offense of second-degree manslaughter. You denied that motion but observed that "the State's evidence of intent is limited," and noted that "defendant's remorse is compelling." You also characterized the case as one involving "idiocy" and "a bunch of drunkards."

On the scheduled day of trial, Lessley filed a motion to waive his right to a jury trial. Immediately after Lessley filed that motion, the State said that it would ask you to remove yourself from the case. The prosecutor said that you "indicated to us in chambers and on the record that this is more of a manslaughter matter. And I think that unfortunately the Court has shown bias toward the defendant in this case, and I respectfully ask that you recuse yourself." You denied the State's motion to recuse yourself from the case.

The State then asked you to deny Lessley's request for a jury trial waiver. Minnesota Rules of Criminal Procedure, Rule 26.01, specifically addresses jury-trial-waiver requests: "The defendant, with the approval of the court may waive jury trial on the issue of guilt provided the defendant does so personally in writing or orally upon the record in open court, after being advised by the court of the right to trial by jury and after having had an opportunity to consult with counsel." How would you rule on this motion? Are the relevant considerations for this decision the same as the factors that inform your ruling on a recusal motion? Cf. State v. Lessley, 779 N.W.2d 825 (Minn. 2010).

B. SELECTION OF JURORS

Jury members are selected in two stages. The first stage involves the selection of the "venire"—the pool of potential jurors. Early in American history, only adult white males who owned a certain amount of property were eligible to serve on a jury. Over time, eligibility for service expanded in steps, first covering white males without property and eventually reaching all adults. As legal eligibility for jury service expanded, however, the actual methods for selecting the jury venire did not keep pace. Under the "key man" selection system used in many states, public officials or prominent citizens served as jury commissioners (the "key men") to nominate potential jurors. Not surprisingly, their nominations did not reflect a demographic cross section of the eligible jurors in the community.

The Supreme Court periodically has decided cases requiring the states to change their selection processes to produce venires that better represent the community. In the first case to deal with the question, Strauder v. West Virginia, 100 U.S. 303 (1880), the Court sustained an equal protection challenge to a statute excluding blacks from the jury venire. In Norris v. Alabama, 294 U.S. 587 (1935), the Court quashed an indictment because blacks were excluded *in fact* from serving on grand juries in the jurisdiction, even though they were legally eligible to participate. In later cases, the Court did not require the defendant to show complete exclusion of a racial group from jury service: A substantial disparity between the racial mix of the county's population and the racial mix of the venire, together with an explanation of how the jury selection process had created this outcome, would be enough to establish a prima facie case of discrimination. The government would then have to rebut the presumption of discrimination. See Turner v. Fouche, 396 U.S. 346 (1970) (underrepresentation of African Americans); Castaneda v. Partida, 430 U.S. 482 (1977) (underrepresentation of Mexican Americans).

The Supreme Court has also recognized a defendant's right to challenge the process of creating the venire, based on the Sixth Amendment's promise of an "impartial jury." In Taylor v. Louisiana, 419 U.S. 522 (1975), the Court held that a Louisiana law placing on the venire only those women who affirmatively requested jury duty violated the Sixth Amendment's requirement that the jury represent a "fair cross section" of the community. Duren v. Missouri, 439 U.S. 357 (1979), summarized the current test followed in both federal and state courts for challenging a venire under the Sixth Amendment and its analogs. The defendant must show that (1) the group allegedly excluded is a "distinctive" group in the community, (2) the representation of this group in venires is not reasonable in relation to the number of such persons in the community, and (3) this underrepresentation is a result of "systematic" exclusion of the group (not necessarily intentional discrimination) in the jury selection process. At that point, the burden of proof shifts to the government to show a "significant state interest" that justifies use of the method that systematically excludes a group. Courts have determined the distinctiveness of groups that are "cognizable" under the Sixth Amendment by looking to the shared attitudes and experiences of the group. By and large, this has meant that racial groups and gender are considered distinctive, while age groups (such as 18- to 24-year-olds) are not. For a sample of the state and federal constitutional cases on the construction of the jury venire, go to the web extension for this chapter at *http:// www.crimpro.com/extension/ch17.*

1. Voir Dire

A second stage of juror selection takes place for each case. From among a large pool of prospective jurors at the courthouse on a given day, a random group will be called to a particular courtroom for a specific case. An initial group of jurors are seated in the jury box, and then the judge and lawyers determine which individuals will serve on the jury for that case. There are two ways to remove a potential juror from the box. First, there are removals "for cause": The judge removes from the panel any jurors who are not qualified to serve or are not capable of performing their duties. Second, the attorneys may remove a limited number of qualified jurors through "peremptory" challenges.

Each of these methods of removing potential jurors requires the judge and the attorneys to learn something about the attitudes and experiences of the individual jurors. Jurors are questioned in a process known as *voir dire* ("to speak the truth," or more literally, "to see to say"). In most jurisdictions, statutes and rules of procedure allow both the judge and the attorneys to formulate the questions; often the judge asks questions proposed by counsel, but sometimes the attorneys query potential jurors directly. Fewer than 10 states allow the attorneys to conduct all the questioning. Some questions are directed to the jurors as a group, while follow-up questions with individual jurors are typical in most places. Regardless of the voir dire process described in statutes or procedure rules, the trial judge retains discretion to control the questions that attorneys can ask at voir dire.

The best approach to voir dire is a subject of great interest among trial attorneys. One influential publication on the topic starts with advice about the basic objectives of the questioner: "Lawyers can approach the voir dire process as an interrogation, [as a] job interview, or as a conversation." A conversational style of questioning, carried out with empathy and friendly interest, is most likely to bring out open and candid answers from jurors. Jeffrey T. Fredrick, Mastering Voir Dire and Jury Selection: Gaining an Edge in Questioning and Selecting a Jury 83-87 (2005). Jurors also tend to like lawyers who are similar to them, and offer more complete and revealing answers to such lawyers. The questioner can encourage this process by pointing out experiences that the juror and the lawyers have shared, such as attendance at the same university or growing up in the same neighborhood.

The juror's ability to identify with the defendant is also critical from the point of view of defense counsel. The legendary trial attorney Clarence Darrow, in a 1936 magazine article, argued that an attorney can make informed guesses on this question by noting the religion and ethnicity of the potential jurors.

> Every knowing lawyer seeks for a jury of the same sort of men as his client; men who will be able to imagine themselves in the same situation and realize what verdict the client wants. . . . In this undertaking, everything pertaining to the prospective juror needs to be questioned and weighed: his nationality, his business, religion, politics, social standing, family ties, friends, habits of life and thought; the books and newspapers he likes and reads, and many more matters that combine to make a man; all of these qualities and experiences have left their effect on ideas, beliefs and fancies that inhabit his mind. . . .
>
> The most important point to learn is whether the prospective juror is humane. This must be discovered in more or less devious ways. As soon as "the court" sees what you want, he almost always blocks the game. Next to this, in having more or less bearing on the question, is the nationality, politics, and religion of the person examined for the jury. . . .
>
> An Irishman is called into the box for examination. There is no reason for asking about his religion; he is Irish; that is enough. We may not agree with his religion, but it matters not, his feelings go deeper than any religion. You should be aware that he is emotional, kindly and sympathetic. If he is chosen as a juror, his imagination will place him in the dock; really, he is trying himself. You would be guilty of malpractice if you got rid of him, except for the strongest reasons. An Englishman is not so good as an Irishman, but still, he has come through a long tradition of individual rights, and is not afraid to stand alone; in fact, he is never sure that he is right unless the great majority is against him. . . .
>
> If a Presbyterian enters the jury box and carefully rolls up his umbrella, and calmly and critically sits down, let him go. He is cold as the grave; he knows right from wrong, although he seldom finds anything right. He believes in John Calvin and eternal punishment. Get rid of him with the fewest possible words before he contaminates the others; unless you and your clients are Presbyterians you probably are a bad lot, and even though you may be a Presbyterian, your client most likely is guilty. . . .
>
> Never take a wealthy man on a jury. He will convict, unless the defendant is accused of violating the anti-trust law, selling worthless stocks or bonds, or something of that kind. Next to the Board of Trade, for him, the penitentiary is the most important of all public buildings. . . .

Clarence Darrow, How to Pick a Jury, Esquire, May 1936.

▮ KEITH FILMORE v. STATE

813 A.2d 1112 (Del. 2003)

STEELE, J.

In October 2001, a Superior Court jury convicted Appellant Keith C. Filmore of Assault in the Third Degree and Disorderly Conduct. Before jury selection, Filmore's counsel filed a written motion requesting five special voir dire questions. Question five requested that the trial judge inquire as follows: "The alleged victims of this offense are White Females. The Defendant is a Black Male. Do you have any prejudice, however slight, against the Defendant which may [affect] your ability to render a fair and impartial verdict?" . . . The State objected and the trial judge refused to put [question five] to the jury venire. We reverse because the trial judge's refusal to put Filmore's question five, or one similar to it, unfairly prejudiced Filmore by failing to place the issue of prospective racial prejudice squarely before the jury as a matter of essential fairness as required by Article I, Section 7, of the Delaware Constitution and our case law. . . .

On the evening of November 21, 2000, Filmore entered a convenience store in Cheswold, Delaware. Filmore asked the store manager if he could use the store telephone. The manager directed Filmore to the pay phone located outside the store. The manager testified that Filmore began entering and leaving the store and asking customers for a ride. When Filmore started to cause a serious disruption and used foul language, the manager telephoned the Delaware State Police and requested assistance with a disorderly customer.

Filmore informed the manager that he wanted to find the bus station and asked the manager to find a telephone number for the bus station. The manager asked Filmore what bus station he wanted, but Filmore did not seem to know and according to the manager: "He picked up the phone book and he said, 'Eat this mother fucker,' and that's when he picked it up, pulled his arm back, and just wailed it at me and hit me right up here on the side of my face. It happened so fast, I didn't have time to move." After throwing the telephone book which struck the manager, Filmore ran out of the store. Two Delaware State Police officers responded to the manager's complaint and testified that the manager had a red mark on her face. The police officers later apprehended and arrested Filmore. . . .

Pursuant to provisions of Del. Super. Ct. Cr. R. 24(a), Filmore's counsel filed a written motion for five special voir dire questions. Before jury selection on the first day of trial, the trial judge conducted a hearing to consider the motion. The State objected to question number five on the basis that the question was covered by a standard bias inquiry. . . . In response to the State's objection to the proposed voir dire question, the trial judge stated: "the standard question is do you have any bias or prejudice for or against the State or the defendant?" The trial prosecutor argued against the inclusion of Filmore's proposed question five as follows:

> The State would ask that the question not be asked. They're already asked if, for any reason, they cannot be fair, and it's going to be obvious to the jury that the defendant is a black male. Injecting—making race an issue by means of this question, the State submits, is not fair. It's not relevant. Nobody is going to make race an issue in this trial. The State is not. Hopefully, the defense will not, although this question seems to be an attempt to do that.

> I mean, one would hope that the jury is going to be color blind in the sense that they're not going to focus on the race of the witnesses or the race of the defendant, they're not going to let that affect their thinking, and certainly the State would hope that that's the case and we're not going to try inject that as an issue. So, why this has to be brought up, I really don't have any idea, but they're going to be asked whether there's any reason they would be partial to one side or the other and I think this makes—it sort of tries to create a racial issue where there is none.

In response to the State's opposition, Filmore's trial counsel argued:

> Your Honor, the reason why it's important is because the case law says that where this is, in fact, the circumstance, it is proper. It is based on the Fourteenth Amendment. The Fourteenth Amendment was passed 125 or some-odd years ago basically to benefit individuals of the black race that they would not be discriminated against, and because of that, this question basically has been accepted for years and years. It is the proper way to be done.
>
> I would also like to assume that individuals are not prejudiced, but I'm also old enough to know that things don't always turn out the way they should in theory. If someone has a particular problem with this defendant for some reason and if they come forward and tell the Court, they should be excused, but it's an appropriate question, is a question which is routinely asked, and we'd ask the Court to give it.

. . . After hearing further comments from the trial prosecutor, the trial judge denied the request and stated: "I don't recall ever giving this instruction. I don't see a need for it at the present time for the reasons that I think [the State] has stated on the record, so I'm not going to give it."

Filmore alleges the trial judge committed reversible error when he denied Filmore's proposed voir dire question concerning racial bias. Specifically, Filmore alleges the trial judge's failure to question prospective jurors on racial prejudice violated his rights under the federal Constitution and the Constitution of this State. We review claims of constitutional violations de novo. With respect to any inquiry into possible racial prejudice, the trial judge retains discretion as to the form and number of questions on the subject.

The United States Supreme Court has held that the United States Constitution does not require a question about juror racial bias unless there are "special circumstances" in the case. Ristaino v. Ross, 424 U.S. 589 (1976). Special circumstances exist if racial issues are "inextricably bound up with the conduct of the trial." . . . The *Ristaino* holding is not an interpretation of the United States Constitution (and therefore neither binding on state courts nor a limitation on state courts' policy to employ more stringent cautions to explore and rule out racial bias), but stems from the Court's supervisory capacity over the federal courts. Rosales-Lopez v. United States, 451 U.S. 182 (1981). In the federal system when racial issues are "inextricably bound up with the conduct of the trial," a voir dire question is mandatory "when requested by a defendant accused of a violent crime and where the defendant and the victim are members of different racial or ethnic groups."

In Feddiman v. State, 558 A.2d 278, 282-83 (Del. 1989), this Court discussed the foregoing precedent and held "the same higher standard is applicable in the courts of this State by virtue of Article I, Section 7 of the Delaware Constitution." A jury convicted Feddiman of knocking a victim off of her bicycle, and taking her away in his automobile to two separate locations. During the course of transporting the victim, and at each location, Feddiman forced the victim to engage in various acts of sexual intercourse. Feddiman's defense counsel submitted a written request for the trial judge to ask a voir dire question concerning possible racial prejudice. The question submitted by defense counsel and later asked by the trial judge was: "The victim in this case is a white person. The defendant is black. Do you have any prejudice, however slight, against black people which would affect you in any way in deciding this case regarding their sexual proclivities?"

In *Feddiman*, we held that Article I, Section 7 of the Delaware Constitution required the trial judge to question prospective jurors about racial prejudice and that the above question met that requirement. [We also noted, however, that "subject to the essential demands of fairness, the trial court has broad discretion in determining the scope and form of question to be asked on voir dire." Thus, the trial judge need not adopt verbatim the question submitted by the defense counsel. Once the trial judge determines an inquiry of racial bias is necessary, the trial judge need only inquire to a degree necessary to ensure the defendant is afforded all of the rights he is entitled to under the federal Constitution and the Constitution of this State.]

If for some reason our holding in *Feddiman* seems unclear, we announce the following bright line rule: Our view that Article I Section 7 of the Delaware Constitution calls for the "essential demands of fairness" requires that the trial judge question prospective jurors about racial prejudice when: (1) the defendant stands accused of a violent crime; (2) the defendant and victim are members of different racial groups; and (3) the defense attorney specifically requests the trial court to question the jurors during voir dire concerning potential racial prejudice.

This case, like *Feddiman*, involves an accusation of violent crime, an African-American defendant, a Caucasian victim, and a specific request by defense counsel for the trial court to question the jurors during voir dire concerning the possibility of racial prejudice. In fact, the very question proposed by Filmore's defense counsel parallels the question asked in *Feddiman*. Our jurisprudence mandates strict adherence to the more sensitive approach for ferreting out racial prejudice set forth in *Feddiman* and reiterated in our holding today. The trial judge should have followed *Feddiman* and the now well established practice in our courts to ask the venire a question on voir dire directly addressing the issue of possible racial prejudice. Race was injected into this case by its factual circumstances and not, as the State argued, by a sensitive question during voir dire seeking to expose bigotry. A broad antiseptic question seeking to explore "bias for or against the defendant or the state" as an institutional entity falls woefully short of a fair and adequate inquiry into the onerous potential taint of racial bigotry present in every case where an alleged victim of a violent crime is a member of another race than that of the accused. Accordingly, the trial judge erred by not making a fair inquiry into the potential of racial prejudice among the prospective jurors consistent with the "demands of essential fairness" mandated by our Constitution. . . .

Notes

1. *Racial bias questions on voir dire: majority position.* As the Delaware opinion in *Filmore* indicates, the federal constitution requires the judge to ask specific voir dire questions about racial prejudice only when "special circumstances" in the case

create a "reasonable possibility" that the jury will be influenced by racial prejudice. Virtually all state courts now agree on this general principle, saying that some "special circumstances" must be present before a trial court is obliged to ask racial prejudice questions on voir dire. See State v. Fernandez, 876 A.2d 221 (N.H. 2005). Older decisions more often declared in general terms a defendant's right to insist on questions about racial prejudice. See Pinder v. State, 8 So. 837 (Fla. 1891) (requiring questions on racial prejudice in murder case because such information is of "most vital import" to defendant). A few state courts operate under a broader rule, either as a matter of state constitutional law or as a ruling under the state court's supervisory powers. They declare that a trial court must ask (or allow the attorneys to ask) a voir dire question related to racial prejudice if one of the parties requests such a question. See Hernandez v. State, 742 A.2d 952 (Md. 1999) (voir dire question related to race is available upon request to a defendant without a showing of special circumstances); Cynthia Lee, A New Approach to Voir Dire on Racial Bias, 5 UC Irvine L. Rev. 843 (2015).

2. *Special circumstances defined.* The exact nature of the "special circumstances" that most courts require before asking a voir dire question about racial prejudice depends on the facts of individual cases. In Ham v. South Carolina, 409 U.S. 524 (1973), an African American civil rights activist, who was charged with a drug offense, defended on the basis that the police framed him in retaliation for his active, and widely known, civil rights activities. A voir dire question related to racial prejudice was required in that case. In Ristaino v. Ross, 424 U.S. 589 (1976), on the other hand, the court ruled that no special circumstances were present. James Ross was tried in a Massachusetts court with two other black men for armed robbery and assault. The victim of the alleged crimes was a white man employed as a uniformed security guard. Under a state statute, the court was required during voir dire to inquire generally into prejudice. Ross asked the judge to question the prospective jurors specifically about racial prejudice. The judge refused to ask the more specific question. The Supreme Court held that a specific inquiry was not required in this case, based on the "mere fact that the victim of the crimes alleged was a white man and the defendants were Negroes." Racial issues were not "inextricably bound up with the conduct of the trial."

Most state courts say that special circumstances must amount to more than the fact that the defendant and the victim (or the arresting officer) are of different races. See Commonwealth v. Moffett, 418 N.E.2d 585 (Mass. 1981). But beyond this, there is little agreement about what qualifies as a "special" circumstance. State courts are split over whether charges of a "violent" crime are enough to invoke racial prejudice questions. Some conclude that a violent crime is enough, but others require some more specific showing. People v. Peeples, 616 N.E.2d 294 (Ill. 1993) (murder, no questions required); Hill v. State, 661 A.2d 1164 (Md. 1995) (narcotics charges, questions required). Rape cases present some of the most compelling cases for questions about racial prejudice. In such cases, courts have concluded more often than not that racial prejudice questions were necessary in the case at hand, even if a blanket rule was not necessary.

Why have so few courts adopted a per se rule allowing the parties to insist on specific voir dire questioning about racial prejudice in any criminal case? Do such questions cause any harm? Do the questions create racial tensions or stereotyping where they would not otherwise appear? Do they allow a party to begin arguing a case before the evidence is introduced, by casting a case in racial terms?

3. *Voir dire questions on other matters.* The trial court has substantial discretion over the content of voir dire questions regarding questions other than race. However, if the particular circumstances of a case make it reasonably likely that some potential jurors will not be able to render an impartial verdict, the court should inquire into those subjects if the parties request it. See Pearson v. State, 86 A.3d 1232 (Md. 2014) (trial court, on request, must ask voir dire question, "Do any of you have strong feelings about [the charged crime]?"). For instance, when a case has received media attention before trial, the judge asks specific questions about the juror's familiarity with the news coverage. Again, however, the trial court has broad discretion to decide how many questions to ask and whether to question jurors individually or as a group.

Problem 17-2. Defendant Bias and Voir Dire

The decomposed body of Delores Jackson, a black female, was found in a wooded area in Riceland County, South Carolina. The pathologist determined that she died from a blow to the head from a blunt instrument. After the media publicized the discovery of the body, several witnesses reported to the authorities that Charles Cason had admitted killing a black woman in October of the previous year. Further investigation led police to other witnesses, who said that Cason had been drinking on the day of the alleged murder. He was angry because his sister-in-law failed to pick him up at work as promised. Jackson jeered at Cason on the bus ride home and during their walk down Decker Boulevard toward their respective homes. Cason's neighbors told police that he had in his possession some of Jackson's personal effects after she disappeared, suggesting a robbery. Two witnesses said that Cason admitted several days later that he killed Jackson, and used appalling language to describe the victim: "I killed a nigger bitch."

Prior to trial, defense counsel requested a specific voir dire to ascertain racial bias on the part of the jury. They requested the specific voir dire because two prosecution witnesses planned to testify at trial about Cason's description of the victim. The prosecutors objected to the voir dire question; they said that they planned to use Cason's pejorative words to show his state of mind and not to show that race was a motive for the crime.

The trial judge refused defense counsel's request for the specific voir dire question about race. Rather, the trial judge asked a general question as to bias or prejudice. The trial judge explained that a specific question related to race is required only when there are "special circumstances creating a constitutionally significant likelihood that, absent questioning about racial prejudice, the jurors would not be indifferent in the matter."

S.C. Code Ann. §14-7-1020 provides in pertinent part as follows:

> The court shall, on motion of either party in the suit, examine on oath any person who is called as a juror therein to know whether he . . . has any interest in the case, has expressed or formed any opinion, or is sensible of any bias or prejudice therein. . . . If it appears to the court that the juror is not indifferent in the cause, he shall be placed aside as to the trial of that cause and another shall be called.

The jury convicted, and Cason appealed. How would you rule? Compare *State v. Cason*, 454 S.E.2d 888 (S.C. 1995).

2. *Dismissal for Cause*

Recall that there are two methods to remove potential jurors from the panel: dismissal of any unqualified jurors "for cause," and dismissal of a limited number of qualified jurors based on "peremptory challenges" by the parties. We now consider the first of these methods of removal.

A potential juror might be unqualified to serve in any cases at all: For instance, the juror might be unable to understand English or might be a felon ineligible for jury duty. The juror might also be qualified to serve in some cases but not in others, as when a juror is closely related to the defendant or the alleged victim. More generally, the judge must dismiss a juror for cause whenever it appears that the juror cannot keep an open mind about the evidence and apply the relevant law. All these standards are straightforward, but they play out in a complex setting. Many jurors would prefer to avoid lengthy jury duty; the judge would prefer to seat the jury as quickly as possible without excusing many potential jurors; and the parties would prefer to convince the judge to remove unsympathetic jurors from the panel rather than using their limited peremptory challenges. Everyone concerned must predict the jurors' future behavior based on brief answers to questions that are continually being rephrased.

■ TEXAS CODE OF CRIMINAL PROCEDURE ART. 35.16

(a) A challenge for cause is an objection made to a particular juror, alleging some fact which renders the juror incapable or unfit to serve on the jury. A challenge for cause may be made by either the state or the defense for any one of the following reasons:

1. That the juror is not a qualified voter in the state and county under the Constitution and laws of the state; provided, however, the failure to register to vote shall not be a disqualification;

2. That the juror has been convicted of misdemeanor theft or a felony;

3. That the juror is under indictment or other legal accusation for misdemeanor theft or a felony;

4. That the juror is insane;

5. That the juror has such defect in the organs of feeling or hearing, or such bodily or mental defect or disease as to render the juror unfit for jury service . . . ;

6. That the juror is a witness in the case;

7. That the juror served on the grand jury which found the indictment;

8. That the juror served on a petit jury in a former trial of the same case;

9. That the juror has a bias or prejudice in favor of or against the defendant;

10. That from hearsay, or otherwise, there is established in the mind of the juror such a conclusion as to the guilt or innocence of the defendant as would influence the juror in finding a verdict. To ascertain whether this cause of challenge exists, the juror shall first be asked whether, in the juror's opinion, the conclusion so established will influence the juror's verdict. If the juror answers

in the affirmative, the juror shall be discharged without further interrogation by either party or the court. If the juror answers in the negative, the juror shall be further examined as to how the juror's conclusion was formed, and the extent to which it will affect the juror's action; and . . . if the juror states that the juror feels able, notwithstanding such opinion, to render an impartial verdict upon the law and the evidence, the court, if satisfied that the juror is impartial and will render such verdict, may, in its discretion, admit the juror as competent to serve in such case. If the court, in its discretion, is not satisfied that the juror is impartial, the juror shall be discharged;

11. That the juror cannot read or write.

No juror shall be impaneled when it appears that the juror is subject to the second, third or fourth grounds of challenge for cause set forth above, although both parties may consent. All other grounds for challenge may be waived by the party or parties in whose favor such grounds of challenge exist. . . .

(b) A challenge for cause may be made by the State for any of the following reasons:

1. That the juror has conscientious scruples in regard to the infliction of the punishment of death for crime, in a capital case, where the State is seeking the death penalty;

2. That he is related within the third degree of consanguinity or affinity [to the defendant]; and

3. That he has a bias or prejudice against any phase of the law upon which the State is entitled to rely for conviction or punishment.

(c) A challenge for cause may be made by the defense for any of the following reasons:

1. That he is related within the third degree of consanguinity or affinity . . . to the person injured by the commission of the offense, or to any prosecutor in the case; and

2. That he has a bias or prejudice against any of the law applicable to the case upon which the defense is entitled to rely, either as a defense to some phase of the offense for which the defendant is being prosecuted or as a mitigation thereof or of the punishment therefor.

■ STATE v. RECHE SMITH

607 S.E.2d 607 (N.C. 2005)

WAINWRIGHT, J.

On 8 March 2002, defendant Reche Smith was convicted of first-degree murder and felony larceny. The jury found defendant guilty of first-degree murder on the basis of malice, premeditation, and deliberation and under the felony murder rule. Following a capital sentencing hearing, the jury recommended a sentence of death for the murder. The trial court accordingly imposed a sentence of death for the murder and further imposed a sentence of fifteen to eighteen months imprisonment for the felony larceny.

The evidence at trial showed [that the victim, Charles King, invited Smith into his home. Smith choked King until he was unconscious. He bound King's wrists and ankles and covered his face with packaging tape. King died of asphyxiation while

Smith collected property to steal from the home. Smith then drove to another town, rented a hotel room, and bought cocaine.]

Defendant first argues the trial court erred by denying his challenge for cause to prospective juror Charles Hassell. During voir dire, Hassell indicated he was strictly against drug use. Defense counsel then asked Hassell the following question: "Your position is such concerning drug use and abuse that in the event evidence came out in this trial that drug use was involved, it would affect or impair—substantially impair your ability to be fair and impartial; is that correct?" Hassell replied "yes" to this question. Defendant then challenged Hassell for cause. In response, the trial court engaged in the following colloquy with Hassell:

> *The Court:* Well let me—Mr. Hassell, let me ask you . . . just a couple of questions if I could. I don't mean to embarrass you. There are no right or wrong answers, and I want to make sure I understand what you're saying, and I'm trying to frame the question in a way that—are you saying to me, sir, that your personal feelings about the use . . . of or possession of drugs is such that it would interfere or prevent you from following the law in this—as I would instruct you as it relates to this case?
>
> *Mr. Hassell:* Well, I could follow the law.
>
> *The Court:* All right. Now—and so I want to make sure what you're saying—you know, many people don't like drugs, don't approve of drugs, and I don't believe that's the question that [the defense attorney] was asking you, and that may have been how—that may have been what you are saying. I don't know one way or the other.
>
> I'm not trying to put words in your mouth, but I—I'm just making sure I understand that's what you were saying or whether what you were saying is you didn't like drugs or are you saying to me that your feeling is such—I'm asking you as to whether or not your personal feelings about particular crimes or particular types of conduct are such that it would overwhelm your reason and common sense and your ability to follow the law as I would instruct you on should we reach some aspect of the case that may relate to the consumption or use or possession of drugs?
>
> *Mr. Hassell:* No. It wouldn't do that.
>
> *The Court:* You would be able and could and would follow the law as I would instruct you on regardless of what your own personal feelings would be as it relates to the use or possession of or consumption of drugs; is that correct?
>
> *Mr. Hassell:* Yes.
>
> *The Court:* Are you sure of that answer, sir?
>
> *Mr. Hassell:* Yeah.
>
> *The Court:* All right. The Challenge for cause is denied.

Defendant properly preserved error by exhausting the peremptory challenges available to him, renewing his challenge to prospective juror Hassell, and having his renewed challenge denied. N.C.G.S. §15A-1214(h). However, in addition to preserving error, defendant must show error by (1) demonstrating that the trial court abused its discretion in denying the challenge, and (2) showing defendant was prejudiced by this abuse of discretion.

Defendant contends the trial court improperly rehabilitated Hassell with leading questions, despite the prohibition against reducing determinations of juror bias "to question-and-answer sessions which obtain results in the manner of a catechism." Wainwright v. Witt, 469 U.S. 412, 424 (1985). However, we conclude that the trial court did not lead Hassell to answer that he would follow the law. Rather, the trial court questioned Hassell in an effort to determine whether, despite Hassell's feelings about drug use, he could follow the law.

We further conclude that the trial court did not abuse its discretion by denying defendant's challenge for cause. As the United States Supreme Court further stated in *Wainwright*:

> What common sense should have realized experience has proved: many veniremen simply cannot be asked enough questions to reach the point where their bias has been made "unmistakably clear"; these veniremen may not know how they will react when faced with imposing the death sentence, or may be unable to articulate, or may wish to hide their true feelings. Despite this lack of clarity in the printed record, however, there will be situations where the trial judge is left with the definite impression that a prospective juror would be unable to faithfully and impartially apply the law. . . . This is why deference must be paid to the trial judge who sees and hears the juror.

Thus, we must give substantial weight to the trial court's determination that Hassell was not biased. We defer to the trial court who could see and hear Hassell, and we conclude that the trial court did not abuse its discretion by denying defendant's challenge for cause. Defendant's assignment of error is overruled.

Next, defendant contends the trial court erred by failing to give him an additional peremptory challenge. Defendant claims he was entitled to an additional peremptory challenge because the trial court removed a seated juror for cause before the end of jury selection and after defendant had used all but one of his remaining peremptory challenges.

After both defendant and the prosecution accepted prospective juror Gloria Cox, Cox brought the trial court a note from her doctor recommending that she be excused from jury duty because serving as a juror would be too stressful for her. The trial court dismissed Cox for cause. Defendant then requested an additional peremptory challenge, stating that he had undergone a substantial portion of jury selection believing that Cox would be a juror. The trial court denied defendant's request.

Defendant contends the trial court erred by failing to use its inherent authority to restore a peremptory challenge to remedy a prejudicial development in jury selection. However, we disagree. Although a trial court must grant a defendant an additional peremptory challenge if, upon reconsideration of the defendant's previously denied challenge for cause, "the judge determines that the juror should have been excused for cause," N.C.G.S. §15A-1214(i), trial courts generally have no authority to grant additional peremptory challenges. In fact, trial courts are "precluded from authorizing any party to exercise more peremptory challenges than specified by statute." State v. Dickens, 484 S.E.2d 553, 561 (N.C. 1997) (holding that the trial court did not err by refusing to grant the defendant an additional peremptory challenge following the reexamination and excusal for cause of a juror). Because the trial court had no authority to provide defendant with additional peremptory challenges, defendant's argument is without merit and we overrule this assignment of error.

Next, defendant contends the trial court failed to comply with the N.C.G.S. §15A-1214(a) requirement for random jury selection when it placed a prospective juror in a specific seat after that juror was randomly called to fill another seat.

Prospective juror Jonas Simpson, who had been summoned in the initial group of venire members to be examined for fitness to serve, was not present when the clerk called his name. The trial court called another prospective juror in Simpson's place. The trial court then examined this prospective juror and two other prospective jurors. Following a recess, Simpson arrived at the courtroom. The trial court placed him in panel A, seat twelve, the panel and seat for which he was originally called. After the trial court and the prosecutor questioned Simpson, the trial court allowed the prosecutor's request to challenge Simpson for cause, finding that Simpson was unequivocally opposed to the death penalty.

Defendant contends the trial court violated the §15A-1214(a) requirement for random jury selection when it placed Simpson in a specific seat. However, defendant has waived review of this issue . . . because he failed to follow the N.C.G.S. §15A-1211(c) procedure for challenging the randomness of jury selection. Subsection 15A-1211(c) states that all such challenges must be in writing, must "specify the facts constituting the ground of challenge," and must be "made and decided before any juror is examined." These challenges must be made at the trial court level. Defendant did not object to the trial court's placement of Simpson in a specific seat. Therefore, defendant has failed to preserve this issue for review, and we overrule his assignment of error. . . .

Notes

1. *Dismissals for cause: majority position.* The judge must confirm that each of the potential jurors meets the general requirements for service, such as residency and literacy requirements. Some states disqualify potential jurors with a prior felony conviction. The judge also evaluates possible sources of bias against the defendant or against the government. The most common source of potential bias is a personal relationship between the juror and some person connected with the case, such as one of the attorneys. The judge might inquire into the prior experiences of the jurors; for instance, the judge might ask if a juror has been a victim of a crime. This ground leads to disqualification less often than do personal relationships. A juror who has learned before trial about the events that will be disputed at trial will receive special scrutiny. Although prior knowledge of the case alone does not disqualify a juror, a judge will sometimes conclude that the juror who has already learned about the events in question will be unable to keep an open mind and base a verdict only on the evidence presented at trial. Even if the judge allows the juror to remain on the panel, one of the parties will almost always remove the knowledgeable juror with a peremptory challenge. Does this special scrutiny of jurors who are aware of the relevant events systematically remove the most informed and intelligent candidates from the jury? Or is this a concern only in cases receiving unusual pretrial publicity?

2. *Excused for hardship.* The judge will at times "excuse" jurors who are qualified in general and who have no particular reason to favor one party or another. Statutes and procedural rules often specify that the judge may exempt jurors for "undue hardship" or "extreme inconvenience." Jurors themselves frequently raise this issue with the judge by describing the financial hardship of jury duty. See Sudler v. State, 611 A.2d 945 (Del. 1992) (trial court's excusal of five jurors based on their unavailability after holiday weekend violated defendant's right to jury trial). H.L. Mencken, the American satirist and journalist of the early twentieth century, defined a jury

with this dynamic in mind: "Jury—A group of twelve men who, having lied to the judge about their hearing, health, and business engagements, have failed to fool him." What behavior might one expect from a juror who faces unusual hardships while serving on a jury? Would the juror predictably favor the prosecution or the defense?

The judge's decision about whether to excuse a juror for hardships interacts with rules about the length of service expected of jurors and the sanctions for citizens who do not appear for jury duty. How do you suppose a judge would react to a juror asking for a hardship excuse in a system requiring 10 days of service from jurors, and where only 5 percent of all citizens who are summoned actually appear for jury duty? Would the judge's response to the hardship request change in a "one day or one trial" system? Under the "one day or one trial" system, prospective jurors serve in a maximum of one trial and complete their service after one day if they are not chosen for a trial.

3. *Dismissals for cause in death penalty cases.* Special problems arise during voir dire in cases in which the prosecutor plans to seek the death penalty. Many jurors have pronounced views about the use of capital punishment, and those who strongly favor or oppose its use may still serve on the jury if they remain able to apply the law that dictates the cases eligible for the death penalty. However, if a juror declares that he would always vote to impose the death penalty, or to recommend against the death penalty, then he will be excluded for cause. See Witherspoon v. Illinois, 391 U.S. 510 (1968); White v. Wheeler, 136 S. Ct. 456 (2015) (state supreme court deserved deference in federal habeas review when it concluded that the exclusion of a juror based on the judge's conclusion that he could not give sufficient assurance of neutrality or impartiality in considering whether the death penalty should be imposed, did not violate the Sixth Amendment). If you were a prosecutor and a juror declares that she believes in the biblical injunction "an eye for an eye," what follow-up questions would you ask?

3. Peremptory Challenges

In addition to removal of jurors for cause, all states allow the parties to "strike" additional jurors without any initial requirement of a reason or explanation. Such strikes are called "peremptory challenges." The following Idaho statute sets out the traditional definition: "A peremptory challenge . . . is an objection to a juror for which no reason need be given, but upon which the court must exclude him." Idaho Stat. §19-2015.

States usually allow a specific number of peremptory challenges, ranging from 2 to 20 or more. In some states, the parties have equal numbers of peremptories, while elsewhere the defense may excuse more jurors than the prosecution.

The procedures for exercising peremptory challenges vary enormously. Statutes and court rules describe the order in which peremptories must be exercised, often establishing a back-and-forth pattern between defense and prosecution. Challenges in some jurisdictions are made in the presence of all the jurors; in some jurisdictions challenges must be made in writing. Generally, to preserve a challenge about jury selection on appeal, a party must exhaust all peremptory challenges. The use of objections for cause and peremptory challenges involves an intense mix of law and trial strategy.

Why allow peremptory challenges? A number of theories have been advanced. Consider the following explanation of the functions of peremptory challenges.

> The peremptory challenge has traditionally served two principal functions. First, the peremptory challenge provides a margin of protection for challenges for cause. [The] difficulties of developing information about bias, together with the risk of error in adjudicating claims of bias, combine to make the peremptory challenge an essential fallback for use when a challenge for cause is rejected. . . .
>
> The second principal function of the peremptory challenge is to provide the parties with an opportunity to participate in the construction of the decision-making body, thereby enlisting their confidence in its decision. To fulfill this function, the peremptory challenge gives the parties the power to exclude jurors who are indisputably free of bias, merely because the parties would prefer to be judged by others instead. . . .

Barbara D. Underwood, Ending Race Discrimination in Jury Selection: Whose Right Is It, Anyway?, 92 Colum. L. Rev. 725 (1992).

It may be helpful to think about a range of potential jurors, some of whom are biased for the prosecution, and others for the defense; indeed it may be helpful to picture the array of jurors along a bell curve (without making any necessary assumptions about the shape of the curve). Some of those biased jurors (and perhaps some unbiased jurors) will be dismissed by the court for "cause," either on the decision of the court or the motion of counsel. But some jurors in the middle of the bell curve will remain who the lawyers believe are likely to favor one side or the other. In theory, peremptory challenges allow the parties to shape a fair jury for their perspective, which may mean both avoiding antagonistic jurors and finding sympathetic ones.

Should lawyers ever be required to explain why they struck a particular juror? Until fairly recent times, these questions had relatively clear answers: peremptory strikes were just that, with no explanation required. Only if prosecutors engaged in a pattern of peremptory strikes across several cases that revealed racial discrimination would a review of those peremptory decisions be allowed. Swain v. Alabama, 380 U.S. 202 (1965). In 1978 California became the first state to prohibit race-based peremptory challenges in individual cases as a matter of state constitutional law, People v. Wheeler, 583 P.2d 748 (Cal. 1978). Massachusetts took a similar position in 1979, Commonwealth v. Soares, 387 N.E.2d 499 (Mass. 1979), as did Florida in 1984, State v. Neil, 457 So. 2d 481 (Fla. 1984). In 1986, the U.S. Supreme Court addressed the claim that the federal constitution prohibited race-based peremptory challenges in Batson v. Kentucky.

■ JAMES BATSON v. KENTUCKY
476 U.S. 79 (1986)

POWELL, J.*

This case requires us to reexamine that portion of Swain v. Alabama, 380 U.S. 202 (1965), concerning the evidentiary burden placed on a criminal defendant who

---

* [Justices Brennan, White, Marshall, Blackmun, Stevens, and O'Connor joined this opinion.—EDS.]

claims that he has been denied equal protection through the State's use of peremptory challenges to exclude members of his race from the petit jury.

I.

Petitioner, a black man, was indicted in Kentucky on charges of second-degree burglary and receipt of stolen goods. On the first day of trial in Jefferson Circuit Court, the judge conducted voir dire examination of the venire, excused certain jurors for cause, and permitted the parties to exercise peremptory challenges. The prosecutor used his peremptory challenges to strike all four black persons on the venire, and a jury composed only of white persons was selected. Defense counsel moved to discharge the jury before it was sworn on the ground that the prosecutor's removal of the black veniremen violated petitioner's rights under the Sixth and Fourteenth Amendments to a jury drawn from a cross section of the community, and under the Fourteenth Amendment to equal protection of the laws. Counsel requested a hearing on his motion. Without expressly ruling on the request for a hearing, the trial judge observed that the parties were entitled to use their peremptory challenges to "strike anybody they want to." The judge then denied petitioner's motion, reasoning that the cross-section requirement applies only to selection of the venire and not to selection of the petit jury itself. The jury convicted petitioner on both counts. . . .

II.

. . . More than a century ago, the Court decided that the State denies a black defendant equal protection of the laws when it puts him on trial before a jury from which members of his race have been purposefully excluded. Strauder v. West Virginia, 100 U.S. 303 (1880). That decision laid the foundation for the Court's unceasing efforts to eradicate racial discrimination in the procedures used to select the venire from which individual jurors are drawn.

[A] defendant has no right to a petit jury composed in whole or in part of persons of his own race. . . . But the defendant does have the right to be tried by a jury whose members are selected pursuant to nondiscriminatory criteria. The Equal Protection Clause guarantees the defendant that the State will not exclude members of his race from the jury venire on account of race, or on the false assumption that members of his race as a group are not qualified to serve as jurors. . . . The harm from discriminatory jury selection extends beyond that inflicted on the defendant and the excluded juror to touch the entire community. Selection procedures that purposefully exclude black persons from juries undermine public confidence in the fairness of our system of justice. . . .

In *Strauder*, the Court invalidated a state statute that provided that only white men could serve as jurors. We can be confident that no State now has such a law. The Constitution requires, however, that we look beyond the face of the statute defining juror qualifications and also consider challenged selection practices to afford protection against action of the State through its administrative officers in effecting the prohibited discrimination. Thus, the Court has found a denial of equal protection where the procedures implementing a neutral statute operated to exclude persons from the venire on racial grounds, and has made clear that the Constitution prohibits all forms of purposeful racial discrimination in selection of jurors. . . .

Accordingly, the component of the jury selection process at issue here, the State's privilege to strike individual jurors through peremptory challenges, is subject to the commands of the Equal Protection Clause. Although a prosecutor ordinarily is entitled to exercise permitted peremptory challenges for any reason at all, as long as that reason is related to his view concerning the outcome of the case to be tried, the Equal Protection Clause forbids the prosecutor to challenge potential jurors solely on account of their race or on the assumption that black jurors as a group will be unable impartially to consider the State's case against a black defendant.

III.

The principles announced in *Strauder* never have been questioned in any subsequent decision of this Court. Rather, the Court has been called upon repeatedly to review the application of those principles to particular facts. A recurring question in these cases, as in any case alleging a violation of the Equal Protection Clause, was whether the defendant had met his burden of proving purposeful discrimination on the part of the State. That question also was at the heart of the portion of Swain v. Alabama we reexamine today. . . .

The record in *Swain* showed that the prosecutor had used the State's peremptory challenges to strike the six black persons included on the petit jury venire. While rejecting the defendant's claim for failure to prove purposeful discrimination, the Court nonetheless indicated that the Equal Protection Clause placed some limits on the State's exercise of peremptory challenges. . . .

To preserve the peremptory nature of the prosecutor's challenge, the Court in *Swain* declined to scrutinize his actions in a particular case by relying on a presumption that he properly exercised the State's challenges. [On the other hand, it] was impermissible for a prosecutor to use his challenges to exclude blacks from the jury "for reasons wholly unrelated to the outcome of the particular case on trial" or to deny to blacks "the same right and opportunity to participate in the administration of justice enjoyed by the white population." [An] inference of purposeful discrimination would be raised on evidence that a prosecutor, "in case after case, whatever the circumstances, whatever the crime and whoever the defendant or the victim may be, is responsible for the removal of Negroes who have been selected as qualified jurors by the jury commissioners and who have survived challenges for cause, with the result that no Negroes ever serve on petit juries." Evidence offered by the defendant in *Swain* did not meet that standard. . . .

A number of lower courts following the teaching of *Swain* reasoned that proof of repeated striking of blacks over a number of cases was necessary to establish a violation of the Equal Protection Clause. Since this interpretation of *Swain* has placed on defendants a crippling burden of proof, prosecutors' peremptory challenges are now largely immune from constitutional scrutiny. . . .

Since the decision in *Swain*, we have explained that [circumstantial] evidence of invidious intent may include proof of disproportionate impact. . . . Moreover, since *Swain*, we have recognized that . . . a defendant may make a prima facie showing of purposeful racial discrimination in selection of the venire by relying solely on the facts concerning its selection in his case. . . . A single invidiously discriminatory governmental act is not "immunized by the absence of such discrimination in the making of other comparable decisions." For evidentiary requirements to dictate that several must suffer discrimination before one could object would be inconsistent with the promise of equal protection to all.

[A] defendant may establish a prima facie case of purposeful discrimination in selection of the petit jury solely on evidence concerning the prosecutor's exercise of peremptory challenges at the defendant's trial. To establish such a case, the defendant first must show that he is a member of a cognizable racial group, and that the prosecutor has exercised peremptory challenges to remove from the venire members of the defendant's race. . . . In deciding whether the defendant has made the requisite showing, the trial court should consider all relevant circumstances. For example, a "pattern" of strikes against black jurors included in the particular venire might give rise to an inference of discrimination. Similarly, the prosecutor's questions and statements during voir dire examination and in exercising his challenges may support or refute an inference of discriminatory purpose. These examples are merely illustrative. We have confidence that trial judges, experienced in supervising voir dire, will be able to decide if the circumstances concerning the prosecutor's use of peremptory challenges creates a prima facie case of discrimination against black jurors.

Once the defendant makes a prima facie showing, the burden shifts to the State to come forward with a neutral explanation for challenging black jurors. Though this requirement imposes a limitation in some cases on the full peremptory character of the historic challenge, we emphasize that the prosecutor's explanation need not rise to the level justifying exercise of a challenge for cause. But the prosecutor may not rebut the defendant's prima facie case of discrimination by stating merely that he challenged jurors of the defendant's race on the assumption—or his intuitive judgment—that they would be partial to the defendant because of their shared race. Just as the Equal Protection Clause forbids the States to exclude black persons from the venire on the assumption that blacks as a group are unqualified to serve as jurors, so it forbids the States to strike black veniremen on the assumption that they will be biased in a particular case simply because the defendant is black. . . . Nor may the prosecutor rebut the defendant's case merely by denying that he had a discriminatory motive or affirming his good faith in making individual selections. . . . The prosecutor therefore must articulate a neutral explanation related to the particular case to be tried. The trial court then will have the duty to determine if the defendant has established purposeful discrimination. . . .

IV.

[We] do not agree that our decision today will undermine the contribution the challenge generally makes to the administration of justice. The reality of practice, amply reflected in many state- and federal-court opinions, shows that the challenge may be, and unfortunately at times has been, used to discriminate against black jurors. By requiring trial courts to be sensitive to the racially discriminatory use of peremptory challenges, our decision enforces the mandate of equal protection and furthers the ends of justice. In view of the heterogeneous population of our Nation, public respect for our criminal justice system and the rule of law will be strengthened if we ensure that no citizen is disqualified from jury service because of his race. . . .

MARSHALL, J., concurring.

I join Justice Powell's eloquent opinion for the Court, which takes a historic step toward eliminating the shameful practice of racial discrimination in the selection of juries. . . . I nonetheless write separately to express my views. The decision today will not end the racial discrimination that peremptories inject into the jury-selection process. That goal can be accomplished only by eliminating peremptory challenges entirely. . . .

Merely allowing defendants the opportunity to challenge the racially discriminatory use of peremptory challenges in individual cases will not end the illegitimate use of the peremptory challenge. . . . First, defendants cannot attack the discriminatory use of peremptory challenges at all unless the challenges are so flagrant as to establish a prima facie case. This means . . . that where only one or two black jurors survive the challenges for cause, the prosecutor need have no compunction about striking them from the jury because of their race. See Commonwealth v. Robinson, 415 N.E.2d 805 (Mass. 1981) (no prima facie case of discrimination where defendant is black, prospective jurors include three blacks and one Puerto Rican, and prosecutor excludes one for cause and strikes the remainder peremptorily, producing all-white jury). Prosecutors are left free to discriminate against blacks in jury selection provided that they hold that discrimination to an "acceptable" level.

Second, when a defendant can establish a prima facie case, trial courts face the difficult burden of assessing prosecutors' motives. Any prosecutor can easily assert facially neutral reasons for striking a juror, and trial courts are ill equipped to second-guess those reasons. How is the court to treat a prosecutor's statement that he struck a juror because the juror had a son about the same age as defendant, or seemed uncommunicative, or "never cracked a smile"? . . .

Nor is outright prevarication by prosecutors the only danger here. . . . A prosecutor's own conscious or unconscious racism may lead him easily to the conclusion that a prospective black juror is "sullen," or "distant," a characterization that would not have come to his mind if a white juror had acted identically. A judge's own conscious or unconscious racism may lead him to accept such an explanation as well supported. . . .

Some authors have suggested that the courts should ban prosecutors' peremptories entirely, but should zealously guard the defendant's peremptory as essential to the fairness of trial by jury. . . . I would not find that an acceptable solution. Our criminal justice system "requires not only freedom from any bias against the accused, but also from any prejudice against his prosecution. Between him and the state the scales are to be evenly held." Hayes v. Missouri, 120 U.S. 68 (1887). We can maintain that balance, not by permitting both prosecutor and defendant to engage in racial discrimination in jury selection, but by banning the use of peremptory challenges by prosecutors and by allowing the States to eliminate the defendant's peremptories as well. . . .

BURGER, C.J., dissenting.*

Today the Court sets aside the peremptory challenge, a procedure which has been part of the common law for many centuries and part of our jury system for nearly 200 years. . . . Permitting unexplained peremptories has long been regarded as a means to strengthen our jury system. . . . One commentator has recognized:

> The peremptory, made without giving any reason, avoids trafficking in the core of truth in most common stereotypes. . . . Common human experience, common sense, psychosociological studies, and public opinion polls tell us that it is likely that

_____
* [Justice Rehnquist joined this opinion.—EDS.]

certain classes of people statistically have predispositions that would make them inappropriate jurors for particular kinds of cases. But to allow this knowledge to be expressed in the evaluative terms necessary for challenges for cause would undercut our desire for a society in which all people are judged as individuals and in which each is held reasonable and open to compromise. . . . Instead we have evolved in the peremptory challenge a system that allows the covert expression of what we dare not say but know is true more often than not.

Babcock, Voir Dire: Preserving "Its Wonderful Power," 27 Stan. L. Rev. 545 (1975). . . . A moment's reflection quickly reveals the vast differences between the racial exclusions involved in *Strauder* and the allegations before us today:

> [Excluding] a particular cognizable group from all venire pools is stigmatizing and discriminatory in several interrelated ways that the peremptory challenge is not. The former singles out the excluded group, while individuals of all groups are equally subject to peremptory challenge on any basis, including their group affiliation. Further, venire-pool exclusion bespeaks a priori across-the-board total unfitness, while peremptory-strike exclusion merely suggests potential partiality in a particular isolated case. . . . To suggest that a particular race is unfit to judge in any case necessarily is racially insulting. To suggest that each race may have its own special concerns, or even may tend to favor its own, is not.

United States v. Leslie, 783 F.2d 541 (5th Cir. 1986) (en banc). [In] making peremptory challenges, both the prosecutor and defense attorney necessarily act on only limited information or hunch. The process cannot be indicted on the sole basis that such decisions are made on the basis of assumption or intuitive judgment. As a result, unadulterated equal protection analysis is simply inapplicable to peremptory challenges exercised in any particular case. A clause that requires a minimum "rationality" in government actions has no application to "an arbitrary and capricious right." *Swain.* . . .

Our system permits two types of challenges: challenges for cause and peremptory challenges. Challenges for cause obviously have to be explained; by definition, peremptory challenges do not. . . . Analytically, there is no middle ground: A challenge either has to be explained or it does not. It is readily apparent, then, that to permit inquiry into the basis for a peremptory challenge would force the peremptory challenge to collapse into the challenge for cause.

[One] painful paradox of the Court's holding is that it is likely to interject racial matters back into the jury selection process, contrary to the general thrust of a long line of Court decisions and the notion of our country as a "melting pot." . . . Today we mark the return of racial differentiation as the Court accepts a positive evil for a perceived one. Prosecutors and defense attorneys alike will build records in support of their claims that peremptory challenges have been exercised in a racially discriminatory fashion by asking jurors to state their racial background and national origin for the record, despite the fact that such questions may be offensive to some jurors and thus are not ordinarily asked on voir dire. . . .

REHNQUIST, J., dissenting.[*]
. . . In my view, there is simply nothing "unequal" about the State's using its peremptory challenges to strike blacks from the jury in cases involving black

---

[*] [Chief Justice Burger joined this opinion.—EDS.]

defendants, so long as such challenges are also used to exclude whites in cases involving white defendants, Hispanics in cases involving Hispanic defendants, Asians in cases involving Asian defendants, and so on. This case-specific use of peremptory challenges by the State does not single out blacks, or members of any other race for that matter, for discriminatory treatment. Such use of peremptories is at best based upon seat-of-the-pants instincts, which are undoubtedly crudely stereotypical and may in many cases be hopelessly mistaken. But as long as they are applied across-the-board to jurors of all races and nationalities, I do not see—and the Court most certainly has not explained—how their use violates the Equal Protection Clause. [Given] the need for reasonable limitations on the time devoted to voir dire, the use of such "proxies" by both the State and the defendant may be extremely useful in eliminating from the jury persons who might be biased in one way or another. . . .

■ PEOPLE v. RENE GUTIERREZ, JR.
395 P.3d 1886 (Cal. 2017)

CUÉLLAR, J.

. . . The mix of Californians who report for jury service across the state changes nearly every day, but the responsibility of courts to assure integrity in the selection of jurors does not. We have long held that discrimination in jury selection based on race, ethnicity, or similar grounds offends constitutional guarantees—and so has the United States Supreme Court. People v. Wheeler, 583 P.2d 748 (Cal. 1978); Batson v. Kentucky, 476 U.S. 79 (1986). It is not only litigants who are harmed when the right to trial by impartial jury is abridged. Taints of discriminatory bias in jury selection—actual or perceived—erode confidence in the adjudicative process, undermining the public's trust in courts.

During jury selection proceedings at trial, defendants Rene Gutierrez, Jr., Gabriel Ramos, and Ramiro Enriquez (collectively, defendants) joined in a *Batson/Wheeler* motion, contending that the prosecutor had improperly excluded prospective jurors on account of Hispanic ethnicity, after the prosecutor exercised 10 of 16 peremptory challenges to remove Hispanic individuals from the jury panel. The trial court found that defendants had established a prima facie case, but denied defendants' motion after finding the prosecutor's reasons to be neutral and non-pretextual. . . . What we conclude is that the record here does not sufficiently support the trial court's denial of the *Batson/Wheeler* motion with respect to one prospective juror. . . . Defendants' resulting convictions must be reversed.

[Around midnight on July 30, 2011, Gabriel Ramos became involved in an altercation with Clarence Langston in the parking lot of a motel in Bakersfield. When Langston left the motel on his bicycle, four associates of Ramos—Rene Gutierrez, Ramiro Enriquez, Kyle Fuller, and Gabriel Trevino—drove an SUV in search of him. Once they found Langston, Gutierrez fired a weapon at him three times; Langston was hit with shotgun pellets and suffered nonfatal wounds to his upper body.

The prosecution believed that the defendants were Sureño gang members, and that the shooting was gang-related. According to the police, Ramos was a member of the Varrio Bakers, a Sureño gang subset based in Bakersfield. Gutierrez, Enriquez, and Trevino were members of two other subsets of the Sureño gang, based in Shafter and Wasco.]

All three defendants are Hispanic, and they joined in a *Batson/Wheeler* motion toward the end of voir dire proceedings. . . . By the time the motion was made, the People had exercised 16 peremptory strikes—10 of them against individuals identified as Hispanic, either based on appearance or surname. The court observed that four of the prosecutor's challenges against Hispanics were consecutive. There were two Hispanic prospective jurors seated on the panel at the time of the motion. . . .

After finding that defendants had established a prima facie case under the *Batson/Wheeler* framework, the court asked the prosecutor to explain the reasons for his challenges. The prosecutor did so for each removed Hispanic panelist. [The court made a global finding that the prosecutor's strikes were neutral and nonpretextual. The final jury, which included one Hispanic individual, convicted Gutierrez of attempted premeditated murder, assault with a firearm, and active participation in a criminal street gang.]

Legal Standard

. . . When a party raises a claim that an opponent has improperly discriminated in the exercise of peremptory challenges, the court and counsel must follow a three-step process. First, the *Batson/Wheeler* movant must demonstrate a prima facie case by showing that the totality of the relevant facts gives rise to an inference of discriminatory purpose. The moving party satisfies this first step by producing evidence sufficient to permit the trial judge to draw an inference that discrimination has occurred. Second, if the court finds the movant meets the threshold for demonstrating a prima facie case, the burden shifts to the opponent of the motion to give an adequate nondiscriminatory explanation for the challenges. To meet the second step's requirement, the opponent of the motion must provide a "clear and reasonably specific" explanation of his "legitimate reasons" for exercising the challenges. *Batson*, 476 U.S. at 98. In evaluating a trial court's finding that a party has offered a neutral basis—one not based on race, ethnicity, or similar grounds—for subjecting particular prospective jurors to peremptory challenge, we are mindful that "unless a discriminatory intent is inherent in the prosecutor's explanation," the reason will be deemed neutral. *Purkett v. Elem*, 514 U.S. 765, 768 (1995).

Third, if the opponent indeed tenders a neutral explanation, the trial court must decide whether the movant has proven purposeful discrimination. In order to prevail, the movant must show it was "more likely than not that the challenge was improperly motivated." *People v. Mai*, 305 P.3d 1175 (Cal. 2013). This portion of the *Batson/Wheeler* inquiry focuses on the subjective genuineness of the reason, not the objective reasonableness. At this third step, the credibility of the explanation becomes pertinent. To assess credibility, the court may consider, among other factors, the prosecutor's demeanor; how reasonable, or how improbable, the explanations are; and whether the proffered rationale has some basis in accepted trial strategy. To satisfy herself that an explanation is genuine, the presiding judge must make "a sincere and reasoned attempt" to evaluate the prosecutor's justification, with consideration of the circumstances of the case known at that time, her knowledge of trial techniques, and her observations of the prosecutor's examination of panelists and exercise of for-cause and peremptory challenges. . . . We recognize that the trial court enjoys a relative advantage vis-à-vis reviewing courts, for it draws on its contemporaneous observations when assessing a prosecutor's credibility. . . .

A trial court's conclusions are entitled to deference only when the court made a sincere and reasoned effort to evaluate the nondiscriminatory justifications offered.

What courts should not do is substitute their own reasoning for the rationale given by the prosecutor, even if they can imagine a valid reason that would not be shown to be pretextual. "[A] prosecutor simply has got to state his reasons as best he can and stand or fall on the plausibility of the reasons he gives. . . . If the stated reason does not hold up, its pretextual significance does not fade because a trial judge, or an appeals court, can imagine a reason that might not have been shown up as false." Miller-El v. Dretke, 545 U.S. 231, 252 (2005).

Overview of Strikes

The prosecutor provided justifications for strikes of 10 Hispanic individuals. As to four of these prospective jurors—Prospective Jurors Nos. 2647624, 2408196, 2732073, and 2632053—the prosecutor cited as at least one reason the fact that they were each either previously affiliated with gangs or had family members who were at some point involved in gang activity. The prosecutor struck Prospective Jurors Nos. 2852410 and 2291529 because they recounted negative experiences with law enforcement. Prospective Juror No. 2468219 was removed because she testified about "living in an area with a lot of gang activity." . . . Below we describe in more depth the circumstances surrounding the strikes of the remaining three Hispanic panelists who were the subject of defendants' *Batson/Wheeler* motion. . . .

A teacher from the City of Wasco, Prospective Juror No. 2723471 was divorced and without children. Her former husband was a correctional officer. She had other relatives in law enforcement positions, including an uncle who worked for California Highway Patrol. Neither she nor anyone close to her had any connections to gangs. The prosecutor's colloquy with Juror 2723471, in its entirety, was as follows:

> [Q]: And starting with Ms. 2723471, are you gangs [sic] that are active in the Wasco area?
> [A]: No.
> [Q]: Do you live in the Wasco area?
> [A]: Yes.
> [Q]: In Wasco itself?
> [A]: Yes, I live in Wasco.

The prosecutor indicated that his decision to challenge Juror 2723471 was "a tough one." The reason for the strike, he said, was that "she's from Wasco and she said that she's not aware of any gang activity going on in Wasco, and I was unsatisfied by some of her other answers as to how she would respond when she hears that Gabriel Trevino is from a criminal street gang, a subset of the Surenos out of Wasco." The prosecutor did not specify which of her "other answers" caused him dissatisfaction. . . .

The prosecutor had broached the Wasco-related justification a few minutes earlier, during his explanation of his strike of a different Hispanic female, Prospective Juror No. 2408196. He said that that panelist's unawareness of Wasco gang activity "causes a moment of pause when she's going to hear . . . Mr. Trevino freely admits that he's a member of the Varrio Wasco." But the prosecutor struck Juror 2408196 because she also had an uncle who was in a gang and had a cousin who had been murdered.

[The court also described the removal of two additional Hispanic prospective jurors. The prosecutor asked Juror No. 2547226 several questions about the jury deliberation process and her understanding of a juror's role. When asked if she would "be able to participate in deliberations and listen to everyone else in speaking your mind," the juror answered "Yes," but later added that "I think I do better at listening than speaking my mind out." When the defendants filed their *Batson/Wheeler* motion, the prosecutor could not recall at first why he struck this panelist. Later, the prosecutor explained that after Juror 2547226 articulated the role of a juror, he was concerned about her ability "strongly to be heard in the course of jury deliberations." During the same round of voir dire questions, the prosecutor also perceived Juror No. 2570137, a non-Hispanic female, to be soft-spoken. Despite her answer of "I hope so" in response to the prosecutor's inquiry as to whether she could speak her mind during jury deliberations, the prosecutor did not further press this panelist on her ability to voice her opinions, and allowed her to remain on the panel.

Prospective Juror 2510083 was an elementary school instructional aide. One of her cousins was in the California Highway Patrol and another cousin worked for the highway patrol in Arizona. During the first week of voir dire proceedings, she informed the court of a potential hardship due to a job interview scheduled the morning of the upcoming Friday, but the next day she reported that her interview had been rescheduled and now presented no conflict. During individual voir dire of this panelist, the prosecutor asked questions about the juror's job as an instructional aide and her prior job in customer service for a telephone company. In explaining why he struck Juror 2510083, the prosecutor stated, "I was concerned about her life experience." In his view, "she came across of being quite young" and "I thought there was a lack of sophistication in some of her answers. And, I believe, she had also asked for release due to a hardship." The prosecutor acknowledged that this strike was a "tough call" because this panelist had relatives in law enforcement.

The trial judge found Juror 2510083 and Juror 2861675, a non-Hispanic who was included on the jury, to be comparable in terms of relative youth and lack of life experience. But the judge found credible the prosecutor's "other reasons" for striking Juror 2510083: a request for release due to hardship and a lack of sophistication. The court did not correct the prosecutor's erroneous assertion that this panelist asked to be excused due to a hardship.]

Neutrality of Explanation

When they assess the viability of neutral reasons advanced to justify a peremptory challenge by a prosecutor, both a trial court and reviewing court must examine only those reasons actually expressed. Defendants argue that the prosecutor's explanation regarding his removal of Juror 2723471 was inadequate because it did not explain why her unawareness of gang activity where she lived made her a bad or undesirable juror. But *Batson* and *Wheeler* do not prescribe such an exacting standard at the second step. We find the reason here to be "clear and reasonably specific," particularly considering that the prosecutor had previously, with respect to another prospective juror, introduced the notion of this Wasco-related rationale and provided somewhat more insight into the logic underlying it.

Defendants also contend that the prosecutor's reasoning was not neutral, because he was effectively using an individual's residence in Wasco as a proxy for Hispanic ethnicity. According to 2010 census data, Wasco is a city of approximately 25,000 residents, 76.7% of whom identify as Hispanic or Latino. Defendants cite *United States v. Bishop*, 959 F.2d 820 (9th Cir. 1992), for the proposition that equal protection principles prohibit the utilization of residence as a surrogate for racial stereotypes during jury selection. In *Bishop*, the prosecutor explained that he felt an eligibility worker who lived in Compton was likely to be hostile to law enforcement and desensitized to violence. The court found discriminatory intent to be inherent in these generic "group-based presuppositions" that "one who lives in an area heavily populated by poor black people could not fairly try a black defendant."

The prosecutor's justification here is distinguishable from the justification at issue in *Bishop*. True: in some ways, the purported basis of unawareness of gang activity in one's neighborhood was particular to Wasco, a city whose population is mostly Hispanic or Latino. After all, the prosecutor did not exercise a strike, for example, against non-Hispanic Prospective Juror No. 2581907, a longtime resident of Tehachapi who was unaware of gang problems in his neighborhood [and yet was seated on the jury]. But such a discrepancy is not altogether inconsistent, given the prosecutor's articulated basis referencing Trevino's Wasco gang affiliation. The reason was thus not inherently based on stereotypical views of Wasco residents.

We find the Wasco reason to be facially neutral. Our conclusion is compelled by the high court's decision in *Purkett*, which held that the second stage of the *Batson/Wheeler* framework "does not demand an explanation that is persuasive, or even plausible. [The] issue is the facial validity of the prosecutor's explanation." Accordingly, we proceed to the third step of the *Batson/Wheeler* inquiry, in order to assess the credibility of the explanations provided. . . .

Credibility of Explanation

At the third step of the *Batson/Wheeler* analysis, the trial court evaluates the credibility of the prosecutor's neutral explanation. Credibility may be gauged by examining factors including but not limited to the prosecutor's demeanor; by how reasonable, or how improbable, the explanations are; and by whether the proffered rationale has some basis in accepted trial strategy. . . .

The prosecutor cited the "Wasco reason" for challenging both Jurors 2723471 and 2408196, the only two panelists who were Wasco residents. This rationale nonetheless applied only to Hispanic panelists—so the notion that the prosecutor "consistently" cited this reason appears minimally probative on the issue of whether the reason offered by the prosecutor was credible. The court . . . made a general finding that the prosecutor had "paid the same attention to all the jurors in terms of questioning whether they are Hispanic or not Hispanic, and he's asked appropriate questions to all the jurors." Yet the prosecutor questioned only Hispanic panelists about gang activity in Wasco, because only Hispanic panelists stated that they lived in Wasco. . . .

The prosecutor's articulated basis for striking Juror 2723471 was derived solely from three responses to yes/no questions, which established that this panelist lived in Wasco and was not aware of gangs active in the Wasco area. The prosecutor may have conveyed the gist of his concern—that he was uncertain how a prospective juror's unawareness of Wasco gang activity might bear on her response to Trevino—but his explanation left some lucidity to be desired. What the People argue on review is that [a potential juror who is unaware] of the activity of gangs in Wasco "could cause that juror to be biased against Trevino who would testify to the contrary." In consideration of the record of voir dire, such a deduction is tenuous. . . . Although it is possible that a juror unaware of gang activity in Wasco would be discomfited by, and skeptical of, a witness who claimed to be member of a gang based in her neighborhood, such a conclusion does not strike us as an obvious or natural inference drawn from this panelist's responses. . . .

The questioning of Juror 2723471 provides little aid in elucidating the reasoning for this strike. The prosecutor asked no follow-up questions to this prospective juror, certainly none about how she would react if she heard that a member of a Wasco gang would testify in this case. . . . The fact that the prosecutor struck Juror 2723471 despite her law enforcement ties—though he expressed his tendency to favor this characteristic with regard to other panelists—is a relevant circumstance in assessing the credibility of the prosecutor's reasoning. . . .

Some neutral reasons for a challenge are sufficiently self-evident, if honestly held, such that they require little additional explication. One example: excusing a panelist because she has previously been victim to the same crime at issue in the case to be tried. Moreover, a peremptory challenge may be based on a broad range of factors indicative of juror partiality, even those which are "apparently trivial" or "highly speculative." People v. Williams 940 P.2d 710 (Cal. 1997). Yet when it is not self-evident why an advocate would harbor a concern, the question of whether a neutral explanation is genuine and made in good faith becomes more pressing. That is particularly so when, as here, an advocate uses a considerable number of challenges to exclude a large proportion of members of a cognizable group. Out of 16 strikes exercised by the prosecution up to that point, 10 were used to remove jurors who shared the same ethnicity as defendants. Four of these challenges against Hispanics were consecutive. And when the motion was made, 10 out of 12 Hispanic panelists (83 percent) who had entered the jury box were peremptorily struck by the prosecution.

Advocates and courts both have a role to play in building a record worthy of deference. . . . When the prosecutor's stated reasons are either unsupported by the record, inherently implausible, or both, more is required of the trial court than a global finding that the reasons appear sufficient. The court here acknowledged the "Wasco issue" justification and deemed it neutral and nonpretextual by blanket statements. It never clarified why it accepted the Wasco reason as an honest one. Another tendered basis for this strike, the reference to the prospective juror's "other answers" as they related to an expectation of her reaction to Trevino, was not borne out by the record—but the court did not reject this reason or ask the prosecutor to explain further. In addition, the court improperly cited a justification not offered by the prosecutor: a lack of life experience. On this record, we are unable to conclude that the trial court made "a sincere and reasoned attempt to evaluate the prosecutor's explanation" regarding the strike of Juror 2723471. . . . Because the prosecutor's reason for this strike was not self-evident and the record is void of any explication from the court, we cannot find under these circumstances that the court made a reasoned attempt to determine whether the justification was a credible one.

Though we exercise great restraint in reviewing a prosecutor's explanations and typically afford deference to a trial court's *Batson/Wheeler* rulings, we can only perform a meaningful review when the record contains evidence of solid value. Providing an adequate record may prove onerous, particularly when jury selection extends over several days and involves a significant number of potential jurors. It can be difficult to keep all the panelists and their responses straight. Nevertheless, the obligation to avoid discrimination in jury selection is a pivotal one. It is the duty of courts and counsel to ensure the record is both accurate and adequately developed.

Excluding by peremptory challenge even a single juror on the basis of race or ethnicity is an error of constitutional magnitude. The trial court's ruling—its finding that defendants had not met their burden of proving intentional discrimination with respect to the prosecutor's exclusion of Juror 2723471—was unreasonable in light of the record of *voir dire* proceedings. Our conclusion renders it unnecessary to determine whether the trial court erred in denying the *Batson/Wheeler* motion as to other Hispanic panelists. Because the court's denial of defendants' motion is unsupported, at least regarding Juror 2723471, we conclude that defendants were denied their right to a fair trial in violation of the equal protection clause of the federal Constitution and their right to a trial by a jury drawn from a representative cross-section of the community under the state Constitution. . . .

LIU, J., concurring.

I agree that the trial court erred in rejecting defendants' claim of racial discrimination in jury selection under Batson v. Kentucky and People v. Wheeler. Today's decision is the first time in 16 years, and the second time in over 25 years, that this court has found a *Batson/Wheeler* violation. The occasion provides an opportunity to review key principles of *Batson/Wheeler* analysis and to make a few observations about the nature of the legal inquiry. . . .

In applying the three-stage *Batson/Wheeler* inquiry, our court and the United States Supreme Court have set forth several important precepts. First, although we generally accord great deference to the trial court's ruling that a particular reason is genuine, we do so only when the trial court has made a sincere and reasoned attempt to evaluate each stated reason as applied to each challenged juror. Second, when illegitimate grounds like race are in issue, a prosecutor's decision to strike a juror must stand or fall on the plausibility of the reasons he gives. It does not matter if a trial judge, or an appeals court, can imagine a reason that might not have been shown up as false; a court's substitution of a reason not given by the prosecutor does nothing to satisfy the prosecutor's burden of stating a racially neutral explanation for his own actions.

Third, at the final stage of *Batson/Wheeler* analysis, courts must consider all relevant circumstances in determining whether a strike was improperly motivated, and this requires a careful review of the entire record. Fourth, comparative juror analysis is an important tool in ferreting out improper discrimination, and the mandate to consider all relevant circumstances means a court must undertake comparative juror analysis even if it is raised for the first time on appeal. [Comparative analysis requires the court to examine any inconsistencies by a party in applying reasons for exclusion to jurors who are similarly situated.]

Today's opinion explains how the trial court . . . ran afoul of these principles in evaluating the prosecutor's strike of Prospective Juror No. 2723471. The trial court did not discharge its duty to make a sincere and reasoned attempt to evaluate the prosecutor's reason for striking this juror. In upholding the strike, the trial court relied on a reason ("lack of life experience") that the prosecutor did not give. [The trial court's ruling did not provide] the careful and thorough examination of the record that today's opinion does in determining whether the prosecutor's stated reason was credible. . . .

The trial court . . . committed similar errors in evaluating the prosecutor's strikes of Prospective Juror No. 2547226 and Prospective Juror No. 2510083. [Justice Liu then explained why he believed that the denial of the defendant's *Batson/Wheeler* motion as to the removal of these two jurors was also legal error.]

I offer a few additional observations to put today's decision in context. As the high court has explained, "the adjudication of a *Batson* claim is, at bottom, a credibility determination." Foster v. Chatman, 136 S. Ct. 1737, 1765 (2016). In some cases, the inquiry turns up information that directly reveals the improper use of race. In *Foster*, the high court noted that "the sheer number of references to race in the prosecution's file is arresting" and that "an 'N' [for 'No'] appeared . . . "next to the name of each black prospective juror on the list of the 42 qualified prospective jurors." . . . But *Foster* [involved a trial] that took place over 30 years ago. I would surmise and hope, though I do not know for sure, that such brazenly unlawful practices are rare today.

More typical are the circumstances in Snyder v. Louisiana, 552 U.S. 472 (2008), which involved a 1996 capital trial. The prosecutor gave two reasons for striking a black juror, Jeffrey Brooks. As to the prosecutor's first reason—"he looked very nervous to me throughout the questioning"—the high court said "we cannot presume that the trial judge credited the prosecutor's assertion that Mr. Brooks was nervous" because the trial court made no "specific finding on the record concerning Mr. Brooks' demeanor." The prosecutor's second concern was that Mr. Brooks had a teaching obligation that might cause him to try "to go home quickly" by returning "a lesser verdict so there wouldn't be a penalty phase." The high court found this reason "suspicious" and "highly speculative" because (among other reasons) Mr. Brooks' "dean stated that he did not think that [Mr. Brooks' jury service] would be a problem." . . . Further, the high court said "the implausibility of this explanation is reinforced by the prosecutor's acceptance of white jurors who disclosed conflicting obligations that appear to have been at least as serious as Mr. Brooks'."

The nature of the case before us is closer to *Snyder* than to *Foster*. . . . Our finding of improper discrimination as to Juror 2723471 is not based on any conduct that is particularly egregious or any evidence that approximates a smoking gun. Instead, the analysis in today's opinion involves a careful and comprehensive review of the record, highlighting the lack of comparable questioning of non-Hispanic jurors, the lack of any indication that the prosecutor thought the juror was untruthful or uninformed, the prosecutor's lack of interest in "meaningfully examining" the Wasco issue with the juror, and the fact that the prosecutor struck Juror 2723471 despite her law enforcement ties "though he expressed his tendency to favor this characteristic with regard to other panelists."

Today's decision is an apt illustration of the "sensitive inquiry" and "review of the entire record" that *Batson/Wheeler* analysis demands. [This] requires a searching review of the record as well as sensitivity to the disproportionate effect that certain reasons—such as the gang-related reasons in this case—may have in excluding members of cognizable groups. . . .

The ultimate issue is whether it was more likely than not that the challenge was improperly motivated. This probabilistic standard is not designed to elicit a definitive finding of deceit or racism. Instead, it defines a level of risk that courts cannot tolerate in light of the serious harms that racial discrimination in jury selection causes to the defendant, to the excluded juror, and to public confidence in the fairness of our system of justice. . . . I do not think the finding of a violation should brand the prosecutor a liar or a bigot. Such loaded terms obscure the systemic values that the constitutional prohibition on racial discrimination in jury selection is designed to serve. With these observations, I join the opinion of the court.

■ WASHINGTON GENERAL RULE 37, JURY SELECTION

(a) *Policy and Purpose.* The purpose of this rule is to eliminate the unfair exclusion of potential jurors based on race or ethnicity.

(b) *Scope.* This rule applies in all jury trials.

(c) *Objection.* A party may object to the use of a peremptory challenge to raise the issue of improper bias. The court may also raise this objection on its own. The objection shall be made by simple citation to this rule, and any further discussion shall be conducted outside the presence of the panel. The objection must be made before the potential juror is excused, unless new information is discovered.

(d) *Response.* Upon objection to the exercise of a peremptory challenge pursuant to this rule, the party exercising the peremptory challenge shall articulate the reasons the peremptory challenge has been exercised.

(e) *Determination.* The court shall then evaluate the reasons given to justify the peremptory challenge in light of the totality of circumstances. If the court determines that an objective observer could view race or ethnicity as a factor in the use of the peremptory challenge, then the peremptory challenge shall be denied. The court need not find purposeful discrimination to deny the peremptory challenge. The court should explain its ruling on the record.

(f) *Nature of Observer.* For purposes of this rule, an objective observer is aware that implicit, institutional, and unconscious biases, in addition to purposeful discrimination, have resulted in the unfair exclusion of potential jurors in Washington State.

(g) *Circumstances Considered.* In making its determination, the circumstances the court should consider include, but are not limited to, the following: (i) the number and types of questions posed to the prospective juror, which may include consideration of whether the party exercising the peremptory challenge failed to question the prospective juror about the alleged concern or the types of questions asked about it; (ii) whether the party exercising the peremptory challenge asked significantly more questions or different questions of the potential juror against whom the peremptory challenge was used in contrast to other jurors; (iii) whether other prospective jurors provided similar answers but were not the subject of a peremptory challenge by that party; (iv) whether a reason might be disproportionately associated with a race or ethnicity; and (v) whether the party has used peremptory challenges disproportionately against a given race or ethnicity, in the present case or in past cases.

(h) *Reasons Presumptively Invalid.* Because historically the following reasons for peremptory challenges have been associated with improper discrimination in jury selection in Washington State, the following are presumptively invalid reasons for a peremptory challenge: (i) having prior contact with law enforcement officers; (ii) expressing a distrust of law enforcement or a belief that law enforcement officers engage in racial profiling; (iii) having a close relationship with people who have been stopped, arrested, or convicted of a crime; (iv) living in a high-crime neighborhood; (v) having a child outside of marriage; (vi) receiving state benefits; and (vii) not being a native English speaker.

(i) *Reliance on Conduct.* The following reasons for peremptory challenges also have historically been associated with improper discrimination in jury selection in Washington State: allegations that the prospective juror was sleeping, inattentive, or staring or failing to make eye contact; exhibited a problematic attitude, body language, or demeanor; or provided unintelligent or confused answers. If any party intends to offer one of these reasons or a similar reason as the justification for a peremptory challenge, that party must provide reasonable notice to the court and the other parties so the behavior can be verified and addressed in a timely manner. A lack of corroboration by the judge or opposing counsel verifying the behavior shall invalidate the given reason for the peremptory challenge.

Notes

1. *Number and theory of peremptory challenges: majority view.* States generally allow the most peremptory challenges in capital cases and the least in misdemeanor cases. In capital cases, most states allow somewhere between 12 and 20 challenges per party. Some of these states grant the defense more challenges than the prosecution. For ordinary noncapital felonies, states allow between 3 (Hawaii and New Hampshire for most felonies) and 20 (New Jersey defendants) peremptory challenges, with about a third of states allowing 6 challenges. As with capital cases, a significant minority of states provide the prosecution with fewer possible challenges than the defense. Bureau of Justice Statistics, State Court Organization 2004, at Table 41 (August 2006, NCJ 212351). In felony cases the federal system currently allows 10 strikes for the defense but only 6 for the prosecution. Fed. R. Crim. P. 24. What explains the greater numbers of challenges allowed in more serious cases?

2. *Stages of a* Batson *claim.* The court in *Batson* sketched the basic procedure for resolving allegations of racial bias in the exercise of peremptory challenges, which largely mirrors federal discrimination claims made under Title VII. First, the defendant must establish a prima facie case of intentional discrimination; second, the prosecutor must offer a neutral explanation for why it struck black jurors; finally, the trial court determines whether or not there has been "purposeful discrimination." As the California Supreme Court explained in *Gutierrez*, the second stage involves an objective evaluation of the nonracial quality of the reason the nonmoving party offers, while the third stage asks the trial judge to determine the subjective credibility of the party's claim that the nonracial reason motivated the decision to strike a juror. In Purkett v. Elem, 514 U.S. 765 (1995), the U.S. Supreme Court held that the government's burden at the second stage is merely a burden of production that can be satisfied by virtually any race-neutral explanation (including a "silly" or "superstitious" explanation), and that it is the moving party who carries the burden of persuasion that purposeful discrimination has in fact occurred.

Trial courts are relatively amenable to finding that a prima facie case has been made, but find purposeful discrimination and grant relief much less often. For a discussion of the empirical research on the success rates of parties who file *Batson* claims, go to the web extension for this chapter at *http://www.crimpro.com/extension/ch17*.

3. *Indicators of pretextual reasons.* The appellate courts that apply *Batson* struggle repeatedly with two situations. The first involves a party who applies inconsistently the purported basis for a strike. When a party explains a peremptory strike based on

a particular nonracial reason, but the party did not use that same reason to strike a juror of a different race, both trial judges and appellate courts tend to treat that as a factor that indicates "pretext" under the third step of *Batson*. Some courts call this a "comparative" juror analysis.

The second high-litigation situation involves a party's invocation of an apparently nonracial reason for a strike, but the reason correlates to some degree with race. For instance, a party who mentions a juror's residence in a "high-crime" neighborhood as a reason to support a strike might attract judicial scrutiny, either as a matter of step two sufficiency or step three credibility. Courts are split on whether the prior arrests or negative police encounters of the prospective juror or the family members of the juror correlate too strongly with race or with racial stereotypes to count as a "nonracial" reason. Compare McCarty v. State, 371 P.3d 1002 (Nev. 2016) (trial court erred when it accepted as race-neutral and nonpretextual the State's contention that it struck prospective juror because someone "close" to her had been "charged with, arrested for, or convicted of any public offense") with Johnson v. State, 809 S.E.2d 769 (Ga. 2018) (striking jurors with family members who had been arrested or tried for criminal offenses qualified as nonracial reason).

Most courts hesitate to accept unarticulated "gut feelings" or "hunches" as a reason to strike a juror, though it is sometimes difficult to distinguish gut feelings from the reasons that are offered. Compare Johnson v. Commonwealth, 450 S.W.3d 696 (Ky. 2014) (prosecutor's explanation that he struck potential juror because he had attended high school with her and had "personal knowledge" about her was not specific enough), with State v. Porter, 179 A.3d 1218 (R.I. 2018) (juror's demeanor, which prosecutor characterized as inattentive and uninterested, qualified as race-neutral reason).

4. *Race-neutral reasons and appellate courts.* The trial court initially evaluates the reasons that a party gives for striking jurors and determines whether the race-neutral reason was a genuine explanation for the strikes. What sort of deference should this finding of the trial judge receive on appellate review? The Supreme Court offered some guidance on the proper role of appellate review in Miller-El v. Dretke, 545 U.S. 231 (2005). The Court described several reasons to treat the prosecutor's race-neutral reason as a pretext:

> Out of 20 black members of the 108-person venire panel for Miller-El's trial, only 1 served. Although 9 were excused for cause or by agreement, 10 were peremptorily struck by the prosecution. The prosecutors used their peremptory strikes to exclude 91% of the eligible African-American venire members. Happenstance is unlikely to produce this disparity. More powerful than these bare statistics, however, are side-by-side comparisons of some black venire panelists who were struck and white panelists allowed to serve. If a prosecutor's proffered reason for striking a black panelist applies just as well to an otherwise-similar nonblack who is permitted to serve, that is evidence tending to prove purposeful discrimination. . . .

The opinion also reviewed the history of overt racial discrimination in the selection of jurors by prosecutors in the jurisdiction and noted systematic differences in the questions that prosecutors asked black and white jurors in this case. The Supreme Court then insisted that every judge evaluating a *Batson* claim—at both the trial and appellate levels—concentrate on the reason that the party gave at the time rather than strengthening the rationale later: "A *Batson* challenge does not call for a mere exercise in thinking up any rational basis. If the stated reason does not hold up, its pretextual significance does not fade because a trial judge, or an appeals court, can imagine a reason that might not have been shown up as false."

When documents are available to shed light on the thinking of the attorneys during jury selection, appellate courts may take a more assertive role in reviewing the case. See Foster v. Chatman, 136 S. Ct. 1737 (2016) (file notes drafted by prosecutors demonstrated they were motived in substantial part by race when they struck African-American jurors from panel). On the other hand, a trial judge who makes specific findings based on the demeanor of the prospective juror and the attorney still receives considerable deference on appeal. See State v. Hollis, 189 A.3d 244 (Me. 2018) (although appellate court may be skeptical of a proffered explanation for striking a juror based on low education level without individual voir dire on intelligence or education, trial judge's decision on discriminatory intent represents a finding of fact of the sort accorded great deference on appeal).

5. *Race and decision making.* Did the Court in *Batson* assume that jurors of different races will systematically reach different judgments? Is such a belief necessary to justify the decision? Researchers in psychology have conducted a number of experiments in an effort to learn about the effects of racial composition on the group decision dynamics of juries and the influence of a juror's and defendant's race on individual juror judgments. A review of this literature appears in Samuel R. Sommers & Omoniyi O. Adekanmbi, Race and Juries: An Experimental Psychology Perspective, in Critical Race Realism: Intersections of Psychology, Race, and Law 78 (Gregory S. Parks, Shayne Jones & W. Jonathan Cardi eds., 2008). For further exploration of this research, go to the web extension for this chapter at *http://www.crimpro.com/extension/ch17*.

6. *Extending* Batson *claims to other groups: majority view.* The U.S. Supreme Court has extended the coverage of *Batson* from jurors who are racial minorities to other groups. A prima facie case of racial discrimination arises when a party uses peremptory strikes to exclude Latinos from the jury. Hernandez v. New York, 500 U.S. 352 (1991). The Court applied the *Batson* framework to claims of gender discrimination in J.E.B. v. Alabama ex rel. T.B., 511 U.S. 127 (1994). State courts disagree about whether *Batson* applies to juror exclusions based on religion. See State v. Fuller, 862 A.2d 1130 (N.J. 2004); State v. Hodge, 726 A.2d 531 (Conn. 1999). The reach of *Batson* extends beyond groups subject to strict scrutiny under equal protection analysis. See, e.g., SmithKline Beecham Corp. v. Abbott Labs., 740 F.3d 471, 484 (9th Cir. 2014) (*Batson* reaches juror exclusions based on sexual orientation); Commonwealth v. Carleton, 641 N.E.2d 1057 (Mass. 1994) (analyzing prosecutor's effort to strike all jurors with Irish-sounding names).

7. *Extending* Batson *to other proceedings and parties.* The federal and state courts have also applied the *Batson* limits on peremptory challenges to parties other than the prosecutor and to proceedings other than a criminal trial. In Powers v. Ohio, 499 U.S. 400 (1991), the Court held that any litigant, regardless of race, could raise a claim of racially discriminatory peremptory challenges. In Edmonson v. Leesville Concrete Co., Inc., 500 U.S. 614 (1991), the Court extended the prohibition against race-based strikes to civil trials. A year after *Edmonson*, the Court accepted challenges by prosecutors to race-based peremptory strikes by defendants in Georgia v. McCollum, 505 U.S. 42 (1992). While *Batson* claims can be made now in civil or criminal cases, and by defendants or prosecutors, criminal defendants still make the majority of *Batson* claims. See Kenneth J. Melilli, *Batson* in Practice: What We Have Learned About *Batson* and Peremptory Challenges, 71 Notre Dame L. Rev.

447 (1996). Do these developments point to the eventual abolition of peremptory challenges, the position that Justice Marshall advocated in his concurring opinion in *Batson*?

8. *Remedies for* Batson *violations*. One of the many complicated questions courts have tried to answer in the wake of *Batson* is the question of the proper remedy. Should the judge start with a fresh venire, or reseat the improperly excluded jurors, or reseat all jurors excluded after the first improper peremptory strike? Some jurisdictions require trial courts, as a general rule, to disallow the strike and reseat the improperly stricken juror. State v. Urrea, 421 P.3d 153 (Ariz. 2018) (trial court's remedy of restoring impermissibly excluded jurors to prior places on venire and forfeiting State's peremptory challenges was sufficient). A few states require the trial court to conduct jury selection from a newly convened venire. Most courts, however, have allowed the trial judge to choose among available remedies, without designating a preferred or required remedy. See People v. Willis, 43 P.3d 130 (Cal. 2002). If the preferred remedy for a *Batson* violation is dismissal of the initial panel and selection of the jury from a fresh venire, would the parties ever have an incentive to create a deliberate *Batson* violation? Which remedy is most consistent with the view that the jury serves important functions for the jurors themselves and for the public at large?

9. *Removal of judges*. Just as jurors can be excluded when they are unable to find the facts impartially, a judge presiding at a trial may be removed from a case if she is not able to preside impartially. A party who questions the judge's impartiality may request that the judge recuse herself from the case. Statutes typically list some specific grounds for mandatory recusal, along with an instruction that the judge recuse herself whenever her "impartiality might reasonably be questioned." See 28 U.S.C. §455 (lists personal knowledge of disputed facts, family relationship with a party or attorney, and financial interest in outcome among the grounds for recusal). These statutory standards give specific content to the constitutional requirement that judges be impartial. See Tumey v. Ohio, 273 U.S. 510 (1927) (due process requires recusal of judge who has direct pecuniary interest in outcome of case).

In addition to challenges for cause and recusal of judges, about 20 states allow defendants to have one automatic strike—a kind of peremptory challenge—to the trial judge. See, e.g., 725 ILCS 5/114-5. Some statutes that appear to require evidence of judicial bias in fact operate as automatic challenge provisions; others that appear on their face to allow peremptory challenges to judges in fact require some evidence of bias. See, e.g., 28 U.S.C. §144; Liteky v. United States, 510 U.S. 540 (1994) (recusal and removal statutes require "extrajudicial source" of bias; bias allegations cannot be sustained solely on rulings by judge or information judge received during judicial proceedings). Is the presumption that judges are neutral stronger than for jurors?

Problem 17-3. The Reach of *Batson*

Defendant Edward Lee Davis, an African American man, was charged with aggravated robbery. No jurors were struck for cause during the jury selection. The defense, however, exercised four of its five peremptory strikes, while the state used one of its three. When the state used the one peremptory to strike a black man from the jury panel, defense counsel objected and asked for a race-neutral explanation.

The prosecutor, in response, stated for the record that the prospective juror would have been a very good juror for the state and that race had nothing to do with her decision to strike. She explained:

> However, it was highly significant to the State that the man was a Jehovah's Witness. I have a great deal of familiarity with the sect of Jehovah's Witness. I would never, if I had a peremptory challenge left, fail to strike a Jehovah's Witness from my jury. In my experience that faith is very integral to their daily life in many ways. At least three times a week he goes to church for separate meetings. The Jehovah's Witness faith is of a mind the higher powers will take care of all things necessary. In my experience Jehovah's Witnesses are reluctant to exercise state authority over their fellow human beings in this Court House.

The prosecutor concluded her statement by saying she did not feel it appropriate "to pry" into this matter with the juror because there was no need to do so when exercising a peremptory on race-neutral grounds. Defense counsel had nothing further to add, and the trial judge ruled the peremptory strike would stand.

The defendant concedes the state's peremptory was exercised for race-neutral reasons but contends that the race-neutral explanation offered by the state is constitutionally impermissible as religious discrimination. How would you rule on appeal? See State v. Davis, 504 N.W.2d 767 (Minn. 1993). Would a ruling in favor of the state here follow the logic of attorney Clarence Darrow (quoted earlier in this chapter) as he described some common qualities of Presbyterians, Englishmen, and Irishmen? And what would be the strongest argument against applying *Batson* in the context of a juror removed on the basis of sexual orientation?

C. JURY DELIBERATIONS AND VERDICTS

Once the jury is seated, the trial begins. In a few jurisdictions, the judge delivers preliminary instructions regarding the task at hand, along with an outline of the procedures for the jury to follow at trial and during deliberation. More often, the jury hears right away the opening statements of the attorneys, followed by the government's case in chief. Assuming that the judge denies the customary defense motion to dismiss the charges at the close of the prosecution's case, the jury then hears the defense evidence, if indeed the defendant chooses to present a defense. After closing statements from the attorneys, the judge instructs the jury on the law relevant to the case, using a combination of standard jury instructions for criminal cases and a few customized instructions that the parties suggest. The case then rests in the hands of the jury. In this section, we consider the rules governing the jury's deliberations.

■ STATE v. RONALD BEAN
149 A.3d 487 (Vt. 2016)

REIBER, C.J.
¶ 1. Defendant appeals his conviction for simple assault, arguing that the trial court erred by instructing the jury to consider simple assault as a lesser-included

offense of domestic assault, the crime for which he was charged. Specifically, defendant contends (1) that—as instructed to the jury—simple assault is not a lesser-included offense of domestic assault and (2) that the court cannot instruct the jury to consider a lesser-included offense over the defendant's objection. We affirm.

¶ 2. The altercation leading to defendant's conviction occurred on July 29, 2014, at a Middlebury residential facility for persons with major mental illnesses. In a sworn statement admitted without objection, the complainant claimed that defendant initiated the altercation by pointing his finger at the complainant. The complainant responded by kicking defendant's hand twice and telling defendant that he "needed a kick in the ass." Suddenly, the complainant experienced blurred vision, pressure, and heat on the left side of his face. Although he initially did not know what had happened, after he saw defendant talking to him, he concluded that defendant had hit him.

¶ 3. Defendant was charged with domestic assault. At trial, he testified that he suffered from schizophrenia and lived at the residential facility. He did not have a complete memory of the altercation and could not remember what started the altercation. The State's case relied on the complainant's sworn statement and the testimony of a staff member of the facility. This staff member said that she was behind defendant as "he reached over with his right hand and punched [the complainant] in the side of the head," and she could "hear the sound of a punch connecting."

¶ 4. Defendant responded with two legal theories. First, defendant argued that he could not be convicted of domestic assault because the complainant was not a "household member" under the domestic assault statute. On this point, defendant's counsel addressed the jury that defendant and the complainant were not part of the same household because the residential facility is "more like a boarding house kind of a situation, where each of these people has their own room." Second, defendant argued that his actions were taken in self-defense because the complainant "kicked at [defendant] twice, by his own statement" and said "something akin to you need to have your ass kicked, I'll kick your ass, words to that effect."

¶ 5. After the State rested, but before defendant rested, the State asked the judge to instruct the jury on simple assault as a lesser-included offense of domestic assault because "all the elements are the same except for the family or household member." Defendant's counsel . . . objected to the possibility of a second charge so far into the trial, saying "We've passed all evidence; the State's rested . . . we would oppose the addition of the lesser-included at this point in time." After closing statements, the court nevertheless instructed the jury on simple assault:

> If you decide that the State has not proven each of the essential elements of domestic assault, then you must consider whether [defendant] is guilty of the lesser-included offense of simple assault. Or if you are unable to agree upon a verdict concerning the charge of domestic assault, after all reasonable efforts to reach a unanimous verdict, then you may move on to consider the offense of simple assault.

This instruction was critical to the case; the jury acquitted defendant of domestic assault but convicted him of simple assault. . . .

¶ 6. Defendant first argues that—as instructed to the jury—simple assault is not a lesser-included offense of domestic assault. [Defendant] emphasizes that he does not refer to simple assault and domestic assault generally, but rather to how the court defined the two offenses in its jury instructions. Specifically, he argues that—again, as instructed to the jury—the elements of simple assault and domestic assault each had an element that the other did not. Defendant primarily contends that (1) the domestic-assault instruction had a "household member" requirement but the simple-assault instruction did not and (2) the simple-assault instruction had a proximate cause requirement but the domestic-assault instruction did not. He secondarily contends that simple assault and domestic assault simply had different intent elements: the domestic-assault instruction had a requirement that defendant acted "willfully" but the simple-assault instruction had a requirement that defendant acted "purposely."

¶ 7. A lesser-included offense is one that is composed exclusively of elements shared with the greater, charged offense but also lacks at least one element of that greater, charged offense. State v. Forbes, 523 A.2d 1232, 1235 (Vt. 1987); see also Blockburger v. United States, 284 U.S. 299, 304 (1932). If two offenses share elements but each also has an element that the other does not, then neither can be a lesser-included offense of the other.

¶ 8. As instructed to the jury, the definitions of the two offenses show that simple assault in this case was composed exclusively of elements shared with domestic assault. Explaining the elements of domestic assault, the court instructed the jury: "The essential elements of domestic assault are . . . (1) defendant; (2) caused bodily injury to the complainant by punching him in the head; (3) he did so willfully; and (4) the person injured . . . was a household member." Explaining the elements of simple assault, the court instructed the jury: "The essential elements of simple assault are . . . (1) defendant; (2) caused bodily injury to the complainant by punching him in the head; and (3) he did so purposely. . . . To cause bodily injury means that defendant's acts produced bodily injury to the complainant in a natural and continuous sequence, unbroken by any efficient, intervening cause." . . .

¶ 9. Defendant correctly notes that the domestic-assault instruction had a "household member" requirement but the simple-assault instruction did not. . . . Of relevance to this case, the "household member" requirement is met if the victim is living or has lived with the assailant, or shares or has shared occupancy of a dwelling with the assailant.

¶ 10. However, defendant incorrectly argues that the simple-assault instruction had a proximate cause requirement but the domestic-assault instruction did not. He notes that the court did not explain "cause bodily injury" in its domestic-assault instruction but did in its simple-assault instruction. . . . But considering the facts as stated in complainant's sworn statement and the testimony of the staff member relating to causation, no reasonable juror could find that there was an "efficient intervening cause" between defendant's punch and complainant's head injury. In other words, the evidence showed that complainant's head injury could be explained only by defendant's punch. A proximate-cause instruction was superfluous for the simple-assault instruction and likewise would have been superfluous for the domestic-assault instruction. Therefore, although a proximate-cause instruction was given as part of the simple-assault instruction, it did not actually add an additional element to simple assault that domestic assault lacked.

¶ 11. Finally, defendant's argument regarding a difference in intent elements likewise fails; we do not agree that simple assault and domestic assault—as instructed—had different intent elements. The court used the term "willfully" to describe the intent element for domestic assault and used the term "purposely" to describe the intent element for simple assault. It explained both terms, and there was no relevant difference between the court's explanations of the two terms. The court explained "willfully" as: "To act willfully means to act intentionally. In other words, it means to act on purpose and not inadvertently because of mistake or by accident." It explained "purposely" as "not inadvertently or because of mistake or by accident . . . it was his conscious objective to cause [the complainant] to be harmed." The explanations are interchangeable: both convey that the jury had to find that defendant caused the harm intentionally rather than by mistake or accident. . . .

¶ 13. Defendant next argues that the court cannot instruct the jury to consider a lesser-included offense over the defendant's objection; in other words, that the defendant—as opposed to the State or the court sua sponte—has sole control over whether a lesser-included instruction is given and can force an "all or nothing decision" whereby the defendant is either convicted on the greater offense or on nothing at all. . . .

¶ 14. [The] Vermont statute regarding lesser-included offenses explicitly authorizes the court to give a lesser-included jury instruction if requested by either party: . . . "If requested by either party, the jury shall be informed of the lesser included offense if supported by the evidence." 13 V.S.A. §14(a). [The court may consider a lesser-included instruction absent a request from either party if supported by the evidence. See 13 V.S.A. §14(b) ("If requested by either party, or in his or her discretion, the judge in a court trial shall consider a lesser included offense if supported by the evidence.").]

¶ 15. This principle aligns with the purposes and traditions underlying lesser-included instructions. See Beck v. Alabama, 447 U.S. 625, 633 (1980) ("At common law the jury was permitted to find the defendant guilty of any lesser offense necessarily included in the offense charged."). The lesser-included instruction "originally developed as an aid to the prosecution in cases in which the proof failed to establish some element of the crime charged." Id. It also has value to the defendant and society:

> The doctrine is a valuable tool for defendant, prosecutor, and society. From a defendant's point of view, it provides the jury with an alternative to a guilty verdict on the greater offense. From the prosecutor's viewpoint, a defendant may not go free if the evidence fails to prove an element essential to a finding of guilt on the greater offense. . . . In addition, the punishment society inflicts on a criminal may conform more accurately to the crime actually committed if a verdict on a lesser included offense is permissible.

State v. Cox, 851 A.2d 1269, 1272 (Del. 2003). . . . We find no Vermont case supporting defendant's position. Affirmed.

Notes

1. *Lesser included offenses and jury deliberations: majority position.* Although most juries reach a unanimous verdict, many start out with divided views among the panel members about the proper outcome. Divisions among jurors may be easier to resolve when juries are presented with a range of offenses, including lesser included charges, that create room for negotiation.

Experimental data suggest that juries presented with alternatives for verdicts other than acquittal or the most serious available charge produce fewer acquittals and fewer hung juries. See Neil Vidmar, Effects of Decision Alternatives on the Verdicts and Social Perceptions of Simulated Jurors, 22 J. Personality & Soc. Psychol. 211 (1972) (in 54 percent of mock homicide trials, jury acquitted when choice of verdict was guilty of first-degree murder or not guilty; when jury had four options, jurors returned verdicts of first-degree murder in 8 percent of the cases, second-degree murder in 64 percent, manslaughter in 21 percent, and not guilty in 8 percent). Depending on the case, as a strategic matter the prosecution or the defense may favor or oppose the judge instructing the jury about lesser included offenses.

In cases involving lesser included offenses or multiple charges, the judge may encourage agreement among jurors by providing instructions on the order for them to consider lesser included offenses. Two instructions are common. Under an "acquittal first" instruction, the judge tells the jury to reach a unanimous decision to acquit on the most serious charge before moving on to consider conviction for a lesser offense. See State v. Tate, 773 A.2d 308 (Conn. 2001) (if jury that has received "acquittal first" instruction asks for clarification about a lesser included offense and then reports itself deadlocked, trial court should first ask jury if it has reached a partial verdict before declaring mistrial). An alternative is the "unable to agree" or "reasonable efforts" instruction, which permits a jury to consider lesser included offenses if, after reasonable efforts, the jury cannot agree on a verdict on the more serious offense. The acquittal-first instruction was the more traditional of the two, but the reasonable efforts instruction is gaining a strong following among state courts. See State v. Thomas, 533 N.E.2d 286 (Ohio 1988). As defense counsel, which of these instructions would you ordinarily prefer? Under what circumstances might you prefer the other instruction?

In some cases, the defendant asks the judge to present the jury with an "all or nothing" choice: they convict the defendant of either the most serious charge, or nothing at all. Because of the jury's traditional freedom to accept or reject evidence selectively, courts usually disfavor such instructions. In other circumstances, the defendant finds the all-or-nothing strategy to be too risky. Where one of the elements of the offense charged remains in doubt, but the defendant is plainly guilty of some offense, the jury might "resolve its doubts in favor of conviction." Keeble v. United States, 412 U.S. 205, 213 (1973). The judge's willingness to discuss lesser included offenses in the jury instructions depends in part on whether the prosecution filed the lesser offenses in the indictment or information, and whether the defense attorney made the lesser offense central to her theory of the case. See Blueford v. Arkansas, 566 U.S. 599 (2012) (defendant in first trial was charged with capital murder and lesser included homicide offenses, and jury was given verdict forms that allowed them to acquit of all charges or to convict of one charge; second trial after mistrial not barred by double jeopardy).

2. *"Dynamite" charges: majority position.* After jurors deliberate for a while and fail to reach a unanimous verdict, they sometimes ask the judge for guidance. Typically, the judge simply tells the jury to continue its deliberations without further instruction. N.Y. Crim. Proc. Law §310.30 (upon request of jury during deliberation, court may return jury to courtroom and, in presence of defendant, give jury information with respect to the law or the substance of any trial evidence). But after some time passes, the judge might issue a "dynamite" charge (or "hammer" charge) to encourage jurors more actively to rethink their positions. This type of jury instruction originated in Commonwealth v. Tuey, 62 Mass. 1 (1851), and came to national attention in Allen v. United States, 164 U.S. 492 (1896). The charge instructs jurors

to reconsider their views in light of the views of the other jurors; it is an instruction designed—like dynamite—to move immoveable objects. The instruction produced verdicts, and its use spread rapidly. The *Allen* opinion summarized the charge as follows:

> [That] in a large proportion of cases absolute certainty could not be expected; that, although the verdict must be the verdict of each individual juror, and not a mere acquiescence in the conclusion of his fellows, yet they should examine the question submitted with candor, and with a proper regard and deference to the opinions of each other; that it was their duty to decide the case if they could conscientiously do so; that they should listen, with a disposition to be convinced, to each other's arguments; that, if much the larger number were for conviction, a dissenting juror should consider whether his doubt was a reasonable one which made no impression upon the minds of so many men, equally honest, equally intelligent with himself. If, upon the other hand, the majority were for acquittal, the minority ought to ask themselves whether they might not reasonably doubt the correctness of a judgment which was not concurred in by the majority.

More recently, many courts have limited or abandoned the *Allen* instruction. About half the states have disapproved dynamite charges, in whole or in part. See People v. Gainer, 566 P.2d 997 (Cal. 1977); State v. Fool Bull, 766 N.W.2d 159 (S.D. 2009). The case law on the subject is extensive. Some courts limit the instruction through procedural devices, such as preventing judges from giving the instruction too early during the jury's deliberations or from giving it more than once. Along these lines, some courts say that an *Allen* charge is acceptable only if the judge delivered an identical charge to the jury at the start of its deliberations. Other courts focus on the content of the instructions. Appellate courts pay special attention to the balance between statements about the need for agreement and statements about the duty of individual jurors to stand by their own considered opinions.

The ABA Criminal Justice Standard 15-5.4(a) (2005) recommends this charge to promote unanimous verdicts:

> Before the jury retires for deliberation, the court may give an instruction which informs the jury: (1) that in order to return a verdict, each juror must agree thereto; (2) that jurors have a duty to consult with one another and to deliberate with a view to reaching an agreement, if it can be done without violence to individual judgment; (3) that each juror must decide the case for himself or herself but only after an impartial consideration of the evidence with the other jurors; (4) that in the course of deliberations, a juror should not hesitate to reexamine his or her own views and change an opinion if the juror is convinced it is erroneous; and (5) that no juror should surrender his or her honest belief as to the weight or effect of the evidence solely because of the opinion of the other jurors, or for the mere purpose of returning a verdict.

Do you believe that the ABA alternative creates a different reaction among jurors than the traditional *Allen* charge? See also Lowenfield v. Phelps, 484 U.S. 231 (1988) (approving charge that does not instruct minority jurors to reconsider in light of majority views but does tell jurors not to hesitate to "reexamine" their views and to "change" their opinion if they are convinced that they are wrong). The dynamite charge has become the subject of some empirical studies that attempt to measure its impact on jury deliberations. For a survey of the state cases and the empirical work, go to the web extension for this chapter at *http://www.crimpro.com/extension/ch17*.

3. *Numerical breakdowns.* When a jury sends out word that it is divided and cannot reach a consensus, two questions spring to mind: How many jurors are "holding out," and which side does the majority favor? Appellate courts usually express concern if a trial judge inquired about the numerical division of the jury, explaining that such inquiries might create undue pressure on the minority jurors to change their votes. However, courts are divided over whether such inquiries, standing alone, constitute legal error. The larger group, including the federal courts, say that a judge's inquiries about the jury's numerical division are per se error. See Brasfield v. United States, 272 U.S. 448 (1926); People v. Wilson, 213 N.W.2d 193 (Mich. 1973). In the other states, this type of inquiry becomes a ground for reversal when combined with other circumstances, such as the judge's further inquiry about whether the majority favors conviction, acquittal, or some other option. On the other hand, if the jury *volunteers* information about its numerical division, the judge typically must inform the parties. Statutes and court rules typically state that the parties must be informed about any statement that the jury makes during its deliberations, and they must have an opportunity to argue to the judge about what she should say to the panel.

4. *Sequestration of juries.* One powerful practical force working in favor of jury agreement is the fact that jurors are forced to remain together in a single room, at least during working hours, until their task is complete. Indeed, for some cases involving an unusual amount of publicity that could taint the jurors, the court will "sequester" the jury and order them to remain together in a hotel during their meals, evenings, and off-days. See Tex. Code Crim. Proc. art 35.23. At one time, this process was much more explicitly designed to produce a verdict. Consider William Blackstone's description of the environment for jury deliberations: "the jury, . . . in order to avoid intemperance and causeless delay, are to be kept without meat, drink, fire, or candle, unless by permission of the judge, till they are all unanimously agreed." Blackstone, 3 Commentaries on the Laws of England 375 (1768).

5. *Prevalence of hung juries.* In the popular imagination, the "hung jury" is a common occurrence. A study of juries in the 1960s found that hung juries occurred in 5.5 percent of the cases studied. Harry Kalven & Hans Zeisel, The American Jury 57 (1966). The rate of deadlocked juries differs from place to place. For instance, rates of hung juries in Los Angeles are higher than in other jurisdictions: 13 to 16 percent in Los Angeles, compared to 6.2 percent nationwide. In federal criminal trials, the rate of hung juries remains around 2 to 3 percent. See Paula L. Hannaford, Valerie P. Hans & G. Thomas Munsterman, How Much Justice Hangs in the Balance?, 83 Judicature 59 (1999). Keep in mind that these rates reflect the number of juries that end their deliberations in deadlock; there are no data on the extent to which juries declare themselves deadlocked and ultimately reach a verdict. What outcomes would you expect during any later retrials of cases that initially produced a hung jury?

6. *Jury size: majority position.* The classic structure for a criminal jury calls for 12 members whose names are known to the parties. The jurors must agree unanimously on a verdict, based on their unaided memory of the testimony and other evidence. What effects might we anticipate from changes to this traditional structure?

Starting in 1970, the Supreme Court permitted experimentation with the size of criminal juries. In Williams v. Florida, 399 U.S. 78 (1970), the Court upheld the use of a 6-person jury in a criminal case; however, in Ballew v. Georgia, 435 U.S. 223

(1978), the Court struck down the use of a 5-person jury as a violation of the Sixth Amendment. For a while, a few states took up this invitation and allowed felonies (other than capital cases) to be tried by juries of either 6 or 8 members. Today, however, general jurisdiction courts in all 50 states use 12-person juries to try felony charges. State Court Organization 2011 at Table 10 (November 2013, NCJ 242850). A small group of states, including Indiana and Massachusetts, allow 6-member juries for felony trials in limited jurisdiction courts but require full 12-member juries in general jurisdiction courts.

In contrast, for misdemeanors, more than half of the states provide for juries with fewer than 12 members. Efforts in a few states to reduce the size of the criminal jury have been rejected on state constitutional grounds. See, e.g., Byrd v. State, 879 S.W.2d 435 (Ark. 1994). Perhaps reducing the expense and difficulty of selecting and maintaining juries makes it possible to offer juries in a broader range of cases. Will a smaller jury function differently? In a predictable direction?

7. *Non-unanimous verdicts.* In Apodaca v. Oregon, 406 U.S. 404 (1972), the Supreme Court reversed earlier cases and interpreted the Sixth Amendment right to jury trial to allow convictions based on 11-1 and 10-2 votes. A companion case, Johnson v. Louisiana, 406 U.S. 356 (1972), upheld a conviction based on a 9-3 vote. However, in Burch v. Louisiana, 441 U.S. 130 (1979), the Court concluded that a conviction based on a 5-1 vote violated the right to a jury trial. States have not rushed into this constitutional opening.

The most famous study of non-unanimous juries is Reid Hastie, Steven D. Penrod & Nancy Pennington, Inside the Jury (1983). The study found several differences between behavior on unanimity-rule and majority-rule juries. Majority-rule juries reach a verdict more quickly; they tend to vote early and conduct discussions in a more adversarial manner; holdouts are more likely to remain at the conclusion of deliberations; members of small groups are less likely to speak; and large factions attract members more quickly. Does democratic theory support any non-unanimous verdict that mimics what a simple majority of society at large would decide in a case? After Louisiana voters in 2018 amended the state constitution to eliminate non-unanimous juries, Oregon is the only state that uses this device.

8. *Different rationales for one verdict.* The unanimity requirement calls for each juror to agree to the group outcome, whether it be conviction or acquittal of each possible charge. Jurors may, however, take different routes to reach the same conclusion. For instance, a statute might list more than one method of committing a crime, and jurors may have differing views about which method the defendant used. In Schad v. Arizona, 501 U.S. 624 (1991), a defendant was indicted for first-degree murder, and the prosecutor argued both premeditated and felony murder theories. It was not clear whether the jurors all agreed on one theory when they returned a guilty verdict. The Court held that there was no due process violation because the state statute treated felony murder and premeditation as alternative *means* of establishing the single criminal element. Thus, the key question is whether the statute makes a particular fact an element of the offense or instead an alternative means of establishing a crime element. State courts have also framed the question in these terms. See State v. Fortune, 909 P.2d 930 (Wash. 1996). However, it has proven difficult to determine which facts are the "means" (over which jurors may disagree) and which are the "elements" (on which jurors must agree). See State v. Boots, 780 P.2d 725 (Or. 1989) (Linde, J.); Richardson v. United States, 526 U.S. 813 (1999) (interpreting the federal Continuing Criminal Enterprise statute to require jury to agree

unanimously on the "violations" that make up the "series of continuing violations" that define the enterprise; violations are elements of the offense, not merely the means of committing an element). For a sampling of the varied state court rulings on this question, go to the web extension for this chapter at *http://www.crimpro.com/extension/ch17*.

9. *Special verdicts: majority position.* Special verdicts require the jury to answer specific questions about its subsidiary findings of fact, and they instruct the jury about the sequence for proceeding from preliminary findings to final conclusions. Although a special verdict allows judicial review of improper verdicts, they are not often used in criminal cases, and some courts have struck down convictions based on special verdicts. See State v. Dilliner, 569 S.E.2d 211 (W. Va. 2002) (use of special interrogatories in criminal case in absence of statutory authorization is reversible error). According to the seminal case on this question, United States v. Spock, 416 F.2d 165 (1st Cir. 1969), special verdicts may coerce a jury into reaching a guilty verdict: "There is no easier way to reach, and perhaps force, a verdict of guilty than to approach it step by step. A juror, wishing to acquit, may be formally catechized." Despite this general disinclination to use special verdicts, some state statutes or procedural rules provide for special verdicts in particular types of cases, such as those in which the defendant presents an insanity defense.

10. *Inconsistent verdicts.* When there are multiple defendants in a trial or multiple counts against a single defendant, the jury could reach inconsistent conclusions for the different defendants or charges. Yet because of the preference for general verdicts, there is no explanation available for how the jury reached its incongruent outcomes. Faced with this situation, the federal courts have decided that consistency among verdicts is not necessary when a defendant is convicted on one or more counts but acquitted on others. Dunn v. United States, 284 U.S. 390 (1932) (Holmes, J.). The incompatible results, these courts conclude, could be a product of jury lenity, but that does not invalidate the guilty verdict the jury did return.

State courts have by and large followed the *Dunn* rule for inconsistent verdicts. People v. Caldwell, 681 P.2d 274 (Cal. 1984); Commonwealth v. Campbell, 651 A.2d 1096 (Pa. 1994). A small minority of state courts still hold that inconsistent verdicts require reversal. Many courts, however, recognize an exception for "logically" inconsistent verdicts (as opposed to "factually" inconsistent verdicts). When a jury has returned verdicts convicting a defendant of two or more crimes, and the existence of an element of one of the crimes negates the existence of a necessary element of the other crime, courts generally say that the verdicts should not be sustained. Why do courts hope to avoid inquiries into the reasons for inconsistent verdicts? If the primary objective is to avoid speculation about the basis for verdicts, would a presumption in favor of dismissing all inconsistent verdicts work just as well as the current majority rule?

11. *Juror note-taking.* Traditionally jurors in criminal cases have been barred from taking notes during trial. However, the majority of states (around 35) and the federal courts have begun to allow note-taking subject to judicial approval. See, e.g., Wash. Superior Ct. Crim. R. 6.8; Mich. R. Crim. P. 6.414. Another group of states authorize note-taking without leaving the decision to the trial court in ordinary cases. See Minn. R. Crim. P. 26.03; Md. Crim. R. 4-326; see also ABA Standards for Criminal Justice: Trial by Jury 15-3.5 (3d ed. 1996). Fewer than a half dozen states still prohibit note-taking. In states where statutes and procedural rules do not address the question, courts often authorize note-taking. See, e.g., People v. Hues, 704 N.E.2d

546 (N.Y. 1998) (survey of cases). Research suggests higher juror satisfaction and no change in outcomes when jurors are allowed to take notes. See Larry Heuer & Steven Penrod, Increasing Juror Participation in Trials Through Note Taking and Question Asking, 79 Judicature 256 (1996).

12. *Authority of jury to nullify: majority position.* During its deliberations, the jury resolves factual disputes based on the evidence the parties present. It then applies the facts to the relevant legal principles that the judge provides in her instructions. But does the jury also have the power to interpret the law in light of its own values and priorities? Judicial opinions on this subject widely recognize that the jurors have the "power" to ignore the law or to interpret the law themselves. This power has come to be known as "jury nullification." Nevertheless, judges usually consider jury nullification to be illegitimate. Hence, most courts refuse to instruct a jury that they have the power to "nullify" the law, and most do not allow defense counsel to make such an argument to the jury.

State constitutions and statutes fall into two camps on the issue of the jury's authority to decide questions of law (and thus to decide not to apply the law when an injustice would result). The state constitutions of Georgia (art. I, §1, para. 11, §A), Indiana (art. I, §19), Maryland (art. XXIII), and Oregon (art. I, §16) declare that the jury has authority over both the factual and legal aspects of each case. Other state statutes take an opposite view. Cal. Penal Code §1126 ("In a trial for any offense, questions of law are to be decided by the court, and questions of fact by the jury").

Some states acknowledge the power of the jury to assess law and facts by the rather subtle shift from general jury instructions directing the jury that if it finds the facts to be true it "must" find the defendant guilty to language suggesting to the jury that it "should" or "may" find the defendant guilty. A handful of states allow the judge to instruct the jury more directly about its power. Some even allow attorneys to argue nullification directly to the jury if the trial judge allows it. See State v. Bonacorsi, 648 A.2d 469 (N.H. 1994).

The jury's power to nullify the law presents profound questions about the connection between public opinion and criminal enforcement in a democratic society. Legal scholars have approached these issues from several intriguing angles. For a sample of these essays, go to the web extension for this chapter at *http://www.crim-pro.com/extension/ch17.*

13. *Juror misconduct during deliberations.* If jurors violate direct instructions from the judge or lie during voir dire, and it comes to light before the jury starts deliberations, those jurors can be removed from the case and alternates put in their place. If their misbehavior comes to light after a verdict has been reached, depending on the nature and severity of the misbehavior, jurors may be prosecuted for jury tampering. California employs a jury instruction that requires jurors to inform the judge whenever a fellow member of the jury refuses to deliberate based on his or her disagreement with the law. People v. Williams, 21 P.3d 1209 (Cal. 2001) (upholding conviction after trial court replaced juror who was reported by fellow juror; replaced juror disagreed with statutory rape law as applied to 18-year-old male defendant and 16-year-old female victim). Another common form of juror misbehavior occurs when a panel member conducts online research about places, people, events, or legal questions at issue in the trial. See Nancy S. Marder, Jurors and Social Media: Is a Fair Trial Still Possible? 67 SMU L. Rev. 617 (2014).

Most states and the federal system place sharp limits on the introduction of evidence about jury deliberations in an effort to protect jury secrecy and maintain a focus on issues of guilt and innocence. For instance, in Tanner v. United States, 483 U.S. 107 (1987), one juror in a wire fraud case alleged after the guilty verdict that other jurors consumed alcohol during lunch breaks at trial, slept through afternoons, and treated the deliberations as "one big party." The Supreme Court upheld the conviction, ruling that the trial judge did not err in denying a defense motion to interview the jurors and to grant a new trial. Under Federal Rules of Evidence 606(b), a juror "may not testify about any statement made or incident that occurred during the jury's deliberations." The rule bars any juror testimony about internal influences on the deliberations.

On the other hand, the Sixth Amendment right to an impartial jury requires an exception to this evidentiary bar when a juror makes a "clear statement" indicating that he or she relied on racial stereotypes or animus to convict a criminal defendant. In Pena-Rodriguez v. Colorado, 137 S. Ct. 855 (2017), a juror in a child sex abuse case said during deliberations that he believed the defendant was guilty because "Mexican men had a bravado that caused them to believe they could do whatever they wanted with women" and "are physically controlling of women because of their sense of entitlement." Faced with allegations of this sort, evidentiary rules meant to shield jury deliberations must give way.

Problem 17-4. Someone Is Not Talking or Someone Is Not Listening

Bin Zhang worked at the Golden Dragon Restaurant in Philadelphia. He received a telephone call requesting a food delivery and when he arrived at the designated address, two men approached him, took his cell phone, and attempted to flee. One man escaped, but Zhang grabbed the clothing of the second man, Benjamin Greer, long enough for police to apprehend him. Zhang suffered a broken ankle during his struggle with Greer. The state charged Greer with criminal conspiracy, aggravated assault, and robbery.

After two days of trial testimony, the jury began deliberations late in the afternoon, breaking after less than an hour that day. The jury resumed deliberations the following morning. At 2:50 P.M., the jury sent to the judge a note, signed by the jury foreperson, entitled "Reason for Hung Jury." The note volunteered that juror number nine was "not convinced" of (1) the police account of how they actually apprehended Greer, and (2) "the discrepancy between" Zhang's testimony and the police testimony; and juror number ten was "not convinced" that the evidence "concluded" that Greer was "the actual perp." The judge informed counsel of the note, revealing that it identified the holdout jurors. The judge also suggested that he make "a comment" to the jury about the importance of unanimous verdicts. The trial judge then brought the jury back into the courtroom and addressed them as follows:

> I received your note. What this indicates to me is either someone is not talking or someone is not listening. You owe that to the parties here. That's why you were picked. You promised us that you would be fair and that you would listen to your fellow jurors, and that you would give us a fair verdict.

A jury verdict is a jury of 12 people speaking as one. And, you know, if it were easy, anybody could do it. But it's not easy.

Now, you're almost there. You're there on one count. But we need your best efforts. We need you to talk. This is not time for people to stand on ego. There's people's lives that are depending on your verdict and on your participation, if you can fairly do so.

Don't ask people to surrender deeply-held beliefs just to get out of here and reach a verdict. On the other hand, each of you has views and just judging by what the note says, you're close, but no cigar. So we need you to go back and try to do and resolve this case. We're going to ask you to go back and try because I think you can do it. But just keep an open mind. Listen to each other.

When the jury returned to deliberations at 3:20 P.M., the defendant objected to the above charge, arguing that it was directed at the two holdout jurors and pressured them to convict. Greer requested that the court declare a hung jury on the two deadlocked counts. The judge rejected the argument. At 3:53 P.M., the jury returned with a unanimous verdict of not guilty on the charge of robbery, and guilty on the charges of criminal conspiracy and aggravated assault.

Did the trial judge commit reversible error? Cf. Commonwealth v. Greer, 951 A.2d 346 (Pa. 2008).

Problem 17-5. Non-Unanimous Verdicts

> A jury too frequently have at least one member, more ready to hang the panel than
> to hang the traitor.
> —Abraham Lincoln to Erastus Corning, June 12, 1863

As in many states, prosecutors and citizens in California have expressed concern that too many trials result in hung juries and that a requirement of unanimity provides radical or irrational jurors with the power to block a just outcome. A Blue Ribbon Commission on Jury System Improvement in California recommended the following jury reform:

> The Legislature should propose a constitutional amendment which provides that, except for good cause when the interests of justice require a unanimous verdict, trial judges shall accept an 11-1 verdict after the jury has deliberated for a reasonable period of time [not less than six hours] in all felonies, except where the punishment may be death or life imprisonment, and in all misdemeanors where the jury consists of twelve persons. . . .

The commission explained that "eliminating the unanimity requirement is intended primarily to address the problem of an 11-1 or 10-2 hung jury where the hold-out jurors are refusing to deliberate, are engaging in nullification, or are simply [being] unreasonable (e.g., ignoring the evidence)." A slight majority of the commission preferred allowing only 11-1 and not 10-2 verdicts because "where *two* jurors share the same minority position, it seems less likely that the basis for the minority position is irrationality rather than a legitimate disagreement."

The commission's recommendation was a version of the "modified unanimity" approach—adopted in England and used in civil cases in several states—that gives judges the power to allow non-unanimous verdicts after a period of time (two hours in England). Opting for a time delay before allowing non-unanimous verdicts "forces the jury to begin its deliberations listening to all jurors and counting the votes of all jurors."

As a legislator in California, would you support a bill implementing the commission's recommendation? See Clark Kelso, Final Report of the Blue Ribbon Commission on Jury System Improvement, 47 Hastings L.J. 1433 (1996).

Problem 17-6. Jury Nullification and Social Justice

Defense counsel has asked the trial judge to instruct the jury as follows:

> The Court instructs the Jury that under the Constitution of the United States, the Jury has a paramount right to acquit an accused person for whatever reason and to find him not guilty, even though the evidence may support a conviction, and this is an important part of the jury trial system guaranteed by the Constitution.
>
> The Court further instructs the Jury that this principle of jury nullification is just as important to the constitutional process as any other instruction which the Court has given to this Jury, and that in the final analysis, you, the members of the Jury, are the sole judges of whether or not it is right and fair to convict the Accused or whether under the totality of the circumstances, the Accused should be found not guilty. In arriving at your verdict you are not compelled to answer to anyone or to the State, nor are you required at any time by the Court or any person or party to give a reason or to be brought to accountability for your decision and vote.

Alternatively, counsel has asked the court for permission to make such an argument to the jury in the closing statement. The prosecutor has objected to the proposed instruction and will object if defense counsel makes such an argument in the closing statement.

This issue has arisen in four cases. In State v. Adams, the defendant is charged with destruction of government property and criminal trespass because she scaled a fence at a military installation and spray-painted antinuclear slogans on military equipment used to maintain nuclear weaponry. In State v. Baker, the defendant is charged with criminal trespass for blocking the doorway to an abortion clinic. He was protesting the practices of the clinic and calling for an end to legal abortions.

In State v. Cunningham, the defendant is charged with robbery in the first degree. The prosecution will present evidence that the defendant took two 12-packs of beer at gunpoint from a convenience store. The minimum sentence for this crime is 10 years. The state has also charged the defendant with being a "persistent felony offender" in the second degree because of his prior felony convictions. If the jury finds him guilty on this charge, the judge will impose a 20-year mandatory minimum sentence.

In State v. Derby, the defendant is an African American man who is charged with distribution of crack cocaine. The government will present evidence that the defendant sold two ounces of crack to an undercover agent. Venue for the trial is set in a location where it is likely that a number of the jurors will be African Americans.

As trial judge in each of these cases, would you grant the motions? What particular circumstances that you do not yet know would influence your decision? Would it matter to you if there were a state constitutional provision stating that the "jury shall have the right to determine the law and the facts"? Compare Davis v. State,

520 So. 2d 493 (Miss. 1988); State v. Wentworth, 395 A.2d 858 (N.H. 1978); Medley v. Commonwealth, 704 S.W.2d 190 (Ky. 1985).

D. THE PUBLIC AS DECISIONMAKER

The Sixth Amendment to the U.S. Constitution provides defendants with a right to a "speedy and public trial," as do analogous state constitutional provisions. A public trial might mean that any person could attend, including reporters. Or the right to a public trial might be a personal right of the defendant, giving the defendant a right *not* to have a public trial—the right to a closed trial—as well.

Courts have recognized both a private and a public interest in open trials. The presumption in favor of an open trial is not absolute, and the courts have wrestled with issues such as when the defense or prosecution has a right to a closed proceeding, and when the media has a right of access to proceedings even against the wishes of both parties. Questions regarding media coverage, particularly with cameras and microphones, have taken a higher profile with the creation of specialized television channels devoted to trials, and the increasing capacity through technology to create much wider access to trials. Consider whether the court in the following case properly balances the prosecutor's request to close the trial during the testimony of one key witness and the defendant's request that the trial remain open.

■ STATE v. MANUEL TURRIETTA
308 P.3d 964 (N.M. 2013)

MAES, C.J.

In a criminal trial, the accused shall enjoy the right to a speedy and public trial. However the right to a public trial is not absolute and may give way in certain cases to other rights or interests. In this case we address whether Manuel Turrietta's right to a public trial was violated when the district court partially closed the courtroom during the testimony of two confidential informants. . . .

Defendant, a member of two gangs known as Bad Boys Krew (BBK) and Thugs Causing Kaos (TCK), shot and killed Alberto Sandoval, a member of the West Side gang. Defendant was found guilty of second degree murder (firearm enhancement), shooting at or from a motor vehicle resulting in great bodily harm, aggravated battery with a deadly weapon, and tampering with evidence.

Following trial, Defendant appealed to the Court of Appeals claiming that "the district court improperly closed the courtroom during the testimony of two confidential informants in violation of [his] right to a public trial under the Sixth Amendment to the United States Constitution and Article II, Section 14 of the New Mexico Constitution. . . ." The Court of Appeals affirmed Defendant's convictions. . . .

We granted certiorari to address whether the Court of Appeals erred under *Presley v. Georgia*, 558 U.S. 209 (2010), by relying on pre-*Presley* circuit authority providing for a less-strenuous constitutional test than *Presley* requires. . . . We hold that the Court of Appeals erred by applying the "substantial reason" standard to a

Sixth Amendment constitutional challenge. Accordingly, we conclude that when a court is deciding whether a closure, partial or full, is constitutional it must analyze the facts using the more strenuous standard articulated in Waller v. Georgia, 467 U.S. 39 (1984)....

ANY CLOSURE OF A COURTROOM, OVER THE OBJECTION OF THE ACCUSED, MUST SATISFY THE WALLER "OVERRIDING INTEREST" STANDARD

The State filed a pre-trial motion requesting that the courtroom be cleared of unnecessary persons during testimony of four cooperating witnesses—David Torrez, George Morales, Brandon Neal and Joshua Ayala—all of whom were former gang members. The State argued that "based on previous trials involving gang members . . . the State [was] fearful that other gang members, and possibly family members, affiliated with the Defendant [would] 'pack' the Courtroom and 'maddog' the witnesses, or even try to physically intimidate [the witnesses] so that they [would] not testify."

Outside of the presence of the jury, the district court held a hearing on the motion. The district court allowed the State to conduct a limited voir dire of the confidential informants recognizing Defendant's constitutional right to a public trial and that the State had the burden to establish a "substantial probability of danger" in order to justify closure. Defendant objected to the closed proceeding, arguing that a closed courtroom, even during a limited voir dire, violated an individual's First Amendment right to be present at a hearing and Defendant's Sixth Amendment right to a public trial.

Torrez, a former member of TCK, testified that after he became an informant against Defendant and another gang member in an unrelated case, he began receiving threats from TCK. Torrez also testified that he was beaten up twice in jail by members of TCK. Morales testified that after TCK learned he had become an informant for the police, a TCK member called him "a rat or a snitch" and threatened to kill him. Morales did not say that the death threat was specifically related to him testifying at Defendant's trial.

Because Neal testified that he was not concerned about the threats, and the State failed to establish that the threats Ayala had received came from Defendant's gang, the district court denied that part of the motion. The district court judge believed there to be a TCK presence in the courtroom after court security twice found the etched moniker "TCK Blast" outside the courtroom doors. Therefore, the district court partially granted the State's motion to close the courtroom during the testimony of Torrez and Morales. The court ordered that the immediate family members of both Defendant and Victim, as well as attorneys, staff members, and press, could remain in the courtroom but that all other members of the public would not be allowed in the courtroom during the testimony of Torrez and Morales "for the purposes of witness protection, as well as the protection of the Defendant and the court." [On this basis, the trial judge excluded more than 30 persons from the courtroom.] Defendant objected, stating that those who would be excluded had a First Amendment right to attend proceedings and that he had a federal and state constitutional right to their presence. The district court overruled Defendant's objection, reasoning that it did not know of any other alternatives except to request the names and social security numbers of each observer to determine whether they were affiliated with any gangs, thus partial closure of the courtroom was the least intrusive and least limiting alternative available.

The Court of Appeals affirmed Defendant's convictions ruling that Defendant's Sixth Amendment right to a public trial was not violated because the specific threats of retaliatory gang violence and evidence of gang presence in the courtroom provided a "substantial reason" for the district court to order a partial closure. The Court did not rely on the *Waller* "overriding interest" standard in upholding the district court's decision. Rather, because the district court only partially closed the courtroom during the testimony of Torrez and Morales, the Court applied the more lenient "substantial reason" standard, which requires the party seeking closure to proffer a "substantial reason" for the partial closure, rather than an "overriding interest."

The Court of Appeals reasoned that "a partial closure satisfies the court's obligation to consider, sua sponte, reasonable alternatives to a complete closure of the proceeding." In applying the more lenient standard in this case, the Court determined that the district court was correct in ordering a partial closure because "Torrez and Morales both testified that TCK gang members had threatened them with death or physical harm in retaliation for their cooperation." In reaching this decision, the Court of Appeals also relied on the fact that there was a "TCK presence" in the courtroom, reflected by the tagging "TCK Blast," found twice by the district court during the trial. . . .

The Court of Appeals went on to state that the partial closure of the courtroom was narrowly tailored to protect the witnesses, Defendant, and the court from specific threats of gang violence. The closure did not extend beyond Torrez' and Morales' testimony and did not exclude the immediate family members of Defendant or Victim, attorneys, staff, or the press from the proceedings. . . .

In a criminal trial, the accused shall enjoy the right to a speedy and public trial. U.S. Const. amend. VI; N.M. Const. art. II, §14. The Supreme Court has uniformly recognized the public-trial guarantee as one created for the benefit of the defendant. The right to a public trial is for the benefit of the accused; that the public may see he is fairly dealt with and not unjustly condemned, and encourages witnesses to come forward while discouraging perjury. The right to a public trial is not absolute and may give way in certain cases to other rights or interests, such as the defendant's right to a fair trial or the government's interest in inhibiting disclosure of sensitive information. However, these circumstances are rare and the balance of interests must be struck with special care.

There are two types of courtroom closures, total courtroom closures and partial courtroom closures. A total courtroom closure occurs when no spectators are allowed in the courtroom and only attorneys and court staff remain. A partial closure occurs when the courtroom is closed to some spectators, but not all. . . .

A total courtroom closure is allowed when there is "an overriding interest based on findings that closure is essential to preserve higher values and is narrowly tailored to serve that interest." . . . *Waller* outlines a four-pronged "overriding interest" standard:

> [1] the party seeking to close the hearing must advance an overriding interest that is likely to be prejudiced, [2] the closure must be no broader than necessary to protect that interest, [3] the [district] court must consider reasonable alternatives

to closing the proceeding, and [4] it must make findings adequate to support the closure.

Several federal circuit courts have applied a less stringent "substantial reason" standard "for closure orders which only partially exclude the public or are otherwise narrowly tailored to specific needs." The reason for this standard, according to the Fifth Circuit Court of Appeals, is because "partial closures do not implicate the same fairness and secrecy concerns as total closures." The Tenth Circuit has utilized the "substantial reason" standard for partial closures as well. . . .

We adopt the "overriding interest" standard as discussed by the Supreme Court in *Waller* for any type of courtroom closure. First, the difference between the two standards is not perfectly clear, other than the fact that the reviewing court knows that the "substantial reason" standard is a more lenient standard than the "overriding interest" standard. Second, within the *Waller* standard, the reviewing court is charged with considering reasonable alternatives to closing the proceeding. Therefore, if a reviewing court is already contemplating a partial closure . . . that analysis seems to already align with the *Waller* standard's requirement that the closure be no broader than necessary. Furthermore, if a party is seeking something less than full closure, the *Waller* standard should still apply as originally intended because any courtroom closure is an infringement on a defendant's Sixth Amendment right to a public trial, and therefore, such a request should not be granted lightly. . . .

THE STATE DID NOT DEMONSTRATE AN OVERRIDING INTEREST FOR CLOSURE THAT IS LIKELY TO BE PREJUDICED

In this case the State's burden was to advance an overriding interest that is likely to be prejudiced. The State must show "a substantial probability that the defendant's right to a fair trial will be prejudiced by publicity that closure would prevent." When dealing with witness intimidation by gang members, the State must show that "the witness has a legitimate fear that might affect his or her ability to testify truthfully." The proponent of a closure must establish a nexus between the particular overriding interest asserted and open-court testimony. . . .

Defendant argues that the State failed to meet its burden because neither witness testified that the threats they received were specifically linked to this case or that intimidation would affect their testimony in court. Defendant further argues that the etched gang moniker does not establish an overriding interest and that speculative and general concerns do not support closure.

Neither Torrez nor Morales ever stated that they were afraid to testify, that their trial testimony would be affected by any received threats, or that having gang members or related family members in the audience would affect their testimony. We are not to assume that the absence of a definitive statement that a witness's testimony would not be affected by an open courtroom means that it automatically would be effected. Further, the State failed to establish whether the threats and violence that Torrez and Morales had experienced prior to trial were directly related to Defendant's case or other cases where both had admitted to snitching. Both Torrez and Morales had received those threats when TCK initially discovered they were assisting the police; the State did not present any evidence that the threats occurred or increased in an effort by TCK members to deter the two informants from testifying. Further, the State never presented any evidence that either Torrez or Morales was aware of the TCK etchings outside of the courtroom. There was insufficient proof that a link existed between the experienced threats and either witnesses' ability or willingness to testify. Without more, the State did not demonstrate an overriding interest that was likely to be prejudiced by an open courtroom. Therefore, the first prong of the *Waller* standard was not satisfied and the closure was unconstitutional. The courtroom closure in this case is deemed unconstitutional because of the failure of the first prong; however, because we are adopting a new standard, we address the remaining three prongs for the purpose of analysis.

THE CLOSURE WAS OVERLY BROAD

Defendant contends that the closure in this case was extreme and overly broad because there was no showing that the thirty plus people excluded were in any way gang-affiliated, had done anything wrong, or posed any threat. Defendant cites to a handful of cases holding that the exclusion of observers without specific justification supports a finding that the closure was overly broad [citing cases from Hawaii, Massachusetts, and Maryland].

The State argues that the closure in this case was narrowly tailored because the court enforced only a partial closure, allowing Defendant's family, Victim's immediate family, attorneys, staff, and members of the press to remain. Further, the State asserts that the closure was not overly broad because it was only enforced during the testimony of Torrez and Morales. However, the State failed to cite to any supporting authority explaining how or why the district court's closure was narrowly tailored so as not to infringe on Defendant's Sixth Amendment right to a public trial.

The second prong of *Waller* requires that the closure "be no broader than necessary to protect [the overriding interest]." A properly tailored closure may exist where a careful balance of interests is struck and only the individuals allegedly involved in the creation of the threat are excluded. Here, both Torrez and Morales testified to the names of specific individuals from TCK who had threatened and intimidated them. The district court could have chosen to exclude those named gang members, possibly creating a narrowly tailored closure. Instead, the district court excluded more than thirty people without knowing how many of them, if any, were gang affiliated. The court also later admitted that as a result of the closure, it had excluded "members of . . . Defendant's family and a few of his friends."

"An accused is at the very least entitled to have his friends, relatives and counsel present." In re Oliver, 333 U.S. 257 (1948). The relationship between those excluded to the defendant must be taken into account when deciding whether a closure is constitutional. Here, some family members and friends were excluded without any finding that they posed a threat, suggesting that the exclusion was overly broad and unconstitutional. Accordingly, the State did not satisfy the second prong of *Waller*.

THE DISTRICT COURT FAILED TO ADEQUATELY ASSESS POSSIBLE ALTERNATIVES TO CLOSURE

The third *Waller* prong requires that the court consider reasonable alternatives to closure. A district court is required to "take every reasonable measure to accommodate public attendance at criminal trials." Even if the parties do not offer alternatives to closure, the court is required to assess whether any reasonable alternatives exist.

The State argues that the district court's granting of a partial closure was a reasonable alternative to a complete closure. [The] State contends that some courts have interpreted the third prong of *Waller* to mean that trial courts need not consider sua sponte any and all alternatives to partial closure, but rather they must only consider sua sponte alternatives to complete closure. . . . Defendant argues that there were a variety of reasonable alternatives to both a partial and complete closure such as screening observers, admonishing spectators of possible criminal sanctions, the wait-and-see method, or increased security in the courtroom, all of which the court in this case chose not to pursue.

We decline to follow the State's interpretation of the third *Waller* prong and instead adopt *Presley*'s rule that a court must consider, sua sponte, all alternatives to any type of closure. Presley v. Georgia, 558 U.S. 209, 214 (2010). Although Defendant did not suggest at trial all of the alternatives to closure that he now argues, the district court had the responsibility to consider as many alternatives as possible. In fact, the judge suggested that screening the spectators and recording names to determine gang affiliation was a possibility, but neglected to do so. As Defendant now suggests there were several other alternatives to closure that the district court did not consider such as using the wait-and-see method or increasing security. Because the district court failed to consider all reasonable alternatives to closure, we hold that the third *Waller* prong was not satisfied.

THE DISTRICT COURT FAILED TO MAKE ADEQUATE FINDINGS UNDER THE WALLER STANDARD TO SUPPORT CLOSURE

The final prong of *Waller* requires that the court make legally adequate findings to justify the closure. It is appropriate to evaluate the amount of evidence required and the level of findings needed to support an overriding interest in closure. When a trial court fails "to make the requisite case-specific findings of fact, closure of the courtroom violates the defendant's right to a public trial."

Defendant argues that the Court of Appeals erred in applying the more lenient "substantial reason" standard . . . and thus its findings are not legally adequate to support closure as analyzed through the *Waller* standard. Defendant asserts that if we were to adopt the less stringent standard for closure, the exception would swallow the rule and fear and intimidation would be rewarded instead of discouraged. . . .

The State maintains that the district court made adequate legal findings in granting the partial closure to support both the "substantial reason" and "overriding interest" tests. The State points to the Court of Appeals' affirmation of the district court's ruling that protection of a witness who claims to be frightened as a result of perceived threats did not violate Defendant's Sixth Amendment right to a public trial. By implementing a narrowly tailored closure, the State argues that violent and threatening spectators are kept out of the courtroom which prevents disruption of the fairness of trials, contrary to Defendant's reasoning.

The district court justified the closure based on "the danger to the witnesses . . . and the fact that there were two etchings outside of the courtroom, indicating that there was a TCK presence that was undetected." This basis however fails to mention any specific threat or possibility of intimidation. In fact, no testimony was ever elicited from Torrez or Morales that either was afraid to testify or that the presence of certain spectators in the courtroom would affect their ability to testify. Similarly, there is nothing in the record that indicates either informant witness was aware of the etchings outside the courtroom. Finally, the district court admitted that it was unable to identify who was gang-affiliated and thus it was unable to ascertain who if anyone posed a real or specific threat. The findings of fact concerning the two etchings and testimony from the informants about past threats were not sufficient to justify closing the courtroom and did not satisfy the fourth *Waller* requirement. As such, Defendant's Sixth Amendment right to a public trial was violated. . . .

Notes

1. *"Public trial": majority view.* The defendant, prosecution, reporters, and the public may all have different interests with respect to whether a trial remains open. The public nature of criminal trials derives both from the express guarantee of the Sixth Amendment and its state analogs and from the First Amendment rights of both the defendant and the press. The presumption of open trials is usually tested when one party wants to close the proceedings and the other does not. A defendant might want to avoid publicity or retribution, exclude people who might provide new evidence, or reduce the risk of a biased jury. The government might want to protect the identity of an informant, undercover police officer, victim, or witness by limiting the number of people who watch the testimony. See, e.g., People v. Jones, 750 N.E.2d 524 (N.Y. 2001) (undercover officer). Courts are often most sympathetic to victim and witness concerns, especially in cases involving children and in cases of sexual assault and abuse. See generally Vivian Berger, Man's Trial, Woman's Tribulation: Rape Cases in the Courtroom, 77 Colum. L. Rev. 1 (1977).

2. *Media access to the courtroom.* Journalists are members of the public and have the same initial rights as any other person to watch trials. In addition to recognizing the right to court access shared by all citizens, the U.S. Supreme Court has enumerated a qualified First Amendment right in the press to attend criminal trials. See Globe Newspaper Co. v. Superior Court for Norfolk County, 457 U.S. 596 (1982); Richmond Newspapers, Inc. v. Virginia, 448 U.S. 555, 572 (1980). According to Smith v. Daily Mail Publishing, 443 U.S. 97 (1979), the First Amendment limits the power of courts to punish the publication of sensitive details from judicial proceedings, such as the name of a juvenile in a delinquency matter. While a judge can close proceedings to the public after making a sufficient showing (as described in Waller v. Georgia, 467 U.S. 39 (1984)), the state cannot punish journalists for publishing information about litigants or the court process that they learn despite the closure of the proceedings.

3. *Defendant's right to fair trial as counterweight.* Although public monitoring of criminal trials normally contributes to fairer procedures and more public confidence in the courts, the press and the public can also become so fixated on a trial that it calls into doubt the fairness of the proceedings. A famous example involved the trial of Dr. Sam Sheppard, charged with murdering his wife in their home in suburban Cleveland. The case attracted intense press coverage prior to trial; Cleveland newspapers published the names and addresses of the prospective jurors in the case. As trial began, the judge assigned dozens of reporters to seats in the small courtroom. The local television station set up broadcasting facilities in the courthouse, next door to the jury room. Witnesses, counsel, jurors, and the defendant were photographed and televised whenever they entered or left the courtroom. During the nine weeks of trial, the movement of reporters in and out of the courtroom caused

so much confusion that, despite a loudspeaker system installed in the courtroom, it was difficult for the witnesses and counsel to be heard. When the jury viewed the scene of the murder on the first day of the trial, hundreds of reporters, cameramen, and onlookers were there (along with a helicopter flying overhead), and one representative of the news media accompanied the jury while it inspected the Sheppard home. Throughout the trial, local media published allegations from relatives and other people who claimed to have relevant information about the murder; some of these claims in local news stories never appeared as testimony in the trial. The judge denied defense motions for change of venue, continuance, and mistrial. The U.S. Supreme Court, however, later decided that the trial violated the Sixth Amendment right of the defendant to a fair trial. See Sheppard v. Maxwell, 384 U.S. 333 (1966). The case formed the basis for a television series and a movie, both titled, "The Fugitive."

4. *Change of venue after pretrial publicity.* The threat to a defendant's right to a fair trial can begin will before the start of trial, when prospective jurors and witnesses hear media reports about the alleged crime and form opinions about the defendant's guilt or innocence on that basis. As a matter of constitutional doctrine and criminal procedure rules, the remedy for pretrial publicity that interferes with a fair trial in that location is a change of venue. See Federal Rule of Criminal Procedure 21 (court "must transfer the proceeding against that defendant to another district if the court is satisfied that so great a prejudice against the defendant exists in the transferring district that the defendant cannot obtain a fair and impartial trial there"); Rideau v. Louisiana, 373 U.S. 723 (1963) (trial judge's refusal of request for change of venue was denial of due process, where video of defendant admitting in detail to committing a robbery, kidnapping, and murder was televised three times in the parish).

5. *Broadcast of trials.* In addition to general claims for access, reporters often want to bring their cameras and microphones with them. Courts have largely rejected claims that the media have a constitutional right to bring cameras and microphones into the courtroom. However, almost all states currently allow cameras at trials (with various limitations on the placement and use of flash), and over 35 states allow trials to be filmed—a dramatic shift since Florida first allowed cameras into its courtrooms in 1977. See Ruth Ann Strickland & Richter H. Moore, Jr., Cameras in State Courts: A Historical Perspective, 78 Judicature 128 (1994). As in North Dakota, state rules often leave the degree of access to the discretion of the trial judge. In contrast, the federal courts have experimented with but largely rejected the use of cameras in the courtroom. Trial judges seem always to face new questions about communications technologies, such as text messages, Twitter updates, and cameras in telephones. For a window into the changing role of communication technologies in the courtroom, go to the web extension for this chapter at *http://www.crimpro.com/extension/ch17.*

6. *What parts of the trial process must be public?* The general requirement of public trials does not mean that all parts of all trials must be open to the public. The trial proceedings may include bench conferences or discussions between judge and counsel in chambers. Submissions will often be made in writing. Physical evidence may be difficult to view at a distance, or in the form presented in court. Does the defendant have a right to make these proceedings public? Pretrial proceedings often reveal information that, if reported, might influence the judgment of jurors at trial, and courts have been more willing to restrict access at this stage. Some

information provided at pretrial proceedings, including detention and competency hearings, may be irrelevant to questions of guilt and innocence. Other proceedings, such as voir dire hearings, are closely linked to trial, and for these proceedings the rules governing media at trial apply. See Presley v. Georgia, 558 U.S. 209 (2010) (trial judges must consider all available methods to preserve public access to jury selection before closing proceedings to public; court should not consider just those alternatives that defendant suggests); Weaver v. Massachusetts, 137 S. Ct. 1899 (2017) (jury voir dire must be in public unless judge states appropriate reason for closing courtroom).

7. *Anonymous jurors.* Based on concerns about the safety and privacy of jurors, trial judges decide from time to time to use numbers rather than names when referring to individual jurors. Sometimes, the jurors remain anonymous to the parties, while in other trials, prosecutors and attorneys for the defense might know the juror names. In either case, the judge prohibits the use of those juror names in the courtroom when other people are present. See United States v. Barnes, 604 F.2d 121 (2d Cir. 1979) (jurors' demeanors and responses to questions regarding their family, education, and other matters would provide substantially the same information as the juror names, religious affiliations, and ethnicity; no violation of defendant's right to an impartial jury). Appellate courts note that this practice poses some risk to the presumption of innocence at trial because it signals to the jury that the defendant is dangerous. They affirm the use of anonymous juries only after a showing of need for juror protection and the use of precautions against jury taint. See United States v. Thomas, 757 F.2d 1359 (2d Cir. 1985) (anonymous jury is warranted only if there is a "strong reason" to believe that the jury needs protection and if the court takes "reasonable precautions" to minimize the impact of anonymity on the jurors' views of the defendant).

8. *Gag orders on prosecutors and defense attorneys.* The professional conduct rules of every state limit the ability of attorneys to comment publicly on judicial proceedings. In particular, the Model Rules of Professional Conduct, Rule 3.6, states a general rule and several safe harbor exceptions regarding attorney statements to the media. The general rule is that a lawyer participating in litigation "shall not make an extrajudicial statement that the lawyer knows or reasonably should know will be disseminated by means of public communication and will have a substantial likelihood of materially prejudicing an adjudicative proceeding in the matter." The rule does authorize the attorney to state publicly the "offense or defense involved" and "information contained in a public record." The rules declare a further set of limits on prosecutors. Under Rule 3.8(f), prosecutors must "refrain from making extrajudicial comments that have a substantial likelihood of heightening public condemnation of the accused." See Vin Bonventre, "Preet Bharara on Sheldon Silver: Prosecutorial Ethics?" Mar. 5, 2015, available at *http://www.newyorkcourtwatcher.com/2015/03/preet-bharara-on-sheldon-silver.html.*

Trial judges can order the attorneys in a case not to address the media, if necessary to assure a fair trial. There are, however, constitutional limits on the power of trial judges and bar authorities to discipline lawyers based on these rules. In Gentile v. State Bar of Nevada, 501 U.S. 1030 (1991), the U.S. Supreme Court overturned discipline against an attorney who held a press conference and made only a brief opening statement about the nature of the criminal charges against his client and declined to answer reporters' questions seeking more detailed comments. The state ethics rule, the Court held, was void for vagueness as applied in this case.

9. *Public access to court records.* To what extent does a commitment to open courts require a commitment to public access to court records? See Commonwealth v. Fujita, 23 N.E.3d 882 (Mass. 2015) (based on common-law right of public access to judicial records, names of jurors must be made public after trial ends unless trial judge can point to reason for confidentiality beyond juror preference). Criminal court records in the state and federal courts are usually open to media and public scrutiny, sometimes in hard copy in the office of the clerk, and sometimes in electronic format. Private information vendors purchase compilations of these records from the courts and repackage the information for resale. Access to juvenile records is more restricted, and states typically allow for the expungement or sealing of arrest and conviction records in selected cases.

This high level of public access to judicial records is not universal. Most continental European countries, for instance, keep criminal records private. Some verdicts are not delivered in open court. And before court cases are published, the government edits the document to remove identifying references to the defendant and other figures in the case. See James B. Jacobs, The Eternal Criminal Record (2015). What public purposes might be served by narrower public access to records about criminal proceedings? Law enforcement records, as opposed to records of judicial proceedings, tend to be exempt from public records laws such as the Freedom of Information Act. See Dept. of Justice v. Reporters Committee for Freedom of the Press, 489 U.S. 749 (1989) (personal privacy exemption protects from disclosure criminal identification records of individuals compiled by FBI).

10. *Public monitoring of criminal proceedings.* Some private groups with particular interest in the work of the criminal courts send members to the courthouse to observe proceedings and to collect information from public records. For instance, "Mothers Against Drunk Driving" (MADD) has monitored and publicized, across several decades, the sentences that judges impose in DWI cases. Some journalists and academics compile databases from hard-copy court records that allow comparisons, across many cases, of charges filed, negotiated guilty pleas, jury selection practices, and sentences. These efforts focus on the investment of the entire community in an accountable criminal justice system. See Jocelyn Simonson, The Criminal Court Audience in a Post-Trial World, 127 Harv. L. Rev. 2173 (2014) (arguing that First and Sixth Amendments together create a right to public criminal adjudication, benefiting local community and extending to trial and nontrial courtroom proceedings).

Problem 17-7. Measures for Justice

The nonprofit organization Measures for Justice collects, curates, and publishes data about the decisions of prosecutors, defense attorneys, judges, and law enforcement officials as reflected in the highly fragmented records of these different contributors to criminal justice in the state courts. As the organization explains, "data collection across a country whose records are maintained differently county by county has required some innovative and old-fashioned methods. MFJ acquires its data by approaching state and local leaders, often traveling county by county. In the process, we solicit feedback on our metrics and counsel on the limitations of the data we're acquiring." See *https://measuresforjustice.org/about/overview/*. The end product is a set of measures that allow for meaningful comparisons across different

counties within a state or comparisons of practices in different states. MFJ reports dozens of "core measures" such as the percentage of cases referred to prosecutors that were not prosecuted, "companion measures" such as the time to disposition for felonies, and "contextual measures" such as the demographics of the local population.

Imagine that you are a lobbyist for Measures for Justice. You approach a state legislator, hoping for passage of a new public records law in the state that will facilitate the recording and dissemination of electronic records about criminal justice in the state courts. A potential template for your proposed bill appears in Florida Stat. §900.05, which requires various criminal justice actors to collect and make available to the public—in digital format on a yearly basis—a range of performance measures. The data collected under this statute include the dates of filing, arraignment, attorney assignment, motions filed, trial, and disposition; number of cases declined for prosecution; the number and types of charges filed; the defendant's date of birth, race or ethnicity, gender, residence zip code, primary language, immigration status, and indigency status; information related to bail or pretrial release determinations; information related to the sentence imposed; information related to the victim of the alleged offense; and the annual felony and misdemeanor caseloads of each trial judge, trial attorney in the office of the prosecutor, and trial attorney in the office of the public defender.

Which measures would you add to the above list, if your objective is to promote meaningful comparisons of performance across different criminal court actors at the county level? Who might argue against the passage of such a statute? What arguments might they raise?

XVIII

■

Witnesses and Proof

A complete understanding of felony trials requires a knowledge of substantive criminal law, the law of evidence, trial strategy, and procedural rules. Yet it is possible to boil down this wide-ranging material into a few core principles of procedure that define criminal trials. At a general level, these principles are familiar to lawyers and nonlawyers alike.

The first core principle—the right to confront witnesses—is our central tool for squeezing truth from the evidence. It is difficult to imagine a system that does not allow a defendant the right to challenge and test witnesses and other evidence.

The defendant can confront any government witness, and the government can confront any defense witness. But can the government call any witness to prove a case? The second principle—the privilege against self-incrimination—recognizes the single great exception to the power of the government to call relevant witnesses. The principle recognizes that a defendant cannot be forced to testify, either by threat of prison or by calling the defendant's silence to the attention of the factfinder. This principle may preclude the government from calling the single person who may know most about the alleged offense.

The third core principle is the presumption of innocence—the idea that a person is not guilty of a crime until the state proves to a factfinder that the person has committed a criminal act with the requisite mental state. The state must prove its case "beyond a reasonable doubt."

This chapter explores these central features of a criminal trial in the United States. It also highlights one of the most important ethical dilemmas in an adversary trial system devoted to finding the truth: What should a defense lawyer do if the lawyer believes the client or a witness is lying? What should a prosecutor do if the prosecutor believes a key witness is lying?

A. CONFRONTATION OF WITNESSES

An adversarial legal system, by its very nature, places great value on the testing of evidence. Cross-examination of witnesses presents the attorneys with their best opportunity to test the reliability of evidence.

State and federal constitutions recognize the importance of this adversarial testing of evidence. Often, however, the constitutional provisions refer to "confrontation" of witnesses rather than to cross-examination. Consider the relevant clause from the Sixth Amendment to the federal constitution: "In all criminal prosecutions, the accused shall enjoy the right . . . to be confronted with the witnesses against him." In this section, we consider the devices available to test evidence.

1. The Value of Confrontation

Ordinarily the prosecution presents witnesses who testify at trial in the presence of the defendant, and the defense counsel cross-examines the witnesses with the defendant present. But does the presence of the defendant add anything? Is there some value in the "confrontation" of witnesses that goes beyond an effective cross-examination? See Richard D. Friedman, Confrontation: The Search for Basic Principles, 86 Geo. L.J. 1011 (1998).

The Texas case reprinted below deals with the tradeoff between the values of confrontation and the human costs of presenting evidence in a format that allows live testimony. As you read the case, reflect on what makes a cross-examination effective and what additional functions confrontation might serve. The second case, an opinion of the European Court of Human Rights, plays a variation on this theme: efforts by investigating judges and prosecutors in the Netherlands to use witnesses whose names remain unknown to the defendant. As you read the case, try to sort out which of the concepts discussed would be familiar to an American court and which would be unthinkable. What does this European decision tell us about criminal justice in the United States?

A word is in order about the European Court of Human Rights. More than 30 nations have signed a treaty known as the European Convention for the Protection of Human Rights and Fundamental Freedoms. The treaty was signed in 1950, after the revelation of outrageous human rights abuses during World War II and during a time when some European nations felt the need to distinguish their democratic forms of government from Communist legal systems during the Cold War.

Under the European Convention, an individual who is convicted in the criminal courts of a signatory nation can challenge that conviction if it was obtained in violation of the convention. The challenge first goes to the European Commission on Human Rights; either the defendant or the government may appeal the commission's decision to the European Court of Human Rights. The judges of the court are drawn from various signatory nations. They interpret the convention in light of broad principles of international and domestic law. The European Court of Human Rights both reflects and develops a consensus among nations about human rights, including the nature of a fair criminal trial.

■ ISRAEL ROMERO v. STATE

173 S.W.3d 502 (Tex. 2005)

KELLER, P.J.

The question before us is whether the defendant's Sixth Amendment right to confront witnesses was violated when a witness testified in disguise. Although this is a very close issue, and one undecided by the United States Supreme Court, we answer that question "yes." . . .

Appellant was indicted for aggravated assault. On the morning of trial, Cesar Hiran Vasquez, one of the State's key witnesses, arrived at the courthouse but refused to enter the courtroom to testify. Vasquez, who had been subpoenaed by the State, notified the State that he "would rather go to jail than testify in this case" because of his fear of appellant. [Vasquez spoke little English, and all of his communications were through an interpreter.] The State informed the trial court of Vasquez's fear and his refusal to testify, and the trial court responded by threatening to fine Vasquez $500 for failing to obey the State's subpoena. Vasquez persisted in his refusal to testify, however, stating that, because he was worried for himself and his children, he "would prefer to pay" the fine rather than testify. The trial court then imposed the fine. Shortly thereafter, Vasquez entered the courtroom wearing dark sunglasses, a baseball cap pulled down over his forehead, and a long-sleeved jacket with its collar turned up and fastened so as to obscure Vasquez's mouth, jaw, and the lower half of his nose. The net effect and apparent purpose of Vasquez's "disguise" was to hide almost all of his face from view. The record reflects that, at the time of trial, appellant was aware of Vasquez's name and address.

Appellant objected to the "disguise" on the basis of his "right to confrontation" and, more generally, his right to a fair trial. The trial court overruled these objections.

The State then called Vasquez to the stand, outside the presence of the jury, to testify regarding appellant's motion to suppress Vasquez's in-court identification of appellant. Vasquez testified that he was operating a taxicab on May 10, 2002, at approximately 1:45 A.M., outside the Cosmos nightclub in Houston, when he saw appellant run toward the nightclub and, for no apparent reason, fire several shots in that direction. Given Vasquez's proximity to the nightclub's entrance, appellant's shots came fairly close to him. A security guard at the nightclub returned fire and hit appellant in the back. Appellant then retreated to a pickup truck and sped away, stopping once to fire again in the direction of the nightclub. Vasquez's testimony continued:

> *Q: [DEFENSE COUNSEL]* If the Court were to order you not to wear your sunglasses, your hat, and your jacket with my client present in the courtroom, are you still going to testify. . . .
> *A:* For my safety, I wouldn't do it. . . .
> *Q: [PROSECUTOR]* Why are you afraid to testify against this defendant?
> *A:* Because of the way that it could be seen that he was going to attack the security guard. It can be seen that he's a person who's dangerous on the street. . . .
> *Q:* What are you afraid that he would do?
> *A:* To take revenge. . . .
> *Q: [DEFENSE COUNSEL]* Well, my client's never threatened you, has he?
> *A:* No.

Q: All right. He's given you no reason to be afraid of him, right?

A: Didn't you see the way he's looking at me? . . .

Q: You just don't like the way he's looking at you, right, basically?

A: No.

Q: Then what is it?

A: The way I saw him attack with the gun. . . .

On direct appeal, appellant . . . argued that the trial court's ruling denied him his Sixth Amendment right to confrontation because Vasquez's "ball cap, large opaque sunglasses and mask [*sic*] prevented a face-to-face confrontation" and hindered the jury's ability to observe Vasquez's demeanor and assess his credibility. [The court of appeals] reversed the judgment of the trial court, and remanded the case to the trial court for further proceedings. . . .

The Sixth Amendment's Confrontation Clause ("In all criminal prosecutions, the accused shall enjoy the right . . . to be confronted with the witnesses against him") reflects a strong preference for face-to-face confrontation at trial. An encroachment upon face-to-face confrontation is permitted only when necessary to further an important public interest and when the reliability of the testimony is otherwise assured.

Reliability

Whether the reliability of the testimony is otherwise assured turns upon the extent to which the proceedings respect the four elements of confrontation: physical presence, oath, cross-examination, and observation of demeanor by the trier of fact. In Maryland v. Craig, 497 U.S. 836 (1990), the Supreme Court found sufficient assurance of reliability in a procedure that denied one of these elements—physical presence—where the remaining three elements were unimpaired. In that case, a child witness testified in front of a one-way closed-circuit monitor that prevented her from seeing the defendant but permitted the judge, jury, and defendant to see the witness. Because the witness was under oath, subject to contemporaneous cross-examination, and her demeanor was on display before the trier of fact, the Supreme Court found that the procedure adequately ensured that the testimony was "both reliable and subject to rigorous adversarial testing in a manner functionally equivalent to that accorded live, in person testimony."

In this case, as with *Craig*, the presence element of confrontation was compromised. Although the physical presence element might appear, on a superficial level, to have been satisfied by Vasquez's taking the witness stand, it is clear that Vasquez believed the disguise would confer a degree of anonymity that would insulate him from the defendant. The physical presence element entails an accountability of the witness to the defendant. The Supreme Court has observed that the presence requirement is motivated by the idea that a witness cannot "hide behind the shadow" but will be compelled to look the defendant "in the eye" while giving accusatory testimony. Coy v. Iowa, 487 U.S. 1012 (1988). In the present case, accountability was compromised because the witness was permitted to hide behind his disguise.

But unlike *Craig*, the present case also involves a failure to respect a second element of confrontation: observation of the witness's demeanor. Although Vasquez's tone of voice was subject to evaluation and some body language might have been observable, the trier of fact was deprived of the ability to observe his eyes and his facial expressions. And while wearing a disguise may itself be an aspect of demeanor that jurors could consider in assessing credibility, that fact cannot by any stretch of the imagination be considered an adequate substitute for the jurors' ability to view a witness's face, the most expressive part of the body and something that is traditionally regarded as one of the most important factors in assessing credibility. To hold otherwise is to remove the "face" from "face-to-face confrontation."

IMPORTANT INTERESTS

While there may be circumstances sufficient to justify a procedure that overrides not just one but two elements of a defendant's right to confrontation, those circumstances should rise above the "important" interests referred to in *Craig* to interests that are truly compelling. But we do not see an important interest served in the present case, much less a compelling one.

One important, even compelling, interest might be to protect a witness from retaliation, but the disguise in this case did little to further such an interest because Vasquez's name and address, but not his face, were already known to the defendant. Although Vasquez might reasonably fear that the defendant would be able to connect his facial features and appearance to his name and address, this connection could easily be made without any in-court appearance. A defendant seeking retaliation could simply knock on the door at the known address and ask for the named person. Moreover, this is not a case in which the defendant gave the victim or the authorities any concrete reason for suspecting retaliation, nor is this a case in which the defendant was shown to belong to a crime syndicate or a street gang from which retaliation might be anticipated.

At best, the disguise worked to allay the witness's subjective fear of retaliation. But some degree of trauma is to be expected in face-to-face confrontations. *Coy*, 487 U.S. at 1020 ("face-to-face presence may, unfortunately, upset the truthful rape victim or abused child; but by the same token it may confound and undo the false accuser, or reveal the child coached by a malevolent adult. It is a truism that constitutional protections have costs"). Calming an adult witness's fears is quite a different thing from protecting a child victim from serious emotional trauma. Adults are generally considered to be made of sterner stuff and capable of looking after their own psychological well-being. And the difference is especially great when the adult witness is not the victim, but merely a bystander who observed events, and when the basis of the witness's fear is simply that the defendant committed a violent crime and gave the witness a bad look. If those circumstances are sufficient to justify infringing on a defendant's right to face-to-face confrontation, then such infringement can be carried out against anyone accused of a violent crime. That outcome would violate the principle that face-to-face confrontation may be deprived only in exceptional situations. . . . We affirm the judgment of the Court of Appeals.

MEYERS, J., dissenting.

Mr. Israel G. Romero, this is your lucky day. You're going to get a new trial. The trial judge erred by allowing an eye witness to your crime to wear a ball cap, jacket, and sunglasses while testifying. . . .

The majority says that two elements of the confrontation clause were compromised—that being presence and demeanor. While I'm unsure what compromise means here, I'm fairly confident that the witness was there face-to-face to testify, was cross-examined, and that his demeanor showed that he was scared to death of the defendant. In Texas, is an accused entitled to more than this? Apparently so. Since Mr. Vasquez spoke through an interpreter, I really think this whole controversy is probably "lost in translation." . . .

The central concern of the Confrontation Clause is to ensure the reliability of the evidence against a criminal defendant by subjecting it to rigorous testing in the context of an adversary proceeding before the trier of fact. [As the Supreme Court noted in its earliest case interpreting the Confrontation Clause]:

> The primary object of the constitutional provision in question was to prevent depositions or ex parte affidavits, such as were sometimes admitted in civil cases, being used against the prisoner in lieu of a personal examination and cross-examination of the witness in which the accused has an opportunity, not only of testing the recollection and sifting the conscience of the witness, but of compelling him to stand face to face with the jury in order that they may look at him, and judge by his demeanor upon the stand and the manner in which he gives his testimony whether he is worthy of belief. Mattox v. United States, 156 U.S. 237, 242-243 (1895). . . .

But here's the catch, the defense basically neutralized the witness's disguise. Mr. Vasquez was the only one in the courtroom who thought he was The Phantom of the Opera. The only effect that wearing a hat and sunglasses had was to make Mr. Vasquez more comfortable on the stand and to limit the trauma he felt when testifying against someone whom he feared. This is similar to the cases cited by the parties, Coy v. Iowa, 487 U.S. 1012 (1988), and Maryland v. Craig, 497 U.S. 836 (1990), in which measures were used to prevent face-to-face contact between the defendant and the witness in order to prevent trauma to the victims. However, unlike the screen in *Coy* and the closed circuit television in *Craig*, in this case, the outfit worn by Mr. Vasquez did not prevent or encroach upon face-to-face contact between the defendant and the witness.

Attorneys often change the appearance of witnesses appearing in court. Drunks are sobered up, addicts are cleaned up, and the homeless are dressed up; prostitutes even appear in business suits. These modifications are intended to persuade the jury that the witness is reliable. Mr. Vasquez's additions were not intended to fool the jury. Rather it was simply a method to allay his fears about testifying. Nothing was compromised—just slightly camouflaged.

I agree with the trial court's decision to allow the witness to appear as secret agent man. Therefore, I respectfully dissent.

HOLCOMB, J., dissenting.

. . . After considering the record and the arguments of the parties, I conclude that an important state interest is implicated in this case. On this record, the trial court could have reasonably concluded that Vasquez's disguise was necessary to further the important state interest in protecting the physical well-being of witnesses who have a well-founded fear of retaliation on the part of the defendant. Vasquez testified that he witnessed appellant engage in an unprovoked, determined, and lethal attack on a nightclub in Houston. Vasquez also [remarked] about how appellant was looking at him in the courtroom, apparently in a threatening manner. On this record, the trial court could have reasonably concluded that Vasquez reasonably believed appellant was a dangerous person, possibly a sociopath, and that Vasquez had a well-founded fear of retaliation on appellant's part. The fact that the trial court made no such finding on the record is not determinative. Nothing in Maryland v. Craig requires that a trial court make explicit, as opposed to implicit, findings regarding the necessity of a special procedure to protect a witness. . . .

Finally, I conclude that the reliability of Vasquez's testimony was otherwise assured, because (1) both parties were aware of his name and residence address, i.e., he was not an anonymous witness; (2) he testified in the courtroom and under oath, thus impressing him with the seriousness of the matter and the possibility of a penalty for perjury; (3) he was able to see appellant's face in the courtroom, thus reducing the risk that he would wrongfully implicate an innocent person; (4) he was subject to cross-examination; and (5) the jury was able to hear his voice and observe his overall demeanor.

Undoubtedly, the Sixth Amendment does not always require that the jurors have the ability to see the witness's eyes or see his mouth move as he talks. In some situations, for example, a witness may be blind and may wear sunglasses over his sightless eyes; in other situations, a witness may testify in sign language. In my view, the Sixth Amendment was satisfied in this case. . . .

■ DÉSIRÉ DOORSON v. NETHERLANDS

22 Eur. Ct. H.R. 330 (1996)

In August 1987 the prosecuting authorities decided to take action against the nuisance caused by drug trafficking in Amsterdam.* The police compiled photographs of persons suspected of being drug dealers, and showed the photos to about 150 drug addicts to collect statements from them. However, most of the witnesses were only prepared to make statements on condition that their identity was not disclosed to the drug dealers they identified. Witnesses who had testified during a similar enforcement effort in 1986 had received threats.

In September 1987 the police received information from a drug addict that Doorson was engaged in drug trafficking. The police then included a 1985 photograph of Doorson in the collection of photographs they showed to other drug addicts. A number of addicts recognized Doorson from his photograph and told police that he had sold drugs. Six of these drug addicts remained anonymous; they were referred to by the police under the code names Y05, Y06, Y13, Y14, Y15 and Y16. The identity of two others was disclosed, namely R and N.

On 12 April 1988 Doorson was arrested on suspicion of having committed drug offenses. During the preliminary judicial investigation, Doorson's lawyer requested an examination of the witnesses referred to in the police report. The investigating judge ordered the police to bring these witnesses before him on 30 May 1988 between 09.30 and 16.00. Doorson's lawyer was notified and invited to attend the questioning of these witnesses before the investigating judge.

On 30 May 1988 Doorson's lawyer arrived at the investigating judge's chambers at 09.30. However, after an hour and a half had elapsed and none of the witnesses had appeared, he concluded that no questioning would take place. The attorney left for another appointment, after the judge promised him that if the witnesses should turn up later that day, they would not be heard but would be required to

---

* [Material in this opinion preceding paragraph 53 has been edited without indication.—Eds.]

appear for questioning at a later date so that he would be able to attend. After the lawyer had left, two of the eight witnesses referred to in the police report turned up and were heard by the investigating judge in the absence of the lawyer, witness Y15 at about 11.15 and witness Y16 at about 15.00. Y15 and Y16 did not keep a promise to return for further questioning on 3 June.

In proceedings before the Regional Court, the named witness N appeared, but R did not. Both the prosecution and the defense were given the opportunity to put questions to N. Asked to identify Doorson, N stated that he did not recognize him. On being shown Doorson's photograph, he said that he recognized it as that of a man who had given him heroin when he was ill. However, towards the end of his examination he stated that he was no longer quite sure of recognizing the man in the photograph; it might be that the man who had given him the heroin only resembled that man. He also claimed that when shown the photographs by the police, he had only identified Doorson's photograph as that of a person from whom he had bought drugs because at the time he had felt very ill and had been afraid that the police might not give him back the drugs which they had found in his possession.

After the Regional Court convicted Doorson of drug trafficking and sentenced him to 15 months' imprisonment, he appealed to the Amsterdam Court of Appeal. Doorson's lawyer requested the procurator general of the Court of Appeal to summon the anonymous witnesses and the named witnesses N and R for questioning at that Court's hearing. The procurator general replied that he would summon N and R but not the anonymous witnesses, because he wished to preserve their anonymity.

The Court of Appeal decided to verify the necessity of maintaining the anonymity of the witnesses and referred the case back to the investigating judge for this purpose. The Court of Appeal also requested the investigating judge to examine the witnesses—after deciding whether their anonymity should be preserved or not—and to offer Doorson's lawyer the opportunity both to attend this examination and to put questions to the witnesses.

On 14 February 1990 the investigating judge heard the witnesses Y15 and Y16 in the presence of Doorson's lawyer. The lawyer was given the opportunity to put questions to the witnesses but was not informed of their identity. The identity of both witnesses was known to the investigating judge.

Both witnesses expressed the wish to remain anonymous and not to appear in court. Witness Y16 stated that he had in the past suffered injuries at the hands of another drug dealer after he had cooperated with the police, and he feared similar reprisals from Doorson. Witness Y15 stated that he had in the past been threatened by drug dealers if he were to talk. He also said that Doorson was aggressive. The investigating judge concluded that both witnesses had sufficient reason to wish to maintain their anonymity and not to appear in open court.

At its next hearing on the case, the Court of Appeal heard the witness N in Doorson's presence and his lawyer was given the opportunity to question the witness. N said that his statement to the police had been untrue and that he did not in fact know Doorson. The named witness R was initially present at these proceedings. Before he was heard, he asked the Court usher who was guarding him for permission to leave for a minute; he then disappeared and could not be found again.

The Court of Appeal decided to refer the case once again back to the investigating judge, requesting her to record her findings as to the reliability of the witnesses Y15 and Y16. On 19 November 1990 the investigating judge drew up a record of her findings regarding the reliability of the statements made to her by Y15 and Y16 on 14 February 1990. She stated in this document that she could not remember the faces of the two witnesses but, having re-read the records of the interrogations, could recall more or less what had happened. She had the impression that both witnesses knew whom they were talking about and had identified Doorson's photograph without hesitation. As far as she remembered, both witnesses had answered all questions readily and without hesitating, although they had made a "somewhat sleepy impression."

On 6 December 1990, the Court of Appeal found Doorson guilty of the deliberate sale of quantities of heroin and cocaine. As regards Doorson's complaint that the majority of the witnesses had not been heard in the presence of Doorson or his lawyer, the Court stated that it had based its conviction on evidence given by the witnesses N, R, Y15 and Y16. Doorson brought this appeal to the European Court of Human Rights.

53. The applicant alleged that the taking of, hearing of and reliance on evidence from certain witnesses during the criminal proceedings against him infringed the rights of the defence, in violation of Article 6(1) and (3)(d) of the Convention, which provide as follows:

> 1. In the determination . . . of any criminal charge against him, everyone is entitled to a fair . . . hearing [by an] impartial tribunal. . . .
> 3. Everyone charged with a criminal offence has the following minimum rights: . . . (d) to examine or have examined witnesses against him and to obtain the attendance and examination of witnesses on his behalf under the same conditions as witnesses against him. . . .

54. The applicant claimed in the first place that, in obtaining the statements of the anonymous witnesses Y15 and Y16, the rights of the defence had been infringed to such an extent that the reliance on those statements by the Amsterdam Court of Appeal was incompatible with the standards of a "fair" trial. . . .

Although he conceded that in the course of the appeal proceedings Y15 and Y16 had been questioned by [the Investigating Judge] in the presence of his Counsel and had identified him from a photograph taken several years previously, that was not a proper substitute for a confrontation with him in person. Not knowing the identity of the persons concerned, he could not himself cross-examine them to test their credibility. Nor could the possibility of mistakes be ruled out. It would, in his submission, have been possible to examine the witnesses in his presence, protecting them, if need be, by the use of disguise, voice-distorting equipment or a two-way mirror.

In fact, he questioned the need for maintaining the anonymity of Y15 and Y16 at all. Both had stated before the investigating judge that they feared reprisals but there was nothing to suggest that they were ever subjected to, or for that matter threatened with, violence at the hands of the applicant. Moreover, the basis of the investigating judge's assessment of the need for anonymity was not made clear to the defence. . . .

55. In the second place, the applicant complained about the reliance on the evidence of the named witness R. Although R had been brought to the hearing of the Court of Appeal for questioning, he had—in the applicant's submission— been allowed to abscond under circumstances which engaged the Court of Appeal's responsibility. . . . Since he—the applicant—had not been able to cross-examine R, his statement to the police should not have been admitted as evidence. . . .

67. The Court of Appeal had been entitled to consider the reliability of the statements of Y15 and Y16 sufficiently corroborated by the findings of the investigating judge, as officially recorded on 19 November 1990, and by the statement in open court of the [investigating police officer] that the witnesses in the case had been under no constraint. In any case, the Court of Appeal had noted in its judgment that it had made use of the anonymous statements with "the necessary caution and circumspection." . . .

69. As the Court has held on previous occasions, the Convention does not preclude reliance, at the investigation stage, on sources such as anonymous informants. The subsequent use of their statements by the trial court to found a conviction is however capable of raising issues under the Convention. See Kostovski v. Netherlands, 12 Eur. Ct. H.R. 344 (1990).

[Under the *Kostovski* judgment, the use of statements by anonymous witnesses is acceptable when the statement is taken down by a judge who (a) is aware of the identity of the witness, (b) has expressed, in the official record of the hearing of such a witness, his reasoned opinion as to the reliability of the witness and as to the reasons for the witness's wish to remain anonymous, and (c) has provided the defence with some opportunity to put questions or have questions put to the witness. This rule is subject to exceptions; thus, according to the same judgment, the statement of an anonymous witness may be used in evidence despite the absence of the safeguards mentioned above if (a) the defence has not at any stage of the proceedings asked to be allowed to question the witness concerned, and (b) the conviction is based to a significant extent on other evidence not derived from anonymous sources, and (c) the trial court makes it clear that it has made use of the statement of the anonymous witness with caution and circumspection.]

70. It is true that Article 6 does not explicitly require the interests of witnesses in general, and those of victims called upon to testify in particular, to be taken into consideration. However, their life, liberty or security of person may be at stake, as may interests coming generally within the ambit of Article 8 of the Convention.* Such interests of witnesses and victims are in principle protected by other, substantive provisions of the Convention, which imply that Contracting States should organise their criminal proceedings in such a way that those interests are not unjustifiably imperilled. Against this background, principles of fair trial also require that in appropriate cases the interests of the defence are balanced against those of witnesses or victims called upon to testify.

71. As the Amsterdam Court of Appeal made clear, its decision not to disclose the identity of Y15 and Y16 to the defence was inspired by the need, as assessed by it, to obtain evidence from them while at the same time protecting them against the possibility of reprisals by the applicant. . . .

Although, as the applicant has stated, there has been no suggestion that Y15 and Y16 were ever threatened by the applicant himself, the decision to maintain their anonymity cannot be regarded as unreasonable per se. Regard must be had to the fact, as established by the domestic courts and not contested by the applicant, that drug dealers frequently resorted to threats or actual violence against persons who gave evidence against them. Furthermore, the statements made by the witnesses

---

* [Article 8 provides: "Everyone has the right to respect for his private and family life, his home and his correspondence."—Eds.]

concerned to the investigating judge show that one of them had apparently on a previous occasion suffered violence at the hands of a drug dealer against whom he had testified, while the other had been threatened. In sum, there was sufficient reason for maintaining the anonymity of Y15 and Y16. . . .

73. In the instant case the anonymous witnesses were questioned at the appeals stage in the presence of Counsel by an investigating judge who was aware of their identity, even if the defence was not. . . . In this respect the present case is to be distinguished from that of *Kostovski*. Counsel was not only present, but he was put in a position to ask the witnesses whatever questions he considered to be in the interests of the defence except in so far as they might lead to the disclosure of their identity, and these questions were all answered. . . .

74. While it would clearly have been preferable for the applicant to have attended the questioning of the witnesses, the Court considers, on balance, that the Amsterdam Court of Appeal was entitled to consider that the interests of the applicant were in this respect outweighed by the need to ensure the safety of the witnesses. More generally, the Convention does not preclude identification—for the purposes of Article 6(3)(d)—of an accused with his Counsel. . . .

76. Finally, it should be recalled that, even when "counterbalancing" procedures are found to compensate sufficiently the handicaps under which the defence labours, a conviction should not be based either solely or to a decisive extent on anonymous statements. That, however, is not the case here: it is sufficiently clear that the national court did not base its finding of guilt solely or to a decisive extent on the evidence of Y15 and Y16.

Furthermore, evidence obtained from witnesses under conditions in which the rights of the defence cannot be secured to the extent normally required by the Convention should be treated with extreme care. The Court is satisfied that this was done in the criminal proceedings leading to the applicant's conviction, as is reflected in the express declaration by the Court of Appeal that it had treated the statements of Y15 and Y16 "with the necessary caution and circumspection." . . .

83. None of the alleged shortcomings considered on their own lead the Court to conclude that the applicant did not receive a fair trial. Moreover, it cannot find, even if the alleged shortcomings are considered together, that the proceedings as a whole were unfair. In arriving at this conclusion the Court has taken into account the fact that the domestic courts were entitled to consider the various items of evidence before them as corroborative of each other. . . . For these reasons, the Court holds, by seven votes to two, that there has been no violation of Article 6(1) taken together with Article 6(3)(d) of the Convention. . . .

RYSSDAL, J., dissenting.

It is not only in drug cases that problems may arise in relation to the safety of witnesses. It is not permissible to resolve such problems by departing from such a fundamental principle as the one that witness evidence challenged by the accused cannot be admitted against him if he has not had an opportunity to examine or have examined, in his presence, the witness in question.

In the instant case the applicant had this opportunity in respect of witness N, who withdrew his earlier statement. The applicant did not have such an opportunity in relation to witness R, who "disappeared," or witnesses Y15 and Y16, who were heard only in the presence of his lawyer. Moreover, Y15 and Y16 were anonymous witnesses whose identity was only known to the investigating judge but not to the applicant and his lawyer, nor to the Regional Court and the Court of Appeal.

Notes

1. *Anonymous witnesses: majority position.* In the United States, a witness is usually required to divulge both his name and address on cross-examination. This is said to allow the defendant to put the witness in a "proper setting" and to test the witness's credibility. See Smith v. Illinois, 390 U.S. 129 (1968). At the same time, the right to cross-examine prosecution witnesses about their identities or addresses is not considered absolute, and a trial court has discretion to restrict cross-examination on such topics if there is an adequate showing that the safety of the witness is at risk. Alvarado v. Superior Court, 5 P.3d 203 (Cal. 2000) (prosecution may not permanently withhold identities of key witnesses; although disclosure may be delayed until trial, safety concerns of prisoner-witnesses must be addressed by means less drastic than anonymous testimony if testimony is crucial to prosecution's case); State v. Vandebogart, 652 A.2d 671 (N.H. 1994) (witness allowed not to reveal address; she was victim of prior assault by defendant). Recall also that the government often may shield the identity of "confidential informants" during the investigation stage.

Courts in a number of nations have upheld convictions based on the testimony of "anonymous witnesses." Legislation in some nations (such as New Zealand) allows undercover police officers to testify without revealing their identities. The general trend has been to allow the use of anonymous witnesses only when accompanied by the sort of safeguards described in the *Doorson* opinion from the European Court of Human Rights. As European nations move toward more of a hybrid between common law and civil law processes (and thus a hybrid between adversarial and inquisitorial development of proof), will they become less likely to rely on devices such as anonymous witnesses?

2. *The value of comparative law.* The concept of confronting witnesses is a familiar one even in civil law legal systems, which are based on an "inquisitorial" model of factfinding (in which the judge takes responsibility for developing facts) rather than an "adversarial" model (in which the parties present their own facts and take responsibility for testing the factual claims of their adversaries). But the confrontation rights of defendants in civil law systems do not exactly track the confrontation rights of defendants in U.S. courts. Do the practices and values of European criminal justice systems have any relevance for American lawyers, legislators, or judges? See Diane Marie Amann, Harmonic Convergence? Constitutional Criminal Procedure in an International Context, 75 Ind. L.J. 809 (2000).

3. *Confrontation of child witnesses: majority position.* Under the federal constitution, some witnesses may testify outside the courtroom and outside the presence of the defendant if the defendant is able to monitor the testimony and communicate with the defense attorney conducting the cross-examination. According to Maryland v. Craig, 497 U.S. 836 (1990), the trial court must make a case-specific finding that the witness would suffer from extreme emotional trauma during traditional testimony that would prevent the witness from reasonably communicating. The Supreme Court held that admission of the child victim's live testimony at the time of trial, transmitted to the courtroom and the trier of fact via one-way closed-circuit television, was consistent with the confrontation clause. The Court found it significant

that Maryland's procedure preserved all of the elements of the confrontation right apart from the physical presence of the witness in the courtroom: "[The] child witness must be competent to testify and must testify under oath; the defendant retains full opportunity for contemporaneous cross-examination; and the judge, jury, and defendant are able to view (albeit by videotape monitor) the demeanor (and body) of the witness as he or she testifies."

Most high state courts to address this issue follow the federal position and allow prosecuting witnesses to testify outside the courtroom (and outside the defendant's physical presence) so long as the arrangement is "necessary to further an important public policy" and "the reliability of the testimony is otherwise assured." People v. Wrotten, 923 N.E.2d 1099 (N.Y. 2009) (two-way video testimony authorized by statute for child witnesses and within inherent authority of trial judge for other witnesses, based on finding of necessity). The cases often require that the defendant be able to monitor the cross-examination from a remote location or from a hidden or screened location in the room. Another group of high state courts (fewer than 10) have concluded that the defendant must be present (and visible to the witness) during the direct testimony and cross-examination. See People v. Fitzpatrick, 633 N.E.2d 685 (Ill. 1994) (striking down statute that allowed cross-examination on closed-circuit television).

The states departing from the federal position, by and large, are those with specific "face to face" provisions in their state constitutions. Almost 30 state constitutions track the language of the Sixth Amendment to the federal constitution and speak of the right of the accused to be "confronted" with adverse witnesses. About 20 state constitutions mention a defendant's right to meet adverse witnesses "face to face." For a sampling of the state court rulings and statutes on this topic, go to the web extension for this chapter at *http://www.crimpro.com/extension/ch18.*

4. *Reliability of out-of-court statements by child witnesses.* Social science and psychology researchers have explored at great length the factors associated most strongly with reliable and unreliable child testimony. As one might expect, older children are more reliable witnesses than younger children. Young children depend more heavily than older children on "recognition memory" (responding to specific questions about an event rather than volunteering information in response to a general question). Suggestive questioning is more likely to influence younger children, and small differences in age can mean large differences in reliability. The number of times a child is questioned before trial also affects reliability. See Stephen Ceci & Maggie Bruck, Suggestibility of the Child Witness: A Historical Review and Synthesis, 113 Psychol. Bull. 403 (1993). Contrary to expectations, promptness in coming forward with an accusation or consistency in the details of a story is not a good indicator of a reliable child witness.

5. *Defendant's presence at trial.* Both federal and state courts have concluded that defendants have a right, both under confrontation clauses and due process clauses, to be present at "every stage" of the trial. Does a defendant waive the right to be present during the trial by engaging in disruptive behavior? See Illinois v. Allen, 397 U.S. 337 (1970) (no constitutional error to remove defendant from courtroom after repeated outbursts, if defendant is allowed to return to courtroom after promise of better behavior). By escaping from jail before trial? Crosby v. United States, 506 U.S. 255 (1993) (interpreting Fed. R. Crim. P. 43 to prevent trial in absentia of defendant who escapes jail before trial begins, but to allow such trials for defendants who escape after trial has begun). By failing to appear on the day set for trial after being

released before trial? See People v. Johnston, 513 N.E.2d 528 (Ill. 1987) (failure to appear at trial, after appearing at pretrial hearing, is waiver of right to be present).

6. *Victims and sequestration of witnesses.* A traditional rule of evidence allows a party to insist that the judge exclude a witness from the courtroom until that witness has testified. This rule of "sequestration of witnesses" makes cross-examination more effective because it prevents the witness from changing her testimony to remain consistent with (or to rebut) the evidence presented up until that time. The judge's power to exclude witnesses existed at common law, and many states now have rules of evidence codifying this discretionary rule. Others, such as Fed. R. Evid. 615, give the parties an absolute right to exclude a witness; the judge has no discretion on the question for most witnesses.

The sequestration rule sometimes conflicts with the notion that the victim of an alleged crime has a special interest in attending a trial. Consider the following typical effort to reconcile these competing principles, contained in Utah R. Evid. 615(1):

> At the request of a party the court shall order witnesses excluded so that they cannot hear the testimony of other witnesses, and it may make the order on its own motion. This rule does not authorize exclusion of . . . a victim in a criminal trial or juvenile delinquency proceeding where the prosecutor agrees with the victim's presence.

Compare Mich. Comp. Laws §780.761(11) ("The victim has the right to be present throughout the entire trial of the defendant, unless the victim is going to be called as a witness. If the victim is going to be called as a witness, the court may, for good cause shown, order the victim to be sequestered until the victim first testifies"). Under these rules and statutes, does the victim now have a right to presence at trial comparable to the defendant's right to be present? Does the presence of the victim in the courtroom influence other witnesses as they testify (creating a sort of "confrontation" right for a crime victim)?

Problem 18-1. Child Testimony

Teresa Brady's father and mother, Michael Brady and Carla Myers, were married at the time of her birth but were divorced a year later. Under a court visitation order, Teresa spent a Friday night and a Saturday night with her father at the home of Michael's mother, Rosemary Brady. Michael returned Teresa to Carla's home on Sunday at 6:00 P.M. Teresa was four years old at the time. On Monday morning, one of Teresa's teachers discovered her hiding in the bathroom closet and complaining about genital pain. A physical examination produced evidence of sexual abuse. During the three months following the discovery of the child's injury, she made several statements to investigators that her father had hurt her. The state filed charges against Michael three months after these events.

Six months later, the State asked the court to order that Teresa's testimony be videotaped for use at trial, using the statutory procedures for recording the testimony of children. The trial court ruled that it was more likely than not that it would be traumatic for Teresa to testify in court and ordered that the videotape testimony be taken. Teresa's videotape testimony was taken and was subsequently admitted at trial over appellant's objection and viewed by the jury. The tape had been taken at home in Teresa's kitchen and bedroom. The judge, prosecutor, defense attorney, investigator, Teresa's mother, and the operator of the video equipment were present during the videotaping. The videotape session lasted approximately two hours. Michael was situated in the garage of the house, and he was able to see and hear Teresa via closed-circuit television as she was questioned. Michael was also able to speak with defense counsel by a microphone hook-up. Teresa was not able to see or hear appellant and was not aware of his presence. All of these arrangements carefully followed the statutory requirements.

Michael Brady maintains that this statute is unconstitutional on its face because it infringes upon his right to confront the witnesses against him as guaranteed by the Sixth Amendment of the United States Constitution and the analogous provision of the state constitution. The statute in question in this case is similar to the Maryland statute that the United States Supreme Court reviewed in Maryland v. Craig, 497 U.S. 836 (1990). The Supreme Court upheld the constitutionality of the Maryland statute as it found that the admission of the child victim's live testimony at the time of trial, transmitted to the courtroom and the trier of fact via one-way closed-circuit television, was consistent with the confrontation clause.

The single significant dissimilarity in the two statutes appears to be that the statute here, unlike the Maryland statute, authorizes the use of videotaped pretrial statements as well as the use of closed-circuit television during trial. How would you rule on Brady's claim? Cf. Brady v. State, 575 N.E.2d 981 (Ind. 1991). Which of the various elements of the classic courtroom confrontation create more reliable testimony? Does it matter that the testimony takes place during a trial rather than during an earlier deposition? Would a cardboard cutout image of the defendant in the courtroom serve the purposes of "confrontation"?

2. Out-of-Court Statements by Unavailable Witnesses

How can a defendant confront the person who accuses her if the accuser is not present in the courtroom? There may be many reasons for a witness or victim's absence from the courtroom. For the most part, the law of evidence dictates when statements made by unavailable witnesses will be admitted at trial—principally through the hearsay rule and its many exceptions. There is, however, a constitutional component to these questions, as well. The confrontation clause of the Sixth Amendment provides that "in all criminal prosecutions, the accused shall enjoy the right . . . to be confronted with the witnesses against him." Crawford v. Washington provides the current framework for analyzing the relationship between the confrontation clause and the hearsay rules: Judges must determine whether the unavailable witness made a "testimonial" statement out of court.

■ MICHAEL CRAWFORD v. WASHINGTON
541 U.S. 36 (2004)

SCALIA, J.*
Petitioner Michael Crawford stabbed a man who allegedly tried to rape his wife, Sylvia. At his trial, the State played for the jury Sylvia's tape-recorded statement to the police describing the stabbing, even though he had no opportunity for

---

* [Justices Stevens, Kennedy, Souter, Thomas, Ginsburg, and Breyer joined this opinion.—EDS.]

cross-examination. The Washington Supreme Court upheld petitioner's conviction after determining that Sylvia's statement was reliable. The question presented is whether this procedure complied with the Sixth Amendment's guarantee that, "[in] all criminal prosecutions, the accused shall enjoy the right . . . to be confronted with the witnesses against him."

I.

On August 5, 1999, Kenneth Lee was stabbed at his apartment. Police arrested petitioner later that night. After giving petitioner and his wife *Miranda* warnings, detectives interrogated each of them twice. Petitioner eventually confessed that he and Sylvia had gone in search of Lee because he was upset over an earlier incident in which Lee had tried to rape her. The two had found Lee at his apartment, and a fight ensued in which Lee was stabbed in the torso and petitioner's hand was cut. Petitioner gave the following account of the fight:

> *Q:* Okay. Did you ever see anything in [Lee's] hands?
> *A:* I think so, but I'm not positive.
> *Q:* Okay, when you think so, what do you mean by that?
> *A:* I coulda swore I seen him goin' for somethin' before, right before everything happened. He was like reachin', fiddlin' around down here and stuff . . . and I just . . . I don't know, I think, this is just a possibility, but I think, I think that he pulled somethin' out and I grabbed for it and that's how I got cut . . . but I'm not positive. . . .

Sylvia generally corroborated petitioner's story about the events leading up to the fight, but her account of the fight itself was arguably different—particularly with respect to whether Lee had drawn a weapon before petitioner assaulted him:

> *Q:* Did Kenny do anything to fight back from this assault?
> *A:* (pausing) I know he reached into his pocket . . . or somethin' . . . I don't know what.
> *Q:* After he was stabbed? . . .
> *A:* Okay, he lifted his hand over his head maybe to strike Michael's hand down or something and then he put his hands in his . . . put his right hand in his right pocket . . . took a step back . . . Michael proceeded to stab him . . . then his hands were like . . . how do you explain this . . . open arms . . . with his hands open and he fell down . . . and we ran (describing subject holding hands open, palms toward assailant).
> *Q:* Okay, when he's standing there with his open hands, you're talking about Kenny, correct?
> *A:* Yeah, after, after the fact, yes.
> *Q:* Did you see anything in his hands at that point?
> *A:* (pausing) um um (no).

The State charged petitioner with assault and attempted murder. At trial, he claimed self-defense. Sylvia did not testify because of the state marital privilege, which generally bars a spouse from testifying without the other spouse's consent. In Washington, this privilege does not extend to a spouse's out-of-court statements admissible under a hearsay exception, so the State sought to introduce Sylvia's tape-recorded statements to the police as evidence that the stabbing was not in self-defense. Noting that Sylvia had admitted she led petitioner to Lee's apartment and thus had facilitated the assault, the State invoked the hearsay exception for statements against penal interest, Wash. Rule Evid. 804(b)(3).

Petitioner countered that, state law notwithstanding, admitting the evidence would violate his federal constitutional right to be "confronted with the witnesses against him." According to our description of that right in Ohio v. Roberts, 448 U.S. 56 (1980), it does not bar admission of an unavailable witness's statement against a criminal defendant if the statement bears "adequate indicia of reliability." To meet that test, evidence must either fall within a "firmly rooted hearsay exception" or bear "particularized guarantees of trustworthiness." The trial court here admitted the statement on the latter ground, offering several reasons why it was trustworthy: Sylvia was not shifting blame but rather corroborating her husband's story that he acted in self-defense or "justified reprisal"; she had direct knowledge as an eyewitness; she was describing recent events; and she was being questioned by a "neutral" law enforcement officer. The prosecution played the tape for the jury and relied on it in closing, arguing that it was "damning evidence" that "completely refutes [petitioner's] claim of self-defense." The jury convicted petitioner of assault.

The Washington Court of Appeals reversed. It applied a nine-factor test to determine whether Sylvia's statement bore particularized guarantees of trustworthiness, and noted several reasons why it did not: The statement contradicted one she had previously given; it was made in response to specific questions; and at one point she admitted she had shut her eyes during the stabbing. . . . The Washington Supreme Court reinstated the conviction [and we] granted certiorari to determine whether the State's use of Sylvia's statement violated the Confrontation Clause.

II.

The Sixth Amendment's Confrontation Clause provides that, "[in] all criminal prosecutions, the accused shall enjoy the right . . . to be confronted with the witnesses against him." . . . Petitioner argues that [the *Roberts*] test strays from the original meaning of the Confrontation Clause and urges us to reconsider it.

The Constitution's text does not alone resolve this case. One could plausibly read "witnesses against" a defendant to mean those who actually testify at trial, those whose statements are offered at trial, or something in-between. We must therefore turn to the historical background of the Clause to understand its meaning.

The right to confront one's accusers is a concept that dates back to Roman times. The founding generation's immediate source of the concept, however, was the common law. English common law has long differed from continental civil law in regard to the manner in which witnesses give testimony in criminal trials. The common-law tradition is one of live testimony in court subject to adversarial testing, while the civil law condones examination in private by judicial officers.

Nonetheless, England at times adopted elements of the civil-law practice. Justices of the peace or other officials examined suspects and witnesses before trial. These examinations were sometimes read in court in lieu of live testimony. . . . The most notorious instances of civil-law examination occurred in the great political trials of the 16th and 17th centuries. One such was the 1603 trial of Sir Walter Raleigh for treason. Lord Cobham, Raleigh's alleged accomplice, had implicated him in an examination before the Privy Council and in a letter. At Raleigh's trial, these were read to the jury. Raleigh argued that Cobham had lied to save himself: "Cobham is absolutely in the King's mercy; to excuse me cannot avail him; by accusing me he may hope for favour." 1 D. Jardine, Criminal Trials 435 (1832). Suspecting that Cobham would recant, Raleigh demanded that the judges call him to appear, arguing that "[the] Proof of the Common Law is by witness and jury: let Cobham be here, let him speak it. Call my accuser before my face. . . ." The judges refused, and, despite Raleigh's protestations that he was being tried "by the Spanish Inquisition," the jury convicted, and Raleigh was sentenced to death. . . .

Through a series of statutory and judicial reforms, English law developed a right of confrontation that limited these abuses. For example, treason statutes required witnesses to confront the accused "face to face" at his arraignment. Courts, meanwhile, developed relatively strict rules of unavailability, admitting examinations only if the witness was demonstrably unable to testify in person. Several authorities also stated that a suspect's confession could be admitted only against himself, and not against others he implicated.

One recurring question was whether the admissibility of an unavailable witness's pretrial examination depended on whether the defendant had had an opportunity to cross-examine him. In 1696, the Court of King's Bench answered this question in the affirmative, in the widely reported misdemeanor libel case of King v. Paine, 87 Eng. Rep. 584. The court ruled that, even though a witness was dead, his examination was not admissible where "the defendant not being present when [it was] taken before the mayor . . . had lost the benefit of a cross-examination." . . .

Controversial examination practices were also used in the Colonies. . . . A decade before the Revolution, England gave jurisdiction over Stamp Act offenses to the admiralty courts, which followed civil-law rather than common-law procedures and thus routinely took testimony by deposition or private judicial examination. Colonial representatives protested that the Act subverted their rights "by extending the jurisdiction of the courts of admiralty beyond its ancient limits." John Adams, defending a merchant in a high-profile admiralty case, argued: "Examinations of witnesses upon Interrogatories, are only by the Civil Law. Interrogatories are unknown at common Law, and Englishmen and common Lawyers have an aversion to them if not an Abhorrence of them."

Many declarations of rights adopted around the time of the Revolution guaranteed a right of confrontation. The proposed Federal Constitution, however, did not. At the Massachusetts ratifying convention, Abraham Holmes objected to this omission precisely on the ground that it would lead to civil-law practices: "The mode of trial is altogether indetermined; . . . whether [the defendant] is to be allowed to confront the witnesses, and have the advantage of cross-examination, we are not yet told. [We] shall find Congress possessed of powers enabling them to institute judicatories little less inauspicious than a certain tribunal in Spain, . . . the *Inquisition*." 2 Debates on the Federal Constitution 110-111 (J. Elliot 2d ed. 1863). . . . The First Congress responded by including the Confrontation Clause in the proposal that became the Sixth Amendment. Early state decisions shed light upon the original understanding of the common-law right. State v. Webb, 2 N.C. 103 (1794) (per curiam), decided a mere three years after the adoption of the Sixth Amendment, held that depositions could be read against an accused only if they were taken in his presence. . . .

III.

This history supports two inferences about the meaning of the Sixth Amendment. . . . First, the principal evil at which the Confrontation Clause was directed was the civil-law mode of criminal procedure, and particularly its use of *ex parte* examinations as evidence against the accused. It was these practices that the Crown deployed in notorious treason cases like Raleigh's; . . . that English law's assertion of a right to confrontation was meant to prohibit; and that the founding-era rhetoric decried. The Sixth Amendment must be interpreted with this focus in mind.

Accordingly, we once again reject the view that the Confrontation Clause applies of its own force only to in-court testimony, and that its application to out-of-court statements introduced at trial depends upon "the law of Evidence for the time being." Leaving the regulation of out-of-court statements to the law of evidence would render the Confrontation Clause powerless to prevent even the most flagrant inquisitorial practices. Raleigh was, after all, perfectly free to confront those who read Cobham's confession in court.

This focus also suggests that not all hearsay implicates the Sixth Amendment's core concerns. An off-hand, overheard remark might be unreliable evidence and thus a good candidate for exclusion under hearsay rules, but it bears little resemblance to the civil-law abuses the Confrontation Clause targeted. On the other hand, *ex parte* examinations might sometimes be admissible under modern hearsay rules, but the Framers certainly would not have condoned them.

The text of the Confrontation Clause reflects this focus. It applies to "witnesses" against the accused—in other words, those who "bear testimony." 1 N. Webster, An American Dictionary of the English Language (1828). "Testimony," in turn, is typically "[a] solemn declaration or affirmation made for the purpose of establishing or proving some fact." An accuser who makes a formal statement to government officers bears testimony in a sense that a person who makes a casual remark to an acquaintance does not. The constitutional text, like the history underlying the common-law right of confrontation, thus reflects an especially acute concern with a specific type of out-of-court statement. . . .

Regardless of the precise [definition of testimonial statements], some statements qualify under any definition—for example, *ex parte* testimony at a preliminary hearing. Statements taken by police officers in the course of interrogations are also testimonial under even a narrow standard. Police interrogations bear a striking resemblance to examinations by justices of the peace in England. . . . In sum, even if the Sixth Amendment is not solely concerned with testimonial hearsay, that is its primary object, and interrogations by law enforcement officers fall squarely within that class.[4] . . .

The historical record also supports a second proposition: that the Framers would not have allowed admission of testimonial statements of a witness who did not appear at trial unless he was unavailable to testify, and the defendant had had a prior opportunity for cross-examination. The text of the Sixth Amendment does

---

4. We use the term "interrogation" in its colloquial, rather than any technical legal, sense. Cf. Rhode Island v. Innis, 446 U.S. 291 (1980). Just as various definitions of "testimonial" exist, one can imagine various definitions of "interrogation," and we need not select among them in this case. Sylvia's recorded statement, knowingly given in response to structured police questioning, qualifies under any conceivable definition.

not suggest any open-ended exceptions from the confrontation requirement to be developed by the courts. Rather, the "right . . . to be confronted with the witnesses against him," is most naturally read as a reference to the right of confrontation at common law, admitting only those exceptions established at the time of the founding. As the English authorities above reveal, the common law in 1791 conditioned admissibility of an absent witness's examination on unavailability and a prior opportunity to cross-examine. The Sixth Amendment therefore incorporates those limitations. . . .

This is not to deny . . . that "[there] were always exceptions to the general rule of exclusion" of hearsay evidence. Several had become well established by 1791. But there is scant evidence that exceptions were invoked to admit testimonial statements against the accused in a criminal case.[6] Most of the hearsay exceptions covered statements that by their nature were not testimonial—for example, business records or statements in furtherance of a conspiracy. . . .

V.

Roberts conditions the admissibility of all hearsay evidence on whether it falls under a "firmly rooted hearsay exception" or bears "particularized guarantees of trustworthiness." This test departs from the historical principles identified above in two respects. First, it is too broad: It applies the same mode of analysis whether or not the hearsay consists of *ex parte* testimony. This often results in close constitutional scrutiny in cases that are far removed from the core concerns of the Clause. At the same time, however, the test is too narrow: It admits statements that *do* consist of *ex parte* testimony upon a mere finding of reliability. This malleable standard often fails to protect against paradigmatic confrontation violations. . . .

Where testimonial statements are involved, we do not think the Framers meant to leave the Sixth Amendment's protection to the vagaries of the rules of evidence, much less to amorphous notions of "reliability." . . . To be sure, the Clause's ultimate goal is to ensure reliability of evidence, but it is a procedural rather than a substantive guarantee. It commands, not that evidence be reliable, but that reliability be assessed in a particular manner: by testing in the crucible of cross-examination. . . .

The Raleigh trial itself involved the very sorts of reliability determinations that *Roberts* authorizes. In the face of Raleigh's repeated demands for confrontation, the prosecution responded with many of the arguments a court applying *Roberts* might invoke today: that Cobham's statements were self-inculpatory, that they were not made in the heat of passion, and that they were not "extracted from [him] upon any hopes or promise of Pardon." It is not plausible that the Framers' only objection to the trial was that Raleigh's judges did not properly weigh these factors before sentencing him to death. Rather, the problem was that the judges refused to allow Raleigh to confront Cobham in court, where he could cross-examine him and try to expose his accusation as a lie.

---

6. The one deviation we have found involves dying declarations. . . . Although many dying declarations may not be testimonial, there is authority for admitting even those that clearly are. We need not decide in this case whether the Sixth Amendment incorporates an exception for testimonial dying declarations. If this exception must be accepted on historical grounds, it is sui generis.

Dispensing with confrontation because testimony is obviously reliable is akin to dispensing with jury trial because a defendant is obviously guilty. This is not what the Sixth Amendment prescribes. . . .

The legacy of *Roberts* in other courts vindicates the Framers' wisdom in rejecting a general reliability exception. . . . Reliability is an amorphous, if not entirely subjective, concept. There are countless factors bearing on whether a statement is reliable; the nine-factor balancing test applied by the Court of Appeals below is representative. See, e.g., People v. Farrell, 34 P.3d 401 (Colo. 2001) (eight-factor test). Whether a statement is deemed reliable depends heavily on which factors the judge considers and how much weight he accords each of them. Some courts wind up attaching the same significance to opposite facts. . . .

Roberts' failings were on full display in the proceedings below. Sylvia Crawford made her statement while in police custody, herself a potential suspect in the case. Indeed, she had been told that whether she would be released depended on "how the investigation continues." In response to often leading questions from police detectives, she implicated her husband in Lee's stabbing and at least arguably undermined his self-defense claim. Despite all this, the trial court admitted her statement, listing several reasons why it was reliable. In its opinion reversing, the Court of Appeals listed several *other* reasons why the statement was *not* reliable. Finally, the State Supreme Court relied exclusively on the interlocking character of the statement and disregarded every other factor the lower courts had considered. The case is thus a self-contained demonstration of *Roberts'* unpredictable and inconsistent application. . . .

We have no doubt that the courts below were acting in utmost good faith when they found reliability. The Framers, however, would not have been content to indulge this assumption. They knew that judges, like other government officers, could not always be trusted to safeguard the rights of the people. . . . By replacing categorical constitutional guarantees with open-ended balancing tests, we do violence to their design. . . .

Where nontestimonial hearsay is at issue, it is wholly consistent with the Framers' design to afford the States flexibility in their development of hearsay law — as does *Roberts,* and as would an approach that exempted such statements from Confrontation Clause scrutiny altogether. Where testimonial evidence is at issue, however, the Sixth Amendment demands what the common law required: unavailability and a prior opportunity for cross-examination. We leave for another day any effort to spell out a comprehensive definition of "testimonial." Whatever else the term covers, it applies at a minimum to prior testimony at a preliminary hearing, before a grand jury, or at a former trial; and to police interrogations. These are the modern practices with closest kinship to the abuses at which the Confrontation Clause was directed. . . .

REHNQUIST, C.J., concurring in the judgment.[*]

I dissent from the Court's decision to overrule Ohio v. Roberts, 448 U.S. 56 (1980). I believe that the Court's adoption of a new interpretation of the Confrontation Clause is not backed by sufficiently persuasive reasoning to overrule long-established precedent. . . .

---

[*] [Justice O'Connor joined this opinion.—EDS.]

The Court's distinction between testimonial and nontestimonial statements, contrary to its claim, is no better rooted in history than our current doctrine. Under the common law, although the courts were far from consistent, out-of-court statements made by someone other than the accused and not taken under oath, unlike *ex parte* depositions or affidavits, were generally not considered substantive evidence upon which a conviction could be based. Testimonial statements such as accusatory statements to police officers likely would have been disapproved of in the 18th century, not necessarily because they resembled *ex parte* affidavits or depositions as the Court reasons, but more likely than not because they were not made under oath. Without an oath, one usually did not get to the second step of whether confrontation was required. Thus, while I agree that the Framers were mainly concerned about sworn affidavits and depositions, it does not follow that they were similarly concerned about the Court's broader category of testimonial statements. . . .

With respect to unsworn testimonial statements, there is no indication that once the hearsay rule was developed courts ever excluded these statements if they otherwise fell within a firmly rooted exception. Dying declarations are one example. . . . It is an odd conclusion indeed to think that the Framers created a cut-and-dried rule with respect to the admissibility of testimonial statements when the law during their own time was not fully settled. . . .

Exceptions to confrontation have always been derived from the experience that some out-of-court statements are just as reliable as cross-examined in-court testimony due to the circumstances under which they were made. . . . That a statement might be testimonial does nothing to undermine the wisdom of one of these exceptions. [Cross-examination] is a tool used to flesh out the truth, not an empty procedure. In a given instance cross-examination may be "superfluous." 5 J. Wigmore, Evidence §1420, at 251 (J. Chadbourn rev. 1974).

[The] thousands of federal prosecutors and the tens of thousands of state prosecutors need answers as to what beyond the specific kinds of "testimony" the Court lists is covered by the new rule. They need them now, not months or years from now. Rules of criminal evidence are applied every day in courts throughout the country, and parties should not be left in the dark in this manner. . . .

Notes

1. *Hearsay exceptions and confrontation: majority position.* Rules of evidence in all jurisdictions exclude out-of-court hearsay statements (that is, statements made out of court by someone other than the witness, offered to prove the truth of the matter addressed in the statement) but then make exceptions to allow into evidence some of the more reliable hearsay statements. Before the Supreme Court decided *Crawford*, federal and state law allowed the government to use hearsay statements of a person who would not testify at trial so long as the evidence fell within a "firmly rooted" exception to the bar on hearsay. When no such exception was available, the confrontation clause prevented use of the evidence unless the judge found some "particularized guarantees of trustworthiness." Ohio v. Roberts, 448 U.S. 56 (1980).

Does the older "reliability" test or *Crawford's* "testimonial" test better capture the modern-day meaning of the Sixth Amendment's text, embodying a right for a defendant "to be confronted with the witnesses against him"? In a world that relies so much on guilty pleas and so little on trials to adjudicate criminal cases, is the right to confront witnesses in the courtroom only one means to an end—reliable evidence to support a conviction?

2. *Timing and motives in domestic violence cases.* What sorts of prosecutions depend most heavily on "testimonial" statements and are thus most affected by *Crawford?* In domestic violence cases, the government traditionally introduces into evidence a recording of the alleged victim's emergency call to the police. This happens even when the victim did not testify at trial. What other crime categories are most affected by the *Crawford* decision's application of confrontation rights to all "testimonial" evidence?

The Supreme Court has reached different outcomes on the "testimonial" nature of statements obtained during investigations of violent crimes. In these cases, the timing of the statement is part of the equation, along with the purposes of the questioner. In Davis v. Washington, 547 U.S. 813 (2006), the Supreme Court declared that a 911 caller's statements about an ongoing domestic assault was not "testimonial," and hence not subject to the confrontation clause. The statement was made under circumstances "objectively indicating" that the primary purpose of the police interrogation was to enable police assistance to meet an "ongoing emergency." It is fair to assume that the motives of the police for obtaining witness statements, along with the witness's motives for providing the statements, are often mixed: They hope for immediate help to prevent an ongoing harm, and to collect evidence for prosecution of the alleged offender. Does this *Davis* test weaken the *Crawford* holding?

The Court reached the opposite conclusion in a companion case to *Davis,* Hammon v. Indiana. When police responded to a domestic violence call, they found "no emergency in progress" because Mr. Hammon was indoors and Mrs. Hammon was outdoors on the porch. Her statement to the officer was intended as evidence of a past crime. Statements that are "formal enough" qualify as "testimonial" and must be tested by cross-examination.

Five years later, in Michigan v. Bryant, 562 U.S. 344 (2011), the Court declared that statements by a shooting victim about the identity and current location of the gunman were not testimonial. The central inquiry, according to the Court, was whether the "primary purpose" of the interrogation was to "establish or prove past events potentially relevant to later criminal prosecution." The ongoing nature of the emergency had some bearing on this question; the location of the victim at the crime scene and the informality of the statement were also relevant.

For a sampling of state court cases that trace this wavering line between testimonial and nontestimonial statements to police during violent crime investigations, go to the web extension for this chapter at *http://www.crimpro.com/extension/ch18.*

3. *Identity of government agent.* Statements to law enforcement officials are more likely to become part of the government's evidence in a criminal trial than statements made to some other categories of government agents, such as teachers. In Ohio v. Clark, 135 S. Ct. 2173 (2015), the Court considered statements that a three-year-old child made to preschool teachers, indicating possible abuse in the home. The Court did not adopt a blanket rule, because "some statements to individuals who are not law enforcement officers could conceivably raise confrontation concerns." But statements to this type of government agent "are much less likely to be testimonial than statements to law enforcement officers."

4. *Scientific evidence and confrontation.* The *Crawford* doctrine also has an enormous practical influence in DUI and drug cases, where the state introduces evidence from a crime laboratory. In Melendez-Diaz v. Massachusetts, 557 U.S. 305

(2009), the Supreme Court decided that sworn reports of analysts for state crime laboratories, describing the results of scientific testing of the state's evidence, are "testimonial." As a result, defendants have a right under the confrontation clause to cross-examine the analysts, and the government cannot prove the facts relevant to the lab tests through the introduction of sworn "certificates of analysis." For states that rely on centralized crime labs with limited staffing, *Melendez-Diaz* creates an obligation for lab analysts to travel extensively around the state for court hearings. See also Bullcoming v. New Mexico, 564 U.S. 647 (2011) (report describing a blood-alcohol analysis was "testimonial" within the meaning of the confrontation clause because the report addressed chain of custody and certified the use of a precise testing protocol with the testing equipment; therefore the defendant in a DWI case had the right to confront at trial the analyst who certified the report); cf. Williams v. Illinois, 567 U.S. 50 (2012) (expert statement about outside laboratory procedures for handling evidence was not "testimonial" because the expert was only explaining the factual assumptions underlying her opinion that the outside lab's DNA profile matched a DNA profile based on a blood sample from defendant; in addition, statement was not testimonial because no suspect had been identified at time of lab work).

5. *Forfeiture by wrongdoing.* If an out-of-court "testimonial" statement becomes unavailable as evidence when the witness is not available to testify at trial, does this give defendants an incentive to prevent prosecution witnesses from appearing at trial? Under the "forfeiture by wrongdoing" doctrine, a defendant who takes action designed to prevent the testimony of a prosecution witness at trial waives the right to confront that witness. See Giles v. California, 554 U.S. 353 (2008) (state must prove intent of defendant to prevent testimony before invoking forfeiture by wrongdoing doctrine); People v. Stechly, 870 N.E.2d 333 (Ill. 2007).

3. Statements by Co-Defendants

Sometimes the government wants to introduce an out-of-court statement by one defendant implicating another defendant during a joint trial. Because the defendant who made the statement can invoke the privilege against self-incrimination, the co-defendant cannot "confront" the witness who made the statement. The holding in Bruton v. United States, 391 U.S. 123 (1968), governs the use of these statements. In the following application of that doctrine, does the Court adopt a realistic view of juror behavior?

■ COMMONWEALTH v. JOHN BACIGALUPO
918 N.E.2d 51 (Mass. 2009)

COWIN, J.

The defendant and a codefendant, Gary Carter, were convicted by a jury in the Superior Court of murder in the first degree on the theory of deliberate premeditation. Both men were also convicted of two counts of armed assault with intent to murder; two counts of assault and battery by means of a dangerous weapon; one count of unlawful possession of a firearm; and one count of unlawful possession of ammunition. The defendant appeals from the convictions and from the denial of his motions for a new trial. We reverse the defendant's convictions because, in contravention of Bruton v. United States, 391 U.S. 123 (1968), the codefendant's extrajudicial confession implicating the defendant was admitted in evidence. . . .

FACTS AND PROCEDURAL BACKGROUND

[We] summarize the evidence in the light most favorable to the Commonwealth. Two shootings occurred in the early morning of November 24, 1996: the first at Club Caravan in Revere at shortly after 1 A.M., and the second outside the Comfort Inn in Saugus at about 1:30 A.M. The two locations were only minutes apart by car at that time of night. Each of the victims of the first shooting, confederate drug dealers Charles McConnell and Vincent Portalla, survived. Robert Nogueira, Portalla's "enforcer," died in the second shooting.

Just after midnight on November 24, 1996, McConnell and Portalla were looking for the defendant and Carter to collect money that they owed to Portalla. They drove to the defendant's home in Winthrop but could not locate him. They then drove to Carter's house, where they found Carter sitting outside in a blue Ford Taurus automobile. Carter was wearing gloves and appeared nervous and "jittery." McConnell became concerned because wearing gloves usually indicated that a person is "up to something." Carter told Portalla that he had heard that Portalla was looking for him and asked if Portalla was "out to hurt [him]." Carter then told the two men to follow him, and they did so, as he drove to Club Caravan in Revere.

Outside the club, Carter and Portalla left their respective automobiles and, for approximately ten minutes, engaged in a heated discussion, which McConnell observed. Carter repeated that he had heard that Portalla had been "looking for us" and wanted to "hurt us." Portalla denied this and pulled up his shirt to indicate that he was unarmed. The men then spoke in normal tones. Shortly thereafter, the defendant "came ripping around the corner" in a black Lincoln Town Car automobile. He put on a glove and jumped out, holding a pistol. Portalla and the defendant wrestled over the gun. When the defendant's pistol discharged into the air, Portalla, who was unarmed, ran into the club. The defendant fired approximately five times at him, hitting him in the buttocks. As McConnell fled in Portalla's car, the defendant and Carter simultaneously fired at McConnell, shooting him in the back and arm. Neither McConnell nor Portalla originally identified the shooters to police. In a recorded conversation with a friend the day after the shootings, McConnell identified the defendant and Carter as his assailants. [The conversation was recorded because, unbeknownst to McConnell, his friend was a federal government informant.]

An employee at Club Caravan ran outside immediately after the shooting. He observed a dark blue or black car going around the rotary. It was a large car, "like a Cadillac or a Continental"; he considered a Lincoln Town Car to be a Continental. When the police responded to Club Caravan, they discovered a blue Ford Taurus rental car in the parking lot. The car had been rented to Carter, and in it was a clip "fully loaded" with nine millimeter ammunition. This ammunition was of the same type as casings found at the scene of the later shooting in Saugus.

As stated, the third victim was Nogueira, Portalla's "enforcer." He "handled" Portalla's "problems," i.e., he collected the money people owed Portalla for drug purchases. Nogueira had a reputation in the community for violence and was "a dangerous guy." On the night of the shooting, Nogueira was at a Comfort Inn on the Revere-Saugus border, where he had been staying for a "good couple of weeks." At about 1 A.M., the night clerk at the Comfort Inn saw Nogueira leave the motel; the clerk heard shots immediately thereafter. Nogueira was shot twenty times.

The ballistics evidence recovered from the body of Nogueira and from the two crime scenes established that two different weapons, one revolver and one semiautomatic firearm, were used in the shootings and that one of the weapons, the semiautomatic, had been used at both locations. State police ballistics evidence indicated that a copper-jacketed bullet found in McConnell's getaway car and a full metal-jacketed bullet recovered from Nogueira's body were fired from the same weapon. Although the ballistics evidence established that a second weapon was used at each scene, no determination could be made whether the second weapon was the same one used at both scenes.

Prior to trial, the defendant moved to sever his trial from Carter's because Carter had earlier recounted to John Patti the roles that he and the defendant played in the shootings. Carter's confession to Patti implicated the defendant, and the Commonwealth planned to call Patti as a witness. The judge denied the motion but stated that, when Carter's confession was introduced, he would exclude any testimony that referred to the defendant. . . .

THE BRUTON ISSUE

The defendant claims that the testimony given by the witness, John Patti, recounting Carter's confession to him shortly after the shootings incriminates the defendant and violates the principle of *Bruton*. Patti's testimony on direct examination referred to the defendant solely as Carter's unnamed "friend" (in compliance with the judge's order) and included statements that the "friend" drove up to Club Caravan and got out of his car immediately before the shooting of Portalla and McConnell. In addition, on cross-examination, Patti agreed that Carter said that "Johnny" shot Nogueira at the Comfort Inn. Earlier in his testimony, Patti had referred to the defendant as "Johnny." The judge instructed emphatically that none of Carter's statements could be used against the defendant.

In *Bruton*, the United States Supreme Court reversed the defendant's conviction because the introduction of a nontestifying codefendant's confession implicating the defendant violated the defendant's right to confront the witnesses against him in contravention of the confrontation clause of the Sixth Amendment to the United States Constitution. The confession added "substantial, perhaps even critical, weight to the Government's case in a form not subject to cross-examination since [the codefendant] did not take the stand. [The defendant] was thus denied his constitutional right of confrontation." The Court also doubted that a curative instruction would alleviate the prejudice and concluded that the risk that the jury may not follow such an instruction is too great. "[We] cannot accept limiting instructions as an adequate substitute for [the defendant's] constitutional right of cross-examination. The effect is the same as if there had been no instruction at all."

The *Bruton* rule was limited by Richardson v. Marsh, 481 U.S. 200 (1987). In *Richardson*, the Court held that "the Confrontation Clause is not violated by the admission of a nontestifying codefendant's confession with a proper limiting instruction when . . . the confession is redacted to eliminate not only the defendant's name, but any reference to his or her existence."[11] The Court specifically declined to consider at that time the admissibility of a confession in which the defendant's name "has been replaced with a symbol or neutral pronoun."

The question whether the use of a symbol or neutral pronoun would violate the *Bruton* rule was resolved in Gray v. Maryland, 523 U.S. 185 (1998). In *Gray*, a nontestifying codefendant's confession was redacted by substituting the word "deleted" or "deletion" each time Gray's name appeared. The Supreme Court held that such a redacted confession was within the class of statements protected by *Bruton* and that the nonconfessing defendant's name could not be replaced with an obvious blank space, a word such as "deleted," a symbol, or other similarly conspicuous type of alteration. Because the redacted confession still referred "directly to the existence of the nonconfessing defendant" and incriminated him, the Court held that it fell within the *Bruton* rule.

Patti's reference to Carter's "friend" suggested to the jury that Carter was referring to the defendant. This implication was strengthened by the fact that only two people were on trial for the shootings that Carter said were committed by himself and a "friend." Thus, the jury logically would have inferred that the "friend" was the defendant. In addition, repeated objections by the defendant's counsel, the judge's forceful instructions that Patti's testimony did not concern the defendant, and the judge's repeated admonitions to Patti on how to respond properly to the questions (to testify only to "what . . . Carter did, not what anybody else did") only emphasized to the jury that the "friend" was indeed the defendant.[12] This is particularly so

---

11. In *Richardson*, a joint murder trial of two defendants, the confession of one defendant, Williams, was redacted to omit all reference to the other codefendant, Marsh. There was no indication in the confession that anyone other than Williams and a third person took part in the crime. The jury were also instructed not to consider the confession against Marsh. As redacted, the confession indicated that only Williams and the third person had discussed the murder in the front seat of a car while driving to the victim's house. There was no suggestion in the confession that Marsh or any other person was in the back seat of the car at the time.

12. The pertinent portions of Patti's testimony are the following (emphasis added):

Q: "What did he tell you happened?"
A: "He said a *friend* of his came flying up in the hot box." . . .
Q: "What did Mr. Carter tell you he did at that point in time, if anything?"
A: "*His friend* was exiting the car that he pulled up in, the hot box. And then he tried to wave *his friend* off. He put his arms up and yelled, no, stop." . . .
Q: "What did Mr. Carter tell you he did?"
A: "*His friend* started — "
THE JUDGE: "No. What did Carter tell you he did."
ATTORNEY FOR DEFENDANT: "I make the same motion again."
THE JUDGE: "Overruled. Now, would you — hold it for just a minute. Let me get this straight. Do you understand his question?"
A: "Yes."
THE JUDGE: "He's asking you what did Carter say that he did, he, Carter did, not what anybody else did, what Carter did. Do you understand that question?"
A: "Yes, I — "
THE JUDGE: "Are you able to answer the question?"
A: "Yeah."
THE JUDGE: "Directly?"
A: "Yes."
THE JUDGE: "All right. Well, answer it, then."
A: "He said he pulled his gun and started firing at Charlie."
Q: "And do you know who Charlie is?"
A: "Charlie McConnell."

given that McConnell's earlier testimony named Carter and the defendant as the two shooters at Club Caravan. Moreover, when Carter's attorney cross-examined Patti, Patti agreed that "Johnny" shot at Nogueira at the Comfort Inn, and Patti had earlier referred in his testimony to the defendant as "Johnny."[13] Pursuant to *Gray*, nicknames fall under the rule of *Bruton* as much as full names. This reference plainly incriminated the defendant. It was just as "blatant and incriminating" as the word "deleted" in the *Gray* case. The fact that the remark was made during cross-examination by the attorney for the codefendant does not reduce its prejudicial effect on the defendant.

Other courts have similarly determined that there was a *Bruton* error in the admission of a nontestifying codefendant's accusation of a "friend." See, e.g., People v. Fletcher, 917 P.2d 187 (Cal. 1996); People v. Hernandez, 521 N.E.2d 25 (Ill. 1988). Most of these decisions preceded the United States Supreme Court's decision in *Gray*, suggesting the logic of the Supreme Court's holding in *Gray*: even if the defendant is not named, out-of-court statements that clearly refer to the defendant should not be admitted.

Having concluded that a *Bruton* error occurred, we consider the effect of this improperly admitted evidence. A *Bruton* error is one of constitutional dimension. Preserved constitutional errors are reviewed to determine whether they are harmless beyond a reasonable doubt. The essential question is whether the error had, or might have had, an effect on the jury and whether the error contributed to or might have contributed to the verdicts. . . .

McConnell, the witness whose testimony was crucial to the defendant's convictions in regard to the Revere shootings, was a convicted felon testifying pursuant to a proffer agreement with the Commonwealth. He did not name his assailants to the government until, four years after the shootings, he was in jeopardy of being charged with serious offenses. Thus, the introduction of an inadmissible confession by a codefendant, naming a "friend" as participating in the shootings, buttressed the testimony of McConnell (testimony that the jury may otherwise have rejected). Identification of one of the shooters of Nogueira as "Johnny" significantly added to the Commonwealth's case against the defendant for Nogueira's murder. Accordingly, we conclude that the error "had, or might have had," an effect on the jury; the evidence of Carter's statement implicated the defendant in each of the shootings and requires reversal of all his convictions. . . .

Notes

1. *Out-of-court statements by co-defendants: majority position.* A co-defendant who has confessed and implicated the defendant may be unavailable for testimony

---

13. On cross-examination, Patti's relevant testimony was as follows:

Q: "Okay. Sir, you told the grand jury that Johnny put his arm out the window, fired a bunch of shots at Bobby and then put two more in his head; right?"
A: "Yes."
Q: "That's what you told the grand jury?"
A: "That's what he told me."
Q: "And that's what Gary Carter told you?"
A: "Exactly."

or cross-examination at trial because of the co-defendant's privilege against self-incrimination. In Bruton v. United States, 391 U.S. 123 (1968), the Court prevented the use of the co-defendant's statement in a joint jury trial, even if the judge cautions the jury to consider the confession as evidence only against the co-defendant. When the co-defendant takes the stand at trial (and is therefore available for cross-examination), the co-defendant's confession may come into evidence.

In many trial settings, the law assumes that judicial instructions to a jury will eliminate the ill effects of the jury's exposure to prejudicial evidence. Why do the courts declare that exposure to a co-defendant statement, untested by cross-examination, is an exception to that usual approach?

2. *Redacted statements.* The decision in Gray v. Maryland, 523 U.S. 185 (1998), considered the types of redactions to a co-defendant confession that would make the statement admissible against the co-defendant in a joint trial. Redactions of a co-defendant's out-of-court statement do not comply with *Bruton* if the context makes it obvious that the statement refers to the defendant. See Jefferson v. State, 198 S.W.3d 527 (Ark. 2004) (in a case involving a small cast of characters, replacing defendant's name in co-defendant's confession did not solve *Bruton* problem). Should it matter whether the co-defendant's attorney (as opposed to the prosecutor) links the defendant to the co-defendant's out-of-court statement? For a survey of the fact-sensitive cases on this topic, go to the web extension for this chapter at *http://www.crimpro.com/extension/ch18.*

Recall from Chapter 14 that joinder and severance rules give trial judges discretion to order separate trials for co-defendants if a joint trial would be prejudicial. Would the need to edit a co-defendant's confession convince you, as a trial judge, to adopt a strong presumption in favor of separate trials? Does the operation of the *Bruton* rule call for any changes in joinder and severance rules?

3. Bruton *and* Crawford. The decisions in Bruton v. United States and Crawford v. Washington both interpret the confrontation clause. Are they consistent with one another? Suppose, for instance, that two co-defendants in a murder case make statements to friends and relatives, and each statement implicates both the speaker and the co-defendant in the crime. Can the government introduce each statement at a joint trial, without redaction, because the statements are not "testimonial"? See Thomas v. United States, 978 A.2d 1211 (D.C. 2009).

4. *Cross-examination about pending charges: majority position.* Rules of evidence control the scope of questions that lawyers can ask during cross-examination. For instance, the rules restrict the cross-examining lawyer to questions related to the subjects covered during direct examination. They also limit questions about prior convictions or pending criminal charges against the witness. However, the constitutional right to confrontation sometimes allows a defendant to go beyond these usual restrictions on cross-examination to ask questions that the prosecuting attorney could not ask. In Delaware v. Van Arsdall, 475 U.S. 673 (1986), the Court held that a defendant's rights secured by the confrontation clause were violated when the trial court prohibited "all inquiry" into the possibility that a witness would be biased after agreeing to testify in exchange for favorable treatment in a different criminal matter. The Court noted that the witness's agreement about the pending charges could show a "prototypical form of bias." The jury "might have received a significantly different impression" of the witness's credibility if defense counsel had been permitted to pursue the proposed line of cross-examination. See also Davis v. Alaska, 415 U.S. 308 (1974) (refusal to allow defendant to cross-examine key prosecution witness to

show his probation status for juvenile offense denied defendant his constitutional right to confront witnesses, notwithstanding state policy protecting anonymity of juvenile offenders).

State courts have also concluded that their constitutions allow defendants to pursue lines of cross-examination that the rules of evidence would not allow for other litigants. About 30 states have endorsed the federal position. Like the Supreme Court in *Van Arsdall*, these courts ask if the proposed questions would explore a "prototypical form of bias." They most often conclude that defense counsel may ask questions about criminal charges pending against the witness. See State v. Mizzell, 563 S.E.2d 315 (S.C. 2002) (trial court violated confrontation rights by forbidding defense counsel to elicit from prosecution witness, charged with same crime as defendant "Tootie" Mizzell, the punishment he could receive if convicted). However, state courts will sometimes uphold a trial court that restricts defense cross-examination on this subject, if the witness asserts that she expects no benefit to flow from testifying. See Marshall v. State, 695 A.2d 184 (Md. 1997). Can an appellate court develop sound rules on this question, or is the issue better left to the discretion of the trial court?

5. *Prior criminal record of prosecution witnesses.* On topics of cross-examination other than pending criminal charges against the witness, trial courts tend to have more discretion to limit cross-examination. This is true, for instance, when defense counsel tries to explore the prior criminal record of prosecution witnesses. Although trial judges often allow at least some cross-examination on this subject, appellate courts uphold most efforts to limit questioning on the topic. Many state courts conclude that the prior convictions of a witness do not demonstrate a "prototypical form" of bias against the defendant, but are simply a generalized attack on the witness's credibility that might confuse the jury. Trial judges can impose reasonable limits on cross-examination to guard against harassment, prejudice, confusion of the issues, or waste of time. See State v. Lanz-Terry, 535 N.W.2d 635 (Minn. 1995). Why do courts treat prior convictions differently from pending criminal charges against a prosecution witness?

6. *Ethics of cross-examination.* Sometimes a judge's evidentiary ruling arrives too late. An attorney's leading question on cross-examination might suggest an answer to the jury, even if the witness never has to answer the question. In response to this problem, rules of legal ethics typically instruct attorneys not to ask a question on cross-examination if there is no reasonable factual basis for the question. See ABA Model Rule of Professional Conduct 3.4(e) (lawyer at trial shall not "allude to any matter that the lawyer does not reasonably believe is relevant or that will not be supported by admissible evidence"). If you were a staff attorney working within the disciplinary body of the state bar, how would you expect to enforce this rule?

7. *Legislative limits on defense evidence.* Our discussion has focused on the defendant's power to "confront" adverse witnesses and test the prosecution's case, mostly through cross-examination of witnesses. Defendants also answer the prosecution's case by presenting their own evidence. As with cross-examination, a range of legal rules can restrict the evidence a defendant might present. Rules of evidence require generally that any evidence be relevant to an issue in controversy and that its probative value outweigh its prejudicial impact. See Fed. R. Evid. 403 ("Although relevant, evidence may be excluded if its probative value is substantially outweighed by the danger of unfair prejudice, confusion of the issues, or misleading the jury, or by considerations of undue delay, waste of time, or needless presentation of cumulative

evidence."). States sometimes enact rules or statutes for a particular subject matter that defendants might try to raise at trial. For instance, most jurisdictions have "rape shield" laws, which limit the power of a defendant in a sexual assault case from inquiring into certain aspects of the sexual history of the victim of the alleged crime.

Statutes and rules of evidence in some jurisdictions also limit the defendant's ability to introduce evidence of voluntary intoxication. In Montana v. Egelhoff, 518 U.S. 37 (1996), the Court upheld the constitutionality of a statute that precluded the jury from considering evidence of intoxication when it determined whether the defendant had the mens rea to commit the crime. The Court indicated that 10 states had enacted similar statutes or rules; since the *Egelhoff* decision appeared, the number has grown. The statute in *Egelhoff* appears to place a new type of limit on defense efforts to present evidence. The Montana legislature did not justify its rule by arguing that intoxication evidence is unreliable, cumulative, privileged, or irrelevant. The state instead adopted the rule to deter irresponsible behavior, to incapacitate those who cannot control violent impulses while drunk, and to express society's moral judgment that persons who voluntarily become intoxicated should remain responsible for their actions.

After *Egelhoff*, is there any legal or practical limit on the legislature's power to prevent the defendant from presenting evidence that many juries might find convincing? See Holmes v. South Carolina, 547 U.S. 319 (2006) (defendant's federal constitutional rights violated by an evidence rule precluding defense from introducing proof that third party committed the crime charged, even if the prosecution has introduced forensic evidence that strongly supports a guilty verdict against the defendant); Clark v. Arizona, 548 U.S. 735 (2006) (upholding state statute limiting defense uses of evidence of defendant's mental illness; statute required defendant to assert affirmative defense of insanity rather than using evidence of paranoid schizophrenia to deny specific intent to shoot a police officer).

8. *Commentary on evidence.* Although judges constantly evaluate evidence and rule on its admissibility, many states have constitutional or statutory provisions that prohibit the judge from "commenting" on the evidence or the credibility of witnesses. See Wash. Const. art. IV, §16; Ga. Code §17-8-57. There is, however, no per se federal constitutional bar to judicial commentary on evidence, and some states do not impose such a bar. See Quercia v. United States, 289 U.S. 466 (1933) (no error for judge to comment on evidence so long as the comment does not "excite [in the jury] a prejudice which would preclude a fair and dispassionate consideration of the evidence"; court here committed error by saying that witness displayed mannerisms of a person who is lying).

B. SELF-INCRIMINATION PRIVILEGE AT TRIAL

Once the prosecution has presented its case in chief, the defendant may present evidence as well. The central strategic question for the defendant at this point is whether to testify. While the defendant might present testimony from other witnesses, that evidence is not likely to carry the same weight as a defendant's personal denial of the crime and personal explanation of the prosecution's key evidence. At the same time, a defendant might not feel capable of making a convincing denial at trial, because of nervousness, concern about charges of perjury, or for some other reason.

In the United States, as in most Western legal systems, the law allows the defendant alone to choose whether to testify at trial. The privilege against self-incrimination allows the defendant to refuse to cooperate during certain phases of an investigation, but the privilege provides the clearest protections during a criminal trial. Professor John Langbein has traced the origins of the privilege to the emergence in the eighteenth century of adversary criminal procedure and a prominent role for defense counsel who could speak for the defendant and challenge the government's evidence. See John Langbein, The Historical Origins of the Privilege Against Self-Incrimination at Common Law, 92 Mich. L. Rev. 1047 (1994).

Because of the privilege against self-incrimination, a criminal defendant may refuse to cooperate in some investigative efforts and may refuse to testify at trial. Is there any price for such refusals? As a practical matter, some disadvantages do flow from invoking the privilege. A jury or judge might infer from a defendant's silence that she is guilty or at least that she has no answer to the government's evidence. But can the prosecutor urge the factfinder to draw such inferences? Should the judge do or say anything to prevent the jury from drawing such conclusions? The *Griffin* case reprinted below announced the bright-line constitutional rule that all American courts follow on this question; the following *Murray* opinion from the European Court of Human Rights describes a position encountered in other Western legal systems.

■ EDDIE DEAN GRIFFIN v. CALIFORNIA

380 U.S. 609 (1965)

DOUGLAS, J.[*]

Petitioner was convicted of murder in the first degree after a jury trial in a California court. He did not testify at the trial on the issue of guilt, though he did testify at the separate trial on the issue of penalty. The trial court instructed the jury on the issue of guilt, stating that a defendant has a constitutional right not to testify. But it told the jury:

> As to any evidence or facts against him which the defendant can reasonably be expected to deny or explain because of facts within his knowledge, if he does not testify or if, though he does testify, he fails to deny or explain such evidence, the jury may take that failure into consideration as tending to indicate the truth of such evidence and as indicating that among the inferences that may be reasonably drawn therefrom those unfavorable to the defendant are the more probable.

It added, however, that no such inference could be drawn as to evidence respecting which he had no knowledge. It stated that failure of a defendant to deny or explain the evidence of which he had knowledge does not create a presumption of guilt nor by itself warrant an inference of guilt nor relieve the prosecution of any of its burden of proof.

Petitioner had been seen with the deceased the evening of her death, the evidence placing him with her in the alley where her body was found. The prosecutor made much of the failure of petitioner to testify:

---

[*] [Justices Black, Clark, Brennan, and Goldberg joined this opinion.—EDS.]

The defendant certainly knows whether Essie Mae had this beat up appearance at the time he left her apartment and went down the alley with her. . . . He would know that. He would know how she got down the alley. He would know how the blood got on the bottom of the concrete steps. He would know how long he was with her in that box. He would know how her wig got off. He would know whether he beat her or mistreated her. He would know whether he walked away from that place cool as a cucumber when he saw Mr. Villasenor because he was conscious of his own guilt and wanted to get away from that damaged or injured woman. These things he has not seen fit to take the stand and deny or explain. And in the whole world, if anybody would know, this defendant would know. Essie Mae is dead, she can't tell you her side of the story. The defendant won't.

The death penalty was imposed and the California Supreme Court affirmed. The case is here on a writ of certiorari which we granted to consider whether comment on the failure to testify violated the Self-Incrimination Clause of the Fifth Amendment which we made applicable to the States by the Fourteenth in Malloy v. Hogan, 378 U.S. 1 (1964). . . .[3]

If this were a federal trial, reversible error would have been committed. Wilson v. United States, 149 U.S. 60 (1893), so holds. It is said, however, that the *Wilson* decision rested not on the Fifth Amendment, but on an Act of Congress, now 18 U.S.C. §3481.[4] That indeed is the fact. . . . But that is the beginning, not the end, of our inquiry. The question remains whether, statute or not, the comment rule, approved by California, violates the Fifth Amendment.

We think it does. It is in substance a rule of evidence that allows the State the privilege of tendering to the jury for its consideration the failure of the accused to testify. No formal offer of proof is made as in other situations; but the prosecutor's comment and the court's acquiescence are the equivalent of an offer of evidence and its acceptance. The Court in the *Wilson* case stated:

> . . . It is not every one who can safely venture on the witness stand though entirely innocent of the charge against him. Excessive timidity, nervousness when facing others and attempting to explain transactions of a suspicious character, and offences charged against him, will often confuse and embarrass him to such a degree as to increase rather than remove prejudices against him. It is not every one, however honest, who would, therefore, willingly be placed on the witness stand. The statute, in tenderness to the weakness of those who . . . may have been in some degree compromised by their association with others, declares that the failure of the defendant in a criminal action to request to be a witness shall not create any presumption against him.

[Comment] on the refusal to testify is a remnant of the inquisitorial system of criminal justice, which the Fifth Amendment outlaws. It is a penalty imposed by courts for exercising a constitutional privilege. It cuts down on the privilege by making its assertion costly. It is said, however, that the inference of guilt for failure to testify as to facts peculiarly within the accused's knowledge is in any event natural

---

3. [Most states do not allow] comment on the defendant's failure to testify. The legislatures or courts of 44 States have recognized that such comment is, in light of the privilege against self-incrimination, "an unwarrantable line of argument."

4. Section 3481 reads as follows: "In [a federal criminal trial] the person charged shall, at his own request, be a competent witness. His failure to make such request shall not create any presumption against him."

and irresistible, and that comment on the failure does not magnify that inference into a penalty for asserting a constitutional privilege. What the jury may infer, given no help from the court, is one thing. What it may infer when the court solemnizes the silence of the accused into evidence against him is quite another. [We] hold that the Fifth Amendment, in its direct application to the Federal Government, and in its bearing on the States by reason of the Fourteenth Amendment, forbids either comment by the prosecution on the accused's silence or instructions by the court that such silence is evidence of guilt. Reversed.

STEWART, J., dissenting.*

. . . Article I, §13, of the California Constitution establishes a defendant's privilege against self-incrimination and further provides: ". . . whether the defendant testifies or not, his failure to explain or to deny by his testimony any evidence or facts in the case against him may be commented upon by the court and by counsel, and may be considered by the court or the jury." In conformity with this provision, the prosecutor in his argument to the jury emphasized that a person accused of crime in a public forum would ordinarily deny or explain the evidence against him if he truthfully could do so. Also in conformity with this California constitutional provision, the judge instructed the jury [that they could draw a negative inference from the defendant's failure to deny to explain evidence or facts if he had the knowledge to make such an explanation].

We must determine whether the petitioner has been "compelled . . . to be a witness against himself." Compulsion is the focus of the inquiry. Certainly, if any compulsion be detected in the California procedure, it is of a dramatically different and less palpable nature than that involved in the procedures which historically gave rise to the Fifth Amendment guarantee. When a suspect was brought before the Court of High Commission or the Star Chamber, he was commanded to answer whatever was asked of him, and subjected to a far-reaching and deeply probing inquiry in an effort to ferret out some unknown and frequently unsuspected crime. He declined to answer on pain of incarceration, banishment, or mutilation. And if he spoke falsely, he was subject to further punishment. Faced with this formidable array of alternatives, his decision to speak was unquestionably coerced.

Those were the lurid realities which lay behind enactment of the Fifth Amendment, a far cry from the subject matter of the case before us. I think that the Court in this case stretches the concept of compulsion beyond all reasonable bounds, and that whatever compulsion may exist derives from the defendant's choice not to testify, not from any comment by court or counsel. . . .

It is not at all apparent to me, on any realistic view of the trial process, that a defendant will be at more of a disadvantage under the California practice than he would be in a court which permitted no comment at all on his failure to take the witness stand. How can it be said that the inferences drawn by a jury will be more detrimental to a defendant under the limiting and carefully controlling language of the instruction here involved than would result if the jury were left to roam at large with only its untutored instincts to guide it, to draw from the defendant's silence broad inferences of guilt? The instructions in this case expressly cautioned the jury that the defendant's failure to testify "does not create a presumption of guilt or by

---

* [Justice White joined this opinion.—EDS.]

itself warrant an inference of guilt"; it was further admonished that such failure does not "relieve the prosecution of its burden of proving every essential element of the crime." . . .

I think the California comment rule is not a coercive device which impairs the right against self-incrimination, but rather a means of articulating and bringing into the light of rational discussion a fact inescapably impressed on the jury's consciousness. The California procedure is not only designed to protect the defendant against unwarranted inferences which might be drawn by an uninformed jury; it is also an attempt by the State to recognize and articulate what it believes to be the natural probative force of certain facts. . . .

No constitution can prevent the operation of the human mind. Without limiting instructions, the danger exists that the inferences drawn by the jury may be unfairly broad. Some States have permitted this danger to go unchecked, by forbidding any comment at all upon the defendant's failure to take the witness stand. Other States have dealt with this danger in a variety of ways, as the Court's opinion indicates. Some might differ, as a matter of policy, with the way California has chosen to deal with the problem, or even disapprove of the judge's specific instructions in this case. But, so long as the constitutional command is obeyed, such matters of state policy are not for this Court to decide. I would affirm the judgment.

■ KEVIN SEAN MURRAY v. UNITED KINGDOM
22 Eur. Ct. H.R. 29 (1996)

. . . The applicant was arrested by police officers at 17.40 on 7 January 1990. . . . Pursuant to Article 3 of the Criminal Evidence (Northern Ireland) Order 1988, he was cautioned by the police in the following terms:

> You do not have to say anything unless you wish to do so but I must warn you that if you fail to mention any fact which you rely on in your defence in court, your failure to take this opportunity to mention it may be treated in court as supporting any relevant evidence against you. If you do wish to say anything, what you say may be given in evidence.

In response to the police caution the applicant stated that he had nothing to say. . . .

13. At 21.27 on 7 January a police constable cautioned the applicant pursuant to Article 6 of the Order, inter alia, requesting him to account for his presence at the house where he was arrested. He was warned that if he failed or refused to do so, a court, judge or jury might draw such inference from his failure or refusal as appears proper. He was also served with a written copy of Article 6 of the Order. In reply to this caution the applicant stated: "nothing to say." . . .

15. The applicant was interviewed by police detectives at Castlereagh Police Office on 12 occasions during 8 and 9 January. In total he was interviewed for 21 hours and 39 minutes. At the commencement of these interviews he was either cautioned pursuant to Article 3 of the Order or reminded of the terms of the caution.

16. During the first 10 interviews on 8 and 9 January the applicant made no reply to any questions put to him. He was able to see his solicitor for the first time at 18.33 on 9 January. At 19.10 he was interviewed again and reminded of the Article 3

caution. He replied: "I have been advised by my solicitor not to answer any of your questions." A final interview, during which the applicant said nothing, took place between 21.40 and 23.45 on 9 January. His solicitor was not permitted to be present at any of these interviews.

17. In May 1991 the applicant was tried by a single judge, the Lord Chief Justice of Northern Ireland, sitting without a jury, for the offences of conspiracy to murder, the unlawful imprisonment, with seven other people, of a certain Mr. L and of belonging to a proscribed organisation, the Provisional Irish Republican Army (IRA).

18. According to the Crown, Mr. L had been a member of the IRA who had been providing information about their activities to the Royal Ulster Constabulary. On discovering that Mr. L was an informer, the IRA tricked him into visiting a house in Belfast on 5 January 1990. He was falsely imprisoned in one of the rear bedrooms of the house and interrogated by the IRA until the arrival of the police and the army at the house on 7 January 1990. It was also alleged by the Crown that there was a conspiracy to murder Mr. L as punishment for being a police informer.

19. In the course of the trial, evidence was given that when the police entered the house on 7 January the applicant was seen by a police constable coming down a flight of stairs wearing a raincoat over his clothes and was arrested in the hall of the house. Mr. L testified that he was forced under threat of being killed to make a taped confession to his captors that he was an informer. He further said that on the evening of 7 January he had heard scurrying and had been told to take off his blindfold. . . . The applicant had told him that the police were at the door and to go downstairs and watch television. While he was talking to him the applicant was pulling tape out of a cassette. On a search of the house by the police . . . a tangled tape was discovered in the upstairs bedroom. The salvaged portions of the tape revealed a confession by Mr. L that he had agreed to work for the police. . . . At no time, either on his arrest or during the trial proceedings, did the applicant give any explanation for his presence in the house.

20. At the close of the prosecution case the trial judge, acting in accordance with Article 4 of the Order, called upon [Murray to give evidence in his own defense]:

> I am also required by law to tell you that if you refuse to come into the witness box to be sworn or if, after having been sworn, you refuse, without good reason, to answer any question, then the court in deciding whether you are guilty or not guilty may take into account against you to the extent that it considers proper your refusal to give evidence or to answer any questions.

21. Acting on the advice of his solicitor and counsel, the applicant chose not to give any evidence. No witnesses were called on his behalf. Counsel . . . submitted, inter alia, that the applicant's presence in the house just before the police arrived was recent and innocent.

22. On 8 May 1991 the applicant was found guilty of the offence of aiding and abetting the unlawful imprisonment of Mr. L and sentenced to eight years' imprisonment. He was acquitted of the remaining charges. . . .

25. In concluding that the applicant was guilty of the offence of aiding and abetting false imprisonment, the trial judge drew adverse inferences against the applicant under both Articles 4 and 6 of the Order. The judge stated that in the

particular circumstances of the case he did not propose to draw inferences against the applicant under Article 3 of the Order. . . .

27. Criminal Evidence (Northern Ireland) Order 1988 includes the following provisions:

Article 3: Circumstances in which inferences may be drawn from accused's failure to mention particular facts when questioned, charged, etc.

(1) Where, in any proceedings against a person for an offence, evidence is given that the accused

(a) at any time before he was charged with the offence, on being questioned by a constable trying to discover whether or by whom the offence had been committed, failed to mention any fact relied on in his defence in those proceedings; or

(b) on being charged with the offence or officially informed that he might be prosecuted for it, failed to mention any such fact, being a fact which in the circumstances existing at the time the accused could reasonably have been expected to mention when so questioned, charged or informed, as the case may be, paragraph (2) applies.

(2) [The] court or jury, in determining whether the accused is guilty of the offence charged, may . . . draw such inferences from the failure as appear proper [and] on the basis of such inferences treat the failure as, or as capable of amounting to, corroboration of any evidence given against the accused in relation to which the failure is material. . . .

Article 4: Accused to be called upon to give evidence at trial . . .

(2) Before any evidence is called for the defence, the court . . . shall tell the accused that he will be called upon by the court to give evidence in his own defence, and . . . shall tell him in ordinary language what the effect of this Article will be if . . . when so called upon, he refuses . . . to answer any question. . . .

(3) If the accused . . . refuses to be sworn, . . . paragraph (4) applies.

(4) The court or jury, in determining whether the accused is guilty of the offence charged, may . . . draw such inferences from the refusal as appear proper [and] treat the refusal as, or as capable of amounting to, corroboration of any evidence given against the accused in relation to which the refusal is material. . . .

Article 6: Inferences from failure or refusal to account for presence at a particular place

(1) Where (a) a person arrested by a constable was found by him at a place or about the time the offence for which he was arrested is alleged to have been committed, and (b) the constable reasonably believes that the presence of the person at that place and at that time may be attributable to his participation in the commission of the offence, and (c) the constable informs the person that he so believes, and requests him to account for that presence, and (d) the person fails or refuses to do so, then if, in any proceedings against the person for the offence, evidence of those matters is given, paragraph (2) applies.

(2) [The] court or jury, in determining whether the accused is guilty of the offence charged, may . . . draw such inferences from the failure or refusal as appear proper [and] treat the failure or refusal as, or as capable of amounting to, corroboration of any evidence given against the accused in relation to which the failure or refusal is material.

(3) Paragraphs (1) and (2) do not apply unless the accused was told in ordinary language by the constable when making the request mentioned in paragraph (1)(c) what the effect of this Article would be if he failed or refused to do so. . . .

40. The applicant alleged that there had been a violation of the right to silence and the right not to incriminate oneself contrary to Article 6(1) and (2) of the Convention. . . . The relevant provisions provide as follows:

1. In the determination of . . . any criminal charge against him, everyone is entitled to a fair and public hearing within a reasonable time by an independent and impartial tribunal. . . .
2. Everyone charged with a criminal offence shall be presumed innocent until proved guilty according to law. . . .

41. In the submission of the applicant, the drawing of incriminating inferences against him under the Criminal Justice (Northern Ireland) Order 1988 violated Article 6(1) and (2) of the Convention. It amounted to an infringement of the right to silence, the right not to incriminate oneself and the principle that the prosecution bear the burden of proving the case without assistance from the accused.

He contended that a first, and most obvious element of the right to silence is the right to remain silent in the face of police questioning and not to have to testify against oneself at trial. In his submission, these have always been essential and fundamental elements of the British criminal justice system. Moreover the Commission in Saunders v. United Kingdom, No. 19187/91, Comm. Rep. 10.5.94 (1994) and the Court in Funke v. France, 1 C.M.L.R. 897 (1993) have accepted that they are an inherent part of the right to a fair hearing under Article 6. In his view these are absolute rights which an accused is entitled to enjoy without restriction.

A second, equally essential element of the right to silence was that the exercise of the right by an accused would not be used as evidence against him in his trial. However, the trial judge drew very strong inferences, under Articles 4 and 6 of the Order, from his decision to remain silent under police questioning and during the trial. Indeed, it was clear from the trial judge's remarks . . . that the inferences were an integral part of his decision to find him guilty.

Accordingly, he was severely and doubly penalised for choosing to remain silent: once for his silence under police interrogation and once for his failure to testify during the trial. To use against him silence under police questioning and his refusal to testify during trial amounted to subverting the presumption of innocence and the onus of proof resulting from that presumption: it is for the prosecution to prove the accused's guilt without any assistance from the latter being required. . . .

43. The Government . . . emphasised that the Order did not detract from the right to remain silent in the face of police questioning and explicitly confirmed the right not to have to testify at trial. They further noted that the Order in no way changed either the burden or the standard of proof: it remained for the prosecution to prove an accused's guilt beyond reasonable doubt. What the Order did was to confer a discretionary power to draw inferences from the silence of an accused in carefully defined circumstances. [The] Order merely allows the trier of fact to draw such inferences as common sense dictates. The question in each case is whether the evidence adduced by the prosecution is sufficiently strong to call for an answer. . . .

45. Although not specifically mentioned in Article 6 of the Convention, there can be no doubt that the right to remain silent under police questioning and the privilege against self-incrimination are generally recognised international standards which lie at the heart of the notion of a fair procedure under Article 6. By providing the accused with protection against improper compulsion by the authorities these immunities contribute to avoiding miscarriages of justice and to securing the aim of Article 6.

46. The Court does not consider that it is called upon to give an abstract analysis of the scope of these immunities and, in particular, of what constitutes in this context "improper compulsion." What is at stake in the present case is whether these immunities are absolute in the sense that the exercise by an accused of the right to silence cannot under any circumstances be used against him at trial or, alternatively, whether informing him in advance that, under certain conditions, his silence may be used, is always to be regarded as "improper compulsion."

47. On the one hand, it is self-evident that [it] is incompatible with the immunities under consideration to base a conviction solely or mainly on the accused's silence or on a refusal to answer questions or to give evidence himself. On the other hand, the Court deems it equally obvious that these immunities cannot and should not prevent that the accused's silence, in situations which clearly call for an explanation from him, be taken into account in assessing the persuasiveness of the evidence adduced by the prosecution. Wherever the line between these two extremes is to be drawn, it follows from this understanding of "the right to silence" that the question whether the right is absolute must be answered in the negative. . . .

48. As regards the degree of compulsion involved in the present case, it is recalled that the applicant was in fact able to remain silent. Notwithstanding the repeated warnings as to the possibility that inferences might be drawn from his silence, he did not make any statements to the police and did not give evidence during his trial. [His] insistence in maintaining silence throughout the proceedings did not amount to a criminal offence or contempt of court. . . .

50. Admittedly a system which warns the accused—who is possibly without legal assistance (as in the applicant's case)—that adverse inferences may be drawn from a refusal to provide an explanation to the police . . . involves a certain level of indirect compulsion. However, since the applicant could not be compelled to speak or to testify, as indicated above, this factor on its own cannot be decisive. The Court must rather concentrate its attention on the role played by the inferences in the proceedings against the applicant and especially in his conviction.

51. In this context, it is recalled that these were proceedings without a jury, the trier of fact being an experienced judge. Furthermore, the drawing of inferences under the Order is subject to an important series of safeguards designed to respect the rights of the defence and to limit the extent to which reliance can be placed on inferences.

In the first place, before inferences can be drawn under Article 4 and 6 of the Order appropriate warnings must have been given to the accused as to the legal effects of maintaining silence. Moreover . . . the prosecutor must first establish a prima facie case against the accused, i.e. a case consisting of direct evidence which, if believed and combined with legitimate inferences based upon it, could lead a properly directed jury to be satisfied beyond reasonable doubt that each of the essential elements of the offence is proved.

The question in each particular case is whether the evidence adduced by the prosecution is sufficiently strong to require an answer. The national court cannot conclude that the accused is guilty merely because he chooses to remain silent. It is only if the evidence against the accused "calls" for an explanation which the accused ought to be in a position to give that a failure to give an explanation "may as a matter of common sense allow the drawing of an inference that there is no explanation and that the accused is guilty." Conversely if the case presented by the prosecution had so little evidential value that it called for no answer, a failure to provide one could not justify an inference of guilt. In sum, it is only common sense inferences which the judge considers proper, in the light of the evidence against the accused, that can be drawn under the Order.

In addition, the trial judge has a discretion whether, on the facts of the particular case, an inference should be drawn. [The] judge must explain the reasons for the decision to draw inferences and the weight attached to them. The exercise of discretion in this regard is subject to review by the appellate courts.

52. In the present case, the evidence presented against the applicant by the prosecution was considered by the Court of Appeal to constitute a "formidable" case against him. It is recalled that when the police entered the house some appreciable time after they knocked on the door, they found the applicant coming down the flight of stairs in the house where Mr. L had been held captive by the IRA. [Soon after the police arrived, the] applicant was pulling a tape out of a cassette. The tangled tape and cassette recorder were later found on the premises. Evidence by the applicant's co-accused that he had recently arrived at the house was discounted as not being credible. . . .

54. In the Court's view, having regard to the weight of the evidence against the applicant, as outlined above, the drawing of inferences from his refusal, at arrest, during police questioning and at trial, to provide an explanation for his presence in the house was a matter of common sense and cannot be regarded as unfair or unreasonable in the circumstances. [The] courts in a considerable number of countries where evidence is freely assessed may have regard to all relevant circumstances, including the manner in which the accused has behaved or has conducted his defence, when evaluating the evidence in the case. [What] distinguishes the drawing of inferences under the Order is that, in addition to the existence of the specific safeguards mentioned above, it constitutes, as described by the Commission, "a formalised system which aims at allowing common sense implications to play an open role in the assessment of evidence." . . .

55. The applicant submitted that it was unfair to draw inferences under Article 6 of the Order from his silence at a time when he had not had the benefit of legal advice. . . . In this context he emphasised that under the Order once an accused has remained silent a trap is set from which he cannot escape: if an accused chooses to give evidence or to call witnesses, he is, by reason of his prior silence, exposed to the risk of an Article 3 inference sufficient to bring about a conviction; on the other hand, if he maintains his silence inferences may be drawn against him under other provisions of the Order.

56. The Court [will not] speculate on the question whether inferences would have been drawn under the Order had the applicant, at any moment after his first interrogation, chosen to speak to the police or to give evidence at his trial or call

witnesses. Nor should it speculate on the question whether it was the possibility of such inferences being drawn that explains why the applicant was advised by his solicitor to remain silent.

Immediately after arrest the applicant was warned in accordance with the provisions of the Order but chose to remain silent. [There] is no indication that the applicant failed to understand the significance of the warning given to him by the police prior to seeing his solicitor. Under these circumstances the fact that during the first 48 hours of his detention the applicant had been refused access to a lawyer does not detract from the above conclusion that the drawing of inferences was not unfair or unreasonable. . . .

57. [The] Court does not consider that the criminal proceedings were unfair or that there had been an infringement of the presumption of innocence. . . . For these reasons, the Court [holds] by 14 votes to 5 that there has been no violation of Article 6(1) and (2) of the Convention arising out of the drawing of adverse inferences on account of the applicant's silence. . . .

WALSH, partly dissenting.

1. In my opinion there have been violations of Article 6(1) and (2) of the Convention. The applicant was by Article 6(2) guaranteed a presumption of innocence in the criminal trial of which he complains. Prior to the introduction of the Criminal Evidence (Northern Ireland) Order 1988 a judge trying a case without a jury could not lawfully draw an inference of guilt from the fact that an accused person did not proclaim his innocence. Equally in a trial with a jury it would have been contrary to law to instruct the jurymen that they could do so. [The] object and effect of the 1988 Order was to reverse that position. . . .

3. . . . To permit such a procedure is to permit a penalty to be imposed by a criminal court on an accused because he relies upon a procedural right guaranteed by the Convention. I draw attention to the decision of the Supreme Court of the United States in Griffin v. California, 380 U.S. 609 (1965), which dealt with a similar point in relation to the Fifth Amendment of the Constitution by striking down a Californian law which permitted a court to make adverse comment on the accused's decision not to testify. . . .

Notes

1. *Commenting on silence: majority position.* The Supreme Court's broad holding in *Griffin* that a prosecutor may not comment on a defendant's silence at trial has taken an even broader form over time in the state and federal courts. The *Griffin* rule applies not only to a prosecutor's statements literally pointing out that a defendant has not testified. It also prevents the prosecutor from calling the defendant to the witness stand to allow the jury to see the defendant invoke the privilege. The principle also covers veiled references to a defendant's failure to testify. See State v. McLamb, 69 S.E.2d 537 (N.C. 1952) (argument that defendant was "hiding behind his wife's coattail" was equivalent to comment on defendant's failure to testify on his own behalf). Most state courts say that the constitutional rule bars any comments "manifestly intended" to note a defendant's silence, or statements that are reasonably likely to draw a jury's attention to the fact that the defendant did not testify. See People v. Arman, 545 N.E.2d 658 (Ill. 1989). If a prosecutor makes an

improper statement and the defense counsel objects, most states require the trial court to give a curative instruction to the jury immediately.

While the prosecutor may usually comment on a defendant's failure to produce *other* witnesses or exculpatory evidence to contradict the government's evidence, even a statement that the government's proof is "uncontradicted" could run afoul of the *Griffin* rule when it is highly unlikely that anyone other than the defendant could rebut the evidence. See Smith v. State, 787 A.2d 152 (Md. 2001) (prosecutor in closing argument improperly commented that the defendant had given "zero" answer to key piece of incriminating evidence; proper test is whether the prosecutor's comment is "susceptible of the inference" by the jurors that they were to consider silence). On the other hand, the prosecutor has a bit more latitude in comments that respond directly to defense attorney claims about the quality of the government's case. See United States v. Robinson, 485 U.S. 25 (1988) (prosecutor may refer to defendant's failure to testify when defense counsel claims in closing argument that government did not allow defendant to explain defendant's side of story); Tate v. State, 20 So. 3d 623 (Miss. 2009) (no error when prosecutor says in closing argument that child sex-abuse cases often amount to "her word against his," responding to defense arguments about daughter's motives to frame her father for the crime). For a sampling of state court cases that carry out the ban on commentary about a defendant's silence at trial, go to the web extension for this chapter at *http://www.crimpro.com/extension/ch18.*

2. *Jury instructions about silence.* The constitutional right to silence at trial encompasses a right to have the judge instruct the jury not to draw any inferences from the defendant's decision not to testify. As the court said in Carter v. Kentucky, 450 U.S. 288, 303 (1981), "No judge can prevent jurors from speculating about why a defendant stands mute in the face of a criminal accusation, but a judge can, and must, if requested to do so, use the unique power of the jury instruction to reduce that speculation to a minimum." Most jurisdictions rely on pattern jury instructions about a defendant's silence, along these lines: "The defendant has an absolute right not to testify. The fact that the defendant did not testify should not be considered by you in any way in arriving at your verdict." As defense counsel, would you rather have the judge deliver this jury instruction, or would you rather not call attention to the defendant's silence?

3. *Defendant silence at sentencing.* In Mitchell v. United States, 526 U.S. 314 (1999), the U.S. Supreme Court held that a sentencing judge may not draw an adverse inference from a defendant's silence in a sentencing hearing. Justice Scalia, characterizing this outcome as an extension of the *Griffin* rule into new territory, dissented and explored some difficulties with the rule:

> The illogic of the *Griffin* line is plain, for it runs exactly counter to normal evidentiary inferences: If I ask my son whether he saw a movie I had forbidden him to watch, and he remains silent, the import of his silence is clear. . . . And as for history, *Griffin*'s pedigree is equally dubious. The question whether a factfinder may draw a logical inference from a criminal defendant's failure to offer formal testimony would not have arisen in 1791, because common-law evidentiary rules prevented a criminal defendant from testifying in his own behalf even if he wanted to do so. That is not to say, however, that a criminal defendant was not allowed to speak in his own behalf, and a tradition of expecting the defendant to do so, and of drawing an adverse inference when he did not, strongly suggests that Griffin is out of sync

with the historical understanding of the Fifth Amendment. Traditionally, defendants were expected to speak rather extensively at both the pretrial and trial stages of a criminal proceeding. The longstanding common-law principle, nemo tenetur seipsum prodere, was thought to ban only testimony forced by compulsory oath or physical torture, not voluntary, unsworn testimony. . . .

The *Griffin* question did not arise until States began enacting statutes providing that criminal defendants were competent to testify under oath on their own behalf. Maine was first in 1864, and the rest of the States and Federal Government eventually followed. Although some of these statutes (including the federal statute, 18 U.S.C. § 3481) contained a clause cautioning that no negative inference should be drawn from the defendant's failure to testify, disagreement with this approach was sufficiently widespread that, as late as 1953, the Uniform Rules of Evidence drafted by the National Conference of Commissioners on Uniform State Laws provided that "[if] an accused in a criminal action does not testify, counsel may comment upon [sic] accused's failure to testify, and the trier of fact may draw all reasonable inferences therefrom." Uniform Rule of Evidence 23(4).

Whatever the merits of prohibiting adverse inferences as a legislative policy, the text and history of the Fifth Amendment give no indication that there is a federal constitutional prohibition on the use of the defendant's silence as demeanor evidence. Our hardy forebears, who thought of compulsion in terms of the rack and oaths forced by the power of law, would not have viewed the drawing of a common-sensical inference as equivalent pressure.

4. *Inferences based on silence at trial: other legal systems.* The European Court of Human Rights, as indicated by the *Murray* opinion, reflects a common position in foreign legal systems. Not all systems allow the defendant to remain silent at trial; even among those allowing silence, most empower the judge to draw inferences against the defendant based on this silence. See Criminal Procedure Act of Norway, ch. 9, §93 ("If the person charged refuses to answer, or states that he reserves his answer, the president of the court may inform him that this may be considered to tell against him."). In the United States, the federal and state constitutions as well as some statutes and rules of evidence prevent the factfinder from drawing inferences based on the defendant's silence at trial. See Conn. Gen. Stat. §54-84(b). Is there any value in preventing comments on silence if the factfinder is a judge rather than a jury? Would it be more consistent with truth-seeking if the judge (but not the prosecutor) could tell the jury it may draw inferences from silence?

5. *Incentives to remain silent.* Do juries act differently when none of the attorneys mention the defendant's silence, or is that something a jury will consider regardless of what the attorneys say? Even if a defendant is convinced that the jury looks unfavorably on a decision not to testify, there are some powerful reasons to remain silent at trial. Once a defendant chooses to take the stand at trial, he may not selectively invoke the privilege to avoid answering the most difficult questions. The defendant is subject to the ordinary scope of cross-examination. For many defendants, this means that the prosecutor can introduce evidence of some prior convictions as a method of impeaching the defendant's credibility as a witness. See Theodore Eisenberg & Valerie P. Hans, Taking a Stand on Taking the Stand: The Effect of a Prior Criminal Record on the Decision to Testify and on Trial Outcomes, 94 Cornell L. Rev. 1353 (2009). There is some experimental evidence to suggest that the negative effects of a defendant's silence at trial and the negative effects of the

jury hearing about the defendant's prior convictions are roughly comparable. See Jeffrey Bellin, The Silence Penalty, 103 Iowa L. Rev. 395 (2018).

6. *Use at trial of pretrial silence.* Although it is clear that a prosecutor cannot make even an indirect reference to the defendant's silence at trial, there is more leeway to comment at trial on some forms of *pretrial* silence by the defendant. The Supreme Court has drawn fine distinctions under the federal constitution. The prosecutor may not comment on any pretrial silence of the defendant *after* arrest and the delivery of *Miranda* warnings. Doyle v. Ohio, 426 U.S. 610 (1976). However, the government can use a defendant's *pre-arrest* silence as a basis for impeachment during the defendant's testimony at trial. The same is true for postarrest silence when there is no indication that *Miranda* warnings were delivered. Fletcher v. Weir, 455 U.S. 603 (1982) (postarrest, pre-*Miranda* silence); Jenkins v. Anderson, 447 U.S. 231 (1980) (pre-arrest silence); cf. Anderson v. Charles, 447 U.S. 404 (1980) (defendant made inconsistent factual statements at trial and during interrogation after waiver of *Miranda* rights; prosecution may properly comment on factual inconsistency). Is there any real difference in the evidentiary value of these various forms of silence?

State courts are about evenly divided between those that follow this cluster of federal rulings and those that depart from one or more of the components. It is most common to find state courts ruling that postarrest unwarned silence cannot be used as impeachment material at trial. These courts base such rulings both on state constitutional provisions and on rules of evidence. See Reynolds v. State, 673 S.E.2d 854 (Ga. 2009) (while federal law allows impeachment use of evidence of pre-arrest, pre-*Miranda* silence, state evidence rules make it improper for prosecutor to comment on defendant's prewarning silence or failure to come forward); Weitzel v. State, 863 A.2d 999 (Md. 2005) (discussing division of authority on question of whether substantive use of pre-arrest silence violates state constitutional rights); State v. Leach, 807 N.E.2d 335 (Ohio 2004) (allowing use of pre-arrest silence for impeachment, but not as substantive evidence of guilt).

In 1994 the British Parliament changed the rule regarding silence before trial. A 1984 statute required the police to inform suspects in custody that they have a right to consult an attorney before any interrogation. Under section 34 of the Criminal Justice and Public Order Act of 1994, a court may draw inferences from the fact that a person is questioned and fails to mention a fact that an innocent person could reasonably be expected to mention during questioning, so long as the constable warns the accused of this fact at the time of questioning.

7. *Compulsory process for defense witnesses.* The defendant who hopes to call witnesses and collect evidence to undermine the prosecution's case receives some significant help from the government. Provisions in the federal constitution and in virtually all state constitutions give the defendant the power of "compulsory process," that is, the power to subpoena witnesses who must inform the court of what they know about the events in question. For instance, the Sixth Amendment to the federal constitution grants to the accused the right "to have compulsory process for obtaining witnesses in his favor." Statutes and rules of procedure also confirm the defendant's power to obtain government support in presenting witnesses.

8. *Threats of perjury charges against defense witnesses.* While it is surely true that the law makes it easier for defendants to obtain favorable testimony, there are also some legal obstacles to finding defense witnesses. To begin with, the defense witnesses might invoke the privilege against self-incrimination. Further, the potential witnesses might fear that if they testify, they will create a risk of perjury charges if

the prosecutor believes that the testimony is not truthful. To what extent can government agents, such as judges or prosecutors, use these incentives to make it more difficult for the defendant to obtain witnesses?

The due process clause of the federal constitution controls the statements of prosecutors and judges about possible criminal charges to be filed against defense witnesses. In the leading Supreme Court decision, Webb v. Texas, 409 U.S. 95 (1972), a trial judge warned the defendant's only witness against committing perjury and explained the consequences of a perjury conviction. The Court held that the judge's statements violated due process. See also State v. Finley, 998 P.2d 95 (Kan. 2000) (right to present defense infringed when prosecutor suggests state will charge potential defense witness with felony murder based on her testimony).

High state courts have read *Webb* flexibly to mean that the judge or prosecutor can sometimes mention possible criminal charges to a defense witness. Applying federal due process principles rather than state constitutional provisions, the courts often condemn a prosecutor for saying that she "will" bring criminal charges against the defense witness if the witness testifies. See Mills v. State, 733 P.2d 880 (Okla. Crim. App. 1985). However, when a prosecutor tells a defense witness that testimony "could" expose the witness to criminal charges, courts are less likely to find a due process violation. The same distinction applies to a trial judge who informs the witness about possible criminal charges which could result from testifying. See Jones v. State, 655 N.E.2d 49 (Ind. 1995). Should it matter whether the prosecutor speaks directly to the defense witness or instead sends a message by way of the defense attorney or some other third party?

Defendants have much less success when they complain that the government has deported aliens whom the defendant planned to call as defense witnesses. United States v. Valenzuela-Bernal, 458 U.S. 858 (1982) (no due process violation in prosecution for illegal transportation of aliens when government deports all aliens who would have testified for defendant). Can you explain why these claims are more difficult to sustain than those dealing with threats of criminal charges against witnesses?

9. *Defense grants of immunity.* If a prosecution witness invokes her privilege against self-incrimination, the prosecutor has the option of "immunizing" the witness from later prosecution based on the testimony, and the court will compel the witness to testify despite the privilege. (Recall the discussion of this issue in Chapter 10.) However, the defense does not have a comparable power to immunize defense witnesses who invoke the privilege. Defendants sometimes ask the court to order the prosecution to grant immunity to a defense witness, but courts routinely deny the requests. See State v. Roy, 668 A.2d 41 (N.H. 1995). Why have defendants been so unsuccessful in obtaining grants of immunity, even for their most crucial witnesses? When a defendant requests a grant of immunity for a witness and does not receive it, should the judge explain to the jury that the defendant had hoped to call a witness who is now "missing" because of the privilege against self-incrimination?

Problem 18-2. Telling the Jury

Two police officers on patrol learned of an activated security alarm around 2:25 A.M. at Pleasants Hardware Store in the Pinewood Shopping Center. As they approached the plaza, the officers observed a car parked about 100 yards from the shopping center facing away from the hardware store. The store was not lit, and the parking lot was empty. When the officers got out of their car and inspected the premises, they noticed a large hole in the concrete block wall at the rear of the building.

After this initial investigation, the officers drove to the location of the car they had seen earlier to obtain license tag numbers but discovered that it was gone. Within two minutes, they observed the car traveling north on Highway 321 at a high speed with its headlights off. After a brief pursuit, the driver of the car pulled over. The driver, Joseph Reid, told the officers he had stopped in the area of the shopping center because his car had run out of gas. When the officers asked why the car was running at that time, Reid said it had started unexpectedly. The officers found a sledgehammer near the location where Reid stopped his car.

Reid was tried in superior court on the charge of breaking and entering with intent to commit the felony of larceny. During the prosecution's closing argument to the jury, the following exchange took place:

The State: Now defendant hasn't taken the stand in this case—
Defense Counsel: Objection to his remarks about that, Your Honor.
The Court: Overruled.
Defense Counsel: Exception.
The State: The defendant hasn't taken the stand in this case. He has that right. You're not to hold that against him. But we have to look at the other evidence to look at intent in this case.

The prosecutor's remark that the defendant had not testified mirrored the North Carolina Pattern Jury Instructions regarding a criminal defend<ant's right not to testify. Did the prosecutor commit reversible error by quoting to the jury from the pattern jury instructions? Compare State v. Reid, 434 S.E.2d 193 (N.C. 1993).

Problem 18-3. Pre-Arrest Silence

At 2:30 A.M., Patrick Easter's Isuzu Trooper collided with a yellow taxicab. Easter was returning from a wedding reception to his home near the accident site. The cab was carrying six university students. Easter suffered injuries in the accident, and four of the students were seriously injured. A test administered shortly after the accident showed Easter's blood-alcohol content was approximately .11. Several days later, Easter was arrested and charged with four counts of vehicular assault.

Easter did not testify at trial. The state and the defense presented evidence supporting different versions of how the accident happened. Officer Fitzgerald's testimony occupied much of the trial, although he did not observe the accident or take a statement from a witness. He testified that he arrived within minutes of the accident and found Easter in the bathroom of a gas station at the intersection, with torn clothes, a cut forehead, and blood on his elbows and knees. He testified that Easter then "totally ignored" him when he asked what happened. He also testified that when he continued to ask questions, Easter looked down, "once again ignoring me, ignoring my questions."

Fitzgerald said that he "felt the defendant was being smart drunk." The officer explained that when he used the term "smart drunk," he meant to say that Easter "was evasive, wouldn't talk to me, wouldn't look at me, wouldn't get close enough for me to get good observations of his breath and eyes, I felt that he was trying to hide or cloak."

Fitzgerald testified he took Easter back to the intersection and told him he would be placed under arrest or he could submit to a voluntary blood-alcohol test at a hospital. Fitzgerald suspected Easter was intoxicated because of Easter's slightly slurred speech, bloodshot eyes, and the odor of alcohol on his breath, although Easter had no coordination problems, walked without difficulty, and produced his license without fumbling or stumbling. After learning that he would be arrested, Easter's attitude changed. He asked for business papers in the truck and for a friend to be telephoned. Easter answered questions about his driver's license and said his home was a mile north of the accident scene.

In closing, the prosecutor argued that the trial testimony was best summed up with the words "smart drunk." He referred several times to testimony that Easter was a "smart drunk" who had ignored Officer Fitzgerald, except when asking about his papers and friend, and concluded, "Easter is a smart drunk." He closed his final argument with these words: "I urge you to find Mr. Easter, the smart drunk in this case, guilty." Did the prosecutor and the prosecution witness improperly comment on the defendant's invocation of his right to silence? See State v. Easter, 922 P.2d 1285 (Wash. 1996).

C. ETHICS AND LIES AT TRIAL

Ethical issues arise at all stages in the prosecution and defense of criminal defendants. Issues before trial include the conduct of interrogations, the grounds for filing charges, and the statements made while negotiating plea bargains. During trial preparation, ethical obligations may require discovery disclosures beyond those required by constitutional doctrine, statutes, or rules of procedure. Throughout the criminal process, ethical dilemmas for defense counsel arise from the tension between the search for truth and the zealous representation of the defendant. For the prosecutor, ethical dilemmas arise from the conflict between the obligation to seek justice on behalf of the public as a whole and the need to consult and defer to the wishes of crime victims.

Some of the most difficult ethical questions in all of legal practice arise when the lawyer believes the client is acting illegally or is lying. Related problems arise when a lawyer believes that a friendly witness is lying. Consider the extent to which the ethical obligations of defense lawyers and prosecutors at trial are—or should be—different. Is this difference on obligations simply an outgrowth of the burden of proof and the beyond-a-reasonable-doubt standard in criminal cases?

■ PEOPLE v. DEREK ANDRADES
828 N.E.2d 599 (N.Y. 2005)

G.B. SMITH, J.

In People v. DePallo, 96 N.Y.2d 437 (N.Y. 2001), we held that defense counsel properly balanced the duties he owed to his client and the duties he owed to the court and to the criminal justice system when, during a jury trial, counsel notified the court that his client had offered perjured testimony and refused to use that testimony in his closing argument to the jury. We left open the question of the propriety of a similar disclosure under circumstances where the court sits as the factfinder. We address that issue in the case now before us and hold that counsel's disclosure to the court, which was open to the inference that his client intended to perjure himself upon taking the stand, did not deprive defendant of a fair hearing or of the effective assistance of counsel.

Defendant became enraged when he heard rumors that Magalie Nieves, a woman with whom he had had a sexual relationship, was infected with the HIV virus. Defendant, with the aid of 14-year-old Ericka Cruz, confronted Nieves and a fight ensued. Subsequently, defendant and Cruz lured Nieves to an isolated area where defendant choked her with a bandana, and he and Cruz stabbed her in the ear and in the breast, killing her. Days later, the police arrested Cruz, who offered a confession of the killing. The next day, defendant was arrested and charged, inter alia, with second degree murder and first degree manslaughter. Upon his arrest, defendant was read his *Miranda* rights and gave both written and videotaped statements in which he admitted to acting in concert with Cruz in killing Nieves.

Defendant moved to suppress his confessions. . . . Prior to the hearing, defendant's attorney asked to be relieved as counsel, stating, "There is an ethical conflict with my continuing to represent [defendant] and I can't go any further than that." The prosecutor opposed the application, citing the age of the case. The court asked defense counsel to state the nature of the ethical dilemma without disclosing privileged information so that the court could make an effective ruling. Counsel stated, however, that he could not elaborate. The court then presumed that counsel's ethical dilemma concerned defendant's right to testify. The court denied counsel's application and told him that if the problem arose, he would have to offer more specific information to the court.

After the People presented their case at the . . . hearing, defense counsel informed the court that defendant intended to testify. Outside defendant's presence, counsel stated:

> As part and parcel of my request to be relieved in this matter, I think I should tell the Court and place on the record that I did tell [defendant] and advise [defendant] that he should not testify at the hearing and as a result of the problem that I'm having, the ethical problem I'm having. What I'm going to do is just basically direct his attention to date, time and location of the statement and let him run with the ball.

The court, recognizing that defense counsel was not permitted to divulge privileged matters to the court, concluded that counsel's conduct complied with his ethical obligations under the disciplinary rules given his anticipation that defendant "could possibly, could commit perjury on the witness stand." The court further concluded that counsel could still afford defendant the effective assistance of counsel. [The court also concluded that it was not necessary for defendant to be present during the conference because it did not constitute a critical stage of his trial.]

Defendant thereafter testified on his own behalf, largely in narrative form, with the court and counsel asking clarifying questions. Defendant testified that at the time he provided his statements to the police, he did not remember the events leading to Nieves's death and specifically did not recall stabbing her. He stated that during his interrogation, the police informed him of Cruz's version of the events, and he believed what she said because he did not think that Cruz would lie about him. Defendant stated that he initially refused to sign the written confession drafted by the police officers because its contents were not true, but that later he signed it only after one of the officers took him into a private room. Defendant further testified that when he gave his videotaped statement, he simply restated Cruz's rendition of the killing as described to him by the officers. Thus, he claimed that this confession was not a recounting of events from his own memory. Finally, defendant stated that by the time he had provided the videotaped confession at approximately 10:00 P.M., he was hungry because he had not eaten all day, and was not permitted food until after he had given that statement.

Defense counsel offered no closing argument, choosing instead to rest on the record and the papers submitted. Following the People's closing statement, the court denied defendant's motion to suppress his confessions. In a subsequent written decision, the court noted that it "did not find the defendant's testimony credible or worthy of belief." The court held that defendant made his written and videotaped statements after voluntarily waiving his constitutional rights. Upon a jury trial, at which defendant largely defended himself, defendant was convicted of second degree murder and sentenced to a prison term of 25 years to life. . . .

In *DePallo*, we recognized that a defense attorney's duty to zealously represent a client must be circumscribed by his or her duty as an officer of the court to serve the truth-seeking function of the justice system. Moreover, as perjury is a criminal offense, defense counsel has a duty to refrain from participating in the client's commission of it. Thus, we stated that while counsel must pursue all reasonable means to reach the objectives of the client, counsel must not in any way assist a client in presenting false evidence to the court. See Nix v. Whiteside, 475 U.S. 157 (1986).

Indeed, New York's Code of Professional Responsibility specifically addresses an attorney's ethical obligations in providing lawful representation. Disciplinary Rule 7-102 expressly states that an attorney may not "knowingly use perjured testimony or false evidence," DR 7-102(a)(4); "knowingly make a false statement of law or fact," DR 7-102(a)(5); "participate in the creation or preservation of evidence when the lawyer knows or it is obvious that the evidence is false," DR 7-102(a)(6); "counsel or assist the client in conduct that the lawyer knows to be illegal or fraudulent," DR 7-102(a)(7); or "knowingly engage in other illegal conduct," DR 7-102(a)(8).

In light of the ethical obligations of an attorney in this state, and in accordance with United States Supreme Court jurisprudence, an attorney faced with a client who intends to commit perjury has the initial responsibility to attempt to dissuade the client from pursuing the unlawful course of action. Nix v. Whiteside, 475 U.S. at 169-170. Should the client insist on perjuring himself, counsel may seek to withdraw from the case. If counsel's request is denied, defense counsel, bound to honor defendant's right to testify on his own behalf, should refrain from eliciting the testimony in traditional question-and-answer form and permit defendant to present his testimony in narrative form. However, in accordance with DR 7-102(a)(4), counsel may not use the perjured testimony in making argument to the court.

Here, defense counsel properly discharged his ethical obligations under the circumstances presented. Counsel clearly advised defendant against lying on the witness stand; indeed, counsel encouraged defendant not to take the stand at all. Yet defendant insisted on testifying at the hearing, and his attorney believed that the evidence he intended to present was false. Thus, it was entirely proper for counsel to seek to withdraw as defendant's attorney prior to the hearing based on his perceived ethical dilemma.

While defendant does not argue the propriety of his attorney's actions up to that point, he does take issue with his attorney's telling the court that the ethical dilemma he faced concerned defendant's right to testify at the hearing. Defendant argues that such a disclosure signifies defendant's intention to commit perjury to the court which sits as the factfinder for the hearing. He contends that such a disclosure inevitably affected the court's ability to assess his credibility in determining the outcome of the hearing.[3] In that same vein, defendant argues that his attorney should not have told the court of his intent to question defendant in the narrative before having done so. Defendant asserts that his attorney should have said nothing, proceeded to question defendant in the narrative, and if counsel's suspicions about defendant's testimony ripened into a reality, counsel could simply refrain from using the perjured testimony in his closing argument.

We disagree. As an initial matter, we note that at no time did counsel ever disclose to the court that defendant intended to commit perjury or otherwise disclose any client secrets. Rather, the court inferred defendant's perjurious intent based upon the nature of counsel's application. However, counsel could have properly made such a disclosure since a client's intent to commit a crime is not a protected confidence or secret. See Nix v. Whiteside, 475 U.S. at 174; Code of Professional Responsibility DR 4-101(c)(3). Moreover, counsel's ethical obligations do not change simply because a judge rather than a jury is sitting as the factfinder. Moreover, as a practical matter, defendant's suggestion would solve nothing because counsel would likely find it difficult to allow defendant to testify in the narrative without prior explanation. Like the direct examination of any witness, defendant's examination must be guided by proper questioning. Had counsel attempted to offer defendant's testimony in the narrative, it would have been subject to objection either by the prosecutor or the court. Even if counsel were permitted to present defendant's testimony in narrative form without objection, the very fact of defendant testifying in such a manner would signify to the court that counsel believes that his client is perjuring himself.

We therefore conclude that defense counsel properly balanced his duties to his client with his duties to the court and the criminal justice system and that in doing so, defendant was not denied his right to a fair hearing. Furthermore, absent a breach of any recognized professional duty, defendant's claim that he was denied the effective assistance of counsel must also fail.

Finally, we reject defendant's contention that he was denied his right to be present during a material stage of the trial because he was absent during the colloquy between the court and the attorneys regarding defense counsel's intent to present defendant's testimony in the narrative. [A] colloquy of this nature involves procedural matters at which a defendant can offer no meaningful input. Therefore, defendant had no right to be present. . . .

---

3. In support of his position, defendant relies on Lowery v. Cardwell, 575 F.2d 727 (9th Cir. 1978). In that case, defendant testified at her bench trial and perjured herself, to the surprise of her attorney. Counsel requested a recess, at which time he unsuccessfully attempted to withdraw from the case. Counsel then ended the defendant's testimony and made no reference to the defendant's perjured testimony during his closing arguments. The [court] held that counsel's actions denied the defendant a fair trial because counsel's actions gave the judge the impression that counsel believed that the defendant had testified falsely. The court . . . suggested that it would have been the better practice for the attorney to have made a record for his own protection in the event that he was ever questioned about his professional conduct. We expressly reject this approach because it requires an attorney to remain silent while the client commits perjury, which is wholly incompatible with counsel's role as an officer of the court and, more specifically, counsel's obligation to reveal fraud perpetrated by a client upon the court.

Notes

1. *Lying clients: majority view.* As the U.S. Supreme Court made clear in Nix v. Whiteside, 475 U.S. 157 (1986), the federal constitutional right to effective counsel does not compel an attorney to remain silent when a client plans to commit perjury during testimony. Nor does the Constitution require the attorney to take any other particular action, such as withdrawing from the case or informing the court of the client's plans. The same can be said for state constitutional rulings: They leave the attorney with several acceptable options. The most pertinent legal requirements in this situation come not from constitutions, but from the rules of legal ethics, sometimes embodied in state statutes. The first ethical duty of the defense attorney who learns that a client might commit perjury at trial is to convince the client not to commit perjury. What exactly does an attorney tell a client accused of a crime who apparently plans to lie during testimony?

Before taking any further steps, the attorney must have sufficient reason to believe that her client plans to lie during testimony, despite her best efforts to convince him otherwise. ABA Model Rule of Professional Conduct 3.3(a)(4) phrases it this way: "A lawyer shall not knowingly offer evidence that the lawyer knows to be false." How will an attorney "know" that a client's testimony will be false? State courts sometimes require the attorney to be convinced "beyond a reasonable doubt" that the client plans to commit perjury. Other formulations include "good cause to believe the defendant's proposed testimony would be deliberately untruthful," a "firm factual basis," a "good-faith determination," and "actual knowledge." See Commonwealth v. Mitchell, 781 N.E.2d 1237 (Mass. 2003) (reviewing standards and adopting "firm basis in fact" because standard of beyond reasonable doubt would "eviscerate" attorney's ethical obligation of candor to tribunal).

2. *Defense counsel responses to perjury.* If the attorney knows that a client plans to commit perjury, or has already committed perjury at trial, several options are open to her under the rules of ethics. One possibility is to withdraw from the case. Ethics rules allow (or even require) the attorney in most pretrial situations to make the motion, although courts often will deny the motion. ABA Model Rule of Professional Conduct 1.16(a)(1) (a lawyer "shall withdraw from the representation of a client if . . . the representation will result in violation of the rules of professional conduct or other law"). What should the attorney say in the motion to withdraw? Suppose the case is set for a bench trial. Does withdrawal prevent any harm from befalling the client or the tribunal?

The attorney who does not withdraw must deal with a "trilemma—that is, the lawyer is required to know everything, to keep it in confidence, and to reveal it to the court." Monroe Freedman, Lawyers' Ethics in an Adversary System 28 (1975). Since the appearance of the ABA's Model Rules of Professional Conduct in 1983 (now adopted in over 40 jurisdictions), the states have moved toward rules requiring counsel to reveal the potential perjury to the court. In the words of Rule 3.3(a)(2), a lawyer "shall not knowingly . . . fail to disclose a material fact to a tribunal when disclosure is necessary to avoid assisting a criminal or fraudulent act by the client."

The defense attorney might allow the client to testify but use a "narrative" form of testimony, in which the attorney asks an open-ended question, such as, "tell us what happened," and the defendant relates his story without further questions from defense counsel. See State v. Chambers, 994 A.2d 1248 (Conn. 2010) (no violation of state constitution or ethics rules). Does this response strike the right balance among the defense lawyer's ethical obligations? Is this an appropriate response to perjury by a defense witness other than the defendant?

3. *Client control over admissions of guilt.* Just as the client ultimately decides whether to testify in his or her own defense, the client controls whether or not to contest guilt. See McCoy v. Louisiana, 138 S. Ct. 1500 (2018) (Sixth Amendment guarantees a defendant the right to choose the objective of his defense and to insist that his counsel refrain from admitting guilt during jury trial, even when counsel's professional opinion is that confessing guilt offers the defendant the best chance to avoid the death penalty.

4. *Lying prosecution witnesses.* Sometimes defendants challenge the validity of a conviction based on false testimony by prosecution witnesses. A prosecutor who knowingly allows prosecution witnesses to present false testimony about a material fact violates the federal due process clause. This is true even if the government attorney who knows about the false testimony is not the same as the trial attorney. Once the prosecution witness has delivered the false testimony, the prosecutor must inform the court of the falsehood. See Giglio v. United States, 405 U.S. 150 (1972); Mooney v. Holohan, 294 U.S. 103 (1935).

Some courts go a step further, and overturn convictions based on false testimony of prosecuting witnesses even if the prosecutor was unaware of the perjury. These courts require a defendant to demonstrate that the perjury came to his attention after trial (despite his due diligence in preparing for trial), and that the jury probably would have acquitted if it had not heard the perjured testimony. Ex parte Chabot, 300 S.W.3d 768 (Tex. Crim. App. 2009).

What inquiries would you expect prosecutors to make about the truthfulness of the testimony from government witnesses? What if the local police department has developed a reputation for "testilying" (providing false testimony to strengthen the prosecution's case)? See Joseph Goldstein, He Excelled as a Detective, Until Prosecutors Stopped Believing Him, N.Y. Times, Oct. 10, 2017.

When prosecutors knowingly rely on false testimony, or when they fail to disclose their agreements to reduce the criminal punishment that a prosecution witness faces, they could face professional discipline. See State ex rel. Oklahoma Bar Association v. Miller, 309 P.3d 108 (Okla. 2013); Duff Wilson, Prosecutor in Duke Case Disbarred by Ethics Panel, N.Y. Times, June 17, 2007.

Problem 18-4. The Do-Not-Call List

Prosecutors are obliged under discovery laws to inform defense attorneys about some types of information that reflect poorly on the truthfulness of law enforcement officers who will testify at trial for the prosecution. In light of this obligation, as well as prosecutors' independent concerns about the quality of the evidence they plan to use, some offices maintain a list of police officers who will not be called as witnesses. Prosecutors in other offices do not maintain a formal list but they do avoid calling certain officers to the stand.

Suppose that a newspaper reporter starts inquiring about these "do not call" lists and files a request for any such list under the state open records law. As the designated press liaison for the local prosecutor's office, how would you respond when the reporter calls? Would you refuse any comment? Provide the number of officers on the list but no further information? The names of the officers and the reasons why they appear on the list? See Eric Dexheimer, Lists of Police Officers with Credibility Issues Often Hidden, Austin American-Statesman, Dec. 12, 2016.

D. BURDEN OF PROOF

Some trial court observers are skeptical about the practical consequences of using various standards of proof in civil and criminal cases. Perhaps jurors would reach the same verdicts whether they were told to decide cases on preponderance-of-the-evidence, "clear and convincing" proof, or beyond-a-reasonable-doubt standards. But the idea (if not the precise language) of the reasonable doubt standard has ancient roots, and the higher burden on the government to obtain a conviction in criminal cases is the cornerstone for principles and practices that appear throughout the criminal trial.

How should we define reasonable doubt? How should judges instruct juries to decide when the government has proven its case "beyond" that point? The very phrase "beyond a reasonable doubt" suggests a tension that makes the concept difficult to grasp: Doubt is a negative concept, but to go "beyond" a given amount of evidence is a positive concept. This tension—between a positive and a negative conception of reasonable doubt—is reflected in various definitions and rules that the states have adopted. Is there a single point at which reasonable doubt is passed, or do these positive and negative notions together define a range for juries to apply?

Some courts simply direct jurors to decide whether the government has proven all elements beyond a reasonable doubt and allow no further explanation of the reasonable doubt concept. A leading nineteenth-century treatise explains this position: "There are no words plainer than reasonable doubt and none so exact to the idea meant." 1 Joel Prentiss Bishop, New Criminal Procedure, §1094 (1895). Most jurisdictions either direct or allow judges to define reasonable doubt more precisely. Should judges be limited to a standard definition? If so, which one?

■ STATE v. DENISE FREI
831 N.W.2d 70 (Iowa 2013)

HECHT, J.

The defendant killed her longtime boyfriend. At trial she raised a defense of justification based on evidence of battered women's syndrome and a defense of insanity based on various diagnoses including depression and an anxiety disorder. She was convicted of first-degree murder. On appeal, she alleges the district court erred in denying her motion for mistrial and by giving improper jury instructions. . . . Finding no error in the record, we affirm the conviction. . . .

In response to a 911 call shortly before 2:00 A.M. on July 19, 2009, police found Denise Frei sitting on the front porch of the home she shared with [her common-law husband] Curtis Bailey in Marengo, Iowa. She had blood on her shirt and hands. Inside, Bailey's dead body lay on the living room floor, beaten severely with blunt objects. Frei told the police she had been upstairs and overheard a drug deal "gone bad" and then found Bailey's body. Later, however, she admitted that she had killed Bailey with the help of her eighteen-year-old son and his girlfriend.

Frei was charged with first-degree murder. At trial, she relied on defenses of justification and insanity. She testified that Bailey subjected her to humiliating and degrading emotional, verbal, and sexual abuse and that he threatened to kill her children and grandchild if she ever left him. She described Bailey as an extremely jealous and controlling person who checked her sales receipts after shopping trips to see if her purchases had been rung up by a male cashier. If the receipts evidenced the involvement of a male cashier, Bailey forced her to return the items for a refund. He allegedly cut her off from her family, including her adult sons and her grandchild. Frei testified that she had tried to leave Bailey at least once and had talked about it on other occasions but that he had threatened to slit the throats of her children and grandchild if she did, and that he had told her that even if she killed herself, he would still harm her family. She testified that she tried to kill Bailey on three previous occasions by giving him doses of morphine and insulin.

Frei devised a plan in early July 2009 to get Bailey drunk enough to pass out and then smother him by wrapping his face in Saran Wrap. She believed that if she suffocated him with the plastic wrap it would leave no marks and it would appear Bailey had died as a consequence of an overdose or heart attack. She sought the help of her eighteen-year-old son, Jacob, and his girlfriend, Jessica. Frei told Bailey that she and Jessica would engage in sex acts together while he watched if he would drink a shot of vodka for each sex act they performed. Bailey agreed and, on the morning of Saturday, July 18, told his work acquaintances about the ménage à trois that was to take place that night.

That night, Frei and Jessica followed their plan, serving Bailey shots of vodka until he passed out in the living room. Jessica summoned Jacob to the house, and Frei bound Bailey's wrists with plastic wrap. As his face was being wrapped, however, Bailey woke up and struggled to free himself. Frei, Jacob, and Jessica each grabbed objects nearby, including a rock and a candy dish, and struck Bailey approximately thirty times until he died. The three cleaned up the scene, and Jacob and Jessica left the house. Frei called 911 and reported a false story about the circumstances surrounding Bailey's death. She told the police that Bailey died during a drug deal gone bad—that while she was upstairs he had let two men into the house to purchase drugs and that she heard them struggle and came down to find Bailey dead. When she later learned that her son had confessed his participation in the incident, she returned to the police station and admitted her own involvement.

Frei offered the trial testimony of Dr. Marilyn Hutchinson, who testified that Frei suffered from depression, posttraumatic stress syndrome (PTSD), battered women's syndrome (BWS), and possibly an anxiety disorder. Dr. Hutchinson explained that she believed Frei had endured a tremendous amount of sexual and emotional abuse from Bailey, childhood sexual and physical abuse, and adult physical abuse from her former husband. She opined this extensive history of abuse distorted Frei's thoughts and feelings and impacted her ability to make rational decisions. . . .

The State offered expert testimony from Dr. Michael Taylor, who concluded that Frei did not suffer from any psychiatric disorder and that she understood the nature and quality of her acts when she plotted to kill Bailey. He specifically rejected Dr. Hutchinson's posttraumatic stress syndrome disorder diagnosis, noting Frei had denied all of the normal symptoms of PTSD during his interview with her. The State also relied on Frei's own admissions to disprove her justification defense—specifically that she planned Bailey's death for a week-and-a-half to two weeks and that she tried to make it look like an accidental death rather than a murder. The State also introduced evidence that she made statements suggesting proceeds from life insurance on Bailey's life would allow her to pay off debts on the restaurant she owned with Bailey.

The jury found Frei guilty. On appeal, she [argues that the district court erroneously] instructed the jury on the definition of reasonable doubt. . . .

Frei requested a jury instruction on reasonable doubt that read as follows:

> The burden is on the State to prove Denise Frei guilty beyond a reasonable doubt. A "reasonable doubt" is such a doubt as fairly and naturally arises in our mind and by reason of which you cannot say that you have a full and abiding conviction of the guilt of the defendant; and if, after considering all of the circumstances as disclosed by the evidence, you find your mind wavering or vacillating, then you have a reasonable doubt, and the defendant is entitled to the benefit of such doubt and you must acquit her. A reasonable doubt may arise from the evidence in the case or it may arise from a lack or failure of evidence produced by the State, and it must be such a doubt as would cause a reasonable, prudent and considerate man to pause and hesitate before acting in the graver and more important affairs of life. But you should not ignore credible evidence to hunt for doubt, and you should not entertain such doubt as is purely imaginary or fanciful or based on groundless conjecture. If, after a careful and impartial consideration of all evidence in the case, you have a full and abiding conviction of the guilt of the defendant, then you are satisfied beyond a reasonable doubt, otherwise you are not satisfied beyond a reasonable doubt.

[This proposed instruction was derived from language found in one of the "Uniform Jury Instructions" drafted by a special committee of the Iowa State Bar Association (ISBA) and published by that association prior to 2004.]

The district court declined to give the instruction requested by Frei, electing instead to give the following instruction on the subject:

> The burden is on the State to prove Denise Leone Frei guilty beyond a reasonable doubt. A reasonable doubt is one that fairly and naturally arises from the evidence or lack of evidence produced by the State.
>
> If, after a full and fair consideration of all the evidence, you are firmly convinced of the defendant's guilt, then you have no reasonable doubt and you should find the defendant guilty. But if, after a full and fair consideration of all the evidence or lack of evidence produced by the State, you are not firmly convinced of the defendant's guilt, then you have a reasonable doubt and you should find the defendant not guilty.[5]

---

5. This instruction given by the district court was derived from language found in the version of the ISBA's uniform instruction on reasonable doubt extant from 2004 to 2009. By the time of the trial of this case in August 2011, the ISBA's uniform instruction on reasonable doubt had been revised to include an additional paragraph which provides:

> A reasonable doubt is a doubt based upon reason and common sense, and not the mere possibility of innocence. A reasonable doubt is the kind of doubt that would make a reasonable person hesitate to act. Proof beyond a reasonable doubt, therefore, must be proof of such a convincing character that a reasonable person would not hesitate to rely and act upon it. However, proof beyond a reasonable doubt does not mean proof beyond all possible doubt.

Iowa Crim. Jury Instruction 100.10 (March 2009).

Frei contends the instruction given by the district court violated her due process rights. We begin our analysis by noting the clearly established proposition that "the Due Process Clause protects the accused against conviction except upon proof beyond a reasonable doubt of every fact necessary to constitute the crime with which he is charged." In re Winship, 397 U.S. 358, 364 (1970). "Taken as a whole, the instructions must correctly convey the concept of reasonable doubt to the jury." Victor v. Nebraska, 511 U.S. 1, 5 (1994) (quoting Holland v. United States, 348 U.S. 121, 140 (1954)). The constitutional question presented here is whether there is a reasonable likelihood that the jury understood the instructions to allow conviction based on proof insufficient to meet the *Winship* standard.

Courts have struggled, however, in settling upon a serviceable definition of the "reasonable doubt" standard. The choice of words accurately communicating the nature and extent of certitude jurors must have [about] a defendant's guilt in order to vote for a conviction is not an easy project. The Due Process Clause provides no definitional guidance as it requires no "particular form of words be used in advising the jury of the government's burden of proof." Victor v. Nebraska, 511 U.S. at 5 (noting "although this standard is an ancient and honored aspect of our criminal justice system, it defies easy explication."). Yet, Supreme Court jurisprudence teaches that a minimum definitional threshold for the standard does exist. For example, a jury instruction characterizing reasonable doubt as "such doubt as would give rise to grave uncertainty" and "an actual substantial doubt" amounting to a "moral certainty" set the bar for the State's burden of proof too low and fell below the due process threshold. Cage v. Louisiana, 498 U.S. 39, 41 (1990).

Other formulations of the reasonable doubt standard have survived due process scrutiny. In *Victor*, the Supreme Court found no due process violation resulted from jury instructions in two consolidated cases. In one of these cases, the California state trial court's instructions defined reasonable doubt as follows:

> It is not a mere possible doubt; because everything relating to human affairs, and depending on moral evidence, is open to some possible or imaginary doubt. It is that state of the case which, after the entire comparison and consideration of all the evidence, leaves the minds of the jurors in that condition that they cannot say they feel an abiding conviction, to a moral certainty, of the truth of the charge.

In the other consolidated case, a Nebraska state trial court defined reasonable doubt as follows:

> "Reasonable doubt" is such a doubt as would cause a reasonable and prudent person, in one of the graver and more important transactions of life, to pause and hesitate before taking the represented facts as true and relying and acting thereon. It is such a doubt as will not permit you, after full, fair, and impartial consideration of all the evidence, to have an abiding conviction, to a moral certainty, of the guilt of the accused. At the same time, absolute or mathematical certainty is not required. You may be convinced of the truth of a fact beyond a reasonable doubt and yet be fully aware that possibly you may be mistaken. You may find an accused guilty upon the strong probabilities of the case, provided such probabilities are strong enough to exclude any doubt of his guilt that is reasonable. A reasonable doubt is an actual and substantial doubt reasonably arising from the evidence, from the facts or circumstances shown by the evidence, or from the lack of evidence on the part of the State, as distinguished from a doubt arising from mere possibility, from bare imagination, or from fanciful conjecture.

The Supreme Court concluded both of these reasonable doubt formulations passed due process muster.

Frei contends the reasonable doubt instruction given by the district court in this case fell short of the applicable due process standard because it failed to "impress upon the factfinder the need to reach a subjective state of near certitude of the guilt of the accused." 511 U.S. at 15 (quoting Jackson v. Virginia, 443 U.S. 307, 315 (1979)). In particular, she posits that the "firmly convinced" formulation of reasonable doubt instructed upon in this case provided no real guidance to the jurors as to the nature or quality of doubt that would require an acquittal, and thus allowed them to convict her with a lesser quantum of certainty than is required by the Federal Constitution.

We approved a very similar formulation of the reasonable doubt standard in State v. McFarland, 287 N.W.2d 162, 163 (Iowa 1980). The relevant instructions in *McFarland* authorized the jury to convict the defendant only if they were "firmly and abidingly convinced" of the defendant's guilt. We concluded the instructions sufficiently "set out an objective standard for measuring the jurors' doubts."

Since *Victor* was decided in 1994, the "firmly convinced" standard has achieved extensive recognition and is likely the formulation of the reasonable doubt standard most widely approved by American jurists, academics, and litigants. Lawrence M. Solan, Refocusing the Burden of Proof in Criminal Cases: Some Doubt About Reasonable Doubt, 78 Tex. L. Rev. 105, 145 (1999) ("The superiority of the firmly convinced instruction comes not from its semantic fidelity to the reasonable doubt standard but from its greater success in promoting important values."); see also Irwin A. Horowitz, Reasonable Doubt Instructions, 3 Psychol. Pub. Pol'y & L. 285, 297-98 (1997) (discussing the superiority of the firmly convinced standard as evidenced by statistical analysis); A Handbook of Criminal Terms 574 (Bryan A. Garner ed., 2000); Black's Law Dictionary 1380 (9th ed. 2009) (defining reasonable doubt as "the doubt that prevents one from being firmly convinced of a defendant's guilt, or the belief that there is a real possibility that a defendant is not guilty.").

In her concurring opinion in *Victor*, Justice Ginsburg stoutly endorsed a reasonable doubt instruction proposed by the Federal Judicial Center (FJC), characterizing it as "clear, straightforward, and accurate." [The FJC Pattern Criminal Jury Instruction 21] embraced firmly convinced language comparable to that used in the instruction challenged in this case: "Proof beyond a reasonable doubt is proof that leaves you firmly convinced of the defendant's guilt. . . . If, based on your consideration of the evidence, you are firmly convinced that the defendant is guilty of the crime charged, you must find him guilty." Six federal courts of appeals have approved the firmly convinced standard, finding that it accurately expresses the degree of certainty required to find a defendant guilty beyond a reasonable doubt. [The court cited decisions from the Tenth, Second, Fifth, Ninth, and D.C. Circuits.]

Numerous state courts have also adopted the FJC pattern instruction and expressly approved its firmly convinced language. State v. Portillo, 898 P.2d 970 (Ariz. 1995) (adopting the FJC firmly convinced standard in all criminal cases); Winegeart v. State, 665 N.E.2d 893 (Ind. 1996) (approving the FJC firmly convinced standard and recommending its use in Indiana courts, "preferably with no supplementation or embellishment"); State v. Reyes, 116 P.3d 305, 314 (Utah 2005) (requiring that Utah trial courts use the FJC instruction).

We find no reversible error in the "firmly convinced" formulation used by the district court in this case. "Firmly" means "steadfastly," "resolutely," "soundly," "solidly," and "strongly." Webster's Third International Dictionary 856 (unabr. ed. 2002). Likewise, "firm" is defined as "immovable," "fixed," "settled," "not easily moved, shaken, excited, or disturbed." The word "firmly" is not arcane or obscure, but rather is a plain, well-understood word commonly used in modern speech. We believe it adequately expressed—within the due process parameters articulated in *Victor*—the extent of certitude the jury must possess to convict a defendant of a crime in this state. [Our determination that the district court did not err in using the "firmly convinced" formulation to define the reasonable doubt standard in this case should not be viewed as a rejection of any other formulation expressing in equivalent terms the state's burden of proof.]

Accordingly, we conclude the district court did not err when it instructed the jury on reasonable doubt. . . .

Notes

1. *Defining reasonable doubt: majority position.* As the Iowa court in *Frei* indicated, the federal constitution requires that the government prove all elements of an offense beyond a reasonable doubt, In re Winship, 397 U.S. 358 (1970), but it does not require that courts define reasonable doubt in a particular way. States have adopted a range of positions specifying both what is required and what is forbidden in defining reasonable doubt.

Several modern definitions trace their wording back to a famous decision by Chief Justice Lemuel Shaw, in Commonwealth v. Webster, 59 Mass. 295, 320 (1850):

> [What] is reasonable doubt? It is a term often used, probably pretty well understood, but not easily defined. It is not mere possible doubt; because every thing related to human affairs, and depending on moral evidence, is open to some possible or imaginary doubt. It is that state of the case, which, after the entire comparison and consideration of all the evidence, leaves the minds of the jurors in that condition that they cannot say they feel an abiding conviction, to a moral certainty, of the truth of the charge.

Some states emphasize the negative perspective, defining reasonable doubt as a doubt that would cause a reasonable person to "hesitate to act in their most important affairs." Other states require the doubt to be "based on reason" or "a valid reason." Roughly 10 states refer to "actual and substantial doubt" or "serious and substantial doubt" or "fair and actual doubt." A handful require that the doubt be articulable, that it be "doubt for which a reason can be given," although some states forbid such formulations because they require jurors to be articulate and place the burden on the defendant to show reasonable doubt. See People v. Antommarchi, 604 N.E.2d 95 (N.Y. 1992).

A growing number of states define reasonable doubt in positive terms, focusing on the "moral certainty of guilt" or saying the juror must be "firmly convinced of guilt." See Commonwealth v. Russell, 23 N.E.3d 867 (Mass. 2015) (updating state jury instruction to clarify "moral certainty" phrase to mean "the highest degree of certainty possible in matters relating to human affairs—based solely on the evidence that has been put before you in this case"); Steve Sheppard, The Metamorphoses of Reasonable Doubt: How Changes in the Burden of Proof Have Weakened the Presumption of Innocence, 78 Notre Dame L. Rev. 1165 (2003) (tracking twentieth-century shift to interpretation that emphasizes assignment of reasons as operational meaning of reasonableness).

State courts also diverge on the question whether to define reasonable doubt at all. About a dozen states allow the trial judge to avoid the issue by providing no definition to the jury, while two states forbid trial judges from giving definitions. Paulson v. State, 28 S.W.3d 570 (Tex. Crim. App. 2000) (best practice is not to define reasonable doubt for jury). More than a dozen states require trial judges to define reasonable doubt in all cases, based either on statutes or case law. A few states require a definition only if the defendant requests it, and another handful require a definition to be given only in complex cases. For a graphic showing the distribution of states on this issue, go to the web extension for this chapter at *http://www.crimpro. com/extension/ch18*.

One danger of using a negative definition of "reasonable doubt" is that it seems to place a burden on the defendant to show reasonable doubt instead of placing the burden on the government to dispel reasonable doubt (or to offer proof "beyond" reasonable doubt). The positive formulation of the instruction—found in the Federal Judiciary Center version of the instruction, which requires a juror to be "firmly convinced that the defendant is guilty of the crime charged"—has gained legal momentum in recent decades. The U.S. Supreme Court has refused to mandate a particular definition for all federal courts, and the circuits have adopted a range of positions parallel to those taken among the states.

2. *Do definitions help?* States that forbid trial courts from defining reasonable doubt, or those that leave the decision to the trial judge, echo the long-standing skepticism of observers like Joel Bishop and John Henry Wigmore. Definitions, they say, do not help jurors decide cases. But the difficulty of applying the concept suggests that if states or individual judges want to leave jurors to use their own conceptions of reasonable doubt, they may be saying more about their view of the jury's role than about reasonable doubt.

Experimental evidence suggests that different descriptions of the reasonable doubt formula in judicial instructions do have an impact on the jury. See Michael D. Cicchini & Lawrence T. White, Testing the Impact of Criminal Jury Instructions on Verdicts: A Conceptual Replication, 117 Colum. L. Rev. Online No. 2 (2017) (experiment finding statistically significant difference in conviction rates between mock jurors who were properly instructed on reasonable doubt, and mock jurors who were instead instructed "to search for the truth," with latter group nearly twice as likely to mistakenly believe they could convict defendant even if they had a reasonable doubt about guilt).

3. *Quantifying reasonable doubt.* Most state and federal courts discourage or prohibit trial judges from efforts to quantify the reasonable doubt standard. See State v. Cruz, 639 A.2d 534 (Conn. 1994). Can the preponderance standard for civil cases be quantified? Don't the preponderance, clear and convincing, and reasonable doubt standards all express degrees of certainty? Some judges have used sports analogies rather than numerical descriptions. What if the judge said that the prosecution had to "take the ball way past the 50-yard line, but you don't have to go a hundred yards for a guilty finding"? See State v. DelVecchio, 464 A.2d 813 (Conn. 1983). Studies conducted in the 1970s found that jurors quantified reasonable doubt at around 86 percent certainty of guilt. See Saul Kassin & Lawrence Wrightsman, On the Requirements of Proof: The Timing of Judicial Instruction and Mock Juror Verdicts, 37 J. Personality & Soc. Psychol. 282 (1979). Another

study suggests that jurors take a wide range of positions, associating the concept of "reasonable doubt" with anything from 50 to 100 percent certainty of guilt. See Terry Connolly, Decision Theory, Reasonable Doubt, and the Utility of Erroneous Acquittals, 11 Law & Hum. Behav. 101 (1987). For a review of the empirical studies of juror understanding of the reasonable doubt standard, go to the web extension for this chapter at *http://www.crimpro.com/extension/ch18.*

4. *Presumption of innocence and burden of proof.* Is the presumption of innocence anything more than another way to refer to the prosecution's burden of proof? In other words, when a defendant is said to be "presumed innocent," does that statement have legal ramifications beyond requiring the state to prove all elements of the offense beyond a reasonable doubt? Does it remind the jury not to place any evidentiary weight on the mere fact that the defendant has been charged with a crime? Most states declare that a separate instruction on presumption of innocence is not necessary in every case, while about 15 states do require a separate instruction. See, e.g., Ohio Rev. Stat. §2938.08 ("The presumption of innocence places upon the state (or the municipality) the burden of proving him guilty beyond a reasonable doubt. In charging a jury the trial court shall state the meaning of the presumption of innocence and of reasonable doubt in each case."). Does the presumption of innocence tell the jury anything about how long the government bears its burden of proof? Consider this typical description from Horn v. Territory, 56 P. 846, 848 (Okla. 1899):

> A defendant's friends may forsake him, but the presumption of innocence, never. It is present throughout the entire trial; and, when the jury go to their room to deliberate, the "presumption of innocence" goes in with them, protesting against the defendant's guilt. And it is only after the jury has given all the evidence in the case a full, fair, and impartial consideration, and have been able to find beyond a reasonable doubt that the defendant is guilty as charged, that the presumption of innocence leaves him.

In Taylor v. Kentucky, 436 U.S. 478 (1978), the Supreme Court found a federal due process violation when a Kentucky judge refused to instruct the jury on the presumption of innocence. The Court cited Coffin v. United States, 156 U.S. 432 (1895), to establish that the presumption of innocence in favor of the accused "is the undoubted law, axiomatic and elementary, and its enforcement lies at the foundation of the administration of our criminal law." A year later, however, the Court held that a presumption-of-innocence instruction was not a constitutional requirement in all cases. Kentucky v. Whorton, 441 U.S. 786 (1979). The instruction was necessary in *Taylor* only because of "skeletal" jury instructions and the prosecutor's repeated suggestions that the defendant's status as a person charged with a crime tended to establish his guilt.

5. *Guilty clothing.* The presumption of innocence can have an impact on the operation of the courtroom beyond the jury instructions. For example, courts generally forbid the state from requiring the defendant to appear in prison garb or surrounded by armed guards. However, the defendant must object to the clothing or other circumstances. Estelle v. Williams, 425 U.S. 501 (1976). Federal and state courts allow the conspicuous use of security guards more readily than they will tolerate shackles or distinctive clothing on the defendant. See Holbrook v. Flynn, 475 U.S. 560 (1986) (upholding four uniformed state troopers sitting in the front spectator row during trial as security measure); Sterling v. State, 830 S.W.2d 114 (Tex.

Crim. App. 1992) (seven uniformed deputies in courtroom). Which option would most defendants prefer: shackles and a heavy presence of security officers, or the use of a glass enclosure around the defendant's seat (a common feature of courtrooms in some parts of the world)?

6. *Rebuttable Presumptions and the government's burden of proof.* Judges instruct juries, and lawyers argue to juries, about evidentiary presumptions—asserting either that the jurors should assume a fact to be true or that if one fact is found then another fact or conclusion is more likely to be true. These presumptions can undermine the requirement that crime elements be proven beyond a reasonable doubt. In Sandstrom v. Montana, 442 U.S. 510 (1979), the U.S. Supreme Court rejected an instruction in a deliberate homicide case where intent was an element of the offense. The instruction said, "the law presumes that a person intends the ordinary consequences of his voluntary acts." The defendant had confessed to the killing, making his mental state the key issue. The Court found that, from the standpoint of the reasonable juror, this instruction shifted the burden of proof from the state to the defendant.

In Francis v. Franklin, 471 U.S. 307 (1985), a Georgia prisoner attempting escape killed a man when he fired a gun through a door at the moment the victim slammed it. Again, the sole defense was lack of intent to kill. The trial court, using an instruction with a long pedigree, instructed the jury that the acts of a "person of sound mind and discretion are presumed to be the product of the person's will, but the presumption may be rebutted. A person of sound mind and discretion is presumed to intend the natural and probable consequences of his acts but the presumption may be rebutted. A person will not be presumed to act with criminal intention but the trier of facts . . . may find criminal intention upon a consideration of the words, conduct, demeanor, motive and all of the circumstances connected with the act for which the accused is prosecuted." The jury was also instructed that the defendant was presumed innocent and that the State was required to prove every element of the offense beyond a reasonable doubt. The Supreme Court again rejected the instruction. Even though the trial court had stated that "the presumption may be rebutted," such qualifying language did not prevent a reasonable juror from believing that the defendant bore the burden of showing he did not intend to kill. The *Franklin* Court distinguished valid and invalid instructions involving evidentiary presumptions as follows:

> The court must determine whether the challenged portion of the instruction creates a mandatory presumption, or merely a permissive inference. A mandatory presumption instructs the jury that it must infer the presumed fact if the State proves certain predicate facts. A permissive inference suggests to the jury a possible conclusion to be drawn if the State proves predicate facts, but does not require the jury to draw that conclusion.

Both federal and state courts have followed the constitutional structure that the U.S. Supreme Court built in *Sandstrom* and *Franklin*. Federal and state courts differ, however, on the particular kinds of language that create an impermissible mandatory presumption. For instance, courts disagree on whether presumptions such as "a person generally intends the consequences of his acts" can be cured by additional language saying that such presumptions are rebuttable. *Sandstrom* claims apply as well to arguments made by the prosecutor in closing arguments.

Despite the best efforts of trial courts instructing juries, *Sandstrom* claims continue to arise. Should legislatures bar the use of all evidentiary presumptions?

Doesn't all circumstantial evidence require reliance on presumptions? Don't all findings about mens rea require jurors to rely on presumptions even if they are unstated?

7. *Reasonable doubt about what?* Every defendant benefits from the requirement that the state prove all elements of any criminal offense beyond a reasonable doubt. But what are "elements" of offenses, and what are "defenses" that the defendant must prove? Can states define crimes any way they want? The U.S. Supreme Court at times has wrestled with the idea that the federal constitution might place some controls on what the state can designate as an element of a crime or a defense to the charges. Current doctrine, however, reinforces the view that states have substantial discretion in defining crimes. In Patterson v. New York, 432 U.S. 197 (1977), the Supreme Court rejected a due process challenge to a New York law that made the defense of extreme emotional disturbance an affirmative defense that the defendant must prove by a preponderance of the evidence. The Court emphasized that "preventing and dealing with crime is much more the business of the States than it is of the Federal Government." The federal constitution limits the capacity of states to define crimes only to the extent that the state law "offends some principle of justice so rooted in the traditions and conscience of our people as to be ranked as fundamental." The Court declined to adopt "as a constitutional imperative, operative countrywide, that a State must disprove beyond a reasonable doubt every fact constituting any and all affirmative defenses related to the culpability of an accused."

Thus, states appear to have substantial discretion within federal constitutional boundaries to define crimes and defenses and to allocate the burden of proving or disproving an element to either the prosecution or the defense. Sometimes the argument is not about whether the state *can* place a particular burden on the state or the defendant, but whether it has in fact done so.

8. *The burden on affirmative defenses: majority view.* States divide on the general issue of whether the prosecution carries the burden of proof on affirmative defenses. Roughly 35 states require the defendant to carry the burden of proof on all affirmative defenses, but they usually require only that the defendant prove the defense by a preponderance of the evidence. See, e.g., Ohio Rev. Code §2901.05 (the burden of proof "for all elements of the offense is upon the prosecution. The burden of going forward with the evidence of an affirmative defense, and the burden of proof, by a preponderance of the evidence, for an affirmative defense, is upon the accused"). A handful of states require the state to carry the burden of proof on all affirmative defenses, though usually the defendant has the burden of going forward with facts sufficient to raise the defense. It is most common for states to require the prosecution to carry the burden on self-defense, while about half the states place the burden of proving insanity and related defenses on the defendant.

9. *Statutory definitions of sufficient evidence.* As we have seen, a legislature is free by and large to define the elements of crimes; it is more limited in its power to declare what inferences about crime elements that a jury must draw from the proven facts. However, the legislature may specify the type of evidence that is *not* sufficient to prove the elements. For instance, some statutes specify the minimum number of witnesses the prosecution must present to support a conviction for a particular crime (e.g., the traditional "two witness rule" for perjury convictions).

Issues about the proper burden of proof and crime definitions draw from a mixture of substantive criminal law, constitutional law, criminal procedure, sentencing law, and evidence, and often from a blend of statutes, case law, and other kinds of legal authority. The mixed nature of questions about defining crimes means that a legislature might accomplish a goal with a rule of evidence that might be invalid as a crime definition. See Montana v. Egelhoff, 518 U.S. 37 (1996) (upholding state statute barring evidence of voluntary intoxication in determining the mental element of an offense).

Problem 18-5. Words and Numbers

Joseph McCullough was charged with possession of a controlled substance (marijuana) and possession of stolen property (a 1974 Chevrolet "Luv" pickup truck). During the voir dire examination of potential jurors, the district judge attempted to illustrate the concept of reasonable doubt with a numerical scale. On a scale of 0 to 10, the judge placed the preliminary hearing standard of probable cause at about 1 and the burden of persuasion in civil trials at just over 5. She then twice described reasonable doubt as about "seven and a half, if you had to put it on a scale." The judge also provided the jurors with the reasonable doubt standard described in Nev. Rev. Stat. §175.211, which provides as follows:

> A reasonable doubt is one based on reason. It is not mere possible doubt, but is such a doubt as would govern or control a person in the more weighty affairs of life. If the minds of the jurors, after the entire comparison and consideration of all the evidence, are in such a condition that they can say they feel an abiding conviction of the truth of the charge, there is not a reasonable doubt. Doubt to be reasonable must be actual and substantial, not mere possibility or speculation.

After introducing the jurors to the reasonable doubt standard provided by the Nevada statute, the judge again noted, "I have tried to give you that on a zero to ten scale." The jury convicted the defendant of both charges. He appeals, claiming that the judge's attempt to quantify reasonable doubt impermissibly lowered the prosecution's burden of proof and confused the jury rather than clarifying the reasonable doubt concept. How would you rule? See McCullough v. State, 657 P.2d 1157 (Nev. 1983).

Problem 18-6. A Doubt with a Reason

At 10:40 P.M. on October 29, Trooper Radford stopped Warren Manning on Highway 34 for a defective headlight. After writing Manning a warning ticket, Radford learned from his dispatcher that Manning was driving with a suspended license. Radford placed Manning under arrest and the two left the scene with Manning in the back seat of the patrol car.

Radford's patrol car was spotted early the next morning half-submerged in Reedy Creek Pond. He had been shot twice through the head with his own revolver and severely pistol-whipped. The prosecutor charged Manning with murder. The State's theory of the case was that Manning used his own .25 caliber pistol to threaten Radford. The prosecutor argued that Manning forced the trooper to drive to Reedy Creek Pond, where Manning murdered him and attempted to submerge the patrol car. Radford's revolver was found in a tobacco barn 75 yards behind Manning's home.

Manning testified on his own behalf that after he and Trooper Radford left in the patrol car, the trooper stopped another car traveling in front of them after a bag was thrown from its window. There were four people in the car. Radford approached the vehicle and while he was talking with the driver, Manning ran away from the patrol car unobserved. He walked to a friend's house and was driven back to his car.

After the close of evidence at trial, the judge gave the following charge on reasonable doubt:

> Beyond a reasonable doubt, in telling you that that is the degree of proof by which the State must prove, that phrase means exactly what it states in the English language, and that is a doubt for which you can give a real reason. That excludes a whimsical doubt, fanciful doubt. You could doubt any proposition if you wanted to. A reasonable doubt is a substantial doubt for which honest people, such as you, when searching for the truth can give a real reason. So it's to that degree of proof that the State is required to establish the elements of a charge.

Later in the charge, the judge added this thought about the meaning of reasonable doubt: "I instruct you to seek some reasonable explanation of the circumstances proven other than the guilt of the Defendant and if such a reasonable explanation can be found you should find the Defendant not guilty." As defense counsel, how would you argue that this charge was invalid? Compare State v. Manning, 409 S.E.2d 372 (S.C. 1991).

Problem 18-7. Presumption in the Fire

James Jubilee, an African American, moved with his family from California to Virginia Beach in April 1998. After a few weeks in the new neighborhood, he asked his new neighbor, Susan Elliott, about shots being fired from behind the Elliott home. Elliott explained to Jubilee that her son shot firearms as a hobby, and used the backyard as a firing range.

A few nights later, Elliott's son Richard drove a truck onto Jubilee's property, planted a cross, and set it on fire. He was trying to "get back" at Jubilee for complaining about the shooting in the backyard. Elliott was not affiliated with the Ku Klux Klan. The next morning, as Jubilee was pulling his car out of the driveway, he noticed the partially burned cross approximately 20 feet from his house. After seeing the cross, Jubilee was very nervous because "a cross burned in your yard tells you that it's just the first round." He worried about the violence that might follow.

A separate cross burning incident took place elsewhere in the state a few months later. One August night, Barry Black led a Ku Klux Klan rally in Carroll County. Twenty-five to 30 people attended this gathering, which occurred on private property with the permission of the owner, who also attended the rally. When the sheriff of the county learned that a Klan rally was occurring in his jurisdiction, he went to observe it from the side of the road. Over the next hour or so, about 40 to 50 cars passed the site, and a few of the drivers stopped to ask the sheriff what was happening on the property.

Eight to 10 houses were located nearby. Rebecca Sechrist, who was related to the owner of the property where the rally took place, sat and watched to see what was going on from the lawn of her in-laws' home. She heard Klan members speak about what they believed in. As she put it, the speakers "talked real bad about the blacks and the Mexicans." One speaker told the assembled gathering that "he would love to take a .30/.30 and just randomly shoot the blacks." The speakers also talked about "President Clinton and Hillary Clinton," and about how their tax money "goes to the black people." This language made Sechrist feel "very scared." At the conclusion of the rally, the crowd circled around a 25- to 30-foot cross, which was placed 325 yards away from the road. As the sheriff and others looked on, the cross went up in flames. The sheriff then went down the driveway, entered the rally, and asked who was responsible for burning the cross. Black responded, "I guess I am because I'm the head of the rally." The sheriff then told Black, "There's a law in the State of Virginia that you cannot burn a cross and I'll have to place you under arrest for this."

Barry Black and Richard Elliott were both charged with violating Virginia's cross burning statute. Section 18.2-423 provides:

> It shall be unlawful for any person or persons, with the intent of intimidating any person or group of persons, to burn, or cause to be burned, a cross on the property of another, a highway or other public place. . . . Any such burning of a cross shall be prima facie evidence of an intent to intimidate a person or group of persons.

At Black's trial, the judge instructed the jury that "intent to intimidate means the motivation to intentionally put a person or a group of persons in fear of bodily harm. Such fear must arise from the willful conduct of the accused rather than from some mere temperamental timidity of the victim." The trial court also instructed the jury that "the burning of a cross by itself is sufficient evidence from which you may infer the required intent." The jury found Black guilty and fined him $2,500.

At Elliott's trial, the court instructed the jury that the Commonwealth must prove that "the defendant intended to commit cross burning," that he "did a direct act toward the commission of the cross burning," and that he "had the intent of intimidating any person or group of persons." The court did not instruct the jury on the meaning of the word "intimidate" or on the prima facie evidence provision of §18.2-423. The jury found Elliott guilty of attempted cross burning and sentenced him to 90 days in jail and a $2,500 fine.

Did either the statute or the judge's instructions in either of the two trials create an unconstitutional presumption of guilt? Cf. Virginia v. Black, 538 U.S. 343 (2003).

PART FOUR

MEASURING PUNISHMENT AND REASSESSING GUILT

Sentencing

Criminal adjudication points toward sentencing. At sentencing, the system finally announces a "bottom line" outcome for those defendants who have proceeded all the way through the criminal process. Along the way, defense counsel, prosecutors, judges, and police make choices with one eye on the possible sentence. This anticipation of sentencing is perhaps most evident in plea bargaining.

Just as much of criminal procedure looks ahead to sentencing, the sentencing phase offers a chance to look back on the earlier steps in the process. At sentencing, the criminal justice system surveys once again all the major decisions it has reached regarding an offender, from investigation through conviction. It also takes a broader view of the offender's past and future, the victim's past and future, and the community's present attitude toward the crime. After this panoramic survey is complete, the sentencing authority selects a sanction. The rules the sentencing authority follows when selecting the sanction can be advisory, but sometimes they are quite specific, as in the following provisions from an ancient criminal code.

CODE OF HAMMURABI

(C.H.W. Johns trans., 1911)

§1: If a man weave a spell and put a ban upon a man, and has not justified himself, he that wove the spell upon him shall be put to death.

§8: If a man has stolen ox or sheep or ass, or pig, or ship, whether from the temple or the palace, he shall pay thirtyfold. If he be a poor man, he shall render tenfold. If the thief has naught to pay, he shall be put to death.

§15: If a man has caused either a palace slave or palace maid, or a slave of a poor man or a poor man's maid, to go out of the gate, he shall be put to death.

§195: If a man has struck his father, his hands one shall cut off.

§196: If a man has caused the loss of a gentleman's eye, his eye one shall cause to be lost.

§197: If he has shattered a gentleman's limb, one shall shatter his limb.

§198: If he has caused a poor man to lose his eye or shattered a poor man's limb, he shall pay one mina of silver.

§209: If a man has struck a gentleman's daughter and caused her to drop what is in her womb, he shall pay ten shekels of silver for what was in her womb.

§210: If that woman has died, one shall put to death his daughter.

§211: If the daughter of a poor man through his blows he has caused to drop that which is in her womb, he shall pay five shekels of silver.

§212: If that woman has died, he shall pay half a mina of silver.

One major puzzle for modern sentencing procedures can be summed up in this question: Why go to all the trouble of following intricate procedures for police and prosecutors, before and during trial, if the last step in the system ignores those procedural protections? This question, however, raises another: If the sentencing authority had to be bound by all determinations made prior to conviction, would convicted offenders receive undue protection, as if they were still presumed innocent?

A. WHO SENTENCES?

In most criminal justice systems, several institutions share the decision about the proper sentence to impose: Legislatures and judges always have a say in the sentence, and juries, parole commissions, or sentencing commissions sometimes participate. But the precise division of labor in deciding on sentencing policy and punishment in particular cases varies a great deal from place to place. We begin with sentencing systems that put the initial choice of sanctions into the hands of case-level actors such as the sentencing judge, followed by review at the systemic level by a parole board. Then we consider alternatives that place more sentencing authority in the hands of legislatures and sentencing commissions as they promulgate general rules.

1. Indeterminate Sentencing

Until recently, sentencing in the United States was an area characterized more by discretion than by procedure. In 1950 every state and the federal system had an "indeterminate" sentencing system. Under this type of system, the legislature prescribed broad potential sentencing ranges, and the trial judge sentenced without meaningful legal guidance and typically without offering any detailed explanation for the sentence. An executive branch agency (usually a parole board) ultimately determined the actual sentence each defendant would serve. There were virtually no judicial opinions explaining or reviewing a sentence, and legal counsel ordinarily made oral arguments at sentencing hearings without any written submissions to the court. The unwritten nature of the arguments and the decisions, together with the unavailability of pre-sentence investigation reports, made it difficult to get a handle on sentencing law and practice in an indeterminate system. Perhaps that reveals the most important point about such a system: Sentencing happened without much law.

The following materials offer a glimpse of indeterminate sentencing systems at work. The U.S. Supreme Court decision in Williams v. New York, which came at the high water mark for indeterminate sentencing, captures not only the huge discretion given to trial judges but also some of the principles underlying that discretion.

■ SAMUEL WILLIAMS v. NEW YORK
337 U.S. 241 (1949)

BLACK, J.[*]

A jury in a New York state court found appellant guilty of murder in the first degree. The jury recommended life imprisonment, but the trial judge imposed sentence of death. In giving his reasons for imposing the death sentence the judge discussed in open court the evidence upon which the jury had convicted stating that this evidence had been considered in the light of additional information obtained through the "Probation Department, and through other sources." [A New York statute authorized the court to consider "any information that will aid the court in determining the proper treatment of such defendant." Williams claimed that the sentence, which was based on information supplied by witnesses, violated due process because the defendant had no chance to confront or cross-examine the witnesses or to rebut the evidence.]

The record shows a carefully conducted trial lasting more than two weeks in which appellant was represented by three appointed lawyers who conducted his defense with fidelity and zeal. The evidence proved a wholly indefensible murder committed by a person engaged in a burglary. . . .

About five weeks after the verdict of guilty with recommendation of life imprisonment, and after a statutory pre-sentence investigation report to the judge, the defendant was brought to court to be sentenced. [The] judge gave reasons why he felt that the death sentence should be imposed. . . . He stated that the pre-sentence investigation revealed many material facts concerning appellant's background which though relevant to the question of punishment could not properly have been brought to the attention of the jury in its consideration of the question of guilt. He referred to the experience appellant "had had on 30 other burglaries in and about the same vicinity" where the murder had been committed. The appellant had not been convicted of these burglaries although the judge had information that he had confessed to some and had been identified as the perpetrator of some of the others. The judge also referred to certain activities of appellant as shown by the probation report that indicated appellant possessed "a morbid sexuality" and classified him as a "menace to society." The accuracy of the statements made by the judge as to appellant's background and past practices were not challenged by appellant or his counsel, nor was the judge asked to disregard any of them or to afford appellant a chance to refute or discredit any of them by cross-examination or otherwise.

The case presents a serious and difficult question. The question relates to the rules of evidence applicable to the manner in which a judge may obtain information to guide him in the imposition of sentence upon an already convicted defendant. . . . To aid a judge in exercising this discretion intelligently the New York procedural policy encourages him to consider information about the convicted person's past life, health, habits, conduct, and mental and moral propensities. The sentencing judge may consider such information even though obtained outside the courtroom from persons whom a defendant has not been permitted to confront or cross-examine. . . .

---

[*] [Chief Justice Vinson and Justices Reed, Frankfurter, Douglas, Jackson, and Burton joined this opinion.—EDS.]

Tribunals passing on the guilt of a defendant always have been hedged in by strict evidentiary procedural limitations. But both before and since the American colonies became a nation, courts in this country and in England practiced a policy under which a sentencing judge could exercise a wide discretion in the sources and types of evidence used to assist him in determining the kind and the extent of punishment to be imposed within limits fixed by law. Out-of-court affidavits have been used frequently, and of course in the smaller communities sentencing judges naturally have in mind their knowledge of the personalities and backgrounds of convicted offenders. . . .

In addition to the historical basis for different evidentiary rules governing trial and sentencing procedures there are sound practical reasons for the distinction. In a trial before verdict the issue is whether a defendant is guilty of having engaged in certain criminal conduct of which he has been specifically accused. Rules of evidence have been fashioned for criminal trials which narrowly confine the trial contest to evidence that is strictly relevant to the particular offense charged. These rules rest in part on a necessity to prevent a time consuming and confusing trial of collateral issues. They were also designed to prevent tribunals concerned solely with the issue of guilt of a particular offense from being influenced to convict for that offense by evidence that the defendant had habitually engaged in other misconduct. A sentencing judge, however, is not confined to the narrow issue of guilt. His task within fixed statutory or constitutional limits is to determine the type and extent of punishment after the issue of guilt has been determined. Highly relevant—if not essential—to his selection of an appropriate sentence is the possession of the fullest information possible concerning the defendant's life and characteristics. And modern concepts individualizing punishment have made it all the more necessary that a sentencing judge not be denied an opportunity to obtain pertinent information by a requirement of rigid adherence to restrictive rules of evidence properly applicable to the trial.

Undoubtedly the New York statutes emphasize a prevalent modern philosophy of penology that the punishment should fit the offender and not merely the crime. The belief no longer prevails that every offense in a like legal category calls for an identical punishment without regard to the past life and habits of a particular offender. This whole country has traveled far from the period in which the death sentence was an automatic and commonplace result of convictions—even for offenses today deemed trivial. . . . Indeterminate sentences, the ultimate termination of which are sometimes decided by nonjudicial agencies, have to a large extent taken the place of the old rigidly fixed punishments. . . . Retribution is no longer the dominant objective of the criminal law. Reformation and rehabilitation of offenders have become important goals of criminal jurisprudence. . . .

Under the practice of individualizing punishments, investigation techniques have been given an important role. Probation workers making reports of their investigations have not been trained to prosecute but to aid offenders. Their reports have been given a high value by conscientious judges who want to sentence persons on the best available information rather than on guesswork and inadequate information. To deprive sentencing judges of this kind of information would undermine modern penological procedural policies that have been cautiously adopted throughout the nation after careful consideration and experimentation. We must recognize that most of the information now relied upon by judges to guide them in the intelligent imposition of sentences would be unavailable if information were restricted to that given in open court by witnesses subject to cross-examination. And the modern probation report draws on information concerning every aspect of a defendant's life. The type and extent of this information make totally impractical if not impossible open court testimony with cross-examination. Such a procedure could endlessly delay criminal administration in a retrial of collateral issues.

The considerations we have set out admonish us against treating the due-process clause as a uniform command that courts throughout the Nation abandon their age-old practice of seeking information from out-of-court sources to guide their judgment toward a more enlightened and just sentence. . . . So to treat the due-process clause would hinder if not preclude all courts—state and federal—from making progressive efforts to improve the administration of criminal justice. We hold that appellant was not denied due process of law.

Affirmed.

MURPHY, J., dissenting.[*]

[Williams] was convicted of murder by a jury, and sentenced to death by the judge. . . . In our criminal courts the jury sits as the representative of the community; its voice is that of the society against which the crime was committed. A judge even though vested with statutory authority to do so, should hesitate indeed to increase the severity of such a community expression.

He should be willing to increase it, moreover, only with the most scrupulous regard for the rights of the defendant. The [evidence here] would have been inadmissible at the trial. Some, such as allegations of prior crimes, was irrelevant. Much was incompetent as hearsay. All was damaging, and none was subject to scrutiny by the defendant.

Due process of law includes at least the idea that a person accused of crime shall be accorded a fair hearing through all the stages of the proceedings against him. I agree with the Court as to the value and humaneness of liberal use of probation reports as developed by modern penologists, but, in a capital case, against the unanimous recommendation of a jury, where the report would concededly not have been admissible at the trial, and was not subject to examination by the defendant, I am forced to conclude that the high commands of due process were not obeyed.

Notes

1. *Informal procedure at sentencing: majority position.* The New York statute discussed in *Williams*, which allowed the sentencing judge to consider evidence inadmissible under the rules of evidence, typifies sentencing practices in most states. See also Tex. Crim. Proc. Code Ann. §37.07(3). The informal presentation of evidence supposedly supports an effort to obtain the most information possible about the offender and the offense and to make an individualized (perhaps even clinical) decision. Many different actors participate over time in the decision about how best to respond to an individual offender. Thus, the indeterminate sentencing system is one of "multiple discretions." Professor Franklin Zimring describes the system as follows:

[*] [Justice Rutledge joined this opinion.—EDS.]

The best single phrase to describe the allocation of sentencing power in state and federal criminal justice is multiple discretion. Putting aside the enormous power of the police to decide whether to arrest, and to select initial charges, there are four separate institutions that have the power to determine criminal sentences—the legislature, the prosecutor, the judge, and the parole board or its equivalent. . . . With all our emphasis on due process in the determination of guilt, our machinery for setting punishment lacks any principle except unguided discretion. Plea bargaining, disparity of treatment and uncertainty are all symptoms of a larger malaise—the absence of rules or even guidelines in determining the distribution of punishments. . . .

Zimring, Making the Punishment Fit the Crime: A Consumer's Guide to Sentencing Reform, 12 Occasional Papers of the University of Chicago Law School (1977). More than half of the states use such an indeterminate sentencing system for large groups of cases, although many of these same states might use more narrowly circumscribed sentencing rules for some crimes.

2. Williams *revisited*. Samuel Titto Williams, a black man, was 18 years old at the time he killed 15 year-old Selma Graff, who surprised him during a burglary. He had no record of prior convictions, but he had been accused of burglary at age 11. The judgment in juvenile court was suspended. The probation report—a report prepared by probation officers prior to sentencing, also called a pre-sentence investigation report—informed the judge that Williams was suspected of (but not charged with) committing 30 burglaries during the two months before the murder. A seven year-old girl who was present during one of those burglaries told the probation department that Williams had molested her sexually. She identified Williams as the perpetrator two weeks after the incident. The probation report also stated that Williams was living with two women, and had brought different men into the apartment for the purpose of having sexual relations with the women. It alleged that he had once gone to a local school to photograph "private parts of young children." Finally, the sentencing judge relied on injuries inflicted on the murder victim's brother during the burglary. The prosecutor had not brought any charges based on the assault. See Kevin Reitz, Sentencing Facts: Travesties of Real-Offense Sentencing, 45 Stan. L. Rev. 523 (1993). Is the problem in Williams the new offender information at sentencing or the defendant's lack of an opportunity to challenge that information?

3. *Capital punishment and informal procedure*. Although the *Williams* Court emphasized that rehabilitative purposes of sentencing required far-reaching information about an offender, the proposed "treatment" for Williams was execution. It brings to mind the statement attributed to the comedian W. C. Fields, who quoted a condemned prisoner on his way to the electric chair, saying, "This will certainly be a lesson to me." *Williams* is still cited with approval in support of informal sentencing procedures generally. However, it has been partially overruled in the context of capital sentencing. In Gardner v. Florida, 430 U.S. 349 (1977), the trial judge sentenced a defendant to death after consulting confidential and unrebutted information in the pre-sentence investigation report. A plurality of the Supreme Court found that due process required, at least in capital cases, that the defendant have access to information that will influence the sentencing judge and have an opportunity to test its reliability.

4. *Recurring themes in discretionary sentencing.* One study of sentences in white-collar crime cases in federal court concluded that judges considered three common principles during sentencing: (1) the harm the offense produced; (2) the blame-worthiness of the defendant, judged both from the defendant's criminal intent and from other details of the crime and defendant's earlier life; and (3) the consequences of the punishment, both for deterring future wrongdoing and for the well-being of the defendant's family and community. Despite the presence of these common principles for sentencing, judges selected very different sentences because they did not agree on how to measure each of the principles or the relative weight to place on each. See Stanton Wheeler, Kenneth Mann & Austin Sarat, Sitting in Judgment: The Sentencing of White-Collar Criminals (1988).

Observers in higher-volume courts, such as state misdemeanor courts, have described a very different reality. During plea bargaining the parties settle quickly on a proper sentence, hinging largely on the charges finally filed and on the parties' interpretation of the facts as reflected in the police reports. These negotiations do not often involve individualized haggling, as in a Middle Eastern bazaar. Rather, they are "more akin to modern supermarkets in which prices for various commodities have been clearly established and labeled." Malcolm Feeley, The Process Is the Punishment: Handling Cases in a Lower Criminal Court 187 (1979).

It is extremely rare for sentencing judges in discretionary systems in the United States to produce written opinions explaining their reasons for selecting a particular punishment. One intriguing exception occurred in the case of Colonel Oliver North, who was prosecuted for crimes connected to his involvement with funding for Nicaraguan military insurgent during the Reagan administration. The attorneys and the sentencing judge in that case produced remarkable documents for those sentencing proceedings, which are available on the web extension for this chapter at *http://www.crimpro.com/extension/ch19.*

5. *Sentencing juries.* In some states, juries not only rule on guilt or innocence but also decide the sentence to impose, even in noncapital cases. In about six of these states, the jury's choice is binding; in a few others, the jury only recommends a sentence to the judge. See Fla. Stat. §921.141 (jury recommends sentence); Tex. Crim. Proc. Code Ann. §37.07 (judge can assess punishment if defendant does not request probation or jury sentence; jury must be instructed about parole and other devices for reducing actual amount of prison time offender must serve). Sentencing juries tend to impose longer prison terms than sentencing judges would impose in comparable cases. See Nancy J. King & Rosevelt L. Noble, Felony Jury Sentencing in Practice: A Three-State Study, 57 Vand. L. Rev. 885 (2004). Even in a system that gives no formal sentencing power to juries, the jury might consider likely punishments as it deliberates on the verdict in the case. The jury might acquit if it believes the sanction is too severe.

Should the sentencing jury be required to vote unanimously for a particular sentence? Should its voting rules be the same as the rules for its vote on guilt and innocence? See Manual for Courts-Martial, Rule 1006(d) (Exec. Order No. 12,473) (members of court martial may propose sentences; panel must consider each proposed sentence from least severe to most severe; unanimous vote needed for death penalty; three-fourths of members must recommend confinement for more than 10 years; two-thirds of members must recommend other sentences).

2. Legislative Sentencing

Although indeterminate sentencing has been the norm in this country for most of the twentieth century, new arrangements have emerged over the past generation. Some of those alternative approaches have put the legislature more firmly in control of sentencing. Legislators have decided for themselves the precise sentence that will attach to various types of offenses; other sentencing institutions such as courts are supposed to carry out the choices of the legislature without adding any meaningful choices of their own.

Sentences dominated by legislative choices go back to some of the earliest recorded sources of law (as in the Code of Hammurabi at the start of this chapter). American legislatures during the eighteenth and nineteenth centuries often set specific sentences for designated crimes. Only in the late nineteenth and early twentieth centuries did the state and federal legislatures routinely create more "indeterminate" sentences, authorizing a range of sentences from which a sentencing judge could select a sentence to impose on a particular offender. Thus when mid-twentieth-century legislatures began to designate the specific punishments for certain crimes, they were returning to earlier practices.

■ U.S. SENTENCING COMMISSION, MANDATORY MINIMUM PENALTIES IN THE FEDERAL CRIMINAL JUSTICE SYSTEM
i-ix, 5-15, 27-32 (1991)

Mandatory minimum sentences are not new to the federal criminal justice system. As early as 1790, mandatory penalties had been established for capital offenses. In addition, at subsequent intervals throughout the 19th Century, Congress enacted provisions that required definite prison terms, typically quite short, for a variety of other crimes. Until recently, however, the enactment of mandatory minimum provisions was generally an occasional phenomenon that was not comprehensively aimed at whole classes of offenses.

A change in practice occurred with the passage of the Narcotic Control Act of 1956, which mandated minimum sentences of considerable length for most drug importation and distribution offenses. . . . In 1970, Congress drew back from the comprehensive application of mandatory minimum provisions to drug crimes enacted 14 years earlier. Finding that increases in sentence length "had not shown the expected overall reduction in drug law violations," Congress passed [legislation] that repealed virtually all mandatory penalties for drug violations.

[Growing criticism of efforts to rehabilitate inmates led lawmakers] to renew support for mandatory minimum penalties. On the state level this trend began in New York in 1973, with California and Massachusetts following soon thereafter. While the trend toward mandatory minimums in the states was gradual, by 1983, 49 of the 50 states had passed such provisions. . . . On the federal level, a comparable but more comprehensive trend was under way. Beginning in 1984, and every two years thereafter, Congress enacted an array of mandatory minimum penalties specifically targeted at drugs and violent crime. . . . Today there are approximately 100 separate federal mandatory minimum penalty provisions located in 60 different criminal statutes. . . . Of the 59,780 cases sentenced under mandatory minimum statutes [between 1984 and 1990], four statutes account for approximately 94 percent of the cases. These four statutes . . . all involve drugs and weapons violations. . . .

REASONS CITED IN SUPPORT OF MANDATORY MINIMUMS

[Field interviews with] judges, assistant United States attorneys, defense attorneys, and probation officers . . . identified six commonly offered rationales for mandatory minimum sentencing provisions.

Retribution or "Just Deserts." Perhaps the most commonly voiced goal of mandatory minimum penalties is the "justness" of long prison terms for particularly serious offenses. Proponents generally agree that longer sentences are deserved and that, absent mandatory penalties, judges would impose sentences more lenient than would be appropriate.

Deterrence. . . . Those supporting mandatory minimums on deterrence grounds point not only to the strong deterrent value of the certainty of substantial punishment these penalties are intended to provide, but also to the deterrent value of sentence severity that these penalties are intended to ensure in the war against crime.

Incapacitation, Especially of the Serious Offender. Mandating increased sentence severity aims to protect the public by incapacitating offenders convicted of serious crimes for definite, and generally substantial, periods of time. Proponents argue that one way to increase public safety, particularly with respect to guns and drugs, is to remove drug dealers and violent offenders from the streets for extended periods of time.

Disparity. Indeterminate sentencing systems permit substantial latitude in setting the sentence, which in turn can mean that defendants convicted of the same offense are sentenced to widely disparate sentences. Supporters of mandatory minimum penalties contend that they greatly reduce judicial discretion and are therefore more fair. Mandatory minimums are meant to ensure that defendants convicted of similar offenses receive penalties that at least begin at the same minimal point.

Inducement of Cooperation. Because they provide specific lengthy sentences, mandatory minimums encourage offenders to assist in the investigation of criminal conduct by others. This is because cooperation—that is, supplying information concerning the activities of other criminally involved individuals—is the only statutorily recognized way to permit the court to impose a sentence below the length of imprisonment required by the mandatory minimum sentence.

Inducement of Pleas. Although infrequently cited by policymakers, prosecutors express the view that mandatory minimum sentences can be valuable tools in obtaining guilty pleas, saving scarce enforcement resources and increasing the certainty of at least some measure of punishment. In this context, the value of a mandatory minimum sentence lies not in its imposition, but in its value as a bargaining chip to be given away in return for the resource-saving plea from the defendant to a more leniently sanctioned charge.

[Now we turn to some of the criticisms of mandatory minimum sentences.]

THE "TARIFF" EFFECT OF MANDATORY MINIMUMS

Years ago, Congress used tariff sentences in sanctioning broad categories of offenses, ranging from quite serious crimes (e.g., homicide) to fairly minor property theft. This tariff approach has been rejected historically primarily because there were too many defendants whose important distinctions were obscured by this single, flat approach to sentencing. A more sophisticated, calibrated approach that takes into account gradations of offense seriousness, criminal record, and level of culpability has long since been recognized as a more appropriate and equitable method of sentencing. . . .

The mandatory minimums set forth in 21 U.S.C. §841(b), applicable to defendants convicted of trafficking in the more common street drugs, are illustrative. For those convicted of drug trafficking under this section, one offense-related factor, and only one, is determinative of whether the mandatory minimum applies: the weight of the drug or drug mixture. Any other sentence-individualizing factors that might pertain in a case are irrelevant as far as the statute is concerned. Thus, for example, whether the defendant was a peripheral participant or the drug ring's kingpin, whether the defendant used a weapon, whether the defendant accepted responsibility or, on the other hand, obstructed justice, have no bearing on the mandatory minimum to which each defendant is exposed. . . .

THE "CLIFF" EFFECT OF MANDATORY MINIMUMS

Related to the proportionality problems posed in mandatory minimums already described are the sharp differences in sentence between defendants who fall just below the threshold of a mandatory minimum compared with those whose criminal conduct just meets the criteria of the mandatory minimum penalty. Just as mandatory minimums fail to distinguish among defendants whose conduct and prior records in fact differ markedly, they distinguish far too greatly among defendants who have committed offense conduct of highly comparable seriousness.

[A] lack of coordination between statutory maximum and mandatory minimum penalties for the same or similar offenses can create dramatic sentencing cliffs among similarly situated defendants. For example, 21 U.S.C. §884 mandates a minimum five-year term of imprisonment for a defendant convicted of first-offense, simple possession of 5.01 or more grams of "crack." . . . However, a first-offender convicted of simple possession of 5.0 grams of crack is subjected to a *maximum* statutory penalty of one year imprisonment. . . .

THE "CHARGE-SPECIFIC" NATURE OF MANDATORY MINIMUMS

. . . In general, a mandatory minimum becomes applicable only when the prosecutor elects to *charge* and the defendant is *convicted* of the specific offense carrying the mandatory sentence. . . . Mandatory minimums employ a structure that allows a shifting of discretion and control over the implementation of sentencing policies from courts to prosecutors. [There] is substantial reason to believe that mandatory minimums are not in fact pursued by prosecutors in all instances that the underlying statutes otherwise would require. . . .

Problem 19-1. The Golf Club Odyssey

Gary Ewing walked into the pro shop of the El Segundo Golf Course in Los Angeles County on March 12, 2000. He walked out with three golf clubs, priced at $399 apiece, concealed in his pants leg. A shop employee, who became suspicious when he saw Ewing limp out of the pro shop, telephoned the police. He was convicted of one count of felony grand theft. Now it's time for sentencing.

Ewing had been in and out of the criminal courts for the past 15 years. Here is a list of his prior offenses, with the incarceration sentence he received for each crime attached:

- 1984: theft (6 months jail, suspended)
- 1988: felony grand theft auto (1 year jail, eventually expunged)
- 1990: petty theft with a prior theft (60 days jail)
- 1992: battery (30 days jail); theft (10 days jail)
- 1993: burglary (60 days jail); possession of drug paraphernalia (6 months jail); receiving stolen property (10 days jail); unlawful possession of a firearm (30 days jail); first degree robbery and three counts of first-degree burglary (9 years and 8 months in prison). While he was still on parole for robbery/burglary, Ewing stole the golf clubs at issue in this case.

California has a "three strikes and you're out" law that was designed "to ensure longer prison sentences and greater punishment for those who commit a felony and have been previously convicted of serious and/or violent felony offenses." Cal. Penal Code §667(b). When a defendant is convicted of a felony, and has previously been convicted of one or more prior felonies defined as "serious" or "violent" in Cal. Penal Code Ann. §§667.5 and 1192.7, sentencing is conducted pursuant to the three-strikes law. If the defendant has two or more prior "serious" or "violent" felony convictions, he must receive 25 years to life imprisonment.

Trial courts may avoid imposing a three-strikes sentence in two ways: first, by reducing certain felonies to misdemeanors (when those felonies do not qualify as serious or violent triggering offenses), and second, by vacating allegations of prior "serious" or "violent" felony convictions.

The prosecutor formally alleges that Ewing has been convicted previously of four serious or violent felonies: the three burglaries and the robbery in 1993. She also points out that he was on parole when he committed his latest offense, which is a factor in aggravation.

You are the sentencing judge, and you have two decisions to make. (1) Should the grand theft of the golf clubs remain a felony, or should you reduce it to a misdemeanor? (This is not a serious or violent felony.) (2) Should the four prior strikes (for the three burglaries and the robbery) stand? If you answer yes to both of these questions, you will have to sentence Ewing under the three-strikes law to 25 years to life. [Note: California recently amended its three-strikes law to require the third felony to be a serious or violent felony, just like the strike felonies; does that seem like an improvement on the law?]

Notes

1. *Federal constitutional limits on legislative choice of sanctions: majority position.* Courts by and large allow legislatures to choose any punishment for a given crime (with the exception of the death penalty) and turn aside most claims that a punishment is "cruel and unusual" or "disproportionate" to the crime. According to the Supreme Court in Ewing v. California, 538 U.S. 11 (2003), the Eighth Amendment

does not require strict proportionality between crime and sentence. Instead, it forbids only extreme sentences that are "grossly disproportionate" to the crime. Courts applying this proportionality test engage in three related inquiries. First, the court weighs the crime committed against the sentence imposed. If this "threshold" inquiry leads to an inference of gross disproportionality, the court then compares sentences imposed on other criminals in the same jurisdiction (the "intrajurisdictional analysis") and sentences imposed for commission of the same crime in other jurisdictions (the "interjurisdictional analysis"). How can the Court assess the first prong of its test—the gravity of the offense and the harshness of the penalty—other than by relying on the second and third prongs to provide an answer?

Does the decision in *Ewing* reflect the predilections of the majority of the Court or a principled assessment of the sentence? Would it have been more honest for the Court to decline proportionality review in imprisonment cases generally? See also Miller v. Alabama, 567 U.S. 460 (2012) (mandatory life imprisonment without parole for defendants under the age of 18 at the time of their crimes violates cruel and unusual punishment clause of Eighth Amendment); Harmelin v. Michigan, 501 U.S. 957 (1991) (because of the severe social harms flowing from illegal drugs, there is no gross disparity between the crime of possession of 650 grams of cocaine and the sentence of life imprisonment).

The Eighth Amendment proportionality assessment of capital punishment for various crimes and types of offenders (such as juveniles and mentally impaired defendants) is a complex topic with its own elaborate jurisprudence. For an overview of these death penalty precedents, go to the web extension for this chapter at *http://www.crimpro.com/extension/ch19.*

2. *Proportionality in the state courts.* State courts have applied the *Ewing* test under the Eighth Amendment to bar some disproportionate sentences. See Bradshaw v. State, 671 S.E.2d 485 (Ga. 2008) (mandatory life sentence for second conviction of failure to register as sex offender violates cruel and unusual punishment ban of the Eighth Amendment; failure to register is a passive felony that causes no harm to society, and crimes such as voluntary manslaughter carry a lighter penalty). But it is more common for state courts to uphold a legislative choice of sanctions in the case at hand, even if they recognize that a proportionality challenge might succeed in theory. State v. Moss-Dwyer, 686 N.E.2d 109 (Ind. 1997) (recognizing possible proportionality challenges under state constitution, but refusing to declare a sentence disproportionate where statute made misinformation on a handgun permit application a greater crime than carrying a handgun without a license). A few state courts have been willing to insist, under various provisions of their state constitutions, that the legislature select a punishment that is proportionate to the crime. See State v. Rodriguez, 217 P.3d 659 (Or. 2009) (mandatory 75-month sentence violated state constitutional ban on cruel and unusual punishment when applied to defendants who touched clothed youths with sexual purpose). Whose standards—those of the state, the nation, or the local community—should apply in determining what shocks the conscience?

Nonconstitutional limitations on imprisonment provide more meaningful day-to-day controls than do constitutional limitations. Sentencing guidelines, for example, set out presumptive sentencing ranges for specific offenses. Other limitations may be imposed by state statutes mandating that certain offenders not be sentenced to prison. Among such legislation is a California law requiring drug treatment rather than imprisonment for first-time, nonviolent drug offenders.

3. *Judicial discretion and mandatory penalties.* Many criticisms of mandatory minimum statutes focus on the loss of judicial discretion in sentencing. Consider, for example, the 1970 statement of then-Representative George Bush:

> Federal judges are almost unanimously opposed to mandatory minimums, because they remove a great deal of the court's discretion. In the vast majority of cases which reach the sanctioning stage today, the bare minimum sentence is levied—and in some cases, less than the minimum mandatory is given. . . . Probations and outright dismissals often result. Philosophical differences aside, practicality requires a sentence structure which is generally acceptable to the courts, to prosecutors, and to the general public.

116 Cong. Rec. H33314, Sept. 23, 1970. These criticisms and others have led some state and federal judges to believe that mandatory minimum statutes too often force them to impose a fundamentally unjust sentence. A 1993 survey found that 90 percent of federal judges and 75 percent of state judges believed that mandatory minimum sentences for drug cases were "a bad idea." More than half of the federal judges believed that mandatory minimums were "too harsh" on first-time offenders. A.B.A. J., October 1993, at 78. Are all mandatory minimums subject to the criticisms about uneven enforcement and loss of judicial discretion?

Can any decisionmaker other than a judge—who decides many individual cases—appreciate the facts about an offender's past that should lead to a lighter sentence? Why do judges sentence below what the legislature might choose as a minimum sentence? Do judges generally share a different political view on crime control?

4. *Mandatory mandatories.* Most mandatory minimum statutes instruct the judge to impose a particular sentence for a particular charge, but they do not require the prosecutor to file a given charge when adequate facts are present. Thus, typical mandatory sentencing statutes give prosecutors considerable bargaining power during plea negotiations; they also offer prosecutors opportunities to avoid mandatory minimum sentences when they believe that such sentences would be unjust or a poor use of resources. Legislatures sometimes constrain this prosecutorial power by passing statutes that require the prosecutor to file charges and that prevent plea bargaining. This sort of "mandatory mandatory" statute, however, is rare. Why do legislators hesitate to pass statutes that remove the prosecutor's discretion to decline charges or to select a charge not subject to the minimum penalty?

5. *Net effects of mandatory minimum penalties.* Studies of mandatory minimum penalties have reached different conclusions about the effect of these laws on the crime rates for the targeted offenses. Some studies have found a deterrent effect for gun crimes and homicides, but other studies have found no such effect on the commission of drug crimes or violent crimes generally. The effects of mandatory minimum penalties on the criminal justice system are clearer. These laws consistently lead to fewer arrests for the designated crimes, fewer charges filed, more dismissals of charges, more trials rather than guilty pleas, and longer sentences imposed and served. See Dale Parent, Terence Dunworth, Douglas McDonald & William Rhodes, Key Legislative Issues in Criminal Justice: Mandatory Sentencing (National Institute of Justice, Research in Action) (January 1997, NCJ 161839).

6. *Self-correcting democratic process.* If mandatory minimum sentences truly produce the ill effects described by critics, won't the democratically elected legislature recognize these flaws after a time and abandon the experiment? There are a few

examples of this happening. In Connecticut in 2001, the legislature granted judges authority to depart from mandatory minimum sentences for certain drug crimes, such as first-time sales or possession within 1,500 feet of a school. Why do legislatures sometimes fail to reconsider self-destructive legislation? Is it a lack of information, a lack of time, or something else?

3. Sentencing Commissions

While the legislature always sets the upper and lower boundaries on the permissible punishments for a crime, those boundaries can still leave open many choices about the sentence in particular cases. Rather than leaving the remaining sentencing choices to the discretion of judges and parole authorities, some state legislatures have empowered permanent "sentencing commissions" to create additional rules to guide judges as they select sentences within the statutory range. These guidelines (some embodied in statutes and others in administrative rules) are different from statutory maximum and minimum punishments because they allow judges, under some circumstances, to go above or below the recommended range so long as the final sentence remains within the statutorily authorized range. Sentencing guidelines can be binding or merely advisory for the sentencing judge depending on the judge's statutory authority to "depart" from the guidelines without risking reversal on appeal.

What are the effects of creating a sentencing commission and asking it to formulate sentencing rules more specific than the outer bounds of the statutory maximum and minimum sentence? Will sentencing commissions produce rules that look systematically different from the sentencing rules a legislature would adopt on its own? Will those sentencing guidelines produce a different pattern of sentences in individual cases than judges would impose, if left to their own devices? Whatever other effects a sentencing commission may have, it is certainly true that commissions (and the guidelines they create) give sentencing courts a more refined vocabulary for discussing sentencing choices and make more explicit the types of considerations that matter to a sentencing court. Indeed, without sentencing guidelines and the judicial decisions applying them, it would be difficult to study sentencing at all as a topic in a criminal procedure course.

Sentencing commissions have created sentencing rules in almost half of the states. The materials below introduce the basic structure and functions of such commissions, with particular attention paid to the sentencing commission in Minnesota, one of the earliest and most influential of these bodies.

■ DALE PARENT, STRUCTURING CRIMINAL SENTENCING
2-5, 28, 51-53, 57-60 (1988)

For centuries, legislative control over the sentencing process fluctuated between two statutory models of how to formulate punishments for crimes. One model prescribed mandatory penalties, such as capital punishment in nineteenth century England for every theft of fifty shillings or more, or a minimum of two years in prison in twentieth century Michigan for anyone convicted of possessing a gun.

The second model prescribed discretionary penalty ranges. [A] person convicted of robbery, for example, could receive probation in the community, or as much as 25 years in prison, or any sanction in between depending on how the facts of the case were assessed in the discretion of the individual judge.

Under the mandatory model, legislatures ousted judges from control over sentencing by stipulating sentences in advance. Every sentencing was required to impose either a stated penalty, or a mandatory minimum sentence, on every offender convicted of the crime, without regard to mitigating circumstances. The judge was permitted no discretion for downward adjustments to reflect either the offender's reduced culpability for the past crime, or his high promise to avoid crime in the future.

The discretionary model exemplified an entirely different approach to the setting of punishment. Under this model, the legislature deferred to the sentencing court's closer opportunity to learn the facts of each crime, to see each offender in person, and to fashion a sentence to fit the particular case. This model left it to the judgment of a single judge to determine how high, or how low, to set the penalty within the authorized sentencing range. The experience or inexperience of the judge, his or her subjective appraisal of the crime's seriousness and the offender's blameworthiness, the decisionmaker's prediction or hunch regarding the offender's likely future conduct—these and similar factors could all influence the discretion to set a severe, moderate, or lenient sentence. . . .

The advantages of each model reflected the disadvantages of the other. By removing all discretion from judges, mandatory sentences sometimes produced punishment that was too severe and disproportionate to the crime. Discretionary sentencing, on the other hand, conferred unguided discretion on judges and inevitably produced unjustifiable discrepancies—unduly lenient sentences for some, undue harshness for others. Whereas mandatory sentences reflected legislative arbitrariness and coerced uniformity, discretionary sentencing power allowed anarchy among judges and produced both arbitrariness and unwarranted disparity.

In at least three major respects, Minnesota's venture altered traditional institutions and concepts in the realm of criminal sentencing:

- It substituted a new system—guided discretion—for the more extreme methods of dividing authority over the punishment process between legislatures and courts.
- It inserted a new governmental entity—the sentencing commission—between the legislature and the judiciary, and authorized the commission to monitor and continuously adjust criminal sentences.
- And it established an unprecedented conceptual connection—known as capacity constraint—between the degree of severity with which guidelines could specify prison sentences and the extent to which state prison resources were available to carry such sentences into effect. . . .

The former system of indeterminate prison sentences set by a judge, subject to the possibility of early release in the discretion of a parole board, was abolished. In its place came a system of determinate sentences, set by the judge under guidance from the sentencing commission, with review by an appellate court. Five key elements were incorporated into this plan:

- First, sentences would be scaled to take account of differences both in the gravity of crimes and the prior records of offenders. Guidance would be specified in the form of sentencing ranges, rather than precise sentences.
- Second, factors relevant to the individualization process would be standardized and weighted in advance. Clear rules would encourage similar outcomes in similar cases. Proportionality among different cases would be facilitated by a carefully constructed hierarchy of offense seriousness.
- Third, a set of departure principles would define the circumstances under which judges could deviate from the guideline sentencing range with good reasons. Judges would thus retain discretion to set the actual sentence, to do justice on a case-by-case basis.
- Fourth, sentencing judges would be required to state reasons for each sentence that differed from the applicable guideline, to assure accountability and reviewability.
- Fifth, all sentences would be subject to review by an appellate court whose written opinions could, over time, evolve finely tuned principles to guide future sentencers. . . .

The [1988 Minnesota] law created a nine-member Sentencing Guidelines Commission, consisting of the chief justice or his designee, two district court judges appointed by the chief justice, the Commission of Corrections, the chairman of the Minnesota Corrections Board, and four gubernatorial appointees—a prosecutor, a public defender, and two citizens. Commission members would serve four-year terms and be eligible for reappointment. The Commission was authorized to hire a director and other staff. . . .

The guidelines . . . were to recommend when state imprisonment was appropriate and to recommend presumptive sentencing durations. The Commission could set ranges of permissible deviation about the fixed sentence of plus or minus 15 percent, which would not constitute departures. The guidelines were to be based on reasonable combinations of offender and offense characteristics. . . . Judges had to give written reasons for sentences that departed from the guidelines recommendation. The state or the defense could appeal any sentence. On appeal, the Supreme Court was to determine if the sentence was illegal, inappropriate, unjustifiably disparate, or not supported by findings of fact. . . .

The Commission sought to assure that guideline punishments would be proportional to the seriousness of offenders' crimes. To achieve that proportionality, it was necessary for the Commission to rank crimes in the order of their seriousness. The seriousness of a crime varies according to the gravity of the offense and the blameworthiness of the offender. Gravity is determined by the harm caused, directly or as a consequence, by the crime. Blameworthiness is determined by the offender's motivation, intent, and behavior in the crime and is enhanced if the offender previously has been convicted of and sentenced for criminal acts. . . .

In devising an offense seriousness ranking, the Commission had to make . . . relatively broad decisions about elements of behavior and intent as they relate to offense seriousness. For example, most would agree that crimes that involve or threaten physical injury generally are more serious than those that involve the loss of property. Case-level judgments involve finer distinctions and are used to distinguish among offenders convicted of similar crimes who have similar prior records.

Although most of us have an intuitive sense of offense seriousness, the concept is highly complex. Most criminal events consist of an offender and a victim linked by an act defined by law as a crime. Thus, judgments about the seriousness of criminal events may involve facts about offenders, victims, and criminal acts.

Some factors can be dismissed because all would agree they are irrelevant to assessing gravity or ascribing blame—for example, that the victim was a Mason or the offender was a Methodist. Some facts are both irrelevant and invidious—such as that the offender and the victim were of the same or different races. But there is a long list of factors that some would consider relevant to assessing harm or ascribing blame.

Most Frequent Offenses in Seriousness Scale

Seriousness Level	*Most Frequent Offenses*
1	Aggravated forgery, less than $100
	Possession of marijuana (more than 1.5 ounces)
	Unauthorized use of a motor vehicle
2	Aggravated forgery, $150 to $2,500
	Sale of marijuana . . .
3	Aggravated forgery, over $2,500
	Arson, third-degree . . .
	Theft crimes, $150 to $2,500
	Sale of cocaine
	Possession of LSD, PCP
4	Burglary, nondwellings and unoccupied dwellings
	Theft crimes, over $2,500
	Receiving stolen goods, $150 to $2,500
	Criminal sexual conduct, fourth-degree
	Assault, third-degree (injury)
5	Criminal negligence (resulting in death)
	Criminal sexual conduct, third-degree
	Manslaughter, second-degree . . .
	Witness tampering
	Simple (unarmed) robbery . . .
6	Assault, second-degree (weapon)
	Burglary (occupied dwelling) . . .
	Criminal sexual conduct, fourth-degree . . .
	Kidnapping (released in a safe place)
	Sale, LSD or PCP
	Sale, heroin and remaining hard narcotics
	Receiving stolen goods, over $2,500
7	Aggravated (armed) robbery
	Arson, first-degree
	Burglary (victim injured)

Most Frequent Offenses in Seriousness Scale

Seriousness Level	Most Frequent Offenses
	Criminal sexual conduct, second-degree
	Criminal sexual conduct, third-degree
	Kidnapping (not released in a safe place)
	Manslaughter, first-degree
	Manslaughter, second-degree
8	Assault, first-degree (great bodily harm)
	Kidnapping (great bodily harm)
	Criminal sexual conduct, first-degree
	Manslaughter, first-degree
9	Murder, third-degree
10	Murder, second-degree

The victim may be a normal healthy adult or a person who may be especially vulnerable due to age or infirmity. In violent crimes the extent of physical injury may vary from a scratch to death. Some victims may recover fully from physical injuries, while others suffer permanent damage or impairment. In property crimes, the victim's loss could range from a small amount to a fortune. The consequences of property loss may vary greatly with the economic status of the victim. The crime may involve one victim or many. A crime might involve an offender acting alone or in concert with others. The offender might have been immature or mentally impaired and easily induced to participate in a crime. He or she might have been the ringleader who induced others. . . .

The list of factors relevant, or arguably relevant, to assessing offense seriousness is large, and the above variations are a mere sample. Their potential combinations are virtually infinite. Given events as complex and diverse as criminal acts, how was the Commission to go about judging their seriousness?

In the initial unsatisfactory effort [to rank offenses,] each member received a randomly arranged deck of sixty offense cards. Each card listed one offense [and] its statutory maximum sentence. . . . Each member arranged his or her deck in decreasing order of seriousness. [For] the most serious person offenses—homicides—the members' individual ranks clustered together, reflecting a high level of consensus. For less serious person offenses—robberies, sexual assaults, and so forth—consensus declined.

[The] Commission expressed concern about the initial ranking exercise [because it] had overloaded members with information. [The Commission created a subcommittee to divide the task into more manageable components. The subcommittee grouped] crimes into 6 categories—violent, arson, sex, drug, property, and miscellaneous—5 of which contained 20 or fewer crimes. . . .

The subcommittee instructed the Commission to focus on the usual or typical case in [a] ranking exercise. . . . In phase one individual Commission members ranked crimes within each of the six categories. . . . Phases two, three, and four relied on identification of differences among members, on the articulation of reasons for those differences, and on debate about those reasons. . . . When differences existed it assured that the basis of the differences would be discovered and scrutinized and that the final rankings would reflect a majority opinion.

[The Commission divided the overall ranking into 10 seriousness levels. The table reprinted here shows the most common types of offenses within each of the 10 seriousness levels.]

■ RICHARD S. FRASE, STATE SENTENCING GUIDELINES: DIVERSITY, CONSENSUS, AND UNRESOLVED POLICY ISSUES
105 Colum. L. Rev. 1190 (2005)

Sentencing guidelines have been adopted in at least eighteen states and the District of Columbia, but the approaches taken are almost as numerous as the jurisdictions adopting them. State guidelines systems differ in their goals, scope of coverage, design, and operation. There are also many similarities, suggesting a substantial degree of consensus on some issues. These similarities also suggest that states can learn and "borrow" from other states; to use a well-worn comparative law metaphor, donor and recipient systems are sufficiently compatible to permit viable "legal transplants." . . . State guidelines are popular because they have proven more effective than alternative sentencing regimes as a means to promote consistency and fairness, set priorities in the use of limited correctional resources, and manage the growth in prison populations. . . .

SUMMARY OF GUIDELINES SYSTEMS

In 1980 Minnesota became the first jurisdiction to implement sentencing guidelines developed by a permanent sentencing commission, an idea that had been proposed by federal judge Marvin Frankel in the early 1970s. A number of other states had previously experimented with state-wide, judicially enacted, voluntary guidelines. . . .

Where they exist, state sentencing commissions are more widely representative than the federal commission, typically including judges, prosecutors, defense attorneys, correctional officials, public members, and sometimes legislators. There are also major variations in the duties, staffing, and budget of state commissions, and in the role of the commission relative to the legislature. For example, the Minnesota enabling statute gave the commission relatively little guidance and provided that the Commission's initial guidelines would become effective unless the legislature voted otherwise; in later years the legislature reclaimed some of the authority it had delegated, but the Minnesota Commission still retains primary control over the formulation of statewide sentencing policy. In contrast, the Arkansas enabling statute provides a detailed mandate, and in Washington State the legislature has dominated the guidelines revision process. . . .

In all states with permanent sentencing commissions, the commission (or occasionally another state agency) assesses the resource impact of proposed sentencing guidelines and statutes, in particular, the predicted effect on prison populations. The greater uniformity of guidelines sentencing makes such impact assessment more accurate than is possible in an indeterminate sentencing system, and the research and planning capacities of a permanent sentencing commission provide the necessary data and staff. . . .

In seven states (Utah, Maryland, Delaware, Virginia, Arkansas, Missouri, and Wisconsin) and the District of Columbia, guidelines are "voluntary" and not subject to appeal. But there are several varieties of "voluntary" guidelines. In some of these states judges are required to give reasons for departure from the guidelines. Moreover, "compliance rates" in some voluntary guidelines jurisdictions are quite high, which suggests that in some jurisdictions peer pressure or other informal processes may effectively substitute for appellate review. For example, in Virginia, trial court judges must be periodically reappointed by the legislature, and many judges apparently fear that a high departure rate will jeopardize their reappointment.

There are also several varieties of "legally binding" guidelines. In Pennsylvania, sentence appeal is available but the standard of review is highly deferential. However, Pennsylvania may have found another way to encourage judicial compliance with guidelines recommendations: Since 1999, judges' departure rates have been made public, and this change appears to have slightly increased compliance rates. In North Carolina, judges have very broad discretion to sentence within the presumptive, aggravated, or mitigated sentencing ranges and sentences are rarely reversed on appeal. [Other guideline states] have more active appellate review, which, particularly in Kansas, Minnesota, and Washington, has generated a substantial body of substantive appellate case law. But trial courts in these states still retain considerable discretion, as to both the type and the severity of sanctions.

[There is] substantial variation in the decisions each system seeks to regulate, including whether the guidelines abolish parole release discretion, regulate the use of intermediate sanctions, apply to sentencing of misdemeanor crimes, or regulate decisions about the revocation of probation or revocation of postprison parole or supervised release. Eleven guidelines states and the District of Columbia have abolished parole release discretion for all or most felons, usually substituting limited "good time" credits for inmates who obey prison rules. Seven states retain parole for all or most offenses, and use guidelines only to regulate judges' decisions about the imposition and duration of prison sentences. . . .

State guidelines systems also differ somewhat in the nature and priority of their punishment and sentencing reform goals. Adoption of a guidelines system is always motivated at least in part by a desire to make sentencing more uniform and to eliminate unwarranted disparities, but some jurisdictions, especially those with voluntary guidelines or those retaining parole discretion, give this objective much less weight. Another goal inherent in commission-based guidelines sentencing is to promote more rational sentencing policy formulation—decisionmaking that is at least partially insulated from short term political pressures and is comprehensive and informed by data. But states differ substantially in their levels of funding of and deference to the commission. States that abolished parole release discretion and substituted limited "good time" credits were seeking not only to reduce disparity but also to achieve "truth in sentencing," the notion that the length of prison sentences imposed by courts should correspond closely to the amount of time inmates actually serve. [In] the federal system and many states, the sentence reduction for good conduct in prison cannot exceed fifteen percent.

A few jurisdictions have more or less "descriptive," or historically based, guidelines: Recommended sentences reflect existing sentencing norms and the goal is simply to get judges to apply these norms more consistently. But even these states usually make some changes in prior norms—especially to reduce racial disparities. Other states, with "prescriptive" guidelines, usually seek to increase sentence severity for certain offenses, particularly violent and drug crimes. Several states, including Minnesota and Kansas, explicitly based their guidelines on retributive, or just deserts, theories of punishment, with increased emphasis on the severity of the current offense and less on offender characteristics. But these and other guidelines states still leave substantial room for offender-based sentences designed to achieve crime control purposes, applying a "limiting retributive" model. For example, under Minnesota's "modified just deserts" approach, rehabilitation, reintegration, and offender risk management remain very important goals, pursued primarily by varying the conditions of probation. The determination of these conditions is not regulated under the Minnesota guidelines, and almost eighty percent of felony sentences are to probation. . . .

Guidelines systems, once enacted, do not remain static. . . . Utah, Maryland, Michigan, and Virginia began with judicially developed guidelines and later established a permanent, legislatively mandated sentencing commission. Delaware's, Virginia's, and Wisconsin's initial guidelines retained traditional parole release discretion, which was later abolished. Michigan's guidelines were initially voluntary, but became enforceable via sentence appeals in 1999. Several of the earlier guidelines states (Utah, Maryland, Florida, Michigan, and Virginia) began using resource impact assessments in later years. In 1994, Pennsylvania added provisions regulating the use of intermediate sanctions. . . .

Sentencing reform goals have also evolved over time. Although offender risk management has always been at least an implicit goal of most guidelines systems, as is reflected in the substantial weight these systems give to prior criminal record, public safety has come to play an increasingly important role. For example, in 1989 the Minnesota legislature amended the guidelines enabling statute to specify that public safety should be the commission's "primary" consideration. The legislature then also passed numerous laws providing increased penalties for dangerous or repeat offenders. Some of the newer state guidelines systems explicitly include public safety as a goal, or provide for individualized risk assessment procedures for certain offenses.

Another important reform goal that Minnesota recognized at the outset, and that almost all other states have now adopted, is to use guidelines sentencing as a resource management tool—in particular to avoid prison overcrowding, set priorities in the use of limited prison capacity, and gain better control over the growth in prison populations and expenditures. . . . As state prison populations began to shoot up in the 1980s, increasing costs and raising problems of overcrowding and court intervention, resource management became the most important reason for adopting guidelines and a sentencing commission. . . .

SIMILARITIES

The discussion above has highlighted the many differences in the designs and aims of state guidelines, but it is important also to note the similarities. There are some matters about which most state systems, especially the ones implemented or revised in recent years, seem to agree. This strong consensus suggests that certain features of guidelines sentencing have proved valuable in practice in multiple jurisdictions. . . .

First, there is broad agreement that sentencing must reflect a wide variety of sentencing theories, reform goals, and systemic needs, and that sentencing and reform purposes must and will evolve over time. Although guidelines are often viewed as deliberately, and perhaps inherently, designed to emphasize retributive goals of proportionality and uniformity, all state guidelines reforms, even at their inception, have also given substantial weight to crime control purposes. As noted above, the latter purposes, along with resource management and truth in sentencing, have received increased emphasis in recent years.

Second, there is strong—but not universal—agreement that sentencing guidelines need to be developed, implemented, monitored, and periodically revised by a permanent, broadly based, independent sentencing commission. One of the most important features of sentencing guidelines reforms is their research component. Most legislatively created guidelines commissions have been charged with the responsibility of collecting and analyzing sentencing data, as background for drafting the initial guidelines and then as a means of monitoring implementation and proposing revisions. This empirical component has become more and more important, as states have begun to focus on resource management goals. Prison and other resource management projections require detailed information on past and current sentencing practices, and the application of sophisticated modeling techniques.

[Another] area of implicit consensus in guidelines states involves the allocation of sentencing authority between various institutions and actors. As Kevin Reitz has shown, sentencing outcomes depend on decisions made both at the systemic level by legislatures and sentencing commissions, and at the case level by the parties, trial and appellate courts, and corrections officials. Kevin R. Reitz, Modeling Discretion in American Sentencing Systems, 20 Law & Pol'y 389 (1998). Reitz argues that the relative influence of these various decisionmakers needs to be kept in balance. He concludes that the federal guidelines have concentrated too much power at the systemic level, both in Congress and the federal sentencing commission, and in the hands of prosecutors. He finds a better balance in state guidelines systems, particularly in Minnesota. State guidelines have generally succeeded in obtaining and preserving broad acceptance by legislators and practitioners; an important reason for this acceptance is that state guidelines allow substantial inputs from all systemic and case-level actors, and avoid concentrations of sentencing power.

A review of state guidelines provisions and their implementation reveals a [final] area of implicit agreement: the importance of keeping guidelines rules relatively simple. Offenders and the public need to be able to understand the rules, and the rules must remain fairly easy for courts and other officials to apply. Complex rules promote errors and disparity; they also waste scarce court and attorney time. . . .

Notes

1. *Sentencing commissions and guidelines: majority position.* Almost half the states use sentencing guidelines created by sentencing commissions. The federal system also operates under sentencing guidelines, created by the U.S. Sentencing Commission. A state sentencing commission typically drafts the initial set of guidelines on behalf of the legislature, which then enacts it as an integrated package of sentencing reforms. In other states, the state judiciary adopts a package of guidelines as procedural rules

or as informal guidance to judges. Some guidelines are truly "voluntary": There is no practical consequence for a judge who decides to sentence outside the range recommended in the guidelines, so long as the judge remains within the statutory maximum and minimum for the crime. Other guidelines, to some degree or another, are "presumptive." That is, a judge who sentences outside the presumed range for sentences encounters more risk of reversal. Perhaps a reviewing court will reverse the sentence if the sentencing judge did not write an explanation for the unusual sentence; in other states, a sentence could be reversed if the judge's reason does not satisfy some legal standard (in Minnesota, a "substantial and compelling" reason is necessary). Why would a legislature ask a commission to create a set of sentencing guidelines? Does a commission have any advantages over a legislature in setting specific sentencing ranges for particular types of offenses and offenders? Does it have any advantages over a sentencing court with complete discretion to sentence offenders within statutory boundaries? See Max M. Schanzenbach & Emerson H. Tiller, Reviewing the Sentencing Guidelines: Judicial Politics, Empirical Evidence, and Reform, 75 U. Chi. L. Rev. 715 (2008).

2. *Amending the rules.* The states that have adopted sentencing guidelines have recognized a need to amend the guidelines over time, and they typically give the leading role in the amendment process to a permanent sentencing commission. However, the extent of the commission's power to amend the guidelines varies. In the largest group of states, the commission only recommends changes to the guidelines, and the legislature (and sometimes the state supreme court) must approve the changes before they become law. Elsewhere, amendments to the guidelines take effect at the end of the commission's administrative rulemaking process or after a waiting period that allows the legislature a chance to pass a statute disapproving of the changes. Do these procedural variations make any difference in the content of sentencing guidelines?

3. *Departures from the rules.* Most guidelines allow the judge to depart from the narrow sentence range designated in the guidelines. The departure could affect either the "disposition" of the sentence (active prison term or nonprison sanctions) or the "duration" of the sentence (the number of months to serve). The departure statutes generally require the judge to explain any departure, and an inadequate explanation can lead to reversal on appeal. Appellate courts in these jurisdictions have developed an extensive case law approving or disapproving of various grounds for departure. However, in theory the sentencing court still retains substantial discretion in deciding whether to depart from the guidelines.

In virtually all the guideline systems, departures have remained well below the number of cases sentenced within the guidelines. For instance, in Minnesota "dispositional" departures have occurred in approximately 10 percent of the total cases sentenced, while "durational" departures have occurred in about 25 percent of the cases involving an active prison term. By what criteria could a sentencing commission decide how many departures are "too many"? A large academic literature explores the departure practices of sentencing judges. To get a sense of these empirical studies, go to the web extension for this chapter at *http://www.crimpro.com/extension/ch19*.

4. *Appellate courts as the source of sentencing guidelines.* Most sentencing statutes provide only the most general guidance to the sentencing court and do not provide for appellate review of any sentence imposed within the broad statutory limits. Indeed, statutes in about half of the states limit appellate courts to the simple task of determining whether the sentence of the trial court fell within the statutory

minimum and maximum for the charged crimes. A second, large group of states create a more searching appellate review of sentences, in which the appellate court confirms both the legality and the "reasonableness" or "proportionality" of the sentence. Minn. Stat. §244.11. Given that judges see so many individual cases and develop such expertise in sentencing, shouldn't judges develop sentencing rules rather than just apply rules that others create? Statutes establishing sentencing commissions often reserve some commission posts for judges. Are there other ways to involve judges in the creation of general sentencing rules?

The law in Great Britain enables the appellate courts themselves to develop more specific guidelines for sentencing, announced in decisions of particular cases. Appellate courts in Great Britain have become one of the main institutions for developing sentencing policy. See R. v. Aramah, 76 Crim. App. Rep. 190 (1982) (conviction for importation of herbal cannabis; court establishes benchmark sentences for importation of various drugs in different amounts); Attorney General's Reference (Number 8 of 2004) (Dawson et al.), 2005 NICA 18 (applying *Aramah* guidelines). What might constitute a proper or persuasive reason for an appellate court to change its own sentencing guidelines? R. v. Bilinski, 86 Crim. App. Rep. 146 (1987) (amending the *Aramah* guidelines to reflect new increased statutory maximum sentences). See also State v. Wentz, 805 P.2d 962 (Alaska 1991) (limiting use of judicially created "benchmark" sentence for assault).

5. *Parole and parole guidelines.* Wherever judges or juries exercise great discretion in selecting criminal sentences, states have found it necessary to give parole or corrections authorities the power to review those decisions at some later date. This later review imposes a centralized perspective on the decisions of judges or juries from all over the state, and it coordinates the sentences with the amount of correctional resources actually available. In that way, a parole board performs some of the same functions as a sentencing commission. However, parole boards decide on the actual time an offender will serve *after* the judge has already announced a sentence. Some parole boards decide cases according to formal parole guidelines, while others make more ad hoc decisions, depending on prison capacity and other factors. What are the advantages and disadvantages of selecting the release date later in the process through a parole board rather than through a judge applying up-front sentencing rules?

Prison officials also have some influence over the amount of a prison sentence served. In most states, prison officials have the power to reduce the sentence by up to one-third or one-half of the maximum sentence set by the judge or the parole authority. Prison authorities use this discretion to reward good behavior by inmates: The reductions are known as "good time." Jim Jacobs has pointed out the anomaly of placing legal controls on other sentencing decisions, while leaving good time decisions unregulated. Jacobs, Sentencing by Prison Personnel: Good Time, 30 UCLA L. Rev. 217 (1982). Which institutions would be best suited to create legal constraints on good time decisions?

B. NEW INFORMATION ABOUT THE OFFENDER AND THE VICTIM

During the sentencing process, the scope of relevant evidence expands. The judge often considers a broad range of information about the offender's past and future, the broader context of the offense, and the viewpoint of the victim. The judge learns about these matters through the work of prosecutors, defense attorneys, and court personnel—especially probation officers—who assemble pre-sentence investigation reports and present their factual claims in a sentencing hearing.

1. Offender Information

Although the offender's involvement in the crime of conviction is critical to a sentence, judges also consider other aspects of the offender's character and past conduct. In this section, we consider the use at sentencing of the offender's prior criminal record, cooperation with the government in other investigations, and other aspects of an offender's personal history and prospects.

a. Criminal History

At sentencing, the court learns about the defendant's life before the crime of conviction took place. The single most influential factor in the offender's past is criminal history: the individual's prior convictions or other encounters with the criminal justice system. Under an unstructured sentencing system, the judge gives the prior criminal record whatever weight she thinks appropriate. Sentencing statutes and guidelines, however, instruct judges in some systems more precisely about the effect that a prior criminal record must have on a sentence.

■ WASHINGTON STATE SENTENCING GUIDELINES
Implementation Manual

The offender score is measured on the horizontal axis of the sentencing guidelines grid. An offender can receive anywhere from 0 to 9+ points on that axis. In general terms, the number of points an offender receives depends on four factors: 1) the number of prior felony criminal convictions; 2) the relationship between any prior offenses(s) and the current offense of conviction; 3) the presence of multiple prior or current convictions; and 4) whether the crime was committed while the offender was on community placement. [A higher number of points translates into a longer prison term or a change from nonprison to prison disposition.] RCW 9.94A.030(12) defines criminal history to include the defendant's prior adult convictions in this state, federal court, and elsewhere, as well as [felonies adjudicated] in juvenile court if [they did not result in a diversion].

"Washout" of Certain Prior Felonies

In certain instances, prior felony convictions are not calculated into the offender score. . . . Prior Class A and sex offense felony convictions are always included in the offender score. Prior Class B felony convictions are not included if 1) the offender has spent ten years in the community; and 2) has not been convicted of any felonies since the most recent of either the last date of release from confinement . . . or the day the sentence was entered. Prior Class C felonies are not included if the offender has spent five years in the community and has not been convicted of any felonies since the most recent of either the last date of release from confinement . . . or the day the sentence was entered.

■ FEDERAL RULES OF CRIMINAL PROCEDURE, RULE 32

(c) Presentence Investigation.

(1) Required Investigation.

(A) *In General.* The probation officer must conduct a presentence investigation and submit a report to the court before it imposes sentence unless . . . the court finds that the information in the record enables it to meaningfully exercise its sentencing authority . . . and the court explains its finding on the record.

(B) *Restitution.* If the law permits restitution, the probation officer must conduct an investigation and submit a report that contains sufficient information for the court to order restitution.

(2) *Interviewing the Defendant.* The probation officer who interviews a defendant as part of a presentence investigation must, on request, give the defendant's attorney notice and a reasonable opportunity to attend the interview.

(d) Presentence Report.

(1) *Applying the Advisory Sentencing Guidelines.* The presentence report must . . . identify all applicable guidelines and policy statements of the Sentencing Commission; . . . calculate the defendant's offense level and criminal history category; . . . state the resulting sentencing range and kinds of sentences available; [and] identify any basis for departing from the applicable sentencing range.

(2) *Additional Information.* The presentence report must also contain the following:

(A) the defendant's history and characteristics, including:

(i) any prior criminal record;

(ii) the defendant's financial condition; and

(iii) any circumstances affecting the defendant's behavior that may be helpful in imposing sentence or in correctional treatment;

(B) information that assesses any financial, social, psychological, and medical impact on any victim;

(C) when appropriate, the nature and extent of nonprison programs and resources available to the defendant;

(D) when the law provides for restitution, information sufficient for a restitution order; [and]

(G) any other information that the court requires. . . .

(e) Disclosing the Report and Recommendation.

. . . The probation officer must give the presentence report to the defendant, the defendant's attorney, and an attorney for the government at least 35 days before sentencing unless the defendant waives this minimum period. . . .

(f) Objecting to the Report.

(1) *Time to Object.* Within 14 days after receiving the presentence report, the parties must state in writing any objections, including objections to material information, sentencing guideline ranges, and policy statements contained in or omitted from the report. . . .

(3) *Action on Objections.* After receiving objections, the probation officer may meet with the parties to discuss the objections. The probation officer may then investigate further and revise the presentence report as appropriate. . . .

(i) *Sentencing.*

(1) *In General.* At sentencing, the court:

(A) must verify that the defendant and the defendant's attorney have read and discussed the presentence report and any addendum to the report; . . .

(C) must allow the parties' attorneys to comment on the probation officer's determinations and other matters relating to an appropriate sentence; and

(D) may, for good cause, allow a party to make a new objection at any time before sentence is imposed.

(2) *Introducing Evidence; Producing a Statement.* The court may permit the parties to introduce evidence on the objections. . . .

(3) *Court Determinations.* At sentencing, the court:

(A) may accept any undisputed portion of the presentence report as a finding of fact;

(B) must—for any disputed portion of the presentence report or other controverted matter—rule on the dispute or determine that a ruling is unnecessary either because the matter will not affect sentencing, or because the court will not consider the matter in sentencing; and

(C) must append a copy of the court's determinations under this rule to any copy of the presentence report made available to the Bureau of Prisons.

(4) Opportunity to Speak.

(A) *By a Party.* Before imposing sentence, the court must:

(i) provide the defendant's attorney an opportunity to speak on the defendant's behalf;

(ii) address the defendant personally in order to permit the defendant to speak or present any information to mitigate the sentence; and

(iii) provide an attorney for the government an opportunity to speak equivalent to that of the defendant's attorney.

(B) *By a Victim.* Before imposing sentence, the court must address any victim of the crime who is present at sentencing and must permit the victim to be reasonably heard. . . .

Notes

1. *Prior convictions, prior arrests, and pending charges: majority position.* In all U.S. sentencing systems, the prior convictions of an offender are among the most important determinants of the sentence imposed. In jurisdictions with detailed sentencing rules, prior convictions for more serious offenses typically increase the sentence more than prior convictions for less serious offenses. In some systems (such as the Washington system, illustrated above), prior convictions that occurred long ago have less impact on the current sentence. Prior convictions for the same type of crime as the current offense can increase a sentence more than prior convictions for unrelated wrongdoing. What purposes do these provisions serve? Are they designed

to deter the offender, or other offenders, from committing future crimes? Are they designed to select a sentence "proportionate" to the crime committed (that is, to give the offender her "just deserts")? Some sentencing judges are more reluctant to increase a sentence based on a prior arrest or a pending unadjudicated criminal charge. Nevertheless, it is highly unusual for sentencing rules to prevent judges from relying on a prior arrest or a pending charge in setting the current sentence. Under the federal sentencing guidelines, a court may depart from the designated range of sentences if the guidelines' calculation of prior criminal record does not adequately account for "similar adult criminal conduct not resulting in a criminal conviction." U.S. Sentencing Guidelines §4A1.3.

2. *Guidelines versus statutes.* Almost all states employ "habitual offender" laws, of the sort we encountered in Problem 19-1 above. These statutes increase sentences by designated amounts for offenders with the necessary prior felony record. The "three strikes and you're out" variety is distinctive for the type of prior record necessary and the amount of increase in the sentence; about half the states have statutes of this type.

The Washington guidelines provisions instruct a sentencing judge on the amount to increase a sentence in light of a prior criminal record; the amount of increase moves up gradually as the prior record becomes more serious. The judge can depart from the guidelines in exceptional cases. Guidelines also do not allow *prosecutors* to choose whether to use the prior record to increase a sentence; most "habitual offender" laws do allow prosecutors to choose whether to charge a defendant as a "habitual offender."

3. *Unreliable prior convictions.* The use of prior convictions to enhance the sentence for the current offense becomes more controversial when there are reasons to question the accuracy of the earlier charges. This is true especially when the earlier conviction occurred without the involvement of defense counsel. The federal constitution bars the use at sentencing of uncounseled prior convictions, but only if the government obtained the prior conviction by violating the defendant's constitutional right to counsel. See Nichols v. United States, 511 U.S. 738 (1994) (sentencing court may consider defendant's previous uncounseled misdemeanor conviction in sentencing him for subsequent offense); United States v. Tucker, 404 U.S. 443 (1972) (conviction obtained in violation of Sixth Amendment rights cannot enhance later sentence). These questions often arise when the prior conviction took place in the juvenile system or when the earlier case dealt with charges of driving while intoxicated. See State v. LaMunyon, 911 P.2d 151 (Kan. 1996) (juvenile); State v. Brown, 676 A.2d 350 (Vt. 1996) (DWI).

4. *Criminal history and pre-sentence investigation reports.* Federal Rule of Criminal Procedure 32, reprinted above, establishes a formal process of preparation and presentation of evidence that is relevant to the judge's selection of an authorized sentence. The process is less formal in many state courts, particularly in less serious crimes. For misdemeanors and the least serious felonies, sentencing sometimes happens immediately after the entry of a guilty plea or a verdict at trial. Even in more serious felonies, state judges do not always have access to probation officer resources to prepare a formal pre-sentence investigation report. See Nancy J. King & Ronald F. Wright, The Invisible Revolution in Plea Bargaining: Managerial Judging and Judicial Involvement in Negotiations, 95 Tex. L. Rev. 325 (2016). Despite these systemic differences in the levels of procedural formality at sentencing hearings,

judges virtually always learn about the prior criminal convictions of the defendant before choosing the appropriate sentence.

5. *Durability of criminal record.* Some state guidelines instruct judges to ignore or discount prior convictions after a designated number of years, when they become "stale." Others make no distinctions between recent convictions and older ones. For discussions of the many ways that prior criminal record influences later defendant contacts with criminal justice, see Richard S. Frase, Julian Roberts, Rhys Hester & Kelly Mitchell, Criminal History Enhancements Sourcebook (2015); James B. Jacobs, The Eternal Criminal Record (2015).

6. *Offender characteristics at sentencing: majority rule.* Criminal defendants are more than the sum of their contacts with the criminal justice system. The sentencing judge in most cases adjusts the sentence in light of the offender's overall character, including the facts known about his or her family, physical or mental health, and prospects for rehabilitation. In an unstructured sentencing system, it is difficult to say which personal characteristics of an offender tend to influence the sentence. Most structured systems do not consider such personal characteristics at all in setting the presumptive guideline sentence. Nevertheless, most do allow (and even encourage) the sentencing judge to depart from the guidelines on the basis of personal characteristics. See Pepper v. United States, 562 U.S. 476 (2011) (sentencing judge, when resentencing a defendant after the initial sentence had been set aside on appeal, can consider evidence of the defendant's efforts at rehabilitation since the time of initial sentencing).

Consider the various grounds the defendant in Problem 19-2, printed below, might assert as reasons to reduce his sentence. How could a sentencing court in this system best insulate a departure sentence from reversal on appeal? See People v. Heider, 896 N.E.2d 239 (Ill. 2008) (sentencing statute listed mental retardation as a mitigating factor; sentence here improper because trial court referred to defendant's mental retardation as a factor making him more dangerous to the public but did not make specific findings about nature of future dangerousness).

7. *Family and community.* Sentencing judges also consider the impact of a proposed sentence on the defendant's family and community. The federal sentencing guidelines attempt to limit this practice by declaring that many personal characteristics of the defendant (including the defendant's "family ties and responsibilities") are "not ordinarily relevant" to a sentence. Appellate courts have upheld departure sentences based on such circumstances only when they are present to an "extraordinary" degree. For a review of the empirical research and the complex case law on this issue, go to the web extension for this chapter at *http://www.crimpro.com/extension/ch19*.

As a staff attorney for a sentencing commission, how would you draft guidance for sentencing courts in identifying the sorts of family circumstances that should lead to a departure up or down from the ordinary sentence? Would one circumstance be the number of children? The likely home for those children if the parent is incarcerated?

Problem 19-2. Personal History and Prospects

Robert Arnautovic broke into a home in Victoria, Arkansas to steal computers and electronic equipment. While he was inside the house, the tenants—Xavier

Haveraux and his three-year-old daughter Kemely—returned home. Arnautovic rushed at Haveraux, striking him on the head three times with a flat instrument similar to a small jemmy bar and causing Haveraux to fall on the floor. While he was on the floor, Arnautovic took his watch and demanded money from him. Arnautovic then asked Haveraux to drive him to get more money but Haveraux talked him out of this. Arnautovic apologized to Kemely, who was present during the entire incident, and left the house. For a week after the attack, Haveraux says, he found it difficult to enter his empty house. He installed an alarm system.

After police arrested Arnautovic for the burglary and assault, they discovered his extensive criminal record: 39 prior convictions for burglary, 57 prior convictions for theft, and eight terms of incarceration. None of these earlier convictions involved violence.

Arnautovic is now 30 years old, the youngest of three children born to parents who separated when he was still a baby. His mother was a heroin addict who now resides in a nursing home after suffering a stroke as a result of a heroin overdose about five years ago. Arnautovic has no contact with his father, who was himself jailed for criminal behavior over the years.

Arnautovic was placed in foster care at age two and remained in that system for the next 13 years. His placements changed every two to three years. At the age of 15 he returned to live with his mother for six months, and she introduced him to heroin. He quickly became addicted and committed crimes to sustain that habit.

After he was released from his most recent prison term, Arnautovic met Rebecca Gibbons, also a heroin user. They had a daughter together, Shakira. She was born with a significant medical condition, Pierre Robin Syndrome, which is associated with abnormal development of the jaw, tongue, and mouth, and children with this condition often have a cleft palate and can have significant problems with breathing and feeding.

For the first 18 months of her life Shakira depended on tube feeding for her growth and nutrition. Arnautovic took charge of his daughter's medical care, accompanying her to weekly visits to the Child Development and Rehabilitation Centre and periodic hospital visits to replace her neo-gastric tube. He entirely ceased heroin use and became Shakira's primary caretaker. Arnautovic and Gibbons are no longer in a relationship and she no longer participates in the care of Shakira.

During the guilty plea hearing, Arnautovic described what he had done to Haveraux and his daughter as the "lowest act" he had committed in his life. He expressed concern that he could have "devastated that little girl" and said that he thought about what he had done all the time. The sentencing judge described her dilemma this way:

> Appallingly, this violent offending, however, took place before the undoubtedly terrified gaze of a three year old child. This offending in particular was abhorrent in the extreme. In the absence of mitigatory material, indeed in the absence of any but the most compelling mitigatory material, the court would, in a case such as this involving the intrusion into a home, a violent attack upon the occupier of the house, the terrifying of a little girl in her own home, watching her father being assaulted, would undoubtedly result in a sentence of imprisonment to be served immediately. Such offending cannot and should not be tolerated. I make it clear to you, Mr. Arnautovic, that I condemn your behaviour and I do so in the strongest

possible terms. The fact of your difficult personal history, the fact of your heroin addiction, are of no moment. This was an appalling and dangerous attack.

The question is whether your undoubted reformation, together with the needs of your highly dependent little daughter, are such that a sentence of imprisonment to be immediately served should be averted. I am satisfied . . . that the hardship which would be faced by Shakira if you were incarcerated would amount to be extreme and exceptional circumstances as demanded by the authority. Shakira is only two and a half years old. She has disabilities that require particular care and this will be ongoing for some four years.

Further, and unusually, Shakira has no meaningful relationships with any adult other than yourself, thus she is in familial terms, apart from yourself, an isolated, disabled toddler, and your removal from her life would see her placed in foster care with strangers.

Do you believe that the sentencing judge should impose a custodial sentence on Arnautovic? If not, what conditions of probation should the judge impose? If ten different judges handle all the criminal sentencing in the division of the court handling this case, would those judges likely disagree among themselves about a proper sentence (assuming that the jurisdiction employs discretionary sentencing laws that give the judge great latitude)? See R. v. Arnautovic, [2007] VCC 597 (9 June 2005), County Court of Victoria, Melbourne Criminal Division.

b. Cooperation in Other Investigations

Just as a defendant's past conduct can influence the sentence, so can the defendant's future conduct. Perhaps the most important future conduct for sentencing purposes is the defendant's ability and willingness to help the government investigate other suspects. The defendant can tell investigators about past events or can agree to take part in future "sting" operations. In the federal system, "substantial assistance" to the government is by far the most common reason judges give for "departing" downward to give a sentence lower than the range specified in the guidelines. It is clear that all sentencing systems allow trial judges to reduce a defendant's sentence based on cooperation. What is less clear is exactly who can determine whether the defendant should benefit from an effort to cooperate, and how much the benefit should be.

◼ TAGGART PARRISH v. STATE

12 P.3d 953 (Nev. 2000)

AGOSTI, J.

[Police] stopped a vehicle in which the appellant, Taggart Parrish, was riding as a passenger. Parrish attempted to flee on foot from the officers. Immediately, several officers gave chase. During the foot pursuit, Parrish attempted to aim a handgun in one officer's direction. Fortunately, the officer knocked the handgun out of Parrish's hand. A lengthy struggle ensued, during which Parrish attempted to reach the handgun numerous times. Finally, the police subdued and arrested Parrish. The police subsequently discovered methamphetamine in the vehicle in which Parrish had been riding.

After Parrish's arrest, detectives assigned to the Consolidated Narcotics Unit ("CNU") met with Parrish at the jail to discuss the possibility that Parrish would provide "substantial assistance" pursuant to NRS 453.3405(2), [which empowers the sentencing judge to reduce sentences for defendants who qualify under the statutory terms]. The detectives testified that Parrish was very cooperative during this meeting. Parrish, in conjunction with his fiancée, provided information concerning fourteen individuals allegedly involved in drug trafficking. The information was detailed and particular, including names and telephone numbers, maps of areas where police could find drug traffickers, information about surveillance, and how the police could protect themselves during later investigations.

The CNU detectives admitted that it was a "large list" and conceded that Parrish had supplied more information than would normally be provided by others attempting to render substantial assistance. . . . However, CNU detectives never investigated the information Parrish gave them. When asked during the sentencing hearing why they had not followed up on these leads, a CNU detective explained [that the unit placed a higher priority on other investigations. Furthermore,] CNU detectives testified that because of the events surrounding Parrish's arrest, they would not work with Parrish because Parrish would present a danger to officers. . . .

The detectives also testified that it is the CNU's opinion that lists, like the one provided by Parrish, do not constitute substantial assistance unless "we fully follow it up and it results in arrest." Furthermore, the detectives stated that their supervisors do not like officers testifying at a defendant's sentencing hearing that the defendant provided substantial assistance unless the information provided resulted in "actual bodies and product. That's their policy." [NRS 453.3405(2) requires that the arresting law enforcement agency be given an opportunity to be heard concerning whether the defendant has rendered substantial assistance.]

In addition to a fine of not more than $500,000, the punishment for trafficking in twenty-eight or more grams of a controlled substance is either: (1) life imprisonment, with the possibility of parole after a minimum of ten years has been served; or (2) a definite term of twenty-five years imprisonment, with the possibility of parole after a minimum of ten years has been served. . . . Parrish was informed by the written plea memorandum, his attorney and the district court at the time he entered his plea of guilty that he was not eligible for probation on the trafficking count unless the district court determined that he had [rendered] substantial assistance to law enforcement officials. The district court heard evidence on Parrish's motion at the sentencing hearing. However, the district court made no finding concerning whether Parrish had or had not provided substantial assistance. Instead, the district court sentenced Parrish to [life imprisonment], the maximum prison sentence allowed for the crime of trafficking in a controlled substance. . . . [The district court sentenced Parrish to a consecutive term of twelve to forty-eight months in prison for obstructing and resisting a public officer with the use of a dangerous weapon.] On appeal, Parrish claims that the district court abused its discretion by failing to find that he rendered substantial assistance. . . .

NRS 453.3405(2) allows the district court, upon proper motion, to reduce or suspend the sentence of the defendant when the district court finds the defendant rendered substantial assistance in the identification or apprehension of other drug traffickers. NRS 453.3405(2) reads:

> The judge, upon an appropriate motion, may reduce or suspend the sentence of any person convicted of violating any of the provisions of NRS 453.3385 [or two other drug statutes] if he finds that the convicted person rendered substantial assistance in the identification, arrest or conviction of any of his accomplices, accessories, coconspirators or principals or of any other person involved in trafficking in a controlled substance in violation of NRS 453.3385 [or two other drug statutes]. The arresting agency must be given an opportunity to be heard before the motion is granted. Upon good cause shown, the motion may be heard in camera.

We note that several other states, as well as the federal system, have similar provisions. See, e.g., U.S. Sentencing Commission, Guidelines Manual §5K1.1; Fla. Stat. Ann. §893.135(4); Ga. Code Ann. §16-13-31(f)(2). Such statutes are obviously intended to provide an incentive to drug-trafficking offenders to cooperate with law enforcement in the investigation of other drug traffickers. . . .

We begin by noting that the district court is afforded wide discretion when sentencing a defendant. As we have acknowledged, "judges spend much of their professional lives separating the wheat from the chaff and have extensive experience in sentencing, along with the legal training necessary to determine an appropriate sentence." We are also cognizant that in this case the legislature has clearly vested the district court with discretion, by stating that the judge "*may* reduce or suspend the sentence . . . *if* he finds that the convicted person rendered substantial assistance." NRS 453.3405(2) (emphasis added). . . .

In addition to the "abuse of discretion" standard, we are also mindful of our holding in Matos v. State, 878 P.2d 288 (Nev. 1994). In *Matos*, the defendant, in an effort to reduce his sentence, offered to assist the police pursuant to NRS 453.3405(2). However, because Matos had threatened to kill several members of the Consolidated Narcotics Unit, and had gone so far as to have a "contract" put out on a former police informant, law enforcement officers refused to accept his assistance. Under the facts of *Matos*, we concluded that since the defendant clearly posed a danger to law enforcement officers, those officers could legitimately reject his offer to render substantial assistance. Furthermore, we observed that on appeal this court would imply findings of fact and conclusions of law if the record clearly supports the district court's ruling. Therefore, we held in *Matos* that even if the district court erred in its technical interpretation of the statute, the district court did not err in concluding the defendant had not rendered substantial assistance.

Today's case does not overrule these sound principles. Rather, Parrish's situation does not present the case where law enforcement officers legitimately rejected his offer to assist drug agents. On the contrary, Parrish was approached by CNU officers after he was arrested and was asked if he was willing to provide substantial assistance. Parrish was willing. CNU detectives testified that they were "definitely interested" in following up on the information Parrish provided. One of the detectives further testified that he believed that the information Parrish provided was reliable since two people on Parrish's list had been arrested for drug offenses subsequent to, but not related to, Parrish's disclosure of their identities. Therefore, unlike *Matos*, this is not a case where detectives legitimately refused to work with the defendant. In contrast to *Matos*, detectives in this case seemed quite willing to extract information from Parrish; they simply did not want to work personally with and in close proximity to Parrish.

Parrish correctly argues that nowhere in NRS 453.3405(2) is there a requirement that the police personally work with a defendant who is attempting to provide substantial assistance. While police may legitimately refuse to work closely with a defendant who, in the view of police officers, poses a danger to themselves or the public, substantial assistance, pursuant to the terms of the statute, may be rendered in other ways. We understand the detectives' unwillingness to utilize Parrish in a controlled buy operation after he engaged in a prolonged physical struggle with law enforcement officers during his arrest and had, during the same incident, drawn a weapon on those officers. However, it is clear in this case that the information Parrish provided could have been investigated in a manner that did not personally involve Parrish. . . . Therefore, the district court could have found that Parrish rendered substantial assistance even though the detectives refused to work closely with Parrish.

What is so troubling about this case is the district court's apparent acceptance of CNU's "policy" concerning substantial assistance. The CNU detectives testified that in their opinion only arrests, or as they put it, information resulting in "actual bodies and product," constituted substantial assistance. Because the district court did not specifically address this interpretation and sentenced Parrish to the maximum sentence allowed, it seems that the district court may have implicitly accepted CNU's "policy" as a correct statement of the law.

CNU's policy clearly constitutes a misinterpretation of the statute. NRS 453.3405(2) plainly states that the district court may find that the defendant rendered "substantial assistance in the identification, arrest *or* conviction" of other drug traffickers. (Emphasis added.) A plain reading of the statute reveals that an arrest is not a necessary prerequisite to a determination that a defendant has rendered substantial assistance. While CNU is free to develop its own internal policy concerning when the agency, in exercising its opportunity to be heard pursuant to NRS 453.3405(2), will recommend that the court reduce or suspend the sentence of an offender, CNU is not free to represent to the court that substantial assistance has not been rendered simply because their internal requirements have not been met. . . .

[We do not hold today] that substantial assistance is rendered as a matter of law whenever a defendant provides law enforcement officers with information. The trial judge is always in the best position to evaluate the sincerity, reliability, quality and value of a defendant's efforts to provide substantial assistance. However, a judicial determination of whether or not substantial assistance has been rendered must be made by application of the statutory requirements to the defendant's efforts. If the district court sets a higher standard than is statutorily required for a finding of substantial assistance, the purpose of the statute is defeated. What is more, offenders who might otherwise be willing to trade information for the possibility of leniency will not do so if the carrot of leniency is illusory.

Those responsible for enforcing the laws of this state, and in turn the public, are benefited when defendants choose to provide the police with information that leads to the "identification, arrest or conviction" of others involved in the drug trade. When offenders perform substantial assistance, it would be unfair to provide no relief under the statute to them unless an articulable reason exists not to reduce or suspend the sentence. . . .

Accordingly, we hold that when evidence is presented to the district court concerning whether or not a defendant has rendered substantial assistance pursuant to NRS 453.3405(2), the district court is required to expressly state its finding concerning whether or not substantial assistance has been provided. Because the district court in this case made no such finding, and because the record does not clearly support a finding that there had been no substantial assistance provided to law enforcement, we vacate Parrish's sentence. We cannot determine from the record in this case whether the district court misinterpreted NRS 453.3405(2) since evidence was presented which could support a finding that Parrish had provided substantial assistance. Based on the foregoing, we affirm Parrish's judgment of conviction but vacate his sentence and remand this case for a new sentencing hearing before a different district judge.

■ U.S. SENTENCING GUIDELINES §5K1.1

Upon motion of the government stating that the defendant has provided substantial assistance in the investigation or prosecution of another person who has committed an offense, the court may depart from the guidelines.

The appropriate reduction shall be determined by the court for reasons stated that may include, but are not limited to, consideration of the following: (1) the court's evaluation of the significance and usefulness of the defendant's assistance, taking into consideration the government's evaluation of the assistance rendered; (2) the truthfulness, completeness, and reliability of any information or testimony provided by the defendant; (3) the nature and extent of the defendant's assistance; (4) any injury suffered, or any danger or risk of injury to the defendant or his family resulting from his assistance; (5) the timeliness of the defendant's assistance.

Notes

1. *Assisting in other investigations: majority position.* In the unstructured sentencing states, cooperation with the government in investigating and trying other criminal cases is generally believed to have some positive effect both on the sentencing court's disposition of the case and on the duration of the sentence imposed. State v. Johnson, 630 N.W.2d 583 (Iowa 2001). Even in highly discretionary sentencing systems, statutes commonly address the sentencing discount a court must give to a defendant who assists the government. See Brugman v. State, 339 S.E.2d 244 (Ga. 1986) (discussing statute). The more structured sentencing states have followed the same route, instructing the judge that cooperation with the government can serve as a basis for departing from the guideline sentence and imposing some lesser sentence. See Or. Criminal Justice Commission R. 213-008-0002.

2. *Substantial in whose eyes?* There is some variation in the amount of control the prosecution has over the use of the "substantial assistance" sentencing factor. If the prosecution refuses to accept a defendant's offer of cooperation, then the sentence usually will not be affected. But what happens if the government accepts the cooperation and later determines that it was not valuable or complete? Section 5K1.1 of the federal guidelines requires a government motion before the court can reduce the sentence based on the defendant's cooperation, while 18 U.S.C. §3553(e) requires the same before a court can reduce a sentence below a statutory mandatory minimum. Should the court have an independent power to reduce a sentence on these

grounds, even in the absence of a government motion? See Wade v. United States, 504 U.S. 181 (1992) (Constitution does not preserve for federal judges the power to depart for "substantial assistance" without permission of the government; only when the defendant makes a "substantial threshold showing" of an unconstitutional prosecutorial motive can the court adjust the sentence without a government motion). State legislatures and courts have been debating this issue for years with regard to their own guidelines. See State v. Sarabia, 875 P.2d 227 (Idaho 1994) (declaring unconstitutional a statute allowing sentence below mandatory minimum only when prosecutor moves for reduction based on substantial assistance).

3. *Nonconstitutional controls on assistance discounts.* The real debate over limiting prosecutorial power in this sphere takes place at the nonconstitutional level. Legislatures and sentencing commissions must decide whether to make a prosecutor's motion a necessary precondition to this sort of sentence reduction. The concern, of course, is that an unsupervised or unscrupulous prosecutor will make the recommendations on arbitrary or inconsistent grounds. In the federal system, prosecutors have attempted to regulate themselves, by creating written policies about which defendants should receive a reduced sentence for substantial assistance. Most federal districts have adopted written guidelines on the subject, and their content is fairly consistent. However, a study sponsored by the U.S. Sentencing Commission found great variety among the 94 federal districts in their granting of substantial assistance motions. The findings of this study and related research receive further attention on the web extension for this chapter at *http://www.crimpro.com/extension/ch19*. As a chief prosecutor, how could you create guidelines within your office that would promote more consistent decisions about sentence discounts for cooperating defendants?

2. New Information About the Victim and the Community

What information not related to the offender or the offense may affect the sentence? This section considers two kinds of information beyond the offense and offender: information about the victim and information about the community.

In a traditional indeterminate sentencing system, victims do not formally address the sentencing court. The trial is seen as a process through which the state prosecutes and punishes individuals for violations of collective norms; individuals are compensated through private law (tort) remedies. Of course, the prosecutor attempts in many cases to bring the victim's concerns or information to the court's attention, and the judge may account for this in imposing a sentence. But until recently, the victim has had little opportunity to speak directly to the sentencing court.

In recent decades, through statutes, state constitutional provisions, and procedural rules, most jurisdictions have created a formal role for victims. Many jurisdictions give victims an opportunity to address the court, both to provide information about the harm caused by the crime and to express an opinion about the proper sentence to impose. But what impact should victims have on individual sentences? Should the personal or family circumstances of the victim matter? Will these factors, if considered, become a means for considering invidious factors such as wealth and race?

■ MICHIGAN CONSTITUTION ARTICLE I, §24

(1) Crime victims, as defined by law, shall have the following rights, as provided by law:

— The right to be treated with fairness and respect for their dignity and privacy throughout the criminal justice process. . . .

— The right to be reasonably protected from the accused throughout the criminal justice process.

— The right to notification of court proceedings.

— The right to attend trial and all other court proceedings the accused has the right to attend.

— The right to confer with the prosecution.

— The right to make a statement to the court at sentencing.

— The right to restitution.

— The right to information about the conviction, sentence, imprisonment, and release of the accused.

(2) The legislature may provide by law for the enforcement of this section.

Notes

1. *Community views at sentencing: majority position.* Judges do not hand down sentences in a vacuum. Judges may respond implicitly to changing societal conceptions of the seriousness of the offense, or to changes in the prevalence of an offense, or to the particular "message" that a sentence may send to the community. But can judges do so openly? Information about community impact is available much less often than information about the impact on specific victims. One problem with considering community impact is identifying the relevant community. Who should express the community's view? Some courts have allowed victims to offer information about broader community impact. For example, the Pennsylvania Supreme Court in Commonwealth v. Penrod, 578 A.2d 486 (Pa. 1990), allowed victims, family members, and friends to testify at sentencing for drunken-driving defendants "regarding the impact of the offense on the victim, the impact on the community generally, and/or the impact on the family members or friends as members of the community." Should representatives of victims' rights organizations be allowed to speak at every sentencing? Should equal time be given to representatives of those who believe sentences are too severe or that imprisonment harms communities by removing vital members?

2. *Victims' rights at sentencing: majority position.* Over the past 30 years, nearly every state has decided to allow victim involvement at sentencing. It is difficult to capture the depth, range, and impact of this dramatic change in sentencing practice. Almost all states allow victim input through the PSI report. Many allow victims a separate opportunity to make a written or oral statement regarding sentencing, often detailing the kinds of information victims may offer. A few states have retained sharper limits: Several allow judges to choose whether to admit or refuse victim impact information; Texas allows a victim to make a statement only after sentencing, Tex. Code Crim. Proc. art. 42.03.

The rich variety of victim rights statutes has not produced a substantial case law regarding victim impact statements in the noncapital context. When defendants challenge the impact of such statements, they often claim that the judge was biased, or unduly influenced, by the information. See Nichols v. Commonwealth, 839 S.W.2d 263 (Ky. 1992); People v. Vecchio, 819 P.2d 533 (Colo. App. 1991) (rejected a claim that the trial judge should have recused himself after the prosecutor filed more than 100 victim impact statements).

3. *Victim impact statements in capital cases.* Courts and legislatures have wrestled with the special problems of integrating victim impact statements with the complex law of capital sentencing. The U.S. Supreme Court limited introduction of victim evidence in capital cases in Booth v. Maryland, 482 U.S. 496 (1987) (victim impact statement in capital cases leads to arbitrary and capricious decisions because sentencing jury's focus would shift away from the defendant and onto the victim and the victim's family), and South Carolina v. Gathers, 490 U.S. 805 (1989) (rejecting prosecutorial argument about victim impact). The Court reversed itself in Payne v. Tennessee, 501 U.S. 808 (1991), holding that the jury could hear victim impact information. In *Payne,* the Court upheld admission of testimony from a murder victim's mother, describing the impact of the killing on the victim's three-year-old son. The Court held that the victim impact statements "illustrated quite poignantly some of the harm that Payne's killing had caused." State courts and state legislatures have overwhelmingly followed the invitation in *Payne* to allow victim impact evidence in capital cases. See State v. Muhammad, 678 A.2d 164 (N.J. 1996). A few states still ban victim evidence in capital cases or limit the topics that victims can address. See Bivins v. State, 642 N.E.2d 928 (Ind. 1994); Mack v. State, 650 So. 2d 1289 (Miss. 1994).

4. *Implementing victims' rights at sentencing.* As a Michigan legislator, how would you draft legislation to enforce section 24 of the Michigan constitution? Would you provide for victim statements prior to the sentencing hearing, along with any statement at the hearing? If the victim is unwilling to testify, would your statute nevertheless allow the defense or prosecution to subpoena the victim and obtain his evidence under oath?

5. *Vulnerable victims.* Structured sentencing rules often instruct a judge to enhance a sentence if the victim of the crimes was "vulnerable" or otherwise worthy of exceptional protection. The Minnesota Sentencing Guidelines authorize the judge to decrease a sentence if "the victim was an aggressor in the incident," and to increase the sentence if the "victim was particularly vulnerable due to age, infirmity, or reduced physical or mental capacity, which was known or should have been known to the offender" or if the "victim was treated with particular cruelty for which the individual offender should be held responsible." Minn. Sentencing Guidelines II.D.2.a.1, II.D.2.b.1-2. The federal guidelines contain a similar provision for enhancement of the sentence by a designated amount if "the defendant knew or should have known that a victim of the offense was unusually vulnerable due to age, physical or mental condition, or that a victim was otherwise particularly susceptible to criminal conduct." U.S. Sentencing Guidelines §3A1.1. A specified increase is also required when the victim is "a government officer or employee" or a law enforcement officer.

6. *Judicial experience and community priorities.* Is it appropriate for judges in the same jurisdiction to weigh community impact differently? Federal Judge Reena Raggi argues that federal guidelines should allow local variation among federal districts because particular crimes may create special harms in some localities and because the judges in that area develop special expertise on certain topics:

I first began to question [the nationally uniform approach of the sentencing guidelines] when I had to impose sentences on a number of defendants who had unlawfully transported firearms into New York from other states. Almost daily my fellow New Yorkers and I would read in the press of the senseless shooting of young children, on the streets, even in their own homes, all victims of random gun fire. . . . Almost invariably the guns used in these crimes, as well as most others unlawfully possessed in this area, had come from out of state. . . . And yet, when it came time for me to impose sentences in my cases . . . I was confronted by a guideline range that rarely exceeded six months' incarceration. . . .

The insight judges have about crimes in their particular districts goes beyond simply recognizing which conduct is more destructive to a community. It also reaches the question of how different levels of conduct contribute to an area's crime problems. For example, despite the fact that no part of the United States is immune from the problem of drugs, few judges have as broad an experience dealing with drug importation and large-scale distribution as my colleagues in the Eastern District of New York. . . . The piers and airports of the district make it, for all intents and purposes, . . . the entry point for a large percentage of the contraband entering this country. . . . District judges should enjoy more discretion—indeed they should be encouraged—to depart from the guidelines to reflect specific local concerns.

Raggi, Local Concerns, Local Insights, 5 Fed. Sentencing Rep. 306 (1993). Consider also the following language from a trial judge in a West Virginia case, State v. Broughton, 470 S.E.2d 413 (W. Va. 1996), imposing an unusually severe sentence for delivery of cocaine and marijuana on a Jamaican national who was not a resident of the state:

We have several convictions of offenses which have caused great difficulty here in this area. We have found ourselves inundated with drugs from outside sources which has created a subculture of crime where there was none before. We even have had a police officer shot and wounded. Sort of things that one would expect in the metropolitan area has come to sleepy little Charles Town. And I don't know if there is any way that we are ever going to be able to stop it, but I do know if the Courts don't lean on these issues when they come up, that we don't have any hope of ever stopping them.

Problem 19-3. The Community as Victim

The Outlaw Crip Killers (OLCK) is a street gang that is an offshoot of the larger Bloods gang; their primary color is red. The OLCKs have a territorial conflict with a Crips affiliated gang, the Native Gangster Crips (NGC); their primary color is blue.

Fred Leoso is an OLCK member. On July 4 he hosted a barbeque in his front yard, attended by a number of family members. Shortly after midnight someone opened fire from a dark blue Chevrolet Suburban sports utility vehicle passing in front of Fred's house. One of the bullets struck Fred's cousin, Issac Pritchard, in the leg. Fred, who had seen the vehicle before, recognized it as an NGC vehicle.

On August 23, the state of Washington charged Angel Bluehorse with one count of drive-by shooting with a gang aggravator in connection with the July 4 shooting. At the trial, witnesses testified that whenever they saw Bluehorse, Bluehorse was wearing all blue clothing and making gang signs with his fingers that identified him as an NGC member or associate. Witnesses did not specify whether these encounters took place in gang-claimed territory, although some of them took place as Bluehorse walked past the Leosos' house.

During closing arguments, the prosecutor said, "this case involves retaliation, back and forth shootings, gangs having motives to shoot at other gang members and affiliates and then retaliate." The prosecutor spoke only briefly about the July 4 drive-by shooting. She discussed evidence showing that Bluehorse was identified as the shooter, and also recounted witnesses' generalized testimony about seeing Bluehorse in the past wearing blue and making gang signs. She referred to generalized testimony about gangs and gang members and closed with this observation:

> When there's a shooting like this, they're walking the walk, they're doing the deeds. They're maintaining their status in the gang. They are active and maintaining that status by doing what some gang members do, which is retaliate and shoot at and hit sometimes other people with firearms.

The jury convicted Bluehorse of the July 4 drive-by shooting. The jury also found that Bluehorse had committed the drive-by shooting in order to maintain or advance his position in a gang.

At sentencing, the trial court determined that Bluehorse's prior record score was zero. But then the prosecutor stated that the State had "grossly undercharged" Bluehorse; she claimed that he also committed an assault and characterized the crime of conviction as "more serious than a simple drive-by." The prosecutor requested that the trial court impose the statutory maximum sentence for a class B felony, 120 months, instead of the 15-20 months (which the normal drive-by would have supported).

The trial court seemed to agree with the prosecutor's assessment of undercharging, and stated that the jury's finding (gang status as motivation) was an aggravating circumstance supporting an exceptional sentence. The trial court noted the danger posed to the community by cycles of gang violence and the danger posed to the July 4 bystanders in particular. The trial court imposed a sentence of 108 months.

Bluehorse appeals his conviction and his exceptional sentence based on a gang aggravator. Bluehorse contends that the record does not support the jury's finding of a gang aggravator. He also argues that the trial court's reasons for imposing an exceptional sentence were not "substantial and compelling" (as required by the sentencing statute) because they violated the "real facts doctrine," which holds that "a trial court may not impose a sentence based on the elements of a more serious crime." State v. Wakefield, 925 P.2d 183 (Wash. 1996). Finally, Bluehorse claims that the exceptional sentence was "clearly excessive." How would you rule? Cf. State v. Bluehorse, 248 P.3d 537 (Wash. App. 2011); State v. Johnson, 873 P.2d 514 (Wash. 1994).

Problem 19-4. Sentencing Hearings, Guilty Plea Hearings

You are the chief judge in the state trial court for felonies in your jurisdiction. The state Administrative Office of the Courts issued a memorandum to you and all the other chief judges in the state, suggesting that you promulgate local rules of practice for sentencing hearings. During consultations with local defense attorneys, you learn that they have some concerns about these hearings. They believe that the preponderance standard of proof is too low, given the importance of some factual findings. They also say that prosecutors should not be able to establish so many sentencing factors based on the hearsay testimony of law enforcement officers or probation officers. Finally (and most important in their view), they believe that probation officers should make available to them, at least 48 hours in advance of the hearing, any pre-sentence investigations and any recommendations they make to the judge about the sentence to impose. Prosecutors, on the other hand, are advocating against any changes in the current practices. They believe that the procedures at a sentencing hearing should resemble the procedures at a guilty plea hearing, and should not be structured to resemble trials.

What rules will you promulgate about the procedures to use at the sentencing hearing for proof of relevant facts and access to probation officer work product? Does Federal Rule of Criminal Procedure 32, reprinted above, offer a sound model for your purposes? To what extent do the comparatively higher case volumes and lower staffing levels of state court systems influence your choices about procedures?

C. REVISITING POINTS IN THE CRIMINAL PROCESS

The sentencing process reconsiders decisions made earlier in the criminal process, from investigation to adjudication. Sentencing courts never explicitly reverse earlier decisions in the same case, but a sentencing court might allow a close or difficult question decided one way at an earlier stage (for or against the defendant) to influence the sentence. This section evaluates the extent to which courts should reconsider investigative and charging decisions in determining a proper sentence.

1. Revisiting Investigations

If some of the defendant's bad acts or statements during investigations are excluded from consideration at a suppression hearing—say because of a *Miranda* violation—should the sentencing judge consider that information after conviction? If some of the government's bad acts during investigations (for example, when government agents propose multiple drug transactions simply to increase the total amount of drugs at issue) do not affect the guilty verdict, should that information nevertheless affect the sentence?

When government agents behave in an outrageous fashion or encourage a person who would not otherwise have committed a crime to do so, the defendant may have a complete defense to the charges, based on entrapment or a due process "outrageous misconduct" claim. But entrapment defenses rarely succeed, even when the government agents control the severity of the defendant's crimes. Entrapment, like other complete defenses, is an all-or-nothing doctrine, allowing no subtlety or gradation in the analysis of government behavior or its effect. Sentencing, defendants claim, is a proper time to make more carefully graded judgments about the relative culpability of the offender (compared to offenders not subject to government encouragement). Claims of "sentencing entrapment" or "sentencing manipulation" often arise in drug cases where the amount of drugs in a transaction can have a major impact on the likely sentence.

■ PEOPLE v. DEON LAMONT CLAYPOOL
684 N.W.2d 278 (Mich. 2004)

TAYLOR, J.

The issue in this case is whether it is permissible for Michigan trial judges, sentencing under the legislative sentencing guidelines pursuant to M.C.L. §769.34, to consider, for the purpose of a downward departure from the guidelines range, police conduct that is described as sentencing manipulation, sentencing entrapment, or sentencing escalation. These doctrines are based on police misconduct, which, alone, is not an appropriate factor to consider at sentencing. Rather, we hold that, pursuant to People v. Babcock, 666 N.W.2d 231 (Mich. 2003), if it can be objectively and verifiably shown that police conduct or some other precipitating cause altered a defendant's intent, that altered intent can be considered by the sentencing judge as a ground for a downward sentence departure. . . .

This case arose from a series of sales of crack cocaine by defendant to an undercover police officer. An acquaintance of defendant's in the drug trade introduced him to an undercover officer as a potential customer. On March 8, 2001, the officer bought 28.35 grams of crack cocaine for $1,100. On March 12, 2001, he bought 49.2 grams for $2,000. Finally, on March 14, 2001, he bought 127.575 grams for $4,000. Defendant was arrested and charged with delivery of 50 or more, but less than 225, grams of cocaine, reflecting the third sale.

Defendant pleaded guilty to this charge. [Although the defendant also pleaded guilty to charges related to the first and second buys, this appeal only deals with the sentence for his third offense.] The offense carries a statutorily mandated minimum sentence of ten years of imprisonment. However, according to the legislative sentencing guidelines and the former M.C.L. §333.7401(4), the statutorily mandated minimum ten-year sentence for this offense can be reduced or "departed from," as it is described, if certain conditions set forth in M.C.L. §769.34(3) are met. [The statute provides as follows:

> A court may depart from the appropriate sentence range established under the sentencing guidelines if the court has a substantial and compelling reason for that departure and states on the record the reasons for departure. . . . The court shall not base a departure on an offense characteristic or offender characteristic already taken into account in determining the appropriate sentence range unless the court finds from the facts contained in the court record, including the presentence investigation report, that the characteristic has been given inadequate or disproportionate weight.]

At the sentencing hearing, the defense requested a downward departure from the statutorily mandated ten-year minimum sentence on the bases that defendant has a limited criminal history (only one criminal conviction for misdemeanor retail fraud) for his age of twenty-six and that he has an addiction to cocaine, which was costly and jeopardized his ability to pay for his home. In this case, defense counsel also argued that the police had manipulated defendant by making repeated purchases for increasing quantities of cocaine and that, by doing so, they "escalated" the sentence to which defendant would be subjected. In particular, defense counsel argued that the undercover police officer did not arrest defendant after either of the initial buys, but went back to him repeatedly to purchase cocaine. The defense argued that the officer even paid defendant at least $500 more than the going rate to persuade him to sell a larger quantity of crack cocaine than he otherwise would have sold.

The prosecutor countered that the officer had legitimate law enforcement reasons for the repeated purchases. Those reasons were that many usual sellers of large amounts only will sell small amounts to new buyers, and, thus, it is only by working up to larger amounts that law enforcement can in fact determine what type of seller the suspect is. The prosecutor, however, did not address the defense's distinct claim that no matter what the police motivation may have been, the fact that the police paid defendant $500 over the market price was the sole reason defendant's intent to sell changed from selling a lesser amount to selling a greater amount.

At the conclusion of these arguments, the trial court found substantial and compelling reasons to depart from the mandatory minimum sentence on the basis of defendant's age, minimal criminal history, and stable employment history of approximately two years, and, finally, on the basis of the fact that, in the court's view, defendant had been "escalated" and precluded from getting substance abuse treatment earlier. . . . The court then departed downward two years from the statutorily mandated minimum sentence of ten years and sentenced defendant to eight to twenty years of imprisonment. . . .

The underlying approach of the guidelines is that the person to be sentenced is first placed in a narrow sentencing compartment based on rigid factors surrounding the offense and offender variable statuses. Then the individual is eligible to be removed from such "default" compartments on the basis of individualized factors. [Statutes] allow a downward departure if the court has a "substantial and compelling reason" for the departure. This Court has determined that this statutory language means that there must be an "objective and verifiable" reason that "keenly or irresistibly grabs our attention"; is of "considerable worth" in determining the appropriate sentence; and "exists only in exceptional cases."

It is clear from the legislative sentencing guidelines that the focus of the guidelines is that the court is to consider *this* criminal and *this* offense. As People v. Babcock, 666 N.W.2d 231 (Mich. 2003), said after discussing the roots of our nation's attachment to the concept of proportionality in criminal sentencing: "The premise of our system of criminal justice is that, everything else being equal, the more egregious the offense, and the more recidivist the criminal, the greater the punishment."

Because of this approach, police misconduct, on which the doctrines of sentencing manipulation, sentencing entrapment, and sentencing escalation are based, is not an appropriate factor to consider at sentencing. Police misconduct, standing alone, tells us nothing about the defendant. However, if the defendant has an enhanced intent that was the product of police conduct or any other precipitating factor, and the enhanced intent can be shown in a manner that satisfies the requirements for a sentencing departure as outlined in *Babcock*, it is permissible for a court to consider that enhanced intent in making a departure.

The trial court in this case concluded, without more, that the defendant was "escalated." It is not clear whether the court was thinking about defendant's intent or the police conduct. Thus, resentencing or rearticulation of the court's reasons for departure on this factor is required because, under M.C.L. §769.34(3), "it is not enough that there *exists* some potentially substantial and compelling reason to depart from the guidelines range. Rather, this reason must be articulated by the trial court on the record." *Babcock*, 666 N.W.2d at 231. Moreover, a trial court must articulate on the record a substantial and compelling reason why its *particular* departure was warranted. The trial court is instructed to do this on remand. . . .

The Chief Justice . . . contends that we are employing the subjective factor of intent to determine whether a sentencing departure is warranted in a particular case. That is, she believes that because intent is subjective, it can never be shown to have been altered in an objective and verifiable way. We disagree. For example, if under surveillance a defendant is importuned to sell more of an illegal substance than he wished and it is clear that he would not have sold it absent the buyer's pleas to do so, the tape of their conversations could well establish in an objective and verifiable fashion the change in the defendant's intent. Similarly, if there is evidence that after a physical assault the assailant helped the victim by securing medical assistance, this could establish objectively and verifiably an immediate repudiation of his previous criminal intent. This is all to say that the trial court cannot depart from the mandatory minimum sentence or guidelines sentence without basing its decision on some actual facts external to the representations of the defendant himself. . . .

We are considering the defendant's intent for the purpose of sentencing. It seems obvious that the sentencing stage is different from the trial stage. Indeed, the latitude for the trial court in sentencing to consider things inadmissible at trial can be found in the Legislature's requirements of what a presentence report can contain. A presentence report . . . can include hearsay, character evidence, prior convictions, and alleged criminal activity for which the defendant was not charged or convicted. Moreover, the sentencing guidelines themselves use this approach by empowering the trial court to consider virtually *any* factor that meets the substantial and compelling standard. . . .

In light of the applicable sentencing statutes and our recent decision in *Babcock*, we . . . remand this case to the trial court for resentencing or rearticulation of the court's reasons for departure, consistent with this opinion.

CORRIGAN, C.J., concurring in part and dissenting in part.

[Sentencing] entrapment or escalation is often used to effectively nullify an element of a crime for which the defendant was convicted by purporting to lessen or eliminate the defendant's intent. This is no different than the application of the entrapment defense before trial. Evidence regarding the nature and extent of defendant's intent is only a proper subject for the case-in-chief, when determining whether the elements of a crime have been established. Reviewing a defendant's subjective intent at sentencing can amount to a nullification of a conviction, or at least an element of a crime, without procedural protections.

In cases in which only a general intent is required, the Legislature has already determined that the specific intent of the individual defendant is irrelevant for the purpose of a conviction. If the intent is irrelevant at the initial stage for the purpose of the conviction, it cannot be used at sentencing as an end-run around the Legislature's decision. Here, the Legislature determined that those who intend to distribute drugs assume the risk of punishment according to the amount distributed. It is not for this Court to make a different policy decision upon sentencing.

[Under the Michigan sentencing guidelines, the trial court is required to choose a sentence within the guidelines range, unless there is a "substantial and compelling" reason for departing from this range.] For a reason to be "substantial and compelling," it must be "objective and verifiable."

Although the majority attempts to conform to the legislative requirements by requiring objective and verifiable proof that police conduct (or any other general cause) influenced the defendant's intent, the fact remains that the departure is, in fact, based on the defendant's intent, which is an inherently *subjective* factor. I cannot fathom how a person's subjective intent can ever be considered objective or verifiable. . . .

Notes

1. *Sentence entrapment and manipulation: majority position.* Indeterminate sentencing statutes do not tell a judge whether to take corrective action if she believes that government agents have attempted to manipulate a sentence. Likewise, most structured sentencing systems have not addressed the issue of "sentencing entrapment" or "manipulation." A few courts have refused to recognize government behavior as a factor at sentencing. More courts have recognized the possibility of taking account of the behavior of government agents but have not found facts that support a departure in a particular case. A few lower state courts in structured sentencing systems, like the trial judge in *Claypool,* have altered sentences because of investigators' choices.

The federal sentencing guidelines have a specific instruction for judges facing a "reverse buy" situation, in which the government agent sells to the target of the investigation: "If, in a reverse sting operation . . . the court finds that the government agent set a price for the controlled substance that was substantially below the market value of the controlled substance, thereby leading to the defendant's purchase of a significantly greater quantity of the controlled substance than his available resources would have allowed him to purchase . . . a downward departure may be warranted." U.S.S.G. §2D1.1 (Application Note 27). Is this policy an adequate response to potential government manipulation of the sentence?

2. *Inadequate self-defense and other "partial" substantive criminal law defenses.* Should courts develop refined or modified versions of substantive criminal law defenses other than entrapment, such as self-defense or duress? For instance, a defendant's self-defense argument may not result in an acquittal, but the court may nevertheless rely on the argument to reduce a sentence. Some state sentencing statutes explicitly recognize "partial" or "near-miss" defenses at sentencing: In Tennessee, the court may reduce a sentence if "substantial grounds exist tending to excuse or justify the defendant's criminal conduct, though failing to establish a defense." Tenn. Code §40-35-113(3). Discussions of criminal law defenses often postpone until sentencing any effort to refine the determination of blameworthiness beyond what is necessary to conclude that a defendant is guilty or not guilty. For additional examples of partial defenses that find some basis in the law of sentencing, go to the web extension for this chapter at *http://www.crimpro.com/extension/ch19.*

3. *Exclusionary rule at the sentencing hearing: majority position.* Most jurisdictions allow sentencing judges to consider evidence obtained in violation of a defendant's constitutional rights, even when that evidence is suppressed at trial. See Smith v. State, 517 A.2d 1081 (Md. 1986). The U.S. Supreme Court held in Estelle v. Smith, 451 U.S. 454 (1981), that a sentencing judge in a capital case could not consider a statement obtained in violation of the Fifth Amendment, but it has never addressed whether the exclusionary rule applies generally in sentencing proceedings. Most lower federal courts have decided that the exclusionary rule does not

apply at sentencing in noncapital proceedings, concluding that (1) exclusion would not deter police misconduct because the evidence is already excluded at trial, and (2) the sentencing court needs as much information as possible about the offense and offender to select a proper sanction. See, e.g., United States v. Torres, 926 F.2d 321 (3d Cir. 1991). A smaller group applies the exclusionary rule at sentencing. See Pens v. Bail, 902 F.2d 1464 (9th Cir. 1990). If the application of the exclusionary rule to sentencing depends on whether procedural rules at sentencing can truly influence law enforcement officers, do the "sentencing manipulation" cases throw any light on this question?

Problem 19-5. Learning a Lesson

Barbara Graham sold a small amount of cocaine to an undercover police officer. The officer selected the location for this sale, an apartment complex that happened to be approximately 650 feet from a private school, but the transaction took place late on a Friday night. Graham had no prior drug arrests or convictions. A Florida statute requires a mandatory minimum term of three years' imprisonment for any offender who sells illicit drugs within 1,000 feet of a school. If you were the court, would you nevertheless sentence the defendant to less than three years? How would you explain such a decision? Would you reduce the sentence whenever the government induces the defendant to commit an act that will enhance the punishment under sentencing statutes or guidelines? Compare Graham v. State, 608 So. 2d 123 (Fla. Dist. Ct. App. 1992).

Problem 19-6. Reversing the Exclusion

Juan Guzon Valera shot and killed his wife and another man after he discovered them engaging in sexual activity in a car. After inadequate *Miranda* warnings, Valera told a Hawaii County Police Officer about the events leading up to the killings, and where he had illegally obtained the gun. Although the trial judge suppressed these statements during the jury trial, he relied on them during sentencing to enhance the sentence after the jury convicted him of manslaughter.

The judge stated: "I think if the jury had heard the evidence which had to be barred because of the way the police questioned Mr. Valera, a different result would have occurred. I think in sentencing, the Court can consider those items which had to be barred. I think in this case, Mr. Valera acted as an executioner. He stalked his victims and shot them one after the other." He sentenced Valera to serve two consecutive 10-year terms of imprisonment for manslaughter, and lesser, concurrent terms of imprisonment for the firearms violations.

Valera argues on appeal that the sentencing judge violated his constitutional rights to due process and to counsel, and his privilege against self-incrimination as guaranteed by article I, sections 5, 14, and 10 of the Hawaii Constitution, by relying almost exclusively upon his suppressed statements in determining his sentence. How would you rule? Compare State v. Valera, 848 P.2d 376 (Haw. 1993).

2. Revisiting Charging Decisions: Relevant Conduct

It might seem obvious that defendants can be punished only for the crimes of which they have been convicted. Obvious, perhaps, but that is not the law in most jurisdictions. To varying degrees, sentencing laws allow defendants to be punished for the "real offense" and not just for the offense of conviction.

How can defendants be punished for acts that are not the basis for a conviction? Under an unstructured sentencing system, the sentencing court can consider any evidence of the offender's wrongdoing, whether or not the conduct formed the basis of the criminal charges. The statutory floor and ceiling for punishing the crime of conviction leave the sentencing judge with plenty of latitude to set a punishment, even if it is based in part on uncharged conduct. It is difficult and perhaps impossible to define offenses with all of the detail necessary to capture facts that affect the assessment of culpability or harm. Even structured sentencing systems tend to allow a *range* of presumptive sentences, and when choosing a sentence within that range, a judge may account for circumstances that the bare bones elements of the crime cannot capture.

Judges receive information about conduct beyond the offense itself from several sources: during trial, from prosecutors, and in pre-sentence investigation reports. Some of this information, although not strictly necessary to establish the elements of the crime of conviction, nonetheless relates directly to the charged offense. The "relevant conduct" might be an element of an offense other than the crime charged, either more or less serious. For instance, the defendant may have used a gun during the robbery, even though the charge was robbery and not armed robbery. Other facts about the offense, such as the defendant's role in a multiparty offense, may receive no mention in the statutory framework.

The extra information could relate to other uncharged offenses committed during the same time period as the charged crime or as part of the same overarching criminal scheme. A court may also consider all suspected criminal conduct in the past, whether or not it led to a conviction. If a prosecutor ignores some wrongdoing, the judge may nevertheless take it into account. Finally, the court might rely on past noncriminal conduct that is nevertheless blameworthy. The sentencing laws allowing the judge to consider uncharged conduct are sometimes called "real offense" systems (as opposed to "charge offense" systems) because the judge sentences based on the "real" criminal behavior, independent of the prosecutor's charging decisions.

Under indeterminate sentencing, it was possible for a judge to consider all of this information, though some judges would reject some or all of it as irrelevant. Structured sentencing has brought the issue of relevant conduct to a more formal and visible level. Legislatures, sentencing commissions, and judges must now decide explicitly which additional facts a sentencing judge may or may not consider and how much impact the uncharged "relevant conduct" should have.

■ U.S. SENTENCING GUIDELINES §1B1.3(A)

[The seriousness of the offense] shall be determined on the basis of the following:

(1) (A) all acts and omissions committed, aided, abetted, counseled, commanded, induced, procured, or willfully caused by the defendant; and

(B) in the case of a jointly undertaken criminal activity (a criminal plan . . . undertaken by the defendant in concert with others, whether or not charged as a conspiracy), all reasonably foreseeable acts and omissions of others in furtherance of the jointly undertaken criminal activity, that occurred during the commission of the offense of conviction, in preparation for that offense, or in the course of attempting to avoid detection or responsibility for that offense. . . .

    (3) all harm that resulted from the acts and omissions specified in [subsection (a)(1)], and all harm that was the object of such acts and omissions. . . .

ILLUSTRATION OF CONDUCT FOR WHICH THE DEFENDANT IS ACCOUNTABLE . . .

Defendants F and G, working together, design and execute a scheme to sell fraudulent stocks by telephone. Defendant F fraudulently obtains $20,000. Defendant G fraudulently obtains $35,000. Each is convicted of mail fraud. Defendants F and G each are accountable for the amount he personally obtained under subsection (a)(1)(A). Each defendant is accountable for the amount obtained by his accomplice under subsection (a)(1)(B) because the conduct of each was in furtherance of the jointly undertaken criminal activity and was reasonably foreseeable in connection with that criminal activity.

■ FLORIDA RULE OF CRIMINAL PROCEDURE 3.701(D)(11)

Departures from the recommended or permitted guideline sentence should be avoided unless there are circumstances or factors that reasonably justify aggravating or mitigating the sentence. Any sentence outside the permitted guideline range must be accompanied by a written statement delineating the reasons for the departure. Reasons for deviating from the guidelines shall not include factors relating to prior arrests without conviction or the instant offenses for which convictions have not been obtained.

■ STATE v. DOUGLAS McALPIN
740 P.2d 824 (Wash. 1987)

CALLOW, J.

Douglas McAlpin received a sentence of 90 months following his plea of guilty to a charge of first degree robbery. [This sentence] exceeded the presumptive sentence range established under the Sentencing Reform Act of 1981 (SRA). The defendant appealed. . . .

Under the SRA the defendant's presumptive sentence range for first degree robbery was 46 to 61 months. This range, which is based on the seriousness of the crime committed and the offender's "criminal history," accounted for: (1) the defendant's two other current convictions for conspiracy and burglary; and (2) two prior juvenile convictions for second degree theft, both crimes being committed while the defendant was between 15 and 18 years of age and both convictions being entered on the same date.

At the defendant's sentencing hearing, it was revealed that his actual record of juvenile crime far exceeded that which was accounted for in determining the standard sentence range. The presentence report confirmed that the defendant had, in fact, amassed a juvenile record of "three files comprising hundreds of pages." The prosecutor supplemented this report with additional information obtained from juvenile court authorities.

The defendant's juvenile record included the following: (1) prior to reaching his 15th birthday he was convicted four times for second degree burglary, and once for taking a motor vehicle without permission (all felonies); (2) between the ages of 15 and 18, he had been found guilty of false reporting and third degree malicious mischief (both misdemeanors); (3) he had been committed to juvenile institutions on four occasions; and (4) he had had "various additional felony arrests which were handled informally."

The presentence report described the defendant as a "textbook sociopath" who had no remorse for his crimes, a long history of drug abuse as a youth, and two episodes in which he had tortured animals. While in the Kitsap County Corrections Center, sharpened toothbrushes were taken away from him. The report aptly characterized the defendant as an "exceedingly dangerous young man." The defendant's counsel did not object to the introduction of the above record at any time prior to the trial court's oral pronouncement of sentence. . . .

In addition to the juvenile record, it was disclosed that the defendant, in entering his guilty plea to the first degree robbery charge, had also signed a plea bargaining agreement. The prosecutor had agreed not to file charges regarding additional crimes to which the defendant had confessed, and for which he had agreed to make restitution.

The prosecutor recommended a sentence of 61 months, the top of the presumptive range. The trial court, however, imposed a 90-month exceptional sentence. The court cited the following reasons for imposing this sentence:

> That the defendant has an extensive criminal history, as set forth in the presentence report. . . . That such criminal history includes at least five felony convictions as a juvenile prior to the defendant's 15th birthday, four commitments to juvenile institutions and various additional felony arrests which were handled informally. That in the course of the police investigations of the instant offenses the defendant also confessed to his involvement in additional burglaries or criminal trespasses with which he was not charged but for which he agreed to make restitution. That such convictions were not computed as prior criminal history and thus the defendant is not being penalized twice for his behavior. . . .

[According to the statute governing appellate review of exceptional sentences,] we must independently determine, as a matter of law, whether the trial court's reasons justify an exceptional sentence. There must be "substantial and compelling" reasons for imposing such a sentence. RCW 9.94A.120(2). . . .

We turn first to the trial court's consideration of the defendant's lengthy record of juvenile felonies. Generally, "criminal history" may not be used to justify an exceptional sentence, because it is one of two factors (the other being the "seriousness level" of the current offense committed) which is used to compute the presumptive sentence range for a particular crime. A factor used in establishing the presumptive range may not be considered a second time as an "aggravating circumstance" to justify departure from the range.

The term "criminal history" as used in the SRA for purposes of the presumptive range calculation includes only certain types of juvenile crimes. Specifically, it is limited to juvenile felonies committed while the defendant was between 15 and 18 years of age. The trial court, recognizing this limitation, did not rely on the defendant's two prior juvenile convictions for second degree theft, both committed while he was between 15 and 18 years of age, as reasons to impose an exceptional sentence. These crimes had already been considered when computing the presumptive sentence range.

On the other hand, the trial court did cite the defendant's five prior pre-age-15 felony convictions as aggravating factors justifying an exceptional sentence. The defendant asserts that this constituted error; he argues that the Legislature, by excluding such crimes from the presumptive range calculation, intended to exclude consideration of them entirely. We disagree.

One of the overriding purposes of the sentencing reform act is to ensure that sentences are proportionate to the seriousness of the crime committed and the defendant's criminal history. This purpose would be frustrated if a court were required to blind itself to a significant portion of a defendant's juvenile criminal record. . . . The trial court here did not err in concluding that a defendant who has amassed an extensive and recent record of pre-age-15 felonies is significantly different from a defendant who has no record at all. . . .

The trial court cited the following two findings as additional aggravating factors:

[1] That [the defendant's] criminal history includes . . . various additional [juvenile] felony arrests which were handled informally.
[2] That in the course of the police investigations of the instant offenses the defendant also confessed to his involvement in additional burglaries or criminal trespasses with which he was not charged but for which he agreed to make restitution.

We agree with the defendant that the trial court improperly relied on the above findings. The sentencing reform act bars the court from considering unproven or uncharged crimes as a reason for imposing an exceptional sentence. RCW 9.94A.370, at the time of sentencing, provided inter alia: "Real facts that establish elements of a higher crime, a more serious crime, or additional crimes cannot be used to go outside the presumptive sentence range except upon stipulation." In David Boerner, Sentencing in Washington §9.16, at 9-49 to 9-50 (1985), the author states:

The policy reasons behind this provision are obvious, and sound. To consider charges that have been dismissed pursuant to plea agreements will inevitably deny defendants the benefit of their bargains. If the state desires to have additional crimes considered in sentencing, it can insure their consideration by refusing to dismiss them and proving their existence. . . .

It is not sufficient that the defendant has a record of arrests which were "handled informally." Nor is it sufficient that the defendant confessed to additional uncharged "burglaries or criminal trespasses." Since these arrests and confessions have not resulted in convictions, they may not be considered at all.

We conclude that some of the trial court's reasons for imposing the exceptional sentence could not be considered as aggravating factors. However, the defendant's lengthy record of pre-age-15 felonies, standing alone, is a substantial and compelling reason and justification for imposing the exceptional sentence. The trial court did not err in deciding to impose a sentence outside the standard range. . . .

Notes

1. *Relevant conduct in state sentencing: majority position.* Sentencing judges in indeterminate sentencing systems have always had the power (but not an obligation) to consider any conduct of the defendant, whether charged or uncharged. This conduct might influence the judge's choice of a maximum or minimum sentence from within the broad statutory range. See People v. Lee, 218 N.W.2d 655 (Mich. 1974) (pending charges mentioned in PSI); People v. Grabowski, 147 N.E.2d 49 (Ill. 1958) (indictments pending for other crimes in same series of events); see also Williams v. New York, 337 U.S. 241 (1949) (death sentence imposed by judge based on pre-sentence report suggesting defendant had been involved in "30 other burglaries" in area of murder).

States with more structured sentencing systems place more restrictions on the use of the defendant's uncharged conduct. Formally, the structured state systems adopt "charge offense" rather than "real offense" sentencing. The charged offense determines a fairly small range of options available to the judge in the normal case. But "real" and "charge" offense concepts define the ends of a spectrum, and all systems allow varying degrees of real offense conduct to affect the sentencing determination. At a minimum, the uncharged conduct is available to influence the judge's selection of a sentence *within* the narrow range that the guidelines designate for typical cases. Some states go further, and allow judges to use uncharged conduct as a basis for a "departure" from the designated normal range of sentences. Other structured sentencing states (like Florida) prevent the judge from using uncharged conduct to depart from the guideline sentence. Commentary to the Minnesota sentencing guidelines states that "departures from the guidelines should not be permitted for elements of alleged offender behavior not within the definition of the offense of conviction." Minn. Sentencing Guidelines cmt. II.D.103.

2. *Relevant conduct in federal sentencing.* In contrast to the states, the federal guidelines create a "modified real offense" system. In a 1995 self-study report, the federal sentencing commission described the tradeoffs at stake in framing a relevant conduct provision:

> If uncharged misconduct is considered, punishment is based on facts proven outside procedural protections constitutionally defined for proving criminal charges, introducing an argument of unfairness. . . . The scope of conduct considered at sentencing will also affect, at least to some extent, the complexity of a sentencing system. The scope can be as limited as the conduct defined by the elements of the offense or as broad as any wrongdoing ever committed by the defendant or the defendant's partners in crime. All things being equal, a large scope of considered conduct will require more fact-finding than a more limited scope. . . . Besides fairness and complexity, the scope of conduct considered at sentencing may have serious implications for the balance between prosecutorial and judicial power in sentencing. For example, if the scope of considered conduct is confined to the offense of conviction, many argue that the sentencing system will provide relatively more power to prosecutors to control sentences. . . . Finding the right balance among fairness, complexity, and the role of the prosecutor has been a struggle for sentencing commissions generally. . . .

Discussion Paper, Relevant Conduct and Real Offense Sentencing (1995). The federal system uses the offense of conviction as a starting point for guidelines calculations, but then calls for adjustments to the "offense level" based on other relevant conduct. The commission explained its support for "real offense" factors on several grounds. First, such a system mirrored prior practices in the indeterminate system. It also gave judges a means to refine and rationalize the chaotic federal criminal code. Finally, the real offense features of the system gave judges a way to check the power of the prosecutor to dictate a sentence based upon the selection of charges.

Critics have attacked the uses of uncharged or dismissed conduct as bad policy, because of the uncertain proof of the uncharged conduct, and the difficulty of achieving uniform practices in deciding how much uncharged conduct is "relevant." They have also raised constitutional questions about whether reliance on such information violates due process, by punishing a person for conduct without proving it beyond a reasonable doubt. See Kate Stith & Jose A. Cabranes, Fear of Judging: Sentencing Guidelines in the Federal Courts 66-77 (1998). Does real offense sentencing shift power back toward judges? Are there other ways for courts, legislatures, or commissions to respond to potential prosecutorial abuse?

3. *Varieties of uncharged conduct.* In *McAlpin*, what difference is there, if any, between the aspects of the juvenile record that were proper for the sentencing judge to consider and those aspects of McAlpin's prior conduct that were improper for the court to consider? Some wrongdoing by defendants could form the basis for additional criminal charges, or more serious criminal charges. Other conduct, while blameworthy, does not affect the charging options available to the prosecutor. For example, under the federal criminal code, a mail fraud that nets $10,000 is eligible for the same punishment as a mail fraud that nets $100,000; under some state codes, however, the value of stolen property might determine the degree of crime the prosecutor can charge. Should it matter to a sentencing judge (or to a sentencing commission creating sentencing guidelines) whether the conduct in question is an element of some crime for which the defendant was not charged? Consider this approach to the problem in Kansas Statutes §38-2371(a)(3): "If a factual aspect of a crime is a statutory element of the crime . . . that aspect of the current crime of conviction may be used as an aggravating or mitigating factor only if [it] is significantly different from the usual criminal conduct captured by the aspect of the crime."

4. *Sentencing for multiple counts.* Defendants are often convicted of multiple offenses arising out of the same transaction or course of conduct. The sentencing judge in an indeterminate system has the discretion to impose separate sentences for the multiple convictions and to decide whether those sentences will be served concurrently (all the terms begin at the same time) or consecutively (a second sentence starts after the first one ends). This gives the judge power to limit the effect of a prosecutor's decision to file multiple charges based on the same conduct. Judges with complete power over the concurrent or consecutive nature of sentences have tended to give what might be termed a "volume discount." Additional convictions will increase the total sentence served, but in decreasing amounts for each additional conviction. Some structured systems limit the judge's ability to adjust a sentence based on multiple convictions. The federal sentencing guidelines have intricate rules for the "grouping" of offenses. See U.S. Sentencing Guidelines ch. 3D. More typical is this provision from the Kansas guidelines, codified in Kan. Stat. §21-6819:

When the sentencing judge imposes multiple sentences consecutively, [the] sentencing judge must establish a base sentence for the primary crime. The primary crime is the crime with the highest crime severity ranking. . . . The total prison sentence imposed in a case involving multiple convictions arising from multiple counts within an information, complaint or indictment cannot exceed twice the base sentence. . . .

For instance, if a defendant is convicted of aggravated assault and three counts of burglary in one proceeding, the sentence would be limited to twice the guideline sentence for aggravated assault (the more serious charge).

5. *Prosecutorial motives and control.* Do rules allowing higher punishment for multiple counts than for a single count give too much power to prosecutors? It is often said that structured sentencing systems shift power from judges to prosecutors. Are there avenues other than "real offense" sentencing to limit these types of prosecutorial control over sentences? In this regard, consider the federal "*Petite* policy" governing successive prosecutions in federal court. See Chapter 14.

When sentencing rules place great weight on the charges and criminal history, the prosecutor has greater influence over the sentence to be imposed. Despite the power of prosecutors to influence sentences in structured sentencing states, research suggests they do not tend to change their charging or plea bargaining practices. Structured systems have not produced dramatically longer sentences or changed rates of guilty pleas. See Terance Miethe, Charging and Plea Bargaining Practices Under Determinate Sentencing: An Investigation of the Hydraulic Displacement of Discretion, 78 J. Crim. L. & Criminology 155 (1987). This is not to say that plea bargains have no effect on the viability or uniformity of sentencing rules. Sometimes the prosecutor and defendant agree to charges and to factual and guideline stipulations that place the sentence outside the range that would ordinarily be prescribed by the guidelines—without asking the judge to depart from the guidelines. See Ilene Nagel & Stephen Schulhofer, A Tale of Three Cities: An Empirical Study of Charging and Bargaining Practice Under the Federal Sentencing Guidelines, 66 S. Cal. L. Rev. 501 (1992).

3. Revisiting Proof at Trial

Just as sentencing provides an opportunity to reconsider the significance of events during investigations and charge selection, it also provides an opportunity to reconsider choices made during the resolution of charges. This section reviews the interaction between the sentence, guilty pleas, and decisions made at trial.

The prosecution carries the burden of proving all the elements of an offense at trial beyond a reasonable doubt or establishing a factual basis in a guilty plea hearing to show that the government *could have* satisfied this burden. But once the government obtains a conviction, the burden of proving new facts relevant to sentencing becomes easier. Generally, the government need only demonstrate the facts at sentencing by a preponderance of the evidence; there are some sentencing facts for which the *defendant* bears the burden of proof, usually also by a preponderance, such as the facts necessary to justify a downward departure from a presumptive sentence. Hence, it is critical to know which facts must be proven at trial and which can wait until the sentencing hearing.

The U.S. Supreme Court and state supreme courts have held that due process requires the government to prove each element of every offense beyond a reasonable doubt. Sullivan v. Louisiana, 508 U.S. 275 (1993); In re Winship, 397 U.S. 358 (1970). The courts have also decided that legislatures are not completely free to shift facts from "element" status to "sentencing" status. In McMillan v. Pennsylvania, 477 U.S. 79 (1986), the Court held that the government did not violate due process by proving facts supporting a "sentencing enhancement" for visibly possessing a firearm using the lower preponderance standard of proof. The Court recognized, however, that legislatures could not freely convert offense elements into sentencing facts, and that in some situations sentencing facts would have to be treated as if they were elements and would have to be proved to the jury beyond a reasonable doubt. The following case develops further the idea that some factfinding must happen at trial rather than at sentencing, regardless of the label the legislature uses.

■ RALPH BLAKELY v. WASHINGTON
542 U.S. 296 (2004)

SCALIA, J.*

Petitioner Ralph Howard Blakely, Jr., pleaded guilty to the kidnaping of his estranged wife. The facts admitted in his plea, standing alone, supported a maximum sentence of 53 months. Pursuant to state law, the court imposed an "exceptional" sentence of 90 months after making a judicial determination that he had acted with "deliberate cruelty." We consider whether this violated petitioner's Sixth Amendment right to trial by jury.

I.

Petitioner married his wife Yolanda in 1973. He was evidently a difficult man to live with, having been diagnosed at various times with psychological and personality disorders including paranoid schizophrenia. His wife ultimately filed for divorce. In 1998, he abducted her from their orchard home in Grant County, Washington, binding her with duct tape and forcing her at knifepoint into a wooden box in the bed of his pickup truck. In the process, he implored her to dismiss the divorce suit and related trust proceedings.

When the couple's 13-year-old son Ralphy returned home from school, petitioner ordered him to follow in another car, threatening to harm Yolanda with a shotgun if he did not do so. Ralphy escaped and sought help when they stopped at a gas station, but petitioner continued on with Yolanda to a friend's house in Montana. He was finally arrested after the friend called the police.

The State charged petitioner with first-degree kidnaping. Upon reaching a plea agreement, however, it reduced the charge to second-degree kidnaping involving domestic violence and use of a firearm. Petitioner entered a guilty plea admitting the elements of second-degree kidnaping and the domestic-violence and firearm allegations, but no other relevant facts.

---

* [Justices Stevens, Souter, Thomas, and Ginsburg joined this opinion.—EDS.]

The case then proceeded to sentencing. In Washington, second-degree kidnaping is a class B felony. State law provides that [a person convicted of a class B felony faces a maximum punishment of 10 years confinement]. Other provisions of state law, however, further limit the range of sentences a judge may impose. Washington's Sentencing Reform Act specifies, for petitioner's offense of second-degree kidnaping with a firearm, a "standard range" of 49 to 53 months. A judge may impose a sentence above the standard range if he finds "substantial and compelling reasons justifying an exceptional sentence." The Act lists aggravating factors that justify such a departure, which it recites to be illustrative rather than exhaustive. . . . When a judge imposes an exceptional sentence, he must set forth findings of fact and conclusions of law supporting it. A reviewing court will reverse the sentence if it finds that under a clearly erroneous standard there is insufficient evidence in the record to support the reasons for imposing an exceptional sentence.

Pursuant to the plea agreement, the State recommended a sentence within the standard range of 49 to 53 months. After hearing Yolanda's description of the kidnaping, however, the judge rejected the State's recommendation and imposed an exceptional sentence of 90 months—37 months beyond the standard maximum. He justified the sentence on the ground that petitioner had acted with "deliberate cruelty," a statutorily enumerated ground for departure in domestic-violence cases.

Faced with an unexpected increase of more than three years in his sentence, petitioner objected. The judge accordingly conducted a 3-day bench hearing featuring testimony from petitioner, Yolanda, Ralphy, a police officer, and medical experts. After the hearing, he issued 32 findings of fact, [and] adhered to his initial determination of deliberate cruelty. Petitioner appealed, arguing that this sentencing procedure deprived him of his federal constitutional right to have a jury determine beyond a reasonable doubt all facts legally essential to his sentence.

II.

This case requires us to apply the rule we expressed in Apprendi v. New Jersey, 530 U.S. 466, 490 (2000): "Other than the fact of a prior conviction, any fact that increases the penalty for a crime beyond the prescribed statutory maximum must be submitted to a jury, and proved beyond a reasonable doubt." This rule reflects two longstanding tenets of common-law criminal jurisprudence: that the "truth of every accusation" against a defendant "should afterwards be confirmed by the unanimous suffrage of twelve of his equals and neighbours," 4 W. Blackstone, Commentaries on the Laws of England 343 (1769), and that "an accusation which lacks any particular fact which the law makes essential to the punishment is . . . no accusation within the requirements of the common law, and it is no accusation in reason," 1 J. Bishop, Criminal Procedure §87, p. 55 (2d ed. 1872). These principles have been acknowledged by courts and treatises since the earliest days of graduated sentencing. . . .

Apprendi involved a New Jersey hate-crime statute that authorized a 20-year sentence, despite the usual 10-year maximum, if the judge found the crime to have been committed "with a purpose to intimidate . . . because of race, color, gender, handicap, religion, sexual orientation or ethnicity." . . .

In this case, petitioner was sentenced to more than three years above the 53-month statutory maximum of the standard range because he had acted with "deliberate cruelty." The facts supporting that finding were neither admitted by petitioner nor found by a jury. The State nevertheless contends that there was no *Apprendi* violation because the relevant "statutory maximum" is not 53 months, but the 10-year maximum for class B felonies in §9A.20.021(1)(b). . . . Our precedents make clear, however, that the "statutory maximum" for *Apprendi* purposes is the maximum sentence a judge may impose solely on the basis of the facts reflected in the jury verdict or admitted by the defendant. In other words, the relevant "statutory maximum" is not the maximum sentence a judge may impose after finding additional facts, but the maximum he may impose without any additional findings. When a judge inflicts punishment that the jury's verdict alone does not allow, the jury has not found all the facts "which the law makes essential to the punishment," Bishop, supra, §87, at 55, and the judge exceeds his proper authority.

The judge in this case could not have imposed the exceptional 90-month sentence solely on the basis of the facts admitted in the guilty plea. Those facts alone were insufficient because, as the Washington Supreme Court has explained, "[a] reason offered to justify an exceptional sentence can be considered only if it takes into account factors other than those which are used in computing the standard range sentence for the offense," State v. Gore, 21 P.3d 262, 277 (Wash. 2001), which in this case included the elements of second-degree kidnaping and the use of a firearm. Had the judge imposed the 90-month sentence solely on the basis of the plea, he would have been reversed. . . .

The State defends the sentence by drawing an analogy to those we upheld in McMillan v. Pennsylvania, 477 U.S. 79 (1986), and Williams v. New York, 337 U.S. 241 (1949). Neither case is on point. *McMillan* involved a sentencing scheme that imposed a statutory minimum if a judge found a particular fact. We specifically noted that the statute "does not authorize a sentence in excess of that otherwise allowed for [the underlying] offense." *Williams* involved an indeterminate-sentencing regime that allowed a judge (but did not compel him) to rely on facts outside the trial record in determining whether to sentence a defendant to death. The judge could have sentenced the defendant to death giving no reason at all. Thus, neither case involved a sentence greater than what state law authorized on the basis of the verdict alone. . . .

III.

Our commitment to *Apprendi* in this context reflects not just respect for long-standing precedent, but the need to give intelligible content to the right of jury trial. That right is no mere procedural formality, but a fundamental reservation of power in our constitutional structure. Just as suffrage ensures the people's ultimate control in the legislative and executive branches, jury trial is meant to ensure their control in the judiciary. *Apprendi* carries out this design by ensuring that the judge's authority to sentence derives wholly from the jury's verdict. Without that restriction, the jury would not exercise the control that the Framers intended.

Those who would reject *Apprendi* are resigned to one of two alternatives. The first is that the jury need only find whatever facts the legislature chooses to label elements of the crime, and that those it labels sentencing factors—no matter how much they may increase the punishment—may be found by the judge. This would mean, for example, that a judge could sentence a man for committing murder even if the jury convicted him only of illegally possessing the firearm used to commit it—or of making an illegal lane change while fleeing the death scene. Not even *Apprendi*'s critics would advocate this absurd result. The jury could not function as circuit-breaker in the State's machinery of justice if it were relegated to making a determination that the defendant at some point did something wrong, a mere preliminary to a judicial inquisition into the facts of the crime the State actually seeks to punish.

The second alternative is that legislatures may establish legally essential sentencing factors within limits—limits crossed when, perhaps, the sentencing factor is a "tail which wags the dog of the substantive offense." *McMillan*, 477 U.S., at 88. What this means in operation is that the law must not go too far—it must not exceed the judicial estimation of the proper role of the judge.

The subjectivity of this standard is obvious. Petitioner argued below that second-degree kidnaping with deliberate cruelty was essentially the same as first-degree kidnaping, the very charge he had avoided by pleading to a lesser offense. . . . Petitioner's 90-month sentence exceeded the 53-month standard maximum by almost 70 percent; the Washington Supreme Court in other cases has upheld exceptional sentences 15 times the standard maximum. Did the court go too far in any of these cases? There is no answer that legal analysis can provide. . . .

Whether the Sixth Amendment incorporates this manipulable standard rather than *Apprendi*'s bright-line rule depends on the plausibility of the claim that the Framers would have left definition of the scope of jury power up to judges' intuitive sense of how far is too far. We think that claim not plausible at all, because the very reason the Framers put a jury-trial guarantee in the Constitution is that they were unwilling to trust government to mark out the role of the jury.

IV.

. . . This case is not about whether determinate sentencing is constitutional, only about how it can be implemented in a way that respects the Sixth Amendment. . . .

Justice O'Connor argues that, because determinate sentencing schemes involving judicial factfinding entail less judicial discretion than indeterminate schemes, the constitutionality of the latter implies the constitutionality of the former. This argument is flawed on a number of levels. First, the Sixth Amendment by its terms is not a limitation on judicial power, but a reservation of jury power. It limits judicial power only to the extent that the claimed judicial power infringes on the province of the jury. Indeterminate sentencing does not do so. It increases judicial discretion, to be sure, but not at the expense of the jury's traditional function of finding the facts essential to lawful imposition of the penalty. . . . In a system that says the judge may punish burglary with 10 to 40 years, every burglar knows he is risking 40 years in jail. In a system that punishes burglary with a 10-year sentence, with another 30 added for use of a gun, the burglar who enters a home unarmed is entitled to no more than a 10-year sentence—and by reason of the Sixth Amendment the facts bearing upon that entitlement must be found by a jury.

But even assuming that restraint of judicial power unrelated to the jury's role is a Sixth Amendment objective, it is far from clear that *Apprendi* disserves that goal. Determinate judicial-factfinding schemes entail less judicial power than indeterminate schemes, but more judicial power than determinate jury-factfinding schemes. Whether *Apprendi* increases judicial power overall depends on what States with determinate judicial-factfinding schemes would do, given the choice between the two alternatives. Justice O'Connor simply assumes that the net effect will favor judges, but she has no empirical basis for that prediction. Indeed, what evidence we have points exactly the other way: When the Kansas Supreme Court found *Apprendi* infirmities in that State's determinate-sentencing regime in State v. Gould, 23 P.3d 801, 809-814 (Kan. 2001), the legislature responded not by reestablishing indeterminate sentencing but by applying *Apprendi*'s requirements to its current regime. The result was less, not more, judicial power.

Justice Breyer argues that *Apprendi* works to the detriment of criminal defendants who plead guilty by depriving them of the opportunity to argue sentencing factors to a judge. But nothing prevents a defendant from waiving his *Apprendi* rights. When a defendant pleads guilty, the State is free to seek judicial sentence enhancements so long as the defendant either stipulates to the relevant facts or consents to judicial factfinding. . . . Even a defendant who stands trial may consent to judicial factfinding as to sentence enhancements, which may well be in his interest if relevant evidence would prejudice him at trial. We do not understand how *Apprendi* can possibly work to the detriment of those who are free, if they think its costs outweigh its benefits, to render it inapplicable.

Nor do we see any merit to Justice Breyer's contention that *Apprendi* is unfair to criminal defendants because, if States respond by enacting "17-element robbery crimes," prosecutors will have more elements with which to bargain. Bargaining already exists with regard to sentencing factors because defendants can either stipulate or contest the facts that make them applicable. If there is any difference between bargaining over sentencing factors and bargaining over elements, the latter probably favors the defendant. Every new element that a prosecutor can threaten to charge is also an element that a defendant can threaten to contest at trial and make the prosecutor prove beyond a reasonable doubt. Moreover, given the sprawling scope of most criminal codes, and the power to affect sentences by making (even nonbinding) sentencing recommendations, there is already no shortage of in terrorem tools at prosecutors' disposal.

Any evaluation of *Apprendi*'s "fairness" to criminal defendants must compare it with the regime it replaced, in which a defendant, with no warning in either his indictment or plea, would routinely see his maximum potential sentence balloon from as little as five years to as much as life imprisonment . . . based not on facts proved to his peers beyond a reasonable doubt, but on facts extracted after trial from a report compiled by a probation officer who the judge thinks more likely got it right than got it wrong. . . .

Justice Breyer's more general argument—that *Apprendi* undermines alternatives to adversarial factfinding—is not so much a criticism of *Apprendi* as an assault on jury trial generally. . . . Ultimately, our decision cannot turn on whether or to what degree trial by jury impairs the efficiency or fairness of criminal justice. One can certainly argue that both these values would be better served by leaving justice entirely in the hands of professionals; many nations of the world, particularly those following civil-law traditions, take just that course. There is not one shred of doubt, however, about the Framers' paradigm for criminal justice: not the civil-law ideal of administrative perfection, but the common-law ideal of limited state power accomplished by strict division of authority between judge and jury. . . .

Petitioner was sentenced to prison for more than three years beyond what the law allowed for the crime to which he confessed, on the basis of a disputed finding that he had acted with "deliberate cruelty." The Framers would not have thought it too much to demand that, before depriving a man of three more years of his liberty, the State should suffer the modest inconvenience of submitting its accusation to "the unanimous suffrage of twelve of his equals and neighbours," 4 Blackstone, Commentaries, at 343, rather than a lone employee of the State. . . .

O'CONNOR, J., dissenting.[*]

The legacy of today's opinion, whether intended or not, will be the consolidation of sentencing power in the State and Federal Judiciaries. The Court says to Congress and state legislatures: If you want to constrain the sentencing discretion of judges and bring some uniformity to sentencing, it will cost you—dearly. Congress and States, faced with the burdens imposed by the extension of *Apprendi* to the present context, will either trim or eliminate altogether their sentencing guidelines schemes and, with them, 20 years of sentencing reform. . . .

I.

. . . Prior to 1981, Washington, like most other States and the Federal Government, employed an indeterminate sentencing scheme. . . . This system of unguided discretion inevitably resulted in severe disparities in sentences received and served by defendants committing the same offense and having similar criminal histories. . . . To counteract these trends, the state legislature passed the Sentencing Reform Act of 1981. The Act had the laudable purposes of making the criminal justice system "accountable to the public," and ensuring that "the punishment for a criminal offense is proportionate to the seriousness of the offense [and] commensurate with the punishment imposed on others committing similar offenses." Wash. Rev. Code Ann. §9.94A.010. The Act neither increased any of the statutory sentencing ranges for the three types of felonies . . . nor reclassified any substantive offenses. It merely placed meaningful constraints on discretion to sentence offenders within the statutory ranges, and eliminated parole. There is thus no evidence that the legislature was attempting to manipulate the statutory elements of criminal offenses or to circumvent the procedural protections of the Bill of Rights. . . .

II.

Far from disregarding principles of due process and the jury trial right, as the majority today suggests, Washington's reform has served them. Before passage of the Act, a defendant charged with second degree kidnaping, like petitioner, had no idea whether he would receive a 10-year sentence or probation. The ultimate sentencing determination could turn as much on the idiosyncrasies of a particular judge as on the specifics of the defendant's crime or background. A defendant did not know what facts, if any, about his offense or his history would be considered relevant by the sentencing judge or by the parole board. After passage of the Act, a defendant charged with second degree kidnaping knows what his presumptive sentence will be; he has a good idea of the types of factors that a sentencing judge can and will consider when deciding whether to sentence him outside that range; he is guaranteed meaningful appellate review to protect against an arbitrary sentence. . . .

---

* [Chief Justice Rehnquist and Justices Breyer and Kennedy joined all portions of this opinion reprinted here.—EDS.]

While not a constitutional prohibition on guidelines schemes, the majority's decision today exacts a substantial constitutional tax. [Facts] that historically have been taken into account by sentencing judges to assess a sentence within a broad range—such as drug quantity, role in the offense, risk of bodily harm—all must now be charged in an indictment and submitted to a jury simply because it is the legislature, rather than the judge, that constrains the extent to which such facts may be used to impose a sentence within a pre-existing statutory range. . . . The majority may be correct that States and the Federal Government will be willing to bear some of these costs. But simple economics dictate that they will not, and cannot, bear them all. To the extent that they do not, there will be an inevitable increase in judicial discretion with all of its attendant failings.

[The] guidelines served due process by providing notice to petitioner of the consequences of his acts; they vindicated his jury trial right by informing him of the stakes of risking trial; they served equal protection by ensuring petitioner that invidious characteristics such as race would not impact his sentence. Given these observations, it is difficult for me to discern what principle besides doctrinaire formalism actually motivates today's decision. . . .

The consequences of today's decision will be as far reaching as they are disturbing. Washington's sentencing system is by no means unique. Numerous other States have enacted guidelines systems, as has the Federal Government. Today's decision casts constitutional doubt over them all and, in so doing, threatens an untold number of criminal judgments. Every sentence imposed under such guidelines in cases currently pending on direct appeal is in jeopardy. . . . What I have feared most has now come to pass: Over 20 years of sentencing reform are all but lost, and tens of thousands of criminal judgments are in jeopardy. I respectfully dissent.

KENNEDY, J., dissenting.*

. . . The Court, in my respectful submission, disregards the fundamental principle under our constitutional system that different branches of government converse with each other on matters of vital common interest. . . . Case-by-case judicial determinations often yield intelligible patterns that can be refined by legislatures and codified into statutes or rules as general standards. As these legislative enactments are followed by incremental judicial interpretation, the legislatures may respond again, and the cycle repeats. This recurring dialogue, an essential source for the elaboration and the evolution of the law, is basic constitutional theory in action. . . . Sentencing guidelines are a prime example of this collaborative process. [Because] the Constitution does not prohibit the dynamic and fruitful dialogue between the judicial and legislative branches of government that has marked sentencing reform on both the state and the federal levels for more than 20 years, I dissent.

BREYER, J., dissenting.**

. . . As a result of the majority's rule, sentencing must now take one of three forms, each of which risks either impracticality, unfairness, or harm to the jury trial right the majority purports to strengthen. This circumstance shows that the majority's Sixth Amendment interpretation cannot be right. . . .

---

* [Justice Breyer joined this opinion.—EDS.]
** [Justice O'Connor joined this opinion.—EDS.]

A.

A first option for legislators is to create a simple, pure or nearly pure "charge offense" or "determinate" sentencing system. In such a system, an indictment would charge a few facts which, taken together, constitute a crime, such as robbery. Robbery would carry a single sentence, say, five years' imprisonment. . . .

Such a system assures uniformity, but at intolerable costs. First, simple determinate sentencing systems impose identical punishments on people who committed their crimes in very different ways. When dramatically different conduct ends up being punished the same way, an injustice has taken place. Simple determinate sentencing has the virtue of treating like cases alike, but it simultaneously fails to treat different cases differently. . . .

Second, in a world of statutorily fixed mandatory sentences for many crimes, determinate sentencing gives tremendous power to prosecutors to manipulate sentences through their choice of charges. Prosecutors can simply charge, or threaten to charge, defendants with crimes bearing higher mandatory sentences. Defendants, knowing that they will not have a chance to argue for a lower sentence in front of a judge, may plead to charges that they might otherwise contest. . . .

B.

A second option for legislators is to return to a system of indeterminate sentencing. . . . When such systems were in vogue, they were criticized, and rightly so, for producing unfair disparities, including race-based disparities, in the punishment of similarly situated defendants. [Under] such a system, the judge could vary the sentence greatly based upon his findings about how the defendant had committed the crime—findings that might not have been made by a "preponderance of the evidence," much less "beyond a reasonable doubt." Returning to such a system would . . . do little to ensure the control of what the majority calls "the people," i.e., the jury, "in the judiciary," since "the people" would only decide the defendant's guilt, a finding with no effect on the duration of the sentence. . . .

C.

A third option is that which the Court seems to believe legislators will in fact take. That is the option of retaining structured schemes that attempt to punish similar conduct similarly and different conduct differently, but modifying them to conform to *Apprendi*'s dictates. Judges would be able to depart downward from presumptive sentences upon finding that mitigating factors were present, but would not be able to depart upward unless the prosecutor charged the aggravating fact to a jury and proved it beyond a reasonable doubt. . . .

This option can be implemented in one of two ways. The first way would be for legislatures to subdivide each crime into a list of complex crimes, each of which would be defined to include commonly found sentencing factors such as drug quantity, type of victim, presence of violence, degree of injury, use of gun, and so on. A legislature, for example, might enact a robbery statute, modeled on robbery sentencing guidelines, that increases punishment depending upon (1) the nature of the institution robbed, (2) the (a) presence of, (b) brandishing of, (c) other use of, a firearm, (3) making of a death threat, (4) presence of (a) ordinary, (b) serious,

(c) permanent or life threatening, bodily injury, (5) abduction, (6) physical restraint, (7) taking of a firearm, (8) taking of drugs, (9) value of property loss, etc.

[Under this option, the] prosecutor, through control of the precise charge, controls the punishment, thereby marching the sentencing system directly away from, not toward, one important guideline goal: rough uniformity of punishment for those who engage in roughly the same real criminal conduct. . . .

This "complex charge offense" system . . . prejudices defendants who seek trial, for it can put them in the untenable position of contesting material aggravating facts in the guilt phases of their trials. Consider a defendant who is charged, not with mere possession of cocaine, but with the specific offense of possession of more than 500 grams of cocaine. Or consider a defendant charged, not with murder, but with the new crime of murder using a machete. Or consider a defendant whom the prosecution wants to claim was a "supervisor," rather than an ordinary gang member. How can a Constitution that guarantees due process put these defendants, as a matter of course, in the position of arguing, "I did not sell drugs, and if I did, I did not sell more than 500 grams" or, "I did not kill him, and if I did, I did not use a machete," or "I did not engage in gang activity, and certainly not as a supervisor" to a single jury? . . .

The majority announces that there really is no problem here because "States may continue to offer judicial factfinding as a matter of course to all defendants who plead guilty" and defendants may stipulate to the relevant facts or consent to judicial factfinding. [The] fairness problem arises because States may very well decide that they will not permit defendants to carve subsets of facts out of the new, *Apprendi*-required 17-element robbery crime, seeking a judicial determination as to some of those facts and a jury determination as to others. . . .

The second way to make sentencing guidelines *Apprendi*-compliant would be to require at least two juries for each defendant whenever aggravating facts are present: one jury to determine guilt of the crime charged, and an additional jury to try the disputed facts that, if found, would aggravate the sentence. Our experience with bifurcated trials in the capital punishment context suggests that requiring them for run-of-the-mill sentences would be costly, both in money and in judicial time and resources. . . . The Court can announce that the Constitution requires at least two jury trials for each criminal defendant—one for guilt, another for sentencing—but only because it knows full well that more than 90% of defendants will not go to trial even once, much less insist on two or more trials.

What will be the consequences of the Court's holding for the 90% of defendants who do not go to trial? The truthful answer is that we do not know. . . . At the least, the greater expense attached to trials and their greater complexity, taken together in the context of an overworked criminal justice system, will likely mean, other things being equal, fewer trials and a greater reliance upon plea bargaining—a system in which punishment is set not by judges or juries but by advocates acting under bargaining constraints. At the same time, the greater power of the prosecutor to control the punishment through the charge would likely weaken the relation between real conduct and real punishment as well. . . .

For more than a century, questions of punishment (not those of guilt or innocence) have reflected determinations made, not only by juries, but also by judges, probation officers, and executive parole boards. Such truth-seeking determinations have rested upon both adversarial and non-adversarial processes. The Court's holding undermines efforts to reform these processes, for it means that legislatures cannot both permit judges to base sentencing upon real conduct and seek, through guidelines, to make the results more uniform. . . .

Notes

1. *Juries and determinate sentencing laws.* The decision in *Blakely* created a great deal of upheaval in the state and federal courts. Defendants can insist that juries rather than judges find any facts that authorize an increase in the legally available range of sentences. The key appears to be appellate review: if a judge could be overturned on appeal for selecting a given sentence without establishing the existence of a given fact, the jury trial right attaches to that fact. This dynamic affects any "upward departures" from sentences designated in guidelines, if those guidelines have "presumptive" authority and are not simply voluntary for judges.

Within a few months, the Supreme Court ruled in United States v. Booker, 543 U.S. 220 (2005), that the federal sentencing guidelines were unconstitutional because they authorized judges to increase the available range of guideline sentences only after finding various facts about the offense, factual findings that a jury must make. The Court fashioned an unexpected remedy for this Sixth Amendment problem: It severed portions of the statute making the guidelines binding on judges, and thus declared the federal guidelines advisory. In so doing, the Court tried to ensure that the guidelines would continue to operate in a manner as close to the old system as possible: "district courts, while not bound to apply the Guidelines, must consult those Guidelines and take them into account when sentencing." Federal courts of appeals were still authorized by statute to review sentences, overturning any sentences that were not "reasonable."

The Supreme Court has remained active in fleshing out the implications of *Blakely* and *Booker* for the federal sentencing system. For a run-down of those decisions, along with a discussion of doctrinal twists such as the "prior record exception," go to the web extension for this chapter at *http://www.crimpro.com/extension/ch19*.

2. *Other factfinding that affects sentences served.* The effects of *Blakely* might not be limited to determinate sentencing structures. Justice Scalia's bold assertion that "every defendant has the *right* to insist that the prosecutor prove to a jury all facts legally essential to the punishment" could ultimately prove to be far reaching. Restitution orders, revocation of probation and parole, and a host of other punishment decisions that rest on nonjury factfinding may be subject to constitutional challenge. The *Apprendi* ruling also has implications for capital sentencing, which requires that "aggravating factors" be found before a court may impose the death penalty. See Ring v. Arizona, 536 U.S. 584 (2002) (jury rather than judge must find an aggravating circumstance necessary for imposing death penalty).

3. *Translation of jury functions to a new context.* For a judge who interprets the Constitution in light of the historical meaning of the text and historical practices, the right to a jury trial in criminal cases presents several challenges. The criminal system has changed enormously in the past few centuries, most recently in the increased role of guilty pleas and the enormous innovations in sentencing rules. How can courts in the twenty-first century give meaning to the constitutional vision of a criminal adjudication process that is bounded by the views of juries about reasonable application of the criminal law? See Montana v. Betterman, 136 S. Ct.

1609 (2016) (speedy trial guarantee protects the accused from arrest or indictment through trial, but does not apply once a defendant is found guilty at trial or pleads guilty to criminal charges).

Consider some of the ways that juries' involvement in sentencing might go beyond *Blakely*'s mandate. First, a legislature might require juries to be the finders of all (or at least all significant) sentencing facts. Second, a legislature might want juries not only to find facts but also to advise judges about appropriate punishments or even to impose specific punishments. Suppose you are advising a sentencing commission in a jurisdiction with sentencing guidelines affected by *Apprendi* and *Blakely*. What changes would you advise the commission to make to comply with these cases?

4. *Minimum sentences, discretionary sentencing, and mitigating adjustments.* The *Blakely* holding now extends to mandatory minimum sentences. In Alleyne v. United States, 570 U.S. 99 (2013), the Court finally confirmed that any fact necessary to support an increased mandatory minimum sentence for a crime is an "element" of the crime that must be submitted to jury, rather than a "sentencing factor." The issue of whether a defendant brandished a firearm in connection with a crime of violence must be resolved by a jury because under federal law it could elevate the mandatory minimum term for a firearms offense from five to seven years.

Despite the breadth of *Blakely*'s holding and dicta, however, the ruling still allows judicial factfinding in an array of sentencing settings. *Blakely* formally distinguished Williams v. New York, 337 U.S. 241 (1949), which permits judges to find facts in the course of making discretionary sentencing determinations. In addition, the *Apprendi* and *Blakely* rulings apply only to facts that increase sentences; judges may still find facts that the law provides as the basis for *decreasing* sentences. Could a jurisdiction, drawing on these gaps in the reach of the *Blakely* rule, construct a sound sentencing system that is still administered principally through judicial factfinding? Should a jurisdiction aspire to do so?

5. *Standard of proof at sentencing: majority position.* In McMillan v. Pennsylvania, 477 U.S. 79 (1986), the Court declared that the federal due process clause allows states to prove some facts affecting the sentence by a preponderance of the evidence. Although *Blakely* changed which facts could be found by a judge at the sentencing hearing rather than by a jury at trial, the Court did not overturn the standard of proof to be used in the sentencing hearing.

Nearly all states have adopted by statute the preponderance standard for facts to be proven at sentencing. Structured sentencing systems in the states typically provide for a presumptive guideline sentence that is set by reference to the facts underlying a conviction, either proven beyond a reasonable doubt at trial or admitted by the defendant in a guilty plea. Yet these guidelines also allow judges, in varying degrees, to depart from the sentence indicated in the guidelines. The departure might be based on facts proven at the sentencing hearing, and most require the prosecution to show these facts only by a preponderance.

6. *Rules of evidence at sentencing.* Williams v. New York established that the rules of evidence for criminal trials need not apply in sentencing hearings. This is true both for indeterminate sentencing systems and for most structured sentencing systems. The Federal Rules of Evidence state this explicitly: "The rules (other than with respect to privileges) do not apply in . . . sentencing." Fed. R. Evid. 1101(d)(3). The federal sentencing guidelines also adopt this position: "any information may be considered, so long as it has sufficient indicia of reliability to support its probable

accuracy." U.S. Sentencing Guidelines §6A1.3(a). The rules do not apply because of the perceived burden they would place on sentencing judges, converting the sentencing hearing into a second trial. Should Congress or the U.S. Sentencing Commission change positions and apply the rules of evidence to sentencing hearings?

4. Revisiting Jury Verdicts and Guilty Pleas

Because the judge decides the defendant's sentence independently, an opportunity exists to revisit questions that were already answered in the jury's verdict after trial or in the defendant's plea of guilty. To what extent should a sentencing judge fashion a sentence to reward a plea of guilty or to punish a decision to go to trial? What should the sentencing judge do when the jury acquits on some counts and convicts on at least one other count, yet the judge believes that the defendant probably committed all the crimes as charged?

■ U.S. SENTENCING GUIDELINES §3E1.1

(a) If the defendant clearly demonstrates acceptance of responsibility for his offense, decrease the offense level by 2 levels.

(b) If the defendant qualifies for a decrease under subsection (a), the offense [is serious enough to qualify for a level 16 or greater], and the defendant has assisted authorities in the investigation or prosecution of his own misconduct by taking one or more of the following steps:

(1) timely providing complete information to the government concerning his own involvement in the offense; or

(2) timely notifying authorities of his intention to enter a plea of guilty, thereby permitting the government to avoid preparing for trial and permitting the court to allocate its resources efficiently, decrease the offense level by 1 additional level.

Notes

1. *Sentencing after refusal to plead guilty: majority position.* In a plea agreement a defendant agrees to waive trial, normally in exchange for some perceived advantage at the time of sentencing. In unstructured sentencing systems, judges almost always accept a plea bargain if offered by the parties, but it is not clear what effect the defendant's willingness to plead guilty has on the sentence. Research has shown that defendants pleading guilty tend to receive substantially lower sentences than defendants who go to trial (in some studies the "plea discount" has been one-third or more off posttrial sentences) but that judges tend to sentence based on the original charges filed rather than the charges forming the basis of the guilty plea. A review of this research appears on the web extension for this chapter at *http://www.crimpro. com/extension/ch19.*

Almost all high state courts say that a sentencing court cannot punish a refusal to plead guilty but can enhance a punishment based on "lack of remorse" or failure

to "accept responsibility" for a crime. Jennings v. State, 664 A.2d 903 (Md. 1995). Courts routinely treat an agreement to plead guilty as an appropriate reason for imposing a less severe sentence. In practice, is there a difference between "punishing the exercise of trial rights" and "rewarding acceptance of responsibility"? Do these rules encourage judges to do anything more than choose their words carefully?

2. *Plea bargaining and structured sentencing rules.* Section 3E1.1 of the federal sentencing guidelines, reprinted above, allows the sentencing judge to reduce a sentence for "acceptance of responsibility," while commentary to that guideline provision insists that courts should not equate acceptance of responsibility with a decision to plead guilty. Rules in various structured sentencing systems give sentencing judges different instructions about the impact of a plea agreement. The possibilities range from rules saying that plea agreements should not change the sentence at all to rules that allow the judge to accept the sentencing recommendations of the parties within certain broad limits. For instance, under the Minnesota sentencing guidelines, judges must impose the sentence indicated in the guideline grid unless there is a valid ground for departure. A plea agreement, standing alone, is not a sufficient reason to depart from the guidelines. In Washington state, statutory guidelines tell the judge to "determine if the agreement is consistent with the interests of justice and with the [statutory] prosecuting standards" and to reject the agreement if it is not. Wash. Rev. Code §9.94A.431. The federal sentencing guidelines also advise judges to limit the impact of a guilty plea at sentencing. The court may accept sentencing recommendations offered in a plea agreement "if the court is satisfied either that: (1) the recommended sentence is within the applicable guideline range; or (2) the recommended sentence departs from the applicable guideline range for justifiable reasons." U.S. Sentencing Guidelines §6B1.2(b).

3. *Sentence enhancements for perjury and obstruction of justice at trial.* Judges who preside at trial also typically impose the sentence on the same defendant after conviction. In United States v. Dunnigan, 507 U.S. 87 (1993), the Court concluded that a sentencing court can enhance a defendant's sentence by a designated amount under the federal guidelines if the court finds that the defendant committed perjury at trial. A defendant's right to testify "does not include a right to commit perjury." To reduce the risk that a court will wrongfully punish a truthful defendant, the court must make "findings to support all the elements of a perjury violation in the specific case." Does the sentencing judge's power to punish perjury without a perjury conviction punish the right to trial? Compare Mitchell v. United States, 526 U.S. 314 (1999) (guilty plea does not extinguish the defendant's Fifth Amendment right to remain silent at sentencing).

4. *Acquitted conduct at sentencing.* Although indeterminate sentencing systems typically allow judges to consider prior misconduct when setting a sentence, many states make an exception for acquitted conduct—conduct that formed the basis for a charge resulting in an acquittal at trial. Judges in many states have developed common law rules preventing the use of acquitted conduct at sentencing. See Bishop v. State, 486 S.E.2d 887 (Ga. 1997); State v. Cobb, 732 A.2d 425 (N.H. 1999). On the other hand, a roughly equal number of states approve the use of acquitted conduct. State v. Huey, 505 A.2d 1242 (Conn. 1986); State v. Leiter, 646 N.W.2d 341 (Wis. 2002). Why do so many states limit the use of acquitted conduct but permit

sentencing judges to consider prior convictions and prior uncharged conduct more generally?

The Supreme Court in United States v. Watts, 519 U.S. 148 (1997), ruled that neither the Constitution nor the federal sentencing statutes or guidelines bar a judge from considering acquitted conduct at sentencing. In that case, police discovered cocaine in a kitchen cabinet and two loaded guns in a bedroom closet of Watts's house. The jury acquitted Watts of the firearms charge but convicted him of drug possession. The judge increased Watts's sentence on the drug charges after finding by a preponderance of the evidence that Watts had possessed the weapons illegally. The Court explained the use of information underlying acquittals in terms of the different standards of proof at trial and sentencing: Evidence that was insufficient to establish guilt beyond a reasonable doubt might nevertheless be enough to convince the judge to enhance a sentence. In effect, this allows the sentencing judge to ignore the verdict of the jury. See also Edwards v. United States, 523 U.S. 511 (1998) (sentencing judge can determine that defendants were trafficking in both crack and powder, even if jury believed defendants were trafficking only in powder). Do the rulings in *Watts* and *Edwards* survive the later decisions in *Apprendi* and *Blakely*?

5. *"Vindictive" sentencing after retrial.* Just as courts insist that a sentence may not be increased to punish a defendant for exercising the right to trial, federal and state courts say that a trial judge may not punish a defendant for exercising the statutory right to appeal. If a defendant successfully appeals a conviction and is convicted again after retrial, a sentence higher than the original sentence imposed is presumed to be a product of "vindictiveness" by the sentencing judge. A sentence motivated by such vindictiveness violates federal due process. The judge must rebut this presumption by placing on the record his reasons for increasing the sentence after the second conviction. See North Carolina v. Pearce, 395 U.S. 711 (1969). According to *Pearce*, those reasons could be based on "objective information concerning identifiable conduct on the part of the defendant occurring after the time of the original sentence proceeding." Later, the Court said that a court could rebut the presumption of vindictiveness by pointing to any "objective information" that the court did not consider during the first sentencing proceeding. Texas v. McCullough, 475 U.S. 134 (1986).

6. *Probation officers.* Judges who sentence a defendant after a guilty plea have not heard an extensive presentation of the evidence at trial and thus depend heavily on the pre-sentence investigation (PSI) report to inform them about the offender and the offense. Especially in structured sentencing systems in which particular facts have an identifiable impact on the sentence, probation officers (who create the PSI reports) are critical players in the sentencing process. How might a prosecutor or a defense attorney influence the recommendations of the probation officer? What institutional or individual biases might the probation officer bring to her assessment (and recommendation) of proper sentences? Compare Simon Halliday et al., Street-Level Bureaucracy, Interprofessional Relations, and Coping Mechanisms: A Study of Criminal Justice Social Workers in the Sentencing Process, 31 Law & Pol'y 405 (2009). For a more complete picture of the role of probation officers in the process of collecting facts relevant to the sentence, go to the web extension for this chapter at *http://www.crimpro.com/ extension/ch19.*

Problem 19-7. Trial Penalty or Reward for Plea?

An experienced police officer watched Milton Coles speak with another person and give that person currency in exchange for a ziploc plastic bag, which the latter retrieved from a hiding place in a nearby tree. A jury found Coles guilty of one count of possessing marijuana. At sentencing, the trial judge made the following statement:

> I never understood why you went to trial in this case, Mr. Coles. Your lawyer did the best he could with no defense at all. I was amazed how successfully he was able to even come up with something plausible. If you had come before the Court and said, "Look, I had a little stuff on me and I needed a little extra money," I would have had some sympathy for you. As it is, though, I don't have any sympathy for you at all. So the Court sentences you to one year.

One year was the maximum available sentence for this offense. Coles has challenged the validity of this sentence, because he claims that the judge penalized him for exercising his constitutional right to stand trial. How would you rule on appeal? Compare Coles v. United States, 682 A.2d 167 (D.C. 1996).

D. RACE AND SENTENCING

Race is an unavoidable part of modern American criminal procedure. Difficult questions arise at all stages of the criminal process: What is the role of race in stops and investigations? Can race be an element in the determination of reasonable suspicion or probable cause? When are racial disparities sufficient to justify challenges to charging practices? What role should race play in jury selection? In arguments at trial?

Previous chapters have explored these and other questions about the role that race plays in decisions throughout the criminal process. But perhaps the most common and visible questions about race arise at the end of the process, in the form of claims that black Americans and other minorities are punished more severely than whites. This section considers the charge that racism is an inherent part of the criminal justice process and that its end product is unequal punishment. In some situations, the responsible decisionmakers may be identifiable; in other situations, the source of racial disparities may be hard to specify even when disparity clearly exists.

Discussion of race and punishment must start with some disquieting facts about prison and jail populations. In 2016, 41 percent of the inmates in state and federal prisons were African American, although African Americans constitute only about 13 percent of the population. The rate of imprisonment for black males was about 1,609 per 100,000, while the rate for Hispanic males was 857 per 100,000; the comparable rate for white males was 274 per 100,000. Bureau of Justice Statistics, Prisoners in 2016 (January 2018, NCJ 251149). After combining the number of young men on probation or parole with the number in prison or jail, almost a third of young black men are under criminal justice supervision on any given day. African American women remain the fastest growing group in prisons and jails. Drug policies have contributed more than any other crimes to the fast growth in the imprisonment rate for African Americans.

These materials provoke a recurring question: Does the criminal justice system exacerbate or mediate larger social problems? Can criminal justice systems respond to intentional or unintentional racial bias in society? If so, what is the proper role for courts, police, prosecutors, and legislators in crafting such a response?

1. Race and the Victims of Crime

The influence of race on punishment has received the most sustained attention in the context of capital punishment. Many facets of the story of race in American capital punishment emerge in the story of Warren McCleskey and his extraordinary trip through the criminal justice system.

On the morning of May 13, 1978, McCleskey drove to pick up Ben Wright, Bernard Dupree, and David Burney. The four men planned to commit a robbery; they drove from Marietta, Georgia, into Atlanta and decided on the Dixie Furniture Store as a target. McCleskey had a .38 caliber Rossi nickel-plated revolver, which he had stolen in an armed robbery of a grocery store a month earlier. Ben Wright carried a sawed-off shotgun, and the two others had blue steel pistols. McCleskey, who was black, entered the front of the store, and the other three came through the rear by the loading dock. He secured the front of the store by forcing all the customers and employees there to lie on the floor while the other robbers rounded up the employees in the rear and began to bind them with tape. A pistol was taken from George Malcom, an employee, at gunpoint. Before all the employees were tied up, Officer Frank Schlatt, answering a silent alarm, stopped his patrol car in front of the building. Officer Schlatt, who was white, entered the front door and proceeded about 15 feet down the center aisle, where he was shot twice, once in the face and once in the chest. The head wound was fatal. The robbers fled. Sometime later, McCleskey was arrested in Cobb County in connection with another armed robbery. He confessed to the Dixie Furniture Store robbery but denied the shooting. Ballistics showed that Schlatt had been shot by a .38 caliber Rossi revolver. The weapon was never recovered.

McCleskey was convicted in 1978. The jury found two aggravating circumstances that authorized the use of the death penalty: (1) the murder was committed while the offender was committing another capital felony (armed robbery), and (2) the murder was committed against a police officer engaged in the performance of his official duties. The jury sentenced McCleskey to death for murder. Co-defendant Burney was sentenced to life imprisonment, while another co-defendant received a 20-year sentence.

On direct appeal in the Georgia courts, McCleskey first raised the claim that the death penalty violates the due process and equal protection provisions of the federal and state constitutions because prosecutorial discretion permits the government to apply the penalty in a racially discriminatory way. The Georgia Supreme Court rejected this claim as follows: "Appellant's argument is without merit. Gregg v. Georgia, 428 U.S. 153 (1976); Moore v. State, 243 S.E.2d 1 (Ga. 1978)." McCleskey v. State, 263 S.E.2d 146 (Ga. 1980).

Eventually, McCleskey took his claims to federal court: The U.S. district court had the power, under the venerable Habeas Corpus Act of 1867, 28 U.S.C. §2254, to invalidate state convictions obtained in violation of the federal constitution. In federal district court, McCleskey presented the findings of a massive statistical study, dubbed the "Baldus" study (named after its principal author, Professor David Baldus of the University of Iowa). The study analyzed almost 2,500 murder and voluntary manslaughter convictions for crimes committed (or for defendants arrested) between 1973 and 1978 in Georgia. For a random sample of these cases, researchers answered more than 500 questions about each case, such as the defendant's mental and physical condition, the defendant's race and other demographic information, the defendant's prior criminal record, the method of killing, the victim's role in the offense, and so forth. Due to the large number of variables, the researchers could not match many cases that differed in only one respect (for instance, cases that were identical in every respect, except one defendant shot the victim twice while the other defendant shot the victim only once). Thus, they used a statistical technique known as "multivariate regression analysis" to estimate the amount of influence each feature of the case had on the ultimate decision of whether the defendant received the death penalty.

The study concluded that the race of the defendant was not a "statistically significant" factor in the outcome, after "controlling" for all the other factors that could influence the outcome. However, the race of the *victim* remained one of the most important influences on the outcome, even after controlling for other factors.

The district court decided that the study did not establish the intentional discrimination necessary to show a violation of equal protection because the study was flawed. For instance, the court pointed to several errors in the collection of data and noted that "the questionnaire could not capture every nuance of every case." The court also suggested that the study had not successfully isolated the effects of race but instead measured the effects of other permissible factors that were "correlated" with race. McCleskey v. Zant, 580 F. Supp. 338 (N.D. Ga. 1984).

The federal court of appeals took a different approach to the question. It was willing to assume that the study successfully demonstrated "what it purports to prove": Defendants who kill a white victim have a greater chance of receiving the death penalty, and part of that increased risk is based on the race of the victim. Nevertheless, the court of appeals said that this statistical evidence was not enough for McCleskey to prove intentional racial discrimination in his case. When a party relies on statistical patterns of discrimination, the court said, it must show such large racial disparities that the evidence "compels a conclusion that . . . purposeful discrimination . . . can be presumed to permeate the system." The estimated effects of the race of the victim on the death penalty decision were not enough to compel such a conclusion. Indeed, the court said, any statistical study would have difficulty making such a showing about a complex process involving many different decisionmakers. McCleskey v. Kemp, 753 F.2d 877 (11th Cir. 1985). McCleskey then appealed to the U.S. Supreme Court.

■ WARREN McCLESKEY v. RALPH KEMP

481 U.S. 279 (1987)

POWELL, J.*

This case presents the question whether a complex statistical study that indicates a risk that racial considerations enter into capital sentencing determinations

---

* [Chief Justice Rehnquist and Justices White, O'Connor, and Scalia joined this opinion.—EDS.]

proves that petitioner McCleskey's capital sentence is unconstitutional under the Eighth or Fourteenth Amendment.

I.

[In support of his habeas claim], McCleskey proffered a statistical study performed by Professors David Baldus, Charles Pulaski, and George Woodworth (the Baldus study) that purports to show a disparity in the imposition of the death sentence in Georgia based on the race of the murder victim and, to a lesser extent, the race of the defendant. The Baldus study is actually two sophisticated statistical studies that examine over 2,000 murder cases that occurred in Georgia during the 1970's. The raw numbers collected by Professor Baldus indicate that defendants charged with killing white persons received the death penalty in 11% of the cases, but defendants charged with killing blacks received the death penalty in only 1% of the cases. . . . Baldus also divided the cases according to the combination of the race of the defendant and the race of the victim. He found that the death penalty was assessed in 22% of the cases involving black defendants and white victims; 8% of the cases involving white defendants and white victims; 1% of the cases involving black defendants and black victims; and 3% of the cases involving white defendants and black victims. . . .

Baldus subjected his data to an extensive analysis, taking account of 230 variables that could have explained the disparities on nonracial grounds. One of his models concludes that, even after taking account of 39 nonracial variables, defendants charged with killing white victims were 4.3 times as likely to receive a death sentence as defendants charged with killing blacks. . . . Thus, the Baldus study indicates that black defendants, such as McCleskey, who kill white victims have the greatest likelihood of receiving the death penalty. . . .

II.

McCleskey's first claim is that the Georgia capital punishment statute violates the Equal Protection Clause of the Fourteenth Amendment.[7] He argues that race has infected the administration of Georgia's statute. . . . McCleskey's claim of discrimination extends to every actor in the Georgia capital sentencing process, from the prosecutor who sought the death penalty and the jury that imposed the sentence, to the State itself that enacted the capital punishment statute and allows it to remain in effect despite its allegedly discriminatory application. [This] claim must fail.

A.

[To] prevail under the Equal Protection Clause, McCleskey must prove that the decisionmakers in his case acted with discriminatory purpose. He offers no evidence

---

7 [We] assume the study is valid statistically without reviewing the factual findings of the District Court. Our assumption that the Baldus study is statistically valid does not include the assumption that the study shows that racial considerations actually enter into any sentencing decisions in Georgia. Even a sophisticated multiple-regression analysis such as the Baldus study can only demonstrate a risk that the factor of race entered into some capital sentencing decisions and a necessarily lesser risk that race entered into any particular sentencing decision.

specific to his own case that would support an inference that racial considerations played a part in his sentence. Instead, he . . . argues that the Baldus study compels an inference that his sentence rests on purposeful discrimination. McCleskey's claim that these statistics are sufficient proof of discrimination, without regard to the facts of a particular case, would extend to all capital cases in Georgia, at least where the victim was white and the defendant is black.

The Court has accepted statistics as proof of intent to discriminate in certain limited contexts. First, this Court has accepted statistical disparities as proof of an equal protection violation in the selection of the jury venire in a particular district. Although statistical proof normally must present a "stark" pattern to be accepted as the sole proof of discriminatory intent under the Constitution, because of the nature of the jury-selection task, we have permitted a finding of constitutional violation even when the statistical pattern does not approach such extremes. Second, this Court has accepted statistics in the form of multiple-regression analysis to prove statutory violations under Title VII of the Civil Rights Act of 1964.

But the nature of the capital sentencing decision, and the relationship of the statistics to that decision, are fundamentally different from the corresponding elements in the venire-selection or Title VII cases. Most importantly, each particular decision to impose the death penalty is made by a petit jury selected from a properly constituted venire. Each jury is unique in its composition, and the Constitution requires that its decision rest on consideration of innumerable factors that vary according to the characteristics of the individual defendant and the facts of the particular capital offense. Thus, the application of an inference drawn from the general statistics to a specific decision in a trial and sentencing simply is not comparable to the application of an inference drawn from general statistics to a specific venire-selection or Title VII case. In those cases, the statistics relate to fewer entities, and fewer variables are relevant to the challenged decisions.

Another important difference between the cases in which we have accepted statistics as proof of discriminatory intent and this case is that, in the venire-selection and Title VII contexts, the decisionmaker has an opportunity to explain the statistical disparity. Here, the State has no practical opportunity to rebut the Baldus study. Controlling considerations of public policy dictate that jurors cannot be called to testify to the motives and influences that led to their verdict. Similarly, the policy considerations behind a prosecutor's traditionally wide discretion suggest the impropriety of our requiring prosecutors to defend their decisions to seek death penalties, often years after they were made.[17] Moreover, absent far stronger proof, it is unnecessary to seek such a rebuttal, because a legitimate and unchallenged explanation for the decision is apparent from the record: McCleskey committed an act for which the United States Constitution and Georgia laws permit imposition of the death penalty.

Finally, McCleskey's statistical proffer must be viewed in the context of his challenge. McCleskey challenges decisions at the heart of the State's criminal justice system. One of society's most basic tasks is that of protecting the lives of its citizens and one of the most basic ways in which it achieves the task is through criminal laws against murder. Implementation of these laws necessarily requires discretionary

---

17. Requiring a prosecutor to rebut a study that analyzes the past conduct of scores of prosecutors is quite different from requiring a prosecutor to rebut a contemporaneous challenge to his own acts. See Batson v. Kentucky, 476 U.S. 79 (1986).

judgments. Because discretion is essential to the criminal justice process, we would demand exceptionally clear proof before we would infer that the discretion has been abused. . . . Accordingly, we hold that the Baldus study is clearly insufficient to support an inference that any of the decisionmakers in McCleskey's case acted with discriminatory purpose. . . .

IV.

B.

[McCleskey also] contends that the Georgia capital punishment system is arbitrary and capricious in application, and therefore his sentence is excessive [and contrary to the Eighth Amendment], because racial considerations may influence capital sentencing decisions in Georgia. . . . To evaluate McCleskey's challenge, we must examine exactly what the Baldus study may show. Even Professor Baldus does not contend that his statistics prove that race enters into any capital sentencing decisions or that race was a factor in McCleskey's particular case. Statistics at most may show only a likelihood that a particular factor entered into some decisions. There is, of course, some risk of racial prejudice influencing a jury's decision in a criminal case. There are similar risks that other kinds of prejudice will influence other criminal trials. The question is at what point that risk becomes constitutionally unacceptable. McCleskey asks us to accept the likelihood allegedly shown by the Baldus study as the constitutional measure of an unacceptable risk of racial prejudice influencing capital sentencing decisions. This we decline to do.

Because of the risk that the factor of race may enter the criminal justice process, we have engaged in "unceasing efforts" to eradicate racial prejudice from our criminal justice system.[30] [However,] McCleskey's argument that the Constitution condemns the discretion allowed decisionmakers in the Georgia capital sentencing system is antithetical to the fundamental role of discretion in our criminal justice system. Discretion in the criminal justice system offers substantial benefits to the criminal defendant. Not only can a jury decline to impose the death sentence, it can decline to convict or choose to convict of a lesser offense. Whereas decisions against a defendant's interest may be reversed by the trial judge or on appeal, these discretionary exercises of leniency are final and unreviewable. Similarly, the capacity of prosecutorial discretion to provide individualized justice is firmly entrenched in American law. As we have noted, a prosecutor can decline to charge, offer a plea bargain, or decline to seek a death sentence in any particular case. Of course, the power to be lenient also is the power to discriminate, but a capital punishment system that did not allow for discretionary acts of leniency would be totally alien to our notions of criminal justice. . . .

---

30. This Court has repeatedly stated that prosecutorial discretion cannot be exercised on the basis of race. Nor can a prosecutor exercise peremptory challenges on the basis of race. More generally, this Court has condemned state efforts to exclude blacks from grand and petit juries. Other protections apply to the trial and jury deliberation process. Widespread bias in the community can make a change of venue constitutionally required. The Constitution prohibits racially biased prosecutorial arguments. If the circumstances of a particular case indicate a significant likelihood that racial bias may influence a jury, the Constitution requires questioning as to such bias. Finally, in a capital sentencing hearing, a defendant convicted of an interracial murder is entitled to such questioning without regard to the circumstances of the particular case.

C.

At most, the Baldus study indicates a discrepancy that appears to correlate with race. Apparent disparities in sentencing are an inevitable part of our criminal justice system. [There] can be no perfect procedure for deciding in which cases governmental authority should be used to impose death. Despite these imperfections, our consistent rule has been that constitutional guarantees are met when the mode for determining guilt or punishment itself has been surrounded with safeguards to make it as fair as possible. Where the discretion that is fundamental to our criminal process is involved, we decline to assume that what is unexplained is invidious. In light of the safeguards designed to minimize racial bias in the process, the fundamental value of jury trial in our criminal justice system, and the benefits that discretion provides to criminal defendants, we hold that the Baldus study does not demonstrate a constitutionally significant risk of racial bias affecting the Georgia capital sentencing process.

V.

Two additional concerns inform our decision in this case. First, McCleskey's claim, taken to its logical conclusion, throws into serious question the principles that underlie our entire criminal justice system. The Eighth Amendment is not limited in application to capital punishment, but applies to all penalties. Thus, if we accepted McCleskey's claim that racial bias has impermissibly tainted the capital sentencing decision, we could soon be faced with similar claims as to other types of penalty. Moreover, the claim that his sentence rests on the irrelevant factor of race easily could be extended to apply to claims based on unexplained discrepancies that correlate to membership in other minority groups, and even to gender. Similarly, since McCleskey's claim relates to the race of his victim, other claims could apply with equally logical force to statistical disparities that correlate with the race or sex of other actors in the criminal justice system, such as defense attorneys or judges. Also, there is no logical reason that such a claim need be limited to racial or sexual bias. If arbitrary and capricious punishment is the touchstone under the Eighth Amendment, such a claim could—at least in theory—be based upon any arbitrary variable, such as the defendant's facial characteristics, or the physical attractiveness of the defendant or the victim, that some statistical study indicates may be influential in jury decisionmaking. As these examples illustrate, there is no limiting principle to the type of challenge brought by McCleskey. . . .

Second, McCleskey's arguments are best presented to the legislative bodies. It is not the responsibility—or indeed even the right—of this Court to determine the appropriate punishment for particular crimes. It is the legislatures, the elected representatives of the people, that are constituted to respond to the will and consequently the moral values of the people. Legislatures also are better qualified to weigh and evaluate the results of statistical studies in terms of their own local conditions and with a flexibility of approach that is not available to the courts. Capital punishment is now the law in more than two-thirds of our States. It is the ultimate duty of courts to determine on a case-by-case basis whether these laws are applied consistently with the Constitution. Despite McCleskey's wide-ranging arguments that basically challenge the validity of capital punishment in our multiracial society, the only question before us is whether in his case the law of Georgia was properly applied. [This] was carefully and correctly done in this case. . . .

BRENNAN, J., dissenting.*

. . . *II.*

At some point in this case, Warren McCleskey doubtless asked his lawyer whether a jury was likely to sentence him to die. A candid reply to this question would have been disturbing. First, counsel would have to tell McCleskey that few of the details of the crime or of McCleskey's past criminal conduct were more important than the fact that his victim was white. Furthermore, counsel would feel bound to tell McCleskey that defendants charged with killing white victims in Georgia are 4.3 times as likely to be sentenced to death as defendants charged with killing blacks. In addition, frankness would compel the disclosure that it was more likely than not that the race of McCleskey's victim would determine whether he received a death sentence: 6 of every 11 defendants convicted of killing a white person would not have received the death penalty if their victims had been black, while, among defendants with aggravating and mitigating factors comparable to McCleskey's, 20 of every 34 would not have been sentenced to die if their victims had been black. Finally, the assessment would not be complete without the information that cases involving black defendants and white victims are more likely to result in a death sentence than cases featuring any other racial combination of defendant and victim. The story could be told in a variety of ways, but McCleskey could not fail to grasp its essential narrative line: there was a significant chance that race would play a prominent role in determining if he lived or died. . . .

III.

C.

Evaluation of McCleskey's evidence cannot rest solely on the numbers themselves. We must also ask whether the conclusion suggested by those numbers is consonant with our understanding of history and human experience. Georgia's legacy of a race-conscious criminal justice system, as well as this Court's own recognition of the persistent danger that racial attitudes may affect criminal proceedings, indicates that McCleskey's claim is not a fanciful product of mere statistical artifice.

For many years, Georgia operated openly and formally precisely the type of dual system the evidence shows is still effectively in place. The criminal law expressly differentiated between crimes committed by and against blacks and whites, distinctions whose lineage traced back to the time of slavery. During the colonial period, black slaves who killed whites in Georgia, regardless of whether in self-defense or in defense of another, were automatically executed. A. Higginbotham, In the Matter of Color: Race in the American Legal Process 256 (1978). By the time of the Civil War, a dual system of crime and punishment was well established in Georgia. See Ga.

---

* [Justices Marshall, Blackmun, and Stevens joined the portions of this opinion reprinted here.— EDS.]

Penal Code (1861). The state criminal code contained separate sections for "Slaves and Free Persons of Color," and for all other persons. . . .

IV.

The Court . . . states that its unwillingness to regard petitioner's evidence as sufficient is based in part on the fear that recognition of McCleskey's claim would open the door to widespread challenges to all aspects of criminal sentencing. Taken on its face, such a statement seems to suggest a fear of too much justice. Yet surely the majority would acknowledge that if striking evidence indicated that other minority groups, or women, or even persons with blond hair, were disproportionately sentenced to death, such a state of affairs would be repugnant to deeply rooted conceptions of fairness. The prospect that there may be more widespread abuse than McCleskey documents may be dismaying, but it does not justify complete abdication of our judicial role. . . .

In fairness, the Court's fear that McCleskey's claim is an invitation to descend a slippery slope also rests on the realization that any humanly imposed system of penalties will exhibit some imperfection. Yet to reject McCleskey's powerful evidence on this basis is to ignore both the qualitatively different character of the death penalty and the particular repugnance of racial discrimination, considerations which may properly be taken into account in determining whether various punishments are "cruel and unusual." Furthermore, it fails to take account of the unprecedented refinement and strength of the Baldus study.

V.

In more recent times, we have sought to free ourselves from the burden of [our history of racial discrimination]. Yet it has been scarcely a generation since this Court's first decision striking down racial segregation, and barely two decades since the legislative prohibition of racial discrimination in major domains of national life. These have been honorable steps, but we cannot pretend that in three decades we have completely escaped the grip of a historical legacy spanning centuries. Warren McCleskey's evidence confronts us with the subtle and persistent influence of the past. His message is a disturbing one to a society that has formally repudiated racism, and a frustrating one to a Nation accustomed to regarding its destiny as the product of its own will. Nonetheless, we ignore him at our peril, for we remain imprisoned by the past as long as we deny its influence in the present. . . .

Notes

1. *Victim's race or defendant's race?* Note that the Baldus study found that the race of the *defendant* had no statistically significant effect on the use of capital punishment. In Furman v. Georgia, 408 U.S. 238 (1972), the Supreme Court struck down several capital punishment statutes, declaring that the death penalty (as administered at that time) was "cruel and unusual punishment" and a violation of the Eighth Amendment. Among the many reasons for this decision discussed in the various concurring opinions, several of the justices argued that capital punishment could not stand because it was imposed disproportionately against the poor and

racial minorities. Would the Supreme Court have reached a different outcome in *McCleskey* if the Baldus study had pointed to racial discrimination based on the race of the defendant rather than the race of the victim? Can a punishment be racially discriminatory if the government imposes it equally on defendants of all races?

2. *Other venues.* Suppose that on the day after the district court issued its order, the NAACP sends a copy of the Baldus study to a member of the Georgia legislature, and that member distributes copies. As the chair of the senate's committee on criminal justice matters, would you hold hearings? If so, what would be the topic of the hearings—the validity of the study or the most appropriate response to the study? If the Supreme Court had concluded instead that the influence of race in Georgia's capital punishment system rendered McCleskey's sentence unconstitutional, how would you advise Georgia legislators and prosecutors to respond? Would a victory for McCleskey mean abolition of the death penalty in Georgia?

3. *Adequate proof of discrimination.* If racial discrimination does influence some decisionmakers, to some degree, in some cases, how might one demonstrate that fact in a court of law? Both the court of appeals and the Supreme Court concluded that a stronger statistical showing would be necessary before racial influences in sentencing would amount to a constitutional problem. What sort of evidence did the courts have in mind? See State v. Harris, 786 N.W.2d 409 (Wis. 2010) (during sentencing of drug defendant, judge remarked on large number of unemployed and uneducated male defendants who lived with women who were working full time and going to school, and referred to defendant's "baby mama"; in determination of whether judge improperly considered race in sentencing, defendant must prove by clear and convincing evidence that the judge actually relied on race, and not simply whether a reasonable observer might perceive that the judge considered race).

The "race of the victim" effect that appeared in the Baldus study in Georgia has also appeared in statistical studies of other states. These claims have gotten very little serious attention from courts; many simply cite *McCleskey* with no further discussion in refusing to consider the studies as relevant evidence of racial discrimination in the use of capital punishment. See People v. Davis, 518 N.E.2d 78 (Ill. 1987). For a review of the most recent statistical studies of the racially disparate impact of capital punishment, go to the web extension for this chapter at *http://www.crimpro.com/extension/ch19.*

4. *Hate crimes.* The substantive criminal code in many jurisdictions directly addresses the race of the victim by increasing penalties for "hate crimes," or crimes motivated in part by the race of the victim. For an in-depth treatment of the subject, see James B. Jacobs & Kimberly Potter, Hate Crimes: Criminal Law and Identity Politics (2000).

2. Race and Discretionary Decisions Affecting Punishment

Racial disparities at sentencing can result from decisions made by actors at early stages of the criminal justice process. A strong bias in investigations or arrests may be passed through and perhaps even validated by studies showing unbiased decision making at a later stage of the process. For example, if whites and blacks who are convicted of a particular offense are punished identically, but members of one race are disproportionately investigated, then the sanction will appear neutral but will in fact be highly disparate, because the investigatory practices do not accurately reflect actual underlying behavior. It is not only police decisions that can generate sharp disparities that are passed through the system: Prosecutors may disproportionately direct cases involving members of one race to state court and identical allegations involving another race to federal court, where very different punishments attach to analogous state and federal charges. Or prosecutors may offer pleas in a racially disproportionate fashion.

This section highlights the difficulty of proving the source of discriminatory effects in large, complicated systems with many participants. Discrimination may be especially hard to unearth when it is the product of repeated, low-level behavior of a large group of individuals, and perhaps the result of unconscious influences on decision making. This section also raises questions about the capacity of the law to change group behavior. It is hard enough to alter the behavior of individuals; the challenge of developing effective rules is multiplied when disfavored outcomes reflect complex decisions by large groups of people.

■ FREDDIE STEPHENS v. STATE
456 S.E.2d 560 (Ga. 1995)

FLETCHER, J.

Freddie Stephens challenges the constitutionality of OCGA §16-13-30(d), which provides for life imprisonment on the second conviction of the sale or possession with intent to distribute a controlled substance. He contends that the provision as applied is irrational and racially discriminatory in violation of the United States and Georgia Constitutions. . . . The challenged statute states:

> [Any] person who violates subsection (b) of this Code section . . . shall be guilty of a felony and, upon conviction thereof, shall be punished by imprisonment for not less than five years nor more than 30 years. Upon conviction of a second or subsequent offense, he shall be imprisoned for life.

Subsection (b) makes it unlawful to "manufacture, deliver, distribute, dispense, administer, sell, or possess with intent to distribute any controlled substance." For a defendant to receive a life sentence for a second conviction, the state must notify the defendant prior to trial that it intends to seek the enhanced punishment based on past convictions.

Stephens contends that the statute as applied discriminates on the basis of race. He argues that this court should infer discriminatory intent from statewide and county-wide statistical data on sentences for drug offenders. In Hall County, where Stephens was convicted, the trial court found that one hundred percent (14 of 14) of the persons serving a life sentence under OCGA §16-13-30(d) are African-American, although African-Americans make up less than ten percent of the county population and approximately fifty to sixty percent of the persons arrested in drug investigations. Relying on evidence provided by the State Board of Pardons and Paroles, the trial court also found that 98.4 percent (369 of 375) of the persons serving life sentences for drug offenses as of May 1, 1994 were African-American, although African-Americans comprise only 27 percent of the state's population. Finally, a 1994 Georgia Department of Corrections study on the persons eligible for a life sentence under subsection (d) shows that less than one percent (1 of 168) of the whites sentenced for two or more convictions for drug sales are serving a life sentence, compared to 16.6 percent (202 of 1219) of the blacks.

In an earlier challenge to death penalty sentencing in Georgia based on statistics showing that persons who murder whites are more likely to be sentenced to death than persons who murder blacks, the United States Supreme Court held that the defendant had the burden of proving the existence of purposeful discrimination and that the purposeful discrimination had a discriminatory effect on him. McCleskey v. Kemp, 481 U.S. 279 (1987). . . .

Stephens concedes that he cannot prove any discriminatory intent by the Georgia General Assembly in enacting the law or by the Hall County district attorney in choosing to seek life imprisonment in this case. His attorney stated at the sentencing hearing: "I cannot prove and I do not feel there is any evidence to show that the district attorney's office is exercising their prosecutorial discretion in a discriminatory manner [and] I don't think I can demonstrate the legislature acted with discriminatory intent in enacting this code section." These concessions preclude this court from finding an equal protection violation under the United States Constitution.

We also conclude that the statistical evidence Stephens presents is insufficient evidence to support his claim of an equal protection violation under the Georgia Constitution. Stephens fails to present the critical evidence by race concerning the number of persons eligible for life sentences under OCGA §16-13-30(d) in Hall County, but against whom the district attorney has failed to seek the aggravated sentence. Because the district attorney in each judicial circuit exercises discretion in determining when to seek a sentence of life imprisonment, a defendant must present some evidence addressing whether the prosecutor handling a particular case engaged in selective prosecution to prove a state equal protection violation. . . .

Stephen's argument about inferring intent from the statistical evidence also ignores that other factors besides race may explain the sentencing disparity. Absent from the statistical analysis is a consideration of relevant factors such as the charges brought, concurrent offenses, prior offenses and sentences, representation by retained or appointed counsel, existence of a guilty plea, circuit where convicted, and the defendant's legal status on probation, in prison, or on parole. Without more adequate information about what is happening both statewide and in Hall County, we defer deciding whether statistical evidence alone can ever be sufficient to prove an allegation of discriminatory intent in sentencing under the Georgia Constitution.

The dissent argues that McCleskey v. Kemp is not the controlling precedent, instead relying on the United States Supreme Court decision on peremptory challenges in jury selections in Batson v. Kentucky, 476 U.S. 79 (1986). We must look to *McCleskey* for a proper analysis of the substantive issue before us, rather than *Batson*, because *McCleskey* dealt with the use of statistical evidence to challenge racial disparity in sentencing, as does this case.

The Supreme Court in *McCleskey* pointed out several problems in requiring a prosecutor to explain the reasons for the statistical disparity in capital sentencing decisions. Many of these same problems exist in requiring district attorneys to justify their decisions in seeking a life sentence for drug offenses based on statewide, and even county-wide, statistics of persons serving life sentences in state prisons for drug offenses.

First, "requiring a prosecutor to rebut a study that analyzes the past conduct of scores of prosecutors is quite different from requiring a prosecutor to rebut a contemporaneous challenge to his own acts. See Batson v. Kentucky, 476 U.S. 79 (1986)." *McCleskey*, 481 U.S. at 296. Second, statewide statistics are not reliable in determining the policy of a particular district attorney. [Even the statistics from Hall County do not accurately reflect the record of the district attorney in this case since she did not assume office until 1993.] Finally, the Court stated that the policy considerations behind a prosecutor's discretion argue against requiring district attorneys to defend their decisions to seek the death penalty. Since district attorneys are elected to represent the state in all criminal cases, it is important that they be able to exercise their discretion in determining who to prosecute, what charges to bring, which sentence to seek, and when to appeal without having to account for each decision in every case. [There] is a rational basis for the sentencing scheme in OCGA §16-13-30(d) and that it does not deprive persons of due process or equal protection under the law.

THOMPSON, J., concurring specially.

[We] are presented once again with the claim that OCGA §16-13-30(d) is being used in a discriminatory fashion. This time, we are introduced to statewide statistical information which must give us pause: From 1990 to 1994, OCGA §16-13-30(d) was used to put 202 out of 1,107 eligible African-Americans in prison for life. During that same period, the statute was used to put 1 out of 167 eligible whites in prison for life. A life eligible African-American had a 1 in 6 chance of receiving a life sentence. A life eligible white had a 1 in 167 chance of receiving a life sentence. An African-American was 2,700 percent more likely to receive a life sentence than a white. . . . These statistics are no doubt as much a surprise to those who work and practice within the judicial system as to those who do not.

Statistical information can inform, not explain. It can tell what has happened, not why. However, only a true cynic can look at these statistics and not be impressed that something is amiss. That something lies in the fact that OCGA §16-13-30(d) has been converted from a mandatory life sentence statute into a statute which imposes a life sentence only in those cases in which a district attorney, in the exercise of his or her discretion, informs a defendant that the State is seeking enhanced punishment.

McCleskey v. Kemp, 481 U.S. 279 (1987), provides a workable test for determining whether the death penalty statute is being applied discriminatorily. *McCleskey* should continue to be applied in death penalty cases where there is a system of checks and balances to ensure that death sentences are not sought and imposed autocratically. Likewise *McCleskey* should be applied in other cases where the courts have discretion to determine the length of time to be served. However, *McCleskey* probably should not be applied where a district attorney has the power to decide whether a defendant is sentenced to life, or a term of years. . . .

I am persuaded that Batson v. Kentucky, 476 U.S. 79 (1986), could be used to supply a general framework in analyzing cases of this kind. . . . Nevertheless, it is my considered view that the judgment in this case must be affirmed because the defendant has failed to meet his burden even under a *Batson*-type analysis.

In order to establish a prima facie case under *Batson*, a defendant must prove systematic discrimination in his particular jurisdiction. Although the statistics presented by defendant are indicative of a statewide pattern of discrimination in the use of OCGA §16-13-30(d), the Hall County statistics are insufficient to make such a case. They simply show that all the persons in Hall County serving a life sentence under OCGA §16-13-30(d) are African-Americans. They do not show how many African-Americans were eligible to receive a life sentence under the statute; nor do they show how many whites were eligible. Moreover, they offer no information concerning the record of the district attorney in this case. Thus, upon careful review, I must conclude that this defendant, in this case and on this record, failed to prove a pattern of systematic discrimination in his jurisdiction. . . .

Statewide, approximately 15 percent of eligible offenders receive a life sentence under OCGA §16-13-30(d). The statistical evidence presented in this case serves as notice to the General Assembly of Georgia that the mandatory life sentence provision of OCGA §16-13-30(d) has been repealed *de facto*. With such notice, there are at least three courses of action the legislature might now choose to pursue.

One. The General Assembly could choose to leave the mandatory life sentence on the books realizing that it is being used in a small percentage of the eligible cases. Militating against this course of action is the fact that all laws passed by the legislature should be followed. Contempt for and failure to follow any law breeds contempt for and failure to follow other laws.

Two. The General Assembly could reaffirm its commitment to a mandatory life sentence by requiring district attorneys to inform all defendants of prior convictions and thus enforce OCGA §16-13-30(d) with respect to all life eligible offenders. Militating against this course of action is the fact that mandatory life sentences are not favored by the prosecuting bar or by the defense bar. That is evidenced by the fact that from 1990 to 1994 only 203 out of 1,274 life eligible defendants actually received a life sentence under OCGA §16-13-30(d). . . .

Three. The General Assembly could choose to change the mandatory life sentence penalty to one of several sentencing options which the court could impose. For example, the penalty for a second or subsequent sale could be imprisonment for not less than 5 nor more than 30 years, or life. . . . It is my concern that these problems be resolved in whatever way the General Assembly deems best and that, thereafter, the prosecutors and the courts carry out that legislative will.

BENHAM, P.J., dissenting.

Of those persons from Hall County serving life sentences pursuant to OCGA §16-13-30(d), which mandates a life sentence for the second conviction for sale of or possession with intent to distribute certain narcotics, 100 percent are African-American, although African-Americans comprise only approximately 10 percent of Hall County's population. In our state prison system, African-Americans represent 98.4 percent of the 375 persons serving life sentences for violating OCGA §16-13-30(d). These statistics were part of the finding of the trial court in this case. In the face of such numbing and paralyzing statistics, the majority say there is no need for inquiry. It is with this determination that I take issue.

[In Batson v. Kentucky, 476 U.S. 79 (1986), the Supreme Court] installed a system that shifted the burden to the prosecutor to give race-neutral reasons for the peremptory challenges once the defendant established facts supporting an inference that the prosecutor's use of peremptory challenges was racially motivated. [The] court in *Batson* stated that an inference of discriminatory intent could be drawn from certain conduct or statistical data. Beyond its effect on peremptory challenges, the importance of *Batson* was that it significantly reduced the burden on one claiming discrimination, recognizing that under certain circumstances, the crucial information about an allegedly discriminatory decision could only come from the one who made the decision.

This is the course of reasoning we need to follow in analyzing the issue in this case rather than the more restrictive course taken in McCleskey v. Kemp and applied by the majority. . . . I am not unmindful or unappreciative of the vital and taxing role district attorneys are called upon to undertake in the ongoing battle against the blight of illicit drug trafficking. Throughout this state, they shoulder an enormous burden of responsibility for advancing the fight against drugs, and to do so successfully, they must be invested with considerable discretion in making decisions about ongoing prosecutions. However, it is the very breadth of that discretion, concentrated in a single decision-maker, which makes it necessary that the one exercising the discretion be the one, when confronted with facts supporting an inference of discriminatory application, to bear the burden of establishing that the discretion was exercised without racial influence. This case is more like *Batson* than *McCleskey* because all the discretion in the sentencing scheme involved in this case resides in the district attorney, to the exclusion of the trial court, whereas in death penalty cases such as *McCleskey*, the spread of discretion among the prosecutor, the trial court, and the jurors introduces variables which call for more rigorous statistical analysis. In addition, the complexity of the death penalty procedure, with its many safeguards and the recurring necessity of specific findings at every stage from the grand jury to the sentencing jury, differentiates it from the relative simplicity of the sentencing scheme applicable to this case.

[The] U.S. Supreme Court recognized in *McCleskey* itself that statistical proof which presents a "stark pattern" may be accepted as the sole proof of discriminatory intent. In distinguishing *McCleskey* from such a case, the Supreme Court mentioned in a footnote two cases in which "a statistical pattern of discriminatory impact demonstrated a constitutional violation." One was Gomillion v. Lightfoot, 364 U.S. 339 (1960), where a city's boundaries were altered so as to exclude 395 of 400 black voters without excluding a single white voter, and the other was Yick Wo v. Hopkins, 118 U.S. 356 (1886), in which an ordinance requiring permits for the operation of laundries was applied so as to exclude all of the over 200 Chinese applicants and only one white applicant. The statistics in those cases presented a "stark pattern," but no more stark than the pattern presented in this case. In the present case, based on evidence from law enforcement officers who testified as to arrest rates and other relevant statistics,[2] the trial court found that 100% of the people from that county who were serving life sentences pursuant to OCGA §16-13-30(d) were African-Americans and that statewide, 98.4% of all the persons serving life sentences pursuant to OCGA §16-13-30(d) were African-Americans. . . .

In some instances we must lead the way. [This] is the time for this Court to draw from our historical strength and our determination that the citizens of this state be treated fairly before the law, and declare that Georgia's constitutional guarantee of equal protection requires that OCGA §16-13-30(d) be applied evenly, in a

---

2. Agent David McIlwraith testified that 50% of the drug investigations involved black males. Investigator Shelly Manny testified that of the 60 drug investigations she conducted in Hall County, only 9 involved blacks and that only 50% of her undercover buys involved black males. Another narcotics investigator testified that since 1989, he had made over 300 cocaine distribution cases in Hall County and only 60% involved black males.

race-neutral fashion. . . . I would hold, therefore, as a matter purely of state constitutional law, that equal protection of the law in the context of OCGA §16-13-30(d) requires that the prosecution be required, when a defendant has made a prima facie showing sufficient to raise an inference of unequal application of the statute, to "demonstrate that permissible racially neutral selection criteria and procedures have produced the monochromatic result." *Batson.* . . .

Because appellant has made a sufficient showing of discriminatory application of OCGA §16-13-30(d) that the State should be required to give race-neutral reasons for the "monochromatic" application of that statute in Hall County, this court should vacate the life sentences and remand this case to the trial court for a hearing. At such a hearing, should the trial court find that the prosecution could not provide race-neutral reasons for the "monochromatic result" of the application of OCGA §16-13-30(d) in Hall County, sentencing for the offenses involved would still be permissible, but not with the aggravation of punishment authorized by OCGA §16-13-30(d). On the other hand, should the trial court find that the State has provided appropriate race-neutral reasons, the life sentences would be reimposed, whereupon appellant would be entitled to a new appeal. . . .

The statistics offered in this case show an enormous potential for injustice, and those statistics are just like the tip of an iceberg, with the bulk lying below the surface, yet to be realized. And unless we reveal or expose this massive obstacle that lies in the shipping lanes of justice, it will . . . tear a gaping hole in the ship of state, just as a gaping hole was ripped in the Titanic. . . .

Notes

1. *Who discriminates against whom?* What discrimination does Freddie Stephens claim? Who did Warren McCleskey claim had discriminated against him? Other than the fact that both McCleskey and Stephens asserted that race was the basis for discrimination, were these similar claims?

2. *Competing analogies.* Did the majority in Stephens v. State think that Stephens's claim was the same as McCleskey's? Were you convinced by the competing analogy to discriminatory jury selection in Batson v. Kentucky? Justice Robert Benham, dissenting in *Stephens*, argued that sentencing under the Georgia drug statute was different from capital punishment because it concentrates the decision in the hands of the district attorney. Do you agree? Are there ways a police officer might influence who receives a life sentence under the statute? Do the voters in the county or in the state have some control over this question?

3. *Constitutional challenges to punishment differentials: majority position.* Racial disparities in the application of criminal laws highlight several distinct forms of discrimination. A law could be discriminatory in intent, either at the point of creation or when it is applied. A criminal sanction could also be discriminatory in effect because of uneven (though not intentionally skewed) application of the law. See United States v. Armstrong, 517 U.S. 456 (1996) (denial of request for discovery after allegation of racial discrimination in charge decisions). But these are not the only dynamics that create racial differences in criminal punishments. Some laws have racially discriminatory effects, even though the people who create and enforce the law do not intend to burden one racial group more than another and even though they apply the law with complete evenhandedness. These effects occur when

the criminal sanctions apply to behavior that people of one race engage in more often than people of other races. Would it ever be unconstitutional for a legislature to criminalize conduct when one racial group is more likely to engage in it?

A number of defendants convicted of trafficking in crack cocaine have argued for a downward departure from the guideline sentence (or an invalidation of the relevant guidelines and statutes) based on an equal protection claim. Federal courts have uniformly rejected this assertion, reasoning that any racial impact of the crack cocaine statutes and guidelines was unintentional. See United States v. Reece, 994 F.2d 277 (6th Cir. 1993) (per curiam). While not often addressing such claims, high state courts have usually rejected the constitutional challenges.

4. *Crack cocaine in the federal system.* For many years, the federal penalty structure punished cocaine powder and crack offenders equally for amounts that differ by a factor of 100—the so-called 100-to-1 ratio. Note that this is not a ratio of penalties but of the amounts of drugs generating similar penalties. Proposals to reduce this ratio flared into combustible debates several times over the years. The sentencing commission amended the federal sentencing guidelines to reduce the differential between the punishments in 1995, but Congress overturned the amendments. In 2002, the commission recommended that Congress itself should reduce the ratio, but the legislators took no action.

Then, in May 2007, the U.S. Sentencing Commission took action on its own, amending the crack cocaine guidelines to eliminate any reliance on a 100-to-1 ratio, even though mandatory minimum penalty statutes remained in place to trump the guideline sentences in some cases. After reviewing the statutory purposes of sentencing under 18 U.S.C. §3553(a), the scientific and medical literature, and its own extensive research into sentencing patterns in drug cases, the commission found that the existing crack penalties failed in several respects:

(1) The current quantity-based penalties overstate the relative harmfulness of crack cocaine compared to powder cocaine.
(2) The current quantity-based penalties sweep too broadly and apply most often to lower level offenders.
(3) The current quantity-based penalties overstate the seriousness of most crack cocaine offenses and fail to provide adequate proportionality.
(4) The current severity of crack cocaine penalties mostly impacts minorities.

Report to the Congress: Cocaine and Federal Sentencing Policy 8 (2007), available at *http://www.ussc.gov/r_congress/cocaine2007.pdf.*

The revised guidelines used different ratios at different offense levels, with higher powder-to-crack ratios operating at higher offense levels. The commission estimated that its modifications to the guidelines would affect 69.7 percent of crack cocaine offenses and would reduce the average sentence of all crack cocaine offenses from 121 months to 106 months.

Congress followed suit with passage of the Fair Sentencing Act of 2010, which adjusted upward the amount of crack needed to trigger mandatory minimum prison terms. Though President Obama's Department of Justice and many public policy groups urged Congress to equalize the sentencing provisions for powder and crack cocaine, Congress settled on a compromise proposal that produced a new 18-to-1 ratio for powder and crack sentences. The Fair Sentencing Act also completely eliminated the mandatory minimum prison term for simple possession of crack cocaine.

What explains the different political outcomes in 1995, 2002, 2007, and 2010? Did the commission manage the 2007 process more effectively, or did an overall change in the political atmosphere or practical experience with drug sentencing make the difference? As for the merits of the proposal, what might explain a ratio between powder and crack that varies, depending on the seriousness of the case?

5. *Race and crack.* Are you persuaded that racial differentials are the central issue in the crack cocaine punishment debate? Do different parts of the criminal world just happen to be controlled by groups of a particular race or ethnicity, as an analogy to the use of racketeering laws against the Mafia suggests? Or do you find convincing the argument that racially disproportionate effects (but not intent) justify reworking the system to start with a 1-to-1 quantity ratio?

Michael Tonry surveyed the various causes of the increasing racial divide in criminal punishments in the United States during the 1980s and 1990s. After tracking the steady increase in the proportion of blacks in the nation's prison population during those years, Tonry notes that the increase did not occur because of increased black participation in serious violent crimes: "The proportions of serious violent crimes committed by blacks have been level for more than a decade. Since the mid-1970s, approximately 45 percent of those arrested for murder, rape, robbery, and aggravated assault have been black (the trend is slightly downward)." Instead, most of the changing racial impact of criminal sentences during this time can be traced to drug law enforcement. According to Tonry, politicians pursued the "War on Drugs" with full knowledge of its likely racial impact. Those policies caused

> the ever harsher treatment of blacks by the criminal justice system, and it was foreseeable that they would do so. Just as the tripling of the American prison population between 1980 and 1993 was the result of conscious policy decisions, so also was the greater burden of punishment borne by blacks. Crime control politicians wanted more people in prison and knew that a larger proportion of them would be black.

Michael Tonry, Malign Neglect: Race, Crime and Punishment in America 52 (1995). Is this the sort of "discriminatory intent" that could form the basis for an equal protection challenge? Does this argument create a politically viable basis for revising penalties for violation of the drug laws?

Problem 19-8. The Crack-Powder Differential

In 1986 the United States Congress passed the Anti-Drug Abuse Act to increase the penalties for various drug crimes. The new law imposed heavier penalties on cocaine base (or "crack") than on cocaine powder, a relationship now called the "100 to 1 ratio." An offense involving mixtures weighing 5 grams or more containing cocaine base was subject to the same punishment as an offense involving mixtures weighing 500 grams or more containing cocaine powder. Congress considered crack cocaine to be more dangerous than cocaine powder because of crack's potency, its more highly addictive nature, and its greater accessibility because of its relatively low cost.

Some of the impetus for the federal law came from the news media. Stories associated the use of crack cocaine with social maladies such as gang violence and parental neglect among user groups. Critics of the federal law, however, argued that these social problems did not result from the drug itself, but instead from the disadvantaged social and economic environment in places where the drug often is used.

In practice, the increased penalties for crack meant that African American defendants received heavier penalties than whites for possession and sale of cocaine. Over 90 percent of all people arrested for sale or possession of crack were African American; roughly 80 percent of all people arrested for sale or possession of powder cocaine were white.

The Minnesota legislature debated the same issue. The legislators considered a bill that would make a person guilty of a third-degree offense if he or she possessed 3 or more grams of crack cocaine. Under the same statute, a person who possessed 10 or more grams of cocaine powder would be guilty of the same offense; someone who possesses less than 10 grams of cocaine powder would be guilty of a fifth-degree offense. The bill became known as the "10 to 3 ratio" law.

The sponsors of the bill argued that this structure facilitated prosecution of "street level" drug dealers. Law enforcement officers who testified at legislative hearings suggested that 3 grams of crack and 10 grams of powder indicated a level at which dealing, not merely using, took place. A person convicted of selling 100 grams of crack may often be characterized as a mid-level dealer (someone who provides the drug to street-level retailers). By comparison, 100 grams of powder usually typifies a low-level retailer; 500 grams is more indicative of a mid-level dealer. However, witnesses from the Department of Public Safety Office of Drug Policy contradicted these estimates for the typical amount of drugs carried by dealers, suggesting that most cocaine powder users are dealers as well.

The customary unit of sales for the two drugs were also different. The normal sales unit of crack was a "rock" weighing. 1 gram and selling on the street for $20 or $25. On the other hand, the customary unit of sale for powder was the "8-ball," 1/8 ounce or about 3.5 grams, which sold for about $350. Ten grams of powder cocaine could be easily converted into more than 3 grams of crack.

Sponsors of the bill also argued that crack is more addictive and dangerous than cocaine powder. Witnesses at the hearings testified that crack cocaine had a more severe effect on the central nervous system and is more addictive than powder cocaine. Other witnesses pointed out, however, that crack and powder cocaine have the same active ingredient, and both produce the same type of pharmacological effects. The differences in effect between the two drugs were based on the fact that cocaine powder is sniffed through the nostrils, while crack cocaine is smoked. If powder cocaine is dissolved and injected, it is just as addictive as crack.

As a member of the Minnesota legislature, would you support the "10 to 3 ratio" bill? What else would you like to know before you vote? Compare State v. Russell, 477 N.W.2d 886 (Minn. 1991).

XX

Appeals

Errors happen in most criminal proceedings. Appellate courts cannot correct every mistake that occurs at the trial level, but they do try to identify and correct the errors that matter most. Depending on the pertinent double jeopardy rules, an appellate court might respond to a trial error by ordering a new trial or a new sentencing proceeding, by remanding the case for further factual findings by the judge (after a bench trial), or by dismissing the charges.

In this chapter, we explore limits on the power or willingness of appellate courts to correct errors in criminal proceedings. The chapter addresses deceptively simple questions: Who should be able to appeal, and when? How much deference should an appellate court show to findings of fact by the trier of fact? When, if ever, should an appellate court allow a judgment to stand even when it believes that an error occurred? What could be more important than getting the right answer in criminal proceedings?

A. WHO APPEALS?

With rare exceptions (notably in capital cases), appeals are not automatic. Cases can be heard on appeal only when at least one of the parties requests an appeal. This section explores the typical legal limits on the power of parties to file an appeal and the circumstances under which parties are willing to do so.

1. Right to Appeal

Most federal and state constitutions do not guarantee criminal defendants any "right to appeal." Instead, statutes and rules of appellate procedure determine who can file an appeal and what issues the parties can raise. What limits do legislatures tend to place on the parties' authority to appeal?

■ ARKANSAS STATUTES §16-91-101

(a) Any person convicted of a misdemeanor or a felony by virtue of a trial in any circuit court of this state has the right of appeal to the Supreme Court of Arkansas. . . .

■ ARKANSAS RULE OF CRIMINAL PROCEDURE 24.3(B)

With the approval of the court and the consent of the prosecuting attorney, a defendant may enter a conditional plea of guilty or nolo contendere, reserving in writing the right, on appeal from the judgment, (i) to review an adverse determination of a pretrial motion to suppress seized evidence or a custodial statement; (ii) to review an adverse determination of a pretrial motion to dismiss a charge because not brought to trial within the time provided in [these rules]; or (iii) to review an adverse determination of a pretrial motion challenging the constitutionality of the statute defining the offense with which the defendant is charged.

■ CALIFORNIA PENAL CODE §1237.5

No appeal shall be taken by the defendant from a judgment of conviction upon a plea of guilty or nolo contendere, or a revocation of probation following an admission of violation, except where both of the following are met:

(a) The defendant has filed with the trial court a written statement, executed under oath or penalty of perjury showing reasonable constitutional, jurisdictional, or other grounds going to the legality of the proceedings.

(b) The trial court has executed and filed a certificate of probable cause for such appeal with the clerk of the court.

■ CALIFORNIA RULE OF COURT 8.304(B)(4)

The defendant need not comply with [the requirement of a written statement under Penal Code §1237.5 if] the appeal is based on [the] denial of a motion to suppress evidence under Penal Code section 1538.5; or [grounds] that arose after entry of the plea and do not affect the plea's validity.

Notes

1. *Nonconstitutional basis for right to appeal.* The Supreme Court held long ago in McKane v. Durston, 153 U.S. 684 (1894), that there is no federal constitutional basis for the right to appeal. That holding still accurately describes the law. State constitutions also do not typically provide for a right to appeal, although there are some exceptions. See Mich. Const. art. I, §20; Wash. Const. art. 1, §22. This is an area dominated by statutes and rules of procedure, which address in some detail the types of cases and claims where appeal is available. All states do provide for at least

some appellate review of criminal convictions. If one could demonstrate that appellate review is far more common and important today than it was in 1894, might that convince a court to find a new constitutional basis for appeal?

2. *Appeal after guilty plea: majority position.* Some states allow appeals after guilty pleas only for those issues expressly reserved for appeal in a conditional plea agreement. Others give either the trial court or the appellate court the power to allow the appeal as a completely discretionary matter. Still others (such as California) give the court discretion to allow the appeal only when the defendant meets certain preconditions specified in statute or rule. What variables would be most important in convincing a court to allow an appeal after a plea of guilty? In light of the numbers of appeals and trials occurring each year, how often do you imagine that discretionary appeals after pleas are allowed? See Class v. United States, 138 S. Ct. 798 (2018) (guilty plea, by itself, does not bar a federal criminal defendant from challenging the constitutionality of the statute of conviction on direct appeal).

3. *Number of appeals.* The number of defendants who file appeals each year tends to exceed the number of defendants who are convicted at trial. Consider the following statistics for the federal system:

Year	Criminal Appeals	Total Convictions	Guilty or Nolo Pleas	Convictions After Trial
1991	9,949	46,768	41,213	5,555
2000	9,162	68,156	64,939	3,217
2013	12,707	82,838	80,710	2,128

To the extent that these numbers are typical of other jurisdictions, they suggest that appeal rights may be important to more defendants than trial rights and that a crucial dimension of appeal rights is the availability of appeals after guilty pleas.

4. *Bail pending appeal.* Most felony defendants, in most places, are released at some point prior to their trials or guilty pleas. After conviction, however, statutes and court rules make it far less likely that a trial court will release an offender while the appeal is pending. See 18 U.S.C. §§3143(b)(2), 3145(c); Ex parte Anderer, 61 S.W.3d 398 (Tex. 2001) (condition placed on postconviction bail—prohibition on operating automobile—was aimed at protecting public and "reasonable" under applicable statute). A convicted person who escapes is ineligible to appeal in most systems, although it may be possible to file an appeal upon recapture. See Ortega-Rodriguez v. United States, 507 U.S. 234 (1993) (nonconstitutional federal law creates no absolute bar to escapee's filing of appeal upon recapture); State v. Troupe, 891 S.W.2d 808 (Mo. 1995) ("escape" rule bars appeal, even for those recaptured).

5. *Motions for new trial.* A defendant may convince a trial judge to reconsider a judgment before taking an appeal to another court. A motion for a new trial is, in effect, an "appeal" to the trial court. The motion is made routinely after convictions at trial, and trial judges deny the motion in the overwhelming majority of cases. If you were drafting rules of appellate procedure, would you require such a motion before allowing a party to file an appeal with the appellate court? Would you require it for some issues but not for others?

2. Appeals by Indigent Defendants

Although defendants have no federal constitutional right to an appeal, the federal equal protection clause does require states to make its chosen appeals process available to all defendants, even those without the financial resources to pay for an appeal. According to Griffin v. Illinois, 351 U.S. 12 (1956), the state must provide a defendant with a free transcript of a trial record, if such a transcript is necessary to file an appeal. In Douglas v. California, 372 U.S. 353 (1963), the Court extended *Griffin* to require the government to provide indigent appellants with an attorney for an initial "appeal as of right." Even when appellate counsel for an indigent defendant believes the defendant could raise only frivolous issues on appeal, she must advise the appellate court of any colorable issue.

■ BRYAN MOSLEY v. STATE
908 N.E.2d 599 (Ind. 2009)

BOEHM, J.

In Anders v. California, 386 U.S. 738 (1967), the Supreme Court of the United States established a procedure permitting appointed counsel to withdraw from "frivolous" criminal appeals. We decline to adopt the *Anders* protocol and hold that in any direct criminal appeal as a matter of right, counsel must submit an advocative brief in accordance with Indiana Appellate Rule 46.

FACTS AND PROCEDURAL HISTORY

Mosley was charged with Count I, class A misdemeanor resisting law enforcement, and Count II, class A misdemeanor criminal trespass. Following a bench trial, Mosley was acquitted of criminal trespass but convicted of resisting law enforcement. Mosley appealed, challenging the sufficiency of the evidence that he resisted arrest. The Court of Appeals affirmed, finding sufficient evidence to support Mosley's conviction. The Court of Appeals then . . . added:

> We understand that a criminal defendant has a right to an appeal of his conviction. But that does not mean that an appeal should be filed in every case. When it is clear that the trial court did not commit reversible error, it is a waste of the resources of this court and the attorney general's office and, most of all, public defender funds, for an appeal to nonetheless be filed. Trying to create issues where there are none leads to the sort of perfunctory, baseless brief we have before us today. When there are no meritorious arguments to be made, the better approach is to file a brief in accordance with our decision in Packer v. State, 777 N.E.2d 733 (Ind. App. 2002), which outlines the proper procedure for such a situation.

ANDERS V. CALIFORNIA

The Fourteenth Amendment to the United States Constitution provides that no state shall "deprive any person of life, liberty, or property, without due process of law; nor deny to any person within its jurisdiction the equal protection of the laws." The Sixth Amendment to the United States Constitution provides that in "all criminal prosecutions, the accused shall enjoy the right . . . to have the Assistance of Counsel for his defence." The Sixth Amendment right to counsel applies to the states via the Due Process Clause of the Fourteenth Amendment, and guarantees the assistance of counsel at critical stages of prosecution up through trial, sentencing, and various post-trial matters. However, the Sixth Amendment does not apply to appellate proceedings. Rather, the Equal Protection and Due Process Clauses of the Fourteenth Amendment are the source of the guarantee to indigent defendants of assistance of counsel on appeal. Douglas v. California, 372 U.S. 353 (1963); Halbert v. Michigan, 545 U.S. 605 (2005). That right attaches in any first appeal granted by state law as a matter of right, but not to discretionary review following initial appeals, Ross v. Moffitt, 417 U.S. 600 (1974), state post-conviction proceedings, Pennsylvania v. Finley, 481 U.S. 551 (1987), or habeas corpus actions, Murray v. Giarratano, 492 U.S. 1 (1989).

There is plainly tension between these rights of defendants and the obligation of attorneys not to "bring or defend a proceeding, or assert or controvert an issue therein, unless there is a basis in law and fact for doing so that is not frivolous, which includes a good faith argument for an extension, modification or reversal of existing law." Model Rules of Prof'l Conduct R. 3.1 (2007).

In Anders v. California, 386 U.S. 738 (1967), the Supreme Court of the United States sought to address this issue by proposing the following protocol for counsel to withdraw from nonmeritorious criminal appeals in a manner that is consistent with the requirements of the federal constitution:

> [If] counsel finds his case to be wholly frivolous, after a conscientious examination of it, he should so advise the court and request permission to withdraw. That request must, however, be accompanied by a brief referring to anything in the record that might arguably support the appeal. A copy of counsel's brief should be furnished the indigent and time allowed him to raise any points that he chooses; the court—not counsel—then proceeds, after a full examination of all the proceedings, to decide whether the case is wholly frivolous. If it so finds it may grant counsel's request to withdraw and dismiss the appeal insofar as federal requirements are concerned, or proceed to a decision on the merits, if state law so requires. On the other hand, if it finds any of the legal points arguable on their merits (and therefore not frivolous) it must, prior to decision, afford the indigent the assistance of counsel to argue the appeal.

The *Anders* procedure has been described as a "prophylactic framework" designed to ensure minimum constitutional protection. Pennsylvania v. Finley, 481 U.S. 551 (1987). It is clear, however, that *Anders* represents "merely one method of satisfying the requirements of the Constitution for indigent criminal appeals. States may . . . craft procedures that, in terms of policy, are superior to, or at least as good as, that in *Anders*." Smith v. Robbins, 528 U.S. 259 (2000).

ANDERS IN INDIANA

The first reference to *Anders* in Indiana jurisprudence appears in Justice DeBruler's concurring opinion in Cline v. State, 252 N.E.2d 793 (Ind. 1969). The defendants in *Cline* were convicted of robbing a drugstore and on appeal challenged the sufficiency of the evidence supporting their convictions. "Appellant Covington's sole contention [was] that there was a failure to prove he was the same

Covington who participated in the robbery." In light of four positive identifications of Covington as one of the perpetrators, the majority concluded that

> This is one of those cases where the evidence in our opinion is overwhelming in support of the conviction. We realize the appellant's attorney had very little to work with in order to make out a good-faith effort in an appeal, yet the decisions of the United States Supreme Court compels [sic] such an appeal, regardless of merit. In our opinion a great deal of useless effort and work has been expended in this case where there was no real or substantial grounds for an appeal. . . .

Justice DeBruler concurred, but noted that

> No fair and constitutional method for screening out perfunctory appeals in criminal cases has as yet been devised. Any such method would necessarily involve a decision by someone that the proposed appeal being considered has no merit at all. The duty to make this decision properly attaches to the appellate tribunal rather than to the trial court, trial counsel, or appellate counsel. A decision, by an appellate tribunal, that a potential appeal has no merit, would be valid only if it were made after consideration of the occurrences at the trial level and arguments of legally trained personnel in support of both sides of the issue of whether or not a meritorious appeal exists. Anders v. California, 386 U.S. 738 (1967). It would require as much time and effort to effectuate a legally sound screening method as it does to operate our present system of freely taking appeals. . . .

Read in its entirety, *Cline* seems to be Indiana's earliest rejection of the *Anders* protocol.

The Court of Appeals addressed the propriety of *Anders* withdrawals more directly in Dixon v. State, 284 N.E.2d 102 (Ind. App. 1972) (per curiam). In *Dixon*, a public defender filed an *Anders* brief and petitioned to withdraw as counsel from the defendant's appeal from the denial of post-conviction relief. The Court of Appeals denied the request and ordered the public defender to file an amended brief. The court rejected *Anders* and adopted the opinion of the American Bar Association that counsel "should not seek to withdraw because he believes that the contentions of his client lack merit, but should present for consideration such points as the client desires to be raised provided he can do so without compromising professional standards." ABA Standards, *Providing Defense Services* §5.3 (Approved Draft 1968).

None of the cases from this Court directly addressed the propriety of an *Anders* brief on direct appeal. In what would serve as the latest major precedent on the subject, the Court of Appeals endorsed *Anders* withdrawals on direct appeal. Packer v. State, 777 N.E.2d 733 (Ind. App. 2002). In *Packer*, the appellant's attorney filed a brief in which counsel repeatedly claimed to be "unable to construct non-frivolous arguments" on the appellant's behalf. There was no indication that counsel had consulted with the appellant or advised her of the positions that would be taken in the brief. The Court of Appeals expressed concern that counsel had provided inadequate representation and explained that a better approach would have been to follow the "dictates" of *Anders*. . . .

REJECTING ANDERS

For the reasons explained below, we disapprove of *Packer* and . . . hold that *Anders* withdrawals are impermissible in Indiana in any direct criminal appeal.

Overall *Anders* is cumbersome and inefficient. An attorney who withdraws pursuant to *Anders* must still review the record, complete at least some legal research, consult and advise the client, and draft a brief for submission to the Court of Appeals. If all this is done, the attorney "may as well submit it for the purposes of an ordinary appeal." Commonwealth v. Moffett, 418 N.E.2d 585, 590-91 (Mass. 1981). Furthermore, the Court of Appeals must conduct a "full examination of all the proceedings" to determine if there are any meritorious issues. Any saving of time and effort by counsel in preparing an *Anders* brief is offset by increased demands on the judiciary, which is to some extent placed in the precarious role of advocate. And if the reviewing court finds any meritorious issues, even more time and money must be spent in substituting new counsel and starting the appeal all over again. Requiring counsel to submit an ordinary appellate brief the first time—no matter how frivolous counsel regards the claims to be—is quicker, simpler, and places fewer demands on the appellate courts.

An *Anders* brief also raises issues of fairness. An *Anders* withdrawal prejudices an appellant and compromises his appeal by flagging the case as without merit, which invites perfunctory review by the court. The result is to jeopardize receptive and meaningful appellate review. We understand the frustration of the Court of Appeals in receiving underdeveloped briefs and poorly substantiated arguments. We also recognize that our decision to prohibit *Anders* withdrawals may in some cases perpetuate the filing of "perfunctory" appeals. But in a direct appeal a convicted defendant is entitled to a review by the judiciary, not by overworked and underpaid public defenders.

The professional obligation to avoid frivolous contentions is expressly "subordinate to federal or state constitutional law that entitles a defendant in a criminal matter to the assistance of counsel in presenting a claim or contention that otherwise would be prohibited." Ind. Professional Conduct Rule 3.1 cmt. The Indiana Oath of Attorneys expands this to permit a defense that the attorney regards as unjust whether or not constitutional rights are at stake.

In sum, we believe that disapproving *Anders* is simpler, more effective, fairer, and less taxing on counsel and the courts. Prohibiting *Anders* withdrawals may also force counsel to be more diligent and locate meritorious issues in a seemingly empty record. And in those few cases that offer no colorable argument of trial court error whatsoever, counsel may still be able to solicit a sentence revision or even a change in the law. Prof. Cond. R. 3.1 cmt. ("[The] law is not always clear and never is static. Accordingly, in determining the proper scope of advocacy, account must be taken of the law's ambiguities and potential for change."). We conclude that in any criminal appeal as a matter of right, counsel may neither withdraw on the basis that the appeal is frivolous nor submit an *Anders* brief to the appellate court. . . .

Notes

1. *Counsel for indigent appellants.* The Supreme Court has read the equal protection clause to require equal access to some aspects of the appeals process for both indigent appellants and those who can afford an attorney and various fees. The Court has now expanded the constitutional bases for the right to counsel on appeal. In Halbert v. Michigan, 545 U.S. 605 (2005), the Court declared that the due process and equal protection clauses prohibit the government from extracting,

as part of a plea agreement, a waiver of the right to appointed counsel on appeal, as this right differentially impacts poor defendants and is largely irrelevant to wealthy defendants. (The government is, however, permitted to extract from defendants a waiver of the right to appeal itself.) As with the right to appointed counsel at trial, many states use their own constitutions, statutes, or rules of procedure to expand the availability of counsel on appeal beyond what the federal constitution requires. Not every stage of the appeals process is available on equal terms to indigent defendants. Under Ross v. Moffitt, 417 U.S. 600 (1974), there is no constitutional requirement to provide counsel for preparation of petitions for discretionary appellate review.

2. *Duties of counsel on appeal.* When appellate counsel for an indigent defendant believes the defendant could raise only frivolous issues on appeal, states still must have some mechanism for bringing potential issues to the court's attention. Those mechanisms can take different forms. The Indiana court defended the traditional duties of appellate counsel. It is also possible, consistent with the federal constitution, for appellate counsel to submit an *Anders* brief, or some variation on that model. In Smith v. Robbins, 528 U.S. 259 (2000), the Court approved a California practice allowing counsel to summarize the procedural and factual history of the case, with citations to the record, to attest to a review of the record, to explain his or her evaluation of the case to the client, to provide the client with a copy of the brief, and to inform the client of his right to file a pro se supplemental brief. Under this process, the court independently examines the record for arguable issues. See also Commonwealth v. Santiago, 978 A.2d 349 (Pa. 2009) (appellate brief for indigent appellant must refer to anything in record that counsel believes arguably supports appeal, and must specify counsel's reasons for concluding that appeal is frivolous); In re Bailey, 992 A.2d 276 (Vt. 2009) (allowing withdrawal of counsel without brief specifying law or argument that arguably supported each claim, or a statement that counsel did not consider petitioner's claims to be warranted by existing law or by a nonfrivolous argument for modification of existing law).

3. *Self-representation on appeal.* In Martinez v. Court of Appeal of California, 528 U.S. 152 (2000), the Supreme Court refused to extend the right of self-representation at trial—established in Faretta v. California, 422 U.S. 806 (1975)—to a direct appeal. The appellate courts may properly appoint counsel for the appellant, even if the appellant objects. One of the Court's reasons to embrace the right of self-representation at trial was "respect for individual autonomy." Are there any differences between the interests of a defendant at trial and the interests of an appellant when it comes to self-representation?

3. Interlocutory Appeals

Appeals usually take place after a final judgment, but on occasion the rules allow for an "interlocutory" appeal of an issue before the proceedings below have reached an end. These interlocutory appeals are especially important to the government. In general, prosecutors have less access to appellate review than defendants. The U.S. Supreme Court noted the state of the common law on prosecutorial appeals in 1892:

> In a few States, decisions denying a writ of error to the State after judgment for the defendant on a verdict of acquittal have proceeded upon the ground that to grant

it would be to put him twice in jeopardy, in violation of a constitutional provision. But the courts of many States, including some of great authority, have denied, upon broader grounds, the right of the State to bring a writ of error in any criminal case whatever, even when the discharge of the defendant was upon the decision of an issue of law by the court, as on demurrer to the indictment, motion to quash, special verdict, or motion in arrest of judgment.

United States v. Sanges, 144 U.S. 310, 312-313 (1892). As the Court suggested in *Sanges*, the double jeopardy clauses of the federal and state constitutions have some bearing on when the prosecutor can appeal: They limit the power of the prosecution to request an appeal after jeopardy "attaches," and they bar virtually any prosecutorial appeal after an acquittal. In light of this common-law presumption against appeals by the state (bolstered by the constitutional limits on double jeopardy), consider the following statute and judicial decision interpreting a rule of appellate procedure.

■ DELAWARE CODE TIT. 10, §§9902, 9903

§9902

(a) The State shall have an absolute right to appeal to an appellate court a final order of a lower court where the order constitutes a dismissal of an indictment or information or any count thereof, or the granting of any motion vacating any verdict or judgment of conviction where the order of the lower court is based upon the invalidity or construction of the statute upon which the indictment or information is founded or the lack of jurisdiction of the lower court over the person or subject matter.

(b) When any order is entered before trial in any court suppressing or excluding substantial and material evidence, the court, upon certification by the Attorney General that the evidence is essential to the prosecution of the case, shall dismiss the complaint, indictment or information or any count thereof to the proof of which the evidence suppressed or excluded is essential. [The] reasons of the dismissal shall be set forth in the order entered upon the record.

(c) The State shall have an absolute right of appeal to an appellate court from an order entered pursuant to subsection (b) of this section and if the appellate court upon review of the order suppressing evidence shall reverse the dismissal, the defendant may be subjected to trial.

§9903

The State may apply to the appellate court to permit an appeal to determine a substantial question of law or procedure, and the appellate court may permit the appeal in its absolute discretion. The appellate court shall have the power to adopt rules governing the allowance of the appeal; but, in no event of such appeals shall the decision or result of the appeal affect the rights of the defendant and he or she shall not be obligated to defend the appeal, but the court may require the Office of Defense Services of this State to defend the appeal and to argue the cause.

■ STATE v. MATTHEW MEDRANO

67 S.W.3d 892 (Tex. Crim. App. 2002)

COCHRAN, J.

The issue in this case is whether article 44.01(a)(5) of the Texas Code of Criminal Procedure[1] permits the State to bring a pretrial appeal of an adverse ruling on a motion to suppress evidence when the trial court does not conclude that the evidence was "illegally obtained." Although this Court, in State v. Roberts, 940 S.W.2d 655 (Tex. Crim. App. 1996), held that the State cannot appeal a pretrial evidentiary ruling unless the defendant claims that the evidence was "illegally obtained," neither the language of the statute nor legislative intent supports this limitation. It is not consistent with the interpretation other state or federal courts have given to the same or similar language in their government-appeal statutes. Moreover, the rule in *Roberts* has proved unworkable in practice. Therefore, we overrule *Roberts* and hold that under article 44.01(a)(5), the State is entitled to appeal any adverse pre-trial ruling which suppresses evidence, a confession, or an admission, regardless of whether the defendant alleges, or the trial court holds, that the evidence was "illegally obtained."

[In a capital murder prosecution,] defense counsel filed a "Motion to Suppress In Court Identification." . . . After a pretrial suppression hearing, the trial judge orally granted the defense motion. Her written order stated that she granted the motion "for the reasons stated on the record" at the hearing and that she also found "said identification was obtained in violation of the 4th, 5th, 6th and 14th Amendments of the United States Constitution and Article I, sections 9, 10, 13, and 19 of the Texas Constitution." The State certified that it could not prosecute the case without Jennifer's testimony and filed an appeal. . . .

Article 44.01 was enacted as a vehicle for the State to challenge "questionable legal rulings excluding what may be legally admissible evidence."[5] The purpose of the statute is to permit the pretrial appeal of erroneous legal rulings which eviscerate the State's ability to prove its case. The Texas legislature, in passing Senate Bill 762 in 1987, clearly intended to provide Texas prosecutors with the same vehicle of appeal for pretrial evidentiary rulings as federal prosecutors.

All fifty states, as well as the District of Columbia, have provisions permitting the government to appeal adverse rulings of a question of law. Many of those

---

1. Article 44.01(a), in pertinent part, provides:

The State is entitled to appeal an order of a court in a criminal case if the order: . . . (5) grants a motion to suppress evidence, a confession, or an admission, if jeopardy has not attached in the case and if the prosecuting attorney certifies to the trial court that the appeal is not taken for the purpose of delay and that the evidence, confession, or admission is of substantial importance to the case.

5. Bill Analysis, S.B. 762, Acts 1987, 70th Leg., ch. 382, §1. The "Background" Section of the bill analysis begins:

The Texas Constitution provides that the State has no right to appeal in a criminal case, making Texas the only state that bans all prosecution appeals. This prohibition is viewed as a serious problem in the administration of justice for several reasons: (1) On occasion, defendants are released because of questionable legal rulings excluding what may be legally admissible evidence; (2) Legal issues that have been wrongly decided by trial courts nevertheless stand as precedent, albeit unbinding, for police, prosecutors, and courts; and (3) Trial judges may have a tendency to resolve doubtful legal questions in favor of the defendant because such a ruling cannot harm the judge's reversal rate.

states [at least 18 of them] use the same or very similar language as that contained in art. 44.01(a)(5), and they permit the State to appeal *any* pretrial ruling suppressing evidence if that evidence is likely to be outcome determinative. [At least 13 other] states explicitly grant the prosecution a broad right to appeal any pretrial suppression, evidentiary or other legal ruling which is likely to determine the outcome of the case. A few states explicitly permit the State to appeal only orders excluding "seized evidence," "evidence illegally obtained," or "evidence seized in violation of the Constitution." A handful of state courts [four of them] have construed their government-appeal statutes to permit only appeals of constitutionally based pretrial rulings excluding evidence. State v. Shade, 867 P.2d 393 (Nev. 1994); State v. Counts, 472 N.W.2d 756 (N.D. 1991). At least one state, Ohio, has judicially broadened its government-appeal statute to permit pretrial appeals of nonconstitutional trial rulings excluding evidence, despite language to the contrary. O.R.C. §2945.67; Ohio Crim. R. 12. Although a few states apply their government-appeal statutes narrowly, the vast majority of courts and legislatures across the nation broadly construe their state's-right-to-appeal statutes. They focus upon the same major themes: 1) Does this pretrial ruling effectively prevent the government from presenting its case to a jury? And 2) Is the ruling based upon an erroneous interpretation or application of law?

In *Roberts*, this Court followed that handful of states which have very narrowly construed their state's right-to-appeal statutes. This Court ruled that it lacked jurisdiction to consider a State's appeal from a trial court's ruling that civil deposition testimony was inadmissible. We held that the phrase "motion to suppress evidence," as used in article 44.01(a)(5), was limited to motions which sought to suppress evidence on the basis that such evidence was "illegally obtained." . . . Texas article 44.01(a)(5) authorizes an appeal from a motion to suppress evidence, but it does not explicitly authorize an appeal from a motion to *exclude* evidence. In *Roberts*, this Court reasoned, "By using the term 'suppress' alone, not in conjunction with the broader term 'exclude,' the Legislature meant to limit the State's appeal to those instances where evidence is suppressed in the technical sense, not merely excluded."

The legislative history of article 44.01 shows otherwise. The legislative intent, explicitly stated in the Bill Analysis, was to permit the State to appeal any "questionable legal rulings excluding what may be legally admissible evidence." Period. . . . There is no logical, legal, or linguistic reason that a single phrase concerning the same pretrial evidentiary motion should bear one meaning for purposes of which pretrial motions a court may consider, but bear a totally different meaning when the State appeals an adverse ruling on that motion. The rule is simple: If the trial court can rule upon a pretrial motion to suppress evidence, the State can appeal it. A motion for the goose is a motion for the gander.

Finally, the rule in *Roberts* is, as this case demonstrates, unworkable. Who decides whether a pretrial motion to suppress evidence is one that seeks to exclude "illegally obtained" evidence? If the defendant labels his motion as one to suppress illegally obtained evidence, is that determinative? If the defendant cites constitutional provisions, is that determinative? If the trial court, in ruling, cites constitutional provisions, is that determinative? Or, as in this case, if the court of appeals determines that, even though both the defendant and trial judge cited constitutional provisions, the motion (and ruling) was not really a motion to suppress illegally obtained evidence? This is a linguistic puzzle that only Humpty Dumpty or a rejection of *Roberts* can resolve. . . .

Womack, J., dissenting.

. . . Today the Court says [our holding in *Roberts*] was wrong because the legislature modeled art. 44.01 after the corresponding federal provision generally, a statute that permits an appeal by the government from suppression or exclusion of evidence. I want to point out four things. First, drafting a statute to apply only to "suppressing" is an odd way of modeling on the federal statute that specifies both "suppressing" and "excluding." Second, our 1996 decision was based on the language of the statute, which is more important than the intentions and interpretations of witnesses who supported the act, which are the primary support for today's decision. "It is the *law* that governs, not the intent of the lawgiver," Antonin Scalia, A Matter of Interpretation 17 (1997), much less the intent of the lawgiver's committee witnesses. But this is only to rehash the 1996 decision of the Court.

In 2002 the more important points are my third and fourth: Today's construction of the ambiguous word increases the scope of the statute, applying it to "excluding" evidence as well as to "suppressing" it. And if that is the correct scope of the statute, the legislature had but to amend the statute by inserting the words "or excluding." Three sessions of the legislature have intervened since our decision, with no action. In this case, that is significant.

If this case were the opposite (if the statute had read "suppressing or excluding evidence," and we had held that it did not apply to the excluding of evidence) legislative inaction might mean little or nothing. What could the legislature do to express more clearly that the statute applied to the excluding of evidence? But when the statute says it applies only to "suppressing" evidence and this Court held that "suppressing" does not mean every "excluding" of evidence, the remedy is quick and easy. If we have misconstrued a statute that is stated clearly, what can the legislature do? Reenact the statute with the additional phrase, "and we really mean it"? When we have misconstrued a criminal-procedure statute that is unambiguous, *stare decisis* has its least force. In such a case we should be more free to overrule our earlier decision. . . .

The Court's other argument that "suppress evidence" means "suppress or exclude evidence" is by reference to Code of Criminal Procedure article 28.01, which provides the procedure for a pretrial hearing like the one that was held in this case. . . . The Court reasons thus: pretrial hearings are to determine motions to suppress evidence; the motion that was filed in this case was decided at a pretrial hearing; therefore it must have been a motion to suppress evidence. . . .

[There are] strong arguments why the State should be allowed to appeal pretrial rulings excluding evidence. But the statute that was enacted did not allow it, and it still does not. We have no authority to change the statute.

Notes

1. *Appeal of pretrial issues by the government: majority position.* Statutes and procedural rules in most states have now expanded beyond the common-law bar on government appeals, granting the government power to appeal certain pretrial rulings. Most of these rules cover a trial judge's decision to dismiss charges before trial or a decision during a suppression hearing to exclude key evidence. See also McCullough v. State, 900 N.E.2d 745 (Ind. 2009) (state constitution allows appellate courts to revise sentences upward or downward, but state has no authority to initiate

an appeal of a criminal sentence; prosecutors may urge more severe sentence without filing cross-appeal if defendant seeks a revised sentence). The federal statute, 18 U.S.C. §3731, allows the government to appeal the dismissal of an indictment or information as well as a decision "suppressing or excluding evidence . . . not made after the defendant has been put in jeopardy." Under this statute, the government may also appeal a decision to release a person from pretrial detention. Appeals of pretrial rulings do not create double jeopardy problems because double jeopardy does not "attach" in the lower court until the start of a trial. See Anne Bowen Poulin, Government Appeals in Criminal Cases: The Myth of Asymmetry, 77 U. Cin. L. Rev. 1 (2008) (government access to appellate review in criminal cases is more extensive today than at most times in the history of the country, based on its ability to challenge range of pretrial or postverdict rulings on appeal, or through petitions for writ of mandamus).

2. *Appeal after jeopardy attaches.* Once a trial has begun, the government will have more difficulty obtaining appellate review for any errors of the trial judge. If the judge's error leads to an acquittal or a dismissal of the charges, double jeopardy clearly would prevent a second trial for the same offense. But can the government suspend the proceedings at trial once a major error has occurred and obtain appellate review before an acquittal or dismissal? Most criminal procedure rules and statutes block such appeals; there is, however, a small and growing number of states willing to allow the government to bring an appeal after trial has begun but before an acquittal or a dismissal takes place. See, e.g., State v. Malinovsky, 573 N.E.2d 22 (Ohio 1991) (allowing prosecutorial appeal of midtrial evidentiary ruling, based on procedural rule allowing appeal of "motion to suppress evidence").

Double jeopardy clearly bars government appeals after an acquittal. Ball v. United States, 163 U.S. 662 (1896). However, that limit does not matter in the great majority of cases: Acquittals occur in 1 percent of all felony cases filed. Dismissals of charges after jeopardy attaches are more common than acquittals, and government appeals after dismissals present more complex legal issues. If a dismissal on a legal question occurs after a conviction, an appellate court can reverse the legal ruling and reinstate the factfinder's verdict without requiring a second trial. For dismissals taking place before a verdict, the government may not appeal if the ruling amounts to a resolution, "correct or not, of some or all of the factual elements of the offense charged." United States v. Scott, 437 U.S. 82, 97 (1978); Smith v. Massachusetts, 543 U.S. 462 (2005) (after trial judge granted motion to dismiss one among several charges based on insufficiency of government's evidence, double jeopardy barred any reconsideration by judge on this count). However, if the preverdict dismissal is based on some legal issue not going to the defendant's guilt or innocence (such as pretrial delay), then a reprosecution after a government appeal is consistent with double jeopardy limits.

When *defendants* appeal after conviction and convince the court to overturn the judgment, the government may ordinarily retry the case without violating double jeopardy. One exception occurs when the factfinder at trial is presented with both a greater and lesser included offense and convicts the defendant only of the lesser offense. In that setting, the "implied acquittal" of the defendant prevents the government from retrying the greater charges if the defendant succeeds on appeal. Green v. United States, 355 U.S. 184 (1957). The government also cannot retry a case after a defendant wins an appeal if the error was the government's failure to present legally sufficient facts to support a conviction. For an evaluation of the

government's asymmetric appeal rights from an economic perspective, go to the web extension for this chapter at *http://www.crimpro.com/extension/ch20.*

3. *Prosecutorial and appellate court screening of appeals.* Most state statutes leave the chief prosecutor with some control over which issues the government may appeal. The chief prosecutor (or some statewide representative of the government, such as the attorney general) must certify to the appellate court that the trial court's ruling dealt with evidence or some other claim critical to the prosecution of the case and that the appeal is not taken "merely" for purposes of delay. Under what circumstances might the chief prosecutor refuse to certify an issue for appeal? Is this a meaningful limitation on the scope of the government's appeal rights? Should appellate courts themselves sort the important claims from the less important ones? Appellate rules of procedure often give courts the discretion to decline to hear government claims that otherwise qualify for appeal. See State v. Doucette, 544 A.2d 1290, 1293 (Me. 1988).

4. *"Moot" appeals by the prosecution.* A few states, such as Kansas, permit the government to appeal from an acquittal to the state supreme court if the legal issue is of statewide interest and vital to the administration of justice. The appellate decision is only advisory; even if the appellate court sustains the government's position, the trial court acquittal remains final. See Kan. Stat. §22-3602(b)(1)-(3); State v. Martin, 658 P.2d 1024 (Kan. 1983); State v. Viers, 469 P.2d 53 (Nev. 1970) (striking down a provision similar to Kansas statute on the ground that an advisory appeal presents no case or controversy under the state constitution). In Canada, the appellate court has discretionary power to hear government claims of legal error leading to an acquittal. See Alan Mewett, An Introduction to the Criminal Process in Canada 209-212 (1988). Will the defense point of view receive adequate representation in such "moot" appeals?

5. *Interlocutory appeals by the defense.* Defendants may also bring interlocutory appeals, although they can do so for fewer issues than the government. Denials of motions for pretrial release and the trial judge's setting of a bail amount are common grounds for defense interlocutory appeals. See Ill. Supreme Ct. R. 604(c). Why do these decisions receive exceptional treatment? What other choices might a defendant most desire to appeal on an interlocutory basis?

B. APPELLATE REVIEW OF FACTUAL FINDINGS

Appellate courts could take a wide range of approaches in selecting which judgments made at trial to review. They could conceivably engage in complete and new ("de novo") review for all issues of fact and law. But this approach would engender huge administrative costs; in effect, the appellate court would retry the entire case. Alternatively, appellate courts might play an extremely limited role in reviewing verdicts, presuming that all judgments of fact and law are correct and reversing only for fundamental failures in process that would undermine confidence in the fairness of the decisionmakers or the ability of the defendant to put on a case (such as a failure to provide counsel, evident bias on the part of the judge, or jury tampering). An even more extreme system might abolish appellate courts altogether, trusting completely in the trial process.

Appellate courts operate under standards that lie somewhere between these conceivable boundaries. Courts distinguish between review of factual findings and legal judgments at trial. The standards of review for factual findings tend to be more deferential because the factfinder at trial (whether a jury or judge) is in a better position to view and weigh evidence. The standard of review on questions of law is different: Appellate courts often assert the same (or greater) competence in assessing legal issues and tend to review questions of law de novo.

The Supreme Court in Jackson v. Virginia, 443 U.S. 307 (1979), announced the standard that most appellate courts now apply when reviewing the sufficiency of the evidence to support a guilty verdict. Jackson had challenged his first-degree murder conviction in both state and federal court on the grounds that the evidence was constitutionally insufficient. Although the Supreme Court opinion addressed the standard of review for factual judgments on federal collateral review of state convictions, state and federal courts have applied this constitutional standard for almost all reviews of factual findings, including on direct appeal:

> [The] relevant question is whether, after viewing the evidence in the light most favorable to the prosecution, any rational trier of fact could have found the essential elements of the crime beyond a reasonable doubt. This familiar standard gives full play to the responsibility of the trier of fact fairly to resolve conflicts in the testimony, to weigh the evidence, and to draw reasonable inferences from basic facts to ultimate facts. Once a defendant has been found guilty of the crime charged, the factfinder's role as weigher of the evidence is preserved through a legal conclusion that upon judicial review all of the evidence is to be considered in the light most favorable to the prosecution. The criterion thus impinges upon "jury" discretion only to the extent necessary to guarantee the fundamental protection of due process of law.

443 U.S. at 317-320. Applying this new standard, the Court concluded that "a rational factfinder could readily have found the petitioner guilty beyond a reasonable doubt of first-degree murder under Virginia law."

States modify the *Jackson* standards in two ways. First, as with many other broad standards applied throughout the criminal process, different legal cultures and groups of judges will apply similar standards differently and will reach consistently different outcomes. Thus, the flexibility of the *Jackson* standard allows for more aggressive or more deferential review. Second, some states have supplemented the *Jackson* standard to require from appellate courts an additional task when reviewing the factual support for the guilty verdict.

■ KELVIN BROOKS v. STATE

323 S.W.3d 893 (Tex. Crim. App. 2010)

HERVEY, J.

We granted discretionary review in this case to address, among other things, whether there is any meaningful distinction between a legal-sufficiency standard under Jackson v. Virginia, 443 U.S. 307 (1979), and a factual-sufficiency standard under Clewis v. State, 922 S.W.2d 126 (Tex. Crim. App. 1996), and whether there is a need to retain both standards. Under the Jackson v. Virginia legal-sufficiency standard, a reviewing court is required to defer to a jury's credibility and weight determinations. In *Clewis*, this Court adopted a factual-sufficiency standard, which is supposed to be distinguished from a Jackson v. Virginia legal-sufficiency standard primarily by not requiring a reviewing court to defer to a jury's credibility and weight determinations. But then *Clewis* contradicted itself by also requiring a reviewing court to apply this standard with deference to these jury determinations "so as to avoid an appellate court's substituting its judgment for that of the jury." After having made several attempts to "clarify" *Clewis* in part to resolve this fundamental contradiction, we eventually came to realize that the *Clewis* factual-sufficiency standard is "barely distinguishable" from the Jackson v. Virginia legal-sufficiency standard. We now take the next small step in this progression and recognize that these two standards have become essentially the same standard and that there is no meaningful distinction between them that would justify retaining them both. We, therefore, overrule *Clewis* and decide that the Jackson v. Virginia legal-sufficiency standard is the only standard that a reviewing court should apply in determining whether the evidence is sufficient to support each element of a criminal offense that the State is required to prove beyond a reasonable doubt. . . .

Is There Any Meaningful Distinction Between Jackson v. Virginia Legal-Sufficiency Review and Clewis Factual-Sufficiency Review?

We begin the discussion by noting that in Watson v. State, 204 S.W.3d 404 (Tex. Crim. App. 2006), this Court recognized that a factual-sufficiency standard is "barely distinguishable" from a legal-sufficiency standard and that "the only apparent difference" between these two standards is that the appellate court views the evidence in a "neutral light" under a factual-sufficiency standard and "in the light most favorable to the verdict" under a legal-sufficiency standard. It is fair to characterize the Jackson v. Virginia legal-sufficiency standard as: "Considering all of the evidence in the light most favorable to the verdict, was a jury rationally justified in finding guilt beyond a reasonable doubt." Compare this to the *Clewis* factual-sufficiency standard which may fairly be characterized as: "Considering all of the evidence in a neutral light, was a jury rationally justified in finding guilt beyond a reasonable doubt."

Viewing the evidence "in the light most favorable to the verdict" under a legal-sufficiency standard means that the reviewing court is required to defer to the jury's credibility and weight determinations because the jury is the sole judge of the witnesses' credibility and the weight to be given their testimony. Viewing the evidence in a "neutral light" under a factual-sufficiency standard is supposed to mean that the reviewing court is not required to defer to the jury's credibility and weight determinations and that the reviewing court may sit as a "thirteenth juror" and disagree with a jury's resolution of conflicting evidence and with a jury's weighing of the evidence. . . .

The final nail in the coffin that made a legal-sufficiency standard "indistinguishable" from a factual-sufficiency standard came in this Court's decision in Lancon v. State, 253 S.W.3d 699 (Tex. Crim. App. 2008). There this Court decided that the reviewing court cannot decide that the evidence is factually insufficient "solely because [it] would have resolved the conflicting evidence in a different way" since "the jury is the sole judge of a witness's credibility, and the weight to be given the testimony." Our current formulation of a factual-sufficiency standard in *Lancon*, recognizing that the jury is "the sole judge of a witness's credibility, and the weight to be given their testimony," entirely eliminates the viewing the evidence in a "neutral light" component of a factual-sufficiency standard and makes the current factual-sufficiency standard indistinguishable from the Jackson v. Virginia legal-sufficiency standard. . . .

DOUBLE-JEOPARDY CONSIDERATIONS

The *Clewis* factual-sufficiency standard being "barely distinguishable" (and now indistinguishable) from a legal-sufficiency standard also raises some troubling double-jeopardy questions under the United States Supreme Court's decision in Tibbs v. Florida, 457 U.S. 31 (1982).

[The] United States Supreme Court decided that double-jeopardy principles do not bar a retrial when an appellate court sits as a "thirteenth juror" and "disagrees with the jury's resolution of the conflicting testimony." In reaching this decision, the United States Supreme Court noted that a reversal based on "insufficiency of the evidence" has the same effect as a jury acquittal "because it means that no rational factfinder could have voted to convict the defendant" and that "the prosecution has failed to produce sufficient evidence to prove its case." The United States Supreme Court further stated that an appellate reversal based on evidentiary weight "no more signifies acquittal than does a disagreement among the jurors themselves" and that an "appellate court's disagreement with the jurors' weighing of the evidence does not require the special deference accorded verdicts of acquittal." . . .

We believe that the *Clewis* factual-sufficiency standard with its remedy of a new trial could very well violate double-jeopardy principles under *Tibbs* if factual-sufficiency review is "barely distinguishable" from legal-sufficiency review. . . . We also note that, were we to decide that reviewing courts must continue to apply a factual-sufficiency standard with its remedy of a new trial in criminal cases, then we must also be prepared to decide that they should apply this standard as "thirteenth jurors" with no deference at all to a jury's credibility and weight determinations in order to avoid these potential federal constitutional double-jeopardy issues. We must also keep in mind that such a nondeferential standard could violate the right to trial by jury under the Texas Constitution. . . .

We believe that these and the reasons given by the Florida Supreme Court for abandoning its factual-sufficiency standard are good reasons for discarding the confusing and contradictory *Clewis* factual-sufficiency standard. We agree with the Florida Supreme Court that:

> . . . Eliminating reversals for evidentiary weight will avoid disparate appellate results, or alternatively our having to review appellate reversals based on evidentiary shortcomings to determine whether they were based on sufficiency or on weight. Finally, it will eliminate any temptation appellate tribunals might have to direct a retrial merely by styling reversals as based on "weight" when in fact there is a lack of competent substantial evidence to support the verdict or judgment and the double jeopardy clause should operate to bar retrial. . . .

TEXAS CONSTITUTION, TEXAS STATUTES AND CASE LAW REVISITED

. . . Article 44.25, Tex. Code Crim. Proc., . . . currently states that direct-appeal courts and this Court "may reverse the judgment in a criminal action, as well upon the law as upon the facts." [When] Article 44.25 was changed to its current version—permitting a case to be reversed only "upon the law as upon the facts"—its statutory predecessor provided that a case could be reversed "upon the law as upon the facts" and also "because the verdict is contrary to the evidence." . . .

The issue thus becomes whether direct-appeal courts' constitutional jurisdiction to review "questions of fact," as also codified in Article 44.25 authorizing direct-appeal courts to reverse a judgment "upon the facts," should now be construed for the first time to mandate direct-appeal courts to sit as "thirteenth jurors" in criminal cases contrary to 150 years of practice in civil and criminal cases. We decline to question over 150 years of criminal and civil jurisprudence in this State and construe constitutional and statutory mandates to review "questions of fact" to also require direct-appeal courts to sit as "thirteenth jurors" in criminal cases.

As the Court with final appellate jurisdiction in this State, we decide that the Jackson v. Virginia standard is the only standard that a reviewing court should apply in determining whether the evidence is sufficient to support each element of a criminal offense that the State is required to prove beyond a reasonable doubt. All other cases to the contrary, including *Clewis*, are overruled. . . .

We must now decide how to dispose of this case. [Having] decided that there is no meaningful distinction between a *Clewis* factual-sufficiency standard and a Jackson v. Virginia legal-sufficiency standard, we could decide that the court of appeals necessarily found that the evidence is legally insufficient to support appellant's conviction when it decided that the evidence is factually insufficient to support appellant's conviction. However, primarily because the confusing factual-sufficiency standard may have skewed a rigorous application of the Jackson v. Virginia standard by the court of appeals, we believe that it is appropriate to dispose of this case by sending it back to the court of appeals to reconsider the sufficiency of the evidence to support appellant's conviction under a proper application of the Jackson v. Virginia standard. . . .

PRICE, J., dissenting.

. . . The plurality frames the question as a policy choice, asserting that we granted discretionary review in order to determine whether "there is a need to retain" factual sufficiency review. But as our opinion less than four years ago in *Watson* demonstrated, the authority to reverse a conviction on the basis of factual insufficiency has been recognized from the beginning to be inherent in the appellate jurisdiction of first-tier appellate courts in Texas. . . .

The plurality's primary justification for overruling *Clewis* is that, because the standards for factual sufficiency and legal sufficiency have essentially melded into one, there is no longer any "meaningful distinction between them that would justify retaining them both." But the plurality's premise is flawed. [The] difference is that the [factual sufficiency standard] views all of the evidence in a "neutral" light rather than, as in the [legal sufficiency standard], "in the light most favorable to the verdict." [The] distinction is a real one.

A holding of legally insufficient evidence—that is, that the evidence is so lacking that federal due process will not tolerate a conviction—has double jeopardy implications. Under the standard established by Jackson v. Virginia for deciding whether the evidence satisfies due process, a reviewing court "faced with a record of historical facts that supports conflicting inferences must presume—even if it does not affirmatively appear in the record—that the trier of fact resolved any such conflicts in favor of the prosecution." But this kind of categorical deference is not required of a reviewing court in Texas when conducting a non-due-process review for factual sufficiency. For a reviewing court to view the evidence in a "neutral" light means that it need not resolve every conflict in the evidence, or draw every inference from ambiguous evidence, in favor of the defendant's guilt just because a rational jury *could* have. Rational juries can also choose to acquit a defendant even when presented with legally sufficient evidence. Factual sufficiency review recognizes that there may be rare cases in which, though some jury might convict, and it would not be irrational for it to do so, most juries would almost certainly harbor a reasonable doubt given the tenuousness of the State's evidence or the weight and apparent credibility and/or reliability of the exculpatory evidence. Under these circumstances, factual sufficiency review in Texas permits a first-tier appellate court to reverse a conviction and remand for a new trial, in the interest of justice, to grant the defendant a second chance to obtain a jury acquittal.

The deference required of the appellate court in a factual sufficiency review is of a different kind than that required by legal sufficiency. It is not, as with legal sufficiency analysis, total deference to the jury's prerogative to resolve all conflicts and ambiguities in the record against the defendant. Instead, it is a qualified deference to the jury's apparent assessment of the weight, credibility, or reliability of the (admittedly legally sufficient) evidence. This deference is important because it respects the jury's fact-finding role at the trial court level. But it is not the absolute deference that legal sufficiency review affords to the jury's resolution of conflicts and ambiguities. It demands that, before a first-tier appellate court may reverse a conviction based upon factually insufficient evidence, it must be able to say, with some objective basis in the record, that the jury's verdict, while legally sufficient, is nevertheless against the great weight and preponderance of the evidence, and therefore "manifestly unjust." This does not grant an appellate judge license to declare the evidence to be factually insufficient simply because, on the quantum of evidence admitted, he would have voted to acquit had he been on the jury. . . .

Notes

1. *Sufficiency of the evidence and weight of the evidence.* The federal due process clause, as we have seen, requires a minimum level of evidentiary support for a conviction. Prior to Jackson v. Virginia, 443 U.S. 307 (1979), appellate courts could affirm a conviction so long as there was "some evidence" to support the judgment. In *Jackson*, the Supreme Court decided that a federal court, when reviewing a state court conviction during postconviction habeas corpus proceedings, must confirm that there was sufficient evidence to support a "reasonable trier of fact" in concluding that the government had proven guilt beyond a reasonable doubt. Does this due process standard for the "sufficiency" of the evidence require the appellate court to consider the inculpatory evidence alone, or to consider it in light of the exculpatory evidence?

The "weight of the evidence" inquiry, discussed in *Brooks*, was more common years ago than it is today, but some states still grant their appellate courts this authority. Is it necessary, now that the *Jackson* test has replaced the "some evidence" test? If you were advising legislators or court personnel in a foreign jurisdiction that has recently introduced the criminal jury to its system, what sort of appellate court factual review would you recommend? See also United States v. Musacchio, 136 S. Ct.

709 (2016) (when a jury instruction sets forth all the elements of the charged crime, but incorrectly adds one more element, a sufficiency challenge should be assessed against the correct statutory elements of the charged crime).

For a discussion of factual review in systems outside the United States, go to the web extension for this chapter at *http://www.crimpro.com/extension/ch20*.

2. *Evidentiary review and double jeopardy.* The precise type of factual review that an appellate court uses can have double jeopardy consequences. According to Tibbs v. Florida, 457 U.S. 31 (1982), a retrial is possible after an appellate court reverses a conviction because it is contrary to the "weight of the evidence." The prosecution, in such a case, has met the constitutional minimum burden of proof during the first trial, and the defendant's appeal therefore does not bar a second trial. If the prosecution fails to present evidence sufficient to meet the *Jackson* standard in the first trial, however, it will not receive a second chance. See Evans v. Michigan, 568 U.S. 313 (2013) (double jeopardy bars retrial after a directed verdict of acquittal, even if the directed verdict resulted from the trial court's erroneous understanding of the crime's elements).

Given this more favorable outcome for the state under the double jeopardy clause, should prosecutors generally favor giving to appellate courts the option of a "weight of the evidence" review? See also State v. Wright, 203 P.3d 1027 (Wash. 2009) (when appellate court reverses conviction under second-degree felony murder statute because statutory scheme did not apply to the conduct at issue, double jeopardy did not bar retrial under second-degree intentional murder statute; because jury was not instructed on intentional murder, conviction for felony murder was not an implicit acquittal on the greater crime).

Problem 20-1. Edited Trials

Suppose all the testimony in a trial were presented to the jury in video-recorded format. The prosecution and defense would present their cases in open court with the defendant present, but without a jury. At the conclusion of the case, questions leading to sustained objections would be deleted from a copy of the tape as would any statements ruled improper in opening or closing arguments. Sidebars and time intensive nontestimonial activities such as legal arguments and the marking of exhibits would also be eliminated from the final tape. At the end of the process, a jury would be empaneled to watch the taped trial and deliberate on the verdict.

Would this innovation at the trial level change practices in the appellate courts? Would appellate judges, after viewing the tapes for themselves, become more willing to question factual findings? Would they become more willing to find reversible error, knowing that an error-free retrial becomes cheaper if the tape could simply be corrected and then shown to a new jury?

C. HARMLESS ERROR

"For every wrong there should be a remedy." This notion entered U.S. legal culture through the words of William Blackstone, conveyed by Chief Justice John Marshall in Marbury v. Madison, 5 U.S. (1 Cranch) 137, 163 (1803) ("it is a settled and invariable principle . . . that every right, when withheld, must have a remedy, and every injury its proper redress") (quoting 3 William Blackstone, Commentaries *109). Indeed, this principle has been crystallized in many state constitutions, which include language such as Illinois Constitution article I, section 12: "Every person shall find a certain remedy in the laws for all injuries and wrongs which he receives to his person, privacy, property or reputation. He shall obtain justice by law, freely, completely, and promptly." Surely if this principle applies anywhere, it should apply to the operation of the justice system itself. If a defendant's rights are violated during trial on criminal charges, the error should be correctable on appeal.

Yet criminal trials are complex events, and few long trials occur without some error. If the remedy for every error at trial were a new trial, no major trial would ever end. Moreover, in cases where the proof is overwhelming, won't the outcome at the retrial be inevitable? Even for substantial errors, if the outcome is inevitable, why drag witnesses, jurors, and judges through a mere charade? The doctrine of harmless error aims to sort out the tension between a desire to be fair to a wronged defendant and the need to have an efficient system that focuses on errors that may have produced a wrong outcome. But if stated too broadly, harmless error rules have the capacity to undermine all other procedural rules, because no error will ever be significant enough to warrant a new trial.

The U.S. Supreme Court took up this challenge in Fahy v. Connecticut, 375 U.S. 85 (1963), where the defendant was charged with willfully injuring a public building by painting swastikas on a synagogue. The Court found that the erroneous admission of an illegally seized can of paint and paintbrush was not harmless because there was "a reasonable possibility that the evidence complained of might have contributed to the conviction."

In Chapman v. California, 386 U.S. 18 (1967), the Court squarely addressed the issue of whether constitutional errors can be considered harmless. At the trial, the prosecutor commented extensively on the decision by both defendants to remain silent; such comments, as we saw in Chapter 18, violate the privilege against self-incrimination. See Griffin v. California, 380 U.S. 609 (1965). In concluding that the denial of the federal rights recognized in *Griffin* amounted to harmless error in Chapman's case, the Court wrote:

> [We] do no more than adhere to the meaning of our *Fahy* case when we hold, as we now do, that before a federal constitutional error can be held harmless, the court must be able to declare a belief that it was harmless beyond a reasonable doubt. [386 U.S. at 22-24.]

While allowing harmless error analysis to apply to some constitutional errors, the *Chapman* Court recognized that other constitutional errors are "so basic to a fair trial that their violation can never be treated as harmless error," and cited Gideon v. Wainwright, 372 U.S. 335 (1963) (right to counsel); Payne v. Arkansas, 356 U.S. 560 (1958) (coerced confession); and Tumey v. Ohio, 273 U.S. 510 (1927) (impartial judge).

In Arizona v. Fulminante, 499 U.S. 279 (1991), the Court reconsidered whether a coerced confession was one of the errors "so basic to a fair trial" that harmless error analysis could not apply. *Fulminante* created a new conceptual divide between "trial errors," which are subject to harmless error analysis, and "structural defects," which are not.

The admission of an involuntary confession—a classic "trial error"—is markedly different from the other two constitutional violations referred to in the *Chapman* footnote as not being subject to harmless-error analysis. One of those violations, involved in Gideon v. Wainwright, was the total deprivation of the right to counsel at trial. The other violation, involved in Tumey v. Ohio, was a judge who was not impartial. These are structural defects in the constitution of the trial mechanism, which defy analysis by "harmless-error" standards. The entire conduct of the trial from beginning to end is obviously affected by the absence of counsel for a criminal defendant, just as it is by the presence on the bench of a judge who is not impartial. Since our decision in *Chapman*, other cases have added to the category of constitutional errors which are not subject to harmless error the following: unlawful exclusion of members of the defendant's race from a grand jury, see Vasquez v. Hillery, 474 U.S. 254 (1986); the right to self-representation at trial, see McKaskle v. Wiggins, 465 U.S. 168 (1984); and the right to public trial, see Waller v. Georgia, 467 U.S. 39 (1993). Each of these constitutional deprivations is a similar structural defect affecting the framework within which the trial proceeds, rather than simply an error in the trial process itself. Without these basic protections, a criminal trial cannot reliably serve its function as a vehicle for determination of guilt or innocence, and no criminal punishment may be regarded as fundamentally fair.

It is evident from a comparison of the constitutional violations which we have held subject to harmless error, and those which we have held not, that involuntary statements or confessions belong in the former category. . . .

States have wrestled with their own harmless error standards, which apply to any errors based in state law. Some apply a unitary rule for constitutional and nonconstitutional errors, while others apply a different standard—usually one that makes it harder to find reversible error—for nonconstitutional errors. Most states have procedural rules that limit reversible error to those errors that affect the outcome or the "substantial rights" of the defendant.

■ FEDERAL RULE OF CRIMINAL PROCEDURE 52

(a) Harmless Error. Any error, defect, irregularity, or variance that does not affect substantial rights must be disregarded.

(b) Plain Error. A plain error that affects substantial rights may be considered even though it was not brought to the court's attention.

■ TENNESSEE RULE OF APPELLATE PROCEDURE 36(B)

Effect of Error. A final judgment from which relief is available and otherwise appropriate shall not be set aside unless, considering the whole record, error involving a substantial right more probably than not affected the judgment or would result in prejudice to the judicial process. When necessary to do substantial justice, an appellate court may consider an error that has affected the substantial rights of a party at any time, even though the error was not raised in the motion for a new trial or assigned as error on appeal.

▮KENTEL WEAVER v. MASSACHUSETTS
137 S. Ct. 1899 (2017)

KENNEDY, J.*

During petitioner's trial on state criminal charges, the courtroom was occupied by potential jurors and closed to the public for two days of the jury selection process. Defense counsel neither objected to the closure at trial nor raised the issue on direct review. And the case comes to the Court on the assumption that, in failing to object, defense counsel provided ineffective assistance.

In the direct review context, the underlying constitutional violation—the courtroom closure—has been treated by this Court as a structural error, i.e., an error entitling the defendant to automatic reversal without any inquiry into prejudice. The question is whether invalidation of the conviction is required here as well, or if the prejudice inquiry is altered when the structural error is raised in the context of an ineffective-assistance-of-counsel claim.

I.

In 2003, a 15-year-old boy was shot and killed in Boston. A witness saw a young man fleeing the scene of the crime and saw him pull out a pistol. A baseball hat fell off of his head. The police recovered the hat, which featured a distinctive airbrushed Detroit Tigers logo on either side. The hat's distinctive markings linked it to 16-year-old Kentel Weaver. He is the petitioner here. DNA obtained from the hat matched petitioner's DNA.

Two weeks after the crime, the police went to petitioner's house to question him. He admitted losing his hat around the time of the shooting but denied being involved. Petitioner's mother was not so sure. Later, she questioned petitioner herself. She asked whether he had been at the scene of the shooting, and he said he had been there. But when she asked if he was the shooter, or if he knew who the shooter was, petitioner put his head down and said nothing. Believing his response to be an admission of guilt, she insisted that petitioner go to the police station to confess. He did. Petitioner was indicted in Massachusetts state court for first-degree murder and the unlicensed possession of a handgun. He pleaded not guilty and proceeded to trial.

The pool of potential jury members was large, some 60 to 100 people. The assigned courtroom could accommodate only 50 or 60 in the courtroom seating. As a result, the trial judge brought all potential jurors into the courtroom so that he could introduce the case and ask certain preliminary questions of the entire venire panel. Many of the potential jurors did not have seats and had to stand in the courtroom. After the preliminary questions, the potential jurors who had been standing were moved outside the courtroom to wait during the individual questioning of the other potential jurors. The judge acknowledged that the hallway was not "the most

---

* [Chief Justice Roberts and Justices Thomas, Ginsburg, Sotomayor, and Gorsuch joined this opinion.—EDS.]

comfortable place to wait" and thanked the potential jurors for their patience. The judge noted that there was simply not space in the courtroom for everybody.

As all of the seats in the courtroom were occupied by the venire panel, an officer of the court excluded from the courtroom any member of the public who was not a potential juror. So when petitioner's mother and her minister came to the courtroom to observe the two days of jury selection, they were turned away.

All this occurred before the Court's decision in Presley v. Georgia, 558 U.S. 209 (2010). *Presley* made it clear that the public-trial right extends to jury selection as well as to other portions of the trial. Before *Presley*, Massachusetts courts would often close courtrooms to the public during jury selection, in particular during murder trials.

In this case petitioner's mother told defense counsel about the closure at some point during jury selection. But counsel "believed that a courtroom closure for [jury selection] was constitutional." As a result, he "did not discuss the matter" with petitioner, or tell him that his right to a public trial included the jury voir dire, or object to the closure.

During the ensuing trial, the government presented strong evidence of petitioner's guilt. Its case consisted of the incriminating details outlined above, including petitioner's confession to the police. The jury convicted petitioner on both counts. The court sentenced him to life in prison on the murder charge and to about a year in prison on the gun-possession charge.

Five years later, petitioner filed a motion for a new trial in Massachusetts state court. As relevant here, he argued that his attorney had provided ineffective assistance by failing to object to the courtroom closure. After an evidentiary hearing, the trial court recognized a violation of the right to a public trial based on the following findings: The courtroom had been closed; the closure was neither de minimis nor trivial; the closure was unjustified; and the closure was full rather than partial (meaning that all members of the public, rather than only some of them, had been excluded from the courtroom). The trial court further determined that defense counsel failed to object because of "serious incompetency, inefficiency, or inattention." On the other hand, petitioner had not "offered any evidence or legal argument establishing prejudice." For that reason, the court held that petitioner was not entitled to relief.

Petitioner appealed the denial of the motion for a new trial to the Massachusetts Supreme Judicial Court. The court consolidated that appeal with petitioner's direct appeal. As noted, there had been no objection to the closure at trial; and the issue was not raised in the direct appeal. The Supreme Judicial Court then affirmed in relevant part. Although it recognized that a violation of the Sixth Amendment right to a public trial constitutes "structural error," the court stated that petitioner had "failed to show that trial counsel's conduct caused prejudice warranting a new trial." On this reasoning, the court rejected petitioner's claim of ineffective assistance of counsel.

There is disagreement among the Federal Courts of Appeals and some state courts of last resort about whether a defendant must demonstrate prejudice in a case like this one—in which a structural error is neither preserved nor raised on direct review but is raised later via a claim alleging ineffective assistance of counsel. . . .

II.

This case requires a discussion, and the proper application, of two doctrines: structural error and ineffective assistance of counsel. The two doctrines are intertwined; for the reasons an error is deemed structural may influence the proper standard used to evaluate an ineffective-assistance claim premised on the failure to object to that error.

A.

The concept of structural error can be discussed first. In Chapman v. California, 386 U.S. 18 (1967), this Court adopted the general rule that a constitutional error does not automatically require reversal of a conviction. If the government can show beyond a reasonable doubt that the error complained of did not contribute to the verdict obtained, the Court held, then the error is deemed harmless and the defendant is not entitled to reversal.

The Court recognized, however, that some errors should not be deemed harmless beyond a reasonable doubt. These errors came to be known as structural errors. The purpose of the structural error doctrine is to ensure insistence on certain basic, constitutional guarantees that should define the framework of any criminal trial. Thus, the defining feature of a structural error is that it affects the "framework within which the trial proceeds," rather than being "simply an error in the trial process itself." For the same reason, a structural error defies analysis by harmless error standards.

The precise reason why a particular error is not amenable to that kind of analysis—and thus the precise reason why the Court has deemed it structural—varies in a significant way from error to error. There appear to be at least three broad rationales.

First, an error has been deemed structural in some instances if the right at issue is not designed to protect the defendant from erroneous conviction but instead protects some other interest. This is true of the defendant's right to conduct his own defense, which, when exercised, "usually increases the likelihood of a trial outcome unfavorable to the defendant." McKaskle v. Wiggins, 465 U.S. 168 (1984). That right is based on the fundamental legal principle that a defendant must be allowed to make his own choices about the proper way to protect his own liberty. See Faretta v. California, 422 U.S. 806 (1975). Because harm is irrelevant to the basis underlying the right, the Court has deemed a violation of that right structural error. See United States v. Gonzalez-Lopez, 548 U.S. 140 (2006).

Second, an error has been deemed structural if the effects of the error are simply too hard to measure. For example, when a defendant is denied the right to select his or her own attorney, the precise "effect of the violation cannot be ascertained." Because the government will, as a result, find it almost impossible to show that the error was "harmless beyond a reasonable doubt," the efficiency costs of letting the government try to make the showing are unjustified.

Third, an error has been deemed structural if the error always results in fundamental unfairness. For example, if an indigent defendant is denied an attorney or if the judge fails to give a reasonable-doubt instruction, the resulting trial is always a fundamentally unfair one. See Gideon v. Wainwright, 372 U.S. 335 (1963) (right to an attorney); Sullivan v. Louisiana, 508 U.S. 275 (1993) (right to a reasonable-doubt instruction). It therefore would be futile for the government to try to show harm-lessness.

These categories are not rigid. In a particular case, more than one of these rationales may be part of the explanation for why an error is deemed to be structural. For these purposes, however, one point is critical: An error can count as structural even if the error does not lead to fundamental unfairness in every case.

B.

As noted above, a violation of the right to a public trial is a structural error. It is relevant to determine why that is so. In particular, the question is whether a public-trial violation counts as structural because it always leads to fundamental unfairness or for some other reason.

In Waller v. Georgia, 467 U.S. 39 (1984), the state court prohibited the public from viewing a weeklong suppression hearing out of concern for the privacy of persons other than those on trial. Although it recognized that there would be instances where closure was justified, this Court noted that "such circumstances will be rare" and that the closure in question was unjustified. Still, the Court did not order a new trial. Instead it ordered a new suppression hearing that was open to the public. If the same evidence was found admissible in that renewed pretrial proceeding, the Court held, no new trial as to guilt would be necessary. This was despite the structural aspect of the violation.

Some 25 years after the *Waller* decision, the Court issued its per curiam ruling in Presley v. Georgia. In that case, as here, the courtroom was closed to the public during jury voir dire. Unlike here, however, there was a trial objection to the closure, and the issue was raised on direct appeal. On review of the State Supreme Court's decision allowing the closure, this Court expressed concern that the state court's reasoning would allow the courtroom to be closed during jury selection "whenever the trial judge decides, for whatever reason, that he or she would prefer to fill the courtroom with potential jurors rather than spectators." Although the Court expressly noted that courtroom closure may be ordered in some circumstances, the Court also stated that it was "still incumbent upon" the trial court "to consider all reasonable alternatives to closure."

These opinions teach that courtroom closure is to be avoided, but that there are some circumstances when it is justified. The problems that may be encountered by trial courts in deciding whether some closures are necessary, or even in deciding which members of the public should be admitted when seats are scarce, are difficult ones. For example, there are often preliminary instructions that a judge may want to give to the venire as a whole, rather than repeating those instructions (perhaps with unintentional differences) to several groups of potential jurors. On the other hand, various constituencies of the public—the family of the accused, the family of the victim, members of the press, and other persons—all have their own interests in observing the selection of jurors. How best to manage these problems is not a topic discussed at length in any decision or commentary the Court has found.

So although the public-trial right is structural, it is subject to exceptions. See Simonson, The Criminal Court Audience in a Post-Trial World, 127 Harv. L. Rev. 2173 (2014) (discussing situations in which a trial court may order a courtroom closure). Though these cases should be rare, a judge may deprive a defendant of his right to an open courtroom by making proper factual findings in support of the decision to do so. The fact that the public-trial right is subject to these exceptions suggests that not every public-trial violation results in fundamental unfairness. . . .

III.

The Court now turns to the proper remedy for addressing the violation of a structural right, and in particular the right to a public trial. [We must decide] what showing is necessary when the defendant does not preserve a structural error on direct review but raises it later in the context of an ineffective-assistance-of-counsel claim. To obtain relief on the basis of ineffective assistance of counsel, the defendant as a general rule bears the burden to meet two standards. First, the defendant must show deficient performance—that the attorney's error was "so serious that counsel was not functioning as the 'counsel' guaranteed the defendant by the Sixth Amendment." Strickland v. Washington, 466 U.S. 668 (1984). Second, the defendant must show that the attorney's error "prejudiced the defense."

The prejudice showing is in most cases a necessary part of a *Strickland* claim. The reason is that a defendant has a right to effective representation, not a right to an attorney who performs his duties "mistake-free." As a rule, therefore, a "violation of the Sixth Amendment right to effective representation is not 'complete' until the defendant is prejudiced."

That said, the concept of prejudice is defined in different ways depending on the context in which it appears. In the ordinary *Strickland* case, prejudice means "a reasonable probability that, but for counsel's unprofessional errors, the result of the proceeding would have been different." But the *Strickland* Court cautioned that the prejudice inquiry is not meant to be applied in a "mechanical" fashion. For when a court is evaluating an ineffective-assistance claim, the ultimate inquiry must concentrate on "the fundamental fairness of the proceeding." Petitioner therefore argues that under a proper interpretation of *Strickland*, even if there is no showing of a reasonable probability of a different outcome, relief still must be granted if the convicted person shows that attorney errors rendered the trial fundamentally unfair. For the analytical purposes of this case, the Court will assume that petitioner's interpretation of *Strickland* is the correct one. In light of the Court's ultimate holding, however, the Court need not decide that question here.

As explained above, not every public-trial violation will in fact lead to a fundamentally unfair trial. Nor can it be said that the failure to object to a public-trial violation always deprives the defendant of a reasonable probability of a different outcome. Thus, when a defendant raises a public-trial violation via an ineffective-assistance-of-counsel claim, *Strickland* prejudice is not shown automatically. Instead, the burden is on the defendant to show either a reasonable probability of a different outcome in his or her case or, as the Court has assumed for these purposes, to show that the particular public-trial violation was so serious as to render his or her trial fundamentally unfair. . . .

The reason for placing the burden on the petitioner in this case . . . derives both from the nature of the error, and the difference between a public-trial violation preserved and then raised on direct review and a public-trial violation raised as an ineffective-assistance-of-counsel claim. As explained above, when a defendant objects to a courtroom closure, the trial court can either order the courtroom opened or explain the reasons for keeping it closed. When a defendant first raises the closure in an ineffective-assistance claim, however, the trial court is deprived of the chance to cure the violation either by opening the courtroom or by explaining the reasons for closure.

Furthermore, when state or federal courts adjudicate errors objected to during trial and then raised on direct review, the systemic costs of remedying the error are diminished to some extent. That is because, if a new trial is ordered on direct review, there may be a reasonable chance that not too much time will have elapsed for witness memories still to be accurate and physical evidence not to be lost. There are also advantages of direct judicial supervision. Reviewing courts, in the regular course of the appellate process, can give instruction to the trial courts in a familiar context that allows for elaboration of the relevant principles based on review of an adequate record. For instance, in this case, the factors and circumstances that might justify a temporary closure are best considered in the regular appellate process and not in the context of a later proceeding, with its added time delays.

When an ineffective-assistance-of-counsel claim is raised in postconviction proceedings, the costs and uncertainties of a new trial are greater because more time will have elapsed in most cases. The finality interest is more at risk, and direct review often has given at least one opportunity for an appellate review of trial proceedings. These differences justify a different standard for evaluating a structural error depending on whether it is raised on direct review or raised instead in a claim alleging ineffective assistance of counsel. . . .

IV.

The final inquiry concerns the ineffective-assistance claim in this case. Although the case comes on the assumption that petitioner has shown deficient performance by counsel, he has not shown prejudice in the ordinary sense, i.e., a reasonable probability that the jury would not have convicted him if his attorney had objected to the closure.

It is of course possible that potential jurors might have behaved differently if petitioner's family had been present. And it is true that the presence of the public might have had some bearing on juror reaction. But here petitioner offered no evidence or legal argument establishing prejudice in the sense of a reasonable probability of a different outcome but for counsel's failure to object.

In other circumstances a different result might obtain. If, for instance, defense counsel errs in failing to object when the government's main witness testifies in secret, then the defendant might be able to show prejudice with little more detail. Even in those circumstances, however, the burden would remain on the defendant to make the prejudice showing, because a public-trial violation does not always lead to a fundamentally unfair trial.

In light of the above assumption that prejudice can be shown by a demonstration of fundamental unfairness, the remaining question is whether petitioner has shown that counsel's failure to object rendered the trial fundamentally unfair. The Court concludes that petitioner has not made the showing. Although petitioner's mother and her minister were indeed excluded from the courtroom for two days during jury selection, petitioner's trial was not conducted in secret or in a remote place. Cf. In re Oliver, 333 U.S. 257 (1948). The closure was limited to the jury voir dire; the courtroom remained open during the evidentiary phase of the trial; the closure decision apparently was made by court officers rather than the judge; there were many members of the venire who did not become jurors but who did observe the proceedings; and there was a record made of the proceedings that does not indicate any basis for concern, other than the closure itself.

There has been no showing, furthermore, that the potential harms flowing from a courtroom closure came to pass in this case. For example, there is no suggestion that any juror lied during voir dire; no suggestion of misbehavior by the prosecutor, judge, or any other party; and no suggestion that any of the participants failed to approach their duties with the neutrality and serious purpose that our system demands. . . .

In sum, petitioner has not shown a reasonable probability of a different outcome but for counsel's failure to object, and he has not shown that counsel's shortcomings led to a fundamentally unfair trial. He is not entitled to a new trial.

In the criminal justice system, the constant, indeed unending, duty of the judiciary is to seek and to find the proper balance between the necessity for fair and just trials and the importance of finality of judgments. When a structural error is preserved and raised on direct review, the balance is in the defendant's favor, and a new trial generally will be granted as a matter of right. When a structural error is raised in the context of an ineffective-assistance claim, however, finality concerns are far more pronounced. For this reason, and in light of the other circumstances present in this case, petitioner must show prejudice in order to obtain a new trial. As explained above, he has not made the required showing. The judgment of the Massachusetts Supreme Judicial Court is affirmed.

BREYER, J., dissenting.[*]

The Court notes that *Strickland*'s prejudice inquiry is not meant to be applied in a mechanical fashion, and I agree. But, in my view, it follows from this principle that a defendant who shows that his attorney's constitutionally deficient performance produced a structural error should not face the additional—and often insurmountable—*Strickland* hurdle of demonstrating that the error changed the outcome of his proceeding. . . .

The Court has recognized that structural errors' distinctive attributes make them defy analysis by harmless-error standards. It has therefore categorically exempted structural errors from the case-by-case harmlessness review to which trial errors are subjected. Our precedent does not try to parse which structural errors are the truly egregious ones. It simply views all structural errors as "intrinsically harmful" and holds that any structural error warrants automatic reversal on direct appeal without regard to its effect on the outcome of a trial.

The majority here does not take this approach. It assumes that some structural errors—those that "lead to fundamental unfairness"—but not others, can warrant relief without a showing of actual prejudice under *Strickland*. While I agree that a showing of fundamental unfairness is sufficient to satisfy *Strickland*, I would not try to draw this distinction.

Even if some structural errors do not create fundamental unfairness, all structural errors nonetheless have features that make them "defy analysis by 'harmless-error' standards." This is why all structural errors—not just the "fundamental unfairness" ones—are exempt from harmlessness inquiry and warrant automatic reversal on direct review. Those same features mean that all structural errors defy an actual-prejudice analysis under *Strickland*. . . .

---

[*] [Justice Kagan joined this opinion.—EDS.]

In my view, we should not require defendants to take on a task that is normally impossible to perform. Nor would I give lower courts the unenviably complex job of deciphering which structural errors really undermine fundamental fairness and which do not—that game is not worth the candle. I would simply say that just as structural errors are categorically insusceptible to harmless-error analysis on direct review, so too are they categorically insusceptible to actual-prejudice analysis in *Strickland* claims. A showing that an attorney's constitutionally deficient performance produced a structural error should consequently be enough to entitle a defendant to relief. I respectfully dissent.

Notes

1. *Harmless error standards: majority position.* State and federal courts vary widely in the details of their harmless error standards, but most courts apply variations on the standards enunciated by the Supreme Court in *Fahy, Chapman,* and *Sullivan.* Was the U.S. Supreme Court correct when it asserted that the *Chapman* standard assessing whether the errors were harmless "beyond a reasonable doubt" was the same as in *Fahy,* where the test of harmless error was "whether there is a reasonable possibility that the evidence complained of might have contributed to the conviction"? Compare the *Chapman* standard to the newer formulation in Sullivan v. Louisiana, 508 U.S. 275 (1993): The inquiry "is not whether, in a trial that occurred without the error, a guilty verdict would surely have been rendered, but whether the guilty verdict actually rendered in this trial was surely unattributable to the error." What other standards might courts use? What factors might argue for a standard even more restrictive than "harmless beyond a reasonable doubt"? See State v. Van Kirk, 32 P.3d 735 (Mont. 2001) (applies "cumulative evidence" approach rather than "overwhelming" weight of evidence approach; question is whether factfinder was presented with admissible evidence that proved same facts as tainted evidence proved). Note that when the issue is noncompliance with *Brady* disclosure rules, courts do not perform harmless error analysis after finding a violation; this is because the *Brady* materiality standard already incorporates a conception of harm that the defense must establish. The same is true for *Strickland* errors under the Sixth Amendment; the prejudice prong of the *Strickland* standard requires the defense to establish harm.

According to Kotteakos v. United States, 328 U.S. 750 (1946), the "harmless error" standard that applies to nonconstitutional errors is slightly different. Nonconstitutional error is harmless only when "the error did not influence the jury, or had but very slight effect." Some states create separate standards for reviewing constitutional and nonconstitutional errors. See State v. Barr, 210 P.3d 198 (N.M. 2009). Most states, however, apply a single standard to both types of error, following the unitary direction of rules like the federal and Tennessee procedure rules printed above. For a fascinating case, predating current issues of police use of deadly force, and emphasizing how much the facts and context matter in deciding harmless error issues in high profile cases, see People v. Budzyn, 566 N.W.2d 229 (Mich. 1997).

2. *Applying the standard.* One striking feature of harmless error review is how often appellate courts apply the concept, without explanation, to affirm judgments after even substantial errors. Even when harmless error is the central question and there is detailed analysis of the facts, courts treat the standard of review as so well established that it does not require restating.

But we can learn as much from what courts do as from what they say. A study by Landes and Posner, based on a sample of over 1,000 federal appeals, identifies patterns in the outcomes of harmless error cases even if the court opinions do not themselves offer much analysis. Intentional prosecutor and judge errors are more likely than inadvertent errors to be found harmful. Appellate courts are more likely to ignore prosecutor errors than judge errors, possibly because judge errors have a greater influence on jurors. William M. Landes & Richard A. Posner, Harmless Error, 30 J. Legal Stud. 161 (2001).

3. *Structural and trial error.* As we have seen, courts classify errors under two headings: "trial" errors, which are subject to harmless error analysis, and "structural" errors, which call for automatic reversal. See Gonzalez-Lopez v. United States, 548 U.S. 140 (2006) (trial court's violation of a defendant's Sixth Amendment right to be represented by paid counsel of choice amounts to structural error; remedy is reversal of conviction without a showing of prejudice). For a sampling of the state court rulings on this issue, go to the web extension for this chapter at *http://www. crimpro.com/extension/ch20.*

One of the most common and difficult harmless error problems arises in assessing the impact of improper jury instructions. The U.S. Supreme Court has wrestled for at least a decade with whether different kinds of instructional error should be subject to harmless error analysis. In Sullivan v. Louisiana, 508 U.S. 275 (1993), a unanimous Court held that a constitutionally defective reasonable-doubt instruction was a "structural error" not subject to harmless error analysis. Most states, however, continue to apply harmless error analysis to most instructional errors. Compare People v. Harris, 886 P.2d 1193 (Cal. 1994) (misinstruction on elements of robbery harmless error), with Commonwealth v. Conefrey, 650 N.E.2d 1268 (Mass. 1995) (harmless error does not apply to failure to give "unanimity" instruction to jury). Other deviations from the usual procedure for empaneling and instructing a jury are very often deemed to be structural errors in the trial. See State v. LaMere, 2 P.3d 204 (Mont. 2000) (summoning jurors by telephone rather than by mail in violation of statute governing juror summonses requires automatic reversal). Why would a violation of the public trial right amount to a structural defect, comparable to denial of counsel, or denial of counsel of choice?

4. *The capacity of harmless error to make procedure irrelevant.* If a harmless error standard allows many cases with clear trial error to be immune from appellate review, then the justice system may lose the shaping function of appellate courts. See Sam Kamin, Harmless Error and the Rights/Remedies Split, 88 Va. L. Rev. 1 (2002). Are not cases that are obvious most likely to be subject to guilty pleas? Are trials—at least difficult or long ones—ever so obvious that the outcome would be the same regardless of how the evidence was presented or the approach taken by the lawyers?

5. *Procedural forfeiture of error.* The defendant typically must object to an error at trial or raise the objection in a posttrial motion for a new trial. If defense counsel fails to take the proper steps at trial (or during pretrial proceedings) to "preserve" the error for appellate review, the appellate courts might never hear the issue. This failure to follow proper procedures at trial can block the appellate court from hearing some errors that could have survived a harmless error test. What purposes could such a limit on appellate review serve? It is commonly justified as a way to give trial judges the chance to correct errors before they become too costly, and to prevent defense counsel from remaining silent about the errors they observe, creating an insurance policy if the jury happens to convict (a strategy known as "sandbagging").

The rules are also said to encourage the creation of complete appellate records. Is this rule about the scope of appellate review too remote from events at trial to have these desired effects?

6. *Plain error.* An error not brought to the attention of the trial judge for immediate correction usually cannot form the basis for a later appeal. However, appellate courts make an exception for "plain error," as described in the Tennessee rule reprinted above. If the error is plain, the appellate court will ignore the procedural failure of the defense counsel to preserve the error at trial. While the "harmless error" doctrine often involves constitutional arguments, "plain error" is treated as a matter of common-law interpretation of the procedural rules. See Puckett v. United States, 556 U.S. 129 (2009) (federal defendant claimed on appeal that government breached plea agreement, but failed to raise issue in district court; defendant must demonstrate plain error under Fed. R. Crim. P. 52); United States v. Cotton, 535 U.S. 625 (2002) (omission from federal indictment of a fact that enhances the statutory maximum sentence does not amount to plain error).

Problem 20-2. Preserving Error

On an October afternoon, two men wearing dark jeans and hooded pullover sweatshirts entered the lobby of a hotel on South Lake Shore Drive in Chicago. According to Angela Eiland, the hotel's front desk supervisor, one man was around six feet tall, and the other man was shorter, "probably around five-five." Though the hoods covered their foreheads, Eiland observed that the taller man had a missing tooth; the shorter man had a darker complexion and an unshaven face. They pointed a gun at her and told her to open the hotel cash register. She complied.

Robert Comanse, the hotel's front officer manager, saw them before they left. He told the police that he had never seen the robbers before but described the man in the back office as 5 feet, 10 inches or 5 feet, 11 inches tall, wearing a black hooded sweatshirt covering his hair but not his face. Comanse said that he viewed the man's face for approximately 20 to 25 seconds before they walked out. He viewed a photo lineup that day but did not identify anyone.

Fifteen months later, Eiland and Comanse participated in lineups. Eiland identified Antonio Durant as the taller man; Comanse identified Malcolm Herron as the shorter man in the robbery.

Durant died before he could be prosecuted, but the state charged Herron with armed robbery. After the close of evidence during Herron's trial, the parties discussed jury instructions. The following exchange occurred:

> *Assistant State's Attorney:*   No. 10 is IPI Criminal No. 3.15.
> *The Court:*   That has all the points in it?
> *Assistant State's Attorney:*   Yes.
> *Defense Counsel:*   Okay. No objection, judge.

The bulk of the State and defense closing arguments centered around the reliability of eyewitness identifications. In instructing the jury, the trial court recited Illinois Pattern Instruction, Criminal, No. 3.15, as follows:

> When you weigh the identification testimony of a witness, you should consider all the facts and circumstances in evidence, including, but not limited to, the following: The opportunity the witness had to view the offender at the time of the offense

or the witness's degree of attention at the time of the offense *or* the witness's earlier description of the offender *or* the level of certainty shown by the witness when confronting the defendant *or* the length of time between the offense and the identification confrontation.

The jury found the defendant guilty of armed robbery. The defendant appealed, arguing that the trial court erred in its reading of the pattern instruction. Specifically, the defendant charged that the trial court's use of the word "or" between the listed factors signaled that the jury could find an eyewitness's testimony reliable based on a single factor. The defendant acknowledged that he did not object to the instruction at trial or in a posttrial motion. Instead, he argued that the appellate court should consider this forfeited issue under the plain-error doctrine.

Will the appellate court hear the argument on the merits? Assuming the legal argument about the jury instruction is correct, will the appellate court reverse the conviction? Cf. People v. Herron, 830 N.E.2d 467 (Ill. 2005).

D. RETROACTIVITY

When lower courts violate rules of law announced in later appellate decisions, appellate courts are sometimes willing to ignore those errors by saying that the new rule of law will not receive "retroactive" application. The question of which appellate decisions should receive retroactive application seems simple—and until the middle of the twentieth century, it was. Common-law systems operated on the assumption that courts "found" the law, and therefore each decision reflected law already in existence. Since the law existed before, during, and after a court's decision, it applied "retroactively" to other active cases, and perhaps (through postconviction review such as habeas corpus) even to defendants who have concluded their direct appeals (sometimes many years ago).

We no longer live in such innocent times. Legal realism has led lawyers and judges to recognize that courts make law, at least interstitially. In light of this honest assessment, some courts have declared that their own rulings will have only prospective application (like statutes) or only limited retroactive effect. The law regarding the retroactivity of rulings typically distinguishes cases on direct or collateral review, and as in many other areas can be different and more expansive under state constitutional and statutory law. Even where retroactivity doctrine is relatively settled, the application of that doctrine can be wildly complex.

▇ GEORGE MEMBRES v. STATE
889 N.E.2d 265 (Ind. 2008)

BOEHM, J.

We hold that Litchfield v. State, 824 N.E.2d 356 (Ind. 2005), does not apply retroactively because it established a new rule of state criminal procedure that does not affect the reliability of the fact-finding process. . . .

In March of 2005, Deputy Scott Wildauer of the Marion County Sheriff's Department was involved in an ongoing investigation into possible drug trafficking at the residence of George Membres III. A confidential informant told Wildauer that he saw another drug dealer at Membres's house and that he was "pretty sure"

Membres was dealing "large quantities" of marijuana from his residence. Although Wildauer had never used information from the informant to obtain a search warrant, Wildauer had used the informant at least forty to fifty times in the past and found his information "solid" and "reliable." Wildauer was uncertain as to the exact number of convictions that resulted from the informant's information, but he believed that it was more than three. Other surveillance officers reported seeing a vehicle that Wildauer associated with a suspected drug dealer at Membres's house.

Based on this information, on March 9, 2005, Wildauer seized the trash from the public area in front of Membres's residence on a routine trash collection day. A search of the trash revealed twenty-five burnt ends of marijuana cigarettes, marijuana, four plastic baggies with corners missing, two empty packages of rolling papers, and mail addressed to Membres. Based on the evidence recovered from Membres's trash, the State obtained a warrant to search Membres's home for "marijuana, controlled substances, U.S. Currency, papers, records, documents, computers, or any other documentation which indicates or tends to indicate a violation or a conspiracy to violate the Indiana Controlled Substances Act, paraphernalia, scales, packing materials, and weapons." A search produced $57,060 in cash, marijuana, rolling papers, paraphernalia, firearms, four Rolex watches and other jewelry, cell phones, and a number of documents.

Several weeks later, the State successfully moved for an order . . . to authorize the transfer of the seized cash, jewelry, and firearms to federal authorities for forfeiture proceedings. Membres moved for a stay of the turnover order and to suppress the evidence, alleging that the search warrant was based on an illegal search of his trash and was overbroad. The trial court initially granted a stay of the turnover order and after a hearing denied the motion to suppress and ordered the property to be turned over to the federal government. A stay of the turnover order was granted to allow Membres to seek appellate review.

Membres appealed, arguing that the turnover was invalid because . . . the search and seizure of his trash was unlawful under Litchfield v. State, 824 N.E.2d 356 (Ind. 2005), which was handed down two weeks after the search. . . .

In California v. Greenwood, 486 U.S. 35 (1988), a majority of the United States Supreme Court concluded that under the Fourth Amendment individuals do not have a reasonable expectation of privacy in garbage left for collection outside the curtilage of a home. Under this standard, the seizure of Membres's trash did not violate the Fourth Amendment. Presumably for that reason, Membres relies on Indiana law. Searches under Indiana law are governed by Article I, Section 11 of the Indiana Constitution. [Although the language of section 11] tracks the language of the Fourth Amendment of the Federal Constitution verbatim, significant differences have evolved between Indiana and federal constitutional law governing searches and seizures, including warrantless searches and seizures of trash. Litchfield v. State, 824 N.E.2d 356, 359 (Ind. 2005).

At the time of Membres's search, the most recent decision of this Court on the subject of trash searches was Moran v. State, 644 N.E.2d 536 (Ind. 1994). In *Moran*, undercover investigators ran a hydroponic equipment supply store in order to identify individuals who might be cultivating marijuana. The *Moran* defendants were patrons of the store and had discussed their growing facilities with the investigators. This resulted in a monitoring of the energy consumption at one of the defendant's homes, which revealed abnormally high electricity consumption. Based on this information, officers seized the trash without a warrant and found marijuana.

In evaluating the legality of the warrantless trash search, *Moran* rejected the federal "reasonable expectation of privacy" test and determined that the legality of warrantless searches, including searches of trash, turns on the reasonableness of the police conduct under the totality of the circumstances. A majority of this Court noted that the police did not trespass on the premises of the defendants, conducted themselves in the same manner as trash collectors when picking up the trash, and did not cause a disturbance. This Court concluded that "given these . . . circumstances, and while realizing that Hoosiers are not entirely comfortable with the idea of police officers casually rummaging through trash left at curbside" the police activity was reasonable under the Indiana Constitution. The search of Membres's trash met this standard.

Membres contends that the search of his trash was unlawful under *Litchfield,* decided two weeks after the search. In *Litchfield,* this Court was again presented with the issue of warrantless trash searches. . . . In an effort to establish more clear lines of permissible police conduct, we expressly stated two factors necessary to establish a reasonable warrantless trash search: (1) "trash must be retrieved in substantially the same manner as the trash collector would take it" and (2) the police must possess "articulable individualized suspicion" that the subject of the trash search was engaged in illegal activity. We explained that articulable individualized suspicion is "essentially the same as is required for a *Terry* stop of an automobile."

Membres argues that Wildauer did not have reasonable suspicion to conduct the search, and it was therefore unlawful under *Litchfield.* The State . . . responds that *Litchfield* is not retroactive and therefore Wildauer did not need reasonable suspicion before searching Membres's trash because the prevailing case law at the time of the search imposed limitations only on the manner in which the trash was retrieved. . . .

[The State's argument proceeds] from the assumption that *Moran* stood for the proposition that warrantless trash searches are valid under the Indiana Constitution as long as the police conduct themselves in the same manner as trash collectors. *Moran* did impose this limitation, but as *Litchfield* noted, *Moran* also held that reasonableness of warrantless trash searches is to be determined based on a totality of the circumstances. *Litchfield* expressly adopted the requirement of "articulable individualized suspicion" as an elaboration of *Moran* but did not overrule *Moran.* Indeed, in *Moran* itself there were grounds for reasonable suspicion based on the electricity consumption and the defendants' avowed interest in growing facilities. *Litchfield* expressly adopted a requirement that was not inconsistent with *Moran* but also was not foreshadowed by *Moran.* In that respect, *Litchfield* represents a new rule of criminal procedure:

> In general, . . . a case announces a new rule when it breaks new ground or imposes a new obligation on the [government or] if the result was not *dictated* by precedent existing at the time the defendant's conviction became final, or if the result is "susceptible to debate among reasonable minds.

State v. Mohler, 694 N.E.2d 1129 (Ind. 1998). Under *Moran* it was debatable what constituted a reasonable trash search. Also, before *Litchfield* there was no express statement that an "articulable individualized suspicion" would be necessary in all warrantless trash searches. . . . *Litchfield* reshaped the understanding of what constitutes a reasonable warrantless trash search.

Membres argues that because his case was not yet final at the time *Litchfield* was decided, *Litchfield's* new rule of criminal procedure applies retroactively to Wildauer's search of his trash. . . . This case deals with a direct appeal, not a collateral attack. We are bound by the Supremacy Clause to apply new rules of federal criminal procedure retroactively to the extent required by federal law. Griffith v. Kentucky, 479 U.S. 314, 328 (1987), establishes the general rule for federal constitutional rules that "a new rule for the conduct of criminal prosecutions is to be applied retroactively to all cases, state or federal, pending on direct review or not yet final. . . ." This sets a minimum requirement for new federal rules, but states may be more generous in giving retroactive effect to new federal rules. . . .

Federal law does not govern retroactivity of a new rule of criminal procedure that derives from the state constitution. Although Indiana has followed federal retroactivity doctrine for post-conviction claims, we have not recently addressed the retroactivity of new constitutional rules in direct appeals. An earlier Indiana case on direct appeal identified three relevant considerations in determining whether to apply new rules of state criminal procedure retroactively: "(a) the purpose to be served by the new standards, (b) the extent of the reliance by law enforcement authorities on the old standards, and (c) the effect on the administration of justice of a retroactive application of the new standards." Enlow v. State, 303 N.E.2d 658 (Ind. 1973). In *Enlow,* this Court differentiated between new criminal principles that go to "the fairness of the trial itself and [are] designed to eliminate a previously existing danger of convicting the innocent" and those that "enforce other constitutional rights not necessarily connected with the fact finding function." The former require retroactive effect, and the latter do not. *Enlow* addressed the point of establishing habitual offender status by proving prior convictions in the course of the trial. This was found to affect the fairness of the proceeding.

We think the exclusionary rule that prohibits introduction into evidence of unlawfully seized materials is an example of a rule that does not go to the fairness of the trial. It is a rule that is, as *Enlow* put it, designed to "enforce other constitutional rights not necessarily connected with the fact finding function." Otherwise stated, we do not exclude the products of unlawful searches and seizures because they are unreliable or immaterial or unduly prejudicial evidence. Indeed, exclusion of this evidence is an obstacle to the truth-finding objective of trials. We nonetheless exclude it because that is the only effective means of deterring improper intrusions into the privacy of all citizens.

Justice Rucker is correct that there is no authority squarely supporting our view, but there is also none opposing it. As both dissents point out, new rules of criminal procedure required by the federal constitution are applied retroactively on collateral attack only in the limited circumstances established in Teague v. Lane, 489 U.S. 288 (1989). And Daniels v. State, 561 N.E.2d 487 (Ind. 1990), adopted the same approach to new rules of criminal procedure under the Indiana Constitution.

Neither the Supreme Court of the United States nor this Court has ever considered whether these general principles of retroactivity apply to the rule requiring exclusion of evidence that is the product of an unconstitutional search or seizure. In *Teague, Daniels,* and every case cited by Justices Rucker and Sullivan, the "new rule" in question was one designed to assure a fair trial by prohibiting the introduction of evidence that was deemed unreliable or otherwise to assure a fair trial. The exclusionary rule for searches and seizures is qualitatively different from all of these rules. For example, Withrow v. Williams, 507 U.S. 680 (1993), explained that although *Miranda*'s rule is in part based on prophylactic considerations, it also serves to guard against the use of unreliable statements at trial." In this respect it is unlike the Fourth Amendment exclusionary rule, which merely serves to deter future constitutional violations and does not improve the reliability of trial evidence. For that reason federal habeas corpus is generally not available to overturn convictions based on unlawfully seized evidence, but is available for *Miranda* violations. In sum, we do not exclude evidence that is unlawfully seized because it is irrelevant or unduly prejudicial. To the contrary, that evidence ordinarily furthers the quest for accurate resolution of the facts of the case. We nevertheless exclude it because we consider it necessary to protect the privacy of all citizens from excessive intrusion by law enforcement. In other words, we accept the obstacle to the truth-seeking function in order to preserve a higher value.

There appear to be few "new rules" in the search and seizure area under other states' constitutions. We do find one authority, State v. Skidmore, 601 A.2d 729 (N.J. App. 1992), that considered the specific issue of retroactive application of a new state constitutional rule on warrantless trash searches. In *Skidmore,* defendants urged the court to retroactively apply a recent holding from the New Jersey Supreme Court that warrantless trash searches without probable cause violated the state constitution. The court used a three-part test similar to that enunciated in *Enlow* for its retroactivity analysis. In evaluating the first criterion—the purpose to be served by retroactive application—the New Jersey court stated "where a new rule is an exclusionary rule, meant solely to deter illegal police conduct, the new rule is virtually never given retroactive effect. The reason is that the deterrent purpose of such a rule would not be advanced by applying it to past misconduct." Evaluating this in light of the other criteria, the court concluded that the new rule of state criminal procedure on warrantless searches of trash should not be applied retroactively, even to cases pending on direct review or not yet final. . . .

In sum, we agree with the *Skidmore* court. Indiana search and seizure jurisprudence, like federal Fourth Amendment doctrine, identifies deterrence as the primary objective of the exclusionary rule. The rule announced in *Litchfield* is designed to deter random intrusions into the privacy of all citizens. Retroactive application of that rule would not advance its purpose for the obvious reason that deterrence can operate only prospectively. Exclusion of the fruit of a random search, although important in protecting Indiana citizens from unreasonable searches and seizures, does not in any way serve to avoid an unjust conviction. To the contrary, exclusion of relevant and otherwise admissible evidence can prevent conviction where reliable evidence supports it. Because there is this cost to enforcing the exclusionary rule, it should be done only where appropriate to advance its purpose. . . .

Finally, we permit retroactivity to a successful litigant, and in that sense applied *Litchfield* retroactively in *Litchfield* itself. Relief, and the incentive to present a novel claim, should not turn on the relative speed with which a specific case reaches appellate resolution. Accordingly, *Litchfield* applies in *Litchfield* itself, and also any other cases in which substantially the same claim was raised before *Litchfield* was decided. But challenges to pre-*Litchfield* searches that did not raise *Litchfield*-like claims in the trial court before *Litchfield* was decided are governed by pre-*Litchfield* doctrine even if the cases were "not yet final" at the time *Litchfield* was decided.

Justice Sullivan is correct that there is some arbitrariness in granting relief under our holding today to some defendants and not to others. But any rule of retroactivity is arbitrary unless it gives full retroactive effect to everyone. Indeed, courts are not required to apply new federal constitutional rules retroactively unless the issue has been preserved and the case is "pending on direct review or not yet final." See *Griffith,* 479 U.S. at 328; United States v. Booker, 543 U.S. 220 (2005) (holding that reviewing courts must still "apply ordinary prudential doctrines, determining, for example, whether the issue was raised below," before applying a rule retroactively). So, under *Griffith,* even if they barely miss the magic date, those unfortunate enough to have appealed and lost or failed to appeal or failed to preserve the issue all get no benefit of a new rule, even one deemed necessary for a fair trial. For prophylactic rules, specifically the exclusionary rule, there is good reason to give relief to those who raised the issue in the trial court because it prevents a race to appellate judgment that could frustrate the orderly resolution of individual cases. But because the evidence in search and seizure cases is usually inherently probative and reliable, we see no reason to exclude it categorically if the issue has not been raised before the new ruling, and the officers seizing the evidence operated under the rules this Court had announced at the time. . . . The trial court's denial of Membres's motion to suppress and its grant of the State's motion for turnover order are affirmed.

SULLIVAN, J., dissenting.

Our long-standing retroactivity rule dictates that new rules of criminal procedure apply to future trials and also to cases pending on direct appeal (or otherwise not yet final) where the issue was properly preserved in the trial court. Smylie v. State, 823 N.E.2d 679 (Ind.2005).

Today the Court announces an exception to that retroactivity rule for cases involving warrantless searches of trash that implicate the new rule of Indiana Constitutional law announced in Litchfield v. State. In such cases, the new rule applies only if the issue was raised in the trial court before the new rule was announced.

The warrantless search of Membres's trash in this case occurred on March 9, 2005. *Litchfield* was decided on March 24, 2005. Under the traditional retroactivity rule, the *Litchfield* rule would apply to Membres's future trial. But under today's decision, whether the defendant gets the advantage of the new rule depends on whether Membres raised the issue in the 14-day window prior to March 24. If so, the new rule applies and the evidence is inadmissible; if not, the evidence comes in. But often a prosecutor does not file charges in such a short time period. And even if the prosecutor here had done so, asking that defense counsel assess the vulnerability of the search and seizure to a novel constitutional challenge simply asks too much. The Court says that relief should not turn on the relative speed with which a specific case reaches appellate resolution. I agree. But neither should relief turn on the relative speed at which an overworked prosecutor gets charges on file or an overworked defense attorney sits down to examine the case. . . .

RUCKER, J., concurring in result in part and dissenting in part.

I agree that the trial court correctly denied Membres' motion to suppress. On this point I concur with the majority opinion. But the majority charts new territory to this Court's longstanding jurisprudence on the question of retroactivity. I would adhere to established precedent and as a result apply Litchfield v. State retroactively. On this issue I respectfully dissent.

In determining whether a new rule of state criminal procedure applies retroactively, the majority relies on Enlow v. State, 303 N.E.2d 658 (Ind. 1973). In that case this

Court applied a three-pronged test: "(a) the purpose to be served by the new standards, (b) the extent of the reliance by law enforcement authorities on the old standards, and (c) the effect on the administration of justice of a retroactive application of the new standards." But *Enlow* quoted Stovall v. Denno, 388 U.S. 293 (1967), for this three-pronged test. And on this precise point *Stovall* has been overruled by Griffith v. Kentucky, 479 U.S. 314 (1987). In essence the majority today adopts as the Indiana rule long abandoned federal precedent on the issue of retroactivity. I see no reason to travel this path.

In a related vein, and perhaps more importantly, although this Court has acknowledged its independence to fashion its own rule of retroactivity, it has declined to do so. Instead this Court has adopted as this state's retroactivity rule the same rule articulated by the United States Supreme Court in Teague v. Lane, 489 U.S. 288 (1989), as refined in Penry v. Lynaugh, 492 U.S. 302 (1989). See Daniels v. State, 561 N.E.2d 487 (Ind. 1990). It is true that *Daniels* involved a case on collateral review. . . . But we have consistently applied the *Teague/Penry* rule to cases pending on direct appeal as well.

Essentially, until today Indiana's rule on retroactivity—which is the same as the federal rule—was well established, "a new rule for the conduct of criminal prosecutions is to be applied retroactively to all cases, state or federal, pending on direct review or not yet final, with no exception for cases in which the new rule constitutes a 'clear break' with the past."

To support its abandonment of this state's long-standing authority on retroactivity the majority says that a different rule should apply where the exclusionary rule is at stake. [Contrary] to the majority's claim, neither this Court nor the federal circuit courts have been hesitant about applying the *Teague* retroactivity rule to cases in which the exclusionary rule was at stake.

In sum, controlling authority simply does not support the majority's rationale for crafting a different rule of retroactivity applicable only to exclusionary rule cases. . . . There appears to be no doubt that *Litchfield* represents a new rule of criminal procedure. . . . And because Membres' case was not yet final when *Litchfield* was decided, I would apply to this case the new rule of criminal procedure we announced in *Litchfield*. . . .

In this case an informant told Officer Wildauer that Membres was dealing marijuana from his home. The reliability of the informant's tip was established by Officer Wildauer's testimony that the informant had given the officer factual and reliable information in the past—in excess of forty to fifty times—and that the information had resulted in convictions on more than three occasions. Combined with the surveillance team's observation that an automobile belonging to a suspected drug dealer was parked at Membres' house, the informant's tip, although not sufficient to establish probable cause for the issuance of a search warrant, was enough under the totality of the circumstance to provide the police with reasonable suspicion that "criminal activity may be afoot." Thus, Officer Wildauer acted well within the dictates of *Litchfield* to conduct a warrantless search of Membres' trash. Accordingly, the trial court properly denied Membres' motion to suppress. On this issue I therefore concur in result.

Notes

1. *Retroactivity of appellate decisions: majority position.* Historically, appellate courts applied their precedents to all litigants bringing appeals to them, even

if the precedents were announced after the proceedings in the trial court were completed. The Warren Court altered the historical approach to retroactivity in Linkletter v. Walker, 381 U.S. 618 (1965), and Stovall v. Denno, 388 U.S. 293 (1967). *Linkletter* dealt with the retroactivity of Mapp v. Ohio, 367 U.S. 643 (1961), which applied the exclusionary rule in state court proceedings for evidence obtained through unconstitutional searches or seizures. Under the new retroactivity doctrine, the appellate court could refuse to give some appellants the benefit of a new constitutional ruling. The defendant in the original appeal would always receive the benefit of the ruling, but other appellants who were complaining on direct appeal about government conduct taking place before the announcement of the new rule might or might not receive the benefit.

These changes in retroactivity doctrine appeared at a time when the Supreme Court was expanding the influence of the federal constitution in state criminal proceedings. What part did the retroactivity doctrine play in the "activism" of the Warren Court? Imagine yourself as one of the Justices who routinely opposed the Court's expansive reading of the Constitution. What would be your views about the new retroactivity doctrine? Did it limit the "damage" of wrongheaded decisions, or did it make them possible? Note the relationship between the expanded Indiana doctrine from trash searches (and the application of the exclusionary rule) to the retroactivity decision in *Membres*. Compare Davis v. United States, 564 U.S. 229 (2011) (exclusion not available as remedy for defendant when police reasonably relied on established precedent before a change in search and seizure doctrine, even if the new doctrine applies retroactively under *Griffith*).

In Griffith v. Kentucky, 479 U.S. 314 (1987), the Supreme Court abandoned the flexible *Linkletter* approach to retroactivity and announced that it would apply its decisions to all cases on direct appeal, even if the new rule of law did not exist at the time of the defendant's trial. In the wake of the *Griffith* case, some state courts have followed suit and have altered their own "retroactivity" standards (which govern the application of state law rulings). See State v. Waters, 987 P.2d 1142 (Mont. 1999) (follows *Griffith*; new rules of criminal procedure are applicable to cases still subject to direct review regardless of whether those rules represent "clear breaks" with the past). It is still common, however, to find state decisions that retain some discretion on the retroactivity question. When courts insist on some flexibility in deciding retroactivity, are they proclaiming an "activist" posture toward constitutional criminal procedure? Are they suggesting that their decisions in this field are more legislative than judicial, in the traditional senses of those terms? See also State v. Mares, 335 P.3d 487 (Wyo. 2014) (constitutional ban on mandatory juvenile sentences of life without parole applies retroactively to cases not final at time of Supreme Court ruling; surveys split of authority); Casiano v. Commissioner, 115 A.3d 1031 (Conn. 2015). In Montgomery v. Louisiana, 136 S. Ct. 718 (2016), the court held that constitutional ban on mandatory life sentences for juveniles was a new substantive federal constitutional rule that was retroactive on state collateral review.

2. *Retroactivity and plain error.* Recall that appellate courts will normally not hear a claim about legal error at trial if defense counsel failed to preserve that error in the trial court; the only exceptions occur when the legal challenge involves a "plain error." How should courts apply this rule when the legal doctrine involved was not explicitly announced until the time interval between the end of trial and the resolution of the appeal? Won't defendants virtually always fail to object at trial to a

failure to observe legal requirements that had not been established at the time of trial? Will defendants actually benefit more if the courts ignore the plain error rule in the context of retroactive changes to the law, but apply the more flexible *Linkletter* approach to retroactivity on direct appeal?

3. *Postconviction procedural issues.* After a direct appeal is complete, the offender can still challenge the validity of the conviction in court. These postconviction review procedures take a variety of names with somewhat different historical roots; the best-known form, used in both federal and state constitutions, is the writ of habeas corpus. Some states structure their postconviction processes around a different historical writ—error coram nobis—which focuses more on new evidence. Others have supplanted the traditional postconviction remedies with broader statutes, often simply labeled "postconviction review" acts. These various postconviction review procedures are referred to under the general heading of "collateral" review, and they are nominally civil proceedings. If the judge in a collateral proceeding becomes convinced that the government obtained the conviction illegally, she sometimes has the power to grant relief to the petitioner and overturn the conviction. See Davila v. Davis, 137 S. Ct. 2058 (2017) (defendant cannot obtain federal habeas corpus relief based on a substantial but procedurally defaulted claim of ineffective assistance of state postconviction counsel).

The web extension for this casebook contains a chapter dealing with collateral review of convictions. The first section of this chapter considers the history and theory behind the common-law writ of habeas corpus. The second section considers some of the basic features of collateral review in the states. Two central questions arise here: What distinguishes collateral review procedures from appeals, and to what extent are such procedures necessary at all? The third section considers the particular and highly political debate about federalism that arises when federal courts review and invalidate convictions obtained in state court. The chapter appears at *http://www.crimpro.com/extension/ch21.*

4. *Retroactivity and collateral review.* Courts usually treat retroactivity questions differently when they arise during postconviction challenges. Federal courts apply decisions retroactively to cases on direct appeal but not to most defendants who have completed their direct appeals and are bringing a postconviction collateral attack on the judgment. According to Teague v. Lane, 489 U.S. 288 (1989), new constitutional rules of criminal procedure may not be applied retroactively on federal habeas review unless they place conduct beyond the states' power to criminalize or are "watershed" rules of criminal procedure. State systems, however, are free to give broader retroactive effect during state proceedings to newly announced federal rules of procedure. See Danforth v. Minnesota, 552 U.S. 264 (2008).

If new legal rules were available for postconviction challenges, would new claims flood the court whenever it announced a new procedural rule? Could this problem be solved by allowing retroactive application of a new rule only for prisoners who have *pending* collateral attacks at the time of the decision? Are there reasons other than sheer numbers of claims to treat those on direct appeal differently from those who have filed (or might file) a collateral attack? See Taylor v. State, 10 S.W.3d 673 (Tex. Crim. App. 2000) (rejects federal retroactivity doctrine and adopts a multifactor approach to determine whether new rules of nonconstitutional state law should be retroactively applied in state postconviction proceedings).

5. *Ex post facto laws and retroactive statutes.* Although the view of judges as law makers has evolved over time, the common law has always recognized legislatures

as law "makers" rather than law "finders," and thus statutes were presumed to apply only prospectively. Constitutional doctrine bolstered this assumption: The "ex post facto clause" of the federal constitution barred legislation that enhanced the punishment for a prior act. The clause provides that "[no] state shall . . . pass any . . . ex post facto law." U.S. Const. art. I, §10, cl. 1. In Calder v. Bull, 3 U.S. (3 Dall.) 386, 390 (1798), the Supreme Court explained that the ex post facto clause prohibited the following kinds of laws:

1. Every law that makes an action done before the passing of the law, and which was innocent when done, criminal, and punishes such action.
2. Every law that aggravates a crime, or makes it greater than it was when committed.
3. Every law that changes the punishment, and inflicts a greater punishment than the law annexed to the crime when committed.
4. Every law that alters the legal rules of evidence, and receives less, or different, testimony than the law required at the time of the commission of the offense in order to convict the offender.

In Thompson v. Utah, 170 U.S. 343 (1898), the Court held that a Utah law reducing the size of a criminal jury from 12 to 8 deprived a defendant of "a substantial right involved in his liberty" and thus violated the ex post facto clause. The Court overruled *Thompson* in Collins v. Youngblood, 497 U.S. 37 (1990), concluding that the ex post facto clause does not apply to every change of procedure that "alters the situation of a party to his disadvantage." It upheld a statute allowing an appellate court to reform an unauthorized verdict without having to remand for retrial, even for crimes committed before the passage of the statute. Does *Collins* give a legislature flexibility on the retroactivity question comparable to that of the *Linkletter* rule?

Most courts limit application of the ex post facto principle to laws that enhance punishment or are found to be "substantive" rather than "procedural." See also Rogers v. Tennessee, 532 U.S. 451 (2001) (state supreme court abolished common-law defense in criminal case and applied new rule retroactively to defendant; due process clause rather than the ex post facto clause controls this situation because it involves judicial rather than legislative action); Stogner v. California, 539 U.S. 607 (2003) (striking down state "revivification" statutes that revive the possibility of prosecution by creating a new and extended statute of limitations after the original time bar has run).

Do legislatures think differently about laws because they are limited to prospective application? Do courts think differently about their rulings if decisions are generally applied retroactively?

Table of Cases

Principal Supreme Court cases are in bold.
Other principal cases are in italic.

Abbate v. United States, 869
Adams v. New York, 346
Adcock v. Commonwealth, 189
Addington v. Texas, 772
Adel, State v., 884
Adkins, People v., 698
Advisory Opinion to the Governor
   (Appointed Counsel), In re, 680
Agnello, State v., 484
Aguilar v. State, 482
Aguilar v. Texas, 162–163, 164, 165, 168,
   171, 173, 175
Agurs, United States v., 916
Ah Sin v. Wittman, 846
Ake v. Oklahoma, 679
Alabama v. Shelton, 676–677
Alabama v. White, 76, 78, 174
Albernaz v. United States, 881
Allen, State v. (31 A.3d), 894
Allen, State v. (294 P.3d), 611
Allen v. Commonwealth, 699
Allen v. United States, 1117–1118
Alleyne v. United States, 1268
Almeida v. State, 533
Alspach, State v., 691
Alston, State v., 385, 386
Alvarez, State v., 883

Alvarado v. Superior Court, 1148
Amazon Indus. Chem. Corp., United
   States v., 632
Ammidown, United States v., 1029
Amrein v. State, 1078
Anchorage Police Dep't Emps. Ass'n v.
   Municipality of Anchorage, 269
Anderer, Ex parte, 1293
Anders v. California, 1294–1298
Anderson, People v., 592, 593–595
Anderson, State v., 8
Anderson v. Charles, 1180
Anderson v. Creighton, 401
Anderson v. State, 947
Andrades, People v., 1183
Andrei, State v., 274
Andresen v. Maryland, 274
Angilau, State v., 830
Antommarchi, People v., 1194
Anyan, State v., 182
Apelt, State v., 149
Apodaca v. Oregon, 1120
Apprendi v. New Jersey, 1259–1263,
   1265–1266, 1267, 1268, 1271
Argersinger v. Hamlin, 676
Arguello, People v., 698
Arizona v. Evans, 370

Arizona v. Fulminante, 483, 566, 1311
Arizona v. Gant, 230, 279, 280, 281,
    282, 371
Arizona v. Hicks, 51
Arizona v. Johnson, 122
Arizona v. Mauro, 545
Arizona v. Roberson, 548
Arizona v. Youngblood, 926
Arkansas v. Sanders, 292, 293, 295
Arkansas v. Sullivan, 326
Arman, People v., 1177
Armstrong, United States v., 86, 844, 850,
    928, 1287
Arvizu, United States v., 76
Ash, United States v., 597
Ashbaugh, State v., 64
Ashcraft v. Tennessee, 476
Ashcroft v. al-Kidd, 89
Ashe v. Swenson, 881, 883, 888, 890,
    893, 897
Askerooth, State v., 325
Atwater v. City of Lago Vista, 322,
    323, 325
Ault, State v., 380
Avant, People v., 489
Azania, State v., 968

Babcock, People v., 1246, 1247–1248
Bacigalupo, Commonwealth v., 1160
Bado v. United States, 1068
Bagley, United States v., 916, 925
Bailey, In re, 1298
Bailey, State ex rel., v. Facemire, 798
Bailey v. State, 298
Bailey v. United States, 190
Baker, State v., 1078
Baldwin v. New York, 1068, 1069
Balicki, Commonwealth v., 149
Ball v. United States, 862, 1303
Ballew v. Georgia, 1119–1120
Bamber, State v., 184
Banks, People v., 131
Banks, State v., 482
Banks, United States v., 188
Banks v. Dretke, 924
Barber, State v., 99
Barboza, State v., 1018
Barker v. Wingo, 962, 964, 965, 966,
    967, 968
Barnes, State v., 701
Barnes, United States v., 1134
Barnett, State v., 578
Barone v. State, 597

Barr, State v., 1320
Barraza, People v., 662
Barron, State v., 565
Bartkus v. Illinois, 863, 871, 872
Barton, State v., 162, 171, 175
Bass, United States v., 850
Batchelder, United States v., 817, 818, 819
Batson v. Kentucky, 1094, 1100–1107,
    1109–1110, 1111–1113, 1276,
    1283–1284, 1285, 1286, 1287
Battis, Commonwealth v., 1063
Bauer, State v., 324
Baust, Commonwealth v., 654
Bayard, State v., 321
Baynes, State v., 814
Baysinger, State v., 316
Beaman, People v., 917
Bean, State v., 1113
Beavers v. Haubert, 961
Beck v. Alabama, 1116
Beecher v. Alabama, 477
Bell v. Clapp, 188, 294
Bell v. Wolfish, 269
Bellamy, State v., 999
Belote v. State, 302
Beltz v. State, 53
Benevento, People v., 729
Benjamin v. State, 542
Benoit, State v., 1076
Benton v. Maryland, 871
Berard, State v., 270
Berger v. New York, 439
Berghuis v. Thompkins, 527, 529, 530,
    531, 532, 533, 534, 538
Berkemer v. McCarty, 511, 513, 514, 515
Best, State v., 267
Betterman v. Montana, 969
Betts v. Brady, 671, 672, 673, 674, 678
Bevel, State v., 556
Bey, State v., 982, 988, 1006
Birchfield v. North Dakota, 225, 230,
    240, 241
Bisaccia, State v., 274
Bishop, United States v., 1103–1104
Bishop v. State, 1270
Biswell, United States v., 256
Bittick, State v., 525
Bivens v. Six Unknown Named Agents of
    Fed. Bureau of Narcotics, 404
Bivins v. State, 1242
Blackledge v. Perry, 851, 989
Blakely v. Washington, 1258,
    1267–1268, 1271

Blanton v. City of N. Las Vegas, 1069–1074
Bleyl, State v., 507
Bloate v. United States, 975
Blockburger v. United States, 552, 557, 869, 874, 875, 876, 878, 879, 881, 883, 884, 886, 890, 1115
Blodgett, Commonwealth v., 944
Blueford v. Arkansas, 1117
Bluehorse, State v., 1244
Blyth, State v., 856
Board of Educ. of Indep. Sch. Dist. No. 92 of Pottawatomie Cty. v. Earls, 259–260, 261, 264
Bobby v. Van Hook, 722
Bobic, State v., 55
Boff, People v., 232
Bolte, State v., 195
Bonacorsi, State v., 1122
Bond v. State, 483
Bond v. United States, 55, 414
Booker, United States v., 1039, 1267, 1328
Boone, People v., 617
Booth v. Maryland, 1242
Boots, State v., 1120
Bordenkircher v. Hayes, 985, 987
Bost v. State, 78
Bouie, State v., 1007
Bouldin v. State, 301, 302
Boulies v. People, 885
Bousman v. District Court, 241
Boyd v. United States, 272, 274, 275, 276, 346
Boykin v. Alabama, 990, 1000, 1009, 1018, 1019
Bradshaw, Commonwealth v., 530
Bradshaw v. State, 1216
Bradshaw v. Stumpf, 998
Brady v. Maryland, 916, 917, 919, 920–921, 923, 924, 925, 927, 928, 929, 930, 933, 934, 940, 954, 1320
Brady v. State, 1151
Brady v. United States, 984, 999, 1000, 1003, 1005, 1006
Bram v. United States, 473, 483, 492
Brant, Commonwealth v., 529
Branzburg v. Hayes, 651
Brasfield v. United States, 1119
Brashars v. Commonwealth, 577
Braswell v. United States, 652
Bravata, United States v., 977
Bravo-Fernandez v. United States, 893
Brazelton, Commonwealth v., 687
Brendlin v. California, 389

Brewer v. Williams, 559
Brigham City v. Stuart, 12
Brignoni-Ponce, United States v., 105, 132
Brimage, State v., 1040, 1044–1045, 1046
Brinegar v. United States, 152, 153
Brisbon v. United States, 492
Broce, United States v., 989
Brooks, State v., 53
Brooks v. State, 1305, 1309
Broughton, State v., 1243
Brown, People v., 148
Brown, State ex rel., v. Dietrick, 178, 181
Brown, State v. (156 S.W.3d 722), 210
Brown, State v. (676 A.2d), 1232
Brown, State v. (783 P.2d), 210
Brown, State v. (792 N.E.2d), 325
Brown, State v. (940 P.2d), 945
Brown v. Illinois, 383
Brown v. Mississippi, 473, 475, 476, 477, 492, 503
Brown v. Ohio, 881, 883
Brown v. State, 198
Brown v. Texas, 81
Brugman v. State, 1239
Bruns, State v., 384, 388
Bruton v. United States, 909, 1160, 1161–1164, 1165
Bryant, State v., 52, 56
Bryant v. State, 172
Buckner v. United States, 151
Budzyn, People v., 1320
Buelow, State v., 827
Bulgin v. State, 976
Bullcoming v. New Mexico, 1160
Bumper v. North Carolina, 209
Bunting, Commonwealth v., 976
Burch v. Louisiana, 1120
Burdeau v. McDowell, 68
Burge, Commonwealth v., 876
Burge v. State, 872
Burns v. Reed, 665
Burrows v. Superior Court, 275, 276
Buza, People v., 456, 466–467
Byrd, State v., 230
Byrd v. State, 1120
Byron, United States v., 854

Cabagbag, State v., 617
Caceres, United States v., 807
Cady v. Dombrowski, 8
Cage v. Louisiana, 1192
Cahan, People v., 349, 355, 358, 359, 361
Calandra, United States v., 359, 371

Calder v. Bull, 1332
Caldwell, People v., 1121
Caldwell v. Mississippi, 679
Caldwell v. State, 211
California v. Acevedo, 290, 296
California v. Beheler, 511, 514
California v. Carney, 283
California v. Ciraolo, 52
California v. Greenwood, 53, 246, 1324
California v. Hodari D., 65
California v. Prysock, 524
Callahan, People v., 988
**Camara v. Municipal Court of San
    Francisco,** 124, 199, 202, 220
Campbell, Commonwealth v., 1121
Campbell, State v., 197
Campfield, State v., 1018
Canino, People v., 1020
Cantre, People v., 172
Capolongo, State v., 445
Cardwell v. Lewis, 283
Carleton, Commonwealth v., 1111
Carlson v. Landon, 772, 773
Caron, State v., 534
Carpenter v. United States, 276, 418,
    425–427, 446, 455, 650
Carper, State v., 289
Carroll v. United States, 154, 155, 156,
    276, 277, 282, 290, 291, 292, 293
Carter v. Kentucky, 1178
Carvajal, State v., 390
Case, State v., 1021
Casey, State v., 1048
Casiano v. Commissioner, 1330
Cason, State v., 1088
Castagnola, State v., 145
Castaneda v. Partida, 1081
Castillo-Alvarez, State v., 577
Ceccolini, United States v., 380–381
Chabot, Ex parte, 1188
Chadwick, United States v., 291, 292, 293,
    294, 295, 296
Chalaire, State v., 1010
Chambers, State v., 1187
Chambers v. Maroney, 276, 277, 282, 290
Champion, People v., 118, 120
Chapman, State v., 535
Chapman v. California, 1311, 1312,
    1315, 1320
Chase v. State, 80
Chenique-Puey, State v., 907
Chenoweth, State v., 150, 171
Chenze, People v., 816

Chimel v. California, 226, 229, 231, 279,
    280, 281
Chippero, State v., 310
Chong, State v., 857–858
Chrisman, State v., 149
Citizen, State v., 735
City of Casper v. Fletcher, 1077
City of Chicago v. Morales (527 U.S.),
    27, 30
City of Chicago v. Morales
    (687 N.E.2d), 30
City of Indianapolis v. Edmond, 124,
    129, 130
City of Los Angeles, United States v., 402
City of Los Angeles v. Lyons, 407
City of Los Angeles v. Patel, 202
City of Panora v. Simmons, 32
City of Ontario v. Quon, 257, 427
City of Sumner v. Walsh, 29
Clark, People v., 534
Clark, State v., 734
Clark v. Arizona, 1167
Clark v. State, 64
Clarke, Commonwealth v., 527, 533, 539
Class v. United States, 1293
Claypool, People v., 1246, 1249
Cleary, State v., 539
Cleckley, Commonwealth v., 208
Clewis v. State, 1305–1308
Clewley v. State, 1021
Cline v. State, 1295–1296
Clopten, State v., 619
Cobbs, People v., 1012
Cobb, State v., 1270
Coffin v. United States, 1196
Cohen v. United States, 652
Coleman v. Alabama, 690
Coleman v. Johnsen, 698
Coleman v. State, 92, 100
Coleman v. Thompson, 964
Coles v. United States, 1272
Collins, Commonwealth v., 529
Collins, People v. (27 P.3d), 1012
Collins, People v. (475 N.W.2d), 455
Collins v. Virginia, 250
Collins v. Youngblood, 1332
Colonnade Catering Corp. v. United
    States, 256
Colorado v. Bertine, 285, 287, 288
Colorado v. Connelly, 493, 534, 535
Colorado v. Spring, 536
Commonwealth v. _____. *See* name of
    defendant

Comstock, United States v., 780–781
Conefrey, Commonwealth v., 1321
Connally v. Georgia, 179, 181
Connecticut v. Barrett, 531
Connick v. Thompson, 927
Consent Decree, United States v. City of
    Los Angeles, 402
Cooks v. State, 690
Coolidge v. New Hampshire, 149,
    178, 248
Corbitt v. New Jersey, 1026
Cornell, State v., 698
Cortez, United States v., 80
Costello v. United States, 857, 858
Cotton, United States v., 1322
Cotton v. State, 190
Counselman v. Hitchcock, 637, 638
Counts, State v., 1301
County of Riverside v.
    McLaughlin, 310, 477
Cowan v. Superior Court, 988
Cox, State v., 1116
Cox v. State, 80
Cox v. United States, 900
Coy v. Iowa, 1140, 1141, 1142
Cozart, State v., 999
Crawford v. Washington, 1151,
    1158–1159, 1165
Crawley, State v., 341
Crayton, Commonwealth v., 608
Creel v. Johnson, 554
Cregan, People v., 230
Crews, United States v., 381
Crimm v. Commonwealth, 854
Crockett v. State, 97
Cronic, United States v., 718, 719,
    731, 732
Crosby v. State, 78
Crosby v. United States, 1149
Crow Dog, Ex parte, 838
Crowell v. State, 130
Cruz, State v., 1195
C.T., In re, 275
Culbreath, State v., 844
Culombe v. Connecticut, 489
Cunningham, People v., 548
Cupp v. Murphy, 227
Cuyler v. Sullivan, 705, 707, 717, 718

Danforth v. Minnesota, 1331
Danh, State v., 984
Daniels v. State, 1326, 1329
D'Antonio, State v., 1014

David S., In re, 302
Davidson, State v., 370
Davie v. People, 999
Davila, State v., 231
Davila, United States v., 1014
Davila v. Davis, 1331
Davis, People v. (208 P.3d), 523
Davis, People v. (518 N.E.2d), 1281
Davis, State v., 1113
Davis v. Alaska, 1165
Davis v. Mississippi, 609
Davis v. State, 1125–1126
Davis v. United States (512 U.S.), 529,
    531, 532, 533
Davis v. United States (564 U.S.),
    371, 1330
Davis v. Washington, 1159
D.B., In re, 850
Dean, State v. (543 P.2d), 99
Dean, State v. (645 A.2d), 72, 75
Defore, People v., 348
DeJohn, Commonwealth v., 366
De La Cruz, State v., 370
Delaraba v. Police Dep't, 269
Delaware v. Prouse, 125, 126, 130
Delaware v. Van Arsdall, 1165–1166
DelVecchio, State v., 1195
Dement, People v., 554
Demore v. Kim, 781
Denehy, Commonwealth v., 975
Deneui, State v., 12
Dennis v. DPP, 793
DePallo, People v., 1183, 1185
Department of Justice v. Reporters
    Comm. for Freedom of the
    Press, 1135
Derricott v. State, 97
Desgranges on Behalf of Kunkeli, People
    ex rel., v. Anderson, 768
DeShields v. State, 567
Devenpeck v. Alford, 305
Devone, People v., 434
DeWolfe v. Richmond, 691
Diaz, Commonwealth v.
    (661 N.E.2d), 524
Diaz, Commonwealth v.
    (730 N.E.2d), 944
Diaz, People v., 118, 120
Dickens, State v., 1091
Dickerson v. United States, 507, 575
DiGiambattista, Commonwealth v., 492
Dilliner, State v., 1121
Dilworth, People v., 268

Dionisio, United States v., 649, 653
Disciplinary Action Against Feland,
    In re, 933
District Court of Black Hawk Cty.,
    State v., 177
District of Columbia v. Heller, 115
Ditter, State v., 1012
Dixon, People v., 594
Dixon, State v., 825
Dixon, United States v., 869, 875, 879,
    881, 883, 884, 886
Dixon v. State (284 N.E.2d), 1296
Dixon v. State (758 A.2d), 302
Dixson, State v., 252
Doctor v. State, 382
Dodson v. State, 161
Doe, United States v., 652
Doe v. United States, 653
Doggett v. United States, 964, 968
Donovan v. Dewey, 203, 256
Doolin, People v., 736
Doorson v. Netherlands, 1143, 1148
Dopp, State v., 897
Dorado, People v., 495
Doucette, State v., 1304
Douglas v. California, 692, 1294, 1295
Dow Chem. Co. v. United
    States, 53, 435
Dowdy v. Commonwealth, 679
Doyle v. Ohio, 1180
Dracon, People v., 511
Drago v. State, 316
Draper, State v., 1000
Draper v. United States, 838
Drayton, United States v., 67, 210
Driscoll, State v., 633
Drope v. Missouri, 700
Dube, State v., 13
Dubose, State v., 608
Duckworth v. Eagan, 524
Dudick, State v., 179
Dudley, State v., 677
Duff, State v., 170
Duhe, State v., 97
Dunaway v. New York, 305
Duncan v. Louisiana, 1068, 1069
Dunn, United States v., 246, 247, 250
Dunn v. State, 525
Dunn v. United States, 1121
Dunnigan, United States v., 1270
Duren v. Missouri, 1081
Durham, Commonwealth v., 942
Dyer, State v., 516

Ealy, People v., 656
Eason, State v., 369
Easter, State v., 1183
Edler, State v., 548
Edmonson v. Leesville Concrete
    Co., 1111
Edmunds, Commonwealth v., 362,
    364–365, 366–367, 368
Edwards v. Arizona, 539, 544, 545, 546,
    548, 556, 559
Edwards v. United States, 1271
El, Commonwealth v., 698
Elerieki, State v., 189
El-Ghazzawy v. Berthiaume, 304
Elison, State v., 449
Elkins v. United States, 360
Elliott, People v., 548
Ellis, Commonwealth v., 842
Ellis, State v., 215
Elmarr, State v., 508, 515
Elson v. State, 371
Emmett, State v., 1051
Engelmann, State v., 1021
England v. State, 662
Engram, People v., 973
Enlow v. State, 1326, 1327, 1328–1329
Entick v. Carrington, 47, 136, 137, 139,
    140, 182, 273, 412
Escobedo v. Illinois, 495, 496, 549
Espinoza v. Martin, 1028
Estelle v. Smith, 515, 691, 1249
Estelle v. Williams, 1196
Estrada, People v., 818
Evans, State v., 115
Evans v. Michigan, 1310
Ewing v. California, 1215, 1216
Ex parte ____. *See* name of defendant.

Fahy v. Connecticut, 1311, 1320
Fair v. State, 288
Falkner v. State, 251
Fanner v. State, 373
Faretta v. California, 693, 694, 695–696,
    697, 698, 699, 700, 1298, 1315
Fare v. Michael C., 535
Farley, State v., 883
Farrell, People v., 1157
Feddiman v. State, 1084–1085
Feliciano, State v., 883
Felix, United States v., 884
Fellers v. United States (397 F.3d), 565
Fellers v. United States (540 U.S.),
    555, 565

Ferguson v. City of Charleston, 270
Fernandes, State v., 830
Fernandez, State v., 1086
Fernandez v. California, 214
Ferris v. State, 210
Fikes v. Alabama, 478, 494
Filion, State v., 389
Filkin, State v., 243
Filmore v. State, 1083, 1085
Finley, State v., 1181
Fisher, State v., 244, 250
Fisher v. State, 1076
Fisher v. United States, 652, 653
Fitzgerald, State v., 73
Fitzpatrick, People v. (633 N.E.2d), 1149
Fitzpatrick, People v. (986 N.E.2d), 325
Fletcher, People v., 1164
Fletcher v. Weir, 1180
Flippo v. West Virginia, 251
Florence v. Bd. of Chosen
    Freeholders, 236, 239
Flores-Montano, United States v., 132
Florida v. Bostick, 67
Florida v. Harris, 158
Florida v. Jardines, 53, 250, 424, 430,
    434–435
Florida v. Jimeno, 211
Florida v. J.L., 76
Florida v. Nixon, 719
Florida v. Powell, 524
Florida v. Riley, 52
Florida v. Royer, 97, 304
Florida v. Wells, 286, 287
Floyd v. City of New York, 115
Flynt v. Commonwealth, 812
Fool Bull, State v., 1118
Forbes, State ex rel., v. Canady, 906
Forbes, State v., 1115
Ford v. State, 189
Fortune, State v., 1120
Foss, State v., 787
Foster v. Chatman, 1107, 1111
Foster v. State, 663
Fox, State v., 537
Fox v. Ohio, 864
Foxman, United States v., 959
Foy, People v., 1077
Francis v. Franklin, 1197
Frank v. Maryland, 199, 200
Franklin, State v., 871
Franks v. Delaware, 150
Fraternal Order of Police, Miami
    Lodge 20 v. City of Miami, 269

Frazier v. Cupp, 492
Frei, State v., 1189, 1194
Friedman v. Commissioner of Pub.
    Safety, 687
Frierson, State v., 383
Frisbie v. Collins, 381
Fry v. State, 778
Fujita, Commonwealth v., 1135
Fuller, State v., 1111
Funke v. France, 1174
Furman v. Georgia, 1280

Gaddis ex rel. Gaddis v. Redford
    Twp., 304
Gagnon v. Scarpelli, 691
Gainer, People v., 1118
Gallagher, People ex rel., v. District
    Court, 633
Gallegos, State v., 887
Galvadon, People v., 253, 256
Garcia, People v., 304
Garcia, State v., 66
Garcia v. State, 377
Gardner v. Florida, 1210
Garrett v. United States, 884
Garrity v. New Jersey, 489
Garvey v. State, 534
Gault, In re, 692, 830
Gentile v. State Bar of Nev., 1134
Georgia v. McCollum, 1111
Georgia v. Randolph, 214, 217, 450, 453
Gerald, State v., 534
Geraw, State v., 455
Gerstein v. Pugh, 310, 477, 690, 772, 783
Gibson, State v. (267 P.3d), 12
Gibson, State v. (514 S.E.2d), 1000
Gideon v. Wainwright, 672, 676, 677, 678,
    698, 705, 715, 724, 729, 730–731, 1311,
    1312, 1315
Giglio v. United States, 917, 924–925,
    930, 931, 933, 1188
Gilbert v. California, 590, 593, 595
Giles v. California, 1160
Gillespie, State v., 161
Giordano, United States v., 444
Gipson, People v., 284, 287
Glass, People v., 857
Globe v. State, 539, 549
Globe Newspaper v. Superior Court for
    Norfolk Cty., 1132
G.O., In re, 484
Go-Bart Importing Co. v. United
    States, 229

Godinez v. Moran, 700, 701, 1021
Goetz, State v., 447
Gomez, People v., 212
Gomillion v. Lightfoot, 1286
Gonzales v. Raich, 832
Gonzalez-Gutierrez, State v., 97, 106
Gonzalez-Lopez v. United
    States, 1315, 1321
Goodwin, United States v., 851
Gordon v. Justice Court for Yuba, 1078
Gore, State v., 1260
Goseland, State v., 522
Gould, State v., 1262
Grabowski, People v., 1255
Grady v. Corbin, 875, 879, 883, 886
Graham, United States v., 977
Graham v. Commonwealth, 617
Graham v. Connor, 336
Graham v. State, 1250
Grand Jury Proceeding, Schofield I,
    In re, 650
Grand Jury Proceedings, In re, 633
Grant, State v., 522
Grant v. State, 95
Grassi v. People, 160
Gravino, People v., 999
Gray, Commonwealth v., 367
Gray, State v., 959
Gray v. Maryland, 1163, 1164, 1165
Green, State v. (79 So. 3d), 232, 326
Green, State v. (471 N.W.2d), 701
Green v. United States, 1303
Greenstreet v. State, 150
Greer, Commonwealth v., 1124
Gregg v. Georgia, 1273
Grier v. State, 302
Griffin v. California, 1168, 1177–1179,
    1311
Griffin v. Illinois, 1294
Griffith, United States v., 158
Griffith v. Kentucky, 1326, 1328,
    1329, 1330
Grigg, United States v., 304
Griggs, State v., 173
Groh v. Ramirez, 148
Grosjean v. American Press Co., 673
Grubbs, United States v., 160
Guevara, United States v., 990
Guilbert, State v., 619
Guillen, State v., 381
Guilty Plea Cases, Re, 1021
Gustine v. State, 1006
Gutierrez, People v., 1100, 1109

Habbena, State v., 371
*Hageman v. Goshen County School District
    No. 1,* 263, 268
Hagemann, State v., 1021
Halbert v. Michigan, 1295, 1297
Haley v. Ohio, 477
Haliburton v. State, 690
Hall, State v. (115 P.3d), 75
Hall, State v. (235 N.W.2d), 858
Ham v. South Carolina, 1086
Hammon v. Indiana, 1159
Hana, People v., 911
Handy, State v., 1019
Hansen, State v., 872
Hargis, State v., 230
Harlow v. Fitzgerald, 401, 405
Harman v. Frye, 841
Harmelin v. Michigan, 1216
Harris, People v., 1321
Harris, State v. (105 P.3d), 476
Harris, State v. (680 N.W.2d), 925
Harris, State v. (786 N.W.2d), 1281
Harris v. Commonwealth, 210
Harris v. New York, 530, 565
Harris v. Oklahoma, 881, 884
Harris v. Roderick, 339
Harris v. State, 90
Harris v. United States, 226, 229
Harris v. Washington, 891
Hartman v. State, 548
Hartwell, United States v., 132
Hauseman, State v., 288
Havens, United States v., 372
Hawkins, Commonwealth v., 75
Hayes v. Florida, 305
Hayes v. Missouri, 1098
Haynes v. State, 400
Heider, People v., 1233
Helton v. Commonwealth, 242
Henderson v. Morgan, 998
Henderson, State v., 269, 598, 607
Henning, State v., 282
Henry v. State, 541
Hernandez, People v. (521 N.E.2d), 1164
Hernandez, People v. (896 N.E.2d), 718
Hernandez, State v., 856
Hernandez v. New York, 1111
Hernandez v. State, 1086
Hernley, Commonwealth v., 56
Herrera, State v., 858
Herrera v. State, 514
Herring v. United States, 362, 363, 365,
    366, 367, 370, 373

Herron, People v., 1323
Hess, State v., 388
Hester v. United States, 249
Hickman, People v., 592
Hickman v. Taylor, 945–946
Hicks, State v. (55 S.W.3d), 130
Hicks, State v. (488 N.W.2d), 82
Hiibel v. Sixth Judicial Dist. Court, 66
Hill, Commonwealth v., 969
Hill v. Lockhart, 711–712, 714, 717, 993
Hill v. State, 1086
Hitch v. Pima Cty. Superior Court, 952
Hobbs, People v., 172
Hobson, State v., 688
Hodge, State v., 1111
Hofmann, State v., 326
Hogan, State v., 858
Holbrook v. Flynn, 1196
Holder v. State, 196
Holland, State v., 193, 195
Holland v. Rosen, 768
Holland v. United States, 1192
Holley, Commonwealth v., 854
Holliday, State v., 679
Hollis, State v., 1111
Holloway, People v., 484
Holmes, State v., 698
Holmes v. South Carolina, 922, 1167
Holt v. State, 80
Hood, United States v., 304
Hope v. Pelzer, 406
Hoppe, State v., 1001
Hopper v. State, 999
Horn v. Territory, 1196
Horne, Commonwealth v., 886
Horton v. California, 148, 149, 248, 249
Howes v. Fields, 514
Hoxworth, State v., 170
Hubbell, United States v., 653
Hudson v. Michigan, 381
Hudson v. Palmer, 269–270
Hues, People v., 1121–1122
Huey, State v., 1270
Hufnagel, State v., 232
Huggins, State v., 924
Hughes, United States v., 304
Huisman, State v., 297
Humboldt Cty., Sheriff of, v. Marcum, 858
Hundley, People v., 286, 287
Hurrell-Harring v. State, 729
Hurtado v. California, 856
Husske v. Commonwealth, 680
Hutchins, State v., 194

Ibarra, In re, 985
Illinois v. Allen, 1149
Illinois v. Caballes, 433, 434
Illinois v. Fisher, 926
Illinois v. Gates, 158, 163, 164, 166, 168,
    169, 171, 173, 175, 177
Illinois v. Krull, 370
Illinois v. Lafayette, 288
Illinois v. Lidster, 131
Illinois v. McArthur, 197
Illinois v. Perkins, 522–523
Illinois v. Rodriguez, 217, 218, 219
Illinois v. Wardlow, 78, 79, 80
Indiana v. Edwards, 701
In re_____. *See* name of defendant.
INS v. Delgado, 257
INS v. Lopez-Mendoza, 371
Interest of A.E., In the, 830
Interest of J.L.H., In re, 536
Interest of S.C., In re, 260–261
Iowa v. Tovar, 714, 998
Irvine v. California, 351, 354
Isiah B. v. State, 271

Jackson, Commonwealth v., 701
Jackson, People v., 593
Jackson, State v., 189
Jackson, United States v., 1026
Jackson v. Indiana, 772
Jackson v. United States, 899
Jackson v. Virginia, 1193, 1305–1308, 1309
Jacobsen, United States v., 56, 69, 433
Jacobson v. United States, 662–663
James v. Illinois, 372
Janis, United States v., 359
Janisczak, State v., 31
Jawad, Commonwealth v., 778
J.D.B. v. North Carolina, 515
J.E.B. v. Alabama ex rel. T.B., 1111
Jeffers, United States v., 217
Jefferson v. State, 1165
Jenkins, People v. (20 N.E.3d), 231
Jenkins, People v. (122 Cal.
    App. 4th), 477
Jenkins v. Anderson, 1180
Jennings v. State, 1270
Jerrell C.J., In re, 577
Jewell v. State, 557
J.H., People v., 633
Jiminez, People v., 536
Johnson, Commonwealth v. (86 A.3d), 362
Johnson, Commonwealth v.
    (650 N.E.2d), 608

Johnson, Ex parte, 988
Johnson, People v. (606 P.2d), 973
Johnson, People v. (647 N.W.2d), 654, 662
Johnson, People v. (929 N.E.2d), 1029
Johnson, State v. (346 A.2d), 208
Johnson, State v. (606 A.2d), 663, 666
Johnson, State v. (630 N.W.2d), 1239
Johnson, State v. (873 P.2d), 1244
Johnson v. Commonwealth, 1110
Johnson v. Louisiana, 1120
Johnson v. State (809 S.E.2d), 1110
Johnson v. State (871 S.W.2d), 377
Johnson v. United States, 3, 234, 250
Johnson v. Zerbst, 206, 678, 698
Johnston, People v., 1150
Johnston v. State, 856
Jones, People v. (750 N.E.2d), 1132
Jones, People v. (810 N.E.2d), 381
Jones, State v. (228 P.3d), 699
Jones, State v. (666 N.W.2d), 258
Jones v. State (655 N.E.2d), 1181
Jones v. State (798 So. 2d), 29
Jones v. United States, 43, 46, 51, 53, 251,
   385–386, 390, 412, 418, 420, 421, 424,
   425, 426, 431, 435
Jordan, State v., 613
J.P., State v., 29
Juillet, People v., 656, 658

Kahlbaun, State v., 859
Kahn, United States v., 443
Kansas v. Crane, 780
Kansas v. Hendricks, 780
Kansas v. Ventris, 565
Karr, United States v., 557
Kastigar v. United States, 566, 636,
   637–639, 640
Katz v. United States, 43, 47, 48, 49, 50,
   135, 243, 249, 254, 283, 385, 412, 414,
   415, 417, 420, 424, 425, 426, 431, 433,
   434, 435, 437, 438, 439, 447
Kaupp v. Texas, 303
Keeble v. United States, 1117
Keith, State v., 535
Kelekolio, State v., 492
Kelley, Ex parte, 157
Kelly, People v., 640
Kent v. United States, 824, 827, 828, 829
Kentucky v. King, 193, 196, 197
Kentucky v. Whorton, 1196
Kentucky Bar Ass'n, United States v., 988
Killackey, Commonwealth v., 197
Killebrew, People v., 1029–1030

Kimbro, State v., 162, 163, 164, 165, 166
Kimbrough v. United States, 1039
King v. Commonwealth, 197
King v. Paine, 1154
Kiper, State v., 310
Kirby, People v., 1078
Kirby v. Illinois, 593, 595
Kirk v. Louisiana, 310
Klopfer v. North Carolina, 967
Knights, United States v., 270
Knotts, United States v., 414, 420
Knowles, State v., 851
Knowles v. Iowa, 231–232, 325–326
Kolender v. Lawson, 29
Kostovski v. Netherlands, 1146, 1147
Kotteakos v. United States, 1320
Kramer, State v., 12
Krause v. Commonwealth, 209
Kuhlmann v. Wilson, 556
Kurylczyk, People v., 611
Kyles v. Whitley, 924
Kyllo v. United States, 426, 435

LaCour, State v., 179
Lacy, State v., 959
Ladson, State v., 87
Lafler v. Cooper, 710, 717
Lagenella, Commonwealth v., 288
La Jeune, United States v., 346
Lamay, State v., 231
LaMere, State v., 1321
LaMunyon, State v., 1232
Lancon v. State, 1306
Landis v. Farrish, 799
Laney v. State, 11
Lanza, United States v., 862, 864
Lanz-Terry, State v., 1166
Lara, United States v., 871
Larocco, State v., 283
Larsen, People v., 692
Larsen, State v., 203
Latimore, Commonwealth v., 1053
Lawson, State v., 608
Layton, State v., 699
Leach, State v., 1180
Ledbetter, State v., 617
Lee, People v. (3 Cal. App. 3d), 947
Lee, People v. (218 N.W.2d), 1255
Lefkowitz, United States v., 226
Leftwich, People v., 171, 373
Lego v. Twomey, 534
LeGrand, People v., 619
Leiter, State v., 1270

Lem Woon v. Oregon, 856

Leon, United States v., 362, 363, 364, 365, 367, 369–370, 373, 406

Leslie, United States v., 1099

Lessley, State v., 1080

Levinson, Commonwealth v., 856

Lewinski, Commonwealth v., 944

Lewis, Commonwealth v., 97

Lewis v. United States, 1077

Leyda, State v., 886

Licari, State v., 214

Linkletter v. Walker, 1330, 1331, 1332

Litchfield v. State, 1324–1326, 1327, 1328, 1329

Liteky v. United States, 1112

Lively, People v., 881

Livingstone, Commonwealth v., 6, 11, 12

L.M., In re, 830

Lockhart, State v., 577

Lo-Ji Sales v. New York, 178, 275

Lombera-Camorlinga, United States v., 525

Long v. United States, 897, 904–905

Lopez, People v., 557

Lopez, United States v., 832, 835

Lotsch, United States v., 904

Loud Hawk, United States v., 969

Lovasco, United States v., 955, 958–959

Lovegren v. State, 9

Lovelace v. Commonwealth, 232, 326

Lowenfield v. Phelps, 1118

Lowery v. Cardwell, 1186

Luong, United States v., 884

Lynch, People v., 698

Lynch, State v., 738

Lynumn v. Illinois, 483

Mabry v. Johnson, 1006, 1007

MacDonald, United States v., 960

Mack v. State, 1242

Maddox, State v., 151

Madison, State v., 598, 601, 603–604, 606

Madson, People v., 305

Maffett, People v., 659

Mai, People v., 1101

Maine v. Moulton, 551, 553, 557

Maldonado, State v., 554

Malinovsky, State v., 1303

Malley v. Briggs, 406

Mallory, State v., 99

Mallory v. United States, 477

Malloy v. Hogan, 1169

Manbeck, United States v., 304

Mancusi v. DeForte, 254, 255

Mandujano, United States v., 515, 633

Manduley v. Superior Court, 830

Manning, State v., 1200

Manns v. State, 553

Manson v. Brathwaite, 598, 601, 603–604, 606, 607

Mantha, United States v., 159

Mapp v. Ohio, 354, 358, 359, 361, 365, 366, 373, 1330

Marbury v. Madison, 732, 1310

Mares, State v., 1330

Marion, United States v., 954, 955, 960, 967

Maristany, State v., 221

Marquez, United States v., 985

Marrero, Commonwealth v., 530

Marron v. United States, 144, 148

Marshall, State v., 148

Marshall v. Barlow's, Inc., 203

Marshall v. State, 1166

Martin, Commonwealth v., 566

Martin, State v. (79 So. 3d), 65

Martin, State v. (367 S.E.2d), 269

Martin, State v. (658 P.2d), 1304

Martinez, People v. (898 P.2d), 151

Martinez, People v. (996 P.2d), 968

Martinez v. Court of Appeal of Cal., 700, 1298

Martinez v. Illinois, 885

Martinez-Fuerte, United States v., 125, 126, 132

Martin-Trigona, People v., 856

Mary Beth G. v. City of Chicago, 240

Maryland v. Buie, 231

Maryland v. Craig, 1140, 1141, 1142, 1143, 1148, 1151

Maryland v. Garrison, 150

Maryland v. King, 227, 234, 455, 458–462, 466–467

Maryland v. Pringle, 159

Maryland v. Shatzer, 545, 548

Maryland v. Wilson, 122

Massiah v. United States, 494–495, 551, 552, 553, 554, 555, 557

Masson v. Netherlands, 780

Master, United States v., 872

Matheny, People v., 511

Matlock, United States v., 212, 217

Matos v. State, 1237

Matson, State v., 31

Matthews v. Commonwealth, 578

Mattox v. United States, 1142

Mavredakis, Commonwealth v., 537
Mayen, People v., 352
Mayes v. City of Columbus, 858
Mazzone, State v., 442
Mbacke, State v., 290
McAdam, State v., 819
McAllister, State v., 427
McAlpin, State v., 1252, 1256
McBratney, United States v., 838
McCann, United States ex rel., v.
    Thompson, 854–855
McCann v. State, 242
McCarter v. State, 690
McCarthy v. United States, 1017, 1018
McCarty v. State, 1110
McCaughey, State v., 219
McCleskey v. Kemp, 1274, 1281,
    1283–1284, 1286
McCleskey v. State, 1273
McCleskey v. Zant, 1274
McCloskey v. Honolulu Police Dep't, 269
McConkie, State v., 492
McCormick, State v., 8
McCoy v. Louisiana, 700, 718, 1188
McCoy v. State, 270
McCray v. Illinois, 172
McCullough v. State (657 P.2d), 1199
McCullough v. State (900 N.E.2d), 1302
McDonald v. City of Chicago, 115
McFarland, State v., 1193
McFarland v. Texas, 716
McGrane, State v., 233
McHugh, People v., 130
McIntosh, People v., 68
McKane v. Durston, 1292
McKaskle v. Wiggins, 694, 695, 697, 699,
    1312, 1315
McKee v. Gratz, 432
McKenna, State v., 515
McKinstry, People v., 360
McKnight, State v., 548
McLamb, State v., 1177
McLees, State v., 219
McMann v. Richardson, 989
McMillan v. Pennsylvania, 1258,
    1260, 1268
McMillian v. State, 622
McNabb v. United States, 477
McNeil v. Wisconsin, 556
McNulty, Commonwealth v., 537
Medford v. State, 303
Medley, State v., 130
Medley v. Commonwealth, 1126

Medlock v. 1985 Ford F-150 Pick
    Up, 1076
Medrano, State v., 1300
Mehner, State v., 148
Melendez-Diaz v. Massachusetts,
    1159–1160
Membres v. State, 1323, 1330
Mempa v. Rhay, 691
Mendenhall, United States v., 58, 62, 64
Mendes, State v., 496
Mendonza v. Commonwealth, 779
Meneese, State v., 268
Menna v. New York, 989
Meredith, People v., 947
Mezzanatto, United States v., 988
Messerschmidt v. Millender, 370, 409
Michigan v. Bryant, 1159
Michigan v. Chesternut, 65
Michigan v. Fisher, 12, 196
Michigan v. Harvey, 565
Michigan v. Jackson, 553, 556
Michigan v. Long, 122, 282
Michigan v. Mosley, 529, 530, 532, 539,
    540–541, 549
Michigan v. Summers, 190
Michigan v. Tucker, 506, 566
Michigan v. Tyler, 225
Michigan Dep't of Police v. Sitz, 125, 126,
    129, 131
Mickens v. Taylor, 718
Mikolinski, State v., 129
Miller v. Alabama, 1216
Miller, People v. (75 P.3d), 370
Miller, People v. (869 N.W.2d), 884
Miller, State v., 75
Miller, United States v., 275, 276, 366,
    415, 418, 420, 421, 423, 424,
    426–427, 446
Miller-El v. Dretke, 1102, 1110
Mills v. State, 1181
Mincey v. Arizona, 251, 565
Minjarez, People v., 512, 525
Minnesota v. Carter, 388, 391
Minnesota v. Dickerson, 118, 119, 120
Minnesota v. Murphy, 515
Minnesota v. Olson, 388, 391
Minnick v. Mississippi, 548
Miranda, State v., 498
Miranda v. Arizona, 206, 225, 383, 485,
    494, 496, 506, 507, 508, 510, 512–541,
    542, 544, 547, 549, 550, 555, 556, 557,
    558, 559, 560–568, 570–575, 578–579,
    633, 681, 1152, 1180, 1184, 1250, 1327

Missouri v. Frye, 991
Missouri v. Hunter, 884
Missouri v. McNeely, 225, 241
Missouri v. Seibert, 560, 564–565
Missouri Pub. Defender Comm'n, State
    ex rel., v. Pratte, 734
Mitchell, Commonwealth v., 1187
Mitchell, People v. (650 N.E.2d), 118
Mitchell, State v. (482 N.W.2d), 525
Mitchell, State v. (592 S.E.2d), 131
Mitchell, State v. (593 S.W.2d), 595
Mitchell v. State, 87
Mitchell v. United States, 1178, 1270
Mizzell, State v., 1166
Moffett, Commonwealth v., 1086, 1297
Mohler, State v., 1325
Molina, Commonwealth v., 311
Molina-Isidoro, United States v., 276
Mollica, State v., 386, 388
Montague v. Commonwealth, 65
Montana v. Betterman, 1267–1268
Montana v. Egelhoff, 1167, 1199
Monteiro, State v., 515
Montejo v. Louisiana, 553, 554,
    556, 557
Montero-Camargo, United States v., 106
Montgomery v. Louisiana, 1330
Montoya de Hernandez, United
    States v., 132
Mooney, State v., 250
Mooney v. Holohan, 475, 916, 1188
Moore v. Commonwealth, 150
Moore v. Illinois, 592, 593, 595, 596
Moore v. Michigan, 999
Moore v. State, 1273
Moran, United States v., 304
Moran v. Burbine, 536, 537
Moran v. State, 1324–1325
More, People v., 241, 243
Moretti, State v., 679
Morris v. Slappy, 701
Morton v. State, 302
Mosley v. State, 1294
Moss-Dwyer, State v., 1216
Muehler v. Mena, 190
Muhammad, State v., 1242
Mullens, State v., 455
Murphy v. Commonwealth, 120
Murphy v. Waterfront Comm'n of N.Y.
    Harbor, 643
Murray v. Giarratano, 692, 1295
Murray v. United Kingdom, 1168, 1171
Murray v. United States, 376, 379

Musacchio, United States v., 1309–1310
Musi, Commonwealth v., 366
Myers v. State, 382

Nachtigal, United States v., 1070, 1074
Napue v. Illinois, 916
National Treasury Emps. Union v. Von
    Raab, 125, 269
Naujoks, State v., 259
Navarette v. California, 76, 173
Neil, State v., 1094
Neil v. Biggers, 598, 601, 603, 607, 608
Neilson, Commonwealth v., 217
Nelson, People v., 959
Nelson, State v. (638 A.2d), 71, 73, 74, 75
Nelson, State v. (941 P.2d), 650
Neuenfeldt v. State, 495
Nevius v. State, 613
New Jersey v. T.L.O., 259, 260, 261,
    262, 267
New York v. Belton, 279, 280, 281, 371
New York v. Burger, 125, 203
New York v. Class, 283
New York v. Quarles, 506, 523
New York Cty. Lawyer's Ass'n v. State, 734
Niblack, State v., 1012
Nichols v. Commonwealth, 1242
Nichols v. United States, 1232
Nielsen, In re, 881
Nieves, State v., 149
Nix v. Whiteside, 1185, 1186, 1187
Nix v. Williams, 379, 382
Nixon, United States v., 645–646
Nixon v. Singletary, 719
Nobles, United States v., 943
Norris v. Alabama, 1080
North v. Russell, 1078
North Carolina v. Alford, 1011, 1014,
    1017, 1018, 1021–1022
North Carolina v. Butler, 534
North Carolina v. Pearce, 1271
North Carolina State Bar v. Nifong, 927
Notti, State v., 380
Nguyen, State v., 434
Nuckols, United States v., 985
Nutt, People v., 878

Ochoa, State v., 98
O'Connor v. Ortega, 254, 256, 257
O'Dell, Commonwealth v., 855
ODonnell v. Harris Cty., 768
Ohio v. Clark, 1159
Ohio v. Johnson, 893

Ohio v. Roberts, 1153, 1156, 1157, 1158

Ohio v. Robinette, 210

Oklahoma Bar Ass'n, State ex rel., v.
    Miller, 1188

Oklahoma Press Publ'g v. Walling, 649

Oles v. State, 289

Oliver, In re, 1130, 1318

Oliver v. United States, 249, 250, 252

Olkon, State v., 858

Olmstead v. United States, 47, 351, 412,
    422, 435, 436, 437, 438, 439

Olwell, State v., 947, 948, 951

Oman v. State, 650

O'Meara, State v., 76

One 1985 Ford Thunderbird Auto.,
    Commonwealth v., 371

Opinion of the Justices (DWI Jury
    Trials), 1076

Oregon v. Bradshaw, 548

Oregon v. Elstad, 562, 563, 564–565

Oregon v. Hass, 565

Oregon v. Mathiason, 511

Ornelas v. United States, 76, 159

Orozco v. Texas, 514

Ortega, State v., 538

Ortega-Rodriguez v. United States, 1293

Ortiz, Commonwealth v., 211

Ortiz, United States v., 132

Osakalumi, State v., 928

Otto, State v., 283

Oyler v. Boles, 846, 850

Packer v. State, 1294, 1296

Padilla v. Kentucky, 716, 993, 999

Page v. State, 690

Palko v. Connecticut, 864

Papachristou v. City of Jacksonville, 29

Parent, State v., 162

Parrish v. State, 1235

Parrow, People v., 879

Partin v. Commonwealth, 699

Patane, United States v., 529, 566

Patrick Y., In re, 260, 267

Patterson v. Illinois, 557

Patterson v. New York, 1198

Patterson v. United States, 29

Paulson v. State, 1195

Payne v. Arkansas, 476, 1311

Payne v. Tennessee, 1242

Payner, United States v., 390

Payton v. New York, 307, 310

Pearson v. State, 1087

Peart, State v., 726, 734–735

Peeples, People v., 1086

Pena-Rodriguez v. Colorado, 1123

Pennellatore, Commonwealth v., 531

Pennsylvania v. Finley, 1295

Pennsylvania v. Mimms, 122

Pennsylvania v. Muniz, 522

Pennsylvania Bd. of Probation & Parole v.
    Scott, 371

Penrod, Commonwealth v., 1241

Penry v. Lynaugh, 1329

Pens v. Bail, 1250

People ex rel. Gallagher v. District
    Court, 633

People v. _____. *See* name of
    defendant

Pepper v. United States, 1233

Perez, Commonwealth v., 477

Perez v. United States, 834

Perham, State v., 288

Perry v. New Hampshire, 598, 614

Peters, State v., 822

Peterson, State v. (110 P.3d), 121

Peterson, State v. (923 A.2d), 566

Petite v. United States, 868, 872–873,
    874, 1257

Petroll, Commonwealth v., 7

Pettingill, People v., 549

Pettitt, State v., 1046

Pinder, State v., 251

Pinder v. State, 1086

Piorkowski, State v., 548

Place, United States v., 126, 426,
    433, 434

Plumhoff v. Rickard, 341, 406

Polander, People v., 511

Poller, United States v., 224

Porter P., Commonwealth v., 215, 219

Porter v. McCollum, 716

Porter, State v., 1110

Portillo, State v., 1193

Portrey, State v., 250

Posey v. Commonwealth, 197

Powell v. Alabama, 670–671, 673, 674,
    705, 715

Powers v. Ohio, 1111

Pratt v. Chicago Hous. Auth., 220

Presha, State v., 484

Presley v. Georgia, 1126, 1131,
    1134, 1314

Provenzano, United States v., 854

Pruss, State v., 250

Puckett v. United States, 1322

Purkett v. Elem, 1101, 1104, 1109

Quarles v. State, 92, 93
Quercia v. United States, 1167
Quick, State v., 884

Rabinowitz, United States v., 226, 229
Rackoff v. State, 687
Rafay, State v., 700
Rakas v. Illinois, 384, 385, 386, 389
Ramirez, State v., 607
Ramirez, United States v., 189
Ramos, State v., 903
Ramos v. Town of Vernon, 29
Randolph v. California, 554
Randy G., In re, 267
Rawlings v. Kentucky, 386, 388
Ray, State v., 281
Recorder's Court Bar Ass'n v. Wayne
    Circuit Court, 739
Reece, United States v., 1288
Reed, State v., 984
Reese v. United States, 755
R. v. Aramah, 1228
R. v. Arnautovic, 1235
R. v. Bilinski, 1228
R. v. Chief Constable of Kent
    ex rel. L, 798
R. v. DPP ex rel. Kebilene, 798
R. v. Grant, 361
Regina v. Turnbull, 620
Reid, State v., 1182
Reid v. Georgia, 93, 94, 97
Renico v. Lett, 885
R. Enters., Inc., United States v., 645–646,
    648, 649
Rey v. State, 679
Reyes, State v., 1193
Reynolds v. State, 1180
Rezk, State v., 483, 609
Rhode Island v. Innis, 517, 522, 545, 1155
Richards v. Wisconsin, 185, 187, 189
Richardson, People v., 476
Richardson v. Marsh, 910, 1162, 1163
Richardson v. State, 447
Richardson v. United States, 1120
Richland Cty. Magistrate's Court,
    In re, 842
Richman, Commonwealth v., 690
Richmond Newspapers v. Virginia, 1132
Rideau v. Louisiana, 1133
Riek, In re, 933
Riley v. California, 226–227, 230, 276, 467
Riley, State v., 382
Rinaldi v. United States, 868

Ring v. Arizona, 1267
Ristaino v. Ross, 1084, 1086
Roberts, State v., 1300–1302
Roberts, United States v., 858
Robertson, Commonwealth v., 231
Robinette, State v., 210
Robinson, Commonwealth v., 1098
Robinson, People v. (224 P.3d), 457,
    460–461
Robinson, People v. (767 N.E.2d), 82, 87, 89
Robinson, United States v. (414 U.S.),
    226, 228, 230, 236, 302, 462
Robinson, United States v. (485 U.S.), 1178
Robinson v. State, 277, 280
Rochin v. California, 241
Rodrigues, State v., 380
Rodriguez, State v. (217 P.3d), 1216
Rodriguez, State v. (921 P.2d), 609
Rodriguez, State v. (945 A.2d), 51
Rodriguez v. United States, 121
Roe v. Flores-Ortega, 716
Rogers, People v., 822
Rogers, State v., 66
Rogers, United States v., 837
Rogers v. Richmond, 490, 492
Rogers v. Tennessee, 1332
Romero v. State, 1139
Rompilla v. Beard, 716
Roquemore v. State, 377
Rosales-Lopez v. United States, 1084
Ross, State v., 1002
Ross, United States v., 280, 291, 292, 293,
    295, 296
Ross v. Moffitt, 692, 1295, 1298
Ross v. State, 1021
Rothgery v. Gillespie Cty., Tex., 596, 685,
    686, 690
Roy, State v., 1181
Rubalcado v. State, 550, 556
Rubin v. State, 951
Ruiz, United States v., 925, 1000
Rusen, State ex rel., v. Hill, 940
Rushing, State v., 120
Russell, Commonwealth v., 1194
Russell, State v., 1290
Russell, United States v., 662, 663
Russo, Commonwealth v., 249
Russo, State v., 428

Sabri v. United States, 832
Sacramento Cty., Cal. v. Lewis, 341
Safford Unified Sch. Dist. #1 v.
    Redding, 267

St. Pierre, Commonwealth v., 855

Salaiscooper v. Eighth Judicial Dist. Court ex rel. Cty. of Clark, 850

Saldana v. State, 446

Salduz v. Turkey, 549

Salerno, United States v., 769, 778, 779, 780

Salvucci, United States v., 385, 386, 390

Sampson, State v., 53

Samson v. California, 234, 270

Sanchez, State v., 130

Sanders, State v., 479

Sandstrom v. Montana, 1197

Sandy v. District Court, 1029

Sanges, United States v., 1299

Santana, United States v., 308

Santiago, Commonwealth v., 1298

Santiago, State v., 526, 565

Santobello v. New York, 987, 1006–1007

Santos v. Frederick Cty. Bd. of Comm'rs, 96

Sapp v. State, 533

Sarabia, State v., 1240

Saunders v. United Kingdom, 1174

Savva, State v., 296

Scales, State v., 577

Scavello, Commonwealth v., 131

Schad v. Arizona, 893, 1120

Schall v. Martin, 772

Scheett, State v., 281

Scher, Commonwealth v., 954, 959

Schmerber v. California, 225, 240, 400, 653

Schneckloth v. Bustamonte, 204, 210, 220

Schreiber v. Rowe, 722

Schultz, State v., 276

Schuster v. Eighth Judicial Dist. Court, 857

Schwarz, State v., 214

Scott, State v., 115

Scott, United States v., 1303

Scott v. Harris, 341, 343

Scott v. Illinois, 676

Scott v. State, 88

Scott v. United States, 444

Screws v. United States, 865

Seaberg, People v., 988

Search Warrants Executed on Apr. 9, 2018, In re, 652

Sears v. State, 275

Sears v. Upton, 717

Secord, State v., 1002

Segura v. United States, 197, 375, 376, 379

Semayne's Case, 184, 188

Senn, State v., 682

Sepulveda, Commonwealth v., 524

Serrano, People v., 171

Shade, State v., 1301

Shadwick v. City of Tampa, 178

Sharpe, United States v., 304

Shelton v. United States, 1005

Sheppard v. Maxwell, 1133

Sheridan, State v., 348

Sheriff of Humboldt Cty. v. Marcum, 858

Sherman v. United States, 662

Shumpert v. Department of Highways, 1026

Sibron v. New York, 75

Siebert, People v., 1030

Sigler, State v., 130

Silva-Santiago, Commonwealth v., 609

Silverman v. United States, 44, 432, 438

Silverthorne Lumber Co. v. United States, 348, 375

Simmons v. United States, 390

Simon, Commonwealth v., 529

Sines, State v., 68

Singer v. United States, 1078

Singleton, United States v., 1064

Sitz v. Department of Police, 129

Sizer v. State, 77, 81, 82

Skelton, State v., 283

Skidmore, State v., 1327

Skinner v. Railway Labor Execs.' Ass'n, 225, 268

Skinner, State v., 427

Smith, Commonwealth v., 565

Smith, State v. (39 S.W.3d), 66

Smith, State v. (184 P.3d), 210

Smith, State v. (488 S.E.2d), 210

Smith, State v. (546 N.W.2d), 514

Smith, State v. (607 S.E.2d), 1089

Smith, State v. (637 A.2d), 122

Smith, State v. (672 P.2d), 1076

Smith, State v. (681 P.2d), 737

Smith, State v. (782 N.W.2d), 211

Smith v. Beckman, 179

Smith v. Cain, 924

Smith v. Daily Mail Publ'g, 1132

Smith v. Hooey, 968

Smith v. Illinois, 529, 544, 1148

Smith v. Maryland, 419, 420, 421, 423, 424, 426–427, 446

Smith v. Massachusetts, 1303

Smith v. Robbins, 1295, 1298

Smith v. State (517 A.2d), 1249
Smith v. State (787 A.2d), 1178
Smith v. State (948 P.2d), 380
SmithKline Beecham Corp. v. Abbott
    Labs., 1111
Smullen, State v., 1018, 1020
Smylie v. State, 1328
Sneed, State v., 170
Snell, United States v., 873
Snyder v. Louisiana, 1107
Soares, Commonwealth v., 1094
Sokolow, United States v., 70, 97
Sorrells v. United States, 659, 661–662
South Carolina v. Gathers, 1242
South Dakota v. Opperman, 285, 287
Spano v. New York, 492, 494
Spencer, State v. (519 N.W.2d), 693,
    698, 700
Spencer, State v. (750 P.2d), 688
Spinelli v. United States, 162, 163, 164,
    165, 166, 168, 171, 173, 175
Spivey, State v., 968
Spock, United States v., 1121
Sprague, State v., 122
Spry v. State, 29
Stack v. Boyle, 754, 773
Stagner, Commonwealth v., 986
Stallworth, Commonwealth v., 231
Standley v. Warden, 1011
Stanert, United States v., 170
Stanley, State v., 525
Stansbury v. California, 511
Staten, State v., 97
State v. ____. *See* name of defendant
Steagald v. United States, 307, 308
Stechly, People v., 1160
Steele v. United States, 147
Stephan v. State, 577
Stephens v. State, 1282, 1287
Sterling v. State, 1196–1197
Steven William T., In re, 477
Stevens, People v. (53 P.2d 133), 717
Stevens, People v. (610 N.W.2d), 988
Stevenson, State v., 158
Stevenson, United States v., 1028
Stewart, People v., 498
Stith, People v., 380
Stogner v. California, 1332
Stoner v. California, 214
Stovall v. Denno, 590, 598, 1329, 1330
Strauder v. West Virginia, 1080, 1095,
    1096, 1099
Strecker, State v., 1030

Strickland v. Washington, 703, 711, 712,
    713, 715, 716, 717, 718, 719, 721, 723,
    729, 730–731, 732, 992, 993, 995–997,
    1317, 1319–1320
Strunk v. United States, 968
Sudler v. State, 1092
Sugar, State v., 380
Sullivan, State v., 326
Sullivan v. Louisiana, 1258, 1315,
    1320, 1321
Swaim, State v., 177
Swain v. Alabama, 1094, 1096, 1099
Swanigan, State v., 478, 484
Swift v. State, 299
Swinehart, Commonwealth v., 636, 640, 642
Syrie, People v., 190

Taccetta, State v., 1018
Tackitt, State v., 451
Tanner v. United States, 1123
Tate, State v., 1117
Tate v. State, 1178
Tattered Cover, Inc. v. City of
    Thornton, 275
Taylor, Ex parte, 888, 893
Taylor, People v. (41 P.3d), 514
Taylor, People v. (541 N.E.2d), 360
Taylor, United States v., 281
Taylor v. Commonwealth, 875
Taylor v. Kentucky, 1196
Taylor v. Louisiana, 1081
Taylor v. State, 1331
Taylor v. Taintor, 755
Taylor v. United States, 316
Teague v. Lane, 1326, 1329, 1331
Telfaire, United States v., 612–613, 617
Tennessee v. Garner, 327, 334–335,
    336, 339
Terry v. Ohio, 57, 59–60, 66, 70, 80,
    81, 87, 107, 114, 115, 116, 117, 118,
    120, 121, 122, 133, 230, 281, 282, 299,
    300–301, 302, 303, 304, 305, 310, 331,
    333, 1325
Terzado-Madruga, United States v., 566
Texas v. Cobb, 556
Texas v. McCullough, 1271
Thomas, People v., 486
Thomas, State v. (124 P.3d), 306, 310
Thomas, State v. (533 N.E.2d), 1117
Thomas, State v. (540 N.W.2d), 148
Thomas, United States v. (757 F.2d), 1134
Thomas v. United States, 1165
Thompson, Commonwealth v., 159

Thompson, People v., 241–242
Thompson, State v., 275
Thompson v. Utah, 1332
Thornton v. United States, 281
Tibbles, State v., 282
Tibbs v. Florida, 1307, 1310
Tiedemann, State v., 926
Tiller v. Corrigan, 643, 649
Tinsley v. Purvis, 557
Todd v. State, 885
Tollett v. Henderson, 989
Topanotes, State v., 380
Torres, People v., 122
Torres, State v., 360
Torres, United States v., 1250
Trammell v. Fruge, 343
Traylor v. State, 507, 540
Troupe, State v., 1293
Trujillo, People v., 511
Trupiano v. United States, 190, 229
Tucker, Ex parte, 157
Tucker, United States v., 1232
Tuey, Commonwealth v., 1117
Tumey v. Ohio, 179, 1112, 1311, 1312
Turmel, State v., 516
Turner, Ex parte, 161
Turner v. Rogers, 690
Turner, People v., 594
Turner v. Fouche, 1081
Turrietta, State v., 1126
Twining v. New Jersey, 474

United States v. _____. *See* name of
    defendant
Urbina, State v., 1015
Urrea, State v., 1112
U.S. Attorneys for E. & W. Dists. of Ky.,
    United States ex rel., v. Kentucky Bar
    Ass'n, 988
Utah v. Strieff, 381
Utterback, State v., 168, 171, 172, 175

Valenzuela-Bernal, United States v., 1181
Vale v. Louisiana, 231
Valera, State v., 1250
Vallejos, State v., 662
Vandebogart, State v., 1148
Van de Kamp v. Goldstein, 927
Van Kirk, State v., 1320
Van Leeuwen, United States v., 97
Vasquez, State v., 1040, 1041, 1042,
    1043, 1044
Vasquez v. Hillery, 1312

Vasquez-Aerreola, State v., 1030
Vecchio, People v., 1242
Vermont v. Brillon, 962, 967
Vernier v. State, 961
Vernonia Sch. Dist. 47J v. Acton, 125,
    259–260, 263, 264, 265, 268, 422
Victor v. Nebraska, 1192, 1193, 1194
Viers, State v., 1304
Vietor, State v., 684
Vilardi, People v., 925
Villalobos, People v., 533
Villamonte-Marquez, United
    States v., 132
Vincent v. Commonwealth, 886
Vinnie, Commonwealth v., 855
Virginia v. Black, 1201
Virginia v. Moore, 325

Wade, United States v. (388 U.S.), 566,
    588, 593, 595, 596, 598, 600–601, 603,
    606, 685–686, 714
Wade v. United States (504 U.S.), 1240
Wainwright v. Witt, 1090–1091
Wakefield, State v., 1012, 1244
Walker, Commonwealth v., 619
Walker, State v., 191
Walker v. City of Calhoun, 768
Wallace v. State, 613
Waller v. Georgia, 1127–1132, 1312, 1316
Ward v. State, 999
Warden v. Hayden, 251, 274
Wardius v. Oregon, 944, 945
Waring v. State, 390
Warner, State v., 1013
Warren, State v., 1030
Washington, United States v., 633
Washington W., Commonwealth v., 850
Waters, State v., 1330
Watson, United States v., 210, 310
Watson v. State, 1306, 1308
Watts, United States v., 1271
Wayte v. United States, 845–846, 850
Weaver, People v., 48, 415
Weaver v. Massachusetts, 1134, 1313
Webb, State v., 1154
Webb v. Texas, 1181
Webster, Commonwealth v., 1194
Weeks v. United States, 346, 348, 355,
    356, 358, 361
Wehrenberg v. State, 374
Weisler, State v., 209
Weiss, People v., 379
Weitzel v. State, 1180

Welfare of D.A.G., In re, 213
Welsh v. Wisconsin, 193, 195, 196, 251, 310
Wentworth, State v., 1126
Wentz, State v., 1228
Werneth v. Idaho, 878
West, State v., 288
Wheeler, People v., 1094, 1100–1107
Wheeler, United States v., 837
Wheeler v. State, 143, 148
White, People v., 878, 879–880, 881
White, United States v., 51, 448, 452, 453–454
White v. Wheeler, 1093
Whitfield, People v., 1000
Whren v. United States, 82, 83, 84, 85, 86, 87, 88, 103, 127, 128
Wickard v. Filburn, 834
Wilcox, Commonwealth v., 853
Wilder v. State, 379
Wilkes v. Wood, 137, 139
Wilkinson, People v. (94 P.3d), 815, 822
Wilkinson, People v. (163 Cal. App. 4th), 69
Wilkins, State v., 122
William M., In re, 830
Williams, Commonwealth v., 535–536
Williams, Ex parte, 548
Williams, People v. (21 P.3d), 1122
Williams, People v. (940 P.2d), 1105
Williams, State v., 304
Williams, United States v., 857
Williams v. Florida, 943, 945, 1119
Williams v. Illinois, 1160
Williams v. New York, 1206, 1207, 1210, 1255, 1260, 1268
Williams v. State, 12
Willis, People v., 1112
Wilson, Commonwealth v., 116, 120
Wilson, People v. (213 N.W.2d), 1119

Wilson, People v. (563 N.W.2d), 888
Wilson, State v., 88–89
Wilson v. Arkansas, 184, 188
Wilson v. Renfroe, 787
Wilson v. State (311 S.W.3d), 492
Wilson v. State (562 S.E.2d), 549
Wilson v. State (745 N.E.2d), 122
Wilson v. State (874 P.2d), 61, 65
Wilson v. United States, 1169
Winegeart v. State, 1193
Winship, In re, 1192, 1194, 1258
Winterstein, State v., 379
Witherspoon v. Illinois, 1093
Withrow v. Williams, 1326
Wojtkowski, People v., 555
Wolf v. Colorado, 142, 348, 350, 355, 356, 357, 358, 373
Wood v. State, 283
Woolverton v. Multi-County Grand Jury Okla. Cty., 653
Wright, People v., 613
Wright, State v., 1310
Wrotten, People v., 1149
Wyman v. James, 220
Wyoming v. Houghton, 141, 281, 296

Yarborough v. Alvarado, 514
Ybarra v. Illinois, 120, 159
Yeager v. United States, 893
Yick Wo v. Hopkins, 846, 850, 1286
York v. Wahkiakum Sch. Dist. No. 200, 268
Young, State v. (172 P.3d), 736
Young, State v. (863 N.W.2d), 684
Young v. State, 608

Zadvydas v. Davis, 781
Zarychta v. State, 371
Zeller, State v., 189
Zhahir, Commonwealth v., 118
Zurcher v. Stanford Daily, 651

Index

Abandoned property, 53–54
Abuse, police tolerating, 29
Acquittal-first instruction, 1117
Acquittal rates, effects of pretrial release on, 766–767
Act of production doctrine, 652
Administrative caretaking functions, 287–288
Administrative searches, 42, 202, 203, 257–271
Administrative search warrants, 198–203
Administrative stops, 123–133. *See also* Roadblocks
  advance notice, 131
  airports, 132–133
  balancing tests, 130
  immigration, 132
  mass transit, 132
  neutral plans, 131
  public transit, 132–133
  reasonableness, 130
  warrants, 133
Adversarial model, 1148
Aerial observation, 56
Affirmative defenses
  burden of proof, 1198
  insanity, 692
Aguilar-Spinelli test, 171
Airlines and drug courier profile, 97

Airports, administrative stops, 132–133
Alford pleas, 1014–1022
  free will, 1021
  truth, 1021–1022
Aliens. *See also* Immigration
  detention of, 781
Allen charges, 1118
Allen Report, 733
Anonymous jurors, 1134
Anonymous tips to stop vehicles, 173–175
Anticipatory search warrants, 197
Anti-Drug Abuse Act, 1289
Anti-gang units, 396–397
Antiquated statutes, 784
Apartment curtilage, 250
Apparent authority rule, 219
Appeals, 1291–1332
  advisory appeals, 1303
  bail pending appeal, 1293
  collateral review, 1331
  counsel, right to, 691–692, 1294–1298
  defense, interlocutory appeals by, 1303
  dismissal of charges after, 1291, 1302–1303
  double jeopardy, 1299, 1303, 1310
  ex post facto laws, 1331–1332
  of factual findings, 1304–1310
  by government, 1302–1303
  guilty plea, after, 1293

1353

Appeals (*continued*)
  harmless error, 1310–1323. *See also*
      Harmless error
  indictments, judicial review of, 858
  indigent appellants, 1294–1298
  interlocutory appeals, 1298–1304
  Jackson standards, 1305
  jeopardy attaches, after, 1303
  joinder/severance decisions, 905
  moot appeals, 1304
  new trial, motions for, 1293
  nonconstitutional basis for, 1292–1293
  number of, 1293
  plain error, 1322, 1330–1331
  postconviction procedural issues, 1331
  preservation of error, 1322–1323
  pretrial issues, 1302–1303
  retrial after reversal, 1310
  retroactivity of decisions, 1323–1332.
      See also Retroactivity of appellate
      decisions
  revivification statutes, 1332
  right to, 1291–1293
  screening of, 1304
  self-representation on, 1298
  statistics concerning, 1293
  structural defects, 1311
  sufficiency of evidence, 1309–1310
  videotaping of trial, 1310
  weight of evidence, 1309–1310
Appearance, initial, 852
Appointed counsel. *See* State-provided
    counsel
Arrests, 297–343
  automatic authorization for search
     incident to arrest, 230
  cell phone review incident to
     arrest, 230, 467
  citations, 319–326. *See also* Citations
  common law arrest powers, 316
  conditions of detention, 304–305
  conversation and stop compared, 57
  domestic abuse, 313–318
  duration of detention, 304
  exigent circumstances, 308–309, 310–311
  experiments concerning, 314–316, 318
  force used in, 326–343. *See also*
     Force, use of
  Frisbie rule, 381
  historical background, 317–318
  in homes, 310
  indoor or outdoor, 311
  location of detention, 305

  motorcycle rider, subduing, 342–343
  police discretion in, 312–319
  pretextual, 326
  prior arrests and sentencing, 1231
  in public places, 310
  quotas, 317
  racial patterns, 318–319
  resisting unlawful, 341–342
  search incident to, 224–233
  search subsequent to, 231, 232
  social science research, 317–318
  stops compared, 297–305
  at third-party's house, 307–308
  time of detention, 304
  warrantless, 310
  warrants, 305–311
Articulable suspicion, 58
Ashcroft Memo, 1038–1039
Attention, 583
Attenuation, 380–381
Attorneys. *See* Counsel
Attrition, 797
Automatic standing rule, 385, 389–390
Automobiles. *See* Motor vehicles
Avoidance of police, 81–82

"Bad neighborhood" as proxy for race, 81
Bags. *See* Containers, searches of
Bail, 757–781
  acquittal rates, 760, 766–767
  appeal, pending, 1293
  appellate court controls, 754
  bond dealers, 755
  bounty hunters, 755
  constitutional litigation, 768
  consultation with victims, 754
  crowded jails and, 765–766
  discretion, 753–754
  disparate impact of bail practices, 768
  domestic assault, 756–757
  Excessive Bail Clause, 754
  failure to appear rates, 766
  Federal Bail Reform Act of 1966, 767
  gender bias in granting, 766
  Manhattan Bail Project, 757–761
  method of release, 748–768
  misconduct during pretrial release, 753
  nonfinancial release conditions, 755–756
  nonfinancial techniques, shift to, 767
  presumption of innocence, 778–779
  pretrial detention, 768–781. *See also*
     Pretrial detention
  pretrial release, 748–768

prosecutors, role of, 753–755
racial bias in granting, 766
reform efforts, 757–768
risk assessment, 761–765, 767–768
rules and discretion, 753–754
schedules, 753
self-incrimination risk, 767
sentencing, 760–761, 767
station-house, 747, 753, 754
surety bonds, 755
victims' rights, 754
who sets, 748–768
wrongful detention, 780
Baldus study, 1273, 1280
Banking records, searches of, 275–276
Bargains. *See* Plea bargains
Barker factors, 968
Batson claims, 1094–1113. *See also*
Peremptory challenges
Belton rule, 279
Bench trials and jury trials
compared, 1068–1080
Betts rule, 678
Bill of particulars, 940
Binoculars. *See* Technological innovations
Bivens actions, 404
Black light examinations, 241
Blockburger test, 874–875
Blood samples, 240–242, 653
Blurting, 523–524
Bodily fluids, 240–242
Body searches at jail, 233–243
Bond dealers, 755
Booking
questions at, 522
searches, 239
Bounty hunters, 755
Brady disclosure requirement, 916
Briefcases. *See* Containers, searches of
Brief police-citizen encounters. *See*
Investigative stops; Searches; Stop
and frisk
Brimage Guidelines, 1044–1045
Bugs. *See* Wiretapping
Burden of proof, 1189–1201
affirmative defenses, 1198
presumptions, 1196, 1197, 1200–1201.
See also Presumptions
reasonable doubt standard, 1189–1200.
See also Reasonable doubt standard
searches, 189–190
search warrants, 189–190
statistical proof, 1195–1196

Capital punishment. *See also* Sentencing
dismissal of jurors for cause in, 1093
informal procedure in, 1210
proportionality, 1215–1216
racial factors, 1280
Caretaker function, 4–13
Cars. *See* Motor vehicles
Cause, dismissal of jurors for, 1088–1093
Cavity searches. *See* Intrusive body
searches
Cell phones
cell-site location information,
418–425, 426
probable cause regarding
ownership, 158
records, search of, 418–425, 426
review incident to arrest, 467
search of, 158, 230, 276, 455, 467
Charge bargaining, 986, 1036–1037, 1058
Charging, 783–859. *See also* Double
jeopardy; Joinder
antiquated statutes, 784
attrition, 797
binding over for trial, 783
crimes requiring indictment, 856
declination, 799–808. *See also*
Declination
de minimis violations, 785
discouraging charges, 799–808
discretion, 784–790, 797, 798
diversion, 808–814. *See also* Diversion
domestic assault, 790–792, 796
encouraging charges, 790–799
family courts, 823–831
federal vs. state justice system, 831–836
in foreign systems, 798
grand jury screening, 852–859
habitual offenders, 820–821
judicial screening, 852–859
Justice Department policy, 803–805, 807
juveniles, 812–813, 823–831. *See also*
Juveniles
juvenile vs. adult justice system,
823–831
mandating charges, 790–799
mandatory charging statutes in United
States, 798–799
new policies in prosecutors'
offices, 797–798
no-drop policies, 790–791, 796
overcharging, 821
police cautions, 788
police-prosecutor cooperation, 788

Charging (*continued*)
  police screening, 787–788
  policies to discourage charges,
      799–808
  policies to encourage or mandate
      charges, 790–799
  pretrial screening, 852–859
  private prosecution, 839–844. *See also*
      Private prosecution
  prosecutorial screening, 790–852
  prosecutorial vindictiveness, 851
  public reasons, 798
  racial patterns in, 850–851
  reform, 822
  selection among charges, 814–822
  selection of system, 822–844
  selective prosecution, 844–852. *See also*
      Selective prosecution
  sentencing, 1251–1257
  specialized units or new policies in
      prosecutors' offices, 797–798
  structuring decision, 819–820
  tribal lands, crime committed on,
      836–838
  victim input into charging
      decisions, 839–844
  victim notice and consultation, 842
  written reasons, 798
Chases, high-speed, 340–341
Checkpoints, 123–133
  advance notice, 131
  airport, 132–133
  balancing tests, 130
  driver's license checks, 130
  effectiveness of, 131
  immigration, 132
  mass transit, 132
  neutral plans, 131
  for particular criminal suspects,
      131–132
  public transit, 132–133
  for safety, 130
Children. *See* Juveniles
"Christian burial speech," 557–559
Citations, 319–326
  pretextual arrests, 326
  race, 326
  as replacement for arrest, 325
  search incident to, 325–326
  as supplement to arrest, 324–325
Citizen/police interactions, 3–39
Citizen review boards, 396

Civility, enforcement of, 31
Cliff effect, 1214
Clothing of accused, 1196–1197
Cocaine, 1288–1290
Code of Hammurabi, 1201–1206, 1212
Collateral estoppel, 888–894
  dual sovereignty, 894
  inconsistent jury verdicts, 893
  parties covered, 894
  proceedings covered, 894
Collateral review, 1331
Collective bargaining, 398
Collective entity doctrine, 652
Collective knowledge doctrine, 160
Community caretaker function, 4–13
Community participation in policing,
      25–26
Community policing, 13–39
  components of, 20–22
  crime control values, 35–36, 38
  day-to-day operations and, 27
  defined, 20–21
  due process values, 36–38
  external operations, 27
  impact on criminal procedure, 38–39
  implications of, 27, 28
  internal operations, 27
  measures of success, 27
  overview, 4
  traditional policing compared, 13–32
Community prosecution model, 807–808
Compliance, 25
Compulsory joinder, 905–906
Compulsory process, 1180
Computers
  computer searches, 438
  impact on policing, 27
  search warrants, 190
  "trash" cans, 54
Confessions, 471, 472–579
  abroad, interrogation techniques,
      493–494
  cellmate confessions, 559–560
  "Christian burial speech," 557–559
  coerced, 566
  coerced-compliant, 485
  coerced-internalized, 485
  deception in obtaining, 485–494
  deliberately eliciting, 555–556
  deprivations, 472–478
  electronic recording of statements,
      policy concerning, 575–577

Escobedo, 495–496
false confessions, 484–485
false evidence, 492
false friends, 492
by innocent people, 484–485
interrogation defined, 522
interrogation techniques abroad,
    493–494
length of interrogation, 476
lies by police, 485–494
Massiah, 494–495
McNabb-Mallory rule, 477
Miranda warnings, 494–579. *See also*
    Miranda warnings
in open court, 565
physical abuse, 472–478
police deception abroad, 493–494
promises, 478–485
recording, 575–579
separate trials, 909
threats, 478–485
torture, 478
videotaping, 575–579
voluntariness of, 472–494. *See also*
    Voluntariness of confessions
vulnerability of suspect, 477–478
Confrontation of witnesses, 1138–1167
anonymous witnesses, 1148
child witnesses, 1148–1149, 1150–1151
co-defendants, statements by,
    1160–1167
comparative law, 1148
defendant's presence at trial,
    1149–1150
domestic violence cases, timing and
    motives in, 1159
ethics, 1166
forfeiture by wrongdoing, 1160
hearsay exceptions, 1158–1159
judges commenting on evidence, 1167
legislative limits, 1166–1167
motive, role of, 1159
nontestimonial vs. testimonial
    statements to police, 1159, 1160
out-of-court statements, 1149,
    1164–1165
particularized guarantees of
    trustworthiness, hearsay and, 1158
pending charges, 1165–1166
prior criminal record of prosecution
    witnesses, 1166
redacted statements, 1165

scientific evidence, 1159–1160
sequestration of witnesses, 1150
testimonial nature of
    statements, 1159, 1160
timing, role of, 1159
unavailable witnesses, 1151–1160
value of, 1138–1151
violent-crime investigations, 1159
Consensual searches, 203–222
apparent authority, 219
consent-to-search form, 208
co-tenants, 213
custody, consent while in, 210
duration of consent, 211
family members, 215
forms and policies, 215
government benefits conditioned on
    consent, 220
group consent, 220–221
inevitability of search, 209–210
intrusive body searches, 242
knock and talk practices, 210
leases, 220–221, 221–222
overview, 42, 57
parent and child, 213–214
presence or absence of target, 214
proof of knowledge, 209
rationality of, 209
reasonableness, 219–220
scope of consent, 211
third-party consent, 212–222
traffic stops, 210–211
unequal interests in property, 214–215
voluntariness, 203–212, 220
withdrawal of consent, 211
Conspiracy, 886–887
Constitutional conventions, 140–141
Containers, searches of, 230, 290–296
digital containers, 158, 230
impoundment of motor vehicles, 288
in motor vehicles, 290, 296
not in cars, 290, 296
overview, 121, 122–123
Controlled Substances Act, 832–836
Conversation, stop and arrest
    compared, 57–58
Convictions, multiple, 821–822
COPS (Community-Oriented Policing
    Services), 20–21
Corporations
declination, 803–805, 808
self-incrimination privilege for, 652

Corruption, 396–397
Counsel, 669–746
  civil-law tradition, 669
  common-law tradition, 669
  defense function standards, 719–720
  effective assistance of counsel,
      703–723. *See also* Effective
      assistance of counsel
  ethics. *See* Ethics
  during investigations, 549–560
  malpractice liability, 722
  public defenders, 722, 724–726,
      733–734
  right to counsel. *See* Right to counsel
  state-provided counsel, 670–692. *See
      also* State-provided counsel
Courts
  drug courts, 811
  family courts, 823–831
  juvenile courts, 823–831
  police courts, 325
  special courts, 678
  youth courts, 812–813, 823–831
Crack cocaine, 1288–1290
CRASH units, 397
Crime control
  by community, 26
  model, 35–36
Crime prevention, 22–23
Crime rates, 23–24
Crime reporting, 58
Crime scene searches, 251
Criminal history information and
      sentencing, 1229–1235
Criminal Justice Act of 1964, 733
Criminal Procedure, border of, 3–39
Criminal prosecutions as remedies, 399–
      409
Cross burning, 1200–1201
Cross-examination, 1138–1167. *See also*
      Confrontation of witnesses
Cruel and unusual punishment, 1215
Curfews
  adult, 29–30
  juvenile, 29
Curtilage
  of home, 53, 244, 250
  searches of, 53, 244, 250
Custody precondition for *Miranda*
      rights, 508–516
  blunt questions, 516
  compelled appearance in legal
      proceedings as, 515

  police assistance, 515–516
  stop vs., 515
  subjective vs. objective test, 514

Databases, government access to,
      455–470
Data transfers, 439
Deadlocked juries, 1117, 1119,
      1123–1124
  "dynamite charges," 1117–1118
  "hammer charges," 1117
  lesser-included offenses, 1116–1117
  numerical breakdowns, 1119
  prevalence of, 1119
  sequestration, 1119
Death penalty. *See* Capital punishment
Declaration of Rights (Virginia), 140
Declination, 799–808
  ad hoc judgment vs., 806
  business organizations, 803–805, 808
  community prosecution model, 807–808
  dismissal after charges filed, 787
  internal consultation, 807
  judicial review, 787
  marijuana, low-level possession of, 806
  office size, effect of, 807
  prevalence of, 786–787
  reasons for, 786
Defense disclosure, 940–946
  consensual discovery, 945
  effective advocacy, 946
  work-product doctrine, 945–946
Delinquency. *See* Juveniles
De minimis violation, 785
Depositions, 939–940
Detainer, 873
Detention. *See also* Stop and frisk; Stops
  excludable aliens, 781
  for fingerprinting, 305
  for identification, 305, 608–609
  post sentence, 780–781
  pretrial, 768–781
  wrongful, 780
Determinate sentencing, 1267
Digital evidence, 940
Digital search, 158, 230, 276, 455, 467
"Digital trespass," 425
Disclosure. *See* Discovery
Discovery, 915–952
  Brady disclosure requirement, 916
  consensual, 945
  defense disclosure, 940–946. *See also*
      Defense disclosure

depositions, 939–940

e-discovery, 940

ethics, 946–952

exculpatory evidence, disclosure
of, 916–934. *See also* Exculpatory
evidence, disclosure of

extent of disclosure violations, 926–927

impeachment evidence, 924–925

inculpatory evidence, disclosure
of, 934–940. *See also* Inculpatory
evidence, disclosure of

materiality standard, 925

open file, 939

perjured testimony, 916

plea bargains, 925, 934, 1002

pre-plea, 1002

preservation of evidence, 925–926

prosecution disclosures, 916–940

reciprocal, 942–946

remedies, 927–928, 940

voluminous, 976–977

witnesses, 938–939

work product, 945–946

Discretionary joinder, 895–907

Discretionary sentencing, 1033, 1211,
1217, 1268

Discrimination in jury eligibility,
1080–1113

Dismissal of jurors for cause, 1088–1093

Diversion, 800, 808–814

authority for, 811–812

felony cases, 810–811

juvenile cases, 810, 812–813

policies and exceptions, 813–814

pretrial diversion agreements, 810

prevalence of, 811

reasons for, 812

youth courts, 812–813

DNA

collection and use of, 456–467

collection vs. use, 466

databases, 455–470

government databases, 467

misuse of private information, reducing
risk of, 467

nontestimonial statement regarding lab
work, 1159–1160

private databases, access to, 467,
469–470

tests, 241

Document subpoenas, 643–654

Dogs

homes, sniffing, 430–435

stopped motor vehicles, sniffing, 158

Domestic abuse and arrest, 313–318

Double jeopardy, 861–894

appeals, 1299, 1302–1303, 1310

collateral estoppel compared, 888–894.
See also Collateral estoppel

conspiracy, 886–887

dual sovereignty exception, 862–874.
See also Dual sovereignty

enhancement of sentencing, 1250,
1255–1257

extradition, 873

federal *Petite* policy, 872–873

included offenses, 883–884

international extradition, 873

Interstate Agreement on
Detainers, 873

manifest necessity exception, 885

mistrial, 885–886

multiple punishment, 884–885

Petite policy, 868–870, 872–873

prosecutorial misconduct, 885–886

RICO, 869

same elements test, 875

same offense requirement, 874–888.
See also Same offense requirement

when claimed, 885

Doubt, 1189–1200. *See also* Reasonable
doubt standard

"Driving while black" (DWB), 100

Driving while intoxicated (DWI)
chemical testing, 400–402

Drones, plain view from, 55–56. *See also*
Plain view doctrine

Drug checkpoints, 129–133

Drug courier profile, 59, 85,
92–94, 95, 97

Drug courts, 811

Drug testing
other contexts, 268–269

pregnant patients, 270

in schools, 268

Drunk driving. *See* Driving while
intoxicated (DWI)

Dual juries, 910

Dual sovereignty, 862–874

collateral estoppel, 894

extradition, 873

Interstate Agreement on
Detainers, 873

Petite policy, 868–870, 872–873

silver platter doctrine, 872

statutes, 871–872

Due process
   entrapment, 664, 665
   incorporation of, 142
   model of community policing, 36–38
DWB ("driving while black"), 100
DWI (driving while intoxicated),
   400–402, 1160

Early intervention systems, 397
Early warning systems, 397
Eavesdropping. *See* Wiretapping
E-discovery, 940
Edwards rule, 548
Effective assistance of counsel, 703–723
   caseload limits, 722
   disqualification as remedy, 722–723
   malpractice liability, 723
   objective standards, 723
   performance, measuring, 715–716
   performance vs. experience, 722
   plea bargains, 991–998, 999–1000
   prejudice, measuring, 717
   presumed prejudice, 717–718
   public vs. private incompetence,
     716–717
   quality of representation, 715
   structural ineffectiveness, 717–718
   test for, 703–710, 715, 719, 729
   waivers of IAC in plea agreements, 988
Eighteen to one (18 to 1) ratio, 1288
Eighth Amendment, 754, 885,
   1215–1216, 1280
Electronic devices, searches of, 158, 230,
   276, 455, 467
Electronic mail (email), 427, 439
Electronic Privacy Information Center
   (EPIC), 446
Electronic recording of statements, policy
   concerning, 575–577
Electronic surveillance. *See* Wiretapping
Email, privacy of, 427, 439
Emergency aid doctrine, 12
Enforcement
   arbitrary, 86
   selective, 86
Entrapment, 654–666. *See also*
     Undercover operations
   due process, 663, 664, 665
   "hybrid" approach, 662
   informants, 664
   "objective" approach, 662, 664
   outrageous government conduct,
     663–664, 665–666

   sentencing entrapment, 1249
   subjective standards, 662–663, 664
   trial strategy, 663
   undercover operations, 664
EPIC (Electronic Privacy Information
   Center), 446
Ethics
   contacting grand jury witness, 633–634
   cross-examination, 1166
   defending criminals, 740–746
   discovery, 946–952
   obligation vs. excuse, 744–745
   perjury, 1183–1189. *See also* Perjury
European Convention for the
     Protection of Human Rights and
     Fundamental Freedoms, 1138
European Court of Human Rights, 597,
   780, 1138, 1179
Evidence
   confrontation of witnesses, 1138–1167.
     See also Confrontation of witnesses
   disclosure by defense, 946–952
   exculpatory evidence, disclosure
     of, 916–934. *See also* Exculpatory
     evidence, disclosure of
   forfeiture by wrongdoing, 1160
   hearsay exceptions, 1158–1159
   inculpatory evidence, disclosure
     of, 934–940. *See also* Inculpatory
     evidence, disclosure of
   judges commenting on, 1167
   limits on defense, 1166–1167
   pending charges, 1165–1166
   perjury, 1183–1189. *See also* Perjury
   pre-arrest silence, comments on,
     1177–1180, 1182–1183
   preservation of, 925–926
   presumptions, 1196, 1197, 1200–1201.
     See also Presumptions
   prior wrongdoing, 1165, 1166
   reasonable doubt standard, 1189–1200.
     See also Reasonable doubt standard
   redacted statements, 1165
   scientific evidence, 1159–1160
   self-incrimination, 1167–1183. *See also*
     Self-incrimination
   sufficiency and weight of, 1198
Excessive Bail Clause, 754
Exclusionary rule
   additions to, 391–409
   administrative remedies, 391–399,
     406, 409
   alternatives to, 391–409

attenuation, 380–381
benefits of, 358–359
costs of, 359
criminal charges and, 407
early warning systems, 397
federal involvement in police
        review, 407
four corners rule, 370
"fruits of the poisonous tree," 348, 373
good faith exception, 362–373. *See also*
        Good faith exception
impeachment exception, 372, 565
independent source rule, 379
inevitable discovery doctrine,
        373–383. *See also* Inevitable
        discovery doctrine
internal vs. external review, 396
international adoption of, 361
judicial integrity, 359
"law of policing," 398
legislative remedies, 409
limitations on, 361–391
media review, 396–397
nonconstitutional "law of policing," 398
objective good faith and perjury,
        369–370
origins of, 345–361
perjury in obtaining warrant, 369–370
police oversight commission, 399
police review boards, 396, 398
proceedings in which evidence
        excluded, 371–372
renegade police officers, 399
revocation of police licenses, 397
sentencing, 1249–1250
silver platter doctrine, 360–361
standing, 383–391
state cases, 348
statutory exclusion, 371
tort actions and, 399–409. *See also* Tort
        actions as remedies for illegal
        searches
Exclusion of identification evidence
    confrontations, 587
    due process grounds, 597–611
    foreign practice, 597
    Kirby rule, 595
    lineups, 586, 587, 595–597, 608,
        610–611
    photographs, 587, 597, 609
    reliability of eyewitness
        identifications, 598–606
    right to counsel grounds, 588–597

showups, 587, 608, 624–625
suggestive identifications, 598–606,
        607–608
at trial, 596–597
unreliability, 608
Wade-Gilbert rule, 595
Exculpatory evidence, disclosure of,
        916–934
    digital evidence, 940
    e-discovery, 940
    extent of disclosure violations, 926–927
    in government hands, 924
    impeachment, 924–925
    interaction among obligations, 933
    internal enforcement practices,
        933–934
    Justice Department policies, 929–933
    materiality of, 925
    plea bargaining, 925
    preserving evidence, 925–926, 928
    remedies for nondisclosure, 927–928
Exigent circumstances
    anticipatory search warrants, 197
    arrests, 308–309, 310–311
    searches, 42
    search warrant "exception," 191–198,
        251–252
Expectation of privacy, 50–51, 52, 53
Expertise, police, 97–98
Experts, provision by state, 680
Ex post facto laws, 1331–1332
Extradition, 873
Eyewitness. *See* Identification

Facial recognition technology,
        429–430, 610
Fair Sentencing Act of 2010, 1288
Family courts, 823–831
Family model, 39
Faretta rights, 698–700
Fast-track programs, 1039
Federal Bureau of Investigation
        (FBI), 338–340
Federal Day, 836
Federalism
    justice system, federal vs. state, 831–836
    wiretapping, 445
Federal Tort Claims Act, 404
"Fellow officer" doctrine, 160
Fields, open fields doctrine, 244, 249–250
Fifth right, 525
Financial records, privacy of, 468
FinCEN, 467–468

Fingerprints, 241, 305, 653
FISC (Foreign Intelligence Surveillance
        Court), 445–446
Flight from police, 65–66
FLIR (forward-looking infrared radar), 426
Fluids, bodily, 240–242
Force, use of
    in arrests, 326–343
    continuum, 336
    deadly force, 334–335, 335–336, 338–340
    excessive force, 334–340, 342–343,
        398–399
    extent of, 340
    FBI policy, 339
    guidance on, 340
    in high-speed chases, 340–341, 343
    historical perspective, 335
    motorcycle riders, 342–343
    racial patterns in, 335–336
    resisting unlawful arrest, 341–342
    Ruby Ridge incident, 338–340
    search warrants, 188
Foreign Intelligence Surveillance Court
        (FISC), 445–446
Forfeiture by wrongdoing, 1160
Forward-looking infrared radar
        (FLIR), 426
Four corners rule, 150, 370
Fourteenth Amendment
    due process clause, 87, 142, 609, 611,
        671, 678, 856, 871, 967, 1068
    incorporation and, 87, 142, 678, 856,
        871, 967, 1068
    lineup, 611
    search as violation of, 649
Fourth Amendment. *See also* Searches
    history in Supreme Court, 141
    language of, 142–143
    origins and analogs, 135–143
    privacy analysis, 41
    search as violation of, 649
    state governments, application to, 142
    text of, 41
Frisbie rule, 381
Frisk. *See* Stop and frisk
"Fruits of the poisonous tree," 348, 373

Gag orders on prosecutors and defense
        attorneys, 1134
Game, inspection of, 130
Gangs
    community as victim, 1243–1244
    loitering by, 25–26

Garbage, searches of, 53–54
Gates totality of circumstances test, 171
Gender, release on bail bias, 756
General search warrants, 136–143
    limits on, 140–141
    writs of assistance, 139–140
Global Positioning System (GPS), 43,
        46–50, 341, 412–417, 419–421, 425
Good faith exception, 362–373
    appellate courts, reliance on, 370–371
    costs, 360
    impeachment, 372
    legislatures, reliance on, 370–371
    objective good faith, 372–373
    perjury, 369–370
    police action, reliance on, 370
    proceedings covered, 371–372
    statutory exclusion, 371
    unwarranted good faith, 373
Government access to databases, 455–470
GPS (Global Positioning System), 43, 43,
        46–50, 341, 412–417, 419–421, 425
GPS darts, 341
Grady same conduct test, 883
Grand juries, 629–654
    contacting represented persons,
        633–634
    debriefing of witnesses, 632–633
    freedom of press, 649
    historical background, 629–630
    immunity for witnesses, 635–643
    independent sources for
        prosecution, 642–643
    indictments. *See* Indictments
    informations, 852, 853
    investigative grand juries, 629–654
    nonadversarial proceedings, 857
    other acts compelled by, 653
    police defendants, 858
    police interrogation vs. witnesses, 633
    preliminary examination vs., 856–857
    pretrial screening, 852–859
    secrecy, 630–632
    selection of, 632
    self-incrimination privilege, 640–642
    staff, 859
    subpoenas, 643–653. *See also*
        Subpoenas
    transactional immunity, 640, 642
    trial jury compared, 857
    use immunity, 640
    warnings to witnesses, 633
    witnesses, 632–633

Guilty clothing, 1196–1197
Guilty pleas, appeals after, 1293
Gun laws' effect on stops and frisks, 115

Habeas corpus, 1309, 1323, 1327, 1331
Habitual offenders, 820–821
Hair samples, 241
Hammurabi, Code of, 1205–1206, 1212
Handwriting samples, 241
Hardship excuse, 1092–1093
Harmless error, 1310–1323
   applying the standard, 1320–1321
   capacity to make procedure
      irrelevant, 1321–1322
   courtroom closure, 1313–1320
   forfeiture of error, 1321–1322
   Miranda warnings, 566
   overview, 1310–1312
   plain error, 1322
   preservation of error, 1322–1323
   procedural forfeiture of error, 1321–1322
   relevance of procedure, 1321
   standards, 1320
   structural error, 1311, 1313–1320, 1321
   trial error, 1321
Hearings, preliminary, 856–857
Hearsay exceptions, 1158–1159
Helicopters, 56, 429–430
Highly regulated industries, 203
High-speed chases, 340–341
Highways as special arena, 88
Holder Memo, 1039
Homelessness, 250
Homicide policies and procedures,
    800–803
Hot pursuit doctrine, 251–252, 309
Houses, searches of, 243–252
   constitutional texts, categories covered
     by, 251
   crime scenes, 251
   curtilage, 53, 244, 250
   homelessness and, 250
   hot pursuit warrantless entry and
     search of homes, 251–252
   impermanent homes, 250
   mobile homes, 283
   open fields, 244, 249–250
   outer boundaries of, 244–252
   special status of, 197–198
Human Rights, European Court of, 597,
    780, 1138, 1179
Hundred to one (100 to 1)
    ratio, 1288, 1289

Hung juries, 1119. *See also*
    Deadlocked juries
Hunting licenses, 130

IAC (ineffective assistance of counsel).
    See also Effective assistance of
    counsel
   courtroom closure, failure to object
     to, 1313–1320
   plea negotiations, 991–998
   publicly provided vs. privately retained
     counsel, 716–717
   test for, 703–710, 715, 719, 729
   waivers in plea agreements, 988
IAD (Interstate Agreement on
    Detainers), 873
Identification, 581–627
   asking for, 66
   best practices, 625, 626
   confrontations, 587
   corroboration of, 620
   cross-racial, 583–584, 611–618
   detention for, 608–609
   due process grounds, exclusion
     on, 597–611
   exclusion of evidence, 587–611. *See
    also* Exclusion of identification
    evidence
   executive guidelines and policies,
     625–626
   expert testimony about, 617–618,
     618–620
   facial recognition databases, 610
   foreign practice, 597
   immigration law in Arizona, 105–106
   jury instructions, 611–618
   Kirby rule, 595
   lineups, 595–597, 608, 609, 610–611,
     621–622, 626. *See also* Lineups
   memory problems, 582–587
   mistaken, 581–587, 622–627. *See also*
    Mistaken identification
   new technology and, 609–610
   nonintrusive identification
     evidence, 241
   nontestimonial evidence, 241
   photographs used for, 587, 597, 609,
     610–611
   preventing mistaken
     identification, 622–627
   prosecutors, role of, 620–621
   reliability of eyewitness testimony,
     598–606, 607–608

Identification (*continued*)
  remedies for improper
    identification, 611–627
  right to counsel, exclusion on grounds
    of, 588–597
  showups, 587, 608
  statutory limits on lineups, 625
  suggestive identification
    procedures, 598–606, 607–608
  technology and, 609–610
  Telfaire instructions, 617
  Terry stops and requests for, 66
  at trial, 596–597
  unreliable measures of reliability, 608
  Wade-Gilbert rule, 595
Immigration
  administrative stops, 132
  checkpoints, 132
  identification law in Arizona, 105–106
  racial profiling, 105–106
  roadblocks, 132
  stop or search, 105–106
Immunity
  self-incrimination, 1181
  for testimony, 1181
  transactional immunity, 640, 642
  use immunity, 640, 642
  witnesses, 635–643
Impeachment exception, 372, 565
Impoundment of motor vehicles, 288
Inadequate self-defense, 1249
Inconsistent verdicts, 1121
Inculpatory evidence, disclosure of,
    934–940
  defendant and codefendant
    statements, 938
  depositions, 939–940
  expert witnesses, 938
  lay witnesses, 938–939
  nonexpert witnesses, 938–939
  open file policies, 939
  potential witnesses, 938–939
  remedies for nondisclosure, 940
Independent source rule, 379
Indeterminate sentencing, 1206–1211
Indictments
  crimes requiring, 856
  judicial review, 858
  overview, 852–853
  waiver of, 857
Indigents. *See* State-provided counsel
Individualized suspicion, 42, 65, 89, 116,
    129, 130, 131, 132, 268, 287

Industries, highly regulated, 203
Ineffective-assistance-of-counsel (IAC).
    See also Effective assistance of
    counsel
  publicly provided vs. privately retained
    counsel, 716–717
  test for, 715, 719
  waivers in plea agreements, 988
Inevitable discovery doctrine, 373–383
  attenuation, 380–381
  illegal stop vs. outstanding
    warrant, 382–383
  improper stops and arrests producing
    additional evidence, 381–382
  independent source rule, 379
  limits on, 380
  search parties, 382
Informants
  anonymous, 173–175
  citizen informants, 172
  entrapment, 665–666
  prevalence of, 172
  privilege, 172–173
  probable cause, supporting, 162–173
  reliability of, 170
Information (data)
  gathering without searching, 43–56
  quality of, 152
Informations (criminal actions), 852
Infrared searches. *See* Technological
    innovations
Initial appearance, 852
Injunctions, 406–407
Innocence, presumption of, 1137, 1196,
    1197, 1206
Inquisitorial model, 1148
Insults, 29
Interlocutory appeals, 1298–1304
Internal affairs, 396
Internet, privacy of, 469
Internet service providers (ISPs), 427
Interrogation precondition for *Miranda*
    rights, 516–524. *See also*
    Confessions
  blurting, 523–524
  booking questions, 522
  defined, 522
  by known government agents, 522
  police self-report survey on, 567–572
  safety as motivation, 523, 524
  torture, use of, 478
  by unknown government agents,
    522–523

Interstate Agreement on Detainers
        (IAD), 873
Intoxication. *See also* Driving while
        intoxicated
    as defense, 1167
    Miranda warnings, 535
Intrusive body searches, 233
    blood tests, 241–242
    consensual searches, 242
    for infractions, 239–240
    for misdemeanors, 239–240
    nonintrusive identification
            evidence, 241
    noninvasive medical search
            techniques, 241–242
    probable cause "plus," 240–241
    substantive standards, 240
Inventory searches
    executive rules on, 289
    impoundment, 288
    investigatory intent, 288
    least intrusive means, 288
    motor vehicles, 287–288, 296
    at police station, 288–289
Investigations
    grand juries, 629–653
    investigative stops. *See*
            Investigative stops
    right to counsel during, 549–560. *See
            also* Right to counsel
    undercover investigations, 654–666.
            See also Entrapment; Undercover
            operations
Investigative grand juries, 629–653
Investigative stops, 57–106
    ambiguous statutory language, 58
    bus passengers, 67–68
    checking for warrants, 65
    close quarters, 67
    consensual encounters and "stops," 58–68
    conversation, stop, and arrest
            compared, 57–58
    definition of "stop," 64
    duration of, 121–122
    name and identification, 66
    pretextual stops, 82–90, 100. *See also*
            Pretextual stops
    prevalence of, 58
    racial profiling, 90–123. *See also* Racial
            profiling
    reasonable person standard, 65, 67
    reasonable suspicion, 70–82. *See also*
            Reasonable suspicion

Invocation of *Miranda* rights, 526–539
    ambiguous assertion, 534
    language barriers, 536
    post-invocation activity by police,
            539–549
    silence by conduct, 527–533
    timing of, 533–534
    unambiguous assertion, 533
    waiver vs., 538
ISPs (Internet service providers), 427

Jackson standards, 1305
Jeopardy. *See* Double jeopardy
Joinder, 894–911
    antagonistic brothers, 910–911
    appellate review, 905
    compulsory, 905–906
    discretionary, 895–907
    effects of, 904
    joint trials of defendants, 907–911
    mandatory, 905
    misjoinder, 905
    overview, 861–862
    permissive, 903–904
    protective orders, 906–907
    rules for, 895
    severance of offenses, 895–907
Joint trials of defendants, 907–911
Judges
    automatic strike to, 1112
    bench trials, 1068–1080
    evidence, commenting on, 1167
    judge shopping, 1079–1080
    jury trial, option of prosecutor or
            judge, 1077
    non-law trained, 1078–1079
    peremptory challenges to, 1112
    removal of, 1112
    shopping for, 1079–1080
Judicial review. *See* Appeals
Juries and jurors
    alternate, 1122
    anonymous jurors, 1134
    deadlock. *See* Deadlocked juries
    death penalty cases, dismissal for cause
            in, 1093
    deliberations and verdicts, 1113–1126
    different rationales for one
            verdict, 1120–1121
    dismissal for cause, 1088–1093
    grand juries. *See* Grand juries
    hardship excuse, 1092–1093
    inconsistent verdicts, 1121

Juries and jurors (*continued*)
   juvenile delinquency
       proceedings, 830–831
   lesser included offenses, 1113–1116,
       1116–1117
   misconduct during
       deliberations, 1122–1123
   non-unanimous verdicts, 1120,
       1124–1125
   note-taking, 1121–1122
   nullification, 1122, 1125–1126
   option of prosecutor or judge, 1077
   peremptory challenges, 1093–1113. *See
       also* Peremptory challenges
   petty offenses, 1075–1076
   selection of, 1080–1113
   sentencing by, 1211, 1267–1268
   sequestration, 1119
   size of, 1119–1120
   special verdicts, 1121
   statutory right to jury trial, 1076
   tampering, 1122
   verdicts, 1120–1121, 1124–1125. *See
       also* Verdicts
   voir dire, 1081–1088. *See also* Voir dire
   waiver of jury trial, 1079–1080
Jurisdiction, state and federal
       overlap, 831–836
Justice Department
   charging policy, 814–815
   exculpatory evidence disclosure
       policies, 929–933
   identification procedure, 624–625
   showups, 624–625
Juvenile courts, 823–831
Juveniles
   curfew, 29
   delinquency proceedings, counsel and
       jury in, 830–831
   Miranda warnings, 535–536
   trying, 812–813, 823–831
   as witnesses, 1148–1149, 1150–1151

Kirby rule, 595
Knock and announce, 188
"Knock and talk" practices, 210

Language barriers and *Miranda*
       warnings, 536
"Law of policing," 398
Lawyers. *See* Counsel
Leases, consensual searches, 220–221,
       221–222

Legislative sentencing, 1212–1218
Limitation, statutes of, 952–961
Lineups, 595–597
   best practices during, 626
   orders for, 241
   overview, 587–588
   photo, 609, 610–611, 627
   showups compared, 608
   statutory limits on, 625
Lockers, searches of, 271
Loitering
   gangs and narcotics-related, 19, 26
   ordinances, 30
Luggage. *See* Containers, searches of

Magistrates, neutral and detached, 178–181
Malpractice, 722
Mandatory joinder, 905
Manhattan Bail Project, 757–761
Marijuana
   low-level possession of, 806
   medical 832–836
Massiah and confessions, 494–495
Mass transit, administrative stops, 132
Material evidence and discovery, 916
Materiality standard, 925
McNabb-Mallory rule, 477
Measures for Justice, 1135–1136
Media access to courtroom, 1132
Media review of police, 396–397
Medical marijuana, 832–836
Medical records, privacy of, 467
Memory, 582–587
Mere evidence rule, 274
Metal detectors. *See* Technological
       innovations
Minors. *See* Juveniles
Miranda warnings, 494–579
   alternatives to, 574–579
   "arrest" vs. "custody," 515
   blurting, 523–524
   booking questions, 522
   capacity to waive, 535–536, 538–539
   clearance rates, 573
   coercive environment, 508, 567
   compelled appearances in legal
       proceedings, 515
   constitutional basis for, 506–507
   convictions, number of, 573–574
   costs and benefits, 574
   custody as trigger, 508–516. *See
       also* Custody precondition for
       Miranda rights

Edwards rule, 548

effect of asserting rights, 539–549

fifth right, 525

foreign practice, 549

form of, 524–526

harmless error, 566

historical background, 496–508

impacts of warning/waiver regime, 567–574

impeachment, use of statements for, 565

infinite regress problem, 508

interrogation as trigger, 516–524. *See also* Interrogation precondition for *Miranda* rights

invocation of rights, 526–539. *See also* Invocation of *Miranda* rights

known government agents, interrogation by, 522

language barriers, 536

Mosley rule, 549

other approaches, 574–579

out-of-court statements after earlier *Miranda* violations, 564–565

physical fruits discovered, 566–567

post-invocation activity by police, 539–549

preventing unlawful interrogations, 574–579

public safety exception, 523, 524

questioning with and without, 572

reforms, 507–508

reversals, frequency of, 574

right to counsel, effect of invoking, 548–549

right to silence, effect of invoking, 549

state adoption and modification of, 507

"stop" vs. "custody," 515

supplementing *Miranda*, 579

systemwide impacts of *Miranda*'s warning/waiver regime, 567–574

tainted leads, 565–566

translation of, 526

triggering, 508–524

unknown government agents, interrogation by, 522–523

unlawful interrogations, impact of, 560–579

variations in, 525

video recording as alternative to, 578

violations at case level, 560–567

vulnerable suspects, warnings for, 526

waiver of rights, 526–539. *See also* Waiver of *Miranda* rights

Misbehavior by jury, 1122

Misconduct

by government, 663, 665–666

by jury, 1122–1123

by police, 391–397

Misjoinder, 905

Mistaken identification

cross-racial, 583–584, 602

memory problems, 582–587

police officers as witnesses, 587

prevention of, 622–627

Mistrial, 885–886

Mobile homes, 283

Moot appeals, 1304

Mosley rule, 549

Motor vehicles

anonymous tips to stop vehicles, 173–175

exception, 296

frisking of driver, 123

high-speed chases, 340–341

impoundment of, 288

inventory searches of, 287–288, 296

mobile homes as, 283

motorcycle riders, 342–343

pretextual stops, 82–90

roadblocks, 341

searches, 290–296. *See also* Motor vehicle searches

stop and search, 100–106, 123

stops, 58, 82–90

Motor vehicle searches

containers, in and out of, 122–123, 283, 290–296

exception to warrant requirement, 296

incident to arrest, 277–283

inventory searches, 287–288, 296

mobile homes, 283

overview, 136

of passengers, 281

search incident landscape, changes in, 281–282

stop and search, 100–106, 123

Terry, application of, 282–283

at traffic stop, 210–211

viewing exterior of vehicle, 283

Multiple punishment, 884–885

Multiple sovereigns. *See* Dual sovereignty

Multiplicity, 886–888

National Commission on Law Observance
and Enforcement, 472–473
National security
warrants, 445–446
wiretaps, 445–446
Neighborhood Defender Service, 739–740
Nemo tenetur seipsum prodere, 640
Neutral and detached magistrates,
178–181
New trial, motions for, 1293
9/11. *See* September 11, 2001, terrorist
attacks
No-drop policies, 790–791, 796
No-knock entry, 188–189
Nolo contendere pleas, 986–987
Non-unanimous verdicts, 1120,
1124–1125
Norms, 23–28
Nullification by jury, 1122, 1125–1126

Obedience, reasons for, 25
Observational viewpoint, 583
Obstruction of justice, sentence
enhancement for, 1270
One-man grand jury, 650
Open fields doctrine, 244, 249–250
Open file discovery, 939
Operating while intoxicated (OWI),
682–689
Order maintenance, 14
Organized crime, RICO
prosecutions, 869
Outrageous government conduct, 663,
665–666
OWI (operating while intoxicated),
682–689

Palm prints, 241, 653
Papers, searches of, 271–276
Boyd doctrine, 274–275
extra particularity in warrants, 275
third parties, records held by, 275–276
Paraffin tests, 241
Parole guidelines, 1228
Passengers, searches of, 281
PATRIOT Act, 443
Patrol function, 27
Patrol officer job description, 5–6
Peace-keeping, 28
PEACE technique, 494
Peep-hole observations, 54–55. *See also*
Plain view doctrine
Pending charges
and cross-examination, 1165–1166
and sentencing, 1231

Pen registers, 366, 446, 447
Peremptory challenges, 1093–1113
appellate review, 1110–1111
defined, 1093
ethnicity-based, 1100–1108
extending *Batson,* 1111–1112
number of, 1109
pretext and truth, 1109–1110
race and decision making, 1111
race-based, 1094–1108
race-neutral reasons, 1110–1111
reasons for, 1094
remedies for *Batson* violations, 1112
removal of judges, 1112
stages of *Batson* claim, 1109
theory of, 1109
Perjury
attorney ethics regarding, 1183–1189
client control over admissions of
guilt, 1188
defense counsel responses to,
1187–1188
discovery, 916
do-not-call list, 1188–1189
obtaining warrant by, 369–370
police officers, 493–494, 1188–1189
prosecution witnesses, 1188–1189
self-incrimination and threat
of, 1180–1183
sentence enhancement for, 1270
threat of charge against defense
witnesses, 1180–1181
Permissive joinder, 903–904
Personal information, privacy of, 467
Petite policy, 868–870, 872–873
Photographs
exclusions of identification
evidence, 587, 596–597, 609
facial recognition databases,
429–430, 610
lineups, 610–611, 627
overview, 241
Plain error, 1322, 1330–1331
Plain view doctrine
abandoned property, 53–54
computer "trash" cans, 54
drones, from, 55–56
garbage, 53–54
helicopters, from, 56
inadvertence, 149
incriminating nature of item, 149
information gathering, 43–56
ladders, from, 55–56
legal entitlement vs. likelihood of
observation, 52

location of item, 51
observation of items in plain
    view, 51
other sense enhancements, 53
peep-hole observations, 54–55
plain feel, 52, 120
plain hearing, 51–52
plain smell, 51–52
police vs. public observation, 52–53
reasonable expectation of privacy,
    50–51, 52
search warrants, 148–150
sense enhancements, 435
squeezes, jurisprudence of, 55
technological innovations, 435
Plea bargains, 979–1065
    Alford pleas, 1014–1022. *See also*
        Alford pleas
    alternatives to, 1053–1065
    Ashcroft Memo, 1038–1039
    breach of contract, 1006–1007
    Brimage Guidelines, 1044–1045
    charge bargaining, 986,
        1036–1037, 1058
    charge vs. sentence, 1025, 1030
    civil consequences, 1006
    codifying plea considerations, 1025
    coercive overcharging, 1006
    as compromise, 1055–1057
    conditional, 986
    as contract, 1063–1064
    direct and collateral effects,
        1001–1002
    discounts, 1003–1007
    discovery, 925, 1000, 1002
    discretionary sentencing, shift away
        from, 1033
    effective assistance of counsel,
        991–998, 999–1000
    efforts to ban, 1064–1065
    essential components of, 991
    fact bargaining, 1033, 1037
    fast-track programs, 1039
    forfeiture of claims, 988–989
    future of, 1053–1065
    good faith presumption, 987
    guilty pleas, validity of, 990–1022
    hearings, 1000–1001
    history of, 1063
    Holder Memo, 1039
    "horizontal" charge bargain, 986
    ineffective-assistance-of-counsel (IAC)
        waivers, 988
    inevitability of, 1063, 1065
    internal review, 1046
    involuntary pleas, 1002–1022
    judicial coercion, 1013
    judicial neutrality, 1013–1014
    judicial overinvolvement,
        1007–1014
    judicial rules, 1026–1030
    lack of knowledge, 990–1002
    large plea discounts, 1003–1007
    legislative limits on, 1022–1026
    legitimacy of, 1053–1065
    nolo contendere pleas, 986–987
    non-waivable claims, 988
    objects of bargaining, 980–988
    "package" deals, 982–986, 1006
    pervasiveness of, 979
    plea discounts, 987, 1005–1006,
        1025–1026
    policy with respect to, 1028–1029
    political accountability, 1038
    popularity of banning, 1064
    prevalence of, 979
    priority crimes, 1046
    professional obligations, 1000
    prosecutorial plea negotiation
        guidelines, 1030–1046
    prosecutor's objections, 1030
    public interest in trials, 1064
    Redbook, 1034, 1036–1037
    rejection, reasons for, 1029
    relevant conduct, 1033
    Reno Bluesheet, 1035, 1037–1038
    restrictions on, 1022–1053
    screening alternative to, 1057–1062
    sentence bargaining, 986,
        1036, 1270
    sentencing guidelines, 1033–1035
    "Sharkfest," 1045–1046
    slow plea, 986
    statewide guidelines, 1044–1045
    stipulated sentences, 1029–1030
    Terwilliger Bluesheet, 1034–1035
    Thornburgh Bluesheet, 1034
    types of, 986–987
    uniformity of guidelines,
        1039–1040, 1046
    unwritten guidance, 1039
    USA PROTECT Act, 1038–1039
    validity of guilty pleas, 990–1022
    "vertical" charge bargain, 986
    victims, 1047–1053
    waiver of appeal, 988, 989–990
    waiver of trial, 986
    witness bribing, 1064
    written guidance, 1039
Plea discounts, 987, 1025–1026

Police
    abuse, tolerating, 29
    caution, 788
    community caretaker function, 4–13
    community control of, 27
    deception, 493–494, 1188–1189
    departments, history of, 142
    federal review, 407
    force used by, 398–399
    interviewing and interrogation, self-
        report survey, 567–572
    "law of policing," 398
    legitimacy, 23–26
    misconduct, 391–397
    Misconduct Provision, 407
    officer job description, 5–6
    oversight commission, 399
    police/citizen interactions, 3–39
    private, 69–70, 468
    review boards, 396, 398
    review by media, 396–397
    revocation of officer's license, 397
    screening, 787–788. See also Charging
    testimonial vs. nontestimonial
        statements to, 1159, 1160. See also
        Confrontation of witnesses
Police courts, 325
Policing
    community policing, 13–32. See also
        Community policing
    organizations, 32–39
    philosophies, 13–32
    traditional and community
        compared, 13–32
Precision Immobilization
    Techniques, 341
Preliminary hearings, 856–857
Preservation of error, 1322–1323
Press, freedom of, 649
Presumptions, 1200–1201
    burden of proof, 1196, 1197–1198
    cross burning, 1200–1201
    of innocence, 1137, 1196, 1197, 1206
    reasonable doubt, 1198
    statutory definitions, 1198–1199
Pretextual arrests, 326
Pretextual stops, 82–90
    arbitrary enforcement, 86
    asset forfeiture, 89–90
    department-level pretext, 89
    federal Constitution, 87–88
    on highways, 88
    police response to claims of, 88–89

state constitutions, 87–88
    technology and, 89
Pretrial detention, 768–781
    compensation for wrongful
        detention, 780
    completion of sentence, after, 780–781
    excludable aliens, 781
    number of defendants detained, 780
    presumption of innocence, 778–779
    preventive detention, 778
    repeat offenders, 779–780
    serious felonies, 779–780
    social science research, 781
    terrorism context, 781
    wrongful detention, 780
Pretrial proceedings, 852–859
Pretrial publicity, change of venue
        after, 1133
Pretrial release, 748–768. See also Bail
    acquittal rates, effects on, 766–767
    bail reform efforts. See Bail
    felony defendants in state courts, 751–753
    gender bias, 766
    nonmonetary conditions, 765
    racial bias, 766
    sentences, effects on, 767
    standard release practices, 748–757
Prior arrests and sentencing, 1231–1232
Prior convictions and sentencing, 1231, 1232
Prior wrongdoing, 1165, 1166
Prisons, searches in, 257–270
    "Fourth-Amendment-free zones," 270
    jail, body searches at, 233–243
    prison and jail cells, 269, 270
    pretrial detainees vs. convicted
        offenders, 269–270
Privacy, 455–470. See also Technological
        innovations
    email, 427, 439
    financial records, 468
    government access to databases, 455–470
    government-held information, 467–468
    on Internet, 469
    medical records, 467
    nongovernmental infringement of, 468
    personal information, 467
    "private privacy," 468
    private security searches, 468
    social guests, 390–391
    tort actions, 468–469
    Web, 469
    workplaces, searches of, 256–257
Privacy Protection Act of 1980, 651

Private papers, 274–276
Private police, 69–70, 468
Private prosecution, 839–844
    charging decisions, 839–844
    complaints, 841–842
    financial aid to public
        prosecution, 842–843
    historical background, 842
    involved citizens, 843–844
    special prosecutors, 843
    victim input into charging
        decisions, 839–844
Probable cause, 151–177
    actual knowledge, 160
    Aguilar-Spinelli test, 171
    anonymous tips supporting, 173–175
    applying standards, 158
    clarification by statute or rule, 175–177
    clarifying statutes and rules, 175–177
    defining, 151–162
    digital search cases, 158
    elements of, 152
    fact-based analysis, 171
    Gates test, 171
    groups of suspects, 159
    informants supporting, 162–173
    intrusive body searches, probable cause
        "plus," 240–241
    legal standards and cultures, 171–172
    police expertise, 159
    probabilities, 158, 159
    reasonable suspicion compared, 70–82
    sources of information for, 162–175
    standards for defining, 151–162
    vehicle stops, 173–174
    wiretapping, 442–443
Probation officers, 1271
Profanity, 29, 31
Profiles
    drug courier, 59, 85, 92–94, 95, 97
    racial, 90–100. *See also* Racial profiling
Proof. *See* Burden of proof
Proportionality, 1215–1216
Pro se counsel, performance standards
        for, 701
Prosecution
    career choice, 745–746
    disclosures, 916–940
    dual and successive, 868–870
    exculpatory evidence, disclosure
        of, 916–934. *See also* Exculpatory
        evidence, disclosure of
    gag orders on prosecutors, 1134

inculpatory evidence, disclosure
        of, 934–940. *See also* Inculpatory
        evidence, disclosure of
    private, 839–844
    selective, 844–852
Prosecutorial vindictiveness, 851
Prosecutors, special, 843
Pro se defense, standby counsel for, 699
Protective sweeps, 231
Psychiatric examinations, 691, 692
Public access to court records, 1135
Public access to trials, 1126–1136
Public as decisionmaker, 1126–1136
Public defenders, 722, 724–726, 733–734,
        739–740. *See also* State-provided
        counsel
Public monitoring of criminal
        proceedings, 1135
Public transit, administrative stops, 132–133
Purses. *See* Containers, searches of
Pursuit, seizure by, 65–66

Questioning
    booking questions, 522
    voir dire, racial bias questions, 1085–1086

Race
    arrest rates based on, 318–319
    "bad neighborhood" as proxy for, 81
    capital punishment, 1280
    citations, 326
    crack cocaine, 1288–1289, 1289–1290
    criminal profiles, 90–100
    cross-racial identification, 583–584,
        602, 611–627
    discretionary decisions affecting
        punishment, 1281–1290
    "driving while black" (DWB), 100
    force, use of in arrests, 335–336
    jury selection, 1080–1113
    in juvenile justice system, 831
    patterns in charging, 850–851
    peremptory challenges, 1092,
        1093–1113. *See also* Peremptory
        challenges
    profiling, 90–100. *See also* Racial
        profiling
    release on bail bias, 756
    selective prosecution, 850–852
    sentencing, 1272–1290
    victims of crime, 1273–1281
    voir dire, 1083–1087
    witness descriptions, 98–99

Racial profiling, 90–100, 100–106
  collecting and reporting stop
      data, 100–106
  collective judgments, 98
  constitutional claims, 103
  crime rates and stop rates, 104–105
  data collection and reporting, 100–106
  discretion, 97
  discriminatory profiling, ending of, in
      Maryland, 94–97
  executive branch policies, 104
  immigration enforcement, 105–106
  legislation, 103–104
  police expertise, 97–98
  stops, 100–106
  subjective standards, 97–98
  terrorism, prevention of, 105
  traffic violations, 100–106
  witness descriptions, 98–99
Racketeer Influenced and Corrupt
    Organizations Act (RICO), 869
Rampart scandal, 396–397
Rape shield laws, 1167
Reasonable doubt standard, 1189–1200
  clothing of accused, 1196–1197
  defined, 1189, 1194–1195
  innocence, presumption of, 1196, 1197
  numerical demonstrations,
      1195–1196, 1199
  presumptions, 1196, 1197, 1200–1201
  quantifying, 1195–1196
Reasonableness Clause, 133
Reasonable person standard, 67
Reasonable suspicion, 70–106
  anonymous tips as basis for, 76
  appellate courts, role of, 76
  avoiding or fleeing police, 81–82
  collecting and reporting stop
      data, 100–106
  collective judgments and expertise, 98
  components of, 74–75
  criminal profiles and race, 90–100,
      100–106
  discretion to stop, 82
  dueling profiles and discretion, 97
  grounds for stops, 70–82
  high crime neighborhood as proxy for
      race, 81
  individualized reasonable
      suspicion, 70–82
  objective basis, 75
  officer expertise, 97–98
  overview, 57–58

  pretextual stops, 82–90
  probable cause compared, 70–82
  race and witness descriptions, 98–88
  seizure by pursuit, 65–66
  seriousness of crime, 75
  stop and frisk, 114
  subjective standards, 97–98
  "totality of circumstances" test, 76
  witness descriptions, 98–99
Redacted statements, 1165
Redbook, 1034, 1036–1037
Rehabilitation, 808–809
Release on own recognizance (R.O.R.),
    756, 758–759
Remedies
  administrative, 391–399
  searches, 345–409
Reno Bluesheet, 1035, 1037–1038
Resisting unlawful arrest, 341–342
Restitution, 808–809
Retardation and *Miranda* warnings, 535
Retrial, 1310
Retroactivity of appellate decisions,
    1323–1332
  collateral review, 1331
  ex post facto laws, 1331–1332
  overview, 1323
  plain error, 1330–1331
  postconviction procedural issues, 1331
  revivification statutes, 1332
Return of warrant, 151
Review boards, 396
Revivification statutes, 1332
RICO, 869
Right to counsel. *See also* Counsel; State-
    provided counsel
  adversarial proceedings, initiation
      of, 689–690
  appeal, during, 1294–1298
  cellmate confessions, 559–560
  charge filing, after, 550–555
  constitutional right, 676–677
  constitutional sources of, 678
  investigations, during, 549–560
  invocation of rights, 556
  in juvenile court, 830
  other offenses, 556–557
  statutory right, 677
  waiver of, 556, 698–699, 700–701,
      702–703
Right to Financial Privacy Act, 276
Roadblocks, 123–133
  advance notice, 131

balancing tests, 130
driver's license checks, 130
effectiveness of, 131
high-speed chases, 341
immigration, 132
neutral plans, 131
particular criminal suspects, to
find, 131–132
for safety, 130
R.O.R. (Release on own
recognizance), 756, 758–759
Ruby Ridge, 338–340

Same elements test, 875
Same episode test, 883
Same evidence test, 883
Same facts test, 883
Same incident test, 883
Same offense requirement, 874–888
Blockburger test, 883–884, 886
consistency, 886
conspiracy, 886–887
greater and lesser included
offenses, 883–884
mistrial, 885–886
multiple punishment, 884–885
multiplicity, 886–888
tests for, 883–884
Same transaction test, 883
Sandbagging, 1321
Satellites. *See also* Surveillance
GPS. *See* Global Positioning
System (GPS)
spy satellites, 426
Schengen Agreement of 1985, 873
Schools, searches in, 257–268
drug testing, 268–269
guns in lockers, 271
lesser protections, 267
school officials as criminal law
enforcers, 267–268
school-owned areas, 267
Scientific evidence, 1159–1160
Screening
as alternative to plea bargaining,
1057–1062
of appeals, 1304
by grand juries, 852–859
by police, 787–788. *See also* Charging
by prosecutors, 784–852. *See also*
Charging
Searches, 135–222. *See also* Stops
of abandoned property, 53–54

administrative caretaking
functions, 257–271, 287
administrative stops and searches, 123–133.
See also Administrative stops
apparent authority rule, 219
arrest, incident to, 224–233, 277–283
arrest, subsequent to, 231, 232
of attorneys, 651–652
automatic authorization for search
incident to arrest, 230
banking records, 275–276
blood and tissue samples, 240–242
body searches at jail, 233–243
brief searches, 106–123, 123–133. *See
also* Stop and frisk
burden of proof, 189–190
cell phones, 230, 455, 467
checkpoints, 123–133. *See also*
Checkpoints
citations, incident to, 231–232,
325–326
in close quarters, 67
consensual, 203–222. *See also*
Consensual searches
constitutional language, 142
of containers, 230, 290–296. *See also*
Containers, searches of
criminal prosecution remedies,
399–409
curtilage, 53
defined, 43–56
digital, 158, 230
DNA databases, 455–470
drug testing, 268–269
effects, 276–296
electronic devices, 276
exclusionary rule. *See* Exclusionary rule
exigent circumstances, 42
frisks for weapons, 107–116
full searches, 135–222
garbage, 53–54
group consent, 220–221
highly regulated industries, 203
historical background, 135–143
hot pursuit, 251–252
houses, 243–252. *See also* Houses,
searches of
incident to arrest, 224–233, 277–283
incident to citation, 325–326
individuals, 106–123
inevitability, consent based on,
209–210
information gathering without, 43–56

Searches (*continued*)
  information held by third parties, 455
  intrusive body searches, 233. *See also*
      Intrusive body searches
  inventory searches, 283–290. *See also*
      Inventory searches
  investigative stops, 57–106. *See also*
      Investigative stops
  jail, body searches at, 233–243
  "knock and talk" practices, 210
  leases, consent through, 220–221,
      221–222
  location of, 243–271
  lockers, 267, 271
  luggage, 230
  mobile homes, 283
  motor vehicles, 277–283, 290–296. *See*
      also Motor vehicle searches
  nighttime, 189
  papers, 271–276. *See also* Papers,
      searches of
  of persons, 224–243
  plain feel, 52, 120
  plain hearing, 51–52
  plain smell, 51–52
  plain view. *See* Plain view doctrine
  police station, inventory at, 288–289
  pre-arrest, 251–252
  pretextual stops, 82–90, 100. *See also*
      Pretextual stops
  prisons, 257–271. *See also* Prisons,
      searches in
  by private parties, 257, 468
  probable cause, 151–177. *See also*
      Probable cause
  protective sweeps, 231
  purses, 230
  racial profiling, 90–100. *See also* Racial
      profiling
  reasonable expectation of privacy,
      50–51, 52
  reasonable suspicion, 70–82. *See also*
      Reasonable suspicion
  recent appearance of police
      departments, 142
  recurring contexts, 223
  remedies, 345–409
  roadblocks, 123–133. *See also*
      Roadblocks
  schools, 257–268. *See also* Schools,
      searches in
  scope of consent to, 211
  seizure by pursuit, 65–66
  self-incrimination, 274

  small areas in search for suspect,
      251–252
  special needs, 198–203
  squeezes, 55
  standing to challenge, 383–391
  stop and frisk, 107–123. *See also* Stop
      and frisk
  stopped cars, *Terry* searches of, 122–123
  subsequent to arrest, 231, 232
  Terry search, scope of, 116–123
  third-party consent, 212–222
  tort actions as remedies, 399–409. *See*
      also Tort actions as remedies for
      illegal searches
  trash, 53–54
  wallets, 230
  warrantless, 41, 190–203
  warrant requirement, 136–190. *See also*
      Search warrants
  weapons, frisks for, 107–116
  "wingspan" rule, 229–230
  witness required, 189
  workplaces, 252–257. *See also*
      Workplaces, searches of
Search warrants, 136–203
  administrative, 198–203
  anticipatory, 197
  burden of proof, 189–190
  challenges to, 150
  compensation for issuance of, 181
  computer searches, 190
  detentions during execution of, 190
  error in, 150–151
  execution of, 181–190
  exigent circumstances, 191–198
  force, use of, 188
  four corners rule, 150
  general search warrants, 136–143. *See*
      also General search warrants
  highly regulated industries, 203
  homes, 197–198
  knock and announce, 188
  motor vehicle exception, 296
  neutral and detached magistrate
      requirement, 178–181
  nighttime execution of, 189
  no-knock entry, 188–189
  obtaining, 135
  papers, extra particularity, 275
  particularity requirement, 143–151
  perjury in obtaining, 369–370
  physical detention during
      execution, 190
  plain view doctrine, 148–150

requirements for obtaining, 136–151
return of, 151
routine check for, 65
small items, 149
special needs, 198–203
status quo, maintaining, 197
strong preference for, 41–42
subpoena compared, 650–651
support by oath or affirmation, 143
telephonic, 198
witnesses, 189
"in writing," 198
wrong jurisdiction, 151
Seat belt laws, 88
Secrecy of grand juries, 630–632
Seizure. *See* Searches
Selection of juries, 1080–1113. *See also*
    Voir dire
Selective enforcement
  prosecutorial vindictiveness, 851
  race-based, 86
Selective prosecution, 844–852
  discovery, 850
  racial patterns, 850–851
Self-defense, inadequate, 1249
Self-incrimination, 1167–1183
  bail, evaluation for, 767
  comparative law, 1179
  compulsory process for defense
    witnesses, 1180
  documents, 652
  grand juries, 640–642
  history of privilege against, 640–641
  immunity, 1181
  inferences from silence, 1179
  jury instructions, 1178
  overview, 1137, 1167–1168
  perjury charges, threat of, 1180–1181
  pre-arrest silence, comments on,
    1177–1180, 1182–1183
  purpose of privilege against, 641–642
  scope of privilege, 635–643
Sentence bargaining, 986, 1036, 1270
Sentencing, 1205–1290
  appellate courts as source of
    guidelines, 1227–1228
  assistance discounts, 1240
  capacity constraint, 1219
  capital punishment. *See* Capital
    punishment
  charging decisions, 1250–1257
  cliff effect, 1214
  cocaine, 1288–1290
  Code of Hammurabi, 1205–1206, 1212

commissions, 1212–1214, 1218–1228,
  1288, 1289
community considerations, 1233,
  1243–1244
cooperation of accused, 1235–1240
crack cocaine, 1288–1290
criminal history information,
  1229–1235
cruel and unusual punishment, 1215
death penalty. *See* Capital punishment
democratic process, effect of,
  1217–1218
determinate sentencing, 1267
discretionary sentencing, 1033, 1211,
  1217, 1268
disproportionate punishment,
  1215–1216
eighteen to one (18 to 1) ratio, 1288
entrapment, 1249
exclusionary rule, 1249–1250
factfinding, 1267
family considerations, 1233
guidelines, 1033–1035, 1218–1228,
  1229, 1251–1252, 1268
guilty pleas, 1269–1272
hundred to one (100 to 1)
  ratio, 1288, 1289
inadequate self-defense, 1249
indeterminate sentencing, 1206–1211
informal procedure at, 1209–1210
interjurisdictional analysis, 1216
intrajurisdictional analysis, 1216
investigations, 1245–1250
judicial experience, effect of,
  1242–1243
by juries, 1211, 1267–1268
jury verdicts, 1269–1272
legislative sentencing, 1212–1218
mandatory minimum, 1212–1214,
  1217, 1268
manipulation, 1245–1250
minimum sentences, 1268
mitigating factors, 1268
multiple counts, 1256–1257
new information about offender and
  victim, effect of, 1228–1245
obstruction of justice, enhancement
  for, 1270
offender characteristics, effect of, 1233
offender information, 1229–1240
parole guidelines, 1228
"partial" defenses, 1249
pending charges, effect of, 1231
perjury, enhancement for, 1270

Sentencing (*continued*)
pleas, 1257, 1270, 1272
points in criminal process, 1245–1280
pretrial release, effects of, 767
prior arrests, effect of, 1231
prior convictions, effect of, 1231, 1232
probation officers, 1271
proof at trial, 1257–1269
proportionality, 1215–1216
prosecutorial motives and
control, 1257
race, effect of, 1272–1290
real vs. charged offense, 1251
relevant conduct, effect of, 1250–1257
remorse, effect of, 1269
right to counsel at, 691
right to stand trial, punishment for
exercising, 1269–1270
rules of evidence, 1268–1269
sentence bargain, 986
speedy, no right to, 969
standard of proof, 1268
stipulated sentences, 1029–1030
structuring of, 1218–1223
suppressed statements, use of, 1250
tariff effect, 1213–1214
ten to three (10 to 3) ratio, 1290
three strikes law, 1214–1215
uncharged conduct, effect of, 1256
victim and community information,
effect of, 1240–1245
vindictive sentencing, 1271
vulnerable victim, 1242
who sentences, 1206–1228
wobblers, 816
Sentencing Reform Act of 1984, 1033
Separate trials, 907–911
September 11, 2001, terrorist attacks
airport checkpoints after, 132–133
detention of suspects after, 781
mass transit security after, 132–133
Sequestration of juries, 1119
Sequestration of witnesses, 1150
Severance
of charges, 861
of offenses, 895–907
Sex offenders
civil detention after sentence
completion, 780–781
plea bargaining restrictions, 1023, 1047
registration of, 999, 1216
sentencing guidelines, 1229
Showups, 587, 608, 624–625

Silence
comparative law, 1179
by conduct, 527–533
incentive for, 1179–1180
inferences from, 1179
invocation of *Miranda* rights, 527–533
jury instructions on, 1178
Miranda warnings, 527–533, 549
pre-arrest silence, comments on,
1177–1180, 1182–1183
Silver platter doctrine, 360–361, 439, 872
Sixth Amendment
exclusion of identification
evidence, 588–597
interrogations, 494–495
invocation of rights, 556
right to counsel, 494, 549–560. *See also*
Right to counsel
waiver of rights, 556
Slow plea, 986
Smart phones, search of, 455, 467. *See
also* Cell phones
Sobriety checkpoints, 129–132
Social guests, privacy interests of,
390–391
Social norms, 28–29
Sources of crime, 28–29
Sovereign immunity and waiver, 406
Special courts, 678
Special needs searches, 198–203
Special prosecutors, 843
Special verdicts, 1121
Speedy trial, 952–977
Barker factors, 968
child victims, 960–961
excluded periods, 975–976
overview, 915
post-accusation delay, 961–977
pre-accusation delay, 953–961
prejudice, 968
preparation time allowed, 975
pretrial hearings, influence of, 969
reasons for delay, 959, 967–968, 969
remedies for violations, 968–969, 976
sentencing, no right to speedy, 969
source of protections, 960
starting the clock, 975
state statutes compared, 969–976
statutes of limitations, 960–961
voluminous discovery, 976–977
victims, 959, 969, 975
Standards, subjective, 97–98
Standing doctrine, 383–391

State-provided counsel, 690–692
  actual imprisonment, 676
  adequacy of, 703–723
  adversarial proceedings, initiation
      of, 689–690
  advice on counsel, 679–680
  on appeal, 691–692, 1294–1298
  bail determination, 691
  challenges to, 736
  client autonomy and control over
      objective of representation, 700
  competence to stand trial, 700–701,
      702–703
  conscripted lawyers, 734–735
  constitutional right, 676–677, 678
  contract attorney systems, 736–737
  critical stage, 690, 691
  determination of indigence, 677
  distribution of offenses, 678
  expert witnesses, 680
  Faretta rights, 698–700
  fees, 737, 738–739
  funding parity, 736
  incentives, 735–736
  incorporation of right, 678
  indigence, 677
  initiation of adversarial
      proceedings, 689–690
  juvenile court proceedings, 692
  law students as, 702
  local variety, 733
  pro se representation, 698, 699, 701
  psychiatric examinations, 691, 692
  recoupment of fees, 677–678
  remedies for failure of, 735
  rights of counsel, 737–738
  selection and rejection, 692–703
  self-help, 735
  at sentencing, 691
  stand-by counsel, 699
  statutory right, 677
  systems for providing, 723–740
  type of proceedings, 681–692
  types of charges, 670–681
  universal appointment, 680–681
  volunteer lawyers, 734–735
  waiver of, 698–699, 700–701, 702–703
Statistical proof, 1195–1196
Statutes of limitation, 952–961
Stop and frisk, 107–123
  arrest compared, 297–305
  courts, role of, 121
  crime control, 115

  duration of stop, 121–122
  foreign systems, 116
  grounds for, 70–82, 114–115
  gun laws, effect of, 115
  immigration, 105–106
  investigative, 57–106
  motor vehicle drivers, 123
  motor vehicles, 122–123, 290
  non-weapons searches, 120
  order to exit vehicle, 122
  plain feel, 120
  prevalence of, 115
  purses, briefcases, and bags, 121
  racial disparities, 115
  scope of, 116–123
  search incident to arrest
      compared, 230
  self-preservation, 115–116
  statutes, 120–121
  stopped cars, searches of, 122–123
  weapons, 114
Stops
  administrative, 123–133
  conversation and arrest compared,
      57–58
  custody compared, 515
  duration of, 121–122, 304
  grounds for, 70–82
  pretextual, 82–90, 100. *See also*
      Pretextual stops
  stop and frisk, 107–123. *See also* Stop
      and frisk
"Stop sticks," 341
Strip searches, 233–243. *See also* Intrusive
    body searches
Structural defects, 1311, 1313–1320,
    1321
Subpoenas
  act of production doctrine, 652
  of attorney, 651–652
  breadth of, 649
  contents of documents, 652
  document, 643–653
  grand juries, 643–653
  justification needed for, 649–650
  negotiation re compliance, 652
  prosecutor, role of, 650
  search warrant compared, 650–651
Substantial assistance motion,
    1239–1240
Substantial threshold showing, 1240
Sufficiency of evidence, 1309–1310
Supremacy Clause, 445, 884

Surveillance. *See also* Wiretapping
  cameras, 426, 429–430
  "digital trespass," 425
  electronic, 425
  GPS, 43, 46–50, 341, 412–417,
    419–421, 425
  "mosaic theory," 425–426
  satellite, 426
  street-level cameras, 426
Suspicion
  articulable, 70
  individualized, 70, 268, 287
  reasonable, 70–106. *See also* Reasonable
    suspicion

Tampering, jury, 1122
Target standing, 390
Tariff effect, 1213–1214
Technological innovations, 411–470
  cell phones, search of, 230, 455, 467
  cell site location, 418–425, 426
  databases, government access to,
    455–470
  dogs, 430–435
  enhancement of senses, 412–435
  facial recognition technology,
    429–430, 610
  government access to databases,
    455–470
  GPS, 43, 46–50, 341, 412–417,
    419–421, 425
  helicopters, 429–430
  homes, 426
  identification, 609–610
  plain view doctrine, 435
  search, defined, 425
  smart phone, search of, 455, 467
  spy satellites, 426
  in surveillance. *See* Surveillance
  thermal imaging, 426
  tracking devices, 425–426
  video cameras, 426, 429–430
  wiretapping, 435–455. *See also*
    Wiretapping
Telfaire instructions, 617
Ten to three (10 to 3) ratio, 1290
Terrorism
  airport checkpoints after September 11
    attacks, 132–133
  detention of suspects after September
    11 attacks, 89, 781
  mass transit security after September 11
    attacks, 132–133

pretextual stops, 89
race and prevention of, 105
racial profiling after September 11
  attacks, 105
suspects, detention of, 89, 781
torture, confessions obtained
  through, 478
wiretapping, 443, 445–446
Terry searches, 107–123. *See also* Stop
  and frisk
Terwilliger Bluesheet, 1034–1035
"Testilying," 1188
Thermal imaging, 426
Third degree, 472, 475–476
Thornburgh Bluesheet, 1034
Three strikes laws, 1214–1215
Tissue samples, 240–242
Tort actions as remedies for illegal
  searches, 399–409
  availability, 404
  costs, 405
  equitable relief, limitations on,
    406–407
  indemnity, 405
  invisibility of claims, 404–405
  qualified good faith immunity,
    405–406
  sovereign immunity, 406
Torture, 478
Totality of circumstances test, 76, 171
Tracking devices, 425–426
Traditional policing, 13–32
Traffic stop, consent to search at,
  210–211
Transactional immunity, 640, 642
Trespass, digital, 425
Trials, 1067–1136
  Allen instruction, 1118
  alternate jurors, 1122
  Batson claims, 1094–1113
  bench trials and jury trials
    compared, 1068–1080
  change of venue after pretrial
    publicity, 1133
  clothing of accused, 1196–1197
  confrontation of witnesses. *See*
    Witnesses
  deadlocked jury, 1119, 1123–1124
  defendant's presence at, 1149–1150
  defendant's right to fair trial,
    1132–1133
  "dynamite charges," 1117–1118
  "hammer charges," 1117

inconsistent verdicts, 1121
juries and jurors. *See* Juries
and jurors
law-trained judges, 1078–1079
lesser included offenses, 1113–1116,
1116–1117
media access to courtroom, 1132
mixed panels, 1079
new trial, motions for, 1293
non-unanimous verdicts, 1120,
1124–1125
obstruction of justice at, 1270
other decisionmakers, 1079
outcome differences, bench vs. jury
trials, 1078
peremptory challenges, 1092,
1093–1113
public as decisionmaker, 1126–1136
public interest in, 1064
"public trial," 1126–1132
removal of judges, 1112
right to jury, 1068–1080
right to stand trial, punishment for
exercising, 1269–1270
self-incrimination privilege, 1167–1183.
See also Self-incrimination
sentencing. *See* Sentencing
separate and joint, 907–911
special courts, 678
special verdicts, 1121
speedy, 952–977. *See also* Speedy trial
televising, 1126–1133
venire, 1080
videotaping of, 1310
voir dire, 1081–1088
waiver of jury trial, 1079–1080
Tribal lands, crime committed
on, 836–838
Two witness rule, 1198

Ultraviolet light examinations, 241
Unavailable witnesses, 1151–1160
"Unconstitutional conditions"
doctrine, 220
Undercover operations, 654, 664–666
ban, 664
entrapment. *See* Entrapment
informants, 664
outrageous government conduct,
665–666
prosecutors, role of, 664–665
regulation, 664
supervision by prosecutors, 664–665

Uniform Arrest Act of 1940, 57
USA PATRIOT Act, 443
USA PROTECT Act, 1038–1039
Use immunity, 640, 642

Vehicles. *See* Motor vehicles
Venire, 1080
Verdicts, 1120–1121, 1124–1125
differing rationales, 1120–1121
inconsistent, 1121
non-unanimous, 1120, 1124–1125
special, 1121
Victims
community as, 1243–1244
impact statements, 1242
notice and consultation, 842
race, 1273–1281
sentencing and victims' rights,
1241–1242
sexual history of, 1167
victims' rights laws, 1053
vulnerable, 1242
Video cameras, 426, 429–430
Video conferencing, 439
Video recording
administrative issues, 578
confessions, 575–579
constitutional requirement, 577
interrogations, 575–579
Miranda, as "alternative" to, 578
police discretion, 577–578
statutory requirement, 577
trial, 1310
Viewpoint, observational, 583
Vindictiveness
prosecutorial, 851
in sentencing, 1271
Voice samples, 241
Voir dire, 1081–1088
defendant bias, 1087–1088
other matters, 1087
racial bias questions, 1085–1087
special circumstances, 1086–1087
Voluntariness of confessions, 472–494
delay in presenting suspect to judicial
officer, 476–477
deprivations, 472–478
length of interrogation, 476
physical abuse, 472–478
third degree, 472–473
torture, 478
vulnerability of suspect, 477–478
Voluntariness of searches, 203–212

Wade-Gilbert rule, 595
Waiver of *Miranda* rights, 526–539
  ambiguous waiver, 534
  capacity to waive, 535–536, 538–539
  informing suspect about available
      retained attorney, 536–537
  intoxication, 535
  invocation vs. waiver, 538
  juveniles, 535–536
  language barriers, 536
  reasons for, 534–535
  standard of proof, 534
  validity of waiver, 536
  voluntary, knowing, and
      intelligent, 536
Waivers
  of appeal, 988, 989–990
  of indictment, 857
  of jury trial, 1079–1080
  Miranda rights, 526–539. *See also* Waiver
      of *Miranda* rights
  of right to counsel, 556, 698–699,
      700–701, 702–703
  of trial, 986
Warrant Clause, 133
Warrantless searches, 190–203, 251–252
Warrant preference, motor vehicle
      searches, 296
Warrants
  anticipatory, 197
  arrest, 305–311
  FISC-issued, 445–446
  homes, special status of, 197–198
  search, 136–203. *See also* Search
      warrants
  telephonic, 198
  "in writing," 198
Web privacy, 469
Weight of evidence, 1309–1310
Whren stops, 82–90
Wickersham Commission, 472–473
"Wingspan" rule, 229–230. *See also*
      Searches
Wiretapping, 435–455
  agents, bugs on, 447–455
  computer searches, 438
  consensual intercepts, 444
  data transfers, 439
  duration of, 444
  email, 439
  exclusion remedy, 444

federalism, 445
federal statute, 445
interpretation, 445
judicial limits on, 436–438
marital communications, 442
minimization, 444–445
national security warrants, 445–446
necessity requirement, 443
pen registers, 366, 446, 447
probable cause, special showing
      of, 442–443
remedy, 444
roving wiretaps and oral intercepts, 443
silver platter doctrine, 439
specifying targeted person and
      facility, 443
state statutes, 444, 445
statutes and federalism, 445
statutory exclusion remedy, 444
statutory procedures, 439–447
terrorism, 443, 445–446
video teleconferencing, 439
Witnesses, 1137–1189
  anonymous, 1148
  children as, 1148–1149, 1150–1151
  compelled by defense, 1180
  confrontation, 1138–1167. *See also*
      Confrontation of witnesses
  defendants as, 1167–1183
  domestic violence cases, timing and
      motives in, 1159
  forfeiture by wrongdoing, 1160
  grand juries, 632–633
  hearsay exceptions, 1158–1159
  immunity for, 635–643
  lying prosecution witnesses, 1188–1189
  out-of-court statements, 1149,
      1164–1165
  pending charges against, 1165–1166
  perjury, 1180–1181, 1183–1189. *See also*
      Perjury
  race, and witness descriptions, 98–99
  redacted statements, 1165
  right to confront, 1137, 1138–1167
  to searches, 189
  self-incrimination, 1167–1183. *See also*
      Self-incrimination
  sequestration, 1150
  sexual history of victim, 1167
  testimony for immunity, 1181
  unavailable witnesses, 1151–1160

Wobblers, 816
Workplaces, searches of, 252–257
    government as employer, 257
    privacy interests, 256–257
    private searches, 257
Work product doctrine, 651, 945–946

Writs of assistance, 138–139, 139–141

X-rays, 241–242

Youth. *See* Juveniles
Youth courts, 812–813, 823–831